CASES AND MATERIALS ON THE LAW OF RESTITUTION

CASES AND MATERIALS ON THE LAW OF RESTITUTION

Second Edition

ANDREW BURROWS

AND

EWAN McKENDRICK

AND

JAMES EDELMAN

OXFORD

UNIVERSITY PRESS

OXFORD
UNIVERSITY PRESS

Great Clarendon Street, Oxford OX2 6DP

Oxford University Press is a department of the University of Oxford.
It furthers the University's objective of excellence in research, scholarship,
and education by publishing worldwide in

Oxford New York

Auckland Cape Town Dar es Salaam Hong Kong Karachi
Kuala Lumpur Madrid Melbourne Mexico City Nairobi
New Delhi Shanghai Taipei Toronto

With offices in

Argentina Austria Brazil Chile Czech Republic France Greece
Guatemala Hungary Italy Japan Poland Portugal Singapore
South Korea Switzerland Thailand Turkey Ukraine Vietnam

Oxford is a registered trade mark of Oxford University Press
in the UK and in certain other countries

Published in the United States
by Oxford University Press Inc., New York

First published 1997

Reprinted 2005

British Library Cataloguing in Publication Data

Data available

Library of Congress Cataloging in Publication Data

Data available

Typeset by RefineCatch Limited, Bungary, Suffolk
Printed in Great Britain
on acid-free paper by
Ashford Colour Press Ltd, Gosport, Hants

ISBN 0-19-929651-0   978-0-19-929651-4

1 3 5 7 9 10 8 6 4 2

ABBREVIATIONS

Burrows	A Burrows, *The Law of Restitution* (2nd edn, 2002)
Goff and Jones	R Goff and G Jones, *The Law of Restitution* (6th edn, 2002)
Virgo	G Virgo, *The Principles of the Law of Restitution* (2nd edn, 2006)

PREFACE

In the nine years since the first edition of this book, the law of restitution has continued to develop apace with many important new cases and numerous academic writings. This is reflected in the fact that extracts from 40 new cases and 25 new academic writings have been included in this second edition.

In our view, it remains important to include cases *and materials*. An exclusive focus on the cases is to tell only half the story. The modern growth of restitution has relied heavily on academic writings and represents a triumph for those who believe in a close working relationship between judges and academics. Having said that, we have found it far from easy to decide how to select even a small number of extracts from the increasingly voluminous scholarly literature. Guided by the assumption that the reader has access to one or more of the standard contemporary texts (by Burrows, Goff and Jones, or Virgo) we have essentially included extracts from materials on the basis that (i) they are seminal articles or (ii) they are articles or notes that neatly summarize a range of views or are particularly helpful in understanding a particular case. Subject to a couple of minor exceptions we have not included extracts from the above standard texts but have referred in each chapter to the relevant pages from those books under the heading of 'General Reading'. Our idea is that this collection should be used along with one, or more, of those texts. In contrast, not least because it takes the form of an extended thesis rather than a standard text, we have included at various stages extracts from the late Peter Birks' *Unjust Enrichment* (2nd edn, 2005).

The style is unchanged from the first edition. The introductory text in each chapter (or section) is designed to give an overview of how the extracted cases and materials fit together. The notes and questions that follow extracts aim to clarify the importance of the case or article, to highlight difficult issues raised by it, and to draw out general themes. As with the first edition, we have not confined ourselves to English cases. Interest in, and recognition of, the law of restitution has been a phenomenon throughout the common law world and we include extracts from cases and materials in the United States, Canada, New Zealand, and Australia.

The structure has been marginally changed to reflect the increasing tendency to distinguish restitution of an unjust enrichment (where unjust enrichment is the cause of action or event) from restitution for wrongs (where the wrong is the cause of action or event). Restitution for wrongs is therefore now dealt with in the final chapter of the book and the defences chapter (now Chapter 14) is concerned only with defences to the cause of action of unjust enrichment.

Chapter 2 includes an examination of Peter Birks' new 'absence of basis' approach to the unjust question and throughout we have asked readers to think about that approach. But our belief remains that an 'unjust factors' approach is to be preferred and the structure of the book continues to reflect that. So after two introductory chapters, Chapters 3–12 are arranged according to the different grounds of restitution/unjust factors. Chapter 13 looks at tracing and proprietary restitution, while Chapter 14 deals with defences. As we have already indicated, Chapter 15 considers restitution for wrongs.

It may be useful for the reader to know that Chapters 1–4, 8, 13, and 15 were primarily the work of Andrew Burrows; Chapters 6–7 and 9–11 were primarily the work of Ewan McKendrick; and Chapters 5, 12, and 14 were primarily the work of James Edelman.

We have been greatly encouraged by the favourable comments we received on the first edition and we would like to thank those who reviewed the book or who wrote to us or to OUP. In relation to this edition, we would like to thank Lyn Hambridge for her secretarial skills and, from OUP, Francesca Griffin and Anna Read.

Given the flow of cases, there is rarely a perfect time to write a book on the law of restitution. At the time of writing, we await the appeal to the House of Lords (due to be heard in July 2006) in *Deutsche Morgan Grenfell Group plc v IRC* on restitution of mistakenly paid tax.

The text was submitted at the end of May 2006 and, subject to a few minor amendments at proof stage, the law is stated as at that date.

ANDREW BURROWS
EWAN McKENDRICK
JAMES EDELMAN
30 June 2006

ACKNOWLEDGEMENTS

We are grateful to all authors and publishers of copyright material used in this book and in particular to the following for permission to reprint from the sources indicated.

Extracts from *Law Commission Reports* (LCR) 121 & 227 and from Law Commission Working Paper no 65, are Crown copyright material and are reproduced under Class Licence Number C01P0000148 with the permission of the Controller of OPSI and the Queen's Printer for Scotland.

American Law Institute: extracts from *Restatement of the Law of Restitution* (1937), © 1937 by the American Law Institute. All rights reserved.

Blackwell Publishing: extracts from *Modern Law Review*: Ewan McKendrick: 'Restitution, Misdirected Funds and Change of Position', (1992) 55 *MLR* 377; S Stoljar: 'Unjust Enrichment and Unjust Sacrifice', (1987) 50 *MLR*; *Legal Studies*: S Hedley: 'Unjust Enrichment as the Basis of Restitution – an Overworked Concept', (1985) 5 *LS* 66; and W J Swadling: 'A New Role for Resulting Trusts', (1996) 16 *LS* 110.

Cambridge Law Review Association and the authors: extracts from *Cambridge Law Journal*: J Hilliard: 'A Case for the Abolition of Legal Compulsion as a Ground of Restitution', *CLJ* (2002) 551; I M Jackman: 'Restitution for Wrongs', (1989) *CLJ* 48; M McInnes: '"At the Plaintiff's Expense": Quantifying Restitutionary Relief', (1998) *CLJ* 472; L D Smith: 'Tracing into the Payment of a Debt', (1995) *CLJ* 54; and A Tettenborn: 'Remedies for the Recovery of Money Paid by Mistake', (1980) *CLJ* 272.

Canada Law Book, a Division of The Cartwright Group Ltd (www.canadalawbook.ca): extracts from the *Dominion Law Reports* [DLR].

Canadian Bar Foundation: extract from D M Paciocco: 'The Remedial Constructive Trust: A Principles Basis for Priorities over Creditors', (1989) 68 *Canadian Bar Review* 315.

Cegla Center for Interdisciplinary Research of the Law, University of Tel Aviv: extract from E Weinrib: 'Restitutionary Damages as Corrective Justice' (2000) 1 *Theoretical Inquiries in Law* 1.

Council of Law Reporting in Victoria: extract from the *Victorian Reports* [VR].

Council of Law Reporting for New South Wales: extracts from the *New South Wales Law Reports* [NSWLR].

Federation Press: extracts from P Birks: *Restitution—The Future* (Federation Press, 1992); I Jackman: *The Varieties of Restitution* (Federation Press, 1998); and J Dietrich: *Restitution —a New Perspective* (Federation Press, 1998).

Harry & Michael Sacher Institute for Legislative Research and Comparative Law:

extracts from P Birks: 'Restitution and Resulting Trusts', in Stephen Goldstein (ed.): *Equity and Contemporary Legal Developments* (1992).

Hart Publishing Ltd: extracts from P Birks: 'Misnomer', Lord Nicholls: 'Knowing Receipt: The Need for a New Landmark', and E McKendrick: 'Work Done in Anticipation of a Contract which does not Materialise', all in W R Cornish, R Nolan, J O'Sullivan and G Virgo (eds): *Restitution, Past, Present and Future: Essays in Honour of Gareth Jones* (Hart, 1998); A Burrows: 'The English Law of Restitution: A Ten-Year Review', and R Chambers: 'Tracing and Unjust Enrichment', both in J W Neyers, M McInnes and S G A Pitel (eds): *Understanding Unjust Enrichment* (Hart, 2004); J Edelman: *Gain-Based Damages* (Hart, 2002); and P Jaffey: *The Nature and Scope of Restitution* (Hart, 2000); and extract from P Birks: 'Failure of Consideration and its Place on the Map', *Oxford University Commonwealth Law Journal* 1 (2002).

Incorporated Council of Law Reporting: extracts from the *Appeal Court Reports* [AC], *Chancery Reports* [Ch], *Industrial Cases Reports* [ICR], *King's Bench Reports* [KB], *Queen's Bench Reports* [QB], and *Weekly Law Reports* [WLR].

Informa Professional, a division of T & F Informa UK Ltd: extracts from *Lloyds Law Reports* and *Building Law Reports*; *Lloyd's Maritime and Commercial Law Quarterly*: K Barker: 'Restitution of Passenger Fare', (1994) *LMCLQ* 291; P Birks: 'Misdirected Funds: Restitution from the Recipient', (1989) *LMCLQ*; P Birks: 'The Travails of Duress', (1990) *LMCLQ* 342; E McKendrick: 'Tracing Misdirected Funds', (1991) *LMCLQ*; A Tettenborn: 'Bank Fraud, Change of Position, and Illegality: The Case of the Innocent Money-Launderer', (2005) *LMCLQ* 6; and R Stevens: 'Why do Agents "Drop Out"?', (2005) *LMCLQ* 101.

Jordan Publishing Ltd: extract from *Bankrupcy and Personal Insolvency Reports* [BPIR].

Law Book Co., part of Thomson Legal & Regulatory Ltd (www.thomson.com.au): extracts from G A Muir: 'Unjust Sacrifice and the Officious Intervener' in P D Finn (ed.): *Essays on Restitution* (Law Book Co, 1990); S Stoljar: *The Law of Quasi-Contract* (2e, Law Book Co, 1989); and *Commonwealth Law Reports* [CLR] and *Australian Law Journal Reports* [ALJR].

LexisNexis Pty Ltd: extract from Australian Law Reports [ALR].

Mansfield Press: extract from P Birks and R Chambers: *Restitution Research Resource* (1994).

New Zealand Council of Law Reporting: extract from *New Zealand Law Reports* [NZLR].

Oxford University Press: extracts from J Beatson: *The Use & Abuse of Unjust Enrichment* (OUP, 1991); P Birks & Chin Nyuk Yin: 'The Nature of Undue Influence' in J Beatson and D Friedman (eds): *Good Faith and Fault in Contract Law* (OUP, 1995); K Barker: 'After Change of Position: Good Faith Exchange in the Modern Law of Restitution', and W J Swadling: 'The Nature of Ministerial Receipt', both in P Birks (ed.): *Laundering and Tracing* (OUP, 1995); P Birks: *Unjust Enrichment* (2e, OUP 2005); P Birks: 'In Defence of

Free Acceptance', and E McKendrick: 'Frustration, Restitution and Loss', both in A Burrows (ed.): *Essays on the Law of Restitution* (OUP, 1991); and P Birks: 'The Necessity of a Unitary Law of Tracing' in Ross Cranston (ed.): *Making Commercial Law: Essays in Honour of Roy Goode* (OUP, 1997).

Oxford University Press, Journals: extracts from *Oxford Journal of Legal Studies*: K Barker: 'Unjust Enrichment: Containing the Beast', (1995) 15 *OJLS* 457; M Garner: 'The Role of Subjective Benefit in the Law of Unjust Enrichment', (1990) *OJLS* 10; R Sharpe & S M Waddams: 'Damages for Lost Opportunity to Bargain', (1982) *OJLS* 2; and L Smith: 'Three-Party Restitution: A Critique of Birks' Theory of Interceptive Subtraction', (1991) 4 *OJLS* 480.

David Paciocco: extract from D M Paciocco: 'The Remedial Constructive Trust: A Principles Basis for Priorities over Creditors', (1989) 68 *Canadian Bar Review* 315.

Province of British Columbia: extracts from *British Columbia Frustrated Contract Act 1996* (RSBC, 1996).

Reed Elsevier (UK) Ltd trading as LexisNexis Butterworths: extracts from P Birks: 'Civil Wrongs: A New World' in *Butterworths Lectures* (1990–91); A Burrows: *The Law of Restitution* (2e, 2002); P Matthews: 'Money Paid Under Mistake of Fact', (1980) *New Law Journal*; and from *All England Law Reports* [All ER], *Property Planning and Compensation Reports* [P & CR] and unreported case from LexisNexis internet *Land Hessen v Gray & Gerrish*, 31 July 1998.

Sellier European Law Publishers: extracts from *Principles of European Law: Study Group on a European Civil Code. Benevolent Intervention in Another's Affairs* prepared by Christian von Bar (Sellier, 2006).

Sweet & Maxwell Ltd: extracts from R Goff & G Jones: *Law of Restitution* (1e, 1966); S Hedley: *Restitution: Its Division and Ordering* (2001), and W R Kennedy: 'Law of Civil Salvage' in D W Steel and F D Rose (eds): *The Law of Civil Salvage* (5e, 1985); *Law Quarterly Review*: J Beatson and G Virgo: 'Contract, Unjust Enrichment and Unconscionability', (2002) 118 *LQR* 352; P Birks & J Beatson: 'Unrequested Payment of Another's Debt', (1976) *LQR* 92; A Burrows: 'Free Acceptance and the Law of Restitution, (1988) *LQR* 576; S Evans: 'Rethinking Tracing and the Law of Restitution', (1999) 115 *LQR* 469; D Friedmann: 'Payment of Another's Debt', (1983) *LQR* 99; W S Holdsworth: 'Unjustifiable Enrichment', (1939) *LQR* 55; G Jones: 'The Recovery of Benefits Gained from a Breach of Contract', (1983) 99 *LQR* 442; B McFarlane & R Stevens: 'In Defence of *Sumpter v Hedges*', (2002) 118 *LQR* 569; A W Scott: 'Constructive Trusts', (1955) *LQR* 71; W A Seavey & A W Scott: 'Restitution', (1983) *LQR* 54; and Westlaw Internet case reports.

Texas Law Review: extracts from L Smith: 'Restitution: The Heart of Corrective Justice', (2001) 79 *Texas L Rev* 2215.

United Kingdom National Committee of Comparative Law: extract from P Birks: 'Change of Position and Surviving Enrichment' in W J Swadling (ed.): *The Limits of Restitutionary Claims* (UKNCCL, 1997).

University of Illinois College of Law: extract from E Sherwin: 'Constructive Trusts in Bankrupcy', (1989) *University of Illinois Law Review* 297.

Ernest J Weinrib: extract from E Weinrib: 'Restitutionary Damages as Corrective Justice' (2000) 1 *Theoretical Inquiries in Law* 1 (Cegla Center for Interdisciplinary Research of the Law, University of Tel Aviv).

Every effort has been made to trace and contact copyright holders but this has not been possible in every case. If notified, the publisher will undertake to rectify any errors or omissions at the earliest opportunity.

CONTENTS

Preface   vii

Acknowledgements   ix

Table of Cases   xxv

Table of Legislation   li

1 UNJUST ENRICHMENT AND COMPETING THEORIES   1

   1 The Contribution of Lord Mansfield   4
      Moses v Macferlan   4

   2 The Implied Contract Theory   6
      Sinclair v Brougham   6
      WS Holdsworth, 'Unjustifiable Enrichment'   9

   3 The Recognition of the Principle against Unjust Enrichment   9
      Restatement of the Law of Restitution ss 1–3, 160 9
      WA Seavey and AW Scott, 'Restitution'   9
      Fibrosa Spolka Akcyjna v Fairbairn Lawson Combe Barbour Ltd   12
      Deglman v Guaranty Trust Co. of Canada and Constantineau   18
      R Goff and G Jones, *The Law of Restitution* (1st edn, 1966)   19
      Pavey and Matthews Pty. Ltd v Paul   22
      Lipkin Gorman v Karpnale Ltd   28
      Westdeutsche Landesbank Girozentrale v Islington London Borough Council   40

   4 Birks' Focus on the Cause of Action of Unjust Enrichment   41
      P Birks, *Restitution—The Future*   41
      P Birks, 'Misnomer'   42
      P Birks, *Unjust Enrichment* (2nd edn, 2005)   46

   5 Corrective Justice and Unjust Enrichment   48
      K Barker, 'Unjust Enrichment: Containing the Beast'   48
      L Smith, 'Restitution: The Heart of Corrective Justice'   50

   6 Modern-Day Sceptics   54
      S Stoljar, 'Unjust Enrichment and Unjust Sacrifice'   54
      S Hedley, 'Unjust Enrichment and the Basis of Restitution—An
        Overworked Concept'   55
      S Hedley, *Restitution: Its Division and Ordering*   59
      I Jackman, *The Varieties of Restitution*   62
      J Dietrich, *Restitution—A New Perspective*   65
      P Jaffey, *The Nature and Scope of Restitution*   69

2 THE ESSENTIAL INGREDIENTS OF A CLAIM FOR RESTITUTION
OF AN UNJUST ENRICHMENT   71

   1 Benefit   71

(1) The 'benefit' issue analysed by the judiciary   72
    BP Exploration Co. (Libya) Ltd v Hunt (No 2)   72
    Procter & Gamble Philippine Manufacturing Corp v Peter Cremer
        GmbH   73
    Peel (Regional Municipality) v Canada   74
    Rowe v Vale of White Horse District Council   76
    Cressman v Coys of Kensington (Sales) Ltd   77
(2) Academic analysis of the 'benefit' issue   84
    A Burrows, 'Free Acceptance and the Law of Restitution'   84
    M Garner, 'The Role of Subjective Benefit in the Law of Unjust
        Enrichment'   86
    J Beatson, *The Use and Abuse of Unjust Enrichment*   90
    P Birks, 'In Defence of Free Acceptance'   93
(3) Unjust sacrifice   101
    S Stoljar, 'Unjust Enrichment and Unjust Sacrifice'   101
    G A Muir, 'Unjust Sacrifice and the Officious Intervener'   103
(4) Two problematic cases   106
    Planché v Colburn   106
    Greenwood v Bennett   107

2 At the Claimant's Expense   109
(1) The correspondence question   110
    M McInnes, ' "At the Plaintiff's Expense": Quantifying
        Restitutionary Relief'   110
    P Birks, *Unjust Enrichment* (2nd edn, 2005)   113
    Re BHT (UK) Ltd   115
(2) The directness question   116

    (i) Interceptive subtraction?   116
         P Birks, *Unjust Enrichment* (2nd edn, 2005)   116
         L Smith, 'Three-Party Restitution: A Critique of Birks' Theory
             of Interceptive Subtraction'   117
    (ii) Leapfrogging?   119
         P Birks, *Unjust Enrichment* (2nd edn, 2005)   119
         Pan Ocean Shipping Ltd v Creditcorp Ltd (The Trident Beauty) 122
         Khan v Permayer   128
         Uren v First National Home Finance Ltd   130

3 Was the Enrichment Unjust?   133
(1) Unjust Factors and Incremental Development from Them   134
    Uren v First National Home Finance Ltd   134
(2) Birks and Chambers' Structuring of the Unjust Factors   135
    P Birks and R Chambers, *The Restitution Research Resource 1997*   135
(3) Birks' New 'Absence of Basis' Scheme   137
    P Birks, *Unjust Enrichment* (2nd edn, 2005)   137
(4) The Canadian Approach to the Unjust Question   138
    Rathwell v Rathwell   138

Garland v Consumers' Gas Co.   140

4   Defences   145

3   **MISTAKE**   147

   1   Mistaken Payments   147

     (1)   Mistakes of fact   147

       Kelly v Solari   147

       Aiken v Short   149

       Morgan v Ashcroft   150

       Barclays Bank Ltd v W J Simms Ltd   153

       P Matthews, 'Money Paid Under Mistake of Fact'   162

       Lloyds Bank plc v Independent Insurance Co. Ltd   163

       Dextra Bank & Trust Co. Ltd v Bank of Jamaica   165

     (2)   Mistakes of law   167

       Bilbie v Lumley   167

       Kleinwort Benson Ltd v Lincoln City Council   167

       Nurdin & Peacock plc v DB Ramsden & Co. Ltd   183

   2   Benefits in Kind Rendered by Mistake   187

     Greenwood v Bennett   187

     Torts (Interference with Goods) Act 1977, ss 1, 3(7) and 6   188

     County of Carleton v City of Ottawa   188

     Banque Financière de la Cité v Parc (Battersea) Ltd   190

   3   Rescission of an Executed Contract Entered Into by Mistake   195

     Newbigging v Adam   196

     Whittington v Seale-Hayne   199

     Car and Universal Finance Co. Ltd v Caldwell   201

4   **IGNORANCE**   203

   1   The Position at Common Law—Strict Liability Subject to Defences   204

     Holiday v Sigil   204

     Banque Belge pour L'Etranger v Hambrouck   204

     Agip (Africa) Ltd v Jackson   209

     E McKendrick, 'Tracing Misdirected Funds'   213

     Lipkin Gorman v Karpnale Ltd   219

     E McKendrick, 'Restitution, Misdirected Funds and Change of Position'   219

   2   The Predominant Position in Equity—Knowing Receipt and Dealing   225

     (1)   Dishonesty required   225

       Carl-Zeiss Stiftung v Herbert Smith & Co. (No 2)   225

       Re Montagu's Settlement Trusts   229

     (2)   Negligence held to be sufficient   232

       Belmont Finance Corp v Williams Furniture Ltd (No 2)   232

     (3)   Unconscionability as the test   233

       BCCI (Overseas) Ltd v Akindele   233

3 The Exceptional Position in Equity—Strict Liability Subject to Defences
   and to Exhausting Remedies Against Defaulting Fiduciary   237
   Ministry of Health v Simpson (sub nom. Re Diplock)   237
4 A Preferable Analysis?: Ignorance and Strict Liability Subject to Defences 239
   P Birks, 'Misdirected Funds: Restitution from the Recipient'   239
   Lord Nicholls, 'Knowing Receipt: The Need for a New Landmark'   245

5 FAILURE OF CONSIDERATION   249
1 The Meaning of Consideration   251
   Roxborough v Rothmans of Pall Mall Ltd   252
   Chillingworth v Esche   254
2 Contracts Discharged for Breach   256
   (1) Claim by the innocent party for the recovery of money paid   257
       Giles v Edwards   257
       Hunt v Silk   257
       Bush v Canfield   259
       Rowland v Divall   261
       Yeoman Credit Ltd v Apps   263
       D O Ferguson & Associates v M Sohl   264
       Baltic Shipping Company v Dillon (The Mikhail Lermontov)   267
   (2) Claim by the innocent party for the value of work done   279
       Planché v Colburn   279
       De Bernardy v Harding   280
       Boomer v Muir   280
       Taylor v Motability Finance Ltd   284
   (3) Claim by the party in breach for the recovery of money paid   287
       Dies v British and International Mining and Finance Co.   287
       Rover International Ltd v Cannon Film Sales Ltd   290
       Stocznia Gdanska SA v Latvian Shipping Co.   294
   (4) Claim by the party in breach for the value of work done   297
       Sumpter v Hedges   298
       Pecuniary Restitution on Breach of Contract (1975) Law Commission
       Working Paper No. 65   302
       Pecuniary Restitution on Breach of Contract (1983) Law Com.
       No. 121   303
       B McFarlane and R Stevens, 'In Defence of *Sumpter v Hedges*'   305
3 Contracts Discharged by Frustration   313
   (1) The Law Reform (Frustrated Contracts) Act 1943   314
       Law Reform (Frustrated Contracts) Act 1943, ss. 1, 2(3)–(5)   314
       BP Exploration Co. (Libya) Ltd v Hunt (No. 2)   316
       Gamerco SA v ICM/Fair Warning (Agency) Ltd   327
   (2) Developments in the Commonwealth   329
       Frustrated Contracts Act 1996 (British Columbia), ss. 5–8   329
       E McKendrick, 'Frustration, Restitution and Loss Apportionment'   330

4 Work Done in Anticipation of a Contract Which Does not Materialize 332
William Lacey (Hounslow) Ltd v Davis 333
British Steel Corporation v Cleveland Bridge and Engineering Co. Ltd 336
Regalian Properties Ltd v London Docklands Development Corporation 337
Countrywide Communications Ltd v ICL Pathway Ltd 343
E McKendrick, 'Work done in Anticipation of a Contract which does not
Materalise' 348
5 Contracts Which are Unenforceable for Want of Formality 355
Thomas v Brown 356
6 Void Contracts 356
Craven-Ellis v Canons Ltd 356
Rover International Ltd v Cannon Film Sales Ltd 358
Westdeutsche Landesbank Girozentrale v Islington London Borough Council 362
Guinness Mahon & Co. Ltd v Kensington and Chelsea Royal London
Borough Council 369
P Birks, Unjust Enrichment (2nd edn, 2005) 382
Goss v Chilcott 384
7 Subsisting Contracts 386
Roxborough v Rothmans of Pall Mall Ltd 386
P Birks, 'Failure of Consideration and its Place on the Map' 389
J Beatson and G Virgo, 'Contract, Unjust Enrichment and
Unconscionability' 390
8 Free Acceptance 392
Rowe v Vale of White Horse District Council 393

6 ILLEGITIMATE PRESSURE 397
1 Duress of the Person 399
Barton v Armstrong 399
2 Duress of Goods 404
Astley v Reynolds 404
Skeate v Beale 404
3 Economic Duress 405
North Ocean Shipping Co. Ltd v Hyundai Construction Co. Ltd (The
Atlantic Baron) 405
Pao On v Lau Yiu Long 411
Universe Tankships of Monrovia v International Transport Workers'
Federation 413
B & S Contracts and Design Ltd v Victor Green Publications Ltd 417
Crescendo Management Pty. Ltd v Westpac Banking Corp. 420
P Birks 'The Travails of Duress' 421
Dimskal Shipping Co. SA v International Transport Workers' Federation 422
CTN Cash and Carry Ltd v Gallaher 426
Huyton SA v Peter Cremer GmbH & Co. 429
R v Attorney-General for England and Wales 433

    4 Threats to Prosecute or Sue or Publish Information 435
       Williams v Bayley 436
       Silsbee v Webber 438
       Mutual Finance Ltd v John Wetton & Sons Ltd 440
       Norreys v Zeffert 442
       P Birks and Chin Nyuk Yin, 'On the Nature of Undue Influence' .. 443

7 UNDUE INFLUENCE AND EXPLOITATION OF WEAKNESS 447
    1 Relational Undue Influence 448
       Allcard v Skinner 448
       Royal Bank of Scotland v Etridge (No 2) 457
       R v Attorney-General for England and Wales 474
       National Commercial Bank (Jamaica) Ltd v Hew 476
    2 The Role of Unconscionable Conduct 480
       Louth v Diprose 480
    3 (Exploitation of) the Mental Inadequacy of the Claimant 486
       Fry v Lane 486
       Creswell v Potter 488
       Boustany v Pigott 490
       Credit Lyonnais Bank Nederland NV v Burch 492
    4 (Exploitation of) the Economic Weakness of the Claimant 494
       Earl of Aylesford v Morris 494
       Alec Lobb (Garages) Ltd v Total Oil (Great Britain) Ltd 495
    5 (Exploitation of) the Difficult Circumstances in Which the Claimant
       Finds Himself 498
       The Medina 498
       The Port Caledonia and The Anna 499
    6 Illegality Designed to Protect the Vulnerable Class, to which the
       Claimant Belongs, from Exploitation 500
       Green v Portsmouth Stadium Ltd 500

8 LEGAL COMPULSION: COMPULSORY DISCHARGE OF ANOTHER'S
   LEGAL LIABILITY 503
    1 C Discharges D's Liability to X in Order to Recover His (C's) Goods ... 504
       Exall v Partridge 504
       Edmunds v Wallingford 505
    2 C Discharges D's Liability to X where C and D are Under a Common
       Liability to X but C's Liability is Secondary 507
       Moule v Garrett 507
       Gebhardt v Saunders 508
       Brook's Wharf and Bull Wharf Ltd v Goodman Brothers 510
       Owen v Tate 512
       Niru Battery Manufacturing Co. v Milestone Trading Ltd (No 2) ... 519

3 No Restitution because No Liability of the Defendant has been
Discharged (i.e. the Defendant has not been Enriched)   523
   *Bonner v Tottenham and Edmonton Permanent Investment Building
Society*   523
   Re Nott and Cardiff Corp.   526
   Metropolitan Police District Receiver v Croydon Corp. 528
   Land Hessen v Gray and Gerrish   531
   Esso Petroleum Ltd v Hall, Russell & Co. Ltd   533
4 When does Payment of Another's Debt Discharge that Debt?   534
   Crantrave Ltd v Lloyds Bank plc   534
   P Birks and J Beatson, 'Unrequested Payment of Another's Debt'   538
   D Friedmann, 'Payment of Another's Debt'   544
   S Stoljar, *The Law of Quasi-Contract*   548
   J Beatson, *The Use and Abuse of Unjust Enrichment*   549
5 Restitution by Contribution   551
   Deering v Earl of Winchelsea   551
   Civil Liability (Contribution) Act 1978, ss 1(1), 2(1), 2(3), 3, 6(1)
and 7(3)   552
6 Rejection of an Unjust Enrichment Analysis   554
   J Hilliard, 'A Case for the Abolition of Legal Compulsion as a Ground
of Restitution'   554

9 NECESSITY   559
1 The 'Traditional' Analysis: No Right of Recovery   561
   Nicholson v Chapman   561
   Falcke v Scottish Imperial Insurance Co.   562
2 Cases in Which English Law Recognizes the Existence of a Right
of Recovery   565
   (1) The burial cases   565
      Jenkins v Tucker   565
      Rogers v Price   566
      Ambrose v Kerrison   567
      Bradshaw v Beard   568
   (2) Salvage   569
      W Kennedy and F Rose, *Law of Salvage* 570
      The Goring   570
   (3) Agency of necessity   573
      Prager v Blatspiel Stamp and Heacock Ltd   573
      China Pacific SA v Food Corporation of India   577
   (4) Provision of necessaries for the incapacitated   581
      In re Rhodes   581
   (5) Miscellaneous cases   584
      Great Northern Railway v Swaffield   584
      Matheson v Smiley   586
      In re Berkeley Applegate Ltd   587

3 The Future Development of the Law   591
   A Burrows, *The Law of Restitution* (2nd edn, 2002)   591
   P Birks, *Unjust Enrichment* (2nd edn, 2005)   592
   Principles of European Law: Study Group on a European Civil Code.
      Benevolent Intervention in Another's Affairs   593

10 ILLEGALITY AS A GROUND FOR RESTITUTION   597

   1 Withdrawal in the *Locus Poenitentiae*   597
      Taylor v Bowers   598
      Kearley v Thomson   600
      Bigos v Bousted   601

11 INCAPACITY AS A GROUND FOR RESTITUTION   607

   1 Infancy   607
      Valentini v Canali   608
      Steinberg v Scala (Leeds) Ltd   608
      Pearce v Brain   610
   2 Mental Illness   612
      Hart v O'Connor   612
   3 A Company Acting *Ultra Vires*   620
      Brougham v Dwyer   620
   4 A Public Authority Acting *Ultra Vires*   621
      Commonwealth of Australia v Burns   621

12 *ULTRA VIRES* DEMANDS BY PUBLIC AUTHORITIES   625

      Woolwich Equitable Building Society v Inland Revenue Commissioners 626

13 TRACING AND PROPRIETARY RESTITUTION   647

   1 Tracing   647

      (1) Tracing at common law   648
           Taylor v Plumer   649
           Banque Belge pour L'Etranger v Hambrouck   650
           Agip (Africa) Ltd v Jackson   650
           Lipkin Gorman v Karpnale Ltd   651
           Trustee of the Property of FC Jones and Sons (a firm) v Jones 651

      (2) Tracing in equity   656

           (i)   Where there is a mixed fund comprising the money of two
                 innocent parties the general equitable tracing rule is
                 'proportionate sharing' subject sometimes to 'first in, first out' 657

Sinclair v Brougham 657
Re Diplock 660
Barlow Clowes International Ltd v Vaughan 667
(ii) Where there is a mixed fund comprising the money of a beneficiary and a fiduciary, who has acted in breach of duty in mixing the moneys, the general equitable tracing rule is proportionate sharing subject to loss to the mixed fund first being borne by the fiduciary 672
Re Hallett's Estate 672
Re Oatway 674
Re Tilley's Will Trusts 676
Foskett v McKeown 678
(iii) The 'intermediate balance' (or 'exhaustion of the fund') rule 687
James Roscoe (Bolton) Ltd v Winder 687
Re Goldcorp Exchange Ltd 689
Bishopsgate Investment Management Ltd v Homan 696
(3) Three academic analyses of tracing 700
L Smith, 'Tracing into the Payment of a Debt' 700
P Birks, 'The Necessity of a Unitary Law of Tracing' 701
S Evans, 'Rethinking Tracing and the Law of Restitution' 703

2 Proprietary Restitution 704
(1) Case law on the scope of proprietary restitution 707
Chase Manhattan Bank NA v Israel-British Bank (London) Ltd 707
A Tettenborn, 'Remedies for the Recovery of Money Paid by Mistake' 711
Lord Napier & Ettrick v Hunter 712
Boscawen v Bajwa 720
Westdeutsche Landesbank Girozentrale v Islington London BC 727
(2) Academic analyses of proprietary restitution 744
A W Scott, 'Constructive Trusts' 744
P Birks, 'Restitution and Resulting Trusts' 750
W Swadling, 'A New Role for Resulting Trusts?' 752
R Chambers, 'Tracing and Unjust Enrichment' 755
E Sherwin, 'Constructive Trusts in Bankruptcy' 756
D Paciocco, 'The Remedial Constructive Trust: A Principled Basis for Priorities over Creditors' 757
A Burrows, 'The English Law of Restitution: A Ten-Year Review' 758

14 DEFENCES 761
1 Change of Position 762
(1) The recognition and basis of change of position 763
Lipkin Gorman v Karpnale Ltd 763
P Birks, Unjust Enrichment (2nd edn, 2005) 763
(2) The scope and application of change of position 765

(i)   Does change of position require reliance by the defendant upon
      the receipt?   765
      Scottish Equitable plc v Derby   765

(ii) How much evidence is required?   769
      Philip Collins Ltd v Davis   769
      Commerzbank AG v Gareth Price-Jones   773

(iii) Do changes of position which anticipate an enrichment count?   781
      Dextra Bank and Trust Co. Ltd v Bank of Jamaica   781

(iv) What is the relevance of fault to the defence?   785
      Niru Battery Manufacturing Co. v Milestone Trading Ltd   786
      Barros Mattos Junior v Macdaniels Ltd   796
      A Tettenborn, 'Bank Fraud, Change of Position and Illegality:
          The Case of the Innocent Money-Launderer'   800

(v)   Can a defendant change her position by purchasing something
      valuable which she still retains?   801
      RBC Dominion Securities Inc. v Dawson   801

(vi) Does change of position apply to claims for proprietary
      restitution?   802
      P Birks, 'Change of Position and Surviving Enrichment'   803

(vii) Does change of position apply to claims other than unjust
      enrichment?   804

2 Estoppel   804
   (1) The traditional position   805
        Avon County Council v Howlett   805
   (2) The future of estoppel and its relationship with change of position   811
        Scottish Equitable plc v Derby   811
        National Westminster Bank plc v Somer International (UK) Ltd   814

3 Bona Fide Purchase   822
   Lipkin Gorman v Karpnale Ltd   822
   Dextra Bank and Trust Co. Ltd v Bank of Jamaica   824

4 Agency   824
   *Australia and New Zealand Banking Group Ltd v Westpac Banking
       Corporation*   825
   Portman Building Society v Hamlyn Taylor Neck (a firm)   828
   W Swadling, 'The Nature of Ministerial Receipt'   831
   R Stevens, 'Why do Agents "Drop Out"?'   835

5 Counter-Restitution Impossible   844
   Clarke v Dickson   844
   Erlanger v New Sombrero Phosphate Co.   845
   Armstrong v Jackson   847
   Spence v Crawford   849
   O'Sullivan v Management Agency and Music Ltd   851
   Guinness plc v Saunders   857
   Cheese v Thomas   861

      Smith New Court Securities Ltd v Scrimgeour Vickers (Asset Management)
         Ltd 866
      Mahoney v Purnell 867
  6 Passing On 870
      Kleinwort Benson Ltd v Birmingham City Council 871
      Commissioner of State Revenue v Royal Insurance Australia Ltd 879
  7 Illegality 883
    (1) Mistake 883
        Oom v Bruce 883
        P Birks, *Unjust Enrichment* (2nd edn, 2005) 884
    (2) Duress and Exploitation of Weakness 885
        Smith v Bromley 885
        Smith v Cuff 885
    (3) Total failure of consideration 886
        Parkinson v College of Ambulance Ltd 886
        Re Cavalier Insurance Co. Ltd 887
        Mohamed v Alaga & Co. 890
    (4) Title Claims 892
        Bowmakers Ltd v Barnet Instruments Ltd 892
        Tinsley v Milligan 894
        Tribe v Tribe 903
        Nelson v Nelson 912
  8 Incapacity 919
    (1) Minors 919
      (i) Liability at common law and in equity 919
          Cowern v Nield 919
          Stocks v Wilson 920
          R Leslie Ltd v Sheill 922
      (ii) Statutory liability 925
          Minors' Contracts Act 1987 s. 3 925
    (2) Local authorities and companies 926

15 **RESTITUTION FOR WRONGS** 929
  1 Three Academic Analyses of When there should be Restitution for
    Wrongs 930
    I Jackman, 'Restitution for Wrongs' 930
    P Birks, 'Civil Wrongs: A New World' 934
    J Edelman, *Gain-Based Damages* 936
  2 Corrective Justice and Restitution for Wrongs 937
    K Barker, 'Unjust Enrichment: Containing the Beast' 937
    E Weinrib, 'Restitutionary Damages as Corrective Justice' 938
  3 Restitution for Torts 942
    (1) Proprietary torts (other than protecting intellectual property) 942

United Australia Ltd v Barclays Bank Ltd   942
Phillips v Homfray   948
Edwards v Lee's Administrators   952
Penarth Dock Engineering Co. Ltd v Pounds   953
Bracewell v Appleby   955
R Sharpe and S Waddams, 'Damages for Lost Opportunity
    to Bargain'   956
Stoke-on-Trent City Council v W & J Wass Ltd   959
Ministry of Defence v Ashman   964
Jaggard v Sawyer   967
    (2) Intellectual property torts   969
        Colbeam Palmer Ltd v Stock Affiliates Pty. Ltd   969
        Patents Act 1977, ss. 61(1), 61(2), and 62(1)   971
        Copyright, Designs and Patents Act 1988, ss. 96(1) and (2),
            97(1), 191I(1) and (2), 191J(1), 229(1)(2), and 233(1)–(3)   972
    (3) Non-proprietary torts   973
        Aggravated, Exemplary and Restitutionary Damages, Law
            Commission Report No 247 (1997) Draft Bill, clauses 12(1),
            (5), 15(6)   974
        Halifax Building Society v Thomas   974

4 Restitution for Breach of Contract   978
    Wrotham Park Estate Co. Ltd v Parkside Homes Ltd   978
    Attorney General v Blake   981
    Experience Hendrix LLC v PPX Enterprises Inc   990
    World Wide Fund for Nature (formerly World Wildlife Fund) v World
        Wrestling Federation Entertainment Inc   995
    G Jones, 'The Recovery of Benefits Gained From a Breach of Contract' 998

5 Restitution for Breach of Fiduciary Duty   1002
    (1) Unauthorised profit   1002
        Regal (Hastings) Ltd v Gulliver   1002
        Boardman v Phipps   1007
        Murad v Al-Saraj   1012
    (2) Bribes   1016
        Reading v Attorney-General   1016
        Attorney-General for Hong Kong v Reid   1018
        Daraydon Holdings Ltd v Solland International Ltd   1023

6 Restitution for Breach of Confidence   1026
    Attorney-General v Guardian Newspapers (No 2)   1026
    LAC Minerals Ltd v International Corona Resources Ltd   1031

Index   1039

TABLE OF CASES

AB Corp v CD Co (The Sine Nomine) [2002]
1 Ll Rep 805 . . . 989

Aberdeen Railway v Blaikie Bros (1854)
1 Macq 461 . . . 1011

Abram Steamship Co Ltd v Westville Shipping Co
Ltd [1923] AC 773; (1923) 16 Ll L Rep 245;
1923 SC (HL) 68; 1923 SLT 613 HL . . . 852

Adam v Newbigging (1888) LR 13 App Cas 308
HL . . . 848–50

Addie v Western Bank of Scotland (1866–69)
LR 1 Sc 145 HL . . . 846–8

Admiralty Commissioners v National Provincial
and Union Bank (1922) 127 LT 452 . . . 838

Agip (Africa) Ltd v Jackson [1991] Ch 547;
[1991] 3 WLR 116; [1992] 4 All ER 451; (1991)
135 SJ 117 CA . . . 203, **209–13**, 216–18, 221,
234, 246, 648, **650**, 653–4, 722, 825, 836, 838–9

Agnew v Commissioners of Inland Revenue
(Brumark) [2001] UKPC 28; [2001] 2 AC 710;
[2001] 3 WLR 454; [2001] Ll Rep Bank 251;
[2001] BCC 259; [2001] 2 BCLC 188 PC . . .
115

Aiken v Short (1856) 1 H & N 210 . . . 127, 147,
149–50, 152, 154, 156, 158–9, 162

Air Canada v British Columbia [1989]
1 SCR 1161 Sup Ct Can . . . 53, 172, 182, 633,
635, 642, 871–2, 875–8, 1032

Alati v Kruger (1955) 94 CLR 216 . . . 851

Alexander v Rayson [1936] 1 KB 169;
114 ALR 357 CA . . . 602–4, 893, 898

Alf Vaughan & Co Ltd (in receivership) v
Royscott Trust Plc [1999] 1 All E.R. (Comm.)
856 Ch D . . . 429

Allcard v Skinner (1887) 36 CHD 245 CA . . .
448–56, 459, 461–2, 469, 471, 475, 478–9,
484–5

Allen v Flood [1898] AC 1 HL . . . 439

Allison, Johnson & Foster Ltd Ex p Birkenshaw
[1904] 2 KB 327 KBD . . . 357

Allison v Bristol Marine Insurance Co (1876)
LR 1 App Cas 209 HL . . . 271

Alton v Midland Railway Co (1865)
34 LJ (CP) 292 . . . 922

Amalgamated Investment & Property Co Ltd
(in liquidation) v Texas Commerce
International Bank Ltd [1982] QB 84; [1981]
3 WLR 565; [1981] 3 All ER 577; [1982]
1 Ll Rep 27; [1981] Com LR 236; 125 SJ
623 CA . . . 808

Ambrose v Kerrison (1851) 10 CB 776 . . . 565,
566, **567–9**

Amec Developments Ltd v Jury's Hotel
Management (UK) Ltd [2002] TCLR 13;
(2001) 82 P & CR 22; [2001] 1 EGLR 81;
[2001] 07 EG 163; [2000] EGCS 138; [2000]
NPC 125 Ch D . . . 996

Ames' Settlement, Re [1946] Ch 217 Ch D . . .
253, 737–9

Amministrazione delle Finanze dello Stato v
San Giorgio SpA (C-199/82) [1983]
ECR 3595; [1985] 2 CMLR 658 ECJ . . . 635,
872, 878

Anglo-Austrian Printing and Publishing Union
(No 3), Re [1985] 2 Ch 891 Ch D . . . 58

Anson v Anson [1953] 1 QB 636; [1953]
1 WLR 573; [1953] 1 All ER 867;
97 SJ 230 QBD . . . 517, 542

Antares, The see Kenya Railways v Antares Co
Pty Ltd (The Antares) (No 1)

Appleby v Myers (1867) LR 2 CP 651 Ex C . . .
327

Arbutus Park Estates Ltd v Fuller (1977)
74 DLR (3d) 257 . . . 957

Archer v Cutler [1980] 1 NZLR 386 . . . 613–17,
619

Armstrong v Jackson [1917] 2 KB 822 KBD . . .
196, 844, **847–8**, 851

Arnhem Technology Ltd v Dudley Joiner
Unreported – 31 January 2001 Ch D . . . 842

Arris v Stukely (1677) 2 Mod 260; 86 ER 1060 . . .
116, 274

Asfar & Co v Blundell [1896] 1 QB 123 CA . . .
306

Ashbury Railway Carriage & Iron Co Ltd v
Riche (1874–75) LR 7 HL . . . 620, 653

Astley v Reynolds (1731) 2 Str 915 KB . . . **404**,
406, 408, 412, 539

Atchison, Topeka & Santa Fe Railway Co v
O'Connor 223 US 280 . . . 631, 636

Athans v Canadian Adventure Camps Ltd (1977)
17 OR (2d) 425 . . . 958

Attfield, Lindsay v Driscoll [1929] 1 KB 470;
[1928] All ER Rep 130 CA . . . 799

Attorney-General's Reference (No 1 of 1985)
Re [1986] QB 491; [1986] 2 WLR 733; [1986]
2 All ER 219; (1986) 83 Cr App R 70; (1986)
150 JP 242; [1986] Crim LR 476; (1986)
150 JPN 287; (1986) 83 LSG 1226; (1986)
130 SJ 299 CA . . . 744

Attorney-General for New South Wales v
Perpetual Trustee Co Ltd [1955] AC 457;
[1955] 2 WLR 707; [1955] 1 All ER 846;
99 SJ 233; 85 CLR 237 HC Aus . . . 529

Attorney-General for Victoria v Commonwealth of Australia (1945) 71 CLR 237 . . . 622

Attorney-General of Hong Kong v Humphrey's Estate Ltd [1987] AC 114 PC . . . 343, 354

Attorney-General of Hong Kong v Reid [1994] 1 AC 324; [1993] 3 WLR 1143; [1994] 1 All ER 1; (1993) 143 NLJ 1569; (1993) 137 SJLB 251; [1993] NPC 144 PC . . . 652, 695, 704, 752, 910, 930, 977, **1018–22**, 1023–5

Attorney-General v Alford (1854) 4 De GM & G 843 . . . 728

Attorney-General v Blake [2001] 1 AC 268; [2000] 3 WLR 625; [2000] 4 All ER 385; [2000] 2 All ER (Comm) 487; [2001] IRLR 36; [2001] Emp LR 329; [2000] EMLR 949; (2000) 23(12) IPD 23098; (2000) 97(32) LSG 37; (2000) 150 NLJ 1230; (2000) 144 SJLB 242 HL . . . 933, 937, 964, **981–89**, 1025

Attorney-General v Guardian Newspapers Ltd (No 2) [1990] 1 AC 109; [1988] 3 WLR 776; [1988] 3 All ER 545; [1989] 2 FSR 181; (1988) 85(42) LSG 45; (1988) 138 NLJ Rep 296; (1988) 132 SJ 1496 HL . . . 931, 975, **1026**

Attorney-General v Wilts United Dairies Ltd (1921) 37 TLR 884 . . . 625, 630

Auckland Harbour Board v The King [1924] AC 318 PC . . . 308, 622–3, 634

Australasian Steam Navigation Co v Morse (1871–73) LR 4 PC 222 PC . . . 574, 576

Australia and New Zealand Banking Group Ltd v Westpac Banking Corp (1988) 78 ALR 157 HC Aus . . . 28, 37, **825–7**, 828, 833, 838, 841

Australian Consolidated Pres v Uren [1969] 1 AC 590; [1967] 3 WLR 1338; [1967] 3 All ER 523; 111 SJ 741 PC . . . 934

Avon CC v Howlett [1983] 1 WLR 605; [1983] 1 All ER 1073; [1983] IRLR 171; 81 LGR 555; (1983) 133 NLJ 377; (1983) 127 SJ 173 CA . . . 36, 766, 770, **805–10**, 811–14, 816–21

Awwad v Geraghty & Co [2001] QB 570; [2000] 3 WLR 1041; [2000] 1 All ER 608; [2000] 1 Costs LR 105; [1999] NPC 148 CA . . . 892

Ayres v Hazelgrove Unreported 9 February 1984 . . . 619

B & S Contracts and Design Ltd v Victor Green Publications Ltd [1984] ICR 419; (1984) 81 LSG 893; (1984) 128 SJ 279 CA . . . **417–19**

B Liggett (Liverpool) Ltd v Barclays Bank Ltd [1928] 1 KB 48 KBD . . . 535–8, 724

Backhouse v Backhouse [1978] 1 WLR 243; [1978] 1 All ER 1158; (1977) 7 Fam Law 212; 121 SJ 710 Fam Div . . . 490, 492

Baden, Delvaux and Lecuit v Société Generale pour Favoriser le Développement du Commerce et de l'Industrie en France SA [1993] 1 WLR 509; [1992] 4 All ER 161 [1983] BCLC 325 Ch D . . . 229–31, 794–6

Bainbrigge v Browne (1881) 18 Ch D 188 Ch D . . . 119

Baker Ltd v Medway Building and Supplies Ltd [1958] 1 WLR 1216; [1958] 3 All ER 540; 102 SJ 877 CA . . . 239

Balian v Joly (1900) 6 TLR 45 . . . 312

Baltic Shipping Co v Dillon (The Mikhail Lermontov) (1993) 176 CLR 344 HC Aus . . . **267–76**, 289

Bamford v Shuttleworth (1840) 11 A & E 926 . . . 842

Bank of Credit and Commerce International (Overseas) Ltd v Akindele [2001] Ch 437; [2000] 3 WLR 1423; [2000] 4 All ER 221; [2000] Ll Rep Bank 292; [2000] BCC 968; [2000] WTLR 1049; (1999–2000) 2 ITELR 788; (2000) 97(26) LSG 36; (2000) 150 NLJ 950 CA . . . 203, **233–7**, 788, 794

Bank of Credit and Commerce International SA v Aboody [1990] 1 QB 923; [1989] 2 WLR 759; [1992] 4 All ER 955; [1990] 1 FLR 354; [1989] CCLR 63; [1989] Fam Law 435; (1988) 132 SJ 1754 CA . . . 460, 469, 471, 862

Bank of New South Wales v Murphett [1983] VR 489 Sup Ct Vic . . . 37

Bankers Trust Co v Shapira [1980] 1 WLR 1274; [1980] 3 All ER 353; 124 SJ 480 CA . . . 738

Banque Belge pour l'Etranger v Hambrouck [1921] 1 KB 321 CA . . . 119, 121, **203–4**, 212–14, 217–18, 221, **649–50**, 654, 877

Banque Financière de la Cité SA v Parc (Battersea) Ltd [1999] 1 AC 221; [1998] 2 WLR 475; [1998] 1 All ER 737; [1998] CLC 520; [1998] EGCS 36; (1998) 95(15) LSG 31; (1998) 148 NLJ 365; (1998) 142 SJLB 101 HL . . . 2, 71, 78, 129–30, 187, **190–4**, 519–20, 522

Banque Keyser Ullmann SA v Skandia (UK) Insurance Co Ltd [1991] 2 AC 249; [1990] 3 WLR 364; [1990] 2 All ER 947; [1990] 2 Ll Rep 377; (1990) 87(35) LSG 36; (1990) 140 NLJ 1074; (1990) 134 SJ 1265 HL . . . 355

Barber v NWS Bank Plc [1996] 1 WLR 641; [1996] 1 All ER 906; [1996] RTR 388; [1996] CCLR 30; (1995) 145 NLJ 1814 CA . . . 263

Barclays Bank Ltd v WJ Simms, Son & Cooke (Southern) Ltd [1980] QB 677; [1980] 2 WLR 218; [1979] 3 All ER 522; [1980] 1 Ll Rep 225; 123 SJ 785 QBD . . . 127, 147, **153–61**, 162–5, 185–7, 224, 232, 536, 543–4, 547, 549, 827, 829

Barclays Bank Plc v Khaira [1992] 1 WLR 623; [1996] 5 Bank LR 196; (1992) 89(17) LSG 50; [1991] NPC 141 Ch D . . . 355

Barclays Bank Plc v O'Brien [1993] QB 109; [1992] 3 WLR 593; [1992] 4 All ER 983; [1993] 1 FLR 124; [1993] 1 FCR 97; (1993) 25 HLR 7; (1993) 66 P & CR 135; (1992) 11 Tr LR 153; [1992] CCLR 37; [1993] Fam Law 62; (1992) 89(27) LSG 34; (1992) 142 NLJ 1040; (1992)

136 SJLB 175; [1992] NPC CA . . . 202, 355, 458, 463–6, 468–70, 472–3, 755, 862

Barlow Clowes International Ltd (In Liquidation) v Vaughan [1992] 4 All ER 22; [1992] BCLC 910 CA . . . **667–71**

Barlow Clowes International Ltd v Eurotrust International Ltd [2005] UKPC 37; [2006] 1 WLR 1476; [2006] 1 All ER 333; [2006] 1 All ER (Comm) 478; [2006] 1 Ll Rep 225; [2005] WTLR 1453; (2005–06) 8 ITELR 347; (2005) 102(44) LSG. 32; [2006] 1 P & CR DG16 PC . . . 231, 796

Barnes, Re (1861) 4 LTNS 60 . . . 539

Barnes v Addy (1873–74) LR 9 Ch App 244; (1874) 22 WR 505; (1874) 43 LJ Ch 513; (1874) 30 LT 4 CA . . . 228, 231–2, 730

Barros Mattos Junior v Macdaniels Ltd [2004] EWHC 1188; [2005] 1 WLR 247; [2004] 3 All ER 299; [2004] 2 All ER (Comm) 501; [2004] 2 Ll Rep 475 Ch D . . . **796–9**, 804

Barton v Armstrong [1976] AC 104; [1975] 2 WLR 1050; [1975] 2 All ER 465; (1973) 119 SJ 286 PC . . . **399–403**, 412, 415, 420–2, 424, 430, 432–4

Baylis v Bishop of London [1913] 1 Ch 127 CA . . . 21, 36, 238, 242, 824, 827, 840

Beatty v Guggenheim Exploration Co (1919) 255 NY 380 . . . 745

Beavan v M'Donnell (1854) 9 Exch 309 . . . 616

Becton Dickinson UK Ltd v Zwebner [1989] QB 208; [1988] 3 WLR 1376; [1989] 13 EG 65; (1988) 132 SJ 1638 QBD . . . 508

Beddoe, Re [1893] 1 Ch 547 CA . . . 590

Bell v Lever Bros Ltd [1932] AC 16 HL . . . 162, 195, 389

Belmont Finance v Williams Furniture Ltd (No 2) [1980] 1 All ER 393 CA . . . 203, 230, **232–3**, 234, 788

Belshaw v Bush (1851) 11 CB 191 . . . 539, 543

Berg v Sadler v Moore [1937] 2 KB 158 CA . . . 602–4, 889

Berkeley Applegate (Investment Consultants) Ltd (No 1), Re [1989] Ch 32; [1988] 3 WLR 95; [1988] 3 All ER 71; (1988) 4 BCC 274; [1989] BCLC 28; [1989] PCC 261; (1988) 132 SJ 896 Ch D . . . 560, **587–90**

Berkley-Freeman v Bishop 2 Atk 39 . . . 487

Berry, Re (1906) 147 Fed 208 . . . 708, 710

Beynon v Cook (1874–75) LR 10 Ch App 389 CA . . . 487

BHT (UK) Ltd, Re [2004] EWHC 201; [2004] BCC 301; [2004] 1 BCLC 569 Ch D . . . 110, **115–16**

Bigos v Bousted [1951] 1 All ER 92 KBD . . . **601–5**, 884, 911

Bilbie v Lumley (1802) 2 East 469; 102 ER 448 . . . 147, **167**, 170–1, 628

Birch v Blagrave (1755) 1 Amb 264 . . . 731

Bishopsgate Investment Management Ltd (in liquidation) v Homan [1995] Ch 211; [1994] 3 WLR 1270; [1995] 1 All ER 347; [1994] BCC 868; (1994) 91(36) LSG 37; (1994) 138 SJLB 176 CA . . . **696–700**

Biss, Re [1903] 2 Ch 40 CA . . . 910

Blaauwpot v Da Costa 1 Ed 130 . . . 716

Blackburn v Smith (1848) 2 Ex 783 . . . 845, 853

Blacklocks v JB Developments (Godalming) Ltd [1982] Ch 183; [1981] 3 WLR 554; [1981] 3 All ER 392; (1982) 43 P & CR 27; 125 SJ 356 Ch D . . . 755

Blake v Mowatt (1856) 21 Beav 603 . . . 848

Blomley v Ryan (1956) 99 CLR 362 . . . 480, 482–3

Blundell, Re (1889) LR 40 Ch D 370 Ch D . . . 227

Boardman v Phipps [1964] 1 WLR 993; [1964] 2 All ER 187; 108 SJ 619 Ch D . . . 588–9, 858, 860, 941, **1007–12**, 1014

Boissevain v Weil [1950] AC 327; [1950] 1 All ER 728; 66 TLR (Pt. 1) 771; 94 SJ 319 HL . . . 891–2

Bolton Partners v Lambert (1889) LR 41 Ch D 295 CA . . . 32

Bone v Eckless 29 LJ (Ex) 440; 5 H & N 925 . . . 599

Bonner v Tottenham and Edmonton Permanent Investment Building Society [1899] 1 QB 161 CA . . . 189, 503, **523–6**

Boodle, Hatfield & Co v British Films Ltd [1986] PCC 176; [1986] Fin LR 134; (1986) 136 NLJ 117 Ch D . . . 193

Bookmakers Afternoon Greyhound Services v Wilf Gilbert (Staffordshire) Ltd [1994] FSR 723 Ch D . . . 394

Boomer v Muir (1933) 24 P 2d 570 . . . 277, **280–4**, 286

Boothby v Boothby 1 Mac & G 604 . . . 487

Borden (UK) Ltd v Scottish Timber Products Ltd [1981] Ch 25; [1979] 3 WLR 672; [1979] 3 All ER 961; [1980] 1 Ll Rep 160; 123 SJ 688 CA . . . 699

Bornmann v Tooke (1808) 1 Camp 376 . . . 311

Boscawen v Bajwa [1996] 1 WLR 328; [1995] 4 All ER 769; (1995) 70 P & CR 391; (1995) 92(21) LSG 37; (1995) 139 SJLB 111 CA . . . 193–4, 251, 656, 706, **720–6**

Boston Deep Sea Fishing and Ice Co v Ansell (1888) LR 39 Ch D 339 CA . . . 305

Boustany v Pigott (1993) 69 P & CR 298 PC . . . **490–1**

Bowes v Foster 2 H & N 779; 27 LJ (Ex) 262 . . . 599

Bowmakers Ltd v Barnet Instruments Ltd [1945]
1 KB 65 CA . . . **892–4**, 894–6, 901–2, 907,
915–17

Box v Midland Bank Ltd [1979] 2 Ll Rep 391
QBD . . . 355

Boys v Chaplin [1971] [1971] AC 356; [1969]
3 WLR 322; [1969] 2 All ER 1085; [1969]
2 Ll Rep 487; 113 SJ 608 HL . . . 425

BP Exploration Co (Libya) Ltd v Hunt (No 2)
[1979] 1 WLR 783 QBD . . . **316–26**, 327

BP Exploration Co (Libya) Ltd v Hunt (No 2)
[1983] 2 AC 352; [1982] 2 WLR 253; [1982]
1 All ER 925 HL . . . **71–3**, 80, 98, 125, 325–6,
329

Bracewell v Appleby [1975] Ch 408; [1975]
2 WLR 282; [1975] 1 All ER 993; (1975)
29 P & CR 204; (1974) 119 SJ 114 Ch D . . .
937, **955–6**, 957, 959, 984, 989

Bradford Advance Co Ltd v Ayers [1924]
WN 152 . . . 365

Bradshaw v Beard (1862) 12 CBNS 344 CCP . . .
568–9

Brennan v Bolt Burdon [2004] EWCA Civ 1017;
[2005] QB 303 CA . . . 183, 642–3

Brewer Street Investments Ltd v Barclays Woollen
Co Ltd [1954] 1 QB 428; [1953] 3 WLR 869;
[1953] 2 All ER 1330; 97 SJ 796 CA . . . 92,
339, 351–2

Bridgewater v Griffiths [2000] 1 WLR 524; [1999]
2 Costs LR 52 QBD . . . 394

Bridgman v Green (1755) 2 Ves Sr 627; Wilm 58
. . . 746

Bristol and West Building Society v Mathew
(t/a Stapley & Co) [1996] 4 All ER 698; [1998]
Ch 1; [1996] CLY 4503 . . . 830

Bristow v Eastman (1794) 1 Peake 291 . . . 243,
922

British American Continental Bank v British
Bank for Foreign Trade [1926] 1 KB 328 CA
. . . 827–8

British and North European Bank Ltd v Zalzstein
[1927] 2 KB 92 KBD8 40

British Motor Trade Association v Gilbert [1951]
2 All ER 641; [1951] 2 TLR 514; [1951]
WN 454; 95 SJ 595 Ch D . . . 986, 1000

British Red Cross Society v Johnson [1914] 2 Ch
419; [1914–15] All ER Rep 459 Ch D . . . 668

British Steel Corp v Cleveland Bridge &
Engineering Co Ltd [1984] 1 All ER 504;
[1982] Com LR 54; 24 BLR 94 QBD . . . 92,
336, 340–1, 346, 394

British Steel Plc v Customs and Excise
Commissioners (No 1) [1997] 2 All ER 366 CA
. . . 641

British Westinghouse Electric & Manufacturing
Co Ltd v Underground Electric Railways Co of
London Ltd (No 2) [1912] AC 673 CA . . .
266, 876

Bromage v Gunning (1617) 1 Rolle 368 . . . 998

Brook v Hook (1904) LR 6 Ex 89 Ex Ct . . . 441

Brooks v MacDonnell (1835) 1 Y & C 500 . . .
717

Brook's Wharf and Bull Wharf Ltd v Goodman
Bros [1937] 1 KB 534; [1936] 3 All ER 696;
(1936) 56 Ll L Rep 71 CA . . . 189, 503,
510–14, 517, 529, 541

Brougham v Dwyer (1913) 108 LT 504 . . . 364,
367, **620–1**

Brown v Jodrell (1827) 3 C & P 30 . . . 615

Brown v Smith (1924) 34 CLR 160 . . . 851

Browning v Morris (1878) 2 Cowp 790 . . . 500,
888

Buller v Harrison (1777) 2 Cowp 565 . . . 824,
826, 833, 838

Bullock v Lloyds Bank Ltd [1955] Ch 317; [1955]
2 WLR 1; [1954] 3 All ER 726; 99 SJ 28 Ch D
. . . 589

Bulman & Dickinson v Fenwick & Co [1894]
1 QB 179 CA . . . 418

Burdick v Garrick (1869–70) LR 5 Ch App 233
CA . . . 728

Burglas v Finance Funds Group Inc 252 So 2d 498
(1971) . . . 103

Burnald v Rodocanachi Sons & Co (1881–82)
LR 7 App Cas 333 HL . . . 717–18

Burns Philp & Co Ltd v Gillespie Brothers Pty
Ltd (1947) 74 CLR 147; (1947) 20 ALJ 490 HC
Aus . . . 576

Burt v Claude Cousins & Co Ltd [1971] 2 QB
426; [1971] 2 WLR 930; [1971] 2 All ER 611;
(1971) 115 SJ 207 CA . . . 842

Bush v Canfield (1818) 2 Conn 485 Sup Ct Conn
. . . **259–61**

Butler v Broadhead [1975] Ch 97; [1974] 3 WLR
27; [1974] 2 All ER 401; (1973) 118 SJ 115 Ch
D . . . 239

Butler v Rice [1910] 2 Ch 277 Ch D . . . 192–3,
548, 724, 727

Butterworth v Kingsway Motors Ltd [1954]
1 WLR 1286; [1954] 2 All ER 694; 98 SJ 717
. . . 263, 270, 277

Byfield (A Bankrupt), Re [1982] Ch 267; [1982]
2 WLR 613; [1982] 1 All ER 249 Ch D . . . 68

CA Stewart & Co v PHS Van Ommeren (London)
Ltd [1918] 2 KB 560 CA . . . 123–4, 126

Cadbury Schweppes Inc v FBI Foods Ltd (1999)
167 DLR (4th) 577 SC Can . . . 1037

Campbell v Campbell (2000) 79 Can Bar Rev 459
. . . 141

Campbell v Hall (1774) 1 Cowp 204 . . . 625, 636

Campbell v Hooper (1855) 3 Sm & Giff 153 . . .
616

Campbell v Mirror Group Newspapers Ltd
[2004] UKHL 22; [2004] 2 AC 457; [2004]

2 WLR 1232; [2004] 2 All ER 995; [2004]
EMLR 15; [2004] HRLR 24; [2004] UKHRR
648; 16 BHRC 500; (2004) 101(21) LSG 36;
(2004) 154 NLJ 733; (2004) 148 SJLB 572 HL
. . . 1030

Canada and Dominion Sugar Co Ltd v Canadian
National (West Indies) Steamship Ltd [1947]
AC 46; (1947) 80 Ll L Rep 13; 62 TLR 666;
[1947] LJR 385 PC . . . 816

Cannan v Meaburn (1923) 1 Bing 243 . . . 574

Canson Enterprises Ltd v Boughton & Co (1991)
85 DLR (4th) 129 . . . 868–9

Cantiere Sen Rocco SA v Clyde Shipbuilding and
Engineering Co Ltd [1924] AC 226; (1923)
16 Ll L Rep 327; 1923 SC (HL) 105; 1923 SLT
624 HL . . . 17

Cantor v Cox (1975) 239 EG 121 . . . 895, 900

Car and Universal Finance Co Ltd v Caldwell
[1965] 1 QB 525; [1964] 2 WLR 600; [1964]
1 All ER 290; 108 SJ 15 CA . . . 196, **201–2**, 706

Cargo ex Argos (1873) LR 5 PC 6 . . . 578, 585

Carl-Zeiss Stiftung v Herbert Smith & Co (No 2)
[1969] 2 Ch 276 CA . . . 203, **225–7**, 231

Carlill v Carbolic Smoke Ball Co [1893] 1 QB 256
CA . . . 306

Carmichael v Old Straight Creek Coal Corp 232
Ky 133; 22 SW (2d) 572 . . . 952

Cassell & Co Ltd v Broome (No 1) [1972] AC
1027; [1972] 2 WLR 645; [1972] 1 All ER 801;
116 SJ 199 HL . . . 934, **973–4**

Castellain v Preston (1883) 11 QBD 380 CA . . .
533–4, 718

Cavalier Insurance Co Ltd, Re [1989] 2 Ll Rep 430
Ch D . . . 501, **887–9**

Cave v Cave (1880) LR 15 Ch D 639 Ch D . . .
822

Chambers v Miller (1862) 143 ER 50; (1862)
13 CBNS 125 . . . 154

Chandler v Webster [1904] 1 KB 493 CA . . . 12,
14, 17–18, 251, 275, 313, 317, 363–4

Chaplin v Leslie Frewin (Publishers) Ltd [1966]
Ch 71; [1966] 2 WLR 40; [1965] 3 All ER 764;
109 SJ 871 CA . . . 611

Chappels v Poles (1837) 2 M & W 867 . . . 833

Chase Manhatten Bank NA v Israel-British Bank
(London) Ltd [1981] Ch 105; [1980] 2 WLR
202; [1979] 3 All ER 1025; 124 SJ 99 Ch D . . .
147, 216, 652, 692, 704, **707–12**, 729, 731, 737,
741, 751–2, 841, 873–4, 1035

Cheese v Thomas [1994] 1 WLR 129; [1994] 1 All
ER 35; [1994] 1 FLR 118; [1995] 1 FCR 162;
(1994) 26 HLR 426; (1995) 69 P & CR 316;
[1994] Fam Law 80; [1993] EGCS 149; (1993)
143 NLJ 1368 CA . . . **861–6**

Chesworth v Farrar [1967] 1 QB 407; [1966]
2 WLR 1073; [1966] 2 All ER 107; 110 SJ 307
QBD . . . 947

Chettiar (Palaniappa) v Chettiar (Arunasalam)
[1962] AC 294; [1962] 2 WLR 548; [1962] 1 All
ER 494; 106 SJ 110 PC . . . 895, 900–1, 903,
905, 909

Chetwynd v Allen [1899] 1 Ch 353 Ch D . . . 193

Chichester Diocesan Fund and Board of Finance
Inc v Simpson [1944] AC 341; [1944] 2 All ER
60 HL . . . 237

Chief Constable of Leicestershire v M [1989]
1 WLR 20; [1988] 3 All ER 1015; (1988) 138
NLJ Rep 295 Ch D . . . 976–7

Childers v Childers (1857) 1 De G & J 482 . . .
731, 895, 909

Chillingworth v Esche [1924] 1 Ch 97; [1923]
All ER Rep 97 CA . . . **254**, 343

China Pacific SA v Food Corp of India
(The Winson) [1982] AC 939; [1981] 3 WLR
860; [1981] 3 All ER 688; [1982] 1 Ll Rep 117;
125 SJ 808 HL . . . **577–81**

Christy v Row (1808) 1 Taunt 300 . . . 585

CHT Ltd v Ward [1965] 2 QB 63 [1963] 3 WLR
1071; [1963] 3 All ER 835; 107 SJ 907 CA . . .
33

CICB Mortgages Plc v Pitt [1994] AC 200; [1994]
CLY 3293 HL . . . 459, 471, 478

Cigna Life Insurance New Zealand Ltd v Westpac
Securities Ltd [1996] 1 NZLR 80 HC NZ . . .
838

Citadel General Assurance Co v Lloyds Bank
Canada [1997] 3 SCR 805; (1997) 152 DLR
(4th) 411 Sup Ct Can . . . 233, 838–9

City Bank of Sydney v McLouglin (1909)
9 CLR 615 . . . 541

City of New Orleans v Fireman's Charitable
Association 9 SO 486 (1891) . . . 999, 1002

City of Philadelphia v Tripple 230 Pa 481;
79 A 703 . . . 281–2

Clark v Manchester 51 NH 594 . . . 282

Clarke v Dickson (1858) El Bl & El 148 . . . 196,
844–5, 848, 851

Clarke v Shee and Johnson (1774) 1 Cowp 197;
Lofft 756 . . . 30–1, 38, 655

Clayton's Case [1814–23] All ER Rep 1; (1816)
1 Mer 572 . . . 660, 666–71, 674, 688

Cleadon Trust, Re [1939] Ch 286 CA . . . 22,
535–7, 539

Close v Phipps (1844) 7 Man & G 566 . . . 407

Clough v London and North Western Railway Co
(1871–72) LR 7 Ex 26 Ex Ch . . . 846–7

Clowes Development (UK) Ltd v Mulchinock
Unreported 24 May 2001 Ch D . . . 289

Colbeam Palmer Ltd v Stock Affiliates Pty Ltd
(1968) 122 CLR 25 HC Aus . . . **969–71**, 973

Cole v Shallet (1693) 3 Lev 41 . . . 311

Coleman v Bucks & Oxon Union Bank [1897]
2 Ch 243 Ch D . . . 838

Collier v Collier [2002] EWCA Civ 1095; [2002] BPIR 1057; [2003] WTLR 617; (2003–04) 6 ITELR 270; [2003] 1 P & CR DG3 CA . . . 912

Colonial Bank v Exchange Bank of Yarmouth, Nova Scotia (1886) LR 11 App Cas 84 PC . . . 157, 211, 838

Combe v Combe [1951] 2 KB 215; [1951] 1 All ER 767; [1951] 1 TLR 811; 95 SJ 317 CA . . . 354

Commercial Bank of Australia v Amadio (1983) 151 CLR 447; (1983) 46 ALR 402 . . . 480–4, 491

Commercial Bank of Scotland v Rhind (1860) 3 Macq HL 643 . . . 840

Commercial Banking Co of Sydney Ltd v Mann [1961] AC 1; [1960] 3 WLR 726; [1960] 3 All ER 482; 104 SJ 846 PC . . . 32, 220

Commercial Union Assurance Co v Lister (1873–74) LR 9 Ch App 483 CA . . . 714, 716

Commerzbank AG v IMB Morgan Plc [2004] EWHC 2771; [2005] 2 All ER (Comm) 564; [2005] 1 Ll Rep 298; [2005] WTLR 1485; [2005] 1 P & CR DG17 Ch D . . . 671

Commerzbank AG v Price-Jones [2003] EWCA Civ 1663; (2003) 147 SJLB 1397; [2004] 1 P & CR DG15 CA . . . 764, **773–80**, 785

Commission of the European Communities v Italian Republic (C-104/86) [1988] ECR 1799 ECJ . . . 873

Commissioner of Stamp Duties (Queensland) v Livingston [1965] AC 694; [1964] 3 WLR 963; [1964] 3 All ER 692; (1964) 43 ATC 325; [1964] TR 351; 108 SJ 820 PC . . . 732

Commissioner of State Revenue v Royal Insurance Australia Ltd (1995) 69 ALJR 51 HC Aus . . . 28, 113, 871–2, **879–83**

Commonwealth of Australia v Burns [1971] VR 825 Sup Ct Aus . . . **621–3**, 811

Commonwealth of Australia v John Fairfax & Sons Ltd 147 CLR 39 HC Aus . . . 1028

Commonwealth of Australia v Kerr [1919] SALR 201 . . . 623

Commonwealth of Australia v Verwayen (1990) 170 CLR 394; (1990) 95 ALR 321 . . . 484, 814

Compagnie Commercial Andre v Artibell Shipping Ltd (No 2) [2001] EC 653 OH . . . 839

Compania Colombiana de Seguros v Pacific Steam-Navigation Co (The Colombiana) [1965] 1 QB 101; [1964] 2 WLR 484; [1964] 1 All ER 216; [1963] 2 Ll Rep 479; 108 SJ 75 QBD . . . 534

Compania Naviera General SA v Kerametal Ltd (The Lorna I) [1983] 1 Ll Rep 373; [1982] Com LR 257; (1983) 80 LSG 36 CA . . . 271

Competitive Insurance Co Ltd v Davies Investments Ltd [1975] [1975] 1 WLR 1240; [1975] 3 All ER 254; 119 SJ 559 Ch D . . . 230–1

Condon Ex p James, Re (1873–74) LR 9 Ch App 609; [1874–80] All ER Rep 388 CA . . . 889

Conkey v Bond (1861) 34 Barb 276 . . . 848

Continental C & G Rubber Co Pty Ltd, Re (1919) 27 CLR 194 . . . 272

Continental Caoutchoc & Gutta Percha Co v Kleinwort Sons & Co (1904) 90 TLR 474 . . . 838

Cook, Re [1948] Ch 212; [1948] 1 All ER 231; 64 TLR 97; [1948] LJR 902; 92 SJ 125 Ch D . . . 732

Cook v Lister (1863) 13 CB NS 543 . . . 539

Cooke, Ex p see Strachen Ex p Cooke

Cooper v Phibbs (1867) LR 2 HL 149 HL . . . 706

Cordell v Second Clanfield Properties Ltd [1969] [1969] 2 Ch 9; [1968] 3 WLR 864; [1968] 3 All ER 746; (1968) 19 P & CR 848; 112 SJ 841 Ch D . . . 775

Cornish v Midland Bank Plc [1985] 3 All ER 513; [1985] FLR 298; (1985) 135 NLJ 869 CA . . . 355

Cory Bros & Co Ltd v Owners of the Turkish Steamship Mecca [1897] AC 286 HL . . . 668

Cotman v Brougham [1918] AC 514 HL . . . 373

Cotnam v Wisdom (1907) 32 Ark 601 . . . 102

Cottington v Fletcher (1740) 2 Atk 155 . . . 915

Coultwas v Swan (1870) 18 WR 746 . . . 908

Countrywide Communications Ltd v ICL Pathway Ltd [2000] CLC 324 QBD . . . **343–7**, 355

County of Carleton v City of Ottawa (1965) 52 DLR (2d) 220 Sup Ct Can . . . 75–6, 162, **187–90**, 543

Cowan de Groot Properties Ltd v Eagle Trust Plc [1992] 4 All ER 700; [1991] BCLC 1045 Ch D . . . 231

Cowern v Nield [1912] 2 KB 419 KBD . . . **919–20**, 922

Cox v Prentice (1815) 3 M & S 344 . . . 826, 838

Cox v Smail [1912] VLR 274 . . . 403

Crabb v Arun District Council [1976] Ch 179; [1975] 3 WLR 847; [1975] 3 All ER 865; (1976) 32 P & CR 70; 119 SJ 711 CA . . . 345, 814–16

Craddock Bros Ltd v Hunt [1923] 2 Ch 136 CA . . . 117

Crantrave Ltd (in liquidation) v Lloyds Bank Plc [2000] QB 917; [2000] 3 WLR 877; [2000] 4 All ER 473; [2000] 2 All ER (Comm) 89; [2000] Ll Rep Bank 181; [2000] CLC 1194; [2001] BPIR 57; (2000) 97(20) LSG 42; (2000) 144 SJLB 219 CA . . . **534–8**, 543

Craven Ellis v Canons Ltd [1936] 2 KB 403 CA . . . 89, 335, **336–8**, **356**, 858, 861

Credit Lyonnais Bank Nederland NV v Burch [1997] 1 All ER 144; [1996] 5 Bank LR 233; [1997] CLC 95; [1997] 1 FLR 11; [1997] 2 FCR 1; (1997) 29 HLR 513; (1997) 74 P & CR 384; [1997] Fam Law 168; (1996) 93(32) LSG 33; (1996) 146 NLJ 1421; (1996) 140 SJLB 158; [1996] NPC 99; (1996) 72 P & CR D33 CA . . . **492–3**

Crescendo Management Pty Ltd v Westpac Banking Corp (1989) 63 ALJ 504; (1988) 19 NSWLR 40 CA NSW . . . 28, **420–1**, 424, 431

Cressman v Coys of Kensington (Sales) Ltd [2004] EWCA Civ 47; [2004] 1 WLR 2775; (2004) 101(10) LSG 29; (2004) 148 SJLB 182 CA . . . 1, 71, **77**, 522, 796

Creswell v Potter [1978] 1 WLR 255 Ch D . . . **488–90**, 492

Crichton v Crichton (1895) 13 R 770 . . . 909

Criterion Properties Plc v Stratford UK Properties Plc [2004] UKHL 28; [2004] 1 WLR 1846; [2004] BCC 570; [2006] 1 BCLC 729; (2004) 101(26) LSG 27; (2004) 148 SJLB 760; [2004] NPC 96 HL . . . **236–7**

Cross v Kirkby [2000] TLR 268 CA . . . 800

Crown Dilmun v Sutton [2004] [2004] EWHC 52; [2004] 1 BCLC 468; [2004] WTLR 497; (2004) 101(7) LSG 34 Ch D . . . 995

Crown House Engineering Ltd v Amec Projects Ltd (1990) 48 BLR 32; (1990) 6 Const LJ 141 CA . . . 337

CTN Cash and Carry Ltd v Gallaher Ltd [1994] 4 All ER 714 CA . . . 134, **426–9**, 431

Culverley v Green (1984) 155 CLR 242 . . . 913

Curtis v Perry (1802) 6 Ves 739 . . . 895, 908, 915

Cutler v Wandsworth Stadium Ltd [1949] AC 398; [1949] 1 All ER 544; 65 TLR 170; [1949] LJR 824; 93 SJ 163 HL . . . 501

Cutter v Powell (1795) 6 TR 320 . . . 298, 313–14

CVG Siderurgicia del Orinoco SA v London Steamship Owners Mutual Insurance Association Ltd (The Vainqueur Jose) [1979] 1 Ll Rep 557 QBD . . . 309

D & C Builders Ltd v Rees [1966] 2 QB 617; [1966] 2 WLR 288; [1965] 3 All ER 837; 109 SJ 971 CA . . . 408

Dakin v Oxley (1864) 15 CB NS 646 . . . 306

Daly v Sydney Stock Exchange Ltd (1986) 160 CLR 371 . . . 977

Dane v Viscountess Kirkwall (1838) 8 C & P 679 . . . 615

Daniel v O'Leary (1976) 14 NBR (2d) 564 . . . 958

Daniell v Sinclair (1880–81) LR 6 App Cas 181 PC . . . 216

Daraydon Holdings Ltd v Solland International [2004] EWHC 622 Ch D . . . 930, **1022–6**

Dart Industries Inc v Decor Corp Pty Ltd (1993) 179 CLR 101 HC Aus . . . 971

David Securities Pty Ltd v Commonwealth Bank of Australia (1992) 175 CLR 353 HC Aus . . . 172, 177, 182, 270, 277, 386–8, 390, 766–7, 789, 793–4

Davis Contractors Ltd v Fareham UDC [1956] AC 696; [1956] 3 WLR 37; [1956] 2 All ER 145; 54 LGR 289; 100 SJ 378 HL . . . 422

Davis v Bryan 6 B & C 651 . . . 369, 372, 377–8, 382

Davis v Duke of Marlborough 2 Sw 108 . . . 487

Davis v Johnson [1979] AC 264; [1978] 2 WLR 553; [1978] 1 All ER 1132; 122 SJ 178 HL . . . 1025

Dawson v Linton (1822) 5 B & Ald 521 . . . 511

de Bernardy v Harding (1853) 8 Ex 822 C Ex . . . 100, **280**

De Vitre v Betts (1873) LR 6 HL 319; (1873) 21 WR 705; (1873) 42 LJ Ch 841 HL . . . 948

Deacon v Transport Regulation Board [1958] VR 458 . . . 409

Debtor (No 627 of 1936), Re [1937] Ch 156 CA . . . 512, 514, 517, 542

Decorative Carpets Inc v State Board of Equalization (1962) 373 P 2d 637 . . . 880

Deering v Earl of Winchelsea (1787) 1 Cox Eq Cas 318; (1787) 2 B & P 270 C Ex . . . 542, **551–2**, 777, 914

Deglman v Guaranty Trust Co of Canada and Constantineau [1954] 3 DLR (2d) 785 Sup Ct Can . . . 2–3, **18–19**, 20, 23, 53, 189, 355, 1034

Derry v Peek (1889) LR 14 App Cas 337; (1889) 5 TLR 625 HL . . . 200

Design Progression Ltd v Thurloe Properties Ltd [2004] EWHC 324; [2005] 1 WLR 1; [2004] 2 P & CR 31; [2004] L & TR 25; [2004] 1 EGLR 121; [2004] 10 EGCS 184; (2004) 101(12) LSG 36 Ch D . . . 974

Deutsch Morgan Grenfell Group Plc v Inland Revenue Commissioners [2005] EWCA Civ 78; [2006] 2 WLR 203 CA . . . 183, 639

Dew v Parsons 2 B & Ald 562 . . . 629, 636

Dewar v Dewar [1975] [1975] 1 WLR 1532; [1975] 2 All ER 728; 119 SJ 681 Ch D . . . 900

Dextra Bank & Trust Co Ltd v Bank of Jamaica [2002] 1 All ER (Comm) 193 PC . . . 165–6, 776–7, **779–80**, **781–5**, 789, **824**, 842

Dies v British & International Mining & Finance Corp Ltd [1939] 1 KB 724 KBD . . . 270, **287–91**, 296, 351, 361

Dillon v Baltic Shipping Co (The Mikhail Lermontov) [1991] 2 Ll Rep 155 CA NSW . . . 28, 268

Dimond v Lovell [2002] [2002] 1 AC 384; [2000] 2 WLR 1121; [2000] 2 All ER 897; [2000] RTR 243; [2000] CCLR 57; 2000 Rep LR 62; (2000)

97(22) LSG 47; (2000) 150 NLJ 740 HL . . . 306

Dimskal Shipping Co SA v International Transport Workers Federation (The Evia Luck) (No 2) [1992] 2 AC 152; [1991] 3 WLR 875; [1991] 4 All ER 871; [1992] 1 Ll Rep 115; [1992] ICR 37; [1992] IRLR 78 HL . . . 403, 405, **422–6**, 430–2

Diplock's Estate, Re [1948] Ch 465 (CA) . . . 656–7, **660–7**, 669, 693, 695, 698–9, 709–11, 725–6, 732, 736, 837

Diprose v Louth (No 2) (1990) 54n SASR . . . 485

Director of Prosecutions for Northern Ireland v Lynch [1975] AC 653; [1975] 2 WLR 641; [1975] 1 All ER 913; (1975) 61 Cr App R 6; [1975] Crim LR 707; 119 SJ 233 HL . . . 420, 432

DO Ferguson & Associates v M Sohl (1962) 62 BLR 95 CA . . . **264–7**

Donaldson v Freeson (1934) 51 CLR 598 . . . 914

Donoghue v Stevenson [1932] AC 562; 1932 SC (HL) 31; 1932 SLT 317; [1932] WN 139 HL . . . 1, 59, 632

Doolittle v McCullough 12 Ohio St 360 . . . 281–3

Doughty v Turner Manufacturing Co Ltd [1964] 1 QB 518; [1964] 2 WLR 240; [1964] 1 All ER 98; (1964) 108 SJ 53 CA . . . 1025

Douglass v Hustler Magazine Inc 769 F 2d 1128 (1985) . . . 934

Downshire Settled Estates, Re [1953] Ch 218; [1953] 2 WLR 94; [1953] 1 All ER 103; (1953) 46 R & IT 64; 97 SJ 29 CA . . . 589

Dowson & Mason Ltd v Potter [1986] 1 WLR 1419; [1986] 2 All ER 418; (1986) 83 LSG 3429; (1986) 130 SJ 841 CA . . . 1037

Drane v Evangelou [1978] 1 WLR 455; [1978] 2 All ER 437; (1978) 36 P & CR 270; (1977) 246 EG 137; 121 SJ 793 CA . . . 974

DSND Subsea Ltd (formerly DSND Oceantech Ltd) v Petroleum Geo Services ASA [2000] BLR 530 QBD . . . 410

Dublin City Distillery Ltd v Doherty [1914] AC 823 HL . . . 693–4

Duke of Norfolk's Settlement Trusts, Re [1982] Ch 61; [1981] 3 WLR 455; [1981] 3 All ER 220; 125 SJ 554 CA . . . 588–90

Duomatic Ltd, Re [1969] 2 Ch 365; [1969] 2 WLR 114; [1969] 1 All ER 161; 112 SJ 922 Ch D . . . 858

Durrant v Ecclesiastical Commissioners for England and Wales (1880) 6 QBD 234 Ex Div . . . 36

Dutch v Warren 1 Stra 406 . . . 260, 274

Eadie v Township of Brantford (1967) 63 DLR (2d) 561 . . . 632

Eagle Trust Plc v SBC Securities Ltd [1993] 1 WLR 484; [1992] 4 All ER 488; [1991] BCLC 438 Ch D . . . 231, 234, 788, 836

Eagle Trust Plc v SBC Securities Ltd (No 2) [1995] BCC 231; [1996] 1 BCLC 121 Ch D . . . 231

Earl of Aylesford v Morris (1872–73) LR 8 Ch App 484 CA . . . 487, **494–6**, 618

Earl of Chesterfield v Janseen 2 Ves Sen 125 . . . 494

Earl of Portman v Taylor 4 Sim 182 . . . 487

Earlanger v New Sombrero Phosphate Co (1878) LR 3 App Cas 1218 HL . . . 845–6

East Fifty-Fourth Street (123) Inc v United States of America (1946) 157 F Rep (2d) 68 . . . 872, 877, 880–2

East India Co v Tritton (1824) 3 B & C 280 . . . 831

Eastgate Ex p Ward, Re [1905] 1 KB 465 KBD . . . 692

Edelsten v Edelsten (1863) 1 De GJ & S 185 . . . 970–1

Edgell v Day (1865) LR 1 CP 80 CCP . . . 842

Edmunds v Wallingford (1884–85) LR 14 QBD 811 CA . . . 503, **505–7**, 513, 515, 541

Edwards, Ex p Chapman, Re (1884) 13 QBD 747 . . . 830

Edwards v Lee's Administrator 96 SW 2d 1028 (Kentucky CA 1936) . . . 114, **952–3**

Eid v Al-Kazemi [2004] EWHC 2129 Ch D . . . 479

El Ajou v Dollar Land Holdings Plc [1993] 3 All ER 717; [1993] BCC 698; [1993] BCLC 735 Ch D; [1994] 2 All ER 685; [1994] BCC 143; [1994] 1 BCLC 464; [1993] NPC 165 CA . . . 119–21, 233, 682–3, 723, 744, 788, 836

Electricity Supply Nominees Ltd v Thorn EMI Retail Ltd and British Telecommunications Plc (1992) 63 P & CR 143; [1991] 2 EGLR 46; [1991] 35 EG 114; [1991] EGCS 48 CA . . . 536

Ellis v Goulton [1893] 1 QB 350 CA . . . 842

Emery's Investment Trusts, Re [1959] Ch 410; [1959] 2 WLR 461; [1959] 1 All ER 577; 103 SJ 257 Ch D . . . 909

England v Marsden (1865–66) LR 1 CP 529 CCP . . . 506–7, 513–14

Equiticorp Industries Group Ltd v R. [1998] 2 NZLR 481 . . . 838

Erlanger v New Sombrero Phosphate Co (1877–78) LR 3 App Cas 1218 CA 196, **845–6**, 847, 849, 851–3, 859, 864

Essery v Cowlard (1884) LR 26 Ch D 191 Ch D . . . 253

Esso Petroleum Co Ltd v Mardon [1976] QB 801; [1976] 2 WLR 583; [1976] 2 All ER 5; [1976] 2 Ll Rep 305; 2 BLR 82; 120 SJ 131 CA 355

Esso Petroleum Co Ltd v Niad Ltd [2001] 2 All ER (D) 324 . . . 991–2

Esso Petroleum Ltd v Hall, Russell & Co Ltd (The Esso Bernicia) [1989] AC 643; [1988] 3 WLR 730; [1989] 1 All ER 37; [1989] 1 Ll Rep 8; 1988 SLT 874; (1988) 85(42) LSG 48; (1988) 132 SJ 1459 HL . . . 503, **533–4**, 549

Eurig Estate, Re [1998] 2 SCR 565 Sup Ct Can . . . 53

Euro-Diam Ltd v Bathurst [1990] [1990] 1 QB 1; [1988] 2 WLR 517; [1988] 2 All ER 23; [1988] 1 Ll Rep 228; [1988] FTLR 242; [1988] Fin LR 27; (1988) 85(9) LSG 45; (1988) 132 SJ 372 CA . . . 917

Evans v Bartlam [1937] AC 473; [1937] 2 All ER 646 HL . . . 816

Evans v Llewellin 1 Cox 333 . . . 487

Ewbank v Nutting (1849) 7 CB 797 . . . 575

Exall v Partridge (1799) 8 TR 308 KBD . . . 101, 503, **504–7**, 513–14, 527, 540–1, 548

Experience Hendrix LLC v PPX Enterprises Inc [2003] EWCA Civ 323; [2003] 1 All ER (Comm) 830; [2003] EMLR 25; [2003] FSR 46; (2003) 26(7) IPD 26046; (2003) 100(22) LSG 29; (2003) 147 SJLB 509 CA . . . 937, **990–4**, 996

F (Mental Patient: Sterilisation), Re [1990] 2 AC 1; [1989] 2 WLR 1025; [1989] 2 All ER 545; [1989] 2 FLR 376; (1989) 139 NLJ 789; (1989) 133 SJ 785 HL . . . 575–6, 583

F v West Berkshire HA see F (Mental Patient: Sterilisation), Re

Fairbanks v Snow (1887) 13 NE 596 . . . 400, 402

Fairhurst v Griffiths Fairhurst v Griffiths Unreported – Isle of Man 4 May 1989 . . . 753

Falcke v Scottish Imperial Insurance Co (1886) LR 34 Ch D 234 CA . . . 536, 560, **562–5**, 573, 587

Farnum v Kennebec Water Dist (CCA) 170 F 173 . . . 281

Favor v State Board of Equalization (1974) 527 P 2d 1153 . . . 881

Federal Power Commission v Hope Natural Gas Co 329 US 591 (1944) . . . 1 03

Federal Sugar Refining Co v United States Sugar Equalization Board 268 F 575 (1920) . . . 953, 976, 1001

Ferret v Hill (1854) 15 CB 207 . . . 898–9

Fibrosa Spolka Akcyjna v Fairbairn Lawson Combe Barbour Ltd [1943] AC 32; [1942] 2 All ER 122; (1942) 73 Ll L Rep 45; 144 ALR 1298 HL . . . 1, **12–18**, 21, 29, 40, 126, 189, 251, 269, 271–3, 275–6, 296-7 , 307, 314, 317, 325, 359, 363–4, 366–8, 371–2, 378, 381, 385, 854

First National Bank Plc v Thompson [1996] Ch 231; [1996] 2 WLR 293; [1996] 1 All ER 140; [1996] 5 Bank LR 113; (1996) 72 P & CR 118; (1995) 92(28) LSG 30; (1995) 139 SJLB 189; [1995] NPC 130; (1996) 71 P & CR D14 CA . . . 816

Fitzpatrick v M'Glone [1897] 2 IR 542 . . . 826

Flood v Irish Provident Assurance Co 46 Ir LT 214; [1912] 2 Ch 597 CA . . . 6, 8, 365

Flower v Sadler (1882) 10 QBD 572 CA . . . 441

Foley v Hill (1848) 2 HL Cas 28 . . . 840

Foran v White (1989) 64 ALJR 1 . . . 95

Forman & Co Pty Ltd v The Liddesdale [1900] AC 190 PC . . . 305

Foskett v McKeown [2001] 1 AC 102; [2000] 2 WLR 1299; [2000] 3 All ER 97; [2000] Ll Rep IR 627; [2000] WTLR 667; (1999–2000) 2 ITELR 711; (2000) 97(23) LSG 44 HL . . . 114, 647–8, **678–87**, 706

Foster v Driscoll [1929] 1 KB 470; [1928] All ER Rep 130 CA . . . 799

Foster v Roberts 29 Beav 467 . . . 487

Fostif Pty Ltd v Campbells Cash & Carry Pty Ltd (2005) 218 ALR 1662 . . . 54

Foxton v Manchester and Liverpool District banking Co (1881) 44 LT 406 . . . 838–9

French Marine v Compagnie Napolitaine d'Eclairage et de Chauffage par le Gaz [1921] 2 AC 494; (1921) 8 Ll L Rep 345 HL . . . 123–4

Friends' Provident Life Office v Hillier Parker May & Fowden (A Firm) [1997] QB 85; [1996] 2 WLR 123; [1995] 4 All ER 260; [1995] CLC 592; (1996) 71 P & CR 286; [1995] EGCS 64; [1995] NPC 63 CA . . . 521–2, 877

Fry, Re (1889) LR 40 Ch D 312 Ch D . . . 483

Fry v Lane (1889) LR 40 Ch D 312 Ch D . . . 483, **486–8**, 487–90, 492, 619

Fung Kai Su v Chan Fui Hing [1951] AC 489; [1951] 2 TLR 47; 95 SJ 431 PC . . . 806

Fyffes Group Ltd v Templeman [2000] 2 Ll Rep 643; (2000) 97(25) LSG 40 QBD . . . 1025

Gafford v Graham (1999) 77 P & CR 73; [1999] 3 EGLR 75; [1999] 41 EG 159; (1999) 96(40) LSG 44; (1998) 95(21) LSG 36; (1998) 142 SJLB 155; [1998] NPC 66; (1998) 76 P & CR D18 CA . . . 997

Gamerco SA v ICM/Fair Warning (Agency) Ltd [1995] 1 WLR 1226; [1995] CLC 536; [1995] EMLR 263 QBD . . . 326, **327–8**

Garland v Consumers' Gas Co [2004] SCC 25 Sup Ct Can . . . **139–42**, 799, 804

Garriock v Walker (1873) 1 R 100 . . . 578

Gascoigne v Gascoigne [1918] 1 KB 223 KBD . . . 900, 909

Gebhardt v Saunders [1892] 2 QB 452 QBD . . . 503, **508–10**, 530, 541

GEC Marconi Systems Pty Ltd v BHP Information Technology Pty Ltd (2003) 128 FCR 1 . . . 284

Ghana Commercial Bank v Chandiram [1960]
AC 732; [1960] 3 WLR 328; [1960] 2 All ER
865; 104 SJ 583 PC . . . 192–3, 724

Gilbert & Partners v Knight [1968] 2 All ER 248;
(1968) 112 SJ 155 CA . . . 394

Giles v Edwards (1797) 7 Term Rep 181 KB . . .
257–8, 274

Gillett v Peppercorne 3 Beav 78 . . . 848

Gillette UK Ltd v Edenwest Ltd [1994] RPC 279
Ch D . . . 971

Gissing v Gissing [1971] AC 886; [1970]
3 WLR 255; [1970] 2 All ER 780; (1970)
21 P & CR 702; 114 SJ 550 HL . . . 899

Goldcorp Exchange Ltd (in receivership),
Re [1995] 1 AC 74; [1994] 3 WLR 199; [1994]
2 All ER 806; [1994] 2 BCLC 578; [1994] CLC
591; (1994) 13 Tr LR 434; (1994) 91(24) LSG
46; (1994) 144 NLJ 792; (1994) 138 SJLB 127
PC . . . 656, **689–96**, 697–9, 733, 759

Golightly v Reynolds (1772) Lofft 88 . . . 81

Gondall v Dillon Newspapers Ltd [2001] RLR 221
CA . . . 966

Goodey and Southwold Trawlers v Garriock,
Mason and Millgate [1972] 2 Ll Rep 369 QBD
. . . 842

Goring, The [1988] AC 831; [1988] 2 WLR 460;
[1988] 1 All ER 641; [1988] 1 Ll Rep 397;
[1988] FTLR 524; (1988) 85(14) LSG 50;
(1988) 138 NLJ Rep 61; (1988) 132 SJ 334 HL
. . . 569, **570–3**, 575

Gorog v Kiss (1977) 78 DLR (3d) 690 . . . 902

Goss v Chilcott [1996] A.C. 788; [1996] 3 WLR
180; [1997] 2 All ER 110; (1996) 93(22) LSG
26; (1996) 140 SJLB 176; [1996] NPC 93 PC
. . . 267, 277, 349, 372, **384–7**, 784, 843

Gowers v Lloyds and National Provincial Foreign
Bank Ltd [1938] 1 All ER 766 CA . . . 623,
826–7, 838

Grant v Edwards [1986] Ch 638; [1986] 3 WLR
114; [1986] 2 All ER 426; [1987] 1 FLR 87;
[1986] Fam Law 300; (1986) 83 LSG 1996;
(1986) 136 NLJ 439; (1986) 130 SJ 408 CA . . .
899

Gray v Johnston (1868) LR 3 HL 1 HL . . . 838

Great Berlin Steamboat Co, Re (1884) LR 26 Ch
D 616 CA . . . 895, 908

Great Northern Railway Co v Swaffield (1873–74)
LR 9 Ex 132 Ex Ct . . . 560, 565, 574, 578, **584**

Great Peace Shipping Ltd v Tsavliris Salvage
(International) Ltd [2002] EWCA Civ 1407;
[2003] QB 679; [2002] 3 WLR 1617; [2002]
4 All ER 689; [2002] 2 All ER (Comm) 999;
[2002] 2 Ll Rep 653; [2003] 2 CLC 16; (2002)
99(43) LSG 34; (2002) 152 NLJ 1616; [2002]
NPC 127 CA . . . 195, 327

Great Western Railway Co v Sutton (1869–70)
LR 4 HL 226 HL . . . 628

Green v Portsmouth Stadium Ltd [1953] [1953]
2 QB 190; [1953] 2 WLR 1206; [1953] 2 All ER
102; 97 SJ 386 CA . . . **500–1**, 888–9

Greenmast Shipping Co SA v Jean Lion et Cie SA
(The Saronikos) [1986] 2 Ll Rep 277 QBD . . .
362

Greenwood v Bennett [1973] QB 195; [1972]
3 WLR 691; [1972] 3 All ER 586; [1972] RTR
535; 116 SJ 762 CA . . . 72, **107–9**, 187

Greenwood v Martins Bank Ltd [1932] 1 KB 371
CA . . . 806–8, 817

Greeves v West India & Pacific Steamship Co Ltd
(1870) 22 LT 6152 . . . 71

Greville v Da Costa 170 ER 213; (1797) Peake
Add Cas 113 . . . 274

Groves v Groves (1829) 3 Y & J 163 . . . 895–6,
908

Groves v John Wunder Co 286 NW 235 (1939)
. . . 999

Grundt v Great Boulder Gold Mines Pty Ltd
(1939) 59 CLR 641 . . . 623, 813, 820

Guardian Ocean Cargoes v Banco de Brazil SA
[1991] 2 Ll Rep 68 QBD8 . . . 42

Guinness Mahon & Co Ltd v Kensington and
Chelsea RLBC [1999] QB 215; [1998] 3 WLR
829; [1998] 2 All ER 272; [1998] Ll Rep Bank
109; [1998] CLC 662; (1998) 95(13) LSG 28;
(1998) 148 NLJ 366; (1998) 142 SJLB 92 CA
. . . 134, 183, 253, 308, **369–83**

Guinness Plc v Saunders [1990] 2 AC 663; [1990]
2 WLR 324; [1990] 1 All ER 652; [1990] BCC
205; [1990] BCLC 402; (1990) 87(9) LSG 42;
(1990) 134 SJ 457 HL . . . 219, 358, 856,
857–61, 1012

Guppys (Bridport) Ltd v Brooking and James
(1984) 14 HLR 1; (1984) 269 EG 846 CA . . .
974

Gwilliam v Twist [1895] 2 QB 84 CA . . . 574

Haigh v Kaye (1871–72) LR 7 Ch App 469 CA . . .
895–6, 901

Hain Steamship Co Ltd v Tate & Lyle Ltd (1934)
49 Ll L Rep 123; 50 TLR 415; 39 Com Cas 259;
151 LT 249 CA . . . **299**, 311–13

Hain Steamship Co Ltd v Tate & Lyle Ltd [1936]
2 All ER 597; (1936) 55 Ll L Rep 159; 52 TLR
617; 41 Com Cas 350; [1936] WN 210 HL . . .
299, 305, 311

Halifax Building Society v Thomas [1996] Ch
217; [1996] 2 WLR 63; [1995] 4 All ER 673;
[1995] NPC 112 CA . . . **974–7**, 1025

Hall & Barker, Re (1878) LR 9 Ch D 538 Ch D . . .
268

Hallett's Estate, Re (1879–80) LR 13 Ch D 696 CA
. . . 174, 206–7, 209, 657, 659, 662–3, **672–6**,
678, 685, 688–9, 701, 703, 710, 723

Hambly v Trott (1776) 1 Cowp 372; 98 ER 1136 ... 113, 950, 952

Hammond v Osborn [2002] EWCA Civ 885; [2002] WTLR 1125; (2002) 99(34) LSG 29; (2002) 146 SJLB 176; [2002] 2 P & CR DG20 CA ... 479

Harbet's (Sir William) Case 2 Co 11 ... 552

Harris v Jenkins (1922) 31 CLR 341 ... 483

Hart v EP Dutton & Co Inc 93 NYS 2d 871 (1949) ... 953

Hart v O'Connor [1985] AC 1000; [1985] 3 WLR 214; [1985] 2 All ER 880; [1985] 1 NZLR 159; (1985) 82 LSG 2658; (1985) 129 SJ 484 PC ... 447, 486, 491, **612–19**

Hastelow v Jackson 8 B & C 221 ... 599

Hastingwood Property Ltd v Saunders Bearman Anselm [1991] Ch. 114; [1990] 3 WLR 623; (1990) 140 NLJ 817; (1990) 134 SJ 1153 Ch D ... 843

Hawtayne v Bourne (1841) 10 LJ Ex 224; 5 Jur 118; 7 M & W 595 ... 574

Haygarth v Wearning (1871) LR 12 Eq 320 Ct Ch ... 487

Hazell v Hammersmith and Fulham LBC [1992] 2 AC 1 [1991] 2 WLR 372; [1991] 1 All ER 545; 89 LGR 271; (1991) 3 Admin LR 549; [1991] RVR 28; (1991) 155 JPN 527; (1991) 155 LG Rev 527; (1991) 88(8) LSG 36; (1991) 141 NLJ 127 HL ... 167–9, 173, 178, 182, 308, 373, 727

Healing Research Trustee Co Ltd, Re [1992] 2 All ER 481; [1991] BCLC 716; [1992] 2 EGLR 231 Ch D ... 508

Hedley Byrne & Co Ltd v Heller & Partners Ltd [1964] AC 465; [1963] 3 WLR 101; [1963] 2 All ER 575; [1963] 1 Ll Rep 485; 107 SJ 454 HL ... 200

Henderson v Folkestone waterworks Co (1885) 1 TLR 329 ... 628

Henderson v Merrett Syndicates Ltd (No 1) [1995] 2 AC 145; [1994] 3 WLR 761; [1994] 3 All ER 506; [1994] 2 Ll Rep 468; [1994] CLC 918; (1994) 144 NLJ 1204 HL ... 285

Herman v Charlesworth [1905] 2 KB 123 CA ... 501, 604

Heywood v Wellers (A Firm) [1976] QB 446; [1976] 2 WLR 101; [1976] 1 All ER 300; [1976] 2 Ll Rep 88; (1975) 120 SJ 9 CA ... 272, 275–6

Hicks v Hicks (1802) 3 East 16 ... 366

Hill v van Erp (1997) 188 CLR 159; (1997) 71 ALJR 487 HC Aus ... 117, 119

Hillsdown Holdings Plc v Pensions Ombudsman [1997] 1 All ER 862; [1996] OPLR 291 QBD ... 231

Hirachand Punamchand v Temple [1911] 2 KB 330 CA ... 539, 543–6

Hirt v Hahn (1876) 61 Missouri 496 ... 265

Hoare's Case (1862) 2 John & H 441; 70 ER 1041 ... 367

Hobbs v Marlowe [1978] AC 16; [1977] 2 WLR 777; [1977] 2 All ER 241; [1977] RTR 253; 121 SJ 272 HL ... 192, 715

Hobourn Aero Components Ltd's Air-Raid Distress Fund, Re [1946] Ch 86 Ch D ... 668

Hodgson v Marks [1971] Ch 892; [1971] 2 WLR 1263; [1971] 2 All ER 684; (1971) 22 P & CR 586; 115 SJ 224 CA ... 756

Hodgson v Sham (1834) 3 My & K 183 ... 540

Hoenig v Isaacs [1952] 2 All ER 176; [1952] 1 TLR 1360 CA ... 269, 298, 306

Hogg v Kirby 8 Ves 215 ... 983

Holiday v Sigil (1826) 2 C & P 176 KB ... 203, **204**, 243

Holland Hannen & Cubitts (Northern) Ltd v Welsh Health Technical Services Organisation (1981) 18 Build LR 80 ... 305

Holland v Manchester and Liverpool District Banking Co (1904) 14 Com Cas 241 ... 840

Holland v Russell (1861) 1 B & S 424 Ex Ct ... 826–7, 829, 837–8

Holman v Johnson (1775) 1 Cowp 341; 98 ER 1120 ... 798, 892, 896–7, 901, 910, 916–17

Holmes v Hall (1841) 9 M & W (1704) Holt 36 ... 15, 274

Holt v Markham [1923] 1 KB 504 CA ... 21, 167, 220, 623, 806–7, 809–10, 812, 817–18, 840

Home v Smith 27 Ch D 89 ... 255

Hooper and Grass' Contract, Re [1949] VLR 369 ... 407

Hooper v Mayor and Corporation of Exeter (1887) 56 LJQB 457 ... 625, 629–30

Hopper v Burness (1876) 1 CPD 137 ... 311

Horsford v Bird [2006] UKPC 3; [2006] 1 EGLR 75; [2006] 15 EG 136; (2006) 22 Const LJ 187; (2006) 103(6) LSG 34 PC ... 966

Horton v Jones (1934) 34 SR (NSW) 359 ... 100

Hospital Products Ltd v United States Surgical Corp (1984) 156 CLR 41 ... 989

Howard v Wood (1678) 2 Lev 245; 83 ER 530 ... 116

Howe v Smith (1884) LR 27 Ch D 89 CA ... 308

Hughes v Liverpool Victoria Legal Friendly Society [1916] 2 KB 482 CA ... 886–7

Huguenin v Baseley (1807) 14 Ves Jr 273 ... 451–2, 481

Hunt v Silk (1804) 5 East 449 KB ... **257–8**, 262–3, 269, 845, 850–1, 853

Hunter Engineering Co v Syncrude Canada Ltd 57 DLR (4th) ... 321, 1034–5

Hunter v Prinsep 10 East 378 ... 943

Hunter v Shell Oil Co 198 F 2d 485 (5th Cir 1952) ... 1000

Hurstwood Developments Ltd v Motor & General & Andersley & Co Insurance Services Ltd [2001] EWCA Civ 1785; [2002] Ll Rep IR

185; [2002] Ll Rep PN 195; [2002] PNLR 10
CA . . . 522

Hussey v Eels [1990] 2 QB 227; [1990] 2 WLR
234; [1990] 1 All ER 449; [1990] 19 EG 77;
[1989] EGCS 168; (1990) 140 NLJ 53 CA . . .
876

Huyton SA v Peter Cremer GmbH & Co [1999]
1 Ll Rep 620; [1999] CLC 230 QBD . . .
429–33

Hydro Electric Commission of the Township of
Nepean v Ontario Hydro (1982) 132 DLR (3d)
193; [1982] 1 SCR 347 CA Can . . . 172, 633

Hyundai Heavy Industries Co Ltd v
Papadopoulos [1980] 1 WLR 1129; [1980]
2 All ER 29; [1980] 2 Ll Rep 1; 124 SJ 592 HL
. . . 271, 289–92, 295

Hyundai Shipbuilding & Heavy Industries Co Ltd
v Pournaras [1978] 2 Ll Rep 502 CA . . . 271

Ibmac Ltd v Marshall (Homes) Ltd (1968) 208
EG 851 CA . . . 305

Imperial Loan Co Ltd v St1 [1892] 1 QB 599 CA
. . . 614, 616–17

India v India Steamship Co Ltd (The Indian
Endurance and The Indian Grace) (No 2)
[1998] AC 878; [1997] 3 WLR 818; [1997] 4 All
ER 380; [1998] 1 Ll Rep 1; [1997] CLC 1581;
[1998] ILP 511; (1997) 94(43) LSG 29; (1997)
147 NLJ 1581; (1997) 141 SJLB 230 HL . . .
816–17

Inland Revenue Commissioners v Hambrook
[1956] 2 QB 641; [1956] 3 WLR 643; [1956]
3 All ER 338; 57 ALR 2d 790; 100 SJ 632 CA
. . . 529

International Sales and Agencies Ltd v Marcus
[1982] 3 All ER 551; [1982] 2 CMLR 46 QBD
. . . 233, 836

Inverugie Investments v Hackett [1995] 1 WLR
713; [1995] 3 All ER 841; [1996] 1 EGLR 149;
[1996] 19 EG 124; [1995] EGCS 37; [1995]
NPC 36; (1995) 69 P & CR D48 PC . . . 966–7

Island Records Ltd v Tring International Plc
[1996] 1 WLR 1256; [1995] 3 All ER 444;
[1995] FSR 560 Ch D . . . 948

J Lauritzen AS v Wijsmuller BV (The Super
Servant 2) [1990] 1 Ll Rep 1 CA . . . 332

J Leslie Engineers Co Ltd (In Liquidation), Re
[1976] 1 WLR 292; [1976] 2 All ER 85; 120 SJ
146 Ch D . . . 239

Jackson v Harrison (1978) 138 CLR 438 . . . 918

Jacob v Allen (1703) 1 Salk 27; 91 ER 26 . . . 116

Jagan v Vivian (1871) LR 6 Ch App 742 . . . 982

Jaggard v Sawyer [1995] 1 WLR 269; [1995] 2 All
ER 189; [1995] 1 EGLR 146; [1995] 13 EG 132;
[1994] EGCS 139; [1994] NPC 116 CA 930,
967–9, 981, 984, 986, 990–1

James Ex p (1803) 8 Ves 337 . . . 1004, 1006

James Roscoe (Bolton) Ltd v Winder [1915]
1 Ch 62 Ch D . . . **687–9**, 694, 696,
698–700

James v Thomas H Kent & Co Ltd [1951] 1 KB
551; [1950] 2 All ER 1099; [1951] 1 TLR 552;
95 SJ 29 CA . . . 23

Jebara v Ottoman Bank [1927] 2 KB 254; (1927)
27 Ll L Rep 294 CA . . . 575

Jenkins v Tucker (1788) 1 Hy Bl 90 CCP . . . 560,
565–7, 569

Jennings and Chapman v Woodman, Matthews &
Co [1952] 2 TLR 409; 96 SJ 561 CA . . . 339,
351

Jestons v Brooke (1778) 2 Cowp 793 . . . 21

John Loudon & Co v Elder's Curator Bonis
(1922) 13 Ll L Rep 500; 1923 SLT 226 OH . . .
620

Johnson v Agnew [1980] AC 367; [1979] 2 WLR
487; [1979] 1 All ER 883; (1979) 38 P & CR
424; (1979) 251 EG 1167; 123 SJ 217 HL . . .
258, 285–6, 957

Johnson v Buttress (1936) 56 CLR 113 . . . 456,
481

Johnson v Gore Wood & Co (No 1) [2002] 2 AC
1; [2001] 2 WLR 72; [2001] 1 All ER 481;
[2001] CPLR 49; [2001] BCC 820; [2001]
1 BCLC 313; [2001] PNLR 18; (2001) 98(1)
LSG 24; (2001) 98(8) LSG 46; (2000) 150 NLJ
1889; (2001) 145 SJLB 29 HL . . . 820

Johnson v Royal Mail Steam Packet Co (1867–68)
LR 3 CP 38 CCP . . . 505–6, 541

Johnson v The King [1904] AC 817 PC . . . 742

Johnsons Tyne Foundry Pty Ltd v Maffra Corp
(1948) 77 CLR 544 . . . 27

Jones, Re 18 ChD 118 . . . 922

Jones v Merionethshire Permanent Benefit
Building Society [1892] 1 Ch 173 CA . . . 441

Jorden v Money (1854) 5 HL Cas 185; [1843–60]
All ER Rep 350 . . . 817

Joseph Thorley Ltd v Orchis Steamship Co Ltd
[1907] 1 KB 660 CA . . . 310–12

Juliana (The) (1822) 2 Dods 504 . . . 915

Kahler v Midland Bank Ltd [1950] AC 24; [1949]
2 All ER 621; 65 TLR 663; [1949] LJR 1687 HL
. . . 799

Kahn v Permayer [2001] BPIR 95 CA . . . 110,
128–30

Kaufman v Gerson [1904] 1 KB 591 CA . . .
441–2, 445

Kayford Ltd (in liquidation), Re [1975] 1 WLR
279; [1975] 1 All ER 604; (1974) 118 SJ 752 Ch
D . . . 690

Kearley v Thomson (1890) LR 24 QBD 74 CA . . .
600–1, 602–6, 911

Keech v Sandford (1726) 25 ER 223; (1726) Sel
Cas Ch 61 . . . 747, 935, 1000, 1003–5, 1019–20

Kelly v Solari (1841) 9 M & W 54 C Ex . . . 15, **147–9**, 154, 157–8, 162, 167, 171, 215–16, 242, 351, 382, 784, 810, 836

Kennedy v Panama, New Zealand and Australian Royal Mail Co (1866–67) LR 2 QB 580 QB . . . 198

Kenya Railways v Antares Co Pte Ltd (The Antares) (No 1) [1987] 1 Ll Rep 424 CA . . . 312

Kerrison v Glyn, Mills, Currie & Co (1912) 17 Com Cas 41 . . . 152, 155–8, 790, 838

Kettlewell v Refuge Assurance Co [1908] 1 KB 545 CA . . . 887

King Construction Co v WM Smith Electric Co (1961) 350 SW 2d 940 . . . 408

King, Re Ex p Unity Joint Stock Mutual Banking Association 3 De G & J 63 . . . 923

King v Leith (1787) 2 Term Rep 141 . . . 945

King v Victoria Insurance Co Ltd [1896] AC 250 PC . . . 717

Kiriri Cotton Co Ltd v Dewani [1960] AC 192; [1960] 2 WLR 127; [1960] 1 All ER 177; 104 SJ 49 PC . . . 501, 884, 888

Kish v Taylor [1912] AC 604 HL . . . 310

KL Tractors, Re (1961) 106 CLR 318 . . . 622

Kleinwort Benson Ltd v Birmingham City Council [1997] QB 380; [1996] 3 WLR 1139; [1996] 4 All ER 733; [1996] CLC 1791 CA . . . 2, 113–14, 116, 642, **870–9**

Kleinwort Benson Ltd v Lincoln City Council [1999] 2 AC 349; [1998] 3 WLR 1095; [1998] 4 All ER 513; [1998] Ll Rep Bank 387; [1999] CLC 332; (1999) 1 LGLR 148; (1999) 11 Admin LR 130; [1998] RVR 315; (1998) 148 NLJ 1674; (1998) 142 SJLB 279; [1998] NPC 145 HL . . . 1, 134–5, 138, 147, 161, 164, **167–87**, 184–5, 394, 639, 643, 767, 789, 793, 796, 836

Kleinwort Benson Ltd v Sandwell BC [1996] AC 669; [1996] 2 WLR 802; [1996] 2 All ER 961; [1996] 5 Bank LR 341; [1996] CLC 990; 95 LGR 1; (1996) 160 JP Rep 1130; (1996) 146 NLJ 877; (1996) 140 SJLB 136 HL . . . 363, 369, 377, 890–1

Kleinwort Benson Ltd v South Tyneside MBC [1994] 4 All ER 972 QBD . . . 770, 777, 818, 845, 873–5

Kleinwort Benson Ltd v Vaughan [1996] CLC 620; [1995] NPC 195 CA . . . 505

Kleinwort, Sons & Co v Dunlop Rubber Co (1907) 97 LT 263 . . . 154–5, 158, 826–7, 838

Knatchbull v Hallett see Hallett's Estate, Re

Knibbs v Hall 1 Esp 84 . . . 404

Knutson v Bourkes Syndicate [1941] 2 DLR 593 . . . 407

Kooratang Nominees Pty Ltd v Austalia and New Zealand Banking Group Ltd [1998] 3 VR 16 . . . 838

Krell v Henry [1903] 2 KB 740 CA . . . 14

Kuwait Airways Corp v Iraqi Airways Co (Nos 4 and 5) [2002] UKHL 19; [2002] AC 883 HL . . . 804, 963–4, 990

LAC Minerals Ltd v International Corona Resources Ltd [1990] FSR 441 Sup Ct Can . . . 749–50, 930, **1031–6**

Lady Hood of Avalon v MacKinnon [1909] 1 Ch 476 Ch D . . . 161, 753

Lagunas Nitrate Co v Lagunas Syndicate [1899] 2 Ch 392 CA . . . 849, 851, 853–4

Lake v Bayliss [1974] 1 WLR 1073; [1974] 2 All ER 1114; (1974) 28 P & CR 209; 118 SJ 532 Ch D . . . 986

Lamine v Dorrell (1701) 2 Ld Ray 1216 . . . 947, 949

Lampleigh v Brathwait (1615) Hobart 105; 80 ER 255 KB . . . 524

Lamplugh Iron Ore Co Ltd, Re [1927] 1 Ch 208 Ch D . . . 518

Land Hessen v Gray and Gerrish Unreported 31 July 1998 QBD . . . **531–2**

Lane v O'Brien Homes Ltd [2004] EWHC 303 QBD . . . 989

Lankshear v ANZ Banking Group [1993] 1 NZLR 481 . . . 839

Lansdowne (Marquis of) v Dowager of Lansdowne 1 Madd 116 . . . 950

Larner v London County Council [1949] 2 KB 683; [1949] 1 All ER 964; 65 TLR 316; 113 JP 300; 47 LGR 533; [1949] LJR 1363; 93 SJ 371 CA . . . 159, 161

Law Society of Upper Canada v Toronto-Dominion Bank (1998) 169 DLR (4th) 353; (1998) 42 OR (3d) 257 CA Ont . . . 699

Leduc v Ward (1888) LR 20 QBD 475 CA . . . 310

Leeds Industrial Co-operative Society Ltd v Slack [1924] AC 851; [1924] All ER Rep 264 HL . . . 980

Lep Air Services Ltd v Rolloswin Investments Ltd [1973] AC 331; [1972] 2 WLR 1175; [1972] 2 All ER 393; 116 SJ 372 HL . . . 285–6

Les Fils de Jules Bianco SA v Directeur General des Douanes et Droits Indirects (C-331/85) [1988] ECR 1099; [1989] 3 CMLR 36 ECJ . . . 872–3, 877

Leuty v Hillas (1858) 2 De G & J 110 . . . 117

Lever v Goodwin (1887) 36 Ch D 1 . . . 984

Lindon v Hooper 1 Cowp 414 . . . 404

Linz v Electric Wire Co of Palestine Ltd [1948] AC 371; [1948] 1 All ER 604; [1948] LJR 1836; 92 SJ 308 PC . . . 366, 380, 382

Lipkin Gorman v Karpnale Ltd [1989] 1 WLR 1340; [1992] 4 All ER 409; [1989] BCLC 756; [1989] Fin LR 137; (1990) 87(4) LSG 40; (1989) 139 NLJ 76; (1990) 134 SJ 234 CA; [1991] 2 AC 548; [1991] 3 WLR 10;

[1992] 4 All ER 512; (1991) 88(26) LSG 31; (1991) 141 NLJ 815; (1991) 135 SJLB 36 HL . . . 1, 8, **28–39**, 40, 71, 83, 119, 121, 134, 144, 162, 164, 171, 203, 209, 218, **219–24**, 235, 239–45, 366–7, 555, 648–9, **651**, 653–5, 701, 721, 743, 761–2, **763–5**, 766–7, 770, 776, 781–3, 785, 787–9, 792–3, 797, 800–1, 804, 811, 818, **822–3**, 837–8, 843, 875, 878

Lister & Co v Stubbs (1890) LR 45 Ch D 1 CA . . . 976–7, 1020–2, 1024–5

Lister v Hodgson (1867) LR 4 Eq 30 Ct Ch . . . 119

Livingstone v Raywards Coal Co (1880) 5 App Cas 25 HL . . . 982

Lloyds Bank Ltd v Brooks (1950) 6 Legal Decisions Affecting Bankers 161 . . . 807, 810, 817, 840

Lloyds Bank Ltd v Bundy [1975] [1975] QB 326; [1974] 3 WLR 501; [1974] 3 All ER 757; [1974] 2 Ll Rep 366; 118 SJ 714 CA . . . 493, 496–8

Lloyds Bank Plc v Independent Insurance Co Ltd [2000] QB 110; [1999] 2 WLR 986; [1999] 1 All ER (Comm.) 8; [1999] Ll Rep Bank 1; [1999] CLC 510; (1999) 96(3) LSG 31 CA . . . 121, 161–2, **163–5**, 761

Lloyds Bank Plc v Rosset [1991] 1 AC 107; [1990] 2 WLR 867; [1990] 1 All ER 1111; [1990] 2 FLR 155; (1990) 22 HLR 349; (1990) 60 P & CR 311; (1990) 140 NLJ 478 HL . . . 899

Lobb (Alec) Garages Ltd v Total Oil (Great Britain) Ltd [1983] 1 WLR 87; [1983] 1 All ER 944; (1983) 133 NLJ 401; 126 SJ 768 Ch D . . . 429, 490, 493, **495–8**

Lobb (Alec) Garages Ltd v Total Oil (Great Britain) Ltd [1985] 1 WLR 173; [1985] 1 All ER 303; [1985] 1 EGLR 33; (1985) 273 EG 659; (1985) 82 LSG 45; (1985) 129 SJ 83 CA . . . 490, **495–8**

Lobb v Vasey Housing Auxiliary (War Widows Guild) [1963] VR 239 . . . 328–9

Lodder v Slowey (1902) 20 NZLR 321 CA NZ; affd [2004] AC 442 PC . . . 90, 100, 284, 286

Lodge v National Union Investment Co Ltd [1907] 1 Ch 300 Ch D . . . 500

London and North Western Railway v Duerden (1916) 32 TLR 315 . . . 574

London and River Plate Bank Ltd v Bank of Liverpool Ltd [1896] 1 QB 7 QBD . . . 36

London Assurance Co v Sainsbury (1873) 2 Doug 245 . . . 716

London County Commercial Reinsurance Office Ltd, Re [1922] 2 Ch 67; (1922) 10 Ll L Rep 370 Ch D . . . 308

London Joint Stock Bank Ltd v Macmillan [1918] AC 777 HL . . . 815–16

London Wine Co (Shippers) Ltd, Re [1986] PCC 122 CA . . . 690

Lord Napier and Ettrick v Hunter [1993] AC 713; [1993] 2 WLR 42; [1993] 1 All ER 385; [1993] 1 Ll Rep 197; (1993) 137 SJLB 44 HL . . . 192, 695, 706, **712–20**, 732, 744

Louth v Diprose (1992) 175 CLR 621 HC Aus . . . 28, 448, **480–5**, 706, 755

Low v Bouverie [1891] 3 Ch 82 CA . . . 815

Lucky Homes Inc v Tarrant Savings Association 379 SW 2d 386 (1964) . . . 103

Lupton v White (1808) 15 Ves Jr 432 . . . 676

Lysaght v Pearson Times 3 March 1879 . . . 298

Macadam, Re [1946] Ch 73; [1945] 2 All ER 664 Ch D . . . 860

McCormick v Grogan (1869) LR 4 HL 82 HL . . . 738, 745–6

McDonald v Coys of Kensington Holdings Ltd [2004] EWCA Civ 47; [2004] 1 WLR 2775; (2004) 101(10) LSG 29; (2004) 148 SJLB 182 CA . . . 72

McDonald v Dennys Lascelles Ltd (1933) 48 CLR 457 . . . 270, 273, 290–2, 296

McDonald v Horn [1995] [1995] 1 All ER 961; [1995] ICR 685; [1994] Pens LR 155; (1994) 144 NLJ 1515 CA . . . 590

McEvoy v Belfast Banking Co Ltd [1935] AC 24; [1934] NI 67 HL . . . 900, 909

Mackenzie v Royal Bank of Canada [1934] AC 468 PC . . . 848

Macklin v Dowsett [2004] EWCA Civ 904; [2004] 2 EGLR 75; [2004] 34 EG 68; [2005] WTLR 1561; [2004] 26 EGCS 193 CA . . . 479

McLaughlin v Daily Telegraph Newspaper Co Ltd (No 2) (1904) 1 CLR 243 . . . 616–17

Macmillan Inc v Bishopsgate Investment Trust (No 3) [1996] 1 WLR 387; [1996] 1 All ER 585; [1996] BCC 453; (1995) 139 SJLB 225 CA . . . 45, 225, 705, 838

Macmillan v Singh 769 F 2d 1128 . . . 934

McRae v Commonwealth Disposals Commission (1951) 84 CLR 377 . . . 275

Maddison v Alderson (1883) LR 8 App Cas 467 HL . . . 777

Mahesan v Malaysia Government Officers' Co-operative Housing Society Ltd [1979] AC 374; [1978] 2 WLR 444; [1978] 2 All ER 405; 122 SJ 31 PC . . . 948

Mahoney v Purnell [1996] 3 All ER 61; [1997] 1 FLR 612; [1997] Fam Law 169 QBD . . . **867–70**

Malory Enterprises Ltd v Cheshire Homes (UK) Ltd [2002] EWCA Civ 151; [2002] Ch 216; [2002] 3 WLR 1; [2002] 10 EGCS 155; (2002) 99(14) LSG 25; (2002) 146 SJLB 61 CA . . . 755

Manley v Sartori [1927] 1 Ch 147 Ch D . . . 1013

Marc Rich & Co v Portman [1996] 1 Ll Rep 430 CA . . . 433

Marine Mansions Co, Re (1867) LR 4 Eq 601
Ct Ch . . . 588–9

Marriot v Hampton 101 ER 969; (1797) 7 Term
Rep 269 . . . 5

Marsh v Keating (1834) Bing (NC) 198 . . . 32,
945

Marston Construction Co Ltd v Kigass Ltd 46
BLR 109; (1990) 15 Con LR 116 QBD . . . 81,
341, 343, 350, 355

Martin v Martin (1959) 110 CLR 297 . . . 914

Martin v Porter (1839) 5 M & W 351 . . . 982

Maskell v Horner [1915] 3 KB 106 CA . . . 406,
412, 415, 628–9

Mason v New South Wales 102 CLR 108 . . . 628,
630, 632, 871–2, 881

Mason v Sainsbury (1782) 3 Doug KB 61 . . .
715–16

Matheson v Smiley [1932] 2 DLR 787; [1932]
1 WWR 758 CA Manit . . . 559–60, **586**, 587

Mayson v Clouet [1924] AC 980; [1924] 3 WWR
211 PC . . . 273, 291–2, 308

Medforth v Blake [2000] [2000] Ch 86; [1999]
3 WLR 922; [1999] 3 All ER 97; [1999] BCC
771; [1999] 2 BCLC 221; [1999] BPIR 712;
[1999] Ll Rep PN 844; [1999] PNLR 920;
[1999] 2 EGLR 75; [1999] 29 EG 119; [1999]
EGCS 81; (1999) 96(24) LSG 39; (1999) 149
NLJ 929 CA . . . 787, 791

Medina, The (1876) 1 P 272 Prob Div . . .
498–9

Mercury Communications Ltd v Director
General of Telecommunications [1996] 1 WLR
48; [1996] 1 All ER 575; [1995] CLC 266;
[1998] Masons CLR Rep 39 HL . . . 641

Merry v Pownall [1898] 1 Ch 306 Ch D . . . 589

Mertens v Home Freeholds Co [1921] 2 KB 526
CA . . . 265

Metall und Rohstoff AG v Donaldson Lufkin and
Jenrette Inc [1990] [1990] 1 QB 391; [1989]
3 WLR 563; [1989] 3 All ER 14; (1989) 133 SJ
1200 CA . . . 737

Metallgesellschaft Ltd v Inland Revenue
Commissioners (C-397/98) [2001] Ch 620;
[2001] 2 WLR 1497; [2001] All ER (EC) 496;
[2001] STC 452; [2001] ECR I-1727; [2001]
2 CMLR 32; [2001] BTC 99; 3 ITL Rep 385;
[2001] STI 498 ECJ . . . 639

Metropolitan Asylum District Managers v Hill
(No 2) (1880–81) LR 6 AC 193; [1881–85]
All ER Rep 536 HL . . . 586

Metropolitan Bank v Heiron (1880) 3 Ex D 319
. . . 1019–21

Metropolitan Police District Receiver v Croydon
Corp [1957] 2 QB 154; [1957] 2 WLR 33;
[1957] 1 All ER 78; 121 JP 63; 55 LGR 18; 101
SJ 60 CA . . . 503, **528–31**

Middle East Banking Co v State Street Bank
International 821 F 2d 897 (1987) . . . 103

Midland Bank Plc v Perry [1988] 1 FLR 161;
[1987] Fin LR 237; (1988) 56 P & CR 202;
[1988] Fam Law 87 CA . . . 119

Midland Bank Trust Co Ltd v Green [1981] AC
513; [1981] 2 WLR 28; [1981] 1 All ER 153;
(1981) 42 P & CR 201; 125 SJ 33 HL . . .
378

Miles v Wakefield MDC [1987] AC 539; [1987]
2 WLR 795; [1987] 1 All ER 1089; [1987] ICR
368; [1987] IRLR 193; [1987] 1 FTLR 533; 85
LGR 649; (1987) 84 LSG 1239; (1987) 137 NLJ
266; (1987) 131 SJ 408 HL . . . 300, 386

Millar's Machinery Co Ltd v David Way & Son
(1934) 40 Com Cas 204 CA . . . 272

Miller, Gibb & Co Ltd, Re [1957] 1 WLR 703;
[1957] 2 All ER 266; [1957] 1 Ll Rep 258; 101
SJ 392 Ch D . . . 714, 717–18

Miller v Race (1758) 1 Burr 452 . . . 31, 205–6,
822

Ministry of Defence v Ashman (1993) 25 HLR
513; (1993) 66 P & CR 195; [1993] 40 EG 144;
[1993] NPC 70 CA . . . 929, 948, **964–6**, 983

Ministry of Defence v Thompson (1993) 25 HLR
552; [1993] 40 EG 148 CA . . . 966

Ministry of Health v Simpson (Diplock, Re)
[1951] AC 251; [1950] 2 All ER 1137; 66 TLR
(Pt 2) 1015; 94 SJ 777 HL . . . 37, 117, 119, 203,
215–16, 235, **237–9**, 246, 709–10, 748, 767

Ministry of Sound (Ireland) Ltd v World Online
Ltd [2003] EWHC 2178; [2003] 2 All ER
(Comm) 823 Ch D . . . 267

Mobil Oil Exploration & Producing SouthEast
Inc v United States 120 S Ct 2423 (2000) US
Sup Ct . . . 261

Modern Engineering (Bristol) Ltd v Gilbert-Ash
(Northern) Ltd [1974] AC 689; [1973] 3 WLR
421; [1973] 3 All ER 195; 1 BLR 73; 72 LGR 1;
117 SJ 745 HL . . . 302, 309–10

Moet v Couston (1864) 33 Beav 578 . . . 970

Mohamed v Alaga & Co [2000] 1 WLR 1815;
[1999] 3 All ER 699; [2000] CP Rep 87; [1999]
2 Costs LR 169 CA . . . **890–2**

Molton v Camroux (1848) 2 Exch 487 . . .
614–17

Monmouthshire CC v Smith [1957] 2 QB 154;
[1957] 2 WLR 33; [1957] 1 All ER 78; 121 JP
63; 55 LGR 18; 101 SJ 60 CA . . . 528

Montagu's Settlement Trusts, Re [1987] Ch 264;
[1987] 2 WLR 1192; [1992] 4 All ER 308;
(1987) 84 LSG 1057; (1987) 131 SJ 411 Ch D
. . . 203, **229–31**, 234, 788

Montana v Crow Tribe of Indians 523 US 696 715
Sup Ct USA . . . 116

Moorgate Mercantile Co Ltd v Twitchings [1976]
QB 225; [1975] 3 WLR 286; [1975] 3 All ER
314; [1975] RTR 528; 119 SJ 559 CA . . .
816–17

Morgan Guaranty Trust Co of New York v
Lothian Regional Council 1995 SC 151; 1995
SLT 299; 1995 SCLR 225 IH . . . 172, 182

Morgan v Ashcroft [1938] 1 KB 49 CA . . . 22, 147, **150–3**, 158–9, 884

Morgan v Palmer 2 B & C 729 . . . 628, 630, 636

Morley v Moore [1936] 2 KB 359; (1936) 55 Ll L Rep 10 CA . . . 719

Morrison-Knudsen Co Inc v British Columbia Hydro & Power Authority (1978) 85 DLR (3d) 186 Sup Ct BC . . . 284

Moses v Macferlan (1760) 2 Burr 1005 . . . 1, **4–5**, 8, 15, 21, 36, 273–4, 276, 743, 764

Moss v Hancock [1899] 2 QB 111 QBD . . . 205

Moule v Garrett (1871–72) LR 7 Ex 101 Ex Ct . . . 189, 503, **507**, 508, 511, 514, 517–18, 520, 523–6, 530, 534, 541

Muckleston v Brown (1801) 6 Ves Jr 52 . . . 915

Muller, Re [1953] NZLR 879 . . . 731

Multiservice Bookbinding v Marden [1979] Ch 84; [1978] 2 WLR 535; [1978] 2 All ER 489; (1978) 35 P & CR 201; 122 SJ 210 Ch D . . . 490, 493, 497–8

Munro v Butt (1858) 8 E & B 738 . . . 298, 302, 305

Munro v Willmott [1949] [1948] 2 All ER 983; 64 TLR 627; [1949] LJR 471; 92 SJ 662 KBD . . . 109

Murad v Al-Saraj [2005] EWCA Civ 959; [2005] WTLR 1573; (2005) 102(32) LSG 31 CA . . . **1012–16**

Murray v Baxter (1914) 18 CLR 622 . . . 216

Muschinski v Dodds (1985) 160 CLR 583 HC Aus . . . 26, 252, 1035–6

Mutual Finance Ltd v John Wetton & Sons Ltd [1937] 2 All ER 657 KBD . . . 428, **440–2**, 444

My Kinda Town Ltd (t/a Chicago Pizza Pie Factory) v Soll and Grunts Investments [1981] Com LR 194; [1982] FSR 147; [1983] RPC 15 Ch D . . . 971

National & Provincial Building Society v United Kingdom (21319/93) [1997] STC 1466; (1998) 25 EHRR 127; 69 TC 540; [1997] BTC 624; [1998] HRCD 34 ECtHR . . . 638

National Bank of New Zealand Ltd v Waitaki International Processing (NI) Ltd [1999] 2 NZLR 211 CA NZ . . . 784–5, 841

National Commercial Bank (Jamaica) Ltd v Hew's Executors [2003] UKPC 51 PC . . . 473, **476–9**

National Employers Mutual General Insurance Association Ltd (in liquidation)[1997] LRLR 159; [1997] 2 BCLC 191 v AGF Holdings (UK) Ltd Ch D . . . 115

National Motor Mail-Coach Co Ltd, Re [1908] 2 Ch 515 CA . . . 513, 517

National Pari-Mutuel Association Ltd v The King 47 TLR 110 . . . 625, 628, 630

National Westminster Bank Ltd v Barclays Bank Ltd [1975] QB 654; [1975] 2 WLR 12; [1974] 3 All ER 834; [1974] 2 Ll Rep 506; 118 SJ 627 QBD . . . 841

National Westminster Bank Plc v Morgan [1985] AC 686; [1985] 2 WLR 588; [1985] 1 All ER 821; [1985] FLR 266; (1985) 17 HLR 360; (1985) 82 LSG 1485; (1985) 135 NLJ 254; (1985) 129 SJ 205 HL . . . 427, 459, 461–2, 471–3, 486, 862

National Westminster Bank Plc v Somer International (UK) Ltd [2001] EWCA Civ 970; [2002] QB 1286; [2002] 3 WLR 64; [2002] 1 All ER 198; [2001] Ll Rep Bank 263; [2001] CLC 1579 CA . . . 765, 779, **814–21**, 822

Neate v Harding (1851) 6 Exch 349 . . . 243

Neesom v Clarkson (1845) 4 Hare 97 . . . 588

Neilson v Betts (1871–72) LR 5 HL 1 HL . . . 948

Nelson v Nelson (1995) 132 ALR 133 . . . 28, **912–18**

Neste Oy v Lloyds Bank Plc (The Tiiskeri, The Nestegas and The Enskeri) [1983] 2 Ll Rep 658; [1983] Com LR 145; (1983) 133 NLJ 597 QBD . . . 692

Newall v Tomlinson (1871) LR 6 CP 405 CCP . . . 840

Newbigging v Adam (1886) 34 ChD 582; (1888) LR 13 App Cas 308 HL . . . **196–9**, 200, 863

Nichols v Jessup [1986] 1 NZLR 226 . . . 484, 491

Nicholson v Chapman [1775–1802] All ER Rep 67; 2 Hy Bl 254 . . . **561–2**, 569, 573–4

Nimmo v Westpac Banking Corp [1993] 3 NZLR 218 . . . 839

Ninety Five Pty Ltd v Banque Nationale de Paris (1988) WAR 132 . . . 233

Nippon Menkwa Kabushiki Kaisha (Japan Cotton Trading Co Ltd) v Dawsons Bank Ltd (1935) (1935) 51 Ll L Rep 147 PC . . . 815

Niru Battery Manufacturing Co v Milestone Trading Ltd [2002] EWHC 1425; [2002] 2 All ER (Comm) 705 QBD . . . 83

Niru Battery Manufacturing Co v Milestone Trading Ltd (No 1) [2003] EWCA Civ 1446; [2004] QB 985; [2004] 2 WLR 1415; [2004] 1 All ER (Comm) 193; [2004] 1 Ll Rep 344; [2004] 1 CLC 647; [2004] WTLR 377; (2003) 100(44) LSG 33 CA . . . 841

Niru Battery Manufacturing Co v Milestone Trading Ltd (No 2) [2004] EWCA Civ 487; [2004] 2 All ER (Comm) 289; [2004] 2 Ll Rep 319; [2004] 1 CLC 882; (2004) 148 SJLB 538 CA . . . 503, **519–23**, 553, **786–96**

Nisbet and Potts Contract, Re [1906] 1 Ch 386 CA . . . 823

Nixon v Furphy (1925) 25 SR (NSW) 151 . . . 407

Nocton v Lord Ashburton [1914] AC 932; [1914–15] All ER Rep 45 HL . . . 868–70

Norfolk (Duke of) v Worthy (1808) 1 Camp 342 . . . 832, 842

Norreys v Zeffert [1939] 2 All ER 187 KBD . . . **442–3**

North Central Wagon Finance Co Ltd v Brailsford [1962] 1 WLR 1288; [1962] 1 All ER 502; 106 SJ 878 . . . 365–6

North Eastern Timber Importers Ltd v Ch Arendt & Sons [1952] 2 Ll Rep 513 QBD . . . 842

North Ocean Shipping Co Ltd v Hyundai Construction Co Ltd (The Atlantic Baron) [1979] QB 705; [1979] 3 WLR 419; [1978] 3 All ER 1170; [1979] 1 Ll Rep 89; 123 SJ 352 QBD . . . **405–9**, 410, 412–13, 419, 424

Norton v Haggett (1952) 117 Vt 130; 85 A 2d 571 . . . 540, 549–50

Norwich Union Fire Insurance Society v William H Price Ltd [1934] AC 455; (1934) 49 Ll L Rep 55 PC . . . 151, 153, 158

Notara v Henderson (1871–72) LR 7 QB 225 Ex Ch . . . 578, 585

Nott and Cardiff Corp, Re [1919] AC 337 HL . . . 503, **526–7**

Nottingham Permanent Benefit Building Society v Thurstan [1903] AC 6 HL . . . 727

Nurdin & Peacock Plc v DB Ramsden & Co Ltd [1999] 1 WLR 1249; [1999] 1 All ER 941; [1999] 1 EGLR 15; [1999] 10 EG 183; [1999] 09 EG 175; [1999] EGCS 19; (1999) 96(8) LSG 29; (1999) 149 NLJ 251; [1999] NPC 17 Ch D . . . 161, **183–6**

Oatesa v Hudson (1851) 6 Ex 346 . . . 834

Oatway, Re [1903] 2 Ch 356 Ch D . . . **674–5**, 676, 723

Occidental Worldwide Investment Corp v Skibs AS Avanti (The Siboen and The Sibotre) [1976] 1 Ll Rep 293 QBD . . . 407–8, 412, 414, 424, 431–2, 986

Ocular Sciences Ltd v Aspect Vision Care Ltd (No 2) [1997] RPC 289; (1997) 20(3) IPD 20022 Ch D . . . 1025

Oelkers v Ellis [1914] 2 KB 139 KBD . . . 848

Official Custodian for Charities v Mackey (No 2) [1985] 1 WLR 1308; [1985] 2 All ER 1016; (1986) 51 P & CR 143; [1985] 1 EGLR 46; (1985) 274 EG 398; 129 SJ 853 Ch D . . . 117

Ogilvie v West Australian Mortgage and Agency Corp Ltd [1896] AC 257 PC . . . 806–8, 817

Olwell v Nye & Nissan Co 26 Wash 2d 282 (1946) . . . 953

Ontario Securities Commission and Greymac Credit Corp, Re (1986) 55 OR (2d) 673 . . . 667, 670

Oom v Bruce (1810) 12 East 225 KB . . . **883–4**

Orakpo v Manson Investments Ltd [1978] AC 95; [1977] 3 WLR 229; (1978) 35 P & CR 1; 121 SJ 632 HL . . . 56, 192–3, 219, 723–4, 727

O'Reilly v Mackman [1983] [1983] 2 AC 237; [1982] 3 WLR 1096; [1982] 3 All ER 1124; 126 SJ 820 HL . . . 641

O'Rorke v Bollingbroke (1877) 2 App Cas 814 HL . . . 483

Orphanos v Queen Mary College [1985] AC 761; [1985] 2 WLR 703; [1985] 2 All ER 233; [1986] 2 CMLR 73; [1985] IRLR 349; (1985) 82 LSG 1787; (1985) 129 SJ 284 HL . . . 390, 392

O'Sullivan v Management Agency and Music Ltd [1985] QB 428; [1984] 3 WLR 448; [1985] 3 All ER 351 CA . . . **851–6**, 861, 865, 868, 870

OTM Ltd v Hydranautics [1981] 2 Ll Rep 221 QBD . . . 336

Oughton v Seppings (1830) 1 B & Ad 241 . . . 947

Owen & Co v Cronk [1895] 1 QB 265 CA . . . 832, 838, 843

Owen v Tate [1976] QB 402; [1975] 3 WLR 369; [1975] 2 All ER 129; (1974) 119 SJ 575 CA . . . 503, **512–18**, 519, 534, 538, 541–4, 547–8, 551, 555

Owners of the Steamship Mediana v Owners of the Lightship Comet [1900] AC 113 HL . . . 961, 983

P v P [1916] IR 400 . . . 253

Pacific National Investments v Victoria [2004] S.C.C. 75; (2004) 245 DLR (4th) 221 Sup Ct Can . . . 144

Palmer v Temple (1839) 9 Ad & E 508 . . . 270, 291–2

Pan Atlantic Insurance Co v Pine Top Insurance Co [1995] 1 AC 501; [1994] 3 WLR 677; [1994] 3 All ER 581; [1994] 2 Ll Rep 427; [1994] CLC 868; (1994) 91(36) LSG 36; (1994) 144 NLJ 1203; (1994) 138 SJLB 182 HL . . . 433

Pan Ocean Shipping Ltd v Creditcorp (UK) Ltd (The Trident Beauty) [1994] 1 WLR 161; [1994] 1 All ER 470; [1994] 1 Ll Rep 365; [1994] CLC 124; (1994) 144 NLJ 1203 HL . . . 110, **122–8**, 286, 306, 312–13, 386, 391

Pao On v Lau Yiu Long [1980] AC 614; [1979] 3 WLR 435; [1979] 3 All ER 65; 123 SJ 319 PC . . . **411–12**, 414–15, 418–19, 421, 424, 430

Papamichael v National Westminster Bank Plc (No 2) [2003] EWHC 164; [2003] 1 Ll Rep 341 QBD . . . 838

Parker, Re [1894] 3 Ch 400 CA . . . 518

Parker v Great Western Railway Co (1844) 7 Man & G 253 . . . 407, 411

Parker v McKenna (1874) LR 10 Ch App 96 . . . 1006

Parkinson v College of Ambulance Ltd [1925] 2 KB 1 KBD . . . 884, **886–7**, 889

Pattinson v Luckley (1875) LR 10 Ex 330 Ex Ct . . . 298–9

Paul v Speirway (in liquidation) [1976] Ch 220; [1976] 2 WLR 715; [1976] 2 All ER 587; (1976)

31 P & CR 353; 120 SJ 331 Ch D . . . 193, 723–5

Pavey and Matthews Pty v Paul (1987) 162 CLR 221; (1990) 6 Const LJ 59 HC Aus . . . 88, 273, 307, 355

Pavey and Matthews Pty v Paul (1990) 6 Const LJ 59 HC Aus . . . 2–3, **22–8**, 40, 387–8, 391

Payne v McDonald (1908) 6 CLR 208 . . . 905

Pearce v Brain [1929] 2 KB 310 KBD . . . 375, **610–11**

Peel (Regional Municipality) v Canada (1993) 98 DLR (4th) 140 Sup Ct Can . . . 72, **74–6**, 141

Pellatt v Boosey (1862) 31 LJCP 281 . . . 539

Penarth Dock Engineering Co Ltd v Pounds [1963] 1 Ll Rep 359 QBD . . . **953–4**, 958, 963, 965, 980, 982, 998

Penley v Watts 7 M & W 601 . . . 524

Pennell v Deffell (1853) 4 De G M & G 372 . . . 672, 674

Perpetual Executors and Trustees Association of Australia Ltd v Wright (1917) 23 CLR 185 . . . 904, 909

Peruvian Guano Co v Dreyfus Bros & Co [1892] AC 166 HL . . . 108–9, 562

Pesticcio v Huet [2004] EWCA Civ 372; [2004] All ER (D) 36 CA . . . 473, 479

Peter Pan Manufacturing Corp v Corsets Silhouette Ltd [1964] 1 WLR 96; [1963] 3 All ER 402; [1963] RPC 45; 108 SJ 97 Ch D . . . 958, 1027, 1030

Peter v Beblow (1993) [1993] 3 WWR 337; 101 DLR (4th) 621 Sup Ct Can . . . 141

Petherpermal Chetty v Muniandi Servai LR 35 Ind App 98 PC . . . 905, 908

Petrinovic & Co Ltd v Mission Française des Transports Maritimes (1941) (1941) 71 Ll L Rep 208 KBD . . . 580

Pettit v Pettit [1970] AC 777; [1969] 2 WLR 966; [1969] 2 All ER 385; (1969) 20 P & CR 991; 113 SJ 344 HL . . . 904

Pettkus v Becker [1980] 2 SCR 834 Sup Ct Can . . . 113, 139–41, 1033–4

Philip Collins Ltd v Davis [2000] 3 All ER 808; [2001] ECDR 17; [2000] EMLR 815 Ch D . . . 767–8, **769–73**, 776–7, 780, 811, 822

Phillips v Ellinson Bros Pty Ltd (1941) 65 CLR 235 . . . 25

Phillips v Homfray (1883) LR 24 Ch D 439 CA . . . 91, 113, **948–50**, 951–2, 957

Phillips v Hunter (1795) 1 H Bl 402 HL . . . 5

Phipps v Boardman [1967] 2 AC 46; [1966] 3 WLR 1009; [1966] 3 All ER 721; 110 SJ 853 HL . . . 247, 851–2, 854, 935, 941

Phoenix Life Assurance Co, Re (1862) 2 J & H 441 . . . 6–8, 308, 365, 375, 926

Photo Production Ltd v Securicor Transport Ltd [1980] AC 827; [1980] 2 WLR 283; [1980] 1 All ER 556; [1980] 1 Ll Rep 545; 124 SJ 147 HL . . . 256, 285–6

Pilcher v Rawlins (1871–72) LR 7 Ch App 259; (1872) 20 WR 281; (1872) 41 LJ Ch 485; (1872) 25 LT 921 CA . . . 822

Pitts v Hunt [1991] 1 QB 24; [1990] 3 WLR 542; [1990] 3 All ER 344; [1990] RTR 290; (1990) 134 SJ 8 CA . . . 917–18

Planché v Colburn (1831) 8 Bing 14; 131 ER 305 . . . 63, 72, 89, 92, 99, **106–7**, **279–80**

Platamone v Staple Coop 250 . . . 896

Polly Peck International Ltd v Nadir (No 2) [1992] 4 All ER 769; [1992] 2 Ll Rep 238; [1993] BCLC 187; (1992) 142 NLJ 671 CA . . . 231, 234, 743, 839

Port Caledonia, The [1903] P 184 Prob Div . . . **499–500**

Porter v Latec Finance (Qld) Pty Ltd (1964) 111 CLR 177; (1964) 38 ALJR 184 HC Aus . . . 158

Portman Building Society v Dusangh [2000] 2 All ER (Comm) 221; [2000] Ll Rep Bank 197; [2001] WTLR 117; [2000] NPC 51; (2000) 80 P & CR D20 CA . . . 493

Portman Building Society v Hamlyn Taylor Neck [1998] 4 All ER 202; [1998] PNLR 664; (1999) 77 P & CR 66; [1998] 2 EGLR 113; [1998] 31 EG 102; (1998) 76 P & CR D16 CA . . . **828–31**, 836–7, 840–1

Potton Ltd v Yorkclose Ltd [1990] FSR 11 . . . 971

Powell v Thompson [1991] 1 NZLR 597 HC NZ . . . 233, 838

Pownal v Ferrand (1827) 6 B & C 439 . . . 511, 513–14

Prager v Blatspiel Stamp and Heacock Ltd [1924] 1 KB 566 KBD . . . **573–5**, 576, 581

President of India v La Pintada Compania Navigacion SA (The La Pintada) [1985] AC 104; [1984] 3 WLR 10; [1984] 2 All ER 773; [1984] 2 Ll Rep 9; [1984] CILL 110; (1984) 81 LSG 1999; (1984) 128 SJ 414 HL . . . 728

Price v Neal (1762) 3 Burr 1355 . . . 36

Price v Strange [1978] Ch 337; [1977] 3 WLR 943; [1977] 3 All ER 371; (1978) 36 P & CR 59; (1977) 243 EG 295; 121 SJ 816 CA . . . 957

Procter & Gamble Philippine Manufacturing Corp v Peter Cremer GmbH (The Manila) [1988] 3 All ER 843 QBD . . . 72, **73–4**, 80–1

Pulbrook v Lawes (1876) 1 QBD 284 QBD . . . 307

Queen (The) v Stewart 12 Ad & E 773; 4 P & D 349 QBD . . . 568

Queens of the River SS Co Ltd v Thames Conservators (1889) 15 TLR 494 . . . 625, 630, 636, 640

Quistclose Investment Ltd v Rolls Razor Ltd (in voluntary liquidation) [1970] AC 567; [1968] 3 WLR 1097; [1968] 3 All ER 651; 112 SJ 903 HL . . . 690, 733, 736

R Leslie Ltd v Sheill [1914] 3 KB 607 CA . . . 367, 738, **922–5**, 924

R (on the application of Rowe) v Vale of White Horse DC [2003] EWHC 388; [2003] 1 Ll Rep 418; [2003] RVR 170; [2003] 11 EGCS 153; [2003] NPC 34 QBD (Admin) . . . 1

R Pagnan & Fratelli v Corbisa Industrial Agropacuaria Ltd [1970] 1 WLR 1306; [1970] 1 All ER 165; [1970] 2 Ll Rep 14; 114 SJ 568 CA . . . 874

R v Attorney-General for England and Wales [2003] UKPC 22; [2003] EMLR 24; (2003) 147 SJLB 354 PC . . . **433–5, 474**, 479

R v Inland Revenue Commissioners Ex p Woolwich Equitable Building Society [1990] 1 WLR 1400; [1991] 4 All ER 92; [1990] STC 682; 63 TC 589; (1990) 134 SJ 1404 HL . . . 626

R v Shadrokh-Cigari [1988] Crim LR 465 CA . . . 744

R v Tower Hamlets LBC Ex p Chetnik Developments Ltd [1988] AC 858; [1988] 2 WLR 654; [1988] 1 All ER 961; 86 LGR 321; [1988] RA 45; [1988] EGCS 36; (1988) 138 NLJ Rep 89; (1988) 132 SJ 4621 HL . . . 625, 627

Rahimtoola v Nizam of Hyderabad [1958] AC 379; [1957] 3 WLR 884; [1957] 3 All ER 441; 101 SJ 901 HL . . . 826–7, 838

Ralli Bros v Cia Navieria Sota v Aznar [1920] 2 KB 287; [1920] All ER Rep 427; (1920) 2 Ll L Rep 550 CA . . . 799

Randal v Cockran (1748) 1 Ves Sen 98 . . . 714, 716

Randall v Randall [2004] EWHC 2258; [2005] WTLR 119; (2004–05) 7 ITELR 340; [2005] 1 P & CR DG4 Ch D . . . 479

Rathwell v Rathwell (1978) 83 DLR (3d) 829 Sup Ct Can . . . **138–9**, 140, 749

Raven Red Ash Coal Co v Ball 39 SE 2d 231 (1946) . . . 953

Rawlins v Wickham 3 De G & I 304 . . . 198

RBC Dominion Securities Inc v Dawson (1994) 111 DLR (4th) 230 CA Newf . . . 768, **801–2**, 811, 822

RE Jones Ltd v Waring and Gillow Ltd [1926] AC 670 HL . . . 15–16, 36, 156–7, 161, 166, 242–3, 766, 807, 810

Reading v Attorney-General [1951] AC 507; [1951] 1 All ER 617; [1951] 1 TLR 480; 95 SJ 155 HL . . . 111, 748–9, **1016–18**, 1027

Redgrave v Hurd (1881–82) LR 20 Ch D 1 CA . . . 197–8

Rees v Hughes [1946] KB 517 CA . . . 566, 569

Reese River Silver Mining Co v Smith (1869) LR 4 HL 64 HL . . . 852

Regal (Hastings) Ltd v Gulliver [1967] 2 AC 134; [1942] 1 All ER 378 HL . . . 851, 856, **1002–7**, 1012–13

Regalian Properties Ltd v London Docklands Development Corp [1995] [1995] 1 WLR 212; [1995] 1 All ER 1005; 45 Con LR 37; (1995) 11 Const LJ 127; [1994] EGCS 176; (1995) 92(4) LSG 34; [1994] NPC 139; (1994) 68 P & CR D29 Ch D . . . **337–42**, 343, 345–6, 350, 354

Regazzioni v KC Sethia (1944) Ltd [1958] AC 301; [1957] 3 WLR 752; [1957] 3 All ER 286; [1957] 2 Ll Rep 289; 101 SJ 848 HL . . . 799

Reid v Rigby & Co [1894] 2 QB 40 QBD . . . 243

Reid-Newfoundland Co v Anglo-American Telegraph Co Ltd [1912] AC 555 . . . 986

Renard Construction (MD) Pty Ltd v Minister for Public Works (1992) 26 NSWLR 234 CA NSW . . . 283–5

Reynell v Sprye (1852) 42 ER 708; (1852) 1 De GM & G 660 . . . 401

Rhodes, Re (1890) LR 44 Ch D 94 CA . . . 25, **581–3**, 586

Rhodes v Bate (1865–66) LR 1 Ch App 252 CA . . . 453

Rice v Reed [1900] 1 QB 54 . . . 946

Rio Tinto Co Ltd v Seed Shipping Co Ltd (1926) 24 Ll L Rep 316 KBD . . . 310

Roberts v Crowe (1872) LR 7 CP 629 CCP . . . 524

Roberts v Roberts Dan 143 . . . 895

Robinson v Harman (1848) 1 Exch 850 . . . 932

Rochdale Canal Co v Brewster [1894] 2 QB 852 CA . . . 526

Rodemer v Gonder 9 Gill (Md) 288 . . . 281–3

Rogers v Price (1829) 3 Y & J 28 Ct Ex . . . 560, **566–7**

Rogers v Ingham (1876) 3 Ch D 351 . . . 216

Rookes v Barnard (No 1) [1964] AC 1129; [1964] 2 WLR 269; [1964] 1 All ER 367; [1964] 1 Ll Rep 28; 108 SJ 93 HL . . . 934, 973

Rothschild v Brookman (1831) 5 Bli NS 165 . . . 848

Rover International Ltd v Cannon Film Sales Ltd [1989] 1 WLR 912; . . . [1989] 3 All ER 423; [1988] BCLC 710 CA . . . 277, **290–3, 358–62**, 366–7, 369, 371–2, 378, 380–1, 621

Rowan v Dann (1992) 64 P & CR 202; [1991] EGCS 138; [1992] NPC 3 CA . . . 908

Rowe v Vale of White Horse DC [2003] EWHC 388; [2003] 1 Ll Rep 418; [2003] RVR 170; [2003] 11 EGCS 153; [2003] NPC 34 QBD . . . 71–2, **76–7**, 78, **393**

Rowland v Divall [1923] 2 KB 500 CA . . . **261–3**, 270, 359, 366, 371, 379–81

Roxborough v Rothmans of Pall Mall Australia
Ltd (2001) 208 ClR 516; (2002) 76 ALJR 203
HC Aus . . . 28, 113, **251–6, 386–9**, 391, 843,
871, 882

Roy v Kensington and Chelsea and Westminister
Family Practitioner Committee [1992] [1992]
1 AC 624; [1992] 2 WLR 239; [1992] 1 All ER
705; [1992] IRLR 233; (1992) 4 Admin LR 649;
[1992] 3 Med LR 177; (1992) 142 NLJ 240;
(1992) 136 SJLB 63 HL . . . 641

Royal Bank of Scotland Plc v Etridge (No 2)
[2001] UKHL 44; [2002] 2 AC 773; [2001]
3 WLR 1021; [2001] 4 All ER 449; [2001] 2 All
ER (Comm) 1061; [2002] 1 Ll Rep 343; [2001]
2 FLR 1364; [2001] 3 FCR 481; [2002] HLR 4;
[2001] Fam Law 880; [2001] 43 EGCS 184;
(2001) 151 NLJ 1538; [2001] NPC 147 HL . . .
457–78, 473–4, 477

Royal British Bank v Turquand [1843–60] All ER
Rep 435; 119 ER 886; (1856) 6 E & B 327 Ex Ch
. . . 235

Royal Brompton Hospital NHS Trust v
Hammond (No 3) [2002] UKHL 14 HL 522;
[2002] 1 WLR 1397; [2002] 2 All ER 801;
[2002] 1 All ER (Comm) 897; [2003] 1 CLC
11; [2002] BLR 255; [2002] TCLR 14; 81 Con
LR 1; [2002] PNLR 37 HL . . . 522

Royal Brunei Airlines Sdn Bhd v Tan [1995]
[1995] 2 AC 378; [1995] 3 WLR 64; [1995]
3 All ER 97; [1995] BCC 899; (1995) 92(27)
LSG 33; (1995) 145 NLJ 888; [1995] 139 SJLB
146; (1995) 70 P & CR D12 PC . . . 231, 234,
246, 791, 838

Rugg v Minett 103 ER 985; (1809) 11 East 210
. . . 14, 17, 372

Rumsey v NE Railway (1863) 14 CB (NS) 641 . . .
91

Rural Municipality of Storthoaks v Mobil Oil
Canada Ltd (1975) 55 DR (3d) 1 . . . 37, 143,
768

Russell-Cooke Trust Co v Prentis (No 1) [2002]
EWHC 2227; [2003] 2 All ER 478; [2003]
WTLR 81; (2002–03) 5 ITELR 532; (2002) 152
NLJ 1719 Ch D . . . 671

Sabemo Pty Ltd v North Sydney Municipal
Council [1977] 2 NSWLR 880 . . . 63, 92,
338–41, 343, 350–1

Sadler v Evans (1766) 4 Burr 1984 . . . 21, 824,
838

St John Shipping Corp v Joseph Rank Ltd [1957]
1 QB 267; [1956] 3 WLR 870; [1956] 3 All ER
683; [1956] 2 Ll Rep 413; 100 SJ 841 QBD . . .
889, 917

Salangor United Rubber Estates Ltd v Cradock
(No 3) [1968] 1 WLR 319; [1968] 1 All ER 567;
112 SJ 108 Ch D . . . 230

Salvation Army Trustee Co Ltd v West Yorkshire
CC (1981) 41 P & CR 179 QBD . . . 343

Sanders & Foster Ltd v A Monk & Co Ltd [1980]
CA Transcript 35 . . . 336

Sandhu v Gill [2005] EWCA Civ 1297; [2006]
Ch 456; [2006] 2 WLR 8; [2006] 2 All ER 22;
[2006] 2 BCLC 38; (2005) 155 NLJ 1713;
(2005) 149 SJLB 1353; [2005] NPC 125 CA . . .
996

Sapsford v Fletcher (1792) 4 TR 511 . . . 541

Sargood Bros v Commonwealth of Australia
11 CLR 258 . . . 628

Saunders v Edwards [1987] 1 WLR 1116; [1987]
2 All ER 651; (1987) 137 NLJ 389; (1987) 131
SJ 1039 CA . . . 917

Say-Dee Pty Ltd v Farah Construction Property
Ltd [2005] NSWCA 309 CA NSW . . . 248

Scandinavian Trading Tanker Co AB v Flota
Petrolera Ecuatoriana (The Scaptrade) [1983]
2 AC 694; [1983] 3 WLR 203; [1983] 2 All ER
763; [1983] 2 Ll Rep 253 HL . . . 730

Scaramanga & Co v Stamp (1880) LR 5 CPD 295
CA . . . 310

Scott v Brown, Doering, McNab & Co [1892]
2 QB 729 CA . . . 893, 902

Scott v Nesbitt 14 Ves Jun 438 . . . 588–9

Scott v Pattison [1923] 2 KB 723 KBD . . . 19

Scott v Scott (1963) 109 CLR 649; (1963)
37 ALJR 345 . . . 685

Scott v Surman (1742) Willes 400 . . . 208, 649

Scottish Equitable Plc v Derby [2001] EWCA Civ
369; [2001] 3 All ER 818; [2001] 2 All ER
(Comm) 274; [2001] OPLR 181; [2001] Pens
LR 163; (2001) 151 NLJ 41 CA . . . 83, **765–9**,
772, 775–8, 780, **811–14**, 817, 819–22

Seager, Re 60 LT 665 . . . 922

Seager v Copydex Ltd (No 1) [1967] 1 WLR 923;
[1967] 2 All ER 415; 2 KIR 828; [1967] FSR
211; [1967] RPC 349; 111 SJ 335 CA . . . 1031

Seager v Copydex Ltd (No 2) [1969] 1 WLR 809;
[1969] 2 All ER 718; [1969] FSR 261; [1969]
RPC 250; 113 SJ 281 CA . . . 958, 1031

Sebel Products Ltd v Customs and Excise
Commissioners [1949] Ch 409; [1949] All ER
729; 65 TLR 107; 65 TLR 207; [1949] LJR 925;
93 SJ 198 Ch D . . . 45, 629

Seear v Cohen 45 LTR 589 . . . 441

Segnit v Cotton Unreported 9 December 1999 CA
. . . 305

Severn Trent Water Ltd v Barnes [2004] EWCA
Civ 570; [2004] 2 EGLR 95; [2004] 26 EG 194;
[2005] RVR 181; (2004) 148 SJLB 693; [2004]
NPC 76 CA . . . 969

Shand v Grant [1863] 15 CB (NS) 324 . . . 838

Shaw v Applegate [1977] 1 WLR 970; [1978]
1 All ER 123; (1978) 35 P & CR 181; 121 SJ 424
CA . . . 997

Shepherd v Cartwright [1995] AC 431 . . . 901

Silsbee v Webber 50 NE 555 (1898) Sup Ct Mass . . . **438–40**, 445

Simms Ex p Trustee, Re [1934] Ch 1 CA . . . 976

Simpson & Co v Thomson (1877) LR 3 App Cas 279; (1877) 5 R (HL) 40 HL . . . 715, 719

Simpson v Eggington (1855) 10 Ex 845 . . . 540, 544

Sims & Co v Midland Railway Co [1913] 1 KB 103 KBD . . . 574

Sinclair v Brougham [1914] AC 398; [1914–15] All ER Rep 622 HL . . . 1, **6–9**, 13, 16, 20–2, 40–1, 150, 153, 205, 207–9, 364–5, 367, 378, 656, **657–9**, 660–3, 667, 671, 689, 692, 709, 729, 731, 734–6, 740, 754–5, 891, 925, 927, 944

Singh v Ali [1960] AC 167; [1960] 2 WLR 180; [1960] 1 All ER 269; 104 SJ 84 PC . . . 901–2, 907, 909

Skeate v Beale (1841) 11 Ad & E 983 . . . 398, **404–5**, 407

Skyring v Greenwood (1925) 4 B & C 281 . . . 806–7, 809–12, 817–18, 840

Slade's Case (1602) 4 Co Rep 92b . . . 274, 944

Slater v Burnley Corp (1888) 59 LTNS 636 . . . 625, 628

Slazenger & Sons v Spalding & Bros [1910] 1 Ch 257 Ch D . . . 970–1

Smith New Court Securities Ltd v Scrimgeour Vickers (Asset Management) Ltd [1997] AC 254; [1996] 3 WLR 1051; [1996] 4 All ER 769; [1997] 1 BCLC 350; [1996] CLC 1958; (1996) 93(46) LSG 28; (1996) 146 NLJ 1722; (1997) 141 SJLB 5 HL . . . 196, **866–7**

Smith v Bromley (1760) 2 Doug 696 KB . . . **885**, 886

Smith v Croft (No 1) [1986] 1 WLR 580; [1986] 2 All ER 551; [1986] BCLC 207; [1986] PCC 412; (1986) 83 LSG 3672; 130 SJ 314 Ch D . . . 590

Smith v Cuff (1817) 6 M & S KB . . . **885–6**

Smith v Land and House Property Corp (1884) LR Ch D 7 CA . . . 355

Smith v William Charlick Ltd (1924) 34 CLR 38 . . . 407, 429

Snepp v United States of America (1980) 444 US 507 . . . 989

Snowden v Davis (1808) 1 Taunt 359 . . . 824, 834

Solle v Butcher [1950] 1 KB 671; [1949] 2 All ER 1107; 66 TLR (Pt 1) 448 CA . . . 195

Soper v Arnold (1889) LR 14 App Cas 429 CA . . . 254–5

Sorochan v Sorochan (1986) 29 DLR (4th) 1 . . . 1034

South of Scotland Electricity Board v British Oxygen Co Ltd [1959] 1 WLR 587; [1959] 2 All ER 225; 1959 SC (HL) 17; 1959 SLT 181; 103 SJ 370 HL . . . 628, 640

South Tyneside MBC v Svenska International Plc [1995] 1 All ER 545 QBD . . . 623, 770, 777, 781, 783, 818, 874–5

Southern Pacific Co v Jensen (1917) 244 US 205 . . . 174

Space Investments Ltd v Canadian Imperial Bank of Commerce Trust Co (Bahamas) Ltd [1986] 1 WLR 1072; [1986] 3 All ER 75; (1986) 83 LSG 2567; (1986) 130 SJ 612 PC . . . 693–700

Spence v Crawford [1939] 3 All ER 271; 1939 SC (HL) 52; 1939 SLT 305 HL . . . 196, **849–51**, 853, 865, 867

Spring Form Inc v Toy Brokers Ltd [2002] FSR 17; (2001) 24(11) IPD 24073 Ch D . . . 948

Springer v Great Western Railway [1921] 1 KB 257; (1920) 4 Ll L Rep 211 CA . . . 574

Staffordshire Gas & Coke Co, Re [1893] 3 Ch 523 Ch D . . . 588

Standard Bank London Ltd v Canara Bank [2002] EWHC 1032 . . . 838

Standard Chartered Bank Ltd v Pakistan National Shipping Corp (No 2) [2002] UKHL 43; [2003] 1 AC 959; [2002] 3 WLR 1547; [2003] 1 All ER 173; [2002] 2 All ER (Comm) 931; [2003] 1 Ll Rep 227; [2002] BCC 846; [2003] 1 BCLC 244; [2002] CLC 1330; (2003) 100(1) LSG 26; (2002) 146 SJLB 258 HL . . . 801

Standard Oil Co v Bollinger (1929) 169 NE 236 . . . 879

Standing v Bowring (1886) LR 31 Ch D 282 CA . . . 900, 908

Stapylton Fletcher Ltd (in administrative receivership), Re [1994] 1 WLR 1181; [1995] 1 All ER 192; [1994] BCC 532; [1994] 2 BCLC 681 Ch D . . . 696

Starling v Lloyds TSB Bank Plc [2000] Ll Rep Bank 8; [2000] 1 EGLR 101; [2000] 01 EG 89; [1999] EGCS 129; (1999) 96(43) LSG 35; [1999] NPC 129; (2000) 79 P & CR D12 CA . . . 787

State Bank of New South Wales Ltd v Swiss Bank Corp [1997] 6 Bank LR 34; (1995) 39 NSWLR 350 CA NSW . . . 793

Stearns v Village Main Reef Gold Mining Co Ltd 10 Com Cas 89 . . . 717

Steele v Tardiani (1946) 72 CLR 386 . . . 100, 269, 306, 313

Steele v Williams (1853) 8 Ex 625 . . . 625, 628–30, 636, 638, 640

Steinberg v Scala (Leeds) Ltd [1923] 2 Ch 453 CA . . . 375–6, 379, **608–10**, 611

Stephens Travel Services International v Qantas Airways (1988) 12 NSWLR 31 . . . 838

Stimpson v Smith [1999] Ch 340; [1999] 1 WLR 1292; [1999] 2 All ER 833; [1999] Ll Rep Bank

131; (1999) 96(15) LSG 29; (1999) 149 NLJ
414; [1999] NPC 35 CA . . . 554–5

Stockloser v Johnson [1954] 1 QB 476; [1954]
2 WLR 439; [1954] 1 All ER 630; 98 SJ 178 CA
. . . 294

Stocks v Wilson [1913] 2 KB 235 KBD . . . 738,
920–2, 923–4

Stocznia Gdanska SA v Latvian Shipping Co
[1998] 1 WLR 574; [1998] 1 All ER 883; [1998]
1 Ll Rep 609; [1998] CLC 540; (1998) 95(15)
LSG 33; (1998) 148 NLJ 330; (1998) 142 SJLB
118 HL . . . **294–7**

Stoke-on-Trent CC v W & J Wass Ltd (No 1)
[1988] 1 WLR 1406; [1988] 3 All ER 394; 87
LGR 129; (1989) 153 LG Rev 586; [1988] EGCS
121; (1988) 85(40) LSG 44; (1988) 132 SJ 1458
CA . . . **959–63**, 964

Strachan Ex p Cooke, (1876–77) LR 4 Ch D 123
CA . . . 207

Strand Electric and Engineering Co v Brisford
Entertainemnts [1952] 2 QB 246; [1952] 1 All
ER 796; [1952] 1 TLR 939; 96 SJ 260 CA . . .
43, 954, 958–60, 962–3, 979, 983

Stray v Russell 1 E & F 888 Ex C . . . 288

Sumitomo Bank Ltd v Kartika Ratna Thahir
[1993] 1 SLR 735 . . . 1021–2

Sumpter v Hedges [1898] 1 QB 673 CA . . . 84,
286, **298–9**, 300–301, 303, 305–12

Sundell v Emm Yannoulatos (Overseas) Pty Ltd
(1955) 56 SR (NSW) 323 . . . 408

Surrey CC v Bredero Homes Ltd [1993] 1 WLR
1361; [1993] 3 All ER 705; [1993] 25 EG 141;
[1993] EGCS 77; 137 SJLB 135; [1993] NPC 63
CA . . . 968, 981, 986, 989–90

Sutton v Sutton [1984] Ch 184; [1984] 2 WLR
146; [1984] 1 All ER 168; [1984] Fam Law 205;
(1984) 81 LSG 591; (1984) 128 SJ 80 Ch D . . .
778

Swain v Wall 1 Ch Rep 149 . . . 552

Swordheath Properties Ltd v Tabet [1979] 1 WLR
285; [1979] 1 All ER 240; (1979) 37 P & CR
327; (1978) 249 EG 439; (1978) 122 SJ 862 CA
. . . 958, 964–5

Symes v Hughes (1870) LR 9 Eq 475 C Ch . . .
905–6, 908–9

T & J Brocklebank Ltd v The King [1925] 1 KB
52; (1924) 19 Ll L Rep 375 CA . . . 628, 630

Talbor v Staniforth 1 J & H 484 . . . 487

Talbot v General Television Corp Pty Ltd [1980]
2 VR 224 Sup Ct Vict . . . 1037

Tang Min Sit v Capacious Investments Ltd [1996]
AC 514; [1996] 2 WLR 192; [1996] 1 All ER
193 PC . . . 947–8

Tappenden v Randall (1801) 2 B & P 467 . . . 606

Target Holdings Ltd v Redferns [1996] AC 421;
[1995] 3 WLR 352; [1995] 3 All ER 785; [1995]
CLC 1052; (1995) 139 SJLB 195; [1995] NPC
136 HL . . . 868, 870

Taylor (Ex parte) 8 DM & G 254 . . . 609

Taylor v Bhail [1996] CLC 377; 50 Con LR 70 CA
. . . 889–90, 892

Taylor v Bowers (1876) LR 1 QBD 291 CA . . .
598–600, 601–6, 906–7, 909

Taylor v Caldwell (1863) 32 LJ QB 164 . . . 12–13

Taylor v Chester (1869) LR 4 BD 309 . . . 888,
893, 898–9

Taylor v Laird (1856) 25 LJ Ex 329 . . . 64, 96,
108, 542

Taylor v Motability Finance Ltd [2004] EWHC
2619 QBD . . . **284–6**

Taylor v Plumer (1815) 3 M & S 562 KBD . . .
205, 207–9, 220, **649–50**, 654, 837

Taylor v Zamira (1816) 6 Taunt 524 . . . 541

TC Industrial Plant Pty Ltd v Robert's
Queensland Pty Ltd (1963) 37 ALFR 289;
[1964] ALR 1083 . . . 276

Tetley & Co v British Trade Corp (1922) 10 Ll L
Rep 678 KBD . . . 574

TH Knitwear (Wholesale) Ltd, Re [1988] Ch 275;
[1988] 2 WLR 276; [1988] 1 All ER 860; [1988]
STC 79; [1987] BCLC 195; [1988] PCC 281;
(1988) 85(4) LSG 35; (1987) 131 SJ 1696 CA
. . . 725

Thackwell v Barclays Bank Ltd [1986] 1 All ER
676 QBD . . . 800

Thomas v Brown (1876) 1 QBD 714 . . . 26, **356**

Thomas v Houston Corbett & Co [1969] NZLR
151 CA . . . 158, 784–5

Thompson, Re [1930] 1 Ch 203 . . . 747

Thompson v Clydesdale Bank Ltd [1893] AC 282
. . . 838

Thorne v Motor Trade Associatiion [1937]
AC 797 HL . . . 415, 427, 431, 434, 442–3

Tilley's Will Trusts, Re [1967] Ch 1179; [1967]
2 WLR 1533; [1967] 2 All ER 303; 111 SJ 237
Ch D . . . **676–7**, 685

Tinker v Tinker [1970] P 136; [1970] 2 WLR 331;
[1970] 1 All ER 540; (1970) 21 P & CR 102;
(1969) 114 SJ 32 CA . . . 895, 897, 900, 909–10

Tinsley v Milligan [1993] [1994] 1 AC 340;
[1993] 3 WLR 126; [1993] 3 All ER 65; [1993]
2 FLR 963; (1994) 68 P & CR 412; [1993]
EGCS 118; [1993] NPC 97 HL . . . 798–800,
894–902, 903–4, 906–10, 912–14, 916–18

Tito v Waddell (No 2) [1977] Ch 106; [1977]
3 WLR 972; [1977] 2 WLR 496; [1977] 3 All ER
129 Ch D . . . 127, 967, 986, 999, 1001

Tonnelier v Smith (1897) 2 Com Cas 258 . . . 123,
126

Torrez, Re (1987) 827 F 2d 1299 . . . 918

Towers v Barret 1 Term Rep 133; 1 Chitty 341 . . .
260

Transport North American Express Inc v New
Solutions Financial Corp [2004] 2 SCR 429;

2004 SCC 7; 235 DLR (4th) 385 Sup Ct Can . . . 142

Transvaal & Delagoa Bay Investment Co Ltd v Atkinson [1944] 1 All ER 579 KBD . . . 221, 244, 825, 834, 838

Tribe v Tribe [1996] Ch 107; [1995] 3 WLR 913; [1995] 4 All ER 236; [1995] CLC 1474; [1995] 2 FLR 966; [1996] 1 FCR 338; (1996) 71 P & CR 503; [1996] Fam Law 29; (1995) 92(28) LSG 30; (1995) 145 NLJ 1445; (1995) 139 SJLB 203; [1995] NPC 151; (1995) 70 P & CR D38 CA . . . 605, **903–12**

Trimis v MINA [1999] NSWCA 140 CA NSW . . . 284

Trustee of the Property of FC Jones & Sons (A Firm) v Jones [1997] Ch 159; [1996] 3 WLR 703; [1996] 4 All ER 721; [1996] BPIR 644; (1996) 93(19) LSG 29; (1996) 140 SJLB 123 CA . . . 113–14, 225, 649–50, **651**, 655, 683

TSB Bank Plc v Camfield [1995] 1 WLR 430; [1995] 1 All ER 951; [1995] 1 FLR 751; [1995] 2 FCR 254; (1995) 27 HLR 205; (1995) 92(3) LSG 37; (1995) 145 NLJ 215; (1995) 139 SJLB 15 CA . . . 856

Turkey v Ahwad [2005] EWCA Civ 507 CA . . . 479

Turner v Bladin (1951) 82 CLR 474 . . . 23, 26

Twinsectra Ltd v Yardley [2002] UKHL 12; [2002] 2 AC 164 HL . . . 231, 248, 787, 791, 838

Twyford v Manchester Corp [1946] Ch 236; [1946] 1 All ER 621; 62 TLR . . . 367; 110 JP 196; [1946] WN 70; [1947] LJR 12; 175 LT 124; 90 SJ 164 Ch D . . . 625, 628, 637, 644

Union Bank of Australia Ltd v McClintock [1922] 1 AC 240 PC . . . 32, 220

United Australia Ltd v Barclays Bank Ltd [1941] AC 1; [1940] 4 All ER 20 HL . . . 16, 95–8, 349, **942–7**, 984

United Overseas Bank v Jiwani [1976] 1 WLR 964; [1977] 1 All ER 733; 120 SJ 329 QBD . . . 840

United Shoe Machinery Corp v Hanover Shoe Inc 392 US 481 (1968) Sup Ct US . . . 871

United States of America v Algernon Blair Inc 479 F 2d 638 (1973) . . . 103

United States of America v Steele (19959) 175 F Supp 24 . . . 840

Universal Thermosensors Ltd v Hibben [1992] 1 WLR 840; [1992] 3 All ER 257; [1992] FSR 361; (1992) 142 NLJ 195 Ch D . . . 1031

Universe Tankships of Monrovia Inc v International Transport Workers' Federation (The Universe Sentinel) [1983] 1 AC 366; [1982] 2 WLR 803; [1982] 2 All ER 67; [1982] 1 Ll Rep 537; [1982] Com LR 149; [1982] ICR

262; [1982] IRLR 200 HL . . . 399, **413–16**, 418–20, 424, 428, 431, 434

Uren v First National Home Finance Ltd [2005] EWHC 2529 Ch D . . . 110, **130–4**

Uren v John Fairfax & Sons Pty Ltd (1966) 117 CLR 118 . . . 934

Vadasz v Pi1er Concrete (SA) Pty Ltd (1955) 184 CLR 102 . . . 856

Valentini v Canali (1889) 24 QBD 166 DC . . . **608**, 611

Valley County v Thomas 109 Mont 345; 97 P 2d 345 (1939) . . . 116

Vandervell v Inland Revenue Commissioners [1967] 2 AC 291; [1967] 2 WLR 87; [1967] 1 All ER 1; 43 TC 519; (1966) 45 ATC 394; [1966] TR 315; 110 SJ 910 HL . . . 732–3

Vandervell's Trusts (No 2), Re [1974] Ch 269; [1974] 3 WLR 256; [1974] 3 All ER 205; 118 SJ 566 CA . . . 733

Vantage Navigation Corp v Suhail and Saud Bahwan Building Materials LLC (The Alev) [1989] 1 Ll Rep 138 QBD . . . 419

Vaughan v Vanderstegen (1854) 2 Drew 363 . . . 923

Vedatech Corp v Crystal Decisions (UK) Ltd (formerly Seagate Software IMG Ltd) [2002] EWHC 818 Ch D . . . 286, 347

Verschures Creameries Ltd v Hull and Netherlands Steamship Co Ltd [1921] 2 KB 608 CA . . . 947

Vigers v Cook [1919] 2 KB 475 CA . . . 305

Vinogradoff, Re [1935] WN 68 . . . 731

Vyse v Foster (1872) LR 8 Ch App 309 CA . . . 1014

Wainwright v Home Office [2003] UKHL 53; [2004] 2 AC 406; [2003] 3 WLR 1137; [2003] 4 All ER 969; [2004] UKHRR 154; 15 BHRC 387; (2003) 100(45) LSG 30; (2003) 147 SJLB 1208 HL . . . 1030

Wakefield v Newbon (1844) 6 QB 276 . . . 407

Walford v Miles [1992] 2 AC 128; [1992] 2 WLR 174; [1992] 1 All ER 453; (1992) 64 P & CR 166; [1992] 1 EGLR 207; [1992] 11 EG 115; [1992] NPC 4 HL . . . 353

Wallersteiner v Moir (No 2) [1975] QB 373; [1975] 2 WLR 389; [1975] 1 All ER 849; 119 SJ 97 CA . . . 590, 728

Walstab v Spottiswoode (1846) 15 M & W 501 . . . 272–3

Walter v James (1871) LR 6 Ex 124 Ex Ct . . . 539–40, 544, 550

Waltons Stores (Interstate) Pty Ltd v Maher (1988) 164 CLR 387 . . . 332, 354, 814

Ward & Co v Wallis [1900] 1 QB 675 QBD . . . 158

Warman v Southern Counties Car Finance Corp
Ltd [1949] 2 KB 576; [1949] 1 All ER 711;
[1949] LJR 1182; 93 SJ 319 KBD . . . 277, 360,
371, 1016

Watkins v Combes (1922) 30 CLR 180 . . . 483

Watson, Laidlaw & Co Ltd v Pott, Cassels &
Williamson (1914) 31 RPC 104 . . . 956, 962,
978, 983

Watts v Cresmell 9 Vin Abr 415 . . . 924

Waverley, The (1869–77) L.R. 3 A & E 369 Ct
Admir . . . 499

Way v Latilla [1937] 3 All ER 759 HL . . . 323, 335

Weatherby v Banham (1832) 5 C & P 228 . . . 84,
98

Weaver, Re (1882) LR 21 Ch D 615 CA . . . 583

Welby v Drake (1825) 1 C & P 557 . . . 539, 543

Weld-Blundell v Synott [1940] 2 KB 107 KBD . . .
153, 158

Wellston Coal Co v Franklin Paper Co 57 Ohio St
182; 48 NE 888 . . . 281, 283

West Sussex Constabulary's Widows, Children
and Benevolent (1930) Fund Trusts, Re
[1971] Ch 1; [1970] 2 WLR 848; [1970] 1 All
ER 544; 114 SJ 92 Ch D . . . 733

Westdeutsche Landesbank Girozentrale v
Islington LBC [1994] 1 WLR 938; [1994] 4 All
ER 890; [1994] CLC 96; 92 LGR 405; (1994)
158 LG Rev. 981; (1994) 91(8) LSG 29; (1994)
138 SJLB 26 CA . . . 363–9, 372, 374, 377–8,
380–1, 385, 638, 642

Westdeutsche Landesbank Girozentrale v
Islington LBC [1996] AC 669; [1996] 2 WLR
802; [1996] 2 All ER 961; [1996] 5 Bank LR
341; [1996] CLC 990; 95 LGR 1; (1996) 160 JP
Rep 1130; (1996) 146 NLJ 877; (1996) 140
SJLB 136 HL . . . 1, 8, **40–1**, 134–5, 182, 251,
362–8, 369, 372, 376, 381, 416, 623, 655, 659,
706, 711, **727–44**, 749, 759, 879, 890–2, 925,
927

Westminster Bank Ltd v Hilton (1926) 43 TLR
124 . . . 211

Westpac Banking Corp v Savin [1985] 2 NZLR 41
CA NZ . . . 233, 836

Whenman v Clark [1916] 1 KB 94 CA . . . 527

Whincup v Hughes (1870–71) LR 6 CP 78 CCP
. . . 17, 269, 303

White v Dobinson (1844) 14 Sim 273;
116 LTOS 233 . . . 714, 716–19

Whitecomb v Jacob (1710) 1 Salk 160 . . . 208,
649

Whiteley (William) v The King (1909) 101 LT 741
. . . 625, 629, 637, 643–4

Whithem v Westminster Co 12 Times LR 318 . . .
952

Whittington v Seale-Hayne (1900) 82 LT 49 . . .
196, **199–200**

Whitwham v Westminster Brymbo Coal and
Coke Co [1896] 2 Ch 538 . . . 954, 959–61,
978–9, 982

Wilder v Pilkington [1956] JPL 739 . . . 842

Wilkinson v Lloyd (1845) 7 QB 27 . . . 261

William Lacey (Hounslow) Ltd v Davis [1957]
1 WLR 932; [1957] 2 All ER 712; 101 SJ 629
QBD . . . 92, 96, **333–7**, 339–40, 343, 347–50,
394

William Watson & Co v Shankland (1871) 10 IH
. . . 17

Williams v Bayley (1866) LR 1 HL 200 HL . . .
436–8, 441, 444

Williams v Roffey Bros & Nicholls (Contractors)
Ltd [1991] 1 QB 1; [1990] 2 WLR 1153; [1990]
1 All ER 512; 48 BLR 69; (1991) 10 Tr LR 12;
(1990) 87(12) LSG 36; (1989) 139 NLJ 1712
CA . . . 398, 413, 421

Williams v Wentworth (1842) 5 Beav 325 . . . 583

Williams v Williams (1881) LR 17 Ch D 437 Ch D
. . . 227

Willis Faber Enthoven (Pty) Ltd v Receiver of
Revenue 1992 (4) SA 202 Sup Ct SA . . . 172,
182

Wilton v Farnworth (1948) 76 CLR 646 . . . 484

Wiluszynski v Tower Hamlets LBC [1989] ICR
493; [1989] IRLR 259; 88 LGR 14; (1989) 133
SJ 628 CA . . . 305

Wiseman v Beake 2 Vern 121 . . . 487

Wittet v Bush (1889) LR 40 Ch D 312 Ch D . . .
483

Woolwich Building Society (formerly Woolwich
Equitable Building Society) v Inland Revenue
Commissioners [1993] AC 70; [1992] 3 WLR
366; [1992] 3 All ER 737; [1992] STC 657 HL
. . . 1, 40, 45, 53,7 6, 173, 176, 363, 370, 375–6,
381, 390, 411, 623, **626–38**, 639–45, 706, 761,
870–2, 878

Woosung, The (1876) 1 P 260 CA . . . 499

Worcester Works Finance Ltd v Cooden
Engineering Co Ltd [1972] 1 QB 210; [1971]
3 WLR 661; [1971] 3 All ER 708; 115 SJ 605 CA
. . . 1025

Workers Trust & Merchant Bank Ltd v Dojap
Investments Ltd [1993] AC 573; [1993] 2 WLR
702; [1993] 2 All ER 370; (1993) 66 P & CR 15;
[1993] 1 EGLR 203; [1993] EGCS 38; (1993)
143 NLJ 616; (1993) 137 SJLB 83; [1993] NPC
33 PC . . . 309

World Wide Fund for Nature (formerly World
Wildlife Fund) v World Wrestling Federation
Entertainment Inc [2006] EWHC 184; [2006]
FSR 38; (2006) 150 SJLB 263 Ch D . . . **995–7**

Wrexham, Mold & Connah's Quay Railway Co,
Re [1899] 1 Ch 440 CA . . . 724

Wright v Vanderplank 8 D M & G 137 . . . 449,
453

Wrotham Park Estate Co Ltd v Parkside Homes
Ltd [1974] 1 WLR 798; [1974] 2 All ER 321;

(1974) 27 P & CR 296; (1973) 118 SJ 420 Ch D
... 937, 955–6, 959–60, 963, 967–9, **978–81**,
985–6, 989, 991, 995–6, 998

X v X (Y and Z Intervening) [2002] [2002] 1 FLR
508; Fam Law 98 Fam Div ... 778

Yango Pastoral Co Pty Ltd v First Chicago
Australia Ltd (1978) 139 CLR 410 ...
916–18

Yardley v Arnold (1843) C & M 434; 174 ER 577
... 116

Yates v White 1 Arn 85; sub nom Yates v Whyte 4
Bing (NC) 272 ... 716

Yeoman Credit Ltd v Apps [1962] 2 QB 508;
[1961] 3 WLR 94; [1961] 2 All ER 281; 105 SJ
567 CA ... **263–4**

York Glass Co Ltd v Jubb (1924) 131 LT 559 ...
614, 617–18

Yorkshire Insurance Co Ltds v Nisbet Shipping
Co Ltd [1962] 2 QB 330; [1961] 2 WLR 1043;
[1961] 2 All ER 487; [1961] 1 Ll Rep 479; 105
SJ 367 QBD ... 715, 717

Zaidan Group Ltd v City of London (1987) 36
DLR (4th) 443 ... 642, 706

Zuhal K, The [1987] 1 Ll Rep 151; [1987] 1 FTLR
76 QBD ... 519

TABLE OF LEGISLATION

AUSTRALIA

Builders Licensing Act 1971 (NSW) . . . 22, 24,
   88–9
   s.3 . . . 22
   s.45 . . . 22, 24–5, 27–8, 89

Commonwealth of Australia Constitution
   s.82 . . . 622
   s.83 . . . 622

Frustrated Contracts Act 1959 (Victoria) . . . 329
Frustrated Contracts Act 1978 (NSW) . . . 331
   s.9–13 . . . 331
Frustrated Contracts Act 1988 (South Australia)
   . . . 330

Minors (Property and Contracts) Act 1970
   (NSW)
   s.37 . . . **925**
   s.37(1) . . . **925**

Repatriation Act 1920
   s.113 . . . 621

Western Australia Law Reform (Property,
   Perpetuities and Succession) Act 1962
   s.23 . . . 172
   s.24 . . . 37
Western Australia Trustee Act 1962
   s.65(8) . . . 37

CANADA

Criminal Code
   s.347 . . . 140, 142–3

Frustrated Contracts Act 1996 (British
   Columbia) . . . **330**
   s.5–8 . . . **329**

Juvenile Delinquents Act 1970 . . . 74

Ontario State of Frauds 1950 . . . 18

Uniform Act (Frustrated Contracts Act) 1948 . . .
   329

EUROPEAN COMMUNITY

EEC Treaty
   Art. 174 . . . 637

HONG KONG

Prevention of Bribery Ordinance . . . 1018

NEW ZEALAND

Frustrated Contracts Act 1944 . . . 329

Illegal Contracts Act 1970 . . . 898
   s.6 . . . 897
   s.7 . . . 897

Judicature Act 1908
   s.94A . . . 172
   s.94A(2) . . . 174
   s.94B . . . 37, 784
Judicature Amendment Act 1958
   s.2 . . . 172, 174
   s.94(A)(1) . . . **182**
   s.94(A)(2) . . . **182**

UK

Administration of Justice Act 1956 . . . 571
   s.1 . . . 571
Admiralty Court Act 1840
   s.VI . . . 571
Annuity Act 1777 . . . 379
Annuity Act 1813 . . . 379

Betting and Lotteries Act 1934 . . . 501, 888
   s.13 . . . 500–1
Bill of Rights 1688 . . . 635

Capital Transfer Tax Act 1984
   s.241 . . . 627
Chancery Amendment Act 1858 (Lord Cairns'
   Act) . . . 954, 956–7, 984, 1027
   s.2 . . . 868
Civil Aviation Act 1949 . . . 571
Civil Aviation Act 1982 . . . 571
Civil Liability (Contribution) Act 1978 . . . 84,
   521–3
   s.1(1) . . . 521–2, **552**
   s.1(4) . . . 547
   s.2(1) . . . **552**
   s.2(3) . . . **552**
   s.3 . . . **552**
   s.6(1) . . . 521–2, **552**
   s.7(3) . . . **552**
Common Law Procedure Act 1852 . . . 943
   s.3 . . . 16, 273
   s.49 . . . 16

Commonwealth of Australia Constitution . . .
    622
  s.53 . . . 622
  s.54 . . . 622
  s.56 . . . 622
  s.81 . . . 621–2
  s.83 . . . 621
Companies Act 1985
  s.30 . . . 308
  s.35(1) . . . 620, 926
Copyright, Designs and Patents Act 1988
  s.96(1) . . . **972**
  s.96(2) . . . **972**
  s.97(1) . . . **972**
  s.191I(1) . . . **972**
  s.191I(2) . . . **972**
  s.191J(1) . . . **972**
  s.229(1) . . . **972**
  s.229(2) . . . **972**
  s.233(1) . . . **972**
  s.233(2) . . . **972**
  s.233(3) . . . **972**
Criminal Justice Act 1988
  Pt.VI . . . 977
Customs and Excise Management Act 1979
  s.137A(3) . . . 879
Customs' Duties Consolidation Act 1876
  s.85 . . . 510

Defence Service Homes Act 1918 . . . 912

Electricity Act 1947
  s.37(8) . . . 640
Exchange Control Act 1947 . . . 601

Fatal Accidents Act 1976
  s.5 . . . 553
Finance Act 1989
  s.24 . . . 627
  s.29 . . . 627
Finance Act 1994
  sch.7 para 8(3) . . . 879
Finance Act 1996
  sch.5 para 14(3) . . . 879
Finance Act 1997
  sch.5 . . . 879
  s.46–47 . . . 645
Finance Act 1998
  s.117(3) . . . 645
Finance Act 2000
  sch.6 . . . 879
Finance Act 2001
  sch.8 . . . 879
Finance (No 2) Act 1992
  s.64 . . . 638

Gaming Act 1845 . . . 150, 223
  s.18 . . . 30, 33, 35, 223
Gaming Acts . . . 34
General Rate Act 1967
  s.9 . . . 627

Hydrocarbon Oil Duties Act 1979
  s.9(1) . . . 641

Income Tax (Building Societies) Regulations 1986
    . . . 626
Infants' Relief Act 1874
  s.1 . . . 608, 610
Insurance Companies Act 1974 . . . 887

Judicature Act 1875 . . . 943
Judicature Acts 1873–5 . . . 5

Larceny Act 1916 . . . 443
Law of Property Act 1925
  s.199 . . . 226
Law Reform (Contributory Negligence) Act 1945
  s.1 . . . 553
Law Reform (Frustrated Contracts) Act 1943 . . .
    72, 80, 98, 123, 314, 316–17, 320, 322, 325–6,
    329, 362
  s.1 . . . **314**
  s.1(1) . . . 316
  s.1(2) . . . 72, 316–18, 321, 324, 325–7
  s.1(3) . . . 73, 93, 316–23, 325, 327
  s.1(3)(a) . . . 319, 321
  s.1(3)(b) . . . 319, 321, 326
  s.1(4) . . . 316
  s.1(6) . . . 316
  s.2(1) . . . 316
  s.2(2) . . . 316
  s.2(3) . . . 316–17, 323–4
  s.2(3)-2(5) . . . **314**
  s.2(5) . . . 316
Law Reform (Married Women and Tortfeasors)
    Act 1935 . . . 566
Limitation Act 1980
  s.32(1) . . . 168–9, 178
  s.32(1)(c) . . . 168–9, 178–9, 183
Lottery Act 1772 . . . 30

Marine Insurance Act 1906
  s.84 . . . 372

Married Women's Property Act 1882 . . . 566
Matrimonial Causes Act 1973
  s.1(2)(d) . . . 778
Matrimonial Proceedings and Property
    Act 1970
  s.37 . . . 95
Mercantile Law Amendment Act 1856
  s.5 . . . 518
Merchant Shipping Act 1854
  s.458 . . . 571
Merchant Shipping Act 1894
  s.546 . . . 571
Minors' Contracts Act 1987 . . . 919
  s.1(a) . . . 608
  s.3 . . . **925**
  s.3(2) . . . **925**

Misrepresentation Act 1967
  s.2(1) . . . 200
  s.2(2) . . . 868

Partnership Act 1890
  s 40 . . . 14
Patents Act 1977
  s.61(1) . . . **971**
  s.61(2) . . . **971**
  s.62(1) . . . **971**
Public Health (Control of Diseases) Act 1984
  s.46(1) . . . 566
Public Health (London) Act 1891 . . . 508
  s.4(1) . . . 508–10
  s.4(3) . . . 509
  s.4(3)(a) . . . 508
  s.4(4) . . . 508–9
  s.11 . . . 508–10
  s.11(1) . . . 508

Road Traffic (NHS Charges) Act 1999 . . . 531

Sale of Goods Act 1893
  s.4 . . . 296
Sale of Goods Act 1979
  s.3(2) . . . 584
  s.53 . . . 261
Sale of Goods (Amendment) Act 1995 . . . 696
Social Security (Recovery of Benefits)
  Act 1997 . . . 531
Stamp Act 1891
  s.13(4) . . . 627
Statute of Frauds 1667 . . . 25–7

Supreme Court Act 1981 . . . 571
  s.35A . . . 626
  s.50 . . . 943

Taxes Management Act 1970
  s.33 . . . 627, 644–5
Torts (Interference with Goods) Act 1977 . . . 187
  s.1 . . . **188**
  s.3(7) . . . **188**
  s.6 . . . **188**
Trade Union and Labour Relations Act 1974
  s.13 . . . 413
  s.13(1) . . . 416

Value Added Tax Act 1994
  s.80 . . . 645
  s.80(3) . . . 879

War Damage Act 1965 . . . 181

US

Restatement of the Law of Contract
  s.468 . . . 17
Restatement of the Law of Restitution 1937 . . . **9,**
    101, 171, 943
  para.1 . . . 21
  para.160 . . . 227
  s.1 . . . 873
  s.33 . . . 165
  s.47 . . . 370
  s.141(2) . . . 804

1

UNJUST ENRICHMENT AND COMPETING THEORIES

The conventional way of defining the law of restitution is that it is the law based on the principle of reversing a defendant's unjust enrichment at the claimant's expense. The bulk of the subject comprises what used to be called quasi-contract, but it also includes areas of equity such as a fiduciary's liability to account for unauthorized profits, rescission of an executed contract (for misrepresentation, undue influence, or duress), tracing, and subrogation.

English law traditionally did not recognize a law of restitution based on the principle of reversing unjust enrichment and obiter dicta of great judges, such as Lord Mansfield in *Moses v Macferlan* (below, 4) and Lord Wright in *Fibrosa* (below, 12), were largely ignored. On the traditional approach, the above areas were treated as having no relationship to each other; and the implied contract theory (hence 'quasi-contract') was primarily put forward to explain most of the relevant common law (see, for example, *Sinclair v Brougham*, below, 6). If a claimant paid a defendant £1,000 under a mistake of fact, his or her legal remedy to recover the £1,000 was said to rest on the defendant's implied promise to pay it back. But such a promise cannot rest on the defendant's actual intention and the implied contract theory provides no explanation for why the promise should be implied.

In 1966 Goff and Jones published *The Law of Restitution* (now in its sixth edition, published in 2002) which attacked the traditional English approach and sought to demonstrate that, looking across both common law and equity, there is a coherent English law of restitution based on the principle of reversing unjust enrichment (below, 19). Although incorporating elements of the law of property as well as the law of obligations, they saw the law of restitution as belonging alongside contract and tort as a third division of the law of obligations. Goff and Jones' thesis slowly gained acceptance in academia and amongst practitioners and judges, culminating in the House of Lords' acceptance of it in 1991 in *Lipkin Gorman v Karpnale Ltd* (below, 28), which can be regarded as the *Donoghue v Stevenson* ([1932] AC 562) of the law of restitution. A year later in *Woolwich Equitable Building Society v IRC*, (below, Chapter 12) their Lordships relied on unjust enrichment reasoning to reach the radical decision that a citizen is entitled as of right to restitution of payments demanded by a public authority *ultra vires*. In *Westdeutsche Landesbank Girozentrale v Islington London BC*, (below, 40) the House of Lords 'unequivocally and finally' rejected the implied contract theory of restitution and formally overruled *Sinclair v Brougham* on this point (as well as in relation to the other 'proprietary' point in the case: see below, Chapter 13). Explicit reference to unjust enrichment as the basis of the restitutionary claim has subsequently been made by judges at all levels in many cases including, for example, *Cressman v Coys of Kensington* on the meaning of benefit (below, 77), *Kleinwort Benson Ltd v Lincoln City Council* on restitution of payments made by mistake of law (below, 167), *Banque Financiere de la Cité v Parc (Battersea) Ltd* on non-contractual subrogation (below, 190) and *Kleinwort Benson v Birmingham CC* rejecting the defence of passing on (below, 871).

It should not be thought that this recognition of unjust enrichment is confined to England. On the contrary, English law has, in this respect, lagged behind much of the common law world (let alone civilian systems, such as Germany and France, where a law of unjust enrichment has long been established). In the United States, restitution based on the principle of reversing unjust enrichment was accepted earlier this century with the publication in 1937 of the *Restatement of Restitution* (below, 9). In Canada, the principle was accepted in *Deglman v Guaranty Trust Co.* (below, 18), and the equivalent landmark case in Australia is *Pavey Matthews Pty. Ltd v Paul* (below, 22). The English law of restitution has much to learn from other systems, and this book contains several extracts from Canadian and Australian cases.

That the law of restitution has only relatively recently been recognized in England does not mean that one has no concern with cases prior to 1991. On the contrary we believe that, whatever the overt language used, the courts have long been applying the principle of reversing unjust enrichment. As regards pre-1991 decisions, the modern approach must therefore be to explain how most of those decisions can be rationalized using the language of unjust enrichment, while acknowledging that the open acceptance of the principle may enable unwarranted traditional restrictions to be evaded more easily.

It has become widely recognized in recent years that there are (at least) two funda-mentally distinct parts to the law of restitution, albeit that the *principle* of reversing unjust enrichment can be regarded as underpinning both. The two parts are distin-guishable by the cause of action (or event) triggering the response of restitution. The first and main part is where the cause of action to which restitution responds is an unjust enrichment of the defendant at the claimant's expense. The second part is where the cause of action to which restitution responds is the commission of a wrong by the defendant against the claimant (such as a breach of contract or tort or breach of fiduciary duty). So the former part is independent of a claim for a wrong (that is, a breach of duty) whereas the latter part is dependent on establishing a wrong. For shorthand purposes, we can refer to the two parts as being, respectively, restitution of unjust enrichments and restitution for wrongs. The importance of this distinction is that, for example, different criteria have to be established for the different causes of action; different legal rules may apply (for example, as regards limitation of actions and conflict of laws); and some of the defences applicable are different (most importantly, change of position applies to the cause of action of unjust enrichment but, it appears, not to wrongs).

In his later writings (below, 41–48), the late Peter Birks took what might be seen as the next logical step in the development of the subject. He argued that, in line with the conventional approach to classification in private law—which is by cause of action (or event) rather than by response—the subject should be confined to the cause of action of unjust enrichment. Restitution for wrongs should instead be studied within the law of wrongs. In so far as there are other events triggering restitution (and Birks argued that there were, for example, consent)[1] they too should be studied with the law governing that event.

---

1 We do not agree with Birks that it is helpful to see consent as triggering restitution: see below, 48, note 2.

But university courses are almost invariably courses on the law of restitution not the law of unjust enrichment and, in particular, include restitution for wrongs. This is consistent with the coverage of all the main textbooks. It also directly reflects the way in which the subject has been developed in the common law world. We have therefore continued to call this book the law of restitution, rather than the law of unjust enrichment, and have continued to include within it restitution for wrongs. Having said that, apart from this introductory chapter we confine our consideration of restitution for wrongs to the final chapter of the book and thereby acknowledge that the bulk of this book concerns restitution for the cause of action (or event) of unjust enrichment.

It follows from what has been said in the last few paragraphs that care must be taken to ensure that one does not confuse the overarching *principle* of reversing unjust enrichment (which can be regarded as including restitution for wrongs) with restitution for the *cause of action* of unjust enrichment (which excludes restitution for wrongs). In this book, unless we make it clear that we are referring to the principle of reversing unjust enrichment (sometimes alternatively referred to as the principle 'against unjust enrichment') our references to unjust enrichment will be to the cause of action (or event) of unjust enrichment.

Restitution scholarship has rarely sought to examine, at a deep theoretical level, the justification for restitution. The emphasis has rather been on establishing the subject's existence in the law and clarifying its internal structure and details. Nevertheless some commentators have explored the question of whether restitution rests on corrective justice. We include extracts on this issue in respect of restitution of unjust enrichment from Barker (below, 48) and Lionel Smith (below, 50) (the latter drawing heavily on the pioneering work of Weinrib). Corrective justice as a justification of restitution for wrongs is explored in Chapter 15.

Not everyone favours the legal recognition of unjust enrichment whether as a principle or as a cause of action. We include in this Chapter extracts from the works of leading sceptics (below, 54–70).

What can cause an unnecessary amount of confusion, especially for beginners to the subject, is that there is a host of different personal (that is, substitutionary) remedies concerned to effect restitution. In an ideal world these would be rationalized. But at the present time one cannot simply talk of claiming personal restitution. Rather differently described personal remedies are applicable to different situations. The most common restitutionary remedy covering the recovery of money paid to the defendant is the action for money had and received to the claimant's use. This is the remedy in issue where, for example, a claimant seeks (personal) restitution of money paid to the defendant by mistake (see Chapter 3) or for a consideration that has totally failed (see Chapter 5). For the value of services rendered one claims a *quantum meruit* (see, for example, *Deglman v Guaranty Trust Co.*, below, 18, and *Pavey & Matthews Pty. Ltd v Paul*, below, 22, both of which concerned services rendered under unenforceable contracts). As we shall see in Chapter 8, where one has discharged another's debt under legal compulsion, one may claim restitution in an action for money paid to the defendant's use or an indemnity. Other examples of personal restitutionary remedies for the cause of action of unjust enrichment include accounting for the value of property received (see Chapter 4) and, in certain contexts, rescission of a contract. Restitutionary remedies for wrongs normally comprise an account of profits, an award of money had and received or restitutionary damages (that is, damages measured by the enrichment of the wrongdoer rather than by the loss of the victim). Restitution for wrongs is the subject matter of Chapter 15.

While this panoply of often archaic-sounding remedies is unfortunate, it should not be allowed to obscure what, in our view, is the straightforward position that, while some of these remedies can be used in other contexts, a claimant choosing one of them is almost always seeking personal restitution of an unjust enrichment or for a wrong.

In addition to personal (substitutionary) remedies, some restitutionary remedies are proprietary (that is, concerned with specific property). The major practical difference between personal and proprietary restitutionary remedies is that the latter, unlike the former, give the claimant priority on the defendant's insolvency. Probable examples of proprietary restitutionary remedies are the equitable lien, some constructive and resulting trusts, rescission of a contract or deed of gift under which title has passed, and subrogation to secured rights. Proprietary restitution of an unjust enrichment is considered in Chapter 13. Proprietary restitution for wrongs is dealt with in Chapter 15.

General Reading

BURROWS, 1–15, 52–53; GOFF AND JONES, 1-001–1-016; VIRGO, 3–18, 51–56

1. THE CONTRIBUTION OF LORD MANSFIELD

• *Moses v Macferlan* (1760) 2 Burr 1005, Court of King's Bench

The claimant (Moses) had endorsed to the defendant (Macferlan) four promissory notes (payable by a third party, Chapman Jacob, to the claimant) of 30s each. The defendant signed an agreement to the effect that the claimant should not be prejudiced by reason of his endorsement. Nevertheless the defendant sued the claimant, as endorser, on each of the four notes. The Court of Conscience thought that the non-prejudice agreement could not be a defence and, without hearing evidence of it, gave judgment for the defendant for £6. After paying it, the claimant brought an action for money had and received to the claimant's use to recover the £6. Lord Mansfield held that, while the Court of Conscience's judgment had technically been correct, nevertheless the action for money had and received should succeed because it was unjust for the defendant to keep the money.

Lord Mansfield (delivering the unanimous decision of the Court): [An objection put to this action was] 'That no assumpsit lies, except upon an express or implied contract: but here it is impossible to presume any contract to refund money, which the defendant recovered by an adverse suit.'

Answer. If the defendant be under an obligation, from the ties of natural justice, to refund; the law implies a debt, and gives this action, founded in the equity of the plaintiff's case, as it were upon a contract ('quasi ex contractu,' as the Roman law expresses it). . . .

[Another objection put was that] [W]here money has been recovered by the judgment of a Court having competent jurisdiction, the matter can never be brought over again by a new action.

Answer. It is most clear, 'that the merits of a judgment can never be over-haled by an original suit, either at law or in equity.' Till the judgment is set aside, or reversed, it is conclusive, as to the subject matter of it, to all intents and purposes.

But the ground of this action is consistent with the judgment of the Court of Conscience. . . .

The ground of this action is not, 'that the judgment was wrong:' but, 'that, (for a reason which the now plaintiff could not avail himself of against that judgment,) the defendant ought not in justice to keep the money.' . . .

This kind of equitable action, to recover back money, which ought not in justice to be kept, is very beneficial, and therefore much encouraged. It lies only for money which, ex æquo et bono, the defendant ought to refund: it does not lie for money paid by the plaintiff, which is claimed of him as payable in point of honor and honesty, although it could not have been recovered from him by any course of law; as in payment of a debt barred by the Statute of Limitations, or contracted during his infancy, or to the extent of principal and legal interest upon an usurious contract, or, for money fairly lost at play: because in all these cases, the defendant may retain it with a safe conscience, though by positive law he was barred from recovering. But it lies for money paid by mistake; or upon a consideration which happens to fail; or for money got through imposition, (express, or implied;) or extortion; or oppression; or an undue advantage taken of the plaintiff's situation, contrary to laws made for the protection of persons under those circumstances.

In one word, the gist of this kind of action is, that the defendant, upon the circumstances of the case, is obliged by the ties of natural justice and equity to refund the money.

Therefore we are all of us of opinion that the plaintiff might elect to wave any demand upon the foot of the indemnity, for the costs he had been put to; and bring this action, to recover the 6l. which the defendant got and kept from him iniquitously.

NOTES

1. The importance of this case lies in Lord Mansfield's obiter dicta articulating (a) the basis of the action for money had and received and (b) some of the situations where that action would, and would not, succeed.

2. In the second paragraph in the above extract, Lord Mansfield was recognizing that the promise that needed to be pleaded for the *indebitatus assumpsit* form of action, used for the action for money had and received, was fictional.

3. The action for money had and received is a common law action in the sense that it was awarded (prior to the Judicature Acts 1873–5) by the common law courts and not the Court of Chancery. Lord Mansfield's reference to it being an 'equitable action' means no more than that he considered the action flexible and concerned to achieve justice.

4. On the face of it the actual decision seems wrong in reversing, through restitution and not by means of an appeal (or by otherwise setting aside a judgment), a decision rendered by a competent court within its jurisdiction. It therefore contradicts the policy of finality in litigation (embodied in, for example, the defence of *res judicata*). A linked criticism is that the decision appears to contradict the general principle that there is no unjust enrichment where a benefit is conferred in accordance with a valid obligation (here a judgment obligation). The decision was subsequently rejected in e.g. *Phillips v Hunter* (1795) 2 H Bl. 402 and *Marriot v Hampton* (1797) 7 TR 269. But in *Unjust Enrichment* (2nd edn, 2005), 14–15 Birks argued that the decision was correct if seen as awarding restitution for breach of contract rather than restitution of an unjust enrichment:

   The difference between unjust enrichment and restitution for wrongs was not articulated in the 18th century, but Lord Mansfield's decision can be defended in retrospect on the ground that it was only the analysis in unjust enrichment, not the action for breach of contract, which encountered objections. Lord Mansfield's premiss was that Moses was indubitably entitled to an action for breach of contract. Such an action was perfectly compatible with respect for the other court's judgment, which, valid as it was, had indeed been obtained in breach of contract.

2. THE IMPLIED CONTRACT THEORY

• *Sinclair v Brougham* [1914] AC 398, House of Lords

The Birkbeck Permanent Benefit Building Society was acting *ultra vires* by carrying on a banking business. In an application by the liquidator on the winding up of the society the question arose, *inter alia*, whether those who had lent money under the *ultra vires* banking facilities (the depositors) could recover that money in an action for money had and received. The House of Lords held that the action should fail (although the depositors' equitable proprietary tracing claim succeeded: see below, 657).

Viscount Haldane LC (with whom **Lord Atkinson** concurred): . . . I propose to consider in the first place the question whether an action for money had and received would have lain against the society on the footing that although its conduct in receiving the depositors' money was ultra vires, it had become improperly, as between itself and the depositors, enriched thereby, so that the amount received was money held to the depositors' use and recoverable as a debt, independently of any right to trace and follow. Two authorities were cited in support of the argument that such an action could have been brought successfully. One of these was a judgment of Sir William Page Wood v-C. in the case of the *Phœnix Life Assurance Co*[1] The other was a decision of the Court of Appeal in Ireland which followed his judgment in *Flood v Irish Provident Assurance Co*[2] In these cases the principle of tracing was not relied on, but it was apparently held that the amount of certain premiums which had been paid in respect of policies, the issue of which was ultra vires, could be recovered as money had and received.

My Lords, if these decisions had related to the recovery of borrowed money I should find it difficult to reconcile them with principle. If it be outside the power of a statutory society to enter into the relation of debtor and creditor in a particular transaction, the only possible remedy for the person who has paid the money would on principle appear to be one in rem and not in personam, a claim to follow and recover specifically any money which could be earmarked as never having ceased to be his property. To hold that a remedy will lie in personam against a statutory society, which by hypothesis cannot in the case in question have become a debtor or entered into any contract for repayment, is to strike at the root of the doctrine of ultra vires as established in the jurisprudence of this country. That doctrine belongs to substantive law and is the outcome of statute, and cannot be made different by any choice of form in procedure.

It is, therefore, binding both at law and in equity. In the jurisprudence of England the doctrine of ultra vires must now be treated as established in a stringent form by Acts of the Legislature and decisions of great authority which have interpreted these Acts. This is a principle which it appears to me must to-day be taken as a governing one, not only at law but in equity. I think it excludes from the law of England any claim in personam based on the circumstance that the defendant has been improperly enriched at the expense of the plaintiff by a transaction which is ultra vires. All analogies drawn from other systems, such as that of the Roman law, appear to me to be qualified in their application by two considerations. The first is that, broadly speaking, so far as proceedings in personam are concerned, the common law of England really recognizes (unlike the Roman law) only actions of two classes, those founded on contract and those founded on tort. When it speaks of actions arising quasi ex contractu it refers merely to a class of action in theory based on a contract which is imputed to the defendant by a fiction of law. The fiction can only be set up with effect if such

---

1 2 J & H 441.   2 46 Ir. LT 214; [1912] 2 Ch 597, n.

a contract would be valid if it really existed. This is a point to which I shall have to return later on in what I have to say. The second consideration is that where an Act of Parliament imposes a restriction on capacity, that restriction is binding in equity as much as at law, the principles of which equity follows.

. . .

My Lords, notwithstanding the wide scope of the [action for money had and received], I think that it must be taken to have been given only, as I have already said, where the law could consistently impute to the defendant at least the fiction of a promise. And it appears to me that as matter of principle the law of England cannot now, consistently with the interpretation which the Courts have placed on the statutes which determine the capacity of statutory societies, impute the fiction of such a promise where it would have been ultra vires to give it. The fiction becomes, in other words, inapplicable where substantive law, as distinguished from that of procedure, makes the defendant incapable of undertaking contractual liability. For to impute a fictitious promise is simply to presume the existence of a state of facts, and the presumption can give rise to no higher right than would result if the facts were actual.

I am accordingly of opinion that while the decisions of Sir William Page Wood and of the Irish Court of Appeal to which I have referred may possibly, notwithstanding that the issue of the policies was ultra vires, be supported on the ground that they related merely to the failure of consideration for the premiums paid (a question on which it is unnecessary for me to express any opinion), they cannot be invoked as authorities for the proposition that an action for money had and received would have lain in a case of borrowing ultra vires. . . .

Lord Dunedin: . . . Let me now examine the position where the money is received under a contract to repay and where that contract is found to be ultra vires. That there can be no resulting proper contractual obligation is clear. . . . It is here that the difficulty comes in in extending the action for money had and received to such a case. For, in the first place, if that action lay it would have the effect of bringing in A., who has, ex hypothesi, no binding contract to urge against B., pari passu with the ordinary creditors of B. who have got binding contracts; and in the second, how is it possible to say that there is a fictional contract which is binding in circumstances in which a real contract is not binding? My Lords, I confess that for a person not bred to the common law to express an opinion as to the true meaning and extent of common law actions is to handle periculosæ plenum opus alææ. But to the best of my comprehension, and notwithstanding the case of *Phœnix Life Assurance Co.*, I have come to the conclusion that the action for money had and received cannot be stretched to meet the situation. . . .

Lord Parker of Waddington: . . . It has been settled . . . that an ultra vires borrowing by persons affecting to act on behalf of a company or other statutory association does not give rise to any indebtedness either at law or in equity on the part of such company or association. It is not, therefore, open to the House to hold that in such a case the lender has an action against the company or association for money had and received. To do so would in effect validate the transaction so far as it embodied a contract to repay the money lent. The implied promise on which the action for money had and received is based would be precisely that promise which the company or association could not lawfully make. At the same time there seems to be nothing in those decisions which would bind the House, if they were considering whether an action would lie in law or in equity to recover money paid under any ultra vires contract which was not a contract of borrowing; for example, money paid to a company or association for the purchase of land which the company had no power to sell and the sale of which was therefore void, or money paid to the company or association by way of subscription for shares which it had no power to issue. In such cases the implied promise on which the action for money had and received depends would form no part of, but would be merely collateral to, the ultra vires contract. It will therefore be well to postpone consideration of such cases as the *Phœnix Life Assurance Co.* and *Flood v Irish Provident Assurance Co.* till the question actually arises. . . .

Lord Sumner: . . . The depositors' case has been put, first of all, as consisting in a right enforceable in a common law action. It is said that they paid their money under a mistake of fact, or for a consideration that has wholly failed, or that it has been had and received by the society to their use. My Lords, in my opinion no such actions could succeed. To hold otherwise would be indirectly to sanction an ultra vires borrowing. All these causes of action are common species of the genus assumpsit. All now rest, and long have rested, upon a notional or imputed promise to repay. The law cannot de jure impute promises to repay, whether for money had and received or otherwise, which, if made de facto, it would inexorably avoid.

. . .

In these straits, Lord Mansfield's celebrated account of the action of money had and received in *Moses v Macferlan* was of course relied upon. It was said that for any one to keep the depositors' money as against them would be unconscientious, while that they should get it back would be eminently ex æquo et bono, though it appeared also that conscience had nothing to say against payment of the depositors in full at the expense of the shareholders, though all alike must be deemed cognizant of the invalidity of the society's banking business. [*After considering, and casting some doubt on* Phœnix Life Assurance Co. *(1862) 2 J & H 441, Lord Sumner continued:*] The other cases cited seem to me insufficient to support the appellants' claim to any common law right. The action for money had and received cannot now be extended beyond the principles illustrated in the decided cases, and although it is hard to reduce to one common formula the conditions under which the law will imply a promise to repay money received to the plaintiff's use, I think it is clear that no authority extends them far enough to help the appellants now.

Resort was then had to equity, and, as I understood it, the argument was that the action for money had and received was founded on equity and good conscience, and imported a head of equity (apart altogether from its possibly too limited application at law), namely, that whenever it is ex æquo et bono for A. to repay money which he has received from B., and would be against conscience for A. to keep it, then B. has an equity to have A. decreed to repay it. For this again Lord Mansfield's authority in the same case was invoked.

My Lords, I cannot but think that Lord Mansfield's language has been completely misunderstood. [*Lord Sumner considered the judgment of Lord Mansfield and its subsequent development and continued:*] There is now no ground left for suggesting as a recognizable 'equity' the right to recover money in personam merely because it would be the right and fair thing that it should be refunded to the payer. . . .

NOTES AND QUESTIONS

1. This case, more than any other, with the Lords' adherence to the implied contract theory, held back the development of a principled law of restitution in England. The implied contract theory was not formally departed from in England until *Lipkin Gorman v Karpnale Ltd* (below, 28). *Sinclair v Brougham* was overruled in *Westdeutsche Landesbank Girozentrale v Islington London BC* (below, 40).

2. Do you think that *Sinclair v Brougham* was wrongly decided (as the House of Lords in the *Westdeutsche Landesbank* case has now laid down) in denying a personal restitutionary remedy for money had and received? If one were seeking to defend *Sinclair v Brougham*, which of the following two lines of argument better justifies the decision:

   (a) there could be no action for money had and received because an actual contract to repay the loan was *ultra vires* and void and the same must apply to an implied contract; or
   (b) although the society was unjustly enriched at the depositors' expense the policy behind

the *ultra vires* doctrine dictated that restitution (as well as contractual enforcement) must be denied?

3. In the following short extract, we see support for the implied contract theory being given by Sir William Holdsworth who feared that overtly resting the law on unjust enrichment thinking would give rise to 'palm tree' justice.

• **WS Holdsworth, 'Unjustifiable Enrichment'** (1939) 55 *LQR* 37, 43, 53

It would seem that there is overwhelming authority for saying that the common law personal remedy for unjustifiable enrichment depends both on the question whether in the circumstances it is fair and right that the defendant should pay, and on the question whether the relations of the defendant and plaintiff to each other are such that the law can imply a contract to repay. . . .

I conclude that the conditions in which English law gives a remedy for unjustifiable enrichment are not unreasonable. It may be that they require amendment in some particulars. If so let them be amended. But it would be a remedy far worse than the disease if the basis of the common law rule was scrapped, and for it was substituted a rule which left the whole matter to the discretion of the judge; and if, in consequence, the equitable modifications of, and supplements to, both the proprietary and the personal remedies given by the common law were left in the air. . . .

Better a system which is too rigid than no system at all.

3. THE RECOGNITION OF THE PRINCIPLE AGAINST UNJUST ENRICHMENT

In the common law world, the United States led the way in recognizing a law of restitution based on the principle of reversing unjust enrichment with the publication by the American Law Institute in 1937 of the Restatement of the Law of Restitution.

• **Restatement of the Law of Restitution** (1937, American Law Institute)

s. 1 Unjust enrichment

A person who has been unjustly enriched at the expense of another is required to make restitution to the other.

s. 2 Officious conferring of a benefit

A person who officiously confers a benefit upon another is not entitled to restitution therefor.

s. 3 Tortious acquisition of a benefit

A person is not permitted to profit by his own wrong at the expense of another.

s. 160 Constructive trust

Where a person holding title to property is subject to an equitable duty to convey it to another on the ground that he would be unjustly enriched if he were permitted to retain it, a constructive trust arises.

Warren Seavey and Austin Scott, the chief reporters on the Restatement of the Law of Restitution, explained the central thinking behind it in the following extract.

• **WA Seavey and AW Scott, 'Restitution'** (1938) 54 *LQR* 29

The most recent product of the American Law Institute is a restatement entitled 'Restitution', a word which to the best of our knowledge is not used as a title in any law digest or treatise. The matters with which it deals are found scattered through many sections of the digests and in treatises on apparently diverse subjects. Your editor has asked us to explain why such a grouping of material was undertaken and why there was given to it a title which is indefinite in connotation and unfamiliar to the profession.

The purpose of the American Law Institute is to analyse the most important topics of the law and to state succinctly the rules which are shown by analysis to represent the predominant American authority. In the restatements already published it has been possible to use familiar names and familiar categories. It so happens, however, that because of the way in which the English law developed, a group of situations having distinct unity has never been dealt with as a unit and because of this has never received adequate treatment. It was for the purpose of making clear the principles underlying this group and of attempting to give to it the individual life and development which its importance demands that the restatement of this subject was undertaken. Although it is a rule of the Institute that no new word should be coined, it is consistent with its practices to use an old word with either a more precise or a more generalized meaning. With this in mind, the word 'restitution' was chosen, a word which has a connotation of the right to recover back something which one once had.

In order to indicate the sweep of the subject and to justify its separate treatment, it may be well to indicate its scope. In brief it includes most of the situations dealt with in the few works on quasi contracts, together with the addition of corresponding matters dealt with in treatises on equity and trusts, including the specific remedy of constructive trust. . . .

In bringing these situations together under one heading, the Institute expresses the conviction that they are all subject to one unitary principle which heretofore has not had general recognition. In this it has recognized the tripartite division of the law into contracts, torts and restitution, the division being made with reference to the purposes which each subject serves in protecting one of three fundamental interests. In this division, the postulate of the law of contracts (or of undertakings) is that a person is entitled to receive what another has promised him or promised another for him. It is to be noted that in this analysis the obligations resulting from trusts are considered as falling within the contract field since they result from an undertaking by the trustee and since the beneficiary is entitled to performance by the trustee in accordance with his undertaking, although the remedies of the beneficiaries of a trust are equitable, whereas the remedies for breach of contract are ordinarily legal. The interest of the promisee or beneficiary which is protected by the law is his reasonable expectation that a promise freely made will be performed. The law requires the promisor, if he fails to perform the promise, to place the other, as far as reasonably can be done, in as good a position as if the promise had been performed. The law of torts is based upon the premise that a person has a right not to be harmed by another, either with respect to his personality or with respect to his interests in things and in other persons. The law protects this right by requiring a wrongdoer to give such compensation to the person harmed as will be substantially equivalent to the harm done. The accent is upon wrong and harm. Beside these two postulates there is a third, sometimes overlapping the others, but different in its purpose. This third postulate, which underlies the rules assembled in the Restatement under the heading 'Restitution', can be expressed thus: A person has a right to have restored to him a benefit gained at his expense by another, if the retention of the benefit by the other would be unjust. The law protects this right by granting restitution of the benefit which otherwise would, in most cases, unjustly enrich the recipient. . . .

Lord Mansfield seems first to have recognized the fundamental principle of restitution in an opinion remarkable for its insight (whether or not a proper result was reached), in which he stated that 'the gist of this kind of action [the action of general *assumpsit*] is that the defendant upon the circumstances of the case, is obliged by the ties of natural justice and equity to refund the money'. But although such a principle has since been sporadically recognized and although it underlies the decisions of many cases, the diverse sources of the individual rules and the adherence by legal treatise writers and law teachers to the divisions of the law created by historical accident rather than by analysis, have prevented its common acceptance and a unified treatment. . . .

In many cases restitution is an alternative remedy for a breach of contract or for a tort, and to this extent there is no necessity for having a separate treatment of the remedy. However, in many of the situations in which there is a right to restitution there is no right upon any theory of the law of contracts or of tort. Thus, where a person pays a debt twice, the recipient being ignorant of the prior payment, it is purely fictional to state that the recipient manifested a promise to pay it back. It is even clearer that where a person in the belief that a duty is his own, performs another's duty, as where he pays taxes upon land which he thinks he owns, but which in fact is owned by another, there is no contract between the two; obviously there has been no prior relation between the parties and no possibility of a manifestation of consent by the beneficiary. Another type of case which has become important in recent years is that where a broker has possession of share certificates owned by a number of customers which he pledges with a third person for a debt of his own, the pledge being valid because the certificates have been endorsed in blank. Here, if the pledgee sells the certificate of one of the customers in order to satisfy the debt of the broker, the customer is entitled to contribution from the others whose certificates were not sold. If it were not for the principle of restitution there would be no remedy.

These cases and numerous others where relief is properly given indicate that a theory of restitution is essential to dealing justly between the parties. If it is alleged, as it frequently has been, that its basic premise is so broad as to be meaningless, it may be answered that the same is equally true of the generalizations made with reference to contracts and torts. Not all promises are required to be performed, and in not every case is the promisee put in substantially as good a position as if the promise had been performed. It requires a large number of individual rules to determine when relief will be given. This becomes even more obvious with reference to the law of torts, although, in general, the postulate suggested for torts satisfies the requirements of the cases. In order to reach an answer we must first define wrong and also harm. It requires no extensive learning to know that wrong does not always mean moral wrong and that harm does not necessarily mean either physical hurt or pecuniary damage. The law of torts has become formalized and the postulate is merely a brief thumb-nail sketch indicating extent rather than giving precise boundaries.

The situation is the same in the case of the fundamental conception of restitution. It requires an extensive set of individual rules to spell out what is meant by 'unjust': . . . as in other branches of the law, the subject of restitution is not properly or adequately described merely by a description of the purpose or interest which gives life to the rules. It is an organism, growing in accordance with the principle which causes it to exist; a statement of the principle is not a description of what it produces. . . .

It may . . . be objected that a number of actions commonly known as tort actions come within the idea of restitution. These are ejectment, replevin, detinue (which, curiously enough, survives in one of the American States) and trover. It is readily conceded that these are restitutionary in nature since all of them are maintainable in situations where the defendant has at least gained possession at the expense of the plaintiff. This proves nothing, however, except that these actions can be looked at either from the standpoint of the harm done or of the value of the benefit received. They are in fact restitutionary tort actions.

At this point it may be asked why it was not thought advisable to use the term 'quasi contract' which, in the form of 'obligationes quasi ex contractu', existed in the Roman law and which has had a considerable usage since the time of Austin. In the first place, as has been frequently pointed out, the term 'quasi contract' is unfortunate in that it connotes that the circumstances give rise to a contract right. That is, of course, not always true since in many of the cases the situation is nothing like that under which a contract arises. In such cases, the only connexion between the quasi-contractual right and the contract right is the historical one that both rights could be enforced in the law Courts by an action of *assumpsit*. A second reason for avoiding 'quasi contract' as a title is that many writers have used it to designate the topic in which are included, on the ground that an action of general *assumpsit* could be brought, actions for failure to pay a judgment, for a breach of statutory duty and even upon an account stated. It may be that for procedural purposes such situations should be classified with those based upon unjust enrichment, but analytically the two groups have little in common. A third reason for not using the term 'quasi contract' is that the phrase has by custom been confined to situations where the right is enforceable in an action at law, and it is desirable to include all situations which involve the restitution postulate, irrespective of the remedy which can be obtained. That there is no fundamental difference between the restitutional rights enforced at law and those enforced in equity can be demonstrated only by a comparison of the cases; such a comparison indicates that the principles used by both Courts are the same, although for various reasons a suitor may not be able to get into one of the Courts or, because of procedural reasons, he may obtain less in one than in the other. . . .

It may be that for many purposes it is desirable still to keep distinct the functions of the two Courts, but certainly it is not rational, except so far as differences in procedure require it, and they seldom do, for two co-ordinate Courts in the same jurisdiction to reach different results upon the same set of facts. A statement of rules stated to be applicable to both will have a tendency to lessen the few remaining differences.

Prior to the 1990s probably the most important case on restitution in England was *Fibrosa*. Lord Wright's speech is especially important.

• *Fibrosa Spolka Akcyjna v Fairbairn Lawson Combe Barbour Ltd*
  [1943] AC 32, House of Lords

The claimants, a Polish company, entered into a written contract with the defendants, an English company, to purchase 'flax-hackling' machines for £4,800. The claimants paid £1,000 in advance under a clause requiring advance payment of a third of the contract price. A couple of months after the making of the contract, and before any of the machinery had been delivered, war broke out between Great Britain and Germany. It was held by the House of Lords that the outbreak of war discharged the contract under the doctrine of frustration but that the claimants were entitled to restitution of the £1,000 in an action for money had and received because there had been a total failure of consideration. 'The loss lies where it falls' approach of *Chandler v Webster* [1904] 1 KB 493 was overruled.

Viscount Simon LC: . . . The locus classicus for the view which has hitherto prevailed is to be found in the judgment of Collins M.R. in *Chandler v Webster*. It was not a considered judgment, but it is hardly necessary to say that I approach this pronouncement of the then Master of the Rolls with all the respect due to so distinguished a common lawyer. When his judgment is studied, however, one cannot but be impressed by the circumstance that he regarded the proposition that money in such cases could not be recovered back as flowing from the decision in *Taylor v Caldwell*.[1] *Taylor v Caldwell*, however, was not a case in which any question arose whether money could be recovered back, for there had been no payment in advance, and there is nothing in the judgment of Blackburn J., which, at any rate in terms, affirms the general proposition that 'the loss lies where it falls.' The application by Collins M.R. of *Taylor v Caldwell* to the actual problem with which he had to deal in *Chandler v Webster*[2] deserves close examination. He said 'The plaintiff contends that he is entitled to recover the money which he has paid on the ground that there has been a total failure of consideration. He says that the condition on which he paid the money was that the procession should

---

1 3 B & S 826.   2 [1904] 1 KB 493, 499.

take place, and that, as it did not take place, there has been a total failure of consideration. That contention does no doubt raise a question of some difficulty, and one which has perplexed the courts to a considerable extent in several cases. The principle on which it has been dealt with is that which was applied in *Taylor v Caldwell* – namely, that where, from causes outside the volition of the parties, something which was the basis of, or essential to the fulfilment of, the contract has become impossible, so that, from the time when the fact of that impossibility has been ascertained, the contract can no further be performed by either party, it remains a perfectly good contract up to that point, and everything previously done in pursuance of it must be treated as rightly done, but the parties are both discharged from further performance of it. If the effect were that the contract were wiped out altogether, no doubt the result would be that money paid under it would have to be repaid as on a failure of consideration. But that is not the effect of the doctrine; it only releases the parties from further performance of the contract. Therefore the doctrine of failure of consideration does not apply.'

It appears to me that the reasoning in this crucial passage is open to two criticisms: *(a)* The claim of a party, who has paid money under a contract, to get the money back, on the ground that the consideration for which he paid it has totally failed, is not based on any provision contained in the contract, but arises because, in the circumstances that have happened, the law gives a remedy in quasi-contract to the party who has not got that for which he bargained. It is a claim to recover money to which the defendant has no further right because in the circumstances that have happened the money must be regarded as received to the plaintiff's use. It is true that the effect of frustration is that, while the contract can no further be performed, 'it remains a perfectly good contract up to that point, and everything previously done in pursuance of it must be treated as rightly done,' but it by no means follows that the situation existing at the moment of frustration is one which leaves the party that has paid money and has not received the stipulated consideration without any remedy. To claim the return of money paid on the ground of total failure of consideration is not to vary the terms of the contract in any way. The claim arises not because the right to be repaid is one of the stipulated conditions of the contract, but because, in the circumstances that have happened, the law gives the remedy. It is the failure to distinguish between (1.) the action of assumpsit for money had and received in a case where the consideration has wholly failed, and (2.) an action on the contract itself, which explains the mistake which I think has been made in applying English law to this subject-matter. . . . Once it is realized that the action to recover money for a consideration that has wholly failed rests, not on a contractual bargain between the parties, but, as Lord Sumner said in *Sinclair v Brougham*,[3] 'upon a notional or imputed promise to repay,' or (if it is preferred to omit reference to a fictitious promise) upon an obligation to repay arising from the circumstances, the difficulty in the way of holding that a prepayment made under a contract which has been frustrated can be recovered back appears to me to disappear. *(b)* There is, no doubt, a distinction between cases in which a contract is 'wiped out altogether,' e.g., because it is void as being illegal from the start or as being due to fraud which the innocent party has elected to treat as avoiding the contract, and cases in which intervening impossibility 'only releases the parties from further performance of the contract.' But does the distinction between these two classes of case justify the deduction of Collins M.R. that 'the doctrine of failure of consideration does not apply' where the contract remains a perfectly good contract up to the date of frustration? This conclusion seems to be derived from the view that, if the contract remains good and valid up to the moment of frustration, money which has already been paid under it cannot be regarded as having been paid for a consideration which has wholly failed. The party that has paid the money has had the advantage, whatever it may be worth, of the promise of the other party. That is true, but it is necessary to draw

---

3 [1914] AC 398, 452.

a distinction. In English law, an enforceable contract may be formed by an exchange of a promise for a promise, or by the exchange of a promise for an act—I am excluding contracts under seal—and thus, in the law relating to the formation of contract, the promise to do a thing may often be the consideration, but when one is considering the law of failure of consideration and of the quasi-contractual right to recover money on that ground, it is, generally speaking, not the promise which is referred to as the consideration, but the performance of the promise. The money was paid to secure performance and, if performance fails the inducement which brought about the payment is not fulfilled.

If this were not so, there could never be any recovery of money, for failure of consideration, by the payer of the money in return for a promise of future performance, yet there are endless examples which show that money can be recovered, as for a complete failure of consideration, in cases where the promise was given but could not be fulfilled: see the notes in Bullen and Leake's *Precedents of Pleading*, 9th ed., p. 263. In this connexion the decision in *Rugg v Minett*[4] is instructive. There the plaintiff had bought at auction a number of casks of oil. The contents of each cask were to be made up after the auction by the seller to the prescribed quantity so that the property in a cask did not pass to the plaintiff until this had been done. The plaintiff paid in advance a sum of money on account of his purchases generally, but a fire occurred after some of the casks had been filled up, while the others had not. The plaintiff's action was to recover the money he had paid as money received by the defendants to the use of the plaintiffs. The Court of King's Bench ruled that this cause of action succeeded in respect of the casks which at the time of the fire had not been filled up to the pre-scribed quantity. A simple illustration of the same result is an agreement to buy a horse, the price to be paid down, but the horse not to be delivered and the property not to pass until the horse had been sold. If the horse dies before the shoeing, the price can unquestionably be recovered as for a total failure of consideration, notwithstanding that the promise to deliver was given. This is the case of a contract de certo corpore where the certum corpus perishes after the contract is made, but, as Vaughan Williams L.J.'s judgment in *Krell v Henry*[5] explained, the same doctrine applies 'to cases where the event which renders the contract incapable of performance is the cessation or non-existence of an express condition or state of things, going to the root of the contract, and essential to its performance.' I can see no valid reason why the right to recover prepaid money should not equally arise on frustration arising from supervening circumstances as it arises on frustration from destruction of a particular subject-matter. The conclusion is that the rule in *Chandler v Webster* is wrong, and that the appellants can recover their 1000*l*.

While this result obviates the harshness with which the previous view in some instances treated the party who had made a prepayment, it cannot be regarded as dealing fairly between the parties in all cases, and must sometimes have the result of leaving the recipient who has to return the money at a grave disadvantage. He may have incurred expenses in connexion with the partial carrying out of the contract which are equivalent, or more than equivalent, to the money which he prudently stipulated should be prepaid, but which he now has to return for reasons which are no fault of his. He may have to repay the money, though he has executed almost the whole of the contractual work, which will be left on his hands. These results follow from the fact that the English common law does not undertake to apportion a prepaid sum in such circumstances—contrast the provision, now contained in s. 40 of the Partnership Act, 1890, for apportioning a premium if a partnership is prematurely dissolved. It must be for the legislature to decide whether provision should be made for an equitable apportion-ment of prepaid moneys which have to be returned by the recipient in view of the frustration of the contract in respect of which they were paid. I move that the appeal be allowed, and that judgment be entered for the appellants.

4 11 East 210.   5 [1903] 2 KB 740, 748.

Lord Wright: My Lords, the claim in the action was to recover a prepayment of 1000*l.* made on account of the price under a contract which had been frustrated. The claim was for money paid for a consideration which had failed. It is clear that any civilized system of law is bound to provide remedies for cases of what has been called unjust enrichment or unjust benefit, that is to prevent a man from retaining the money of or some benefit derived from another which it is against conscience that he should keep. Such remedies in English law are generically different from remedies in contract or in tort, and are now recognized to fall within a third category of the common law which has been called quasi-contract or restitution. The root idea was stated by three Lords of Appeal, Lord Shaw, Lord Sumner and Lord Carson, in *R.E. Jones, Ltd v Waring & Gillow, Ltd,*[6] which dealt with a particular species of the category, namely, money paid under a mistake of fact. Lord Sumner referring to *Kelly v Solari,*[7] where the money had been paid by an insurance company under the mistaken impression that it was due to an executrix under a policy which had in fact been cancelled, said: 'There was no real intention on the company's part to enrich her.' Payment under a mistake of fact is only one head of this category of the law. Another class is where, as in this case, there is prepayment on account of money to be paid as consideration for the performance of a contract which in the event becomes abortive and is not performed, so that the money never becomes due. There was in such circumstances no intention to enrich the payee. This is the class of claims for the recovery of money paid for a consideration which has failed. Such causes of action have long been familiar and were assumed to be common-place by Holt C.J. in *Holmes v Hall*[8] in 1704. Holt C.J. was there concerned only about the proper form of action and took the cause of the action as beyond question. He said: 'If A give money to B to pay to C upon C's giving writings, etc., and C will not do it, indebit will lie for A against B for so much money received to his use. And many such actions have been maintained for earnests in bargains, when the bargainor would not perform, and for premiums, for insurance, when the ship, etc., did not go the voyage.' The Chief Justice is there using earnest as meaning a prepayment on account of the price, not in the modern sense of an irrevocable payment to bind the bargain, and he is recognizing that the indebitatus assumpsit had by that time been accepted as the appropriate form of action in place of the procedure which had been used in earlier times to enforce these claims such as debt, account or case.

By 1760 actions for money had and received had increased in number and variety. Lord Mansfield C.J., in a familiar passage in *Moses v Macferlan*, sought to rationalize the action for money had and received, and illustrated it by some typical instances. 'It lies,' he said, 'for money paid by mistake; or upon a consideration which happens to fail; or for money got through imposition (express, or implied;) or extortion; or oppression; or an undue advantage taken of the plaintiff's situation, contrary to laws made for the protection of persons under those circumstances. In one word, the gist of this kind of action is, that the defendant, upon the circumstances of the case, is obliged by the ties of natural justice and equity to refund the money.' Lord Mansfield prefaced this pronouncement by observations which are to be noted. 'If the defendant be under an obligation from the ties of natural justice, to refund; the law implies a debt and gives this action [sc. indebitatus assumpsit] founded in the equity of the plaintiff's case, as it were, upon a contract ("quasi ex contractu" as the Roman law expresses it).' Lord Mansfield does not say that the law implies a promise. The law implies a debt or obligation which is a different thing. In fact, he denies that there is a contract; the obligation is as efficacious as if it were upon a contract. The obligation is a creation of the law, just as much as an obligation in tort. The obligation belongs to a third class, distinct from either contract or tort, though it resembles contract rather than tort. This statement of Lord Mansfield has been the basis of the modern law of quasi-contract, notwithstanding the criticisms which have been launched against it. Like all large generalizations, it has needed and received qualifications in practice. There is, for

---

6 [1926] AC 670, 696.   7 (1841) 9 M & W 54.   8 (1704) Holt 36.

instance, the qualification that an action for money had and received does not lie for money paid under an erroneous judgment or for moneys paid under an illegal or excessive distress. The law has provided other remedies as being more convenient. The standard of what is against conscience in this context has become more or less canalized or defined, but in substance the juristic concept remains as Lord Mansfield left it.

The gist of the action is a debt or obligation implied, or, more accurately, imposed, by law in much the same way as the law enforces as a debt the obligation to pay a statutory or customary impost. This is important because some confusion seems to have arisen though perhaps only in recent times when the true nature of the forms of action have become obscured by want of user. If I may borrow from another context the elegant phrase of Viscount Simon L.C. in *United Australia, Ltd v Barclays Bank, Ltd*,[9] there has sometimes been, as it seems to me, 'a misreading of technical rules, now happily swept away.' The writ of indebitatus assumpsit involved at least two averments, the debt or obligation and the assumpsit. The former was the basis of the claim and was the real cause of action. The latter was merely fictitious and could not be traversed, but was necessary to enable the convenient and liberal form of action to be used in such cases. This fictitious assumpsit or promise was wiped out by the Common Law Procedure Act, 1852. As Bullen and Leake (*Precedents of Pleading*, 3rd ed., p. 36) points out, this Act, by s. 3, provided that the plaintiff was no longer required to specify the particular form of action in which he sued, and by s. 49 that (*inter alia*) the statement of promises in indebitatus counts which there was no need to prove were to be omitted; 'the action of indebitatus assumpsit,' the authors add, 'is [that is by 1868] virtually become obsolete.' Lord Atkin in the *United Australia* case,[10] after instancing the case of the blackmailer, says: 'The man has my money which I have not delivered to him with any real intention of passing to him the property. I sue him because he has the actual property taken.' He adds: 'These fantastic resemblances of contracts invented in order to meet requirements of the law as to forms of action which have now disappeared should not in these days be allowed to affect actual rights.' Yet the ghosts of the forms of action have been allowed at times to intrude in the ways of the living and impede vital functions of the law. Thus in *Sinclair v Brougham*,[11] Lord Sumner stated that 'all these causes of action [sc. for money had and received] are common species of the genus assumpsit. All now rest, and long have rested, upon a notional or imputed promise to repay.' This observation, which was not necessary for the decision of the case, obviously does not mean that there is an actual promise of the party. The phrase 'notional or implied promise' is only a way of describing a debt or obligation arising by construction of law. The claim for money had and received always rested on a debt or obligation which the law implied or more accurately imposed, whether the procedure actually in vogue at any time was debt or account or case or indebitatus assumpsit. Even the fictitious assumpsit disappeared after the Act of 1852. I prefer Lord Sumner's explanation of the cause of action in *Jones's* case.[12] This agrees with the words of Lord Atkin which I have just quoted, yet serious legal writers have seemed to say that these words of the great judge in *Sinclair v Brougham* closed the door to any theory of unjust enrichment in English law. I do not understand why or how. It would indeed be a reductio ad absurdum of the doctrine of precedents. In fact, the common law still employs the action for money had and received as a practical and useful, if not complete or ideally perfect, instrument to prevent unjust enrichment, aided by the various methods of technical equity which are also available, as they were found to be in *Sinclair v Brougham*.

Must, then, the court stay its hand in what would otherwise appear to be an ordinary case for the repayment of money paid in advance on account of the purchase price under a contract for the sale of goods merely because the contract has become impossible of performance and the consideration has failed for that reason? The defendant has the plaintiff's money. There was no intention to enrich

---

9 [1941] AC 1, 21.   10 [1941] AC 1, 29.   11 [1914] AC 398, 452.   12 [1926] AC 670, 696.

him in the events which happened. No doubt, when money is paid under a contract it can only be claimed back as for failure of consideration where the contract is terminated as to the future. Characteristic instances are where it is dissolved by frustration or impossibility or by the contract becoming abortive for any reason not involving fault on the part of the plaintiff where the consideration, if entire, has entirely failed, or where, if it is severable, it has entirely failed as to the severable residue, as in *Rugg v Minett*. The claim for repayment is not based on the contract which is dissolved on the frustration but on the fact that the defendant has received the money and has on the events which have supervened no right to keep it. The same event which automatically renders performance of the consideration for the payment impossible, not only terminates the contract as to the future, but terminates the right of the payee to retain the money which he has received only on the terms of the contract performance . . . .

The decision reached in *Chandler v Webster* is criticized by Williston on Contracts: s. 1954, p. 5477: see, too, s. 1974, p. 5544, and has not been followed in most of the States of America. Nor is it adopted in the Restatement of the Law of Contract by the American Law Institute, s. 468, pp. 884, et seq. Indeed, the law of the United States seems to go beyond the mere remedy of claims for money had and received and allow the recovery of the value of the benefit of any part performance rendered while performance was possible. Such and similar claims should be recognized in any complete system of law, but it is not clear how far they have been admitted in English law. The Scots law upheld in *Cantiare Sen Rocco S.A. v Clyde Shipbuilding and Engineering Co. Ltd*[13] may seem to be generally like the English law and to be limited to recovery of money payments. The opinion which I have been stating perhaps brings the two laws into substantial accord, though in the passage quoted by Lord Birkenhead in the *Cantiare* case from Lord President Inglis's judgment in *William Watson & Co. v Shankland*[14] that judge seems to accept that the payer who had paid in advance should give credit to the extent that he is lucratus by any part performance. I do not wish to discuss how far, if at all, this is open in English law. That was a case of advance freight, which Scots law treats as a prepayment on account, but I think it is clear both in English and Scots law that the failure of consideration which justifies repayment is a failure in the contract performance. What is meant is not consideration in the sense in which the word is used when it is said that in executory contracts the promise of one party is consideration for the promise of the other. No doubt, in some cases the recipient of the payment may be exposed to hardship if he has to return the money though before the frustration he has incurred the bulk of the expense and is then left with things on his hands which become valueless to him when the contract fails, so that he gets nothing and has to return the prepayment. These and many other difficulties show that the English rule of recovering payment the consideration for which has failed works a rough justice. It was adopted in more primitive times and was based on the simple theory that a man who has paid in advance for something which he has never got ought to have his money back. It is further imperfect because it depends on an entire consideration and a total failure Courts of equity have evolved a fairer method of apportioning an entire consideration in cases where a premium has been paid for a partnership which has been ended before its time: Partnership Act, s. 40, contrary to the common law rule laid down in *Whincup v Hughes*.[15] Some day the legislature may intervene to remedy these defects. . . .

Lords Atkin, **Russell**, **Macmillan**, **Roche** and **Porter** also delivered speeches allowing the claimants' appeal.

---

13 [1924] AC 226, 233.   14 10 M 142, 152.   15 L R 6 C P 78.

NOTES AND QUESTIONS

1. What was the '*Chandler v Webster* heresy' rejected in this case? (See also below, 313.)

2. Their Lordships recognized that to allow the restitution of money for a total failure of consideration might not produce perfect justice? What possible injustices remained?

3. How does Viscount Simon LC explain why there should be restitution of money paid for a consideration that totally fails?

4. Only Lord Wright used the language of unjust enrichment. It follows that, although his speech is of importance, it could not be said that *Fibrosa* established an English law of restitution based on the principle against unjust enrichment.

5. Legislation to deal with remedies following the frustration of a contract came more quickly than their Lordships might have anticipated. Under the Law Reform (Frustrated Contracts) Act 1943 it is no longer necessary, in relation to contracts covered by the Act, to show a total failure of consideration in order to recover money paid. Restitution for non-monetary benefits may also be awarded and to some extent expenses may be retained or recovered: see below, 314.

6. It appears from the decision of the Court of Appeal in this case [1942] 1 KB 12 that, prior to the frustrating event, the defendants had completed two machines but that those machines could be sold without loss.

The case that follows was the first case in which the Supreme Court of Canada expressly rejected the implied promise theory of restitution and recognized that the obligation to make restitution was imposed by law to prevent unjust enrichment.

• *Deglman v Guaranty Trust Co. of Canada and Constantineau*
[1954] 3 DLR 785, Supreme Court of Canada

The claimant (the respondent) entered into an oral agreement with his aunt by which, in return for his performing various personal services for her (e.g. doing odd jobs, taking her out on trips, and running errands), she promised to leave him a house in her will. He performed the services but she failed to leave him the house. He therefore sued her estate. The contract was unenforceable at law because it was not evidenced in writing as required by the Ontario Statute of Frauds 1950. Moreover it was held by the Supreme Court of Canada, reversing the lower courts, that the contract was not specifically enforceable under the doctrine of part performance. On the other hand the claimant was held entitled to a restitutionary *quantum meruit* for the value of the services which he had rendered.

Rand J: There remains the question of recovery for the services rendered on the basis of a *quantum meruit*. On the findings of both Courts below the services were not given gratuitously but on the footing of a contractual relation: they were to be paid for. The statute in such a case does not touch the principle of restitution against what would otherwise be an unjust enrichment of the defendant at the expense of the plaintiff. This is exemplified in the simple case of part or full payment in money as the price under an oral contract; it would be inequitable to allow the promisor to keep both the land and the money and the other party to the bargain is entitled to recover what he has paid. Similarly is it in the case of services given. . . . [T]he respondent is entitled to recover for his services and outlays what the deceased would have had to pay for them on a purely business basis to any other person in the position of the respondent. The evidence covers generally and perhaps in the only way possible the particulars, but enough is shown to enable the Court to make a fair determination of the amount called for; and since it would be to the benefit of the other beneficiaries to bring an end to this litigation, I think we should not hesitate to do that by fixing the amount to be allowed. This I place at the sum of $3,000 . . .

Cartwright J: It remains to consider the respondent's alternative claim to recover for the value of the services which he performed for the deceased. . . .

I agree with the conclusion of my brother Rand that the respondent is entitled to recover the value of these services from the administrator. This right appears to me to be based, not on the contract, but on an obligation imposed by law. . . .

In *Scott v Pattison*, [1923] 2 KB 723, the plaintiff served the defendant under a contract for service not to be performed within one year which was held not to be enforceable by reason of the *Statute of Frauds*. It was held that he could nonetheless sue in *assumpsit* on an implied contract to pay him according to his deserts. While I respectfully agree with the result arrived at in *Scott v Pattison* I do not think it is accurate to say that there was an implied promise . . . .

In the case at bar all the acts for which the respondent asks to be paid under his alternative claim were clearly done in performance of the existing but unenforceable contract with the deceased that she would devise 548 Besserer St. to him, and to infer from them a fresh contract to pay the value of the services in money would be . . . to draw an inference contrary to the fact.

In my opinion when the *Statute of Frauds* was pleaded the express contract was thereby rendered unenforceable, but the deceased having received the benefits of the full performance of the contract by the respondent, the law imposed upon her, and so on her estate, the obligation to pay the fair value of the services rendered to her . . . .

Runfret CJC and **Tascherau J** concurred with **Rand J**: **Estey**, **Locke** and **Fauteux JJ** concurred with **Cartwright J**.

NOTE

Nowadays the law of restitution in Canada is well developed. Other Canadian cases covered in this book include *Peel (Regional Municipality) v Canada* (below, 74), *Rathwell v Rathwell*, (below, 138), *Garland v Consumers' Gas Co.* (below, 140), *County of Carleton v City of Ottawa* (below, 136), *Lac Minerals Ltd v International Corona Resources Ltd* (below, 1031). See, generally, P Maddaugh and J McCamus, *The Law of Restitution* (2nd edn, 2004); L Smith, R Chambers, M McInnes, J Neyers and S Pitel, *The Law of Restitution in Canada* (2004).

In England the campaign for recognition of a law of restitution based on the principle of reversing unjust enrichment was led by Robert Goff and Gareth Jones in their brilliant book, *The Law of Restitution*, first published in 1966. What follows are a few extracts from that book which set out some of the authors' central theoretical thinking.

• R Goff and G Jones, *The Law of Restitution* (1st edn, 1966), 4–14

1 RESTITUTION AND QUASI-CONTRACT

. . . Quasi-contractual claims are, therefore, those which fall within the scope of the actions for money had and received or for money paid, or of *quantum meruit* or *quantum valebat* claims, and which are founded upon the principle of unjust enrichment. There are, however, other claims of different origin which are also founded on that principle. So, for example, there are claims in equity analogous to quasi-contractual claims to recover money paid under a mistake; and equitable relief from undue influence is a rational extension of the limited relief which the common law provides in cases of duress. Some restitutionary claims outside the scope of quasi-contract were known to both law and equity; these include two of the most important topics in restitution, namely, contribution and subrogation. Other restitutionary claims, notably generally average and salvage, were developed by the Court of Admiralty. But the substantive link between these and quasi-contractual claims was hidden by the artificial barriers erected by the forms of action. It is now almost a century since the forms of action were abolished, and there is no reason why they should be allowed any longer to obstruct a unified treatment of all claims founded on the principle of unjust enrichment. The law of restitution is the law relating to all claims, quasi-contractual or otherwise, which are founded upon that principle.

2 THE LEGACY OF HISTORY: THE 'IMPLIED CONTRACT THEORY'

Just as the unified treatment of the law of torts was at first received with scepticism, the contents of this volume will no doubt be regarded by some as no more than a heterogeneous collection of unrelated topics. It may even be suggested that quasi-contractual claims should, on principle, receive separate treatment from the other matters considered in this book on the ground that it is the special characteristic of these claims that they are founded upon an implied contract by the defendant to pay to the plaintiff the money claimed by him.

The 'implied contract theory,' as it is usually called, has little or no immediate attraction. There are, it is true, some contexts in which an implied contract for repayment can, with not too much artificiality, be imputed to the parties. So if the plaintiff has paid money to the defendant under a contract, subsequently discharged by reason of the defendant's breach, it can be argued that the defendant should be taken to have impliedly contracted that, in such an event, he would repay the money to the plaintiff. But in most situations recourse to the theory becomes so absurd that serious doubts about its validity are aroused. It is difficult to understand, for example, how the recipient of money paid under a mistake, still less a thief who has stolen money, could be held to have impliedly contracted to repay it.

. . .

[T]he assertion that the requirement of implied contract leads to certainty is unintelligible. When is a contract to be implied? No logical answer can be given to the question when recourse should be had to a fiction. Moreover, study of the cases reveals that emphasis on implied contract, and the spurious connection with contract which it implies, has inhibited discussion of substantive issues. In *Sinclair v Brougham*,[1] the House of Lords held that money deposited under contracts of deposit which were *ultra vires* the 'banking' company were not recoverable in an action for money had and received because, *inter alia*, 'the law cannot *de jure* impute promises to repay, whether for money had and received or otherwise, which, if made *de facto*, it would inexorably avoid.'[2] This resort to implied contract prevented any discussion of the real point at issue, namely, whether the rule of policy which precludes unjust enrichment should override the rule of policy which underlies the *ultra vires* doctrine . . . .

In our view, the concept of implied contract is, in this context, a meaningless, irrelevant and misleading anachronism . . . .

3 THE PRINCIPLE OF UNJUST ENRICHMENT

Most mature systems of law have found it necessary to provide, outside the fields of contract and civil wrongs, for the restoration of benefits on grounds of unjust enrichment.[3] There are many circumstances in which a defendant may find himself in possession of a benefit which, in justice, he should restore to the plaintiff. Obvious examples are where the plaintiff has himself conferred the benefit on the defendant through mistake or compulsion. To allow the defendant to retain such a benefit would result in his being unjustly enriched at the plaintiff's expense, and this, subject to certain defined limits, the law will not allow. 'Unjust Enrichment' is, simply, the name which is commonly

1 [1914] AC 398.
2 [1914] AC 398, 452, *per* Lord Sumner.
3 *Fibrosa Spolka Akcyjna v Fairbairn Lawson Combe Barbour* [1943] AC 32, 61, *per* Lord Wright.

given to the principle of justice which the law recognises and gives effect to in a wide variety of claims of this kind.

It has been said that the principle of unjust enrichment is too vague to be of any practical value. Nevertheless, most rubrics of the law disclose, on examination, an underlying principle which is almost invariably so general as to be incapable of any precise definition. Moreover, in a search for unifying principle at this level we should not expect to find any precise 'common formula,' but rather an abstract proposition of justice. *Pacta sunt servanda* is no less vague a principle than unjust enrichment; yet without it the modern law of contract would fall apart. The search for principle should not be confused with the definition of concepts.

The principle of unjust enrichment is placed in the forefront of the American *Restatement of Restitution*. Paragraph 1 provides that 'a person who has been unjustly enriched at the expense of another is required to make restitution to the other.' Similar statements of principle had been made by Lord Mansfield in a number of cases[4] concerning the action for money had and received. His conclusion was that 'the gist of this kind of action is, that the defendant, upon the circumstances of the case, is obliged by the ties of natural justice and equity to refund the money.'[5] We have only to substitute 'make restitution' for the last three words of his statement to make it appropriate for the whole law of restitution.

For many years Lord Mansfield's views gained wide acceptance. But the change of climate which encouraged or accompanied the advance of the implied contract theory also led to a reaction against his enunciation of principle. Scrutton L.J., no doubt with Lord Mansfield's influence in mind, went so far as to describe the history of the action for money had and received as a 'history of well-meaning sloppiness of thought.'[6] Earlier, in 1913, Hamilton L.J. had said that 'whatever may have been the case 146 years ago, we are not now free in the twentieth century to administer that vague jurisprudence which is sometimes attractively styled "justice as between man and man." '[7]

Such remarks are merely pejorative. Others are more revealing of the error under which these critics were labouring. In *Sinclair v Brougham*, Lord Sumner confessed[8] that 'it is hard to reduce to one common formula the conditions upon which the law will imply a promise to repay money received to the plaintiff's use,' a sentiment with which Scrutton L.J. was later to express agreement.[9] It is indeed impossible to produce any such common formula in this, as in other, branches of the law. Moreover, there is nothing in what Lord Mansfield said to indicate that he regarded his enunciation of principle as a 'common formula' or touchstone which would enable judges to decide future cases. The inference that he was giving his successors *carte blanche* to adjudicate upon disputes in accordance with their own ideas of justice is, we suggest, unjustified. He was simply describing the fundamental notion of justice which underlay the action for money had and received. Acceptance of the principle of unjust enrichment is not, of course, inconsistent with recognition that, in restitution as in other fields, recourse must be had to the decided cases to determine the prospects of success or failure of any particular claim. As Lord Wright once said[10] of Lord Mansfield's statement: 'Like all large generalisations, it has needed and received qualifications in practice. . . . The standard of what is against conscience has become more or less canalised or defined, but in substance the juristic concept remains as Lord Mansfield left it.'

---

4 See, e.g., *Moses* v *Macferlan* (1760) 2 Burr 1005, 1012; *Sadler* v *Evans* (1766) 4 Burr 1984, 1986; *Jestons* v *Brooke* (1778) 2 Cowp 793, 795.

5 *Moses* v *Macferlan* (1760) 2 Burr 1005, 1012.

6 *Holt* v *Markham* [1923] 1 KB 504, 513.

7 *Bavlis* v *Bishop of London* [1913] 1 Ch 127, 140, referring to *Sadler* v *Evans* (1766) 4 Burr 1984, 1986, *per* Lord Mansfield. Hamilton LJ later became Lord Sumner.

8 [1914] AC 398, 454.

9 *Holt* v *Markham* [1923] 1 KB 504, 514.

10 *Fibrosa Spolka Akcyjna* v *Fairbairn Lawson Combe Barbour* [1943] AC 32, 62–3.

In fact, as one might expect, close study of the law of restitution reveals, as with contract and tort, a highly developed and reasonably systematic complex of rules. But, though all restitutionary claims are unified by *principle*, English law has not as yet recognised any generalised *right* to restitution in every case of unjust enrichment. Whether any such general right will emerge is a matter for speculation. Lord Sumner's opinion[11] that the scope of the action for money had and received was fixed by the decided cases can now be balanced against more recent authority that the common law is not 'condemned . . . to no further growth in this field.'[12] The cases provide good evidence that this growth is in fact taking place, and is likely to continue. The law of restitution should not lightly be presumed to be past the age of child-bearing.

Although not all would agree, the following decision, in our view, constitutes the acceptance in Australia of a law of restitution based on unjust enrichment.

• *Pavey and Matthews Pty. Ltd v Paul* (1986) 162 CLR 217, High Court of Australia

The claimant builders had renovated a cottage for the defendant pursuant to a contract by which they were to be remunerated according to prevailing rates. When the work was done the defendant paid the claimants $36,000. The claimants maintained that she should pay nearly twice that sum. The contract was unenforceable by them because it was not in writing as required for building contracts to be enforceable by builders under the Builders Licensing Act 1971 (New South Wales). Nevertheless it was held by the High Court of Australia, reversing the Court of Appeal of New South Wales, that the claimants were entitled to recover a non-contractual *quantum meruit*.

Mason and Wilson JJ: The important issue in this appeal is whether a builder may bring an action in indebitatus assumpsit for the value of work done and materials supplied under an oral building contract, notwithstanding the provisions of s. 45 of the *Builders Licensing Act* 1971 (N.S.W.) ('the Act'). That section provides:

> A contract (in this section referred to as a 'building contract') under which the holder of a licence undertakes to carry out, by himself or by others, any building work or to vary any building work or the manner of carrying out any building work, specified in a building contract is not enforceable against the other party to the contract unless the contract is in writing signed by each of the parties or his agent in that behalf and sufficiently describes the building work the subject of the contract.

Section 3 of the Act defines, subject to the existence of any contrary intention, the expression 'building work' to mean:

> (1) . . .
>
> (a) the work involved in the carrying out of the construction of, the making of alterations or additions to, or the repairing, renovation, decoration or painting of, a dwelling, where that work does not consist solely of work of one class or description that is prescribed for the purposes of the definition of 'trade work' in this subsection; or
>
> (b) trade work,
>
> but does not include any work, or work of any class or description, that is prescribed for the purposes of this definition. . . .

---

11 *Sinclair v Brougham* [1914] AC 398, 453.

12 *Re Cleadon Trust* [1939] Ch 286, 314, *per* Scott LJ; see also *Morgan v Ashcroft* [1938] 1 KB 49, 74, *per* Scott LJ.

The appellant, which holds a builders' licence under the Act, sued the respondent in the Supreme Court of New South Wales for $26,945.50 being an amount claimed to be due and payable under a quantum meruit. The appellant calculated this amount as the sum payable, after alleging that the amount of $62,945.50 'represents a reasonable sum for the work done and materials provided' and giving credit for a payment of $36,000. The respondent, after putting in issue some allegations of fact in the appellant's statement of claim and denying the reasonableness of the charges, pleaded that the contract was a building contract and as such was unenforceable by reason of s. 45.

. . .

The Court of Appeal in this case . . . considered that an action in indebitatus assumpsit to recover the agreed remuneration for building work done pursuant to an oral contract that was wholly executed was an action to enforce that contract. Their Honours arrived at this conclusion after a very lengthy review of the history of indebitatus assumpsit as a result of which they found that in order to succeed in the action the plaintiff must plead and prove the special contract for building work under which he claims remuneration. Their Honours reinforced the conclusion reached in this way by invoking considerations of legislative policy which, they thought, supported a legislative intention to prevent a builder from recovering any remuneration in respect of building work unless the contract is in writing and complies with the statutory requirements.

. . .

Deane J., whose reasons for judgment we have had the advantage of reading, has concluded that an action on a quantum meruit, such as that brought by the appellant, rests, not on implied contract, but on a claim to restitution or one based on unjust enrichment, arising from the respondent's acceptance of the benefits accruing to the respondent from the appellant's performance of the unenforceable oral contract. This conclusion does not accord with the acceptance by Williams, Fullagar and Kitto JJ. in *Turner v Bladin*[1] of the views expressed by Lord Denning in his articles in the *Law Quarterly Review*, vol. 41 (1925), p. 79, and vol. 55 (1939), p. 54, basing such a claim in implied contract. These views were a natural reflection of prevailing legal thinking as it had developed to that time. The members of this Court were then unaware that his Lordship had, in his judgment in *James v Thomas H. Kent & Co. Ltd*,[2] as reported in the authorized reports, discarded his earlier views in favour of the restitution or unjust enrichment theory. Since then the shortcomings of the implied contract theory have been rigorously exposed (see Goff and Jones, *The Law of Restitution*, 2nd ed. (1978), pp. 5–11) and the virtues of an approach based on restitution and unjust enrichment, initially advocated by Lord Mansfield and later by Fuller and Perdue (see 'The Reliance Interest in Contract Damages', *Yale Law Journal*, vol. 46 (1936–37), pp. 52, 373, esp. at p. 387), widely appreciated (Goff and Jones, op. cit., p. 15 et seq.; and see *Deglman v Guaranty Trust*[3]). We are therefore now justified in recognizing, as Deane J. has done, that the true foundation of the right to recover on a quantum meruit does not depend on the existence of an implied contract.

Once the true basis of the action on a quantum meruit is established, namely execution of work for which the unenforceable contract provided, and its acceptance by the defendant, it is difficult to regard the action as one by which the plaintiff seeks to enforce the oral contract. True it is that proof of the oral contract may be an indispensable element in the plaintiff's success but that is in order to show that (a) the benefits were not intended as a gift, and (b) that the defendant has not rendered the promised exchange value: Fuller and Perdue, loc. cit., p. 387 n. 125. The purpose of proving the contract is not to enforce it but to make out another cause of action having a different foundation in law.

If the effect of bringing an action on a quantum meruit was simply to enforce the oral contract in some circumstances only, though not in all the circumstances in which an action on the contract

---

1 (1951) 82 CLR at 474.   2 [1951] 1 KB 551.   3 [1954] 3 DLR 785, at 794–5.

would succeed, it might be persuasively contended that the action on a quantum meruit was an indirect means of enforcing the oral contract. So, if all the plaintiff had to prove was that he had fully executed the contract on his part and that he had not been paid the contract price, there would be some force in the suggestion that the proceeding amounted to an indirect enforcement of the contractual cause of action. However, when success in a quantum meruit depends, not only on the plaintiff proving that he did the work, but also on the defendant's acceptance of the work without paying the agreed remuneration, it is evident that the court is enforcing against the defendant an obligation that differs in character from the contractual obligation had it been enforceable. . . .

Deane J: At material times, the appellant company ('the builder') was the holder of a licence under the *Builders Licensing Act* 1971 (N.S.W.) ('the Act'). It carried out the work and supplied the materials involved in the renovation of a cottage at Swansea Heads in New South Wales for the respondent, Mrs. Paul. It is common ground that the work was 'building work' within the meaning of s. 45 of the Act and that it was carried out pursuant to an oral contract, between the builder and Mrs. Paul, to the effect that the builder would do the work requested by Mrs. Paul and that Mrs. Paul would pay the builder 'a reasonable remuneration for that work, calculated by reference to prevailing rates of payment in the building industry'. After the work had been completed and Mrs. Paul had accepted the benefit of it and taken up occupation of the renovated cottage, the builder instituted proceedings in the Supreme Court of New South Wales for what is claimed to be the balance (after giving credit for $36,000 already paid) owing to it in respect of the work. Its claim was for money payable as on a quantum meruit and corresponded with the old common indebitatus count for work done and materials provided. By her (amended) statement of defence, Mrs. Paul put in issue certain matters of fact and denied the reasonableness of the charges. She also pleaded that the contract pursuant to which the work had been carried out was a building contract which was not enforceable by the builder by reason of the provisions of s. 45 of the Act. By consent, it was ordered in the Supreme Court that the issue raised by the defence based on s. 45 be determined, upon agreed facts, as a separate preliminary issue. It is with that issue that the present appeal is concerned.

Section 45 of the Act relevantly provides that a contract under which a licensed builder 'undertakes to carry out . . . any building work . . . is not enforceable against the other party to the contract' unless it 'is in writing signed by each of the parties or his agent in that behalf and sufficiently describes the building work the subject of the contract'. Plainly enough, the oral contract between the builder and Mrs. Paul was of the kind described in the section and failed to satisfy its requirements. The issue between the parties on the present appeal is whether the words of the section should be construed as applying to preclude the builder from suing to recover recompense for building work completed under an oral contract in circumstances where the work has been fully completed by the builder and accepted by the building owner. Whatever may be the merits of the present case, where Mrs. Paul claims to have already paid all that is reasonably due, such a construction of the section would inevitably lead to injustice in those cases where a builder had discharged all his obligations under the building contract only to find that he was unable to recover any payment at all by reason of some innocent failure to ensure that the contract satisfied the requirements of the section. Since the section does not preclude enforcement of the contract against the licensed builder, that broad construction could also give rise to the oppressive situation in which a builder was contractually bound to continue and complete building work under a contract in circumstances where the section operatated to preclude recovery by him of any recompense at all on completion of the work. A likelihood of consequential injustice and oppression does not, of course, warrant a refusal to give effect to the legislative intent disclosed by the relevant words of the Statute. It does, however, call for careful scrutiny of those words to determine whether any such legislative intent can properly be discerned in them.

At first instance in the Supreme Court, Clarke J. resolved the preliminary issue in favour of the builder. His Honour upheld a submission that the action was not one to enforce the oral contract which was rendered unenforceable by s. 45 of the Act for the reason that the builder's claim was 'quite independent of the contract and based upon the fact that the consideration moving from the plaintiff had been fully executed'. Mrs. Paul appealed from Clarke J.'s decision on the preliminary issue to the Court of Appeal. There, a contrary view prevailed. J was held that the words of s. 45, in the context of the legislative policy to be discerned in the Act as a whole, precluded any action by the builder to recover payment for the work done under the unenforceable building contract. That determination of the preliminary issue disposed of the builder's claim and the Court of Appeal ordered that judgment be entered in Mrs. Paul's favour. The appeal to this Court is from the judgment and orders of the Court of Appeal.

. . .

[T]he basis of the obligation to make payment for an executed consideration given and received under an unenforceable contract should now be accepted as lying in restitution or unjust enrichment . . . In such a case, the underlying obligation or debt for the work done, goods supplied, or services rendered does not arise from a genuine agreement at all. It is an obligation or debt imposed by operation of law which 'arises from the defendant having taken the benefit of the work done, goods supplied, or services rendered . . .' (per Starke J., *Phillips v Ellinson Bros. Pty. Ltd*[4]) and which can be enforced '*as if* it had a contractual origin' (emphasis added) (*In re Rhodes, per* Lindley L.J.[5]) . . . [I]t is clear that the old common indebitatus count could be utilised to accommodate what should be seen as two distinct categories of claim: one to recover a debt arising under a genuine contract, whether express or implied; the other to recover a debt owing in circumstances where the law itself imposed or imputed an obligation or promise to make compensation for a benefit accepted. In the first category of case; the action was brought upon the genuine agreement regardless of whether it took the form of a special or a common count. It follows from what has been said above that the cases in which a claimant has been held entitled to recover in respect of an executed consideration under an agreement upon which the Statute of Frauds precluded the bringing of an action should be seen as falling within the second and not the first category. In that second category of case, the tendency of common lawyers to speak in terms of implied contract rather than in terms of an obligation imposed by law . . . should be recognized as but a reflection of the influence of discarded fictions, buried forms of action and the conventional conviction that, if a common law claim could not properly be framed in tort, it must necessarily be dressed in the language of contract. That tendency should not be allowed to conceal the fact that, in that category of case, the action was not based upon a genuine agreement at all. Indeed, if there was a valid and enforceable agreement governing the claimant's right to compensation, there would be neither occasion nor legal justification for the law to super-impose or impute an obligation or promise to pay reasonable remuneration. The quasi-contractual obligation to pay fair and just compensation for a benefit which has been accepted will only arise in a case where there is no applicable genuine agreement or where such an agreement is frustrated, avoided or unenforceable. In such a case, it is the very fact that there is no genuine agreement or that the genuine agreement is frustrated, avoided or unenforceable that provides the occasion for (and part of the circumstances giving rise to) the imposition by the law of the obligation to make restitution.

To identify the basis of such actions as restitution and not genuine agreement is not to assert a judicial discretion to do whatever idiosyncratic notions of what is fair and just might dictate. The circumstances in which the common law imposes an enforceable obligation to pay compensation for a benefit accepted under an unenforceable agreement have been explored in the reported cases and

---

4 (1941) 65 CLR, at 235.   5 (1890) 44 ChD 94, at 107.

in learned writings and are unlikely to be greatly affected by the perception that the basis of such an obligation, when the common law imposes it, is preferably seen as lying in restitution rather than in the implication of a genuine agreement where in fact the unenforceable agreement left no room for one. That is not to deny the importance of the concept of unjust enrichment in the law of this country. It constitutes a unifying legal concept which explains why the law recognizes, in a variety of distinct categories of case, an obligation on the part of a defendant to make fair and just restitution for a benefit derived at the expense of a plaintiff and which assists in the determination, by the ordinary processes of legal reasoning, of the question whether the law should, in justice, recognize such an obligation in a new or developing category of case: see *Muschinski v Dodds*;[6] Goff & Jones, op. cit., p. 11ff. In a category of case where the law recognizes an obligation to pay a reasonable remuneration or compensation for a benefit actually or constructively accepted, the general concept of restitution or unjust enrichment is, as is pointed out subsequently in this judgment, also relevant, in a more direct sense, to the identification of the proper basis upon which the quantum of remuneration or compensation should be ascertained in that particular category of case.

The fact that the action which can be brought on a common indebitatus count consistently with the Statute of Frauds is founded on an obligation arising independently of the unenforceable contract does not mean that the existence or terms of that contract are necessarily irrelevant. In such an action, it will ordinarily be permissible for the plaintiff to refer to the unenforceable contract as evidence, but as evidence only, on the question whether what was done was done gratuitously. In many cases, such as where the claim is for money lent or paid, the obligation to make restitution will plainly involve the obligation to pay the precise amount advanced or paid. In those cases where a claim for a reasonable remuneration or price is involved, the unenforceable agreement may . . . be referred to as evidence, but again as evidence only, on the question of the appropriate amount of compensation. If the unenforceable contract has not been rescinded by the plaintiff or otherwise terminated, the defendant will be free to rely on it as a defence to the claim for compensation in a case where he is ready and willing to perform his obligations under it: see *Thomas v Brown*.[7] The defendant will also be entitled to rely on the unenforceable contract, if it has been executed but not rescinded, to limit the amount recoverable by the plaintiff to the contractual amount in a case where that amount is less than what would constitute fair and reasonable remuneration.

. . .

It was submitted on behalf of Mrs. Paul that the cases establishing the right of a claimant to recover compensation for an executed consideration under an agreement upon which the bringing of an action is precluded by the Statute of Frauds could not be applied, by analogy, to sustain the right of the builder to sue her on a common indebitatus count in the present case to recover a liquidated amount representing reasonable remuneration for the work done and materials provided under the contract which was rendered unenforceable against her by the provisions of s. 45 of the Act. The primary basis of this submission was the distinction between a provision precluding the bringing of an action by either party upon an agreement (such as the Statute of Frauds) and a provision that an agreement is not enforceable by a designated part against the other party to it (such as s. 45 of the Act).

On the approach accepted in *Turner v Bladin*,[8] namely that the action which could be brought consistently with the Statute of Frauds was a common indebitatus assumpsit count based on the fictional promise to pay the actual debt arising under the agreement, there was obvious force in this submission since it would not necessarily follow from an acceptance of the view that such an action was not technically brought 'upon' the unenforceable agreement that the action could not properly be seen as none the less brought to enforce it. Once the approach in *Bladin* is rejected, however, the

---

6 (1985) 160 CLR 583, at 619–20.   7 (1876) 1 QBD 714.   8 (1951) 82 CLR 463.

force in the submission disappears. The common indebitatus count for compensation does not involve enforcing an agreement which is unenforceable by the builder under s. 45 of the Act any more than it involves bringing an action upon an agreement upon which the bringing of an action is precluded by the Statute of Frauds. As has been seen, the basis of such an action lies not in agreement but in restitution and the claim in restitution involves not enforcing the agreement but recovering compensation on the basis that the agreement is unenforceable.

. . .

There is no apparent reason in justice why a builder who is precluded from enforcing an agreement should also be deprived of the ordinary common law right to bring proceedings on a common indebitatus count to recover fair and reasonable remuneration for work which he has actually done and which has been accepted by the building owner: cf. *Johnsons Tyne Foundry Pty. Ltd v Maffra Corporation.*[9] Nor, upon a consideration of the words of s. 45 in their context in the Act, am I able to identify any legislative intent to deprive the builder of that ordinary common law right. The section does not make an agreement to which it applies illegal or void Nor do its words disclose any legislative intent to penalise the builder beyond making the agreement itself unenforceable by him against the other party. It may be that the bringing of an action as on a common indebitatus count would conflict with the apparent legislative policy underlying s. 45 if the claimant in such an action were entitled as of right to recover the amount which the building owner had agreed to pay under the unenforceable agreement. I am, however, unpersuaded that the bringing by a builder of an action on the common indebitatus count in which he can recover no more than what is fair and reasonable in the circumstances as compensation for the benefit of the work which he has actually done and which has been accepted by the building owner conflicts with any discernible legislative policy. Plainly enough, the survival of the ordinary common law right of the builder to recover, in an action founded on restitution or unjust enrichment, reasonable remuneration for work done and accepted under a contract which is unenforceable by him does not frustrate the purpose of the section to provide protection for a building owner. The building owner remains entitled to enforce the contract. He cannot, however, be forced either to comply with its terms or to permit the builder to carry it to completion. All that he can be required to do is to pay reasonable compensation for work done of which he has received the benefit and for which in justice he is obligated to make such a payment by way of restitution. In relation to such work, he can rely on the contract, if it has not been rescinded, as to the amount of remuneration and the terms of payment. If the agreed remuneration exceeds what is reasonable in the circumstances, he can rely on the unenforce-ability of the contract with the result that he is liable to pay no more than what is fair and reasonable.

The tendency in some past cases to see the rationale of the right to recover remuneration for a benefit provided and accepted under an unenforceable contract as contract or promise rather than restitution has tended to distract attention from the importance of identifying the basis upon which the quantum of the amount recoverable should be ascertained. What the concept of monetary restitution involves is the payment of an amount which constitutes, in all the relevant circumstances, fair and just compensation for the benefit or 'enrichment' actually or constructively accepted. Ordinarily, that will correspond to the fair value of the benefit provided (e.g. remuneration calculated at a reasonable rate for work actually done or the fair market value of materials supplied). In some categories of case, however, it would be to affront rather than satisfy the requirements of good conscience and justice which inspire the concept or principle of restitution or unjust enrichment to determine what constitutes fair and just compensation for a benefit accepted by reference only to what would represent a fair remuneration for the work involved or a fair market value of materials supplied. One such category of case is that in which unsolicited but subsequently accepted work is

9 (1948) 77 CLR 544, at 565.

done in improving property in circumstances where remuneration for the unsolicited work calculated at what was a reasonable rate would far exceed the enhanced value of the property. More relevant for present purposes is the special category of case where restitution is sought by one party for work which he has executed under a contract which has become unenforceable by reason of his failure to comply with the requirements of a statutory provision which was enacted to protect the other party. In that category of case, it would be contrary to the general notions of restitution or unjust enrichment if what constituted fair and just compensation for the benefit accepted by the other party were to be ascertained without regard to any identifiable real detriment sustained by that other party by reason of the failure of the first party to ensure that the requirements of the statutory provision were satisfied. Thus, if it is established on the hearing of the present case that Mrs. Paul has sustained an identifiable real detriment by reason of the failure of the builder to ensure that there was a written memorandum of the oral contract which satisfied the requirements of s. 45 of the Act, that would be an important factor in determining what constituted fair and just restitution in the circumstances of the case for the work done and materials supplied of which she has accepted the benefit. The mere fact that the reasonable remuneration for the building work done at Mrs. Paul's request exceeded Mrs. Paul's expectations would not, however, of itself constitute any such identifiable real detriment since it is not necessary for the purposes of s. 45 of the Act that a written contract contain either an agreed price for the building work or an estimate of what the cost of it to the building owner will ultimately be.

Dawson J delivered a judgment also allowing the appeal. **Brennan J** delivered a dissenting judgment: his reasoning was that the unenforceability of the building contract under the 1971 Act ruled out a 'quasi-contractual' claim for work done under the contract both as a matter of legal theory and policy.

NOTES AND QUESTIONS

1. Their Honours reasoned that Mrs Paul had accepted the benefit of the builders' work. What did they mean by this and should such acceptance have had any legal significance?

2. Was restitution awarded in this case because a benefit had been rendered for a consideration that had failed?

3. Although in this case the High Court accepted a law of restitution based on unjust enrichment, many Australian judges, practitioners, and academics remain sceptical about the merits of that approach. This may in part reflect the very strong influence in Australia of *Meagher, Gummow, and Lehane's Equity—Doctrine and Remedies* (4th edn, 2002 by Meagher, Heydon and Leeming) which seeks to uphold and maintain the separation of equity from the common law. Mason and Carter, *Restitution Law in Australia* (1995) is the first book devoted to the Australian law of restitution. See also J Edelman and E Bant, *Unjust Enrichment in Australia* (2006). In addition to the *Pavey & Matthews* case, Australian cases set out in this book include *Baltic Shipping Co. v Dillon (The Mikhail Lermontov)* (below, 267); *Roxborough v Rothmans of Pall Mall (Australia) Ltd* (below, 252, 386); *Crescendo Management Pty. Ltd v Westpac Banking Corp.* (below, 420); *Louth v Diprose* (below, 480); *Australia and New Zealand Banking Group Ltd v Westpac Banking Corporation* (below, 825); *Commissioner of State Revenue (Victoria) v Royal Insurance (Australia) Ltd* (below, 879); *Nelson v Nelson* (below, 912).

- *Lipkin Gorman v Karpnale Ltd* [1991] 2 AC 548, House of Lords

Cass, a partner in the claimant firm of solicitors, had drawn on the partnership account at Lloyds Bank (he was an authorized signatory) to pay for his gambling at the Playboy Club. The partners had thereby suffered a loss of some £220,000. The club had overall won £154,695 from the money stolen and used for gambling by Cass, i.e. although the stolen money staked by Cass was a lot higher, the club had paid out winnings to Cass thereby reducing its net gain. The solicitors succeeded before the House of Lords (over-turning the decision of the Court of Appeal) in being awarded £150,960 in an action for money had and received against the club. The club was also held liable to pay the solicitors damages of £3,735 for conversion of a banker's draft that on one occasion had been used for gambling by Cass instead of cash.

Lord Bridge of Harwich: . . . I agree with my noble and learned friend, Lord Goff of Chieveley, that it is right for English law to recognise that a claim to restitution, based on the unjust enrichment of the defendant, may be met by the defence that the defendant has changed his position in good faith. I equally agree that in expressly acknowledging the availability of this defence for the first time it would be unwise to attempt to define its scope in abstract terms, but better to allow the law on the subject to develop on a case by case basis. In the circumstances of this case I would adopt the reasoning of my noble and learned friend, Lord Templeman for the conclusion that the club can only rely on the defence to the extent that it limits the club's liability to the solicitors to the amount of their net winnings from Cass which must have been derived from the stolen money.

Lord Templeman: . . . [T]he law imposes an obligation on the recipient of stolen money to pay an equivalent sum to the victim if the recipient has been 'unjustly enriched' at the expense of the true owner. In *Fibrosa Spolka Akcyjna v Fairbairn Lawson Combe Barbour Ltd* [1943] AC 32, 61, Lord Wright said:

> It is clear that any civilised system of law is bound to provide remedies for cases of what has been called unjust enrichment or unjust benefit, that is to prevent a man from retaining the money of or some benefit derived from another which it is against conscience that he should keep.

The club was enriched as and when Cass staked and lost to the club money stolen from the solicitors amounting in the aggregate to £300,000 or more. But the club paid Cass when he won and in the final reckoning the club only retained £154,695 which was admittedly derived from the solicitors' money. The solicitors can recover the sum of £154,695 which was retained by the club if they show that in the circumstances the club was unjustly enriched at the expense of the solicitors.

In the course of argument there was a good deal of discussion concerning tracing in law and in equity. In my opinion in a claim for money had and received by a thief, the plaintiff victim must show that money belonging to him was paid by the thief to the defendant and that the defendant was unjustly enriched and remained unjustly enriched. An innocent recipient of stolen money may not be enriched at all; if Cass had paid £20,000 derived from the solicitors to a car dealer for a motor car priced at £20,000, the car dealer would not have been enriched. The car dealer would have received £20,000 for a car worth £20,000. But an innocent recipient of stolen money will be enriched if the recipient has not given full consideration. If Cass had given £20,000 of the solicitors' money to a friend as a gift, the friend would have been enriched and unjustly enriched because a donee of stolen money cannot in good conscience rely on the bounty of the thief to deny restitution to the victim of the theft. Complications arise if the donee innocently expends the stolen money in reliance on the validity of the gift before the donee receives notice of the victim's claim for restitution. Thus if the donee spent £20,000 in the purchase of a motor car which he would not have purchased but for the gift, it seems to me that the donee has altered his position on the faith of the gift and has only been unjustly enriched to the extent of the secondhand value of the motor car at the date when the victim of the theft seeks restitution. If the donee spends the £20,000 in a trip round the world, which he would not have undertaken without the gift, it seems to me that the donee has altered his position on the faith of the gift and that he is not unjustly enriched when the victim of the theft seeks restitution. In the present case Cass stole and the club received £229,908.48 of the solicitors' money. If the club was in the same position as a donee, the club nevertheless in good faith allowed Cass to gamble with the solicitors' money and paid his winnings from time to time so that when the solicitors' sought restitution, the club only retained £154,695 derived from the solicitors. The question is whether the club which was enriched by £154,695 at the date when the solicitors sought restitution was unjustly enriched.

. . .

If Cass had been gambling with his own money, the gaming system operated by the club would have ensured that Cass paid his gambling losses contemporaneously and that the club paid their gambling losses in arrears. The gaming contracts were void but section 18 of the Act of 1845 does not, as between gamblers, prevent a gambling loss from being paid contemporaneously or in arrears. A gambling loss, whenever paid, is a completed voluntary gift from the loser to the winner. But Cass was gambling with the money of the solicitors who have never gambled and never made a voluntary gift to the club.

. . .

When Cass lost and paid £154,695 to the club as a result of gaming contracts, he made to the club a completed gift of £154,695. The club received stolen money by way of gift from the thief; the club, being a volunteer, has been unjustly enriched at the expense of the solicitors from whom the money had been stolen and the club must reimburse the solicitors. . . .

Lord Goff: . . .

The solicitors' appeal

I turn then to the solicitors' appeal in respect of the money, which they claim from the respondents as money had and received by the respondents to their use. To consider this aspect of the case it is, in my opinion, necessary to analyse with some care the nature of the claim so made.

The solicitors' claim is, in substance, as follows. They say, first, that the cash handed over by the bank to Chapman in exchange for the cheques drawn on the solicitors' client account by Cass was in law the property of the solicitors. That is disputed by the respondents who say that, since the cheques were drawn on the bank by Cass without the authority of his partners, the legal property in the money immediately vested in Cass; that argument was however rejected by the Court of Appeal. If that argument is rejected, the respondents concede for present purposes that the cash so obtained by Cass from the client account was paid by him to the club, but they nevertheless resist the solicitors' claim on two grounds: first, that they gave valuable consideration for the money in good faith, as held by a majority of the Court of Appeal; and second that, in any event, having received the money in good faith and having given Cass the opportunity of winning bets and, in some cases, recovering substantial sums by way of winnings, it would be inequitable to allow the solicitors' claim.

At the heart of the solicitors' claim lies *Clarke v Shee and Johnson*, 1 Cowp. 197; Lofft 756. In that case the plaintiff's clerk received money and negotiable notes from the plaintiff's customers, in the ordinary course of the plaintiff's trade as a brewer, for the use of the plaintiff. From the sums so received by him, the clerk paid several sums, amounting to nearly £460, to the defendant 'upon the chances of the coming up of tickets in the State Lottery of 1772,' contrary to the Lottery Act 1772. The Court of Queen's Bench held that the plaintiff was entitled to recover the sum of £460 from the defendant as money had and received by him for the use of the plaintiff. The judgment of the court was delivered by Lord Mansfield. He said, at pp. 199–201:

'This is a liberal action in the nature of a bill in equity; and if, under the circumstances of the case, it appears that the defendant cannot in conscience retain what is the subject matter of it, the plaintiff may well support this action . . . the plaintiff does not sue as standing in the place of Wood his clerk: for the money and notes which Wood paid to the defendants, are the identical notes and money of the plaintiff. Where money or notes are paid bona fide, and upon a valuable consideration, they never shall be brought back by the true owner; but where they come mala fide into a person's hands, they are in the nature of specific property; and if their identity can be traced and ascertained, the party has a right to recover. It is of public benefit and example that it should: but otherwise, if they cannot be followed and identified, because there it might be inconvenient and open a door to fraud. *Miller v Race*, 1 Burr. 452: and in *Golightly v Reynolds* (1772) Lofft 88 the identity was traced through different hands and shops. Here the plaintiff sues for his identified property, which has come to the hands of the defendant iniquitously and illegally, in breach of the Act of Parliament, therefore they have no right to retain it; and consequently the plaintiff is well entitled to recover.'

It is the solicitors' case that the present case is indistinguishable from *Clarke v Shee and Johnson*. In each case, the plaintiff's money was stolen—in that case by his servant, and in the present case by a partner—and then gambled away by the thief; and the plaintiff was or should be entitled to recover his money from the recipient in an action for money had and received. It is the respondents' case that the present case is distinguishable on one or more of the three grounds I have mentioned. I shall consider those three grounds in turn.

Title to the money

The first ground is concerned with the solicitors' title to the money received by Cass (through Chapman) from the bank. It is to be observed that the present action, like the action in *Clarke v Shee and Johnson*, is concerned with a common law claim to money, where the money in question has not been paid by the appellant directly to the respondents—as is usually the case where money is, for example recoverable as having been paid under a mistake of fact, or for a consideration which has failed. On the contrary, here the money had been paid to the respondents by a third party, Cass; and in such a case the appellant has to establish a basis on which he is entitled to the money. This (at least, as a general rule) he does by showing that the money is his legal property, as appears from Lord Mansfield's judgment in *Clarke v Shee and Johnson*. If he can do so, he may be entitled to succeed in a claim against the third party for money had and received to his use, though not if the third party has received the money in good faith and for a valuable consideration. The cases in which such a claim has succeeded are, I believe, very rare: see the cases, including *Clarke v Shee and Johnson*, collected in *Goff and Jones, The Law of Restitution*, 3rd ed. (1986), p. 64, note 29. This is probably because, at common law, property in money, like other fungibles, is lost as such when it is mixed with other money. Furthermore, it appears that in these cases the action for money had and received is not usually founded upon any wrong by the third party, such as conversion; nor is it said to be a case of waiver of tort. It is founded simply on the fact that, as Lord Mansfield said, the third party cannot in conscience retain the money—or, as we say nowadays, for the third party to retain the money would result in his unjust enrichment at the expense of the owner of the money.

So, in the present case, the solicitors seek to show that the money in question was their property at common law. But their claim in the present case for money had and received is nevertheless a personal claim; it is not a proprietary claim, advanced on the basis that money remaining in the hands of the respondents is their property. Of course there is no doubt that, even if legal title to the money did vest in Cass immediately on receipt, nevertheless he would have held it on trust for his partners, who would accordingly have been entitled to trace it in equity into the hands of the respondents. However, your Lordships are not concerned with an equitable tracing claim in the present case, since no such case is advanced by the solicitors, who have been content to proceed at common law by a personal action, viz, an action for money had and received. I should add that, in the present case, we are not concerned with the fact that money drawn by Cass from the solicitors' client account at the bank may have become mixed by Cass with his own money before he gambled it away at the club. For the respondents have conceded that, if the solicitors can establish legal title to the money in the hands of Cass, that title was not defeated by mixing of the money with other money of Cass while in his hands. On this aspect of the case, therefore, the only question is whether the solicitors can establish legal title to the money when received by Cass from the bank by drawing cheques on the client account without authority.

Before your Lordships, and no doubt before the courts below, elaborate argument was advanced by counsel upon this issue. The respondents relied in particular upon two decisions of the Privy Council as showing that where a partner obtains money by drawing on a partnership bank account without authority, he alone and not the partnership obtains legal title to the money so obtained. These cases, *Union Bank of Australia Ltd v McClintock* [1922] 1 AC 240 and *Commercial Banking Co. of Sydney Ltd v Mann* [1961] AC 1, were in fact concerned with bankers' cheques; but for the respondents it was submitted that the same principle was applicable in the case of cash. The solicitors argued that these cases were wrongly decided, or alternatively sought to distinguish them on a number of grounds. I shall have to examine these cases in some detail when I come to consider the respondents' cross-appeal in respect of the banker's draft; and, as will then appear, I am not prepared to depart from decisions of such high authority as these. They show that, where a banker's cheque payable to a third party or bearer is obtained by a partner from a bank which has received the authority of the partnership to pay the partner in question who has, however, unknown to the bank, acted beyond the authority of his partners in so operating the account, the legal property in the banker's cheque thereupon vests in the partner. The same must a fortiori be true when it is not such a banker's cheque but cash which is so drawn from the bank by the partner in question. Even so, I am satisfied that the solicitors are able to surmount this difficulty, as follows.

It is well established that a legal owner is entitled to trace his property into its product, provided that the latter is indeed identifiable as the product of his property. Thus, in *Taylor v Plumer* (1815) 3 M & S 562, where Sir Thomas Plumer gave a draft to a stockbroker for the purpose of buying exchequer bills, and the stockbroker instead used the draft for buying American securities and doubloons for his own purposes, Sir Thomas was able to trace his property into the securities and doubloons in the hands of the stockbroker, and so defeat a claim made to them by the stockbroker's assignees in bankruptcy. Of course, 'tracing' or 'following' property into its product involves a decision by the owner of the original property to assert his title to the product in place of his original property. This is sometimes referred to as ratification. I myself would not so describe it, but it has, in my opinion, at least one feature in common with ratification, that it cannot be relied upon so as to render an innocent recipient a wrongdoer (cf. *Bolton Partners v Lambert* (1889) 41 ChD 295, 307, *per* Cotton LL: 'an act lawful at the time of its performance [cannot] be rendered unlawful, by the application of the doctrine of ratification.')

I return to the present case. Before Cass drew upon the solicitors' client account at the bank, there was of course no question of the solicitors having any legal property in any cash lying at the bank. The relationship of the bank with the solicitors was essentially that of debtor and creditor; and since the client account was at all material times in credit, the bank was the debtor and the solicitors were its creditors. Such a debt constitutes a chose in action, which is a species of property; and since the debt was enforceable at common law, the chose in action was legal property belonging to the solicitors at common law.

There is my opinion no reason why the solicitors should not be able to trace their property at common law in that chose in action, or in any part of it, into its product, i.e. cash drawn by Cass from their client account at the bank. Such a claim is consistent with their assertion that the money so obtained by Cass was their property at common law. Further, in claiming, the money as money had and received, the solicitors have not sought to make the respondents liable on the basis of any wrong, a point which will be of relevance at a later stage, when I come to consider the defence of change of position.

Authority for the solicitors' right to trace their property in this way is to be found in the decision of your Lordships' House in *Marsh v Keating* (1834) 1 Bing. (NC) 198. Mrs. Keating was the proprietor of £12,000 interest or share in joint stock reduced 3 per cent. annuities, standing to her credit in the books of the Bank of England, where the accounts were entered in the form of debtor and creditor accounts in the ledgers of the bank. Under what purported to be a power of attorney given by Mrs. Keating to the firm of Marsh, Sibbard & Co., on which Mrs. Keating's signature was in fact forged by Henry Fauntleroy, a partner in Marsh, Sibbard & Co., an entry was made in the books of the Bank of England purporting to transfer £9,000 of Mrs. Keating's interest or share in the stock to William Tarbutt, to whom, on the instructions of Henry Fauntleroy, the stock had been sold for the sum of £6,018 15s. In due course, the broker who conducted the sale accounted for £6,013 2s. 6d. (being the sale price less commission) by a cheque payable to Marsh & Co. Upon the discovery of the forgery, Mrs. Keating made a claim upon the Bank of England; and the bank requested Mrs. Keating to prove in the bankruptcy of the partners in Marsh & Co. in respect of the sum so received by them. Mrs. Keating then commenced an action, pursuant to an order of the Lord Chancellor, for the purpose of trying the question whether the partners in Marsh & Co. were indebted to her, in which she claimed the sum so received by Marsh & Co. as money had and received to her use. The opinion of the judges was taken, and their opinion was to the effect that Mrs. Keating was entitled to succeed in her claim. Your Lordships' House ruled accordingly. It must follow a fortiori that the solicitors, as owners of the chose in action constituted by the indebtedness of the bank to them in respect of the sums paid into the client account, could trace their property in that chose in action into its direct product, the money drawn from the account by Cass. It further follows, from the concession made by the respondents, that the solicitors can follow their property into the hands of the respondents when it was paid to them at the club.

Whether the respondents gave consideration for the money

There is no doubt that the respondents received the money in good faith; but, as I have already recorded, there was an acute difference of opinion among the members of the Court of Appeal whether the respondents gave consideration for it. Parker LJ was of opinion that they did so, for two reasons. (1) The club supplied chips in exchange for the money. The contract under which bets were placed at the club; and the contract for the chips was not avoided as a contract by way of gaming and wagering under section 18 of the Gaming Act 1845. (2) Although the actual gaming contracts were void under the Act, nevertheless Cass in fact obtained in exchange for the money the chance of winning and of then being paid and so received valuable consideration from the club. May LJ agreed with the first of these two reasons. Nicholls LJ disagreed with both.

I have to say at once that I am unable to accpet the alternative basis upon which Parker LJ held that consideration was given for the money, viz. that each time Cass placed a bet at the casino, he obtained in exchange the chance of winning and thus of being paid. In my opinion, when Cass placed a bet, he received nothing in return which constituted valuable consideration. The contract of gaming was void; in other words, it was binding in honour only. Cass knew, of course, that, if he won his bet, the club would pay him his winnings. But he had no legal right to claim them. He simply had a confident expectation that, in fact, the club would pay; indeed, if the club did not fulfil its obligations binding in honour upon it, it would very soon go out of business. But it does not follow that, when Cass placed the bet, he received anything that the law recognises as valueable consideration. In my opinion he did not do so. Indeed, to hold that consideration had been given for the money on this basis would, in my opinion, be inconsistent with *Clarke v Shee and Johnson*, 1 Cowp. 197. Even when a winning bet has been paid, the gambler does not receive a valuable consideration for his money. All that he receives is, in law, a gift from the club.

However, the first basis upon which Parker and May LJJ decided the point is more difficult. To that I now turn.

In common sense terms, those who gambled at the club were not gambling for chips: they were gambling for money. As Davies LJ said in *C.H.T. Ltd v Ward* [1965] 2 QB 63, 79:

'People do not game in order to win chips; they game in order to win money. The chips are not money or money's worth; they are mere counters or symbols used for the convenience of all concerned in the gaming.'

The convenience is manifest, especially from the point of view of the club. The club has the gambler's money up front, and large sums of cash are not floating around at the gaming tables. The chips are simply a convenient mechanism for facilitating gambling with money. The property in the chips as such remains in the club, so that there is no question of a gambler buying the chips from the club when he obtains them for cash.

But this broad approach does not solve the problem, which is essentially one of analysis. I think it best to approach the problem by taking a situation unaffected by the impact of the Gaming Acts.

Suppose that a large department store decides, for reasons of security, that all transactions in the store are to be effected by the customers using chips instead of money. On entering the store, or later, the customer goes to the cash desk and obtains chips to the amount he needs in exchange for cash or a cheque. When he buys goods, he presents chips for his purchase. Before he leaves the store, he presents his remaining chips, and receives cash in return. The example may be unrealistic, but in legal terms it is reasonably straightforward. A contract is made when the customer obtains his chips under which the store agrees that, if goods are purchased by the customer, the store will accept chips to the equivalent value of the price, and further that it will redeem for cash any chips returned to it before the customer leaves the store. If a customer offers to buy a certain item of goods at the store, and the girl behind the counter accepts his offer but then refuses to accept the customer's chips, the store will be in breach of the contract for chips. Likewise if, before he leaves the store, the customer hands in some or all of his chips at the cash desk, and the girl at the cash desk refuses to redeem them, the store will be in breach of the contract for chips.

Each time that a customer buys goods, he enters into a contract of sale, under which the customer purchases goods at the store. This is a contract for the sale of goods; it is not a contract of exchange, under which goods are exchanged for chips, but a contract of sale, under which goods are bought for a price, i.e. for a money consideration. This is because, when the customer surrenders chips of the appropriate denomination, the store appropriates part of the money deposited with it towards the purchase. This does not however alter the fact that an independent contract is made for the chips when the customer originally obtains them at the cash desk. Indeed that contract is not dependent upon any contract of sale being entered into; the customer could walk around the store and buy nothing, and then be entitled to redeem his chips in full under the terms of his contract with the store.

But the question remains: when the customer hands over his cash at the cash desk, and receives his chips, does the store give valuable consideration for the money so received by it? In common sense terms, the answer is no. For, in substance and in reality, there is simply a gratuitous deposit of the money with the store, with liberty to the customer to draw upon that deposit to pay for any goods he buys at the store. The chips are no more than the mechanism by which that result is achieved without any cash being handed over at the sales counter, and by which the customer can claim repayment of any balance remaining of his deposit. If a technical approach is adopted, it might be said that, since the property in the money passes to the store as depositee, it then gives consideration for the money in the form of a chose in action created by its promise to repay a like sum, subject to draw-down in respect of goods purchased at the store. I however prefer the common sense approach. Nobody would say that the store has purchased the money by gaming to repay it: the promise to repay is simply the means of giving effect to the gratuitous deposit of the money with the store. It follows that, by receiving the money in these circumstances, the store does not for present purposes give valuable consideration for it. Otherwise a bank with which money was deposited by an innocent donee from a thief could claim to be a bona fide purchaser of the money simply by virtue of the fact of the deposit.

Let me next take the case of gambling at a casino. Of course, if gaming contracts were not void under English law by virtue of section 18 of the Gaming Act 1845, the result would be exactly the same. There would be a contract in respect of the chips, under which the money was deposited with the casino; and then separate contracts would be made when each bet was placed, at which point of time part or all of the money so deposited would be appropriated to the bets.

However, contracts by way of gaming or wagering are void in English law. What is the effect of this? It is obvious that each time a bet is placed by the gambler, the agreement under which the bet is placed is an agreement by way of gaming or wagering, and so is rendered null and void. It follows, as I have said, that the casino, by accepting the bet, does not thereby give valuable consideration for the money which has been wagered by the gambler, because the casino is under no legal obligation to honour the bet. Of course, the gambler cannot recover the money from the casino on the ground of failure of consideration; for he has relied upon the casino to honour the wager – he has in law given the money to the casino, trusting that the casino will fulfil the obligation binding in honour upon it and pay him if he wins his bet – though if the casino does so its payment to the gambler will likewise be in a law a gift. But suppose it is not the gambler but the true owner of the money (from whom the gambler has perhaps, as in the present case, stolen the money) who is claiming it from the casino. What then? In those circumstances the casino cannot, in my opinion, say that it has given valuable consideration for the money, whether or not the gambler's bet is successful. It has given no consideration if the bet is unsuccessful, because its promise to pay on a successful bet is void; nor has it done so if the gambler's bet is successful and the casino has paid him his winnings, because that payment is in law a gift to the gambler by the casino.

For these reasons I conclude, in agreement with Nicholls LJ, that the respondents did not give valuable consideration for the money. But the matter does not stop there; because there remains the question whether the respondents can rely upon the defence of change of position.

Change of position

I turn then to the last point on which the respondents relied to defeat the solicitors' claim for the money. This was that the claim advanced by the solicitors was in the form of an action for money had and received, and that such a claim should only succeed where the defendant was unjustly enriched at the expense of the plaintiff. If it would be unjust or unfair to order restitution, the claim should fail. It was for the court to consider the question of injustice or unfairness, on broad grounds. If the court thought that it would be unjust or unfair to hold the respondents liable to the solicitors, it should deny the solicitors recovery. Mr. Lightman, for the club, listed a number of reasons why, in his submission, it would be unfair to hold the respondents liable. There were (1) the club acted throughout in good faith, ignorant of the fact that the money had been stolen by Cass; (2) although the gaming contracts entered into by the club with Cass were all void, nevertheless the club honoured all those contracts; (3) Cass was allowed to keep his winnings (to the extent that he did not gamble them away); (4) the gaming contracts were merely void not illegal; and (5) the solicitors' claim was no different in principle from a claim to recover against an innocent third party to whom the money was given and who no longer retained it.

I accept that the solicitors' claim in the present case is founded upon the unjust enrichment of the club, and can only succeed if, in accordance with the principles of the law of restitution, the club was indeed unjustly enriched at the expense of the solicitors. The claim for money had and received is not, as I have previously mentioned, founded upon any wrong committed by the club against the solicitors. But it does not, in my opinion, follow that the court has carte blanche to reject the solicitors' claim simply because it thinks it unfair or unjust in the circumstances to grant recovery. The recovery of money in restitution is not, as a general rule, a matter of discretion for the court. A claim to recover money at common law is made as a matter of right; and even though the underlying principle of recovery is the principle of unjust enrichment, nevertheless, where recovery is denied, it is denied on the basis of legal principle.

It is therefore necessary to consider whether Mr Lightman's submission can be upheld on the basis of legal principle. In my opinion it is plain, from the nature of his submission, that he is in fact seeking to invoke a principle of change of position, asserting that recovery should be denied because of the change in position of the respondents, who acted in good faith throughout.

Whether change of position is, or should be, recognised as a defence to claims in restitution is a subject which has been much debated in the books. It is however a matter on which there is a remarkable unanimity of view, the consensus being to the effect that such a defence should be recognised in English law. I myself am under no doubt that this is right.

Historically, despite broad statements of Lord Mansfield to the effect that an action for money had and received will only lie where it is inequitable for the defendant to retain the money (see in particular *Moses v Macferlan* (1760) 2 Burr. 1005), the defence has received at most only partial recognition in English law. I refer to two groups of cases which can arguably be said to rest upon change of position: (1) where an agent can defeat a claim to restitution on the ground that, before learning of the plaintiff's claim, he has paid the money over to his principal or otherwise altered his position in relation to his principal on the faith of the payment; and (2) certain cases concerned with bills of exchange, in which money paid under forged bills has been held irrecoverable on grounds which may, on one possible view, be rationalised in terms of change of position: see, e.g. *Price v Neal* (1762) 3 Burr. 1355, and *London and River Plate Bank Ltd v Bank of Liverpool* [1896] 1 QB 7. There has however been no general recognition of any defence of change of position as such; indeed any such defence is inconsistent with the decisions of the Exchequer Division in *Durrant v Ecclesiastical Commissioners for England and Wales* (1880) 6 QBD 234, and of the Court of Appeal in *Baylis v Bishop of London* [1913] 1 Ch 127. Instead, where change of position has been relied upon by the defendant, it has been usual to approach the problem as one of estoppel: see, e.g. *R. E. Jones Ltd v Waring and Gillow Ltd* [1926] AC 670 and *Avon Council v Howlett* [1983] 1 WLR 605. But it is difficult to see the justification for such a rationalisation. First, estoppel normally depends upon the existence of a representation by one party, in reliance upon which the representee has so changed his position that it is inequitable for the representor to go back upon his representation. But, in cases of restitution, the requirement of a representation appears to be unnecessary. It is true that, in cases where the plaintiff has paid money directly to the defendant, it has been argued (though with difficulty) that the plaintiff has represented to the defendant that he is entitled to the money; but in a case such as the present, in which the money is paid to an innocent donee by a thief, the true owner has made no representation whatever to the defendant. Again, it was held by the Court of Appeal in *Avon County Council v Howlett* that estoppel cannot operate protanto, with the effect that if, for example, the defendant has innocently changed his position by disposing of part of the money, a defence of estoppel would provide him with a defence to the whole of the claim. Considerations such as these provide a strong indication that, in many cases, estoppel is not an appropriate concept to deal with the problem.

In these circumstances, it is right that we should ask ourselves: why do we feel that it would be unjust to allow restitution in cases such as these? The answer must be that, where an innocent defendant's position is so changed that he will suffer an injustice if called upon to repay or to repay in full, the injustice of requiring him so to repay outweighs the injustice of denying the plaintiff restitution. If the plaintiff pays money to the defendant under a mistake of fact, and the defendant then, acting in good faith, pays the money or part of it to charity, it is unjust to require the defendant to make restitution to the extent that he has so changed his position. Likewise, on facts such as those in the present case, if a thief steals my money and pays it to a third party who gives it away to charity, that third party should have a good defence to an action for money had and received. In other words, bona fide change of position should of itself be a good defence in such cases as these. The principle is widely recognised throughout the common law world. It is recognised in the United States of America (see *American Law Institute, Restatement of the Law, Restitution* (1937), section 142, pp. 567–78 and

Palmer, The Law of Restitution (1978), vol. III, para. 16.8); it has been judicially recognised by the Supreme Court of Canada (see *Rural Municipality of Storthoaks v Mobil Oil Canada Ltd* (1975) 55 DR, (3d) 1); it has been introduced by statute in New Zealand (Judicature Act 1908, section 94B (as amended)), and Western Australia (see Western Australia Law Reform (Property, Perpetuities and Succession) Act 1962, section 24, and Western Australia Trustee Act 1962, section 65(8), and it has been judicially recognised by the Supreme Court of Victoria: see *Bank of New South Wales v Murphett* [1983] 1 VR 489. In the important case of *Australia and New Zealand Banking Group Ltd v Westpac Banking Corporation* (1988) 78 ALR 157, there are strong indications that the High Court of Australia may be moving towards the same destination (see especially at pp. 162 and 168, *per curiam*). The time for its recognition in this country is, in my opinion, long overdue.

I am most anxious that, in recognising this defence to actions of restitution, nothing should be said at this stage to inhibit the development of the defence on a case by case basis, in the usual way. It is, of course, plain that the defence is not open to one who has changed his position in bad faith, as where the defendant has paid away the money with knowledge of the facts entitling the plaintiff to restitution; and it is commonly accepted that the defence should not be open to a wrongdoer. These are matters which can, in due course, be considered in depth in cases where they arise for consideration. They do not arise in the present case. Here there is no doubt that the respondents have acted in good faith throughout, and the action is not founded upon any wrongdoing of the respondents. It is not however appropriate in the present case to attempt to identify all those actions in restitution to which change of position may be a defence. A prominent example will, no doubt, be found in those cases where the plaintiff is seeking repayment of money paid under a mistake of fact; but I can see no reason why the defence should not also be available in principle in a case such as the present, where the plaintiff's money has been paid by a thief to an innocent donee, and the plaintiff then seeks repayment from the donee in an action for money had and received. At present I do not wish to state the principle any less broadly than this: that the defence is available to a person whose position has so changed that it would be inequitable in all the circumstances to require him to make restitution, or alternatively to make restitution in full. I wish to stress however that the mere fact that the defendant has spent the money, in whole or in part, does not of itself render it inequitable that he should be called upon to repay, because the expenditure might in any event have been incurred by him in the ordinary course of things. I fear that the mistaken assumption that mere expenditure of money may be regarded as amounting to a change of position for present purposes has led in the past to opposition by some to recognition of a defence which in fact is likely to be available only on comparatively rare occasions. In this connection I have particularly in mind the speech of Lord Simonds in *Ministry of Health v Simpson* [1951] AC, 251, 276.

I wish to add two further footnotes. The defence of change of position is akin to the defence of bona fide purchase; but we cannot simply say that bona fide purchase is a species of change of position. This is because change of position will only avail a defendant to the extent that his position has been changed; whereas, where bona fide purchase is invoked, no inquiry is made (in most cases) into the adequacy of the consideration. Even so, the recognition of change of position as a defence should be doubly beneficial. It will enable a more generous approach to be taken to the recognition of the right to restitution, in the knowledge that the defence is, in appropriate cases, available; and while recognising the different functions of property at law and in equity, there may also in due course develop a more consistent approach to tracing claims, in which common defences are recognised as available to such claims, whether advanced at law or in equity.

I turn to the application of this principle to the present case. In doing so, I think it right to stress at the outset that the respondents, by running a casino at the club, were conducting a perfectly lawful business. There is nothing unlawful about accepting bets at a casino; the only relevant consequence of the transactions being gambling transactions is that they are void. In other words, the transactions as such give rise to no legal obligations. Neither the gambler, nor the casino, can go to court to enforce a gaming transaction. That is the legal position. But the practical or business position is that, if a casino does not pay winnings when they are due, it will simply go out of business. So the obligation in honour to pay winnings is an obligation which, in business terms, the casino has to comply with. It is also relevant to bear in mind that, in the present case, there is no question of Cass having gambled on credit. In each case, the money was put up front, not paid to discharge the balance of an account kept for gambling debts. It was because the money was paid over, that the casino accepted the bets at all.

In the course of argument before your Lordships, attention was focused upon the overall position of the respondents. From this it emerged, that, on the basis I have indicated (but excluding the banker's draft), at least £150,960 derived from money stolen by Cass from the solicitors was won by the club and lost by Cass. On this approach, the possibility arose that the effect of change of position should be to limit the amount recoverable by the solicitors to that sum. But there are difficulties in the way of this approach. Let us suppose that a gambler places two bets with a casino, using money stolen from a third party. The gambler wins the first bet and loses the second. So far as the winning bet is concerned, it is readily understandable that the casino should be able to say that it is not liable to the true owner for money had and received, on the ground that it has changed its position in good faith. But at first sight it is not easy to see how it can aggregate the two bets together and say that, by paying winnings on the first bet in excess of both, it should be able to deny liability in respect of the money received in respect of the second.

There are other ways in which the problem might be approached, the first narrower and the second broader than that which I have just described. The narrower approach is to limit the impact of the winnings to the winning bet itself, so that the amount of all other bets placed with the plaintiff's money would be recoverable by him regardless of the substantial winnings paid by the casino to the gambler on the winning bet. On the broader approach, it could be said that each time a bet is accepted by the casino, with the money up front, the casino, by accepting the bet, so changes its position in good faith that it would inequitable to require it to pay the money back to the true owner. This would be because, by accepting the bet, the casino has committed itself, in business terms, to pay the gambler his winnings if successful. In such circumstances, the bookmaker could say that, acting in good faith, he had changed his position, by incurring the risk of having to pay a sum of money substantially larger than the amount of the stake. On this basis it would be irrelevant whether the gambler won the bet or not, or, if he did win the bet, how much he won.

I must confess that I have not found the point an easy one. But in the end I have come to the conclusion that on the facts of the present case the first of these three solutions is appropriate. Let us suppose that only one bet was placed by a gambler at a casino with the plaintiff's money, and that he lost it. In that simple case, although it is true that the casino will have changed its position to the extent that it has incurred the risk, it will in the result have paid out nothing to the gambler, and so prima facie it would not be inequitable to require it to repay the amount of the bet to the plaintiff. The same would, of course, be equally true if the gambler placed a hundred bets with the plaintiff's money and lost them all; the plaintiff should be entitled to recover the amount of all the bets. This conclusion has the merit of consistency with the decision of the Court of King's Bench in *Clarke v Shee and Johnson*, 1 Cowp. 197. But then, let us suppose that the gambler has won one or more out of one hundred bets placed by him with the plaintiff's money at a casino over a certain period of time, and that the casino has paid him a substantial sum in winnings, equal, let us assume, to one half of the amount of all the bets. Given that it is not inequitable to require the casino to repay to the plaintiff the amount of the bets in full where no winnings have been paid, it would, in the circumstances I have just described, be inequitable, in my opinion, to require the casino to repay to the plaintiff more than one half of his money. The inequity, as I perceive it, arises from the nature of gambling itself. In gambling only an occasional bet is won, but when the gambler wins he will receive much more than the stake placed for his winning bet. True, there may be no immediate connection between the bets. They may be placed on different occasions, and each one is a separate gaming contract. But the point is that there has been a series of transactions under which all the bets have been placed by paying the plaintiff's money to the casino, and on each occasion the casino has incurred the risk that the gambler will win. It is the totality of the bets which yields, by the laws of chance, the occasional winning bet; and the occasional winning bet is therefore, in practical terms, the result of the casino changing its position by incurring the risk of losing on each occasion when a bet is placed with it by the gambler. So, when in such circumstances the plaintiff seeks to recover from the casino the amount of several bets placed with it by a gambler with his money, it would be inequitable to require the casino to repay in full without bringing into account winnings paid by it to the gambler on any one or more of the bets so placed with it. The result may not be entirely logical; but it is surely just.

For these reasons, I would allow the solicitors' appeal in respect of the money, limited however to the sum of £150,960.

Lords Griffiths and **Ackner** gave speeches concurring with **Lords Templeman** and **Goff**.

NOTES AND QUESTIONS

1. This was the first case in which the House of Lords fully recognized the principle against unjust enrichment: not only did their Lordships use the language of unjust enrichment but, more specifically, the defence of change of position was accepted for the first time and that defence can only be rationalized through unjust enrichment reasoning.

2. The case is a difficult one involving, as it does, the notoriously complex situation of a benefit being conferred by a third party (Cass) rather than by the claimants (the solicitors). This 'third party issue' goes to the 'at the expense of the claimant' element of the cause of action of unjust enrichment. A standard way of showing that a gain is at the claimant's expense, rather than at the expense of the person (the third party) who has directly conferred the benefit, is for the claimant to show that the asset was the claimant's prior to its transfer by the third party to the defendant. But in *Lipkin Gorman* the House of Lords refused to overrule the Privy Council cases which laid down that the money drawn out by Cass, as an authorized signatory on the partnership account, belonged to Cass not to the solicitors. How then did the solicitors establish that the club's enrichment was at their expense rather than at the expense of Cass?

3. Assuming that the club was enriched at the solicitors' expense, why was the enrichment *unjust*? (see below, 221).

4. For notes and questions concerning the acceptance of the defence of change of position in this case, see below, 763.

5. Although Lord Bridge preferred Lord Templeman's reasoning on the application of change of position to the facts, it is not clear that there is any major difference between the speeches of Lords Goff and Templeman on this point. Of the two, Lord Goff's reasoning is surely to be preferred, in that he clarifies the dilemma posed where the club's payment out of winnings could not be specifically related to particular payments by Cass.

6. What are the differences between the defence of *bona fide* purchase and change of position? Why did the former defence fail, and the latter (partially) succeed? (See below, Chapter 14.)

7. In what sense, if any, was Lord Templeman correct to say that the club *retained* £150,960 of stolen money (or £154,695 if one includes the value of the banker's draft)?

8. For helpful case-notes on the *Lipkin Gorman* case see, for example, P Birks, 'The English Recognition of Unjust Enrichment' [1991] LMCLQ 473; and E McKendrick, 'Restitution, Misdirected Funds and Change of Position' (1992) 55 *MLR* 377 (below, 219).

- *Westdeutsche Landesbank Girozentrale v Islington London Borough Council*
  [1996] 2 WLR 802, House of Lords

For the facts, see below, 727. We are here concerned solely with their Lordships' over-ruling of *Sinclair v Brougham* (above, 6) on the personal claim for money had and received.

Lord Browne-Wilkinson [*in a section of his speech dealing with relevant cases, and having considered the facts of* Sinclair v Brougham, *continued*]: The House of Lords was unanimous in rejecting the claim by the ultra vires depositors to recover in quasi-contract on the basis of moneys had and received. In their view, the claim in quasi-contract was based on an implied contract. To imply a contract to repay would be to imply a contract to exactly the same effect as the express ultra vires contract of loan. Any such implied contract would itself be void as being ultra vires.

Subsequent developments in the law of restitution demonstrate that this reasoning is no longer sound. The common law restitutionary claim is based not on implied contract but on unjust enrich-ment: in the circumstances the law imposes an obligation to repay rather than implying an entirely fictitious agreement to repay: *Fibrosa Spolka Akcyjna v Fairbairn Lawson Combe Barbour Ltd.* [1943] AC 32, 63–4, *per* Lord Wright; *Pavey & Matthews Pty. Ltd v Paul* (1987) 162 CLR 221, 227, 255; *Lipkin Gorman v Karpnale Ltd* [1991] 2 AC 548, 578c; *Woolwich Equitable Building Society v Inland Revenue Commissioners* [1993] AC 70. In my judgment, your Lordships should now unequivocally and finally reject the concept that the claim for moneys had and received is based on a implied contract. I would overrule *Sinclair v Brougham* on this point.

It follows that in *Sinclair v Brougham* the depositors should have had a personal claim to recover the moneys at law based on a total failure of consideration. The failure of consideration was *not* partial: the depositors had paid over their money in consideration of a promise to repay. That promise was ultra vires and void; therefore the consideration for the payment of the money wholly failed. So in the present swaps case (though the point is not one under appeal) I think the Court of Appeal were right to hold that the swap moneys were paid on a consideration that wholly failed. The essence of the swap agreement is that, over the whole term of the agreement, each party thinks he will come out best: the consideration for one party making a payment is an obligation on the other party to make counter-payments over the whole term of the agreement.

If in *Sinclair v Brougham* the depositors had been held entitled to recover at law, their personal claim would have ranked pair passu with other ordinary unsecured creditors, in priority to the members of the society who could take nothing in the liquidation until all creditors had been paid.

Lord Goff (dissenting): For present purposes, I approach this case in the following way. First, it is clear that the problem which arose in *Sinclair v Brougham*, viz. that a personal remedy in restitution was excluded on grounds of public policy, does not arise in the present case, which is not of course concerned with a borrowing contract. Second, I regard the decision in *Sinclair v Brougham* as being a response to that problem in the case of ultra vires borrowing contracts, and as not intended to create a principle of general application. From this it follows, in my opinion, that *Sinclair v Brougham* is not relevant to the decision in the present case. In particular it cannot be relied upon as a precedent that a trust arises on the facts of the present case, justifying on that basis an award of compound interest against the council.

But I wish to add this. I do not in any event think that it would be right for your Lordships' House to exercise its power under the *Practice Statement (Judicial Precedent)* [1966] 1 WLR 1234 to depart from *Sinclair v Brougham*. I say this first because, in my opinion, any decision to do so would not be material to the disposal of the present appeal, and would therefore be obiter. But there is a second reason of substance why, in my opinion, that course should not be taken. I recognise that nowadays cases of incapacity are relatively rare, though the swaps litigation shows that they can still occur. Even so, the question could still arise whether, in the case of a borrowing contract rendered void because it was ultra vires the borrower, it would be contrary to public policy to allow a personal claim in restitution. Such a question has arisen in the past not only in relation to associations such as the Birkbeck Permanent Benefit Building Society, but also in relation to infants' contracts. Moreover there is a respectable body of opinion that, if such a case arose today, it should still be held that public policy would preclude a personal claim in restitution, though not of course by reference to an implied contract. That was the opinion expressed by Leggatt LJ in the Court of Appeal in the present case [1994] 1 WLR 938, 952E–F, as it had been by Hobhouse J; and the same view has been expressed by Professor Birks (see *An Introduction to the Law of Restitution* (1985), p. 374). I myself incline to the opinion that a personal claim in restitution would not indirectly enforce the ultra vires contract, for such an action would be unaffected by any of the contractual terms governing the borrowing, and moreover would be subject (where appropriate) to any available restitutionary defences. If my present opinion were to prove to be correct then *Sinclair v Brougham* will fade into history. If not, then recourse can at least be had to *Sinclair v Brougham* as authority for the proposition that, in such circumstances, the lender should not be without a remedy. Indeed, I cannot think that English law, or equity, is so impoverished as to be incapable of providing relief in such circumstances. Lord Wright, who wrote in strong terms ('*Sinclair v Brougham*' [1938] CLJ 305) endorsing the just result in *Sinclair v Brougham*, would turn in his grave at any such suggestion. Of course, it may be necessary to reinterpret the decision in that case to provide a more satisfactory basis for it; indeed one possible suggestion has been proposed by Professor Birks (see *An Introduction to the Law Restitution*, pp. 396 et seq.). But for the present the case should in my opinion stand, though confined in the manner I have indicated, as an assertion that those who are caught in the trap of advancing money under ultra vires borrowing contracts will not be denied appropriate relief.

Lords Slynn and **Lloyd** agreed with **Lord Browne-Wilkinson**. **Lord Woolf** in his dissenting speech did not touch on the personal claim in *Sinclair v Brougham*.

4. BIRKS' FOCUS ON THE CAUSE OF ACTION OF UNJUST ENRICHMENT

- P Birks, *Restitution—The Future* (1992), 1–2

The most important division in the law of restitution is between that part which is substantive and that part which is purely remedial. However, these words 'substance' and 'remedy' are dangerous. They need to be defined by every person who seeks to use them. The remedial part of the law of restitution is concerned with the question whether the victim of a wrong can obtain restitution of gains made by the wrongdoer through the wrong. It is called remedial because it is not concerned to describe and define any cause of action but only to ask whether causes of action defined in the law of civil wrongs trigger by way of remedy a right to restitution. To take the commonest case, it is not the business of the law of restitution to define the tort of conversion, but it is its business to find out whether and why that tort gives rise not merely to compensation but also to restitution.

By contrast the substantive part of the law of restitution focuses on causes of action which are not defined in other categories. They are causes of action specifically in unjust enrichment and nothing else. Substance here means causes of action. Causes of action are sets of facts, here sets of facts which give rise to a right to restitution of the defendant's enrichment at the plaintiff's expense. For example, just as conversion is a specific cause of action within the familiar generic terms 'tort' or 'wrong', so failure of consideration is a specific cause of action within the still somewhat less familiar genus 'unjust enrichment'.

The key to the difference lies in the phrase 'at the plaintiff's expense'. If the plaintiff has to rely on that phrase in the sense 'by committing a wrong against', or if he chooses to rely on the phrase in that sense, he identifies himself as the victim of a wrong. Since the connection between him and the enrichment which he seeks to recover is then the wrong, the wrong is clearly the ultimate foundation of his claim. All he is doing is asking for a restitutionary remedy for the wrong. But if he can and does use the subtractive sense of the phrase, saying only that his wealth has passed to the defendant, he is not identifying himself as the victim of a wrong but rather as the person whose minus accounts for the plaintiff's plus. That subtraction is now the connection between him and the wealth which is in question. He has only to show that the enrichment of the defendant by subtraction from him happened in circumstances which the law regards as actionably 'unjust' or, in other words, as requiring that restitution be made. By identifying a sufficient unjust factor he will establish a cause of action in unjust enrichment. Such causes of action are always compounded of a subtractive enrichment and an unjust factor calling for the enrichment to be reversed.

- **P Birks, 'Misnomer' in _Restitution, Past, Present & Future_** (1998, eds W Cornish, R Nolan, J O'Sullivan, G Virgo), 1

The whole thrust of the law of restitution is towards defining and analysing the event which most commonly brings it about. Generically, that event is unjust enrichment. Most of us most of the time, when we talk of the law of restitution, do in fact mean to refer to the law of unjust enrichment. We treat the two terms as forming a perfect square, the one being the effect of the cause, and the other the cause of the effect. Restitution is the response to unjust enrichment, and unjust enrichment is the event which triggers restitution. This paper will try to say that we ought to allow the name of the event to predominate over the name of the response. In other words, we ought to call our subject unjust enrichment. This is partly a matter of elegance. The dominant categories of our law are categories of event. The series 'contract (or, larger, consent), wrongs, unjust enrichment, and other causative events' is on its face a well-dressed series in which every term is of the same kind. It is a classification of the events which generate legal rights and duties. When we substitute restitution for unjust enrichment, we appear to have invited a cuckoo into the nest. One term now refers, not to a cause, but to an effect. On the assumption of perfect quadration between restitution and unjust enrichment, there is in fact no cuckoo at all, merely the appearance of one. That is mere inelegance. But it would be worth preferring unjust enrichment to restitution even if it were only a matter of avoiding a mildly misleading inelegance. However, the paper goes on to say that the danger of preferring restitution is greater. It argues that the perfect quadration is artificial and tries to show that in that artificality are hidden a number of intellectual traps . . .

  . . .

The truth is that the quadration of unjust enrichment and restitution is not naturally perfect. It can be made perfect only by artificially imposing a restricted meaning upon the word 'restitution'. We have to assert that the word means only that yielding up which is precipitated by unjust enrichment. In the law such artificiality, within limits, is commonplace. But it is always dangerous. The natural meaning is hard to keep at bay. There must be a compelling reason to justify the attempt. And here there is none. Unjust enrichment triggers restitution, but, naturally, restitution is triggered by events other than the analytically distinct event called unjust enrichment. This means that, unless we are to remain constantly on guard against infringing the line between the natural and the artificial meanings and resolve never to use 'restitution' except in its artifically restricted sense, it will never be certain that a claim which we describe as restitutionary does indeed arise from unjust enrichment.

It may be that those who spend a large part of their lives in this subject can fall easily enough into habitual vigilance against this danger. But it is too much to expect every judge and every author to be similarly alive to it. 'The claim . . . is not based on loss to the plaintiff . . . It resembles therefore an action for restitution, rather than an action in tort.'[1] What does this kind of sentence mean? Does the speaker mean that the cause of action is unjust enrichment rather than tort, or that, the cause of action remaining the tort, the claim is for restitution rather than compensation? Our present practice offers no escape from this kind of ambiguity. There are artificialities and artificialities. Otherwise we could have no terms of art. But the unnatural restriction must be easily grasped. This one is too subtle and deceptive.

The rest of this paper assumes, without further argument, the classification of rights by reference to their causative events. All rights, whether *in personam* or *in rem*, arise from events which happen in the world and, further, these causative events divide into four genera, namely consent, wrongs, unjust enrichment, or other events. In this series, 'consent' includes not only contracts, but also other manifestations of consent such as conveyances, wills, and declarations of trust. When the series is arranged in this order, the line between consent and the others distinguishes between rights conceded by a person and rights raised by operation of law; in the language of the will, the *voluntas*, that is the line between voluntary and involuntary. The series can be rearranged. If one puts wrongs first, the line between wrongs and the rest distinguishes between wrongs and not-wrongs. In that order it helps us remember that many claims and their correlative liabilities arise independently of wrongdoing . . .

There are two further points about this series which it is necessary to insist upon without the argument which they deserve. First, each member of the series is analytically distinct from all the others. Any given set of facts may be susceptible of two or more analyses, but each analysis then stands alone. In other words a plaintiff may have a choice between two causes of action. For example, a plaintiff who pays money by reason of a misrepresentation may sometimes be able to choose between unjust enrichment and wrongs.

The misrepresentation will nearly always operate as an unjust factor entitling the plaintiff to restitution, but the misrepresentation may also be a civil wrong entitling the plaintiff to recover damages. The plaintiff then has a choice whether to base himself on the wrong or, ignoring that characterization of the facts, on the unjust enrichment. Secondly, accepting that in a loose sense every plaintiff who comes to court does so because he feels that he has suffered a wrong and needs a remedy (a word more abused than any other), it is essential to take great care in identifying the precise sense in which 'wrongs' are analytically distinct from all other causative events in the fourterm series. This is difficult. In this paper I take a 'wrong' to be any breach of duty, so that it follows that a right arises from a wrong where, in order to establish it, the plaintiff must so analyse the facts as to disclose a breach of duty. Although fault of some kind is very commonly a necessary ingredient of such an analysis, fault is not a reliable indicator. Some wrongs—some breaches of duty—can be committed without fault, and, the other way around, the fact that a defendant appears to be at fault is not a sure guide to his having committed a wrong.

It follows from the analytical independence of the four causative events that a plaintiff who relies on a wrong cannot, whatever measure of liability he seeks to impose, be claiming under any one of the other three heads. He cannot, for example, be suing in unjust enrichment, not even if that which he is seeking is correctly described as restitution. To be suing in unjust enrichment he must be able to drop the analysis of the facts as a breach of duty. That is, he must move into the land of not-wrongs and, in particular, into the not-wrong which is, generically, unjust enrichment.

. . .

WRONGS

Every acquisitive wrong can be loosely described as an unjust enrichment at the expense of the plaintiff, but, where the plaintiff relies on the wrong, the invocation of that language does not alter

---

1 *Strand Electric and Engineering* Co. v *Brisford Entertainments* [1952] 2 QB 246, 254, Denning LJ. His Lordship certainly meant that the claim was for restitution rather than for compensation. No cause of action had been advanced other than tort.

the fact that the causative event upon which he is relying is the wrong, not unjust enrichment. As we have seen, when we affirm that rights arise from wrongs or from not-wrongs and, among not-wrongs, from contract, unjust enrichment and other events, we necessarily affirm at the same time that each member of the series is analytically distinct from every other. The independence of each causative event is essential to the nature and function of the series. However, if we say that profits taken from an infringement of patent or the tort of passing-off constitute an unjust enrichment and, as such, give rise to restitution, we ignore the line between wrongs and the not-wrong which is unjust enrichment.

'Unjust enrichment' is short for 'unjust enrichment at the expense of the plaintiff'. When connection between the plaintiff and the enrichment which he seeks to recover is a wrong, the phrase 'at the expense of the plaintiff' means 'by doing wrong to the plaintiff'. Whenever a plaintiff relies on that sense of 'at the expense of', his cause of action is the wrong itself. If you are paid to beat me up, your profit is an enrichment obtained by doing wrong to me. The language of unjust enrichment will not alter the fact that my claim to your profit can only be made out through the battery, you were enriched at my expense only in that sense. By contrast, a mistaken payment is an enrichment from the payer, rendered unjust by the mistake. In the series of independent causative events, unjust enrichment at the plaintiff's expense must conform to that subtractive model in which 'at the plaintiff's expense' means 'from the plaintiff'.

In our series of causative events, the topic which we identify as 'restitution for wrongs' thus belongs under wrongs, not under unjust enrichment. It tends to be addressed in books and courses on restitution. But it belongs in the books and courses on torts or civil wrongs, for it is no more than an inquiry into the consequences of wrongs. Which wrongs give punitive damages? Which wrongs give aggravated damages? These questions are obviously part of the law of tort. It should be no less obvious that the inquiry into gain-based awards belongs there too. Which wrongs give restitutionary damages? That question belongs in the same series. The phrase 'restitutionary damages' tends to set some jurists' teeth on edge. There is no imperative need to court a hostile reaction. There are a variety of money obligations which can be generated by a wrong. It would be useful to be able to use one word for all, but it is enough to say that the consequence of civil wrongs is in general that the wrongdoer must pay money to the victim. The quantification of the amount payable belongs to the law of wrongs.

It is worth pausing on the meaning of 'belongs to' in that last sentence. Our series of causative events exists because of the need to know from what events rights arise. The terms in the series do not identify mere contextual categories: all the law about wrongs, contract, and so on. There is no objection, of course, to turning them into contextual categories, so long as one is conscious of doing so. In practice, that conversion happens rather easily. Thus most books on contract contextualize the causative event and do present all the law about contract. We might by the same convenient technique justify discussing restitution for wrongs in a book or course on unjust enrichment, but the justification for doing so would have to be based on the convenience of treating the causative category as a contextual category. In an unannounced way, that has been the effect of calling the subject restitution. The response-oriented name has invited us to speak of rather more than the causative event unjust enrichment. When we say, therefore, that restitution for wrongs belongs to wrongs and not to unjust enrichment, we say it on the assumption that we are talking of pure causative categories.

. . .

CONSENT

This need not detain us very long. Restitution can sometimes be consent-based. A contractual right can be restitutionary. That is, it can be contractual in origin and restitutionary in purpose and effect . . .

It is . . . possible, when money is claimed of you, for you to hand it over in exchange for a promise by the other to return it in certain events. There might be a doubt about its being due. You can take a promise that it shall be returned if and when the doubt is resolved against the recipient. These are contracts to make restitution. Nor does the horrible history of this subject, and in particular its long subjugation to the implied contract theory of restitution, mean that such a contract can never be genuinely implied. In earlier litigation not unlike the *Woolwich* case Vaisey J felt able to conclude that the Customs and Excise Commissioners had impliedly made such a promise.[2] He may have leaned over a little too far to find that agreement. There is a hint in the *Woolwich* case to that effect.[3] However, so long as we are sure that use of the word 'restitution' does not point inexorably back to the event 'unjust enrichment', we have no reason to resist the notion that a restitutionary obligation can sometimes be the creature of contract.

. . .

MISCELLANEOUS OTHER EVENTS

We have so far shown that restitutionary rights can be brought into existence, not only by unjust enrichment from the plaintiff, but also by wrongs and by consent. This section shows that it is necessary to accept that restitution can also be triggered by an event which cannot be fitted in any of the first three categories and must therefore belong in the miscellaneous fourth. This can be illustrated from *Macmillan v Bishopsgate Investment Trust*.[4]

The case arose from the collapse of the Maxwell empire. Maxwell so pulled the strings that Macmillan, an American member of the empire, transferred its shares in the Berlitz language school within the empire to Bishopsgate. After the transfer Bishopsgate expressly acknowledged that it held the Berlitz shares on trust for Macmillan. Maxwell then started using them as security for huge loans. But this borrowing failed to save the day. After the collapse, the Berlitz shares were found in the hands of numerous lending institutions, all claiming to hold free of the Macmillan equitable interest. The finance houses relied on their having acquired as bona fide purchasers of the legal estate without notice. There were complex issues in the conflict of laws. It suited Macmillan to argue that English law should apply. The attraction of English law was that it took a relatively narrow view of what it meant to be a bona fide purchaser.

The easiest path to the application of English law seemed to Macmillan to be through unjust enrichment. It argued that the claim to recover its shares should be analysed as a claim to restitution of unjust enrichment and should therefore be subject to the law of the place where the enrichment had been received, namely London. The courts appear to have accepted that Macmillan's claim was a claim in restitution.[5] They nevertheless escaped the conclusion that English law applied. We do not need to pursue the conflicts questions. What matters here is only that the case illustrates a claim which is indeed restitutionary but which not only does not arise from unjust enrichment but does on analysis arise from an event in the fourth category, namely the receipt of a *res* which belongs in equity to another.

It is necessary to distinguish two elements of Macmillan's contention. The first is that which the Romans would have recognized as a *vindicatio* and more specifically the distinctive *intentio* of that kind of action: 'Those shares are ours!' The common law recognizes no such claim, but equity does. A plaintiff can ask for a declaration that the defendant holds on trust for him. 'Please say they are mine in equity!' It comes to the same thing. The essence of the *vindicatio* is the direct assertion of a

2 *Sebel Products Ltd v Customs and Excise Commissioners* [1949] Ch 409.
3 [1993] AC 70, 165–6.
4 [1996] 1 All ER 585, [1996] BCC 453, CA. The appeal has only dealt with the issue of the applicable law.
5 [1996] 1 All ER 585, 596 (Staughton LJ), 614 (Aldous LJ); [1995] 1 WLR 978, 988–90 (Millett J).

proprietary right. The second element derives from the inert nature of that assertion of any pure proprietary claim. Differently from a judicial declaration of any obligation ('The defendant ought to pay the plaintiff 100') a declaration of a proprietary right implies no imperative ('The shares belong to Macmillan'). Something more has to be tacked on. What, if anything, will the court make the defendant do? In classical Roman law the plaintiff would in the last analysis have to put up with a money judgment. In equity, provided that the plaintiff asks for something more than a declaration, a successful *vindicatio* will end in an order for specific transfer to the plaintiff.

. . .

The mere receipt of an asset belonging to another is neither a contract nor a wrong. We might jiggle it into the defintion of a wrong if we had to, but it belongs more naturally in either category three, unjust enrichment, or category four, miscellaneous other events. If we locate this obligation under unjust enrichment, we will encounter a huge difficulty. The subsidiary obligation will become subject to the defence of change of position. We do not want every *vindicatio* to be subject to that defence. It would mean that, simply because of their inert nature and their need to be enlivened by this ancillary obligation to deliver, all property rights, even those not born of unjust enrichment, would at one stage removed be subjected to the characteristic and essential weakness of rights which are born of unjust enrichment. That is not the law. Nor is it desirable that it should be.

As we learn to live without the idea of a perfect quadration between restitution and unjust enrichment, it will become easier to accept that the restitutionary obligation to transfer which underpins every *vindicatio* is not an obligation which arises from unjust enrichment. It is an obligation which arises in category four, the miscellaneous residue of causative events. The mere receipt of another's thing is not a contract, not a wrong, and not an unjust enrichment. It is one among the 'various other events'.

. . .

CONCLUSION

The great achievement of *Goff and Jones on Restitution*, building on the American *Restatement of Restitution*, has been to identify in the common law legal family an analytically distinct cause of action known to the civil law family as unjust or unjustified enrichment. There was already a copious case law, but its unity had been obscured by layer on layer of impenetrable language. Each fragment had therefore acquired a life of its own. The elementary business of treating like cases alike had to be left more or less to chance. The exercise of unification was achieved under the name 'restitution'. Despite the choice of that name, oriented to the response rather than to the causative event, it was constantly evident that the central mission was to define the event and all the sub-events which were the species of that genus. The hard, response-oriented name served as a bulwark against fears that 'unjust enrichment' might invite the courts into a soft and dangerous world inhabited by moral and political philosophers. That unreal fear having been laid aside, it is possible to face up to the very real dangers of naming an event by the response which it provokes.

This paper has been an attempt to show, and to accept, that restitution is a response which is sometimes triggered by and within the other three categories of causative event. Restitution can on occasion arise, not from unjust enrichment from the plaintiff, but from consent, wrongs, and miscellaneous other events. So far as we continue to speak in terms of a law of restitution, we must take care to ensure that that marginal diversity of causative event is not concealed. Very little in fact changes. In the centre there is still the identification and analysis of unjust enrichment as an independent member of the series of causative events. . . .

- P Birks, *Unjust Enrichment* (2nd edn, 2005), 3–5

Of the subjects which form the indispensable foundation of private law, unjust enrichment is the only one to have evaded the great rationalization achieved since the middle of the 19th century in both England and America by the writers of textbooks. Its fragments, obscurely named, were instead tucked under the edges of contract and trusts. The consequence is that even at the beginning of the 21st century unjust enrichment is still unfamiliar to most common lawyers. It will have played no independent part in their intellectual formation. Its modern name, adapted from civilian equivalents, is slightly disconcerting. Suspicion of the unfamiliar is therefore compounded by instinctive aversion to the hint of revolutionary doctrine. In fact it has no tendencies of that kind. Neglect has certainly left it difficult and untidy, but the example of the civilian jurisdictions shows that it is not by nature disruptive. In this chapter it is introduced through one core case. The law of unjust enrichment is the law of all events materially identical to the mistaken payment of a non-existent debt.

Such a payment gives rise to a right to restitution. The law of restitution is the law of gain-based recovery, just as the law of compensation is the law of loss-based recovery. Thus a right to restitution is a right to a gain received by the defendant, while a right to compensation is a right that the defendant make good a loss suffered by the claimant. The word 'restitution' is not entirely happy in this partnership with 'compensation'. It has had to be manoeuvred into that role. 'Disgorgement', which has no legal pedigree, might be said to fit the job more easily and more exactly. . . . At the end of this chapter we will return to the difficult question whether the right which arises from an unjust enrichment not only is, but can only be, a right to restitution. In English law it always is.

The law of restitution is better known than the law of unjust enrichment because it was under that name, starting in America in the 1930s, that the first serious attempts were made to overcome the problems of misdescription and misclassification which deprived unjust enrichment of its own place on the map of the law. The outcome was the American Law Institute's *Restatement of the Law of Restitution*.[1]

In England the law of restitution has attracted an enormous amount of attention since 1966. That year saw the publication of the first edition of the path-breaking textbook by Goff and Jones . . .[2]

However, the very success of the law of restitution is now itself impeding the recognition of the law of unjust enrichment. The reason is simply stated. The law of gain-based recovery is larger than the law of unjust enrichment. Every unjust enrichment gives rise to a right to restitution and therefore belongs in the law of restitution. But that proposition cannot be turned around, because, quite often, a right to gain-based recovery is the law's response to some other causative event.

It is a grave but all too tempting error to suppose that every instance of gain-based recovery is also an instance of unjust enrichment. Restitution is not mono-causal . . . Unjust enrichment is a distinct causative event, while restitution is a multi-causal response. To be properly understood unjust enrichment needs books to itself. That is not to deny that it will always occupy a large part of any book on the law of restitution, but only to assert that its distinct nature as an independent causative event cannot be securely made apparent unless and until it is also treated in isolation from other instances of gain-based recovery.

NOTES AND QUESTIONS

1. While critical of some aspects of it, M McInnes, 'Misnomer: A Classic' [2004] *RLR* 79 argued that Birks' article 'Misnomer' was the most important article on restitution in the (then) previous decade (1994–2004). The central message of 'Misnomer' is that the law of restitution has been concealing by a false name, on the face of it focussing on a response, that the subject is essentially concerned with the cause of action or event of unjust enrichment. In line with the conventional method of classifying private law by reference to causes of action, the subject

---

1 A Scott and W Seavey (reporters), *Restatement of the Law of Restitution* [:] *Quasi Contracts and Constructive Trusts* (American Law Institute St Paul 1937).

2 R Goff and G Jones, *The Law of Restitution* (Sweet & Maxwell London 1966), now G Jones (ed.), Lord Goff of Chieveley and G Jones, *The Law of Restitution* (6th edn Sweet & Maxwell London 2002).

should be renamed the law of unjust enrichment; and restitution for wrongs is better examined under the law of wrongs.

2. Birks' view that restitution can be consent-based is problematic. He gives as an illustration a contractual obligation to repay a loan. But surely that obligation is no different from any other primary obligation to perform a contractual duty. If we regard a contractual promise to pay a price for goods as triggering an action for the agreed sum (where property in the goods has been transferred)—and one may describe that as a response of 'specific enforcement' or 'perfection'—why should one treat a promise to repay a loan as triggering the different response of restitution? Does this suggest that there is an interplay between event and response that Birks' clinical separation of the two may conceal?

3. Many commentators would accept (as this book does) that restitution is multi-causal in the sense that it can be triggered by wrongs as well as by the cause of action of unjust enrichment. But like Birks, some commentators go further. Particularly influential has been Graham Virgo's multi-causal view. Virgo includes 'vindication of proprietary rights' as a third 'principle' triggering restitution. He writes in *The Principles of the Law of Restitution* (2006), 17:

[T]he law of restitution should properly be analysed in the following way. The law of restitution is concerned with all claims where the remedy which the plaintiff seeks is a restitutionary remedy which is assessed by reference to the defendant's gain. Restitutionary remedies are available in three situations: first, where it can be shown that the defendant has been unjustly enriched—here the only remedies which are available are personal restitutionary remedies; secondly, where the defendant has committed a wrong for which restitutionary relief may be available—here the remedy may be restitutionary but it can also be compensatory; finally, where the plaintiff wishes to vindicate his or her property rights—here the remedy is typically restitutionary and, depending on whether or not the defendant retains property in which the plaintiff has a proprietary interest, the restitutionary remedy will either be proprietary or personal.

A major problem with Virgo's principle of 'vindication of proprietary rights' is that it elides a crucial distinction, explained further in Chapter 13 below, between the vindication of pre-existing proprietary rights and the creation of new proprietary rights which effect restitution in response to an unjust enrichment or a wrong. Birks himself made clear that distinction by arguing that: (i) proprietary rights may be created to effect restitution of an unjust enrichment (as well as being created in response to other events); (ii) proposition (i) is to be distinguished from a *vindicatio* claim for restitution which is triggered not by unjust enrichment but by the 'other event' of the receipt (or, it might be preferable to say, retention) of property belonging to another (above, 45–6). Indeed one might go further away from Virgo's approach than Birks by arguing that the *vindicatio* claim for restitution does not involve a new (personal) right triggered by a new event but is simply the application of the claimant's pre-existing proprietary right to the return of one's property.

5. CORRECTIVE JUSTICE AND UNJUST ENRICHMENT

• K Barker, 'Unjust Enrichment: Containing the Beast' (1995) 15 *OJLS* 457

. . .

Where a defendant unjustly makes a gain at the expense of a plaintiff by subtracting wealth from him, the restitutionary response which ensues can relatively straightforwardly be justified by reference to corrective justice. This form of justice demands that, where one party wrongly upsets an existing distribution of resources between himself and another, he be called upon to rectify (literally 'set straight')[1] the imbalance. This is achieved, in the Aristotelian conception at least, by a direct transfer of resources by the wrongdoer to the party who has been wronged.

In cases in which the defendant's unjust gain can be traced to a loss on the part of the plaintiff, restitution of the gain therefore forms part of a juridical process which is primarily retrospective (aimed at setting right the past), not purposive (aimed at securing broad aims in the future). It colludes with the compensatory response to reinforce a direct tie of moral responsibility between individuals falling within a correlative relationship of wrongful gain and loss. The individual nature of this tie of responsibility explains the two-party structure of litigation with which we are so familiar: it explains why it is the plaintiff and the plaintiff *alone* who has the moral authority to bring a claim; and why it is only the defendant who has any moral obligation to respond to it.

There is just one complication that has to be overcome if we are to accept this rationalization of unjust enrichment by subtraction. How can such cases be concerned with 'correcting wrongs,' we must ask ourselves, when the defendant's liability to give up a benefit is frequently strict and (more importantly) always independent of any showing that he has breached a primary legal duty? How can we maintain, for example, that the receipt of a mistaken payment constitutes a 'wrongful' gain calling for reversal under corrective justice, when the defendant breached no civil law duty by receiving, and was entirely innocent of the mistake?

At first sight, this obstacle looks a little daunting, since Aristotle himself appears to have contemplated a corrective justice duty of rectification only where the defendant was guilty of a deliberate wrong.[2] In fact, however, it is not as problematic as it seems. As Posner has observed in a different context, corrective justice in its Aristotelian conception is a *form* of justice which does not necessarily entail any particular substantive *content*.[3] The crucial idea is that wrongful transactions should be rectified without regard to the respective needs or merits of the individual parties, not that wrongfulness be defined in any particular way. This leaves it open to other theorists to provide alternative definitions of what it is that constitutes 'wrongful' gain or loss, without losing faith with the central intuition that the aims of the law in a given case are 'corrective'.

It is at this point that the invaluable work of the restitution writers can now usefully be tied in. Most obviously, the list of 'factors' which Birks and Burrows identify as rendering the receipt of a substantive enrichment 'unjust', can slide neatly in to provide the substantive content for Aristotle's corrective justice form. None of these 'factors' involves the breach of any primary civil law duty by the defendant; and many are independent of fault—but these facts are, in the light of Posner's observations, largely unproblematic. Strict liability is in no sense antithetical to corrective justice theory. And the simple fact that the defendant has committed no civil law wrong has no bearing upon the independent force of a plaintiff's moral claim to relief in the cases at issue. The factors identified describe sound reasons why, independently of any question of the defendant's culpability, the plaintiff is entitled to claim the benefit which the defendant has substracted from her.

The point, then, is that the concept of 'wrongful' gain in corrective justice theory is a flexible and open-textured one. On the view endorsed here, it can include gains which are 'unjust' in the sense that there is an individualistic reason why they should not have been made (for example, because there was a volitional defect in their transfer) even if these gains have not been attained via the breach of any primary legal duty. Following this premise to its logical conclusion, corrective justice embraces the broad objective of rectifying *individual injustices*, not simply the (narrower) concern to rectify *wrongdoing*. It is in this way that it can accommodate a restitutionary response in the mistake case posited above: where a party—even a party who is entirely innocent of any breach of legal duty—obtains title to property without the full and informed consent of the original owner, she has

1 'Diorthotikos' in the original Greek.
2 *Nicomachean Ethics*, Book V, chapter 8.
3 Posner, 'The Concept of Corrective Justice in Recent Theories of Tort Law' (1981) 10 JLS 187.

an individual duty in justice to return it. The duty is unique to her, flows from the transaction which has occurred between them, and endorses a corrective or restorative aim.

This may be a wider vision of corrective justice than that entertained by Aristotle in the *Nicomachean Ethics*, but it does not contradict the basic premise of his theory; which is simply that the law should set right unjust transactions between individuals. Nor, incidentally, is this vision the widest one possible. Posner's own approach is that the concept of a 'wrongful' transaction in corrective justice theory is so open-textured that its definition can quite legitimately (and consistently with that theory) be influenced by broad social considerations.[4] . . .

Not everyone will be prepared to go as far as Posner. I, for one, would resist any suggestion that the receipt of a gain in the law of restitution can be 'unjust' simply because it defeats the aim of maximizing wealth in society. But there is nonetheless a great deal of value in his basic observation that corrective justice is a *form* of justice which has no *a priori* attachment to a given conception of wrongdoing. This intuition enables us simultaneously to develop both our understanding of the law of restitution and our understanding of corrective justice theory. We can now appreciate how a plaintiff's causes of action in unjust enrichment by subtraction can be truly 'autonomous' (independent of civil law 'wrongs'); and (reciprocally) we find ourselves spurred to the novel, but intellectually satisfying conclusion that corrective justice is a form of justice which concerns the rectification of unjust transactions, not just the rectification of some narrower conception of wrongdoing.

NOTE

For extracts from this article dealing with restitution for wrongs, see below, 937. For Barker's later view that, while corrective justice dominates, deterrent and (more rarely) distributive factors are relevant in unjust enrichment by subtraction (as well as in restitution for wrongs), see 'Understanding the Unjust Enrichment Principle in Private Law: A Study of the Concept and its Reasons' in *Understanding Unjust Enrichment* (eds J Neyers, M McInnes and S Pitel, 2004), 79.

• L Smith, 'Restitution: The Heart of Corrective Justice' (2001) 79 *Texas LR* 2115

Weinrib[1] presents his theory of corrective justice as capable of explaining the main features of private law. There are two difficulties with squaring this theory with the law of restitution. First, the book does not clearly distinguish between the two distinct parts of the law of restitution: (a) claims that the defendant must disgorge some gain achieved through a wrong against the plaintiff ('disgorgement for wrongdoing') and (b) claims that the defendant must make restitution of a benefit received from the plaintiff ('autonomous' or 'subtractive unjust enrichment'). The two kinds of claims are fundamentally distinct. In disgorgement for wrongdoing, the plaintiff builds her claim on the wrongful conduct of the defendant. The plaintiff need not show a loss; her entitlement to the gain is based on her being the victim of the wrong. By contrast, in a claim in autonomous unjust enrichment, the plaintiff needs to show that the defendant's gain corresponds to a deprivation on the part of the plaintiff. Moreover, such a claim does not depend on any wrongdoing; it is based on an autonomous cause of action, the elements of which do not include any fault on the defendant's part. This leads to the second difficulty: Weinrib's theory in general presupposes that private-law liability depends on wrongdoing by defendants. In this regard, it does not seem to square with the law of autonomous unjust enrichment.

The first problem has now been addressed by Weinrib himself. He has treated the problem of disgorgement for wrongdoing separately and provided a convincing explanation of how and to what

---

4 It is in this way that he is able to argue, (above n 3 at 201) that an economic theory of law is compatible with the concept of corrective justice.

1 'Earnest J. Weinrib, *The Idea of Private Law* (1995) [hereinafter Weinrib, *Private Law*].

extent it can be subsumed within his theory of corrective justice[2] The primary aim of this Article is to address the second problem: fitting autonomous unjust enrichment within Weinrib's theory of corrective justice. It will be argued that it is possible to fit into Weinrib's theory an understanding of unjust enrichment liability that does not depend on any wrongdoing by the defendant . . .

Weinrib's theory of corrective justice is a magnificent intellectual achievement. Built upon Aristotle's *Nicomachean Ethics*, mediated by the work of Kant, the theory shows us how to understand a large body of our private law as an internally intelligible system which protects and defends that which is common to all of us: our ability to make choices in our lives and our corresponding duty to allow others to do the same. A remarkable feature of the theory is that it understands private law in its own terms and on its own terms. It therefore permits the rejection of functionalist understandings, which view the role of private law as the promotion of some external goal, such as increasing economic efficiency or deterring undesirable conduct.

The theory is built on three foundational theses. First, the correct approach to understanding private law as internally intelligible is a formal approach—one that insists that legal relationships have a certain form or structure. This makes the subject matter coherent on its own terms, as opposed to being coherent only by reference to some external desideratum. Second, the unifying structure of private law is Aristotle's conception of corrective justice. This provides the form that the first thesis requires. Third, the normative content of corrective justice (which Aristotle did not specify) is Kant's concept of right. Kant's understanding of the basis of ethical behavior is that we must treat others as ends in themselves, not as means for obtaining our own ends. It is this understanding that allows one to take the formal structure presented by Aristotle and use it to understand private law as it actually is.

. . .

Weinrib [understands] corrective justice as being concerned not with material gains and losses but with normative gains and losses.[3] And it is Kantian right that identifies normative gains and losses. 'The correlative gains and losses of corrective justice compare what the parties have with what they ought to have under a Kantian regime of rights and corresponding duties.'[4] The framework that Weinrib ultimately develops is Aristotle's corrective justice, seen through a Kantian lens.

In setting out the distinction between normative gains and losses on the one hand, and factual gains and losses on the other, Weinrib says that '[a]ll the possible combinations are recognized in sophisticated systems of private law.'[5] He then sets out four combinations. First, he notes that a party may realize a normative gain but no factual gain, such as when he inflicts a negligent injury; clearly the party in question is the defendant, who is liable. Second, he says that a party may realize a factual gain but no normative gain, such as when his driveway has been paved mistakenly by another; again, he is referring to the defendant, and he says here that there will be no liability. In his third case, a party may suffer a normative loss, but no material loss, as in the case of nondamaging trespass to land. Here the party is the plaintiff, who will be awarded nominal damages to vindicate a right. Finally, he supposes a party who suffers a factual loss but no normative loss, such as in the case of an injury inflicted without fault. Again, the party here must be the plaintiff; here there is no liability. So it is normative gains and losses that are crucial. All of the elements of Weinrib's developed theory of corrective justice—breach of duty generating normative gain, violation of correlative right causing normative loss, and reversal by liability—come together in the following passage:

> The defendant realizes a normative gain through action that violates a duty correlative to the plaintiff's right; liability causes the disgorgement of this gain. The plaintiff realizes a normative loss

---

2 *See* Ernest J Weinrib 'Restitutionary Damages as Corrective Justice' (2000) 1 *Theoretical Inquiries in Law* 1.

3 *See* Weinrib, *Private Law, supra* note 1, at 115–20.

4 *Id.* at 125.   5 *Id.* at 116.

when the infringed right is within the scope of the duty violated; liability causes the reparation of this infringement. Since the normative gain is morally correlative to the normative loss, disgorgement of the gain takes the form of reparation of the loss. And because of the mutual moral reference of the infringement of the right and the breach of the duty, the amount of the gain is necessarily identical to the amount of the loss. Hence the transfer of a single sum annuls both the defendant's normative gain and the plaintiff's normative loss.[6]

This passage and others show that Weinrib's central conceptualization of corrective justice includes the idea that it is activated only by wrongdoing. This idea will be questioned in what follows.

. . .

The simplest case of unjust enrichment liability is the mistaken payment. The plaintiff, thinking she owes the defendant $100, pays that amount, but in fact she does not owe anything. But the transfer takes effect as such, so that the defendant becomes the owner of the money. There is an enrichment of the defendant, a corresponding deprivation of the plaintiff, and a reason for restitution in the plaintiff's mistake. The material gains and losses are clear. The plaintiff has also suffered a normative loss because she did not fully assent to the transfer of wealth; the transfer was made on the basis of bad information. It was not a free expression of self-determining agency. The question is how we can say that the defendant achieved a normative gain without doing anything wrong. As we should expect, the answer appears to lie in the constitutive elements of unjust enrichment liability, which differentiate it from civil wrongs. Unjust enrichment includes both a material gain by the defendant and a material loss by the plaintiff. Moreover, the loss and gain do not come together by random chance. They are two sides of the same coin—that coin being a transfer of wealth from plaintiff to defendant. There is a nexus of exchange between the parties. This nexus gives an 'articulated unity'[7] to their bilateral relationship in a transaction which is paradigmatically within Aristotle's conception of corrective justice. The transactional unity is far tighter than in a case of carelessness causing loss or profitable wrongful conduct. The single transfer of wealth, lost by the plaintiff and gained by the defendant, functions normatively just as the owned thing in the case of the *vindicatio*. Before the transfer, the wealth is an external projection of the plaintiff's agency. If the transfer is normatively flawed from the plaintiff's end, then the plaintiff suffers a normative loss. Because the defendant's enrichment is nothing other than the plaintiff's normative deprivation, the defendant's material gain is also a normative gain. Hence, corrective justice is violated, and a duty to make restitution arises without the need to find any breach of duty on the part of the defendant.

However, it should be stressed that, unlike in the case of the *vindicatio*, there need not be anything that passed from plaintiff to defendant. The transfer of wealth might have been in the form of services, or the payment of the defendant's debt, or the saving of the defendant's health or property through the consumption of food or other property of the plaintiff. It might have been in the promotion of the defendant's mortgage above that of the plaintiff, through a mistaken discharge. And, even if there were something that passed, after the transfer it belongs to the defendant. In unjust enrichment, the nexus between the parties is not a particular tangible thing belonging to the plaintiff but possessed by the defendant; instead, it is a flow of wealth, measured abstractly even if it was locked up in a tangible thing, which has moved from the plaintiff's patrimony to that of the defendant.

The same understanding can apply to other reasons for restitution. It applies directly to other vitiations of the plaintiff's consent, such as transfers of which the plaintiff was entirely ignorant or which she was compelled to make. These same reasons can undermine contracts. If the plaintiff makes a contract under a mistake induced by the defendant, it is voidable at the election of the plaintiff, even if the defendant did no wrong. The contract satisfies the rules of contract formation,

---

6 Weinrib, *Private Law, supra* note 1, at 125–6.   7 Weinrib, *Private Law, supra* note 1, at 123.

just as the transfer of wealth in a mistake case may satisfy the rules of transfer. But, it is violative of corrective justice, even without wrongdoing, so the plaintiff has the power to undo it. Sometimes the plaintiff's consent to a transaction is not so much defective as merely conditional. An example is the *Deglman* case.[8] The same reasoning will cover these cases.

. . .

Some reasons for restitution turn on neither a shortcoming in the plaintiff's consent to the transfer, nor on any shabby conduct by the defendant. Birks calls these 'policy-based restitution.'[9] Even these claims seem explicable under corrective justice. The crucial difference is that the flaw in the trans-action, which makes the material gain and loss into a normative gain and loss, is not a violation of Kantian right. Rather, it is a violation of some other norm. Often it is a norm of public law. For example, the law in England and Wales is that a payment of tax under *ultra vires* legislation is recoverable, even if the plaintiff made no mistake and was under no compulsion, and the defendant did nothing wrong.[10] This liability supports the constitutional principle that there should be no taxation without legislative authority. The public-law nature of this liability is made clear by the opposite rule which has been suggested for Canada, that to protect the public purse from 'fiscal chaos,' there should be a bar to recovery of any taxes paid pursuant to *ultra vires* legislation.[11] Similarly, claims might be allowed to encourage people to withdraw from illegal transactions.[12] In other cases, the policy is less clearly public, but ultimately it appears to be so. For example, assume that both the plaintiff and defendant are under a legal liability to pay a sum of money to a third party, but between plaintiff and defendant, the defendant is primarily liable; the plaintiff is a surety or in the character of one. If the plaintiff pays the third party, she has an action in unjust enrichment against the defendant. This is usually classified in the texts as a case of pressure, under the subcategory 'legal pressure.' The problem with this is that pressure only generates liability if it is illegitimate. The third party, using or threatening legal process against the plaintiff, does not use an illegitimate form of pressure. In fact, the claim will lie even if the plaintiff had yet to come under any legal liability. It does not rest on faulty consent but simply on the law's ensuring that the burden of the liability falls on the right person. Corrective justice does not resolve the question of who is the 'right person.' In the case of a guarantor and a primary debtor, the right person is the primary debtor. That may be by agree-ment, in which case the allocation merely reflects the agreement. As we have seen, a contract is not a product of corrective justice, although it is clearly a private-law matter reflecting Kantian right. If there is no agreement, the same result will follow, apparently because the primary debtor is the one who had the benefit of the loan. Assigning burdens to go with benefits appears to be distributive justice, although again the context here is private law. The role of distributive justice is even clearer in the case of multiple coguarantors: the 'right' result is that they should bear the burden equally, unless their guarantees have different limits, in which case their burdens must reflect the proportions of their guarantee limits. So in all of these cases of policy-based unjust enrichment, we seem to have a relationship which fits Aristotle's formal structure, but the normative input that identifies the transfer as violative of corrective justice is non-Kantian.

. . .

---

8 *Deglman v Guar. Trust Co. of Can.* [1954] SCR 725, 728–9.

9 Birks, *An Introduction to the Law of Restitution* (rvsd edn, 1989), at 294.

10 See *Woolwich Equitable Bldg. Soc'y v Inland Revenue Comm'rs*, [1993] AC 70 (HL 1992).

11 Proposed obiter by three of six judges in *Air Canada v British Columbia* [1989] 1 SCR 1161, but now doubted by the majority in *Re Eurig Estate* [1998] 2 SCR 565, 586–7.

12 Birks, *supra* note 9, at 299–303.

NOTES

1. For criticism of Lionel Smith's corrective justice analysis, see Stephen Smith, 'Justifying the Law of Unjust Enrichment' (2001) 79 *Texas LR* 2177. M McInnes, 'Unjust Enrichment: A Reply to Professor Weinrib' [2001] *RLR* 29 also argues that Weinrib's theory of corrective justice does not explain restitution of an unjust enrichment.

2. In a wide-ranging exploration of the subject's normative underpinnings H Dagan, *The Law and Ethics of Restitution* (2004) argues that unjust enrichment serves as a loose framework structuring the law of restitution's commitment to autonomy, utility, and community. For reviews of Dagan's book see, e.g., E Weinrib, 'Restoring Restitution' (2005) 91 *Va L Rev* 861; K Barker, 'Theorising Unjust Enrichment Law: Being Realist(ic)?' (2006) 26 *OxJLS* 609.

6. MODERN-DAY SCEPTICS

• **S Stoljar, 'Unjust Enrichment and Unjust Sacrifice'** (1987) 50 *MLR* 603

Many years ago I advanced the thesis that quasi-contract, or unjust enrichment or restitution (the two latter now the more current names), may be better explained by what I called a proprietary theory.[1] The theory has serious limitations, or what appear to be limitations, as we shall later see. But it also has this important opening advantage that it helps us understand what, over a significant area, the subject is really about—assuming we wish to deal with a genuine subject, one constituting a distinctive source of obligations, separate from but comparable to contract, tort or trusts, a subject therefore with a core, not just a repository of residual unclassifieds.

Now the point of the proprietary theory was not that unjust enrichment should become part of the 'law of property,' neither that quasi-contractual recovery of money is like the recovery of an ordinary *res*, for clearly it is not. The point is rather that the recovery of anything, whether money or land or chattels, rests on the claimant (P) being able to show that what he seeks to recover in fact 'belongs' to him, having a better 'title' to it than the person (D) from whom recovery is sought. P, more particularly, has to show that D came to the money ('had and received it') without any sort of transmissive consent from P, whether consent in the form of a gift or contract or bailment or some trust established by P. A basic theme running through our private law, perhaps any system of private law, surely is that, apart from assets distributed by public allocation or by operation of law, things or money cannot validly pass from one person to another without the former's sufficient consent either before or after the event. This is what property essentially means, at least importantly means amongst other things.

So seen, a proprietary theory can better pick out the various claims with which quasi-contract is preoccupied. Instead of P claiming recovery merely on the ground that D is 'unjustly' enriched (so even incurring a charge of making claims based on a 'sloppy' jurisprudence, a charge still rife not so long ago), we can now say D's enrichment is indeed unjust: it is unjust precisely because D retains money without title, having got it without P's consent, so that P now has a claim on straightforward proprietary grounds. Thus if D were to dispute his claim, P can say: 'I claim this money because it is mine.' Certainly D is also unjustly enriched; but in confirming that he is, we are not so much activating our sense of justice in response to an allegedly undue benefit (though we may do that too) as rather stating that D is retaining money which, being non-consensually acquired, 'belongs' to P. The injustice here lies in the retention of assets demonstrably belonging to someone else.

. . .

If the proprietary theory thus identifies the situations in which a claim for recovery lies, what it does identify makes for a surprisingly short list. The list includes items like payment by mistake (A paying B

---

1 S Stoljar, *The Law of Quasi-Contract* (Sydney, 1964), ch 1 and *passim*.

instead of C), following or tracing one's money (into mixed funds or third hands), and perhaps . . . waiver of tort; as a strictly separate subject, or distinctive source of obligation, however, we have hardly anything else. Admittedly, we still have to consider restitution for unsolicited services, but this depends on quite different considerations—broadly such as I shall later describe as 'unjust sacrifice.' But unjust enrichment itself transpires as a decidedly 'small' subject,—not surprisingly, since many more frequent (which is not to say more typical) instances of unjust benefits are taken care of by more familiar topics in private law. Unfortunately this is not the currently fashionable view. The modern tendency is to regard unjust enrichment as a large, even growing, conglomerate, one out of all proportion to the material in fact available to it.

NOTES AND QUESTIONS

1. For further elaboration of his 'proprietary' theory, see Stoljar, *The Law of Quasi-Contract* (2nd edn, 1989), 5–9, 113, 250. On 'unjust sacrifice' see below, 101.
2. If P pays money by mistake to D, is Stoljar correct that P is entitled to restitution only where P retains title to the money? Is not the classic example of unjust enrichment precisely one where D does obtain good title to the mistaken payment?

- **S Hedley, 'Unjust Enrichment as the Basis of Restitution—An Overworked Concept'** (1985) 5 *Legal Studies* 56

The proposition that 'Restitution is based on unjust enrichment' is usually the first that a student of Restitution is presented with. It is a claim at several different levels: as to the terminology we should use in discussing Restitution; as to the sort of rules the subject contains; and as to the way these rules have been developing or should develop in the future. Nor is this confusion of claims particularly surprising. Much of the work of the academic lawyer consists of interpreting the judgements of the higher courts; it is not really very odd when those courts' ambivalent approach to whether they are making the law, or simply applying it, rubs off. 'Restitution is based on unjust enrichment' is really a collection of subsidiary propositions about Restitution; and it is clear that, of those who believe that Restitution is so based, not all would subscribe to every one of the subsidiary propositions.

The matter is more important than it might otherwise appear, for recent years have seen the establishment of Restitution as an academic discipline in its own right, and the beginnings of its recognition by the courts. And whatever the precise meaning or meanings of 'Restitution is based on unjust enrichment', it has been the rallying-call of those academics most deeply committed to the study of Restitution. The only English textbook so far produced, Goff and Jones' *Law of Restitution*, regards the 'principle of unjust enrichment' as central; and the concept of unjust enrichment may fairly be said to represent academic orthodoxy in this area. This is even being carried to the extent that leading writers regard attacks on the concept of 'unjust enrichment' as attacks on Restitution itself, as if the two were simply different sides of the same coin.

My standpoint is this: I am happy to have the law of Restitution studied as one unit, on the basis that we have to split up the law of Obligations on some basis or it will swamp us. I would also accept that, speaking in very loose and general terms, Restitution can be said to concern the recovery of benefits unjustly retained. But the natural desire of Restitution lawyers to gain accept-ance for their subject has led them to make far wider claims for its coherence and internal consist-ency than is justified. If the claim that 'Restitution is based on unjust enrichment' were made on the basis that it was simply one possible approach to the subject, no better than others but no worse either, then I would have no quarrel with it. But the claim has not been made in those terms. Unjust enrichment has been put forward as a *uniquely* satisfactory approach; and it is this view I regard as misguided.

. . .

THE FIRST ISSUE: WHETHER 'UNJUST ENRICHMENT' SHOULD BE USED TO DEFINE THE SUBJECT-MATTER OF RESTITUTION

The view of the 'unjust enrichment' supporters on this issue is clear: Restitution must be seen as the study of unjust enrichment, otherwise the subject is simply a meaningless jumble. Thus we have Burrows' assertion that 'the principle of reversing unjust enrichment provides the only rational explanation for a large body of law'.[1] He purports to prove this by pointing out the absurdities of the legal fictions of 'implied contracts' and 'fiduciary duties', which he sees as the only possible rivals for the position of *the* 'rational explanation' of Restitution. He deduces from this that the judges are in fact already applying the 'principle of unjust enrichment', and all that is needed is for them to do it 'overtly' rather than 'covertly'.[2]

The difficulty with this argument, though it is one I have had problems in getting 'unjust enrichment' supporters to see, is its circularity. *If* Restitution forms one coherent whole, *if* there are principles underlying and uniting all Restitution cases, then quite arguably 'unjust enrichment' is the best pattern for it, the best explanation of its internal coherence. But this is a massive assumption. The alleged internal coherence of Restitution is not a proven fact; it is an *assumption* of the 'unjust enrichment' supporters, which they have to prove.

One possible explanation for the failure of 'unjust enrichment' supporters to justify it is that they do not see it as an assumption at all, but as an obvious fact – too obvious to require proof. One exchange of views where this appears to have been the case was that between Lord Diplock and Burrows. Lord Diplock's attack was as follows: 'My Lords, there is no general doctrine of unjust enrichment recognised in English law. What it does is to provide specific remedies in particular cases of what might be classified as unjust enrichment in a legal system that is based upon the civil law.'[3] The challenge is clear: that English law possesses no coherent category of claims based on unjust enrich-ment, and that it is nothing to the point that many claims within it could accurately be described as 'unjust enrichment' claims, or that in other systems they *would* form part of a coherent category. Yet Burrows plainly regarded it as a sufficient answer to dispose of the claims of *other* theories to be the basis of Restitution.[4] The idea that Lord Diplock might be saying that *no* theory would do, that there was in this sense no such thing as a 'basis' for Restitution, does not seem to have occurred to him.

Rather more sophisticated, but resting on the same sort of disagreement, is the exchange between Professor Atiyah and Professor Birks. Atiyah's attack went as follows: '. . . it must be said that there is little sign yet of any wholehearted acceptance by English lawyers of a new branch of law entitled the Law of Restitution, and based on unjust enrichment ideas. The reality is that unjust enrichment has become a more important underlying idea of the law, for it is only another phrase for the concept of benefit-based liability, but the developments have been occurring interstitially in all branches of the law. In contract, in tort, in family law, in the law of property, in company law, the same development has been occurring. The various cases show little signs of coming together to cohere into one new body of law, and this may be just as well'[5] Again, the challenge is clear: 'unjust enrichment' cannot be used as a criterion for dividing Restitution from other areas of the law, for unjust enrichment ideas play a major role in those areas too. Birks' reply falls into much the same trap as does Burrows', though in a more rigorous way: he carefully constructs meanings for 'Restitution', 'Contract' and 'Property' with sufficient precision to enable him to maintain the three are distinct.[6] Again, the unjust enrichment supporter reacts as if the criticism raised was, 'Of course Restitution is a distinct category,

---

1 'Contract, Tort and Restitution — A Satisfactory Division or Not?' (1983) 99 LQR 217, 233.
2 *Loc. cit.* 234.
3 *Orakpo v Manson Investments Ltd* [1978] AC 95, 104cd.
4 Burrows, *loc. cit.* at 232–4.
5 P Atiyah, *The Rise and Fall of Freedom of Contract* (1979), 768.
6 Birks 'Restitution and the Freedom of Contract' [1983] CLP 141, 143–6 and 149–56.

but your theory does not unite it'. It is taken for granted that there must be a theory of Restitution; arguments to the contrary are treated, quite wrongly, as assertions that there should be a *different* theory. As such, Birks fails to meet the main thrust of Atiyah's argument, that unjust enrichment *exerts influence* over many branches of the law, while providing the *complete explanation* of none.[7]

. . .

What, then, can 'Restitution' mean to one who does not hold the pre-conception that there are principles underlying it, principles which do not underlie other areas too? I am quite happy to leave this question in the air, for if there is no proof of underlying principles, there is equally no need to define the areas within which these principles are to operate. 'Restitution' can simply join that vast class of English words with fuzzy edges—concepts whose main outlines are clear but which tend to fade away in any protracted argument about their 'true' or 'real' meaning. . . .

THE SECOND ISSUE: CLASSIFICATION OF CONCEPTS WITHIN RESTITUTION

. . .

Specifically, then, I have two objections to the *exclusive* use of 'unjust enrichment' terminology to describe Restitution. Firstly, it obscures the fact that the majority of Restitution cases are the recovery of a *loss suffered* as much as they are the recovery of a benefit gained. And secondly, it encourages legal fictions as absurd as the ones Restitution lawyers sought to escape by dropping the 'implied contract' theory of obligation.

Firstly, the problem of loss. A substantial number of Restitution cases are situations which could equally be described as the recovery of a loss suffered or of a benefit gained. Neither can be made out as a better description than the other, for they both describe the same thing from two different viewpoints.

. . .

Secondly, there is the increasing use of legal fictions in relation to 'benefit'. Again, I am not decrying the use of the expression 'benefit' in Restitution, but only its use as a straight-jacket into which *everything* must be fitted. A particular instance is the 'free acceptance' cases. These are cases where a benefit is transferred to the defendant; the defendant does not promise to pay, but freely accepts in the knowledge that payment is expected. The defendant is liable for the reasonable price of the benefit. The similarity with Contractual liability is obvious, and its strengths and weaknesses have been well described by Birks.[8] But his and others' attempts to see this as a simple example of the value of a benefit run into a conceptual morass. Why is the defendant liable for the *reasonable price*, and not for the amount by which he is actually better off, whether this is less or more than the reasonable price? Why is it no defence to show that the benefit was accidentally destroyed before the defendant could take advantage of it, or that for some other reason he has in no real sense been benefited? Approaches based solely on benefit seem to suggest that the rule is simply wrong.

'Unjust enrichment' theorists have used two devices to escape from this. The problem of the benefit accidentally destroyed is seen as one of Remoteness. Once the benefit is transferred, it is argued, it is no concern of the plaintiff's whether or not the defendant makes valuable use of it[9] But while I see no fundamental objection to such an infusion of concepts from the law of Damages, the use of 'remoteness' in this way is inept. 'Remoteness' is a tool for *limiting* damages, for excusing a defendant from the full consequences of a wrong on the ground that they could not have been foreseen. It is perverse to turn the notion on its head and use it to *increase* liability by a pretence that a gain has been made.

---

7 See especially Birks' treatment of Atiyah's concept of 'benefit-based liability', *loc. cit.* at 147–9.
8 'Restitution for Services' [1974] CLP 13, 15.
9 For the concept of 'remoteness of gain', see generally Birks 'Restitution and Wrongs' [1982] CLP 53.

The problem of lack of economic benefit is dealt with in another way, by the device of 'subjective valuation'. The usual problem case is that of the house-owner with appalling taste, who invites a decorator to do work on his house according to the owner's plans. The work is done perfectly, but because the owner's taste is so poor the overall effect is to *reduce* the value of the house. All concede that in those circumstances the workman can sue for the market rate for decorating work, provided only that the owner knew he intended to charge, as would no doubt readily be inferred. This result is fitted into the concept of 'benefit' by saying that while *objectively* the workman has not conferred a benefit, *subjectively* he has done so—the work is a 'benefit' because the owner thinks it is. With the greatest of respect to all concerned, this is nonsense. An enquiry into the owner's view of what constitutes a 'benefit' is neither practicable nor relevant. Can it seriously be suggested that it would make a difference if the owner's taste changed while the work was in progress, so that by the time it was complete he too was of opinion that it did not constitute a benefit? The owner is liable because he created an expectation of payment and encouraged detrimental reliance on that expect-ation. We can describe this as Contract, or as Restitution, or as both together, but to describe it as 'benefit' is simply a random departure from the meaning of that word. Metaphors are unavoidable, but the only reason for *this* metaphorical use of 'benefit' appears to be a refusal to admit that the ordinary meaning has no application.

And more generally, there is a tendency to describe various recoveries as the recovery of a 'benefit' where what is meant is that a *loss* is recovered *because* a benefit was transferred. Common examples are the recovery of expenses incurred by an Agent of Necessity or by a Necessitous Intervener. The result is, I think, tolerably clear: 'benefit' is a vital concept in Restitution, but only *one* vital concept out of several.

THE THIRD ISSUE: THE USE OF 'UNJUST ENRICHMENT' TO RATIONALISE THE LAW OF RESTITUTION

This use of the 'unjust enrichment' concept veers more sharply in the direction of law reform. It is used as a weapon against results in the older cases which now seem outmoded or absurd. The Victorian 'implied contract' theory of obligation, for example, leads to quite absurd results if taken too literally, if only because the policy reasons for allowing or refusing liability in Contract can differ sharply from those for allowing or refusing Restitutionary liability. References to 'unjust enrichment' in policy arguments have their uses. If one party has in fact gained an unjust enrichment at the expense of the other, this can be an important fact, which should not be submerged in fictions about 'implied contracts'.

But if this is the justification for the reference to 'unjust enrichment' in this area, two con-sequences follow. Firstly, that we should not neglect other approaches to the practical realities of the fact-situation, if we wish to make a realistic policy decision. Secondly, we should carefully watch the 'unjust enrichment' approach, lest it too leads us away from reality instead of towards it.

. . .

To sum up [on this third issue], 'unjust enrichment' reasoning on policy issues is sometimes useful. Certainly it is better than mechanical application of any 'implied contract' dogma. But it is no substitute for a completely open-ended policy debate, untrammelled by conformity to any one theory of liability.

THE FOURTH ISSUE: SHOULD A GENERALISED RIGHT TO RESTITUTION FOR UNJUST ENRICHMENT BE INTRODUCED?

This final issue is rather more controversial *within* the 'unjust enrichment' camp. The argument for the introduction of such a right rests heavily on analogies drawn from other areas. Just as the academics and judges in the late 19th century generalised the cases on contracts into a single law of Contract, and just as Lord Atkin in *Donoghue v Stevenson*[10] generalised cases on the duty of care in Tort into a single 'neighbour principle' based on foreseeability, so (runs the argument) some judge today should recognise the existence of a broad general principle of 'unjust enrichment' which would enable the courts to grant a remedy in new situations, not covered by any previous authority.

. . .

It is difficult to take a view on this fourth issue without having already taken a view on the previous three. It will be plain that I would regard the introduction of a generalised right of Restitution for unjust enrichment as a far greater change in the law than would the 'unjust enrichment' supporters. It amounts to freeing the concepts of 'unjust' and 'enrichment' from the vital constraint that they must conform to the case law. But, whether the change be thought large or small, why is it thought desirable at all? The argument from 'logical consequences' or from other areas where generalisation has occurred in the past is simply *permissive*—it shows that such a generalisation could be achieved, but does not explain why it *should* be. The courts could indeed use existing materials to create a broad principle of 'unjust enrichment'. But why would the world be a better place if they did? Positive reasons in favour of such a reform have not been put forward. And if the terms 'unjust' and 'enrichment' are no longer tied to the cases, the charge that they are too vague to be of practical use really comes home to roost. What situations are there, which cry out for a remedy to reverse an enrichment but where there is today no remedy? The generalisation of the concept of the 'duty of care' in Tort provided solutions for cases where real injustice would be done if no remedy was available. Is Restitution similar in that sense? There is no evidence on the point. And if situations exist which need a new 'unjust enrichment' remedy, is the best approach to create a general right, or a more specific right tailored to that problem area? The onus in this matter must be on those who seek to introduce a general right to Restitution for unjust enrichment; and I cannot see that they have satisfied it.

CONCLUSION

The concept of unjust enrichment, then, is of some use within the law of Restitution. But its use as the universal solvent to all problems within Restitution leads to disaster. It simply does not work. To find the way forward, 'unjust enrichment' lawyers must retreat, and recognise that their concept is only one amongst several of value in Restitution.

It has been suggested to me that the difference between myself and the 'unjust enrichment' camp consists of an irreconcilable difference in approach – a totally different attitude to the way judges decide cases. But I think this puts it too strongly. It would be truer to put it this way: the 'unjust enrichment' camp think that I am ignoring consistent patterns of judicial thought, ignoring the judicial tendency to use 'unjust enrichment' concepts even when it stares me in the face. But I do not ignore it. What I think the 'unjust enrichment' camp forget is that the judge who decides a Restitution case on the Monday may decide a Contract case on the Tuesday and a Tort case on the Wednesday. Judicial thought does indeed display consistent patterns. All the less reason, then, for trying to treat Restitution cases as distinct from other cases within the law of Obligations. The judges' wish to prevent unjust enrichment is not something they turn on when they decide Restitution cases and turn off again when they decide Contract and Tort cases. No well-read Tort or Contract lawyer would suppose that 'unjust enrichment' concepts are irrelevant to Tort or to Contract. Why, then, is it supposed that 'unjust enrichment' is the explanation of *everything* in Restitution?

- **S Hedley, *Restitution: Its Division and Ordering* (2001) 224–232**

(In this extract from the final chapter of the book, the author summarizes much of what he has argued in more detail in earlier chapters.)

---

10 [1932] AC 562.

A NEW THEORY OF RESTITUTION

In the view of this author, restitution is a collection of legal doctrines at the fringes of the common law and equity. Like many other legal subjects, its boundaries have fluctuated over time, and are largely set by convention rather than strict logic; though of course debates over what the boundaries should be have sometimes employed logical arguments. Like many other subjects, it was created by dragging together doctrines from a number of different, seemingly disparate, areas. There is currently no agreement on the precise scope of the subject—and no mechanism for encouraging such agreement—but nonetheless there are four sets of doctrines which are repeatedly said to be major parts of it.

(*i*) First, the law on consensual transfers of value. These situations concern situations either related to a contract or strongly analogous to contract, and are best seen as an outgrowth of contract law. A common approach up to now has been to put sharp boundaries around contract: either a particular remedy claimed is 'contractual' or it is 'non-contractual'. But in fact the supposedly non-contractual remedies are not so dissimilar from the contractual ones, and in my view deserve to be treated together.

'Contract' was a broad notion indeed in the middle ages, and was used extensively to describe the liabilities arising out of consensual arrangements. Yet when the notion came to be incorporated into legal textbooks in the late nineteenth century, a very rigorous and narrow definition was adopted (requiring the familiar 'offer and acceptance'). This affords a high degree of systematisation of the law, but we pay a high price for it. In particular, broader and more sophisticated notions of liability have to struggle with the burden of 'not really' being part of contract, even though they too plainly concern consensual transactions. So negligence, equity, 'good faith' and a host of other notions have had to be dragged in to deal with the deficiencies of contract. As I have argued above, I think that much of the confusion here can be resolved by recognising a broader notion of contract than has traditionally been allowed for. The law can be perfectly adequately stated on that basis, and indeed in many respects rather better than it can by reference to 'unjust enrichment'. And once this recognition has been made, the notion that 'unjust enrichment' represents something different from contract falls away; the ancient notion that restitutionary liability is 'quasi-contractual' has more truth in it than falsehood.

As an example, consider the classic restitutionary liability, the payment of a debt wrongly supposed to be due. This is clearly a consensual arrangement; payor and payee are *ad idem* on the purpose of the payment. And the remedy—the return of the payment—reflects that consensual arrangement precisely. One side did not receive the thing they were meant to have, so the law unravels the bargain which cannot be enforced. There are of course objections to treating this situation as consensual, but here as elsewhere these arguments prove too much. You will usually struggle to find an offer and an acceptance (but so you would in many cases which are well recognised as contracts). And it is impossible to show that this remedy was actually *intended* by either party (but this is usually the case with contractual remedies). There are always cases on the borderline of consensuality. The basic argument for treating them as consensual is that this makes sense of the remedies the law affords.

(*ii*) Secondly, notions of damages for wrongs have also begun to develop holes. The virtual disappearance of the civil jury in the decades surrounding 1900 allowed for greater sophistication in damages calculations. One long-term effect of this greater sophistication is the build-up of anomalous cases, which (as the calculations become more precise) are rightly seen as in need of a different explanation. The truth is that different measures may be needed for different types of claim. Whether any of these measures can best be explained by reference to unjust enrichment is a much-debated matter, on which I have given my views above; suffice it to say that the number of cases that can be so explained seems to be small, if indeed there are any. In my view, it is impossible to form a sensible view on whether or when these exceptional measures should be available without considering the normal measure, and its utility in various situations. For example, I argue that it is only the inadequacy of conventional damages in intellectual property actions that accounts for the proliferation of damages on these unusual measures. Accordingly, these cases should be seen as an outgrowth of the law of wrongs and their remedies, and it makes no sense to corral the few 'enrichment' cases away from the others. Accordingly, this area should be seen as an outgrowth of the law of wrongs and their remedies.

(*iii*) Thirdly, some aspects of the law on property. The cases concern claimants who try to recover their lost property from wherever it has ended up. It seems natural to treat this as an outgrowth of property law. And while it is not too surprising that attempts to claim the property from a recipient are described as claims to prevent that party's 'unjust enrichment', it is far from obvious that this way of putting it adds any new insights. Nor have attempts to define a stable category of 'restitutionary property rights' based on unjust enrichment yielded any clear results. While there is plainly room for further systematisation of the law, attempts to find it through 'unjust enrichment' have not so far yielded useful results.

. . .

(*iv*) Fourthly and finally, there are the cases where the claimant has paid a debt which should rightly have been paid by the defendant, and the claimant seeks redress from the defendant. The basic principle here is simple enough, that (subject to a few exceptions) the claimant may exercise the same remedies against the defendant that the defendant's creditor could have exercised had the debt not been paid. An attempt has been made to rationalise the law here, by explaining the various liabilities in terms of the unjust enrichment of the defendant by the payment of the debt. But as I have shown, not only is this theory very complex, it gives no added explanatory power. To the extent that it suggests novel rules or liabilities, they are not supported by the case law. There therefore seems to be no advantage to the theory.

. . .

'UNJUST ENRICHMENT' UNCHAINED?

So where is 'restitution' headed? Much depends on what restitution is supposed to be for. The vision of the 'unjust enrichment' theorists has been to make it a *foundational* subject. The object has not been to solve any particular practical problem—as we have seen, the response to practical difficulties has uniformly been to argue that they are not the theorists' concern. That vision of the subject, as I have argued, is ultimately futile. The foundations of legal system should not be torn up and replaced except for reasons for dire necessity; attempts to install 'unjust enrichment', and then to claim that it was there all along, are merely a waste of effort.

But 'unjust enrichment' as a legal doctrine has another use: to identify areas where traditional concepts lead to an unsatisfactory result, and to suggest remedies to deal with this. Are there areas that call for this? There is every reason to suppose that new candidates for inclusion in restitution will emerge. The problem of unmarried couples' property rights will perhaps one day return to the subject; and in the maelstrom of the modern law of intellectual property, there are always some who see 'unjust enrichment' as the solution to some problem or other. The law of restitution has not been static ever since its creation, and so there is no reason to suppose that it will start now. And there will always be arguments for using it as a tool to develop this area or that; its great merit has always been its flexibility. So if the idea of 'unjust enrichment' has a purpose, it is this. But it cannot fulfil that purpose within the structure of ideas used up to this point.

SUMMARY

The various cases usually thought to constitute 'restitution' are in fact linked by little except their ejection from the traditional mega-theories of private law. To leave them as pariah doctrines is unacceptable; the question is, where they should go. In accordance with the analysis in previous chapters, I here suggest that they should fairly be divided into four groups: some to be returned to contract law, some to wrongs, some to property, and the remainder to the law of adjustment of liabilities. The notion of 'unjust enrichment' has not proved successful in uniting the four; its possible utility for other purposes is discussed.

NOTES AND QUESTIONS

1. For similar views, criticizing the 'unjust enrichment' theory, see Hedley, 'Unjust Enrichment' [1995] 54 *CLJ* 578; 'Implied Contract and Restitution' [2004] *CLJ* 435. See also his valuable book, *A Critical Introduction to Restitution* (2001) in which he describes and analyses, applying various approaches, the main areas within what has traditionally been called the law of restitution.

2. For a direct reply to Hedley's article above, see P Birks, 'Unjust Enrichment—A Reply to Mr Hedley' (1985) 5 *Legal Studies* 67.

3. Do you agree with Hedley that what is now treated as the law of restitution is an incoherent 'rag-bag'; and that a proper and broader understanding of contract, wrongs and property, along with recognizing a law on 'adjustment of liabilities', would swallow up that 'rag-bag' and explain it better than does the unjust enrichment theory?

4. It is important to appreciate that on Hedley's approach, there is nothing (or, at best, very little) to be gained by recognizing either a *principle* of reversing unjust enrichment or a *cause of action/event* of unjust enrichment.

• I Jackman, *The Varieties of Restitution* (1998), 1–5, 9–10

In what circumstances is a person liable to repay money received from another, in the absence of any contractual or tortious duty to do so? In what circumstances is a person liable to remunerate or reimburse another for benefits in kind provided by that other person, again in the absence of any contractual or tortious duty to do so? In what circumstances is the defendant who has committed a wrong against the plaintiff liable to pay an amount representing the benefit to the defendant from committing the wrong, rather than an amount representing the plaintiff's loss?

These are the main questions which the law of restitution addresses. The general theme of this book is that the answers to these three questions relate to fundamentally distinct categories of legal thought. These are, in turn, the reversal of non-voluntary transactions, the fulfilment of non-contractual promises and the protection of facilitative institutions of private law. Because each of those concepts is distinct, it is not feasible to force uniformity on them in terms of the so-called unifying principle of 'unjust enrichment at the plaintiff's expense'.

This is not a currently fashionable position. Most modern writers on the subject take as their starting-point that the law of restitution can (and should) be analysed in terms of 'unjust enrichment at the plaintiff's expense', and with varying degrees of equivocation and dissent, that view has been adopted by the House of Lords, the High Court of Australia, and the Supreme Court of Canada. As those decisions demonstrate, the law of restitution comprises various non-statutory legal principles which cannot be explained satisfactorily within the law of contract and the law of tort. But that proposition in itself does not demonstrate that the law of restitution is a distinct category of legal thought, unified by a single concept, and one of the aims of the present work is to identify the shortcomings of that position.

There are two main ways in which the proposition that the law of restitution is explicable as unified by the concept of unjust enrichment at the plaintiff's expense is open to challenge. One way, though the less important, is semantic. Most modern writers on the subject propound the theory that a restitutionary action consists of four elements: (i) an enrichment; (ii) an unjust factor; (iii) expense to the plaintiff; and (iv) the inapplicability of any defences. But in a number of areas, cases which are commonly regarded as restitutionary do not fit within that formulation. For example, it is commonly recognised that in a large topic of the law of restitution, namely restitution for wrongs . . . the plaintiff may be awarded a pecuniary remedy even where he or she has not been made materially worse off, so that in that area the third element listed above is not satisfied. Some writers then try to avoid the problem with a fiction that the plaintiff can be treated as being worse off because a wrong has been committed, even though he or she has not suffered any loss or expense. That fiction, like any legal fiction, is a feeble basis on which to construct a coherent set of legal principles. Similarly, in a different area of the law of restitution, namely remuneration or reimbursement for benefits in kind, there have been cases of restitution where there was no enrichment in any material sense, for example, where a quantum meruit was awarded for a literary work or an architectural plan which the defendant would never use.[1] Accordingly, one finds occasionally judicial recognition of the proposition that, in the context of claims based on a quantum meruit, the notion of benefit to the defendant is irrelevant or fictional. If enrichment to the defendant is treated as an essential element of a restitutionary cause of action, then the law of restitution is necessarily narrowed so as to exclude these cases from its ambit, with the risk that cases which are relevant to the proper formulation of the relevant principles have been artificially excluded from the analysis. A third example concerns claims for the repayment of money where the defendant's gain is not at the plaintiff's expense because the plaintiff has been able to pass on the loss to others and is therefore no worse off than before the transaction . . . the plaintiff may still succeed in recovering the money in restitution, even though the supposed requirement that the defendant's gain be at the plaintiff's expense is not satisfied.

The second, and more fundamental, line of attack is to ask what are the concepts of injustice which inform the law of restitution. This approach is the more important of the two, because it does not merely falsify the 'unjust enrichment' theory, but also points in a constructive way towards an alternative analysis. Unifying principles in the common law arise only by the analogical technique of treating like cases alike, yet none of the proponents of the 'unjust enrichment' principle suggests that there is only a single concept of injustice at stake in the cases which that so-called principle is used to explain. In this book it is contended that there are three principal concepts of injustice involved in the law of restitution. First, in the case of money received by the defendant from the plaintiff . . . the injustice lies in the non-voluntary conferring of an incontrovertible benefit, the non-voluntariness arising on grounds such as mistake, duress, undue influence or total failure of consideration. This reasoning extends also to restitution for necessitous benefits in kind which are not voluntarily conferred . . . for the necessity makes the benefit incontrovertible (and thus akin to money) and the non-voluntariness of its provision makes it unjust for the defendant not to pay for it. Second, in the case of benefits in kind which are voluntarily conferred . . . the injustice lies in the defendant's failure to fulfil a genuine, but typically implicit, promise to pay for the benefit in question. And third, in the case of restitution for wrongs . . . the injustice lies in the need to protect the integrity of certain facilitative institutions of private law (such as private property or fiduciary relationships) from those who seek the benefits of those institutions without submitting to their burdens.

There are two major distinctions in the law of restitution which further define these categories. The first, which has already been mentioned, is that between restitution where the plaintiff has been made materially worse off by the transaction in question, and restitution for wrongs, where the plaintiff may be entitled to a pecuniary remedy even though the defendant's conduct has not caused him or her any harm. In cases concerning restitution for wrongs, the plaintiff seeks to disgorge the benefit derived by the defendant by means of the defendant's wrongdoing, rather than seeking restoration of a loss

---

1 As in *Planché v Colburn* (1831) 8 Bing 14; 131 ER 305; *Sabemo Pty. Ltd v North Sydney Municipal Council* [1977] 2 NSWLR 880.

actually suffered. That distinction is accepted by the mainstream of current academic writing as a major division in the law of restitution, exemplified by Professor Birks' terminology of 'unjust enrichment by subtraction' (where the plaintiff has suffered a loss) as opposed to 'unjust enrichment by a wrong' (where loss to the plaintiff is not a necessary ingredient in the cause of action).

The second major distinction is between restitution for payments of money and restitution for the value of benefits in kind. The latter category comprises principally goods and services but also . . . extends to the payment of another's debt. A fundamental reason for this distinction, suggested by the leading academic writing, concerns the question of whether the defendant has received a benefit which as a matter of justice should be paid for. The receipt of money, being the universal measure of value, is indisputably a benefit, and an obligation to give restitution to the payer ordinarily arises where money has been paid non-voluntarily, for example, where it has been paid by mistake, duress, legal compulsion or upon a total failure of consideration. By contrast, the value of goods and services to a particular recipient depends upon the individual tastes and budget of the particular person. Thus the mere fact that a person has received a benefit in kind cannot generate an obligation to pay for it. As Pollock CB said in *Taylor v Laird*, 'One cleans another's shoes; what can the other do but put them on?'[2]
. . .

The theme of Chapter 5 of this book (which deals with the voluntary provision of benefits in kind) is that the law of restitution for non-monetary benefits which are voluntarily conferred should be considered as founded upon promissory obligations which subsist outside the law of contract. Although the quantification of the relevant liability in terms of a reasonable amount is imposed by operation of law, the liability itself is founded on a genuine promise by the defendant to pay for the particular benefit. Accordingly, Blackstone was correct to regard Lord Mansfield's rejection of the implied promise as directed to actions for the repayment of money. But the relevant promissory obligation is not contractual; rather, it arises in situations where there is no applicable contract and it is defeated by the existence of an enforceable contractual allocation of risk. This is not to suggest that the entire law of restitution is founded on promissory obligations. Rather the operation of promissory obligations is confined to non-monetary benefits which have been conferred otherwise than as a matter of compulsion or necessity. In this field, the fact of an implied, though genuine, promise to pay for the benefit explains (if it is necessary to do so) both why the goods or services can be regarded as subjectively benefiting the defendant, and why it is unjust for the defendant not to pay for them.

The undifferentiated use of the term 'unjust enrichment at the plaintiff's expense' masks the fundamentally disparate nature of the various concepts of justice which comprise the law of restitution. Moreover, by the vagueness of the term, it invites judicial idiosyncrasy and speculative litigation. The approach taken in this book is to inquire in respect of each kind of restitutionary cause of action which concept of injustice is at stake in the formulation of the relevant legal principles. That approach reveals that it is misleading and cumbersome to insist on the separate identification of 'enrichment' to the defendant and 'expense' to the plaintiff in every kind of case. For example, if the basis of the cases concerning the voluntary provision of benefits in kind is the finding of an implicit promise to pay for goods or services, it does not matter whether the defendant has been made materially better off by performance of what was promised, as in the illustrations already referred to of a writer composing a work or an architect preparing plans which the defendant decides not to use. Accordingly, the academic debate over whether the provision of a 'pure service' (with no tangible end-product in the accretion of wealth to the defendant) is a 'benefit' to the defendant is a matter of irrelevance if the real question is whether the service is one which the defendant promised to pay for but has failed to do so.

---

2 (1856) 25 LJ Ex 329 at 332.

NOTES

1. Putting to one side restitution for wrongs (which most commentators accept is fundamentally distinct from restitution for the cause of action of unjust enrichment), Jackman's criticism of the unjust enrichment approach is that the law is better explained as based on two different principles: (i) the reversal of a non-voluntary transfer of money or another incontrovertible benefit; and (ii) the fulfilment of non-contractual promises where benefits in kind have been voluntarily conferred on the promisor. But this criticism seems to miss the point that as regards (i) we need to explain *why* the law reverses non-voluntary transfers; and as regards (ii) while it may be that the law should move, or has moved, to enforcing non-contractual promises there is still a role for the (less controversial) reversal of the value of unjust benefits in kind received at the claimant's expense.

2. For a critical analysis of Jackman's views, see Birks, 'Equity, Conscience and Unjust Enrichment' (1999) 23 *Melbourne ULR* 1.

• J Dietrich, *Restitution—A New Perspective* (1998), 92–99

Demonstrably, there are problems with unjust enrichment jurisprudence. The endeavours of the theorists to give content to unjust enrichment are less than convincing. Such theorists seek to utilise unjust enrichment in a critically important way – as a tool for analysing liability rules in restitution – despite the many problems of attempting to give content to the most important constituent parts of the unjust enrichment formulation: those of 'unjust' and 'enrichment' . . . It is not the purpose of this book to attempt to solve such problems, nor even to analyse restitution within the conceptual confines of unjust enrichment theory. Instead, such problems invite a consideration of alternative theoretical frameworks for restitution. It is time to consider restitution from a new and different perspective.

. . .

This writer's focus upon the recurrent general themes of liability rules activated by similar causative events, has resulted in the identification of four broad categories within which liability rules claimed for restitution can be grouped . . .

(1) FAULT-BASED LIABILITY: BREACH OF CONTRACT-LIKE OR TORT-LIKE DUTIES

In the first category . . . liability rules are activated by *conduct* of the defendants. In all such cases, a defendant's conduct will have resulted in some detriment to a plaintiff, who may have incurred financial losses, performed services, paid money, entered a contractual relationship he or she may otherwise not have, or in some way changed his or her position detrimentally. Such detriment is a precondition for an obligation being imposed upon a defendant. But the remedial responses to such detriment are not limited to making good the detriment (though usually this will be a plaintiff's minimum entitlement) and may vary considerably as to the measure of the defendant's liability. A plaintiff's reasonable or actual expectations may be fulfilled, or restitution may be awarded. Where restitution is awarded, however, it should be noted that since losses and gains will usually be equal, the effect of a restitutionary remedy will be to return the plaintiff to his or her previous position.

Within this broad category, it is possible to identify two sub-categories of liability rules. Although there are considerable points of overlap, the liability rules within each sub-category emphasise different types of conduct giving rise to an obligation.

The first sub-category of liability rules is principally concerned with conduct which, contract-like, amounts to an assumption of an obligation or of a risk by a defendant. Characteristically, the parties will have reached some mutual agreement or at least tacit understanding which results in a plaintiff acting upon an expectation as to the defendant's future conduct. Although such an agreement or understanding may not in law amount to a legally enforceable contract (it may be 'void', 'voidable', 'illegal' or 'unenforceable'), the courts will nevertheless give at least limited recognition to the relationship should the defendant subsequently breach his or her agreement or contract-like duty resulting in losses to the plaintiff as measured by reference to the plaintiff's original position. The term 'limited recognition' highlights the fact that in many of these cases, a completed agreement is non-contractual because some statutory or common law rules preclude the contract being enforced. Consequently, in order to give effect to the policies of such statutory or common law rules, the courts may limit recovery to the restoration of the plaintiff's status quo ante, by means of compensation or restitution. In some cases, the relevant policy may preclude *any* remedy – restitutionary, compensatory or otherwise – being granted. The operation of 'illegality' in some contexts best demonstrates the latter type of case. In other cases, however, full recognition of the parties' agreement may ensue, with a plaintiff's expectations being fulfilled. In effect, a full 'contractual' remedy may be awarded. In such contract-like cases of liability, then, the reason for the contract not being enforceable (or 'void', 'voidable' or 'illegal') will be a significant factor in shaping the availability and extent of remedial relief.

In this sub-category, both equitable and quasi-contractual liability rules may give rise to the obligation. Examples of the former include many cases of proprietary estoppel; and examples of the latter include most cases of quasi-contractual relief arising from unenforceable, or anticipated contracts, both for services rendered (quantum meruit), goods delivered (quantum valebat) and money had and received.

In the second sub-category, the principal concern is with tort-like conduct causing loss to a plaintiff. Consistently with the tort-like nature of a defendant's conduct – examples might be conduct akin to negligence or fraud, or an abuse of position or power – the remedy in such cases, as in tort proper, characteristically aims at restoring the plaintiff to his or her status quo ante. This end may be achieved by means of either compensatory remedies, the specific restitution of money or property, or the rescission of contracts entered into.

Tort-like conduct may be caught by equitable or, less typically, quasi-contractual doctrines or rules. Many equitable doctrines, such as unconscionability and undue influence, fall within such a sub-category of liability rules. In such cases, the law in effect appears to be expanding legal notions of what amounts to a breach of duty to one's neighbours: a defendant has acted or omitted to act as a reasonable person ought to have done in the circumstances, given the detrimental consequences to the plaintiff which foreseeably could follow such act or omission. Although there will have been no breach of duty in tort (the requirements of tort law not having been met), nonetheless an obligation to restore the plaintiff to his or her previous position will be imposed, usually by means of rescission of the transaction entered into.

(2) THE CONSEQUENCES OF UNPROVIDED FOR CONTINGENCIES ON PARTIES WITH A COMMON INTEREST (PRINCIPLE OF JUST SHARING)

In the second category of liability rules, obligations may arise despite the absence of any conduct on a defendant's part which has caused the problems which a plaintiff seeks to have remedied. But where a plaintiff and defendant share a 'common interest', or perhaps a 'community of interest', they may owe a responsibility to share losses and gains arising as a result of some unprovided for contingencies which affect their common interest . . . [A] variety of factual assumptions are envisaged. For example, the parties may be linked in a common endeavour, such as a commercial joint venture or domestic relationship, which endeavour fails, breaks down or is frustrated; or the parties may be involved in a contract which is frustrated; or the parties may be linked fortuitously by a common interest, such as where strangers all own cargo being carried on the same ship which is wrecked, and consequently, all have a common interest in the safe completion of the voyage. Likewise, two co-sureties, unknown to each other, may have guaranteed the same debt, yet only one co-surety is called upon to pay the debt. In such an example, the unprovided for contingency is that recourse has only been had against one of the co-sureties, when both were liable to meet the obligation.

In all such cases, the unprovided for contingency, whether it be a frustrating event, a failure of a relationship or some other unforeseen event, results in burdens being borne by one party but not the other, or benefits being obtained by one party but not the other. Given the parties' common interest, the law characteristically responds by imposing a principle of just sharing. Burdens and benefits resulting from the contingency are required to be distributed justly, which often means proportionally, according to each party's contribution to the matter in which they have the common interest. Although restitutionary remedies may be utilised to effect loss and gain sharing (where plaintiffs' losses and defendants' gains are equal), nonetheless, it will be argued that benefit disgorgement is not, or ought not to be, the main purpose of the liability rules under consideration and that unjust enrichment is therefore an inappropriate rubric for such liability.

These liability rules are diverse. Topics to be considered include the dissolution of partnerships and joint ventures; the division of de facto property upon the break-up of the relationship; the doctrine of contribution between co-sureties; and the doctrine of general average contribution in maritime law.

The frustration of contracts will also be considered, even though a governing principle of loss and gain sharing has not been openly recognised in the common law relating to the frustration of contracts; nevertheless, many decisions are consistent with such a principle. Some decisions which are not consistent with a principle of sharing have been subjected to academic and, at times, judicial criticism. Further, recent statutory regimes introduced in a number of jurisdictions are based on principles of loss and gain sharing.

(3) JUSTIFIABLE SACRIFICE: ALLOCATING THE COSTS OF JUSTIFIABLE CONDUCT.

In the third category . . . liability rules are activated in circumstances in which the law considers that a plaintiff's unsolicited intervention in another's affairs is justifiable. Consequently, any reasonable 'costs' incurred by the plaintiff whilst intervening are allocated to the defendant where the law considers the defendant to be the more 'appropriate' party in the circumstances to bear those costs. Thus, the salvor of a sinking ship and its cargo, or the rescuer of an accident victim, may be entitled to recover reasonable costs incurred. The recovery of reasonable 'costs' incorporates both reimbursement of the actual expenses incurred by a plaintiff, the most common remedial response, but also in more exceptional cases, remuneration for services rendered.

Liability in cases of justifiable intervention does not depend on any culpable or wrongful conduct on the defendant's part. Instead, a plaintiff's costs will be allocated to the defendant in those limited circumstances in which a plaintiff's actions are considered to be consistent with the promotion of certain desirable social goals and policies. Social policy considerations are at the crux of liability in this category. Although in many cases, the defendant will have received some benefit as a result of the plaintiff's actions, such a benefit is not a precondition for liability.

Although the common law courts have accepted that certain unsolicited interventions are justifiable and ought not be discouraged, liability in such cases has not been recognised as part of a single, coherent doctrine of justifiable intervention, or negotiorum gestio, as is recognised in civil law. Instead, liability arises for the most part in a diverse but numerically small collection of seemingly anomalous decisions and isolated instances. The obvious exceptions are maritime salvage, an ancient and well-developed doctrine involving much detailed learning, and 'agency of necessity'. Nevertheless, one can draw from these instances sufficient common principles to provide us with some guidelines as to the limits of available relief. Also to be considered are cases of self-interested intervention by a plaintiff, say, to pay a defendant's debt in order to protect the plaintiff's own property interests. Significantly, a distinguishing feature of the concerns addressed by the liability rules in this category is their very unlikeness to other concerns recurrent in property law, contract, tort or equity.

(4) 'INNOCENT' RECIPIENTS

The fourth category of liability rules . . . is perhaps the most difficult. Whereas in the above three categories, the conduct of a defendant, the common interests of a plaintiff and a defendant, or the promotion of desirable social goals provide the foundations for the imposition of an obligation upon a defendant, this fourth category is characterised by the absence of any of the above factors. The concern here is with circumstances in which money, goods or services of a plaintiff have been conferred on an 'innocent' defendant not legally responsible for such conferral. Where no requisite intention existed or now exists on the part of the plaintiff to 'transfer' to the defendant such money, goods or services, a plaintiff may seek to undo the consequences of the 'transfer' and seek to impose liability of some kind on the defendant, even despite the innocence of that defendant. Two significant types of case, though not the only ones to be considered, in which liability is sought to be imposed on an innocent defendant, are where a plaintiff has acted under a mistake or has 'transferred' money, goods or services upon a condition, which condition has failed.

Taking the former example, as a result of a mistaken belief, a plaintiff may have entered or completed certain transactions, or modified his or her existing position or status, in a way in which he or she would not have done but for the mistake. But our discussion is limited to mistakes of a very specific kind: 'spontaneous' mistakes of a plaintiff, as they will be called, in no way created by or knowingly allowed to continue by the defendant. Thus, we are not here concerned with cases where, for example, a plaintiff's mistaken belief was the result of some active inducement by, or negligence or unconscionably acquiescent conduct of, the defendant: proprietary estoppel cases provide a good example of this type of mistake and would fall within the first category of liability rules considered above.

To be included for consideration in this fourth category of liability rules are the topics of mistaken payments of money, the mistaken improvement of another's land or goods and the mistaken payment of another's debt or performance of another's duty.

This category presents considerable difficulties for any generalisation seeking to encompass the rules governing these topics. Certainly, in the mistaken payment of money cases, the 'siren song'[1] of unjust enrichment sounds its most persuasive. For clearly, the defendant will have been enriched at the time of the receipt. In many circumstances, the receipt of such money and its retention, barring some countervailing consideration such as a change of position, would appear 'unjust'. Hence, unjust enrichment may well prove to be a rationalising idea of continuing force and of some utility in this area. It should be noted, though, that unjust enrichment still appears to be a statement of conclusion (albeit an appealing one) which does not indicate the processes of reasoning followed to reach that conclusion.

Substantial conceptual difficulties arise, however, if unjust enrichment is sought to be used to explain not only money cases, but non-money (that is, service) cases as well. Mistaken 'transfers' of things other than money are often difficult to analyse in terms of the receipt of a benefit and, where recovery is allowed, in terms of benefit *disgorgement*. At the level of practical decision making, there is no uniformity between 'money' and 'service' cases and no single principle can be used to explain both sub-categories of case. At best, it is possible to identify only an idea or notion which, at a very general level, informs the law and specific liability rules in both sub-categories of case, without purporting to provide a uniform explanation of all cases of spontaneous mistake. The informing idea, or perhaps ideal to which the law strives, which will be advanced in Chapter 9 is that of achieving 'fair outcomes'.

---

1 *Re Byfield* [1982] Ch 267 at 276.

. . .

The notion of fair outcomes . . . encapsulates two competing concerns of the law: (1) to restore plaintiffs as near as possible to their position before a 'vitiated' transfer (2) without disadvantaging innocent defendants. It is not intended to operate as an *explanatory* principle of the specific liability rules, though such liability rules may achieve (more or less) fair outcomes, in the sense of balancing the two competing concerns. Since 'fair outcomes' is not an explanatory principle in each of money and service cases, specific principles, doctrines and rules need to be identified. Recovery of mistaken payments of money provides the most generous scope for recovery because the receipt of money is best seen as a receipt of an *economic advantage*. Consequently, restitution of that economic advantage may be possible, provided such economic advantage survives in the defendant's hands. As with goods or land, a refusal by the defendant to part with the economic advantage which he or she still retains will amount, in a broad sense, to a retention of the plaintiff's 'property'. Consequently, many mistake cases have a strong proprietary flavour and a property principle will be identified as having considerable explanatory force. But as the service cases will demonstrate, recovery is not limited to restitution. It may be possible to achieve a fair outcome by means of imaginative remedies which are merely akin to or in the nature of specific restitution, and thus do not disadvantage the defendant.

NOTES

1. It is hard to understand why Dietrich regards his 'fair outcomes' as a better explanation of his fourth category than unjust enrichment.

2. As regards his first three categories, the acceptance that the defendant's behaviour might be classified as a civil wrong triggering compensation is not incompatible with the less controversial proposition that, without being recognised as a wrong, there is a claim for restitution of an unjust enrichment.

3. For a review of Dietrich's book, see C Rotherham [2000] *RLR* 254.

• P Jaffey, *The Nature and Scope of Restitution* (2000), 6

[V]arious claims are generally understood to form the heart of the modern law of restitution. In each case, according to the theory of unjust enrichment, the claim operates to reverse the unjust enrichment of the defendant at the plaintiff's expense. It is certainly true that in all such cases the claim is 'benefit-based', or at least 'benefit-related', in the sense that the receipt of a benefit by the defendant is an essential element of the plaintiff's claim. The theory of unjust enrichment is considered below; but, first, the next section sets out the approach adopted in this book, according to which these various claims should be understood as instances of three distinct claims that are not reducible to a single underlying principle. These are the claim for restitution for a vitiated transfer, the non-contractual or restitutionary claim for reasonable payment under an 'imputed contract', and the claim for disgorgement. As will appear, each of the three types of claim has a natural affinity for, and a disputed boundary with, a related area of law: for restitution for a vitiated transfer, this is the law of property; for the claim for reasonable payment it is the law of contract; and for disgorgement it is what might be called the law of legal responses, and in particular punishment. It follows that what is now regarded as the law of restitution is not a single body of law equivalent to, say, contract or tort.

NOTES

1. Putting to one side restitution, or disgorgement, for a wrong, Jaffey's two categories of case are restitution for a vitiated transfer and reasonable payment under an 'imputed contract'. It is hard to see why the first is not merely a more specific mode of formulating what at root

is driven by a concern to reverse an unjust enrichment. Put another way, to talk of there being restitution for a vitiated transfer does not explain what triggers that restitution. And the second category of claim relies on a fictional imputed contract which, like the rejected implied contract theory, does not explain why a contract to make reasonable payment is imputed.

2. For a review of Jaffey's book, see K Barker [2001] *RLR* 232.

2

THE ESSENTIAL INGREDIENTS OF A CLAIM FOR RESTITUTION OF AN UNJUST ENRICHMENT

The recognition of unjust enrichment does not mean that English law has moved to a discretionary system whereby the judges simply ask themselves, 'is this enrichment unjust?' On the contrary, the approach of the courts is still very much an incremental one, whereby what is meant by unjust enrichment is heavily dependent on past cases (see Lord Goff's speech in *Lipkin Gorman v Karpnale Ltd*, above, 28).

In seeking to link the black letter law laid down in the cases to the cause of action of unjust enrichment, the most rational and helpful approach is to analyse any claim for restitution of an unjust enrichment in terms of four distinct questions.

1. Has the defendant been *benefited* (i.e., enriched)?
2. Was the enrichment *at the claimant's expense*?
3. Was the enrichment *unjust*?
4. Are there any *defences*?

If the first three questions are answered affirmatively and the fourth negatively the claimant will be entitled to restitution.

That these are the four questions to be answered in an unjust enrichment claim was confirmed by Lord Steyn in *Banque Financière de la Cité v Parc (Battersea) Ltd* (below, 190), Lightman J in *Rowe v Vale of White Horse DC* (below, 76) and Mance LJ in *Cressman v Coys of Kensington* (below, 77).

These four stages constitute the fundamental conceptual structure of an unjust enrichment claim. Each of the four stages will be examined in turn in this chapter.

1. BENEFIT

The benefit is usually the receipt of money but it can be the receipt of, for example, services, goods or land.

Where the benefit is the receipt of money, there is no great difficulty. If C pays D £100 D is clearly benefited, and benefited to the tune of £100 (plus interest).

Much more problematic (as emphasized by Robert Goff J in *BP Exploration Co. (Libya) Ltd v Hunt*; below, 72) are non-money benefits (that is, benefits in kind), especially services. If C increases the objective market value of D's land by building something on it,

D may well say that what C has built is of no value to D or, at least, is not worth to D the objective value. Or if C cleans D's car, D may legitimately say that he did not want it cleaned or did not want it cleaned at the price that C is demanding. This is the argument that Birks has labelled 'subjective devaluation', terminology that has since been used by the judiciary (in, e.g. *Cressman v Coys of Kensington*; below, 77).

Whether using that label or not, the courts do accept that defendants are entitled subjectively to devalue objective benefits. This means that where benefits in kind are in issue, claimants must identify facts that overcome the subjective devaluation argument. What those facts are is a matter of dispute among academic writers. Goff and Jones, followed by Birks, have suggested two tests of whether the defendant (i) has been *incontrovertibly benefited* or (ii) has *freely accepted* the benefit. These ideas have been referred to and, as regards incontrovertible benefit, used by the courts (see *BP v Hunt* (below, 72), *Procter & Gamble Philippine Manufacturing Corp. v Peter Cremer GmbH* (below, 73), the Canadian case of *Peel v Canada* (below, 74), *Rowe v Vale of White Horse DC* (below, 76), *Cressman v Coys of Kensington* (below, 77)). Free acceptance is controversial and, as recognised by Mance LJ in *Cressman v Coys,* has spawned an extensive academic debate (see, e.g., the extracts, below, 84–101, from Burrows, Garner, Beatson, and Birks). This debate links to a wider argument (espoused by e.g. Beatson, Stoljar, and Muir; below, 101–106) that, particularly in respect of services, the law is better explained in terms of 'unjust sacrifice' or 'reliance loss' than unjust enrichment.

Two cases which have been much discussed in academic writings on the 'benefit' issue—and which are particularly problematic on this question—are considered at the end of this section (*Planché v Colburn*, below, 106, and *Greenwood v Bennett*, below, 107).

General Reading

BURROWS, 16–25; GOFF AND JONES 1-017–1-039; VIRGO, 62–104.

(1) THE 'BENEFIT' ISSUE ANALYSED BY THE JUDICIARY

- **BP Exploration Co. (Libya) Ltd v Hunt (No 2)** [1979] 1 WLR 783, Queen's Bench Division; [1981] 1 WLR 232, Court of Appeal; [1983] 2 AC 352, House of Lords

For the facts, see below, 316.

Robert Goff J: . . . [I]t is always necessary to bear in mind the difference between awards of restitution in respect of money payments and awards where the benefit conferred by the plaintiff does not consist of a payment of money. Money has the peculiar character of a universal medium of exchange. By its receipt, the recipient is inevitably benefited; and (subject to problems arising from such matters as inflation, change of position and the time value of money) the loss suffered by the plaintiff is generally equal to the defendant's gain, so that no difficulty arises concerning the amount to be repaid. The same cannot be said of other benefits, such as goods or services. By their nature, services cannot be restored; nor in many cases can goods be restored, for example where they have been consumed or transferred to another. Furthermore the identity and value of the resulting benefit to the recipient may be debatable. From the very nature of things, therefore, the problem of restitution in respect of such benefits is more complex than in cases where the benefit takes the form of a money payment. . . .

The principle underlying the [Law Reform (Frustrated Contracts) Act 1943] is prevention of the unjust enrichment of the defendant at the plaintiff's expense. Where, as in cases under section 1(2), the benefit conferred on the defendant consists of payment of a sum of money, the plaintiff's expense and the defendant's enrichment are generally equal; and, subject to other relevant factors, the award of restitution will consist simply of an order for repayment of a like sum of money. But where the benefit does not consist of money, then the defendant's enrichment will rarely be equal to the plaintiff's expense. In such cases, where (as in the case of a benefit conferred under a contract thereafter frustrated) the benefit has been requested by the defendant, the basic measure of recovery in restitution is the reasonable value of the plaintiff's performance—in a case of services, a quantum meruit or reasonable remuneration, and in a case of goods, a quantum valebat or reasonable price. Such cases are to be contrasted with cases where such a benefit has not been requested by the defendant. In the latter class of case, recovery is rare in restitution; but if the sole basis of recovery was that the defendant had been incontrovertibly benefited, it might be legitimate to limit recovery to the defendant's actual benefit—a limit which has (perhaps inappropriately) been imported by the legislature into section 1(3) of the Act. . . .

NOTES AND QUESTIONS

1. In the above two passages, Robert Goff J makes clear that: (i) non-money benefits raise more complex issues than where the benefit comprises a payment; (ii) restitution is rare where non-money benefits have not been requested by the defendant, although restitution may be granted, irrespective of request, where the defendant has been incontrovertibly benefited.

2. What does Robert Goff J mean, and do you agree with him, when he says that where the defendant has been incontrovertibly benefited 'it might be legitimate to limit recovery to the defendant's actual benefit'?

3. For more detailed discussion of this case, see below, 316.

- **Procter & Gamble Philippine Manufacturing Corp v Peter Cremer GmbH**
  [1988] 3 All ER 843, Queen's Bench Division

The claimants had contracted to buy copra cake from the defendant sellers. The goods were being shipped on board *The Manila*. The shipowners were insolvent and, in order to ensure that the vessel sailed on time from the Philippines to Rotterdam, the claimants paid additional freight to the shipowners. It transpired that the relevant bills of lading were incorrectly dated, so that the claimants were entitled to reject the goods and to recover their purchase money. But in addition the claimants sought restitution from the defendants of the additional freight paid to the shipowners. This aspect of the claim succeeded before the Board of Appeal of the Grain and Feed Trade Association but was overturned by Hirst J.

Hirst J: . . . The relevant principles are common ground between the two parties, and are conveniently set out in the leading textbook on the law of restitution, Goff and Jones *The Law of Restitution* (3rd edn, 1986) p 148, as follows:

'The general principle should be that restitution should always be granted when, as a result of the plaintiff's services, the defendant has gained a financial benefit readily realisable without detriment to himself or has been saved expense which he inevitably must have incurred'.

This forms part of a section headed 'Restitutionary Claims; where the defendant has gained an incontrovertible benefit', a neat phrase which in my judgment epitomises the whole doctrine under consideration here.

Counsel for the buyers submits that the board of appeal have found, and rightly found, that the sellers did indeed obtain an incontrovertible benefit, in that, as a result of the buyers' funding the extra freight, they had the advantage of being able to sell the goods in Rotterdam rather than locally, and were saved expense.

In my judgment this is not a proper interpretation of the supplemental award. I am unable to derive any findings from it that an incontrovertible benefit was conferred; at most it amounted to the finding that, in the difficult circumstances of the shipowners' insolvency, [Recourse and Recovery Bureau MV of Rotterdam], on behalf of the (presumably European) cargo interests collectively, formed the view that, to make the best of a bad job, the most favourable solution all round was for the vessel to sail to Rotterdam. This falls far short even of a general finding of incontrovertible benefit, still less of a finding (which in my judgment would be essential to justify relief under this heading) that the present sellers viewed in isolation received an incontrovertible benefit. It is not surprising that the board of appeal did not focus on this critical point, since the question of restitution was, it seems clear, never argued before them. Nor is there any finding that the sellers were saved any expense which they would 'inevitably have incurred'; indeed it is by no means clear that such was the case, since, as a corporation themselves based in the Philippines, they might well have thought it prudent from their own point of view to withdraw the cargo there in the hope of an upturn in the market. It follows, in my judgment, that there was no proper basis for the award based on restitution.

QUESTIONS

Is the passage cited by Hirst J from Goff and Jones a correct statement of the law? Even if the sellers had been enriched (incontrovertibly) were they unjustly enriched?

- *Peel (Regional Municipality) v Canada*
(1993) 98 DLR (4th) 140, Supreme Court of Canada

Under the Juvenile Delinquents Act 1970, courts were empowered to order the municipality to which a juvenile delinquent belonged to contribute to the cost of that juvenile's support where placed in, for example, foster homes or a charitable institution. In accordance with such orders, the Regional Municipality of Peel under protest paid for the support of a number of juveniles in homes run by (nonstate) bodies but then successfully established that the empowering legislation was *ultra vires* and void. It sought restitution from the provincial and federal governments on the basis that it had discharged their liabilities. The Supreme Court dismissed that restitutionary claim because the claimant had not established that the provincial or federal governments had been incontrovertibly benefited by the claimant's payments (i.e. no legal liability had been discharged nor had any inevitable or likely expense been saved).

McLachlin J: . . . The question thus reduces to this: how should 'benefit' in the general test for recovery for unjust enrichment be defined? More particularly, can it encompass payments which fall short of discharging the defendant's legal liability?

We have been referred to no cases in Canada or the commonwealth where a 'negative' benefit has been found in the absence of an underlying legal liability on the defendant. . . .

Notwithstanding the absence of authority, some scholars (Goff and Jones, and Maddaugh and McCamus) perceive a 'whittling away' of the hard and fast rule barring recovery absent proof of a defendant's legal obligation to undertake the expense or perform the act which the plaintiff claims to have accomplished on the defendant's behalf. They suggest that where the plaintiff has conferred on the defendant an 'incontrovertible benefit', recovery should be available even in the absence of a defendant's legal liability. . . .

An 'incontrovertible benefit' is an unquestionable benefit, a benefit which is demonstrably apparent and not subject to debate and conjecture. Where the benefit is not clear and manifest, it would be wrong to make the defendant pay, since he or she might well have preferred to decline the benefit if given the choice. According to Justice Gautreau of the District Court of Ontario, where an unjust benefit is found 'one discharges another's debt that is owed to a third party or discharges another's contractual or statutory duty': J. R. Maurice Gautreau, 'When Are Enrichments Unjust.' (1988–89) 10 Adv. Q 258. The late Justice Gautreau cites this court's decision in *County of Carleton v City of Ottawa* as an example of such a case but adds the following pertinent remarks at pp. 270–1:

> While the principle of freedom of choice is ordinarily important, it loses its force if the benefit is an incontrovertible benefit, *because it only makes sense that the defendant would not have realistically declined the enrichment*. For example, choice is not a real issue if the benefit consists of money paid to the defendant or paid to a third party to satisfy the debt of the defendant that was owing to the third party. In either case there has been an *unquestionable* benefit to the defendant. In the first case, he can return it or repay it if he chooses; in the second, he had no choice but to pay it, the only difference is that the payee has changed. Likewise, the principle of freedom of choice is a spent force if the benefit covers an expense that the defendant would have been put to in any event, and, as an issue, it is weak if the defendant subsequently adopts and capitalizes on the enrichment by turning it to account through sale or profitable commercial use.
>
> The principle of incontrovertible benefit is not the antithesis of freedom of choice. It is not in competition with the latter, rather, it exists when freedom of choice as a problem is absent.

(Emphasis added.)

Justice Gautreau's comment takes us back to the terms of the traditional test; the discharge of a legal liability creates an 'unquestionable' benefit because the law allowed the defendant no choice. Payment of an amount which the defendant was under no legal obligation to discharge is quite another matter.

The same requirement of inevitable expense is reflected in McInnes' discussion of the notion of incontrovertible benefit: McInnes, ['Incontrovertible Benefits and the Canadian Law of Restitution' (1990–91) 12 Adv. Q 323]. He asserts, at p. 346, that 'restitutionary relief should be available to one who has saved another an inevitable or necessary expense (whether factually or legally based)'. *Arguendo*, he suggests that recovery may lie where one 'has discharged an obligation which the obligee *would likely have paid* another to discharge' [emphasis added]. He goes on, at p. 347, to caution that 'although otherwise warranted, restitutionary relief should be denied if the benefit was conferred officiously, or if liability would amount to a hardship for the recipient of the benefit'. McInnes concludes at p. 362 that the case law provides only theoretical and not express support for the incontrovertible benefit doctrine and suggests that, as such relief is 'somewhat extraordinary', it 'should not be imposed unless the equities of the circumstances demand it'.

It is thus apparent that any relaxation of the traditional requirement of discharge of legal obligation which may be effected through the concept of 'incontrovertible benefit' is limited to situations where it is clear on the facts (on a balance of probabilities) that had the plaintiff not paid, the defendant would have done so. Otherwise, the benefit is not incontrovertible.

Where does this discussion of 'benefit' in the doctrine of unjust enrichment bring us? Accepting for the purposes of argument that the law of restitution should be extended to incontrovertible benefits, the municipality still falls short of the law's mark. The benefit conferred is not incontrovertible in the sense in which Goff and Jones define that concept; the municipality has not shown that either level of government being sued 'gained a demonstrable financial benefit or has been saved an inevitable expense'. Nor is it 'unquestionable', to use Justice Gautreau's test; the federal and provincial governments were under no legal obligation and their contention that they were not benefited at all, or in any event to the value of the payments made, has sufficient merit to require, at the least, serious consideration. It was neither inevitable nor likely, in McInnes' phrase, that in the absence of a scheme which required payment by the municipality the federal or provincial government would have made such payments; an entirely different scheme could have been adopted, for example. . . .

La Forest, **Sopinka**, **Gonthier** and **Cory JJ** concurred with **McLachlin J**. **Lamer CJC** delivered a short judgment agreeing with McLachlin J.

NOTES AND QUESTIONS

1. Had the claimant sought restitution of the money from the (non-state) bodies to which it was paid, it would have had no difficulty establishing the defendant's enrichment. However, it might have had difficulty establishing an unjust factor (although one possibility would have been the *ultra vires* nature of the demand, in line with *Woolwich Equitable Building Society v IRC*, see below, Chapter 12, albeit that no demands were made by the recipient bodies). In any event those bodies would presumably have been able to raise the defence of change of position (see below, 762).

2. Had the claimant been able to establish that the federal or provincial governments were enriched, would it have been able to show that they were *unjustly* enriched? I.e. was there an unjust factor? Consider, for example, mistake (cf. *County of Carleton v Ottawa*, below, 188), legal compulsion (below, Chapter 7), or an *ultra vires* demand (cf. the *Woolwich* case, below, Chapter 12).

- ● *Rowe v Vale of White Horse District Council*
  [2003] EWHC 388 (Admin), [2003] 1 Lloyd's Rep 418, Queen's Bench Division

The defendant district council supplied sewerage services to the claimant, Mr Rowe, over a number of years without charging for them. The council's explanation for their failure to charge was that, between 1982–1995, it had made an administrative error; and that between 1995–2001 it was unsure whether it had the legal power to operate the sewerage station by which it was providing the services and hence was unsure whether it could charge for the services. In 2001, it was clarified that it did have that power and so in March 2001, the council wrote to the defendant saying that it would be charging for the future for sewerage services and demanding payment for those services provided for the previous six years (1995–2001). The claimant refused to pay for the previous six years saying that he had previously had no intimation that there was to be a charge for those sewerage services over and above what he had paid through council and water rates. He brought an application for judicial review although the proceedings were treated by Lightman J as a trial of the private law question of whether the Council was entitled to the payments demanded for 1995–2001. He held that they were not so entitled because there was no unjust factor. That aspect of the judgement is set out below at 393. We here focus on the 'benefit' issue.

Lightman J: . . .

11. It is now authoritatively established that there are four essential ingredients to a claim in restitution:

(i)   a benefit must have been gained by the defendant;

(ii) the benefit must have been obtained at the claimant's expense;

(iii) it must be legally unjust, that is to say there must exist a factor (referred to as an unjust factor) rendering it unjust, for the defendant to retain the benefit;

(iv) there must be no defence available to extinguish or reduce the defendant's liability to make restitution.

12. It is common ground between the parties that the first two and the fourth conditions are satisfied, for Mr. Rowe obtained the benefit of the sewerage services provided by the Council and there is no defence available e.g. of change of position. Originally in a case such as the present of a supply of services, it was necessary in order to satisfy the second condition to establish a request by the defendant for the services. But under the developing law of restitution it is now enough if either of two principles are brought into play. The first principle is that the second condition is to be deemed to be satisfied if the defendant has freely accepted (or acquiesced in the supply for consideration of) the services rendered. The second principle is that in exceptional circumstances the second condition is to be deemed satisfied if the defendant has been incontrovertibly benefited from their receipt: see Goff & Jones. The Law of Restitution, 6th ed., par. 1002. The Council in this action contends that Mr. Rowe freely accepted the sewerage services rendered and by reason of such free acceptance in accordance with the first principle the second condition is to be deemed satisfied. An essential ingredient for application of the principle of free acceptance is acquiescence by the defendant in the supply of the services for a consideration (a matter to which I turn when I consider the third condition). In the absence of proof of such acquiescence, the principle of free acceptance cannot be invoked to satisfy the second condition. But it is common ground that the receipt of the services constituted an incontrovertible benefit and that the second condition is to be deemed to be satisfied for this reason.

NOTES

1. In his discussion of 'benefit' Lightman J appeared to accept that free acceptance is a valid principle for establishing the defendant's benefit, albeit that on the facts free acceptance could not be made out. But this is all obiter dicta because Mr Rowe conceded that the provision of the sewerage services was an incontrovertible benefit.

2. In paragraph 12, it would appear that Lightman J's references to his 'second condition' are better understood as references to his 'first condition'.

- ### *Cressman v Coys of Kensington (Sales) Ltd*
  [2004] EWCA Civ 47, [2004] 1 WLR 2775, Court of Appeal

The late Mr T A Cressman owned a Mercedes 280 SL car with the personalized registration number, TAC 1. After his death his executors (Mr and Mrs Cressman) instructed Coys of Kensington, who were car auctioneers, to sell the car but without its personalized registration number. Mr McDonald was the successful bidder when Coys auctioned the car. He bought the car for £20,290 without its personalized number plate. The trial judge had valued that personalized number plate at £15,000. However, because of an administrative error by Coys in not retaining the registration mark before the car was sold, Mr McDonald became statutorily entitled to have the car and the personalized number plate registered in his own name which he duly did. Mr and Mrs Cressman brought an action against Coys for the loss of the personalised number plate. Coys settled that claim for £13,608 and were assigned the Cressmans' rights against Mr McDonald. Coys brought this action to recover £13,608 as 100 per cent contribution from Mr McDonald (on the basis of Mr McDonald's liability in unjust enrichment to the Cressmans) plus £1,392 as assignees of the Cressmans' cause of action against Mr McDonald in unjust enrichment. The action succeeded at trial (for £15,000 overall) and was upheld in this appeal.

Mance LJ: . . .

Restitution—general

22. The issue which is basic to all aspects of this appeal is whether the circumstances gave the Cressmans any claim against Mr McDonald based on unjust enrichment. It is common ground that four questions arise when considering a claim for unjust enrichment. (1) Has the defendant benefited or been enriched? (2) Was the enrichment at the expense of the claimant? (3) Was the enrichment unjust? (4) Is there any specific defence available to the defendant (such as change of position)? See *Banque Financière de la Cité v Parc (Battersea) Ltd* [1999] 1 AC 221, 227a, *per* Lord Steyn, and *Row e v Vale of White Horse District Council* [2003] 1 Lloyd's Rep 418, paras 10–11 *per* Lightman J.

The statutory scheme

23.   The first proposition advanced on Mr McDonald's behalf is that Mr McDonald's acquisition of the registration mark was a consequence of the statutory scheme, and of his performance of his contractual obligations in ignorance of any problem about the mark, and that 'it would be wrong, and it is submitted contrary to public policy, to hold an individual liable for the consequences, which he did not seek, of the administration of the vehicle registration scheme'.

24.   It was the statutory scheme that meant that Mr McDonald acquired the registration mark. That does not mean that there was no enrichment or no unjust enrichment. On the contrary, it is the reason why there may have been. His potential enrichment consisted in his acquisition of a car carrying with it a potentially valuable registration mark. Any such enrichment must have been at the expense of the estate of Mr TA Cressman. Mr Swirsky, who appears for Mr McDonald, does not seriously dispute that.

25.   Further, it was legally unjust for Mr McDonald to keep the registration mark, since it was an express term of the auction contract that he would not receive the vehicle's existing mark (whatever that might be), but would instead get an age-related mark, and he only obtained the old, cherished mark as the result of a mistaken failure by Coys to operate the statutory scheme correctly on behalf of the estate, about which mistake Mr McDonald soon became aware. Subject to any points arising from any transfer to his partner, Mr McDonald could easily have cooperated with the Cressmans and Coys as they invited, and could have arranged for the mark TAC 1 to be retransferred, in which connection Coys would no doubt have been only too pleased to resolve the matter by meeting any retransfer costs, and Mr McDonald would have received instead from the DVLA the age-related mark which he had expected. There is nothing in the suggestion that the statutory scheme means that principles of unjust enrichment can have no application.

Benefit

26.   On this basis, the next submission advanced on Mr McDonald's behalf is that his receipt of the mark was insufficient to amount to a benefit or enrichment. What was necessary was either realisation of its value or at the least proof of an intention to benefit by realising its value. Our attention was drawn to the discussion on the nature of the benefit required in leading academic works, particularly *Birks, An Introduction to the Law of Restitution* (1985), pp 114–128, *Goff & Jones, The Law of Restitution*, 6th ed. (2002), paras 1-017–1-032 and *Burrows, The Law of Restitution*, 2nd ed. (2002), pp 16–25.

27.   Arguments about the respective merits of the differing approaches taken in these works were not very fully developed before us, and we were not shown the articles to which I refer in the next paragraph of this judgment. So far as possible, I shall therefore avoid expressing positive conclusions favouring any one of the approaches. But they contain much common ground and give considerable guidance as to the type of factors which are likely to be relevant when determining whether a defendant has received a sufficient benefit to enable a claimant to assert that he has been enriched for the purposes of a claim for unjust enrichment. It seems to me, however, that the parties' submissions failed generally to give due weight to the fact that the academic debate in the passages cited about 'free acceptance' and 'indisputable benefit' relates primarily to situations (typically the supply of services) where any benefit is not readily returnable.

28. The law's general concern is with benefit to the particular defendant, or so-called 'subjective devaluation'. Mr McDonald has not actually realised or received any monetary benefit from the mark. Professor Birks and *Goff & Jones* both identify (a) free acceptance and (b) incontrovertible benefit as two main categories of case in which a defendant who has not realised any actual monetary benefit may be treated as unjustly enriched. Professor Birks (in response to a critique by Professor Burrows) has stressed that 'free acceptance' should not be understood as meaning that the recipient values the thing in question, but as unconscientious conduct precluding him or her from exercising the usual right to assert that he or she was not subjectively benefited: see 'In Defence of Free Acceptance' in *Burrows, Essays on the Law of Restitution* (1991), pp 105–146 Professor Burrows disagrees about the possibility of free acceptance—cf. 'Free Acceptance and the Law of Restitution' (1988) 104 LQR 576 and *Burrows, The Law of Restitution*, pp 20–23—basically because free acceptance may amount to 'nothing more than indifference to the objective benefit being rendered'. Consistently with that objection, he suggests that 'reprehensible seeking-out' (where a recipient's conduct clearly shows that he wants the benefit, but also that he is unwilling to pay for it) should suffice as a test of benefit: ibid, at pp 24–25. Citing some extreme examples (holding a pistol to a doctor's head and demanding medical treatment, stealing goods and intentionally using another's land without permission), he goes on, at p 25:

'Although there are no authorities specifically on this point, the defendant in such situations must be regarded as benefited (by the objective value of the subject matter). He cannot rationally say that he was indifferent to receiving the thing: and he cannot be allowed to raise the argument "I was not willing to pay" because his reprehensible conduct shows a disregard for the bargaining process (i e, the market system).'

In a footnote he comments at this point:

'It is arguable that the "seeking-out" alone is sufficient to outweigh the subjective devaluation objection. But as the argument for this test is one of principle, without direct support from the case law, it has been considered preferable to focus on the stronger case where the conduct is also reprehensible.'

It is of interest to recall that Professor Birks's explanation of the theory of 'free acceptance' is that the recipient's 'unconscientious conduct' precludes him or her from denying subjective benefit. Professor Burrows's text continues, at p 25:

'Clearly this test runs close to free acceptance. But it is crucially distinct because in requiring a "seeking-out" of the benefit rather than a "standing-by" it overcomes the indifference argument. Moreover this test is a test of benefit only. It is not intended to establish that the enrichment is unjust.'

29. 'Free acceptance' and 'reprehensible seeking out' represent tests focusing on the circumstances under which Mr McDonald came to have a car carrying the registration mark TAC 1, while 'incontrovertible benefit' focuses on the subjective value to him of the mark once acquired, regardless of those circumstances. Here, because of Coys' mistake, Mr McDonald acquired a car on 12 December 2000 which had, under the statutory scheme, a right to the mark TAC 1. His acquisition of the car on that date cannot have involved any 'free acceptance' of either the mark or the right to it. Mr Brownlee of Coys had reminded or told him and he knew on 12 December that he was *not* to get the old mark. But the process by which Mr McDonald came to have a car carrying that mark can, I think, be regarded as extending beyond 12 December 2000. In order to register himself as keeper he applied for a registration document, entering on the form V62 the mark TAC 1 in the knowledge that this would lead to the car being registered in his name with that mark. Notes B, C and

E to the Retention of Vehicle Registration Number form V778/1 (trial document E14) indicate that Mr McDonald could, even on 13 December 2000, have applied to retain the mark, with a view to re-transferring it to the estate or its order. But he made, so far as appears, no inquiry and certainly did not pursue the obvious possibility that such a step could be taken.

30. Further, on 3 January 2001, it is clear that his discussion with the DVLA covered the possibility of retention by the sellers, and he must have been aware that this was also a course open to him. By 5 January 2001, Mr McDonald was aware that the estate and Coys would be pursuing claims against him in relation to the mark. Notwithstanding that, he still did not make any application to retain the mark, with a view to its re-transfer to the estate. Only on or about 10 January 2001 did the DVLA register him as the keeper of the car with the mark TAC 1, so that he had every opportunity to correct the position before the mistake made in his favour was consolidated.

31. It is a salient feature of this case that Mr McDonald could have exercised a right of 'retention' so as to retransfer the registration mark to the Cressmans' order, and would then in lieu have received from the DVLA the age-related mark which he had expected; he could have done this at any stage after his acquisition of the car—at least until its gift to his partner which, [on my view of the evidence], cannot have been before 8 February 2001; and he refused to do this knowing that he had received the mark by mistake contrary to the auction bargain. The mark was here not just realisable, but easily returnable. The case lies outside the scope of Pollock CB's aphorism in *Taylor v Laird* (1856) 25 LJ Ex 329, 332: 'One cleans another's shoes; what can the other do but put them on?'

32. If the case turned on whether there was 'free acceptance' or 'reprehensible seeking-out', it would be borderline. Bearing in mind the circumstances in which Mr McDonald came to register in his name a car carrying the mark TAC 1, it could, I think, be regarded as falling within the general principle of free acceptance advocated by Professor Birks and *Goff & Jones*. On and after 13 December 2000 Mr McDonald was acting unconscientiously in seeking and in insisting upon such registration, in the knowledge that this was not in accordance with the bargain made and that there had been an obvious mistake. Professor Burrows's test of 'reprehensible seeking-out' is on its face more stringent. But it is designed to overcome any suggestion of indifference, and it could be consistent with this rationale if the test were, if necessary, given a slightly wider reformulation to cover circumstances such as the present. The qualification 'reprehensible' derives from what Professor Burrows himself describes as 'the stronger case' where the defendant shows a 'disregard for the bargaining process'. Mere 'seeking-out' might in his view suffice. Here, there was positive conduct aimed at the registration in his name of his car with the old cherished mark contrary to the known bargain. What happened involved sufficient elements of knowledge, choice and action to overcome any suggestion of indifference, and can once again be seen as reprehensible in so far as it was in conscious disregard of the prior bargain. However, the case does not need to turn on whether or not its facts can be brought within a concept of 'free acceptance' or '[reprehensible] seeking-out'.

33. The alternative basis of restitutionary recovery on which Coys rely is 'incontrovertible benefit'. This does not depend on analysis of the circumstances in which the benefit came to be acquired and fully enjoyed. It depends on the nature and value of the benefit as and when acquired. This basis of recovery was approved in principle by Hirst J in a dictum in *Procter & Gamble Philippine Manufacturing Corpn v Peter Cremer GmbH & Co. (The Manila)* [1988] 3 All ER 843. In *BP Exploration Co. (Libya) Ltd v Hunt (No 2)* [1979] 1 WLR 783, 805D Robert Goff J used a similar phrase in relation to the Law Reform (Frustrated Contracts) Act 1943, which he explained, at p 799D, as grounded on principles of unjust enrichment. Professor Birks suggests as the test of incontrovertible benefit whether 'no reasonable man would say that the defendant was not enriched': *An Introduction to the Law of Restitution*, at p 116. However, he emphasises the major difference, in his view, between this and 'the adoption of a straightforward objective standard of value', at p 116, and identifies two main cases in which the test should, in his view, be satisfied. They are cases of necessary expenditure (not here in issue) and cases of realised benefit. While he also identifies, at p 124, under a third heading of '(c) Others', some cases in which courts 'simply took the view that the recipient's benefit was "obvious" ', he evidently regards them as incompletely explained and exceptional cases of recourse to an objective standard.

34. In contrast, *Goff & Jones* in addressing incontrovertible benefits submit that it should be sufficient 'that the benefit is *realisable*' and that it should not be necessary to show that it has been *realised: The Law of Restitution*, para. 1–023. They comment:

'It is said that the principle of respect for the subjectivity of value would be subverted if this were accepted. But it may not be unreasonable, in some circumstances, to compel a person to sell an asset which another has mistakenly improved.'

Goff & Jones recognise that not every financial gain may be said to be realisable, and refer in this connection to the landowner who 'subject to the equitable doctrine of acquiescence, is not obliged to make restitution to the mistaken improver even though the land can, of course, be sold or mortgaged'. In *The Manila* [1988] 3 All ER 843, 855F Hirst J recorded that it had been common ground between the parties that the test in cases of receipt of services was appropriately set out in *Goff & Jones* as being whether the defendant had 'gained a financial benefit readily realisable without detriment to himself'. In *Marston Construction Co. Ltd v Kigass Ltd* (1989) 46 BLR 109, Judge Bowsher QC preferred *Goff & Jones's* to Professor Birks's approach.

35. Professor Burrows advocates an approach lying midway between realisation and realisability. He suggests as the test of benefit whether it is reasonably certain that the defendant will realise the positive benefit in the future. He puts the position as follows, *The Law of Restitution*, p 19:

'A problem with the narrow Birks view is that the date of trial is made crucial. Realisation of the benefit after trial is ignored and wily defendants may therefore be encouraged simply to wait before realising the benefit. *Goff & Jones's* view avoids this problem but has its own weakness because what is realisable cannot depend just on whether it is land or a chattel that is improved. The circumstances of the individual are also relevant. An improvement to a car is not realisable to the person who cannot afford to sell it and buy a suitable replacement. An improvement to land may be realisable to an owner who does not live on the land. In any event if it is clear that the defendant will not realise the benefit can it be said that he is so obviously benefited just because he *could* easily realise it? The best approach seems to be to take Birks's realised test but to add that the defendant will also be regarded as incontrovertibly benefited where the court regards it as reasonably certain that he will realise the positive benefit. Assessment of the defendant's future conduct is necessarily speculative but the courts commonly have to predict future conduct in assessing damages for loss, precisely to avoid the nonsense of rigidly cutting off loss at the date of trial.'

Mr Purchas for Coys supports *Goff & Jones's* approach, while Mr Swirsky submits on behalf of Mr McDonald that we should adopt Professor Burrows's intermediate approach. However, I think that Professor Burrows's approach might perhaps be open to the comment that it is too restrictive, and that a requirement of proof of intention might itself also encourage tactical stances or manoeuvring not too dissimilar to that which he fears on Professor Birks's approach.

36. Here, Mr McDonald received the mark. He did not realise any financial benefit from it, so if one were to treat Professor Birks's suggested requirement of actual *realisation* as relevant, it would not be met. However, Mr McDonald could easily have arranged for re-transfer of the mark to any car nominated by the estate and its financial value was easily realisable on the market, if he had so wished. If the test suggested by *Goff & Jones* were accepted, there would of course be no difficulty in concluding that Mr McDonald received a readily realisable benefit. That he subsequently gave it away to his partner could go at most to a possible defence of change of position. Professor Burrows's modified approach, requiring us to consider whether it was also reasonably certain that Mr McDonald would realise the financial benefit, would seem difficult to apply in or adapt to the present situation. It would fit a case where the defendant retains the alleged benefit at trial, not a case where he has apparently chosen to give it away, in knowledge of the relevant facts and claims (unless perhaps one could treat the gift away as the realisation of a benefit). Even if one were to attempt to ignore the gift away, it would be difficult, if not impossible, to consider what a defendant's intention would have been regarding realisation, if he had not given the benefit away, when giving it away is what he actually chose to do.

37. Looking at the matter generally, I have no doubt that justice requires that a person, who (as a result of some mistake which it becomes evident has been made in the execution of an agreed bargain) has a benefit or the right to a benefit for which he knows that he has not bargained or paid, should reimburse the value of that benefit to the other party if it is readily returnable without substantial difficulty or detriment and he chooses to retain it (or give it away to a third party) rather than to retransfer it on request. Even if realisable benefit alone is not generally sufficient, the law should recognise, as a distinct category of enrichment, cases where a benefit is readily returnable. A person who receives another's chattel must either return it or pay damages, commonly measured by reference to its value. The mark is not a chattel, and it was not suggested before us that its return could at any stage (even before the gift to the partner) have been enforced, or that its nonreturn could sound in damages. (There were allegations below of implied duties to co-operate in the return of the mark, but the judge did not accept them, and there is no appeal in that respect.) However, Mr McDonald's insistence on keeping the mark and the absence of any obvious means of compelling its retransfer are reasons for analysing this case in terms of unjust enrichment. Mr McDonald knew that he had not bargained or paid for the mark. The mark or its benefit was in practice easily returnable. If Mr McDonald chose to keep it, then I see every reason for treating him as benefited.

38. It also seems to me unrealistic to suppose that Mr McDonald did not in the circumstances himself attach value to the mark. By refusing to effect a retransfer, and by later giving the car with its mark away to his partner, Mr McDonald was exercising a deliberate preference to give himself and/or his partner the practical enjoyment of the mark for the meantime and the possibility of realising its monetary value in the longer term. Before giving the car to his partner, he could have retransferred the mark to the estate's order, or he could have given her the car on the understanding that she would retransfer the mark to the estate's order, if he so required. Further, although I would not go as far as the judge did in equating Mr McDonald and his partner for all purposes, the practical effect of their relationship and of Mr McDonald's evidence about it cannot be ignored. They were living together with a young family, and the car was for their joint use. The expectation would have been that both would continue to benefit both by the supposed cachet and by any future sale of the mark.

39. Mr McDonald's responses under cross-examination were to the general effect that the registration mark was a matter of indifference to him and to his partner. If that had been so, then, as the judge said, it would be difficult to understand why he took the attitude he did and did not co-operate in a retransfer to the estate. To my mind, Mr McDonald's attitude in and after December 2000, and his conduct in giving his partner the mark. with the car, show that he attached and attaches a value to the mark. Whatever their motives, numbers of car-owners pay good money to have a personalised plate. The inference is that Mr McDonald, despite his denials, attached real value to the mark, and determined that it should be retained for that reason.

40. In these circumstances, and in agreement with the judge, I would conclude that Mr McDonald received an incontrovertible benefit in the market value of the mark. Viewing the matter in the terms in which counsel presented it, there could be no difficulty in reaching this conclusion on the simple test of realisability advocated by *Goff & Jones*. Even if realisability is not alone generally sufficient, the ability to realise the mark in the future, coupled with the enjoyment of its possession and use in the meantime, seem to me considerable arguments in favour of a conclusion that

Mr McDonald regarded himself as subjectively benefited by the mark and should be treated as benefited by its value. I would regard Professor Birks's test of realised benefit, if it were to be applied to this situation, as overly narrow, and Professor Burrows's test as inappropriate and inapplicable in the present context (unless in each case one were to treat the gift to the partner as a realisation of benefit, which seems artificial). In my view, however, the law must in any event recognise as a distinct category of enrichment cases of readily returnable benefit, of which the present is an example. I therefore conclude that Mr McDonald did obtain a benefit which he should prima facie reimburse, if not in kind then in cash.

Change of position

41. To rebut this prima facie conclusion, Mr Swirsky repeated before us the submission advanced below to the effect that Mr McDonald had changed his position and deprived himself of any benefit by giving the car with its mark to his partner. The wide view of the doctrine of change of position is that it 'looks to a change of position, causally linked to the mistaken receipt, which makes it inequitable for the recipient to be required to make restitution': *Scottish Equitable plc v Derby* [2001] 3 All ER 818, para. 30 *per* Robert Walker LJ. Assuming this to be the correct view, still there can be nothing in the suggested defence in this case. . . . By the time Mr McDonald gave the car away, he knew that there had been a mistaken failure to obtain any right of retention under the statutory scheme and that both the estate and Coys would be pursuing him to recover the mark or its value. This negatives both any causal link and any inequity. A gift away made in such circumstances cannot have been made in reliance on the validity of the original receipt of the mark and cannot be regarded as having been made 'in good faith', so there can be no defence of change of position: see *Lipkin Gorman v Karpnale Ltd* [1991] 2 AC 548, 560c, *per* Lord Templeman and, at p 580c, *per* Lord Goff of Chieveley, and *Niru Battery Manufacturing Co. v Milestone Trading Ltd* [2002] 2 All ER (Comm) 705, paras 134–135 *per* Moore-Bick J, approved [2004] QB 985. Even if I had found that the gift to the partner took effect on the evening of 13 December 2000, I would also have considered that Mr McDonald was by then in possession of sufficient knowledge to exclude causal reliance and inequity or good faith . . .

42. It follows that Mr McDonald became liable to the estate for unjust enrichment, to the extent of £15,000. The trial below proceeded on the basis that all but £1,391.88 of that liability was met by Coys' settlement payment to the estate in March 2003; and that any further recovery by Coys could only be sought by way of contribution under the [Civil Liability (Contribution) Act 1978].

. . .

48. [I]t was . . . open to the judge to treat both parties as causally responsible for the same damage. Bearing in mind that it is Mr McDonald who received the benefit of the mark, and that the whole proceedings would have been unnecessary had he retransferred the mark to the estate's order as he should have done, the judge's conclusion that Coys should recover 100 per cent contribution from him appears to me unassailable in this court.

. . .

Wilson J and **Thorpe LJ** concurred.

NOTES AND QUESTIONS

1. For useful notes on this case, see G Virgo, 'Enrichment: The case of the Cherished Mark' [2004] *CLJ* 280; E Bant, 'Identifying Enrichment' [2004] *RLR* 151.

2. Mance LJ held that Mr McDonald was benefited because he had chosen to retain (or had given away) property which was readily returnable without substantial difficulty or detriment. Is this a test of benefit separate from incontrovertible benefit or free acceptance or reprehensible seeking-out?

3. Consider whether the following are illustrations of Mance LJ's principle:

(i) The award of the value of the materials left behind and used by the owner of the building in *Sumpter v Hedges* (below, 298).

(ii) The award of the value of the magazines in *Weatherby v Banham* (1832) 5 C & P 228. In that case, the claimant successfully recovered, in an action for goods sold and delivered, the price of issues of the 'Racing Calendar' sent to a subscriber who, unknown to the claimant, had in fact died. The defendant, who had moved into the deceased's house which he had inherited, had received the magazines over a two-year period and had never offered to return them. Lord Tenterden CJ's short judgment was as follows: 'If the defendant receive the books, and use them, I think that the action is maintainable. These books come addressed to the deceased gentleman, whose estate has come to the defendant, and he keeps the books. I think that the defendant is clearly liable in this form of action'.

4. Mance LJ treated the test he was applying as showing that Mr McDonald was 'incontrovertibly benefited' because it dealt with circumstances after the number plate was acquired. This was contrasted (see para. 29) with 'free acceptance' or 'reprehensible seeking-out' because they were dealing with the circumstances in which the number plate was acquired. But the concept of an 'incontrovertible benefit' was not conceived by the academics who devised it (see below 85) as being linked to the timing of the relevant circumstances. Rather it was devised as isolating where the defendant is obviously benefited putting to one side any conduct indicating, or precluding denial of, subjective value. So, for example, the receipt of money is the clearest example of an incontrovertible benefit. It would seem, therefore, that Mance LJ's test or principle is not best viewed as showing that the number plate was an incontrovertible benefit. Rather it refers to conduct showing that Mr McDonald subjectively valued the number plate.

5. Why was the defence of change of position rejected on the facts? See below, 796.

6. Mance LJ was prepared to assume, without deciding the point (which had not been raised in the appeal), that contribution was available in respect of restitutionary liability under the Civil Liability (Contribution) Act 1978. For the controversy in the cases on this point, see below, 552 and 519.

(2) ACADEMIC ANALYSIS OF THE 'BENEFIT' ISSUE

In the following extract, Burrows attacks the idea that 'free acceptance' establishes that the defendant is benefited and suggests instead a test of whether the performance has been bargained for.

• A Burrows, 'Free Acceptance and the Law of Restitution' (1988) *LQR* 576

It is over 21 years since the first edition of Goff and Jones' *The Law of Restitution*. An important part of their approach to unjust enrichment was a restitutionary concept which they identified and labelled as 'free acceptance'. More recently Peter Birks has similarly, albeit with added refinement, made free acceptance a central pillar in his exposition of restitution's theoretical structure in *An Introduction to the Law of Restitution*. The thesis of this article is that these scholars are mistaken and that neither on principle nor authority does free acceptance have a place within the law of restitution. This is not meant to suggest, however, that the cases which Goff and Jones and Birks explain as restitutionary because of free acceptance belong outside the law of restitution. On the contrary it is believed that they can nearly all be explained as restitutionary, but on grounds other than free acceptance.

What then is free acceptance? Goff and Jones in their first edition (although this does not appear in their second or third editions, where they simply refer to free acceptance without further elaboration) explain the idea as follows: '. . . the defendant will not usually be regarded as having been benefited by the receipt of services or goods unless he has accepted them (or, in the case of goods, retained them) with an opportunity of rejection and with actual or presumed knowledge that they were to be paid for. For convenience we shall refer to a person who has so acted as having *freely accepted* the services or goods in question.'[1] In Birks' words, 'A free acceptance occurs where a recipient knows that a benefit is being offered to him non-gratuitously and where he, having the opportunity to reject, elects to accept.'[2]

. . .

It is helpful to [have in mind] the hypothetical example which Birks gives to illustrate . . . free acceptance. 'Suppose that I see a window-cleaner beginning to clean the windows of my house. I know that he will expect to be paid. So I hang back unseen till he has finished the job; then I emerge and maintain that I will not pay for work which I never ordered. It is too late, I have freely accepted the service. I had the opportunity to send him away. I chose instead to let him go on. I must pay the reasonable value of his work.' For Birks this provides 'a clear and simple example.' But for the present author it was the start of the feeling that something had gone awry with the reasoning. . . .

The general question of when a defendant is benefited is surprisingly complex; but in order to challenge the role of free acceptance it is necessary to give some indication straightaway of an approach to the answer. It is submitted that as a matter of fact a person may be benefited either negatively—that is by being saved an expense—or positively—that is by making a gain—and that as a matter of policy one may judge the issue on a range from total subjectivity (solely through the defendant's own eyes) through to total objectivity (solely through the eyes of the reasonable man, which in this context means the market). The problem with a purely subjective approach is that one can never be sure what the defendant is thinking and, in any event, one would probably not wish to prejudice the plaintiff according to the eccentricities of the defendant. On the other hand, the problem with a purely objective approach is that it may involve a complete sacrifice of the individual's values for those of society. It would seem therefore that the best approach is one that takes a line somewhere between these two extremes.

Half of Goff and Jones' and Birks' approach to the problem of benefit sits happily with this suggestion. Hence the concept of an 'incontrovertible benefit,' which Birks amplifies as resting on a 'no reasonable man' test, is vitally important and stresses that the courts do largely take an approach between the two extremes. So, for example, the receipt of a sum of money by a defendant is regarded as a benefit because no reasonable man would deny that a sum of money benefits him. Any subjective devaluation argument by the defendant to the effect that the receipt of money is of no benefit to him is therefore ignored. Similarly a defendant who has had legally required expenses paid by the plaintiff is regarded as being benefited even though he may argue that he would not have paid those expenses. No reasonable man would make that argument. Clearly at its parameters the concept of an incontrovertible benefit is open-textured and allows a more or a less objective approach to be adopted. So, for example, necessary expenses saved can range from legally to mere factually necessary expenses. Similarly positive incontrovertible gains can range from those which have been *realised* to those which are merely *realisable*. But the importance of the concept should not be obscured by its open-textured nature.

However, the other half of Goff and Jones' and Birks' approach to benefit is free acceptance. Even where a defendant is not incontrovertibly benefited, they regard him as benefited where he freely accepts the plaintiff's goods or services. But why is this thought correct? The answer would appear to be that free acceptance shows that the defendant regards himself as benefited, and therefore ordering him to pay does not undermine respect for the individuality of values. But the problem with this is that, even accepting that the defendant's inner wishes must be judged according to his

---

1 *The Law of Restitution* (1966), 30–1.
2 *An Introduction to the Law of Restitution* (1985), 265. See also 104.

outward conduct,[3] there is no reason why one should assume that a freely accepting defendant actually regards himself as being benefited by what the plaintiff has conferred. On the contrary a defendant is just as likely to accept what the plaintiff is conferring on him where he considers it neither beneficial nor determental as where he considers it beneficial.

So if we return to Birks' window-cleaning example, the fact that the householder freely accepts does not establish that he regards himself as being better off by having his windows cleaned. For even if it is a fair inference that he would have stopped the window-cleaning if he had regarded the cleaning of his windows as detrimental to him, he is acting perfectly rationally if he allows the cleaning to continue on the grounds that he is neither being benefited nor harmed. In short, he may be indifferent to the cleaning of his windows. Free acceptance cannot therefore be regarded as establishing the defendant's enrichment.

An alternative way of looking at this is to ask whether the defendant would have otherwise paid for goods or services of the kind provided by the plaintiff so that the plaintiff's intervention has now saved him incurring that expense. It is submitted that free acceptance gives no sound indication that the defendant would have otherwise been willing to pay for the goods or services provided, and hence does not establish that the defendant has been benefited by being saved expense.

[Instead of free acceptance, the most important principle, apart from incontrovertible benefit] is that a defendant can be regarded as negatively benefited where the plaintiff performs what the defendant contracted or bargained[4] for, although it is debatable whether his expense saved should be judged objectively by the market price of the services or goods or subjectively by the contract or bargain price. The reasoning behind this 'bargained-for' principle of benefit[5] is that where the defendant has 'promised' to pay for a particular performance, the outward appearance is that he regards that performance as beneficial or, put in an alternative way, that he has been saved expense that he would otherwise have been willing to incur. By the same token even if the defendant receives only part of what he bargained for, it can be presumed that he regards himself as benefited by what he has received and that he has been saved part of the expense that he would otherwise have incurred.[6]

In the following extract, Garner rejects not only free acceptance (other than where an imperfect contract has been fully performed) but also Burrows' presumption of benefit where the defendant receives part of what he bargained for. In other words, he advocates a more objective approach than Goff and Jones, Birks or Burrows.

- **M Garner, 'The Role of Subjective Benefit in the Law of Unjust Enrichment'** (1990) 10 *OJLS* 42

INTRODUCTION

The boundaries of the law of unjust enrichment are only now being drawn. The way has been pioneered by Goff and Jones and Birks, and in the spirit of true frontiersmen they have sought

---

3 This aspect of objectivity should not be confused with that used earlier in this paragraph and in the preceding one where it refers to judging benefit by the values of the reasonable man in contrast to the values of the individual.

4 The wider term bargain is necessary so as to include cases where a contract is void, unenforceable, incomplete or anticipated.

5 Arguably one could talk instead of a 'request' principle of benefit: but it would seem that this would not go quite far enough to establish the defendant's benefit, because request does not necessarily indicate reciprocity (i.e. 'payment' by the defendant).

6 The presumption is rebuttable; for example if to complete performance would now cost the defendant as much as the original bargain (or market) price for full performance.

to annex as much territory as possible. Much of the ground claimed by them has been taken legitimately. But in certain areas they have transgressed. In particular, it is submitted that by adopting an overinclusive concept of subjective benefit through the vehicle of 'free acceptance' they have staked too great a claim. And that threatens not only the conceptual purity of the developing doctrine of unjust enrichment, but also its status as a legitimate legal event having as much a place in English law as contract and tort.

Broadly speaking, a plaintiff who asserts a claim in unjust enrichment must do two things— establish benefit and demonstrate that its receipt is 'unjust'. This article is concerned only with the former. Its purpose is to consider the role of free acceptance, or any other subjective benefit substitute, in the law of restitution.

FREE ACCEPTANCE, BARGAINED-FOR BENEFIT AND 'SUBJECTIVE REVALUATION'

In Birks' words 'a free acceptance occurs where a recipient knows that a benefit is being offered to him non-gratuitously and where he, having the opportunity to reject, elects to accept'. Birks argues that free acceptance establishes a benefit because the recipient's conduct shows that he values what is being offered to him. He therefore cannot have resort to the principle of 'subjective devaluation', which is based on the argument from freedom of choice.[1] For he has exercised that freedom and made his choice.

Burrows[2] criticizes this notion of benefit. He argues that free acceptance gives no sound indication that the recipient regards what is conferred on him as beneficial, because he may be indifferent to it. Burrows therefore concludes that free acceptance does not establish enrichment of the recipient. He argues that something more is needed. In his view, the additional element is request. For unlike acceptance or acquiescence, both of which are passive, request negatives indifference. Burrows asserts that a defendant can be regarded as negatively benefited where the plaintiff performs what the defendant contracted or bargained for. . . .

Thus two theories of subjective benefit are advanced: 'free acceptance benefit', which is based on acceptance or acquiescence, and 'bargained-for benefit', which is based on request. Both theories are designed to do the same work. They provide an alternative to incontrovertible benefit, which is measured objectively. Both rely on the argument that benefit may be established if a defendant concedes or acknowledges that what he received was valuable to him. The theories only differ on what amounts to a concession or acknowledgment of benefit.

Thus a defendant may 'subjectively revalue' something done for him by the plaintiff even though the plaintiff's work may be objectively worthless. Subjective revaluation is the corollary of subjective devaluation. Both principles appeal to the argument from freedom of choice. Subjective revaluation simply says that the defendant has exercised his freedom to choose and has thereby indicated what *he* values.

A defendant may seek subjective devaluation of an objective benefit conferred on him by the plaintiff in two ways. First, he can appeal to his own personal, and perhaps perverse, tastes. While the 'reasonable man' might like his house to have clean windows, the defendant may assert that he prefers his dirty. So if a window cleaner does work on his house by mistake, he may resist the window cleaner's restitutionary claim simply by denying that he has received a benefit. Clean windows are of no value to *him*. He has the right to be perverse. Alternatively, he may appeal to a particular (and not

---

1 See Birks, 'Restitution For Services', (1974) 27 *CLP* 13, 19. The argument finds judicial expression in two oft cited *dicta*: 'One cleans another's shoes; what can the other do but put them on'. (Pollock CB in *Taylor v Laird* (1856) 25 LJ Ex 329); and 'Liabilities are not to be forced upon people behind their backs anymore than you can confer a benefit upon a man against his will'. (Bowen LJ in *Falcke v Scottish Imperial Insurance Co.* (1886) 34 Ch.1) 234.)

2 'Free Acceptance and the Law of Restitution', (1988) 104 *LQR* 576.

necessarily perverse) expenditure priority. He might concede that he likes his windows clean. However, he may have preferred to have done the job himself rather than pay somebody else to do it for him. He might have more important things on which to spend his money. Or he may have been willing to pay for the work, but only if he had sufficient funds left after meeting expenses associated with higher-priority matters. The argument from freedom of choice therefore allows a defendant to resist a restitutionary claim notwithstanding that the receipt of a benefit in his hands is established. And this is so even if the plaintiff can negative voluntariness and officiousness and establish that the enrichment was 'unjust'; thus the principle of incontrovertible benefit. Putting to one side claims for the return of money, that principle allows a restitutionary claim in the case of established objective benefit only if the plaintiff's work has saved the defendant from an inevitable expense or, perhaps, if that work has resulted in a readily realizable financial gain.[3]

If the argument from freedom of choice permits subjective devaluation of an objective benefit, *a fortiori* that argument must be countered by a plaintiff who relies on subjective revaluation to establish his claim in unjust enrichment. Thus free acceptance and bargained-for benefit must do *more* than simply establish a conceded or acknowledged benefit; they must meet also the arguments based on willingness to pay and priority. And this they can seldom do.

THE AREAS OF OPERATION OF SUBJECTIVE BENEFIT

According to Goff and Jones, Birks and Burrows there are three main areas in which the principles of free acceptance and bargained-for benefit operate. The first is mistaken improvement of another's land. The second is services rendered or goods supplied under a contract discharged because of breach or frustration. And the third is services rendered under a void, unenforceable, incomplete or anticipated contract. The last two categories may be conveniently considered together under the heading 'Imperfect Contracts'. [*After considering the mistaken improvement of another's land, Garner continued:*]

Imperfect contracts (i) *Full performance*. It will assist by considering first the case where nothing goes wrong; the plaintiff does all the work contracted for and the defendant is ready and willing to pay him the full contract price. Here all of the elements of subjective benefit are made out. The contract itself is clear evidence that the defendant values the plaintiff's full performance and the contract consideration demonstrates the defendant's willingness to pay for that performance as a present priority. However, there is no room for benefit-based recovery if the defendant is willing to perform his side of the bargain. A plaintiff who provides full performance is limited to enforcement of the contract where that gives him the very thing he bargained for in return for his performance. There are two reasons for this. First, he has agreed to accept the contract price—and nothing more or less—for his work. Benefit-based recovery is expressly excluded by the contract. Secondly, the response of restitution, which is backward-looking, is wholly inconsistent with the policy of contract, which looks forward. The law, out of deference to the principle of free choice, gives primacy to bargains. It gives effect to the forward-looking policy of contract by respecting and protecting the parties' prospective rights and obligations and by providing compensation for breaches of past obligations on an expectation loss basis. Therefore, so long as a contract subsists, backward-looking restitution is necessarily excluded.

But if there is full performance of a contract which unbeknown to the parties is unenforceable, restitution may assume a role, and subjective benefit can provide the necessary enrichment. Thus in *Pavey and Matthews Pty. Ltd v Paul*[4] a builder fully completed work under a contract which was unenforceable for want of writing by virtue of section 45 of the Builders Licensing Act 1971 (New

---

3 See Birks, *Introduction*, 116–17 and Goff and Jones, *The Law of Restitution* (3rd edn), 19–22.
4 (1987) 162 CLR 221.

South Wales). The owner of the property on which the work was done refused to pay under the oral contract. The High Court of Australia held that the builder was entitled to rescind the contract and recover fair and just compensation for the work done. Deane J said that the builder's claim was in unjust enrichment:

> The quasi-contractual obligation to pay fair and just compensation for a benefit which has been accepted will arise in a case where there is no applicable genuine agreement or where such an agreement is frustrated, avoided or unenforceable. In such a case, it is the very fact that there is no genuine agreement or that the genuine agreement is frustrated, avoided or unenforceable that provides the occasion for (and part of the circumstances giving rise to) the imposition by the law of the obligation to make restitution.

The benefit therefore was determined subjectively on the basis of free acceptance. Further, in the Court's view, the restitutionary claim did not undermine the policy of section 45 of the Builders Licensing Act.

In theory, an unjust subjective enrichment claim might lie also in the case of full performance of a void contract. However, often the factor invalidating the contract precludes an inference that the defendant has freely accepted or requested the plaintiff's services.[5]

(ii) *Part performance.* By itself and without more, part performance of a contract discharged because of breach of frustration affords no basis for the identification of a subjective benefit. There is no free acceptance by the defendant, because he never had an opportunity to accept or decline the plaintiff's part performance.[6] Nor did he request or bargain for it.[7] True, he must have valued full performance. But the job only part done may be of no benefit to him. Thus the *quantum meruit* claim allowed in *Planché v Colburn*[8] was not restitutionary. And this was not just because the defendant had not received any part of the book which the plaintiff was writing for him. For subjectively determined benefit does not require an end-product. But it does require an acknowledgment or concession of benefit, and there was none in *Planché v Colburn*. The proper explanation of the case is that contractual damages were awarded on a reliance loss basis, it not being possible to prophesy the plaintiff's expectation loss and the defendant having failed to show that the plaintiff made a bad bargain.

Birks has suggested that objective valuation might be allowed against a party in breach, or perhaps against any wrongdoer:

> More cautiously it might be said that a party in breach of a contract cannot push the argument from subjective devaluation to extremes. [If I have built half a house when our contract ends] there is at least 'limited acceptance' in the sense that what you have received is part of a project which you certainly did want. It may therefore be that, at least against a party in breach, 'limited acceptance' is sufficient to turn aside any attempt at subjective devaluation.[9]

---

5 See, e.g., *Craven Ellis v Canons Ltd* [1936] 2 KB 403, where the restitutionary relief granted is better explained on the basis of objectively measured incontrovertible benefit: see Birks, 'Negotiorum Gestio and The Common Law', (1971) 24 *CLP* 110, 120–2.

6 See Birks, *Introduction*, 126.

7 Burrows' bargained-for benefit' explanation of part performance cases is based on a fallacious jump in reasoning. He argues that, where a defendant promises to pay for a particular performance, the outward appearance is that he regards that performance as beneficial. That much makes good sense. But it does not follow that 'if the defendant receives only part of what he bargained for, it can be presumed that he regards himself as benefited by what he has received and that he has been saved part of the expense that he would otherwise have incurred'. ('Free Acceptance and the Law of Unjust Enrichment', 582–3.) For as Burrows himself acknowledges (at 588) 'the defendant has only agreed to pay under a contract for completion of the job'.

8 (1831) 8 Bing 14.   9 *Introduction*, 126–7.

[But this argument must be] rejected on the basis that unconscionability or wrongfulness should not trump the argument from subjective devaluation.

Sometimes, however, the defendant's conduct *after* the repudiatory breach amounts to a concession by him that he was benefited by the plaintiff's part performance. This is what happened in *Lodder v Slowey*.[10] There the plaintiff was sub-contracted by the defendants to construct works on land owned by a New Zealand municipal corporation. Part way through the project, the plaintiff was wrongfully excluded from the land by the defendants' agent, the municipal corporation's engineer, who took possession of the site for the purpose of completing the works. In these circumstances, the defendants could not argue that the part-finished project was of no benefit to them, because their agent went ahead and completed the job. Further, their willingness to pay for the works as a present priority was clearly established by the contract. The Privy Council, affirming the decision of the New Zealand Court of Appeal, held that the plaintiff had the right to treat the contract as at an end and to sue on a *quantum meruit* for work and labour done instead of suing for damages for breach of contract. The plaintiff's part performance, coupled with the defendants' post-repudiation conduct, established the necessary subjective benefit.

. . .

CONCLUSION

There is a limited role for subjective benefit in the law of unjust enrichment. But a subjective benefit should not be found where none exists. Only where the defendant truly has acknowledged or conceded that he has received a benefit should enrichment be determined subjectively, and then only if the defendant has manifested a willingness to pay for that benefit as a present priority. The doctrine of unjust enrichment should not be too greedy lest it leave itself open to the familiar attack that it is based on nothing more than broad and uncertain considerations of 'fairness' and 'justice', a charge that threatens its status as a legitimate legal event having a place in the framework of English law alongside contract and tort.

In the next extract, Beatson rejects the view that the performance of pure services can constitute a benefit. He therefore regards the remedy given to those who perform pure services (outside the context of a valid contract) as resting on the principle of injurious reliance (cf. 'unjust sacrifice' discussed below at 101–106) and not on the principle against unjust *enrichment*.

- **J Beatson, *The Use and Abuse of Unjust Enrichment*** (1991), 22–3, 31–5, 44.

My concern is with services and the extent to which remedies given in respect of services rendered or received should be seen as based on the unjust enrichment of the defendant or as recompense for reliance losses.

. . .

The main forms which services may take are:

(i)   those that *result* in improvements to property or in a marketable residuum in the hands of the defendant;

(ii) those where, although there is no marketable residuum, a necessary expense of the defendant is anticipated or avoided (as where a debt is paid or other obligation met by the plaintiff);

(iii) those with no marketable residuum in the hands of the recipient but an increase in his human capital (as where a teacher gives a lesson to an able pupil), and;

(iv) those where there is neither marketable residuum nor increase in human capital (as where an actor or a musician performs his art or where the teacher's lesson falls on deaf ears).

---

10 (1902) 20 NZLR 321 (New Zealand Court of Appeal); aff'd. [1904] AC 442 (PC).

I shall concentrate on (iii) and (iv) which are forms of 'pure' service. Both Birks and Goff and Jones treat certain pure services as within the category of enrichment. . . .

If exchange-value, transferability, or capacity to produce income are the hallmarks of wealth it is difficult to see how pure services qualify, at any rate when one is asking whether they are wealth in the hands of the recipient. Services may be the *source* of wealth or they may be its *product*. Services may be a source of wealth where they result in an end-product or an improvement to property, as where a tailor makes a suit or a builder constructs a house. Services may also be the product of wealth; in the above examples the services are products of the skills constituting the human capital of the tailor and the builder. These are very different items of wealth from that which may result from the service. A service can be the product but not the source of wealth as where a physician treats a patient or a lawyer advises a client without success. The *right to a service* may in some cases be a form of wealth, although the non-assignability of rights to personal services means that even this proposition requires qualification. But the service itself does not fit comfortably into this notion of wealth; it ceases to exist when it has been rendered and cannot be exchanged, transferred, or turned to account in any other way. . . .

For Birks and Goff and Jones, however, the receipt of services can constitute a clear example of enrichment; i.e. of the receipt of wealth. Why is this? They have two primary tests of enrichment; incontrovertible benefit and 'free acceptance'. In the context of non-monetary enrichment, incontrovertible benefit is either the anticipation of *necessary* expenditure, or the realization or realizability in money of a benefit.

Necessary expenditure is anticipated where, for instance, the plaintiff pays the defendant's debt to a third party. A non-monetary benefit which does not anticipate a necessary expenditure may nevertheless become 'incontrovertible' by its realization in money, for instance, where the defendant sells property the plaintiff has improved. In certain situations a non-monetary benefit which is realizable in money may be treated as incontrovertible by the adoption of a less subjective view.

The second test of enrichment, free acceptance, is satisfied 'where a recipient knows that a benefit is being offered to him non-gratuitously and where he, having the opportunity to reject, elects to accept'. The person who, seeing a window-cleaner beginning to clean the windows of his house, hangs back unseen till the window-cleaner has finished the job has freely accepted the service and cannot maintain that he does not have to pay for work which he never ordered On this approach showing that a defendant has freely accepted an intervention establishes both that he has been 'enriched' by defeating the possibility of subjective devaluation and that there is a ground for restitution; i.e. that the enrichment is 'unjust'.

The two cases of incontrovertible benefit are not problematic. The 'realization in money' and 'realizability' categories satisfy the exchange-value test by treating as the enrichment, i.e. as wealth, not the pure service itself but its product. Interventions in anticipation or avoidance of necessary expenditure . . . also satisfy the exchange-value test. This is clearly so where the plaintiff pays the defendant's debt to a third party and it may also be so even where the intervention is a service rendered, as where the plaintiff clears the defendant's overflowing drains, abating his nuisance. But for the intervention, the defendant's assets ('wealth') would necessarily have been reduced and, as the intervention has prevented this it has enhanced his stock of assets with exchange-value, i.e. his wealth. The one case in which this might not be so is where the defendant would have abated the nuisance by his own labour and, in this case, it is arguable that the test of anticipation of necessary *expenditure* is not satisfied. Cases on the wrongful use of the property of another also satisfy the 'negative' enrichment aspect if the use of the property is necessary to the defendant's enterprise.[1]

---

1 Getting coal to the surface as on the facts of *Phillips v Homfray* (1883) 24 Ch D 439 or getting one's luggage from Scarborough to Whitby as in *Rumsey v NE Ry.* (1863) 14 CB (NS) 641.

It should be noted that the exchange value test would not be satisfied by loose use of the word 'necessary', for instance to include expenditure which the defendant *might* have incurred.

So far, therefore, the treatment of enrichment is consistent with the exchange-value test. The difficulty arises with the second test of enrichment: 'free acceptance'. This test establishes that there is an enrichment (a benefit, a receipt of wealth) by reference to the consent or acquiescence of the defendant to an act of injurious reliance on the part of the plaintiff. There is no concern with the utility of the intervention (i.e. objective benefit) or with its realizability. On this test of enrichment, a pure service would count as an enriching intervention whether or not it results in any physical or human capital in the hands of the recipient. Viewed from the perspective of the renderer of services and prospectively, it may be plausible to argue that the ability to render service has exchange value. Physicians, lawyers, and other professionals can after all agree to exchange their services for payment and are (subject to professional etiquette) free to refuse to do so. Arguably this is what Birks does. In the discussion of positive and negative enrichment he states that 'saving man's dignity, his work is the user or enjoyment obtainable from him over time. It is referred to as his 'time' and he 'markets' his time (time in himself) just as he hires out time in his corporeal property'.[2] But to look at the matter this way is in effect to make the opportunity-loss of the unrequested renderer of services the source of the obligation whereas the hallmark of a restitution-ary claim is the gain to the receiver. Viewed from the perspective of the receiver of the service (the patient or the client) and retrospectively there is no question of pure service satisfying the exchange-value test.

It is clear that a person who has rendered services requested, accepted, or acquiesced in by the defendant is entitled to recompense whether or not the defendant gained from the services. Thus, recompense has been given in respect of plans prepared in the anticipation of the conclusion of a contract by a developer but rendered useless when the landowner decided not to proceed.[3] Recompense has also been given in *Brewer Street Investments v Barclays Woollen Co. Ltd*, in respect of alterations to property effected by the owner at the request of prospective tenants when the negotiations for a lease broke down.[4] This case is particularly striking since the work was done on the *plaintiff's* property. The basis of the obligation in these cases is the request or representation and the consequent (or induced) reliance. The same reasoning is used even where the services do lead to an increase in the defendant's assets. Thus, in *British Steel Corporation v Cleveland Bridge & Engineering Co. Ltd*,[5] where BSC manufactured and delivered cast-steel nodes to Cleveland pursuant to a letter of intent but in anticipation of a contract, the basis of the obligation was said to be Cleveland's *request* that BSC undertake the work and BSC's consequent *compliance* with that request, rather than the receipt and use of the nodes by Cleveland. These cases are all seen by Birks as examples of unjust enrichment by free acceptance. The irrelevance of the exchange-value test in these cases is also illustrated by *Planché v Colburn*, a case which uses identical reasoning but which is classified by Birks as enrichment by reason of 'limited' as opposed to 'free' acceptance.[6] In *Planché v Colburn* an author had contracted to write a book on Costume and Ancient Armour for The Juvenile Library, a series to be published by the defendant. The series was abandoned after the plaintiff had started to work and the publisher was obliged to recompense him by a *quantum meruit* for the

---

2 129. See also Endnote 3 to paperback edition, 451.

3 *Sabemo v North Sydney Municipal Council* (1977) 2 NSWLR 880. *William Lacey (Hounslow) Ltd v Davis* [1957] 2 All ER 712 is another example although not unequivocally so because the defendant did use the estimates prepared by the plaintiff-builder in negotiating for compensation from the War Damage Commission. But this does not appear to have played a part in the decision, see 719.

4 [1953] 2 All ER 1330 (CA). In fact only Denning LJ based his judgement on restitution, but the case is seen by Birks as an example of 'free acceptance', 283–4.

5 [1984] 1 All ER 504.   6 (1831) 8 Bing 14.

work he had done, even though the manuscript had not been completed or tendered. These cases are concerned with 'consent', 'acquiescence', 'reliance', 'fault', and 'risk' rather than 'enrichment' or 'benefit'.

. . .

[In conclusion] it has been argued [in this essay] that the concept of 'enrichment' or 'benefit' by free acceptance developed by Birks and goff and Jones is overinclusive. The consequent lack of conceptual purity and functional homogeneity leads either to inappropriate rules or to the development of fictions. These might be tolerated on a subjective view of contractual consent and in the absence of a developed principle of injurious reliance. But England law does not have a subjective view of contract and is increasingly recognizing the principle of injurious reliance.

The issue is not therefore whether relief should or should not be granted but what is the appropriate basis for that relief. Those who argue for a category of enrichment which includes pure services need to explain the inadequacies of reliance as a basis. For once reliance is recognized we should not permit an overinclusive concept of 'unjust enrichment' to marginalize it; just as we should not allow the imperial claims of the reliance principle to marginalize unjust enrichment. Another consequence of treating freely accepted services as 'enrichment' is that the distinction between independent and dependent claims becomes very difficult to sustain. It is submitted that the exchange-value test of enrichment is a theoretically attractive and practical method of identifying the ambit of the principle of unjust enrichment and, that freely accepted pure services do not satisfy it. Birks and Goff and Jones should therefore give up a small part of the territory they claim for the principle of unjust enrichment and accord more recognition to the principle of injurious reliance.

In the following extract, Birks strongly defends 'free acceptance' as a test of benefit against its critics. (Cf. below, 392 where it is explained that, in contrast to his continued belief that it was a valid test of benefit, Birks ultimately conceded that free acceptance was not an unjust factor.)

- P. Birks, 'In Defence of Free Acceptance' in Burrows (ed.) *Essays on the Law of Restitution* (1991), 127–35, 137–41.

ESTABLISHING THE ENRICHMENT

This is as difficult as it is important. It may be best to start with some secure propositions.

1 Six Uncontentious Propositions

(1) If the receipt by the defendant is a receipt of value expressible in money—a *valuable* benefit, in the language of section 1(3) of the Law Reform (Frustrated Contracts) Act, 1943—the causes of action which entitle the plaintiff to restitution in respect of money must support the same entitlement when the value is received in a form other than money.

(2) In the case of a non-money receipt it is not easy to establish that the recipient has obtained a valuable benefit.

(3) The source of that additional difficulty is the subjectivity of value, meaning by that the fact that different people value different things differently according to their own tastes and priorities.

(4) Notwithstanding that difficulty, in some circumstances a court can reach the conclusion, even in the extreme case in which the recipient had no knowledge that the benefit was being conferred, that the recipient did receive an incontrovertibly valuable benefit, as for instance where it would be wholly unrealistic to deny that, had the plaintiff not furnished it, the recipient would have laid out money to secure it, or where, whether he would have done so or not, its value was realizable in money and he has so realized it.

(5) A legal system might decide to override the difficulty arising from the subjectivity of value by peremptorily insisting that the question be decided—even, that is, in cases where the receipt is not incontrovertibly valuable—by reference to the market.

(6) The common law has not opted for that peremptory strategy.

2. Six More Propositions: How Free Acceptance Works

Where what was received was not incontrovertibly valuable, in what circumstances will the common law hold that it was nevertheless a valuable benefit? The general answer is, wherever the benefit has an objective (i.e. market) value *and* for some reason the recipient cannot evade that objective valuation by an appeal to the argument from the subjectivity of value (in shorthand, he cannot subjectively devalue). Here we are only concerned with the thesis that one case where the recipient cannot subjectively devalue is that in which he has freely accepted. Just as, in relation to the unjust factor, the phrase 'free acceptance' can only be given meaning in the light of the larger question whether in all the circumstances the defendant's receipt was unconscientious, so here, in relation to the issue of enrichment, its meaning is determined by the larger question whether the court could in all the circumstances reasonably allow the defendant to resort to subjective devaluation. So far as the word 'unconscientious' can be used in both cases, the question *quoad* the unjust factor is whether in the given circumstances it was unconscientious to receive; *quoad* the issue of enrichment it is whether it would be unconscientious to resort to subjective devaluation.

Both Burrows and, even more emphatically, Garner take the view that the law's commitment to the subjectivity of value is such that a valuation in money is only possible if the recipient has manifested a positive desire to have the thing in question at a money price. Burrows observes that the inference from the facts of free acceptance falls short of this. Often one could infer no more than that the recipient did not care whether the work was done or not. Garner calls this 'the indifference argument'. Burrows insists on a request as the foundation for an inference that the recipient wanted and bargained for the benefit, while Garner says, more explicitly, that the plaintiff must show that the defendant wanted the thing, was willing to pay for it, and attached immediate priority to getting it. Both defer to people's freedom of economic choice more than is reasonably required for that freedom to be amply protected. The six propositions which follow seek to secure a less extreme position.

(1) Free acceptance never indicates that the recipient does value the thing in question, much less values it at a particular sum of money.

(2) A free acceptance only settles the enrichment issue by interposing an obstacle to the argument from the subjectivity of value, with the effect that the freely accepting recipient must acknowledge the objective valuation of the benefit.

The first of these propositions accepts the initial step in 'the indifference argument'. The second denies that the inference of indifference leaves the recipient free to evade the market valuation. Indifferent or not, the freely accepting party may be unconscientious in subsequently appealing to the subjectivity of value.

(3) Automatic market valuation of the freely accepted benefit is qualified to the extent that the free acceptance was itself qualified. For example, where a defendant accepted in the belief that the thing with a market value of £20 was being offered at £10, the valuation cannot exceed £10.

This is not a true exception to the previous proposition, the truth being that in such circumstances it is not unconscientious in the defendant to appeal to subjective devaluation to defeat any valuation above £10. A defendant who accepts in the belief that the thing is offered as a gift will not be barred from subjective devaluation. A defendant who accepts believing the price of the thing is £10 will not be barred in respect of any sum by which the market valuation exceeds £10. This can create the illusion that acceptance operates other than as an obstacle to the attempt to evade the market valuation.

(4) When the argument from the subjectivity of value (subjective devaluation) is available, it does not consist in an appeal to and proof of the tastes and priorities of the particular recipient but, on the contrary, only requires the recipient to show he made no choice to receive the benefit: 'I did not choose this.' Even hypotheses as to what might have been the tastes and priorities of the recipient are strictly speaking superfluous.

(5) The recipient's argument is none the less called 'subjective devaluation' because, if someone were to ask why it mattered whether he chose or not, the explanation would be in terms of the subjectivity of value. The argument derives its force from the need to protect people generally from the danger implicit in obligatory market valuation, namely that their choices will be dictated to them by their being made to pay for what they themselves do not value.

These two propositions vigorously protect freedom of economic choice. For a party who can conscientiously make the 'I did not choose it' argument thereby evades the market valuation. *Vis-à-vis* those whose appeal to that argument would be unconscientious, the law has no reason to deny the objective value of the benefit for which the other seeks to be paid.

(6) A system which, to defend freedom of choice, does accept the possibility of subjective devaluation, and correspondingly does not peremptorily impose objective (market) valuation where subjective devaluation is possible, is bound to produce conclusions which will be very surprising to some or even most people.

In the present state of the debate about the issue of enrichment, this sixth proposition is especially important. The startling nature of some of the results easily distracts the observer from the strength of the logic by which they are dictated. In the eye of a beholder who does subscribe to the demand which creates the market for, say, garages, a conclusion that a garage is not valuable will seem perverse. Yet such a conclusion will be reached where the defendant can and does evade the objective valuation by appeal to the subjectivity of value. And one who does not subscribe to the market in fur-styling for poodles will be affronted in the contrary case. It was no doubt in response to the startling nature of some results that Deane, J., recently coined the phrase 'constructive enrichment'.[1] The word 'constructive' has an awkward history in this subject and implies 'deemed' or 'fictitious'. Rather than distinguish between actual and constructive, it would be better, while distinguishing money or money's worth, to give a warning that, as the market itself proves, conclusions as to money's worth will reflect the diversity of people's tastes.

Suppose that a woman returns from abroad to find that a garage has been built beside her house. Let it be given that it has not been built by her spouse. If it had been our example would be located in a statutory exception to the normal deference to subjectivity of value.[2] Suppose the woman's neighbour built it, either thinking the land was his or that the woman would let him have it. Let it also be true that the garage cost £2,000 to build and that the land is now worth £3,000 more on the market than it was without the garage. Is the woman enriched? It would be very difficult to hold that a garage was an incontrovertibly valuable benefit, since very many people with means and space for a garage prefer to have a greenhouse or leave things as they are and use their buying-power to take holidays abroad. So this woman is not enriched. She uses the garage. That changes nothing. 'One

---

1 *Foran v White* (1989) 64 ALJR 1, 24 E.

2 Matrimonial Proceedings and Property Act, 1970, s. 37. The improving spouse acquires an interest without regard to the other's wishes. The trust for sale effects *ipso iure* a notional, and perhaps ultimately actual, realization in money.

man cleans another's shoes, what can the other do but put them on?'[3] Privately she is delighted to have the garage, and it is the case that she might very well have decided to pay for one to be built. Subject to one hitherto unexplored argument which we cannot pursue,[4] that makes no difference either. All she has to show (it not being incontrovertibly valuable) is that in fact she made no choice to have it. She might have wanted to use her money differently. The hypothetical 'might' protects everyone's liberty to arrange priorities according to taste. But the objection will be made that she has an asset which can be sold for more. That too is irrelevant (unless she voluntarily chooses to realize the asset and the excess attributable to the £2,000 input is still identifiable when she does so). She cannot be forced to realize the asset. She might—again merely hypothetically—be fond of the house for non-economic reasons. Once more the hypothetical nature of the observation protects the freedom of choice of all of us. The conclusion is that this woman, returning from abroad and presented with a new garage, has not received a valuable benefit. We were warned by our sixth proposition to expect startling conclusions.

Suppose now that the same woman comes back early and sees the work beginning. Knowing what mistake or misprediction the neighbour has made she decides to withdraw to her country cottage until the work is finished, so as to be able to take advantage of it under the doctrines in the preceding paragraph. She returns when the garage is finished. This time she is enriched. The reason is that she cannot conscientiously assert, 'Oh, but I did not choose to have this garage built'. She had her opportunity to say so earlier. It is not that her neglect of that opportunity affirmatively indicates that she attached value to the garage; it merely makes it impossible for her to get to her appeal to the subjectivity of value. It would be outrageous in the circumstances if she were allowed to evade objective valuation by calling for a defence of the right to freedom of economic choice.

It would be tedious to work through another example in fine detail. In brief therefore, suppose that in a *William Lacey* situation[5] the pre-contractual work were the demolition of a building or the guarding of a store or the playing of a violin. These are chosen as labours which leave no end-product. To this type of 'pure service' we shall later return. It needs to be said here . . . that there is nothing in the logic of the propositions enunciated above which excludes such services from the category of enrichment. This is true even if the service immediately redounds to the benefit of a third party, as for instance where the imperfect contract is for demolition of a building on land owned by a third party. I am negotiating a contract under which you will play before an audience of which I will not form part. You do give that concert, but your agent and I had in fact never agreed your fee. There is a market for this labour. I cannot evade that market's valuation, since I cannot in these circumstances say, 'Oh, but I did not choose to have you play.' Clearly I did. Situations of this kind contain special problems, to which we will return.

3. Pure Services: Beatson's Objection

In Beatson's view most of the assertions in the preceding subsection fail *in limine* because, except in very limited circumstances, a service cannot be an enrichment. His position differs from that of both Burrows and Garner in that he thinks that what he calls 'pure services' only qualify as enrichments if and so far as they anticipate necessary expenditure. In short not even a request made with appropriate knowledge and intent will save them.

---

3 *Taylor v Laird*, (1856) 25 LJ Ex 329.

4 There might be a subjective version of incontrovertible value. Cf. Garner's concept of 'subjective revaluation'. . . . In cases of incontrovertible value it is unconscientious to appeal to freedom of choice because it is for practical purposes certain that people so placed would have incurred the expenditure in question. The untested argument would seek to add that it is similarly unconscientious to appeal to freedom of choice when you yourself, given your own tastes and priorities, would have chosen to incur the expenditure if you had had the opportunity to choose.

5 [*William Lacey (Hounslow) Ltd v Davis* [1957] 1 WLR 932 is set out at 333 below.]

Having made a sensitive and acute analysis of the nature of enrichment, Beatson concludes that work, as opposed to its end-product, can only qualify as an enrichment if it satisfies the 'exchange-value' test, which is only passed if it leaves the recipient directly or indirectly with more money than he would otherwise have. Since work (as opposed to its end-product, if there is one) is in itself evanescent, it cannot satisfy that test other than negatively. A pure service—that is to say, a service which leaves no end-product—can only be an enrichment if it saves money which would otherwise have been laid out. That is, the service passes the exchange-value test by saving expenditure of money (negatively, because of money not expended) rather than positively by adding money or money's worth to the defendant's stock of wealth: 'Interventions in anticipation or avoidance of necessary expenditure, termed "negative enrichments" . . . satisfy the exchange-value test.' On the other hand, to count a pure service as an enrichment on the basis of free acceptance is artificial and 'overinclusive': 'The difficulty arises with the second test of enrichment: "free acceptance." . . . On this test . . . a pure service would count as an enriching intervention whether or not it results in any physical or human capital [i.e. any end-product] in the hands of the recipient. Viewed from the perspective of the renderer of services and prospectively, it may be plausible to argue that the ability to render service has exchange value. . . . Viewed from the perspective of the receiver of the service (the patient or the client) and retrospectively, there is no question of pure service satisfying the exchange-value.'

Common sense, not always a reliable guide, says this must be wrong. It means that many of the things we all pay money for—the products of service industries as opposed to manufacturing industries—are at one stroke almost completely excluded from the law of unjust enrichment on the ground that they can hardly ever confer an enrichment equivalent to payment of money. This comes very close to affirming, if it does not actually do so, that though we all pay money for them they are very rarely 'money's worth'. The exceptional case is that in which they are necessary, in the sense that we have no realistic choice whether or not to lay out money on them, for then we are enriched by the amount of money we would have laid out but have not. Not never, therefore, but hardly ever. The VAT man, however, thinks on common-sense lines, for all those who charge fees for making music, giving lectures, hiring out halls, washing clothes, and so on, have to pay the value added tax. It cannot be that these are not valuable services, services the receipt of which counts as value received. On the other hand, Beatson's case is carefully argued, and no fallacy lies patient.

There is none the less a false step. It consists in assuming that the exchange-value test is only negatively satisfied in the case of services which are judged incontrovertibly valuable on the ground that they anticipate necessary expenditure. Test it by this example. A company offers a round-the-world holiday as a prize for a simple competition. The holiday is advertised as 'worth £10,000'. It is true that, booked through a travel agent in the ordinary way, that is what it would cost. Friends of the woman who wins, sharing her excitement, allow themselves to suggest that she is better off by £10,000. Wary of the attendant obligations, she puts the figure at more like £3,000, that being the cost of the holiday she would otherwise have taken. This difference of opinion implicitly accepts Beatson's exchange-value test of enrichment. The measure by which the winner is better off is put by one side at the market value—the sum which would have had to be paid across a travel agent's counter. The measure used by the winner is the amount she would have spent if she had been choosing her own trip. Neither is determined by a standard of incontrovertible value. Let us suppose that a court would hold that no reasonable person would deny that a woman in the winner's circumstances would have spent £1,000 on an annual holiday. Here £10,000 is the objective market value; £3,000 is value as ordered by the particular person's priorities; £1,000 is the value determined as incontrovertible benefit.

This example shows that, if the law were to adopt a rigid and invariable objective standard (market value in all cases), all services with a market value would satisfy the exchange-value test. The law will in fact adopt that objective valuation provided an appeal to subjective devaluation is barred. Free acceptance does bar that argument. It follows that where a benefit is freely accepted, so that the market valuation applies, the exchange-value test is passed.

A much shorter version of this proof: the proposition that a service has negative exchange-value asserts only that it has a money value; it has a money value if there is a demand for it on the market; that money value on the market is the measure of the recipient's enrichment in every case, unless the recipient can evade it by subjective devaluation.

If this were wrong, the problems would not be confined to services as conventionally understood. A four-star restaurant works to produce an ephemeral end-product. But the diners in the restaurant are not to be distinguished from the people in the concert hall across the street. Again, a newspaper is not valued for its durable end-product, twenty sheets of paper, but for the ephemeral consumable which it bears, the news while new. In *Weatherby v Banham*[6] where the plaintiff had mistakenly sent issues of *The Racing Calendar* to the defendant, the defendant barred himself from subjective devaluation by freely accepting, but the market value which he thereby became unable to evade was not the value of the paper but the price to the public of the ephemeral racing news—that is, the price at which new issues were sold. Even money can become problematical, easily lost or rashly spent.

It is only when the claim is made in the second measure of restitution that there is any inquiry into what the plaintiff still holds. The first measure of restitution is concerned with the enrichment received, not the enrichment retained.[7] Two propositions are important. On the one hand a service with a fleeting end-product or none at all—a song, a meal, or prospecting for gold—can all be enrichments for the purpose of such claims. And even where there is an endproduct—a gold-field discovered—in first-measure claims it is the value of the work which ultimately counts. The discovery of a gold-field on my land, however it may be enriching, is not an enrichment at the prospectors' expense save by the amount of their input. And films dubbed to tap the market in another country are likewise enrichments of their owner at the expense of the dubber only to the value of the dubber's work.

Finally, *BP Exploration Co. (Libya) Ltd v Hunt (No 2)*[8] is, as Beatson admits, difficult for his position. In that case the exploration work on which the plaintiffs had embarked in the Libyan desert had been crowned with success before the frustration of their contract with Hunt. It was in their interest that the ceiling below which the court might award a just sum by way of restitution be constituted by the end-product (the enormously enhanced value of the right to drill for oil once oil had been found and had begun to flow) rather than by the work of finding and developing the field. If there is to be a ceiling, one obviously wants it as high as possible. Given the richness of the Libyan oilfield, the ceiling set by the end-product would be so high as never to depress any likely measure of recovery. Robert Goff, J., acceded to B.P.'s argument: in an appropriate case, the Act did require the court to treat the end-product as the ceiling. Beatson says, 'The difficulty I face is that he [Robert Goff, J.] would have preferred the legislature to have treated the services themselves as the benefit.' The difficulty is more formidable. Robert Goff, J., only held that, where a service does leave the other with an end-product, the Act 'in an appropriate case' requires the court to take the end-product rather than the service itself as the ceiling. The judgment unequivocally favours the view that in other cases, even as the Act now stands, pure services such as transport of goods can be regarded as the enrichment to be valued as the ceiling for the award.

---

6 (1832) 5 Car & P 228.
7 For this distinction in more detail, Birks, *Introduction*, 75–7, 358.
8 [1979] 1 WLR 783.

4. Special Problems

. . .

Receiving Part of an Entire Performance This subsection concerns only the special problem of part performance of a unit of work due under a contract. Here *Planché v Colburn*[9] has caused unnecessary trouble, for much the same reason as the window cleaner—because, that is, it is an insecure example of that which it has been used to illustrate. It is essential to begin by observing the importance of a preliminary issue of construction.

When a contract is terminated by frustration or breach by either side and it happens that a party who expected to be paid, had all gone well, has already, to use as neutral a phrase as possible, done something referable to that contract, that something may be of one of two kinds. It may be part of the contractual performance. Or it may be preliminary or ancillary to the performance. One who pays a pianist to play a sonata at a private function will not usually think of the pianist's time and money spent travelling to the venue as being part of the contractual performance rather than preliminary to it; but, if the pianist has played two movements of the sonata when a bomb scare puts an end to the concert, that will certainly count as part of the contractual performance. Similarly with a contract to build. Laying the foundations is part performance, but transporting the workforce to the site each day is ancillary.

It will require an exercise of construction in each case to determine what counts as part performance and what as expenditure in or for performance of the contract. Work which is *dehors* the contractual performance cannot be regarded as done for the paying party. A building company which transports its workers to the site is more accurately seen as providing a service for itself, albeit because it wants to perform the contract with the paying party.

The common-sense impression is that an incomplete performance, building three-quarters of the house or playing two movements of the sonata, is a valuable benefit to the recipient, even though he only promised to pay for a whole house or complete concert. That does not means, of course, that a fractional performance measured by, say, volume or duration should be counted conferring exactly the same fraction of value; on the contrary, a three-quarter performance will generally be worth much less than 75 per cent of the value of the completed project. Can this impression be substantiated?

There is unlikely to be room for a finding of incontrovertible value, since only special circumstances will ever serve to show that the work was such that the recipient must needs have ordered it elsewhere if it had not been done by the plaintiff.[10] Nor in this kind of situation can it be shown that the defendant expressly manifested any intent to have anything less than the full performance. Garner, who takes a more extreme view even than Burrows of the way in which subjective devaluation works, therefore argues that a part performance can hardly ever be an enrichment, because the very fact that what the defendant has received is not what he asked for means that none of the three *probanda* can be established: that he actually wanted it, was willing to pay for it, and regarded that expenditure as an immediate priority. From this general negative, Garner can only except the case in which the recipient, having asked for the whole performance and received part, goes in and finishes it himself.

The principal argument against this position is to be found in the attempted refutation above of the super-subjective interpretation of the way in which free acceptance and subjective devaluation work. However, Burrows, somewhat surprisingly in view of his basic position, affirms that there is enrichment in these part performance cases because the initial 'bargain' for the whole performance supports a presumption that the recipient regards himself as benefited by the part. The customer is

---

9 (1831) 8 Bing 14.

10 If the party to pay was a property development company and the incomplete house was to have been sold in the course of business, the contrary finding might be possible.

enriched because he has shown by his 'bargain' that he would have laid out that money anyhow. It is worth setting out his statement of principles:

> Otherwise [sc. outside, incontrovertibly valuable benefits] the most important principle is that a defendant can be regarded as negatively benefited where the plaintiff performs what the defendant contracted or bargained for. . . . The reasoning behind this 'bargained-for' principle of benefit is that where the defendant has 'promised' to pay for a particular performance, the outward appearance is that he regards the performance as beneficial or, put in an alternative way, that he has been saved expense that he would otherwise have been willing to incur. By the same token even if the defendant receives only part of what he had bargained for, it can be presumed that he regards himself as benefited by what he has received and that he has been saved part of the expense that he would otherwise have incurred.[11]

Though Burrows denies the sufficiency of free acceptance without request, within the terms of his own request-based doctrine this is not in fact much different from my infelicitous 'limited acceptance'.[12] The idea behind that label was that there is in these cases a sufficient acceptance of the part-performance to bar recourse to subjective devaluation even though it would be difficult to say that there was an acceptance from which you could spell out any unjust factor. That is, the acceptance in these cases is not such as to indicate an unconscientious receipt. On the other hand, if the unjust factor is . . . supplied by failure of consideration, the acceptance in these cases is sufficient to bar subjective devaluation.

Where the part performance is one which can be and has been completed by the recipient, this approach is easily applied.[13] It is also easy to apply where the defendant has prevented the plaintiff from completing or rectifying the incomplete performance.[14] Where the performance has not been completed or prevented, typically in cases therefore in which the contract has been frustrated or terminated for the plaintiff's own breach, it is less obvious that recourse to subjective devaluation is barred. It is crucial to recall at this point that a decision in favour of the plaintiff on this enrichment issue does not in itself satisfy all the conditions for restitution. Bearing that in mind and thus isolating the enrichment question, it is easier to conclude that one who has asked for a whole house to be built cannot conscientiously say that three-quarters of a house should be regarded as valueless to him because he never chose to have it. In other words, the plaintiff builder in *Sumpter v Hedges*[15] should not be regarded as having lost on the ground that the defendant was not enriched.

Planché v Colburn is exceptionally difficult. The plaintiff had worked on the writing of a book which the defendant had contracted to pay for. The defendant had then repudiated, without ever receiving the manuscript. The plaintiff was allowed a *quantum meruit*. Beatson, Burrows, and Garner, and even Jones,[16] say that this cannot be regarded as a claim based on the enrichment of the defendant.

This depends first on the exercise of construction which decides whether the plaintiff conferred part of the contractual performance or merely put himself to preparatory trouble and expense. If the latter, Plancé worked for himself, not for the defendant, and on no test could the defendant be said to have been enriched. Further, if that was the right construction, the plaintiff could not possibly have brought his *assumpsit* for *quantum meruit*; his only remedy would have been damages.

On the other hand, if the right construction was that Colburn commissioned not merely the book

---

11 (1988) 104 *LQR* 576, 582–3.

12 Cf. Birks, *Introduction*, 126–7, 132.   13 As in *Lodder v Slowey* [1904] AC 442.

14 Subject to the observations below on the issue of construction, *Planché v Colburn* (1831) 8 Bing 14 can be so explained. More clearly, *De Bernardy v Harding* (1853) 8 Ex. 822; *Horton v Jones* (1934) 34 SR (NSW) 359. *Steele v Tardiani* (1946) 72 CLR 386 is in the same family, despite the breach on the side of the claimant.

15 [See below 298.]

16 G Jones, 'Claims Arising out of Anticipated Contracts Which Do Not Materialize' (1980) 18 *UW Ontario LR*, 447, 458.

but the work of researching and writing the book, the objection to the analysis of the decision as based on enrichment must be grounded on either (1) surprise of the kind warned against above, which the analyst simply has to overcome unless and until the law takes a fundamentally different approach to enrichment, or (2) rejection of the proposition, just discussed, that one who receives part of a contractual performance is not able to appeal to the argument from subjective devaluation, above all not when he has himself prevented completion. Neither (1) nor (2) is a tenable ground for denying enrichment. The jurist who, while accepting the construction that what Planché did was indeed part of what Colburn asked for, does nevertheless deny that Colburn was enriched, will find the form of the action unobjectionable. But the claim, assuming it still succeeds, will not then be based on unjust enrichment and cannot be described as restitutionary.

(3) UNJUST SACRIFICE

Stoljar and Muir (see, similarly, Beatson, above, 90) have argued that, because of the difficulty of establishing that the defendant is benefited by unsolicited services, a principle of unjust sacrifice is a better explanation of unsolicited services cases than is the principle against unjust enrichment.

• S Stoljar, 'Unjust Enrichment and Unjust Sacrifice' (1987) 50 *MLR* 603

We turn to situations for which unjust enrichment is neither a comfortable, nor even an acceptable niche. These are situations of unsolicited services by A to B, that is, services so wholly unrequested as to fall outside any sort of implied contract or implied authority, yet services for which A may nevertheless make a claim for reward or recompense. Civil law knows this as *negotiorum gestio*, a not inconsiderable if complicated area. . . . Anglo-American law, as everyone knows, has however been quite dismissive about such claims, at any rate on the face of things, with unsolicited services being generally regarded as officious, as offered by an intermeddler or volunteer, and hence beyond reward. Thus the Restatement of Restitution, after stating one 'underlying principle' to the effect that a person unjustly enriched at the expense of another is required to make restitution to the other, immediately adds that a person officiously conferring a benefit upon another is not entitled to restitution thereof, a qualification which indeed expresses a countervailing principle of justice according to which an officious enrichment cannot be regarded as unjust.[1]

Still it is not true that all unsolicited services are necessarily officious, nor the case that the common law rejects all such claims. Of the three main items usually included in the civilian *negotiorum gestio*, i.e. payment of another's debt, supply of necessaries, and preservation of another's property,[2] the common law, too, admits claims for the supply of necessaries (claims against a breadwinner defaulting in the support of his family), although it has consistently refused to allow claims by an unsolicited payor of another's debt or by an unsolicited preserver of another's property, however urgent the payment or necessary the preservation. A few exceptions exist even here. The payment of another's debt does give rise to a claim for reimbursement if the payment was made under compulsion, under the doctrine of *Exall v Partridge*,[3] i.e. where the payor only intervenes to save his own property from distress. However a payor recovers nothing if the payment is intended to help the defendant rather than himself, even if the defendant is thereby enriched on account of saving his own money owed to the creditor. The law also recognises a claim for preserving another's property if

---

1 See *Restatement*, ss. 1 and 2 and Comments thereto.
2 The civil law also includes claims for the rescue of another where the rescuer in injured or dies; but this may be omitted for present purposes.
3 (1799) 8 TR 308.

the claim is one for maritime salvage and (this fully only in American law) for finding and keeping property an owner has lost. But, so far, the common law has not gone further than this.

It can well be argued that some of the older cases denying reward were wrongly analysed, or that the notion of officiousness was taken much too strictly, or that some newer cases in fact support a new approach, or that salvage might still be extended to non-maritime situations, and so on. But we need not pursue this now since, for present purposes, it suffices to confine ourselves to the supply of necessaries, claims which the common law does admit and which furnish a good enough instance of unsolicited services being legally recognised. It may be said that this recognition is not really surprising, given that such supplies cannot be regarded as officious services. But the same can of course be said of urgent payments of another's debt or of necessary acts of preservation of another's property, although the law still continues to reject claims of reimbursement in either case. However this may be, our more crucial point now is that any claim for unsolicited services, even one for the supply of necessaries, is a claim of quite different character compared with the actions [for the restitution of money].

In a claim for money paid by mistake, for example, there can be restitution on clear proprietary grounds, provided the defendant's position has not changed. In a claim for unsolicited services, on the other hand, the claim is for reimbursement or recompense for services voluntarily or deliberately done by A for B, albeit without B's knowledge and authority. Hence what A now seeks is not restitution *of* some thing or money retained by B, but recompense *for* services rendered, for his sacrifice of time, effort and expense on behalf of B. It follows that while in an 'ordinary' quasi-contractual claim (as for payment by mistake), the restitution of the money merely restores the parties' *status quo ante*, as B merely surrenders money which is not his but A's, in a claim for recompense for services, B has nothing to restore, for services cannot be restored: thus B must pay on the claim out of his own pocket, which further means that B becomes exposed to a new financial liability just as though he had hired A's services. This is one reason why civil law often treats *negotiorum gestio* as a sort of extended agency.

This is not all. As regards services, B, the defendant, does not even have to be enriched to be liable to reward. Suppose A medically attends to B's child injured in an accident, but the child dies. There is an American precedent for saying that A, as a doctor, can recover his usual fee, even if B cannot be said to have been enriched.[4] To say he is enriched would not only be odd, it would not be very relevant. For A's recompense is calculated by the normal worth of *his* services or supplies, not by their actual benefit to B. So while, to repeat, in ordinary quasicontract, recovery ceases at the point of B's change of position, or at the point of B's having to pay his own money rather than paying back what is A's, in *negotiorum gestio*-style restitution, recovery takes place in spite of B's position being changed inasmuch as B can only reimburse or recompense with his own money, for here B has no money to give back. This, too, explains why A's claims have to be kept within strict bounds; his services must at all times be urgent and necessary, for unless they are B's position and autonomy could be too easily— indeed 'officiously'—altered by A.

The upshot is that we then have two sorts of claims: restitution of money and restitution for services, each resting on considerations rather special to itself. If the former claim raises questions of unjust enrichment, but in a proprietary way that separates its causes of action from those booked by contract, tort or trust, the gestor's claim (for reward) does not necessarily concern unjust enrichment, for the simple reason that no enrichment need occur. Again, where the former sort of restitution necessarily gives the plaintiff a claim for his money, if though only if the defendant is in fact enriched, the second kind of restitution calls for special safeguards, even where the defendant is actually enriched, for the question is no longer whether B is enriched, but whether A's services, though

---

4 Cf *Cotnam v Wisdom* (1907) 32 Ark 601.

unsolicited, are nevertheless manifestly necessary or urgent or useful for B so as to escape any charge of officiousness.

As regards unsolicited services, it is therefore clear, a proprietary theory cannot really help; nonetheless proprietary considerations, in a wider sense, need not be completely absent. To say that A as gestor has a right to reward is but to say that the law will not let him sacrifice his time, effort or money performing services for another, unsolicited though these services are. For such services, though rendered kindly, are nonetheless not given *animo donandi*; even if rendered for urgent and useful purposes, they are also given in the expectation that they will be paid, simply because they are not the sort of services we give as gifts, involving as they often do considerable expense and effort which most of us cannot afford to give away without being reimbursed. In the final analysis, therefore, *negotiorum gestio*, even in its so far sparse common law manifestations, protects a person's labour, protecting it as though it were his property—it is work or labour which, if unrewarded, would constitute an unjust sacrifice by A. So we may, if we wish, speak again of a proprietary theory, although 'property' now has an obviously different sense, since property nwo means not a right to things or money, but a right in respect of work, or work done seen as an asset to be protected. Still, whether or not we call this property is perhaps not very important. What nevertheless is important is the more basic realisation that in dealing with quasi-contract or restitution we are dealing not with one but with what are virtually two subjects—closely related certainly, yet each responding to considerations which significantly diverge.

- **G Muir, 'Unjust Sacrifice and the Officious Intervener' in Finn (ed.), *Essays on Restitution* (1990), 297, 301–2, 305–6, 308, 350–1**

A defendant is unjustly enriched when the plaintiff confers a benefit upon him which in the circumstances it is unjust for him to retain. A plaintiff makes an unjust sacrifice when he expends time or effort for the benefit of the defendant in circumstances in which the defendant should be obliged to pay the plaintiff for his intervention. With an unjust enrichment claim, benefit is the gist of the action, and the appropriate remedy is disgorgement. In an unjust sacrifice claim the conferral of a benefit is incidental and should be largely irrelevant to establishing the cause of action.

The unjust sacrifice claim is a paper tiger. The term 'unjust sacrifice' does not appear in one reported case in the common law world. Its synonymic counterpart 'unjust impoverishment' is recorded seven times.[1] The cases discussed in this essay are, however, real enough, but they are squeezed into the unjust enrichment cause of action. To do this, benefit to the defendant is 'discovered' even when it does not exist, and the tensions created by this exercise are not easily disguised.

. . .

There is an entrenched practice of eliding benefit as describing a positive accretion to wealth with benefit denoting a motive for acting, and an equally misleading tendency to cast both legal and economic conceptions of benefit into the same analysis without distinction. In doing this the fundamental nature of the restitution action is, not surprisingly, lost sight of. To prevent this it is submitted that the following uses of the term 'benefit' should be carefully distinguished:

1. An action for the benefit of the defendant. This looks to the motive of the plaintiff in acting. It is usually fatal to the plaintiff's claim that his primary motive was to benefit himself.

---

1 *Federal Power Commission v Hope Natural Gas Co.*, 320 US 591 (1944); *Middle East Banking Co. v State Street Bank International*, 821 F 2d 897 (1987); *United States of America v Algernon Blair Inc*, 479 F 2d 638 (1973); *Cooper v Union Bank*, 507 P 2d 609 (1973); *Louisiana State Mineral Board v Alborado*, 180 So 2d 700 (1965); *Burglass v Finance Funds Group Inc.*, 252 So 2d 498 (1971); *Lucky Homes Inc. v Tarrant Savings Assoc.*, 379 SW 2d 386 (1964).

2. An action which confers a benefit upon the defendant. There is no difficulty with this concept. It is a necessary element in any claim to disgorgement founded upon enrichment. It refers to a transfer of wealth. The transfer may either be directly from the plaintiff to defendant, which is sometimes called a 'subtractive benefit', or it may consist of the defendant intercepting a benefit which flows from a third party and which should rightly have been received by the plaintiff. This benefit could be called an 'intercepted benefit'.

3. An action of benefit to the defendant. This is the most difficult and misleading usage. It encompasses not only the positive enrichment referred to in (2) above, but any intervention which improves, maintains, or minimises the dissipation of the wealth of the defendant. In an economic sense, any expense which the plaintiff incurs is a benefit to the defendant provided the defendant would have himself incurred it given the opportunity, although of course the sum he would have paid for it might be exceedingly small if the intervention denies him an opportunity otherwise open to act himself.

. . . [S]ituations in which an action is a benefit to the defendant without involving the conferral of a benefit upon him require, in the writer's view, a compensatory remedy rather than disgorgement, yet this alleged truism has been largely obscured. The immediate explanation for this is that a residual category of compensation beyond the traditional torts has not yet been recognised.

If disgorgement then is only an appropriate remedy where there has been a positive accretion to wealth, some of the claims for the scope of the unjust enrichment action begin to look suspect. The following are the most significant.

SERVICES AS BENEFITS

Most restitutionary writers regard the performance of services as capable of conferring a benefit upon the recipient of a type susceptible to disgorgement. It might be asked, however, whether this is not fundamentally misconceived. Services may create wealth but they never transfer it. And in most cases services disspipate immediately when measured against the yardstick of value created. Of course if services are performed which the recipient knows the performer intended to be paid for, the appropriate cause of action is in or akin to contract . . .

USE AS BENEFIT

Quasi-contract had common counts for money conferred, property transferred, and services performed, but largely ignored the category of 'property used'. Modern unjust enrichment writers have largely followed this tradition. This is hardly surprising, because use, unlike services, can never involve an indirect increase in the value of the defendant's assets.

SAVING AS INEVITABLE EXPENDITURE

If the plaintiff meets a liability of the defendant, then he has demonstrably conferred no positive benefit upon the defendant, although his action was certainly of benefit. It is easy in these circumstances to explain why the defendant may be required to compensate the plaintiff, but has there been an enrichment? The position of the defendant has not been altered by the payment excepting that the law may now require him to pay the plaintiff rather than the creditor discharged. It is not denied that the saving of an inevitable expenditure may be construed as a positive benefit to the defendant in practical if not logical terms, in order to ensure that substance does not prevail over form, and a wrong is not left unremedied. One must ask, however, of logic should yield to common sense in this way, if a cause of action based on compensation for the defendant was recognised as already available.

. . .

[*Muir then considers the notion of 'incontrovertible benefit' before turning to the question of how one should divide the law of obligations*].

The law of obligations forms the most complex portion of the common law corpus juris, and different analyses to which it may be subject are legion. Traditionally quasi-contract/restitution has been relegated to a miscellany category, suffering a hybrid existence, not an independent branch of obligation, half contract but different from a proper contract. Like the fortunes of Mouton-Rothschild however, the wheel of legal history has turned favourably for quasi-contract, which has now been elevated into a first growth in the law of obligations, an independent body of rules under the appellation of 'unjust enrichment' or 'restitution'. The evolution of unjust enrichment is not, however, complete. Where it has previously expanded it is now suggested it must to some extent contract in order to make room for unjust sacrifice as an independent cause of action.

The miscellany in the law of obligations known as quasi-contract itself contained a miscellany which it is hoped the discussion of benefit has hinted at although not yet fully exposed. This further body of obligations, collected under the rubric of 'unjust sacrifice' or 'unjust impoverishment' is as different from unjust enrichment as tort is from contract. The standard texts of unjust enrichment make no such claims; 'necessity', 'negotiorum gestio', and 'the obligation to reward' all describe obligations which have been contorted to comply with the benefit based model where disgorgement is the appropriate remedy. In fairness, however, there is an evident unease in dealing with these types of reward based obligations, a half-acknowledgment that they are sui generis, but a realisation that unjust enrichment must make something of them if they are not to fall through the cracks between the different branches of the law of obligations.

. . .

With unjust sacrifice, the basis of loss distribution is not conveniently discovered in the action of the defendant who, as can be seen with hindsight, 'should have' done something which he did not. It is in fact very difficult to explain why there is any obligation to reward or compensate an unjust sacrifice and the reality is probably that no one explanation is sufficient. The following are tentative suggestions:

1. The plaintiff should be compensated for loss when he has acted for the benefit of the defendant, and the law wishes to creates incentives to encourage such conduct in the future. Compensation in this category is often known as 'the obligation to reward'.
2. The plaintiff should be compensated for loss where he has not acted officiously in performing services or doing some act which has (knowingly or unknowingly to the defendant) been of benefit to him. In such circumstances the result may be to distribute part of the loss to the defendant by requiring the defendant to compensate the plaintiff to the extent to which he is positively benefited from the plaintiff's action, or to fully compensate the plaintiff whichever is the less.
3. The plaintiff should be compensated for loss where he has acted non-officiously in spending money or time or has suffered some diminution in his own wealth in order to save the defendant an outgoing or loss. Here the defendant should compensate the plaintiff to the extent that he has been saved an outgoing or expenditure himself (in circumstances in which he would have been primarily liable to incur that liability) unless this is greater than the loss suffered by the plaintiff, or, in circumstances in which the loss could have fallen randomly upon either party, to equalise the risk by sharing a proportion of the loss suffered.

Obviously these categories are tentative and there will be some overlaps. For example, the obligation to reward would normally consist of a payment to the plaintiff for his services. In the second category, likewise, the plaintiff will be rewarded for his services. What distinguishes the two categories is first, and most obviously, that the second category has been claimed as part of mainstream unjust enrichment while the first category has been regarded as something of an anomaly. Secondly, the right to compensation is seen as more compelling in category (1) than category (2). Therefore, a reward may be available even if there has been no positive 'benefit' to the defendant, whereas in category (2) the latter must be identified.

In all cases the plaintiff must not have thrust himself officiously upon the defendant, and here there are obvious parallels with the unjust enrichment action. In the categories other than relating to reward, the concept of acting non-officiously is an integral part of the plaintiff's successful claim. In relation to reward it is less important, as the plaintiff will never act officiously where the law wishes to create incentives to encourage such action.

[*Muir goes on, in 41 pages, to discuss, in the light of his theory, the case law in three specific categories: rewarding necessitous intervention, compensating for the non-officious conferral of services, and compensating for the payment of another's debt. He then concludes:*]

We have confined our discussion of unjust sacrifice to three specific categories. Is there any room for further growth? The first point to note is that the action is not a claim for reliance damages in a disguised form. There is no suggestion that the defendant has necessarily acted wrongfully, nor that he should be compensated for the total amount of his loss. Rather we are looking at a judicial solution to problems where loss must be distributed, and no disgorgeable benefit is being conferred. Two examples not previously discussed immediately spring to mind. The first occurs where the defendant makes a representation as to a future course of action which does not in itself give rise to a contract. If he resiles from that representation not knowing that it has already been relied upon the court is faced with the position that as between two innocent parties loss must be distributed. Would it not be possible to formulate an action in unjust sacrifice to compensate the plaintiff for his reasonable loss? The present resort to estoppel in these circumstances provides far less certain remedial guidelines.

The other possibility is misrepresentation, mistake, or frustration under a contract. In these circumstances a contract is abandoned and the court is faced with the claims of two innocent parties and the allocation of loss between them. In the past one remedial response has been to force disgorgement of benefits conferred, and the courts have been far less ready to distribute losses as between the parties. The *Frustrated Contracts Act* 1978 (N.S.W.) indicates that it should not be beyond the imagination of the common law to formulate appropriate rules in these and other circumstances in which not only benefit conferred but loss suffered must be brought into the remedial equation.

NOTES AND QUESTIONS

1. Do you agree with Stoljar and Muir that the law recognizes (or ought to recognize) a principle of unjust sacrifice?

2. If there is a valid legal principle of unjust sacrifice, it is our view that, by definition, it belongs outside the law of unjust enrichment and should be seen as the basis of a fourth major branch of the law of obligations (alongside contract, tort, and unjust enrichment).

(4) TWO PROBLEMATIC CASES

We include here two cases which have been much discussed in academic writings on the 'benefit' issue: *Planché v Colburn* and *Greenwood v Bennett*.

● *Planché v Colburn* (1831) 8 Bing 14, Court of Common Pleas

The claimant was contracted for £100 to write a book on Costume and Ancient Armour for the defendant's 'Juvenile Library' series. After starting the book, but before the claimant tendered any part of it, the claimant terminated the contract for the defendant's repudiatory breach in abandoning publication of the series. The Court of Common Pleas upheld the award to the claimant of £50 (as damages or on a *quantum meruit*).

Tindal CJ: In this case a contract had been entered into for the publication of a work on Costume and Ancient Armour in 'The Juvenile Library'. The considerations by which an author is generally actuated in undertaking to write a work are pecuniary profit and literary reputation. Now, it is clear that the latter may be sacrificed, if an author, who has engaged to write a volume of a popular nature, to be published in a work intended for a juvenile class of readers, should be subject to have his writings published as a separate and distinct work, and therefore liable to be judged of by more severe rules than would be applied to a familiar work intended merely for children. The fact was, that the Defendants not only suspended, but actually put an end to, 'The Juvenile Library;' they had broken their contract with the Plaintiff; and an attempt was made, but quite unsuccessfully, to shew that the Plaintiff had afterwards entered into a new contract to allow them to publish his book as a separate work.

I agree that, when a special contract is in existence and open, the Plaintiff cannot sue on a quantum meruit: part of the question here, therefore, was whether the contract did exist or not. It distinctly appeared that the work was finally abandoned; and the jury found that no new contract had been entered into. Under these circumstances the Plaintiff ought no to lose the fruit of his labour; and there is no ground for the application which has been made.

Bosanquet J: The Plaintiff is entitled to retain his verdict. The jury have found that the contract was abandoned; but it is said that the Plaintiff ought to have tendered or delivered the work. It was part of the contract, however, that the work should be published in particular shape; and if it had been delivered after the abandonment of the original design, it might have been published in a way not consistent with the Plaintiff's reputation, or not at all.

Gaselee and **Alderson JJ** concurred.

NOTES AND QUESTIONS

Was the remedy awarded in *Planché v Colburn* restitutionary? If not, what was its basis? See on these questions the views of Garner, Beatson, and Birks (above, 86, 90, and 93). Do you agree with G Virgo's suggestion in *The Principles of the Law of Restitution* (2nd edn, 2006), 90–93 that, in cases like this, the defendant is estopped by his wrongful behaviour from denying that the claimant's work has enriched him? See also the notes and questions below, 279.

- *Greenwood v Bennett* [1973] QB 195, Court of Appeal

Harper had repaired a car (spending £226 on labour and materials), that he had bought for £75 from Searle, thinking that he had acquired good title to it. In fact the car belonged to the owners of a garage managed by Bennett and Bennett had entrusted it to Searle who had agreed to repair it for £85. Harper had subsequently sold the car for £450 to a finance company which had let it on hire purchase to Prattle. In interpleader proceedings taken out by the police to determine the parties' rights, Harper claimed that he ought to be paid £226 for the cost of the improvements he had made to the car. The judge held that Harper was not entitled to anything for the work he had done and ordered the police to hand the car over to Bennett, who resold it for £400. Harper successfully appealed to the Court of Appeal.

Lord Denning MR: . . . The judge held that Mr. Bennett's company was entitled to the car, and that Mr. Harper was entitled to nothing for the work he had done on it. He had that Mr. Harper had no lien and no remedy. The judge said: 'It seems to me that the loss here must lie where it falls. . . . Mr. Harper must be left with his worthless remedy against Mr. Searle.' So the judge ordered the car to be handed over to Mr. Bennett's company. The chief constable obeyed that order. It was handed over, and Mr. Bennett's company have resold it for £400 or so. Mr. Harper now appeals to this court. He asks that he should be paid £226 for the work he did on the car and of which the company have had the benefit.

. . .

[I]f Mr. Bennett's company had brought an action against Mr. Prattle for specific delivery of the car, it is very unlikely that an order for specific delivery of the car would be made. But if it had been, no court would order its delivery unless compensation was made for the improvements. There is a valuable judgment by Lord Macnaghten in *Peruvian Guano Co. v Dreyfus Brothers & Co.* [1892] AC 155, 176, where he said:

> 'I am not aware of any authority upon the point, but I should doubt whether it was incumbent upon the court to order the defendant to return the goods in specie where the plaintiff refused to make a fair and just allowance.'

So if this car was ordered to be returned to Mr. Bennett's company, I am quite clear the court in equity would insist upon a condition that payment should be made to Mr. Harper for the value of the improvements which he put on it.

Applying the principles stated by Lord Macnaghten, I should have thought that the county court judge here should have imposed a condition on the plaintiffs. He should have required them to pay Mr. Harper the £226 as a condition of being given delivery of the car.

But the judge did not impose such a condition. The plaintiffs have regained the car, and sold it. What then is to be done? It seems to me that we must order the plaintiffs to pay Mr. Harper the £226; for that is the only way of putting the position right.

Upon what principle is this to be done? [Counsel for Harper] has referred us to the familiar cases which say that a man is not entitled to compensation for work done on the goods or property of another unless there is a contract express or implied, to pay for it. We all remember the saying of Pollock CB: 'One cleans another's shoes; what can the other do but put them on?': *Taylor v Laird* (1856) 25 LJ Ex. 329, 332. That is undoubtedly the law when the person who does the work knows, or ought to know, that the property does not belong to him. He takes the risk of not being paid for his work on it. But it is very different when he honestly believes himself to be the owner of the property and does the work in that belief. . . . Here we have an innocent purchaser who bought the car in good faith and without notice of any defect in the title to it. He did work on it to the value of £226. The law is hard enough on him when it makes him give up the car itself. It would be most unjust if the company could not only take the car from him, but also the value of the improvements he has done to it—without paying for them. There is a principle at hand to meet the case. It derives from the law of restitution. The plaintiffs should not be allowed unjustly to enrich themselves at his expense. The court will order the plaintiffs, if they recover the car, or its improved value, to recompense the innocent purchaser for the work he has done on it. No matter whether the plaintiffs recover it with the aid of the courts, or without it, the innocent purchaser will recover the value of the improvements he has done to it.

In my opinion, therefore, the judge ought not to have released the car to the plaintiffs except on condition that the plaintiffs paid Mr. Harper the £226. But now that it has been released to them and they have sold it, we should order Mr. Bennett's company to pay Mr. Harper £226 in respect of the improvements he made to the car. I would allow the appeal accordingly.

Phillimore LJ: I agree. This was a case in which I should have thought that in the ordinary way no order for specific restitution of the chattel would have been made, because this was an ordinary commercial article; but the judge has, in effect, dealt with it as if by an order of specific restitution in allowing Mr. Bennett to take the car back. In those circumstances it seems to me perfectly clear that on equitable principles someone who has improved the car since it was originally converted and who is not himself a wrongdoer—and it is not suggested that Mr. Harper was in any way a wrongdoer— should be credited with the value of the work which he had put into the car by way of improving it. It was not seriously disputed in this case that the £226 had improved the value of the car, making its value far above what it was; and I entirely agree with Lord Denning MR that the judge having failed to allow Mr. Harper's claim to be repaid his £226 as a condition of Mr. Bennett recovering the motor car, the only course which this court can now take is to make an order that Mr. Bennett should pay directly to Mr. Harper that sum which indeed ought to have been a condition of Mr. Bennett being allowed to take possession.

I agree therefore that this appeal should succeed to that extent.

Cairns LJ: I agree. The main issue in this appeal is one on which there is no authority directly in point. The matter has been very well argued on both sides in this court. If the car had, before any proceedings were brought, reached the hands of Mr. Bennett, it is difficult to see that Mr. Harper could have had any claim against him for the expenditure that he was put to in making the repairs to it. If, on the other hand, the car had remained in the possession of Mr. Prattle and Mr. Bennett had sued Mr. Harper, then it appears to me that probably the action would have had to be in conversion, and that in assessing the damages for conversion a deduction would have to be made for the expenditure that Mr. Harper had incurred. Alternatively, if there could have been an action for detinue against Mr. Harper, then similarly, on the principles laid down in *Munro v Willmott* [1949] 1 KB 295 and in the speech of Lord Macnaghten in *Peruvian Guano Co. v Dreyfus Brothers & Co.* [1892] AC 166, 175–7, Mr. Harper's expenditure would have had to be allowed. It appears to me that in interpleader proceedings similar considerations come into play as those which would affect an action for detinue; and an order for delivery of the car to Mr. Bennett now having been made and carried out, it seems to me that the result must be that Mr. Harper ought to receive from Mr. Bennett the amount of his expenditure on the car. I agree, therefore, that the appeal should be allowed and that the order proposed ought to be made.

NOTES AND QUESTIONS

1. To what extent does Lord Denning's judgment go beyond those of Phillimore and Cairns L JJ?

2. Was the garage company benefited by Harper's work and by how much? On such facts, how is the 'subjective devaluation' argument overcome?

3. For further issues relating to this case, see below, 187.

4. The question whether Mr Bennett was enriched is examined in detail by Ewan McKendrick, 'Restitution and the Misuse of Chattels' in N Palmer and E McKendrick (eds), *Interests in Goods* (1993), 603–6.

2. AT THE CLAIMANT'S EXPENSE

It was explained at the start of this book that there is an important distinction between restitution of unjust enrichments (where the unjust enrichment is the cause of action) and restitution for wrongs (where the wrong is the cause of action).

If one sees both as being linked by an overarching principle of reversing an unjust enrichment at the claimant's expense, it is clear that 'at the claimant's expense' must be used in two very different senses. In relation to restitution of an unjust enrichment, 'at the claimant's expense' means by subtraction from the claimant's wealth. For example, if the claimant mistakenly pays the defendant £100, the defendant's gain of £100 represents a subtraction from the claimant's wealth of £100. In contrast, in relation to restitution for wrongs, 'at the claimant's expense' means simply 'by committing a wrong to the claimant.' So if D is paid £1,000 by X to beat up C, C's only possible claim to the £1000 from

D is by claiming restitution for the wrong of trespass to the person. There is no unjust enrichment by subtraction from the claimant's wealth.

In this book, our consideration of restitution for wrongs is confined to the final chapter. For the rest of the book, where we are concerned with the cause of action of unjust enrichment, 'at the expense of' therefore means by subtraction from the claimant's wealth.

In recent years, there has been a burgeoning literature on two difficult issues that arise in relation to 'at the expense of' in its subtractive sense. First, the 'correspondence' question. Does one need a correspondence or equivalence between the claimant's loss and the defendant's gain? Secondly, the 'directness' question. Can the claimant have restitution from the defendant where the benefit has been conferred by a third party? We here include extracts from academic analyses of each question (below, 110–121); from *Re BHT (UK) Ltd* on correspondence (below, 115); and from *Pan Ocean Shipping Ltd v Creditcorp Ltd, Kahn v Permayer* and *Uren v First National Home Finance Ltd* on 'leapfrogging' (below, 122–133).

General Reading

BURROWS, 25–41; GOFF AND JONES, 1-044–1-051; VIRGO, 105–16.

(1) THE CORRESPONDENCE QUESTION

- **M McInnes, ' "At the Plaintiff's Expense": Quantifying Restitutionary Relief'** [1998] *CLJ* 472

Consider the following scenario.

> Pam deals in second-hand cars. Dave parks his vehicle on the street opposite Pam's premises and leaves the keys in the glove box. Mistakenly believing that the car is part of her stock, Pam inspects it and discovers that it requires certain repairs. Although those repairs would cost £1000 on the market, her brother, Tom, a mechanic, provides them to Pam at a price of £250. Indeed, Tom routinely provides the same service to his sister at that reduced rate and is willing to do so as often as she asks. Dave eventually discovers what has occurred and resumes possession of his vehicle. Delighted to have the benefit of the repairs, he sells the car in its improved state and thereby obtains £1000 as a result of the work performed by Tom.

The issue addressed in this article pertains to the proper measure of relief to which Pam is entitled in an action in unjust enrichment. There is no doubting her ability to establish the constituent elements of that action. Dave was *enriched* by the receipt of an incontrovertible benefit because he realised a financial gain from the services rendered. That enrichment was derived at Pam's *expense* (at least in part) because she paid for the repairs. And Dave's enrichment was *unjust* because Pam's intention in rendering the benefit was vitiated by her mistaken belief that the car was hers. However, it is unclear whether she should be awarded £1000 (reflecting Dave's gain) or £250 (reflecting her loss). The specific question that arises is whether the second element of the principle of unjust enrichment ('at the plaintiff's expense') merely determines Pam's standing to sue or whether it also limits her measure of relief. It is suggested, contrary to a growing body of opinion, that the latter alternative is preferable.

. . . .

It is clear that restitutionary relief sometimes is not limited by the extent of the plaintiff's loss. That fact flows from the ambiguity inherent in the second element of the generic principle of unjust enrichment. Typically, as in Pam and Dave's case, the defendant is enriched 'at the plaintiff's expense' because he receives a benefit subtracted from her; the accretion to his wealth results from a diminution of hers. In such circumstances, the plaintiff's claim lies in an autonomous action in unjust enrichment and the measure of relief (according to the arguments presented in this article) is limited to the lesser of his gain and her loss. Exceptionally, however, the defendant is enriched 'at the plaintiff's expense' because he receives a benefit as a result of committing a wrong against her. In such circumstances, the applicable action lies not in unjust enrichment, but rather in some other area of civil obligations; the law of restitution is relevant only remedially in so far as it reveals that the applicable action supports a gain-based remedy. For present purposes, the significant point is that a claimant may rely upon an enrichment by wrong, and seek disgorgement in a cause of action other than unjust enrichment, even if the benefit that the defendant acquired by reason of his breach was derived from a third party and never could have been acquired by the plaintiff[1] And because that is true, it logically follows that the plaintiff's measure of relief is limited only by the amount of the defendant's gain; the extent of her own loss, if any, simply is irrelevant.

As a matter of policy, it makes perfectly good sense to preclude the plaintiff in a subtractive enrichment case from recovering more than she lost, even though the same limitation does not apply in a case of wrongful enrichment. In the latter situation, there is a strong social value in stripping the defendant of his ill-gotten gain: no person should be able to profit from his own wrongdoing. And while the plaintiff who suffered no loss may find it difficult to adduce a positive reason why she should be the recipient of the defendant's disgorgement, the law properly allows her to reap that windfall as a means of encouraging her to bring a claim that will vindicate that overriding social value. There is no other party with whom an effective action might lie,[2] and as between the wrongdoer and his victim, it certainly is preferable that the innocent party enjoy the benefit.

A different set of considerations applies with respect to claims arising from subtractive enrichments. Thus, in the scenario provided at the beginning of this article, Pam makes no allegation of wrongdoing against Dave; rather, she simply seeks restoration of the enrichment that passed from her to him. It is consequently more difficult to justify judicial redistribution of the £750 windfall that arose from Tom's agreement to provide work to Pam at a reduced price. Indeed, as between two innocents, there is no apparent reason why the party who did not lose the disputed enrichment should receive disgorgement from the party who acquired it fortuitously.

That point is illustrated best through an examination of the principle of corrective justice that underlies an action in unjust enrichment. The Aristotelian conception is premised upon a notion of correlativity. As a result of a single event, the plaintiff suffers a loss and the defendant reaps a gain. Those two effects inextricably are tied: the plaintiff suffers the loss only because the defendant enjoys the gain and vice versa. The same correlation recurs in the legal response to the triggering event: the plaintiff is entitled to recover her loss and the defendant is compelled to give up his gain. Moreover, the nexus forged by the triggering event uniquely identifies each party as the proper object of the other's remedial response. Thus, the mere fact that the plaintiff suffered an unjustifiable loss may indicate that she should enjoy recompense, but in isolation it cannot reveal the defendant to be the appropriate source of such relief. The remedy equally might come from the state or from some third party who is considered to possess more than he deserves. However, by proving that the defendant acquired a benefit correlative to her loss, the plaintiff justifiably is able to point the remedial arrow at him. Similarly, the mere fact that the defendant holds more than he ought to possess may indicate that he should give up the unjustified wealth, but in isolation it cannot reveal the plaintiff to be the appropriate beneficiary of his divestment. He might equally pay the value of the enrichment over to the state or to some needy third party. It is only by proving that

---

1 See *e.g. Reading v Attorney-General* [1951] AC 507 (HL).

2 It might be thought desirable to allow the state to claim the benefit of the wrongdoer's disgorgement. In practical terms, however, the state often would have neither the wherewithal to discover the wrong nor the motivation to prosecute an action.

the defendant's enrichment was subtracted from her that the plaintiff can establish herself as the appropriate recipient.

In most instances, that analysis provides a simple and complete explanation for an award of restitutionary relief.[3] However, a difficulty arises when, as in Pam and Dave's case, the value of the plaintiff's loss and the defendant's gain do not coincide. Given the corrective justice goal of restoring the status quo of both parties, how should the law respond when the disequilibrium created by the triggering event affects the two parties differently? While Dave's acquisition of a mistakenly conferred benefit reveals that he perhaps should be required to give it up, can Pam establish a connection that would justify her receipt of the full measure of his enrichment? Or does her participation in the triggering event justify her recovery of only so much as she actually lost?

Those questions have received insufficient attention within the law of restitution. However, an emerging view appears to proceed largely on normative grounds and to give remedial priority to the defendant's gain over the plaintiff's loss. On that approach, the claimant simply is required, at a threshold level, to prove a nexus (in the form of an unjust factor) between the fact that she suffered a subtractive deprivation and the fact that the defendant received an enrichment. More specifically, she need not prove that she suffered a loss equivalent to his gain; while there must be a causally related plus and minus, the sum of the two need not be zero. If able to establish that, at least initially, the defendant had more than he ought to have had and that she had less than she ought to have had, the plaintiff is entitled (subject to defences) to *all* of his enrichment on the ground that she suffered *some* expense.

That approach is open to several objections. Most significantly, contrary to general principles, it allows the autonomous action in unjust enrichment to generate relief that is not truly restitutionary. The legal response of restitution consists of requiring the defendant to 'give back' to the plaintiff that which he unjustly gained at her expense. Of course, the logical corollary of the defendant's 'giving back' is the plaintiff's 'getting back'. And the notion of 'getting back' presupposes that the claimant previously held that to which she judicially is entitled. If she did not, then her entitlement is not restitutionary. The point is illustrated by the hypothetical. The value of Dave's enrichment, as realised through the sale of the vehicle in its enhanced condition, was £1000. However, because she acquired the services from Tom at a reduced cost, and because she never was in a position to sell Dave's car and thereby to realise the market value of the repairs for herself, Pam's corresponding expense was only £250. Consequently, to award her the full measure of Dave's enrichment (£1000) would allow her to 'get back' that which he gained and that which she previously held (£250), but it also would allow her simply to 'get' that which she never previously held (£750). The latter result would not be restitutionary.

To award relief in excess of the plaintiff's loss in a case of subtractive enrichment also is objectionable in so far as it leads to public cost without concomitant public benefit. Given that neither Dave nor Pam positively deserves the £750 surplus resulting from the reduced rate that Tom gave to his sister, why should the community be forced to pay to transfer that wealth from the defendant to the plaintiff? Why should Pam be encouraged to activate the legal process, and to generate societal expense, in order to achieve the socially neutral effect of redistributing the windfall from Dave to herself?[4] Granted, in a case of enrichment of wrong, the promise of such redistribution is held out as a means of encouraging the claimant to effectuate the social goals of deterrence and

---

3 Suppose that the plaintiff mistakenly pays £500 to the defendant. The single event of subtractive enrichment reveals why the plaintiff is entitled to recover £500, why the defendant is liable to pay £500, and how those remedial responses are interdependent.

4 Pam admittedly enjoys an action in unjust enrichment even if her relief is limited by the extent of her loss. However, she is more likely to institute legal proceedings, and Dave less likely to settle her claim, if she stands to receive £1000, rather than £250.

condemnation. In a case of subtractive enrichment, however, those concepts are attenuated, if not entirely absent.

. . .

• P Birks, *Unjust Enrichment* (2nd edn, 2005), 79, 82–4

(a) AN ARGUMENT FINELY BALANCED

Under French influence transmitted through Quebec the law of Canada now uses words which appear to insist that the claimant must always have suffered . . . a corresponding loss.[1] However, 'from' does not necessarily imply loss, and English law appears not to insist that the claimant must have suffered one.

Suppose that when I am taking my summer holidays you use my bicycle for a month without my permission, then put it back in perfect condition; or that you stow away on my ship intending to take a free ride across the Atlantic. In these cases you have gained a valuable benefit but I have suffered no loss. I am no worse off. As long ago as 1776 in *Hambly v Trott* Lord Mansfield indicated that a claim for the value of these benefits would lie.[2] Such a claim might be explained as restitution for a wrong, but it is not obvious that it should be and it is very unlikely that Lord Mansfield was thinking on those lines.

There is other evidence that a claimant in unjust enrichment need not have suffered a loss. Attempts have been made to forge a defence out of facts which show that, if the claimant suffered a loss initially, he has since eliminated it. These arguments have been thrown out in Australia[3] and England.[4] One reason has been that loss is beside the point, an action in unjust enrichment being concerned with gains not losses. This is also what the German jurists say.[5]

. . .

(b) FROM MY PROPERTY

It is clear that if I invest your money and double it, you are entitled to the doubled proceeds. That is the law. This is what happened in *FC Jones (Trustee in Bankruptcy) v Jones*.[6] There Mr Jones had transferred money from the firm's bank account to Mrs Jones. As the law then stood, in the firm's insolvency the account then vested retrospectively in the trustee in bankruptcy. She multiplied the money she had received fivefold by speculation in potato futures. The trustee in bankruptcy recovered all that she had made. There is no hint that the outcome turned on wrongdoing. The only satisfactory explanation is that she was unjustly enriched at his expense to the extent of the whole sum.

---

1 *Pettkus v Becker* [1980] 2 SCR 217, 227–8; M McInnes, 'The Measure of Restitution' (2002) 52 U Toronto LJ 163; M McInnes, 'At the Plaintiff's Expense: Quantifying Restitutionary Relief' [1998] CLJ 472. This Canadian position is vigorously supported by RB Grantham and CEF Rickett, 'Disgorgement for Unjust Enrichment' [2003] CLJ 159.

2 (1776) 1 Cowp 371, 375, 98 ER 1136, 1138. The later refusal in *Phillips v Homfray* (1883) 24 ChD 439 (CA) to treat use, and hence saving of expense, as an enrichment is roundly repudiated by Goff and Jones [36–003]. Compare the case of the stowaway on the plane to New York BGH NJW 609 (7.1.1971) translated by G Dannemann in B Markesinis, W Lorenz, and G Dannemann, *German Law of Obligations Vol 1 The Law of Contracts and Restitution: A Comparative Introduction* (OUP Oxford 1997) 771.

3 *Roxborough v Rothmans of Pall Mall Australia Ltd* (2002) 76 ALJR 203 (HCA), Kirby J dissenting; *Commissioner of State Revenue v Royal Insurance Australia Ltd* (1994) 182 CLR 51 (HCA), where Mason ACJ adopted the view of Windeyer J in *Mason v NSW* (1959) 102 CLR 108, 146.

4 *Kleinwort Benson v Birmingham City Council* [1996] 4 All ER 733 (CA).

5 'In this area of law only the enrichment of the person liable is relevant. Whether the enrichment-creditor has been impoverished is of no significance. . . . It would therefore be a serious mistake to withhold a claim founded on unjust enrichment on the ground that the enrichment-creditor had suffered no detriment' HJ Wieling, *Bereicherungsrecht* (Springer Berlin 1993) 1–2 (my translation).

6 [1997] Ch 159 (CA).

More recently ... the House of Lords has held, in *Foskett v McKeown*,[7] that, where a trustee misappropriates trust property, the beneficiaries under a trust are entitled to choose between a security interest and a beneficial interest in the traceable proceeds. In the case itself they thus obtained many times what they had lost. This outcome is fully compatible with, if not dictated by, the law relating to resulting trusts based on contributions to the purchase price of a house or other asset.

The taxonomy of these cases is disputed. They fit the unjust enrichment analysis if we say that the earning opportunities inherent in an asset are attributed to its owner. Anyone who takes those opportunities intercepts what is already attributed in law to that owner. In speculating with the firm's money Mrs Jones intercepted the firm's earning opportunities. The actual loss to the firm and its trustee was one fifth of that which they recovered from her. The fivefold increase was from the firm's property and therefore from it.

(c) THE FUTURE

There is a great deal at stake. The taxonomic disputes surrounding such cases as *Jones* and *Foskett* will determine the scope of the English law of unjust enrichment. Are these cases in which the defendant was enriched 'at the expense of the claimant' within the way that the law understands the 'from' sense of that phrase? Or, bearing in mind that we are not construing a statutory phrase, are they cases in which the connection between the claimant and the enrichment is sufficient to keep them within the logic which drives the recovery of the mistaken payment of a non-existent debt? If they are, the reach of the law of unjust enrichment is much longer than we thought.

...

Edwards v Lee's Administrator,[8] the case of the Great Onyx Cave in Kentucky, was an example of a profitable trespass. Edwards found on his land the entrance to a wonderful scenic cave. He started up a thriving tourist business. Unfortunately one third of the cave extended into Lee's neighbouring land. Far below the surface the trespassing tourists caused no loss, but profits were being made from the use of his land. Edwards had to pay Lee's estate one-third of his profits.

The result is easily explained as restitution for the trespass itself. In that light it is an instance of gain-based recovery for a wrong. Can it be understood, by alternative analysis, as restitution of unjust enrichment at Lee's expense? The language used by the court is equivocal, not to say muddled, but once we break away from the requirement of corresponding loss the answer must be that it can. *Jones* and *Foskett* tell us that we have, unequivocally, made that break.

NOTES AND QUESTIONS

1. *FC Jones (Trustee in Bankruptcy) v Jones* is set out below, 651. *Foskett v McKeown* is set out below, 678. *Edwards v Lee's Administrators* is set out below, 952.

2. Do you agree with Birks that English law has 'unequivocally' made the break from any requirement of a correspondence of loss and gain so that 'at the expense of' (in its subtractive sense) means simply from the claimant's wealth/from the claimant?

3. R Grantham and C Rickett, 'Disgorgement for Unjust Enrichment' [2003] CLJ 159 take a very similar view to McInnes. That is, they argue that restitution is about 'giving back' a gain, whereas 'disgorgement' is about 'giving up' a gain. In their view, the cause of action of unjust enrichment triggers restitution not disgorgement.

4. Does the rejection of the passing on defence—which was rejected in England in *Kleinwort Benson v Birmingham City Council*, below, 871—represent a rejection of the need for a correspondence of loss and gain?

---

7 [2000] AC 51 (HL).   8 96 SW 2d 1028 (Kentucky CA 1936).

5. Can McInnes' insistence on a correspondence of loss and gain explain the award of interest in addition to restitution of a principal sum paid?

6. C mistakenly pays D £10. D purchases 10 lottery tickets. She would not have purchased any lottery tickets had she not received the mistaken payment. One of the lottery tickets is the winning ticket and D wins £5 million. Does C have a claim against D in unjust enrichment for the £5 million?

7. D owes X £1000. C discharges D's debt with X for £800 (i.e. at a discount). Assuming C has a claim for unjust enrichment against D for the discharge of D's debt (e.g. because paid under legal compulsion) is C entitled to £800 or £1000?

8. If D steals C's bicycle, and sells it, can C recover the proceeds of sale by claiming: (a) restitution of an unjust enrichment; (b) restitution for the wrong of conversion; (c) compensation for the wrong of conversion?

• Re BHT (UK) Ltd
[2004] EWHC 201 (Ch); [2004] 1 BCLC 568, Chancery Division

The administrative receiver of a company paid out money (from the realisation of book debts) to Natwest Finance Ltd (NFL) in the mistaken belief that it had a fixed charge over the book debts. That was a mistake of law because, as clarified by the Privy Council subsequent to the payments in *Agnew v Commissioners of Inland Revenue* ('Brumark') [2001] 2 AC 710, NFL's charge was a floating and not a fixed charge. The correct recipients of the proceeds should therefore have been the company's preferential creditors and not NFL. The liquidator of the company, on behalf of the company, sought restitution from NFL of the mistakenly paid money. This was denied primarily on the grounds that NFL's enrichment was not at the expense of the company because the company had suffered no loss.

Kevin Garnett QC: . . .

[**19**] As it emerged in Mr Chaisty's skeleton argument [on behalf of the liquidator] and then more clearly during the hearing, the basis of the applicant's potential claim is solely one for repayment to the company on the basis of unjust enrichment. If the charge was a floating charge, Mr Chaisty argues, NFL was not entitled to receive the book debt realisations from the receivers, and they were only paid to NFL based on a mistaken view of the law. NFL should therefore return the money to the company because it has been unjustly enriched. Mr Chaisty made it clear that the claim was not being made on behalf of the preferential creditors and that no remedy under the Insolvency Act 1986 was relied on. Indeed, he argued that had there been no liquidation the company would have been just as entitled to bring the claim.

. . .

[**21**] Mr Moss's riposte [on behalf of NFL], leaving aside for the moment any defence on the facts which NFL might have to an unjust enrichment claim, was that such a claim required that any enrichment be at the expense of the claiming party: see *Banque Financière de la Cité v Parc (Battersea) Ltd* [1998] 1 All ER 737 at 740, [1999] 1 AC 221 at 227 *per* Lord Steyn. In this case this condition was not satisfied . . .

[**25**] Mr Moss submits . . . that since anything recovered from NFL would, subject no doubt to any unpaid costs of recovery, go straight to the preferential creditors, the company has suffered no loss. Its balance sheet position is unaffected by what has happened. He points to the decision of *National Employers' Mutual General Insurance Association Ltd (in liq) v AGF Holdings (UK) Ltd* [1997] 2 BCLC 191 where, on the very complicated facts of that case, Lightman J held that the liquidator's claim for breach of contract should be struck out because the company had suffered no loss. The only parties to have suffered loss were certain creditors of the company and it was not sufficient for the purposes

of a breach of contract claim that the liquidator would apply certain reinsurance proceeds amongst all the creditors in accordance with the statutory scheme. The company had been made no worse off by any breach.

[26] Mr Chaisty submits that that case was one for breach of contract whereas the present claim would be for unjust enrichment, but that does not seem to me to be a material difference. The company here suffered no loss by any wrongful payment to NFL. I accept Mr Moss's submission.

[27] This is not a case in which, if there has been a wrong, there is no remedy. The preferential creditors are perfectly well able to pursue whatever claims they may have against NFL.

. . .

NOTES AND QUESTIONS

1. The money was paid by the company and in that sense there was an initial loss to the company. Even if one does regard 'at the expense of' as requiring loss, rather than being satisfied by the gain coming from the claimant's wealth, it would therefore seem that the element of loss was present. The fact that the loss was as a matter of law, *ultimately* borne by the preferential creditors rather than the company (because the company should have paid the preferential creditors and would be bound to do so if the money were now recovered) should surely have been irrelevant in the light of the Court of Appeal's rejection of a passing on defence in *Kleinwort Benson v Birmingham CC* (below, 871).

2. The judge left open the possibility of claims by the preferential creditors against NFL. Leaving aside any statutory claims, would the preferential creditors have had a claim in unjust enrichment against NFL? (See below 116 on interceptive subtraction.)

(2) THE DIRECTNESS QUESTION

(i) INTERCEPTIVE SUBTRACTION?

- **P Birks, *Unjust Enrichment* (2nd edn, 2005), 75–7**

In the standard case the asset moves from the claimant's possession to that of the defendant. Is it sufficient that it was on its way from a third party to the claimant when the defendant intercepted it? Where there is an interceptive subtraction the enriching assets are never reduced to the ownership or possession of the claimant. They will have been on their way, in fact or law, to the claimant when the defendant intercepted them. The choice has gone in favour of accepting the sufficiency of interceptive subtractions, albeit without much analysis and hence with many untidy loose ends.

. . .

One early example was where *D* usurped an office of profit which ought to have been occupied by *C*. *D* thus received fees which ought to have been paid to *C*. *C* could claim those profits intercepted by *D*.[1] In 1998 in *Montana v Crow Tribe of Indians* the Supreme Court of the United States upheld the principle, although on the facts the majority found that it did not apply, that where authority *D* has wrongfully levied a tax payable to authority *C*, *C* can recover from *D*.[2] Similarly, a self-appointed executor or administrator who receives what was due to the estate is liable to make restitution to the incoming rightful personal representative.[3] Again, if *D* receives rent from *X* which was due to *C*, he

---

1 *Arris v Stukely* (1677) 2 Mod 260, 86 ER 1060; *Howard v Wood* (1679) 2 Lev 245, 83 ER 530. Although these provide a root for waiver of tort, they do not need to be analysed as instances of wrongful enrichment.

2 523 US 696 (1998) 715–16 (Souter and O'Connor JJ dissenting, 722–3). Both majority and minority approved *Valley County v Thomas* 109 Mont 345, 97 P 2d 345 (1939) where one county recovered vehicle tax levied by another.

3 *Jacob v Allen* (1703) 1 Salk 27, 91 ER 26; *Yardley v Arnold* (1842) C & M 434, 174 ER 577.

will have to account to C.[4] Of the same kind but rather more difficult are the cases, which are discussed by Professor Chambers, of land intended to be conveyed by X to C being mistakenly conveyed to D. In such a case C has sometimes been allowed to claim against D.[5]

However, the claimant has a heavy onus when his case rests on a factual rather than a legal inevitability the enrichment was en route to him. In *Hill v van Erp*[6] a solicitor's negligence caused a will to be invalid. The solicitor was liable in tort, but it was said that the intended beneficiaries could not sue the next of kin to whom the estate had gone. They could not say that those who benefited under the intestacy had intercepted assets which were on their way to those who, but for its invalidity, were entitled under the will.

If the boot had been on the other foot and the money been paid out under the invalid will, the mispaid beneficiaries would have been held to have intercepted money destined to those who were indisputably entitled as a matter of law, as in *Ministry of Health v Simpson*.[7] There, failing to notice the nullity of the bequest, the executors of Caleb Diplock had paid to charities sums which ought as a matter of law to have gone to the next of kin. The next of kin recovered directly from the charities. The money which the charities received was, as a matter of law, destined to go to them.

- **L Smith, 'Three-Party Restitution: A Critique of Birks' Theory of Interceptive Subtraction'** (1991) 4 *OJLS* 480

(In the earlier part of this article, Smith set out Birks' theory of interceptive subtraction. He referred to an example of X paying D mistakenly thinking that he was discharging his (X's) debt to C. Rather than D being enriched by interceptive subtraction from C, Smith argued that *in the general case* there was no subtraction from C because C could still sue X for the debt. Similarly X could sue D for return of the mistaken payment.)

We can now consider the cases in which the plaintiff's claim for restitution was allowed. Some of these are used by Birks in the presentation of the theory of interceptive subtraction. He relies on the cases which deal with usurpers of offices, and the cases dealing with the receipt of rents.[1] He also relies on *Re Diplock*.[2]

It will be recalled that, when presenting the general fact pattern for this class of cases, I said that *in the general case* the plaintiff has suffered no expense. Before the third party paid the defendant, the plaintiff was owed money by the third party. After the payment, the plaintiff is owed the same amount of money. I also said that *in the general case*, the third party will have a restitutionary claim against the defendant. It is the third party who has suffered a subtractive loss; he is poorer by the payment he has made, and his debt to the plaintiff still exists. Hence, the defendant's enrichment has been at the expense of the third party.

---

4 *Official Custodian for Charities v Mackey (No 2)* [1985] 1 WLR 1308, where Nourse J acknowledged the principle but found it not to apply on the particular facts.

5 *Leuty v Hillas* (1858) 2 De G & J 110; *Craddock Brothers v Hunt* [1923] 2 Ch 136 (CA). R Chambers, *Resulting Trusts* (OUP Oxford 1997) 127.

6 (1997) 188 CLR 159 (HCA).

7 [1951] AC 251 (HL).

1 *Introduction*, 134, 142–3.

2 [1948] Ch 465, [1948] 2 All ER 318, 429 (CA), affirmed [1951] AC 251. This case is cited by Birks in the *Introduction*, 143.

But not every case is the general case. Sometimes, when the third party pays the defendant in an attempt to discharge his debt to the plaintiff, he succeeds. This can happen for several reasons . . . But consider the consequences of this result, which we will call the special case.[3]

Let us hypothesize that the third party has paid £100 to the defendant, attempting to discharge the debt of £100 he owes to the plaintiff. For whatever reason, he succeeds; this is an example of the special case. Now, the third party has not suffered any loss. He has parted with £100, but he has also negated his debt to the plaintiff. He has lost an asset and an equivalent liability. He has suffered no expense, and has no claim in restitution. As for the defendant, her position is the same as in the general case. She has been enriched by £100.

We know that subtraction is a zero-sum game. We have seen that an enrichment of £100 cannot cause subtractive losses of £200. Equally, such an enrichment cannot cause subtractive losses of zero pounds. If the defendant has been enriched by £100, someone else has been impoverished in the same amount. In the general case, it was the third party. In the special case, it is the plaintiff.

Why is this? By hypothesis, the third party no longer owes the plaintiff £100. So the plaintiff has lost this debt. He has lost an asset, and has received nothing in return. This has come about via the payment by the third party to the defendant of £100. In other words, the defendant has been enriched at the expense of the plaintiff, and so the plaintiff may have restitution against the defendant.

What is more, the enrichment has occurred as a result of a straightforward, direct subtraction. The defendant's gain is necessarily equal to the plaintiff's loss. That gain and loss are two sides of the same coin. The coin is the transaction between the third party and the defendant.

My thesis with respect to these cases is that they may all be analysed and explained as simple, direct subtractions. In the *general case*, the defendant has been enriched by direct subtraction from the third party. The latter thus has a restitutionary claim against the former. The plaintiff continues to be owed money by the third party. His position is unchanged; he has suffered no expense; he has no claim in restitution. In the *special case*, the defendant has been enriched by direct subtraction from the plaintiff. The plaintiff thus has a cause of action in restitution against the defendant. The position of the third party has changed—he has satisfied his obligation to the plaintiff—but he has suffered no expense. He has no claim in restitution.

Since all of the cases in this category are examples of either the general or of the special case, I contend that the theory of interceptive subtraction is superfluous for these cases. We need not ask questions about whether it was or was not certain that the wealth would arrive in the plaintiff. We merely examine the legal effect of the transfer of money to determine who has been impoverished by it. It is at the expense of that person that the defendant has been enriched. If the payment has discharged the third party's obligation to the plaintiff (the special case), then the plaintiff has been impoverished by the payment. If the payment has not discharged that obligation (the general case), then the payer third party is the one who has been impoverished.

NOTES AND QUESTIONS

1. Birks' view was that, where it was factually or legally certain that, had D not intercepted, X would have benefited C, D's enrichment is at C's expense. D has been enriched by interceptive subtraction from C. Smith's view is that the cases appearing to accept interceptive subtraction are in reality ones where the payment received by D from X is at C's expense in the subtractive sense because, by reason of X's payment to D, X's liability to C is legally discharged and C therefore loses its prior entitlement to sue X.

---

3 The 'special case' actually arises more frequently in the reports than does the 'general case'. The labels are meant to indicate that the general case is a straightforward triangular fact pattern, whereas the special case contains a critical complication in the effect of the third party's payment to the plaintiff.

2. In a part of his article subsequent to the above extract, Smith argued that *Ministry of Health v Simpson* (*sub nom Re Diplock*, below, 237) only allowed C (the next of kin) to pursue D (the charities) where C's legal claims against X (the personal representatives) were factually unsatisfied so that, at that point, D's enrichment was at C's expense. On Smith's view, therefore, the much-criticised proviso in *Ministry of Health v Simpson*—that the next-of-kin first exhausted their claims against the personal representatives—was justified: on Birks' view, it was unjustified.

3. Say a donor has drawn up a deed of gift mistakenly favouring D rather than C. If X died before realising his mistake, could C apply for rectification of the gift in his favour? Obiter dicta of Lord Romilly MR in *Lister v Hodgson* (1867) LR 4 Eq 30, 34 suggests that he can (although obiter dicta of Gummow J in *Hill v Van Erp* (1997) 188 CLR 159 suggests the contrary). What would Birks and Smith say about this situation?

(ii) LEAPFROGGING?

- **P Birks, *Unjust Enrichment*** (2nd edn, 2005), 86–87, 89–90, 93–94

THE IMMEDIATE ENRICHEE

It is usually perfectly obvious who is enriched at whose expense. The reason is that in most cases there are only two parties in view. Even when there are more than two players it is often obvious who is whose immediate enrichee. I pay you money by mistake; you make a present of it to X. We can arrange these three parties in a straight line. You are my immediate enrichee, and X is your immediate enrichee. So far as X can be said to be enriched at my expense, he is a secondary or remote enrichee. Immediacy matters. I can only sue a remote enrichee if the rules of leapfrogging do not forbid it. 'At the expense of the claimant' means, in the first instance, 'immediately at the expense of the claimant'. Thereafter the problems of leapfrogging set in. It is essential to be able to recognize the immediate enrichee. One cannot otherwise tell whether the claimant faces leapfrogging problems.

1. The proprietary connection

There is one recurrent three-party situation in which the intervention of a third hand makes no difference at all. If the defendant has received the claimant's property, it does not matter how many intermediate hands it has passed through. There is an illusion of leapfrogging, but in reality there is none. In *Lipkin Gorman v Karpnale Ltd*[1] a partner in a firm of solicitors who was addicted to gambling fed his addiction from the firm's client account. He gambled the money away at the defendant's casino. There was no point in suing the gambler. He was penniless and in prison. The firm succeeded in recovering from the casino, seemingly leapfrogging the addicted gambler. Although the facts were actually more complex, the model from which the House of Lords worked was this. If X takes C's money without C's consent and gives it to D, then, subject to possible defences, D becomes indebted to C in the sum received.

A number of cases show that the model holds good where the claimant's interest in the thing is a power to avoid a voidable title. In *Banque Belge pour l'Étranger v Hambrouck*[2] the bank had paid out money to a fraudster who had forged cheques. On the strength of its power to avoid his title, it was able to go against his mistress, to whom he had given some of the money. On a larger scale *El Ajou v Dollar Land Holdings plc*[3] is structurally similar. The claimant was the victim of a huge share-selling

---

1 [1991] 2 AC 548 (HL).

2 [1921] 1 KB 321 (CA). Cf. undue influence: *Bainbrigge v Browne* (1881) 18 Ch D 188, 196–7; *Midland Bank v Perry* [1988] 1 FLR 161, 167.

3 [1993] 3 All ER 717 (Millett J) rev'd on one point as to attribution of knowledge [1994] 2 All ER 685 (CA). In the CA the defendants were no longer seen as bona fide purchasers.

fraud. He was able to reach across a world-wide money laundering operation to the defendant company in cooperation with which the rogues had invested in the development of New Covent Garden.

It is necessary to bear in mind the operation of the defence of bona fide purchase. Where bona fide purchase destroys prior property rights, there will be no proprietary connection between the claimant and the bona fide purchaser, and in the case of money bona fide purchase always does clear off earlier interests.[4] In *El Ajou v Dollar Land Holdings plc* the defendant developers were found to have known of the provenance of the funds in question. They were not bona fide purchasers. Subject to that caveat, where there is a sufficient proprietary connection there are no remote recipients. If I find your wallet it makes no difference whether I am the first recipient or the second or the twenty-second. Suppose a pickpocket took it and, in alarm, threw it down, and then I found it. My position would be exactly the same as if your wallet had fallen from your pocket into the road in front of me without your noticing its loss. A receipt of your money is always a receipt directly from you.

2. Enrichments conferred by one but procured by another

Appearances can deceive. It is quite often true that a defendant is not the immediate enrichee of the person who actually conferred the enrichment. This happens where that person, in conferring the enrichment, acts at the behest of and on the credit of another. If I want to pay off a debt to you or build you a garage, I will almost certainly do it through another person. To pay my debt to you, I will draw a cheque in your favour which my bank will honour. To build the garage, I will employ a builder to do the work. The builder works under a contract with me and on my credit. Likewise my bank in making the payment to you. In such cases you appear at first sight to be immediately enriched by the builder and the bank, but the builder and bank act for me and look to me to pay them. You are my immediate enrichee.

. . .

LEAPFROGGING

. . .

The picture seems to be that there is one common case in which leapfrogging is ruled out. For the rest the policy of the law is not hostile to leapfrogging. It leaves remote recipients to the protection of normal defences.

1. Initially valid contracts

At this point we return to those cases in which one party confers an enrichment which is procured by another. Where a defendant receives a benefit from or because of the performance of a contract between two others and the party making the performance and thus conferring the benefit had a valid contractual right to be paid for that performance by the other party to the contract, the recipient of the enrichment is the immediate enrichee of the latter party, the party bound to pay, and the remote enrichee of the former, the party conferring the enrichment. In such a case the former, who procured the performance, may never be leapfrogged by the latter, who conferred it. Leapfrogging out of an initially valid contract is not allowed. One may never attack one's contractual counter-party's immediate enrichee.

A simple model is an unsecured loan. If a bank extends overdraft facilities to a customer, and the customer thus has funds enough to give £1,000 to his son, the bank will have no recourse against the son. If the father becomes insolvent, the bank will have to line up with the other unsecured creditors. One reason for not allowing the bank to sue the son is precisely that the bank must not

---

4 [Below, 822].

wriggle round the risk of insolvency inherent in its contract with the father. Contracts entail the risk of insolvency.

. . .

2. No initial contract

. . .

Leapfrogging supposes a claimant who could, however unsatisfactorily, sue an immediate enrichee but who wants to sue a remote enrichee instead, on the ground that, but for the unjust enrichment of the first recipient, the remote recipient would not have been enriched. In the previous subsection we saw that there is no hope of leapfrogging out of an initially valid contract with the immediate enrichee. But in the absence of any such contract, it seems that such leapfrogging is permitted. This is controversial. Professor Burrows assumes a general principle against actions against anyone but the immediate enrichee, but recognizes a series of exceptions.[5] Professor Tettenborn takes a strongly negative stance. He puts this case:

> C inadvertently overpays his creditor A by £1000; A, pleasantly surprised on reading his next bank statement but entirely unsuspicious . . ., proceeds to give £1000 from his other account to his son B. . . . A can almost certainly plead change of position as a defence. Hence the potential significance of a direct claim by C against B; can C say (in effect): 'I have paid money by mistake; but for this B would not have been enriched; therefore B has been unjustifiably enriched at my expense and ought to refund'?[6]

His answer is no. In German law it is certainly yes, for this very case is provided for in the BGB.[7] The answer must also be yes in English law.

NOTES AND QUESTIONS

1. *Lipkin Gorman v Karpnale Ltd* is set out above, 28 (and especially look again at note 2 under that case); *Banque Belge pour l'Etranger v Hambrouck* is set out below, 650; Millett J's decision in *El Ajou v Dollar Land Holdings plc* is discussed below, 744.

2. Birks goes on, at 95–8, to argue controversially, that the 'yes' answer he has given at the end of the above extract is supported by the 'real state of things' in the *Lipkin Gorman* case and by some subrogation cases.

3. C pays £100 to X who, as a consequence of believing that she has extra money, gives a different £100 to D as a gift. Is C entitled to restitution of £100 from X and/or from D? What was Birks' answer?

4. On Birks' view a sub-contracting builder who performs work on an employer's land under a contract with a head-contractor engaged by the employer has no claim for restitution of an unjust enrichment against the employer. This is because: (i) the enrichment is at the direct expense of the head-contractor not the builder; and (ii) the builder cannot leapfrog over the head-contractor and claim against the employer because one cannot, on grounds of policy (eg upsetting insolvency rules) leapfrog out of an initially valid contract.

5. Does Birks' approach explain the denial of restitution in *Lloyds Bank plc v Independent Insurance Co. Ltd* (below, 163)?

---

5 Burrows, *The Law of Restitution* (2nd edn) 31–41. His basic rule is not specific to leapfrogging. It is much wider: 'the claimant is not entitled to the restitution of benefits conferred by a third party rather than himself' 32.

6 A Tettenborn, 'Lawful Receipt—A Justifying Factor' [1997] *RLR* 1, 1. Cf. Burrows (n 5 above) 41.

7 822 BGB: If the recipient disposes of the thing received to a third party gratuitously, then, so far as the first recipient's restitutionary obligation is thereby barred, the third party incurs a restitutionary obligation just as though the disposition had been made to him by the creditor without legal ground (my translation).

- *Pan Ocean Shipping Ltd v. Creditcorp Ltd (The Trident Beauty)*
  [1994] 1 WLR 161, House of Lords

Pan Ocean chartered the vessel, the *Trident Beauty*, from the Trident Shipping Company Ltd. By the terms of the time charter, the hire was payable fifteen days in advance. In order to finance its business, Trident had arranged credit facilities with Creditcorp Ltd which, in turn, entered into the facility agreement on behalf of a group of investors. Trident 'irrevocably and exclusively' assigned to the investors, 'free of all encumbrances and third party interests' its right, title, and interest in and to the receivables, including the sums which were payable for the charter of the vessel. Creditcorp notified Pan Ocean of the assignment and Pan Ocean paid the monthly hire direct to Creditcorp. On 31 May 1991 Pan Ocean paid the sum of $93,600 to Creditcorp in respect of the hire of the vessel from 31 May to 15 June. In fact the vessel was off hire from 27 May because it had to undergo repairs and, when the repairs were completed, the vessel was still unavailable to Pan Ocean because Trident was unable to pay for the repairs. In these circumstances Pan Ocean concluded that Trident had repudiated the time charter and on 10 July they accepted the breach and brought the contract to an end. Trident was not, by this stage, worth suing and so Pan Ocean sought to recover the hire paid on 31 May to Creditcorp on the ground that it had been paid for a consideration which had wholly failed. The House of Lords, dismissing Pan Ocean's appeal, held that it was not entitled to recover the hire so paid: its remedy was against Trident, not Creditcorp.

Lord Goff of Chieveley: . . . Pan Ocean is not seeking to recover the hire instalment from Trident, because it does not consider Trident worth suing. Instead, it seeks to recover the money from Creditcorp on the ground of total failure of consideration, since the vessel was off-hire for the whole of the period in respect of which the relevant hire instalment was paid. In an unreserved judgment the judge held that Pan Ocean was entitled to succeed in its claim. His decision was however unanimously reversed by the Court of Appeal.

To consider the question whether Pan Ocean is entitled to recover the money from Creditcorp on this ground, it is necessary first to turn to the time charter which governed the relationship between Trident and Pan Ocean. Under the charter the hire was, as normal, payable in advance—here 15 days in advance. Provision was made, also as normal, for the vessel to be off-hire in certain specified circumstances. This is to be found in the usual off-hire clause, clause 15 in the printed form. In addition, other circumstances were specified in some of the additional typed clauses, under which the vessel would or might be off hire (see clauses 37, 56, 61, 74 and 79). In another typed clause (clause 59), there was provision for the hire to be reduced pro rata in certain circumstances. I should also record that, again as normal, the charter contained an arbitration clause (clause 17 of the printed form), providing for any dispute to be referred to arbitration in the manner there prescribed.

Now, given the circumstances that the charter hire was payable in advance and that the vessel might be off hire under one or other of the relevant clauses during a period in respect of which hire had been paid, it was inevitable that, from time to time, there might have to be an adjustment of the hire so paid. Such adjustments are a normal feature of the administration of time charters. The usual practice is, I understand, for an adjustment to be made when the next instalment of hire falls due, by making a deduction from such instalment in respect of hire previously paid in advance which has not been earned; in the present charter, provision is to be found to that effect in clause 29(f), one of the additional typed clauses. If the relevant period is the last hire period under the charter, such a deduction may not be possible. Any overpayment will then have to be repaid by the shipowner, and no doubt this will normally be taken care of in the final account drawn up at the end of the charter period.

Sometimes, the event which gives rise to the charter being deprived of the services of the vessel, in whole or in part, which in its turn renders the vessel off hire under one of the applicable clauses, may constitute a breach of contract by the shipowner. If so, the character will have a claim for damages for breach of contract, which may embrace the amount of hire paid in advance in respect of the period during which the vessel was off hire. But this need not be so; and in any event the charter will usually make express provision for the repayment of hire which has been overpaid. In the present charter, such a provision is to be found in clause 18 of the printed form, which provides that 'any overpaid hire' is 'to be returned at once.' This provision gives rise to a contractual debt payable in the relevant circumstances by the shipowner to the character. But even in the absence of any such express contractual provision, advance hire which proves to have been paid in respect of a period during which the vessel was rendered off hire under a term of the contract must ordinarily be repaid, and if necessary a term will be implied into the contract to that effect. That such an implied obligation may arise is implicit in such early cases as *Tonnelier* v. *Smith* (1897) 2 Com. Cas. 258, and *C. A. Stewart & Co.* v. *Phs. Van Ommeren (London) Ltd* [1918] 2 KB 560. This will of course be dealt with in the ordinary case as a matter of administration of the time charter; if any dispute should persist, it will fall to be resolved by arbitration.

All this is important for present purposes, because it means that, as between shipowner and character, there is a contractual regime which legislates for the recovery of overpaid hire. It follows that, as a general rule, the law of restitution has no part to play in the matter; the existence of the agreed regime renders the imposition by the law of a remedy in restitution both unnecessary and inappropriate. Of course, if the contract is proved never to have been binding, or if the contract ceases to bind, different considerations may arise, as in the case of frustration (as to which see *French Marine* v. *Compagnie Napolitaine d'Eclairage et de Chauffage par le Gaz* [1921] 2 AC 494, and now the Law Reform (Frustrated Contracts) Act 1943). With such cases as these, we are not here concerned. Here, it is true, the contract was prematurely determined by the acceptance by Pan Ocean of Trident's repudiation of the contract. But, before the date of determination of the contract, Trident's obligation under clause 18 to repay the hire instalment in question had already accrued due; and accordingly that is the relevant obligation, as between Pan Ocean and Trident, for the purposes of the present case.

It follows that, in the present circumstances and indeed in most other similar circumstances, there is no basis for the charterer recovering overpaid hire from the shipowner in restitution on the ground of total failure of consideration. It is true that sometimes we find in the cases reference to there having been in such circumstances a failure of consideration (see, e.g., *C. A. Stewart & Co.* v. *Phs. Van Ommeren (London) Ltd* [1918] 2 KB 560, 563, *per* Scrutton LJ). But it should not be inferred that such statements refer to a quasi-contractual, as opposed to a contractual, remedy. Consistently with this view, the remedy is not limited to the recovery of money paid for a consideration which has *wholly* failed. A contractual remedy is not, of course, so circumscribed and so, in *C. A. Stewart & Co.* v. *Phs. Van Ommeren (London) Ltd* itself, overpaid hire was recoverable where it was recognised that there had been a partial failure of consideration—see 562, *per* R.A. Wright KC arguendo.

It is against this background that we have to consider Pan Ocean's claim now made against Creditcorp for repayment of the hire instalment paid to it as assignce of the charter hire. First, although the benefit of the contract debt had been assigned to Creditcorp, with the effect that payment to Creditcorp by Pan Ocean constituted a good discharge of the debt, nevertheless the burden of the contract remained upon Trident. From this it follows that Trident remained contractually bound to repay to Pan Ocean any overpaid hire, notwithstanding that such hire had been paid not to Trident but to Creditcorp as assignee. Mr Hirst, for Pan Ocean, accepted in argument that this was so; but he nevertheless maintained that Pan Ocean had alternative courses of action open to it—either to proceed against Trident in contract, or to proceed against Creditcorp in restitution. His argument proceeded on the basis that, in ordinary circumstances, a charterer has alternative remedies against the shipowner for the recovery of overpaid hire, either in contract or in restitution; and that here, since the hire had been paid to Creditcorp as assignee, Pan Ocean's remedy in restitution lay against Creditcorp in place of Trident. However, for the reasons I have already given, I am unable to accept this argument. This is because, in my opinion, Pan Ocean never had any remedy against Trident in restitution on the ground of failure of consideration in the present case, its only remedy against Trident lying under the contract.

In these circumstances, Pan Ocean was thrown back on the arguments canvassed below which, although accepted by the judge, were rejected by the Court of Appeal. Of these, the principal argument was to the effect that, since a payment in advance of time charter hire has been described as a 'provisional' or 'conditional' payment, therefore the hire payment must be regarded as having that character in the hands of an assignee, as it does in the hands of the shipowner, with the consequence that the assignee is liable to repay the hire to the charterer to the extent that it proves to have not been earned. I myself agree with the Court of Appeal that this argument is not well founded, because it rests on a misconception as to what is meant by the terms 'provisional' or 'conditional' in this context. As I understand the position, in a case such as the present they mean no more than that the payment is not final since under the contract there is an obligation, express or implied, to repay to the charterer any part of the hire payment which has not been earned. If this is not clear (as I believe it to be) from the judgments of Bankes and Scrutton L JJ in *G. A. Stewart & Co. v. Phs. Van Ommeren (London) Ltd* [1918] 2 KB 560, 563–4, it was made clear by Lord Sumner in *French Marine* v. *Compagnie Napolitaine d'Eclairage et de Chauffage par le Gaz* [1921] 2 AC 494, 517. In truth, all that happened in the present case was that the benefit of receiving the hire payment was assigned to Creditcorp and, in accordance with the terms of the charter, Trident remained liable to repay to Pan Ocean any part of the hire so paid to Creditcorp which was not earned. Under the charter there were two separate contractual obligations—an obligation on Pan Ocean to pay instalments of hire in advance, and an obligation on Trident to repay any part of any such instalment which was not earned. The assignment to Creditcorp of Trident's right to receive advance hire payments left undisturbed Trident's obligation to repay any hire which was unearned; and I cannot see that in these circumstances the assignment to Creditcorp can have carried with it any obligation upon Creditcorp, additional to the contractual obligation imposed upon Trident, to repay unearned hire on the ground of failure of consideration. As Neill LJ said in the Court of Appeal [1993] 1 Lloyd's Rep. 443, 449:

'No doubt it would be possible to construct a tripartite agreement whereby the assignee of a debt from a creditor would acknowledge that the sum assigned might be repayable in whole or in part to the debtor in specified circumstances. In the present case, however, by the terms of the assignment Creditcorp were assured that the receivables were not subject to any set off or any counterclaim. The debts assigned were not of trust moneys or subject to any form of quasi-trust. The fact that the payment may have been 'provisional' as between Pan Ocean and Trident did not mean, as I see it, that the moneys retained some special characteristic when they reached the hands of a third party.'

I am of course well aware that writers on the law of restitution have been exploring the possibility that, in exceptional circumstances, a plaintiff may have a claim in restitution when he has conferred a benefit on the defendant in the course of performing an obligation to a third party (see, e.g., *Goff and Jones on the Law of Restitution*, 4th edn. (1993), 55 ff, and (for a particular example) *Burrows on the Law of Restitution* (1993), 271–2). But, quite apart from the fact that the existence of a remedy in restitution in such circumstances must still be regarded as a matter of debate, it is always recognised that serious difficulties arise if the law seeks to expand the law of restitution to redistribute risks for which provision has been made under an applicable contract. Moreover, it would in any event be unjust to do so in a case such as the present where the defendant, Creditcorp, is not the mere recipient of a windfall but is an assignee who has purchased from Trident the right to receive the contractual debt which the plaintiff, Pan Ocean, is now seeking to recover from Creditcorp in restitution despite the facts that the relevant contract imposes on the assignor (Trident) an obligation of repayment in the circumstances in question, and that there is nothing in the assignment which even contemplates, still less imposes, any additional obligation on the assignee (Creditcorp) to repay. This is the point which, as I understand it, concerned Neill LJ in the Court of Appeal, when he said that 'Creditcorp were in a position analogous to that of a bona fide purchaser for value:' see [1993] 1 Lloyd's Rep. 443, 449.

For these reasons, I would dismiss the appeal.

Lord Woolf: . . .

The time charter makes it clear that as between Pan Ocean and Trident, Pan Ocean was required to make payments 15 days in advance. If, after the hire has been paid in advance, there occurred an event which caused the vessel to be off-hire during the period for which the hire had been paid, then part or all of the hire paid in advance would not have been earned. In that situation an adjustment of account between the parties would have to be made. The necessary adjustment could be achieved by deducting an appropriate amount from the *next* payment of advance hire or, if there would be no further payment due, by Trident making a repayment to Pan Ocean. The fact that such an adjustment or repayment would have to be made would not alter the fact that under the time charter Trident had been contractually entitled to receive payment in advance, in full, of the instalment which was to be paid prior to the occurrence of the event. Although after the happening of that event Pan Ocean would have a right of set-off as against a future instalment of hire or a right of repayment, the right to receive the payment of the hire instalment was separate and distinct from the right to receive credit for hire which had been paid but not earned and those rights would give rise to independent causes of action.

This being the position between the immediate parties to the time charter, as Trident had only assigned its rights under the time charter to Creditcorp, you would expect (a) that Creditcorp would be entitled to receive the third instalment of hire or at least part of that sum; and (b) that Pan Ocean's right to repayment would be confined to enforcing their contractual rights against Trident since the burden of the contract had not been assigned to Creditcorp. (As Neill LJ points out, the vessel had been off-hire since 27 May so that at the time of payment of the third instalment Pan Ocean may have been entitled to withhold a proportion of the instalment.)

Mr Hirst on behalf of Pan Ocean vigorously disputes that this should be the result. He concedes that Pan Ocean would not be entitled to enforce its contractual rights to receive a repayment against Creditcorp since the assignment by Trident of its right to receive payment of the hire instalments to Creditcorp would not involve a transfer to Creditcorp of Trident's contractual obligations under the time charter. However, Mr Hirst submits that where a person receives, as of right, a payment in advance, it is liable to be repaid if the payment is not earned since it is a condition of retaining the payment that the consideration for which it is paid is provided. He contends that if there had been no assignment, Pan Ocean would have had bath a contractual right of repayment and a right of restitution as against Trident. That while after the notice of the assignment and payment to Creditcorp, Pan Ocean's contractual rights would still only be against Trident, there would also be a personal right of restitution which would then be against Creditcorp. The personal right would arise, so it is argued, because Creditcorp, once it had given notice of assignment, was entitled to receive the advance payment as of right from Pan Ocean and the payment being an advance payment was one which was conditional or provisional on the payment being earned. If at the end of the period for which the payment was made all or part of the hire had not been earned Pan Ocean would be entitled to the return of that part of the payment which had not been earned in the same way as it could admittedly be deducted from a future instalment of hire not yet paid.

In support of his contentions, Mr Hirst was not able to rely upon any authorities which involved an assignment but he submitted that he could derive support from *Tonnelier* v. *Smith* (1897) 2 Com. Cas. 258, *C. A. Stewart & Co.* v. *Phs. Van Ommeren (London) Ltd* [1918] 2 KB 560 and *Fibrosa Spolka Akcyjna* v. *Fairbairn Lawson Combe Barbour Ltd.* [1943] AC 32. The two earlier cases both involved charterparties where the charterer was required to pay for the hire in advance. In the *Tonnelier* case it was held by a majority that the charterer was liable to pay the monthly hire to the owners at the beginning of each month, even if it was obvious that the vessel would be redelivered to the owners before the month had expired. However, although the payments were to be made in advance, in the words of the judgment of the majority (Lord Esher MR and Rigby LJ at 265), they were 'to be provisional only and not final and the charterer was entitled to have repaid all moneys paid in advance and not earned. In *Stewart's* case [1918] 2 KB 560 the Court of Appeal applied the decision in the *Tonnelier* case and Bankes LJ stated, at 562, that under the charterparty the payment was to be:

'made of a fixed sum on a fixed date in each month in advance for the opportunity of using the ship for every day in that month, but upon the terms that in certain events, which are named, if the charterers are deprived of that opportunity for any of those days, the owners are liable to repay the amount attributable to those days.'

In *Stewart's* case it was an express term of the charterparty that hire paid in advance and not earned should be returned to the charterers. Mr Hirst therefore relies on the statement of Scrutton LJ (at 564) that if the ship during a month, in respect of which hire had been paid, came off hire, 'there is a failure of consideration for the payment' for the days upon which the ship is off-hire and the sum paid for those days can be recovered by action.

The *Fibrosa* case [1943] AC 32 is relied on for what was said by their Lordships as to the position with regard to payments in advance which, because a contract was frustrated by a super-vening event, were not earned. The House held that a party who has paid money under a contract in advance, which is frustrated, is entitled to recover the money on the ground that the consideration for which the sum had been paid wholly failed. In that situation as Viscount Simon LC said, at 46:

'[the claim] is not based on any provision contained in the contract, but arises because, in the circumstances that have happened, the law gives a remedy in quasi-contract to the party who has not got that for which he bargained. It is a claim to recover money to which the defendant has no further right because in the circumstances that have happened the money must be regarded as received to the plaintiff's use.'

While it is understandable that Mr Hirst should submit that support for his submissions is provided by these cases, the statements on which he relies were made in a different context and it is disputed by Mr Glennie, on behalf of Creditcorp, that they can be applied to the advance payment here so that unearned hire can be recovered not from the other party to the contract but from the other party's assignee to whom the payment was made.

To this issue the cases really provide no direct assistance. The claims in quasi-contract with which they deal arise as a result of the failure of the other party to the contract to provide the consideration for which the payment was made. It is one thing to require the other party to the contract to repay if he does not provide the consideration which under the contract he was under obligation to supply, it is another to make the assignee, who was never intended to be under any obligation to supply the consideration liable to make the repayment. It is conceded that there is no right to trace moneys which are paid to an assignee and there is never any question of their being any restriction on the assignee preventing him dealing with the money as his own. There is no justification for subjecting an assignee, because he has received a payment in advance, to an obligation to make a repayment because of the non-performance of an event for which he has no responsibility.

Mr Hirst also referred to general statements of principle which were made by Sir Robert Megarry V-C in *Tito* v. *Waddell (No 2)*, [1977] Ch. 106. In that case, under the heading 'Benefit and burden' the Vice-Chancellor considered conditional benefits and independent obligations. In a passage of his judgment on which Mr Hirst relies, the Vice-Chancellor drew a distinction between what 'for brevity may be called conditional benefits, on the one hand, and on the other hand independent obligations.' The Vice-Chancellor stated, at 290:

'An instrument may be framed so that it confers only a conditional or qualified right, the condition or qualification being that certain restrictions shall be observed or certain burdens assumed, such as an obligation to make certain payments. Such restrictions or qualifications are an intrinsic part of the right: you take the right as it stands, and you cannot pick out the good and reject the bad. In such cases it is not only the original grantee who is bound by the burden: his successors in title are unable to take the right without also assuming the burden. The benefit and the burden have been annexed to each other ab initio, and so the benefit is only a conditional benefit. In the other class of case the right and the burden, although arising under the same instrument, are independent of each other.'

This statement of principle by the Vice-Chancellor only helps Mr Hirst if Creditcorp's right to receive payment in advance was a conditional right or what the Vice-Chancellor describes as a 'conditional benefit.' In fact the right was not conditional. There was nothing qualified about the right, notwithstanding the fact that if a payment in advance was made but not earned an independent right to be repaid the unearned advance instalment would accrue to Pan Ocean.

Mr Hirst drew our attention to an interesting article reviewing the decision in this case in the Court of Appeal by Mr Tettenborn in 1993 *Cambridge Law Journal* 220. The article endorses the approach of Judge Diamond QC. Mr Tettenborn, in the article, asks what he describes as the fundamental question, at 222:

'Having paid Creditcorp for something they did not get, why should Pan Ocean not have got their money back? There is every reason in justice why they should: the Court of Appeal, it it suggested, has given no reason why they should not.'

With respect to Mr Tettenborn, he has not given sufficient credit to the reasoning of the judgments, in particular of Neill LJ, in the Court of Appeal. Pan Ocean are in exactly the same position as against Trident as they would have been if there had been no assignment to Creditcorp of the right to receive payment. The assignment occurred quite independently of Pan Ocean's contract with Trident. If Pan Ocean were entitled to recover from Creditcorp, the consequence would be that they would have two different parties instead of a single party from whom they could recover; on Mr Hirst's argument, against Trident under the contract and against Creditcorp for money had and received. It is equally possible to frame a different fundamental question. Why should Pan Ocean have two alternative parties to whom to look for a repayment merely because Trident as part of their own financial arrangements, have assigned their right to receive payment to a third party, Creditcorp?

I should also refer to the fact that Mr Hirst criticises the reliance which Beldam LJ made in his judgment in the Court of Appeal on *Aiken* v. *Short* (1856) 1 H & N 210 and *Barclays Banks Ltd* v. *W.J. Simms Son & Cooke (Southern) Ltd* [1980] QB 677, which were apparently not considered in the course of argument. Those cases were dealing with payments made by mistake and I would not, myself, rely on them in order to come to the conclusion that this appeal has to be dismissed.

Finally, I should indicate that I make no comment about Creditcorp's second line of defence. Their Lordships did not feel it necessary to hear argument in support of this second line of defence. This defence is that Creditcorp could not be called upon to make repayment since Creditcorp, after receiving the third instalment, had altered its position without notice of the claim of Pan Ocean by paying out the money received in the ordinary course of its business.

For the reasons I have given I would dismiss this appeal with costs.

Lord Keith and **Lord Slynn** agreed with **Lord Woolf**, while **Lord Lowry** agreed with both **Lord Woolf** and **Lord Goff**.

NOTES AND QUESTIONS

1. The correct analysis of this case has proved elusive. Some of the reasoning of their Lordships is unpersuasive: e.g. Lord Woolf's view that failure of consideration can only be claimed against the contracting party responsible for that failure; and Lord Goff's primary reasoning that there was an express contractual term governing overpaid hire which ousted restitution. Is Lord Goff's secondary reasoning—that restitution for Pan Ocean from Creditcorp would undermine the contract of assignment between Trident and Creditcorp—more convincing?

2. According to Birks none of their Lordships pointed to the true reason for the denial of restitution. In his view, Creditcorp's enrichment was 'at the expense of' Trident and not 'at the expense of' Pan Ocean. Although the money was paid directly by Pan Ocean to Creditcorp that was in accordance with the terms of an initially valid contract between Pan Ocean and Trident. It did not matter that by reason of the assignment, Pan Ocean were bound to pay Creditcorp. He wrote in *Unjust Enrichment* (2nd edn, 2005), 92: 'Can it be that a payer liable to the payee was not in an immediate enricher-enrichee relationship with the payee? The answer is yes, because recourse to the machinery of assignment does not alter the facts that the payment to Creditcorp was procured by the owners on the faith of their either earning it or repaying it, and that to allow the restitutionary claim against Creditcorp would be to allow Pan Ocean to wriggle out of the risk of insolvency which their contract with the owners entailed. The fact that their contract contained a term for repayment may make this extra-clear. But the result would have been the same without it. What we know from this case, although we could have worked it out without its help, is that the veto on leapfrogging out of an initially valid contract is very strong, strong enough to protect even an assignee'.

3. For case notes, see K Barker, 'Restitution and Third Parties' [1994] *LMCLQ* 305 and A Burrows, 'Restitution from Assignees' [1994] *RLR* 52.

• *Khan v Permayer* [2001] BPIR 95, Court of Appeal

The claimant (Mr Khan) ran a restaurant with his business partner (Mr El-Mahdi). They wanted to sell the restaurant and the lease of its premises to X (Mr Eaves). The defendant landlord, Mr Permayer, made it a condition of the assignment of the lease that a debt of £40,000 owed to him by the claimant was repaid. It was agreed that X would repay that debt. X did so and the claimant then reimbursed X. Later it emerged that the supposed debt of £40,000 did not exist: it had been discharged in earlier insolvency proceedings. The claimant therefore sought to recover £40,000 from the defendant on the basis of unjust enrichment. This claim succeeded at trial and the appeal by the defendant was dismissed.

Morritt LJ: . . .

(32) Miss Reed [counsel for Permayer] relied on passages from the 5th Edition of *Goff & Jones on Restitution*. Thus at p 38 it is pointed out that:

'Where the payment to the defendant was made by a third party it cannot normally be recovered by the claimant.'

(33) The authors added on p 39:

'The conclusion that P has no claim against D is, as a general rule, a wise one. At one time it was held that P's claim failed because there was no "privity" between P and D. As Professor Dawson said, the invocation of the fiction of privity reflected a "dimly felt situation that it was a mistake to become involved in these multi-party confusions when quasi-contract would short circuit a series of interconnected transactions, without joinder of the parties at intermediate stages".'

(34) Later on the same page the authors recognised that:

'There are situations where P has successfully recovered from D the sum which T paid to D and where D's gain was commensurate with P's loss.'

(35) The examples given in the succeeding pages of Goff & Jones are usurpation of office, attornment, mistaken bequests, secret trusts and bribes paid to a fiduciary. As Miss Reed pointed out none of these cases of exception would appear to cover this case.

(36) However, in a recent decision of the House of Lords, it is recognised, if not first established, that subrogation is an equitable remedy available in cases of unjust enrichment: see *Banque Financiere de la Cité v Parc (Battersea) Ltd* [1999] 1 AC 221.

. . .

(38) On behalf of Mr Permayer it is submitted by Miss Reed that the case of *Banque Financiere v (Battersea) Ltd* is of little help. She submits that it has always been recognised that subrogation exists as a remedy and that that case was a classic example of subrogation to the rights of the creditor who had been partially repaid . . . She points out (which is undoubtedly the case) that unlike *Parc (Battersea)* it would not be possible here to follow or trace the money from Mr Khan through Mr Eaves into the hands of Mr Permayer. She submits that—and this is where I disagree—in this case the transactions between Mr Khan and Mr El-Mahdi on the one hand and Mr Eaves on the other were separate and independent from the transactions between Mr Eaves on the one hand and Mr Permayer on the other.

(39) It appears to me that Mr Khan, Mr El-Mahdi and Mr Eaves were severally liable for the same debt they mistakenly thought was due to Mr Permayer. They agreed between them that the debt would be paid by Mr Eaves, but the cost of it would be borne by Mr Khan and Mr El-Mahdi.

(40) It appears to me that *Parc Battersea* does establish that a payment made by a third party under a mistaken belief which gives rise to unjust enrichment of the defendant may be recoverable by the person at whose ultimate expense it was paid if that person is also acting under the same mistake as the third party. In this case Mr Khan and Mr El-Mahdi bore the ultimate expense of the payment Mr Eaves made to Mr Permayer. On the judge's findings, all three of them, that is to say Mr Khan, Mr El-Mahdi and Mr Eaves, were acting under the same mistaken belief that there was a debt due to Mr Permayer from Mr Khan and Mr El-Mahdi secured on the subunderlease. The loss to Mr Khan and Mr El-Mahdi is precisely commensurate with the payment by Mr Eaves to Mr Permayer and there are no intermediate rights in favour of third parties capable of giving rise to the multi-party confusions to which Professor Dawson referred in the passage quoted in Goff & Jones to which I have referred earlier.

(41) The judge considered the limits to the restitutionary remedy relied on, but not, I think, the decision of the House of Lords in *Parc (Battersea)*. He said:

'There was, in my judgment, first of all a wrongful demand; secondly, there were the two elements of mistake and, I think, a degree of compulsion, but certainly mistake; thirdly the debt was not paid voluntarily; fourthly, in my judgment there was unjust enrichment in that it is unconscionable for the defendant to keep what he was never entitled to demand in the first place; fifthly, the money was obtained at the plaintiff's expense. In case it is necessary, I add that it is the plaintiff's money that ultimately has gone to the defendant.'

(42) For my part I agree . . .

Sir Christopher Staughton delivered a concurring judgment.

NOTES AND QUESTIONS

1. The Court of Appeal justified the decision by reference to the law on subrogation. Although unclear, it would appear that the subrogation in mind was that C (Khan) was subrogated to X's (Eaves') rights against D (Permayer) because, mistakenly, C had paid for the discharge of D's liability to X. On this analysis, what created D's liability to X? For the *Banque Financière* case, see below, 190.

2. Birks, *Unjust Enrichment* (2nd edn, 2005), 88 argued that this was a straightforward case of direct subtraction. As X had been procured by C to pay D, D was the immediate enrichee of C (not the immediate enrichee of X). No question of leapfrogging therefore arose. Leapfrogging would have arisen (and would 'almost certainly' have been ruled out because of the valid agreement between C and X) if X had been seeking restitution from D.

3. For an alternative justification in terms of avoiding circuity of action—based on X having an action for mistaken payment against D, and C having an action against X—see Burrows, *The Law of Restitution* (2nd edn, 2002), 40–41.

- **Uren v First National Home Finance Ltd**
  [2005] EWHC 2529 (Ch), Chancery Division

The claimant wanted to buy two flats in a new development being built in Tenerife. In part payment of the purchase price, he paid £50,000 to the development company called Arrish Ltd. Loans to Arrish for the development were provided by the defendant bank. When Arrish defaulted, the defendant bank appointed receivers and the development property was acquired by a subsidiary of the defendant's, called Pitchcott Ltd. Pitchcott in turn was purchased by Santa Barbara Ltd. The claimant paid the remaining balance of £75,000 due on the flats to Pitchcott/Santa Barbara in order for the work to be completed. The defendant bank continued to provide loans for the development. When the development had been substantially completed, the defendant called in its loans, took over the development and sold it to a company called LSI (which was experienced in time-shares). That sale enabled the bank to recoup its loans and in addition it was guaranteed by LSI future profitable loan business. The claimant argued that the defendant had in bad faith engineered the receiverships and sought to recover £125,000 from the defendant bank on the ground of the latter's unjust enrichment. The defendant's application for reverse summary judgment succeeded because the claimant had no reasonable prospect of success at trial. Mann J said, in obiter dicta, that there was no *unjust* enrichment of the bank (see below, 134). But even if there had been, he held that that enrichment was not *at the claimant's expense*.

Mann J: . . . 21. Mr Hibbert's [counsel for the defendant] point is that, even given whatever injustice may be said to have been perpetrated in the defendant's plans, what is not demonstrated as a result of all that is that there has been anything which the law of unjust enrichment would regard as an enrichment of the defendant at the expense of the claimant. There is no sufficient nexus between the payment of Mr Uren's money, the acts of the defendant bank and the benefits flowing from the arrangements with LSI. Mr Matthias [counsel for the claimant] says there is a sufficient link. Mr Uren has paid 125,000. It has gone into the development. The defendant has embarked on a course of conduct which reduced the development into its hands, and it has have now made a profit from it in the amount of the sums paid by LSI over and above the amount necessary to discharge the original debt owed by Pitchcott. He points out, and relies on, the fact that the defendant from time to time indicated that it was going to protect, or have regard to, the interests of the purchasers by getting an ultimate purchaser of the development to acknowledge their rights to flats. It has reneged on those indications. It is only because the bank had the advantage of the contributions of people like Mr Uren that it had an asset that it could sell at such a value. It has behaved unjustly in order to put itself in that position; therefore he can make out the ingredients of a claim in unjust enrichment as those ingredients are set out by Lord Steyn in the [*Banque Financière* case, below, 190].

22. I am afraid that I do not accept those submissions on the part of Mr Matthias. I have approached this question with all the caution required of a court considering a defendant's summary judgment application, or a defendant's application to strike out. I must be satisfied that at the trial there will be nothing emerging, or likely to emerge, which will assist the claimant. However, making all due allowances, and giving full effect to the assumed facts (which put the case at the highest level at which Mr Uren can hope to establish it at a trial) Mr Uren is still bound to fail. The reason is that one can only say that the defendant had been enriched at the expense of Mr Uren in an unjust way by a very loose and generalised use of language and concepts which are not appropriate to a legal analysis of the situation. The answer to the point lies in an appreciation that the benefits to the bank do not, in law, amount to an enrichment at the expense of Mr Uren. Let it be allowed for the moment that the bank had indeed been enriched in the sense that it is financially better off at the end of the sequence of events than it was at the beginning, and that it has achieved that by the terms on which it realised its (or its subsidiaries) interest in the development. It cannot, in my view, be said that that was done at the expense of Mr Uren. Mr Uren's first 50,000 became lost to him at the latest when Arrish Limited became insolvent (as it apparently did) and went into receivership. The property was then sold away from Arrish Limited. At that point Mr Uren had (presumably) the benefit of a worthless unsecured claim against Arrish Limited. He had no claim against the bank at that stage. At that stage, the bank has not acquired the benefit of his money by any unjust means, even though it then acquired the property by taking it into a subsidiary. Mr Uren's next tranche of money (the 75,000) was first paid into the fighting fund. I assume that it was in no way dissipated there and survived intact so that it could be passed on at the next stage. That next stage was when the fighting fund provided the money to Santa Barbara Limited so that it could be used to discharge an outstanding indebtedness of Pitchcott to the bank (presumably arising when Pitchcott borrowed money to buy the development from Arrish Limited). At this stage Pitchcott probably owed the 75,000 to Mr Uren, or to someone else on his behalf. Although it was apparently intended at some stage that the purchasers should have shares, that never happened. When Mr Uren provided his money to the fighting fund, the fund either held it beneficially for him or he lent it to the fighting fund. When the money was passed into Santa Barbara Limited/Pitchcott, it seems likely to me that the transaction became one of loan. It may be that an alternative analysis would be that it was treated as an advance payment of the purchase price. Whichever analysis is the case, Mr Uren got whatever it was that the transaction gave rise to some cause of action against Pitchcott (probably) but absolutely no relationship with the bank. It is true that there is a pleading (which is assumed to be true for these purposes) that the bank encouraged the fighting fund to put its money into Pitchcott, but that money did not go to pay for the development: it went to repay an indebtedness to the bank.

23. So at this stage of the analysis neither sum of money has gone to enrich the bank (or at least not in any material way). It has been used as advance payments or as loans. All the usual instances of

unjust enrichment involve the payment of money, or the transfer of property, by the claimant to or for the benefit of the defendant, which of itself either at that time or by the operation of intended facts, produces some form of benefit to the defendant amounting to enrichment. Nothing like that has happened in the present case. What has happened in this case is that Mr Uren has spent his money, and lost his money, in and towards the development of land. That developed land has come into the hands of the defendant, and (on the assumed facts) it has come into the hands of the defendant as the result of an injustice. There is not, however, the necessary link between the first set of events and the second set to enable Mr Uren to be able to say that the enrichment of the defendant is at the expense of him. It is not enough to say that the defendant has had the benefit of the expenditure by the claimant; there must, in my view, be some causal connection or nexus.

24. The point can be developed by reference to the speech of Lord Clyde in *Banque Financière* at page 237F:

> Without attempting any comprehensive analysis, it seems to me that the principle [of unjust enrichment] requires at least that the plaintiff should have sustained a loss by the provision of something for the benefit of some other person with no intention of making a gift, that the defend-ant should have received some form of enrichment, and that the enrichment has come about because of the loss. The loss may be an expenditure which has not met with the expected return.

The some other person in that citation is, in my view, clearly the same person as the defendant otherwise the citation contains no causal connection between the events at all. If that is right, then the application of that analysis demonstrates why it is that Mr Uren fails in this case. If one breaks it down, one has the following elements:

(i)   the plaintiff has sustained a loss;
(ii)   he has done so by providing something for the benefit of some other person. That other person in this case was two people first Arrish Limited and second Pitchcott. It was not the bank.
(iii) With no intention of making a gift Mr Uren satisfies that.
(iv)   That the defendant should have received some form of enrichment the bank has, on these facts, received some form of enrichment, but only in a generalised sense.
(v)   That enrichment has come about because of the loss this is not established. The enrichment has come about because the bank, through its subsidiary, acquired the development property and then turned a profit on a subsequent sale. It has not achieved that enrichment because of the loss to Mr Uren.

. . .

26. In analysing the matter in this way I would not wish to suggest that it is necessary to come within some strict form of words. What is, however, necessary is to bring the case within justifiable legal concepts. The passage from Lord Steyn clearly suggests, not surprisingly and in accordance with what one would normally expect to be the principles applicable, that there should be some proper connection between the payment of the money and the enrichment. That is usually achieved in unjust enrichment cases by demonstrating money flowing from A to B, or money flowing from A to Bs benefit because, for example, it has been spent on Bs property. That sort of flow, or something like it, is simply not demonstrated in the present case. Mr Uren's first 50,000 was lost when Arrish Limited went into receivership. His next 75,000 was lost when Pitchcott became insolvent. When it was lost the bank was not thereby enriched.

27. Accordingly, on this basis, Mr Uren's case fails. . . .

28. This does not mean of course that there is no remedy on the supposed facts of this case (though the passage of time may in fact mean there is no remedy). If the bank has behaved as badly as is alleged, then there would almost certainly be remedies vested in Pitchcott, and conceivably Santa Barbara Limited. If the banks refusal to honour the loan arrangements properly was a breach

of contract, then any loss flowing would sound in damages. If the bank has contrived a situation which enabled it to acquire the property at an undervalue and then turn it to advantage, then again Pitchcott, as the owner of the property, would presumably have a remedy. Those claims may or may not be without their own difficulties, but if wrongs were committed then those claims ought to exist. I am told that the receivers of Pitchcott have declined to pursue the bank. I do not know the extent to which that is true, or if it is true what the reasons for it are. However, if it is the case, then that is very unfortunate for the purchasers (if they would otherwise have benefited from such claims) but that misfortune cannot be overcome by seeking to fashion a remedy based on unjust enrichment in order to overcome the inconveniences of the chain of contracts and incorporation that exist in this case and which have their own consequences. The purchasers may feel that the bank has been enriched, that it has behaved unfairly, and that they have lost, but it is not appropriate to put all those ingredients in some melting pot, give it a stir and pull out a newly cast unjust enrichment claim. A proper degree of analysis is required.

. . .

NOTES AND QUESTIONS

1. This case clearly shows that factual causation is insufficient to establish the required nexus between claimant and defendant. That is, it was insufficient in establishing that the defendant's gain was *at the claimant's expense* to prove that the defendant bank's enrichment would not have occurred but for the claimant's (and other purchasers') loss.

2. Is the decision best explained by saying: (i) the defendant bank was not the direct enrichee of the claimant and, apart from inapplicable rare situations, restitution against indirect enrichees is not allowed; or (ii) leapfrogging against indirect enrichees is permissible but an exception to that is that one cannot leapfrog out of an initially valid contract (see Birks above, 120)?

3. WAS THE ENRICHMENT UNJUST?

This is the question which requires the most detailed analysis of past cases because the decision as to when enrichment at the claimant's expense is unjust is not a matter for a judge's (or commentator's) individual discretion, but must essentially be gleaned from the existing case law. As regards the cause of action of unjust enrichment, the main *unjust factors* can be listed as follows:

mistake, ignorance, failure of consideration, illegitimate pressure, undue influence, exploitation of weakness, legal compulsion, necessity, illegality, incapacity, and *ultra vires* demands by public authorities.

It is those factors that, *at a general level*, establish that the defendant's enrichment at the claimant's expense is unjust. But to isolate those unjust factors is merely the start of the investigation. Only detailed examination of the cases will reveal, for example, what types of mistake have been held to trigger restitution or what the law means by failure of consideration and in what factual contexts it operates. It is primarily with the task of elucidating the details of *unjust* enrichment that Chapters 3–12 are concerned.

The heavy reliance on past cases is not meant to suggest that there is no scope for an expansion of the cause of action of unjust enrichment. On the contrary, we believe that the above categories of unjust factor are not closed (the decision in *Woolwich Equitable Building Society v IRC*, see below, Chapter 12, can be regarded as proving this); and that, within the categories, the open recognition of the underlying principle against unjust enrichment in *Lipkin Gorman v Karpnale Ltd* (above, 28) makes it easier for the courts to discard unwarranted historical restrictions (the rejection in *Kleinwort Benson Ltd v Lincoln City Council* (below, 167) of the mistake of law rule can be regarded as showing this). In *CTN Cash and Carry Ltd v Gallaher Ltd* (below, 426) Sir Donald Nicholls V-C expressly said, 'The categories of unjust enrichment are not closed'.

On the other hand, as obiter dicta in *Uren v First National Home Finance Ltd* (below, 134) clearly shows, it is insufficient for a claimant simply to plead an unjust enrichment at the claimant's expense without pointing to facts that fall within an existing category or can be seen as a justifiable development from that category.

Although Birks subsequently preferred an entirely different approach, he and Chambers (below, 135) earlier regarded it as useful to take the unjust factors back to three higher-level ideas, namely (i) that the claimant did not mean the defendant to have the enrichment; (ii) that the receipt was unconscientious; (iii) that there is a policy favouring restitution.

In his final book, *Unjust Enrichment* (2nd edn, 2005) (below, 137) Birks abandoned the common law 'unjust factors' approach to the unjust question, that he himself had done so much to develop and refine, in favour of a civilian-style 'absence of basis' approach. According to this, restitution is awarded (subject to defences) if an enrichment at the claimant's expense is without a legal basis. Birks saw his scheme as 'an English version of the civilian "sine causa" approach' (preface p ix). In shorthand terms, the legal bases in mind are, most importantly, a valid obligation or, if no obligation, a trust or gift or (anticipated) contract. So, for example, if C pays money to D mistakenly believing that it is bound to do so, C is entitled to restitution simply because it thought there was a legal obligation to pay and in reality that basis was absent. Birks went so far as to argue that the English courts through *Westdeutsche Landesbank Girozentrale v Islington London BC* (below, 362) and *Guinness Mahon & Co. Ltd v Kensington and Chelsea RLBC* (below, 369) have already moved to the absence of basis approach but this seems a far-fetched and inaccurate interpretation. On the other hand, there are significant advantages, as well as major disadvantages, to the new Birksian scheme and debate rages as to its merits. Throughout Chapters 3–12, the reader should reflect on how cases would be decided applying the Birksian approach. So while the traditional unjust factors approach is adhered to in this book, it is believed that Birks' 'civilian' scheme can operate as a useful cross-check in novel or difficult cases.

We also examine in this section the 'modified civilian approach' to the unjust question that has been adopted by the Supreme Court of Canada.

General Reading

BURROWS, 41–51; GOFF AND JONES, 1-052–1-091; VIRGO, 119–130.

(1) UNJUST FACTORS AND INCREMENTAL DEVELOPMENT FROM THEM

- *Uren v First National Home Finance Ltd*
  [2005] EWHC 2529 (Ch), Chancery Division

For the facts, see above, 130.

Mann J: . . .

16. . . . It seems to me that it has not been established that the authorities have yet moved to a

position in which it can be said that there is a freestanding claim of unjust enrichment in the sense that a claimant can get away with pleading facts which he says leads to an enrichment which he says is unjust. The authorities, and at least some academic opinion, still support the view that on the present state of the authorities, the law has not yet got that far. It seems to me to be clear that that is the present state of the law. Were it necessary to decide the case on this basis, I would be likely to decide that despite the undeniable fact that the law of restitution is still developing. It has not developed and is unlikely to develop (at least in the foreseeable future) to that extent. A claimant still has to establish that his facts bring him within one of the hitherto established categories of unjust enrichment, or some justifiable extension thereof. Were it otherwise, then why did the claimants in the *West Deutsche* case have to go to such lengths to establish that their facts fell within one of the then established categories or recovery bases (by extension)? The same is true of *Kleinwort Benson v Lincoln City Council* [1999] 1 AC 349. That case established that it was no longer true to say that a payment made under a mistake of law was irrecoverable. I think that if there had been a general ground of recovery based on unjust enrichment which it could invoke by pleading facts and alleging injustice, then the speeches in that case would have taken a rather different form.

. . .

18. Accordingly, had I had to decide the point in this case, I would be likely to have decided against the claimant and Mr Matthias. That being the case, it would follow that the claim fails because it does not plead facts which are capable of bringing the case within one of the established restitutionary claims or some justifiable extension of them. By that I do not mean merely that it fails to incorporate some particular form of words. If the facts were sufficient it would not matter that there is no pleading of some particular category of restitutionary claim. I mean that the facts themselves do not come sufficiently close to the required objective. When asked which established claim he would rely on if necessary Mr Matthias could only suggest unconscionability (not enough by itself) or an extension of the claim for the money paid for a consideration which has wholly failed. This latter point will not assist him. It might describe a claim against the developer companies, but it cannot begin to describe the claim against the defendant.

19. However, because of my views on the other limbs of the case, I do not have to decide this point and can base my decision on those other points. . . .

(2) BIRKS AND CHAMBERS' STRUCTURING OF THE UNJUST FACTORS

- P Birks and R Chambers, *The Restitution Research Resource 1997*, 2–3

What [this diagram] suggests is that the law of restitution is sharply divided as between restitution for wrongs and autonomous unjust enrichment . . . Restitution for wrongs is a remedial inquiry about the availability of restitutionary (i.e. gain-based) damages for wrongs. This part of the law of restitution can equally be considered to be part of the law of wrongs and part of the law of remedies. However, autonomous unjust enrichment is a study of causes of action in unjust enrichment. The word 'autonomous' is put in to make clear that here the cause of action arises, not in the law of wrongs (torts, breaches of contract, breaches of equitable or statutory duty), but in the independent category of unjust enrichment. . . .

[The diagram] then subdivides autonomous unjust enrichment according to the nature of the fact which renders the enrichment unjust. We think that there are only three families of such fact, though a cautious classifier might add a fourth, namely 'others.' The first family of 'unjust factors' is quite numerous but all its members have in common that they entitle the plaintiff to say, in effect, 'I did not mean the defendant to have this value.' The second family is 'unconscientious receipt.' Here the reason for restitution is that the defendant behaved badly in receiving the value in question. The third family of unjust factors have nothing to do with either the impairment of the plaintiff's intention to give or the quality of the defendant's behaviour in receiving; it includes all of what might be called 'overriding reasons' for restitution, where the law judges that a given policy objective is best pursued by ensuring that there is restitution of the value in question. The three families of unjust factor can be represented in nursery terms as: 1) I didn't mean it; 2) it was bad of you to receive it; and 3) Mother says give it back anyway.

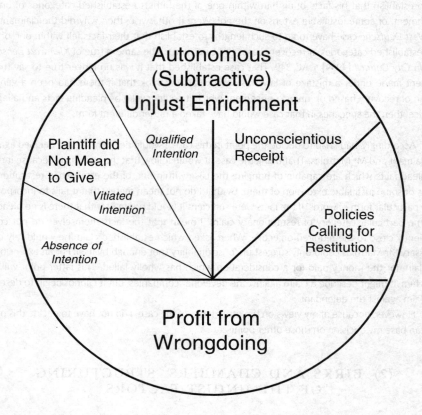

The lines which divide the first of these families represent important sub-divisions of the 'I didn't mean it' group. Moving clockwise, in the first of the three segments 'I didn't mean it' is true because the plaintiff had no intent at all that value should pass from him to the defendant. This may be because the plaintiff (a) was unaware that value was passing (e.g. he transported goods or a person secretly hidden on his train or dropped money without knowing it), (b) was powerless to prevent it passing (e.g. he saw his money being taken but was too far away to intervene), (c) was absolutely incapable of making the decision to pass the value or (d) may have intended to pass the legal title, but did not intend to give the defendant a beneficial interest in the property. In the second segment, the integrity of the plaintiff's decision to transfer the value was impaired, as by a mistake or because of illegitimate pressure. In the third segment the reason why the plaintiff can say that he did not mean the defendant to have the value in question is not because his decision to give was impaired but because it was initially conditional and in the event the condition has not been purified. If I give you £10,000 because you have agreed to build me a garage and in the event no garage is built, I can fairly say that, in the events which have happened, I did not mean you to have the £10,000.

The reasons for restitution are therefore either the fact that an acquisitive wrong is of a kind which the law recognizes as giving rise to a restitutionary award or that a subtractive enrichment was received in circumstances in which it was not intended, or in which it was shabby of the defendant to receive it, or in which, outside the parties, there is an overriding reason why the money should be given back.

NOTE

The existence and content of 'unconscientious receipt' are controversial and largely turn on whether one believes that free acceptance is an unjust factor (see below, 392). Even Birks came to regard 'unconscientious receipt' as relevant only where there was a consent-based factor and not as an independent category: see P Birks, *The Foundations of Unjust Enrichment* (2002), 48, 68; and *Unjust Enrichment* (2nd edn, 2005), 42.

(3) BIRKS' NEW 'ABSENCE OF BASIS' SCHEME

• P Birks, *Unjust Enrichment* (2nd edn, 2005) 113–14, 129–130

The swaps cases show that the invalidity of a contract is in itself the reason why there has to be restitution of enrichments transferred under it. The invalidity means that those enrichments have no explanatory basis. They are transferred *sine causa*. After the swaps cases English law is bound to use this civilian method of answering the third question. In a system which was getting used to consent-based and policy-based unjust factors it has been tempting to absorb this conclusion by adding absence of basis to the list. That cannot be done.

. . .

In most situations the 'no basis' test works with a surgical simplicity which the lists of unjust factors could not emulate.

Every enrichment comes about either with or without the participation of the claimant. Non-participatory transfers are those over which the claimant has no control, as where a pickpocket takes money from his pocket. Such an enrichment at the claimant's expense almost invariably has no explanatory basis.

Participatory enrichments are perceived as either obligatory or voluntary. If the purpose is discharge of an obligation and there is indeed a valid obligation which is discharged, the enrichment has an explanatory basis and cannot be unjust. If there turns out to be no valid obligation discharged, the enrichment is inexplicable. It has no explanatory basis. Voluntary enrichments are those which are transferred without obligation but in order to achieve some outcome. If that purpose is achieved, the basis has not failed. If it is not achieved, the enrichment has no explanatory basis.

The previous paragraph can be restated in the form of three questions which will resolve nearly all cases. (1) Was the enrichment perceived to be obligatory? If it was, its basis will have failed if there was in fact no obligation. (2) If it was not obligatory but voluntary, what end was it intended to achieve or depend upon and, in particular, was it intended to bring about or depend upon a contract, trust, gift or other outcome? If that outcome did not come about, the basis of the enrichment will have failed. (3) If the enrichment was acquired without the participation of the claimant or his agents, was there any legal authority for its acquisition by the defendant? The premiss of the third question is that in general enrichments of that kind necessarily have no basis.

In relation to both 1) and 2) it is tempting to enter an immediate caveat, namely that the claimant must not have knowingly taken the risk that the desired outcome would not be achieved. But that caveat is actually supererogatory, for one who takes such a risk desires one outcome but intends two. A busker desires to be paid for his music but intends a gift to those who choose not to pay. It follows without more that, in relation to the latter, there is no failure of basis.

NOTES AND QUESTIONS

1. For Birks' full formulation of his new scheme, see *Unjust Enrichment* (2nd edn, 2005), Chapters 5–6. For an evaluation of it see, e.g., R Stevens' review of those chapters of Birks' book in [2004] *RLR* 270–273; A Burrows, 'Absence of Basis: The New Birksian Scheme' in *Mapping the Law: Essays in Memory of Peter Birks* (eds A Burrows and Lord Rodger, 2006), 33–48.

2. What are the respective advantages and disadvantages of the traditional common law unjust factors approach and the new Birksian scheme? Would the application of Birks' new scheme lead to different decisions in cases?

3. Birks' new scheme seems particularly problematic in two respects. First, it relies on a very broad notion of 'gift' to deny restitution in cases where one would not want it: e.g. C heats his flat and thereby, because of the heat rising, benefits D who lives in the upstairs flat and whose heating bills are reduced (see Birks, *Unjust Enrichment*, 158–160). Secondly, Birks regards there as being an absence of basis triggering the right to restitution of all benefits conferred where a contract is voidable or terminable even though it has not yet been avoided or terminated by the innocent party (see Birks, *Unjust Enrichment*, 125–127).

4. Is Birks correct to say that English law has already moved to his 'absence of basis' scheme? Does not the emphasis on mistake in, e.g., *Kleinwort Benson v Lincoln CC* (below, 167) contradict Birks' claim? Indeed in that case, Lord Hope (below, 180) specifically contrasted the common law approach of looking for unjust factors with the 'absence of legal justification' civilian approach.

(4) THE CANADIAN APPROACH TO THE UNJUST QUESTION

- *Rathwell v Rathwell* (1978) 83 DLR (3d) 289, Supreme Court of Canada

The parties had been married for over thirty years when they separated. During their married life all their money went into a joint account, and for most of their married life they worked together in a farming business. The farm was bought from the joint account and was put into the defendant husband's name. The claimant sought a declaration that she had a half interest in her husband's real and personal property. Her action succeeded before the Court of Appeal for Saskatchewan and the Supreme Court of Canada.

Dickson J: ... The constructive trust ... comprehends the imposition of trust machinery by the Court in order to achieve a result consonant with good conscience. As a matter of principle, the Court will not allow any man unjustly to appropriate to himself the value earned by the labours of another. That principle is not defeated by the existence of a matrimonial relationship between the parties; but, for the principle to succeed, the facts must display an enrichment, a corresponding deprivation, and the absence of any juristic reason—such as a contract or disposition of law—for the enrichment. Thus, if the parties have agreed that the one holding legal title is to take beneficially an action in restitution cannot succeed. ...

It seems to me that Mrs. Rathwell must succeed whether one applies classical doctrine or constructive trust. Each is available to sustain her claim. The presumption of common intention from her contribution in money and money's worth entitles her to succeed in resulting trust. Her husband's unjust enrichment entitles her to succeed in constructive trust. ...

Laskin CJC and **Spence J** concurred with **Dickson J. Ritchie** and **Pigeon JJ** agreed that the husband's appeal should be dismissed but only on the basis of a resulting and not a constructive trust.

Martland J, with whom **Judson**, **Beetz**, and **de Grandpré JJ** concurred, dissented and would have allowed the husband's appeal.

NOTES AND QUESTIONS

1. Dickson J's reasoning was in this case concurred with by only two of his colleagues (albeit that he was in the majority in dismissing the husband's appeal). Subsequently his approach to unjust enrichment was repeated and supported by a majority of the Supreme Court of Canada in *Pettkus v Becker* (1980) 117 DLR (3d) 257. His three-stage analysis has provided the conceptual structure for the Canadian law of restitution. But his language of 'absence of juristic basis' is civilian terminology and it is unclear why he chose this phrase. Perhaps the answer lies in his being influenced by the civil law of unjust enrichment applied in Quebec.

2. In practice, it appears that the Canadian courts have often paid lip-service to 'absence of juristic basis' and have instead often decided cases by applying the traditional common law approach of looking for positive reasons for restitution of an unjust enrichment. In 'The Mystery of "Juristic Reason" '(2000) 12 SCLR (2d) 211, Lionel Smith called for the Supreme Court of Canada to clarify the position by confirming the correctness of the common law approach. At 244 he wrote:

   > The time has come for firm guidance from the Supreme Court of Canada. We may never know why Dickson CJC chose the phrase 'absence of juristic reason.' But his own judgments, and later decisions of the Supreme Court of Canada, show that it remains acceptable for the common law to operate as it always has, by seeking reasons for restitution. They show, in other words, that 'absence of juristic reason' need not be taken literally. The argument in this paper goes further, and suggests that it should not be taken literally. If it were, then the concept of 'juristic reason' would be required to do too much. We would effectively be starting from scratch in a fundamental field of the common law. The right outcome appears to be this: that 'absence of juristic reason' must be understood to mean 'a positive reason for reversing the defendant's enrichment.' Only so can the mystery be solved.

   But in the most important recent Canadian case on this issue, *Garland v Consumers' Gas Co.* (below, 140), the position has been rendered more complex because the Supreme Court has laid down that courts should consider not only established juristic reasons but also the parties' reasonable expectations and public policy.

3. The difference between the traditional common law and civilian approaches has often been expressed by reference to the former requiring proof of a positive reason while the latter requires proof of a negative reason. Lionel Smith, in the article referred to above, contrasts 'reasons for plaintiffs to have restitution' with 'reasons for defendants to keep enrichments.' In the first edition of this book, at 94–6, we referred to an alternative approach to that of unjust factors of 'unjust enrichment unless . . .' which seems to reflect the same idea.

4. Turning away from the general debate about the 'injustice' question triggered by Dickson J in *Rathwell* there are some more specific issues raised by his reasoning.

   (a) In the matrimonial or quasi-matrimonial context, is the remedy concerned to reverse an enrichment? Or is it better viewed as either fulfilling one party's expectations or as pursuing a social policy of joint ownership of matrimonial or quasi-matrimonial property?

   (b) Dickson J regarded the resulting trust in this context as resting on a presumed common intention of the parties whereas the constructive trust rested on unjust enrichment. Is this the true difference (if any) between resulting and constructive trusts (at least in the sphere of matrimonial or quasi-matrimonial property)? See also below, 749.

   (c) If the decision did rest on unjust enrichment, was it appropriate for the court to 'award' the claimant a half share of the property rather than a personal monetary remedy for the amount of money paid, or value of services rendered, to the defendant on the unfulfilled expectation that the defendant would transfer half the property?

- *Garland v Consumers' Gas Co.*
  (2004) 237 DLR (4th) 385, Supreme Court of Canada

The defendant, the Consumers' Gas Co., sold gas in Ontario under regulations established by the Ontario Energy Board (OEB). The OEB devised a pricing scheme, implemented by regulations, that turned out to be criminal. This was because the rate of interest charged under, what were termed, 'late payment penalties' (LPPs), was more than that permitted (that is, it was in excess of 60 per cent per annum) under section 347 of the Criminal Code. The claimant sought restitution on the basis of unjust enrichment on behalf of himself and a class of claimants numbering as many as 500,000. The claim failed in the lower courts. But the Supreme Court of Canada held that the claimant was entitled to restitution of the interest paid that was over 60 per cent per annum but only where paid after the action was commenced in 1994. The payments of excessive interest paid between 1981–1994 were held to be irrecoverable even though contrary to section 347 of the Criminal Code.

Iacobucci J delivered the judgment of the court comprising himself and **Major**, **Bastarache**, **Binnie**, **LeBel**, **Deschamps** and **Fish JJ**.

UNJUST ENRICHMENT

. . .

(i) General Principles

[38] In his original formulation of the test for unjust enrichment in *Rathwell v Rathwell* [above 138] (adopted in *Pettkus v Becker* (1980) 117 DLR (3d) 257), Dickson J. (as he then was) held in his minority reasons that for an action in unjust enrichment to succeed:

> . . . the facts must display an enrichment, a corresponding deprivation, and the absence of any juristic reason—such as a contract or disposition of law—for the enrichment.

. . .

[40] The 'juristic reason' aspect of the test for unjust enrichment has been the subject of much academic commentary and criticism. Much of the discussion arises out of the difference between the ways in which the cause of action of unjust enrichment is conceptualized in Canada and in England. While both Canadian and English causes of action require an enrichment of the defendant and a corresponding deprivation of the plaintiff, the Canadian cause of action requires that there be 'an absence of juristic reason for the enrichment', while English courts require 'that the enrichment be unjust' (see discussion in L. D. Smith, 'The Mystery of "Juristic Reason" ' (2000), 12 *S.C.L.R.* (2d) 211, at pp. 212–13). It is not of great use to speculate on why Dickson J. in *Rathwell, supra,* expressed the third condition as absence of juristic reason but I believe that he may have wanted to ensure that the test for unjust enrichment was not purely subjective in order to be responsive to Martland J.'s criticism in his reasons that application of the doctrine of unjust enrichment contemplated by Dickson J. would require 'immeasurable judicial discretion' (p. 473). The importance of avoiding a purely subjective standard was also stressed by McLachlin J. in her reasons in *Peel, v Canada* [above 74], in which she wrote that the application of the test for unjust enrichment should not be 'case by case "palm tree" justice'.

[41] Perhaps as a result of these two formulations of this aspect of the test, Canadian courts and commentators are divided in their approach to juristic reason. . . . In his article, 'The Mystery of "Juristic Reason" ', *supra* . . ., Professor Smith suggests that it is not clear whether the requirement of 'absence of juristic reason' should be interpreted literally to require that plaintiffs show the absence of a reason for the defendant to keep the enrichment or, as in the English model, the plaintiff must show a reason for reversing the transfer of wealth. Other commentators have argued that in fact there

is no difference beyond semantics between the Canadian and English tests (see, for example, M. McInnes, 'Unjust Enrichment—Restitution—Absence of Juristic Reason: *Campbell v Campbell*' (2000), 79 *Can. Bar Rev.* 459).

[42] Professor Smith argues that, if there is in fact a distinct Canadian approach to juristic reason, it is problematic because it requires the plaintiff to prove a negative, namely the absence of a juristic reason. Because it is nearly impossible to do this, he suggests that Canada would be better off adopting the British model where the plaintiff must show a positive reason that it would be unjust for the defendant to retain the enrichment. In my view, however, there is a distinctive Canadian approach to juristic reason which should be retained but can be construed in a manner that is responsive to Smith's criticism.

[43] It should be recalled that the test for unjust enrichment is relatively new to Canadian jurisprudence. It requires flexibility for courts to expand the categories of juristic reasons as circumstances require and to deny recovery where to allow it would be inequitable. As McLachlin J. wrote in *Peel*, [above 74], the Court's approach to unjust enrichment, while informed by traditional categories of recovery 'is capable, however, of going beyond them, allowing the law to develop in a flexible way as required to meet changing perceptions of justice'. But at the same time there must also be guidelines that offer trial judges and others some indication of what the boundaries of the cause of action are. The goal is to avoid guidelines that are so general and subjective that uniformity becomes unattainable.

[44] The parties and commentators have pointed out that there is no specific authority that settles this question. But recalling that this is an equitable remedy that will necessarily involve discretion and questions of fairness, I believe that some redefinition and reformulation is required. Consequently, in my view, the proper approach to the juristic reason analysis is in two parts. First, the plaintiff must show that no juristic reason from an established category exists to deny recovery. By closing the list of categories that the plaintiff must canvass in order to show an absence of juristic reason, Smith's objection to the Canadian formulation of the test that it required proof of a negative is answered. The established categories that can constitute juristic reasons include a contract (*Pettkus*, *supra*), a disposition of law (*Pettkus*, *supra*), a donative intent (*Peter v Beblow*, (1993) 101 DLR (4th) 621), and other valid common law, equitable or statutory obligations (*Peter*, *supra*). If there is no juristic reason from an established category, then the plaintiff has made out a *prima facie* case under the juristic reason component of the analysis.

[45] The *prima facie* case is rebuttable, however, where the defendant can show that there is another reason to deny recovery. As a result, there is a *de facto* burden of proof placed on the defendant to show the reason why the enrichment should be retained. This stage of the analysis thus provides for a category of residual defence in which courts can look to all of the circumstances of the transaction in order to determine whether there is another reason to deny recovery.

[46] As part of the defendant's attempt to rebut, courts should have regard to two factors: the reasonable expectations of the parties, and public policy considerations. It may be that when these factors are considered, the court will find that a new category of juristic reason is established. In other cases, a consideration of these factors will suggest that there was a juristic reason in the particular circumstance of a case but which does not give rise to a new category of juristic reason that should be applied in other factual circumstances. In a third group of cases, a consideration of these factors will yield a determination that there was no juristic reason for the enrichment. In the latter cases, recovery should be allowed. The point here is that this area is an evolving one and that further cases will add additional refinements and developments.

[47] In my view, this approach to the juristic reason analysis is consistent with the general approach to unjust enrichment endorsed by McLachlin J. in *Peel*, *supra*, where she stated that courts must effect a balance between the traditional 'category' approach according to which a claim for restitution will succeed only if it falls within an established head of recovery, and the modern

'principled' approach according.to which relief is determined with reference to broad principles. It is also, as discussed by Professor Smith, *supra*, generally consistent with the approach to unjust enrichment found in the civil law of Quebec (see, for example, arts. 1493 and 1494 of the *Civil Code of Quebec*, S. Q. 1991, c. 64).

(ii) Application

[48] In this case, the only possible juristic reason from an established category that could be used to justify the enrichment is the existence of the OEB orders creating the LPPs under the 'disposition of law' category. The OEB orders, however, do not constitute a juristic reason for the enrichment because they are rendered inoperative to the extent of their conflict with s. 347 of the *Criminal Code*. The plaintiff has thus made out a *prima facie* case for unjust enrichment.

. . .

[54] The second stage of juristic reason analysis requires a consideration of reasonable expectations of the parties and public policy considerations.

[55] When the reasonable expectations of the parties are considered, Consumers' Gas's submissions are at first blush compelling. Consumers' Gas submits, on the one hand, that late payers cannot have reasonably expected that there would be no penalty for failing to pay their bills on time and, on the other hand, that Consumers' Gas could reasonably have expected that the OEB would not authorize an LPP scheme that violated the *Criminal Code*. Because Consumers' Gas is operating in a regulated environment, their reliance on OEB orders should be given some weight. An inability to rely on such orders would make it very difficult, if not impossible, to operate in this environment. At this point, it should be pointed out that the reasonable expectation of the parties regarding LPPs is achieved by restricting the LPPs to the limit prescribed by s. 347 of the *Criminal Code* and also would be consistent with this Court's decision in *Transport North American Express Inc. v New Solutions Financial Corp.*, [2004] 1 s. C.R. 249, 2004 SCC 7, 235 D.L.R. (4th) 385.

[56] Consumers' Gas's reliance on the orders would not provide a defence if it was charged under s. 347 of the *Criminal Code* because they are inoperative to the extent of their conflict with s. 347. However, its reliance on the orders is relevant in the context of determining the reasonable expectations of the parties in this second stage of the juristic reason analysis.

[57] Finally, the overriding public policy consideration in this case is the fact that the LPPs were collected in contravention of the *Criminal Code*. As a matter of public policy, a criminal should not be permitted to keep the proceeds of their crime . . .

[58] In weighing these considerations, from 1981–1994, Consumers' Gas's reliance on the inoperative OEB orders provides a juristic reason for the enrichment. As the parties have argued, there are three possible dates from which to measure the unjust enrichment: 1981, when s. 347 of the *Criminal Code* was enacted, 1994, when this action was commenced, and 1998, when this Court held in *Garland* #1 that the LPPs were limited by s. 347 of the *Criminal Code*. For the period between 1981 and 1994, when the current action was commenced, there is no suggestion that Consumers' Gas was aware that the LPPs violated s. 347 of the *Criminal Code*. This militates in favour of Consumers' Gas during this period. The reliance of Consumers' Gas on the OEB orders, in the absence of actual or constructive notice that the orders were inoperative, is sufficient to provide a juristic reason for Consumers' Gas's enrichment during this first period.

[59] However, in 1994 when this action was commenced, Consumers' Gas was put on notice of the serious possibility that it was violating the *Criminal Code* in charging the LPPs. This possibility became a reality when this Court held that the LPPs were in excess of the s. 347 limit. Consumers' Gas could have requested that the OEB alter its rate structure until the matter was adjudicated in order to ensure that it was not in violation of the *Criminal Code* or asked for contingency arrangements to be made. Its decision not to do this, as counsel for the appellant pointed out in oral submissions, was a 'gamble'. After the action was commenced and Consumers' Gas was put on notice that there was a

serious possibility the LPPs violated the *Criminal Code*, it was no longer reasonable for Consumers' Gas to rely on the OEB rate orders to authorize the LPPs.

[60] Moreover, once this Court held that LPPs were offside, for purposes of unjust enrichment, it is logical and fair to choose the date on which the action for redress commenced. Awarding restitution from 1981 would be unfair to the respondent since it was entitled to reasonably rely on the OEB orders until the commencement of this action in 1994. Awarding restitution from 1998 would be unfair to the appellant. This is because it would permit the respondent to retain LPPs collected in violation of s. 347 after 1994 when it was no longer reasonable for the respondent to have relied on the OEB orders and the respondent should be presumed to have known the LPPs violated the *Criminal Code*. Further, awarding restitution from 1998 would deviate from the general rule that monetary remedies like damages and interest are awarded as of the date of occurrence of the breach or as of the date of action rather than the date of judgment.

[61] Awarding restitution from 1994 appropriately balances the respondent's reliance on the OEB orders from 1981–1994 with the appellant's expectation of recovery of moneys that were charged in violation of the *Criminal Code* once the serious possibility that the OEB orders were inoperative had been raised. As a result, as of the date this action was commenced in 1994, it was no longer reasonable for Consumers' Gas to rely on the OEB orders to insulate them from liability in a civil action of this type for collecting LPPs in contravention of the *Criminal Code*. Thus, after the action was commenced in 1994, there was no longer a juristic reason for the enrichment of the respondent, so the appellant is entitled to restitution of the portion of moneys paid to satisfy LPPs that exceeded an interest rate of 60 per cent, as defined in s. 347 of the *Criminal Code*.

DEFENCES

[62] Having held that the appellant's claim for unjust enrichment is made out for LPPs paid after 1994, it remains to be determined whether the respondent can avail itself of any defences raised. It is only necessary to consider the defences for the period after 1994, when the elements of unjust enrichment are made out, and thus I will not consider whether the defences would have applied if there had been unjust enrichment before 1994. I will address each defence in turn.

(a) Change of Position Defence

[63] Even where the elements of unjust enrichment are made out, the remedy of restitution will be denied where an innocent defendant demonstrates that it has materially changed its position as a result of an enrichment such that it would be inequitable to require the benefit to be returned (*Storthoaks Mobil Oil Canada* (1975) 55 DLR (3d) 1). In this case, the respondent says that any 'benefit' it received from the unlawful charges was passed on to other customers in the form of lower gas delivery rates. Having 'passed on' the benefit, it says, it should not be required to disgorge the amount of the benefit (a second time) to overcharged customers such as the appellant. The issue here, however, is not the ultimate destination within the regulatory system of an amount of money equivalent to the unlawful overcharges, nor is this case concerned with the net impact of these overcharges on the respondent's financial position. The issue is whether, as between the overcharging respondent and the overcharged appellant, the passing of the benefit on to other customers excuses the respondent from having overcharged the appellant.

[64] The appellant submits that the defence of change of position is not available to a defendant who is a wrongdoer and that, since the respondent in this case was enriched by its own criminal misconduct, it should not be permitted to avail itself of the defence. I agree. The rationale for the change of position defence appears to flow from considerations of equity. G.H.L. Fridman writes that '[o]ne situation which would appear to render it inequitable for the defendant to be required to disgorge a benefit received from the plaintiff in the absence of any wrongdoing on the part of the defendant would be if he has changed his position for the worse as a result of the receipt of the

money in question' (*Restitution* (2nd ed. 1992), at p. 458). In the leading British case on the defence, *Lipkin Gorman (a firm) v Karpnale Ltd*, [1992] 4 All E.R. 512 (H.L.), Lord Goff stated (at p. 533):

> [I]t is right that we should ask ourselves: why do we feel that it would be unjust to allow restitution in cases such as these [where the defendant has changed his or her position]? The answer must be that, where an innocent defendant's position is so changed that he will suffer an injustice if called upon to repay or to repay in full, the injustice of requiring him so to repay outweighs the injustice of denying the plaintiff restitution.

[65] If the change of position defence is intended to prevent injustice from occurring, the whole of the plaintiff's and defendant's conduct during the course of the transaction should be open to scrutiny in order to determine which party has a better claim. Where a defendant has obtained the enrichment through some wrongdoing of his own, he cannot then assert that it would be unjust to return the enrichment to the plaintiff. In this case, the respondent cannot avail itself of this defence because the LPPs were obtained in contravention of the *Criminal Code* and, as a result, it cannot be unjust for the respondent to have to return them.

[66] Thus, the change of position defence does not help the respondent in this case. Even assuming that the respondent would have met the other requirements set out in *Storthoaks, supra*, the respondent cannot avail itself of the defence because it is not an 'innocent' defendant given that the benefit was received as a result of a *Criminal Code* violation. It is not necessary, as a result, to discuss change of position in a comprehensive manner and I leave a fuller development of the other elements of this defence to future cases. . . .

NOTES AND QUESTIONS

1. The approach taken to the 'unjust question' in this case was a novel one. One might label it a 'modified civilian approach'. One is looking for an absence of basis but that basis may be found, outside existing categories, by reference to the parties' expectations and/or public policy. So here the starting point was that there was an absence of basis in that the payments of 60 per cent interest were not due because illegal. But that starting point was countered, and a basis was found for the payments prior to 1994, by reference to the reasonable expectations of the parties, especially the defendant's reasonable expectation, prior to the claim being brought, that the OEB's regulations would be valid.

2. This modified civilian approach gives considerable discretion to the courts in finding a basis that lies in the parties' reasonable expectations and/or public policy.

3. Applying an unmodified civilian approach or a common law unjust factors approach, it would seem that, subject to defences (e.g. limitation), restitution should have been granted of all the excessive interest payments since 1981. That money was not due, because illegal or, on the common law approach, there was an unjust factor (most obviously, mistake of law or illegality designed to protect a weaker class).

4. The change of position defence (in relation to which 'passing on' terminology was unhelpfully applied) was here rejected because the defendant was a criminal wrongdoer in collecting the excessive interest. This is discussed further below, 799. (The other 'defences' considered by Iacobucci J are not set out in the above extract. They were not of general interest (e.g. particular statutory provisions)).

5. The modified civilian approach of the Supreme Court of Canada has been criticised in notes on this case by, e.g., M McInnes 'Juristic Reasons and Unjust Factors in the Supreme Court of Canada' (2004) 120 *LQR* 554; J Neyers, 'One Step Forward, Two Steps Back: Unjust Enrichment in the Supreme Court of Canada' [2004] *LMCLQ* 435. But that approach was confirmed and applied by the Supreme Court of Canada in *Pacific National Investments v Victoria* (2004) 245 DLR (4th) 211. There restitution of the value of land improvements was granted to a

developer under what was thought to be a valid contract with the local authority but which in reality was *ultra vires* the local authority. See, on that case, R Grantham, 'Absence of Juristic Reason in the Supreme Court of Canada' [2005] *RLR* 102.

4. DEFENCES

Even if the claimant establishes that the defendant has been enriched at the claimant's expense, and that that enrichment was unjust, the defendant may still be able to avail himself of a defence. The general restitutionary defences are examined in detail in Chapter 14 and include change of position, estoppel, counter-restitution impossible, incapacity, illegality, and *bona fide* purchase.

Of greatest significance, both in practice and in theory is change of position. In essence the defence protects the defendant to the extent that he has in good faith lost the benefit received. The defence was accepted for the first time in England in *Lipkin Gorman v Karpnale Ltd* (above, 28) and some would argue that it was premature to talk of an English law of restitution based on unjust enrichment until a proper defence of change of position had been so recognized. Certainly the defence has a pivotal role to play in counterbalancing the sweep of *prima facie* unjust enrichment liability. Now that it has been recognized, the courts may feel less constrained in pushing forward the range and content of the unjust factors knowing that defendants have the security of receipt guaranteed by the defence. What precisely should constitute a change of position was left open for case law development by their Lordships in *Lipkin Gorman*.

General Reading

BURROWS, 51; GOFF AND JONES, 39-001; VIRGO, 665–7.

3

MISTAKE

1. MISTAKEN PAYMENTS

A mistaken payment is generally regarded as the central example of an unjust enrichment. The unjust factor is the mistake which negatives the voluntariness of the payor. The enrichment is the money, which is an incontrovertible benefit. And the enrichment is at the claimant's expense in its subtractive sense. Subject to defences therefore, one might expect there to be wide recovery of mistaken payments. Yet traditionally this was not so: restitution was restricted in two major ways. First, for mistakes of fact, claimants generally needed to satisfy a 'supposed liability' test (see *Kelly v Solari, Aiken v Short, Morgan v Ashcroft*: below, 147–153). Secondly, no recovery was generally allowed for mistakes of law (see *Bilbie v Lumley*, below, 167). More recently, both restrictions have been removed. As regards mistakes of fact, Robert Goff J in *Barclays Bank v W. J Simms* (below, 153) adopted a *prima facie* test (i.e. subject to defences) of whether the mistake *caused* the payment. And the mistake of law bar was abolished in *Kleinwort Benson Ltd v Lincoln City Council* (below, 167).

It is sometimes difficult to draw the line between unjust enrichment and contract in the sphere of mistake. One important point is that, where there is a valid contractual obligation to render the benefit, restitution of the benefit would almost always contradict that contractual obligation and is hence unwarranted. It follows that the restitutionary rules on mistake are only applicable where any purported contract (or contractual term) requiring the rendering of the benefit is void, or unenforceable, or has been discharged, or is voidable and the claimant has chosen to rescind. The *Kleinwort Benson* case is an example of restitution of money paid by mistake (of law) under a contract that was void (because outside the powers of the local authority). Restitution through rescission of an executed contract is discussed in the third section of this Chapter.

Although we defer discussion until Chapter 13, the very controversial case of *Chase Manhattan Bank NA v Israel-British Bank (London) Ltd*, below, 707, can be regarded as exemplifying *proprietary* restitution of a payment made by mistake.

General Reading

BURROWS, 128–159; GOFF AND JONES, chs 4–5; VIRGO, ch 8.

(1) MISTAKES OF FACT

• *Kelly v Solari* (1841) 9 M & W 54, Court of Exchequer

The claimant insurance company paid over money to the defendant, a widow, on a life insurance policy taken out by her deceased husband, apparently forgetting that the policy had lapsed because her husband had failed to pay a premium. At trial the claimant succeeded in recovering the money in an action for money had and received. On appeal the Court of Exchequer ordered a new trial.

Lord Abinger CB: . . . [I]f the party makes the payment with full knowledge of the facts, although under ignorance of the law, there being no fraud on the other side, he cannot recover it back again. There may also be cases in which, although he might by investigation learn the state of facts more accurately, he declines to do so, and chooses to pay the money notwithstanding; in that case there can be no doubt that he is equally bound. Then there is a third case, and the most difficult one,— where the party had once a full knowledge of the facts, but has since forgotten them. I certainly laid down the rule too widely to the jury, when I told them that if the directors once knew the facts they must be taken still to know them, and could not recover by saying that they had since forgotten them. I think the knowledge of the facts which disentitles the party from recovering, must mean a know-ledge existing in the mind at the time of payment. I have little doubt in this case that the directors had forgotten the fact, otherwise I do not believe they would have brought the action; but as [counsel for the defendant] certainly has a right to have that question submitted to the jury, there must be a new trial.

Parke B: I entirely agree in the opinion just pronounced by my Lord Chief Baron, that there ought to be a new trial. I think that where money is paid to another under the influence of a mistake, that is, upon the supposition that a specific fact is true, which would entitle the other to the money, but which fact is untrue, and the money would not have been paid if it had been known to the payer that the fact was untrue, an action will lie to recover it back, and it is against conscience to retain it; though a demand may be necessary in those cases in which the party receiving may have been ignorant of the mistake. . . . If, indeed, the money is intentionally paid, without reference to the truth or falsehood of the fact, the plaintiff meaning to waive all inquiry into it, and that the person receiving shall have the money at all events, whether the fact be true or false, the latter is certainly entitled to retain it; but if it is paid under the impression of the truth of a fact which is untrue, it may, generally speaking, be recovered back, however careless the party paying may have been, in omitting to use due diligence to inquire into the fact. In such a case the receiver was not entitled to it, nor intended to have it.

Rolfe B: I am of the same opinion. With respect to the argument, that money cannot be recovered back except where it is unconscientious to retain it, it seems to me, that wherever it is paid under a mistake of fact, and the party would not have paid it if the fact had been known to him, it cannot be otherwise than unconscientious to retain it. But I agree that [counsel for the defendant] has a right to go to the jury again, upon two grounds: first, that the jury may possibly find that the directors had not in truth forgotten the fact; and secondly, they may also come to the conclusion, that they had determined that they would not expose the office to unpopularity, and would therefore pay the money at all events; in which case I quite agree that they could not recover it back.

Gurney B concurred.

NOTES AND QUESTIONS

1. Which of the judgments lays down a 'supposed liability' test?

2. What facts or situations did the judges have in mind when they said that the company could not have recovered the money if it had chosen to pay/waived all inquiry/paid the money at all events?

3. Parke B emphasized that the mistaken payor's carelessness does not generally bar restitution. Should it do so?

4. On Birks' new 'absence of basis' approach (above, 137), the question of whether the insurance company was mistaken was not of central importance. The defendant was, on the face of it, unjustly enriched simply because the money was not due (and Birks refers to the ambiguous final sentence of Parke B's judgment in which he said 'the receiver was not entitled to it' as well as saying 'nor intended to have it'). But for Birks restitution does not automatically follow on the payment not being due because of the possibility that the insurance company intended a gift rather than to discharge an obligation; and it is on that secondary issue (discharge of an obligation or gift?) that the payer's mistaken state of mind would be relevant. See Birks, *Unjust Enrichment* (2nd edn, 2005), 103–4, 132.

- *Aiken v Short* (1856) 1 H & N 210, Court of Exchequer

The claimant bank, believing that it had bought certain property from George Carter, subject to a charge securing a £200 debt owed in favour of Short, paid to Short's executrix (the defendant) the £200 plus interest to release the charge, thereby making the property more saleable. It transpired that George Carter had not inherited the relevant property under the true will of Edwin Carter and that Short had therefore had no charge securing the debt owed to him by George Carter. The claimants action for money had and received, to recover the money paid to the defendant by mistake of fact, failed.

Pollock CB: . . . The defendant's testator, Short, had a claim on Carter,—a bond and a security on property which Carter afterwards mortgaged to the Bank. The defendant, who was the executrix of Short, applied to Carter for payment. He referred her to the Bank, who, conceiving that the defendant had a good equitable charge, paid the debt, as they reasonably might do, to get rid of the charge affecting their interest. In consequence of the discovery of a later will of Edwin Carter, it turned out that the defendant had no title. The Bank had paid the money in one sense without any consideration, but the defendant had a perfect right to receive the money from Carter, and the bankers paid for him. They should have taken care not to have paid over the money to get a valueless security; but the defendant has nothing to do with their mistake. Suppose it was announced that there was to be a dividend on the estate of a trader, and persons to whom he was indebted went to an office and received instalments of the debts due to them, could the party paying recover back the money if it turned out that he was wrong in supposing that he had funds in hand? The money was, in fact, paid by the Bank, as the agents of Carter.

Platt B: I am of the same opinion. The action for money had and received lies only for money which the defendant ought to refund ex æquo et bono. Was there any obligation here to refund? There was a debt due to Short, secured by a bond and a supposed equitable charge by way of collateral security. The property on which Short had the charge was conveyed by Carter to the Bank. Short having died, the defendant, his executrix, applied to George Carter for payment of the debt due to her husband, the testator. Carter referred her to the Bank, who paid the debt, and the bond was satisfied. The money which the defendant got from her debtor was actually due to her, and there can be no obligation to refund it.

Bramwell B: My brother Martin, before he left the Court, desired me to say that he was of the same opinion, and so am I. In order to entitle a person to recover back money paid under a mistake of fact, the mistake must be as to a fact which, if true, would make the person paying liable to pay the money; not where, if true, it would merely make it desirable that he should pay the money. Here, if the fact was true, the bankers were at liberty to pay or not, as they pleased. But relying on the belief that the defendant had a valid security, they, having a subsequent legal mortgage, chose to pay off the defendant's charge. It is impossible to say that this case falls within the rule. The mistake of fact was, that the Bank thought that they could sell the estate for a better price. It is true that if the plaintiff could recover back this money from the defendant, there would be no difficulty in the way of the defendant suing Carter . . . . But that does not shew that the plaintiffs can maintain this action, and I am of opinion they cannot, having voluntarily parted with their money to purchase that which the defendant had to sell, though no doubt it turned out to be different to, and of less value than, what they expected.

NOTES AND QUESTIONS

1. What is the ratio of this case?

2. Was there a contract between the claimant and defendant? Was there consideration for the claimant's payment? Was any purported contract void for common mistake?

3. Is it justifiable to limit recovery according to the 'supposed liability' test applied by Bramwell B?

4. Assuming one rejects the 'supposed liability' restriction, was this case nevertheless correctly decided in favour of the defendant?

5. Did the bank have a valid restitutionary claim against George Carter for having mistakenly discharged his debt to Short?

6. There is a slightly different and fuller report of Bramwell B's judgment in (1856) 25 LJ Ex 321, 324.

- • *Morgan v Ashcroft* [1938] 1 KB 49, Court of Appeal

The claimant bookmaker (the respondent) mistakenly paid the defendant (the appellant) twice on a bet. The bookmaker's claim to recover the overpayment failed. One ground of reasoning concerned the Gaming Act 1845 and an illegality defence (see generally on illegality as a defence, 883–919 below, and especially 884). The other ground, relevant to this Chapter, was that the type of mistake in question did not entitle the claimant to restitution.

Sir Wilfrid Greene MR: . . . The plaintiff's claim is for money had and received, and it is based upon what the learned county court judge found to be a mistake of fact. The question which arises is, Can such a claim succeed in the circumstances of this case? In my opinion it cannot. The nature of the claim to recover money paid under a mistake, and the limits within which it can be made, have been the subject of much controversy and the difficulties involved in providing a comprehensive solution to these problems have not as yet been overcome. Two propositions can, I think, be put forward with certainty. The first is that the claim cannot now be said to be based on some rule of aequum et bonum by virtue of which a man must not be allowed to enrich himself unjustly at the expense of another. Lord Mansfield's views upon those matters, attractive though they be, cannot now be accepted as laying the true foundation of the claim. The second proposition is that the claim is based upon an imputed promise to repay. . . .

So much is I think clear. But the question still remains, In what circumstances will the law impute a promise to repay where the payment was made under a mistake? That it will not do so in all circumstances is manifest. In general, no such promise can be imputed where the payment is made under a mistake of law. Nor can a promise to repay be imputed which, to quote Lord Sumner's words in *Sinclair v Brougham*,[1] 'if made de facto' the law 'would inexorably avoid.' . . .

A great part of the argument was concentrated on the words used by Bramwell B in *Aiken v Short*.[2] [*He considered the judgment of Bramwell B and continued*:] Now it is to be observed that in that case

---

1 [1914] AC 398, 452.　　2 1 H & N 210, 215.

the bank, although contractually bound to its supposed grantor to pay off the charge, was under no such liability towards the holder of the charge herself; and although the payment was thought by the bank to be beneficial to itself in that it was, as it thought, discharging a contractual obligation and freeing its property from an incumbrance, yet it was not under any mistaken belief that the payee could demand payment. In other words, the payment was in any event, whether or not the supposed facts were true, a voluntary payment as between payer and payee.

The passage which I have quoted from Bramwell B.'s judgment has been referred to with approval by several learned judges, but always I think by way of dictum. [*He cited a number of cases and continued:*] The last case in which the matter was considered was *Norwich Union Fire Insurance Society v William H. Price, Ltd,*[3] decided by the Privy Council, and I will quote two passages from the judgment of the Judicial Committee in that case, which was delivered by Lord Wright:[4] 'The facts which were misconceived were those which were essential to liability and were of such a nature that on well-established principles any agreement concluded under such mistake was void in law, so that any payment made under such mistake was recoverable. The mistake, being of the character that it was, prevented there being that intention which the common law regards as essential to the making of an agreement or the transfer of money or property.' Later on he said:[5] 'It is true that in general the test of intention in the formation of contracts and the transfer of property is objective; that is, intention is to be ascertained from what the parties said or did. But proof of mistake affirmatively excludes intention. It is, however, essential that the mistake relied on should be of such a nature that it can be properly described as a mistake in respect of the underlying assumption of the contract or transaction or as being fundamental or basic.'

. . . It is, I think, instructive to consider the words of Bramwell B referred to above in the light of these authorities. In the first case which he mentions, namely, that where the supposed fact if true would have made the person paying liable to pay the money, the mistake is a mistake as to the nature of the transaction. The payer thinks that he is discharging a legal obligation whereas in truth and in fact he is making a purely voluntary payment. Such a mistake is to my mind unquestionably fundamental or basic and may be compared, at least by way of analogy, with the class of case in which mistake as to the nature of the transaction negatives intention in the case of contract. But the second case which he mentions, namely, that where the supposed fact would, if true, merely make the payment desirable from the point of view of the payer, is very different. In that case the payment is intended to be a voluntary one and a voluntary payment it is whether the supposed fact be true or not. It appears to me that a person who intends to make a voluntary payment and thinks that he is making one kind of voluntary payment whereas upon the true facts he is making another kind of voluntary payment, does not make the payment under a mistake of fact which can be described as fundamental or basic. The essential quality of the payment, namely its voluntary character, is the same in each case. If a father, believing that his son has suffered a financial loss, gives him a sum of money, he surely could not claim repayment if he afterwards discovered that no such loss had occurred; and (to take the analogous case of contract) if instead of giving him money, he entered into a contract with his son, he surely could not claim that the contract was void. To hold the contrary would almost amount to saying that motive and not mistake was the decisive matter.

I come therefore to the conclusion that the observations of Bramwell B., supported as they are by much weight of judicial opinion, are, so far as regards the class of mistake with which he was dealing, in agreement with the more recent authorities, and I propose to follow them. It was said on behalf of the respondent that these observations do not correctly state the law. I do not agree, although I am disposed to think that they cannot be taken as an exhaustive statement of the law but must be confined to cases where the only mistake is as to the nature of the transaction. For example, if A makes a voluntary payment of money to B under the mistaken belief that he is C, it may well be

3 [1934] AC 455.   4 *Ibid.* 461.   5 *Ibid.* 463.

that A can recover it. Bramwell B, was not dealing with a case such as that, since he was assuming that there was no such error in persona. If we are to be guided by the analogous case of contract, where mistake as to the person contracted with negatives the intention to contract, the mistake in the case which I have mentioned ought to be held to negative the intention to pay the money and the money should be recoverable.

But it is not necessary to pursue this matter further. It is sufficient to say that in my opinion the present case falls within principles laid down both by Bramwell B. and in the more recent authorities. In making the payment the respondent was, it is true, under a mistake as to the nature of the transaction. He thought that a wagering debt was due from himself to the appellant, whereas in fact it was not. But if the supposed fact had been true, the respondent would have been under no liability to make the payment which therefore was intended to be a voluntary payment. Upon the true facts the payment was still a voluntary payment; and there is in my opinion no such fundamental or basic distinction between the one voluntary payment and the other that the law can for present purposes differentiate between them and say that there was no intention to make the one because the intention was to make the other. . . .

Scott LJ: . . . In none of the . . . cases . . . not even in *Aiken v Short*, was there a decision of the Court that the action failed simply because the mistake did not induce a belief of liability. And indeed in *Kerrison v Glyn, Mills, Currie & Co.*[6] it was definitely decided by Hamilton J and by the House of Lords that the plaintiff was entitled to recover a payment made to the defendants for the purpose of meeting an anticipated liability although he then knew that no actual liability had yet attached to him. The decision of the House of Lords seems to me conclusive that the rule as stated in *Aiken v Short* cannot be regarded as final and exhaustive in the sense that no mistake, which does not induce in the mind of the payer a belief that payment will discharge or reduce his liability, can ground an action for money had and received. It is, of course, obvious that such a belief must in fact have been induced in a very high percentage of mistaken payments giving rise to a dispute; in human affairs the vast majority of payments made without any fresh consideration are made to perform an obligation or discharge a liability; and I doubt not that performance of an obligation would be accounted discharge of a liability for the purpose of the *Aiken v Short* proposition. For this reason of human nature, that proposition is very often—and perhaps usually—a crucial test of the question whether the payment was in truth made by reason of a mistake or was merely voluntary and therefore irrecoverable. But I agree with the view of the Master of the Rolls that the final demarcation of the boundaries of the old action of money had and received has not yet been achieved, and that their final delineation can only be worked out as concrete cases arise and bring up new points for decision. And in refusing assent to the appellant's argument that the *Aiken v Short* proposition is of itself necessarily sufficient to fix the boundary, I desire to keep clearly open the possibility of the common law treating other types of payment in mistake as falling within the scope of the action for money had and received. Without expressing any opinion, I recognize, for instance, the possibility that there may be cases of charitable payments or other gifts made under a definite mistake of person to be benefited, or of the substantial nature of the transaction, where on consideration the old principles of the action might still, in spite of limiting decisions, be held to cover such circumstances. . . .

An additional reason for keeping the door open is the very heterogeneous list of causes of action which unquestionably fall within this field of implied contracts. They are so various in kind as almost irresistibly to invite the inference that there may be one or more unifying principles upon which they rest. If one takes the action for money had and received by way of illustration of this point, one finds assembled under that heading the following wholly different types of causes: (1.) money paid in mistake of fact; (2.) money paid for a consideration which has failed; (3.) money paid because it was

6 (1912) 17 Com Cas 41.

extorted colore officii, or by duress, etc.; (4.) cases where the plaintiff has had an actionable wrong done him by the defendant, and 'waiving the tort' sues in assumpsit—whether any of his money has actually passed from himself to the defendant or not. In this context I venture humbly and respectfully to doubt whether the criterion suggested by Viscount Haldane LC in *Sinclair v Brougham*[7] that 'the fiction' (i.e., the common law fiction of an implied contract) 'can only be set up with effect if such a contract would be valid if it really existed' is consistent with the common law history of these implied contracts; for some of them are quite incapable of formulation as real—i.e., consensual—contracts.

But I am in complete agreement with the Master of the Rolls that there is a plain principle applicable to all those cases of payments in mistake of fact, and that is that the mistake must be in some aspect or another fundamental to the transaction. On the facts of this case there was no fundamental mistake. To pay 24*l.* for a betting debt is just as much in the eye of the law a purely voluntary gift as a wedding present of 24*l.*: the law prevents the plaintiff from saying that he intended anything but a present. I agree that the appeal must be allowed.

NOTES AND QUESTIONS

1. The mistake in question was not one of supposed liability because wagering contracts do not create legally binding obligations.

2. Does this decision support or reject the 'supposed liability' approach?

3. Is a test of whether the mistake was 'fundamental' preferable to a 'supposed liability' or 'causation' test?

4. Sir Wilfred Greene MR cited Lord Wright's judgment in *Norwich Union Fire Insurance Society v W H Price Ltd* [1934] AC 455. In that case the claimant insurance company paid up on a policy insuring lemons in the mistaken belief that the lemons had been damaged by an insured event. In fact the lemons had started to ripen because of a delay in transit which was not covered by the policy. Although the mistake in question was one as to supposed liability, Lord Wright, giving the judgment of the Privy Council, thought that what was important was that the mistake was fundamental. His approach can be criticized, *inter alia*, for seeking to assimilate the approach to mistake for contract, unjust enrichment, and the passing of title in property (see Burrows, 107).

5. Scott LJ, in contrast to Sir Wilfred Greene MR, rejected the 'implied contract' theory of restitution. Did this difference between them affect their approach to the right to recover mistaken payments?

- ### *Barclays Bank Ltd v W J Simms Ltd* [1980] 1 QB 677, Queen's Bench Division

The claimant bank overlooked a stop instruction on a cheque for £24,000 drawn by its customer (the Royal British Legion Housing Association Ltd) in favour of the defendant company for building work done. The claimant sought restitution of the £24,000 from the defendant company and its receiver (who had been appointed by National Westminster Bank under the terms of a mortgage debenture granted to it by the defendant company) as having been paid under a mistake of fact. That claim succeeded.

Robert Goff J: . . .

The principles upon which money is recoverable on the ground that it has been paid under a mistake of fact

Nearly 40 years ago, Asquith J. stated that 'it is notoriously difficult to harmonise all the cases dealing with payment of money under a mistake of fact,': see *Weld-Blundell v Synott* [1940] 2 KB 107, 112.

---

7 [1914] AC 398, 415.

This is indeed true, and it does not make easy the task of the trial judge, whose duty it is both to search for guiding principles among the authorities, and to pay due regard to those authorities by which he is bound. I have however come to the conclusion that it is possible for me, even in this field, to achieve both these apparently irreconcilable objectives. The key to the problem lies, in my judgment, in a careful reading of the earliest and most fundamental authorities, and in giving full effect to certain decisions of the House of Lords. It is necessary therefore for me to review the leading authorities.

I shall go straight to three early cases, the first of which provided the basis of the modern law on this topic. That is *Kelly v Solari* (1841) 9 M & W 54. [*He set out the facts of the case, quoted from the judgments of Parke B (above, 100) and Rolfe B (above, 101) and continued:*] [I]t would not, in my judgment, be right to infer that Parke B was stating that money paid under a mistake of fact was only recoverable in cases where the plaintiff's mistake led him to believe that he was under a liability to the defendant to pay the money to him. There is nothing to indicate that the first part of his statement of principle was intended so to restrict the right of recovery; indeed later in his judgment he stated the principle of recovery in broader terms, as did Rolfe B, which appears to indicate that it is sufficient to ground recovery that the plaintiff's mistake has caused him to make the payment.

The second of these cases is *Aiken v Short* (1856) 1 H & N 210. [*He set out the facts and continued:*] It is a crucial fact in the case that, the payment having been authorised by Carter, it was effective to discharge the debt which was in fact owed by Carter to the defendant; the defendant therefore gave consideration for the payment which was, for that reason, irrecoverable. This was the basis of the decision of both Pollock CB and Platt B; it seems likely, from interventions in the argument, that Martin B (who was absent when judgment was given) would have decided the case on the same basis. . . . The case is however remembered principally for an obiter dictum of Bramwell B. He said, at p. 215:

'In order to entitle a person to recover back money paid under a mistake of fact, the mistake must be as to a fact which, if true, would make the person paying liable to pay the money; not where, if true, it would merely make it desirable that he should pay the money.'

. . . It appears from the rather fuller report in 25 LJ Ex. 321, 324 that Bramwell B did not necessarily regard his statement of principle as comprehensive. But, strictly construed, it appears to restrict the right of recovery more narrowly than did Parke B in *Kelly v Solari*. It purports to exclude recovery in cases where the plaintiff's mistake did not lead him to believe that he was liable to pay the money to the defendant; and it appears in particular to exclude recovery in a case where the plaintiff had paid the money to the defendant in the mistaken belief, not that he was liable to the defendant to pay it, but that he was under an obligation to a third party to pay it to the defendant, even when the payment did not discharge a debt owing to the defendant who therefore gave no consideration for it. . . .

The third of the early cases to which I must refer is *Chambers v Miller* (1862) 13 CBNS 125. [*He considered the case and continued:*]

Such are the early cases most frequently cited on this topic. I propose to go next to three cases in the House of Lords, in which the law on this subject was authoritatively established. . . . . . . The first is *Kleinwort, Sons & Co. v Dunlop Rubber Co* (1907) 97 LT 263. A firm called Messrs. Kramrisch were rubber merchants, who were financed both by the appellants Messrs. Kleinworts, and by another merchant bank, Messrs. Brandts. Kramrisch supplied the respondents, the Dunlop Rubber Co., with a quantity of rubber, directing them to pay the price to Brandts, who had an equitable mortgage upon it. The respondents mistakenly paid it to the appellants, who received it in good faith. Messrs. Kramrisch failed and the respondents were subsequently held liable to pay the money to Messrs. Brandts. They claimed to recover from the appellants the money they had mistakenly paid to them.

It was held that they were entitled to recover it as having been paid under a mistake of fact. The main question in the case was whether the appellants could rely upon the defence of change of position; but that plea was conclusively negatived by the answers of the jury at the trial. For present purposes, the interest of the case lies in two matters. First, there was no question of the respondents mistakenly believing that they were under any liability to the appellants to pay the money to them. Second, Lord Loreburn LC stated the principle of recovery in very broad terms. He said, at p. 264:

> '. . . it is indisputable that, if money is paid under a mistake of fact and is redemanded from the person who received it before his position has been altered to his disadvantage, the money must be repaid in whatever character it was received.'

The second of these cases is *Kerrison v Glyn, Mills, Currie & Co.* (1911) 81 LJKB 465. The appellant paid a sum of money to the respondents, for the account of a New York bank called Kessler & Co., in anticipation of a liability to recoup Kessler & Co. for advances made by them to a mining company in Mexico in which the appellant was interested. Unknown to the appellant or the respondents, Kessler & Co. were insolvent at the time of the payment. The money was not paid over by the respondents to Kessler & Co.; but since Kessler & Co. were indebted to them, the respondents claimed to be entitled to retain the money and declined to refund it to the appellant. It was held that the appellant was entitled to recover the money from the respondents. Two questions arose in the case. First, whether the arrangements between the appellant and Kessler & Co. were such that he was indebted to Kessler & Co. in the sum of money; it was held by the House of Lords (differing from the Court of Appeal on this point) that he was not, and that the money was paid only in anticipation of a future liability. Had the appellant been so indebted, it was recognised by the House of Lords that the money would have been paid in discharge of an existing debt and would have been irrecoverable, despite the fact that the appellant had paid it under the misapprehension that Kessler & Co. were solvent. Lord Atkinson, who delivered the leading speech, said, at p. 470:

> [The appellant] lodged the money in the belief that Kessler & Co. were a living commercial entity able to carry on their business as theretofore, that they were in a position to honour and would honour the drafts of the Bote Mining Co. up to the sum which he, in anticipation, sent to recoup them for their repeated advances. Kessler & Co. had, in fact, ceased to be in that position.'

The second question was whether the fact that the respondents were bankers enabled them to resist the appellant's claim, on the ground that money once paid in to a bank ceases altogether to be the money of the payer. That was held to be irrelevant.

This decision, too, is therefore inconsistent with the proposition that the only mistake which will ground recovery is a mistake which leads the payer to believe that he is liable to the payee to pay it to him. But the case is also of interest for present purposes because of statements in the speeches of their Lordships relating to the type of mistake which will ground recovery. These are in very broad terms. Lord Atkinson said, at p. 470:

> 'I cannot doubt but that on general principles . . . [the appellant] would be entitled to recover back money paid in ignorance of these vital matters as money paid in mistake of fact.'

Lord Shaw of Dunfermline said, at p. 471:

> 'The money was paid . . . under the mistake of fact—which was material, and was indeed the only reason for payment—that Kessler & Co. could perform their obligations.'

Lord Mersey said, at p. 472, that the facts brought the case directly within the terms of the judgment of Lord Loreburn LC in *Kleinwort, Sons & Co. v Dunlop Rubber Co.*, and then quoted the passage from that judgment which I have set out above. He went on to dismiss an attempt by the respondents 'to take the case out of this plain and simple rule of law.' It is to be observed that Lord Loreburn LC was a member of the Judicial Committee in *Kerrison v Glyn, Mills, Currie & Co.*, and concurred, as did the Earl of Halsbury.

It thus appears that, provided the plaintiff's mistake is 'vital' or 'material,' which I understand to mean that the mistake caused the plaintiff to pay the money, the money is prima facie recoverable; but that if the payment discharged an existing debt owing to the payee (or to a principal on whose behalf the payee is authorised to receive the payment), it is irrecoverable. Such a conclusion is, if I may say so with respect, entirely consistent with the decision in *Aiken v Short*, though not with the dictum of Bramwell B in that case.

The third decision of the House of Lords to which I must refer is *R. E. Jones Ltd v Waring and Gillow Ltd* [1926] AC 670. The facts of the case are complicated and somewhat unclear, due in part to the curious way in which they were found, since they appear to have been taken by the trial judge from the opening speech of the plaintiff's counsel. In summary, a rogue named Bodenham obtained from the respondents furniture and other effects to a value of over £13,000 on hire purchase terms, under which the down payment was to be £5,000. It appears that Bodenham defaulted in making the down payment, and that the respondents then repossessed the goods. Bodenham then approached the appellants, informing them that he represented a firm of motor manufacturers called International Motors who had control of a car called the 'Roma' car, and he persuaded the appellants to accept an appointment as agents for the sale of the car in certain parts of this country, one term of the agency being the payment of a deposit of £5,000 (£10 for each of 500 cars). Bodenham told the appellants that the people who were financing the thing and who were the principals behind him in the matter were the respondents, and that the deposit might be paid to them. The appellants then made out two cheques payable to the order of the respondents, one for £2,000 and one for £3,000, and handed them to Bodenham; he handed them to the respondents, who received them from him in respect of his deposit under the hire purchase agreement. The respondents' accountant observed that the cheques bore the signature of only one director; he then arranged with the appellants to exchange them for one cheque for £5,000 duly signed. This exchange was effected in good faith, nothing being said about the nature of the transaction. The cheque for £5,000 was cashed by the respondents, who then restored to Bodenham the furniture they had seized, and let him have some more. Subsequently, the fraud came to light, and it transpired that there was no International Motors and no 'Roma' car. The respondents resumed possession of the furniture. The appellants claimed repayment of the sum of £5,000 from the respondents.

The trial judge gave judgment for the appellants; but his judgment was reversed by the Court of Appeal [1925] 2 KB 612. The reasons given by the members of the court vary; but for present purposes the significant judgment is that of Pollock MR. He held that the appellants' claim to recover the money as paid under a mistake of fact must fail, because the mistake was not a mistake *as between* the appellants and the respondents. He referred to the dicta of Parke B in *Kelly v Solari*, and of Bramwell B in *Aiken v Short*; he also referred to the decision in *Chambers v Miller*, 13 CBNS 125, and to the dictum of Erlc CJ in that case (in the version reported in 32 LJ CP 30, 32). He concluded, at p. 632:

> 'The plaintiffs and the defendants were each of them under misapprehensions . . . and different mistakes of fact. It appears to me, therefore, that it is not possible for the plaintiffs to recover the money as having been paid under a mistake of fact.'

The House of Lords were however unanimous in concluding that the appellants' mistake of fact was sufficient to ground recovery, though a minority considered that the respondents had a good defence to the claim because they had changed their position in good faith. The House accordingly allowed the appeal. For present purposes, I am only concerned with the nature of the mistake which will ground recovery. Viscount Cave LC (with whose speech Lord Atkinson agreed) stated the principle in very broad terms, which show that he considered it sufficient for the plaintiff to show that he suffered under a mistake of fact which caused the payment. He said, at pp. 679–680:

'The plaintiffs were told by Bodenham that he represented a firm called International Motors which was about to be formed into a company, that the firm had control of a car called the "Roma" car which he described as an existing car, and that the defendants were financing the firm and were the principals behind him and behind International Motors in the matter. Believing these statements to be true, the plaintiffs entered into an agreement which bound them to pay a deposit of £5,000 on 500 Roma cars; and still believing them to be true, and that the respondents as the nominees of International Motors could give a good receipt for the £5,000, they paid that sum to the respondents. In fact the statements were untrue from beginning to end; and the money was, therefore, paid under a mistake of fact induced by the false statements of a third party and, apart from special circumstances, could be recovered. As to the general principle, it is sufficient to refer to the well known case of *Kelly v Solari*, and to the more recent decisions in *Colonial Bank v Exchange Bank of Yarmouth, Nova Scotia* and *Kerrison v Glyn, Mills, Curres & Co.*'

It is significant that Viscount Cave LC did not consider it necessary to identify the precise capacity in which the appellants supposed that the respondents received the money; it was enough for him that the appellants supposed that the respondents were 'nominees' of International Motors who could give a good receipt for the money—a purely neutral term. It follows that he did not regard it as necessary that the appellants should have supposed that they were liable to the respondents to pay the money to them, as is borne out by his citation of *Colonial Bank v Exchange Bank of Yarmouth, Nova Scotia*, 11 App. Cas. 84 and of *Kerrison v Glyn, Mills, Currie & Co.*. It is scarcely surprising that Lord Atkinson, who delivered the leading speech in *Kerrison's* case, agreed with Viscount Cave LC on this aspect of the case. Lord Shaw of Dunfermline also agreed with Viscount Cave LC that the money was paid under a mistake of fact. He concluded, at p. 686, that it seemed quite clear that the appellants would never have parted with the money if they had had any knowledge of the real truth, and that the money was recoverable. It appears from his statement of the facts that he did not consider that the appellants mistakenly believed that they were liable to the respondents to pay the money to them. Lord Sumner, at pp. 691–692, stated the facts in terms which show that he considered that the appellants supposed that, in paying the money, they were discharging an obligation to International Motors, not an obligation to the respondents. Lord Carson, in agreeing with Viscount Cave LC that the money was paid under a mistake of fact, cited and relied upon both the dictum of Parke B and the very broad dictum of Rolfe B in *Kelly v Solari*, of which at least the latter requires only that the plaintiff's mistake should have caused him to pay the money.

I wish to make three comments on the decision of the House of Lords in *R. E. Jones Ltd v Waring and Gillow Ltd*. First, the House of Lords must have rejected the view, expressed by Pollock MR, that to ground recovery the mistake must have been 'as between' payer and payee, in the sense of having been a mistake shared by both parties. Second, it is implicit in the speeches of all their Lordships that it is not a prerequisite of recovery that the plaintiff must have mistakenly believed that he was liable to the defendant to pay the money to him. Third, as I understand their Lordships' speeches, in particular the speech of Viscount Cave LC (with which Lord Atkinson agreed) and the speeches of Lord Shaw and Lord Carson, it is sufficient to ground recovery that the plaintiff's mistake should have caused him to pay the money to the payee.

. . .

From this formidable line of authority certain simple principles can, in my judgment, be deduced: (1) If a person pays money to another under a mistake of fact which causes him to make the payment, he is prima facie entitled to recover it as money paid under a mistake of fact. (2) His claim may however fail if (a) the payer intends that the payee shall have the money at all events, whether the fact be true or false, or is deemed in law so to intend; or (b) the payment is made for good consideration, in particular if the money is paid to discharge, and does discharge, a debt owed to the payee (or a principal on whose he is authorised to receive the payment) by the payer or by a third party by whom he is authorised to discharge the debt; or (c) the payee has changed his position in good faith, or is deemed in law to have done so.

To these simple propositions, I append the following footnotes: (a) *Proposition* 1. This is founded upon the speeches in the three cases in the House of Lords, to which I have referred. It is also consistent with the opinion expressed by Turner J in *Thomas v Houston Corbett & Co.* [1969] NZLR 151, 167. Of course, if the money was due under a contract between the payer and the payee, there can be no recovery on this ground unless the contract itself is held void for mistake (as in *Norwich Union Fire Insurance Society Ltd v Wm. H. Price Ltd* [1934] AC 455) or is rescinded by the plaintiff. (b) *Proposition* 2 (a). This is founded upon the dictum of Parke B in *Kelly v Solari*. I have felt it necessary to add the words 'or is deemed in law so to intend' to accommodate the decision of the Court of Appeal in *Morgan v Ashcroft* [1938] 1 KB 49, a case strongly relied upon by the defendants in the present case, the effect of which I shall have to consider later in this judgment. (c) *Proposition* 2 (b). This is founded upon the decision in *Aiken v Short*, and upon dicta in *Kerrison v Glyn, Mills, Currie & Co.* However, even if the payee has given consideration for the payment, for example by accepting the payment in discharge of a debt owed to him by a third party on whose behalf the payer is authorised to discharge it, that transaction may itself be set aside (and so provide no defence to the claim) if the payer's mistake was induced by the payee, or possibly even where the payee, being aware of the payer's mistake, did not receive the money in good faith: cf. *Ward & Co. v Wallis* [1900] 1 QB 675, 678–679, *per* Kennedy J. (d) *Proposition* 2 (c). This is founded upon the statement of principle of Lord Loreburn LC in *Kleinwort, Sons & Co. v Dunlop Rubber Co.* I have deliberately stated this defence in broad terms, making no reference to the question whether it is dependent upon a breach of duty by the plaintiff or a representation by him independent of the payment, because these matters do not arise for decision in the present case. . . . (c) I have ignored, in stating the principle of recovery, defences of general application in the law of restitution, for example where public policy precludes restitution. (f) The following propositions are inconsistent with the simple principle of recovery established in the authorities: (i) That to ground recovery, the mistake must have induced the payer to believe that he was liable to pay the money to the payee or his principal. (ii) That to ground recovery, the mistake must have been 'as between' the payer and the payee. Rejection of this test has led to its reformulation (notably by Asquith J in *Weld-Blundell v Synott* and by Windeyer J in *Porter v Latec Finance (Qld.) Pty. Ltd* (1964) 111 CLR 177, 204) in terms which in my judgment mean no more than that the mistake must have caused the payment.

In the case before me, Mr. Evans Lombe submitted on behalf of the defendants that I could not proceed on the basis of the simple principles I have stated, because I was precluded from so doing by binding authority, viz. the decision of the Court of Appeal in *Morgan v Ashcroft*. . . . Mr. Evans Lombe relied in particular on a passage in the judgment of Sir Wilfrid Greene MR, in which he stated, at p. 66:

'. . . a person who intends to make a voluntary payment and thinks that he is making one kind of voluntary payment whereas upon the true facts he is making another kind of voluntary payment, does not make the payment under a mistake of fact which can be described as fundamental or basic.'

That passage Mr. Evans Lombe identified as being the crucial passage in Sir Wilfrid Greene MR's judgment on this point; and he submitted further that the expression 'voluntary payment' must here be understood as a payment made without legal obligation, so that, generally speaking, a person who makes a payment without the intention of discharging a legal obligation cannot recover the money from the payee although it has been paid under a mistake of fact except possibly in circumstances where the mistake can be described as fundamental, for example where the mistake is as to the identity of the payee.

It is legitimate to observe the consequences of Mr. Evans Lombe's submission. If he is right, money would be irrecoverable in the following, by no means far-fetched, situations. (1) A man, forgetting that he has already paid his subscription to the National Trust, pays it a second time. (2) A substantial charity uses a computer for the purpose of distributing small benefactions. The computer runs mad, and pays one beneficiary the same gift one hundred times over. (3) A shipowner and a character enter into a sterling charterparty for a period of years. Sterling depreciates against other currencies; and the charterer decides, to maintain the goodwill of the shipowner but without obligation, to increase the monthly hire payments. Owing to a mistake in his office, the increase in one monthly hire payment is paid twice over. (4) A Lloyd's syndicate gets into financial difficulties. To maintain the reputation of Lloyd's, other underwriting syndicates decide to make gifts of money to assist the syndicate in difficulties. Due to a mistake, one syndicate makes its gift twice over. It would not be difficult to construct other examples. The consequences of Mr. Evans Lombe's submission are therefore so far-reaching that it is necessary to examine the ratio decidendi of this part of the decision in *Morgan v Ashcroft* to ascertain whether it produces the result for which Mr. Evans Lombe contends.

Only two judges sat to hear the appeal in *Morgan v Ashcroft*—Sir Wilfrid Greene MR and Scott LJ. Furthermore, there are considerable differences between their two judgments on this part of the case. [*He set out the differences and continued:*] [I]t is by no means easy to determine the ratio decidendi of this part of the case. It may well be found in the opinion of both judges that an overpayment of betting debts by a bookmaker is not made under a mistake of fact sufficiently fundamental to ground recovery, apparently on the basis that the payment is in any event intended to be a purely voluntary gift, because 'the law prevents the plaintiff from saying that he intended anything but a present' (see p. 77, *per* Scott LJ), and the plaintiff is therefore deemed in law to intend that the payee shall be entitled to retain the money in any event.

That the ratio decidendi is not to be found in the passage from Sir Wilfrid Greene MR's judgment on which Mr. Evans Lombe relied is shown by the fact that the subsequent decision of the Court of Appeal in *Larner v London County Council* [1949] 2 KB 683 is, in my judgment, inconsistent with that passage. In that case, the London County Council had resolved to pay all their employees who went to the war the difference between their war service pay and their civil pay until further order. Mr. Larner was an ambulance driver employed by the council, who was called up in 1942. As a result of his failure to keep the council accurately informed about changes in his war service pay, the council overpaid the difference. In contending that the overpayment was irrecoverable, Mr. Larner's counsel relied upon the dictum of Bramwell B in *Aiken v Short*. The Court of Appeal however held that the money was recoverable. Denning LJ who delivered the judgment of the court, declined to follow that dictum, because he said, at p. 688, '. . . that dictum, as Scott LJ pointed out in *Morgan v Ashcroft*, cannot be regarded as an exhaustive statement of the law.' He pointed out that the council

'made a promise to the men which they were in honour bound to fulfil. The payments made under that promise were not mere gratuities. They were made as a matter of duty . . .'

but he went on to state that it was irrelevant that the council's promise was unsupported by consideration or unenforceable by action. It was enough that the council would never have paid the money to Mr. Larner had they known the true facts: see p. 688 of the report. It is doubtful if the decision in *Larner v London County Council* is one of which Sir Wilfrid Greene MR would have approved; but, if I may say so with respect, it is entirely consistent with the principles of recovery established in the earlier decisions of the House of Lords to which I have referred. Accordingly it is those principles which I intend to apply in the present case.

Where a bank pays a cheque drawn upon it by a customer of the bank, in what circumstances may the bank recover the payment from the payee on the ground that it was paid under a mistake of fact?

It is a basic obligation owed by a bank to its customer that it will honour on presentation cheques drawn by the customer on the bank, provided that there are sufficient funds in the customer's account to meet the cheque, or the bank has agreed to provide the customer with overdraft facilities sufficient to meet the cheque. Where the bank honours such a cheque, it acts within its mandate, with the result that the bank is entitled to debit the customer's account with the amount of the cheque, and further that the bank's payment is effective to discharge the obligation of the customer to the payee on the cheque, because the bank has paid the cheque with the authority of the customer.

In other circumstances, the bank is under no obligation to honour its customer's cheques. If however a customer draws a cheque on the bank without funds in his account or agreed overdraft facilities sufficient to meet it, the cheque on presentation constitutes a request to the bank to provide overdraft facilities sufficient to meet the cheque. The bank has an option whether or not to comply with that request. If it declines to do so, it acts entirely within its rights and no legal consequences follow as between the bank and its customer. If however the bank pays the cheque, it accepts the request and the payment has the same legal consequences as if the payment had been made pursuant to previously agreed overdraft facilities; the payment is made within the bank's mandate, and in particular the bank is entitled to debit the customer's account, and the bank's payment discharges the customer's obligation to the payee on the cheque.

In other cases, however, a bank which pays a cheque drawn or purported to be drawn by its customer pays without mandate. A bank does so if, for example, it overlooks or ignores notices of its customer's death, or if it pays a cheque bearing the forged signature of its customer as drawer, but, more important for present purposes, a bank will pay without mandate if it overlooks or ignores notice of countermand of the customer who has drawn the cheque. In such cases the bank, if it pays the cheque, pays without mandate from its customer, and unless the customer is able to and does ratify the payment, the bank cannot debit the customer's account, nor will its payment be effective to discharge the obligation (if any) of the customer on the cheque, because the bank had no authority to discharge such obligation.

It is against the background of these principles which were not in dispute before me, that I have to consider the position of a bank which pays a cheque under a mistake of fact. In such a case, the crucial question is, in my judgment, whether the payment was with or without mandate. The two typical situations, which exemplify payment with or without mandate, arise first where the bank pays in the mistaken belief that there are sufficient funds or overdraft facilities to meet the cheque, and second where the bank overlooks notice of countermand given by the customer. In each case, there is a mistake by the bank which causes the bank to make the payment. But in the first case, the effect of the bank's payment is to accept the customer's request for overdraft facilities; the payment is therefore within the bank's mandate, with the result that not only is the bank entitled to have recourse to its customer, but the customer's obligation to the payee is discharged. It follows that the payee has given consideration for the payment; with the consequence that, although the payment has been caused by the bank's mistake, the money is irrecoverable from the payee unless the transaction of payment is itself set aside. Although the bank is unable to recover the money, it has a right of recourse to its customer. In the second case, however, the bank's payment is without mandate. The bank has no recourse to its customer; and the debt of the customer to the payee on the cheque is not discharged. Prima facie, the bank is entitled to recover the money from the payee, unless the payee has changed his position in good faith, or is deemed in law to have done so.

. . .

Application of the foregoing principles to the present case

In the light of the above principles, it is plain that in the present case the plaintiff bank is entitled to succeed in its claim. First, it is clear that the mistake of the bank, in overlooking the drawer's instruction to stop payment of the cheque, caused the bank to pay the cheque. Second, since the drawer had in fact countermanded payment, the bank was acting without mandate and so the payment was not effective to discharge the drawer's obligation on the cheque; from this it follows that the payee gave no consideration for the payment, and the claim cannot be defeated on that ground. Third, there is no evidence of any actual change of position on the part of either of the defendants or on the part of the National Westminster Bank; and, since notice of dishonour is not required in a case such as this, the payee is not deemed to have changed his position by reason of lapse of time in notifying them of the plaintiff's error and claiming repayment.

I must confess that I am happy to be able to reach the conclusion that the money is recoverable by the plaintiff bank. If the bank had not failed to overlook its customer's instructions, the cheque would have been returned by it marked 'Orders not to pay,' and there would have followed a perfectly bona fide dispute between the association and the receiver on the question, arising on the terms of the building contract, whether the association was entitled to stop the cheque—which ought to be the real dispute in the case. If the plaintiff bank had been unable to recover the money, not only would that dispute not have been ventilated and resolved on its merits but, in the absence of ratification by the association, the plaintiff bank would have had no recourse to the association. Indeed, if under the terms of the building contract the money had not been due to the defendant company, non-recovery by the plaintiff bank would have meant quite simply a windfall for the preferred creditors of the defendant company at the plaintiff bank's expense. As however I have held that the money is recoverable, the situation is as it should have been; nobody is harmed, and the true dispute between the association and the receiver can be resolved on its merits. . . .

NOTES AND QUESTIONS

1. Robert Goff J's statement of principles was applied, with the focus being on what was meant by proposition 2(b), by the Court of Appeal in *Lloyds Bank plc v Independent Insurance Co. Ltd* (below, 163). A causation approach was also approved in the reasoning of the majority of the House of Lords (albeit not directly mentioning the *Simms* case) in *Kleinwort Benson Ltd v Lincoln City Council* (below, 167).

2. On the facts as it believed them to be, the claimant bank would have been under a legal obligation to pay the £24,000 to the defendant. Why, then, was the decision for the claimant not more simply and conventionally reached by an application of the 'supposed liability' test? Could *Jones v Waring and Gillow Ltd* and *Larner v London County Council* have been interpreted as supporting a 'supposed liability' rather than a causation test? Is Robert Goff J's causation approach preferable to the 'supposed liability' or 'fundamental' tests? If so, why?

3. Although not mentioned by Robert Goff J, further support in the authorities for a rejection of a 'supposed liability' test derives from cases on the rescission of formal gifts for mistake (see, e.g., *Lady Hood of Avalon v MacKinnon* [1909] 1 Ch 476).

4. No explicit reference was made to the test for determining whether a mistake is causative. However, a 'but for' causation test for mistaken payments (whether of fact or law) was approved in the reasoning of the majority of the House of Lords in *Kleinwort Benson Ltd v Lincoln City Council* (below, 167). See also Neuberger J in *Nurdin & Peacock plc v DB Ramsden & Co. Ltd* (below, 183) favouring a prima facie but for test for all mistakes, whether of fact or law.

5. In Robert Goff J's statement of principles (above, 157) what is meant by proposition 2(a)?

6. Where do payments made under a contract entered into by mistake fit into Robert Goff J's scheme? Consider, for example, what the restitutionary consequences would have been if the

House of Lords in *Bell v Lever Bros* [1932] AC 16] had decided that the contract was void for common mistake. And take cases on the rescission of an executed contract for misrepresentation, non-disclosure, or mistake (below, 195–202). Does the restitution of money paid, through the remedy of rescission of an executed contract entered into by mistake, fall within Robert Goff J's scheme?

7. Robert Goff J was careful to explain (in relation to proposition 2(c) of his statement of principles) that he was leaving open the question whether there was a 'change of position' defence beyond estoppel. Twelve years later in *Lipkin Gorman v Karpnale Ltd* (above, 28) he was able authoritatively to determine that question in favour of recognizing the wider defence.

8. Without casting doubt on Robert Goff J's scheme for mistake of fact, it can be argued that his decision was incorrect in relation to his conclusion that the customer's debt to the defendant was not discharged by the bank's payment (so that the defendant provided no consideration and had not changed its position). If one takes the view that payment of another's debt that is accepted by the creditor as discharging that debt discharges the debt automatically without the consent of the debtor, the bank's restitutionary claim would have lain against its customer (in an action for money paid to the defendant's use): see generally below, Chapter 8. *County of Carleton v City of Ottawa* (below, 188) is a mistake case consistent with the automatic discharge view. See also Goode 'The Bank's Right to Recover Money Paid on a Stopped Cheque' (1981) 97 *LQR* 254 who argues that, applying normal agency principles, the debt should have been regarded as discharged because the bank had the customer's apparent authority to pay.

9. Tettenborn rejects a straightforward 'but for' causation test. He writes in Tettenborn, *The Law of Restitution in England and Ireland* (3rd edn, 2002), 76, 'Assume I give £1000 to my niece as a birthday present, not realising that she has just married a man I privately detest. It seems instinctively odd that a footling or idiosyncratic error like that should entitle me to repent of my generosity and recover my money, even if I can prove by impeccable evidence that had I known the relevant facts, I would not have made the gift in the first place'.

10. A few commentators have criticized Robert Goff J's approach by arguing that restitution for a mistake of fact is merely part of the wider ground for restitution of failure of consideration: see Butler, 'Mistaken Payments, Change of Position and Restitution' in *Essays on Restitution* (1990) Finn (ed.), chapter 4; and the following extract from a short article by Matthews.

• P Matthews, 'Money Paid Under Mistake of Fact' (1980) *NLJ* 587

In the recent case of *Barclays Bank Ltd v W. J. Simms Son and Cooke (Southern) Ltd* Robert Goff J examined the right to recover payments made under mistake of fact. It is here suggested that the learned judge's analysis, rather than clarifying the position, managed to obfuscate it, even if the ultimate result is otherwise justifiable. . . .

The recovery of payments made under mistake of fact is in truth another manifestation of the quasi-contractual doctrine of failure of consideration . . .

In *Kelly v Solari*, the consideration which the plaintiff paid to secure totally failed, because the liability the plaintiff sought to discharge in fact never existed. (If the plaintiff did not discharge his liability under the contract he could not retain the premium paid by the defendant, who would be entitled to sue for its return, again as money paid on a total failure of consideration: *Hong Kong Fir* case [1962] 2 QB 26.) On the other hand, in *Aiken v Short* the plaintiff agreed to pay and did pay the defendant to discharge a debt owed by a third party to the defendant, and thereby to increase the value of property held by them as security for a debt owed them also by the third party. Since the debt was discharged by the payment, there was no failure of consideration. The use of the word 'liable' in *Aiken*, as also the use of the word 'entitle' in *Kelly*, is quite apposite to demonstrate that supposed contractual liability is the motive for the payment, and that the consideration intended to be secured by that payment will only be so secured and retainable as against the defendant if that liability is discharged. If, contrary to the plaintiff's belief, there is no liability anyway, the plaintiff is paying to secure a consideration to which he is already entitled. His payment secures nothing: there is a failure of consideration. The plaintiff's mistake is crucial, not to bring some independent quasi-contractual doctrine into play, but to demonstrate that the payment was made for a particular consideration that has failed and not as an out-and-out gift.

Now, why does a bank pay the holder of a cheque, whether payee or indorsee? It cannot be in order to discharge its customer's liability to the holder, for not only will there be none in many cases (except on the cheque itself) to be discharged, but also the bank will not be concerned to know whether there is such a liability. The fact that in a particular case no liability was discharged could not ground an action for recovery by the bank as money paid on a total failure of consideration. On the other hand, the bank does pay the holder of a cheque to secure a consideration from its customer, that is, a release pro tanto of the debt owing to the customer (or an increase pro tanto in the indebtedness of the customer). Payment to a third party nominated by the customer is agreed to be the consideration flowing from the bank. If A pays B expecting a consideration in return but receiving none, A can recover. Why should it make a difference if A pays X believing B to have requested this, and expecting a consideration from B, which in fact never materialises? This is exactly the instant case.

. . .

. . . Whilst the results in the more recent Commonwealth cases, as in the *Simms* case itself, are to be supported, it is to be hoped that, should the matter come before the highest courts, they will take the opportunity to set the plaintiff's right to recover on a more sound and principled footing.

NOTES AND QUESTIONS

1. Do you agree with Matthews that it is preferable to analyse mistakes of fact as being an aspect of failure of consideration? (see Burrows, 145–6).

2. Is it not a disadvantage of Matthews' view that it imports into mistake cases the difficult requirement that the failure of consideration be total (see Chapter 5)?

3. Is Matthews advocating the same as Birks' 'absence of basis' approach (above, 149, note 4)?

- *Lloyds Bank plc v Independent Insurance Co. Ltd*
  [2000] 1 QB 110, Court of Appeal

WF Insurance Co. Ltd (WF) owed the defendant insurance company £162,388 (comprising premiums it had collected for the defendant). WF requested its bank, the claimant, to pay that sum to the defendant's account. In the mistaken belief that three cheques for £172,132 in total payable to WF had been cleared, the claimant bank made a credit transfer of £162,388 to the defendant's account. In fact one of the three cheques which was for £168,000 had not been cleared so that WF's account was substantially overdrawn. The claimant bank sought restitution from the defendant of £107,388 (which was the £162,388 paid minus £55,000 which was subsequently paid into WF's account). In allowing the appeal, the Court of Appeal refused restitution on the ground that the claimant bank's payment to the defendant, albeit made by a mistake of fact, had discharged a debt owed by WF to the defendant.

Waller LJ: . . .

Does the fact that the bank was authorised prevent a restitutionary remedy?
Mr. Hapgood on behalf of the bank boldly submits that condition 2(b) as set out by Robert Goff J. in *Barclays Bank Ltd v W. J. Simms Son & Cooke (Southern) Ltd* [1980] Q.B. 677, 695, is inaccurately

expressed. He indeed submitted in his skeleton argument that part of condition 2(b) is obiter. Condition 2(b) provides that a claim may fail where (at p. 695):

> 'the payment is made for good consideration, in particular if the money is paid to discharge, and does discharge, a debt owed to the payee . . . by the payer *or by a third party by whom he is authorised to discharge the debt* . . .' (Emphasis added.)

The submission is that because Robert Goff J. found that in that case the bank was unauthorised the italicised words are obiter.

. . .

I follow in one sense the point that it can be said that even an authorised payment leaves Independent enriched at the expense of the bank. But clearly one of the points that lay at the root of Robert Goff J.'s reasoning in the *Simms* case [1980] Q.B. 677 was the recognition that restitution would not be ordered where the payment made under a mistake had in fact discharged an existing debt. If restitution could be ordered even where a debt was discharged, it would have been quite unnecessary to consider whether the bank in that case was acting within its authority. But Robert Goff J. recognised that if a payment by an agent (the bank in that case as in this) did discharge a debt, that would provide a payee with a defence to a restitutionary claim. That being fundamental to his reasoning it is inaccurate to suggest that his formulation of the principle expressing that view was obiter. . . . It also seems to me that the proposition that *if* the debt was discharged the payee would have a defence to a restitutionary claim in fact simply applies basic principles relating to restitutionary remedies. There are, as I see it, two bases which support the fundamental proposition in restitutionary terms. First, arguably, where the debt has been discharged the payment has been made for good consideration. That is the basis expressed in Robert Goff J.'s formulation in *Barclays Bank Ltd v W. J. Simms Son & Cooke (Southern) Ltd* [1980] Q.B. 677. *Goff & Jones, The Law of Restitution*, 4th ed., p. 134 could be said not to support that basis with wholehearted conviction. But the second basis does have *Goff & Jones's* support in the same paragraph. If a payment has discharged the debt, then unless an order to return the money reinstates the debt, the payee will have changed his position in no longer having a remedy against the debtor.

. . .

Peter Gibson LJ: . . .

My principal objection to Mr. Hapgood's contentions relates to his assertion that Independent has been unjustly enriched by the payment made to it by the bank. In my judgment that cannot be said of a payment made to discharge a debt, absent the special factors referred to by Robert Goff J. in his qualification of his proposition (b). In *Kleinwort Benson Ltd v Lincoln City Council* [1999] 2 A.C. 349, 407, Lord Hope of Craighead posed as the third of three questions raised by a claim for restitution of money paid under a mistake: 'Did the payee have a right to receive the sum which was paid to him?' He said [1999] 2 A.C. 349, 408:

> 'The third question arises because the payee cannot be said to have been unjustly enriched if he was entitled to receive the sum paid to him. The payer may have been mistaken as to the grounds on which the sum was due to the payee, but his mistake will not provide a ground for its recovery if the payee can show that he was entitled to it on some other ground.'

So here. Independent was entitled to receive the sum paid to it in discharge of the debt owed to it by W.F. That, in my view, is not affected by the fact that the payment was made by the bank as W.F.'s agent.

I would add that I cannot accept that the defence of bona fide purchase has been overtaken by or subsumed in the defence of change of position. Both defences may coexist: see *Lipkin Gorman v Karpnale Ltd* [1991] 2 A.C. 548, 580–581.

It is interesting to note that the conclusion that a payment made under a mistake but in discharge of a debt is irrecoverable is consistent with the *American Law Institute, Restatement of the Law, Restitution* (1937), to which Mr. Sumption took us. In section 33 it is stated that the holder of a cheque or other bill of exchange who, having paid value in good faith therefor, receives payment from the drawee without reason to know that the drawee is mistaken is under no duty of restitution to him although the drawee pays because of a mistaken belief that he has sufficient funds of the drawer. The commentary states that the payee is entitled to retain the money which he has received as a bona fide purchaser, and the illustrations given by way of typical cases include the payment by a bank of a cheque drawn on it by a customer who has insufficient funds to cover the cheque, the payment going to discharge a mortgage debt.

For these reasons as well as those given by Waller L.J. I would reject the bank's contentions on [this] issue.

Thorpe LJ delivered a concurring judgment.

NOTES AND QUESTIONS

1. The judges put forward several justifications for qualification 2(b) in Robert Goff J's judgment in *Barclays Bank Ltd v W J Simms*: (i) payee entitled to be paid; (ii) bona fide purchase/good consideration; (iii) change of position. Which of these, if any, is the best justification? Peter Gibson LJ, in a passage not set out above, said that 'in this part of his formulation, Robert Goff J is basing himself on the defence of good consideration and not of change of position, which is the separate subject of para (c) of his formulation.'

2. How does one distinguish this case (no restitution) from *Barclays Bank Ltd v W J Simms* (restitution granted)?

- *Dextra Bank & Trust Co. Ltd v Bank of Jamaica*
  [2002] 1 All ER (Comm) 193, Privy Council

Dextra Bank drew a cheque on its bankers for $US 2,999,000 in favour of the Bank of Jamaica (BOJ). Both Dextra Bank and the BOJ had been deceived by fraudsters. Dextra Bank were led to believe that the BOJ had asked for a loan; and that the sum lent had been secured by its agent having received a signed promissory note from the BOJ. The BOJ in turn believed that the money received was for foreign currency purchased by its agents and they reimbursed those (fraudulent) agents in advance of actual receipt of the $US 2,999,000. Dextra Bank sought restitution of the $US 2,999,000 but the Privy Council held that its claim failed for two reasons. The first, which we look at here, is that Dextra Bank had made no relevant mistake of fact but had rather made a misprediction. The second, examined below, 781, is that the BOJ had changed its position.

Lord Bingham of Cornhill and **Lord Goff of Chieveley** (giving the judgment of the Privy Council comprising themselves, **Lord Hobhouse of Woodborough**, **Sir Martin Nourse** and **Sir Patrick Russell**): . . .

Mistake of fact
[28] Their Lordships turn to Dextra's claim to recover its money as having been paid to the BOJ under a mistake of fact. To succeed in an action to recover money on that ground, the plaintiff has to identify a payment by him to the defendant, a specific fact as to which the plaintiff was mistaken in making the payment, and a causal relationship between that mistake of fact and the payment of the money: see *Barclays Bank Ltd v W J Simms Son & Cooke (Southern) Ltd* [1979] 3 All ER 522 at 534, [1980] QB 677 at 694. In the opinion of their Lordships, there are difficulties with regard to the second and third of these elements in the present case.

[29] Their Lordships turn then to the second element, viz that Dextra must have paid the money to

the BOJ under a mistake of fact. It is the contention of Dextra that the money was paid under a mistake, in that Dextra had intended to make a loan. The difficulty with this proposition is that this does not appear to have been a mistake as to a specific fact, like for example a mistake as to the identity of the defendant, but rather a misprediction as to the nature of the transaction which would come into existence when the Dextra cheque was delivered to the BOJ, which is a very different matter: see Birks *An Introduction to the Law of Restitution* (1985) pp 147–148. In that passage, Professor Birks explains the rationale of this distinction in terms relevant to the present case, as follows:

'The reason is that restitution for mistake rests on the fact that the plaintiff's judgment was vitiated in the matter of the transfer of wealth to the defendant. A mistake as to the future, a misprediction, does not show that the plaintiff's judgment was vitiated, only that as things turned out it was incorrectly exercised. A prediction is an exercise of judgment. To act on the basis of a prediction is to accept the risk of disappointment. If you then complain of having been mistaken you are merely asking to be relieved of a risk knowingly run . . .

The safe course for one who does not want to bear the risk of disappointment which is inherent in predictions is to communicate with the recipient of the benefit in advance of finally committing it to him. He can then qualify his intent to give by imposing conditions, or sometimes by making a trust . . .'

Here, unfortunately, Dextra failed to communicate directly with the BOJ to make sure that the BOJ understood that the money was being offered as a loan. Instead, it left the communication of this vital matter to its agent, Phillips. Dextra's misplaced reliance on Phillips led it to assume that a loan would result; and this prediction proved to be mistaken. But a misprediction does not, in their Lordships' opinion, provide the basis for a claim to recover money as having been paid under a mistake of fact.

[**30**] Dextra did, however, argue that it suffered under a mistake of fact when it was deceived by Wildish into believing that the BOJ had previously agreed to take a loan from Dextra. In fact, the BOJ had not so agreed. But, although this can be regarded as a mistake of fact on the part of Dextra, it cannot be said to have caused Dextra's payment to the BOJ. This is because it was overtaken by the specific instructions given by Dextra to Phillips that the cheque was not to be handed over to the BOJ except against the delivery to him of a promissory note evidencing the loan and its terms. It was upon the compliance by Phillips with this instruction that Dextra relied to ensure that a loan was made upon the terms acceptable to it. The significance of the earlier deception by Wildish was only that it contributed to Dextra instructing Phillips to ensure that the cheque was handed over as a loan. Dextra's payment was not, however, caused by any such mistake of fact as that now alleged by Dextra; it was caused by a misprediction by Dextra that Phillips would carry out his instructions and that a loan would eventuate.

. . .

NOTES AND QUESTIONS

1. Do you agree that Dextra Bank's payment was the consequence of a misprediction rather than a mistake? Why could one not say that at the time the cheque was delivered to the BOJ, Dextra Bank mistakenly believed that the BOJ had signed a promissory note in its favour? Or, alternatively, why could one not say that Dextra Bank was mistaken as to the trustworthiness of its agent (which was a relevant mistake not merely at the time the cheque was handed to its agent but also, importantly, when the cheque was subsequently delivered by its agent to the BOJ)?

2. Can the denial of a claim for mistake in this case be reconciled with the acceptance of such a claim in *RE Jones Ltd v Waring & Gillow Ltd* [1926] AC 670 (above, 149)?

3. Is restitution for mispredictions always denied?

4. Birks, *Unjust Enrichment* (2nd edn, 2005), 145–6 wrote the following: 'The "no basis" approach

suggests that . . . the *Dextra* case was wrongly decided so far as its claim was excluded under question three (unjust). There was no basis for the *Dextra* payment. In view of the Bank of Jamaica's defence, no damage was done. If the third question had been put entirely independently of the fifth question (defences), the probable error would immediately have been revealed. The factual premiss would then have been that the Bank of Jamaica's assets were still swollen by the $3M. It would have been difficult to conclude that Dextra had no cause of action'.

(2) MISTAKES OF LAW

- *Bilbie v Lumley* (1802) 2 East 469, Court of King's Bench

The claimant underwriter had paid £100 to the defendant under an insurance policy for loss of the defendant's ship. As a matter of law, the claimant had not been liable to pay because of a non-disclosure by the defendant (at the time the contract was made) of a material letter relating to the time of sailing of the insured ship. Yet the claimant had had that letter before him at the time of making the pay-out (i.e. he knew all the facts). The claim for restitution of the £100 on the ground that it had been paid by mistake failed because the mistake was one of law.

Lord Ellenborough CJ asked the plaintiff's counsel whether he could state any case where if a party paid money to another voluntarily with a full knowledge of all the facts of the case, he could recover it back again on account of his ignorance of the law? [No answer being given, his Lordship continued;] Every man must be taken to be cognizant of the law; otherwise there is no saying to what extent the excuse of ignorance might not be carried. It would be urged in almost every case. In *Lowrie v Bourdieu*,[1] money paid under a mere mistake of the law (was endeavoured to be recovered back), and there Buller J observed that ignorantia juris non excusat, &c.

NOTES AND QUESTIONS

1. Does the maxim 'ignorance of the law is no defence' justify denying restitution of money paid by mistake of law?

2. It has been suggested that, irrespective of the mistake of law bar, *Bilbie v Lumley* may have been correctly decided on the basis that the claimant submitted to an honest claim (see, e.g., Goff and Jones, (5th edn, 1998) 213–5). Do you agree? If *Bilbie v Lumley* was a case of submission to an honest claim, should the same not also be said of *Kelly v Solari* (above, 147)? For discussion of the meaning, and role, of 'submission to an honest claim' see S Arrowsmith, 'Mistake and the Role of the "Submission to an Honest Claim" 'in *Essays on the Law of Restitution* (ed. A Burrows, 1991), 17; Burrows, 138–40.

3. Another case applying a mistake of law bar to recovery was *Holt v Markham* [1923] 1 KB 504, see below, 809.

- *Kleinwort Benson Ltd v Lincoln City Council*
  [1999] 2 AC 349, House of Lords

The claimant bank had made payments to several local authorities (the defendants) under interest rate swap agreements (for an explanation of the nature of these, see below, 727). The agreements had been fully performed by both parties (i.e. the swaps were 'closed'). Then it was decided by the House of Lords in *Hazell v Hammersmith and Fulham Borough Council* [1992] 2 AC 1 that interest rate swap agreements were void as

---

1 Dougl. 467.

being outside the powers of local authorities. The claimant had made net payments to the local authorities of £811,208. The local authorities were willing to pay back the £388,114 which had been paid to them within six years of the date of the issue of the writ. But they were not willing to pay back the £423,094 that had been paid prior to the six years, arguing that a claim for such repayment was statute-barred. The claimant bank sought restitution of the £423,094 on the basis that it had paid under a mistake of law and that, therefore, under s. 32(1) of the Limitation Act 1980 the six year limitation period did not start to run until the claimant discovered, or could with reasonable diligence have discovered, the mistake. And that mistake of law was not discoverable until the decision of the House of Lords in the *Hazell* case. By a three to two majority the House of Lords held that that restitutionary claim should succeed.

Lord Browne-Wilkinson (dissenting): My Lords, I have had the advantage of reading in draft the speech of my noble and learned friend, Lord Goff of Chieveley which contains yet another major contribution to the law of restitution.

Were it not for one matter, I would be in full agreement with his views. But unfortunately he and the majority of your Lordships take the view that when established law is changed by a subsequent decision of the courts, money rightly paid in accordance with the old established law is recoverable as having been paid under a mistake of law. I take the view that the moneys are not recoverable since, at the time of payment, the payer was not labouring under any mistake.

The majority view is that *Hazell v Hammersmith and Fulham London Borough Council* [1992] 2 A.C. I established that the swaps agreements were void; that although the decision in *Hazell* postdated the last of the payments made by the bank to the local authorities the decision operated retrospectively so that under the law as eventually established the bank were labouring under a mistake at the time they made each payment in thinking that they were liable to make such payment. Therefore, in their view, the bank can recover payments made under a mistake of law. My view, on the other hand, is that although the decision in *Hazell* is retrospective in its effect, retrospection cannot falsify history: if at the date of each payment it was settled law that local authorities had capacity to enter into swap contracts, the bank were not labouring under any mistake of law at that date. The subsequent decision in *Hazell* could not create a mistake where no mistake existed at the time.

. . .

My Lords, in these circumstances I find myself in a quandary. I am convinced that the law should be changed so as to permit moneys paid under a mistake of law to be recovered. I also accept, for the reasons given by my noble and learned friend, Lord Goff of Chieveley, that the relevant limitation period applicable to such a claim would be that laid down by section 32(1)(c) of the Limitation Act 1980, i.e. six years from the date on which the mistake was, or could with reasonable diligence have been, discovered. The majority of your Lordships consider that such claim will arise when the law (whether settled by existing authority or by common consensus) is changed by a later decision of the courts. The consequence of this House in its judicial capacity introducing such a fundamental change would be as follows. On every occasion in which a higher court changed the law by judicial decision, all those who had made payments on the basis that the old law was correct (however long ago such payments were made) would have six years in which to bring a claim to recover money paid under a mistake of law. All your Lordships accept that this position cannot be cured save by primary legislation altering the relevant limitation period. In the circumstances, I believe that it would be quite wrong for your Lordships to change the law so as to make money paid under a mistake of law recoverable since to do so would leave this gaping omission in the law. In my judgment the correct course would be for the House to indicate that an alteration in the law is desirable but leave it to the Law Commission and Parliament to produce a satisfactory statutory change in the law which, at one and the same time, both introduces the new cause of action and also properly regulates the limitation period applicable to it.

I would dismiss these appeals.

Lord Goff of Chieveley: My Lords, there are before your Lordships consolidated appeals in four actions, each of which arises from the unravelling of one or more interest rate swap transactions which, following the decision of this House in *Hazell v Hammersmith and Fulham London Borough Council* [1992] 2 A.C. 1, proved to be void. The process of unravelling transactions of this kind has produced a host of problems, so much so that Professor Andrew Burrows stated in 1995 (see [1995] R.L.R. 15) that 'it is no exaggeration to say that one could write a book on the restitutionary consequences of the decision in *Hazell*.' I fear that any such book will be growing in length as the cases, including the present appeals, pass through the courts.

The nature of an interest rate swap transaction is now very well known. The description usually referred to is that of the Divisional Court in *Hazell's* case [1990] 2 Q.B. 697, 739–741, the transactions in the present cases being of the simple type there described. The essence of such a transaction is that one party, known as the fixed rate payer, agrees to pay to the other party over a certain period interest at a fixed rate on a notional capital sum; and the other party, known as the floating rate payer, agrees to pay to the former over the same period interest on the same notional sum at a market rate determined in accordance with a certain formula. In practice, a balance is struck at each relevant date and the party who then owes the greater sum will pay the difference to the other party.

Interest rate swaps can fulfil many purposes, ranging from pure speculation to more useful purposes such as the hedging of liabilities. One form of interest rate swap involves an upfront payment, i.e. a capital sum paid at the outset by one party to the other, which will be balanced by an adjustment of the parties' respective liabilities. The practical result of this is to achieve a form of borrowing. It appears that it was this feature which, in particular, attracted local authorities to enter into transactions of this kind, since they enabled local authorities subject to rate-capping to obtain upfront payments uninhibited by the relevant statutory controls, though they must in the process have been storing up trouble for themselves in the future.

The appellant in each of the four consolidated appeals is Kleinwort Benson Ltd, a bank which was an early participant in the market for interest rate swaps. Each of the respondents is a local authority. They may be described in brief as Birmingham City Council, Southwark London Borough Council, Kensington and Chelsea Royal London Borough Council and Lincoln City Council. The bank entered into interest rate swap transactions with each of the authorities. Following the decision of this House in *Hazell*, the bank commenced proceedings against each of the authorities claiming restitution of the sums it had paid to them under these transactions. The total of the net payments made under them by the bank was £811,208.90.

There are two features of these transactions which are of particular relevance to the present appeals, no doubt flowing from the fact that the bank participated in interest rate swaps at an early stage. The first is that, at the time when proceedings were commenced by the bank, each of the transactions was fully performed by both parties according to its terms across the whole of the agreed period. The second is that not all of the sums paid by the bank to the authorities were paid within the six-year limitation period expiring with the date of the issue of the writs. Of the net sum of £811,208.90 paid by the bank, £388,114.72 was paid within the six-year period, and £423,094.18 represented earlier payments. The former sum has been paid by the relevant local authorities to the bank. The latter sum is in issue, and is the subject of the cases now under appeal.

The claim of the bank in each of these cases is that the money in question was paid by it under a mistake, viz. a mistaken belief that it was paid pursuant to a binding contract between it and the relevant local authority. The claims have been formulated in this way to avoid the six-year time limit by bringing them within section 32(1)(*c*) of the Limitation Act 1980. Section 32(1) provides:

'Subject to subsections (3) and (4A) below, where in the case of any action for which a period of limitation is prescribed by this Act . . . (*c*) the action is for relief from the consequences of a mistake

... the period of limitation shall not begin to run until the plaintiff has discovered the ... mistake ... or could with reasonable diligence have discovered it.'

It is plain however that here the mistake relied upon is a mistake of law; and under the law as it stands at present restitution will in general not be granted in respect of money paid under a mistake of that kind. It follows that, in the present proceedings, the bank is seeking a decision that that long-established rule should no longer form part of the English law of restitution—a decision which, as all parties to the present litigation recognise, can only be made by your Lordships' House.

...

Issue (1): Whether the present rule, under which in general money is not recoverable in restitution on the ground that it was paid under a mistake of law, should be maintained as part of English law

In argument before the appellate committee the bank presented in its written case a fully developed argument for the abrogation of what I will, for convenience, call the mistake of law rule. This did not however evoke a comparable argument by the authorities in defence of the rule. On the contrary, their submission was not that the rule should be retained, but rather that it should be reformulated. Their primary argument was that the House should not itself embark upon any such reformulation, but should leave that task to the Law Commission which already has the matter under consideration. Such a course would benefit the local authorities because, quite apart from the fact that it is uncertain when, if ever, the Law Commission's proposed reforms will be enacted, they would not, if enacted as proposed, be retrospective in effect. Their secondary argument was that, if the House did decide to abrogate the present rule, it should do so in terms which provided a defence in cases in which the money has been paid under a settled understanding of the law, or in which the money has been the subject of an honest receipt by the defendant. Such defences would recognise that the payee has, in such circumstances, a legitimate interest in retaining the payment, based on the need for certainty and finality in transactions.

Faced with this situation, it might be thought that your Lordships need do no more than accept that the present rule should no longer remain in its present form, and then proceed to consider whether reformulation of the rule should be undertaken by this House or by the Law Commission and, if the former, whether the newly recognised right to recover money paid under a mistake of law should be subject to certain special limits as proposed by the authorities. I myself do not consider that such a course would be appropriate. What is in issue at the heart of this case is the continued existence of a long-standing rule of law, which has been maintained in existence for nearly two centuries in what has been seen to be the public interest. It is therefore incumbent on your Lordships to consider whether it is indeed in the public interest that the rule should be maintained, or alternatively that it should be abrogated altogether or reformulated. Having said this, however, your Lordships are fully entitled to recognise that the local authorities are in truth adopting a realistic stance that, in the light of prolonged criticism of the rule by scholars working in the field of restitution, and of recent decisions by courts in other major common law jurisdictions, the case for retention of the rule in its present form can no longer sensibly be advanced before your Lordships' House. In these circumstances I do not have to consider this aspect of the case in as much depth as might otherwise be regarded as appropriate, though I have discovered that consideration of the case as a whole has cast light on the formulation of the limits to the right of recovery which lie at the heart of the case as presented to your Lordships' House.

How the rule became established

The origin of the rule is, as is very well known, the decision of the Court of King's Bench in *Bilbie v Lumley* (1802) 2 East 469.

...

Criticism of the rule ...   The main criticisms of the rule are now widely perceived as threefold (see the Law Commission's Consultation Paper No 120 on Restitution of Payments Made Under a Mistake of Law (1991), paras. 2.24–2.26). First, the rule allows the payee to retain a payment which would not have been made to him but for the payer's mistake, whereas justice appears to demand that money so paid should be repaid unless there are special circumstances justifying its retention. Second, the distinction drawn between mistakes of fact (which can ground recovery) and mistakes of law (which cannot) produces results which appear to be capricious. It is usual here to compare the results in *Bilbie v Lumley*, 2 East 469 and *Kelly v Solari*, 9 M. & W. 54, each concerned with an action by an underwriter to recover back money paid under an insurance policy under a mistake. In the former case, where he did not appreciate that the law enabled him to repudiate a policy for non-disclosure, his action failed; but in the latter, where he forgot that the premium had not been paid and so the policy had lapsed, his action was successful. The same comment can be made of the exceptions and qualifications to which the rule became subject. These are usefully listed in paras. 2.5–2.15 of the Law Commission's Report, 'Restitution: Mistakes of Law and Ultra Vires Public Authority Receipts and Payments' (1994) (Law Com. No 227). They are well-known, and it is unnecessary for me to rehearse them in this opinion. It is however legitimate to comment that, apart from limits such as the recently recognised defence of change of position and an as yet undefined limit in cases in which the payment has been made in settlement of an honest claim, these exceptions and qualifications are heterogeneous and in truth betray an anxiety to escape from the confines of a rule perceived to be capable of injustice; and that, as a result, the law appeared to be arbitrary in its effect. Third, as a result of the difficulty in some cases of drawing the distinction between mistakes of fact and law, and the temptation for judges to manipulate that distinction in order to achieve practical justice in particular cases, the rule became uncertain and unpredictable in its application.

Rejection of the mistake of law rule in the common law world

It is perhaps easier for us now to see that the policy underlying the rule can best be achieved, consistently with justice, by the recognition of a right of recovery subject to specified defences to cater for the fears which formerly appeared to require a blanket exclusion of recovery. However, the blossoming of scholarly interest in the development of a coherent law of restitution did not occur in the common law world until the middle of the 20th century, inspired by the pioneering work of Professors Seavey and Scott in the *American Law Institute, Restatement of the Law, Restitution* (1937). We may regret that it was not until late in the long history of the common law that this should have occurred, but now the judges are able to welcome the assistance which they receive from a number of distinguished writers on the subject. There can be no doubt that it is this scholarly work which has provided the prime cause for the rejection of the mistake of law rule, either by legislation or by judicial decision, in countries throughout the common law world. This is due not only to specific criticism of the mistake of law rule as such, but still more to the combined effect of two fundamental changes in the law: first, recognition that there exists a coherent law of restitution founded upon the principle of unjust enrichment, and second, within that body of law, recognition of the defence of change of position. This is due essentially to the work of scholars. Once that work had been published and widely read it was, I believe, inevitable that in due course both doctrines would be recognised by the judges, the time of such acceptance depending very much on the accidents of litigation. In fact, in England both were accepted by this House in 1991, in the same case, *Lipkin Gorman v Karpnale Ltd* [1991] 2 A.C. 548. Once both had been recognised it became, in my opinion, also inevitable that the mistake of law rule should be abrogated, or at least reformulated, so that there should be a general right of recovery of money paid under a mistake, whether of fact or law, subject to appropriate defences. This is because a blanket rule of non-recovery, irrespective of the justice of the case, cannot sensibly survive in a rubric of the law based on the principle of unjust enrichment; and because recognition of a defence of change of position demonstrates that this must be proved in fact if it is to justify retention, in whole or in part, of money which would otherwise be repayable on the ground that the payee was unjustly enriched by its receipt. The combined effect is not only that the mistake of law rule can no longer be allowed to survive, but also that the law must evolve appropriate defences which can, together with the defence of change of position, provide protection where appropriate for recipients of money paid under a mistake of law in those cases in which justice or policy does not require them to refund the money. It is this topic which lies at the centre of the present appeals. As the argument before the appellate committee has demonstrated, the identification of such defences is by no means easy and, whatever your Lordships' House may decide, the topic is likely to continue to engage the attention of judges, scholars and law reformers for some years to come.

I have referred to the fact that the mistake of law rule has already been abrogated in other common law jurisdictions, either by legislation or by judicial decision. This material is, of course, well known to lawyers in this country, and has, I know, been studied by all members of the appellate committee, not of course for the first time, and is regarded with great respect. However, since it is conceded in these appeals by the respondent authorities that the mistake of law rule must at least be reformulated in the manner indicated by them, I trust that I will be forgiven if I do not lengthen this opinion by an express consideration of, in particular, the relevant judicial pronouncements. I refer, of course, to the dissenting opinion of Dickson J., with whom Laskin C.J. agreed, in *Hydro Electric Commission of the Township of Nepean v Ontario Hydro* [1982] 1 S.C.R. 347, 357–370, later to be adopted by La Forest J., with whom (on this point) Lamer, Wilson and L'Heureux-Dubé JJ. agreed, in *Air Canada v British Columbia* [1989] 1 S.C.R. 1161; 59 D.L.R. (4th) 161 and *David Securities Pty. Ltd v Commonwealth Bank of Australia* (1992) 175 C.L.R. 353. (I shall have to refer in particular to the dissenting judgment of Brennan J. in this case at a later stage, when I come to consider the proposed defence of honest receipt.) From countries which, on this topic, apply a system of law based on the civil law, I refer to the decisions of the Appellate Division of the Supreme Court of South Africa in *Willis Faber Enthoven (Pty.) Ltd v Receiver of Revenue*, 1992 (4) S.A. 202, and of the Inner House of the Court of Session in *Morgan Guaranty Trust Co. of New York v Lothian Regional Council*, 1995 S.C. 151, each of whom also rejected the mistake of law rule. The same conclusion was reached at an earlier date by legislation in New Zealand (see section 94A of the Judicature Act 1908, inserted by section 2 of the Judicature Amendment Act 1958) and Western Australia (see section 23 of the Law Reform (Property, Perpetuities and Succession) Act 1962). I shall have to refer to the New Zealand and Western Australian legislation at a later stage, when I come to consider the proposed exclusion of recovery in cases where payments have been made under a settled understanding of the law subsequently departed from by judicial decision. I should add that the mistake of law rule either never applied, or has been abrogated, in a number of states of the United States of America.

The Law Commission

The Law Commission has, in its Report on the subject (to which I have already referred), recommended that the mistake of law rule should be abrogated (see paragraphs 3.1 et seq., and clause 2 of the draft Bill appended to the report). For the reasons set out in paragraphs 3.8–3.12 the Commission has recommended that this change should be introduced by legislation. This is a matter to which I will have to return later in this opinion.

Comparative law

The appellate committee was helpfully provided with material showing the policy adopted in a number of civil law systems on the continent of Europe towards the recovery of money paid under a mistake of law.

. . .

For present purposes . . . the importance of this comparative material is to reveal that, in civil law systems, a blanket exclusion of recovery of money paid under a mistake of law is not regarded as necessary. In particular, the experience of these systems assists to dispel the fears expressed in the early English cases that a right of recovery on the ground of mistake of law may lead to a flood of litigation, while at the same time it shows that in some cases a right of recovery, which has in the past been denied by application of the mistake of law rule, may likewise be denied in civil law countries on the basis of a narrower ground of principle or policy.

Conclusion on the first issue

For all these reasons, I am satisfied that your Lordships should, if you decide to consider the point yourselves rather than leave it to the Law Commission, hold that the mistake of law rule no longer forms part of English law. I am very conscious that the Law Commission has recommended legislation. But the principal reasons given for this were that it might be some time before the matter came before the House, and that one of the dissentients in the *Woolwich* case (Lord Keith of Kinkel) had expressed the opinion that the mistake of law rule was too deeply embedded to be uprooted judicially: [1993] A.C. 70. 154. Of these two reasons, the former has not proved to be justified, and the latter does not trouble your Lordships because a more robust view of judicial development of the law is, I understand, taken by members of the appellate committee hearing the present appeals. Moreover, especially in the light of developments in other major common law jurisdictions, not to mention South Africa and Scotland, the case for abrogation is now so strong that the respondents in these appeals have not argued for its retention. In these circumstances I can see no good reason for postponing the matter for legislation, especially when we do not know whether or, if so, when Parliament may legislate. Finally I believe that it would, in all the circumstances, be unjust to deprive the appellant bank of the benefit of the decision of the House on this point. I would therefore conclude on issue (1) that the mistake of law rule should no longer be maintained as part of English law, and that English law should now recognise that there is a general right to recover money paid under a mistake, whether of fact or law, subject to the defences available in the law of restitution.

Issue (1A): Payments made under a settled understanding of the law

I turn now to a central question in these appeals. This relates to the fact that the payments of which recovery is sought in these cases were made under contracts which at the time were understood by all concerned to be valid and binding, so that the payments themselves were believed to be lawfully due under those contracts. This misunderstanding was, of course, removed by the decision of this House in *Hazell's* case [1992] 2 A.C. 1 that the contracts were beyond the powers of the local authorities is involved and so void. The argument now advanced by the authorities is that payments so made on the basis of a settled understanding of the law which is later changed by a judicial decision should not be recoverable on the ground of mistake of law.

This argument is based upon a view propounded by the Law Commission in Consultation Paper No 120, paragraphs 2.57–2.65 and, after consultation, adopted by the Commission in its Report, paragraph 5.3, and in clause 3(1) of its draft Bill.

. . .

[C]lause 3 of the draft Bill (at p.196 of the Report) provides:

'(1) An act done in accordance with a settled view of the law shall not be regarded as founding a mistake claim by reason only that a subsequent decision of a court or tribunal departs from that view. (2) A view of the law may be regarded for the purposes of this section as having been settled at any time notwithstanding that it was not held unanimously or had not been the subject of a decision by a court or tribunal.'

The Law Commission's consultation paper and Report are, of course, concerned with legislative proposals for changes in the law, proposals which find their origin in a New Zealand statutory provision (section 94A(2) of the Judicature Act 1908, inserted by section 2 of the Judicature Amendment Act 1958) to which I shall refer later. In these appeals, however, your Lordships are concerned with the common law, albeit on the basis that the common law should now recognise that restitution may be granted in respect of money paid under a mistake of law. I therefore ask myself first whether, on the ordinary principles of the common law, any such provision as that proposed by the Law Commission should be held to apply. This raises the question of what is meant by the declaratory theory of judicial decisions, which has long been held to underlie judicial decision-making.

The declaratory theory of judicial decisions

Historically speaking, the declaratory theory of judicial decisions is to be found in a statement by Sir Matthew Hale over 300 years ago, viz. that the decisions of the courts do not constitute the law properly so called, but are evidence of the law and as such 'have a great weight and authority in expounding, declaring, and publishing what the law of this Kingdom is:' see *Hale's Common Law of England*, 6th ed. (1820), p. 90. To the like effect, *Blackstone Commentaries*, 6th ed. (1774), pp. 88–89, stated that 'the decisions of courts are the evidence of what is the common law.' In recent times, however, a more realistic approach has been adopted, as in Sir George Jessel M.R.'s celebrated statement that rules of equity, unlike rules of the common law, are not supposed to have been established since time immemorial, but have been invented, altered, improved and refined from time to time: see *In re Hallett's Estate; Knatchbull v Hallett* (1880) 13 ChD 696, 710. There can be no doubt of the truth of this statement; and we all know that in reality, in the common law as in equity, the law is the subject of development by the judges—normally, of course, by appellate judges. We describe as leading cases the decisions which mark the principal stages in this development, and we have no difficulty in identifying the judges who are primarily responsible. It is universally recognised that judicial development of the common law is inevitable. If it had never taken place, the common law would be the same now as it was in the reign of King Henry II; it is because of it that the common law is a living system of law, reacting to new events and new ideas, and so capable of providing the citizens of this country with a system of practical justice relevant to the times in which they live. The recognition that this is what actually happens requires, however, that we should look at the declaratory theory of judicial decision with open eyes and reinterpret it in the light of the way in which all judges, common law and equity, actually decide cases today.

When a judge decides a case which comes before him, he does so on the basis of what he understands the law to be. This he discovers from the applicable statutes, if any, and from precedents drawn from reports of previous judicial decisions. Nowadays, he derives much assistance from academic writings in interpreting statutes and, more especially, the effect of reported cases; and he has regard, where appropriate, to decisions of judges in other jurisdictions. In the course of deciding the case before him he may, on occasion, develop the common law in the perceived interests of justice, though as a general rule he does this 'only interstitially,' to use the expression of O. W. Holmes J. in *Southern Pacific Co. v Jensen* (1917) 244 U.S. 205, 221. This means not only that he must act within the confines of the doctrine of precedent, but that the change so made must be seen as a development, usually a very modest development, of existing principle and so can take its place as a congruent part of the common law as a whole. In this process, what Maitland has called the 'seamless web,' and I myself (*The Search for Principle*, Proc. Brit. Acad. vol. LXIX (1983) 170, 186) have called the 'mosaic,' of the common law, is kept in a constant state of adaptation and repair, the doctrine of precedent, the 'cement of legal principle,' providing the necessary stability. A similar process must take place in codified systems as in the common law, where a greater stability is provided by the code itself; though as the years pass by, and decided cases assume a greater importance, codified systems tend to become more like common law systems.

Occasionally, a judicial development of the law will be of a more radical nature, constituting a departure, even a major departure, from what has previously been considered to be established principle, and leading to a realignment of subsidiary principles within that branch of the law. Perhaps the most remarkable example of such a development is to be found in the decisions of this House in the middle of this century which led to the creation of our modern system of administrative law. It is into this category that the present case falls; but it must nevertheless be seen as a development of the law, and treated as such.

Bearing these matters in mind, the law which the judge then states to be applicable to the case before him is the law which, as so developed, is perceived by him as applying not only to the case before him, but to all other comparable cases, as a congruent part of the body of the law. Moreover when he states the applicable principles of law, the judge is declaring these to constitute the law relevant to his decision. Subject to consideration by appellate tribunals, and (within limits) by judges of equal jurisdiction, what he states to be the law will, generally speaking, be applicable not only to the case before him but, as part of the common law, to other comparable cases which come before the courts, whenever the events which are the subject of those cases in fact occurred.

It is in this context that we have to reinterpret the declaratory theory of judicial decision. We can see that, in fact, it does not presume the existence of an ideal system of the common law, which the judges from time to time reveal in their decisions. The historical theory of judicial decision, though it may in the past have served its purpose, was indeed a fiction. But it does mean that, when the judges state what the law is, their decisions do, in the sense I have described, have a retrospective effect. That is, I believe, inevitable. It is inevitable in relation to the particular case before the court, in which the events must have occurred some time, perhaps some years, before the judge's decision is made. But it is also inevitable in relation to other cases in which the law as so stated will in future fall to be applied. I must confess that I cannot imagine how a common law system, or indeed any legal system, can operate otherwise if the law is be applied equally to all and yet be capable of organic change.

. . .

Was the bank mistaken when it paid money to the local authorities under interest swap agreements which it believed to be valid?

It is in the light of the foregoing that I have to ask myself whether the Law Commission's 'settled understanding of the law' proposal forms part of the common law. This, as I understand the position, requires that I should consider whether parties in the position of the appellant bank were mistaken when they paid money to local authorities under interest swap agreements which they, like others, understood to be valid but have later been held to be void. To me, it is plain that the money was indeed paid over under a mistake, the mistake being a mistake of law. The payer believed, when he paid the money, that he was bound in law to pay it. He is now told that, on the law as held to be applicable at the date of the payment, he was not bound to pay it. Plainly, therefore, he paid the money under a mistake of law, and accordingly, subject to any applicable defences, he is entitled to recover it.

. . .

The same view is expressed by Professor Burrows in *The Law of Restitution*, pp. 118–119, where he points out that in the common law the jurisprudential tradition is that 'changes' are retrospective. He continues:

'On this retrospective view the payor did make a mistake of law at the time he made the payment and, in accordance with the proposed abolition of the mistake of law bar, he would prima facie be entitled to restitution.'

He then proceeds to rehearse the arguments for and against legislative change of the law in this respect.

Should the House recognise a limit to recovery on the lines of the Law Commission's proposal?

The question then arises whether, having regard to the fact that the right to recover money paid under a mistake of law is only now being recognised for the first time, it would be appropriate for your

Lordships' House so to develop the law on the lines of the Law Commission's proposed reform as a corollary to the newly developed right of recovery. I can see no good reason why your Lordships' House should take a step which, as I see it, is inconsistent with the declaratory theory of judicial decision as applied in our legal system, under which the law as declared by the judge is the law applicable not only at the date of the decision but at the date of the events which are the subject of the case before him, and of the events of other cases in pari materia which may thereafter come before the courts. I recognise, of course, that the situation may be different where the law is subject to legislative change. That is because legislation takes effect from the moment when it becomes law, and is only retrospective in its effect to the extent that this is provided for in the legislative instrument. Moreover even where it is retrospective, it has the effect that as from the date of the legislation a new legal provision will apply retrospectively in place of that previously applicable. It follows that retrospective legislative change in the law does not necessarily have the effect that a previous payment was, as a result of the change in the law, made under a mistake of law at the time of payment . . . As I have already pointed out, this is not the position in the case of a judicial development of the law. But, for my part, I cannot see why judicial development of the law should, in this respect, be placed on the same footing as legislative change. In this connection, it should not be forgotten that legislation which has an impact on previous transactions can be so drafted as to prevent unjust consequences flowing from it. That option is not, of course, open in the case of judicial decisions.

At this point it is, in my opinion, appropriate to draw a distinction between, on the one hand, payments of taxes and other similar charges and, on the other hand, payments made under ordinary private transactions. The former category of cases was considered by your Lordships' House in *Woolwich Equitable Building Society v Inland Revenue Commissioners* [1993] A.C. 70, in which it was held that at common law taxes exacted ultra vires were recoverable as of right, without the need to invoke a mistake of law by the payer.

. . .

Two observations may be made about the present situation . . . The first observation is that, in our law of restitution, we now find two separate and distinct regimes in respect of the repayment of money paid under a mistake of law. These are (1) cases concerned with repayment of taxes and other similar charges which, when exacted ultra vires, are recoverable as of right at common law on the principle in *Woolwich*, and otherwise are the subject of statutory regimes regulating recovery; and (2) other cases, which may broadly be described as concerned with repayment of money paid under private transactions, and which are governed by the common law. The second observation is that, in cases concerned with overpaid taxes, a case can be made in favour of a principle that payments made in accordance with a prevailing practice, or indeed under a settled understanding of the law, should be irrecoverable. If such a situation should arise with regard to overpayment of tax, it is possible that a large number of taxpayers may be affected; there is an element of public interest which may militate against repayment of tax paid in such circumstances; and, since ex hypothesi all citizens will have been treated alike, exclusion of recovery on public policy grounds may be more readily justifiable.

In the present case, however, we are concerned with payments made under private transactions. It so happens that a significant number of payments were in fact made under interest rate swap agreements with local authorities before it was appreciated that they were void; but the number is by no means as great as might conceivably occur in the case of taxes overpaid in accordance with a prevailing practice, or under a settled understanding of the law. Moreover the element of public interest is lacking. In cases such as these I find it difficult to understand why the payer should not be entitled to recover the money paid by him under a mistake of law, even if everybody concerned thought at the time that interest rate swap agreements with local authorities were valid.

Of course, I recognise that the law of restitution must embody specific defences which are concerned to protect the stability of closed transactions. The defence of change of position is one such defence; the defences of compromise, and settlement of an honest claim (the scope of which is a matter of debate), are others. It is possible that others may be developed from judicial decisions in the future. But the proposed 'settled understanding of the law' defence is not, overtly, such a defence. It is based on the theory that a payment made on that basis is not made under a mistake at all. Once that reasoning is seen not to be correct, the basis for the proposed defence is, at least in cases such as the present, undermined.

. . .

Issue (1 B): Honest receipt

This issue arises from a principle proposed by Brennan C.J. (then Brennan J.) in *David Securities Pty. Ltd v Commonwealth Bank of Australia* (1992) 175 C.L.R. 353, 399. It reads:

> 'It is a defence to a claim for restitution of money paid or property transferred under a mistake of law that the defendant honestly believed, when he learnt of the payment or transfer, that he was entitled to receive and retain the money or property.'

This principle was expressly proposed in order to achieve a degree of certainty in past transactions. As Brennan J. said, at p. 398: 'Unless some limiting principle is introduced, the finality of any payment would be as uncertain as the governing law.'

In this part of the law there has long been concern, among common law judges, about what is sometimes called the finality of transactions, and sometimes the security of receipts. This concern formed a significant part of the amalgam of concerns which led to the rule that money paid under a mistake of law was irrecoverable on that ground. Now that that rule has been abrogated throughout the common law world, attention has of course shifted to the formulation of appropriate defences to the right of recovery. The principle proposed by Brennan J. is, I believe, the most far-reaching of the defences to the right of recovery that has yet been proposed.

. . .

In my opinion, it would be most unwise for the common law, having recognised the right to recover money paid under a mistake of law on the ground of unjust enrichment, immediately to proceed to the recognition of so wide a defence as this which would exclude the right of recovery in a very large proportion of cases. The proper course is surely to identify particular sets of circumstances which, as a matter of principle or policy, may lead to the conclusion that recovery should not be allowed; and in so doing to draw on the experience of the past, looking for guidance in particular from the analogous case of money paid under a mistake of fact, and also drawing upon the accumulated wisdom to be found in the writings of scholars on the law of restitution. However, before so novel and far-reaching defence as the one now proposed can be recognised, a very strong case for it has to be made out; and I can discover no evidence of a need for so wide a defence as this. In particular, experience since the recognition of the right of recovery of money paid under a mistake of law in the common law world does not appear to have revealed any such need.

For these reasons, with all respect to Brennan J., I am unable to accept that the defence proposed by him forms part of the common law.

Issue (2): Completed transactions

This issue . . . arose from a footnote to an article by Professor Peter Birks entitled 'No Consideration: Restitution after Void Contracts' (1993) 23 U.W.A.L.R. 195. . . . In this he said:

> 'None the less there is one good argument against allowing restitution in this situation on the ground of this particular kind of mistake, namely the transferor's mistaken belief in his/her liability to make the transfer and the liability of the other to reciprocate. It is that after the execution of the supposed contract the force of this type of mistake is spent . . . Therefore, even though it is true, as is admitted in the text above, that the mistake will have been causative at the time of the

performance, that mistake cannot on this reasoning be relied upon when matters have progressed to the point at which it can clearly be seen that the only prejudice which it might have entailed never in fact eventuated.'

The question for consideration on this issue is whether the thesis contained in the footnote is well founded.

. . .

[T]he only possible basis for the thesis in Professor Birks's footnote would seem to be that, in the context of void contracts, failure of consideration should be allowed to trump mistake of law as a ground for recovery of benefits conferred. However an equally strong argument may perhaps be made in favour of mistake of law trumping failure of consideration, though either approach is antagonistic to the usual preference of English law to allow either of two alternative remedies to be available, leaving any possible conflict to be resolved by election at a late stage. Neither of these two solutions was however relied upon in argument in the present case; and it is in any event difficult to see how Professor Birks's proposal in his footnote can here be reconciled with the consequences of invalidity arising from the application of the ultra vires doctrine. As a result, following the decision of the House of Lords in *Hazell* [1992] 2 A.C. 1, it was ordered and declared that the items of account (irrespective whether they represented payments or receipts) appearing in the capital markets fund account of the local authority in that case (Hammersmith and Fulham London Borough Council) for the years under challenge were contrary to law (see pp. 43H–44A, *per* Lord Templeman, with whose opinion the other members of the appellate committee agreed). Of the interest rate swap transactions entered into by the council, some were closed transactions, and a number were profitable, but no exceptions were made for these in the declarations so made. As Mr. Southwell submitted on behalf of the bank, it is incompatible with the ultra vires rule that an ultra vires transaction should become binding on a local authority simply on the ground that it has been completed. Moreover the ultra vires rule is not optional; it applies whether the transaction in question proves to have been profitable or unprofitable. If the argument in Professor Birks's footnote is right, the result would be that effect would be given to a contract which public policy has declared to be void.

In my opinion, these points are unanswerable; and they are reinforced by further arguments advanced by Professor Burrows in his article entitled 'Swaps and the Friction between Common Law and Equity' [1995] R.L.R. 15, 18–19. I would accordingly decide this issue in favour of the bank.

Issue (3): Does section 32(1)(c) of the Limitation Act 1980 apply to mistakes of law?

Section 32(1) of the Limitation Act 1980 provides:

'Subject to subsections (3) and (4A) below, where in the case of any action for which a period of limitation is prescribed by this Act, either—(a) the action is based upon the fraud of the defendant; or (b) any fact relevant to the plaintiff's right of action has been deliberately concealed from him by the defendant; or (c) the action is for relief from the consequences of a mistake; the period of limitation shall not begin to run until the plaintiff has discovered the fraud, concealment or mistake (as the case may be) or could with reasonable diligence have discovered it.'

The question which arises under this issue is whether the actions brought by the bank for the recovery on the ground of mistake of law of money paid to the authorities under void interest swaps agreements are actions for relief from the consequences of a mistake within section 32(1)(c).

. . .

I recognise that the effect of section 32(1)(c) is that the cause of action in a case such as the present may be extended for an indefinite period of time. I realise that this consequence may not have been fully appreciated at the time when this provision was enacted, and further that the recognition of the right at common law to recover money on the ground that it was paid under a mistake of law may call for legislative reform to provide for some time limit to the right of recovery in such cases. The Law Commission may think it desirable, as a result of the decision in the present case, to give consideration to this question; indeed they may think it wise to do so as a matter of some urgency. If they do so, they may find it helpful to have regard to the position under other systems of law, notably Scottish and German law. On the section as it stands, however, I can see no answer to the submission of the bank that their claims in the present case, founded upon a mistake of law, fall within the subsection.

Conclusion

In the result, I would answer the questions posed for your Lordships under the various issues as follows.

Issue (1). The present rule, under which in general money is not recoverable in restitution on the ground that it has been paid under a mistake of law, should no longer be maintained as part of English law, from which it follows that the facts pleaded by the bank in each action disclose a cause of action in mistake.

Issue (1A). There is no principle of English law that payments made under a settled understanding of the law which is subsequently departed from by judicial decision shall not be recoverable in restitution on the ground of mistake of law.

Issue (1B). It is no defence to a claim in English law for restitution of money paid or property transferred under a mistake of law that the defendant honestly believed, when he learnt of the payment or transfer, that he was entitled to retain the money or property.

Issue (2). There is no principle of English law that money paid under a void contract is not recoverable on the ground of mistake of law because the contract was fully performed.

Issue (3). Section 32(1)(c) of the Limitation Act 1980 applies in the case of an action for the recovery of money paid under a mistake of law.

It follows that [the] appeals must be allowed with costs.

Lord Hope of Craighead: . . . .

Was there a mistake?

Subject to any defences that may arise from the circumstances, a claim for restitution of money paid under a mistake raises three questions. (1) Was there a mistake? (2) Did the mistake cause the payment? And (3) did the payee have a right to receive the sum which was paid to him?

The first question arises because the mistake provides the cause of action for recovery of the money had and received by the payee. Unless the payer can prove that he acted under a mistake, he cannot maintain an action for money had and received on this ground. The second question arises because it will not be enough for the payer to prove that he made a mistake. He must prove that he would not have made the payment had he known of his mistake at the time when it was made. If the payer would have made the payment even if he had known of his mistake, the sum paid is not recoverable on the ground of that mistake. The third question arises because the payee cannot be said to have been unjustly enriched if he was entitled to receive the sum paid to him. The payer may have been mistaken as to the grounds on which the sum was due to the payee, but his mistake will not provide a ground for its recovery if the payee can show that he was entitled to it on some other ground.

In the present case the second and third questions do not appear to present any difficulty. But the first question raises an issue of very real importance. The answer which is given to it will have significant implications for the future development of the law of restitution on the ground of unjust enrichment.

In my opinion the proper starting point for an examination of this issue is the principle on which the claim for restitution of these payments is founded, which is that of unjust enrichment. The essence of this principle is that it is unjust for a person to retain a benefit which he has received at the expense of another, without any legal ground to justify its retention, which that other person did not intend him to receive. This has been the basis for the law of unjust enrichment as it has developed both in the civilian systems and in Scotland, which has a mixed system—partly civilian and partly common law. On the whole, now that the common law systems see their law of restitution as being based upon this principle, one would expect them to apply it, broadly speaking, in the same way and to reach results which, broadly speaking, were similar: *Zweigert and Kötz, An Introduction to Comparative Law,* 2nd ed. (1987), vol. II, pp. 262–263, 267.

What, then, is the function of mistake in the field of restitution on the ground of unjust enrichment? The answer, one may say, is that its function is to show that the benefit which has been received was an unintended benefit. A declaration of intention to confer the benefit, even if unenforceable, will be enough to justify the retention of the enrichment. A mistake, on the other hand, will be enough to justify the restitutionary remedy, on the ground that a benefit which cannot be legally justified should not be retained where it was a mistaken and thus unintended benefit.

It may be helpful to mention the material we were given to illustrate its function in the civilian systems. The details vary as between the major civil codes. But in simple terms, the law looks for the absence of a legal justification for the enrichment: *Zweigert and Kötz,* p. 232. If the payer paid in the mistaken belief that he was under a duty to pay, it is prima facie unjust that the payee should be allowed to retain what he received. But the burden of proving that the payer knew that there was no duty, and was not mistaken, is on the recipient: *England, International Encyclopedia of Comparative Law* (1991), vol. X, pp. 8–9, para. 5-13. Mistake in this context means lack of knowledge, and it makes no difference whether this is of fact or of law: *England,* p. 18, para. 5-30. As for the concept of enrichment, a person is enriched when he receives a payment which the payer was not bound by any obligation to make to him. The payee is entitled to retain the payment if it was made to him voluntarily, as in the case of a gift. The enrichment is unjust if the person who made the payment did not do so voluntarily and there was no obligation to confer the benefit: *Zweigert and Kotz,* p. 261.

The approach of the common law is to look for an unjust factor, something which makes it unjust to allow the payee to retain the benefit: *Birks, An Introduction to the Law of Restitution,* 2nd ed. (1989), pp. 140 et seq. It is the mistake by the payer which, as in the case of failure of consideration and compulsion, renders the enrichment of the payee unjust. The common law accepts that the payee is enriched where the sum was not due to be paid to him, but it requires the payer to show that this was unjust. Whereas in civilian systems proof of knowledge that there was no legal obligation to pay is a defence which may be invoked by the payee, under the common law it is for the payer to show that he paid under a mistake. My impression is that the common law tends to place more emphasis on the need for proof of a mistake. But the underlying principle in both systems is that of unjust enrichment. The purpose of the principle is to provide a remedy for recovery of the enrichment where no legal ground exists to justify its retention. But does it matter whether the mistake is one of fact or one of law?

To answer this question one must have in mind both the state of mind of the payer and the state of the facts or the law about which there is said to have been a mistake. The state of mind of the payer must be related to the time when the payment was made. So also must the state of the facts or the law. That is the time as at which it must be determined whether the payment was or was not legally justified . . . The point of the inquiry is to show that, had the payer known the true state of the facts or the law at that time, he would not have made the payment to the payee.

The inquiry will not be a difficult one, where the mistake is said to have been one of fact, if the facts have not changed since the date of the payment and the payer is able to show that he paid due to a misunderstanding of them, to incorrect information or to ignorance. In such a case the requirements for recovery will normally be satisfied. Nor is it difficult to deal with the case where the facts have changed. In such a case proof that the alleged state of the facts at the time did not emerge until afterwards will usually be sufficient to show that there was, at the time of payment, no mistake. The case may be more difficult where the mistake is said to have been a mistake of law. But I do not think that there is any essential difference in principle. A question of law may be as capable of being answered as precisely and with as much certainty as a question of fact, or it may be—as are some questions of fact—a matter of opinion.

Nor is there any essential difference as between fact and law in regard to the payer's state of mind. This may vary from one of complete ignorance to a state of ample knowledge but a misapplication of what is known to the facts. The mistake may have been caused by a failure to take advice, by omitting to examine the available information or by misunderstanding the information which has been obtained. Or it may have been due to a failure to predict correctly how the court would determine issues which were unresolved at the time of the payment, or even to foresee that there was an issue which would have to be resolved by the court. . . .

Cases where the payer was aware that there was an issue of law which was relevant but, being in doubt as to what the law was, paid without waiting to resolve that doubt may be left on one side. A state of doubt is different from that of mistake. A person who pays when in doubt takes the risk that he may be wrong—and that is so whether the issue is one of fact or one of law. As for mistake, this may arise where there is no suggestion that the law has changed since the payment was made. If it can be demonstrated by reference to statute or to case law that the law was overlooked or was applied wrongly, the position will be the same as that where the mistake was one as to the state of the facts. It is very unusual for a statute to provide for the law to be changed retrospectively, but this is not unknown: see the War Damage Act 1965. If the law is changed retrospectively by statute, so that a payment which was legally due when it was paid has now become undue, the correct analysis will be that there was no mistake at the time when it was made. The enrichment will have been due to the fact that the law was changed retrospectively by the statute.

What then is the position where the fact that the payment was not legally due at the time when it was made was only revealed later by subsequent case law? In posing this question I am not dealing with the situation where a judgment of the court that a sum is due has become final and been acted upon, but is afterwards overruled by a higher court in a different case. The law of unjust enrichment does not disturb transactions of that kind. Where the payment is made because the court has held that the sum is due to be paid to the payee, the obligation to pay is to be found in the order which has been made by the court. I am dealing with the case where the payment was made on the understanding that the law on the point was settled and that understanding was shown by sub-sequent case law to have been wrong.

The answer to this question may be said to depend upon whether the decision in question has changed the law or has merely declared what the law always was. We were reminded of Lord Reid's observation that to say that the judges never change the law is a fairy tale: 12 J.S.P.T.L. 22. Experience has shown that the judges do from time to time change the law, in order to adapt it to changed social conditions or in response to other factors which show that the law has become out of date. But it would be equally wrong to say that the judges never declare the law. It may simply be that there was a gap which needed to be filled, or that there was a defect in thinking which needed to be revealed so that a point could be clarified. And to overturn an established line of authority is one thing. It is quite another where there was no previous decision on a point which no one had sought to bring before the court previously. It may be said that a view of the law can be regarded as settled even where there is no case law at all on the subject, because all those interested in it have acted on a common understanding of what the law requires. But I would find it difficult to accept that a judge who said that that common understanding was wrong, and that the law was different from what everyone previously had thought it was, had changed the law. It would seem to be more accurate to say that, as it was for the judge to say what the law was he was merely declaring what the law was and that he was not changing it.

On the whole it seems to me to be preferable to avoid being drawn into a discussion as to whether a particular decision changed the law or whether it was merely declaratory. It would not be possible to lay down any hard and fast rules on this point. Each case would have to be decided on what may in the end be a matter of opinion, about which there may be room for a good deal of dispute. It is better to face up to the fact that every decision as to the law by a judge operates retrospectively, and to concentrate instead on the question—which I would regard as the critical question—whether the payer would have made the payment if he had known what he is now being told was the law. It is the state of the law at the time of the payment which will determine whether or not the payment was or was not legally due to be paid, and it is the state of mind of the payer at the time of payment which will determine whether he paid under a mistake. But there seems to me to be no reason in principle why the law of unjust enrichment should insist that that mistake must be capable of being demonstrated at the same time as the time when the payment was made. A mistake of fact may take some time to discover. If there is a dispute about this, the question whether there was a mistake may remain in doubt until the issue has been resolved by a judge. Why should this not be so where the mistake is one of law?

In the present case we have no evidence about the state of the law at the time of the payments other than what can be derived from the agreed facts. But the background, as it can be discovered from the judgment of Hobhouse J. in the *Westdeutsche* case [1994] 4 All E.R. 890, is reasonably clear. He said, at p. 931e, that the effect of the statutory provisions of which the relevant bank had previously been unaware was subsequently 'declared' by the Divisional Court and the House of Lords in the *Hazell* case [1992] 2 A.C. 1. His choice of language seems to me to have been entirely appropriate. There had been no previous judicial decision on the point until the practice in the money markets was challenged for the first time in that case by the district auditor. Nor is it suggested that an opinion had been expressed about it which could be regarded as authoritative in the sense that it was binding on all parties including the auditor. If it were necessary to decide this point, I do not think that it would be right to say that the decision in the *Hazell* case 'changed' the law. What it did was to clarify a point which had been overlooked and was in need of determination by the court. But the situation seems to me to be no different in principle from one where the facts are shown, as a result of inquiries which at the time of the payment were overlooked or not thought to be necessary, to have been different from what they had been thought to be at the time of the payment by the payer. Prima facie the bank is entitled to restitution on the ground of mistake.

. . .

In the result I would answer each of the questions under the issues which are before us in the terms proposed by my noble and learned friend, Lord Goff of Chieveley. I, too, would allow these appeals.

Lord Hoffmann delivered a speech concurring with **Lord Goff**.

Lord Lloyd of Berwick delivered a dissenting speech.

NOTES AND QUESTIONS

1. This decision removed the mistake of law bar in England. As Lord Goff's speech makes clear, the mistake of law bar was earlier removed judicially in Canada in *Air Canada v British Columbia* (1989) 59 DLR (4th) 161, in Australia in *David Securities Pty. Ltd v Commonwealth Bank of Australia* (1992) 175 CLR 353, in South Africa in *Willis Faber Enthoven (Pty) Ltd v Receiver of Revenue* (1992) 4 SA 202 and in Scotland in *Morgan Guaranty Trust Co. of New York v Lothian Regional Council* 1995 SLT 299. In New Zealand the mistake of law bar was abolished by statute by the Judicature Amendment Act 1958, s. 94(A)(1) which went on, in section 94(A)(2) to say:

   'Nothing in this section shall enable relief to be given in respect of any payment made at a time when the law requires or allows, or is commonly understood to require or allow, the payment to be made or enforced, by reason only that the law is subsequently changed or shown not to have been as it was commonly understood to be at the time of the payment'

2. The majority of their Lordships approved a prima facie 'but for' causation test for restitution

of mistaken payments, whether of fact or law. See Lord Goff at 171 above and Lord Hope at 179 above. See also Lord Hoffmann [1999] 2 AC 349, 399.

3. Do you agree with the majority that Kleinwort Benson had made a mistake of law in paying under the (void) interest-rate swap agreements? In answering this, consider the view of Birks, 'Mistakes of Law' [2000] CLP 205 that Kleinwort Benson had made a misprediction not a mistake because the basis on which it had paid could not be demonstrated to be true or false at the time of payment. It could only be shown to be false subsequently.

4. For the civilian view that the restitution was here justified because the money was not due (because the contract was void), rather than because of any mistake by the payor, see the case-note by S Meier and R Zimmermann, 'Judicial development of the law, error iuris and the law of unjustified enrichment' (1999) 115 *LQR* 556. That was also the view ultimately favoured by Birks: see *Unjust Enrichment* (2nd edn, 2005), 108–13, 135, 239–40 and above, 137, 149.

5. For support for the majority's view that the bank was mistaken and for Lord Goff's 'reinter-preted' declaratory theory, see the case-note by J Finnis, 'The Fairy Tale's Moral' (1999) 115 *LQR* 170.

6. Do you agree with the majority's rejection of a 'settled view of the law' defence?

7. Has the minority's fear of a flood of restitutionary claims for mistake, consequent on judicial 'changes' to the law, been borne out in practice? Are adequate controls in place to allay this fear?

8. Although not mentioned by their Lordships, the fear of never-ending claims for payments made by mistakes of law would be removed if the Law Commission's recommendations (in *Limitation of Actions*, Report No 270, 2001) for reform of limitation of actions were enacted. These would remove section 32(1)(c) Limitation Act 1980 while introducing a general dis-coverability starting date for the running of a standard three-year limitation period. But, crucially, this would be subject to a ten-year long-stop from the date of payment.

9. In *Brennan v Bolt Burdon* [2004] EWCA Civ 1017, [2005] QB 303, it was held that, after the *Kleinwort Benson* case, a common mistake of law, as well as of fact, can render a contract void. But it was emphasised that it would be very rare for a contract *of compromise* to be void for a common mistake of law consequent on a development or clarification of the law because, in a compromise, the parties normally take the risk of such development or clarification. On the facts of the case, a contract of compromise had been reached in respect of a personal injuries claim arising from alleged carbon monoxide poisoning from a faulty gas boiler. The com-promise was reached because both parties believed that the claim form had been served out of time and was therefore invalid. Subsequent to the compromise a Court of Appeal decision made clear that that assumption was incorrect and that the claim form had been served in time (because service on a Monday counted if the four months time limit fell at the week-end). It was held that that contract of compromise was not void for common mistake.

10. Where a bank sought restitution of money paid under a void interest-rate swap agreement, what were the grounds for restitution (i) in an open swap and (ii) in a closed swap? Consider in addition to mistake, failure of consideration and the controversial ground of 'absence of consideration' (on which see the *Westdeutsche* case below, 362 and *Guinness Mahon & Co. Ltd v Kensington and Chelsea Royal London Borough Council* below, 369). A local authority might alternatively have based its claim for restitution on its own incapacity (see below, Chapter 11).

11. For the question of whether restitution of overpaid taxes can be grounded on mistake of law, see *Deutsche Morgan Grenfell Group plc v IRC* [2005] EWCA Civ 78, [2006] 2 WLR 203, discussed below, 639.

• *Nurdin & Peacock plc v DB Ramsden & Co. Ltd*
[1999] 1 WLR 1249, Chancery Division

The defendant landlord increased the rent owing by the claimant tenant in respect of business premises. Although acting in good faith, the landlord was not entitled to do this because there had been no rent review. Nevertheless the claimant tenant paid the first five instalments demanded ('the first five overpayments') without complaint because it had overlooked or forgotten about the need for a rent review. It then received advice that, because there had been no rent review, it was not bound to pay the extra rent. Nevertheless it paid five more instalments ('the last five overpayments') at the higher rate because it had been legally advised that, if overpaying, it would be entitled to restitution of the overpayment. Neuberger J held that all ten overpayments were recoverable. The first five were straightforward after *Kleinwort Benson*: they had been paid by a mistake of fact but it now made no difference if one characterized the mistake as one of law. As regards the last five overpayments, Neuberger J held that four of them (but not the May 1997 overpayment) were repayable because there was a contractual agreement to that effect. Moreover, all five were recoverable in the law of restitution as paid by a mistake of law even though the claimant knew that those five payments were not owing.

Neuberger J: . . .

Nurdin's argument based on a mistake of law

Nurdin's main remaining argument in relation to the May 1997 overpayment (and its alternative main argument in relation to the last four overpayments) is that any such overpayment was made under a mistake of law, and, following the decision of the House of Lords in *Kleinwort Benson Ltd v Lincoln City Council* [1998] 3 W.L.R. 1095, it is now recoverable on that basis, albeit that, until the decision in the *Kleinwort Benson* case, it was rightly accepted on behalf of Nurdin that it would not have been so recoverable.

Nurdin's argument proceeds thus. The May 1997 overpayment was made by Nurdin to D.B.R. on the basis of a belief on the part of Nurdin that, if D.B.R. failed in its argument on construction and on rectification, the overpayments would be repayable by D.B.R. It is accepted by Mr. Brock on behalf of Nurdin that, at least in the absence of any other factors, a payment is irrecoverable if it is made in circumstances where it is not due, and where the payer is aware that the payment may not be due, and, indeed, knows the basis upon which he may be able to defend his liability to make the payment. In other words, Nurdin accepts that, while the House of Lords has decided that money is not irrecoverable because it was paid under a mistake of law pursuant to a bona fide demand, the decision does not go so far, at least in the absence of special facts, to enable a person who has made a payment which is not due to recover it where he was aware that he might not be liable to pay.

That this concession is rightly made is perhaps most easily appreciated by considering what Lord Hope of Craighead said in the *Kleinwort Benson* case, at p. 1147:

'Cases where the payer was aware that there was an issue of law which was relevant but, being in doubt as to what the law was, paid without waiting to resolve that doubt may be left on one side. A state of doubt is different from that of mistake. A person who pays when in doubt takes the risk that he may be wrong—and that is so whether the issue is one of fact or one of law.'

The special fact in the present case upon which Mr. Brock relies as justifying repayment of the May 1997 overpayment is that it was made pursuant to a mistake of law on the part of Nurdin, and that mistake was Nurdin's belief that it would be entitled to recover that overpayment if the court found in its favour on the issues of construction and rectification. That mistake, says Mr. Brock, is a mistake of law, and, as the May 1997 overpayment would not have been paid had that mistake not have been made, that overpayment was, he says, made under a mistake of law, and is therefore recoverable following the decision of the House of Lords in the *Kleinwort Benson* case.

. . .

Against this, Mr. Nugee contends on behalf of D.B.R. that nothing in the decision of the House of Lords in the *Kleinwort Benson* case affects the previous law so far as the May 1997 overpayment is concerned. This is because the May 1997 overpayment was not made by Nurdin under a mistake as to whether or not it was liable to make it, but under a mistake as to Nurdin's right to get it back. Mr. Nugee contended that the decision in the *Kleinwort Benson* case is only concerned with a case where a payment is made under a mistake of law by the payer as to whether or not he is liable to make the payment.

Mr. Nugee attractively argued that Nurdin's claim for repayment is logically unsustainable. The argument proceeds thus. Either the May 1997 overpayment is recoverable or else it is not. If Mr. Brock succeeds in his argument, and the overpayment is recoverable, there was no mistake; on the other hand, if Mr. Brock is wrong in his argument and the overpayment is not recoverable, then that is the end of the matter. Accordingly, D.B.R. contends, the question of according Nurdin relief for the consequences of mistake simply does not arise in relation to the May 1997 overpayment.

. . .

In my judgment, Nurdin's argument on this point is correct. First, as a matter of principle, it seems to me that the correct question for the court to ask itself when considering whether money was paid under a mistake of law (and is therefore prima facie recoverable) would at least normally be whether the payment would have occurred if the payer had not made the alleged mistake. It is hard to see a good reason, either in principle or in practice, for holding that a person should be entitled to recover a payment made under a mistake if that mistake relates to the question of his liability, but that he should not be entitled to recover the payment if the mistake was of some other nature. As I see it, if there was a mistake, and particularly if it related directly and closely to the payment and to the relationship between payer and payee, and, above all, if the mistake had not been made there would have been no payment, then the payment in question is prima facie recoverable. I would hesitate, particularly so soon after the decision in the *Kleinwort Benson* case, before trying to lay down any general principle, but it does seem to me clear that in order to found a claim for repayment of money paid under a mistake of law it is necessary for the payer to establish not only that the mistake was made but also that, but for the mistake, he would not have paid the money. It may be that the payer must go further and establish, for instance, that the mistake was directly connected to the overpayment and/or was connected to the relationship between payer and payee. I doubt whether such further requirements, if they exist, would take matters any further in most cases. However, if such further requirements do exist, I believe that they are satisfied here in relation to the May 1997 overpayment (and indeed would be satisfied in relation to the last four overpayments).

Secondly, I derive assistance in reaching this conclusion from the commonsense approach (if I may so characterise it) of Lord Hoffmann in the *Kleinwort Benson* case. In relation to a client seeking advice from a solicitor on a somewhat different type of distinction, he said, at p. 1138:

'it seems to me that the imaginary client would have great difficulty in understanding how these distinctions can arise out of a rule giving a remedy for unjust enrichment. In each case he thought that the obligation was valid and it has subsequently turned out that it was not. In principle, the question should not turn upon what other people might have thought was the law but upon what he thought was the law.'

So, here, I believe that it would be surprising if the payee was unjustly enriched because the payer thought he was liable to make the payment, but that he would not be unjustly enriched if the payer, knowing that there was an argument as to whether he was liable or not, made the payment in the clear belief that he thought it would be recoverable if it turned out not to have been due as a matter of law. For the issue of recoverability to turn upon a nice analysis as to the precise nature of the mistake of law appears to me to be almost as undesirable as it is for recoverability to turn upon whether the mistake made by the payer was one of fact or law.

Thirdly, it seems to me that my conclusion is supported by the reasoning [of Robert Goff J] in *Barclays Bank Ltd v W. J. Simms Son & Cooke (Southern) Ltd.* . . .

'it is not a prerequisite of recovery that the plaintiff must have mistakenly believed that he was liable to the defendant to pay the money to him . . . it is sufficient to ground recovery that the plaintiff's mistake should have caused him to pay the money to the payee.'

That case was, of course, decided some 20 years before *Kleinwort Benson Ltd v Lincoln City Council* [1998] 3 W.L.R. 1095, and therefore at a time when it was thought that money paid under a mistake of law was irrecoverable. However, whether one looks at it as a matter of logic, as a matter of authority or as a matter of common sense, it seems to me that the test propounded by Robert Goff J. in *Barclays Bank Ltd v W. J. Simms Son & Cooke (Southern) Ltd.* [1980] Q.B. 677 should apply equally to a case where the money was paid under a mistake of law. Given that a claim for money paid under a mistake, whether of fact or law, is a claim based on restitution (*per* Lord Hope) it is hard to see in logic why there should be any difference; given the reasoning of Lord Goff in the *Kleinwort Benson* case, it would effectively be contrary to authority not to hold that the same principles applied to cases involving mistake of law as to cases involving mistake of fact; the robust approach of Lord Hoffmann similarly points firmly in favour of the view that the same principle should apply in each case.

It may be said that the mistake did not 'cause' the payment, and it is fair to say that the concept of causation is one of which the courts and writers have had much to say in many areas of law. As I have mentioned already, I consider that the 'but for' test (possibly coupled with a requirement for a close and direct connection between the mistake and the payment and/or a requirement that the mistake impinges on the relationship between payer and payee) is sufficient, in my judgment, to found a claim based on mistake. This seems to me to receive some support from the words used in earlier authorities, 'material' and 'vital,' to describe the necessary quality of the mistake.

It may also be said that my conclusion involves wrong advice turning out to be right, a logical paradox of the type illustrated by the fictional Cretan who said that all Cretans were liars. That is on the basis that the advice to Nurdin was that the overpayments were recoverable, the advice was wrong, Nurdin followed that advice, therefore Nurdin paid under a mistake of law, therefore the advice was right; therefore, no mistake was made. This is really another way of putting Mr. Nugee's argument that Nurdin's case is logically unsustainable. The trouble with this argument is that it appears to me to amount to a classic vicious circle, because, if one follows the last step in the argument, the overpayment is not repayable, in which case the advice given to Nurdin, upon which it relied, was wrong, in which case the overpayment was made pursuant to a mistake. In my judgment, at least following the decision in the *Kleinwort Benson* case, and in light of the factors I have already discussed, it seems to me that the right point at which to cut the vicious circle is at the point where one concludes that Nurdin made the May 1997 overpayment under a mistake of law. In other words, while I accept that the particular nature of the mistake in the present case does present an unusual logical problem in relation to the payer's claim for repayment, I do not think that it should stand in the way of the conclusion I have reached.

In those circumstances, applying the test laid down by Robert Goff J., it appears to me that the mistake in question 'caused' Nurdin to make the May 1997 overpayment. If I am wrong on the question of a contract so far as the last four overpayments are concerned, then for the same reasons, the same conclusion would apply to them. It therefore follows, in my judgment, that the last four overpayments would be recoverable on this alternative ground, and that the May 1997 overpayment is recoverable on this ground.

. . .

NOTES AND QUESTIONS

1. Neuberger J here explicitly rejected a supposed liability test for restitution of payments made by mistake of law and favoured a prima facie but for causation test for all mistakes, whether of fact or law.

2. G Virgo in a case-note [1999] *CLJ* 478 criticizes this decision (as regards restitution of the last five overpayments) because the tenant then knew that the increased rent was not due. The payments were therefore voluntary and a mistake of law as to one's right to recover over-payments should not count as a relevant mistake. Do you agree with this criticism? If you agree with Virgo that mistake should not here have grounded restitution, was there any other ground for restitution?

2. BENEFITS IN KIND RENDERED BY MISTAKE

In principle, provided the argument of subjective devaluation can be overcome, restitution for benefits in kind should be granted as it is for a mistaken payment. The nature of the benefit should not affect the 'unjust factor'. In practice, there are very few cases, outside the realm of executed contracts being rescinded for misrepresentation (as in, for example, *Whittington v Seale-Hayne*, below, 199), which clearly illustrate restitution of benefits in kind rendered by mistake. (This is particularly so once one recognizes, as we believe one must, that proprietary estoppel cases have rarely been concerned to award restitution for the mistaken improvement of land as opposed to protecting the promisee's expectation or reliance interests.)

A leading case in *Greenwood v Bennett* (below, 187) which concerned the mistaken improvement of a car. Also of importance is the Canadian case of *County of Carleton v City of Ottawa* (below, 188) which was concerned with the mistaken discharge of another's liability. Discharge of a liability, although involving a payment of money, is a benefit in kind to the person whose liability is discharged. Discussion of the difficult question of when the unrequested payment of another's debt discharges that debt is postponed until Chapter 7. We further include here—because it concerned a mistakenly rendered benefit in kind—the leading case on non-contractual subrogation, *Banque Financière de la Cité v Parc (Battersea) Ltd* (below, 190).

General Reading

BURROWS, 162–168; GOFF AND JONES, chapters 6–8; VIRGO, 78–81.

- *Greenwood v Bennett* [1973] 1 QB 195, Court of Appeal

See above, 107.

NOTES AND QUESTIONS

1. There was no question in *Greenwood v Bennett* of the mistake by the improver having to be one of supposed liability. This adds further support to the causation approach for mistaken payments in *Barclays Bank v W J Simms* (above, 153).

2. For a libertarian critique of Lord Denning's approach in *Greenwood v Bennett*, see P Matthews, 'Freedom, Unrequested Improvements and Lord Denning' [1981] 40 *CLJ* 340.

3. The Torts (Interference with Goods) Act 1977 was enacted subsequent to *Greenwood v Bennett*. Although the interpretation of the Act on this issue is not straightforward, it provides in certain circumstances for an allowance to be given to a mistaken improver of goods. But it does not give the improver an active claim. Moreover, as there was no action for wrongful interference with goods, it would appear that the Act would not have applied on the facts of *Greenwood v Bennett*.

- **Torts (Interference with Goods) Act 1977 sections 1, 3(7) and 6**

Definition of 'wrongful interference with goods'

1. In this Act 'wrongful interference', or 'wrongful interference with goods', means—

    (a)   conversion of goods (also called trover),

    (b)   trespass to goods,

    (c)   negligence so far as it results in damage to goods or to an interest in goods,

    (d)   subject to section 2, any other tort so far as it results in damage to goods or to an interest in goods. . . .

Forms of judgment where goods are detained

3.—(7) Where under subsection (1) or subsection (2) of section 6 an allowance is to be made in respect of an improvement of the goods, and an order is made [for delivery of the goods], the court may assess the allowance to be made in respect of the improvement, and by the order require, as a condition for the delivery of the goods, that allowance to be made by the claimant.

Allowance for improvement of the goods

6.—(1) If in proceedings for wrongful interference against the person (the 'improver') who has improved the goods, it is shown that the improver acted in the mistaken but honest belief that he had a good title to them, an allowance shall be made for the extent to which, at the time as at which the goods fall to be valued in assessing damages, the value of the goods is attributable to the improvement.

(2) If, in proceedings for wrongful interference against a person ('the purchaser') who has purported to purchase the goods—

    (a)   from the improver, or

    (b)   where after such a purported sale the goods passed by a further purported sale on one or more occasions, or any such occasion,

it is shown that the purchaser acted in good faith, an allowance shall be made on the principle set out in subsection (1).

For example, where a person in good faith buys a stolen car from the improver and is sued in conversion by the true owner the damages may be reduced to reflect the improvement, but if the person who bought the stolen car from the improver sues the improver for failure of consideration, and the improver acted in good faith, subsection (3) below will ordinarily make a comparable reduction in the damages he recovers from the improver.

(3) If in a case within subsection (2) the person purporting to sell the goods acted in good faith, then in proceedings by the purchaser for recovery of the purchase price because of failure of consideration, or in any other proceedings founded on that failure of consideration, an allowance shall, where appropriate, be made on the principle set out in subsection (1).

(4) This section applies, with the necessary modifications, to a purported bailment or other disposition of goods as it applies to a purported sale of goods.

- ***County of Carleton v City of Ottawa***
  (1965) 52 DLR (2d) 220, Supreme Court of Canada

Carleton (the appellant) was under a statutory duty to provide care for its residents who were insane. Not having its own home, it sent them to Lanark and paid Lanark for providing care for them. When Ottawa (the respondent) annexed part of Carleton, Ottawa should have taken over paying Lanark for Norah Baker, who was an insane resident of one of the annexed areas. By an oversight her name was omitted from the list of those for whom Ottawa would be responsible and Carleton mistakenly carried on paying for her. When Carleton discovered its mis- take, it sought reimbursement from Ottawa of the payments it had made to Lanark for Norah Baker's care. The Supreme Court of Canada held that it was so entitled.

Hall J giving the joint judgment of the Court (**Cartwright**, **Judson**, **Ritchie**, **Hall** and **Spence JJ**): . . . The amounts claimed by the County of Carleton from the City of Ottawa totalling $9,833.01 for the period from January 1, 1950, until October 31, 1962, are not disputed and if the City of Ottawa is liable the county is entitled to judgment for the amount claimed plus the cost for care and mainten- ance subsequent to October 31, 1962.

The County of Carleton bases its claim against the City of Ottawa on the doctrine of restitution. Lord Wright, MR, in *Brook's Wharf and Bull Wharf, Ltd v Goodman Bros.*, [1937] 1 KB 534, discussed this doctrine at p.544 as follows:

> The principle has been applied in a great variety of circumstances. Its application does not depend *on privity* of contract. Thus in *Moule v Garrett*, L.R. 7 Ex. 101, which I have just cited, it was held that the original lessee who had been compelled to pay for breach of a repairing covenant was entitled to recover the amount he had so paid from a subsequent assignce of the lease, notwithstanding that there had been intermediate assignces. In that case the liability of the lessee depended on the terms of his covenant, but the breach of convenant was due to the default of the assignee, and the payment by the lessee under legal compulsion relieved the assignee of his liability.
>
> That class of case was discussed by Vaughan Williams LJ in *Bonner v Tottenham and Edmonton Permanent Investment Building Society*, [1899] 1 QB 161, where *Moule v Garrett*, LR 7 Ex. 101 was distinguished. The essence of the rule is that there is a liability for the same debt resting on the plaintiff and the defendant and the plaintiff has been legally compelled to pay, but the defendant gets the benefit of the payment, because his debt is discharged either entirely or protanto, whereas the defendant is primarily liable to pay as between himself and the plaintiff. The case is analogous to that of a payment by a surety which has the effect of discharging the principal's debt and which, therefore, gives a right of indemnity against the principal.

And, at p. 545:

> These statements of the principle do not put the obligation on any ground of implied contract or of constructive or notional contract. The obligation is imposed by the Court simply under the circum- stances of the case and on what the Court decides is just and reasonable, having regard to the relationship of the parties. It is a debt or obligation constituted by the act of the law, apart from any consent or intention of the parties or any privity of contract.

And again in *Fibrosa Spolka Akcyjna v Fairbairn Lawson Combe Barbour, Ltd* [1943] AC 32 at p. 61.

Lord Wright's statement in *Fibrosa* was approved by Cartwright, J, in *Deglman v Guaranty Trust Co. of Canada and Constanlineau* [1954] 3 DLR, 785, where at p. 794, he quotes from *Fibrosa* as follows:

> 'It is clear that any civilized system of law is bound to provide remedies for cases of what has been called unjust enrichment or unjust benefit, that is to prevent a man from retaining the money of or some benefit derived from another which it is against conscience that he should keep. Such remedies in English law are generically different from remedies in contract or in tort, and are now recognized to fall within a third category of the common law which has been called quasi-contract or restitution.'

And again:

> 'Lord Mansfield does not say that the law implies a promise. The law implies a debt or obligation which is a different thing. In fact, he denies that there is a contract; the obligation is as efficacious as if it were upon a contract. The obligation is a creation of the law, just as much as an obligation in

tort. The obligation belongs to a third class, distinct from either contract or tort, though it resembles contract rather than tort.'

Norah Baker was an indigent for whose care the appellant was responsible prior to January 1, 1950, when the area in question was annexed by the respondent. The respondent by the act and fact of annexation ... assumed responsibility for the social service obligations of the appellant to the residents of the area annexed, and the fact that one welfare case was inadvertently omitted from the list cannot permit the respondent to escape the responsibility for that case. To paraphrase Lord Wright, it is against conscience that it should do so.

I am in agreement with the conclusion reached by the learned trial Judge that the appellant is entitled to recover from the respondent the sum of $9,833.01, being the amount claimed to October 31, 1962. The appellant is also entitled to recover from the respondent the cost of maintaining the said Norah Baker from November 1, 1962. ... The appeal will, accordingly, be allowed and the judgment of Grant J, varied accordingly.

NOTES AND QUESTIONS

1. The *Brook's Wharf* case is set out below, 510.

2. In what sense was Ottawa benefited in this case? In particular, did Ottawa have a duty to provide for Norah Baker? (See on this the judgments in the courts below: (1964) 46 DLR (2d) 432, CA; (1963) 39 DLR (2d) 11, 14–15, Grant J). And if its duty was merely a contractual one owed to Lanark, can this decision be reconciled with the traditional view that the mistaken payment of another's debt does not automatically discharge that debt (see below 534)?

- *Banque Financière de la Cité v Parc (Battersea) Ltd*
  [1999] 1 AC 221, House of Lords

The claimants, a Swiss bank (BFC) loaned DM30 million to Parc who used it to pay off a loan to another bank (RTB). RTB's loan had been secured by a first charge over Parc's development land at Battersea. The defendant (OOL) had a second charge over that property securing a loan made by it to Parc. The claimants obtained no security for their loan to Parc but had been promised in a 'postponement letter' that other companies in the group to which Parc belonged, which included the defendant, would not demand repayment of their loan until the claimants had been paid. But that promise was made without the authority of the defendant and was therefore not binding on the defendant. The claimants did not know this and therefore mistakenly believed that they had priority as against the defendant (albeit not against RTB). On Parc's insolvency, the claimants claimed to be subrogated to the rights of the first chargee (RTB) so that they had priority against the defendant. The House of Lords held that the claimants were indeed entitled, as against the defendant, to be subrogated to the right of the first chargee so that they had priority against the defendant.

Lord Steyn: . . . My Lords, both the judge and Morritt L.J. invoked the vocabulary of unjust enrichment or restitution. Nevertheless both courts ultimately treated the question at stake as being whether B.F.C. is entitled to be subrogated to the rights of R.T.B. On the present appeal counsel adopted a similar approach. That position may have seemed natural at a stage when B.F.C. apparently claimed to be entitled to step in the shoes of R.T.B. as chargee with the usual proprietary remedies. On appeal to your Lordships' House counsel for B.F.C. attenuated his submission by making clear that B.F.C. only seeks a restitutionary remedy against O.O.L. In these circumstances it seems sensible to consider directly whether the grant of the remedy would be consistent with established principles of unjust enrichment. O.O.L. committed no wrong: it cannot therefore be a case of unjust enrichment by wrongdoing. If it is a case of unjust enrichment, it must in the vivid terminology of Professor Peter Birks, *An Introduction to the Law of Restitution* (1985), be unjust enrichment by subtraction. If the case is approached in this way it follows that B.F.C. is either entitled to a restitutionary remedy or it is not so entitled. After all, unjust enrichment ranks next to contract and tort as part of the law of obligations. It is an independent source of rights and obligations.

Four questions arise. (1) Has O.O.L. benefited or been enriched? (2) Was the enrichment at the expense of B.F.C.? (3) Was the enrichment unjust? (4) Are there any defences? The first requirement is satisfied: the repayment of £10m. of the loan pro tanto improved O.O.L.'s position as chargee. That is conceded. The second requirement was in dispute. Stripped to its essentials the argument of counsel for O.O.L. was that the interposition of the loan to Mr. Herzig meant that the enrichment of O.O.L. was at the expense of Mr. Herzig. The loan to Mr. Herzig was a genuine one spurred on by the motive of avoiding Swiss regulatory requirements. But it was nevertheless no more than a formal act designed to allow the transaction to proceed. It does not alter the reality that O.O.L. was enriched by the money advanced by B.F.C. via Mr. Herzig to Parc. To allow the interposition of Mr. Herzig to alter the substance of the transaction would be pure formalism.

That brings me to the third requirement, which was the ground upon which the Court of Appeal decided against B.F.C. Since no special defences were relied on, this was also the major terrain of debate on the present appeal. It is not seriously disputed that by asking for a letter of postponement B.F.C. expected that they would obtain a form of security sufficient to postpone repayment of loans by all companies in the Omni Group until repayment of the B.F.C. loan. In any event, that fact is clearly established. But for B.F.C.'s mistaken belief that it was protected in respect of intra-group indebtedness B.F.C. would not have proceeded with the refinancing. In these circumstances there is in my judgment a principled ground for granting a restitutionary remedy.

Counsel for O.O.L. challenged the view that restitutionary liability is prima facie established by submitting that there was no mutual intention that B.F.C. should have priority as against O.O.L. Restitutionary liability is triggered by a range of unjust factors or grounds of restitution. Defeated bilateral expectations are a prime source of such liability. But sometimes unilateral defeated expectations may be sufficient, e.g. payments made under a unilateral mistake of fact where the ground of liability is the mistake of one party. I would reject the idea that in a case such as the present a test of mutuality must be satisfied.

. . .

In my view, on an application of established principles of unjust enrichment B.F.C. are entitled to succeed against O.O.L. But, if it were necessary to do so, I would reach the same conclusion in terms of the principles of subrogation. It would admittedly not be the usual case of subrogation to security rights in rem and in personam. The purpose of the relief would be dictated by the particular form of security, involving rights in personam against companies in the group, which B.F.C. mistakenly thought it was obtaining. It is true that no decided case directly in point has been found. But distinguished writers have shown that the place of subrogation on the map of the law of obligations is by and large within the now sizeable corner marked out for restitution: see *Goff & Jones, The Law of Restitution*, 4th ed. (1993), pp. 526, 531; *Birks, An Introduction to the Law of Restitution*, p. 93 et seq.; *Burrows, The Law of Restitution* (1993), p. 92; *Mitchell, The Law of Subrogation* (1994), p. 4. And there can be no conceptual impediment to the remedy of subrogation being allowed not in respect of both rights in rem and rights in personam but only in respect of rights in personam.

For these reasons, as well as the reasons contained in the speech of my noble and learned friend, Lord Hoffmann, I would allow the appeal.

Lord Hoffmann. My Lords, this appeal raises, in unusual circumstances, a question on the scope of the equitable remedy of subrogation. The appellant, the Banque Financière de la Cité, made an advance of DM30m. for the purpose of enabling Parc (Battersea) Ltd to repay part of a loan from another bank secured by a first charge upon its property. The transaction did not contemplate that Parc would provide any security. It was however an express condition of the advance that other companies in the group to which Parc belonged would not demand repayment of their loans until B.F.C. had been repaid. One such company was Omnicorp Overseas Ltd which was owed £26.25m. secured by a second charge over the property. Unfortunately the persons who negotiated the transaction had no authority to commit O.O.L. to such an undertaking and it was not binding upon it. Parc is insolvent and if B.F.C. has no priority over O.O.L.'s second charge, it is unlikely to be repaid. The question is whether, as against O.O.L., B.F.C. is entitled to be subrogated to the first charge to the extent that its money was used to repay the debt which it secured. The judge, Robert Walker J., decided that the remedy was available. The Court of Appeal, in a judgement delivered by Morritt L.J., decided that it was not. Against that decision B.F.C. appeals to your Lordships' House.

The striking feature of this case, which distinguishes it from familiar cases on subrogation to which it bears a partial resemblance such as *Butler v Rice* [1910] 2 Ch 277 and *Ghana Commercial Bank v Chandiram* [1960] A.C. 732 is that B.F.C. did not contemplate that Parc would provide it with any security at all. As against Parc, it was content to be an unsecured creditor. What was contemplated was a negative form of protection from certain of Parc's other creditors, namely the other companies in the group, in the form of an undertaking that they would not enforce any claims they might have against Parc in priority to B.F.C. It is this distinction which is principally relied upon by the respondents for their submission, which found favour in the Court of Appeal, that subrogation is not available. To allow B.F.C. to be subrogated to the first charge would mean, it is said, giving it far greater security than it ever bargained for.

. . .

My Lords, the subject of subrogation is bedevilled by problems of terminology and classification which are calculated to cause confusion. For example, it is often said that subrogation may arise either from the express or implied agreement of the parties or by operation of law in a number of different situations: see, for example, Lord Keith of Kinkel in *Orakpo v Manson Investments Ltd.* [1978] A.C. 95, 119. As a matter of current terminology, this is true. Lord Diplock, for example, was of the view that the doctrine of subrogation in contracts of insurance operated entirely by virtue of an implied term of the contract of insurance (*Hobbs v Marlowe* [1978] A.C. 16, 39) and although in *Lord Napier and Ettrick v Hunter* [1993] A.C. 713 your Lordships rejected the exclusivity of this claim for the common law and assigned a larger role to equitable principles, there was no dispute that the doctrine of subrogation in insurance rests upon the common intention of the parties and gives effect to the principle of indemnity embodied in the contract. Furthermore, your Lordships drew attention to the fact that it is customary for the assured, on payment of the loss, to provide the insurer with a letter of subrogation, being no more nor less than an express assignment of his rights of recovery against any third party. Subrogation in this sense is a contractual arrangement for the transfer of rights against third parties and is founded upon the common intention of the parties. But the term is also used to describe an equitable remedy to reverse or prevent unjust enrichment which is not based upon any agreement or common intention of the party enriched and the party deprived. The fact that contractual subrogation and subrogation to prevent unjust enrichment both involve transfers of rights or something resembling transfers of rights should not be allowed to obscure the fact that one is dealing with radically different institutions. One is part of the law of contract and the other part of the law of restitution. Unless this distinction is borne clearly in mind, there is a danger that the contractual requirement of mutual consent will be imported into the conditions for the grant of the restitutionary remedy or that the absence of such a requirement will be disguised by references to a presumed intention which is wholly fictitious. There is an obvious parallel with the confusion caused by classifying certain restitutionary remedies as quasi-contractual and importing into them features of the law of contract.

In this case there was plainly no common intention as between O.O.L., the party enriched, and B.F.C., the party deprived. O.O.L. had no knowledge of the postponement letter or reason to believe that the advance to Parc of the money provided by B.F.C. was otherwise than unsecured. But why should this necessarily exclude subrogation as a restitutionary remedy? I shall refer to five authorities which in my view demonstrate the contrary.

. . .

[*After referring to* Chetwynd v Allen *[1899] 1 Ch 353,* Butler v Rice *[1910] 2 Ch 277,* Ghana Commercial Bank v Chandiram *[1960] AC 732,* Paul v Speirway Ltd *[1976] Ch 220 and* Boscawen v Bajwa, *below, 720, Lord Hoffmann continued:*]

These cases seem to me to show that it is a mistake to regard the availability of subrogation as a remedy to prevent unjust enrichment as turning entirely upon the question of intention, whether common or unilateral. Such an analysis has inevitably to be propped up by presumptions which can verge upon outright fictions, more appropriate to a less developed legal system than we now have. I would venture to suggest that the reason why intention has played so prominent a part in the earlier cases is because of the influence of cases on contractual subrogation. But I think it should be recognised that one is here concerned with a restitutionary remedy and that the appropriate questions are therefore, first, whether the defendant would be enriched at the plaintiff's expense; secondly, whether such enrichment would be unjust; and thirdly, whether there are nevertheless reasons of policy for denying a remedy. An example of a case which failed on the third ground is *Orakpo v Manson Investments Ltd.* [1978] A.C. 95, in which it was considered that restitution would be contrary to the terms and policy of the Moneylenders Acts.

This does not of course mean that questions of intention may not be highly relevant to the question of whether or not enrichment has been unjust. I would certainly not wish to question the proposition of Oliver J. in *Paul v Speirway Ltd.* [1976] Ch 220 that, as against a borrower, subrogation to security will not be available where the transaction was intended merely to create an unsecured loan. I do not express a view on the question of where the burden of proof lies in these matters. Oliver J., following the dictum of Lord Jenkins in *Ghana Commercial Bank v Chandiram* [1960] A.C. 732, 745 which I have quoted, held that if the plaintiff's money was used to discharge a secured liability, he was presumed to 'intend that the mortgage shall be kept alive for his own benefit' and this presumption was applied by Nicholls J. in *Boodle, Hatfield & Co. v British Films Ltd.*, 1986 P.C.C. 176. However, if it is recognised that the use of the plaintiff's money to pay off a secured debt and the intentions of the parties about whether or not the plaintiff should have security are only materials upon which a court may decide that the defendant's enrichment would be unjust, it could be argued that on general principles it is for the plaintiff to make out a case of unjust enrichment.

In this case, I think that in the absence of subrogation, O.O.L. would be enriched at B.F.C.'s expense and that prima facie such enrichment would be unjust. The bank advanced the DM30m. upon the mistaken assumption that it was obtaining a postponement letter which would be effective to give it priority over any intra-group indebtedness. It would not otherwise have done so . . . B.F.C. failed to obtain that priority over intra-group indebtedness which was an essential part of the transaction under which it paid the money. It may have attached more importance to the pledge of the shares but the provision of the postponement letter was a condition of completion. The result of the transaction is that B.F.C.'s DM30m. has been used to reduce the debt secured by R.T.B.'s first charge and that this reduction will, by reason of O.O.L.'s second charge, enure wholly to the latter's advantage.

. . .

In my view, the phrase 'keeping the charge alive' needs to be handled with some care. It is not a literal truth but rather a metaphor or analogy: see Birks, *An Introduction to the Law of Restitution*, pp. 93–97. In a case in which the whole of the secured debt is repaid, the charge is not kept alive at all. It is discharged and ceases to exist. In a case like the present, in which part of the secured debt is repaid, the charge remains alive only to secure the remainder of the debt for the benefit of the original chargee. Nothing can affect his rights and there is no question of competition between him and the party claiming subrogation. It is important to remember that, as Millett L.J. pointed out in *Boscawen v Bajwa* [1996] 1 W.L.R. 328, 335, subrogation is not a right or a cause of action but an equitable remedy against a party who would otherwise be unjustly enriched. It is a means by which the court regulates the legal relationships between a plaintiff and a defendant or defendants in order to prevent unjust enrichment. When judges say that the charge is 'kept alive' for the benefit of the plaintiff, what they mean is that his legal relations with a defendant who would otherwise be unjustly enriched are regulated *as if* the benefit of the charge had been assigned to him. It does not by any means follow that the plaintiff must for all purposes be treated as an actual assignee of the benefit of the charge and, in particular, that he would be so treated in relation to someone who would not be unjustly enriched.

This, I interpose, is the real reason why there is no 'conceptual problem' about treating B.F.C. as subrogated to part of the R.T.B. secured debt. The equitable remedy is available only against O.O.L., which is the only party which would be unjustly enriched. As between R.T.B. and B.F.C., subrogation has no part to play. R.T.B. is entitled to its security and B.F.C. is no more than an unsecured creditor. The same is true as between B.F.C. and any secured or unsecured creditor of Parc other than the members of the Omni Group. The transaction contemplated that as against non-group creditors. B.F.C. would incur no more than an unsecured liability, evidenced by the promissory note issued to Mr. Herzig and assigned by him to B.F.C. As against such creditors, therefore, the remedy of subrogation is not available. Nor is it available against Parc itself, so as to give B.F.C. the rights of sale, foreclosure etc. which would normally follow from B.F.C. being treated as if it were an assignee of the R.T.B. charge.

It follows that subrogation *as against* O.O.L., which is all that B.F.C. claims in the action, would not give it greater rights than it bargained for. All that would happen is that O.O.L. would be prevented from being able to enrich itself to the extent that B.F.C.'s money paid off the R.T.B. charge. This is fully within the scope of the equitable remedy. I would therefore allow the appeal. Robert Walker J. made a declaration that B.F.C. 'is and has since 28 September 1990 been entitled to the benefit of' the R.T.B. charge and the priority agreement of 13 February 1990. I think that this declaration goes further than is justified. As against Parc, B.F.C. is not entitled to such a declaration. I would therefore insert after the words 'entitled to' the words 'be treated as against O.O.L. as if it had.' Subject to that amendment, I would restore the declaration made by the judge.

Lord Hutton delivered a concurring speech. **Lord Clyde** delivered a speech concurring with Lord Hoffmann. **Lord Griffiths** agreed with Lord Hoffmann.

NOTES AND QUESTIONS

1. This case is of fundamental importance in authoritatively accepting that non-contractual subrogation is concerned to reverse, or prevent, unjust enrichment. Moreover, Lord Steyn (and, in very similar language, Lord Hoffmann) explicitly approached the unjust enrichment enquiry according to the steps set out in Chapter 2 above.

2. Subrogation is a difficult technique. Although this case concerned a mistake, subrogation is very wide-ranging and has been applied in respect of many different unjust factors. At root it is concerned with the *taking over* of another's present or former rights and remedies. It has two forms that have been helpfully labelled by C Mitchell, *The Law of Subrogation* (1994), 4–6 as 'simple' and 'reviving' subrogation (see also his article 'The Law of Subrogation' [1992] *LMCLQ* 483). Simple subrogation is less common and most obviously illustrated by an indemnity insurer's right to take over the assured's 'live' rights against a wrongdoer. In contrast, reviving subrogation is where a person has discharged (or his money has been used to discharge) another's liability to a third party and takes over the third party's *former* rights and

remedies against that other party (i.e., the discharged liability is revived). For example, where money has been borrowed by D from C and D has used it to discharge its liability to a third party (X), reviving subrogation may entitle C to take over X's former rights and remedies, including secured rights, against D.

3. The *Banque Financière* case was significantly more complex than the standard example of a lender's (reviving) subrogation rights (where the enrichment is normally the discharge of the defendant's liability to another). The case is considered here because it involved a mistakenly rendered enrichment where the enrichment was the enhancement in value of OOL's second charge over land by reason of the claimant's money being used to discharge RTB's first charge over that land.

4. A further unusual feature of the case is that normally, in the context of lenders' rights, subrogation effects *proprietary* restitution (as in *Boscawen v Bajwa* below, 720) by giving the claimant the former secured rights that the principal lender had against the debtor. But in this case BFC would not have been entitled to the secured rights that RTB had against Parc. Rather it was seeking repayment by Parc of the loan paid and it successfully argued that that personal claim should have priority over the rights of OOL against Parc in order to prevent OOL's unjust enrichment. Put another way, this was an unusual lenders' subrogation case where *proprietary* restitution against the debtor (Parc) was unnecessary in order for the claimant to succeed.

5. Lord Steyn's analysis shows that one could have arrived at the same result by reasoning straight from unjust enrichment to the result without involving the language of (reviving) subrogation.

3. RESCISSION OF AN EXECUTED CONTRACT ENTERED INTO BY MISTAKE

The remedy of rescission of a contract is one of the most difficult remedies to analyse. While it is (arguably) always a contractual remedy (because it wipes away and allows escape from a contract), it is also a remedy reversing unjust enrichment where a contract has been wholly or partly executed and where the effect of the rescission is therefore to restore benefits to the contracting parties. The rescission may effect personal restitution (for example, by entitling the payor to the repayment of a purchase price or by requiring the payment of the value of work done); but it is also commonly a proprietary restitutionary remedy in that it revests the proprietary rights to goods or land transferred under the contract. (For further discussion of proprietary restitution through rescission, see below, 706, 744.) In a nutshell, therefore, rescission is difficult to analyse because it may combine:- (i) contract and unjust enrichment; (ii) personal and proprietary restitution; (iii) restitution of payments and restitution for benefits in kind.

As far as rescission of a contract *for mistake* is concerned, the traditional approach has been to distinguish between rescission for misrepresentation (where the mistake is induced by a false statement of fact); rescission for non-disclosure (where there is a duty on the non-mistaken party to disclose the true facts to the mistaken party); and rescission for common mistake (where both parties make the same 'fundamental' mistake). But in *Great Peace Shipping Ltd v Tsavliris Salvage (Int) Ltd* [2002] EWCA Civ 1407, [2003] QB 679, the Court of Appeal controversially overruled *Solle v Butcher* [1950] 1 KB 671 and cases following it as being inconsistent with *Bell v Lever Bros* [1932] AC 161. It laid down that there is no equitable doctrine of common mistake i.e. there can be no rescission for common mistake. The only effect of common mistake is to make a contract void (not voidable). This means that we are purely concerned here with rescission of an executed contract for misrepresentation or non-disclosure.

There are four main bars to rescission: *restitutio in integrum* being impossible; affirmation; lapse of time; and third party rights. Of these bars, the most significant from a restitutionary perspective is the first, which we discuss as an aspect of the general restitutionary defence of 'counter-restitution impossible' in Chapter 14. Leading cases on that bar are the misrepresentation cases of *Clarke v Dickson*, *Armstrong v Jackson*, *Spence v Crawford*, and *Smith New Court Securities Ltd v Scrimgeour Vickers (Asset Management) Ltd* (see below, 844, 847, 849, 866); and the non-disclosure case of *Erlanger v New Sombrero Phosphate Co.*, below, 845. The details of rescission of contracts for misrepresentation and non-disclosure are well-covered in standard contract text-books and case-books. We include here three cases which can serve as general examples of restitutionary rescission of contracts entered into by misrepresentation or non-disclosure: *Newbigging v Adam* (below, 196), *Whittington v Seale-Hayne* (below, 199) and *Car and Universal Finance Co. Ltd v Caldwell* (below, 201).

We should emphasize that, while we consider it convenient to treat rescission for mistake separately in this section, the approach to restitution through rescission should be consistent with restitution through other restitutionary remedies.

General Reading
BURROWS, 56–60, 168–181; GOFF AND JONES, 9-002–9-056, VIRGO, 28–36.

- *Newbigging v Adam* (1886) 34 ChD 582, Court of Appeal

The claimant was induced to give up his commission in the army and to enter into a contract of partnership with the defendants by non-fraudulent repesentations of the state of the business. The claimant contributed £9,700 to the partnership and discharged partnership debts of £324. At first instance, the claimant was held entitled to rescind the contract, and the defendants were ordered to repay the £9,700 plus £324, minus the sums that that he had received from the partnership, making a balance payable of £9,279 6s. He was also held entitled to be indemnified against all other outstanding debts or liabilities of the partnership. The defendants appealed unsuccessfully against that decision.

Cotton LJ: . . . The Plaintiff, then, is entitled to be put back into his old position. How is that to be done? . . . [T]he moneys brought in by the Plaintiff were brought in to assist and support the business, and even if they did not go directly to pay any liabilities of the old business, the Plaintiff would be entitled, on the contract of partnership being set aside, to have paid back to him the sum which under that contract he brought into the business. But the Vice-Chancellor has given more. He has directed that there should be an indemnity given by the *Adams* to the Plaintiff, and the question is, Was he right in so doing?

Undoubtedly the statements made, as I have already stated, by the *Adams* were not such as would enable the Plaintiff to recover damages in an action of deceit, and Mr. *Rigby* [Counsel for the defendants] contended that it would not be right in an action of this kind to make the Defendants, whose misstatement had enabled the Plaintiff to set aside the contract, undertake liabilities for which they were never subject antecedently to the contract, for that this was really giving damages in another way. I differ from that proposition. In my opinion it is not giving damages in consequence of the deceit, it is working out the proper result of setting aside a contract in consequence of misrepresentation. This is a very different thing, because although the damages which would have been obtained in an action of deceit if the misstatement had been made fraudulently, or with such reckless negligence as to bring about the same consequences, might have been the same as what the

Plaintiff will get under the indemnity, they might have been much more. The Plaintiff here does not recover damages as in an action of deceit, but gets what is the proper consequence in equity of setting aside the contract into which he has been induced to enter. In my opinion it cannot be said that he is put back into his old position unless he is relieved from the consequences and obligations which are the result of the contract which is set aside. That is a very different thing from damages. The Plaintiff may have been induced by these misstatements to give up a commission in the army, and if the misstatements had been such that an action of deceit would lie he could have recovered damages for the loss of his commission, but he could not in such an action as the present obtain any relief in respect of it. The indemnity to which he is entitled is only an indemnity against the obligations which he has contracted under the contract which is set aside, and, in my opinion, the requiring the Defendant whose misstatements, though not fraudulent, have been the cause of setting aside the contract, to indemnify the Plaintiff from those obligations, is the only way in which the Plaintiff can be restored to his old position in an action like this, but I entirely disclaim any intention of giving damages in an action of this nature.

The case of *Redgrave v Hurd* [20 ChD 1] was relied upon by Mr. *Haldane* [junior Counsel for the defendants] in support of the contention of himself and Mr. *Rigby* on this point, but in my opinion that case does not support it. What was there claimed by the defendant in his counter-claim was not merely to have the contract rescinded, and the deposit of £100 returned to him, but also to have £100 damages for his loss and trouble in removing from *Stroud to Birmingham*, and £200 damages for having given up his practice at *Stroud*, and for further relief. Now those two last items were simply damages. If an action had been brought for damages on intentional misrepresentation they might have been considered as coming within the proper rule as to damages—that the damages should be such as to indemnify the party against loss, but they could not be claimed in a proceeding to set aside a contract on the ground of misrepresentation not so made as to support an action for deceit. . . .

Bowen LJ: . . . [E]quity will set aside this contract, and the only question remaining is, upon what terms, and what is the extent and nature of the relief which ought to be given to the Plaintiff. The Vice-Chancellor has in the first place ordered repayment of the sum of £9700 brought by the Plaintiff into the partnership, and also of the sum of £324, which, although not brought in *eo nomine* into the partnership, was in substance brought into it, because it was applied by the Plaintiff in discharge of debts of the firm. He has ordered these sums to be repaid after deducting certain moneys received by the Plaintiff, the balance being £9279 6s., and he has further declared that the Defendants Messrs. *Adam*, as well as Mr. *Townend*, are bound to indemnify the Plaintiff against all outstanding debts, claims, demands, and liabilities which the Plaintiff has become or may become subject to, or be liable to pay, for or on account of or in respect of the dealings and transactions of the partnership. I dwell at some length on this part of the case, because I conceive it to be important that we should lay down exactly the line on which our judgment proceeds, and decide nothing more than is necessary for the decision of the case, leaving open any points which it is not necessary to decide.

Now, in the first place, in considering the question to what extent Mr. *Newbigging* is entitled to demand an indemnity from *Adam & Co.*, one must consider the doctrine of equity as to the relief which will be given in cases of fraud and misrepresentation. A contract obtained by fraud, being voidable and not void, remains until it is set aside, and when it is set aside it is treated both at law and in equity as non-existing. It appears that equity, as has been pointed out in the case of *Peek v Gurney* [LR 13 Eq. 79], has a concurrent jurisdiction with law to give relief in cases of fraud. Common law recognised a rescission if the case shaped itself so that a Court of Common Law had jurisdiction to decide whether there should be a rescission or not, but, besides this, the common law gave damages for deceit, and in my opinion gave them, not as an alternative remedy, but as an alternative or cumulative remedy as the case might be. The Court of Chancery had a concurrent jurisdiction, and in cases of fraud, so far as I know, there can be no doubt that complete indemnity could be given by a Court of Equity to the person who had been defrauded, so as to protect him as fully in equity as he could have been protected in law.

If we turn to the question of misrepresentation, damages cannot be obtained at law for misrepresentation which is not fraudulent, and you cannot, as it seems to me, give in equity any indemnity which corresponds with damages. If the mass of authority there is upon the subject were gone through I think it would be found that there is not so much difference as is generally supposed between the view taken at common law and the view taken in equity as to misrepresentation. At common law it has always been considered that misrepresentations which strike at the root of the contract are sufficient to avoid the contract on the ground explained in *Kennedy v Panama, New Zealand, and Australian Royal Mail Company* [LR 2 QB 580], but when you come to consider what is the exact relief to which a person is entitled in a case of misrepresentation it seems to me to be this, and nothing more, that he is entitled to have the contract rescinded, and is entitled accordingly to all the incidents and consequences of such rescission. It is said that the injured party is entitled to be replaced in *statu quo*. It seems to me that when you are dealing with innocent misrepresentation you must understand that proposition that he is to be replaced *in statu quo* with this limitation—that he is not to be replaced in exactly the same position in all respects, otherwise he would be entitled to recover damages, but is to be replaced in his position so far as regards the rights and obligations which have been created by the contract into which he has been induced to enter. [*Bowen LJ then discussed the judgment of Sir George Jessel MR in* Redgrave v Hurd *(1881) 20 ChD 1, 12–13 and, after pointing out that the Master of the Rolls treated the relief as being the giving back by the party who made the misrepresentation of the advantages he obtained by the contract, he continued:*] Now those advantages may be of two kinds. He may get an advantage in the shape of an actual benefit, as when he receives money; he may also get an advantage if the party with whom he contracts assumes some burthen in consideration of the contract. In such a case it seems to me that complete rescission would not be effected unless the misrepresenting party not only hands back the benefits which he has himself received—but also re-assumes the burthen which under the contract the injured person has taken upon himself. Speaking only for myself I should not like to lay down the proposition that a person is to be restored to the position which he held before the misrepresentation was made, nor that the person injured must be indemnified against loss which arises out of the contract, unless you place upon the words 'out of the contract' the limited and special meaning which I have endeavoured to shadow forth. Loss arising out of the contract is a term which would be too wide. It would embrace damages at common law, because damages at common law are only given upon the supposition that they are damages which would naturally and reasonably follow from the injury done. I think *Redgrave v Hurd* shews that it would be too wide, because in that case the Court excluded from the relief which was given the damages which had been sustained by the plaintiff in removing his business, and other similar items. There ought, as it appears to me, to be a giving back and a taking back on both sides, including the giving back and taking back of the obligations which the contract has created, as well as the giving back and the taking back of the advantages. There is nothing in the case of *Rawlins v Wickham* [3 Deb & J 304] which carries the doctrine beyond that. In that case, one of three partners having retired, the remaining partners introduced the plaintiff into the firm, and he, under his contract with them, took upon himself to share with them the liabilities which otherwise they would have borne in their entirety. That was a burthen which he took under the contract and in virtue of the contract. It seems to me, therefore, that upon this principle indemnity was rightly decreed as regards the liabilities of the new firm. I have not found any case which carries the doctrine further, and it is not necessary to carry it further in order to support the order now appealed from. A part of the contract between the Plaintiff and *Adam & Co.* was that the Plaintiff should become and continue for five years partner in a new firm and bring in £10,000. By this very contract he was to pledge his credit with his partners in the new firm for the business transactions of the new firm. It was a burthen or liability imposed on him by the very contract. It seems to me that the £9000 odd, and, indeed, all the moneys brought in by him or expended by him for the new firm up to the £10,000, were part of the actual moneys which he undertook by the true contract with *Adam & Co.* to pay. Of course be ought to be indemnified as regards that. I think, also, applying the same doctrine, he ought to be indemnified against all the liabilities of the firm, because they were liabilities which under the contract he was bound to take upon himself.

Fry LJ: . . . The only other point upon which I will say anything is with regard to the indemnity, and in this case it is obvious that my learned Brothers, although arriving at the same conclusion, have arrived at that conclusion by different roads. It is perhaps enough to say that I agree in their conclusion, and so escape from an inquiry of a very nice and subtle kind. I will only say this, that the inclination of my opinion is towards the view of Lord Justice *Cotton*; that I am inclined to hold that the Plaintiff is entitled to an indemnity in respect of all obligations entered into under the contract when those obligations are within the necessary or reasonable expectation of both of the contracting parties at the time of the contract. I hesitate to adopt the view of Lord Justice *Bowen*, that the obligations must be created by the contract, and I feel a little doubt whether the obligation in question in the present suit can be said to have been so created.

It appears to me, however, to be plain that the Plaintiff having been induced by the Defendants to enter into the contract of partnership, it must have been in the contemplation of the contracting parties that the new partner would under that new contract of partnership become liable to the ordinary partnership obligations, and the obligations against which indemnity is sought are such ordinary partnership obligations.

NOTES AND QUESTIONS

1. An appeal to the House of Lords, *Adam v Newbigging* (1888) 13 App. Cas. 308, was dismissed, albeit that there was some variation of the order made at first instance to reflect concessions made by the claimant. In particular, the payment of the £324 by the claimant to discharge liabilities of the partnership was no longer in dispute; and there was no need for their Lordships to consider the validity of the general indemnity ordered because it was accepted by the claimant that the firm had no outstanding general liabilities.

2. The line between rescission and an indemnity, on the one hand, and damages, on the other, can be regarded as the line between a restitutionary remedy and a compensatory remedy. The crucial difference is whether the incurring of the loss was a benefit to the defendants. The discharge of a defendant's liabilities is an incontrovertible benefit to that defendant.

3. Was there a difference between Bowen LJ and Cotton LJ on the scope of an indemnity? If so, which view is to be preferred?

• *Whittington v Seale-Hayne* (1900) 82 LT 49, Chancery Division

The claimants entered into a lease of a farm which they wished to use for the purpose of breeding prize poultry. The claimants were induced to take the lease by the defendant's non-fraudulent misrepresentation that the premises were in a thoroughly sanitary condition and in a good state of repair. As a result of the water supply being poisoned the claimants' manager became seriously ill and the poultry either died or became valueless. The claimants sought rescission of the lease plus an indemnity for all losses that had been suffered as a result of the misrepresentation (for example, the loss of the poultry, the consequent loss of profits, and the medical expenses incurred on behalf of the manager). It was not in dispute that the claimants were entitled to recover the rent paid and to an indemnity for the rates and the repairs carried out in conformity with a local authority order. But Farwell J held that they were not entitled to the other losses claimed because they fell outside the ambit of an indemnity and could only have been compensated if damages were recoverable which they were not as the representation was non-fraudulent.

Farwell J: . . . The plaintiffs' action is one for the rescission of a lease on the ground of innocent misrepresentation, and the claim also asks for damages and an indemnity against all costs and charges incurred by the plaintiffs in respect of the lease and the insanitary condition of the premises. The suggestion was made that I should assume for the purpose of argument that innocent mis-representations were made sufficient to entitle the plaintiffs to rescission. The question then arises to what extent the doctrine, that a plaintiff who succeeds in an action for rescission on the ground of innocent misrepresentation is entitled to be placed *in statu quo ante*, is to be applied. Counsel for the plaintiffs say that in such a case the successful party is to be placed in exactly the same position as if he had never entered into the contract. The defendant admits liability so far as regards anything which was paid under the contract, but not in respect of any damages incurred by reason of the contract; and I think the defendant's view is the correct one. The question is one of some difficulty, because the various authorities have left the point to be decided rather at large. Lord Watson, in *Adam v Newbigging* (13 App. Cas. 308, at p. 324), stated it to be one of great nicety and some difficulty. When the plaintiffs say they are entitled to have the misrepresentations made good, it may mean one of two things. It may mean that they are entitled to have the whole of the injury incurred by their entering into the contract made good, or that they are entitled to be repaid what they have paid under their contract—e.g., to make good in the present case would mean to have the drains put right, but to make good by way of compensation for the consequences of the misrepresentations is the same thing as asking for damages. Having regard to *Derry v Peek* (1889) 14 App. Cas. 337, it is doubtful whether the old doctrine that damages occasioned by misrepresentation should be made good can be enforced now. . . . This brings me back to the case of *Newbigging v Adam* (34 Ch Div. 582), and the difficulty which I have is that the judgments in the Court of Appeal do not agree, and I have therefore to choose between them. I think Bowen LJ's is the correct view. [*Farwell J discussed the judgments of Bowen and Cotton LJJ in* Newbigging v Adam *and continued*] Having regard to the fact that it was only a question of indemnity which was being considered in *Newbigging v Adam*, I do not think that Cotton LJ intended to go further than Bowen LJ. If he did, I prefer to agree with Bowen LJ. But Fry LJ certainly went further. [*Farwell J cited the first paragraph of Fry LJ's judgment extracted above, 144, and continued*:] Fry LJ was pointing at cases under the head of damages. His is an entirely different proposition to what Bowen LJ puts, and he says so. This being so, the point I have here to consider is what is the limit of the liabilities which are within the indemnity. [Counsel for the defendant] admits that the rents, rates, and repairs under the covenants in the lease ought to be made good; but he disputes, and I agree with him, that the plaintiff is entitled to what is claimed by paragraph 11 of the statement of claim which is really damages pure and simple.

NOTES AND QUESTIONS

1. The payment of rates and the carrying out of necessary repairs were (incontrovertibly) beneficial to the defendants in that they were expenses that they would otherwise have had to incur. They therefore fell within the scope of a restitutionary indemnity. The other losses claimed were not of benefit to the defendants and therefore fell within the scope of compensatory damages which could not be awarded in the absence of a tort.

2. It is likely that the claimants on similar facts would now have a claim for damages either at common law following *Hedley Byrne & Co. Ltd v Fletter & Partners Ltd* [1964] AC 465 or under section 2(1) of the Misrepresentation Act 1967.

- *Car and Universal Finance Co. Ltd v Caldwell* [1965] 1 QB 525, Court of Appeal

The defendant (Caldwell) was the owner of a Jaguar car. He sold it for £975 to Norris, who took the car away leaving a deposit of £10 and a cheque for £965. Norris was a fraudster and the cheque was dishonoured the following day (13 January). The defendant immediately informed the police and the Automobile Association of the fraudulent transaction. Norris subsequently sold the car to a firm of dealers and it was subsequently sold on a number of times and eventually to the claimants who bought in good faith and without any defect in title. In interpleader proceedings to determine whether the claimants or the defendant owned the car, the central question at issue was whether the defendant had validly rescinded the contract on 13 January before the car had been acquired by a *bona fide* purchaser for value without notice. Lord Denning MR, sitting as an additional judge of the Queen's Bench Division, held that the contract had been validly rescinded and this decision (although not all the reasoning) was upheld by the Court of Appeal.

Sellers LJ: This appeal raises a primary point in the law of contract. The question has arisen whether a contract which is voidable by one party can in any circumstances be terminated by that party without his rescission being communicated to the other party. Lord Denning MR has held in the circumstances of this case that there can be rescission without communication where the seller of a motor car, who admittedly had the right to rescind the contract of sale on the ground of fraudulent misrepresentation, terminated the contract by an unequivocal act of election which demonstrated clearly that he had elected to rescind it and to be no longer bound by it. The general rule, no doubt, is that where a party is entitled to rescind a contract and wishes to do so the contract subsists until the opposing party is informed that the contract has been terminated. The difficulty of the seller in this case was that, when he learnt of the fraud and, therefore, ascertained his right to terminate the bargain, he could not without considerable delay find either the fraudulent buyer or the car which had been sold. Such circumstances would not appear to be so rare in transactions in motor cars (or horses in earlier days) that they would not, it might be thought, have given rise to litigation and an authoritative decision, but it seems that over the years the point in issue has not been decided in any reported cases in similar or comparable circumstances.

. . .

The position has to be viewed, as I see it, between the two contracting parties involved in the particular contract in question. That another innocent party or parties may suffer does not in my view of the matter justify imposing on a defrauded seller an impossible task. He has to establish, clearly and unequivocally, that he terminates the contract and is no longer to be bound by it. If he cannot communicate his decision he may still satisfy a judge or jury that he had made a final and irrevocable decision and ended the contract. I am in agreement with Lord Denning MR who asked 'How is a man in the position of Caldwell ever to be able to rescind the contract when a fraudulent person absconds as Norris did here?' and answered that he can do so '. . . if he at once, on discovering the fraud, takes all possible steps to regain the goods even though he cannot find the rogue nor communicate with him.'

. . .

Upjohn LJ: . . . If one party, by absconding, deliberately puts it out of the power of the other to communicate his intention to rescind which he knows the other will almost certainly want to do, I do not think he can any longer insist on his right to be made aware of the election to determine the contract. In these circumstances communication is a useless formality. I think that the law must allow the innocent party to exercise his right of rescission otherwise than by communication or repossession. To hold otherwise would be to allow a fraudulent contracting party by his very fraud to prevent the innocent party from exercising his undoubted right. I would hold that in circumstances such as these the innocent party may evince his intention to disaffirm the contract by overt means falling short of communication or repossession.

. . .

Davies LJ: . . . On the facts of this case Norris must be taken to have known that the defendant might, on ascertaining the fraud, wish to rescind the contract. Norris disappeared; and so did the car. The defendant could, therefore, neither communicate with Norris nor retake the car. It must, therefore, I think, be taken to be implied in the transaction between Norris and the defendant that in the event of the defendant's wishing to rescind he should be entitled to do so by the best other means possible. Lex non cogit ad impossibilia. It is true that it was conceivably possible that the defendant might decide not to rescind but to sue on the cheque instead; but it is most doubtful whether on the facts of this case such a possibility could have occurred to Norris as a real one. The fact that Norris knew that he was a rogue and that, therefore, the defendant was likely to be after him distinguishes this case from that of an innocent misrepresentor. It would not occur to the latter that the other party to the contract would have any right or desire to rescind, so that there would be no such implication as that which I have suggested arose in the present case.

It was argued that the defendant's action in going to the police and the Automobile Association was not an unequivocal act, since it was open to him to have changed his mind on the next day if, to use [Counsel for the plaintiffs'] phrase, Norris had suddenly won a football pool and so have become a worthwhile defendant to an action on the cheque. That again, in my opinion, is an unrealistic view of the facts. The defendant was, as I think, declaring to the world: 'I have been swindled and I want my car back.' He was declaring his intention as clearly as if he had seen the car in the street and seized it.

. . .

NOTES AND QUESTIONS

1. In this case, the rescission revested in the defendant the proprietary rights to the car that had been transferred to the fraudster, and thence to the third party claimants. This is therefore a good example of rescission being a proprietary restitutionary remedy (see below, 201). The following passage from Lord Denning's judgment at first instance [1965] 1 QB 525, 532 summarizes particularly clearly the proprietary effect of the rescission:

   [W]here a seller of goods has a right to avoid a contract for fraud, he sufficiently exercises his election if he at once, on discovering the fraud, takes all possible steps to regain the goods even though he cannot find the rogue or communicate with him. That is what Caldwell did here by going to the police and asking them to get back the car. I, therefore, hold that on January 13 the contract of sale to these rogues was avoided and Caldwell then became the owner of the car again. It was only after he avoided it (so that it was once again his property), that these rogues purported to sell it to Motobella and Motobella purported to sell it to G & C Finance. Those sales were ineffective to pass the property because it had already been revested in Caldwell.

2. In the cases that have been considered in this section, rescission was being based on the misrepresentation of the other contracting party. A more complex situation is where a third party's misrepresentation induces the claimant to enter into a contract with the defendant. For an example of this, see *Barclays Bank plc v O'Brien* [1994] 1 AC 180 (below, 458) where the situation is discussed alongside the much more common situation where it is the *undue influence* of a third party that induces the claimant to enter into a contract with the defendant.

4

IGNORANCE

The role and content of unjust enrichment in this area are highly controversial. The courts have never overtly recognized an unjust factor of ignorance and, on a traditional analysis, the equity and common law cases have not been seen as sharing a common basis. The typical, but by no means only, situations in play are where there has been a breach of fiduciary duty or some sort of fraud and the defendant has received money or other property from the fiduciary or fraudster. The question is whether the owner/defrauded party has a cause of action in unjust enrichment against the defendant.

As the cases reveal, there is inconsistency in the answer given, not only between common law and equity but also within equity. At common law (in an action for money had and received) restitutionary liability is strict subject to defences (see *Banque Belge pour l'Etranger v Hambrouck, Agip (Africa) Ltd v Jackson, Lipkin Gorman v Karpnale*; below, 204–19). In equity the predominant approach has been to require that the defendant has knowledge in order to fix him with a personal liability to account for the value of the money or property received and the main dispute has been whether knowledge extends beyond dishonesty to negligence (see *Carl-Zeiss Stiftung v Herbert Smith & Co. (No 2), Re Montagu's Settlements, Belmont Finance v Williams* below, 225–233). In *BCCI (Overseas) Ltd v Akindele* (below, 233) 'unconscionability' was favoured as the appropriate test. Yet in *Ministry of Health v Simpson* (below, 237) strict personal liability was imposed in equity.

The analogy to cases of mistaken payments, in which the restitutionary liability is clearly strict, suggests that the common law model of strict liability, subject to defences, is to be preferred, with the most obvious unjust factor being the claimant's absence of consent to his loss (i.e. ignorance). This is also supported by the rare two-party case of the claimant losing money that is found by the defendant (as in *Holiday v Sigil*, below, 204). The fact that most of the cases in this area involve three parties should not affect the unjust factor or the standard of liability, albeit that the range of defences may be wider (i.e. the defence of *bona fide* purchase for value without notice comes into play) and there may be more difficulty in establishing that the defendant's benefit is at the expense of the claimant rather than at the expense of the person (e.g. the fraudster) who immediately transferred it to the defendant. It was in a path-breaking article by Birks in 1989 that the strict liability/ignorance restitutionary approach was first advocated (see below, 239). Birks' thesis has been accepted, albeit with an important refinement (which Birks himself subsequently agreed with), by Lord Nicholls writing extra-judicially (below, 245).

General Reading

Burrows, chapter 4; Goff and Jones, 4-001–4-002, 30-001–30-003, 33-027–33-032; Virgo ch 7, 646–54.

1. THE POSITION AT COMMON LAW—STRICT LIABILITY SUBJECT TO DEFENCES

In nearly all the cases considered in this Chapter the facts involved three parties: that is, X transferred the claimant's (legal or equitable) property to the defendant. But in the case that follows two parties only were involved: that is, the claimant lost his money which was found by the defendant.

- *Holiday v Sigil* (1826) 2 C & P 176, Court of King's Bench

The defendant found a £500 note that had been dropped by the claimant. He was held liable for £500 in the claimant's action for money had and received.

Abbott CJ (to the jury): The question to be considered is, whether you are satisfied that the plaintiff lost this note, and that the defendant found it; for if you are, the plaintiff is entitled to your verdict. I should observe, that it is scarcely possible for a plaintiff, when his property is stolen, or accidentally lost, to prove the loss by direct evidence; and, therefore, that must in almost all cases be made out by circumstances.

NOTES AND QUESTIONS

1. The facts of *Holiday v Sigil* could not have been more straightforward. Can the same be said of the legal analysis of the case? Was the claim dependent on establishing a tort by the defendant?

2. On Birks' new 'absence of basis' model, there is an *unjust* enrichment in the cases in this chapter because, where there is no consent at all, there is no possible basis (not even a putative one) for the enrichment. This is what he termed a 'non-participatory enrichment': see *Unjust Enrichment* (2nd edn, 2005), 129, 154–8.

- *Banque Belge pour L'Etranger v Hambrouck* [1921] 1 KB 321, Court of Appeal

Hambrouck forged a number of cheques so that £6,000 was debited from his employer's (Mr Pelabon's) account at the claimant bank and credited to his own account at Farrow's bank. From that account Hambrouck drew sums which he paid to his mistress, Mlle Spanoghe, the second defendant, who provided no consideration for them. She paid that money into her deposit account at the London Joint City and Midland Bank, the third defendant. At the time of the action, £315 stood to her credit in that account. The claimant bank brought an action for a declaration that the £315 was its property and should be paid out to them. The London Joint City and Midland Bank paid the money into court. The claimant succeeded before Salter J and, on appeal by Mlle Spanoghe, that decision was upheld by the Court of Appeal.

Bankes LJ: . . . The action was brought against the London Joint City and Midland Bank as well as against Hambrouck and the appellant, but by an order made in the action proceedings were stayed against the Bank on their paying the 315*l.* into Court. No evidence was given in the Court below as to the exact means by which Hambrouck defrauded M. Pelabon. The statement of claim alleges that he obtained payment of the cheques by fraudulently representing that they were drawn by M. Pelabon's authority. For the purposes of my judgment I will assume that Hambrouck obtained a voidable title to the proceeds of the cheques. Whatever the position of the plaintiff Bank may have been in relation to their customer, M. Pelabon, in the event of the Bank being unable to recover the moneys which they had paid out when the cheques were presented to them for payment, it is I think clear that the moneys which were so paid out were the moneys of the plaintiff Bank which they were entitled to recover if they could. This conclusion disposes of the point raised by [counsel for the appellant] that the action would not lie, because the Bank were, at the time of the trial, claiming that as between themselves and M. Pelabon the loss must fall upon him.

Had the claim been for the recovery of a chattel sold instead of for a sum of money alleged to be given, the appellant's counsel do not dispute that, in order to retain the chattel, the appellant must establish that she gave value for it without notice that it had been obtained by the vendor by fraud; but they attempt to distinguish the present case from the case of the sale of a chattel by saying: (a) that the appellant, who had no notice of Hambrouck's fraud, obtained a good title to the money, because it was a gift to her from Hambrouck; (b) that the rule applicable to a chattel has no application to currency; (c) that the fact that the appellant had paid the money into her banking account prevented any following of the money by the plaintiff Bank, and that an action for money had and received would therefore not lie.

In my opinion the first contention cannot be supported either upon the facts or in law. The facts show that the payments made by Hambrouck to the appellant were made without valuable consideration, and for an immoral consideration. Even if they could be appropriately described as gifts, a gift without valuable consideration would not give the appellant any title as against the plaintiff Bank.

The second contention also cannot be supported in law. It rests upon a misconception as to the meaning which has been attached to the expression 'currency' in some of the decisions which have been referred to. In *Miller v Race*[1] Lord Mansfield in dealing with the question whether money has an earmark says: 'The true reason is upon account of the currency of it; it cannot be recovered after it has passed in currency.' The learned judge is there using the expression in the same sense at that in which Channell J uses it in *Moss v Handcock*[2] where he says: 'If the coin had been dealt with and transferred as current coin of the realm, as, for instance, in payment for goods purchased or in satisfaction of a debt, or bona fide changed as money for money of a different denomination.' Where the word 'currency' is used merely as the equivalent of coin of the realm, then for present purposes the difference between currency and a chattel personal is one of fact and not of law. This was the view of Lord Ellenborough in *Taylor v Plumer*,[3] in the passage in which he deals with the difficulty of tracing money which has become part of an undivided and undistinguishable mass of current money, and which in this respect differs from marked coins or money in a bag. With regard to the latter he says that the rule for the purpose we are considering in this appeal is the same as that which applies to every other description of personal property. Dealing with this point in *Sinclair v Brougham*[4] Lord Haldane says: 'The common law, which we are now considering, did not take cognizance of such duties. It looked simply to the question whether the property had passed, and if it had not, for instance, where no relationship of debtor and creditor had intervened, the money could be followed, not withstanding its normal character as currency, provided it could be earmarked or traced into assets acquired with it.' To accept either of the two contentions with which I have been so far dealing would be to assent to the proposition that a thief who has stolen money, and who from fear of detection hands that money to a beggar whom he happens to pass, gives a title to the money to the beggar as against the true owner—a proposition which is obviously impossible of acceptance.

The last contention for the appellant cannot in my opinion be supported. The law on the subject has been so fully discussed recently in *Sinclair v Brougham* that I need only point out that the law as laid down by Lord Ellenborough in *Taylor v Plumer* as to the right of an owner to recover property in the common law Courts from a person who can show no title to it, where the property was capable of

1 1 Burr 452, 457.   2 [1899] 2 QB 111, 118.   3 3 M & S 562, 575.
4 [1914] AC 398, 420.

being traced, whether in its original form or in some substituted form, was fully accepted, and it was explained that the rule in equity which was applied in *Hallett's Case*[5] was only introduced to meet cases where the money sought to be traced could no longer be identified owing to its having become merged in the Bank's assets, and the relationship of debtor and creditor, between the customer who had paid the money into the Bank and the Bank into which the money had been paid, having intervened.

The facts in the present case in my opinion remove any difficulty in the way of the plaintiff Bank recovering, without having recourse to the equity rule. The money which the Bank seeks to recover is capable of being traced, as the appellant never paid any money into the Bank except money which was part of the proceeds of Hambrouck's frauds, and the appellant's Bank have paid all the money standing to the appellant's credit into Court, where it now is. Even if it had been necessary to apply the rule in *Hallett's Case* to enable the plaintiff Bank to establish their right to the money they claim, I see no difficulty in applying the rule to the facts as found by the learned judge in the Court below.

In my opinion the appeal fails. . . .

Scrutton LJ: . . . The ground of the decision below is that the 315*l.* is traced to the money which Hambrouck obtained by fraud from the Bank; that this money was never Hambrouck's property, and as Mlle Spanoghe gave no legal consideration of past or future cohabitation, she cannot acquire a title to the money as a purchaser for value without notice of any defect in the transferor's title.

The first objection taken is that the Bank are not the proper plaintiffs, as Pelabon is not now objecting to the Bank's debiting his account with the cheques. It is clear, however, that the money actually obtained by Hambrouck was the Bank's money, even if they might debit their payments to the account of another, and the Bank therefore can sue for the money if it was obtained by fraud on them. Secondly, it was said that as Hambrouck paid the stolen money into a bank, he had only a creditor's right to be paid with any money, not the particular money he paid in; so that when he drew some money out of the bank and paid it to Mlle Spanoghe, he did not make her the recipient of the money he had obtained from the Banque Belge, and therefore an action for money had and received would not lie. It was further said that Mlle Spanoghe received the money as a gift without notice of any defect in title and that therefore no action would lie against her.

This last objection is, I think, bad. At common law, a man who had no title himself could give no title to another. Nemo potest dare quod non habet. To this there was an exception in the case of negotiable chattels or securities, the first of which to be recognized were money and bank notes: *Miller v Race*; and if these were received in good faith and for valuable consideration, the transferee got property though the transferor had none. But both good faith and valuable consideration were necessary, as Lord Mansfield says:[6] 'in the case of money stolen, the true owner cannot recover it after it has been paid away fairly and honestly upon a valuable and bona fide consideration'; but before money has passed in currency an action may be brought for the money itself. In the present case, it is clear that this money came to Mlle Spanoghe either as savings out of house-keeping allowance, or as a gift to a mistress for past or future cohabitation. In the first case she would hold it as agent for Hambrouck; in the second for no consideration that the law recognized. If then the money that came to her was the money of the Banque Belge, she got no title to it, as Hambrouck against the Banque Belge had no title. The defence is that it was not the money of the Banque Belge, for payment into Hambrouck's bank, and his drawing out other money in satisfaction, had changed its identity.

I am inclined to think that at common law this would be a good answer to a claim for money had and received, at any rate if the money was mixed in Hambrouck's bank with other money. But it is clear that the equitable extension of the doctrine as based on *In re Hallett's Estate* and explained in

---

5　13 Ch D 696.　　　6　1 Burr 457.

Sinclair v Brougham enables money though changed in character to be recovered, if it can be traced. As Lord Parker says in the latter case[7] on equitable principles, the original owner would be entitled 'to follow the money as long as it or any property acquired by its means could be identified.' In that case there was an equitable charge on the substituted fund or property, if it could be traced to the stolen money. As Bramwell JA puts it in *Ex parte Cooke*:[8] 'A difficulty in tracing money often arises from the circumstance that payments now are not usually made in gold, but by cheques which go into a banking account, so that the sum is mixed up with the other moneys of the customer. But if this payment were made by a bag of gold which the broker put into his strong box, and then misapplied part of the money, leaving the rest in the bag, there would be no doubt that what was so left could be claimed as the money of the client. The use of cheques may make difficulties in tracing money, but that, so far as it can be traced, it may be claimed as the property of the client, appears to me to be covered both by the reason of the thing and by the authority of *Taylor v Plumer*.' If that is the test to apply it is clear that the 315*l.* in Mlle Spanoghe's account and now in Court, can all clearly be traced to the money obtained by Hambrouck by fraud or forgery from the Bank, and as she gave for it no valuable consideration, she cannot set up a title derived from Hambrouck, who had no title against the true owner.

For these reasons, in my opinion the appeal fails. . . .

Atkin LJ: . . . The money was obtained from the plaintiff Bank by the fraud of Hambrouck. It does not appear to be necessary for this case to determine whether Hambrouck stole the money or obtained it by false pretences. At present it appears to me that the plaintiff Bank intended to pass the property in and the possession of the cash which under the operations of the clearing house they must be taken to have paid to the collecting bank. I will assume therefore that this is a case not of a void but of a voidable transaction by which Hambrouck obtained a title to the money until the plaintiffs elected to avoid his title, which they did when they made their claim in this action. The title would then revest in the plaintiffs subject to any title acquired in the meantime by any transferee for value without notice of the fraud.

The appellant however contends that the plaintiffs cannot assert their title to the sum of money which was on a deposit account: 1. because it has passed through one if not two bank accounts and therefore cannot be identified as the plaintiffs' money; 2. because in any case a transfer to an innocent donee defeats the original owner's claim. The course of the proceedings in this case is not quite clear. The statement of claim alleges specifically that the money is the property of the plaintiffs which they are entitled to follow, and the relief asked is not for a money judgment against the defendants, but an order that the sum paid into Court by the defendant Bank should be paid out to the plaintiffs. In giving judgment however, the learned judge has treated the claim as one for money had and received, and the judgment entered is an ordinary judgment against the appellant on a money claim for 315*l.* together with an order that the sum in Court should be paid out to the plaintiffs in part satisfaction. The two forms of relief are different, and though in this case there is no substantial difference in the result, the grounds upon which relief is based might have been material.

First, does it make any difference to the plaintiffs' rights that their money was paid into Farrow's Bank, and that the money representing it drawn out by Hambrouck was paid to the defendant Bank on deposit? If the question be the right of the plaintiffs in equity to follow their property, I apprehend that no difficulty arises. The case of *In re Hallett's Estate* makes it plain that the Court will investigate a banking account into which another person's money has been wrongfully paid, and will impute all drawings out of the account in the first instance to the wrongdoer's own moneys, leaving the

---

7 [1914] AC 447.   8 (1876) 4 Ch D 123, 128.

plaintiff's money intact so far as it remains in the account at all. There can be no difficulty in this case in following every change of form of the money in question, whether in the hands of Hambrouck or of the appellant, and it appears to me that the plaintiffs were, on the grounds alleged in the statement of claim, entitled to a specific order for the return of the money in question, and, as it is now represented by the sum in Court, to payment out of Court of that sum.

The question whether they are entitled to a common law judgment for money had and received may involve other considerations. I am not without further consideration prepared to say that every person who can in equity establish a right to have his money or the proceeds of his property restored to him, can, as an alternative, bring an action against the person who has been in possession of such money or proceeds for money had and received; still less that he can always bring trover or detinue. But the common law rights are large and are admirably stated in *Taylor v Plumer*,[9] which was a case stated for the opinion of the Court of King's Bench after trial before Lord Ellenborough at the London Sittings. The facts are significant. Sir Thomas Plumer wishing to invest in exchequer bills gave his broker, Walsh, a draft on his bankers for 22,200*l.* to be invested accordingly. Walsh cashed the draft, receiving bank notes. He bought 6500*l.* exchequer bills. With the balance he bought certain American securities, paying for them with the actual notes received from the bank. But he gave one of the notes to his brother-in-law, from whom he received a draft on the brother-in-law's bankers for 500*l.* With this draft he bought bullion—namely 71½ doubloons—intending to abscond to North America via Lisbon. Sir Thomas Plumer's attorney overtook Walsh at Falmouth, and secured from him a return of the American securities and the bullion. Walsh, who was afterwards indicted, tried, found guilty subject to the opinion of the judges and pardoned without judgment having been passed, was made bankrupt on an act of bankruptcy alleged to have been committed before he returned the property. His assignees in bankruptcy brought trover against Sir Thomas Plumer. It was held by Lord Ellenborough delivering the judgment of the Court that the defendant was entitled to succeed, for he had repossessed himself of that which he never ceased to be the lawful proprietor. 'The plaintiff,' he says, '. . . is not entitled to recover if the defendant has succeeded in maintaining these propositions in point of law—viz., that the property of a principal entrusted by him to his factor for any special purpose belongs to the principal, notwithstanding any change which that property may have undergone in point of form, so long as such property is capable of being identified, and distinguished from all other property. . . . It makes no difference in reason or law into what other form, different from the original, the change may have been made, whether it be into that of promissory notes for the security of the money which was produced by the sale of the goods of the principal, as in *Scott v Surman*,[10] or into other merchandise, as in *Whitecomb v Jacob*,[11] for the product of or substitute for the original thing still follows the nature of the thing itself, as long as it can be ascertained to be such, and the right only ceases when the means of ascertainment fail, which is the case when the subject is turned into money, and mixed and confounded in a general mass of the same description.' I notice that in *Sinclair v Brougham*[12] Lord Haldane LC in dealing with this decision says: 'Lord Ellenborough laid down, as a limit to this proposition, that if the money had become incapable of being traced, as, for instance, when it had been paid into the broker's general account with his banker, the principal had no remedy excepting to prove as a creditor for money had and received,' and proceeds to say 'you can, even at law, follow, but only so long as the relation of debtor and creditor has not superseded the right in rem.' The words above 'as for instance' et seq. do not represent and doubtless do not purport to represent Lord Ellenborough's actual words; and I venture to doubt whether the common law ever so restricted the right as to hold that the money became incapable of being traced, merely because paid into the broker's general account with his banker. The question always was, Had the means of

---

9 3 M & S 562, 574.   10 (1742) Willes 400.   11 (1710) 1 Salk 160.
12 [1914] AC 398, 419.

ascertainment failed? But if in 1815 the common law halted outside the bankers' door, by 1879 equity had had the courage to lift the latch, walk in and examine the books: *In re Hallett's Estate*. I see no reason why the means of ascertainment so provided should not now be available both for common law and equity proceedings. If, following the principles laid down in *In re Hallett's Estate* it can be ascertained either that the money in the bank, or the commodity which it has bought, is 'the product of, or substitute for, the original thing,' then it still follows 'the nature of the thing itself.' On these principles it would follow that as the money paid into the bank can be identified as the product of the original money, the plaintiffs have the common law right to claim it, and can sue for money had and received. In the present case less difficulty than usual is experienced in tracing the descent of the money, for substantially no other money has ever been mixed with the proceeds of the fraud. Under the order of the Court in this case I think the money paid into Court must be treated as paid in on behalf of the defendant Spanoghe, and the money judgment, together with the order for payment out to the plaintiffs, effectually secures their rights.

Secondly, so far as it is contended that the bankers are entitled to retain possession where they have not given value, I think that has been concluded by what I have already said as to valuable consideration.

I agree that the appeal should be dismissed.

NOTES AND QUESTIONS

1. Why was tracing necessary given that the judges regarded a personal remedy only as being in issue? (For help on this question, see below, Chapter 13; and see below, 672, 649, 657, for *Re Hallett's Estate*, *Taylor v Plumer*, and *Sinclair v Brougham*, which were mentioned by all three of the judges.)

2. Why was Hambrouck's initial enrichment and, consequently, Mlle Spanoghe's enrichment regarded as being at the expense of the claimant bank rather than at the expense of M Pelebon? Is this aspect of the decision inconsistent with *Agip (Africa) Ltd v Jackson* (see below, 650)?

3. To what extent do the judgments of Scrutton and Atkin L JJ support the view that the tracing rules at common law and equity are fused? See on this, Birks, *An Introduction to the Law of Restitution* (rvsd. edn, 1989) 361–2; Burrows, 87; and the comments of Fox LJ in the *Agip* case (below, 213).

4. How does one best explain tracing at common law into and through a bank account? Was it important that no sums, other than the proceeds of fraud, had been paid into Mlle Spanoghe's account?

5. Was the unjust factor, the claimant bank's mistake or ignorance (or some other factor)?

6. A peculiarity of this case is that, although the judges treated the action as one for money had and received (a personal remedy), the claimant was concerned only with the £315 that was retained by the defendant bank and that had been paid into court. On the face of it, the claimant was *prima facie* entitled to the higher sums received by Mlle Spanoghe (although since the recognition of a change of position defence in *Lipkin Gorman v Karpnale*—see above, 28—she might now have been able to reduce her liability to a sum close to the amount she retained).

- *Agip (Africa) Ltd v Jackson* [1991] Ch 547, Court of Appeal

Zdiri, an employee of the claimant company, fraudulently altered the name of the payee, to Baker Oil Services Ltd, on a payment order of some $518,000 from the claimant. The $518,000 was transferred from the claimant's account with the Banque du Sud in Tunisia to Baker Oil's account with Lloyds Bank in London. Baker Oil was a puppet company which had been set up and was controlled by the defendants, who were chartered accountants. Throughout they were acting on the instructions of clients. The $518,000 was transferred to accounts of the defendants' accountancy firm and all but $43,000 was paid on to unknown parties. Millett J held that the claimant had an equitable proprietary claim to the $43,000 and was entitled to compensation for the defendants' 'knowing assistance in a breach of trust'; but that the claimant could not succeed in its alternative claims based on the receipt of the money either at common law (because the claimant's money could not be traced at common law into Baker Oil's account with Lloyds Bank as it had been transferred electronically rather than physically) or in equity (because those defendants who had received the money had done so as agents and not for their own benefit). The Court of Appeal upheld Millett J's decision on the equitable proprietary claim and on the defendants' equitable compensatory liability for knowing assistance. On the claimant's cross-appeal on the common law action for money had and received, the Court of Appeal again upheld Millett J's decision because the claimant's money had been mixed in the New York clearing system and could not therefore be traced at common law. (There was no cross-appeal against Millett J's dismissal of the claimant's equitable receipt claim.)

Fox LJ: . . .

THE RIGHT TO SUE

Agip's claim was for money paid under a mistake of fact. The defendants' contention was that Agip had disclosed no title to sue. The basis of that contention was that the relationship between banker and customer was one of debtor and creditor. When the customer paid money into the bank, the ownership of the money passed to the bank. The bank could do what it liked with it. What the bank undertook to do was to credit the amount of the money to the customer's account, and to honour his drafts or other proper directions in relation to it. Thus, it was said, when Banque du Sud paid Baker Oil it had no authority to do so on behalf of Agip because the order for payment was forged. Further, the Banque du Sud paid with its own money.

In terms of the mechanism of payment, what happened was no different from what would have happened if the order was not forged but genuine. Banque du Sud paid the collecting bank and debited Agip's account at Banque du Sud. In practical terms the Banque du Sud paid with Agip's money in both cases and, indeed, in both cases intended to do so. In both cases the substance of the matter was that money standing to the credit of Agip's account was paid to a third party in accordance with the order or supposed order, as the case may be, of Agip. The direction was to pay from Agip's account. To say that the payment was made out of the Banque du Sud's own funds, while true as far as it goes, only tells half the story. The banker's instruction is to pay from the customer's account. He does so by a payment from his own funds and a corresponding debit. The reality is a payment by the customer, at any rate in a case where the customer has no right to require a re-crediting of his account. Nothing passes in specie. The whole matter is dealt with by accounting transactions partly in the paying bank and partly in the clearing process.

It does not advance the matter to say that the Banque du Sud had no mandate from Agip to make the payment at Agip's expense. What actually happened was that Banque du Sud did so. Moreover, when Agip sued Banque du Sud in the Tunisian courts—and I take it that Tunisian law was the proper law of the banking relationship between Agip and Banque du Sud—to have its account re-credited, it failed to obtain that relief. In those circumstances, to regard Agip as not having paid Baker Oil is highly unreal. Banque du Sud had no intention of paying with its own money. The substance of its intention, which it achieved, was to pay with Agip's money. The order, after all, was an order to pay with Agip's money. I agree, therefore, with the view of Millett J [1990] Ch 265, 283h that 'the fact remains that the Banque du Sud paid out the plaintiffs' money and not its own.' If Banque du Sud paid away Agip's money, Agip itself must be entitled to pursue such remedies as there may be for its recovery. The money was certainly paid under a mistake of fact.

It was said that the difference between this case and a case where the bank paid with the authority (though given under a mistake of fact) of the customer, was that, in the latter case, the bank paid as agent of the customer and that, accordingly, either the principal or agent could sue. Thus, it was contended that where, as here, there was a claim to recovery money paid by mistake of fact, the mistake must be that of the plaintiff or of his agent. That, it was contended, could not be established here. There was no mistake by Agip, which was simply the victim of a fraud. The only mistake was that of Banque du Sud, which paid in the mistaken belief that it had Agip's authority to do so. Banque du Sud, it was said, did not pay as the agent of Agip because it had no authority to pay. In *Westminster Bank Ltd v Hilton* (1926) 43 TLR 124, 126, Lord Atkinson said:

> 'It is well established that the normal relation between a banker and his customer is that of debtor and creditor, but it is equally well established that quoad the drawing and payment of the customer's cheques as against money of the customer's in the banker's hands the relation is that of principal and agent. The cheque is an order of the principal's addressed to the agent to pay out of the principal's money in the agent's hands the amount of the cheque to the payee thereof.'

The defendants, as I understand it, would accept the proposition as to agency but say that Banque du Sud did not pay as agent of Agip because of lack of authority. The order was forged. It seems to me, however, Banque du Sud plainly intended to pay as agent of Agip. Thus, it paid in accordance with the order as presented to it and debited Agip's account accordingly. There was no reason why it should do anything else. The order as presented to it appeared perfectly regular.

But, accepting the intention, can the Banque du Sud properly be regarded as having paid as agent of Agip? The defendants say the absence of authority concluded the point against Agip. The judge met that by saying that Banque du Sud had general authority from Agip to debit the account in accordance with instructions. That is correct but it was said that there were no instructions because the order was bad. I do not feel able to accept that. The order emanated from within Agip; it was properly signed and the amount had not been altered. Banque du Sud had no reason at all to doubt its authenticity. The Tunisian court refused to order Banque du Sud to re-credit Agip's account. For practical purposes, therefore, the order was given effect to according to its tenor as if it were a proper order. Everything that was done (i.e. the payments and the debit) stands good so far as the banking transaction is concerned. Agip cannot recover from Banque du Sud. And Banque du Sud does not seek to recover from Baker Oil. It seems to me, therefore, that the order must be regarded as having been paid by Banque du Sud as agent for Agip. That, however, does not alter the circumstance that it was money paid under a mistake of fact. The defendants accepted that a principal could recover where there was either (i) mistaken payment by an authorised agent within his instructions or (ii) mistaken payment in breach of instructions by using money entrusted to the agent by the principal. The present case can be brought within, at any rate, the first of these.

The judge referred to the decision in *Colonial Bank v Exchange Bank of Yarmouth, Nova Scotia* (1885) 11 App. Cas. 84, 91. In that case it was held that the bank had a sufficient interest to recover the money, if only to obtain relief from the consequences of its liability to its customer. Millett J thought the decision was inconsistent with any suggestion that, far from being the wrong plaintiff, the bank was the only plaintiff. The present point, however, was not before the Privy Council in that case and I think the decision gives only limited assistance.

Looking at the whole matter, however, it seems to me that the judge correctly concluded that Agip's right to sue was made out.

TRACING AT COMMON LAW

The judge held that Agip was not entitled to trace at law. Tracing at law does not depend upon the establishment of an initial fiduciary relationship. Liability depends upon receipt by the defendant of the plaintiff's money and the extent of the liability depends on the amount received. Since liability depends upon receipt the fact that a recipient has not retained the asset is irrelevant. For the same reason dishonesty or lack of inquiry on the part of the recipient are irrelevant. Identification in the defendant's hands of the plaintiff's asset is, however, necessary. It must be shown that the money received by the defendant was the money of the plaintiff. Further, the very limited common law remedies make it difficult to follow at law into mixed funds. The judge's view [1990] Ch 265, 286 of the present case was that the common law remedy was not available. He said:

'The money cannot be followed by treating it as the proceeds of a cheque presented by the collecting bank in exchange for payment by the paying bank. The money was transmitted by telegraphic transfer. There was no cheque or any equivalent. The payment order was not a cheque or its equivalent. It remained throughout in the possession of the Banque du Sud. No copy was sent to Lloyds Bank or Baker Oil or presented to the Banque du Sud in exchange for the money. It was normally the plaintiff's practice to forward a copy of the payment order to the supplier when paying an invoice but this was for information only. It did not authorise or enable the supplier to obtain payment. There is no evidence that this practice was followed in the case of forged payment orders and it is exceedingly unlikely that it was. Nothing passed between Tunisia and London but a stream of electrons. It is not possible to treat the money received by Lloyds Bank in London or its correspondent bank in New York as representing the proceeds of the payment order or of any other physical asset previously in its hands and delivered by it in exchange for the money.'

[*After examining the facts and reasoning of the Court of Appeal in* Banque Belge pour L'Etranger v Hambrouck *(above, 204), which was relied on by Agip, Fox LJ continued:*] Now, in the present case, the course of events was as follows. (1) The original payment order was in December signed by an authorised signatory. (2) The name of the payee was then altered to Baker Oil. (3) The altered order was then taken to Banque du Sud who complied with it by debiting the account of Agip with $518,822.92 and then instructing Lloyds Bank to pay Baker Oil. Banque du Sud also instructed Citibank in New York to debit its account with Citibank and credit Lloyds Bank with the amount of the order. (4) Lloyds Bank credited the money to Baker Oil's account on the morning of 7 January. (5) On 8 January, Lloyds Bank in pursuance of instructions from Baker Oil transferred the $518,822.92, which was the only sum standing to the credit of Baker Oil's account, to an account in the name of Jackson & Co. (6) Immediately before the transfer from Baker Oil, Jackson & Co.'s account was $7,911.80 in credit. In consequence of the transfer it became $526,734.72 in credit.

The inquiry which has to be made is whether the money paid to Jackson & Co's account 'was the product of, or substitute for, the original thing.' In answering that question I do not think that it matters that the order was not a cheque. It was a direction by the account holder to the bank. When Atkin LJ referred in the *Banque Belge* case to the 'original money' he was, I assume, referring to the money credited by Banque Belge (the plaintiff) to Hambrouck's account. Money from that account was the only money in Mlle Spanoghe's deposit account. It was not, therefore, difficult to say that the money in issue (i.e. the residue of Mlle Spanoghe's account) could be identified as the product of the original money. There were no complexities of tracing at all. Everything in Mlle Spanoghe's account could be identified as the product of the original money. There were no complexities of tracing at all. Everything in Mlle Spanoghe's account came from Hambrouck's account and everything in Hambrouck's account came from the credit in respect of the fraudulent cheque.

The position in the present case is much more difficult. Banque du Sud can be regarded as having paid with Agip's money but Lloyds Bank, acting as directed by Banque du Sud, paid Baker Oil with its own money. It had no other and, accordingly, took a delivery risk. It was, in the end, put in funds, but it is difficult to see how the origin of those funds can be identified without tracing the money through the New York clearing system. The money in the present case did get mixed on two occasions. The first was in the New York clearing system and the second was in Jackson & Co.'s own account. The judge held that the latter was of no consequence. I agree. The common law remedy attached to the recipient of the money and its subsequent transposition does not alter his liability. The problem arises at an earlier stage. What did Jackson & Co. receive which was the product of Agip's asset? Baker Oil was controlled for present purposes by Jackson & Co. but Baker Oil was paid by Lloyd's Bank which had not been put in funds from New York. It was subsequently recouped. But it is not possible to show the source from which it was recouped without tracing the money through the New York clearing system. The judge said [1990] Ch 265, 286:

> 'Unless Lloyds Bank's correspondent bank in New York was also Citibank, this involves tracing the money through the accounts of Citibank and Lloyds Bank's correspondent bank with the Federal Reserve Bank, where it must have been mixed with other money. The money with which Lloyds Bank was reimbursed cannot therefore, without recourse to equity, be identified as being that of the Banque du Sud.'

I respectfully agree with that view. Accordingly, it seems to me that the common law remedy is not available.

I should add this. Atkin LJ's approach in the *Banque Belge* case amounts virtually to saying that there is now no difference between the common law and equitable remedies. Indeed, the common law remedy might be wider because of the absence of any requirement of a fiduciary relationship. There may be a good deal to be said for that view but it goes well beyond any other case and well beyond the views of Bankes and Scrutton L JJ. And in the 70 years since the *Banque Belge* decision it has not been applied. Whether, short of the House of Lords, it is now open to the courts to adopt it I need not consider. I would in any event feel difficulty in doing so in the present case where, as I indicate later, it seems to me that the established equitable rules provide an adequate remedy in relation to this action . . .

Butler-Sloss and **Beldam LJJ** concurred.

NOTES AND QUESTIONS

1. Was Fox LJ correct in asserting that the money was paid under a mistake. If not, what was the 'unjust factor'?

2. Why was it necessary for the claimant to satisfy the rules of tracing? (For further discussion of the approach to tracing at common law in this case, see below, 650.)

3. Was the Court of Appeal correct to conclude that Agip, rather than the Banque du Sud, had title to sue?

4. In the following extract, Ewan McKendrick criticizes much of the reasoning of the Court of Appeal in the *Agip* case.

• E McKendrick, 'Tracing Misdirected Funds' [1991] *LMCLQ* 378

TITLE TO SUE

The defendants' first argument was that Agip did not have title to sue because it was their bank, Banque du Sud, which was the proper plaintiff. The defendants argued that, in paying $518,000 to Baker Oil, Banque du Sud had acted without authority from Agip because the order for payment was a forgery. The relationship between a banker and customer, being one of debtor and creditor, and the bank having had no authority from Agip to pay Baker Oil, the defendants argued that it followed that the bank had paid Baker Oil with their own money and were not entitled to debit Agip's account. The Court of Appeal, adopting a pragmatic approach, rejected the defendants' argument. They held that 'in practical terms' the bank had paid Baker Oil with Agip's money and that the 'substance of the matter' was that money standing to the credit of Agip had been paid to Baker Oil in accordance with the (supposed) order. This conclusion appears to be inconsistent with *Banque Belge pour l'Etranger v Hambrouck*,[1] where the defendants argued[2] that the bank were not entitled to recover the proceeds of Hambrouck's fraud because, as between themselves and M. Pelabon, they were arguing that M. Pelabon must bear the loss. The Court of Appeal rejected this argument, Scrutton LJ, stating that it was 'clear . . . that the money actually obtained by Hambrouck was *the Bank's money*, even if they might debit their payments to the account of another'.[3] Yet in *Agip* the Court of Appeal bent over backwards to conclude that it was Agip's money and not the bank's money which had been paid to Baker Oil. It is suggested that the Court of Appeal in *Hambrouck* was correct to conclude that it was the bank's money which had been paid out, because it is a fundamental principle of banking law that a banker who pays money without a mandate cannot debit the customer's account. And, if the bank cannot debit the customer's account, then it must be the bank's money and not the customer's money which is paid out. Given the confusion which surrounds this issue and since its resolution was crucial to the success of Agip's claim, it is very difficult to understand why the House of Lords has refused leave to appeal and has thrown away the opportunity to consider these issues at the highest level.

The refusal of the House of Lords to grant leave to appeal strongly suggests that the House was of the opinion that the decision of the Court of Appeal on this point was correct. If this is so, what are the limits of the decision? In particular, what is the significance of the fact that Agip has unsuccessfully brought proceedings against Banque du Sud in Tunisia to have its account re-credited? There is some evidence that this factor weighed heavily with the Court of Appeal; thus Fox LJ, stated, the 'reality is a payment by the customer *at any rate in a case where the customer has no right to require a re-crediting of his account*'.[4] But is the bringing of such a claim against the bank a prerequisite to bringing a claim against the recipient of the money or does the customer now have a free choice; either he can sue his own bank to have his account recredited or the third party recipient? For example, in *Banque Belge v Hambrouck*, could M. Pelabon have brought an action against Mlle Spanoghe? Unless the bringing of a claim against the bank is a prerequisite, it would appear that he could have done.[5] Furthermore, what would have been the case in *Agip* if Banque du Sud had brought an action against the defendants? On the basis of *Banque Belge*, it would appear that their claim to recover the money would, subject to their ability to trace, have been successful. The fact that they were refusing to re-credit Agip's account would appear to be irrelevant, because in *Banque Belge* the bank were entitled to bring a claim even though it seemed that they had debited M. Pelabon's account and were refusing to re-credit it.[6] Therefore, both the bank and the customer would now appear to have a cause of action against the recipient, although, presumably, the recipient cannot be required to pay out twice.

Finally, can a bank now use *Agip* as authority to justify a refusal to re-credit a customer's account on the ground that, where it does so refuse, the customer has a cause of action against the recipient of the money or persons who knowingly assist in its dissipation? It is suggested that it is extremely improbable that the Court of Appeal intended by its decision to enable a bank to refuse, with

---

1 [1921] 1 KB 321.   2 *Ibid.* 323.   3 *Ibid.* 328–9 (emphasis added).
4 Emphasis added.
5 It would appear that M. Pelabon did actually commence an action against *Banque Belge* but, according to Atkin LJ (*ibid.* 331), the action had been withdrawn.
6 *Ibid.* 328 (Scrutton LJ) and 331 (Atkin LJ).

justification, to re-credit a customer's account in a case such as this. But the difficulty with the decision of the Court of Appeal is that it simply does not face up to these and other difficult questions; its emphasis is confined to the 'realities' of the situation. But an appellate court has responsibilities which transcend the facts of the case before it. It must explain how its decision is consistent with other established principles of law, its relationship with these principles and the limits of the new principle which it has laid down. In the present case the Court of Appeal has signally failed to do this.

THE GROUND OF RESTITUTION

The second issue relates to the ground upon which Agip sought restitution of the money paid. Both Millett, J, and the Court of Appeal held that, at least in relation to the claim at common law, the ground was mistake. There are two points which must be considered here. The first is whether the ground of claim was indeed mistake. The difficulty with this view is that, as the defendants pointed out, Agip were not mistaken at all; they were 'simply the victim of a fraud'. But the Court of Appeal held that the bank were Agip's agents and that Agip were entitled to recover a mistaken payment made by an authorized agent acting within its instructions. The difficulty with this view is the obvious one, namely that Banque du Sud did not pay as Agip's agent, because the payment order was a forgery and so the bank had no authority from Agip to pay. Once again, the Court of Appeal returned to the so-called 'realities' of the situation; the bank 'intended to pay as agent of Agip', the payment order emanated from within Agip, the bank had no reason to doubt its authenticity and it had refused to re-credit Agip's account. But, while it may be true to say that, as a matter of fact, the payment order was given effect to 'as if it were a proper order', the conclusion does not follow, as the Court of Appeal thought it did, that the 'Order must be regarded as having been paid by [the bank] as agent for Agip'. This is to confuse what happened in fact with what happened in law. As a matter of law, it was not a proper payment order and it is suggested that the bank did not act as the authorized agent of Agip in making the payment.

This strained line of reasoning could have been avoided if the Court of Appeal had accepted the argument put forward by Professor Birks[7] that the ground of claim is not mistake but ignorance; that is to say, Agip were ignorant of the payment of their money to Baker Oil and, on that ground, were entitled to the return of the money paid. It is suggested that the adoption of this line of reasoning ought to have led to the conclusion that the liability of the recipient was strict because, given that the liability of the recipient of a mistaken payment is strict,[8] the party who is entirely unaware of the transfer of his money should not, logically, be in a worse position than the party who knows of the transfer but is mistaken. This approach also avoids the artificiality involved in stating that Agip were mistaken or in arguing that the bank paid as authorized agents of Agip. The importance of this argument is not confined to *Agip*. It can be applied to cases such as *Re Diplock*,[9] the ground of claim there being the ignorance of the next of kin of the payment to the charities of money to which they were entitled.[10] The difficulty with Professor Birks' view is that English law has not yet recognized ignorance as a ground of restitution, although it does not appear that the argument has ever been put to an English court. But it is difficult to deny the logic of the argument and it needs to be explored by the English courts.

---

7 'Misdirected Funds: Restitution from the Recipient' [1989] *LMCLQ* 296.

8 *Kelly v Solari* (1841) 9 M & W 54.

9 [1948] Ch 465, aff'd. as *Ministry of Health v Simpson* [1951] AC 251.

10 The difficulty with the mistake argument in its application to *Diplock* is two-fold. The first is that the next of kin were not mistaken, the second that the executors' mistake was one of law and such mistakes do not generally give rise to a right of recovery. Both difficulties are avoided by the adoption of the 'ignorance' argument.

There is, however, a second point. Let it be assumed that the ground of claim was indeed mistake. Now, a further problem arises because, in the case of a mistaken payment, the knowledge of the recipient is irrelevant, because it is clear from cases such as *Kelly v Solari*[11] that innocence of the payee is no defence even against a payor who is careless. The difficulty for Agip was that, although they had a cause of action at law (mistake), they could not trace because it was held that the common law could not identify the proceeds of the fraud in the hands of the defendants. But the plaintiffs were held to be entitled to trace in equity, and could they not have argued that their ground of claim in equity was also mistake? The point was not argued and it is a noticeable feature of the case that mistake is discussed only in relation to the claim at law; when we turn to the claim in equity, the talk is of 'knowing receipt' and 'knowing assistance'. This is odd because, having worked so hard to turn the case into one of mistake, the argument from mistake is instinctively abandoned whenever we enter into the realms of equity. The plaintiff orientation of the common law claim is thus turned into the defendant orientation of the equitable claim, without this switch being explained or even noticed. Analytically, this is very difficult to explain. Once it was concluded that Agip were mistaken they remained mistaken whether the claim was brought at law or in equity. On the other hand, the defendants in *Chase Manhattan Bank N.A. Ltd v Israel-British Bank (London) Ltd*[12] argued that a person who pays money to another as a result of a mistake of fact does not have in equity any right or remedy against the payee. Goulding, J, responded by placing reliance upon the following passage from Story's *Commentaries on Equity and Jurisprudence as Administered in England and America*,[13] which he said was in accord with the general principles of equity as applied in England:

> [i]t is true that courts of law now entertain jurisdiction in many cases of [mistake] where formerly the remedy was solely in Equity; as, for example, in an action of assumpsit for money had and received, where the money cannot conscientiously be withheld by the party . . . But this does not oust the general jurisdiction of Courts of Equity over the subject-matter, which had for many years before been in full exercise, although it renders a resort to them for relief less common, as well as less necessary than it formerly was.

Therefore, it is suggested that there is support for the view that a mistaken payment can be recovered in equity, although many of the cases are cases of payments made under a mistake of law[14] or where the plaintiff switches to a claim in equity because he wishes to make a proprietary claim.[15] And so it is suggested that, if Agip were indeed mistaken, they ought to have had a claim to the return of the sum paid, irrespective of the knowledge of the defendants.

COMMON LAW TRACING

The third issue relates to the scope of common law tracing, which emerges from *Agip* considerably reduced in significance. At first instance Millett, J, held that common law tracing served an 'evidential purpose',[16] which enabled the defendant to be identified as the recipient of the plaintiff's money. The crucial and traditional limitation upon common law tracing is that it cannot trace into a mixed fund. But in *Agip* that was not a problem because the money was not mixed, there being no other money in the Baker Oil account. Nevertheless, both Millett, J, and the Court of Appeal held that Agip could not trace at common law.

---

11 (1841) 9 M & W 54.   12 [1981] Ch 105, 113.   13 Vol. 2 (2nd edn), para. 1256.
    14 *Daniell v Sinclair* (1881) 6 App Cas 181, 190–1; *Murray v Baxter* (1914) 18 CLR 622, 630; *Rogers v Ingham* (1876) 3 Ch D 351, 356; *Re Diplock* [1948] Ch 465.
    15 As in *Chase Manhattan Bank NA Ltd v Israel—British Bank (London) Ltd* [1981] Ch 105.
    16 [1990] Ch 264, 285.

The first reason given by Millett, J, was that the money was transmitted by telegraphic transfer and '[n]othing passed between Tunisia and London but a stream of electrons'.[17] There was no physical asset which the common law could follow and the common law was thus paralysed by modern technology. This view requires one to draw a clear distinction between a cheque and an electronic transfer because there is a physical asset (the cheque) in the former case but not in the latter case. Although the Court of Appeal quoted this section of the judgment of Millett, J, without express disapproval, Fox LJ, also stated that he did not think that, in deciding whether the money paid to Jackson & Co. was 'the product of or substitute for the original thing', it mattered that the payment order was not a cheque. Had Fox LJ, been in agreement with Millett, J, the distinction would have been vital. It therefore remains unclear whether the common law can trace funds transferred by telegraphic transfer.

The second objection to common law tracing lay in the argument that the common law could not trace through the New York clearing system. The crucial factor, according to the Court of Appeal, was that Lloyds Bank, in taking a delivery risk, had paid Baker Oil with their own money. Although Lloyds were subsequently reimbursed by Citibank, the money received by Lloyds could not be identified with the money which left Citibank without tracing through the New York clearing system, which the common law could not do. The difficulty with this view lies in reconciling it with *Banque Belge v Hambrouck*, where the plaintiffs were held to be entitled to trace into the bank account of Mlle Spanoghe. The Court of Appeal in *Agip* emphasized that Mlle Spanoghe did not mix the money received from Hambrouck with any other money in her account and that everything in Hambrouck's account came from the proceeds of his fraud. But how did the court know that everything in Hambrouck's account came from the proceeds of his fraud? It must be remembered that Hambrouck paid the cheques into his account at Farrow's Bank and that Farrow's Bank cleared the cheques through the London and South Western Bank which, in turn, collected the cheques from Banque Belge. In order to reach the conclusion that everything in Hambrouck's account came from the proceeds of his fraud, did Banque Belge not have to trace through the clearing system? Writing extra-judicially, Sir Peter Millett has conceded that in *Banque Belge* it was assumed that it was possible to trace through the clearing system, although he notes that the contrary was not argued.[18] If this is so, what is the difference between *Agip* and *Banque Belge*? The view of Millett, J, is that the common law could follow the cheque in *Banque Belge* but that in *Agip* there was no physical asset which the common law could follow. The difficulty with this view is, as we have noted, that the Court of Appeal does not appear to have accepted it. The view of the Court of Appeal was that the crucial factor in *Agip* was that Lloyds had paid Baker Oil with their own money before being reimbursed. But in *Banque Belge* there was no enquiry as to whether Farrow's Bank had allowed Hambrouck to draw against the cheques before they collected them. The matter was treated as being irrelevant and, if it was irrelevant in *Banque Belge*, it is not at all clear why it should be a relevant factor in *Agip*. The relationship between these two cases is therefore in need of further consideration.

MONEY HAD AND RECEIVED AND SUBSEQUENT RECIPIENTS

A related issue which arose for consideration was whether an action for money had and received could lie against a subsequent recipient of misdirected funds. There are a number of possible views; it may never lie, only sometimes, always, or only in the second measure (that is, for the value retained rather than the value received). The nub of this issue would appear to relate to the nature of a tracing claim. Writing extra-judicially, Sir Peter Millett has expressed the view that tracing at common law served an evidential purpose, that the cause of action was for money had and received and that the

---

17 *Ibid.* 286.   18 (1991) 107 *LQR* 71, 74 n. 7.

'common law claim for money had and received is a personal and not a proprietary claim'.[19] He has argued that there is 'something distinctly odd about a purely personal receipt-based remedy lying against successors in title of the original recipient'[20] and he denies that there is such a thing as a 'proprietary claim with a personal remedy'.[21] The difficulty with this argument relates to the words 'proprietary claim'. Sir Peter Millett appears to assume that a claim against a subsequent recipient must necessarily be proprietary, so that, for example, in *Banque Belge* the only sum which could be recovered from Mlle Spanoghe was the sum remaining in her bank account. But, if the function of tracing is simply identification, that is to say to identify the money in the hands of the defendant as having been the money paid out by the plaintiff, then the identification of the money of itself tells us nothing about the remedy to which the plaintiff is entitled. He may ask for a proprietary remedy or a personal remedy. As Professor Birks has argued, 'even the personal claim does require an element of tracing, to the extent necessary to show that the recipient did receive the money'.[22] There is therefore nothing anomalous about seeking a personal remedy after completing the tracing exercise.

But let us assume that Sir Peter Millett is correct and that a claim does not lie against a subsequent recipient who has parted with the money. A vital question now arises which is: who is a subsequent recipient? Professor Birks has argued that the distinction between a first and a subsequent recipient is 'quite arbitrary' because it 'turns on how the fund happens to be misdirected'.[23] Writing extra-judicially, Sir Peter Millett has conceded this point but only 'if the dishonest employee himself is treated as the first recipient'.[24] He continues by arguing that there is a real distinction 'between the immediate recipient from the dishonest employee and later recipients' because the 'action against the immediate recipient is based on the fraud of the defendant or of the person through whom he claims; the claim against the later recipient is not'. This re-definition of a 'subsequent recipient' has considerable implications for *Banque Belge v Hambrouck*. In his judgment in *Agip* Millett, J, appeared to be of the opinion that Mlle Spanoghe was a subsequent recipient, because he interpreted the case as authority for the proposition that 'an action for money had and received is not limited to the immediate recipient or his principal but may be brought against a *subsequent transferee* into whose hands the money be followed and who still retains it'.[25] But, if the dishonest employee, Hambrouck, is not treated as the first recipient, then Mlle Spanoghe becomes the first recipient and an action for money had and received should lie against her for the amount received ('the first measure of restitution') and not simply for the amount retained ('the second measure'). Yet this is the very point which Millett, J, denies in his judgment. And, if an action lies against Mlle Spanoghe, why not any later recipient? The subsequent recipient is as innocent as the first and the action against the sub-sequent recipient is as much based on fraud as is the action against the immediate recipient. The point is that the common law has not recognized innocence as a defence; the defence is bona fide purchase *for value*. It is the interposition of an innocent purchaser for value which defeats the claim, not the interposition of a mere innocent recipient. For example, in *Lipkin Gorman v Karpnale Ltd* it was not doubted that the defendants were innocent; the issue which was before the House of Lords was whether or not they had provided value. Thus, the relevant distinction should not be between a first and a subsequent recipient but between a purchaser who has provided value and one who has not. Nevertheless, it must be conceded that most recent cases have been brought against the first recipient from the dishonest party and it is difficult to find an example of a successful claim against a later recipient who has parted with the money. The point may therefore be regarded as an open one but it is suggested that there is no insuperable barrier to the recognition of such a claim.

The fact that there is no insuperable barrier to the recognition of such a claim suggests that the reasons behind these restrictions upon the common law claim lie not in logic but in reasons of policy.

---

19 (1991) 107 *LQR* 71, 76.   20 *Ibid*. 77.   21 *Ibid*.   22 Birks [1989] *LMCLQ* 296, 311.
23 *Ibid*. 339.   24 (1991) 107 *LQR* 71, 79.   25 [1990] Ch 264, 287 (emphasis added).

Both Millett, J, and the Court of Appeal were of the opinion that the principles which had been worked out in equity were more 'appropriate' than the common law rules. Thus, it was argued that: liability at common law is 'fortuitous', because it depends on whether or not the money has been mixed prior to its receipt; it is strictly receipt-based and therefore does not apply to those who participate in the fraud but do not receive the proceeds; liability is strict, not fault-based; and, finally, there are no adequate defences, principally because English law had not at that time recognized a defence of change of position. These arguments are all contestable (and their consideration lies beyond the scope of the present paper) but the point which must be grasped is that this is a deliber-ate policy choice by the courts. They have chosen to place greater reliance upon those cases in equity which support the imposition of fault-based liability, thus narrowing the scope of the common law rules and leaving out of account those cases in equity, such as *Re Diplock*,[26] which support the imposition of strict liability.

[*The article goes on to discuss tracing in equity, knowing receipt and knowing assistance*].

- *Lipkin Gorman v Karpnale Ltd* [1991] 2 AC 548, House of Lords

See above, 28–39 (including the notes and questions).

In the following extract, Ewan McKendrick analyses the *Lipkin Gorman* case in terms of the four essential ingredients of an unjust enrichment claim.

- E McKendrick, 'Restitution, Misdirected Funds and Change of Position'
  (1992) 55 *MLR* 377

A LAW OF RESTITUTION BASED ON UNJUST ENRICHMENT

The point of greatest significance which emerges from the speeches of their Lordships is their clear recognition of an independent law of restitution based upon unjust enrichment. This recognition has been slow in coming and, as recently as 1977, Lord Diplock stated that 'no general doctrine of unjust enrichment is recognised in English law.'[1] Nor were the sceptics confined to the judiciary; Professor Atiyah, writing about the same time, also expressed hostility to the recognition of an independent law of restitution. For many years the modern law of restitution was hidden away under the label of quasi-contract, which led many to believe that the law of restitution (or quasi-contract) was in fact part of the law of contract. Indeed, signs of this confusion were evident as recently as 1990, when, in *Guinness plc v Saunders*,[2] Lord Templeman stated that a claim for a *quantum meruit* was in fact 'based on an implied contract' so that a bar to the recognition of an enforceable contract also operated as a bar to the restitutionary claim. This analysis was given a frosty reception within the academic community but was not, at the time, expressly refuted by any of their Lordships. Yet, just over a year later, the 'implied contract' theory of restitution has been clearly rejected by the House of Lords. With the exception of Lord Griffiths, who simply concurred with the judgments of Lord Goff and Lord Templeman, all of their Lordships invoked the language of unjust enrichment and recognised that the basis of a restitutionary claim lies in the fact that the defendant has been unjustly enriched at the expense of the plaintiff. Accordingly, the implied contract theory of restitution can be laid to rest and judges, practitioners and academics must now recognise and begin to come to grips with an independent law of restitution based upon unjust enrichment. Law teachers must now justify, if they can, their focus on contract and tort to the virtual exclusion of the law of restitution.

---

26 [1948] Ch 465.

1 *Orakpo v Manson Investments Ltd* [1978] AC 95, 104.
2 [1990] 2 AC 663, 689F–H, 692A and 693E–F.

THE STRUCTURE OF THE CLAIM

The existence of a law of restitution based upon unjust enrichment having been recognised, attention must now be focused upon the structure of a restitutionary claim. A clear structure is important because restitution lawyers have, in the past, been accused of 'well-meaning sloppiness of thought.'[3] Lord Goff was alive to this criticism when he said that:

> the recovery of money in restitution is not, as a general rule, a matter of discretion for the court. A claim to recover money at common law is made as a matter of right; and even though the underlying principle of recovery is the principle of unjust enrichment, nevertheless, where recovery is denied, it is denied on the basis of legal principle.

Restitution scholars have often recognised that there are four distinct stages to a restitutionary claim. At the first stage, the defendant must be enriched; at the second, it must be shown that that enrichment was 'at the expense of' the plaintiff; third, it must be shown that there is an 'unjust' factor, that is to say, there is some identifiable and principled basis upon which it can be said that the continued retention of the benefit by the defendant is unjust; finally, consideration must be given to whether any defences exist, either in whole or in part, to the restitutionary claim.

The first stage of this inquiry was easily satisfied because the defendants received money, and money, being the very measure of value, is incontrovertibly an enrichment. But problems emerged at the other three stages and these difficulties will be briefly highlighted in the remaining sections of this note.

'AT THE EXPENSE OF'

Adopting a 'common-sense' approach, one could readily conclude that the defendants were enriched 'at the expense of' the plaintiffs; Cass had stolen money from the plaintiffs which belonged to them and had gambled it away at the defendants' club. The difficulty in the way of this analysis was that there was Privy Council authority, which the House of Lords declined the invitation to overrule, for the proposition that, when Cass obtained money by drawing on the partnership bank account without authority, it was Cass and not the partnership who acquired legal title to the cash.[4] This conclusion appeared to place an insurmountable obstacle in the plaintiffs' path, but Lord Goff managed to find a way round it. He noted that the partnership bank account was in credit, thus constituting the bank the debtor of the partnership. He held that this debt created a chose in action which belonged to the plaintiffs at common law and that, on the basis of *Taylor v Plumer*,[5] the plaintiffs were entitled, or had a power, to follow that chose in action into its proceeds, namely the cash which was drawn by Cass from the client account. But at this point a further problem emerges because it must surely have been very likely that Cass mixed the sum which he drew out of the client account with his own money before he paid any money over to the club, and it is an established rule that the common law cannot trace into a mixed fund. Yet, astonishingly, the defendants conceded that, if the plaintiffs could 'establish legal title to the money in the hands of Cass, that title was not defeated by the mixing of the money with other money of Cass while in his hands.'[6] It is impossible, on the facts as they appear in the law reports, to ascertain the basis for such a concession because the defendants seem to have thrown away one of their strongest arguments. In fact, the whole shape of the argument before the House of Lords is skewed because the plaintiffs' claim was argued solely at law, although a claim in equity had been made at first instance. Indeed, the success of the common law claim contrasts rather oddly with the determined effort on the part of Millett J and the Court of

---

3 *Holt v Markham* [1923] 1 KB 504, 514, *per* Scrutton LJ.

4 Following *Union Bank of Australia Ltd v McClintock* [1922] 1 AC 240 and *Commercial Banking Co. of Sydney Ltd v Mann* [1961] AC 1.

5 (1815) 3 M & S 562.   6 [1991] 2 AC 548, 572H.

Appeal in *Agip (Africa) Ltd v Jackson*[7] to cut back on the scope of common law tracing, preferring to invoke the more 'appropriate' rules which have evolved in equity. The concessions made by the parties are, in fact, an extremely disappointing aspect of the case: we cannot tell the basis upon which the defendants' concession was made, and the effect of the plaintiffs' decision to proceed at common law only deprived the House of Lords of the opportunity to consider the relationship between common law and equitable tracing.

THE 'UNJUST' FACTOR

It is suggested that one of the most worrying features of *Lipkin Gorman* is the failure of the House of Lords to identify with any real clarity the 'unjust' factor or the ground of restitution. Indeed, Lord Templeman does not appear to identify any unjust factor at all. He posed the right question in that he asked himself whether the defendant club, which was enriched by the receipt of the money, was *unjustly* enriched, but he never answered his own question. He does refer to the fact that the defendants received the money under a contract with Cass which was void. But the voidness of a contract has never been recognised as a ground of restitution, as can be seen from a glance at cases on illegality and *ultra vires*, where the void nature of the contract does not, of itself, ground a restitutionary claim.

There were, in fact, a number of possible grounds of restitution. One, recently favoured by the Court of Appeal in *Agip (Africa) Ltd v Jackson*, was mistake but, as Lord Goff pointed out, the plaintiffs did not know that their money had been paid over to the defendants, so it could hardly be said that their intention to give was vitiated by mistake. The most obvious ground was, in fact, the one put forward by Professor Birks, namely ignorance,[8] that is to say, the plaintiffs were ignorant of the payment of their money to the club and, on that ground, were, subject to defences, entitled to the return of the money paid. But, disappointingly, no express reference was made by the House of Lords to this possible ground of restitution.

Lord Goff did, however, establish a ground of restitution, although that ground is not, perhaps, immediately obvious. He affirmed the need for the plaintiffs to 'establish a basis on which [they are] entitled to the money' and this he found on the ground that they could show that the money was their 'legal property.' So, where a plaintiff can establish that the money is his legal property, he 'may be entitled to succeed in a claim against the third party for money had and received to his use, though not if the third party has received the money in good faith and for a valuable consideration.' It is suggested that there are a number of objections to 'legal property' as a ground of restitution.

The first is that, as Lord Goff recognised, it will be a rare ground of claim because at common law a plaintiff cannot establish property in money after it has been mixed with other money. This is a significant practical limitation. For example, this ground would not have been available to the plaintiffs in *Agip v Jackson* because there it was held that the plaintiffs could not trace at law, either because the money was transmitted by telegraphic transfer or because the common law could not trace through the New York clearing system.

The second is that it can be misunderstood as a proprietary claim. Although the ground of claim was that the money was the legal property of the plaintiffs, Lord Goff was careful to emphasise that this was a personal claim and not a proprietary claim. The judgment of Lord Templeman is more ambiguous on this point because of his reliance upon and treatment of *Banque Belge pour l'Etranger v Hambrouck* and *Transvaal & Delagoa Bay Investment Co. Ltd v Atkinson*. The fact that he attached significance to the point that the club 'retained' the money can also be understood as support for the view that it was a proprietary claim. But the claim was clearly a personal one based upon the

---

7 [1990] Ch 265 (Millett J); aff'd [1991] Ch 547 (CA).

8 See, in particular, P. Birks, 'Misdirected Funds: Restitution from the Recipient' [1989] *LMCLQ* 296.

defendants' receipt of the plaintiffs' money and, once it was proved that the defendants had received the plaintiffs' money, what subsequently happened to the actual money received was irrelevant. In so far as Lord Templeman's judgment can be taken to support the view that this was a proprietary claim, then it is suggested that it is clearly wrong and must be rejected.

The third objection is that it overlaps with other unjust factors, such as mistake, and so cuts across the existing category of unjust factors. So, where the plaintiff's mistake is sufficiently fundamental to prevent property passing to the defendant, it would appear that the plaintiff now has two grounds of restitution, namely mistake and 'legal property.'

The fourth objection is that the plaintiffs could not actually show that the money was their legal property; the money was the legal property of Cass, and it was only 'traceably' theirs in the sense that, as a result of their power to trace, they could follow their chose in action into the money drawn by Cass from their account. So the ground of restitution must, on the facts of *Lipkin Gorman*, read 'traceably legal property.' And this leads us into a further objection which is that it is difficult to accept that establishing title to money at law is itself a ground of action. Tracing at common law simply performs an evidential function, namely to identify the defendant as the recipient of the plaintiff's money; it is not a cause of action, nor is it a remedy. Surely it is preferable to say that it is the fact that the plaintiff did not consent to or was ignorant of the transfer of his money which is the unjust factor, and not simply that the money can be identified in the defendant's hands as belonging to the plaintiff. But, accepting for the moment that identification at law of the plaintiff's money in the hands of the defendant is a ground of restitution, is it also a ground of restitution to establish that the money belongs to the plaintiff in equity? In one sense it is hard to say why it is not because, if a plaintiff can identify his property in the hands of a defendant, why should it matter that in one case the identification is carried out at law, but that in another it is carried out in equity? On the other hand, it can be argued that Lord Goff was concerned only with a common law claim, money had and received, and not a claim in equity and his ground of restitution is not 'property' but '*legal* property.' It can also be argued that 'equitable property' cannot, in itself, be a ground of restitution because the preponderance of authority in equity favours the view that the liability of a recipient is fault-based, or based on dishonesty, and is not strict. Unless one is prepared to subscribe to the view that liability in equity is strict, the ground of restitution would have to be described as 'dishonest (or negligent) receipt of the plaintiff's equitable property.' At this point, 'property' begins to look a rather unwieldy ground of restitution and it may also entrench the traditional, historical distinction between claims at law and claims in equity, with the former, as *Lipkin Gorman* demonstrates, being in principle strict and the latter being arguably fault-based or based upon dishonesty. This dichotomy can be explained in historical terms but is very difficult to justify analytically. Admittedly, the same conflict of authority both within equity and between common law and equity has to be resolved if 'ignorance' is accepted as the ground of restitution, but the title 'ignorance' does not in any way reflect the law—equity division and so a court applying ignorance as a ground of restitution is, it is suggested, less likely to accept the proposition that liability at law is strict, whereas liability in equity is based upon dishonesty or fault. It is therefore suggested that the 'property' analysis adopted by Lord Goff, while having its adherents, is not without its difficulties and further analysis may well demonstrate that it should be discarded in favour of 'ignorance.'

DEFENCES

At the fourth stage of the enquiry there were two defences in issue, namely *bona fide* purchase for value and change of position. We shall consider each of them briefly in turn.

(i) Bona Fide Purchase for Value

The defendants argued that they were not under an obligation to repay the money which they had received because they had acted *bona fide* and they were not volunteers; they had provided consideration for the cash received from Cass in the form of the gambling services which they provided at the club and the chips which Cass had used in the club. But the House of Lords rejected their arguments.

The first point considered by Lord Goff was whether the supply of chips in exchange for money constituted the provision of consideration. Lord Goff considered this issue in two stages. The first was whether the exchange of chips for cash constituted the provision of consideration; the second was the impact of s. 18 of the Gaming Act 1845 which renders contracts by way of gaming and wagering void.

In relation to the first point, Lord Goff gave an example of chips being used in a shop on the same basis as chips were used in the casino. He held that, when the shop gave customers chips in exchange for cash, the transaction was analysed as a gratuitous deposit and so the shop gave no consideration for the money proffered by the customer. Although it could be argued that the shop gave consideration in the form of a promise to repay the sum received subject to a draw-down in relation to the goods purchased from the store, this was dismissed as a 'technical' approach, Lord Goff preferring to adopt a 'common sense' approach. This 'common sense' approach has considerable practical significance for banks because it was held that a bank with which money was deposited by an innocent donee from a thief cannot claim to be a *bona fide* purchaser of money simply by virtue of the fact of the deposit of the money. If the liability of the recipient is indeed strict, then this appears to create difficulties for banks because the defence of *bona fide* purchase is removed from them, although they may be able to argue that they were not recipients of the money (because they did not receive the money beneficially), or they may be able to avail themselves of the defence of change of position.

In relation to the effect of s. 18 of the Gaming Act, it was held that the club could not argue that they had provided consideration where the bet was unsuccessful because the promise to pay on a successful bet was void and so could not constitute consideration and, where the bet was successful, the club could not argue that it had provided consideration because the club was under no legal obligation to pay the money, and so in law it was a gift to the gambler by the casino. Yet this is to take the 'technical' approach which Lord Goff expressly refused to take in relation to the exchange of chips for cash; the 'common sense' approach would surely state that the money paid by the casino to the gambler was paid as a matter of obligation, not gift.

This leads us to the second argument, an argument which found favour with Parker LJ in the Court of Appeal, namely that every time Cass placed a bet he obtained in exchange the chance of winning and of being paid, and that the club therefore did provide value. This, too, was rejected by Lord Goff on the same 'technical' ground that a gambler has no 'legal right' to the winnings, which are, in law, paid to him as a matter of gift. Again, it is suggested, it would have been more consistent with 'common sense' or reality to conclude that the provision of gambling services did constitute the provision of value rather than conclude that the making of bets and the payment of winnings were two unrelated gifts.

Therefore, it is suggested that, subject to two possible counter-arguments, the defence of *bona fide* purchase should have been available to the defendants. The first is that it has been argued that *bona fide* purchase cannot operate as a defence to a personal restitutionary claim but that it is, in fact, a species of change of position.[9] But Lord Goff expressly rejected this argument, although he did concede that change of position was 'akin' to *bona fide* purchase. The second argument is derived from the policy of the legislation, namely that the policy behind the Gaming Act 1845 prevented the defendants from bringing the value which they had provided into account. The difficulty with this view is that the defendants were permitted, for the purposes of the defence of change of position, to bring the value of their services into account in the form of the winnings which they had paid to Cass, and it

---

9 See Sir Peter Millett, 'Tracing the Proceeds of Fraud' (1991) 107 *LQR* 71, at 82.

is not at all easy to formulate the policy in terms that permitted the defendants to bring into account the winnings which they had paid to Cass but not other services which they had provided for him.

(ii) The Defence of Change of Position

Finally, the defendants argued that they had changed their position as a result of the receipt of the plaintiffs' money. The difficulty which the defendants faced here was that the authorities were against the recognition of such a defence. But these authorities were swept aside by Lord Goff, and the defence was welcomed into English law on the ground that 'where an innocent defendant's position is so changed that he will suffer an injustice if called upon to repay or to repay in full, the injustice of requiring him to repay outweighs the injustice of denying the plaintiff restitution.' At this point in time, it is rather difficult to assess the likely impact of the recognition of the defence because their Lordships stated that it is to be developed on a case by case basis. But there are a number of pointers given in the judgment of Lord Goff. The first is that the mere fact that the recipient has spent the money does not, of itself, entitle him to invoke the defence because the expenditure might have been incurred by him in any case in the ordinary course of events. Second, the defence will not be available to a person who changes his position in bad faith or to a person who is a wrongdoer. Third, the existence of the defence might encourage the recognition of a right to restitution in a broader range of circumstances than is the case at present, because a court will be secure in the knowledge that it has available to it a defence of change of position which can protect the defendant's interest in the stability of his receipts. Thus, future courts might be more inclined to follow the more liberal approach to the recovery of money paid under a mistake of fact adopted by Robert Goff J (as he then was) in *Barclays Bank Ltd v W. J. Simms & Son*,[10] or even to conclude that mistake of law can, in principle, ground a restitutionary claim. Finally, the recognition of the defence might encourage a 'more consistent approach to tracing claims' with common defences being recognised to claims whether they are brought at law or in equity.

A number of problems remain to be resolved in the future. The first is that the basis of the defence remains unclear and it must not be allowed to depend upon the discretion of the individual judge. The second is that its relationship with estoppel must be worked out. It is suggested that estoppel will not wither away in the light of the recognition of the defence of change of position. Plaintiffs may still have an interest in invoking estoppel because it cannot operate *pro tanto* and because the detrimental reliance necessary to trigger an estoppel may be less than that required for a change of position. The final problem lies in applying the defence to the facts of any given case, and the application of the defence to the facts of *Lipkin Gorman* was, actually, extremely problematic. Lord Templeman, joined on this point by Lord Bridge and Lord Ackner, adopted a robust approach and held that, in ascertaining the extent to which the club was enriched, its winnings and losses had to be aggregated so that the club was bound to repay to the plaintiffs the sum of £154,685, which represented its net winnings. Lord Goff was more troubled by this aspect of the case, in particular whether the club was entitled to bring into account each winning payment they had made to Cass, or whether each bet was a separate transaction so that the winnings paid out on one bet could not be set against another bet. After some hesitation, Lord Goff concluded that, 'on the facts of the present case,'[11] the fairest approach was to aggregate the bets so that the club was entitled to bring into account the winnings which had been paid to Cass and it was therefore only liable to repay the net winnings.

---

10 [1980] QB 677.

11 There may, however, be other cases where this conclusion will not be appropriate. One example, provided by Professor Birks, [1991] *LMCLQ* 473, 493, arises where the gambler steals money from two different people and places a winning bet with the money stolen from one party and a losing bet with the money stolen from the other. In such a case, it may be more 'appropriate' to treat the bets separately from each other and not aggregate them.

NOTES AND QUESTIONS

1. Do you agree with McKendrick's suggestion that Lord Goff's 'property' analysis should be discarded in favour of 'ignorance'?

2. In a note on *Macmillan Inc. v Bishopsgate Investment Trust plc (No 3)* [1996] 1 WLR 387 in (1996) 10 *Trust Law Int.* 20, Graham Virgo briefly analyses *Lipkin Gorman* and concludes, at 24:

   Lipkin Gorman v Karpnale, the leading case on the law of restitution which recognised that there is an independent body of law based on the principle of reversing unjust enrichment, should not be regarded as having anything to do with unjust enrichment at all. The cause of action should have been treated as proprietary with restitutionary remedies being awarded to vindicate the plaintiff's continuing proprietary interest, an interest which continued beyond the point where the defendant received the money from the thief.

   For the same point, see Virgo, *The Principles of the Law of Restitution* (2006), 13. (For a similar approach, see Swadling's essay in W. Swadling (ed.), *The Limits of Restitutionary Claims* (1997).) Do you agree? Is it not fictional to say that the claim was based on a vindication of pre-existing proprietary rights? How, on this approach, can one explain the defence of change of position which was accepted by all their Lordships?

3. Is a problem with regarding ignorance as the unjust factor that the knowledge of Cass might be attributed to his fellow-partners?

4. Birks, *Introduction*, 174 argued that alongside 'ignorance' one must logically recognize an unjust factor of 'powerlessness'. This is needed in order to cover situations where, although there is no standard factor vitiating consent, such as mistake or duress, the claimant plainly does not consent to the defendant's enrichment at his expense and yet knows of it (for example, if Cass' fellow-partners had known of his stealing but were too terrified to stop it).

5. In *Trustees of the Property of FC Jones v Jones* (below, 651) a partner, after the partnership's bankruptcy and hence after the trustee in bankruptcy had taken title to the partnership's property, drew money from the partnership account and paid it to his wife. She used that money to trade on the potato futures market at a profit. The Court of Appeal held that the trustee in bankruptcy was entitled to that money (including the profit) which was in the wife's account. As can be seen at 651–5, Millett LJ reasoned simply that the husband, and hence the wife, had no title (legal or equitable) to the money. The title was in the trustee in bankruptcy who was therefore entitled to the money and to its traceable product. He therefore regarded the cause of action as 'legal title.' But is 'legal title' or 'interference with legal title' a recognized cause of action? Is it better to say that the claim was for unjust enrichment where the unjust factor was the ignorance or powerlessness of the other partners or the trustee in bankruptcy?

2. THE PREDOMINANT POSITION IN EQUITY—KNOWING RECEIPT AND DEALING

(1) DISHONESTY REQUIRED

- *Carl-Zeiss Stiftung v Herbert Smith & Co. (No 2)*
  [1969] 2 Ch 276, Court of Appeal

The Carl Zeiss company based in East Germany (the claimant) claimed to be equitable owner of the assets of the Carl Zeiss company based in West Germany. In this action the claimant sought to establish that the solicitors (the defendants) acting for the West

German company were personally liable to account as constructive trustees for the legal fees (allegedly belonging to the claimant) received from the West German company. The action was dismissed at first instance by Pennycuick J and the claimant's appeal was unsuccessful.

Sachs LJ: . . . I now turn to the issues raised by the plaintiffs' claim. When so doing I propose to assume that the plaintiffs will in the main action succeed in establishing that the relevant moneys are either their own property or held in trust for them by the West German foundation. The initial issue then for consideration is as follows. Upon the facts as alleged in the present statement of claim, had the defendant solicitors at the date of action brought such cognisance of the true ownership of the property or of the trusts as would make an ordinary stranger a constructive trustee of the relevant moneys?

. . .

The rule, as I understand it, is that no stranger can become a constructive trustee merely because he is made aware of a disputed claim the validity of which he cannot properly assess. Here it has been rightly conceded that no one can foretell the result of the litigation even if the plaintiffs were to prove all the facts they allege.

Thus, to my mind, the plaintiffs fail at an early stage in their attempt to fix the defendant solicitors with appropriate cognisance. It seems to me, however, that in order to succeed they would also have to overcome further obstacles which are insurmountable. . . .

The first obstacle emerges upon an examination of the submission for the plaintiffs that to fix a stranger with the appropriate responsibility it is sufficient to show that he has notice of the type exemplified by the terms of section 199 of the Law of Property Act, 1925; that is to say, to show that the existence of the trusts would have come to his knowledge if such inquiries had been made as ought reasonably to have been made by him. On the assumption that this is the right test (a point to which I will return) it is to be noticed that in many cases, and in particular in the present case, knowledge of the existence of a trust depends on knowledge first of the relevant facts and next of the law applicable to that set of facts. As to facts alleged in a statement of claim, Mr. Kerr [counsel for the defendants] was, to my mind, correct in submitting that a defendant's solicitor is under no duty to the plaintiffs to inquire into their accuracy for the purposes urged by Mr. Harman [counsel for the plaintiff], nor, where there is a likelihood of a conflict of evidence between his client's witnesses and those of the plaintiffs is he under any such duty to assess the result. . . . As to the law, they were similarly under no duty to the plaintiffs in such a complex matter either to make inquiries or to attempt to assess the result. . . .

Thus the plaintiffs fail again at this point to show that the defendant solicitors should be deemed to be cognisant of the trusts. . . .

The next point strongly pressed by Mr. Kerr was that in order to succeed the plaintiffs would have had to allege either fraud, or improper conduct as a solicitor, or wilful use of the moneys in breach of trust. In this behalf it has been Mr. Harman's case that once it was shown that the moneys were in law being used in breach of trust the section 199 test was once more decisive when considering whether a stranger is fixed with liability.

It does not, however, seem to me that a stranger is necessarily shown to be both a constructive trustee and liable for a breach of the relevant trusts even if it is established that he has such notice. As at present advised, I am inclined to the view that a further element has to be proved, at any rate in a case such as the present one. That element is one of dishonesty or of consciously acting improperly, as opposed to an innocent failure to make what a court may later decide to have been proper inquiry. That would entail both actual knowledge of the trust's existence and actual knowledge that what is being done is improperly in breach of that trust—though, of course, in both cases a person wilfully shutting his eyes to the obvious is in no different position than if he had kept them open. . . .

If, . . . it were right that the plaintiffs must establish fraud or improper dealing or wilful breach of trust in the sense that I have used those words, then, of course, they are bound to fail also on that point. . . .

I have thus come to the conclusion that the plaintiffs could not possibly . . . succeed in their claim against the defendant solicitors: they cannot establish that the defendant solicitors were cognisant either of the relevant trusts or of the moneys being employed in breach thereof. . . .

Edmund Davies LJ: The basic question raised by this appeal is whether the defendant solicitors hold the moneys of the plaintiffs as constructive trustees. The American Restatement of the Law of Restitution (1937) sets out to define a constructive trust by declaring in paragraph 160, p.640, that:

'Where a person holding title to property is subject to an equitable duty to convey it to another on the ground that he would be unjustly enriched if he were permitted to retain it, a constructive trust arises.'

English law provides no clear and all-embracing definition of a constructive trust. Its boundaries have been left perhaps deliberately vague, so as not to restrict the court by technicalities in deciding what the justice of a particular case may demand. But it appears that in this country unjust enrichment or other personal advantage is not a sine qua non. . . . Nevertheless, the concept of unjust enrichment has its value as providing one example among many of what, for lack of a better phrase, I would call 'want of probity,' a feature which recurs through and seems to connect all those cases drawn to the court's attention where a constructive trust has been held to exist. *Snell's Principles of Equity* expresses the same idea by saying, 26th edn (1966) at p. 201, that:

'A possible definition is that a constructive trust is a trust which is imposed by equity in order to satisfy the demands of justice and good conscience, without reference to any express or presumed intention of the parties.'

It may be objected that, even assuming the correctness of the foregoing, it provides no assistance, inasmuch as reference to 'unjust enrichment,' 'want of probity' and 'the demands of justice and good conscience' merely introduces vague concepts which are in turn incapable of definition and which therefore provide no yardstick. I do not agree. Concepts may defy definition and yet the presence in or absence from a situation of that which they denote may be beyond doubt. The concept of 'want of probity' appears to provide a useful touchstone in considering circumstances said to give rise to constructive trusts, and I have not found it misleading when applying it to the many authorities cited to this court. It is because of such a concept that evidence as to 'good faith,' 'knowledge' and 'notice' plays so important a part in the reported decisions. It is true that not every situation where probity is lacking gives rise to a constructive trust. Nevertheless, the authorities appear to show that nothing short of it will do. Not even gross negligence will suffice. [*Edmund Davies LJ then referred to* Williams v Williams *17 Ch D 437*; In re Blundell *40 Ch D 370*] The foregoing cases are but two illustrations among many to be found in the reports of that want of probity which, to my way of thinking, is the hall-mark of constructive trusts, however created.

The proposition which the plaintiffs' counsel described as fundamental to his case was stated in these terms: that a man who receives property which he knows (or ought to know) is trust property and applies it in a manner which he knows (or ought to know) is inconsistent with the terms of the trust is accountable in a suit by the beneficiaries of the trust. Although the soundness of that proposition was from the beginning accepted without qualification by the defendant solicitors, count-less cases were cited to demonstrate its validity. But it turned out that their citation was far from being a sleeveless errand, for it emerged that in not one of those cases was there any room for doubt that a trust already existed. None of them dealt with the fundamental assertion which has here been so strongly contested, and which Pennycuick J summarised by saying that:

'Counsel for the [plaintiffs] contends that [the defendant solicitors] have notice of the trust and if, at the end of the day, the trust is established in the main action, they will be accountable as constructive trustees for all moneys comprised in that trust which they have received from the West German company.'

But, as admittedly the West German foundation hold nothing for the plaintiffs under an express trust, and as, even despite the 13 long years that litigation between them has been proceeding, there has been no determination that any trust does exist, Mr. Harman has found himself compelled to go further if this appeal is to be put on its feet. He asserts, in effect, that for present purposes claims are the same as facts. More amply stated, he submits that it is sufficient to render the defendant solicitors accountable to the plaintiffs that they have (a) knowledge that the plaintiffs are claiming that the West German foundation holds all their assets in trust for them; (b) knowledge of the nature of the allegations advanced by the plaintiffs which (if established) are said to justify that claim; and (c) knowledge that all sums paid to them by the West German foundation must be and are derived solely and entirely from those assets which are the subject-matter of the plaintiffs' claim to be beneficial owners. Such knowledge on the part of the defendant solicitors being established, submits Mr. Harman, the preliminary issue raised by this appeal must here and now be determined in favour of the plaintiffs, and it matters not that, as he concedes, the defendant solicitors do not and cannot know for some time to come whether the plaintiffs will succeed in the main action in establishing their claim to a trust. He submits that it is equally immaterial that the plaintiffs accept that the defendant solicitors have throughout acted honestly as solicitors of the West German foundation and received fees, costs and disbursements solely in that capacity and proper in amount.

Like Sachs LJ, I am prepared for present purposes to assume that the plaintiffs will ultimately and at some unknown date succeed in establishing in the main action that the moneys in question are either their own property or are held in trust for them by the West German foundation. Nevertheless, in my judgment, none of the cases cited affords support for the contention that in the present circumstances the defendant solicitors are accountable to the plaintiffs, and it would be supererogation for me to attempt to add to my Lord's analysis of those cases.

. . .

Mr. Kerr gave the court a helpful distillation of the numerous authorities to which reference has already been made by my Lords. Their effect, he rightly submits, may be thus stated. (A). A solicitor or other agent who receives money from his principal which belongs at law or in equity to a third party is not accountable as a constructive trustee to that third party unless he has been guilty of some wrongful act in relation to that money. (B). To act 'wrongfully' he must be guilty of (i) knowingly participating in a breach of trust by his principal; or (ii) intermeddling with the trust property otherwise than merely as an agent and thereby becomes a trustee de son tort; or (iii) receiving or dealing with the money knowing that his principal has no right to pay it over or to instruct him to deal with it in the manner indicated; or (iv) some dishonest act relating to the money. These are, indeed, but variants or illustrations of that 'want of probity' to which I have earlier referred.

Do the demands of justice and good conscience bring the present case within any of the foregoing categories? In my judgment, the question is one which demands a negative answer. The law being reluctant to make a mere agent a constructive trustee, as Lord Selborne LC put it in *Barnes v Addy*, 9 Ch App. 244, 251–2, mere notice of a claim asserted by a third party is insufficient to render the agent guilty of a wrongful act in dealing with property derived from his principal in accordance with the latter's instructions unless the agent knows that the third party's claim is well-founded and that the principal accordingly had no authority to give such instructions. The only possible exception to such exception arises where the agent is under a duty to inquire into the validity of the third party's claim and where, although inquiry would have established that it was well-founded, none is instituted. But, as it is conceded by the plaintiffs that the defendant solicitors are under no such duty of inquiry, that further matter does not now call for consideration.

Danckwerts LJ delivered a concurring judgment.

NOTES AND QUESTIONS

1. Edmund Davies LJ and, more tentatively, Sachs LJ thought that 'want of probity' (that is, dishonesty) was required to render someone liable as a constructive trustee. But Sachs LJ and Danckwerts LJ held that the claim should fail, in any event, because the defendants could not be fixed with even constructive notice of the relevant *facts*.

2. The claim was for the value of the legal fees received by the solicitors. Is it helpful to describe the liability of the defendants in terms of their being liable *as constructive trustees?* That is, do those words add anything to saying that the liability is to account for the money (or other property) received? If not, is it preferable to avoid those words? Ask the same question after reading each of the next three cases.

● **Re Montagu's Settlement Trusts** [1987] Ch 264, Chancery Division

In breach of trust, trustees transferred a number of settled chattels (for example, furniture and pictures) to the tenth Duke of Manchester, who disposed of several of them. In an action brought by the eleventh Duke against the trustees of the family settlement and the executor of the tenth Duke, one issue that arose was whether the tenth Duke had been personally liable, as a constructive trustee, for the value of the chattels he had received and sold off (so that his estate was now liable). It was held that the tenth Duke had not been so liable.

Sir Robert Megarry V-C: . . . There is no suggestion that anyone concerned in the matter was dishonest. There was a muddle, but however careless it was, it was an honest muddle. Further, I do not think that the Duke was at any relevant time conscious of the fact that he was not entitled to receive the chattels and deal with them as beneficial owner. . . .

At the outset, I think that I should refer to *Baden, Delvaux and Lecuit v Société Generale pour Favoriser le Développement du Commerce et de l'Industrie en France SA* [1983] BCLC 325, a case which for obvious reasons I shall call 'the *Baden* case.' That case took 105 days to hear, spread over 7 months, and the judgment of Peter Gibson J is over 120 pages long. It was a 'knowing assistance' type of constructive trust, as distinct from the 'knowing receipt or dealing' type which is in issue before me. I use these terms as a convenient shorthand for two of the principal types of constructive trust. Put shortly, under the first of these heads a person becomes liable as a constructive trustee if he knowingly assists in some fraudulent design on the part of a trustee. Under the second head, a person also becomes liable as a constructive trustee if he either receives trust property with knowledge that the transfer is a breach of trust, or else deals with the property in a manner inconsistent with the trust after acquiring knowledge of the trust. It will be seen that the word 'knowledge' occurs under each head; and in the *Baden* case, at p. 407, the judge in effect said that 'knowledge' had the same meaning under each head.

. . .

Now until recently I do not think there had been any classification of 'knowledge' which corresponded with the classification of 'notice.' However, in the *Baden* case, at p. 407, the judgment sets out five categories of knowledge, or of the circumstances in which the court may treat a person as having knowledge. Counsel in that case were substantially in agreement in treating all five types as being relevant for the purpose of a constructive trust; and the judge agreed with them: p. 415. These categories are (i) actual knowledge; (ii) wilfully shutting one's eyes to the obvious; (iii) wilfully and recklessly failing to make such inquiries as an honest and reasonable man would make; (iv) knowledge of circumstances which would indicate the facts to an honest and reasonable man; and (v) knowledge of circumstances which would put an honest and reasonable man on inquiry. . . .

Of the five categories of knowledge set out in the *Baden* case, [Counsel for both sides in this case] accepted the first three. What was in issue was nos. (iv) and (v), namely, knowledge of circumstances which 'would indicate the facts to an honest and reasonable man' or 'would put an honest and reasonable man on inquiry.' On the view that I take of the present case I do not think that it really matters whether or not categories (iv) and (v) are included, but as the matter has been argued at length, and further questions on it may arise, I think I should say something about it.

[*After discussing the difference between notice and knowledge, and cases such as* Salangor United Rubber Estates Ltd v Cradock (No 3) *[1968] 1 WLR 1555,* Karak Rubber Co. Ltd v Burden (No 2) *[1972] 1 WLR 602,* Competitive Insurance Co. Ltd v Davies Investments Ltd *[1975] 1 WLR 1240, and* Belmont Finance Corp. Ltd v Williams Furniture Ltd (No 2) *[1980] 1 All ER 393, Sir Robert Megarry V–C continued:*]

I shall attempt to summarise my conclusions. In doing this, I make no attempt to reconcile all the authorities and dicta, for such a task is beyond me; and in this I suspect I am not alone. Some of the difficulty seems to arise from judgments that have been given without all the relevant authorities having been put before the judges. All I need do is to find a path through the wood that will suffice for the determination of the case before me, and to assist those who have to read this judgment.

(1) The equitable doctrine of tracing and the imposition of a constructive trust by reason of the knowing receipt of trust property are governed by different rules and must be kept distinct. Tracing is primarily a means of determining the rights of property, whereas the imposition of a constructive trust creates personal obligations that go beyond mere property rights.

(2) In considering whether a constructive trust has arisen in a case of the knowing receipt of trust property, the basic question is whether the conscience of the recipient is sufficiently affected to justify the imposition of such a trust.

(3) Whether a constructive trust arises in such a case primarily depends on the knowledge of the recipient, and not on notice to him; and for clarity it is desirable to use the word 'knowledge' and avoid the word 'notice' in such cases.

(4) For this purpose, knowledge is not confined to actual knowledge, but includes at least knowledge of types (ii) and (iii) in the *Baden* case [1983] BCLC 325, 407, i.e. actual knowledge that would have been acquired but for shutting one's eyes to the obvious, or wilfully and recklessly failing to make such inquiries as a reasonable and honest man would make; for in such cases there is a want of probity which justifies imposing a constructive trust.

(5) Whether knowledge of the *Baden* types (iv) and (v) suffices for this purpose is at best doubtful; in my view, it does not, for I cannot see that the carelessness involved will normally amount to a want of probity.

(6) For these purposes, a person is not to be taken to have knowledge of a fact that he once knew but has genuinely forgotten: the test (or a test) is whether the knowledge continues to operate on that person's mind at the time in question.

(7) (a) It is at least doubtful whether there is a general doctrine of 'imputed knowledge' that corresponds to 'imputed notice.' (b) Even if there is such a doctrine, for the purposes of creating a constructive trust of the 'knowing receipt' type the doctrine will not apply so as to fix a donee or beneficiary with all the knowledge that his solicitor has, at all events if the donee or beneficiary has not employed the solicitor to investigate his right to the bounty, and has done nothing else that can be treated as accepting that the solicitor's knowledge should be treated as his own. (c) Any such doctrine should be distinguished from the process whereby, under the name 'imputed knowledge,' a company is treated as having the knowledge that its directors and secretary have.

(8) Where an alleged constructive trust is based not on 'knowing receipt' but on 'knowing assist-ance,' some at least of these considerations probably apply; but I need not decide anything on that, and I do not do so.

From what I have said, it must be plain that in my judgment the Duke did not become a construct-ive trustee of any of the chattels. I can see nothing that affected his conscience sufficiently to impose a constructive trust on him: and even if, contrary to my opinion, all of the five *Baden* types of knowledge are in point, instead of only the first three, I do not think that he had any such knowledge. . . . Accordingly, I hold that the Duke never became a constructive trustee of any of the chattels.

NOTES AND QUESTIONS

1. Other cases favouring a dishonesty standard (that is, the first three points on the *Baden* scale) for 'knowing receipt' include *Competitive Insurance Co. Ltd v Davies Investments Ltd* [1975] 1 WLR 1240 (Goff J); *Eagle Trust plc v SBC Securities Ltd* [1992] 4 All ER 488 (Vinelott J, although the judgment is not easy to interpret on this issue); *Cowan de Groot Properties Ltd v Eagle Trust plc* [1992] 4 All ER 700 (Knox J); *Eagle Trust plc v SBC Securities Ltd (No 2)* [1996] 1 BCLC 121 (Arden J). That standard was also tentatively favoured by Scott LJ in *Polly Peck International plc v Nadir (No 2)* [1992] 4 All ER 769. In *Hillsdown Holdings plc v Pensions Ombudsman* [1997] 1 All ER 862 the defendants did not realize that what they were instigating constituted a breach of trust. Nevertheless they had full knowledge of it and took a very active part in it. Knox J was therefore able to conclude that they were less innocent than the defendants in the *Carl-Zeiss* and *Re Montagu* cases. The Pension Ombudsman was therefore correct to have regarded them as liable for knowing receipt.

2. At two points in the above extract, Sir Robert Megarry VC refers to the distinction between 'knowing receipt' (which this case was concerned with) and 'knowing assistance'. This distinction derives from Lord Selborne LC's famous obiter dictum in *Barnes v Addy* (1874) LR 9 Ch App. 244, 251–2:

> [S]trangers not are to be made constructive trustees merely because they act as the agents of trustees in transactions within their legal powers, transactions, perhaps of which a Court of Equity may disapprove, unless those agents receive and become chargeable with some part of the trust property, or unless they assist with knowledge in a dishonest and fraudulent design on the part of the trustees.

'Knowing assistance', unlike 'knowing receipt', does not necessitate the receipt of property and is essentially concerned with compensation for a wrong that is secondary or accessory to the breach of trust. This distinction was clearly brought out by Lord Nicholls, giving the judgment of the Privy Council, in *Royal Brunei Airlines Sdn Bhd v Tan* [1995] 2 AC 378. He said, at 386:

> It is not necessary [in this case] to . . . consider the essential ingredients of recipient liability. The issue on this appeal concerns only the accessory liability principle. Different considerations apply to the two heads of liability. Recipient liability is restitution-based, accessory liability is not.

The Privy Council went on to clarify that: (i) the necessary state of mind for knowing assistance (that is, the accessory liability principle) is dishonesty; (ii) there is no need for there to be a dishonest and fraudulent breach of trust; a breach of trust is sufficient and, accordingly, Lord Selborne's formulation in *Barnes v Addy* should be departed from; (iii) it is preferable to talk of a principle of 'dishonestly procuring or assisting a breach of trust or fiduciary obligation' rather than 'knowing assistance'; (iv) the term 'unconscionable' is better avoided in this con-text; (v) the scale of knowledge put forward in the *Baden* case is best forgotten. *Tan* was approved and applied in respect of 'dishonest assistance' in *Twinsectra Ltd v Yardley* [2002] UKHL 12, [2002] 2 AC 164. In examining what is meant by dishonesty in this context, the Privy Council in *Barlow Clowes International Ltd v Eurotrust International Ltd* [2005] UKPC 37, [2006] 1 All ER 333 has clarified that, contrary to what appeared to have been said in *Twinsectra*, dishonesty is to be assessed objectively. If by ordinary standards the defendant's mental state was dishonest, that is sufficient and it is irrelevant that the defendant has different standards.

(2) NEGLIGENCE HELD TO BE SUFFICIENT

- *Belmont Finance Corp v Williams Furniture Ltd (No 2)*
  [1980] 1 All ER 393, Court of Appeal

City Industrial Finance Ltd owned all the shares in Belmont. Mr James was chairman of the board of directors of City and Belmont. In breach of fiduciary duty, and contrary to the statutory bar on a company providing financial assistance for the purchase of its own shares, Belmont's directors paid £500,000 of Belmont's money under a scheme to help a company called Maximum (which was owned and controlled by a Mr Grosscurth) to buy shares in Belmont from City. Ultimately City received £489,000 of that money. Belmont successfully claimed that City was liable to account as a constructive trustee for that sum.

Buckley LJ: . . . I now come to the constructive trust point. If a stranger to a trust (a) receives and becomes chargeable with some part of the trust fund or (b) assists the trustees of a trust with knowledge of the facts in a dishonest design on the part of the trustees to misapply some part of a trust fund, he is liable as a constructive trustee (*Barnes v Addy per* Lord Selborne LC).

A limited company is of course not a trustee of its own funds: it is their beneficial owner; but in consequence of the fiduciary character of their duties the directors of a limited company are treated as if they were trustees of those funds of the company which are in their hands or under their control, and if they misapply them they commit a breach of trust. . . . So, if the directors of a company in breach of their fiduciary duties misapply the funds of their company so that they come into the hands of some stranger to the trust who receives them with knowledge (actual or constructive) of the breach, he cannot conscientiously retain those funds against the company unless he has some better equity. He becomes a constructive trustee for the company of the misapplied funds. . . .

In the present case, the payment of the £500,000 by Belmont to Mr Grosscurth, being an unlawful contravention of [statute], was a misapplication of Belmont's money and was in breach of the duties of the directors of Belmont. £489,000 of the £500,000 so misapplied found their way into the hands of City with City's knowledge of the whole circumstances of the transaction. It must follow, in my opinion, that City is accountable to Belmont as a constructive trustee of the £489,000 under the first of Lord Selborne LC's two heads. . . .

Goff LJ: . . . I turn next to the first limb of Belmont's case on constructive trust, that is to say, 'knowing receipt'. This is now relevant as against City only. As I have said, this does not depend on proof of fraud, nor in my judgment is Mr James's belief that 'the agreement was a good commercial proposition for Belmont to purchase Maximum's shares for £500,000' any answer.

What Belmont has to show is that the payment of the £500,000 was a misfeasance, which for this purpose is equivalent to breach of trust, that City received all or part of this money, and that it did so knowing, or in circumstances in which it ought to know, that it was a breach of trust. In fact City received £489,000 and that is the basic measure of any liability under this head. . . .

Then was the payment of the £500,000 a breach of trust? In my judgment it was, on two counts. First, and obviously, because, as I have held, the agreement was unlawful and the payment was made by Belmont for an illegal purpose, namely to facilitate the purchase by Grosscurth and his associates of Belmont shares. [*Goff LJ went on, secondly, to explain the conflict of interest and hence breach of fiduciary duty involved (by, e.g., the directors of Belmont to Belmont).*]

Then did City know, or ought it to have known, of the misfeasance or breach of trust? In my judgment the answer to that question must plainly be Yes, for they are fixed with all the knowledge that Mr James had. Now, he had actual knowledge of all the facts which made the agreement illegal and his belief that the agreement was a good commercial proposition for Belmont can be no more a defence to City's liability as constructive trustees than in conspiracy.

Apart from this, clearly, in my judgment, Mr James knew or ought to have known all the facts that I have rehearsed, showing that there was in any event a misfeasance apart from illegality. He knew of the conflict of interest. . . .

In my judgment, therefore, City are liable in damages as constructive trustees. 'The long arm of equity' is long enough to catch this sort of transaction . . .

Waller LJ concurred with **Buckley** and **Goff LJJ**.

NOTES AND QUESTIONS

1. There were official resolutions of the Belmont board authorizing the directors' activities and, in other parts of their judgments, Buckley LJ and Goff LJ make clear that the innocent directors were told what to do. In such circumstances, what is the 'unjust factor'? Can it be ignorance?

2. An alternative claim to render, *inter alia*, City liable as a constructive trustee under the second head of *Barnes v Addy* (that is, for knowing assistance in a dishonest and fraudulent scheme) failed because there had been no dishonest scheme on the part of the directors of Belmont, who genuinely believed that the scheme was a sound and *bona fide* commercial one. But this aspect of the decision cannot now stand with the Privy Council's judgment in *Royal Brunei Airlines v Tan* (above, 231, note 2) to the effect that there is no need for the breach of trust or fiduciary duty to be dishonest or fraudulent.

3. Other cases favouring a negligence standard for knowing receipt include *International Sales and Agencies Ltd v Marcus* [1982] 3 All ER 551; *Westpac Banking Corp. v Savin* [1985] 2 NZLR 41; *Powell v Thompson* [1991] 1 NZLR 597, 607–10; *Ninety Five Pty. Ltd v Banque Nationale de Paris* (1988) WAR 132, 176; *Citadel General Assurance Co. v Lloyds Bank Canada* (1997) 152 DLR (4th) 411. In *El Ajou v Dollar Land Holdings plc* [1993] 3 All ER 717, the claimant's money was held by an investment manager, Mr Murad. In breach of fiduciary duty he was bribed to invest the claimant's money, without the claimant's authority, in fraudulent share selling schemes operated by three Canadians. The proceeds of the fraudulent schmes were invested in the defendant company (DLH). The claimant sought restitution from DLH of the money it had received from the Canadians on the basis that it was a knowing recipient in equity. Millett J was prepared to assume (at 739) that a negligence, rather than a dishonesty, standard triggered liability in equity for knowing receipt. His decision that the recipient company did not have the requisite knowledge was overturned by the Court of Appeal [1994] 2 All ER 688 which adopted a different analysis of a company's knowledge.

(3) UNCONSCIONABILITY AS THE TEST

- *BCCI (Overseas) Ltd v Akindele* [2001] Ch 437, Court of Appeal

The defendant, Chief Akindele, entered into an agreement with ICIC Overseas Ltd, a company owned by the BCCI group, for the purchase of shares in the BCCI Group's holding company (BCCI Holdings). The agreement guaranteed the defendant a return of 15 per cent *per* annum on his investment of $US10 million. Unknown to the defendant, this agreement was part of a fraudulent scheme by officers of the BCCI group enabling the holding company to buy its own shares. In line with the agreement, BCCI Overseas Ltd paid the defendant $16,679 million. The liquidator of BCCI Overseas Ltd, the claimant, sought to hold the defendant liable to account for the $16,679 million as a constructive trustee for knowing receipt (and knowing assistance). The Court of Appeal held that the defendant was not liable.

Nourse LJ: . . . While a knowing recipient will often be found to have acted dishonestly, it has never been a prerequisite of the liability that he should.

. . .

Belmont Finance Corpn Ltd v William Furniture Ltd (No 2) 1 All ER 393 is clear authority for the proposition that dishonesty is not a necessary ingredient of liability in knowing receipt. There have been other, more recent, judicial pronouncements to the same effect. Thus in *Polly Peck International plc v Nadir (No 2)* [1992] 4 All ER 769, 777D Scott LJ said that liability in a knowing receipt case did not require that the misapplication of the trust funds should be fraudulent. While in theory it is possible for a misapplication not to be fraudulent and the recipient to be dishonest, in a practice such a combination must be rare. Similarly, in *Agip (Africa) Ltd v Jackson* [1990] Ch 265, 292A Millett J said that in knowing receipt it was immaterial whether the breach of trust was fraudulent or not. The point was made most clearly by Vinelott J in *Eagle Trust plc v SBC Securities Ltd* [1993] 1 WLR 484, 497:

> 'What the decision in *Belmont (No 2)* [1980] 1 All ER 393 shows is that in a "knowing receipt" case it is only necessary to show that the defendant knew that the moneys paid to him were trust moneys and of circumstances which made the payment a misapplication of them. Unlike a "knowing assistance" case it is not necessary, and never has been necessary, to show that the defendant was in any sense a participator in a fraud.'

. . .

The seminal judgment, characteristically penetrative in its treatment of authority and, in the best sense, argumentative, is that of Sir Robert Megarry V-C in *In re Montagu's Settlement Trusts* [1987] Ch 264. It was he who first plumbed the distinction between notice and knowledge.

. . .

The effect of Sir Robert Megarry V-C's decision, broadly stated, was that, in order to establish liability in knowing receipt, the recipient must have actual knowledge (or the equivalent) that the assets received are traceable to a breach of trust and that constructive knowledge is not enough.

. . .

In *Royal Brunei Airlines Sdn Bhd v Tan* [1995] 2 AC 378, which is now the leading authority on knowing assistance, Lord Nicholls of Birkenhead, in delivering the judgment of the Privy Council, said, at p 392G, that 'knowingly' was better avoided as a defining ingredient of the liability, and that in that context the *Baden* categorisation was best forgotten. Although my own view is that the categorisation is often helpful in identifying different states of knowledge which may or may not result in a finding of dishonesty for the purposes of knowing assistance, I have grave doubts about its utility in cases of knowing receipt. Quite apart from its origins in a context of knowing assistance . . . any categorisation is of little value unless the purpose it is to serve is adequately defined, whether it be fivefold, as in the *Baden* case [1993] 1 WLR 509, or twofold, as in the classical division between actual and constructive knowledge, a division which has itself become blurred in recent authorities.

What then, in the context of knowing receipt, is the purpose to be served by a categorisation of knowledge? It can only be to enable the court to determine whether, in the words of Buckley LJ in *Belmont Finance Corpn Ltd v Williams Furniture Ltd (No 2)* [1980] 1 All ER 393, 405, the recipient can 'conscientiously retain [the] funds against the company' or, in the words of Sir Robert Megarry V-C in *In re Montagu's Settlement Trusts* [1987] Ch 264, 273, '[the recipient's] conscience is sufficiently affected for it to be right to bind him by the obligations of a constructive trustee'. But, if that is the purpose, there is no need for categorisation. All that is necessary is that the recipient's state of knowledge should be such as to make it unconscionable for him to retain the benefit of the receipt.

For these reasons I have come to the view that, just as there is now a single test of dishonesty for knowing assistance, so ought there to be a single test of knowledge for knowing receipt. The recipient's state of knowledge must be such as to make it unconscionable for him to retain the benefit of the receipt. A test in that form, though it cannot, any more than any other, avoid difficulties of application, ought to avoid those of definition and allocation to which the previous categorisations have led. Moreover, it should better enable the courts to give commonsense decisions in the commercial context in which claims in knowing receipt are now frequently made. . . .

Knowing receipt—a footnote We were referred in argument to 'Knowing Receipt: The Need for a New Landmark', an essay by Lord Nicholls of Birkenhead in *Restitution Past, Present and Future* (1998) p 231, a work of insight and scholarship taking forward the writings of academic authors, in particular those of Professor Birks, Professor Burrows and Professor Gareth Jones. It is impossible to do justice to such a work within the compass of a judgment such as this. Most pertinent for present purposes is the suggestion made by Lord Nicholls, at p 238, in reference to the decision of the House of Lords in *Lipkin Gorman v Karpnale Ltd* [1991] 2 AC 548:

> 'In this respect equity should now follow the law. Restitutionary liability, applicable regardless of fault but subject to a defence of change of position, would be a better-tailored response to the underlying mischief of misapplied property than personal liability which is exclusively fault-based. Personal liability would flow from having received the property of another, from having been unjustly enriched at the expense of another. It would be triggered by the mere fact of receipt, thus recognising the endurance of property rights. But fairness would be ensured by the need to identify a gain, and by making change of position available as a defence in suitable cases when, for instance, the recipient had changed his position in reliance on the receipt.'

Lord Nicholls goes on to examine the *In re Diplock* [1948] Ch 465 principle, suggesting, at p 241, that it could be reshaped by being extended to all trusts but in a form modified to take proper account of the decision in *Lipkin Gorman v Karpnale Ltd* [1991] 2 AC 548.

No argument before us was based on the suggestions made in Lord Nicholls's essay. Indeed, at this level of decision, it would have been a fruitless exercise. We must continue to do our best with the accepted formulation of the liability in knowing receipt, seeking to simplify and improve it where we may. While in general it may be possible to sympathise with a tendency to subsume a further part of our law of restitution under the principles of unjust enrichment, I beg leave to doubt whether strict liability coupled with a change of position defence would be preferable to fault-based liability in many commercial transactions, for example where, as here, the receipt is of a company's funds which have been misapplied by its directors. Without having heard argument it is unwise to be dogmatic, but in such a case it would appear to be commercially unworkable and contrary to the spirit of the rule in *Royal British Bank v Turquand* (1856) 6 E & B 327 that, simply on proof of an internal misapplication of the company's funds, the burden should shift to the recipient to defend the receipt either by a change of position or perhaps in some other way. Moreover, if the circumstances of the receipt are such as to make it unconscionable for the recipient to retain the benefit of it, there is an obvious difficulty in saying that it is equitable for a change of position to afford him a defence.

Knowing receipt—the facts of the present case I return to the facts of the present case, in order to determine whether the defendant is liable in knowing receipt to repay (together with interest) US$6.679m of the sum received by him pursuant to the divestiture agreement, being the excess over the US$10m he paid to ICIC Overseas pursuant to the 1985 agreement. (By a decision whose forensic good sense dispensed with an analysis of its juristic foundation the claimants abandoned a claim for the full US$16.679m.) The answer to that question depends on whether the judge's findings, though made in the course of an inquiry as to the defendant's honesty, are equally supportive of a conclusion that his state of knowledge was not such as to make it unconscionable for him to retain the benefit of the receipt.

I start with the defendant's state of knowledge at the date of the 1985 agreement. As to that, the judge found that there was no evidence that anyone outside BCCI had reason to doubt the integrity of its management at that time. More specifically, it is clear that the judge was of the view that the defendant had no knowledge of the underlying frauds within the BCCI group either in general or in relation to the 1985 agreement. He found that the defendant saw it simply as an arm's length business transaction. Moreover, he was not prepared to draw the conclusion that the high rate of interest and the artificial nature of the agreement were sufficient to put an honest person in the defendant's position on notice that some fraud or breach of trust was being perpetrated. He said that the defendant would have had no reason to question the form of the transaction.

Those findings, expressed in language equally appropriate to an inquiry as to constructive notice, appear to me to be consistent only with the view that the defendant's state of knowledge at the date of the 1985 agreement was not such as to make it unconscionable for him to enter into it.

. . .

There having been no evidence that the defendant was aware of the internal arrangements within BCCI which led to the payment to him of the US$16.679m pursuant to the divestiture agreement, did the additional knowledge which he acquired between July 1985 and December 1988 make it unconscionable for him to retain the benefit of the receipt? In my judgment it did not. The additional knowledge went to the general reputation of the BCCI group from late 1987 onwards. It was not a sufficient reason for questioning the propriety of a particular transaction entered into more than two years earlier, at a time when no one outside BCCI had reason to doubt the integrity of its management and in a form which the defendant had no reason to question. The judge said that the defendant was entitled to take steps to protect his own interest, and that there was nothing dishonest in his seeking to enforce the 1985 agreement. Nor was there anything unconscionable in his seeking to do so. Equally, had I thought that that was still the appropriate test, I would have held that the defendant did not have actual or constructive knowledge that his receipt of the US$6.79m was traceable to a breach or breaches of fiduciary duty by Mr Naqvi, Mr Hafeez and Mr Kazmi.

Ward and **Sedley LJJ** concurred.

NOTES AND QUESTIONS

1. Was Nourse LJ here accepting that constructive knowledge is sufficient to trigger liability for 'knowing receipt'?

2. Does a test of unconscionability help in resolving the traditional uncertainty as to whether constructive knowledge is sufficient for 'knowing receipt'?

3. Is there a difference between a scale of dishonesty and negligence on the one hand, and actual and constructive knowledge on the other?

4. Were Nourse LJ's tentative reasons for rejecting a model of strict liability subject to defences convincing? For extracts from Lord Nicholls' essay, referred to by Nourse LJ, see below, 245.

5. 'Knowing receipt' has traditionally been viewed as relevant only in three-party cases. Yet the facts of *Akindele* indicate that the line between two-party and three-party cases may be unclear. One could analyse *Akindele* as a case where, because of a breach of fiduciary duty by its directors, the claimant company paid money to the defendant under a contract that was void (or voidable) because the directors were acting outside their authority. On that analysis it was a two-party contract case and, as with all questions of restitution under invalid contracts, liability should have been strict and based on an unjust factor of, e.g., failure of consideration or mistake or ignorance or powerlessness. That that is a possible analysis is supported by the speech of Lord Nicholls in *Criterion Properties plc v Stratford UK Properties plc* [2004] UKHL 28, [2004] 1 WLR 1846, noted by R Stevens, 'The Proper Scope of Knowing Receipt' [2004]

LMCLQ 421. Criterion had there entered into a 'poison-pill' agreement with a partner company, Oaktree. That agreement required Criterion to buy out Oaktree on very favourable terms to Oaktree, in certain events. The aim of the agreement was to put off a potential takeover of Criterion. Criterion subsequently sought to set aside the agreement and the lower courts thought that the claim turned on the 'knowing receipt' unconscionability test applied in *Akindele*. The House of Lords held that that had been the wrong approach on these facts where what was in issue was the setting aside of an executory agreement for want of authority. The leading speech was given by Lord Scott. But Lord Nicholls went further and criticised *Akindele* itself as having been a case where unconscionable receipt was irrelevant. Instead the relevant principles should have been those applicable to restitution under void (or voidable) contracts. He said at paras 3–4:

> [3] Unfortunately, in the courts below this 'want of authority' issue was approached on the basis that the outcome turned on whether Oaktree's conduct was unconscionable. This seems to have been the test applied by the Court of Appeal in *Bank of Credit and Commerce International (Overseas) Ltd v Akindele* [2001] Ch 437 both to questions of 'want of authority' and to liability for what traditionally has been labelled 'knowing receipt'.
>
> [4] I respectfully consider the Court of Appeal in *Akindele's* case fell into error on this point. If a company (A) enters into an agreement with B under which B acquires benefits from A, A's ability to recover these benefits from B depends essentially on whether the agreement is binding on A. If the directors of A were acting for an improper purpose when they entered into the agreement, A's ability to have the agreement set aside depends upon the application of familiar principles of agency and company law. If, applying these principles, the agreement is found to be valid and is therefore *not* set aside, questions of 'knowing receipt' by B do not arise. So far as B is concerned there can be no question of A's assets having been misapplied. B acquired the assets from A, the legal and beneficial owner of the assets, under a valid agreement made between him and A. If, however, the agreement *is* set aside, B will be accountable for any benefits he may have received from A under the agreement. A will have a proprietary claim, if B still has the assets. Additionally, and irrespective of whether B still has the assets in question, A will have a personal claim against B for unjust enrichment, subject always to a defence of change of position. B's personal accountability will not be dependent upon proof of fault or 'unconscionable' conduct on his part. B's accountability, in this regard, will be 'strict'.

3. THE EXCEPTIONAL POSITION IN EQUITY— STRICT LIABILITY SUBJECT TO DEFENCES AND TO EXHAUSTING REMEDIES AGAINST DEFAULTING FIDUCIARY

- *Ministry of Health v Simpson (sub nom. Re Diplock)*
  [1951] AC 251, House of Lords

In breach of their fiduciary duty to the next of kin, and by a mistake of law, the personal representatives of a testator had distributed his residuary estate to certain charities (the appellant defendants) in accordance with a trust in the will requiring payment to 'charitable or benevolent' objects. That trust was held by the House of Lords in *Chichester Diocesan Fund and Board of Finance Incorporated v Simpson* [1944] AC 341 to be invalid. The House of Lords in this case upheld the decision of the Court of Appeal that the next of kin (the respondent claimants), who would otherwise be entitled to the residuary estate, were entitled, *inter alia*, to a personal equitable remedy against the charities to recover the monies paid subject to exhausting their claim against the personal representatives.

Lord Simonds: . . . The problem for determination can be simply stated and it is perhaps surprising that the sure answer to it is only to be found by examination of authorities which go back nearly 300 years. Acting under a mistake the personal representatives of a testator whose residuary disposition is invalid distribute his residuary estate upon the footing that it is valid. Have the next of kin a direct claim in equity against the persons to whom it has been wrongfully distributed? I think that the authorities clearly established that, subject to certain qualifications which I shall state, they have such a claim.

[*He considered the authorities which in his view established that the next of kin were entitled to recover subject to exhausting their claim against the personal representatives and continued:*] I come to the argument upon which counsel for the appellant laid the greatest stress, relying not only on the judgment of Wynn-Parry, J, but upon the other cases which have yet to be examined. It was that the equitable remedy was subject at least to this qualification, that it was not applicable where the wrongful payment was made in error of law. It was said that in every case where it had been applied the wrongful payment had been made under a mistake of fact and that wherever the principle had been stated without any such qualification, it must be read, nevertheless, as subject to it. I think, my Lords, that this argument which found favour with the judge is mis-conceived.

. . .

[T]he most satisfactory reason for the distinction [between a mistake of fact and a mistake of law] rests in the maxim, itself probably taken from the criminal law, ignorantia juris neminem excusat: see *Baylis v Bishop of London*.[1] The man who makes a wrong payment because he has mistaken the law may not plead his own ignorance of the law and so cannot recover what he has wrongfully paid. It is difficult to see what relevance this distinction can have, where a legatee does not plead his own mistake or his own ignorance but, having exhausted this remedy against the executor who has made the wrongful payment, seeks to recover money from him who has been wrongfully paid. To such a suit the executor was not a necessary party and there was no means by which the plaintiff could find out whether his mistake was of law or of fact or even whether his wrongful act was mistaken or deliberate. He could guess and ask the court to guess but he could prove nothing. I reject therefore the suggestion that the equitable remedy in such circumstances was thus restricted and repeat that it would be a strange thing if the Court of Chancery, having taken upon itself to see that the assets of a deceased person were duly administered, was deterred from doing justice to creditor, legatee or next of kin because the executor had done him wrong under a mistake of law. If in truth this were so, I think that the Father of Equity would not recognize his child.

. . .

Finally, my Lords, I must say some words on an argument of a more general character put forward on behalf of the appellant. The Court of Chancery, it was said, acted upon the conscience, and, unless the defendant had behaved in an unconscientious manner, would make no decree against him. The appellant or those through whom he claimed, having received a legacy in good faith and having spent it without knowledge of any flaw in their title, ought not in conscience to be ordered to refund. My Lords, I find little help in such generalities. Upon the propriety of a legatee refusing to repay to the true owner the money that he has wrongly received I do not think it necessary to express any judgment. It is a matter on which opinions may well differ. The broad fact remains that the Court of Chancery, in order to mitigate the rigour of the common law or to supply its deficiencies, established the rule of equity which I have described and this rule did not excuse the wrongly paid legatee from repayment because he had spent what he had been wrongly paid. No doubt the plaintiff might by his conduct and particularly by laches have raised some equity against himself; but if he had not done so,

1 [1913] 1 Ch 127.

he was entitled to be repaid. In the present case the respondents have done nothing to bar them in equity from asserting their rights. . . .

Lords Normand, **Oaksey**, **Morton of Henryton**, and **MacDermott** concurred.

NOTES AND QUESTIONS

1. In the Court of Appeal it was also decided that the next of kin had equitable *proprietary* tracing claims against the charities (see below, 660) but that was not raised on the appeal to the Lords.

2. In so far as the decision rejected a change of position defence by the charities, it can no longer stand in the light of the acceptance of that defence in *Lipkin Gorman v Karpnale Ltd* (see above, 28).

3. The qualification that the next of kin should first exhaust their remedies against the personal representatives is a controversial one. But for a defence of it see Lionel Smith, 'Three-Party Restitution; A Critique of Birks' Theory of Interceptive Subtraction' (1991) 11 *OJLS* 481 (see above, 119, note 2).

4. There has been no attempt in the equity cases to resolve the apparent inconsistency between the strict liability imposed in this case and the requirement of knowledge or unconsciability insisted on in the 'knowing receipt' cases. It is hardly satisfactory to treat *Re Diplock* as solely concerning the administration of estates and indeed there are cases in which the decision has been applied outside that context: see, most importantly, *Baker Ltd v Medway Building and Supplies Ltd* [1958] 2 All ER 532 (Danckwerts J); [1958] 3 All ER 540, CA. (See also dicta in *Butler v Broadhead* [1975] Ch 97 and *Re J Leslie Engineers Ltd* [1976] 1 WLR 292).

4. A PREFERABLE ANALYSIS?: IGNORANCE AND STRICT LIABILITY, SUBJECT TO DEFENCES

- P Birks, 'Misdirected Funds: Restitution from the Recipient'
[1989] *LMCLQ* 296

1. INTRODUCTION

When large sums of money are misdirected, it often happens that the person immediately responsible is not worth suing. The natural instinct is then to cast around for a defendant with a longer purse. The liability of a remoter recipient to return misapplied funds is thus a matter of some importance to any business but above all to banks and building societies, who are not only specially attractive defendants but also specially exposed to the risk of receiving, and identifiably receiving, misdirected funds. Some recent decisions in equity have begun to make it moire difficult for the person properly entitled to reach the ultimate recipient of his funds. The merits of that policy are open to debate, but the method is suspect. It is beginning to be done by insisting that this restitutionary liability cannot attach in the absence of a high degree of fault.

This incipient but still patchy trend towards a liability which is not only fault-based but based on a high degree of fault conflicts with choices which the law has already made. It has only been able to creep in because, in the immaturity of the law of restitution, neither judges nor jurists have been able to see a clear view of the nature and the rationale of the recipient's liability. The very idea that liability might be strict may surprise. A relevant analogy, though only an analogy, is the law of conversion. Suppose my car is stolen. It may pass through a dozen honest hands. No general defence of innocent receipt protects them from liability in conversion.

The law of restitution imposes a similar strict liability on the recipient of misdirected funds. For special circumstances, as we shall see, there are special defences, but there is no general defence of innocent receipt. Such a liability invariably stands in need of explicit explanation. It will otherwise inevitably gravitate towards fault, simply because a fault-based liability is easier to understand. The immediate purpose of this article is to counter that tendency by showing not only that the law has opted for strict liability but also that that option is rationally defensible.

There is also a larger purpose which has to do with the structure of the law of restitution. The structural proposition is, as will emerge in the discussion, that in the sequence of causes for restitution—enrichment unjust by reason of mistake, compulsion, failure of consideration, and so on—much more serious attention should be paid to a cause which so far has no conventional name but which can be called 'ignorance': i.e., enrichment which is unjust by reason of the plaintiff's being wholly unaware of a transfer of a value from himself to the defendant. This involves a sub-plot. The recipient's liability is for the moment predominantly perceived as a baffling complexity on the fringes of the law of trusts. This perception can be replaced by another, which will make it instead a relatively straightforward topic central to the law of restitution. This happens naturally when the sequence of causes for restitution is revised.

The article was written by way of response to *Lipkin Gorman v Karpnale Ltd.*[1] Indeed it grew out of a note on that decision, as it became apparent that the main issues had more radical structural implications for the law of restitution than could be treated in a few pages. That case nevertheless still remains the focus.

2. PATTERNS OF FACTS AND PRINCIPAL ISSUES

There are many variations of the situation with which we are concerned. Expressed somewhat abstractly, the relevant pattern of facts is that in which money to which one person is entitled is misdirected, without his knowledge, to another. The recipient may have given value or may be a volunteer. The question is whether he must make restitution to the person entitled to the funds before the misdirection. 'Misdirected' is intended to be neutral as to the moral quality of the mis-application. The most graphic case is the thief who steals the plaintiff's money and gives it to the defendant. But an honest mistake may equally underlie the misdirection, as where trustees misunderstand their duty and pay to the defendant money which ought to go to the plaintiff. The plaintiff is described as 'the person entitled' and, for present purposes, we may assume that that means the owner, at law or in equity, of the money misdirected. . . .

These examples suppose some third party doing the misdirecting, but in fact the case is frequently the same even without the intervention of a third hand. If I lose money and you find it and give it to another, the pattern of facts is exactly as in the examples just given. Yours is the third hand misdirecting my money to the ultimate recipient. But if you pocket the money yourself your position in relation to me is not materially different from, in the other case, that of the person who received from you: both you in the one case and he in the other are recipients of my money without my knowledge. It would be possible, but is not necessary, to bring out the similarity between the two cases by saying, where you keep the money yourself, that it is misdirected not by a third hand but by circumstances, or that you misdirect it to yourself.

When restitution is sought from the recipient, the facts may be such that the plaintiff can show that all or some of the money received, or its identifiable proceeds, are still in the recipient's hands. If he is able and willing to take on this difficult exercise of identification, he will be in a position to claim in the second measure of restitution (value surviving) and to argue for his claim to be regarded as proprietary (*in rem*). If he is unwilling or unable to engage in that exercise, the plaintiff will be

---

1 [1987] 1 WLR 987 (Alliott, J); reversed in part by the Court of Appeal, as yet unreported.

confined to a personal claim (*in personam*) in the first measure of restitution (value received). There is no mystery about this. It is simply impossible to claim the surviving enrichment unless you are prepared to show what survives, and it is equally impossible to assert a proprietary right unless you are prepared to identify the subject-matter in which you say your right subsists. Hence, without the exercise of identification, the claim cannot but be *in personam* and in the first measure: it must consist in an assertion that the defendant owes the plaintiff the amount received. It is with this personal claim that we shall be primarily concerned.

In equity it is customary to say that this species of personal liability involves 'accountability as a constructive trustee'. There are few, if any, contexts in which that language is necessary or helpful. At common law (where the notion of a fault-based liability has not so far caught on) the language is almost equally uninformative—'money had and received (to the use of the plaintiff)' or, more rarely, 'money paid (to the use of the defendant)'. It would help if the question could always be put simply in terms of personal restitutionary liability, at law or in equity. Another equitable label must also be mentioned. *Snell* names the recipient's liability by reference to the facts which are supposed to generate it and calls it a liability for 'knowing receipt'.[2] But one has only to read a handful of the relevant cases to know that that term contains an obvious *petitio principii*. Whether the recipient's liability turns on his knowing of the misdirection (and hence on fault) is the question.

In that misdirection of funds often, even if not always, involves dishonest behaviour on the part of the person who effects the misdirection, alongside the recipient's liability there is frequently encountered a question about the possible liability of an accessory to the fraudulent misdirection. *Snell* calls this 'knowing assistance'.[3] It ought to be possible to keep the two species of liability clearly distinct, but in the past this has not been done. In the result, although the accessory's liability is not restitutionary and is not immediately germane to our enquiry, we shall have to touch on it incidentally. . . .

In the context of this paper 'fault' is a function of the defendant's knowledge of the misapplication or his culpable failure to acquire that knowledge. It is convenient, therefore, to introduce at this early stage what will subsequently be referred to as 'the *Baden Delvaux* scale'. In *Baden, Delvaux and Lecuit v Société Générale pour Favoriser le Développement du Commerce et de l'Industrie en France S.A.*, Peter Gibson J, worked out a five-point differentiation of 'knowledge'.[4] The first three points indicate shades of dishonesty, the last two shades of carelessness. The scale is as follows:

(1) actual knowledge;
(2) wilfully shutting one's eyes to the obvious;
(3) wilfully and recklessly failing to make such enquiries as an honest and reasonable man would make;
(4) knowledge of circumstances which would indicate the facts to an honest and reasonable man;
(5) knowledge of circumstances which would put an honest and reasonable man on enquiry and failure to make such enquiries.

3. *LIPKIN GORMAN v KARPNALE LTD*

[*In this section Birks first examines the facts in* Lipkin Gorman *and the decisions of Alliott J and of the Court of Appeal. He points to the conflict in the judgments between the strict liability common law approach and the fault-based approach in equity.*]

No doubt because the widely different language of law and equity conceals the underlying common sense and makes the whole subject look much more technical and obscure than it really is, this

---

2 *Snell's Principles of Equity* (28th edn, eds P Baker and P St.J Langan, London, 1982), 194.
3 *Ibid.*
4 [1983] BCLC 325.

conflict between a strict and a fault-based version of the recipient's liability is not even examined. Nevertheless, when it does fall to be examined, the position of the Court of Appeal should prevail: the recipient's personal liability to make restitution is strict, subject to defences for some types of receipt.

After one preliminary matter has been dealt with in the next section, the sections which follow attempt to explain why this is so. . . .

4. SPECIAL DEFENCES

We will see below that one source of the false notion that the recipient's liability is fault-based is the failure to distinguish between fault relevant to the defendant's liability and fault relevant to his disqualification from a defence to which his particular circumstances might have entitled him. The antidote to this confusion is to be sensitive to the principal special defences at the outset.

[Birks goes on to discuss the defences of bona fide purchase, 'ministerial receipt', and change of position.]

5. PARALLELS WITH MISTAKE

The task of this section is to show that there is a very close relationship between the restitutionary liability of our recipient and restitutionary liability in respect of mistaken payments, such that the conditions of the liability to return mistaken payments must apply a fortiori to our case.

(a) Mistake and 'ignorance' It is evident, as a matter of positive law, that a payment by mistake is recoverable against a completely innocent recipient. So far is this true that a carelessly mistaken payor can recover from an innocent payee.[5] And an innocent recipient of a mistaken payment, if he cannot get himself within the defence of ministerial receipt (or some other special defence), remains liable even when out of possession and after having changed his position for the worse.[6] In short, liability is strict or, in other words, there is no defence of innocent receipt.

How does this bear on our case? The situation with which we are concerned is exemplified in the following facts. I drop my wallet, and a thief who picks it up misdirects the money in it. Let us say that he gives £100 as a present to a friend, R1, who spends it. Compare my situation in relation to R1 with the case of a simple mistaken payment made by myself to R2, who also spends the money. What is in common between the two cases? Both R1 and R2 have been enriched at my expense. Here 'at my expense' means 'by subtraction from me'. So both examples fall within the field of subtractive enrichment, where the plus to the recipient is an immediately corresponding minus to the plaintiff seeking restitution. In cases of subtractive enrichment there is a family of causes for restitution, and mistake is one example, where the factor calling for restitution, and thus rendering the enrichment 'unjust', is the vitiation of the plaintiff's intention to enrich the defendant. Thus, here my claim against R2 is made out because he has been enriched at my expense by the receipt of my money and my decision to make the transfer was impaired by my mistake. And we know that I can have restitution from him without any inquiry into the moral quality of his receipt, for, as we have already noticed, there is no defence of innocent receipt, not even of innocent receipt associated with change of position. My claim against R1 must succeed a fortiori. For as against him I am not talking about a merely impaired decision to transfer the money; as against R1 there was no decision at all: I knew nothing whatever of the transfer to him.

Without elegance but for the sake of balancing the terminology, we may say that, just as R2 is a case of mistake, so R1 is a case of 'ignorance'. And this is invariably true of the kind of situation under

5 *Kelly v Solari* (1841) 9 M & W 54; *Baylis v Bishop of London* [1913] 1 Ch 127; *R E Jones Ltd v Waring & Gillow Ltd* [1926] AC 670; *Barclays Bank Ltd v W J Simms & Son* [1980] QB 677.
6 e.g. (an extreme case but still the law) *Baylis v Bishop of London* [1913] 1 Ch 127.

consideration in this article. The 'recipient's liability' whose nature we are discussing is, when aligned with mistake, coercion, and the other causes for restitution, nothing other than the case of 'ignorance': subtractive enrichment by a defendant at the expense of a plaintiff who was completely unaware of (hence 'ignorant' of) the passage of wealth from himself to that defendant.

It will be apparent from this that, given that the liability of the mistaken payee is strict and not fault-based, it is unlikely to prove possible, without inconsistency and contradiction, to advance any arguments for a more relaxed, fault-based liability for the recipient who receives the plaintiff's funds quite without his knowledge. In terms of impairment of the intention to transfer, 'ignorance' is obviously *a fortiori* from mistake. It would be artificial, and pointless, to try to break this logic by insisting on some kind of 'privity' between restitutionary plaintiff and defendant or, which is the same idea in different words, limiting restitutionary rights to cases in which some shadow of a *negotium* has taken place between the parties.[7]

(b) Linear and triangular configurations It would not be necessary to press this point further, were there not an insistent temptation to perceive receipt from a third hand as a separate category. Subject to one crucial proviso [*namely, that tracing is required to establish that the defendant has been enriched at the expense of the plaintiff rather than the third party*], receipt from a third hand requires no special treatment, though it will often be the case that such recipients, if they have given value, will be able to avail themselves of the defence emanating from *bona fide* purchase. However, the temptation to believe the contrary obliges us to demonstrate the factual, as opposed to the merely logical, proximity of mistake and 'ignorance'. This can be done by illustrating the proposition that, in both mistake and 'ignorance', the intervention of a third hand may or may not be part of the factual story.

In cases of 'ignorance' the third hand provides the commonest explanation of how the money reached the defendant without the knowledge of the plaintiff; but simple two-party situations are also possible. Thus, where the thief is himself the defendant, the claim against him is capable of analysis, without reference to the character of his conduct as a wrong or to his guilty state of mind, as a simple, two-party subtractive enrichment absolutely without the plaintiff's knowledge.[8] In *Lipkin Gorman* the claim against the errant partner himself, had he been worth suing, would have been of that kind. Correspondingly, though most mistakes involve a two-party situation, some do involve a third hand. In *R. E. Jones Ltd v Waring and Gillow Ltd*[9] the plaintiffs paid the defendants by mistake, but they were led into the mistake by the fabrications of the rogue, Bodenham, who induced them to believe they were securing an agency to sell a new model of car which was being sponsored by the defendants. Correctly analysed as a case of mistaken payment, it is also, factually, an example of a misdirection of the plaintiffs' funds by the intervention of a third party. The plaintiffs were duped by Bodenham, and it was fortuitous that the duping took the form of his getting control of cheques drawn in favour of the defendants rather than of cash to misdirect. To take an extreme variant, it would be very odd indeed if the result had been different if, instead, Bodenham had simply taken their money without their knowledge and paid it over to the defendants, in which case substantially the same story would have had to be analysed as a case of 'ignorance': enrichment of the defendants by subtraction from the plaintiffs without their knowledge (through the act of a third party).

Very similar is *Reid v Rigby & Co.*[10] The defendants' workforce had been paid with the plaintiffs' money. It was accepted that, one way or another, the men's claims had been discharged. The

---

7 Many cases in the past did include such a requirement, to be regarded now as an outwork of the implied contract heresy. The requirement of privity was never lucid; see R Jackson, *The History of Quasi-Contract in English Law* (Cambridge, 1936), 102–3, 120–1.

8 Examples are: *Bristow v Eastman* (1794) 1 Peake 291; *Holiday v Sigil* (1826) 2 Car & P 177; *Neate v Harding* (1851) 6 Exch 349.

9 [1926] AC 670.   10 [1894] 2 QB 40.

defendants were thus incontrovertibly enriched, and at the plaintiffs' expense. What was the 'unjust' factor? A third party, in fact the defendants' manager but technically a stranger in that he had no authority from the defendants, had borrowed the money from the plaintiffs for the defendants and had applied it to pay the men's wages. The plaintiffs thought that they were lending to the defendants; they were mistaken as to the authority of the immediate borrower to bind the defendants. The intervention of the third party thus led them to benefit the defendants by mistake. Hence, this was another case in which the plaintiffs obtained restitution for a mistake when the effective agency for the transfer of the money had been a third party. A different result could hardly have been reached if the plaintiff had had no knowledge of the defendant at all, as for instance if the third party had named some alien principal or had secretly taken the plaintiff's money and given it to the defendant or applied it on his behalf.

The same is true of the facts in *Transvaal and Delagoa Bay Investment Co. v Atkinson*,[11] . . . . The rogue in that case slipped extra cheques into a pile which he knew would be signed as a matter of routine. [One can] treat the facts as an illustration of 'ignorance', not mistake. But the truth is that it is quite difficult to decide which classification to use, and the difficulty shows that, whatever the classification and absent some powerful reason to the contrary,[12] the result should be the same. Could a difference of result turn on whether the fraudulent cheques were blank when signed and then misdirected by the rogue (ignorance) or already made out to payees owed nothing (mistake)? The case of computer malfunction poses the same problem. If I pay you a second time, forgetting the first payment, which alone was due, no doubt the second payment is impaired by mistake; but, in an automated system, if a computer repeats a transfer, I might find it more natural to say that the second payment happened entirely without my knowledge, a case therefore of 'ignorance' rather than mistake.

The aim of this section has been, first, to show that, logically, a system which allows restitution from mistaken payees without inquiring into the moral quality of their receipt cannot refuse restitution in the absence of fault from those who have received the plaintiff's money absolutely without his knowledge. 'Ignorance' is *a fortiori* from mistake. Then, secondly, an attempt has been made to show that, factually, there is no real contrast between two-party and three-party situations: some cases of mistake involve triangular situations, and some cases of 'ignorance' do not.

[*Birks goes on in the next sections to deal with numerous cases which have considered the recipient's restitutionary liability for money received without the knowledge of the person entitled to it. He attempts to show that the cases can be analysed as resting on strict liability, with fault being relevant only to defences.*]

CONCLUSION

The personal liability of the recipient of misdirected funds is a strict restitutionary liability. It is based on the proposition that the defendant (the recipient) has been enriched at the expense (in the subtraction sense) of the plaintiff, in circumstances in which that enrichment is unjust by reason of the plaintiff's not having consented to it. The 'unjust' factor can be named 'ignorance', signifying that the plaintiff, at the time of the enrichment, was absolutely unaware of the transfer from himself to the defendant. 'Ignorance' is similar to but, as a factor calling for restitution, stronger than mistake, for in cases of mistake the plaintiff's decision is impaired but in cases of 'ignorance' impairment is an understatement: there is no decision at all. The relationship between mistake and 'ignorance' is analogous to that between money got by threats of violence (duress) and money taken from the pocket of a victim already bound and gagged or tetraplegic (helplessness), the one case a vitiated

---

11 [1944] 1 All ER 579.
12 As may be present when the misdirecting third party's mistake is of law, not fact.

decision to transfer, the other a transfer never the subject of any decision at all. It would be as irrational to make the conditions for restitution stricter for 'ignorance' than mistake as it would be to make it more difficult to obtain restitution for 'helplessness' than for duress.

The strict quality of the recipient's liability does not exclude the possibility that some recipients may be able to take advantage of special defences. In particular, a ministerial recipient out of possession in accordance with his principal's instructions is entitled to refer the plaintiff to the principal for whom he received; and a recipient who has given value may have a defence arising out of *bona fide* purchase. Here the words 'arising out of' are probably to be taken seriously. The defence to the personal claim is likely to turn out to be, not *bona fide* purchase as such, but the plaintiff's inability to comply with the *bona fide* purchaser's right to insist on counter-restitution.

The personal liability in equity of an accessory to a misapplication arises in the law of wrongs, not the law of unjust enrichment. It is always to be carefully distinguished from the recipient's liability, and is unintelligible in the absence of fault on the part of the alleged accessory. The degree of fault required is currently uncertain. But, even though it will mean overruling a number of recent cases, the better interpretation of the earlier authority, arguably the better common sense, and certainly the only way to avoid contradictions in the case law between tort, and that part of the law of wrongs still handled separately in equity, is to hold that this liability requires dishonesty or (which means the same) want of probity (nothing less than point 3 on the *Baden Delvaux* scale).

NOTES

1. While tangential to his central thesis, Birks' view, as set out in the final paragraph above, is that an accessory's (non-restitutionary) liability should rest on dishonesty. That view, shared by several other commentators, has since been accepted by the Privy Council and the House of Lords (see above, 231, note 2).

2. In a subsequent essay, P Birks, 'Receipt' in *Breach of Trust* (eds Birks and Pretto, 2002), 212–40, Birks argued that he had been wrong to argue in the above article that 'knowing receipt' was *simply* a species of unjust enrichment which should have been imposing strict liability subject to defences. Rather 'knowing receipt' concealed two different kinds of liability: one for the wrong of misappropriation of equitable property (where the relevant standard of liability should probably be dishonesty) and the other for unjust enrichment (where the liability was strict). As Birks recognized, this was to accept the strategy of Lord Nicholls in his seminal article, extracted below.

- **Lord Nicholls, 'Knowing Receipt: The Need for a New Landmark' in *Restitution, Past, Present & Future* (eds Cornish, Nolan, O'Sullivan and Virgo) 1998, 231**

. . .

The decision in *Lipkin Gorman v Karpnale*[1] has been rightly described as a catalyst for the evolution of a more rational remedial structure.[2] Encouraged by this major development in the law, the restitutionary approach has been widely hailed as showing the way forward for recipient liability. At least two standard textbooks have seized upon this decision accordingly.[3]

---

1 [1991] 2 AC 548.

2 Harpum in Birks (ed.), *The Frontiers of Liability* (1994), Vol 1, at p. 17.

3 *Underhill and Hayton on the Law Relating to Trusts and Trustees*, 15th edn, pp. 409, 415–16, and Hanbury and Martin, *Modern Equity*, 15th edn, p. 300. See generally also Sir Peter Millett, "Tracing the Proceeds of Fraud" (Sydney 1985), 107 LQR 71, 85; Austin in Finn (ed.), *Essays in Equity*, p. 217; and the powerful writing of Professor Birks in "Misdirected funds: restitution from the recipient" [1989] *LMCLQ* 296 and "Trusts in the recovery of misapplied assets: Tracing, Trusts and Restitution" in McKendrick (ed.) *Commercial Aspects of Trusts and Fiduciary Obligations*, pp. 159–66.

There is force in this view. In this respect equity should now follow the law. Restitutionary liability, applicable regardless of fault but subject to a defence of change of position, would be a better-tailored response to the underlying mischief of misapplied property than personal liability which is exclusively fault-based. Personal liability would flow from having received the property of another, from having been unjustly enriched at the expense of another. It would be triggered by the mere fact of receipt, thus recognising the endurance of property rights. But fairness would be ensured by the need to identify a gain, and by making change of position available as a defence in suitable cases when, for instance, the recipient had changed his position in reliance on the receipt.

. . .

The restitutionary approach would represent a significant development in the law relating to recipient liability. It would be wrong, however, to regard this as the introduction of a wholly alien concept into the field of equity. Equity would not be forging a completely new tool. In one area historically equity did impose personal liability on even the fault-free recipient. For the last half century, languishing largely unloved in the comparative obscurity of the law relating to the administration of deceased persons' estates, is the principle applied in the proceedings arising from the invalidity of the charitable bequests in Caleb Diplock's will. In *Ministry of Health v Simpson*[4] the House of Lords affirmed the continuing existence of an equitable principle whereby those to whom a deceased's estate has been erroneously distributed are personally liable to repay the persons rightfully entitled to the deceased's property whether as creditors or beneficiaries.

. . .

The *Diplock* principle is at hand and available to be reshaped, by being extended to all trusts but in a form modified to take proper account of the subsequent decision of the House of Lords in *Lipkin Gorman v Karpnale*. The modification would make the *Diplock* principle more acceptable, by softening its rigour with the defence arising from change of position. At the same time the opportunity should be taken to decide that this form of relief is no longer subject to a pre-condition that a plaintiff must first exhaust his remedy against the trustees. A soundly-based restitutionary claim presupposes that the recipient was enriched by a windfall gain and that no change of position defence is available to him. When this is so, justice requires the recipient to disgorge the gain before the defaulting trustees are compelled to put their hands into their own pockets and personally bear the loss.

. . .

[We now turn to] third party recipients . . . who acted dishonestly. Their position can be taken shortly, because no difficulty of substance arises here. They are subject to the two-fold personal liabilities of making good losses caused by their misapplication of trust property and accounting for profits received in the form of or by virtue of the trust property. There is no reason to suppose that these swingeing liabilities, which travel far beyond making restitution of an unjust gain, are inappropriate in cases of dishonesty.

It must be said, however, that the use of the constructive trust concept for this head of liability is not altogether comfortable. Dishonest receipt and dishonest assistance are two instances of similarly wrongful conduct: dishonest participation by third parties in a breach of trust. Both cases concern personal liability for participation by a third party in a breach of trust. In both cases liability is triggered by the same degree of fault: dishonesty, conduct which an honest person would regard as dishonest behaviour.[5] In both cases the issue, which is essentially a jury question,[6] is whether the third party, placed as he was and acting as he did for the reason he did, attained the standards of an honest person. The personal liability imposed by equity is the same in the two cases.

---

4 [1951] AC 251.
5 See the *Brunei Airlines* case at 389–91, and Gardner (1996), 112 *LQR* 56, 66.
6 Per Millett J in *Agip (Africa) Ltd v Jackson* [1990] Ch 265, 293.

The traditional approach to these two classes of wrongdoers involves interposing a deemed ("constructive") trusteeship between the wrongful conduct (dishonest participation) and the remedy (liability in equity). This intermediate step seems otiose and, indeed, confusing. It prays in aid the trustee concept, but by doing so distorts the ordinary principles of trusteeship. Holding property is one of the hallmarks of a trustee, but dishonest assistants need receive no property of which they can become trustees. Liability arises irrespective of whether they obtained any property. In the case of dishonest recipients, liability is not confined to the value of the property received. Receipt of property is incidental, in the sense that it is merely the form which the dishonest participation takes.

The law is perhaps now sufficiently mature to dispense with an ill-fitting deemed trusteeship as the source of liability. A more direct approach is to recognise that breach of trust and dishonest participation in a breach of are two species of equitable wrongs. Dishonest participation in a breach of trust, whether by receiving trust property or otherwise, is itself an equitable wrong, rendering the participants accountable in equity. It is the equitable counterpart of the common law tort of interfering with contractual relations.

This direct approach also provides a more coherent jurisprudential basis for the dishonest recipient's obligation to account for profits even though, had the transfer not taken place, the profits would not have been received by the beneficial owner. This might arise if the property were land and the recipient used the land to carry on a business. The rationale underpinning the ordinary trust principle concerning accountability for secret profits, encapsulated in authorities such as *Phipps v Boardman*,[7] does not fit easily onto a third party recipient. An express trustee agrees to undertake fiduciary obligations. The ordinary trust principle buttresses the due performance of these obligations by not permitting the trustee to be so placed that his fiduciary duty and his personal interest may conflict. But the third party recipient has not agreed to undertake any trust obligations. The rationale is not applicable in his case.

This difficulty disappears once it is accepted that dishonest participation is itself an equitable wrong. The way is then open to invoke the established principle that a wrongdoer should not be permitted to benefit from his wrong. This is a somewhat nebulous principle but, given the dishonest nature of the wrong, its application in this circumstance is compelling.

THE NEED FOR A NEW LANDMARK

If recipient liability is to have a firmer basis for the future, the attempt to formulate one single principle of personal liability should be abandoned. Instead, personal liability should be based on the combination of two separate principles of liability. First, recipient liability should cover all third party recipients. This would be a principle of strict liability in that it would apply to every recipient with an impeachable title irrespective of fault, but it would be restitutionary in nature. It would be confined to restoring an unjust gain. Change of position would be available as a defence accordingly. Secondly, dishonest recipients should be personally liable to make good losses as well as accounting for all benefits.

This development in the law can be achieved readily, first, by fashioning the *Diplock* principle into an improved remedy of general application and, secondly, in conjunction with this and as a counterbalance to this extension in personal liability, by preferring and adopting the more restricted view of what has hitherto been labelled constructive trusteeship but for the future may be better regarded as an instance of the equitable wrong of dishonest participation in a breach of trust.

---

7 [1967] 2 AC 46.

NOTES AND QUESTIONS

1. Lord Nicholls refers to the relevant equitable wrong as dishonest participation in a breach of trust. On his view, it sits alongside 'dishonestly assisting or procuring a breach of fiduciary duty' (i.e. the wrong recognised in *Tan*, above, 231) as the 'equitable counterpart of the common law tort of interfering with contractual relations.' Birks in his essay 'Receipt' referred to above, 245, prefers to label the equitable wrong as equitable misappropriation, with the analogous common law wrong being the tort of conversion. Which of these two views of the wrong is to be preferred?

2. In seeking to formulate an appropriate wrong, one should not lose sight of the more important aspect of the Birks/Nicholls approach, namely that in the equity 'knowing receipt' cases there should have been recognition of the cause of action in unjust enrichment (subject to defences). Reliance on a wrong would be necessary only if the claimant was seeking compensation or a measure of restitution beyond that available for the cause of action of unjust enrichment.

3. In *Twinsectra Ltd v Yardley* [2002] AC 164, which was a dishonest assistance case, Lord Millett, in obiter dicta, said of 'knowing receipt' at para. 105,

> There is no basis for requiring actual knowledge of the breach of trust, let alone dishonesty, as a condition of liability. Constructive notice is sufficient, and may not even be necessary. There is powerful academic support for the proposition that the liability of the recipient is the same as in other cases of restitution, that is to say strict but subject to the change of position defence.

For other judicial support for strict liability see *Say-Dee Pty. Ltd v Farah Constructions Property Ltd* [2005] NSWCA 309. In that case, in breach of fiduciary duty to its partner in a joint venture, land was transferred by the fiduciary to his wife and daughters. They were held to hold half the land on constructive trust for the claimant. The New South Wales Court of Appeal expressly applied the Birksian strict liability approach to the unauthorized receipt of trust property.

5

FAILURE OF CONSIDERATION

The recovery of money paid on a total failure of consideration is a well-established ground of unjust enrichment. In its development it has been confined to money claims: when we turn to non-money claims, the restitutionary claim has traditionally been discussed under the labels of *quantum meruit* and *quantum valebat*. Yet it is our contention that this restriction upon the failure of consideration claim cannot be justified in analytical terms. The distinction between a money claim and a non-money claim is of importance in terms of establishing that the defendant has been enriched, but it should not have any relevance to the identification of the unjust factor that is in play. In essence, our argument is that, if failure of consideration can apply to money claims (as it undoubtedly does), then logically it must also be capable of application to non-money claims. But, thus far, English law has refused to take this step. It is at this point that we run up against the legacy of the forms of action. The forms of action did not recognize that failure of consideration could apply outside the money context and the courts have, thus far, not been prepared to cast off the shackles of the forms of action and acknowledge that the emergence of an independent law of unjust enrichment demands that these old classifications be subjected to fresh examination and, when found wanting, dispensed with. So it is that the scope of the claim to recover the value of a benefit conferred upon a consideration that has (totally) failed is one of the most interesting of the current debates in the law of unjust enrichment. In the course of this Chapter we shall explore a number of issues and it might be helpful at the outset to identify the principal issues which we shall examine. The principal issues which should be borne in mind when reading the extracts which follow are:

(i)   What is meant by 'consideration'? One of the most contentious issues here is the question whether consideration inevitably means 'contractual consideration'. There are cases (examined at 254–256) where there is no contract between the parties but the restitutionary analysis appears to be identical to the cases in which there is a contract between the parties. If the argument is accepted that failure of consideration extends beyond cases in which the parties are in a contractual relationship, then it might be more helpful to label the unjust factor 'failure of basis' so as to avoid the misunderstandings which are likely to arise from the use of a word, such as 'consideration', which lawyers tend to regard as a purely contractual concept. Yet it should not be thought that the meaning of 'consideration' gives rise to difficulty only when it is sought to apply it to a case where the parties are not in a contractual relationship: it has caused considerable problems even when the parties are in a contractual relationship. Two such problems may be mentioned here. The first is: must the contract be set aside *ab initio* before a claim based on total failure of consideration can be brought (discussed in more detail at 313–314 and 386–392)? The second is: can a claim based on failure of consideration be brought by a contract breaker, or is the claim only available to the innocent party (discussed in more detail at 287–313)?

(ii) What is meant by the requirement that the failure of consideration must be *total*? Further, why does the law insist that the failure be total? Should a partial failure of consideration suffice to ground a claim for restitution of unjust enrichment?

(iii) Is failure of consideration confined to money claims? This is certainly the traditional understanding of the law, which is derived from the language of the forms of action. But, as we have noted above, a powerful argument can be made, based on the need for symmetry, for its application to non-money claims. The answer to this question may reveal a great deal about the methodological approach which is utilized when seeking to develop the law. It could be said that this area of law illustrates the traditional incremental development of the common law: the law has generally reached the right answer but without resort to any broad, underlying principle. On the other hand, a more rigorous analytical approach, which seeks to build a logical and symmetrical body of law, will wish to sweep away the old divisions and erect in their place a unified law based on the recovery of benefits conferred on a consideration which has failed.

(iv) What is meant by the requirement that the consideration must *fail*? We have seen that, in his final book, Peter Birks argued that absence of basis (consideration) subsumed all other unjust factors (137–138). What is the difference between 'absence of consideration' or 'no consideration' and failure of consideration? Does 'failure' mean initial failure or subsequent failure or both? Can failure of consideration be applied to the case of a claimant who makes a mistaken payment? Can failure of consideration be applied to cases of void contracts when both parties have fully performed?

(v) Where the parties are in a contractual relationship, does a claimant have a free choice between an unjust enrichment claim and a claim in contract, or is that choice circumscribed in any way? Further, can a claimant combine a claim in contract with an unjust enrichment claim, or must the claimant elect between the two claims?

(vi) An issue which recurs at a number of points in this Chapter concerns the test which is applied when seeking to identify and measure the enrichment which it is asserted that the defendant has obtained at the expense of the claimant. We have examined the enrichment issue in some detail in Chapter 2 and will not traverse the same ground in this Chapter. But the issues raised in Chapter 2 should be borne in mind when reading the cases which follow. A question which arises at various points in the Chapter concerns the relevance, if any, of the terms of the contract to the measurement of the benefit which the defendant has obtained. The critical issue can be summed up in the following question: can an unjust enrichment claim be used to escape from the consequences of a bad bargain, or does the measure of recovery in the contractual claim act as a ceiling upon the unjust enrichment claim?

(vii) A further issue of controversy concerns the possible role of 'free acceptance' as the basis for an unjust enrichment claim (cf. the discussion of free acceptance as a test of enrichment at 84–101 above). Free acceptance was originally suggested by Goff and Jones as an explanation for a number of older cases. In 1985 in *An Introduction to the Law of Restitution*, Birks explained (at 266) that free acceptance was unique in being both an unjust factor and a test for enrichment. Although it was referred to in one English decision in which the requirements were not met (see below, 393–395). Birks subsequently rejected free acceptance as an unjust factor (see *Unjust Enrichment* (2nd edn, 2005), 42–3). Although free acceptance, if it exists, is analytically distinct from failure of consideration, it is incorporated into this chapter because it is linked to the scope of failure of consideration as an unjust factor. If the argument is accepted that failure of consideration can apply to non-money claims, then there is no scope for an unjust factor of free acceptance. But if courts continue to adhere to the view that failure of consideration can apply only to money claims, then a number of non-money claims will be left without any obvious unjust factor and courts may be compelled to have resort to 'free acceptance' in an effort to explain the unjust factor in these cases. Recent cases have gone in both directions.

(viii) We defer until Chapter 14 discussion of whether failure of consideration can ever give rise to a *proprietary* restitutionary claim. Suffice it to say here that that question can be regarded as the central issue in dispute in the House of Lords in *Westdeutsche Landesbank Girozentrale v Islington LBC* (see below, 727–744) and that the subrogation case of *Boscawen v Bajwa* (below, 720) has been interpreted as an example of restitution for failure of consideration (see note below, 727)

General Reading

Burrows, chapter 10; Goff and Jones, chapters 20–2 and 26; Virgo, 121–4, chapter 12.

1. THE MEANING OF CONSIDERATION

The word 'consideration' tends to be viewed by many lawyers as a contractual concept, where mutual promises are common and treated as consideration. For many years, English law approached consideration in the law of unjust enrichment in the same way. In *Chandler v Webster* [1904] 1 KB 493, money was paid in advance for a room from which to view the coronation of Edward VII. When the coronation was cancelled, a claim for restitution was brought. The Court of Appeal refused the claim because, in the words of the Master of the Rolls, it was only 'if the effect were that the contract were wiped out altogether, . . . the money paid under it [would] have to be repaid as on a failure of consideration' (at 499). In *Fibrosa Spolka Akcyjna v Fairbairn Lawson Combe Barbour Ltd* [1943] AC 32 (above, 12) that decision was overruled by the House of Lords and a new definition of consideration was adopted. Viscount Simon LC said that 'in the law relating to the formation of contract, the promise to do a thing may often be the consideration, but when one is considering the law of failure of consideration . . . it is, generally speaking, not the promise which is referred to as the consideration, but the performance of the promise' (at 48). In 1985, Birks argued that a broader approach to the meaning of consideration was required and that failure of consideration was not confined to non-performance of contractual obligations. Although he said that the most common case was failure of contractual reciprocation (the example given by Viscount Simon), Birks argued that this was only one species of failure of consideration. The generic meaning of failure of consideration, he argued, was the failure to materialize or sustain itself of 'the state of affairs contemplated as the basis or reason for the payment' (P Birks, *Introduction to the Law of Restitution* (1985), 223). This meaning was adopted by the High Court of Australia in *Roxborough v Rothmans of Pall Mall Ltd* (2001) 208 CLR 516 (below).

- *Roxborough v Rothmans of Pall Mall Ltd*
  (2001) 208 CLR 516, High Court of Australia

Roxborough was a tobacco retailer that purchased cigarettes from Rothmans of Pall Mall Ltd. The purchase price included an itemized amount representing the tax due from the wholesalers to the New South Wales government. It was later discovered that the tax was unconstitutional and that the wholesaler did not have to pay it to the government. Roxborough sought restitution of tax payments made to the wholesaler under the contracts. A majority of the High Court allowed the claim.

Gleeson CJ, Gaudron and **Hayne JJ**: . . . [14] The appellants based their case, in part, upon the principles underlying the common indebitatus count for money had and received by the defendant to the use of the plaintiff. The notes to the 1868 edition of Bullen and Leake's *Precedents of Pleadings*, giving examples of cases where such a count would lie, said:[1]

> Money paid by the plaintiff for a *consideration that has failed*, may be thus recovered . . .
>
> . . .
>
> The failure of consideration must be complete in order to entitle the plaintiff to recover the money paid for it . . .; but where the consideration is severable, complete failure of part may form a ground for recovering a proportionate part of the money paid for it . . .; as where a quantity of goods were ordered at a certain rate of payment, and only a portion was delivered. [emphasis in original]

[15] Mason and Carter, in *Restitution Law in Australia*, point out that cases decided in relation to the common indebitatus counts, although they involved an implied contract analysis which is now out of date, 'form the precedents which make up the legal matrix of restitution law'[2] Lord Mansfield, in *Moses v Macferlan*,[3] referred to money paid 'upon a consideration which happens to fail' as an example of money which, ex aequo et bono, a defendant ought to refund and, therefore, money for the recovery of which the count for money had and received lies.

[16] Failure of consideration is not limited to non-performance of a contractual obligation, although it may include that. The authorities referred to by Deane J, in his discussion of the common law count for money had and received in *Muschinski v Dodds*,[4] show that the concept embraces payment for a purpose which has failed as, for example, where a condition has not been fulfilled, or a contemplated state of affairs has disappeared[5] Deane J, referring to 'the general equitable notions which find expression in the common law count', gave as an example 'a case where the substratum of a joint relationship or endeavour is removed without attributable blame and where the benefit of money or other property contributed by one party on the basis and for the purposes of the relationship or endeavour would otherwise be enjoyed by the other party in circumstances in which it was not specifically intended or specially provided that that other party should so enjoy it'.[6] In the case of money paid pursuant to a contract, it would involve too narrow a view of those 'general equitable notions' to limit failure of consideration to failure of contractual performance. In the present case, the amount of the net total wholesale cost referable to the tax was, from one point of view, part of the money sum each appellant was obliged to pay to obtain delivery of the tobacco products. But there was more to it than that. The tax was a government imposition, in the form of a fee payable

---

1 Bullen and Leake, *Precedents of Pleadings*, 3rd edn, 1868, pp 48–9.
2 Mason and Carter, *Restitution Law in Australia*, 1995, p 73.
3 (1760) 2 Burr 1005 at 1012; 97 ER 676 at 680–1.
4 (1985) 160 CLR 583 at 619–20; 62 ALR 429 at 454–5.
5 See Birks, *An Introduction to the Law of Restitution*, 1985, p 223.
6 (1985) 160 CLR 583 at 619–20; 62 ALR 429 at 454–5.

under a licensing scheme. The nature of the scheme was such that the licensed wholesaler, or, if not the wholesaler, then the licensed retailer, would pay the amount referable to particular tobacco products. The respondent, anticipating liability for the fee, required the appellants, when purchasing products by wholesale, to pay an amount equal to the fee. The appellants, in turn, had an interest in the respondent paying the fee to the revenue authorities, for they were thereby relieved of a corresponding liability. There was a purpose involved in the making of the requirement that the appellants pay the amounts described as 'tobacco licence fee', and in the compliance with that requirement. To describe those amounts as nothing more than an agreed part of the price (or, to use the language of the parties, cost) of the goods, is to ignore an important aspect of the facts.

[17] In a contract for the sale of goods, the total amount which the buyer is required to pay to the seller may be expressed as one indivisible sum, even though it is possible to identify components which were taken into account by the parties in arriving at a final agreed figure. The final figure itself may have been the result of negotiation, making it impossible to relate a cost component to any particular part of that figure. Or there may be other factors which prevent even a notional apportionment. But there are cases, of which the present is an example, where it is possible, both to identify that part of the final agreed sum which is attributable to a cost component, and to conclude that an alteration in circumstances, perhaps involving a failure to incur an expense, has resulted in a failure of a severable part of the consideration. Here, the buyers, the retailers, were required to bear, as a component of the total cost to them of the tobacco products, a part of the licence fees which the seller, the wholesaler, was expected to incur at a future time, and which was referable to the products being sold. It was in the common interests of the parties that the fees, when so incurred, would be paid to the revenue authorities by the seller, and it was the common intention of the parties (and the revenue authorities) that the cost of the goods would include the fees. In the events that happened, the anticipated licence fees were not incurred by the seller. The state of affairs, which was within the contemplation of the parties as the basis of their dealings, concerning tax liability, altered. And it did so in circumstances which permitted, and required, severance of part of the total amount paid for the goods. . . .

Gummow and **Callinan JJ** delivered concurring judgments and **Kirby J** dissented.

NOTES AND QUESTIONS

1. The judgment of Gleeson CJ, Gaudron, and Hayne JJ quoted from Birks and described the meaning of consideration as 'the state of affairs, which was within the contemplation of the parties as the basis of their dealings'. In his concurring judgment, Gummow J explained that consideration meant 'the failure to sustain itself of the state of affairs contemplated as a basis for the payments'. The state of affairs contemplated as the basis for performance of a contract will generally be the receipt of counter-performance and this Chapter focuses primarily on such cases. However, the majority joint judgment in *Roxborough* explained that this would not always be the case. For instance, money paid in contemplation of a marriage which does not take place can be recovered (*Essery v Cowlard* (1884) 26 Ch D 191) or in respect of a marriage which is subsequently declared to be a nullity (see *Re Ames' Settlement* [1946] Ch 217 and *P v P* [1916] *IR* 400). Another possible example, considered below is the difficult decision of *Guinness Mahon & Co. Ltd v Kensington and Chelsea Royal London Borough Council* [1999] QB 215 (at 369–384) in which restitution was given of the net payments made by one party to a void contract despite complete counter-performance by the other party.

2. What is the difference between failure of basis and the absence of basis approach which Birks has adopted to describe all claims in unjust enrichment (see above, 137–138)?

3. How would the decision in *Roxborough* be treated on Birks' new absence of basis approach?

4. Why did the High Court of Australia insist upon a shared basis? In her article 'A new conception of failure of basis' [2004] *RLR* 96 at 101, Felicity Maher argues that 'the rationale for a

shared basis requirement is that, if the claimant transfers a benefit on a basis which the defendant does not share, the claimant takes the risk of the basis failing. Restitution is justified only when the basis is shared and the risk shifts to the defendant.' A similar approach is taken by Grantham and Rickett (*Enrichment and Restitution in New Zealand* (2000), 148). Do you agree?

5. Is the basis or contemplated state of affairs to be determined subjectively or objectively? In *Fostif Pty. Ltd v Campbells Cash & Carry Pty. Ltd* (2005) 218 ALR 166, a class action by tobacco retailers which was brought after *Roxborough v Rothmans of Pall Mall Ltd,* and involved very similar facts, the New South Wales Court of Appeal held that the basis for the payments was to be determined objectively so that it was not necessary for all of the members of a class action to give evidence of their subjective intentions. Do you agree with this approach?

• *Chillingworth v Esche* [1924] 1 Ch 97, Court of Appeal

The claimants agreed to purchase freehold land from the defendant for £4,800 'subject to a proper contract to be prepared by the vendor's solicitors' and they paid the defendant the sum of £240 as 'a deposit and in part payment of the said purchase money'. The vendor's solicitors subsequently prepared a contract for the sale of the property and the contract was approved by the claimants' solicitors. The contract was executed by the defendant and sent to the claimants' for execution. The claimants refused to proceed with the purchase and instead sought to recover the £240 which they had paid to the defendant. It was held that they were entitled to recover the pre-payment, as it had been paid on condition that a binding contract would subsequently be concluded between the parties and that, in the absence of such a contract, they were entitled to recover their money.

Pollock MR: . . . It has been said that this case is one of general interest and application in other cases where the words of a document are very similar, but for my own part I do not think that this case can be of wide application, as the decision depends on this particular document and the particular circumstances under which it was signed. [*He considered these matters and continued*:]

I think when you look at the words here used that what was intended was that the whole document should be conditional on the execution of a proper contract, to be prepared by the vendor's solicitors. I think it is not possible to hold that those words were merely the expression of a desire for a further contract. In my opinion the word 'proper' must be given its full meaning, and I think that the intention of the parties was that the full conditions should be considered in a further contract, and that until that further contract was executed there should be no binding contract for the purchase of the property.

. . .

I have come to the conclusion that we must hold that until a proper contract had been prepared, concluded and executed there was no agreement at all.

My Luxmoore says that the result of such a finding is that the money paid on deposit is recoverable, on the ground that there never was a contract, and I think that prima facie he is right, and that the deposit is recoverable and ought to be repaid to the plaintiffs. This 240*l.* was paid 'as deposit and in part payment of the said purchase money.' It is clear that the purchase money might never become payable, so the character of part payment was lost. But then it is said that it had the character of a deposit, and never lost that character, and therefore the vendor is entitled to retain it. As to the meaning of 'deposit,' Lord Macnaghten in *Soper v Arnold*[1] says: 'Everybody knows what a deposit is. The purchaser did not want legal advice to tell him that. The deposit serves two purposes—if the purchase is carried out it goes against the purchase-money—but its primary purpose is this, it is a

---

1 14 App. Cas. 429, 435.

guarantee that the purchase means business; and if there is a case in which a deposit is rightly and properly forfeited, it is, I think, when a man enters into a contract to buy real property without taking the trouble to consider whether he can pay for it or not.' It is said here that this 240*l.* was a guarantee that the purchasers meant business, and as, through their action, business did not result, the deposit should be forfeited, on the ground that the purchasers should have executed the contract tendered to them. It is, however, no part of the business of this Court to concern itself with the question why the negotiations in this case came to an end and whether any one is to blame in the matter, but the duty of the Court is to note that as no contract was entered into the deposit would prima facie be returnable. What ground is there then for saying that the purchasers who were entitled to break off negotiations have thereby lost the deposit? It is said that they could not seriously enter into these negotiations and then break them off without reason, but that is not for us to consider. That they were entitled not to complete the purchase seems clear, and I do not accept the view that the purchasers were paying the deposit as a guarantee or earnest of good faith that they would complete the purchase, because they could have revoked what had up to that time been agreed upon at any moment. It seems to me that when once the negotiations came to an end the rights of the parties were gone, and the purchasers were entitled to receive their money back. . . .

Warrington LJ: . . . I am clearly of opinion that this document of July 10, 1922, was nothing more than a conditional offer and acceptance, and would only ripen into a contract when a formal document was signed.

Both parties therefore being at liberty to determine the negotiations, is the vendor entitled to retain the deposit? The purchasers, in determining the negotiations, committed no wrong. They did what they were quite entitled to do. Yet it is said that though they were entitled to do what they did, they could do so only under pain of forfeiting the deposit. Whether a vendor is entitled to retain a deposit depends in each case upon the construction of the document under which that deposit is made. The authority for that proposition is to be found in *Home v Smith*,[2] where Bowen LJ said: 'The question as to the right of the purchaser to the return of the deposit money must, in each case, be a question of the conditions of the contract. In principle it ought to be so, because of course persons may make exactly what bargain they please as to what is to be done with the money deposited. We have to look at the documents to see what bargain was made.' Then after referring to *Palmer v Temple*[3] he quoted the following observations of Lord Denman CJ in delivering the judgment of the Court in that case: 'The ground on which we rest this opinion is, that, in the absence of any specific provision, the question, whether the deposit is forfeited, depends on the intent of the parties to be collected from the whole instrument.' Fry LJ made statements to the same effect.

Two rival views have been put before us. On behalf of the vendor it is said that the deposit must be taken to be a guarantee for the conduct by the purchasers of the negotiations so as to bring them to their legitimate conclusion, that is, the signing of a proper contract, and that it was intended to prevent the purchasers from breaking off negotiations for other reasons than default of the vendor. I have great difficulty in arriving at such a conclusion. If the document were a binding contract, there would of course be no doubt as to the result. In *Soper v Arnold*[4] Lord Herschell said: 'The deposit is given as a security for the performance of the contract. The appellant admittedly cannot recover that deposit if it was through his default that the transaction was not completed.' And when Lord Macnaghten describes the nature of a deposit in somewhat more popular language I think he means the same thing. But where, as here, there is no binding contract, where the whole matter is left indefinite, it seems impossible to say that the purchasers pay the deposit as a guarantee to carry out the bargain, when by the document they have entered into they have not bound themselves to carry

2 27 Ch D 89, 97.   3 (1839) 9 Ad & E 508, 520.
4 14 App Cas 429, 433.

out any bargain. Where there is no legal relation, how can it be said that the purchasers have done something which they ought not to have done, or have abstained from doing something which they ought to have done? Then it is said that unless the consequence of the payment of a deposit amounts to a guarantee to complete the purchase the payment of it is perfectly futile. I do not agree, because the purchaser by payment of a deposit shows that he means business. The purchaser has not bound himself, but in order to show a definite intention he is willing to part with money, and run the risk of the vendor spending the money and being unable to return it if negotiations are broken off. The purchasers contend that this is a deposit paid in anticipation of a final contract and nothing more. That seems to me to be the true view. The decision of Astbury J I think is wrong and ought to be reversed. . . .

Sargant LJ concurred.

NOTES AND QUESTIONS

1. What was the basis upon which the pre-payment was made?
2. What was the precise ground upon which the claimants obtained restitution of their pre-payment?
3. Would it have made a difference if the deposit had been paid pursuant to a binding contract, which was immediately repudiated by the claimants?

2. CONTRACTS DISCHARGED FOR BREACH

When a repudiatory breach of contract has been accepted by the innocent party as a discharge of the contract, the parties are released from their future obligations to perform under the contract and the party in breach has imposed upon him a secondary obligation to pay damages to the innocent party (see *Photo Production Ltd v Securicor Transport Ltd* [1980] AC 827). The innocent party may seek to recover damages, the aim of which is to put him in the position which he would have been in had the contract been performed according to its terms. Such a claim is the preserve of the law of contract, not the law of unjust enrichment. But this is not to say that the law of contract is the sole repository of the law relating to the financial consequences of the discharge of contracts. Once the contract has been discharged, the law of unjust enrichment may be invoked by the parties in an effort to recover the value of benefits which have been conferred upon the other party in the performance of the now discharged contract.

The approach which we have taken in this section is to consider first the restitutionary claim of the innocent party (that is to say, the party who is not in breach of contract). In so doing, we distinguish between money claims and non-money claims. As we have already noted, the courts have not traditionally recognized that non-money claims can be restitutionary claims in unjust enrichment for failure of consideration. Although we divide the cases below between money claims and non-money claims, this should not be taken as acceptance that such a division is valid. On the contrary, we believe that the only relevance of the distinction between money claims and non-money claims relates to the difficulties in the latter context of identifying and measuring the enrichment. It should have no relevance to the reason for restitution which, in both instances, we believe to be based on (total) failure of consideration. Where the benefit conferred is a monetary one, then the law is relatively straightforward: the money is recoverable only upon a total failure of consideration. A partial failure does not suffice. Yet, this is a controversial issue. Should the law allow the recovery of money upon a partial failure of consideration?

The position is rather more complicated in the case of non-money claims because here the law has not recognized with any precision the reason for restitution, nor has it worked out the relationship between the contractual claim and the claim for unjust enrichment.

Having considered the claim of the innocent party, we then analyse the claims which the law gives to the contract-breaker. Here the principal difficulty can be identified as follows: what is the ground upon which the contract-breaker seeks restitution? Is it failure of consideration or is it something else? If it is something else, what is this 'something else'? As in the case of the innocent party, we distinguish between money claims and non-money claims, but, again, the distinction is employed for expository purposes only and does not imply acceptance of the argument that the law should distinguish between the two types of claim when identifying the unjust factor.

(1) CLAIM BY THE INNOCENT PARTY FOR THE RECOVERY OF MONEY PAID

- *Giles v Edwards* (1797) 7 Term Rep 181, Court of King's Bench

The parties entered into a contract under which the defendant agreed to sell to the claimants all his cordwood. It was a custom for the seller to cord the wood and for the buyer to re-cord it before it became the property of the buyer. The defendant cut sixty cords. He corded ten of them and the claimants re-corded half a cord. The claimants then paid the defendant 20 guineas, but the defendant failed to cord the rest of the wood and so the claimants brought an action to recover the 20 guineas they had paid on the ground that the consideration for the payment had failed. The defendant argued that the claimants could not abandon the contract because they had acted under it. The trial judge rejected the argument on the ground that the claimants could not be considered to have executed the contract in part because they had simply measured the wood and re-corded a very small part of it. Verdict was therefore given for the claimants. The defendant sought to set aside that verdict but the court upheld the directions at trial.

Lord Kenyon Ch.J: . . . this was an entire contract; and as by the defendant's default the plaintiffs could not perform what they had undertaken to do, they had a right to put an end to the whole contract and recover back the money that they had paid under it; they were not bound to take a part of the wood only.

QUESTIONS
1. Was there a total failure of consideration on the facts?
2. Why did the claimants claim restitution of the money paid rather than damages for breach of contract?

- *Hunt v Silk* (1804) 5 East 449, Court of King's Bench

Hunt, the claimant, entered into an agreement with Silk, the defendant, under which Hunt agreed to pay Silk £10 and Silk, in return, agreed to let a house to Hunt and also to put the premises in complete repair and to execute a lease within ten days of concluding the agreement. Hunt paid the £10 and moved into the house, but Silk did not carry out the repairs, despite the protests of Hunt. Some days after the ten-day period had elapsed, Hunt left the premises, gave notice to Silk that he had rescinded the agreement as a result of Silk's default, and brought an action in money had and received to recover back the £10 which he had paid. His claim failed.

Lord Ellenborough CJ: Without questioning the authority of [*Giles v Edwards*[1]] which I admit to have been properly decided, there is this difference between that and the present; that there by the terms of the agreement the money was to be paid antecedent to the cording and delivery of the wood, and here it was not to be paid till the repairs were done and the lease executed. The plaintiff there had no opportunity by the terms of the contract of making his stand to see whether the agreement were performed by the other party before he paid his money, which the plaintiff in this case had; but instead of making his stand, as he might have done, on the defendant's non-performance of what he had undertaken to do, he waved his right, and voluntarily paid the money; giving the defendant credit for his future performance of the contract; and afterwards continued in possession notwithstanding the defendant's default. Now where a contract is to be rescinded at all, it must be rescinded in toto, and the parties put in statu quo. But here was an intermediate occupation, a part execution of the agreement, which was incapable of being rescinded. If the plaintiff might occupy the premises two days beyond the time when the repairs were to have been done and the lease executed, and yet rescind the contract, why might he not rescind it after a twelvemonth on the same account. This objection cannot be gotten rid of: the parties cannot be put in statu quo.

Lawrence J: In the case referred to, where the contract was rescinded, both parties were put in the same situation they were in before. For the defendant must at any rate have corded his wood before it was sold. But that cannot be done here where the plaintiff has had an intermediate occupation of the premises under the agreement. If indeed the 10l. had been paid specifically for the repairs, and they had not been done within the time specified, on which the plaintiff had thrown up the premises, there might have been some ground for the plaintiff's argument that the consideration had wholly failed: but the money was paid generally on the agreement, and the plaintiff continued in possession after the ten days, which can only be referred to the agreement.

Le Blanc J: The plaintiff voluntarily consented to go on upon the contract after the defendant had made the default of which he now wishes to avail himself in destruction of the contract. But the parties cannot be put in the same situation they were in, because the plaintiff has had an occupation of the premises under the agreement.

Grose J concurred.

NOTES AND QUESTIONS

1. Why might the claimant have brought a claim for money had and received rather than an action for damages for breach of contract? What advantages can be obtained by bringing a claim for money had and received?

2. Goff and Jones (at 508) rationalize *Hunt v Silk* 'as an example, perhaps harsh, of the principle of affirmation. Hunt was held to have affirmed the contract, because he had remained in possession of the land 'some days after' he knew of Silk's breach.' Can the case be so explained? What are the consequences of rationalizing the case on this basis?

3. To what extent was the decision of the court influenced by the perception that, in order to rescind a contract, it must be set aside *in toto* and the parties returned to their pre-contract position? Now that the courts recognize that discharge for breach operates prospectively but not retrospectively (see, for example, *Johnson v Agnew* [1980] AC 367), what impact should this recognition have on the decision in *Hunt*?

---

1 7 Term Rep 181.

• *Bush v Canfield*
(1818) 2 Conn 485, Supreme Court of Errors of State of Connecticut

The claimant agreed to buy 2,000 barrels of flour for seven dollars a barrel and made a prepayment of $5,000. The defendant failed to supply the flour, even though the contract had turned out to be an extremely good one for him (the price of flour having dropped to five dollars and fifty cents a barrel at the time of delivery). The claimant successfully sued to recover the $5,000 prepayment.

Swift Ch.J: Where a man contracts to deliver any articles besides money, and fails to do it, the rule of damages is the value of the article at the time and place of delivery, and the interest for the delay. Though the promisee may have suffered a great disappointment and loss, by the failure to fulfill the contract; yet these remote consequences cannot in such cases, be taken into consideration by courts, in estimating the damages. It is always supposed, that the party could have supplied himself with the article at that price; and if he intends to provide against the inconvenience arising from such a disappointment, he must make a contract adapted to such objects. In the present case, if the plaintiffs had paid to the defendants the full sum for the two thousand barrels of flour contracted for, then they would have been entitled to recover the value of it at *New-Orleans* where it was to have been delivered. If the price had risen between the time of purchase and delivery, they would have made a profitable speculation; otherwise, if it had fallen. If they had paid nothing, if the flour had advanced in price, they would have been entitled to recover the amount of such advance. If the price had fallen, they would have been entitled to recover nominal damages for the breach of the contract; though they might have been subjected to a great loss, if the contract had been fulfilled. This proves, that the actual damages suffered by a party cannot always be the rule of estimating damages for a breach of contract.

In this case, the plaintiffs advanced a part of the purchase money; that is, the sum of five thousand dollars; and no parallel case has been adduced to shew what ought to be the rule of damages for not delivering the flour. I think the one adopted by the court at the circuit, to be just and reasonable. The defendant has violated his contract; and it is not for him to say, that if he had fulfilled it, the plaintiffs would have sustained a great loss, and that this ought to be deducted from the money advanced. It is not for him to say, that the plaintiffs shall only recover the reduced value of a part of the flour which was to have been delivered, in proportion to the advanced payment. The contract was for the delivery of an entire quantity of flour; and no rule can be found for an apportionment in such manner. The plaintiffs have been disappointed in their arrangements; the defendant has neglected his duty; and retains in his hands, five thousand dollars of the money of the plaintiffs, without consideration. Nothing can be more just than that he should refund it; and I am satisfied, that a better rule cannot be adopted in similar cases.

Trumbull J: concurred, substantially, in this opinion. He remarked, that the plaintiffs, by paying the 5,000 dollars, have performed all that the contract required them to do, before the receiving of the flour. As the flour was not delivered, they were not bound, by the contract, to pay any more. The defendant, on the other hand, has wholly failed of performance, at the time stipulated. He is liable for the breach; and it will be conceded, that if the plaintiffs had done nothing, they would be entitled to judgment, with nominal damages. Shall they not now recover what they have advanced upon the contract, previous to the breach? This sum is the actual loss, which they have sustained, by the breach. Complete justice has been done; and no new trial ought to be granted.

Hosmer J (dissenting): . . . Had the contracts been rescinded, in an action for money had and received to recover the sum advanced, the charge to the jury would have been precisely correct. The agreement, however, was open; the action is founded upon it, and damages are demanded for the breach of it. So long as the agreement is open, it must be stated specially (*Weston v Downs, Doug.*

23. *Towers v Barret*, 1 Term Rep. 133. 1 *Chitty*, 341.) and the consideration paid cannot be recovered. The case of *Dutch v Warren*, 1 Stra. 406, cited in 2 Burr. 1011, does not contravene, but supports, the latter branch of the above proposition. Although an action for money had and received was sustained, (in my opinion, illegally,) while the agreement remained in full force; yet the rule of damages, deliberately settled, was, not the money advanced, but the damages in not transferring the stock, at the time prefixed. The sum paid by the plaintiff was 262*l*. 10*s*. The stocks, however, having fallen before it was to have been transferred, the verdict, being the price of stock at the infraction of the contract, was for 175*l*. only.

The jury should have been directed to give the plaintiffs the damages sustained by the breach of the agreement, on the day when it should have been performed. . . . There have been many determinations for not transferring stock pursuant to contract; and the established rule of damages is, the price of it at the time of trial, or on the day when it should have been transferred. . . .

He who controverts the principle advanced in the cases cited, must supply a better. If he would sustain the charge to the jury in this case, he must contend, that for breach of contract the sum to be recovered is, not the damages sustained by the non-performance, but the consideration which the plaintiff may have advanced. A rule so unwarranted as this, so opposed to familiar practice, and numerous decisions, so arbitrary, bearing not at all on the contract of the parties, and mistaking the very ground of the complaint, cannot be supported.

It is contended, that the plaintiffs have not recovered a greater sum than is due to them; and that justice does not require a new trial. To this proposition I cannot accede. If the benefit derivable to the plaintiffs from a compliance with the agreement, can be ascertained, we shall possess an infallible criterion of the damages sustained. Now the facts stated, furnish unquestionable *data*, and reduce the inquiry to a mere question of calculation. The damages sustained, were, the price of flour when the contract was first broken; that is, the sum of 11,000 dollars. If the contract is to be considered as mutual and independent, the plaintiffs are entitled to that sum, and are bound to pay the defendant 14,000 dollars, the sum stipulated for the purchase. But, if the agreement is dependent on the prior performance of the contract by the defendant, there must be deducted from the above mentioned sum, the balance which would be payable to him on delivery of the flour, that is, 9,000 dollars. The effect of this would be precisely the same, as if the flour had been delivered, and the plaintiffs had performed the agreement on their part. *Quacunque via data*, the verdict is not conformable to legal justice. This view of the subject makes it unnecessary to consider what was the precise character of the contract.

That the plaintiffs have sustained a considerable loss on the supposed legal result, is unquestionably manifest. A fallacy has existed in not ascribing it to the right cause. It did not arise from the non-performance of the defendant's agreement. Before the period had arisen when the flour was to have been delivered, the loss had accrued by the fall of it in the market. It is equally obvious, that the defendant had derived a correspondent benefit. The verdict of the jury, in opposition to the contract of the parties, reverses their condition. It rescues the plaintiffs from their loss, and deprives the defendant of his gain. In effect, it arbitrarily subjects the defendant to a warranty, that flour shall not sink in price, and renders him the victim of the plaintiffs' unfortunate speculation.

It has been contended, that inasmuch as the defendant did not fulfil his contract, he ought not to derive a profit from it. To this I reply, that the obligations of the parties depend exclusively upon their own voluntary agreement. There was a hazard accompanying the contract. If flour rose in the market, the defendant would become, proportionably, a loser; and if it fell he would be a gainer. The event on which the result was suspended, was favourable to him; and of this he cannot be deprived, unless it is the duty of courts to *make* contracts, *not to enforce* them.

I am clear in my opinion, that a new trial ought to be granted.

Edmonds, Smith, Brainard and **Peters JJ** concurred with the judgment of **Swift Ch J**.

NOTES AND QUESTIONS

1. The claimant's action was one for damages and not an action for money had and received to recover the sum which he had paid to the defendant. Had the action been for money had and received, then Hosmer J. would have joined with the majority because his dissent was based upon the inappropriateness of the action which the claimant had actually brought.

2. Clearly a court is going to be reluctant to allow a defendant to retain any benefit which he has obtained under the contract while refusing to perform any part of his obligations. Edelman, *Gain-based Damages* (2002), 177–8, relies on the explanation of this case in the *Restatement (Second) of Contracts* s. 373, and argues that this is an example of restitutionary damages for breach of contract. For the cases and commentary related to restitution for the wrong of breach of contract, see 978–1002. This explanation of *Bush v Canfield* does not exclude an alternative analysis of the case as one in unjust enrichment for failure of consideration: see *Mobil Oil Exploration & Producing SouthEast Inc. v United States* 120 S Ct 2423 (2000).

3. Should the claimant have been allowed to escape from a bad bargain by bringing a restitutionary claim? Could it not be said that the effect of the decision was to reverse the contractual allocation of risk?

4. It would appear that an English court would come to the same conclusion as that reached in *Bush v Canfield*. In *Wilkinson v Lloyd* (1845) 7 QB 27 the claimant agreed to purchase from the defendant shares in a mining company. The claimant paid for the shares but the directors of the company refused to transfer any of the defendant's shares because, at the time, the defendant was engaged in litigation with the company. The claimant brought an action to recover the purchase price which he had paid to the defendant on the ground that there had been a total failure of consideration. His action was successful even though by the time of the action the shares had fallen in value. Patteson J. stated (at 44) that the objection that 'the contract could not be rescinded because the shares had fallen, can hardly arise where the complaint of the plaintiff is that he never has had the shares he purchased at all'.

5. If a claimant can escape from a bad bargain in cases of total failure of consideration, *should* she be able to do so where the failure of consideration is only partial?

- *Rowland v Divall* [1923] 2 KB 500, Court of Appeal

The facts are set out in the judgment of Bankes LJ. The claimant was held to be entitled to recover the price paid for the car on the ground that there had been a total failure of consideration.

Bankes LJ: . . . The facts are shortly these. The plaintiff bought a motor car at Brighton from the defendant in May, 1922. He took possession of it at once, drove it to his place of business at Blandford, where he exhibited it for sale in his shop, and ultimately sold it to a purchaser. It was not discovered that the car was a stolen car until September, when possession was taken of it by the police. The plaintiff and his purchaser between them had possession of it for about four months. The plaintiff now brings his action to recover back the price that he paid to the defendant upon the ground of total failure of consideration. As I have said, it cannot now be disputed that there was an implied condition on the part of the defendant that he had a right to sell the car, and unless something happened to change that condition into a warranty the plaintiff is entitled to rescind the contract and recover back the money. The Sale of Goods Act itself indicates in s. 53 the circumstances in which a condition may be changed into a warranty: 'Where the buyer elects, or is compelled, to treat any breach of a condition on the part of the seller as a breach of warranty' the buyer is not entitled to reject the goods, but his remedy is in damages. Mr. Doughty contends that this is a case in which the buyer is compelled to treat the condition as a warranty within the meaning of that section, because, having had the use of the car for four months, he cannot put the seller in statu quo and therefore cannot now rescind, and he has referred to several authorities in support of that contention. But when those authorities are looked at I think it will be found that in all of them the buyer got some part of what he contracted for . . . In *Hunt v Silk*[1] Lord Ellenborough went upon the ground that the plaintiff had received part of what he bargained for. He said: 'Where a contract is to be rescinded at all, it must be rescinded in toto, and the parties put in statu quo. But here was an intermediate occupation, a part execution of the agreement, which was incapable of being rescinded.' . . . But in the present case it cannot possibly be said that the plaintiff received any portion of what he had agreed to buy. It is true that a motor car was delivered to him, but the person who sold it to him had no right to sell it, and therefore he did not get what he paid for – namely, a car to which he would have title; and under those circumstances the user of the car by the purchaser seems to me quite immaterial for the purpose of considering whether the condition had been converted into a warranty. In my opinion the plaintiff was entitled to recover the whole of the purchase money, and was not limited to his remedy in damages as the judge below held.

Scrutton LJ: . . . Mr. Doughty argues that there can never be a rescission where a restitutio in integrum is impossible, and that here the plaintiff cannot rescind because he cannot return the car. To that the buyer's answer is that the reason of his inability to return it—namely, the fact that the defendant had no title to it—is the very thing of which he is complaining, and that it does not lie in the defendant's mouth to set up as a defence to the action his own breach of the implied condition that he had a right to sell. In my opinion that answer is well founded, and it would, I think, be absurd to apply the rule as to restitutio in integrum to such a state of facts. No doubt the general rule is that a buyer cannot rescind a contract of sale and get back the purchase money unless he can restore the subject matter. There are a large number of cases on the subject, some of which are not very easy to reconcile with others. Some of them make it highly probable that a certain degree of deterioration of the goods is not sufficient to take away the right to recover the purchase money. However I do not think it necessary to refer to them. It certainly seems to me that, in a case of rescission for the breach of the condition that the seller had a right to sell the goods, it cannot be that the buyer is deprived of his right to get back the purchase money because he cannot restore the goods which, from the nature of the transaction, are not the goods of the seller at all, and which the seller therefore has no right to under any circumstances. For these reasons I think that the plaintiff is entitled to recover the whole of the purchase money as for a total failure of consideration, and that the appeal must be allowed.

Atkin LJ: I agree. It seems to me that in this case there has been a total failure of consideration, that is to say that the buyer has not got any part of that for which he paid the purchase money. He paid the money in order that he might get the property, and he has not got it. It is true that the seller delivered to him the de facto possession, but the seller had not got the right to possession and consequently could not give it to the buyer. Therefore the buyer, during the time that he had the car in his actual possession had no right to it, and was at all times liable to the true owner for its conversion. . . . It seems to me that in this case there must be a right to reject, and also a right to sue for the price paid as money had and received on failure of the consideration, and further that there is no obligation on the part of the buyer to return the car, for ex hypothesi the seller had no right to receive it. Under those circumstances can it make any difference that the buyer has used the car before he found out that there was a breach of the condition? To my mind it makes no difference at all. The buyer accepted the car on the representation of the seller that he had a right to sell it, and

---

1 (1804) 5 East 449.

inasmuch as the seller had no such right he is not entitled to say that the buyer has enjoyed a benefit under the contract. In fact the buyer has not received any part of that which he contracted to receive—namely, the property and right to possession—and, that being so, there has been a total failure of consideration. The plaintiff is entitled to recover the 334*l*. which he paid.

NOTES AND QUESTIONS

1. Why did the claimant seek restitution of the price paid rather than damages for breach of contract?

2. *Rowland* was followed by Pearson J in *Butterworth v Kingsway Motors Ltd* [1954] 1 WLR 1286 and by the Court of Appeal in *Barber v NWS Bank plc* [1996] 1 WLR 641. Those cases involved, respectively, a hire-purchase agreement and a conditional purchase agreement in which the claimants had the use and enjoyment of a car for ten months (*Butterworth*) and more than a year (*Barber*).

3. Should the intermediate use of the car by the claimant have prevented there being a total failure of consideration? Would it be true to say that the claimant had bargained for the use of the car as well as title to it and that, by ignoring the use which the claimant obtained, the court demonstrated that the law has an 'excessive preoccupation with title' (M Bridge, 'The Title Obligations of the Seller of Goods' in N Palmer and E McKendrick (eds), *Interests in Goods* (1993), 157) and that it ignores the economic and practical realities of sales transactions?

4. Can *Rowland* be reconciled with *Hunt v Silk*? If so, how?

5. If the claimant did obtain a benefit through his use of the car, was that benefit obtained 'at the expense of' the defendant or 'at the expense of' the true owner of the car?

- **Yeoman Credit Ltd v Apps** [1962] 2 QB 508, Court of Appeal

The claimant hire-purchase company entered into a hire-purchase agreement with the defendant relating to a second-hand car. The hire-purchase agreement excluded all liability for the condition of the car. The car was delivered at night outside the defendant's house but it had such a variety of defects that it was unusable, unroadworthy, and unsafe. The defendant protested to the claimants about the condition of the car, but he nevertheless kept the car and paid three instalments under the hire-purchase agreement. He then failed to pay the next two instalments, whereupon the claimants determined the agreement and resumed possession of the car. The claimants then brought an action to recover the arrears of rental instalments and damages, while the defendant sought to recover the three instalments which he had paid on the ground that there had been a total failure of consideration. It was held that the defendant could recover damages as a result of the claimants' breaches of their obligations under the contract, but that the defendant was not entitled to recover any of the instalments which he had paid as he could not show that there had been a total failure of consideration.

Holroyd Pearce LJ: . . . I cannot, however, with all respect, agree with the judge that there was a total failure of consideration. The defendant was plainly entitled to reject the car, to accept the plaintiff's repudiation of the contract by their delivery of such a car, and to rescind the contract. Had he done so, there would have been a total failure of consideration, and he would have recovered the sums paid. But, as the judge found, he made no serious effort to return the car. He kept it for five or six months, and approbated the contract by paying three instalments. He intended (to quote his evidence) 'to keep the car, and hoped Goodbody [the dealer] would pay half the cost.' He tried to find out from the plaintiffs what he could do to make Goodbody carry out the work. In those circumstances he was at that stage continuing with the agreement while protesting against the state of the car which was due to a breach of condition by the plaintiffs. This is not a case like *Rowland v Divall*[1] where title was lacking, and the defendant never had lawful possession. Here the defendant had the possession of the car and its use, such as it was. In evidence he said: 'That month I got copy of agreement. I had had the car by that time. I had been able to drive it—very poor.' Admittedly the use was of little (if any) value, but in my view that use, coupled with possession, and his continuance of the hiring agreement with the intention of keeping the car and getting Goodbody to pay half the repairs, debars the defendant from saying that there was a total failure of consideration. . . .

. . .

Davies LJ: . . . The second point on which I would say just one word relates to the question whether or not there was a total failure of consideration. I was, I confess, for some time attracted by the argument of Mr. Stephen Chapman that if there had been any consideration moving to the hirer (if 'moving' is an apt word in connection with this motor-car at all), it was de minimis. But I think it is impossible to say that. The defendant actually had the vehicle in his possession for some months— the vehicle which albeit on little or no inspection, he had agreed to take—and he was hoping, of course, that Goodbody (the dealer) would remedy the refects. The vehicle was not worthless; it fetched £210 in the trade eventually. It would go, though very badly indeed. The defendant retained it, as I have said, and paid the three instalments that he did pay. He had work done upon the car by Mr. Watson in order to take it to Goodbody's premises. And it was not, as my Lord has said, until at any rate August that eventually his patience became exhausted, and he told the plaintiffs: 'I am not paying any more. You had better take it back.' . . .

Harman LJ concurred.

QUESTION

Why is there a total failure of consideration when a party obtains possession but not title of a car which is in good working order, but no total failure of consideration when he obtains good title to a car which is so defective that it is unroadworthy?

● *D O Ferguson & Associates v M Sohl* (1992) 62 BLR 95, Court of Appeal

Sohl employed Ferguson to carry out building works to a shop for a total contract price of £32,194. Before the work was completed, and after having been paid £26,738, Ferguson repudiated the contract. Sohl was able to complete the work for less than the amount which remained unpaid under the contract. However, he sued Ferguson for breach of contract and for restitution for a total failure of consideration. The Court of Appeal held that Sohl had suffered no loss so damages for breach of contract were nominal. However, the value of the work completed by Ferguson (at contract rates) was only £22,065 and the Court of Appeal upheld the trial judge's order for restitution of the overpayment (£4673) on the basis that it had been made for a consideration which totally failed.

Hirst LJ: . . . The questions which we have to decide really come down to this in a nutshell. Was the judge right, as the respondent contends, in awarding the defendant a refund of £4,673 for the money overpaid, as the learned judge held it had been, together with the £1 damages? Was he right to approach this case on the footing that there were two separate causes of action – one which was successful for the refund and the other which was only nominally successful for the £1 general damages. Or, as has been submitted by Mr Armstrong in his able argument before the

---

1 [1923] 2 KB 500, CA.

court today, should the learned judge have viewed the case overall and, since the plaitiff's 'saving' was more than the £4,673, awarded him only £1 nominal damages, on the footing that his correct claim was simply and solely one for common law damages, and that he did not have a valid cause of action for restitution?

The basis for that is, of course, as Mr Armstrong put it, that in the event the defendant was not a penny worse off overall than if the contract had been properly performed. The other side of the coin, of course, is that if the judge was wrong and Mr Armstrong was right, the plaintiff builders are entitled to hold on to £4,673 for work they never did, and which they failed to perform in breach of their own obligations under the contract.

Mr Armstrong, in support of his argument, raises a number of points which are based on decided authorities and textbook citations. I will go through them in more detail in a moment, but perhaps the clearest statement on which he relies is that quoted from *Chitty on Contracts*, in the current edition [26th] at page 1115 in paragraph 1771:

'Damages for a breach of contract committed by the defendant are a compensation to the plaintiff for the damage, loss or injury he has suffered through that breach. He is, as far as money can do it, to be placed in the same position as if the contract had been performed. This implies a 'net loss' approach in which the gains made by the plaintiff as the result of the breach (eg savings made because he is [absolved] from performing his side of a contract which has been terminated for breach; savings in taxation; benefits obtained from partial performance; or the salvage value of something left in his hands).'

That, of course, is a very well-established and irrefutable principle for the assessment of general damages for breach of contract under the first of the two limbs of the rule in *Hadley v Baxendale* (1854) 9 Exch 341. But the key point here is that the £4,673 was not awarded as damages for breach of contract, but in restitution for monies paid for work that had never been done to which according to the judge's finding, the defendant was clearly entitled, and which cannot be affected by the fate of the parallel claim for damages for breach of contract since the two causes of action are separate and give rise to two separate claims.

Mr Armstrong submits that the learned judge's conclusion was, to use his own words, a novel departure from the general principle, and he relies not only on the passage in *Chitty* which I have just quoted, but also on passages laying out the same principle in the current edition of *McGregor on Damages*, paragraph 1086, page 673, where, under the heading 'Failure to Build At All Or In Part', the learned editor states as follows:

'The normal measure of damages is the cost to the owner of completing the building in a reasonable manner less the contract price.'

There are similar statements of principle in *Hudson on Building Contracts*, page 585, and in *Emden*, which is another work on building contracts, paragraph 155; the *Hudson* text says:

'The general rule is that basis (a) is adopted, and the employer is entitled to recover from the contractor the cost of rectifying the defects, such cost to be assessed at the time it was reasonable for him to carry out the work.'

Mr Armstrong also relied on the Court of Appeal case of *Mertens v Home Freeholds Company* [1921] 2 KB 526 where Lord Sterndale referred to an American case as being a correct guide to the English law. That was the case of *Hirt v Hahn* (1876) 61 Missouri 496 which Lord Sterndale, Master of the Rolls, quoted from as follows at page 535:

'B agreed to erect a house for the plaintiff according to plans by a certain day. The defendants were B's sureties. After partly completing, B ceased work, and the plaintiff, after giving notice to the sureties, entered and completed and sued the sureties. Held, that the measure of damages was what it cost the plaintiff to complete the house substantially as it was originally intended, and in a reasonable manner, less any amount that would have been [and those words are significant] due and payable to B by the plaintiff had B completed the house at the time agreed by the terms of his contract.'

In Younger LJ's judgment at page 541 the following appears:

'The plaintiff, accordingly, is entitled to have partially built that house which the defendant was bound so to build for him and has not built, and the damages which the plaintiff has sustained by reason of the defendant's breach is naturally and properly, as it seems to me, as it does also to the other members of the court, the cost to which the plaintiff was put in reasonably carrying out, by himself and for himself, that work which the defendant had failed to do, less only the sum which the plaintiff was bound to pay the defendant under the contract for carrying out the same work.'

Mr Armstrong submitted that all those cases and all those passages in the textbooks really rule out reliance on two causes of action because they make reference solely to this one formula for general damages. In my judgment, that really is not a valid point, because in none of those passages was the judge or the editor considering, or even contemplating, the question which arises here today, where there has been a separate claim to recover an overpayment in addition to the other claim for damages for breach of contract.

Mr Armstrong then referred to the well-known rule as to the obligation of the injured party to mitigate his loss as laid down in the classic passages in the House of Lords' case of *British Westinghouse Electric v Underground Electric Railways Company of London Ltd* [1912] AC 673. In my judgment, that case does not assist Mr Armstrong either, because in that case also the two separate causes of action were not under consideration, and in fact in the present case full mitigation has already been given by the defendant for his savings, through the reduction of his general damages to the nominal sum of £1.

Finally, there are a number of passages on which Mr Armstrong relies from the leading textbook on restitution (that is the textbook of Lord Goff of Chievely and Professor Gareth Jones on *Restitution* in the third and current edition), stating the well-known principle (which is strongly criticised by the editors as worthy of reform) that where there is only a partial failure of consideration then, as the law at present stands, an injured party cannot claim restitution, but is only entitled to claim for general damages for breach of contract.

But here again Mr Armstrong, in my judgment, derives no assistance because, *ex hypothesi*, the learned judge's finding is that for the £4,673 there was indeed a total failure of consideration because £4,673 was paid by the defendant for work that was never done at all. The plaintiffs rightly recovered their £22,000 odd for work which they had done, including their profit, and there is no question of rolling back the carpet so far as that payment is concerned. But for the sum actually claimed in restitution there was, in my judgment, no consideration at all, and it matters not, though Mr Armstrong sought to argue the contrary, that at some stage or other that sum of money formed part of a larger instalment.

In those circumstances the learned judge was, in my judgment, correct in upholding two separate causes of action, and awarding restitution in the amount that he did on the first, and only nominal damages on the second.

For all these reasons I would dismiss this appeal.

Nourse LJ delivered a short concurring judgment.

NOTES AND QUESTIONS

1. Cunnington, 'Failure of Basis' [2004] *LMCLQ* 234, 246, has argued that 'the Court of Appeal effectively broke up the consideration pound by pound to enable them to find a total failure of the severed part. Such analysis removes any real distinction between partial and total failure of consideration.' Similarly, in *Ministry of Sound (Ireland) Ltd v World Online Ltd* [2003] EWHC 2178 (Ch) at [63], Nicholas Strauss QC said:

   Whilst the traditional view is that a party to a contract (whether the innocent party or the contract breaker) can only recover payments made under it where there has been a total failure of consideration, the dictum of Lord Goff in *Goss v Chilcott* . . . suggests that this may no longer be so, and recent authority suggests that there may be circumstances in which recovery for partial failure may be allowed: see *D.O. Ferguson & Associates v Sohl* (1992) 62 B.L.R. 95 (C.A.) in which, as the editorial note indicates, Hirst L.J. 'robustly' described as a total failure of consideration what might more conventionally have been seen as a partial failure.

   In contrast, Birks argued that 'a claimant seeking to establish that an enrichment has no basis must establish a total failure of its basis. There is no such thing as a partial failure of basis' (*Unjust Enrichment* (2nd edn, 2005), 120). Do you agree?

2. Would the award of restitution have been the same if the Court of Appeal had ordered that Ferguson should repay Sohl all payments made (£26,738) subject to counter-restitution of the value of the work done? Would it make a difference if the work was valued at market rates instead of contract rates?

3. Should Sohl's claim for damages for breach of contract have had an impact upon his claim for restitution? Given that the award of damages for breach of contract is to protect the claimant's expectation interest, could it not be argued that the ability of a claimant such as Mr Sohl to protect his disappointed expectations (if they exist) via a damages claim results in there being no failure of consideration (whether total or partial) because the claimant's expectations have been fulfilled, whether by performance or by the payment of damages? (see further E McKendrick, 'Total failure of Consideration and Counter-Restitution: Two issues or One?' in P Birks (ed.), *Laundering and Tracing* (1995), 217).

- *Baltic Shipping Company v Dillon (The Mikhail Lermontov)*
  (1993) 176 CLR 344, High Court of Australia

The claimant (respondent), Mrs Dillon, booked a cruise on board the defendant's (appellant's) vessel, the *Mikhail Lermontov*. The cruise began on 7 February 1986 from Sydney and was scheduled to end in Sydney on 21 February. The vessel struck a shoal off the South-East coast of New Zealand on 16 February and it sank, causing the claimant loss both to her possessions and her person. The trial judge, Carruthers J, awarded the claimant damages under a number of different heads, namely restitution of the part of the fare which the defendants had not returned to her (they had returned the 'unused portion of [the] passage money' but Mrs Dillon wished to recover the rest of the fare which she had paid), loss of valuables, compensation for disappointment and distress, damages for personal injury, and interest. In total she was awarded damages of some $51,000. The defendants appealed unsuccessfully to the New South Wales Court of Appeal and from there to the High Court of Australia. The appeal to the High Court was successful in that it was held that the claimant was not entitled to recover the balance of the fare as there had been no total failure of consideration and, further, it was held that the claimant could not combine an action to recover the balance of the fare with an action for damages for breach of contract.

Mason CJ:

THE CLAIM FOR RESTITUTION OF THE FARE

Basis on which the claim is advanced

By cl. 12 of her further amended writ of summons in personam, the respondent claimed: 'return of the full fare in the sum of $2,205.00 as for a total failure of consideration.' By cl. 7 of the defence, the appellant simply denied that there had been a total failure of consideration. At trial, the respondent's claim was refined so as to extend only to the balance of the fare not already refunded by the appellant, that balance being $1,417.50.

Carruthers J held that the contract of passage was an entire one[1] and said:[2]

'In reality, the plaintiff got no benefit from this contract. It is true that she did have eight days cruising on the vessel and visited the Bay of Islands, Auckland, Tauranga, Wellington and Picton, but those benefits were entirely negated by the catastrophe which occurred upon departure from Picton. Thus, I would allow the amount claimed under this head.'

In the Court of Appeal, the appellant challenged the finding that there was a total failure of consideration. The challenge was rejected. Kirby P,[3] with whom Gleeson CJ agreed on this point,[4] noted that the appellant had urged that there was no total failure of consideration as '[t]he respondent had had the benefit of eight of fourteen days of an idyllic cruise.' He concluded that the contract of carriage was an entire one. His Honour said:

'On this point it is my view that Carruthers J reached the right conclusion. The respondent did not contract with the appellant for an eight-day cruise, still less for an eight-day cruise interrupted by the disaster which befell the *"Mikhail Lermontov"*. What she contracted for was a relaxing holiday experience. It is this that she failed to secure. The contract of carriage was properly categorized as an entire contract. I agree with the judge that there is a good analogy to Sir George Jessel MR's statement in *Re Hall & Barker*:[5] ". . . If a shoemaker agrees to make a pair of shoes, he cannot offer you one shoe, and ask you to pay one half of the price." '

He then observed that, in order to avoid over-compensation, a claim for restitution of money paid on a total failure of consideration will succeed only if accompanied by counter-restitution of benefits bargained for and received by the claimant.

In the Court of Appeal, the appellant also relied upon cl. 9 of the printed ticket terms and conditions. That clause incorporated a right to proportional return of the consideration in certain circumstances. Kirby P held that the clause, while it could exclude the right to restitution in certain circumstances, was inapplicable for two reasons: first, the clause was not incorporated into the contract of carriage; secondly, by reason of the admission of negligence by the appellant, the reason for the impossibility of continuation of the voyage was not 'beyond the control' of the appellant and, therefore, a precondition of its operation was not satisfied. Gleeson CJ agreed generally that the ticket terms and conditions were not incorporated. However, he said that sufficient notice may have been given of some terms and conditions printed on the ticket so as to incorporate them. He did not consider cl. 9 separately.

Accordingly, the Court of Appeal, by majority, held that the respondent was entitled to restitution of the balance of the fare.

In this Court, the appellant contends that the majority in the Court of Appeal erred in holding that

---

1   *Dillon v Baltic Shipping Co.* (1989), 21 NSWLR, 614, at 667.   2   *Ibid.*, 668.
3   (1991) 22 NSWLR, at 26.   4   *Ibid.*, 7.   5   (1878) 9 ChD 538, at 545.

the respondent was entitled to restitution of the whole of the fare. In support of this contention, the appellant submits that there was not a total failure of consideration arising from the fact that the contract of carriage was entire. The appellant also submits that a plaintiff cannot pursue both a claim for restitution of the consideration paid under a contract and a claim for damages for breach of that contract. It seems that this argument was not presented to, or considered by, the courts below. The merits of this argument, which will be considered below, do not necessarily depend on the availability of damages for disappointment and distress. That is but one head of damages whose recoverability is in question. However, if restitution is available and such damages are recoverable, questions of double compensation arise.

Is the fare recoverable on the ground of total failure of consideration or otherwise?

An entire contract or, perhaps more accurately, an entire obligation is one in which the consideration for the payment of money or for the rendering of some other counter-performance is entire and indivisible. In *Steele v Tardiani*,[6] Dixon J cited the general proposition stated in E. V. Williams' *Notes to Saunders' Reports*:[7]

> 'Where the consideration for the payment of money is entire and indivisible, as where the benefit expected by the defendant under the agreement is to result from the enjoyment of every part of the consideration jointly, so that the money payable is neither apportioned by the contract, nor capable of being apportioned by a jury, no action is maintainable, if any part of the consideration has failed; for, being entire, by failing partially, it fails altogether.'

The concept of an entire contract is material when a court is called upon to decide whether complete performance by one party is a condition precedent to the other's liability to pay the stipu-lated price or to render an agreed counter-performance.[8] If this were a case in which the appellant sought to enforce a promise to pay the cruise fare at the conclusion of the voyage the concept would have a part to play; then, if the appellant's obligations were entire, on the facts as I have stated them, the appellant's incomplete performance of its obligations would not entitle it to recover.

When, however, an innocent party seeks to recover money paid in advance under a contract in expectation of the entire performance by the contract-breaker of its obligations under the contract and the contract-breaker renders an incomplete performance, in general, the innocent party cannot recover unless there has been a total failure of consideration.[9] If the incomplete performance results in the innocent party receiving and retaining any substantial part of the benefit expected under the contract, there will not be a total failure of consideration.

In the context of the recovery of money paid on the footing that there has been a total failure of consideration, it is the performance of the defendant's promise, not the promise itself, which is the relevant consideration.[10] In that context, the receipt and retention by the plaintiff of any part of the bargained-for benefit will preclude recovery, unless the contract otherwise provides or the circum-stances give rise to a fresh contract. So, in *Whincup v Hughes*,[11] the plaintiff apprenticed his son to a watchmaker for six years for a premium which was paid. The watchmaker died after one year. No part of the premium could be recovered. That was because there was not a total failure of consideration.[12]

---

6 (1946) 72 CLR 386, at 401.

7 6th edn (1845), vol. 1: *Pordage v Cole* (1669), 1 Wms Saund. 319, at 320, n. (c) [85 ER 449, at 453].

8 *Hoenig v Isaacs* [1952] 2 All ER 176, at 180–1; Glanville Williams, 'Partial Performance of Entire Contracts' (1941) 57 *Law Quarterly Review* 373; Beck, 'The Doctrine of Substantial Performance: Conditions and Conditions Precedent' (1975) 38 *Modern Law Review* 413.

9 Goff and Jones, *The Law of Restitution* (3rd edn, 1986), 449; Birks, *An Introduction to the Law of Restitution* (rev. edn, 1989), 242–8.

10 *Fibrosa Spolka Akeyjna v Fairbairn Lawson Combe Barbour Ltd* [1943] AC 32, at 48.

11 (1871) LR 6 CP 78.   12 See also *Hunt v Silk* (1804) 5 East 449 [102 ER 1142].

A qualification to this general rule, more apparent than real, has been introduced in the case of contracts where a seller is bound to vest title to chattels or goods in a buyer and the buyer seeks to recover the price paid when it turns out that title has not been passed. Even if the buyer has had the use and enjoyment of chattels or goods purportedly supplied under the contract for a limited time, the use and enjoyment of the chattels or goods has been held not to amount to the receipt of part of the contractual consideration. Where the buyer is entitled under the contract to good title and lawful possession but receives only unlawful possession, he or she does not receive any part of what he or she but gained for. And thus, it is held, there is a total failure of consideration.[13] As this Court stated in *David Securities Pty. Ltd v Commonwealth Bank of Australia*:[14] 'the notion of total failure of consideration now looks to the benefit bargained for by the plaintiff rather than any benefit which might have been received in fact.'

An alternative basis for the recovery of money paid in advance pursuant to a contract in expectation of the receipt of the consideration to be provided by the defendant may arise when the defendant's right to retain the payment is conditional upon performance of his or her obligations under the contract. This basis of recovery has a superficial, but not a close, resemblance to the concept of an entire contract. In this class of case the plaintiff may be entitled to recover so long as the payment remains conditional.

So, in *Dies v British & International Mining & Finance Corporation*,[15] the plaintiff bought arms for the price of £135,000, paying £100,000 in advance. Though unwilling or unable to take delivery, the plaintiff succeeded in recovering the payment, notwithstanding that Stable J held that there was not a total failure of consideration. There can, of course, be no such failure when the plaintiff's unwilling-ness or refusal to perform the contract on his or her part is the cause of the defendant's non-performance. The decision is explicable either on the ground that the seller accepted the plaintiff's repudiation and thus itself effected the discharge of the contract[16] or on the ground that the payment was a mere part payment, the right to which depended upon performance of the contract and was thus conditional.[17] Of the two explanations, the second is to be preferred because it is in closer accord with the judgment of Stable J. His Lordship said:[18]

'[W]here the language used in a contract is neutral, the general rule is that the law confers on the purchaser the right to recover his money, and that to enable the seller to keep it he must be able to point to some language in the contract from which the inference to be drawn is that the parties intended and agreed that he should.'

This statement in turn accords with the distinction drawn by Lord Denman CJ (to which Stable J referred) in *Palmer v Temple*[19] between a deposit which was to be forfeited if the plaintiff should not perform the contract and a mere part payment the right to which depended upon performance of the contract. The statement also accords with the point made by Dixon J in *McDonald v Dennys Lascelles Ltd*, where he said:[20]

'When a contract stipulates for payment of part of the purchase money in advance, the purchaser relying only on the vendor's promise to give him a conveyance, the vendor is entitled to enforce payment before the time has arrived for conveying the land; yet his title to retain the money has been considered not to be absolute but conditional upon the subsequent completion of the contract.'

---

13 *Rowland v Divall* [1923] 2 KB 500; *Butterworth v Kingsway Motors Ltd* [1954] 1 WLR 1286; [1954] 2 All ER 694.
14 (1992) 175 CLR 353, at 381–3.   15 [1939] 1 KB 724.
16 Birks, 237.   17 Beatson, *The Use and Abuse of Unjust Enrichment* (1991), 54.
18 [1939] 1 KB at 743.   19 (1839) 9 Ad. & E 508, at 520–1 [112 ER 1304, at 1309].
20 (1933) 48 CLR 457, at 477.

The question whether an advance payment, not being a deposit or earnest of performance, is absolute or conditional is one of construction. In determining that question it is material to ascertain whether the payee is required by the contract to perform work and incur expense before completing this performance of his or her obligations under the contract. If the payee is so required then, unless the contract manifests a contrary intention, it would be unreasonable to hold that the payee's right to retain the payment is conditional upon performance of the contractual obligations.[21]

I have come to the conclusion in the present case that the respondent is not entitled to recover the cruise fare on either of the grounds just discussed. The consequence of the respondent's enjoyment of the benefits provided under the contract during the first eight full days of the cruise is that the failure of consideration was partial, not total. I do not understand how, viewed from the perspective of failure of consideration, the enjoyment of those benefits was 'entirely negated by the catastrophe which occurred upon departure from Picton',[22] to repeat the words of the primary judge.

Nor is there any acceptable foundation for holding that the advance payment of the cruise fare created in the appellant no more than a right to retain the payment conditional upon its complete performance of its entire obligations under the contract. As the contract called for performance by the appellant of its contractual obligations from the very commencement of the voyage and continuously thereafter, the advance payment should be regarded as the provision of consideration for each and every substantial benefit expected under the contract. It would not be reasonable to treat the appellant's right to retain the fare as conditional upon complete performance when the appellant is under a liability to provide substantial benefits to the respondent during the course of the voyage. After all, the return of the respondent to Sydney at the end of the voyage, though an important element in the performance of the appellant's obligations, was but one of many elements. In order to illustrate the magnitude of the step which the respondent asks the Court to take, it is sufficient to pose two questions, putting to one side cl. 9 of the printed ticket terms and conditions. Would the respondent be entitled to a return of the fare if, owing to failure of the ship's engines, the ship was unable to proceed on the last leg of the cruise to Sydney and it became necessary to airlift the respondent to Sydney? Would the fare be recoverable if, owing to a hurricane, the ship was compelled to omit a visit to one of the scheduled ports of call? The answer in each case must be a resounding negative.

The respondent sought to derive support from authorities relating to the contracts for the carriage of goods by sea which hold that freight is due on the arrival of the goods at the agreed destination. More to the point is the principle that an advance by the shipper on account of the freight to be earned is, in the absence of any stipulation to the contrary, 'an irrevocable payment at the risk of the shipper of the goods'.[23] The result of this rule is that an advance on account of freight may be retained, notwithstanding that, because of a failure to complete the voyage and to deliver the goods, the freight remains unearned[24] and that a payment due as an advance on account of freight is recoverable (if not duly paid) even after frustration of the voyage.[25] This rule, although it has been said to be a stipulation introduced into such contracts by custom and not the result of applying some abstract principle,[26] would certainly exclude a restitutionary claim on facts analogous to those in the present case.

---

21 See *Hyundai Shipbuilding & Heavy Industries Co. Ltd v Pournaras* [1978] 2 Lloyd's Rep. 502; *Hyundai Heavy Industries Co. Ltd v Papadopoulos* [1980] 1 WLR 1129; [1980] 2 All ER 29; and the discussion in Beatson, 56–7.

22 (1989) 21 NSWLR at 668.

23 *Allison v Bristol Marine Insurance Co.* (1876), 1 App Cas 209, at 253, *per* Lord Selborne; see also *Greeves v West India & Pacific Steamship Co. Ltd* (1870), 22 LT 615.

24 See *Compania Naviera General SA v Kerametal Ltd (The 'Lorna I')* [1983] 1 Lloyd's Rep 373

25 See Goff and Jones, 451, n.14. This does not mean that freight is earned prior to delivery: it will be earned upon shipment only if the parties expressly so stipulate.

26 *Fibrosa* [1943] AC at 43.

The combination of a claim for restitution and a claim for damages

In view of my conclusion that the respondent cannot succeed in her restitutionary claim for recoupment of the fare, there is no necessity for me to consider whether the two claims can be maintained. However, as the question has been argued, I should record my view of the question. There is authority to suggest that the claims are alternative and not cumulative.[27] But Lord Denning MR was clearly of the view that the claims may be concurrent. In *Heywood v Wellers (a firm),*[28] he said:

'[The plaintiff] could recover the £175 as money paid on a consideration which had wholly failed. She was, therefore, entitled to recover it as of right. And she is entitled to recover as well damages for negligence. Take this instance. If you engage a driver to take you to the station to catch a train for a day trip to the sea, you pay him £2—and then the car breaks down owing to his negligence. So that you miss your holiday. In that case you can recover not only your £2 back but also damages for the disappointment, upset and mental distress which you suffered.'

Lord Denning was speaking of negligence in the sense of breach of a contractual obligation of due care. He noted a qualification to the entitlement to maintain the two claims:[29]

'Some reduction should be made for the fact that if the [defendants] had done their duty . . . it would have cost her something.'

That reduction was accordingly made to the damages for breach of contract.

Similarly, in *Millar's Machinery Co. Ltd v David Way & Son,*[30] the Court of Appeal dismissed an appeal from a decision of Branson J in which such a dual award was made. The case concerned a contract for supply of machinery. It was held that there had been a total failure of consideration and that the purchasers were entitled to recover the amount paid on account. In addition, the purchasers were held to be entitled to damages, the proper measure of which was:[31] 'the sum which the [purchasers] had to spend to put themselves in the position [in] which they would have been if the [suppliers] had carried out their contract.' That amount was the difference between the contract price and the amount which they had to pay to another supplier for a similar machine.

And Treitel says in relation to claims for loss of bargain, reliance loss and restitution:[32]

'There is sometimes said to be an inconsistency between combining the various types of claim . . .

The true principle is not that there is any logical objection to combining the various types of claim, but that the plaintiff cannot combine them so as to recover more than once for the same loss. . . . The point has been well put by Corbin: "*full* damages and *complete* restitution . . . will not both be given for the same breach of contract"[33].'

The action to recover money paid on a total failure of consideration is on a common money count for money had and received to the use of the plaintiff.[34] The action evolved from the writ of indebitatus assumpsit.[35] It is available only if the contract has been discharged, either for breach or

---

27 e.g., *Walstab v Spottiswoode* (1846), 15 M & W 501, at 514 [153 ER 947, at 953], *per* Pollock CB.

28 [1976] Q 46, at 458.

29 [1976] QB at 459.   30 (1935) 40 Com Cas 204.   31 *Ibid.,* at 208.

32 *Law of Contract* (8th edn 1991), 834. However, elsewhere he appears to treat the claims as alternatives: 932–3.

33 *Corbin on Contracts* (1952), §1221. Emphasis added by Treitel.

34 *Fibrosa* [1943] AC at 61–3. To the extent that it is necessary to say so, this decision correctly reflects the law in Australia and, to the extent that it is inconsistent, should be preferred to the decision of this Court in *In re Continental C. & G. Rubber Co. Pty. Ltd* (1919) 27 CLR 194.

35 See Lücke, 'Slade's Case and the Origin of the Common Courts—Part 3' (1966) 82 *Law Quarterly Review* 81.

following frustration,[36] and if there has been a total, and not merely partial, failure of consideration.[37] It is now clear that, in these cases, the discharge operates only prospectively, that is, it is not equivalent to rescission ab initio. Nor is rescission ab initio a precondition for recovery.[38] Unconditionally accrued rights, including accrued rights to sue for damages for prior breach of the contract,[39] are not affected by the discharge. Prepayments can, in general, be recovered, but the position of deposits or earnests is not entirely clear, the better view being that they are not recoverable if paid to provide a sanction against withdrawal.[40]

In 1846, when Pollock CB held in *Walstab v Spolliswoode* that it was not possible to combine a claim for damages with one for restitution, the restitutionary action was brought on the writ of indebitatus assumpsit.[41] Subsequently, Lord Wright said in *Fibrosa Spolka Akcyjna v Fairbairn Lawson Combe Barbour Ltd*:[42]

'The writ of indebitatus assumpsit involved at least two averments, the debt or obligation and the assumpsit. The former was the basis of the claim and was the real cause of action. The latter was merely fictitious and could not be traversed, but was necessary to enable the convenient and liberal form of action to be used in such cases.'

The action was, as Lord Mansfield said in *Moses v Macferlan*,[43] 'quasi ex contractu' and founded on an obligation imposed by law and accommodated within the system of formal pleading by means of the fictitious assumpsit or promise. It was necessary to plead the fictitious assumpsit until the enactment of s. 3 of the *Common Law Procedure Act* 1852 (Eng.). And even then its influence continued. The abolition of the forms of action inspired an analysis of the sources of obligation in the common law in terms of a rigid dichotomy between contract and tort. In that context, there was little room for restitutionary obligation imposed by law except as a 'quasi-contractual' appendix to the law of contract. As a result, until recently, restitutionary claims were disallowed when a promise could not be implied in fact.[44] However, since *Pavey & Matthews Pty. Ltd v Paul*,[45] such an approach no longer represents the law in Australia.

But, in the circumstances prevailing in 1846, it is not difficult to see that a plaintiff would necessarily be put to an election between the real and fictitious promises. In cases of tort it is equally plain that there had to be a choice between an action on a fictitious assumpsit (waiving the tort) and seeking damages for the tort.

The decision in *Walstab v Spottiswoode* may also be seen as a consequence of two historical threads. The first is the competition in the latter part of the sixteenth century between the judges of the King's Bench and those of the Common Pleas as to the relationship between debt and assumpsit.

---

36 Goff and Jones, 449, states that the law in either case is 'fundamentally similar'. The House of Lords in *Fibrosa* drew no distinction.

37 The action in debt based on a partial failure of consideration (*Anon* (1293), Y.B. 21–22 Edw. I. (R.S.) 110–11) disappeared in the middle ages. See Stoljar, *A History of Contract at Common Law* (1975), 7.

38 *Fibrosa* [1943] AC at 49, 53, 57, 60, 70, 73, 83.

39 *McDonald v Dennys Lascelles Ltd* (1933), 48 CLR at 477, *per* Dixon J.

40 Birks, 223–4; *Mayson v Clouet* [1924] AC 980.

41 Stoljar, 116–17, notes that the availability of *indebitatus assumpsit* (from the late seventeenth century) in such quasi-contractual situations supplementing and eventually supplanting debt and account (see Jackson, *The History of Quasi-Contract in English Law* (1936), 18 ff. and Stoljar, 181), was essentially a procedural development, simplifying recovery and providing a more convenient or more summary remedy.

42 [1943] AC at 63.

43 (1760) 2 Burr 1005, at 1008 [97 ER 676, at 678].

44 Birks and McLeod trace civil law origins of the implied contract approach: 'The Implied Contract Theory of Quasi-Contract: Civilian Opinion Current in the Century Before Blackstone' (1986) 6 *Oxford Journal of Legal Studies* 46.

45 (1987) 162 CLR 221.

The critical decision in the resolution of the conflict was *Slade's Case*.[46] While the precise contemporary import of the decision is a matter of controversy,[47] it was taken in the seventeenth century as deciding that indebitatus assumpsit lay as well as debt to recover sums due under a contract in the absence of an express subsequent promise to pay.[48] The assumpsit or promise was founded 'not upon any fiction of law, but upon an interpretation of facts by the court which led it to the genuine conclusion that the parties had actually agreed [to make the payment]'.[49]

The second is the decision at around the same time that indebitatus assumpsit lay in circumstances where the assumpsit was necessarily imputed rather than genuinely implied from the facts.[50] *Arris v Stukely*[51] is an example. In that case, the defendant, who had been granted by letters patent the office of comptroller of the customs at the port of Exeter, continued to pretend title to that office after its termination and grant to the plaintiff. The Court held that indebitatus assumpsit lay to recover the profits received by the defendant after the grant of the office to the plaintiff. In *Holmes v Hall*,[52] Holt CJ refused to nonsuit the plaintiff who sued on an indebitatus assumpsit to recover moneys he paid as executor to the defendant who held certain writings of the testator. The defendant failed to perform his promise to deliver up the writings.[53]

But it was recognized early on that cases like *Holmes v Hall* were equally cases of breach of contract in which a special assumpsit lay, and the question was raised whether the plaintiff should be required to bring his or her action in that form. In *Moses v Macferlan*, Lord Mansfield said[54] that the plaintiff would be permitted to proceed on an indebitatus assumpsit, although an action for damages in covenant or on a special assumpsit was available. He continued:

'If the plaintiff elects to proceed in this favourable way [on the indebitatus assumpsit], it is a bar to his bringing another action upon the agreement; though he might recover more upon the agreement, than he can by this form of action.'

He referred to *Dutch v Warren* where the general principles were re-stated as follows:[55]

'[T]he defendant by a refusal to execute, or by a complete and selfevident inability to perform, or by a fraudulent execution he has given the plaintiff an option to disaffirm the contract, and recover the consideration he was paid for it in the same manner as if it had never existed . . . But then the contract must be totally rescinded, and appear unexecuted in every part at the time of bringing the action; since otherwise, the contract is affirmed by the plaintiff's having received part of that equivalent for which he has paid his consideration, and it is then reduced to a mere question of damages proportionate to the extent to which it remains unperformed.'

See also *Greville v Da Costa*.[56]

---

46 (1602) 4 Co. Rep 92b [76 ER 1074]; also reported as *Slade v Morley*, Yelv 21 [80 ER 15], Moo KB 433 [72 ER 677].

47 See Lücke, 'Slade's Case and the Origin of the Common Courts' (1964) 81 *Law Quarterly Review* 422 and 539; (1966) 82 *Law Quarterly Review* 81; Baker, 'New Light on *Slade's Case*', [1971] *Cambridge Law Journal* 51 and 213; Ibbetson, 'Sixteenth Century Contract Law: *Slade's Case* in Context' (1984) 4 *Oxford Journal of Legal Studies* 295.

48 See Ibbetson, *op. cit.*

49 Winfield, *The Law of Quasi-Contracts* (1952), 7.

50 See Winfield, *op. cit.*, 8; Jackson, *op. cit.*, 40–1.

51 (1677) 2 Mod 260 [86 ER 1060].

52 (1704) 6 Mod 161 [87 ER 918]; Holt KB 36 [90 ER 917].

53 According to the *Modern Reports*, the plaintiff was nonsuited when it became clear that the money was paid in discharge of a debt owed by the testator to the defendant: (1704) 6 Mod, at 161 [87 ER at 919].

54 (1760) 2 Burr at 1010 [97 ER at 679–80].

55 (1720) 1 Stra 406, at 406 [93 ER 598, at 599].

56 (1797) Peake Add Cas 113 [170 ER 213]; cf. *Giles v Edwards* (1797), 7 TR 181 [101 ER 920].

This insistence on rescission or the non-existence of an 'open' contract makes it easier to understand how the decision in *Chandler v Webster*[57] was reached. We now know the effect of discharge to be different and, as *Fibrosa* indicates, nothing more than that usual effect is necessary to ground the action to recover money paid on a total failure of consideration.

Conclusion: the respondent cannot recover the fare and damages for breach of contract

The old forms of action cannot provide the answer today. But, in my view, *Walstab v Spottiswoode* and the earlier cases support the view expressed by Corbin and Treitel that full damages and complete restitution will not be given for the same breach of contract. There are several reasons. First, restitution of the contractual consideration removes, at least notionally, the basis on which the plaintiff is entitled to call on the defendant to perform his or her contractual obligations. More particularly, the continued retention by the defendant is regarded, in the language of Lord Mansfield, as 'against conscience' or, in the modern terminology, as an unjust enrichment of the defendant because the condition upon which it was paid, namely, performance by the defendant may not have occurred.[58] But, equally, that performance, for deficiencies in which damages are sought, was conditional on payment by the plaintiff. Recovery of the money paid destroys performance of that condition. Secondly, the plaintiff will almost always be protected by an award of damages for breach of contract, which in appropriate cases will include an amount for substitute performance or an amount representing the plaintiff's reliance loss. It should be noted that nothing said here is inconsistent with *McRae v Commonwealth Disposals Commission*.[59]

I would therefore conclude that, even if the respondent had an entitlement to recover the cruise fare, Carruthers J and the majority of the Court of Appeal erred in allowing restitution of the balance of the fare along with damages for breach of contract. The consequences of this conclusion will be considered below in light of the conclusion to be reached with regard to the award of damages for disappointment and distress. . . .

Deane and **Dawson JJ** . . . There can be circumstances in which there is, for relevant purposes, a complete failure of consideration under a contract of transportation notwithstanding that the carrier has provided sustenance, entertainment and carriage of the passenger during part of the stipulated journey. For example, the consideration for which the fare is paid under a contract for the transportation of a passenger by air from Sydney to London would, at least prima facie, wholly fail if, after dinner and the inflight film, the aircraft were forced to turn back due to negligent maintenance on the part of the carrier and if the passenger were disembarked at the starting point in Sydney and informed that no alternative transportation would be provided. Thus, *Heywood v Wellers*, Lord Denning MR regarded it as self-evident that, in some circumstances where part of a journey had been completed, money paid to the carrier or 'driver' was recoverable 'as of right' for the reason that it was 'money paid on a consideration which had wholly failed'.[60]

However, the promised consideration in the present case was not, as a matter of substance, the transportation of Mrs Dillon from Sydney to Sydney. As has been said, it was the provision of all that was involved in the promised pleasure cruise as a holiday experience. Even on the assumption that that promised consideration was entire and indivisible, it did not wholly fail. Baltic provided and Mrs Dillon accepted and enjoyed eight complete days of the cruise. It is true that Mrs Dillon would have been entitled to decline to board the ship or to accept only part of the promised consideration if it could have, and had, been known in advance that all the Baltic would in fact provide was eight days of cruising culminating in the sinking of the ship off New Zealand as a result of

---

57 [1904] 1 KB 493. It was overruled in *Fibrosa*.
58 See *Fibrosa* [1943] AC at 65–6, *per* Lord Weight.
59 (1951) 84 CLR 377.   60 [1976] QB 446, 458.

Baltic's breach of its contractual duty to take reasonable care. If, in that necessarily hypothetical situation, Mrs Dillon had wisely decided to stay at home, the consideration for the fare would have failed completely and, subject to any applicable provisions of the contract between herself and Baltic,[61] she would have been entitled to succeed in an action in unjust enrichment for the recovery of the whole fare. In circumstances where Mrs Dillon accepted and enjoyed the major portion of the pleasure cruise, however, there was no complete failure of the consideration for which she paid the fare. The catastrophe of the ship wreck and its consequences undoubtedly outweighed the benefits of the first eight complete days. It did not, however, alter the fact that those benefits, which were of real value, had been provided, accepted and enjoyed.

There is a further reason, which would appear not to have been raised in argument in the courts below, why Mrs Dillon's action for restitution of the fare paid to Baltic must fail. It is that she has sought and obtained an order against Baltic for compensatory damages for Baltic's failure to perform its contractual promises to her. In particular, she has received a refund of a proportionate part of the fare and has obtained and will retain (see below) the benefit of an award of damages for the disappointment and distress which she sustained by reason of Baltic's failure to provide her with the full pleasure cruise which it promised to provide. In these circumstances, Mrs Dillon has indirectly enforced, and indirectly obtained the benefit of, Baltic's contractual promises.

Ordinarily, as has been seen, 'when one is considering the law of failure of consideration and of the ... right to recover money on that ground, it is ... not the promise which is referred to as the consideration, but the performance of the promise'.[62] That statement has nothing to say, however, to the situation which exists when the promise has sought and obtained an award of full compensatory damages for the failure to perform the promise. In that situation, the damages are awarded and received as full compensation for non-performance or breach of the promise and represent the indirect fruits of the promise. That being so, it would be quite wrong to say either that the only quid pro quo which has been obtained for the payment by the promisee is the bare promise or that the promise and the recovery of compensatory damages for its breach can realistically be seen as representing no consideration at all. In such a case, the promise has been indirectly enforced and the award of compensation has, as a matter of substance, been received in substitution for the promised consideration. In those circumstances, the promisee, having received full compensation for non-performance of the promise, is not entitled to a refund of the price upon payment of which the performance of the promise was conditioned.[63] Were it otherwise, the promisee 'would have the equivalent' of performance of the contractual promise 'without having borne the expense' which he or she had agreed to pay for it.[64] ...

Brennan, Toohey, Gaudron, and **McHugh JJ** delivered concurring judgments.

NOTES AND QUESTIONS

1. It is suggested that the High Court of Australia was correct to conclude that there had been no total failure of consideration, but the more difficult question, and the question which the High Court was not required to answer, was whether the claimant should have been able to recover even upon a partial failure of consideration. The High Court did not need to answer this question because Mrs Dillon had already been refunded the proportionate part of her fare (corresponding to the days of the cruise lost) by Baltic Shipping. But both English and

---

61 See, e.g. *Fibrosa* [1943] AC at 67. 62 *Ibid.* 48, *per* Viscount Simon I.C.
63 See, e.g., *Moses v Macferlan* (1760), 2 Burr at 1010 [97 ER at 679].
64 See *TC Industrial Plant Pty. Ltd v Robert's Queensland Pty. Ltd* (1963), 37 ALJR 289, at 293; [1964] ALR 1083, at 1090.

Australian law still formally insist that the failure of consideration be total, although there are signs that the courts may be prepared to allow recovery in the case of a partial failure of consideration where the apportionment can be carried out without difficulty (see *Goss v Chilcott* (below, 384) and *David Securities Pty. Ltd v Commonwealth Bank of Australia* (1992) 175 CLR 353, 383, HCA).

2. The case for recognizing a partial failure of consideration as a sufficient ground for a restitutionary claim has been made by K Barker ('Restitution of Passenger Fare' [1994] *LMCLQ* 291, 293–4) in the following terms:

> If the lower courts were indeed straining to grant restitution for partial failure, why did not the High Court reconsider the requirement that failures of consideration must be total? The simple answer, of course, is that no argument was put before it upon the issue, but this in itself is no justification. Indeed, it is difficult to find a cogent reason for the traditional rule.
>
> One justification sometimes offered is that the requirement avoids difficulties over counter-restitution. If plaintiffs only ever have a cause of action when they have received no performance, the courts are relieved of the often tricky task of valuing counter-restitutionary awards. This is unconvincing. For one thing, a plaintiff may be willing to allow the court a liberal approach to valuation; if so, it seems unfair to bar his claim. More importantly, however, if there is a problem over counter-restitution, it can (and should) be dealt with at the defence, not the cause of action, stage.
>
> Secondly, it is said that the requirement, by restricting restitution, indirectly protects the law of contract, and in particular the presumption that the normal remedy for breach should be compensatory damages. This point is also misconstrued. Restitution poses no internal threat to contractual remedies, because in this context it is not founded upon breach, but operates autonomously, outside the boundaries of contract law. Nor does it greatly undermine contractual remedies externally, because its availability is contingent upon the (relatively rare) event of contractual discharge. Furthermore, once it is accepted that the restitutionary cause of action *is* autonomous, an automatic policy of contractual protectionism appears to be unjustified. There is no *a priori* reason why, just because contract law gives a compensatory remedy by way of response to a given set of facts, the plaintiff should be debarred from seeking a restitutionary remedy provided by the law of unjust enrichment.
>
> There is now a considerable number of cases where restitution has been granted in what are best viewed as instances of partial failure.[1] Moreover, the regime under the Law Reform (Frustrated Contracts) Act 1943 expressly recognizes partial failure as a good restitutionary cause of action. There is sense in this, since the plaintiff's moral case for relief is much the same as where the failure is total. Her consent to the defendant's retaining the money, originally qualified by reference to a condition, has, with the failure of that condition, been vitiated. This being so, the moral imperative for relief is established and it can make no difference that some part of the requested performance has been received.
>
> In the event, the High Court's failure to acknowledge that partial failures disclose a good cause of action is regrettable. The development is long overdue.

3. What would have been the position if the contract between Mrs Dillon and Baltic Shipping had contained a liquidated damages clause making provision for the sum payable to Mrs Dillon in the event of a breach by Baltic? Would, or should, Mrs Dillon have been able to bring a claim to recover the balance of the fare on the ground of a partial failure of consideration, notwithstanding the presence of the liquidated damages clause in the contract? Would the effect of such a clause be that the parties had thereby contracted out of restitution?

4. The High Court of Australia was also of the view that Mrs Dillon could not combine her claim for damages in contract with her restitutionary claim to recover the fare: she had to elect between them. This aspect of the decision has been criticized by K Barker [1994] *LMCLQ* 291, 294–6 in the following terms:

---

1 See, e.g., *Boomer v Muir* (1933) 24 P 2d 570; *Rover International Ltd v Cannon Film Sales Ltd* [1989] 1 WLR 912; *Butterworth v Kingsway Motors Ltd* [1954] 1 WLR 1286; *Warman v Southern Counties Car Finance Corp. Ltd* [1949] 2 KB 576.

The High Court appears to have offered two lines of justification for its conclusion that Mrs Dillon could not successfully maintain both an action for damages for breach of contract and an action to recover her fare. One was that the two forms of action were logically inconsistent on the facts; the other that they could not be combined for reasons of policy.

Logical inconsistency

At one point, it was suggested that an award of compensation for breach eradicates a plaintiff's restitutionary cause of action: since damages for breach of contract represent a form of substitute performance or 'consideration', it is not open to a plaintiff who has received them to argue that the consideration for her payment has totally failed. She *has* received something for her money—namely, damages.

A mirror argument, that an award of restitution extinguishes a plaintiff's contractual cause of action, was also used. Since Mrs Dillon's right to demand performance from Baltic was itself conditional upon the payment of her fare, restitution of the fare removed her entitlement to demand contract performance and, with it, the right to recover compensatory damages for breach.

Both of these arguments are misconstrued. The first overlooks the fact that Mrs Dillon wanted primary performance (a cruise), not secondary performance (damages). To obtain compensation is never *to receive part of* that for which one has bargained; it is to have one's *loss* of bargain made good. The second argument plays tricks with time. If Mrs Dillon had a contractual cause of action at the time the *Mikhail Lermontov* sank (which she did), it cannot be that giving her money back would retroactively eradicate this ground of complaint. The wrong done to her at the time would remain until her losses were fully compensated. A restitutionary award would do nothing, in other words, to 'rectify' or 'extinguish' the contractual wrong. Moreover, the consequence of the second argument would be ludicrous. To take an extreme example, the recovery of a 50p bus-fare would automatically preclude a passenger from suing in contract for spinal injuries caused to her by the driver's culpable negligence.

A third argument sometimes put is not so much that contract damages eradicate the restitutionary cause of action, as that the objectives of compensatory and restitutionary remedies are logically incompatible. Damages for breach are designed to 'enforce' a contract, taking the plaintiff 'forward' to a notional post-performance position, while restitution forms part of the process of its 'rescission', and aims to restore a plaintiff to the pre-contractual position. One cannot, it is said, go forwards and backwards at the same time. Logical though this proposition may seem, it is founded upon artificial considerations. For one thing, contract damages do not always take the plaintiff 'forward', since reliance damages aim to restore the plaintiff to the position he would have been in if the contract had never been made. More generally, the perceived contrast between 'enforcement' and 'restitution' is largely the product of loose thinking. Contract damages, remember, do not, 'enforce' a contract in any real sense; they compensate a loss.[2] So the appropriate principles to compare, when deciding upon the logical compatibility of damages and the action for money had and received, are not the principles of 'enforcement' and 'rescission' (whatever these may mean) but those of 'compensation' and 'restitution'; the rectification of unjust losses and the restoration of unjust gains. Once this is realized, and the misleading imagery of a plaintiff's moving forwards and backwards in time is removed, it becomes apparent that the two actions are not incompatible at all. It is quite feasible, on one set of facts, both to eradicate a loss and to restore a gain, though one must always be careful that, in so doing, the plaintiff is not compensated twice.

The logical compatibility of restitutionary awards and contract damages appears now to have been widely acknowledged.

Policy

The more popular reservation about combining the two remedies is that this may contravene the law's policy against double recovery for the same loss. This is always a danger in cases such as the present, because there is at least a partial correspondence between the plaintiff's loss and the defendant's gain. If Mrs Dillon were awarded both 'full' (gross) compensation and restitution of her fare, she would 'have the equivalent of performance of the contractual promise without having borne the expense which . . . she

---

2 Albeit that this loss may be assessed by reference to different notional positions: pre-contractual and post-contractual. The only real 'enforcement' remedy in this context is specific performance.

had agreed to pay for it'. Her fare might be recovered once within the restitutionary award, and again as part of the loss occasioned by the defendant's breach. The argument is nonetheless strictly limited. It holds true only if the plaintiff's loss of bargain is valued gross; that is, without subtracting from the award the amount she would have had to pay to secure the promised performance. Provided losses are assessed net of this sum, compensation and restitution are perfectly compatible. The policy argument does not debar combined claims for restitution and contract damages at all. It merely requires a downward adjustment of the latter to take account of the former.

(2) CLAIM BY THE INNOCENT PARTY FOR THE VALUE OF WORK DONE

- *Planché v Colburn* (1831) 8 Bing. 14, Court of Common Pleas

See 106–107 above.

NOTES AND QUESTIONS

1. The history of this decision is considered by C Mitchell and C Mitchell 'Planche v Colburn' in C Mitchell and P Mitchell (eds), *Landmark Cases in the Law of Restitution* (2006), 65. Mitchell and Mitchell observe that although the reports of *Planché* do not specify whether the claimant was awarded £50 on the *quantum meruit* count or as damages for breach of contract, in a later case Lord Campbell argued that Tindal CJ 'is reported as if he considered the plaintiff entitled to recover on the *quantum meruit*' (*Goodman v Pocock* (1850) 15 QB 576, 582–3).

2. Were the defendants enriched? If so, what test was used to establish the existence and extent of the enrichment (see the notes and questions at 107 above)?

3. It has been argued (Burrows, 343, n4) that *Planché* 'is better viewed as non-restitutionary with the *quantum meruit* awarded being the equivalent of contractual damages (whether expectation or reliance)', see also M. Garner, above, 86). Do you agree? In this context it should also be noted that Goff and Jones (426, n35) doubt whether *Planché* was actually a claim in 'quasi-contract', pointing out that a '*quantum meruit* claim could also lie as a remedy on a special contract.'

4. What was the unjust factor in this case? Could it have been 'failure of consideration'? The proposition that failure of consideration can apply to a non-money claim at first sight seems a strange one because, historically, it was tied to the action for money had and received. The suggestion that failure of consideration can apply to non-money claims was first made by A. Burrows ('Free Acceptance and the Law of Restitution' (1988) 104 *LQR* 576), albeit that he did not apply it to *Planché*. The argument is analytically persuasive but has to overcome the legacy of the forms of action. Birks ('In Defence of Free Acceptance' in A Burrows (ed), *Essays on the Law of Restitution*, (1991) 112) rationalized the argument for the application of failure of consideration to non-money claims in the following terms:

> It is, of course, still extremely unusual to talk of recovering the value of services or goods on [the ground of failure of consideration], which is historically linked with money had and received. It was within that action that the judges worked out this unjust factor (or borrowed it, for there is the strongest probability that 'a consideration which fails' is no more than the English for the cause of indebtedness called *causa data causa non secuta* in Justinian's *Digest*). Correspondingly, no English judge ever referred to failure of consideration in an *assumpsit* for *quantum meruit* or *quantum valebat*. Nevertheless, it is right to insist that, once the forms of actions were abolished, there remained no logical reason for confining the causes of action in money had and received solely to money. Although it might be easier to establish 'value received' when the recipient had received money, as a matter of logic the law could not be different according to the different forms in which value might be received. Hence, if and when the hurdle of establishing value received is crossed, all the unjust factors worked out in relation to money, including

failure of consideration, must be equally effective in triggering restitution in respect of value received in other forms. Indeed, unless the enrichment question can never be answered positively (which nobody has suggested) there must be cases where restitution should be so explained. Otherwise there would be inexplicable asymmetry in our law of restitution, which, adapting and transcending the old actional language, is no more or less than the law of 'value received'.

• *De Bernardy v Harding* (1853) 8 Exch. 822, Court of Exchequer

After the death of the Duke of Wellington, the defendant began to erect seats for the purpose of letting them to enable members of the public to view the funeral procession. He entered into a contract with the claimant under which the claimant agreed to advertise the funeral abroad and to sell tickets for the seats. The claimant was to be paid by an allowance of 10 per cent on the amount of the tickets which he sold. After the claimant had expended money in advertising the funeral, but before he had sold any tickets, the defendant decided that he wished to sell the tickets himself and so dispensed with the claimant's services. The defendant paid the printers and others who had been employed by the claimant, but he refused to pay the claimant himself. The claimant brought an action upon a *quantum meruit*, to which the defendant objected on the ground that he should have brought a claim for breach of contract. The judge accepted the argument of the defendant but on appeal it was held that the claimant was, in principle, entitled to bring a claim upon a *quantum meruit* and that the issue should have been left to the jury.

Pollock CB: This rule must be absolute. It was a question for the jury, whether under the circumstances, the original contract was not abandoned, and whether there was not an implied understanding between the parties that the plaintiff should be paid for the work actually done as upon a quantum meruit.

Alderson B: I also think that it ought to have been left to the jury to say whether the special contract was abandoned. Where one party has absolutely refused to perform, or has rendered himself incapable of performing, his part of the contract, he puts it in the power of the other party either to sue for a breach of it, or to rescind the contract and sue on a quantum meruit for the work actually done.

Platt B concurred.

QUESTIONS
1. Was the defendant enriched at the expense of the claimant?
2. How would you classify the unjust factor in this case?

• *Boomer v Muir* 24 P (2d) 570 (1933), District Court of Appeal of California

R C Storrie & Co., which was a co-partnership composed of Muir and Storrie, entered into a contract with a power company under which they agreed to build a massive hydro-electric project, one part of which involved the construction of a dam. Storrie & Co. subcontracted the work of construction of the dam to Boomer. But the parties' relationship proved to be a difficult one, almost from the commencement of the work in May 1926. Boomer repeatedly complained to Storrie & Co. about delays in providing him with the materials which he needed to complete the work, with the result that his progress was slowed and his costs were increased. Eventually, in December 1927, there having been no improvement in the supply of materials, Boomer walked off the job, leaving the dam incomplete. Boomer had been paid for the work in stages as it had been completed and, at the time at which he walked off the site, only a further $20,000 remained to be paid to him under the terms of the contract. So Boomer elected to treat the contract as discharged for Storrie's breach and sued upon a *quantum meruit* for the reasonable value of the work which he had done. It was held that Boomer was entitled to walk off the site because of Storrie's fundamental breach of contract in failing to supply him with materials sufficiently expeditiously, and that Boomer was entitled to recover the sum of $258,000 as the reasonable value of the work which he had done.

Dooling J: . . .

[1] It is well settled in California that a contractor who is prevented from performing his contract by the failure of the other party to furnish materials has a choice of three remedies: He may treat the contract as rescinded and recover upon a quantum meruit so far as he has performed; he may keep the contract alive, offering complete performance, and sue for damages for delay and expense incurred; or he may treat the repudiation as putting an end to the contract for purposes of performance and sue for the profits he would have realized. . . . Storrie & Co. and Storrie's sureties admit this rule, but claim that the evidence will not support a finding that Boomer was prevented from performance by Storrie & Co.'s failure to furnish materials. [*He set out the facts, considered the instruction to the jury and continued*:]

Under this instruction the jury must have found that Boomer intended to proceed if materials were furnished. We are satisfied that under the evidence this was a question of fact for the determination of the jury, and that their implied finding on this point is not without substantial support in the evidence.

. . .

It is further urged that, 'assuming that prevention of performance was shown, the contractor may not, where the contract has been fully liquidated up to a given stage, reopen the part of the contract which has been fully executed on both sides and seek to have his past work revalued.' In this connection it is pointed out that, at the time Boomer left the job in December, 1927, the monthly estimates provided for in the contract had been made up to November 25, 1927, and Boomer had been paid in full for all work covered by these estimates, with the exception of the retained percentage of 10 per cent, for three months after May, 1927, in which months Boomer had not placed 40,000 cubic yards of material in the dam as provided in the supplemental agreement. It is conceded that the general rule, and the one followed in California, is that, where a contract has been rescinded for prevention of performance, the plaintiff may recover the reasonable value of what he has done or supplied under the contract, even though such recovery may exceed the contract price. . . . It is insisted, however, that this general rule does not apply in cases where specific payment is provided in the contract for specific portions of the work, and such portions have been fully performed and payment for which has been fully ascertained and liquidated prior to the breach by the adverse party. In support of this contention are cited *Rodemer v Gonder*, 9 Gill (Md.) 288; *Doolittle v McCullough*, 12 Ohio St. 360; *Wellston Coal Co. v Franklin Paper Co.*, 57 Ohio St. 182, 48 N. E. 888; *City of Philadelphia v Tripple*, 230 Pa. 481, 79 A. 703; and *Farnum v Kennebec Water Dist.* (C.C.A.) 170 F. 173. [*He considered the cases and continued*:]

It will thus be seen from this examination of the cases relied on by Storrie & Co. and Storrie's sureties that in only three of them is the rule contended for by them actually applied, and in only two, the *Rodemer Case* and the *Doolittle Case*, was the application of the rule necessary to the decision; since under the law of Maine the recovery would have been limited to the contract rates in the Farnum Case in any event.

We are not impressed by the rule announced in these two cases. It being settled as the general rule that upon prevention of performance the injured plaintiff may treat the contract as rescinded and recover upon a quantum meruit without regard to the contract price, why should he be limited to the contract price in case payments for portions of the entire contract have been made or liquidated? Those payments were received in full only on condition that the entire contract be performed. But, if the contract is rescinded, the prices fixed by the contract are also rescinded. As aptly said by the Pennsylvania Supreme Court in the passage quoted supra from *City of Philadelphia v Tripple*: 'Where the defendant undertakes to limit the plaintiff's recovery by treating the contract price as a limitation upon such recovery, he is asserting a right under the very contract which he himself has discharged.'

To hold that payments under the contract may limit recovery where the contract is afterwards rescinded through the defendant's fault seems to us to involve a confusion of thought. A rescinded contract ceases to exist for all purposes. How then can it be looked to for one purpose, the purpose of fixing the amount of recovery? 'A contract is extinguished by its rescission.' Civ. Code, §1688. 'Generally speaking, the effect of rescission is to extinguish the contract. The contract is annihilated so effectually that in contemplation of law it has never had any existence, even for the purpose of being broken.' . . . In *Clark v Manchester*, 51 N H 594, a case wherein payments for a portion of the services had been made according to the contract, the court said: 'The contract being entire, the defendants cannot break one part of it and still insist upon the performance of the other part. When the defendants rescinded the contract, they put it out of their power to enforce it upon the other party, but the other party may consider it as rescinded and claim pay just as though it had never existed.'

. . . .

In *Woodward on Quasi-Contracts*, §269, the author has this to say of the *Rodemer* and *Doolittle Cases*: 'This rule is doubtless a sound one when applied to an agreement which is severable in the sense that it really constitutes two or more separate contracts. But the propriety of its application to cases like *Rodemer v [Gonder &] Hazelhurst* and *Doolittle v McCullough* is at least questionable. Payments pro tanto in such cases are not received in extinguishment of the defendant's liability; or, at most, the extinguishment is subject to the condition that the contractor be allowed to complete the job and receive compensation, at the contract rate, for the whole of it. This is very clearly pointed out in a New Hampshire case, *Clark v Manchester* (1872) 51 N H 594.

. . . .

We conclude that the rule of the *Rodemer* and *Doolittle Cases* is illogical and not supported by reason; that a contract rescinded is no longer in existence for any purpose; that the defendant, by his own wrong having put an end to the contract, cannot insist on its terms to limit the recovery even though part payments have been made for part performance because the payments are received as satisfaction only on condition that the entire contract be performed according to its terms; but that, the contract having been rescinded through defendant's fault, he should place the plaintiff as nearly as possible in statu quo by paying the reasonable value of plaintiff's performance.

Storrie & Co. and Storrie's sureties say that to permit such recovery in this case is to allow Boomer to recover over $250,000, when if he had completed the contract, he would have received no more than $20,000. The answer to this is found in the language of *City of Philadelphia v Tripple*, quoted supra:

'Let it be assumed that, in an extreme case, a builder has actually expended in the course of his work a sum in excess of the contract price and has not yet completed performance. If, under such circumstances, the builder finishes his work, the owner, upon paying the contract price, will receive the benefit of a large expenditure actually made, in return for the payment of a smaller sum of money. . . .

Let it further be supposed, however, that the owner, who finds himself in this position of advantage, voluntarily puts an end to his contract rights in the premises. . . .

The situation which then presents itself is one in which the builder has in good faith expended money in the course of work done for the benefit of the owner, and has, in the absence of contract, an equitable claim to be reimbursed. The owner, on the other hand, has deprived himself of the legal right which would have sufficed to defeat the equity. He accordingly stands defenseless in the presence of the builder's claim.'

Even if it were true, then, that Boomer would only have received an additional $20,000 for the completion of his contract, we are of the opinion that that does not prevent him from recovering the reasonable value of his services upon its rescission for Storrie & Co.'s breach. But Boomer points out that he had large claims for damages against Storrie & Co. for continued delays and increased expense of operation due to their misconduct. If this is so, it would furnish an additional reason for disregarding the rule of the *Rodemer* and *Doolittle Cases* even if we felt disposed to follow them. It was stated in the *Wellston Case* that the rule of the *Doolittle Case* should only be applied where it was equitable to do so. Upon the rescission of the contract, it ceased to exist for all purposes, including the purpose of relying upon its terms for the purpose of recovering damages for any breach. 13 C. J. 623, §684. If Boomer had valid claims for damages arising under the contract by reason of the fact that his cost of operation had been wrongfully increased, it would seem inequitable to limit him to the recovery of the contract price upon a rescission for Storrie & Co.'s failure of performance. . . .

Spence, Acting PJ and **Sturtevant J** concurred.

NOTES AND QUESTIONS

1. A central plank in the reasoning of the court in *Boomer* was that, once the contract was set aside, it was set aside for all purposes. Given that English law does not accept the proposition that rescission for breach operates retrospectively, does this undermine the reasoning of the court or can it be supported on other grounds?

2. Goff and Jones state that the award in *Boomer* was incongruous and they argue (at 513–514) that it is 'difficult to contemplate with equanimity "wind-fall" awards, such as the award in *Boomer v Muir*, particularly when, if the innocent party has substantially or fully performed, the common law rule is that the contract price is the limit of his recovery, even though the defendant has wrongfully repudiated the contract.' Do you agree?

3. How could the claimant in *Boomer* show that the defendant was enriched by the work which he had done? The enrichment angle of this case was not considered by the court, yet it may in fact turn out to hold the key to the resolution of the case. If the claimant had invoked the bargained-for (or similar) test of benefit, would he not have been forced to have regard to the terms of the contract for the purpose of establishing what it was that the defendant had bargained for? If this is correct, should the contract price not then have acted as a pro-rata valuation ceiling on the claimant's claim? On the other hand, if the claimant could have demonstrated that the defendant had been incontrovertibly benefited, the market value of the services which he had performed would have been of more obvious relevance than the contract price. But the difficulty must surely lie in showing that, on the facts, the defendant was incontrovertibly benefited (on which see further above, 72–84). This solution to the enrichment question in *Boomer*, and the problems of showing incontrovertible benefit, are considered by M McInnes, 'The Measure of Restitution' (2002) 52 *UTLJ* 163, 210–18. The contract valuation ceiling point was also considered by the Court of Appeal in *Rover International Ltd v Cannon Film Sales Ltd* (below, 290).

4. In *Renard Construction (MD) Pty. Ltd v Minister for Public Works* (1992) 26 *NSWLR* 234, 276–8 (New South Wales Court of Appeal) Meagher JA stated that the option given to the innocent party to sue for damages for breach of contract or to bring a restitutionary claim presupposes

   a choice between different remedies, which presumably may lead to different results. The nature of these different remedies renders it highly likely that the results will be different. If the [contractual] remedy is chosen the innocent party is entitled to damages amounting to the loss of profit which he would have made if the contract had been performed rather than repudiated; it has nothing to do with reasonable-ness. If the [restitutionary] remedy is chosen, he is entitled to a verdict representing the reasonable cost of the work he has done and the money he has expended; the profit he might have made does not enter into that exercise. There is nothing anomalous in the notion that two different remedies, proceeding on entirely different principles, might yield different results.

But it does not follow that Meagher JA was of the view that the contract price should necessarily be irrelevant because he stated that the 'most one can say is that the amount contractually agreed is evidence of the reasonableness of the remuneration claimed on a quantum meruit; strong evidence, but certainly not conclusive evidence'. He concluded his judgment by saying that it 'would be extremely anomalous if the defaulting party when sued on a quantum meruit could invoke the contract which he has repudiated in order to impose a ceiling on amounts otherwise recoverable'. Although the High Court of Australia refused special leave to appeal from the decision in *Renard Constructions*, its correctness has been doubted in later cases (see *Trimis v MINA* [1999] NSWCA 140 at [54] and *GEC Marconi Systems Pty. Ltd v BHP Information Technology Pty. Ltd* (2003) 128 FCR 1 at [660]–[666], [1569]). See J Edelman and E Bant, *Unjust Enrichment in Australia* (2006) at 260–4.

5. Where the innocent party elects to continue with the work in the face of the defendant's breach of contract then it appears that the innocent party is confined to his remedy under the contract and cannot bring a claim in unjust enrichment in an attempt to recover a sum in excess of the contract price (*Morrison-Knudsen Co. Inc. v British Columbia Hydro & Power Authority* (1978) 85 DLR (3d) 186, 224–35).

- *Taylor v Motability Finance Ltd*
  [2004] EWHC 2619 (Comm), Queen's Bench Division

Motability Finance Ltd employed Taylor as a finance director. During his employment Taylor was involved in negotiating a highly successful insurance settlement. When Mota-bility subsequently terminated his employment contract he sued for breach of contract for wrongful termination and, in the alternative, restitution for the value of the work he did on the insurance settlement. Although Taylor's contract did not provide for a bonus entitlement, bonuses were given as a matter of discretion and Taylor alleged that a negotiation consultant would have charged 0.5 per cent of the settlement (£375,000). Cooke J treated Taylor's claim as a claim in unjust enrichment for restitution of the value of services conferred on a consideration which failed. Cooke J held that a claim for failure of consideration could not be brought, even after a contract had been terminated, if the contractual rights had already accrued and summary judgment was granted to Motability Finance.

Cooke J: . . .

18. In paragraph 50 the Claimant seeks a restitutionary remedy amounting to 0.5 per cent of the RVI settlement. In the prayer for relief this is still expressed as damages for breach of contract but I regard that matter as one which is capable of cure and therefore put that out of my mind. The essential question is whether or not a restitutionary claim can be maintained as a matter of law in the circumstances of this case, on the agreed or uncontrovertible facts or, where there is a real issue on the facts, the facts put forward by the Claimant.

19. The plea proceeds on the basis of the wrongful termination of the contract by the Defendant on 31st May 2003 when the Claimant's dismissal became effective. In these circumstances the Claimant argued that a claim in restitution would lie outside the terms of the contract. In the Claimant's skeleton argument a large number of authorities were referred to and in oral argument reference was made to *Lodder v Slowey* [1904] AC 442, a decision of the Privy Council in relation to an appeal from New Zealand and the more recent decision of the Court of Appeal in New

South Wales in *Renard Constructions (ME) BTY Limited v Minister for Public works* (1992) 26 NSWLR 34.

20. Mr. Goudie QC also sought to rely on textbook writers such as Professor Burrows at page 343–345 in the Law of Restitution but, as a matter of fundamental principle, in accordance with decisions of the House of Lords in this country, I can see no basis for any claim arising outside the terms of the contract on the facts which obtain here.

21. There is no plea in the Re-Amended Particulars of Claim to the effect that any work done by the Claimant fell outside the terms of his contractual duties. Although his statement seeks to suggest that the negotiation of the RVI claim fell outside his contractual duties and there is a proposed amendment to the Particulars of Claim to allege this, such an allegation has no realistic prospect of success. I have referred to the contractual documents which make such a plea untenable, before having any regard to the Defendant's evidence. The Claimant's evidence, such as it is on this point, does not support the argument that he would wish to make, with the result that the current debate must proceed on the basis that the Claimant did what he was required to do under his contract of employment.

22. The position then is that, on the Claimant's own case, he was wrongfully dismissed on 22nd May 2003 with effect from 31st May 2003. By this time he had not only fulfilled all his contractual duties with regard to the RVI claim, in respect of which he seeks a bonus payment, but had also been paid for those services in the shape of his salary. If there was a repudiatory breach of contract, then the contract was wrongly terminated as at 31st May 2003 but all rights which had accrued to the Claimant by that point were vested in him. He had on his case fulfilled the terms of the contract and was therefore entitled to damages in respect of its breach, including damages for breach of the implied term of trust and confidence in failing to award him a bonus in line with his legitimate expectation.

23. The Claimant sought to argue that there was room for concurrent remedies in contract and restitution, relying on the decision of the House of Lords in *Henderson v Merrett* [1995] 2AC 145 at page 193 where Lord Goff said that there was nothing antithetical in principle to concurrent remedies in contract and tort. On this basis it was argued that the same position would obtain as between contract and restitution. Lord Goff went on however to say that there would not be room for concurrent liability in contract and tort where the tortious duty was so inconsistent with the applicable contract that such tortious liability had to be taken as excluded. In the context of contract and restitution, it is clear that the parties, in agreeing a contract, intend that to apply and there is therefore no room for restitution at all where there is full contractual performance by one party and, even on the Claimant's own case part performance by the other. Not only is it true to say that, historically, restitution has emerged as a remedy where there is no contract or no effective contract, but there is no room for a remedy outside the terms of the contract where what is done amounts to a breach of it where ordinary contractual remedies can apply and payment of damages is the secondary liability for which the contract provides.

24. The decisions of the House of Lords in *Johnson v Agnew* [1980] AC 3677, *Photo Products v Securicor Transport* [1980] AC 827 and *Lep Air Services Limited v Rolloswin Investments Limited* [1973] AC 331 establish the position where there is a repudiation of the contract which is accepted or which is effective to bring the contract to an end. In those circumstances the contract is not rescinded ab initio, but future obligations are discharged from the moment the contract comes to end. All accrued rights remain in being and, so far as executory elements are concerned, the primary obligation to perform is replaced by a secondary obligation to pay damages.

25. The position is wholly different from that where money is paid for a consideration which wholly fails. In such a case there is a total failure of consideration and the money is recoverable. Although this means that the payer may escape from the consequences of a bad bargain, there is

no room for extending this to a situation where both parties have performed substantially and there is a full and adequate remedy for breach of contract which will compensate the Claimant for any loss suffered. The point is clearly set out in Goff & Jones – The Law of Restitution at paragraphs 20-007 and between paragraphs 20-019 and 20-023. The authors there say that there is no English authority to suggest that an innocent party, who has rendered services or supplied goods, may elect to sue in restitution if he has performed or substantially performed his part of the contract. If therefore he can claim under the contract whether in debt or in damages, that is the true measure of his entitlement, because it is that which he bargained for. If it were otherwise, not only would the Claimant be able to recover more than his contractual entitlement in respect of bonus, but he could also seek to establish that he was underpaid in terms of salary, despite his agreement thereto.

26. Moreover, notwithstanding the California case of *Boomer v Muir* 24 p. 2d 570 (1933) there can also be no justification, even if a restitutionary claim is available, for recovery in excess of the contract limit. Such recovery in itself would be unjust since it would put the innocent party in a better position than he would have been if the contract had been fulfilled. In deciding any quantum meruit regard must be had to the contract as a guide to the value put upon the services and also to ensure justice between the parties (compare the comments of Jacob J at paragraphs 76–79 in *Vedatech Corporation v Crystal Decisions* EWHC 818 (CH).

27. Notwithstanding therefore the multiplicity of authority to which the Claimant's skeleton made reference and the academic treatises in which the view is express that the law should move in a different direction, in my judgment the current state of the law is clear both as a matter of principle and by reference to the decisions of the House of Lords to which I have referred. Whilst restitution is undoubtedly a developing area of law and factual questions are important in the context of deciding such issues, here the essential facts which matter are clear and, on the Claimant's own case he is entitled to pursue a contractual claim in circumstances where he has fully performed and the Defendant has partly performed. I therefore accede to the Defendant's application for summary judgment in respect of the claim pleaded in paragraph 50 of the Particulars of Claim.

NOTES AND QUESTIONS

1. In paragraphs [23] and [24], Cooke J appears to suggest that unless a contract is rescinded *ab initio* there can be no room for a restitutionary remedy (referring to decisions of the House of Lords which established that discharge of a contract for breach terminates contractual rights *in futuro* but does not affect accrued rights: (*Johnson v Agnew* [1979] 1 All ER 833, *Photo Productions Ltd v Securicor Transport Ltd* [1980] 1 All ER 556, and *LEP Air Services Ltd v Rolloswin Investments Ltd* [1972] 2 All ER 393). But in paragraph [25], Cooke J says that the position is 'wholly different' in cases of total failure of consideration although his Lordship does not explain why such an exception to his approach should exist in cases of total failure of consideration. A possible explanation, consistent with Cooke J's approach, is that restitution should only be permitted if the defendant's right to the claimant's performance has not accrued: see B McFarlane and R Stevens, 'In Defence of *Sumpter v Hedges*' (2002) 118 *LQR* 569 (below at 305–313).

2. A less technical approach to the role of a contract in claims based on failure of consideration was taken by Lord Goff in *Pan Ocean Shipping v Creditcorp Ltd, The Trident Beauty* [1994] 1 WLR 161 (above, 122). Lord Goff denied a claim for restitution of hire payments in that case because there was an express contractual term governing overpaid hire and also because to grant restitution would have undermined the contractual regime. Do you think that these are valid reasons why a restitutionary claim for failure of consideration should be denied?

3. How does Cooke J deal with *Lodder v Slowey* [1904] AC 442 (see above at 90)?

4. In obiter dicta, Cooke J suggested that even if a claim for restitution were available it should

not exceed the total contract price (this is different from the argument that the contract price should form a pro-rata valuation ceiling for the work done). This would prevent escape from a bad bargain. However, Gordon and Frankel have argued that in many contracts the allocation of price and risk is on the basis that the contract could be entirely performed. A claimant might have included in the contract price non-price benefits of entire performance such as reciprocal treatment by the defendant, further contracts or reputation (W Gordon and T Frankel, 'Enforcing Coasian Bribes for Non-Price Benefits' (1994) 67 *S Cal L Rev* 1519). Do you think that the contract price should always be a pro-rata valuation ceiling?

(3) CLAIM BY THE PARTY IN BREACH FOR THE RECOVERY OF MONEY PAID

- *Dies v British and International Mining and Finance Co.*
[1939] 1 KB 724, King's Bench Division

The claimant contracted to purchase ammunition from the defendant and made a pre-payment of £100,000. In breach of contract the claimant refused to take delivery. The defendants terminated the contract on the ground of the claimant's breach and the claimant sued to recover the £100,000 pre-payment. It was held that the claimant was entitled to recover the money so paid.

Stable J: . . . [T]he plaintiffs' contention can, I think, be fairly summarized as follows: Where there is a contract for the sale of goods, and a part payment for the goods is made, but no goods are delivered or tendered by reason of the default of the buyer, the seller's only remedy is to recover damages for the default, while the buyer, notwithstanding that it is by reason of his default that the contract has not been performed, is entitled to recover the purchase price that he has paid, subject possibly to the right of the seller to set off against that claim the damages to which he can establish his title.

In support of this contention a number of authorities were cited to me. The form of declaration or count which it was said embraced a claim of this nature was the old common count for money had and received . . .

In my judgment, the question whether the right exists cannot be determined by inquiring whether the action for money had and received is the appropriate form of plea. If the right exists, the form of plea is appropriate enough. If the right does not exist, it cannot be enforced, no matter how attractively it be disguised by the pleader.

The question is not now one of the appropriate form in which to clothe the right, but whether or not the right exists, although the absence of any clothing that fits may be an indication of the non-existence of the right. In support of his submission that the right exists Mr. Pritt cited three cases. [*He considered the cases and continued*:]

In the present case, neither by the use of the word 'deposit' or otherwise, is there anything to indicate that the payment of 100,000*l*. was intended or was believed by either party to be in the nature of a guarantee or earnest for the due performance of the contract. It was a part payment of the price of the goods sold and was so described.

On behalf of the defendant corporation it was contended that on the true construction of the contract the part payment was agreed to be regarded as an earnest for the performance of the contract, inasmuch as, since the clause which I have already read provided for the return of a part of the payment to the plaintiffs in one event only, it must have been the intention of the parties that in every other event the money was to be retained by the defendant corporation.

I do not so construe the contract. The clause, in my judgment, deals with one situation, and one situation only—namely, the frustration of the performance of the contract. It was . . . designed to confer on the defendant corporation certain rights additional to the rights which the law alone in the absence of agreement would have given in the event of the performance of the contract being frustrated. Beyond that field its implications ought not to be extended, and the doctrine 'expressum facit cessare tacitum' has no application. The argument under this head is double-edged, since it might be argued on behalf of the plaintiffs that, as the contract expressly conferred on the corporation the right in one event to retain 13,500*l.*, it cannot have been intended that in another event they were to have the right of retaining 100,000*l.*

It was said further that the rule which under certain circumstances enables a purchaser in default to recover a payment or part payment of the purchase price is a rule applicable to the sale of land only and must not be extended to the sale of goods, but no authority for this latter proposition was cited to me, and I was referred to certain passages in the Seventh Edition of *Benjamin on Sale*, at 989, 994 and 995, which state the rule as being of general application.

At 989 the principle is summarized in these words: 'In ordinary circumstances, unless the contract otherwise provides, the seller, on rescission following the buyer's default, becomes liable to repay the part of the price paid.'

If this passage accurately states the law as, in my judgment, it does where the language used in a contract is neutral, the general rule is that the law confers on the purchaser the right to recover his money, and that to enable the seller to keep it he must be able to point to some language in the contract from which the inference to be drawn is that the parties intended and agreed that he should.

The argument on behalf of the defendant corporation was supported by the submission that the action for money had and received would not lie, since on the present facts the only possible basis was a total failure of consideration, which basis was ruled out by the fact that it was the purchaser who had made default.

In support of this proposition was cited the case of *Stray v Russell*,[1] a case decided in the Court of Queen's Bench and affirmed on error in the Exchequer Chamber. When the facts of that case are examined it is clear that the plaintiff had contracted to buy shares for which he had paid, and the shares which he had contracted to buy had been tendered to him. He refused to take them, and then sued for the return of his money on the basis of a total failure of consideration. The decision of the Court rested on this, that there had been neither total nor partial failure of consideration inasmuch as the defendants had always been able, ready and willing to do everything which they had contracted to do. The contract in that case never was rescinded in any sense of the word, and it is in relation to these facts that the passages in the judgments which were cited to me have to be considered.

I was, however, quite satisfied that in the present case the foundation of the right, if right there be, is not a total failure of consideration. There was no failure of consideration, total or partial. It was not the consideration that failed but the party to the contract.

This objection, in my judgment, really goes to a question of form and not of substance, for if under the present circumstances there is a right in the buyer to recover a payment he has made in part, it is wholly immaterial in point of form whether the basis of right depends on a total failure of consideration, or something else. In my judgment, the real foundation of the right which I hold exists in the present case is not a total failure of consideration but the right of the purchaser, derived from the terms of the contract and the principle of law applicable, to recover back his money.

I am fortified in the view I have formed by the consideration that, in cases where the parties have agreed that a certain sum shall in the event of a breach represent the liquidated damages to be paid, the Court can, if satisfied that the agreed amount is not damages but a penalty, relieve one or other of the parties against his inequitable and improvident bargain. In my judgment there would be a

---

1 1 E & F 888: in Exch Ch at 916.

manifest defect in the law if, where a buyer had paid for his goods but was unable to accept delivery, the vendor could retain the goods and the money quite irrespective of whether the money so retained bore any relation to the amount of the amount of the damage, if any, sustained as a result of the breach. The seller is already amply protected, since he can recover such damage as he has sustained and can, it seems, set off his claim for damages against the claim for the return of the purchase price . . .

NOTES AND QUESTIONS

1. In *Clowes Development (UK) Ltd v Mulchinock* (Unreported, Chancery Division, 24 May 2001 at [3]–[4]) John Martin QC, sitting as a High Court judge, treated *Dies* as a case where recovery was allowed because of a total failure of consideration. In order to explain the result in *Dies*, is it necessary to reject the remark of Stable J that the foundation of the right to restitution was not a total failure of consideration? What was the basis on which Stable J decided the case?

2. What did Stable J mean when he said that 'it was not the consideration that failed but the party to the contract'? Can failure of consideration ever be invoked by a party who is in breach of contract? If not, why not?

3. The argument that failure of consideration can be invoked by a party who is himself in breach of contract found judicial support in the judgment of McHugh J in the High Court of Australia in *Baltic Shipping Company v Dillon (The Mikhail Lermontov)* (1993) 176 CLR 344, 390–1 in the following terms:

   Moreover, 'once it does appear that the condition for retaining the money has failed the fact that it failed in response to the payer's own breach does not matter'.[1] As Birks says,[2] this is the best explanation of the much discussed case of *Dies v British & International Mining & Finance Corporation*[3] where a buyer in default was held entitled to recover instalments of the purchase price of guns and ammunition. Once the seller elected to accept the buyer's repudiation and terminate the contract, the consideration for the advance payment had wholly failed because the seller retained the guns and ammunition.

   However, when a contractual payment is not subject to any condition or the condition for its retention has been fulfilled, discharge of the contract does not entitle the payer to the return of money advanced even though the payee is in breach of a promise going to the root of the contract. In such a case, the payer's remedy is for breach of contract for non-performance of the promise and not for restitution of the payment . . .

   Whether or not a payment is the subject of a condition at the time a contract is discharged depends upon the express and implied terms of the contract. As a general rule, however, absent an indication to the contrary, a payment, made otherwise than to obtain the title to land or goods, should be regarded as having been made unconditionally, or no longer the subject of a condition, if the payee has performed work or services or incurred expense prior to the completion of the contract. If the payment has been made before the work has been performed or expense incurred, it should be regarded as becoming unconditional once work is performed or expense incurred. In that situation, the advance payment is ordinarily made in order to provide a fund from which the payee can meet the cost of performing the work or services or meeting the expenditure incurred or to be incurred before the completion of the contract. *Hyundai Heavy Industries Co. Ltd v Papadopoulos*[4] illustrates the point. A shipbuilder agreed to construct a ship under a contract which provided for the payment of instalments of the purchase price during the progress of the work and gave the builder the right to terminate the contract if an instalment was unpaid. The House of Lords unanimously held that the builder, after terminating the contract for failure to pay an instalment, was entitled to recover the price of the instalment from a guarantor. All their Lordships held that the guarantor was liable having regard to the terms of the guarantee. But a majority of their Lordships

---

1 Birks, *Introduction,* 238.   2 *Ibid.* 236–7.   3 [1939] 1 KB 724.
4 [1980] 1 WLR 1129; [1980] 2 All ER 29.

held that the guarantor was also liable because the buyer itself was still liable to pay the unpaid instalment even though the contract had been terminated. The right to be paid the instalment was an unconditional right which was not affected by the subsequent discharge of the contract. Lord Fraser of Tullybelton's speech[5] makes it plain that the right to the instalment was unconditional because its purpose was to compensate the builder who 'was bound to incur considerable expense in carrying out his part of the contract long before the actual sale could take place'. It would have been a fortiori the case if the buyer had sought to recover an instalment which it had paid prior to breach. The builder would have had an unconditional right to retain the instalment.

• *Rover International Ltd v Cannon Film Sales Ltd*
[1989] 1 WLR 912, Court of Appeal

In 1985 Proper Films Ltd entered into a contract with Thorn EMI for the exhibition of films on Italian television. Under the terms of the contract EMI granted a licence to Proper to exhibit nine films on Italian television, with up to seven transmissions in each case, for a total licence fee of $1,800,000. Thorn EMI warranted that at the time of delivery of each film it would have a good right to grant the licence for its transmission. The licence fee was to be paid in three instalments with the final instalment of $900,000 being payable on 30 September 1986. Cannon took over Thorn EMI in May 1986 and thereafter relations between the parties deteriorated. In the light of the disputes which existed between the parties, Proper refused to pay the $900,000 which fell due for payment on 30 September direct to Cannon and insisted that the money be paid into a joint account of the parties' solicitors pending the outcome of the litigation between them. Cannon refused to accept this proposal and it elected to terminate the contract, one of the grounds for the termination being Proper's failure to pay the sum due on 30 September. Cannon sued to recover the $900,000 but it was held that it was not entitled to recover it on the ground that, had the sum been paid by Proper prior to the determination of the contract, it would have been recoverable by them from Cannon on the basis that there had been a total failure of consideration (Proper had not received any of the films at the date of discharge). It therefore followed that Cannon was not entitled to recover the $900,000 from Proper.

Kerr LJ: . . . The relevant principles were stated by Dixon J in the High Court of Australia in *McDonald v Dennys Lascelles Ltd* (1933) 48 CLR 457, 476–8. Part of this judgment was cited by Lord Edmund-Davies in *Hyundai Heavy Industries Co. Ltd v Papadopoulos* [1980] 1 WLR 1129, 1141, but for present purposes it is helpful to quote a fuller extract:

'When a party to a simple contract, upon a breach by the other contracting party of a condition of the contract, elects to treat the contract as no longer binding upon him, the contract is not rescinded as from the beginning. Both parties are discharged from the further performance of the contract, but rights are not divested or discharged which have already been unconditionally acquired. Rights and obligations which arise from the partial execution of the contract and causes of action which have accrued from its breach alike continue unaffected. . . . But when a contract, which is not void or voidable at law, or liable to be set aside in equity, is dissolved at the election of one party because the other has not observed an essential condition or has committed a breach going to its root, the contract is determined so far as it is executory only and the party in default is liable for damages for its breach. . . . *It does not, however, necessarily follow from these principles that when, under an executory contract for the sale of property, the price or part of it is paid or*

5 *Ibid.* 1148; 44.

payable in advance, the seller may both retain what he has received, or recover overdue instalments, and at the same time treat himself as relieved from the obligation of transferring the property to the buyer. When a contract stipulates for payment of part of the purchase money in advance, the purchaser relying only on the vendor's promise to give him a conveyance, the vendor is entitled to enforce payment before the time has arrived for conveying the land; yet his title to retain the money has been considered not to be absolute but conditional upon the subsequent completion of the contract. 'The very idea of payment falls to the ground when both have treated the bargain as at an end; and from that moment the vendor holds the money advanced to the use of the purchaser' (*Palmer v Temple* (1839) 9 Ad. & E 520, 521). . . . *It is now beyond question that instalments already paid may be recovered by a defaulting purchaser when the vendor elects to discharge the contract (Mayson v Clouet* [1924] AC 980) . . .' (Emphasis added.)

Subject to Mr Pardoe's reliance on the *Hyundai* decision, to which I turn in a moment, it is clear from the passages which I have emphasised that if Proper had paid the disputed instalment of $900,000, and if the contract had thereafter been rescinded by Cannon for whatever reason, Proper would have been entitled to recover this sum; and if the reason for the rescission of the contract had been a breach on the part of Proper, then Cannon would still not have been entitled to retain this sum but would have been limited to a claim in damages. The fact that the present contract is not one of sale cannot affect the position in principle.

In the present case Proper do not claim repayment, but Cannon claim that the liability to pay survives the rescission of the contract. Clearly that cannot make any difference to the outcome; on the contrary, it must be a fortiori from the point of view of Proper, who are merely resisting Cannon's claim. Dixon J in *McDonald v Dennys Lascelles Ltd*, 48 CLR 457, dealt with this situation a little later on when he said, at 479:

'It appears to me inevitably to follow from the principles upon which instalments paid are recoverable that an unpaid overdue instalment ceases to be payable by the purchasers when the contract is discharged.'

The situation envisaged by Dixon J in the main passage, at 476–8, which I have quoted, arose in *Dies v British and International Mining and Finance Corporation Ltd* [1939] 1 KB 724. [*He considered the case and continued*] That decision was distinguished by a majority of the House of Lords in *Hyundai Heavy Industries Co. Ltd v Papadopoulos* [1980] 1 WLR 1129. The case arose from a ship-building contract which provided that the builders should 'build, launch, equip and complete' the vessel and that its construction should proceed continuously from keel laying to delivery. The price was payable by instalments and it was a term that the builders' yard should have the right to cancel the contract in the event of the buyers' failure to pay an instalment. That is what happened. The builders thereupon brought an action against the guarantor, on the same lines as Cannon's claim against Monitor in the [associated appeal in the] present case, and the House of Lords held unanimously that the defendant was liable under the terms of the guarantee irrespective of the liability of the buyers. But three of their Lordships also dealt with the question whether the buyers' liability to pay the instalment in question survived the consequent cancellation of the contract by the builders. They held that it did, in effect because this was not a contract which merely provided for the sale and delivery of the ship, but because it was in the nature of a building contract under which the yard was obliged to continue with the construction of the vessel throughout. By continuing to work upon the ship during the period since the payment of the previous instalment, the builders had accordingly provided consideration for the instalment in question, with the result that it remained due despite the builders' cancellation of the contract.

The issue in the present case, as I see it, is accordingly whether it falls on the side of cases such as *Dies v British and International Mining and Finance Corporation Ltd* [1939] 1 KB 724, or whether the terms of the contract and the facts lead to the conclusion that it is to be assimilated to the situation in *Hyundai Heavy Industries Co. Ltd v Papadopoulos* [1980] 1 WLR 1129. Had Thorn EMI/Cannon provided any consideration under the contract for which the instalment of $900,000 was payable or was this instalment payable merely as an advance for the obligations which Thorn EMI/Cannon had agreed to perform thereafter? When referring to the provision of consideration in this context, in the same way as in the context of a failure of consideration discussed earlier in the Rover appeal, one is not referring to the original promise to perform the contract. The question is whether there was any consideration in the nature of part performance for which the instalment was payable, as in *Hyundai Heavy Industries Co. Ltd v Papadopoulus* [1980] 1 WLR 1129, or whether the instalment was payable in advance of any performance which was required from Thorn EMI/Cannon.

In my view the present case falls clearly into the latter category and is indistinguishable in principle from the situations examined by Dixon J in *McDonald v Dennys Lascelles Ltd*, 48 CLR 457, and the decision in *Dies v British and International Mining and Finance Corporation Ltd*. It is true that *Dies* appears to have been a contract for the sale of unascertained goods whereas the present contract deals with specific films in relation to which Thorn EMI/Cannon had to possess or to acquire the necessary rights. It is also true that they were precluded from transferring these rights to anyone other than Proper. But that is not a situation whereby Thorn EMI/Cannon provided anything in the nature of part performance under the contract. It merely meant that they had to arrange matters so as to enable them to perform their contractual obligations at the time when these would become due. Thus, it is clear from *Palmer v Temple*, 9 Ad. & E 508, and the judgment of Dixon J in *McDonald v Dennys Lascelles Ltd*, 48 CLR 457, that the principle that advance payments made on account of the price are recoverable applies even where the contract relates to a specific piece of land which the vendor must either acquire or retain in order to perform the contract. The fact that he is bound to the contract in that way does not alter the character of the payment being in the nature of an advance for a consideration to be provided in the future.

In the present case it is entirely clear, in my view, that this instalment was payable in advance of any consideration for the payment which fell to be provided from the side of Thorn EMI/Cannon. Indeed, when Proper declined to pay it, it was rightly pointed out on behalf of Cannon that nothing in the way of performance was as yet due from their side. This instalment would accordingly have been recoverable by Proper if it had been paid, and it is therefore irrecoverable by Cannon for the same reason. The only claim open to them would have been a claim for damages if they had shown that they had suffered any as the result of the termination of the contract. It follows that Cannon's counterclaim should in my view have been dismissed, and that Proper's appeal should also be allowed.

Dillon LJ: . . . There is no doubt that the $900,000 was not payable by way of deposit or earnest. It was merely payable as the final instalment of the price for the licence under the Proper agreement. Consequently, if the Proper agreement had been a contract for the sale of land which went off through Proper's default before the land had been conveyed to Proper, there is no doubt that the $900,000 instalment, if paid, could have been recovered by Proper from Cannon subject to set-off only of Cannon's actual damage from Proper's default: *Mayson v Clouet* [1924] AC 980 and *Palmer v Temple*, 9 Ad. & E 508. So equally if it had been a contract for the sale of goods, property in which had not passed to Proper: *Dies v British and International Mining and Finance Corporation Ltd* [1939] 1 KB 724. That would not have been the case if the $900,000 represented, in part, consideration to Proper for things that Proper had done under the Proper agreement before 30 September or 3 October 1986; see *Hyundai Heavy Industries Co. Ltd v Papadopoulos* [1980] 1 WLR 1129. The crux therefore, as I see it, on the cases is whether at 30 September or 3 October 1986 (and on the facts it matters not which) the Proper agreement was wholly executory on the part of Cannon, or, to put it another way, whether by that date Proper had received any of the consideration moving from Cannon under the Proper agreement.

It was urged for Cannon that the agreement was not wholly executory on the part of Proper, and conversely Proper had received benefit, in that (i) because of the agreement Cannon had refrained between the date of the Proper agreement and 3 October 1986 from granting licence rights to any third party to show any of the nine films on Italian television; and (ii) after the Proper agreement was made, Cannon had paid a substantial sum to a third party which might otherwise have entitled the third party to restrain Cannon, when the time came, from performing its part under the Proper agreement. It is also said that the television rights in respect of a film are a wasting asset as the film gets older, and therefore the analogy of a sale of land or non-perishable goods is not apposite.

I am unable to accept any of these arguments.

The argument that, before 3 October, Cannon had not granted the television rights to anyone else would apply equally if there was a contract for the sale of land and pending repudiation by the first purchaser the vendor had refrained from selling the same land to a second purchaser. It comes to no more than that until Proper repudiated the Proper agreement Cannon itself had not broken that agreement. It has never been suggested that it is an answer to a claim by a 'guilty' purchaser, who has broken his contract, to recover instalments of purchase money (as opposed to a deposit) that the vendor was 'innocent' and had not broken the contract.

As for the payment made by Cannon to buy back rights granted to a third party, that too could happen under a contract for the sale of land, if the vendor made payments to get in an outstanding interest or otherwise put his title in order. The payment could enure to the benefit of the vendor, and would be no concern of the purchaser provided the title was in order by the time for completion. Indeed, that is precisely the attitude Cannon took up in the present case when, at an earlier stage before 30 September 1986, Proper complained that, because of the rights granted to the third party, Cannon was not in a position to grant Proper the Italian television rights to the most important film among the nine, 'Passage to India;' Cannon urged emphatically and correctly that the complaint was premature as Cannon had until the time came for delivery of the film to take whatever steps might be necessary to ensure that it was able to deliver.

Finally, whatever validity the point that the goods were perishable or a depreciating asset might have in other cases, it has none, in my judgment, on the facts of the present case. At 3 October 1986 the date for delivery of each film still lay far ahead. There is no evidence that the value of the television rights had been depreciating with the passage of time since the Proper agreement had been made; on the contrary the whole emphasis was that the television rights should not be exercised too soon before the theatre (or cinema) rights had been fully exploited throughout Italy. Indeed the delivery date for each film is defined in the Proper agreement as '*not earlier than* two years from the date of first theatrical release in the Territory.' (My emphasis.)

For these reasons, I would, with every respect to the judge who thought otherwise, allow the appeal of Proper, set aside the judgment entered against Proper, and order instead that there be judgment for Proper against Cannon for damages to be assessed.

Nicholls LJ concurred with both judgments.

NOTES AND QUESTIONS

1. For further discussion see J Beatson, 'Discharge for Breach: Instalments, Deposits and Other Payments Due Before Completion' in *The Use and Abuse of Unjust Enrichment* (1991), 45.

2. If Proper had actually paid the $900,000 as a deposit or earnest, it seems clear that they would not have been able to recover it (subject to the possibility of being able to claim relief against forfeiture). Would this have been because, in such a case, the consideration for the payment would not have failed (because it was paid as a security for performance and that basis had not failed; on the contrary, it had been fulfilled) or because the parties had contracted out of restitution? Does it matter which view is taken?

3. The courts can, in certain circumstances, grant relief against the forfeiture of a deposit (see, for example, *Stockloser v Johnson* [1954] 1 QB 476). Can this jurisdiction to grant relief be explained in terms of restitution of unjust enrichment.

4. Cannon had, in fact, spent a substantial sum of money in buying back rights in the films which had previously been given to a third party. Why did this expenditure not prevent there being a total failure of consideration? Is sufficient protection given to detrimental expenditure by a payee when that expenditure is not perceived to be part of the bargained-for performance?

• *Stocznia Gdanska SA v Latvian Shipping Co.* [1998] 1 WLR 574, House of Lords.

The claimants were shipbuilders who entered into six contracts for the design, building and delivery of ships for the defendant. The contracts provided that the title to the ships did not pass until delivery. The contracts provided that the price was to be paid in four instalments. The second instalment was 20 per cent of the total price and it was payable within five days from the time the claimants gave notice to the defendant that the keel had been laid. The claimants served notice in relation to two of the ships but the defendants did not pay so the claimants terminated the contracts for those two ships for this breach by the defendant. The claimants sought summary judgment on their claim for payment of the second instalment for the two ships. The defendant argued that these payments, if made, would have been immediately recoverable because the ships had not been delivered and so the instalments would be paid for a consideration which totally failed. The House of Lords rejected this defence of total failure of consideration because, on a proper construction, the contract was not just for the delivery of the ship but also for the design and building of it and therefore the consideration did not totally fail.

Lord Goff:. . . It was recognised by Mr. Glennie for the buyers that the second (keel-laying) instalments of the price payable in respect of vessels 1 and 2 accrued due under clause 5.02(*b*). However he submitted that, after rescission of the contracts, an action by the yard for the recovery of the instalments must fail because, if paid, the instalments would immediately be recoverable by the buyers on the ground that they had been paid for a consideration which had wholly failed. It was Mr. Glennie's submission that there would in such circumstances have been a total failure of consideration, because the buyers would have received nothing under the contract, no property in the vessel or any part of it having been transferred to them. The relevant question was: had the buyers received the benefit of any part of that which they had bargained for? The answer to that question must be in the negative, because any time or money spent by the yard in building the keels enured solely for the benefit of the yard, in whom the property remained. The situation was therefore different from that under an ordinary building contract, where the building as it is erected belongs to the building owner as the owner of the land on which it is being built.

This submission was challenged by Mr. Cordara for the yard, both on principle and authority. He relied in particular on the fact that, under the contracts in question, the yard was bound not merely to transfer the property in the vessels, when built, to the buyers. On the contrary it was bound to design, build, complete and deliver the vessels which were to be built in accordance with the agreed specification. The contracts were not therefore contracts of sale simpliciter, but 'contracts for work and materials,' though they included an obligation to transfer the property in the finished product to the buyers. The contractual performance of the yard began with the translation of the agreed specification into a design which complied with its requirements, the next stage in the performance being the translation of the design into a completed vessel, subject of course to amendments to the design agreed by the parties in the course of construction. Only at a late moment would the title in the completed vessel pass to the buyers.

Before addressing the rival submissions of the parties, I pause to observe that these were both founded on the premise that the issue was simply one of total failure of consideration. I am, of course, well aware of the continuing debate among scholars and law reformers as to the circumstances in which, and the basis on which, a party in breach of contract can recover a benefit conferred by him on the innocent party under the contract before it was terminated by reason of his breach, as to which see, for example, the admirable discussion by Professor Jack Beatson in *The Use and Abuse of Unjust Enrichment* (1991), ch. 3. However, I am content to approach this aspect of the case on the premise, common to both parties, that the issue is one of total failure of consideration since, as I understand it, this is consistent with the approach of the majority in *Hyundai Heavy Industries Co. Ltd v Papadopoulos* [1980] 1 W.L.R. 1129, which is directly in point on this aspect of the case.

I find myself to be in agreement with Mr. Cordara's submission on this point. I start from the position that failure of consideration does not depend upon the question whether the promisee has or has not received anything under the contract like, for example, the property in the ships being built under contracts 1 and 2 in the present case. Indeed, if that were so, in cases in which the promisor undertakes to do work or render services which confer no direct benefit on the promisee, for example where he undertakes to paint the promisee's daughter's house, no consideration would ever be furnished for the promisee's payment. In truth, the test is not whether the promisee has received a specific benefit, but rather whether the promisor has performed any part of the contractual duties in respect of which the payment is due. The present case cannot, therefore, be approached by asking the simple question whether the property in the vessel or any part of it has passed to the buyers. That test would be apposite if the contract in question was a contract for the sale of goods (or indeed a contract for the sale of land) simpliciter under which the consideration for the price would be the passing of the property in the goods (or land). However before that test can be regarded as appropriate, the anterior question has to be asked: is the contract in question simply a contract for the sale of a ship? or is it rather a contract under which the design and construction of the vessel formed part of the yard's contractual duties, as well as the duty to transfer the finished object to the buyers? If it is the latter, the design and construction of the vessel form part of the consideration for which the price is to be paid, and the fact that the contract has been brought to an end before the property in the vessel or any part of it has passed to the buyers does not prevent the yard from asserting that there has been no total failure of consideration in respect of an instalment of the price which has been paid before the contract was terminated, or that an instalment which has then accrued due could not, if paid, be recoverable on that ground.

I am satisfied that the present case falls into the latter category. This was what the contracts provided in their terms. Moreover, consistently with those terms, payment of instalments of the price was geared to progress in the construction of the vessel. That this should be so is scarcely surprising in the case of a shipbuilding contract, under which the yard enters into major financial commitments at an early stage, in the placing of orders for machinery and materials, and in reserving and then occupying a berth for the construction of the vessel. Indeed if Mr. Glennie's argument is right, it would follow that no consideration would have been furnished by the yard when instalments of the price fell due before the moment of delivery, notwithstanding all the heavy and irreversible financial commitments then undertaken by the yard.

As authority for the construction of the contracts in question, Mr. Cordara was able to invoke the decision of your Lordship's House in *Hyundai Heavy Industries Co. Ltd v Papadopoulos* [1980] 1 W.L.R. 1129, to which I have already referred, which was concerned with a shipbuilding contract in substantially the same form as that under consideration in the present case. In that case the question at issue was whether the defendant's liability as guarantor continued in existence despite the termination of the contract. All five members of the Appellate Committee held that it did. But the basis on which three members of the Committee reached that conclusion was that the instalment of the price in question remained due notwithstanding the termination of the contract. Viscount Dilhorne, at p. 1136 put on one side cases of contracts for the sale of land or goods. I interpolate that in such cases it has been held that the buyer's remedy is contractual, the seller's title to retain the money being conditional upon his completing the contract: see, e.g., *Dies v British and International Mining and Finance Corporation Ltd.* [1939] 1 K.B. 724 (sale of goods), and the much-quoted judgment of Dixon J. in *McDonald v Dennys Lascelles Ltd* (1933) 48 C.L.R. 457, 475–479 (sale of land). Viscount Dilhorne did not find it necessary to consider whether the decision in *Dies* was correct, since he was satisfied that in the case before him the contract was not just for the sale of a ship. His conclusion [1980] 1 W.L.R. 1129, 1136 was that:

'save in the case of sales of land and goods and where there has been a total failure of consideration. . . cancellation or rescission of a contract in consequence of a repudiation did not affect accrued rights to the payment of instalments of the contract price unless the contract provided that it was to do so.'

He further concluded, at 1137F, that in the case before him, despite the cancellation of the contract, the buyer remained liable for the second instalment which had accrued due, there having been no total failure of consideration for the payment.

The position was put very clearly by Lord Fraser of Tullybelton when he said, at 1148–1149:

'Much of the plausibility of the argument on behalf of the guarantor seemed to me to be derived from the assumption that the contract price was simply a *purchase* price. That is not so, and once that misconception has been removed I think it is clear that the shipbuilding contract has little similarity with a contract of sale and much more similarity, so far as the present issues are concerned, with contracts in which the party entitled to be paid had either performed work or provided services for which payment is due by the date of cancellation. In contracts of the latter class, which of course includes building and construction contracts, accrued rights to payment are not (in the absence of express provisions) destroyed by cancellation of the contract'

In such a case, therefore, contrary to the submission of Mr. Glennie, there can be no total failure of consideration, notwithstanding that the buyer has received no specific benefit under the contract in the sense of property in the vessel being transferred to him, in whole or in part. Lord Edmund-Davies, at 1140–1141, expressly rejected as unacceptable an argument by the guarantor that, under the terms of the shipbuilding contract, the builders on cancellation of the contract lost their accrued right to recover the relevant instalment of the price, and fortified this conclusion with 'sound commercial reasons.' The other members of the Appellate Committee, Lord Russell of Killowen and Lord Keith of Kinkel, while doubting the conclusion of the majority on the issue of construction of the contract (though not specifying the reasons for their doubt), held that, even so, the cancellation of the contract did not bring to an end the guarantor's obligation under his guarantee.

Faced with this authority, Mr. Glennie submitted first that your Lordships were not bound by that decision, on the ground that the view on the construction of the contract expressed by Viscount Dilhorne and Lord Fraser of Tullybelton was not shared by Lord Edmund-Davies. Like Clarke J., however, I do not so read the opinion expressed by Lord Edmund-Davies. Mr. Glennie next invited your Lordship's House to depart from the decision of the majority in that case, in exercise of the power under the Practice Statement. I however consider that it would not be appropriate to do so, having regard to the recent date of the decision and the reasoning of the majority.

Mr. Glennie advanced a number of particular arguments in support of the latter submission. He relied on the fact that contracts for the manufacture and sale of chattels had been characterised as contracts for the sale of goods for the purposes of, for example, the now repealed section 4 of the Sale of Goods Act 1893 (56 & 57 Vict. c. 71). I do not, however, consider that these cases are directly in point, since they do not address the particular question under consideration in the present case. He referred in particular to the decision of your Lordship's House in *Fibrosa Spolka Akcyjna v Fairbairn*

Lawson Combe Barbour Ltd [1943] A.C. 32, in which a contract for the supply by the respondents of special machinery to be manufactured by them was treated as an ordinary contract for the sale of goods. However, the fact that the relevant contract involves the manufacture of the goods by the supplier does not necessarily mean that the manufacture constitutes part of the contract consideration; and it was held that on the facts of that case, in which incidentally the only advance instalment of the price was payable with the order, the contract was simply one of sale. Finally, Mr. Glennie referred to certain academic criticisms of the decision in the *Hyundai* case but these seem to be directed not so much to the conclusion that the construction of the vessel constituted part of the contractual consideration, as to the consequences of the rule that, for money to be recovered on the ground of failure of consideration, the failure must be total. This rule has been subject to considerable criticism in the past; but it has to be said that in a comparatively recent Report (Law Com. No 121 (1983) concerned with Pecuniary Restitution on Breach of Contract) the Law Commission has declined to recommend a change in the rule, though it was there considering recovery by the innocent party rather than by the party in breach. I for my part am unpersuaded by matters such as these to exercise the power under the Practice Statement (Judicial Precedent) [1966] 1 W.L.R. 1234 to depart from the decision in the *Hyundai* case.

For these reasons, I am unable to accept the argument of the buyers on this point.

Lords Hoffmann, Hope and **Hutton** agreed. **Lord Steyn** delivered a concurring speech.

NOTES AND QUESTIONS

1. Goff and Jones (at 531) state that 'the inquiry, whether a party to the contract has received any part of the bargained for performance, may depend on how anxious the court is to grant restitution. For the terms of the contract may provide only equivocal guidance in determining what is the bargained-for performance.' Do you agree?

2. Do you agree with the distinction drawn by Lord Goff between *Stocznia* and the decision in *Fibrosa Spolka Akcyjna v Fairbairn Lawson Combe Barbour Ltd* [1943] AC 32?

3. Goff and Jones prefer to rely on a presumption, employed by Stable J in *Dies*, that 'where the language of the contract is neutral, the general rule is that the law confers on the purchaser the right to recover his money'. Is this a preferable solution to the problem? What is being presumed?

4. Although the case was argued (and decided) on the basis that a total failure of consideration had to be shown, would the result have been different if a partial failure of consideration had been claimed in the alternative? (See *Goss v Chilcott*, below at 384 and the note above at 294 (n4).)

(4) CLAIM BY THE PARTY IN BREACH FOR THE VALUE OF WORK DONE

The position is rather more complicated where the party in breach has conferred a non-monetary benefit on the other party prior to the discharge of the contract. Where his obligations are divisible, the party in breach will generally be entitled to recover under the contract in respect of the complete performance of each divisible obligation but not in respect of an obligation which has only been partially performed. Where, however, an obligation of the party in breach is entire (often referred to, somewhat misleadingly, as the 'entire contracts rule'), then the party in breach cannot generally make any claim for payment under the contract, because the other party's obligation to pay for the work done only arises when the work has been completed. It is true that the courts have created some exceptions to the general rule of no-recovery (the most controversial of which is that the party in breach can recover the contract price, subject to a counter-claim for damages for breach of contract, where he has substantially performed his obligations under the contract: see, for example, *Hoenig v Isaacs* [1952] 2 All ER 176), but the outlook, as far as the law of contract is concerned, remains a bleak one for the party in breach. As we shall see, his restitutionary rights are also very weak, although there has been some dissatisfaction expressed with the limited restitutionary rights which are given to the party in breach.

- *Sumpter v Hedges* [1898] 1 QB 673, Court of Appeal

The claimant entered into a contract to erect buildings on the defendant's land, payment to be made on completion of the work. The claimant failed to complete the work having become insolvent, and the defendant finished the work using the claimant's materials. The trial judge gave judgment for the claimant in respect of the value of the materials used by the defendant in completing the work, but held that the claimant was not entitled to recover in respect of his part performance of his contractual duties. The claimant appealed unsuccessfully to the Court of Appeal.

A L Smith LJ: In this case the plaintiff, a builder, entered into a contract to build two houses and stables on the defendant's land for a lump sum. When the buildings were still in an unfinished state the plaintiff informed the defendant that he had no money, and was not going on with the work any more. The learned judge has found as a fact that he abandoned the contract. Under such circumstances, what is a building owner to do? He cannot keep the buildings on his land in an unfinished state for ever. The law is that, where there is a contract to do work for a lump sum, until the work is completed the price of it cannot be recovered. Therefore the plaintiff could not recover on the original contract. It is suggested however that the plaintiff was entitled to recover for the work he did on a quantum meruit. But, in order that that may be so, there must be evidence of a fresh contract to pay for the work already done. With regard to that, the case of *Munro v Butt*[1] appears to be exactly in point. That case decides that, unless the building owner does something from which a new contract can be inferred to pay for the work already done, the plaintiff in such a case as this cannot recover on a quantum meruit. In the case of *Lysaght v Pearson*,[2] to which we have been referred, the case of *Munro v Butt* does not appear to have been referred to. There the plaintiff had contracted to erect on the defendant's land two corrugated iron roofs. When he had completed one of them, he does not seem to have said that he abandoned the contract, but merely that he would not go on unless the defendant paid him for what he had already done. The defendant thereupon proceeded to erect for himself the second roof. The Court of Appeal held that there was in that case something from which a new contract might be inferred to pay for the work done by the plaintiff. That is not this case . . .

Chitty LJ: I am of the same opinion. The plaintiff had contracted to erect certain buildings for a lump sum. When the work was only partly done, the plaintiff said that he could not go on with it, and the judge has found that he abandoned the contract. The position therefore was that the defendant found his land with unfinished buildings upon it, and he thereupon completed the work. That is no evidence from which the inference can be drawn that he entered into a fresh contract to pay for the work done by the plaintiff. If we held that the plaintiff could recover, we should in my opinion be overruling *Cutter v Powell*,[3] and a long series of cases in which it has been decided that there must in such a case be some evidence of a new contract to enable the plaintiff to recover on a quantum meruit. There was nothing new in the decision in *Pattinson v Luckley*,[4] but Bramwell B there pointed

---

1 8 E & B 738.   2 *The Times*, 3 Mar 1879.   3 (1795) 6 TR 320.
4 (1875) LR 10 Ex 330.

out with his usual clearness that in the case of a building erected upon land the mere fact that the defendant remains in possession of his land is no evidence upon which an inference of a new contract can be founded. He says: 'In the case of goods sold and delivered, it is easy to shew a contract from the retention of the goods; but that is not so where work is done on real property.' I think the learned judge was quite right in holding that in this case there was no evidence from which a fresh contract to pay for the work done could be inferred.

Collins LJ: I agree. I think the case is really concluded by the finding of the learned judge to the effect that the plaintiff had abandoned the contract. If the plaintiff had merely broken his contract in some way so as not to give the defendant the right to treat him as having abandoned the contract, and the defendant had then proceeded to finish the work himself, the plaintiff might perhaps have been entitled to sue on a quantum meruit on the ground that the defendant had taken the benefit of the work done. But that is not the present case. There are cases in which, though the plaintiff has abandoned the performance of a contract, it is possible for him to raise the inference of a new contract to pay for the work done on a quantum meruit from the defendant's having taken the benefit of that work, but, in order that that may be done, the circumstances must be such as to give an option to the defendant to take or not to take the benefit of the work done. It is only where the circumstances are such as to give that option that there is any evidence on which to ground the inference of a new contract. Where, as in the case of work done on land, the circumstances are such as to give the defendant no option whether he will take the benefit of the work or not, then one must look to other facts than the mere taking the benefit of the work in order to ground the inference of a new contract. In this case I see no other facts on which such an inference can be founded. The mere fact that a defendant is in possession of what he cannot help keeping, or even has done work upon it, affords no ground for such an inference. He is not bound to keep unfinished a building which in an incomplete state would be a nuisance on his land. I am therefore of opinion that the plaintiff was not entitled to recover for the work which he had done.

NOTES AND QUESTIONS

1. Was the defendant enriched (see, for example, Birks, above, 100)? Is it true to say that the defendant was presumptively benefited by receiving a part of what he had bargained for? Does it matter that the defendant went on to complete the building?

2. What was the 'unjust factor' which was relied upon by the claimant?

3. Why did the defendant have to pay for the value of the materials which he used in the completion of the work?

4. Some support can be found in the cases for a more generous right of action for the party in breach. Take the example of the shipowner who deviates from the prescribed route for the delivery of the goods, but nevertheless delivers the goods to the cargo owner at the port of discharge which is named in the contract. The cargo owner terminates the contract on the ground of the shipowner's repudiatory breach of contract, as he is entitled to do. Can the shipowner nevertheless bring a claim to recover a reasonable remuneration in respect of the services which he has performed? The Court of Appeal in *Hain Steamship Co. Ltd v Tate and Lyle Ltd* (1934) 39 Com. Cas. 259, 271–2, 285 and 290 thought not, but in the House of Lords [1936] 2 All ER 597, both Lord Wright and, albeit less strongly, Lord Maugham inclined, obiter dicta, to the view that the shipowner ought to have claim in such circumstances. They expressed their views in the following way:

> **Lord Wright**: . . . Let me put a quite possible case: A steamer carrying a cargo of frozen meat from Australia to England deviates by calling at a port outside the usual or permitted route: it is only the matter of a few hours extra steaming: no trouble ensues except the trifling delay. The cargo is duly delivered in England at the agreed port. The goods owner has had for all practical purposes the benefit

of all that his contract required; he has had the advantages, of the use of a valuable ship, her crew, fuel, refrigeration and appliances, canal dues, port charges, stevedoring. The shipowner may be technically a wrongdoer in the sense that he has once deviated, but otherwise over a long period he has been performing the exacting and costly duties of a carrier at sea. I cannot help thinking that epithets like 'unlawful' and 'unauthorised' are not apt to describe such services; it may be that by the maritime law the relationship of carrier and goods owner still continues despite the deviation, though subject to the modifications consequent on the deviation. Nor can I help feeling that the court would not be slow to infer an obligation when the goods are received at destination to pay, not indeed the contract freight, but a reasonable remuneration . . .

Lord Maugham: Finally, on the general question whether a consignee is liable to pay freight after a deviation which has been treated as putting an end to the contract of affreightment I would only observe that that question does not now arise for decision; but I am strongly inclined to doubt the correctness of the view suggested in the Court of Appeal. As I have already indicated, I do not agree with the proposition that the shipowner (apart from any step taken by the consignee) ought to be regarded as a volunteer or a wrongdoer, and I am of opinion that a claim on the footing of *quantum meruit* must depend on all the circumstances of the case, including the question whether the goods have been delivered at the agreed port and without injury or substantial delay. Bearing in mind a well-known adage and your Lordships' abstention from expressing any final opinion on this matter I do not propose to express any further view of my own on it.

Were a shipowner to be held entitled to bring such a claim, how would it be classified? Would it be a claim for restitution of unjust enrichment? If so, what would be the unjust factor and how could it be reconciled with *Sumpter v Hedges*?

5. Further possible support for the availability of a restitutionary claim for unjust enrichment to a party who is in breach of contract can be found in obiter dicta of Lord Brightman and Lord Templeman in the relatively recent decision of the House of Lords in *Miles v Wakefield MDC* [1987] AC 539. Here the claimant was employed by the defendant council as a superintendent registrar of births, deaths, and marriages. He engaged in industrial action which took the form of a refusal to conduct marriage ceremonies on Saturday mornings, although he carried out his other duties on these mornings. The defendants informed him that they would not pay him for any work he did on Saturday mornings unless he was prepared to carry out the full range of his contractual duties. The claimant refused and so the defendants withheld the part of his salary which was attributable to his work on Saturday mornings. The claimant sued to recover the amount which the defendants withheld but his claim was dismissed by the House of Lords on the ground that, in an action to recover his salary under his contract of employment, he had to aver and prove that he was ready and willing to perform his obligations under his contract of employment and this he could not do. One of the issues which was considered by their Lordships in the course of their judgment was whether or not an employee who had rendered only a part of his contractual obligations was entitled to bring a *quantum meruit* claim to recover the reasonable value of the services which he had performed.

Lord Bridge: . . . Industrial action can take many different forms and there are a variety of options open to an employer confronted by such action. In particular I should, for my part, have preferred to express no opinion on questions arising in the case of an employee who deliberately 'goes slow' or otherwise does his work in a less than satisfactory way, when the employer nevertheless acquiesces in his continuing to work the full number of hours required under his contract. There may be no single, simple principle which can be applied in such cases irrespective of differences in circumstances. But I find it difficult to understand the basis on which, in such a case, the employee in place of remuneration at the contractual rate would become entitled to a quantum meruit. This would presuppose that the original contract of employment had in some way been superseded by a new agreement by which the employee undertook to work as requested by the employer for remuneration in a reasonable sum. This seems to me to be contrary to the realities of the situation.

Lord Brightman: If an employee offers partial performance, as he does in some types of industrial conflict falling short of a strike, the employer has a choice. He may decline to accept the partial performance that is offered, in which case the employee is entitled to no remuneration for his unwanted services, even if they are performed. That is the instant case. Or the employer may accept the partial performance. If he accepts the partial performance as if it were performance which satisfied the terms of the contract, the employer must pay the full wage for the period of the partial performance because he will have precluded or estopped himself from asserting that the performance was not that which the contract required. But what is the position if the employee offers partial performance and the employer, usually of necessity, accepts such partial performance, the deficient work being understood by the employer and intended by the employee to fall short of the contractual requirements and being accepted by the employer as such? There are, as it seems to me, two possible answers. One possible answer is that the employer must pay the full wage but may recover by action or counterclaim or set off damages for breach of contract. The other possible answer is that the employee is only entitled to so much remuneration as represents the value of the work he has done, i.e. quantum meruit. My noble and learned friend Lord Templeman prefers the latter solution, and so do I. My reason is this. One has to start with the assumption that the employee sues for his pay; the employer is only bound to pay the employee that which the employee can recover by action. The employee cannot recover his contractual wages because he cannot prove that he has performed or ever intended to perform his contractual obligations. If wages and work are interdependent, it is difficult to suppose that an employee who has voluntarily declined to perform his contractual work can claim his contractual wages. The employee offers partial performance with the object of inflicting the maximum damage on the employer at the minimum inconvenience to himself. If, in breach of his contract, an employee works with the object of harming his employer, he can hardly claim that he is working under his contract and is therefore entitled to his contractual wages. But nevertheless in the case supposed the employee has provided *some* services, albeit less than the contract required, and the employer has received those (non-contractual) services; therefore the employer must clearly pay something—not the contractual wages because the contractual work has deliberately not been performed. What can he recover? Surely the value of the services which he gave and which the employer received, i.e. quantum meruit.

. . .

Lord Templeman: . . . I agree with my noble and learned friend Lord Bridge of Harwich that industrial action can take many forms and that the legal consequences of industrial action will depend on the rights and obligations of the worker, the effect of the industrial action on the employer and the response of the employer. For my part, however, I take the provisional view that on principle a worker who, in conjunction with his fellow workers, declines to work efficiently with the object of harming his employer is no more entitled to his wages under the contract than if he declines to work at all. The worker whose industrial action takes the form of 'going slow' inflicts intended damage which may be incalculable and non-apportionable but the employer, in order to avoid greater damage, is obliged to accept the reduced work the worker is willing to perform. In those circumstances, the worker cannot claim that he is entitled to his wages under the contract because he is deliberately working in a manner designed to harm the employer. But the worker will be entitled to be paid on a quantum meruit basis for the amount and value of the reduced work performed and accepted. In the present case, the council by their letter dated 18 October 1981 refused to accept any work from the plaintiff unless he worked normally and discharged all his duties. The plaintiff offered to work inefficiently on Saturday but could not compel the council to accept that offer, and upon their refusal to accept that offer he ceased to be entitled to be paid for Saturday.

Lord Brandon and Lord Oliver expressly reserved their opinion on the question whether an employee engaged in certain forms of industrial action may be entitled to claim remuneration on a *quantum meruit* basis for the work actually done.

6. Notwithstanding these developments, there is a case to be made for a more general reform of this area of the law, as is shown in the following extracts from papers of the Law Commission.

• **Pecuniary Restitution on Breach of Contract** (1975), Law Commission Working Paper No 65 paragraphs 18–20

(B) JUSTIFICATION OF THE PRESENT LAW

18. The justification of the present law as it applies to entire contracts is that 'it holds men to their contracts'.[1] The contractor who has agreed to do a job for an all-in price, to be paid when the work is completed, may not then insist on payments on account; much less may he break the contract by leaving the work half-finished and recover payment for what he has done.

By refusing him redress except as provided by the contract the law gives him an incentive to see the job through. It may be argued that this incentive would be greatly reduced if he were to be entitled to payment otherwise than under the contract in respect of benefits conferred by partial performance. The contractor would, it may be said, do as much work under the contract as suited him and then claim payment for the benefit conferred; indeed he might take on contracts that he intended from the outset to break. Two points may therefore be made in favour of maintaining the rule on entire contracts in its present form. First a relaxation of it could lead to a lowering of standards of commercial morality which would be against the public interest. Second the removal of the hardship that the present rule may cause to some could result in more serious and more general hardship to others whom it benefits.

(C) CRITICISMS OF THE PRESENT LAW

19. The principal criticism of the rule on entire contracts is its lack of flexibility. In some situations the application of the rule prevents injustice. For example, it prevents the contractor who has stipulated for an all-in price, payable on completion, from insisting on payments being made on account while the contract is still on foot. It also works satisfactorily where the damage caused by the breach of contract exceeds the value of the benefit conferred by partial performance: no 'net' benefit has been conferred so there is no injustice in leaving the party in breach without a remedy. There are however situations in which the party in breach is unable to complete the work required of him—whether because this is a physical impossibility or because the other party has accepted his breach as a repudiation of the contract—and the value of the benefit conferred by partial performance is greater than the damage caused by the breach. Here the application of the rule on entire contracts allows the party on whom the benefit has been conferred to make and to keep a profit at the expense of the party in breach; he gets something for nothing. This is, arguably, an injustice. Where the net value of the benefit is small the injustice that the present law causes to the party in breach may be slight. Where however the benefit conferred by partial performance is out of all proportion to the damage caused by the breach the forfeiture of 'the fruit of his labour' may appear penal. The court's jurisdiction to relieve against penalties may have some relevance here. Let us say that a building contract provides that money is payable when certified due by a named architect but that the other party may nevertheless withhold all payment if he has a counterclaim against the builder for damages for breach of contract. The court would probably hold the latter provision to be unenforceable as a penalty in which case the damages recoverable on the counterclaim would be set off against the sum certified due and the builder would be entitled to the difference.[2] Yet the effect of the rule on entire contracts is to allow the party receiving a benefit from partial (but not substantial) performance to withhold all payment where the builder is unable to perform further even though no loss or damage has resulted from his breach.

20. Another criticism of the present law on entire contracts is that it leads to different results in given situations depending on whether money happens to have been paid to the party in breach

---

1 *Munro v Butt* (1858) 8 E & B 735, 754; 120 ER 275, 280, *per* Campbell CJ.
2 *Modern Engineering (Bristol) Ltd v Gilbert-Ash (Northern) Ltd* [1974] AC 689.

before the benefit has been conferred. The party in breach may not claim payment for the benefit conferred, but, if he has in fact been paid, and provided that the other party has obtained a benefit from the partial or defective performance of the contract, the money so paid does not have to be returned.[3] For example, in *Sumpter v Hedges*[4] Mr Sumpter had in fact received part payment before he left the site: Mr Hedges did not counterclaim for the repayment of what he had paid but if he had done so his claim would have failed. He might have counterclaimed for damages for breach of contract but if Mr Hedges had been able to complete the work without incurring further expense damages would probably have been assessed at a purely nominal figure . . .

[T]he point we are making now is that the present law on entire contracts can produce anomalous results: the party in breach who has already received payment is in a markedly better position, in fact *and in law*, than the party who has not. It may be argued, in support of a change in the present law, that the rights and remedies of the party in breach ought to be broadly the same in either case.

After engaging in a process of consultation, the Law Commission published its Report (No 121 (1983), on which see A Burrows (1984) 47 *MLR* 76) in which it maintained the view which it had earlier canvassed in its Working Paper and put forward proposals for reform together with a Draft Law Reform (Lump Sum Contracts) Bill which it appended to its report. The essence of the Law Commission's proposal can be found in the following extract from its report.

- **Pecuniary Restitution on Breach of Contract**
  (1983), Law Com No 121, paragraphs 2.37–2.40

(i) Our proposed remedy in outline

2.37 . . . The party who has conferred the benefit shall be entitled as against the other party to such sum as represents the value of what he has done under the contract to the person who has the benefit of it. The remedy will not be available either where the contract is still on foot or, subject to one exception [*where the benefit obtained by the innocent party consists of returnable goods which are retained in circumstances in which a fresh contract to pay for them is implied*], where the party who has failed to complete has a remedy under the present law. The party in breach can, of course, only have a remedy in respect of work done under the contract, though the person who benefits from this work will not necessarily be the other party to the contract. The benefit obtained by the innocent party must be a benefit obtained *in terms of* the contract. The sum payable pursuant to the remedy should not exceed the sum representing the proportion that what has been done under the contract bears to what was promised to be done. The normal rules relating to remoteness of damage and mitigation of damages should continue to apply with regard to any set-off (or counterclaim) which the innocent party makes against the party in breach. It should be open to the parties to exclude the new remedy but in order to do so it will be necessary to show that the parties both adverted to the possibility of less than complete performance and provided for it.

2.38 The new remedy should apply in the same way to cases where there is no breach of contract. Where the contract is not entire but is severable into parts, our remedy should apply to any of the severable parts which are themselves entire.

2.39 We have considered an alternative method of curing the mischief which we have identified in the present law. This approach would simply involve the removal of the present presumption that the mere postponement of payment until the completion of performance leads to no liability at all being imposed on one party until the other has rendered complete performance. The attraction of such an approach lies in its simplicity. However we have concluded that it would not be desirable to adopt

---

3 Cf. *Whincup v Hughes* (1871) LR 6 CP 78.   4 [1898] 1 QB 673.

such an approach. We think it would fail adequately to protect the innocent party. For example, there would be no provision, . . . that to the extent that the innocent party seeks to set-off his damages for breach of contract against a claim made by the other party pursuant to our new remedy, any clauses which would otherwise limit or exclude those damages should not be given effect to. In our view a provision of this type is essential if justice is to be done between the parties, but the simple approach which we have just outlined would not include this or any other balancing factor.

2.40 Another alternative method of curing the mischief which we have identified in the present law would be to adopt the principles of section 1(3) of the Law Reform (Frustrated Contracts) Act 1943. In our view such a course would not be desirable for one important reason. Our proposals and the 1943 Act are intended to achieve different objectives in different types of cases. An obvious example of where this difference 'bites' is that, for the reason given in paragraph 2.39 above, the 1943 Act would fail adequately to balance the interests of the innocent party with those of the partial performer.

However, the Lord Chancellor (Hailsham) did not accept the recommendations of the Law Commission and, consequently, the report has never been implemented. In deciding not to proceed to legislation, the Lord Chancellor was, in all probability, heavily influenced by the Note of Dissent prepared by one of the Law Commissioners, Mr Brian Davenport. He dissented on the following grounds:

I have the misfortune to differ from my colleagues both as regards the principal policy conclusion reached in this report and as to the manner of its implementation. In almost all contracts of any substance today under which one party promises to carry out certain work in return for a consideration to be given by the other, the contract will make provision for stage payments of one sort or another. The facts of modern economic life have demonstrated that payments on account while the work proceeds are a necessity. Both printed and specially prepared contracts will therefore, in almost every case, provide for such payments. Where a written contract does not provide for such payments, the reason may well be that the parties intended that payment would be due if, but only if, the contractor finished the work. The so-called mischief which the report is intended to correct is therefore likely only to exist in relation to small, informal contracts of which the normal example will be a contract between a householder and a jobbing builder to carry out a particular item of work. Experience has shown that it is all too common for such builders not to complete one job of work before moving on to the next. The effect of the report is to remove from the householder almost the only effective sanction he has against the builder not completing the job. In short, he is prevented from saying with any legal effect, 'Unless you come back and finish the job, I shan't pay you a penny'. In my view, the disadvantages in practice of the recommendations contained in the report outweigh the advantages to be gained from the search for theoretically perfect justice between the parties. If the report's recommendations are implemented, the jobbing builder can leave the site and, when the irate and exasperated householder finally brings the contract to an end, send in a bill for the work done up to the time when he abandoned the site. It will then be for the householder to dispute the amount and calculate his counter-claim for damages. To put the burden on the householder in this manner is, in my view, to put him in a disadvantageous position where he negotiates from a position of weakness. It must not be forgotten that it is the builder who has broken the contract, not the householder, and that the contract is one under which the parties agreed that payment would be by lump-sum only when the work was done.

At present, the courts have a good deal of flexibility in determining what the intention of the parties was and the number of reported cases on the subject do not seem to show that there is any great call for reform. The 'intention of the parties' always tends to vary according as to which party is asked what his intention was. The presumed common intention, where the parties have agreed a lump-sum contract, cannot be too readily assumed to be that if the contractor, in breach of contract, fails to complete his contract the innocent party is nevertheless liable to pay him for what he has done and mount a counter-claim for his damages. It was pointed out to us on consultation that most householders in practice do not insist upon the pound of flesh and are willing to negotiate a reasonable sum. Nevertheless, this sum is negotiated against a background of legal rights which, in my view, provide a juster solution in the great majority of cases than would in my view mentation of the report.

If the basic policy in the report were to be implemented, it would in my view be better that this were done by adopting the principles of the law reform (Frustrated Contracts) Act 1943. No doubt, that Act is not perfect but in the vast majority of cases its provisions seem to work satisfactorily, for there are almost no reported cases illustrating difficulties. To create a new, and perforce complicated, set of rules such as is contained in the draft Bill annexed to the report does not seem to me a satisfactory way of simplifying the law to achieve justice in practice, especially having regard to the fact that the draft Bill will largely have to be operated in County Courts and small claims courts.

In the following extract, McFarlane and Stevens defend the rule from *Sumpter v Hedges* by arguing that a *quantum meruit* claim should be precluded where the claimant's obligation is entire. The core of their argument is that any enrichment of the defendant in such a case is not unjust.

- B McFarlane and R Stevens, 'In Defence of *Sumpter v Hedges*' (2002) 118 *LQR* 569, 569–71, 574–7, 580–1, 592–4

. . .

As will be seen[1] this article does not attempt to support all the reasoning of the Court of Appeal in *Sumpter v Hedges*. Rather, it aims to support the general rule, applied in that case, that a party in breach cannot claim for the value of services rendered or for the value of goods supplied under a contract unless he has an accrued contractual entitlement to be paid.[2]

. . . it is the central thesis of this article that the criticisms made are misplaced. The part performance of an entire obligation should not *by itself* entitle the part performer to payment. Even where the party in breach confers a benefit upon the other party by the part performance of an entire obligation there is nothing unjust about such enrichment. It will be argued that the one clear exception to the rule, the *quantum meruit* claim to freight after a deviation proposed by the House of Lords in *Hain SS. Co. Ltd v Tate & Lyle Ltd*,[3] does not undermine the validity of the rule. Rather, it suggests that any disapproval of the effects of the rule should focus not on the rule itself but on the anterior question of which obligations should be viewed as entire.

. . .

To understand the rule it is necessary to examine the distinction between entire and severable obligations. Wherever it is agreed that full performance of an obligation is necessary before the right to payment or other counter-performance is to be earned, then that obligation is entire. If A agrees to carry B's goods from Oxford to Glasgow with payment at the destination, A is under an entire obligation to carry the goods to their destination. Taking them as far as Carlisle is not enough.

In contrast, if an obligation to do building work were said to be severable then, whilst complete performance would still be necessary before the full price could be claimed, partial performance

---

1 *infra* text.

2 *Munro v Butt* (1858) 8 E & B 738; *Bostom Deep Sea Fishing and Ice Co. v Ansell* (1888) 39 ChD. 339; *Sumpter v Hedges, supron; Forman & Co. Pty. Ltd v The Liddesdale* [1900] AC 190; *Vigers v Cook* [1919] 2 KB 475: *Ibmac Ltd v Marshall (Homes) Ltd*, CA (1968) 208 EG 851; *Bolton v Mahadeva* [1972] 1 WLR 1009; *Holland Hannen & Cubitts (Northern) Ltd v Welsh Health Technical Services Organisation* (1981) 18 Build LR 80; *Wiluszynski v Tower Hamlets LBC* [1989] ICR 493; *Segnit v Cotton*, CA, December 9, 1999; Sale of Goods Act 1979, s. 30(1).

3 (1936) 41 Com Cas 350.

would still earn some payment under the contract. The obligation to build may be fully severable, so that part payment becomes due on a rateable basis according to the extent of performance rendered. However, a severable obligation may itself consist of a number of entire stages. For example, in a building contract part payment might be earned on completion of each of a number of stages of the work. In that case, the obligation to complete the work as a whole could be seen as severable, yet the obligation to complete each specific stage as entire.[4]

Not all contractual obligation can be described as either entire or severable. The distinction is used to classify those contractual obligations, the performance of which can trigger a duty of counter-performance. It classifies them on the basis of the degree of performance necessary to trigger that duty. It is only, however, in those cases where a duty to counter-perform has not been triggered that the issue arises of the party in breach claiming resitution for the value of services rendered or the value of goods supplied.[5] Where the party in breach has a contractual action in debt for the services rendered or goods supplied this will be determinative of his rights.[6]

Some cases and commentators refer not to entire and severable obligations, but rather to entire and severable contracts.[7] However, Professor Treitel's insistence on using the terms to classify obligations rather than contracts is to be preferred.[8] A contract may contain both entire and non-entire obligations. If a carrier performs the (entire) obligation to carry goods to the agreed destination he is entitled to be paid even though he is in breach of another obligation under the contract of carriage (e.g. to carry the goods with reasonable care).[9] However, a breach of the obligation to carry the goods with reasonable care may be so severe as to prevent performance of the obligation to deliver the goods as described in the contract[10] Similarly, under a contract for the sale of goods, the obligation as to quantity may be entire but the obligation as to quality may not be.

Steele v Tardiani[11] also shows that there is room for further refinement. The plaintiffs agreed to cut firewood into sections of a particular length and width. Payment was to be made according to the tonnage cut. Both parties were free to terminate the contract at any time. Hence, the wood-cutters were under no obligation to cut wood at all.[12]

Steele v Tardiani illustrates an important distinction between *promissory* conditions and *contingent* conditions.[13] The wood-cutters' right to be paid was *contingent* upon their cutting wood. They had not, however, promised to cut any quantity of wood. This is a familiar conclusion in the context of unilateral contracts. In the classic case of *Carlill v Carbolic Smoke Ball Co.*[14] Mrs Carlill was under no obligation to use the smoke ball as directed but only then would she be entitled to payment if she caught influenza. Similarly in *Sumpter v Hedges* the essential reason why the builders were not entitled to be paid was not because they were in breach of contract but because they had not fulfilled the condition entitling them to payment. Those acts which a party needs to perform if he wants to trigger a duty of counter-performance can be categorised as entire or severable, even if there is no contractual obligation on that party to perform at all. Indeed, it is more accurate to explain the rule in *Sumpter v Hedges* without any

---

4 There is a sense in which even fully severable obligations can be viewed as consisting of an infinite number of distinct entire obligations, using the same conceptual model as Zeno of Elea's paradox of Achilles and the Tortoise (discussed by Aristotle, *Physics* 239b 14–8: see Barnes, *Presocratic Philosophers* (1999) 242 at p. 273).

5 *Hoenig v Isaacs* [1952] 2 All ER 176 at p. 181.

6 cf. *Pan Ocean Shipping Ltd v Creditcorp Ltd (The Trident Beauty)* [1994] 1 WIR 161.

7 *e.g.* Williams: *Hoenig v Isaacs* [1952] 2 All ER 176. *per* Somervell LJ at p. 177, *per* Denning LJ at p. 181 and *per* Romer LJ at p. 182; *Dimond v Lovell* [2002] 1 AC 384 *per* Lord Hoffmann at p. 394: Goff and Jones at pp. 513–515; Birks at p. 231.

8 Treitel at pp. 728–730.   9 *Dakin v Oxley* (1864) 15 CB (NS) 647.

10 *Asfar & Co. v Blundell* [1896] 1 QB 123.   11 (1946) 72 CLR 386.

12 *per* Latham CJ at p. 393.

13 *Chitty on Contracts*, Beale ed., (28th ed. *cf.* n. 98, 1999), Vol. 1 at para. 2-135.

14 [1893] 1 QB 256.

reference to the obligation to perform. If a party fails to meet any conditions necessary to gain a contractual right to payment then the fact that he has benefited the other party to the contract in attempting to meet those conditions will not in itself give rise to a claim against that other party.

. . .

'UNJUST'

Three potential reasons why the defendant's enrichment is unjust have been suggested: free acceptance, failure of consideration and unconscionability.[15]

(i) FREE ACCEPTANCE

'Free acceptance' is not a principle which has been expressly adopted in case law but was introduced by Goff and Jones as the best explanation for a number of cases where the defendant receives services from another without request but is required to make restitution. The principle is said to operate where the defendant 'as a reasonable man, should have known that the plaintiff who rendered the services expected to be paid for them, and yet he did not take a reasonable opportunity open to him to reject the proffered services'.[16]

The existence of such a principle has been doubted[17] but regardless of whether it is accepted or not, it has no application in the current context. At the time the services are rendered the defendant expects complete performance under the contract. He will clearly not, therefore, reject the services proffered. There is nothing unfair about the conduct of a defendant who accepts work expecting to be obliged to pay when it is completed but who refuses to do so when it is not.

(ii) FAILURE OF CONSIDERATION

Claims based upon a 'total failure of consideration' were developed as a cause of action to the count in *assumpsit* for money had and received. 'Consideration' is given a different meaning from that used in the context of contract formation. The most famous judicial definition of failure of consideration is that of Viscount Simon L.C. in *Fibrosa Spolka Akcyjna v Fairbairn, Lawson, Combe Barbour Ltd*[18]

'. . . when one is considering the law of failure of consideration . . . it is, generally speaking, not the promise which is referred to as the consideration, but the performance of the promise. The money was paid to secure performance and, if performance fails, the inducement which brought about the payment is not fulfilled.'

If E agrees to paint F's house, F paying £100 in advance, and E subsequently refuses to begin painting F may recover his money on the basis of a total failure of consideration: *i.e.* because of E's failure of counter-performance.

Failure of consideration has never been applied by the courts as a ground for the recovery of benefits other than money. Several important commentators have argued that money and non-money benefits should receive the same treatment within the law of unjust enrichment and that the same factors should trigger recovery regardless of the nature of the enrichment[19] Indeed, there are cases awarding restitution for the value of services conferred which, whilst not adopting the terminology 'failure of consideration', can be explained as basing recovery upon that ground.[20]

If it is accepted that 'failure of consideration' may be a ground for the recovery of benefits

---

15 Goff and Jones at p. 553.   16 Goff and Jones at p. 18.

17 Burrows at pp. 315–320; Birks and Mitchell, *English Private Law* at p. 548.

18 [1943] A C 32 at p. 48.

19 Birks at pp. 226–234; Burrows at pp. 299–304; Goff and Jones at p. 44.

20 *Pulbrook v Lawes* (1876) 1 QBD 284; *Pavey and Matthews Pty. Ltd v Paul* (1987) 162 CLR 221. See Birks at pp. 226–234.

other than money, can it be a basis for recovering the value of the part performance of an entire obligation?

At first it might seem that there is a clear failure of consideration: the claimant performed the work expecting to be paid and that contractual reciprocation has failed to materialise. If failure of consideration can always be taken to mean failure of contractual counter-performance, then it would be possible to say the recipient of part performance is unjustly enriched.

However, failure of counter-performance whilst generally sufficient is not an accurate definition of the meaning of failure of consideration. Indeed, Viscount Simon L.C. said that it was only true 'generally speaking'. A more subtle approach to failure of consideration would be to see it as equivalent to the civilian concept *causa data causa non secuta* (things given upon a basis, that basis having failed)[21] Where there is a failure of consideration the reason for recovery is that the basis upon which the enrichment has been transferred has failed.

Indeed, there are situations in which counter-performance is not received and yet there is no failure of basis and hence no unjust enrichment. This is perhaps most apparent in the case of deposits. If payment in advance is construed as a deposit it forms part of the basis of the payment that it is to be forfeited if the purchaser refuses to go ahead with the transaction.[22] It is irrelevant that the purchaser has received no counter-performance for his money. He cannot recover.

Conversely there are situations in which counter-performance is received and yet there is a failure of basis. In *Re Phoenix Life Assurance Co. Ltd*[23] a company entered into marine insurance policies which it had no capacity to contract. Today, the doctrine of *ultra vires* as applicable to companies has been effectively abolished and the contracts would have been valid.[24] In 1862, however, the contracts were void and the policy holders were entitled to recover their premiums on the basis that 'they did not get anything for them'.[25] It was irrelevant that there was no failure of counter-performance. In other words, it did not matter that no monies became due under the policies. Even if the Phoenix Life Assurance Company had paid out losses, these could have been recovered because of its lack of capacity.[26] The basis upon which the money was paid to the Phoenix Life Assurance company was that they were 'on risk', and they never were.

The same reasoning might have been employed to achieve the result reached in *Guinness Mahon & Co. Ltd v Kensington and Chelsea R.L.B.C.*[27] The Court of Appeal were faced with one of the many cases concering the unravelling of an interest rate swap. Like contracts of insurance, interest rate swaps are a form of gambling. Both serve the potentially useful commercial function of passing risk from one party to another. An interest rate swap is an agreement whereby each party agrees to pay to the other different rates of interest, usually one fixed and one fluctuating, on a notional principal sum over a given period. In *Hazell v Hammersmith L.B.C.*[28] all such transactions were found to be *ultra vires* local authorities and consequently void *ab initio*. After *Hazell* payments under those swaps entered into by local authorities ceased. Under swaps where payments were outstanding and performance incomplete ('open swaps') it was possible to say that there was a failure of consideration due to the failure of counter-performance. The party who in net terms had paid money under the swap could

---

21 Zimmermann. *The Law of Obligations: Roman Foundations of the Civilian Tradition* (1990) at pp. 843–844; Birks at pp. 227–228.

22 *Mayson v Clouet* [1924] AC 980; *Howe v Smith* (1884) 27 ChD. 89.

23 (1862) 2 J & H 441, 70 ER 1131: *cf. Re London County Commercial Reinsurance Office Ltd* [1922] 2 ChD. 67.

24 Companies Act 1985, s. 30.

25 (1862) 31 LJ. Ch 749 at p. 752. In one report the claim is said to be due to 'no consideration' having been received for the payments: (1862) 2 J. & H. 441 at p. 448. These words do not appear in the other reports: (1862) 31 LJ Ch 749; (1862) 7 L.T 191.

26 *Auckland Harbour Board v R.* [1924] AC 318.   27 [1998] QB 215.

28 [1992] 2 AC 1.

therefore recover on this basis. It was argued, however, that where all payments had been made, there was no failure of consideration: the parties got all that they bargained for.[29] This was rejected. The court held that there was a failure of consideration, the consideration being the legally enforceable obligation to be paid. It might be objected to this that what a party desires is performance and that once he has received this he is no longer concerned with the fact that at some time in the past he could not have compelled performance.[30] It is submitted that a more satisfactory explanation as to why there was a failure of consideration is to focus on the fact that, whatever happened, the local authority could always recover money it paid out on the ground of its lack of capacity. It was never on risk and could never lose under the bet. The other party bargained for the opportunity to win under the bet and it never could. Receiving counter-performance is of little comfort if the local authority is always entitled to get it back.

Given these nuances, we can return to the question of defining the basis on which the performance of an entire obligation is undertaken. Where a contract imposes an entire obligation, work is done in the expectation that it will be paid for *when complete*. There is no shared expectation that part performance is to be rewarded. There is hence no failure of basis if the part performer is not paid.[31] Crucially, and contrary to the argument of Goff and Jones,[32] concluding that an obligation is entire bars not only a contractual claim by a part performer but also an unjust enrichment claim grounded on failure of consideration.

(iii) UNCONSCIONABILITY

Whilst admitting that it is not currently possible to recognise that there is a general principle allowing relief from bargains upon the basis of 'unconscionability',[33] Goff and Jones suggest that relief may be granted in a case like *Sumpter v Hedges* because 'the defendant's reliance on the terms of the contract to deny the plaintiff any recompense may be said to be unconscionable; it is unjust to penalise the party in breach, when the value of the benefit conferred by him is out of all proportion to the loss which the innocent party suffered'.[34]

It seems that Goff and Jones are not suggesting that the contract should not bind the parties because of any impropriety in the bargaining process. There are some situations in which an enrichment can be said to be unjust because of a need to protect parties from the consequences of bargains which are felt to be substantively unfair. For example, money paid pursuant to a deposit which is found to be penal must be returned.[35] Why parties of equal bargaining power should not be free, absent impropriety, to agree to penal clauses if they see fit is an issue which cannot be explored here. However, the validity of an analogy between the rule applied in *Sumpter v Hedges* and existing jurisdictions to give relief against penal clauses will be examined.[36]

Certain critics of the rule applied in *Sumpter v Hedges* have condemned it on the basis that, like a penal deposit or other penalty clause, its sole function is to encourage contractual performance.[37] Support for the view can be gained from *Gilbert-Ash (Northern) Ltd v Modern Engineering (Bristol) Ltd*[38] Under a building contract between a main contractor and a sub-contractor the main contractor was entitled to 'suspend or withhold payment' if the sub-contractor failed to

---

29 Birks (1993) 23 *UWALR* 195 at pp. 206–208.   30 White (1999) 115 LQR 380.

31 *contra* Palmer, *Law of Restitution* (1978) at p. 573: Goff and Jones at p. 553: MacQueen [1994] JR 137: Birks at p. 234: Burrows at p. 276.

32 at p. 513.   33 Goff and Jones at p. 45.   34 Goff and Jones at p. 553.

35 *Workers Trust & Merchant Bank Ltd v Dojap Investments Ltd* [1993] AC 573 at p. 578: Treitel at p. 940

36 *cf.* Corbin, *Corbin on Contracts* (1950), s.1122.

37 *e.g.* Corbin. *supra*, n. 72 and Ballantine, *supra*, n. 21: Williams at p. 396; Burrows (1984) 47 *MLR* 76 at p. 78.

38 [1974] AC 689; *cf. The Vaingueur José* [1979] 1 Lloyd's Rep 557 at p. 578.

'comply with any of the provisions' of the contract. This entitlement was said to be invalid as a penalty[39]

Certainly, any attempt to justify the rule as *simply* based on providing a deterrent to breaches of contract will be doomed to failure. This is partly why the Law Commission had no qualms in proposing modifications of the rule, as this was the principal argument they considered in its favour.[40] However, the fact that the rule precludes recovery for part performance of any condition precedent to payment, be it a promissory condition or a contingent condition, shows that the sole rationale for the rule cannot be the need to promote adherence to contractual obligations. Hence there is no valid analogy between rules which allow the recovery of penal deposits, or other sums paid under penalty clauses. The rule applied in *Sumpter v Hedges* is not a form of forfeiture for breach of contract, and therefore should not be subject to a regime giving relief against such forfeiture.

A simple example may illustrate the point.

J agrees with K that he will build K a shed for £100. J quits after putting up the walls but failing to put on the roof.

L promises M that if he builds L a shed he will pay him £100. M quits after putting up the walls but failing to put on the roof.

In both cases the entitlement to be paid does not accrue because the shed is not finished. It would be strange indeed if J could claim that the withholding of payment to him was penal and invalid because he was in breach whereas M could not because he was not in breach of any obligation to build.

The result in *Gilbert-Ash (Northern) Ltd v Modern Engineering (Bristol) Ltd* is not inconsistent with the rule applied in *Sumpter v Hedges*. The clause found to be penal in that case attempted to remove the subcontractor's accrued right to be paid if he committed any breach of contract, however minor. It was, therefore, functionally equivalent to a penalty payable upon breach of contract. However, if the parties had drafted the contract so as to make the right to payment conditional on full performance, then no such right would have accrued. Whilst there may seem to be little difference in practice between a clause which prevents a right to payment accuring following a minor breach and a clause which attempts to remove an accrued right following such a breach, only the latter can be characterised as penal. As the argument based on 'unconscionability' cannot be supported by reference to cases on penalty clauses, it amounts to a blunt argument that it is unfair to hold parties to what they have agreed.

...

DEVIATION

In a contract for the carriage of goods by sea, a deliberate,[41] unauthorised[42] and unjustifiable[43] departure from the agreed or usual route constitutes a deviation and will be a breach of the contract of carriage. Compliance with the duty not to deviate is a condition precedent to recovery of the agreed freight.[44] Therefore *any* deviation will be sufficient to bar a contractual claim for freight, even

---

39 [1974] AC 689, *per* Lord Reid at p. 698. Lord Morris at p. 703. Lord Dilhome at p. 711 and Lord Salmon at p. 728.

40 Law Com. No 121 (1983) at para. 2.25.

41 *Rio Tinto Co. v Seed Shipping Co.* (1926) 42 TLR 381.

42 Clauses purporting to authorise a departure from the contract route will be narrowly interpreted: e.g. *Leduc v Ward* (1888) 20 QBD 475.

43 Departures necessary to save life or to preserve the venture will be justifiable: e.g. *Scaramanga v Stamp* (1880) 5 CPD 295; *Kish v Taylor* [1912] AC 604. Art IV, r. 4 of the Hague-Visby Rules also justifies departures which are necessary to save property of others and any 'reasonable' departure.

44 *Joseph Thorley Ltd v Orchis SS. Co. Ltd* [1907] 1 KB 660.

one which does not prevent or unduly delay the arrival of the goods at the agreed destination.[45] Of course, if the conduct of the goods owner reveals a waiver of the deviation, entry into a new contract, or receipt of an unjust enrichment, then the carrier will have a claim. However, it may well be the case that the goods owner does not know of the deviation until after the carriage has been completed. In such circumstances, it will be impossible to argue that the goods owner has waived the breach or entered into a new contract simply by taking delivery of his goods. Further, the mere acceptance of his own goods when they are discharged should not be sufficient grounds on which to claim the goods owner is unjustly enriched. The goods owner has no more choice in accepting such perform-ance than the defendant in *Sumpter v Hedges*.

The situation following a deviation should thus exactly resemble that where the carrier does not complete the stipulated voyage but instead delivers the goods at an intermediate port. A condition precedent to the duty to pay the agreed freight has not been performed, and acceptance of the goods when they are discharged cannot by itself justify a *quantum meruit* award.[46] Once performance of the duty not to deviate is taken so seriously as to be a condition precedent of the duty to pay the agreed freight, then, as Scrutton L.J. stated in the Court of Appeal in *Hain SS. Co. Ltd v Tate & Lyle Ltd,* a *quantum meruit* claim must fail 'as a matter of logic'.[47]

However, as was noted in the House of Lords in *Hain,* this logic can produce seemingly harsh results. Lord Wright thought that the approach of the Court of Appeal would 'have startling con-sequences' in cases, where, despite the deviation, the goods arrived at their agreed destination with only a trifling delay. His Lordship thought that in such a case, as 'the goods owner has had, for all practical purposes, the benefit of all that his contract required . . . the court would not be slow to infer an obligation when the goods are received at destination to pay, not indeed the contract freight, but a reasonable remuneration'.[48] Such statements in *Hain* are *obiter* in as much as it was decided that on the facts of the case no obligation to pay reasonable freight could be imposed,[49] but it is generally accepted that where goods are carried to their destination after a deviation, a restitutionary claim for freight will prima facie be available.[50]

The claim for reasonable freight as envisaged in *Hain* does constitute a genuine exception to the rule that part performance of entire obligation by itself cannot give rise to a claim in unjust enrichment. One possible response is to argue that the claim should therefore not be allowed. After all, the factor stressed by Lord Wright and Lord Maugham, that the claimant received a benefit at the expense of the defendant, is not in itself enough to justify recovery. Another response is to argue that the chain of logic in the Court of Appeal decision can be broken at an earlier stage. Once it is accepted that performance of the duty not to deviate is a condition precedent to a contractual claim for freight, then the logical result is that no claim can be brought. However, this view of the duty not to deviate has not always been accepted.[51] In *Bornmann v Tooke,*[52] for example, the plaintiff brought an action of *indebitatus assumpsit* to recover the agreed freight having carried goods from Riga to Portsmouth. The defendant argued that the plaintiff had not proceeded direct to Portsmouth but had unnecessarily put

45 *Hain SS. Co. Ltd v Tate & Lyle Ltd* (1936) 41 Com Cas 350 *per* Lord Wright M.R. at p. 367.

46 *Hopper v Burness* (1876) 1 CPD 137.

47 (1934) 39 Com. Cas. 259 at pp. 271–272.

48 (1936) 41 Com Cas 350 at p. 368. Lord Maugham takes the same stance at p. 373.

49 The possible *quantum meruit* claim discussed in *Hain* was against an indorsee of the bill of lading. The original charterer was liable to pay the agreed freight, having waived the deviation.

50 *Scrutton on Charterparties and Bills of Lading,* ed. Boyd (20th ed., 1996), Art. 127 at p. 260: *Joseph Thorley Ltd v Orchis SS. Co. Ltd* [1907] 1 KB 660, *per* Collins MR at p. 667 and *per* Fletcher-Moulton LJ at p. 669.

51 e.g. *Cole v Shallet* (1693) 3 Lev 41. Recovery of agreed freight was allowed despite a deviation on a return journey from Barcelona to London. The court held that the breach of the covenant not to deviate could not be pleaded in bar of an action on the covenant to pay the freight.

52 (1808) 1 Camp 376.

in to Copenhagen, causing the defendant to incur extra expense in insuring the cargo. Lord Ellenborough expressly denied that the duty not to deviate was a condition precedent to recovery of the agreed freight and held that the defendant would have to bring a cross-action for any loss he may have suffered through this breach. He took the view that 'to hold that any short delay in setting sail or trifling departure from the direct course of the voyage would entirely destroy the plaintiff's right to be remunerated for transporting the cargo, would indeed be going *inter apices facti*'.[53]

Lord Ellenborough's reasoning seems persuasive. In a contract of carriage, the duty not to deviate should be on a par with the duty to take reasonable care of the cargo. Failures to perform such duties may give rise to a claim for damages, but should not impede the claim for freight, unless they are so severe as to interfere with the key duty to deliver the goods to the agreed destination, or to give the owner of the goods the right to terminate the contract before the goods have been delivered.[54] The solution to the supposed harshness of the Court of Appeal's view in *Hain* is to re-classify the duty not to deviate, not to interfere with the logic which dictates the result of a failure to perform a condition precedent. This seems to be the real gist of the arguments of Lord Wright and Lord Maugham.[55] Like the judges in *Hoenig v Isaacs*, they focus on the fact that the defendant has received what amounts to full performance. Indeed, it does not seem right that a claim for reasonable freight should be advocated: the reasoning of the House of Lords points towards a restoration of the former principle that a deviation by itself does not prevent a claim for the agreed freight.[56]

The views of the House of Lords in *Hain* should not be interpreted as casting doubt on the existence or justice of the rule in *Sumpter v Hedges*. Rather, they question the validity of deciding that the duty not to deviate is a condition precedent to recovery of the agreed freight. A closer examination of which contractual duties can truly be said, as a matter of construction, to be conditions precedent to receiving counter-performance may well be the correct response in other cases where it is felt that the rule applied in *Sumpter v Hedges* operates unfairly.

NOTES AND QUESTIONS

1. The Law Commission identified the mischief of the rule in *Sumpter v Hedges* as 'the rule that postponement of payment until completion of performance leads to the result that there is no liability at all until the other party has rendered complete performance' (above, 303). Referring to this in a part of their article not extracted, McFarlane and Stevens argue that the Law Commission's 'real complaint . . . is with the courts' readiness to find that particular obligations are entire, and thereby to trigger the application of the rule. Given this diagnosis of the mischief, it is surprising that the Law Commission recommended abrogating the rule itself, rather than simply emphasising that postponement of payment does not necessarily make full performance a condition precedent to earning payment'. Do you agree?

2. If restitution cannot be awarded where it would be inconsistent with the contractual regime to do so (as the House of Lords said in *Pan Ocean Shipping v Creditcorp Ltd, The Trident Beauty*

---

53 *ibid.* at p. 378.   54 *cf.* Baughen [1991] *LMCLQ* 70 at p. 88.

55 There is a tension between this argument and the acceptance by Lord Wright M.R. that 'unjustified deviation is a fundamental breach of a contract of affreightment . . . any deviation changes the adventure'. It could however be argued that the alteration in risk caused by a deviation prevents exemption clauses applying as a matter of interpretation (e.g. Lloyd LJ in *The Antares* [1987] I Lloyd's Rep. 424 at p. 430) or as a rule derived from the general law of hailment (e.g. Coote in *Lex Mercatoria* (Rose ed., 2000)). Indeed, as Coote suggests, a number of the well-known problems in the law of deviation may stem from a mistaken desire to explain the effect of deviation on the application of exemption clauses by arguing that a deviation prevents the carrier from relying on *any* terms of the contract of carriage.

56 The preference for a *quantum meruit* in *Hain* may well be linked to the view that although the deviation prevents the express contract from applying, it leaves intact a basic implied contract arising from the act of a requested carriage: *e.g. Balian v Joly* (1900) 6 TLR 45 and *Thorley Ltd v Orchis SS. Co. Ltd* [1907] 1 KB 660.

[1994] 1 WLR 161), is the approach of McFarlane and Stevens anything more than saying that restitution will be denied when, on the proper construction of the contract, the parties intended that full performance was a condition precedent to recovery (and therefore an award of restitution would be inconsistent with the contract)?

3. Do any of the judgments in *Sumpter v Hedges* (above, 298–299) refer to the obligation as entire?

4. Do you agree with McFarlane and Stevens' explanation of the obiter dicta in *Hain Steamship Co. Ltd v Tate and Lyle Ltd* (above, 299–300)?

5. In *Steele v Tardiani* (1946) 72 CLR 386, the claimants were three Italian internees who were released from internment and given permission to work for the defendant. According to the terms of the contract between them (as found by the trial judge), the claimants were required to cut firewood into lengths, each length being six feet long and six inches in diameter. Payment was to be made at the rate of eight shillings *per* ton. The trial judge found that the amount of the timber which had been cut by the claimants was 1,500 tons, but also found that most of it had not been split to a diameter of six inches (it varied from six to fifteen inches in diameter). The High Court of Australia held the obligation to cut to the dimensions provided was an entire obligation but that the claimants were entitled to recover on a *quantum meruit*. Dixon J explained that this was because there was 'either a dispensation from precise performance or an implication at law of a new obligation to pay the value of the work done' (at 405). If the first explanation is rejected (because the High Court of Australia made an award of remuneration at a reasonable rate rather than contract rates) and the case is seen as one of an imposed (unjust enrichment) obligation, is this case inconsistent with McFarlane and Stevens' theory? Do you agree with their argument that this case is one that can be explained as performance being offered, and accepted on the basis that it was substitute performance for the strict contractual requirements?

3. CONTRACTS DISCHARGED BY FRUSTRATION

Once a contract has been discharged by a frustrating event, attention must be given to the remedial consequences of the frustration of the contract. The effect of frustration is to discharge the contract automatically and to release both parties from their future obligations to perform under the contract. But the law of contract does not make provision for the payment of monetary compensation, there having been no breach of the contract. It is within the law of unjust enrichment that we find the source of the law relating to the financial consequences of the frustration of a contract.

The law concerning the restitutionary consequences of frustration in England has developed in three distinct stages (see further E McKendrick, 'Frustration, Restitution and Loss Apportionment' in A Burrows (ed.), *Essays on the Law of Restitution*, (1991, 147). The first stage was to let the loss occasioned by the frustration of the contract lie where it fell. While the Court of Appeal in *Chandler v Webster* [1904] 1 KB 493 recognized that money could be recovered upon a total failure of consideration, they held that such a total failure could only arise when the contract had been set aside *ab initio*. Given that frustration discharges a contract prospectively, but not retrospectively, a frustrated contract could not be set aside *ab initio* so as to give rise to a right of recovery based upon a total failure of consideration. The loss also lay where it fell in the case of services provided prior to the frustration of the contract. In *Cutter v Powell* (1795) 6 TR 320 Cutter was employed by Powell as second mate on a journey from Jamaica to England. Powell promised to pay Cutter the sum of thirty guineas ten days after the ship arrived in Liverpool provided that Cutter 'proceeds, continues and does his duty as second mate, in the said ship from [Kingston, Jamaica] to the port of Liverpool'. Cutter died during the course of the voyage. His widow brought an action to recover the wages which she alleged were payable in respect of the work which Cutter had done prior to his death. Her action failed because Cutter was not entitled to payment until the completion of the voyage.

The second stage in the development of the law was the decision of the House of Lords in the great case of *Fibrosa Spolka Akcyjna v Fairbairn Lawson Combe Barbour Ltd* (above, 12). Essentially the House of Lords rejected the proposition that a total failure of consideration could only arise when the contract was set aside *ab initio* and overruled *Chandler*. Instead it was held that a total failure of consideration simply meant that the basis upon which the money had been paid must have wholly failed. Although *Fibrosa* marked an important stage in the development of the law, it did not leave the law in an entirely satisfactory state. Two principal defects arguably arose. The first was that the payee in *Fibrosa* was compelled to return the pre-payment but was not permitted to bring into account the expenditure which it had incurred in the performance of the contract. Such a payee might now be protected by the defence of change of position (see below, 761–804) but the defence was not recognized at the time *Fibrosa* was decided. The second possible defect was that the failure of consideration had to be total: a partial failure of consideration did not suffice to generate a restitutionary claim.

The third stage was the enactment of the Law Reform (Frustrated Contracts) Act 1943. The origin of this Act was in a report of the Law Revision Committee (chaired by Lord Wright, who also sat as a Law Lord in *Fibrosa*) which was commissioned in 1937. However, the outbreak of war delayed the Act until four years after the Committee reported, by which time *Fibrosa* had been decided. It is suggested that the Act enacts a scheme of mutual restitution and that it does not seek to apportion the loss caused by the frustration of a contract. This proposition is, however, a contestable one and it has been argued by some (see, for example, A. M. Haycroft and D. M. Waksman, 'Frustration and Restitution' [1984] *JBL* 207) that the Act does give the courts a flexible discretion to adjust losses. This debate should be borne in mind when examining the Act and the limited case law to which it has given rise.

(1) THE LAW REFORM (FRUSTRATED CONTRACTS) ACT 1943

- Law Reform (Frustrated Contracts) Act 1943, sections 1, 2(3)–(5)

Adjustment of rights and liabilities of parties to frustrated contracts

1.—(1) Where a contract governed by English law has become impossible of performance or been otherwise frustrated, and the parties thereto have for that reason been discharged from the further performance of the contract, the following provisions of this section shall, subject to the provisions of section two of this Act, have effect in relation thereto.

(2) All sums paid or payable to any party in pursuance of the contract before the time when the parties were so discharged (in this Act referred to as 'the time of discharge') shall, in the case of sums so paid, be recoverable from him as money received by him for the use of the party by whom the sums were paid, and, in the case of sums so payable, cease to be so payable:

Provided that, if the party to whom the sums were so paid or payable incurred expenses before the time of discharge in, or for the purpose of, the performance of the contract, the court may, if it considers it just to do so having regard to all the circumstances of the case, allow him to retain or, as the case may be, recover the whole or any part of the sums so paid or payable, not being an amount in excess of the expenses so incurred.

(3) Where any party to the contract has, by reason of anything done by any other party thereto in, or for the purpose of, the performance of the contract, obtained a valuable benefit (other than a payment of money to which the last foregoing subsection applies) before the time of discharge, there shall be recoverable from him by the said other party such sum (if any), not exceeding the value of the said benefit to the party obtaining it, as the court considers just, having regard to all the circumstances of the case and, in particular,—

(a) the amount of any expenses incurred before the time of discharge by the benefited party in, or for the purpose of, the performance of the contract, including any sums paid or payable by him to any other party in pursuance of the contract and retained or recoverable by that party under the last foregoing subsection, and

(b) the effect, in relation to the said benefit, of the circumstances giving rise to the frustration of the contract.

(4) In estimating, for the purposes of the foregoing provisions of this section, the amount of any expenses incurred by any party to the contract, the court may, without prejudice to the generality of the said provisions, include such sum as appears to be reasonable in respect of overhead expenses and in respect of any work or services performed personally by the said party.

(5) In considering whether any sum ought to be recovered or retained under the foregoing provisions of this section by any party to the contract, the court shall not take into account any sums which have, by reason of the circumstances giving rise to the frustration of the contract, become payable to that party under any contract of insurance unless there was an obligation to insure imposed by an express term of the frustrated contract or by or under any enactment.

(6) Where any person has assumed obligations under the contract in consideration of the conferring of a benefit by any other party to the contract upon any other person, whether a party to the contract or not, the court may, if in all the circumstances of the case it considers it just to do so, treat for the purposes of subsection (3) of this section any benefit so conferred as a benefit obtained by the person who has assumed the obligations as aforesaid.

2.— . . .

(3) Where any contract to which this Act applies contains any provision which, upon the true construction of the contract, is intended to have effect in the event of circumstances arising which operate, or would but for the said provision operate, to frustrate the contract, or is intended to have effect whether such circumstances arise or not, the court shall give effect to the said provision and shall only give effect to the foregoing section of this Act to such extent, if any, as appears to the court to be consistent with the said provision.

(4) Where it appears to the court that a part of any contract to which this Act applies can properly be severed from the remainder of the contract, being a part wholly performed before the time of discharge, or so performed except for the payment in respect of that part of the contract of sums which are or can be ascertained under the contract, the court shall treat that part of the contract as if it were a separate contract and had not been frustrated and shall treat the foregoing section of this Act as only applicable to the remainder of that contract.

(5) This Act shall not apply—

(a) to any charterparty, except a time charterparty or a charterparty by way of demise, or to any contract (other than a charterparty) for the carriage of goods by sea; or

(b) to any contract of insurance, save as is provided by subsection (5) of the foregoing section; or

(c) to any contract to which [section 7 of the Sale of Goods Act 1979] (which avoids contracts for the sale of specific goods which perish before the risk has passed to the buyer) applies, or to any other contract for the sale, or for the sale and delivery, of specific goods, where the contract is frustrated by reason of the fact that the goods have perished.

- **BP Exploration Co. (Libya) Ltd v Hunt (No 2)**
[1979] 1 WLR 783, Queen's Bench Division

Mr Hunt was the owner of an oil concession granted by the Libyan government. He did not have the resources to develop the concession himself, so he entered into a joint venture with BP under which BP were to carry out the exploration and development of the site and they also agreed to transfer to Mr Hunt certain 'farm-in' contributions in cash and in oil. In return Mr Hunt agreed to grant BP a half share of the concession and further agreed to repay, over a period of time, 125 per cent of BP's 'farm-in' contributions and his half share of the expenditure incurred in the exploration and development of the fields. Payment was to be made in the form of three-eighths of Mr Hunt's share of the oil produced from the field until such time as the reimbursement was complete. A giant oil field was discovered and the field came on stream in 1967. Once the field came on stream it was agreed that the costs of production would be divided equally between the parties. In 1971 BP's interest in the oilfield was expropriated by the Libyan government and, in 1973, Mr Hunt's interest was also expropriated. At this point BP had received approximately one-third of their reimbursement oil. BP claimed that the expropriation of the interests in the oilfield had frustrated the contract between the parties and that they were entitled to the award of a 'just sum' under section 1(3) of the Law Reform (Frustrated Contracts) Act 1943.

Robert Goff J:
. . .

II. THE PRINCIPLES GOVERNING CLAIMS UNDER THE ACT OF 1943

The Law Reform (Frustrated Contracts) Act 1943 is described as an Act to amend the law relating to the frustration of contracts. In fact, it is concerned not with frustration itself, but with the consequences of frustration; and it creates statutory remedies, enabling the court to award restitution in respect of benefits conferred under contracts thereafter frustrated.

Section 1(1) of the Act sets out the circumstances in which the Act applies, namely, that a contract governed by English law has become impossible of performance or been otherwise frustrated, and the parties thereto have for that reason been discharged from the further performance of the contract. However, section 2(5) excludes from the operation of the Act certain contracts, which are immaterial for the purposes of the present case; and section 2(4) provides that, where part of a contract can properly be severed from the remainder, the severed part having before the time of discharge been either wholly performed or so performed except for payment of ascertained or ascertainable sums, the court shall treat the severed part as a separate contract which has not been frustrated, the Act being applicable only to the remainder.

The most important subsections are subsections (2) and (3) of section 1, which set out the statutory remedies, the former being concerned with cases where the benefit conferred under the contract consists of money, and the latter with cases where the benefit does not consist of money. These subsections are of such importance that I shall set them out in full: . . .

Of the remaining provisions of the Act, section 2(1) and (2) are of no materiality to the present case, nor is section 1(6). Section 1(4) provides that, in estimating expenses incurred, sums may be included for overhead expenses, and for work or services performed personally. Section 2(3) is, however, of considerable importance. I shall quote the subsection in full: . . .

There remains section 1(5), which is possibly related to section 2(3). This subsection provides that the court is not to take into account any sums which have by reason of the circumstances giving rise to the frustration of the contract become payable under any contract of insurance, unless there was an obligation to insure imposed by an express term of the frustrated contract or by or under any enactment.

Such, in summary, is the Act. The historical background of the Act is well known. At one time, money paid under a contract thereafter frustrated was held to be irrecoverable. This was known as the rule in *Chandler v Webster* [1904] 1 KB 493. The results of this rule were so obviously harsh that, following severe criticism, the rule was referred to the Law Revision Committee which, in its seventh interim report (Rule in *Chandler v Webster*) (1939) (Cmd. 6009), recommended that (with exceptions relating to freight pro rata itineris and advance freight) money paid in pursuance of a contract there-after frustrated (or, where a severable part of such a contract had been performed, money paid in pursuance of the remainder) should be recoverable, subject to a deduction of such sum as repre-sented a fair allowance for expenditure incurred by the payee in the performance of or for the purpose of performing the contract. However in 1942, before this recommendation had been implemented, *Chandler v Webster* was overruled by the House of Lords in *Fibrosa Spolka Akcyjna v Fairbairn Lawson Combe Barbour Ltd* [1943] AC 32. The effect of that decision was that money paid under a contract thereafter frustrated was recoverable, but only if the consideration for the payment had wholly failed. It was, however, considered by certain members of the House of Lords that, even with the rule in *Chandler v Webster* [1904] 1 KB 493 out of the way, the common law remedy was imperfect; attention was drawn in particular to the fact that there could be no recovery if the con-sideration had only partially failed, and that no allowance could be made for expenses incurred by the payee: see 49–50, *per* Viscount Simon; 54–5, *per* Lord Atkin; and 71–2 *per* Lord Wright. Further-more, the *Fibrosa* case was, like the report of the Law Revision Committee, concerned only with the recovery of money. Neither touched upon the more difficult question of restitution where the benefit conferred under a contract was a benefit other than a payment of money: in such cases, the old strict common law doctrine of entire contracts provided a formidable obstacle to restitution. At all events, no doubt stimulated by the observations made in the *Fibrosa* case, in the following year the legislature enacted the Act of 1943.

It was suggested in argument that I might have regard to the report of the Law Revision Committee in construing the Act of 1943. I do not, however, consider that the report is of any assistance to me. Its terms of reference were limited to consideration of the rule in *Chandler v Webster* [1904] 1 KB 493; that case was overruled by the House of Lords in the period between the date of the report and the passing of the Act, and the scope of the Act is considerably wider than that of the report.

I turn, therefore, to the construction of the Act itself. Much argument was directed towards the problem of construction, and in particular to the effect to be given to section 1(2) and (3) and section 2(3) of the Act. I shall now set out my conclusions on the effect to be given to these subsections.

(1) The principle of recovery

(a) The principle, which is common to both section 1(2) and (3), and indeed is the fundamental principle underlying the Act itself, is prevention of the unjust enrichment of either party to the contract at the other's expense. It was submitted by Mr Rokison, on behalf of BP, that the principle common to both subsections was one of restitution for net benefits received, the net benefit being the benefit less an appropriate deduction for expenses incurred by the defendant. This is broadly correct so far as section 1(2) is concerned; but under section 1(3) the net benefit of the defendant simply provides an upper limit to the award—it does not measure the amount of the award to be made to the plaintiff. This is because in section 1(3) a distinction is drawn between the plaintiff's performance under the contract, and the benefit which the defendant has obtained by reason of that performance—a distinction about which I shall have more to say later in this judgment; and the net benefit obtained by the defendant from the plaintiff's performance may be more than a just sum payable in respect of such performance, in which event a sum equal to the defendant's net benefit would not be an appropriate sum to award to the plaintiff. I therefore consider it better to state the principle underlying the Act as being the principle of unjust enrichment, which underlies the right of recovery in very many cases in English law, and indeed is the basic principle of the English law of restitution, in which the Act forms part.

(*b*) Although section 1(2) and (3) is concerned with restitution in respect of different types of benefit, it is right to construe the two subsections as flowing from the same basic principle and therefore, so far as their different subject matters permit, to achieve consistency between them. Even so, it is always necessary to bear in mind the difference between awards of restitution in respect of money payments and awards where the benefit conferred by the plaintiff does not consist of a payment of money. Money has the peculiar character of a universal medium of exchange. By its receipt, the recipient is inevitably benefited; and (subject to problems arising from such matters as inflation, change of position and the time value of money) the loss suffered by the plaintiff is generally equal to the defendant's gain, so that no difficulty arises concerning the amount to be repaid. The same cannot be said of other benefits, such as goods or services. By their nature, services cannot be restored; nor in many cases can goods be restored, for example where they have been consumed or transferred to another. Furthermore the identity and value of the resulting benefit to the recipient may be debatable. From the very nature of things, therefore, the problem of restitution in respect of such benefits is more complex than in cases where the benefit takes the form of a money payment; and the solution of the problem has been made no easier by the form in which the legislature has chosen to draft section 1(3) of the Act.

(*c*) The Act is *not* designed to do certain things: (i) It is not designed to apportion the loss between the parties. There is no general power under either section 1(2) or section 1(3) to make any allowance for expenses incurred by the plaintiff (except, under the proviso to section 1(2), to enable him to enforce pro tanto payment of a sum payable but unpaid before frustration); and expenses incurred by the defendant are only relevant in so far as they go to reduce the net benefit obtained by him and thereby limit any award to the plaintiff. (ii) It is not concerned to put the parties in the position in which they would have been if the contract had been performed. (iii) It is not concerned to restore the parties to the position they were in before the contract was made. A remedy designed to prevent unjust enrichment may not achieve that result; for expenditure may be incurred by either party under the contract which confers no benefit on the other, and in respect of which no remedy is available under the Act.

(*d*) An award under the Act may have the effect of rescuing the plaintiff from an unprofitable bargain. This may certainly be true under section 1(2), if the plaintiff has paid the price in advance for an expected return which, if furnished, would have proved unprofitable; if the contract is frustrated before any part of that expected return is received, and before any expenditure is incurred by the defendant, the plaintiff is entitled to the return of the price he has paid, irrespective of the consideration he would have recovered had the contract been performed. Consistently with section 1(2), there is nothing in section 1(3) which necessarily limits an award to the contract consideration. But the contract consideration may nevertheless be highly relevant to the assessment of the just sum to be awarded under section 1(3); this is a matter to which I will revert later in this judgment.

(2) Claims under section 1(2)

Where an award is made under section 1(2), it is, generally speaking, simply an award for the repayment of money which has been paid to the defendant in pursuance of the contract, subject to an allowance in respect of expenses incurred by the defendant. It is not necessary that the consideration for the payment should have wholly failed: claims under section 1(2) are not limited to cases of total failure of consideration, and cases of partial failure of consideration can be catered for by a cross-claim by the defendant under section 1(2) or section 1(3) or both. There is no discretion in the court in respect of a claim under section 1(2), except in respect of the allowance for expenses; subject to such an allowance (and, of course, a cross-claim) the plaintiff is entitled to repayment of the money he has paid. The allowance for expenses is probably best rationalised as a statutory recognition of the defence of change of position. True, the expenses need not have been incurred by reason of the plaintiff's payment; but they must have been incurred in, or for the purpose of, the performance of the contract under which the plaintiff's payment has been made, and for that reason it is just that they should be brought into account. No provision is made in the subsection for any increase in the sum recoverable by the plaintiff, or in the amount of expenses to be allowed to the defendant, to allow for the time value of money. The money may have been paid, or the expenses incurred, many years before the date of frustration; but the cause of action accrues on that date, and the sum recoverable under the Act as at that date can be no greater than the sum actually paid, though the defendant may have had the use of the money over many years, and indeed may have profited from its use. Of course, the question whether the court may award interest from the date of the accrual of the cause of action is an entirely different matter, to which I shall refer later in this judgment.

(3) Claims under section 1(3)

(a) General

In contrast, where an award is made under section 1(3), the process is more complicated. First, it has to be shown that the defendant has, by reason of something done by the plaintiff in, or for the purpose of, the performance of the contract, obtained a valuable benefit (other than a payment of money) before the time of discharge. That benefit has to be identified, and valued, and such value forms the upper limit of the award. Secondly, the court may award to the plaintiff such sum, not greater than the value of such benefit, as it considers just having regard to all the circumstances of the case, including in particular the matters specified in section 1(3)(a) and (b). In the case of an award under section 1(3) there are, therefore, two distinct stages—the identification and valuation of the benefit, and the award of the just sum. The amount to be awarded is the just sum, unless the defendant's benefit is less, in which event the award will be limited to the amount of that benefit. The distinction between the identification and valuation of the defendant's benefit, and the assessment of the just sum, is the most controversial part of the Act. It represents the solution adopted by the legislature of the problem of restitution in cases where the benefit does not consist of a payment of money; but the solution so adopted has been criticised by some commentators as productive of injustice, and it certainly gives rise to considerable problems, to which I shall refer in due course.

(b) Identification of the defendant's benefit. In the course of the argument before me, there was much dispute whether, in the case of services, the benefit should be identified as the services themselves, or as the end product of the services. One example canvassed (because it bore some relationship to the facts of the present case) was the example of prospecting for minerals. If minerals are discovered, should the benefit be regarded (as Mr Alexander contended) simply as the services of prospecting, or (as Mr Rokison contended) as the minerals themselves being the end product of the successful exercise? Now, I am satisfied that it was the intention of the legislature, to be derived from section 1(3) as a matter of construction, that the benefit should in an appropriate case be identified as the end product of the services. This appears, in my judgment, not only from the fact that section 1(3) distinguishes between the plaintiff's performance and the defendant's benefit, but also from section 1(3)(b) which clearly relates to the product of the plaintiff's performance. Let me take the example of a building contract. Suppose that a contract for work on a building is frustrated by a fire which destroys the building and which, therefore, also destroys a substantial amount of work already done by the plaintiff. Although it might be thought just to award the plaintiff a sum assessed on a quantum meruit basis, probably a rateable part of the contract price, in respect of the work he has done, the effect of section 1(3)(b) will be to reduce the award to nil, because of the effect, in relation to the defendant's benefit, of the circumstances giving rise to the frustration of the contract. It is quite plain that, in section 1(3)(b), the word 'benefit' is intended to refer, in the example I have given, to the actual improvement to the building, because that is what will be affected by the frustrating event; the subsection therefore contemplates that, in such a case, the benefit is the end product of the plaintiff's services, not the services themselves. This will not be so in every case, since in some cases the services will have no end product; for example, where the services consists of doing such work as surveying, or transporting goods. In each case, it is necessary to ask the question: what benefit has the defendant obtained by reason of the plaintiff's contractual performance? But it must not be forgotten that in section 1(3) the relevance of the value of the benefit is to fix a ceiling to the award. If, for example, in a building contract, the building is only partially completed, the value of the partially completed building (i.e. the product of the services) will fix a ceiling for the award; the stage of the work may be such that the uncompleted building may be worth less than the value of the work and materials that have gone into it, particularly as completion by another builder may cost more than completion by the original builder would have cost. In other cases, however, the actual benefit to the defendant may be considerably more than the appropriate or just sum to be awarded to the plaintiff, in which event the value of the benefit will not in fact determine the quantum of the award. I should add, however, that, in a case of prospecting, it would usually be wrong to identify the discovered mineral as the benefit. In such a case there is always (whether the prospecting is successful or not) the benefit of the prospecting itself, i.e. of knowing whether or not the land contains any deposit of the relevant minerals; if the prospecting is successful, the benefit may include also the enhanced value of the land by reason of the discovery; if the prospector's contractual task goes beyond dis-covery and includes development and production, the benefit will include the further enhancement of the land by reason of the installation of the facilities, and also the benefit of in part transforming a valuable mineral deposit into a marketable commodity.

I add by way of footnote that all these difficulties would have been avoided if the legislature had thought it right to treat the services themselves as the benefit. In the opinion of many commentators, it would be more just to do so; the services in question have been requested by the defendant, who normally takes the risk that they may prove worthless, from whatever cause. In the example I have given of the building destroyed by fire, there is much to be said for the view that the builder should be paid for the work he has done, unless he has (for example by agreeing to insure the works) taken upon himself the risk of destruction by fire. But my task is to construe the Act as it stands. On the true construction of the Act, it is in my judgment clear that the defendant's benefit must, in an appropriate case, be identified as the end product of the plaintiff's services, despite the difficulties which this construction creates, difficulties which are met again when one comes to value the benefit.

(c) *Apportioning the benefit.* In all cases, the relevant benefit must have been obtained by the defendant by reason of something done by the plaintiff. Accordingly, where it is appropriate to identify the benefit with an end product and it appears that the defendant has obtained the benefit by reason of work done both by the plaintiff and by himself, the court will have to do its best to apportion that benefit, and to decide what proportion is attributable to the work done by the plaintiff. That proportion will then constitute the relevant benefit for the purposes of section 1(3) of the Act.

(d) *Valuing the benefit.* Since the benefit may be identified with the product of the plaintiff's performance, great problems arise in the valuation of the benefit. First, how does one solve the problem which arises from the fact that a small service may confer an enormous benefit, and conversely, a very substantial service may confer only a very small benefit? The answer presumably is that at the stage of valuation of the benefit (as opposed to assessment of the just sum) the task of the court is simply to assess the value of the benefit to the defendant. For example, if a prospector after some very simple prospecting discovers a large and unexpected deposit of a valuable mineral, the benefit to the defendant (namely, the enhancement in the value of the land) may be enormous; it must be valued as such, always bearing in mind that the assessment of a just sum may very well lead to a much smaller amount being awarded to the plaintiff. But conversely, the plaintiff may have undertaken building work for a substantial sum which is, objectively speaking, of little or no value— for example, he may commence the redecoration, to the defendant's execrable taste, of rooms which are in good decorative order. If the contract is frustrated before the work is complete, and the work is unaffected by the frustrating event, it can be argued that the defendant has obtained no benefit, because the defendant's property has been reduced in value by the plaintiff's work; but the partial work must be treated as a benefit to the defendant, since he requested it, and valued it as such. Secondly, at what point in time is the benefit to be valued? If there is a lapse of time between the date of the receipt of the benefit, and the date of frustration, there may in the meanwhile be a substantial variation in the value of the benefit. If the benefit had simply been identified as the services rendered, this problem would not arise; the court would simply award a reasonable remuneration for the services rendered at the time when they were rendered, the defendant taking the risk of any subsequent depreciation and the benefit of any subsequent appreciation in value. But that is not what the Act provides: section 1(3)(b) makes it plain that the plaintiff is to take the risk of depreciation or destruction by the frustrating event. If the effect of the frustrating event upon the value of the benefit is to be measured, it must surely be measured upon the benefit as at the date of frustration. For example, let it be supposed that a builder does work which doubles in value by the date of frustration, and is then so severely damaged by fire that the contract is frustrated; the valuation of the residue must surely be made on the basis of the value as at the date of frustration. However, does this mean that, for the purposes of section 1(3), the benefit is always to be valued as at the date of frustration? For example, if goods are transferred and retained by the defendant till frustration when they have appreciated or depreciated in value, are they to be valued as at the date of frustration? The answer must, I think, generally speaking, be in the affirmative, for the sake of consistency. But this raises an acute problem in relation to the time value of money. Suppose that goods are supplied and sold, long before the date of frustration does the principle that a benefit is to be valued as at the date of frustration require that allowance must be made for the use in the meanwhile of the money obtained by the disposal of the goods, in order to obtain a true valuation of the benefit as at the date of frustration? This was one of the most hotly debated matters before me, for the very good reason that in the present case it affects the valuation of the parties' respective benefits by many millions of dollars. It is very tempting to conclude that an allowance should be made for the time value of money, because it appears to lead to a more realistic valuation of the benefit as at the date of frustration; and, as will appear hereafter, an appropriate method for making such an allowance is available in the form of the net discounted cash flow system of accounting. But I have come to the conclusion that, as a matter of construction, this course is not open to me. First, the subsection limits the award to the value of the benefit obtained by the defendant; and it does not follow that, because the defendant has had the money over a period of time, he has in fact derived any benefit from it. Secondly, if an allowance was to be made for the time value of the money obtained by the defendant, a comparable allowance should be made in respect of expenses incurred by the defendant, i.e. in respect of the period between the date of incurring the expenditure and the date of frustration, and section 1(3)(a) only contemplates that the court, in making an allowance for expenses, shall have regard to the 'amount of [the] expenses.' Thirdly, as I have already indicated, no allowance for the time value of money can be made under section 1(2); and it would be inconsistent to make such an allowance under section 1(3) but not under section 1(2).

Other problems can arise from the valuation of the defendant's benefit as the end product; I shall come to these later in the consideration of the facts of the present case. But there is a further ther problem which I should refer to, before leaving this topic. Section 1(3)(a) requires the court to have regard to the amount of any expenditure incurred before the time of discharge by the benefited party in, or for the purpose of, the performance of the contract. The question arises—should this matter be taken into account at the stage of valuation of the benefit, or of assessment of the just sum? Take a simple example. Suppose that the defendant's benefit is valued at £150, and that a just sum is assessed at £100, but that there remain to be taken into account defendant's expenses of £75; is the award to be £75 or £25? The clue to this problem lies, in my judgment, in the fact that the allowance for expenses is a statutory recognition of the defence of change of position. Only to the extent that the position of the defendant has so changed that it would be unjust to award restitution, should the court make an allowance for expenses. Suppose that the plaintiff does work for the defendant which produces no valuable end product, or a benefit no greater in value than the just sum to be awarded in respect of the work; there is then no reason why the whole of the relevant expenses should not be set off against the just sum. But suppose that the defendant has reaped a large benefit from the plaintiff's work, far greater in value than the just sum to be awarded for the work. In such circumstances it would be quite wrong to set off the whole of the defendant's expenses against the just sum. The question whether the defendant has suffered a change of position has to be judged in the light of all the circumstances of the case. Accordingly, on the Act as it stands, under section 1(3) the proper course is to deduct the expenses from the value of the benefit with the effect that only in so far as they reduce the value of the benefit below the amount of the just sum which would otherwise be awarded will they have any practical bearing on the award.

Finally, I should record that the court is required to have regard to the effect, in relation to the defendant's benefit, of the circumstances giving rise to the frustration of the contract. I have already given an example of how this may be relevant, in the case of building contracts; and I have recorded the fact that this provision has been the subject of criticism. There may, however, be circumstances where it would not be just to have regard to this factor—for example if, under a building contract, it was expressly agreed that the work in progress should be insured by the building-owner against risks which include the event which had the effect of frustrating the contract and damaging or destroying the work.

(e) *Assessment of the just sum.* The principle underlying the Act is prevention of the unjust enrichment of the defendant at the plaintiff's expense. Where, as in cases under section 1(2), the benefit conferred on the defendant consists of payment of a sum of money, the plaintiff's expense and the defendant's enrichment are generally equal; and, subject to other relevant factors, the award of restitution will consist simply of an order for repayment of a like sum of money. But where the benefit does not consist of money, then the defendant's enrichment will rarely be equal to the plaintiff's expense. In such cases, where (as in the case of a benefit conferred under a contract thereafter frustrated) the benefit has been requested by the defendant, the basic measure of recovery in restitution is the reasonable value of the plaintiff's performance—in a case of services, quantum meruit or reasonable remuneration, and in a case of goods, a quantum valebat or reasonable price. Such cases are to be contrasted with cases where such a benefit has not been requested by the defendant. In the latter class of case, recovery is rare in restitution; but if the sole basis of recovery was that the defendant had been incontrovertibly benefited, it might be legitimate to limit recovery to the defendant's actual benefit—a limit which has (perhaps inappropriately) been imported by the legislature into section 1(3) of the Act. However, under section 1(3) as it stands, if the defendant's actual benefit is less than the just or reasonable sum which would otherwise be awarded to the plaintiff, the award must be reduced to a sum equal to the amount of the defendant's benefit.

A crucial question, upon which the Act is surprisingly silent, is this: what bearing do the terms of the contract, under which the plaintiff has acted, have upon the assessment of the just sum? First, the terms upon which the work was done may serve to indicate the full scope of the work done, and so be relevant to the sum awarded in respect of such work. For example, if I do work under a contract under which I am to receive a substantial prize if successful, and nothing if I fail, and the contract is frustrated before the work is complete but not before a substantial benefit has been obtained by the defendant, the element of risk taken by the plaintiff may be held to have the effect of enhancing the amount of any sum to be awarded. Secondly, the contract consideration is always relevant as providing some evidence of what will be a reasonable sum to be awarded in respect of the plaintiff's work. Thus if a prospector, employed for a fee, discovers a gold mine before the contract under which he is employed is frustrated (for example, by illegality or by his illness or disablement) at a time when his work was incomplete, the court may think it just to make an award in the nature of a reasonable fee for what he has done (though of course the benefit obtained by the defendant will be far greater), and a rate able part of the contract fee may provide useful evidence of the level of sum to be awarded. If, however, the contract had provided that he was to receive a stake in the concession, then the just sum might be enhanced on the basis that, in all the circumstances, a reasonable sum should take account of such a factor: cf. *Way v Latilla* [1937] 3 All ER 759. Thirdly, however, the contract consideration, or a rateable part of it, may provide a limit to the sum to be awarded. To take a fairly extreme example, a poor householder or a small businessman may obtain a contract for building work to be done to his premises at considerably less than the market price, on the basis that he cannot afford to pay more. In such a case, the court may consider it just to limit the award to a rateable part of the contract price, on the ground that it was the understanding of the parties that in no circumstances (including the circumstances of the contract being frustrated) should the plaintiff recover more than the contract price or a rateable part of it. Such a limit may properly be said to arise by virtue of the operation of section 2(3) of the Act. But it must not be forgotten that, unlike money, services can never be restored, nor usually can goods, since they are likely to have been either consumed or disposed of, or to have depreciated in value; and since, ex hypothesi, the defendant will only have been prepared to contract for the goods or services on the basis that he paid no more than the contract consideration, it may be unjust to compel him, by an award under the Act, to pay more than that consideration, or a rateable part of it, in respect of the services or goods he has received. It is unnecessary for me to decide whether this will always be so; but it is likely that in most cases this will impose an important limit upon the sum to be awarded – indeed it may well be the most relevant limit to an award under section 1(3) of the Act. The legal basis of the limit may be section 2(3) of the Act; but even if that subsection is inapplicable, it is open to the court, in an appropriate case, to give effect to such a limit in assessing the just sum to be awarded under section 1(3), because in many cases it would be unjust to impose upon the defendant an obligation to make restitution under the subsection at higher than the contract rate.

(4) The effect of section 2(3) of the Act

The court has always to bear in mind the provisions of section 2(3) of the Act. It was submitted by Mr Rokison that effect should only be given to this subsection where the relevant contractual provision was clearly intended to have effect in the event of the frustrating circumstances. I can see no good reason for so qualifying the express words of the subsection. In my judgment the effect of the subsection depends, as it expressly provides, simply upon applying the ordinary principles of construction. If the contract contains any provision which, upon the true construction of the contract, is intended to have effect in the circumstances specified in the subsection, then the court can only give effect to section 1 of the Act to such extent as is consistent with such provision.

Examples of such provisions may be terms which have the effect of precluding recovery of any award under the Act, or of limiting the amount of any such award, for example, by limiting the award to the contractual consideration or a rateable part thereof. Similarly, the parties may contract upon the terms that the plaintiff shall not be paid until the occurrence of an event, and by reason of the frustration of the contract that event does not or cannot occur; then, if upon a true construction of the contract the court concludes that the plaintiff has taken the risk of non-payment in the event of such frustration the court should make no award by virtue of section 2(3) of the Act. Such may be the conclusion if the contract contains an express term imposing upon the plaintiff an obligation to insure against the consequences of the frustrating event. Another example considered in argument was a loan of money advanced to a businessman on the terms that it was to be repaid out of the profits of his business. Such a term should not automatically preclude an award in the event of frustration, for example, if the businessman is incapacitated the day after the loan is made; but if the business consists, for example, of a ship, which strikes a reef and sinks, then it may be that the court, having regard to the terms of the contract and the risk taken thereunder by the lender, would make no award. But in such cases the court should only refuse to make an award if it is satisfied that the plaintiff has, by the contract, taken the risk of the consequences of the frustrating event. The principle is the same as in those cases where the contract consideration controls the amount or basis of the award under the Act – the court should not act inconsistently with the contractual intention of the parties applicable in the events which have occurred. But, such cases apart, the court is free to make an award which differs from the anticipated contractual performance of the defendant. I have already referred to the fact that, under section 1(2) at least, the effect of an award under the Act may be to rescue the plaintiff from a bad bargain. Again, the contract may provide that the plaintiff is to receive goods or services; the court may nevertheless make an award in money. The contract may provide for the plaintiff to receive money at a certain place or in a certain currency; frustration may render that impossible (for example, in a case of supervening illegality), and the court may make an award for payment which takes effect at a different place or in a different currency. Most striking of all, in most frustrated contracts under which the claim is made in respect of a benefit other than money, the time for payment will not yet have come – the contract, or a severable part of it, will be 'entire' in the old strict sense of that term; I do not, however, consider that such a provision should automatically preclude an award under section 1(3). If it were intended to do so, there would be few awards under section 1(3), and the matter would surely be the subject of an express provision if it was the intention that so fundamental a qualification was to be imposed upon the power of the court under this subsection. Certainly, no such qualification is imposed in section 1(2), and no such result can be achieved in relation to an award under that subsection since, generally speaking, the plaintiff is entitled to the return of his money. In my judgment, only if upon a true consideration of the contract the plaintiff has contracted on the terms that he is to receive no payment in the event which has occurred, will the fact that the contract is 'entire' have the effect of precluding an award under the Act.

(5) Cross-claims

There may, in any particular case, be not merely a claim by the plaintiff against the defendant under the Act, but also a cross-claim by the defendant against the plaintiff. This may occur if each party has obtained a benefit by reason of the performance of the other, whether the benefit does or does not consist of a payment of money. The cross-claim may or may not be under the same subsection as the claim; indeed, claims, or cross-claims, or both, may be made under both subsections. Of course, where each party has conferred a benefit on the other, the effect may be that the lesser claim is extinguished by the greater, in the sense that in the final result the party who has conferred the greater benefit may recover the balance; in particular, in a case under section 1(3), the assessment of the just sum to be awarded to either party should take into account the receipt of any part of the contractual consideration from the other. Even so the court must take care, in making its award, that neither party gains an unjust benefit by taking advantage of the same item twice over. Section 1(3)(a) of the Act recognises the existence of the problem of 'double-counting' by providing that the defendant to a claim under section 1(3) may bring into account, as expenses incurred by him, any sum paid or payable by him in pursuance of the contract and retained or recoverable by the payee under section 1(2).

(6) The relevance to a claim under the Act of a prior breach by the plaintiff

If the plaintiff in an action in which he claims an award of restitution under the Act has committed a breach of the relevant contract prior to frustration, the only relevance of such breach is that, since the defendant will have an accrued right to damages, the defendant's claim to damages may be the subject of a set-off or counterclaim in the action. I cannot see that the breach of contract can have any other relevance. It certainly cannot otherwise affect a claim for repayment of money under section 1(2), since the court has (subject to an allowance for expenses, or the effect of section 2(3), or a cross-claim or set-off) no option but to order repayment in an appropriate case. Nor, in my judgment, can any such breach of contract have any other relevance to the award of a just sum under section 1(3); the basis of such an award is that the defendant has been unjustly enriched at the plaintiff's expense, and the mere fact that the plaintiff has committed a prior breach of contract does not affect the question whether the defendant has been unjustly enriched, which depends upon the quite separate question whether he has received a benefit in respect of which he ought, in justice, to make restitution. The appropriate way of enforcing a claim for damages for breach of contract is by an action for damages, or (where appropriate) by a counterclaim or set-off; such proceedings are, of course, subject to the ordinary rules relating to limitation of actions. If a defendant allows such a claim to become time-barred, I cannot see why he should be able to revive his claim by the back-door by inviting a court to take it into account when assessing a just sum to be awarded to the other party under section 1(3) of the Act. A fortiori, I cannot see any possible justification for the award of a just sum under section 1(3) being reduced on the ground that the plaintiff, acting reasonably, might have acted in a manner more favourable to the defendant; quite apart from the fact that such action might have enhanced the benefit received by the defendant (and so have raised the limit to an award to the plaintiff), I cannot see how any such matter can have the slightest bearing on the question whether the defendant has, in the events which occurred, been unjustly enriched at the plaintiff's expense. . . .

Both parties appealed to the Court of Appeal ([1981] 1 WLR 232) on various points and the defendants further appealed to the House of Lords ([1983] 2 AC 352). The grounds of appeal generally concerned issues which were either points of detail relating to the application of the law to the complex facts of the case or concerned points of law which are not of direct significance to us in the present context. But the following passage from the judgment of Lawton LJ in the Court of Appeal is worth setting out in full for the purpose of comparing it with the approach adopted by Robert Goff J at first instance. Lawton LJ stated:

The Act of 1943 was passed shortly after the decision of the House of Lords in *Fibrosa Spolka Akcyjna v Fairbairn Lawson Combe Barbour Ltd* [1943] AC 32, which overruled *Chandler v Webster* [1904] 1 KB 493. The earlier case had been regarded as authority for the proposition that, on the occurrence of an event which frustrates the performance of a contract, the loss lies where it falls and that money paid by one party to the contract to the other party is to be retained by the party in whose hands it is. The object of the Act was to make the operation of the law more fair when a contract governed by English law . . . has become impossible of performance and the parties to it have for that reason been discharged from further performance. This was to be done by adjusting the rights and liabilities of the parties in the ways set out: see section 1(1).

Section 1(2) dealt with payments of money. They were to be recoverable as money received for the use of the payer; but an adjustment could be made for expenses incurred by the recipient before the time of discharge in, or for the purpose of, the performance of the contract. The amount of the adjustment was to be such as the court considered just, having regard to all the circumstances of the case. In section 1(3) the Act provided for the case where one party had obtained a valuable benefit (other than a payment of money) before the time of discharge. . . .

Before the court can make an award under this subsection it must be satisfied that one party to a contract has obtained a valuable benefit by reason of something done by the other. In this case the plaintiffs did a great deal for the defendant and he obtained, before the frustrating events happened, a most valuable benefit from what they had done for him, which was so great that it was incapable of any exact valuation. This part of the problem presented no difficulties for the judge. What was difficult was the assessment of the sum which the court considered just, having regard to all the circumstances of the case. Save for what is mentioned in paragraphs (a) and (b), the subsection gives no help as to how, or upon what principles, the court is to make its assessment or as to what factors it is to take into account. The responsibility lies with the judge: he has to fix a sum which he, not an appellate court, considers just. This word connotes the mental processes going to forming an opinion. What is just is what the trial judge thinks is just. That being so, an appellate court is not entitled to interfere with his decision unless it is so plainly wrong that it cannot be just. The concept of what is just is not an absolute one. Opinions among right thinking people may, and probably will, differ as to what is just in a particular case. No one person enjoys the faculty of infallibility as to what is just. It is with these considerations in mind that we approach this case.

. . .

The judge assessed the just sum on what can be described as a reimbursement basis, that is to say, by ensuring as far as was practicable that the plaintiffs got back what they had paid out on the defendant's behalf before the frustrating events happened. . . .

Mr Rokison, on behalf of the plaintiffs, accepted that there could be more than one way of assessing a just sum. He pointed out that there was nothing in the Act to indicate that its purpose was to enable the judge to apportion losses or profits, or to put the parties in the positions which they would have been in if the contract had been fully performed or if it had never been made. This we accept. He submitted that the concept behind the Act was to prevent unjust enrichment. This is what the judge had thought. We get no help from the use of words which are not in the statute. . . . In our judgment, this court would not be justified in setting aside the judge's way of assessment merely because we thought that there were better ways. Mr Rokison tried to show that the judge's way was wrong and palpably wrong. . . . In our judgment, it cannot be said that the judge went wrong, and certainly not palpably wrong, in assessing a just sum by reference to the concept of reimbursing the plaintiffs.

NOTES AND QUESTIONS

1. Applying the principles he had set out to the extremely complicated facts of the case, Robert Goff J concluded that the 'valuable benefit' which Mr Hunt obtained as a result of the work done by BP prior to the frustration of the contract was the 'end product' of the services provided by BP, namely the enhancement in the value of Mr Hunt's concession. When valuing that benefit he held that section 1(3)(b) required him to take account of the circumstances giving rise to the frustration of the contract which, on the facts, had the effect of reducing the value of the benefit to the value of the oil which Mr Hunt had actually obtained from the oil-field and the financial settlement which he had reached with the Libyan government. In assessing the 'just sum' BP were, essentially, awarded the costs and expenses which they had incurred on Mr Hunt's account plus the 'farm-in' contributions in cash and oil given to Mr Hunt minus the reimbursement oil which BP had received. In essence, the just sum was the reasonable value of the services rendered and goods supplied by BP with counter-restitution being made for the value of the oil received by BP.

2. Was Robert Goff J correct to state that the 'fundamental principle underlying the Act itself, is prevention of the unjust enrichment of either party to the contract at the other's expense'? What did Lawton LJ mean when he said that the court got 'no help from the use of words which are not in the statute'?

3. Is the Act designed to provide a flexible machinery for the adjustment of loss or would it be true to say that loss apportionment is not explicitly addressed within the Act except to the extent that the court has a discretion to allow the claimant to recover so much of the benefit as appears to the court to be just?

4. One of the most notable features of the Act is its elimination of the total failure require-ment. What problems are the courts likely to experience now that the requirement has been abolished? Can the Act be used as a model for the development of the common law in this respect or will the courts view the Act as an isolated example of the intervention of Parliament which cannot be used as an analogy when seeking to develop the common law?

5. Was Robert Goff J correct to characterize the proviso to section 1(2) of the Act as a 'statutory recognition of the defence of change of position'? Section 1(2) was not directly in point at first instance in *BP v Hunt* and so the comments of Robert Goff J were strictly obiter dicta (contrast the approach of Garland J in *Gamerco SA v ICM/Fair Warning (Agency) Ltd*, below, 327).

6. Was Robert Goff J correct to conclude that section 1(3) of the Act required him to hold 'in an appropriate case' that it was the end-product of the claimant's services which was to be regarded as the benefit? Is this approach consistent with the common law approach to the identification of an enrichment in cases where the enrichment is asserted to have taken the form of a service (see Birks, above, 93)? When is it not 'appropriate' to regard the end-product as the benefit? How would a case such as *Appleby v Myers* (1867) LR 2 CP 651 be decided under the Act? In this case the claimants contracted to make and erect machinery in the defendant's factory and to maintain the machinery for a period of two years. After part of the machinery had been erected, an accidental fire destroyed the factory and the machinery and frustrated the contract. The claimants sought to recover payment in respect of the work which they had done prior to the frustration of the contract, but it was held that they were not entitled to any payment. Would the same result now be reached under the 1943 Act?

7. Why does the Act distinguish between the identification of the benefit, its valuation and the award of a just sum? Is each stage in the inquiry necessary? What approach should the courts adopt when considering what constitutes a just sum? Do you agree with the suggestion of the Court of Appeal in *Great Peace Shipping Ltd v Tsavliris (International) Ltd* [2003] QB 679, 726 (see above, 195) that the Act gives 'flexibility' to the courts?

- *Gamerco SA v ICM/Fair Warning (Agency) Ltd*
  [1995] 1 WLR 1226, Queen's Bench Division

A contract to promote a rock concert was held to have been frustrated when the permit to hold the concert at a sports stadium in Madrid was suddenly withdrawn because of safety fears about the stadium. The claimant promoters had paid the defendant group the sum of $412,500 prior to the frustration of the contract and both parties had incurred expenditure in preparing for the concert. It was held that the claimants were entitled to the return of the prepayment which they had made under section 1(2) of the Law Reform (Frustrated Contracts) Act 1943 and that no deduction should be made under the proviso to that subsection. The claimants were therefore entitled to recover $412,500.

Garland J:

...

RECOVERY AND EXPENSES

The contract, having been discharged by frustration, the plaintiffs were entitled to recover from the second defendants the advance payment of U.S. $412,500 (less the sum returned by the first defendants) by virtue of section 1(2) of the Act of 1943. . . .

In addition the balance net of tax, $362,500, ceases to be payable.

The issue which I have to decide is whether and, if so, to what extent, the defendants can set off against the U.S.$412,500 expenses incurred before the time of discharge in or for the purpose of the performance of the contract. It is perhaps surprising that over a period of 50 years there is no reported case of the operation of section 1(2), although it was considered obiter by Robert Goff J in *BP Exploration Co. (Libya) Ltd v Hunt (No 2)* [1979] 1 WLR 783, 800. The section has, of course, received the attention of textbook writers, most recently that of Professor Treitel in *Frustration and Force Majeure* (1994). . . . [*He set out the proviso together with subsections (4) and (5) and continued*:]

I therefore turn to the proviso and subsection (4). The defendants' claim for expenses was set out as a schedule to their defence and counterclaim. . . . [*He considered the schedule and continued*:]

THE APPROACH TO THE PROVISO

The following have to be established: (1) that the defendants incurred expenses paid or payable (2) before the discharge of the contract on 2 July (3) in performance of the contract (which is not applicable) or (4) for the purposes of the performance of the contract, and (5) that it is just in all the circumstances to allow them to retain the whole or any part of the sums so paid or payable.

The onus of establishing these matters must lie on the defendant. It is, in the broad sense, his case to be made out and I am assisted by the Victorian case of *Lobb v Vasey Housing Auxiliary (War Widows Guild)* [1963] VR 239 under the corresponding Victorian Act of 1959, which is in very similar terms to the Act of 1943.

I have already dealt with (1), (2) and (4) so far as the evidence allows. I turn to (5). I take the following matters into consideration. (a) My assumption that the relevant expenses of U.S.$50,000 was undisputed. (b) It was undisputed that the plaintiffs incurred expenses in excess of 52m. pesetas (approximately £285,000 or U.S.$450,000). (c) Neither party conferred any benefit on the other or on a third party, so that subsections (3) and (6) did not apply. (d) The plaintiffs' expenditure was wholly wasted, as was the defendants'. (e) The plaintiffs were concerned with one contract only. The defendants were concerned with the last of 20 similar engagements, neither party being left with any residual benefit or advantage. (f) As already stated, I entirely ignore any insurance recoveries in accordance with subsection (5).

Various views have been advanced as to how the court should exercise its discretion and these can be categorised as follows.

(1) *Total retention.* This view was advanced by the Law Revision Committee in 1939 (Cmd. 6009) on the questionable ground 'that it is reasonable to assume that in stipulating for pre-payment the payee intended to protect himself from loss under the contract.' As the editor of *Chitty on Contracts*, 27th edn (1994), vol. 1, 1141, para. 23-060, note 51, (Mr E. G. McKendrick) comments: 'He probably intends to protect himself against the possibility of the other party's insolvency or default in payment.' To this, one can add: 'and secure his own cash flow.' [*He then considered two passages from the judgment of Robert Goff J set out at 251–61 above, and continued:*]

I do not derive any specific assistance from the *BP Exploration Co.* case. There was no question of any change of position as a result of the plaintiff's advance payment.

(2) *Equal division.* This was discussed by Professor Treitel in *Frustration and Force Majeure*, 555–6, paras. 15-059 and 15-060. There is some attraction in splitting the loss, but what if the losses are very unequal? Professor Treitel considers statutory provisions in Canada and Australia but makes the point that equal division is unnecessarily rigid and was rejected by the Law Revision Committee in the 1939 report to which reference has already been made. The parties may, he suggests, have had an unequal means of providing against the loss by insurers, but he appears to overlook subsection (5). It may well be that one party's expenses are entirely thrown away while the other is left with some realisable or otherwise usable benefit or advantage. Their losses may, as in the present case, be very unequal. Professor Treitel therefore favours the third view.

(3) *Broad discretion.* It is self-evident that any rigid rule is liable to produce injustice. The words, 'if it considers it just to do so having regard to all the circumstances of the case,' clearly confer a very broad discretion. Obviously the court must not take into account anything which is not 'a circumstance of the case' or fail to take into account anything that is and then exercise its discretion rationally. I see no indication in the Act, the authorities or the relevant literature that the court is obliged to incline towards either total retention or equal division. Its task is to do justice in a situation which the parties had neither contemplated nor provided for, and to mitigate the possible harshness of allowing all loss to lie where it has fallen.

I have not found my task easy. As I have made clear, I would have welcomed assistance on the true measure of the defendants' loss and the proper treatment of overhead and non-specific expenditure. Because the defendants have plainly suffered some loss, I have made a robust assumption. In all the circumstances, and having particular regard to the plaintiffs' loss, I consider that justice is done by making no deduction under the proviso. . . .

NOTES AND QUESTIONS

1. Is the approach of Garland J preferable to that adopted by Robert Goff J in *BP v Hunt* (above)?

2. Garland J stated that the onus of proof lay upon the defendant and that, in so concluding, he derived assistance from the Victorian case of *Lobb v Vasey Housing Auxiliary* [1963] VR 239. The latter case underlines the significance of the location of the onus of proof. The defendants were paid £1,250 by Mrs Smith for an exclusive licence to occupy a flat in a block of flats which they were building. Mrs Smith died before her flat was completed. The defendants refused to return the £1,250. Her executrix sued to recover it. It was held that the death of Mrs Smith frustrated the contract between the parties and that the onus of proof was on the defendants to show that it was just in all the circumstances of the case for them to retain any part of the pre-payment. This they could not do and the trial judge remarked that in the normal case one would expect the defendants to sell the right to occupy the flat to someone else and so recover their expenses in that way.

(2) DEVELOPMENTS IN THE COMMONWEALTH

The impact of the Law Reform (Frustrated Contracts) Act 1943 was to extend beyond England and Wales. The Act was used as a model for legislation in New Zealand (Frustrated Contracts Act 1944), the state of Victoria in Australia (Frustrated Contracts Act 1959) and it was used by the Commissioners on Uniformity of Legislation in Canada as the basis for a model Act (The Uniform Act [Frustrated Contracts Act], recommended in 1948), which was subsequently enacted in every Canadian Province with the exceptions of Nova Scotia, British Columbia, and Saskatchewan. The widespread adoption of the 1943 Act did not, however, exempt it from criticism by a number of law reform commissions in the Commonwealth. The principal criticism levelled against the Act was that it was deficient in so far as it failed to address the question of the apportionment of any loss caused by the frustration of the contract. An example of an approach which seeks to bring the apportionment of loss into the equation is provided by the British Columbian Frustrated Contracts Act 1974 (which has since formed the basis for a new Uniform Act that has been adopted in Canada), the central provisions of which provide:

- **Frustrated Contracts Act 1996 (British Columbia), sections 5–8**

ADJUSTMENT OF RIGHTS AND LIABILITIES

5. (1) In this section, 'benefit' means something done in the fulfillment of contractual obligations, whether or not the person for whose benefit it was done received the benefit.

(2) Subject to section 6, every party to a contract to which this Act applies is entitled to restitution from the other party or parties to the contract for benefits created by the party's performance or part performance of the contract.

(3) Every party to a contract to which this Act applies is relieved from fulfilling obligations under the contract that were required to be performed before the frustration or avoidance but were not performed, except in so far as some other party to the contract has become entitled to damages for consequential loss as a result of the failure to fulfil those obligations.

(4) If the circumstances giving rise to the frustration or avoidance cause a total or partial loss in value of a benefit to a party required to make restitution under subsection (2), that loss must be apportioned equally between the party required to make restitution and the party to whom the restitution is required to be made.

EXCEPTION

6. (1) A person who has performed or partly performed a contractual obligation is not entitled to restitution under section 5 in respect of a loss in value, caused by the circumstances giving rise to the frustration or avoidance, of a benefit within the meaning of section 5 if there is

(a)   a course of dealing between the parties to the contract,
(b)   a custom or a common understanding in the trade, business or profession of the party so performing, or
(c)   an implied term of the contract,

to the effect that the party performing should bear the risk of the loss in value.

(2) The fact that the party performing the obligation has in respect of previous similar contracts between the parties effected insurance against the kind of event that caused the loss in value is evidence of a course of dealing under subsection (1).

(3) The fact that persons in the same trade, business, or profession as the party performing the obligations, on entering into similar contracts, generally effect insurance against the kind of event that caused the loss in value is evidence of a custom or common understanding under subsection (1).

CALCULATION OF RESTITUTION

7. (1) If restitution is claimed for the performance or part performance of an obligation under the contract, other than an obligation to pay money, in so far as the claim is based on expenditures incurred in performing the contract, the amount recoverable must include only reasonable expenditures.

(2) If performance under subsection (1) consisted of or included delivery of property that could be and is returned to the performer within a reasonable time after the frustration or avoidance, the amount of the claim must be reduced by the value of the property returned.

8. In determining the amount to which a party is entitled by way of restitution or apportionment under section 5, account must not be taken of

(a)   loss of profits, or
(b)   insurance money that becomes payable

because of the circumstances that give rise to the frustration or avoidance, but account must be taken of any benefits which remain in the hands of the party claiming restitution.

The British Columbian Act is not the only attempt which has been made to take account of losses incurred as well as benefits conferred. In the following extract a brief account is given of other Commonwealth attempts to devise a solution which takes account of losses incurred and an attempt is made to evaluate the arguments for and against such a development of the law.

- **E McKendrick, 'Frustration, Restitution and Loss Apportionment' in A Burrows (ed.), *Essays on the Law of Restitution*, (1991), 166–9**

The South Australian Frustrated Contracts Act 1988 produces similar practical results to the British Columbian Act but, in structural terms, is very different. Broadly speaking, the Act requires that the parties aggregate both benefits received and costs incurred in the performance of the contract up to the date of the frustration of the contract. The latter sum is then subtracted from the former and the remainder is 'notionally divided between the parties in equal shares'. In this way both benefits received and costs incurred are explicitly and equally taken into account and the loss occasioned by the frustration of the contract split between the parties.

The New South Wales Frustrated Contracts Act 1978 enacts a more complex scheme of loss adjustment. The Act distinguishes between cases in which the payee's part performance has been received by the payer and cases where it has not been received. Where the payer has received the part performance, the payee is, subject to one exception, entitled to recover an amount equal to the attributable value of the performance, that is the rateable proportion of the contract price minus any loss in value caused by the frustrating event. But, where the loss caused by the frustrating event has the consequence that the attributable value of performance is now less than its attributable cost (generally calculated by reference to the costs reasonably incurred by the party who has provided the partial performance), then the payee is entitled to recover a sum equal to 'one-half of the amount by which the attributable cost of the performance exceeds its attributable value'. On the other hand, where the payee's partial performance is not received by the payer and in consequence the payee has suffered a 'detriment', the payee is entitled to recover an amount equal to 'one-half of the amount that would be fair compensation for the detriment suffered' by him in providing the partial performance.

It is suggested that the solution adopted in South Australia and, to a lesser extent, in British Columbia is simpler and more attractive than the cumbersome and difficult scheme enacted in New South Wales. The New South Wales Act seeks to provide for as many contingencies as possible but, by enabling the court to adjust the operation of sections 9–13 where their operation leads to conclusions which are 'manifestly inadequate or inappropriate', would cause 'manifest injustice', or would be 'excessively difficult or expensive', it tacitly admits that it cannot provide for all possible eventualities.

Yet it can be argued that all three Acts go too far in so far as they require that the losses occasioned by the frustration of the contract be divided between the parties. In the first place, the common law has generally set its face against loss apportionment. There is no general principle known to the common law which requires that losses be shared between the parties. It has been left to Parliament to introduce loss apportionment schemes in areas where it has been thought to be desirable. Parliament in 1943 did not think that loss apportionment was desirable in the case of frustration and there is no sign of a change of heart. Secondly, parties enter into contracts to further their own interests and not in a 'spirit of mutual welfare'[1] and that, restitution in respect of benefits conferred apart, leaving the loss to lie where it falls is 'more in accordance with business ethics and commercial expectations'.

On the other hand, there are arguments in favour of apportioning the loss between the parties. The first is that apportionment of loss is 'economically sounder' because 'each of the two parties may be able to bear half the loss without serious consequences when the whole loss might come close to ruining him'. The second argument is that a failure to take explicit account of the reliance interest may lead to the adoption of an unnatural definition of benefit. Restitution lawyers have been warned about adopting an 'over-inclusive concept of enrichment'[2] and of 'marginalising' the 'principle of injurious reliance'. The classic example of this process is, of course, the British Columbian Frustrated Contracts Act which, as we have noted, defines a benefit as 'something done in the fulfilment of contractual obligations whether or not the person for whose benefit it was done received the benefit'. To force losses incurred into the language of benefit distorts the concept of benefit and hinders the development of a principle of injurious reliance in English law.

---

1 A Stewart and J Carter 'Frustrated Contracts and Statutory Adjustment: The Case for a Reappraisal' [1992] *CLJ* 66.

2 See J Beatson, 'Benefit, Reliance and the Structure of Unjust Enrichment' in *The Use and Abuse of Unjust Enrichment* (Oxford, 1991), 21.

The final argument is that the situation with which frustrated contracts legislation is concerned 'is the familiar one in which one of two parties has to suffer loss for which neither is responsible' and that in the 'normal case' the just course 'would be to order the retention or repayment of half the loss incurred'. The 'justice' involved in being required to share in the losses of the other party may not be readily apparent. But, while it may be true to say that contracting parties enter into contracts to serve their own interests, it should not be assumed that upholding the pursuit of self-interest is the basis of the doctrine of frustration. On the contrary, Bingham LJ has stated that the 'doctrine of frustration has evolved to mitigate the rigour of the common law's insistence on literal performance of absolute promises' and that its object is to 'give effect to the demands of justice' and 'to do what is reasonable and fair . . . after a significant change in circumstances'.[3] It must also be remembered that the frustrating event which has occurred is one which neither party has foreseen and neither party has assumed the risk of its occurrence. Moreover, neither party has been at fault. The expenditure was incurred justifiably in the pursuance of what was at the time a valid and subsisting contract. Justice and reasonableness surely demand that such expenditure be brought into account so that, on the frustration of a contract, the position is reached whereby both parties are discharged from their obligations to perform in the future (the expectation interest of neither party being protected), benefits conferred must be paid for (thus protecting the restitution interest), and losses suffered as a result of wasted expenditure be apportioned between the parties (thus taking account of the reliance interest).

NOTES AND QUESTIONS

1. Do you think the law should take account of losses incurred in the performance of a frustrated contract and, if so, would this development be seen as part of the law of restitution or would its justification lie outside of the law of restitution? Or would it be more accurate to say that 'the case for loss apportionment is as yet unproven and that restitution achieves sufficient justice following frustration' (Burrows, 366)?

2. These issues are further discussed by A Stewart and J Carter, 'Frustrated Contracts and Statutory Adjustment: The Case for a Reappraisal' [1992] CLJ 66.

4. WORK DONE IN ANTICIPATION OF A CONTRACT WHICH DOES NOT MATERIALIZE

As a general rule, a party can withdraw from pre-contractual negotiations without incurring any liability for so doing. English law knows of no general duty to act in good faith in the process of contractual negotiations. This is not to say, however, that negotiating parties have complete freedom to withdraw from negotiations without liability: they do not. In a number of cases the courts have imposed liability upon a party who simply walks away from the negotiations. Some of these cases are examples of the imposition of restitutionary liability, but some are not (an example in the latter category is provided by the decision of the High Court of Australia in *Waltons Stores (Interstate) Ltd v Maher* (1988) 164 CLR 387, where a promise was recognised, and damages awarded, even though no formal contract had been concluded between the parties). Here we shall confine our attention to those cases which, in our view, belong within the fold of the law of unjust enrichment.

---

3 *J Lauritzen A S v Wijsmuller BV (The Super Servant Two)* [1990] 1 Lloyd's Rep 1, 8.

There are a number of cases in which the courts have held that a party who withdraws from negotiations prior to the conclusion of a contract is under a restitutionary obligation to pay the other party the reasonable value of benefits which he has obtained from that party in the course of these negotiations. The courts have experienced a number of difficulties in this context. The first lies in ascertaining the scope of the restitutionary claim: given that the general rule is that a party can withdraw from pre-contractual negotiations without incurring any liability, what is the scope of the restitutionary claim and when is it triggered? The second relates to the test which is to be applied when seeking to ascertain the existence and extent of any enrichment. Indeed, one might go further and question whether or not there is any enrichment in these cases at all: are they not in fact examples of claims for the recovery of reliance expenditure (cf. Chapter 2 on unjust sacrifice)? The final difficulty relates to the reason for restitution or the existence of the unjust factor. In the cases which follow the courts do not spell out with any precision the basis for the restitutionary claim. It is our contention that failure of consideration supplies the most convincing explanation for the intervention of the courts, but it must be conceded that the courts have not yet adopted this analysis.

- • *William Lacey (Hounslow) Ltd v Davis* [1957] 1 WLR 932, Queen's Bench Division

The defendant was the owner of premises which had been damaged during the Second World War and which he proposed to rebuild. The claimant builders submitted a tender for the reconstruction of the building and they claimed that they were led to believe that they would be awarded the contract. They were then asked to carry out a substantial amount of further work by the defendant. They prepared estimates of the steel and timber requirements for the purpose of obtaining the necessary licences, they submitted an estimate for a reconstruction of the premises as they were before the war damage so that the defendant could negotiate a 'permissible amount' with the War Damage Commission and they had to prepare a revised estimate in accordance with new specifications for which they had to prepare their own bills of quantities. All of this work had no connection with any scheme of reconstruction then contemplated by the defendant. After they had done the work the defendant informed the claimants that he proposed to employ another firm of builders but he actually sold the premises to another party. The claimants brought an action for damages for breach of contract but their claim was rejected because it was found that no contract had been concluded between the parties. However they succeeded in their alternative claim which was to recover a reasonable remuneration for the work which they had done on a *quantum meruit*.

Barry J: In elaborating his argument . . . Mr Daniel [counsel for the plaintiffs] rightly conceded that if a builder is invited to tender for certain work, either in competition or otherwise, there is no implication that he will be paid for the work—sometimes the very considerable amount of work—involved in arriving at his price: he undertakes this work as a gamble, and its cost is part of the overhead expenses of his business which he hopes will be met out of the profits of such contracts as are made as a result of tenders which prove to be successful. This generally accepted usage may also—and I think does also—apply to amendments of the original tender necessitated by bona fide alterations in the specification and plans. If no contract ensues, the builder is, therefore, without a remedy. Mr Daniel, however, contends that no such principle applies if the builder's tender is sought and used not to ascertain the cost of erecting or reconstructing some genuinely contemplated building project, but for some extraneous or collateral purpose for which the building owner may require it. In such circumstances, Mr Daniel suggests that the builder is entitled to recover a reasonable payment for his work. It may also happen—as it certainly did happen in the present case—that when a builder is told that his tender is the lowest and led to believe that the building contract is to be given to him, he, the builder, is prepared to perform other incidental services at the request of the building owner without any intention of charging for them as such. He is not—Mr Daniel suggests—rendering these services gratuitously, but is content to be recompensed for them out of the profit which he will make under the contract. If, without default on the builder's part, no contract supervenes, then, says Mr Daniel, the law will imply a contract to pay a reasonable sum for these services. His contention is that, for one or other of these two reasons, the defendants are under a legal obligation to pay for all the work itemised in the schedule.

Mr Lawson's [counsel for the defendants] answer can be put quite shortly. He does not deny that a considerable amount of work was done by the plaintiffs but he says that it was all done—on [the plaintiffs'] own admission—in the expectation and hope that they would receive the building contract. They did not do so and, although the consequences to them are, of course, unfortunate, there can be no room for an implication that they were to be paid for services for which they never intended to charge. As an alternative, Mr Lawson somewhat tentatively questioned the plaintiffs' allegation that their services were rendered at the defendant's request and, further, he suggested that even if requests for these services were in fact made by Day, the latter had no authority from the defendant to make any such requests.

[*His Lordship examined the facts in detail and continued*:] Now, on this evidence, I am quite satisfied that the whole of the work covered by the schedule fell right outside the normal work which a builder, by custom and usage, normally performs gratuitously, when invited to tender for the erection of a building. In the absence of any evidence called by the defendants, I can only find that the earlier estimates were given for work which it was never intended to execute. It is possible that, in the very latest stages, the defendant was intending to erect the type of building for which the plaintiffs were giving their quotation, but having obtained, without charge, an initial estimate for a purely notional building, Mr Davis could hardly expect the builders to go on giving free estimates when a state of reality was at last approached. The earlier estimates, as the correspondence shows, were in fact used, and used for some purpose, in the defendant's negotiations with the War Damage Commission and, as an apparent result of the plaintiffs' efforts, not only were the reconstruction plans approved, but a much higher 'permissible amount' was also agreed with the War Damage Commission. It is perhaps justifiable to surmise that these facts, especially the reconstruction plans and the increase in the permissible amount, had at least some influence upon the price of the damaged building which the defendant obtained when it was ultimately sold by him. The work itemised in the schedule which does not relate to estimation, as I think, falls even more clearly outside the type of work which any builder would be expected to do without charge when tendering for a building contract.

The plaintiffs are carrying on a business and, in normal circumstances, if asked to render services of this kind, the obvious inference would be that they ought to be paid for so doing. No one could expect a business firm to do this sort of work for nothing, and again, in normal circumstances, the law would imply a promise to pay on the part of the person who requested the services to be performed. Mr Lawson, however, submits that no such promise can be implied in the circumstances of the present case. The existence, he submits, of a common expectation that a contract would ultimately come into being and that the plaintiffs' services would be rewarded by the profits of that contract leaves no room, in his submission, and, indeed, wholly negatives any suggestion, that the parties impliedly agreed that these services would be paid for in any other way.

This, at first sight, is a somewhat formidable argument which, if well founded, would wholly defeat the plaintiffs' alternative claim. If such were the law it would, I think, amount to a denial of justice to the plaintiffs in the present case, and legal propositions which have that apparent effect must always be scrutinised with some care. In truth, I think that Mr Lawson's proposition is founded upon too narrow a view of the modern action for quantum meruit. In its early history it was no doubt a genuine action in contract, based upon a real promise to pay, although that promise had not been expressed in words, and the amount of the payment had not been agreed. Subsequent developments have, however, considerably widened the scope of this form of action, and in many cases the action is now founded upon what is known as quasi-contract, similar, in some ways, to the action for money had and received. In these quasi-contractual cases the court will look at the true facts and ascertain from them whether or not a promise to pay should be implied, irrespective of the actual views or intentions of the parties at the time when the work was done or the services rendered. [*He considered the case of* Craven-Ellis v Canons Ltd *below, 281.*]

I am unable to see any valid distinction between work done which was to be paid for under the terms of a contract erroneously believed to be in existence, and work done which was to be paid for out of the proceeds of a contract which both parties erroneously believed was about to be made. In neither case was the work to be done gratuitously, and in both cases the party from whom payment was sought requested the work and obtained the benefit of it. In neither case did the parties actually intend to pay for the work otherwise than under the supposed contract, or as part of the total price which would become payable when the expected contract was made. In both cases, when the beliefs of the parties were falsified, the law implied an obligation—and, in this case, I think the law should imply an obligation—to pay a reasonable price for the services which had been obtained. I am, of course, fully aware that in different circumstances it might be held that work was done gratuitously merely in the hope that the building scheme would be carried out and that the person who did the work would obtain the contract. That, I am satisfied, is not the position here. In my judgment, the proper inference from the facts proved in this case is not that this work was done in the hope that this building might possibly be reconstructed and that the plaintiff company might obtain the contract, but that it was done under a mutual belief and understanding that this building was being reconstructed and that the plaintiff company was obtaining the contract.

. . .

I have, therefore, come to the conclusion that the defence to the alternative claim fails and that the court should imply a condition or imply a promise that the defendant should pay a reasonable sum to the plaintiffs for the whole of these services which were rendered by them. As to amount, I have considered the plaintiffs' charges as set out in the schedule with some care. On the rather scanty information available to me, I have come to the conclusion that while some of the items may well be undercharged, certain of the large items cannot be fully justified. The plaintiffs are entitled to a fair remuneration for the work which they have done, but they cannot, in my view, quantify their charges by reference to professional scales. Doing the best I can, I think the plaintiffs would be fairly recompensed if I deducted £100 from the amount claimed, leaving a balance of £250 13s 5d.

NOTES AND QUESTIONS

1. Goff and Jones state, 658, that in *William Lacey*, '. . . The reality is that the award concealed a claim for loss suffered in anticipation of a contractual agreement which never materialised'. Do you agree? If the claim is one for the recovery of a loss can it be classified as a restitutionary claim? If it cannot, how should it be classified? For a more detailed exposition of this loss-based view see Gareth Jones, 'Claims Arising Out of Anticipated Contracts Which Do Not Materialize' (1980) 18 *Univ of Western Ontario LR* 447 and see also J Beatson, above, 90.

2. Was Barry J correct to say that he could not see a valid distinction between work done which was to be paid for under the terms of a contract erroneously believed to be in existence and work done which was to be paid for out of the proceeds of a sale which both parties erroneously believed was about to be made? Is one not a mistake and the other a misprediction?

3. If the unjust factor was not mistake, what was it? Could it have been failure of consideration?

4. It has been suggested that the case would have been better resolved through the law of contract and such an approach was in fact adopted by the House of Lords in *Way v Latilla* [1937] 3 All ER 759. Do you agree?

- **British Steel Corporation v Cleveland Bridge and Engineering Co. Ltd**
  [1984] 1 All ER 504, Queen's Bench Division

The parties entered into negotiations for the manufacture by the claimants of steel nodes for the defendants. The defendants sent the claimants a letter of intent, which stated their intention to place an order for the steel nodes and proposed that the contract be on the defendants' standard terms. The claimants refused to contract on these terms. Detailed negotiations then took place over the specifications of the steel nodes, but no agreement was reached on matters such as progress payments and liability for loss arising from late delivery, and no formal contract was ever concluded. After the final node was delivered the defendants refused to pay for them, so the claimants brought an action against the defendants. Their claim in contract was dismissed on the ground that no contract had ever been concluded between the parties, but the claimants were able to recover upon a *quantum meruit*. The defendants' counterclaim for damages for breach of contract for delivery of the nodes in the wrong sequence was dismissed because of the lack of a contract between the parties.

Robert Goff J: . . . In my judgment, the true analysis of the situation is simply this. Both parties confidently expected a formal contract to eventuate. In these circumstances, to expedite performance under that anticipated contract, one requested the other to commence the contract work, and the other complied with that request. If thereafter, as anticipated, a contract was entered into, the work done as requested will be treated as having been performed under that contract; if, contrary to their expectation, no contract was entered into, then the performance of the work is not referable to any contract the terms of which can be ascertained, and the law simply imposes an obligation on the party who made the request to pay a reasonable sum for such work as has been done pursuant to that request, such an obligation sounding in quasi contract or, as we now say, in restitution. Consistently with that solution, the party making the request may find himself liable to pay for work which he would not have had to pay for as such if the anticipated contract had come into existence, e.g. preparatory work which will, if the contract is made, be allowed for in the price of the finished work (cf. *William Lacey (Hounslow) Ltd v Davis* [1957] 1 WLR 932). This solution moreover accords with authority: see the decision in *Lacey v Davis*, the decision of the Court of Appeal in *Sanders & Forster Ltd v A. Monk & Co. Ltd* [1980] CA Transcript 35, though that decision rested in part on a concession and the crisp dictum of Parker J in *OTM Ltd v Hydranautics* [1981] 2 Lloyd's Rep. 211 at 214, when he said of a letter of intent that 'its only effect would be to enable the defendants to recover on a quantum meruit for work done pursuant to the direction' contained in the letter. I only wish to add to this part of my judgment the footnote that, even if I had concluded that in the circumstances of the present case there was a contract between the parties and that that contract was of the kind I have described as an 'if' contract, then I would still have concluded that there was no obligation under that contract on the part of BSC to continue with or complete the contract work, and therefore no obligation on their part to complete the work within a reasonable time. However, my conclusion in the present case is that the parties never entered into any contract at all.

. . .

It follows that BSC are entitled to succeed on their claim and the CBE's set-off and counterclaim must fail. . . .

NOTES AND QUESTIONS

1. At a later point in his judgment Robert Goff J stated that 'an obligation to deliver in a certain sequence could only have arisen from an express term of the contract'. Is this statement correct? Should the wishes of the defendants not have been taken into account when assessing the value of the benefit which they had obtained?

2. How should the law of unjust enrichment respond where the work done, or the material which is supplied, is defective? In *Crown House Engineering Ltd v Amec Projects Ltd* (1990) 48 BLR 32, the issue was briefly considered by Slade LJ and Bingham LJ in the following terms:

> **Slade LJ**: . . . I am not convinced that either [Goff and Jones on the Law of Restitution], or any of the other reported cases cited to us, affords a clear answer to the crucial question of law: On the assessment of a claim for services rendered based on a quantum meruit, may it in some circumstances (and, if so, what circumstances) be open to the defendant to assert that the value of such services falls to be reduced because of their tardy performance, or because the unsatisfactory manner of their performance has exposed him to extra expense or claims by third parties?
>
> In my judgement, this question of law is a difficult one, the answer to which is uncertain and may depend on the facts of particular cases. If, as the learned judge apparently considered, the answer to it is an unqualified 'No, never', I cannot help thinking that, at least in some circumstances, there would result injustice of a nature which the whole law of restitution is intended to avoid. . . .

> **Bingham LJ**: . . . The doctrine of unjust enrichment from which, as I understand, the restitutionary remedy of quantum meruit, in part at least, derives does no doubt require that in the absence of contract a customer should not take the benefit of a contractor's services rendered at his request without making fair recompense to the contractor, but it does not so obviously require that assessment of that recompense should be made without regard to acts or omissions of the contractor when rendering those services which have served to depreciate or even eliminate their value to the customer. This question seems to me to have been little explored, and I would profess myself an agnostic. In my judgment it is a classical example of the kind of question unsuitable for resolution without full legal argument in the context of facts agreed or fully explored.

3. What was the unjust factor which was recognized by Robert Goff J?

- *Regalian Properties Ltd v London Docklands Development Corporation*
  [1995] 1 WLR 212, Chancery Division

The claimant property developers entered into negotiations with the defendant corporation, which was set up by statute and which had as its object the regeneration of the Docklands Area of London. In 1986 LDDC invited tenders for the development of four pieces of land. The claimants submitted a tender of £18.5 million which was accepted by the defendant in July 1986 in a letter which was headed 'SUBJECT TO CONTRACT'. The defendant then experienced great difficulty in obtaining vacant possession and the fluctuations in the property market caused both parties to look again at the terms on which they were prepared to contract. Eventually the gulf between the parties was so great that it was clear that no contract was going to materialise. The claimant insisted that it was entitled to be paid for the work which it had done in furtherance of the aborted project. It brought a claim for £2,891 million for fees which it had paid to various professionals in respect of the proposed development. There being no contract between the parties, the claimant was compelled to claim in unjust enrichment, but the claim failed because the work had been carried out on a 'subject to contract' basis.

Rattee J: [*His Lordship considered the facts and judgment of Barry J in* William Lacey v Davis *[1957] WLR 932 and continued:*]

In my judgment, one important distinction between the facts in that case and those in the present case is that the work for which the plaintiffs claimed in that case was not work done for the purposes of the expected contract, but was rather . . . 'for some extraneous or collateral purpose.' It was for the wholly separate purpose of enabling the defendant to negotiate a claim made by the defendant to the War Damage Commission. In the present case, by contrast, the expenditure for which Regalian claims recompense was, I find, all for the purpose either of satisfying the requirements of the proposed contract as to planning permission and the approval of the designs for the development by L.D.D.C., or of putting Regalian into a position of readiness to start the development in accordance with the terms of the proposed contract. In other words it was expenditure made for the purpose of enabling Regalian to obtain and perform the expected contract.

Although I have to say, with respect, that I do not find the reasoning of Barry J entirely easy to follow, the result seems to me to make perfectly good sense on the facts of that case. At the request of the defendant the plaintiffs had done work which had clearly benefited the defendant, quite outside the ambit of the anticipated contract, and had only not charged for it separately, as one would otherwise have expected them to do, because they thought they would be sufficiently recompensed by what they would be paid by the defendant under the contract. In those circumstances it is not surprising that the law of restitution found a remedy for the plaintiffs when the contract did not materialise. I do not consider that the decision lends any real support to the claim made by Regalian in the present case for compensation for expenditure incurred by it for the purpose of enabling itself to obtain and perform the intended contract at a time when the parties had in effect expressly agreed by the use of the words 'subject to contract' that there should be no legal obligation by either party to the other unless and until a formal contract had been entered into. It was frankly accepted by Mr Goldstone of Regalian that he knew and intended that this should be the effect of the use of the phrase 'subject to contract,' and indeed Regalian admits in its pleadings that those words were not intended to have any unusual meaning in the present case. As Mr Goldstone, whom I found an honest and indeed impressive witness, put it in his evidence, he knew that either party was free to walk away from the negotiations, although he confidently expected that this would not happen.

I should mention at this point the only question of fact on which there was any real issue between the parties. That is whether the expenditure for which Regalian claims recompense produced any benefit for L.D.D.C. Regalian contended that the production of designs and obtaining of detailed planning permission for the proposed development did benefit L.D.D.C. in that it enhanced the value of the Hermitage sites and also other adjacent land belonging to L.D.D.C. Despite the evidence of Mr Warner, a surveyor called to give expert evidence on behalf of Regalian, I am not satisfied that any such or any other ascertainable benefit accrued to L.D.D.C. L.D.D.C. did not own the copyright in the designs. It could not have used them itself or enabled any other developer to do so. More important was the fact that by the time the negotiations between the parties fell through the fall in the residential property market had been such that Regalian was not, and no-one else would have been, interested in buying the land concerned to carry out the sort of development for which designs had been produced.

The second authority on which Mr Coulson [counsel for Regalian] relied was a decision of the Supreme Court of New South Wales, *Sabemo Pty. Ltd v North Sydney Municipal Council* [1977] 2 NSWLR 880. The facts of that case have a certain similarity to the facts of the present case. The plaintiff company ('Sabemo') tendered for a building lease of land on which the defendant local authority ('the council') wished to carry out development. The council accepted Sabemo's tender and negotiations for the lease followed. According to the headnote (which contains the only statement of the facts of the case):

> 'It was agreed that the acceptance of the tender did no more than bring the parties together so that they could plan the project until a point was reached where they would enter into a contractual relationship, namely, the proposed building lease.'

Sabemo carried out a lot of detailed work on the plans for the proposed development, and at one point actually raised (apparently inconclusively with the council) the question of compensation before it worked on any revised design. Eventually the council decided to abandon the proposed development scheme altogether. Sabemo sued the council for $426,000 which it said was the cost of work done by it for the council in connection with the proposed development. Sabemo succeeded. Sheppard J said, at 900–1:

'In a judgment of this kind it would be most unwise, and in any event impossible, to fix the limitations which should circumscribe the extent of the right to recover. It is enough for me to say that I think that there is one circumstance here which leads to the conclusion that the plaintiff is entitled to succeed. That circumstance is the fact that the defendant deliberately decided to drop the proposal. It may have had good reasons for doing so, but they had nothing to do with the plaintiff, which, in good faith over a period exceeding three years, had worked assiduously towards the day when it would take a building lease of the land and erect thereon the civic centre which the defendant, during that long period, has so earnestly desired. In the *William Lacey* case, [1957] 1 WLR 932 too, the defendant made a unilateral decision not to go on, but to sell its land instead. I realise that, in looking at the matter in this way, I am imputing a degree of fault to the defendant. To some this may seem to be, at least in English law, somewhat strange. It has long been the law that parties are free to negotiate such contract as they may choose to enter into. Until such contract comes about, they are in negotiation only. Each is at liberty, no matter how capricious his reason to break off the negotiations at any time. If that occurs that is the end of the matter and, generally speaking, neither party will be under any liability to the other. But the concept that there can be fault in such a situation was adopted both by Somervell and Romer L JJ in the *Bremer Street* case [1954] 1 QB 428, 434, 438, 439 the latter, so it seems to me, basing his judgment upon it. Denning LJ [1954] 1 QB 428, 435, 437 did not in fact find fault in that case, but it would seem that he thought it could sometimes exist in negotiating situations, as distinct from contractual ones, although there had not in fact been fault in the case with which he was immediately concerned. To my mind the defendant's decision to drop the proposal is the determining factor. If the transaction had gone off because the parties were unable to agree, then I think it would be correct, harking back to the expressions used by the judges in the *Jennings v Chapman* case [1952] 2 TLR 409, 413, 414, 415, and in the *Bremer Street* case [1954] 1 QB 428, 436, 437, 438, to say that each party had taken a risk, in incurring the expenditure which it did, that the transaction might go off because of the bona fide failure to reach agreement on some point of substance in such a complex transaction. But I do not think it right to say that that risk should be so borne, when one party has taken it upon itself to change its mind about the entirety of the proposal.'

Sheppard J described the principle he was applying, at 902–3:

'In my opinion, the better view of the correct application of the principle in question is that, where two parties proceed upon the joint assumption that a contract will be entered into between them, and one does work beneficial for the project, and thus in the interests of the two parties, which work he would not be expected, in other circumstances, to do gratuitously, he will be entitled to compensation or restitution, if the other party unilaterally decides to abandon the project, not for any reason associated with bona fide disagreement concerning the terms of the contract to be entered into, but for reasons which, however valid, pertain only to his own position and do not relate at all to that of the other party.'

Sheppard J appears from other passages in his judgment to have considered that he was applying the decision in *William Lacey (Hounslow) Ltd v Davis* [1957] 1 WLR 932. In my judgment *Sabemo*'s claim was distinguishable from that in *William Lacey (Hounslow) Ltd v Davis* on similar grounds to those on which I have already explained I think Regalian's claim in the present case is distinguishable—namely that in *William Lacey (Hounslow) Ltd v Davis* the work the subject matter of the claim was quite outside the ambit of the intended contract.

I will deal a little later in this judgment with the question whether the principle enunciated by Sheppard J in the *Sabemo* case [1977] 2 NSWLR 880 should be held to apply in English law.

Irrespective of the answer to that question, in my judgment it would not apply to the facts of the present case, for the reason for the breakdown of negotiations between L.D.D.C. and Regalian was their inability to agree on an essential term of the intended contract, namely the price. It was not because one party 'unilaterally decided to abandon the project' in the words of Sheppard J in the *Sabemo* case.

In this context Regalian placed reliance on the letter of 8 July 1987 from Mr Ward, Chief Executive of L.D.D.C., to Mr Goldstone, which I have already quoted, in which Mr Ward said that 'the delay in our providing vacant possession will not create the situation under which we would seek to amend the terms of our disposal of the site to you.' Regalian submitted that in the end that was just what L.D.D.C. did try to do—namely increase the price because of the alleged change in market value during the period of delay in L.D.D.C.'s obtaining vacant possession. I see some force in this submission, despite L.D.D.C.'s response that in the interim Regalian itself had sought successfully to alter the terms of the deal to take account of the vacant possession problem. However, I cannot see that the submission helps Regalian's claim as formulated in this action, even if the principle enunciated by Sheppard J in the *Sabemo* case is to be applied, for it does not alter the fact that negotiations broke down because the parties could not ultimately agree on price. It may be that the letter of 8 July 1987 could have been relied on as giving rise to some sort of estoppel disentitling L.D.D.C. from seeking to renegotiate the price, but no such estoppel is relied on by Regalian for the obvious reason that presumably the result of such a plea, if successful, would be a contract between the parties at the price agreed subject to contract before L.D.D.C. tried to increase it and otherwise on the other terms agreed between the parties. This would be a result totally unwanted by Regalian, because in the light of market changes since mid-1988 such a contract would be financially very unattractive to Regalian.

The third authority particularly relied on by Mr Coulson is a decision of Judge Peter Bowsher QC sitting on official referee's business in *Marston Construction Co. Ltd v Kigass Ltd* (1989) 15 Con. LR 116. In that case the defendant had invited tenders for the rebuilding of a factory which had been burned down. The plaintiff tendered for the work. Its tender was accepted. It was made clear by the defendant to the plaintiff that no contract for the rebuilding would be entered into unless and until the defendant had succeeded in obtaining from an insurance claim sufficient money to finance the rebuilding. Both the plaintiff and the defendant confidently expected that sufficient insurance moneys would be forthcoming and that accordingly a contract between them would result. In this confident expectation the plaintiff carried out substantial preparatory works the cost of which, if a contract had materialised, would have been included in the contract price. At one point the plaintiff sought an assurance from the defendant that the plaintiff's costs incurred before the expected contract was signed would be met by the defendant. No such assurance was forthcoming. The defendant's insurance claim did not produce sufficient to cover the cost of the proposed rebuilding and no contract was entered into between the parties. The plaintiff sought recompense for the preparatory works. Judge Bowsher QC referred, at 126, to *William Lacey (Hounslow) Ltd v Davis* [1957] 1 WLR 932 and cited the passage, at 939, which I have already cited from the judgment of Barry J. He then referred to a dictum of Robert Goff J in *British Steel Corporation v Cleveland Bridge and Engineering Co. Ltd* [1984] 1 All ER 504, 511, to which I shall refer a little later in this judgment. Then Judge Bowsher QC said, 15 *Con.LR* 116, 127:

'I find that the facts of the present case, although different in important respects are similar in kind to the facts in *William Lacey (Hounslow) Ltd v Davis* [1957] 1 WLR 932. There was a request to do the work, though the request in respect of the bulk of the work was implied rather than express. It was contemplated that the work would be paid for out of the contemplated contract. Both parties believed that the contract was about to be made despite the fact that there was a very clear condition which had to be met by a third party if the contract was to be made. The defendants obtained the benefit of the work in my judgment, though Mr Raeside submitted that they did not.'

Judge Bowsher QC expressed his conclusion in favour of the plaintiff in the following terms, at 129:

'The preliminary works requested were undoubtedly done for the benefit of the defendants and were only done for the benefit of the plaintiffs in the sense that they hoped to make a profit out of them. As a result of the works some progress was made towards getting consents and in the end the defendants had in the hands of their agent some designs and working drawings (though not a complete set) together with an implied licence to build to those drawings even though that licence be limited as I think (without having heard argument) to a licence to have the factory built by the plaintiffs. Whether the defendants decide ultimately to build a factory or to sell the land, they have a benefit which is realisable.

Conclusion. I therefore conclude that there was no agreement as alleged in paras. 5 to 8 of the statement of claim. I find that there was an express request made by the defendants to the plaintiffs to carry out a small quantity of design works and that there was an implied request to carry out preparatory works in general and that both the express and the implied requests gave rise to a right of payment of a reasonable sum.'

I have to say, with all respect for Judge Bowsher QC, that I find this a surprising decision, not least because, as I have recited from his findings of fact, the plaintiff had earlier requested and been refused an assurance that it would be compensated for the preparatory work concerned. In this respect I agree with the critical commentary on Judge Bowsher's decision by the editor of the Building Law Reports (1989) 46 BLR 109. However, whether the decision be right or wrong, I do not feel obliged to apply it in the present case, which is distinguishable on the facts in two particular respects. First, in the present case, unlike the *Marston Construction Co* case, even if a contract had materialised no part of any costs incurred or work done by Regalian in connection with the contract would have been paid for by L.D.D.C. The only obligation on L.D.D.C. would have been to grant the building lease. Secondly, as I have already said, I am not satisfied in the present case that the preparatory works resulted in any benefit to L.D.D.C.

I referred a little earlier to the citation by Judge Bowsher QC in the *Marston Construction Co* case of a dictum of Robert Goff J in *British Steel Corporation v Cleveland Bridge and Engineering Co. Ltd* [1984] 1 All ER 504, 511. [*He set out the facts of the case and considered the judgment of Robert Goff J before continuing:*]

I do not consider that this decision lends any real support to Regalian's claim in the present case. I can well understand why Robert Goff J concluded that, where one party to an expected contract expressly requests the other to perform services or supply goods that would have been performable or suppliable under the expected contract when concluded, in advance of the contract, that party should have to pay a quantum meruit if the contract does not materialise. The present case is not analogous. The costs for which Regalian seeks reimbursement were incurred by it not by way of accelerated performance of the anticipated contract at the request of L.D.D.C., but for the purpose of putting itself in a position to obtain and then perform the contract.

Mr Coulson relied on the last part of the dictum of Robert Goff J at 511, which I have cited, in which he pointed out that the application of the principle of restitution which he applied in that case can result in one party to an anticipated contract which does not materialise finding himself liable to pay the other party for preparatory work for which he would not have had to pay under the contract, because under the contract it would have been allowed for in the overall contract price. I do not think the judge had in mind (because he was not concerned with such a claim) that a landowner intending to contract to grant a building lease could find itself liable to pay the intending lessee developer for preparatory work done by the lessee for the purpose of putting itself in a position to obtain and perform the contract.

I must return now to the statement of principle made by Sheppard J in the *Sabemo* case [1977] 2 NSWLR 880, 900–1, 902–3 which I have cited earlier, for the essence of Mr Coulson's submissions on behalf of Regalian is that that principle should be applied in the present case. For convenience I repeat here the relevant passage from the judgment of Sheppard J at 902–3:

'In my opinion, the better view of the correct application of the principle in question is that, where two parties proceed upon the joint assumption that a contract will be entered into between them, and one does work beneficial for the project, and thus in the interests of the two parties, which work he would not be expected, in other circumstances, to do gratuitously, he will be entitled to compensation or restitution, if the other party unilaterally decides to abandon the project, not for any reason associated with bona fide disagreement concerning the terms of the contract to be entered into, but for reasons which, however valid, pertain only to his own position and do not relate at all to that of the other party.'

I have already said that the principle as so stated would not, in my judgment, apply in any event to the facts of this case, because the reason the contract did not materialise was that the parties could not agree on the price, and not that either party decided to abandon the project. However, in case I am wrong on this, I should say that in my respectful opinion the principle enunciated by Sheppard J in the passage I have cited is not established by any English authority. I appreciate that the English law of restitution should be flexible and capable of continuous development. However I see no good reason to extend it to apply some such principle as adopted by Sheppard J in the *Sabemo* case to facts such as those of the present case, where, however much the parties expect a contract between them to materialise, both enter negotiations expressly (whether by use of the words 'subject to contract' or otherwise) on terms that each party is free to withdraw from the negotiations at any time. Each party to such negotiations must be taken to know (as in my judgment Regalian did in the present case) that pending the conclusion of a binding contract any cost incurred by him in preparation for the intended contract will be incurred at his own risk, in the sense that he will have no recompense for those costs if no contract results. In other words I accept in substance the submission made by Mr Naughton for L.D.D.C., to the effect that, by deliberate use of the words 'subject to contract' with the admitted intention that they should have their usual effect, L.D.D.C. and Regalian each accepted that in the event of no contract being entered into any resultant loss should lie where it fell.

Regalian, under the leadership of Mr Goldstone, was a very experienced operator in the property development market. To his considerable credit Mr Goldstone did not pretend that he was not aware that L.D.D.C., like any other party to negotiations 'subject to contract,' was free to walk away from those negotiations, however little he expected it to do so. Regalian incurred the costs concerned in that knowledge. Though it is perhaps not strictly relevant, I see nothing inequitable in those circumstances in the loss resulting from the breakdown of negotiations lying where it fell, particularly bearing in mind that, in the light of the slump in the residential property market that followed the attempt by L.D.D.C. in May 1988 to renegotiate the price for the proposed building leases, Regalian has good reason to be thankful that it did not find itself having to take those leases on the terms previously proposed.

In my judgment Regalian has failed to make good its claim based on the principles of restitution. It having, rightly, in my view, abandoned its alternative pleaded claim based on alleged misrepresentation, its action fails and must be dismissed.

NOTES AND QUESTIONS

1. Was the LDDC enriched by the work of the claimant? If so, what test was (or should have been) used to establish the enrichment?

2. What 'unjust factor' might have been relevant in this case?

3. Was the fact that the work was done 'subject to contract' relevant to the existence or otherwise

of (a) an enrichment or (b) the unjust factor? Can any useful analogy be drawn between *Regalian* and *Chillingworth v Esche* (above, 254)?

4. How did Rattee J distinguish *William Lacey* and *British Steel v Cleveland Bridge*? Do you find his analysis of these cases convincing?

5. Do you agree with Rattee J's criticisms of the *Marston Construction* case?

6. *Sabemo Pty. Ltd v North Sydney Municipal Council* [1977] 2 NSWLR 880, which is discussed by Rattee J, is a difficult case to classify. Sheppard J expressly stated (at 897) that it was not a 'case of unjust enrichment' and added that 'there are cases not founded on contract, nor in tort, nor upon the application of any equitable doctrine or principle, where there may be recovery.' The 'principle' which he identifies (set out by Rattee J above, 339) does not appear to be based on any category known to the law. Yet the approach has its supporters. J Davies ('What's in a Title?' (1981) 1 *OJLS* 300, 305) has suggested that Sheppard J comes out 'on top' because 'he accepts that the law imposes liabilities outside the traditional categories. By so doing he reduces artificiality and places emphasis where it belongs. There is no ascription of facts to categories of which they are not a natural part. There is no expansion of categories to fill all needs. Instead, there is analysis of the facts; and this ensures that the legitimate grounds for imposing liability emerge. There is no word magic; and any labels, or titles, that then get used to describe the results will be less liable to confuse. This seems the best way of developing a comprehensible body of law.' Do you agree?

7. The Privy Council in *Attorney-General of Hong Kong v Humphrey's Estate Ltd* [1987] AC 114 held that the claimants were not estopped from withdrawing from negotiations which had been entered into on a 'subject to contract' basis. What is the relationship between this case and *Regalian*? Why was it not cited to Rattee J? Why do some claimants bring a restitutionary claim and others an estoppel claim in identical fact situations? Can the streams of authority be reconciled? The estoppel cases are also of interest because they suggest that the fact that negotiations are conducted on a subject to contract basis will not necessarily prevent one party from being estopped from withdrawing from the negotiations where, by its conduct, it has led the other party to believe that it will not do so (see, for example, *Salvation Army Trustee Co. Ltd v West Yorkshire Metropolitan City Council* (1980) 41 P & CR 179).

- ● *Countrywide Communications Ltd v ICL Pathway Ltd*
  [2000] CLC 324, Queens Bench Division

Girobank was a member of a consortium of companies bidding for a contract to supply a card and computerized payment system. Girobank asked Countrywide Communications Ltd to do public relations work for the bid on the basis that, if the consortium were successful, Countrywide would be appointed as public relations consultants to the project. A company called ICL Pathway Ltd was established as the entity which would make the bid. Girobank subsequently withdrew from the consortium. After winning the tender, ICL Pathway appointed a different company (Financial Dynamics) to the project instead of Countrywide. Countrywide alleged that (1) ICL Pathway was bound by a contract to appoint it when Girobank invited it to commence work; (2) ICL Pathway was estopped from denying the existence of that contract as ICL Pathway had induced Countrywide's expectation of an appointment and had allowed that expectation to continue, and (3) if no contract had been entered into, a *quantum meruit* should be awarded in respect of the work done in anticipation of a contract. The trial judge, Nicholas Strauss QC rejected (1) and (2) but allowed the *quantum meruit* claim. His Lordship held that the general rule was that a person who carries out work in the hope of gaining a contract does so at his own risk. However, this did not apply here because Countrywide was induced to carry out work by an assurance that ICL Pathway would negotiate a contract if the bid succeeded and because Countrywide had done work far beyond what would normally be expected free of charge. Because the work was outside the various risks of working without remuneration and because Country-wide's services provided ICL Pathway with a benefit for which it would otherwise have had to pay, it would be unjust for ICL Pathway to enrich itself by not paying for Countrywide's work.

Nicholas Strauss QC . . . Countrywide claimed a quantum meruit for the work done in anticipation of the contract which in the end was not awarded to them. There is no doubt that, in most cases, a person who carries out work in the hope of obtaining a contract, for example a builder who prepares an estimate, cannot claim the cost of doing so. In general, parties are free to withdraw from negotiations at any time before a contact is entered into for good or bad reasons, or for none at all, without incurring liability. If it were otherwise, persons seeking quotes for work might routinely find themselves liable for the expenses of several disappointed bidders. In most cases prospective contractors expressly (for example by offering a free estimate or when negotiations are 'subject to contract') or impliedly do the work at their own risk.

. . .

[*Nicholas Strauss QC then considered the authorities and academic commentary in detail and continued*]

I have found it impossible to formulate a clear general principle which satisfactorily governs the different factual situations which have arisen, let alone those which could easily arise in other cases. Perhaps, in the absence of any recognition in English law of a general duty of good faith in contractual negotiations, this is not surprising. Much of the difficulty is caused by attempting to categorise as an unjust enrichment of the defendant, for which an action in restitution is available, what is really a loss unfairly sustained by the plaintiff. There is a lot to be said for a broad principle enabling either to be recompensed, but no such principle is clearly established in English law. Undoubtedly the court may impose an obligation to pay for benefits resulting from services performed in the course of a contract which is expected to, but does not, come into existence. This is so, even though, in all cases, the defendant is ex hypothesi free to withdraw from the proposed contract, whether the negotiations were expressly made 'subject to contract' or not. Undoubtedly, such an obligation will be imposed only if justice requires it or, which comes to much the same thing, if it would be unconscionable for the plaintiff not to be recompensed.

Beyond that, I do not think that it is possible to go further than to say that, in deciding whether to impose an obligation and if so its extent, the court will take into account and give appropriate weight to a number of considerations which can be identified in the authorities. The first is whether the services were of a kind which would normally be given free of charge. Secondly, the terms in which the request to perform the services was made may be important in establishing the extent of the risk (if any) which the plaintiffs may fairly be said to have taken that such services would in the end be unrecompensed. What may be important here is whether the parties are simply negotiating, expressly or impliedly 'subject to contract', or whether one party has given some kind of assurance or indication that he will not withdraw, or that he will not withdraw except in certain circumstances. Thirdly, the nature of the benefit which has resulted to the defendants is important, and in particular whether such benefit is real (either 'realised' or realisable') or a fiction, in the sense of Traynor C.J's dictum. Plainly, a court will at least be more inclined to impose an obligation to pay for a real benefit, since otherwise the abortive negotiations will leave the defendant with a windfall and the plaintiff out of pocket. However, the judgment of Denning L.J. in the *Brewer Street* case suggests that the perform-ance of services requested may of itself suffice amount to a benefit or enrichment. Fourthly, what may often be decisive are the circumstances in which the anticipated contract does not materialise and in particular whether they can be said to involve 'fault' on the part of the defendant, or (perhaps of more relevance) to be outside the scope of the risk undertaken by the plaintiff at the outset. I agree with the view of Rattee J. that the law should be flexible in this area, and the weight to be given to each of these factors may vary from case to case.

There is in my view considerable doubt whether an obligation can be imposed in a case in which the plaintiff has not provided a benefit of any kind, even of the 'fictional' kind discussed earlier of performing services at the request of the defendant albeit without enriching him in any real sense. Thus I doubt whether an obligation can be imposed on a contracting party to repay a plaintiff for expense incurred, reasonably or even necessarily, in anticipation of a contract which does not materialise, where this is not in the course of providing services requested by the defendant. Such an obligation would not be restitutionary, and there is no English authority which would clearly support its imposition, except perhaps in circumstances similar to those suggested in the *Humphreys Estate* and *Walton's* cases where the defendant is precluded by estoppel from denying the existence of a binding contract. If it were otherwise, there would often be a remedy against gazumpers, against whom it could always or at least usually be said that the buyer did not take the risk of expenditure wasted through the seller's decision to withdraw, having earlier accepted an offer 'subject to contract', not for a reason connected with the negotiation of the contract, but because he had been offered more by someone else. Similarly, in some cases there might be a remedy where 'gazundering' has caused a contract to go off. There is an interesting suggestion by Mr. Paul Key in 111 L.Q.R. at 180 that, even if the effect of an estoppel would not be to preclude denial of a binding contract, the court could do 'the minimum equity' necessary to meet the circumstances, on the basis of the Court of Appeal decision in *Crabb v Arun District Council* [1976] Ch 179 and that this could include compensation for 'reliance loss'. However, in view of my conclusions set out below, I do not need to reach a decision on this difficult question.

CONCLUSIONS ON *QUANTUM MERUIT* IN THIS CASE

I would regard it as most unjust if Countrywide were not appropriately recompensed for their work before and after the submission of the bid in March 1996. Put shortly, this is because (1) they were induced to provide their services free of charge by an assurance, ultimately dishonoured, that ICL Pathway would be prepared to negotiate a contract with them if the bid succeeded, and (2) their services provided ICL Pathway with a benefit for which (in the absence of such an assurance) they would otherwise have had to pay reasonable fees for time spent, namely advice and assistance in connection with the public relations and communications issues during the bid and subsequently. As I have already found, the members of the consortium had a policy from the outset of seeking the services of potential sub-contractors during the bid process free, on the basis that they would be assured of being rewarded by a sub-contract if they gave their help until the final bid was submitted and if it succeeded. Such an assurance was given by Mr. Jones at the outset, and repeated by Mr. Hodgson in about April 1995, when ICL Pathway was formed. This is important for two reasons. In the first place, the formulation of this approach, and the giving of the assurance to Countrywide, suggest that the work which was to be expected from potential sub-contractors, and in particular from Countrywide, went beyond that which might be expected to be provided free by a sub-contractor who, if the bid succeeded, would merely be given a chance of bidding for the sub-contract. Secondly, such an assurance takes the case as far from a typical 'subject to contract' case, in which each party may be taken to have accepted the risk of withdrawal by the other and consequent waste of expenditure, as it could possibly be taken short of an actual contract. *Regalian* is clearly distinguishable on this ground.

As to the risk which Countrywide may be said to have accepted of unrecompensed work, clearly a degree of risk was accepted. Countrywide accepted the risk that their work would be unrewarded if it was found to be unsatisfactory at any time before a final bid was submitted, if the bid failed, or if negotiations failed with ICL Pathway for the sub-contract. As to the last, I think that it is most unlikely that this would have happened. It is true that Ms. Campopiano [of Countrywide] would not have accepted the terms suggested in Mr. Orme's [of ICL Pathway] letter of 23rd May, 1996, or Countrywide's standard conditions, but I have no doubt that Mr. Orme would never have insisted on these terms, and would have been as flexible as necessary to obtain an important sub-contract of this kind. It may be arguable that Countrywide also accepted other risks, for example that the consortium would decide not to proceed at all, or that BA/POCL would decide to do all the public relations/communication work themselves, and certainly they could not expected to be employed if their work was seriously defective at any stage. But Countrywide did not accept the risk that they would be dismissed, following a change of personnel within ICL Pathway, because their reputation was now not considered to be satisfactory. This is something which Countrywide were entitled to expect to be considered either by the consortium when they made their proposal in early 1995, or by ICL Pathway at the latest before the final tender was submitted. They cannot fairly be said to have taken the risk of being dismissed for this reason not only after the final tender had been submitted, but after having provided further help in preparation for the implementation of the work for a further two or three months.

On the question of benefit, the underlying position is not quite the same as in cases involving building contracts. Countrywide were not bidding for specific work. Rather, they were assisting ICL Pathway to formulate the correct approach to the public relations and communications work and to provide an estimate of costs for which allowance would be made in ICL Pathway's final tender. The details of the scope of the work, and of Countrywide's remuneration, were always going to be negotiated after the bid succeeded. From ICL Pathway's point of view, what they needed at this stage was advice and assistance, rather than a detailed final budget, and some of the work done before 21st March 1996 (for example attendance at meetings which were essentially so that Countrywide were up to date and in a position to advise on any issues which might arise suddenly), and all the work done after that date, was done principally to assist ICL Pathway, and not in the preparation of a bid or proposal for the sub-contract work. Indeed, all the work done between April 1995 and the submission of the final tender on 21st March 1996 can be said to have been done for a dual purpose. It was done to assist ICL Pathway in the formulation of their initial proposal and final tender, and therefore also, by enhancing the prospects of success of the latter, insofar as this depended upon its public relations content, to enhance the prospects of Countrywide being awarded the sub-contract. Countrywide's work was of value to ICL Pathway, not merely because they performed services at ICL Pathway's request, but because these services provided ICL Pathway with advice which they needed, and for which (in the absence of an assurance of the kind they gave), they would probably have had to pay either Countrywide or some other public relations consultant. Therefore, ICL Pathway was, in a real sense, enriched by Countrywide's work. The gain was realised, not merely realisable.

On the issue of benefit, this case is therefore distinguishable from *Regalian*, in which no benefit was conferred on the defendant. It is less easy to distinguish it from *Lacey*. It is true that Countrywide's work cannot be said to have conferred a benefit on ICL Pathway 'quite outside the ambit of the anticipated contract', which Rattee J. said ([1995] 1 W.L.R. at 225A) was the basis on which *Lacey* was correctly decided. However, I do not understand Rattee J. to have held that it was in all cases necessary that a benefit should have been conferred by the proposed contractor on the proposed employer which was 'outside the ambit' of the anticipated contract. Clearly, this was not true of the benefit conferred on the defendants in the *British Steel Corporation* case. Indeed was it only partly true of the benefit conferred in Lacey. In that case, the work connected with the war damage claim, which was based upon a notional reconstruction of the building in its original state, was outside the ambit of the proposed building work. But the plaintiffs also recovered on a quantum meruit for revised estimates for the actual rebuilding, which was the subject matter of the anticipated contract.

Finally, with reference to the circumstances in which the anticipated contract failed to materialise, I have already found that the principal reasons for this were Ms. Campopiano's distrust of Countrywide, from her own experience and from what she had heard from within ICL, and the availability of another contractor, Financial Dynamics, in whom she did have trust. One could perhaps with some justice say that ICL Pathway (as opposed to Ms. Campopiano personally, who was not fully aware of the background and was simply following Mr. Foley's instructions) was 'at fault' for not honouring the assurance which they had given. But I think that the more logical question to ask is whether Countrywide took the risk of ICL Pathway reaching this conclusion after all the preparatory work, and indeed some work towards the implementation of the project, had been done. Of course, in a sense, it follows from the very fact that no binding agreement was concluded that the plaintiffs did take this risk, but the effect of the authorities cited above is to require a broader view to be taken. Otherwise no claim of this kind could ever succeed. In my view, what happened was outside the various risks of working without recompense which Countrywide can fairly be said to have accepted. Therefore I think that it is unjust that ICL Pathway have enriched themselves by not paying for Countrywide's services. I would have held otherwise, if I had found that the, or even a, substantial reason for ICL Pathway's failure to offer Countrywide the sub-contract was a disagreement about terms. I would also have held otherwise, if the reason had been that Countrywide offered work which, in the circumstances in which it was offered, was seriously defective. However, they merely failed to provide work which was of sufficient excellence to overcome Ms. Campopiano's predisposition to recommend Financial Dynamics. There was never much chance of their securing Ms. Campopiano's support if Financial Dynamics were available.

NOTES AND QUESTIONS

1. Like Goff and Jones' comment on *William Lacey* (above, 333), Nicholas Strauss QC suggests that in many cases 'difficulty is caused by attempting to categorise as an unjust enrichment of the defendant, for which an action in restitution is available, what is really a loss unfairly sustained by the plaintiff.' In *Vedatech Corporation v Crystal Decisions (UK) Ltd* [2002] EWHC 818 (Ch), work was done by a Japanese company for an English company and its subsidiary in Japan. A proposed agreement never materialized. The English company conceded that the Japanese company was entitled to a *quantum meruit* for the time spent by the Japanese workers. The Japanese company argued that the enterprise was intended to be a joint one and the *quantum meruit* should include some part of the future earnings of the English company. Jacob J held that the reason for recovery was unjust enrichment but that this was a flexible concept and it should include a 'share of the action' because 'it was that sort of basis which had been contemplated by the parties' (at [76], [82]). If the award is focused upon fulfilling the expectations of the parties is it not a loss-based rather than a restitutionary award?

2. Although Nicholas Strauss QC does not identify an unjust factor, he refers to four considerations which a court will take into account: (1) whether the services were of a kind which would normally be given free of charge; (2) the terms in which the request to perform the services was made; (3) the nature of the benefit which has resulted to the defendants is important, and in particular whether such benefit is 'realised' or 'realisable' or if services requested have been performed; (4) whether the circumstances in which the anticipated contract does not materialise involve 'fault' on the part of the defendant or are outside the scope of the risk undertaken by the claimant. Although Nicholas Strauss QC held that no contract had been entered into, Jaffey ([2000] *RLR* 270) has argued that the solution to the case lies in recognizing that the four factors identified show that a contract did exist and that the remedy awarded protected a reliance loss from contracting. Do you agree? Alternatively, could it be said that (1), (2), and (4) are concerned with the basis/consideration upon which the work has been performed (and whether that basis has failed) and (3) is concerned with enrichment?

3. ICL Pathway was required to make restitution because Countrywide's work was outside the risks of working without remuneration. But Nicholas Strauss QC accepted that Countrywide had taken the risk that their work would be unrewarded if it was found to be unsatisfactory at any time before a final bid was submitted, if the bid failed, or if negotiations failed with ICL Pathway for the sub-contract. Does this create too fine a distinction about when a claimant will have borne the risk of working without remuneration?

4. Do you agree with Nicholas Strauss QC that, in the case of a 'gazumper' (a vendor who sells his house for a higher offer after having entered a 'subject to contract' agreement) no obligation arises in relation to the first offeror because the first offeror is never enriched? Would there be any unjust factor in relation to the first offeror that takes the risk?

5. Nicholas Strauss QC said that in the anticipated contracts cases 'an obligation will be imposed only if justice requires it or, which comes to much the same thing, if it would be unconscionable for the plaintiff not to be recompensed'. In the following extract, McKendrick criticizes a criterion of unconscionability because 'there is a real danger that principles will be abandoned and hard questions ducked by conferring a broad and largely unstructured discretion on the courts'. In the extract McKendrick examines and assesses each of the different alternative suggestions by which these cases can be explained.

- E McKendrick, 'Work Done in Anticipation of a Contract which does not Materialise' in W Cornish and others (eds), *Restitution: Past, Present and Future*, (1998), 181–90

. . .

INJUSTICE

What is it in these cases which leads us to the conclusion that the defendant was *unjustly* enriched? Here the *quantum meruit* label proves to be something of a hindrance because it can be used to absolve the court from explaining the ground for recovery. The plaintiff succeeds simply because he is deserving. Some judges have, however, been more forthcoming. In *William Lacey* Barry J stated that he was 'unable to see any valid distinction between work done which was to be paid for under the terms of a contract erroneously believed to be in existence, and work which was to be paid for out of the proceeds of a contract which both parties erroneously believed was about to be made'.[1] The difficulty with this passage is that there is a vital distinction between the two cases. The former is an example of a mistake which may suffice to generate a restitutionary claim, whereas the latter is merely a misprediction. And a failure to predict the future course of events does not, of itself, give rise to a restitutionary claim.

An alternative analysis, which has proved to be very influential, is that the injustice lies in the fact that the defendant requested, or freely accepted the work and has not paid for it. There is no doubt that the terms of the defendant's request are of great importance in deciding whether or not, and to what extent, the defendant was enriched.[2] The difficulty lies in determining whether or not the fact that the defendant requested the work to be done can be used to establish that the enrichment was unjust. Where, at the time of making the request, the defendant has no actual intention of paying for the work then a basis for declaring the enrichment to be unjust can be discerned.[3] On the other hand, where the defendant did have an intention to pay for the work at the time of the request, but has subsequently changed his mind, it is not easy to see why the terms of the initial request should

---

1 [1957] 1 WLR 932, 939.   2 See above pp. 172–3.

3 This has been termed 'initial unconscionability' by Birks using terminology originally employed in a slightly different context by M Garner, 'The Role of Subjective Benefit in the Law of Unjust Enrichment' (1990) 10 *OJLS* 42, 48.

give rise to a claim for payment. The request, when made, did not generate a restitutionary obligation to pay for the work done because the parties at this stage believed that payment would be made through the completion of the contract. What is suggested is the basis for intervention is the expectation of both parties that a contract would be concluded and the fact that that expectation has not been fulfilled. Thus Professor Burrows has argued that the reason for restitution in *William Lacey* is failure of consideration, namely the failure of the expected payment through the main contract.[4] There are two difficulties with this view. The first is that the ground of consideration presently known to the law is *total* failure of consideration and not simply failure of consideration. While this is true, it should be noted that the total failure requirement has few academic supporters[5] and it may not survive further judicial scrutiny.[6] The second is that the claim to recover upon a (total) failure of consideration is a claim to recover money. It does not apply to a claim to recover in respect of services rendered. The latter claim is a claim to recover upon a *quantum meruit*. To a large extent, the resolution of this issue turns on the extent to which the forms of action should be allowed to dictate the shape of the modern law. The analysis of Professor Burrows has great analytical merits, but it runs into the practical difficulty that, historically, failure of consideration has been treated as a money claim which cannot be applied to goods or services. But, as *Goff and Jones* themselves state, 'historical accident is an unsatisfactory basis for classification'.[7] To adapt the words of Lord Atkin,[8] the ghosts of the past should not be allowed to stand in the path of the coherent development of the law. The distinction between a money and a non-money claim is very relevant to the existence of an enrichment, but it should not be relevant to the reason for restitution. On the money side of the equation we require the reason for restitution to be spelt out. The same should hold true for non-money claims. Just as failure of consideration can ground a money claim, so it should be able to ground a non-money claim.

One objection to the failure of consideration analysis is that it has contractual overtones and so should be analysed in contractual terms. If the consideration (or, to use less contractual language, the 'basis') upon which the work was done was that the work done would be paid for out of the contract which was expected to materialise, can it not be said that the obligation to repay the money also arises from that basis and so can be said to be contractual in nature? In other words, there is in these cases an implied agreement or understanding between the parties that work done will be paid for if a contract fails to materialise. This is a possible analysis but in many cases it is likely to be an implausible construction of what has taken place. While the parties may both have expected a contract to materialise, they are unlikely to have considered expressly what is to happen if a contract fails to materialise. The obligation to pay for the work done is one which is imposed on the parties and not one which is attributable to their will; hence it is a restitutionary obligation and not a contractual obligation.

However, cases can arise in which it is difficult to work out the 'basis' upon which the work was done. In many cases the basis will be that the work is done at the risk of the party doing the work. The contractor takes a 'gamble, and its cost is part of the overhead expenses of his business which he hopes will be met out of the profits of such contracts as are made as a result of tenders which prove to be successful'.[9] In such a case, the contractor will have no claim because the failure of the contract to materialise does not affect the basis upon which the work was done. Similarly, where the work is done on a 'subject to contract' basis then no restitutionary claim should generally arise because in

---

4 A Burrows, 'Free Acceptance and the Law of Restitution' (1988) 104 *LQR* 576, 596.

5 The arguments are conveniently summarised by P Birks, 'Failure of Consideration' in F Rose (ed.) *Consensus Ad Idem: Essays on the Law of Contract in Honour of Guenter Treitel* (London, Sweet & Maxwell, 1996) p. 179.

6 See, in particular the speech of Lord Goff in *Goss v Chilcott* [1996] AC 788, 798.

7 *Goff and Jones* p. 4.   8 In *United Australia Ltd v Barclays Bank Ltd* [1941] AC 1, 28–9.

9 *William Lacey (Hounslow) Ltd v Davis* [1957] 1 WLR 932, 934.

such a case the basis, or consideration, upon which the work is done is that each party is free to withdraw from the negotiations without penalty, so that it cannot be said that the basis on which the work was done has failed when one party does so withdraw.[10] But the volume or the nature of the work done may lead a court to put a different construction upon the understanding of the parties. Thus where the work done is exceptionally onerous[11] or is done for a purpose which is 'quite outside the ambit of the anticipated contract'[12] then the court may conclude that the only basis upon which the work was done was that it would be paid for by the defendant under the contract which both parties expected to materialise. The exact point at which a court will conclude that this was the basis upon which the work was done ultimately depends on a careful examination of the facts of the case.

A case which illustrates the difficulties is *Marston Construction Co. Ltd v Kigass Ltd*[13] The plaintiffs were building and engineering contractors. The defendants were factory owners whose factory was destroyed in a fire. They invited tenders for a design and build contract to provide a replacement factory. The plaintiffs' tender offered the best value for money, but more detailed negotiations had to take place before a contract could be concluded and the defendants were anxious to proceed as quickly as possible. During these negotiations, the defendants made it clear to the plaintiffs that no contract could be concluded for the rebuilding of the factory unless and until they had obtained the insurance money to meet the cost. The plaintiffs were given an assurance that they would get the contract but they were not given an assurance which they sought that their pre-contract expenditure would be met by the defendants in the event of the insurance money being insufficient to meet the cost. On the other hand, the defendants did not expressly inform the plaintiffs that, in the event of the insurance money being insufficient to meet the cost, the preparatory work would be at the expense of the plaintiffs. The defendants reasonably expected that the proceeds of their insurance policy would pay for the work but their expectations were dashed when the local authority required certain additional work to be carried out which added considerably to the cost and meant that the project was no longer viable. Judge Bowsher QC held that in these circumstances the plaintiffs were entitled to recover in respect of the work which they had done. The decision has been described as a 'surprising'[14] one and the difficulty is to be found in the following crucial sentence in the judgment of Judge Bowsher QC:

'Both parties believed that the contract was about to be made despite the fact that there was a very clear condition which had to be met by a third party if the contract was to be made'.[15]

If the basis upon which the work was done was that 'no contract for the rebuilding would be entered into unless and until the defendant had succeeded in obtaining from an insurance claim sufficient money to finance the rebuilding'[16] then it seems clear that there should have been no claim because there was no failure of basis. As the editor of Building Law Reports notes, the result of the case was

---

10 Or, to put in slightly different terms, the relevance of the 'subject to contract' stipulation was that the parties had contracted out of restitution by making it clear that each party was able to withdraw from negotiations without incurring any liability to the other party.

11 A case which could fall within this category is *Sabemo Pty. Ltd v North Sydney Municipal Council* [1977] 2 NSWLR 880, although it was not so categorised by Sheppard J.

12 *Regalian Properties plc v London Docklands Development Corporation* [1995] 1 WLR 212, 225, *per* Rattee J, where he was seeking to explain the decision in *William Lacey (Hounslow) Ltd v Davis* [1979] 1 WLR 932.

13 (1989) 46 BLR 109.

14 *Regalian Properties plc v London Docklands Development Corporation* [1995] 1 WLR 212, 229 *per* Rattee J, agreeing in this respect with the 'critical commentary' of the decision by the editor of the Building Law Reports, on which see (1989) 46 BLR 109, 111–13. The criticism is expressed in rather strong terms, with the editor concluding that the decision 'apparently flies in the face of the contractual negotiations between the parties'.

15 (1989) 46 BLR 109, 124.   16 [1995] 1 WLR 212, 228.

that the defendant 'was required to do the one thing it had made clear it was unwilling to do – pay out any sums in the absence of payment from insurers'.[17] On the other hand, if the basis was the belief that a contract would materialise then there was a failure of basis and so a ground of claim. The difficulty is that, in the absence of an express stipulation as to the basis upon which pre-contract work is carried out, it is not easy to discern the basis upon which work is done. Professor Birks states that there is a failure of consideration where 'the person performing was entitled in the circumstances to assume that the other knew, as indeed the other did know, that the work was being done on the basis that arrangements would be agreed for it to be rewarded'.[18] Given that the plaintiffs had failed to obtain the sought-for assurance that they would be paid for the work done, the finding that they were entitled to be paid appears to be highly questionable.

One final point which merits brief examination is whether or not it is relevant that the breakdown in the negotiations was attributable to the fault of the party bringing the claim. There are signs in the cases that fault is a relevant factor, but, as *Goff and Jones* point out, fault is a 'shadowy signpost'.[19] The clearest example is perhaps *Jennings and Chapman Ltd v Woodman, Matthews & Co.*[20] The plaintiffs, who were themselves lessees of premises, proposed to lease part of the premises to the defendant. The plaintiffs agreed to alter the premises to suit the needs of the defendant. They carried out the work but no sub-lease was ever granted because the landlord refused to agree to the division of the premises in the manner proposed. The plaintiffs' action to recover the value of the work which they had done failed. One factor which weighed heavily with the Court of Appeal was that the plaintiffs knew, but the defendant did not, that the consent of the landlord was required to the works.[21] The fault or lack of care of the plaintiffs therefore appeared to act as a bar to their claim. Yet it could be said that they had satisfied all the elements of a restitutionary claim in that, assuming the existence of an enrichment (which is admittedly a dubious assumption),[22] the basis upon which the work was done was that a contract would materialise and none had materialised. Is the precise cause of the failure of the contract to materialise a relevant factor? Is there some notion of 'self-induced' failure at work here which operates to bar the claim which would otherwise lie? Fault on the part of the plaintiff does not generally operate to bar a restitutionary claim which would otherwise arise,[23] and it has been argued that a claim based on failure of consideration can be brought by a contract-breaker[24] so why have regard to the fault of the plaintiff in this case? It is also

---

17 (1989) 46 BLR 109, 113.

18 P Birks, 'In Defence of Free Acceptance' in A Burrows (Ed), *Essays on the Law of Restitution* (1991) at p. 114.

19 *Goff and Jones* p. 558. Although at p. 555 it is pointed out that 'the reasons why the negotiations collapsed' has proved to be one of the 'critical' factors in the cases.

20 [1952] 2 TLR 409. Another example is provided by *Sabemo Pty. Ltd v North Sydney Municipal Council* [1977] 2 NSWLR 880.

21 Thus Denning LJ noted that the position might well have been different had the defendant been at fault for the breakdown of the negotiations. *Jennings* can, of course, be contrasted with the later decision of the Court of Appeal in *Brewer Street Investments Ltd v Barclays Woollen Co. Ltd* [1954] 1 QB 428, discussed in more detail at p. 178 above.

22 If it is accepted that there was a benefit on the facts of *Brewer Street Investments Ltd v Barclays Woollen Co. Ltd* [1954] 1 QB 428, discussed in more detail at p. 178 above, then it would seem to follow that there was an enrichment on the facts. Given the conclusion expressed above that there was no enrichment on the facts in *Brewer*, then it should equally follow that there was no enrichment on the present facts either.

23 *Kelly v Solari* (1841) 9 M & W 54.

24 See *Dies v British and International Mining and Finance Co. Ltd* [1939] 1 KB 724 which a number of commentators have argued should be seen as an example of a claim based on a failure of consideration, notwithstanding the fact that the plaintiff had committed a repudiatory breach of contract. On the other hand it can be argued that the case is not really analogous with the situation under discussion because the cause of the failure in *Dies* was not the plaintiff's breach, but the defendant's decision to accept the repudiation and terminate further performance of the contract.

very difficult to define fault and to distinguish it from a genuine failure to reach agreement.[25] It is therefore suggested that the cause of the failure of the contract to materialise should not be a relevant factor where a plaintiff is otherwise able to establish all the ingredients of a restitutionary claim.[26]

OTHER GROUNDS OF LIABILITY

There are a number of other grounds upon which liability can be imposed on a party who withdraws from negotiations prior to the conclusion of a contract. It is not possible to deal with these alternative grounds in any detail in this paper. These possible grounds are tort, estoppel, unjust sacrifice, *culpa in contrahendo* and breach of a duty of good faith and fair dealing. While they are all deserving of fuller analysis, it is suggested that they can be grouped together on the basis that they focus to a greater or lesser extent on the conduct of the defendant. That conduct varies from case to case and can be classified on a sliding-scale of 'wrongfulness' but, before seeking to set out such a sliding-scale, three important preliminary points must be made.

The first is that, in terms of classification, some of these doctrines are of dubious pedigree. This is most obviously so in relation to *culpa in contrahendo*. There is a temptation to look enviously across the Channel at our civilian counterparts who are able to invoke the doctrine of *culpa in contra-hendo* to regulate the conduct of the parties during the negotiation process.[27] But this confidence in civilian doctrines is not entirely justified because closer analysis shows that *culpa in contrahendo* is, and probably always has been, a doctrine which lacks stability. Thus Professor Zimmermann concludes that it 'falls squarely into the grey area between the law of contract and the law of delict, and there is much to be said for the proposition that it does not fit neatly into either of these, but rather forms an integral part of a third 'track' of liability'.[28] According to Rudolf von Jhering, who is generally credited with the 'discovery' of the doctrine, it was a contractual form of liability, but it protected only the reliance interest in the case of pre-contractual negligence. But some of the cases which fall under the rubric of *culpa in contrahendo* in German law would be regarded by an English lawyer as straightforward claims in tort[29] and the use of the 'contractual' doctrine of *culpa in contrahendo* provides an example of a system having to 'turn to its law of contract in order to remedy the shortcomings of its law of tort'.[30] Some of the reasoning smacks of artificiality, especially when extended to a plaintiff who

---

25 A good example is provided by *Brewer Street Investments Ltd v Barclays Woollen Co. Ltd* [1954] 1 QB 428, where Somervell and Romer LJJ thought that the defendants were at fault, while Denning LJ thought that they were not.

26 The position might be otherwise if the law were to recognise the existence of an obligation of good faith and fair dealing in the negotiation process, see p. 188 below.

27 See generally F Kessler and E Fine, 'Culpa in Contrahendo, Bargaining in Good Faith, and Freedom of Contract: A Comparative Study' (1964) 77 *Harv L Rev* 401; J Spencer, 'A Call for a Common Law Culpa in Contrahendo Counterpart' (1981) 15 *University of San Francisco Law Rev* 587; G Kuhne, 'Reliance, Promissory Estoppel and Culpa in Contrahendo: A Comparative Analysis' (1990) 10 *Tel Aviv University Studies in Law* 279.

28 R Zimmermann, *The Law of Obligations-Roman Foundations of the Civilian Tradition* (Oxford, Clarendon Press, 1996) p. 245. See also B Markesinis, *The German Law of Obligations Volume 1: Contracts and Restitution* (Oxford, Clarendon Press, 1997) p. 64; Y Ben-Dor 'The Perennial Ambiguity of Culpa in Contrahendo' (1983) 27 *American Journal of Legal History* 142.

29 See, for example, RGZ 78, 239 where a prospective purchaser was held to be entitled to bring a claim in contract when she suffered injury in a shop when she was hit by a linoleum carpet which had been negligently handled by a store employee: see B Markesinis, *A Comparative Introduction to the German Law of Torts*, 3rd edn (Oxford, Clarendon Press, 1994) pp. 774–6.

30 B Markesinis (n. [29] above) p. 687.

was not in any sense of the word a negotiating party.[31] The importation of a doctrine which straddles the contract/tort divide in such an uncertain fashion would do little to improve the current state of English law. Better to search out a doctrine which has secure foundations. The same point can be made about the pedigree of the suggestion that there is a 'developing civil wrong of unconscionable conduct in pre-contractual negotiations'.[32] Can there be such a wrong while English law refuses to recognise the existence of a duty of good faith and fair dealing when negotiating a contract? If there is such a civil wrong, is it a tort or an equitable wrong? Does it matter? The conceptual basis of this suggested wrong and the remedial consequences of its breach must be made clear.

The second point is that doctrines, such as *culpa in contrahendo*, have proven to be difficult to apply in practice. When will a withdrawal from negotiations constitute '*culpa*'? Kessler and Fine, writing in 1964, pointed out that the case law and literature has generally rejected the proposition that 'once parties have entered into negotiations for a contract neither party can break them off "arbitrarily" without compensating the other party for his reliance damages'[33] on the ground that 'if the utility of contract as an instrument of self-government is not to be seriously weakened, parties must be free to break off preliminary negotiations without being held to an accounting'.[34] Something more is required that simply breaking off negotiations without a good reason. The position would appear to be the same in France, this time via a 'duty of good faith or honesty and fair dealing in pre-contractual negotiations'.[35] Thus examples can be found of cases in which a party has been held liable for breaking off negotiations in a 'brutal and unilateral way'[36] when the negotiations were at an advanced stage and it was known that the plaintiff had already incurred considerable expenditure. It would appear that the liability this time is delictual, but the 'fault' must be 'obvious and beyond dispute' otherwise 'there would be grave interference with freedom of contract and the security of commercial transactions'.[37] It is therefore tolerably clear that the standard required of defendants by continental jurisprudence is not high, but the exact point at which it is broken remains unclear.

The third point is that the status of some of these doctrines in English law is, at best uncertain. As we have seen, *culpa in contrahendo* has no place in English law. Nor does English law presently recognise a doctrine of good faith and fair dealing in pre-contractual negotiations.[38] It has been suggested that consideration should be given to the proposition that 'parties should be subject to a duty of good faith in the bargaining process so that neither is at liberty . . . to withdraw for unjustifiable reasons'[39] but there is no sign of judicial recognition of such a doctrine. Unjust sacrifice also has its academic supporters in this context[40] but equally it has not found its way into the case law. An unjust sacrifice is made where a plaintiff 'expends time or effort for the benefit of the defendant in

---

31 The best example is, perhaps, provided by BGHZ 66, 51 where the plaintiff was a 14-year-old girl who was held to be entitled to sue the owners of a self-service store when she slipped on a vegetable leaf and was injured. The defendant had breached his duty to provide safe access: see B Markesinis (n. 115 above) pp. 776–80.

32 A Wyvill (1993) 11 Aust Bar Rev 93, 129.   33 Kessler and Fine (n. [27] above) p. 412.

34 *Ibid.* To the same effect see B Markesinis (n. [28] above) p. 69.

35 B Nicholas, *The French Law of Contract*, 2nd edn (Oxford, Clarendon Press, 1992) p. 70.

36 Com 20.3.1972, JCP 1973.II.17543, discussed by B Nicholas (n. [35] above) pp. 70–1.

37 Nicholas (n. [35] above) p. 71.

38 See, for example, *Walford v Miles* [1992] 2 AC 128. For critical commentary see J Paterson, 'The Contract to Negotiate in Good Faith: Recognition and Enforcement' (1996) 10 *JCL* 120 and, for a more general assessment of the role of good faith, see J Carter and M Furmston, 'Good Faith and Fairness in the Negotiation of Contracts' (1994) 8 *JCL* 1 and 93.

39 Sir A Mason and S Gageler, 'The Contract' in P Finn (ed.), *Essays on Contract* (Sydney, Law Book Co, 1989) p. 15.

40 E Pegoraro, 'Recovery of Benefits Conferred Pursuant to Failed Anticipated Contracts-Unjust Enrichment, Equitable Estoppel or Unjust Sacrifice?' (1995) 23 *Australian Business Law Review* 117.

circumstances in which the defendant should be obliged to pay the plaintiff for his intervention'.[41] The difficulty with this argument is that its doctrinal foundation remains insecure. If the plaintiff does work which is of benefit to the defendant but does not actually result in a benefit to the defendant, why should the defendant pay for the cost of the work done?

While estoppel is clearly a part of English law and cases can be found in which it has been invoked in the context of work done in anticipation of a contract which fails to materialise,[42] the limits on the doctrine, particularly the fact that it cannot act as a sword,[43] have inhibited its utility for plaintiffs. Nevertheless, it has been argued that estoppel provides a better foundation for these cases because it places the emphasis where it belongs, namely on the conduct of the defendant, and it gives the court remedial flexibility.[44] Professor Jones has also maintained that the analogy of proprietary estoppel is a 'simpler and more elegant method of solving the problem' because it 'avoids any analysis of the meaning of "benefit", or of "fault" or "bona fide disagreement" '.[45] Thus, it has been argued that the common thread running through these cases is 'the court's willingness to found a remedy based on the injurious reliance of the plaintiff in circumstances where it would be unconscionable for the defendants to withdraw from the transaction'.[46] Notwithstanding these arguments, it is suggested that there are two problems with the invocation of estoppel in this context. The first relates to the meaning of the word 'unconscionability'. Goff and Jones conclude that the principles enunciated in the estoppel cases, 'particularly the elaboration of the concept of unconscionability, should be of significant assistance to future courts when confronted with comparable problems'.[47] While some undoubtedly value the flexibility given to the courts in the absence of a settled meaning of unconscionability, it is suggested that there is a real danger that principles will be abandoned and hard questions ducked by conferring a broad and largely unstructured discretion on the courts. The second problem relates to the location of estoppel in a classificatory scheme. Where does it reside? It could be located within the law of contract, on the ground that the defendant is estopped from denying the existence of a contract so that his promise is enforceable and he is liable for breach of contract. Alternatively, it could lie within the law of restitution on the ground that the defendant is prevented from denying that he is enriched, so as to trigger a liability in restitution. The third possibility is that the estoppel arises from some unconscionable dealing and

---

41 G Muir, 'Unjust Sacrifice and the Officious Intervener' in P Finn (ed.), *Essays on Restitution* (Sydney, Law Book Co, 1990) p. 297. The origin of this doctrine is to be found in the work of Professor Stoljar, see in particular S Stoljar, 'Unjust Enrichment and Unjust Sacrifice' (1987) 50 *MLR* 603.

42 See, for example, *Attorney-General of Hong Kong v Humphreys Estate Ltd* [1987] AC 114 where the Privy Council held that the plaintiffs were not estopped from withdrawing from negotiations which had been entered into on a 'subject to contract' basis. The fact that the defendants had acted to their detriment to the knowledge of the plaintiffs was not sufficient to found an estoppel when it could not be shown that the plaintiffs had created or encouraged a belief in the defendants that they would not withdraw from the negotiations. Rather surprisingly, the case was not considered by Rattee J in *Regalian Properties plc v London Docklands Development Corporation* [1995] 1 WLR 212, notwithstanding its factual similarities. The omission is particularly surprising given the earlier citation by Rattee J of chapter 25 of *Goff and Jones*, in which the subject of anticipated contracts which do not materialise is discussed. *Goff and Jones* place considerable reliance upon *Humphreys Estate* (see pp. 559–63) in their discussion of the principles which they think should underpin these cases

43 *Combe v Combe* [1951] 2 KB 215. The Australian courts have cast off this limitation (*Walton Stores (Interstate) Ltd v Maher* (1988) 164 CLR 387) and consequently estoppel has the potential to play a greater role in cases of work done in anticipation of a contract which fails to materialise.

44 See, for example, J Carter, 'Contract, Restitution and Promissory Estoppel' (1989) 12 *UNSW Law Journal* 30.

45 G Jones, (1980) 18 *UWOLR* 447 at p. 457.

46 S Christensen, 'Recovery for Work Performed in Anticipation of Contract: Is Reliance an Element of Benefit?' (1993) 11 *Aust Bar Rev* 144, 161 (emphasis in original).

47 *Goff and Jones* p. 562.

so should be located within the law of wrongs. The doctrinal basis of estoppel is in need of further elaboration.[48]

Tort law also clearly exists, but it has consistently stopped short of imposing a duty of care on a negotiating party.[49] One party may, by virtue of his position in relation to the other, be required to advise[50] or to warn[51] the other party about the risks or disadvantages inherent in a particular course of action. Thus, where one party assumes, or is held to have assumed the role of an adviser to the other party, the court may conclude that, where the adviser has greater knowledge and expertise than the advisee, the statements made by the adviser to the advisee during the negotiation period must be made with reasonable care and skill[52] or that the adviser knows facts which justify his opinion.[53] But to state that obligations are owed to each other by negotiating parties (whether in the form of a duty of disclosure or a duty to advise) is not the same thing as saying that there is an obligation not to withdraw from negotiations. While a party subject to a duty to disclose or to advise must not *enter* into a contract unless he has discharged his obligations, the law of tort has consistently stopped short of imposing a duty not to *withdraw* from negotiations. The principal difficulty which must be overcome if liability is to be imposed is the location of the breach of duty which is committed by a person who withdraws from negotiations. If the law recognised the existence of a duty to negotiate in good faith, then a sudden, unexplained withdrawal from negotiations, might give rise to liability in tort but, in the absence of such a duty, there can surely be no general liability in tort.

NOTES AND QUESTIONS

1. Which of the different possibilities identified by McKendrick do you prefer?
2. Is the result in *Marston Construction Co. Ltd v Kigass Ltd* (1989) 46 BLR 109, which McKendrick discusses, consistent with the analysis of risk in *Countrywide Communications* (above)?
3. Do you agree with McKendrick that the fault of the defendant in the failure of the contract to materialize should not, in itself, be a relevant factor?

5. CONTRACTS WHICH ARE UNENFORCEABLE FOR WANT OF FORMALITY

The leading cases in this area are the decisions of the Supreme Court of Canada in *Deglman v Guaranty Trust Co. of Canada and Constantineau* (above, 18) and the High Court of Australia in *Pavey and Matthews Pty. Ltd v Paul* (above, 22). Both cases have been

---

48 See further P Birks (1996) 26 UWALR 1 at pp. 61–2.

49 *Banque Keyser Ullmann SA v Skandia (UK) Insurance Co. Ltd* [1990] 3 WLR 364, 374. For a more expansive view see H Collins, *The Law of Contract*, 3rd edn (London, Butterworths, 1997) ch. 10 and G Cauchi, 'The Protection of the Reliance Interest and Anticipated Contracts Which Fail to Materialize' (1981) 19 *Univ of Western Ontario LR* 237.

50 In *Cornish v Midland Bank plc* [1985] 3 All ER 513, 523 Kerr LJ stated, obiter, that he inclined to the view that, on the facts of that case, the bank would have owed its customer a duty to 'proffer her some adequate explanation of the nature and effect of the document which she had come to sign'. His inclination has not found support in subsequent cases: *Barclays Bank plc v Khaira* [1992] 1 WLR 623, 637, *Barclays Bank plc v O'Brien* [1993] QB 109, 140–1.

51 See generally J Logie, 'Affirmative Action in the Law of Tort: The Case of the Duty to Warn' [1989] *CLJ* 115.

52 See, for example, *Esso Petroleum Co. Ltd v Mardon* [1976] QB 801; *Box v Midland Bank Ltd* [1979] 2 Lloyd's Rep 391, although in this instance Lloyd J was careful to point out (at 398) that liability was not limited to negligent advice but covered 'negligent statements generally including pre-contractual statements of the kind which grounded liability in *Esso Petroleum Co. Ltd v Mardon*'.

53 *Smith v Land and House Property Corp* (1884) Ch D 7.

analysed in an earlier chapter of the book and we shall not set out any further extracts from the judgments at this point. However, you should look again at the extracts which we have taken from these cases and consider, in particular, the following questions: what was the unjust factor which was recognised by the courts in these cases? Could it have been failure of consideration or was it free acceptance (on the latter point see below, 392–395).

There is, however, one further issue which should be considered at this point. Assume that the agreement which the parties have concluded is legally ineffective, but the defendant nevertheless remains ready, able, and willing to perform his (legally ineffective) promise. Can the claimant recover the value of any benefit which he has conferred upon the defendant under this legally ineffective transaction on the ground that the consideration for his payment (or work) has failed? This issue was considered in the following case.

• *Thomas v Brown* (1876) 1 QBD 714, Queen's Bench Division

The claimant signed a contract for the purchase of a leasehold shop from the defendant and paid a deposit of £70. She subsequently decided that she wished to withdraw from the transaction and brought an action to recover the sum which she had paid. The court was prepared to assume that the contract between the parties was unenforceable under the Statute of Frauds because it did not disclose the identity of the vendor, but it nevertheless held that the claimant was not entitled to recover the deposit because the defendant remained ready, able, and willing to complete and because she had paid the deposit in the knowledge that the vendor's name was not disclosed on the contract.

Quain J: . . . I decide this cause on the ground that it is an action by an unwilling vendee against a willing vendor, and that it cannot be said that the consideration has failed so as to entitle the plaintiff to recover. By the 10th paragraph of the case it appears that the defendant has always been ready and willing to assign the purchased property to the plaintiff in pursuance of the contract; in short, to give the plaintiff all that was bargained for. Now where, upon a verbal contract for the sale of land, the purchaser pays the deposit and the vendor is always ready and willing to complete, I know of no authority to support the purchaser in bringing an action to recover back the money.

6. VOID CONTRACTS

• *Craven-Ellis v Canons Ltd* [1936] 2 KB 403, Court of Appeal

On 14 April 1931 the claimant was appointed managing director of Canons Ltd and the terms of his remuneration were also contained in that agreement. The agreement was void because neither the claimant nor the other 'directors' who were parties to the agreement were qualified to appoint the claimant, as they did not obtain their qualification shares as required by the articles of association. The claimant worked for the company but the company refused to pay for the work done. The claimant was held to be entitled to recover the value of the work which he had carried out on a *quantum meruit*.

Greer LJ: . . . The company, having had the full benefit of these services, decline to pay either under the agreement or on the basis of a quantum meruit. Their defence to the action is a purely technical defence, and if it succeeds the Messrs du Cros as the principal shareholders in the company, and the company, would be in the position of having received and accepted valuable services and refusing, for purely technical reasons, to pay for them.

As regards the services rendered between December 31, 1930, and April 14, 1931, there is, in my judgment, no defence to the claim. These services were rendered by the plaintiff not as managing director or as a director, but as an estate agent, and there was no contract in existence which could present any obstacle to a claim based on a quantum meruit for services rendered and accepted.

As regards the plaintiff's services after the date of the contract, I think the plaintiff is also entitled to succeed. The contract, having been made by directors who had no authority to make it with one of themselves who had notice of their want of authority, was not binding on either party. It was, in fact, a nullity, and presents to obstacle to the implied promise to pay on a quantum meruit basis which arises from the performance of the services and the implied acceptance of the same by the company.

. . .

It was contended by Mr Croom-Johnson on behalf of the respondents that, inasmuch as the services relied on were purported to be done by the plaintiff under what he and the directors thought was a binding contract, there could be no legal obligation on the defendants on a quantum meruit claim. The only one of the numerous authorities cited by Mr Croom-Johnson that appears to support his contention is the judgement of a Divisional Court in *In re Allison, Johnson & Foster, Ld.; Ex parte Birkenshaw.*[1] The Court consisted of Lord Alverstone, Wills and Kennedy JJ, and the judgment was delivered by Kennedy J. In giving judgment that learned judge, expressing not merely his own opinion, but that of the other two judges, said: 'There can be no implied contract for payment arising out of acceptance of the work done where the work was done upon an express request which turns out to be no request at all, but which down to the time when the whole of the work had been done was supposed by both parties to be valid and operative.' This passage appears to involve the proposition that in all cases where parties suppose there is an agreement in existence and one of them has performed services, or delivered goods in pursuance of the suppositious agreement there cannot be any inference of any promise by the person accepting the services or the goods to pay on the basis of a quantum meruit. This would certainly be strictly logical if the inference of a promise to pay on a quantum meruit basis were an inference of fact based on the acceptance of the services or of the goods delivered under what was supposed to be an existing contract; but in my judgment the inference is not one of fact, but is an inference which a rule of law imposes on the parties where work has been done or goods have been delivered under what purports to be a binding contract, but is not so in fact.

. . .

In my judgment, the obligation to pay reasonable remuneration for the work done when there is no binding contract between the parties is imposed by a rule of law, and not by an inference of fact arising from the acceptance of services or goods. It is one of the cases referred to in books on contracts as obligations arising quasi ex contractu, of which a well known instance is a claim based on money had and received. Although I do not hold that the decision of the Court in *Ex parte Birkenshaw* was wrong, I think that the passage I read from the judgment is not a correct statement of the law.

I accordingly think that the defendants must pay on the basis of a quantum meruit not only for the services rendered after December 31, 1930, and before the date of the invalid agreement, but also for the services after that date. I think the appeal should be allowed, and judgment given for such a sum as shall be found to be due on the basis of a quantum meruit in respect of all services rendered by the plaintiff to the company until he was dismissed. The defendants seem to me to be in a dilemma. If the contract was an effective contract by the company, they would be bound to pay the remuneration provided for in the contract. If, on the other hand, the contract was a nullity and not

---

1 [1904] 2 KB 327.

binding either on the plaintiff or the defendants, there would be nothing to prevent the inference which the law draws from the performance by the plaintiff of services to the company, and the company's acceptance of such services, which, if they had not been performed by the plaintiff, they would have had to get some other agent to carry out.

Greene LJ and **Talbot J** concurred.

NOTES AND QUESTIONS

1. Was the company enriched by the claimant's work? Could the company have requested or bargained-for the work which the claimant had carried out? If not, was it incontrovertibly benefited?

2. What was the unjust factor in this case?

3. Where the effect of the claim for restitution of unjust enrichment would be to contradict the rule that a director must not make an unauthorized profit from his position as a director then the claim should be denied. It is suggested that this is the best explanation for the decision of the House of Lords in *Guinness plc v Saunders*, below, 857.

• *Rover International Ltd v Cannon Film Sales Ltd*
[1989] 1 WLR 912, Court of Appeal

In this case there were two separate claimants, Proper and Rover, who were bringing entirely separate claims. We have dealt with Proper's claim above at 290–294. Here we deal with Rover's claim. Thorn EMI (which was later taken over by Cannon Film Sales Ltd) entered into negotiations with the Italian film distributors, Monitor, with a view to entering into a joint venture for the dubbing and distribution of films in Italian cinemas. Under the terms of the joint venture, it was anticipated that EMI would supply master prints of the films and all other necessary materials, which would remain their property, and that Monitor would arrange for the dubbing of the films into Italian and carry out the artwork and related matters. It was further anticipated that Monitor would make substantial advances to EMI and that Monitor would be reimbursed through their share of the gross receipts of the films when they were shown in the cinemas. However, for fiscal reasons, it was found to be necessary for Monitor to interpose between itself and EMI a company, Rover International Ltd, which was to be incorporated in the Channel Islands. So it was Rover, and not Monitor, who entered into the agreement with EMI and assumed the obligation to pay the advances to EMI. EMI was then taken over by Cannon Film Sales Ltd Relations between the parties subsequently deteriorated and Cannon became very anxious to find a way out of the agreement so concluded with Rover. Eventually Cannon found that Rover had breached the terms of the agreement by releasing a film, called 'Highlander', before the agreed date for release, and they also discovered that Rover was not incorporated at the time at which it purported to enter into the agreement with EMI. So Cannon terminated the agreement with Rover on the ground of the later's breach of contract, but without prejudice to their allegation that the contract was in any event non-existent because of the failure to incorporate Rover at the time of entry into the contract. As part of a complex web of litigation between the parties, Rover brought an action against Cannon to recover five instalments, totalling $312,500, which it had paid to Cannon under the agreement and also to recover on a *quantum meruit* for the distribution expenses which it had incurred in relation to the films which were released and also to recover reasonable remuneration for the work which they had done. Both of their claims succeeded.

Kerr LJ: . . .

TOTAL FAILURE OF CONSIDERATION

The claim for repayment of the five instalments of the advance on this ground was rejected by the judge in the following terms [1987] BCLC 540, 546:

> 'As for the claim for money had and received, the answer is plain. The consideration, if there had been a contract, had not failed at all. Rover has had several films, including 'Highlander,' and distributed them in Italy for payment no doubt of substantial sums. To allow it now to get back the moneys which it paid to Cannon would be grossly unjust. There is no claim in law here for moneys had and received to the use of Rover.'

This passage strongly supports my impression that the judge did not have in mind the full financial consequences which would flow from his judgment. But that is of no direct relevance at this juncture. The important point is that in my view the judge could not have expressed himself in this way if his attention had been directed to the correct approach in principle. The question whether there has been a total failure of consideration is not answered by considering whether there was any consideration sufficient to support a contract or purported contract. The test is whether or not the party claiming total failure of consideration has in fact received any part of the benefit bargained for under the contract or purported contract.

The relevant principles are set out in *Chitty on Contracts*, 25th edn (1983), vol. 1, 1091–2, para. 1964 and the authorities there cited, to which we understand the judge was not referred. It is convenient to quote the following passages from the text:

> 'Where money has been paid under a transaction that is or becomes ineffective the payer may recover the money provided that the consideration for the payment has totally failed. Although the principle is not confined to contracts most of the cases are concerned with ineffective contracts. In that context failure of consideration occurs where the payer has not enjoyed the benefit of any part of what he bargained for. Thus, the failure is judged from the payer's point of view and "when one is considering the law of failure of consideration and of the quasi-contractual right to recover money on that ground, it is generally speaking, not the promise which is referred to as the consideration, but the performance of the promise." The failure has to be total . . . Thus, any performance of the actual thing promised, *as determined by the contract*, is fatal to recovery under this heading.
>
> The role of the contractual specification means that it is not true to say that there can be a total failure of consideration only where the payer received no benefit at all in return for the payment. The concept of total failure of consideration can ignore real benefits received by the payer if they are not the benefit bargained for. . . .'

The quotation was taken from the speech of Viscount Simon LC in *Fibrosa Spolka Akcyjna v Fairbairn Lawson Combe Barbour Ltd* [1943] AC 32, 48. It is not necessary to refer to this or the other authorities cited in support of this passage, but I should refer to two authorities by way of illustration.

In *Rowland v Divall* [1923] 2 KB 500 the plaintiff bought a car from the defendants. He had the use of it for several months but then discovered that the seller had no title, with the result that he had to surrender the car to the true owner. He sued for the return of the price on the ground that there had been a total failure of consideration. The defendant denied this, pointing out that the plaintiff had had the use of the car for a substantial time. This contention succeeded at first instance, leaving the plaintiff only with a claim for damages, but this court unanimously upheld the plaintiff's claim. The consideration for which he had bargained was lawful possession of the car and a good title to it, neither of which he got. Although the car had been delivered to him pursuant to the contract and he had had its use and enjoyment for a considerable time, there was a total failure of consideration because he had not got any part of what he had bargained for.

The decision of Finnemore J in *Warman v Southern Counties Car Finance Corporation Ltd* [1949] 2 KB 576 was to the same effect. The plaintiff was buying a car on hire purchase when he became aware that a third party was claiming to be the true owner of the car. But he nevertheless went on paying the remaining instalments and then the necessary nominal sum to exercise his option to purchase. When the true owner then claimed the car he surrendered it and sued the finance company for the return of everything he had paid. He succeeded on the ground that there had been a total failure of consideration. He had not bargained for having the use of the car without the option to purchase it.

The position of Rover in the present case is a fortiori to these cases. Admittedly, as the judge said, they had several films from Cannon. But the possession of the films was merely incidental to the performance of the contract in the sense that it enabled Rover/Monitor to render services in relation to the films by dubbing them, preparing them for release on the Italian market and releasing them. These were onerous incidents associated with the delivery of the films to them. And delivery and possession were not what Rover had bargained for. The relevant bargain, at any rate for present purposes, was the opportunity to earn a substantial share of the gross receipts pursuant to clause 6 of the schedule, with the certainty of at least breaking even by recouping their advance. Due to the invalidity of the agreement Rover got nothing of what they had bargained for, and there was clearly a total failure of consideration.

This equally disposes of Mr Pardoe's ingenious attempt to convert his concession of a quantum meruit, in particular the element of reasonable remuneration, into consideration in any relevant sense. Rover did not bargain for a quantum meruit, but for the benefits which might flow from clause 6 of the schedule. That is the short answer to this point.

It follows that in my view Rover's claim for the repayment of the five instalments of the advance totalling $312,500 succeeds on the basis of a total failure of consideration.

MISTAKE OF FACT

In my view Rover are equally entitled to recover these instalments as having been paid to Cannon under a mistake of fact. . . .

QUANTUM MERUIT

As already mentioned, shortly after the opening of the appeal the plaintiffs' entitlement to a quantum meruit was agreed, and it was also agreed that its quantification in figures should be dealt with at the same time as the accounts and inquiries relating to the gross receipts. We therefore asked the parties to formulate an agreement statement defining the measures of the quantum meruit so far as possible. It then transpired that a number of points of disagreement remained. We were accordingly supplied with a document which indicated the extent of the agreement and also some minor points raised by one side or the other which were not agreed and on which we were asked to rule. I therefore set out below what I consider to be the appropriate terms defining the quantum meruit to which the plaintiffs are entitled. I have emphasised the words about which the parties were not in agreement to the extent that I consider that they should form part of the definition. This is as follows: 'Cannon agrees that in the account to be taken, Rover can recover on a quantum meruit for work done for Cannon by *Rover and/or* Monitor Srl in respect of the distribution of the films supplied by Cannon, together with disbursements reasonably incurred by *Rover and/or* Monitor in connection therewith, such recovery: (a) to include such element of profit as is reasonable (b) not to be in excess of the gross receipts of distribution in Italy of the said films supplied by Cannon, such gross receipts to be calculated in accordance with clause 12(a) of the theatrical agreement (c) not to include any work done or disbursements incurred prior to 6 February 1986 (d) to include the reasonable dubbing *and other* expenses incurred in connection with "Link".'

As can be seen from the emphasised words, the only disagreement of substance was on the question whether the quantum meruit should relate to any services rendered by Rover as well as

Monitor. In my view it is right to refer to both; Rover were the parties to the intended contract and it was always envisaged that the work in Italy would be done by Monitor as their agents. For this reason I also conclude that the element of profit referred to in (a) should not be limited to Monitor, as Cannon had suggested. But that is only how I see the position in principle. It may well turn out that nothing at all can justifiably be claimed on behalf of Rover, because it was a mere 'front' and shell; and there could certainly be no question of any duplicated claim. As regards the expenses incurred in connection with the film 'Link,' I can see no good ground for confining these to the dubbing. If and to the extent that additional expenses preparatory to the release of this film had also been reasonably incurred, it seems to me that these should be recoverable.

However, this leaves one further major area of disagreement between the parties to which I have already referred; the so-called 'ceiling' point. The question is whether the quantum meruit should in any event be limited to such amount, if any, as Rover would have been entitled to retain out of the gross receipts by 13 October 1986, when Cannon terminated the (purported) agreement pursuant to clauses 16 and 17, the 'default' and 'termination' provisions. As already mentioned, Cannon's right to invoke these clauses on the ground of the unauthorised release of 'Highlander' on 10 October was upheld below, and there has been no appeal against this part of the judgment.

This raises an issue of principle of some general importance. Cannon submit that the plaintiffs would be unjustly enriched if they recovered more by way of a quantum meruit than what would have been their entitlement under the purported contract, bearing in mind that it was their breach which led to its termination. They rely on the famous dictum of Lord Mansfield in *Moses v Macferlan* (1760) 2 Burr. 1005, 1010, that the defendant

> 'may defend himself by every thing which shows that the plaintiff, ex aequo et bono, is not entitled to the whole of his demand, or to any part of it.'

The problem only arises in cases where a contract has been rescinded by an 'innocent' party without a prior breach by the other party. Where there has been a prior breach, as in somewhat similar situations in which pre-payments may be recoverable such as *Dies v British and International Mining and Finance Corporation Ltd* [1939] 1 KB 724 . . . the 'innocent' party can of course sue for damages. But where the contract was void ab initio or has come to an end without breach, e.g., by frustration, all remedies must necessarily lie in the area of restitution.

The contention on behalf of Cannon is at first sight attractive, that Rover's recovery of a quantum meruit should be subject to a 'ceiling' which would take account of their breach and the consequent right of Cannon, which was in fact invoked, to terminate under the 'default' clause, but for the fact that the contract has been void ab initio. However, on further consideration I have reached the clear conclusion that this would not be a correct analysis, for a number of reasons.

First, there are purely pragmatic reasons which militate against the justice of a superficially attractive solution on these lines. Thus, it is not simply a case of a contract which was void ab initio without the knowledge of either party and which was then broken by Rover. It was a case where the invalidity of the contract was discovered by Cannon, no doubt with considerable satisfaction, and relied upon by them. If they had wished to do so they could have affirmed the contract, since the cause of its invalidity had no practical significance for the parties' bargain. But they chose to rely on the invalidity, and when they first invoked it there had been no breach on the side of Rover; merely unfounded allegations of breaches and other unattractive conduct from the side of Cannon. In these circumstances it does not appear unjust that Cannon cannot have the best of both worlds: reliance on the invalidity of the contract ab initio as well as upon a subsequent breach on the part of Rover. Moreover, the suggested 'ceiling' would be unjust, since its operation would be one-sided. The quantum meruit in favour of Rover would be limited, and indeed disappear entirely on the facts of this case, whereas the benefits of the restitutionary position in favour of Cannon would be without limit, since no 'ceiling' would be applicable to their entitlement to the gross receipts.

Secondly, I do not think that the contention in favour of a 'ceiling' is in accordance with principle. It would involve the application of provisions of a void contract to the assessment of a quantum meruit which only arises due to the non-existence of the supposed contract. Albeit on very different facts, a similar mixture between a contract and an extra-contractual quantum meruit was rightly rejected by Saville J in *Greenmast Shipping Co. SA v Jean Lion et Cie SA* [1986] 2 Lloyd's Rep. 277.

Moreover, as pointed out in *Goff and Jones, The Law of Restitution*, 3rd edn (1986), 691, there has been reluctance to accept the full breadth of Lord Mansfield's dictum in *Moses v Macferlan*, 2 Burr. 1005, 1010. As shown by this chapter, the concept of restitution in the face of what would otherwise be unjust enrichment has been limited by defences protecting the party from whom restitution is claimed; not by considering the merits or demerits of the party which has made a payment under a mistake or for a consideration which has wholly failed.

Finally, if the imposition of a 'ceiling' in the present case were accepted, then the consequences could be far-reaching and undesirable in other situations which it would be impossible to distinguish in principle. It would then follow that an evaluation of the position of the parties to a void contract, or to one which becomes ineffective subsequently, could always be called for. We know that this is not the position in the case of frustrated contracts, which are governed by the Law Reform (Frustrated Contracts) Act 1943. It would cause many difficulties if the position were different in relation to contracts which are void ab initio. By analogy to Cannon's submission in the present case, in deciding on the equities of restitution the court could then always be called upon to analyse or attempt to forecast the relative position of the parties under a contract which is ex hypothesi non-existent. This is not an attractive proposition, and I can see no justification for it in principle or upon any authority.

I therefore conclude that Cannon must accept the primary basis on which they have succeeded, the invalidity of the contract ab initio, and that they cannot also rely on Rover's breach of this non-existent contract. It follows that for the purposes of assessing an appropriate quantum meruit I would order an account to be taken on the basis of the terms set out above. . . .

Dillon LJ considered that Rover's case was a 'classic case of money paid under a mistake of fact' and therefore did not find it necessary to 'express any opinion on the question of total failure of consideration'. **Nicholls LJ** agreed with the judgments of both **Kerr LJ** and **Dillon LJ**.

NOTES AND QUESTIONS

1. Did the Court of Appeal take an 'artificial view of total failure' (Burrows, 330)? Should the court have recognized that the failure of consideration was only partial but that Rover was nonetheless entitled to recover the five instalments it had paid provided that it made counter-restitution to Cannon for any benefit which it had obtained from Cannon?

2. The unjust factor in the money claim was either (total) failure of consideration or mistake of fact. But when he turned to the services claim, Kerr LJ simply described the claim as a '*quantum meruit*'? Why did he not find it necessary to identify an unjust factor in relation to the services claim? What, if any, was the unjust factor?

3. Kerr LJ's reasons for holding that the '*quantum meruit*' claim should not be limited by the contract ceiling have been described as being 'both pragmatic and principled' (J Beatson (1989) 105 *LQR* 179, 180). Is this so?

- *Westdeutsche Landesbank Girozentrale v Islington London Borough Council* [1994] 4 All ER 890, Queen's Bench Division, [1994] 1 WLR 938, Court of Appeal, [1996] AC 669, House of Lords

This decision, at first instance, involved two cases which were heard together. Both involved claimant banks and defendant local authorities that entered into interest rate swap transactions. In the lead action (*Westdeutsche*) the interest rate swap transaction was 'open' (that is, it had not been completed when the payments stopped). In the other action (*Sandwell*) the interest rate swap transaction was 'closed' (that is, all payments had been made by both parties under the putative agreement). The House of Lords had held that these transactions were *ultra vires* local authorities with the result that they were void and unenforceable. The banks sought to recover the sums which they had paid to the local authorities under these void swap transactions. It was held that the banks were entitled to recover the net sums which they had paid to the local authorities (a fuller account of the facts is set out below, at 727). In this extract we are concerned only with the ground on which the courts held that the banks were entitled to restitution of the money which they had paid to the local authorities. The other aspects of the case concerning proprietary restitution are dealt with below, at 727.

Hobhouse J:

. . .

(2) MONEY HAD AND RECEIVED

(a) Total failure of consideration

The phrase 'failure of consideration' is one which in its terminology presupposes that there has been at some stage a valid contract which has been partially performed by one party. It is essentially a concept for use in the law of contract and provides a common law remedy governed by rigid rules granted as of right where the contract becomes ineffective through breach or otherwise. The rules that govern the application of the principle include the technical concept of an 'entire' consideration, what amounts in law to a total failure of consideration, and the absence of defences to the action for the recovery of money paid for a consideration which has wholly failed. In the case of ultra vires transactions such as those with which I am concerned where there is not and never has been any contract, I prefer to use the phrase 'absence of consideration'. I note that this was the phrase used by the House of Lords in the *Woolwich* case, [1993] AC 70 and has been used by other judges in the past, although it is right to say that the phrase 'failure of consideration' has very frequently been used in connection with void contracts (see e.g. the argument in *Fibrosa Spolka Akcyjna v Fairbairn Lawson Combe Barbour Ltd* [1943] AC 32 at 36).

Adopting for the moment the contractual approach, what amounts to a total failure of consideration was authoritively considered by the House of Lords in the *Fibrosa* case. That case concerned a frustrated contract under which the buyer had made an advance payment of the price but had not received any goods or actual benefit in return and under which, prior to its frustration, the seller had incurred expense in starting to manufacture the goods which would, after the completion of their manufacture, have become the subject of the sale. It was argued that the consideration for the advance payment was the promises of the seller and that they had been valid promises; it was said that the principle was confined to cases where the contract was avoided (so that the promises were avoided as well). Viscount Simon, having referred to the opinion expressed in *Chandler v Webster* [1904] 1 KB 493 that the doctrine of failure of consideration only applied to contracts which had been avoided as opposed to frustrated, and having distinguished contracts under seal, continued ([1943] AC 32 at 48):

'. . . when one is considering the law of failure of consideration and of the quasi-contractual right to recover money on that ground, it is, generally speaking, not the promise which is referred to as the consideration, but the performance of the promise. The money was paid to secure performance and, if performance fails, the inducement which brought about the payment is not fulfilled.'

Accordingly the relevant failure of consideration for the application of this principle is the failure of performance on the part of the opposite party. If the opposite party has at least partially performed his obligations under the contract so as to confer some benefit upon the claimant, then the claimant cannot rely upon the principle. Further, it is clear from the speeches in the House of Lords and the overruling of *Chandler v Webster* that, whilst the principle was properly applied in cases where contracts had been avoided ab initio, it was not confined to such cases.

Applying the principle stated in the *Fibrosa* case, the banks cannot say that the contractual principle enables them to recover on any of the contracts save for the third and fourth Sandwell swaps. On the third and fourth Sandwell swaps there were only payments one way and there was never any performance by Sandwell. Accordingly, in respect of those two transactions, Kleinwort Benson is entitled to say, on the basis of the contractual principle, that there has been a total failure of consideration and that they should be entitled to recover all sums paid under those two swaps at common law as money had and received. As regards the Islington swap and the second Sandwell swap, there has been partial performance by both sides and both sides have received benefits under the 'contract'. As regards the first Sandwell swap the contemplated contract was in fact fully performed and neither party can, on the contractual approach, say that there was any failure of consideration, let alone any total failure. Therefore the contractual principle of total failure of consideration does not suffice to give any right to recover the sums paid under those contracts.

(b) Void contracts and absence of consideration

To get round the difficulty that they could not satisfy the test stated in the *Fibrosa* case, the plaintiffs advanced various arguments which all in the end amounted to the proposition that, where there has never been any contract in law, as is the case where the purported contracted is ultra vires one party, any sums paid under that contract can in principle be recovered. They recognised that if ordering the repayment of sums paid amounted to indirectly enforcing the ultra vires contract, as was the case in *Sinclair v Brougham*, the prima facie right to repayment could not be recognised, but they relied in particular upon what was said by Lord Parker, which expressly recognised that where no question of indirectly enforcing an ultra vires contract was involved there might well be a right of recovery (see [1914] AC 398 at 440).

They were also able to rely upon the decision of the Divisional Court in *Brougham v Dwyer* (1913) 108 LT 504. This case also involved the ultra vires banking business of the Birkbeck Building Society. The plaintiff was the liquidator of the society and the defendant was a customer of the supposed bank. It appears that the defendant had had an active current account with the society for some time and that at the date of the liquidation the account was £32 2s 2d overdrawn. The county court judge had declined to distinguish between ultra vires and illegality and had given judgment for the defendant. The Divisional Court allowed the appeal and held that the plaintiff was entitled to recover the amount of the overdraft as money had and received by the defendant to the use of the society. The distinction between ultra vires and illegality was underlined, and the basis of recovery was spelt out by Lush J (at 505):

'It turned out that in point of law the building society were incompetent to make such a contract, and it followed that the contract which the directors thought they were making was not a contract at all, but was simply a transaction which in point of law did not exist. The consequence was that the defendant had received moneys belonging to the building society under a transaction which had no validity of any sort or kind. If the matter stood there, I should have thought it plain that there being no contract an action for money had and received would lie. The case appears to me to be on all fours with one in which money has been advanced on something which was thought to be a contract, but as to which it turns out there has been a total failure of consideration ... the action was maintainable, and the defendant had no answer to it. It was an action brought for money lent under a transaction which was thought to be valid but which was in fact not valid. On principle I can see no possible reason why such an action should not be maintainable, and the Court of Appeal in *Re Coltman* ((1881) 19 Ch D 64) clearly decided that in a case such as the present assuming the contract not to be illegal, there would be no answer to the action.'

What Lush J says must of course be read subject to what was said by the House of Lords in *Sinclair v Brougham*, but it confirms the basic proposition that in the absence of some special factor money paid under an ultra vires contract can be recovered as money had and received in the same manner as can money paid for a consideration that has totally failed. This is so even though no question of mistake of fact arises and there were mutual dealings under the supposed contract which would preclude the application of what I have chosen to characterise as the ordinary contractual principle.

The same conclusions are also powerfully supported by the annuity cases and, in particular, *Hicks v Hicks*.

The two cases referred to in the speeches in *Sinclair v Brougham*, that is to say *Re Phoenix Life Assurance Co, Hoare's Case* (1862) 2 John & H 441, 70 ER 1041 and *Flood v Irish Provident Assurance Co. Ltd* [1912] 2 Ch 597n, were concerned with purported insurance contracts which were entered into ultra vires the powers of the relevant insurance company. In the *Phoenix Life Assurance* case the claimants were allowed to prove in the liquidation for the premiums that they had paid on the basis that they would have been recoverable at law as money had and received. *Flood's* case was similar save that the insurance company was not in liquidation. The premiums paid on the void policies were held to be recoverable as being money paid without consideration. The *Phoenix Life Assurance* case was cited and treated as having been decided upon the same basis. These cases are accordingly consistent with both sides' submissions. The language used assists the banks; the facts show that the application of the *Fibrosa* test would have led to the same conclusion.

The banks also relied upon the decision of Cairns J in *North Central Wagon Finance Co. Ltd v Brailsford* [1962] 1 WLR 1288. The facts were somewhat complicated. In summary they were that in 1955 the defendant, Brailsford, entered into what purported to be a hire-purchase contract with the plaintiffs in respect of an Albion lorry which was in fact already owned by the defendant. Under that agreement the plaintiffs advanced £1,000, which was used by the defendant to purchase a second lorry. Matters then proceeded for some two and a half years on the basis of the supposed hire-purchase agreement and variations of it. Substantial payments were made by or on behalf of the defendant to the plaintiffs. However, by the beginning of 1958 there was still money apparently owing by the defendant to the plaintiffs. The plaintiffs sued for the money outstanding under the supposed hire-purchase agreement. The defendant objected that it was in truth an unregistered bill of sale and therefore void. The court upheld that contention and it followed that the claim on the supposed contract could not succeed. However, an alternative claim for the repayment of the £1,000 as money had and received by the defendant to the use of the plaintiffs was allowed. Cairns J dealt with the point very shortly. He said ([1962] 1 WLR 1288 at 1293–1294):

'I now turn to the plaintiffs' alternative claim for money had and received. In *Davies v Rees* ((1886) 17 QBD 408), it was held that a bill of sale which is void for want of form is void for all purposes, but nevertheless it was held at first instance, and not contested on appeal, that the money could be recovered by the lender with reasonable interest. In *Bradford Advance Co., Ltd v Ayers* ([1924] WN 152), Bailhache, J, held that the money could be recovered, not on the basis of any oral agreement leading up to the bill of sale, but as money had and received. In my view, the same considerations apply where money is advanced on a bill of sale which is void for non-registration.'

Cairns J held that the plaintiffs were entitled to recover from the defendant the sum advanced, 'less repayments and other proper credits, with interest' (see [1962] 1 WLR 1288 at 1295). This case will not stand up to any analysis on the basis of satisfying the *Fibrosa* test. Benefits had been given and received and the approach of the court was not to deny the remedy. Similarly, it is not a case which was based in any way upon any mistake of fact.

The argument of the banks was formulated in a number of ways. The simplest was that contained in the skeleton argument of Mr Southwell QC for Kleinwort Benson: 'Payments made under a void contract do not amount to consideration for the purposes of the law of restitution.' In support of that proposition he cites two Gaming Act cases, which in my judgment do not assist since payments for honour are in law gifts (see the *Lipkin Gorman* case), and *Brailsford's* case and *Hicks v Hicks*, which are clear authorities in favour of the proposition. The argument developed by Mr Sumption QC was that it is necessary to ask whether the payer got the benefit for which he bargained. 'What the bank bargained for was payments which would discharge a legal obligation and which the bank was entitled lawfully to receive. What it obtained were payments made under a void agreement which Islington was prima facie entitled to recover back.'

In support of that submission Mr Sumption relied primarily upon two cases. The first, *Rowland v Divall* [1923] 2 KB 500, in which the purchaser of a motor car was suing the seller for the return of the price on the basis that, although the motor car had been delivered to the buyer and in fact on-sold by him, the seller had never passed a good title in the car to him. The price was held to be recoverable as money paid for a consideration that had wholly failed and the benefit which he had had through having the possession of the motor car for a period of time was disregarded. I do not find that case of assistance. It has to be contrasted with the decision of the Privy Council in *Linz v Electric Wire Co. of Palestine Ltd* [1948] AC 371, where a similar claim failed on the ground that there was not a total failure of consideration. In *Linz's* case what the plaintiff had paid for was a number of preference shares which had been invalidly issued. Such decisions depend upon an analysis of whether the defendant's breach was fundamental to the particular contractual transaction and, by necessary implication, whether the plaintiff was in the circumstances precluded from treating the contract as rescinded. In *Linz's* case it was held that 'she got exactly that which she bargained to get'; (see [1948] AC 371 at 377). In *Rowland v Divall* it was considered that the buyer did not get what he bargained for. This is very different from the present case where there was in truth no bargain at all and problems of deciding what was the essential part of the bargain do not arise and there can be no question whether the plaintiff's conduct has affected his right to treat the contract as rescinded.

The second case relied upon by Mr Sumption was more helpful and, indeed, was illustrative of a principle recognised in a number of other cases. The case was *Rover International Ltd v Cannon Film Sales Ltd (No 3)* [he considered the case and continued:]

This case illustrates that for the purposes of the law of failure of consideration it is contractual performance that must be looked at and that collateral benefits received do not deprive the payer of his remedy. Similarly, compensation by way of quantum meruit or under some form of quasi contract is not a relevant benefit at all. It does not arise under the relevant contract. It is awarded by the court independently, on the basis that there is no effective contract and has been no contractual compensation. However, again, the analysis of Kerr LJ is essentially contractual.

In my judgment, the correct analysis is that any payments made under a contract which is void ab initio, in the way that an ultra vires contract is void, are not contractual payments at all. They are payments in which the legal property in the money passes to the recipient, but in equity the property in the money remains with the payer. The recipient holds the money as a fiduciary for the payer and is bound to recognise his equity and repay the money to him. This relationship and the consequent obligation have been recognised both by courts applying the common law and by Chancery courts. The principle is the same in both cases: it is unconscionable that the recipient should retain the money. Neither mistake nor the contractual principle of total failure of consideration are the basis for the right of recovery.

Where payments both ways have been made the correct view is to treat the later payment as, pro tanto, a repayment of the earlier sum paid by the other party. The character of the remedy, both in law and equity, is restitution, that is to say putting the parties back into the position in which they were before. Accordingly, the remedy is only available to a party on the basis that he gives credit for any benefit which he has received. He must give credit for any payments which have been made by the opposite party to him and, where the court thinks appropriate, pay a quantum meruit or quantum valebat. The same conclusion follows from the application of the principle of unjust enrichment: in so far as the recipient has made cross-payments to the payer, the recipient has ceased to be enriched.

This formulation is explicitly the basis of the decisions in the annuity cases and the decision of the Divisional Court in *Brougham v Dwyer* (1913) 108 LT 504. It is implicit in the decision in *Brailsford's* case [1962] 1 WLR 1288. It is also fully consistent with the many judicial statements of the general principle which underlies the law of restitution and unjust enrichment which are typified by the statement, already quoted, of Lord Wright in the *Fibrosa* case [1943] AC 32 at 61.

The application of the principle is subject to the requirement that the courts should not grant a remedy which amounts to the direct or indirect enforcement of a contract which the law requires to be treated as ineffective. Since the obligation which law and equity require the conscience of the receiver to recognise is in effect an obligation to repay money, it is hard to think of any situation where this qualification will be relevant save where the void contract was one which purported to create a debtor and creditor relationship, as was the case in *Sinclair v Brougham*. Since *Sinclair v Brougham* was decided on the basis of applying this qualification, it is a decision which tends to confirm the formulation. The existence of the qualification and its relevance in *Sinclair v Brougham* was repeated by Lord Sumner in *R. Leslie Ltd v Sheill* [1914] 3 KB 607 at 613.

The right to recover payments is also subject to any available defences. Generally speaking, those are any defences which affect the equity. This is again either explicit or implicit in the annuity cases and, since the *Lipkin Gorman* case, includes, as an application of that approach, the defence of change of position.

Since the right of recovery, although based on equitable principles, has been recognised by the common law courts and has been held to be capable of founding an action for money had and received, it can form a proper basis for a legally recognised right of recovery in personam in the present cases. If, contrary to my view, there were some distinction to be drawn between the right to restitution as recognised in law and in equity, any such distinction should not now affect the outcome of a case where no question of insolvency arises; the principles of both law and equity should be applied in a unified fashion so as to provide the appropriate remedy.

This decision is sufficient to establish the prima facie right of the plaintiffs to recover in both of the actions which are before me. It also follows from the fact that I consider that the correct analysis is absence of consideration and not failure of consideration that it is not open to Kleinwort Benson to assert an absolute right of recovery on the third and fourth Sandwell swaps on the basis of a right to recover money paid for a contractual consideration that has wholly failed to which there are no defences; it will be open to Sandwell to seek to raise a defence of change of position. Likewise, it follows that it is irrelevant to the existence of a cause of action in connection with the payments made under the first Sandwell swap that the supposed contract was in fact fully performed and there was no failure of consideration at all in the contractual sense. . . .

The defendant local authority in the *Westdeutsche* (open swap) case appealed to the Court of Appeal, who dismissed the appeal ([1994] 1 WLR 938) and upheld the analysis of Hobhouse J. The defendant local authority further appealed to the House of Lords, but this time the appeal was only in relation to the award of compound rather than simple interest. Although the unjust factor was not actually in issue in the House of Lords, the point was considered by Lord Goff in the following terms.

Lord Goff of Chieveley:

(1) TOTAL FAILURE OF CONSIDERATION

There has long been a desire among restitution lawyers to escape from the unfortunate effects of the so-called rule that money is only recoverable at common law on the ground of failure of consideration where the failure is total, by reformulating the rule upon a more principled basis; and signs that this will in due course be done are appearing in judgments throughout the common law world, as appropriate cases arise for decision. It is fortunate however that, in the present case, thanks (I have no doubt) to the admirable researches of counsel, a line of authority was discovered which had escaped the attention of the scholars who work in this field. This line of authority was concerned with contracts for annuities which were void if certain statutory formalities were not complied with. They were not therefore concerned with contracts void by reason of the incapacity one of the parties. Even so, they were concerned with cases in which payments had been made, so to speak, both ways; and the courts had to decide whether they could, in such circumstances, do justice by restoring the parties to their previous positions. They did not hesitate to do so, by ascertaining the balance of the account between the parties, and ordering the repayment of the balance. Moreover the form of action by which this was achieved was the old action for money had and received—what we nowadays call a personal claim in restitution at common law. With this precedent before him, Hobhouse J felt free to make a similar order in the present case; and in this he was self-evidently right.

The most serious problem which has remained in this connection is the theoretical question whether recovery can here be said to rest upon the ground of *failure* of consideration. Hobhouse J thought not. He considered that the true ground in these cases, where the contract is void, is to be found in the absence, rather than the failure, of consideration; and in this he was followed by the Court of Appeal. This had the effect that the courts below were not troubled by the question whether there had been a total failure of consideration.

The approach so adopted may have found its origin in the idea, to be derived from a well known passage in the speech of Viscount Simon LC in *Fibrosa Spolka Akcyjna v Fairbairn Lawson Combe Barbour Ltd* [1943] AC 32, 48, that a failure of consideration only occurs where there has been a failure of performance by the other party of his obligation under a contract which was initially binding. But the concept of failure of consideration need not be so narrowly confined. In particular it appears from the annuity cases themselves that the courts regarded them as cases of failure of consideration; and concern has been expressed by a number of restitution lawyers that the approach of Hobhouse J is contrary to principle and could, if accepted, lead to undesirable consequences: see Professor Birks, 'No Consideration: Restitution after Void Contracts' (1993) 23 *UWALR* 195; Mr W.J. Swadling, 'Restitution for No Consideration' [1994] *RLR* 73; and Professor Burrows, 'Swaps and the Friction between Common Law and Equity' [1995] *RLR* 15. However since there is before your Lordships no appeal from the decision that the bank was entitled to recover the balance of the payments so made in a personal claim in restitution, the precise identification of the ground of recovery was not explored in argument before the Appellate Committee. It would therefore be inappropriate to express any concluded view upon it. Even so, I think it right to record that there appears to me to be considerable force in the criticisms which have been expressed; and I shall, when considering the issues on this appeal, bear in mind the possibility that it may be right to regard the ground of recovery as failure of consideration.

NOTES AND QUESTIONS

1. Lord Browne-Wilkinson also engaged in a brief analysis of the ground of restitution in his discussion of *Sinclair v Brougham* above, 6. Having concluded that the depositors in *Sinclair v Brougham* should have had a personal claim to recover the moneys at law based on a total failure of consideration, he held that the Court of Appeal in the present case 'were right to hold that the swap moneys were paid on a consideration that wholly failed. The essence of the swap agreement is that, over the whole term of the agreement, each party thinks he will come out best: the consideration for one party making a payment is an obligation on the other party to make counter-payments over the whole term of the agreement.'

2. Was the basis for restitution (a) absence of consideration, (b) total failure of consideration, (c) partial failure of consideration or, (d) some other factor?

3. In the *Sandwell* case (at first instance) the swap had been fully executed, yet restitution was ordered. Should restitution have been awarded in this case of a closed swap?

4. Was Hobhouse J correct to state that the phrase ' "failure of consideration" is one which in its terminology presupposes that there has been at some stage a valid contract which has been partially performed by one party' (see further above, 251)?

5. The claim that 'absence of consideration' should be recognized as a ground for restitution was the subject of considerable criticism in the academic literature (see, for example, P Birks (1993) 23 *UWALR* 195; W Swadling [1994] *RLR* 195, and A Burrows [1995] *RLR* 15). The issue arose again, in the context of a closed swap, before the Court of Appeal in the next case.

- • *Guinness Mahon & Co. Ltd v Kensington and Chelsea Royal London Borough Council* [1999] QB 215, Court of Appeal

The local authority entered into an interest rate swap under which all payments had been made (the agreement 'was closed') when the House of Lords held that these swap agreements were *ultra vires*. The Court of Appeal held that the local authority was entitled to restitution of the net payments it had made on the ground of total failure of consideration. However, the different judgments gave different explanations for why there had been a total failure of consideration.

Morritt LJ [*referred to the decision in* Westdeutsche *at trial and on appeal to the Court of Appeal and House of Lords and continued*] . . . Except for the decision of Hobhouse J. in Sandwell all these conclusions were reached in the case of an open swap whereas this case concerns a closed swap. For the council Mr. Béar, in his excellent argument, submitted that this makes all the difference. He pointed out that the only interest the bank had ever had in the capacity of the council was to ensure performance of the swap agreement but once it had been completed the bank was in exactly the same position as it would have been if the council had had the necessary capacity. He submitted that there were two stages to the consideration of any question of restitution: first, did the circumstances give rise to a case of unjust enrichment which should prima facie lead to a recovery; if so, did the circumstances give rise to a defence or bar to recovery negativing the prima facie case of unjust enrichment, for example, in the circumstances it was not unjust? He submitted that there is no authority binding on this court on the question whether full performance of a void contract precluded a claim for recovery which would have succeeded in the case of partial performance. He submitted that the decision of Hobhouse J. in Sandwell was in conflict with the observation of Bayley J. in *Davis v Bryan*. He suggested that to answer the question in the negative would fail to give effect to *Rover International Ltd v Cannon Film Sales Ltd* [1989] 1 W.L.R. 912. Quite apart from authority, he argued that there was nothing unjust in refusing recovery for the 'enrichment' of the council which would result because it would be exactly that for which the parties had bargained. He sought support for his arguments from the statements in Goff & Jones, *The Law of Restitution*, 4th ed. (1993), p. 61:

'No doubt it is right that a party who has received the very thing which he has contracted to receive should be unable to reopen the transaction to recover his money'

and in Professor Birks's article, 'No Consideration: Restitution after Void Contracts' (1993) 23 W.A.L.R. 195, 206:

'if we stand back from authority, there is in fact no compelling reason to allow a plaintiff to recover the value of his performance if he has received in exchange for it all that he expected. His ground for restitution, if it exists, must be purely technical.'

He pointed out that acceptance of his argument would align the law of England and Wales with the American Law Institute, Restatement of the Law of Restitution (1937), p. 192, section 47, in which it is stated:

'A person who, in order to obtain the performance of a promise given or believed to have been given by another and in exchange therefor, has conferred upon the other a benefit other than the performance of services or the making of improvements to the land or chattels of the other, is entitled to restitution from the other if the transferor, because of a mistake of law, (a) erroneously believed the promise to be binding upon him and (b) did not obtain the benefit expected by him in return.'

The notes to that section state, at p. 194:

'If the transfer receives what he expected to receive in exchange for what he gave, his right to resitution is discharged, as where the other party ratifies the act of an unauthorised agent with whom the transferor had dealt . . . or where a married woman, not bound by her promises, gives what she had promised . . .'

Mr. Béar's concluding submission was to the effect that if the argument for the bank was right it would amount to giving a right in restitution to repayment of money on the sole ground that its original payment had not been due. This, he contended, would be contrary to the proposition expressed by Lord Goff of Chieveley in *Woolwich Equitable Building Society v Inland Revenue Commissioners* [1993] A.C. 70, 172 that English law did not recognise such a cause of action.

Before considering these submissions in greater detail it is helpful to consider the position of the parties to an open swap and a closed swap. I assume a swap period of five years with swap payments between the bank and local authority every six months. The penultimate payments made 4 1/2 years after the date of the agreement have given rise to a net balance in favour of the local authority of £100,000. *Westdeutsche* establishes that if the original swap agreement was ultra vires the local authority the bank would have a cause of action for repayment of that balance as money had and received or for restitution at common law. Then I assume that six months later the final swap payments are made by a net payment from the bank to the local authority of a further £50,000. The argument for the council, if accepted, would deny the bank any right of recovery. But if the restitutionary principle requires the recognition of a cause of action for recovery of £100,000 when the penultimate payments were made it is difficult to see on what basis it denies any claim at all when on the final payments the balance in favour of the local authority rises to £150,000.

It was not suggested that the position differed depending on which party was the net winner. Thus I assume the converse case. After 4 1/2 years the balance of £100,000 is in favour of the bank. That sum is recoverable by the local authority because it had no capacity to enter into the agreement under which the various sums making up the balance were paid. On the last payment the balance in favour of the bank is increased by a further £50,000. That payment was made by the local authority with the same lack of capacity as all the earlier ones. It is hard to see any basis of logic or justice which would justify allowing the claim of the local authority to the balance due after the penultimate swap but denying it in respect of the final balance. The council seeks to justify the distinction on two theoretical legal bases.

The first theoretical basis on which the case for the council is put is that because over the whole of the term of the swap agreement the parties paid and received exactly what they had bargained for there can be no failure of consideration in the case of the closed swap. By contrast, in the case of the open swap one or more of the swaps envisaged has not been carried out; therefore, it is said, there is a total failure of consideration, for the parties have not received all that for which they bargained. But this argument assumes that in the case of a swap contract the relevant bargain was for the payments which were actually made rather than the legal obligation to make them. It is true that in *Fibrosa Spolka Akcyjna v Fairbairn Lawson Combe Barbour Ltd* [1943] A.C. 32 Viscount Simon L.C. said, at p. 48:

'when one is considering the law of failure of consideration and of the quasi-contractual right to recover money on that ground, it is, generally speaking, not the promise which is referred to as the consideration, but the performance of the promise.' But that case concerned a contract originally valid but subsequently frustrated due to the outbreak of war and not a contract void from the outset. In any event the statement was not intended to be exhaustive as is apparent from the qualification introduced by the words 'generally speaking.'

In *Rover International Ltd v Cannon Film Sales Ltd* [1989] 1 W.L.R. 912 the relevant agreement was invalid from the start because the party with which it was expressed to be made had not been incorporated at the time it was executed. The consequence was that Rover was not entitled to the benefit of the profit-sharing agreement it contained. The judge had rejected the claim of Rover to recover sums it had advanced in the belief that it was a valid and effective agreement on the ground that 'the consideration, if it had been a contract, had not failed' because Rover had received some of the benefits for which the contract provided. Kerr L.J. considered that the judge had adopted the wrong test. He said, at p. 923:

'The question whether there has been a total failure of consideration is not answered by consider-ing whether there was any consideration sufficient to support a contract or purported contract. The test is whether or not the party claiming total failure of consideration has in fact received any part of the benefit bargained for under the contract or purported contract.'

Kerr L.J. then considered the passage from the speech of Viscount Simon L.C. in *Fibrosa Spolka Akcyjna v Fairbairn Lawson Combe Barbour Ltd* [1943] A.C. 32, 48 which I have already quoted the decision of the Court of Appeal in *Rowland v Divall* [1923] 2 K.B. 500 and of Finnemore J. in *Warman v Southern Counties Car Finance Corporation Ltd* [1949] 2 K.B. 576. Kerr L.J. considered that in the latter two cases what was bargained for was lawful possession and a good title to the car and the use of and option to purchase the car. He concluded, in relation to the case before him, at p. 925:

'The relevant bargain, at any rate for present purposes, was the opportunity to earn a substantial share of the gross receipts pursuant to clause 6 of the schedule, with the certainty of at least breaking even by recouping their advance. Due to the invalidity of the agreement Rover got nothing of what they had bargained for, and there was clearly a total failure of consideration.'

Dillon L.J. did not find it necessary to consider the claim based on a total failure of consideration. Nicholls L.J. agreed with the reasoning of both Kerr L.J. and Dillon L.J. I accept, as Mr. Béar argued, that this case concerned a contract void from the start. But I do not accept Mr. Béar's further sub-mission that Kerr L.J. was considering only the performance of the promise. It seems to me that he was considering whether Rover obtained the legal rights for which it had stipulated as well as the fruits of such rights.

But whether or not my reading of the judgment of Kerr L.J. is correct one principle clearly established by the Court of Appeal in *Westdeutsche* [1994] 1 W.L.R. 938 is that in the case of a contract void from the start there must for that reason have been a total failure of consideration: *per* Dillon L.J., at p. 945h, and Leggatt L.J., at p. 953e. To the same effect is the speech of Lord Browne-Wilkinson in the House of Lords [1996] A.C. 669, 710h–711a. These passages, which I have already quoted, demonstrate that it is the very fact that the contract is ultra vires which constitutes the total failure of consideration justifying the remedy of money had and received or restitution for unjust enrichment. If partial performance of that assumed obligation in the case of an open swap does not preclude a total failure of that consideration then there is no basis on which complete performance of a closed swap could do so.

The second theoretical basis on which the council tries to justify the distinction between an open swap and a closed swap for which it contends is by reference to the principle of the severability or apportionment of consideration. Such a concept was referred to by Lord Wright in *Fibrosa Spolka Akcyjna v Fairbairn Lawson Combe Barbour Ltd.* [1943] A.C. 32, 64. He considered that where the entire consideration was severable there might be a total failure of consideration as to a severed part. The authority relied on was *Rugg v Minett*, 11 East 210 which was referred to by Dillon L.J. in *Westdeutsche*. The principle was further explained and applied in *Goss v Chilcott* [1996] A.C. 788, 797–798. Mr. Béar sought to apply that principle by severing each six-monthly swap both from the overall agreement and also from each of the others. In this manner he drew a distinction between the open swap, where it was suggested that there was a total failure of consideration with regard to the outstanding swap, and the closed swap, where there was no such failure because all had been performed. But a distinction cannot in my view be drawn on those lines. On that basis each six-monthly swap would be severable. If the relevant consideration for each swap was the *performance* of the obligation each party thought it was under in respect of that swap then each swap would be fully performed and neither party could recover from the other, either during the term of the swap agreement or thereafter, the amount by which what he paid exceeded what he received. If on the other hand the consideration for each swap was the *benefit* of the contractual obligation then there was a total failure of consideration in the case of each swap either before or after the term of the agreement had elapsed, thereby entitling the loser to recover the balance under a closed swap as well as an open one. Thus, neither horn of the dilemma justifies a distinction between a closed swap and an open swap. As Mr. Leggatt submitted for the bank, the proposition proved either too much or too little.

Mr. Leggatt also relied by way of analogy on the provisions of section 84 of the Marine Insurance Act 1906 and cases decided thereunder. I do not think that it is necessary to deal with them further, for I do not think that his argument requires any such support. I should for completeness add that I am not sure that the field of insurance is necessarily analogous with regard to claims paid under a policy made void by the section. In many such cases the insurer's claim for repayment of the insurance moneys paid would be likely to be met by the defence of change of position. No such defence is suggested in this case.

For these reasons I do not accept either of the theoretical bases on which the council seeks to justify a distinction between an open swap agreement and a closed swap agreement. In dealing with the first of them I have covered the criticism of the judgment of Hobhouse J. based on the judgment of Kerr L.J. in *Rover International Ltd v Cannon Film Sales Ltd* [1989] 1 W.L.R. 912. It is necessary then to consider the remaining criticism of the judgment of Hobhouse J., namely, that based on the judgment of Bayley J. in *Davis v Bryan*, 6 B. & C. 651, one of the annuity cases the application of which was expressly approved by Lord Goff of Chieveley in *Westdeutsche* [1996] A.C. 669, 683. The council contends that the conclusion of Hobhouse J. is contrary to that judgment. In *Davis v Bryan* the defendant had sold to the deceased an annuity for the life of the latter, whose estate was represented by the plaintiff, for a capital sum. The defendant had paid the annuity until the death of the annuitant. But as no memorial of the grant of the annuity had been registered the original grant was void. The plaintiff sought to recover the sum paid for the purchase of the annuity. He failed. Bayley J. said, at pp. 655–656:

'This appears to be a clear case on principles both of law and honesty. This is an action for money had and received, and I learned many years ago that such an action could not be maintained, if it were against equity and good conscience that the money should be recovered. Here a bargain was made, and the testator paid a consideration of £300, and the defendant agreed for that to pay a certain annuity. The testator received the whole of that which he bargained for, and now his representative says that the contract was void from the beginning. Is there anything like good conscience in the claim? Then is the contract void? The Act of Parliament says, that unless a memorial be duly enrolled, the deed of which no memorial is enrolled shall be void; but in many cases such words have been held to make the instrument voidable only at the will of the party, and I think we are at liberty to put that construction upon them in the present case.'

Holroyd J. gave as an additional ground the fact that the agreement had been fully executed. Littledale J. concurred. Hobhouse J. observed that that case appeared to be based on three grounds but had subsequently been regarded as authority for only the second, namely, that the grantee who had failed to register the transaction could not unilaterally avoid it. He concluded that it did not establish any proposition of assistance to Sandwell in relation to the closed swap save that in an action for money had and received it is always necessary to have regard to considerations of equity and good conscience. I agree with Hobhouse J. The grant of the annuity had not, according to the decision of the court, been void from the start because the grantor had never sought to avoid it and the grantee could not rely on his own failure to register. Accordingly there had not been a total failure of consideration because not only had the annuity been paid in full but also the grant had never been avoided by the grantor. Thus that case is distinguishable from that of a contract void from the start because it was ultra vires.

It must be borne in mind that the ultra vires doctrine exists for the protection of the public. This was stated in relation to limited companies by Lord Parker of Waddington and Lord Wrenbury in *Cotman v Brougham* [1918] A.C. 514, 520, 522, and in relation to statutory corporations by Lord Templeman in *Hazell v Hammersmith and Fulham London Borough Council* [1992] 2 A.C. 1, 36. It is true, as Hobhouse J. observed in *Westdeutsche*, that once the transaction has been held to have been void from the start the effect of the doctrine has been exhausted so far as the corporation is concerned for no illegality is involved, though it may have further implications and effect on the officers of the corporation. But that does not mean that the court should apply the law of restitution so as to minimise the effect of the doctrine. If, as the council contends, there is no claim for money had and received in the case of a completed swap then practical effect will be given to a transaction which the doctrine of ultra vires proclaims had no legal existence. The House of Lords declined so to do in *Sinclair v Brougham* [1914] A.C. 398 on the theory, now discredited, that the restitutionary claim was based on an implied promise. If the contractual promise was void because it was ultra vires, how could the law imply a promise to the like effect? Though the basis of the implied promise may now have gone, in my view the general principle must remain that an ultra vires transaction is of no legal effect. It must follow that the recipient of money thereunder has no right to it. If he keeps it he will be enriched. If he does not then or subsequently obtain a right to keep it such enrichment will be unjust. The claim for money had and received may be defeated by the defence of change of position. But in the absence of such a defence, and none was suggested in this case, it seems to me to be no answer to the claim to say that once the transaction has been fully performed the bank no longer has any interest in the capacity of the corporation, or that both parties have received the expected return. Nor does it appear to me to be accurate to describe the party's ability to recover his net payments as a windfall. If any of those factors, not amounting to the defence of change of position, was an answer to the claim it would attribute some effect to the transaction the law had declared to have none.

The passage in Goff & Jones, *The Law of Restitution*, 4th ed., p. 401 which I quoted earlier is not specifically related to payments made in purported performance of an ultra vires contract. Nor, with respect to Professor Birks, do I agree that there is no compelling reason to allow the bank to recover the value of its performance. The bank did not get in exchange for that performance all it expected, for it did not get the benefit of the contractual obligation of the local authority. Likewise, in reference to section 47 of the American Restatement, the bank did not get the benefit it expected in the form of a contractual obligation.

I agree with Hobhouse J. that there is no principle which could justify drawing a distinction between a closed swap and an open swap. I can summarise my reasons for that conclusion in the following propositions. (1) A contract which is ultra vires one of the parties to it is and always has been devoid of any legal contractual effect. (2) Payments made in purported performance thereof are necessarily made for a consideration which has totally failed and are therefore recoverable as money had and received. Thus, at the first stage of the inquiry suggested in the submissions of Mr. Béar, the circumstances do give rise to a case of unjust enrichment which should prima facie lead to a recovery. (3) A party to an apparent swap contract which is void because ultra vires one party is entitled so to recover the amount by which what he paid exceeds what he received, whether or not the apparent contract has been completely performed, for there is a total failure of consideration whether it is regarded as entire or severable. (4) The fact that the swap contract, though ultra vires and void, has been fully performed does not constitute a defence or bar to the recovery of the net payment as money had and received, for the recipient had no more right to receive or retain the payment at the conclusion of the contract than he did before. Thus, at the second stage of the inquiry suggested by Mr. Béar, there are no grounds negativing the prima facie case of unjust enrichment. (5) Proposition (1) is not disputed. Propositions (2) and (3) are established by the decision of the Court of Appeal in Westdeutsche and supported by dicta in the House of Lords in the same case. Proposition (4) is inherent in that decision and those dicta and is a necessary corollary of the principle of ultra vires and the purpose for which it exists.

I would dismiss this appeal.

Waller LJ: I agree that this appeal should be dismissed, essentially for the reasons given by Morritt L.J. I would however like to express shortly certain thoughts of my own.
I need not repeat Morritt L.J.'s analysis of the facts or his full history of the litigation relating to 'swaps' and I will gratefully adopt his terminology.

Although I think Morritt L.J. is right that the general statements he quotes from the judgments of Dillon and Leggatt L.JJ. in the Court of Appeal in *Westdeutsche* [1994] 1 W.L.R. 938 are decisive of this case, I have at certain stages had some doubt about it. I am furthermore doubtful whether the passages quoted from the speeches of Lord Goff and Lord Browne-Wilkinson in the House of Lords in the same case [1996] A.C. 669 can be taken as supporting fully the basis on which Hobhouse J. and the Court of Appeal formulated the grounds for recovery for money had and received in the swaps context. This may not be important in the open swaps situation but could be relevant in the closed swaps case.

The Court of Appeal and the House of Lords were of course dealing only with an 'open swap' situation, and it seems to me that Lord Goff was clearly sounding a note of caution as to whether the basis for recovery was correctly analysed in a way that might make a difference in the 'closed swaps' context.

Lord Goff refers, at p. 683d-h, to Professor Birks's article, 'No Consideration: Restitution after Void Contracts' (1993) 23 W.A.L.R. 195 and other articles. He ends that passage recognising the fact that there was not before the Appellate Committee any appeal as to the correctness or otherwise of the decision relating to the basis of recovery but saying:

'. . . I think it right to record that there appears to me to be considerable force in the criticisms which have been expressed; and I shall, when considering the issues on this appeal, bear in mind the possibility that it may be right to regard the ground of recovery as failure of consideration.'

Because only 'open swaps' were under consideration that statement should not, as it seems to me, be taken as endorsement necessarily that 'closed swaps' could be analysed on the basis that there had been a failure of consideration. Reference to Professor Birks's article and approval of the criticisms should, if anything, be taken as an indication to the contrary.

I was much persuaded by Mr. Béar's arguments, expanding on Professor Birks's article, that there should be a distinction between 'open' and 'closed' swaps. There is in my view great force in the argument that 'absence' of consideration as opposed to 'failure' of consideration should not by itself be a ground for restitution. If one applies the concept of failure as opposed to absence of consideration, failure of consideration still provides a ground for restitution in relation to an open swap. This much is clearly recognised by Lord Goff and was accepted by Mr. Béar. If, however, the proper concept is failure, and not absence, the position may well be different in relation to a 'closed swap,' although—and this seems to me important in the context of this case—Professor Birks would suggest, depending on the circumstances, that there may be some other basis for restitution.

I follow the force of the 'absurdity' argument that Morritt L.J. relies on for suggesting that there should be no difference between an 'open swap' and a 'closed swap.' But, prima facie, the right which A has to reclaim money paid flows from the fact that B has been able to refuse to perform the contract, or been released or prevented from performing or obtaining performance of the contract, but if the remedy of restitution is not allowed, that will leave B unjustly enriched at the expense of A. I have serious doubts as to whether simply because a party can show that a contract between them duly completed was void for whatever reason, that should automatically lead to the court being prepared simply to unravel the contract.

I can illustrate the point I wish to make by reference to one of the cases cited to us and referred to in Professor Birks's article, *In re Phoenix Life Assurance Co.* (1862) 2 J. & H. 441; 31 L.J.Ch. 749. In that case the court was concerned with an insurance company acting ultra vires by issuing marine policies when its powers were only to issue life policies. Three points had to be dealt with. First, could those insureds under marine policies prove for their claims under those policies? The answer was 'No.' Second, could insureds prove on judgments already obtained and on bills of exchange already issued? One report (2 J. & H. 448) would suggest 'Yes,' but the other report (31 L.J.Ch. 752) would suggest there was a change of mind by Sir W. Page Wood V.-C. Third, could the insureds reclaim the premiums paid? The answer was 'Yes.' The case does not deal with whether the insurance company would have been able to reclaim moneys actually paid out on claims under the void marine policies, but the impression one gains from the debate on the judgments and the bills of exchange is that it was not contemplated that they could do so. My instinct would further suggest that even now with the further recognition of restitutionary remedies, and even in the absence of a change of position defence, the court would be reluctant to allow the insurance company to recover, there being nothing unconscionable in the insureds retaining the benefit of the claims which they received, not being aware of the ultra vires point and believing the same to be due for the premiums paid. There was little argument before us by reference to those cases demonstrating that payments made to 'close a transaction' are regarded as voluntary payments and irrecoverable: see, for example, Lord Goff's speech in *Woolwich Equitable Building Society v Inland Revenue Commissioners* [1993] A.C. 70, 165g. But it may be that would be a basis on which recovery would be refused.

In my view authorities also referred to in Professor Birks's article, such as *Pearce v Brain* [1929] 2 K.B. 310 (a case relating to a contract at that time absolutely void under which an infant had exchanged his motorcycle for a car, but where despite the nullity of the contract the court did not order restitution and counter-restitution) and *Steinberg v Scala (Leeds) Ltd.* [1923] 2 Ch 452 a case where an infant under a contract by this time voidable avoided the contract and then surrendered the shares to avoid further calls but could not recover the price) also point in the direction of there not being a simple principle that if a contract is void, but completed as expected, there is still a right to restitution and counter-restitution so as to unravel the contract. That principle would seem to be contrary to the principles recognised by Lord Goff in the *Woolwich* case, at pp. 165d, 172d. What is more, if the principle were so simple and straightforward—voidness equals rights on both sides simply to have returned to them that which has been transferred—why had that not been spelled out clearly in some authority prior to *Westdeutsche*.

But the fact that there is no general principle entitling one party to a void contract to obtain restitution and an unravelling of the contract on that basis does not mean that the court should never provide that remedy in a situation in which a contract is held to be void ab initio. Professor Birks indeed does not suggest that there may or should not be restitutionary remedies available where void contracts have been entered into and completed in certain circumstances. He simply argues for the basis of the remedy being accurately recognised and described so that recovery is only allowed in appropriate situations. One difficulty for Mr. Béar seems to me to be that Professor Birks would suggest that in the swaps cases the banks should be entitled to recover even on a 'closed swap.' The first basis suggested is that of mistake. It is of course recognised that English law would have to be liberalised to achieve that result since 'mistake of law' is still not a recognised basis for recovery despite criticisms: see Lord Goff in the *Woolwich* case, at p. 164d. The other alternative suggested by Professor Birks as a basis of recovery would be, as he puts it at one stage, 'some policy transcending both the plaintiff's intentions and the defendant's conduct which requires that restitution be granted:' 23 W.A.L.R. 195, 206.

It is, I think, of interest that one can recognise in the judgment of, for example, Leggatt L.J. in the Court of Appeal in *Westdeutsche* support for the view he is taking being gained from policy considerations. The passage with which his judgment starts, at p. 951, is pure policy:

'The parties believed that they were making an interest swaps contract. They were not, because such a contract was ultra vires the council. So they made no contract at all. The council say that they should receive a windfall, because the purpose of the doctrine of ultra vires is to protect council taxpayers whereas restitution would disrupt the council's finances. They also contend that it would countenance "unconsidered dealings with local authorities." If that is the best that can be said for refusing restitution, the sooner it is enforced the better. Protection of council taxpayers from loss is to be distinguished from securing a windfall for them. The disruption of the council's finances is the result of ill-considered financial dispositions by the council and its officers. It is not the policy of the law to require others to deal at their peril with local authorities, nor to require others to undertake their own inquiries about whether a local authority has power to make particular contracts or types of contract. Any system of law, and indeed any system of fair dealing, must be expected to ensure that the council do not profit by the fortuity that when it became known that the contract was ineffective the balance stood in their favour. In other words, in circumstances such as these they should not be unjustly enriched.'

There is also, dare I say it, a hint in the above passage, and indeed in a later passage of Leggatt L.J., at p. 953e, being influenced by the fact that the bank was under a mistaken belief that the contract was valid. It follows that thus, for long periods while the contracts were being worked out, the bank was exposed to the possibility that if payments came in its direction it might have to repay them.

I wholeheartedly agree with the passage in Leggatt L.J.'s judgment quoted above and would suggest that there is no injustice in the council being bound to repay. Indeed in one sense it can be said that the council was 'unjustly' enriched, though the sense seems to me slightly different from the unjust enrichment usually relied on.

We may in one sense be at a crossroads. Hobhouse J. has held that the bank should succeed on a 'closed swap.' possibly stretching the lack—to use a neutral word—of consideration basis in order to do so. That basis has in fact been approved by the Court of Appeal and we are bound by it. I have no compunction in dismissing the appeal not only because of the binding nature of that decision but because although I feel, if the matter were considered at a higher level, there may well be further elaboration of the appropriate basis, the result will be the same.

Robert Walker LJ: I have had the advantage of reading in draft the judgment of Morritt L.J. I agree that this appeal should be dismissed, very largely for the reasons set out in the judgment of Morritt L.J., but I add some comments in my own words.

I gratefully adopt Morritt L.J.'s summary of the facts and of the course of the proceedings in Westdeutscheand Sandwell. As Morritt L.J. says, this appeal is in substance, though not in form an appeal from the decision of Hobhouse J. on the first closed swap in *Sandwell* [1994] 4 All E.R. 890. Hobhouse J. dealt with that point quite shortly, at pp. 923–924, and in summaries, at pp. 936, 954. He said of the fully performed annuity case, *Davis v Bryan*, 6 B. & C. 651, at p. 924:

> '[it] does not establish any proposition of assistance to Sandwell in relation to the first Sandwell swap save that in any action for money had and received it is always necessary to have regard to considerations of equity and good conscience.'

The Court of Appeal [1994] 1 W.L.R. 938 upheld Hobhouse J.'s conclusions in *Westdeutsche* both as to the personal restitutionary remedy (money had and received) and as to the proprietary restitutionary remedy (no passing of property in equity). Had that case not proceeded to the House of Lords [1996] A.C. 669 on the narrow issue of compound interest, the resolution of the present appeal would, I think, have presented little difficulty. This court would have been bound by its previous decision (which in turn rested on the decision of the House of Lords in *Sinclair v Brougham* [1914] A.C. 398) that the recipient of a net payment under a swaps transaction received money which belonged in equity to the payer. On that basis retention of the payer's money would on the face of it be unconscionable, subject to any defence of change of position, whether or not the swaps transaction had run its course. It is understandable that Hobhouse J., having concluded that he was not bound by any contrary principle in *Davis v Bryan*, 6 B. & C. 651, dealt with the point so shortly. It is, however, noteworthy that the learned article by Professor Birks (1993) 23 W.A.L.R. 195 relied on by the council was published before *Westdeutsche* had proceeded to either higher court. The House of Lords, although concerned only with the issue of compound interest, departed from *Sinclair v Brougham* as to the passing of property in equity, and so upset the symmetry between the claims at law and in equity which is a salient feature of the judgment of Hobhouse J., especially at p. 929 and again at p. 955:

> The plaintiff is entitled to recover that sum either as money had and received by the defendant to the use of the plaintiff or as money which in equity belongs to the plaintiff . . .'

See also, in this court, Dillon L.J., at pp. 946–947, and Leggatt L.J., at p. 952. In the House of Lords it was the opinion of Lord Browne-Wilkinson, at pp. 711–714, that *Sinclair v Brougham* should be departed from on the equitable proprietary claim, and Lord Slynn, Lord Woolf and Lord Lloyd agree on that point, at pp. 718, 720, 738. Lord Goff would not have departed from *Sinclair v Brougham* although he contemplated, at pp. 688–689, that it might 'fade into history' or be reinterpreted. Lord Goff had already referred, at p. 683, to Professor Birks's article and thought it right to record that he saw considerable force in its criticisms of Hobhouse J.'s approach on 'absence of consideration.' The other members of their Lordships' House did not refer to this point, except for a short passage in the speech of Lord Browne-Wilkinson, at pp. 710–711.

Since the *Westdeutsche* litigation evolved in that way, and the appeal to this court in Sandwell was compromised, the resolution of this appeal is not a short or simple matter, despite the excellent submissions from counsel on both sides. Three different lines of approach can be discerned in both sides' submissions: first impression, legal principle and authority.

(1) As a matter of first impression, the council's best point is that the swap transaction was carried through to completion just as the parties intended. One party ended up better off than the other (subject to any 'passing on') but that was always predictable. The council was enriched but it was not unjustly enriched. The bank's best point, as a matter of first impression, is the apparent absurdity pointed out in the judgment of Morritt L.J.: after 4 1/2 years one party might be £100,000 down and able to recover. What justice is there in denying it recovery if it is £150,000 down after five years?

(2) As a matter of legal principle, it is debatable whether the 'injustice' of the defendant's enrich-ment depends on the fact that (what was supposed to be) an entire contract has been interrupted before it has run its course, or simply on the invalidity of the supposed contract. The council argues for the former, calling in aid Professor Birks's article, 23 W.A.L.R. 195, 206: 'his ground for restitution, if it exists, is purely technical.' The bank argues for the latter, calling in aid Professor Birks's textbook, *An Introduction to the Law of Restitution* (1985), p. 223:

> 'Failure of the consideration for a payment . . . means that the state of affairs contemplated as the basis or reason for the payment has failed to materialise or, if it did exist, has failed to sustain itself.'

(3) As a matter of authority, the council submits that the case is concluded in this court by its decision in *Rover International Ltd v Cannon Film Sales Ltd* [1989] 1 W.L.R. 912; the bank submits that the case is concluded in this court by its decision in *Westdeutsche*, untouched (so far as the claim for money had and received is concerned) by the House of Lords' departure from *Sinclair v Brougham*. The council also relies on *Davis v Bryan* but the bank says that Hobhouse J. was right to treat it as largely irrelevant.

Although I have referred to these as different lines of approach they cannot easily be kept distinct. The tracks soon begin crossing and recrossing. I make two brief preliminary points, one on severance and the other on absurdity.

I do not find the notion of severance helpful to the resolution of this appeal. A swaps contract must, it seems to me, be regarded as an entire contract. That is obviously correct for a transaction (such as the Islington transaction described in *Westdeutsche*, at pp. 900–905) which provides for an 'upfront' payment by the bank. It is also correct, it seems to me, for a series of matched payments, since the transaction as a whole involves the parties taking a view as to the trend of short-term or medium-term interest rates over the whole period of the transaction. It is no more capable of dissection into separate obligations than a term policy at annual premiums on human life.

Moreover, it is in the stark financial nature of a swaps transaction that one party or the other will be seen, with the benefit of hindsight, to have got the better of the transaction; and if the other party is doing badly six months before the end of the transaction it is quite likely (but not, of course, certain) that it will be found to have done even worse when the transaction period comes to an end. That diminishes, but does not entirely remove, the force of the argument based on absurdity.

In the *Rover* case this court held, in relation to a void contract, that one party's claim to recover advance payments as money had and received was not barred by the defendant's plea that there had been no total failure of consideration. In *Westdeutsche* this court preferred Hobhouse J.'s formulation, in relation to a void contract, of 'absence of consideration.' This difference of approach calls for examination, although it may not in the end provide a clear answer to the issue raised in this appeal.

In English law the expression 'consideration' has at least three possible meanings. Its primary meaning is the 'advantage conferred or detriment suffered' (*Midland Bank Trust Co. Ltd v Green* [1981] A.C. 513, 531) which is necessary to turn a promise not under seal into a binding contract. In the context of failure of consideration, however, it is, in the very well known words of Viscount Simon L.C. in *Fibrosa Spolka Ackyjna v Fairbairn Lawson Combe Barbour Ltd.* [1943] A.C. 32, 48: 'generally speaking, not the promise which is referred to as the consideration, but the performance of the promise.' Then there is the older and looser, and potentially very confusing, usage of 'consideration' as equivalent to the Roman law 'causa' reflected in the traditional conveyancing expression, 'in consideration of natural love and affection:' see Professor Birks's textbook, p. 223. Professor Birks appears, at least superficially, to have moved his position in the last part of his more recent article, 23 W.A.L.R. 195, 233–234.

Where a contract is void ab initio there is in the eyes of the law no contract at all and so speaking of failure of consideration, in the sense of failure of contractually promised performance, may be confusing. That is why Hobhouse J. [1994] 4 All E.R. 890 preferred, as he explained at p. 924, to speak of 'absence of consideration' in the case of a purported contract which was void because ultra vires. If on the other hand a plaintiff (of full age and capacity) has got all that he bargained for, that is at first blush the opposite of failure of consideration. The proposition that such a plaintiff cannot complain because he has got all that he bargained for has a simple and direct appeal. It is a proposition which has been stated, more or less in those terms, in a number of otherwise disparate cases several of which were cited in argument.

Davis v Bryan, 6 B. & C. 651 was one of the cases of annuities void for non-registration under the Annuity Act 1813 (53 Geo. 3, c. 41) (re-enacting the Annuities Act 1777). The claim (for repayment of the purchase price) was made after the annuitant's death by his executrix. It failed. Bayley J. said, at p. 655:

'The testator received the whole of that which he bargained for, and now his representative says that the contract was void from the beginning. Is there anything like good conscience in the claim?'

In that case there had been a bargain, and its statutory avoidance for non-registration within 20 days (the obligation being treated as one which fell on the grantee) seems to have been treated as making the annuity voidable ab initio by the grantor. That is one of the grounds of decision discernible in *Davis v Bryan* and, in the view of Hobhouse J., that has emerged as the main ground of decision.

In *Steinberg v Scala (Leeds) Ltd.* [1923] 2 Ch 452 the plaintiff, a minor, had paid for shares allotted to her and sought to recover the payment on the ground of total failure of consideration. The shares had been registered in her name and she could have sold them. Lord Sterndale M.R. said, at p. 459:

'If the plaintiff were a person of full age suing to recover the money back on the ground, and the sole ground, that there had been a failure of consideration it seems to me it would have been impossible for her to succeed, because she would have got the very thing for which the money was paid and would have got a thing of tangible value.'

This is the case referred to in Goff & Jones, *The Law of Restitution*, 4th ed., p. 61 in a footnote to a sentence on which the council strongly relies:

'No doubt it is right that a party who has received the very thing which he has contracted to receive should be unable to reopen the transaction to recover his money.'

That is not in a section of the work dealing with void contracts.

In *Rowland v Divall* [1923] 2 K.B. 500 a car dealer had bought a car to which the seller had no title. The dealer succeeded in his claim to recover the purchase price on the ground of total failure of consideration. Atkin L.J. said, at p. 506:

'in this case there has been a total failure of consideration, that is to say that the buyer has not got any part of that for which he paid the purchase money. He paid the money in order that he might get the property, and he has not got it. It is true that the seller delivered to him the de facto possession, but the seller had not got the right to possession and consequently could not give it to the buyer.'

The vendor had gone through the motions of performance of his contract by handing over a car, but in the eyes of the law that was no performance because the car was stolen.

Then there is the decision, referred to by Goff & Jones, at p. 402, as anomalous, of the Privy Council in *Linz v Electric Wire Co. of Palestine Ltd.* [1948] A.C. 371. The appellant had been allotted what purported to be preference shares in the defendant company. Unlike the plaintiff in the Scala case, she was of full age but her case, which the Privy Council assumed to be correct, was that the company had no power under its memorandum and articles to issue the preference shares. After four years she sold her preference shares at a loss, still apparently unaware of the defect in title. Then another shareholder raised the issue in proceedings which were compromised, and the company made an offer to all its registered preference shareholders including, presumably, the plaintiff's successor in title to repay the amounts paid up on the shares. That offer was not made to the plaintiff herself, and she sued for repayment on the ground of total failure of consideration. The Privy Council rejected the claim. Lord Simonds said, echoing language which is becoming familiar, at p. 377:

'having been duly registered as a shareholder and having parted for value with her shares by a sale which the company recognised . . . she got exactly that which she bargained to get.'

He rejected the plaintiff's counsel's reliance on *Rowland v Divall*:

'That case might have assisted him, if the fact was that the appellant still held the shares . . . But it does not avail him in a case where the shareholder has sold his shares.'

In fact the car dealer in *Rowland v Divall* had resold the stolen car to a customer and had very properly returned the purchase money to the customer. In *Westdeutsche* [1994] 4 All E.R. 890, 928 Hobhouse J. treated *Linz*'s case and *Rowland v Divall* as depending on an analysis of whether the defendant's breach was 'fundamental to the particular contractual transaction.' That was, he said, 'very different from the present case where there was in truth no bargain at all and problems of deciding what was the essential part of the bargain do not arise . . .'

In *Rover International Ltd v Cannon Film Sales Ltd* [1989] 1 W.L.R. 912 a complicated commercial contract was void because one of the parties, Rover, had not been incorporated at the date of the purported contract. Non-existence is the most extreme form of incapacity. Rover had made a series of payments to Cannon in the expectation of a share of substantial profits from the distribution of cinema films in Italy. The parties fell out and the invalidity of the supposed contract was discovered before Rover had received any share of profits. It was conceded that Rover was entitled to a quantum meruit. But it was argued that Rover could not recover its payments because it had obtained possession of films and would get a quantum meruit payment. Kerr L.J. said, at p. 923:

'The test is whether or not the party claiming total failure of consideration has in fact received any part of the benefit bargainedfor under the contract or purported contract.'

Then he applied that test to the facts, at pp. 924–925:

'And delivery and possession were not what Rover had bargained for. The relevant bargain, at any rate for present purposes, was the opportunity to earn a substantial share of the gross receipts pursuant to clause 6 of the schedule, with the certainty of at least breaking even by recouping their advance. Due to the invalidity of the agreement Rover got nothing of what they had bargained for, and there was clearly a total failure of consideration. This equally disposes of [Cannon's counsel's] ingenious attempt to convert his concession of a quantum meruit, in particular the element of reasonable remuneration, into consideration in any relevant sense. Rover did not bargain for a quantum meruit, but for the benefits which might flow from clause 6 of the schedule. That is the short answer to this point.'

Dillon L.J., at p. 933, saw the case as a classic case of money paid under a mistake of fact. He expressed no view on the issue of total failure of consideration. Nicholls L.J. agreed with both judgments.

In *Westdeutsche* Hobhouse J. discussed the *Rover* case in some detail and differed from Kerr L.J.'s 'essentially contractual' analysis. He said, at p. 929:

'In my judgment the correct analysis is that any payments made under a contract which is void ab initio, in the way that an ultra vires contract is void, are not contractual payments at all. They are payments in which the legal property in the money passes to the recipient, but in equity the property in the money remains with the payer.'

In the Court of Appeal [1994] 1 W.L.R. 938 Dillon L.J. made no reference to the *Rover* case.

Leggatt L.J. did, at pp. 952–953, and agreed with Hobhouse J.'s approach, although he also agreed with Kerr L.J.'s statement of the test as being whether the plaintiff had in fact received any 'benefit bargained for under the contract *or purported contract*.' (Emphasis supplied.)

It may be important to note that the *Rover* case [1994] 1 W.L.R. 912 was an appeal to this court after a three-week trial [1987] B.C.L.C. 540 which appears to have concentrated on issues of fact and, so far as the law was concerned, on estoppel by convention. The judge dealt very shortly indeed, at pp. 545–546, with the issues which occupied this court's attention. In this court Kerr L.J. referred to Viscount Simon L.C.'s well known statement in the Fibrosa case and to *Rowland v Divall*, both cases where there had initially been a valid contract. He was concerned to point out that Rover's position was clearer and stronger. His earlier reference, at p. 923, to 'the contract or purported contract' cannot have been intended in the context to make any general equation of valid and void contracts in relation to failure of consideration.

I am not therefore persuaded that there is any serious difference in principle between the decisions of this court in the *Rover* case and *Westdeutsche*, and the fact that Dillon L.J. was a member of both constitutions but did not advert to a difference tends to confirm that there is none. The point was more fully considered in *Westdeutsche*, especially by Leggatt L.J. in the passages at pp. 952–953, to which I have already referred. Leggatt L.J., after referring to the part of Hobhouse J.'s judgment at 929e–f, concluded: 'There can have been no consideration under a contract void abinitio. So it is fallacious to speak of the failure of consideration having been partial.' I respectfully agree with that. Either there was total failure of consideration, in that neither side to the supposed contract undertook any valid obligation, or there was, in Hobhouse J.'s preferred expression, absence of consideration. The choice between the two expressions may be no more than a matter of which is the apter terminology. When *Westdeutsche* was in the House of Lords [1996] A.C. 669 Lord Goff pointed out, at p. 683, that 'the concept of failure of consideration need not be so narrowly confined.' It becomes more than a matter of terminology only if the expression 'absence of consideration' is supposed to take the case right out of any contractual context and into a claim to recover a payment simply because it was not due, a broader ground of recovery than has so far been recognised by English law: see *Woolwich Equitable Building Society v Inland Revenue Commissioners* [1993] A.C. 70, especially at pp. 166–172.

Where there is initially a valid contract total failure of consideration connotes a failure by one contracting party to perform any part of his essential obligation under the contract, as the vendor failed in *Rowland v Divall* even though he had delivered a car to the purchaser. Where a supposed contract is void ab initio, or an expected contract is never concluded, as in *Chillingworth v Esche* [1924] 1 Ch 97, no enforceable obligation is ever created but the context of a supposed or expected contract is still relevant as explaining what the parties are about. An advance payment made in such circumstances is not a gift and is not to be treated as a gift. A net payment under an ultra vires swaps transaction has this much at least in common with the purchase of a stolen car, that the recipient thinks he is getting a clean title but he is wrong. That conclusion is not affected by the House of Lords' decision that property in the net payment passes in equity as well as at law. The recipient's title is still overshadowed by the payer's personal restitutionary claim, and if that shadow is there throughout the period of the transaction it would be paradoxical if it vanished at the moment when, and simply because, the contract, had it been a valid contract, would then have been fully performed. With a valid contract total failure of consideration and full performance are at the opposite ends of the spectrum. The same is not true of a void contract. That is to my mind the real force of the argument based on absurdity. The injustice of the council's enrichment does not vanish because the term of the void contract ran its course.

I am in full agreement with Morritt L.J.'s observations on *Davis v Bryan*, 6 B. & C. 651. On the facts of that case it would have been remarkable, and unconscionable, if the executrix had been able to recover. The reasoning in the *Linz* case [1948] A.C. 371 is difficult to understand and the case is probably best regarded, as suggested by *Goff & Jones*, as anomalous.

For those reasons, and for the reasons given in the judgment of Morritt L.J., I agree that this appeal should be dismissed.

NOTE

This decision was one of the central cases relied upon by Birks for his argument that English law had changed direction and adopted a civilian-type approach to unjust enrichment (above, 137–138). In the following extract Birks explains the importance of the closed swap cases, like *Guinness Mahon*, to his view.

• P Birks, *Unjust Enrichment* (2nd edn 2005), 114–16

ABSENCE OF BASIS IS NOT ANOTHER UNJUST FACTOR

The list of unjust factors was already miscellaneous. In principle it could admit another reason for restitution, just as tort can admit new wrongs. But absence of basis is not a deficiency of consent; nor is it a policy dictating that the enrichment should be reversed; it is also not a reason for restitution independent of the other members of the list. This means that it cannot join either of the two groups of unjust factors, and it cannot make a third group of its own. One could not smuggle 'vertebrates' into a list of mammals. In the same way absence of basis cuts across the list of unjust factors.

The first group comprises all the intent-based unjust factors. Absence of basis cannot go in that group. We have already seen that the mistake in *Kelly v Solari* can be used as an impairment of intent or as the reflection of a non-existent basis for the enrichment. It would be absurd to suggest, as would be suggested by including absence of basis in the list of unjust factors, that by demonstrating two approaches applicable to that case that we have revealed the presence of two different causes of action. Then, when we look down the list of the unjust factors in this group, one after another they all invalidate the contract or gift which would otherwise provide the explanatory basis of the recipient's enrichment—no consent, spontaneous mistake, mistake induced by misrepresentation, pressure, undue influence, and so on. These cannot stand beside absence of basis, only under it.[1]

The other group of unjust factors comprises policies which call for restitution. Policies behind invalidity can fit in the list of reasons why an enrichment should be given up. The effect of treating the policy behind the invalidity as the reason for restitution is to select certain invalidities as meriting that response and thus to prevent all invalidities from automatically presenting themselves in that

---

1 '[I]t is remarkable that these unjust factors do nothing else than mirror the reasons why the contract is invalid': S Meier in P Birks and F Rose (eds), *Lessons of the Swaps Litigation* (LLP Mansfield London 2000) 168, 211.

character. Invalidity is then not a reason for restitution unless the policy behind it is one which is reinforced by and not undermined by restitution. There are hints in *Guinness Mahon v Kensington & Chelsea Royal London BC* that the courts could have made restitution under void interest swaps turn on such a policy. They could have said that it was essential in the longer-term interests of the community to compel respect for the limits put upon the authorities' powers by ordering restitution of money obtained beyond those powers: public authorities had to learn that they must not play ducks and drakes with the limits on their powers.[2]

However, that is not how the case was decided. Except perhaps in the judgment of Waller LJ, the outcome is squarely rested on the invalidity of the swaps contract and the attendant absence of basis for the payments made under it. Absence of basis tells us that invalidity is a reason for restitution in itself. In that state of affairs the group of policy-motivated unjust factors becomes redundant. Invalidity in itself destroys the basis of the enrichment. It is obvious therefore that absence of basis cannot be integrated into this group.

If absence of basis cannot be assigned to either of the two groups of unjust factors, the list could only admit it as constituting a third group of its own. That possibility is shut out by the fact that it is also not independent of the two groups but, on the contrary, is instantiated in every member of the intent-based group, and it overwhelms and enlarges the policy-based group. In the end, therefore, there is no question of integrating absence of basis anywhere in the list of unjust factors. Its recognition and application in the swaps cases is a rejection of the approach through unjust factors. They are incompatibly alternative methods of deciding which enrichments are unjust.

Absence of basis is now the only unjust factor in English law. This makes for lawyer's law. No passenger on the Clapham omnibus ever demanded restitution for want of legally sufficient basis. But the change of course is not a disaster. Nor is it to be regarded as dictated only by the doctrine of precedent. The civilian method at which our courts have arrived, although it too leaves room for many arguments in difficult cases, is efficient, tried, and tested. We borrowed some of it in the 18th century, only to be diverted into the heresy of implied contract.

Emerging from that nonsense, we attempted a more homely development of what we then borrowed. It served us well enough but occasionally led us into severe difficulties, even into downright error. The dangers which Evans foresaw in the civilian method will one way or another be overcome under the fifth question. Defences are infinitely more vigorous than they were even 20 years ago. The best course will be to welcome the change. Surgeons now operate on babies *en ventre*. In effect the law of unjust enrichment has been repaired even before finally escaping from the law of restitution.

NOTES AND QUESTIONS

1. Do you agree with Birks that, except for the judgment of Waller LJ, the outcome of the case 'is squarely rested on the invalidity of the swaps contract'? How can this explain the quotation by Morritt LJ and Robert Walker LJ, with approval, from *Rover International Ltd v Cannon Film Sales* that 'the test is whether or not the party claimaing total failure of consideration has in fact received any part of the benefit bargained for'?

2. If, as Morritt LJ suggests, the *ultra vires* doctrine exists for the protection of the public, and if this means that the local council was always entitled to restitution of any net payments made to the bank, then did the bank (which could never win from the swap) receive any part of the benefit bargained for?

3. One case which was referred to with approval by Morritt LJ, in the course of rejecting the second basis upon which the local authority sought to distinguish between the

---

2 *Guinness Mahon* [1999] QB 215, 229 (Morritt LJ), 232–3 (Waller LJ).

open and closed swap cases, was the decision in *Goss v Chilcott* [1996] AC 788. In that case, which is extracted immediately below, Lord Goff explained that the 'consideration' failed because no payments of the capital sum had been made, not because the agreement was void.

- ● *Goss v Chilcott* [1996] AC 788, Privy Council

A finance company agreed to lend the defendants, Mr and Mrs Goss, the sum of $30,000 for three months on the security of a mortgage over their nursery property. The defendants in turn agreed to lend $30,000 to Mr Haddon, a director of the finance company, who was the brother of Mrs Goss, and it was agreed that he would repay the advance and have the security cancelled. The finance company paid the $30,000 to a firm of solicitors, Haddon Marshall & Co., for the credit of the defendants, and it was retained by the solicitors until the defendants executed the mortgage, at which time the money was paid over at the defendants' direction to Mr Haddon. While the mortgage instrument was in the hands of Mr Haddon he altered it without the knowledge or authority of the defendants by extending the time for repayment to twelve months. Two interest payments were subsequently made but the advance was never repaid. The claimant, the liquidator of the finance company, then brought an action against the defendants claiming the principal and interest which remained due under the mortgage. His claim failed in the High Court of New Zealand where Neazor J held that an action could not be brought on the mortgage because it had been avoided by the alteration made by Mr Haddon. He also held that the claimant was not entitled to bring an action in money had and received because the consideration for the payment had not totally failed. The claimant appealed to the New Zealand Court of Appeal where it was held that the claimant was entitled to rely on the advance and the agreement to repay in order to recover the outstanding balance. On the defendants' appeal to the Privy Council it was held that the claimant could not rely upon the advance to recover the money because that had become merged in and superceded by the mortgage instrument (which had been avoided) but that the claimant was entitled to recover the balance on the ground that there had been a total failure of consideration.

Lord Goff (delivering the advice of the Privy Council): . . .

As their Lordships have already recorded, Neazor J held that the company could not succeed on its claim in restitution, because he considered that there had been no total failure of consideration for the loan, the defendants having furnished consideration for it in the form of the mortgage instrument. With this conclusion, their Lordships are unable to agree.

The advance was in fact paid by the company to Haddon Marshall & Co., as solicitors, but having regard to the terms on which they received it from the company, was retained by them in their trust account until after the defendants had executed the mortgage instrument. It was then available to the defendants but was in fact received by Mr Haddon, as agreed between him and the defendants. In these circumstances the loan appears in fact to have been advanced to the defendants pursuant to the terms of the mortgage instrument, the consideration for the advance being expressed to be the personal covenants by the defendants to repay the advance upon those terms. Even if (which their Lordships doubt) the loan had been paid pursuant to a preceding oral agreement between the company and the defendants, it must have been paid in consideration for the defendants' promise to repay it, though the ensuing loan contract would (as their Lordships have already indicated) have become merged in and superseded by the contract contained in the mortgage instrument.

But the consideration there referred to, necessarily implicit if not explicit in every loan contract, was the consideration necessary for the formation of the contract; and, as Viscount Simon LC observed in a much-quoted passage in his speech in *Fibrosa Spolka Akcyjna v Fairbairn Lawson Combe Barbour Ltd* [1943] AC 32, 48:

> 'when one is considering the law of failure of consideration and of the quasi-contractual right to recover money on that ground, it is, generally speaking, not the promise which is referred to as the consideration, but the performance of the promise. . . . If this were not so, there could never be any recovery of money, for failure of consideration, by the payer of the money in return for a promise of future performance, yet there are endless examples which show that money can be recovered, as for a complete failure of consideration, in cases where the promise was given but could not be fulfilled.'

Of course, in the case of a loan of money any failure by the borrower to repay the loan, in whole or in part, by the due date, will in ordinary circumstances give rise to a claim in contract for repayment of the part of the loan which is then due. There will generally be no need to have recourse to a remedy in restitution. But in the present case that course is, exceptionally, not open to the company, because the defendants have been discharged from their obligations under the mortgage instrument; and so the company has to seek recovery in restitution. Let it however be supposed that in the present case the defendants had been so discharged from liability at a time when they had paid nothing, by way of principal or interest, to the company. In such circumstances their Lordships can see no reason in principle why the company should not be able to recover the amount of the advance made by them to the defendants on the ground that the money had been paid for a consideration which had failed, viz. the failure of the defendants to perform their contractual obligation to repay the loan, there being no suggestion of any illegality or other ground of policy which precluded recovery in restitution in such circumstances.

In the present case however, although no part of the principal sum had been repaid by the defendants, two instalments of interest had been paid; and the question arises whether these two payments of interest precluded recovery on the basis that in such circumstances the failure of consideration for the advance was not total. Their Lordships do not think so. The function of the interest payments was to pay for the use of the capital sum over the period for which the loan was outstanding, which was separate and distinct from the obligation to repay the capital sum itself. In these circumstances it is, in their Lordships' opinion, both legitimate and appropriate for present purposes to consider the two separately. In the present case, since it is unknown when the mortgage instrument was altered, it cannot be known whether, in particular, the second interest instalment was due before the defendants were discharged from their obligations under the instrument. Let it be supposed however that both interest payments had fallen due before that event occurred. In such circumstances, there would have been no failure of consideration in respect of the interest payments rendering them recoverable by the defendants; but that would not affect the conclusion that there had been a total failure of consideration in respect of the capital sum, so that the latter would be recoverable by the company in full on that ground. Then let it be supposed instead that the second interest payment did not fall due until after the avoidance of the instrument. In such circumstances the consideration for that interest payment would have failed (at least if it was payable in advance), and it would prima facie be recoverable by the defendants on the ground of failure of consideration; but that would not affect the conclusion that the capital sum would be recoverable by the company also on that ground. In such a case, therefore, the capital sum would be recoverable by the lender, and the interest payment would be recoverable by the borrower; and doubtless judgment would, in the event, be given for the balance with interest at the appropriate rate: see *Westdeutsche Landesbank Girozentrale v Islington London Borough Council* [1994] 1 WLR 938. In either event, therefore, the amount of the loan would be recoverable on the ground of failure of consideration. In the present case, since no part of the capital sum had been repaid, the failure of consideration for the capital sum would plainly have been total. But even if part of the capital sum had been repaid, the law would not hesitate to hold that the balance of the loan outstanding would be recoverable on the ground of failure of consideration; for at least in those cases in which apportionment can be carried out without difficulty, the law will allow partial recovery on this ground: see *David Securities Pty. Ltd v Commonwealth Bank of Australia* (1992) 175 CLR 353, 383. . . .

NOTES AND QUESTIONS

1. Was the finding that there had been a total failure of consideration not rather artificial?

2. Should the courts now openly recognize that a partial failure of consideration can suffice to generate a restitutionary claim?

7. SUBSISTING CONTRACTS

In *Miles v Wakefield* [1987] AC 539 (above, 300–301) Lords Templeman and Brightman considered, obiter dicta, that an employee that took part in 'go slow' industrial action would not be entitled to wages but would be entitled to a *quantum meruit* for the reduced value of the work done. Their Lordships did not suggest that the contract must be terminated before such a restitutionary claim could be brought. In contrast, Lord Bridge found it 'difficult to understand the basis on which, in such a case, the employee in place of the remuneration at the contractual rate would become entitled to a quantum meruit'. The obiter dicta of Lords Templeman and Brightman was criticized by some commentators particularly because allowing restitution while a contract subsists fails to respect the parties' allocation of risk (e.g. J Beatson, 'Restitution and Contract: Non-Cumul?' (2000) 1 *Theoretical Inquiries in Law* 83; Burrows, 323–4; Goff and Jones, 525, 551). As Lord Goff said in *Pan Ocean Shipping v Creditcorp Ltd, The Trident Beauty* [1994] 1 WLR 161 at 166, 'serious difficulties arise if the law seeks to expand the law of restitution to redistribute risks for which provision has been made under an applicable contract'. However, a minority academic view argued that a subsisting contract should not prevent a claim for restitution where the terms of the contract are not inconsistent with restitutionary recovery (A Tettenborn, 'Subsisting contracts and failure of consideration—A Little Scepticism' [2004] *RLR* 2–3) or the contract did not govern the payment for the work done (G Mead 'Restitution within Contract?' (1991) 11 *LS* 172 at 186). In the following extract this issue is considered by two Justices of the High Court of Australia. Kirby J (in dissent) preferred the dominant academic view that restitution should not be allowed while a contract subsists. Callinan J rejected the view that restitution was only available if a contract is frustrated, discharged for breach, or held to be unenforceable or otherwise avoided.

- *Roxborough v Rothmans of Pall Mall Ltd* (2001) 208 CLR 516, High Court of Australia

The facts are considered above at 252.

Kirby J . . .

THE CLAIM TO RESTITUTION FOR A FAILURE OF CONSIDERATION

[165] The final ground upon which the retailers claimed relief was for restitution on the basis of a failure of consideration. The payments made by the retailers to the wholesaler were made in dis-

charge of express contractual obligations agreed between them. The wholesaler discharged its part of such obligations by supplying the goods in question to the retailers. Those goods were supplied in accordance with an agreed price. That price, in each instance, subsumed, and included within it, various component parts, only one of which was that of the licence fees. No doubt it also included component parts for notional charges for acquisition of raw tobacco product, warehousing, packaging, processing, transport, overheads and the like. The separate appearance of the component for the tobacco licence fees on the wholesaler's invoices was doubtless convenient for accounting purposes. It permitted the ready aggregation of the licence fees then thought to be payable under the Act. But the *legal* obligation of the retailers to the wholesaler was to pay the price of the goods in full. This was a single aggregate amount referable to each occasion of supply.[1] Indeed, until such payment was 'made in full' to the wholesaler, the property in the goods supplied remained with the wholesaler. The retailers then agreed to hold such goods in a fiduciary capacity as bailee.[2]

[166] In the foregoing circumstances, it is impossible to assert that there has been a total failure of consideration. The individual contracts between the wholesaler and the retailers were uncontestably valid. They were not ineffective. Nor were they terminated. Far from attempting to terminate the contracts for the supply of goods by the wholesaler, the retailers actually accepted the goods in every case. They onsold them to consumers, thereby recovering the component for licence fees about which they now complain. The law of restitution only rarely operates in the context of an effective contract.[3] The present, in my opinion, is not a case that falls within one of the recognised exceptions.

[167] The retailers nonetheless claimed to recover under a 'unifying principle' of restitution for unjust enrichment at their expense.[4] They did so on the basis that, notwithstanding that consideration had not *totally* failed, some *part* of the consideration could be separately identified, apportioned and then seen as having failed.[5] This submission should be rejected.

[168] By their terms, the contracts between the wholesaler and the retailers left the obligation of the wholesaler to pay the tobacco licence fee to the government entirely out of account. It was unsurprising that this should have been so. At the time the contracts were agreed to, the obligation to pay the tobacco licence fees arose not by any *contractual* agreement at all but by the operation of *statute* law, namely pursuant to the duties purportedly imposed by the Act. As the majority in the Full Court explained,[6] the retailers could succeed in a claim for restitution on the ground of failure of consideration only if the wholesaler was bound to them by the promise to pay the amount identified as being for the licence fees and such promise was wholly unperformed.

[169] In light of the then understanding of the obligations of the Act, it borders on the surreal to suggest that the wholesaler 'promised' the retailers that it would pay the licence fees to the government, in default of which payment there would be a failure of consideration in respect of that part of the price paid. Not only does this hypothesis defy the express terms upon which the parties traded with each other. It also contradicts the historical fact that the obligation of the wholesaler to pay the tax was an obligation imposed on the wholesaler not by private contract but by the terms of the Act.

[170] I therefore agree with the Full Court that the basis for asserting a right to recover at common law was not established. The moneys were not had and received by the wholesaler to

---

1 cl 6: see reasons of Callinan J at [187].   2 cl 10: see reasons of Callinan J at [187].

3 *Pavey & Matthews Pty. Ltd v Paul* (1987) 162 CLR 221 at 256; 69 ALR 577 at 604; Mason and Carter, *Restitution Law in Australia*, 1995, pp 83–4 [315]; cf. Beatson, 'Restitution and Contract: Non-Cumul?' (2000) 1 *Theoretical Inquiries in Law* 83 at 88.

4 Jones, 'Restitution: Unjust Enrichment as a Unifying Concept in Australia?' (1989) 1 *Journal of Contract Law* 8.

5 *David Securities* (1992) 175 CLR 353 at 382–3; 109 ALR 57 at 78–9; *Goss v Chilcott* [1996] AC 788 at 797–8; [1997] 2 All ER 110 at 116–17.

6 *Roxborough* (1999) 95 FCR 185 at 200 [52]; 167 ALR 326 at 340.

the use of the retailers. Properly analysed, they were had and received in discharge of a contractually stipulated price payable in full in exchange for the supply of specified goods which were duly delivered.

[171] This is not a surprising conclusion. Nor is it an application of the law of restitution different from the way that body of law has developed in Australia. The ghost of implied contract as the basis for restitution may indeed have been exorcised following the decision of this court in *Pavey & Matthews Pty. Ltd v Paul.*[7] But it is still necessary to demonstrate a legal foundation for any enforceable obligation to make restitution. Relevantly, the retailers propounded a partial failure of consideration for the contracts they entered with the wholesaler. But when this proposition fails, by reference to the analysis of the evidence and of the applicable legal principles, what is left? To establish an entitlement to restitution, at the least, some requirement in law and justice must be shown to displace the clear legal obligation that the retailers assumed to pay the wholesaler in full a price, meaning the entire price, for the supply of the goods duly received.

Callinan J . . . [197] I would reject the respondent's submission that it is only in cases in which contracts have been frustrated, discharged for breach, or held to be unenforceable, or otherwise avoided, that a party may obtain restitution. Gyles J answered that submission, correctly, in my opinion, in this way:[8]

> The contract [here] has been executed in all respects save for payment of the licence fee by the respondent. The licence fee is no longer payable. It cannot and will not be paid by the respondent. That is the end of the matter. Performance is no longer possible. If formal termination by the appellants is necessary, then bringing these proceedings is sufficient.

[198] This is also a case of the kind referred to by Mason CJ, Deane, Toohey, Gaudron and McHugh JJ in *David Securities Pty. Ltd v Commonwealth Bank of Australia:*[9]

> In cases where consideration can be apportioned or where counter-restitution is relatively simple, insistence on total failure of consideration can be misleading or confusing. In the present case, for instance, it is relatively simple to relate the additional amounts paid by the appellants to the supposed obligation under cl 8(b) of the loan agreements. The appellants were told that they were required to pay withholding tax and the payments that they made were predicated on the fact that, by doing so, they were discharging their obligation. Such an approach is no different in effect from the cases under the old statutes of usury whereby a borrower could recover from the lender the *excess interest* which the lender was prohibited from stipulating or receiving. [original emphasis]

[199] Accordingly, I am of the opinion that the appellants have made out a case for the recovery of the money paid on the basis that relevantly there has been a total failure of consideration, that is to say, a failure in respect of a discrete, clearly identified component of the consideration.

NOTES AND QUESTIONS

1. This case is not an example of restitution being allowed despite a subsisting contract because, as Callinan J observed, the contract had been discharged by complete performance. Nevertheless, the case squarely raises the issue, which arises in cases of subsisting contracts, of whether a claim in unjust enrichment can be brought despite the risk allocation of the

---

7 (1987) 162 CLR 221; 69 ALR 577; see Jones, 'Restitution: Unjust Enrichment as a Unifying Concept in Australia?' (1989) 1 *Journal of Contract Law* 8 at 14.

8 (1999) 95 FCR 185 at 214 [106]; 167 ALR 326 at 354.

9 (1992) 175 CLR 353 at 383; 109 ALR 57 at 79 (footnote omitted).

contract remaining entirely undisturbed. Although only Kirby and Callinan JJ discussed this issue explicitly, in their joint judgment Gleeson CJ, Gaudron and Hayne JJ also said that allowing restitution for failure of that basis would not subvert contractual risk because the tax was externally imposed, and was not the subject of negotiation.

2. The approach of Kirby J suggests that the basis for the payment of the price by the retailers (including the licence fee) was the delivery of the tobacco. The other members of the court treat the basis of the payment of the licence fee as being for the liability of the wholesaler to the NSW Government. Is it possible for different payments under a contract to be made on different bases?

3. Tettenborn ([2002] *RLR* 1 at 2) gives the following example: I agree to buy a rare stamp from your collection and pay you £1,000 in advance. A couple of days later I change my mind and tell you I do not want the stamp. Tettenborn suggests that it is 'clearly absurd' to suggest that you can keep the £1000 by affirming the contract and maintaining that you remain willing and able to perform. Do you agree? Does it make a nonsense of contracting if, at any time, I can insist upon *either* a refund of my money or specific performance (and delivery) of the stamp?

4. In the next two extracts the same approach is taken to this issue: Birks, Beatson and Virgo all suggest that restitution should only be allowed whilst a contract subsists if it would not disturb the legitimate hopes and fears inherent in the bargain. However, they reach different conclusions in the application of this approach to *Roxborough*.

- ## P Birks, 'Failure of consideration and its Place on the Map'(2002) *OUCLJ* 1, 4–5

THE VALID CONTRACT

This is the really difficult point. The orthodox doctrine is that an enrichment transferred under a valid contract cannot be recovered unless the contract is rescinded or terminated.[1] In this case the parties made a valid contract of sale. The contract had indeed been discharged, but only by full performance. Kirby J, dissenting, sees this difficulty but is either unable or unwilling to overcome it. For him the validity of the sale under which the full price, including the tax, was paid constitutes an absolute bar to the retailers' claim.[2]

The majority judgments appear to take the line that this element of orthodox doctrine is indistinguishable from the old rule that there could be no recovery for failure of consideration unless the consideration failed totally. The requirement of total failure has been very much weakened.[3] Severance and apportionment are now more widely acceptable. The majority judgments appear to assume that by adopting and adhering to that relatively new position they escape the orthodoxy which bars restitution of benefits transferred under a valid contract.[4]

That will not quite do. A mistake which would otherwise indisputably require restitution will be ineffectual if the value in question passed under a contract. The claimant will then succeed only if he or she can show that the mistake destroyed the contract itself.[5] By parity of reasoning, in the very rare case that a failure of consideration can be made out despite the validity and indeed the performance

---

1 G Jones (ed) Lord Goff of Chieveley and G Jones *The Law of Restitution* (5th edn Sweet & Maxwell London 1998) 47–48; A Burrows *The Law of Restitution* (Butterworths London 1993) 271–72; K Mason and J Carter *Restitution Law in Australia* (Butterworths Sydney 1995) [909].

2 *Roxborough* (above) [165]–[166].

3 E McKendrick 'Total Failure of Consideration and Counter-Restitution: Two Doctrines or One' in P Birks (ed) *Laundering and Tracing* (OUP Oxford 1995) 217; P Birks 'Failure of Consideration' in F Rose (ed) *Consensus* ad Idem (Sweet & Maxwell London 1996) 179.

4 14 App Cas 429, 433.   5 *Bell v Lever Bros Ltd* [1932] AC 161 (HL).

of the contract, the contract remains an obstacle to the claim to restitution.[6] The rationale behind the bar can be expressed in the proposition that contracts must not be subverted or that irreconcilable contradictions between the law of contract and the law of restitution cannot be tolerated.

Orthodoxies are sometimes stated too widely. This one has been much discussed.[7] Professor Beatson has argued, rightly, that a more sophisiticated analysis would conclude that the bar is not absolute. In particular he says that a distinction should be drawn between cases in which restitution would disturb legitimate hopes and fears inherent in the bargain and others where it would not. In the latter the orthodox rule should give way.[8] That seems to be exactly the right way to approach this case. The crucial fact is that neither the payment of the tax nor the amount of that payment were viewed as negotiable. There were no hopes and fears in that regard. No tax, no payment. As between the parties there is no doubt whatever that restitution of the tax returned them to exactly the position they would have been in if, to their knowledge, the tax had been annulled or repealed before the payment.[9]

If in this way the orthodox rule proves more flexible than has been thought, serious attention will have to be paid to the outcome of *Orphanos v Queen Mary College*.[10] In that case a student who should have been charged fees on the home scale was charged on the higher overseas scale. When the mistake was discovered he sought to recover the difference. The House of Lords rejected his claim. The contract between him and the college was not invalidated by the mistake. Yet there was again no element of bargaining. There were simply two scales, and he had mistakenly been charged according to the wrong one.

- ● J Beatson and G Virgo, 'Contract, Unjust Enrichment and Unconscionability' (2002) 118 *LQR* 352, 355–7.

Failure of consideration

In many cases where a claimant has paid tax which is not due, the restitutionary claim lies against the revenue authority which has received the payment, so the ground of restitution would be that recognised by the House of Lords in *Woolwich Equitable Building Society v I.R.C.* [1993] A.C. 70, namely *ultra vires* receipt. This ground of restitution was not available in *Roxborough* because the licence fee had not been paid over to the revenue authority but remained with the wholesaler. This was, therefore, simply a private law restitutionary claim. However, the High Court concluded (Kirby J. dissenting) that the relevant ground for ordering restitution of the payment was failure of consideration. The validity of this conclusion is doubtful.

The doubtfulness stems from the fact that a fundamental principle relating to the application of the ground of total failure of consideration in particular, and unjust enrichment generally, is that the law

---

6 SA Smith 'Concurrent Liability in Contract and Unjust Enrichment: The Fundamental Breach Requirement' (1999) 115 Law Quarterly Review 245, 247–48, rightly distinguishing the requirement of total failure from that of discharge of the contract.

7 G Mead 'Restitution within Contract' (1991) 11 Legal Studies 172; D Friedmann 'Valid, Voidable, Qualified and Non-Existing Obligations: An Alternative Perspective on the Law of Restitution' in A Burrows *Essays on the Law of Restitution* (OUP Oxford 1991) 247; S Smith (n 6 above); J Beatson 'The Temptation of Elegance: Concurrence of Restitutionary and Contractual Claims' in W Swadling and G Jones *The Search for Principle: Essays in Honour of Lord Goff of Chieveley* (OUP Oxford 1999) 142.

8 J Beatson (n 7 above) 142, especially 151–54.

9 One important paragraph brings these factors together: [2001] HCA 68, (2001) 185 ALR 335 (HCA) [21] (Gleeson CJ, Gaudron and Hayne JJ) and could be taken as in effect endorsing the approach of Beatson (n 7 above).

10 [1985] AC 761 (HL). Cf. *David Securities Pty. Ltd v Commonwealth Bank of Australia* (1992) 175 CLR 353 (HCA) where there was also no need to protect the bargain, not because the mistaken payment had not been bargained for but because the matter was not as a matter of law open to private bargaining.

of restitution is subordinate to the law of contract. It follows that restitutionary remedies are generally only available in a contractual context once the contract has been set aside, for example for breach, frustration or because it is unenforceable (see *Pan Ocean Shipping Co. Ltd v Creditcorp Ltd* [1994] 1 W.L.R. 161; *Pavey and Matthews v Paul* (1987) 162 C.L.R. 221 at p. 256 (Deane J.)). So was this requirement satisfied in *Roxborough*? Although the majority recognised that the purchase price for the cigarettes incorporated the wholesale cost of the cigarettes and a distinct sum as payment for the licence fee, this sum was paid pursuant to a contract which remained valid, despite the invalidity of the statute which it was thought required the payment of a licence fee (*cf.* the English interest rate swap cases where the contracts themselves were null and void by virtue of the incapacity of local authorities to enter into such contracts). Alternatively, it might be argued that the failure of the respondents to pay the licence fee to the revenue authority was a breach of contract; but it seems that the respondents did not promise to do this, so there was no breach.

It appears therefore, that the contract had not been terminated. It was for this reason that Kirby J. concluded that the ground of failure of consideration could not be established and this was one reason why he dissented. As regards the majority, all bar one failed to consider the requirement that the contract must have been terminated before restitutionary relief can be awarded. Callinan J. did consider this matter. He suggested that restitution would be available as long as performance was not possible and, if formal termination of the contract was required, then bringing proceedings for restitution would be sufficient. But this in effect means that restitution is no longer subordinate to contract and surely this will involve the unnecessary, and unprincipled, usurpation of the law of contract by the law of restitution.

On a theoretical level one of us has argued that there may be exceptional circumstances where restitutionary relief can be awarded even though the contract had not been terminated, but only where this would not subvert the contractual allocation of risk: Beatson (2000) 1 Theoretical Inquiries in Law 83 at p. 88. But there was no evidence in *Roxborough* that the risk of the licence fee being invalid had been placed on the wholesaler rather than the retailers. Surely the burden of proving that the allocation of risk has not been undermined should be placed on the retailers who sought restitution. It will only be the most exceptional case where this burden could be discharged. It may be that that the majority's failure to address these issues stems from their view of the foundation of the claim as equitable and, in Gummow J.'s case, as based on unconscionability.

The fact that the licence fee had been paid pursuant to a valid and enforceable contract also defeated any argument that the fee could be recovered on the ground of mistake of law. This was recognised by Kirby J. but not mentioned by any of the other judges. If the contract remains valid, it is not for the law of restitution to intrude and say that there had been an operative mistake which would justify restitution. Such an argument can only succeed once the contract has been terminated.

It follows that no ground of restitution was applicable and so the restitutionary claim should not have succeeded.

NOTES AND QUESTIONS

1. The difference between the views of Birks, on the one hand, and Beatson and Virgo on the other hand, appears to lie in the view of Beatson and Virgo that there was no evidence that the risk of the licence fee being invalid lay on the wholesaler rather than the retailer. But if this risk of the basis failing had not been allocated by the contract what objection is there to allowing a claim for restitution subject to the defence of change of position?

2. Does it make a difference that the parties, or their legal advisers who devised the contracts, should have realized that there was a real chance that these licence fees were invalid (especially because there had been numerous constitutional decisions, expressing different views on this point for several decades previously).

3. Birks suggested that if the *Roxborough* approach to failure of consideration is applied to mistakes cases then *Orphanos v Queen Mary College* [1985] AC 761 may need to be reconsidered. Do you agree? Or do you prefer the solution proposed by Beatson and Virgo that 'if the contract remains valid, it is not for the law of restitution to intrude and say that there has been an operative mistake which would justify restitution'?

8. FREE ACCEPTANCE

In this section we shall focus on free acceptance as a potential unjust factor (its role as a test for enrichment has already been considered in Chapter 2). Free acceptance, which was first recognized as a ground of restitution by Goff and Jones, has been defined by Professor Birks (*Future* (1992), 53) in the following terms (see also above, 93):

Free acceptance occurs when someone has the opportunity to accept or reject a benefit, knows that the benefit is not being offered as a gift, and elects to accept it. He allows the other to fall into a trap when he might have saved him. The focus is avowedly on the quality of the defendant-recipient's conduct, not on the integrity of the plaintiff's decision to transfer the value in question, nor on a policy independent of the intentions and behaviour of either party. Free acceptance turns out, on analysis, to be a true case of fault-based restitutionary liability. But it is also a highly controversial one.

But in 1988 it was argued both on principle and as a matter of authority, that free acceptance has no place within the law of restitution (A Burrows, 'Free Acceptance and the Law of Restitution' (1988) 104 *LQR* 576). After referring to Birks' notorious window-cleaning example (see above, 85), Burrows continued:

. . . For Birks this provides 'a clear and simple example.' But for the present author it was the start of the feeling that something had gone awry with the reasoning. For while (assuming, for the present, that the enrichment issues is solved) the injustice is fairly obvious if the window-cleaner had been acting non-voluntarily, for example by mistake, the crucial importance of free acceptance for Birks is that it would allow restitution to the window-cleaner even if he had been acting merely in the hope that I would pay; that is, even if the window-cleaner was a disappointed risk-taker. Yet surely on any common sense view there would be no injustice in my not paying a risk-taker. For even if I can be said to have acted shabbily, this is matched by the fact that the plaintiff was a risk-taker—without any inducement, he gambled on my willingness to pay. Why should we now want to protect him against the very risk that he undertook? In short, the plaintiff's risk-taking cancels out any shabbiness in my free acceptance. As such, free acceptance cannot be regarded in principle as an unjust factor.

This attack on the role of free acceptance within the law of restitution was quickly followed up by G. Mead, 'Free Acceptance: Some Further Considerations' (1989) 105 *LQR* 460. Birks subsequently conceded that free acceptance played a much smaller role as an unjust factor than he initially envisaged and was 'needed in only a handful of cases' where failure of consideration (which Burrows had suggested was a better explanation of many of the older free acceptance cases) could not apply (P Birks, 'In Defence of Free Acceptance' in A Burrows (ed.), *Essays on the Law of Restitution* (1991)). Birks abandoned his window cleaner example and said that the few cases where free acceptance was the unjust factor was where there was some initial unconscionability by the defendant. One example of this was 'secret acceptance' where the claimant knows that the defendant knows that the claimant expects to be paid. In a review of that essay, Graham Virgo said that ((1992) 12 *LS* 253, 256) '[i]n an otherwise excellent essay, in which Birks defends the doctrine of free acceptance, the doctrine has surely become too vague when he says that, whether a secret acceptance amounts to an unjust enrichment, depends on unjustness in the recipient's conduct, or unconscionability.'

In *Unjust Enrichment* ((2nd edn 2005), 42) Birks finally abandoned free acceptance altogether in relation to the 'unjust' enquiry. He said that free acceptance 'proved to be the result of muddled thinking . . . There is no doubt that Professor Burrows was right to eliminate this defendant-sided category.' However, Birks maintained that free acceptance still had a role as a test for enrichment (above, 93–101). The authority, in the older cases, for free acceptance as an unjust factor was always weak. Indeed, the cases which contained the broadest statements referring to free acceptance (e.g. *Leigh v Dickeson* (1884) 15 QBD 60, 64–5; *Falcke v Scottish Imperial Insurance Co.* (1886) 34 Ch D 234; *Re Cleadon Trust Ltd* [1939] 1 Ch 286) all denied restitution and, being decisions prior to the recognition of unjust enrichment, naturally did not explain whether the references to acceptance of a benefit were relevant to the question of enrichment or the unjust factor.

However, prior to Birks' recanting on free acceptance as an unjust factor, it received the first explicit judicial recognition (albeit obiter dicta) as an unjust factor in an English case.

- *Rowe v Vale of White Horse DC* [2003] EWHC 388 (Admin); [2003] 1 Lloyd's Rep 418, Queen's Bench Division

For the facts, see above, 76.

Lightman J: . . . [13] The critical question is whether the third condition [the existence of an unjust factor] is satisfied. The Council cannot suggest the existence of any unjust factor (e.g. a mistake on the part of the Council in providing the service or a failure of consideration). Paragraph 1-019 of Goff & Jones above reads as follows:

. . . a defendant who is not contractually bound may have benefited from services rendered in circumstances in which the court holds him liable to pay for them. Such will be the case if he freely accepts the services. In our view he will be held to have benefited from the services rendered if he, as a reasonable man, should have known that the [claimant] who rendered the services expected to be paid for them and yet he did not take a reasonable opportunity open to him to reject the proffered services. Moreover in such a case he cannot deny that he has been unjustly enriched. In a word free acceptance may satisfy not only the second, but also the third condition.

[14] On the facts of any ordinary case, a householder who receives and uses services from a supplier such as the Council must reasonably expect to pay for such services and will know that he has the option to reject them, and he will accordingly be liable under the principle of free acceptance to pay for them. This conclusion will in nowise be affected by the mere fact that the householder is unaware of the identity of the supplier: he may reasonably expect to pay the supplier whoever he may be. But the facts of this case are far removed from the ordinary case. Most particularly in the circumstances of this case and by reason of the administrative oversight of the Council over the period 1982 to 1995 and what can only be described as the extraordinary error of judgement by the Council between 1995 and 2001, the Council created and perpetuated the totally reasonable belief on the part of consumers of its services (and most particularly its former tenants) that there was no payment to be paid (beyond what was already paid to the Council and the TWA) in respect of the sewerage services and there arose no occasion for Mr. Rowe to reject the services. The Council cannot establish (in the language of Goff & Jones) that Mr. Rowe should have known that the Council or other supplier of the sewerage service expected to be paid for them anything beyond what was already paid to the Council and TWA. It is scarcely open to the Council to dispute this fact since on its own case the Council was ignorant until 2001 whether it could charge for the services and this ignorance was the occasion for its

silence on the whole question. Where (as in this case) for good reason the defendant as a reasonable person should not have known that the claimant who rendered the services expected to be paid or paid extra for them, as a matter of principle the third condition cannot be satisfied and no claim can lie in restitution. Support for this view is provided by three authorities which establish that no claim lies against a defendant where there is a common understanding between the claimant and the defendant that a third party shall alone be liable to pay for the services supplied: (consider *Bridge-water v Griffiths* [2000] 1 WLR 524 at 532); or where the claimant continues to foist his services on an unwilling defendant after the defendant has insisted that, if he does so, the defendant will not pay for them: (see *Bookmakers Afternoon Greyhound Services v Gilbert* [1994] FSR 723); or where an architect, having agreed a fee for specified services, renders additional services where the client when he accepted them was reasonably entitled to assume that the architect was undertaking them for no additional charge: (see *Gilbert v Knight* [1968] 2 All ER 248). In this case it does not matter that Mr. Rowe has no defence of change of position. Under English law (unlike Continental law) it is a requirement of a claim in restitution that the claimant establishes the factor rendering it unjust for the defendant to retain the benefit of the services he has received: it is not incumbent on the defendant as a defence to the claim to establish that it is unjust for the liability to be imposed upon him: see Lord Hope in Kleinwort Benson Ltd v Lincoln City Council, [1999] 2 AC 349 at 408–409 and Mindy Chen-Wishart, 'In Defence of Unjust Factors', Johnston and Zimmerman, 'Unjustified Enrichment', Cambridge 2002, 159–193. There was no free acceptance and accordingly there was no unjust factor. The third condition for a claim in restitution being absent, the Council has no claim in private law against Mr. Rowe.

[15] I accordingly hold that the Council has no legal right to the arrears which it claims. The Council is the author of its own discomfort. It was folly and short-sighted to place and deliberately leave the residents of its former Council houses in the dark. Its duty in its dealing with users of its services was to be transparent and disclose what might be in store from the beginning rather than to spring a surprise and later claim payment of arrears. By its failure the Council forfeited the right to charge Mr. Rowe for its services. The consequences may have to be borne in the form of higher charges by other users. The burden of those higher charges may be a cause of complaint by those who have to pay them against the Council and its officers, but cannot make good the absence of an essential element in the Council's cause of action against Mr. Rowe.

NOTES AND QUESTIONS

1. Lightman J considered that the unjust factor of free acceptance would have been established if the Council had expected to be paid for the sewage services and Mr Rowe had known of this. But if this were the case, surely the unjust factor of failure of consideration would have been established. The services would have been provided on a shared basis (that they would be paid for) which failed.

2. Goff and Jones are reluctant to accept that failure of consideration can apply to claims for goods or services (see Chapter 20). For them, as for many practitioners, failure of consideration applies exclusively to money claims. Thus Goff and Jones continue to rely extensively on free acceptance. However, both Birks and Burrows, influenced by the argument from symmetry, insist that the unjust factor, failure of consideration, must logically apply both to money and non-money claims. If English law continues to adhere to the view that failure of consideration can only apply to money claims, then the scope for free acceptance as an unjust factor might be greater because cases such as *William Lacey* (above, 333) and *British Steel v Cleveland Bridge* (above, 336) would then be left without explanation. If, on the other hand, the view is accepted that failure of consideration can apply to non-money claims, then the role for free acceptance as an unjust factor is, at best, a small one.

3. K Mason and J Carter (*Restitution Law in Australia*, 1995) prefer to use the phrase 'failure of the agreed return' instead of 'failure of consideration' (see paragraph 922). But they nevertheless reject the claim that failure of the agreed return, to use their terminology, can be the unjust factor in cases involving non-money benefits. In non-money claims they insist that it is free acceptance which is operative as the principal unjust factor and they defend their claim in the following way (paragraph 928):

> We regard acceptance of benefit as the principal criterion in relation to non-monetary benefits. Apart from the fact that it is supported by authority, acceptance is in our view the relevant criterion. Failure of the agreed return—as an unjust factor—works if the enrichment of the defendant is not in issue. It is because money is always regarded as a benefit that it is generally unnecessary to consider the conduct of the defendant in receiving it. But in cases where restitution in respect of a non-monetary benefit is claimed, enrichment is a matter of debate. There is an ellipsis in the transfer of failure of the agreed return to non-monetary benefits, since it assumes an objective concept of benefit which the law has not embraced. In other words, we cannot apply failure of the agreed return unless benefit is established, and the plain fact is that acceptance has always, at least under Australian law, been regarded as the principal criterion for benefit.

As a matter of (a) logic and (b) policy, should the nature of the enrichment dictate the test to be applied in determining whether or not a particular enrichment is unjust? Take the example of a claimant who improves the goods of the defendant in the mistaken belief that they are his. Are we forced to conclude that the unjust factor is free acceptance (which in most cases it cannot be because the defendant is unaware of the claimant's intervention) simply because the benefit (if there is one) is non-monetary?

6

ILLEGITIMATE PRESSURE

The focus of this Chapter is upon the restitutionary rights given by the law to a claimant who has conferred a benefit on the defendant as a result of the application of illegitimate pressure by the defendant. The central idea is clear. If X compels Y to pay him £500 by threatening to kill him if he does not do so, then Y will be entitled to bring an action to recover the money paid as a result of this illegitimate threat. But the appearance of clarity is deceptive because the limits of, and the basis for, the intervention of the court in these cases has proved to be a matter of some difficulty and controversy. The following are examples of the controversies which you should bear in mind when reading the extracts from the cases and materials in this Chapter.

(i) *What significance, if any, should be attached to the division between common law and equity?* At common law the courts have evolved a doctrine of duress to regulate the use of pressure to obtain benefits from other parties, while in equity the courts have developed a doctrine of undue influence. It is customary for textbooks to discuss the ambit of duress and then to consider the scope of undue influence without analysing the relationship between the two doctrines. Yet the question has to be asked: what, if any, is the relationship between duress and undue influence? Are they both concerned with the same issue, namely the application of illegitimate pressure? Or do they serve different functions? These questions cannot be answered solely by reference to the different jurisdictional origins of the doctrines. Jurisdictional origins cannot be allowed to mask difficult substantive issues. It is our contention that the divide in the cases is between the pressure cases (which are made up of the duress cases and some of the actual undue influence cases) and cases where the reason for intervention is the excessive dependence of the claimant or the defendant's exploitation of the claimant's weakness (this category encompasses the presumed undue influence cases and possibly some of the actual undue influence cases).

(ii) *Is the focus of inquiry in these cases upon the claimant or the defendant or upon both?* Professor Birks has been prominent in arguing that relief in these cases is claimant-sided; that is to say, the reason for restitution is the claimant's vitiated voluntariness (see, for example, *Introduction*, 173 ff.). He holds this view in relation to both the duress cases and the undue influence cases. A second view is that these cases are examples of defendant-sided relief, that is to say, the justification for intervention is the defendant's bad behaviour. On one view this could lead to the classification of these cases as examples of 'restitution for wrongs' (see, for example, P Maddaugh and J McCamus, *The Law of Restitution* (1990) where 'compulsion' is included in a section of the book entitled 'Profit from Wrongdoing'). But it should not be thought that a defendant-sided view of the cases necessarily results in the adoption of a view that the cause of action is a wrong. It can be maintained that the focus of the inquiry is upon the behaviour of the defendant, but that it is nevertheless an example of subtractive unjust enrichment. A third view is that the inquiry must look both to the state of mind of the claimant (in the sense that there must be a causal link between the pressure and the actions of the claimant) and to the nature of the conduct in which the defendant has engaged. It is this latter view which, in our opinion, finds strongest support in the case law.

(iii) *Do common principles apply to all types of pressure or does the law distinguish between, for example, threats of violence to the person and threats of an economic nature?* The law in this area has evolved rather slowly. We begin our analysis with cases of duress of the person where relief has always been available. When we move to the category of duress of goods we find that the law initially adopted a more restrictive approach by refusing to set aside a contract on the ground of duress of goods (see *Skeate v Beale*, below, 404). But, with the recognition of the doctrine of economic duress and of the fact that economic duress can suffice to set aside a contract, the old view in *Skeate* could no longer stand. Yet the law may still want to differentiate between the different types of duress so that, for example, a claimant might be expected to show greater fortitude in the face of economic pressure than in the case of threats of violence to his person. Or the test for the sufficiency of the causal link between the pressure and the actions of the claimant may vary as between the different types of duress. Alternatively, the law could now be viewed as a unified whole, so that the criteria for recovery should be the same for duress of the person, duress of goods, and economic duress.

(iv) *What types of pressure are to be treated as 'illegitimate'?* Where the pressure applied takes the form of threats of violence to the person, then the issue is relatively straight-forward. But it is much more difficult where the coercion consists of economic pressure (such as threats to break a contract or to refuse to contract) or threats to prosecute or to sue unless a demand is met.

(v) *What impact must the illegitimate pressure have on the claimant before the courts will conclude that the benefit has been conferred as a result of the illegitimate pressure?* The central issue to be resolved here relates to the test for causation. Must the pressure be 'a' cause, 'the' cause, or 'a significant' cause before it suffices to give rise to a claim for recovery of the benefit concerned? Other questions can also arise here. For example, what significance is to be attached to the fact that, at the time at which the pressure was applied, the claimant had available to it an alternative remedy (such as resort to the courts or the availability of another supplier)? And what is the significance to be attached to the presence or absence of protests on the part of the victim at the time at which the benefit was conferred or promised?

(vi) *Does (or should) the law distinguish between the case in which the claimant seeks to set aside a contract on the ground of duress and the case in which the claimant seeks to recover a non-contractual payment made or a benefit conferred under duress?* We have already seen in the context of mistaken payments (see 147) that the law does treat these two cases differently and that the scope of the right to recover in the latter context is broader than in the case of the former. The reason for this is, in essence, that the concern to protect the sanctity of contracts does not arise in the latter group of cases. However it cannot be said with any confidence that the same proposition holds good in the case of duress. Indeed, it has been argued that it is 'unhelpful to treat separately payments made under contracts entered into under duress' (Burrows, 215). It is said to be unhelpful principally because it can be difficult to distinguish the contractual from the non-contractual case, particularly in the case where the threat takes the form of a threat to break a contract. It is true that the uncertain scope of the doctrine of consideration can make it difficult to ascertain whether the promise of payment is supported by consideration (and hence contractual) or not (see in particular *Williams v Roffey Bros and Nicholls (Contractors) Ltd* [1991] 1 QB 1). But, on the other hand, the fact that it can

sometimes be difficult to distinguish the two cases does not mean that we should necessarily abandon all attempts to draw the distinction or to deal separately with the case
where it is clear that there is no contract between the parties (see further E McKendrick
'The Further Travails of Duress' in A Burrows and Lord Rodger of Earlsferry (eds)
Mapping the Law: Essays in Memory of Peter Birks (2006), 181, esp 194–6). Take the case of
a payment of £1,000 made under duress and where there is no promised counter-
performance. This is a promise to confer a gift on another party. There is no contract to
set aside and so why should the claimant have to satisfy the standard that would be
applicable had a contract been concluded?

(vii) *Should duress remain as a discrete 'unjust factor' or should it be included within
a broader justification for intervention based upon 'unconscionability'?* It is no easy task
to separate out the pressure cases from those based upon 'excessive dependence' or
'exploitation of weakness' (on which see Chapter 7) and, in turn, to distinguish them
from the incapacity cases (on which see Chapter 11). One approach to this difficulty
might be to abandon the attempts to distinguish between the different categories as
fruitless and to formulate a broader and more flexible ground for intervention. We reject
the latter approach as tending to lead to a situation where all sight of the principles which
guide us is lost, where the cases quickly become irreconcilable and where 'palm tree
justice' becomes the order of the day. However difficult it may be, we maintain that the
attempt to mark out the reasons for, and the limits of, intervention should not be abandoned. This can best be done by separating out the pressure cases from the other cases.

(viii) A final question to consider, although it is not directly considered in any of the
cases within the chapter (with the possible exception of *Universe Tankships of Monrovia v
International Transport Workers' Federation*, below, 413 and in particular note 4 at 416), is
whether a person who confers a benefit on another under duress has a restitutionary
proprietary claim against the recipient of the benefit. Goff and Jones state at 10–057 that
'there is much to be said for the view that the equitable title to property transferred
should revert and, if the status quo cannot be restored, then the threatened party should
be deemed to retain the equitable title in the property transferred. The threatener's
conduct is unquestionably unconscionable. On his insolvency, when this question will
arise, the claims of his creditors are less appealing than those of the threatened party.' Do
you agree?

General Reading

BURROWS, chapter 5; GOFF AND JONES, chapter 10; VIRGO, 187–220.

1. DURESS OF THE PERSON

• *Barton v Armstrong* [1976] AC 104, Privy Council

Armstrong and Barton were the major shareholders in a company, Landmark Corporation Ltd, which was involved in the development of a building estate which was to be
known as 'Paradise Waters'. Armstrong was the chairman and Barton was the managing
director: they were locked in a power struggle for control of the company which, over the
years, became increasingly bitter. Barton initially succeeded in obtaining the removal of
Armstrong as chairman of the company, and then negotiations began as to the terms on
which Armstrong's interest was to be bought out. Armstrong demanded that Landmark
repay to him a loan of $400,000 which was stated to be payable forthwith in the event of

Armstrong being removed from the chairmanship of Landmark. Barton hoped to be able to pay off Armstrong by negotiating a loan from United Dominions Corporation (Australia) Ltd (UDC) but UDC, despite initial appearances to the contrary, refused to provide the loan. In these circumstances Barton entered into negotiations with a representative of Armstrong, and these negotiations resulted in a deed of 17 January 1967 under which Barton agreed, *inter alia*, to repay the loan of $400,000, to pay Armstrong $140,000, and to buy his shares for $180,000. An order for the winding up of Landmark was made on 11 January 1968 but on 10 January Barton commenced a suit in equity in which he alleged that he had been coerced by Armstrong into agreeing to the terms of the deed by threats that he would be murdered and by the exertion of other unlawful pressure over him. He therefore sought a declaration that the deed was 'void' so far as concerned him. The trial judge found that Armstrong had indeed threatened Barton and his family, but held that Barton's primary and predominant reason for entering into the transaction was a commercial one, namely to ensure the survival of the company by ridding it of Armstrong. The Court of Appeal of New South Wales dismissed Barton's appeal. Barton appealed to the Privy Council who, by a majority (Lord Wilberforce and Lord Simon of Glaisdale dissenting), allowed the appeal on the ground that Armstrong's threats were a reason for Barton entering into the agreement and that he was entitled to relief even though he might well have entered into the contract had Armstrong not threatened him in the way in which he had done. The deeds in question were therefore declared to be void so far as they concerned Barton.

Lord Cross of Chelsea (delivering the judgment of the majority of their Lordships): . . . Their Lordships turn now to consider the question of law which provoked a difference of opinion in the Court of Appeal Division. It is hardly surprising that there is no direct authority on the point, for if A threatens B with death if he does not execute some document and B, who takes A's threats seriously, executes the document it can be only in the most unusual circumstances that there can be any doubt whether the threats operated to induce him to execute the document. But this is a most unusual case and the findings of fact made below do undoubtedly raise the question whether it was necessary for Barton in order to obtain relief to establish that he would not have executed the deed in question but for the threats. In answering this question in favour of Barton, Jacobs JA relied both on a number of old common law authorities on the subject of 'duress' and also—by way of analogy—on later decisions in equity with regard to the avoidance of deeds on the ground of fraud. Their Lordships do not think that the common law authorities are of any real assistance for it seems most unlikely that the authors of the statements relied on had the sort of problem which has arisen here in mind at all. On the other hand they think that the conclusion to which Jacobs JA came was right and that it is supported by the equity decisions. The scope of common law duress was very limited and at a comparatively early date equity began to grant relief in cases where the disposition in question had been procured by the exercise of pressure which the Chancellor considered to be illegitimate—although it did not amount to common law duress. There was a parallel development in the field of dispositions induced by fraud. At common law the only remedy available to the man defrauded was an action for deceit but equity in the same period in which it was building up the doctrine of 'undue influence' came to entertain proceedings to set aside dispositions which had been obtained by fraud: see *Holdsworth, A History of English law*, vol. V (1924), 328–9. There is an obvious analogy between setting aside a disposition for duress or undue influence and setting it aside for fraud. In each case—to quote the words of Holmes J in *Fairbanks v Snow* (1887) 13 NE 596, 598—'the party has been subjected to an improper motive for action.' Again the similarity of the effect in law of metus and dolus in connection with dispositions of property is noted by Stair in his *Institutions of the Law of Scotland*, New edn (1832), Book IV, title 40.25. Had Armstrong made a fraudulent misrepresentation to Barton for the purpose of inducing him to execute the deed of January 17, 1967, the answer to the problem which has arisen would have been clear. If it were established that Barton did not allow the representation to affect his judgment then he could not make it a ground for relief even though the representation was designed and known by Barton to be designed to affect his judgment. If on the other hand Barton relied on the misrepresentation Armstrong could not have defeated his claim to relief by showing that there were other more weighty causes which contributed to his decision to execute the deed, for in this field the court does not allow an examination into the relative importance of contributory causes.

'Once make out that there has been anything like deception, and no contract resting in any degree on that foundation can stand': *per* Lord Cranworth LJ in *Reynell v Sprye* (1852) 1 De GM & G 660, 708—see also the other cases referred to in *Cheshire and Fifoot's Law of Contract*, 8th edn (1972), 250–1. Their Lordships think that the same rule should apply in cases of duress and that if Armstrong's threats were 'a' reason for Barton's executing the deed he is entitled to relief even though he might well have entered into the contract if Armstrong had uttered no threats to induce him to do so.

It remains to apply the law to the facts. What was the state of Barton's mind when he executed the deed is, of course, a question of fact and a question the answer to which depended largely on Barton's own evidence. The judge who heard him give evidence was in a better position than anyone else to decide whether fear engendered by Armstrong's threats was 'a' reason for his executing the deed. It was submitted that the decision of Street J in favour of Armstrong amounted to a finding that fear engendered by the threats was not such a reason and that as that decision had been affirmed by a majority of the Appeal Division the Board should not disturb it. But this case, as their Lordships see it, is not one to which the rule as to 'concurrent findings' is applicable. In the first place some of the findings of fact made by the judge were varied by the Appeal Division. In particular they held that he was wrong in finding that Barton did not think that Armstrong's threats were being made with a view to inducing him to execute the agreement. Again there appears to have been little discussion of the law before Street J and it is by no means clear that he directed his mind to the precise question which was debated in the Appeal Division and before the Board. Consequently one cannot be sure that if he had applied to the facts found by him as modified by the Appeal Division what their Lordships think to be the correct principle of law he would have reached the conclusion which he did reach. He might have done so but equally he might not have done so. The judges in the Appeal Division approached the case no doubt in the light of what their Lordships assume to be the right findings of fact but the majority applied to them what in their Lordships' judgment was a wrong principle of law. In these circumstances their Lordships think that they can properly, and indeed should, reach their own conclusion by applying the law as they understand it to the facts found by the judge as modified by the Appeal Division. They proceed then on the footing that although, when he learnt that UDC had decided no longer to finance the Paradise Waters project, Barton was at first despondent as to its future he soon came to share Bovill's view that UDC would change its mind when once Armstrong was out of the way; that the confidence as to the eventual success of the project to which he gave expression to Smith and others during the negotiations and shortly after the execution of the documents was genuine; that he thought that the agreement with Armstrong was a satisfactory business arrangement both from the point of view of Landmark and also from his own point of view; and that the evidence which he gave at the trial, though possibly honest, was a largely erroneous reconstruction of his state of mind at the time. But even so Barton must have realised that in parting with all Landmark's liquid assets to Armstrong and in agreeing himself to buy Armstrong's shares for almost twice their market value in the hope that when Armstrong was out of the way UDC would once more provide finance he was taking a very great risk. It is only reasonable to suppose that from time to time during the negotiations he asked himself whether it would not be better either to insist that any settlement with Armstrong should be conditional on an agreement with UDC or to cut his own and Landmark's losses on the Paradise Waters project altogether rather than to increase the stakes so drastically. If Barton had to establish that he would not have made the agreement but for

Armstrong's threats, then their Lordships would not dissent from the view that he had not made out his case. But no such onus lay on him. On the contrary it was for Armstrong to establish, if he could, that the threats which he was making and the unlawful pressure which he was exerting for the purpose of inducing Barton to sign the agreement and which Barton knew were being made and exerted for this purpose in fact contributed nothing to Barton's decision to sign. The judge has found that during the 10 days or so before the documents were executed Barton was in genuine fear that Armstrong was planning to have him killed if the agreement was not signed. His state of mind was described by the judge as one of 'very real mental torment' and he believed that his fears would be at an end when once the documents were executed. It is true that the judge was not satisfied that Vojinovic [*who was alleged by Barton to have been hired by Armstrong to kill him*] had been employed by Armstrong but if one man threatens another with unpleasant consequences if he does not act in a particular way, he must take the risk that the impact of his threats may be accentuated by extraneous circumstances for which he is not in fact responsible. It is true that on the facts as their Lordships assume them to have been Armstrong's threats may have been unnecessary; but it would be unrealistic to hold that they played no part in making Barton decide to execute the documents. The proper inference to be drawn from the facts found is, their Lordships think, that though it may be that Barton would have executed the documents even if Armstrong had made no threats and exerted no unlawful pressure to induce him to do so the threats and unlawful pressure in fact contributed to his decision to sign the documents and to recommend their execution by Landmark and the other parties to them. It may be, of course, that Barton's fear of Armstrong had evaporated before he issued his writ in this action but Armstrong—understandably enough—expressly disclaimed reliance on the defence of delay on Barton's part in repudiating the deed.

In the result therefore the appeal should be allowed and a declaration made that the deeds in question were executed by Barton under duress and are void so far as concerns him. . . .

Dissenting judgment by **Lord Wilberforce** and **Lord Simon of Glaisdale:** The reason why we do not agree with the majority decision is, briefly, that we regard the issues in this case as essentially issues of fact, issues moreover of a character particularly within the sphere of the trial judge bearing, as they do, upon motivation and credibility. On all important issues, clear findings have been made by Street J and concurred in by the Court of Appeal—either unanimously or by majority. Accepted rules of practice and, such rules apart, sound principle should, in our opinion, prevent a second court of appeal from reviewing them in the absence of some miscarriage of justice, or some manifest and important error of law or misdirection. In our view no such circumstance exists in this case.

Before stating those findings of fact, which are to our mind conclusive, we think it desirable to define in our own way the legal basis on which they rest.

The action is one to set aside an apparently complete and valid agreement on the ground of duress. The basis of the plaintiff's claim is, thus, that though there was apparent consent there was no true consent to the agreement: that the agreement was not voluntary.

This involves consideration of what the law regards as voluntary, or its opposite; for in life including the life of commerce and finance, many acts are done under pressure, sometimes overwhelming pressure, so that one can say that the actor had no choice but to act. Absence of choice in this sense does not negate consent in law: for this the pressure must be one of a kind which the law does not regard as legitimate. Thus, out of the various means by which consent may be obtained—advice, persuasion, influence, inducement, representation, commercial pressure—the law has come to select some which it will not accept as a reason for voluntary action: fraud, abuse of relation of confidence, undue influence, duress or coercion. In this the law, under the influence of equity, has developed from the old common law conception of duress—threat to life and limb—and it has arrived at the modern generalisation expressed by Holmes J—'subjected to an improper motive for action': *Fairbanks v Snow*, 13 NE Reporter 596, 598.

In an action such as the present, then, the first step required of the plaintiff is to show that some illegitimate means of persuasion was used. That there were threats to Barton's life was found by the judge, though he did not accept Barton's evidence in important respects. We shall return to this point in detail later.

The next necessary step would be to establish the relationship between the illegitimate means used and the action taken. For the purposes of the present case (reserving our opinion as to cases which may arise in other contexts) we are prepared to accept, as the formula most favourable to the appellant, the test proposed by the majority, namely, that the illegitimate means used was *a* reason (not *the* reason, nor the *predominant* reason, nor the *clinching* reason) why the complainant acted as he did. We are also prepared to accept that a decisive answer is not obtainable by asking the question whether the contract would have been made even if there had been no threats because, even if the answer to this question is affirmative, that does not prove that the contract was not made because of the threats.

Assuming therefore that what has to be decided is whether the illegitimate means used was a reason why the complainant acted as he did, it follows that his reason for acting must (unless the case is one of automatism which this is not) be a conscious reason so that the complainant can give evidence of it: 'I acted because I was forced.' If his evidence is honest and accepted, that will normally conclude the issue. If, moreover, he gives evidence, it is necessary for the court to evaluate his evidence by testing it against his credibility and his actions.

In this case Barton gave evidence—his was, for practical purposes, the only evidence supporting his case. The judge rejected it in important respects and accepted it in others. The issues as to Barton's motivations were issues purely of fact (that motivation is a question of fact hardly needs authority, but see *Cox v Smail* [1912] VLR 274 *per* Cussen J): the findings as to motivation were largely, if not entirely, findings as to credibility. It would be difficult to find matters more peculiarly than these within the field of the trial judge who saw both contestants in the box, and who dealt carefully and at length with the credibility, or lack of credibility, of each of them.

...

In our opinion the case is far from being one in which a second appellate court should reverse findings made below and endorsed by a Court of Appeal. Respect for such findings—particularly where the issues depend so much upon credibility and an estimate of rival personalities—appears to us to be a central pillar of the appellate process. It is perhaps otiose, but also fair to the judges below, to say that we have no ground for thinking that the factual conclusions which they reached after so prolonged a search did not represent the truth of the situation—or at least the nearest approximation to truth that was attainable.

We would dismiss the appeal.

QUESTIONS

1. What was the test for causation adopted by (a) the majority and (b) the minority?
2. Why was the onus of proof on Armstrong to show that the threats which he had made had 'contributed nothing' to Barton's decision to sign? Should the same approach to causation be adopted in cases of duress of goods and economic duress?
3. Cases post-*Barton* have, however, displayed a marked reluctance to follow this liberal approach to causation. Instead, the courts have inclined towards a test which requires the establishment of a greater link between the pressure applied by the defendant and the claimant's decision to enter into the contract (see, for example, *Dimskal Shipping Co. SA v International Transport Workers' Federation (The Evia Luck (No 2)* [1992] 2 AC 152, below, 422).

2. DURESS OF GOODS

- *Astley v Reynolds* (1731) 2 Str 915, Court of King's Bench

The claimant pawned plate to the defendant for £20. Three years later the defendant refused to allow the claimant to redeem the goods unless he paid him interest of £10. The claimant tendered £4 but the defendant refused to accept it and refused to release the plate. The claimant eventually paid the £10 in order to get his goods back, and then brought the present action to recover the excess which he had paid over the legal interest which the defendant was entitled to charge. It was held that the claimant was entitled to the recovery of the money so paid under compulsion.

Holt CJ: . . . We think that this is a payment by compulsion; the plaintiff might have such an immediate want of his goods, that an action of trover would not do his business: where the rule volenti non fit injuria is applied, it must be where the party had his freedom of exercising his will, which this man had not: we must take it he paid the money relying on his legal remedy to get it back again.

QUESTIONS

1. What significance, if any, was attached to the fact that the claimant had an alternative remedy, in the form of a claim in trover?
2. How would this case be decided applying Birks's 'absence of basis' approach (above, 137) to the unjust question?

- *Skeate v Beale* (1841) 11 Ad & E 983, Court of King's Bench

The claimant distrained for arrears of rent, claiming that £19 10s was due from the defendant. The defendant agreed that, if the distress was withdrawn, he would pay £3 7s immediately and the outstanding £16 2s 6d within a month. He failed to pay the sum so promised and the claimant sued to recover the outstanding amount. The defendant argued that the seizure had been wrongful as the only sum due was £3 7s and that he entered into the agreement only to prevent the claimant from carrying out his threat to sell the goods. It was held that the defendant was not entitled to set aside the transaction and that the claimant was entitled to judgment for the sum claimed.

Lord Denman CJ (delivering the judgment of the court): . . . We consider the law to be clear, and founded on good reason, that an agreement is not void because made under duress of goods. There is no distinction in this respect between a deed and an agreement not under seal; and, with regard to the former, the law is laid down . . . and the distinction pointed out between duress of, or menace to, the person, and duress of goods. The former is a constraining force, which not only takes away the free agency, but may leave no room for appeal to the law for a remedy: a man, therefore, is not bound by the agreement which he enters into under such circumstances: but the fear that goods may be taken or injured does not deprive any one of his free agency who possesses that ordinary degree of firmness which the law requires all to exert. It is not necessary now to enter into the consideration of cases in which it has been held that money paid to redeem goods wrongfully seized, or to prevent their wrongful seizure, may be recovered back in an action for money had and received: for the distinction between those cases and the present, which must be taken to be that of an agreement, not compulsorily but voluntarily entered into, is obvious. *Lindon v Hooper* (1 Cowp. 414), and *Knibbs v Hall* (1 Esp. 84), are, however, authorities to shew that, even if the money had been paid in this case, instead of the agreement to pay it entered into, no action for money had and received could have been sustained by the now defendant. For, although there is a difference in the circumstances, and, the distress having been made, and some rent admitted to be in arrear, no replevin could have been successfully made, yet if the plaintiff distrained goods of the value of 20l. when little more than 3l. were due, there is no doubt that, on payment of the value of the goods, or the sum claimed, an action would have lain for the excessive distress. And it is of great importance that parties should be holden to those remedies for injuries which the law prescribes, rather than allowed to enter into agreements with a view to prevent them, intending at the time not to keep their contracts. In the argument for the defendant, reliance was placed on the facts that the agreement was entered into under protest, and that the plaintiff must have known that only the smaller amount of rent was due. It is unnecessary to consider what the effect of these would have been; for neither of them is alleged in the plea. As, therefore, this plea relies solely on the menace as to the goods, under which the agreement was made, for avoiding it, we think it discloses no answer to the declaration . . .

NOTES AND QUESTIONS

1. Was Lord Denman right to draw a distinction between cases of duress of the person and duress of goods when it is sought to set aside a contract?

2. Sir Jack Beatson ('Duress, Restitution and Contract Renegotiation' in *The Use and Abuse of Unjust Enrichment* (1991), especially 99–109) argues (at 100–1) that in cases where the wrongfulness of the acquisition of the chattel is not unequivocal or where it is not clear whether the claimant was under a duty to pay the sum claimed 'the duress doctrine tends to overlap with two other rules. The first states that money paid under process of law is irrecoverable, and the second states that agreements compromising disputed claims are enforceable even if the claim proves to be unfounded, provided that certain conditions are satisfied.' He further points out (at 105) that the authority cited to the court in *Skeate* further supports the proposition that 'Lord Denman CJ was dealing with either a compromise of, or a submission to, a claim'. Do you agree?

3. Goff and Jones, 10–013 point out that *Skeate v Beale* requires a distinction to be drawn between the following two cases:

   (1) A demands a sum of money from B under duress of goods. B pays the money. He can recover it.
   (2) A extracts from B under similar duress a promise to pay a sum of money. Provided that there is some consideration for the promise, B is bound to pay the money.

Goff and Jones maintain that it is 'very difficult to support a distinction of this kind since there must have been a *scintilla temporis* when A must have agreed to pay before making the payment'. There has also been a judicial reluctance to apply *Skeate* and, indeed, in the light of the critical comments of Lord Goff in *Dimskal Shipping Co. SA v International Transport Workers' Federation* (below, 413) it is highly unlikely that *Skeate* remains good law in England. Do you agree with this criticism of *Skeate*? Is Goff and Jones' argument (that one should not distinguish between payments made under a contract and non-contractual payments) valid (a) in all cases of duress; and (b) in cases of mistake?

3. ECONOMIC DURESS

• *North Ocean Shipping Co. Ltd v Hyundai Construction Co. Ltd (The Atlantic Baron)* [1979] QB 705, Queen's Bench Division

In 1972 the defendants entered into a contract under which they agreed to construct a tanker for the claimants. The contract stated that the price, which was to be paid in US dollars, was not to be subject to adjustment except in certain specific circumstances (which did not occur). In June 1983, after the devaluation of the dollar by 10 per cent, the defendants demanded that they be paid an extra 10 per cent for the work done under the contract. The claimants refused to pay the money so demanded on the ground that there was no basis in law for the demand, and they suggested that the matter be referred to arbitration. The defendants refused to agree to this suggestion and they threatened to terminate the contract if the sum was not paid. The claimants were advised that the defendants were not entitled to make such a demand under the terms of the contract but, as a result of an advantageous sub-contract into which they had entered, they were anxious to obtain delivery of the tanker at the agreed time, and so they promised to pay the extra sum demanded. They paid the additional 10 per cent on each of the remaining instalments, and the ship was delivered to the plaintiffs in November 1974. In July 1975 the claimants sought to recover the extra 10 per cent on the ground that there was no consideration for their payment and that they had agreed to make the payment only when subject to duress. The court held that there was consideration to support the agreement but that the claimants had entered into the contract as a result of duress. However the claimants were held not to be entitled to set aside the contract because they had affirmed the contract by making the final payments without protest and by their delay in making their claim for repayment.

Mocatta J (having found that the agreement to pay the additional 10 per cent was supported by consideration, continued): Having reached the conclusion that there was consideration for the agreement made on June 28 and 29, 1973, I must next consider whether even if that agreement, varying the terms of the original shipbuilding contract of April 10, 1972, was made under a threat to break that original contract and the various increased instalments were made consequently under the varied agreement, the increased sums can be recovered as money had and received. Mr Longmore [counsel for the plaintiffs] submitted that they could be, provided they were involuntary payments and not made, albeit perhaps with some grumbling, to close the transaction.

Certainly this is the well-established position if payments are made, for example, to avoid the wrongful seizure of goods where there is no prior agreement to make such payments. The best known English case to this effect is probably *Maskell v Horner* [1915] 3 KB 106, where the plaintiff had over many years paid illegal tolls on his goods offered for sale in the vicinity of Spitalfields Market. The plaintiff had paid under protest, though the process was so prolonged, that the protests became almost in the nature of jokes, though the plaintiff had in fact suffered seizures of his goods when he had not paid. Lord Reading CJ did not say that express words of protest were always necessary, though they might be useful evidence to negative voluntary payments; the circumstances taken as a whole must indicate that the payments were involuntary. Buckley LJ at 124, regarded the making of a protest before paying to avoid the wrongful seizure of one's goods as 'a further factor,' which went to show that the payment was not voluntary. Pickford LJ at 126 likewise regarded the fact of protest as 'some indication' that the payer intended to resist the claim.

There are a number of well-known examples in the books of English cases where the payments made have been involuntary by reason of some wrongful threatened action or inaction in relation to goods and have subsequently been recovered, but where the issue has not been complicated by the payments having been made under a contract. Some of these cases have concerned threats to seize, seizure or wrongful detention of goods, *Maskell v Horner* being the best known modern example of the former two categories and *Astley v Reynolds* (1731) 2 Str. 915 a good example of the latter category, where a pawnbroker refused to release plate when the plaintiff tendered the money lent and, on demand, more than the legal rate of interest, since without this the pawnbroker would not release the plaintiff's plate. The plaintiff recovered the excess, as having paid it under compulsion and it was held no answer that an alternative remedy might lie in trover.

Mr Longmore referred me to other cases decided in this country bordering upon what he called economic duress as distinct from duress to goods. Thus in *Parker v Great Western Railway Co.* (1844) 7 Man. & G 253, approved in *Great Western Railway Co. v Sutton* (1869) LR 4 HL 226, it was held that the railway was not entitled to differentiate adversely between charges on goods made against one carrier or packer using the railway and others. Excess charges payable by such persons were recovered. In advising the House of Lords in the latter case, Willes J said, at 249:

'. . . I have always understood that when a man pays more than he is bound to do by law for the performance of a duty which the law says is owed to him for nothing, or for less than he has paid, there is a compulsion or concussion in respect of which he is entitled to recover the excess by condictio indebiti, or action for money had and received. This is every day's practice as to excess freight.'

Another case, decided in 1844, on which Mr Longmore relied was *Close v Phipps* (1844) 7 Man. & G 586, in which the attorney of a mortgagee threatened to sell the mortgaged property unless certain costs, to which he was not entitled, were paid in addition to the mortgage money. The additional costs were paid under protest and were subsequently recovered as money had and received. It was stressed in argument, rightly I think, that this was a case of money paid under duress, the duress being a threatened breach of contract, though in Goff and Jones, *The Law of Restitution* (1966), 149 the case is categorised as an example of duress of goods. . . .

There has been considerable discussion in the books whether, if an agreement is made under duress of goods to pay a sum of money and there is some consideration for the agreement, the excess sum can be recovered. The authority for this suggested distinction is *Skeate v Beale* (1841) 11 Ad. & El. 983. It was there said by Lord Denman CJ that an agreement was not void because made under duress of goods, the distinction between that case and the cases of money paid to recover goods wrongfully seized being said to be obvious in that the agreement was not compulsorily but voluntarily entered into. In the slightly later case of *Wakefield v Newbon* (1844) 6 QB 276, Lord Denman CJ referred to cases such as *Skeate v Beale* as 'that class where the parties have come to a voluntary settlement of their concerns, and have chosen to pay what is found due.' Kerr J in *Occidental Worldwide Investment Corporation v Skibs A/S Avanti (The Siboen and The Sibotre)* [1976] 1 Lloyd's Rep. 293, 335, gave strong expression to the view that the suggested distinction based on *Skeate v Beale* would not be observed today. He said, though obiter, that *Skeate v Beale* would not justify a decision:

'For instance, if I should be compelled to sign a lease or some other contract for a nominal but legally sufficient consideration under an imminent threat of having my house burnt down or a valuable picture slashed, though without any threat of physical violence to anyone, I do not think that the law would uphold the agreement.'

I was referred to a number of cases decided overseas. *Nixon v Furphy* (1925) 25 SR (NSW) 151; *Knutson v Bourkes Syndicate* [1941] 3 DLR 593 and *In re Hooper and Grass' Contract* [1949] VLR 269, all of which have a similarity to *Close v Phipps*, 7 Man. & G 586. Perhaps their greatest importance, however, is the quotation in the first mentioned from the judgment of Isaacs J in *Smith v William Charlick Ltd* (1924) 34 CLR 38, 56 where he said:

'It is conceded that the only ground on which the promise to repay could be implied is "compulsion." The payment is said by the respondent not to have been "voluntary" but "forced" from it within the contemplation of the law . . . "Compulsion" in relation to a payment of which refund is sought, and whether it is also variously called "coercion," "exaction" or "force," includes every species of duress or conduct analogous to duress, actual or threatened, exerted by or on behalf of the payee and applied to the person or the property or any right of the person who pays . . . Such compulsion is a legal wrong, and the law provides a remedy by raising a fictional promise to repay.'

These cases do not, however, expressly deal with the position arising when the threat or compulsion result in a new or varied contract. This was, or something very like it, however, the position in *Sundell's* case, 56 SR (NSW) 323. . . . It would seem . . . that the Australian courts would be prepared to allow the recovery of excess money paid, even under a new contract, as the result of a threat to break an earlier contract, since the threat or compulsion would be applied to the original contractual right of the party subject to the compulsion or economic duress. This also seems to be the view in the United States, where this was one of the grounds of decision in *King Construction Co. v W. M. Smith Electric Co.* (1961) 350 SW 2d 940. This view also accords with what was said in *D. & C. Builders Ltd v Rees* [1966] 2 QB 617, 625, *per* Lord Denning MR: 'No person can insist on a settlement procured by intimidation.'

. . .

I may here usefully cite a further short passage from the valuable remarks of Kerr J in *The Siboen and The Sibotre* [1976] 1 Lloyd's Rep. 293, 336, where, after referring to three of the Australian cases I have cited, he said:

'It is true that in [*D & C Builders Ltd v Rees*], and in all the three Australian cases, it was held that there had been no consideration for the settlement which the courts reopened. But I do not think that it would have made any difference if the defendants in these cases had also insisted on some purely nominal but legally sufficient consideration. If the contract is void the consideration would be recoverable in quasi-contract; if it is voidable equity could rescind the contract and order the return of the consideration.'

It is also interesting at this point to quote a few sentences from an article entitled 'Duress As A Vitiating Factor in Contract' by Mr Beatson, Fellow of Merton College, Oxford in (1974) 33 *Cambridge Law Journal* 97, 108:

'It is submitted that there is no reason for making a distinction between actual payments and agreements to pay. If that is so there is nothing to prevent a court from finding that duress of goods is a ground upon which the validity of a contract can be impeached . . . The law was accurately stated by the courts of South Carolina as early as 1795, when it was said that ". . . whenever assumpsit will lie for money extorted by duress of goods, a party may defend himself against any claim upon him for money to be paid in consequence of any contract made under similar circumstances." '

Before proceeding further it may be useful to summarise the conclusions I have so far reached. First, I do not take the view that the recovery of money paid under duress other than to the person is necessarily limited to duress to goods falling within one of the categories hitherto established by the English cases. I would respectfully follow and adopt the broad statement of principle laid down by Isaacs J cited earlier and frequently quoted and applied in the Australian cases. Secondly, from this it follows that the compulsion may take the form of 'economic duress' if the necessary facts are proved. A threat to break a contract may amount to such 'economic duress.' Thirdly, if there has been such a form of duress leading to a contract for consideration, I think that contract is a voidable one which can be avoided and the excess money paid under it recovered.

I think the facts found in this case do establish that the agreement to increase the price by 10 per cent reached at the end of June 1973 was caused by what may be called 'economic duress.' The Yard were adamant in insisting on the increased price without having any legal justification for so doing and the owners realised that the Yard would not accept anything other than an unqualified agreement to the increase. The owners might have claimed damages in arbitration against the Yard with all the inherent unavoidable uncertainties of litigation, but in view of the position of the Yard vis-à-vis their relations with Shell it would be unreasonable to hold that this is the course they should have taken: see *Astley v Reynolds* (1731) 2 Str. 915. The owners made a very reasonable offer of arbitration coupled with security for any award in the Yard's favour that might be made, but this was refused. They then made their agreement, which can truly I think be said to have been made under compulsion, by the telex of June 28 without prejudice to their rights. I do not consider the Yard's ignorance of the Shell charter material. It may well be that had they known of it they would have been even more exigent.

If I am right in the conclusion reached with some doubt earlier that there was consideration for the 10 per cent increase agreement reached at the end of June 1973, and it be right to regard this as having been reached under a kind of duress in the form of economic pressure, then what is said in *Chitty on Contracts*, 24th edn (1977), vol. 1, para. 442, to which both counsel referred me, is relevant, namely, that a contract entered into under duress is voidable and not void:

'... consequently a person who has entered into a contract under duress, may either affirm or avoid such contract after the duress has ceased; and if he has so voluntarily acted under it with a full knowledge of all the circumstances he may be held bound on the ground of ratification, or if, after escaping from the duress, he takes no steps to set aside the transaction, he may be found to have affirmed it.' ...

No protest of any kind was made by the owners after their telex of June 28, 1973. . . . There was . . . a delay between November 27, 1974, when the *Atlantic Baron* was delivered and July 30, 1975, before the owners put forward their claim.

The owners were, therefore, free from the duress on November 27, 1974, and took no action by way of protest or otherwise between their important telex of June 28, 1973, and their formal claim for the return of the excess 10 per cent paid of July 30, 1975. . . . One cannot dismiss this delay as of no significance, though I would not consider it conclusive by itself. I do not attach any special importance to the lack of protest made at the time of the assignment, since the documents made no reference to the increased 10 per cent. However, by the time the *Atlantic Baron* was due for delivery in November 1974, market conditions had changed radically . . . and the owners must have been aware of this. . . . I have come to the conclusion that the important points here are that since there was no danger at this time in registering a protest, the final payments were made without any qualification and were followed by a delay until July 31, 1975, before the owners put forward their claim, the correct inference to draw, taking an objective view of the facts, is that the action and inaction of the owners can only be regarded as an affirmation of the variation in June 1973 of the terms of the original contract by the agreement to pay the additional 10 per cent. In reaching this conclusion I have not, of course, overlooked the findings in paragraph 45 of the special case, but I do not think that an intention on the part of the owners not to affirm the agreement for the extra payments not indicated to the Yard can avail them in their view of their overt acts. As was said in *Deacon v Transport Regulation Board* [1958] VR 458, 460 in considering whether a payment was made voluntarily or not: 'No secret mental reservation of the doer is material. The question is—what would his conduct indicate to a reasonable man as his mental state.' I think this test is equally applicable to the decision this court has to make whether a voidable contract has been affirmed or not, and I have applied this test in reaching the conclusion I have just expressed.

I think I should add very shortly that having considered the many authorities cited, even if I had come to a different conclusion on the issue about consideration, I would have come to the same decision adverse to the owners on the question whether the payments were made voluntarily in the sense of being made to close the transaction.

NOTES AND QUESTIONS

1. The article by J Beatson, which is cited by Mocatta J, has since been revised and updated: see 'Duress, Restitution and Contract Renegotiation' in Beatson, *The Use and Abuse of Unjust Enrichment* (1991), 95.

2. Is the fact that the devaluation of the dollar was beyond the control of the parties of any relevance to the presence or absence of economic duress?

3. Was Mocatta J correct to conclude that the shipbuilder's ignorance of the Shell charter was not a material factor?

4. Why was the defendant's threatened breach of contract held to be illegitimate? What does illegitimate mean? Does it mean (a) that it was made in bad faith, or (b) that the cause of the threat was an event which was outside the control of the defendant, or (c) simply that a breach of contract has been threatened, on the basis that all breaches of contract are wrongful, or (d) that the terms of the threatened renegotiation were substantively unfair? The danger here is that the courts will simply draw up a list of factors which are stated to be relevant but fail to state why they are relevant or explain the extent to which they are relevant. Signs of this approach can be seen in the judgment of Dyson J in *DSDN Subsea Ltd v Petroleum Geo-Services ASA* [2000] BLR 530, 545 when he stated that:

> In determining whether there has been illegitimate pressure, the court takes into account a range of factors. These include whether there has been an actual or threatened breach of contract; whether the person allegedly exerting the pressure has acted in good or bad faith; whether the victim had any realistic practical alternative but to submit to the pressure; whether the victim protested at the time; and whether he affirmed and sought to rely on the contract. These are all relevant factors. Illegitimate pressure must be distinguished from the rough and tumble of the pressures of normal commercial bargaining.

While authority can be found to support the proposition that these are all relevant factors, it is not clear that they are all relevant to the question whether the pressure applied was illegitimate. In particular, the existence of 'any realistic practical alternative' would seem to be more relevant to the existence of a sufficient causal link than to the legitimacy of the pressure applied.

5. Were the defendants in bad faith? Does it matter whether or not they were in bad faith? Can a breach of contract threatened in good faith ever constitute duress?

6. Burrows suggests, 233 that:

> A threatened breach of contract should be regarded as illegitimate if concerned to exploit the claimant's weakness rather than solving financial or other problems of the defendant. To this can be added two supplementary or clarificatory ideas. . . . First, a threat should not be considered illegitimate (made in bad faith) if the threat is a reaction to circumstances that almost constitute frustration. And, secondly, a threat should not be considered illegitimate (made in bad faith) if it merely corrects what was always clearly a bad bargain.

Do you agree?

7. Should any significance be attached to the fact that the court was being asked to set aside a contract, rather than merely order the return of a payment made as a result of duress?

8. M Ogilvie ('Economic Duress, Inequality of Bargaining Power and Threatened Breach of Contract' (1981) 26 *McGill LJ* 289, 318–19) states that

> Economic duress by threatened breach of contract is the unconscionable abuse of a superior bargaining position to place the victim of the threats in the position of having no commercially viable alternatives to submission to the threats. To determine whether there is economic duress, the courts must first explore the factual question of what alternatives are available other than submission and if they discover that none are available short of serious consequences such as insolvency or personal bankruptcy, they must assure themselves either that the absence is the actual result of the exertion of an unacceptable amount of pressure or that the superior party has exploited the absence of viable alternatives, regardless of its explanation, in an unconscionable manner. What is unconscionable in other circumstances, whether they be commercial or consumer, will be unconscionable here. It should be added that, in itself, unjust enrichment provides no basis for redress: restitution of ill-gotten gains should follow the law, not be the law.

Do you agree?

9. In the course of his judgment Mocatta J discussed the case of *Parker v Great Western Railway Co.* (1844) 7 Man. & G 253, which was described by counsel as a case 'bordering upon . . . economic duress'. It can be argued that *Parker* is an example of a broader category of duress where the duress takes the form of illegitimate threats made to support a demand for payment in excess of what is permitted by statute (see Burrows, 223–4). There is an obvious overlap here with the decision of the House of Lords in *Woolwich Equitable Building Society v Inland Revenue Commissioners* (below, 626), where it was held that payments made pursuant to a demand for tax which was *ultra vires* because of the invalidity of the subordinate legislation upon which the demand was based were recoverable. The recognition of the latter right of recovery reduces the need for claimants to establish a case of duress, but it should not be thought that its effect is to render the duress analysis wholly redundant. Thus Lord Goff stated that, particularly in the light of the development of economic duress, it would not be right 'to regard the categories of compulsion for present purposes as closed'.

- *Pao On v Lau Yiu Long* [1980] AC 614, Privy Council

The claimants were the owners of all the shares of a company called Shing On, while the defendants were the majority shareholders in Fu Chip, a company which 'went public' on 9 February 1973. The principal asset owned by Shing On was a building which the defendants wished to acquire. At the same time, the claimants wished to realize the value of the property by selling the shares in Shing On. So the parties agreed that the claimants would sell the shares in Shing On to the defendants, the price payable to be met by the allotment to the claimants of 4.2 million ordinary shares of $1 each in Fu Chip. It was agreed that the market value of each Fu Chip share was to be deemed to be $2.50, and the claimants also agreed that they would not, before the end of April 1974, sell or transfer 2.5 million of the shares so transferred. This restriction was imposed in order to prevent a depression in the value of Fu Chip shares caused by heavy selling of the shares. The difficulty which this restriction posed for the claimants was that their inability to sell the shares exposed them to the risk of any drop in their value. In order to reduce this exposure, the parties entered into a subsidiary agreement under which the defendants agreed, on or before the end of April 1974, to buy back the shares at $2.50 *per* share. However, this agreement operated to the advantage of the defendants because they could require the claimants to sell them the shares for $2.50 even if the market value of the shares had risen beyond $2.50. When the claimants discovered this, they informed the defendants that they would not perform the main agreement unless the subsidiary agreement was cancelled and replaced by a guarantee which only came into operation in the event of the price of the shares falling below $2.50. The defendants were anxious to complete the transaction so that public confidence in the newly formed company was not undermined, and so they agreed to the terms proposed by the claimants and the guarantee was duly executed. The price of Fu Chip shares subsequently slumped on the market and the claimants sought to enforce the guarantee against the defendants. The defendants maintained that the guarantee was unenforceable because it was not supported by consideration and had been procured by duress. The Privy Council rejected the defendants' argument and held that the guarantee was supported by consideration and that there had been no operative duress because the defendants could not show that their will had been coerced such as to vitiate their consent.

Lord Scarman (delivering the judgment of the Board)
Duress, whatever from it takes, is a coercion of the will so as to vitiate consent. Their Lordships

agree with the observation of Kerr J in *Occidental Worldwide Investment Corporation v Skibs A/S Avanti* [1976] 1 Lloyd's Rep. 293, 336 that in a contractual situation commercial pressure is not enough. There must be present some factor 'which could in law be regarded as a coercion of his will so as to vitiate his consent.' This conception is in line with what was said in this Board's decision in *Barton v Armstrong* [1976] AC 104, 121 by Lord Wilberforce and Lord Simon of Glaisdale— observations with which the majority judgment appears to be in agreement. In determining whether there was a coercion of will such that there was no true consent, it is material to inquire whether the person alleged to have been coerced did or did not protest; whether, at the time he was allegedly coerced into making the contract, he did or did not have an alternative course open to him such as an adequate legal remedy; whether he was independently advised; and whether after entering the contract he took steps to avoid it. All these matters are, as was recognised in *Maskell v Horner* [1915] 3 KB 106, relevant in determining whether he acted voluntarily or not.

In the present case there is unanimity amongst the judges below that there was no coercion of the first defendant's will. In the Court of Appeal the trial judge's finding ... that the first defend- ant considered the matter thoroughly, chose to avoid litigation, and formed the opinion that the risk in giving the guarantee was more apparent than real was upheld. In short, there was com- mercial pressure, but no coercion. Even if this Board was disposed, which it is not, to take a different view, it would not substitute its opinion for that of the judges below on this question of fact.

It is, therefore, unnecessary for the Board to embark upon an inquiry into the question whether English law recognises a category of duress known as 'economic duress.' But, since the question has been fully argued in this appeal, their Lordships will indicate very briefly the view which they have formed. At common law money paid under economic compulsion could be recovered in an action for money had and received: *Astley v Reynolds* (1731) 2 Str. 915. The compulsion had to be such that the party was deprived of 'his freedom of exercising his will' (see 916). It is doubtful, however, whether at common law any duress other than duress to the person sufficed to render a contract voidable: see *Blackstone's Commentaries*, Book 1, 12th edn 130–1 and *Skeate v Beale* (1841) 11 Ad. & E 983. American law (*Williston on Contracts*, 3rd edn) now recognises that a contract may be avoided on the ground of economic duress. The commercial pressure alleged to constitute such duress must, however, be such that the victim must have entered the contract against his will, must have had no alternative course open to him, and must have been confronted with coercive acts by the party exerting the pressure: *Williston on Contracts*, 3rd edn, vol. 13 (1970), section 1603. American judges pay great attention to such evidential matters as the effectiveness of the alternative remedy avail- able, the fact or absence of protest, the availability of independent advice, the benefit received, and the speed with which the victim has sought to avoid the contract. Recently two English judges have recognised that commercial pressure may constitute duress the pressure of which can render a contract voidable: Kerr J in *Occidental Worldwide Investment Corporation v Skibs A/S Avanti* [1976] 1 Lloyd's Rep. 293 and Mocatta J in *North Ocean Shipping Co. Ltd v Hyundai Construction Co. Ltd* [1979] QB 705. Both stressed that the pressure must be such that the victim's consent to the contract was not a voluntary act on his part. In their Lordships' view, there is nothing contrary to principle in recognising economic duress as a factor which may render a contract voidable, pro- vided always that the basis of such recognition is that it must amount to a coercion of will, which vitiates consent. It must be shown that the payment made or the contract entered into was not a voluntary act.

NOTES AND QUESTIONS

1. Is the 'coercion of the will' test a satisfactory basis for the development of the law relating to economic duress? What is the difference between 'commercial pressure' and 'coercion'?

2. What is the significance of the fact that (a) the party alleged to have been coerced did not protest; (b) independent advice was available to the coerced party; and (c) an alternative remedy was available to that party?

3. Was Lord Scarman of the view that a threatened breach of contract is always regarded as illegitimate pressure?

4. What significance, if any, should be attached to the fact that the claimants were seeking to correct what was clearly a bad bargain for them? In such a case, should a court be more inclined to accept that a threatened breach of contract is legitimate?

5. What is the relationship between consideration and duress? In *Williams v Roffey Brothers & Nicholls (Contractors) Ltd* [1991] 1 QB 1 the defendants, who had entered into a contract to renovate a block of flats, subcontracted the carpentry work to the claimant for a price of £20,000. During the course of the work the claimant discovered that he had fixed the price too low. It was in the defendants' interest to ensure that the work was completed on time because, if it was not, they would be liable to pay compensation under a 'penalty clause' contained in the main contract. So the defendants arranged a meeting with the claimant, at which it was agreed that they would pay the claimant an extra £10,300 at the rate of £575 *per* flat on completion to ensure that the work was completed on time. The claimant sued the defendants to recover a proportion of the additional promised payment but the defendants argued, *inter alia*, that there was no consideration to support their promise to pay the additional sum as the claimant had only done what he was already contractually obliged to do, namely finish the work on time (see, for example, *Stilk v Myrick* (1809) 2 Camp. 317). The Court of Appeal, adopting a pragmatic approach to the identification of consideration, found that the defendants' promise to pay was supported by consideration because they obtained a practical benefit as a result of the claimant's promise to complete on time in that, *inter alia*, it enabled them to avoid liability under the penalty clause in the main contract. In shifting the focus of attention from consideration to duress, Glidewell LJ relied on dicta of Lord Scarman (set out above, 412), while Purchas LJ stated (at 21) that the 'modern cases tend to depend more on the defence of duress in a commercial context rather than lack of consideration for the second agreement'. Duress was not in issue in *Roffey* because it had not been pleaded by the defendants, but Purchas LJ stated (at 21) that it did not lie in the mouth of the defendants to assert a defence of duress because the initiative in coming to the second agreement had emanated from them. Does this inevitably rule out a finding of duress? See further P Birks, 'The Travails of Duress' [1990] *LMCLQ* 342 (below, 421).

- *Universe Tankships of Monrovia v International Transport Workers' Federation* [1983] 1 AC 366, House of Lords

The claimants' vessel, the *Universe Sentinel*, was 'blacked' by the defendant trade union while it was docked at Milford Haven. The blacking took the form of an instruction to the tugmen at the harbour to refuse to operate their tugs. This refusal constituted a breach by the tugmen of their contracts of employment with the Harbour Authority. Negotiations then took place between the parties. The defendants demanded that the plaintiffs pay the crew of the ship $80,000 in back-pay and pay a further sum of $6,480 to the defendants' welfare fund. The claimants paid the money in order to obtain the release of their vessel and then brought the present action to recover the $6,480 (but not the back-pay) which they had paid. It was conceded that the circumstances in which the payment was made amounted to economic duress but the defendants maintained that they were nevertheless entitled to retain the money because they were acting under an immunity conferred by Parliament in section 13 of the Trade Union and Labour Relations Act 1974. The House of Lords, by a majority (Lord Scarman and Lord Brandon dissenting), held that the defendants did not have the immunity which they asserted and that the money was therefore recoverable.

Lord Diplock: . . . My Lords, I turn to the second ground on which repayment of the $6,480 is claimed, which I will call the duress point. It is not disputed that the circumstances in which ITF demanded that the shipowners should enter into the special agreement and the typescript agreement and should pay the moneys of which the latter documents acknowledge receipt, amounted to economic duress upon the shipowners; that is to say, it is conceded that the financial consequences to the shipowners of the *Universe Sentinel* continuing to be rendered off-hire under her time charter to Texaco, while the blacking continued, were so catastrophic as to amount to a coercion of the shipowners' will which vitiated their consent to those agreements and to the payments made by them to ITF. This concession makes it unnecessary for your Lordships to use the instant appeal as the occasion for a general consideration of the developing law of economic duress as a ground for treating contracts as voidable and obtaining restitution of money paid under economic duress as money had and received to the plaintiffs' use. That economic duress may constitute a ground for such redress was recognised, albeit obiter, by the Privy Council in *Pao On v Lau Yiu Long* [1980] AC 614. The Board in that case referred with approval to two judgments at first instance in the commercial court which recognised that commercial pressure may constitute duress: one by Kerr J in *Occidental Worldwide Investment Corporation v Skibs A/S Avanti* [1976] 1 Lloyd's Rep. 293, the other by Mocatta J in *North Ocean Shipping Co. Ltd v Hyundai Construction Co. Ltd* [1979] QB 705, which traces the development of this branch of the law from its origin in the eighteenth and early nineteenth-century cases.

It is, however, in my view crucial to the decision of the instant appeal to identify the rationale of this development of the common law. It is not that the party seeking to avoid the contract which he has entered into with another party, or to recover money that he has paid to another party in response to a demand, did not know the nature or the precise terms of the contract at the time when he entered into it or did not understand the purpose for which the payment was demanded. The rationale is that his apparent consent was induced by pressure exercised upon him by that other party which the law does not regard as legitimate, with the consequence that the consent is treated in law as revocable unless approbated either expressly or by implication after the illegitimate pressure has ceased to operate on his mind. It is a rationale similar to that which underlies the avoidability of contracts entered into and the recovery of money exacted under colour of office, or under undue influence or in consequence of threats of physical duress.

Commercial pressure, in some degree, exists wherever one party to a commercial transaction is in a stronger bargaining position than the other party. It is not, however, in my view, necessary, nor would it be appropriate in the instant appeal, to enter into the general question of the kinds of circumstances, if any, in which commercial pressure, even though it amounts to a coercion of the will of a party in the weaker bargaining position, may be treated as legitimate and, accordingly, as not giving rise to any legal right of redress. In the instant appeal the economic duress complained of was exercised in the field of industrial relations to which very special considerations apply [*He considered some of these special considerations, in particular the role of the immunities provided by Parliament and continued*].

The use of economic duress to induce another person to part with property or money is not a tort *per se*; the form that the duress takes may, or may not, be tortious. The remedy to which economic duress gives rise is not an action for damages but an action for restitution of property or money exacted under such duress and the avoidance of any contract that had been induced by it; but where the particular form taken by the economic duress used is itself a tort, the restitutional remedy for money had and received by the defendant to the plaintiff's use is one which the plaintiff is entitled to pursue as an alternative remedy to an action for damages in tort.

[*He considered the relevant statutory provisions and concluded that they afforded an 'indication' which the judges should respect 'of where public policy requires that the line should be drawn between what kind of commercial pressure by a trade union upon an employer in the field of industrial relations ought to be treated as legitimised despite the fact that the will of the employer is thereby coerced, and what kind of commercial pressure in that field does amount to economic duress that entitles the employer victim to restitutionary remedies'. He concluded that the action taken by the defendants in the present case did not fall within the scope of the immunity provided by the legislation, with the consequence that the pressure was not 'legitimised' and so the defendants were liable to repay the money to the claimants.*]

Lord Scarman (dissenting): It is, I think, already established law that economic pressure can in law amount to duress; and that duress, if proved, not only renders voidable a transaction into which a person has entered under its compulsion but is actionable as a tort, if it causes damage or loss: *Barton v Armstrong* [1976] AC 104 and *Pao On v Lau Yiu Long* [1980] AC 614. The authorities upon which these two cases were based reveal two elements in the wrong of duress: (1) pressure amounting to compulsion of the will of the victim; and (2) the illegitimacy of the pressure exerted. There must be pressure, the practical effect of which is compulsion or the absence of choice. Compulsion is variously described in the authorities as coercion or the vitiation of consent. The classic case of duress is, however, not the lack of will to submit but the victim's intentional submission arising from the realisation that there is no other practical choice open to him. This is the thread of principle which links the early law of duress (threat to life or limb) with later developments when the law came also to recognise as duress first the threat to property and now the threat to a man's business or trade. . . .

The absence of choice can be proved in various ways, e.g. by protest, by the absence of independent advice, or by a declaration of intention to go to law to recover the money paid or the property transferred: see *Maskell v Horner* [1915] 3 KB 106. But none of these evidential matters goes to the essence of duress. The victim's silence will not assist the bully, if the lack of any practicable choice but to submit is proved. The present case is an excellent illustration. There was no protest at the time, but only a determination to do whatever was needed as rapidly as possible to release the ship. Yet nobody challenges the judge's finding that the owner acted under compulsion. . . .

The real issue in the appeal is, therefore, as to the second element in the wrong duress: was the pressure applied by the ITF in the circumstances of this case one which the law recognises as legitimate? For, as Lord Wilberforce and Lord Simon of Glaisdale said in *Barton v Armstrong* [1976] AC 104, 121**d**: 'the pressure must be one of a kind which the law does not regard as legitimate.'

As the two noble and learned Lords remarked at 121**d**, in life, including the life of commerce and finance, many acts are done 'under pressure, sometimes overwhelming pressure': but they are not necessarily done under duress. That depends on whether the circumstances are such that the law regards the pressure as legitimate.

In determining what is legitimate two matters may have to be considered. The first is as to the nature of the pressure. In many cases this will be decisive, though not in every case. And so the second question may have to be considered, namely, the nature of the demand which the pressure is applied to support.

The origin of the doctrine of duress in threats to life or limb, or to property, suggests strongly that the law regards the threat of unlawful action as illegitimate, whatever the demand. Duress can, of course, exist even if the threat is one of lawful action: whether it does so depends upon the nature of the demand. Blackmail is often a demand supported by a threat to do what is lawful, e.g. to report criminal conduct to the police. In many cases, therefore, 'What [one] has to justify is not the threat, but the demand . . .': see *per* Lord Atkin in *Thorne v Motor Trade Association* [1937] AC 797, 806.

The present is a case in which the nature of the demand determines whether the pressure threatened or applied, i.e. the blacking, was lawful or unlawful. If it was unlawful, it is conceded that the owner acted under duress and can recover. If it was lawful, it is conceded that there was no duress and the sum sought by the owner is irrecoverable. The lawfulness or otherwise of the demand depends upon whether it was an act done in contemplation or furtherance of a trade dispute. If it was, it would not be actionable in tort: section 13(1) of the Act. Although no question of tortious liability arises in this case and section 13(1) is not, therefore, directly in point, it is not possible, in my view, to say of acts which are protected by statute from suit in tort that they nevertheless can amount to duress. Parliament having enacted that such acts are not actionable in tort, it would be inconsistent with legislative policy to say that, when the remedy sought is not damages for tort but recovery of money paid, they become unlawful.

In order to determine whether the making of the demand was an act done in contemplation or furtherance of a trade dispute, it is necessary to refer to section 29 which sets out the statutory meaning of 'trade dispute.'

The issue therefore is reduced to the one question. Was the demand for contributions to the welfare fund connected with one or more of the matters specified in section 29 of the Act? It is common ground that unless the demand was connected with 'terms and conditions of employment' it was not within the section. [*After examining the relevant provisions he concluded that the demand was related to the terms and conditions of employment and so was a legitimate exercise of pressure and did not constitute duress.*]

Lord Russell and **Lord Cross** delivered speeches agreeing that the appeal should be allowed. **Lord Brandon** dissented.

QUESTIONS

1. What use, if any, did their Lordships make of the 'coercion of the will' test?
2. Was the claimants' claim based on the defendants' wrong of inducing breach of contract?
3. What was the relationship between the trade dispute legislation and the claimants' restitutionary right to recover the sum paid?
4. The claimants also claimed that they were entitled to the return of the money paid to the welfare fund on the ground that the money paid was held by the defendants on a resulting trust for the claimants. The welfare fund was set up to 'help provide welfare, social and recreational facilities in ports around the world for seafarers of all nations, especially those serving in flag-of-convenience ships'. The rules provided that the money belonging to the fund should be spent only in accordance with the rules and the rules themselves made no provision for their alteration. The claimants argued that the money paid was held on a trust which was void because it was a non-charitable purpose trust which failed to comply with the certainty of objects test. This argument was rejected by the House of Lords on the ground that the money had been paid by way of contract and not trust, so that the claimants could not be said to have retained an equitable interest in the money which had been paid to the defendants. But could the claimants have argued that, since the money was paid as the result of the application of illegitimate pressure, immediately on its receipt it was held on a resulting trust designed to reverse the unjust enrichment of the defendants at the expense of the claimants? This would appear to be the view of Professor Birks (below, 750) but his argument must now be read in the light of the decision of the House of Lords in *Westdeutsche Landesbank Girozentrale v Islington LBC* (below, 727).

- **B & S Contracts and Design Ltd v Victor Green Publications Ltd**
  [1984] ICR 419, Court of Appeal

The claimants agreed to erect stands at Olympia for the defendants. The contract between the parties contained a force majeure clause which stated that, while 'every effort will be made to carry out a contract based on an estimate' . . . its due performance was 'subject to variation or cancellation owing to . . . strikes . . . work-to-rule or go-slow or overtime bans, lock-outs . . . or any other cause beyond [the claimants'] control'. The claimants experienced difficulties with their work-force, who refused to erect the stands unless they were paid £9,000 severance pay. The claimants offered the workmen £4,500, but this was rejected. The defendants were informed of the position and Mr Barnes, a director of the defendant company, offered to pay £4,500 as an advance payment to enable the claimants to meet the claim of their workforce. This offer was rejected by the claimants' financial director, Mr Fenech, who informed Mr Barnes that the claimants would be unable to perform the contract unless the men could be persuaded to stay at work. Mr Barnes then said to Mr Fenech 'Well, you have me over a barrel' and so the defendants paid the extra £4,500 to the claimants. The contract was duly performed but, when the claimants presented the defendants with the bill, the defendants deducted the £4,500 from the contract price and paid the balance. The claimants sued for £4,500 as due under the contract, and the defendants counterclaimed for the same amount as paid under duress. Sir Douglas Frank QC, sitting as a deputy judge of the High Court, dismissed the claimants' claim on the ground that the money had been paid under duress. The claimants appealed unsuccessfully to the Court of Appeal who also found that the money had been paid under duress.

Eveleigh LJ: . . . For the purpose of this case it is sufficient to say that if the claimant has been influenced against his will to pay money under the threat of unlawful damage to his economic interest he will be entitled to claim that money back, and as I understand it that proposition was not dissented from.

In this case the plaintiffs say that there was no threat; that Mr Fenech was really stating the obvious, stating the factual situation, namely, that unless they could retain the workforce they would be unable to perform their contract. I have had some difficulty in deciding whether or not the evidence in this case did disclose a threat, but on a full reading of the evidence of Mr Fenech and Mr Barnes and the cross-examination of Mr Fenech I have come to the conclusion that the judge was right in the way in which he put it. There was here, as I understand the evidence, a veiled threat although there was no specific demand, and this conclusion is very much supported, as I see it, by Mr Barnes's reaction which must have been apparent to Mr Fenech when Mr Barnes said, 'You have got me over a barrel.' On 18 April what was happening was this. Mr Fenech was in effect saying, 'We are not going on unless you are prepared to pay another £4,500 in addition to the contract price,' and it was clear at that stage that there was no other way for Mr Barnes to avoid the consequences that would ensue if the exhibition could not be held from his stands than by paying the £4,500 to secure the workforce. But, the plaintiffs now say, 'Even so, this was not an unlawful threat or a threat of unlawful action because seeing that there was a strike the strike clause—the force majeure clause—applied and the plaintiffs were entitled to take advantage of that clause and to cancel the contract, and so there was here no threat of unlawful action.' [he considered the force majeure clause and concluded that it did not apply to the present facts] . . .

Griffiths LJ: I agree. The law on economic pressure creating a situation which will be recognised as duress is in the course of development, and it is clear that many difficult decisions lie ahead of the courts. Many commercial contracts are varied during their currency because the parties are faced with changing circumstances during the performance of the contract, and it is certainly not on every occasion when one of the parties unwillingly agrees to a variation that the law would consider that he had acted by reason of duress. The cases will have to be examined in the light of their particular circumstances. But two recent decisions of the highest authority—the decision of the Privy Council in *Pao On v Lau Yiu Long* [1980] AC 614 and *Universe Tankships Inc. of Monrovia v International Transport Workers' Federation* [1982] ICR 262—establish that a threatened breach of contract may impose such economic pressure that the law will recognise that a payment made as a result of the threatened breach is recoverable on the grounds of duress.

The facts of this case appear to me to be as follows. The plaintiffs intended to break their contract, subject to the effect of the force majeure clause, by allowing their workforce to walk off the job in circumstances in which they could not possibly replace it with another workforce. The defendants offered to advance the sum of £4,500 on the contract price, which would have enabled the plaintiffs to pay the men a sufficient extra sum of money to induce them to remain on the job. The plaintiffs refused this sum of money. There is no question that they refused to pay as a matter of principle. They refused to pay because they did not want to reduce the sum they would receive for the contract. They said to the defendants, 'If you will give us £4,500 we will complete the contract.' The defendants, faced with this demand, were in an impossible position. If they refused to hand over the sum of £4,500 they would not be able to erect the stands in this part of the exhibition, which would have clearly caused grave damage to their reputation and I would have thought might have exposed them to very heavy claims from the exhibitors who had leased space from them and hoped to use those stands in the ensuing exhibition. They seem to me to have been placed in the position envisaged by Lord Scarman in the Privy Council decision, *Pao On v Lau Yiu Long* [1980] AC 614, in which they were faced with no alternative course of action but to pay the sum demanded of them. It was submitted to us that there was no overt demand, but it was implicit in negotiations between the parties that the plaintiffs were putting the defendants into a corner and it was quite apparent to the defendants, by reason of the plaintiffs' conduct, that unless they handed over £4,500 the plaintiffs would walk off the job. This is, in my view, a situation in which the judge was fully entitled to find in the circumstances of this case that there was duress. As the defendants' director said, he was over a barrel, he had no alternative but to pay; he had no chance of going to any other source of labour to erect the stands. That being so, the only fall-back position for the plaintiffs was the force majeure clause. Clauses of this kind have to be construed upon the basis that those relying on them will have taken all reasonable efforts to avoid the effect of the various matters set out in the clause which entitle them to vary or cancel the contract: see *Bulman & Dickson v Fenwick & Co.* [1894] 1 QB 179, in the speech of Lord Esher MR at 185. Quite apart from that general principle this particular clause starts with the following wording: 'Every effort will be made to carry out any contract based on an estimate,' which is saying in express terms that which the law will imply when construing such a clause.

There is no doubt that the plaintiffs were faced with a strike situation and the question is, did they behave reasonably when faced with this situation? I, like Eveleigh LJ, am far from saying that whenever a contracting party with such a clause is faced with a strike situation he must give in to it in order to perform his contract. If that were the situation the clause would be absolutely worthless. But the special circumstances of this case, as I see it, are as follows. The plaintiffs were going to close down their subsidiary company; they had already dismissed the workforce and the men were working out their time. There is no question here of any ongoing industrial situation between the plaintiffs' subsidiary company and the workforce. There was no question of principle at stake; the plaintiffs were perfectly prepared to pay what the men were demanding save for the fact, they said, they did not have the money available. Well, then there came the offer of the defendants to make the money available by giving them an advance. In those circumstances I can see no reason why they should not have accepted the money and paid the workforce save their own immediate economic interests, and they chose not to do that but to put pressure on the defendants by refusing the offer and indicating that the only way out was for the defendants to hand over the £4,500 as a gift rather than as an advance.

I think that was thoroughly unreasonable behaviour, and that being so they are not entitled to rely upon the force majeure clause, and for these reasons I agree this appeal fails.

Kerr LJ: . . . In the light of the authorities it is perhaps important to emphasise that there is no question in this case of the defendants having subsequently approbated this payment or failed to seek to avoid it, which in some cases (such as the *North Ocean Shipping Co. Ltd v Hyundai Construction Co. Ltd* [1979] QB 705, a decision of Mocatta J, to which Eveleigh LJ has referred) would be fatal. In the present case the defendants took immediate action by deducting that £4,500 from the invoice price.

I also bear in mind that a threat to break a contract unless money is paid by the other party can, but by no means always will, constitute duress. It appears from the authorities that it will only constitute duress if the consequences of a refusal would be serious and immediate so that there is no reasonable alternative open, such as by legal redress, obtaining an injunction, etc. I think that this is implicit in the authorities to which we have been referred, of which the most recent one is *Universe Tankships Inc. of Monrovia v International Transport Workers' Federation* [1982] ICR 262. I would only refer to one passage from the speech of Lord Scarman, not because he states anything that differs from what was stated elsewhere, but because I wonder whether this passage may not contain a typographical error. Lord Scarman is reported at 288–9 as having said—and it applies to the facts of this case:

> 'The classic case of duress is, however, not the lack of will to submit but the victim's intentional submission arising from the realisation that there is no other practical choice open to him.'

I wonder whether 'the lack of will to submit' should not have been 'the lack of will to resist' or 'the lack of will in submitting.' However that may be, there was no other practical choice open to the defendants in the present case, and accordingly I agree that this is a case where money has been paid under duress, which was accordingly recoverable by the defendants provided they acted promptly as they did, and which they have recovered by deducting it from the contract price. In these circumstances the plaintiffs' claim for this additional sum must fail.

NOTES AND QUESTIONS

1. Is the availability of an alternative remedy relevant (i) as evidence of coercion, and so little more than a re-formulation of the coercion of the will theory, (ii) because it is a prerequisite to a finding of duress, or (iii) because it is relevant in the determination of whether the victim's response to the undoubted coercion was reasonable? In cases such as *Pao On* it seems clear that it is performing an evidential function, but in later cases such as *B & S Contracts* and *Vantage Navigation Corporation v Suhail and Saud Bahwan Building Materials LLC (The Alev)* [1989] 1 Lloyd's Rep. 138, 146–7 it seems to be given a greater role, approximating more closely to a substantive prerequisite to a finding of duress. See further E MacDonald, 'Duress by Threatened Breach of Contract' [1990] *JBL* 460.

2. What would have been the position if the court had concluded that the claimants were entitled to terminate the contract under the *force majeure* clause? Would the demand for payment have been 'illegitimate'?

3. Where a contractor does not have the means of ensuring that the contract is performed, will his passing on of information to the other party that he cannot perform always amount to a threat sufficient to constitute duress? Could it not be seen as an attempt to mitigate his liability for breach?

- *Crescendo Management Pty. Ltd v Westpac Banking Corp.*
  (1988) 19 NSWLR 40, New South Wales Court of Appeal

The claimant sought to set aside a mortgage entered into with the defendants on the ground that it had been executed under economic duress. It was held that he was not entitled to set aside the mortgage because the court was satisfied that any pressure exerted by the defendants had played no part in the execution of the mortgage. The majority of the court (Samuels JA and Mahoney JA) found it unnecessary to go any further and express a view about the conceptual basis of duress, but McHugh JA chose to embark upon a broader analysis of economic duress in the following terms.

McHugh JA: . . . The rationale of the doctrine of economic duress is that the law will not give effect to an apparent consent which was induced by pressure exercised upon one party by another party when the law regards that pressure as illegitimate: *Universe Tankships Inc. of Monrovia v International Transport Workers' Federation* [1983] 1 AC 366 at 384, *per* Lord Diplock. As his Lordship pointed out, the consequence is that the 'consent is treated in law as revocable unless approbated either expressly or by implication after the illegitimate pressure has ceased to operate on his mind' (at 384). In the same case Lord Scarman declared (at 400) that the authorities show that there are two elements in the realm of duress: (a) pressure amounting to compulsion of the will of the victim and (b) the illegitimacy of the pressure exerted. 'There must be pressure', said Lord Scarman 'the practical effect of which is compulsion or the absence of choice'.

The reference in *Universe Tankships Inc. of Monrovia v International Transport Workers' Federation* and other cases to compulsion 'of the will' of the victim is unfortunate. They appear to have overlooked that in *Director of Public Prosecutions for Northern Ireland v Lynch* [1975] AC 653, a case concerned with duress as a defence to a criminal proceeding, the House of Lords rejected the notion that duress is concerned with overbearing the will of the accused. The Law Lords were unanimous in coming to the conclusion, perhaps best expressed (at 695) in the speech of Lord Simon of Glaisdale 'that duress is not inconsistent with act and will, the will being deflected, not destroyed'. Indeed, if the true basis of duress is that the will is overborne a contract entered into under duress should be void. Yet the accepted doctrine is that the contract is merely voidable.

In my opinion the overbearing of the will theory of duress should be rejected. A person who is the subject of duress usually knows only too well what he is doing. But he chooses to submit to the demand or pressure rather than take an alternative course of action. The proper approach in my opinion is to ask whether any applied pressure induced the victim to enter into the contract and then ask whether that pressure went beyond what the law is prepared to countenance as legitimate? Pressure will be illegitimate if it consists of unlawful threats or amounts to unconscionable conduct. But the categories are not closed. Even overwhelming pressure, not amounting to unconscionable or unlawful conduct, however, will not necessarily constitute economic duress.

In their dissenting advice in *Barton v Armstrong* [1973] 2 NSWLR 598; [1976] AC 104, Lord Wilberforce and Lord Simon of Glaisdale pointed out (at 634; 121):

'. . . in life, including the life of commerce and finance, many acts are done under pressure, sometimes overwhelming pressure, so that one can say that the actor had no choice but to act. Absence of choice in this sense does not negate consent in law: for this the pressure must be one of a kind which the law does not regard as legitimate. Thus, out of the various means by which consent may be obtained—advice, persuasion, influence, inducement, representation, commercial pressure—the law has come to select some which it will not accept as a reason for voluntary action: fraud, abuse of relation of confidence, undue influence, duress or coercion.'

In *Pao On v Lau Yiu Long* [1980] AC 614, the Judicial Committee accepted (at 635) that the observations of Lord Wilberforce and Lord Simon in *Barton v Armstrong* were consistent with the majority judgment in that case and represented the law relating to duress.

It is unnecessary, however, for the victim to prove that the illegitimate pressure was the sole reason for him entering into the contract. It is sufficient that the illegitimate pressure was one of the reasons for the person entering into the agreement. Once the evidence establishes that the pressure exerted on the victim was illegitimate, the onus lies on the person applying the pressure to show that it made no contribution to the victim entering into the agreement: *Barton v Armstrong* (at 633; 120), *per* Lord Cross. . . .

In the following extract, Birks applies the analysis of McHugh JA to the facts of *Williams v Roffey Brothers* (above, 413).

• P Birks, 'The Travails of Duress' [1990] *LMCLQ* 342

Suppose, for example, that great importance were attached to encouraging responsibility in bidding for contracts. It might be said that the interest of the customer and the interest of competitors of the bidder concur in requiring this priority. Competitors have a grievance if an irresponsible bidder takes the business by bidding too low, confident of later renegotiation. The customer has an interest in knowing that a bid is something better than the beginning of negotiations. If discipline in the process of bidding were expressly the priority, a renegotiated price, if promised, would rarely be actionable and, if paid, would usually be recoverable. In short, duress would be easily found. If, on the other hand, the priority were to minimize the waste and inconvenience between parties already embarked on a project, and to bring projects safely to a conclusion without interruptions and unnecessary ill-will, renegotiations would generally be upheld, whether executory or executed. In short, duress would then be rather difficult to establish.

McHugh, JA's conception of duress in *Crescendo*, brought to bear on the facts of *Williams v Roffey*, turns out to reflect the first priority, responsibility in the bidding process. The defendants perceived a pressure which indisputably contributed to their decision to pay more. So far as that pressure was applied by the plaintiffs, it was applied unlawfully and therefore illegitimately because, the contract not having been frustrated, late or incomplete performance would be a breach. It would seem to follow that, applying this analysis of duress without modification, the only reason why the plaintiff might have been outside its terms was (if indeed it be the case) that he did not 'apply' the pressure to the defendants. So far as one can see from the report, he did not take the initiative by telling the defendants that he was going to stop or finish late unless an extra payment was made.

However, it is unlikely that the Court of Appeal meant this to be the reason why Williams was not guilty of duress. For, factually, it will be a rare case, in which a person in Williams's position does not tell the other what is about to happen; and, legally, the distinction between 'telling' the other of impending breach and applying pressure by threatening breach is probably too fine and too easily abused to serve as the foundation for doctrine. Furthermore, one judgment, that of Purchas LJ, expressly says that it was open to the plaintiff, without necessarily being guilty of duress, to opt 'to be in deliberate breach of contract in order to "cut his losses" commercially'. This suggests that the court was working from a different concept of duress altogether, inarticulately dictated by the other priority (accommodation between parties).

If this is right, and the priority has indeed been set in favour of accommodation, the *Crescendo* analysis cannot apply to duress by threatened breach of contract without modification. There are two narrower options. One is to say that a threatened breach of contract is not for these purposes illegitimate unless accompanied by bad faith or malice—the deliberate exploitation of difficulties of the other party. The other is to insist that the pressure in this case must be, not merely a factor, but the overwhelming factor in the decision to give or promise the extra payment. This probably amounts to the same thing as saying that the defendant must have had no reasonable alternative. This route, by either description, leads back towards the 'coercion of the will' approach, and it obliges us to say that Lord Scarman in *Pao On* meant to distinguish and depart from *Barton v Armstrong*, not to follow it.

As between these two, the former is much preferable. The inquiry into the question whether the plaintiff was overwhelmed, or whether he had any other reasonable response, is bound to be so difficult and inscrutable as to become nothing more than a vehicle for inarticulate discretion. The other inquiry into bad faith, which need not necessarily be understood as assimilating economic duress to common law fraud, is of a more familiar and manageable kind. If and when this question goes to the Lords, these two options should not exclude a third, namely to give priority to responsibility in the formation of contract and therefore to apply without modification the general law of duress as stated by McHugh, JA.

These uncertainties cannot be resolved without a considered choice between the competing priorities. The old law, it might be said, was simply inconsistent, for the refusal to enforce a promise of a surcharge favoured discipline in formation, while denial of restitution of a surcharge paid favoured accommodation between parties. But, if one once became persuaded that the old law, properly understood, did not intend to deny restitution of a surcharge paid, one would be bound to admit, taking *Davis Contractors Ltd v Fareham U.D.C.* also into consideration, that the choice of priorities had in fact been consistently made in favour of responsible contracting and against subsequent accommodation. The only counter-argument would then be that this commitment was utterly undermined by the possibility of artificially discovering consideration for the surcharge.

Do you agree?

- **Dimskal Shipping Co. SA v International Transport Workers' Federation**
  [1992] 2 AC 152, House of Lords

The claimants were the owners of the *Evia Luck* and they were informed by the defendants that they would be 'blacked' in port in Sweden unless they entered into ITF contracts of employment with their crew. The defendants demanded that the claimants additionally pay ITF entrance fees, membership fees, a contribution towards the ITF welfare fund, and back pay to the crew calculated in accordance with ITF rates. The claimants also agreed to provide a bank performance guarantee of $200,000 and to sign a letter of undertaking which stated that they would comply with certain other demands made of them by ITF. The letter of undertaking was stated to be subject to English law and the jurisdiction of the English courts. The claimants sought to recover the sum of $111,743 which they alleged had been paid to the defendants under duress and (in the lower courts but not the House of Lords) they also sought to recover damages in tort. The difficulty which the claimants faced was that the action which the defendants had taken was carried out in Sweden, and such action was lawful according to the law of Sweden, and was only unlawful according to the law of England. The House of Lords held (Lord Templeman dissenting) that the claimants were entitled to recover the moneys so paid on the ground that the right of recovery was to be determined according to the proper law of the contract, which was English law. The action in which the defendants had engaged was unlawful according to the law of England and so constituted illegitimate pressure entitling the claimants to the recovery of the $111,743 which they had paid.

Lord Templeman (dissenting): . . . In my opinion the owners are not entitled to succeed in this country. In the first place the courts of this country should not concern themselves with industrial action lawfully carried out in the place where that action occurred. In the second place as Lord

Diplock pointed out [in *Universe Tankships*] there is no difference between tort and restitution. Moneys paid as a result of conduct lawful where committed and irrecoverable in this country under the law of tort should not be recoverable in this country under the law of restitution. The contents of a bottle cannot be changed by altering the label.

. . . .

Lord Goff of Chieveley: . . . In the present action, the owners claimed declarations that they had lawfully avoided all the above contracts on the ground of duress, including the contracts with the ITF and the contracts with the Filipino seamen. They claimed restitution in respect of the payments made to the ITF, including the backdated wages for the Filipino seamen, and the entrance fees, membership fees and welfare fund contributions; these sums were claimed as having been paid under duress. They also claimed the total sum of U.S.$140,067.31 as damages in tort, the torts relied on being intimidation and interference with contractual rights. It was agreed between the parties that (1) the agreement for payment was governed by English law as its proper law; (2) the contractual documents concluded between the parties were governed by English law as their proper law; (3) the question whether the agreement for payment and the contractual documents had been avoided for duress fell to be determined according to English law; and (4) the question whether the owners were entitled to restitution of the moneys paid fell to be determined according to English law. The agreement between the parties did not extend to the proper law of the new contracts of employment of the Filipino seamen. Phillips J held that this was Philippine law, as the system of law with which those contracts had their closest connection. The judge decided however that he should not make any declarations in respect of those contracts, since the crew members were not before the court.

It is a crucial feature of the present case that, on the findings of the judge, the pressure exerted by the ITF upon the owners at Uddevalla, although by English law it amounted to economic duress which was not at the relevant time legitimised by any applicable statutory provision in this country, was lawful under Swedish domestic law. On that basis, the judge dismissed the owners' claim in tort, because the acts committed by the ITF in Sweden were not actionable by the law of that country. That claim was not pursued by the owners in the Court of Appeal. Accordingly the Court of Appeal, like your Lordships' House, was concerned only with the owners' claim so far as it related to avoidance of the relevant contract and recovery in restitution of the money paid thereunder to the ITF. It appears to have been common ground between the parties that under English law the pressure exerted by the ITF which induced the owners to enter into the contract under which they made the payments to the ITF would amount to duress unless such pressure was legitimised under the relevant system of law. The point at issue between the parties related to the identity of the legal system by reference to which the question whether such pressure had been so legitimised had to be answered. For the owners, it was submitted that it had to be answered by reference to English law as the proper law of the contract, which at the relevant time did not legitimise such action. For the ITF, on the other hand, it was submitted that the relevant system of law was Swedish law, as the law of the country where the pressure was exerted; and, as I have recorded, at the relevant time such pressure was lawful by Swedish law. . . .

It was common ground between the parties before your Lordships that the money in respect of which the owners claimed restitution was paid to the ITF under a contract, albeit a contract which the owners claim to have been voidable by them, and indeed to have been avoided by them, on the ground of duress. It follows that, before the owners could establish any right to recover the money, they had first to avoid the relevant contract. Until this was done, the money in question was paid under a binding contract and so was irrecoverable in restitution. But once the contract was avoided, the money paid under it was recoverable in restitution, on the ground either of duress or possibly of failure of consideration. It was not, in my opinion, necessary for the owners, even if the duress relied upon by them was in fact tortious, to base their claim on waiver of tort (see the note by Ewan

McKendrick in [1990] *ILJ* 195), nor have they done so. The present case is, however, concerned with the anterior question whether the pressure exerted by the ITF constituted duress enabling the owners to avoid the contract on that ground, as they claim to have been entitled to do.

We are here concerned with a case of economic duress. It was at one time thought that, at common law, the only form of duress which would entitle a party to avoid a contract on that ground was duress of the person. The origin for this view lay in the decision of the Court of Exchequer in *Skeate v Beale* (1841) 11 Ad. & El. 983. However, since the decisions of Kerr J in *Occidental Worldwide Investment Corporation v Skibs A/S Avanti (The Siboen and The Sibotre)* [1976] 1 Lloyd's Rep. 293, of Mocatta J in *North Ocean Shipping Co. Ltd v Hyundai Construction Co. Ltd* [1979] QB 705, and of the Judicial Committee of the Privy Council in *Pao On v Lau Yiu Long* [1980] AC 614, that limitation has been discarded; and it is now accepted that economic pressure may be sufficient to amount to duress for this purpose, provided at least that the economic pressure may be characterised as illegitimate and has constituted a significant cause inducing the plaintiff to enter into the relevant contract (see *Barton v Armstrong* [1976] AC 104, 121, *per* Lord Wilberforce and Lord Simon of Glaisdale (referred to with approval in *Pao On v Lau Yiu Long* [1980] AC 614, 635, *per* Lord Scarman) and *Crescendo Management Pty. Ltd v Westpac Banking Corporation* (1988) 19 NSWLR 40, 46, *per* McHugh JA). It is sometimes suggested that the plaintiff's will must have been coerced so as to vitiate his consent. This approach has been the subject of criticism; see *Beatson, The Use and Abuse of Unjust Enrichment* (1991), 113–17; and the notes by Professor Atiyah in (1982) 98 *LQR* 197–202, and by Professor Birks in [1990] 3 *LMCLQ* 342–51. I myself, like McHugh JA, doubt whether it is helpful in this context to speak of the plaintiff's will having been coerced. It is not however necessary to explore the matter in the present case. Nor is it necessary to consider the broader question of what constitutes illegitimate economic pressure, for it is accepted that blacking or a threat of blacking, such as occurred in the present case, does constitute illegitimate economic pressure in English law, unless legitimised by statute. The question which has fallen for decision by your Lordships is whether, in considering the question whether the pressure should be treated as legitimised, the English courts should have regard to the law of Sweden (where the relevant pressure was exerted on the owners by the agents of the ITF) under which such pressure was lawful.

The starting point for the consideration of this question is the decision of your Lordships' House in *The Universe Sentinel* [1983] 1 AC 366, and in particular the speech in that case of Lord Diplock, who delivered the leading speech for the majority. . . .

It is not necessary for present purposes to explore the basis of this decision. It appears to bear some affinity to the principle underlying those cases in which the courts have given effect to the inferred purpose of the legislature by holding a person entitled to sue for damages for breach of a statutory duty, though no such right of suit has been expressly created by the statute imposing the duty. It is enough to state that, by parity of reasoning, not only may an action of restitution be rejected as inconsistent with the policy of a statute such as that under consideration in *The Universe Sentinel* [1983] 1 AC 366, but in my opinion a claim that a contract is voidable for duress by reason of pressure legitimised by such a statute may likewise be rejected on the same ground.

It is against the background of that decision that the problem in the present case falls to be considered. However, that problem did not arise in the case of *The Universe Sentinel*. There, all relevant events took place within the jurisdiction of the English courts; and by common consent, English law was the only relevant system of law. In the present case, although the payments to the ITF were made, as is agreed, under a contract governed by English law, nevertheless the pressure which induced the [owners] to enter into that contract was effected in Sweden, and by Swedish law such pressure was lawful. And so, as I have said, the question which your Lordships have to consider is whether, and if so to what extent, regard should be had in such circumstances to Swedish law.

I start from the generally accepted proposition, embodied in rule 184 set out in Dicey & Morris, *The Conflict of Laws*, 11th edn (1987), vol. 2, 1213, that the material or essential validity of a contract is governed by the proper law of the contract, which in the present case is English law. Rule 184 is one of a group of rules (rules 181–187) concerned with the scope of application of the proper law of a contract. It is expressed to be subject to two exceptions. The first exception asserts that a contract is generally invalid in so far as its performance is unlawful by the law of the place of performance; with that exception we are not, in my opinion, here concerned. The second (which is not strictly an exception to rule 184) concerns the primacy of what used to be called the distinctive policy of English law over any provision of foreign law, in so far as such provision might be relevant to the validity or invalidity of a contract; to that topic, I will briefly return in a moment.

Accordingly in the present case we look to English law, as the proper law, to discover whether the contract may, as a matter of principle, be affected by duress and, if so, what constitutes duress for this purpose; what impact such duress must have exercised upon the formation of the contract; and what remedial action is available to the innocent party. We know, of course, that by English law a contract induced by duress is voidable by the innocent party; and that one form of duress is illegitimate economic pressure, including the blacking or the threat of blacking of a ship. I can see no reason in principle why, prima facie at least, blacking or the threat of blacking a ship should not constitute duress for this purpose, wherever it is committed—whether within the English jurisdiction or overseas; for in point of fact its impact upon the contract does not depend upon the place where the relevant conduct occurs.

It follows therefore that, prima facie at least, whether or not economic pressure amounts to duress sufficient to justify avoidance of the relevant contract by the innocent party is a matter for the proper law of the contract, wherever that pressure has been exerted. Here, of course, the proper law is English law. Moreover in the present case there was at the relevant time no applicable statutory provision of English law which required that blacking or the threat of blacking should not be regarded as duress. So, unencumbered by any such provision, we are left simply with an English contract which is voidable by the innocent party if the formation of the contract has been induced by duress in the form of blacking or the threat of blacking a vessel. The question then arises whether there is any basis in law for rejecting this simple approach, on the ground that the conduct in question was lawful by the law of the place where it occurred, viz. Swedish law.

Before your Lordships, it was the primary submission of Mr Burton on behalf of the ITF that in relation to any duress abroad, in English law the court should, subject to overriding questions of public policy, look to the law of the place of duress to test its lawfulness or legitimacy. I of course accept that, if Mr Burton's submission is correct, it must be subject to the qualification that, if it was inconsistent with the distinctive policy of English law to treat the relevant conduct as lawful, the English courts (consistently with the second exception to rule 184 in Dicey & Morris, *The Conflict of Laws*) would refuse to do so. But the question is whether Mr Burton's submission is correct. I have to say that I know of no authority which supports his submission which, if correct, would require the recognition and formulation of a fresh exception to rule 184 in Dicey & Morris.

Before your Lordships, as in the courts below, the ITF relied upon the analogy of tort. Under English law, since the decision of your Lordships' House in *Boys v Chaplin* [1971] AC 356, conduct in a foreign country is only actionable as a tort in this country if it is both so actionable in English law (i.e. would be so actionable if the relevant conduct had occurred in this country), and so actionable by the law of the foreign country where the relevant conduct occurred: see rule 205 of Dicey & Morris, vol. 2, 1365 ff. and cases there cited. So, it was suggested, by parity of reasoning regard should be paid to the law of Sweden in the present case, in order to decide whether the conduct of the ITF constituted duress rendering an English contract voidable on that ground. I am bound to say however that I do not find the analogy compelling. In the first place it is not to be forgotten that conduct does not have to be tortious to constitute duress for the purpose of English law; this is so even at common law, and still more so if one has regard to the equitable doctrine of undue influence as an extended form of duress. It is by no means difficult to envisage categories of duress or undue influence which might render a contract voidable by English law as the proper law of the contract, but would not do so by the law of some other country where the relevant conduct in fact occurred. It is difficult to see what relevance the analogy of the English rule of the conflict of laws applicable in the case of tort can have to such a case. More fundamentally, however, there is a basic difference between the case of a foreign tort, and a case such as the present. In the case of a foreign tort, not only has the relevant conduct ex hypothesi occurred outside the jurisdiction of the English court, but the only fact which brings in English law at all is the fact that the defendant is amenable to the jurisdiction of the English court. In the present case, however, there is another English connection of great importance, which is that the dispute relates to a contract whose proper law is English law, and the relevant incidents of which are therefore governed by English law. Some cogent reason has to be produced why in such a case the English courts should not simply apply the principles of English law in deciding whether or not the relevant conduct constitutes duress capable of rendering the contract voidable. I do not find the analogy of tort sufficiently apposite or compelling to achieve that result.

What other reason can be adduced? The judge was impressed by another argument advanced on behalf of the ITF, which was that a man ought to be able safely to regulate his conduct by complying with the laws of the country in which he finds himself. This may be true so far as the criminal law is concerned; but I cannot see that it applies in the case of matters which may affect the validity of a contract governed by some other system of law. If a person enters into such a contract, he has for most purposes to accept the regime of the proper law of the contract; and if under that regime a particular form of conduct constitutes duress, or for that matter undue influence, rendering the contract voidable wherever the relevant conduct occurs, he has in my opinion to accept the consequences of his conduct under that system of law. He should not assume that, simply because his conduct is lawful in the place overseas where it is performed, it cannot for that reason render an English contract voidable for duress.

Lord Lowry delivered a speech concurring with **Lord Goff**. **Lord Keith** and **Lord Ackner** concurred with **Lord Goff**.

NOTES AND QUESTIONS

1. Lord Goff stated that the illegitimate pressure must constitute a 'significant cause inducing the plaintiff to enter into the relevant contract'. Is this consistent with *Barton v Armstrong*? Should it be consistent?

2. Has the overborne will theory survived the decision of the House of Lords?

3. What is the proper relationship between the claimants' restitutionary claim and their claim in tort? Was Lord Templeman correct to say that the 'contents of a bottle cannot be changed by altering the label'?

- *CTN Cash and Carry Ltd v Gallaher* [1994] 4 All ER 714, Court of Appeal

The claimants' agreed to buy a consignment of cigarettes from the defendants. The defendants mistakenly delivered the cigarettes to the claimants' Burnley warehouse instead of their Preston warehouse. When the mistake was discovered the defendants agreed to collect the cigarettes from Burnley and deliver them to Preston. Before they could do so, the cigarettes were stolen from the Burnley warehouse. The defendants insisted that the claimants pay for the stolen cigarettes, maintaining that the cigarettes were at the claimants' risk at the time they were stolen. The trial judge found that the defendants believed in all good faith that the cigarettes were at the claimants' risk, but that there was no legal basis for their belief. In subsequent negotiations, the defendants made clear to the claimants that, unless they paid for the cigarettes, the defendants would withdraw the credit facilities which the claimants had hitherto enjoyed. The defendants were under no obligation to provide the claimants with credit. The claimants paid the money and then sought to recover the money on the ground that it had been paid under duress. The claimants' claim failed both at first instance and in the Court of Appeal.

Steyn LJ (with whom **Farquharson LJ** agreed): . . . It is necessary to focus on the distinctive features of this case, and then to ask whether it amounts to a case of duress.

The present dispute does not concern a protected relationship. It also does not arise in the context of dealings between a supplier and a consumer. The dispute arises out of arm's length commercial dealings between two trading companies. It is true that the defendants were the sole distributors of the popular brands of cigarettes. In a sense the defendants were in a monopoly position. The control of monopolies is, however, a matter for Parliament. Moreover, the common law does not recognise the doctrine of inequality of bargaining power in commercial dealings (see *National Westminster Bank plc v Morgan* [1985] 1 All ER 821, [1985] AC 686). The fact that the defendants were in a monopoly position cannot therefore by itself convert what is not otherwise duress into duress.

A second characteristic of the case is that the defendants were in law entitled to refuse to enter into any future contracts with the plaintiffs for any reason whatever or for no reason at all. Such a decision not to deal with the plaintiffs would have been financially damaging to the defendants, but it would have been lawful. A fortiori, it was lawful for the defendants, for any reason or for no reason, to insist that they would no longer grant credit to the plaintiffs. The defendants' demand for payment of the invoice, coupled with the threat to withdraw credit, was neither a breach of contract nor a tort.

A third, and critically important, characteristic of the case is the fact that the defendants bona fide thought that the goods were at the risk of the plaintiffs and that the plaintiffs owed the defendants the sum in question. The defendants exerted commercial pressure on the plaintiffs in order to obtain payment of a sum which they bona fide considered due to them. The defendants' motive in threatening withdrawal of credit facilities was commercial self-interest in obtaining a sum that they considered due to them.

Given the combination of these three features, I take the view that none of the cases cited to us assist the plaintiffs' case. Miss Heilbron [counsel for the claimant] accepted that there is no decision which is in material respects on all fours with the present case. It is therefore unnecessary to disinter all those cases and to identify the material distinctions between each of those decisions and the present case. But Miss Heilbron rightly emphasised to us that the law must have a capacity for growth in this field. I entirely agree.

I also readily accept that the fact that the defendants have used lawful means does not by itself remove the case from the scope of the doctrine of economic duress. Professor Birks, in *An Introduction to the Law of Restitution* (1989) 177, lucidly explains:

'Can lawful pressures also count? This is a difficult question, because, if the answer is that they can, the only viable basis for discriminating between acceptable and unacceptable pressures is not positive law but social morality. In other words, the judges must say what pressures (though lawful outside the restitutionary context) are improper as contrary to prevailing standards. That makes the judges, not the law or the legislature, the arbiters of social evaluation. On the other hand, if the answer is that lawful pressures are always exempt, those who devise outrageous but technically lawful means of compulsion must always escape restitution until the legislature declares the abuse unlawful. It is tolerably clear that, at least where they can be confident of a general consensus in favour of their evaluation, the courts are willing to apply a standard of impropriety rather than technical unlawfulness.'

And there are a number of cases where English courts have accepted that a threat may be illegitimate when coupled with a demand for payment even if the threat is one of lawful action (see *Thorne v*

Motor Trade Association [1937] 3 All ER 157 at 160–1, [1937] AC 797 at 806–7, *Mutual Finance Ltd v John Wetton & Sons Ltd* [1937] 2 All ER 657, [1937] 2 KB 389 and *Universe Tankships Inc. of Monrovia v International Transport Workers' Federation* [1982] 2 All ER 67 at 76, 89, [1983] 1 AC 366 at 384, 401). On the other hand, Goff and Jones, *Law of Restitution* (3rd edn 1986), 240 observed that English courts have wisely not accepted any general principle that a threat not to contract with another, except on certain terms, may amount to duress.

We are being asked to extend the categories of duress of which the law will take cognisance. That is not necessarily objectionable, but it seems to me that an extension capable of covering the present case, involving 'lawful act duress' in a commercial context in pursuit of a bona fide claim, would be a radical one with far-reaching implications. It would introduce a substantial and undesirable element of uncertainty in the commercial bargaining process. Moreover, it will often enable bona fide settled accounts to be reopened when parties to commercial dealings fall out. The aim of our commercial law ought to be to encourage fair dealing between parties. But it is a mistake for the law to set its sights too highly when the critical inquiry is not whether the conduct is lawful but whether it is morally or socially unacceptable. That is the inquiry in which we are engaged. In my view there are policy considerations which militate against ruling that the defendants obtained payment of the disputed invoice by duress.

Outside the field of protected relationships, and in a purely commercial context, it might be a relatively rare case in which 'lawful act duress' can be established. And it might be particularly difficult to establish duress if the defendant bona fide considered that his demand was valid. In this complex and changing branch of the law I deliberately refrain from saying 'never'. But as the law stands, I am satisfied that the defendants' conduct in this case did not amount to duress.

It is an unattractive result, inasmuch as the defendants are allowed to retain a sum which at the trial they became aware was not in truth due to them. But in my view the law compels the result.

For these reasons, I would dismiss the appeal.

Sir Donald Nicholls V-C: I also agree. It is important to have in mind that the sole issue raised by this appeal and argued before us was duress. The plaintiff claims payment was made by it under duress and is recoverable accordingly. I agree, for the reasons given by Steyn LJ, that that claim must fail. When the defendant company insisted on payment, it did so in good faith. It believed the risk in the goods had passed to the plaintiff company, so it considered it was entitled to be paid for them. The defendant company took a tough line. It used its commercial muscle. But the feature underlying and dictating this attitude was a genuine belief on its part that it was owed the sum in question. It was entitled to be paid the price for the goods. So it took the line: the plaintiff company must pay in law what it owed, otherwise its credit would be suspended.

Further, there is no evidence that the defendant's belief was unreasonable. Indeed, we were told by the defendant's counsel that he had advised his client that on the risk point the defendant stood a good chance of success. I do not see how a payment demanded and made in those circumstances can be said to be vitiated by duress.

So that must be an end to this appeal. I confess to being a little troubled at the overall outcome. At a late stage of the trial the defendant's counsel accepted that the risk in the goods had not in law passed to the plaintiff. Hence, and this must follow, the defendant company was not, and never had been, entitled to be paid for the goods. The risk remained throughout on the defendant. What also follows is that the basis on which the defendant had sought and insisted on payment was then shown to be false.

In those circumstances I confess to being a little surprised that a highly reputable tobacco manufacturer has, so far, not reconsidered the position. A claim for restitution based on wrongful retention of the money, once the risk point had been established, was not pursued before us, no doubt for good reasons. But on the sketchy facts before us, and I emphasise that we have heard argument only from the plaintiff, it does seem to me that prima facie it would be unconscionable for the defendant company to insist on retaining the money now. It demanded the money when under a mistaken belief as to its legal entitlement to be paid. It only made the demand because of its belief that it was entitled to be paid. The money was then paid to it by a plaintiff which, in practical terms, had no other option. In broad terms, in the end result the defendant may be said to have been unjustly enriched. Whether a new claim for restitution now, on the facts as they have since emerged, would succeed is not a matter I need pursue. I observe, as to that, only that the categories of unjust enrichment are not closed.

I too would dismiss this appeal.

NOTES AND QUESTIONS

1. What would have been the outcome if the defendants had not been in good faith in their belief that the cigarettes were at the claimants' risk?

2. If a good faith threat to refuse to contract does not constitute duress, does it follow that a good faith threat to break a contract also does not constitute duress?

3. Should the claimants have been entitled to recover their money on the ground that the defendants had acted unconscionably in retaining the money once the true facts had come to light? Is there, or should there be, a ground of restitution based on 'unjust retention'?

4. The conclusion that a refusal to contract will not generally constitute duress has also been reached in Australia in the case of *Smith v William Charlick Ltd* (1924) 34 CLR 38. The courts have also held that a refusal to waive an existing contractual obligation does not amount to the application of illegitimate pressure (*Alec Lobb (Garages) Ltd v Total Oil (Great Britain) Ltd* [1983] 1 WLR 87, 94) nor is it illegitimate for an owner of goods let on hire-purchase to threaten to repossess the goods when the hirer is in default and has not attempted to obtain relief against forfeiture (*Alf Vaughan & Co. Ltd v Royscot Trust plc* [1999] 1 All ER (Comm) 856).

5. Applying Birks's 'absence of basis' approach (above, 137), would not the decision in this case have straight forwardly been that the claimants were entitled to restitution?

• *Huyton SA v Peter Cremer GmbH & Co* [1999] 1 Lloyd's Rep 620, Queen's Bench Division

The defendant sellers agreed to sell a quantity of wheat to the claimant buyers on fob terms. Payment was stated to be cash against listed documents. The defendants presented shipping documents to the claimants' bank but they were rejected because they contained a number of discrepancies. The defendants nevertheless demanded payment. The claimants maintained that they had properly cancelled the contract on its repudiation by the defendants but later offered to pay the invoice subject to deductions in respect of demurrage and bank guarantee charges subject to the condition that the defendants irrevocably withdrew their demand to arbitrate these issues. Four days later the defendants responded that, while they found the claimants' attitude to be 'completely unreasonable', they concluded that they had 'no real choice but to accept your terms for obtaining payment'. Approximately one week later the defendants informed the claimants that they did not consider themselves to be bound by the agreement to allow the deductions and to give up their right to arbitrate these issues. The claimants then sought injunctive relief to prevent the defendants from pursuing their claims in respect of demurrage and guarantee expenses. One of the grounds on which the defendants sought to resist the claimants' claim was that they had entered into the agreement under economic duress and were entitled to set aside the agreement. It was held that the agreement had not been entered into under duress because no illegitimate pressure had been applied by the claimants. In any event there was found to be no sufficient causal link between any pressure applied and the decision of the defendants to enter into the contract. Accordingly, the claimants were held to be entitled to the relief which they sought.

Mance J [*having considered the evidence, concluded that the defendants had been unable to establish that the claimants had applied illegitimate pressure. Given the defendants' failure to tender conforming documents, the claimants were not liable to pay the price and so their failure to pay the price could not be said to be illegitimate. He then proceeded to consider the case on the basis of a 'contrary assumption', namely that the claimants were liable to pay the price of the wheat so that its refusal to pay was unjustified*]

I start with the requirement that the illegitimate pressure must, in cases of economic duress, constitute 'a significant cause' (cf. *per* Lord Goff in *The Evia Luck* at p 165). This is contrasted in Goff and Jones on *The Law of Restitution* (4th ed.) p. 251, footnote 59 with the lesser requirement that it should be 'a' reason which applies in the context of duress to the person. The relevant authority in the latter context is *Barton v Armstrong* [1976] AC 104 . . .

[*he considered* Barton *in some detail and continued*]

The use of the phrase 'a significant cause' by Lord Goff in *The Evia Luck*, supported by the weighty observation in the footnote in Goff & Jones, suggests that this relaxed view of causation in the special context of duress to the person cannot prevail in the less serious context of economic duress. The minimum basic test of subjective causation in economic duress ought, it appears to me, to be a 'but for' test. The illegitimate pressure must have been such as actually caused the making of the agreement, in the sense that it would not otherwise have been made either at all or, at least, in the terms in which it was made. In that sense, the pressure must have been decisive or clinching. There may of course be cases where a common-sense relaxation, even of a but for requirement is necessary, for example in the event of an agreement induced by two concurrent causes, each otherwise sufficient to ground a claim of relief, in circumstances where each alone would have induced the agreement, so that it could not be said that, but for either, the agreement would not have been made. On the other hand, it also seems clear that the application of a simple 'but for' test of subjective causation in conjunction with a requirement of actual or threatened breach of duty could lead too readily to relief being granted. It would not, for example, cater for the obvious possibility that, although the innocent party would never have acted as he did, but for the illegitimate pressure, he nevertheless had a real choice and could, if he had wished, equally well have resisted the pressure and, for example, pursued alternative legal redress.

I turn therefore to consider other ingredients of economic duress. One possibility, harking back for example to a word used by the minority in *Barton*, is that the pressure should represent the 'predominant' cause. Professor Birks in *An Introduction to the Law of Restitution* (1985), pp. 182–183 has suggested that, in cases such as *Pao On v Lau Yiu Long* [1980] AC 614 where relief was refused on the ground that there had been 'commercial pressure but no coercion' (p 635), the Court was, in effect, insisting 'on a more severe test of the degree of compulsion than is found in *Barton v Armstrong*', securing what he describes as 'a concealed discretion to distinguish between reasonable and unreasonable, legitimate and illegitimate applications of this species of independently unlawful pressure.' His own preference, he indicated, was for 'the simplest and more open course . . . to restrict the right to restitution to cases in which one party sought, mala fide to exploit the weakness of the other.' These comments highlight the extent to which any consideration of causation in economic duress interacts with consideration of the concept of legitimacy. Mr. Males [counsel for the plaintiff] adopts the same approach as Professor Birks in relation to apparent contractual compromises for good consideration, suggesting that here at least bad faith ought to be a pre-condition to relief. The law will of course be cautious about re-opening an apparent compromise made in good faith on both sides. But it seems, on the one hand, questionable whether a 'compromise' achieved by one party who does not believe that he had at least an arguable case is a compromise at all—though it may be upheld if there is other consideration (cf. *Occidental Worldwide Investment Corporation v Skibs A/S Avanti (The Siboen and The Sibotre)* [1976] 1 Lloyd's Rep 293 at p334, col 2); and, on the other hand, difficult to accept that illegitimate pressure applied by a party who believes bona fide in his case could never give grounds for relief against an apparent compromise. Another commentator, Professor Burrows, in *The Law of Restitution* (1993) pp. 181–182, has suggested that the concept of legitimacy is open to some flexibility or at least qualification, so that a threatened or actual breach of contract may not represent illegitimate pressure if there was a reasonable commercial basis for the threat or breach, e.g. because circumstances had radically changed. This suggestion too, is by no means uncontentious.

As to authority, in *The Siboen and The Sibotre*, one of the early cases on economic duress, Mr. Justice Kerr indicated at p. 335, col. 1—in rejecting a contrary submission by Mr. Robert Goff, QC as he was—that he did not think that bad faith had any relevance at all. On the other hand, in McHugh, JA's judgment in the Supreme Court of New South Wales in *Crescendo Management Pty. Ltd v Westpac Banking Corporation*, (1988) 19 NSWLR 40 at p. 46, referred to by Lord Goff in *The Evia Luck*, McHugh, J.A. said that 'Pressure will be illegitimate if it consists of unlawful threats or amounts to unconscionable conduct.' It is also clear that illegitimate pressure may exist, although the threat is of action by itself lawful, if in conjunction with the nature of the demand, it involves potential blackmail: see *Thorn v Motor Trade Association* [1937] AC 797, especially at pp 806–807, cited in Lord Scarman's dissenting judgment in *Universe Tankships Inc. v International Transport Workers' Federation* [1982] 1 Lloyd's Rep 537, 555 and *C.T.N. Cash and Carry Ltd v Gallagher Ltd.*, [1994] 4 All ER 713. And in this last case, Lord Justice Steyn, as he was, contemplated the possibility that unconscionable conduct might have a yet wider ambit. He said:

'Outside the field of protected relationships, and in a purely commercial context, it might be a relatively rare case in which "lawful act duress" can be established. And it might be particularly difficult to establish duress if the defendant bona fide considered that this demand was valid. In this complex and changing branch of the law I deliberately refrain from saying "never".'

That good or bad faith may be particularly relevant when considering whether a case might represent a rare example of 'lawful act duress' is not difficult to accept. Even in cases where the pressure relied on is an actual or threatened breach of duty, it seems to me better not to exclude the possibility that the state of mind of the person applying such pressure may in some circumstances be significant, whether or not the other innocent party correctly appreciated such state of mind. 'Never' in this context also seems too strong a word.

In *The Evia Luck*, Lord Goff did not speak in absolute terms. He said, with reference to the previous authorities, that—

'. . . it is now accepted that economic pressure may be sufficient to amount to duress for this purpose, provided at least that the economic pressure may be characterised as illegitimate and has constituted a significant cause inducing the plaintiff to enter the relevant contract.'

This description itself leaves room for flexibility in the characterization of illegitimate pressure and of the relevant causal link. Lord Goff was identifying minimum ingredients, not ingredients which, if present, would inevitably lead to liability. The recognition of some degree of flexibility is not, I think, fairly open to the reproach that it introduces a judicial 'discretion'. The law has frequently to form judgments regarding inequitability or unconscionability, giving effect in doing so to the reasonable expectations of honest persons. It is the law's function to discriminate, where discrimination is appropriate, between different factual situations—as it does, to take one example, when deciding whether or not to recognize a duty of care. The present context is intervention in relation to bargains or payments in relatively extreme situations. Lord Justice Steyn in *C.T.N. Cash and Carry* cited, albeit in the context of threats involving no unlawful act, an aphorism of Oliver Wendell Holmes 'that general propositions do not solve concrete cases' and went on:

'It may only be a half-truth, but in my view the true part applies to this case. It is necessary to focus on the distinctive features of this case, and then to ask whether it amounts to a case of duress.'

A similar approach appears to me to be appropriate in the present context.

In older authorities, relief against economic duress was said to require illegitimate pressure coercing the innocent party's will and vitiating consent (cf. *The Siboen and The Sibotre* at p 336 and *Pao On v Lau Yiu Long* at p 635). Lord Goff in *The Evia Luck* doubted whether it was helpful to speak in such terms, and referred to McHugh, JA's comments to that effect in the *Crescendo* case. The approach there adopted by McHugh, JA, at p. 45, was based on statements by the House of Lords in *DPP v Lynch* [1975] AC 653, to the effect that, in cases of duress, 'the will [is] deflected, not des-troyed'. Even on this more generous formulation, a simple enquiry whether the innocent party would have acted as he did 'but for' an actual or threatened breach of contract cannot, I think, be the hallmark of deflection of will. Whether because the specific ingredients identified by Lord Goff should be interpreted widely or because it is implicit in the flexibility of Lord Goff's formulation and the underlying rationale of the law's intervention to prevent unconscionability, relief must, I think, depend on the Court's assessment of the qualitative impact of the illegitimate pressure, objectively assessed. It is not necessary to go so far as to say that it is an inflexible third essential ingredient of economic duress that there should be no or no practical alternative course open to the innocent party. But it seems, as I have already indicated, self-evident that relief may not be appropriate, if an innocent party decides, as a matter of choice, not to pursue an alternative remedy which any and possibly some other reasonable persons in his circumstances would have pursued. Relief may perhaps also be refused, if he has made no protest and conducted himself in a way which showed that, for better or for worse, he was prepared to accept and live with the consequences, however unwelcome. Factors such as these are referred to as relevant to relief against duress in both *The Siboen and The Sibotre* and *Pao On*, although in some contexts it may also be possible to rationalize them by reference to other doctrines such as affirmation or estoppel. The emphasis, now to be discarded, in such cases on coercion of will does not, it seems to me, mean that such factors are no longer relevant. Taking, for example, *Pao On*, the complainant there was able, in the face of the illegitimate pressure, to consider its position, to take alternative steps if it wished, and to decide, as it apparently did (and however wrongly with hindsight), that the substitute arrangements proposed were of no real concern or risk to it and that it was preferable to agree to them, rather than become involved in litigation. Although there would have been no re-negotiation at all 'but for' illegitimate pressure, the relationship between the illegitimate pressure applied and the substitute arrangements made was not of a nature or quality, or sufficiently significant in objective terms in deflecting the will, to justify relief. Examination of the same relationship may also involve taking into account the extent to which the party applying illegitimate pressure intended or could reasonably foresee that pressure which he applied would lead to the agreement or payment made, or at least the extent to which factors extraneous to that party played any important role.

The onus of proof in respect of economic duress is another relatively unexplored area. McHugh, JA in *Crescendo* assumed that it would be reversed in accordance with the principle applied by the Privy Council in *Barton v Armstrong*. That was a case of threats to kill, where the Privy Council took as an analogy dispositions induced by fraud. With such threats, as the Privy Council pointed out, it is only in the most unusual circumstances that there can be any doubt whether the threats operated to achieve their intended aim or known effect. The Privy Council's recognition of, not merely the prima facie factual inference, but of an apparent shifting of the legal onus, cannot, I think, be transposed automatically to the context of the more recently developed tort of economic duress. Threats to the person are, by definition, mala fide acts. Economic duress, as this case shows, embraces situations where the party applying what can, at least with hindsight, be shown to have been economic pressure held the view quite reasonably at the time that he was entitled to do so. There is, also, as indicated above, a major difference between the substantive test of causation in cases of threats to the person and in cases of economic duress. Leaving aside cases of fraud and fraudulent misrepresentation, mentioned in *Barton v Armstrong*, the law normally treats the party seeking relief in respect of a breach of contract or seeking to set aside a bargain on grounds, such as innocent misrepresentation, as under a legal onus to prove his case on causation. The particular facts may give rise to an inference of loss or inducement, which may shift a factual onus to the other party, but the underlying legal onus remains at the end of the day on the party seeking relief (cf. e.g. *Marc Rich & Co. v Portman* [1996] 1 Lloyd's Rep 430 at p 442, considering *Pan Atlantic Insurance Co. v Pine Top Insurance Co. Ltd* [1994] 2 Lloyd's Rep 427 on misrepresentation and non-disclosure in relation to insurance contracts). It would seem to me, as presently advised, that this could represent the appropriate general approach in cases of economic duress. I am conscious that the question of onus of proof was only briefly touched on before me without citation of authority from outside the field of economic duress, but in view of my other conclusions I have not felt it necessary or appropriate to call for further submissions on it.

[*Applying these principles to the facts of the case, Mance J concluded that, 'even if there had been illegitimate pressure, [the defendants'] case on economic duress should still, I believe, have failed, on the ground that there was no sufficient deflection of will or no sufficiently significant causal link—between such pressure and the agreement—to make it unconscionable for [the claimants] to insist on the agreement.'*]

NOTES AND QUESTIONS

1. What test did Mance J apply when deciding whether or not there had been a sufficient causal connection between any duress and the decision of the defendants to enter into the agreement?

2. Do you agree with the proposition that the 'more relaxed' approach to causation taken in *Barton* cannot be applied in cases of economic duress? What is to be done in the case where one party threatens the other's physical and economic well-being? If we are to distinguish between duress to the person and economic duress in this way, what test should be applied in cases of duress of goods?

3. What significance did Mance J attach to the availability of an alternative remedy?

4. Why does the onus of proof remain with the claimant in cases of economic duress but not in cases of duress of the person?

5. To what extent does Mance J attempt to inject a degree of flexibility into the law relating to economic duress? Do you agree with his approach?

• *R v Attorney-General for England and Wales* [2003] UKPC 22, Privy Council

The appellant, known simply as 'R', was a member of the SAS and, during the Gulf War of 1991, he was a member of the Bravo Two Zero patrol that was dropped behind enemy lines in Iraq in order to find Scud missiles and cut communication lines. After the war was over there was considerable concern within the SAS, and the Ministry of Defence more generally, about books written by former members of the SAS in which they gave an account (the accuracy of which was contested) of their experience as members of the Bravo Two Zero patrol. The Ministry of Defence decided to respond to this state of affairs by requiring existing SAS members to sign a confidentiality contract under which the soldiers covenanted, *inter alia*, not to 'disclose without express prior authority in writing from MOD any information, document or other article relating to the work of, or in support of, the United Kingdom Special Forces which is, or has been in my possession by virtue of my position as a member of any of those Forces'. The appellant signed the contract but shortly afterwards left the Army, having applied for premature voluntary release. The appellant returned to his native New Zealand and in 1998 he entered into a contract with New Zealand publishers for the publication of his own account of life as a member of the Bravo Two Zero patrol. The New Zealand publishers offered the UK rights to Hodder & Stoughton, who passed a copy of the manuscript on to the Ministry of Defence. The Attorney-General, on behalf of the Crown, then commenced proceedings in the High Court of New Zealand, in which he sought an injunction to restrain publication of the book, damages and an account of profits. The New Zealand Court of Appeal refused to grant an injunction to restrain publication of the book, but made an order for an account of profits and an assessment of damages. The appellant appealed to the Privy Council.

The appellant defended the Crown's claim for damages and an account of profits on a number of grounds, one of which was that he had entered into the contract under duress. The appellant submitted that he had signed the contract because, if he did not, he would be returned to unit ('RTU') and would no longer be a member of the SAS. Involuntary RTU was 'normally imposed as a penalty for some disciplinary offence or on grounds of professional unsuitability for the SAS' and it involved exclusion from the social life of the regiment and loss of its higher rates of pay. The Privy Council concluded that the Crown had not applied pressure on the appellant which could be described as illegitimate so that, on the facts, the doctrine of duress did not provide the appellant with a defence to the claim brought against him.

Lord Hoffmann (delivering the majority judgment of the Privy Council):

15. In *Universe Tankships Inc. of Monrovia v International Transport Workers' Federation* [1983] 1 AC 366, 400 Lord Scarman said that there were two elements in the wrong of duress. One was pressure amounting to compulsion of the will of the victim and the second was the illegitimacy of the pressure. R says that to offer him the alternative of being returned to unit, which was regarded in the SAS as a public humiliation, was compulsion of his will. It left him no practical alternative. Their Lordships are content to assume that this was the case. But, as Lord Wilberforce and Lord Simon of Glaisdale said in *Barton v Armstrong* [1976] AC 104, 121:

'in life . . . many acts are done under pressure, sometimes overwhelming pressure, so that one can say that the actor had no choice but to act. Absence of choice in this sense does not negate consent in law: for this the pressure must be one of a kind which the law does not regard as legitimate.'

16. The legitimacy of the pressure must be examined from two aspects: first, the nature of the pressure and secondly, the nature of the demand which the pressure is applied to support: see Lord Scarman in the *Universe Tankships* case, at p 401. Generally speaking, the threat of any form of unlawful action will be regarded as illegitimate. On the other hand, the fact that the threat is lawful does not necessarily make the pressure legitimate. As Lord Atkin said in *Thorne v Motor Trade Association* [1937] AC 797, 806:

'The ordinary blackmailer normally threatens to do what he has a perfect right to do—namely, communicate some compromising conduct to a person whose knowledge is likely to affect the person threatened . . . What he has to justify is not the threat, but the demand of money.'

17. In this case, the threat was lawful. Although return to unit was not ordinarily used except on grounds of delinquency or unsuitability and was perceived by members of the SAS as a severe

penalty, there is no doubt that the Crown was entitled at its discretion to transfer any member of the SAS to another unit. Furthermore, the judge found, in para. 123:

> 'The MOD could not be criticised for its motivation in introducing the contracts. They were introduced because of the concerns about the increasing number of unauthorised disclosures by former UKSF personnel and the concern that those disclosures were threatening the security of operations and personnel and were undermining the effectiveness and employability of the UKSF. Those are legitimate concerns for the MOD to have.'

18. It would follow that the MOD was reasonably entitled to regard anyone unwilling to accept the obligation of confidentiality as unsuitable for the SAS. Thus the threat was lawful and the demand supported by the threat could be justified. But the judge held that the demand was unlawful because it exceeded the powers of the Crown over a serviceman under military law. It was an attempt to restrict his freedom of expression after he had left the service and was no longer subject to military discipline.

19. The judge's reasoning was that R had signed the contract because he had been ordered to do so. The MOD could not give a serviceman an order which, as a matter of military law, he was obliged to obey after he had left the service and therefore it was an abuse of power for the MOD to try to extend the temporal reach of its orders by ordering the serviceman to sign a contract which could be enforced after he had left.

20. If R had signed the contract because as a matter of military law he had been obliged to do so, their Lordships would see much force in this reasoning. But they agree with the Court of Appeal that this was not the case. There was no order in the sense of a command which created an obligation to obey under military law. Instead, R was faced with a choice which may have constituted 'overwhelming pressure' but was not an exercise by the MOD of its legal powers over him. The legitimacy of the pressure therefore falls to be examined by normal criteria and as neither of the courts in New Zealand considered either the threat to be unlawful or the demand unreasonable, it follows that the contract was not obtained by duress.

Lord Scott dissented but not on the application of the doctrine of duress to the facts of the case.

NOTES AND QUESTIONS

1. Lord Hoffmann in *R* refers to the 'wrong of duress'. The description of duress as a 'wrong' is potentially dangerous in so far as it suggests that duress can give rise to a claim for compensatory damages. The question whether or not duress gives rise to a claim for compensatory damages is analytically distinct from the question whether or not duress creates a right to recover the value of a benefit conferred upon the defendant. It is the latter issue with which we have been concerned in this chapter, not the former (on the relationship between the two see further E McKendrick, 'The Further Travails of Duress' in A Burrows and Lord Rodger of Earlsferry (eds) *Mapping the Law: Essays in Memory of Peter Birks* (2006), 181, 196–8).

2. When, according to Lord Hoffmann, will pressure be regarded as 'illegitimate'? How, if at all, does his approach differ from that taken in previous cases?

4. THREATS TO PROSECUTE OR SUE OR PUBLISH INFORMATION

This group of cases is, perhaps, the most difficult to stabilize and it involves difficult issues of policy about the extent to which it is permissible to have resort to the legal process to support a demand which is believed to be legitimate. The general rule is that a threat to sue to recover a sum of money which is genuinely (but erroneously) believed to be due by the party claiming it is not illegitimate. The reason for this is that, if the law were otherwise, out-of-court settlements would become extremely vulnerable. The law responds differently, however, to threats to prosecute unless money is paid. Here the courts are much more likely to find that such a threat is illegitimate, albeit that there is some difficulty in establishing the precise circumstances in which such a threat is illegitimate. Unlike previous sections of this chapter, we also draw on cases in equity as well as cases at law. It is here (principally in *Williams v Bayley* (1866) LR 1 HL 200, below) that we can put to the test the claim that some actual undue influence cases are concerned with the application of illegitimate pressure just as they are in cases of common law duress. We end this Chapter with an extract from a powerful article by P Birks and Chin Nyuk Yin ('On the Nature of Undue Influence' in J Beatson and D Friedmann (eds), *Good Faith and Fault in Contract Law*, (1995)) in which they maintain, *inter alia*, that all cases of pressure, whatever their jurisdictional origin, should be litigated as pressure or duress cases.

• *Williams v Bayley* (1866) LR 1 HL 200, House of Lords

The claimant's son gave the defendant bankers promissory notes upon which he had forged the claimant's signature. When the defendants discovered what had taken place they met with the claimant and during the course of the meeting they informed him that they had it within their power to prosecute the claimant's son. The claimant was legally advised during the meeting but his solicitor left the meeting when the claimant was asked to meet his son's debts. The claimant then agreed to enter into a mortgage to pay off the debts of his son, which mortgage he later sought to set aside. It was held by the House of Lords that the claimant was entitled to set aside the mortgage in equity.

Cranworth LC: . . . Now the question is, what was the sort of influence which they exercised on the mind of the father to induce him to take on himself the responsibility of paying these notes? Was it merely, we do not know these to be forgeries, we do not believe them to be so, but your son is responsible for them, and if you do not help him we must sue him for the amount? Or was it, if you do not pay these notes we shall be in a position to prosecute him for forgery, and we will prosecute him for forgery? What is the fair inference from what took place?

I do not know what may be the opinion of the rest of your Lordships, but I very much agree with the argument of Sir *Hugh Cairns*, that it is not pressure in the sense in which a Court of equity sets aside transactions on account of pressure, if the pressure is merely this: 'If you do not do such and such an act I shall reserve all my legal rights, whether against yourself, or against your son.' If it had only been, 'if you do not take on yourself the debt of your son, we must sue you for it,' I cannot think that that amounts to pressure, when the parties are at arms' length, and particularly when, as in this case, the party supposed to be influenced by pressure had the assistance of his solicitor, not, indeed, on the first occasion, but afterwards, before anything was done. But if what really takes place is this: If you do not assist your son, by taking on yourself the payment of these bills and notes on which there are signatures which are said, at least, to be forgeries, you must not be surprised at any course we shall take, meaning to insinuate, if not to say, we shall hold in our hands the means of criminally prosecuting him for forgery. I say, if it amounts to that, that it is a very different thing. [*He then set out the facts and continued*:] The father, then, was acting in this matter under the notion that if he did not interfere to save his son, the latter would be liable to be prosecuted, and, probably, would be prosecuted for forgery, and so be transported for life. . . .

That being so, I think the case in point of fact is this:—Here are several forged notes. The bankers, in the presence of the father and of the person who forged them, both being persons of apparent respectability in the country, carrying on business as tradesmen, and the father having the presence and the assistance of his solicitor, the bankers say to him what amounts to this: 'Give us security to the amount of these notes, and they shall all be delivered up to you; or do not give us security, and then we tell you we do not mean to compound a felony; in other words, we mean to prosecute.' That is the fair inference from what passed. Now is that a transaction which a Court of equity will tolerate, or is it not? I agree very much with a good deal of the argument of Sir *Hugh Cairns* as to this doctrine of pressure. Many grounds on which a Court of equity has acted in such cases do not apply in this case. The parties were not standing in any fiduciary relation to one another; and if this had been a legal transaction I do not know that we should have thought that there was any pressure that would have warranted the decree made by the Vice-Chancellor. But here was a pressure of this nature. We have the means of prosecuting, and so transporting your son. Do you choose to come to his help and take on yourself the amount of his debts—the amount of these forgeries? If you do we will not prosecute; if you do not, we will. That is the plain interpretation of what passed. Is that, or is it not, legal? In my opinion, my Lords, I am bound to go the length of saying that I do not think it is legal. I do not think that a transaction of that sort would have been legal even if, instead of being forced on the father, it had been proposed by him and adopted by the bankers. . . .

Lord Chelmsford: My Lords, I agree with my noble and learned friend on the woolsack, that the object of the arrangement between the parties was to save *William Bayley* from a prosecution for forgery; and I make that the foundation of the opinion which I have formed with regard to the agreement having been extorted from the father by undue pressure. It appears to me to be quite clear that the negotiations between the parties proceeded upon the footing of forgery having been committed by *William Bayley*, and of his being liable to a criminal prosecution; and that the bankers, both personally, and by means of their agents, Mr *Thursfield* their solicitor and Mr *Deakin* their manager, availed themselves of the fears of the father for the safety of his son, to press the arrangement upon him.

. . .

[I]n my opinion, this negotiation proceeded upon an understanding between the parties that the agreement of *James Bayley*, to give security for the notes, would relieve *William Bayley* from the consequences of his criminal act; and the fears of the father were stimulated and operated on to an extent to deprive him of free agency, and to extort an agreement from him for the benefit of the bankers. It appears to me, therefore, that the case comes within the principles on which a Court of equity proceeds in setting aside an agreement where there is inequality between the parties, and one of them takes unfair advantage of the situation of the other, and uses undue influence to force an agreement from him. . . .

Lord Westbury: . . . The question, therefore, my Lords, is, whether a father appealed to under such circumstances, to take upon himself an amount of civil liability, with the knowledge that, unless he does so, his son will be exposed to a criminal prosecution, with the certainty of conviction, can be regarded as a free and voluntary agent? I have no hesitation in saying that no man is safe, or ought to be safe, who takes a security for the debt of a felon, from the father of the felon, under such circumstances. A contract to give security for the debt of another, which is a contract without consideration, is, above all things, a contract that should be based upon the free and voluntary agency of the individual who enters into it. But it is clear that the power of considering whether he ought to do it or not, whether it is prudent to do it or not, is altogether taken away from a father who is brought into the situation of either refusing, and leaving his son in that perilous condition, or of taking on himself the amount of that civil obligation.

I have, therefore, my Lords, in that view of the case, no difficulty in saying that, as far as my opinion is concerned, the security given for the debt of the son by the father under such circumstances, was not the security of a man who acted with that freedom and power of deliberation that must, undoubtedly, be considered as necessary to validate a transaction of such a description.

My Lords, I would add to that, the great folly, nay, impropriety, of the bankers proceeding to take this security from the defenceless old man after his solicitor had left him, protesting in such an emphatic manner against the proceedings which he knew they were about to enter upon. The Respondent's solicitor remained so long as a valid contract, namely, that touching the property of *William Bayley*, was regarded as possible. When that was impossible, and the bankers began to exert pressure on the father, the solicitor left, remonstrating with all parties against the impropriety of what they were about to do.

My Lords, there remains the other aspect of the case, which is this: Was the transaction, regarded independently of pressure, an illegal one, as being contrary to the settled rules and principles of law. [*His Lordship considered the matter and concluded that the transaction was indeed illegal.*]

My Lords, I regard this as a transaction which must necessarily, for purposes of public utility, be stamped with invalidity, because it is one which undoubtedly, in the first place, is a departure from what ought to be the principles of fair dealing between man and man, and it is also one which, if such transactions existed to any considerable extent, would be found productive of great injury and mischief to the community. I think, therefore, that the decree which has been made in this case is a perfectly correct decree.

I do not mean for one single moment, by anything I have said, to cast any imputation on the character of these gentlemen. I am only dealing with abstract principles of law. They might, perhaps, fairly have thought that they were doing the best for the family of Mr *William Bayley* and for the father. I beg particularly that it may not be understood that I mean to convey, by any words that I have used, any reproach on their character. I have used those words as necessary to vindicate the policy and justice of the rule of law, and to shew how highly requisite it is that a Court of equity should undo a transaction such as this, whether it is regarded as proceeding from a father who cannot be considered as a voluntary agent, or, taking the other aspect of it, as violating the rules of law which prescribe the duties of individuals under such circumstances. On both of these grounds I think that this is a transaction which ought to be set aside.

NOTES AND QUESTIONS

1. It should be noted that an alternative ground for the decision of the House of Lords was that the mortgage should be set aside on the ground of illegality.

2. Were the facts of this case to recur today, could the claimant plead duress as a ground for setting aside the mortgage?

• *Silsbee v Webber* 50 NE 555 (1898), Supreme Judicial Court of Massachusetts

While the claimant's son was in the employment of the defendant, he was accused of stealing from his employer. He signed a confession and agreed to give security for $1,500. The defendant further threatened to inform the claimant's husband, who was in poor health, of the events which had taken place. The claimant was afraid that such knowledge would make her husband insane and so she assigned to the defendant her share of her father's estate. The claimant sued to recover the money which the defendant had collected under the assignment. It was held that the question of whether or not there had been duress was a question for the jury.

Holmes J: . . . In the opinion of a majority of the court, if the evidence above stated was believed, we cannot say that the jury would not have been warranted in finding that the defendant obtained and knew that he was obtaining the assignment from the plaintiff solely by inspiring the plaintiff with fear of what he threatened to do; that the ground for her fear was, and was known to be, her expectation of serious effects upon her husband's health if the defendant did as he threatened; that the fear was reasonable, and a sufficiently powerful motive naturally to overcome self-interest; and, therefore, that the plaintiff had a right to avoid her act.

It is true that it has been said that the duress must be such as would overcome a person of ordinary courage. We need not consider whether, if the plaintiff reasonably entertained her alleged belief, the well-grounded apprehension of a husband's insanity is something which a wife ought to endure, rather than to part with any money, since we are of opinion that the dictum referred to is taken literally in an attempt to apply an external standard of conduct in the wrong place. If a party obtains a contract by creating a motive from which the other party ought to be free, and which, in fact, is, and is known to be, sufficient to produce the result, it does not matter that the motive would not have prevailed with a differently constituted person, whether the motive be a fraudulently created belief or an unlawfully created fear. Even in torts,—the especial sphere of external standards,—if it is shown that in fact the defendant, by reason of superior insight, contemplated a result which the man of ordinary prudence would not have foreseen, he is answerable for it; and, in dealing with contributory negligence, the personal limitations of the plaintiff, as a child, a blind man, or a foreigner unused to our ways, always are taken into account. Late American writers repudiate the notion of a general external measure for duress, and we agree with them.

The strongest objection to holding the defendant's alleged action illegal duress is that, if he had done what he threatened, it would not have been an actionable wrong. In general, duress going to motives consists in the threat of illegal acts. Ordinarily, what you may do without liability you may threaten to do without liability. See . . . *Allen v Flood* [1898] App. Cas. 1, 129, 165. But this is not a question of liability for threats as a cause of action; and we may leave undecided the question whether, apart from special justification, deliberately and with foresight of the consequences, to tell a man what you believe will drive him mad, is actionable if it has the expected effect. If it should be held not to be, contrary to the intimations in the cases cited, it would be only on the ground that a different rule was unsafe in the practical administration of justice. If the law were an ideally perfect instrument, it would give damages for such a case as readily as for a battery. When it comes to the collateral question of obtaining a contract by threats, it does not follow that, because you cannot be made to answer for the act, you may use the threat. In the case of the threat, there are no difficulties of proof, and the relation of cause and effect, is as easily shown as when the threat is of an assault. If a contract is extorted by brutal and wicked means, and a means which derives its immunity, if it have immunity, solely from the law's distrust of its own powers of investigation, in our opinion the contract may be avoided by the party to whom the undue influence has been applied. Some of the cases go further, and allow to be avoided contracts obtained by the threat of unquestionably lawful acts.

In the case at bar there are strong grounds for arguing that the plaintiff was not led to make the assignment by the duress alleged. They are to be found in the fact that the plaintiff sought the defendant; in her testimony that when she made the assignment she wanted the defendant to have full security for all her son owed him; and in the plaintiff's later conduct; but we are considering whether there was a case of duress for the jury. . . .

Knowlton J (dissenting): . . . The cases in which it is held, in this jurisdiction and elsewhere, that one whose will is overcome, and who is induced to execute a contract by threats of prosecution and imprisonment for a crime, made by one who reasonably believes him to be guilty of the crime, may avoid the contract on the ground of duress, rest upon the principle that it is an abuse of process, and a misuse of the machinery of the law, which the law will not permit, to extort the collection of a private debt, or to procure any other private benefit by proceedings intended only to impose punishment in the interest of the public. It is equally a wrong and an injury to accomplish the same result through threats of such an abuse of process.

The burden of proof is on the plaintiff to show that the defendant obtained the contract by threatening to inflict injury upon her husband. A fair interpretation of the evidence indicates that the defendant's reference to her husband was in no sense a threat, but merely a natural statement, when the plaintiff offered inadequate security, that he should see whether the young man's father, who was an owner of houses and lands, was willing to furnish the security which his son had promised. If it was more than that, and was also a legitimate appeal to a motive which the plaintiff might have had to save her husband from the grief and sorrow that knowledge of the facts would be likely to bring to him, or to save herself from additional pain by sharing her husband's trouble, it would hardly be contended that the contracts would thereby be rendered voidable. A party endeavoring to obtain a contract from another may legitimately appeal to all proper motives which will induce the other to agree to his terms.

. . . .

It is a familiar rule of law that fraud or wrong of any kind is never to be presumed. It cannot be inferred from evidence which is as consistent with right as with wrong. I can see nothing in the evidence that tends to show that the defendant was guilty of any wrong towards the plaintiff. . . .

- *Mutual Finance Ltd v John Wetton & Sons Ltd* [1937] 2 KB 389, King's Bench Division

The claimant finance company entered into a contract of hire-purchase with a friend of Joseph Wetton. As a condition of entering into the agreement, the claimants required a counter-guarantee from the defendant company. Joseph Wetton who had previously been a director of the company, forged the signature of his brother, Percy, and father, William (who were directors of the company), on to the guarantee. When the friend defaulted the claimants agreed that another purchaser could take over the contract, but insisted that the defendant company take over the guarantee, which it did. The claimants did not utter any explicit threats that they would prosecute Joseph if a guarantee was not given, but they knew that Percy would never have signed the guarantee had it not been for the fact that his father was in very poor health and that he, Percy, believed that the shock of any such prosecution might endanger his father's life. When there was a further default on the hire-purchase contract the claimants sought to enforce the guarantee against the defendant company. It was held that they could not do so and that the defendants were entitled to avoid the guarantee on the ground that it had been procured by undue influence.

Porter J: . . . Prima facie the plaintiffs are entitled to recover. They have a guarantee deliberately made and in due form. But it is said that that guarantee is voidable because it was obtained by duress or by undue influence. If the question were whether there was any such duress as the common law would recognize, I should unhesitatingly answer, No. But the right to avoid a contract is not at the present time confined to questions of duress. It depends on the much wider relief given on principles originally evolved in the Chancery Courts under the name of undue influence.

The problem is, I think, well stated in Salmond on Contracts, 1927 edn, p. 259: 'Assuming, then, that the common law of duress has been thus superseded by the equitable doctrine of undue influence, the question remains, What forms of coercion, oppression, or compulsion amount to undue influence invalidating a contract as between strangers between whom there exists no fiduciary relation? How is the line to be now drawn between those forms of coercion or persuasion which are permissible and those which the law recognizes as unlawful and as a ground of contractual invalidity? To this question it is impossible, as the authorities at present stand, to give any definite or confident reply. In the case already cited of *Kaufman v Gerson*[1] it is suggested that the line should be drawn by reference to general considerations of public policy, the question in each case being: 'Is the coercion or persuasion by which this contract was procured of such a nature that the enforcement of a contract so obtained would be contrary to public policy?' Just as a contract may be invalid because it is contrary to public policy in its substance or its purposes, so it may be invalid because it is contrary to public policy in respect of the coercive method of its procurement. If this is the true underlying principle, it is for the law in its future development to reduce this general principle so far as possible to the form of specific rules in respect of divers methods of coercion, just as the requirements of public policy have been similarly made specific in respect of illegal and nugatory contracts. Where the instrument of coercion is the doing or threatening of a wilfully illegal act of any description, it may be anticipated that, notwithstanding the limits of the older common law of duress, a contract so procured will in general be held invalid. But even although the instrument of coercion is not thus in itself illegal, as in the case of a threat of prosecution, the enforcement of a contract so procured may nevertheless be held in appropriate cases to be contrary to public policy.' That states the problem, but by no means solves it.

Duress at common law could only be pleaded where the end arrived at was achieved by the use of something in the nature of unlawful force or the threat of unlawful force against the person of the other contracting party. Undue influence in the Chancery Courts might exist where a promise was extracted by a threat to prosecute certain third persons unless the promise were given. It is not necessary that there should be any direct threat. The headnote in *Williams v Bayley*[2] setting out the principle deduced from the speech of Lord Westbury is, I think, a correct exposition of the law.

Not only is no direct threat necessary, but no promise need be given to abstain from a prosecution. It is enough if the undertaking were given owing to a desire to prevent a prosecution and that desire were known to those to whom the undertaking was given. In such a case one may imply (as I do here) a term in the contract that no prosecution should take place: see *Jones v Merionethshire Permanent Benefit Building Society*.[3]

Kaufman v Gerson[4] is another example of the principle applied in *Williams v Bayley*, but in the former case the underlying threat was the prosecution of the husband, while in the latter case it was of a son. In *Seear v Cohen*[5] the same principle was applied in a case where the underlying threat was against the son of one of the defendants and the nephew of the other, and in *Brook v Hook*[6] against the brother-in-law of the defendant.

Is the principle wide enough to cover the case where the persons involved are the brother and father of the alleged criminal? I think it is. It is not necessary to determine the exact bounds beyond which the doctrine would not be applied, but I should myself be inclined to say that it extended to any case where the persons entering into the undertaking were in substance influenced by the desire to prevent the prosecution or possibility of prosecution of the person implicated, and were known and intended to have been so influenced by the person in whose favour the undertaking was given. Nor do I think it matters that Percy Wetton would not have cared, if he alone were concerned, whether his brother went to prison or not. In fact he did care, and Lopresti knew that he cared, owing to his fear of the effect on his father's health. If the known object was to prevent the prosecution of his brother for whatever reason, that, I think, is enough.

But it is said that in all the cases cited the sole consideration was to stifle a prosecution, whereas in the present case the agreement which was made concerned four parties—namely, the plaintiffs, the defendants, Gregory, and the sellers—and that just as a debtor may secure his debt though the object be to avoid a prosecution, as in *Flower v Sadler*,[7] because there is a further consideration, so, an

1 [1904] 1 KB 591.   2 (1866) LR 1 HL 200, 216.   3 [1892] 1 Ch 173.
4 [1904] 1 KB 591.   5 45 LTR 589.   6 (1871) LR 6 Ex 89.
7 (1882) 10 QBD 572.

agreement which results in the sale of a lorry by one person to another, the hiring by that other to a third person, and the guarantee of the hirer's debt by a fourth, is a perfectly legitimate transaction, though the result may be and was intended to be the stifling of a prosecution.

In my view, however, the question is what was the person giving the guarantee in substance, to the knowledge of the person to whom the guarantee was given, doing and intending to do? In the present case the defendants gained no benefit for themselves and, as I find, were known by the plaintiffs to be gaining no benefit. The sellers had the same knowledge as the plaintiffs, and the fact that Gregory had a lorry delivered to him on hire purchase at an excessive price does not, in my view, affect the right of the debtor to avoid the contract.

It was further argued before me that the defendants' guarantee, if obtained by undue influence, was voidable and not void, and that as it was not repudiated at the earliest possible moment the defendants had affirmed it. But what is the earliest possible moment? In my view it is the earliest moment at which the undue influence has ceased to operate: see *per* Collins MR in *Kaufman v Gerson*.[8]

In the present case, up to the issue of the writ the defendants were always subject to the fear of a prosecution of Joseph Wetton and were never free agents. I think that they did avoid the contract in time. For these reasons I think that the defendants are entitled to avoid the guarantee. There will be judgment for the defendants, with costs.

QUESTION

Were the facts of the case to recur today could the defendants have avoided the guarantee on the ground that it had been procured by duress?

- *Norreys v Zeffert* [1939] 2 All ER 187, King's Bench Division

The defendant defaulted on various horse racing bets and, in consequence, owed money to the claimant. The claimant put the matter in the hands of the National Turf Protection Society and, during the course of an interview with the defendant, the secretary of the society threatened to report the defendant's default to Tattersals, to trade protection societies, and to the defendant's social club. The defendant responded by stating that he was expecting an improvement in his financial plight and that, if he was given a further month, he would make a proposal which would ensure payment within three months. Upon his failure to do so, the claimant brought an action to enforce his promise to pay. It was held that he could not do so because the defendant had not actually promised to pay; he had merely expressed a hope of being able to pay. It was further held that, even if such a promise had been made, the court would not enforce it because of the threats which had been used to obtain the promise.

Atkinson J: . . . Even if all this happened, and if such a promise was obtained, a serious question arises as to whether or not a promise so obtained is one which the court will enforce. There has been a good deal of difference of opinion as to how far agreements to pay money obtained by threats are enforceable. The cases, and particularly, I think, *Thorne v Motor Trade Assocn.*,[1] seem to establish the proposition that, if the threat is a threat to take a step in lawful furtherance of the creditor's business interests, the refraining from taking such step may be good consideration for a promise to pay money not otherwise recoverable, however seriously the person threatened would be injured by the carrying out of the threat. On the other hand, if the threat is only an injuring threat, in order to induce

---

8   [1904] 1 KB 591, 596.

1   [1937] AC 797.

payment of money, the refraining from carrying out the threat will not in general be good consideration for a promise to pay. The mere fact that a person may have a legal right to do something which will injure another is not sufficient justification for the demand of money as the price of not doing it. The opinion of Scrutton LJ, to the contrary was expressly dissented from by the House of Lords in *Thorne v Motor Trade Assocn.*, where Lord Atkin said, at 806, 807 ([1937] 3 All ER at 160):

> ... the mere fact that the threat is to do something a person is entitled to do either causes the threat not to be a 'menace' within the Larceny Act, 1916, or in itself provides a reasonable or probable cause for the demand.

In the same case, Lord Wright says, at 817, 818 ([1937] 3 All ER at 167):

> I think the word 'menace' is to be liberally construed, and not as limited to threats of violence but as including threats of any action detrimental to or unpleasant to the person addressed. ... I think the jury should be directed by the judge that the respondent association had a legal right to put the person's name on the stop list, so long as they did so in order to promote the trade interests of the association and its members and not with intent to injure, and so long as the money, fine or penalty demanded was reasonable and not extortionate. In other words, the jury would have to answer the question suggested by Lord Dunedin, 'Whether there was a conspiracy to injure or only a set of acts dictated by business interests.'

Of course, there is no question of conspiracy here, but it merely illustrates, I think, the dividing line between legitimate business threats and threats which are not legitimate. ... In my opinion, the threat to report to Tattersalls was a threat which the plaintiff, through Carpenter, was entitled to make, and a promise to refrain from thus reporting the defendant would be good consideration. It would be merely taking a step in accordance with the recognised practice of bringing the matter before an independent committee, and the plaintiff, through Carpenter, would in no way be responsible for the consequences which automatically followed any finding of the committee. ... [S]o long as a promise to pay is made in consideration of refraining from taking the recognised step, the recognised procedure, which exists for the protection of the interests of the creditor of this class, the agreement may be a good one. It certainly would be in accordance with the principle laid down in *Thorne's* case. Such a step is one primarily aimed at protecting and furthering the interests of book-makers, but threats that the National Turf Protection Society would notify members of a social club and the trade protection societies are, in my view, threats to defame, which are threats to injure, and seem to me to come within that class of threats which, according to *Thorne's* case, the creditor is not entitled to make. They are aimed merely at injuring. As Lord Atkin said, at 807 ([1937] 3 All ER at 160):

> He must no doubt be acting not for the mere purpose of putting money in [the plaintiff's] pocket, but for some legitimate purpose other than the mere acquisition of money.

... I have dealt with what seems to me to be the law as it was argued. I have no doubt that it is all *obiter*, because I am not satisfied that any contract was in fact made in this case. ...

- **P Birks and Chin Nyuk Yin, 'On the Nature of Undue Influence' in J Beatson and D Friedmann (eds), *Good Faith and Fault in Contract Law*, (1995), 63–7**

SEPARATING THE PRESSURE CASES

Some years ago Professor Malcolm Cope suggested that all cases of duress should be treated as undue influence.[1] We believe the decanting should go the other way: all cases of pressure should

---

1 M Cope, *Duress, Undue Influence and Unconscientious Bargains* (1985), para. 125.

be treated as duress. It is unfortunate if this must still be expressed as transferring them from equity to common law. It is time that in this field we overcame the old jurisdictional duality. It would be better to say simply that pressure should be litigated as pressure, or as 'duress' if that synonym is preferred. The reasons are, first, that pressure or duress is a relatively easily understood and distinct notion; secondly, that pressure has been allowed to dominate the picture and has concealed the nature of relational undue influence; and, thirdly, whatever the precise future of the requirement of manifest disadvantage in the context of undue influence, nobody has ever suggested that it has any role whatever in duress.

A consolidation of the law relating to pressure would not have been possible in earlier times because of the narrowness of the concept of operative duress. Duress to goods and other economic duress was thought not to give relief from a contract. Thanks in large measure to an influential article by Professor Beatson, that picture has been transformed. Nowadays it is clear that duress includes all illegitimate pressure and that all forms of duress can ground relief from a contract. The defendant must have done or threatened to do something 'illegitimate', a word which is chosen precisely because it has softer edges than, say, 'unlawful', with a view to inducing action by the plaintiff. In addition, action or threat must have induced the plaintiff to act or, more accurately, must have been one of his reasons for so acting.

It is now difficult to conceive of any pressure which will not be relieved satisfactorily, if it should be relieved at all, within the category of duress. To suggest otherwise would be to claim relief for a species of pressure which could not be characterized as illegitimate. That point will be revisited below, where it will be suggested that a legitimate pressure can never ground a claim whether framed as duress or as undue influence.

There are a number of cases where relief for pressure has in the past been given under the head of undue influence. In *Williams v Bayley*,[2] for example, the aged plaintiff-respondent had yielded to pressure to give security over his colliery for the repayment of losses inflicted on the appellant bankers by his son's habitually forging his signature on promissory notes accepted by the appellants. Lord Chelmsford summed up the basis on which the father would be relieved in this way:

> [T]his negotiation proceeded upon an understanding between the parties that the agreement of James Bayley, to give security for the notes, would relieve William Bayley [the son] from the consequences of his criminal acts; and the fears of the father were stimulated and operated on to an extent to deprive him of free agency, and to extort an agreement from him for the benefit of the bankers. It appears to me, therefore, that the case comes within the principles on which a court of equity proceeds in setting aside an agreement where there is an inequality between the parties, and one of them takes an unfair advantage of the situation of the other, and uses undue influence to force an agreement from him.[3]

We need not analyse the precise angle of Lord Chelmsford's approach to the relief. It is sufficient to say that a case such as this can and should be litigated as illegitimate pressure.

Mutual Finance Ltd v John Wetton & Sons Ltd[4] is similar. In connection with the hire-purchase of a lorry by a friend, one of the Wetton brothers, Joseph, had forged a guarantee so that it appeared to have been given by the Wetton company. When the friend defaulted, the finance company agreed that another purchaser could take the contract over but, now knowing of the forgery, felt in a position to insist upon a new guarantee from the company. No explicit threats were made that Joseph would be prosecuted if no guarantee were forthcoming, but the other brother gave the company's guarantee feeling that the threat of prosecution or exposure existed and that his elderly father's fragile health would be endangered if he discovered the facts. The narrowness of the common law's

---

2 (1866) LR 1 HL 200.   3 *Ibid.* 215–16.   4 [1937] 2 All ER 657.

prevailing concept of duress obliged Porter J expressly to negative duress. He rested the relief on undue influence. Nowadays we should not hesitate to reclassify the case as one of pressure and hence of duress. In *Kaufman v Gerson*[5] where the pressure was not dissimilar, there is indeed already some instability in the language used to describe it. Collins MR speaks chiefly of undue influence but he also uses the word 'duress.'[6]

A Presumption of Duress?

If we say that pressure cases should be litigated as duress, we have nevertheless to enter one possible caveat. An obvious advantage of litigating under the head of undue influence is that the plaintiff may be able to take the advantage of a presumption that the decision or transfer in question was attributable to undue influence. The next section will argue that the facts which support the presumption hardly ever have anything to do with pressure. However, there is a rare exception where a particular relationship is characterized by a history of violence.

. . . It is an intriguing question whether, in order to gain the benefit of the presumption, plaintiffs . . . who face some difficulty in proving a causal nexus between a transfer and a particular episode of violence or other illegitimate pressure, must invoke undue influence, rather than duress, there being no tradition of a presumption of duress from a history of violence within a relationship. The rational step would be to hold that, if the presumption is justified under one label, it must be no less justified under the other. There is in any case a fine line between the presumption and a simple shifting of the onus of proof. Nevertheless, it must be admitted that, in a less than perfectly rational world, the familiar availability of the presumption in association with undue influence may still constitute, in some cases, a practical reason for describing a case of pressure as a case of undue influence. Even if that is right, it provides no argument against the distinctness of the concept of illegitimate pressure, nor against the desirability on the grounds of intellectual order of drawing a line between all cases of pressure and all other cases of undue influence.

QUESTIONS

Are Birks and Chin Nyuk Yin correct to maintain that all pressure cases 'should be litigated as duress'? Can their approach be applied satisfactorily to all of the cases in this section? How would it apply to the facts of *Silsbee v Webber*?

---

5 [1904] 1 KB 591. Cf. *Silsbee v Webber*, 171 Mass. 378, 50 NE 555 (1898).
6 *Ibid*. 596–7.

7

UNDUE INFLUENCE AND EXPLOITATION OF WEAKNESS

The cases discussed in this Chapter are notoriously difficult to classify. The difficulty lies not in discerning whether or not the defendant has been enriched, nor in establishing whether that enrichment was 'at the expense' of the claimant. Rather, the difficulty lies in identifying the nature and scope of the 'unjust factor' in play. Broadly speaking, there are three different views of the cases. The first is a 'claimant-sided' version, in that it looks to the characteristics of the claimant. It locates the unjust factor in the claimant's weakness (including, in the undue influence cases, the claimant's 'excessive dependence' upon the defendant), albeit that that weakness falls short of incapacity. In this version there is no requirement that the defendant has knowingly taken advantage of the claimant's weakness. The second version looks instead to the conduct of the defendant and finds the unjust factor in the defendant's exploitation, or taking advantage of the claimant's weakness (with the difficult question being whether the exploitation must be in bad faith). We have elected to employ the term 'exploitation' because its principal competitor, 'unconscionable', is notoriously unstable and is used, as we shall see, in many different senses by commentators and courts. An intermediate position is that the unjust factor is neither exclusively claimant-sided nor exclusively defendant-sided, in that it looks to both the claimant and to the defendant and relies on a mix of the claimant's vulnerability and the defendant's taking advantage of that vulnerability.

A further difficulty relates to the role of substantive unfairness in the setting aside of such transactions. What role, if any, does the fairness of the terms have on the decision to set aside, or not to set aside, the transaction? The issue has proved to be particularly troublesome in the context of the law relating to undue influence.

It is also difficult to say where these cases end and the (human) incapacity cases begin (the incapacity cases are discussed in Chapter 11). This problem is most acute where the claimant is elderly and seeks to recover a benefit which he has conferred upon the defendant. In such a case is the claimant entitled to recover on the ground of his weakness or lack of capacity or on the ground of the defendant's exploitation of his infirmity? As we shall see, English law has taken the latter view (see, for example, *Hart v O'Connor*, below, 612) and therefore these cases should, arguably, have been included within this Chapter.

The exploitation by the defendant, or the weakness of the claimant, may be of (at least) four different types. It may relate to:

(i) the relationship between the claimant and the defendant (this is the area covered by undue influence, once one removes those cases of actual undue influence concerned with illegitimate pressure: on which see Chapter 6);

(ii) the mental inadequacy of the claimant;

(iii) the vulnerable financial position of the claimant; and

(iv) the difficult circumstances (other than financial) of the claimant.

There are also examples of contracts being rendered illegal an order to protect a vulnerable class, to which the claimant belongs, from exploitation.

We should emphasize, however, that this fivefold categorization is not a rigid one. It is used only for the purposes of exposition and should not be seen as an encouragement to compartmentalization of this area of the law. Indeed, one of the issues which needs to be explored is the extent to which these seemingly disparate areas of the law have common themes and whether or not a common doctrine can be derived from the cases. To that end, after our discussion of the undue influence cases, we shall stop to consider the decision of the High Court of Australia in *Louth v Diprose*, below, 480, a case which, arguably, straddles the first two categories and which explicitly looks to the unconscionable conduct of the defendant as the justification for providing relief.

General Reading

BURROWS, chapter 6; GOFF AND JONES, chapters 11 and 12; VIRGO, chapter 10.

1. RELATIONAL UNDUE INFLUENCE

In the previous Chapter we argued that some of the actual undue influence cases are, in fact, examples of the application of illegitimate pressure and so should be treated alongside the duress cases. In this section we are concerned with those actual undue influence cases which are not based on pressure (if there are any such cases), and also the presumed undue influence cases. When reading the extracts which follow, it might be helpful to bear in mind the following questions:

(i) What does the word 'undue' mean? Does it mean 'too much', 'illegitimate' (in the sense that that word is used in the context of duress), 'unconscionable', or something else?

(ii) What does 'influence' mean? Does it mean 'pressure', 'domination', 'exploitation', 'dependence', or something else?

(iii) Where the presumption of undue influence is invoked, what is it that is being presumed? Is it illegitimate pressure, exploitation, excessive dependence or something else?

(iv) The principal way in which the presumption of undue influence can be rebutted is through showing that the party subject to the 'influence' was independently advised. Does this suggest that the focus of the presumption is upon excessive dependence rather than exploitation by the defendant?

(v) In these cases is the focus of inquiry upon the excessive dependence of the claimant or the exploitation by the defendant, or elements of both?

• *Allcard v Skinner* (1887) 36 ChD 145, Court of Appeal

In 1868, the claimant was introduced by her 'spiritual director and confessor', Rev. D Nihill, to the defendant, who was the lady superior of the sisterhood of St Mary at the Cross. In July of the same year, the claimant became an associate of the sisterhood, and at that time promised to devote her property to the service of the poor. She subsequently became a postulant, and then a novice, before, in 1871, she joined the sisterhood. On becoming a sister the claimant became subject to the rules of the sisterhood. These rules demanded her implicit obedience to the lady superior, whose voice was stated to be 'the voice of God', and they also stated that she must not 'seek advice of any entern without the Superior's leave'. She also took a vow of poverty, which required her to give away all her property. Although there was no requirement that she give her property to the sisterhood, it was found that there was an expectation to that effect. The claimant left the sisterhood in 1879 and revoked her will under which she had left her property to the sisterhood. In 1885 the claimant sought to recover certain items of property which she had transferred to the sisterhood. Her claim was rejected by the Court of Appeal, affirming the decision of Kekewich J. Although she was able to show that the property had been transferred while she was under the undue influence of the defendant, it was held, Cotton LJ dissenting on this point, that her claim was barred by virtue of her delay after leaving the sisterhood in bringing proceedings (and for this purpose the majority found it unnecessary to decide whether the appropriate label for the defence was acquiesence, laches or affirmation). In the extracts which follow we are concerned solely with the ground on which the claimant was entitled to bring her claim and not with the scope of the defences.

Cotton LJ: . . . The question is—Does the case fall within the principles laid down by the decisions of the Court of Chancery in setting aside voluntary gifts executed by parties who at the time were under such influence as, in the opinion of the Court, enabled the donor afterwards to set the gift aside? These decisions may be divided into two classes—First, where the Court has been satisfied that the gift was the result of influence expressly used by the donee for the purpose; second, where the relations between the donor and donee have at or shortly before the execution of the gift been such as to raise a presumption that the donee had influence over the donor. In such a case the Court sets aside the voluntary gift, unless it is proved that in fact the gift was the spontaneous act of the donor acting under circumstances which enabled him to exercise an independent will and which justifies the Court in holding that the gift was the result of a free exercise of the donor's will. The first class of cases may be considered as depending on the principle that no one shall be allowed to retain any benefit arising from his own fraud or wrongful act. In the second class of cases the Court interferes, not on the ground that any wrongful act has in fact been committed by the donee, but on the ground of public policy, and to prevent the relations which existed between the parties and the influence arising therefrom being abused.

Both the Defendant and Mr Nihill have stated that they used no influence to induce the Plaintiff to make the gift in question, and there is no suggestion that the Defendant acted from any selfish motive, and it cannot be contended that this case comes under the first class of decisions to which I have referred. The question is whether the case comes within the principle of the second class, and I am of opinion that it does. At the time of the gift the Plaintiff was a professed sister, and, as such, bound to render absolute submission to the Defendant as superior of the sisterhood. She had no power to obtain independent advice, she was in such a position that she could not freely exercise her own will as to the disposal of her property, and she must be considered as being, to use the words of Lord Justice Knight Bruce in *Wright v Vanderplank*,[1] 'not, in the largest and amplest sense of the term—not, in mind as well as person—an entirely free agent.' We have nothing to do with the Plaintiff's reasons for leaving the sisterhood; but, in my opinion, when she exercised her legal right to do this she was entitled to recover so much of the fund transferred by her as remained in the hands of the Defendant, on the ground that it was property the beneficial interest in which she had never

---

1 8 D M & G 137.

effectually parted with. But it was urged that it would be contrary to public policy to grant the Plaintiff relief, on the ground that it would be a hindrance to the charitable work in which the Plaintiff and the sisterhood were engaged, and that it would be better to shew those who were desirous of leaving the work that they could not take with them any part of their property. But in my opinion it would be wrong to put such pressure on those who may wish to leave. Such work to be effectual must be done with a willing mind, and in my opinion it would be productive of evil to attempt to retain in such a society as the sisterhood, by the pressure of loss of property, those whose hearts and will are no longer in the work, and who desire to exercise their legal right of withdrawing.

But it is contended, and Mr Justice *Kekewich* decided against the Plaintiff on this ground, that she had competent advice, that of her brother, before she joined the sisterhood, and that she then formed the resolution (as Mr *Nihill* stated in his evidence) to give everything to the sisterhood, and that this prevents the subsequent transfer being set aside. In my opinion even if there were evidence that she had, before she joined the sisterhood, advice on the question of how she should deal with her property, that would not be sufficient. The question is, I think, whether at the time when she executed the transfer she was under such influences as to prevent the gift being considered as that of one free to determine what should be done with her property. No reliance can be placed on the promise made to Mr *Nihill*. This could not be enforced, and did not in any way bind her in law, or pass the property; and the title of the Defendant depends solely on the transfer made in 1874. In my opinion, when the Plaintiff left the sisterhood in 1879, she was entitled to set aside the transfer, and to have re-transferred to her the fund still held by the Defendant. . . .

Lindley LJ: . . . It is important . . . to bear in mind that the fetter . . . placed on the Plaintiff was the result of her own free choice. There is no evidence that pressure was put upon her to enter upon the mode of life which she adopted. She chose it as the best for herself; she devoted herself to it, heart and soul; she was, to use her own expression, infatuated with the life and with the work. But though infatuated, there is no evidence to shew that she was in such a state of mental imbecility as to justify the inference that she was unable to take care of herself or to manage her own affairs.

The rule against obtaining advice from externs without the consent of the lady superior invites great suspicion. It is evidently a rule capable of being used in a very tyrannical way, and so as to result in intolerable oppression. I have carefully examined the evidence to see how this rule practically worked, but I can find nothing on the subject. I can find nothing to shew one way or the other what would have been the effect, for example, of a request for leave to consult a friend, or to obtain legal or other advice respecting any disposition of property, or respecting leaving the sisterhood. There, however, is the rule, and a very important one it is. I shall have occasion to refer to it again hereafter. Such being the nature of the vows and rules which the Plaintiff had taken, and to which she had submitted herself, and by which she felt herself bound by the highest religious sanctions, it is necessary to examine what she did with her property, and the circumstances under which she gave it to the sisterhood.

The evidence shews that her brother, who was one of her trustees, kept her fully informed of what her property consisted of, and he remitted to her from time to time cheques and transfers of railway stock and other securities to which she was entitled. The brother's letters and the cheques and transfers all passed through the hands of the lady superior, it being the rule that she should see all letters to sisters. The Plaintiff gave all the cheques to the lady superior, after indorsing them, and also transferred to her all the railway stock and securities as they were received. The cheques were handed over to Mr *Nihill*, who was the treasurer of the sisterhood, and were paid by him into a bank to an account kept in his own name, and on which he alone could draw. The sisterhood was building an hospital in which the Plaintiff took great interest, and most of the Plaintiff's money was spent in defraying the expenses of the building. I have examined the evidence with care in order to see whether any pressure was put upon the Plaintiff in order to induce her to give her property to the sisterhood, or whether any deception was practised upon her, or whether any unfair advantage was taken of her, or whether any of her money was applied otherwise than *bonâ fide* for the objects of the sisterhood, or for any purpose which the Plaintiff could disapprove. The result of the evidence convinces me that no pressure, except the inevitable pressure of the vows and rules, was brought to bear on the Plaintiff; that no deception was practised upon her; that no unfair advantage was taken of her; that none of her money was obtained or applied for any purpose other than the legitimate objects of the sisterhood. Not a farthing of it was either obtained or applied for the private advantage of the lady superior or Mr *Nihill*; nor indeed did the Plaintiff ever suggest that such had been the case. The real truth is that the Plaintiff gave away her property as a matter of course, and without seriously thinking of the consequences to herself. She had devoted herself and her fortune to the sisterhood, and it never occurred to her that she should ever wish to leave the sisterhood or desire to have her money back. In giving away her property as she did she was merely acting up to her promise and vow and the rule of the sisterhood, and to the standard of duty which she had erected for herself under the influences and circumstances already stated.

. . .

By her action the Plaintiff sought to recover the whole of the money back which she had given to the sisterhood, amounting to nearly £8500. Mr Justice *Kekewich* tried the action, and gave judgment for the Defendant. From this judgment the Plaintiff has appealed, but she has limited her appeal to two sums of £500 and £1171, railway stock transferred by her to the lady superior, and still standing in her name.

Two questions are raised by the appeal, namely, 1st, Whether the gifts made by the Plaintiff to the sisterhood were revocable or irrevocable when made? 2nd, Whether, assuming them to have been revocable when made, it was competent for the Plaintiff to revoke them when she did?

The first question is one of great importance and difficulty. Its solution requires a careful consideration of the legal effect of gifts by persons of mature age who feel bound by vows and rules to give away their property, but who have taken the vows and submitted to the rules voluntarily and without pressure, and who are subject to no other coercion or influence than necessarily result from the vows and rules themselves, and from the state of their own mind.

There is no statutory law in this country prohibiting such gifts unless what is given is land or money to be laid out in land. These are provided for by the *Mortmain* and *Charitable Uses* Acts. But they have no application to this case. The common law, as distinguished from equity, does not invalidate such gifts as these. There being no duress or fraud, the only ground for impeaching such gifts at law would be want of capacity on the part of the donor; and although the Plaintiff was a religious enthusiast, no one could treat her as in point of law *non compos mentis*. There is no authority whatever for saying that her gifts were invalid at law. It is to the doctrines of equity, then, that recourse must be had to invalidate such gifts, if they are to be invalidated. The doctrine relied upon by the Appellant is the doctrine of undue influence expounded and enforced in *Huguenin v Baseley*[2] and other cases of that class. These cases may be subdivided into two groups, which, however, often overlap.

First, there are the cases in which there has been some unfair and improper conduct, some coercion from outside, some overreaching, some form of cheating, and generally, though not always, some personal advantage obtained by a donee placed in some close and confidential relation to the donor. . . . The evidence does not bring this case within this group.

The second group consists of cases in which the position of the donor to the donee has been such that it has been the duty of the donee to advise the donor, or even to manage his property for him. In

---

2 14 Ves 273.

such cases the Court throws upon the donee the burden of proving that he has not abused his position, and of proving that the gift made to him has not been brought about by any undue influence on his part. In this class of cases it has been considered necessary to shew that the donor had independent advice, and was removed from the influence of the donee when the gift to him was made. *Huguenin v Baseley* was a case of this kind. The defendant had not only acquired considerable spiritual influence over the plaintiff, but was intrusted by her with the management of her property. His duty to her was clear, and it was with reference to persons so situated that Lord *Eldon* used the language so often quoted and so much relied on in this case. He said: 'Take it that she (the plaintiff) intended to give it to him (the defendant): it is by no means out of the reach of the principle. The question is, not, whether she knew, what she was doing, had done, or proposed to do, but how the intention was produced: whether all that care and providence was placed round her, as against those, who advised her, which, from their situation and relation with respect to her, they were bound to exert on her behalf. This principle has been constantly recognised and acted upon in subsequent cases, but in all of them, as in *Huguenin v Baseley* itself, it was the duty of the donee to advise and take care of the donor. Where there is no such duty the language of Lord *Eldon* cases to be applicable.

. . .

I have not been able to find any case in which a gift has been set aside on the ground of undue influence which does not fall within one or other or both of the groups above mentioned. Nor can I find any authority which actually covers the present case. But it does not follow that it is not reached by the principle on which the Court has proceeded in dealing with the cases which have already called for decision. They illustrate but do not limit the principle applied to them.

The principle must be examined. What then is the principle? Is it that it is right and expedient to save persons from the consequences of their own folly? or is it that it is right and expedient to save them from being victimised by other people? In my opinion the doctrine of undue influence is founded upon the second of these two principles. Courts of Equity have never set aside gifts on the ground of the folly, imprudence, or want of foresight on the part of donors. The Courts have always repudiated any such jurisdiction. *Hugenin v Baseley* is itself a clear authority to this effect. It would obviously be to encourage folly, recklessness, extravagance and vice if persons could get back property which they foolishly made away with, whether by giving it to charitable institutions or by bestowing it on less worthy objects. On the other hand, to protect people from being forced, tricked or misled in any way by others into parting with their property is one of the most legitimate objects of all laws; and the equitable doctrine of undue influence has grown out of and been developed by the necessity of grappling with insidious forms of spiritual tyranny and with the infinite varieties of fraud.

As no Court has ever attempted to define fraud so no Court has ever attempted to define undue influence, which includes one of its many varieties. The undue influence which Courts of Equity endeavour to defeat is the undue influence of one person over another; not the influence of enthusiasm on the enthusiast who is carried away by it, unless indeed such enthusiasm is itself the result of external undue influence. But the influence of one mind over another is very subtle, and of all influences religious influence is the most dangerous and the most powerful, and to counteract it Courts of Equity have gone very far. They have not shrunk from setting aside gifts made to persons in a position to exercise undue influence over the donors, although there has been no proof of the actual exercise of such influence; and the Courts have done this on the avowed ground of the necessity of going this length in order to protect persons from the exercise of such influence under circumstances which render proof of it impossible. The Courts have required proof of its non-exercise, and, failing that proof, have set aside gifts otherwise unimpeachable. In this particular case I cannot find any proof that any gift made by the Plaintiff was the result of any actual exercise of power or influence on the part of the lady superior or of Mr *Nihill*, apart from the influence necessarily incidental to their position in the sisterhood. Everything that the Plaintiff did is in my opinion referable to her own willing submission to the vows she took and to the rules which she approved, and to her own enthusiastic devotion to the life and work of the sisterhood. This enthusiasm and devotion were nourished, strengthened and intensified by the religious services of the sisterhood and by the example and influence of those about her. But she chose the life and work; such fetters as bound her were voluntarily put upon her by herself; she could shake them off at any time had she thought fit, and had she had the courage so to do; and no unfair advantage whatever was taken of her. Under these circumstances it is going a long way to hold that she can invoke the doctrine of undue influence to save her from the consequences of her own acts, and to entitle her to avoid the gifts she made when in a state of mind different from that in which she now is. I am by no means insensible of the difficulty of going so far.

Nevertheless, consider the position in which the Plaintiff had placed herself. She had vowed poverty and obedience, and she was not at liberty to consult externs without the leave of her superior. She was not a person who treated her vows lightly; she was deeply religious and felt bound by her promise, by her vows, and by the rules of the sisterhood. She was absolutely in the power of the lady superior and Mr *Nihill*. A gift made by her under these circumstances to the lady superior cannot in my opinion be retained by the donee. The equitable title of the donee is imperfect by reason of the influence inevitably resulting from her position, and which influence experience has taught the Courts to regard as undue. Whatever doubt I might have had on this point if there had been no rule against consulting externs, that rule in my judgment turns the scale against the Defendant. In the face of that rule the gifts made to the sisterhood cannot be supported in the absence of proof that the Plaintiff could have obtained independent advice if she wished for it, and that she knew that she would have been allowed to obtain such advice if she had desired to do so. I doubt whether the gifts could have been supported if such proof had been given, unless there was also proof that she was free to act on the advice which might be given to her. But the rule itself is so oppressive and so easily abused that any person subject to it is in my opinion brought within the class of those whom it is the duty of the Court to protect from possible imposition. The gifts cannot be supported without proof of more freedom in fact than the Plaintiff can be supposed to have actually enjoyed.

The case is brought within the principle so forcibly expressed by the late Lord Justice *Knight Bruce* in *Wright v Vanderplank*, in which a gift by a daughter to her father was sought to be set aside. If any independent person had explained to the Plaintiff that her promise to give all her property to the sisterhood was not legally binding upon her, and that her vows of poverty and obedience had no legal validity, and that if she gave her property away and afterwards left the sisterhood she would be unable to get her property back, it is impossible to say what she might or might not have done. In fact she never had the opportunity of considering this question.

Where a gift is made to a person standing in a confidential relation to the donor, the Court will not set aside the gift if of a small amount simply on the ground that the donor had no independent advice. In such a case, some proof of the exercise of the influence of the donee must be given. The mere existence of such influence is not enough in such a case; see the observations of Lord Justice *Turner* in *Rhodes v Bate*.[3] But if the gift is so large as not to be reasonably accounted for on the ground of friendship, relationship, charity, or other ordinary motives on which ordinary men act, the burden is upon the donee to support the gift. So, in a case like this, a distinction might well be made between gifts of capital and gifts of income, and between gifts of moderate amount and gifts of large sums, which a person unfettered by vows and oppressive rules would not be likely to wish to make. In this case the Plaintiff gave away practically all she could, although, having a life interest in other property, she did not reduce herself to a state of poverty.

3 Law Rep 1 Ch 258.

As I have already stated, I believe that in this case there was in fact no unfair or undue influence brought to bear upon the Plaintiff other than such as inevitably resulted from the training she had received, the promise she had made, the vows she had taken, and the rules to which she had submitted herself. But her gifts were in fact made under a pressure which, whilst it lasted, the Plaintiff could not resist, and were not, in my opinion, past recall when that pressure was removed. When the Plaintiff emancipated herself from the spell by which she was bound, she was entitled to invoke the aid of the Court in order to obtain the restitution from the Defendant of so much of the Plaintiff's property as had not been spent in accordance with the wishes of the Plaintiff, but remained in the hands of the Defendant. The Plaintiff now demands no more.

. . .

Bowen LJ: . . . It seems to me that it is of essential importance to keep quite distinct two things which in their nature seem to me to be different – the rights of the donor, and the duties of the donee and the obligations which are imposed upon the conscience of the donee by the principles of this Court. As to the rights of the donor in a case like the present I entertain no doubt. It seems to me that persons who are under the most complete influence of religious feeling are perfectly free to act upon it in the disposition of their property, and not the less free because they are enthusiasts. Persons of this kind are not dead in law. They are dead indeed to the world so far as their own wishes and feelings about the things of the world are concerned; but such indifference to things external does not prevent them in law from being free agents. In the present instance there was no duress, no incompetency, no want of mental power on the part of the donor. It seems to me that, so far as regards her rights, she had the absolute right to deal with her property as she chose. Passing next to the duties of the donee, it seems to me that, although this power of perfect disposition remains in the donor under circumstances like the present, it is plain that equity will not allow a person who exercises or enjoys a dominant religious influence over another to benefit directly or indirectly by the gifts which the donor makes under or in consequence of such influence, unless it is shewn that the donor, at the time of making the gift, was allowed full and free opportunity for counsel and advice outside—the means of considering his or her worldly position and exercising an independent will about it. This is not a limitation placed on the action of the donor; it is a fetter placed upon the conscience of the recipient of the gift, and one which arises out of public policy and fair play. If this had been the gift of a chattel, therefore, the property then would have passed in law, and the gift of this stock may be treated upon a similar method of reasoning. Now, that being the rule, in the first place, was the Plaintiff entitled to the benefit of it? She had vowed in the most sacred and solemn way absolute and implicit obedience to the will of the Defendant, her superior, and she was bound altogether to neglect the advice of externs—not to consult those outside the convent. Now I offer no sort of criticism on institutions of this sort; no kind of criticism upon the action of those who enter them or of those who administer them. In the abstract I respect their motives, but it is obvious that it is exactly to this class of case that the rule of equity which I have mentioned ought to be applied if it exists. It seems to me that the Plaintiff, so long as she was fettered by this vow—so long as she was under the dominant influence of this religious feeling—was a person entitled to the protection of the rule. Now, was the Defendant bound by this rule? I acquit her most entirely of all selfish feeling in the matter. I can see no sort of wrongful desire to appropriate to herself any worldly benefit from the gift; but, nevertheless, she was a person who benefited by it so far as the disposition of the property was concerned, although, no doubt, she meant to use it in conformity with the rules of the institution, and did so use it. I pause for one moment to say a word as to Mr Justice *Kekewich's* view, which is not altogether consistent with the above. He seems to have thought that the question turned on the original intention of the donor at the time she entered the convent, and that what passed subsequently could be treated as if it were a mere mechanical performance of a complete mental intention originally formed. I entirely agree with the view presented to us by the Appellant as to that part of Mr Justice *Kekewich's* judgment. It seems to me that the case does not turn upon the fact that the standard of duty was originally created by the Plaintiff herself, although her original intention is one of the circumstances, no doubt, which bear upon the case, and is not to be neglected. But it is not the crucial fact. We ought to look, it seems to me, at the time at which the gift was made, and to examine what was then the condition of the donor who made it. For these reasons I think that without any interference with the freedom of persons to deal with their property as they please, we can hold but one opinion, that in 1879 the Plaintiff could have set this gift aside. . . .

NOTES AND QUESTIONS

1. In contrast with most of the cases on undue influence, this case concerned a gift and not a contract.

2. How would this case be decided applying Birks's 'absence of basis' approach (above, 137) to the unjust question?

3. What did Lindley LJ mean when he said that undue influence is based on the principle that 'it is right and expedient to save [people] from being victimized by other people'?

4. Was the Mother Superior guilty of unconscionable conduct in failing to ensure that the claimant was given independent advice? Was the Mother Superior at fault? Does it matter?

5. What would have been the outcome if the claimant had given her property to her sister in 1871? Would she have been able to recover it had she brought a claim against her sister shortly afterwards?

6. Leaving aside cases of illegitimate pressure, what falls within the first category of undue influence (actual undue influence) identified by Cotton and Lindley LJJ?

7. Birks and Chin Nyuk Yin ('On the Nature of Undue Influence' in J Beatson and D Friedmann (eds), *Good Faith and Fault in Contract Law* (1995), 57) maintain that *Allcard* is best understood, not as a case of wrongdoing by the Mother Superior but as a case in which the ground for relief was to be found in the claimant's excessive dependence upon the Mother Superior. They then use the case to build a claimant-based analysis of undue influence in the following terms (see 67–8 and 79–80 and 86–8):

THE CASES: PRESUMED RELATIONAL UNDUE INFLUENCE

In cases in which the presumption is relied upon, it is clear time and again that facts upon which it arises suggest excessive dependence. The relationships do not suggest pressure, and the fact presumed is neither pressure nor misconduct by the defendant. In *Allcard v Skinner* the plaintiff had left an Anglican convent to become a Roman Catholic. She sought to recover some of the wealth which she had surrendered to the Mother Superior of the convent at and after the time when she became a full member. She failed, but only because she had let the claim lie too long after she left the order. In presuming the undue influence the Court of Appeal was not presuming recourse to threats, express or implied, either by the Mother Superior or by the clergyman who had been the co-founder of the convent. The plaintiff had been under a spell compounded of her enthusiasm for the sisterhood and devotion to its rules, which included an obligation to seek advice only within the order. Her weakness consisted in her impaired capacity *vis-à-vis* the head of the order to judge her own best interests. She was excessively dependent or, if 'dependent' is a shade wrong, she was excessively spell-bound. Either way, her autonomy was impaired to an exceptional degree.

This type of analysis must also apply to other nominate relationships which are nowadays said to support the presumption of undue influence without further evidence. The relations between doctor and patient, solicitor and client, and parent and child typically contain strong elements of dependence, trust and gratitude, together in each case with a similar tendency to exclude others from the relationship and from the matters passing between the parties to it. It would be unreasonable to analyse the presumption in such cases as resting on a common experience of illegitimate threats. The relief based on the presumption is founded on the contrary upon the common experience of impaired autonomy within such relationships. They are relationships in which the patient, client or child is excessively dependent. . . .

There are some passages in *Allcard v Skinner*, especially in the judgment of Lindley LJ, which do suggest the contrary analysis, namely that undue influence is a matter of improper behaviour on the part of the defendant. Lindley LJ went out of his way to say that the law does not relieve a person from the consequences of folly, imprudence or lack of foresight. These passages can be read as supporting the view that relief must be based on the wrongful, exploitative conduct on the part of the defendant, not on the weak or crippled judgment of the plaintiff. However, that is an incorrect construction of their meaning. Lindley LJ was in no doubt that the Mother Superior was the model of rectitude. Closer examination shows that these passages bear on the ultimate justification for the intervention.

The ultimate justification of the relief is here presented as the need to meet the danger of wicked exploitation to which foolish or fixated people are exposed. Lindley LJ's meaning was not that the party seeking relief must prove wicked exploitation by the other, but only that it was to obviate the danger of wicked exploitation that relief was given, without proof of wicked exploitation, to those whose capacity to make judgments was impaired by relational influence. In other words, in his view, the justification for relieving the weak has to be found in prophylaxis against abuse by the strong. The case itself shows that the relief thus justified remains entirely plaintiff-sided.

The same prophylactic justification for the relief was expressed by Dixon J in *Johnson v Buttress*,[1] when he said:

> The basis of the equitable jurisdiction to set aside an alienation of property on the ground of undue influence is the *prevention* [emphasis added] of an unconscientious use of any special capacity or opportunity that may exist or arise of affecting the alienor's will or freedom of judgment in reference to such a matter.

Dixon J was a master of the English language. When he used the word 'prevention' he intended it to bear its proper meaning: the jurisdiction was designed to anticipate the danger of exploitation. It was not based on proof of exploitation in the particular case but on what Dixon J referred to as the impairment of the alienor's 'free act'. . . .

The ideas involved in this area of law are elusive. It is always difficult to find the right language, and always dangerous to make too much of any single word or phrase. 'Undue influence' itself is difficult. Judges have fought shy of definition, even of exposition. A tendency to circularity can be detected: the requirements of relief for undue influence are that there must be influence and that it must be undue. In struggling towards a more stable understanding, it must be acknowledged that the phrase's natural orientation is to the defendant's side, i.e. it tends to draw the mind towards the person who has influence. At the same time, despite having that tendency, it is not wholly inappropriate to describe, neutrally or bi-polarly, the relationship in which one is dependent or otherwise easily led, while the other has the power to influence. Dependence and influence are two sides of the same coin. The phrase 'undue influence' is not unsuitable to describe the entirety of such a relationship. Its tendency to draw the mind to active abuse of influence is distracting, but it is not so powerful as to necessitate a change of terminology. We should therefore say, first, that the phrase 'undue influence' supposes the existence of two parties and, secondly, that the word 'influence' indicates, in relation to some decision to be taken or some class of such decisions, a degree of reduced autonomy on the part of the one and a corresponding degree of control or ascendancy on in the other.

---

1 (1936) 56 CLR 113.

Next, the ambiguity of the word 'undue' is awesome. It is naturally capable of meaning both 'excessive' and 'unfitting' or 'improper'. Worse, there is a point where, in general usage, that which is excessive also becomes improper or unacceptable. A person who is unduly talkative talks too much and, in doing so, offends the canons of social behaviour. The excess is also out of place. This ambiguity must be resolved in favour of 'excessive.' If the question is whether the plaintiff's autonomy was impaired by the relationship to a degree which deprived him of the capacity for self-management which the law attributes to the generality of adults, and if no inquiry has to be made about the wickedness of the defendant, there is, logically, no warrant for saying that the influence must be 'undue' in any sense other than 'excessive.'

The same conclusion follows from another proposition, namely that a moderate loss of autonomy cannot found relief even if attributable to an influence exercisable or exercised by the other which can be qualified as improper. Appetites, even far short of addiction, create a degree of dependence, and some appetites, as for illicit commodities, invite improper influence. But a rich man who wants ivory or rhinoceros horn does not, in equity's sense, thereby come under the undue influence of the poachers. Whatever the precise quality of the contract by which he pays a vast price, it is not voidable for undue influence. It is not the impropriety of the influence upon which the relief is based, but the excessive and exceptional degree of lost autonomy.

'Undue influence' is therefore too much influence, too much to be compatible with the general presumption that adults all have the standard common law capacity to manage their own affairs. Where there is too much influence on one side there is insufficient autonomy on the other, and it is that insufficient autonomy on which the relief is founded. 'Too much' and 'insufficient' are matters of degree, but the degree in question is exceptional. Although adults are in reality of widely differing intelligence and personality, by and large they must be presumed equally able to cope with their own affairs. Similarly, adults come under all sorts of different influences, and again they have to be assumed able to cope. The law relieves only an extreme loss of autonomy.

Finally, there is the word 'exercise.' Is it correct to speak of exercising undue influence or to ask of a defendant whether it can be said of him that he 'exercised undue influence' so as to obtain an advantage? In pressure cases the application of pressure can of course be described as an exercise of undue influence. However, the usage which derives from those cases should not be allowed to spread into all other examples of undue influence. We have shown that, where undue influence is presumed, the presumption concedes causation, so that it falls to the defendant to show that the plaintiff's want of autonomy did not cause the transfer, usually done by showing that independent advice emancipated the plaintiff from his or her excessive dependence.

In a pressure case 'causation' and 'exercise' are the same thing, but in other cases the causation which the presumption concedes does not imply activity on the party of the defendant. Similarly, where a plaintiff renounces the presumption to avoid affirmative proof that the bargain was disadvantageous or ill-advised, the usage based on the pressure cases should not carry over a requirement of active causation to actual relational influence. The plaintiff renounces the concession of causation and must therefore prove that the excessive dependence (or other shade of lost autonomy) did cause the transfer. We have argued that the Court of Appeal in *Aboody* ought not to have added additional facts to the plaintiff's voluntarily assumed evidential onus. Renouncing the presumption, Miss Allcard a century ago . . . would have had to have proved only that [her] want of autonomy caused the transfer, not that [her] defendant 'exercised undue influence' to obtain it.

- *Royal Bank of Scotland plc v Etridge (No 2)* [2001] UKHL 44; [2002] 2 AC 773, House of Lords

The House of Lords heard eight appeals. Each case arose out of a transaction in which a wife charged her interest in her home in favour of a bank as security for her husband's indebtedness or the indebtedness of a company through which he carried on business. In seven of the appeals the bank sought to enforce the charge signed by the wife. The wife raised a defence that the bank was on notice that her concurrence in the transaction had been procured by her husband's undue influence. In the eighth appeal the wife claimed damages from a solicitor who advised her before she entered into a guarantee obligation under the undue influence of her husband. For present purposes our concern is solely with the identification of the legal rules relating to undue influence held by the House of Lords to be applicable to the cases before them; we are not concerned to apply these principles to the facts of the eight appeals. In some cases the wife was held to have a defence (or a potential defence) to the claim by the bank, while in others it was held that she had no defence based upon her claim that she had entered into the contract as a consequence of the undue influence exercised by her husband.

Lord Bingham of Cornhill

3. . . . While the opinions of Lord Nicholls and Lord Scott show some difference of expression and approach, I do not myself discern any significant difference of legal principle applicable to these cases, and I agree with both opinions. But if I am wrong and such differences exist, it is plain that the opinion of Lord Nicholls commands the unqualified support of all members of the House.

Lord Nicholls of Birkenhead

5. My Lords, before your Lordships' House are appeals in eight cases. Each case arises out of a transaction in which a wife charged her interest in her home in favour of a bank as security for her husband's indebtedness or the indebtedness of a company through which he carried on business. The wife later asserted she signed the charge under the undue influence of her husband. In *Barclays Bank plc v O'Brien* [1994] 1 A.C. 180 your Lordships enunciated the principles applicable in this type of case. Since then, many cases have come before the courts, testing the implications of the *O'Brien* decision in a variety of different factual situations. Seven of the present appeals are of this character. In each case the bank sought to enforce the charge signed by the wife. The bank claimed an order for possession of the matrimonial home. The wife raised a defence that the bank was on notice that her concurrence in the transaction had been procured by her husband's undue influence. The eighth appeal concerns a claim by a wife for damages from a solicitor who advised her before she entered into a guarantee obligation of this character.

Undue influence

6. The issues raised by these appeals make it necessary to go back to first principles. Undue influence is one of the grounds of relief developed by the courts of equity as a court of conscience. The objective is to ensure that the influence of one person over another is not abused. In everyday life people constantly seek to influence the decisions of others. They seek to persuade those with whom they are dealing to enter into transactions, whether great or small. The law has set limits to the means properly employable for this purpose. To this end the common law developed a principle of duress. Originally this was narrow in its scope, restricted to the more blatant forms of physical coercion, such as personal violence.

7. Here, as elsewhere in the law, equity supplemented the common law. Equity extended the reach of the law to other unacceptable forms of persuasion. The law will investigate the manner in which the intention to enter into the transaction was secured: 'how the intention was produced', in the oft repeated words of Lord Eldon L.C., from as long ago as 1807 (*Huguenin v Baseley* 14 Ves. 273, 300). If the intention was produced by an unacceptable means, the law will not permit the transaction to stand. The means used is regarded as an exercise of improper or 'undue' influence, and hence unacceptable, whenever the consent thus procured ought not fairly to be treated as the expression of a person's free will. It is impossible to be more precise or definitive. The circumstances in which one person acquires influence over another, and the manner in which influence may be exercised, vary too widely to permit of any more specific criterion.

8. Equity identified broadly two forms of unacceptable conduct. The first comprises overt acts of improper pressure or coercion such as unlawful threats. Today there is much overlap with the principle of duress as this principle has subsequently developed. The second form arises out of a relationship between two persons where one has acquired over another a measure of influence, or ascendancy, of which the ascendant person then takes unfair advantage . . .

9. In cases of this latter nature the influence one person has over another provides scope for misuse without any specific overt acts of persuasion. The relationship between two individuals may be such that, without more, one of them is disposed to agree a course of action proposed by the other. Typically this occurs when one person places trust in another to look after his affairs and interests, and the latter betrays this trust by preferring his own interests. He abuses the influence he has acquired. In *Allcard v Skinner* (1887) 36 ChD 145, a case well known to every law student, Lindley L.J., at p 181, described this class of cases as those in which it was the duty of one party to advise the other or to manage his property for him . . .

10. The law has long recognised the need to prevent abuse of influence in these 'relationship' cases despite the absence of evidence of overt acts of persuasive conduct. The types of relationship, such as parent and child, in which this principle falls to be applied cannot be listed exhaustively. Relationships are infinitely various. Sir Guenter Treitel Q.C. has rightly noted that the question is whether one party has reposed sufficient trust and confidence in the other, rather than whether the relationship between the parties belongs to a particular type: see Treitel, *The Law of Contract*, 10th ed. (1999), pp 380–381. For example, the relation of banker and customer will not normally meet this criterion, but exceptionally it may: see *National Westminster Bank plc v Morgan* [1985] A.C. 686, 707–709.

11. Even this test is not comprehensive. The principle is not confined to cases of abuse of trust and confidence. It also includes, for instance, cases where a vulnerable person has been exploited. Indeed, there is no single touchstone for determining whether the principle is applicable. Several expressions have been used in an endeavour to encapsulate the essence: trust and confidence, reliance, dependence or vulnerability on the one hand and ascendancy, domination or control on the other. None of these descriptions is perfect. None is all embracing. Each has its proper place.

12. In *CIBC Mortgages plc v Pitt* [1994] 1 A.C. 200 your Lordships' House decided that in cases of undue influence disadvantage is not a necessary ingredient of the cause of action. It is not essential that the transaction should be disadvantageous to the pressurised or influenced person, either in financial terms or in any other way. However, in the nature of things, questions of undue influence will not usually arise, and the exercise of undue influence is unlikely to occur, where the transaction is innocuous. The issue is likely to arise only when, in some respect, the transaction was disadvantageous either from the outset or as matters turned out.

Burden of proof and presumptions

13. Whether a transaction was brought about by the exercise of undue influence is a question of fact. Here, as elsewhere, the general principle is that he who asserts a wrong has been committed must prove it. The burden of proving an allegation of undue influence rests upon the person who claims to have been wronged. This is the general rule. The evidence required to discharge the burden of proof depends on the nature of the alleged undue influence, the personality of the parties, their relationship, the extent to which the transaction cannot readily be accounted for by the ordinary motives of ordinary persons in that relationship, and all the circumstances of the case.

14. Proof that the complainant placed trust and confidence in the other party in relation to the management of the complainant's financial affairs, coupled with a transaction which calls for explanation, will normally be sufficient, failing satisfactory evidence to the contrary, to discharge the burden of proof. On proof of these two matters the stage is set for the court to infer that, in the absence of a satisfactory explanation, the transaction can only have been procured by undue

influence. In other words, proof of these two facts is prima facie evidence that the defendant abused the influence he acquired in the parties' relationship. He preferred his own interests. He did not behave fairly to the other. So the evidential burden then shifts to him. It is for him to produce evidence to counter the inference which otherwise should be drawn . . .

16. Generations of equity lawyers have conventionally described this situation as one in which a presumption of undue influence arises. This use of the term 'presumption' is descriptive of a shift in the evidential onus on a question of fact. When a plaintiff succeeds by this route he does so because he has succeeded in establishing a case of undue influence. The court has drawn appropriate inferences of fact upon a balanced consideration of the whole of the evidence at the end of a trial in which the burden of proof rested upon the plaintiff. The use, in the course of the trial, of the forensic tool of a shift in the evidential burden of proof should not be permitted to obscure the overall position. These cases are the equitable counterpart of common law cases where the principle of res ipsa loquitur is invoked. There is a rebuttable evidential presumption of undue influence.

17. The availability of this forensic tool in cases founded on abuse of influence arising from the parties' relationship has led to this type of case sometimes being labelled 'presumed undue influence'. This is by way of contrast with cases involving actual pressure or the like, which are labelled 'actual undue influence': see *Bank of Credit and Commerce International SA v Aboody* [1990] 1 Q.B. 923, 953, and *Royal Bank of Scotland plc v Etridge (No 2)* [1998] 4 All E.R. 705, 711–712, paras. 5–7. This usage can be a little confusing. In many cases where a plaintiff has claimed that the defendant abused the influence he acquired in a relationship of trust and confidence the plaintiff has succeeded by recourse to the rebuttable evidential presumption. But this need not be so. Such a plaintiff may succeed even where this presumption is not available to him; for instance, where the impugned transaction was not one which called for an explanation.

18. The evidential presumption discussed above is to be distinguished sharply from a different form of presumption which arises in some cases. The law has adopted a sternly protective attitude towards certain types of relationship in which one party acquires influence over another who is vulnerable and dependent and where, moreover, substantial gifts by the influenced or vulnerable person are not normally to be expected. Examples of relationships within this special class are parent and child, guardian and ward, trustee and beneficiary, solicitor and client, and medical adviser and patient. In these cases the law presumes, irrebuttably, that one party had influence over the other. The complainant need not prove he actually reposed trust and confidence in the other party. It is sufficient for him to prove the existence of the type of relationship.

19. It is now well established that husband and wife is not one of the relationships to which this latter principle applies . . . there is nothing unusual or strange in a wife, from motives of affection or for other reasons, conferring substantial financial benefits on her husband. Although there is no presumption, the court will nevertheless note, as a matter of fact, the opportunities for abuse which flow from a wife's confidence in her husband. The court will take this into account with all the other evidence in the case. Where there is evidence that a husband has taken unfair advantage of his influence over his wife, or her confidence in him, 'it is not difficult for the wife to establish her title to relief' . . .

Independent advice

20. Proof that the complainant received advice from a third party before entering into the impugned transaction is one of the matters a court takes into account when weighing all the evidence. The weight, or importance, to be attached to such advice depends on all the circumstances. In the normal course, advice from a solicitor or other outside adviser can be expected to bring home to a complainant a proper understanding of what he or she is about to do. But a person may understand fully the implications of a proposed transaction, for instance, a substantial gift, and yet still be acting under the undue influence of another. Proof of outside advice does not, of itself, necessarily show that the subsequent completion of the transaction was free from the exercise of undue influence. Whether it

will be proper to infer that outside advice had an emancipating effect, so that the transaction was not brought about by the exercise of undue influence, is a question of fact to be decided having regard to all the evidence in the case.

Manifest disadvantage

21. As already noted, there are two prerequisites to the evidential shift in the burden of proof from the complainant to the other party. First, that the complainant reposed trust and confidence in the other party, or the other party acquired ascendancy over the complainant. Second, that the transaction is not readily explicable by the relationship of the parties.

22. Lindley L.J. summarised this second prerequisite in the leading authority of *Allcard v Skinner*, 36 ChD 145, where the donor parted with almost all her property. Lindley L.J. pointed out that where a gift of a small amount is made to a person standing in a confidential relationship to the donor, some proof of the exercise of the influence of the donee must be given. The mere existence of the influence is not enough. He continued, at p 185: 'But if the gift is so large as not to be reasonably accounted for on the ground of friendship, relationship, charity, or other ordinary motives on which ordinary men act, the burden is upon the donee to support the gift.' . . .

24. . . . The second prerequisite, as expressed by Lindley L.J., is good sense. It is a necessary limitation upon the width of the first prerequisite. It would be absurd for the law to presume that every gift by a child to a parent, or every transaction between a client and his solicitor or between a patient and his doctor, was brought about by undue influence unless the contrary is affirmatively proved. Such a presumption would be too far-reaching. The law would be out of touch with everyday life if the presumption were to apply to every Christmas or birthday gift by a child to a parent, or to an agreement whereby a client or patient agrees to be responsible for the reasonable fees of his legal or medical adviser. The law would be rightly open to ridicule, for transactions such as these are unexceptionable. They do not suggest that something may be amiss. So something more is needed before the law reverses the burden of proof, something which calls for an explanation. When that something more is present, the greater the disadvantage to the vulnerable person, the more cogent must be the explanation before the presumption will be regarded as rebutted.

25. This was the approach adopted by Lord Scarman in *National Westminster Bank plc v Morgan* [1985] A.C. 686, 703–707. He cited Lindley L.J.'s observations in *Allcard v Skinner* 36 ChD 145, 185, which I have set out above. He noted that whatever the legal character of the transaction, it must constitute a disadvantage sufficiently serious to require evidence to rebut the presumption that in the circumstances of the parties' relationship, it was procured by the exercise of undue influence. Lord Scarman concluded, at p.704:

> 'the Court of Appeal erred in law in holding that the presumption of undue influence can arise from the evidence of the relationship of the parties without also evidence that the transaction itself was wrongful in that it constituted *an advantage taken of the person subjected to the influence which, failing proof to the contrary, was explicable only on the basis that undue influence had been exercised to procure it.*' (Emphasis added.)

26. Lord Scarman attached the label 'manifest disadvantage' to this second ingredient necessary to raise the presumption. This label has been causing difficulty. It may be apt enough when applied to straightforward transactions such as a substantial gift or a sale at an undervalue. But experience has now shown that this expression can give rise to misunderstanding. The label is being understood and applied in a way which does not accord with the meaning intended by Lord Scarman, its originator.

27. The problem has arisen in the context of wives guaranteeing payment of their husband's business debts. In recent years judge after judge has grappled with the baffling question whether a wife's guarantee of her husband's bank overdraft, together with a charge on her share of the matrimonial home, was a transaction manifestly to her disadvantage.

28. In a narrow sense, such a transaction plainly ('manifestly') is disadvantageous to the wife. She undertakes a serious financial obligation, and in return she personally receives nothing. But that would be to take an unrealistically blinkered view of such a transaction. Unlike the relationship of solicitor and client or medical adviser and patient, in the case of husband and wife there are inherent reasons why such a transaction may well be for her benefit. Ordinarily, the fortunes of husband and wife are bound up together. If the husband's business is the source of the family income, the wife has a lively interest in doing what she can to support the business. A wife's affection and self-interest run hand-in-hand in inclining her to join with her husband in charging the matrimonial home, usually a jointly-owned asset, to obtain the financial facilities needed by the business. The finance may be needed to start a new business, or expand a promising business, or rescue an ailing business.

29. Which, then, is the correct approach to adopt in deciding whether a transaction is disadvantageous to the wife: the narrow approach, or the wider approach? The answer is neither. The answer lies in discarding a label which gives rise to this sort of ambiguity. The better approach is to adhere more directly to the test outlined by Lindley L.J. in *Allcard v Skinner* 36 ChD 145, and adopted by Lord Scarman in *National Westminster Bank plc v Morgan* [1985] A.C. 686, in the passages I have cited.

30. I return to husband and wife cases. I do not think that, in the ordinary course, a guarantee of the character I have mentioned is to be regarded as a transaction which, failing proof to the contrary, is explicable only on the basis that it has been procured by the exercise of undue influence by the husband. Wives frequently enter into such transactions. There are good and sufficient reasons why they are willing to do so, despite the risks involved for them and their families. They may be enthusiastic. They may not. They may be less optimistic than their husbands about the prospects of the husbands' businesses. They may be anxious, perhaps exceedingly so. But this is a far cry from saying that such transactions as a class are to be regarded as prima facie evidence of the exercise of undue influence by husbands.

31. I have emphasised the phrase 'in the ordinary course'. There will be cases where a wife's signature of a guarantee or a charge of her share in the matrimonial home does call for explanation. Nothing I have said above is directed at such a case.

A cautionary note

32. I add a cautionary note. . . It concerns the general approach to be adopted by a court when considering whether a wife's guarantee of her husband's bank overdraft was procured by her husband's undue influence. Undue influence has a connotation of impropriety. In the eye of the law, undue influence means that influence has been misused. Statements or conduct by a husband which do not pass beyond the bounds of what may be expected of a reasonable husband in the circumstances should not, without more, be castigated as undue influence. Similarly, when a husband is forecasting the future of his business, and expressing his hopes or fears, a degree of hyperbole may be only natural. Courts should not too readily treat such exaggerations as misstatements.

33. Inaccurate explanations of a proposed transaction are a different matter. So are cases where a husband, in whom a wife has reposed trust and confidence for the management of their financial affairs, prefers his interests to hers and makes a choice for both of them on that footing. Such a husband abuses the influence he has. He fails to discharge the obligation of candour and fairness he owes a wife who is looking to him to make the major financial decisions.

The complainant and third parties: suretyship transactions

34. The problem considered in *O'Brien's* case and raised by the present appeals is of comparatively recent origin. It arises out of the substantial growth in home ownership over the last 30 or 40 years and, as part of that development, the great increase in the number of homes owned jointly by husbands and wives. More than two-thirds of householders in the United Kingdom now own their own homes. For most home-owning couples, their homes are their most valuable asset. They must

surely be free, if they so wish, to use this asset as a means of raising money, whether for the purpose of the husband's business or for any other purpose. Their home is their property. The law should not restrict them in the use they may make of it. Bank finance is in fact by far the most important source of external capital for small businesses with fewer than ten employees. These businesses comprise about 95 percent of all businesses in the country, responsible for nearly one-third of all employment. Finance raised by second mortgages on the principal's home is a significant source of capital for the start-up of small businesses.

35. If the freedom of home-owners to make economic use of their homes is not to be frustrated, a bank must be able to have confidence that a wife's signature of the necessary guarantee and charge will be as binding upon her as is the signature of anyone else on documents which he or she may sign. Otherwise banks will not be willing to lend money on the security of a jointly owned house or flat.

36. At the same time, the high degree of trust and confidence and emotional interdependence which normally characterises a marriage relationship provides scope for abuse. One party may take advantage of the other's vulnerability. Unhappily, such abuse does occur. Further, it is all too easy for a husband, anxious or even desperate for bank finance, to misstate the position in some particular or to mislead the wife, wittingly or unwittingly, in some other way. The law would be seriously defective if it did not recognise these realities.

37. In O'Brien's case this House decided where the balance should be held between these competing interests . . .

38. The jurisprudential route by which the House reached its conclusion in O'Brien's case has attracted criticism from some commentators. . . Lord Browne-Wilkinson prayed in aid the doctrine of constructive notice. In circumstances he identified, a creditor is put on inquiry. When that is so, the creditor 'will have constructive notice of the wife's rights' unless the creditor takes reasonable steps to satisfy himself that the wife's agreement to stand surety has been properly obtained: see [1994] 1 A.C. 180, 196.

39. Lord Browne-Wilkinson would be the first to recognise this is not a conventional use of the equitable concept of constructive notice. The traditional use of this concept concerns the circumstances in which a transferee of property who acquires a legal estate from a transferor with a defective title may nonetheless obtain a good title, that is, a better title than the transferor had. That is not the present case. The bank acquires its charge from the wife, and there is nothing wrong with her title to her share of the matrimonial home. The transferor wife is seeking to resile from the very transaction she entered into with the bank, on the ground that her apparent consent was procured by the undue influence or other misconduct, such as misrepresentation, of a third party (her husband). She is seeking to set aside her contract of guarantee and, with it, the charge she gave to the bank.

40. The traditional view of equity in this tripartite situation seems to be that a person in the position of the wife will only be relieved of her bargain if the other party to the transaction (the bank, in the present instance) was privy to the conduct which led to the wife's entry into the transaction. Knowledge is required:. . . The law imposes no obligation on one party to a transaction to check whether the other party's concurrence was obtained by undue influence. But O'Brien has introduced into the law the concept that, in certain circumstances, a party to a contract may lose the benefit of his contract, entered into in good faith, if he ought to have known that the other's concurrence had been procured by the misconduct of a third party.

41. There is a further respect in which O'Brien departed from conventional concepts. Traditionally, a person is deemed to have notice (that is, he has 'constructive' notice) of a prior right when he does not actually know of it but would have learned of it had he made the requisite inquiries. A purchaser will be treated as having constructive notice of all that a reasonably prudent purchaser would have discovered. In the present type of case, the steps a bank is required to take, lest it have constructive notice that the wife's concurrence was procured improperly by her husband, do not consist of making inquiries. Rather, O'Brien envisages that the steps taken by the bank will reduce, or even eliminate,

the risk of the wife entering into the transaction under any misapprehension or as a result of undue influence by her husband. The steps are not concerned to discover whether the wife has been wronged by her husband in this way. The steps are concerned to minimise the risk that such a wrong may be committed.

42. These novelties do not point to the conclusion that the decision of this House in *O'Brien* is leading the law astray. Lord Browne-Wilkinson acknowledged he might be extending the law. . . Some development was sorely needed. The law had to find a way of giving wives a reasonable measure of protection, without adding unreasonably to the expense involved in entering into guarantee transactions of the type under consideration. The protection had to extend also to any misrepresentations made by a husband to his wife. In a situation where there is a substantial risk the husband may exercise his influence improperly regarding the provision of security for his business debts, there is an increased risk that explanations of the transaction given by him to his wife may be misleadingly incomplete or even inaccurate.

43. The route selected in *O'Brien* ought not to have an unsettling effect on established principles of contract. *O'Brien* concerned suretyship transactions. These are tripartite transactions. They involve the debtor as well as the creditor and the guarantor. The guarantor enters into the transaction at the request of the debtor. The guarantor assumes obligations. On the face of the transaction the guarantor usually receives no benefit in return, unless the guarantee is being given on a commercial basis. Leaving aside cases where the relationship between the surety and the debtor is commercial, a guarantee transaction is one-sided so far as the guarantor is concerned. The creditor knows this. Thus the decision in *O'Brien* is directed at a class of contracts which has special features of its own . . .

The threshold: when the bank is put on inquiry

44. . . . For practical reasons the level is set much lower than is required to satisfy a court that, failing contrary evidence, the court may infer that the transaction was procured by undue influence. Lord Browne-Wilkinson said [1994] 1 A.C. 180, 196:

> 'Therefore in my judgment a creditor in put on inquiry when a wife offers to stand surety for her husband's debts by the combination of two factors: (a) the transaction is on its face not to the financial advantage of the wife; and (b) there is a substantial risk in transactions of that kind that, in procuring the wife to act as surety, the husband has committed a legal or equitable wrong that entitles the wife to set aside the transaction.'

In my view, this passage, read in context, is to be taken to mean, quite simply, that a bank is put on inquiry whenever a wife offers to stand surety for her husband's debts . . .

46. I do not understand Lord Browne-Wilkinson to have been saying that, in husband and wife cases, whether the bank is put on inquiry depends on its state of knowledge of the parties' marriage, or of the degree of trust and confidence the particular wife places in her husband in relation to her financial affairs. That would leave banks in a state of considerable uncertainty in a situation where it is important they should know clearly where they stand. . . I read (a) and (b) as Lord Browne-Wilkinson's broad explanation of the reason why a creditor is put on inquiry when a wife offers to stand surety for her husband's debts. These are the two factors which, taken together, constitute the underlying rationale.

47. The position is likewise if the husband stands surety for his wife's debts. Similarly, in the case of unmarried couples, whether heterosexual or homosexual, where the bank is aware of the relationship. . . Cohabitation is not essential . . .

48. As to the type of transactions where a bank is put on inquiry, the case where a wife becomes surety for her husband's debts is, in this context, a straightforward case. The bank is put on inquiry. On the other side of the line is the case where money is being advanced, or has been advanced, to husband and wife jointly. In such a case the bank is not put on inquiry, unless the bank is aware the loan is being made for the husband's purposes, as distinct from their joint purposes . . .

49. Less clear cut is the case where the wife becomes surety for the debts of a company whose shares are held by her and her husband. Her shareholding may be nominal, or she may have a minority shareholding or an equal shareholding with her husband. In my view the bank is put on inquiry in such cases, even when the wife is a director or secretary of the company . . .

The steps a bank should take

50. . . . In *O'Brien* [1994] 1 A.C. 180, 196–197 Lord Browne-Wilkinson said that a bank can reasonably be expected to take steps to bring home to the wife the risk she is running by standing as surety and to advise her to take independent advice. That test is applicable to past transactions. All the cases now before your Lordships' House fall into this category. For the future a bank satisfies these requirements if it insists that the wife attend a private meeting with a representative of the bank at which she is told of the extent of her liability as surety, warned of the risk she is running and urged to take independent legal advice. In exceptional cases the bank, to be safe, has to insist that the wife is separately advised . . .

53. . . . it is plainly neither desirable nor practicable that banks should be required to attempt to discover for themselves whether a wife's consent is being procured by the exercise of undue influence of her husband. This is not a step the banks should be expected to take. Nor, further, is it desirable or practicable that banks should be expected to insist on confirmation from a solicitor that the solicitor has satisfied himself that the wife's consent has not been procured by undue influence . . .

54. The furthest a bank can be expected to go is to take reasonable steps to satisfy itself that the wife has had brought home to her, in a meaningful way, the practical implications of the proposed transaction. This does not wholly eliminate the risk of undue influence or misrepresentation. But it does mean that a wife enters into a transaction with her eyes open so far as the basic elements of the transaction are concerned . . .

55. . . . A bank may itself provide the necessary information directly to the wife . . . But . . . provided a suitable alternative is available, banks ought not to be compelled to take this course . . . It is not unreasonable for the banks to prefer that this task should be undertaken by an independent legal adviser . . .

56. . . . Ordinarily it will be reasonable that a bank should be able to rely upon confirmation from a solicitor, acting for the wife, that he has advised the wife appropriately.

57. The position will be otherwise if the bank knows that the solicitor has not duly advised the wife or, I would add, if the bank knows facts from which it ought to have realised that the wife has not received the appropriate advice. In such circumstances the bank will proceed at its own risk.

The content of the legal advice

. . .

61. . . . it is not for the solicitor to veto the transaction by declining to confirm to the bank that he has explained the documents to the wife and the risks she is taking upon herself. If the solicitor considers the transaction is not in the wife's best interests, he will give reasoned advice to the wife to that effect. But at the end of the day the decision on whether to proceed is the decision of the client, not the solicitor. A wife is not to be precluded from entering into a financially unwise transaction if, for her own reasons, she wishes to do so.

62. That is the general rule. There may, of course, be exceptional circumstances where it is glaringly obvious that the wife is being grievously wronged. In such a case the solicitor should decline to act further. . . In identifying what are the solicitor's responsibilities the starting point must always be the solicitor's retainer . . . As a first step the solicitor will need to explain to the wife the purpose for which he has become involved at all. He should explain that, should it ever become necessary, the bank will rely upon his involvement to counter any suggestion that the wife was overborne by her husband or

that she did not properly understand the implications of the transaction. The solicitor will need to obtain confirmation from the wife that she wishes him to act for her in the matter and to advise her on the legal and practical implications of the proposed transaction.

65. When an instruction to this effect is forthcoming, the content of the advice required from a solicitor before giving the confirmation sought by the bank will, inevitably, depend upon the circumstances of the case. Typically, the advice a solicitor can be expected to give should cover the following matters as the core minimum. (1) He will need to explain the nature of the documents and the practical consequences these will have for the wife if she signs them. She could lose her home if her husband's business does not prosper. Her home may be her only substantial asset, as well as the family's home. She could be made bankrupt. (2) He will need to point out the seriousness of the risks involved. The wife should be told the purpose of the proposed new facility, the amount and principal terms of the new facility, and that the bank might increase the amount of the facility, or change its terms, or grant a new facility, without reference to her. She should be told the amount of her liability under her guarantee. The solicitor should discuss the wife's financial means, including her understanding of the value of the property being charged. The solicitor should discuss whether the wife or her husband has any other assets out of which repayment could be made if the husband's business should fail. These matters are relevant to the seriousness of the risks involved. (3) The solicitor will need to state clearly that the wife has a choice. The decision is hers and hers alone. Explanation of the choice facing the wife will call for some discussion of the present financial position, including the amount of the husband's present indebtedness, and the amount of his current overdraft facility. (4) The solicitor should check whether the wife wishes to proceed. She should be asked whether she is content that the solicitor should write to the bank confirming he has explained to her the nature of the documents and the practical implications they may have for her, or whether, for instance, she would prefer him to negotiate with the bank on the terms of the transaction. Matters for negotiation could include the sequence in which the various securities will be called upon or a specific or lower limit to her liabilities. The solicitor should not give any confirmation to the bank without the wife's authority.

66. The solicitor's discussion with the wife should take place at a face-to-face meeting, in the absence of the husband. It goes without saying that the solicitor's explanations should be couched in suitably non-technical language. It also goes without saying that the solicitor's task is an important one. It is not a formality.

67. The solicitor should obtain from the bank any information he needs. If the bank fails for any reason to provide information requested by the solicitor, the solicitor should decline to provide the confirmation sought by the bank . . .

Independent advice

69. I turn next to the much-vexed question whether the solicitor advising the wife must act for the wife alone. . . A requirement that a wife should receive advice from a solicitor acting solely for her will frequently add significantly to the legal costs. Sometimes a wife will be happier to be advised by a family solicitor known to her than by a complete stranger. Sometimes a solicitor who knows both husband and wife and their histories will be better placed to advise than a solicitor who is a complete stranger. . . The advantages attendant upon the employment of a solicitor acting solely for the wife do not justify the additional expense this would involve for the husband. When accepting instructions to advise the wife the solicitor assumes responsibilities directly to her, both at law and professionally. These duties, and this is central to the reasoning on this point, are owed to the wife alone. In advising the wife the solicitor is acting for the wife alone. He is concerned only with her interests. I emphasise, therefore, that in every case the solicitor must consider carefully whether there is any conflict of duty or interest and, more widely, whether it would be in the best interests of the wife for him to accept instructions from her. If he decides to accept instructions, his assumption of legal and professional responsibilities to her ought, in the ordinary course of things, to provide sufficient assurance that he

will give the requisite advice fully, carefully and conscientiously. Especially so, now that the nature of the advice called for has been clarified. If at any stage the solicitor becomes concerned that there is a real risk that other interests or duties may inhibit his advice to the wife he must cease to act for her.

Agency

75. . . . The next question concerns the position when a solicitor has accepted instructions to advise a wife but he fails to do so properly. . . in advising the wife the solicitor is acting for the wife and no one else. The bank does not have, and is intended not to have, any knowledge of or control over the advice the solicitor gives the wife. The solicitor is not accountable to the bank for the advice he gives to the wife. To impute to the bank knowledge of what passed between the solicitor and the wife would contradict this essential feature of the arrangement. The mere fact that, for its own purposes, the bank asked the solicitor to advise the wife does not make the solicitor the bank's agent in giving that advice.

78. In the ordinary case, therefore, deficiencies in the advice given are a matter between the wife and her solicitor. The bank is entitled to proceed on the assumption that a solicitor advising the wife has done his job properly . . .

Obtaining the solicitor's confirmation

79. I now return to the steps a bank should take when it has been put on inquiry and for its protection is looking to the fact that the wife has been advised independently by a solicitor.

(1) . . . the bank should take steps to check *directly with the wife* the name of the solicitor she wishes to act for her. To this end, in future the bank should communicate directly with the wife, informing her that for its own protection it will require written confirmation from a solicitor, acting for her, to the effect that the solicitor has fully explained to her the nature of the documents and the practical implications they will have for her. She should be told that the purpose of this requirement is that thereafter she should not be able to dispute she is legally bound by the documents once she has signed them. She should be asked to nominate a solicitor whom she is willing to instruct to advise her, separately from her husband, and act for her in giving the necessary confirmation to the bank. She should be told that, if she wishes, the solicitor may be the same solicitor as is acting for her husband in the transaction. If a solicitor is already acting for the husband and the wife, she should be asked whether she would prefer that a different solicitor should act for her regarding the bank's requirement for confirmation from a solicitor.

The bank should not proceed with the transaction until it has received an appropriate response directly from the wife.

(2) . . . the bank must provide the solicitor with the financial information he needs. . . What is required must depend on the facts of the case. Ordinarily this will include information on the purpose for which the proposed new facility has been requested, the current amount of the husband's indebtedness, the amount of his current overdraft facility, and the amount and terms of any new facility. If the bank's request for security arose from a written application by the husband for a facility, a copy of the application should be sent to the solicitor. The bank will, of course, need first to obtain the consent of its customer to this circulation of confidential information. If this consent is not forthcoming the transaction will not be able to proceed.

(3) Exceptionally there may be a case where the bank believes or suspects that the wife has been misled by her husband or is not entering into the transaction of her own free will. If such a case occurs the bank must inform the wife's solicitors of the facts giving rise to its belief or suspicion.

(4) The bank should in every case obtain from the wife's solicitor a written confirmation to the effect mentioned above.

80. These steps will be applicable to future transactions. In respect of past transactions, the bank

will ordinarily be regarded as having discharged its obligations if a solicitor who was acting for the wife in the transaction gave the bank confirmation to the effect that he had brought home to the wife the risks she was running by standing as surety.

A wider principle

82. . . . the law does not regard sexual relationships as standing in some special category of their own so far as undue influence is concerned. Sexual relationships are no more than one type of relationship in which an individual may acquire influence over another individual. The *O'Brien* decision cannot sensibly be regarded as confined to sexual relationships, although these are likely to be its main field of application at present. What is appropriate for sexual relationships ought, in principle, to be appropriate also for other relationships where trust and confidence are likely to exist.

83. The courts have already recognised this. Further application, or development, of the *O'Brien* principle has already taken place . . .

84. The crucially important question raised by this wider application of the *O'Brien* principle concerns the circumstances which will put a bank on inquiry. A bank is put on inquiry whenever a wife stands as surety for her husband's debts. It is sufficient that the bank knows of the husband-wife relationship. That bare fact is enough. The bank must then take reasonable steps to bring home to the wife the risks involved. What, then, of other relationships where there is an increased risk of undue influence, such as parent and child? . . . a bank cannot be expected to probe the emotional relationship between two individuals, whoever they may be . . . there is no rational cut-off point, with certain types of relationship being susceptible to the *O'Brien* principle and others not . . . the only practical way forward is to regard banks as 'put on inquiry' in every case where the relationship between the surety and the debtor is non-commercial. The creditor must always take reasonable steps to bring home to the individual guarantor the risks he is running by standing as surety. As a measure of protection, this is valuable. But, in all conscience, it is a modest burden for banks and other lenders. It is no more than is reasonably to be expected of a creditor who is taking a guarantee from an individual. If the bank or other creditor does not take these steps, it is deemed to have notice of any claim the guarantor may have that the transaction was procured by undue influence or mis-representation on the part of the debtor.

88. Different considerations apply where the relationship between the debtor and guarantor is commercial, as where a guarantor is being paid a fee, or a company is guaranteeing the debts of another company in the same group. Those engaged in business can be regarded as capable of looking after themselves and understanding the risks involved in the giving of guarantees.

Lord Clyde

92. I question the wisdom of the practice which has grown up, . . . of attempting to make classifications of cases of undue influence. That concept is in any event not easy to define. . . It is something which can be more easily recognised when found than exhaustively analysed in the abstract. Correspondingly the attempt to build up classes or categories may lead to confusion. The confusion is aggravated if the names used to identify the classes do not bear their actual meaning. Thus on the face of it a division into cases of 'actual' and 'presumed' undue influence appears illogical. It appears to confuse definition and proof. There is also room for uncertainty whether the presumption is of the existence of an influence or of its quality as being undue. I would also dispute the utility of the further sophistication of subdividing 'presumed undue influence' into further categories. All these classifications to my mind add mystery rather than illumination.

93. There is a considerable variety in the particular methods by which undue influence may be brought to bear on the grantor of a deed. They include cases of coercion, domination, victimisation and all the insidious techniques of persuasion. Certainly it can be recognised that in the case of certain relationships it will be relatively easier to establish that undue influence has been at work than in other cases where that sinister conclusion is not necessarily to be drawn with such ease.

English law has identified certain relationships where the conclusion can prima facie be drawn so easily as to establish a presumption of undue influence. But this is simply a matter of evidence and proof. In other cases the grantor of the deed will require to fortify the case by evidence, for example, of the pressure which was unfairly applied by the stronger party to the relationship, or the abuse of a trusting and confidential relationship resulting in for the one party a disadvantage and for the other a collateral benefit beyond what might be expected from the relationship of the parties. At the end of the day, after trial, there will either be proof of undue influence or that proof will fail and it will be found that there was no undue influence. In the former case, whatever the relationship of the parties and however the influence was exerted, there will be found to have been an actual case of undue influence. In the latter there will be none . . .

Lord Hobhouse of Woodborough

O'BRIEN

(1) Presumed undue influence

103. The division between presumed and actual undue influence derives from the judgments in *Allcard v Skinner*. Actual undue influence presents no relevant problem. It is an equitable wrong committed by the dominant party against the other which makes it unconscionable for the dominant party to enforce his legal rights against the other. It is typically some express conduct overbearing the other party's will. It is capable of including conduct which might give a defence at law, for example, duress and misrepresentation. . . Actual undue influence does not depend upon some preexisting relationship between the two parties though it is most commonly associated with and derives from such a relationship. He who alleges actual undue influence must prove it.

104. Presumed undue influence is different in that it necessarily involves some legally recognised relationship between the two parties. As a result of that relationship one party is treated as owing a special duty to deal fairly with the other. It is not necessary for present purposes to define the limits of the relationships which give rise to this duty. Typically they are fiduciary or closely analogous relationships. . .

Such legal relationships can be described as relationships where one party is legally presumed to repose trust and confidence in the other—the other side of the coin to the duty not to abuse that confidence. But there is no presumption properly so called that the confidence has been abused. It is a matter of evidence. . . Thus, at the trial the judge will decide on the evidence whether he is in fact satisfied that there was no abuse of confidence. It will be appreciated that the relevance of the concept of 'manifest disadvantage' is evidential. It is relevant to the question whether there is any issue of abuse which can properly be raised. It is relevant to the determination whether in fact abuse did or did not occur. It is a fallacy to argue from the terminology normally used, 'presumed undue influence', to the position, not of presuming that one party reposed trust and confidence in the other, but of presuming that an abuse of that relationship has occurred; factual inference, yes, once the issue has been properly raised, but not a presumption.

105. The Court of Appeal in *Aboody* [1990] 1 Q.B. 923 and Lord Browne-Wilkinson [in *O'Brien*] classified cases where there was a legal relationship between the parties which the law presumed to be one of trust and confidence as 'presumed undue influence: class 2(A)'. They then made the logical extrapolation that there should be a class 2(B) to cover those cases where it was proved by evidence that one party had in fact reposed trust and confidence in the other. It was then said that the same consequences flowed from this factual relationship as from the legal class 2(A) relationship. Lord Browne-Wilkinson said [1994] 1 A.C. 180, 189–190:

'In a Class 2(B) case therefore, in the absence of evidence disproving undue influence, the complainant will succeed in setting aside the impugned transaction merely by proof that the complainant reposed trust and confidence in the wrongdoer without having to prove that the wrongdoer exerted actual undue influence or otherwise abused such trust and confidence in relation to the particular transaction impugned.'

There are difficulties in the literal application of this statement. It describes the other party as a 'wrongdoer' without saying why when it is expressly postulated that no wrongdoing may have occurred. He treats trust and confidence as indivisible. His actual words are: 'a relationship under which the complainant *generally* reposed trust and confidence in the wrongdoer' (emphasis supplied). But a wife may be happy to trust her husband to make the right decision in relation to some matters but not others; she may leave a particular decision to him but not other decisions. Nor is it clear why the mere 'existence of such relationship raises the presumption of undue influence'. Where the relevant question is one of fact and degree and of the evaluation of evidence, the language of presumption is likely to confuse rather than assist and this is borne out by experience.

106. That there is room for an analogous approach to cases concerning a wife's guarantee of her husband's debts is clear and no doubt led to Lord Browne-Wilkinson saying what he did. The guarantee is given by the wife at the request of the husband. The guarantee is not on its face advantageous to the wife, doubly so where her liability is secured upon her home. The wife may well have trusted the husband to take for her the decision whether she should give the guarantee. If he takes the decision in these circumstances, he owes her a duty to have regard to her interests before deciding. He is under a duty to deal fairly with her. He should make sure that she is entering into the obligation freely and in knowledge of the true facts. His duty may thus be analogous to that of a class 2(A) fiduciary so that it would be appropriate to require him to justify the decision. If no adequate justification is then provided, the conclusion would be that there had been an abuse of confidence. But any conclusion will only be reached after having received evidence. This evidence will inevitably cover as well whether there has in fact been an abuse of confidence or any other undue influence. The judge may have to draw inferences. He may have to decide whether he accepts the evidence of the wife and, if so, what it really amounts to, particularly if it is uncontradicted. Since there is no legal relationship of trust and confidence, the general burden of proving some form of wrongdoing remains with the wife, but the evidence which she has adduced may suffice to raise an inference of wrong-doing which the opposite party may find itself having to adduce evidence to rebut. If at the end of the trial the wife succeeds on the issue of undue influence, it will be because that is the right conclusion of fact on the state of the evidence at the end of the trial, not because of some artificial legal presumption that there must have been undue influence.

107. In agreement with what I understand to be the view of your Lordships, I consider that the so-called class 2(B) presumption should not be adopted. It is not a useful forensic tool. The wife or other person alleging that the relevant agreement or charge is not enforceable must prove her case. She can do this by proving that she was the victim of an equitable wrong. This wrong may be an overt wrong, such as oppression; or it may be the failure to perform an equitable duty, such as a failure by one in whom trust and confidence is reposed not to abuse that trust by failing to deal fairly with her and have proper regard to her interests. Although the general burden of proof is, and remains, upon her, she can discharge that burden of proof by establishing a sufficient prima facie case to justify a decision in her favour on the balance of probabilities, the court drawing appropriate inferences from the primary facts proved. sufficient to displace that conclusion. Provided it is remembered that the burden is an evidential one, the comparison with the operation of the doctrine res ipsa loquitur is useful.

Lord Scott of Foscote

Undue influence

151. Undue influence cases have, traditionally, been regarded as falling into two classes, cases where undue influence must be affirmatively proved (Class 1) and cases where undue influence will be

presumed (Class 2). The nature of the two classes was described by Slade L.J. in *Bank of Credit and Commerce International SA v Aboody* [1990] 1 Q.B. 923, 953:

'Ever since the judgments of this court in *Allcard v Skinner* . . . clear distinction has been drawn between (1) those cases in which the court will uphold a plea of undue influence only if it is satisfied that such influence has been affirmatively proved on the evidence (commonly referred to as cases of "actual undue influence" . . . "Class 1" cases); (2) those cases (commonly referred to as cases of "presumed undue influence" . . . "Class 2" cases) in which the relationship between the parties will lead the court to presume that undue influence has been exerted unless evidence is adduced proving the contrary, e g by showing that the complaining party has had independent advice.'

152. This passage provides, if I may respectfully say so, an accurate summary description of the two classes. But, like most summaries, it requires some qualification.

153. First, the Class 2 presumption is an evidential rebuttable presumption. It shifts the onus from the party who is alleging undue influence to the party who is denying it. Second, the weight of the presumption will vary from case to case and will depend both on the particular nature of the relationship and on the particular nature of the impugned transaction. Third, the type and weight of evidence needed to rebut the presumption will obviously depend upon the weight of the presumption itself . . .

154. The onus will, of course, lie on the person alleging the undue influence to prove in the first instance sufficient facts to give rise to the presumption. The relationship relied on in support of the presumption will have to be proved.

155. In *National Westminster Bank plc v Morgan* [1985] A.C. 686, 704 Lord Scarman, referring to the character of the impugned transaction in a Class 2 case, said: 'it must constitute a disadvantage sufficiently serious to require evidence to rebut the presumption that in the circumstances of the relationship between the parties it was procured by the exercise of undue influence.' Lord Scarman went on:

'In my judgment, therefore, the Court of Appeal erred in law in holding that the presumption of undue influence can arise from the evidence of the relationship of the parties without also evidence that the transaction itself was wrongful in that it constituted an advantage taken of the person subjected to the influence which, failing proof to the contrary, was explicable only on the basis that undue influence had been exercised to procure it.'

With respect to Lord Scarman, the reasoning seems to me to be circular. The transaction will not be 'wrongful' unless it was procured by undue influence. Its 'wrongful' character is a conclusion, not a tool by which to detect the presence of undue influence. On the other hand, the nature of the transaction, its inexplicability by reference to the normal motives by which people act, may, and usually will, constitute important evidential material.

156. Lord Browne-Wilkinson in *CIBC Mortgages plc v Pitt* [1994] 1 A.C. 200 pointed out, plainly correctly, that if undue influence is proved, the victim's right to have the transaction set aside will not depend upon the disadvantageous quality of the transaction. Where, however a Class 2 presumption of undue influence is said to arise, the nature of the impugned transaction will always be material, no matter what the relationship between the parties. . . It is, in my opinion, the combination of relationship and the nature of the transaction that gives rise to the presumption and, if the transaction is challenged, shifts the onus to the transferee.

157. In *Bank of Credit and Commerce International SA v Aboody* [1990] 1 Q.B. 923 Slade L.J. split the Class 2 cases into two subdivisions. He categorised, at p.953, the 'well established categories of relationships, such as a religious superior and inferior and doctor and patient where the relationship as such will give rise to the presumption' as Class 2A cases, and confirmed that neither a husband/wife

relationship nor a banker/customer relationship would normally give rise to the presumption. (See also *National Westminster Bank plc v Morgan* [1985] A.C. 686, 703 and *Barclays Bank v O'Brien* [1994] 1 A.C. 180, 190.) He continued, at p 953:

> 'Nevertheless, on particular facts (frequently referred to in argument as "Class 2B" cases) relationships not falling within the "Class 2A" category may be shown to have become such as to justify the court in applying the same presumption.'

In *O'Brien* Lord Browne-Wilkinson adopted Slade L.J.'s Class 2B category for the purpose of the surety wife cases that he was considering. He said, at pp.189–190:

> 'Even if there is no relationship falling within Class 2(A), if the complainant proves the de facto existence of a relationship under which the complainant generally reposed trust and confidence in the wrongdoer, the existence of such relationship raises the presumption of undue influence. In a Class 2(B) case therefore, in the absence of evidence disproving undue influence, the complainant will succeed in setting aside the impugned transaction merely by proof that the complainant reposed trust and confidence in the wrongdoer without having to prove that the wrongdoer exerted actual undue influence or otherwise abused such trust and confidence in relation to the particular transaction impugned.'

158. In my respectful opinion, this passage, at least in its application to the surety wife cases, has set the law on a wrong track. First, it seems to me to lose sight of the evidential and rebuttable character of the Class 2 presumption. The presumption arises where the combination of the relationship and the nature of the transaction justify, in the absence of any other evidence, a conclusion that the transaction was procured by the undue influence of the dominant party. Such a conclusion, reached on a balance of probabilities, is based upon inferences to be drawn from that combination. There are some relationships, generally of a fiduciary character, where, as a matter of policy, the law requires the dominant party to justify the righteousness of the transaction. These relationships do not include the husband wife relationship. In the surety wife cases, the complainant does have to prove undue influence: the presumption, if it arises on the facts of a particular case, is a tool to assist him or her in doing so. It shifts, for the moment, the onus of proof to the other side.

159. Second, the passage cited appears to regard a relationship of trust and confidence between a wife and husband as something special rather than as the norm. For my part, I would assume in every case in which a wife and husband are living together that there is a reciprocal trust and confidence between them. In the fairly common circumstance that the financial and business decisions of the family are primarily taken by the husband, I would assume that the wife would have trust and confidence in his ability to do so and would support his decisions. I would not expect evidence to be necessary to establish the existence of that trust and confidence. I would expect evidence to be necessary to demonstrate its absence. In cases where experience, probably bitter, had led a wife to doubt the wisdom of her husband's financial or business decisions, I still would not regard her willingness to support those decisions with her own assets as an indication that he had exerted undue influence over her to persuade her to do so. Rather I would regard her support as a natural and admirable consequence of the relationship of a mutually loyal married couple. The proposition that if a wife, who generally reposes trust and confidence in her husband, agrees to become surety to support his debts or his business enterprises a presumption of undue influence arises is one that I am unable to accept. To regard the husband in such a case as a presumed 'wrongdoer' does not seem to me consistent with the relationship of trust and confidence that is a part of every healthy marriage.

160. There are, of course, cases where a husband does abuse that trust and confidence. He may do so by expressions of quite unjustified over-optimistic enthusiasm about the prospects of success of his business enterprises. He may do so by positive misrepresentation of his business intentions, or of the nature of the security he is asking his wife to grant his creditors, or of some other material matter.

He may do so by subjecting her to excessive pressure, emotional blackmail or bullying in order to persuade her to sign. But none of these things should, in my opinion, be presumed merely from the fact of the relationship of general trust and confidence. More is needed before the stage is reached at which, in the absence of any other evidence, an inference of undue influence can properly be drawn or a presumption of the existence of undue influence can be said to arise.

161. For my part, I doubt the utility of the Class 2B classification. Class 2A is useful in identifying particular relationships where the presumption arises. The presumption in Class 2B cases, however, is doing no more than recognising that evidence of the relationship between the dominant and subservient parties, coupled with whatever other evidence is for the time being available, may be sufficient to justify a finding of undue influence on the balance of probabilities. The onus shifts to the defendant. Unless the defendant introduces evidence to counteract the inference of undue influence that the complainant's evidence justifies, the complainant will succeed. In my opinion, the presumption of undue influence in Class 2B cases has the same function in undue influence cases as res ipsa loquitur has in negligence cases. It recognises an evidential state of affairs in which the onus has shifted.

162. In the surety wife cases it should, in my opinion, be recognised that undue influence, though a possible explanation for the wife's agreement to become surety, is a relatively unlikely one. *O'Brien* itself was a misrepresentation case. Undue influence had been alleged but the undoubted pressure which the husband had brought to bear to persuade his reluctant wife to sign was not regarded by the judge or the Court of Appeal as constituting undue influence. The wife's will had not been overborne by her husband. Nor was *O'Brien* a case in which, in my opinion, there would have been at any stage in the case a presumption of undue influence.

NOTES AND QUESTIONS

1. While their Lordships discuss the doctrine of undue influence in some detail, they do not attempt to define it in comprehensive terms. The emphasis in the speeches is very much upon the facts and circumstances of the individual case (see, for example, paragraphs [10], [11] and [13]), although there are indications that some form of 'abuse' on the part of the defendant may be a necessary ingredient of an undue influence claim (see, for example, paragraphs [6] and [32]). However references can be found in the speeches both to the position of the claimant and to the conduct of the defendant and so it is perhaps not surprising to find that courts in subsequent cases have not adopted a consistent interpretation of *Etridge,* with some giving greater emphasis to the position of the claimant (see, for example, *Pesticcio v Huet* [2004] EWCA Civ 372; [2004] All ER (D) 36 (April), see below, 479) while others focus more closely on the conduct of the defendant (see, for example, *National Commercial Bank (Jamaica) Ltd v Hew* [2003] UKPC 51, see below, 476).

2. Their Lordships affirmed the continued existence of the distinction between cases of actual and presumed undue influence (with the apparent exception of Lord Clyde at [92]). How did their Lordships analyse cases of actual undue influence (see, for example, paragraphs [8] and [103]) and what is the relationship between the conception of actual undue influence which emerges from this case and the doctrine of duress?

3. In the case of presumed undue influence, it would appear that the presumption is a rebuttable evidential one (see [16]) and it still has a role to play in what are termed class 2A cases (see [18]) but that there is no longer a category of case known as the class 2B presumption (see, for example, [92], [107], and [161]).

4. The House of Lords in *National Westminster Bank v Morgan* [1985] AC 686 held that 'manifest disadvantage' was a necessary ingredient of a presumed undue influence case. This test did not survive scrutiny in *Etridge* (see, in particular, [29]). Why has the test been abandoned and what has replaced it?

5. In cases of presumed undue influence, what is it that is being presumed? Is it dependence? Is it exploitation? Or are there different presumptions which operate in different ways? For example, some relationships appear to give rise to a presumption of trust and confidence, but this would not appear to be the same thing as a presumption of undue influence.

6. When is a bank put on inquiry that a transaction may have been entered into as a result of the exercise of undue influence and what steps must it take when it has been put on notice? Do the steps which a bank is required to take once it has been put on notice tell us anything about the nature of undue influence?

• **R v Attorney-General for England and Wales** [2003] UKPC 22, Privy Council

The facts of this case are set out at 433 above. One of the grounds on which R sought to challenge the validity of the contract was that it had been obtained as a result of the exercise of undue influence. The Privy Council, by a majority, rejected his claim.

Lord Hoffmann (giving the judgment of the majority): 21. The subject of undue influence has recently been re-examined in depth by the House of Lords in *Royal Bank of Scotland plc* v. *Etridge (No 2)* [2002] 2 AC 773. Their Lordships summarise the effect of the judgments. Like duress at common law, undue influence is based upon the principle that a transaction to which consent has been obtained by unacceptable means should not be allowed to stand. Undue influence has concentrated in particular upon the unfair exploitation by one party of a relationship which gives him ascendancy or influence over the other.

22. The burden of proving that consent was obtained by unacceptable means is upon the party who alleges it. Certain relationships—parent and child, trustee and beneficiary, etc—give rise to a presumption that one party had influence over the other. That does not of course in itself involve a presumption that he unfairly exploited his influence. But if the transaction is one which cannot reasonably be explained by the relationship, that will be prima facie evidence of undue influence. Even if the relationship does not fall into one of the established categories, the evidence may show that one party did in fact have influence over the other. In such a case, the nature of the transaction may likewise give rise to a prima facie inference that it was obtained by undue influence. In the absence of contrary evidence, the court will be entitled to find that the burden of proving unfair exploitation of the relationship has been discharged.

23. The absence of independent legal advice may or may not be a relevant matter according to the circumstances. It is not necessarily an unfair exploitation of a relationship for one party to enter into a transaction with the other without ensuring that he has obtained independent legal advice. On the other hand, the transaction may be such as to give rise to an inference of undue influence even if the induced party was advised by an independent lawyer and understood the legal implications of what he was doing.

24. In the present case it is said that the military hierarchy, the strong regimental pride which R shared and his personal admiration for his commanding officer created a relationship in which the Army as an institution or the commanding officer as an individual were able to exercise influence over him. Their Lordships are content to assume that this was the case. But the question is whether the nature of the transaction was such as to give rise to an inference that it was obtained by an unfair exploitation of that relationship. Like the Court of Appeal, their Lordships do not think that the confidentiality agreement can be so described. As in the case of duress, their Lordships think that the finding that it was an agreement which anyone who wished to serve or continue serving in the SAS could reasonably have been required to sign is fatal to such a conclusion. The reason why R signed the agreement was because, at the time, he wished to continue to be a member of the SAS. If facing him with such a choice was not illegitimate for the purposes of duress, their Lordships do not think that it could have been an unfair exploitation of a relationship which consisted in his being a member

of the SAS. There seems to their Lordships to be some degree of contradiction between R's claim, in the context of duress, that he signed only because he was threatened with return to his unit and his claim, for the purposes of undue influence, that he signed because of the trust and confidence which he reposed in the Army or his commanding officer.

25. The question which has troubled their Lordships is the absence of legal advice . . .

26. . . . the New Zealand courts made a finding that R had not been able to obtain legal advice which their Lordships of course accept. In any event they think it a matter for regret that members of SAS were not told explicitly that arrangements could be made for them to obtain legal advice . . .

27. The legal question, however, is whether failing to provide an opportunity for obtaining legal advice made the transaction one in which the MOD had unfairly exploited its influence over R. Here it is important to note that R does not allege that he did not understand the implications of what he was being asked to do. The contract was in simple terms and the explanatory memorandum even plainer. He does say that he had originally thought that it would only prevent publication of matter which remained confidential. However, a moment's thought would have told him that this would not have prevented the publications to which he and other members of the SAS most objected, namely *The One That Got Away* and the film which followed. In any case, when he saw the actual contract he knew what it meant.

28. In these circumstances, their Lordships do not think that the absence of legal advice affected the fairness of the transaction. The most that R can say is that a lawyer might have advised him to reflect upon the matter and, as in fact he changed his mind within a fairly short time after signing, that might have led to his not signing at all. But that is a decision which he could have made without a lawyer's advice.

Lord Scott of Foscote (dissenting)

[*He set out the principles which he derived from the decision of the Court of Appeal in* Allcard v Skinner *(1887) 36 ChD 145 (448, above) and continued*]

41. Are these principles ones that should be applied to the contract in the present case? I think they are. The appellant was not, of course, an unworldly man in a secluded religious order. He was a soldier in a highly trained and efficient fighting unit. The essence of efficiency in a military unit is obedience to orders. The Armed Services operate on a hierarchical basis. Each rank looks to the rank or ranks above for direction and, having received that direction, is expected to comply with it. It is, in my opinion, entirely artificial to draw sharp distinctions between orders from senior officers that are military orders breach of which will be an offence under military law and may attract court martial sanctions and 'orders' from senior officers couched as requests or as recommendations. It has become a music-hall joke for a sergeant-major to say to the troops under him 'I want three volunteers; you, you and you'. The hierarchical culture of the Armed Services and the deference and obedience to senior officers, both commissioned and non-commissioned, which is part of that culture are the essential background to the circumstances in which the appellant was asked to sign the contract in the present case.

42. It is to be borne in mind that members of Her Majesty's Armed Services do not, unlike ordinary employees, enter into contracts with their employers. They are engaged and can be dismissed under the Royal Prerogative. It is their agreement to serve, not any contract, that subjects them to military discipline and military law. The Board was told by counsel for the Attorney-General that there had been no other example of members of a unit of the Armed Services being asked to enter into a contract with the Ministry of Defence.

43. This background requires, in my opinion, that any contract between a member of the Armed Forces and the Ministry of Defence be looked at very carefully to see whether the benefit conferred by it on the Ministry of Defence was a benefit that the Ministry of Defence was entitled in equity to maintain.

44. The circumstances in which the contract in the present case came to be signed by the appellant were the subject of evidence at trial and the trial judge, Salmon J, formed a number of important conclusions:

(1) The judge concluded that the appellant signed because he had been ordered to do so. An analysis of the 'order' that disqualifies it from constituting a military order and regards it, no doubt correctly, merely as a recommendation or a direction is, in my opinion, of no more than marginal significance if the possibility of undue influence is being considered. What is important is how the appellant regarded it. The appellant regarded it as an order.

(2) The judge found that 'the defendant was not told the terms of the contract before signing [and] was not offered any legal advice' (para. 39).

(3) He found, also, that the appellant was not permitted to show the contract to a legal adviser (para. 139). The weight of this finding is not diminished by evidence from the senior officer in command of the Regiment to the effect that soldiers would have been permitted to show the contract to approved legal advisers if they had asked. What is important is the perception of the appellant, and, as to that, Salmon J's finding stands.

45. In my opinion, the relationship between the appellant and his senior officers and the circumstances, as found by the judge, in which the contract came to be signed by the appellant produced a classic 'relationship' case in which undue influence should be presumed. No evidence was introduced to rebut that presumption. Legal advice was not available to the appellant. As in *Allcard v Skinner*, where no suggestion of fraud or indeed any impropriety was made against the lady superior to whom the plaintiff had transferred her assets, no such suggestion has been, or could be, made against any of the appellant's senior officers who play a part in the story. It is the relationship, produced by the background to which I have referred, between a soldier and that part of the Armed Services of which he is a member, that introduces the potentially vitiating element into the contract. If the Ministry of Defence wants to impose contractual obligations on soldiers by which they will be bound when they leave the service, it must, in my opinion, at the least make available to them independent legal advice. Fairness, in my view, requires it and I think the law requires it. In this case it was not done. I would have allowed the appeal.

NOTES AND QUESTIONS

1. Lord Hoffmann attempts to draw an analogy between undue influence and common law duress. Is the analogy an appropriate one?

2. Does Lord Hoffmann adopt a defendant sided version of undue influence, a claimant sided version or does he have regard to the position of both the claimant and the defendant?

3. The difference between the analysis of Lord Scott and that employed by the majority appears to lie in the fact that Lord Scott focused on the nature of the relationship between the parties, whereas the majority placed greater emphasis on the need for some wrongdoing on the part of the Ministry of Defence.

4. Do you agree with Lord Scott's view that *Allcard v Skinner* is a suitable factual analogy for the present case?

5. What weight was given to the fact that the claimant did not receive legal advice? What weight should have been given to this fact?

• **National Commercial Bank (Jamaica) Ltd v Hew** [2003] UKPC 51, Privy Council

The claimant bank brought a claim against Mr Stephen Hew and his son in which they sought to recover the sum of $32,527,952.98 due on an overdraft facility together with interest at 54 per cent per annum from 3rd May 1996 until payment. Mr Hew obtained the overdraft facility when he was 74 years old. He was 'a businessman of many years' experience and a builder in a small way of business.' He owned various plots of land in Jamaica. Two of the plots of land are relevant for our purposes. The first was a parcel of land known as Ironshore and the second was referred to as Barrett Town. Mr Hew had long harboured a dream of borrowing £1 million (which represented 9 million Jamaican dollars). Over time he developed 'a close and cordial personal relationship' with Mr Cobham, the branch manager of the claimant bank. In September 1989 the branch manager approved an overdraft facility of $3 million, of which $2 million was for property development and $1 million was to provide a guarantee to prospective purchasers who wished to withdraw from the development and asked for the return of their deposits. The court accepted that the money had been advanced for the purpose of developing the land at Barrett Town. Mr Hew gave evidence to the effect that his preference was to develop the Ironside plot but the loan was in fact given for the purpose of enabling him to develop the Barrett Town site.

At the date when the new facility was formally approved Mr Hew's account was already overdrawn by $1 million. In April 1990 that overdraft had increased to $2 million and it stood at $3 million by the end of 1991. When the overdraft reached $6 million Mr Cobham refused to allow any further drawings. At this point only two houses on the development at Barrett Town were complete, three were partly built but there was no electricity or effective water supply and no roads had been constructed. No houses had been sold and no deposits taken. While Mr Hew had made some repayments to the claimant, little inroad had been made into the principal sum. In 1995 the bank brought proceedings to recover the principal sum and interest. Mr Hew admitted that the loan had been made but, *inter alia*, sought to have the agreement set aside on the ground of undue influence. The Privy Council held that he was not entitled to set aside the agreement.

Lord Millett

29. Undue influence is one of the grounds on which equity intervenes to give redress where there has been some unconscionable conduct on the part of the defendant. It arises whenever one party has acted unconscionably by exploiting the influence to direct the conduct of another which he has obtained from the relationship between them. As Lord Nicholls of Birkenhead observed in *Royal Bank of Scotland plc v Etridge (No 2)* [2002] 2 AC 773 at p 794–5:

'Undue influence is one of the grounds of relief developed by the courts of equity as a court of conscience. The objective is to ensure that the influence of one person over another is not abused. . . .

. . . [It] arises out of a relationship between two persons where one has acquired over another a measure of influence, or ascendancy, of which the ascendant person then takes unfair advantage.'

30. Thus the doctrine involves two elements. First, there must be a relationship capable of giving rise to the necessary influence. And secondly the influence generated by the relationship must have been abused.

31. The necessary relationship is variously described as a relationship 'of trust and confidence' or 'of ascendancy and dependency'. Such a relationship may be proved or presumed. Some relationships are presumed to generate the necessary influence; examples are solicitor and client and medical adviser and patient. The banker-customer relationship does not fall within this category. But the existence of the necessary relationship may be proved as a fact in any particular case . . .

33. But the second element is also necessary. However great the influence which one person may

be able to wield over another equity does not intervene unless that influence has been abused. Equity does not save people from the consequences of their own folly; it acts to save them from being victimised by other people: see *Allcard v Skinner* (1887) 36 Ch D 145, 182.

34. Thus it must be shown that the ascendant party has unfairly exploited the influence he is shown or presumed to possess over the vulnerable party. It is always highly relevant that the transaction in question was manifestly disadvantageous to the person seeking to set it aside; though this is not always necessary: see *C I B C Mortgages plc v Pitt* [1994] 1 AC 200. But 'disadvantageous' in this context means 'disadvantageous' as between the parties. Unless the ascendant party has exploited his influence to obtain some unfair advantage from the vulnerable party there is no ground for equity to intervene. However commercially disadvantageous the transaction may be to the vulnerable party, equity will not set it aside if it is a fair transaction as between the parties to it.

35. Their Lordships have looked in vain for any evidence that the transaction of loan was unfair as between the Bank and Mr Hew. The Bank derived no unfair advantage from it, nor any benefit which it would not have sought to obtain from an ordinary arms' length transaction with a commercial borrower. The Court of Appeal identified several features of the transaction which they described as disadvantageous to Mr Hew. These were (i) the fact that the money had to be applied in the development of Barrett Town; (ii) the inadequacy of the funding to finance more than the initial infrastructure; and (iii) the excessive security taken by the Bank (since the Bank, already fully secured on the Ironshore lands, also took a deposit of the titles to the Barrett Town lands when they became available).

36. Their Lordships consider that the Court of Appeal confused the question whether the transaction was commercially disadvantageous to Mr Hew with the very different question whether it was unfair as between him and the Bank. It was not the Bank's responsibility to save Mr Hew from the consequences of embarking upon an unwise project. Its sole responsibility was not to take unfair advantage of the relationship between Mr Cobham and Mr Hew [he examined the facts further and concluded].

41. Their Lordships conclude that it has not been shown that the Bank took unfair advantage of the relationship of trust and confidence which must be taken to have existed between Mr Cobham and Mr Hew. They recognise that in reaching this conclusion they are departing from what may be said to be concurrent findings of fact below; but where they are satisfied that those findings are not supported by the evidence they are not only entitled but bound to reject them . . . It follows that Mr Hew's claim to have the transaction set aside for undue influence must also be dismissed . . .

NOTES AND QUESTIONS

1. Lord Millett clearly adopts a defendant-sided version of the doctrine to the extent that he insists that there must have been an 'abuse' by the defendant of the influence generated by the relationship between the parties.

2. This emphasis on wrongdoing has not been universally welcomed. Professor Birks (2004) 120 *LQR* 34 has sounded a warning in relation to the difficulties that are likely to arise from an insistence on wrongdoing in all cases. In particular, while the emphasis on wrongdoing may open the prospect of the award of compensatory damages in an undue influence claim, it may also shut out the possibility of relief in the case where the claimant cannot establish wrongdoing on the part of the defendant. *Allcard v Skinner* (448, above) may well come into this category (notwithstanding Lord Millett's citation of *Allcard* in support of his analysis in *Hew* at [33]). This is important where the claimant seeks relief in the form of rescission of the contract. In such a case, why does the claimant have to prove some element of wrongdoing on the part of the defendant? There is no such requirement in the law of innocent misrepresentation. Similarly, Professor Birks asserts that not all cases of undue influence can be regarded as

cases of wrongs. He therefore maintains that English law should continue to recognise a category of 'innocent undue influence' (that is to say, the claimant is subject to too much influence in the sense that his volition is impaired but there is no advantage-taking by the defendant). He concludes (at 37) as follows:

> As with misrepresentation, undue influence may be a wrong in aggravating circumstances. That is largely unexplored territory. It is certainly not always a wrong. A party who makes no claim to shift a loss from himself to another but merely requires that other to return to the *status quo* does not need to find and prove those extra facts. A misrepresentee can rely for that same limited purpose on an innocent mis-representation whether because the representation really was innocent or because he does not need to and does not choose to prove the aggravating facts. The same applies to one whose autonomy is impaired by the fact that another has excessive influence over him. It would be odd if, in triggering rescission and return to the *status quo*, relational paralysis were less potent than misrepresentation.

3. Professor Birks' point has been taken up by Mummery LJ in *Pesticcio v Huet* [2004] EWCA Civ 372; [2004] All ER (D) 36 (April). Mummery LJ (at [20]) objected to the defendant-sided conception of undue influence in the following terms:

> The insistence of [counsel] that Maureen [the person alleged to have exercised undue influence over her brother] had 'done nothing wrong' is an instance of the 'continuing misconceptions' mentioned by Sir Martin Nourse in *Hammond* [*v Osborn* [2002] EWCA Civ 885] about the circumstances in which gifts will be set aside on the ground of presumed undue influence. Although undue influence is sometimes described as an 'equitable wrong' or even as a species of equitable fraud, the basis of the court's interven-tion is not the commission of a dishonest or wrongful act by the defendant, but that, as a matter of public policy, the presumed influence arising from the relationship of trust and confidence should not operate to the disadvantage of the victim, if the transaction is not satisfactorily explained by ordinary motives: *Allcard v Skinner* (1887) 36 Ch D 145 at 171. The court scrutinises the circumstances in which the transaction, under which benefits were conferred on the recipient, took place and the nature of the continuing relationship between the parties, rather than any specific act or conduct on the part of the recipient. A transaction may be set aside by the court, even though the actions and conduct of the person who benefits from it could not be criticised as wrongful. The presumption arising from the trust and confidence of their relationship made it unnecessary, for example, for Bernard [the party seeking to set aside the deed of gift] to prove that Maureen actually had influence over him in relation to the gift of the house, let alone that she in fact exercised undue influence or applied improper pressure to obtain the Deed of Gift.

4. Where do we stand in the light of these cases? It can be seen that the cases do not speak with one voice. Sometimes the courts have not looked for wrongdoing on the part of the defendant (and have even stated that the presence of such wrongdoing is not a necessary ingredient of the claim) but have instead focused attention on the position of the claimant and the claim-ant's ability to make a free choice in relation to the transfer of the benefit (see, for example, *Hammond v Osborn* [2002] EWCA Civ 885, *Macklin v Dowsett* [2004] EWCA Civ 904 and *Pesticcio v Huet* [2004] EWCA Civ 372; [2004] All ER (D) 36 (April), above). In other cases (particularly the decisions of the Privy Council in *R v Attorney-General for England and Wales* [2003] UKPC 22, above and *National Commercial Bank (Jamaica) Ltd v Hew* [2003] UKPC 51, above) the courts have looked for some form of wrongdoing on the part of the defendant (see also *Eid v Al-Kazemi* [2004] EWHC 2129). There is still another group of cases in which the courts appear to have looked at both elements and not made an explicit choice between the two schools of thought (see, for example, *Randall v Randall* [2004] EWHC 2258 and *Turkey v Ahwad* [2005] EWCA Civ 507). The academic commentators similarly do not speak with one voice. We have already set out the view defended by Birks and Chin Nyuk Yin that undue influence is claimant-sided and arises from the excessive dependence of the claimant upon the defendant, but others have argued that undue influence consists of a form of wrongdoing on the part of the defendant (see, for example, R Bigwood, 'Undue Influence: "Impaired Consent" or "Wicked Exploitation"?' (1996) 16 *OJLS* 503 and 'Contracts by Unfair Advantage: From Exploitation to Transactional Neglect' (2005) 25 *OJLS* 65). The vast majority of undue

influence cases will involve some advantage-taking on the part of the defendant (albeit that the advantage-taking will assume different forms). But we should not exclude the possibility that, exceptionally, a claimant may be able to demonstrate that he or she was so dependent upon the defendant that a finding of undue influence can be made, even in the absence of specific wrongdoing on the part of the defendant.

2. THE ROLE OF UNCONSCIONABLE CONDUCT

Thus far in this chapter we have been looking at the development of the doctrine of undue influence in equity and seeking to establish the principle which underpins the doctrine. Before examining cases in which the ground for intervention is the (exploitation of the) claimant's mental inadequacy, we must stop to consider an important decision of the High Court of Australia in which the court adopted a rather broader analysis based upon the unconscionable conduct of the defendant.

• *Louth v Diprose* (1992) 175 CLR 621, High Court of Australia

The claimant, Louis Diprose, was infatuated with the defendant, Carol Louth. Although she had previously rejected his proposal of marriage, such was his infatuation that he gave up his legal practice in Tasmania and followed her to Adelaide. She was in very difficult financial circumstances and told Diprose that she had contemplated committing suicide. He responded by bestowing a number of gifts on her and paying her household bills from time to time. She lived in a house owned by her sister and brother-in-law but, when they separated, they told her that she could not assume that she could continue to live in the house on a permanent basis. Louth informed Diprose of this development, adding that if she were forced to vacate the house she would commit suicide. He responded by agreeing to purchase the house for $58,000, which he did, in her name. Some time later the parties fell out, and Diprose demanded that Louth transfer the house to him and pay rent for her occupation of it. She refused. He sought a declaration that he was beneficially entitled to the land, on the ground that it would be unconscionable to allow her to retain it. His claim succeeded at trial. The defendant appealed unsuccessfully to the Court of Appeal (although the majority of the court did vary the order made by the trial judge) and from there to the High Court. The High Court by a majority (Toohey J dissenting) dismissed the defendant's appeal. A crucial factor in the success of Diprose's claim were findings of fact by the trial judge that Louth had exploited Diprose's emotional dependence on her by, *inter alia*, manufacturing an atmosphere of crisis and that her manipulation of him constituted dishonesty on her part. Much of the judgment of the High Court is concerned with the question of whether or not the trial judge was entitled to make this finding and, indeed, Toohey J dissented on this point.

Brennan J: The jurisdiction of equity to set aside gifts procured by unconscionable conduct ordinarily arises from the concatenation of three factors: a relationship between the parties which, to the knowledge of the donee, places the donor at a special disadvantage vis-à-vis the donee; the donee's unconscientious exploitation of the donor's disadvantage; and the consequent overbearing of the will of the donor whereby the donor is unable to make a worth while judgment as to what is in his or her best interest.[1] A similar jurisdiction exists to set aside gifts procured by undue influence. In

---

1 *Commercial Bank of Australia Ltd v Amadio* (1983) 151 CLR 447, at 461, 462, 474–5, 489; *Blomley v Ryan* (1956) 99 CLR 362, at 415.

Commercial Bank of Australia Ltd v Amadio,[2] Mason J distinguished unconscionable conduct from undue influence in these terms:

'In the latter the will of the innocent party is not independent and voluntary because it is over-borne. In the former the will of the innocent party, even if independent and voluntary, is the result of the disadvantageous position in which he is placed and of the other party unconscientiously taking advantage of that position.'

Deane J[3] identified the difference in the nature of the two jurisdictions:

'Undue influence, like common law duress, looks to the quality of the consent or assent of the weaker party ... Unconscionable dealing looks to the conduct of the stronger party in attempting to enforce, or retain the benefit of, a dealing with a person under a special disability in circumstances where it is not consistent with equity or good conscience that he should do so.'

Although the two jurisdictions are distinct, they both depend upon the effect of influence (presumed or actual) improperly brought to bear by one party to a relationship on the mind of the other whereby the other disposes of his property. Gifts obtained by unconscionable conduct and gifts obtained by undue influence are set aside by equity on substantially the same basis. In *White and Tudor's Leading Cases in Equity*,[4] the notes to *Huguenin v Baseley*[5] treat the principle applied in cases of unconscionable conduct as an extension of the principle applied in cases of undue influence:[6]

'The principle upon which equity will give relief as against the persons standing in [the categories of confidential] relations to the donor, will be extended and applied *to all the variety of relations in which dominion may be exercised by one person over another*.'

The ground for setting aside a gift obtained by unconscientious exploitation of a donor's special disadvantage, as explained in *Amadio*, can be compared with the ground for setting aside a gift obtained by undue influence, as explained by Dixon J in *Johnson v Buttress*:[7]

'The basis of the equitable jurisdiction to set aside an alienation of property on the ground of undue influence is the prevention of an *unconscientious use of any special capacity* or opportunity that may exist or arise *of affecting the alienor's will or freedom of judgment* in reference to such a matter. The source of power to practise such a domination may be found in no antecedent relation but in a particular situation, or in the deliberate contrivance of the party. If this be so, facts must be proved showing that the transaction was *the outcome of such an actual influence over the mind of the alienor* that it cannot be considered his free act. But the parties may antecedently stand in a relation that gives to one an authority or influence over the other from the abuse of which it is proper that he should be protected.' (Emphasis added.)

The similarity between the two jurisdictions gives to cases arising in the exercise of one jurisdiction an analogous character in considering cases involving the same points in the other jurisdiction.

THE RELATIONSHIP

There are some categories of confidential relationships from which a presumption of undue influence arises when a substantial gift is made by one party to the relationship to the other—relationships such as solicitor and client, physician and patient, parent and child, guardian and ward, superior and member of a religious community. Public policy creates a presumption of undue influence in cases

---

2 (1983) 151 CLR at 461. 3 *Ibid.*, 474. 4 9th edn (1928), vol. 1, 203 ff.
5 (1807) 14 Ves Jun 273 [33 ER 526]. 6 *White and Tudor*, 227.
7 (1936) 56 CLR 113, at 134.

where the relationship falls into one of the recognized categories. Those categories do not exhaust the cases in which it may be held that it is contrary to conscience for a donee to retain a gift. In cases where the relationship is not one of confidentiality, a gift may be impeached where the evidence shows that in fact it was procured by unconscionable conduct. Where a gift is impeached on the ground that it was obtained by unconscionable conduct consisting in an unconscionable exploitation of an antecedent relationship, the relationship is one in which one party stands in a position of special disadvantage vis-à-vis the other. Such relationships are infinitely various, the common feature being that the donor is, to the knowledge of the donee, in a position of *special* disadvantage vis-à-vis the donee: that is to say, in matters in which their interests do not coincide, the donor's capacity to make a decision as to his or her own best interest is peculiarly susceptible to control or influence by the donee. As Mason J said in *Amadio*:[8]

'I qualify the word "disadvantage" by the adjective "special" in order to disavow any suggestion that the principle applies whenever there is some difference in the bargaining power of the parties and in order to emphasize that the disabling condition or circumstance is one which seriously affects the ability of the innocent party to make a judgment as to his own best interests, when the other party knows or ought to know of the existence of that condition or circumstance and of its effect on the innocent party.'

The relevant relationship may exist because of some weakness in the donor. Thus Fullagar J in *Blomely v Ryan*[9] took as instances of weakness 'poverty or need of any kind, sickness, age, sex, infirmity of body or mind, drunkenness, illiteracy or lack of education, lack of assistance or explanation where assistance or explanation is necessary'. And McTiernan J said that '[t]he essence of such weakness is that the party is unable to judge for himself'.[10] It is unnecessary to show that the donee contributed to that weakness. In the present case ... the relationship between the plaintiff (respondent) and the defendant (appellant) was so different in degree as to be different in kind from the ordinary relationship of a man courting a woman. It was found that the personal relationship between them was such that the plaintiff was extremely susceptible to influence by the defendant, as the defendant knew. ...

EXPLOITATION OF THE DONOR'S DISADVANTAGE

Equity intervenes 'whenever one party to a transaction is at a special disadvantage in dealing with the other party . . . and the other party unconscientiously takes advantage of the opportunity thus placed in his hands'.[11] Citing this passage in *Amadio*,[12] Dawson J said:

'What is necessary for the application of the principle is exploitation by one party of another's position of disadvantage in such a manner that the former could not in good conscience retain the benefit of the bargain.'

What his Honour said of a bargain can be said equally of a gift.

In the present case, King CJ made explicit findings of an unconscientious exploitation by the defendant of the plaintiff's weakness.

. . .

THE DONOR'S WILL AND JUDGMENT

When a donor who stands in a relationship of special disadvantage vis-à-vis a donee makes a substantial gift to the donee, slight evidence may be sufficient to show that the gift has been procured

---

8 (1983) 151 CLR at p. 462.   9 (1956) 99 CLR at p. 405.

10 *Ibid.*, at p. 392; see *Amadio* (1983), 151 CLR, at pp. 476–77, *per* Deane J.

11 *Blomley v Ryan* (1956), 99 CLR at 415, *per* Kitto J.

12 (1983) 151 CLR, at 489; and see also 462, 474.

by unconscionable conduct. Whether that finding should be made depends on the circumstances. In *Watkins v Combes*[13] Isaacs J said:

'It is not the law, as I understand it, that the mere fact that one party to a transaction who is of full age and apparent competency reposed confidence in, or was subject to the influence of, the other party is sufficient to cast upon the latter the onus of demonstrating the validity of the transaction. Observations which go to that extent are too broad.'

But where it is proved that a donor stood in a specially disadvantageous relationship with a donee, that the donee exploited the disadvantage and that the donor thereafter made a substantial gift to the donee, an inference may, and often should, be drawn that the exploitation was the effective cause of the gift. The drawing of that inference, however, depends on the whole of the circumstances. . . . Such an inference must arise, however, from the facts of the case; it is not a presumption which arises by operation of law. The inference may be drawn unless the donee can rely on countervailing evidence to show that the donee's exploitative conduct was not a cause of the gift. At the end of the day, however, it is for the party impeaching the gift to show that it is the product of the donee's exploitative conduct. This is the final and necessary link in the chain of proof of unconscionable conduct leading to a decree setting aside the gift.[14]

The plaintiff discharged that onus in the present case. . . .

Deane J (with whom Mason CJ, Dawson, Gaudron and McHugh JJ agreed): . . . It has long been established that the jurisdiction of courts of equity to relieve against unconscionable dealing extends generally to circumstances in which (i) a party to a transaction was under a special disability in dealing with the other party to the transaction with the consequence that there was an absence of any reasonable degree of equality between them and (ii) that special disability was sufficiently evident to the other party to make it prima facie unfair or 'unconscionable' that that other party procure, accept or retain the benefit of, the disadvantaged party's assent to the impugned transaction in the circumstances in which he or she procured or accepted it. Where such circumstances are shown to have existed, an onus is cast upon the stronger party to show that the transaction was fair, just and reasonable: 'the burthen of shewing the fairness of the transaction is thrown on the person who seeks to obtain' or retain the benefit of it.[15]

The adverse circumstances which may constitute a special disability for the purposes of the principle relating to relief against unconscionable dealing may take a wide variety of forms and are not susceptible of being comprehensively catalogued.[16] In *Blomley v Ryan*,[17] Fullagar J listed some examples of such special disability: 'poverty or need of any kind, sickness, age, sex, infirmity of body or mind, drunkenness, illiteracy or lack of education, lack of assistance or explanation where assistance or explanation is necessary.' As Fullagar J remarked, the common characteristic of such adverse circumstances 'seems to be that they have the effect of placing one party at a serious disadvantage vis-à-vis the other'.

On the findings of the learned trial judge in the present case, the relationship between the respondent and the appellant at the time of the impugned gift was plainly such that the respondent was under a special disability in dealing with the appellant. That special disability arose not merely from the respondent's infatuation. It extended to the extraordinary vulnerability of the respondent in the false 'atmosphere of crisis' in which he believed that the woman with whom he was 'completely

---

13 (1922) 30 CLR 180, at 193; and see *Harris v Jenkins* (1922) 31 CLR 341, at 367–8, *per* Starke J.

14 See *White and Tudor, op. cit.*, 240.

15 See *O'Rorke v Bolingbroke* (1877) 2 App. Cas. 814, at 823, *per* Lord Hatherley; *Fry v Lane, Re Fry*; *Whittet v Bush* (1888), 40 ChD 312, at 322; *Blomley v Ryan* (1956) 99 CLR 362, at 428–9; *Commercial Bank of Australia Ltd v Amadio* (1983) 151 CLR 447, at 474.

16 *Ibid.* 474.   17 (1956) 99 CLR, at 405.

in love' and upon whom he was emotionally dependent was facing eviction from her home and suicide unless he provided the money for the purchase of the house. The appellant was aware of that special disability. Indeed, to a significant extent, she had deliberately created it. She manipulated it to her advantage to influence the respondent to make the gift of the money to purchase the house. When asked for restitution she refused. From the respondent's point of view, the whole transaction was plainly a most improvident one.

In these circumstances, the learned trial judge's conclusion that the appellant had been guilty of unconscionable conduct in procuring and retaining the gift of $59,206.55 was not only open to him. In the context of his Honour's findings of fact, it was inevitable and plainly correct. On those findings, the case was not simply one in which the respondent had, under the influence of his love for, or infatuation with, the appellant, made an imprudent gift in her favour. The case was one in which the appellant deliberately used that love or infatuation and her own deceit to create a situation in which she could unconscientiously manipulate the respondent to part with a large proportion of his property. The intervention of equity is not merely to relieve the plaintiff from the consequences of his own foolishness. It is to prevent his victimization.[18]

. . . .

Toohey J (dissenting):

. . .

CONCLUSIONS

Although the concept of unconscionability has been expressed in fairly wide terms, the courts are exercising an equitable jurisdiction according to recognized principles. They are not armed with a general power to set aside bargains simply because, in the eyes of the judges, they appear to be unfair, harsh or unconscionable. This is in contrast to some legislation which 'permits the courts to exercise a broad discretion to control harsh, oppressive, unconscionable or unjust contracts'.[19] The equitable jurisdiction exists when one of the parties 'suffers from some special disability or is placed in some special situation of disadvantage'.[20] In some cases, for instance where there is unfamiliarity with written English as in *Amadio* or unintelligence and deafness as in *Wilton v Farnworth*,[21] the special situation of disadvantage may be readily apparent. But that is not the present case.

Although the appellant's attack on the findings of the trial judge is generally persuasive, it is not necessary to make contrary findings in order to reach a contrary conclusion. For the most part the findings are of a general nature, bearing upon the relationship between the parties. The appellant's complaint that those findings focus unduly on the position of the respondent and fail to pay due regard to the overall relationship of the parties is, I think, well founded. In particular, his Honour's assessment that the appellant's 'manufacture of an atmosphere of crisis where no crisis existed was dishonest and smacked of fraud'[22] is not so much a finding as an inference. In either case, it does not find great support in the evidence.

But the important thing is that the respondent failed to make good the proposition that his relationship with the appellant placed him in some special situation of disadvantage so that he should be recognised as the beneficial owner of the Tranmere house. The relationship was one which might be thought to have little to offer him but it was one in which he was content to persist and which the appellant in no way misrepresented or disguised. The respondent was well aware of all the

---

18 See, e.g., *Allcard v Skinner* (1887) 36 ChD 145, at 182; *Nichols v Jessup* [1986] 1 NZLR 226, at 227–9; *The Commonwealth v Verwayen* (1990) 170 CLR 394, at 440.

19 Cope, *Duress, Undue Influence and Unconscientious Bargains* (1985), 188. For a review of the relevant statutory powers, see 174–208.

20 *Amadio* (1983) 151 CLR at 461, *per* Mason J.

21 (1948) 76 CLR 646.   22 (1990) 54 SASR, at 448.

circumstances and of his actions and their consequences. This applies particularly with respect to the purchase of the house. That knowledge and his clear appreciation of the consequences of what he was doing run directly counter to a conclusion that he was suffering from some special disability or was placed in some special situation of disadvantage. It is clear that the respondent was emotionally involved with the appellant. But it does not follow that he was emotionally dependent upon her in any relevant legal sense.[23]

As appears from the judgment of Matheson J, the respondent accepted that, if he could not make good a case founded on unconscionability, it would be 'almost impossible to succeed'[24] on the ground of undue influence. And before this Court he did not attempt to sustain a case on that ground.

I would allow the appeal.

NOTES AND QUESTIONS

1. Would the facts of *Allcard v Skinner* fall within the two criteria for setting aside transactions set out by Deane J and the three (slightly differently expressed) criteria set out by Brennan J? Are there situations that fall within undue influence but outside the High Court of Australia's principle of unconscionable conduct?

2. Is Brennan J correct to assert that 'gifts obtained by unconscionable conduct and gifts obtained by undue influence are set aside by equity on substantially the same basis'?

3. What would have been the outcome if the claimant had sought the return of the money on the ground of undue influence?

4. How would an English court have resolved this case? What cases would it have relied upon in reaching its conclusion?

5. The trial judge, King CJ, granted the claimant (Diprose) a declaration that he was beneficially entitled to all the right title and interest in the land, and that the defendant as registered proprietor held it on trust for the claimant and he ordered the defendant to transfer her interest in the land to the claimant within thirty days ((1990) 54 SASR 438). On appeal the majority of the Court of Appeal varied the order of the judge ((1990) 54 SASR 450). Jacobs ACJ (with whom Legoe J agreed) was of the opinion that it would have been more appropriate to declare that the defendant was obliged to repay the sum of $59,206 to the claimant, such repayment to be charged on the property by way of a first mortgage in favour of the claimant. However, in the event, the order that was made by consent was that the defendant execute a memorandum of transfer in favour of the claimant, albeit that the defendant was given a longer period in which to execute the transfer. In the High Court of Australia the parties did not attempt to challenge the order which had been made by the trial judge so that the claimant was entitled to an order that the defendant held the house in trust for him. What justifications (if any) can be adduced to support this form of relief? Why did a personal remedy to reverse the unjust enrichment of the defendant not suffice? In what circumstances is proprietary relief appropriate in cases where the ground of restitution is undue influence or unconscionability (see further Chapter 13)?

6. Goff and Jones, 11-015, state:

> The victim of undue influence may rescind any transaction if she can restore the status quo ante. But it is open to doubt whether in consequence she acquires a proprietary right which is superior, on an insolvency, to the rights of the defendant's general creditors. It is even more uncertain whether she can establish a proprietary claim to a fund, which represents value transferred, in the hands of the wrongdoer. The payer of money under a mistake of fact was said in *Chase Manhattan Bank N.N. v Israel-British Bank Ltd* to retain equitable title to the money paid, but its authority has been questioned. However, the House of Lords has held that a person who exercises undue influence is deemed to be in equity a wrongdoer. So,

---

23 See *Diprose v Louth (No 2)* (1990) 54 SASR, at 480, *per* Matheson J.   24 *Ibid.* 482.

a court may be persuaded to hold, if he has exercised *actual* undue influence, that he has behaved unconscionably and that, consequently, the vulnerable party will be deemed to have retained the equitable title to the value transferred by him. In contrast, a person who is presumed to have exercised undue influence may or may not act unconscionably. If he has so acted, then his position should be no different from one who is held to have exercised actual undue influence.

Do you agree?

3. (EXPLOITATION OF) THE MENTAL INADEQUACY OF THE CLAIMANT

For many years now courts have granted relief to claimants who suffer from some mental inadequacy but the precise ground for intervention has never been clear. To some extent this imprecision has been deliberately created by the courts. As Lord Scarman put it in *National Westminster Bank plc v Morgan* [1985] AC 686, 709

A court in the exercise of this equitable jurisdiction is a court of conscience. Definition is a poor instrument when used to determine whether a transaction is or is not unconscionable: this is a question which depends on the particular facts of the case.

While this view has many supporters, it is not a view with which we can agree. The courts must make greater efforts to spell out the basis or bases upon which they intervene to grant relief. Once again a number of possible analyses can be put forward.

(i) The first is based upon the mental weakness of the claimant. This weakness is not confined to a particular relationship (as in the undue influence cases) but is of a more general nature. It may be attributable to the claimant's mental illness (see further *Hart v O'Connor* below, 612) or general lack of intelligence. This focus on the weakness of the claimant can lead to the adoption of a strict liability approach because the ground for intervention can apply irrespective of the knowledge of the defendant.

(ii) The second view is based upon the conduct of the defendant: that is to say what we are looking for is some unconscionable attempt by the defendant to exploit, or take advantage of, the weakness of the claimant.

(iii) The third view is that the ground for intervention looks both to the weakness of the claimant and the conduct of the defendant.

• *Fry v Lane* (1888) 40 ChD 312, Chancery Division

The claimants were two brothers. One was a laundryman and the other worked for a plumber. They sold their reversionary interests in the estate of John Fry to the defendant for £170 and £270 respectively. When they entered into the transaction, the claimants were advised by an inexperienced solicitor who was acting for both parties. The property which was the subject of their interest was later sold for £3,848, of which the claimants' share would have been £730 each. The proceeds of the sale were paid into court. An actuary stated that J.B. Fry's contingent interest in the £730 would have been valued at £475 at the date of the transaction. The claimants' claim to set aside the transaction with the defendant was successful.

Kay J: . . . I reserved judgment that I might more carefully consider the facts of the case, and the law which is applicable to them since the passing of the statute 31 Vict. c. 4.

Long before the passing of that Act it was settled that the Court of Chancery would relieve against a sale of or other dealing with a remainder or reversion at an undervalue on that ground alone, and this even where the remainderman was of mature age and accustomed to business: *Wiseman v Beake*;[1] *Berkley-Freeman v Bishop*;[2] *Davis v Duke of Marlborough*;[3] *Earl of Portmore v Taylor*;[4] *Boothby v Boothby*;[5] *Foster v Roberts*;[6] *Beynon v Cook*.[7] In such cases it was held that the onus lay upon the purchaser to shew that he had given the 'fair' value as it was called in *Earl of Aldborough v Trye*,[8] or 'the market value': *Talbor v Staniforth*.[9]

By the 31 Vict. c. 4, reciting that it was expedient to amend the law as administered in Courts of Equity with respect to sales of reversions, it was enacted (by sect. 1) that 'no purchase, made *bonâ fide* and without fraud or unfair dealing, of any reversionary interest in real or personal estate shall hereafter be opened or set aside merely on the ground of undervalue,' and by sect. 2 the word 'purchase' in the Act is to include 'every kind of contract, conveyance, or assignment, under or by which any beneficial interest in any kind of property may be acquired.' This Act came into operation on the 1st day of January, 1868.

It is obvious that the words 'merely on the ground of undervalue' do not include the case of an undervalue so gross as to amount of itself to evidence of fraud, and in *Earl of Aylesford v Morris*[10] Lord *Selborne* said that this Act 'leaves undervalue still a material element in cases in which it is not the sole equitable ground for relief. These changes of the law have in no degree whatever altered the *onus probandi* in those cases, which, according to the language of Lord *Hardwicke*, raise "from the circumstances or conditions of the parties contracting—weakness on one side, usury on the other, or extortion, or advantage taken of that weakness"—a presumption of fraud. Fraud,' says Lord *Selborne*, 'does not here mean deceit or circumvention; it means an unconscientious use of the power arising out of these circumstances and conditions; and when the relative position of the parties is such as *primâ facie* to raise this presumption, the transaction cannot stand unless the person claiming the benefit of it is able to repel the presumption by contrary evidence, proving it to have been in point of fact fair, just, and reasonable.'

The most common case for the interference of a Court of Equity is that of an expectant heir, reversioner, or remainderman who is just of age, his youth being treated as an important circumstance. Another analogous case is where the vendor is a poor man with imperfect education, as in *Evans v Llewellin*;[11] *Haygarth v Wearing*.[12]

In the case of a poor man, in distress for money, a sale, even of property in possession, at an undervalue has been set aside in many cases. [*His Lordship discussed the cases and continued*:] The result of the decisions is that where a purchase is made from a poor and ignorant man at a considerable undervalue, the vendor having no independent advice, a Court of Equity will set aside the transaction.

This will be done even in the case of property in possession, and *à fortiori* if the interest be reversionary.

The circumstances of poverty and ignorance of the vendor, and absence of independent advice, throw upon the purchaser, when the transaction is impeached, the onus of proving, in Lord *Selborne's* words, that the purchase was 'fair, just, and reasonable.'

Upon the evidence before me I cannot hesitate to conclude that the price of £170 in *J. B. Fry's* case and £270 in *George Fry's* case were both considerably below the real value. The property has been subjected to the costs of appointing new trustees, and also to part of the costs of an administration suit, and yet the net produce of one-fifth share is £730. Managed in a more careful manner it might have produced more.

Both *J. B. Fry* and his brother *George* were poor, ignorant men, to whom the temptation of the

1 2 Vern 121.   2 2 Atk 39.   3 2 Sw 108, 143.   4 4 Sim 182.
5 1 Mac & G 604; S.C. 15 Beav 212.   6 29 Beav 467.   7 Law Rep 10 Ch 389.
8 7 Cl & F 436, 456.   9 1 J & H 484, 503.   10 Law Rep 8 Ch 484, 490.
11 1 Cox 333.   12 Law Rep 12 Eq. 320.

immediate possession of £100 would be very great. Neither of them in the transaction of the sale of his share, was, in the words of Sir *J. Leach*, 'on equal terms' with the purchaser. Neither had independent advice. The solicitor who acted for both parties in each transaction seems, from the *Law List*, to have been admitted in March, 1877. In October, 1878, at the time of completing the sale of *J. B. Fry's* share, he had not been much more than a year and a-half on the roll. His inexperience probably in some degree accounts for his allowing himself to be put in the position of solicitor for both parties in such a case. I think in each transaction he must have been considering the purchaser's interest too much properly to guard that of the vendors. . . . I regret that I must come to the conclusion that, though there was a semblance of bargaining by the solicitor in each case, he did not properly protect the vendors, but gave a great advantage to the purchasers, who had been former clients, and for whom he was then acting. The circumstances illustrate the wisdom and necessity of the rule that a poor, ignorant man, selling an interest of this kind, should have independent advice, and that a purchase from him at an undervalue should be set aside, if he has not. The most experienced solicitor, acting for both sides, if he allows a sale at an undervalue, can hardly have duly performed his duty to the vendor. To act for both sides in such a case, and permit a sale at an undervalue, is a position in which no careful practitioner would allow himself to be placed. . . .

NOTES AND QUESTIONS

1. If the defendant was not guilty of any wrongdoing, what was the justification for the intervention of the court?

2. Why must the claimant be both 'poor' and 'ignorant'? Why does 'ignorance' not suffice?

3. Why must the sale be at a 'considerable undervalue'?

● *Creswell v Potter* [1978] 1 WLR 255, Chancery Division

On the break-up of her marriage to the defendant, the claimant, a telephonist, released and conveyed to the defendant her interest in the matrimonial home in return for an indemnity against liability under the mortgage. The defendant later sold the former matrimonial home and made a profit of £1,400 on the sale. The claimant sought to set aside the release on the ground that it was exercised in circumstances which amounted to unfair dealing. Her claim was successful.

Megarry J: . . . [*He considered the judgment of Kay J in* Fry v Lane *and continued:*] The judge thus laid down three requirements. What has to be considered is, first, whether the plaintiff is poor and ignorant; second, whether the sale was at a considerable undervalue; and third whether the vendor had independent advice. I am not, of course, suggesting that these are the only circumstances which will suffice; thus there may be circumstances of oppression or abuse of confidence which will invoke the aid of equity. But in the present case only these three requirements are in point. Abuse of confidence, though pleaded, is no longer relied on; and no circumstances of oppression or other matters are alleged. I must therefore consider whether the three requirements laid down in *Fry v Lane* are satisfied.

I think that the plaintiff may fairly be described as falling within whatever is the modern equivalent of 'poor and ignorant.' Eighty years ago, when *Fry v Lane* was decided, social conditions were very different from those which exist today. I do not, however, think that the principle has changed, even though the euphemisms of the 20th century may require the word 'poor' to be replaced by 'a member of the lower income group' or the like, and the word 'ignorant' by 'less highly educated.' The plaintiff has been a van driver for a tobacconist, and is a Post Office telephonist. The evidence of her means is slender. The defendant told me that the plaintiff probably had a little saved, but not much; and there was evidence that her earnings were about the same as the defendant's, and that these were those of a carpenter. The plaintiff also has a legal aid certificate.

In those circumstances I think the plaintiff may properly be described as 'poor' in the sense used in *Fry v Lane*, where it was applied to a laundryman who, in 1888, was earning £1 a week. In this context, as in others, I do not think that 'poverty' is confined to destitution. Further, although no doubt it requires considerable alertness and skill to be a good telephonist, I think that a telephonist can properly be described as 'ignorant' in the context of property transactions in general and the execution of conveyancing documents in particular. I have seen and heard the plaintiff giving evidence, and I have reached the conclusion that she satisfies the requirements of the first head.

The second question is whether the sale was at a 'considerable undervalue.' Slate Hall cost £1,500, £1,200 of the price being provided by the mortgage. The release recited that £1,196 13s. 5d remained outstanding on the mortgage, so that very little had been paid off the capital sum due. Nevertheless, all that the plaintiff was getting for giving up her half interest in Slate Hall was the release from her liability under the mortgage. If Slate Hall was worth no more than it cost, she was giving up her half share in any equity worth £300; and, after all, the mortgage was a recent mortgage to a well-known building society. If she had sought advice it is unlikely in the extreme that she would have been told that there was any real probability that the value of the property would be less than the sum due under the mortgage. There can be little doubt that she was getting virtually nothing for £150.

In fact, as is now known, within a little over two years the property fetched £3,350, so that at the time in question the plaintiff's share of the equity may have been worth appreciably more than £150. It is true, as Mr Balcombe pointed out on behalf of the defendant, that there was no valuation evidence before me, and that any valuation of the property must rest upon inferences from the prices for which the property was sold. I do not think it right to assume, without evidence, that there was a dip in the value of the property between its purchase in November 1958, and the sales in December 1960, and September 1961; and without such a dip it seems to me that the probabilities point to the property having a value in August 1959, which at all events substantially exceeded the sum due under the mortgage for £1,200. The more valuable the equity, of course, the less valuable would be the indemnity against the mortgage. It seems to me that by the release the plaintiff parted with her interest in Slate Hall at an undervalue which cannot be dismissed as being trifling or inconsiderable. In my judgment the undervalue was 'considerable.'

As for independent advice, from first to last there is no suggestion that the plaintiff had any. The defendant, his solicitor and the inquiry agent stood on one side; on the other the plaintiff stood alone. This was, of course, a conveyancing transaction, and English land law is notoriously complex. I am certainly not saying that other transactions, such as hire-purchase agreements, are free from all difficulty. But the authorities put before me on setting aside dealings at an undervalue all seem to relate to conveyancing transactions, and one may wonder whether the principle is confined to such transactions, and, if so, why. I doubt whether the principle is restricted in this way; and it may be that the explanation is that it is in conveyancing matters that, by long usage, it is regarded as usual, and, indeed, virtually essential, for the parties to have the services of a solicitor. The absence of the aid of a solicitor is thus, as it seems to me, of especial significance if a conveyancing matter is involved. The more usual it is to have a solicitor, the more striking will be his absence, and the more closely will the courts scrutinise what was done.

Mr Balcombe points out that the plaintiff was not bereft of possible legal assistance; for on or before July 28, 1959, when she was having difficulty in getting some furniture and effects from Slate Hall, she consulted a Colchester firm of solicitors, who wrote a letter dated July 28, 1959, that produced the required result. If she wanted legal advice, he said, this shows that she knew how to get it. However, what matters, I think, is not whether she could have obtained proper advice but whether in fact she had it; and she did not. Nobody, of course, can be compelled to obtain independent advice: but I do not think that someone who seeks to uphold what is, to him, an advantageous conveyancing transaction can do so merely by saying that the other party could have obtained independent advice, unless something has been done to bring to the notice of that other party the true nature of the transaction and the need for advice.

. . . .

At the end of the day, my conclusion is that this transaction cannot stand. In my judgment the plaintiff has made out her case, and so it is for the defendant to prove that the transaction was 'fair, just, and reasonable.' This he has not done. The whole burden of his case has been that the requirements of *Fry v Lane*, 40 ChD 312, were not satisfied, whereas I have held that they were. . . .

NOTES AND QUESTIONS

1. Is Megarry J's interpretation of *Fry* a legitimate one? Would it be true to say that it has breathed 'new life' into *Fry v Lane*?

2. For an interesting extension of *Creswell v Potter* see the decision of Balcombe J in *Backhouse v Backhouse* [1978] 1 WLR 243.

• *Boustany v Pigott* (1995) 69 P & CR 298, Privy Council

In 1977 Miss Pigott leased property to Mrs Boustany for a period of five years at a monthly rent of $833.33. Miss Pigott was 'quite slow', and her affairs were managed by her cousin, George Pigott. In 1980 Mrs Boustany discussed the possibility of a new lease with George Pigott but no agreement was reached. Later that year, while George Pigott was away, Mrs Boustany went to the chambers of a certain Mr Kendall and presented him with a copy of a new lease which was for ten years at a monthly rent of $1,000, renewable at the same rent at the option of Mrs Boustany. Mr Kendall demanded to see Miss Pigott together with Mr and Mrs Boustany and, during the course of the interview, he pointed out to Miss Pigott various aspects of the agreement which were not in her best interests but she insisted that he draw up the agreement. He did so. When George Pigott discovered what had happened he protested to Mrs Boustany, who was unmoved and so he asked for a declaration that the lease was an unconscionable bargain which should be declared null and void. The Privy Council, upholding the decision of the Court of Appeal of the Eastern Caribbean States, set aside the lease as an unconscionable bargain.

Lord Templeman: . . . In a careful and thoughtful submission, Mr Robertson, who appeared before the Board on behalf of Mrs Boustany, made the following submissions with which their Lordships are in general agreement:

(1) It is not sufficient to attract the jurisdiction of equity to prove that a bargain is hard, unreasonable or foolish; it must be proved to be unconscionable, in the sense that 'one of the parties to it has imposed the objectionable terms in a morally reprehensible manner, that is to say, in a way which affects his conscience': *Multiservice Bookbinding v Marden*.[1]

(2) 'Unconscionable' relates not merely to the terms of the bargain but to the behaviour of the stronger party, which must be characterised by some moral culpability or impropriety: *Lobb (Alec) (Garages) Limited v Total Oil (Great Britain) Limited*.[2]

(3) Unequal bargaining power or objectively unreasonable terms provide no basis for equitable interference in the absence of unconscientious or extortionate abuse of power where exceptionally, and as a matter of common fairness, 'it was not right that the strong should be allowed to push the weak to the wall': *Lobb (Alec) (Garages) Limited v Total Oil (Great Britain) Limited*.[3]

---

1 [1979] Ch 84, 110.   2 [1983] 1 WLR 87, 94.   3 [1985] 1 WLR 173, 183.

(4) A contract cannot be set aside in equity as 'an unconscionable bargain against a party innocent of actual or constructive fraud. Even if the terms of the contract are "unfair" in the sense that they are more favourable to one party than the other ("contractual imbalance"), equity will not provide relief unless the beneficiary is guilty of unconscionable conduct: *Hart v O'Connor*[4] applied in *Nichols v Jessup*.[5]

(5) 'In situations of this kind it is necessary for the plaintiff who seeks relief to establish unconscionable conduct, namely that unconscientious advantage has been taken of his disabling condition or circumstances': *per* Mason J in *Commercial Bank of Australia Ltd v Amadio*.[6]

Mr Robertson submitted that Miss Pigott had received independent advice from Mr Kendall, that she had been made aware by Mr Kendall that the terms of the 1980 lease were disadvantageous to her, that Miss Pigott could not be described as poor or ignorant and that the judge did not find and could not, consistently with the evidence, have found unconscionable behaviour on the part of Mrs Boustany.

The crucial question in this case is—what brought Miss Pigott to the chambers of Mr Kendall in September 1980? That question was not answered by direct evidence because Miss Pigott was not able to give evidence and Mrs Boustany and her husband chose not to do so. The trial judge inferred unconscionable conduct by Mrs Boustany after careful consideration of a number of features which he held were only consistent with unconscientious conduct on the part of Mrs Boustany. The management of the property had been given up by Miss Pigott because of her incapacity. The properties were managed by Mr George Pigott and there was no reason why Miss Pigott should interfere in the management of this one property leased to Mrs Boustany. There was no evidence of any personal attachment between Miss Pigott and her tenant. Mrs Boustany had negotiated with Mr George Pigott and knew that he was the representative of Miss Pigott. No advice was sought by Miss Pigott; she turned up not at her family's solicitors but to Mr Kendall who knew nothing about her save that he had prepared the 1976 lease. Miss Pigott gave to Mr Kendall, according to his evidence, absurd reasons for the grant of a new lease and no reason for the grant of a lease for 20 years on disadvantageous terms.

Miss Pigott must have been under a total misapprehension of the facts when she represented that she might be worried about the property and about the repair of the property while she was away. Mr Kendall forcibly pointed out not only to Miss Pigott but also to Mrs Boustany and her husband the disadvantages to Miss Pigott of the new lease but Mrs Boustany and her husband gave no explanation and offered no concessions. They were content to allow Miss Pigott ostensibly to insist on the unjustifiable terms which they must have already persuaded her to accept. When a writ was issued Mrs Boustany did not write to the solicitor but sought out Miss Pigott and obtained a disclaimer which the court in due course rejected. The inference which the trial judge drew, and which he was entitled to draw, was that Mrs Boustany and her husband had prevailed upon Miss Pigott to agree to grant a lease on terms which they knew they could not extract from Mr George Pigott or anyone else. When they were summoned by Mr Kendall and the unfairness of the lease was pointed out to them, they did not release Miss Pigott from the bargain which they had unfairly pressed on her. In short Mrs Boustany must have taken advantage of Miss Pigott before, during and after the interview with Mr Kendall and with full knowledge before the 1980 lease was settled that her conduct was unconscionable.

4 [1985] AC 1000.   5 [1986] NZLR 226.   6 (1983) 46 ALR 402, 413.

NOTES AND QUESTIONS

1. Was the conduct of Mrs Boustany 'unconscionable'? If so, in what respects?

2. Are the various 'submissions' generally accepted by the Privy Council internally consistent? Do they suggest the need for subjective wrongdoing or objective wrong-doing?

3. Lord Templeman stated that Mr Kendall 'forcibly pointed out' to Miss Pigott 'the disadvantages' of the new lease. Why did this independent advice not suffice to negate the claim?

4. The case is helpfully discussed by N Bamforth in 'Unconscionability as a Vitiating Factor' [1995] *LMCLQ* 538. He maintains (at 559) that unconscionability has 'now emerged as a distinct vitiating factor, and four elements must be present for a transaction to be set aside— special or serious disadvantage, actual or constructive fraud, lack of independent advice, and disadvantageous terms'. Do you think this approach is (a) helpful and (b) explains the outcome in *Pigott*?

- *Credit Lyonnais Bank Nederland NV v Burch* [1997] 1 All E.R. 144, Court of Appeal

The defendant, an 18 year old, was asked by her employer, Mr Pelosi, to mortgage her flat as security for an increase in the company's overdraft (which was in the region of £250,000). She agreed to this request and she entered into a transaction with the plaintiff bank under which she gave them a second charge over the flat and gave the bank an all moneys unlimited guarantee. No attempt was made by the bank to explain to her the nature of the transaction into which she was entering. She was advised to obtain independent advice but did not do so. The company went into liquidation and the bank brought proceedings against the defendant in which they sought possession of the flat. The defendant successfully defended the proceedings. The Court of Appeal set aside the transaction on the ground of undue influence but they also gave brief consideration to the existence of a wider equitable jurisdiction to set aside the transaction.

Nourse LJ: . . . the recorder identified, although without pejorative comment, the truly astonishing feature of this case. Under the terms of the legal charge, Miss Burch was required not simply to pledge her home as security for the £20,000 extension; she was required to pledge it without limit. Worse than that, she was required to enter into a personal covenant guaranteeing not simply repayment of the additional £20,000, nor even repayment up to the new limit of £270,000; she was required to guarantee without limit repayment of all API's borrowings from the bank, present and future and of whatever kind, together with interest, commission, charges, legal and other costs, charges and expenses. All that was required as the price of extending the limit by no more than £20,000 and, be it remembered, of someone who was a mere employee of API, to whom the only detriment in API's collapse would have been the loss of her job. It could not have helped the bank to say that it used its standard form. A mortgagee who uses such a form without regard to its impact on the individual case acts at his peril.

On that state of facts it must, I think, have been very well arguable that Miss Burch could, directly against the bank, have had the legal charge set aside as an unconscionable bargain. Equity's jurisdiction to relieve against such transactions, although more rarely exercised in modern times, is at least as venerable as its jurisdiction to relieve against those procured by undue influence.

[*he considered* Fry v Lane *and continued*]

The decision of Megarry J. in *Cresswell v Potter* [1978] 1 W.L.R. 255 at 257 where he suggested that the modern equivalent of 'poor and ignorant' might be 'a member of the lower income group . . . less highly educated', demonstrates that the jurisdiction is in good heart and capable of adaptation to different transactions entered into in changing circumstances. See also the interesting judgment of Balcombe J. in *Backhouse v Backhouse* [1978] 1 W.L.R. 243 at 250–252, where he suggested that these cases may come under the general heading which Lord Denning M.R. referred to in *Lloyds Bank Ltd v Bundy* [1975] Q.B. 326 at 339 as 'inequality of bargaining power'.

Millett LJ

No court of equity could allow such a transaction to stand. The facts which I have recited are sufficient to entitle Miss Burch to have the transaction set aside as against Mr Pelosi and the company. Every one of those facts was known to the bank when it accepted the security. The bank must accordingly be taken to have had notice of Miss Burch's equity, and must submit to the transaction being set aside against it also.

An eighteenth century Lord Chancellor would have contented himself with saying as much. It is an extreme case. The transaction was not merely to the manifest disadvantage of Miss Burch; it was one which, in the traditional phrase, 'shocks the conscience of the court'. Miss Burch committed herself to a personal liability far beyond her slender means, risking the loss of her home and personal bankruptcy, and obtained nothing in return beyond a relatively small and possibly temporary increase in the overdraft facility available to her employer, a company in which she had no financial interest. The transaction gives rise to grave suspicion. It cries aloud for an explanation.

Miss Burch did not seek to have the transaction set aside as a harsh and unconscionable bargain. To do so she would have had to show not only that the terms of the transaction were harsh or oppressive, but that 'one of the parties to it has imposed the objectionable terms in a morally reprehensible manner, that is to say, in a way which affects his conscience' (see *Multiservice Bookbinding Ltd v Marden* [1979] Ch 84 at 110 *per* Browne-Wilkinson J. and *Alec Lobb (Garages) Ltd v Total Oil GB Ltd* [1983] 1 W.L.R. 87 at 95, where I pointed out that there must be some impropriety, both in the conduct of the stronger party and in the terms of the transaction itself, but added that 'the former may often be inferred from the latter in the absence of an innocent explanation').

Swinton Thomas LJ delivered a concurring judgment.

NOTES AND QUESTIONS

1. Nourse LJ appears to suggest that the unfairness of the charge, combined with an inequality of bargaining power, would have been enough to set aside the transaction with the bank. The judgment of Millett LJ is more cautious in that he stated that, in order to set aside the transaction on this ground, it would have been necessary for Miss Burch to show some impropriety on the part of the bank.

2. The Court of Appeal in *Portman Building Society v Dusangh* [2000] 2 All ER (Comm.) 221 distinguished *Burch* on the ground that the transaction in *Dusangh*, although improvident, was not 'overreaching and oppressive' and there was no evidence that the building society in that case had acted in 'a morally reprehensible manner'. This suggests that *Burch* will be confined within very narrow limits. In *Dusangh* the defendant, an elderly, illiterate man, living on a low income, agreed to mortgage his home in order to enable his son to acquire a supermarket. The supermarket business was not a success and the building society was held to be entitled to a declaration that it was entitled to a charge by way of a legal mortgage over the defendant's home. Ward LJ stated (at 232):

   > The salient features here are that the son had committed himself to the purchase of the small supermarket business. There is no reason to think that he did not believe that it would be a profitable venture which would turn out to his advantage. He needed money to complete the purchase. He persuaded his father to lend it. On the findings of the judge there was no undue influence and no misrepresentation. So it was a case of father coming to the assistance of his son. True it is that it was a financially unwise venture because, absent good profit from the business, there was never likely to be the income to service the borrowing and the father's home was at risk. But there was nothing, absolutely nothing, which comes close to morally reprehensible conduct or impropriety. No unconscientious advantage has been taken of the father's illiteracy, his lack of business acumen or his paternal generosity. True it may be that the son

gained all the advantage and the father took all the risk, but this cannot be stigmatised as impropriety. There was no exploitation of father by son such as would prick the conscience and tell the son that in all honour it was morally wrong and reprehensible.

4. (EXPLOITATION OF) THE ECONOMIC WEAKNESS OF THE CLAIMANT

This ground for intervention is often linked to the previous category, but there is in fact a good case for treating it separately (although it must be conceded that it is difficult, if not impossible, to draw a hard and fast line between the two groups of cases). The reason for seeking to distinguish between these two categories is that the reason for the intervention of the court is not based (necessarily) on the mental weakness of the claimant, but rather looks to the vulnerable economic position in which the claimant finds himself or herself. The classic example of this group of case is the 'expectant heir' who expects to inherit his estate from his father but has, as yet, inherited nothing. Such heirs were often young and inexperienced and were easy prey for money-lenders. The courts were quick to grant relief to such 'expectant heirs' when they entered into harsh transactions. However, as we shall see, the courts have been extremely reluctant to extend this doctrine to more general commercial transactions.

- **Earl of Aylesford v Morris** (1873) 8 Ch App 484, Court of Appeal

The claimant, when he was a young man of 22, had run up a large number of debts. His father was in poor health and he stood to inherit a large amount of property on the death of his father. His creditors were pressing for payment, and the defendant money lender agreed to lend him money to pay off his debts. The claimant received no independent advice and the rate of interest which the defendant demanded was over 60 per cent. The claimant applied to have the defendants' actions for payment restrained. It was held that he was entitled to have the action restrained and an order for delivery up of the bills and policy which he had advanced by way of security for the loan was made on payment by the claimant of the sums actually advanced and interest at 5 per cent.

Lord Selborne LC: There is hardly any older head of equity than that described by Lord *Hardwicke* in *Earl of Chesterfield v Janssen*[1] as relieving against the fraud 'which infects catching bargains with heirs, reversioners, or expectants, in the life of the father,' &c. 'These (he said) have been generally mixed cases,' and he proceeded to note two characters always found in them. 'There is always fraud presumed or inferred from the circumstances or conditions of the parties contracting—weakness on one side, usury on the other, or extortion, or advantage taken of that weakness. There has been always an appearance of fraud from the nature of the bargain.'

. . .

Fraud does not here mean deceit or circumvention; it means an unconscientious use of the power arising out of these circumstances and conditions; and when the relative position of the parties is such as *primâ facie* to raise this presumption, the transaction cannot stand unless the person claiming the benefit of it is able to repel the presumption by contrary evidence, proving it to have been in point of fact fair, just, and reasonable.

---

1 2 Ves. Sen. 125, 157.

This is the rule applied to the analogous cases of voluntary donations obtained for themselves by the donees, and to all other cases where influence, however acquired, has resulted in gain to the person possessing at the expense of the person subject to it. Lord *Cranworth*, in a recent case in the House of Lords (*Smith v Kay*[2]), said that no influence can be more direct, more intelligible, or more to be guarded against than that of a person who gets hold of a young man of fortune, 'and takes upon himself to supply him with means, pandering to his gross extravagance during his minority, and extorting from him, or at least obtaining from him, for every advance that he has made, a promise that the moment he comes of age it shall all be ratified, so as to make the securities good.' The circumstances of the particular case in which these words were spoken differed widely from those of the case now before us; the element of personal influence is here wanting. But it is sufficient for the application of the principle, if the parties meet under such circumstances as, in the particular transaction, to give the stronger party dominion over the weaker; and such power and influence are generally possessed, in every transaction of this kind, by those who trade upon the follies and vices of unprotected youth, inexperience, and moral imbecility.

In the cases of catching bargains with expectant heirs, one peculiar feature has been almost universally present; indeed, its presence was considered by Lord *Brougham* to be an indispensable condition of equitable relief, though Lord *St. Leonards*, with good reason, dissents from that opinion.[3] The victim comes to the snare (for this system of dealing does set snares, not, perhaps, for one prodigal more than another, but for prodigals generally as a class), excluded, and known to be excluded, by the very motives and circumstances which attract him, from the help and advice of his natural guardians and protectors, and from that professional aid which would be accessible to him, if he did not feel compelled to secrecy. He comes in the dark, and in fetters, without either the will or the power to take care of himself, and with nobody else to take care of him. Great Judges have said that there is a principle of public policy in restraining this; that this system of undermining and blasting, as it were, in the bud the fortunes of families, is a public as well as a private mischief; that it is a sort of indirect fraud upon the heads of families from whom these transactions are concealed, and who may be thereby induced to dispose of their means for the profit and advantage of strangers and usurers, when they suppose themselves to be fulfilling the moral obligation of providing for their own descendants.

Whatever weight there may be in any such collateral considerations, they could hardly prevail, if they did not connect themselves with an equity more strictly and directly personal to the Plaintiff in each particular case. But the real truth is, that the ordinary effect of all the circumstances by which these considerations are introduced, is to deliver over the prodigal helpless into the hands of those interested in taking advantage of his weakness; and we so arrive in every such case at the substance of the conditions which throw the burden of justifying the righteousness of the bargain upon the party who claims the benefit of it. . . .

Sir G. Mellish LJ concurred.

- *Alec Lobb (Garages) Ltd v Total Oil (Great Britain) Ltd* [1985] 1 WLR 173,
  Court of Appeal

The defendant oil company advanced money to the claimant company for the purpose of its garage and petrol filling station business and took mortgages on its property as security. In 1969 the company was in financial difficulty and so it entered into fresh negotiations with the defendants. Contrary to the advice of its solicitors, the claimant entered into an agreement with the defendants under which the claimant company

2 7 HLC 750, 771.

3 Sug. V & P 11th edn., 316.

agreed to grant a lease of the property to the defendants for fifty-one years for a £35,000 premium and a peppercorn rent and the defendants agreed to grant the second and third claimants (who were the directors of the claimant company) a lease-back at a rent of £2,250 *per annum* and a tie to the defendants to supply all the petrol for the whole term of the lease-back. In 1979 the claimants sought to set aside the 1969 agreement on the grounds that it was in restraint of trade and that it was an unconscionable bargain. It was held (both at first instance and in the Court of Appeal) that the lease and lease-back were not in restraint of trade, that the transaction was not unconscionable, and that, in any case, the claimants' claim was barred by laches.

Dillon LJ: . . . I turn therefore to the appellants' case on equitable grounds. The basis of the contention that the transaction of the lease and lease-back ought to be set aside in equity is that it is submitted, and in the court below was accepted on behalf of Total, that during the negotiations for the lease and lease-back the parties did not have equal bargaining power, and it is therefore further submitted that a contract between parties who had unequal bargaining power can only stand and be enforced by the stronger if he can prove that the contract was in point of fact fair, just and reasonable. The concept of unequal bargaining power is taken particularly from the judgment of Lord Denning MR in *Lloyds Bank Ltd v Bundy* [1975] QB 326. The reference to a contract only standing if it is proved to have been in point of fact fair, just and reasonable is taken from the judgment of Lord Selborne LC in *Earl of Aylesford v Morris* (1873) LR 8 Ch App. 484, 490–1. Lord Selborne was not there seeking to generalise; he was dealing only with what he regarded as one of the oldest heads of equity, relieving against fraud practised on heirs or expectants, particularly fraud practised on young noblemen of great expectations, considerable extravagance and no ready money. It is none the less submitted that the logic of the development of the law leads to the conclusion that Lord Selborne LC's test should now be applied generally to any contract entered into between parties who did not have equal bargaining power.

In fact Lord Denning MR's judgment in *Lloyds Bank Ltd v Bundy* merely laid down the proposition that where there was unequal bargaining power the contract could not stand if the weaker did not have legal advice. In the present case Mr Lobb and the company did have separate advice from their own solicitor. On the facts of this case, however, that does not weaken the appellants' case if the general proposition of law which they put forward is valid. Total refused to accept any of the modifications of the transaction as put forward by Total which the company's and Mr Lobb's solicitor suggested, and in the end the solicitor advised them not to proceed. Mr Lobb declined to accept that advice because his and the company's financial difficulties were so great, and, it may be said, their bargaining power was so small, that he felt he had no alternative but to accept Total's terms. Because of the existing valid tie to Total which had, as I have said, three to four years to run, he had no prospect at all of raising finance on the scale he required from any source other than Total. There is no suggestion that there was any other dealer readily available who could have bought the property from him subject to the tie. The only practical solutions open to him were to accept the terms of the lease and lease-back as put forward by Total on which Total was not prepared to negotiate, or to sell the freehold of the property to Total and cease trading. In these circumstances, it would be unreal, in my judgment, to hold that if the transaction is otherwise tainted it is cured merely because Mr Lobb and the company had independent advice.

But on the deputy judge's findings can it be said that the transaction is tainted? Lord Selborne LC dealt with the case before him as a case of fraud. He said, at pp. 490–1:

'The usury laws, however, proved to be an inconvenient fetter upon the liberty of commercial transactions; and the arbitrary rule of equity as to sales of reversions was an impediment to fair and reasonable, as well as to unconscionable, bargains. Both have been abolished by the legislature; but the abolition of the usury laws still leaves the nature of the bargain capable of being a note of fraud in the estimation of this court; and the Act as to sales of reversions (31 Vict. c. 4) is carefully limited to purchases 'made bona fide and without fraud or unfair dealing,' and leaves under-value still a material element in cases in which it is not the sole equitable ground for relief. These changes of the law have in no degree whatever altered the onus probandi in those cases, which, according to the language of Lord Hardwicke, raise "from the circumstances or conditions of the parties contracting—weakness on one side, usury on the other, or extortion, or advantage taken of that weakness"—a presumption of fraud. Fraud does not here mean deceit or circumvention; it means an unconscientious use of the power arising out of these circumstances and conditions; and when the relative position of the parties is such as prima facie to raise this presumption, the transaction cannot stand unless the person claiming the benefit of it is able to repel the presumption by contrary evidence, proving it to have been in point of fact fair, just, and reasonable.'

The whole emphasis is on extortion, or undue advantage taken of weakness, an unconscientious use of the power arising out of the inequality of the parties' circumstances, and on unconscientious use of power which the court might in certain circumstances be entitled to infer from a particular—and in these days notorious—relationship unless the contract is proved to have been in fact fair, just and reasonable. Nothing leads me to suppose that the course of the development of the law over the last 100 years has been such that the emphasis on unconscionable conduct or unconscientious use of power has gone and relief will now be granted in equity in a case such as the present if there has been unequal bargaining power, even if the stronger has not used his strength unconscionably. I agree with the judgment of Browne-Wilkinson J, in *Multiservice Bookbinding Ltd v Marden* [1979] Ch 84, which sets out that to establish that a term is unfair and unconscionable it is not enough to show that it is, objectively, unreasonable.

In the present case there are findings of fact by the deputy judge that the conduct of Total was not unconscionable, coercive or oppressive. There is ample evidence to support those findings and they are not challenged by the appellants. Their case is that the judge applied the wrong test; where there is unequal bargaining power, the test is, they say, whether its terms are fair, just and reasonable and it is unnecessary to consider whether the conduct of the stronger party was oppressive or unconscionable. I do not accept the appellants' proposition of law. In my judgment the findings of the judge conclude this ground of appeal against the appellants.

Inequality of bargaining power must anyhow be a relative concept. It is seldom in any negotiation that the bargaining powers of the parties are absolutely equal. Any individual wanting to borrow money from a bank, building society or other financial institution in order to pay his liabilities or buy some property he urgently wants to acquire will have virtually no bargaining power; he will have to take or leave the terms offered to him. So, with house property in a seller's market, the purchaser will not have equal bargaining power with the vendor. But Lord Denning MR did not envisage that any contract entered into in such circumstances would, without more, be reviewed by the courts by the objective criterion of what was reasonable: see *Lloyds Bank Ltd v Bundy* [1975] QB 326, 336. The courts would only interfere in exceptional cases where as a matter of common fairness it was not right that the strong should be allowed to push the weak to the wall. The concepts of unconscionable conduct and of the exercise by the stronger of coercive power are thus brought in, and in the present case they are negatived by the deputy judge's findings.

Even if, contrary to my view just expressed, the company and Mr and Mrs Lobb had initially in 1969 a valid claim in equity to have the lease and lease-back set aside as a result of the inequality of bargaining power, that claim was, in my judgement, barred by laches well before the issue of the writ in this action.

. . .

Dunn LJ:

...

EQUITABLE RELIEF

Mr Cullen conceded that he could not bring himself within any of the established categories of equitable relief, but relied on the dictum of Lord Denning MR in *Lloyds Bank Ltd v Bundy* [1975] QB 326, 339 and submitted that the circumstances of this case disclosed a classic case of inequality of bargaining power of which the defendants had taken advantage by entering into the transaction, although he did not suggest any pressure or other misconduct on their part. He submitted that if it was necessary to categorise the grant of relief sought, it was an unconscionable bargain. He reminded us that the categories of unconscionable bargains are not closed (*per* Browne-Wilkinson J in *Multiservice Bookbinding Ltd v Marden* [1979] Ch 94, 110) and sought to distinguish the instant case from that case by submitting that here the plaintiffs were under a compelling necessity to accept the loan, so that misconduct by the defendants was unnecessary. The fact of their impecuniosity, that they were already tied to the defendants by mortgages, that there was no other source of finance, and that they could not sell the equities of redemption under the mortgages without giving up trading, coupled with the knowledge of the defendants of those facts, rendered the transaction unconscionable, and placed the onus upon the defendants to show that its terms were fair and reasonable.

I find myself unable to accept those arguments. Mere impecuniosity has never been held a ground for equitable relief. In this case no pressure was placed upon the plaintiffs. On the contrary the defendants were reluctant to enter into the transaction. The plaintiffs took independent advice from their solicitors and accountants. They went into the transaction with their eyes open, and it was of benefit to them because they were enabled to continue trade from the site for a number of years. In my view the judge was right to refuse equitable relief.

Waller LJ delivered a concurring judgment.

QUESTIONS

1. What are the differences between *Alec Lobb* and *Earl of Aylesford v Morris*?
2. Why were the defendants found not to have taken undue advantage of the weakness of the claimants in *Alec Lobb*?

5. (EXPLOITATION OF) THE DIFFICULT CIRCUMSTANCES IN WHICH THE CLAIMANT FINDS HIMSELF

Once again it is difficult to draw a clear line between this group of cases and the previous two groups. But the essential idea is that the claimant has found himself or herself in a situation of great difficulty or danger. The defendant offers to free the claimant from that difficulty or danger but asks a very high price for the performance of his services. In such a case is the claimant entitled to relief? Once again we encounter the same problem of discerning whether the ground for intervention lies in the weakness of the claimant or whether it can be located in the unconscionable conduct of the defendant.

• **The Medina** (1876) 1 P 272, Probate Division

Sir Robert Phillimore: The circumstances of this case are very singular; but it is one in which the Court really feels no doubt as to the judgment which it ought to give. It is not necessary that I should go into an examination of the authorities which I recently referred to in the case of *The Cargo Ex Woosung*,[1] and which I also referred to in the case of *The Waverley*.[2] But I may state the result of them to be this, that it is the practice of this Court, partly for the protection of absent owners and partly on the grounds of general policy, to control agreements made by masters when an examination of those agreements shews that they are clearly inequitable. In the present case there were upwards of five hundred pilgrims on a rock which is just six feet above water. Their ship had gone to pieces, and the plaintiffs' vessel, the *Timor*, came up close without any difficulty or danger at all; because the evidence is that the water was quite deep up to the rock; she came up and her captain, in effect, says, I will not relieve you from this situation, which a few hours of bad weather might convert into one of most imminent danger, indeed into your total destruction. I will not take you away unless you give me 4000*l*. Now, what is 4000*l*. with regard to the matter saved, which is human life? On the other hand, however, 4000*l*. is the whole sum that was to be paid for conveying the pilgrims to Jedda, and in my opinion if the master of the *Timor* had not taken these pilgrims off the rock in the circumstances stated, and bad weather had come on, and they had lost their lives in consequence, he would hardly have been in a better position than a pirate. Nevertheless, it was certainly a valuable salvage service according to the principles upon which such services have always been considered in this Court, but I am of opinion that 4000*l*. is a great deal too much, and I shall award 1800*l*. As to the costs there has been no tender, and I shall leave each party to pay their own costs. If there had been a sufficient tender, I should have given the defendants their costs. I shall not give costs on either side.

- **The *Port Caledonia* and the *Anna*** [1903] P 184, Probate Division

The *Port Caledonia* and the *Anna* were sheltering in Holyhead Harbour from a storm when the *Port Caledonia* began to be dragged towards the *Anna*. The master of the *Port Caledonia* signalled for a tug, but the master of the tug demanded '£1,000 or no rope'. The master of the *Port Caledonia* initially objected but agreed to pay the money. The tug then towed the vessel back to its original berth. The master of the tug brought a claim to recover the £1,000. The court set aside the agreement to pay £1,000 on the ground that it was extortionate, and the claimants were awarded instead the sum of £200 for the services which they had rendered.

Bucknill J: . . . With the 1000*l*. agreement on one side, and that which I think was the value of the services on the other, I have to ask myself whether the bargain that was made was so inequitable, so unjust, and so unreasonable that the Court cannot allow it to stand?

The first question to consider is, What was the position of the two persons who made the agreement? The position was this. One man was in a position to insist upon his terms, and the other man had to put up with it. He could not help himself. He says in his letter to his owners: 'He demanded 1000*l*. to take me away. I offered him 100*l*., or to leave it to the owners; but he would not agree, so I agreed to give 1000*l*. rather than foul the *Anna*.' He appreciated the possibility of fouling the *Anna* if the weather had remained bad, and if the wind had remained in the S.W., neither of which things happened. So he found himself obliged to give way to a person who would not move him, and who would have allowed him and the *Anna* to drift towards the rocks, and who would, I think, have seen them go there without putting a hawser on board unless he got a promise of 1000*l*.

I have expressed my opinion about the matter. This opinion is shared by the Elder Brethren, and I hold that this agreement cannot be allowed to stand, and I set it aside.

---

1 (1876) 1 P 260.
2 Law Rep 3 A & E 369.

I hope that those who perform such grand services in tugs from time to time, in worse weather than this, and, in peril of their own lives, save property around the coast, will note that this Court will keep a firm hand over them if they attempt to do what has been done in this case.

This was an inequitable, extortionate, and unreasonable agreement, and I think that the services rendered will be well rewarded by the sum of 200*l.*, and with county court costs.

. . .

QUESTIONS

Can this case and *The Medina* be generalized into some wider ground of relief? If so, how would you define that ground of relief? If not, what is so special about the saving of life or property at sea which prevents these cases from being used to create a broader principle?

6. ILLEGALITY DESIGNED TO PROTECT THE VULNERABLE CLASS, TO WHICH THE CLAIMANT BELONGS, FROM EXPLOITATION

We put forward this ground of restitution with some hesitation. The material could equally be said to lie in Chapter 10, where we discuss the circumstances in which illegality acts as a ground of restitution. Dicta can be found to support the proposition that the law gives a right of recovery to a claimant who is a member of a class of persons for whose protection the illegality of the contract was created (see, for example, *Browning v Morris* (1778) 2 Cowp 790, 792 and *Lodge v National Union Investment Co. Ltd* [1907] 1 Ch 300, 306). The case for the recognition of such a restitutionary right has been set out in the following terms (Burrows, 269):

The reason why a particular contract is illegal may be to protect the claimant as a member of a vulnerable class. For the same reason the claimant may be entitled to 'rescission' of the illegal contract and restitution of benefits conferred under it. At first sight such class protection might appear to be nothing more than another standard example of exploitation of weakness. But actual exploitation requires that the terms of the contract are substantively unfair, whereas the protection here is more extensive. The illegality protects members of a class even if the terms are substantively fair. In other words, protection against possible, rather than actual, exploitation is in mind here.

The following case is an example of one in which the claimant argued, in the event unsuccessfully, that he fell within the class of persons for whose benefit the illegality had been created.

• *Green v Portsmouth Stadium Ltd* [1953] 2 QB 190, Court of Appeal

Over a period of years the claimant bookmaker paid the defendant stadium owners £2 each time he went on to the racecourse. He alleged that this charge was contrary to section 13 of the Betting and Lotteries Act 1934 on the ground that it was more than the maximum sum authorized by that section. On the trial of the preliminary issue it was held by the Court of Appeal that the section was enforceable only by criminal proceedings so that the plaintiff was not entitled to the return of the money paid.

Denning LJ . . . In considering whether the statement of claim discloses a cause of action, it must be observed that there is no allegation that the plaintiff was under any mistake of fact. Nor is there any allegation that he was under a mistake of law, or that he was oppressed or imposed on in any way. We must assume, on the pleading, that the plaintiff knew that the lawful charge was 11s. 3d., and that, nevertheless, he voluntarily chose to pay £2 to the defendants, and now he seeks to recover the excess paid. He does not, and cannot, claim for money paid on a consideration that has wholly failed, as he has had the consideration, i.e., he has gone into the track and conducted his bookmaking operations there. The only ground on which he claims the money is that there was a breach of s. 13 of the Act of 1934, in that he was charged more than the amount permitted by s. 13 (1) . . .

[he considered the statutory provisions in more detail and noted the decision of the House of Lords in *Cutler v Wandsworth Stadium Ltd* [1949] AC 398 in which it was held that the breach of the relevant statutory provision did not give rise to a civil claim and continued]

Applying that decision to this case, it is clear that a breach of s. 13 does not give rise to an action for damages. But the point which impressed Parker J., was that this was not an action for a declaration, or for an injunction, or for damages. It was an action for money had and received, to which different considerations might apply. Reference was made to the judgment of Lord Mansfield in *Browning v Morris* 2 Cowp 790, 792 where he said: 'But, where contracts or transactions are prohibited by positive statutes, for the sake of protecting one set of men from another set of men; the one, from their situation and condition, being liable to be oppressed or imposed upon by the other; there, the parties are not in pari delicto; and in furtherance of these statutes, the person injured, after the transaction is finished and completed, may bring his action and defeat the contract.' In my judgment, those observations of Lord Mansfield apply only to cases where the statute, on its true construction, contemplates the possibility of a civil action. He said that it was 'in furtherance of the statutes' that the action for money had and received could be brought. Just as in an action for damages, so, also, in an action for money had and received, it is a question of the true interpretation of the statute whether an action lies so as to recover the overcharge. I see nothing in the Act of 1934 to authorise such an action.

I can conceive of cases where bookmakers might themselves aid and abet a breach of the statute. Some rich bookmakers might willingly pay more than the statutory amount to get a privileged position for themselves as against their poorer brethren. Clearly, such people could not recover the overpayments. Nor can the plaintiff here. The breach of s. 13, standing by itself, does not give rise to a claim for repayment.

Hodson LJ concurred.

NOTES AND QUESTIONS

1. Had the claimant's claim been allowed, what would have been the ground of restitution?

2. Would it be true to say that restitution based on class protection is arguably excessively protectionist and should not be given a wider ambit than absolutely necessary?

3. Do cases such as *Kiriri Cotton Co. Ltd v Dewani* [1960] AC 192, *Re Cavalier Insurance Co. Ltd*, below, 887 and *Hermann v Charlesworth* [1905] 2 KB 123 (see below, 601) fall within the cases discussed in this chapter or the cases discussed in Chapter 10?

8

LEGAL COMPULSION: COMPULSORY DISCHARGE OF ANOTHER'S LEGAL LIABILITY

Legal compulsion is shorthand for 'legitimate application of the legal process'. Restitution for legal compulsion is a difficult topic for three main reasons. First, the precise injustice in play is not easy to pinpoint. It would seem that the injustice is not so much the claimant's non-voluntariness as the policy of ensuring that the legal process does not compel the 'wrong' person ultimately to bear a liability. For the view (which we disagree with) that unjust enrichment has no role to play, see the extract from Hilliard (below, 554).

Secondly, legal compulsion is only an unjust factor in *three-party cases*: by definition legal compulsion is legitimate pressure as between the person exerting the pressure and the person against whom it is exerted (although where legal process is applied improperly there may be restitution for 'duress' as discussed in Chapter 6). Legal compulsion (by X) leads to injustice only where it causes the claimant (C) to discharge a legal liability to X of the defendant (D): if in that circumstance C had no legal liability to discharge but paid X to recover his (C's) goods (as in *Exall v Partridge* and *Edmunds v Wallingford*, see below, 504–7), or if C's legal liability is secondary to that of D (as in *Moule v Garrett*, *Gebhardt v Saunders*, *Brook's Wharf and Bull Wharf Ltd v Goodman Bros.*, *Owen v Tate*, and the *Niru Battery (No 2)* case, see below, 507–23) one can say that, as between C and D, the legal compulsion should more appropriately have been borne by D than C.

Thirdly, the benefit in play in this area is the discharge of another's legal liability (for cases where there was held to have been no liability discharged, see *Bonner v Tottenham and Edmonton Permanent Building Soc.*, *Re Nott and Cardiff Corp.*, *Metropolitan Police District Receiver v Croydon Corp.*, *Esso Petroleum Ltd v Hall, Russell & Co. Ltd*, below, 523–34). While that form of benefit is normally an incontrovertible benefit, particular difficulties are caused by the traditional doctrine that, other than where the debtor has requested C to intervene, it is only where C's payment has been made by legal compulsion that C's payment to X discharges C's debt to X (on this controversy see the extracts from Birks and Beatson, Friedmann, Stoljar, and Beatson: below, 538–51).

Restitution from D of the whole sum paid by C (which occurs where liability to X ought to rest entirely on D) is, in this area, often referred to as recoupment or reimbursement. The same legal principles explain (or should explain) where the law awards restitution from D of part of the sum paid by C (which occurs where C and D are liable in the same degree to X). Restitution in that situation is referred to as contribution.

General Reading

BURROWS, chapter 8; GOFF AND JONES, chapters 13–15; VIRGO, 220–242

1. C DISCHARGES D'S LIABILITY TO X IN ORDER TO RECOVER HIS (C'S) GOODS

In the following case, C's goods had been lawfully seized by X as distress for rent owed by D.

- *Exall v Partridge* (1799) 8 Term Rep 308, Court of King's Bench

The claimant had left his carriage on the defendants' premises for repair by one of the defendants (Partridge) who was a coachbuilder. The defendants were co-tenants of the premises, albeit that Partridge alone was in occupation, having been assigned the interests of his co-tenants. The rent had not been paid. The landlord, Welch, lawfully seized the claimant's carriage as distress for rent. In order to recover the carriage, the claimant paid the rent due. The claimant successfully brought an action against the defendants for money paid to their use.

Lord Kenyon ChJ: Some propositions have been stated, on the part of the plaintiff, to which I cannot assent. It has been said, that where one person is benefited by the payment of money by another, the law raises an assumpsit against the former; but that I deny: if that were so, and I owed a sum of money to a friend, and an enemy chose to pay that debt, the latter might convert himself into my debtor, nolens volens. . . . I admit that where one person is surety for another, and compellable to pay the whole debt, and he is called upon to pay, it is money paid to the use of the principal debtor, and may be recovered in an action against him for money paid, even though the surety did not pay the debt by the desire of the principal: but none of those points affect the present question. As the plaintiff put his goods on the premises, knowing the interests of the defendants, and thereby placed himself in a situation where he was liable to pay this money, without the concurrence of two of the defendants, I thought at the trial that it was money paid to the use of [Partridge] only; but on that point I have since doubted; and I rather think that the opinion I gave at the trial was not well founded.

Grose J: The question is, whether the payment made by the plaintiff, under these circumstances, were such a one from which the law will imply a promise by the three defendants to repay? I think it was. All the three defendants were originally liable to the landlord for the rent: there was an express covenant by all, from which neither of them was released. One of the defendants only being in the occupation of these premises, the plaintiff put his goods there, which the landlord distrained for rent, as he had a right to do; then, for the purpose of getting back his goods, he paid the rent to the landlord, which all the three defendants were bound to pay. The plaintiff could not have relieved himself from the distress without paying the rent: it was not therefore a voluntary, but a compulsory payment. Under these circumstances, the law implies a promise by the three defendants to repay the plaintiff; and, on this short ground, I am of opinion that the action may be maintained.

Lawrence J: One of the propositions stated by the plaintiff's counsel certainly cannot be supported, that whoever is benefited by a payment made by another, is liable to an action of assumpsit by that other; for one person cannot, by a voluntary payment, raise an assumpsit against another: but here was a distress for rent, due from the three defendants; the notice of distress expressed the rent to be due from them all; the money was paid by the plaintiff in satisfaction of a demand on all, and it was paid by compulsion; therefore I am of opinion that this action may be maintained against the three defendants. The justice of the case indeed is, that the one who must ultimately pay this money, should alone be answerable here: but as all the three defendants were liable to the landlord for the rent in the first instance, and as by this payment made by the plaintiff, all the three were released from the demand of the rent, I think that this action may be supported against all of them.

Le Blanc J: The three defendants were all by their covenant bound to see that the rent was paid; by their default in not seeing that it was paid, the plaintiff's goods were distrained for a debt due from the three defendants to Welch; by compulsion of law he was obliged to pay that debt; and, therefore, I think he has his remedy against the three persons who by law were bound to pay, and who did not pay this money.

NOTES AND QUESTIONS

1. If, after this decision, one of the two non-occupying tenants had satisfied the claimant's judgment, would he have had a claim against Partridge for money paid to Partridge's use on the basis of legal compulsion?

2. Do you agree with Grose J that the question at issue was whether there was an implied promise by the defendants to repay the claimant?

3. For a case applying the same principle as *Exall v Partridge* in respect of a mortgagee of a ship recovering from the mortgagor the wages paid to the ship's crew, so as to release the ship, see *Johnson v Royal Mail Steam Packet Co.* (1867) LR 3 CP 38. See also *Kleinwort Benson Ltd v Vaughan* [1996] CLC 620 in which the claimant paid off the defendants' debt, secured by a legal charge over a house, in a situation where the claimant had traced money stolen from it by the defendants into the house.

4. On Birks' new 'absence of basis' model, there is an *unjust* enrichment in the cases in this chapter because there is no basis for the enrichment of the defendant. This is an example of a 'non-participatory enrichment.' Birks, *Unjust Enrichment* (2nd edn, 2005), 159 said the following: 'The discharged debtor can offer no explanation at all as to why he should retain his enrichment. It is an enrichment without any explanatory basis. This is one area in which "no basis" does come close to lay usage, for the truth is that the reason why we think the defendant should reimburse or contribute is that there was no reason at all why he should reap the by-benefit'.

In the next case, C's goods had been lawfully seized and sold to pay off D's debts to X. Although C did not actually seek to recover the goods by paying off D's debts, the situation was analogous in that C's goods were used to pay off D's debts.

- *Edmunds v Wallingford* (1885) 14 QBD 811, Court of Appeal

The defendant bought an ironmongers' shop for his sons. Certain goods belonging to the sons were lawfully seized from the shop by the sheriff in execution of a judgment against the defendant by a creditor. The claimant, the trustee in bankruptcy for the sons, sought an indemnity from the defendant of the whole value of the goods sold (£1,300). Upholding Huddleston B's judgment at first instance, the Court of Appeal held, applying the principle of *Exall v Partridge*, that the claimant was entitled to recover £1,300 (albeit that judgment was entered for £1,200 as the sum the defendant had promised to pay, and the claimant was content to accept, if liability were established).

Lindley LJ (delivering the judgment of Lord Coleridge, CJ, Sir James Hannen and himself): . . . The first question is the liability incurred by the defendant to his sons by reason of the seizure of what he has deliberately asserted to be their goods for his debt. That as between the father and the sons, the goods were theirs, we consider established by the father's own statements. Speaking generally, and excluding exceptional cases, where a person's goods are lawfully seized for another's debt, the owner of the goods is entitled to redeem them and to be reimbursed by the debtor against the money paid to redeem them, and in the event of the goods being sold to satisfy the debt, the owner is entitled to recover the value of them from the debtor. . . . [As examples of this general proposition], reference may be made to the case of a person whose goods are lawfully distrained for rent due from some one else, as in *Exall v Partridge*; to the case of a surety paying the debt of his principal; to the case where the whole of a joint debt is paid by one only of the joint debtors; to the case where the joint property of a firm is seized for the separate debt of one of the partners. The right to indemnity or contribution in these cases exists, although there may be no agreement to indemnify or contribute, and although there may be, in that sense, no privity between the plaintiff and the defendant: sec *Johnson v Royal Mail Steam Packet Co.* But it is obvious that the right may be excluded by contract as well as by other circumstances. . . .

[An] exception to the general rule has been held to exist, where the owner of the goods has left them for his own convenience, where they could be lawfully seized for the debt of the person from whom he seeks indemnity: *England v Marsden*.[1] The plaintiff in that case seized the defendant's goods under a bill of sale, but did not remove them from the defendant's house. The plaintiff left them there for his own convenience, and they were afterwards distrained by the defendant's landlord. The plaintiff paid the rent distrained for, and brought an action to recover the money from the defendant. The Court, however, held that the action would not lie as the plaintiff might have removed his goods before, and could not under the circumstances be considered as having been compelled to pay the rent. This appears to us a very questionable decision. The evidence did not shew that the plaintiff's goods were left in the defendant's house against his consent; and although it is true that the plaintiff only had himself to blame for exposing his goods to seizure, we fail to see how he thereby prejudiced the defendant, or why, having paid the defendant's debt in order to redeem his own goods from lawful seizure, the plaintiff was not entitled to be reimbursed by the defendant. . . . [W]e think the decision ought not to be followed. Be the case of *England v Marsden*, however, right or wrong, it is distinguishable in its facts from the case now before us.

In order to bring the present case within the general principle alluded to above, it is necessary that the goods seized shall have been lawfully seized; and it was contended before us that the sons' goods were in this case wrongfully seized, and that the defendant, therefore, was not bound to indemnify them. But when it is said that the goods must be lawfully seized, all that is meant is that as between the owner of the goods and the person seizing them, the latter shall have been entitled to take them. It is plain that the principle has no application, except where the owner of the goods is in a position to say to the debtor that the seizure ought not to have taken place; it is because as between them the wrong goods have been seized that any question arises. Now, in this case it has been decided between the owners of the goods seized (i.e., the sons), and the sheriff seizing them, that the goods were rightfully seized; and although the defendant is not estopped by this decision, and is at liberty, if he can, to shew that the seizure was one which the sheriff was not justified in making, he has not done so. Indeed, the defendant's connection with his sons' business was such as to justify the inference that the sheriff had a right to seize the goods for the defendant's debt, and if, in truth, any mistake was made by the sheriff, the defendant had only himself to thank for it. His own conduct led to the seizure, and although he did not in fact request it to be made, he brought the seizure about, and has wholly failed to shew that the seizure was wrongful on the part of the sheriff.

The case, therefore, stands thus: goods which the defendant has admitted in writing to be his sons', have, owing to his conduct, been legally taken in execution for his debt, and the proceeds of sale have

---

1 Law Rep. 1 CP 529.

been impounded as a security for what is due from him to the execution creditors. The defendant, therefore, was liable to repay to his sons the amount realized by the sale of the goods. This liability the plaintiff, as the sons' trustee in bankruptcy, was in a position to enforce, and he has never released it or agreed so to do except upon payment of £1200. . . . The plaintiff is content to take the £1200 expressly promised to be paid instead of insisting on his right to the £1300; and Huddleston, B, has properly given the plaintiff judgment accordingly.

QUESTION

Do you agree with the Court of Appeal that *England v Marsden* was wrongly decided?

2. C DISCHARGES D'S LIABILITY TO X WHERE C AND D ARE UNDER A COMMON LIABILITY TO X BUT C'S LIABILITY IS SECONDARY

In the following case the common liability in question was on a sub-tenant and head-tenant to keep leasehold property in repair.

• *Moule v Garrett* (1872) LR 7 Exch 101, Court of Exchequer Chamber

The claimant was the tenant of certain premises. The lease contained a covenant to keep the property in repair. The claimant assigned the lease to Bartley who assigned it to the defendants. Whilst the defendants were in possession, they committed breaches of the repair covenant, in respect of which the landlord recovered damages from the claimant. The claimant successfully sought reimbursement of the damages in an action for money paid to the defendants' use.

Cockburn CJ: . . . [T]he premises which are the subject of the lease being in the possession of the defendants as ultimate assignees, they were the parties whose duty it was to perform the covenants which were to be performed upon and in respect of those premises. It was their immediate duty to keep in repair, and by their default the lessee, though he had parted with the estate, became liable to make good to the lessor the conditions of the lease. The damage therefore arises through their default, and the general proposition applicable to such a case as the present is, that where one person is compelled to pay damages by the legal default of another, he is entitled to recover from the person by whose default the damage was occasioned the sum so paid. This doctrine, as applicable to cases like the present, is well started by Mr Leake in his work on Contracts, 41: 'Where the plaintiff has been compelled by law to pay, or, being compellable by law, has paid money which the defendant was ultimately liable to pay, so that the latter obtains the benefit of the payment by the discharge of his liability; under such circumstances the defendant is held indebted to the plaintiff in the amount.'

Whether the liability is put on the ground of an implied contract, or of an obligation imposed by law, is a matter of indifference: it is such a duty as the law will enforce. The lessee has been compelled to make good an omission to repair, which has arisen entirely from the default of the defendants, and the defendants are therefore liable to reimburse him.

Mellor, Brett and **Grove JJ** concurred with **Cockburn CJ. Willes** and **Blackburn JJ** also delivered judgments in favour of the claimant.

NOTES AND QUESTIONS

1. Could the claimant have successfully sought reimbursement of the damages in an action against Bartley? Would that claim have been contractual or for restitution of an unjust enrichment?

2. Why was the claimant's liability secondary to that of the defendants?

3. For more recent examples of the application of *Moule v Garrett*, see *Becton Dickinson UK Ltd v Zwebner* [1989] QB 208 and *Re Healing Research Trustee Co. Ltd* [1992] 2 All ER 481.

4. By the Landlord and Tenant (Covenants) Act 1995, sections 3 and 5, the head-tenant is generally released from covenants in leases granted after 1995, once the lease has been assigned. Contrary to the legal position at the time of *Moule v Garrett* and prior to 1996, there is therefore generally now no common liability on a sub-tenant and head-tenant to keep leasehold property in repair. But under section 16 of the 1995 Act a head-tenant still remains liable where he or she has entered into an 'authorized guarantee agreement' to guarantee compliance with the covenants by the assignee.

In the next case, the common liability was on a tenant and a landlord to abate a nuisance.

- *Gebhardt v Saunders* [1892] 2 QB 452, Queen's Bench Division Divisional Court

The claimant, who was the tenant of a house belonging to the defendants, was served with a notice by the local sanitary authority addressed to the owner or occupier requiring the abatement of a nuisance arising from the drains. It transpired that the nuisance arose from a structural defect in the drains. Under the relevant Act (the Public Health (London) Act 1891) nuisances arising from a structural defect were the responsibility of owners, but at the time the notice was served the precise cause of the nuisance in question was not known. Having complied with the order by having the necessary work carried out, the claimant sought reimbursement of the expenses incurred from the defendants as money paid to the defendants' use, either at common law or under s. 11 of the 1891 Act. The decision at first instance to deny the claim was overturned by the Divisional Court on appeal.

Relevant provisions of the 1891 Act were as follows:

Section 4(1): 'On the receipt of any information respecting the existence of a nuisance liable to be dealt with summarily under this Act, the sanitary authority shall, if satisfied of the existence of a nuisance, serve a notice on the person by whose act, default, or sufference the nuisance arises or continues . . .'

Section 4(3)(a): 'Where the nuisance arises from any want or defect of a structural character, or where the premises are unoccupied, the notice shall be served on the owner.'

Section 4(4): 'Where a notice has been served on a person under this section, and . . . such person makes default in complying with any of the requisitions of the notice within the time specified, he shall be liable to a fine not exceeding £10 for each offence . . .'

Section 11(1): 'All reasonable costs and expenses incurred . . . in carrying the order into effect shall be deemed to be money paid for the use and at the request of the person on whom the order is made . . .'

Day J: I am of opinion that this appeal must be allowed. The action is brought by the occupier of a house to recover from the defendants, who are the owners and landlords, the costs necessarily incurred by him in abating a nuisance caused by a structural defect in the drains, and the plaintiff was nonsuited by the learned judge by reason of a defect in the service of notices under the Act. I think that that nonsuit was wrong, and that the plaintiff may recover as of right without proof of the matters relied on on behalf of the defendants. There can be no doubt that in consequence of the defective construction of the drains a serious nuisance did exist in the plaintiff's house, to which the plaintiff very properly called the attention of the sanitary authority; the officer of the authority went to the house and satisfied himself of the existence of a nuisance requiring immediate abatement. Being unable to determine at the time whether the nuisance arose from defective construction of the drains or from their mismanagement by the plaintiff, the officer took a sound view of the position; he saw that there was an accumulation of sewage in the lower part of the house dangerous to health and possibly to life, and he immediately served a notice on the premises requiring the owner or occupier (he not being then in a position to say whether the owner or the occupier might subsequently turn out to be responsible) to forthwith abate the nuisance arising from the defect in or stoppage of the drain. In that notice he does not define whether the nuisance is caused by the drain being defective or by its being stopped; but it was due to one of the two. The plaintiff had already very properly given notice of the defective state of the drain to the defendants, who however did nothing; common sense and the necessity of the case made it necessary for something to be done forthwith, and as either the plaintiff or the defendants was bound to do that something the plaintiff proceeded to do it; had he not done so he would have been liable under s. 4, sub-s. 4, of the Act of 1891 to a penalty of 10*l.* He then brings this action to recover the expenses from the defendants.

The difficulty in the present case is no greater than that which one ordinarily expects to find in the construction of a modern statute. The gist of the enactment is this: where there is a nuisance injurious to life or health measures are to be taken to secure its speedy abatement; the expenses of abating the nuisance are cast on the person who caused it by his acts or defaults. This is a reasonable scheme; is it carried out by the different sections of the statute? In my opinion, whatever criticisms may be passed upon their wording, the sections do contain such a provision. By s. 4, sub-s. 1, a notice is to be served on the occupier or owner, and, by sub-s. 4, disobedience to such notice entails a fine of 10*l.* a day. It is urged on behalf of the defendants that if the occupier does the work which the owner ought to have done, and the owner has not been served at his place of abode with a notice under sub-s. 3 requiring him to abate the nuisance, the occupier must do it at his own cost. I have rarely heard a proposition so unreasonable. The gist of s. 11 is that, if the occupier does the work in order to abate a nuisance for which the owner is responsible, he may recover from the latter the expenses incurred in carrying in doing it. It is true that the section provides in terms only for the expenses incurred in carrying 'the order' into effect, and that one would have expected it to have said 'the notice or the order'; but the word 'order' must clearly be taken to include 'notice,' for disobedience to the notice entails a penalty; the section, therefore, applies to the expenses incurred in carrying out the notice or order in the sense of doing the work. If two people are required to do certain work under a penalty in case of disobedience, and one does the work, and it turns out afterwards that the other ought to have done it, the expenses are properly money paid at the request of the person who was primarily liable, but who neglected to do the work. There are no merits in this defence; and as the technical points upon which the defence was based have failed, judgment must be entered for the plaintiff.

Charles J: . . . The first question is, Was the plaintiff legally compellable to do this work? I think he was. It seems that there was in the plaintiff's house a drainage defect which, being latent, was one of which the sanitary authority may reasonably be held to be unable to find the author; they were, therefore, warranted in serving notice under s. 4, sub-s. 1, on the occupier or owner to abate the nuisance. Such a notice was served upon the plaintiff's premises, requiring the abatement of the nuisance forthwith. Did that notice impose upon the plaintiff the legal liability to obey it? Having regard to the provisions of sub-s. 4, for the imposition of a penalty for default in compliance, I am clearly of opinion that it did. It is contended, however, that the plaintiff was not legally liable to do the work, because in the result it turned out that the defects were structural. Now, there is no doubt that under the proviso in s. 4, sub-s. 3, where the defects are structural, notice is to be served on the owner; it turned out in the present case that they were structural: hence the defendants' contention. It is impossible, having regard to the language of sub-s. 1, to assent to this argument; looking at that sub-section it seems clear that, if on inspection the cause of the nuisance cannot be found, it is right to serve the notice on the occupier. This first question must, therefore, be answered in the affirmative.

The second question is whether the defendants were legally compellable to do the work. The jury found that the nuisance was caused by a structural defect; the moment that that defect was discovered the defendants were the proper persons to do the work, and were bound to do it. I think, therefore, that it having been proved that a nuisance existed, and that it arose from a structural defect in the drain, the defendants were legally compellable to set it right. In my opinion the ordinary principle of law is applicable to this case apart from the statute, the principle applicable to cases where one man has been legally compelled to expend money on what another man ought to have done, and, without having recourse to s. 11, the plaintiff is entitled to recover from the defendants as having been legally compelled to incur expense in abating a nuisance which the defendants themselves ought to have abated. As to the construction of s. 11, I agree with my brother Day. It is a difficult section to construe; but I think that a reasonable construction to place upon it is that where no order for the abatement of a nuisance is actually made, but the nuisance is abated in obedience to a notice from the sanitary authority, the expenses of abatement must be borne by the person causing the nuisance. Beyond all doubt the owners are here the persons responsible for the existence of this nuisance, and ought to pay for its abatement. It is contended that the section only applies where a nuisance order has been obtained; but I feel no difficulty in reading it otherwise so as to apply it to the expenses of serving a notice and carrying the notice into effect. In a sense, indeed, the notice is an order, for it is a requirement that certain things shall be done. I think, therefore, that both apart from and in accordance with s. 11, the plaintiff has proved his case.

NOTES AND QUESTIONS

1. There has been some debate whether, on a true reading of the statute, the tenant was liable to a fine for not abating the nuisance, given that it arose from a structural defect (see, e.g., Birks, *An Introduction to the Law of Restitution* (rvsd edn 1989) 191; *Hackett v Smith* [1917] 2 IR 508, 528–9, *per* Sir James Campbell CJ). If legal compulsion was not a valid unjust factor, alternative unjust factors that could have grounded restitution were mistake of fact and necessity.

2. In the light of the controversy (see below, 450–63) as to whether payment of another's *debt* discharges that debt automatically (i.e. without the debtor's consent), *Gebhardt v Saunders* is a useful illustration of the discharge of a liability that does not comprise a debt. Clearly the defendants' liability was automatically discharged (i.e. the nuisance was abated) and there could be no question of that discharge turning on whether the act was done under legal compulsion or not.

In the case that follows the common liability was on the importers of goods, and the storers of the goods, to pay import duties.

- ### *Brook's Wharf and Bull Wharf Ltd v Goodman Brothers*
  [1937] 1 KB 534, Court of Appeal

The defendants were furriers who had imported from Russia squirrel skins which they had stored in the claimants' bonded warehouse. Without any negligence by the claimants, the skins were stolen from the warehouse. The defendants were liable to pay import duties on the skins but the customs, as they were statutorily entitled to do (under the Customs' Duties Consolidation Act 1876, section 85) in respect of goods removed from the warehouse, demanded payment of the import duties on the skins (£823 17s 10d) from the claimants. The claimants paid, and then successfully sought restitution from the defendants in a claim for money paid to the defendants' use.

Lord Wright MR: . . . [T]he plaintiffs claim that they are entitled to recover from the defendants the amount which they have paid to the Customs in respect of duties due on the defendants' goods. They make their claim as for money paid to the defendants' use on the principle stated in Leake on Contracts. The passage in question is quoted in the Exchequer Chamber by Cockburn CJ in *Moule v Garrett*, and is in these terms: 'Where the plaintiff has been compelled by law to pay, or, being compellable by law, has paid money which the defendant was ultimately liable to pay, so that the latter obtains the benefit of the payment by the discharge of his liability; under such circumstances the defendant is held indebted to the plaintiff in the amount.' This passage remains, with a slight verbal alteration, in the eighth edition of Leake on Contracts at 46.

The principle has been applied in a great variety of circumstances. Its application does not depend on privity of contract. Thus in *Moule v Garrett*, which I have just cited, it was held that the original lessee who had been compelled to pay for breach of a repairing covenant was entitled to recover the amount he had so paid from a subsequent assignee of the lease, notwithstanding that there had been intermediate assignees. In that case the liability of the lessee depended on the terms of his covenant, but the breach of covenant was due to the default of the assignee, and the payment by the lessee under legal compulsion relieved the assignee of his liability.

. . . The essence of the rule is that there is a liability for the same debt resting on the plaintiff and the defendant and the plaintiff has been legally compelled to pay, but the defendant gets the benefit of the payment, because his debt is discharged either entirely or pro tanto, whereas the defendant is primarily liable to pay as between himself and the plaintiff. The case is analogous to that of a payment by a surety which has the effect of discharging the principal's debt and which, therefore, gives a right of indemnity against the principal.

I need not refer to more than two of the numerous cases in which this principle has been applied. In *Pownal v Ferrand*,[1] an endorser of a bill had been compelled on default by the acceptor to make a payment on account to the holder. He used the acceptor for the money so paid as money paid to his use. The money so paid was a part only of the amount of the bill. He was held entitled to recover. Lord Tenterden CJ said:[2] 'I am of opinion that he is entitled to recover upon the general principle, that one man, who is compelled to pay money which another is bound by law to pay, is entitled to be reimbursed by the latter.' As an instance of money payable under a statute I may refer to *Dawson v Linton*,[3] where a tax was due from the landlord, but there was power to enforce payment by distress, if necessary, from the tenant. Abbott CJ said: 'It is clear that this tax must ultimately fall on the landlord, and that the plaintiff has paid his money in discharge of it; he has therefore a right to call upon the landlord to repay it to him.'

These statements of the principle do not put the obligation on any ground of implied contract or of constructive or notional contract. The obligation is imposed by the Court simply under the circumstances of the case and on what the Court decides is just and reasonable, having regard to the relationship of the parties. It is a debt or obligation constituted by the act of the law, apart from any consent or intention of the parties or any privity of contract.

It is true that in the present case there was a contract of bailment between the plaintiffs and the defendants, but there is no suggestion that the obligation in question had ever been contemplated as between them or that they had ever thought about it. The Court cannot say what they would have agreed if they had considered the matter when the goods were warehoused. All the court can say is what they ought as just and reasonable men to have decided as between themselves. The defendants would be unjustly benefited at the cost of the plaintiffs if the latter, who had received no extra

---

1 6 B & C 439.   2 6 B & C 443.   3 (1822) 5 B & Ald 521, 523.

consideration and made no express bargain, should be left out of pocket by having to discharge what was the defendants' debt.

I agree with the learned judge in holding that this principle applies to the present case. As I have explained, the duties were due from the importer. There is nothing in the machinery of the Customs Act which had removed this liability from him when the warehousemen paid the duties, as they were compelled to do under s. 85. The payment relieved the importer of his obligation. The plaintiffs were no doubt liable to pay the Customs, but, as between themselves and the defendants, the primary liability rested on the defendants. The liability of the plaintiffs as warehousemen was analogous to that of a surety. It was imposed in order to facilitate the collection of duties in a case like the present, where there might always be a question as to who stood in the position of importer. The defendants as actual importers have obtained the benefit of the payment made by the plaintiffs and they are thus discharged from the duties which otherwise would have been payable by them. It may also be noted that the goods which were stolen were the defendants' goods and the property remained in them after the theft. If the goods had been recovered, the defendants could have claimed them as their own and would have been free to apply them for home use without further payment of duty.

. . .

I agree with the learned judge that the claim for the amount of the duties succeeds. I think that the judgment of learned judge should be affirmed and the appeal as a whole dismissed with costs.

Romer LJ and **Macnaghten J** concurred.

The controversial decision in the following case deals with whether a 'voluntary surety' (i.e. one who has not been requested to act as a surety by the primary debtor) is entitled to restitution from the primary debtor for discharge of the primary debt.

• *Owen v Tate* [1976] QB 402, Court of Appeal

The defendants had taken out a loan of £350 from Lloyds Bank which was secured by a mortgage on the property of a Miss Lightfoot, the title deeds of that property being surrendered to the bank. Miss Lightfoot wanted to be released from that mortgage and to recover her title deeds. The claimant offered to help her and did so by guaranteeing to the bank, without consultation with the defendants, the repayment of the defendants' loan of £350 in consideration of the bank releasing the mortgage. Over a year later the bank used £350, which the claimant had deposited with the bank in support of the guarantee, to repay the defendants' debt. The claimant subsequently sought an indemnity from the defendants for the debt paid. The Court of Appeal, upholding the decision in the county court, refused the claim.

Scarman LJ: . . . Mr Unwin, who argued the case for the plaintiff, the appellant in this court, makes this submission. He says that one who without being asked to do so guarantees payment of another's debt is entitled upon paying the debt to be indemnified, and he submits that this is a rule that brooks of no exceptions. He gives as the reason for the rule that, at the time when the obligation to pay arises, that is to say, when the guarantor is called by the creditor to pay the debt, he, the guarantor, is compelled by law to make the payment sought by the creditor. He relies on a dictum of Greene LJ in *In re A Debtor* [1937] Ch 156, 166:

> 'A question may arise as to the application of the subsection [that is the subsection being considered in that case] . . . where a guarantee is given without any antecedent request on the part of the debtor. That case is merely one example of a number of cases where the law raises an obligation to indemnify irrespective of any actual antecedent contractual relationship between the parties.'

Mr Stephenson, who has argued the case for the defendants, who are the respondents to this appeal, says that there is no such general rule as that for which Mr Unwin contends. He takes his stand upon the general rule that a volunteer cannot claim repayment of that which he has purely voluntarily paid, or in respect of which he has purely voluntarily assumed the obligation to pay.

. . .

. . . As I understand the law, there are two general rules, both of them well known. The first is conveniently set out in *Chitty on Contracts*, 23rd edn (1968), vol. 1, para. 1736, on which Mr Stephenson, for the defendants, naturally strongly relied. There it is said: 'If the payment is regarded by the law as voluntary, it cannot be recovered.' The editors then quote a passage from the judgment of Swinfen Eady J in *In re National Motor Mail-Coach Co. Ltd* [1908] 2 Ch 515, 520. I quote from that judgment one sentence. The judge said: 'If A voluntarily pays B's debt, B is under no obligation to repay A.' That is the first of the two general rules.

The second general rule which calls for consideration in this appeal was stated authoritatively by Lord Wright MR in *Brook's Wharf and Bull Wharf Ltd v Goodman Brothers* [1937] 1 KB 534. The rule applied in that case was formulated by Lord Tenterden CJ in an earlier case [*Pownal v Ferrand* (1827) 6 B & C 439] in language which received the express approval of Lord Wright MR. I take Lord Tenterden's words from 545 of the reports in the *Brook's Wharf* case. Lord Tenterden CJ said, at 443:

'. . . one man, who is compelled to pay money which another is bound by law to pay, is entitled to be reimbursed by the latter.'

This appeal requires us to consider the interaction of the two rules in the particular circumstances of this case. Before turning to those circumstances, I would add that neither rule can be treated as one to which there can conceivably be no exception. The first rule, that a volunteer who makes a payment on behalf of another cannot obtain repayment, does appear to me to have been one to which over the centuries the common law recognised exceptions. The exceptions have been constructed by the judges through a readiness to imply from the circumstances of the case a request or an authority to make the payment. Good illustrations of that readiness are to be found in the books. I would refer only to a decision of Lord Kenyon CJ in *Exall v Partridge* (1799) 8 Term. Rep. 308. There is another illustration in the comment of Lindley LJ in *Edmunds v Wallingford* (1885) 14 QBD 811 on *England v Marsden* (1866) LR 1 CP 529. I need not at this stage do more than just refer to those two cases, in each of which one sees the point being considered whether in the circumstances of the case the law could imply a request, consent or some sort of authority for the payment made.

When one turns to the second general rule, namely, the rule that where a person is compelled by law to make a payment for which another is primarily liable he is entitled to be indemnified, notwithstanding the lack of any request or consent, one again finds that the law recognises exceptions. This rule has been subjected to very careful treatment in *Goff and Jones, The Law of Restitution* (1966), 207. The authors say, after stating the rule in general terms:

'To succeed in his claim, however, the plaintiff must satisfy certain conditions. He must show (1) that he has been compelled by law to make the payment; (2) that he did not officiously expose himself to the liability to make the payment; (3) that his payment discharged a *liability* of the defendant; and (4) that both he and the defendant were subject to a common demand by a third party, for which, as between the plaintiff and the defendant, the latter was primarily responsible.'

In the present case we are very much concerned with the first two of those conditions: whether the plaintiff had been compelled by law to make the payment, and whether he did or did not officiously expose himself to the liability to make the payment.

The editors, at 214, discuss the exceptions to the general rule which fall under their second condition, namely, the officious assumption of a liability to make the payment. If they are right—as I think they are, and as I think the cases show that they are—then there are exceptions to the second general rule; that is to say, the law does recognise that there may be exceptions, even when a man is legally liable to pay the debt of another, to the general rule that he has a right to an indemnity.

I think that the case law supporting the existence of such exceptions is really epitomised in the *Brook's Wharf* case to which I have already referred. Lord Wright MR, having quoted the passage from Lord Tenterden CJ's judgment that I have already quoted, *Pownal v Ferrand*, explains the principle of the matter in these words [1937] 1 KB 534, 545:

'These statements of the principle do not put the obligation on any ground of implied contract or of constructive or notional contract. The obligation is imposed by the court simply under the circumstances of the case and on what the court decides is just and reasonable, having regard to the relationship of the parties. It is a debt or obligation constituted by the act of the law, apart from any consent or intention of the parties or any privity of contract.'

The breadth of those words is, in my judgment, important. 'The obligation is imposed ... simply under the circumstances of the case and on what the court decides is just and reasonable, ...' That means clearly that circumstances alter cases. One may have a general rule such as Lord Wright MR had just previously stated, but that general rule derives from the principle of what is just and reasonable in all the circumstances of the case.

We are, therefore, in this appeal faced with two recognised and well-established general rules, each of which admits of exceptions. It is not necessary, therefore, in my judgment, to enter into the minutiae of factual analysis that Mr Unwin for the plaintiff invited us to undertake. In particular, he invited this court to answer the question raised obiter by Greene LJ in *In re A Debtor*, the question being: at what stage in a transaction of guarantee does the guarantor become under an obligation to make the payment? The broad analysis of a guarantor situation suffices, and it is this: if, as in this case, there is no antecedent request, no consideration or consensual basis for the assumption of the obligation of a guarantor, he who assumes that obligation is a volunteer. That, of course, is not the end of the transaction. The time comes, or may come, and in this case did come, when the guarantor is called upon by the creditor to honour his guarante. At that moment undoubtedly the guarantor, having entered into his guarantee, is under an obligation by law, or, in the words of the old cases, 'is compelled by law' to make the payment.

Mr Unwin invited this court to look exclusively at the situation as it existed when, in December 1970 or thereabouts, the plaintiff was called upon to pay. At that moment the plaintiff was undoubtedly compelled by law to make payment. Mr Stephenson invited us to look at the antecedent transaction and at the circumstances in which the plaintiff assumed the obligation of a guarantor. Of course, at that moment the plaintiff was, on the judge's findings, a pure volunteer.

For myself, I think the reconciliation (if that is what is needed) of the two general rules is easily achieved. I doubt whether it is necessary to consider in any case, and certainly I do not think it necessary to consider in this case, at what moment the volunteer guarantor becomes compellable at law to make the payment on behalf of the principal debtor. A right of indemnity is a right of restitution. It can arise, as the cases reveal, notwithstanding the absence of any consensual basis. For instance, in *Moule v Garrett* (1872) LR 7 Ex. 101 an original lessee, who was of course in privity of contract with his lessor, was compelled to pay for breach of a repairing covenant by a subsequent assignee. He was held to be entitled to an indemnity notwithstanding the absence of any privity of contract between him and the subsequent assignee.

In the two cases to which I have already referred, *Exall v Partridge*, and *England v Marsden*, the courts were faced with the owner of goods who had deposited them on the land of another, and that other had failed to pay either rates or rent, with the result that a distraint was levied, and the owner in order to release his goods paid their value to the distrainer. In *Exall v Partridge* Lord Kenyon CJ was at pains to discover in the circumstances an implied request or authority from the mere fact that the goods were on the land with the consent of the occupier. In *England v Marsden* no such consent was spelt out by implication by the court. But in *Edmunds v Wallingford*, Lindley LJ said it should have been. We can, therefore, take that class of case as an illustration of where the law will grant a right of indemnity notwithstanding the absence really of any consensual basis. In the *Brook's Wharf* case a warehouseman who paid import duties for which his customer—the owner of the goods—was primarily liable, and did so because of an obligation imposed by statute and without any prior request from the owner of the goods, was also held to be entitled to an indemnity.

These cases, to my mind, amply support the proposition that a broad approach is needed to the question whether in circumstances such as these a right of indemnity arises, and that broad approach requires the court to look at all the circumstances of the case. It follows that the way in which the obligation came to be assumed is a relevant circumstance. If, for instance, the plaintiff has conferred a benefit upon the defendant behind his back in circumstances in which the beneficiary has no option but to accept the benefit, it is highly likely that the courts will say that there is no right of indemnity or reimbursement. But (to take the other extreme) if the plaintiff has made a payment in a situation not of his own choosing, but where the law imposes an obligation upon him to make the payment on behalf of the principal debtor, then clearly the right of indemnity does arise. Not every case will be so clear-cut: the fundamental question is whether in the circumstances it was reasonably necessary in the interests of the volunteer or the person for whom the payment was made, or both, that the payment would be made—whether in the circumstances it was 'just and reasonable' that a right of reimbursement should arise.

I think now one can see the importance to this case of Greene LJ's dictum upon which Mr Unwin so strongly relied. In this case it matters not when the obligation to make the payment arose. What is important to Mr Unwin's case is that the dictum recognises that, even when an obligation is voluntarily assumed, the volunteer may be entitled at law to a right of indemnity.

Adopting this broad approach, I now come to consider in more detail than I have yet done the two phases of the transaction of guarantee which appear to me to be of critical importance. The first phase consists of the circumstances in which the plaintiff entered into the guarantee; the second phase consists of the circumstances in which the plaintiff made the payment.

It is enough to refer to the judge's findings of fact to know that the plaintiff assumed the obligation of a guarantor behind the back of the defendants, against their will, and despite their protest. At that moment he was interested, as the judge has found, not to confer a benefit upon the defendants; he was interested to confer a benefit upon Miss Lightfoot. Using the language of the old common law, I would say that the plaintiff was as absolute a volunteer as one could conceivably imagine anyone to be when assuming an obligation for the debt of another.

What of the second phase? Mr Unwin, rightly I think, relied strongly on two letters; and Mr Stephenson, also rightly, I think, invited us to consider a third. I now turn to those letters. The first letter on which Mr Unwin relied was a letter of July 1, 1970, addressed by the defendants' solicitors to the bank, who at the time held not only the plaintiff's signed guarantee, but the deposit of £350. Mr Unwin invited the court to read that letter as one in which the defendants were pressing the bank to clear their overdraft by recourse to the money deposited by the plaintiff: and there is no doubt that that is exactly what the defendants at that moment were doing. On November 10 they once more invited the bank to clear their overdraft by recourse to the plaintiff. Mr Unwin submits that if one looks at those two letters, and at the whole history of the case, one reaches this situation: that by the time those letters were written the defendants were well aware, although they had not known it at first, that the plaintiff had guaranteed their account up to the sum of £350 and had deposited this sum with the bank. The defendants' case, of course, is that this was an uncovenanted benefit, if benefit it was, and the fact that the plaintiff had conferred this benefit imposed upon them no duty to indemnify him when he made the payment. But, says Mr Unwin, if that is their position, they had a perfectly good opportunity in 1970 of telling the bank that on no account was it to have recourse to the plaintiff; that the plaintiff had interfered without their consent in their affairs, and that they proposed to deal with the matter of their overdraft without the support of the plaintiff's guarantee. No doubt had they either paid off the overdraft or made some suitable arrangements for securing it, the bank would not have had recourse to the plaintiff. But they chose at that moment to encourage the bank to have recourse to the plaintiff.

Mr Unwin has, as one might expect, put his point in a number of different verbal ways—authority, ratification, adoption—all terms really borrowed from different transactions and different legal situations. But he is entitled to make the point under the general principle to which I have referred; he is entitled to rely on the circumstances of payment as part of the total circumstances of the case and to use them to support an argument that it would in all the circumstances be just and reasonable for the plaintiff to have his right of indemnity. But these letters have to be looked at in all the circumstances; and the circumstances, of course, include the earlier history. We learn from the third letter which was introduced before us by Mr Stephenson, and to which I need not refer in terms, something of the earlier history. When the defendants learnt that the bank were proposing to release Miss Lightfoot's deeds because they had accepted a guarantee and a cash deposit, the defendants strongly objected. The bank, no doubt quite properly, did not tell the defendants that the guarantor was the plaintiff—who was of course, a stranger to the Lightfoot/Tate transaction. When the Tates protested strongly the bank replied that they were, as no doubt they were, entitled to disregard the protest, and were going to release, as in fact they did release, to Miss Lightfoot the deeds and rely upon the guarantee and deposit. At the time there was nothing to suggest to the defendants who the guarantor was, or that he was a stranger to the previous transaction. That being the case, must one read the subsequent letters to the bank to which I have referred as an adoption by the defendants of a benefit conferred upon them by the plaintiff? They never wished to lose the security of Miss Lightfoot's deeds. They lost it through circumstances outside their control and notwith-standing their protest. When the bank decided to call in the debt the defendants no longer had the security for the overdraft which was acceptable to them: they had to put up with a security which without their consent or authority had been substituted by the plaintiff for that which was, or had been, acceptable to them and agreed by them. I do not criticise the defendants, nor do I think they can be reasonably criticised, for making the best of the situation in which they then found themselves, a situation which they did not desire, and one which I doubt ever appeared to them as beneficial.

Looking, therefore, at the circumstances as a whole, and giving weight to both phases of the transaction, I come to the conclusion that the plaintiff has failed to make out a case that it would be just and reasonable in the circumstances to grant him a right to reimbursement. Initially he was a volunteer; he has, as I understand the findings of fact of the judge and as I read the documents in the case, established no facts, either initially when he assumed the obligation, or later when he was called upon to make the payment, such as to show that it was just and reasonable that he should have a right of indemnity. I think, therefore, that on the facts as found this appeal fails.

In my judgment, the true principle of the matter can be stated very shortly, without reference to volunteers or to the compulsions of the law, and I state it as follows. If without an antecedent request a person assumes an obligation or makes a payment for the benefit of another, the law will, as a general rule, refuse him a right of indemnity. But if he can show that in the particular circumstances of the case there was some necessity for the obligation to be assumed, then the law will grant him a right of reimbursement if in all the circumstances it is just and reasonable to do so. In the present case the evidence is that the plaintiff acted not only behind the backs of the defendants initially, but in the interests of another, and despite their protest. When the moment came for him to honour the obliga-tion thus assumed, the defendants are not to be criticised, in my judgment, for having accepted the benefit of a transaction which they neither wanted nor sought.

I therefore think the county court judge was right in the conclusion that he reached, and I would dismiss the appeal.

Stephenson LJ: I agree with the judgment of Scarman LJ. On March 19, 1969, the plaintiff guaranteed the defendants' overdraft with Lloyds Bank, Sunderland, up to £350 and made £350 available to the bank. He was not asked to do that by the defendants. He was asked to do it by Miss Lightfoot, and did it to oblige her and to enable her to recover title deeds which she had deposited with the bank when charging certain property on February 26, 1965, to secure a loan by the bank to the defendants up to £500. The defendants did not know of the plaintiff's guarantee and deposit of £350 with the bank until later. The correspondence shows that on March 20, 1969, their solicitors were told that someone had given a guarantee supported by cash, and by July 1, 1970, they heard that that someone was the plaintiff. They preferred Miss Lightfoot's legal charge and deposit of deeds to the plaintiff's guarantee and deposit of cash; but on getting the latter the bank felt bound to Miss Lightfoot to release her deeds, and the defendants' solicitors asked the bank on July 1, 1970, and again on November 10, 1970, in the letters to which Scarman LJ has referred, to clear the defendants' overdraft by recourse to the plaintiff's deposit.

On those facts I am driven to the conclusion that the plaintiff has not got a guarantor's ordinary right to be indemnified by the principal debtor, the defendants, against his liability to pay their debt. He voluntarily took upon himself the liability to pay their debt to the bank without any previous request from them, express or implied. He cannot, therefore, recover what he has paid: *In re National Motor Mail-Coach Co. Ltd* [1908] 2 Ch 515, 520, 523. He could have recovered if he had already been compellable by law to pay: *Moule v Garrett*, LR 7 Ex. 101, 104 and *Brook's Wharf and Bull Wharf Ltd v Goodman Brothers* [1937] 1 KB 534. Nor can he recover because his apparently generous act—whether or not it is correctly described or unfairly denigrated as 'officious'—has enabled the creditor to discharge the debt at the request of the principal debtor. The subsequent request to the creditor cannot give rise to any antecedent request to the guarantor.

There may be cases where a guarantee given without any antecedent request by the debtor gives rise in law to an obligation by the debtor to repay the guarantor. Greene LJ in *In re A Debtor* [1937] Ch 156, 166 and Pearson J in *Anson v Anson* [1953] 1 QB 636, 642–3 clearly thought so. But I wish that they had indicated what those cases were. Perhaps they were cases of necessity as indicated by *Goff and Jones, The Law of Restitution* (1966), 214.

There may be cases where it is obviously unjust that the debtor should be enriched by accepting the benefit, though unasked and even unneeded, of a guarantor's payment of his debt without indemnifying his benefactor, and the court may be able to do justice by compelling the debtor to make restitution to the guarantor. I shall imitate the reticence of Greene LJ and Pearson J and give no instances. But I cannot see in the circumstances of loan and guarantee as far as they emerged at this trial any sufficient reason for imposing that obligation to indemnify on this debtor in favour of this guarantor.

I agree with the statement in *Cheshire and Fifoot's Law of Contract*, 8th edn (1972), 632:

> 'At common law . . . the mere volunteer, officious or benevolent, has no right of action Only if the plaintiff has paid money under constraint is he entitled to sue the defendant for restitution. The nature of the constraint varies with the circumstances.'

The plaintiff was not under such constraint as may be one of the ways of creating a right which it is just and reasonable that a guarantor should have, as a general rule, to be indemnified by the debtor whose debt he has discharged.

I therefore reject Mr Unwin's admirable argument for the plaintiff; I would uphold the judge's judgment, and I agree that the appeal should be dismissed.

Ormrod LJ: I agree, and I have only two observations to add. It seems to me that the crucial question in this area of the law is whether the plaintiff is truly a volunteer in the proper sense of the word, or whether he has been compelled to make the payments. I think the two rules car be reconciled quite easily with one another on that footing.

The second observation that I would make is this. This case demonstrates clearly, in my view, the wisdom of the common law approach to the volunteer, which may be cautious, and perhaps unkind, if not cynical, because looked at superficially this case could be said to be one in which the defendants had acquired a considerable benefit from the acts of the plaintiff and had given nothing in return. But a glance through the correspondence indicates that the transaction in this case is only a part of a much more complex series of transactions which have been going on between various people for some years. Speaking for myself, on the material which was before the county court judge—and I do not criticise that there was not more material—I find it quite impossible to sort out the rights and wrongs in this case, and certainly quite impossible to say whether or not the defendants in fact received a benefit by the plaintiff undertaking an obligation of guarantor which had previously been undertaken by Miss Lightfoot. It seems to me it is possible that the defendants' position was worsened, to use a general word, by the intrusion of the plaintiff rather than helped, and consequently I think it right to take a cautious view towards volunteers in the sense that perhaps the old proverb about 'Greeks bearing gifts' may be applicable.

The only other point I would make is that, for my part, I would prefer to reserve any opinion about guarantors who enter into guarantees without the request of the principal debtor until a specific case comes forward for consideration, because I find it difficult to imagine the circumstances which the Lords Justices had in mind in making the observations which have been referred to. I agree that the appeal should be dismissed.

NOTES AND QUESTIONS

1. Does this decision lay down that a 'voluntary surety' is never entitled to restitution from the primary debtor for discharge of the primary debt? If not, in what circumstances would such a claim succeed?

2. Can this decision be reconciled with *Moule v Garrett* (above, 507)?

3. Was the controversy in *Owen v Tate* one that went to the unjust factor or to the defendants' enrichment?

4. Section 5 of the Mercantile Law Amendment Act 1856 reads as follows:

> **5 Surety who discharges the liability to be entitled to assignment of all securities held by the creditor, and to stand in the place of the creditor**
>
> Every person who, being surety for the debt or duty of another, or being liable with another for any debt or duty, shall pay such debt or perform such duty, shall be entitled to have assigned to him, or to a trustee for him, every judgment, specialty, or other security which shall be held by the creditor in respect of such debt or duty, whether such judgment, specialty, or other security shall or shall not be deemed at law to have been satisfied by the payment of the debt or performance of the duty, and such person shall be entitled to stand in the place of the creditor, and to use all the remedies, and, if need be, and upon a proper indemnity, to use the name of the creditor, in any action or other proceeding, at law or in equity, in order to obtain from the principal debtor, or any co-surety, co-contractor, or co-debtor, as the case may be, indemnification for the advances made and loss sustained by the person who shall have so paid such debt or performed such duty, and such payment or performance so made by such surety shall not be pleadable in bar of any such action or other proceeding by him: Provided always, that no co-surety, co-contractor, or co-debtor shall be entitled to recover from any other co-surety, co-contractor, or co-debtor, by the means aforesaid, more than the just proportion to which, as between those parties themselves, such last-mentioned person shall be justly liable.

Does this provision mean that *Owen v Tate* was wrongly decided in that the claimant should have been held subrogated (by reviving subrogation: see above, 194, note 2) to the bank's former rights against the defendants?

5. For cases on section 5 of the Mercantile Law Amendment Act 1856, see, for example, *Re Parker* [1894] 3 Ch 400; *Re Lamplugh Iron Ore Co. Ltd* [1927] 1 Ch 308. As is made clear by section 5,

the surety is entitled to take over the creditor's securities: in other words, the reviving subrogation is proprietary as well as personal. For discussion of proprietary restitution through reviving subrogation, see below, 726–7.

6. *Owen v Tate* was distinguished, but its reasoning applied, in *The Zuhal K* [1987] 1 Lloyd's Rep 151, noted by P. Watts [1989] *LMCLQ* 7.

7. For further discussion of *Owen v Tate*, see the extract from Birks and Beatson, below, 538.

• *Niru Battery Manufacturing Co. v Milestone Trading Ltd (No 2)*
[2004] EWCA Civ 487, [2004] 2 Lloyd's Rep 319, Court of Appeal

The main facts of the first *Niru* case are set out below, 786: CAI was held liable to Niru Battery (and to Bank Sepah Iran) to make restitution of its unjust enrichment and change of position was held not to be a defence. In that first case, SGS, which had negligently drawn up the inspection certificate, was also held liable to Niru (in the tort of negligence). Although both CAI and SGS were therefore held liable to Niru, Niru had proceeded to satisfaction of judgment solely against SGS. In this second case, SGS now sought restitution from CAI of what it had paid Niru to satisfy judgment. This claim succeeded in the Court of Appeal on the basis of subrogation, recoupment and 100 per cent contribution.

Clarke LJ: . . .

SUBROGATION

[22] Miss Andrews' submissions [on behalf of SGS] both before the judge and before us may be summarised in this way. Having satisfied the judgment, SGS was entitled to be subrogated to Niru's rights against CAI (except in so far as the judgment related to costs) and was thus entitled to obtain a full indemnity in respect of the sum it had paid. SGS had been compelled by law to compensate Niru in full; by doing so it conferred a benefit on CAI by relieving it from any obligation to pay Niru; CAI was initially unjustly enriched at the expense of Niru and was now unjustly enriched at the expense of SGS; accordingly, SGS should be granted the remedy of subrogation in order to prevent that unjust enrichment.

[23] As the judge observed ([2003] 2 All ER (Comm) 365 at [28]) this argument depends, at least in part, on the proposition that CAI continued to be unjustly enriched as a result of receiving the funds transferred to it by Bank Sepah. Mr Bloch [for CAI] resisted the submission on several bases but the judge ultimately accepted Miss Andrews' submissions after considering a number of authorities, notably *Banque Financière de la Cité v Parc (Battersea) Ltd* [1998] 1 All ER 737, [1999] 1 AC 221.

[24] He expressed his conclusions in this way at [54]:

'If SGS were denied relief in the present case CAI would in my view be unjustly enriched at its expense, CAI was unjustly enriched by the receipt of the money from Bank Sepah and as a result became liable to restore it, CAI did not cease to be liable when it parted with the money: on the contrary, it remained liable because it had received a benefit which it was bound to restore. That liability merged in the judgment and came to an end only when, and by reason of the fact that, the judgment was satisfied in full by SGS. SGS was not responsible for CAI's decision to part with the money: that was the result of a combination of Mr Mahdavi's insistence that the bank follow his instructions and its own failure to act in good faith. CAI has been relieved of liability at the expense of SGS and as a party liable to make restitution on the grounds of unjust enrichment I do not think that in relation to SGS it can be treated as if it did not receive the benefit on which its liability was based, any more than it could in relation to Niru.'

[25] That reasoning seems to me to be compelling and, for my part, absent any authority to the contrary, I would follow it. Moreover, I agree with the view expressed by the judge at [55] that the point can be tested by reference to the position which would have arisen if CAI had retained the money which it had received from Bank Sepah instead of paying it away in accordance with Mr Mahdavi's instructions.

. . .

[49] . . . Mr Bloch relies upon the judge's observation that it may be that in a broad sense SGS and CAI were equally to blame as being inconsistent with the conclusion that CAI should bear 100 per cent of the loss. However, as I read the judgment as a whole, the judge was saying that when all the circumstances are taken into account, a solution which left CAI bearing the whole of the loss was a just result. In any event, I have reached the conclusion that that is indeed the just solution.

[50] It seems to me that, whether by the route of subrogation, recoupment or the operation of the 1978 Act (assuming it applies) the just result is that CAI should bear the whole of the loss. This too can be tested by considering the position if CAI still retained the moneys. In that case, I do not think that there can be any doubt that the just result would be that the whole of the sum paid should be repaid either to Niru or, in circumstances in which SGS had discharged its liability under the judgment, to SGS. To my mind the position is no different in circumstances where CAI has paid the moneys away otherwise than in good faith . . . Thus, notwithstanding the views expressed by the judge the first time round, I would not accept the central thrust of Mr Bloch's submission that SGS and CAI were equally liable for Niru's loss, albeit under different causes of action.

. . .

[63] It might be objected that it is inappropriate to describe SGS as being subrogated to Niru's rights against CAI because, once SGS discharged CAI's obligation under the judgment, Niru no longer had any rights against CAI to which SGS could be subrogated. However, that would be to view the matter too technically. The principle upon which the judge relied was that of restitution by reason of unjust enrichment and, if the remedy of subrogation were not available, the correct course would not be to hold that SGS was not entitled to recover from CAI but to describe its remedy as a direct restitutionary right to payment enforceable against CAI. However, as Lord Clyde put it in the *Banque Financière* case [1999] AC 221 at 237, the remedy may vary with the circumstances of the case, the object being to effect a fair and just balance between the rights and interests of the parties concerned and in my opinion it is appropriate to describe the remedy available to SGS as subrogation.

[64] In any event, I would uphold the judge's conclusion that SGS is entitled to recover the amount it paid to Niru in discharge of the judgment in accordance with the principles of the law of restitution, whether the remedy is correctly described as subrogation or not.

[65] I would only add this. In the course of his submissions Mr Bloch suggested that it might be possible to hold that SGS's right or remedy should be limited to something less than the whole of the liability to reflect a just balance between the parties on the facts of this particular case. Having regard to my conclusion that the just result is that CAI should meet the whole of the judgment (except on costs), this point does not arise and I say nothing further about it.

RECOUPMENT

[66] Miss Andrews submits that the judge was wrong to hold that SGS's claim against CAI does not satisfy the principles of recoupment. Although, in the light of my conclusions on subrogation, it is not necessary to decide this question, I will shortly state my opinion on it since it was the subject of argument. The relevant principles were stated by Cockburn CJ in *Moule v Garrett* (1872) LR 7 Exch 101, [1861–73] All ER Rep 135 as follows:

'Where the plaintiff has been compelled by law to pay, or, being compellable by law, has paid, money which the defendant was ultimately liable to pay, so that the latter obtains the benefit of the payment by the discharge of his liability: under such circumstances the defendant is held indebted to the plaintiff in the account.'

[67] The judge set out that passage and added that the principle depends upon the compulsory discharge of a liability which rested *primarily* on the defendant (my emphasis). He referred to para. 15–001 of Goff and Jones *The Law of Restitution* (5th edn, 1998), where the position was put as follows:

'In general, anybody who has under compulsion of law made a payment whereby he has discharged the primary liability of another is entitled to be reimbursed by that other . . .

To succeed in his claim for recoupment, the plaintiff must satisfy certain conditions. He must show:

(1) that he was compelled, or was compellable, by law to make the payment;
(2) that he did not officiously expose himself to the liability to make the payment; and
(3) that his payment discharged a liability of the defendant.'

[68] The judge held that the payment by SGS to Niru pursuant to the judgment was a compulsory discharge of CAI's liability under the judgment and that CAI thus obtained the benefit of it. Miss Andrews submits that, having correctly so held, the judge should have asked himself whether, as between SGS and CAI, CAI was primarily or ultimately liable to pay Niru, that he should have considered how to answer that question by reference to the underlying circumstances and that, having done so, he should have answered the question Yes.

[69] I would accept those submissions. It seems to me that, for all the reasons already given under the heading of subrogation, the ultimate or primary liability as between CAI and SGS was indeed that of CAI. This case is a far cry from joint (or indeed several) tortfeasors responsible for the same damage. The crucial distinction is [that already referred to, namely] the fact that CAI was at no time entitled to retain or make use of the moneys which it had received by mistake. If it had acted in good faith it would have repaid the moneys and SGS would not have been liable at all. In these circumstances both law and equity should in my opinion regard CAI as primarily or ultimately liable as between itself and SGS, as that expression is used in the cases.

. . .

[72] For the reasons given at [69], above I would hold that SGS was entitled to recover by way of recoupment as well as by way of subrogation.

CONTRIBUTION

[73] I have already expressed my view as to the appropriate result on the assumption that the 1978 Act applies, namely that CAI should pay the whole amount of the judgment save as to costs. This conclusion makes it unnecessary to consider whether the 1978 Act applies. I will therefore add only this.

[74] It is not easy to know how we should approach the problem. (As indicated earlier) In *Friends' Provident Life Office v Hillier Parker May & Rowden (a firm)* [1997] QB 85 this court held that the 1978 Act enabled contribution to be claimed as between a tortfeasor and a person liable in restitution. That conclusion was based upon what was held to be the true construction of ss. 1(1) and 6(1) of the Act, which provide as follows:

1.—(1) Subject to the following provisions of this section any person liable in respect of any damage suffered by another person may recover contribution from any other person liable in respect of the same damage (whether jointly with him or otherwise) . . .

6.—(1) A person is liable in respect of any damage for the purposes of this Act if the person who suffered it . . . is entitled to recover compensation from him in respect of that damage (whatever the legal basis of his liability, whether tort, breach of contract, breach of trust or otherwise).'

[75] This court held in the *Friends' Provident* case that in a case like the present CAI and SGS were liable in respect of the 'same damage' within the meaning of s. 1(1) of the 1978 Act, namely the loss sustained by Niru, and Niru was entitled to recover 'compensation' from both SGS and CAI within the meaning of s. 6(1). The court gave 'compensation' a broad and purposive interpretation, which was followed in *Hurstwood Developments Ltd v Motor & General & Andersley & Co. Insurance Services Ltd (H B Boring & Co. Ltd (Pt 20 defendants)* [2001] EWCA Civ 1785, [2002] Lloyd's Rep IR 185.

[76] In [*Royal Brompton Hospital NHS Trust v Hammond* [2002] UKHL 14] Lord Steyn considered the problem in some detail and agreed with the view expressed in Goff and Jones (5th edn) p 396 that a restitutionary claim is not one for 'damage suffered' and that a claim for restitution cannot be said to be a claim to recover 'compensation' within the meaning of the Act: see in particular at [26]–[30], [33] and [34].

[77] Although Lord Steyn described the views of Auld LJ in the *Friends' Provident* case as dicta, it was common ground between the parties in the instant case that they were part of the decision. By contrast, it was common ground between the parties that the views of Lord Steyn were obiter dicta and not necessary for the decision in the *Royal Brompton* case. If that is correct, (as it may well be) the strict position appears to be that we remain bound by the decision in the *Friends' Provident* case.

[78] In these circumstances, although both parties made detailed submissions on the question whether a claim for restitution is a claim for 'compensation', I do not think that it would be appropriate for me to express my own view on the point, at any rate unless it were necessary to do so in order to resolve the issues in this appeal. In the light of the conclusions which I expressed earlier it is not necessary to express such an opinion. I have already expressed my conclusion that if the 1978 Act applies the just result would be to order CAI to pay a contribution of 100 per cent, as was done in the *Coys* case [*above* 77] and for similar reasons. No question of any possible conflict between the effects of subrogation, recoupment and contribution therefore arises. On the other hand, if the Act does not apply, the result is the same, namely that SGS is entitled to recover in full from CAI by way of subrogation or recoupment. In these circumstances, it is not necessary or appropriate for me further to lengthen this judgment by my own analysis of the meaning of 'compensation' in s. 6(1) of the 1978 Act.

. . .

CONCLUSION

[80] For the reasons I have given I would dismiss this appeal and uphold the conclusion of the judge that SGS is entitled to recover the whole of the amount which it paid to Niru in respect of principal and interest. I would do so on the basis that SGS is entitled to restitution and that the appropriate remedy is the equitable remedy of subrogation, although I would also do so by the application of the principles of recoupment. If the 1978 Act applies, I would hold that CAI should contribute 100 per cent of the same amount on the basis that it would be just and equitable having regard to CAI's responsibility for Niru's loss. Finally, I would like to thank counsel for their assistance in this interesting case.

- **Dame Elizabeth Butler-Sloss P** agreed with **Clarke LJ. Sedley LJ** delivered a concurring judgment.

NOTES AND QUESTIONS

1. The subrogation in issue was what has been termed 'reviving' subrogation: see above, 194, note 2.

2. Following the *Banque Financière case*, above, 190, the Court of Appeal treated the subrogation as being concerned to effect restitution of an unjust enrichment. But, as with Lord Steyn's analysis in that leading case, Clarke LJ's judgment shows that one could arrive at the same

result by reasoning from unjust enrichment—here relying on discharge of another's liability under legal compulsion—without resorting to the language of subrogation.

3. For the Civil Liability (Contribution) Act 1978, see below, 552.

4. For a critical case-note, see G Virgo, 'Subrogation, Recoupment and Contribution: Principles not Included' [2005] *CLJ* 35. But while it is true that recourse to subrogation was unnecessary, Virgo's major criticism (that, instead of awarding recoupment and 100 per cent contribution, liability should have been divided equally) involves rejecting Clarke LJ's clear view that, as between CAI and SGS, CAI was primarily/100 per cent responsible. Do you agree with Clarke LJ on this assessment?

3. NO RESTITUTION BECAUSE NO LIABILITY OF THE DEFENDANT HAS BEEN DISCHARGED (I.E. THE DEFENDANT HAS NOT BEEN ENRICHED)

- *Bonner v Tottenham and Edmonton Permanent Investment Building Society*
  [1899] 1 QB 161, Court of Appeal

The claimants were tenants of certain premises. They assigned their lease to Price, who mortgaged it to the defendants. On Price's bankruptcy, the defendant mortgagees took possession of the premises but in breach of their contract with Price they failed to pay any rent. The landlord (Moore) enforced the claimants covenant to pay the rent and the claimants sought to recover the amount paid from the defendant mortgagees. The action failed.

AL Smith LJ: . . . This is an action by plaintiffs who are lessees of premises for a long term to recover from the defendants 97*l.*, being rent they have had to pay to their lessor under the covenant in their lease, which rent accrued during the time the defendants were in possession of the premises as mortgagees by way of demise from an assignee of the term. Between the plaintiffs and the defendants there exists neither contract nor privity of estate; the defendants were not liable to pay to the plaintiffs the rent in question, nor were they liable to pay it to the plaintiff's lessor. In these circumstances my brother Channell gave judgment for the defendants, being of opinion that the action was not maintainable, and that the principle of the decision in *Moule v Garrett* did not apply, the defendants being underlesses and not assigners of the term as in the case cited. My brother Channell held, as I read his judgment that no request by the defendants to the plaintiffs to pay their lessor the rent in question on their behalf could be implied whereon to maintain the action, and I am of opinion that he was right.

. . .

It is clear that no contract or privity of estate exists between the plaintiffs and the defendants, or between the original lessor, Moore, and the defendants; and, unless there be circumstances from which a request to pay can be implied, or, in other words, a contract can be implied between the defendants and the plaintiffs that the defendants would indemnify the plaintiffs if they paid to their landlord the rent accruing whilst they, the defendants, were in possession, there are no circumstances which will support an action by the plaintiffs against the defendants to recover the amount so paid. It is true that Moore could sue the plaintiffs, his lessees, upon their covenant with him in the lease. It is also true that the plaintiffs, the lessees, could sue their assignee, Price, upon his covenant with them. It is also true that Price could sue the defendants, his underlessees, upon their covenant with him. But how can the plaintiffs sue the defendants? I omit Price's trustee in bankruptcy, for he, in my opinion, does not affect this case. It is said that the case of *Moule v Garrett* shews that the plaintiffs can sue the defendants to recover what they have been compelled to pay to their lessor, and that this case falls within the principle of that case. Now what was the case of *Moule v Garrett?* It was a case in which there had been two assignments of the term, the defendants being the second assignees thereof. First of all there was, as here, a lease from a lessor to the lessee, Moule, the plaintiff in the action, containing the usual covenants by a lessee. Moule afterwards assigned the term to Bartley, who afterwards assigned the term to the defendants, Garrett & Co., who then committed breaches of covenants in the lease. Moule, having been compelled under his covenant with his lessor to pay to him damages for these breaches committed by the defendants, Garrett & Co., the assignees of Bartley, sued Garrett & Co. to recover the amount so paid by him, Moule, to his lessor. It was held that, inasmuch as both the plaintiff and the defendants were compellable to pay to the original lessor the damages accruing to him for the breaches of covenant by the defendants whilst assignees of the term, the former by reason of his covenant with the original lessor and the latter by reason of their being assignees of the term and having committed the breaches whilst assignees, and inasmuch as the plaintiff had been compelled to pay damages to his lessor for these breaches of covenant by the defendants, for which the defendants were also compellable under privity of estate to pay to the lessor, they, the defendants, were liable to indemnify the plaintiff in respect of these payments of which the defendants had had the benefit. For, as Willes J puts it in *Roberts v Crowe*,[1] the lessee is liable for breaches of covenant committed by the assignee, but being only secondarily liable he has his remedy over against the person primarily liable—that is, the assignee. The ratio decidendi of *Moule v Garrett* is this: If A is compellable to pay B damages which C is also compellable to pay B, then A, having been compelled to pay B, can maintain an action against C for money so paid, for the circumstances raise an implied request by C to A to make such payment in his ease. In other words, A can call upon C to indemnify him. See the notes to *Lampleigh v Brathwait*,[2] and cases there cited. To raise this implied request, both A and C must, in my judgment, be compellable to pay B; other-wise, as it seems to me, the payment by A to B so far as regards C is a voluntary payment, which raises no implication of a request by C to A to pay . . . In the present case the defendants are underlessees of an assignee of the term, and are not liable at all to the original lessor for rent whenever it accrued, there being between them and the original lessor neither contract nor privity of estate, and there is no suggestion that there were goods upon the demised premises available for distress other than the goods of the mortgagor Price, even if this would have sufficed to maintain the action, about which I say nothing, for it is not before me. The above, in my judgment, is what was decided in *Moule v Garrett*, and the present case, as it appears to me, is an attempt to stretch the decision of that case, and to say that the principle therein laid down applies equally to the case of an underlessee of an assignee who is not compellable to pay the original lessor as to the case of an assignee who is compellable to pay the original lessor. It will be seen upon looking at the case of *Penley v Watts*[3] that Parke B deals with this exact point. He says: 'The lessee and his assignee are liable to precisely the same extent, and the assignee is a surety for the lessee, but that is not the case in a sub-lease.' And, again, in *Moule v Garrett*,[4] in the Exchequer Chamber, when it was suggested that the case of an underlessee of an assignee and an assignee of an assignee were the same, Blackburn J said: 'No, because the underlessee has never come under any obligation to the lessor, but here the defendant, by taking the same estate which the plaintiff had, has become liable to the same obligation,' and this is the foundation of the judgment of the Court of Exchequer delivered by Channell B, and the ground upon which the judgment was upheld in the Exchequer Chamber. The fact that in this case the defendants covenanted with Price, the assignee, that if they, the defendants, became mortgagees in

1 (1872) LR, 7 CP 629, at 637.   2 1 Sm. LC 9th edn, 160.   3 7 M & W 601, at 608.
4 LR 7 Ex. 101, at 102.

possession they would pay the rent, gives Price a remedy against them subject to any set-off which may exist between him and them and does not give the present plaintiffs a right of action against them.

In my judgment, for the reasons above, this action is not maintainable . . .

Vaughan Williams LJ: . . .

The question raised in this case, namely, whether an underlessee, who is a mortgagee by way of demise from an assignee of the lessee, and who is in possession of the demised lands, can be sued for money paid by the lessee, who has been compelled according to his covenant to pay the rent reserved by the principal lease, has not, so far as I know, been directly determined until now. . . . The case of *Moule v Garrett* does not determine the question, although it goes far to define the principles upon which the question must be decided. In *Moule v Garrett* the defendants were not underlessees, but assignees of the term, and the ground upon which they were held to be liable was that, the lessee and the defendants both being liable to the lessor upon all the covenants in the lease, which ran with the land, the former by contract and the latter by privity of estate, the defendants, having had the whole benefit for which the covenant was entered into by the plaintiff as lessee, were liable to recoup to the plaintiff the amount which he had been compelled to pay the lessor for breaches of covenant occurring during the defendants' possession. [*He considered the judgments in* Moule v Garrett *and continued:*] Now what (according to the judgments of Channel B, Blackburn J, and Willes J) were the conditions upon which the liability of the defendants to the plaintiff was based? First, that the plaintiff and defendants were both liable to be sued by the lessor for the same breaches of the same covenant. Secondly, that the defendants had had at the date of those breaches the whole benefit of the land the subject of the lease containing that covenant.

These being the conditions upon which the defendants in *Moule v Garrett*, the sub-assignees of the lease, were held liable, it is necessary to consider whether one finds these conditions in principle present in a case in which lessees, who have been compelled to pay the rent reserved by the lease, are seeking to get recoupment from the underlessees of an assignee of the lease, who are in possession as mortgagees. Now first, as to the common liability of the lessee and underlessee, they clearly are not both liable to be sued by the lessor for rent. The lessee alone can be sued, and the underlessee is only liable to the lessor in the sense that the lessor has a remedy in rem by distress on goods on the property demised and by the power of re-entry for non-payment of rent or breach of covenant. It is in this sense only that the underlessee can be said to be liable to the lessor for the rent, and, so far as distress is concerned, his direct liability is limited to cases in which he happens to have goods on the land, although he may have an indirect liability to indemnify against distress those who by his licence having goods on the land have been compelled to redeem their goods from distraint. Is this a common liability within the reason upon which the condition is based? I think it is not. I am now dealing only with the principle upon which the common law liability is based. There is a common law principle of liability, and also a principle of liability in equity, and these two principles differ. The common law principle requires a common liability to be sued for that which the plaintiff had to pay, and an interest of the defendant in the payment in the sense that he gets the benefit of the payment, either entirely, as in the case of the assignee of a lease, or pro tanto, as in the case of a surety who has paid, and has his action for contribution against his co-surety. The principle in equity seems wide enough to include cases in which there is community of interest in the subject-matter to which the burden is attached, which has been enforced against the plaintiff alone, coupled with benefit to the defendant, even though there is no common liability to be sued. In such a case it seems to me a plaintiff may recover in equity, although there is no common liability to be sued. [*He considered the scope of the equitable right of recovery and continued:*] The equitable principle seems to me based upon natural justice requiring that equity should neutralise 'inter se' the accident that the burden has been borne by one for the benefit of others associated with him in interest, whether such incidence of burden is the result of election of a plaintiff who might have sued all those interested, or whether it is the result of the requirements of the law as to the parties to actions, or whether it is the result of what may be more properly called 'accident' like the 'jettison' of a part of a cargo severally owned, or the seizure of wines on behalf of the Crown in right of prisage. In each of these cases the application of the equitable principle depends on community of interest in something in respect of which one has borne a burden for the benefit of another or others. The covenant in accordance with which a lessee pays rent or expends money in repairs is a covenant in a lease in which the underlessee has no interest. . . .

In conclusion, in my judgment the defendants have not, within either the equitable or common law principle, such an interest in the lease that it can be said that the payment by the lessees of the rent reserved by the lease was a payment for their benefit or relief. . . .

Rigby LJ delivered a concurring judgment.

NOTES AND QUESTIONS

1. In contrast to the facts of *Moule v Garrett* (above, 507) the defendant (D) had no legal liability to pay rent to the head-landlord (X) because D was not a subtenant of the head-tenant (C) but a mortgagee of the sub-tenant of C.

2. Does Vaughan Williams LJ's judgment envisage a wider scope for recovery than A Smith LJ's judgment?

3. Was it correct to say that the defendants derived no benefit from the claimants' payment?

• Re Nott and Cardiff Corp [1918] 2 KB 146, Court of Appeal

The claimant, a builder, entered into a contract with the defendant corporation to build a reservoir. One of the clauses of the contract required the claimant to take over a railway and put it in repair. The contract did not deal with who should pay the rates on the railway. The rating authority placed the claimant in the rate book as the occupier of the railway and hence liable to pay the rates for it. While disputing his liability to do so, the claimant paid the rates demanded and then sought to recover them from the defendant. The dispute was referred to arbitration. The arbitrator found that the claimant was not the occupier of the railway and that the defendant was bound to repay him the rates. This was affirmed by Bray J. The defendant appealed successfully to the Court of Appeal.

Pickford LJ: . . . The arbitrator has found . . . so far as it is a question of fact for him, that the corporation, and not the contractor, were in occupation of the railway, and that in those circumstances, as the contractor, in order to avoid interference with the works, was obliged to pay the rates, there is an implied obligation on the corporation to repay him, and Bray J has upheld this finding. I regret that I cannot take the same view. I am by no means sure that there was any dispute about the facts, and that the question of occupation does not depend upon the terms of the contract, or that those terms gave such control of the corporation as to bring the case within the decision in *Rochdale Canal Co. v Brewster*,[1] but I do not think it is necessary to decide the question. The facts as found were these. The rating authorities communicated with the corporation as to the rates, and they referred them to the contractor. There is no reason to suppose that this was not done in the bona fide belief that the contractor was the occupier and the person liable to be rated. The rating authorities, I assume after proper consideration, placed the contractor on the rate-book as occupier, and he

1 [1894] 2 QB 852.

informed the corporation, who refused to pay the rates. The contractor, if he were not the occupier, could dispute his liability either by appeal or by opposing the issue of a warrant of distress: see *Whenman v Clark*.[2] According to the arbitrator's finding in clause 4(i) he did in 1911 give notice to the corporation that he was about to appeal, but the award is silent as to the exact steps that he took. He may not have appealed at all; he may not have appealed on that ground, but only on the question of amount; he may have withdrawn his appeal, or it may have been dismissed. Whatever he did or did not do, the appeal did not succeed, and he remained on the rate-book and continued to pay the rates until the stop-page of the work, giving notice to the corporation that he disputed his liability. I can find no term in the contract which binds the corporation to repay the amount to him, but it is contended that such a term must be implied. In the first place this implication is said to arise from the terms of the contract itself because there is no agreement by the contractor to pay the rates and no mention of them in the bills of quantities, whereas there are agreements by him to pay certain charges, e.g., fees to local authorities in clause 7 of the contract, and wayleaves and charges in clause 82 of the specification. It is also contended that the implication must arise from the fact that the corporation were really the occupiers, and therefore there must be an implication that they would repay what was really their debt. I do not think either of these contentions is sound. As to the first, there is nothing in the terms expressed to suggest that in order to carry out the contract it must be implied that the corporation will bear all other expenses, e.g., I cannot see how it can be implied that they agreed to pay the rates on the huts to be constructed under clause 97 of the specification. A much more probable explanation is that this question of rates was not present to the mind of either party. With regard to the second contention, this liability for rates was never the liability of the corporation at all, as in such cases as *Exall v Partridge*. The person liable for rates is the person placed upon the rate-book by the rating authority, and so long as the contractor remained on the rate-book he had to pay the rates. He had his remedy as already pointed out, and if he neglected to pursue that remedy, or if it were decided that he was wrong in pursuing it, he cannot, as it seems to me, claim to be repaid. The corporation were throughout, as I read the award, refusing to repay him, and such refusal must have been on the ground that he who had been placed on the rate-book by the responsible authority was the occupier and liable, and not the corporation. I cannot see, even if they were wrong, how these facts raise an implied agreement or obligation to repay him. I think, therefore, the contractor's claim fails on this point also.

The result is that in my opinion the question in the award should be answered that the arbitrator ought not to have awarded any sum to be paid by the employers on any of the said claims. . . .

Bankes LJ: . . . So long as the contractor remains on the rate-book, whether rightly or wrongly so long, in my opinion, will he continue liable to pay the rates, and without any right to call upon the corporation to repay him. The debt is his debt, and the principle of such cases as *Exall v Partridge* does not apply. . . .

Neville J delivered a concurring judgment.

QUESTION

While he is out of the country for three months, C decides to let his house to D. C had intended to have the telephone transferred into D's name but forgot to do so. The telephone bill for rental and calls made for those three months is £300. British Telecom demands payment from C which C pays. Is C entitled to reimbursement from D?

---

2 [1916] 1 KB 94.

• *Metropolitan Police District Receiver v Croydon Corp.*
[1957] 2 QB 154, Court of Appeal

While directing traffic, a policeman was injured owing to the negligence of the defendants. As a result, the policeman was prevented from working for several months. During that time the claimant police authority continued to pay his wages, as it was statutorily bound to do. The policeman brought a claim against the defendants which was settled out of court, but that claim and settlement did not include anything for loss of earnings. The claimant sought to recover from the defendant the wages paid to the policeman for the period of his incapacity. This claim succeeded before Slade J. But in the parallel case of *Monmouthshire County Council v Smith* Lynskey J refused such a claim. The Court of Appeal heard both appeals together and reversed Slade J, while affirming Lynskey J.

Lord Goddard CJ: . . . The first thing to remember in this case is that under the statutes and the statutory regulations made thereunder by which the police forces, both in the metropolis and in the counties, are governed, it is accepted that the police authority is obliged to pay a constable his full wages and allowances, though he may be off duty by reason of an injury received in the course of his service. A time may come when the police officer has to retire because his injuries may have rendered him unfit to remain in the police force; and in that case he will receive a pension, but so long as he is in the police force, he is paid whether he is fit for duty or not, so long as the unfitness for duty is caused by an accident arising out of his duties as a policeman.

In the Croydon case, as in the Monmouthshire case, the police officer in question was injured while regulating traffic. In the Croydon case the injury kept him off his duties for something like seven months. He was paid full wages during that time, and received all the other emoluments to which he was entitled. Both police constables brought actions in which they made no claim for loss of wages as part of the damage which they had sustained, because they had not sustained a loss of wages. Their wages had been paid to them during incapacity, and, therefore, the damages which they recovered against the respective defendants were not so large as they would have been if they had been entitled to claim wages.

It is said that the respective defendants have received a benefit by reason of the fact that the receiver and the county council paid the wages during the period of incapacity, and that therefore they, the defendants, have not had to pay damages as great as they would otherwise have had to pay. For example, in the case of an ordinary man who was in receipt of a weekly wage, and who was injured, the negligent defendant would have had to pay as part of the special damage the wages which the injured man had lost.

Slade J has treated the case as one which depends upon the doctrine of unjust enrichment. He has held that inasmuch as the defendants escaped paying these wages because of the payments made by the receiver, they have received a benefit and must now pay the receiver the amount of those wages. That seems to me to be a misconception, because I cannot see that the defendants have been in any way enriched. Indeed, the matter was dealt with by Earl Jowitt in his speech in *British Transport Commission v Gourley*:[1] 'It is, I think, if I may say so with the utmost respect, fallacious to consider the problem as though a benefit were being conferred upon a wrongdoer by allowing him to abate the damages for which he would otherwise be liable. The problem is rather for what damages is he liable and if we apply the dominant rule, we should answer: "He is liable for such damages as, by reason of his wrongdoing, the plaintiff has sustained." ' It will be remembered that in *Gourley's* case the question was whether, in compensating a man for loss of earnings, one was to take into account his gross earnings or his net earnings after tax; the latter was held to be the right measure.

---

1 [1956] AC 185, 202.

In both cases, the constables sustained certain damage for which they have been compensated. That damage, as I say, did not include wages, because they had already been paid their wages. What is the result of that? The receiver in the one case, and the county council in the other case, have not been called upon to pay anything which they would not otherwise have had to pay. Their obligation is to pay police officers during the time when they are off duty through disablement, provided that the disablement arose in the course of their service. Therefore I cannot see that the receiver or the county council are any worse off than they would have been if these accidents had never taken place. It is their duty to pay a policeman so long as he is in their service.

Once that point is realized it follows that the only loss which the police authorities have sustained is that they have had to pay the police officers, although they were deprived of their services. That loss is exactly the loss which was recoverable, and in certain limited cases is still recoverable, in an action *per* quod servitium amisit. The old action of *per* quod was given to a master because he was deprived of the services of his servant. However, in *Attorney-General for New South Wales v Perpetual Trustee Co. Ltd*[2] it was held by the Judicial Committee that in the case of a police officer, a *per* quod action will not lie because the officer is not a servant of the police authority but of the Crown, for he may have to act independently of the police authority. This court, in *Inland Revenue Commissioners v Hambrook*,[3] applied that judgment to the case of an injury to a civil servant, and expressed the view that a *per* quod action must nowadays be confined to the case of what is generally known as a menial servant. Therefore, it follows that police authorities are not entitled to claim now for loss of their police officers' services against the person who injures them.

In order, therefore, to maintain this action, it must be shown that the legal liability rests on some other principle. The principle that is prayed in aid here is the principle that money which constitutes unjust enrichment of a person may be recovered in an action for money had and received, or money paid to the use of the person. In these cases both judges considered with great care the decision of this court in *Brook's Wharf and Bull Wharf Ltd v Goodman Brothers*. [*He considered that case and continued*:] To my mind, that case, and the large number of cases which were cited there and have been cited in this case, have no bearing on the latter which we have to decide. The obligation of the defendants here was to compensate the injured men, and to pay them the damage which they had sustained. If a man's employer has agreed to pay him wages, whether he is well or wether he is ill, it seems to me that that affords a benefit in one sense to a defendant, because he does not have to pay the damage which he would have had to pay if that agreement had not been made. That simply means that he does not have to compensate the plaintiff for an injury which he has not suffered. The obligation is, in the words of Earl Jowitt, simply to pay 'such damages as, by reason of his [the defendant's] wrongdoing, the plaintiff has sustained.'[4] Having paid that, his obligation seems to me to be at an end.

. . .

For these reasons, I think that the judgment of Lynskey J was perfectly right when he held that there was no obligation on the part of the defendant to pay the police authority the amount of the wages which the police authority had paid, and I do not think that the cases which have been cited to us, and which were before the judges, need be reviewed.

Morris LJ: . . . It is said that the defendants have benefited. It seems to me that the answer to that is that they have not benefited. It is said that their obligation to Bowman was reduced pro tanto; again it seems to me the answer to that is that their obligation has not been reduced at all. Their obligation was to pay what Bowman lost, and they have been adjudged to pay what they were liable to pay. It seems to me, therefore, that the real position in this case is that what has been lost, probably not by the plaintiff but by someone else, is the benefit of the services that the police officer Bowman would

2 [1955] AC 457.   3 [1956] 2 QB 641.   4 [1956] AC 185, 202.

have rendered during the time when he was incapacitated. It can be said with some force that the wrongdoer has been fortunate in that he has injured someone who must be paid whether he is injured or not, whereas those entitled to his services are during the period of incapacity denied those services. It might be said that a case could be put forward for consideration as to whether there might be some change in the law in regard to this matter so as to permit of the recovery of wages payable and paid in reference to a period of incapacity caused by a wrongdoer. But it does not seem to me that the defendants have in this case benefited or received an advantage.

The claim is put partly in reliance upon the principles referred to in the *Brook's Wharf* case. In his judgment in that case Lord Wright MR said this:[5] 'The essence of the rule is that there is a liability for the same debt resting on the plaintiff and the defendant and the plaintiff has been legally compelled to pay, but the defendant gets the benefit of the payment, because his debt is discharged either entirely or pro tanto, whereas the defendant is primarily liable to pay as between himself and the plaintiff.' I agree, if I may say so, with [counsel for the plaintiff] that it is never wise to take a passage out of a judgment, and to treat it as though it were statutory enactment. Lord Wright is there merely stating the essence of the rule. But it does not seem to me that the plaintiff brings himself within that rule, because there was no liability on the defendants for the wages, for the reason that the policeman did not lose them.

Reference was made to *Moule v Garrett*. In that case the plaintiff was a lessee, and the defendant was a sub-assignee who was in possession; he failed to comply with a covenant to repair. The lessee was made liable; he met the demand of the lessor for damages for breach of the covenant to repair. The lessee then sued the sub-assignee; there was no privity of contract between them, but they were both liable to the lessor. The plaintiff was held entitled to recover, and amongst the reasons was that given by Channell B, who said that the lessee was really in the position of a surety vis-a-vis the assignee. So in the *Brook's Wharf* case both the importer and the warehouseman were liable for the payment of the customs dues, the importer as between the two of them being primarily liable.

But [counsel for the plaintiff], in inviting us not to take the words of Lord Wright as being an all-inclusive statement of the legal principle, invites us to say that the law is adaptable, and that within its framework can be found a principle which entitles him to recover in this case. He has adopted as part of his argument a statement from Sir Percy Winfield's book on The Law of Quasi-contracts, 1st edn (1952), 63. The passage reads: 'In spite of our endeavour to extract from the decided cases some broad general principle underlying the law as to compulsion in quasi-contract, the utmost we can do is to enlarge our conclusion that, where A, under what the law regards as compulsion, has paid money to B or to C in such circumstances that the law considers that its retention by B (where the payment was to B), or B's failure to recoup A (where the payment was to C) would constitute an unjust benefit to B at the expense of A, A can recover the amount of payment from B.' Again it does not seem to me that [counsel for the plaintiff] can bring himself within any such principle, for the whole basis of it is that there must be some unjust benefit. I cannot see that there was any unjust benefit here received by the defendants when they have been held liable for all that they were in law liable to pay.

. . .

[Counsel for the plaintiff] referred us to *Gebhardt v Saunders*, . . . [Counsel for the plaintiff] cited that as one illustration of the cases that he referred to as the nuisance cases. But again, it does not seem to me that they carry [counsel for the plaintiff], and for the same reason, that it is not shown that the defendants in this case received a benefit. If an employer makes a contract for a fixed period with a servant, and agrees to pay him a fixed sum, possibly in advance, whether the servant is ill or well, fit or unfit, and if the servant is injured by a wrongdoer and is away for a week, the servant has

---

5 [1937] 1 KB 534, 544.

not then suffered any loss of pay, and the wrongdoer cannot be liable for what the servant has not lost.

Vaisey J delivered a concurring judgment.

NOTES AND QUESTIONS

1. This decision has had an important impact on the approach in English law to the question whether collateral benefits obtained by tort victims should be deducted in assessing damages for personal injury. For if there is no possible restitutionary claim against the tortfeasor by the provider of the benefit, the courts may not be keen to deduct collateral benefits given that deduction will then merely enure to the benefit of the tortfeasor.

2. Slade J's judgment at first instance repays examination: see [1956] 1 WLR 1113.

3. The recoupment scheme for social security benefits contained in the Social Security (Recovery of Benefits) Act 1997 may be regarded as a rejection of the *Croydon Corporation* approach. This Act allows the state, which has paid social security benefits to an injured party thereby reducing the tortfeasor's liability to pay, to recoup (through the Compensation Recovery Unit) those payments from the tortfeasor. However, there is now to be no deduction of social security benefit from damages awarded for non-pecuniary loss. That change from the original recoupment scheme (introduced in 1989) marks an important theoretical shift because, while the original scheme could have been entirely explained on the (unjust enrichment) basis that the state's recoupment was in respect of compulsorily relieving a liability of the defendant, the new scheme goes beyond that and in effect holds the defendant liable for the pure economic loss caused to the state by the tort. See also the Road Traffic (NHS Charges) Act 1999 giving the NHS the right to recover from tortfeasors the costs of treatment provided to victims of motor accidents.

● *Land Hessen v Gray and Gerrish,* 31 July 1998 unreported, Queen's Bench Division

In a road traffic accident two German teachers were injured. One of them subsequently died from her injuries. The claimant (Land Hessen) is one of the constituent states of Germany and employed the two teachers. It was required by German law to make various payments to them, and to the widower and children of the deceased. Land Hessen asserted a restitutionary right to recover the value of the payments from those whose negligence had allegedly caused the accident. Sachs J held that the claimant did indeed have a restitutionary right to recover some of the payments made but left the decision about exactly which for a later hearing.

Sachs J: . . .

RESTITUTION

It was submitted on behalf of the Plaintiff that the law of restitution involves the Plaintiff satisfying three requirements. The Plaintiff relies on Goff and Jones, The Law of Restitution (4th ed.) at Ch 14, p 343 where it states

'The classic statement of the common law principle is to be found in a passage from the first edition of Leake on Contracts, which was quoted by Cockburn C.J. in *Moule v Garrett* in 1872:

"Where the plaintiff has been compelled by law to pay, or being compellable by law, has paid money which the Defendant was ultimately liable to pay, so that the latter obtains the benefit of the payment by the discharge of his liability; under such circumstances the Defendant is held to be indebted to the Plaintiff for that amount." '

Also at Page 344 it states

'To succeed in his claim for recoupment, the Plaintiff must satisfy certain conditions. He must show:

    (1) that he has been compelled, or was compellable, by law to make the payment.

    (2) that he did not officiously expose himself to the liability to make the payment; and

    (3) that his payment discharged a liability of the Defendant.

The Plaintiff enforces his right to reimbursement by recovering his money paid to the Defendant's use.'

. . .

I am satisfied that the current statement of the law relied on by the Plaintiff as stated in Goff and Jones is correct. The Defendants . . . contend that the Plaintiff does not satisfy the . . . three conditions.

First they deny that the Plaintiff was compelled by law to make the payments . . .

Dr Carl and Dr Dannemann [the experts on German law] both made it plain that the payments made to the victims by the Plaintiff were under compulsion of German law.

The Defendants make a further attack on the Plaintiff's claim for restitution saying it officiously exposed them to liability. There is absolutely no merit in the argument advanced in support of that contention.

As to the final requirement, namely that by the payments the Plaintiff discharged a liability of the Defendants, clearly whilst the Plaintiff has discharged this liability the Defendants have been freed from an obligation which otherwise they would have had to discharge.

It is conceded by the Plaintiff that I am bound by the decision of the Court of Appeal in *Receiver of the Metropolitan Police District v Croydon Corporation* [1957] 2 QB 154, [1957] 1 All ER 78. That was a case where two police officers were injured on duty due to the negligence of the Defendants and as a result they were incapacitated from performing their duties for several months. The Police Authorities acting under statutory regulation paid the officers their full wages and allowances. The Defendants were sued by the Receiver who claimed damages for loss of wages.

In the Court of Appeal this submission on behalf of the Plaintiff was on the basis of unjust benefit against the Defendants.

The Court of Appeal dismissed the appeal saying there was no unjust benefit and that the Police Authorities had paid what they were in any event obliged to do.

That decision only binds me to the extent of the Plaintiff's claim to emoluments. It does not bind me in relation to the other parts of the Plaintiff's claim not covered by the decision of the Court of Appeal and which the Plaintiff was liable to pay in consequence of this accident . . .

Further the Defendants complain that the claim in restitution is not pleaded. The Plaintiff denies that and relies on para. 8 of the Statement of Claim which reads, so far as relevant

'The Plaintiff has paid and/or is and/or will be liable to pay some or all of the said losses to or for the benefit of the first victim's estate and/or dependants and/or heirs and to or for the benefit of the second victim under compulsion of German law and has discharged and/or will discharge the first and/or second Defendant's liability therefore to the extent thereof.'

In my view that is an entirely sufficient pleading of the issue of restitution and the submissions to the contrary have no merit.

That finding means the Plaintiff is entitled to recover but what losses it recovers is for future determination.

NOTES AND QUESTIONS

1. Presumably Sachs J meant by 'emoluments' the wages of the two teachers; and (although this is also not made clear) that the other payments were for, e.g., medical costs or non-pecuniary loss.
2. Can one sensibly distinguish, for the purpose of the restitutionary claim, between the wages paid (no restitution from the 'tortfeasors') and the other payments made (restitution granted from the 'tortfeasors')? Was the reasoning in the *Croydon Corpn.* case confined to wages or did it extend to all payments made by a third party which thereby 'relieved' the tortfeasors' liability?

In the context of a claim for subrogation, the following extract makes it clear that payment by an indemnity insurer to its assured, following a tort, does not discharge the tortfeasor's liability to the assured.

- **Esso Petroleum Ltd v Hall, Russell & Co. Ltd (The Esso Bernicia)**
  [1989] AC 643, House of Lords (Scotland)

Esso had entered into an agreement with a large number of other tanker owners ('TOVALOP': Tanker Owners' Voluntary Agreement Concerning Liability for Oil Pollution) whereby each participating owner agreed with the others that, in the event of oil escaping from its tanker and causing oil pollution damage to a third party, the participating party would compensate the third party irrespective of any negligence on its part. Pursuant to that, Esso paid over half a million pounds to crofters in respect of damage to sheep due to pollution of the foreshore from the discharge of oil from their ship. Esso alleged that the damage was the consequence of the negligence of the boat builders, Hall Russell. Esso unsuccessfully sought to recover from Hall Russell, *inter alia* on the basis of subrogation, the sums paid to the crofters.

Lord Goff: . . . The primary submission of [counsel for Esso] was that Esso was entitled to be subrogated to the crofters' claims in tort against Hall Russell, and further that Esso was entitled to pursue such claims against Hall Russell in its own name. In my opinion, this submission is not well founded.

In considering this submission, I proceed on the basis (which appears to have been common ground throughout the case) that there is for present purposes no material distinction between Scots law and English law. Now, let it be assumed that the effect of Esso's payment to the crofters was to indemnify the crofters in respect of loss or damage suffered by them by reason of the wrongdoing of Hall Russell. If such a payment were made under a contract of indemnity between Esso and the crofters, there can be no doubt that Esso would upon payment be subrogated to the crofters' claims against Hall Russell. This would enable Esso to proceed against Hall Russell in the names of the crofters; but it would not enable Esso to proceed, without more to enforce the crofters' claims by an action in its own name against Hall Russell.

The reason for this is plain. It is that Esso's payment to the crofters does not have the effect of discharging Hall Russell's liability to them. That being so, I do not see how Esso can have a direct claim against Hall Russell in respect of its payment. . . . There can of course be no direct claim by Esso against Hall Russell in restitution, if only because Esso has not by its payment discharged the liability of Hall Russell, and so has not enriched Hall Russell; if anybody has been enriched, it is the crofters, to the extent that they have been indemnified by Esso and yet continue to have vested in them rights of action against Hall Russell in respect of the loss or damage which was the subject matter of Esso's payment to them. All that is left is the fact that the crofters' rights of action against Hall Russell continued to exist (until the expiry of the relevant limitation period), and that it might have been inequitable to deny Esso the opportunity to take advantage of them—which is the classic basis of the doctrine of subrogation in the case of contracts of indemnity (see *Castellain v Preston* (1883) 11 QBD

380). In normal cases, as for example under contracts of insurance, the insurer will on payment request the assured to sign a letter of subrogation, authorising the insurer to proceed in the name of the assured against any wrongdoer who has caused the relevant damage to the assured. If the assured refuses to give such authority, in theory the insurer can bring proceedings to compel him to do so. But nowadays the insurer can short-circuit this cumbrous process by bringing an action against both the assured and the third party, in which (1) he claims an order that the assured shall authorise him to proceed against the third party in the name of the assured, and (2) he seeks to proceed (so authorised) against the third party. But it must not be thought that, because this convenient method of proceeding now exists, the insurer can without more proceed in his own name against the third party. He has no right to do so, so long as the right of action he is seeking to enforce is the right of action of the assured. Only if that right of action is assigned to him by the assured can he proceed directly against the third party in his own name (see, e.g., *Compania Colombiana de Seguros v Pacific Steam Navigation Co.* [1965] 1 QB 101). I have no doubt that the like principles apply in the present case. It follows that Esso could only proceed directly in its own name against Hall Russell in respect of the crofters' claims against Hall Russell if, on paying the crofters, it received from them a valid and effective assignation of their claims. I cannot think that, in practice, Esso would have met with difficulty if it had, at the time of payment to the crofters, asked each of them for a receipt which operated either as an assignation or as an authority to proceed against the third party in the name of the crofters concerned; if any such practical difficulty should exist, it could surely be overcome in future by an appropriate amendment to TOVALOP.

For these reasons . . . I would reject Esso's claim based upon subrogation . . .

Lord Jauncey delivered a concurring judgment. **Lords Keith** and **Brandon** agreed with **Lord Jauncey**. **Lord Templeman** agreed with both **Lords Jauncey** and **Goff**.

NOTES AND QUESTIONS

1. Esso's alternative claim against Hall Russell based on recovering the payment to the crofters under the tort of negligence, as being consequent on physical damage to Esso's tanker, failed on the ground that the payment was not truly consequential on that physical damage, and instead constituted irrecoverable pure economic loss.

2. Lord Goff equated the payment made by Esso under TOVALOP to one made by an insurer to his assured under a contract of indemnity. The payment was therefore treated as being made under legal compulsion (albeit legal compulsion under a contract voluntarily entered into as in, e.g., *Moule v Garrett or Owen v Tate*). Cf. Goff and Jones, para. 15-002.

3. The case shows that indemnity insurance payments and the like are exceptions to the normal position that payments under legal compulsion automatically discharge the third party's liability (irrespective of the third party's consent). The tortfeasor's liability is treated as still alive irrespective of the insurer's payment. The relevant unjust enrichment to which the subrogation responds is therefore that of the assured and not that of the tortfeasor. This type of subrogation has been labelled 'simple', in contrast to the more usual 'reviving', subrogation (see above, 194, note 2).

4. WHEN DOES PAYMENT OF ANOTHER'S DEBT DISCHARGE THAT DEBT?

- *Crantrave Ltd v Lloyds Bank plc* [2000] QB 917, Court of Appeal

Two judgment creditors of Crantrave Ltd obtained a garnishee order nisi over the funds of Crantrave, held by the bank. Although the garnishee order was not made absolute, the defendant bank paid £13,497 to those two judgment creditors and then debited Crantrave's account for that amount. Crantrave's liquidator, the claimant, sought repayment of that amount on the ground that, as the payment had not been authorized, no debt of Crantrave's had been discharged. That claim succeeded in the Court of Appeal.

Pill LJ: . . . The judge declined to order summary judgment on the basis that the legal point raised on the authority of *B. Liggett (Liverpool) Ltd v Barclays Bank Ltd* [1928] 1 K.B. 48 was arguable.

. . .

In the *Liggett* case, the defendant bank negligently and contrary to instructions paid cheques to their customers which had been signed by one director only when two signatures were required. The cheques were drawn in favour of trade creditors of the company in payment for goods supplied to the company. Wright J. stated as a general principle of equity [1928] 1 K.B. 48, 61:

'that those who pay legitimate demands which they are bound in some way or other to meet, and have had the benefit of other people's money advanced to them for that purpose, shall not retain that benefit so as, in substance, to make those other people pay their debts.'

Wright J. applied that principle as between banker and customer, at pp. 63–64:

'In such a case there is obviously no conversion, but there is misapplication, under an honest mistake as to the validity of the authority, of the credits which constitute the medium of exchange in place of cash. Under these circumstances I think that the equity I have referred to ought to be extended even in the case where the cheque was paid out of the credit balance, and was not paid by way of overdraft, so that the banker will be entitled to the benefit of that payment if he can show that that payment went to discharge a legal liability of the customer. The customer in such a case is no worse off, because the legal liability which has to be discharged is discharged, though it is discharged under circumstances which at common law would not entitle the bank to debit the customer. The result is that I must order an inquiry, because I have not the facts before me sufficiently to come to a conclusion whether the rule of equity which I have stated does apply, and if so to what extent.'

The *Liggett* case is cited in *Chitty on Contracts*. 28th ed. (1999) vol. 2, p. 304, para. 34–317, as authority for 'the equitable doctrine that a person who pays the debts of another without authority is allowed the benefit of such payment.' In *Halsbury's Laws of England*, 4th ed. reissue, vol. 3(1) (1989), p. 153, para. 175 it is cited to support the proposition that 'if such a cheque is paid in discharge of the customer's debts, the banker is entitled to take credit for it.'

The *Liggett* case was considered in this court in *In re Cleadon Trust Ltd* [1939] Ch 286. One of the two directors of a company paid money in discharge of debts owed by two subsidiary companies and guaranteed by the company in the expectation that the company which benefited thereby would repay him. Its liability under the guarantee would be discharged. The directors were also the directors of the subsidiary companies. A resolution was passed purporting to confirm some of the advances but the resolution was invalid by the company's articles of association. The company and the subsidiary companies went into liquidation but the assets of the subsidiary companies were insufficient to discharge their liabilities. It was held that there was neither knowledge nor acquiescence on the part of the company rendering it liable at common law under an implied contract to repay the director and, by a majority, Sir Wilfrid Greene M.R. dissenting, there was no equitable principle which imposed any liability on the company because it had never had anything to do with the transactions and the director was not entitled to recover the sums advanced by him.

Scott L.J. stated that the company had, at p. 315:

'never decided to forestall its liabilities as guarantor. It did not do these things, because in the state of legal paralysis in which it was it had no mind, and could not do any one of these things, the legal reason being that they were all matters appertaining to the management of the company and requiring a decision of the board.'

Scott L.J. explained the *Liggett* case on the basis that the discharge of the company's debts must be taken to have been made under [its director] Mr. Liggett's authority to pay current debts when he had money of the firm's with which to pay them. Clauson L.J. stated, at pp. 321–322:

'Since the decision in this Court in *Falcke v Scottish Imperial Insurance Co.* (1886) 34 ChD 234, 248, it is, I conceive, not open to this court to hold that a person who by paying money confers an unsought benefit on another thereby entitles himself to an equitable right of recoupment as against that other.'

Clauson L.J. added, at pp. 323–324:

'It is to be observed that the equity cannot operate against C (the company or the principal) merely because C has in fact received a benefit from B's action in providing the money: that fact alone, as *Falcke's* case has settled (so far as this court is concerned), would not set up an equity against C. The equity must, it would seem, arise from the fact that C, by himself or by a person authorised to act, in the manner of payment of C's debts, for C, has used the money so as to obtain a benefit for C. The benefit has not been an unsought benefit conferred on C behind his back. It is a benefit which C has obtained for himself by using (either himself or by his agent) A's money as his own. It is his conduct in so using A's money which makes it unconscientious that he should retain the benefit while refusing recognition of A's just claim to recoupment.'

Clauson L.J. also explained the *Liggett* case on the basis that Mr. Liggett had authority to pay the company's debts. Having referred to the *Liggett* case, Clauson L.J. stated that the principle asserted could not be extended, at pp. 327–328:

'so as to cover not only a case where the money provided had been expended by the quasi-borrower or by an agent authorised by him to pay his legitimate debts, but also the case of the money being expended by an outsider with no authority either direct or indirect to pay the quasi-borrower's debts . . . In my judgment it results from a survey of the cases upon which the appellants sought to establish the equity on which they rely that no principle can be deduced from them which enables this court to hold that the mere facts that Mr. Creighton made payments which enured to the benefit of the company established an equity in his favour against the company to have recoupment from their funds.'

(It appears to have been assumed that the subsidiaries' liabilities to their creditors had been discharged in law by the appellant's payment.)

Applying the *Cleadon* case to the present facts, I regard it as authority for the proposition that, in the absence of authorisation or ratification by the company of the bank's payment to the third party, the 'mere fact' that the bank's payment enured to the benefit of the company does not establish an equity in favour of the bank against the company. Moreover, even upon Wright J.'s formulation in the *Liggett* case, in order to establish the equity, the bank would have to show that the payment discharged (at least partially) a legal liability of the customer. In the absence of evidence that the bank's payment has been made on the customer's behalf or subsequently ratified by him, the payment to the creditor will not of itself discharge the company's liability to the creditor: see *Goff & Jones. The Law of Restitution*, 5th ed. (1998), p. 17, and cases there cited including *Barclays Bank v W. J. Simms Son & Cooke (Southern) Ltd* [1980] Q.B. 677 and *Electricity Supply Nominees Ltd v Thorn EMI Retail Ltd.* (1991) 63 P. & C.R. 143, 148, *per* Fox L.J. It is not established in this case that the company's legal liability to the company's creditor had been discharged by the voluntary payment by the bank. While stating that the rule appears to be of 'little merit' *Goff and Jones* by reference to authority state that, at p. 17: 'it is not easy to discharge another's debt in English law. This will occur only if the debtor authorised, or subsequently ratified, the payment.' Thus the two principles coincide and authorisation or ratification is necessary.

It is unnecessary in this appeal to decide general questions as to the circumstances in which another's debt may be discharged. In present circumstances, the onus is on the bank to set up any equity they assert to defeat their customer's claim for the return of his money. They may do so by evidence of authorisation or ratification of a payment to a third party but those features are missing in this case. That being so I would decide the case on the basis that, in the absence of such authorisation or ratification, payment to a third party cannot of itself defeat the customer's claim. However even if, contrary to the *Cleadon* case, there may be a defence in the absence of authorisation or ratification, there must at least be evidence that the payment had the effect of discharging the customer's debt. Merely to assert the absence of loss is not sufficient.

In relation to a banker, the principle applied appears to me to be soundly based. It is a startling proposition that bankers can pay sums to a third party out of a customer's account because they believe the customer to be indebted to that third party. I see no difference in principle between a judgment debt and other perceived debts. As against a customer, a contrary principle would place the bank in a position to act as debt collector for creditors of the customer. It would be for a customer who contested a creditor's claim then to seek relief. The bank could decide in what priority the claims of creditors were to be met out of the sums in the account, without the customer having recourse against the bank. A bankruptcy or liquidation may occur shortly after a payment, as in this case, with possible effects on the rights of creditors generally.

There will be circumstances in which a court may intervene to prevent unjust enrichment either by the customer in having his money from the bank as well as having the claim of his creditor met, or by the creditor who has double payment of the debt. The onus is in my judgment on the bank to establish the unjust enrichment on the evidence. In this case not only is there no evidence of authorisation or ratification of the payment to the third party by the customer but there is no evidence of unjust enrichment by the customer. In the absence of authorisation or ratification of the payment, the bank must in my judgment meet this claim and recoup the sum paid, if they can, from the third party to which it was paid.

. . .

I find nothing undesirable in a bank which pays money from a customer's account without authority having an onus placed upon it to establish facts which may enable the bank to escape liability for its wrongful act.

I would allow the appeal.

May LJ: I agree that this appeal should be allowed for the reasons given by Pill L.J.

Subject to particular banking arrangements, the customer of a bank is entitled to require payment to him by the bank of the full balance credited to his account. It is, in my view, obvious that the bank cannot, without the customer's authority or unless there is an obligation imposed on the bank by due process of law, unilaterally choose to pay money to a creditor of the customer and then reduce the credit balance in the customer's account by debiting the amount of the payment. If the bank purported to do this, the customer would remain entitled to require payment of the full unreduced credit balance. This would be a claim for payment of an amount to which the customer is contractually entitled, not a claim for damages for breach of contract. The customer does not have to prove a loss to justify requiring the bank to pay the full balance of his account.

In the present case, the defendant bank had no authority, and no purported authority (such as there was in *B. Liggett (Liverpool) Ltd v Barclays Bank Ltd.* [1928] 1 K.B. 48), of their customer to make the payment in question and there was no obligation imposed on them by due process of law to make the payment, since the garnishee order had not been made absolute. It was a gratuitous payment and the bank had no defence to the claim unless they established additional facts. No equity arises from the circumstances of the payment itself. The bank simply made a mistake.

In another case, it might be possible to establish that the customer ratified the gratuitous payment either expressly or by taking advantage of it; or there might conceivably be circumstances not amounting to ratification in which it would nevertheless be unconscionable to allow the customer to recover from the bank the balance of his account without deduction of a payment which the bank had made gratuitously. But I agree with Pill L.J. that no such circumstances were established in this case.

NOTES AND QUESTIONS

1. Is *Crantrave* reconcilable with the *Liggett* case referred to in Pill LJ's judgment?

2. Was Pill LJ deciding when a debt is discharged? On the one hand, he said, 'In the absence of evidence that the bank's payment has been made on the customer's behalf or subsequently ratified by him, the payment to the creditor will not of itself discharge the [customer's] liability to the creditor . . .' On the other hand he went on to say, 'It is unnecessary in this appeal to decide general questions as to the circumstances in which another's debt may be discharged.'

3. The traditional view, as applied in *Crantrave* and adhered to by Goff and Jones, 1–018 is fully articulated by Birks and Beatson in the following extract and defended further by Beatson in a postscript to this article (below, 549). That view is that the unrequested (by the debtor) payment of another's debt only discharges that debt without the debtor's acceptance where it was paid under legal compulsion or, probably, by necessity. The unjust factors that can be linked to the incontrovertible benefit of the discharge of a debt are therefore restricted to legal compulsion and necessity: free acceptance by the debtor is otherwise required for a restitutionary claim to succeed against the debtor.

• P Birks and J Beatson, 'Unrequested Payment of Another's Debt' (1976) 92 *LQR* 188

The proposition which is fundamental to this article is that the problems which arise in the law of restitution when one person pays another's debt cannot be solved in the absence of a stable analysis of the effects of such a payment on the relationship between the creditor and the debtor. Recently, in *Owen v Tate*, the Court of Appeal, deciding that a voluntary surety had no right to restitution from the principal debtor, omitted to supply that analysis. Our aim is to show that the omission can be supplied, largely from nineteenth-century cases, and, ultimately, to suggest that the decision in *Owen v Tate* then becomes open to question.

The situation with which we are concerned is that of which the common sense view would be that one person, whom we shall call the intervener, has by payment or other satisfaction, extinguished the debt of another without having been asked to do so. The discussion will fall into three parts. In the first we shall seek to answer the question whether the debt is in law discharged and, if so, precisely how. In the second the question will be whether the intervener can recover the amount of his payment from the debtor or from the creditor whom he has paid. In both these parts we shall avoid discussing the special facts of *Owen v Tate* itself. The third part will be devoted to that case.

We shall throughout be primarily concerned with the voluntary intervener and shall draw on the law relating to the non-volunteer, which is more settled, only so far as is necessary to avoid presenting an incomplete picture. We shall not consider at all, unless incidentally, either the case of an intervener who was jointly or jointly and severally liable with the debtor whom he claims to have discharged or the right to contribution which an intervener who was liable to make the payment has against those liable in the same degree.

I. IS THE DEBT DISCHARGED?

(a) Volunteers

The Roman rule was that payment of another's debt discharged the debt, even if the intervener paid voluntarily and against the will of the debtor. Although that rule has been pressed on English courts,[1] and found favour with Willes J[2] it has not been accepted.[3] . . .

The question was squarely raised . . . by *Belshaw v Bush*.[4] [*They consider the case and continue:*]

The law as stated in *Belshaw v Bush* can be summed up as follows: where a voluntary intervener pays the debt or part of the debt of another, then, provided he pays for and on account of the debt, the debtor may obtain his discharge or *pro tanto* discharge by subsequently adopting the payment, which he may do by his plea to an action brought by the creditor after the intervener's payment. It is not the intervener's payment but its adoption by the debtor which effects the discharge.

The law so stated was applied in a number of cases after *Belshaw v Bush*. . . .

(b) Non-Volunteers

Where the intervener is not a volunteer a distinction must be made between cases in which the voluntary character of his payment is negatived by reason of a secondary liability, whether personal or proprietary, itself not voluntarily incurred, and cases in which it is negatived by some other factor.

Where the intervener is not a volunteer because of his secondary liability to make the payment, the debt is automatically discharged by his payment. . . .

Where the intervener is not a volunteer by reason of a factor other than a secondary liability, his payment does not discharge the debt. This proposition is subject to one insecure exception.

The cases which allow the intervener reimbursement irrespective of the debtor's assent to the intervention do not, subject to the exception shortly to be mentioned, go beyond non-volunteers who are such because of secondary liability. That means that a non-volunteer who, for instance, is compelled to pay by duress or who pays by mistake cannot move straight to reimbursement from the debtor. And, if he cannot, although not a volunteer, the reason can only be that the debt is not discharged by his payment.

The explanation is that such payments can be recovered from the creditor directly. Thus, slightly varying the facts of *Astley v Reynolds*,[5] if a pawnbroker will not release pledges unless the pledgor pays his brother's debt as well as his own, and the pledgor is thus constrained to pay in order to obtain his property, he may recover from the pawnbroker. If the pledgor chooses to leave the money with the pawnbroker, his election to do so, unlike his original payment, is a voluntary act and puts him back, *quoad* the debtor, in the position of a voluntary intervener. Applying the ordinary rule for volunteers, the debt will then be discharged when the debtor assents.

The insecure exception relates to cases in which the intervener is constrained to act by necessity. It is arguable that he is then entitled to claim reimbursement from the debtor on the same basis as if he had paid under the constraint of a secondary liability. If that is so, it follows that, here too, the payment must automatically discharge the debt.

A payment by necessity has in common with payments under the compulsion of secondary liability the fact that there is no question of immediate recovery from the creditor. If it is right that a payment by necessity is to be treated on the same ground as one made by reason of a secondary liability, there

---

1 *Walter v James* (1871) LR 6 Ex. 124, 125; *James v Isaacs* (1852) 12 CB 791, 797.

2 In *Pellatt v Boosey* (1862) 31 LJCP 281, 284; *Cook v Lister* (1863) 13 CB (NS) 543, 594–5.

3 *Welby v Drake* (1825) 1 C & P 557; *Re Barnes* (1861) 4 LTNS 60; *Hirachand Punamchand v Temple* [1911] 2 KB 330; *Re Cleadon Trust Ltd* [1939] Ch 286, 311, 319, 321 (where the point is assumed without investigation) come closest to accepting this.

4 (1851) 11 CB 191.   5 (1731) 2 Str. 915.

is some basis for saying that the true rule is that every non-voluntary payment of another's debt discharges the debt, unless the factor negativing the voluntary character of the payment is such as to allow the intervener an immediate right of recovery against the creditor.

. . .

II. CAN THE INTERVENER RECOVER?

(a) Volunteers

Where the intervener's payment was voluntary and the debtor by assenting chooses to perfect his discharge, the intervener cannot recover from the creditor but can claim reimbursement from the debtor provided that the debtor, when he assents, knows that the intervener, when he paid, did not intend to make him a gift of his discharge. The cases in which an assenting debtor comes under no obligation to reimburse the intervener are: (i) where he assents believing that the intervener acted *donandi animo*; (ii) where—if such a case exists—the intervener's payment, although voluntary, automatically discharged the debt so that the debtor's assent is not the exercise of a choice whether or not to accept the benefit.

. . .

Where the debtor chooses to repudiate the voluntary intervener's payment, the intervener can recover from the creditor. Although this restitutionary right is not copiously supported in authority,[6] it is consistent with principle in that, once the debtor negatives his discharge, the consideration for which the intervener paid totally fails. On the debtor's repudiation the situation therefore returns to the *status quo*: the creditor can sue the debtor and the intervener can sue the creditor. . . .

It is often said that the volunteer should not be allowed to make himself the debtor's creditor.[7] If that means that he should not be allowed to make himself creditor against the debtor's will, it does not mean much; for the rules of assignment allow precisely that. What is important, however, is that the volunteer should not, unless the debtor assents, be able to substitute himself as creditor without the creditor's consent. For the relationship between debtor and creditor may be such that the creditor would accept discharge from a person to whom he would not assign. Thus, in *Norton v Haggett*[8] the plaintiff, after a dispute with the defendant, deliberately took steps to find out that the latter was in debt. He then approached the creditor, with whom the debtor was on good terms, and offered to discharge the debt. His offer accepted, the plaintiff then moved against the defendant in order to get even with him. The Supreme Court of Vermont rightly frustrated his revenge. Having paid for discharge, not assignment, he had acquired no right of action against the debtor.

. . .

(b) Non-Volunteers

Where the intervener has not paid voluntarily but the factor negativing the voluntary character of his payment is such as to allow him to recover as of right from the creditor, as where the creditor obtained the payment by duress, the intervener's position in relation to the debtor is exactly as if he had paid voluntarily. That is because his choosing to leave the payment with the creditor is itself a voluntary act *quoad* the debtor. Thus, if the debtor then adopts the payment he must reimburse the intervener; if he repudiates, the intervener can recover from the creditor.

Where the intervener has paid under the compulsion of a secondary liability, itself not voluntarily incurred, he cannot recover from the creditor; but there is no doubt that he can recover from

---

6 *Walter v James* (1871) LR 6 Ex 124; *Simpson v Eggington* (1855) 10 Exch 845 (*arguendo*).

7 See especially *Exall v Partridge* (1799) 8 TR 308, 310, 311 (*per* Lord Kenyon CJ and Grose J respectively); *Hodgson v Sham* (1834) 3 My & K 183, 190 (*per* Lord Brougham LC).

8 (1952) 117 Vt. 130; 85 A.2d 571. See also Dawson and Palmer, *Cases on Restitution* (2nd edn), 79–81.

the debtor, irrespective of the debtor's assent.[9] If, as seems possible, the intervener can also claim reimbursement where the voluntary character of his payment is negatived by necessity, not by secondary liability,[10] this proposition should read, as indeed it ought to if it is to be symmetrical with the last, that, where the intervener's payment is not voluntary by reason of a factor giving no immediate right of recovery from the creditor, the intervener is entitled to reimbursement from the debtor.

This restitutionary right is based on the conjunction of two elements, first, that the debtor-defendant has received an unequivocal benefit; second, that the benefit was not conferred voluntarily by the intervener-plaintiff. It is a right whose genesis is wholly independent of the will of the defendant and which is incapable of contractual analysis. It should be contrasted with the right which a voluntary intervener has against an assenting debtor, which depends on the will of the defendant, manifested in his assent, and which will frequently be capable of analysis in terms of genuine implied contract. To facilitate the contrast between these differently generated rights, one of us has suggested the labels 'strong quasi-contract' for the former, and 'weak quasi-contract' for the latter.[11] It is a serious criticism of *Owen v Tate*, even if its result be right, that it does not adequately distinguish between these two different bases of the appellant's case. The Court of Appeal did not observe that even a volunteer, who initially takes the risk of getting no return, may be relieved of that risk by the acquiescence of his beneficiary who, provided he has an opportunity to choose, 'is bound by all the rules of honesty not to be quiescent but actively to dissent, when he knows that others have for his benefit put themselves in a position of disadvantage from which, if he speaks or acts at once, they can extricate themselves, but from which, after a lapse of time, they can no longer escape.'[12]

III. *OWEN v TATE*

[*They consider the facts of the case and continue:*] The Court of Appeal treated the appellant's case as resting solely on strong quasi-contract and, in particular, on the question whether secondary liability, however incurred, was invariably sufficient to negative the voluntary character of the payment. That question was answered against the appellant, it being held that in the circumstances he was a volunteer. With that holding we respectfully agree, even though the position thus taken is different from that of the American Restatement.[13] For there is no basis for adversely distinguishing the position of one who voluntarily assumes an obligation to pay and then pays from that of one who merely pays. Restitutionary consequences ought not to be affected by the machinery which the intervener happens to have used, whether immediate payment or promise followed by payment.

As a volunteer the appellant could not succeed in strong quasi-contract, but, since the respondent had approved his payment, there remained the possibility of a claim in weak quasi-contract, the general rule being that the volunteer can recover from an assenting debtor, unless the assent is given in the belief that the intervener acted *donandi animo* or is not material to the perfection of the discharge.

Assuming this was not a case in which the debtor could say that his assent was based on a belief that the intervener intended to make him a gift, the reason why the claim in weak quasi-contract could not succeed can only be that the respondent's assent was not material to his discharge and was not therefore an election to receive the benefit. While it is true that, when the respondent first

9 *Sapsford v Fletcher* (1792) 4 TR 511; *Exall v Partridge* (1799) 8 TR 308; *Taylor v Zamira* (1816) 6 Taunt 524; *Edmunds v Wallingford* (1885) 14 QBD 811; *Moule v Garrett* (1872) LR 7 Ex 101; *Johnson v Royal Mail Steam Packet Co.* (1867) LR 3 CP 38; *Gebhardt v Saunders* [1892] 2 QB 452; *Brook's Wharf v Goodman* [1937] 1 KB 534.

10 *Owen v Tate* [1975] 2 All ER 129, 135, 136 (*per* Scarman and Stephenson LJJ respectively). Although these dicta refer to one who becomes a surety by necessity, the same reasoning should apply to one who actually pays a debt under necessity.

11 Birks (1974) 27 CLP 13, 14–19.

12 *City Bank of Sydney v McLouglin* (1909) 9 CLR 615, 625 (*per* Griffiths CJ).

13 *Restatement of Restitution* (1937), Art. 78b and comment at 116.

approved—immediately before payment—he was not in a position to decide whether the appellant should or should not pay, it could not be said that continued assent after payment did not constitute a free choice to accept the discharge, unless, contrary to the usual rule, this voluntary payment automatically discharged the debt. Assent after perfect discharge could not connote choice: 'One cleans another's shoes; what can the other do but put them on?'[14] But if the payment did not automatically discharge the debt, the respondent's discharge lay in his own election and his assent satisfied the conditions for the weak quasi-contractual claim. The crucial question is whether payment by a voluntary surety does or does not automatically discharge the debt.

That is a question which appears never to have been fully considered, although the assumption has been, as in *Owen v Tate*, that, so far as concerns discharge as opposed to reimbursement, volunteer and non-volunteer sureties are not to be distinguished.[15] It would be regrettable if that assumption were to prevail, without regard to its restitutionary consequences, since the natural grouping is of all volunteers, not all sureties.

Automatic discharge in this case cannot be supported by reference to cases of requested intervention, since *ex hypothesi* the volunteer surety is not a requested intervener. Nor can it be supported by reference to cases of intervention lawfully compelled, since those cases assimilate only non-volunteers to requested interveners. Nor can it be supported from cases of joint or joint and several liability,[16] since the voluntary surety's liability is several. Moreover, its restitutionary consequences are savage. For if the appellant in *Owen v Tate* had merely paid off the respondent's debt, instead of first becoming his surety and then paying, the respondent's assent would have compelled him to repay and his repudiation would have enabled the appellant to recover from the bank. The machinery of promise followed by payment makes the extreme difference that the intervener can get no restitutionary rights in the event of either assent or repudiation. In another area of restitution [duress] the same unintelligible distinction has been much criticised.

If we are wrong to argue that the voluntary surety's payment does not automatically discharge the principal debt, we think that he ought nevertheless to be subrogated to the creditor's rights against the debtor in order to recoup his payment. Such a right of subrogation would conflict with a basic principle of restitution, namely that a volunteer cannot recover from his beneficiary unless the conditions of the weak quasi-contractual claim are satisfied. It would therefore be an anomaly within the law of restitution, the justification for which would be that the denial of restitution is equally anomalous since, from the narrower perspective of the law relating to voluntary discharge, the unintended consequence of the rule decreeing automatic discharge is to render the position of the voluntary surety uniquely hard.

Such a cure for the conceptual accident of which the voluntary surety would otherwise be the victim is rendered doubly necessary by the fact that if any distinction ought to be drawn between this volunteer and all others it ought to be drawn in his favour. For, so far as the objection to allowing the volunteer direct access to the debtor is that assignment must not masquerade as discharge, because the creditor might accept discharge from a person to whom he would not assign, the volunteer surety is outside that mischief. When a creditor accepts such a surety, there is almost no question of any masquerade, for he must know, at least unless he has clear indication to the contrary, that he is dealing with a person who, if he ultimately pays the debt, will expect to be able to seek reimbursement from the debtor. The voluntary surety therefore ought, if anything, to be in a better position *vis à vis* the debtor than other volunteers. Even if it stood alone, that conclusion should raise a question against the decision in *Owen v Tate*.

---

14 *Taylor v Laird* (1856) 25 LJ Ex 329, 332 (*per* Pollock CB).
15 *Re Debtor (No 627 of 1936)* [1937] Ch 156, 166; *Anson v Anson* [1953] 1 QB 636, 642–3.
16 *Deering v Winchelsea (Earl)* (1787) 1 Cox Eq Cas 318; 2 Bos & Pul 270.

IV. CONCLUSIONS

To sum up:

1. Payment by a voluntary intervener does not discharge the debt unless and until the debtor assents, the assent then operating, not through agency, but simply as the acceptance of a benefit.

2. Payment by a non-volunteer, where the factor negativing voluntariness is not such as to give an immediate right of recovery against the creditor, automatically discharges the debt.
   This proposition is not established beyond doubt, except where the factor negativing voluntariness is a secondary liability, itself not voluntarily incurred.

3. Payment by a non-volunteer, where the factor negativing voluntariness is such as to give an immediate right of recovery from the creditor, does not discharge the debt unless the intervener chooses to leave his payment with the creditor and the debtor assents to his discharge.

4. A voluntary intervener has a right to be reimbursed by the debtor if the latter assents to his discharge, provided that that assent is given in the knowledge that the intervener did not intend to act gratuitously and is (as, subject to proposition 8, it always must be) material to the discharge.

5. A voluntary intervener can recover from the creditor if the debtor, by repudiating, causes a total failure of the consideration for which the intervener paid. If the debtor's repudiation causes only a partial failure of that consideration, the intervener ought to be subrogated to the creditor's right against the debtor.

6. A non-volunteer who could recover his payment from the creditor but chooses not to (proposition 3) has the same restitutionary rights as a volunteer (propositions 4 and 5).

7. A non-volunteer who on payment gets no immediate restitutionary right against the creditor (proposition 2) is entitled to be reimbursed by the debtor, whether or not the debtor assents.
   This is subject to the same uncertainty as proposition 2.

8. An intervener who pays by reason of a secondary liability voluntarily incurred is a volunteer and ought, contrary to *Owen v Tate*, to be subject to the same rules as all other volunteers (propositions 1, 4, 5). But it may be that, contrary to proposition 1, his payment automatically discharges the debt and thus excludes the restitutionary rights in propositions 4 and 5. If that is so, he ought, also contrary to *Owen v Tate*, to be allowed an exceptional restitutionary right against the debtor except in the case in which, in assuming his liability, he manifests an intention to act gratuitously.

In addition to *Belshaw v Bush* (1851) 11 CB 191 and other cases cited by Birks and Beatson, their approach is consistent with *Barclays Bank Ltd v WJ Simms* (above, 153) and *Crantrave Ltd v Lloyds Bank plc* (above, 534) in both of which it was held that a mistaken payment to a creditor by the intervener did not discharge the debtor's debt.

But there are also cases that do not appear to be consistent with the traditional view (see, e.g., *Welby v Drake* (1825) 1 C & P 557 and *Hirachand Punamchand v Temple* [1911] 2 KB 330; see also *County of Carleton v City of Ottawa* above, 188–190). An opposing theory—which rests on the view that a payment made to discharge a debt and accepted by the creditor as discharging that debt ought to discharge that debt automatically (i.e. without the debtor's acceptance)—is put forward by Friedmann in the following extract (see also Burrows at 293–302). If an 'automatic discharge' theory is correct, the unjust factors linked to discharge of another's debt can extend to, for example, mistake or duress or undue influence.

• D Friedmann, 'Payment of Another's Debt' (1983) 99 *LQR* 534

POWER OF A STRANGER TO DISCHARGE ANOTHER'S DEBT

It was established rather early in English law that if a stranger offers to pay another's debt, the creditor is not bound to accept it. The question rarely arises. It is generally in the interest of the creditor to accept payment by whoever it is offered. The ordinary rule of business is that payment is always welcome. It does not, however, follow that because the third party has no power to make legal tender, his payment, if accepted, does not discharge the debt. Nevertheless, the theory that unauthorised payment does not discharge the debt was adopted in a number of cases,[1] though this trend has by no means been uniform.[2] Indeed it will be suggested that most cases which adopted the approach that unauthorised payment does not discharge the debt (unless ratified) are cases in which either the payment was not intended to protect the debtor or the creditor and the third party co-operated in an attempt to compel the debtor to pay. More recently, leading writers [Goff and Jones; Birks and Beatson] have accepted the theory that such payment does not discharge the debt and have used it as a cornerstone in analysing the payor's right to restitution. A similar approach was recently adopted by Goff J in *Barclays Bank v Simms*[3] in which a bank paid under mistake a stopped cheque. The bank was allowed to recover its payment from the payee and the decision was predicated on the ground that since the payment was unauthorised it did not discharge the debt.

It is, however, submitted that analysis of the restitution issue from this angle is not very helpful. It is obvious that payment does not discharge the debt if the payor is entitled to recover it from the creditor and, in fact, does so. But this reasoning is, at best, circular and does not reveal the actual ground for recovery. It is clear that the mere fact that the payor acted without the debtor's authority does not entitle him to restitution from the creditor. There may, of course, be instances of mistake, fraud or duress in which recovery from the creditor is allowed. In these circumstances, the original debt remains outstanding. But to treat this as the ground for recovery is to put the proposition the wrong way round. Rather it is because recovery is allowed that the debt cannot be treated as having been extinguished.

This reasoning is not alien to the common law. Thus, it is generally recognised that where the third party was compelled by law to pay the debt, his payment operates to discharge it although he was not authorised by the debtor to do so. The reason is obvious. The creditor has a right to demand the payment and is entitled to keep it. The inescapable conclusion is that the payment discharges the debt. This reasoning is of broader application. It is submitted that whenever the creditor is entitled to keep the payment, which he received in discharge of the debt, the debt must be treated as having been discharged, even if the creditor was not entitled to demand the payment from the person who made it.

In other words, from the point of view of the creditor the debt has been discharged (even if payment was not authorised) if the following conditions are fulfilled: First, the creditor is entitled to keep the payment he received from the third party. Secondly, the creditor is no longer entitled to sue the debtor for his own benefit.

. . .

It has been suggested [by Birks and Beatson] that if the debtor repudiates the payment, the payor can recover it from the creditor on the ground of total failure of consideration. The argument is predicated on the theory that the unauthorised payment did not discharge the debt and that such a

---

1 *Simpson v Eggington* (1855) 10 Ex. 845; *Walter v James* (1871) LR 6 Ex 124.

2 *Hirachand Punamchand v Temple* [1911] 2 KB 330 (CA); *Owen v Tate* [1976] QB 402 in which Stephenson LJ at 412–13 clearly assumed that the payment by the plaintiff, who became a surety without the debtor's request, discharged the debt.

3 [1980] QB 677.

discharge was the sole consideration promised by the creditor in exchange for the payment. It is not, however, convincing. If the creditor abstains from pursuing his debtor and treats the debt as having been discharged, he does all that is and can be expected of him. It is unlikely that the parties had anything else in mind. It is, of course, conceivable that payment was made and received on condition that the debtor will assent to it. But there is no reason to imply such a condition. Under this view, there will be a failure of consideration only if the creditor actually sues the debtor without the payer's consent.

The creditor's right to keep the payment is (unless otherwise agreed) ... not affected by the position which the debtor chooses to adopt. In fact, the debtor, if he first learns about the payment after it was made, is not required to adopt any position and is free to remain passive. But even if he does raise an objection the creditor may disregard it. Indeed, the debtor has neither a moral right nor legal power to compel the creditor to refund the money to the payor. If the debtor still insists upon paying his own debt to the original creditor, it is unlikely that a serious problem will arise. But the creditor will have to transfer it to the third party from whom he received payment.[4] In any event, it seems obvious that the creditor is entitled to disregard the debtor's repudiation of the third party's payment (as well as a demand to refund the money) if such a repudiation is not accompanied by a tender of payment of the same debt.

A somewhat similar situation exists where the unauthorised payor has prima facie a right to restitution (e.g. on the ground of mistake) but the creditor has a defence (e.g. estoppel or change of position). It seems clear that the debtor cannot by repudiating the payment deprive the creditor of his defence. And yet, although the payment was unauthorised it is hardly conceivable that the creditor, who keeps the payment, can still maintain an action, for his own benefit, against the debtor on the theory that the debt has not been extinguished.

The issue can be further examined in instances in which the obligation once performed by a stranger cannot, as a practical matter, be performed again by the debtor. A possible example is that of an unauthorised performance of an obligation to repair a bridge or to extinguish a fire. In these instances, there can be little doubt that an unauthorised performance by a third party discharges the obligation. At first glance, this type of a case seems, for mere practical reasons, different from the ordinary case of payment of a monetary obligation. Yet, the ground for treating the unauthorised performance as a discharge is in both instances similar. It is because the creditor cannot be compelled to restore that which he received that the obligation is discharged. In one instance, he cannot be compelled to do so because as a matter of fact it is hardly feasible. In the other instance, he is not required to do so because legally he is entitled to keep that which he received.

The concept that a stranger cannot discharge the debt of another has been used to explain the denial of recovery by the payor from the debtor who, in theory, received no benefit since his debt remains outstanding. The argument is, however, a little unreal because ordinarily a creditor who has been paid in full has no interest in pursuing his original claim, nor does he have a legal right to recover the same amount twice. If he does sue the debtor he will in all probability fail,[5] unless he returned the money to the payor. In fact, the only person who can benefit from an action by the creditor against the debtor is the payor. If the creditor recovers, he will be accountable to the payor. If the debtor relies upon the payment in his defence, he will, presumably, be regarded as having ratified it and, thus, become liable to the payor. In this particular instance the concept that unauthorised payment does not discharge the debt (unless ratified) might facilitate recovery against the debtor. However, in order to take advantage of this possibility the co-operation of the creditor is required, and it seems that the payor has no means of forcing the creditor to sue the debtor. Indeed, providing such means

4 *Hirachand Punamchand v Temple* [1911] 2 KB 330, 337, 392 (CA).
5 *Hirachand Punamchand v Temple* [1911] 2 KB 330 (CA).

would actually amount to recognising the payor's right to restitution from the debtor by way of subrogation. But the mere fact that one person pays the debt of another does not entitle him to subrogation. Additional elements must be shown in order for subrogation to be granted.

Hence, the paid creditor can compel the debtor to pay, though, in effect, his act will inure to the benefit of the payor who might otherwise have no right of recovery. *Walter v James*[6] provides a striking example of co-operation between the creditor and the payor, following which the payor received back his payment, while the debtor was compelled to honour his obligation. In that case, the third party acted as an attorney for the defendant but his authority to pay the debt was revoked by the defendant. Nevertheless, the third party felt that he was under a moral obligation to see that the plaintiff was paid and paid him £60 in discharge of the debt. The defendant did not ratify the payment and when the plaintiff learned that the money was paid without the defendant's authority he returned it to the third party. It was held that the plaintiff was entitled to sue on the original claim. It seems clear that the plaintiff would not have been able to succeed if he had not returned the payment to the third party. Indeed, the essence of the case is that the creditor and the third party were competent 'to undo what they had done.'[7] Only by rescinding the transaction it became possible for the creditor to sue upon the original debt.

This provides the clue to resolving the conflict between the rules that permit the creditor to keep the unauthorised payment and prevent him from suing the debtor for his own benefit and the concept that unauthorised payment does not discharge the debt. The answer lies in the possibility of revival. It is submitted that the unauthorised payment, which the creditor is entitled to keep, discharges the debt. However, if the debtor does not adopt the payment, the creditor can by co-operating with the payor, revive the debt. By adopting the payment or relying upon it against the creditor, the debtor renders himself liable to the payor. The adoption of this payment is not a mere reliance on the situation created by the payment (discharge of the debt). It has the additional consequence of preventing the possibility of the original debt being revived. . . .

SUMMARY AND CONCLUSIONS

Discharge of the debt

(1) An unauthorised payment of another's debt, if accepted by the creditor in discharge of the debt, operates to discharge it.
(2) If, however, the debtor does not subsequently ratify the unauthorised payment the creditor and the payor can revive the debt. A possible way of reviving it is by a refund of the payment by the creditor to the payor. The mere fact that an unauthorised payment was made does not, however, entitle the payor to subrogation nor does it entitle him to compel the creditor to co-operate with him in order to revive the debt or to sue the debtor for the benefit of the payor.
(3) If the debtor ratifies the payment, revival of the debt is no longer possible, but such ratification will render him liable to the payor.
(4) Where the payment does not merely discharge the debt, but also imposes upon the creditor an obligation towards the debtor, a demand or an acceptance by the debtor of the performance of this obligation constitutes ratification of the payment. It prevents the possibility of revival of the original debt and it also prevents the possibility of rescinding the creditor's duty of performance towards him on the ground that he did not make the payment upon which the duty of performance was dependent. Ratification will impose upon the debtor a duty of restitution towards the payor.

6 (1871) LR 6 Ex 124.
7 *Ibid.* 127, *per* Kelly CB.

Restitution from the creditor

(5) The mere fact that the payment was not authorised does not entitle the payor to recover it from the creditor. Indeed, where payment was by way of a settlement or was otherwise voluntary, recovery from the creditor is precluded. In such an instance, the payor is similarly not entitled to demand that the creditor will co-operate with him in order to revive the debt (proposition (2) *supra*).

(6) In cases of mistake, the payor is entitled to recover his payment from the creditor in accordance with the general rules which apply to recovery of payments made under mistake, subject to the following:

(a) where the creditor accepted the payment in good faith in discharge of another's debt and was unaware of the payor's mistake, he is not liable to restitution, provided the payor realised that his payment to the creditor is accepted in discharge of such debt;

(b) the payor is, however, entitled to restitution on the ground of mistake if he did not realise that his payment would be accepted in discharge of another's debt even if the creditor believed in good faith that payment is made to him in discharge of such debt. The payor is similarly entitled to restitution on the ground of mistake if he paid in order to discharge a non-existing debt of one person, even if the creditor believed that payment was made to him on account of an existing debt of another person.[8]

(7) In *Barclays Bank v Simms*, it was held, contrary to proposition 6(a), that the payor is entitled to restitution from a bona fide creditor if his mistake related to the existence of the debtor's authority to pay. It was, thus, held that a bank which paid under mistake a countermanded cheque is entitled to restitution from the bona fide payee. It is, however, submitted that if the amount involved was due to the payee by the drawer, restitution from the payee ought to have been denied.

Restitution from the debtor

(8) The unauthorised payment confers a benefit upon the debtor because, unless the debt is revived (proposition (2) *supra*) or unless the creditor is liable to refund the payment to the payor, the debt is discharged and the creditor is not entitled to sue the debtor for his own benefit.

(9) The right of the unauthorised payor to restitution from the debtor for the benefit conferred is determined in accordance with the rules relating to unsolicited benefits. These rules, which subject to a number of exceptions, generally deny recovery for unsolicited payment of another's debt, were in some instances modified by statute.[9] There are also indications that the strict rule regarding unsolicited benefits may be relaxed in the case of services rendered. This approach has not yet been reflected in court decisions dealing with the discharge of another's debt.[10] The payor will, however, be entitled to restitution from the debtor if the debtor ratifies the payment, since ratification prevents the possibility of the debt being revived and thus constitutes an acceptance of the benefit (propositions (3) and (4) *supra*).

(10) Where the mistaken payor has no right to restitution from the creditor because of the rule relating to bona fide discharge (proposition 6(a) *supra*) or because of another defence available to the creditor (e.g. estoppel) restitution from the debtor ought to be allowed. The debtor will, however, be entitled to rely on any defence which was available to him against the original creditor. The test regarding the nature of the mistake which provides ground for recovery should be assimilated to that which would have applied had the money been handed directly by the payor to the debtor.

---

8 Unless, of course, the creditor has another defence such as estoppel.

9 S. 1(4) of the Civil Liability (Contribution) Act 1978.

10 *Owen v Tate* [1976] QB 402.

Alternative remedies

(11) It seems that under English law the mistaken payor will not be allowed to recover from the debtor if he is entitled to restitution from the creditor. It is, however, submitted that *de lege ferenda* the possibility of an alternative remedy against the debtor ought to be recognised.

In the following passage, Stoljar implicitly accepts an automatic discharge view but in the context of his more radical theory that a volunteer who pays off another's debt or liability is entitled to reimbursement so long as not manifestly officious. (For criticism of 'officiousness' as an approach to *unjust* enrichment, see Burrows, at 43–4, 275).

- **S Stoljar,** *The Law of Quasi-Contract* (2nd edn, 1989), 172–4

Suppose D is on holiday when his telephone bill arrives, and suppose the bill is left with D's neighbour (P) who is also told that unless the bill is paid within three days (long before D's announced return), the phone will be disconnected and not reconnected without a substantial penalty. P decides to pay D's bill immediately, to save him from unnecessary trouble later on. We assume of course that P acts without authority yet with a sort of calculated altruism as he advances money to help D but not to make a gift of it. Concomitantly we assume that P's payment is unquestionably beneficial to D, constituting as it does an urgent and even necessary intervention not only because D is in the circumstances unable to act for himself, P's intervention also saved D from having to pay a heavy penalty. Now in *Owen v Tate*, the volunteer principle is certainly repeated in traditional wide terms under which a person is denied reimbursement unless he acts under some request or some form of constraint. Yet this decision, as quite a few others like it, did not actually rest, or at any rate did not have to rest, on so narrow a ground. Indeed Scarman LJ there conceded that even a volunteer may be entitled to an indemnity at law, the 'fundamental question' being whether P's intervention was 'reasonably necessary' or there was 'some necessity' for it in the interests of P or D or both. What is more, the court made a detailed inquiry into all the consequences to D of P's payment or guarantee to C, an inquiry clearly superfluous had the volunteer principle been accepted to its full nominal extent.

Combining these openings with some of the wider (or, more exactly, less strict or literal) views of compulsion . . . as well as with the broader approaches in equity (especially those indicated by *Butler v Rice*[1] or the equitable treatment of contribution . . .), P's right of reimbursement might then even be stated in bolder terms: that, subject to the significant exception of P's actions constituting manifest officiousness, P can recover money paid by him to discharge D's debt or liability to C, even where P is technically a volunteer. P, in other words, can recover without his payment having to be justifiable either on the ground of common law compulsion or on the basis of special equitable doctrines like quasi-assignment or subrogation. Not that under a broader principle the detailed instances of reimbursement discussed before would become entirely redundant; they would still represent instances where P's intervention is both typically and demonstrably non-officious and justified. But they would rather be instances of a wider principle, not closed instances confined to their own facts. Even the equitable doctrines are, after all, but devices to facilitate reimbursement, and so eminently susceptible of merging with other instances in the law all serving the same end.

Putting the various approaches together, the combined principle would simply put D under a duty to reimburse P if the financial liability that P discharged is ultimately, or is originally or primarily, upon D, not P. Precisely this, as we have seen, is the principle very early suggested by Lawrence J.[2] Indeed had this principle been followed ever since, it would have provided a far simpler and more coherent basis for the whole development of money paid, just as it would have been clearer all along that, in

---

1 [1910] 2 Ch 277.   2 *Exall v Partridge* (1799) 8 TR 308 at 311.

final analysis, there are here but two countervailing questions facing the courts: whether P's payment is merely one of an intermeddler, or whether, on the contrary, his payment, if not reimbursed, would entail D's unjustifiable enrichment together with P's unjust sacrifice.

In the extract that follows Beatson defends his earlier views (see above, 538) against an 'automatic discharge' theory, particularly that espoused by Friedmann.

• J Beatson, *The Use and Abuse of Unjust Enrichment* (1991), 200–5

The questions of whether the non-compulsory payment of another's debt discharges the debtor's obligation and, if so, whether the intervener has a restitutionary claim against the debtor involve complex issues. Quite apart from the question of the nature of the benefit, if any, to the debtor, which is not as simple as might appear at first sight, there is the fact that granting the intervener a restitutionary remedy can involve short-circuiting complex multiparty transactions. In a multiparty situation one has to cut the Gordian knot and begin the analysis somewhere but [my and Birks' article] has met with criticism. First there are those who argue that, apart from *Norton v Haggett*[1] officiousness, the intervener should always be subrogated to the creditor's claim.[2] Secondly, it has also been argued, more radically, that unauthorized payment does discharge the debt and should, in principle, give rise to a restitutionary remedy.[3]

Even Professor Birks, my co-author, while accepting that in English law the general rule is that a voluntary payment does not discharge the debt or other liability unless and until the discharge is accepted by the debtor, nevertheless now believes that a different rule, namely, that the debt is discharged, 'would provide a much more stable basis from which to begin the enquiry'.[4] This has attractions from the point of view of the overall symmetry of this body of law since compulsory and voluntary payments would have the same effect. It is also the case that since payments made under necessity are increasingly being regarded as non-voluntary, the category of cases in which a payment is considered voluntary, and therefore as not discharging the debt, is shrinking. However, the English rule concerning voluntary payments has been affirmed[5] and gains support from one argument from principle and a number of more pragmatically based considerations based on the need to protect the debtor. Where there is compulsion, both principle and the pragmatic considerations are met with and overcome by a countervailing policy to protect the intervener who does not act voluntarily.

As a preliminary, the argument that even a voluntary payment should discharge the debt relies on an assumption. This is that in nearly all cases the intervener will be unable to recover the payment from the creditor.[6] On this assumption there is a consequent factual benefit to the debtor who is unlikely to be sued by a creditor who has been paid off[7] and who should therefore be subject to a restitutionary claim by the intervener. The argument advanced in the article that, where the intervention is repudiated by the debtor, the payer can recover the payment from the creditor on the ground of total failure of consideration is rejected as unconvincing. Professor Friedmann states that:

> If the creditor abstains from pursuing his debtor and treats the debt as having been discharged, he does all that is and can be expected of him. It is unlikely that the parties had anything else in mind. It is, of course, conceivable that payment was made and received on condition that the debtor will

1 85 A 2d 571 (1952).

2 Goff & Jones, The Law of Restitution (3rd edn) 317, 529–31; McCamus, (1978) 16 *Osgoode HLJ* 517, 551–8. Cf. Stoljar, The Law of Quasi-Contract (2nd edn) 167–9.

3 Friedmann, (1983) 99 *LQR* 534. See also Stoljar, 166.

4 Birks, *An Introduction to the Law of Restitution* 191.

5 *Barclays Bank Ltd v W J Simms Son & Cooke (Southern) Ltd* [1980] QB 677; *Esso Petroleum Co. Ltd v Hall Russell & Co. Ltd* [1989] AC 643, 663.

6 Friedmann, (1983) 99 *LQR* 534, 537.   7 *Ibid.* 535.

assent to it. But there is no reason to imply such a condition. Under this view, there will be a failure of consideration only if the creditor actually sues the debtor without the payer's consent.[9]

But this takes a *performance* based view of payment rather than an *effect* based view. There is no compelling reason for this. It is surely arguable that a payment made to discharge or settle the debt of another is made on the basis that the debt is in fact discharged and is conditional on such discharge being achieved. If, as is submitted, the intervener is able to recover from the creditor, the assumption upon which the view that payment should discharge is based falls away. Furthermore, a scheme which makes discharge and the liability of the debtor to the intervener depend on the irrecoverability of the payment from the creditor reflects attention from what ought to be the central enquiry; whether the defendant has been unequivocally enriched. This is because it focuses on the position of a third party: the creditor.

What of the arguments favouring the no-discharge rule? The first of these is that the view that payment discharges the debt only works by assuming that it is possible for the creditor and intervener to revive the debt if the debtor does not adopt the payment.[10] *Walter v James*[11] is, despite its reasoning, explained as an instance of revival of the debt. But countenancing revival of the debt is wrong in principle because it permits parties to impose a burden on a non-consenting third party. Secondly, revival would create difficulties in practice. What would the position be if the debtor paid the creditor after the intervention and the creditor took the payment? It would be necessary for principles similar to those governing assignments to be developed so as to protect the position of a debtor who has no notice of the intervener's payment.

The main practical difficulties with the discharge view relate to the consequent assumption that as a general rule the intervener should be accorded restitution against the debtor as a matter of course save on a *Norton v Haggett* fact situation. There are several difficulties with this. First, as the law provides for assignment and imposes certain requirements before a valid assignment, to allow a payment which does not satisfy those requirements to have the same effect as an assignment constitutes a subversion of the policy of the law. It might be said that, if the contract is assignable, there is no harm in permitting the intervener a remedy. In fact, however, this could not be done without replicating the safeguards, for instance those concerning notice, which govern the law of assignment. If it is necessary to do this then it is arguable that to 'reinvent the wheel' within a restitutionary remedy is unnecessary. A perfectly good mechanism exists.

Secondly, the position of a debtor who has a defence or a counterclaim against the creditor must be considered. Where the debtor has a defence he will be able to resist restitution on the ground that there was no benefit conferred on him. However, this would involve determining whether the defence is made out in proceedings to which the creditor would not necessarily be a party. This is not an insuperable objection since it is not unreasonable for the intervener to take the risk of either the debtor establishing a defence or the creditor not co-operating. However, in the case of counterclaims this argument does not apply. If the debtor is able to plead a counterclaim then in effect what the intervener is getting is a subrogation remedy. The debt is not in fact discharged but transferred to the intervener whose claim is, as an assignment would be, 'subject to equities'. If, however, the debtor is not able to plead a counterclaim against the intervener then he is forced to institute separate proceedings against his creditor rather than being able to settle all issues in one action. This would constitute a real procedural disadvantage.

Recognition that a voluntary payment does not discharge the debt is therefore preferable because it does not involve the unprincipled and artificial possibility of permitting the creditor and intervener to revive the debt without recourse to the debtor and because it deals more satisfactorily with the position of debtors who have defences or counterclaims. If one started from the position that the

---

9 (1983) 99 *LQR* 534, 539.   10 Friedmann, *op.cit.* at 542.   11 (1871) LR 6 Ex 127.

debt was always discharged one would have to build into the law of restitution safeguards similar to those developed in the context of assignment in order to protect the position of the debtor. If the effect would be to remove some ofthe requirements of assignment while keeping those which are regarded as important, it is surely arguable that the better way forward is by direct reform of the law of assignment rather than by the law of restitution which, in this respect, is a green-field site.

The alternative way forward, to give the non-officious volunteer derivative rights by subrogating him to the position of the creditor, appears less objectionable. This is because subrogation, which means 'substitution', puts the intervener in the creditor's shoes for the purpose of taking over claims previously maintainable by the creditor. This means that, like the assignee, the intervener will be in no better position than the creditor and most of the dangers of a direct and independent restitution-ary claim discussed above, i.e. defences, counterclaims, and the revival of discharged debts, disappear. It is for this reason that it is not possible to regard restitutionary subrogation as only semantically different from the imposition of direct restitutionary obligations. [My and Birks' article] rejected the applicability of subrogation except in the case where the consideration for the payment by the intervener had not wholly failed. The reason for this was fear that the creditor might accept a payment from a person to whom he would not assign. There is also the possibility, not discussed in the article, that the debt was not assignable. While there may be subrogation of a non-assignable claim, as where an insurer is subrogated to the assured's claim against a tortfeasor, if the debt is not assignable the case for a restitutionary remedy in favour of a volunteer, whether direct or by way of subrogation, is much weaker. However, it is certainly arguable that it is not necessary to deny a subrogation claim entirely in order to protect the debtor. The debtor would have sufficient protection if he was able to show by way of defence to a subrogated claim that the creditor would not have assigned the debt to the intervener who is now seeking a restitutionary subrogation. In *Owen v Tate* the bank could not do this. It had agreed to accept the intervener as a substitute *guarantor*, i.e. as a person who would look to the debtor for reimbursement and there was thus no bar to subrogation.

5. RESTITUTION BY CONTRIBUTION

Where C and D are under a common liability to X, and yet one cannot say that C's liability is secondary to D's (i.e. they are liable in the same degree), and C, under legal compulsion, pays more than, as between C and D, he should be responsible for, C is entitled to contribution from D of that part of the award that constitutes the overpay-ment. The law is now largely contained in the Civil Liability Contribution Act 1978, the main sections of which are reproduced below (at 552). But the 1978 Act does not affect the common law on contribution where there is a common liability to pay the same debt. *Deering v Earl of Winchelsea* (below) deals with that situation.

• *Deering v Earl of Winchelsea* (1787) 2 Bos. & P 270, Court of Exchequer

The claimant was the surety for a bond of £4,000 given by his brother. The two defendants were the sureties on two other of the brother's bonds of £4,000 each. On the insolvency of the brother, the Crown enforced the bond against the claimant for £3883 14s 8½d. The claimant successfully claimed contribution from the defendants (of £1294 11s 6¼d each).

Lord Chief Baron Eyre [*giving the opinion of the court (comprising himself and Hotham and Perrins BB), after stating the case, observed that:*] [C]ontribution was resisted on two grounds; first, that there was no foundation for the demand in the nature of the contract between the parties, the counsel for the Defendants considering the title to contribution as arising from contract expressed or implied;

secondly, that the conduct of Sir Edward Deering had deprived him of the benefit of any equity which he might have otherwise had against the Defendants.

[*After dismissing the second objection, the Lord Chief Baron considered the first objection*]. The real point is, Whether there shall be contribution by sureties in distinct obligations?

It is admitted that if they had all joined in one bond for 12,000*l* there must have been contribution. But this is said to be on the foundation of contract implied from their being parties in the same engagement, and here the parties might be strangers to each other. And it was stated that no man could be called upon to contribute who is not a surety on the face of the bond to which he is called to contribute. The point remains to be proved that contribution is founded on contract. If a view is taken of the cases, it will appear that the bottom of contribution is a fixed principle of justice, and is not founded in contract. Contract indeed may qualify it as in *Swain v Wall*, 1 Ch Rep. 149, where three were bound for H in an obligation, and agreed if H failed to bear their respective parts. Two proved insolvent, the third paid the money, and one of the others becoming solvent, he was compelled to pay a third only.

. . .

In *Sir Wm. Harbet's case*, 3 Co. 11 b. many cases are put of contribution at common law. The reason is, they are all in æquali jure, and as the law requires equality they shall equally bear the burden. This is considered as founded in equity; contract is not mentioned. The principle operates more clearly in a court of equity than at law. . . .

In the particular case of sureties, it is admitted that one surety may compel another to contribute to the debt for which they are jointly bound. On what principle? Can it be because they are jointly bound? What if they are jointly and severally bound? What if severally bound by the same or different instruments? In every one of those cases sureties have a common interest and a common burthen. They are bound as effectually quoad contribution, as if bound in one instrument, with this difference only that the sums in each instrument ascertain the proportions, whereas if they were all joined in the same engagement they must all contribute equally.

In this case Sir E. Deering, Lord Winchelsea, and Sir J. Rous were all bound that Thomas Deering should account. At law all the bonds are forfeited. The balance due might have been so large as to take in all the bonds; but here the balance happens to be less than the penalty of one. Which ought to pay? He on whom the crown calls must pay to the crown: but as between themselves they are in æquali jure, and shall contribute. This principle is carried a great way in the case of three or more sureties in a joint obligation; one being insolvent, the third is obliged to contribute a full moiety. This circumstance and the possibility of being made liable to the whole has probably produced several bonds. But this does not touch the principle of contribution where all are bound as sureties for the same person.

There is an instance in the civil law of average, where part of a cargo is thrown overboard to save the vessel, Show. Parl. Cas. 19 Moor, 297. The maxim applied is qui sentit commodum sentire debet et onus. In the case of average there is no contract express or implied, nor any privity in an ordinary sense. This shews that contribution is founded on equality, and established by the law of all nations.

There is no difficulty in ascertaining the proportions in which the parties ought to contribute. The penalties of the bonds ascertain the proportions. . . .

- ● *Civil Liability (Contribution) Act 1978, sections 1(1), 2(1), 2(3), 3, 6(1) and 7(3)*

ENTITLEMENT TO CONTRIBUTION

1.—(1) Subject to the following provisions of this section, any person liable in respect of any damage suffered by another person may recover contribution from any other person liable in respect of the same damage (whether jointly with him or otherwise). . . .

ASSESSMENT OF CONTRIBUTION

2.—(1) Subject to subsection (3) below, in any proceedings for contribution under section 1 above the amount of the contribution recoverable from any person shall be such as may be found by the court to be just and equitable having regard to the extent of that person's responsibility for the damage in question.

. . .

(3) Where the amount of the damages which have or might have been awarded in respect of the damage in question in any action brought in England and Wales by or on behalf of the person who suffered it against the person from whom the contribution is sought was or would have been subject to—

(a) any limit imposed by or under any enactment or by any agreement made before the damage occurred;

(b) any reduction by virtue of section 1 of the Law Reform (Contributory Negligence) Act 1945 or section 5 of the Fatal Accidents Act 1976; or

(c) any corresponding limit or reduction under the law of a country outside England and Wales;

the person from whom the contribution is sought shall not by virtue of any contribution awarded under section 1 above be required to pay in respect of the damage a greater amount than the amount of those damages as so limited or reduced. . . .

PROCEEDINGS AGAINST PERSONS JOINTLY LIABLE FOR THE SAME DEBT OR DAMAGE

3.—Judgment recovered against any person liable in respect of any damage shall not be a bar to an action, or to the continuation of and action, against any other person who is (apart from any such bar) jointly liable with him in respect of the same debt or damage.

INTERPRETATION

6.—(1) A person is liable in respect of any damage for the purposes of this Act if the person who suffered it (or anyone representing his estate or dependants) is entitled to recover compensation from him in respect of that damage (whatever the legal basis of his liability, whether tort, breach of contract, breach of trust or otherwise). . . .

SAVINGS

7.—(3) The right to recover contribution in accordance with section 1 above supersedes any right, other than an express contractual right, to recover contribution (as distinct from indemnity) otherwise than under this Act in corresponding circumstances; but nothing in this Act shall affect—

(a) any express or implied contractual or other right to indemnity; or

(b) any express contractual provision regulating or excluding contribution;

which would be enforceable apart from this Act (or render enforceable any agreement for indemnity or contribution which would not be enforceable apart from this Act).

NOTES AND QUESTIONS

1. For a detailed examination of the 1978 Act, see C Mitchell, 'The Civil Liability (Contribution) Act 1978' [1997] *RLR* 27. See also C Mitchell, *The Law of Contribution and Reimbursement* (2003), paras 4.20–4.50.

2. Is the law on contribution consistent with that on compulsory discharge of another's primary liability? For a useful bridge between the two, see the *Niru Battery (No 2)* case, above, 519.

3. For the controversy as to whether liability for 'damage' in the 1978 Act includes liability to make restitution, see the discussion of the relevant cases in the *Niru Battery (No 2)* case, above, 521–2.

6. REJECTION OF AN UNJUST ENRICHMENT ANALYSIS

- **J Hilliard, 'A Case for the Abolition of Legal Compulsion as a Ground of Restitution'** [2002] *CLJ* 551

I. Introduction

I agree to act as surety in return for a hefty sum, knowing full well that I might be called upon to pay out in the future. If I am called upon to pay out and do so, why can I recover from the primary debtor? Despite the fact that I chose to assume the liability, the restitutionary explanation of recovery focuses on the fact that I was compelled to pay. It explains recovery by reference to the application of a particular type of pressure upon the transferor, which has come to be known as legal compulsion. In the words of Graham Virgo, '[l]egal compulsion will arise where the plaintiff is compelled to transfer a benefit to someone in circumstances in which, if the plaintiff does not transfer the benefit, it will be taken from him or her by recourse to the legal process'.[1] It will be argued that this focus is misleading and that it is inappropriate to resort to unjust enrichment to explain such relief. Rather than examining the transferor's intent, we should ask whether a remedy is necessary to distribute fairly the burden of discharging the obligation in question. With slight refinement, this rationale can provide a simpler and more accurate explanation of the case law without the need to resort to notions of unjust enrichment.

II. A misnomer

Let us focus on the example of the surety described in the Introduction. When the primary debtor defaults, why does the surety have to pay up? The answer is obvious: he has a legal obligation to do so. So any payment made will be made because the surety was *obliged* by the law to make it. In light of this, it is tempting to emphasise the surety's lack of choice as to whether he pays or not, using the language of 'compulsion'. However, this is a misleading way to view the situation, because it overlooks why the surety came to have such a legal obligation to pay in the first place. He chose, voluntarily, to assume the legal obligation. This deliberate choice is the root cause of the payment. 'Compulsion' is an inaccurate description of what is going on here.

III. Insufficient, unusual and unneccesary

. . .

There are three reasons why it is misleading to group legal compulsion with other unjust factors that vitiate the claimant's intent. Most importantly, where the transfer is made pursuant to a prior legal obligation, the interference with the transferor's autonomy is less serious than where the transferor has made a mistake or is placed under duress for example. The reason for this is explained in Part II above: in many cases, the transferor has deliberately assumed the legal obligation, and so the transfer is consistent with his earlier choice, despite the fact that he may not want to pay up when the time comes to do so. Legal compulsion provides little, if any, justification for relief.

. . .

Secondly, legal compulsion is by itself insufficient: something more is required. A threat to have recourse to legal process is not objectionable, quite the reverse in fact. If A makes such a threat to B, this is not unjust. Some additional policy reason is required.

Thirdly, it appears that actual legal compulsion is unnecessary so long as the claimant could have been compelled—see the recent decision of the Court of Appeal in *Stimpson v Smith*[2] . . .

---

1 G Virgo, *The Principles of the Law of Restitution* (Oxford 1999) (hereafter Virgo, *Principles*), p. 224.
2 [1999] 2 WLR 1292.

What additional policy reason is required? Moran suggests that the compulsion must be 'wrongful'[3] It is submitted that this is slightly inaccurate—can it really be said to be wrongful for a person to threaten to have recourse to legal process to get another to pay him what he is owed? A better word to use might be 'inequitable'. It is inequitable not because someone has demanded a payment to which he is entitled but that the burden of payment has fallen unfairly as between the co-obligors. It is only where two parties are liable in respect of the same damage or debt and the payment of one discharges the liability of the other that the unjust factor comes into play. One of the two has paid more than is fair as regards the other. Therefore, one co-obligor is allowed to recover from another co-obligor, rather than from the party who is entitled to the benefit of the obligation.

Once, however, we have defined the policy reason in this way, the measure of relief is already clear: the defendant must pay however much is required to distribute the burden of the joint liability fairly between the co-obligors. So if it would be equitable for each of the parties to pay the same amount, then the claimant can recover half of the payment he has made, for example. This rationale is sufficient in itself both to determine the measure of relief and explain why such relief should be granted. It is unnecessary to go on to enquire as to the extent of the defendant's gain, whether such gain was at the claimant's expense and whether any defences are available: the rationale above takes care of everything. The other three limbs of Birks's four stage analysis are at best superfluous. The concept of equitable distribution of liability does all the work necessary.

Unjust enrichment is an expositive device: it should be used only where it explains areas of the law better than existing doctrine. No such clearer explanation is forthcoming here. Not only does it offer no improvement here but it adds needless complexity, replacing a one stage process (Is the distribution of liability equitable?) with a four stage version (Is the defendant enriched? Is this at the claimant's expense? etc.). Unjust enrichment is both unnecessary and undesirable here.

IV. The authorities

...

A decade after in *Lipkin Gorman v Karpnale*[4] we still await a case that bases the right of contribution on unjust enrichment. Why? The reason is simple. The judges have no need for such concepts here. The principle of the fair distribution of liabilities allows them to reach the desired result, so why should they make life more difficult for themselves by applying a more complicated set of concepts, the meaning of which remain far from clear?

V. Equitable distribution of the burden of liability

Let me elaborate upon this principle that I have put forward. Three conditions must usually be satisfied in order for it to operate. First, the claimant and defendant must be liable in respect of the same loss or debt to the same right-holder. Second, the claimant must commit an act that discharges an obligation owed by the defendant to a third party. This second requirement is not an absolute one. In the case of simple subrogation, the obligation owed by the defendant is not discharged, yet as argued below, the unusual way in which the claimant obtains relief does not mean that simple subrogation should be treated any differently from situations in which both conditions are satisfied. Thirdly, there must be a valid commerically understandable reason both for the assumption of the liability in the first place (where it was voluntarily assumed) and for the act that discharges the defendant's obligation. This explains *Owen v Tate*, where there was no such reason for the claimant to assume the liability, and it is also consistent with *Stimpson v Smith*, where the reasonable expectation

---

3 M Moran 'Rethinking Winnipeg Condominium: Restitution, Economic Loss, and Anticipatory Repairs' (1997) 47 *University of Toronto Law Journal* 115, 145.

4 [1991] 2 AC 548.

on the part of the claimant that a demand for payment was imminent provided a commercially understandable reason for the transfer.

...

VI. Simple subrogation

An area in which the problems of using unjust enrichment, and more specifically legal compulsion, to explain relief are particularly noticeable, is simple subrogation. Take the following example. A commits a tort against B, causing him £10 of loss. C, the insurer of B, pays B £10 in respect of this loss under the contract of indemnity insurance between them. Two features mark this situation out as an example of simple subrogation. Firstly, in the eyes of the law, this payment does not discharge A's obligation to compensate B. Secondly, C is allowed to take over B's live rights against A. Why is this? An investigation of the reason for relief highlights the inadequacies of unjust enrichment here.

Legal compulsion seems the obvious explanation. C has made a payment under legal compulsion and is allowed to recover the amount he has paid out by suing A in B's name. However, who is the party who is unjustly enriched? B has been enriched by C's payment, but his receipt of the payment is in no way unjust: as discussed in Part III, legal compulsion does not allow recovery from the party to whom the liability or obligation was owed; A has not been enriched at all, because he is still liable to B for the same amount as before. So such relief cannot be framed as the reversal of an enrichment unjustly acquired through legal compulsion, despite C being allowed to, in effect, recover the amount that he transferred under legal compulsion.

This difficulty forces unjust enrichment theorists to characterise the aim of such relief as the prevention, rather than the reversal, of unjust enrichment. . . . Describing simple subrogation in terms of prevention draws a distinction between such relief and the relief in cases such as *Gebhard*, which are portrayed as reversing unjust enrichment. It means that the reasons for relief in the two situations are portrayed as being crucially different. It is argued below that relief in the two situations is in fact better viewed as being founded on the same rationale.

Whatever merits it may have, using unjust enrichment here leads to an extremely complex and descriptively problematic explanation . . . . A rationale based on the equitable distribution of burden of liability overcomes both these problems. The purpose of simple subrogation is to ensure that the wrongdoer A pays, rather than C, who has committed no legal wrong. As between A and C, A should be made to bear the whole burden of liability. We can describe A as being primarily liable and C secondarily liable. Allowing C to sue in B's name is simply a device for ensuring that wherever possible, the burden ultimately falls on A rather than C.

...

NOTES AND QUESTIONS

1. Within an unjust enrichment analysis, it is now generally accepted that 'legal compulsion' is not always a factor vitiating consent (analogous to, for example, duress or mistake). This is most obviously because one can voluntarily put oneself in a position where legal compulsion is likely to be imposed (e.g. where one is a voluntary surety). The better explanation may be, therefore, that it is a policy-motivated unjust factor concerned to ensure restitution where the legal process has compelled the wrong person to pay or to pay too much. Charles Mitchell, *The Law of Contribution and Reimbursement* (2003), para. 3.28 expresses this policy-based explanation as follows: 'In cases where a claimant and a defendant are both legally liable to a creditor, and the creditor is forbidden to accumulate recoveries by enforcing his rights against them both, the law must reconcile two conflicting objectives. On the one hand, the law aims to make the defendant bear an appropriate share of the burden of paying the creditor, but on the other hand the law also aims to give the creditor the fullest possible means of recovering what is due to him. To achieve both objectives, the law therefore gives the creditor the right to recover from either the claimant or the defendant in full. In the event that the creditor

chooses to recover from the claimant, the law then gives the claimant the right to recover an appropriate contribution (or full reimbursement) from the defendant . . .'.

2. Hilliard's analysis goes one stage beyond seeing the unjust factor as being policy-motivated rather than vitiation of consent because he denies that any unjust enrichment analysis is appropriate.

3. Is not all civil law concerned with the principle of the 'equitable distribution of the burden of liability'? If so, is this a helpful organising principle?

4. Is change of position a relevant defence to a claim for 'compulsory discharge of another's liability'? If so, is Hilliard correct to say that 'The other three limbs of Birks's four stage analysis are at best superfluous. The concept of equitable distribution of liability does all the work necessary'.

9

NECESSITY

A man notices that water is seeping through the ceiling of his neighbour's house. The pipes have burst and considerable damage will be done to the contents of the house if a plumber is not called urgently. However the neighbour is away on holiday and cannot be contacted. So the man calls a plumber and pays him £120 to repair the pipes and make good the damage which has been caused. Can the man recover the £120 from his neighbour? Alternatively, suppose that he does the work himself. Can he recover the value of his services from his neighbour? The traditional answer which English law has given is that no claim lies in such circumstances. However there are groups of cases where English law has allowed a claim to succeed in what appear to us to be analogous circumstances. The tension between the traditional view and the line of cases where recovery has been allowed has never been satisfactorily resolved in English law. A number of issues await authoritative resolution in the courts. The first relates to the circumstances in which the intervener can bring a claim. What factors should the courts take into account in deciding whether or not a claim should lie? The second relates to the basis of the claim in those circumstances in which the law does recognize a claim. Is the basis of the claim the unjust enrichment of the defendant or is the aim to compensate the claimant irrespective of the benefit to the defendant? In other words, do these cases belong within the law of restitution at all or are they examples of some other head of liability (such as 'unjust sacrifice', on which see above, 101–106)? Our focus will be upon the issues raised by these cases in so far as they concern the law of unjust enrichment and we shall only touch upon alternative analyses in the concluding section of this chapter. In terms of an analysis of the case law in unjust enrichment terms, a number of problems arise.

The first is whether or not the defendant has been enriched by the intervention of the claimant. In most of the cases, the defendant has not requested or freely accepted the work, and so the test for deciding whether or not there has been a benefit is that of 'incontrovertible benefit', namely the saving of a necessary expense. But there are some cases, of which *Matheson v Smiley* (below, 586) may be said to be one, in which there does not appear to be any benefit to the defendant. Are these cases best viewed as examples of unjust sacrifice (see S. Stoljar, 'Unjust Enrichment and Unjust Sacrifice', above, 101, and G. Muir, 'Unjust Sacrifice and the Officious Intervener', 103).

The second difficulty is whether it can always be said that the enrichment of the defendant is 'at the expense of' the claimant. What of the amateur rescuer who spends time saving the defendant's property? Can it be said that the defendant's enrichment was at the expense of such a claimant? 'At the expense of' normally means that the defendant's gain represents a loss to the claimant: in other words, that there is a correlation of loss and gain. Is this so in these cases here? A further problem is created by the salvage cases: does the element of reward given by the courts to the successful salvor take these cases outside of the law of unjust enrichment?

The third difficulty relates to the identification of the unjust factor. Broadly speaking, there are two problems which arise here. The first is whether or not the law should impose a restitutionary obligation at all. There do exist cases which appear to deny the existence of such a claim (see *Nicholson v Chapman* (below, 561) and *Falcke v Scottish Imperial Insurance Co.* (below, 562)). On the other hand, there are also cases in which such a right of action has been recognized (see, for example, *Jenkins v Tucker* (below, 565), *Great Northern Railway v Swaffield* (below, 584), *Matheson v Smiley* (below, 586), and *Re Berkeley Applegate (Investment Consultants) Ltd* (below, 587)). Which line of cases is to be preferred, or can the cases be reconciled? Could they be said to strike a reasonable balance in terms of general policy (that is to say, encouraging intervention when it is most needed)? The second problem lies in identifying precisely the nature of the 'unjust factor' involved. Professor Birks has argued that it is called 'moral compulsion' (see *Introduction*, 193–202). But there are difficulties with this view, particularly in its application to the case of the professional rescuer or salvor. Alternatively, it could be maintained that the unjust factor rests on 'the policy-motivated desire of the law to encourage people to intervene to preserve the health or property of others' (Burrows, 315).

It is suggested that the latter view is the preferable one, and that cases such *Rogers v Price* (below, 566) cannot be explained in terms of moral compulsion. The difficulty which then arises lies in fleshing out the policy which entitles the claimant to bring a claim for the benefit conferred on the defendant in the course of his intervention. A number of factors appear to be at work in the cases which follow, and it is difficult to stabilize them. However the core idea appears to be that there must be an emergency which affects the defendant, his property, or those for whom he is legally responsible. It is an unresolved question whether it must have been impossible or impracticable for the claimant to have obtained the defendant's consent prior to his intervention. Attention then switches to the justification for the claimant taking upon himself the task of inter-vening in the defendant's affairs. It is not clear whether the claimant must prove that he was an appropriate person to intervene or whether the burden lies on the defendant to show that the claimant was an inappropriate person to intervene (it is suggested that the latter view is the preferable one). In deciding whether or not the claimant is an appropri-ate person to intervene the courts will inquire into the motives which prompted the claimant to intervene, whether or not he had an intention to charge for his intervention, and the qualifications which he possessed which made him an appropriate person to intervene (i.e. was he a professional or not?).

The final difficulty relates to the defences available to a claim in unjust enrichment. We point out at a number of stages in this book that the defences are playing an increasingly important role in modern cases, yet, at the present time, the scope of the defences is difficult to ascertain with any degree of precision. This difficulty is compounded by the fact that commentators do not agree on which factors are relevant as defences, and which are relevant to the identification of the cause of action or the unjust factor. For example, is it a defence for the defendant to show that the intervention of the claimant was 'officious'? Can the intervener recover where he knew or ought to have known that the defendant would not have welcomed his intervention? Must the intervener have intended to charge for his services? Is it a defence to show that there was a more suitable person who could have intervened? Should it be a defence that the services were unavailing? Does it matter that the defendant was insured against damage to his property but that he was not insured against the risk of having to make restitution to the intervener? The difficulty which is encountered in seeking to answer these questions in terms of defences is that they do not correspond with defences generally known to the law of unjust enrichment. It is therefore suggested that these questions raise issues which should be regarded as relevant to the identification of the unjust factor.

We have divided our examination of the cases into three sections. In the first section we consider the cases which reflect the traditional understanding of English law, namely that the law does not recognize the existence of a right of recovery based on necessity. Then we move on in the second section to discuss the (allegedly) exceptional cases in which English law does recognize the existence of a right of recovery. While we have attempted to put the cases into groups, it must be emphasized that the division has been made for the purpose of ease of exposition and cannot claim to be universally accepted. Finally, in the third section, we conclude with some questions which might be borne in mind when considering the future development of the law.

General Reading

Burrows, chapter 9; Goff and Jones, chapters 17 and 18; Virgo, chapter 11.

1. THE 'TRADITIONAL' ANALYSIS: NO RIGHT OF RECOVERY

- *Nicholson v Chapman* (1793) 2 H BI. 254, Court of Common Pleas

Timber, belonging to the claimant and placed in a dock on the banks of the Thames, was accidentally loosened and carried downstream, where it was left at low tide upon a towing path. The defendant was employed by a bailiff to remove the timber to a place of safety. When the claimant sought to recover his timber, the defendant refused to return it to him unless he was paid £6, which the claimant refused to pay. The jury found that two guineas would have been a reasonable charge to have made in the circumstances. The claimant brought an action of trover against the defendant. It was held that the defendant had no lien over the timber and was therefore liable to an action in trover. The judgment of the court was given by Eyre CJ.

Eyre CJ (after considering the salvage cases and concluding that the present case did not fall within its scope, continued): this is not a case of damage-feasance; the timber is found lying upon the banks of the river, and is taken into the possession, and under the care of the Defendant, without any extraordinary exertions, without the least personal risk, and in truth, with very little trouble. It is therefore a case of mere finding, and taking care of the thing found (I am willing to agree) for the owner. This is a good office, and meritorious, at least in the moral sense of the word, and certainly intitles the party to some reasonable recompence from the bounty, if not from the justice of the owner; and of which, if it were refused, a court of justice would go as far as it could go, towards enforcing the payment. So it would if a horse had strayed, and was not taken as an estray by the lord under his manorial rights, but was taken up by some good-natured man and taken care of by him, till at some trouble, and perhaps at some expence, he had found out the owner. So it would be in every other case of finding that can be stated (the claim to the recompence differing in degree, but not in principle); which therefore reduces the merits of this case to this short question, whether every man who finds the property of another, which happens to have been lost or mislaid, and voluntarily puts himself to some trouble and expence to preserve the thing, and to find out the owner, has a lien upon it for the casual, fluctuating and uncertain amount of the recompence which he may reasonably deserve? It is enough to say, that there is no instance of such a lien having been claimed and allowed; the case of the pointer-dog (2 Black. 1117), was a case in which it was claimed and disallowed, and it was thought too clear a case to bear an argument. Principles of public policy and commercial necessity support the lien in the case of salvage. Not only public policy and commercial necessity did not require that it should be established in this case, but very great inconvenience may be apprehended from it, if it were to be established. The owners of this kind of property, and the owners of craft upon the river which lie in many places moored together in large numbers, would not only have common accidents from the carelessness of their servants to guard against, but also the wilful attempts of ill-designing people to turn their floats and vessels adrift, in order that they might be paid for finding them. I mentioned in the course of the cause another great inconvenience, namely, the situation in which an owner seeking to recover his property in an action of trover will be placed, if he is at his peril to make a tender of a sufficient recompence, before he brings his action: such an owner must always pay too much, because he has no means of knowing exactly how much he ought to pay, and because he must tender enough. I know there are cases in which the owner of property must submit to this inconvenience; but the number of them ought not to be increased: perhaps it is better for the public that these voluntary acts of benevolence from one man to another, which are charities and moral duties, but not legal duties, should depend altogether for their reward upon the moral duty of gratitude. But at any rate, it is fitting that he who claims the reward in such case should take upon himself the burthen of proving the nature of the service which he has performed, and the quantum of the recompence which he demands, instead of throwing it upon the owner to estimate it for him, at the hazard of being nonsuited in an action of trover.

Judgment for the Plaintiff.

NOTES AND QUESTIONS

1. This was a claim by the defendant for a lien over the property; it was not a claim for reimbursement of the expenses incurred in saving the claimant's property. Goff and Jones state (17–010, n. 67) that 'there is a great difference between claims for a lien and for reimbursement' and cite in support of this argument a dictum of Lord Macnaghten in *Peruvian Guano Co. v Dreyfus Bros. & Co. (1887)* [1892] AC 166, 177.

2. If the defendant had brought a claim to recover the expenses which he had incurred in saving the claimant's timber, would his claim have succeeded? P. Birks 'Negotiorum Gestio and the Common Law' [1971] *CLP*, 110, 111–12, states that 'as for the simple obligation to repay expenses, *Nicholson v Chapman* had, if anything, rather favoured such a claim'. Do you agree?

• *Falcke v Scottish Imperial Insurance Co.* (1886) 34 ChD 234, Court of Appeal

In 1877 Emanuel purchased a life assurance policy which had been taken out on the life of the Duchess de Bauffremont for £29,000 at an annual premium, payable on 31st July, of £1,211 19s 2d. Emanuel subsequently mortgaged the policy on a number of occasions, one of which was to Falcke who had lent Emanuel £6,000. In 1883 Emanuel became insolvent and filed a petition for liquidation. An arrangement was subsequently reached with Emanuel's creditors, and he was discharged in March 1883. But, crucially, the arrangement did not encompass Falcke because secured creditors were not party to the arrangement. Emanuel's equity of redemption in the policy also survived the bankruptcy.

After obtaining his discharge, Emanuel entered into negotiations with Davis, who had acted for Falcke and other encumbrancers of the policy in the liquidation proceedings, with a view to repurchasing the policy. Emanuel claimed that he purchased the equity of redemption in the policy and paid the premium which was due in July 1883 after Davis had informed him that none of the encumbrancers would be able to pay the premium.

Falcke died in 1885, and later in the year his executrix commenced an action to enforce the security. Meanwhile Davis had absconded and not only was he bankrupt, but it was discovered that he had had no authority from Falcke to act, nor was Falcke aware of what he had purported to agree. The policy was then sold and the proceeds paid into court. After payment of the claims of the insurance company, the sum of £1,722 18s 10d remained in court and the claimants were Emanuel and Falcke's executrix. Emanuel claimed that he was entitled to a lien on the policy entitling him to repayment of the premium in priority to the claims of Falcke's executrix because he had paid the premium 'with the knowledge or privity or with the acquiescence of all parties claiming an interest in the policy, including Falcke, for the purpose of keeping on foot the policy, which would otherwise have been lost'. It was held that Emanuel was not entitled to such a lien and that the entirety of the premiums was therefore ordered to be paid to Falcke's executrix.

Cotton LJ: . . . Now let us see what the general law is. It is not disputed that if a stranger pays a premium on a policy that payment gives him no lien on the policy. A man by making a payment in respect of property belonging to another, if he does so without request, is not entitled to any lien or charge on that property for such payment. If he does work upon a house without request he gets no lien on the house for the work done. If the money has been paid or the work done at the request of the person entitled to the property, the person paying the money or doing the work has a right of action against the owner for the money paid or for the work done at his request. If here there had been circumstances to lead to the conclusion that there was a request by *Falcke* that this premium should be paid by *Emanuel*, then there would be a claim against *Falcke* or his representative for the money, and I do not say that there might not be a lien on the policy. But in my opinion there is no evidence upon which we should be justified in coming to the conclusion that there was any request expressed or implied by *Falcke* to *Emanuel* to pay this money. An express request is not suggested. Was there an implied request? I think that in a case of this sort, when money is paid in order to keep alive property which belongs to another, a request to make that payment might be implied from slight circumstances, but in my opinion there is no circumstance here in evidence from which such a request can be implied.

. . .

   [W]hat was the position of *Emanuel* at the time? He was, in my opinion, owner of the ultimate equity of redemption. Does that give him a right to have this sum paid by him for premium repaid to him out of the moneys arising from the policy? In my opinion it does not. It would be strange indeed if a mortgagor expending money on the mortgaged property could establish a charge in respect of that expenditure in priority to the mortgage. It is true that here the mortgagor, the ultimate owner of the equity of redemption, was no longer personally liable to pay the sums charged on the policy and was not bound by the covenant to pay the premium, but he pays it as the owner of the equity of redemption entitled to the ultimate interest in the property, although not personally bound to pay the debt or provide for the premium. It must be considered, in my opinion, that he paid it not so as to get any claim in priority to the incumbrancer, but in order to retain the benefit of the interest which would come to him if the property proved sufficient to pay off the previous incumbrancers. In my opinion it would be utterly wrong to say that a mortgagor, the owner of the equity of redemption, can under those circumstances defeat the incumbrancers on the estate. Suppose the mortgaged property is a mine, and the owner of the equity of redemption were to spend large sums of money in order to prevent the mine being flooded or otherwise destroyed, could he have in respect of that expenditure a lien on the estate as against the persons having charges and mortgages on that estate? In my opinion, no. . . .

Bowen LJ: I am of the same opinion. The general principle is, beyond all question, that work and labour done or money expended by one man to preserve or benefit the property of another does not according to English law create any lien upon the property saved or benefited, nor, even standing alone, create any obligation to repay the expenditure. Liabilities are not to be forced upon people behind their backs any more than you can confer a benefit upon a man against his will.

There is an exception to this proposition in the maritime law. I mention it because the word 'salvage' has been used from time to time throughout the argument, and some analogy is sought to be established between salvage and the right claimed by the Respondents. With regard to salvage, general average, and contribution, the maritime law differs from the common law. That has been so from the time of the Roman law downwards. The maritime law, for the purposes of public policy and for the advantage of trade, imposes in these cases a liability upon the thing saved, a liability which is a special consequence arising out of the character of mercantile enterprises, the nature of sea perils, and the fact that the thing saved was saved under great stress and exceptional circumstances. No similar doctrine applies to things lost upon land, nor to anything except ships or goods in peril at sea.

With regard to ordinary goods upon which labour or money is expended with a view of saving them or benefiting the owner, there can, as it seems to me, according to the common law be only one principle upon which a claim for repayment can be based, and that is where you can find facts from which the law will imply a contract to repay or to give a lien. It is perfectly true that the inference of an understanding between the parties—which you may translate into other language by calling it an implied contract—is an inference which will unhesitatingly be drawn in cases where the circumstances plainly lead to the conclusion that the owner of the saved property knew that the other party was laying out his money in the expectation of being repaid. In other words, you must have circumstances from which the proper inference is that there was a request to perform the service. It comes to the same thing, but I abstain the using the word 'request' more than is necessary, for fear of plunging myself into all the archaic embarrassments connected with the cases about requests. But wherever you find that the owner of the property saved knew of the service being performed, you will have to ask yourself (and the question will become one of fact) whether under all the circumstances there was either what the law calls an implied contract for repayment or a contract which would give rise to a lien?

Now in the present case how can it be said that Mr. *Falcke*, whose representative is claiming the benefit of this policy, so conducted himself as to justify any inference of the kind on the part of Mr *Emanuel*? There is absolutely no fact from which any such inference, as it seems to me, can be drawn at common law.

. . .

What have we here to take this case out of the general rule? Mr *Emanuel* was the owner of the equity of redemption. Does the mere fact that the owner of the equity of redemption paid premiums to keep alive the policy give him a right against the mortgagees to have the moneys which he so expended paid in priority to their debt? He paid in his own interest; he did not pay in the interest of the mortgagees. There can be no question here of acquiescence. The mortgagor does not pay under a mistake of fact or any mistake as to his own title. The mortgagee does not stand by and allow him to pay under such a mistake, and as regards any notion that he was allowed to pay under the expectation that he would be repaid again, or would have a lien for the money upon the policy, I have examined that already in the first part of the observations I have been making. If there were any acquiescence of this last kind, it would be an acquiescence from which in common law you would draw the inference of a contract; but, as I said before, there is no fact that leads to that.

Then, what equity is there that can be relied upon? It is not even a case where the owner of the saved property requires the assistance of a Court of Equity, or the name of the person who has paid that money to get the property back. Here the simple question is whether there are any facts from which we can say that it is unjust or inequitable that Mr *Falcke's* representatives should be allowed to have that which is their own? If you state the case in that way the answer is obvious, that one cannot see anything of the kind.

Fry LJ concurred.

NOTES AND QUESTIONS

1. Birks states (*Introduction*, 195) that '*Falcke* is at most authority to the effect that an intervention to serve the intervener's own interest, in circumstances in which the benefit of the intervention is necessarily shared by another, does not give rise to restitution.' Do you agree? Are the broad dicta of Bowen LJ part of the ratio of *Falcke*?

2. Does the judgment of Bowen LJ distinguish between the test to be applied when (a) ascertaining the existence of an enrichment and (b) identifying the existence of an unjust factor?

3. If Bowen LJ's dictum set out in the opening paragraph of his judgment was to be applied to the facts of (a) *Ambrose v Kerrison* (below, 567) and (b) *Great Northern Railway v Swaffield* (below, 584), would it change the result in these cases?

4. Should Emanuel have been able to recover the premium on the ground of mistake?

5. Professor Birks ('In Defence of Free Acceptance' in A Burrows (ed.), *Essays on the Law of Restitution*, above) used dicta from the judgment of Bowen LJ in support of his claim, which he later abandoned, that English law does recognize the existence of a doctrine of free acceptance. Can these dicta form the basis for the recognition of a doctrine of free acceptance in English law (see further below, 392–395)?

2. CASES IN WHICH ENGLISH LAW RECOGNIZES THE EXISTENCE OF A RIGHT OF RECOVERY

(1) THE BURIAL CASES

• *Jenkins v Tucker* (1788) 1 H Bl. 90, Court of Common Pleas

A father paid the expenses of his daughter's funeral. He brought an action to recover the expenses from his daughter's husband, who was in Jamaica at the time of her death. It was held that the father was entitled to succeed in his claim.

Lord Loughborough: ... I think there was a sufficient consideration to support this action for the funeral expences, though there was neither request nor assent on the part of the defendant, for the plaintiff acted in discharge of a duty which the defendant was under a strict legal necessity of himself performing, and which common decency required at his hands; the money therefore which the plaintiff paid on this account, was paid to the use of the defendant. A father also seems to be the proper person to interfere in giving directions for his daughter's funeral in the absence of her husband. There are many cases of this sort, where a person has paid money which another was under a legal obligation to pay, though without his knowledge or request, may maintain an action to recover back the money so paid: such as in the instance of goods being distrained by the commissioners of the land-tax, if a neighbour should redeem the goods, and pay the tax for the owner, he might maintain an action for the money against the owner.

Gould J: It appears from this demurrer, that the defendant was possessed of a plantation in Jamaica, from the time he left his wife, till her death, which annually produced above 120 hogsheads of sugar, the value of which, at a moderate estimation, amounted to near 3000*l.* a year. He was therefore bound to support her in a manner suitable to his degree; and the expenses were such as were suitable to his degree and situation in life. The law takes notice of things suitable to the degree of the husband in the paraphernalia of the wife, and in other respects. In the present case, the demurrer admits that the money was expended on account of the wife, and being for things suitable to the degree of the husband, the law raises a consideration, and implies a promise to pay it.

Heath and **Wilson JJ** concurred.

NOTES AND QUESTIONS

1. When considering the nature of the benefit which the defendant obtained as a result of the intervention of the claimant, it must be remembered that *Jenkins* was decided on the basis of a common law rule (which is no longer applicable) that the husband was liable for the funeral expenses of his wife. The basis of this rule was that the 'wife being by marriage completely identified with her husband and having at law no property of her own, and no separate power of disposition, the duty of burying her body inevitably fell at common law on her surviving husband' (*per* Scott LJ in *Rees v Hughes* [1946] 1 KB 517, 523–4). In *Rees v Hughes* the Court of Appeal held that, in the light of legislation such as the Married Women's Property Act 1882 and the Law Reform (Married Women and Tortfeasors) Act 1935, married women were to be treated on the same basis as a feme sole or a man, so that the old common law rule is no longer applicable. So, were *Jenkins* to recur today, the claimant's claim would lie against the personal representatives of the deceased and not her husband.

2. Statute now imposes a duty upon local authorities to cause to be buried or cremated the body of any person who has died or been found dead in their area in any case where it appears to the authority that no other suitable arrangements for the disposal of the body have been or are being made (Public Health (Control of Diseases) Act 1984, section 46(1)) and the authority is entitled to recover the expenses so incurred from the estate of the deceased person (section 46(5)).

3. On the assumption that the husband was liable for the funeral expenses of his wife, how would a modern court characterize the benefit which the defendant obtained as a result of the intervention of the claimant?

4. What was the unjust factor in this case?

5. Lord Loughborough refers to the claimant as a 'proper person to interfere in giving directions for his daughter's funeral in the absence of her husband'. Who is a 'proper person' to interfere? Can a stranger ever be a proper person for this purpose? Can this dicta be reconciled with the approach later taken in *Ambrose v Kerrison* (below, 567)?

6. It should also be noted that the claimant's claim also included sums which he had expended in discharging his daughter's debts while the defendant was in Jamaica. But the court was not ultimately asked to consider whether or not the claimant was entitled to recover in respect of such sums. Had the issue been argued before the court, how should it have been resolved?

7. Could the claimant have recovered at all if the sums which he had expended in burying his daughter were greater than was suitable for the 'rank and fortune' of the defendant?

● *Rogers v Price* (1829) 3 Y & J 28, Court of Exchequer

The deceased, Davies, died at the home of his brother, who called the claimant, an undertaker. The claimant made the arrangements for the burial of the deceased and it was conceded that the funeral was suitable to the deceased's status. But no agreement was concluded between the claimant and the brother for payment in respect of the services provided and the claimant did not at the time know who the executor of the deceased was. The claimant brought a claim against the deceased's executor, seeking to recover 'for work and labour as an undertaker and materials furnished for the funeral of Davies'. The claimant's claim succeeded.

Garrow B: . . . I am of opinion that the plaintiff is entitled to recover, and that therefore this rule must be made absolute. The simple question is, notwithstanding many ingenious views of the case have been presented, who is answerable for the expenses of the funeral of this gentleman. In my opinion, the executor is liable. Suppose a person to be killed by accident at a distance from his home; what, in such a case, ought to be done? The common principles of decency and humanity, the common impulses of our nature, would direct every one, as a preliminary step, to provide a decent funeral, at the expense of the estate; and to do that which is immediately necessary upon the subject, in order to avoid what, if not provided against, may become an inconvenience to the public. Is it necessary in that or any other case to wait until it can be ascertained whether the deceased has left a will, or appointed an executor; or, even if the executor be known, can it, where the distance is great, be necessary to have communication with that executor before any step is taken in the performance of those last offices which require immediate attention? It is admitted here that the funeral was suitable to the degree of the deceased and upon this record it must be taken that the defendant is executor with assets sufficient to defray this demand; I therefore think that, if the case had gone to the jury, they would have found for the plaintiff, and that therefore this rule should be made absolute.

Hullock B: . . . If the executor had kept the body unburied, and the undertaker had come and said, I insist on burying it, he could not have recovered. But there is no evidence here that the person by whom this body was interred knew whether there was or was not an executor. It is the duty of the executor to dispose of the testator in the usual manner, viz. by burying him. It is not that sort of duty which can be enforced by mandamus or other proceedings at law; but it is a duty which decency and the interest of society render incumbent upon the executor. . . .

Vaughan B concurred.

NOTES AND QUESTIONS

1. Although it was the deceased's brother who contacted the claimant, they proceeded upon the assumption that there was no understanding between parties that the work was done upon the credit of the brother.

2. Can it be said that the unjust factor in this case is 'moral compulsion', when the claimant was acting in the course of his business in burying the body?

- **Ambrose v Kerrison** (1851) 10 CB 776, Court of Common Pleas

The claimant was 'distantly connected' with the deceased, who was the wife of the defendant. The defendant and his wife had separated some time before her death. The claimant made arrangements for the funeral after having been summoned by a friend of the deceased. The claimant did not know where the defendant lived (although the friend who had summoned him did know) and thus did not communicate with him until about ten days after the funeral. The defendant argued that the claimant was not entitled to recover because he was a total stranger and a volunteer. The objection was overruled and so the claimant was entitled to recover the expenses which he had incurred.

Jervis CJ: . . . It is admitted by the counsel for the defendant, that, if he was under any legal liability to pay this demand, no question can be raised as to the reasonableness of the amount: nor need we discuss the propriety of incurring the expense of removing the deceased to Kelvedon for interment. This being so, the point for our consideration simply is, whether a husband living apart from his wife is liable to a third person for expenses incurred by him for the decent and suitable interment of his wife. There can be no question that an undertaker who performs a funeral may recover from the executor of the deceased (having assets) the reasonable and necessary expenses of such funeral, without any specific contract. That liability in the executor is founded upon the duty which is imposed upon him by the character he fills, and a proper regard to decency, and to the comfort of others. And I think that the same reasons which call upon the executor to perform that duty, cast at least an equal responsibility upon the husband of a deceased wife, and, without any express authority or request on his part, compel him to recoup one who has performed the funeral. I see no difference in principle between the case of an undertaker and that of a third person who takes upon himself to employ and to pay the undertaker. In point of fact, the undertaker does not do all the work himself: he employs others to assist him. If, therefore, the circumstances of this case would cast a duty upon the husband to pay an undertaker,—which I think they do,—it seems to me, upon the reason of the thing, as well as upon the authority of *Jenkins v Tucker*, that this plaintiff, though a volunteer, is equally entitled to maintain an action against the husband for money paid.

Cresswell J: I am of the same opinion. Whatever observations one or two of the expressions in Lord Loughborough's judgment in the case cited, may fairly be open to, I think the decision was right: and I fully adopt the language of Heath, J, who says,—'The defendant was clearly liable to pay the expenses of his wife's funeral.' This is not exactly the case of a payment made by a mere volunteer: the plaintiff is the party who performed the funeral at his own expense.

Williams and **Talfaurd JJ** concurred.

• *Bradshaw v Beard* (1862) 12 CBNS 344, Court of Common Pleas

The defendant's wife left him after they had quarrelled and she went to live with her sister and her husband, the claimant, who lived approximately one mile away. Some ten years later the defendant's wife died. The claimant did not communicate with the defendant (although it was found that the defendant knew what was taking place and had decided not to interfere) but, instead, employed an undertaker to bury the defendant's wife. The claimant successfully sought to recover the expenses which he had incurred from the defendant.

Willes J: . . . It seems to me not to be at all unreasonable, but on the contrary, quite reasonable and proper, that the husband should be bound to provide Christian burial for his wife. According to our law, every person is entitled to a place where his bones may be at rest. Prima facie, every person has a right to be buried in the churchyard of the parish in which he dies. In *The Queen v Stewart*, 12 Ad. & E 773, 4 P & D 349, it was held by the court of Queen's Bench that every person dying in this country, and not within certain ecclesiastical prohibitions, is entitled to Christian burial; and, where no such prohibition attaches, it seems that every householder in whose house a dead body lies is bound by the common law to inter the body decently; and that, upon this principle, where a body lies in the house of a parish or union, the parish or union must provide for the interment. The law, therefore, has provided not only for the place where the burial is to take place, but also who shall be charged with the performance of the duty. Where the deceased has a husband, the performance of that last act of piety and charity devolves upon him. The law makes that a legal duty which the laws of nature and society make a moral duty. And, upon his default, the law obliges him to recoup the reasonable expenses of the person who performs it for him. I do not refer to the case of an executor, which stands upon a totally different footing. I am not, therefore, surprised to find that there are two authorities in this court, *Jenkins v Tucker*, 1 H Bl. 91, and *Ambrose v Kerrison*, 10 CB 776, which support this view; and I feel no alarm that this doctrine may induce a stranger to thrust himself in between husband and wife for the mere purpose of preventing the husband from performing that duty himself. Generally speaking, parties are not allowed to claim in respect of moneys expended for others without request. If the plaintiff here had been shewn to have been guilty of any fraud, in concealing from the husband the fact of his wife's death, and so preventing him from performing the last duty to her remains, the case would have presented a very different aspect. But I see no reason for imputing any such misconduct to the plaintiff. Therefore I think the plaintiff is entitled to recover the reasonable expense incurred by him in the performance of that duty which the defendant ought to have discharged, but has failed to discharge.

Byles and **Keating JJ** concurred.

NOTES AND QUESTIONS

1. Can *Ambrose* and *Bradshaw* be reconciled with *Jenkins v Tucker* (above)? Further support for the proposition that a 'stranger' can maintain a claim in such circumstances can be found in the judgments of the Court of Appeal in *Rees v Hughes* [1946] 1 KB 517 (see 523 (Scott LJ) and 527 (Tucker LJ)).

2. Could the claimants in both *Ambrose* and *Bradshaw* be described as officious on the ground that they did not communicate with the defendant when it was possible for them to have done so? What obligations should there be upon a claimant to seek out the person primarily responsible for the burial, before intervening himself? Should it be for the defendant to prove that the claimant was 'officious', or should the onus of proof lie on the claimant to show that he was a 'proper person' to intervene in the circumstances?

3. Is the focus of the courts in these cases upon the defendant's moral or legal obligation to ensure that the deceased is buried, or is it upon the moral obligation which impels the claimant to intervene? Or are the courts concerned with both these factors?

4. Can unjust sacrifice provide a better explanation for the burial cases?

(2) SALVAGE

Historically, salvage cases have been treated separately from other necessitous intervention cases. The Court of Admiralty has always adopted a much more generous attitude towards those who intervene at sea to save property. Indeed, such has been the willingness of the courts to encourage intervention that they have been prepared to give a reward to those salvors who succeed in saving or recovering property in danger on the high seas. Three particular problems emerge from the salvage cases.

The first is whether they can be recognized as restitution cases at all: in particular, it is very difficult, if not impossible, to say that the reward which the courts give to salvors represents the reversal of the enrichment of the defendant at the expense of the claimant. The second problem is that it is not at all clear that one can reason by analogy with the salvage cases in an effort to recognize the existence of a more general right of recovery. The courts have tended to be either unwilling to assimilate the facts at hand with the salvage jurisdiction (see, for example, the judgment of Eyre CJ in *Nicholson v Chapman* (above, 561)) or they have regarded the salvage cases as *sui generis* and thus, not a useful source of assistance in terms of developing the common law. The third problem is that Parliament has now intervened to extend the original salvage jurisdiction and one effect of this intervention has been to inhibit the judges in their own development of the salvage rules (see *The Goring*, below, 570).

In this section we confine ourselves to a summary of the principles of law which apply to a salvage claim and then we move on to consider one of the leading (and controversial) modern salvage cases.

- W Kennedy and F Rose, *Law of Salvage* (6th edn, 2002, by F Rose), 1–2

ELEMENTS OF THE LAW OF SALVAGE

The law of maritime salvage is an ancient and important part of the wider law governing marine perils and safety at sea. The definition of salvage is considered below. It suffices to indicate here the elements of the law of salvage considered in this book. The law of salvage applies where (i) there is a recognised *subject of salvage* (ii) which has come into a position of *danger* necessitating a *salvage service* to preserve it from loss or damage and (iii) a person falling within the classification of *salvors* (traditionally called a *volunteer*) (iv) is successful or meritoriously contributes to *success* in preserving the subject from danger. In the days of sail, salvage was frequently effected by various individual acts, without the conclusion of a contractual relationship between the parties. But the availability of instantaneous means of communication and the increased use of steam- and, more recently, motor-driven vessels has resulted in services in the nature of salvage having come more frequently to be governed in part at least by an *agreement* or *contract*. In either case, both the provider and the recipient of salvage services have been held to owe *duties* to each other. These were much less defined before the role of contract increased but the court has always been alert to discourage *misconduct* during salvage operations.

On termination of salvage services, the *salved values* of the preserved property can be calculated. These provide the upper limit of the salvor's *reward* and the most fundamental of all the relevant factors which must be considered in its *assessment*, if not already the subject of a binding agreement. The award to the salvor is intended to represent a reasonable *remuneration* for his efforts, *reimbursement* for his loss or expenditure, plus an additional element of *reward* to reflect the judicially promoted *public policy* of encouraging individuals to salve property imperilled at sea. All recognised *beneficiaries* of salvage services must in principle make a *contribution* to the reward, although special rules apply to proceedings concerning the Crown and the immunity of foreign sovereign Sates. The reward should be *apportioned* amongst the various salvors who have participated in the successful salvage.

Salvors' *remedies* for enforcing their claim include a maritime lien in support of a right to proceed *in rem* or *in personam*. Salvage claims are the subject of the court's *Admiralty jurisdiction*, although it has become overwhelmingly more common over the last century for salvage claims to be dealt with not judicially but by *arbitration*.

- *The Goring* [1988] AC 831, House of Lords

The facts of the case, together with the reasons for the failure of the claimants' claim are set out in the speech of Lord Brandon below.

Lord Brandon of Oakbrook: My Lords, the question for decision in this appeal is whether there is under English law a cause of action for salvage in respect of services rendered to a ship in danger in a navigable non-tidal part of an English river. The question does not appear to have arisen for decision before and its difficulty is shown by the fact that the four judges who have considered it in the two courts below have been divided equally in their opinions upon it.

The way in which the question has arisen is as follows. It is alleged by the appellants that shortly before midnight on 14 September 1984 the *Goring*, a passenger vessel owned by the respondents, broke free of her moorings in the river Thames up-river of Reading Bridge. She was unmanned and her downward drift, if not checked, would have caused her to collide with a line of moored vessels and afterwards taken her on to Reading Bridge and the weir beyond. The appellants were a group of five persons who were members or employees of the Bohemian Club, the premises of which are situated on De Montford island in the middle of the river. With the help of the club's ferry boat they managed to put one of their number on board the *Goring*, thereby making it possible to get a line from her to the island, to check her drift and thereafter to haul her to a vacant mooring where she was made fast.

Two matters are agreed. The first matter is that the Thames above Reading Bridge is not tidal. The second matter is that, if services of the kind which the appellants allege that they rendered to the *Goring* had been rendered further down the river where it is tidal, the appellants would have a cause of action against the respondents for salvage in respect of them. This second matter is agreed because the services as alleged contained, apart from the question of the place in which they were rendered, all four of the classic ingredients necessary to salvage services. First, the appellants were volunteers; secondly, the *Goring*, being a ship, was a recognised subject matter of salvage services; thirdly, she was in danger; and, fourthly, the services were successful in saving her from that danger.

On 22 July 1985 the appellants began in the Admiralty Court an action in rem against the *Goring* in which they claimed salvage remuneration for the services to her described above . . .

My Lords, the cause of action for salvage is an ancient one, derived from the maritime law and peculiar to it. [*His Lordship then examined the historical development of the cause of action for salvage, with particular reference to the various statutes which have been enacted by Parliament. The claimants relied in particular upon section VI of the Admiralty Court Act 1840 and section 1 of the Administration of Justice Act 1956 but, after giving careful consideration to both provisions Lord Brandon concluded that they did not give the claimants the cause of action which they asserted. He then continued:*]

Counsel for the appellants, rightly in my view, did not contend that a cause of action for salvage in respect of services rendered to a ship in non-tidal inland waters of the United Kingdom existed prior to 1840. He did, however, contend, as I said earlier, that such a cause of action was created either by section VI of the Admiralty Court Act 1840 or alternatively by section 1 of the Administration of Justice Act 1956. I have earlier given reasons why I cannot interpret these provisions as having had the effect for which counsel for the appellants contended. My view that they did not have such effect is strongly reinforced by the way in which the legislature has from time to time stipulated in what places in the United Kingdom services require to have been rendered in order to qualify as salvage services. The requirement laid down for services for a ship, her cargo or apparel by section 458 of the Merchant Shipping Act 1854 was that the services should have been rendered on the shore of any sea or tidal water in the United Kingdom. The requirement laid down for services to a ship, her cargo or apparel by section 546 of the Merchant Shipping Act 1894 was that the services should have been rendered where any vessel was wrecked, stranded or in distress on or near the coasts of the United Kingdom or any tidal water within the limits of the United Kingdom. The requirement laid down for services to an aircraft by the Civil Aviation Act 1949 was that they should have been rendered in, on or over the sea or any tidal water, or on or over the shores of the sea or any tidal water. That requirement was repeated in the Civil Aviation Act 1982, after the passing of the Administration of Justice Act 1956 and the Supreme Court Act 1981. It seems to me that the repeated stipulation of requirements of this kind by the legislature is wholly inconsistent with there having been in existence, at the time when such requirements were stipulated, a cause of action for salvage services rendered in non-tidal inland waters.

Counsel for the appellants relied strongly on the existence of a substantial number of reported cases, in which services to ships in an enclosed dock were treated as salvage services. He said that such cases showed that services could qualify as salvage services, although rendered to ships lying in water which, because they were separated from tidal water by lock gates, were non-tidal. Counsel for the respondents did not argue that these cases were wrongly decided. It is difficult to be sure of the legal basis on which the services concerned were treated as salvage services, because the question whether they should be so treated or not does not ever appear to have been raised. The most likely explanation is that the waters in which the services were rendered, though not themselves tidal, were adjacent to and closely connected with waters which were, and formed part of the complex of a basically tidal port or harbour.

Bingham LJ, with whom Ralph Gibson LJ agreed, reached the conclusion that the appellants had no cause of action in this case on two grounds. The first ground was that the *Goring*, being a pleasurecraft, was not capable of being the subject matter of salvage services. The second ground was that the services on which the appellants' claim was founded were rendered in non-tidal inland waters. Counsel for the respondents did not seek to support the first ground, accepting that the *Goring*, being a vessel used in navigation, was capable of being the subject matter of salvage services if rendered at sea or in tidal waters. I think that he was right to make this concession. For the reasons which I have given earlier, however, I think that, in so far as Bingham LJ based his decision on the second ground, he was right in law.

My Lords, counsel for the appellants submitted that, even if the cause of action for salvage had not up till now been extended to services rendered in navigable non-tidal waters, it should now be so extended, by way of analogy and for reasons of public policy, by the process of judicial decision. In support of that submission reliance was placed on certain observations contained in the judgments of Sheen J and Sir John Donaldson MR [1978] QB 687. Sheen J said, at 693:

'If a ship or her cargo is in danger in non-tidal waters it is highly desirable, as a matter of public policy, that other ships should be encouraged to go to her assistance without hesitation.'

Sir John Donaldson MR said, at 706–7:

'In the end I believe that I have to seek a rational basis of confining the cause of action to tidal waters and I can find none. It is, of course, a maritime remedy and the public policy considerations which support it are directed at commercial shipping and seagoing vessels. But that said, I can see no sense in a cause of action which will remunerate the salvors of an ocean-going vessel inward bound for Manchester up to the moment when the vessel enters the Manchester Ship Canal, but no further. Some of the perils facing the vessel in the canal may be different from those facing it at sea, but many, such as fire, will be the same. The need to encourage assistance otherwise than under contract may be greater at sea, but the skills required of the salvors will be the same or at least similar. The vessel is not intended to sail only on tidal waters. The voyage over tidal and non-tidal waters is a single maritime adventure and should not attract wholly different rights and obligations by reference to the tidality of the water in which the vessel is for the time being sailing.'

These are forceful passages. The majority in the Court of Appeal, however, took a different view, expressed with similar force. Their view was that, since salvage was a cause of action peculiar to the maritime law, and unknown to the common law in respect of services voluntarily rendered to property in danger on land, it would be wrong to extend its scope to non-tidal waters. They further considered that the need for such an extension for reasons of public policy had not been established.

In my view, since the scope of the cause of action for salvage has to be determined by reference to the statutory provisions which I examined earlier, it is not open to your Lordships' House, if it concludes that those provisions have the effect of limiting the scope of that cause of action to services rendered at sea or in tidal waters, to extend that scope by the process of judicial decision. If any such extension is to be made, it must, in my opinion, be left to the legislature to make it.

Lord Bridge, Lord Fraser, Lord Ackner and **Lord Oliver** concurred.

NOTES AND QUESTIONS

1. Birks states (*Introduction*, 456) that 'this was not a case in which an action for restitution would have yielded anything, since the plaintiffs had suffered no expense, neither in money paid out nor in remunerative, but unremunerated, work'. Do you agree? Can a

non-professional intervener ever bring a claim to recover the value of the benefit which he has conferred?

2. In terms of principle, can a distinction be drawn between services provided by a salvor to a vessel in danger on the high seas and a vessel in danger in the Manchester Ship Canal?

3. Can the willingness of the courts to grant the salvor a reward be reconciled with the requirements of the law of restitution?

4. Why does the law not allow a claim to be brought by a salvor who has attempted unsuccessfully to save the defendant's property? Could it not be said that the defendant has benefited from the labour which the claimant has expended in seeking to save his property, in the sense that he would have been prepared to pay for the services had he been asked beforehand if he wished the claimant to intervene in an effort to save his property?

5. Are the salvage cases explained more satisfactorily in terms of unjust sacrifice?

6. Why do the courts recognize the existence of a maritime lien in salvage cases (see Kennedy and Rose, above, 570), but refuse to recognize the existence of a lien in cases such as *Nicholson v Chapman* (above, 561) and *Falcke v Scottish Imperial Insurance Co.* (above, 562)? When should necessitous intervention give rise to (a) a (restitutionary) proprietary claim and (b) a personal (restitutionary) claim?

(3) AGENCY OF NECESSITY

Every agency textbook contains a discussion of the rules relating to agency of necessity (see, for example, W Bowstead and FMB Reynolds, *on Agency* (18th edn, 2006), chapter 4). These rules are now relatively well-developed and, while there is some controversy about their exact scope, their existence is not in doubt. We are not here concerned to explain the exact scope of the doctrine. Rather, our task is to consider whether the basis of this doctrine can be said to lie within the law of unjust enrichment and, if so, to ask whether these cases can be relied upon in an attempt to prove that the common law does, in fact, recognise the existence of a right to restitution based on necessitous intervention.

- *Prager v Blatspiel Stamp and Heacock Ltd* [1924] 1 KB 566, King's Bench Division

In 1915 and 1916 the defendants, who were fur merchants in London, agreed to purchase skins as agents for the claimants, who were fur merchants in Bucharest. The claimants paid for the skins but the occupation of Roumania by the Germans during the first World War made it impossible for the defendants to send the skins to Roumania or to communicate with the claimants. So in 1917 and 1918 the defendants sold the skins, which had increased in value. In January 1919, after the war was over, the claimants wrote to the defendants asking them to send the skins. When they were informed of the fact that the defendants had sold the skins, the claimants repudiated the transaction and brought a claim in conversion against the defendants. The defendants claimed that they had acted as the claimants' agents of necessity in selling the skins, but the defence was rejected because there was no necessity to sell the skins and because it had not been shown that the defendants had acted *bona fide* in reselling the skins. The defendants were therefore liable to the claimants.

McCardie J: . . .

Now the first question of law is this: Can the facts as I have outlined them afford a possible legal basis on which to rest an agency of necessity? The defendants say yes; the plaintiff says no. The doctrine of agency of necessity doubtless took its rise from marine adventure. Hence the numerous decisions set out in Carver's Carriage by Sea, 6th edn, s. 294, and following sections. The substance of the matter as stated in that book is that in cases of necessity the master of a ship has power and it is his duty to sell the goods in order to save their value or some part of it: see s. 297. In *Hawtayne v Bourne*[1] Parke B expressed a view that agency of necessity could not arise save in the case of a master of a ship and of the acceptor of a bill of exchange for the honour of the drawer.[2] He added[3] that: 'The authority of the master of a ship rests upon the peculiar character of his office.' In *Gwilliam v Twist*[4] Lord Esher said: 'I am very much inclined to agree with the view taken by Eyre CJ in the case of *Nicholson v Chapman*,[5] and by Parke B in the case of *Hawtayne v Bourne* to the effect that this doctrine of authority by reason of necessity is confined to certain well-known exceptional cases, such as those of the master of a ship or the acceptor of a bill of exchange for the honour of the drawer.' If the dicta I have cited be correct then the defendants in the case now before me cannot justify their acts of sale. In my humble opinion, however, those dicta are not the law to-day. In *Great Northern Ry. Co. v Swaffield*,[6] more than twenty years before the dictum of Lord Esher, the Court of Exchequer (Kelly CB, Pigott, Pollock, and Amphlett BB) had applied the doctrine of agency of necessity to a land carrier. They applied to him the principle of the shipping cases. I think too that *London and North Western Ry. v Duerden*[7] is in substance an application of the same principle. In *Sims & Co. v Midland Ry. Co.*[8]—the sale of butter case—the Divisional Court (Ridley and Scrutton JJ) again recognized that the principle of the shipping cases might apply to land carriers. See also Macnamara on *Carriers by Land*, 2nd edn, art. 189 (n.). In *Springer v Great Western Ry.*[9] the Court of Appeal approved the principle stated in *Sims' Case*.

The decisions I have already cited show that the dictum of Lord Esher in *Gwilliam v Twist* is not the law of to-day. Agency of necessity is not confined to shipmaster cases and to bills of exchange. . . .

I see nothing which as a matter of strict law prevents the defendants here from seeking to rely on the doctrine of agency of necessity. In *Tetley v British Trade Corporation*[10] Bailhache J applied the doctrine of agency of necessity to the case of an agent who, whilst in Russian Georgia, found himself, through violent events, unable to deal with goods in accordance with his instructions and equally unable to communicate with his principals. A like ruling has been given, on substantially similar facts, in other cases (unreported) in the King's Bench Division. Upon the first point I rule in the defendants' favour.

I must refer briefly to several other features of the doctrine of agency of necessity in a case where, as here, the agent has, without orders, sold the goods of his principal. In the first place, it is, of course, clear that agency of necessity does not arise if the agent can communicate with his principal. This is established by all the decisions: see Carver on *Carriage by Sea*, 6th edn, arts. 295, 299; Scrutton on *Charterparties*, 11th edn, art. 98; and *Springer v Great Western Ry.*[11] The basis of this requirement is, I take it, that if the principal's decision can be obtained the agent should seek it ere acting. In the present case it is admitted that the agents could not communicate with the principal. In the next place it is essential for the agent to prove that the sale was necessary. What does this mean? In *Cannan v Meaburn*[12] Park J said: 'The master cannot sell except in a case of inevitable necessity.' In *Australian Steam Navigation Co. v Morse*,[13] however, Sir Montague Smith said: 'The word "necessity," when applied to mercantile affairs, where the judgment must, in the nature of things, be exercised, cannot of course mean an irresistible compelling power—what is meant by it in such cases is, the force of circumstances which determine the course a man ought to take.' Later on he refers to 'commercial necessity.' . . . In substance I may say that the agent must prove an actual and definite commercial necessity for the sale. In the third place, I think that an alleged agent of necessity must

1 (1841) 7 M & W 595.   2 7 M & W 599.   3 *Ibid.* 600.
4 [1895] 2 QB 84, 87.   5 (1793) 2 H Bl 254.   6 (1874) LR 9 Ex 132.
7 (1916) 32 TLR 315.   8 [1913] 1 KB 103.   9 [1921] 1 KB 257.
10 (1922) Unreported. See 10 Lloyd's List Rep 678.
11 [1921] 1 KB 257.   12 (1823) 1 Bing 243, 247.   13 (1872) LR 4 PC 222, 230.

satisfy the court that he was acting bona fide in the interests of the parties concerned. In *Ewbank Nutting*[14] Coltman J said during the argument: 'Does not the authority of the master extend to acts such as he, in the exercise of an honest judgment, thinks the best for the interest of the owner of both ship and goods?' . . . Bona fides, in my opinion, is an essential condition for the exercise of the power of sale.

I have now stated the principles of law which, in my view, apply to this case.

I can now state quite briefly my conclusions of fact after carefully weighing the whole of the evidence, the correspondence and arguments. I hold in the first place that there was no necessity to sell the goods. They had been purchased by the plaintiff in time of war and not of peace. He bought them in order that he might be ready with a stock of goods when peace arrived. He had refused, by letters to the defendants, several profitable offers for some of them before the cessation of correspondence between the defendants and himself. The goods were not perishable like fruit or food. . . . I see no adequate reason for the sale by the defendants, for I am satisfied that there was nothing to prevent the defendants from putting them into cold storage, and certainly nothing to prevent them from keeping them with proper care in their own warehouse. The expense of cold or other storage would have been slight compared with the value of the furs. . . .

In the second place I decide, without hesitation, that the defendants did not act bona fide. . . . I hold that the defendants were not in fact agents of necessity, that the sales of the plaintiff's goods were not justified, and that the defendants acted dishonestly. In the result I give judgment for the plaintiff for 1822*l.* with costs.

NOTES AND QUESTIONS

1. If the salvage jurisdiction does not extend to non-tidal waters (see *The Goring*, above, 570), was McCardie J entitled to extend the scope of agency of necessity beyond cases of carriage of goods by sea to cases on land?

2. One of the most important practical limitations upon the scope of the doctrine of agency of necessity is that there must be a pre-existing legal relationship between the parties (see, for example, *In re F (Mental Patient: Sterilisation)* [1990] 2 AC 1, 75). This does not emerge with any clarity from the judgment of McCardie J but the need for such a relationship was subsequently emphasized by Scrutton LJ in *Jebara v Ottoman Bank* [1927] 2 KB 254, 271 when he stated that:

    The expansion desired by McCardie J becomes less difficult when the agent of necessity develops from an original and subsisting agency, and only applies itself to unforeseen events not provided for in the original contract, which is usually the case where a ship-master is agent of necessity. But the position seems quite different when there is no pre-existing agency, as in the case of a finder of perishable chattels or animals, and still more difficult where there is a pre-existing agency, but it has become illegal and void by reason of war, and the same reason will apply to invalidate any implied agency of necessity.

3. Is the 'pre-existing legal relationship' requirement a necessary one? Could it not be said that the true function of the requirement was simply to show that the intervener was a 'proper person' to intervene in the circumstances? If this is so, can it not be argued that this function would be better achieved by a rule which stated that the claimant cannot recover where his intervention was 'officious'?

4. *Prager* demonstrates that the doctrine of agency of necessity serves purposes beyond the law of restitution in that it can, where it is applicable, provide the agent with a defence to a claim in tort (as it was sought to do in *Prager* itself), and it can also be invoked to create a contractual relationship between the agent's principal and the third party with whom the agent contracted in the emergency. But our concern is with the agent's right to reimbursement against his

---

14 (1849) 7 CB 797, 804.

principal. Does the claim that such a right is restitutionary in nature lead to the proposition that an agent's right to claim reimbursement from his principal is always restitutionary in nature? If so, can such a proposition be defended?

5. Latham CJ, in a dissenting judgment in the High Court of Australia in *Burns Philp & Co. Ltd v Gillespie Brothers Pty. Ltd* (1947) 74 CLR 148, 175, sought to rationalize the basis of agency of necessity in the following terms:

> the phrase 'agency of necessity' is, in my opinion, only a convenient expression used in rationalizing to some extent the rights and obligations which are created in certain circumstances of emergency. It is a 'shorthand' method of saying that such circumstances may create an authority to act in relation to the property of another person or to impose a liability upon him which would not exist in ordinary circumstances. Thus in some circumstances a wife may be an agent of necessity to pledge her husband's credit for necessaries. She may have no express authority to bind him, and the husband may even expressly repudiate her authority. But he cannot effectively do so. The authority is said to be irrevocable. . . . In such a case there is no express or implied agreement that the wife shall be the agent of the husband. The phrases of the law of agency are used to describe, not the means of constituting the relationship which enables the wife to create a liability in her husband, but the result which follows from the marital relationship in certain circumstances of necessity. The so-called agency arises as what has been described an irrebutable presumption of law. . . . Agency of necessity arises from action in circumstances of necessity and not from any real or presumed agreement between the person who becomes an 'agent of necessity' and the person in whose interest he has acted.

6. A rather more modern analysis of the nature of the principle or principles which underpin agency of necessity was provided by Lord Goff in *In re F (Mental Patient: Sterilisation)* [1990] 2 AC 1, 75–6 in the following terms:

> We can derive some guidance as to the nature of the principle of necessity from the cases on agency of necessity in mercantile law. When reading those cases, however, we have to bear in mind that it was there considered that (since there was a pre-existing relationship between the parties) there was a duty on the part of the agent to act on his principal's behalf in an emergency. From these cases it appears that the principle of necessity connotes that circumstances have arisen in which there is a necessity for the agent to act on his principal's behalf at a time when it is in practice not possible for him to obtain his principal's instructions so to do. In such cases, it has been said that the agent must act bona fide in the interests of his principal: see *Prager v Blatspiel Stamp & Heacock Ltd* [1924] 1 KB 566, 572, *per* McCardie J. A broader statement of the principle is to be found in the advice of the Privy Council delivered by Sir Montague Smith in *Australian Steam Navigation Co. v Morse* (1872) LR 4 PC 222, 230, in which he said:
>
> > 'when by the force of circumstances a man has the duty cast upon him of taking some action for another, and under that obligation, adopts the course which, to the judgment of a wise and prudent man, is apparently the best for the interest of the persons for whom he acts in a given emergency, it may properly be said of the course so taken, that it was, in a mercantile sense, necessary to take it.'
>
> In a sense, these statements overlap. But from them can be derived the basic requirements, applicable in these cases of necessity, that, to fall within the principle, not only (1) must there be a necessity to act when it is not practicable to communicate with the assisted person, but also (2) the action taken must be such as a reasonable person would in all the circumstances take, acting in the best interests of the assisted person.
>
> On this statement of principle, I wish to observe that officious intervention cannot be justified by the principle of necessity. So intervention cannot be justified when another more appropriate person is available and willing to act; nor can it be justified when it is contrary to the known wishes of the assisted person, to the extent that he is capable of rationally forming such a wish. On the second limb of the principle, the introduction of the standard of a reasonable man should not in the present context be regarded as materially different from that of Sir Montague Smith's 'wise and prudent man,' because a reasonable man would, in the time available to him, proceed with wisdom and prudence before taking action in relation to another man's person or property without his consent.

• *China Pacific SA v Food Corporation of India* [1982] AC 939, House of Lords

The defendants chartered the *Winson* from its owners to carry a cargo of wheat from United States Gulf ports to ports in India. In January of 1975 the vessel was stranded on a reef in the South China Sea. On 22 February 1975 the ship's managing agents entered into a salvage agreement on Lloyd's open form with the claimant salvors. The claimants succeeded in saving over 15,000 tons of wheat which belonged to the defendants. The salvage operations were suspended on 15 April because of the Vietnam War. On 24 April the shipowner abandoned the voyage and notified the defendants accordingly. On 20 May, the war having made it impractical to continue with the salvage operations, the claimants formally terminated their salvage services. The defendants accepted that they were obliged to pay the storage expenses incurred by the claimants in storing the wheat from 24 April until 5 August, but maintained that it was the responsibility of the shipowners to meet these charges between 22 February and 24 April. The defendants' argument failed on the ground that a direct relationship of bailor and bailee was created between the parties as soon as the cargo was loaded on to vessels provided by the salvor to carry it to a place of safety and that the claimants' obligations as bailees to take care of the goods gave to them a correlative right to charge the defendant cargo owners with the expenses which they had reasonably incurred in discharging their duty.

Lord Diplock: . . . My Lords, it is not suggested that there is any direct authority on the question of law that is posed in this appeal. In my opinion the answer is to be found by applying to the unusual circumstances of the instant case well known and basic principles of the common law of salvage, of bailment and of lien.

. . .

My Lords, with modern methods of communication and the presence of professional salvors within rapid reach of most parts of the principal maritime trade routes of the world, nearly all salvage of merchant ships and their cargoes nowadays is undertaken under a salvage contract in Lloyd's open form. The contract is one for the rendering of services; the services to be rendered are of the legal nature of salvage and this imports into the contractual relationship between the parties to the contract by necessary implication a number of mutual rights and obligations attaching to salvage of vessels and their cargo under common law, except in so far as such rights and obligations are inconsistent with express terms of the contract.

Lloyd's open form is expressed by clause 16 to be signed by the master 'as agent for the vessel her cargo and freight and the respective owners thereof and binds each (but not the one for the other or himself personally) to the due performance thereof.' The legal nature of the relationship between the master and the owner of the cargo aboard the vessel in signing the agreement on the latter's behalf is often though not invariably an agency of necessity. It arises only when salvage services by a third party are necessary for the preservation of the cargo. Whether one person is entitled to act as agent of necessity for another person is relevant to the question whether circumstances exist which in law have the effect of conferring on him authority to create contractual rights and obligations between that other person and a third party that are directly enforceable by each against the other. It would, I think, be an aid to clarity of legal thinking if the use of the expression 'agent of necessity' were confined to contexts in which this was the question to be determined and not extended, as it often is, to cases where the only relevant question is whether a person who without obtaining instructions from the owner of goods incurs expense in taking steps that are reasonably necessary for their preservation is in law entitled to recover from the owner of the goods the reasonable expenses incurred by him in taking those steps. Its use in this wider sense may, I think, have led to some confusion in the instant case, since where reimbursement is the only relevant question all of those conditions that must be fulfilled in order to entitle one person to act on behalf of another in creating direct contractual relationships between that other person and a third party may not necessarily apply. . . .

Upon the assumption, whether correct or not, to which I have already referred as being that upon which this case has been argued throughout, that the salvage services which the salvors had contracted to render to the cargo owner came to an end as respects each parcel of salved wheat when it arrived at a place of safety in Manila Harbour, the legal relationship of bailor and bailee between cargo owner and salvors nevertheless continued to subsist until possession of the wheat was accepted by the cargo owner from the depositaries who had been the salvors' sub-bailees. Subject always to the question of the salvors' right to the provision of security before removal of the salved wheat from Manila, with which I shall deal separately later, the bailment which up to the conclusion of the salvage services had been a bailment for valuable consideration became a gratuitous bailment; and so long as that relationship of bailor and bailee continued to subsist the salvors, under the ordinary principles of the law of bailment too well known and too well-established to call for any citation of authority, owed a duty of care to the cargo owner to take such measures to preserve the salved wheat from deterioration by exposure to the elements as a man of ordinary prudence would take for the preservation of his own property. For any breach of such duty the bailee is liable to his bailor in damages for any diminution in value of the goods consequent upon his failure to take such measures; and if he fulfils that duty he has, in my view, a correlative right to charge the owner of the goods with the expenses reasonably incurred in doing so.

My Lords, as I have already said, there is not any direct authority as to the existence of this correlative right to reimbursement of expenses in the specific case of a salvor who retains possession of cargo after the salvage services rendered by him to that cargo have ended; but Lloyd J discerned what he considered to be helpful analogous applications of the principle of the bailee's right to reimbursement in *Cargo ex Argos* (1873) LR 5 PC, 134, from which I have taken the expression 'correlative right,' and in *Great Northern Railway Co. v Swaffield* (1874) LR 9 Ex. 132. Both these were cases of carriage of goods in which the carrier/bailee was left in possession of the goods after the carriage contracted for had terminated. Steps necessary for the preservation of the goods were taken by the bailee in default of any instructions from owner/bailor to do otherwise. To these authorities I would add *Notara v Henderson* (1872) LR 7 QB 225, in which the bailee was held liable in damages for breach of his duty to take steps necessary for the preservation of the goods, and the Scots case of *Garriock v Walker* (1873) 1 R. 100 in which the bailee recovered the expenses incurred by him in taking such steps. Although in both these cases, which involved carriage of goods by sea, the steps for the prevention of deterioration of the cargo needed to be taken before the contract voyage was completed, the significance of the Scots case is that the cargo owner was on the spot when the steps were taken by the carrier/bailee and did not acquiesce in them. Nevertheless, he took the benefit of them by taking delivery of the cargo thus preserved at the conclusion of the voyage.

In the instant case the cargo owner was kept informed of the salvors' intentions as to the storage of the salved wheat upon its arrival in Manila; it made no alternative proposals; it made no request to the salvors for delivery of any of the wheat after its arrival at Manila, and a request made by the salvors to the cargo owner through their solicitors on February 25, 1975, after the arrival of the second of the six parcels, to take delivery of the parcels of salved wheat on arrival at Manila remained unanswered and uncomplied with until after notice of abandonment of the charter voyage had been received by the cargo owner from the shipowner.

The failure of the cargo owner as bailor to give any instructions to the salvors as its bailee although it was fully apprised of the need to store the salved wheat under cover on arrival at Manila if it was to be preserved from rapid deterioration was, in the view of Lloyd J, sufficient to attract the application of the principle to which I have referred above and to entitle the salvors to recover from the cargo owner their expenses in taking measures necessary for its preservation. For my part I think that in this he was right and the Court of Appeal, who took the contrary view, were wrong. It is, of course, true that in English law a mere stranger cannot compel an owner of goods to pay for a benefit bestowed upon him against his will; but this latter principle does not apply where there is a pre-existing legal relationship between the owner of the goods and the bestower of the benefit, such as that of bailor and bailee, which imposes upon the bestower of the benefit a legal duty of care in respect of the preservation of the goods that is owed by him to their owner.

In the Court of Appeal Megaw LJ, as I understand his judgment, with which Bridge and Cumming-Bruce L JJ expressed agreement, was of opinion that, in order to entitle the salvors to reimbursement of the expenses incurred by them in storing the salvaged wheat at Manila up to April 24, 1975, they would have to show not only that, looked at objectively, the measures that they took were necessary to preserve it from rapid deterioration, but, in addition, that it was impossible for them to communicate with the cargo owner to obtain from him such instructions (if any) as he might want to give. My Lords, it may be that this would have been so if the question in the instant case had been whether the depositaries could have sued the cargo owner directly for their contractual storage charges on the ground that the cargo owner was party as principal to the contracts of storage made on its behalf by the salvors as its agents of necessity; for English law is economical in recognising situations that give rise to agency of necessity. In my view, inability to communicate with the owner of the goods is not a condition precedent to the bailee's own right to reimbursement of his expenses. The bailor's failure to give any instructions when apprised of the situation is sufficient.

So, on the cargo owner's main propositions of law in this appeal, I think it fails and that on these points the Court of Appeal was wrong in reversing Lloyd J. . . .

Lord Simon of Glaisdale: My Lords, I have had the privilege of reading in draft the speech delivered by my noble and learned friend on the Woolsack. Since I am in general agreement with it, and particularly with its argument and conclusion that the salvor is entitled to succeed by reason of his bailment, what follows is by way of marginal comment. . .

The Lloyd's open form. I would myself, like Lloyd J, also come to the same conclusion by implication from the salvage contract, the argument running closely parallel to that on bailment. It was common ground that the contract is incomplete without implication of a term stipulating to whom delivery should be tendered when cargo salved separately from its carrying vessel is brought to a place of safety. I agree with my noble and learned friend that, in the case of bulk cargo the owner of which is known to the salvor, the person entitled to delivery is the cargo owner. The shipowner, by becoming party to and implementing the salvage contract, gives up his possessory lien; and I know of no principle entitling him to repossession merely to reassert a possessory lien: As for his option to on-carry, he can exercise it merely by communication with the cargo owner.

But there is a further matter requiring provision which is not covered by the express terms of the Lloyd's open form: namely, what is the duty of a salvor in respect of the cargo after it, or part of it, has been brought to a place of safety but before delivery to whoever is entitled to receive it? In my view, if cargo, or part of it, is salved separately from the carrying vessel, it is the duty of the salvor, owed to the cargo owner, to take reasonable steps on its arrival at the place of safety to prevent its deterioration. It is also, in my view, a necessary implication that, if the salvor incurs expense in fulfilling that duty, he is entitled to be reimbursed by the cargo owner. What I venture to submit hereafter, under the heading of '*Bailment*,' about the correlation of the performance of the duty to safeguard the goods on the one hand and the entitlement to reimbursement of expenses incurred thereby on the other, is relevant here; but it would be particularly unreasonable not to imply such correlationship in the context of the commercial nexus constituted by the Lloyd's open form.

. . .

Bailment. Counsel for the cargo owner contended that, even if the salvor as bailee owes the duty to the cargo owner as bailor to take reasonable steps to safeguard his goods, there was no correlative right to claim reimbursement of reasonable expenses in so acting: neither a bailee for reward nor a gratuitous bailee has any such general right to indemnity. Counsel for the cargo owner adopted the view of the Court of Appeal that, apart from specific contractual obligation, a bailee's right to reimbursement

> '. . . depends on there being something which can properly be called an element of necessity that the bailee should so act in order to preserve the goods.' [1981] QB 403, 423.

I agree that there is no general right of a bailee to be reimbursed expenses incurred in fulfilling his duty to safeguard bailed goods; and I agree that there was an element of necessity in the cases relied on by the salvor under this head. But I think that it puts it too narrowly to say that such are the only circumstances in which the law will import an obligation to reimburse—unless, indeed, one is prepared to go further and argue that only a bailee who is an agent of necessity is entitled to reimbursement. No authority so stipulates. The relevance of necessity in the cases relied on by the salvor is, in my view, that justice calls for reimbursement in such circumstances: the emergency imposes obligations on the bailee beyond what will generally be contemplated on a bailment.

But such are not the only circumstances in which justice demands indemnity. In my view the following circumstances in the instant appeal import a correlative obligation to reimburse expenses: (1) the contract of bailment was a commercial one; (2) it came to an end when the salved goods were brought to a place of safety, which, it has been the common assumption, was the entry into the port of Manila (though I must not be taken as necessarily endorsing this view); (3) the bailee then continued in possession as a gratuitous bailee; (4) he incurred reasonable expenses in safeguarding and preserving the goods, to the benefit of the bailor; (5) the bailor stood by, knowing that the bailee was so acting to his (the bailor's) benefit.

Agency of Necessity. Lloyd J decided in favour of the salvor on the further ground that he was the cargo owner's agent of necessity and as such entitled to reimbursement of the expenses in issue. The Court of Appeal held that there was no agency of necessity.

One of the ways in which an agency of necessity can arise is where A is in possession of goods the property of B, and an emergency arises which places those goods in imminent jeopardy: If A cannot obtain instructions from B as to how he should act in such circumstances, A is bound to take without authority such action in relation to the goods as B, as a prudent owner, would himself have taken in the circumstances. The relationship between A and B is then known as an 'agency of necessity,' A being the agent and B the principal. This was the situation described by Lloyd J and denied by the Court of Appeal.

Issues as to agency of necessity generally arise forensically when A enters into a contract with C in relation to the goods, the question being whether B is bound by that contract. The purely terminological suggestion that, in order to avoid confusion, 'agent of necessity' should be confined to such contractual situations does not involve that other relevant general incidents of agency are excluded from the relationship between A and B. In particular, if A incurs reasonable expenses in safeguarding B's goods in a situation of emergency, A is entitled to be reimbursed by B: see *Bowstead on Agency*, 14th edn (1976), art. 67; *Chitty on Contracts*, 23rd edn (1968), vol. 2, para. 119; *Petrinovic & Co. Ltd v Mission Française des Transports Maritimes* (1941) 71 Ll.L Rep. 208, 220.

To confine 'agent of necessity' terminologically to the contractual situations is justified by the fact that the law of bailment will often resolve any issue between alleged principal and agent of necessity, as it has done here. But sometimes the law of agency will be more useful: for example, if available here it would obviate any problem about the correlation of performance of a duty of care with a claim for reimbursement, since an agent is undoubtedly entitled to an indemnity for expenses incurred reasonably to benefit his principal.

However, I respectfully agree with the Court of Appeal [1981] QB 403, 424 that

'The relevant time, for the purpose of considering whether there was a necessity, or an emergency ... is ... the time when the existence of the supposed emergency became apparent. The emergency would be the arrival, or expected arrival, of salved cargo at Manila, with no arrangements for its off-loading or for its preservation in proper storage having been made or put in hand. There never was, so far as one can ascertain from the evidential matter here, such an emergency.'

In addition to the factual difficulty in treating the case as one of agency of necessity, there are legal difficulties in the way of the salvor. For an agency of necessity to arise, the action taken must be necessary for the protection of the interests of the alleged principal, not of the agent; the alleged agent must have acted bona fide in the interests of the alleged principal: *Bowstead on Agency*, 14th edn, p. 668; *Prager v Blatspiel, Stamp and Heacock Ltd* [1924] 1 KB 566, 571, 572, 573. The Court of Appeal [1981] QB 403, 425 held that the salvor's purpose in storing the salved cargo was to maintain his lien on it. This was assuredly at least in part the salvor's purpose. The law does not seem to have determined in this context what ensues where interests are manifold or motives mixed: it may well be that the court will look to the interest mainly served or to the dominant motive. In view of the opinion I have formed on the rights arising by implication from the Lloyd's open form and from the common law bailment, it is unnecessary to come to any conclusion on these issues.

Nor is it necessary to express any view on the arguments based on quasi-contract or estoppel.

Lord Keith of Kinkel, Lord Roskill and **Lord Brandon of Oakbrook** concurred with the speech of **Lord Diplock.**

NOTES AND QUESTIONS

1. It is the speech of Lord Diplock which represents the majority opinion. What differences are there between the speech of Lord Diplock and that of Lord Simon of Glaisdale (see the valuable analysis of the case by Palmer in *Bailment* (2nd edn, 1991), 584–91)?

2. What limitations did (a) Lord Diplock and (b) Lord Simon impose on the right of a bailor to recover his custodial expenses? In particular, must there be an 'emergency' or 'necessity' before the right of recovery can arise?

3. Professor Palmer has stated (*Bailment*, 583) that the 'facts of *The Winson* were highly specialized and far removed from the conventional case of a gratuitous safekeeping'. In what respects is this true?

4. What differences (if any) exist between the right of a gratuitous bailee to recover his custodial expenses and the right of an agent of necessity to be reimbursed in respect of his expenses incurred in the course of his agency?

5. Is Lord Diplock's suggested refinement of the use of the phrase 'agent of necessity' likely to prove a beneficial one? Is there any justification for laying down one set of rules for the 'external' aspects of agency and another for the 'internal' aspects of the agency relationship?

6. If the case ultimately rests on principles derived from the law of bailment, does it shed any light on the existence or scope of a restitutionary right of recovery?

(4) PROVISION OF NECESSARIES FOR THE INCAPACITATED

• *In re Rhodes* (1890) 44 ChD 94, Court of Appeal

Eliza Charlotte Rhodes was a lady of unsound mind, but she had never been found to be a lunatic by inquisition. She was in the 'social position of a lady' and had an income of under £96 a year. From 1855 until her death in 1881 she was looked after in a private lunatic asylum, where she had been placed by her brother. The cost of this care was £140 a year. Until his death in 1875, Miss Rhodes' brother applied her income towards the cost of her care and he made up the deficiency out of his own pocket. After his death, this practice was carried on by the defendant, his son, who, in addition to employing his own money, also received contributions from his brother and sisters. The defendant did not make any claim on Miss Rhodes during her lifetime, nor was there any evidence that an account had been kept. But, after her death, he claimed to be entitled to retain from the estate the sums which he and his family had expended in looking after Miss Rhodes. This claim was successfully resisted by the claimants, who were some of Miss Rhodes' next of kin, on the ground that the court was, on the facts, unable to imply an obligation that Miss Rhodes would reimburse the defendant for the sums which had been expended by himself and other members of his family.

Cotton LJ: . . . [The] question is, whether there can be an implied contract on the part of a lunatic not so found by inquisition to repay out of her property sums expended for necessaries supplied to her. Now the term 'implied contract' is a most unfortunate expression, because there cannot be a contract by a lunatic. But whenever necessaries are supplied to a person who by reason of disability cannot himself contract, the law implies an obligation on the part of such person to pay for such necessaries out of his own property. It is asked, can there be an implied contract by a person who cannot himself contract in express terms? The answer is, that what the law implies on the part of such a person is an obligation, which has been improperly termed a contract, to repay money spent in supplying necessaries. I think that the expression 'implied contract' is erroneous and very unfortunate. . . .

But, then, although there may be an implied obligation on the part of the lunatic, the necessaries must be supplied under circumstances which would justify the Court in implying an obligation to repay the money spent upon them.

I have no difficulty as to the question of the expenditure being for necessaries, for the law is well established that when the necessaries supplied are suitable to the position in life of the lunatic an implied obligation to pay for them out of his property will arise. But then the provision of money or necessaries must be made under circumstances which would justify the Court in implying an obligation. Here the lady, who was never found a lunatic, was confined in a private asylum, in 1855, at a cost of £140 a year, and her brother from that time down to the time of his death supplied her with the sums required to make good the necessaries for her maintenance. After his death the Appellant, who was his father's executor, and his brother and sisters, contributed towards the expense of her maintenance. I do not so much rely on the circumstance that there is no evidence to shew that the father intended this to be a debt. But we must look to the facts of the case in order to see whether the payments for the lunatic were made with the intention of constituting thereby a debt against the lunatic's estate. It is said that the father and the brother and sisters always intended to be recouped. And, no doubt, at the time the payments were made, the persons making them were the next of kin, or some of the next of kin, of the lady, and it is very probable that, although they did it as relations, they, no doubt, in making such payments did look to the fact that, as next of kin, they would ultimately come into the lunatic's property. No books have been produced, but we must assume that the Appellant kept no account between himself and his brother and sisters. And the observation occurs that, if it had been intended by the Appellant that these payments should constitute an obligation in his favour, as against the estate of the lunatic, he would not have asked his brother and sisters to contribute, but would have paid the money himself. The certificate has, no doubt, found that the sisters had no intention of making a gift, and this in favour of the Appellant. But although they had no particular intention of making a gift, they contributed the money; and, if they intended to be repaid, it is very strange that they make no claim on their own behalf, but leave their brother to make it for them. In my opinion, the true effect of the evidence is that all these persons—the Appellant, and his brother and sisters, and the father—did provide this money under circumstances from which no implied obligation could arise.

Lindley LJ: . . . The question whether an implied obligation arises in favour of a person who supplies a lunatic with necessaries is a question of law, and in *In re Weaver*[1] a doubt was expressed whether there is any obligation on the part of the lunatic to repay. I confess I cannot participate in that doubt. I think that that doubt has arisen from the unfortunate terminology of our law, owing to which the expression 'implied contract' has been used to denote not only a genuine contract established by inference, but also an obligation which does not arise from any real contract, but which can be enforced as if it had a contractual origin. Obligations of this class are called by civilians *obligationes quasi ex contractu*.

. . .

Now, in order to raise an obligation to repay, the money must have been expended with the intention on the part of the person providing it that it should be repaid. I think that that intention is not only not proved, but is expressly negatived in the present case. I do not believe that the brother ever intended to constitute himself a creditor of his sister so as to render her estate liable to repay him. He was a kind and affectionate brother; but if he had had any such an intention, being a man of business, he would naturally have kept some kind of account between himself and his sister. There is no real ground for saying that he ever dreamt of repayment. Since his death his children maintained this lady by contribution, and, while there is no direct evidence to shew that the money contributed was a gift, there is still less evidence to shew any intention to be repaid.

Upon the facts, then, I come to the conclusion that the constitution of a debt between themselves and the lunatic was the last thing that the persons who made the payments contemplated.

Lopes LJ delivered a concurring judgment.

NOTES AND QUESTIONS

1. Why should the provider of the service be required to show that he had an intention to be repaid when providing the services? Should it not be for the recipient to prove that the provider should not recover because the work was done gratuitously?

2. What was the alleged unjust factor in this case?

3. If the defendant could have persuaded the court that he had an intention to charge, it is clear that the claim would have succeeded: see *Williams v Wentworth* (1842) 5 Beav. 325.

4. Must there be an 'emergency' before a restitutionary claim can arise or does it suffice that the intervention of the claimant was 'necessary' in the circumstances? If an 'emergency' is a prerequisite, can it be said, in any meaningful sense that there was an 'emergency' in a case such as *Re Rhodes*? In *re F (Mental Patient: Sterilisation)* [1990] 2 AC 1, 74–5 Lord Goff stated:

   the historical origins of the principle of necessity do not point to emergency as such as providing the criterion of lawful intervention without consent. The old Roman doctrine of negotiorum gestio pre-supposed not so much an emergency as a prolonged absence of the dominus from home as justifying intervention by the gestor to administer his affairs. The most ancient group of cases in the common law, concerned with action taken by the master of a ship in distant parts in the interests of the shipowner likewise found its origin in the difficulty of communication with the owner over a prolonged period of time—a difficulty overcome today by modern means of communication. In those cases, it was said that there had to be an emergency before the master could act as agent of necessity; though the emergency could well be of some duration. But when a person is rendered incapable of communication either

1 21 ChD 615.

permanently or over a considerable period of time (through illness or accident or mental disorder), it would be an unusual use of language to describe the case as one of 'permanent emergency'—if indeed such a state of affairs can properly be said to exist. In truth, the relevance of an emergency is that it may give rise to a necessity to act in the interests of the assisted person, without first obtaining his consent. Emergency is however not the criterion or even a pre-requisite; it is simply a frequent origin of the necessity which impels intervention. The principle is one of necessity, not of emergency.

5. Section 3(2) of the Sale of Goods Act 1979 provides that 'where necessaries are sold and delivered to a minor or a person who by reason of mental incapacity or drunkenness is incompetent to contract, he must pay a reasonable price for them'. Is this liability restitutionary or contractual?

(5) MISCELLANEOUS CASES

- *Great Northern Railway v Swaffield* (1874) LR 9 Ex. 132, Court of Exchequer

The defendant sent a horse by the claimants' railway to Sandy station. The horse was consigned to the defendant himself, the fare having being pre-paid. When the horse arrived at the station, there was no representative of the defendant there to receive it. So the station-master took the horse to a livery stable for safe-keeping. The next day an employee of the defendant arrived to collect the horse, but the station-master informed him that he could only collect it if the livery charges, which were admitted to be reasonable, were paid. The employee refused to make any such payment. The following day, the defendant himself came to complain to the station-master and, after some negotiation, the station-master offered to pay the charges out of his own pocket but the defendant refused to accept the offer. Negotiations continued between the parties but the defendant maintained that he would not accept delivery of the horse at his farm unless it was accompanied by payment of 30s to cover his expenses in the matter. The horse remained in the livery stables for a further four months until the station-master arranged for its collection and sent it to the defendant, who accepted it. No demand was made at that time for payment. The claimants then paid the livery charges of £17 and sought to recover that sum from the defendant. Their claim failed in the County Court but succeeded in the Court of Exchequer.

Kelly CB: . . . I am clearly of opinion that the plaintiffs are entitled to recover. My Brother Pollock has referred to a class of cases which is identical with this in principle, where it has been held that a shipowner who, through some accidental circumstance, finds it necessary for the safety of the cargo to incur expenditure, is justified in doing so, and can maintain a claim for reimbursement against the owner of the cargo. That is exactly the present case. The plaintiffs were put into much the same position as the shipowner occupies under the circumstances I have described. They had no choice, unless they would leave the horse at the station or in the high road to his own danger and the danger of other people, but to place him in the care of a livery stable keeper, and as they are bound by their implied contract with the livery stable keeper to satisfy his charges, a right arises in them against the defendant to be reimbursed those charges which they have incurred for his benefit.

. . .

Pollock B: I am of the same opinion. If the case had rested on what took place on the night when the horse arrived, I should have thought the plaintiffs wrong, for this reason, that although a common carrier has by the common law of the realm a lien for the carriage, he has no lien in his capacity as warehouseman; and it was only for the warehousing or keeping of this horse that the plaintiffs could have made any charge against the defendant.

But the matter did not rest there; for it is the reasonable inference from what is stated in the case, that on the next day, when the defendant himself came, he could have had the horse without the payment of anything; but he declined to take it, and went away. Then comes the question, first, What was the duty of the plaintiffs, as carriers, with regard to the horse? and secondly, If they incurred any charges in carrying out that duty, could they recover them in any form of action against the owner of the horse? Now, in my opinion it was the duty of the plaintiffs, as carriers, although the transit of the horse was at an end, to take such reasonable care of the horse as a reasonable owner would take of his own goods; and if they had turned him out on the highway, or allowed him to go loose, they would have been in default. Therefore they did what it was their duty to do. Then comes the question, Can they recover any expenses thus incurred against the owner of the horse? As far as I am aware, there is no decided case in English law in which an ordinary carrier of goods by land has been held entitled to recover this sort of charge against the consignee or consignor of goods. But in my opinion he is so entitled. It had been long debated whether a shipowner has such a right, and gradually, partly by custom and partly by some opinions of authority in this country, the right has come to be established. It was clearly held to exist in the case of *Notara v Henderson*,[1] where all the authorities on the subject are reviewed with very great care; and that case, with some others, was cited and acted upon by the Privy Council in the recent case of *Cargo ex Argos*.[2] The Privy Council is not a Court whose decisions are binding on us sitting here, but it is a Court to whose decisions I should certainly on all occasions give great weight; and their judgment on this point is clearly in accordance with reason and justice. It was there said[3] (after referring to the observations of Sir James Mansfield, CJ, in *Christy v Row*[4]), 'The precise point does not seem to have been subsequently decided, but several cases have since arisen in which the nature and scope of the duty of the master, as agent of the merchant, have been examined and defined.' Then, after citing the cases, the judgment proceeds: 'It results from them, that not merely is a power given, but a duty is cast on the master, in many cases of accident and emergency, to act for the safety of the cargo in such manner as may be best under the circumstances in which it may be placed; and that, as a correlative right, he is entitled to charge its owner with the expenses properly incurred in so doing.' That seems to me to be a sound rule of law. That the duty is imposed upon the carrier, I do not think any one has doubted; but if there were that duty without the correlative right, it would be a manifest injustice. Therefore, upon the whole of the circumstances, I come to the conclusion that the claim of the company was a proper one, and that the judgment of the learned judge of the county court must be reversed.

Pigott B and **Amphlett B** delivered concurring judgments.

NOTES AND QUESTIONS

1. Was the defendant enriched by the intervention of the claimants? What test should be applied in deciding whether or not the defendant was enriched? If the test for establishing a benefit is that the defendant was saved a necessary expense, in what sense was this true of the defendant here?
2. What was the unjust factor in this case?
3. Is this case an example of agency of necessity? It is so treated by Goff and Jones (17–003 n.20, cf. Burrows, 305), yet it is not expressly so classified by the court, where the agency of necessity cases were invoked merely by way of analogy.
4. Were the claimants obliged by the terms of the contract of carriage to look after the horse until it was collected? Would it matter if they were not? Suppose that I find your dog in the street. It is clearly extremely hungry and so I take it home and feed it. Can I recover my expenses from you?

----

1 Law Rep 7 QB 225, at 230–5.   2 Law Rep 5 PC 134.   3 Law Rep 5 PC, at 164.
4 I Taunt 300.

● *Matheson v Smiley* [1932] 2 DLR 787, Manitoba Court of Appeal

The defendant, Smiley, shot himself in a suicide bid. He was found by two of his friends while he was still alive but in a serious condition. One of them summoned a doctor who considered that a surgeon was required. Smiley was taken into hospital, where the claimant surgeon attended to him, in the event unsuccessfully. The claimant brought an action against the estate of Smiley and recovered the sum of $150, which he claimed was the value of the services which he had rendered.

Robson JA: . . . Defendant here says there was no request to plaintiff binding upon the defendant. There has been no promise by defendant for a past consideration even if that would be of avail to plaintiff. Smiley was conscious and did say something to plaintiff but it is clear that he was in such an extreme condition that no words of his then should be construed as a request for the plaintiff's services or as an acquiescence in their being rendered on a contractual footing. Smiley was in no shape for that. But that does not seem to me to end the matter. I think it is not within reason that even in such circumstances as are revealed here a person in such a plight should simply be allowed to die without an effort being made by those in contact with him and without resort to all reasonable means to secure his recovery that may be at hand to them. And surely the person to pay should be the person for whose benefit the service is rendered. I hardly think it an answer to say in any case there was no hope. In such circumstances no one gives up while a spark remains.

The common law takes notice of such emergencies and declares to be a duty what is almost invariably done upon human impulse. [*He considered* Metropolitan Asylum District v Hill *(1884) 6 App. Cas. 193, 204 and* Re Rhodes *(1890) 44 ChD 94 and continued:*]

I think it is clear that the principle thus laid down applies to the case of any person 'who by reason of disability cannot himself contract' and that it does not apply solely to cases of lunacy.

. . .

I think the friends of deceased present, Wright and Cousins, only acted within their duty in calling in Dr Condell and that his calling the plaintiff was merely a natural sequence in the nature of the case.

. . .

I look upon the surgeon's service here as a necessary for Smiley even though the effort was unavailing. I therefore think a right to recover from defendant's estate exists in favour of the plaintiff.

This leaves the question of reasonableness of the plaintiff's charge still to be considered.

[*After reviewing the evidence, he concluded that it was impossible to say that the trial judge was wrong in finding that $150 was a reasonable sum.*]

NOTES AND QUESTIONS

1. What is the significance of the fact that the claimant's intervention was (a) unsuccessful and (b) rendered contrary to the will of the defendant? In relation to the first of these issues it is interesting to contrast the salvage cases, where it is clear that the fact that the intervention was unsuccessful is a bar to a right of recovery.

2. What would have been the outcome if Smiley had been a Jehovah's Witness who required a blood transfusion to save his life but, because of his religious views, refused to allow the transfusion to be carried out? Would a doctor who nevertheless carried out the transfusion be entitled to recover the value of his services from Smiley?

3. What would be the significance of the fact that, were this case to occur in Britain, the defendant, in so far as he expected to be treated at all, would expect to be treated free of charge on the National Health Service?

4. Burrows, 320 note 13 states that *Matheson* is 'probably best viewed as compensating the surgeon's loss and not reversing unjust enrichment'. If this is so, how can the claimant's cause of action best be classified?

5. Does unjust sacrifice provide a more satisfactory explanation for *Matheson*?

• *In re Berkeley Applegate Ltd* [1989] Ch 32, Chancery Division

An investment company went into voluntary liquidation. The company had operated as follows: investors paid money to the company which the company would then lend to approved borrowers subject to a mortgage and the mortgage was taken in the name of the company. Before money was advanced to borrowers, it was placed in a client account where it earned interest. At the commencement of the winding up the assets standing in the name of the company consisted of, *inter alia*, £1.2 million in the clients' accounts, together with interest of £29,508, and loans of some £10.2 million made by the company and secured by mortgages. It was held that these assets were held by the company on trust for the investors. The assets of the company which were not subject to any trust were of uncertain value but it was clear that the expenses and remuneration of the liquidator were very considerable and likely greatly to exceed the value of the free assets of the company. So the liquidator took out a summons seeking to determine whether or not he was entitled to be paid any part of his expenses or remuneration out of the trust assets. There was no statutory authority for the payment of such sums out of the trust assets, but it was held that the court had an equitable jurisdiction to require an allowance to be made for the costs incurred and skill and labour expended in the administration of the estate and that the liquidator was entitled to be compensated out of the trust funds to the extent that the company's assets were insufficient to compensate him for his proper expenses and remuneration.

Edward Nugee QC (sitting as a deputy High Court judge): . . . The order which the liquidator now seeks is an order for the payment to him as remuneration and/or fees, expenses, costs, disbursements and liabilities in such sum as to the court shall seem just, out of the assets of the company and out of the funds in the clients' accounts and the sums realised from the mortgages or from the investors if and to the extent that the mortgages are not realised; and as a less satisfactory alternative, an order that the company be entitled to be paid and retain such sums as the court shall think fit by way of remuneration as trustee of the trust assets. The question which I am now asked to determine is the question of principle, namely, whether any part of the liquidator's expenses or remuneration can be paid out of the trust assets, either directly or by way of payment to the company. If the answer to that question is yes, I am not asked at this stage to decide how the expenses and remuneration should be borne as between the company's assets and the trust assets, nor am I asked to determine whether any particular item of expenses or remuneration claimed by the liquidator should be allowed. Both these questions will require consideration in due course if payment can properly be made out of the trust assets, but there is not sufficient evidence to enable them to be decided at present. The liquidator is, however, entitled to know before he incurs further expense whether his proper expenses and proper remuneration for his work will be met from the trust assets in the event of the company's own assets proving insufficient.

There is no reported authority directly in point. . . .

In my judgment Mr de Lacy's submissions are based on too narrow a view of the principles on which the court acts. It is true that the legal title to the mortgages and to the clients' accounts is not vested in the liquidator but remains in the company; but the investors still need the assistance of a court of equity to secure their rights. In this respect their position is different from that of the claimant in *Falcke v Scottish Imperial Insurance Co.*, 34 ChD 234, where Bowen LJ said, at 251: 'It is not even a case where the owner of the saved property requires the assistance of a court of equity . . . to get the property back.' As a condition of giving effect to their equitable rights, the court has in my judgment a discretion to ensure that a proper allowance is made to the liquidator. His skill and labour may not have added directly to the value of the underlying assets in which the investors have equitable interests; but he has added to the estate in the sense of carrying out work which was necessary before the estate could be realised for the benefit of the investors. As was the case in *Scott v Nesbitt*, 14 Ves. Jun. 438, if the liquidator had not done this work, it is inevitable that the work, or at all events a great deal of it, would have had to be done by someone else, and on an application to the court a receiver would have been appointed whose expenses and fees would necessarily have had to be borne by the trust assets. On the evidence before me, the beneficial interests of the investors could not have been established without some such investigation as has been carried out by the liquidator.

The allowance of fair compensation to the liquidator is in my judgment a proper application of the rule that he who seeks equity must do equity.

'That . . . is a rule of unquestionable justice, but which decides nothing in itself; for you must first inquire what are the equities which the defendant must do, and what the plaintiff ought to have:' *Neesom v Clarkson* (1845) 4 Hare 97, 101 *per* Wigram V.-C.

'The rule means that a man who comes to seek the aid of a court of equity to enforce a claim must be prepared to submit in such proceedings to any directions which the known principles of a court of equity may make it proper to give; he must do justice as to the matters in respect of which the assistance of equity is asked:' *Halsbury's Laws of England*, 4th edn, vol. 16 (1976), 874, para. 1303, which in my judgment correctly states the law.

The authorities establish, in my judgment, a general principle that where a person seeks to enforce a claim to an equitable interest in property, the court has a discretion to require as a condition of giving effect to that equitable interest that an allowance be made for costs incurred and for skill and labour expended in connection with the administration of the property. It is a discretion which will be sparingly exercised; but factors which will operate in favour of its being exercised include the fact that, if the work had not been done by the person to whom the allowance is sought to be made, it would have had to be done either by the person entitled to the equitable interest (as in *In re Marine Mansions Co.*, LR 4 Eq. 601 and similar cases) or by a receiver appointed by the court whose fees would have been borne by the trust property (as in *Scott v Nesbitt*, 14 Ves. Jun. 438); and the fact that the work has been of substantial benefit to the trust property and to the persons interested in it in equity (as in *Phipps v Boardman* [1964] 1 WLR 993). In my judgment this is a case in which the jurisdiction can properly be exercised.

It seems to me that this principle is entirely consistent with the basis upon which the Court of Appeal acted in *In re Duke of Norfolk's Settlement Trusts* [1982] Ch 61. What the Court of Appeal held in that case was that, if the increase of the trustees' remuneration was beneficial to the trust administration, there was an inherent jurisdiction to require the beneficiaries to accept, as a condition of effect being given to their equitable interests, that such an increase in remuneration should be authorised. The court there was concerned with the good administration of a settlement of a conventional kind; but the jurisdiction which was held to be exercisable in that case is in my judgment equally exercisable in other cases in which a person seeks to enforce an interest in property to which he is entitled in equity. The principles on which a court of equity acts are not divided into watertight compartments but form a seamless whole, however necessary it may be for the purposes of exposition to attempt to set them out under distinct headings. I have already referred to the way in which Kekewich J in *In re Staffordshire Gas and Coke Co.* [1893] 3 Ch 523 treated expenditure on the preservation of trust property as coming under the head of 'salvage,' and the petitioning creditor in *In re Anglo-Austrian Printing and Publishing Union* [1895] 2 Ch 891 sought to persuade Vaughan Williams J to do the same. It is of interest that in *In re Duke of Norfolk's Settlement Trusts* [1979] Ch 37,

59B–C, Walton J regarded the cases in which the court authorises additional remuneration in order to secure the services of a particular trustee as also being 'closely analogous to "salvage".' I think this can fairly be regarded as confirmation of the underlying unity of the inherent jurisdiction which is exercised in such diverse circumstances as those which existed in *In re Marine Mansions Co.*, LR 4 Eq. 601; *Scott v Nesbitt*, 14 Ves. Jun. 438; *Phipps v Boardman* [1964] 1 WLR 993 and *In re Duke of Norfolk's Settlement Trusts* [1982] Ch 61.

Another example of the exercise of the inherent jurisdiction which seems to me to fall within the same principle occurs when the court sets aside a settlement for undue influence or on the bankruptcy of the settlor. Although there is no longer any property subject to the settlement, the court has a discretion to allow the trustees to take their costs out of the fund before handing it over to the successful litigant: see *Merry v Pownall* [1898] 1 Ch 306, 310–11 and *Bullock v Lloyds Bank Ltd* [1955] Ch 317, 327.

The particular aspect of the inherent jurisdiction which is sometimes referred to as 'salvage' was said by Evershed MR and Romer LJ in *In re Downshire Settled Estates* [1953] Ch 218, 235, to be exercisable

'where a situation has arisen in regard to the [trust] property (particularly a situation not originally foreseen) creating what may be fairly called an "emergency"—that is a state of affairs which has to be presently dealt with, by which we do not imply that immediate action then and there is necessarily required—and such that it is for the benefit of everyone interested under the trusts that the situation should be dealt with by the exercise of the administrative powers proposed to be conferred for the purpose.'

The situation which existed in the present case immediately before the commencement of the winding up could similarly fairly be called an emergency; and although the observations of Evershed MR and Romer LJ were directed to the court's jurisdiction to confer administrative powers upon trustees, the cases to which I have referred show that the inherent jurisdiction is wider than this and extends to making an allowance for costs incurred and skill and labour expended by those who have acted without obtaining the prior authority of the court.

I should notice three particular objections which were made to the existence of the jurisdiction in the present case. First it was said that the liquidator was not in the position of a trustee in that the legal interest in the trust assets remained throughout in the company and did not vest in him. In my judgment this does not preclude the court from making an allowance to him out of the trust assets in respect of his expenses and remuneration, although it is no doubt a factor to consider when determining to what extent compensation for his expenditure of money, skill and labour should be borne by the trust assets rather than the company's own assets. In several of the cases to which I have referred the person to whom the court made an allowance was not in the ordinary sense a trustee, although like the liquidator he was subject to fiduciary obligations; and the fact that he was not a trustee did not prevent the court from making a payment to him out of the trust assets. The salvage jurisdiction referred to in *In re Downshire Settled Estates* [1953] Ch 218 was described in terms which were restricted to the conferment of powers on trustees; but Evershed MR and Romer LJ recognised that salvage was only one aspect of the inherent jurisdiction, and the court's powers are clearly not exercisable only in favour of those who hold office as express trustees.

Secondly it was said that the contract between the company and the investors relieved the investors from any liability for further payments. I have referred in my earlier judgment to the summary of the investment scheme which was provided to all investors, and which stated, *inter alia* that 'No costs whatsoever are incurred by the investor.' While this is again a factor to consider when the court comes to determine how any costs and remuneration of the liquidator should be borne, and would no doubt carry much weight if the question was whether the company itself should be entitled to payment of any part of the expenses incurred by it out of the trust assets, it does not in my judgment preclude the court from exercising the inherent jurisdiction in favour of the liquidator. It is significant that in *In re Duke of Norfolk's Settlement Trusts* [1982] Ch 61 an argument that the trustees' remuneration could not be increased because it was based upon contract and the court had no power to vary the terms of a contract was rejected by the Court of Appeal. The circumstances in that case were of course different from those existing here; but if the terms of a settlement do not prevent the court from exercising its inherent jurisdiction in favour of the trustees in a proper case, I do not consider that the terms of the investment scheme in the present case prevent it from doing so in favour of the liquidator.

Thirdly, it was said that the business carried on by the company was contrary to section 1 of the Banking Act 1979, and that this is a ground for declining to exercise the inherent jurisdiction. It is not necessary for me to express any view on the legality of the company's business, which appears to be a question of some difficulty. I am satisfied that even if it was illegal, this does not preclude the court from exercising the jurisdiction in favour of the liquidator, whose own conduct is blameless in this respect.

Accordingly I propose to declare that the liquidator is entitled to be paid his proper expenses and remuneration out of the trust assets if the assets of the company are insufficient. I am not deciding how such expenses and remuneration should be borne as between the company's assets and the trust assets, nor as between the different classes of trust assets, nor whether any part of them should be borne by the trust assets if the company's own assets should in the end prove sufficient to meet them. It is premature to determine questions of incidence when the full extent of the liquidator's claims to expenses and remuneration are not yet known and the assets of the company may yet be swelled as a result of the litigation in which it is engaged. But the liquidator is entitled to know at this stage that his proper expenses and remuneration will be paid if necessary out of the trust assets, and that he will not be left at the end of the winding up with the possibility of receiving no recompense for his work or of having to bear part of the expenses out of his own pocket.

NOTES AND QUESTIONS

1. Can this claim properly be classified as a restitutionary claim? If so, what is the unjust factor? If not, what is the nature of the claim which was advanced?

2. Goff and Jones state (17–008, note 57) that 'it is doubtful whether these facts can be characterised as examples of necessitous intervention. The court has an inherent jurisdiction to remunerate and reimburse a trustee and liquidator for costs incurred and skill and labour expended in connection with the administration of property'. In his judgment in *In re Duke of Norfolk's Settlement Trusts* [1982] Ch 61, 79 Fox LJ stated that the basis of the court's inherent jurisdiction was 'the good administration of trusts'. Is it possible to frame a ground of restitution in such terms?

3. In *Wallersteiner v Moir (No 2)* [1975] QB 373 the Court of Appeal held that, in certain strictly defined circumstances (as further refined in *Smith v Croft* [1986] 1 WLR 580), a minority shareholder is entitled to be indemnified by the company against all costs and expenses reasonably incurred by him in the course of a derivative action on behalf of the company. Lord Denning stated that the indemnity 'does not arise out of contract, express or implied, but arises on plainest principles of equity'. A similar procedure exists whereby a trustee may be entitled to an indemnity from the beneficiaries of the trust in respect of the costs incurred by the trustee in bringing an action on behalf of the trust (see *Re Beddoe* [1893] 1 Ch 547) and this procedure has been extended to enable beneficiaries under a pension scheme to obtain an indemnity over a limited period from the pension fund in respect of the costs of litigation brought against those responsible for the administration of the pension fund (*McDonald v Horn* [1995] ICR 685). Can such cases be classified as restitutionary? If so, what is the unjust factor? Do they share any common features with *Berkeley Applegate*?

3. THE FUTURE DEVELOPMENT OF THE LAW

The fundamental issue which English law has to face is whether or not it should continue to adhere to its traditional view that altruism should be its own reward or whether it should build on the existing exceptions set out in section 2 and recognize the existence of a general right of recovery.

The case for rationalization (one way or the other) is made stronger by the fact that it is very difficult, if not impossible, to rationalize the cases in section 2. Is there any common thread which runs through these cases? L Aitken has argued ('Negotiorum Gestio and the Common Law: A Jurisdictional Approach' (1988) 11 *Sydney LR* 566, 568) that the 'common historical element, in bills of exchange, ship-masters, salvage and burial is the court in which these questions were first considered. The first three were connected with the Court of Admiralty, while the fourth fell under the aegis of the Ecclesiastical Courts.' The significance of these courts is that they were all 'under the control of judges whose training and outlook was pre-eminently civilian' and hence they were more receptive to the recognition of *negotiorum gestio*. But even Aitken is forced to concede that this analysis is not ultimately 'intellectually satisfying' (569) and it does not displace the need for the English courts to rethink this area of law and put it on a principled foundation (on which see F Rose, 'Restitution for the Rescuer' (1989) 9 *OJLS* 167 and, more generally, J Kortmann, *Altruism in Private Law: Liability for Nonfeasance and Negotiorum Gestio* (2005), chapters 11–13). In seeking to do this, it is necessary to consider the competing arguments which are summarized in the following passage:

- **A Burrows, *The Law of Restitution*,** (2nd edn 2002) 317–19

Apart from enabling one to clarify more specific principles, recognition that the encouragement of 'rescue' is the clear policy goal enables one to face squarely the central question of whether the law should build on the existing categories to give more widespread recovery for necessitous interveners. On the one hand, it can be argued that, given the availability of public services in the modern welfare state, there is no need for the judiciary to encourage private 'rescue': rather the law should be frozen at its existing position which, while perhaps not entirely rational, reflects the historical need for private intervention in certain spheres. Subject to the existing exceptions, altruism should remain its own reward.

Ranged against that—and more persuasive—is the view that, as the present categories do not even apply to all straightforward emergencies (e.g. saving a drowning child, or the repair of an absent neighbour's roof) and as there is no rational reason to distinguish the excluded situations from those where a remedy is now given, the law should be extended. Private 'rescue' should be encouraged because the public services cannot adequately deal with all situations in which another's health or property are in danger. The public services do not cover all types of emergency and, in any event, there may simply be inadequate time to call them out. . . . .

The two sides of the debate are neatly reflected in the differing judicial approaches in *The Goring*. Sheen J and Sir John Donaldson MR rejected as irrational the distinction between rescue on tidal waters, to which the law of salvage did apply, and rescue on non-tidal waters, where there was no salvage remedy; and in Sheen J's words, 'If a ship or her cargo is in danger in nontidal waters it is highly desirable, as a matter of public policy, that other ships should be encouraged to go to her assistance without hesitation.' In contrast the majority of the Court of Appeal and the House of Lords preferred to retain the restriction to tidal waters on the basis, *inter alia*, that the need for extension of the law on the ground of public policy had not been established.

It may be that this issue should be linked to the question, hotly debated by tort lawyers, as to the extent to which tort liability is, or should be, imposed for a failure to intervene to prevent another's injury or property damage. By and large there is no such tort liability. An argument can be put forward that the law should not impose such liability unless it is also prepared to award the necessitous intervener a restitutionary or other remedy. More controversially it can also be reasoned that, if the law were to award a remedy to a necessitous intervener, based on the policy of encouraging 'rescue', it ought to go further and to impose tort liability for failure to 'rescue'.

Before moving on, the views of Maddaugh and McCamus merit examination. They reject the idea that the law on necessitous intervention is primarily to be explained by the policy of encouraging intervention. 'The optimistic view that the granting of restitutionary relief might encourage altruism may provide additional support for the imposition of liability but the unjust enrichment principle is engaged merely by the existence of an unofficiously conferred windfall benefit.'

But the fact that a necessitous intervener is non-officious cannot be the root explanation for regarding the enrichment conferred as unjust. An initial difficulty is what one means by non-officious. The United States Restatement of Restitution, s. 2 vaguely defines the concept of officiousness as 'interference in the affairs of others not justified by the circumstances under which the interference takes place.' Much more helpful is Maddaugh and McCamus' suggestion that a person acts officiously if he acts maliciously or frivolously or 'confers unrequested benefits on another for the exclusive purpose of attempting to exploit for profit the needs of the other.'

Using that as a working definition, it is plain that non-officiousness is too wide an idea to explain necessity. It encompasses not only restitutionary recovery under other standard grounds outside necessity (for example, mistaken payments) but also situations where the law does not award restitution. For example, all gifts and benefits conferred under contracts are non-officious, yet there is no prospect of restitution unless the contract or gift is invalidated in some way. Again if a person indirectly confers a benefit on another while freely acting in self-interest he is not entitled (and should not be entitled) to restitution albeit that he is acting non-officiously.

With respect, therefore, while necessity is undoubtedly a fuzzy-edged concept, officiousness is of no assistance in understanding and clarifying its ambit.

There is, however, a second difficulty which must be faced and that relates to the nature of the claim that is being advanced in these cases. Can these claims be characterized as restitutionary claims or does their basis lie elsewhere? We have seen at various points in this chapter the difficulties which arise in attempting to explain these cases in restitutionary or unjust enrichment terms. These difficulties eventually led Professor Birks to abandon the attempt so to explain these cases. Thus he stated:

- **P Birks, *Unjust Enrichment*** (2nd edn, 2005), 23–4

Negotiorum gestio is not properly regarded as a species of unjust enrichment. There is no doubt that the intervener's right to reimbursement turns on the utility of the intervention, not on its success. There is no inquiry at all into the enrichment of the beneficiary and hence no tie between enrichment of the beneficiary and the amount he must pay. The measure of recovery is not gain-based. Moreover, the event has wider consequences. It binds the intervener to execute his intervention with due care and skill and to surrender anything he obtains in the course of his intervention . . . Even in relation to the intervener's right to reimbursement, *negotiorum gestio* belongs in the fourth column of causative events, miscellaneous other events, not in the third, unjust enrichment. Moreover, the intervener's right is not even a right to restitution. It should appear in the compensation stripe, not in the restitution stripe. That being so, *negotiorum gestio* belongs neither in the law of unjust enrichment (an event-based category) nor in the law of restitution (a response-based category).

It is nonetheless true that, if English law really had no *negotiorum gestio*, some particular instances of uninvited intervention would be found to conform to analysis as unjust enrichments, and those few cases would then form the kernel of a much narrower doctrine of necessitous intervention within the law of unjust enrichment. That is another story. It cannot be pursued here. It may never be pursued, because, as had been said, the old proposition denying the intervener any general right to reimbursement has probably been swallowed up by its numerous so-called exceptions.

Negotiorum gestio makes a brief appearance at this point only to illustrate the need to keep the fourth column of the grid in mind and to avoid overloading the third event-based column (unjust enrichment) under the illusion that non-contractual, non-tortious causative events can find no other home. Uninvited intervention is not a contract, a wrong, or an unjust enrichment. It belongs in the miscellaneous fourth column. In addition, the intervener's right is not a right to restitution.

In this extract Professor Birks refers to the fact that *negotiorum gestio* has 'wider consequences' and, in particular, to the duties which the doctrine imposes upon the intervener. This is true and it is important not to divorce the rights of the intervener from the duties which the law imposes on him. The law must be seen as a coherent whole. A modern attempt to codify the law of *negotiorum gestio* (or, as it is called, benevolent intervention in another's affairs) has been provided by the Study Group on a European Civil Code. The Articles are set out below and it can be seen that they deal both with the rights and the duties of the intervener and it can be seen that the subject matter of the text extends beyond the law of restitution or the law of unjust enrichment as we describe it in this book.

- **Principles of European Law: Study Group on a European Civil Code. Benevolent Intervention in Another's Affairs (prepared by Christian von Bar)** (2006)

CHAPTER 1: SCOPE OF APPLICATION

ARTICLE 1:101: INTERVENTION TO BENEFIT ANOTHER

(1) This Book applies where a person (the intervener) acts with the predominant intention of benefiting another (the principal); and

- (a) the intervener has a reasonable ground for acting; or
- (b) the principal approves the act without such undue delay as would adversely affect the intervener.

(2) The intervener does not have a reasonable ground for acting if the intervener:

- (a) has a reasonable opportunity to discover the principal's wishes but does not do so; or
- (b) knows or ought to know that the intervention is against the principal's wishes.

ARTICLE 1:102: INTERVENTION TO PERFORM ANOTHER'S DUTY

Where an intervener acts to perform another person's duty, the performance of which is due and urgently required as a matter of overriding public interest, and the intervener acts with the predominant intention of benefiting the recipient of the performance, the person whose duty the intervener acts to perform is a principal to whom this Book applies.

ARTICLE 1:103: EXCLUSIONS

This Book does not apply where the intervener:

- (a) is authorised to act under a contractual or other duty to the principal;
- (b) is authorised, other than under this Book, to act independently of the principal's consent or
- (c) is under a duty to a third party to act.

CHAPTER 2: DUTIES OF INTERVENER

ARTICLE 2:101: DUTIES DURING INTERVENTION

(1) During the intervention, the intervener must

    (a) act with reasonable care;

    (b) except in relation to a principal within article 1:102, act in a manner which the intervener knows or ought reasonably to assume accords with the principal's wishes; and

    (c) so far as possible and reasonable, inform the principal about the intervention and seek the principal's consent to further acts.

(2) The intervention may not be discontinued without good reason.

ARTICLE 2:102: DUTIES AFTER INTERVENTION

(1) After intervening the intervener must without undue delay report and account to the principal and hand over anything obtained as a result of the intervention.

(2) If at the time of intervening the intervener lacks full legal capacity, the duty to hand over is subject to the defences which would be available in the law of unjustified enrichment. . . .

ARTICLE 2:103: REPARATION FOR DAMAGE CAUSED BY BREACH OF DUTY

(1) The intervener is liable to make reparation to the principal for damage caused by breach of a duty set out in this Book if the damage resulted from a risk which the intervener created, increased or intentionally perpetuated.

(2) The intervener's liability is reduced or excluded in so far as this is fair and reasonable, having regard to, among other things, the intervener's reasons for acting.

(3) An intervener who at the time of intervening lacks full legal capacity is liable to make reparation only in so far as that intervener is also liable to make reparation under the law of non-contractual obligations arising out of damage caused to another. . . .

CHAPTER 3: RIGHTS AND AUTHORITY OF INTERVENER

ARTICLE 3:101: RIGHT TO INDEMNIFICATION OR REIMBURSEMENT

The intervener has a right against the principal for indemnification or, as the case may be, reimbursement in respect of an obligation or expenditure (whether of money or other assets) in so far as reasonably incurred for the purposes of the intervention.

ARTICLE 3:102: RIGHT TO REMUNERATION

(1) The intervener has a right to remuneration in so far as the intervention is reasonable and under-taken in the course of the intervener's profession or trade.

(2) The remuneration due is the amount, so far as reasonable, which is ordinarily paid at the time and place of intervention in order to obtain a performance of the kind undertaken.

ARTICLE 3:103: RIGHT TO REPARATION

An intervener who acts to protect the principal, or the principal's property or interests, against danger has a right against the principal for reparation for loss caused as a result of personal injury or property damage, suffered in acting, if:

    (a) the intervention created or significantly increased the risk of such injury or damage; and

    (b) that risk, so far as foreseeable, was in reasonable proportion to the risk to the principal

ARTICLE 3:104: REDUCTION OR EXCLUSION OF INTERVENER'S RIGHTS

(1) The intervener's rights are reduced or excluded in so far as the intervener at the time of acting did not want to demand indemnification, reimbursement, remuneration or reparation, as the case may be.

(2) These rights are also reduced or excluded in so far as this is fair and reasonable, having regard among other things to whether the intervener acted to protect the principal in a situation of joint danger, whether the liability of the principal would be excessive and whether the intervener could reasonably be expected to obtain appropriate redress from another.

ARTICLE 3:105: OBLIGATION OF THIRD PERSON TO INDEMNIFY OR REIMBURSE THE PRINCIPAL

If the intervener acts to protect the principal from damage, a person who would be accountable under . . . for the causation of such damage to the principal is obliged to indemnify or, as the case may be, reimburse the principal's liability to the intervener.

ARTICLE 3:106: AUTHORITY OF INTERVENER TO ACT IN THE NAME OF THE PRINCIPAL

(1) The intervener may conclude legal transactions or perform other juridical acts in the name of the principal in so far as this is reasonable to benefit the principal.

(2) However, a unilateral juridical act by the intervener in the name of the principal has no effect if a third person to whom it is addressed rejects the act without undue delay.

NOTES AND QUESTIONS

When thinking about what the law on necessity should be and the nature of the claim which is being made, it might be useful to consider the following questions.

1. If the aim of the law is to encourage people to perform necessary services for others, does the law of restitution offer a sufficient incentive for people to intervene? Should the courts not have the power to give a 'reward' to interveners, as in the salvage cases? If such a power were to be given to the courts, could this body of law still be analysed as (i) part of the law of restitution, (ii) an example of unjust sacrifice, or (iii) would it become an area of law which is *sui generis*?

2. While Anthea is away on holiday, Belinda, her neighbour notices water seeping out from under Anthea's front door. She calls a plumber and pays him £250 to cover the labour and material involved in repairing the pipe which had burst. Belinda also spends her weekend cleaning the carpets and generally trying to make good the damage caused by the flood. Anthea has now returned from holiday and, while she is grateful to Belinda for the work which she has done, she refuses to make any payment to Belinda on the ground that her boyfriend, Craig, was looking after the house in her absence and that he would have carried out the work free of charge had Belinda not intervened. Advise Belinda.

3. David went on a six-month holiday back-packing round Europe. He asked his friend Eric to look after his house in his absence. Three months after David's departure, Eric opened a letter addressed to David which was marked 'Urgent' (although he has not been asked by David to open his mail). It was a letter from an insurance company informing David that he had not paid his annual premium of £700 on a policy and that, if he failed to do so within three weeks, the policy (which was a valuable one) would lapse. So Eric paid the premium. David has now returned from his holiday and is refusing to reimburse Eric. Advise Eric.

10

ILLEGALITY AS A GROUND FOR RESTITUTION

The traditional approach to illegality cases is to commence the analysis with the invocation of two maxims. The first is *ex turpi causa non oritur actio* (no action can be based on a disreputable cause) and the second is *in pari delicto potior est conditio defendentis* (where both parties are equally at fault, the position of the defendant is stronger). The effect of these maxims is, broadly speaking, to allow the loss to lie where it falls and so to deny recovery of benefits conferred in the performance of an illegal contract. Having identified the general rules, the traditional approach then proceeds to examine the exceptional cases in which recovery is, in fact, allowed. There are three such exceptions: where the parties are not *in pari delicto*, where the claimant withdraws from the transaction during the *locus poenitentiae* (a space or time for repentance) and, finally, where the claimant can establish that the defendant retains his property, whether at law or in equity, without having to rely upon the illegality.

In our view this approach is defective in that it fails to distinguish between illegality (or, more exactly, the fact that the parties are not equally responsible for the illegality) operating as a ground for restitution and illegality functioning as a defence to a standard ground for restitution such as mistake, duress, (total) failure of consideration, etc. (see Birks, *An Introduction to the Law of Restitution* 299–303 and 424–32).

Although we believe that this distinction is an important one (and therefore we have separated off all the discussion of illegality except withdrawal in the *locus poenitentiae*—into the chapter on defences, see below, 883–919), it is not always an easy one to draw. Moreover, it is not a distinction which has been expressly adopted by the judges when deciding particular cases and Goff and Jones, chapter 22, do not rely on it but instead discuss all the illegality cases in a chapter entitled 'Illegal Contracts' which itself is included in a section entitled 'Ineffective Transactions'.

General Reading

Burrows, chapter 12; Goff and Jones, 24–007 and 24–008; Virgo, 352–355

1. WITHDRAWAL IN THE *LOCUS POENITENTIAE*

The one situation in which, in our view, it is clear that illegality does not play the role of a defence arises where the claimant abandons the illegal purpose during the *locus poenitentiae*. Such cases cannot be analysed as ones in which the claimant seeks recovery on the basis of a failure of consideration, because the claimant is entitled to recover even though the defendant remains ready, able, and willing to perform his side of the bargain (which he would not be able to do if the claim was analysed in terms of failure of consideration). The ground of restitution must therefore be found in the fact that the law wishes to encourage contracting parties to resile from performing illegal contracts and, to that end, it enables such a party to make a restitutionary claim in respect of benefits which he has bestowed on the other party to the contract.

Nevertheless, the courts have experienced considerable difficulty in establishing the limits of this claim. A number of difficult questions have arisen. For example, up to what point in time can the claimant resile from the transaction (must it be before performance has begun, or can it be at any time before performance has been completed)? And does the motive of the party seeking to recover the benefit matter (in other words, does it matter that the reason for seeking to withdraw from the contract is that the party has discovered that the deal was a bad one from his point of view or that the other party is unlikely to perform his side of the bargain)? Analysis is made more difficult by the fact that the courts appear to have had a change of heart over the course of the last 100 years. Cases in the nineteenth century appear to adopt a more liberal approach to the scope of the claim than has been evident since the middle of this century. Indeed, the scope of the claim can now be said to be so narrow that it is unlikely to be invoked with much success in the courts today.

- *Taylor v Bowers* (1876) 1 QBD 291, Queen's Bench Division and Court of Appeal

The claimant went to America in 1868 and left his wife and son in possession of his stock-in-trade. He returned the following year to discover that his son had incurred debts which appeared to threaten the viability of the business. The claimant consulted his nephew, Alcock, who advised the claimant to assign his stock-in-trade to him and that he, Alcock, would give him fictitious bills of exchange as the pretended consideration for the assignment. It was not clear what Alcock stood to gain from the transaction, but there was no doubt that the claimant's purpose was to prevent his creditors from asserting claims over the goods in order to discharge the debts which the claimant owed to them. Once he had reached agreement with his creditors, the claimant presumably intended that Alcock should re-convey the goods to him. But no agreement was in fact reached with the creditors, and Alcock deceived the claimant by executing a bill of sale of the goods to the defendant, one of the claimant's creditors. When the claimant discovered what had happened, he brought an action in detinue against the defendant for the value of the goods which had been made over to the defendant. The claimant's claim succeeded both in the Queen's Bench Division and in the Court of Appeal on the ground that the fraudulent purpose had not been carried out and that it was not necessary for him to rely upon the illegal transaction in order to recover damages.

Cockburn CJ: . . . In the present case nothing has been done to carry out the fraudulent or illegal object beyond the delivery of the goods to Alcock and their removal to Stafford. We put aside the bill of sale to the defendant, as the plaintiff was not a party to it, nor did it form part of the original arrangement. The next fact is, that before anything was done, and before the sale by auction, the plaintiff repudiated the whole transaction, and demanded back his goods from Alcock and the defendant. Under these circumstances, we think that the plaintiff is entitled to recover back his property from the defendant. The action is not founded upon the illegal agreement, nor brought to enforce it, but, on the contrary, the plaintiff has repudiated the agreement, and his action is founded on that repudiation.

Now it seems to us well established that where money has been paid, or goods delivered, under an unlawful agreement, but there has been no further performance of it, the party paying the money or delivering the goods may repudiate the transaction, and recover back his money or goods.

In *Hastelow v Jackson*[1] Littledale, J says: 'If two parties enter into an illegal contract, and money is paid upon it by one to the other, that may be recovered back before the execution of the contract, but not afterwards.' And in *Bone v Eckless*,[2] Bramwell, B, referring to *Hastelow v Jackson*,[3] says: 'Clearly an authority to pay over money for an illegal purpose may be revoked before the money is paid over. In *Hastelow v Jackson* that proposition of law was laid down, although there the plaintiff had to prove, as part of his case, that he had entered into an illegal contract; he did not, however, seek to recover upon it. . . . The law is in favour of undoing or defeating an illegal purpose, and is therefore in favour of the recovery of the money before the illegal purpose is fulfilled, not afterwards.'
. . .

The defendant appealed to the Court of Appeal.

James LJ: . . . Now the rule is, that a man certainly cannot recover goods in respect of which he is obliged to state a fraud of his own as part of his title. But that is not, according to my view, the position of this plaintiff. All the plaintiff has got to say is: 'These were my goods. I was possessed of these goods in 1868. I have never parted with them to anybody. They are my goods still. I never sold them, and I have never given them to anybody in such a way as to deprive myself of the right to possession of them.' It is the defendant who has got really to shew the fraud. He says, I claim these goods under a bill of sale by Alcock to me, and Alcock claims them under an assignment from the plaintiff to him by means of an inventory given to him with possession. Thus it is the defendant who has got to make out his title to the goods from the transaction which is a fraud, and which it seems he was a party to, in fact the defendant has got to make out his title from the fraudulent possession that was given to Alcock; and there would be no title in the defendant independently of that. So that if it was merely a question for the first time to be determined upon principle, without authority, I should have no doubt in saying that the plaintiff was not obliged to rely upon the fraud for the purpose of recovering back the goods, the legal possession of which in effect had never been parted with by him. But, to mention no other cases, the case of *Bowes v Foster*[4] seems to me entirely upon all fours with this case. In this case Bowers took from Alcock with the knowledge of Alcock's title, so he was in fact a party to the whole transaction from beginning to end. Therefore Bowers, if that question were open upon this rule, can be in no better position than Alcock.

It appears to me, therefore, that the judgment of the Queen's Bench Division was right, and should be affirmed.

Mellish LJ: . . . But the illegal transaction was not carried out; it wholly came to an end. To hold that the plaintiff is enabled to recover does not carry out the illegal transaction, but the effect is to put everybody in the same situation as they were before the illegal transaction was determined upon, and before the parties took any steps to carry it out. That, I apprehend, is the true distinction in point of law. If money is paid or goods delivered for an illegal purpose, the person who had so paid the money or delivered the goods may recover them back before the illegal purpose is carried out; but if he waits till the illegal purpose is carried out, or if he seeks to enforce the illegal transaction, in neither case can be maintain an action; the law will not allow that to be done. In the present action the facts come within the first alternative; and I am of opinion that the Queen's Bench Division has properly held, that the plaintiff does not require the aid of the illegal transaction, but is really bringing the action to set it aside.

Grove J: . . . the plaintiff is not setting up his own fraud in order to make a title, but he is repudiating the fraud and setting up his own prior rightful claim as owner of the goods. No doubt he is admitting

---

1 8 B & C 221, 226.   2 29 LJ (Ex) at 440; 5 H & N 925.   3 8 B & C 221, 226.
4 2 H & N 779; 27 LJ (Ex) 262.

that the goods got into Alcock's hands through his, the plaintiff's, own sham transfer for the fraudulent purpose of deceiving the creditors, but he is not setting up that fraudulent purpose in order to get the goods, but, on the contrary, he is setting it aside. I am, therefore, of opinion that the judgment ought to be affirmed.

Baggallay JA concurred with **Mellish LJ**.

● *Kearley v Thomson* (1890) 24 QBD 742, Court of Appeal

The claimant, who was a friend of a bankrupt, Clarke, offered to pay to the defendant solicitors, who were representing the petitioning creditors, the sum of £40 if they agreed not to appear at the public examination of Clarke and not to oppose his order of discharge. The defendants agreed to this, notwithstanding the fact that the agreement was illegal on the ground that it interfered with the course of justice. The claimant paid the sum of money and the defendants kept their side of the bargain and did not appear at the public examination, which Clarke passed. But, before any application had been made for Clarke's discharge, the claimant brought an action to recover the £40 from the defendants. It was held that, the contract having been partly performed, the claimant was not entitled to recover the money paid.

Fry LJ [*after setting out the general rule of no-recovery, then turned to the exceptions to the general rule:*] As a general rule, where the plaintiff cannot get at the money which he seeks to recover without shewing the illegal contract, he cannot succeed. In such a case the usual rule is potior est conditio possidentis. There is another general rule which may be thus stated, that where there is a voluntary payment of money it cannot be recovered back. It follows in the present case that the plaintiff who paid the 40*l.* cannot recover it back without shewing the contract upon which it was paid, and when he shews that he shews an illegal contract. . . . To that general rule there are undoubtedly several exceptions, or apparent exceptions. . . .

There is suggested to us a third exception, which is relied on in the present case, and the authority for which is to be found in the judgment of the Court of Appeal in the case of *Taylor v Bowers*.[1] In that case Mellish LJ, in delivering judgment, says at 300: 'If money is paid, or goods delivered for an illegal purpose, the person who has so paid the money or delivered the goods may recover them back before the illegal purpose is carried out.' It is remarkable that this proposition is, as I believe, to be found in no earlier case than *Taylor v Bowers*, which occurred in 1867, and, notwithstanding the very high authority of the learned judge who expressed the law in the terms which I have read, I cannot help saying for myself that I think the extent of the application of that principle, and even the principle itself, may, at some time hereafter, require consideration, if not in this Court, yet in a higher tribunal: and I am glad to find that in expressing that view I have the entire concurrence of the Lord Chief Justice. But even assuming the exception to exist, does it apply to the present case? What is the condition of things if the illegal purpose has been carried into effect in a material part, but remains unperformed in another material part? As I have already pointed out in the present case, the contract was that the defendants should not appear at the public examination of the bankrupt or at the application for an order of discharge. It was performed as regards the first; but the other application has not yet been made. Can it be contended that, if the illegal contract has been partly carried into effect and partly remains unperformed, the money can still be recovered? In my judgment it cannot be so contended with success. Let me put an illustration of the doctrine contended for, which was that partial performance did not prevent the recovery of the money. Suppose a payment of 100*l.* by A to B on a contract that the latter shall murder C and D. He has murdered C, but not D. Can the money

---

1 QBD 291.

be recovered back? In my opinion it cannot be. I think that case illustrates and determines the present one.

I hold, therefore, that where there has been a partial carrying into effect of an illegal purpose in a substantial manner, it is impossible, though there remains something not performed, that the money paid under that illegal contract can be recovered back. . . .

Lord Coleridge CJ and **Lord Esher MR** concurred.

- *Bigos v Bousted* [1951] 1 All ER 92, King's Bench Division

The defendant was advised by his doctor to send his daughter abroad for as long as possible in an effort to avoid her suffering a recurrence of pleurisy. He decided to send his wife and daughter to Italy for a period of time but, because of restrictions on English currency, he was unable to obtain a sufficient allowance to maintain them for the duration of their proposed stay in Italy. So he entered into an agreement with the claimant, in contravention of the Exchange Control Act 1947, under which the claimant agreed to supply the defendant's wife and daughter with £150 worth of Italian lire when they were in Italy and the defendant promised to repay her with English money in England. The defendant deposited a share certificate with the claimant as a security for his promise. The claimant failed to make the promised lire available and the defendant's wife and daughter had to return home earlier than planned. The defendant asked the claimant for the return of the share certificate but she refused to return it and brought an action to recover the £150 which she alleged she had paid to him. But she abandoned her claim at the commencement of the hearing, and the only issue before the court was the defendant's counterclaim for the return of the share certificate. It was held that the defendant was not entitled to recover the certificate because the reason for the non-performance of the contract was not the repentance of the defendant but the frustration of the contract by the refusal of the claimant to perform her side of the bargain.

Pritchard J (after setting out the facts of *Taylor v Bowers* and *Kearley v Thomson* continued) *Kearley v Thomson* appears to me to be easily distinguishable from *Taylor v Bowers* in that whereas the reason for the decision in *Taylor v Bowers* was that nothing had been done in pursuance of the illegal agreement, in *Kearley v Thomson* the report makes it quite clear that the plaintiff failed because something had been done in pursuance of the illegal agreement, and, therefore, I do not regard *Kearley v Thomson* as in any way conflicting with the decision in *Taylor v Bowers*, although, of course, the observations made by Fry LJ, in *Kearley v Thomson* on the rule as laid down by Mellish LJ, in *Taylor v Bowers* deserve attention, and, as I pointed out, occur again in subsequent cases.

In 1905 the Court of Appeal considered this question again in *Hermann v Charlesworth*, in connection with an illegal marriage brokerage contract. The plaintiff in that case had promised to pay £250 to the defendant if and when he introduced her to a gentleman who should marry her. She also paid to the defendant £52 which was called 'a client's fee.' The defendant thereupon introduced her to several men, but no marriage took place, and eventually the plaintiff brought an action to recover the £52. The action was remitted to the county court where the county court judge gave judgment for the plaintiff on the ground that, although the contract was a marriage brokerage contract and, therefore, illegal, the parties were not *in pari delicto*, as the defendant, who was out for money, was more blameworthy than the plaintiff, who was out for a husband. The defendant appealed to the Divisional Court who took the view that the contract did not come within the mischief which the law attributes to marriage brokerage contracts and allowed the appeal. The plaintiff appealed to the Court of Appeal who took the view that the Divisional Court was wrong, and that the contract was an illegal contract. Therefore, it became necessary for them to discuss the question with which I am concerned in the present case, and they allowed the plaintiff's appeal, with the result that she recovered her £52. The reason which the Court of Appeal gave for their decision was that, the object of the contract being to bring about a marriage, it could not be performed in part, and, therefore, as nothing had been done in the performance of the contract, the plaintiff was entitled to recover the money back, although she had paid it under an illegal contract. The facts in that case were peculiar, but, on the whole, it appears to me that the reason for the decision seems to support *Taylor v Bowers* and to disregard the criticism of that case which was made by Fry LJ, in *Kearley v Thomson*.

Lastly, *Alexander v Rayson* and *Berg v Sadler and Moore*, two comparatively recent cases, were cited to me, and it was argued on behalf of the plaintiff that they seriously affect the authority of *Taylor v Bowers*. In *Alexander v Rayson* the defendant, in 1929, rented a flat from the plaintiff at a rent of £1,200 a year, which was to include certain services. The plaintiff required the agreement for that letting to be in two documents. One document was the lease which contained a provision for certain services which were to be rendered by the lessor [the plaintiff], and the rent together with the benefit of the services was stated to be £450 a year. The other document, which provided for virtually the same services as that provided in the first document, stated that the consideration for those services should be £750 *per* year. The rent was paid quarterly, the defendant paying £300 in each quarter, i.e., at the rate of £1,200 a year, until Mid-summer, 1934. The defendant refused to pay £300 in respect of the quarterly instalment falling due on Sept. 29, 1934, because, as she alleged, the plaintiff had failed to provide the services which he had contracted to provide. She tendered, however, one quarter's rent under the lease, i.e., £112 10s., but the plaintiff claimed £300 under the two agreements. The plaintiff's purpose in having those two documents prepared was purely to deceive and to defraud the assessment committee who had to assess the rates of the premises. It was proved that that attempt failed because the assessment committee were not deceived, and, therefore, prevented themselves from being defrauded. In those circumstances, the Court of Appeal decided that the plaintiff could not maintain his action. The judgment of the Court of Appeal was prepared by Romer LJ, and read by Scott LJ, and it contains a passage ([1936] 1 KB 190) which, it is said, seriously affects the authority of *Taylor v Bowers*:

'Plaintiff's counsel further contended that inasmuch as the plaintiff had failed in his attempted fraud, and could therefore no longer use the documents for an illegal purpose, he was now entitled to sue upon them. The law, it was said, would allow to the plaintiff a *locus poenitentiae*. So, perhaps, it would have done, had the plaintiff repented before attempting to carry his fraud into effect: see *Taylor v Bowers*. But, as it is, the plaintiff's repentance came too late—namely, after he had been found out. Where the illegal purpose has been wholly or partially effected the law allows no *locus poenitentiae*: see *Salmond and Winfield's Law of Contract*, 152. It will not be any the readier to do so when the repentance, as in the present case, is merely due to the frustration by others of the plaintiff's fraudulent purpose.'

The 'others' referred to were the assessment committee, who were not parties to the illegal agreement, but who found out the purpose of that agreement in time to save themselves from being defrauded.

In *Berg v Sadler and Moore* the plaintiff was a tobacconist who had been a member of the Tobacco Association but had been put on the 'stop list' of that association for a breach of its rules, and, as a result, he could not obtain supplies of cigarettes from members of the association. The plaintiff arranged with a member of the association called Reece, that Reece should order in his own name, but really on behalf of the plaintiff, cigarettes from the defendants, Sadler & Moore, who were members of the association. Reece did so, and the plaintiff sent his representative, accompanied by a representative of Reece, to receive the cigarettes from the defendants. The plaintiff's representative paid for the cigarettes with the plaintiff's money, but the defendants, being suspicious about the transaction, refused to deliver the cigarettes or to return the money which the plaintiff's representative had paid to them. Thereupon, the plaintiff sued the defendants for the return of the money. The case was tried, in the first instance, by Macnaghten, J, who held that the plaintiff was guilty of an attempt to obtain the cigarettes by false pretences and that the court would not assist him to recover his money. The plaintiff appealed, but the decision of Macnaghten, J, was upheld by the Court of Appeal. The judgments in the Court of Appeal contain some strong expressions of opinion as to what the courts ought to do in these and similar circumstances. Lord Wright, MR, based his judgment on *Kearley v Thomson*, which he discussed at some length. He then said ([1937] 1 All ER 642):

> 'Fry LJ [in *Kearley v Thomson*] goes on . . . to distinguish . . . *Taylor v Bowers*, where recovery was allowed, as I understand the decision, on the ground that the illegal purpose had been abandoned, and that the plaintiff had so repented that he was not debarred from recovering what he had paid.'

That passage shows the importance which Lord Wright, MR, attributed to the decision in *Taylor v Bowers*, and to the allegation of repentance on behalf of the plaintiff in that case, although it was not actually mentioned in the case itself. Lord Wright, MR, then said (*ibid.*):

> 'Some such argument was put forward in this case, but I should like to add to the expression of opinion of Fry LJ, on that point the observations which are contained in a judgment of this court in *Alexander v Rayson* . . .'

Lord Wright, MR, then cited the passage which I have already read from *Alexander v Rayson*. Romer, J, gave a very short judgment in *Berg v Sadler & Moore*, but it does contain a principle. He said (*ibid.*, 644):

> 'I entirely agree, and, once the facts of this case are understood, it is abundantly plain that no court in this country would lift a finger to help the plaintiff to recover from the defendants the money which the plaintiff paid to them. The money was paid by the plaintiff to the defendants in the course, and for the purposes, of an attempt, on the part of the plaintiff, to defraud the defendants; the fact that, owing to the vigilance of the defendants, the attempt was frustrated is, in my opinion, wholly immaterial.'

Finally, Scott LJ, dealt with the matter, first, by setting out the passage from the original judgment of Macnaghten, J, which was stated in very clear terms, and could leave no doubt as to what the learned judge meant. Macnaghten, J, said ([1936] 2 All ER 461):

> 'I have no hesitation in saying that in this case Mr Berg attempted, although the attempt failed, by deceit to induce a course of action on the part of the defendants, Messrs. Sadler & Moore, which would have been an action to their grave injury. If in fact they had supplied goods to Mr Berg, he being on the "Stop List", the consequences to them might have been consequences of a very serious character in their business. It seems to me that it is a plain case of . . . an attempt to obtain goods by false pretences, and it is nothing to the purpose to say that the fraudulent person who was attempting to commit that crime was in fact willing to pay to the persons he was attempting to defraud the full price of the goods. Now those being the facts as I find them to be, the question arises, can Mr Berg under those circumstances, having paid this money with the intention of obtaining goods by this false pretence, now maintain an action in this court to recover the money? No case has been cited to me where the court has ever entertained any such action. If dishonest people pay money for a dishonest purpose, and then by good fortune the offence which they designed to commit is not committed, are they entitled in this court to come and ask for recovery of the money? In my opinion, they are not. It would be a bad example if this court were to entertain an action by a man for money dishonestly paid for the purpose of committing an offence against the criminal law, and he were allowed to claim from the court an order that the money should be repaid.'

After quoting this passage, Scott LJ, continued ([1937] 1 All ER 644):

> 'I entirely agree with that judgment, which I have adopted as my own. At the same time, I agree with what Lord Wright, MR, has said, that the facts of this case involve a slightly new application of the rule, but *ubi eadem ratio ibi jus*. The principle which forbids the assistance of the court to a plaintiff who asks it in order to effect a dishonest purpose extends, in my opinion, to the case of a request for the court's assistance in order to extricate himself from a pecuniary difficulty in which he has placed himself by an incomplete performance of a dishonest course of action.'

I now have to consider how the authorities to which I have referred should be applied to the facts of the present case. I confess that there was a time when I thought it would be right to apply to the facts of this case the reasoning of the decision in *Taylor v Bowers*, but, having considered all the authorities, I do not take that view. I think that what is to be extracted from the authorities may be stated as follows. I think that they show, first, that there is a distinction between what may, for convenience, be called the repentance cases, on the one hand, and the frustration cases, on the other hand. If a particular case may be held to fall within the category of repentance cases, I think the law is that the court will help a person who repents, provided his repentance comes before the illegal purpose has been substantially performed. If I were able in this case, to take the view that the defendant had brought himself within that sphere of the authorities, it might well be that I would have been able to help him by saying that his repentance had come before the illegal purpose had been substantially performed, but I do not take that view. I think, however, that this case falls within the category of cases which I call the frustration cases, and that it is proper to regard it as in the same category as *Alexander v Rayson*, and *Berg v Sadler & Moore*, rather than as in the category of cases such as *Taylor v Bowers* and *Kearley v Thomson*, and, to some extent, *Hermann v Charlesworth*.

In *Alexander v Rayson* the illegal contract was made between the plaintiff and the defendant. It was frustrated by third parties and, as there was no repentance by the plaintiff before the frustration by others of his fraudulent purpose, he was held disentitled to succeed. In *Berg v Sadler & Moore* the illegal contract was entered into between the plaintiff and a third party, and was frustrated by the defendants, and the plaintiff was held disentitled to succeed. In the present case the illegal contract was entered into between the plaintiff and the defendant. The defendant is in the position in which the plaintiff was in all the other cases which I have mentioned, and the performance of that illegal contract was frustrated by the other party to it, namely, the plaintiff. For that reason this is, I think, a frustration case and not a case of repentance.

On the return of the defendant's wife and daughter from Italy the whole project fell to the ground. There was no repentance which caused the contract not to be carried out. The defendant desired that it should be carried out until the plaintiff failed to do so, and, when she failed, the wife and daughter had to return to England because, as the result of the plaintiff's failure, they could no longer afford to stay in Italy. By the plaintiff's failure the whole venture was frustrated, and, in those circumstances, I do not think that the reason for this illegal contract not having come to fruition was the repentance of the defendant. The reason was that the whole object of the contract was frustrated by the failure on the part of the plaintiff to provide the lire which she had contracted to provide in Italy. In those circumstances, I have come to the conclusion that the words of Macnaghten, J, ([1936] 2 All ER 462) in *Berg v Sadler & Moore*, which were cited with approval by Scott LJ, in the Court of Appeal, should be applied to this case:

> 'If dishonest people pay money for a dishonest purpose, and then by good fortune the offence which they designed to commit is not committed, are they entitled in this court to come and ask for recovery of the money? In my opinion they are not. It would be a bad example if this court were to entertain an action by a man for money dishonestly paid for the purpose of committing an

offence against the criminal law, and he were allowed to claim from the court an order that the money should be repaid.'

That is the view which I take in this case and, for those reasons, I have come to the conclusion that this is not a case where the defendant showed himself to be within the exception of which *Taylor v Bowers* is an example. In all the circumstances, I think that the defendant's counterclaim must fail, and, accordingly, there must be judgment for the defendant on the claim and his counterclaim must be dismissed.

NOTES AND QUESTIONS

1. These cases are discussed in more detail by R. Merkin, 'Restitution by Withdrawal from Executory Illegal Contracts' (1981) 97 *LQR* 420.

2. What was the basis of the decision of the Court of Appeal in *Taylor v Bowers*? One view is that the plaintiff could recover because he could prove his title to the goods independently of the fraudulent transaction. Yet, how could the claimant have done this? In *Tribe v Tribe* [1996] Ch 107, 125, Millett LJ said of *Taylor* that:

   > [i]t is too late now to hold that it was an illegitimate application of a contractual doctrine to a claim for restitution. But the proposition that the plaintiff did not need to rely on the illegality could not be supported today. It is explicable only on the basis that the rule that title can pass under an illegal contract had not yet been clearly established. Nowadays we would say that Alcock, or his successor in title, did not need to rely on the illegal nature of the contract pursuant to which the goods were delivered because the title passed to him despite the illegality and want of consideration; but the plaintiff did. In order to recover the goods as goods received and held to his own use he had to show that they had not been delivered by way of gift or pursuant to an enforceable contract. This required him to show that they had been delivered pursuant to an illegal contract which he had repudiated; and he could not repudiate the contract once the illegal purpose had been wholly or partly achieved.

   Which view is the more persuasive?

3. Can *Taylor v Bowers* and *Kearley v Thomson* be reconciled? How does Pritchard J attempt to reconcile the two cases in *Bigos v Bousted*? Can this rationalization be reconciled with the facts of *Bigos*? One attempt at reconciliation has been put forward in the following terms by Sir Jack Beatson (1975) 91 *LQR* 313, 314: 'If . . . the principle to be applied is that recovery should only be allowed where the application of the general rule would increase the probability of the illegal purpose being achieved, it is submitted that all the decisions can be justified.'

4. Must the claimant have genuinely repented of the illegality? Birks (*An Introduction to the Law of Restitution*, 302) states that 'there must be both a change of mind and a change of heart'. Do you agree? How can *Taylor v Bowers* be reconciled with this approach? On the other hand, Professor Grodecki has stated ('In Pari Delicto Potior Est Conditio Defendentis' (1955) *LQR* 254, 263) that it is 'odd to see the late emergence of the somewhat elusive moral concept of repentance in a field where the dictates of morality have never been much heeded'. The latter view has received the support of Millett LJ in *Tribe v Tribe* (below, 903), when he said that he 'would hold that genuine repentance is not required. Justice is not a reward for merit; restitution should not be confined to the penitent . . . voluntary withdrawal from an illegal transaction when it has ceased to be needed is sufficient.' Do you agree?

5. Consideration must be given to the effect of the repentance on the rights to the goods which are the subject-matter of the contract. Thus Birks, states, 303: 'Presumably, the effect of repentance is to extinguish the property which passed under the contract. It must, therefore, be a species of common law rescission analogous to rescission for fraud, so that during the *locus poenitentiae* the recipient has a voidable title. The second part of the problem is as to the nature of the relief which the penitent then gets. The rescission is itself restitutionary. The

penitent revests the *res* in himself. But in *Taylor v Bowers* the claim which the plaintiff maintained was then simply in tort, for detinue. Presumably, therefore, the correct analysis is that the plaintiff has a restitutionary right *in rem* which, once it has been exercised, puts him in a position to make all the usual claims in respect of tortious interference with chattels.'

Another view put forward by Professor Enonchong ((1995) 111 *LQR* 135, 156) is that it is the passage of title which determines the limits of the *locus poenitentiae* doctrine. Thus he states '[a]s soon as title has passed it is impossible to recant, even though the contract has not been fully performed'. Thus he states that *Taylor v Bowers* can be explained on the basis that property had not passed to the defendants (but contrast the view of Millett LJ in *Tribe v Tribe* set out in question 2 above), whereas in *Kearley v Thomson* title to the money had passed to the defendant and he concludes that '[a]fter the point at which title has passed, recovery can only be allowed on the grounds of some other exception, as where the parties are not *in pari delicto* and the plaintiff is less blameworthy'.

6. In *Tappenden v Randall* (1801) 2 B & P 467, 471, Heath J stated that a *locus poenitentiae* cannot be given if the contract is 'too grossly immoral for the court to enter into any discussion of it'. The example which he gave was of money which was paid to another to commit a murder (an example which is also employed by Fry LJ in his judgment in *Kearley v Thomson*, above). Is this limitation on the right of recovery a useful one?

7. Could it be said that the 'withdrawal principle allows restitution for total failure of consideration', albeit that restitution can be granted even though the defendant remains able and willing to perform (see G Virgo *The Principles of the Law of Restitution*, pp. 352–355, but contrast Burrows, 425–6). If this approach is accepted, does it mean that illegality can only ever operate as a defence to a restitutionary claim and never as part of the cause of action?

8. How would the cases on withdrawal in the *locus poenitentiae* fit into Birks' new 'absence of basis' scheme (above, 137)?

11

INCAPACITY AS A GROUND FOR RESTITUTION

As was the case with illegal contracts, so in the case of contracts which are affected by incapacity on the part of one of the parties to it, we seek to distinguish those cases in which incapacity operates as a ground for restitution and those cases in which incapacity operates as a defence to a claim brought on one of the other, standard grounds of restitution. Once again, we should point out that this is not a view which is universally shared. Goff and Jones, for example, devote a chapter to the restitutionary consequences of contracts which are affected by incapacity without ever drawing a distinction between incapacity as a ground for restitution and incapacity as a defence.

The principal difficulty which emerges from a study of these cases is whether or not incapacity, of itself, should give rise to a claim in unjust enrichment (subject to defences) or whether there must be something else before a claim in unjust enrichment can arise. Infancy provides an example. Should an infant be able to recover a benefit conferred upon the defendant simply by proving that he or she was an infant at the time of entry into the contract, or should the infant only be able to rely on an unjust factor which would be available to an adult? Alternatively, must the infant show that the defendant in some way exploited the infant's weakness or inexperience before he or she is entitled to restitution? And does the answer which the law gives in the context of infancy also apply to other forms of incapacity, such as mental incapacity and corporate incapacity?

General Reading
BURROWS, chapter 11; GOFF AND JONES, chapter 25; VIRGO, chapter 13.

1. INFANCY

A minor (historically referred to as an 'infant') is a person who has not yet reached the age of 18. He or she has limited contractual capacity (so that, for example, a minor can validly contract for necessaries or enter into a beneficial contract of service). But these contracts are the exception, not the rule. A limited category of contracts, such as contracts to buy shares in a company, entered into with a minor are voidable (that is to say, the minor can avoid liability by repudiating the contract before majority or within a reasonable time thereafter) but the vast majority of contracts do not bind the minor unless he has ratified them. In this section it is not our concern to explain the law relating to the contractual capacity of minors (on which see G Treitel, *The Law of Contract* (11th edn, 2003, 539–57). Our focus is upon the scope of the restitutionary rights which the law affords to a minor in the case of those contracts which are not binding upon him.

● *Valentini v Canali* (1889) 24 QBD 166, Divisional Court

The claimant infant agreed to become a tenant of a house and to purchase the furniture in the house for £102. He paid £68 on account. After he had occupied the premises and used the furniture for some months, he sought to recover the £68 which he had paid to the defendant. His claim failed.

Lord Coleridge CJ: I am of opinion that this appeal should be dismissed. Under the contract in question, which was one for his advantage, the plaintiff, an infant, undertook to pay the defendant a sum of money. He paid the defendant part of this sum, and gave him a promissory note for the balance. The judge satisfied himself that the plaintiff was an infant at the time when he entered into the contract, and, having satisfied himself of this, did, in my opinion, justice according to law. He set aside the contract, and he ordered the promissory note to be cancelled.

It is now contended that, in addition to this relief, the plaintiff was entitled to an order for the re-payment of the sum paid by him to the defendant as money paid under a contract declared to be void. No doubt the words of s. 1 of the Infants' Relief Act, 1874, are strong and general, but a reasonable construction ought to be put upon them. The construction which has been contended for on behalf of the plaintiff would involve a violation of natural justice. When an infant has paid for something and has consumed or used it, it is contrary to natural justice that he should recover back the money which he has paid. Here the infant plaintiff who claimed to recover back the money which he had paid to the defendant had had the use of a quantity of furniture for some months. He could not give back this benefit or replace the defendant in the position in which he was before the contract. The object of the statute would seem to have been to restore the law for the protection of infants upon which judicial decisions were considered to have imposed qualifications. The legislature never intended in making provisions for this purpose to sanction a cruel injustice. The defendant therefore could not be called upon to repay the money paid to him by the plaintiff, and the decision appealed against is right.

Bowen LJ concurred.

NOTES AND QUESTIONS

1. Section 1 of the Infants' Relief Act 1874 provided that 'All contracts, whether by specialty or by simple contract, henceforth entered into by infants for the repayment of money lent or to be lent, or for goods supplied or to be supplied (other than contracts for necessaries) and all accounts stated with infants shall be absolutely void; provided always that this enactment shall not invalidate any contract into which an infant may, by any existing or future statute or by the rules of common law or equity, enter, except such as now by law are voidable.' The section was repealed by section 1(a) of the Minors' Contracts Act 1987.

2. Note that no significance was attached to the question whether or not the adult knew that the claimant was an infant.

3. Did the claim fail because the claimant could not establish a total failure of consideration or because he was unable to make counter-restitution? What are the practical differences between these two interpretations of the case?

● *Steinberg v Scala (Leeds) Ltd* [1923] 2 Ch. 452, Court of Appeal

The infant claimant, the respondent, bought shares in a company. She subsequently repudiated the contract and her allotment of shares was set aside. She sought the return of the money which she had paid for the shares. Her claim failed because she was unable to show that the consideration for her payment had wholly failed.

Lord Sterndale MR: . . . I think the argument for the respondent has rather proceeded upon the assumption that the question whether she can rescind and the question whether she can recover her money back are the same. They are two quite different questions, as is pointed out by Turner LJ in his judgment in *Ex parte Taylor*.[1] He there says: 'It is clear that an infant cannot be absolutely bound by a contract entered into during his minority. He must have a right upon his attaining his majority to elect whether he will adopt the contract or not.' Then he proceeds: 'It is, however, a different question whether, if an infant pays money on the footing of a contract, he can afterwards recover it back. If an infant buys an article which is not a necessary, he cannot be compelled to pay for it, but if he does pay for it during his minority he cannot on attaining his majority recover the money back.' That seems to me to be only stating in other words the principle which is laid down in a number of other cases that, although the contract may be rescinded the money paid cannot be recovered back unless there has been an entire failure of the consideration for which the money has been paid. Therefore it seems to me that the question to which we have to address ourselves is: Has there here been a total failure of the consideration for which the money was paid?

Now the plaintiff has had the shares; I do not mean to say she had the certificates; she could have had them at any time if she had applied for them; she has had the shares allotted to her and there is evidence that they were of some value, that they had been dealt in at from 9s. to 10s. a share. Of course her shares were only half paid up and, therefore, if she had attempted to sell them she would only have obtained half of that amount, but that is quite a tangible and substantial sum.

In those circumstances is it possible to say that there was a total failure of consideration? If the plaintiff were a person of full age suing to recover the money back on the ground, and the sole ground, that there had been a failure of consideration it seems to me it would have been impossible for her to succeed, because she would have got the very thing for which the money was paid and would have got a thing of tangible value.

The argument for the respondent is I think to this effect: That it is necessary, in order to show that the consideration has not entirely failed, to prove that the plaintiff has not only had something which was worth value in the market and for which she could have obtained value, but that she has in fact received that value. It was admitted that if she had in this case sold the shares and received the 125*l.* which would have been receivable according to one of the prices mentioned in evidence she could not have recovered the money back, but it is said that as she did not in fact do that and had only an opportunity of receiving that benefit, there has been a total failure of consideration. I cannot see that. If she has obtained something which has money's worth then she has received some consideration, that is, she has received the very thing for which she paid her money, and the fact that, although it has money's worth, she has not turned that money's worth into money, does not seem to me to prevent it being some valuable consideration for the money which she has paid. I cannot see any difference when you come to consider whether there has been consideration or not between the position of a person of full age and an infant. The question whether there has been consideration or not must, I think, be the same in the two cases. . . .

Warrington LJ: . . . The only question we have to deal with is the repayment of the money she has already paid on those shares. The only ground upon which she asserts that she is entitled to have the money repaid is that there has been a total failure of consideration, and that she is therefore entitled to be repaid that money as in the ordinary case where a man has paid money and the consideration for that payment has wholly failed. In my judgment it cannot be said in the present case that there has been a total failure of consideration. She has in fact got the very thing she bargained for, and, not only the thing she bargained for, but the thing which every other applicant for shares in this company

1 8 D M & G 254, 257, 258.

bargained for. She was placed in exactly the same position as every other shareholder except that, being an infant, she was entitled if she pleased to repudiate the contract and so escape from any future liability. So far as the defendant company is concerned she has received neither more nor less than any other shareholder in the company. Under those circumstances it seems to me impossible to say that there has been a total failure of consideration. . . .

Younger LJ: . . . I think, therefore, we have here to ask ourselves the question whether, during the period when the plaintiff did not elect to repudiate her contract, the consideration for that contract as between herself and the company had wholly failed. To my mind it had not in any sense failed. There was some detriment to the company; and there was substantial consideration being enjoyed by herself, either actual or in possibility, during the whole of the period. She had the tangible advantage of being in a position to sell and transfer, if she had been so minded, her shares for a consideration which would, at least, have been substantial. She might, had she chosen, have attended meetings of the company. In these circumstances I think that the condition imposed upon an infant before she can recover money paid has not been complied with by the respondent. . . . I think the question is not: Has the infant derived any real advantage? but the question is: Has the consideration wholly failed? In my judgment in this case the consideration has not wholly failed on either side, and accordingly the action, as my Lord has said, must be dismissed and judgment entered for the defendants.

- ### *Pearce v Brain* [1929] 2 KB 310, King's Bench Division

The claimant infant exchanged his motor-cycle and side-car for a second-hand motor-car belonging to the defendant. After he had driven the car about seventy miles, the car broke down because of a defect in the back axle. The claimant then repudiated the contract with the defendant on the ground that he was an infant when he entered into the contract. He claimed the return of the motor-cycle and side-car or their value in money and he offered to return the damaged car to the defendant. It was held that, although the contract was void, the claimant was entitled to recover only if there had been a total failure of consideration. Being unable to show that there had been a total failure of consideration, the claimant's claim failed.

Swift J: . . . The only point left is the contention of the plaintiff that, as he was an infant at the time the contract was entered into, the contract was rendered void by s. 1 of the Infants Relief Act, 1874. It was said that the property in the motor bicycle never passed from the plaintiff to the defendant and that the plaintiff was entitled to have it back by virtue of s. 1 of the Act, which provided: 'All contracts, • whether by specialty or by simple contract, henceforth entered into by infants for the repayment of money lent or to be lent, or for goods supplied or to be supplied (other than contracts for necessaries), and all accounts stated with infants, shall be absolutely void: Provided always, that this enactment shall not invalidate any contract into which an infant may, by any existing or future statute, or by the rules of common law or equity, enter, except such as now by law are voidable.'

In his able argument counsel for the plaintiff contended that the transaction was one which was void under that section, and that therefore the plaintiff had never ceased to be the owner of the motor bicycle and was entitled to have it back. I am quite clear that the transaction was, as the county court judge has found, a contract of exchange of goods. But it comes within the words 'goods supplied or to be supplied,' which are as much applicable to exchange as to sale.

If I were at liberty to decide this case without authority, I should be inclined to accept the argument for the plaintiff and decide that the contract being by way of exchange it was void under the Act and that no property passed. But I cannot see any difference in principle between the recovery of a chattel given in exchange and the recovery of money paid as the purchase price of goods. If the contract were void by statute I should have thought, apart from authority, that money paid could have been recovered as money had and received to the use of an infant plaintiff. Money paid under a merely voidable contract is in a very different position. But there is direct authority that money paid under a void contract cannot be recovered unless there is a total failure of consideration. In *Valentini v Canali*,[1] which was decided by Lord Coleridge CJ, and Bowen LJ sitting as a Divisional Court, Lord Coleridge said: 'The construction which has been contended for on behalf of the plaintiff would involve a violation of natural justice. When an infant has paid for something and has consumed or used it, it is contrary to natural justice that he should recover back the money which he has paid. Here the infant plaintiff who claimed to recover back the money which he had paid to the defendant had had the use of a quantity of furniture for some months. He could not give back this benefit or replace the defendant in the position in which he was before the contract. The object of the statute would seem to have been to restore the law for the protection of infants upon which judicial decisions were considered to have imposed qualifications. The legislature never intended in making provisions for this purpose to sanction a cruel injustice.'

That case the county court judge treated as binding on him and adopted as the basis of his decision. He came to the conclusion that the plaintiff had had the benefit of the contract and that, although he had not had everything which he expected to get, there was not a total failure of consideration.

In view of *Valentini v Canali* I think his decision was right. I cannot distinguish between the recovery of a specific chattel under a void contract and the recovery of money. If the latter cannot be recovered, neither can the former. In order to succeed here it was incumbent on the plaintiff to show a complete failure of consideration; this he has failed to do, and in my view the decision of the county court judge was right and the appeal must be dismissed.

Acton J: I agree.

NOTES AND QUESTIONS

1. Did Swift J misinterpret the ratio of *Valentini v Canali* (see question 3, at 608 above)?

2. Had there been a total failure of consideration, could the title to the motorcycle and the side-car have been revested in the claimant? Is there any justification for awarding the claimant more than a personal remedy for the value of the motor-cycle and side-car? In *Chaplin v Leslie Frewin (Publishers) Ltd* [1966] Ch. 71 the claimant sought an interlocutory injunction to restrain the defendant from publishing the manuscript of his memoirs as the parties had previously agreed. The Court of Appeal held that he was not entitled to an injunction because the contract was for his benefit, and so was binding on him, and, further that even if the contract was not binding on him, the claimant could not recover the copyright which he had transferred to the defendant under the terms of the agreement. Danckwerts LJ stated (at 94) that 'if an infant revokes a contract, the property and interests which have been previously transferred by him cannot be recovered by the infant ... the transfers of property made by [the infant] remain effective against him, even if the contract is otherwise revocable.'

3. In *Chaplin v Leslie Frewin* (above) Lord Denning dissented and held that cases such as *Valentini v Canali* (above), *Steinberg v Scala (Leeds) Ltd* and *Pearce v Brain* (above) were cases in which:

   the infant had taken the benefit of a contract, and afterwards sought to recover the money which he had paid, or the goods he had handed over in exchange, contrary to the justice of the case. That he was not permitted to do. Those cases are to be confined, I think, to money or goods handed over by an infant which pass on delivery and where it is unjust that he should recover them back. They have no application

---

to a disposition which requires a deed or writing in order to be effective. They cannot be used so as to nullify the firmly established rule that such a disposition is voidable. For the protection of the young and the foolish, the law holds that a disposition by deed or writing can be avoided by the infant at any time before he comes of age. At any rate a disposition is voidable when it is made in pursuance of a contract which is not for the benefit of the infant.

4. Should infancy in itself (subject to defences) suffice to give rise to a restitutionary claim, or should a minor only have a restitutionary claim where he can show that there has been a (total) failure of consideration, albeit that he is relieved of the need to show that the other party is not ready, able and willing to perform?

5. How do the cases on infancy (and incapacity generally) fit into Birks's new 'absence of basis scheme' (above, 137)?

2. MENTAL ILLNESS

• *Hart v O'Connor* [1985] AC 1000, Privy Council

The defendant, Mr Hart, agreed to purchase farm land from Mr Jack O'Connor, who was the sole trustee of his father's estate and who farmed the land in partnership with his brothers. Mr O'Connor was then aged 83 but, unknown to the defendant, was of unsound mind. He agreed to sell land to the defendant under an agreement which was drawn up by the defendant's solicitor. The agreement stated that the price to be paid was the market value of the land as determined by a named independent valuer. The claimants, who were one of Mr O'Connor's brothers and his two sons, sought a declaration that the agreement should be set aside on the ground of the vendor's lack of capacity and also on the ground that it was an unconscionable bargain. The trial judge held that the agreement was unenforceable but that the transaction could not be set aside because the defendant was entitled to invoke the defence of laches. The Court of Appeal allowed the claimants' appeal and held that laches was inapplicable. On the defendant's appeal to the Privy Council it was held that the claimants were not entitled to set aside the transaction because there was no ground on which an adult could set aside the transaction, there had been no unconscionable dealing by the defendant and the transaction could not be set aside on the ground of the vendor's lack of capacity because the defendant was unaware of the lack of capacity on the part of the vendor.

Lord Brightman: . . . It is important to appreciate that no imputations whatever are made by the plaintiffs against the integrity of the defendant, and rightly so. The defendant's conduct leading up to the sale was above reproach . . .

The defendant now appeals to Her Majesty in Council. He does not challenge the finding of the vendor's mental incapacity, nor the Court of Appeal's finding on the question of laches. The plaintiff trustees for their part do not contend that the defendant knew or ought reasonably to have known of the vendor's incapacity. Apart from questions arising out of the defendant's claim for compensation, the issues raised by the parties on this appeal are as follows: (A) Whether *Archer v Cutler* [1980] 1 NZLR 386 was rightly decided; that is to say, whether a contract by a person of unsound mind, whose incapacity is unknown to the other contracting party, can be avoided (at law) on the ground that it is 'unfair' to the party lacking capacity (or those whom he represents), there being no imputations against the conduct of the other contracting party. (B) If *Archer v Cutler* was rightly decided, whether the High Court and the Court of Appeal were correct in finding that the sale agreement was 'unfair' to the vendor. (C) If *Archer v Cutler* was wrongly decided, whether the plaintiffs were entitled to have the contract set aside (in equity) as an 'unconscionable bargain' notwithstanding the complete innocence of the defendant. (D) If *Archer v Cutler* was rightly decided, and the courts below correctly found that the sale agreement was 'unfair,' whether the sale agreement would escape rescission because it was impossible to achieve restitutio in integrum.

In order to avoid unnecessary prolongation of the hearing and with a view to saving the parties expense, their Lordships invited counsel to confine their submissions to issues (A) and (C), leaving issues (B) and (D) for subsequent argument if necessary.

Their Lordships turn first to a consideration of *Archer v Cutler* [1980] 1 NZLR 386. Their Lordships attach importance to three factors. First, this decision was accepted by both sides as correct when the case was argued at first instance. Secondly, the Court of Appeal in a strong judgment affirmed without hesitation that the law there set out was the law of New Zealand. Thirdly the Court of Appeal, when they gave judgment on the compensation appeal, underlined their previous statement of the law in the following important passage [1984] 1 NZLR 754, 755:

'In that case [*Archer v Cutler*] it was held that there were no considerations of policy or principle precluding the court from holding that a contract entered into by a person of unsound mind is voidable at his option if it is proved either that the other party knew of his unsoundness of mind or, whether or not he had that knowledge, the bargain was unfair. On the basis that this principle should be adopted for New Zealand this court expressly approved *Archer v Cutler*. In the result it made a declaration that the agreement for sale and purchase was rescinded.'

If *Archer v Cutler* is properly to be regarded as a decision based on considerations peculiar to New Zealand, it is highly improbable that their Lordships would think it right to impose their own inter-pretation of the law, thereby contradicting the unanimous conclusions of the High Court and the Court of Appeal of New Zealand on a matter of local significance. If however the principle of *Archer v Cutler*, if it be correct, must be regarded as having general application throughout all jurisdictions based on the common law, because it does not depend on local considerations, their Lordships could not properly treat the unanimous view of the courts of New Zealand as being necessarily decisive. In their Lordships' opinion the latter is the correct view of the decision.

Archer v Cutler was a purchaser's action for specific performance of a contract for the sale of land. By way of defence the vendor pleaded first that she was of unsound mind to the knowledge of the purchaser, secondly that she was induced to enter into the agreement by the undue influence of the purchaser, and thirdly, at 388, 'that the contract should be set aside as a catching and unconscientious bargain.' The facts were briefly as follows. The vendor and the purchaser were adjoining land owners. The purchaser had a problem over access to his land, which would be solved if he acquired the vendor's land. He knew the vendor had already given a purchase option to a friend, but he made known to the vendor his interest in acquiring her land should the opportunity occur. At some later time the vendor got in touch with the purchaser, and inquired if he was still interested in buying, as her friend had decided not to exercise her option. He called on her next day to discuss the matter. The vendor suggested a price of $15,000. The purchaser thought that $17,000 would be a fairer figure and he offered to pay it subject to his being able to arrange finance. He put his offer in writing, and she wrote out her acceptance. A week later he told her that he had arranged finance and that the sale was therefore unconditional. McMullin J held that an informed vendor would have expected to receive at least $24,000; that there was however no evidence that the purchaser knew the true value of the land, and that it was understandable that two persons with no professional expertise should fix a value of $17,000 as being a fair price. He also found that the vendor was suffering from advanced senile dementia at the time of the agreement which rendered her incapable of understanding the bargain, but that the purchaser was unaware of this. The agreement represented a sale at a substan-tial undervalue. It was held that contractual incapacity was established; that a contract entered into by a person of unsound mind was voidable at that person's option if the other party knew of the incapacity or, whether or not he knew, if the contract was 'unfair' to the person of unsound mind; and that the contract was unfair, the indicia of unfairness being (i) a price significantly below the true value, (ii) the absence of independent legal advice for the vendor, and (iii) the difference in bargaining positions resulting from the disparity in their respective mental capacities.

If a contract is stigmatised as 'unfair', it may be unfair in one of two ways. It may be unfair by reason of the unfair manner in which it was brought into existence; a contract induced by undue influence is unfair in this sense. It will be convenient to call this 'procedural unfairness.' It may also, in some contexts, be described (accurately or inaccurately) as 'unfair' by reason of the fact that the terms of the contract are more favourable to one party than to the other. In order to distinguish this 'unfairness' from procedural unfairness, it will be convenient to call it 'contractual imbalance.' The two concepts may overlap. Contractual imbalance may be so extreme as to raise a presumption of procedural unfairness, such as undue influence or some other form of victimisation. Equity will relieve a party from a contract which he has been induced to make as a result of victimisation. Equity will not relieve a party from a contract on the ground only that there is contractual imbalance not amounting to unconscionable dealing. Of the three indicia of unfairness relied upon by the judge in *Archer v Cutler* (assuming unfairness to have existed) the first was contractual imbalance and the second and third were procedural unfairness.

The judgment in *Archer v Cutler* [1980] 1 NZLR 386 contains, if their Lordships may be permitted to say so, a most scholarly and erudite review by the judge of the textbook authorities and reported cases on the avoidance of a contract made by a person of unsound mind. For present purposes the key passages in the judgment are, at 400:

> 'From these authorities, it would seem that the English law on the subject is ill-defined. The case of *Imperial Loan Co. Ltd v Stone* [1892] 1 QB 599 widely accepted as being a statement of the law on avoidance of contracts made with persons of unsound mind would, save in the judgment of Lopes LJ, seem to regard unfairness of the contract as being of no moment. Proof of unsoundness of mind and the other party's knowledge of that unsoundness alone will avoid the contract. But the passage cited from the judgment of Lopes LJ and the dicta of Pollock CB in *Molton v Camroux* (1848) 2 Exch. 487, of Patteson J on appeal in the same case, of Sir Ernest Pollock MR in *York Glass Co. Ltd v Jubb* (1924) 131 LT 559 and of Sargant LJ in the same case would suggest that proof of unfairness of a bargain entered into by a person of unsound mind, even though that unsoundness be not known to the other party, will suffice to avoid it.'

And, at 401:

> 'I find nothing in policy or principle to prevent me from holding that a contract entered into by a person of unsound mind is voidable at his option if it is proved either that the other party knew of his unsoundness of mind or, whether or not he had that knowledge, the contract was unfair to the person of unsound mind.'

Their Lordships apprehend that in these passages the judge is dealing indifferently with procedural unfairness and contractual imbalance, either of which, or both of which in combination, may enable the contract to be avoided against a contracting party ignorant of the mental incapacity of the other.

The original rule at law, and still the rule in Scotland, was that a contract with a person of unsound mind was void, because there could be no consensus ad idem. This was later qualified by a rule that a person could not plead his own unsoundness of mind in order to avoid a contract he had made. This in turn gave way to a further rule that such a plea was permissible if it could be shown that the other contracting party knew of the insanity.

Their Lordships turn to the three cases mentioned in the first citation from *Archer v Cutler*. The starting point for a consideration of the modern rule is *Molton v Camroux* (1848) 2 Exch. 487, and, on appeal, (1849) 4 Exch. 17, which was heard first in the Court of Exchequer, and later in the Court of Exchequer Chamber. It arose out of the purchase by a person of unsound mind of annuities from a life assurance society. The society had granted the annuities in the ordinary course of its business. After referring to earlier authorities that a plea of insanity would not prevail unless the other contracting party knew of it, the courts said, 2 Exch. 487, 502–3:

'We are not disposed to lay down so general a proposition, as that all executed contracts bona fide entered into must be taken as valid, though one of the parties be of unsound mind; we think, however, that we may safely conclude, that when a person, apparently of sound mind, and not known to be otherwise, enters into a contract for the purchase of property which is fair and bona fide, and which is executed and completed, and the property, the subject matter of the contract, has been paid for and fully enjoyed, and cannot be restored so as to put the parties in statu quo, such contract cannot afterwards be set aside, either by the alleged lunatic, or those who represent him.'

The case was then heard by the Court of Exchequer Chamber, 4 Ex. 17. The court identified the issue as, at 19:

'whether the mere fact of unsoundness of mind, which was not apparent, is sufficient to vacate a *fair contract* executed by the grantee, by payment of the consideration money, and intended bona fide to be executed by the grantor, by payment of the annuity.'

The answer was:

'the modern cases show, that when that state of mind was unknown to the other contracting party, and *no advantage was taken of the lunatic*, the defence cannot prevail, especially where the contract is not merely executory, but executed in whole or in part, and the parties cannot be restored altogether to their original position.'

In the foregoing passages and in certain other citations from the authorities, their Lordships find it convenient to emphasise references to 'fairness' and 'not taking advantage' and the like.

The judge in *Archer v Cutler* read these passages from *Molton v Camroux* as emphasising the importance of fairness as an ingredient in an enforceable contract with a lunatic whose condition of mind is unknown to the other party; see 396 and 397. However their Lordships respectfully think that *Molton v Camroux* is not an authority for the proposition that contractual imbalance, or procedural unfairness short of unconscionable conduct or equitable fraud, enables a person of unsound mind to escape from the contract.

In *Molton v Camroux*, 2 Exch. 487, 503, Pollock CB listed the circumstances which would enable the courts safely to conclude that a contract with a lunatic apparently of sound mind should be upheld. One such circumstance was that the contract was 'fair and bona fide.' This was an appropriate qualification for the purpose of excluding cases where the other contracting party, though ignorant of the insanity, was guilty of fraud. It does not, their Lordships respectfully think, support the proposition that the court is entitled to embark on a balancing exercise before upholding such a contract, in order to see where the balance of advantage lies; and if it is thought that the advantage lies, or at the time of the contract lay, substantially in favour of the innocent party of sound mind, then the contract can be set aside. This seems apparent from the earlier passages in the judgment of Pollock CB. At 502 he equated 'fairness' with 'made in good faith' when discussing counsel's distinction between the executed and the executory contract of a lunatic. In the quotations he selected from *Brown v Jodrell* (1827) 3 C & P 30 and *Dane v Viscountess Kirkwall* (1838) 8 C & P 679 the person of unsound mind can have the contract set aside if the other party 'imposed' upon him, or 'took advantage of' his unsoundness of mind. These references seem to their Lordships to demonstrate that it was procedural unfairness to which Pollock CB was directing his mind and not contractual imbalance. The same is to be said of the judgment of the Court of Exchequer Chamber. Their Lordships find nothing in *Molton v Camroux* to suggest that contractual imbalance, falling short of some species of fraud, entitles a person of unsound mind, whose mental impairment is not apparent, to have the contract avoided.

In *Imperial Loan Co. Ltd v Stone* [1892] 1 QB 599 a person of unsound mind was sued on a promissory note which he had signed as surety. The jury found that he was insane when he signed the note but there was no finding as to the creditor's knowledge of such insanity. Nevertheless the judge entered a verdict against the creditor. On appeal it was submitted that there was no authority that a man could be sued and made liable on an executory contract which he had made when of unsound mind, except in the case of a contract for necessaries. This submission was rejected, and a new trial was directed. Lord Esher MR said, at 601:

'When a person enters into a contract, and afterwards alleges that he was so insane at the time that he did not know what he was doing, and proves the allegation, the contract is as binding on him in every respect, whether it is executory or executed, as if he had been sane when he made it, unless he can prove further that the person with whom he contracts knew him to be so insane as not to be capable of understanding what he was about.'

Fry LJ said, at 602:

'It thus appears that there has been grafted on the old rule the exception that the contracts of a person who is non compos mentis may be avoided when his condition can be shewn to have been known to the plaintiff. So far as I know, that is the only exception.'

Lopes LJ introduced the word 'fair' into his statement of the rule, at 603:

'In order to avoid a *fair* contract on the ground of insanity, the mental incapacity of the one must be known to the other of the contracting parties. A defendant who seeks to avoid a contract on the ground of his insanity, must plead and prove, not merely his incapacity, but also the plaintiff's knowledge of that fact, and unless he proves these two things he cannot succeed.'

The judge in *Archer v Cutler* [1980] 1 NZLR 386 relied on the statement of Lopes LJ that the mental incapacity of a lunatic must be known to the other contracting party 'in order to avoid a *fair* contract on the ground of insanity', as implying that such knowledge is unnecessary in order to avoid a contract which is unfair in the sense of contractual imbalance. But in their Lordships' view 'fair' was quite appropriately used by Lopes LJ so as to except the case of the apparently sane person who is imposed upon in a manner which equity regards as unconscionable, and was not intended to permit an inquiry into the balance of the terms of the contract. The quotation from Lopes LJ which the judge in *Archer v Cutler* relied upon, at 398, omits the succeeding sentence where Lopes LJ repeats the rule without any reference to 'fairness' and says in unqualified terms [1892] 1 QB 599, 603:

'A defendant who seeks to avoid a contract on the ground of his insanity, must plead and prove, not merely his incapacity, but also the plaintiff's knowledge of that fact, and unless he proves these two things he cannot succeed.'

In the face of that statement of the rule, it seems to their Lordships impossible to suppose that Lopes LJ regarded proof of contractual imbalance as a permissible alternative to knowledge of insanity where a person of unsound mind seeks to set aside an agreement which was made in good faith. (Indeed, how is one to judge a contract of suretyship in terms of contractual balance?) This approach is in line with two cases which shortly followed *Molton v Camroux*, namely *Beavan v M'Donnell* (1854) 9 Exch. 309, 314, 'the contract *was entered* into by the defendant and the money received, fairly and in good faith'; and *Campbell v Hooper* (1855) 3 Sm. & Giff. 153, 159, 'the money was honestly paid, and *no advantage taken* by the plaintiff, nor any knowledge by him of the lunacy.'

Imperial Loan Co. Ltd v Stone [1892] 1 QB 599 was considered and accepted as correct by the High Court of Australia in *McLaughlin v Daily Telegraph Newspaper Co. Ltd (No 2)* (1904) 1 CLR 243, where

Griffith CJ delivering the judgment of the court said of the *Imperial Loan* case and its predecessor *Molton v Camroux*, at 272:

'The principle of the decision seems, however, to be the same in both cases, which, in our judgment, establish that a contract made by a person actually of unsound, but apparently of sound, mind with another who deals with him directly, and who has no knowledge of the unsoundness of mind, is as valid as if the unsoundness of mind had not existed. If the man dealing with the person of unsound mind is aware of his insanity, the contract is voidable at the option of the latter, but the party who takes advantage of the other cannot himself set up the incapacity. In this respect the matter is treated on the same footing as cases of fraud inducing a contract. There is, indeed, authority for saying that the equitable doctrines governing the validity or invalidity of a contract made with an insane person are only a particular instance of the general doctrines relating to fraudulent contracts. In the cases last mentioned no unfairness of dealing could be imputed to the persons who sought to take advantage of the contract, which was, in fact, made, in each case, with an apparently sane person. The principle appears to be that the validity of a contract made with an apparently sane person is to be determined by the application of the same rules as are applied in ordinary cases.'

The third case mentioned by the judge in the key passage which their Lordships have quoted from his judgment in *Archer v Cutler* [1980] 1 NZLR 386, 400, was *York Glass Co. Ltd v Jubb* (1924) 131 LT 559, and on appeal (1925) 134 LT 36. This was a vendor's action for breach of contract against the committee of the estate of a person of unsound mind. The purchaser pleaded first that he was of unsound mind to the knowledge of the defendant, secondly (by a late amendment) that the vendor knew that he was infirm of mind and body and incapable of managing his affairs reasonably and properly, that the price was excessive, that he had no legal advice and that there was no reasonable degree of equality between the contracting parties. The first plea was a plea at law. The second plea was relied upon as raising a case in equity for the rescission of the contract upon the grounds alleged, that is to say, on the assumption that at law there was a valid and binding contract but that it was one which a court of equity under the old practice, when the two courts were separate, would have rescinded and set aside and would have granted an injunction and restrained the plaintiff from enforcing at law; see the manner in which these two pleas were distinguished by Sir Ernest Pollock MR, 134 LT 36, 37, Warrington LJ, at 41, and Sargant LJ, at 43. Issues (A) and (C) in the instant appeal reflect the same differentiation between the plea at law and the plea in equity.

P. O. Lawrence J, 131 LT 559, 561, had no doubt as to the rule at law:

'It is well settled that where the defendant in an action of contract sets up the defence of his insanity at the date of the contract he must, in order to succeed, show that the plaintiff knew of his insanity.'

That plea failed, because the judge held that the company did not know of the unsoundness of mind. When, throughout his judgment, the judge refers to 'fairness', it is plain that he was doing so in the context of the second plea, the plea in equity, as is apparent from the following passage, also at 561:

'In the result, after having carefully considered the whole of the evidence in support of this part of the case, I have come to the conclusion and hold as a fact that there was no want of fairness either in the terms of the contract itself or in the circumstances under which it was made, and I acquit all the persons concerned in the transaction on behalf of the plaintiff company from the charge made against them of having overreached or exercised any undue influence over the defendant.'

He held that the contract was accordingly valid.

This decision was upheld on appeal, 134 LT 36; the contract was valid at law because the vendor was unaware of the unsoundness of mind. The contract was not impeachable in equity because the purchaser failed to establish any of the four circumstances on which he relied in order to establish the plea in equity. It is however necessary to look a little closely at the argument of Sargant LJ. He identified three issues, at 43; first, whether there was a concluded contract apart from lunacy; if so, secondly, was that contract enforceable at law; thirdly:

> 'if it was enforceable at law, was there any case for saying that equity would restrain the enforcement of the contract, that is to say, is the case one in which, prior to the Judicature Act, a bill would have lain for an injunction to prevent the plaintiff enforcing his remedies at law?'

There was plainly a concluded contract. In dealing with the second question, whether the contract was enforceable at law, which he held it was, he added, at 43–4:

> 'It is possible a question may arise in some future case, with which we have not to deal at present, whether, in the case of a contract which is not a reasonable one and which is made by an insane person that contract can be enforced, the other person not knowing of the insanity. I have looked through a number of cases and I have not found a single case in which a contract has in fact been binding except where the contract was an ordinary reasonable contract. I do not in any way want to attempt to express my own view on this point because the point has not been argued before us. . . . I only want to guard myself by saying that my mind is entirely open on the question whether the fairness of the bargain is an essential element to the enforceability of the bargain against a person who was in fact a lunatic although not known to be such by the other contracting party.'

He then turned to the third point, the plea in equity, and held that it failed.

York Glass Co. Ltd v Jubb then was a case in which the court considered a lunatic's contract from the point of view of the position at law and separately from the point of view of equity; but Sargant LJ, also posed, but did not answer (because it did not arise and was not argued) the question whether on the first aspect a court of common law would have enforced a contract by a person of unsound but apparently sound mind, the terms of which were not 'reasonable' or 'fair.'

In the opinion of their Lordships it is perfectly plain that historically a court of equity did not restrain a suit at law on the ground of 'unfairness' unless the conscience of the plaintiff was in some way affected. This might be because of actual fraud (which the courts of common law would equally have remedied) or constructive fraud, i.e. conduct which falls below the standards demanded by equity, traditionally considered under its more common manifestations of undue influence, abuse of confidence, unconscionable bargains and frauds on a power. (cf. *Snell's Principles of Equity*, 27th edn (1973), 545 ff.) An unconscionable bargain in this context would be a bargain of an improvident character made by a poor or ignorant person acting without independent advice which cannot be shown to be a fair and reasonable transaction. 'Fraud' in its equitable context does not mean, or is not confined to, deceit; 'it means an unconscientious use of the power arising out of these circumstances and conditions' of the contracting parties; *Earl of Aylesford v Morris* (1873) LR 8 Ch. App. 484, 491. It is victimisation, which can consist either of the active extortion of a benefit or the passive acceptance of a benefit in unconscionable circumstances.

Their Lordships have not been referred to any authority that a court of equity would restrain a suit at law where there was no victimisation, no taking advantage of another's weakness, and the sole allegation was contractual imbalance with no undertones of constructive fraud. It seems to their Lordships quite illogical to suppose that the courts of common law would have held that a person of unsound mind, whose affliction was not apparent, was nevertheless free of his bargain if a contractual imbalance could be demonstrated which would have been of no avail to him in equity. Nor do their Lordships see a sufficient foundation in the authorities brought to their attention to support any such proposition . . .

In the opinion of their Lordships, to accept the proposition enunciated in *Archer v Cutler* that a contract with a person ostensibly sane but actually of unsound mind can be set aside because it is 'unfair' to the person of unsound mind in the sense of contractual imbalance, is unsupported by authority, is illogical and would distinguish the law of New Zealand from the law of Australia . . . for no good reason, as well as from the law of England from which the law of Australia and New Zealand and other 'common law' countries has stemmed. In so saying their Lordships differ with profound respect from the contrary view so strongly expressed by the New Zealand courts.

To sum the matter up, in the opinion of their Lordships, the validity of a contract entered into by a lunatic who is ostensibly sane is to be judged by the same standards as a contract by a person of sound mind, and is not voidable by the lunatic or his representatives by reason of 'unfairness' unless such unfairness amounts to equitable fraud which would have enabled the complaining party to avoid the contract even if he had been sane.

Their Lordships turn finally to issue (C), whether the plaintiffs are entitled to have the contract set aside as an 'unconscionable bargain.' This issue must also be answered in the negative, because the defendant was guilty of no unconscionable conduct. Indeed, as is conceded, he acted with complete innocence throughout. He was unaware of the vendor's unsoundness of mind. The vendor was ostensibly advised by his own solicitor. The defendant had no means of knowing or cause to suspect that the vendor was not in receipt of and acting in accordance with the most full and careful advice. The terms of the bargain were the terms proposed by the vendor's solicitor, not terms imposed by the defendant or his solicitor. There was no equitable fraud, no victimisation, no taking advantage, no overreaching or other description of unconscionable doings which might have justified the intervention of equity to restrain an action by the defendant at law. The plaintiffs have in the opinion of their Lordships failed to make out any case for denying to the defendant the benefit of a bargain which was struck with complete propriety on his side.

For these reasons their Lordships have tendered to Her Majesty their humble advice that the appeal should be allowed.

NOTES AND QUESTIONS

1. The issues raised by *Hart* are discussed in more detail by A. H. Hudson, 'Mental Incapacity Revisited' [1986] Conv. 178.

2. Why is knowledge of the incapacity the crucial ingredient in cases of mental incapacity, but irrelevant in the case of infancy?

3. Is the test of knowledge actual or constructive? One consequence of the decision in *Hart* might be to tempt the courts to strain the evidence to find that the defendant did have knowledge of the claimant's incapacity. An example of the latter phenomenon is arguably provided by *Ayres v Hazelgrove*, unreported, 9 February 1984 (discussed by Birks, *Restitution—The Future*, 50–1) in which Lady Ayres, who suffered from senile dementia, sold paintings to Hazelgrove for a fraction of their true value. He visited her at home when she was alone, but he denied that he had any knowledge of her condition. Russell J inferred that Hazelgrove must have known of her lack of capacity and he set aside the sales of the paintings. He also held that the transactions could be set aside under the rule in *Fry v Lane* (1888) 40 Ch D 312 (above, 486).

4. Professor Birks has suggested (*Restitution—The Future*, 50–2) that the rule in *Hart* can be justified on the ground that it does not infantilise the elderly. Do you agree? What consideration should be given to the interests of the relatives of people such as Mr O'Connor who wish to protect them against the consequences of entering into disadvantageous transactions?

5. What was the basis of the decision of McMullin J in *Archer v Cutler* [1980] 1 NZLR 386? Do you find the reasons given for its rejection by the Privy Council convincing? What is the relationship between *Hart* and *Fry v Lane* (1888) 40 Ch D 312 and the other unconscionable transaction cases discussed in Chapter 7 (especially above, 486–498)?

6. Should mental incapacity of itself (that is to say, irrespective of the knowledge of the other party) suffice to give rise to a claim in restitution? This is the rule in Scots law: see *John Loudon & Co. v Elder's Curator Bonis*, 1923 SLT 226.

3. A COMPANY ACTING *ULTRA VIRES*

Ultra vires is now of limited practical significance in the corporate context because of section 35(1) of the Companies Act 1985 which states that 'the validity of an act done by a company shall not be called into question on the ground of lack of capacity by reason of anything in the company's memorandum'. Yet the *ultra vires* doctrine has not been eliminated in its entirety. In the few cases in which it remains applicable does the fact that the contract is *ultra vires* and hence void (*Ashbury Railway Carriage and Iron Co. Ltd v Riche* (1875) LR 7 HL 653) give to the company the right to recover benefits conferred upon the other party to the *ultra vires* transaction?

• *Brougham v Dwyer* (1913) 108 LT 504, Divisional Court

The Birkbeck Permanent Benefit Building Society had been carrying on an *ultra vires* banking business. The defendant was a customer of that business who had an overdraft of £35 2s 2d. The liquidator of the Building Society brought an action to recover the amount of the overdraft. The trial judge rejected the liquidator's claim on the ground that the transaction was illegal and *ultra vires*. On the liquidator's appeal to the Divisional Court it was held that the transaction was *ultra vires* but not illegal, and that the liquidator was entitled to recover the sum in an action for money had and received.

Lush J: . . . When one considers the real meaning of the expression that it was *ultra vires* on the part of the building society to enter into this transaction, the whole case becomes plain. The directors of the society purporting to act on behalf of the building society, and to make a contract on its behalf, lent the society's money to the defendant by way of an overdraft. It turned out that in point of law the building society were incompetent to make such a contract, and it followed that the contract which the directors thought they were making was not a contract at all, but was simply a transaction which in point of law did not exist. The consequence was that the defendant had received moneys belonging to the building society under a transaction which had no validity of any sort or kind. If the matter stood there, I should have thought it plain that there being no contract an action for money had and received would lie. The case appears to me to be on all fours with one in which money has been advanced on something which was thought to be a contract, but as to which it turns out that there has been a total failure of consideration. A defence was raised to the plaintiff's claim to which the learned judge gave effect, that this transaction being *ultra vires* had the same consequences in point of law as if it had been an illegal transaction. If the transaction had been illegal, of course no action would lie, because the court would not allow a person to set up as part of his cause of action something which was necessarily an illegal contract. The learned judge took the view that to all intents and purposes this was an illegal contract, and he also appears to have taken the view that the plaintiff was suing upon such a contract. If that had been the case, the defendant would have had a complete answer to the claim. But when one remembers the meaning of *ultra vires* the position is different. The contract was only no contract because the building society were unable to enter into it. There was nothing wrong in the contract itself or anything illegal in its nature, but the society being incompetent to make it, it did not exist in point of law. That being so the action was maintainable, and the defendant had no answer to it. It was an action brought for money lent under a transaction which was thought to be valid but which was in fact not valid. On principle I can see no possible reason why such an action should not be maintainable, and the Court of Appeal in *Re Coltman* 45 LT Rep. 392 clearly decided that in a case such as the present assuming the contract not to be illegal, there would be no answer to the action. I am therefore of opinion that there was no defence to the present action, and the appeal must accordingly be allowed.

Ridley J concurred.

NOTES AND QUESTIONS

1. What was the unjust factor in this case? Was it (a) mistake, (b) (total) failure of consideration, (c) absence of consideration or (d) the incapacity of the building society?

2. Should the incapacity of the company suffice of itself to give rise to a restitutionary claim?

3. Does the fact that the contract was void of itself give rise to a restitutionary claim (see the discussion of 'void contracts', above, at 356–386)?

4. Can an analogy be drawn between *Brougham v Dwyer* and *Rover International Ltd v Cannon Film Sales Ltd* [1989] 1 WLR 912 (above, 358) where the contract between the parties was void because the claimant company was not incorporated at the time of entry into the contract? Is the same unjust factor at work in both cases? If so, what is it? See also the discussion of *Brougham* by Hobhouse J in *Westdeutsche Landesbank Girozentrale v Islington London Borough Council* (above, 364).

4. A PUBLIC AUTHORITY ACTING *ULTRA VIRES*

• *Commonwealth of Australia v Burns* [1971] VR 825, Supreme Court of Victoria

The claimant sought to recover the sum of $6,459 from the defendant in respect of pension moneys paid to the defendant over a period of five years. The defendant's father had been entitled to a pension, and he had nominated the defendant to collect the pension on his behalf. The defendant's father died in October 1960 and the pension ceased to be paid. But in January 1961 the claimant resumed payment of the pension. On two occasions, the defendant informed the claimant of the fact that her father had died, but she was told that the matter had been looked into and that she must be entitled to the money. The defendant assumed that her father must have been entitled to make the pension over to her. In January 1966 the claimant discovered the mistake and sought to recover the sums which had been paid to the defendant. The defendant refused to repay the money, *inter alia*, on the ground that she had spent a large proportion of the money for her own purposes. It was held that the claimant was entitled to recover the sums which had been paid to the defendant and that the defendant was not entitled to rely on estoppel as a defence to the claimant's claim.

Newton J: . . . I am satisfied that all the payments made to Mrs Burns were made without statutory or other lawful authority, and were also made by reason of a mistake on the part of the officers of the Repatriation Department who were concerned in the matter.

The primary contention on behalf of the Commonwealth was that it must inevitably follow from this conclusion that Mrs Burns is liable to the Commonwealth to repay the sum of $6459. In my opinion, this contention is correct.

The payments made to Mrs Burns were made out of Consolidated Revenue: see s. 113 of the Repatriation Act, and ss. 81 and 83 of the Commonwealth of Australia Constitution. See too the relevant provisions of the Supply and Appropriation Acts relating to the period in question. In my opinion, the authorities establish that money paid out of Consolidated Revenue without statutory or other lawful authority is recoverable by the Crown from the recipient, at all events if paid without any consideration. And, in my opinion, the position is *a fortiori* where, as here, the payments are the result of a mistake. I consider that the principle, which I have just stated, is a special overriding principle applicable to public moneys in the sense of moneys of the Crown forming part of Consolidated Revenue; the principle is of wider scope than the principles relating to the recovery as between subject and subject of moneys paid under a mistake of fact or for a consideration which has failed. The principle is, in my view, based on public policy. In my statement of the principle I have used the words 'at all events if paid without any consideration', because special problems might arise with respect to unauthorized payments of public moneys in return for valuable consideration such as goods or services: cf. *Re K. L. Tractors Ltd* (1961) 106 CLR 318, especially at 334, 335. In the present case Mrs Burns gave no consideration for any of the payments which were made to her.

In *Auckland Harbour Board v R.* [1924] AC 318, Viscount Haldane, speaking for the Privy Council, said at 326, 327: '. . . it has been a principle of the British Constitution now for more than two centuries, a principle which their Lordships understand to have been inherited in the Constitution of New Zealand with the same stringency, that no money can be taken out of the consolidated fund into which the revenues of the State have been paid, excepting under a distinct authorization from Parliament itself. The days are long gone by in which the Crown, or its servants, apart from Parliament, could give such an authorization or ratify an improper payment. *Any payment out of the consolidated fund made without Parliamentary authority is simply illegal and ultra vires, and may be recovered by the Government if it can, as here, be traced*. . . . to invoke analogies of what might be held in a question between subject and subject is hardly relevant.' (Italics are mine.)

By the words 'if it can, as here, be traced' Viscount Haldane was, in my opinion, not referring to tracing in the equitable or proprietary sense, but to tracing the identity of the recipient of the money. The principle stated by his Lordship in the passage which I have set out was applied in the *Auckland Harbour Board Case* itself, notwithstanding that there was no evidence that the sum of £7,500 there in question was at any relevant time still identifiable in the hands of the recipient, the Auckland Harbour Board. And that case was stronger than the present case, because the sum of £7,500 had not been paid by mistake of fact. Reference may also be made to the report of counsel's argument ([1924] AC at 320), where distinguished counsel for the Crown submitted that 'when a subject receives public money without authority he becomes a debtor to the Crown to that extent'. See also the report of the *Auckland Harbour Board Case* in the Court of Appeal of New Zealand in [1919] NZLR 419, especially at 437, 438 *per* Hosking, J, and at 424, 425, *per* Sir John Salmond *arguendo*.

The principle set out in the passage which I have cited from Viscount Haldane's judgment in the *Auckland Harbour Board Case* has never since been questioned, so far as I have discovered. On the contrary it has been referred to in later cases without disapproval and has on occasion been applied. . . .

Since the conclusion of the hearing in the present case I have discovered that a similar principle is well recognized in the United States of America. . . .

Subject to two qualifications, to which I shall refer in a moment, it was not suggested that there was anything in the Commonwealth of Australia Constitution or in relevant Commonwealth legislation to exclude the application to the present case of the general principle formulated by Viscount Haldane in the *Auckland Harbour Board Case, supra*, in the passage already set out. And in my opinion, the true position is that the application of the principle is confirmed by ss. 81, 82 and 83 of the Commonwealth of Australia Constitution: see too ss. 53, 54 and 56; and *Attorney-General for Victoria v Commonwealth* (1945) 71 CLR 237. [*He considered the two qualifications, concluded that neither was applicable and continued:*]

On behalf of Mrs Burns it was finally submitted that the Commonwealth was estopped from alleging that the payments in question had been made to her without lawful authority. It was submitted that the officer of the Repatriation Department with whom she had the second telephone conversation had represented to her that she was entitled to the payments, and that this representation was confirmed by the continuance of the payments. It was further submitted that Mrs Burns had spent the money now sought to be recovered in reliance upon the representation, so that a requirement that she repay the money would operate unjustly to her detriment: see, for example, *Holt v Markham*, [1923] 1 KB 504; [1922] All ER Rep. 134, and *Grundt v Great Boulder Gold Mines Pty. Ltd* (1939) 59 CLR 641, especially at 674–7 *per* Dixon, J. But a sufficient answer to this submission is, in my view, to be found in the well-established rule that a party cannot be assumed by the doctrine of estoppel to have lawfully done that which the law says that he shall not do: as earlier stated, nobody had, or could have had, any lawful authority to make the payments in question to Mrs. Burns: . . .

In the end Mr Fagan did not seek to rely on any defence based on the assertion that Mrs Burns received the payments in question as agent for Mr Wilton. And since she kept the money for herself, it is clear that no such defence would be valid: see, for example, *Gowers v Lloyds and National Foreign Bank Ltd* [1938] 1 All ER 766, especially at 772, 773 . . .

Having regard to the conclusions which I have reached, it is unnecessary to consider whether the amount in question would be recoverable by the Commonwealth as money paid under mistake of fact, which was in the end the only other basis upon which Mr Jenkinson sought to place the Commonwealth's claim: cf. *Commonwealth of Australia v Kerr* [1919] SALR 201 (where the principle upon which I have decided the present case was not raised).

There will be judgment for the plaintiff for $6,459.

NOTES AND QUESTIONS

1. The only English authority on point is the decision of the Privy Council in *Auckland Harbour Board v R.* [1924] AC 318, which is discussed by Newton J in his judgment. The Law Commission considered the case for reform (*Restitution: Mistakes of Law and Ultra Vires Public Authority Receipts and Payments*, Law Com. No 227 (1994)) but recommended that there should be no alteration to the present common law rule.

2. In *Auckland Harbour Board v R.* [1924] AC 318, 327, Viscount Haldane stated that 'any payment out of the consolidated fund made without Parliamentary authority is simply illegal and ultra vires and may be recovered by the Government if it can . . . be traced'. Newton J interpreted this reference to tracing as a reference to the identification of the recipient rather than to the money which had been paid over, but in *Woolwich Equitable Building Society v Inland Revenue Commissioners* (below, 626) Lord Goff interpreted it as a reference to a proprietary claim? Is there any justification for giving the State a proprietary rather than a personal claim (see Chapter 12, especially below, 642)?

3. Is the principle set out by Newton J confined to payments made out of 'Consolidated Revenue'? Can any justification be put forward to support such a limitation?

4. Is the principle at work in *Burns* the same as the principle that was at stake in *Westdeutsche Landesbank Girozentrale v Islington London Borough Council* [1996] AC 669 (above, 362 and below, 727)? Although *Westdeutsche Landesbank* was a case brought *against* a local authority rather than *by* a local authority, the reasoning in *Westdeutsche Landesbank* has been held to be applicable to claims brought *by* local authorities (see *South Tyneside Metropolitan Borough Council v Svenska International plc* [1995] 1 All ER 545, 556–8). If the principle is not the same, why are the two treated differently and what is it that justifies the difference in treatment?

5. Why was the defendant not entitled to rely on the defence of estoppel? Could she have relied on the defence of change of position (see below, 763–804)?

6. Should a public authority's incapacity in itself constitute a ground for restitution?

7. Can a unified approach to incapacity be adopted, encompassing all of the cases discussed in this Chapter?

12

ULTRA VIRES DEMANDS BY PUBLIC AUTHORITIES

The decision of the House of Lords in *Woolwich Equitable Building Society v Inland Revenue Commissioners* (below, 626) is one of great significance in the development of the law of unjust enrichment because, for the first time, English law clearly recognized the existence of a common law right to recover money exacted under an *ultra vires* demand by a public authority.

Two points are worthy of note by way of introduction. The first is that, prior to *Woolwich*, the cases did not speak with one voice. There was a line of authority which appeared to recognize the existence of a general right to recover unlawfully demanded taxes or other imposts (the principal cases being *Campbell v Hall* (1774) 1 Cowp. 204; *Steele v Williams* (1853) 8 Ex. 625; *Queens of the River SS Co. Ltd v Thames Conservators* (1889) 15 TLR 474; *Hooper v Mayor and Corporation of Exeter* (1887) 56 LJQB 457; *A.G. v Wilts Dairies Ltd* (1921) 37 TLR 884; and *R. v Tower Hamlets L.B.C. ex p. Chetnik Developments Ltd* [1988] A.C. 858), but there was also a line of authority which appeared to deny the existence of such a right (the principal cases in this category being *Slater v Burnley Corporation* (1888) 59 LT 636; *William Whiteley v The King* (1909) 101 LT 741; *Twyford v Manchester Corporation* [1946] Ch. 236; and *National Pari-Mutuel Association Ltd v The King* (1930) 47 TLR 110). It was probably true to say that the general under-standing of the legal community was that, absent a standard ground for restitution such as mistake or duress, the rule was one of no-recovery (as exemplified in the case of *William Whiteley v The King*) but, in a powerful essay ('Restitution from the Executive: A Tercentenary Footnote to the Bill of Rights' in P. Finn (ed.), *Essays on Restitution*, (1990) chapter 6), Birks argued that, properly understood, the cases did recognize the existence of a general right of recovery. It was this conflict of authority which led their Lordships in *Woolwich* to devote considerable time and effort to an examination of the earlier authorities, in an effort to identify the true common law rule.

The second point relates to the scope of the new right which the majority of the House of Lords recognized. Here a number of difficult questions arise and, as yet, most of them still await an answer. What was the unjust factor which was recognized by their Lord-ships? What is its scope? What is its relationship with other unjust factors? What defences exist to the claim? These questions should be borne in mind when reading the extracts from the speeches of their Lordships.

General Reading

BURROWS, chapter 13; GOFF AND JONES, chapter 27; VIRGO, chapter 14.

- *Woolwich Equitable Building Society v Inland Revenue Commissioners*
  [1993] AC 70, House of Lords

The claimants, Woolwich, made three payments, totalling some £56.998 million, to the Revenue in response to a tax demand issued under the Income Tax (Building Societies) Regulations 1986. Although Woolwich paid the sums demanded, it disputed the validity of the regulations from the outset. It paid the first sum on 16 June 1986 because it feared that it would incur penalties and adverse publicity if it did not do so, but it commenced judicial review proceedings by notice of application of the following day. At first instance, Nolan J held that the regulations were *ultra vires* and void (this finding was reversed by the Court of Appeal but was subsequently upheld by the House of Lords in *R. v Inland Revenue Commissioners, ex p. Woolwich Building Society* [1990] 1 WLR 1400). The Revenue returned the capital sum together with interest from the date of judgment but refused to pay interest from the date of receipt.

In the meantime, Woolwich had commenced a second action against the Revenue, in which it sought to recover the capital sum together with interest. The capital sum having been recovered, the claim proceeded as one to recover the interest on the capital sum. In order to claim interest under the Supreme Court Act 1981, section 35A, Woolwich had to show that it was entitled to restitution as of right from the moment of receipt of the money by the Revenue. However, Nolan J dismissed its claim, holding that the Revenue had impliedly promised to return the sum of money paid if the regulations were held to be *ultra vires* but, that apart, were under no restitutionary obligation to repay the capital sum. Woolwich appealed to the Court of Appeal which, by a majority, held that Woolwich was entitled to recover interest from the date of payment on the ground that English law recognizes 'a general principle of repayment of tax unlawfully demanded'. The Revenue appealed to the House of Lords but, by a majority (Lord Keith and Lord Jauncey dissenting), their Lordships dismissed the appeal and held that Woolwich was entitled to recover interest because it had established the existence of a right to recover the money at the moment of its receipt by the Revenue.

Lord Keith (dissenting, reviewed the authorities and continued): The foregoing review of the native authorities satisfies me that they afford no support for Woolwich's major proposition. The principle to be derived from them, in my opinion, is that payments not lawfully due cannot be recovered unless they were made as a result of some improper form of pressure. Such pressure may take the form of duress, as in *Maskell v Horner* [1915] 3 KB 106. It may alternatively take the form of withholding or threatening to withhold the performance of some public duty or the rendering of some public service unless a payment is made which is not lawfully due or is greater than that which is lawfully due, as was the position in the colore officii cases. The mere fact that the payment has been made in response to a demand by a public authority does not emerge in any of the cases as constituting or forming part of the ratio decidendi. Many of the cases appear to turn upon a consideration of whether the payment was voluntary or involuntary. In my opinion that simply involves that the payment was voluntary if no improper pressure was brought to bear, and involuntary if it was. In the present case no pressure to pay was put upon Woolwich by the revenue. Woolwich paid because it calculated that it was in its commercial interest to do so. It could have resisted payment, and the revenue had no means other than the taking of legal proceedings which it might have used to enforce payment. The threat of legal proceedings is not improper pressure. There was no improper pressure by the revenue and in particular there was no duress.

To give effect to Woolwich's proposition would, in my opinion, amount to a very far reaching exercise of judicial legislation. That would be particularly inappropriate having regard to the considerable number of instances which exist of Parliament having legislated in various fields to define the circumstances under which payments of tax not lawfully due may be recovered, and also in what situations and upon what terms interest on overpayments of tax may be paid. Particular instances are section 33 of the Taxes Management Act 1970 as regards overpaid income tax, corporation tax, capital gains tax and petroleum revenue tax; section 24 of the Finance Act 1989 as regards value added tax; section 29 of the Finance Act 1989 as regards excise duty and car tax; section 241 of the Capital Transfer Tax Act 1984 as regards inheritance tax; and section 13(4) of the Stamp Act 1891 (54 & 55 Vict. c. 39) as regards stamp duty. Mention may also be made of section 9 of the General Rate Act 1967 which, as described above, was considered by this House in *Reg. v Tower Hamlets London Borough Council, Ex parte Chetnik Development Ltd* [1988] AC 858. It is to be noted that the section only applies where overpayment of rates is not otherwise recoverable, and it plainly did not occur to the House in that case that the overpayment might be recoverable apart from the section. It seems to me that formulation of the precise grounds upon which overpayments of tax ought to be recoverable and of any exceptions to the right of recovery, may involve nice considerations of policy which are properly the province of Parliament and are not suitable for consideration by the courts. In this connection the question of possible disruption of public finances must obviously be a very material one. Then it is noticeable that existing legislation is restrictive of the extent to which interest on overpaid tax (described as 'repayment supplement') may be recovered. A general right of recovery of overpaid tax could not incorporate any such restriction.

I would add that although in the course of argument some distinction was sought to be drawn between overpayment of tax under regulations later shown to be ultra vires and overpayment due to the erroneous interpretation of a statute, no such distinction can, in my view, properly be drawn.... My Lords, for these reasons I would allow this appeal.

Lord Goff of Chieveley: ....

There can be no doubt that this appeal is one of considerable importance. It is certainly of importance to both parties—to the revenue, which is concerned to maintain the traditional position under which the repayment of overpaid tax is essentially a matter for its own discretion; and to Woolwich, which adopted a courageous and independent stance about the lawfulness of the underlying regulations, and now adopts a similar stance about the obligation of the revenue to repay tax exacted without lawful authority. In addition, of course, there is a substantial sum of money at stake. But the appeal is also of importance for the future of the law of restitution, since the decision of your Lordships' House could have a profound effect upon the structure of this part of our law. It is a reflection of this fact that there have been cited to your Lordships not only the full range of English authorities, and also authorities from Commonwealth countries and the United States of America, but in addition a number of academic works of considerable importance. These include a most valuable Consultation Paper (Law Com. No. 120) published last year by the Law Commission, entitled 'Restitution of Payments Made Under a Mistake of Law,' for which we owe much to Mr Jack Beatson and also, I understand, to Dr Sue Arrowsmith; and a series of articles by academic lawyers of distinction working in the field of restitution. I shall be referring to this academic material in due course. But I wish to record at once that, in my opinion, it is of such importance that it has a powerful bearing upon the consideration by your Lordships of the central question in the case.

My first task must be to review the relevant authorities.... I propose to encapsulate their effect in a number of propositions which can, I believe, be so stated as to reflect the law as it is presently understood with a reasonable degree of accuracy. The law as so stated has, I think, been so understood for most of this century, at least at the level of the Court of Appeal; but it has been the subject of increasing criticism by academic lawyers, and has been departed from in significant respects in some Commonwealth countries, both by legislation and by judicial development of the law. A central question in the present case is whether it is open to your Lordships' House to follow their judicial brethren overseas down the road of development of the law; and, if so, whether it would be appropriate to do so, and which is the precise path which it would then be appropriate to choose. But the answers to these fundamental questions must follow a review of the law as understood at present, which I would express in the following propositions.

(1) Whereas money paid under a mistake of fact is generally recoverable, as a general rule money is not recoverable on the ground that it was paid under a mistake of law. This principle was established in *Bilbie v Lumley* (1802) 2 East 469. It has however been the subject of much criticism, which has grown substantially during the second half of the present century. The principle had been adopted in most, if not all, Commonwealth countries; though in some it has now been modified or abandoned, either by statute or by judicial action. No such principle applies in civil law countries, and its adoption by the common law has been criticised by comparative lawyers as unnecessary and anomalous. This topic is the subject of the Consultation Paper No. 120 published by the Law Commission last year, in which serious criticisms of the rule of non-recovery are rehearsed and developed, and proposals for its abolition are put forward for discussion.

(2) But money paid under compulsion may be recoverable. In particular: (a) money paid as a result of actual or threatened duress to the person, or actual or threatened seizure of a person's goods, is recoverable. For an example of the latter, see *Maskell v Horner* [1915] 3 KB 106. Since these forms of compulsion are not directly relevant for present purposes, it is unnecessary to elaborate them; but I think it pertinent to observe that the concept of duress has in recent years been expanded to embrace economic duress.

(b) Money paid to a person in a public or quasi-public position to obtain the performance by him of a duty which he is bound to perform for nothing or for less than the sum demanded by him is recoverable to the extent that he is not entitled to it. Such payments are often described as having been demanded colore officii. There is much abstruse learning on the subject (see, in particular, the illuminating discussion by Windeyer J in *Mason v New South Wales*, 102 CLR 108, 139–2), but for present purposes it is not, I think, necessary for us to concern ourselves with this point of classification. Examples of influential early cases are *Morgan v Palmer*, 2 B & C 729 and *Steele v Williams*, 8 Ex. 625; a later example of some significance is *T. and J. Brocklebank Ltd v The King* [1925] 1 KB 52.

(c) Money paid to a person for the performance of a statutory duty, which he is bound to perform for a sum less than that charged by him, is also recoverable to the extent of the overcharge. A leading example of such a case is *Great Western Railway Co. v Sutton*, LR 4 HL 226; for a more recent Scottish case, also the subject of an appeal to this House, see *South of Scotland Electricity Board v British Oxygen Co. Ltd* [1959] 1 WLR 587.

(d) In cases of compulsion, a threat which constitutes the compulsion may be expressed or implied, a point perhaps overlooked in *Twyford v Manchester Corporation* [1946] Ch. 236.

(e) I would not think it right, especially bearing in mind the development of the concept of economic duress, to regard the categories of compulsion for present purposes as closed.

(3) Where a sum has been paid which is not due, but it has not been paid under a mistake of fact or under compulsion as explained under (2) above, it is generally not recoverable. Such a payment has often been called a voluntary payment. In particular, a payment is regarded as a voluntary payment and so as irrecoverable in the following circumstances.

(a) The money has been paid under a mistake of law: see (1) above. See e.g., *Slater v Burnley Corporation*, 59 LT 636 and *National Pari-Mutuel Association Ltd v The King*, 47 TLR 110.

(b) The payer has the opportunity of contesting his liability in proceedings, but instead gives way and pays: see e.g., *Henderson v Folkestone Waterworks Co.* (1885) 1 TLR 329, and *Sargood Brothers v The Commonwealth*, 11 CLR 258, especially at 301, per Isaacs J. So where money has been paid under pressure of actual or threatened legal proceedings for its recovery, the payer cannot say that for that reason the money has been paid under compulsion and is therefore recoverable by him. If he chooses to give way and pay, rather than obtain the decision of the court on the question whether the money is due, his payment is regarded as voluntary and so it not recoverable: see e.g., *William Whiteley Ltd v The King*, 101 LT 741.

(c) The money has otherwise been paid in such circumstances that the payment was made to close the transaction. Such would obviously be so in the case of a binding compromise; but even where there is no consideration for the payment, it may have been made to close the transaction and so be irrecoverable. Such a payment has been treated as a gift: see *Maskell v Horner* [1915] 3 KB 106, 118, *per* Lord Reading CJ.

(4) A payment may be made on such terms that it has been agreed, expressly or impliedly, by the recipient that, if it shall prove not to have been due, it will be repaid by him. In that event, of course, the money will be repayable. Such was held to be the case in *Sebel Products Ltd v Customs and Excise Commissioners* [1949] Ch. 409 (although the legal basis upon which Vaisey J there inferred the existence of such an agreement may be open to criticism). On the other hand, the mere fact that money is paid under protest will not give rise of itself to the inference of such an agreement; though it may form part of the evidence from which it may be inferred that the payee did not intend to close the transaction: see *Maskell v Horner* [1915] 3 KB 106, 120, *per* Lord Reading CJ.

The principles which I have just stated had come to be broadly accepted, at the level of the Court of Appeal, at least by the early part of this century. But a formidable argument has been developed in recent years by leading academic lawyers that this stream of authority should be the subject of reinterpretation to reveal a different line of thought pointing to the conclusion that money paid to a public authority pursuant to an ultra vires demand should be repayable, without the necessity of establishing compulsion, on the simple ground that there was no consideration for the payment. I refer in particular to the powerful essay by Professor Peter Birks (in the volume *Essays on Restitution* (1990), edited by Professor Finn, at 164 ff.) entitled 'Restitution from the Executive: a Tercentenary Footnote to the Bill of Rights.' I have little doubt that this essay by Professor Birks, which was fore-shadowed by an influential lecture delivered by Professor W. R. Cornish in Kuala Lumpur in 1986 (the first Sultan Azlan Shah Law Lecture (1987) *J Mal. & Comp L* 41), provided the main inspiration for the argument of Woolwich, and the judgments of the majority of the Court of Appeal, in the present case.

I have a strong presentiment that, had the opportunity arisen, Lord Mansfield would have seized it to establish the law in this form. His broad culture, his knowledge and understanding of Roman law, his extraordinary gift for cutting through technicality to perceive and define principle, would surely have drawn him towards this result. Mr Gardiner, for Woolwich, relied upon *Campbell v Hall*, 1 Cowp. 204 as authority that he did in fact reach that very conclusion. But that case was the subject of research by Mr Glick and his team, and was revealed (from the reports in Lofft 655 and in 20 St. Tr. 239) to be a cause célèbre in which the great issue (of immense public interest) related to the power to levy taxes in the island of Grenada following its capture from the French King, it being accepted by the Crown without argument that the relevant taxes, if not duly levied, must be repaid. Lord Mansfield's judgment in the case, adverse to the Crown, became known as the Magna Carta of the Colonies. The fact that the basis of recovery was not in issue, and indeed was overshadowed by the great question in the case, must detract from its importance in the present context; even so, the simple fact remains that recovery was stated to be founded upon absence of consideration for the payment. Furthermore there are other cases in the late 18th and early 19th centuries, of which *Dew v Parsons*, 2 B & Ald. 562 is a significant example, which support this approach.

Later cases in the 19th century upon which Professor Birks places much reliance are *Steele v Williams*, 8 Ex. 625, and *Hooper v Exeter Corporation*, 56 LJQB 457. In *Steele v Williams*, the judgment of Martin B was certainly on the basis that the money, having been the subject of an ultra vires demand by a public officer, was as such recoverable. That approach seems also to have provided considerable attraction for Parke B; but although the point was left open by him, the case was decided by the majority (Parke and Platt BB) on the ground of compulsion. Both of them treated the case as one in which there was an implied threat by the defendant to deprive the plaintiff's clerk of his right to take extracts from the parish register for no charge; and both appear to have concluded that, in the circumstances, although that threat was made before the plaintiff's clerk obtained the extracts he needed, nevertheless it was causative of the payment which was therefore recoverable on the ground of compulsion. In *Hooper v Exeter Corporation*, 56 LJQB 457 Professor Birks is perhaps on stronger ground, although the basis on which the court proceeded is not altogether clear. The plaintiff sought to recover dues paid by him for landing stone for which, unknown to him, he was not liable because the stone was covered by an exemption. It was argued on his behalf that the payment was not voluntary, citing *Morgan v Palmer*, 2 B & C 729 (a case of compulsion). Reliance was also placed upon the power of absolute and immediate distress in the statute. The court accepted the plaintiff's argument. Both Lord Coleridge CJ and Smith J relied on *Morgan v Palmer*; Smith J also invoked *Steele v Williams*, 8 Ex. 625, without however referring to the judgment of Martin B. Neither referred to the power of immediate distress. The case, brief and obscure though it is, might well have provided a basis upon which judges could later have built to develop a principle that money demanded ultra vires by a public authority was prima facie recoverable.

Professor Birks also places reliance upon *Queens of the River Steamship Co. Ltd v Conservators of the River Thames*, 15 TLR 474, and an obiter dictum of Atkin LJ in *Attorney-General v Wilts United Dairies Ltd*, 37 TLR 884, 887. The former case, so far as it goes is undoubtedly consistent with his thesis; but it is very briefly reported, without any indication of the arguments advanced or cases cited, and the conclusion is encapsulated in one brief sentence. The dictum of Atkin LJ is to the effect that such a payment is, if paid under protest, recoverable on the simple ground that it was a sum received by the public authority to the use of the citizen. However, the subsequent decision of the Court of Appeal in *T. and J. Brocklebank Ltd v The King* [1925] 1 KB 52 shows that, in circumstances similar to those of the *Wilts United Dairies* case, recovery could be, and indeed there was, founded upon compulsion and not upon the simple fact that the money was paid pursuant to an ultra vires demand: see [1925] 1 KB 52, 61–2, 67, 72 *per* Bankes LJ (accepting the opinion of the trial judge, Avory J [1924] 1 KB 647, 652–3), and *per* Scrutton and Sargant I. JJ. So the question of the soundness of Atkins LJ's dictum did not arise for decision in that case. Even so, a similar approach to that of Atkin LJ is to be found in an obiter dictum of Dixon CJ in *Mason v New South Wales*, 102 CLR 108, 117 which was to the effect that he had not been able completely to reconcile himself to the view that, if the weight of a de facto governmental authority manifested in a money demand is not resisted, the money belongs to the Crown unless the payment was made under certain specific forms of compulsion.

In all the circumstances, it is difficult to avoid the conclusion that in this country, at the level of the Court of Appeal (see, in particular, the decisions of that court in *T. and J. Brocklebank Ltd v The King* [1925] 1 KB 52 and *National Pari-Mutuel Association Ltd v The King*, 47 TLR 110), the law had settled down in the form which I have indicated. I have little doubt that a major force in the moulding of the law in this form is to be found in the practitioners' text books of the time, notably *Bullen & Leake's Precedents of Pleadings*, 3rd edn (1868), 50, and *Leake's Law of Contracts*, 5th edn (1906), 61; we can see this reflected in the form of the arguments advanced in the cases, and the manner in which the court reacted to submissions by counsel challenging the accepted view. I fear that the courts sorely missed assistance from academic lawyers specialising in this branch of the law; but the law faculties in our universities were only beginning to be established towards the end of the 19th century. It can however be said that the principle of justice, embodied in Martin B's judgment in *Steele v Williams*, 8 Ex. 625 and perhaps also in *Hooper v Exeter Corporation*, 56 LJQB 457, and expressed in the dicta of Lord Atkin and Sir Owen Dixon, still calls for attention; and the central question in the present case is whether your Lordships' House, deriving their inspiration from the example of those two great judges, should rekindle that fading flame and reformulate the law in accordance with that principle. I am satisfied that, on the authorities, it is open to your Lordships' House to take that step. The crucial question is whether it is appropriate for your Lordships to do so.

. . .

I now turn to the submission of Woolwich that your Lordships' House should, despite the authorities to which I have referred, reformulate the law so as to establish that the subject who makes a payment in response to an unlawful demand of tax acquires forthwith a prima facie right in restitution to the repayment of the money. This is the real point which lies at the heart of the present appeal; in a sense, everything which I have said so far has done no more than set the stage for its consideration.

The justice underlying Woolwich's submission is, I consider, plain to see. Take the present case. The revenue has made an unlawful demand for tax. The taxpayer is convinced that the demand is unlawful, and has to decide what to do. It is faced with the revenue, armed with the coercive power of the state, including what is in practice a power to charge interest which is penal in its effect. In addition, being a reputable society which alone among building societies is challenging the lawfulness of the demand, it understandably fears damage to its reputation if it does not pay. So it decides to pay first, asserting that it will challenge the lawfulness of the demand in litigation. Now, Woolwich having won that litigation, the revenue asserts that it was never under any obligation to repay the money, and that it in fact repaid it only as a matter of grace. There being no applicable statute to regulate the position, the revenue has to maintain this position at common law.

Stated in this stark form, the revenue's position appears to me, as a matter of common justice, to be unsustainable; and the injustice is rendered worse by the fact that it involves, as Nolan J pointed out [1989] 1 WLR 137, 140, the revenue having the benefit of a massive interest-free loan as the fruit of its unlawful action. I turn then from the particular to the general. Take any tax or duty paid by the citizen pursuant to an unlawful demand. Common justice seems to require that tax to be repaid, unless special circumstances or some principle of policy require otherwise; prima facie, the taxpayer should be entitled to repayment as of right.

To the simple call of justice, there are a number of possible objections. The first is to be found in the structure of our law of restitution, as it developed during the 19th and early 20th centuries. That law might have developed so as to recognise a condictio indebiti—an action for the recovery of money on the ground that it was not due. But it did not do so. Instead, as we have seen, there developed common law actions for the recovery of money paid under a mistake of fact, and under certain forms of compulsion. What is now being sought is, in a sense, a reversal of that development, in a particular type of case; and it is said that it is too late to take that step. To that objection, however, there are two answers. The first is that the retention by the state of taxes unlawfully exacted is particularly obnoxious, because it is one of the most fundamental principles of our law—enshrined in a famous constitutional document, the Bill of Rights 1688—that taxes should not be levied without the authority of Parliament; and full effect can only be given to that principle if the return of taxes exacted under an unlawful demand can be enforced as a matter of right. The second is that, when the revenue makes a demand for tax, that demand is implicitly backed by the coercive powers of the state and may well entail (as in the present case) unpleasant economic and social consequences if the taxpayer does not pay. In any event, it seems strange to penalise the good citizen, whose natural instinct is to trust the revenue and pay taxes when they are demanded of him. The force of this answer is recognised in a much-quoted passage from the judgment of Holmes J in *Atchison, Topeka & Santa Fe Railway Co. v O'Connor*, 223 US 280, 285–6, when he said:

'when, as is common, the state has a more summary remedy, such as distress, and the party indicates by protest that he is yielding to what he cannot prevent, courts sometimes perhaps have been a little too slow to recognise the implied duress under which payment is made. But even if the state is driven to an action, if at the same time the citizen is put at a serious disadvantage in the assertion of his legal, in this case of his constitutional, rights, by defence in the suit, justice may require that he should be at liberty to avoid those disadvantages by paying promptly and bringing suit on his side. He is entitled to assert his supposed right on reasonably equal terms.'

This particular answer might however point at first sight to a development of the common law concept of compulsion, rather than recognition of the broad principle of justice by which Woolwich contends. This was what in fact occurred in the leading Australian case of *Mason v New South Wales* 102 CLR 108. It is impossible to summarise the effect of that complicated case in a few lines, but in practical terms the High Court of Australia found duress to exist in the possibility that the state might seize the plaintiff's property. A similar tendency to expand the concept of compulsion is to be discovered in the majority judgment of the Supreme Court of Canada in *Eadie v Township of Brantford* (1967) 63 DLR (2d) 561 (though events of a more dramatic character have since occurred in that jurisdiction, to which I will refer in a moment). This type of approach has also been advocated by Mr Andrew Burrows in his interesting essay entitled 'Public Authorities, Ultra Vires and Restitution' in *Essays on the Law of Restitution* (1991), edited by Mr Burrows, at 39 ff. We may expect that in any event the common law principles of compulsion, and indeed of mistake, will continue to develop in the future. But the difficulty with this approach for the present case is that Woolwich was in reality suffering from no mistake at all, so much so that it was prepared to back its conviction that the revenue was acting ultra vires by risking a very substantial amount of money in legal costs in establishing that fact; and, since the possibility of distraint by the revenue was very remote, the concept of compulsion would have to be stretched to the utmost to embrace the circumstances of such a case as this. It is for this reason that Woolwich's alternative claim founded upon compulsion did not loom large in the argument, and is difficult to sustain. In the end, logic appears to demand that the right of recovery should require neither mistake nor compulsion, and that the simple fact that the tax was exacted unlawfully should prima facie be enough to require its repayment.

There is however a second objection to the recognition of such a right of recovery. This is that for your Lordships' House to recognise such a principle would overstep the boundary which we traditionally set for ourselves, separating the legitimate development of the law by the judges from legislation. It was strongly urged by Mr Glick, in his powerful argument for the revenue, that we would indeed be trespassing beyond that boundary if we were to accept the argument of Woolwich. I feel bound however to say that, although I am well aware of the existence of the boundary, I am never quite sure where to find it. Its position seems to vary from case to case. Indeed, if it were to be as firmly and clearly drawn as some of our mentors would wish, I cannot help feeling that a number of leading cases in your Lordships' House would never have been decided the way they were. For example, the minority view would have prevailed in *Donoghue v Stevenson* [1932] AC 562; our modern law of judicial review would have never developed from its old, ineffectual, origins; and *Mareva* injunctions would never have seen the light of day. Much seems to depend upon the circumstances of the particular case. In the present case Mr Glick was fully entitled to, and did, point to practical considerations to reinforce his argument. The first was that a case such as the present was so rare that it could not of itself call for a fundamental reformulation of the underlying principle—a point which I find unimpressive, when I consider that our task is essentially to do justice between the parties in the particular case before us. Second, however, he asserted that, if your Lordships' House were to accept Woolwich's argument, it would be impossible for us to set the appropriate limits to the application of the principle. An unbridled right to recover overpaid taxes and duties subject only to the usual six-year time bar was, he suggested, unacceptable in modern society. Some limits had to be set to such claims; and the selection of such limits, being essentially a matter of policy, was one which the legislature alone is equipped to make.

My reaction to this submission of Mr Glick is to confess (to some extent) and yet to avoid. I agree that there appears to be a widely held view that some limit has to be placed upon the recovery of taxes paid pursuant to an ultra vires demand. I would go further and accept that the armoury of common law defences, such as those which prevent recovery of money paid under a binding compromise or to avoid a threat of litigation, may be either inapposite or inadequate for the purpose; because it is possible to envisage, especially in modern taxation law which tends to be excessively complex, circumstances in which some very substantial sum of money may be held to have been exacted ultra vires from a very large number of taxpayers. It may well therefore be necessary to have recourse to other defences, such as for example short time limits within which such claims have to be advanced. An instructive example of this approach is to be found in German law, in which we find a general right of recovery which is subject to the principle that an administrative act is, even if in fact unlawful, treated as legally effective unless and until it is cancelled, either by the authority itself or by an administrative court. Furthermore a citizen can only enforce the cancellation by making a formal objection within one month of notification; and if that objection is rejected by the authority, the citizen cannot benefit from the successful formal objection of another citizen; he must object in due time himself. Such draconian time limits as these may be too strong medicine for our taste; but the example of a general right of recovery subject to strict time limits imposed as a matter of policy is instructive for us as we seek to solve the problem in the present case.

At this stage of the argument, I find it helpful to turn to recent developments in Canada. First, in a notable dissenting judgment (with which Laskin CJC concurred) in *Hydro Electric Commission of Township of Nepean v Ontario Hydro* (1982) 132 DLR (3d) 193, 201–211, Dickson J subjected the rule against recovery of money paid under a mistake of law to a devastating analysis and concluded that the rule should be rejected. His preferred solution was that, as in cases of mistake of fact, money paid under a mistake of law should be recoverable if it would be unjust for the recipient to retain it. Next, in the leading case of *Air Canada v British Columbia*, 59 DLR (4th) 161, the question arose whether money in the form of taxes paid under a statute held to be ultra vires was recoverable. It is impossible for me, for reasons of space, to do more than summarise the most relevant parts of the judgments of the Supreme Court of Canada. Of the seven judges who heard the appeal, four thought it necessary to consider whether the taxes paid were recoverable at common law. The leading judgment was delivered by La Forest J, with whom Lamer and L'Heureux-Dube JJ agreed. First, he decided, at 192, to follow Dickson J's lead, and to hold that the distinction between mistake of fact and mistake of law should play no part in the law of restitution. This did not however imply that recovery would follow in every case where a mistake had been shown to exist: 'If the defendant can show that the payment was made in settlement of an honest claim, or that he has changed his position as a result of the enrichment, then restitution will be denied.' However he went on to hold, at 193, that, where 'unconstitutional or ultra vires levies' are in issue, special considerations arose. These were twofold. First, if the plaintiff had passed on the relevant tax to others, the taxing authority could not be said to have been unjustly enriched at the plaintiff's expense, and he was not therefore entitled to recover. As La Forest J said, at 193: 'The law of restitution is not intended to provide windfalls to plaintiffs who have suffered no loss.' On that basis alone, he held that the plaintiff's claim in the case before the court must fail. However, he went on to hold that the claim failed on another ground, viz., that as a general rule there will, as a matter of policy, be no recovery of taxes paid pursuant to legislation which is unconstitutional or otherwise invalid. Basing himself on authority from the United States, La Forest J concluded that any other rule would at best be inefficient, and at worst could lead to financial chaos: see 194–7. The rule against recovery should not however apply where a tax is exacted, not under unconstitutional legislation, but through a misapplication of the law. He added, at 198, that, in his opinion, if recovery in all cases is to be the general rule, then that was best achieved through the route of statutory reform.

Wilson J dissented. She did not think it necessary to consider whether the old rule barring recovery of money paid under mistake of law should be abolished, though had she thought it necessary to do so, she would have followed the approach of Dickson J. She considered, at 169, that money paid under unconstitutional legislation was generally recoverable:

'The taxpayer, assuming the validity of the statute as I believe it is entitled to do, considers itself obligated to pay. Citizens are expected to be law-abiding. They are expected to pay their taxes. Pay first and object later is the general rule. The payments are made pursuant to a perceived obligation to pay which results from the combined presumption of constitutional validity of duly enacted legislation and the holding out of such validity by the legislature. In such circumstances I consider it quite unrealistic to expect the taxpayer to make its payments 'under protest.' Any taxpayer paying taxes exigible under a statute which it has no reason to believe or suspect is other than valid should be viewed as having paid pursuant to the statutory obligation to do so.'

Furthermore, she was unable to accept the view of La Forest J that the principle of recovery should be reversed for policy reasons. She spoke in forthright terms, at 169:

'What is the policy that requires such a dramatic reversal of principle? Why should the individual taxpayer, as opposed to taxpayers as a whole, bear the burden of government's mistake? I would respectfully suggest that it is grossly unfair that X, who may not be (as in this case) a large corporate enterprise, should absorb the cost of government's unconstitutional act. If it is appropriate for the courts to adopt some kind of policy in order to protect government against itself (and I cannot say that the idea particularly appeals to me), it should be one that distributes the loss fairly across the public. The loss should not fall on the totally innocent taxpayer whose only fault is that it paid what the legislature improperly said was due.'

She also rejected, at 169–70, the proposed defence of 'passing on.' Accordingly in her opinion the taxpayer should be entitled to succeed.

I cannot deny that I find the reasoning of Wilson J most attractive. Moreover I agree with her that, if there is to be a right to recovery in respect of taxes exacted unlawfully by the revenue, it is irrelevant to consider whether the old rule barring recovery of money paid under mistake of law should be abolished, for that rule can have no application where the remedy arises not from error on the part of the taxpayer, but from the unlawful nature of the demand by the revenue. Furthermore, like Wilson J, I very respectfully doubt the advisability of imposing special limits upon recovery in the case of 'unconstitutional or ultra vires levies.' I shall revert a little later to the defence of passing on.

In all the circumstances, I do not consider that Mr Glick's argument, powerful though it is, is persuasive enough to deter me from recognising, in law, the force of the justice underlying Woolwich's case. Furthermore, there are particular reasons which impel me to that conclusion The first is that this opportunity will never come again. If we do not take it now, it will be gone forever. The second is that I fear that, however compelling the principle of justice may be, it would never be sufficient to persuade a government to propose its legislative recognition by Parliament; caution, otherwise known as the Treasury, would never allow this to happen. The third is that, turning Mr Glick's argument against him, the immediate practical impact of the recognition of the principle will be limited, for (unlike the present case) most cases will continue for the time being to be regulated by the various statutory regimes now in force. The fourth is that, if the principle is to be recognised, this is an almost ideal moment for that recognition to take place. This is because the Law Commission's Consultation Paper is now under active consideration, calling for a fundamental review of the law on this subject, including a fresh look at the various, often inconsistent, statutory régimes under which overpaid taxes and duties either may or must be repaid. The consultation may acquire a greater urgency and sense of purpose if set against the background of a recognised right of recovery at common law. But in addition there is an immediate opportunity for the authorities concerned to reformulate, in collaboration with the Law Commission, the appropriate limits to recovery, on a coherent system of principles suitable for modern society, in terms which can (if it is thought right to do so) embrace the unusual circumstances of the present case. In this way, legislative bounds can be set to the common law principle, as Mr Glick insists that they should. Fifth, it is well established that, if the Crown pays money out of the consolidated fund without authority, such money is ipso facto recoverable if it can be traced: see *Auckland Harbour Board v The King* [1924] AC 318. It is true that the claim in such a case can be distinguished as being proprietary in nature. But the comparison with the position of the citizen, on the law as it stands at present, is most unattractive.

There is a sixth reason which favours this conclusion. I refer to the decision of the European Court of Justice, in *Amministrazione delle Finanze dello Stato v SpA San Giorgio* (Case 199/82) [1983] ECR 3595, which establishes that a person who pays charges levied by a member state contrary to the rules of community law is entitled to repayment of the charge, such right being regarded as a consequence of, and an adjunct to, the rights conferred on individuals by the Community provisions prohibiting the relevant charges: see paragraph 12 of the judgment of the court, at 3612. The *San Giorgio* case is also of interest for present purposes in that it accepts that Community law does not prevent a national legal system from disallowing repayment of charges where to do so would entail unjust enrichment of the recipient, in particular where the charges have been incorporated into the price of goods and so passed on to the purchaser. I only comment that, at a time when Community law is becoming increasingly important, it would be strange if the right of the citizen to recover overpaid charges were to be more restricted under domestic law than it is under European law.

I would therefore hold that money paid by a citizen to a public authority in the form of taxes or other levies paid pursuant to an ultra vires demand by the authority is prima facie recoverable by the citizen as of right. As at present advised, I incline to the opinion that this principle should extend to embrace cases in which the tax or other levy has been wrongly exacted by the public authority not because the demand was ultra vires but for other reasons, for example because the authority has misconstrued a relevant statute or regulation. It is not however necessary to decide the point in the present case, and in any event cases of this kind are generally the subject of statutory regimes which legislate for the circumstances in which money so paid either must or may be repaid. Nor do I think it necessary to consider for the purposes of the present case to what extent the common law may provide the public authority with a defence to a claim for the repayment of money so paid; though for the reasons I have already given, I do not consider that the principle of recovery should be inapplicable simply because the citizen has paid the money under a mistake of law. It will be a matter for consideration whether the fact that the plaintiff has passed on the tax or levy so that the burden has fallen on another should provide a defence to his claim. Although this is contemplated by the European Court of Justice in the *San Giorgio* case, it is evident from *Air Canada v British Columbia*, 59 DLR (4th) 161 that the point is not without its difficulties; and the availability of such a defence may depend upon the nature of the tax or other levy. No doubt matters of this kind will in any event be the subject of consideration during the current consultations with the Law Commission.

For these reasons, I would dismiss the appeal with costs.

Lord Jauncey of Tullichettle [(dissenting) *having examined the authorities and concluded that they did not support the existence of a right to recover* ultra vires *payments, continued*:] There is in theory a good deal to be said for the submission of Professor Birks in his *Introduction to the Law of Restitution* (1985), 295, that a payer should be able to recover payments demanded ultra vires by a public authority on the sole ground that retention of such payment would infringe the principle of 'no taxation without Parliament' enshrined in the Bill of Rights. However it is clear that in practice some limitation would have to be imposed on any such principle. During the course of argument Mr Gardiner suggested certain alternative modifications to the Woolwich principle as initially enunciated by him. First and foremost he maintained that a mistake of law would be no defence to the application of the principle but as alternatives he submitted that the principle would be subject to the mistake of law defence or that the defence of mistake of law should be abrogated altogether. He also sought to draw a distinction between an unlawful demand made under an ultra vires instrument and one made under an intra vires instrument which was misconstrued or misapplied. A distinction which I consider to be without a difference. Public authorities are creatures of statute and can do no more than the statute permits them to do. A demand by such an authority under an ultra vires regulation is no more or no less unlawful than a demand under a valid regulation which does not apply to the situation in which the demand is made. I mention these matters because they show that to accept the Woolwich principle in one or other of its forms would appear to involve a choice of what the law should be rather than a decision as to what it is.

To apply the Woolwich principle as initially enunciated without limitation could cause very serious practical difficulties of administration and specifying appropriate limitations presents equal difficulties. For example, what, if any, knowledge is required on the part of a payer at the time of payment to entitle him to recovery at a later date? Or how long should any right to repayment last? Is it in the public interest that a public authority's finance should be disrupted by wholly unexpected claims for repayment years after the money in question has been received? These are all matters which would arise in any reform of the law to encompass some such principle as Woolwich contend for and are matters with which the legislature is best equipped to deal.

Lord Browne-Wilkinson: . . .

As in so many other fields of English law, the occasions on which recovery is permitted have been built up on a case by case basis. For present purposes there are in my judgment two streams of authority relating to moneys wrongly extracted by way of impost. One stream is founded on the concept that money paid under an ultra vires demand for a tax or other impost has been paid without consideration. The other stream is based on the notion that such payments have been made under compulsion, the relative positions and powers of the two parties being unequal.

The stream based on the concept of payment without consideration stems from what Lord Mansfield said in *Campbell v Hall*, 1 Cowp. 204 and is reflected in the decision in *Dew v Parsons*, 2 B & Ald. 562. In *Steele v Williams*, 8 Ex. 625, 632, Martin B said that the payment in that case was not a voluntary payment but was 'more like the case of money paid without consideration.' In *Queens of the River Steamship Co. Ltd v Conservators of the River Thames* 15 TLR 474, Phillimore J founded his decision on the fact that there was no consideration for the payment. Although this stream seems subsequently to have run into the sand, I find the approach attractive: money paid on the footing that there is a legal demand is paid for a reason that does not exist if that demand is a nullity. There is in my view a close analogy to the right to recover money paid under a contract the consideration for which has wholly failed.

The other stream, based on compulsion, stems from *Morgan v Palmer*, 2B & C 729 and the majority decision in *Steele v Williams*. In their inception, these authorities were based on the fact that the payer and payee were not on an equal footing and it was this inequality which gave rise to the right to recovery. However, most of the cases which arose for decision were concerned with payments extracted ultra vires by persons who in virtue of their position could insist on the wrongful payment as a precondition to affording the payer his legal rights i.e. they were payments colore officii. In consequence, the courts came to limit the cases in which recovery of an ultra vires impost was allowed to cases where there had been an extraction colore officii. I can see no reason in principle to have restricted the original wide basis of recovery to this limited class of case. In my judgment, as a matter of principle the colore officii cases are merely examples of a wider principle, viz. that where the parties are on an unequal footing so that money is paid by way of tax or other impost in pursuance of a demand by some public officer, these moneys are recoverable since the citizen is, in practice, unable to resist the payment save at the risk of breaking the law or exposing himself to penalties or other disadvantages.

In my view the principle is correctly expressed by Holmes J in *Atchison, Topeka & Santa Fe Railway Co. v O'Connor*, 223 U.S. 280, 285–6, [*he then proceeded to quote from the judgment of Holmes J, which quotation is set out in the speech of Lord Goff above, 631.*]

In cases such as the present both the concept of want of consideration and payment under implied compulsion are in play. The money was demanded and paid for tax, yet no tax was due: there was a payment for no consideration. The money was demanded by the state from the citizen and the inequalities of the parties' respective positions is manifest even in the case of a major financial institution like Woolwich. There are, therefore, in my judgment sound reasons by way of analogy for establishing the law in the sense which Lord Goff proposes. I agree with him that the practical objections to taking this course are not sufficient to prevent this House from establishing the law in accordance with both principle and justice. I, too, therefore would dismiss this appeal.

Lord Slynn of Hadley: . . .

I do not consider that the fact that Parliament has legislated extensively in this area means that no principle of recovery at common law can or should at this stage of the development of the law be found to exist. If the principle does exist that tax paid on a demand from the Crown when the tax was the subject of an ultra vires demand can be recovered as money had and received then, in my view, it is for the courts to declare it. In so doing they do not usurp the legislative function. I regard the proper approach as the converse. If the legislative finds that limitations on the common law principle are needed for reasons of policy or good administration then they can be adopted by legislation, e.g. by a short limitation period, presumptions as to validity, even (which I mention but do not necessarily think appropriate since the matter has not been discussed) a power in the courts to limit the effects of any order for recovery comparable to that conferred on the European Court of Justice by article 174 of the EEC Treaty (Cmnd. 5179–II). Because of the other legislative provisions dealing with repayment of various taxes it seems in any event that the number of cases where any principle of common law would need to be relied on is likely to be small. The 'flood gates' argument is therefore not a persuasive one in this case. If it were a risk, then the revenue would need to consider appropriate legislation.

Finally, the revenue has contended that the proper procedure was for Woolwich to seek to challenge its decision not to pay interest by way of judicial review, although it would of course contend that no order should be made on such a review in the present case. I do not accept this. If a claim lies for money had and received, judicial review adds nothing. . . .

The cases cited, and referred to in depth by my noble and learned friends, have proceeded on the basis that on the one hand money paid under a mistake of fact or under duress or as it is said 'colore officii' can be recovered, whereas money paid under a mistake of law or voluntarily 'to close a transaction' or to avoid threatened litigation cannot. The present case does not fall clearly into any of these separate categories.

. . . .

Yet in my view there is nothing in the authorities which precludes your Lordship's House from laying down that money paid by way of tax following an ultra vires demand by the revenue is recoverable. On the other hand, there are in some cases statements of principle in general terms, which do not form part of the ratio decidendi and in others statements in dissenting judgments which it seems to me should be considered when the present question has to be resolved.

. . .

Although as I see it the facts do not fit easily into the existing category of duress or of claims colore officii, they shade into them. There is a common element of pressure which by analogy can be said to justify a claim for repayment.

. . .

I find it quite unacceptable in principle that the common law should have no remedy for a taxpayer who has paid large sums or any sum of money to the revenue when those sums have been demanded pursuant to an invalid regulation and retained free of interest pending a decision of the courts.

It is said that *William Whiteley Ltd v The King*, 101 LT 741 and *Twyford v Manchester Corporation* [1946] Ch. 236. are authorities to the contrary. I consider that they are cases where payments were made to close a transaction and are to be treated as cases of voluntary payments. If they were not, in my view they were wrongly decided and they should not influence your Lordships' decision.

Accordingly I consider that Glidewell and Butler-Sloss L JJ were right to conclude that money paid to the revenue pursuant to a demand which was ultra vires can be recovered as money had and received. The money was repayable immediately it was paid.

I do not agree that this principle cannot apply where there is a mistake of law. That is the situation where the relief is most likely to be needed and if it is excluded not much is left.

This is not, however, a case where the demand was based on an erroneous interpretation of legislation by the revenue; my provisional view is that there is no distinction between such a case and a case like the present where the demand is based on an invalid regulation and is therefore ultra vires. That does not have to be decided in this case, nor is it necessary to consider what defences would be open to such a claim for recovery of the money paid if it lay.

My Lords, for the reasons given I would however dismiss this appeal.

NOTES AND QUESTIONS

1. The issues which are raised by this case are discussed in more detail by J Beatson, (1993) 109 *LQR* 401, P Birks [1992] *PL* 580, and E McKendrick [1993] *LMCLQ* 88. Reference should also be made to the influential academic articles which are cited by Lord Goff in his speech. The Law Commission has now produced a report (Law Com. No. 227, '*Restitution: Mistakes of Law and Ultra Vires Public Authority Receipts and Payments*', especially 51–181) which includes a valuable discussion of *Woolwich* and makes a number of proposals for reform in the light of the decision of the House of Lords.

2. On 16 July 1992, legislation was passed (amending section 64 of the Finance (No 2) Act 1992) which provided, with retrospective effect, that the Treasury Orders held to be *ultra vires* in *Woolwich* 'shall be taken to be and always to have been effective'. The effect of the new section 64 was to extinguish proceedings lodged by any other applicants for judicial review and restitution. In *National & Provincial Building Society v United Kingdom* (1998) 25 EHRR 127 the European Court of Human Rights held that this retrospective legislation was not inconsistent with the European Convention on Human Rights.

3. Some of the obiter dicta in this case seem to provide support for Birks' 'absence of basis' approach to unjust enrichment. For instance, Lord Browne-Wilkinson said that there was a stream of authority 'founded on the concept that money paid under and *ultra vires* demand for a tax or other impost has been paid without consideration'. This obiter dictum was relied upon by Hobhouse J and the Court of Appeal in *Westdeutsche Landesbank Girozentrale v Islington London Borough Council* [1994] 1 WLR 938, 944–5, 953 (above, 362–367). The decision of Hobhouse J, based upon absence of consideration, was one of the reasons Birks said that English law had 'changed direction'. Lord Goff also referred to the 'formidable argument' that 'money paid to a public authority pursuant to an *ultra vires* demand should be repayable . . . on the simple ground that there was no consideration for the payment.' However, Lord Goff also said that English law 'might have developed so as to recognise a *condictio indebiti*—an action for the recovery of money on the ground that it was not due. But it did not do so'.

4. Even if mistake of law had been a recognized unjust factor in 1993, *Woolwich* could not have relied upon mistake as the unjust factor because it had disputed the validity of the regulations from the outset. If it is accepted that in English law an unjust factor is required, was the unjust factor in *Woolwich*

     (a) duress? In particular, Lord Slynn suggested that the facts of the case 'shaded into' duress. Lord Goff analysed *Steele v Williams* as a case in which there was an '*implied* threat by the defendant to deprive the plaintiff's clerk of his right to take extracts from the parish register for no charge' (emphasis added) although his Lordship also said that 'logic appears to demand that the right of recovery should require neither mistake nor compulsion'. Lord Browne-Wilkinson also suggested that 'both the concept of want of consideration and implied compulsion are in play.'

(b) failure of consideration? Lord Browne-Wilkinson suggested that there was 'a close analogy to the right to recover money paid under a contract the consideration for which has wholly failed.' Did Lord Browne-Wilkinson mean that the *basis* upon which the payments were made—for a tax—had failed (see the discussion of the meaning of failure of consideration, above, 251)?

(c) a policy-motivated unjust factor based upon the *ultra vires* nature of the demand by the Revenue? In particular, Lord Goff relied upon 'one of the most fundamental principles of our law . . . that taxes should not be levied without the authority of Parliament.'

5. If the *Woolwich* principle is an independent unjust factor, can a claimant bring an alternative claim for restitution based on a different unjust factor such as mistake of law? This was the issue that arose in *Deutsche Morgan Grenfell Group plc v Inland Revenue Commissioners* [2005] EWCA Civ 78; [2006] Ch 243. Deutsche Morgan Group (DMG) made payments of income tax in 1993, 1995 and 1996. Provisions in the *Income and Corporation Taxes Act 1988* allowed companies with a UK parent to make an election to defer those payments but DMG's parent company was German so it could not make an election. In March 2001, the European Court of Justice in *Metallgesellschaft Ltd v Inland Revenue Commissioners and Attorney General and Hoechst AG v Inland Revenue and Attorney General* C–397/98 and C–410/98 [2001] STC 452 held that the group income election provisions of ICTA contravened freedom of establishment provisions in the EC Treaty. DMG brought an action for restitution of interest on the money for the period for which it would have deferred payment to the Revenue. One issue before the Court of Appeal was whether DMG's 1993 payment was time-barred. The claim was brought in October 2000, more than 6 years after the payment. DMG relied upon the decision of the House of Lords in *Kleinwort Benson Ltd v Lincoln City Council* [1999] 2 AC 349 (above, 167) and argued that its claim fell within an extension period in section 32(1)(c) of the *Limitation Act* because it was seeking relief from the consequences of a mistake. However, the Court of Appeal accepted the argument of the Commissioners that DMG had a (statute-barred) claim under the *Woolwich* principle and that if a *Woolwich* claim could be brought then it was not possible to bring an alternative action based on mistake of law. Therefore, the extended limitation period was unavailable because this was not an action involving relief from the consequences of a mistake. In their judgments in the Court of Appeal, Jonathan Parker LJ and Buxton LJ (Rix LJ agreeing with both on this issue) relied heavily on an obiter dictum of Lord Goff in *Kleinwort Benson Ltd v Lincoln City Council* (above, 167) where Lord Goff said that

> in our law of restitution we now find two separate and distinct regimes in respect of the requirement of money paid under a mistake of law. These are (1) cases concerned with the repayment of taxes and other similar charges which, when exacted ultra vires, are recoverable as of right at common law under the principle in *Woolwich*, and otherwise are the subject of statutory regimes regulatory recovery; and (2) other cases, which may broadly be described as concerned with repayment of money paid under private transactions, and which are governed by the common law.

However, as the trial judge, Park J, said ([2003] EWHC 79 (Ch)), if Lord Goff had had that in his mind he would surely have said so in his discussion of the operation of mistake of law rather than in three paragraphs relating to a 'settled understanding of the law' defence. Rather, Park J stated that (at [18])

> In the context I do not believe that Lord Goff was saying that there could never be a restitutionary claim for tax paid by mistake. Rather he was observing that, although there could be such a claim, the courts might at some future time have to consider whether there was also a settled law defence.

At the time of writing it is anticipated that the House of Lords will hear an appeal in July 2006 from the decision of the Court of Appeal. The argument before the House of Lords on this issue—that there should be a rigid separation of the private and public law of unjust enrichment—is supported by R Williams, 'The Beginnings of a Public Law of Unjust

Enrichment' (2005) 16 *KCLJ* 194 who argues that the existence of the public law action should exclude the private law one. On the other hand, A Burrows, 'Restitution in respect of mistakenly paid tax' (2005) 121 *LQR* 540, 542–3 and J Edelman, 'Limitation periods and the theory of unjust enrichment' (2005) 68 *MLR* 849, 851 argue that there is no reason of principle why one unjust factor should exclude another.

6. Professor Beatson states (1993) 109 *LQR* 401, 403) that *Woolwich* itself concerned 'payments made pursuant to (a) a demand for, (b) tax that was, (c) *ultra vires* because of, (d) the invalidity of the relevant subordinate legislation'. Which, if any, of these requirements are essential ingredients of a *Woolwich*-type claim? Must there be:

(a) *A demand.* In most cases, as in *Woolwich* itself, the payment will have been preceded by a demand for payment. But what is the position of the payer who takes the initiative and makes the payment before any demand is made of her? This may seem an unlikely scenario but it is likely to become a more regular occurrence in a self-assessment tax system. If we adhere to the principle that there should be 'no taxation without Parliament' does the fact that there has been no demand for the payment really matter? On the other hand, can it be said that a person who pays in anticipation of a demand has thereby waived her right to recover the payment?

(b) *Tax.* How far, if at all, does the principle extend beyond demands for payments other than tax? Lord Browne-Wilkinson in his speech referred to 'a tax or other impost'. What is the difference between a tax and an impost? And can they, in turn, be distinguished from a 'levy'. The possible range of charges can be demonstrated by reference to the cases which were discussed in *Woolwich* itself. Thus *Steele v Williams* (1853) 8 Ex. 625 concerned an unlawful charge for taking extracts from a parish register, while *Queens of the River Steamship Co. Ltd v Conservators of the River Thames* (1889) 15 TLR 474 concerned an excessive charge for making use of pier facilities. Do these cases fall within the scope of the *Woolwich* principle? Another instructive example is provided by *South of Scotland Electricity Board v British Oxygen Co. Ltd* [1959] 1 WLR 587, in which the pursuers, who were 'high voltage' consumers (as opposed to 'low voltage' consumers), claimed that the Electricity Board had exercised 'undue discrimination' against them and other high voltage consumers, contrary to section 37(8) of the Electricity Act 1947. The House of Lords allowed a proof before answer on the issue of 'undue discrimination' but they also held that, if such a claim were made out, the pursuers were entitled to recover the amounts which they had been overcharged. Lord Goff treated this as a case which fell within the following principle: 'money paid to a person for the performance of a statutory duty, which he is bound to perform for a sum less than that charged by him, is also recoverable to the extent of the overcharge'. On the other hand, Lord Keith and Lord Jauncey appeared to suggest that the case was closer to duress (a payment to avoid 'unpleasant consequences') or to the *colore officii* line of cases. But does this case fall within the *Woolwich* principle?

The vital question may be asked in different ways. Is it the nature of the body or the nature of the payment which is relevant? For example, is a local authority within the scope of the principle for all cases or does it fall within the scope of the principle only when it is acting as a 'public body' and not when it is acting in a 'commercial capacity'? What is the position of a nationalized industry or a public utility which levies a charge which is in excess of that which has been authorized? It can be argued that the degree of inequality between an individual and a multi-national or other large commercial entity is as great as the inequality which exists between an individual and a public authority. On the other hand, it may be said that this invocation of inequality as the vital factor misses the point. It can be argued that the reasoning of the House of Lords in *Woolwich* gives 'primacy to the principle of legality and the need to ensure adherence to the jurisdictional limits of the power of the state and its emanations rather than to a broad notion of inequality' (Beatson, (1993) 109 *LQR* 401, 412) and that the *Woolwich* principle should apply 'to . . . public bodies whose authority to charge is subject to and limited by public law principles, and to other bodies whose authority to charge is solely the product of statute, and thus limited' (Beatson, 417–18). Another formulation of the potential scope of the principle was set out by Glidewell LJ in the Court of Appeal in *Woolwich* in the following terms (79):

> I think it right to draw a distinction between cases in which a plaintiff claims restitution, i.e. repayment from a defendant who is a private citizen or body or who, although acting on behalf of a public body, had received the payment in the course of a commercial transaction between them, and cases in which the defendant is an instrument or officer of central or local government, exercising a power to require payment of a tax, customs duty, licence fee or other similar impost. Cases in the first category are clearly part of ordinary private law. Cases in the second category, however, seem to me properly to fall in the sphere of what is now called public law. The main distinguishing feature between the two types of case is that in the public law cases there is no question of the defendant having given, offered or purported to give any consideration for the payment by the plaintiff. The payment is required under what purports to be a statutory power entitling the defendant to claim such a payment, sometimes in return for a licence, in other cases simply as part of a general power to levy a tax or customs duty.

Butler-Sloss LJ agreed with Glidewell LJ in the following terms (138): 'In the category of public law, someone with actual or ostensible authority to require payment in respect of tax, duty, licence fee or other payment on behalf of central or local government makes the demand for payment by a private individual or company or other organisation.' Do these dicta provide a sensible basis for ascertaining the scope of the *Woolwich* principle?

(c) and (d): *Ultra vires because of invalidity of the relevant subordinate legislation.* A number of questions arise here. Does the cause of the *ultra vires* matter? What is the position where the *ultra vires* quality of the demand stems from an error of law, an abuse of discretion, or possibly procedural unfairness? The inclination of the House of Lords was not to draw a distinction between the invalidity of the subordinate legislation and the misconstruction of a statute. This seems to be right: the issue should be the *ultra vires* nature of the demand, not the cause of the *ultra vires*.

7. If the claim is based on the *ultra vires* nature of the demand issued by the defendant, is the claim a public law one which is therefore governed by public law rules? Is judicial review a necessary preliminary to such a restitutionary claim and do the rules of procedure set out in CPR Part 54 (previously RSC Ord 53) apply to such a claim? The speech of Lord Goff is rather ambivalent on this point but Lord Slynn stated that 'if a claim lies for money had and received, judicial review adds nothing'. The latter view, namely that judicial review is not a prerequisite, appears to be more in line with the more relaxed approach to the *O'Reilly v Mackman* [1983] 2 AC 236 exclusivity doctrine adopted by the House of Lords in *Roy v Kensington and Chelsea and Westminster Family Practitioner Committee* [1992] 1 AC 624 (a case which is discussed in more detail by P Cane [1992] PL 193 and S Fredman and G Morris (1992) 108 *LQR* 353) and *Mercury Communications Ltd v Director General of Telecommunications* [1996] 1 WLR 250. The approach which their Lordships have taken is to consider whether it would be an 'abuse of process' to litigate the claim by ordinary private law means. The application of this approach to *Woolwich*-type claims for restitution was confirmed in *British Steel plc v Customs and Excise Commissioners* [1997] 2 All ER 366. British Steel paid excise duty on hydrocarbon oil used in its blast furnaces. The payment was accompanied by a protest by the company that pursuant to section 9(1) of the Hydrocarbon Oil Duties Act 1979 entitled it relief from the duty on the ground that the oil was not used as fuel. The Commissioners of Customs & Excise rejected the protest. British Steel challenged

this result by bringing a private law action for restitution of the excise duty which it claimed had been unlawfully demanded. A preliminary issue was whether it was open to the claimant to challenge the Commissioners' decision otherwise than by way of judicial review. The trial judge held that the claim could only be pursued in proceedings for judicial review. The Court of Appeal disagreed. Sir Richard Scott VC (Saville LJ agreeing and Millett LJ delivering a concurring judgment) held that British Steel was not restricted to such repayment remedy as is provided by the Act and could bring a common law action for restitution (at 376):

> In the present case, if the demands for excise duty were unlawful, the payer would, in my judgment, have a prima facie common law right to repayment. I would not construe section 9(4) as removing that common law right. First, the common law right is not expressly removed. Second, section 9(4) does not purport to constitute a comprehensive statutory scheme for recovery of excise duty paid but not due.

A useful note on this decision is N Bamforth, 'Restitution and the scope of judicial review' [1997] *PL* 603.

8. Could Woolwich have brought a proprietary claim against the Inland Revenue? In *Zaidan Group Ltd v City of London* (1987) 36 DLR (4th) 443, the claimant overpaid municipal taxes. At trial Barr J held that the City was a constructive trustee of the overpayment for the claimant so that the claimant was entitled to recover the interest which the City had earned on the money. However, the constructive trust argument was abandoned in the Ontario Court of Appeal, (1990) 64 DLR (4th) 514, and so the point was never resolved (the claimant's personal restitutionary claim also failed on the facts because it was held that the common law had been superceded by the statutory regime). On what basis (if any) could Woolwich have argued that it was entitled to bring a proprietary claim (see further Chapter 13)?

9. What defences should exist to this claim? The issue was not before their Lordships in *Woolwich* and so must await another day for definitive resolution. One of the key defences is likely to be change of position (discussed in more detail in Chapter 14), but the application of this defence to public authorities is by no means easy (see, for example, *Westdeutsche Landesbank Girozentrale v Islington London Borough Council* [1994] 4 All ER 890, 946–54) and, indeed the Law Commission in its report (cited above, note 1) recommended that there should be no provision for the defence in its proposed statutory scheme (paragraphs 11.10–17 and 11.31). Another possible defence is 'passing on' (discussed in more detail below, at 870–883) but, in the light of the decision of the Court of Appeal in *Kleinwort Benson Ltd v Birmingham City Council* (see below, 871), it seems unlikely that the defence will have any role to play in English law. Another defence, favoured by Birks ([1992] *PL* 580, 590), is 'a relatively short period of limitation' which, he argues, 'will provide the best means of reconciling the competing interests'.

It is also noteworthy that jurisdictions which have recognized the existence of more generous rights of recovery have often confined that right within very narrow compass (to the point of emasculating the new right), through the recognition of generous defences in an effort to ensure that public finances are not subject to excessive disruption. A good example of this process is provided by *Air Canada v British Columbia* [1989] ISCR 1161 (a case which is usefully analysed by Lord Goff in his speech). Should the English courts adopt a similar approach?

10. One of the most difficult defences to apply is the defence of 'honest settlement of a claim' (which is discussed in more detail by S Arrowsmith, 'Mistake and the Role of the Submission to an Honest Claim' in A Burrows (ed.), *Essays on the Law of Restitution* (1991), chapter 2, and see also above, 167, note 2). The defence of honest settlement of a claim might be seen as lying on a scale of defences concerned with finality of transactions. At one extreme is compromise of a claim which leads to the entry of a judgment by consent in favour of one party. The judgment will stand as a *res judicata* defence to a claim by the other party including for restitution of unjust enrichment. A related defence might apply where litigation is settled and the action merely discontinued by agreement. In *Brennan v Bolt Burdon (a firm)* [2004] EWCA Civ 1017; [2005] QB 303 (see above, 183) at 317 [23], Maurice Kay LJ said that

although counsel had not sought to argue that a mistake of law can never vitiate such an agreement, 'I suspect that there is scope for a substantive exception to the ambit of mistake of law as a matter of policy in such circumstances'. Bodey J (at 322 [52]) agreed that such a defence 'might well have provided a more simple answer to this appeal.' At the other extreme of possible defences concerned with finality is an 'honest belief in entitlement'. Such a defence was rejected by the House of Lords in *Kleinwort Benson Ltd v Lincoln City Council* [1999] 2 AC 349 (above, 167). The defence of honest settlement of a claim lies closer on this spectrum to recognized defences of *res judicata* and discontinuance of a claim than to the rejected defence of honest belief in entitlement. Indeed, in *Brennan v Bolt Burdon (a firm)*, Sedley LJ (at 323 [61]) said that he could see no principled way of distinguishing between a settlement of threatened litigation (the usual case of honest settlement of a claim) and settlement and discontinuance of extant litigation.

Woolwich itself was obviously not a case in which the payment was made in honest settlement of a claim because Woolwich always challenged the validity of the regulation and it applied for judicial review on the day after it made the first payment. The vast majority of claimants will not be so assiduous. But will a delay in challenging the validity of the demand lead to the conclusion that the payment was made in honest settlement of a claim? Leaving aside arguments about the scope of the defence, can it be argued that this defence ought not to have any role to play in these cases at all? It has been argued (A Burrows, 'Public Authorities, Ultra Vires and Restitution' in A Burrows (ed), *Essays on the Law of Restitution* (1991), 61) that 'if the *ultra vires* theory holds good on the ground that there should be no taxation without Parliament the voluntariness of the payor should be irrelevant'. Do you agree? A useful case to consider when contemplating the possible role of a defence of submission to an honest claim is *William Whiteley v The King* (1909) 101 LT 741, where the suppliants sought to recover taxes which they had paid to the Inland Revenue in respect of cooks and waiters in their employment whom the Revenue had insisted were 'male servants'. The suppliants paid the sums demanded for a period of time, feeling that they had no alternative but to do so. Eventually, however, they decided to resist payment. In the resultant proceedings it was held by the Divisional Court that the employees were not 'male servants'. The suppliants then brought a petition of right to recover the sums which they had overpaid. Walton J held that they were not entitled to recover the sums so overpaid.

Walton J: Those being the facts, I have to decide whether under those circumstances the duties so paid during those six years can be recovered back. Undoubtedly the moneys were paid under a mistaken belief on the part of Messrs Whiteley Limited that they were bound to pay them; but there is no general rule that if duties are paid to the Inland Revenue by mistake as to liability—by mistake as to law—they can be recovered back. In fact the general rule is the other way—namely, that if they have been voluntarily paid under a mistake, a mistake not of fact but a mistake of law, then they cannot be recovered back. It is not suggested in this case that there was any mistake in fact, and as I understand the position taken by the suppliants, they admit that if these duties had been paid, without any communication with the officials of Inland Revenue and merely by mistake on the part of the suppliants as to their liability, they could not be recovered back. Therefore the question is whether, having regard to what did take place between the suppliants and the officers of Inland Revenue, which I have, I think, stated quite fully, the suppliants can recover these moneys back. There is doubt as to the general rule stated in Leake on Contracts to which I have already referred, that money paid voluntarily—that is to say, without compulsion or extortion or undue influence, and, of course, I may add without any fraud on the part of the person to whom it is paid, and with knowledge of all the facts, though paid without any consideration, or in discharge of a claim not due, or a claim which might have been successfully resisted, cannot be recovered back. There is no doubt, and no question raised, that that is an accurate statement of the general rule. But on the other hand, if the payment is not voluntary a different rule applies which may be stated, perhaps, as it is stated in Leake on Contracts (5th edit., 61), that money extorted by a person for doing what he is legally bound to do without payment, or for a duty which he fails to perform, may be recovered back; as in the cases of illegal or excessive fees and payments extorted in the discharge of an office; and money paid under duress either of the person or of goods may be recovered back (58, 59). In all those cases the payment is not voluntary. The question which I have to decide here is whether the payments made during the years which I have mentioned—from 1900 to 1905—were or were not voluntary payments. Was there any duress here? I cannot find any evidence of duress or compulsion beyond this, that the supervisor, the officer of Inland Revenue, told Messrs Whiteley Limited that in the opinion of the Commissioners of Inland Revenue these duties were payable, and that if they were not paid proceedings would be taken for penalties. That is the only evidence of anything which could be called duress or compulsion. The suppliants knew all the facts. They had present to their minds plainly, when these payments were made, that there was a question as to whether upon such servants as those in question duty was payable. They themselves raised that question and they paid the duties. They could have resisted payment. They must have known that if proceedings were taken for penalties it would be open to them in such proceedings to raise the question as to whether the duties were payable or not, as they did, in fact, in 1906. They must have known and must have had present to their minds all that. I think the most that took place was this, that the officer of Inland Revenue told the suppliants that in his opinion and in the opinion of the Commissioners of Inland Revenue the duties were payable. The suppliants knew that that was only an expression of opinion. They knew that the Commissioners of Inland Revenue could not determine whether the duties were payable or not. They could take no action if the duties were not paid except by legal proceedings. They could not distrain if the suppliants did not make a declaration in respect of these servants. In these circumstances I have come to the conclusion that there was nothing in this case which amounted to compulsion. But it was suggested that the case came within that class of cases in which money has been held to be recoverable back if it has been paid in discharge of a demand illegally made under colour of an office. Those cases are referred to in Bullen and Leake, 3rd edit., 1868, 50, in the notes to the counts for money received. The rule as to money paid in discharge of a demand and made under colour of an office is, I think very clearly explained by the paragraph in the notes which says (50): 'This count will lie for money paid by the plaintiff in discharge of a demand illegally made under colour of an office; as excessive fees paid to the steward of a manor for admission to copyholds; excessive fees paid to a broker under a distress; overcharges paid to a carrier to induce him to carry goods, an excessive charge paid to an arbitrator to take up an award; money improperly exacted as a toll at a turnpike'. Those seem to me all to come within that class of cases to which I have just referred, which is described in Leake on Contracts (5th edit., 61) in these words: 'Money extorted by a person for doing what he is legally bound to do without payment, or for a duty which he fails to perform, may be recovered back.' In all those cases in order to have that done which the person making the payment was entitled to have done without a payment, he had to make the payment, and someone who was bound to do something which the person paying the money desired to have done, refused to do his duty unless he was paid the money. If in those circumstances money is paid, then it can be recovered back. There is there an element of duress. I need not go through the cases or refer to them in detail. I am satisfied that this case does not fall within that class of cases, and that neither on that ground nor on the ground that this was a compulsory payment are the suppliants entitled to recover back the moneys which they paid in the circumstances which I have described. I think, therefore, that this petition must be dismissed and there must be judgment for the Crown.

In the light of the decision of the House of Lords in *Woolwich* was *William Whiteley v The King* (a) wrongly decided or (b) an example of a payment in honest settlement of a claim? If the latter, what evidence is there that the suppliants paid in settlement of the claim made? How did Lord Goff and Lord Slynn interpret the case? Another case which is worthy of fresh examination is *Twyford v Manchester Corporation* [1946] Ch 236. How would it be decided today?

11. One of the most important questions is: how can the new common law right in *Woolwich* be reconciled with the existing patchwork of statutory rights to recover taxes which have been overpaid? This issue did in fact surface before their Lordships as one of the issues which they had to consider was whether or not Woolwich had a statutory right to the return of the money together with interest. Their Lordships concluded that Woolwich did not have such a statutory right because section 33 of the Taxes Management Act 1970 was inapplicable since, *inter alia*, there had been no assessment made by the Revenue as required by the section. But the relationship between the statutory rights of recovery and the new restitutionary right is a

difficult one and it is helpfully discussed by J Beatson (1993) 109 LQR 401, 418–25. The consequence is that the law is left in an unsatisfactory state and, as Lord Goff acknowledged, it may well be that the task of producing 'appropriate limits to recovery, on a coherent system of principles suitable for modern society' is one which can be carried out most effectively by the 'authorities . . . in collaboration with the Law Commission'.

In 1994 the Law Commission produced a report in which this issue was considered (cited above, note 1). Although the recommendations of the Law Commission have not been implemented (and although there have been some minor amendments to the relevant legislation since the Law Commission's Report, e.g. section 117(3) of the Finance Act 1998 has amended section 33 of the Taxes Management Act 1970 and section 80 of the Value Added Tax Act 1994 has been amended by the Finance Act 1997, ss. 46–47) those recommendations are useful to consider as a suggestion for a coherent regime to replace the existing patchwork of legislation. The Law Commission did not recommend codification of the *Woolwich* right of recovery because of difficulties of definition (paragraph 8.14). Instead, it advocated a threefold approach. First, a single legislative regime should apply in relation to overpaid central and local government taxes and income tax paid under the self-assessment scheme and a similar regime should apply for inheritance tax and stamp duty. This regime would allow recovery of overpaid tax subject to defences including defences of non-exhaustion of statutory remedies and rights of appeal (proposed section 33AA(2),(3)), contractual compromise and submission to proceedings brought by the Inland Revenue Commissioners (proposed section 33AA(4)) passing on (proposed section 33AA(5)) and a defence broadly concerned with payments made in accordance with a settled view of the law (proposed section 33AA(6)). Second, the current regime in relation to revenue laws such as VAT should remain separate and regulated by separate statutory provisions as a 'complex body of revenue law already exists' (paragraph 8.24). The present law in this area was framed closely to accord with European Community law and the Commissioner of Customs and Excise was satisfied with the operation of the law (paragraph 14.19). However, the Law Commission recommended that some revenue laws, such as excise duties, should be governed by similar legislative provisions to section 80 of the Value Added Tax Act 1994. Third, in relation to *ultra vires* receipts by public authorities which do not fall within the scope of specific statutory provisions, these should be governed by the common law rules developed from the *Woolwich* and subsequent cases.

13

TRACING AND
PROPRIETARY RESTITUTION

While we find it convenient to link together, in this single Chapter, tracing and propri-etary restitution (because equitable tracing commonly leads to proprietary restitution), we must emphasize at the outset that the two are not inextricably linked. A claimant who is seeking a personal restitutionary remedy may have to satisfy the tracing rules and, indeed, at common law, tracing leads to a personal, and not a proprietary, restitutionary remedy (normally the award of money in an action for money had and received).

1. TRACING

Tracing can perhaps best be described as the technique or process by which a person can identify property as being a *substitute* for property that he 'owned' (or still 'owns'). Where a person's property has been replaced by other property, the rules of tracing lay down whether the 'replacement' property counts in law as a substitute for the person's original property.

Lionel Smith, *The Law of Tracing* (1997) (and below, 700) has convincingly argued (and this was explicitly accepted by Lord Millett in *Foskett v McKeown*, below, 678) that tracing is to be distinguished from 'following' and 'claiming'.

If B steals A's bike and gives it to C and C gives it to D, A may be able to 'follow' the bike into D's hands. But this is not tracing because the property is the same (the bike) and A is simply following it into a new person's hands. Tracing is concerned with new property, not new people. Tracing must also be distinguished from 'claiming' because being able to identify property that is a substitute does not necessarily mean that the claimant has any rights/remedies in relation to that substitute property. Nor does it tell you whether the claimant's rights/remedies in relation to the substitute are personal or proprietary nor what the basis is of those rights/remedies.

In our view, tracing is part of the law of restitution reversing an unjust enrich-ment where a claimant is given a proprietary or personal right/remedy in respect of substitute property provided the substitution has been *unauthorized*. The substitutionary connection (sometimes referred to as the 'transactional link') to the claimant's original property goes to establish that the defendant's receipt or retention of property was *at the expense of the claimant* in the subtractive sense. The fact that the substitution was unauthorized, rather than consensual, means that the unjust factor normally in play is (we would argue) ignorance or powerlessness (that is, the claimant does not know about, or is powerless to prevent, his property being substituted). Ignorance as an unjust factor has been explained in detail in Chapter 4 above: for powerlessness, see above, 225, note 4.

It is an important linked point that for the traceable substitute to be at the claimant's expense, rather than at the expense of the person who has effected the substitution (whether the defendant or a third party), the claimant must establish that it had (legal or equitable) title to the property in the substituting person's hands immediately prior to the substitution. Say, for example, C transfers £1,000 to D by a mistake which is not a sufficient mistake to prevent legal title in the £1,000 passing to D. D obtains a car worth £5,000 in exchange for the £1,000. Even if the tracing rules are satisfied, C has no claim to the car, or its value, against D (or against a third party to whom D has given the car). The reason is that the substitute property (the car) was not gained at the expense of C. This is because C did not have title to the £1,000 in D's hands immediately prior to its substitution by the car. If the mistake was sufficiently fundamental to prevent legal title to the £1,000 passing to D, the position would be different. Then, if the tracing rules are satisfied, C would prima facie have a claim in unjust enrichment to the car or its value, against D. The car would have been retained, or received, at C's expense.

Tracing to an unauthorized substitute is normally invoked by a claimant who seeks proprietary restitution (whether through a trust or equitable lien) in respect of the substitute property retained by the defendant. But it may also be invoked with the aim of seeking personal restitution (for example, an award of money had and received or an equitable accounting) in respect of the substitute property received by the defendant (where that property has reached the defendant from a third party). Many of the cases in Chapter 4, including *Lipkin Gorman v Karpnale Ltd*, therefore involved tracing even though personal restitution only was sought.

Unfortunately the House of Lords in *Foskett v McKeown* (below, 678) rejected an unjust enrichment justification of tracing to unauthorised substitutes. Their Lordships instead viewed tracing as an aspect of 'property law not unjust enrichment' and as explicable by nothing more than the persistence of pre-existing proprietary rights.

General Reading

BURROWS, 78–104; GOFF AND JONES, 2-021 to 2-053; VIRGO, 619–635.

(1) TRACING AT COMMON LAW

While money can be traced at common law into its substitute product, the conventional wisdom is that one cannot trace money at common law once the money has been mixed with other money (see, for example, *Agip (Africa) Ltd v Jackson*, below, 650). To adopt Lionel Smith's terminology of 'clean' and 'mixed' substitutions in *The Law of Tracing* (1997), 133–4, the conventional wisdom is that the common law recognizes only clean substitutions. This is traditionally thought to contrast with tracing in equity where one can trace into a mixed fund (i.e. mixed substitutions are recognized). Such a difference of approach between law and equity is irrational and obiter dicta of Lord Steyn and Lord Millett in *Foskett v McKeown* (below, 678) support the fusion of the tracing rules (enabling equity's more generous rules to be applied to common law claims). Unfortunately one cannot yet say that differences between tracing at common law and in equity have been authoritatively abolished. So at the present time it would appear to remain the law that, if the defendant steals £1,000 from the claimant and uses the same £1,000 to buy a car, the claimant can trace at common law into the car. But if the defendant steals £1,000 from the claimant, mixes it with £100 of his own, and uses the £1,100 to buy a car, the claimant cannot trace at common law into either the £1,100 or the car. Even accepting that traditional restriction, however, cases like *Banque Belge v Hambrouck*, *Lipkin Gorman v Karpnale*, and *Jones v Jones*, below, 650–651, indicate that common law tracing may have a more vital role than is sometimes thought. In these cases, common law tracing into and through bank accounts was held to be possible. It should also be noted that while, after tracing, proprietary remedies in respect of money can be awarded in equity, this is not so at common law (that is, there is no common law proprietary remedy for the restitution of money, the action for money had and received being a personal remedy).

- *Taylor v Plumer* (1815) 3 M & S 562, King's Bench Division

Sir Thomas Plumer (the defendant) gave his broker, Walsh, a bank draft for £22,000 for the express purpose of investing the money in Exchequer bills. Walsh had become insolvent and decided to abscond with the money. He therefore invested only £6,500 in bills which he deposited with the bank, and used the rest to buy US securities and bullion. He was apprehended at Falmouth prior to boarding a ship to the United States and Plumer's agent seized the securities and bullion. The claimants, Walsh's assignees in bankruptcy, brought an action in trover (now the tort of conversion) claiming that the securities and bullion belonged to Walsh, and hence to them, and not to the defendant. Their claim failed.

Lord Ellenborough CJ: . . . [T]he plaintiff in this case is not entitled to recover if the defendant has succeeded in maintaining these propositions in point of law, viz. that the property of a principal entrusted by him to his factor for any special purpose belongs to the principal, notwithstanding any change which that property may have undergone in point of form, so long as such property is capable of being identified, and distinguished from all other property. And, secondly, that all property thus circumstanced is equally recoverable from the assignees of the factor, in the event of his becoming a bankrupt, as it was from the factor himself before his bankruptcy. And, indeed, upon a view of the authorities, and consideration of the arguments, it should seem that if the property in its original state and form was covered with a trust in favour of the principal, no change of that state and form can divest it of such trust, or give the factor, or those who represent him in right, any other more valid claim in respect to it, than they respectively had before such change. An abuse of trust can confer no rights on the party abusing it, nor on those who claim in privity with him. The argument which has been advanced in favour of the plaintiffs, that the property of the principal continues only so long as the authority of the principal is pursued in respect to the order and disposition of it, and that it ceases when the property is tortiously converted into another form for the use of the factor himself, is mischievous in principle, and supported by no authorities of law. And the position which was held out in argument on the part of the plaintiffs, as being the untenable result of the arguments on the part of the defendant, is no doubt a result deducible from those arguments: but unless it be a result at variance with the law, the plaintiffs are not on that account entitled to recover. The contention on the part of the defendant was represented by the plaintiff's counsel as pushed to what he conceived to be an extravagant length, in the defendant's counsel being obliged to contend, that 'if A is trusted by B with money to purchase a horse for him, and he purchases a carriage with that money, that B is entitled to the carriage.' And, indeed, if he be not so entitled, the case on the part of the defendant appears to be hardly sustainable in argument. It makes no difference in reason or law into what other form, different from the original, the change may have been made, whether it be into that of promissory notes for the security of the money which was produced by the sale of the goods of the principal, as in *Scott v Surman*, Willes, 400, or into other merchandize, as in *Whitecomb v Jacob*, Salk. 160, for the product of or substitute for the original thing still follows the nature of the thing itself, as long as it can be ascertained to be such, and the right only ceases when the means of ascertainment fail, which is the case when the subject is turned into money, and mixed and confounded in a general mass of the same description. The difficulty which arises in such a case is a difficulty of fact and not of law, and the dictum that money has no ear-mark must be understood in the same way; i.e. as predicated only of an undivided and undistinguishable mass of current money. But money in a bag, or otherwise kept apart from other money, guineas, or other coin marked (if the fact were so) for the purpose of being distinguished, are so far earmarked as to fall within the rule on this subject, which applies to every other description of personal property whilst it remains, (as the property in question did,) in the hands of the factor, or his general legal representatives. [*Lord Ellenborough then considered the authorities and continued:*] He [Plumer] has repossessed himself of that, of which, according to the principles established in the cases I have cited, he never ceased to be the lawful proprietor; and having so done we are of opinion, that the assignees cannot in this action recover that which, if an action were brought against them the assignees by the defendant, they could not have effectually retained against him, inasmuch as it was trust property of the defendant, which, as such, did not pass to them under the commission. If this case had rested on the part of the defendant on any supposed adoption and ratification on his part of the act of converting the produce of the draft or bank-notes of the defendant into these American certificates, we think, it could not have been well supported on that ground, inasmuch as the defendant, by taking a security by bond and judgment to indemnify himself against the pecuniary loss he had sustained by that very act, must be understood to have disapproved and disallowed that act instead of adopting and confirming it; but upon the other grounds above stated, we are of opinion that the defendant is entitled to retain the subjects of the present suit, and of course that a nonsuit must be entered.

NOTES AND QUESTIONS

1. This case is often regarded as showing: (i) that one can trace at common law into substitute property but (ii), applying Lord Ellenborough's dicta on 'identification', that one cannot trace at common law into a mixed fund. Lionel Smith, 'Tracing in *Taylor v Plumer*, Equity in the Court of King's Bench' [1995] *LMCLQ* 240 argues that the decision was based on the assertion of equitable proprietary rights in the proceeds of a disposition by a defaulting fiduciary and therefore says nothing about common law tracing. This thesis was explicitly accepted by Millett LJ in *Jones v Jones*, see below, 651. A similar conclusion is arrived at by S Khurshid and P Matthews, 'Tracing Confusion' (1979) 95 *LQR* 78: but while their approach is to dismiss common law tracing into substitutes as having no sound basis, Smith's agenda is to show that common law and equitable tracing are not as different as is traditionally thought.

2. In this case the questions of tracing and unjust enrichment arose in respect of Walsh's unjust enrichment at the expense of Plumer. Plumer's self-help remedy in taking the securities and bullion was consequently held to be justified so that he had a defence to an action in tort for wrongful interference with these goods. Is the best analysis that Walsh was unjustly enriched at Plumer's expense because, unknown to Plumer, Walsh had taken his money and substituted it for securities and bullion (that is, an 'unjust factor' of ignorance with tracing being relevant to establish that the securities were gained at the expense of Plumer)?

- *Banque Belge pour l'Etranger v Hambrouck* [1921] 1 KB 321, Court of Appeal

See above, 204.

- *Agip (Africa) Ltd v Jackson* [1991] Ch 547, Court of Appeal

See above, 209.

NOTES AND QUESTIONS

At first instance in *Agip*, Millett J had held that tracing at common law was not possible because the payment from Banque du Sud to Lloyds Bank was by telegraphic transfer, so that only 'a stream of electrons' and not a physical asset had passed between the banks. Fox LJ appeared to disapprove of this when he said, 'I do not think that it matters that the order was not a cheque. It was a direction by the account holder to the bank': see above, 212. Why, then, according to Fox LJ was Millett J's conclusion correct that tracing at common law was not possible (see E McKendrick above, 216–217)?

- *Lipkin Gorman v Karpnale Ltd* [1991] 2 AC 548, House of Lords

See above, 28.

NOTES AND QUESTIONS

1. It was conceded by the defendants that the money drawn out by Cass was not mixed with other money by Cass. Had that 'astonishing' concession not been made (see E McKendrick, 220 above), Lord Goff would, it seems, have taken the conventional view, that common law tracing would have been defeated.

2. How does Lord Goff's reasoning on common law tracing help to explain why tracing into and through a bank account is possible at common law?

- *Trustee of the Property of F C Jones and Sons (a firm) v Jones*
  [1996] 3 WLR 703, Court of Appeal

The partners in a potato-growing firm became bankrupt. After the act of bankruptcy, one of the partners (FWJ Jones) drew three cheques totalling £11,700 on the partnership account. He paid that money to his wife (Mrs Jones) who used it to trade on the potato futures market so that the £11,700 was turned into £50,760. She paid that sum into a deposit account at Raphaels & Sons plc. Mr F. W. J. Jones withdrew £900 from the account leaving a balance of £49,860. The Official Receiver informed Raphaels of his claim to that money and Raphaels interpleaded and paid the money into court. The rival claimants to the money were the trustee in bankruptcy (the claimant) and Mrs Jones (the defendant). At first instance the judge found in favour of the claimant. The defendant unsuccessfully appealed against that decision.

Millett LJ: . . . The trustee's case, as presently formulated, is simplicity itself. The money in court represents the proceeds of the defendant's successful speculation with the £11,700 which she received from her husband. The £11,700, in turn, was paid to her out of the joint account of two of the partners who were afterwards adjudicated bankrupt. The money was drawn from the joint account after the date of the act of bankruptcy on which the receiving order was made. All this is undisputed. But, says the trustee, the money in the joint account had already vested in him, for under section 37 of the Bankruptcy Act 1914 his title to the assets of the bankrupts related back to the date of the act of bankruptcy. Accordingly the defendant never acquired any title to the money. The money which she received from her husband belonged to the trustee, and the money in court represents the proceeds of her successful speculation with his money.

. . . .

Counsel for the defendant . . . concedes that the trustee's claim is bound to succeed in relation to the original sum of £11,700 with interest thereon. But, he submitted, the trustee cannot recover the profits which the defendant made by the use of the money because he cannot maintain a proprietary claim in equity, and he cannot maintain a proprietary claim in equity because he cannot establish the existence of a fiduciary relationship between the defendant and the trustee.

Counsel for the defendant submitted that all claims by a trustee or liquidator to recover payments to third parties, whether as fraudulent preferences (which are voidable) or as dispositions by a company made after the commencement of the winding up (which are void), must be made by way of an action for money had and received; that this, being an action at law, is a personal claim; that it does not matter whether the transaction which is impugned was void or merely voidable; and that, in the absence of a constructive trust or fiduciary relationship which would justify the intervention of equity, the trustee cannot recover the proceeds of the profitable investment by the recipient of the money which he received.

The judge thought that the defendant was a constructive trustee. He said:

'... the trustee really has no problem in establishing a fiduciary relationship. In my view where, as here (due to the effect of the doctrine of relation back), A pays B's money to C, B retains the beneficial title to the money and C becomes a bare trustee (see *Chase Manhattan Bank v Israel-British Bank* [1981] 1 Ch 105, 119.'

Founding himself on that reasoning, the deputy judge applied the equitable rules of tracing.

It is, however, in my view plain that the defendant did not receive the money in a fiduciary capacity and that she did not become a constructive trustee. The deputy judge's conclusion pre-supposes that A, who in this case is the bankrupt, had a legal title to transfer. In the present case, however, the bankrupts had been divested of all title by statute. Mr F. W. J. Jones had no title at all in law or equity to the money in the joint account at Midland Bank, and could confer no title on the defendant. While, however, I accept the submissions of counsel for the defendant that she did not become a constructive trustee, I do not accept the proposition that the trustee in bankruptcy is unable to recover the profits which the defendant made by the use of his money unless she can be shown to have received it in one or other of the two capacities mentioned; nor do I consider it necessary for him to invoke the assistance of equity in order to maintain his claim. In short, I do not accept the main submission of counsel that the only action at law which was available to the trustee was an action against the defendant for money had and received.

It is, in my view, unhelpful to categorize the payment of the £11,700 to the defendant as either 'void' or 'voidable'. Neither term is strictly accurate. In order to see why this is so it is necessary to consider the effect of the doctrine of relation back under the old bankruptcy law. [*Millett LJ considered cases on relation back in bankruptcy and continued*:]

Accordingly, as from the date of the act of bankruptcy the money in the bankrupts' joint account at the Midland Bank belonged to the trustee. The account holders had no title to it at law or in equity. The cheques which they drew in favour of the defendant were not 'void' or 'voidable' but, in the events which happened, they were incapable of passing any legal or equitable title. They were not, however, without legal effect, for the bank honoured them. The result was to affect the identity of the debtor but not the creditor and to put the defendant in possession of funds to which she had no title. . . .

What is the result? If the cheques had passed the legal title to the defendant but not the beneficial ownership, she would have received the money as constructive trustee and be liable to a proprietary restitutionary claim in equity (sometimes, though inaccurately, described as a tracing claim). The defendant would have been obliged, not merely to account for the £11,700 which she had received, but to hand over the £11,700 *in specie* to the trustee. Her position would have been no different from that of an express trustee who held the money in trust for the trustee; or from that of Mr Reid in *Attorney-General for Hong Kong v Reid* [1994] 1 AC 324, whose liability to account for the profits which he made from investing a bribe was based on his obligation to pay it over to his principal as soon as he received it. The existence of any such obligation has been disputed by commentators, but no one disputes that, if the obligation exists, it carries with it the duty to pay over or account for any profits made by the use of the money.

But the defendant was not a constructive trustee. She had no legal title to the money. She had no title to it at all. She was merely in possession, that is to say, in a position to deal with it even though it did not belong to her. Counsel for the defendant says that it follows that she cannot be made liable to any kind of proprietary claim. [*After distinguishing cases relied on by counsel for Mrs Jones, Millett LJ continued*:] The present case is entirely different. The defendant had no title at all, at law or in equity. If she became bankrupt, the money would not vest in her trustee. But this would not be because it was trust property: it would be because it was not her property at all. If she made a profit, how could she have any claim to the profit made by the use of someone else's money? In my judgment she could not. If she were to retain the profit made by the use of the trustee's money, then, in the language of the modern law of restitution, she would be unjustly enriched at the expense of the trustee. If she were a constructive trustee of the money, a court of equity, as a court of conscience, would say that it was unconscionable for her to lay claim to the profit made by the use of her beneficiary's money. It would, however, be a mistake to suppose that the common law courts disregarded considerations of conscience. Lord Mansfield CJ, who did much to develop the early law of restitution at common law, founded it firmly on the basis of good conscience and unjust enrichment. It would, in my judgment, be absurd if a person with no title at all were in a stronger position to resist a proprietary claim by the true owner than one with a bare legal title. In the present case equity has no role to play. The trustee must bring his claim at common law. It follows that, if he has to trace his money, he must rely on common law tracing rules, and that he has no proprietary *remedy*. But it does not follow that he has no proprietary *claim*. His claim is exclusively proprietary. He claims the money because it belongs to him at law or represents profits made by the use of money which belonged to him at law.

The trustee submits that he has no need to trace, since the facts are clear and undisputed. The defendant did not mix the money with her own. The trustee's money remained identifiable as such throughout. But of course he does have to trace it in order to establish that the money which he claims represents his money. Counsel for the defendant acknowledges that the trustee can successfully trace his money into her account at Raphaels, for his concession in respect of the £11,700 acknowledges this. . . .

[I]n my judgment the concession that the trustee can trace the money at common law is rightly made. There are no factual difficulties of the kind which proved fatal in this court to the common law claim in *Agip (Africa) Ltd v Jackson* [1991] Ch 547. It is not necessary to trace the passage of the money through the clearing system or the London potato futures market. The money which the defendant paid into her account with the commodity brokers represented the proceeds of cheques which she received from her husband. Those cheques represented money in the bankrupts' joint account at the Midland Bank which belonged to the trustee.

In *Lipkin Gorman v Karpnale Ltd* [1991] 2 AC 548, 573 Lord Goff of Chieveley held that the plaintiffs could trace or follow their 'property into its product' for this 'involves a decision by the owner of the original property to assert title to the product in place of his original property'. In that case the original property was the plaintiffs' chose in action, a debt owed by the bank to the plaintiffs. Lord Goff held, at 574, that the plaintiffs could: '. . . trace their property at common law in that chose in action, or in any part of it, into its product, i.e. cash drawn by Cass from their client account at the bank.'

Accordingly, the trustee can follow the money in the joint account at Midland Bank, which had been vested by statute in him, into the proceeds of the three cheques which the defendant received from her husband. The trustee does not need to follow the money from one recipient to another or follow it through the clearing system; he can follow the cheques as they pass from hand to hand. It is sufficient for him to be able to trace the money into the cheques and the cheques into their proceeds.

In *Agip (Africa) Ltd v Jackson* [1990] Ch 265, 285 I said that the ability of the common law to trace an asset into a changed form in the same hands was established in *Taylor v Plumer* (1815) 3 M. & S. 562. Lord Ellenborough CJ in that case had said, at 575:

> 'The product of or substitute for the original thing still follows the nature of the thing itself as long as it can be ascertained to be such and the right only ceases when the means of ascertainment fails, which is the case when the subject is turned into money and confined within the general mass of the same description.'

In this it appears that I fell into a common error, for it has since been convincingly demonstrated that, although *Taylor v Plumer* was decided by a common law court, the court was in fact applying the rules of equity: see Lionel Smith: 'Tracing in *Taylor v Plumer*: Equity in the King's Bench' (1995) *LMCLQ* 240.

But this is no reason for concluding that the common law does not recognize claims to substitute assets or their products. Such claims were upheld by this court in *Banque Belge Pour l'Etranger v Hambrouck* [1921] 1 KB 321 and by the House of Lords in *Lipkin Gorman v Karpnale Ltd* [1991] 2 AC 548. It has been suggested by commentators that these cases are undermined by their mis-understanding of *Taylor v Plumer*, 3 M. & S. 562, but that is not how the English doctrine of *stare decisis* operates. It would be more consistent with that doctrine to say that, in recognizing claims to substituted assets, equity must be taken to have followed the law, even though the law was not declared until later. Lord Ellenborough CJ gave no indication that, in following assets into their exchange products, equity had adopted a rule which was peculiar to itself or which went further than the common law.

There is no merit in having distinct and differing tracing rules at law and in equity, given that tracing is neither a right nor a remedy but merely the process by which the plaintiff establishes what has happened to his property and makes good his claim that the assets which he claims can properly be regarded as representing his property. The fact that there are different tracing rules at law and in equity is unfortunate though probably inevitable, but unnecessary differences should not be created where they are not required by the different nature of legal and equitable doctrines and remedies. There is, in my view, even less merit in the present rule which precludes the invocation of the equitable tracing rules to support a common law claim; until that rule is swept away unnecessary obstacles to the development of a rational and coherent law of restitution will remain.

Given that the trustee can trace his money at Midland Bank into the money in the defendant's account with the commodity brokers, can he successfully assert a claim to that part of the money which represents the profit made by the use of his money? I have no doubt that, in the particular circumstances of this case, he can. There is no need to trace through the dealings on the London potato futures market. If the defendant, as the nominal account holder, had any entitlement to demand payment from the brokers, this was because of the terms of the contract which she made with them. Under the terms of that contract it is reasonable to infer that the brokers were authorized to deal in potato futures on her account, to debit her account with losses and to credit it with profits, and to pay her only the balance standing to her account. It is, in my opinion, impossible to separate the chose in action constituted by the deposit of the trustee's money on those terms from the terms upon which it was deposited. The chose in action, which was vested in the defendant's name but which in reality belonged to the trustee, was not a right to payment from the brokers of the original amount deposited but a right to claim the balance, whether greater or less than the amount deposited; and it is to that chose in action that the trustee now lays claim.

Given, then, that the trustee has established his legal claim to the £11,700 and the profits earned by the use of his money, and has located the money, first, in the defendant's account with the commodity brokers and, later, in the defendant's account at Raphaels, I am satisfied that the common law has adequate remedies to enable him to recover his property. He did not need to sue the defendant; and he did not do so. He was entitled to bring an action for debt against Raphaels and obtain an order for payment. When he threatened to do so, Raphaels interpleaded, and the issue between the trustee and the defendant was which of them could give a good receipt to Raphaels. That depended upon which of them had the legal title to the chose in action. The money now being in court, the court can grant an appropriate declaration and make an order for payment.

In my judgment the trustee was entitled at law to the money in the joint account of the bankrupts at Midland Bank, which had vested in him by statute. He was similarly entitled to the balance of the money in the defendant's account with the commodity brokers, and the fact that it included profits made by the use of that money is immaterial. He was similarly entitled to the money in the defendant's account at Raphaels and able to give them a good receipt for the money. The defendant never had any interest, legal or equitable, in any of those moneys. The trustee is plainly entitled to the money in court and the judge was right to order that it be paid out to him.

I would dismiss the appeal

Nourse LJ: I also agree that the appeal must be dismissed.

I recognize that our decision goes further than that of the House of Lords in *Lipkin Gorman v Karpnale Ltd* [1991] 2 AC 548, in that it holds that the acton for money had and received entitles the legal owner to trace his property into its product, not only in the sense of property for which it is exchanged, but also in the sense of property representing the original and the profit made by the defendant's use of it.

Millett LJ has explained how that extension is justified on the particular facts of this case. But there is, I think, a broader justification to be found in the seminal judgment of Lord Mansfield CJ in *Clarke v Shee and Johnson* (1774) 1 Cowp. 197, 199–200, where he said of the action for money had and received:

> 'This is a liberal action in the nature of a bill in equity; and if, under the circumstances of the case, it appears that the defendant cannot in conscience retain what is the subject matter of it, the plaintiff may well support this action.'

In my view the defendant cannot in conscience retain the profit any more than the original £11,700. She had no title to the original. She could not have made the profit without her use of it. She cannot, by making a profit through the use of money to which she had no title, acquire some better title to the profit.

Beldam LJ delivered a concurring judgment.

NOTES AND QUESTIONS

1. Millett LJ, writing extra-judicially, 'Tracing the Proceeds of Fraud' (1991) 107 *LQR* 71, had earlier argued that 'in all but the simplest cases recourse to the common law should be abandoned, that attempts to rationalise and develop the common law rules are unlikely to succeed and should no longer be pursued, and that attempts should be made instead to develop a unified restitutionary remedy based on equitable principles'. Does his decision in *Jones v Jones* indicate a change of mind? Is it significant that his 1991 article preceded the House of Lords' decision in *Lipkin Gorman v Karpnale*?

2. The Court of Appeal disagreed with the judge's reasoning that Mrs Jones was a constructive trustee of the £11,700. This was on the basis that legal title to the money was statutorily vested in the trustee in bankruptcy so that Mr FWJ Jones had no title in the money to confer on Mrs Jones. This should be contrasted with the point made by Lord Browne-Wilkinson in *Westdeutsche Landesbank Girozentrale v Islington BC* (see below, 738) that a thief is a constructive trustee of the property he has stolen.

3. For a general analysis of tracing, focussing on *Jones v Jones*, see P Birks, 'On Taking Seriously the Difference between Tracing and Claiming' (1997) 11 *Trusts Law International* 2.

(2) TRACING IN EQUITY

On a conventional view, tracing in equity has two great advantages for claimants over common law tracing: (i) it enables the claimant to trace money into mixed funds; (ii) where the claimant can trace in equity into substitute property still held by the defendant, the claimant can be granted a proprietary, rather than merely a personal, remedy to effect restitution. It is this second feature that has led to the commonly-held (but in our opinion, inaccurate) view that equitable tracing is *always* concerned with *proprietary* restitution.

On the other hand, the conventional view is that equitable tracing is more restricted than common law tracing to the extent that an essential prerequisite for equitable tracing is that the claimant had an equitable interest in the property prior to the substitution: or, as otherwise expressed, that the property must have passed through the hands of someone who held that property as a fiduciary for the claimant.

The extracts from the cases in this part of this chapter are primarily concerned to examine what are sometimes termed 'the identification rules' of equitable tracing: that is, the rules by which one property is identified as a substitute for another where the (unauthorized) substitution is mixed rather than clean. It is subdivided into three subsections in accordance with those rules:

(a) Where there is a mixed fund comprising the money of two innocent parties (for example, two beneficiaries or a beneficiary and an innocent volunteer) the general equitable tracing rule is 'proportionate sharing' subject sometimes to 'first in, first out'.

(b) Where there is a mixed fund comprising the money of a beneficiary and a fiduciary who has acted in breach of duty in mixing the moneys, the general equitable tracing rule is proportionate sharing subject to loss to the mixed fund first being borne by the fiduciary.

(c) The 'intermediate balance' (or 'exhaustion of the fund') rule.

Several of the extracts also emphasize the prerequisite for equitable tracing of an equitable proprietary interest or that the property was held in a fiduciary capacity; see, for example, *Sinclair v Brougham* (below, 657), *Re Diplock* (below, 660), and *Re Goldcorp Exchange Ltd* (below, 689).

In all of the extracts the right/remedy in question was proprietary rather than personal. For examples of personal equitable remedies following equitable tracing, see the so-called 'knowing receipt' cases and *Ministry of Health v Simpson (sub. nom. Re Diplock)* in Chapter 4: although the courts in those cases may not have used the language of tracing in relation to the personal (as opposed to any proprietary) claims, it is our view that the claimant in those cases had to rely on equitable title and tracing to establish that the property received by the defendant was received 'at the expense of' the claimant even though it was transferred to the defendant by a third party rather than by the claimant.

(i) WHERE THERE IS A MIXED FUND COMPRISING THE MONEY OF TWO INNOCENT PARTIES (FOR EXAMPLE, TWO BENEFICIARIES OR A BENEFICIARY AND AN INNOCENT VOLUNTEER) THE GENERAL EQUITABLE TRACING RULE IS 'PROPORTIONATE SHARING' SUBJECT SOMETIMES TO 'FIRST IN, FIRST OUT'

- *Sinclair v Brougham* [1914] AC 398, House of Lords

The Birkbeck Permanent Building Society was acting *ultra vires* by carrying on a banking business. In an application by the liquidator, on the winding up of the society, one of the two major questions that arose was whether the depositors could trace in equity into the funds of the society. The House of Lords held that the depositors and shareholders of the society, as innocent parties, were entitled to trace their payments into the mixed fund and to claim a proportionate share of that mixed fund.

Viscount Haldance LC (with whom **Lord Atkinson** concurred): [*After rejecting the depositors' action for money had and received (see above, 6) his Lordship continued:*] [T]he depositors in the present case will not succeed unless they are able to trace their money into the hands of the society or its agents as actually existing assets. The question is whether they are able to establish enough to succeed upon this footing. Their claim cannot be in personam and must be in rem, a claim to follow and recover property with which, in equity at all events, they had never really parted.

[*After considering common law tracing and regarding it as unavailable where, as here, a relationship of debtor and creditor had arisen, Viscount Haldane went on to examine the approach in equity:*] The Court of Chancery could and would declare . . . that there was what it called a charge on the banker's debt to the person whose money had been paid into the latter's bank account in favour of the person whose money it really was. And, as Jessel MR pointed out in *Hallett's Case*,[1] this equity was not confined to cases of trust in the strict sense, but applied at all events to every case where there was a fiduciary relationship. It was, as I think, merely an additional right, which could be enforced by the Court of Chancery in the exercise of its auxiliary jurisdiction, wherever money was held to belong in equity to the plaintiff. If so . . . I see no reason why the remedy explained by Jessel MR in *Hallett's Case*, of declaring a charge on the investment in a debt due from bankers on balance, or on any mass of money or securities with which the plaintiff's money had been mixed, should not apply in the case of a transaction that is ultra vires. The property was never converted into a debt, in equity at all events, and there has been throughout a resulting trust, not of an active character, but sufficient, in my opinion, to bring the transaction within the general principle.

. . .

In the present case the investment was not made in breach of a fiduciary duty on the part of the society, and it was actually made with the authority of the depositors. What was a material point in *Hallett's Case*, therefore, does not occur here. No doubt it was ultra vires of the society to undertake to repay the money. But it was none the less intended that in consideration of giving such an undertaking the society should be entitled to deal with it freely as its own. The consideration failed and the depositors had the right to follow the money so far as invalidly borrowed into the assets in which it had been invested, whether these assets were mere debts due to the society or ordinary securities, but that was their only right.

As to the part of the assets which was acquired with money paid by the shareholders, the case appears to me to be free from difficulty. The money paid to the society by the sharcholders was paid

---

1 (1880) 13 ChD 696.

as the consideration for the shares which were issued to them. That money, therefore, beyond question, became the money of the society. A large part of it has probably been applied ultra vires in the acquisition of the assets of the banking business. These assets can accordingly be claimed only by the society itself as belonging to it, and the shareholders have no direct title to them.

The total mass of assets which the liquidator has to distribute thus represents in part money which the depositors are entitled to follow and in part money which the society is entitled to follow. If the present value of these assets was equivalent to the total amount of such money, there would be no difficulty; the assets would be apportioned according to the sources from which they came. Does it make a difference that the value has shrunk so that the two sets of claimants cannot be paid in full? I do not think so. The position of the society is different from that of the agent in *Hallett's Case*. The depositors have no alternative right in this case to disaffirm the transaction to the extent of claiming on the footing that their money has been applied in breach of trust. All they can do is to adopt the dealings with the money that they handed over, under circumstances in which it never really ceased to be theirs, and claim the part of the mass of assets which represents it as belonging to them in equity.

There has been no breach of fiduciary duty on the part of the society, and it appears to me that this circumstance is material in distinguishing the consequences here from those which followed in *Hallett's Case* on the footing that there the agent could not gain, at the expense of the principal, an advantage for himself or his general creditors by in effect setting up a breach of duty. The depositors can, in my opinion, only claim the depreciated assets which represent their money, and nothing more. It follows that the principle to be adopted in the distribution must be apportionment on the footing that depreciation and loss are to be borne pro rata. I am, of course, assuming in saying this that specific tracing is not now possible.

What is there must be apportioned accordingly among those whose money it represents, and the question of how the apportionment should be made is one of fact. In the present case the working out of a proper apportionment based on the principle of tracing not only would involve immense labour but would be unlikely to end in any reliable result. The records necessary for tracing the dealings with the funds do not exist. We have therefore, treating the question as one of presumption of fact, to give such a direction to the liquidator as is calculated to bring about a result consistent with the principles already laid down.

I think that this direction should be that, without disturbing anything that has up to now been settled or agreed, he should apportion the entirety of the remaining assets (including mortgages and loans) between the depositors and the shareholders in proportion to the amounts paid by the depositors and the shareholders respectively. In this way I am of opinion that the nearest approach praticable to substantial justice will be done. I think that this is the utmost extent to which, consistently with well-established principles, a Court of justice can go in compelling the society to restore that of which it has become possessed through its ultra vires transactions. . . .

I move that the judgments of the Courts below be varied so as to give effect to a declaration that, subject to matters which have already been settled by the consent of the parties, and subject to any application which may be made by any individual depositor or shareholder with a view of tracing his own money into any particular asset, and subject to the payment of all proper costs, charges, and expenses, the liquidator ought to proceed in distributing the remaining assets of the society between the depositors and the unadvanced shareholders on the principle of distributing them pari passu in proportion to the amounts properly credited to them respectively in the books of the society in respect of their advances at the date of the commencement of the winding-up, and that the case be remitted to the Court of first instance to apply this principle. . . .

Lord Dunedin: . . . Neither party is here in any fiduciary position to the other. It is a mere question of evidence. What has happened is truly this. The directors of the society have taken the moneys of the shareholders which they had a right to receive, and the moneys of the depositors which they had not, and mixed them so that they cannot be discriminated from each other, and have put them, so to speak, in the society's strong-box, where the mixed mass is found by the liquidator. . . . There being no direct evidence, the only equitable means is to let each party bear the shrinkage proportionately to the amount originally contributed, and this is the judgment of my noble and learned friend on the woolsack, in which I concur. . . .

Lord Parker of Waddington: . . . The case . . . presents itself in this way. Here is a mass of assets arising in the course of an ultra vires business carried on by the directors and agents of the society. There are, on the other hand, liabilities, how or for what purpose incurred is not in evidence. No one claims any interest in the assets except the ultra vires lenders, the members of the society and the creditors, in respect of the liabilities to which I have referred. The ultra vires lenders and the members are willing that these liabilities and the costs of the liquidation, which are in effect costs of administering the fund, shall be first paid. If this is done, what is left may be taken to represent in part the moneys of the ultra vires lenders and in part the moneys of the society wrongfully employed in the business. The equities of the ultra vires lenders and of the society are equal, and it follows that the remainder of the assets ought to be divided between the ultra vires lenders and the society rateably, according to the capital amount contributed by such lenders and the society respectively. . . .

Lord Sumner: . . . My Lords, I agree, without recapitulating reasons, that the principle on which *Hallett's Case* is founded justifies an order allowing the appellants to follow the assets, not merely to the verge of actual identification, but even somewhat further in a case like the present, where after a process of exclusion only two classes or groups of persons, having equal claims, are left in and all superior claims have been eliminated. Tracing in a sense it is not, for we know that the money coming from A went into one security and that coming from B into another, and that the two securities did not probably depreciate exactly in the same percentage, and we know further that no one will ever know any more. Still I think this well within the 'tracing' equity, and that among persons making up these two groups the principle of rateable division of the assets is sound.

NOTES AND QUESTIONS

1. For the case of *Re Hallett's Estate*, which was extensively referred to by their Lordships, see below, 672.

2. The House of Lords was willing to presume, subject to evidence to the contrary, that the depositors and shareholders could trace the payments they had made into the funds held by the society. Having thereby established that the fund represented the monies of those two groups of innocent claimants, the rule applied was one of proportionate sharing.

3. An example may make the rule of proportionate sharing clearer. Say £1,000 of C's money is mixed with £2,000 of X's money. C can trace through to a third of the mixed fund and X to two thirds. How much that one third or two thirds share will be worth depends on whether the fund declines in value (for example, by dissipation of money from it) or increases in value (for example, by the profitable investment of the fund in a substitute product). So if half of the mixed fund is dissipated and it therefore declines to £1,500, C will be entitled to £500 and X to £1,000. If it doubles in value (for example, by the purchase of shares which are then sold) C will be entitled to £2,000 and X to £4,000.

4. *Sinclair v Brougham* was overruled, eighty years on, by the House of Lords in *Westdeutsche Landesbank Girozentrale v Islington BC* (see below, 727). The overruling extended to both the proprietary claim (with which we are here concerned) and the personal claim for money had and received (see above, 40). Their Lordships indicated that they were not meaning to cast doubt on the proportionate sharing approach for innocent parties, applied in *Sinclair v Brougham*, but rather on the finding of the prerequisite for equitable tracing of an equitable

proprietary interest. Although it follows that we no longer need to agonize about this, it would appear that the prerequisite for equitable tracing of an equitable proprietary interest was established by treating the society as receiving the payments of the depositors as resulting trustees based on the failure of the purpose for which the payments were given: see Viscount Haldane LC's speech, above, at 6, and the analysis of *Sinclair v Brougham* given in *Re Diplock* by the Court of Appeal (below, 660). Certainly the obscurity of the reasoning of their Lordships in *Sinclair v Brougham* on the finding of a proprietary interest means that few will mourn its passing.

• *Re Diplock* [1948] Ch 465, Court of Appeal

In breach of their fiduciary duty to the claimant next of kin, and by a mistake of law as to the validity of a clause in a will, the personal representatives of a testator had distributed his residuary estate to various charities. The charities (who were innocent volunteers) had mixed that money with their own money. On the claimants' appeal from the decision of Wynn-Parry J it was held by the Court of Appeal that, in addition to having a personal equitable remedy against the charities (on which see above, 237), the claimants were entitled to an equitable proprietary remedy following equitable tracing, in respect of the mixed funds held by the charities. As regards the mixed funds not held in current accounts (for example, the funds of the Royal Sailors Orphan Girls' School and Home) it was held that the claimants were entitled to a proportionate share. As regards the funds held in current accounts (for example, the funds of Dr Barnardo's Homes) a rule of 'first in, first out' derived from *Clayton's Case* (1816) 1 Mer. 572 was applied. But no tracing was thought possible in respect of money drawn from the mixed funds and used by the charities to improve or erect new buildings.

Lord Greene MR giving the judgment of himself, **Wrottesley** and **Evershed L JJ**: . . . It will be seen that the only claims which in our view can be supported on the basis of the so-called equitable doctrine of tracing are of a strictly limited character.

We shall endeavour to explain our views as to the basis on which the doctrine must now be taken to rest. In this connexion we regard the case of *Sinclair v Brougham* as of fundamental importance. That decision, in our view, did not so much extend as explain the doctrine of *Hallett's* case, which now must be regarded not, so to speak, as a genus but as a species in a genus where equity works on the same basic principles but selects what on the particular case is the equitable method of applying them in practice. It will be found that our views as to the meaning and effect of the speeches in *Sinclair v Brougham* differ from those expressed by Wynn-Parry J. We should, however, be lacking in candour rather than showing respect if we refrained from saying that we find the opinions in *Sinclair v Brougham* in many respects not only difficult to follow but difficult to reconcile with one another.

Before passing to a consideration of the case of *Sinclair v Brougham* we may usefully make some observations of our own as to the distinction between the attitude of the common law and that of equity to these questions.

The common law approached them in a strictly materialistic way. It could only appreciate what might almost be called the 'physical' identity of one thing with another. It could treat a person's money as identifiable so long as it had not become mixed with other money. It could treat as identifiable with the money other kinds of property acquired by means of it, provided that there was no admixture of other money. It is noticeable that in this latter case the common law did not base itself on any known theory of tracing such as that adopted in equity. It proceeded on the basis that the unauthorized act of purchasing was one capable of ratification by the owner of the money (see *per* Lord Parker in *Sinclair v Brougham*.)

Equity adopted a more metaphysical approach. It found no difficulty in regarding a composite fund as an amalgam constituted by the mixture of two or more funds each of which could be regarded as having, for certain purposes, a continued separate existence. Putting it in another way, equity regarded the amalgam as capable, in proper circumstances, of being resolved into its component parts.

Adapting, for the sake of contrast, the phraseology which we have used in relation to the common law, it was the metaphysical approach of equity coupled with and encouraged by the far-reaching remedy of a declaration of charge that enabled equity to identify money in a mixed fund. Equity, so to speak, is able to draw up a balance sheet on the right-hand side of which appears the composite fund and on its left-hand side the two or more funds of which it is to be deemed to be made up.

Regarded as a pure piece of machinery for the purpose of tracing money into a mixed fund or into property acquired by means of a mixed fund, a declaration of charge might be thought to be a suitable means of dealing with any case where one person has, without legal title, acquired some benefit by the use of the money of another—in other words, any case of what is often called 'unjust enrichment.' The opinion of Lord Dunedin in *Sinclair v Brougham* appears to us to come very nearly to this, for he appears to treat the equitable remedy as applicable in any case where a superfluity, expressed or capable of being expressed in terms of money, is found to exist. Such a view would dispense with the necessity of establishing as a starting point the existence of a fiduciary or quasi-fiduciary relationship or of a continuing right of property recognized in equity. We may say at once that, apart from the possible case of Lord Dunedin's speech, we cannot find that any principle so wide in its operation is to be found enunciated in English law. . . . The equitable remedies pre-suppose the continued existence of the money either as a separate fund or as part of a mixed fund or as latent in property acquired by means of such a fund. If, on the facts of any individual case, such continued existence is not established, equity is as helpless as the common law itself. If the fund, mixed or unmixed, is spent upon a dinner, equity, which dealt only in specific relief and not in damages, could do nothing. If the case was one which at common law involved breach of contract the common law could, of course, award damages but specific relief would be out of the question. It is, therefore, a necessary matter of consideration in each case where it is sought to trace money in equity, whether it has such a continued existence, actual or notional, as will enable equity to grant specific relief.

. . .

The first question which appears to us to fall for decision on this part of the present appeals may, we think, be thus formulated: Did the power of equity to treat Diplock 'money' as recoverable from the charity, which undoubtedly existed down to the moment when the cheque was paid by the bank on which it was drawn, cease the moment that the 'money' by the process of 'mixture' came to be represented by an accretion to or an enlargement of the chose in action consisting of a debt already owing to the charity by its own bankers? Wynn-Parry J, in effect, decided that it did. His reason for taking this view, shortly stated, was as follows: The principle applicable was to be extracted from the decision in *Hallett's* case and that principle was in no way extended by the decision in *Sinclair v Brougham*. The principle can operate only in cases where the mixing takes place in breach of a trust, actual or constructive, or in breach of some other fiduciary relationship and in proceedings against the trustee or fiduciary agent: here the mixing was not of this character, since it was effected by an innocent volunteer: there is no ground on which, according to principle, the conscience of such a volunteer can be held in equity to be precluded from setting up a title adverse to the claim: in every case, therefore, where a 'mixture' has been carried out by the charity, the claim, whether it be against a mixed monetary fund or against investments made by means of such a mixed fund, must fail in limine.

Now we may say at once that this view of the inability of equity to deal with the case of the volunteer appears to us, with all respect to Wynn-Parry J to be in conflict with the principles expounded, particularly by Lord Parker, in *Sinclair v Brougham*. . . . [W]e may conveniently summarize what we consider to be the effect of [Lord Parker's observations] as follows: Where an innocent volunteer (as distinct from a purchaser for value without notice) mixes 'money' of his own with 'money' which in equity belongs to another person, or is found in possession of such a mixture, although that other person cannot claim a charge on the mass superior to the claim of the volunteer he is entitled, nevertheless, to a charge ranking pari passu with the claim of the volunteer. And Lord Parker's reasons for taking this view appear to have been on the following lines: Equity regards the rights of the equitable owner as being 'in effect rights of property' though not recognized as such by the common law. Just as a volunteer is not allowed by equity in the case, e.g., of a conveyance of the legal estate in land, to set up his legal title adversely to the claim of a person having an equitable interest in the land, so in the case of a mixed fund of money the volunteer must give such recognition as equity considers him in conscience (as a volunteer) bound to give to the interest of the equitable owner of the money which has been mixed with the volunteer's own. But this burden on the conscience of the volunteer is not such as to compel him to treat the claim of the equitable owner as paramount. That would be to treat the volunteer as strictly as if he himself stood in a fiduciary relationship to the equitable owner which ex hypothesi he does not. The volunteer is under no greater duty of conscience to recognize the interest of the equitable owner than that which lies upon a person having an equitable interest in one of two trust funds of 'money' which have become mixed towards the equitable owner of the other. Such a person is not in conscience bound to give precedence to the equitable owner of the other of the two funds.

　　We may enlarge upon the implications which appear to us to be contained in Lord Parker's reasoning. First of all, it appears to us to be wrong to treat the principle which underlies *Hallell's* case as coming into operation only where the person who does the mixing is not only in a fiduciary position but is also a *party to the tracing action*. If he is a party to the action he is, of course, precluded from setting up a case inconsistent with the obligations of his fiduciary position. But supposing that he is not a party? The result cannot surely depend on what equity would or would not have allowed him to say if he had been a party. Suppose that the sole trustee of (say) five separate trusts draws 100*l.* out of each of the trust banking accounts, pays the resulting 500*l.* into an account which he opens in his own name, draws a cheque for 500*l.* on that account and gives it as a present to his son. A claim by the five sets of beneficiaries to follow the money of their respective trusts would be a claim against the son. He would stand in no fiduciary relationship to any of them. We recoil from the conclusion that all five beneficiaries would be dismissed empty handed by a court of equity and the son left to enjoy what in equity was originally their money. Yet that is the conclusion to which the reasoning of the learned judge would lead us. Lord Parker's reasoning, on the other hand, seems to us to lead to the conclusion that each set of beneficiaries could set up its equitable interest which would prevail against the bare legal title of the son as a volunteer and that they would be entitled to share pari passu in so much of the fund or its proceeds as remained identifiable.

　　An even more striking example was admitted by [Counsel for the charities] to be the result of his argument, and he vigorously maintained that it followed inevitably from the principles of equity involved. If a fiduciary agent takes cash belonging to his principal and gives it to his son, who takes it innocently, then so long as the son keeps it unmixed with other cash in one trouser pocket, the principal can follow it and claim it back. Once, however, the son, being under no fiduciary duty to the principal, transfers it to his other trouser pocket in which there are reposing a coin or two of his own of the same denomination, the son, by a sort of process of accretion, acquires an indefeasible title to what the moment before the transfer he could not have claimed as his own. This result appears to us to stultify the beneficent powers of equity to protect and enforce what it recognizes as equitable rights of property which subsist until they are destroyed by the operation of a purchase for value without notice.

　　The error into which, we respectfully suggest, the learned judge has fallen is in thinking that what, in *Hallett's* case, was only the method (there appropriate) of bringing a much wider-based principle of equity into operation—viz., the method by which a fiduciary agent, who has himself wrongfully mixed the funds, is prohibited from asserting a breach of his duty—is an element which must necessarily be present before equity can afford protection to the equitable rights which it has brought into existence. We are not prepared to see the arm of equity thus shortened.

It is now time to examine in some detail the case of *Sinclair v Brougham*. . . . [*The court examined the case and continued:*]

[L]ike Lord Parker, Lord Haldane bases the remedy available in equity upon a right of property recognized by equity as vested in the plaintiff throughout, not lost by payment into a banking account, nor by the mixture of moneys nor by merger in a mass of assets. In all these cases the equitable remedy by way of declaration of charge is available.

It is to be observed that neither Lord Parker nor Lord Haldane suggests that the equitable remedy extends to cover all cases where A becomes possessed of money belonging to B, a view which Lord Dunedin seemed inclined to accept if he did not actually do so. Lord Parker and Lord Haldane both predicate the existence of a right of property recognized by equity which depends upon there having existed at some stage a fiduciary relationship of some kind (though not necessarily a positive duty of trusteeship) sufficient to give rise to the equitable right of property. Exactly what relationships are sufficient to bring such an equitable right into existence for the purposes of the rule which we are considering is a matter which has not been precisely laid down. Certain relationships are clearly included, e.g., trustee (actual or constructive) and cestui que trust; and 'fiduciary' relationships such as that of principal and agent. *Sinclair v Brougham* itself affords another example. There, a sufficient fiduciary relationship was found to exist between the depositors and the directors by reason of the fact that the purposes for which the depositors had handed their money to the directors were by law incapable of fulfilment.

. . .

We have now to consider how the principles which we have outlined are to be applied to the facts of the individual cases which are before us. We deal first of all with what appear to be the most important claims from the point of view of amount. They are cases in which the money received from the Diplock executors was used in the execution of works upon land or buildings already belonging to the charities. The appellants claim in each case declarations of charge on land of the charity in respect of these amounts. [*The court set out the nature of the claims and continued:*]

Where the contribution of a volunteer to a mixed fund or the acquisition of what we may call a 'mixed asset' is in the form of money, it is, as we hope to have shown, inequitable for him to claim the whole fund or the whole asset. The equitable charge given to the other claimant in respect of the money contributed by him results merely in the division of the mixed fund between the two of them or the reduction of the asset by sale to its original components, i.e. money which is then divisible in the same manner. The volunteer gets back what he put in, i.e. money. On this basis, if a charity had used a mixed fund, consisting in part of its own money and in part of Diplock money, in the acquisition of property, whether (for example) land or stock, the application of the equitable remedy would have presented no particular difficulty. The Diplock money and the charity money could each have been traced. A charge enforced by sale and distribution would have been effective as well as fair to both parties. The charity would not, as the result of the mixture, have been deprived of anything that it had before.

In the present cases, however, the charities have used the Diplock money, not in combination with money of their own to acquire new assets, but in the alteration and improvement of assets which they already owned. The altered and improved asset owes its existence, therefore, to a combination of land belonging to the charity and money belonging to the Diplock estate. The question whether tracing is possible and if so to what extent, and also the question whether an effective remedy by way of declaration of charge can be granted consistently with an equitable treatment of the charity as an innocent volunteer, present quite different problems from those arising in the simple case above stated. In the case of the purchase of an asset out of a mixed fund, both categories of money are, as we have said, necessarily present throughout the existence of the asset in an identifiable form. In the case of adaptation of property of the volunteer by means of trust money, it by no means necessarily follows that the money can be said to be present in the adapted property. The beneficial owner of the trust money seeks to follow and recover that money and claims to use the machinery of a charge on the adapted property in order to enable him to do so. But in the first place the money may not be capable of being followed. In every true sense, the money may have disappeared. A simple example suggests itself. The owner of a house who, as an innocent volunteer, has trust money in his hands given to him by a trustee uses that money in making an alteration to his house so as to fit it better to his own personal needs. The result may add not one penny to the value of the house. Indeed, the alteration may well lower its value; for the alteration, though convenient to the owner, may be highly inconvenient in the eyes of a purchaser. Can it be said in such cases that the trust money can be traced and extracted from the altered asset? Clearly not, for the money will have disappeared leaving no monetary trace behind: the asset will not have increased (or may even have depreciated) in value through its use.

But the matter does not end here. What, for the purposes of the inquiry, is to be treated as 'the charity property'? Is it to be the whole of the land belonging to the charity? or is it to be only that part of it which was altered or reconstructed or on which a building has been erected by means of Diplock money? If the latter, the result may well be that the property, both in its original state and as altered or improved, will, when taken in isolation, have little or no value. What would be the value of a building in the middle of Guy's hospital without any means of access through other parts of the hospital property? If, on the other hand, the charge is to be on the whole of the charity land, it might well be thought an extravagant result if the Diplock estate, because Diplock money had been used to reconstruct a corner of it, were to be entitled to a charge on the entirety.

But it is not merely a question of locating and identifying the Diplock money. The result of a declaration of charge is to disentangle trust money and enable it to be withdrawn in the shape of money from the complex in which it has become involved. This can only be done by sale under the charge. But the equitable owner of the trust money must in this process submit to equality of treatment with the innocent volunteer. The latter too, is entitled to disentangle his money and to withdraw it from the complex. Where the complex originates in money on both sides there is no difficulty and no inequity. Each is entitled to a charge. But if what the volunteer has contributed is not money but other property of his own such as land, what then? You cannot have a charge for land. You can, it is true, have a charge for the value of land, an entirely different thing. Is it equitable to compel the innocent volunteer to take a charge merely for the value of the land when what he has contributed is the land itself? In other words, can equity, by the machinery of a charge, give to the innocent volunteer that which he has contributed so as to place him in a position comparable with that of the owner of the trust fund? In our opinion it cannot.

In the absence of authority to the contrary our conclusion is that as regards the Diplock money used in these cases it cannot be traced in any true sense; and, further, that even if this were not so, the only remedy available to equity, viz., that of a declaration of charge would not produce an equitable result and is inapplicable accordingly.

[*Lord Greene MR considered five other claims and continued*:]

In the case of Dr Barnardo's Homes . . ., the case presented to us as we understood it was limited to a claim to trace the sum of 3,000*l.* granted by the executors and paid into the charity's general current account on December 14, 1936, into a sum of 40,000*l.* 2¾ per cent. Funding Loan purchased for 39,341*l.* 13s. 9d. on December 23, 1936, and paid for by a cheque drawn on the same account and cleared on December 24. The precise manner in which the entries in the bank pass book ought to be interpreted is not, we think, entirely clear, but for the purpose of explaining the principle which we consider would be applicable we start with the position at the close of business on December 14,

1936. The position then was that the credit balance of 49,771*l*. 4*s*. 11*d*. represented, as to 3,000*l*., Diplock money, and as to the remainder, namely, 46,711*l*. 4*s*. 11*d*. charity money.

If the whole of this charity money is treated (as for the purpose of our explanation we are treating it) as having been paid in before the Diplock 3,000*l*. was paid in, it would follow, if the principle of *Clayton's* case were applicable as between the claimants and the charity, that the first 46,771*l*. 4*s*. 11*d*. drawn out would be charity money. Now, as we have said, the cheque for 39,341*l*. 13*s*. 9*d*. was cleared and debited to the account on December 24. Meanwhile a number of withdrawals had taken place, namely:

	£	s.	d.	
December 15	682	3	2	(6 cheques)
December 17	2	0	0	
December 17	20,123	6	0	(7 cheques)
December 18	27	11	4	
December 19	841	9	1	(28 cheques)
December 21	447	1	8	(10 cheques)
December 22	66	16	10	(4 cheques)
December 23		16	0	
December 24	3	3	0	
Totalling	£22,194	7	1	

In the pass book the next withdrawal is the 39,341*l*. 13*s*. 9*d*. with which we have to deal. Taking, therefore, the starting figure of 46,771*l*. 4*s*. 11*d*. and deducting from it the 22,194*l*. 7*s*. 1*d*. withdrawn which, on *Clayton's* case must be regarded as charity money, there remained 24,576*l*. 17*s*. 10*d*. The result would be that sum of 39,341*l*. 13*s*. 9*d*. must be regarded as having consisted, as to the first 24,576*l*. 17*s*. 10*d*. of charity money, as to the next 3,000*l*. of Diplock money, and as to the remainder, of charity money. On this basis the appellants would be entitled to a charge on the funding loan in respect of their claim to 3,000*l*.

The above result would only follow if *Clayton's* case applies. It might be suggested that the corollary of treating two claimants on a mixed fund as interested rateably should be that withdrawals out of the fund ought to be attributed rateably to the interests of both claimants. But in the case of an active banking account this would lead to the greatest difficulty and complication in practice and might in many cases raise questions incapable of solution. What then is to be done? In our opinion, the same rule as that applied in *Clayton's* case should be applied. This is really a rule of convenience based upon so-called presumed intention . . .

The Royal Sailors Orphan Girls' School and Home . . . received a grant of 2,000*l*. sent to them on March 20, 1937, and paid it into their current account. By a contract dated March 24, 1937, they contracted to purchase a sum of 1,943*l*. 18*s*. 5*d*. 3½ per cent War Stock. This stock costing (with expenses) the sum of 2,000*l*. was paid for by cheque on the account on April 6 1937. It is admitted in para. 5 of the defence that this 2,000*l*. was the 2,000*l*. received from the Diplock executors.

. . . [W]e think that, for the purposes of the equitable doctrine, this 2,000*l*. and any investment shown to represent it must be regarded as belonging to the Diplock estate. But there is a further complication, since it is argued that there is no investment which can in any true sense be said to represent the 2,000*l*. of Diplock money. At the date of the purchase of the War Stock the charity already owned 9,747*l*. 10*s*. 2*d*. like stock. Both sums of stock were uncertified inscribed stock, and according to the method of accounting adopted by the Bank of England, the 1,943*l*. 18*s*. 5*d*. was added to the existing holding. This, by itself, would not, in our opinion, affect the power of equity to trace the Diplock money and secure its return to the estate in the shape of a proportionate part of the total holding. Unlike the case already discussed, where the Diplock money was expended in works on charity land, no injustice would be done to the charity as volunteers by carrying out the necessary process of dissection.

But there are further complications. Subsequently to the addition of the 1,943*l*. 18*s*. 5*d*. to the existing holding, two further sums of stock amounting respectively to 50*l*. 6*s*. 6*d*. and 47*l*. 10*s*. 9*d*. were purchased by the charity and these sums it would be entitled to have taken into account on a division of the holding. So far, still, there is no difficulty. But in addition to purchases, certain sales took place amounting to 3,509*l*. 11*s*. 4*d*., the purchase price being expended for the general purposes of the charity. Of these sales, the last for 434*l*. 11*s*. 2*d*. was effected on December 23, 1939, i.e., after the receipt of the warning letter and must, we think, be treated as referable solely to the charity's own interest. The other sales covered a period between November 10, 1938, and August 10, 1939. To what interest ought these sales to be attributed? Entirely to the charity's own interest, say the claimants, leaving the Diplock interest intact in the stock remaining unsold. They suggest that a principle analogous to that of *Clayton's* case ought to be applied, with the result that the stock first brought into the mass which was the charity's own stock ought to be treated as having been first drawn out.

We do not accept the view that the case ought to be treated as though it were subject to the rule in *Clayton's* case. We see no justification for extending that rule beyond the case of a banking account. Here, before the sales took place, the mass of stock, if the question had then been raised, would have been regarded in equity as belonging rateably to the charity and to the Diplock estate. The only equitable way of treating the situation appears to us to be to regard each sum of stock withdrawn from the mass as having been made up in the same proportions. In so far as, upon this principle, withdrawals represented in part Diplock money and the sums received on the sale of the stock withdrawn were expended on general purposes and cannot now be traced into any existing asset, that amount of Diplock money must be regarded as having disappeared. But in respect of so much of the Diplock interest as is not thus accounted for, we are of opinion that the claim to a rateable proportion of the stock still held is established . . .

NOTES AND QUESTIONS

1. The 'first in, first out' rule derives from *Clayton's Case* (1816) 1 Mer 572 where, at 608, Sir William Grant MR said the following:

   > [T]his is the case of a banking account, where all the sums paid in form one blended fund, the parts of which have no longer any distinct existence. Neither banker nor customer ever think of saying, this draft is to be placed to the account of the £500 paid in on *Monday*, and this other to the account of the £500 paid in on *Tuesday*. There is a fund of £1000 to draw upon, and that is enough. In such a case there is no room for any other appropriation than that which arises from the order in which the receipts and payments take place, and are carried into the account. Presumably, it is the sum first paid in, that is first drawn out. It is the first item on the debit side of the account, that is discharged, or reduced, by the first item on the credit side. The appropriation is made by the very act of setting the two sides against each other. Upon that principle, all accounts current are settled . . .

   We shall see in the next case that the 'first in, first out' rule of *Clayton's Case*, applied by the Court of Appeal in *Re Diplock* in respect of Dr Barnardo's Homes, is now under attack as a tracing identification rule so that the general rule of 'proportionate sharing' may apply even to active bank accounts.

2. An important distinction drawn by the Court of Appeal was between imposing an equitable charge as a means of reversing any unjust enrichment and imposing an equitable charge only where the defendant's enrichment continues to exist.

3. The Court of Appeal stressed that the necessary starting point for equitable tracing—of property being held for a beneficiary by a fiduciary—need not necessarily involve a trust (although it usually will do).

4. Is there a difference between saying that the defendant holds a mixed fund in proportionate shares and saying that the mixed fund is subject to the claimant's right to a declaration of charge for a proportionate share? That is, is the relevant proprietary remedy following tracing into a mixed fund, always a charge?

5. Is proportionate sharing the correct approach where an innocent volunteer has mixed his own money with a beneficiary's and the mixed fund has increased in value? (See below, 687, note 2.)

- **_Barlow Clowes International Ltd v Vaughan_** [1992] 4 All ER 22, Court of Appeal

An investment company, which had promoted and managed certain investment plans including in particular two plans known as Portfolios 28 and 68, went into liquidation. The funds paid in by investors had been misapplied and largely dissipated. There was a conflict between 'the late investors' (the respondents) who contended that the remaining available assets should be distributed on the basis that withdrawals from the investment fund had been made on a 'first in, first out' basis; and 'the early investors' (the appellants) who argued that the 'first in, first out' rule should not apply and that there should be distribution _pari passu_ amongst all unpaid investors irrespective of the dates on which the investors made their investments. Peter Gibson J applied the 'first in, first out' rule but this was reversed on appeal. (Between the judgment at first instance and the appeal, the Secretary of State for Trade and Industry settled the claims of the vast majority of investors. The Secretary of State pursued the appeal by way of subrogation.)

Dillon LJ: ... The argument put by Mr Walker QC for the appellant is that instead of tracing or any application of _Clayton's Case_ the available assets and moneys should be distributed pari passu among all unpaid investors rateably in proportion to the amounts due to them. This is the basis of distribution which—subject to any application which might be made by any individual depositor or shareholder with a view to tracing his own money into any particular asset—was directed by the House of Lords in _Sinclair v Brougham_ [1914] AC 398, as between the shareholders in a building society which was being wound up and depositors who had made deposits in an ultra vires banking business which the building society had developed and carried on for many years. It is not in doubt that that basis of distribution ought to be adopted if distribution by tracing in accordance with _Clayton's Case_ is not to be preferred.

We were indeed referred in the course of the argument to a third possible basis of distribution, which was called the 'rolling charge' or 'North American' method. This has been preferred by the Canadian and United States courts to tracing in accordance with _Clayton's Case_, as more equitable: see for instance the decision of the Ontario Court of Appeal in _Re Ontario Securities Commission and Greymac Credit Corp._ (1986) 55 OR (2d) 673. This method goes on the basis that where funds of several depositors, or sources, have been blended in one account, each debit to the account, unless unequivocally attributable to the moneys of one depositor or source (eg as if an investment was purchased for one), should be attributed to all the depositors so as to reduce all their deposits pro rata, instead of being attributed, as under _Clayton's Case_, to the earliest deposits in point of time. The reasoning is that if there is an account which has been fed only with trust moneys deposited by a number of individuals, and the account holder misapplies a sum from the account for his own purposes, and that sum is lost, it is fair that the loss should be borne by all the depositors pro rata, rather than that the whole loss should fall first on the depositor who made the earliest deposit in point of time. The complexities of this method would, however, in a case where there are as many depositors as in the present case and even with the benefits of modern computer technology be so great, and the cost would be so high, that no one has sought to urge the court to adopt it, and I would reject it as impracticable in the present case.

...

[The rule in *Clayton's Case*] will apply to the appropriation of payments between any trader and his customer where there is an account current or running account. But it will not apply unless there is a running account—see *per* Lord Halsbury LC in *Cory Bros. & Co. Ltd v Turkish Steamship Mecca (owners), The Mecca* [1897] AC 286 at 290–1,—and even in relation to the appropriation of payments it is not, as Lord Halsbury LC said, an invariable rule: '. . . the circumstances of a case may afford ground for inferring that transactions of the parties were not so intended as to come under this general rule . . .'

One case in which it was held that the nature and circumstances of a fund showed that the parties could not have intended *Clayton's Case* to be applied when the surplus in the fund fell to be returned to the subscribers is *Re British Red Cross Balkan Fund, British Red Cross Society v Johnson* [1914] 2 Ch 419, a decision of Astbury J. There a fund had been collected by public subscription in 1912 for assisting the sick and wounded in the Balkan war of that time. By 1913 there remained a balance in the fund which was no longer required for the purposes of the fund and it was assumed that the surplus fell to be returned to the subscribers. Astbury J held that *Clayton's Case*, which would involve the attribution of the first payments out of the fund to the earlier contributions to it was not to be applied; he said ([1914] 2 Ch 419 at 421: '. . . the rule is obviously inapplicable.'

The actual decision is suspect, since the objects of the fund would seem to have been charitable, and if they were charitable then, as the surplus did not come about through a failure of the charitable objects ab initio, the surplus should have been applied cy-près for other charitable purposes. If however for some reason the fund was not devoted to charity, the decision was plainly right. It was followed, in the case of a winding up of a non-charitable fund, by Cohen J in *Re Hobourn Aero Components Ltd's Air-Raid Distress Fund, Ryan v Forrest* [1946] Ch 86 at 97; Cohen J's decision was affirmed by this court, but the only issue on the appeal was whether or not the fund was charitable (see [1946] Ch 194).

There are many other cases in the books in which the court has been concerned with the distribution of the surplus on the winding up of a non-charitable benevolent fund and no one has suggested that *Clayton's Case* should be applied.

Mr Walker has accordingly submitted for the appellant in the present case, by what he called his narrower submission, that all investors who contributed to the two portfolios in question in the present case were contributing to common funds in which all investors were to participate and that, by analogy with *Re British Red Cross Balkan Fund* and *Re Hobourn Aero Components Ltd's Air-Raid Distress Fund, Clayton's Case* should not be applied.

. . .

I . . . accept Mr Walker's narrower submission and would hold that *Clayton's Case* is not to be applied in the distribution of the available assets and moneys.

Mr Walker's wider submission is to the effect that, while the rule in *Clayton's Case* is valid and useful, subject to the observations in *The Mecca* [1897] AC 286, where what is in question is the appropriation of payments as between the parties to a running account, it is illogical and unfair to the earlier contributors to apply the rule as between innocent beneficiaries whose payments to a third party, BCI, have been paid by that third party into a bank account in which, at the end of the day, there are—for whatever reason—not enough moneys left to meet all claims.

. . .

[T]he decisions of this court, in my judgment, establish and recognise a general rule of practice that *Clayton's Case* is to be applied when several beneficiaries' moneys have been blended in one bank account and there is a deficiency. It is not, in my judgment, for this court to reject that long-established general practice. A fortiori it is not appropriate to reject it in the present case, when the more logical method, the North American method, which is the basis for criticising the application of *Clayton's Case* is accepted to be impracticable. Therefore I would not accept Mr Walker's wider submission.

However as I would accept his narrower submission I would allow this appeal, and set aside the order of the judge and I would declare that the rule in *Clayton's Case* is not to be applied on the distribution of the moneys in the bank accounts specified in schedules A and B to the judge's order or of the proceeds of sale of the additional assets. Instead these were held on trust for all unpaid investors pari passu rateably in proportion to the amounts due to them.

Woolf LJ: ... Mr Walker QC submitted that there are three possible solutions for resolving the competing claims of the investors to the assets which have been recovered. The first solution, which is the one which was adopted by the judge, depends on the rule in *Clayton's Case, Devaynes v Noble* (1816) 1 Mer. 572. ...

In addition to relying upon the arbitrary results which follow from the 'mechanistic' application of the rule Mr Walker relies upon the expense and time which will be involved in having to apply the rule. With the advent of computer technology it cannot be said the task is impossible but it is clearly complex. The costs involved will result in a depletion of the assets available to the investors. In determining the appropriateness of the machinery used for resolving the claims of the investors among themselves, surely this should be a relevant consideration.

The second solution for resolving the claims of the investors among themselves is the rolling charge or North American solution ('North American' because it is the solution adopted or favoured in preference to the rule in *Clayton's Case* in certain decisions of the courts in the United States and Canada because it is regarded as being manifestly fairer). This solution involves treating credits to a bank account made at different times and from different sources as a blend or cocktail with the result that when a withdrawal is made from the account it is treated as a withdrawal in the same proportions as the different interests in the account (here of the investors) bear to each other at the moment before the withdrawal is made. This solution should produce the most just result, but in this case, as counsel accept, it is not a live contender, since while it might just be possible to perform the exercise the costs involved would be out of all proportion even to the sizeable sums which are here involved.

The third solution (and the only other solution canvassed in argument) is the pari passu ex post facto solution. This involves establishing the total quantum of the assets available and sharing them on a proportionate basis among all the investors who could be said to have contributed to the acquisition of those assets, ignoring the dates on which they made their investment. Mr Walker submits this is the solution which is appropriate in this case. It has the virtue of relative simplicity and therefore relative economy and also the virtue of being in this case more just than the first solution. It would have the effect of sharing the pool of assets available proportionately among the thousands of investors in a way which reflected the fact that they were all the victims of a 'common misfortune'. [*He considered the authorities and continued:*]

The decision in *Re Diplock's Estate* must be considered together with the other judgements to which I have referred. When this is done, short of the House of Lords, it is settled law that the rule in *Clayton's Case* can be applied to determine the extent to which, as between each other, equally innocent claimants are entitled in equity to moneys which have been paid into a bank account and then subject to the movements within that account. However, it does not, having regard to the passages from the judgments in the other authorities cited, follow that the rule has always to be applied for this purpose. In a number of different circumstances the rule has not been applied. The rule need only be applied when it is convenient to do so and when its application can be said to do broad justice having regard to the nature of the competing claims. *Re Hallett's Estate* shows that the rule is displaced where its application would unjustly assist the trustee to the disadvantage of the beneficiaries. In *Re Diplock's Estate* the rule would have been displaced by the trustee subsequently earmarking the beneficiary's funds. It is not applied if this is the intention or presumed intention of the beneficiaries. The rule is sensibly not applied when the cost of applying it is likely to exhaust the fund available for the beneficiaries.

...

[T]he approach, in summary, which I would adopt to resolving the issues raised by this appeal are as follows.

(1) While the rule in *Clayton's Case* is prima facie available to determine the interests of investors in a fund into which their investments have been paid, the use of the rule is a matter of convenience and if its application in particular circumstances would be impracticable or result in injustice between the investors it will not be applied if there is a preferable alternative.

(2) Here the rule will not be applied because this would be contrary to either the express or inferred or presumed intention of the investors. If the investments were required by the terms of the investment contract to be paid into a common pool this indicates that the investors did not intend to apply the rule. If the investments were intended to be separately invested, as a result of the investments being collectively misapplied by BCI a common pool of the investments was created. Because of their shared misfortune, the investors will be presumed to have intended the rule not to apply.

(3) As the rule is inapplicable the approach which should be adopted by the court depends on which of the possible alternative solutions is the most satisfactory in the circumstances. If the North American solution is practical this would probably have advantages over the pari passu solution. However, the complications of applying the North American solution in this case make the third solution the most satisfactory.

(4) It must however be remembered that any solution depends on the ability to trace and if the fund had been exhausted (ie the account became overdrawn) the investors whose moneys were in the fund prior to the fund being exhausted will not be able to claim against moneys which were subsequently paid into the fund.

Their claims will be limited to following, if this is possible, any of the moneys paid out of the fund into other assets before it was exhausted.

Leggatt LJ: . . . Logic seems to dictate that as between banker and customer the rule in *Clayton's Case* will apply. As between trustee and beneficiary the trustee will be presumed to draw his own money out of a mixed account before trust money. As between beneficiaries to whom money in an account belongs, they should share loss in proportion to their interest in the account immediately before each withdrawal. The fairness of that course is obvious. It is exemplified by the judgment of the court in *Re Ontario Securities Commission and Greymac Credit Corp.* (1986) 55 OR (2d) 673. But if, as here, that calculation is too difficult or expensive, the beneficiaries should in my judgment share rateably. It seems to me that the rule in *Clayton's Case* has nothing to do with tracing and therefore provides no help in the present action. . . .

As soon as the money of two or more investors was mixed together it became part of a common fund that was diminished only when it was used other than for the purchase of gilts. Such investors cannot be presumed to have intended that losses incurred would be borne other than rateably. All the money was paid into a fund, which already was, or which became, depleted. When paid into the fund it ceased to be earmarked or identifiable as the money of individual investors. They did not expect to incur any loss, but when they found that they had done so they would have had no reason to expect that they would be repaid other than pari passu with other investors whose money was held in the same way.

In my judgment the so-called 'rule of convenience' [i.e. the rule in *Clayton's Case*] would be exceedingly inconvenient in its application here. A glance at the judge's order shows how complex it would be to apply. It would also be, in the words of the editors of Goff and Jones, *Law of Restitution* (3rd edn., 1986) 75, 'capricious and arbitrary'. The use of this fiction, as Judge Learned Hand termed it, for the amelioration of a common misfortune would not be justifiable. It is another case on the facts of which the rule is inapposite and therefore inapplicable. All the moneys, which were provided by the investors, were treated by Barlow Clowes as a common pool to which they could have resort for their own purposes. Since all the investors have equitable charges, and their equities are equal, and they presumably intended their money to be dealt with collectively, they should share rateably what is left in the pool, as did the claimants in *Sinclair v Brougham* [1914] AC 398, and in other cases in which for a variety of reasons the rule has not been applied.

NOTES AND QUESTIONS

1. When will the 'first in, first out' rule be applied, rather than 'proportionate sharing', according to: (i) Woolf LJ; (ii) Dillon and Leggatt LJJ?
2. What was the difference between the rejected North American solution and the favoured approach?
3. Was Woolf LJ being consistent in favouring 'rough and ready' proportionate sharing while insisting that 'any solution depends on the ability to trace' so that proportionate sharing could not be applied once the fund had been exhausted?
4. In *Russell-Cooke Trust Co. v Prentis* [2002] EWHC 2227 (Ch), [2003] 2 All ER 478 a solicitor, in alleged breach of fiduciary duty, had mixed investors' monies in his client account and withdrawn and spent some of that money. Lindsay J applied *Barlow Clowes* in holding that the appropriate approach was pari passu not 'first in, first out'. He said, at paras 55–56,

> It is plain from all three of the judgments in the *Barlow Clowes* case . . . that the rule can be displaced by even a slight counterweight. Indeed, in terms of its actual application between beneficiaries who have in any sense met a shared misfortune, it might be more accurate to refer to the exception that is, rather than the rule in, *Clayton's Case*. Here . . . there is, in my view, an available counterweight: it is quite plain that payments out of the . . . account over the period of its operation showed a pattern of allocation or appropriation such that one could not say that payments in led to allocations by way of payments out in the same sequence. On the contrary, allocation was on occasion completely out of step with the sequence in which payments in had been made. That, as it seems to me, was only to be expected and could reasonably have been foreseen by investors from the publicity material I have described . . . It is, as I see it, one thing to apply a 'first in, first out' rule where it *might* have been expected or intended by the investors to be applied and where nothing is known inconsistent with its being so expected or intended but quite another to presume it as an intention where both a reasonable contemplation of what was intended and the known facts can be seen to be inconsistent with it.

5. Woolf LJ's approach in *Barlow Clowes* and *Russell-Cooke Trust Co. v Prentis* were applied to displace *Clayton's* case in *Commerzbank Aktiengesellschaft v IMB Morgan plc* [2004] EWHC 2771 (Ch), [2005] 2 All ER (Comm) 564. Here money of innocent claimants could be traced into correspondent bank accounts with Commerzbank in the name of IMB Morgan. The claimants' monies had been mixed in those accounts and there had been withdrawals from them. Lawrence Collins J said, at paras 49–50,

> '[I]t would be an extremely onerous (and perhaps impossible) task to determine what sums IMB Morgan has paid away. That is because the nature of a correspondent bank account is such that debits to the account may not necessarily be equated with payments out by IMB Morgan. Some of the debits may be payments to another account held by IMB Morgan, or payments to persons who hold on behalf of IMB Morgan. . . . I am satisfied that the rule in *Clayton's Case* should not apply here, because it would be both impracticable and unjust to apply it. The only fair way to share the balances on each of the accounts would be in proportion to the claims on the respective accounts'.

(ii) WHERE THERE IS A MIXED FUND COMPRISING THE MONEY OF A BENEFICIARY AND A FIDUCIARY, WHO HAS ACTED IN BREACH OF DUTY IN MIXING THE MONEYS, THE GENERAL EQUITABLE TRACING RULE IS PROPORTIONATE SHARING SUBJECT TO LOSS TO THE MIXED FUND FIRST BEING BORNE BY THE FIDUCIARY

- *Re Hallett's Estate* (1880) 13 Ch D 696, Court of Appeal

A solicitor (Hallett), holding bonds for his client (Mrs Cotterill), had wrongfully sold them and had paid the proceeds into his current bank account, where the proceeds were mixed with his own money. Payments then went into and out of that account and, at the date of his death, stood at £3,000. On the administration of his estate following his death, Mrs Cotterill claimed to be entitled to trace in equity the proceeds of her bonds (some £2,145) into the account. On a first appeal from Fry J, the central question at issue was whether Mrs Cotterill could trace in equity, given that the bonds were held by Hallett as a bailee and not under a trust strictly speaking. Dismissing the appeal, the Court of Appeal held that the fiduciary relationship between Hallett and Mrs Cotterill was sufficient to allow tracing into the proceeds of sale of the bonds that had been wrongfully sold. On a second appeal, the central issue was whether the 'first in, first out' rule of *Clayton's Case* should be applied (as it had been by Fry J following *Pennell v Deffell* (1853) 4 De G M & G 372). If that rule were applied it was clear that a large portion of the client's money would have been paid out. A majority of the Court of Appeal (Thesiger LJ dissenting) reversed Fry J and held that the clients were entitled to an equitable charge of £2,145 over the fund. A presumption was applied that a fiduciary is acting honestly and therefore intends to dissipate his own money and not that of the beneficiary.

THE FIRST APPEAL

Jessel MR: . . . [Hallett] was bailee of the bonds, and an agent to receive the dividends on the bonds. There is no doubt, therefore, that Mr *Hallett* stood in a fiduciary position towards Mrs *Cotterill*. Mr *Hallett*, before his death, I regret to say, improperly sold the bonds and put the money to his general account at his bankers. It is not disputed that the money remained at his bankers mixed with his own money at the time of his death; that is, he had not drawn out the money from his bankers. In that position of matters Mrs *Cotterill* claimed to be entitled to receive the proceeds, or the amount of the proceeds, of the bonds out of the money in the hands of Mr *Hallett's* bankers at the time of his death, and that claim was allowed by the learned Judge of the Court below, and I think was properly so allowed . . . . The modern doctrine of Equity as regards property disposed of by persons in a fiduciary position is a very clear and well-established doctrine. You can, if the sale was rightful, take the proceeds of the sale, if you can identify them. If the sale was wrongful, you can still take the proceeds of the sale, in a sense adopting the sale for the purpose of taking the proceeds, if you can identify them. There is no distinction, therefore, between a rightful and a wrongful disposition of the property, so far as regards the right of the beneficial owner to follow the proceeds. But it very often happens that you cannot identify the proceeds. The proceeds may have been invested together with money belonging to the person in a fiduciary position, in a purchase. He may have bought land with it, for instance, or he may have bought chattels with it. Now, what is the position of the beneficial owner as regards such purchases? I will, first of all, take his position when the purchase is clearly made with what I will call, for shortness, the trust money, although it is not confined, as I will shew presently, to express trusts. In that case, according to the now well-established doctrine of Equity, the beneficial owner has a right to elect either to take the property purchased, or to hold it as a security for the amount of the trust money laid out in the purchase; or, as we generally express it, he is entitled at his election either to take the property, or to have a charge on the property for the amount of the trust money. But in the second case, where a trustee has mixed the money with his own, there is this distinction, that the *cestui que trust*, or beneficial owner, can no longer elect to take the property, because it is no longer bought with the trust-money simply and purely, but with a mixed fund. He is, however, still entitled to a charge on the property purchased, for the amount of the trust-money laid out in the purchase; and that charge is quite independent of the fact of the amount laid out by the trustee. The moment you get a substantial portion of it furnished by the trustee, using the word 'trustee' in the sense I have mentioned, as including all persons in a fiduciary relation, the right to the charge follows. That is the modern doctrine of Equity. Has it ever been suggested, until very recently, that there is any distinction between an express trustee, or an agent, or a bailee, or a collector of rents, or anybody else in a fiduciary position? I have never heard, until quite recently, such a distinction suggested. . . . It can have no foundation in principle, because the beneficial ownership is the same, wherever the legal ownership may be. If you have goods bargained and sold to a man upon trust to sell and hand over the net proceeds to another, that other is the beneficial owner; but if instead of being bargained and sold, so as to vest the legal ownership in the trustee, they are deposited with him to sell as agent, so that the legal ownership remains in the beneficial owner, can it be supposed, in a Court of Equity, that the rights of the beneficial owner are different, he being entire beneficial owner in both cases? I say on principle it is impossible to imagine there can be any difference. . . .

Baggallay and **Thesiger LJJ** delivered judgments also dismissing the appeal.

THE SECOND APPEAL

Jessel MR: . . . The question we have to consider depends on very few facts. I will first state all those which I think material, and on which it appears to me my judgment ought to be based. A Mr *Hallett*, a solicitor, was a trustee of some bonds. Without authority and improperly he sold them, and on the 14th of November, 1877, by his direction the proceeds of these bonds were paid to his credit at Messrs. *Winnings' Bank*, and there mixed with moneys belonging to himself, to the credit of the same banking account, and he also drew out by ordinary cheque moneys from the banking account, which he used for his own purposes. He died in February, 1878, and at his death the account stood in this way: that there was more money to the credit of the account than the sum of trust money paid into it; but if you applied every payment made after November, 1877, to the first items on the credit side in order of date, a large portion of the trust money would have been paid out. The question really is, whether or not, under these circumstances, the beneficiaries—that is, the persons entitled to the trust moneys, who are the present Appellants—are or are not entitled to say that the moneys subsequently drawn out—that is, drawn out by Mr *Hallett* subsequently to November, 1877—and applied for his own use, are to be treated as appropriated to the repayment of his own moneys, or whether the Respondents, the executors, are right in their contention that they are to be treated as appropriated in the way I have mentioned, so as to diminish the amount now applicable to the repayment of the trust funds.

. . . Now, first upon principle, nothing can be better settled, either in our own law, or, I suppose, the law of all civilised countries, than this, that where a man does an act which may be rightfully performed, he cannot say that that act was intentionally and in fact done wrongly. . . .

When we come to apply that principle to the case of a trustee who has blended trust moneys with his own, it seems to me perfectly plain that he cannot be heard to say that he took away the trust money when he had a right to take away his own money. The simplest case put is the mingling of trust moneys in a bag with money of the trustee's own. Suppose he has a hundred sovereigns in a bag, and he adds to them another hundred sovereigns of his own, so that they are commingled in such a way that they cannot be distinguished, and the next day he draws out for his own purposes £100, is it tolerable for anybody to allege that what he drew out was the first £100, the trust money, and that he misappropriated it, and left his own £100 in the bag? It is obvious he must have taken away that which he had a right to take away, his own £100. What difference does it make if, instead of being in a bag, he deposits it with his banker, and then pays in other money of his own, and draws out some money for his own purposes? Could he say that he had actually drawn out anything but his own money? His money was there, and he had a right to draw it out, and why should the natural act of simply drawing out the money be attributed to anything except to his ownership of money which was at his bankers.

It is said, no doubt, that according to the modern theory of banking, the deposit banker is a debtor for the money. So he is, and not a trustee in the strict sense of the word. At the same time one must recollect that the position of a deposit banker is different from that of an ordinary debtor. Still he is for some purposes a debtor, and it is said if a debt of this kind is paid by a banker, although the total balance is the amount owing by the banker, yet considering the repayments and the sums paid in by the depositor, you attribute the first sum drawn out to the first sum paid in. That was a rule first established by Sir *William Grant* in *Clayton's Case*; a very convenient rule, and I have nothing to say against it unless there is evidence either of agreement to the contrary or of circumstances from which a contrary intention must be presumed, and then of course that which is a mere presumption of law gives way to those other considerations. Therefore, it does appear to me there is nothing in the world laid down by Sir *William Grant* in *Clayton's Case*, or in the numerous cases which follow it, which in the slightest degree affects the principle, which I consider to be clearly established. . . .

Baggallay LJ delivered a judgment agreeing with Jessel MR. Thesiger LJ dissented on the ground that the court was bound by *Pennell v Deffell* (1853) 4 De G M & G 372 to apply the 'first in, first out' rule.

• *Re Oatway* [1903] 2 Ch 356, Chancery Division

A trustee (Oatway) of a trust set up under the will of Charles Skipper wrongly mixed £3,000 of trust money with £4,000 of his own. After using £2,137 from the fund to buy shares in the Oceana company, he dissipated the rest. On Oatway's death the question arose whether the beneficiaries under the Skipper trust were entitled to trace to the proceeds of sale of the shares (£2,475) which were standing in Oatway's name at his death. Joyce J held that they were so entitled.

Joyce J: . . . It is a principle settled as far back as the time of the Year Books that, whatever alteration of form any property may undergo, the true owner is entitled to seize it in its new shape if he can prove the identity of the original material: see Blackstone, vol. ii, p. 405, and *Lupton v White*.[1] But this rule is carried no farther than necessity requires, and is applied only to cases where the compound is such as to render it impossible to apportion the respective shares of the parties. Thus, if the quality of the articles that are mixed be uniform, and the original quantities known, as in the case of so many pounds of trust money mixed with so many pounds of the trustee's own money, the person by whose act the confusion took place is still entitled to claim his proper quantity, but subject to the quantity of the other proprietor being first made good out of the whole mass: 2 Stephen's Commentaries (13th ed.), 20. Trust money may be followed into land or any other property in which it has been invested; and when a trustee has, in making any purchase or investment, applied trust money together with his

---

1 (1808) 15 Ves 432.

own, the cestuis que trust are entitled to a charge on the property purchased for the amount of the trust money laid out in the purchase or investment. Similarly, if money held by any person in a fiduciary capacity be paid into his own banking account, it may be followed by the equitable owner, who, as against the trustee, will have a charge for what belongs to him upon the balance to the credit of the account. If then, the trustee pays in further sums, and from time to time draws out money by cheques, but leaves a balance to the credit of the account, it is settled that he is not entitled to have the rule in *Clayton's Case* applied so as to maintain that the sums which have been drawn out and paid away so as to be incapable of being recovered represented pro tanto the trust money, and that the balance remaining is not trust money, but represents only his own moneys paid into the account. *Brown v Adams*[2] to the contrary ought not to be followed since the decision in *In re Hallett's Estate*. It is, in my opinion, equally clear that when any of the money drawn out has been invested, and the investment remains in the name or under the control of the trustee, the rest of the balance having been afterwards dissipated by him, he cannot maintain that the investment which remains represents his own money alone, and that what has been spent and can no longer be traced and recovered was the money belonging to the trust. In other words, when the private money of the trustee and that which he held in a fiduciary capacity have been mixed in the same banking account, from which various payments have from time to time been made, then, in order to determine to whom any remaining balance or any investment that may have been paid for out of the account ought to be deemed to belong, the trustee must be debited with all the sums that have been withdrawn and applied to his own use so as to be no longer recoverable, and the trust money in like manner be debited with any sums taken out and duly invested in the names of the proper trustees. The order of priority in which the various withdrawals and investments may have been respectively made is wholly immaterial. I have been referring, of course, to cases where there is only one fiduciary owner or set of cestuis que trust claiming whatever may be left as against the trustee. In the present case there is no balance left. The only investment or property remaining which represents any part of the mixed moneys paid into the banking account is the Oceana shares purchased for 2137*l*. Upon these, therefore, the trust had a charge for the 3000*l*. trust money paid into the account. That is to say, those shares and the proceeds thereof belong to the trust.

It was objected that the investment in the Oceana shares was made at a time when Oatway's own share of the balance to the credit of the account (if the whole had been then justly distributed) would have exceeded 2137*l*., the price of the shares; that he was therefore entitled to withdraw that sum, and might rightly apply it for his own purposes; and that consequently the shares should be held to belong to his estate. To this I answer that he never was entitled to withdraw the 2137*l*. from the account, or, at all events, that he could not be entitled to take that sum from the account and hold it or the investment made therewith, freed from the charge in favour of the trust, unless or until the trust money paid into the account had been first restored, and the trust fund reinstated by due investment of the money in the joint names of the proper trustees, which never was done.

The investment by Oatway, in his own name, of the 2137*l*. in Oceana shares no more got rid of the claim or charge of the trust upon the money so invested, than would have been the case if he had drawn a cheque for 2137*l*. and simply placed and retained the amount in a drawer without further disposing of the money in any way. The proceeds of the Oceana shares must be held to belong to the trust funds under the will of which Oatway and Maxwell Skipper were the trustees.

NOTES AND QUESTIONS

1. This case shows that, where the mixed fund comprises money of a beneficiary and the defaulting fiduciary, the correct tracing principle is not that the money first withdrawn is the

---

2 LR 4 Ch 764.

fiduciary's (on a presumption of honesty) but rather that, before a proportionate sharing rule is applied, losses to the mixed fund should first be borne by the fiduciary (cf. *Re Hallett's Estate*, above, 672).

2. The contrast to the straightforward proportionate sharing principle that is applied where the mixed fund comprises the money of two innocent parties can be illustrated by the following example (cf. above, 659, note 3). If £1,000 of C's money was mixed in breach of trust by a trustee (X) with £2,000 of X's money, and X dissipates £900 so that the value of the fund falls to £2,100 C can trace to (and has an equitable lien for) the £1,000 rather than being confined to a proportionate share of £2,100.

- ## *Re Tilley's Will Trusts* [1967] 1 Ch 1179, Chancery Division

Mrs Tilley received £2,237 on trust for her daughter and son. In breach of trust she mixed it with her private funds and used the mixed fund to purchase houses so that at her death the fund stood at £94,000. The question at issue (in an action by the personal representative of her deceased daughter) was whether the daughter and son were entitled to a proportionate share of the higher mixed fund or were limited to the £2,237. Ungoed-Thomas J held that normally a beneficiary would be entitled to a proportionate share even in the case of a mixed fund which has increased in value but that, on the facts, this was displaced by the trustee's intention to use only her own money or overdraft facilities to make the (profitable) purchases. The daughter was therefore merely entitled to a charge on the defendant's bank account for half of £2,237 (plus interest).

Ungoed-Thomas J: . . .

In Snell's *Principles of Equity*, 26th edn (1966), the law is thus stated at page 315:

> 'Where the trustee mixes trust money with his own, the equities are clearly unequal. Accordingly, the beneficiaries are entitled to a first charge on the mixed fund, or on any land, securities or other assets purchased with it. Thus if the trustee purchases shares with part of the mixed fund, leaving enough of it to repay the trust moneys, and then dissipates the balance, the beneficiaries' charge binds the shares; for although under the rule in *In re Hallett's Estate* the trustee is presumed to have bought the shares out of his own money, the charge attached to the entire fund, and could be discharged only by restoring the trust moneys. Where the property purchased has increased in value, the charge will be not merely for the amount of the trust moneys but for a proportionate part of the increased value. Thus if the trustee purchases land with £500 of his own money and £1,000 of trust moneys, and the land doubles in value, he would be profiting from his breach of trust if he were entitled to all except £1,000; the beneficiaries are accordingly entitled to a charge on the land for £2,000.'

For the defendants it has been rightly admitted that if a trustee wrongly uses trust money to pay the whole of the purchase price in respect of the purchase of an asset a beneficiary can elect either to treat the purchased asset as trust property or to treat the purchased asset as security for the recouping of the trust money. It was further conceded that this right of election by a beneficiary also applies where the asset is purchased by a trustee in part out of his own money and in part out of the trust moneys, so that he may, if he wishes, require the asset to be treated as trust property with regard to that proportion of it which the trust moneys contributed to its purchase.

. . .

The principle in *Lupton v White*[1] is not applicable to this bank account as the amount of trust moneys paid into the mixed bank account is distinguishable as £2,237 and can be readily separated

---

1 15 Ves. 432 [see the reference to the principle of this case in *Re Oatway*, above, 674].

from Mrs Tilley's personal moneys. In the circumstances of this case there would be a charge on the properties purchased by Mrs Tilley out of the bank account as security for repayment of the £2,237 trust moneys paid into her bank account in accordance with the principle in *In re Oatway*, but that would be immaterial as the £2,237 is readily available out of Mrs Tilley's estate.

But can the beneficiary claim the proportion of the proceeds of sale of 11, Church Street which £179 approximately bears to its purchase price of £1,000, and the proportion of the proceeds of sale of 17–17A, High Street for which £82 10s. bears to the purchase price of approximately £2,050, plus costs? These trust moneys bore a small proportion to the purchase price of the properties. Mrs Tilley had ample overdraft facilities to pay the price without relying on these trust sums at the time of the High Street purchase, for she had an overdraft of over £22,000 apparently within her own overdraft facilities, and presumably properly secured, and this would make any contribution of £82 10s. negligible. She had throughout mixed her personal finances and those of her husband's estate, whether paying that estate's debts when it was without ready money or paying its proceeds of sale into her account. The £179 and the £82 10s. were clearly not trust moneys deliberately taken by Mrs Tilley out of the trust fund for the purpose of investing in property in her name. They merely avoided, to the extent of their amount, the use of Mrs Tilley's ample overdraft facilities, and in the case of the £179 that advantage was lost after two months by her bank account showing a credit, although it went into debit again 17 months later. And no interest in these trust sums was lost to any other beneficiary as Mrs Tilley was herself the life-tenant.

All these considerations appear to me to indicate overwhelmingly that Mrs Tilley was not deliberately using trust moneys to invest in or contribute towards or otherwise buy properties in her own name and the whole course of dealing with the trust funds and the bank accounts and the properties purchased and their history, which I have mentioned, indicate that what happened was that Mrs Tilley mixed the trust moneys and her own in the bank account but did not rely on the trust moneys for any of the purchases. If, as it was suggested for the defendants, the correct test whether a beneficiary is entitled to adopt a purchase by a trustee to which his trust moneys have contributed and thus claim a due proportion of its profits, is a subjective test, depending on the trustee's intention to use the trust moneys to contribute to the purchase, then in my view there was no such intention and the beneficiary is not so entitled. But my conclusions about the trustee's intention is based not on any direct evidence but on the circumstantial evidence which I have mentioned. If, of course, a trustee deliberately uses trust money to contribute with his own money to buy property in his own name, then I would see no difficulty in enabling a beneficiary to adopt the purchase and claim a share of any resulting profits. But the subjective test does not appear to me to be exclusive, or indeed adequate, if it is the only test.

It seems to me that if, having regard to all the circumstances of the case objectively considered, it appears that the trustee has in fact, whatever his intention, laid out trust moneys in or towards a purchase, then the beneficiaries are entitled to the property purchased and any profits which it produces to the extent to which it has been paid for out of the trust moneys. But, even by this objective test, it appears to me that the trust moneys were not in this case so laid out. It seems to me, on a proper appraisal of all the facts of this particular case, that Mrs Tilley's breach halted at the mixing of the funds in her bank account. Although properties bought out of those funds would, like the bank account itself, at any rate if the moneys in the bank account were inadequate, be charged with repayment of the trust moneys which then would stand in the same position as the bank account, yet the trust moneys were not invested in properties at all but merely went in reduction of Mrs Tilley's overdraft which was in reality the source of the purchase-moneys.

The plaintiff's claim therefore fails and he is entitled to no more than repayment of the half of the £2,237, interest not being in issue. £2,237 is readily available, which makes the existence of any charge for its security immaterial.

NOTES AND QUESTIONS

1. This decision is, on its facts, controversial because it cuts back the logical application of the tracing rules by taking into account that the claimant could have used other funds to make the same investment.

2. Ungoed-Thomas J, in earlier parts of his judgment, rejected the view that there was anything in Jessel MR's judgment in *Re Hallett's Estate* (see above, 672) to contradict his view that a beneficiary was entitled to a proportionate share of a more valuable fund.

3. Ungoed-Thomas J's view that an innocent claimant is entitled to a proportionate share of a more valuable fund (at least where the mixing and investment have been carried out by a defaulting fiduciary) was subsequently approved in *Foskett v McKeown* (below).

- ### *Foskett v McKeown* [2001] 1 AC 102, House of Lord

A fraudulent trustee (Murphy) had taken £20,440 from a trust fund held by him for the claimant beneficiaries (who were purchasers of plots of land in Portugal). In breach of trust he used the money to pay the fourth and fifth premiums on a policy insuring his life. The first two and, it was assumed, the third premiums had been paid entirely from his own money. When he later committed suicide, the defendants (his children) were paid out £1M under the insurance policy. The claimants argued that they were entitled to a 2/5ths share of the £1M proportionate to the premiums that, in breach of trust, had been paid using the trust money. The Court of Appeal had held that the claimants were entitled only to a lien over the proceeds of the policy to secure repayment of the amount of the fourth and fifth premiums. But this was reversed by the House of Lords, by a three-two majority, which held that the claimants were entitled to a proportionate share of the £1M.

Lord Browne-Wilkinson: . . .

The crucial factor in this case is to appreciate that the purchasers are claiming a proprietary interest in the policy moneys and that such proprietary interest is not dependent on any discretion vested in the court. Nor is the purchasers' claim based on unjust enrichment. It is based on the assertion by the purchasers of their equitable proprietary interest in identified property.

. . .

This case does not depend on whether it is fair, just and reasonable to give the purchases an interest as a result of which the court in its discretion provides a remedy. It is a case of hard-nosed property rights.

Can then the sums improperly used from the purchaser's moneys be traced into the policy moneys? Tracing is a process whereby assets are identified. I do not now want to enter into the dispute whether the legal and equitable rules of tracing are the same or differ. The question does not arise in this case. The question of tracing which does arise is whether the rules of tracing are those regulating tracing through a mixed fund or those regulating the position when moneys of one person have been innocently expended on the property of another. In the former case (mixing of funds) it is established law that the mixed fund belongs proportionately to those whose moneys were mixed. In the latter case it is equally clear that money expended on maintaining or improving the property of another normally gives rise, at the most, to a proprietary lien to recover the moneys so expended.

. . .

The speech of my noble and learned friend, Lord Millett, demonstrates why the analogy with moneys mixed in an account is the correct one.

. . .

The contrary view appears to be based primarily on the ground that to give the purchasers a rateable share of the policy moneys is not to reverse an unjust enrichment but to give the purchasers a wholly unwarranted windfall. I do not myself quibble at the description of it being 'a windfall' on the facts of this case. But this windfall is enjoyed because of the rights which the purchasers enjoy under the law of property. A man under whose land oil is discovered enjoys a very valuable windfall but no one suggests that he, as owner of the property, is not entitled to the windfall which goes with his property right. We are not dealing with a claim in unjust enrichment.

. . .

Lord Steyn (dissenting): . . . There are four considerations which materially affect my approach to the claim of the purchasers. First the relative moral claims of the purchasers and the children must be considered. The purchasers emphasise that their claim is the result of the deliberate wrongdoing of Mr Murphy. This is a point in favour of the purchasers. Moreover the case for the children is not assisted by the fact that Mr Murphy sought to make provision for his family. The legal question would be the same if the beneficiary under the express trust was a business associate of Mr Murphy. On the other hand, it is an important fact that the children were wholly unaware of any wrongdoing by their father. Secondly, it is clear that in the event the premiums paid in 1989 and 1990 added nothing of value to the policy. The policy was established and the children acquired vested interests (subject to defeasance) before Mr Murphy pursuant to the rights acquired by the children before 1989. The entitlement of the children was not in any way improved by payment of the 1989 and 1990 premiums. Thirdly, the purchasers have no claim in unjust enrichment in a substantive sense against the children because the payment of the 1989 and 1990 premiums conferred no additional benefit on the children. They were not enriched by the payment of those premiums: they merely received their shares of the sum assured in accordance with their pre-existing entitlement. The fourth point is that the children, as wholly innocent parties, can cogently say that, if they had become aware that Mr Murphy planned to use trust money to pay the fourth and fifth premiums, they would have insisted that he did not so pay those premiums, with the result that they would still have received the same death benefit. . . .

In arguing the merits of the proprietary claim counsel for the purchasers from time to time invoked 'the rules of tracing'. By that expression he was placing reliance on a corpus of supposed rules of law, divided into common law and equitable rules. In truth tracing is a process of identifying assets: it belongs to the realm of evidence. It tells us nothing about legal or equitable rights to the assets traced. In a crystalline analysis Professor Birks ('The Necessity of a Unitary Law of Tracing', essay in *Making Commercial Law, Essays in Honour of Roy Goode* (1997), pp 239–258) explained, at p 257, that there is a unified regime for tracing and that 'it allows tracing to be cleanly separated from the business of asserting rights in or in relation to assets successfully traced'. Applying this reasoning Professor Birks concludes, at p 258:

> 'that the modern law is equipped with various means of coping with the evidential difficulties which a tracing exercise is bound to encounter. The process of identification thus ceases to be either legal or equitable and becomes, as is fitting, genuinely neutral as to the rights exigible in respect of the assets into which the value in question is traced. The tracing exercise once success-fully completed, it can then be asked what rights, if any, the plaintiff can, on his particular facts, assert. It is at that point that it become relevant to recall that on some facts those rights will be personal, on others proprietary, on some legal, and on others equitable.'

I regard this explanation as correct. It is consistent with orthodox principle. It clarifies the correct approach to so-called tracing claims. It explains what tracing is about without providing answers to controversies about legal or equitable rights to assets so traced.

. . .

There is in principle no difficulty about allowing a proprietary claim in respect of the proceeds of an insurance policy. If in the circumstances of the present case the stolen moneys had been wholly or partly causative of the production of the death benefit received by the children there would have been no obstacle to admitting such a proprietary claim. But those are not the material facts of the case.

. . .

Given that the moneys stolen from the purchasers did not contribute or add to what the children received, in accordance with their rights established before the theft by Mr Murphy, the proprietary claim of the purchasers is not in my view underpinned by any considerations of fairness or justice. And, if this view is correct, there is no justification for creating by analogy with cases on equitable interests in mixed funds a new proprietary right to the policy moneys in the special circumstances of the present case.

. . .

Lord Hoffmann My Lords, I have had the advantage of reading in draft the speech of my noble and learned friend, Lord Millett. I agree with him that this is a straightforward case of mixed substitution (what the Roman lawyers, if they had had an economy which required tracing through bank accounts, would have called confusio). I agree with his conclusion that Mr Murphy's children, claiming through him, and the trust beneficiaries whose money he used, are entitled to share in the proceeds of the insurance policy in proportion to the value which they respectively contributed to the policy. This is not based upon unjust enrichment except in the most trivial sense of that expression. It is, as my noble and learned friend says, a vindication of proprietary right.

. . .

Lord Hope (dissenting) . . . On the agreed facts it is plain that the purchasers can trace their money through the premiums which were paid with it into the policy. When the insurers paid out the agreed sum by way of death benefit, the sum which they paid to the trustees of the policy was paid in consideration of the receipt by them of all the premiums. As *Smith, The Law of Tracing* (1997), p 235, has explained, the policy proceeds are the product of a mixed substitution where the value being traced into a policy of life assurance has provided a part of the premiums. In my opinion that is enough to entitle the purchasers, if they cannot obtain more, at least to obtain reimbursement of their own money with interest from the proceeds of the policy. There can be no doubt as to where the equities lie on the question of their right to recover from the proceeds the equivalent in value of that which they lost when their money was misappropriated.

. . .

I do not think that the purchasers can demonstrate on these facts that they have a proprietary right to a proportionate share of the proceeds. They cannot show that their money contributed to any extent to, or increased the value of, the amount paid to the trustees of the policy. A substantially greater sum was paid out by the insurers as death benefit than the total of the sums which they received by way of premium. A profit was made on the investment. But the terms of the policy show that the amount which produced this profit had been fixed from the outset when the first premium was paid. It was attributable to the rights obtained by the life assured when he paid the first premium from his own money. No part of that sum was attributable to value of the money taken from the purchasers to pay the additional premiums.

. . .

There remains the question which Mr Mawrey raised in his alternative argument, which is whether the purchasers have a remedy in unjust enrichment.

. . .

These questions were not fully explored in the course of the argument, but I think that it is not necessary to do more than to make a few basic points in order to show why I consider that the purchasers cannot obtain what they want by invoking this remedy. If it could be shown that the children had consciously participated in the life assured's wrongdoing and that, having done so, they had profited from his subtraction from the purchasers of the money used to pay the premiums, the answer would be that the law will not allow them to retain that benefit. A remedy would lie against them in unjust enrichment for the amount unjustly subtracted from the purchasers and for any profit attributable to that amount. But in this case it is common ground that the children are innocent of any wrongdoing. They are innocent third parties to the unjust transactions between the life assured and the purchasers. In my opinion the law of unjust enrichment should not make them worse off as a result of those transactions than they would have been if those transactions had not happened.

The aim of the law is to correct an enrichment which is unjust, but the remedy can only be taken against a defendant who has been enriched. The undisputed facts of this case show that the children were no better off following payment of the premiums which were paid with the money subtracted from the purchasers than they would have been if those premiums had not been paid. This is because, for the reasons explained by Hobhouse LJ [1998] Ch 265, 286d–f, the insurers would have been entitled to have recourse to the premiums already paid to keep up the policy and because the premiums paid from the purchasers' money did not, in the events which happened, affect the amount of the sum payable in the event of the insured's death. The argument for a claim against them in unjust enrichment fails on causation. The children were not enriched by the payment of these premiums. On the contrary, they would be worse off if they were to be required to share the proceeds of the policy with the purchasers. It is as well that the purchasers' remedy in respect of the premiums and interest does not depend upon unjust enrichment, otherwise they would have had to have been denied a remedy in respect of that part of their claim also.

. . .

Lord Millett My Lords, this is a textbook example of tracing through mixed substitutions. At the beginning of the story the plaintiffs were beneficially entitled under an express trust to a sum standing in the name of Mr Murphy in a bank account. From there the money moved into and out of various bank accounts where in breach of trust it was inextricably mixed by Mr Murphy with his own money. After each transaction was completed the plaintiffs' money formed an indistinguishable part of the balance standing to Mr Murphy's credit in his bank account. The amount of that balance represented a debt due from the bank to Mr Murphy, that is to say a chose in action. At the penultimate stage the plaintiffs' money was represented by an indistinguishable part of a different chose in action, viz, the debt prospectively and contingently due from an insurance company to its policyholders, being the trustees of a settlement made by Mr Murphy for the benefit of his children. At the present and final stage it forms an indistinguishable part of the balance standing to the credit of the respondent trustees in their bank account.

Tracing and following

The process of ascertaining what happened to the plaintiffs' money involves both tracing and following. These are both exercises in locating assets which are or may be taken to represent an asset belonging to the plaintiffs and to which they assert ownership. The processes of following and tracing are, however, distinct. Following is the process of following the same asset as it moves from hand to hand. Tracing is the process of identifying a new asset as the substitute for the old. Where one asset is exchanged for another, a claimant can elect whether to follow the original asset into the hands of the new owner or to trace its value into the new asset in the hands of the same owner. In practice his choice is often dictated by the circumstances. In the present case the plaintiffs do not seek to follow the money any further once it reached the bank or insurance company, since its identity was lost in the hands of the recipient (which in any case obtained an unassailable title as a bona fide purchaser for value without notice of the plaintiffs' beneficial interest). Instead the plaintiffs have chosen at each stage to trace the money into its proceeds, viz, the debt presently due from the bank to the account holder or the debt prospectively and contingently due from the insurance company to the policy holders.

Having completed this exercise, the plaintiffs claim a continuing beneficial interest in the insurance money. Since this represents the product of Mr Murphy's own money as well as theirs, which Mr Murphy mingled indistinguishably in a single chose in action, they claim a beneficial interest in a proportionate part of the money only. The transmission of a claimant's property rights from one asset to its traceable proceeds is part of our law of property, not of the law of unjust enrichment. There is no 'unjust factor' to justify restitution (unless 'want of title' be one, which makes the point). The claimant succeeds if at all by virtue of his own title, not to reverse unjust enrichment. Property rights are determined by fixed rules and settled principles. They are not discretionary. They do not depend upon ideas of what is 'fair, just and reasonable'. Such concepts, which in reality mask decisions of legal policy, have no place in the law of property.

A beneficiary of a trust is entitled to a continuing beneficial interest not merely in the trust property but in its traceable proceeds also, and his interest binds every one who takes the property or its traceable proceeds except a bona fide purchaser for value without notice. In the present case the plaintiffs' beneficial interest plainly bound Mr Murphy, a trustee who wrongfully mixed the trust money with his own and whose every dealing with the money (including the payment of the premiums) was in breach of trust. It similarly binds his successors, the trustees of the children's settlement, who claim no beneficial interest of their own, and Mr Murphy's children, who are volunteers. They gave no value for what they received and derive their interest from Mr Murphy by way of gift.

Tracing

We speak of money at the bank, and of money passing into and out of a bank account. But of course the account holder has no money at the bank. Money paid into a bank account belongs legally and beneficially to the bank and not to the account holder. The bank gives value for it, and it is accordingly not usually possible to make the money itself the subject of an adverse claim. Instead a claimant normally sues the account holder rather than the bank and lays claim to the proceeds of the money in his hands. These consist of the debt or part of the debt due to him from the bank. We speak of tracing money into and out of the account, but there is no money in the account. There is merely a single debt of an amount equal to the final balance standing to the credit of the account holder. No money passes from paying bank to receiving bank or through the clearing system (where the money flows may be in the opposite direction). There is simply a series of debits and credits which are causally and transactionally linked. We also speak of tracing one asset into another, but this too is inaccurate. The original asset still exists in the hands of the new owner, or it may have become untraceable. The claimant claims the new asset because it was acquired in whole or in part with the original asset. What he traces, therefore, is not the physical asset itself but the value inherent in it.

Tracing is thus neither a claim nor a remedy. It is merely the process by which a claimant demonstrates what has happened to his property, identifies its proceeds and the persons who have handled or received them, and justifies his claim that the proceeds can properly be regarded as representing his property. Tracing is also distinct from claiming. It identifies the traceable proceeds of the claimant's property. It enables the claimant to substitute the traceable proceeds for the original asset as the subject matter of his claim. But it does not affect or establish his claim. That will depend on a number of factors including the nature of his interest in the original asset. He will normally be able to maintain the same claim to the substituted asset as he could have maintained to the original asset. If he held only a security interest in the original asset, he cannot claim more than a security interest in its proceeds. But his claim may also be exposed to potential defences as a result of intervening transactions. Even if the plaintiffs could demonstrate what the bank had done with their money, for example, and could thus identify its traceable proceeds in the hands of the bank, any claim by them to assert ownership of those proceeds would be defeated by the bona fide purchaser defence. The successful completion of a tracing exercise may be preliminary to a personal claim (as in *El Ajou v*

Dollar Land Holdings plc [1993] 3 All ER 717) or a proprietary one, to the enforcement of a legal right (as in *Trustees of the Property of F C Jones & Sons v Jones* [1997] Ch 159) or an equitable one.

Given its nature, there is nothing inherently legal or equitable about the tracing exercise. There is thus no sense in maintaining different rules for tracing at law and in equity. One set of tracing rules is enough. The existence of two has never formed part of the law in the United States: see *Scott on Trusts*, 4th ed. (1989), section 515, at pp 605–609. There is certainly no logical justification for allowing any distinction between them to produce capricious results in cases of mixed substitutions by insisting on the existence of a fiduciary relationship as a precondition for applying equity's tracing rules. The existence of such a relationship may be relevant to the nature of the claim which the plaintiff can maintain, whether personal or proprietary, but that is a different matter. I agree with the passages which my noble and learned friend, Lord Steyn, has cited from Professor Birks's essay 'The Necessity of a Unitary Law of Tracing', and with Dr Lionel Smith's exposition in his comprehensive monograph *The Law of Tracing* (1997): see particularly pp 120–130, 277–279 and 342–347.

This is not, however, the occasion to explore these matters further, for the present is a straightforward case of a trustee who wrongfully misappropriated trust money, mixed it with his own, and used it to pay for an asset for the benefit of his children. Even on the traditional approach, the equitable tracing rules are available to the plaintiffs. There are only two complicating factors. The first is that the wrongdoer used their money to pay premiums on an equity-linked policy of life assurance on his own life. The nature of the policy should make no difference in principle, though it may complicate the accounting. The second is that he had previously settled the policy for the benefit of his children. This should also make no difference. The claimant's rights cannot depend on whether the wrongdoer gave the policy to his children during his lifetime or left the proceeds to them by his will; or if during his lifetime whether he did so before or after he had recourse to the claimant's money to pay the premiums. The order of events does not affect the fact that the children are not contributors but volunteers who have received the gift of an asset paid for in part with misappropriated trust moneys.

The cause of action

As I have already pointed out, the plaintiffs seek to vindicate their property rights, not to reverse unjust enrichment. The correct classification of the plaintiffs' cause of action may appear to be academic, but it has important consequences. The two causes of action have different requirements and may attract different defences.

A plaintiff who brings an action in unjust enrichment must show that the defendant has been enriched at the plaintiff's expense, for he cannot have been unjustly enriched if he has not been enriched at all. But the plaintiff is not concerned to show that the defendant is in receipt of property belonging beneficially to the plaintiff or its traceable proceeds. The fact that the beneficial ownership of the property has passed to the defendant provides no defence; indeed, it is usually the very fact which founds the claim. Conversely, a plaintiff who brings an action like the present must show that the defendant is in receipt of property which belongs beneficially to him or its traceable proceeds, but he need not show that the defendant has been enriched by its receipt. He may, for example, have paid full value for the property, but he is still required to disgorge it if he received it with notice of the plaintiff's interest.

Furthermore, a claim in unjust enrichment is subject to a change of position defence, which usually operates by reducing or extinguishing the element of enrichment. An action like the present is subject to the bona fide purchaser for value defence, which operates to clear the defendant's title.

The tracing rules

The insurance policy in the present case is a very sophisticated financial instrument. Tracing into the rights conferred by such an instrument raises a number of important issues. It is therefore desirable to set out the basic principles before turning to deal with the particular problems to which policies of life assurance give rise.

The simplest case is where a trustee wrongfully misappropriates trust property and uses it exclusively to acquire other property for his own benefit. In such a case the beneficiary is entitled *at his option* either to assert his beneficial ownership of the proceeds or to bring a personal claim against the trustee for breach of trust and enforce an equitable lien or charge on the proceeds to secure restoration of the trust fund. He will normally exercise the option in the way most advantageous to himself. If the traceable proceeds have increased in value and are worth more than the original asset, he will assert his beneficial ownership and obtain the profit for himself. There is nothing unfair in this. The trustee cannot be permitted to keep any profit resulting from his misappropriation for himself, and his donees cannot obtain a better title than their donor. If the traceable proceeds are worth less than the original asset, it does not usually matter how the beneficiary exercises his option. He will take the whole of the proceeds on either basis. This is why it is not possible to identify the basis on which the claim succeeded in some of the cases.

Both remedies are proprietary and depend on successfully tracing the trust property into its proceeds. A beneficiary's claim against a trustee for breach of trust is a personal claim. It does not entitle him to priority over the trustee's general creditors unless he can trace the trust property into its product and establish a proprietary interest in the proceeds. If the beneficiary is unable to trace the trust property into its proceeds, he still has a personal claim against the trustee, but his claim will be unsecured. The beneficiary's proprietary claims to the trust property or its traceable proceeds can be maintained against the wrongdoer and anyone who derives title from him except a bona fide purchaser for value without notice of the breach of trust. The same rules apply even where there have been numerous successive transactions, so long as the tracing exercise is successful and no bona fide purchaser for value without notice has intervened.

A more complicated case is where there is a mixed substitution. This occurs where the trust money represents only part of the cost of acquiring the new asset. As James Barr Ames pointed out in 'Following Misappropriated Property into its Product' (1906) 19 HarvLRev 511, consistency requires that, if a trustee buys property partly with his own money and partly with trust money, the beneficiary should have the option of taking a proportionate part of the new property or a lien upon it, as may be most for his advantage. In principle it should not matter (and it has never previously been suggested that it does) whether the trustee mixes the trust money with his own and buys the new asset with the mixed fund or makes separate payments of the purchase price (whether simultaneously or sequentially) out of the different funds. In every case the value formerly inherent in the trust property has become located within the value inherent in the new asset.

The rule, and its rationale, were stated by Samuel Williston in 'The Right to Follow Trust Property when Confused with other Property' (1888) 2 Harv L Rev 28, 29:

> 'If the trust fund is traceable as having furnished in part the money with which a certain investment was made, and the proportion it formed of the whole money so invested is known or ascertainable, the cestui que trust should be allowed to regard the acts of the trustee as done for his benefit, in the same way that he would be allowed to if all the money so invested had been his; that is, he should be entitled in equity to an undivided share of the property which the trust money contributed to purchase—such a proportion of the whole as the trust money bore to the whole money invested. The reason in the one case as in the other is that the trustee cannot be allowed to make a profit from the use of the trust money, and if the property which he wrongfully purchased were held subject only to a lien for the amount invested, any appreciation in value would go to the trustee.'

If this correctly states the underlying basis of the rule (as I believe it does), then it is impossible to distinguish between the case where mixing precedes the investment and the case where it arises on and in consequence of the investment. It is also impossible to distinguish between the case where the investment is retained by the trustee and the case where it is given away to a gratuitous donee. The donee cannot obtain a better title than his donor, and a donor who is a trustee cannot be allowed to profit from his trust.

In *In re Hallett's Estate; Knatchbull v Hallett* (1880) 13 Ch D 696, 709 Sir George Jessel MR acknowledged that where an asset was acquired exclusively with trust money, the beneficiary could either assert equitable ownership of the asset or enforce a lien or charge over it to recover the trust money. But he appeared to suggest that in the case of a mixed substitution the beneficiary is confined to a lien. Any authority that this dictum might otherwise have is weakened by the fact that Sir George Jessel MR gave no reason for the existence of any such rule, and none is readily apparent. The dictum was plainly obiter, for the fund was deficient and the plaintiff was only claiming a lien. It has usually been cited only to be explained away: see for example *In re Tilley's Will Trusts* [1967] Ch 1179, 1186, *per* Ungoed-Thomas J; *Burrows, The Law of Restitution* (1993), p 368. It was rejected by the High Court of Australia in *Scott v Scott* (1963) 109 CLR 649: see the passage at pp 661–662 cited by Morritt LJ below [1998] Ch 265, 300–301. It has not been adopted in the United States: see the *American Law Institute, Restatement of the Law, Trusts* 2d (1959) at section 202(h). In *Primeau v Granfield* (1911) 184 F 480, 482 Learned Hand J expressed himself in forthright terms: 'On principle there can be no excuse for such a rule.'

In my view the time has come to state unequivocally that English law has no such rule. It conflicts with the rule that a trustee must not benefit from his trust. I agree with Burrows that the beneficiary's right to elect to have a proportionate share of a mixed substitution necessarily follows once one accepts, as English law does, (i) that a claimant can trace in equity into a mixed fund and (ii) that he can trace unmixed money into its proceeds and assert ownership of the proceeds.

Accordingly, I would state the basic rule as follows. Where a trustee wrongfully uses trust money to provide part of the cost of acquiring an asset, the beneficiary is entitled *at his option* either to claim a proportionate share of the asset or to enforce a lien upon it to secure his personal claim against the trustee for the amount of the misapplied money. It does not matter whether the trustee mixed the trust money with his own in a single fund before using it to acquire the asset, or made separate payments (whether simultaneously or sequentially) out of the differently owned funds to acquire a single asset.

Two observations are necessary at this point. First, there is a mixed substitution (with the results already described) whenever the claimant's property has contributed in part only towards the acquisition of the new asset. It is not necessary for the claimant to show in addition that his property has contributed to any increase in the *value* of the new asset. This is because, as I have already pointed out, this branch of the law is concerned with vindicating rights of property and not with reversing unjust enrichment. Secondly, the beneficiary's right to claim a lien is available only against a wrongdoer and those deriving title under him otherwise than for value. It is not available against competing contributors who are innocent of any wrongdoing. The tracing rules are not the result of any presumption or principle peculiar to equity. They correspond to the common law rules for following into physical mixtures (though the consequences may not be identical). Common to both is the principle that the interests of the wrongdoer who was responsible for the mixing and those who derive title under him otherwise than for value are subordinated to those of innocent contributors. As against the wrongdoer and his successors, the beneficiary is entitled to locate his contribution in any part of the mixture and to subordinate their claims to share in the mixture until his own contribution has been satisfied. This has the effect of giving the beneficiary a lien for his contribution if the mixture is deficient.

Innocent contributors, however, must be treated equally inter se. Where the beneficiary's claim is in competition with the claims of other innocent contributors, there is no basis upon which any of the claims can be subordinated to any of the others. Where the fund is deficient, the beneficiary is not entitled to enforce a lien for his contributions; all must share rateably in the fund.

The primary rule in regard to a mixed fund, therefore, is that gains and losses are borne by the contributors rateably. The beneficiary's right to elect instead to enforce a lien to obtain repayment is an exception to the primary rule, exercisable where the fund is deficient and the claim is made against the wrongdoer and those claiming through him. It is not necessary to consider whether there are any circumstances in which the beneficiary is confined to a lien in cases where the fund is more than sufficient to repay the contributions of all parties. It is sufficient to say that he is not so confined in a case like the present. It is not enough that those defending the claim are innocent of any wrongdoing if they are not themselves contributors but, like the trustees and Mr Murphy's children in the present case, are volunteers who derive title under the wrongdoer otherwise than for value. On ordinary principles such persons are in no better position than the wrongdoer, and are liable to suffer the same subordination of their interests to those of the claimant as the wrongdoer would have been. They certainly cannot do better than the claimant by confining him to a lien and keeping any profit for themselves.

. . .

[In the Court of Appeal] Hobhouse LJ adopted a different approach. He concentrated on the detailed terms of the policy, and in particular on the fact that in the event the payment of the fourth and fifth premiums with the plaintiffs' money made no difference to the amount of the death benefit. Once the third premium had been paid, there was sufficient surrender value in the policy, built up by the use of Mr Murphy's own money, to keep the policy on foot for the next few years, and as it happened Mr Murphy's death occurred during those few years. But this was adventitious and unpredictable at the time the premiums were paid. The argument is based on causation and as I have explained is a category mistake derived from the law of unjust enrichment. It is an example of the same fallacy that gives rise to the idea that the proceeds of an ordinary life policy belong to the party who paid the last premium without which the policy would have lapsed. But the question is one of attribution not causation. The question is not whether the same death benefit would have been payable if the last premium or last few premiums had not been paid. It is whether the death benefit is attributable to all the premiums or only to some of them. The answer is that death benefit is attributable to all of them because it represents the proceeds of realising the policy, and the policy in turn represents the product of all the premiums.

. . .

It is true that the last two premiums were not needed to provide the death benefit in the sense that in the events which happened the same amount would have been payable even if those premiums had not been paid. In other words, with the benefit of hindsight it can be seen that Mr Murphy made a bad investment when he paid the last two premiums. It is, therefore, superficially attractive to say that the plaintiffs' money contributed nothing of value. But the argument proves too much, for if the plaintiffs cannot trace their money into the proceeds of the policy, they should have no proprietary remedy at all, not even a lien for the return of their money. But the fact is that Mr Murphy, who could not foresee the future, did choose to pay the last two premiums, and to pay them with the plaintiffs' money; and they were applied by the insurer towards the payment of the internal premiums needed to fund the death benefit. It should not avail his donees that he need not have paid the premiums, and that if he had not then (in the events which happened) the insurers would have provided the same death benefit and funded it differently.

. . .

NOTES AND QUESTIONS

1. In applying the proportionate share approach Lords Hoffmann and Browne-Wilkinson took the simple approach of apportioning the final insurance pay-out according to the premiums paid. Lord Millett was content to accept this although he himself favoured a more complex proportionate sharing which attributed particular premiums to units of the insurance policy.

2. Although the claim was not being brought against the defaulting trustee (or his estate) Lord Millett stressed that the children could be in no better position than the defaulting trustee. The relevant tracing rules were, therefore, those applicable where an innocent party's funds have been mixed with those of a defaulting trustee. Although not entirely clear (and there is no direct authority) it appears that a proportionate share approach would also be applied where an innocent party mixes a beneficiary's money with his own and invests the mixed fund profitably.

3. Lord Millett's speech is of fundamental importance in its acceptance of Lionel Smith's thesis that tracing is different from following and claiming (see above, 647 and below, 700). The obiter dicta of Lords Steyn and Millett accepting the logic of a fusion of common law and equitable tracing rules are also of great importance.

4. The House of Lords treated the case as concerning the vindication of property rights not the reversal of an unjust enrichment. In particular, they regarded the proprietary right in the traced asset as being the same proprietary right that existed in relation to the original asset. Birks, *Unjust Enrichment* (2nd edn, 2005), 34–6 has criticized this for (a) falsely contrasting property and unjust enrichment, thereby missing the point that unjust enrichment can itself trigger proprietary rights and (b) relying on a 'fiction of persistence' to explain the proprietary right in the traced asset. In his view, the correct analysis was that a new proprietary right in the traced asset was being created to reverse the children's unjust enrichment at the claimants' expense. See also P Birks, 'Property, Unjust Enrichment and Tracing' (2001) 54 *CLP* 231; A Burrows, 'Proprietary Restitution: Unmasking Unjust Enrichment' (2001) 117 *LQR* 412.

5. It appears (especially from Lord Hope's dissenting speech) that the way in which the claimants presented their case may have contributed to their Lordships' view that vindication of property rights and unjust enrichment were two different ways of making the claim. Their Lordships seemed to think that there was a causation objection to an unjust enrichment analysis, i.e. the fourth and fifth premiums did not causally contribute to the insurance pay-out because that pay-out would have been made even if only the first two premiums had been paid. Is that a valid objection to an unjust enrichment analysis? In answering that, consider whether restitution of an unjust enrichment would be granted in the following example: A pays £1,000 by mistake to B; C would have paid B £1,000 had A not done so; and C will still do so if A is given restitution of £1,000 (so that there has been no change of position by A).

(iii) THE 'INTERMEDIATE BALANCE' (OR 'EXHAUSTION OF THE FUND') RULE

- *James Roscoe (Bolton) Ltd v Winder* [1915] 1 Ch 62, Chancery Division

The defendant, who was purchasing the claimant company, agreed to pay over to the claimant all moneys received by a certain date on account of book debts owing to the claimant. The defendant collected £455 of book debts but, in breach of the agreement and contrary to his fiduciary duty, kept the £455 in his own account. He then dissipated all but £25 of it before mixing his own money so that at his death the balance in the account stood at £358. The question was whether the claimant was entitled to trace to £358 or merely to £25. Sargant J held that the claimant could trace to only £25.

Sargant J: . . .
What is now claimed in the present action (because one or two other points have been given up) is a charge upon the 358*l.* 5*s.* 5*d.* remaining to the credit of the debtor's account at the time of his death, for the sum of 455*l.* 18*s.* 11*d.* received by him in respect of these book debts and paid into his banking account. That is the strict legal way of putting the claim, but, of course, practically it amounts to claiming the full sum of 358. 5*s.* 5*d.*, since that sum is less than the amount of the charge claimed.

The first point that was taken against the claim was that no trust was created by the agreement as to the book debts to be collected under it. In my opinion, that objection cannot be sustained. . . .

That being so, we have a case where, as in *In re Hallett's Estate*, the banking account of the debtor comprised not only moneys belonging to himself for his own purposes, but also moneys belonging to him upon trust for some one else, and that being so, and apart from the circumstances I am going to mention, it seems to me clear that the plaintiffs would be entitled to the charge they claim, and to receive the whole balance of 358*l.* 5*s.* 5*d.* standing to the debtor's credit at the time of his death, and that although there had been payments out of the account which, under the rule in *Clayton's Case*, would have been attributable to the earlier payments in.

In re Hallett's Estate, which would but for the circumstance I am going to mention entirely conclude this case, decided two clear points: First, that when a trustee mixes trust moneys with private moneys in one account the cestuis que trust have a charge on the aggregate amount for their trust fund; and, secondly, that when payments are made by the trustee out of the general account the payments are not to be appropriated against payments in to that account as in *Clayton's Case*, because the trustee is presumed to be honest rather than dishonest and to make payments out of his own private moneys and not out of the trust fund that was mingled with his private moneys.

But there is a further circumstance in the present case which seems to me to be conclusive in favour of the defendant as regards the greater part of the balance of 358*l.* 5*s* 5*d.* It appears that after the payment in by the debtor of a portion of the book debts which he had received the balance at the bank on May 19, 1913, was reduced by his drawings to a sum of 25*l.* 18*s.* only on May 21. So that, although the ultimate balance at the debtor's death was about 358*l.*, there had been an intermediate balance of only 25*l.* 18*s.* The result of that seems to me to be that the trust moneys cannot possibly be traced into this common fund, which was standing to the debtor's credit at his death, to an extent of more than 25*l.* 18*s.*, because, although prima facie under the second rule in *In re Hallett's Estate* any drawings out by the debtor ought to be attributed to the private moneys which he had at the bank and not to the trust moneys, yet, when the drawings out had reached such an amount that the whole of his private money part had been exhausted, it necessarily followed that the rest of the drawings must have been against trust moneys. There being on May 21, 1913, only 25*l.* 18*s.*, in all, standing to the credit of the debtor's account, it is quite clear that on that day he must have denuded his account of all the trust moneys there—the whole 455*l.* 18*s.* 11*d.*—except to the extent of 25*l.* 18*s.*

Practically, what counsel for the plaintiffs have been asking me to do . . . is to say that the debtor, by paying further moneys after May 21 into this common account, was impressing upon those further moneys so paid in the like trust or obligation, or charge of the nature of a trust, which had formerly been impressed upon the previous balances to the credit of that account. No doubt, counsel for the plaintiffs did say 'No. I am only asking you to treat the account as a whole, and to consider the balance from time to time standing to the credit of that account as subject to one continual charge or trust.' But I think that really is using words which are not appropriate to the facts. You must, for the purpose of tracing, which was the process adopted in *In re Hallett's Estate*, put your finger on some definite fund which either remains in its original state or can be found in another shape. That is tracing, and tracing, by the very facts of this case, seems to be absolutely excluded except as to the 25*l.* 18*s.*

Then, apart from tracing, it seems to me possible to establish this claim against the ultimate balance of 358*l.* 5*s.* 5*d.* only by saying that something was done, with regard to the additional moneys which are needed to make up that balance, by the person to whom those moneys belonged, the debtor, to substitute those moneys for the purpose of, or to impose upon those moneys a trust equivalent to, the trust which rested on the previous balance. Of course, if there was anything like a separate trust account, the payment of the further moneys into that account would, in itself, have been quite a sufficient indication of the intention of the debtor to substitute those additional moneys for the original trust moneys, and accordingly to impose, by way of substitution, the old trusts upon those additional moneys. But, in a case where the account into which the moneys are paid is the general trading account of the debtor on which he has been accustomed to draw both in the ordinary course and in breach of trust when there were trust funds standing to the credit of that account which were convenient for that purpose, I think it is impossible to attribute to him that by the mere payment into the account of further moneys, which to a large extent he subsequently used for purposes of his own, he intended to clothe those moneys with a trust in favour of the plaintiffs.

Certainly, after having heard *In re Hallett's Estate* stated over and over again, I should have thought that the general view of that decision was that it only applied to such an amount of the balance ultimately standing to the credit of the trustee as did not exceed the lowest balance of the account during the intervening period. That view has practically been taken, as far as I can make out, in the cases which have dealt with *In re Hallett's Estate*. *In re Oatway*, a decision of Joyce J, was cited to me in support of the plaintiffs' case, but I do not find anything in it to help them. All that Joyce J did in that case was to say that, if part of the mixed moneys can be traced into a definite security, that security will not become freed from the charge in favour of the trust, but will, together with any residue of the mixed moneys, remain subject to that charge. I am sure that nothing which he said was intended to mean that the trust was imposed upon any property into which the original fund could not be traced. . . . And certainly in the recent case of *Sinclair v Brougham* I can see nothing in any way to impeach the doctrine as to tracing laid down in *In re Hallett's Estate*.

In my opinion, therefore, the only part of the balance of 358*l*. 5*s*. 5*d*. which can be made available by the plaintiffs is the sum of 25*l*. 18*s*., being the smallest amount to which the balance, to the credit of the account had fallen between May 19, 1913, and the death of the debtor.

- **Re Goldcorp Exchange Ltd** [1995] 1 AC 74, Privy Council

The claimants bought gold bullion from a company. Under the terms of the purchase contract with most of them (the 'non-allocated claimants') the gold bullion bought was not to be separated and delivered to the purchasers but was to be kept unallocated as part of the company's overall stock of bullion. The purchasers were given the right on seven days' notice to take physical delivery of the bullion purchased. The company promised that the stock of bullion from which purchasers could call for delivery would always be sufficient to meet its obligations under all outstanding contracts of sale. The contractual arrangements with a class of claimants known as the 'Walker & Hall claimants' was different: the bullion purchased was kept entirely separate and the title and risk in that bullion passed to the purchaser. The company became hopelessly insolvent. In competition with a bank, which had a floating charge over all the company's assets, the claimants sought proprietary tracing remedies in respect of either the remaining stock of bullion (starting from the bullion purchased) or in respect of the company's general assets (starting from the purchase moneys paid). At first instance Thorp J rejected the claims of the non-allocated claimants but held that the Walker & Hall claimants were able to trace to the lowest intermediate balance of metal held. In contrast the New Zealand Court of Appeal, by a majority, held that all the claimants were able to trace their purchase moneys into the company's general assets, so that they had a charge over the company's assets ranking in priority to the bank's charge. On appeal by the bank and receivers the Privy Council overturned that decision and also restored Thorp J's decision as regards the Walker & Hall claimants.

Lord Mustill

[Having concluded, in agreement with all the judges in New Zealand, that the non-allocated claimants had not established a proprietary interest in the bullion]:

PROPRIETARY INTERESTS DERIVED FROM THE PURCHASE PRICE

Their Lordships now turn to the proposition, which first emerged during argument in the Court of Appeal, and which was not raised in *In re London Wine Co. (Shippers) Ltd* [1986] PCC 121, that a proprietary interest either sprang into existence on the sales to customers, or should now be imposed retrospectively through restitutionary remedies, in relation not to bullion but to the moneys originally paid by the customers under the contracts of sale. Here at least it is possible to pin down the subject matter to which the proprietary rights are said to relate. Nevertheless, their Lordships are constrained to reject all the various ways in which the submission has been presented, once again for a single comparatively simple reason.

  The first argument posits that the purchase moneys were from the outset impressed with a trust in favour of the payers. That a sum of money paid by the purchaser under a contract for the sale of goods is capable in principle of being the subject of a trust in the hands of the vendor is clear. For this purpose it is necessary to show either a mutual intention that the moneys should not fall within the general fund of the company's assets but should be applied for a special designated purpose, or that having originally been paid over without restriction the recipient has later constituted himself a trustee of the money: see *Quistclose Investments Ltd v Rolls Razor Ltd* [1970] AC 567, 581–2. This requirement was satisfied in *In re Kayford Ltd (In Liquidation)* [1975] 1 WLR 279 where a company in financial difficulties paid into a separate deposit account money received from customers for goods not yet delivered, with the intention of making withdrawals from the account only as and when delivery was effected, and of refunding the payment to customers if an insolvency made delivery impossible. The facts of the present case are, however, inconsistent with any such trust. This is not a situation where the customer engaged the company as agent to purchase bullion on his or her behalf, with immediate payment to put the agent in funds, delivery being postponed to suit the customer's convenience. The agreement was for a sale by the company to, and not the purchase by the company for, the customer. The latter paid the purchase price for one purpose alone, namely to perform his side of the bargain under which he would in due course be entitled to obtain delivery. True, another part of the consideration for the payment was the collateral promise to maintain separate cover, but this does not mean that the money was paid for the purpose of purchasing gold, either to create the separate stock or for any other reason. There was nothing in the express agreement to require, and nothing in their Lordships' view can be implied, which constrained in any way the company's freedom to spend the purchase money as it chose, or to establish the stock from any source and with any funds as it thought fit. This being so, their Lordships cannot concur in the decision of Cooke P. [1993] 1 NZLR 257, 272, 273, that the purchase price was impressed with a continuing beneficial interest in favour of the customer, which could form the starting point for a tracing of the purchase moneys into other assets.

  The same insuperable obstacle stands in the way of the alternative submission that the company was a fiduciary. If one asks the inevitable first question—What was the content of the fiduciary's duty?—the claimants are forced to assert that the duty was to expend the moneys in the purchase and maintenance of the reserved stock. Yet this is precisely the obligation which, as just stated, cannot be extracted from anything express or implied in the contract of sale and the collateral promises. In truth, the argument that the company was a fiduciary (as regards the money rather than the bullion) is no more than another label for the argument in favour of an express trust and must fail for the same reason.

  Thus far, all the arguments discussed have assumed that each contract of sale and collateral promises together created a valid and effective transaction coupling the ordinary mutual obligations of an agreement for the sale of goods with special obligations stemming from a trust or fiduciary relationship. These arguments posit that the obligations remain in force, albeit unperformed, the claimants' object being to enforce them. The next group of arguments starts with the contrary proposition that the transactions were rendered ineffectual by the presence of one or more of three vitiating factors:

namely, misrepresentation, mistake and total failure of consideration. To these their Lordships now turn.

It is important at the outset to distinguish between three different ways in which the existence of a misrepresentation, a mistake or a total failure of consideration might lead to the existence of a proprietary interest in the purchase money or its fruits superior to that of the bank.

1. The existence of one or more of these vitiating factors distinguished the relationship from that of an ordinary vendor and purchaser, so as to leave behind with the customer a beneficial interest in the purchase moneys which would otherwise have passed to the company when the money was paid. This interest remained with the customer throughout everything that followed, and can now be enforced against the general assets of the company, including the bullion, in priority to the interest of the bank.

2. Even if the full legal and beneficial interest in the purchase moneys passed when they were paid over, the vitiating factors affected the contract in such a way as to revest the moneys in the purchaser, and, what is more, to do so in a way which attached to the moneys an interest superior to that of the bank.

3. In contrast to the routes just mentioned, where the judgment of the court would do no more than recognise the existence of proprietary rights already in existence, the court should by its judgment create a new proprietary interest, superior to that of the bank, to reflect the justice of the case.

With these different mechanisms in view, their Lordships turn to the vitiating factors relied upon. As to the misrepresentations these were presumably that (in fact) the company intended to carry out the collateral promise to establish a separate stock and also that (in law) if this promise was performed the customer would obtain a title to bullion. Whether the proprietary interests said to derive from this misrepresentation were retained by the customers from the moment when they paid over the purchase moneys, or whether they arose at a later date, was not made clear in argument. If the former, their Lordships can only say that they are unable to grasp the reasoning for if correct the argument would until that even in respect of those contracts which the company ultimately fulfilled by delivery the moneys were pro tempore subject to a trust which would have prevented the company from lawfully treating them as its own. This cannot be right. As an alternative it may be contended that a trust arose upon the collapse of the company and the consequent non-fulfilment of the contracts. This contention must also be rejected, for two reasons. First, any such proprietary right must have as its starting point a personal claim by the purchaser to the return of the price. No such claim could exist for so long as the sale contract remained in existence and was being enforced by the customer. That is the position here. The customers have never rescinded the contracts of sale, but have throughout the proceedings asserted various forms of proprietary interest in the bullion, all of them derived in one way or another from the contracts of sale. This stance is wholly inconsistent with the notion that the contracts were and are so ineffectual that the customers are entitled to get their money back. As a last resort the non-allocated claimants invited the Board to treat the contracts as rescinded if their claims for a proprietary interest in bullion were rejected. There is however no mechanism which would permit the claimants to pause, as it were, half way through the delivery of the present judgment and elect at last to rescind; and even if such a course were open, the remedies arising on rescission would come too late to affect the secured rights of the bank under its previously crystallised floating charge.

Furthermore, even if this fatal objection could be overcome, the argument would, in their Lordships' opinion, be bound to fail. Whilst it is convenient to speak of the customers 'getting their money back' this expression is misleading. Upon payment by the customers the purchase moneys became, and rescission or no rescission remained, the unencumbered property of the company. What the customers would recover on rescission would not be 'their' money, but an equivalent sum. Leaving aside for the moment the creation by the court of a new remedial proprietary right, to which totally different considerations would apply, the claimants would have to contend that in every case where a purchaser is misled into buying goods he is automatically entitled upon rescinding the contract to a proprietary right superior to those of all the vendor's other creditors, exercisable against the whole of the vendor's assets. It is not surprising that no authority could be cited for such an extreme proposition. The only possible exception is *In re Eastgate; Ex parte Ward* [1905] 1 KB 465. Their Lordships doubt whether, correctly understood, the case so decides, but if it does they decline to follow it.

Similar objections apply to the second variant, which was only lightly touched upon in argument: namely, that the purchase moneys were paid under a mistake. Assuming the mistake to be that the collateral promises would be performed and would yield a proprietary right, what effect would they have on the contracts? Obviously not to make them void ab initio, for otherwise it would mean that the customers had no right to insist on delivery. Perhaps the mistake would have entitled the customers to have the agreements set aside at common law or under statute, and upon this happening they would no doubt have been entitled to a personal restitutionary remedy in respect of the price. This does not, however, advance their case. The moneys were paid by the customers to the company because they believed that they were bound to pay them; and in this belief they were entirely right. The situation is entirely different from *Chase Manhattan Bank NA v Israel-British Bank (London) Ltd* [1981] Ch 105, to which much attention was given in the Court of Appeal and in argument before the Board. It may be—their Lordships express no opinion upon it—that the *Chase Manhattan* case correctly decided that where one party mistakenly makes the same payment twice it retains a proprietary interest in the second payment which (if tracing is practicable) can be enforced against the payees' assets in a liquidation ahead of unsecured creditors. But in the present case, the customers intended to make payment, and they did so because they rightly conceived that that was what the contracts required. As in the case of the argument based on misrepresentation, this version conceals the true nature of the customers' complaint: not that they paid the money, but that the goods which they ordered and paid for have not been delivered. As in the case of the misrepresentation, the alleged mistake might well have been a ground for setting aside the contract if the claimants had ever sought to do so; and in such a case they would have had a personal right to recover the sum equivalent to the amount paid. But even if they had chosen to exercise this right, it would not by operation of law have carried with it a proprietary interest.

Their Lordships are of the same opinion as regards the third variant, which is that a proprietary interest arose because the consideration for the purchase price has totally failed. It is, of course, obvious that in the end the consideration did fail, when delivery was demanded and not made. But until that time the claimants had the benefit of what they had bargained for, a contract for the sale of unascertained goods. Quite plainly a customer could not on the day after a sale have claimed to recover the price for a total failure of consideration, and this at once puts paid to any question of a residuary proprietary interest and distinguishes the case from those such as *Sinclair v Brougham* [1914] AC 398, where the transactions under which the moneys were paid were from the start ineffectual; and *Neste Oy v Lloyds Bank Plc* [1983] 2 Lloyd's Rep 658, where to the knowledge of the payee no performance at all could take place under the contract for which the payment formed the consideration.

There remains the question whether the court should create after the event a remedial restitutionary right superior to the security created by the charge. The nature and foundation of this remedy were not clearly explained in argument. This is understandable, given that the doctrine is still in an early stage and no single juristic account of it has yet been generally agreed. In the context of the present case there appear to be only two possibilities. The first is to strike directly at the heart of the problem and to conclude that there was such an imbalance between the positions of the parties that if orthodox methods fail a new equity should intervene to put the matter right, without recourse to further rationalisation. Their Lordships must firmly reject any such approach. The bank relied on the floating charge to protect its assets; the customers relied on the company to deliver the bullion and to put in place the separate stock. The fact that the claimants are private citizens whereas their opponent is a commercial bank could not justify the court in simply disapplying the bank's valid security. No case cited has gone anywhere near to this, and the Board would do no service to the nascent doctrine by stretching it past breaking point.

Accordingly, if the argument is to prevail some means must be found, not forcibly to subtract the moneys or their fruits from the assets to which the charge really attached, but retrospectively to create a situation in which the moneys never were part of those assets. In other words the claimants must be deemed to have a retained equitable title: see *Goff and Jones, The Law of Restitution*, 4th edn., 94. Whatever the mechanism for such deeming may be in other circumstances their Lordships can see no scope for it here. So far as concerns an equitable interest deemed to have come into existence from the moment when the transaction was entered into, it is hard to see how this could coexist with a contract which, so far as anyone knew, might be performed by actual delivery of the goods. And if there was no initial interest, at what time before the attachment of the security, and by virtue of what event, could the court deem a proprietary right to have arisen? None that their Lordships are able to see. Although remedial restitutionary rights may prove in the future to be a valuable instrument of justice they cannot in their Lordships' opinion be brought to bear on the present case.

For these reasons the Board must reject all the ways in which the non-allocated claimants assert a proprietary interest over the purchase price and its fruits. This makes it unnecessary to consider whether, if such an interest had existed, it would have been possible to trace from the subject matter of the interest into the company's present assets. Indeed it would be unprofitable to do so without a clear understanding of when and how the equitable interest arose, and of its nature. Their Lordships should, however, say that they find it difficult to understand how the judgment of the Board in *Space Investments Ltd v Canadian Imperial Bank of Commerce Trust Co. (Bahamas) Ltd* [1986] 1 WLR 1072, on which the claimants leaned heavily in argument, would enable them to overcome the difficulty that the moneys said to be impressed with the trust were paid into an overdrawn account and thereupon ceased to exist: see, for example, *In re Diplock* [1948] Ch 465. The observations of the Board in the *Space Investments* case were concerned with a mixed, not a non-existent, fund.

. . .

THE WALKER & HALL CLAIMS

These claims are on a different footing. It appears that until about 1983 the bullion purchased by customers of the predecessor of Walker & Hall Commodities Ltd was stored and recorded separately. Thereafter, the bullion representing purchases by customers was stored en masse, but it was still kept separate from the vendor's own stock. Furthermore, the quantity of each kind of bullion kept in this pooled mass was precisely equal to the amount of Walker & Hall's exposure to the relevant categories of bullion and of its open contracts with customers. The documentation was also different from that received by the customers who later became the non-allocated claimants. The documents handed to the customer need not be quoted at length, but their general effect was that the vendor did not claim title in the bullion described in the document and that the title to that bullion, and the risk in respect of it, was with the customer. The document also stated that the vendor held the bullion as custodian for the customer in safe storage. These arrangements ceased when the shares of Walker & Hall were purchased by the company, and the contractual rights of the customers were transferred.

The features just mentioned persuaded Thorp J at first instance to hold, in contrast to his conclusion in relation to the non-allocated claimants . . ., that there had been a sufficient ascertainment and appropriation of goods to the individual contracts to transfer title to each customer; and that thereafter the customers as a whole had a shared interest in the pooled bullion, which the vendors held on their behalf. The *Dublin City Distillery* case [1914] AC 823 was cited in support of this conclusion. It followed that when the company absorbed the hitherto separated bullion into its own trading stock upon the acquisition of Walker & Hall's business, and thereafter drew upon the mixed stock, it wrongfully dealt with goods which were not its own.

Thus far, the decision of Thorp J was favourable to the Walker & Hall claimants. There remained, however, the question of relief. Here, the judge applied conventional principles of tracing and concluded that the proprietary recoveries of the Walker & Hall claimants and those in a similar position could not exceed the lowest balance of metal held by the company between the accrual of their rights and the commencement of the receivership: see *James Roscoe (Bolton) Ltd v Winder* [1915] 1 Ch 62 and the passages from *Ford and Lee's Principles of the Law of Trusts*, 2nd edn (1990), 738–68, paras. 1716–1730, and *Goff and Jones, The Law of Restitution*, 3rd edn (1986), 74 cited by the judge.

Although the Walker & Hall claimants had succeeded on liability the bank was not unduly concerned, since the limitation of the claim to the lowest intermediate balance meant that it was of comparatively small financial significance. The bank therefore did not appeal against this part of Thorp J's judgment when the unsuccessful claimants appealed to the Court of Appeal against other aspects of that judgment. A rather confusing situation then arose. Because the bank had not appealed in relation to the Walker & Hall claimants the Court of Appeal had no occasion to consider whether these claimants really were, as the judge had held, in a different position from the non-allocated claimants . . ., although some brief observations by Gault J in his judgment [1993] 1 NZLR 257, 277, appeared to indicate some doubt on this score. When, however, the court had turned to the question of quantum, and ordered that the non-allocated claimants . . . were entitled to charges on the remaining bullion assets of the company in priority to the charge of the bank, it concluded its declaration with the words 'and the successful claimants in the High Court are in the same position as the present appellants to the extent they cannot recover under the judgment of Thorp J.' This enhancement of the remedy available to the Walker & Hall claimants made Thorp J's adverse judgment much more serious for the bank, and accordingly the bank desired to appeal to this Board not only on the ground that the Court of Appeal had wrongly enlarged the remedy but also (in case it should be held that in principle the decision of the court on the availability of a remedy should be upheld) on the ground that Thorp J had been in error when holding that the Walker & Hall claimants had any proprietary rights at all. To this the Walker & Hall claimants objected, on the ground that since the bank had never appealed to the Court of Appeal on the issue of liability it could not appeal to the Board. The bank responded that it was not they but the claimants who had set the appellate procedure in motion and if the judgment of Thorp J was to be reopened at all, it ought to be reconsidered in full.

In the event, a lengthy investigation by the Board of what had happened in the Court of Appeal was avoided by a sensible arrangement between the parties, whereby the bank accepted its willingness to abide by the decision of Thorp J on liability (although without making any concession upon it) in the event that the Board restored the judge's decision on the measure of recovery. To this issue, therefore, their Lordships will immediately turn.

On the facts found by the judge the company as bailee held bullion belonging to the individual Walker & Hall claimants, intermingled the bullion of all such claimants, mixed that bullion with bullion belonging to the company, withdrew bullion from the mixed fund and then purchased more bullion which was added to the mixed fund without the intention of replacing the bullion of the Walker & Hall claimants. In these circumstances the bullion belonging to the Walker & Hall claimants which became held by the company's receivers consisted of bullion equal to the lowest balance of metal held by the company at any time: see *James Roscoe (Bolton) Ltd v Winder* [1915] 1 Ch 62.

The Walker & Hall claimants now seek to go further and ask the court to impose an equitable lien on all the property of the company at the date of the receivership to recover the value of their bullion unlawfully misappropriated by the company. Such a lien was considered by the Board in *Space Investments Ltd v Canadian Imperial Bank of Commerce Trust Co. (Bahamas) Ltd* [1986] 1 WLR 1072.

In that case the Board held that beneficiaries could not claim trust moneys lawfully deposited by a bank trustee with itself as banker in priority to other depositors and unsecured creditors. But Lord Templeman considered the position which would arise if a bank trustee unlawfully borrowed trust moneys. He said, at 1074:

'A bank in fact uses all deposit moneys for the general purposes of the bank. Whether a bank trustee lawfully receives deposits or wrongly treats trust money as on deposit from trusts, all the moneys are in fact dealt with and expended by the bank for the general purposes of the bank. In these circumstances it is impossible for the beneficiaries interested in trust money misappropriated from their trust to trace their money to any particular asset belonging to the trustee bank. But equity allows the beneficiaries, or a new trustee appointed in place of an insolvent bank trustee to protect the interests of the beneficiaries, to trace the trust money to all the assets of the bank and to recover the trust money by the exercise of an equitable charge over all the assets of the bank.'

These observations were criticised by Professor Goode in his Mary Oliver Memorial Address (1987) 103 *LQR* 433, 445–7, as being inconsistent with the observations of the Court of Appeal in *In re Diplock* [1948] Ch 465, 521, where it was said:

'The equitable remedies presuppose the continued existence of the money either as a separate fund or as part of a mixed fund or as latent in property acquired by means of such a fund. If, on the facts of any individual case, such continued existence is not established, equity is as helpless as the common law itself. If the fund, mixed or unmixed, is spent upon a dinner, equity, which dealt only in specific relief and not in damages, could do nothing. If the case was one which at common law involved breach of contract the common law could, of course, award damages but specific relief would be out of the question. It is, therefore, a necessary matter for consideration in each case where it is sought to trace money in equity, whether it has such a continued existence, actual or notional, as will enable equity to grant specific relief.'

In the case of a bank which employs all borrowed moneys as a mixed fund for the purpose of lending out money or making investments, any trust money unlawfully borrowed by a bank trustee may be said to be latent in the property acquired by the bank and the court may impose an equitable lien on that property for the recovery of the trust money.

The imposition of such an equitable lien for the purpose of recovering trust money was more favourably regarded by Professor Peter Birks in *An Introduction to the Law of Restitution* (1989), 377 ff., and by *Goff and Jones, The Law of Restitution*, 4th edn., especially at 73–5.

The law relating to the creation and tracing of equitable proprietary interests is still in a state of development. In *Attorney-General for Hong Kong v Reid* [1994] AC 324 the Board decided that money received by an agent as a bribe was held in trust for the principal who is entitled to trace and recover property representing the bribe. In *Lord Napier and Ettrick v Hunter* [1993] AC 713, 738, 739, the House of Lords held that payment of damages in respect of an insured loss created an equitable charge in favour of the subrogated insurers so long only as the damages were traceable as an identifiable fund. When the scope and ambit of these decisions and the observations of the Board in the *Space Investments* case fall to be considered, it will be necessary for the history and foundations in principle of the creation and tracing of equitable proprietary interests to be the subject of close examination and full argument and for attention to be paid to the works of Paciocco (1989) 68 *Cas Bar Rev.* 315, *Maddaugh and McCamus, The Law of Restitution* (1990), Emily L. Sherwin's article 'Constructive Trusts in Bankruptcy' (1989) *U Ill. L Rev.* 297, 335, and other commentators dealing with equitable interests in tracing and referring to concepts such as the position of 'involuntary creditors' and tracing to 'swollen assets.'

In the present case it is not necessary or appropriate to consider the scope and ambit of the observations in the *Space Investments* case [1986] 1 WLR 1072 or their application to trustees other than bank trustees because all members of this Board are agreed that it would be inequitable to impose a lien in favour of the Walker & Hall claimants. Those claimants received the same certificates and trusted the company in a manner no different from other bullion customers. There is no evidence that the debenture holders and the unsecured creditors at the date of the receivership benefited directly or indirectly from the breaches of trust committed by the company or that Walker & Hall bullion continued to exist as a fund latent in property vested in the receivers.

In these circumstances the Walker & Hall claimants must be restored to the remedies granted to them by the trial judge.

Their Lordships will accordingly humbly advise Her Majesty that the appeal ought to be allowed, the judgment of the Court of Appeal of New Zealand of 30 April 1992 set aside and the judgment of Thorp J of 17 October 1990 restored. Their Lordships were informed that the parties had been able to agree the matter of costs in any event and therefore make no order in that regard.

NOTES AND QUESTIONS

1. As regards the non-allocated claimants, the Privy Council's primary ground of reasoning was that they had no equitable proprietary interest in the purchase moneys so as to be able to trace. The opinion that, in any event, the non-allocated claimants could not satisfy the identification rules of tracing—because the mixed fund had been exhausted—was *obiter dicta*. Similarly, as regards the Walker & Hall claimants (who did have an equitable proprietary interest in the bullion), the Privy Council did not go quite as far as to say that their claims failed because, applying *Roscoe v Winder*, they could not satisfy the identification rules of tracing except in respect of the lowest intermediate balance of metal held by the company. Rather, at the end of the judgment, the Privy Council preferred to distinguish *Space Investments* on the ground that, on the instant facts, it would be inequitable to apply it.

2. For extracts from the articles by Paciocco and Sherwin, referred to by Lord Mustill, see below, 756–757.

3. For notes on this case, see P Birks, 'Establishing A Proprietary Base' [1994] *RLR* 93; E McKendrick (1994) 110 *LQR* 509.

4. For a case that is similar to *Re Goldcorp*, see *Re Stapylton Fletcher Ltd* [1995] 1 All ER 192 in which the judgment was given while the *Goldcorp* appeal was pending. Judge Paul Baker said, at 213–14, 'The court must be very cautions in devising equitable interests and remedies which erode the statutory scheme for distribution on insolvency. It cannot do it because of some perceived injustice arising as a consequence of the insolvency.'

5. The Sale of Goods (Amendment) Act 1995 has amended the law on the sale of goods by bulk. But the amendment would not affect the facts of *Re Goldcorp* because of the absence of an identified bulk.

- **Bishopsgate Investment Management Ltd v Homan**
  [1995] Ch 211, Court of Appeal

Money from pension funds belonging to Bishopsgate Investment Management Ltd (BIM) was wrongly transferred by Robert Maxwell into Maxwell Communication Corporation plc (MCC). On an application for directions by MCC's administrators BIM claimed that it was entitled to an equitable charge over all MCC's assets for the amount of the moneys transferred and giving BIM priority over unsecured creditors of MCC. This claim was rejected by the Court of Appeal, upholding Vinelott J's decision, on the ground that the tracing chain between the misappropriated money and the present assets of MCC could not be established, in that the misappropriated money had been paid into an account of MCC that was, at the time of payment, overdrawn or subsequently became so. The mixed fund at that point was exhausted.

Dillon LJ: . . . In essence Vinelott J held that B.I.M. could only claim an equitable charge on any assets of M.C.C. in accordance with the recognised principles of equitable tracing and these principles do not permit tracing through an overdrawn bank account whether an account which was already overdrawn at the time the relevant moneys were paid into it or an account which was then in credit, but subsequently became overdrawn by subsequent drawings.

The judge reserved, however, the position if it were shown that there was a connection between a particular misappropriation of B.I.M.'s moneys and the acquisition by M.C.C. of a particular asset. The judge gave as an instance of such a case what he called 'backward tracing'—where an asset was acquired by M.C.C. with moneys borrowed from an overdrawn or loan account and there was an inference that when the borrowing was incurred it was the intention that it should be repaid by misappropriations of B.I.M.'s moneys. Another possibility was that moneys misappropriated from B.I.M. were paid into an overdrawn account of M.C.C. in order to reduce the overdraft and so make finance available within the overdraft limits for M.C.C. to purchase some particular asset.

By a respondent's notice by way of cross-appeal, the administrators ask us to overrule these reservations of the judge, and hold that even if the possible facts which the judge envisages were clearly proved that could not in law give B.I.M. any equitable charge on the particular asset acquired. For my part I would not interfere at all with this aspect of the judge's exercise of his discretion. In my judgment, if the connection he postulates between the particular misappropriation of B.I.M.'s money and the acquisition by M.C.C. of a particular asset is sufficiently clearly proved, it is at least arguable, depending on the facts, that there ought to be an equitable charge in favour of B.I.M. on the asset in question of M.C.C.

But the main claims of B.I.M. are put much more widely as claims to an equitable charge on all the assets of M.C.C. These claims are not founded on proving any particular intention of Robert Maxwell or others in charge of M.C.C. but on general principles which it is said that the court ought to apply. They are founded primarily on certain observations of Lord Templeman in giving the judgment of the Privy Council in *Space Investments Ltd v Canadian Imperial Bank of Commerce Trust Co. (Bahamas) Ltd* [1986] 1 WLR 1072. In particular, in that case Lord Templeman said, at 1074:

> 'In these circumstances it is impossible for the beneficiaries interested in trust money misappropriated from their trust to trace their money to any particular asset belonging to the trustee bank. But equity allows the beneficiaries, or a new trustee appointed in place of an insolvent bank trustee . . . to trace the trust money to all the assets of the bank and to recover the trust money by the exercise of an equitable charge over all the assets of the bank. . . . that equitable charge secures for the beneficiaries and the trust priority over the claims of the customers . . . and . . . all other unsecured creditors.'

What Lord Templeman there said was strictly obiter, in that on the facts the Privy Council held that the bank trustee was authorised by the trust instruments to deposit trust money with itself as banker and so there had been no misappropriation. The beneficiaries or their new trustee therefore could merely prove with the other general creditors of the insolvent bank trustee for a dividend in respect of the moneys so deposited.

Vinelott J rejected the submissions of B.I.M. founded on the *Space Investments* case. He considered that Lord Templeman could not have intended to effect such a fundamental change to the well-understood limitations to equitable tracing; Lord Templeman was only considering the position of an insolvent bank which had been taking deposits and lending money.

. . .

As I read the judgment of the Privy Council in *In re Goldcorp Exchange Ltd* delivered by Lord Mustill, it makes it clear that Lord Templeman's observations in the *Space Investments* case [1986] 1 WLR 1072 were not concerned at all with the situation we have in the present case where trust moneys have been paid into an overdrawn bank account, or an account which has become overdrawn. Lord Mustill said in the clearest terms, [1995] 1 AC 74, 104–5:

'Their Lordships should, however, say that they find it difficult to understand how the judgment of the Board in *Space Investments Ltd v Canadian Imperial Bank of Commerce Trust Co. (Bahamas) Ltd* [1986] 1 WLR 1072, on which the claimants leaned heavily in argument, would enable them to overcome the difficulty that the moneys said to be impressed with the trust were paid into an overdrawn account and thereupon ceased to exist: see, for example, *In re Diplock* [1948] Ch 465. The observations of the Board in the *Space Investments* case were concerned with a mixed, not a non-existent, fund.'

Thus the wide interpretation of those observations put forward by Cooke P [in the Court of Appeal in New Zealand in *Re Goldcorp*], which is the basis of the first ground of appeal in the present case, is rejected. Instead the decision of the Court of Appeal in *In re Diplock; Diplock v Wintle* [1948] Ch 465 is endorsed. There it was said, at 521:

'The equitable remedies presuppose the continued existence of the money either as a separate fund or as part of a mixed fund or as latent in property acquired by means of such a fund. If, on the facts of any individual case, such continued existence is not established, equity is as helpless as the common law itself.'

Also endorsed, in my judgment, in the decision of the Board delivered by Lord Mustill is the long-standing first instance decision in *James Roscoe (Bolton) Ltd v Winder* [1915] 1 Ch 62, which Mr Heslop for B.I.M., in his submissions in March, invited us to overrule. That was a decision that, in tracing trust moneys into the bank account of a trustee in accordance with *In re Hallett's Estate; Knatchbull v Hallett* (1880) 13 ChD 696, tracing was only possible to such an amount of the balance ultimately standing to the credit of the trustee as did not exceed the lowest balance of the account during the intervening period. Thus as is said in the headnote to the report [1915] 1 Ch 62:

'Payments into a general account cannot, without proof of express intention, be appropriated to the replacement of trust money which has been improperly mixed with that account and drawn out.'

That reflects the statement by Sargant J in the *James Roscoe* case, at 69:

'It is impossible to attribute to him'—i.e. the account holder—'that by the mere payment into the account of further moneys, which to a large extent he subsequently used for purposes of his own, he intended to clothe those moneys with a trust in favour of the plaintiffs.'

... B.I.M: claims (as it has been explained to us) to be entitled to an equitable charge as security for its claims against M.C.C. (i) over any moneys standing to the credit at the time of the appointment of the administrators of M.C.C. of any banking account maintained by M.C.C. into which any moneys of B.I.M. or the proceeds of any assets of B.I.M. misappropriated from it were paid and (ii) over any assets acquired out of any such bank account, whether or not in credit as at the date such assets were acquired.

So far as (i) is concerned, the point is that the National Westminster Bank account into which the misappropriated B.I.M. trust moneys were paid happened to be in credit when the administrators were appointed. B.I.M. therefore claims a lien on that credit balance in the National Westminster Bank account for the amount of the misappropriated trust moneys. It is difficult to suppose, however, in the circumstances of Robert Maxwell's last days—and I know no evidence—that Robert Maxwell intended to make good the misappropriation of the B.I.M. pension moneys by the cryptic expedient of arranging to put M.C.C.'s account with National Westminster Bank into credit—but without repaying the credit balance this created to B.I.M. But in the absence of clear evidence of intention to make good the depradations on B.I.M. it is not possible to assume that the credit balance has been clothed with a trust in favour of B.I.M. and its beneficiaries: see *James Roscoe (Bolton) Ltd v Winder* [1915] 1 Ch 62.

As to (ii), this seems to be going back to the original wide interpretation of what Lord Templeman said in the *Space Investments* case [1986] 1 WLR 1072 and applying it to an overdrawn account because the misappropriated moneys that went into the account were trust moneys and thus different from other moneys that may have gone into that account. But the moneys in the *Space Investments* case were also trust moneys, and so, if argument (ii) is valid in the present case, it would also have been valid, as a matter of law, in the *Space Investments* case. But that was rejected in *In re Goldcorp Exchange Ltd* [1995] 1 AC 74 because equitable tracing, though devised for the protection of trust moneys misapplied, cannot be pursued through an overdrawn and therefore non-existent fund. Acceptance of argument (ii) would, in my judgment, require the rejection of *In re Diplock* [1948] Ch 465, which is binding on us, and of Lord Mustill's explanation of Lord Templeman's statement in the *Space Investments* case in *In re Goldcorp Exchange Ltd* [1995] 1 AC 74, 104.

It is not open to us to say that because the moneys were trust moneys the fact that they were paid into a overdrawn account or have otherwise been dissipated presents no difficulty to raising an equitable charge on assets of M.C.C. for their amount in favour of B.I.M. The difficulty Lord Mustill referred to is not displaced.

Leggatt LJ: . . . [A]s this court asserted in *In re Diplock* [1948] 1 Ch 465, . . . it is only possible to trace in equity money which has continued existence, actual or notional. That was why in *James Roscoe (Bolton) Ltd v Winder* [1915] 1 Ch 62, where trust funds had been mixed with private moneys in a bank account and the credit balance reduced at one point to £25 18s. 0d. before being replenished, Sargant J held that the beneficiary's charge extended only to that sum. As Buckley LJ said in *Borden (U.K.) Ltd v Scottish Timber Products Ltd* [1981] Ch 25, 46: 'it is a fundamental feature of the doctrine of tracing that the property to be traced can be identified at every stage of its journey through life.'

For the same reason there can be no equitable remedy against an asset acquired *before* misappropriation of money takes place, since ex hypothesi it cannot be followed into something which existed and so had been acquired before the money was received and therefore without its aid.

. . .

[The *Space Investments* case] is authority for no wider proposition than that, where a bank trustee wrongly deposits money with itself, the trustee can trace into all the bank's credit balances. . . . Lord Mustill, delivering the judgment of the Board in *In re Goldcorp Exchange Ltd* [1995] 1 AC 74, 104, stated that their Lordships found it difficult to understand how it would enable the claimants in that case to 'overcome the difficulty that the moneys said to be impressed with the trust were paid into an overdrawn account and thereupon ceased to exist.' Lord Mustill emphasised that the observations of the Board were concerned with a mixed, not a non-existent, fund. He also cited with approval *James Roscoe (Bolton) Ltd v Winder* [1915] 1 Ch 62 as conventionally exemplifying the principles of tracing.

I therefore consider that the judge came to the right conclusion, though I do not accept that it is possible to trace through an overdrawn bank account or to trace misappropriated money into an asset bought before the money was received by the purchaser.

Henry LJ agreed.

NOTES AND QUESTIONS

1. For notes on this case, see L Gullifer, 'Recovery of Misappropriated Assets: Orthodoxy Re-Established' [1995] *LMCLQ* 446; and L Smith, 'Tracing, "Swollen Assets" and the Lowest Intermediate Balance' (1994) 8 *Trusts Law International* 102. For Smith's criticism of the Ontario Court of Appeal's abrogation of the lowest intermediate balance rule in *Law Society of Upper Canada v Toronto-Dominion Bank* (1998) 169 DLR (4th) 353, see his article, 'Tracing in Bank Accounts: The Lowest Intermediate Balance Rule on Trial' (2000) 33 *Can Bus LJ* 75.

2. What does Dillon LJ mean by 'backward tracing'? Can it enable one to trace through an exhausted or non-existent fund? Did Leggatt LJ agree that 'backward tracing' might be possible? L Smith, 'Tracing into the Payment of a Debt' [1995] *CLJ* 290 argues powerfully that backward tracing must be possible. He gives the following example. Say D uses £500 stolen from C to buy a car. There is no doubt that C can trace to the car. What then if D has already bought a car on credit and uses the £500 stolen from C to pay off the debt. Surely, argues Smith, the same should apply. He writes, at 292–3, 'There is no substantial change in the transaction; the period of credit might be reduced to a minute or a second the better to make this point. If that is right, then when money is used to pay a debt, it is traceable into what was acquired in exchange for the incurring of the debt'.

3. Did BIM have an equitable proprietary interest in the money before it was misappropriated? If not, why was it able to trace in equity?

4. In the *Barlow Clowes* case, Woolf LJ appeared to reject the intermediate balance rule as being too complex to apply on the facts, while accepting that one cannot trace once a fund has been exhausted (see above, 670 and question 3 on 671).

5. The upholding of the 'intermediate balance' rule of *Roscoe v Winder* in *Bishopsgate* represents a rejection (except, perhaps, where the defendant is a bank trustee) of the views of Lord Templeman in *Space Investment Ltd v Canadian Imperial Bank of Commerce Trust Co. (Bahamas) Ltd* [1986] 1 WLR 1072, 1074 to the effect that a claimant can be entitled to an equitable lien over the defendant's general assets despite a break in the strict tracing chain. That looser approach is sometimes labelled 'the swollen asset' theory. Although the precise content of that theory is not clear the central idea appears to be that provided the defendant received assets, which at the time of receipt the claimant could trace, and provided the defendant cannot prove that the assets it still holds could not possibly include those traceable assets of the claimant's or their product, the claimant is entitled to an equitable lien over the defendant's general assets despite a break in the strict tracing chain. See also 696, note 1, above.

(3) THREE ACADEMIC ANALYSES OF TRACING

- **L Smith, 'Tracing into the Payment of a Debt'** [1995] 54 *CLJ* 290*

[In this article, Smith argues that, contrary to the conventional view that the discharge of a debt constitutes a dissipation for the purposes of tracing, one can trace into the payment of a debt. Here, however, we extract only the first two pages of that article in which he sets out very clearly his conception of the nature of tracing.] A plaintiff who is deprived of a thing might seek out that very thing in order to assert his rights. The victim of a car thief tries to find the car. This is a natural response to such a misfortune, although it is not necessarily a fruitful one. Alternatively, the plaintiff might find that the original thing has been used to acquire some new asset: for example, the thief has swapped the car for a motorcycle. In that case, especially if for some reason the plaintiff will be unlikely or unable to establish a claim in relation to the car, the plaintiff might choose to assert a claim in relation to the motorcycle.

In these two cases, the processes by which the plaintiff identifies an asset to which he will make a claim are very different. The first process involves finding the original thing. In this paper, it will be called 'following'. The second process involves identifying a new asset which was acquired in exchange for the original thing. That process is called 'tracing'. The process of tracing allows us to determine when one asset stands, for certain legal purposes, in the place of another. When a thing is

---

* [See also L Smith, *The Law of Tracing* (1997), 8–14, 46–7.]

used in an exchange transaction, following and tracing take one in different directions. When the thief swaps the car for a motorcycle, following sticks to the car; it bring a new person into the picture. Tracing, on the other hand, points towards the motorcycle; it brings a new asset into the picture.

Tracing and following are, in one sense, opposites.[1] The object of 'follow' is 'thing'. The object of 'trace' is 'value', because we cease to be concerned with a particular physical thing and instead focus on different physical manifestations of the value which was inherent in the original thing. Nonetheless, tracing and following also have certain features in common. Both are processes which identify assets in relation to which a plaintiff might wish to make a claim. Both processes are analytically distinct from the question of what claims might be made to the assets which they identify. If I sell my car, I can follow it in the same way as if it had been stolen; having followed it, however, I will have no claim to it. Tracing is similar; I might be able to trace my value into some proceeds, but whether or not I have a claim to those proceeds is another question.

Tracing and following are also similar in that they can permit the establishment of different sorts of claims. If a thief steals my car and then goes bankrupt, I will try to follow the car in order to establish that I hold proprietary rights in it; this will permit me to remove it from the bankruptcy proceedings. Alternatively, I might only seek to establish a personal right against the thief, say in conversion. So it is with tracing. A plaintiff might trace to establish a currently existing proprietary right, in order to obtain priority in an insolvency[2] or, she might trace to establish a personal right.[3]

These comparisons point to one final parallel which must be drawn between tracing and following. The type of claim which a litigant seeks to establish will have an important bearing on how far she must trace or follow. If the objective is to establish a currently existing proprietary right, in order to obtain a priority or perhaps an order for transfer of possession, then naturally the exercise (be it following or tracing) must be carried forward to the current moment. On the other hand, a personal right depends on establishing that past events have generated the right. A plaintiff might follow his car to show that at some point in the past, the defendant committed the tort of conversion. In that case, there is no need to follow the car after the commission of the tort; it is no part of the claim to show where the car is now. Similarly, a plaintiff might be trying to establish a personal right which depends on the defendant's receipt, at some point in the past, of value which was traceably the plaintiff's. In that case, there is no need to trace past the point of receipt by the defendant.

- **P Birks, 'The Necessity of a Unitary Law of Tracing' in *Making Commercial Law* (ed R Cranston, 1997) 239, 243–4, 258**

. . .

An exercise of identification either can or cannot be conducted. It would be absurd to suppose that it could be conducted vigorously and resourcefully only on Mondays and Thursdays, and it is *prima facie* no less absurd to assert that it can be so conducted only by a plaintiff who has managed to attract the attention of equity. 'Equity' is not a reason. The *prima facie* absurdity can only be displaced by finding a convincing reason why some plaintiffs, but not others, should be allowed to overcome routine evidential difficulties.

So far as there is resistance to this point of view it derives from past failures to distinguish tracing, the exercise of identification, from claiming, the assertion of rights in respect of assets into which value has been successfully traced. It may indeed be that some species of claim are recognized only

---

1 When one traces, and thus identifies a substitute asset, one is not identifying the original asset in a 'changed form': one is ignoring the original asset and concentrating on what was acquired in exchange for it. See P Birks, 'Mixing and Tracing[:] Property and Restitution' (1992) 45(2) CLP 69, 85, 86.

2 *Re Hallett's Estate* (1880) 13 ChD 696 (CA).

3 *Lipkin Gorman v Karpnale Ltd* [1991] 2 AC 548 (HL).

in equity. For example, the common law appears never to have recognized a non-possessory lien, and it does not recognize a tenancy in common of land. But tracing and claiming are distinct matters. If a tracing exercise is successful, a question has to be asked as to the nature of the rights, if any, which the plaintiff can assert in relation to the assets into which he has successfully traced. Those rights may be legal or equitable, personal or proprietary. Their availability will vary according to the nature of the facts, not in the sense that the facts give rise to a discretionary response but, quite to the contrary, that different facts give rise to different rights and, sometimes, to no rights at all. However, the tracing exercise itself is essentially mechanical, neutral as to rights. There is nothing to be said, or nothing has hitherto been convincingly said, for the view that this exercise of identification must be conducted according to different rules at law and in equity.

Suppose that a thief steals money from its legal owner and that that money happens to be trust money held by the legal owner for another. The thief then passes the money through a bank account in which it is mixed with other money. After he has operated the account for a few months, it is evident that he has bought from it a number of durable and valuable assets. It would be a curious system which concluded that the question whether the stolen money could be traced to those durable assets, and, if so, to which, must be answered quite differently depending on whether the exercise was attempted by the legal or the equitable victim of the theft—that is, by the trustee or by the beneficiary. Or suppose that the thief stole from the trustee both trust money and other money which was entirely the trustee's own. It would be difficult to defend the application of different rules for tracing the two different parcels.

The removal of the threshold requirement of a fiduciary relationship appears to contain within it an assurance that this nonsense will not be allowed to happen so long as there is some other factor sufficient to attract the attention of equity. In the case of the thief, that factor is said to be fraud. The examples in the previous paragraph may therefore be secure. Nevertheless, the risk of a similar nonsense will persist in other fact-situations so long as it is supposed that common law and equity do have different tracing rules.

The only sensible position for the modern law is to have a unitary regime for identifying the location of value at whatever moments of time are relevant. That unitary regime must be consistently seen as absolutely neutral as to rights. That is to say, there must be no relapse to a situation in which tracing was thought to imply rights and had to be controlled as though it did imply rights. As for the question, 'When can a person trace?' the only possible answer, on that assumption, is, 'Always', or, 'Whenever he likes'. If tracing is neutral as to rights, there is no point in selecting people who may and may not trace. Selection comes at the next stage. When it comes to asserting rights, it will of course appear that people with different facts have different rights, and that some people who have success-fully traced have no rights at all.

. . .

[T]he modern law is equipped with various means of coping with the evidential difficulties which a tracing exercise is bound to encounter. The process of identification thus ceases to be either legal or equitable and becomes, as is fitting, genuinely neutral as to the rights exigible in respect of the assets into which the value in question is traced. The tracing exercise once successfully completed, it can then be asked what rights, if any, the plaintiff can, on his particular facts, assert. It is at that point that it becomes relevant to recall that on some facts those rights will be personal, on others proprietary, on some legal, and on others equitable.

NOTE

It can be seen in the above extract that for Birks, as for Smith (above, 700), one does not trace a thing; rather one traces value from one asset to another. In 'Overview: Tracing, Claiming and Defences' in P Birks (ed.), *Laundering and Tracing* (1995), 290, Birks wrote the following: 'The key question is . . . whether the value inherent in the one asset has in whole or in part been used to acquire the other. What is traced is value, and the identification rules can be said to determine whether and to what extent value held in one asset at one point of time is located in another asset at some later time relevant to the plaintiff's claim'.

- **S Evans, 'Rethinking Tracing and the Law of Restitution'**
  (1999) 115 *LQR* 469, 471–2

. . .

Whatever the historical confusion about the *nature* of the tracing process, in practical terms the law of tracing has traditionally been regarded as being about substitutions. In particular, the law of tracing has dealt in substitutions that occurred as the result of transactions. The tracing rules meant that where a defendant exchanged, say, £1,000 for 100 shares in a company, any proprietary interest that the claimant had in the money in the hands of the defendant would be replaced by a proprietary interest in the shares. Tracing could be regarded as a matter of adopting and applying to unauthorised transactions similar transactional rules to those that applied to authorised transactions. So, just as the beneficiary could claim the proceeds of sale when a trustee sold trust assets in accordance with the terms of the trust, if the sale was wrongful the beneficiary could still take the proceeds of sale, 'in a sense adopting the sale for the purpose of taking the proceeds'.[1] Equally, if a trustee bought an asset for himself or herself with trust money, the beneficiary could 'in a sense' adopt the purchase and treat the purchased asset as having been bought on behalf of the trust. A wrongdoing trustee would be prevented from saying that a transaction that could have been carried out in accordance with the terms of the trust was in fact carried out wrongfully for his or her own benefit.[2] On this approach to tracing, the result of the tracing rules resembles the result of the rules regarding the passing of title under authorised transactions. It identifies surviving enrichment as the traceable proceeds of an earlier enrichment if there is a transactional chain that links the items of property that represent the initial and surviving enrichments. In this article, this approach to tracing will be referred to as the transactional approach.

Some commentators now assert that the law of tracing is part of the law of restitution, though this is contested by some others. Whether or not the tracing process forms part of the law of restitution, it is a process that has particular significance for restitutionary claims that depend on the claimant identifying value (an enrichment) surviving in the defendant's hands. The tracing process is essential to establishing such claims whenever the defendant has received the value from a third party and not directly from the claimant and whenever the defendant has substituted or transformed the asset representing the value he or she initially received. It is convenient, therefore, to refer to this approach to tracing, which focuses on identifying value surviving in the defendant's hands, as the restitutionary approach to tracing. This approach identifies a surviving enrichment as the traceable proceeds of an earlier enrichment if there is a causal connection between the initial and surviving enrichments.

The distinction between the transactional and restitutionary approaches to tracing is fundamental to the argument made in this article that the rules of tracing should be made more consistent and more coherent with the claiming rules they complement.

. . .

NOTES

1. Having made the above distinction between the transactional and restitutionary approach to tracing, Evans goes on to argue that it is only the former approach that requires transactional

1 *In re Hallett's Estate* (1879) 13 Ch.D. 696, CA, at 708–709 *per* Jessel MR.
2 (1879) 13 Ch D 696 at 727.

links between the deprivation of the claimant and the surviving enrichment. In contrast, the restitutionary approach to tracing, in his view, requires only a causal link between the claimant's deprivation and the surviving enrichment. In other words, Evans regards only a causal approach to tracing as compatible with an unjust enrichment analysis. In our view, that is incorrect. Requiring transactional links is as compatible with an unjust enrichment analysis as is requiring causal links but the former is considerably narrower than the latter. To base tracing not on transactional links but on mere causation would, in our view, extend the law of unjust enrichment too far.

2. Other important academic contributions to the debate about tracing include R Maudsley, 'Proprietary Remedies for the Recovery of Money' (1959) 75 *LQR* 234; D Hayton, 'Equity's Identification Rules' in P Birks (ed.), *Laundering and Tracing* (1995), 1–21; S Moriarty, 'Tracing, Mixing and Laundering' in P Birks (ed.), *Laundering and Tracing*, 73–94; C Rotherham, *Proprietary Remedies in Context* (2002), ch 5; C Rotherham, 'Tracing' in *The Law of Restitution* (eds S Hedley and M Halliwell, 2002), ch 4; R Chambers, 'Tracing and Unjust Enrichment' in *Understanding Unjust Enrichment* (eds J Neyers, M McInnes, and S Pitel, 2004), 263–309; L Smith, 'Tracing' in *Mapping the Law: Essays in Memory of Peter Birks* (eds A Burrows and Lord Rodger, 2006), 119–39.

2. PROPRIETARY RESTITUTION

The bulk of the law of restitution is concerned with *personal* rights/remedies which reverse unjust enrichment *received* by defendants irrespective of whether they still retain particular property. They do not afford priority on the defendant's insolvency. In contrast, *proprietary* rights/remedies afford priority on the defendant's insolvency and are dependent on the defendant's *retention* of particular property. Perhaps the most difficult question in the law of restitution is the extent to which unjust enrichment triggers, or should trigger, proprietary rights/remedies (which we can for shorthand label 'proprietary restitution') rather than the usual personal rights/remedies ('personal restitution').

A fundamental, and perhaps unappreciated, difficulty is that different commentators appear to have approached the question of proprietary restitution at different levels of enquiry.

On one view, most obviously associated with Graham Virgo, *The Principles of the Law of Restitution* (2nd edn, 2006), it appears that the cause of action or event of unjust enrichment is seen as relevant only within the law of obligations. Hence the *creation* of proprietary rights is outside the focus of one's direct enquiry. In contrast, the protection (or in Virgo's terminology, vindication) of proprietary rights through the law of obligations is within one's focus. And the law of restitution is seen as wide enough to include all situations where one person seeks the return of, or the monetary value of, property that still belongs to him, or belonged to him when received by the defendant. The restitutionary remedy given in response to a claim to vindicate one's proprietary rights may be personal (for the monetary value of the asset) or 'proprietary' in the sense that the defendant must give up a specific asset. But on this approach, one is not directly concerned within the law of restitution with whether, for example, proprietary rights were correctly created in *Chase Manhattan Bank NA v Israel-British Bank (London) Ltd* (below, 707) in response to a mistaken payment; or with whether proprietary rights were correctly created in *Attorney General for Hong Kong v Reid* (below, 1018) as a response to the wrong of breach of fiduciary duty. Rather one takes the creation of proprietary rights as a given and the law of restitution is then concerned with the protection of those existing proprietary rights. Similarly tracing is essentially seen as relevant to vindicating proprietary rights in an original asset and not as being relevant to the creation of new proprietary rights in the substitute asset. It is when one looks at the issues at this level of enquiry that one may conclude that one is concerned only with the law of property and not the law of unjust enrichment.

The different view which we favour is that the above approach, by failing to engage with what creates proprietary rights, misses out a fundamentally important level of enquiry and fails to see that unjust enrichment and wrongs (as well as, for example, consent) are events that trigger proprietary rights. To analyse the law on the restitution of mistaken payments without addressing the question of whether proprietary rights are, or should be, created to reverse the mistaken payee's unjust enrichment seems to us to be looking at only half of the picture.

The approach taken in this book, therefore, is to examine when, if ever, the event (or cause of action) of unjust enrichment triggers proprietary rights to effect restitution; and in Chapter 15 we will similarly address whether wrongs trigger proprietary rights to effect restitution. On our approach it is a nonsense to say that one is concerned with the law of property and not the law of unjust enrichment precisely because unjust enrichment may be an event triggering proprietary, as well as personal, rights.

It also follows from what we have said above that we are not concerned in this book with the protection of pre-existing proprietary rights other than where that protection is indirectly given through personal restitution in response to unjust enrichment and wrongs. In particular, we are not concerned with a *vindicatio* claim for the return of one's property (for example, for ejectment from land or for an order to transfer one's equitable property) which rests on the claimant's pre-existing proprietary right to that property. This is sometimes referred to as a 'pure proprietary claim'.[1] Rather we are concerned with the creation of a new proprietary right—sometimes referred to as a 'restitutionary proprietary claim'—in response to an unjust enrichment or, in Chapter 15, in response to a wrong.

In our view, a long-established area of proprietary rights created in response to unjust enrichment is equitable proprietary rights created following equitable tracing. Although it may be tempting to regard those equitable rights as responding to the defendant retaining property that previously belonged in equity to the claimant (so that these are 'pure proprietary claims'), we think that these rights are better viewed as *restitutionary* proprietary rights. They involve the creation of new proprietary rights over property that does not already belong to the claimant but is rather a substitution of property *previously owned* in equity by the claimant. So if one is entitled to trace from a pig to a horse to a car one cannot say, without invoking fiction, that one has proprietary rights in the car merely

---

1 In our view, the claim in *MacMillan Inc. v Bishopsgate Investment Trust plc (No 3)* ([1996] 1 WLR 387, Court of Appeal was purely proprietary—for the return of shares that had from the start belonged in equity to the claimant—so that the decision that the ownership of the shares should be decided by the law of the *lex situs* should have been a straightforward one. There was no tracing into substitutes involved and the claim was not therefore a restitutionary proprietary one (contra were the views of Millett J, [1995] 1 WLR 978, and of the majority of the Court of Appeal, Staughton and Aldous L JJ, who were willing to treat the claim as restitutionary). In contrast, restitutionary issues would have been directly in play had the claimant sought a personal remedy for the value of the shares received by the defendants (the unjust factor being 'ignorance': see Chapter 4 above). Then the approach of the above judges of characterizing the *issue*—the application of the *bona fide* purchase defence—as in any event governed by 'proprietary' rather than 'restitutionary' choice of law rules would have been directly relevant. For helpful notes on this case, see J Bird [1995] *LMCLQ* 308, [1996] *LMCLQ* 57; W. Swadling [1996] *LMCLQ* 63; J Stevens (1996) 59 *MLR* 741.

because one owned the pig which is now represented by the car. The truth is that one's ownership of the pig which has (without authority) been substituted by the car entitles one to claim *de novo* ownership of the car because the owner of the car is unjustly enriched *at one's expense* (the tracing rules being invoked to show that the subtraction of one's pig has become the defendant's enrichment in the form of the car). In our view, therefore, the cases on equitable tracing extracted above in which equitable proprietary rights were recognised (above, 657–687) all exemplify proprietary restitution triggered by unjust enrichment. Although more work needs to be done on clarifying the unjust factor, we would regard it as normally being ignorance (or powerlessness): see above, 647. It should be stressed, however, that the analysis we favour of rights after tracing was rejected by the House of Lords in *Foskett v McKeown* (above, 678).

If one puts to one side equitable proprietary rights following tracing, are there other examples of proprietary restitution (that is, of proprietary rights created *de novo* in response to unjust enrichment)?

In our view, the following are examples:

(i)   The trust imposed on the mistaken payment in *Chase Manhattan Bank NA v Israel-British Bank (London) Ltd* (below, 707) albeit that one must recognize that the reasoning (albeit not the result) in the case was rejected by the House of Lords in *Westdeutsche Landesbank Girozentrale v Islington London BC* (below, 727).

(ii) Some examples of subrogation: see section 5 of the Mercantile Law Amendment Act 1856 (above, 518–519); *Lord Napier v Hunter* (below, 712); and *Boscawen v Bajwa* (below, 720).

(iii) Equitable liens over mistakenly improved land (see *Cooper v Phibbs* (1867) LR 2 HL 149) and maritime liens over property saved by a salvor (see the brief discussion above, 573).

(iv) Rescission of an executed contract which has revested the proprietary rights to goods or land transferred under the contract (see, for example, *Car and Universal Finance Co. Ltd v Caldwell*, above, 201).

(v)   The trust held to exist in *Louth v Diprose* on the basis of undue influence/unconscionable behaviour (see above, 480).

[See also the first instance decision in *Zaidan Group Ltd v City of London* (1987) 36 DLR (4th) 443, discussed above, 642; the brief discussion of restitutionary proprietary claims for duress, above, 399; and the view of Lord Goff in *Woolwich Equitable Building Society v IRC*, above, 634–635 (and see also above, 623) that a public authority which has paid away money *ultra vires* has a proprietary restitutionary remedy to recover it.]

This section is divided into two subsections. In the first, we include extracts from three cases on proprietary restitution that have not been extracted earlier in this book, namely *Chase Manhattan*, *Lord Napier v Hunter*, *Boscawen v Bajwa* (the latter two cases concerning proprietary restitution through subrogation), and *Westdeutsche Landesbank* (in which proprietary restitution for failure of consideration was rejected). The central question that one should be asking in examining those cases, and in putting them alongside the other cases and examples listed in the last two paragraphs and the cases on proprietary restitution following equitable tracing (see above, 657–687), is whether the law on the scope of proprietary restitution is coherent.

In the second subsection, we extract some academic analyses of what the law is, and/or should be, on proprietary restitution. These range from doctrinal examinations of the link between unjust enrichment and constructive or resulting trusts (see, e.g., the extracts from Scott, Birks, Swadling and Chambers) through to the idea that proprietary restitution is justified, as a matter of policy, when the claimant has not taken the risk of the defendant's insolvency (see, e.g., the extracts from Sherwin, Paciocco and Burrows).

General Reading

BURROWS, 60–75, 159–162, 207–210, 409–411; GOFF AND JONES, 2-001–2-020; VIRGO, 569–619, chapter 21.

(1) CASE LAW ON THE SCOPE OF PROPRIETARY RESTITUTION

- *Chase Manhattan Bank NA v Israel-British Bank (London) Ltd*
  [1981] Ch 105, Chancery Division

On 3 July 1974, the claimant, a New York bank, mistakenly made two payments of some $2M, instead of one, to another New York bank, for the account of the defendant, an English bank. On 5 July 1974 the defendant knew, or should have known, of the mistake. Shortly afterwards the defendant became insolvent. The claimant proved, and received a dividend, in the winding up based on its personal restitutionary claim to the mistaken payment. But it now sought a declaration that the defendant became a trustee of the second $2M payment. Goulding J granted that declaration (that is, that the defendant was a trustee of that sum from receipt of it on 3 July 1974). Apart from difficult questions on the English (domestic) law of restitution, the case is complicated by the fact that the payments were made in New York. It therefore raised issues on the correct choice-of-law rule in private international law (otherwise known as the conflict of laws). While it was common ground that, as far as substantive law was concerned, New York law governed, the defendant argued that the trust and right to trace in issue were matters of procedural (or adjectival) law rather than substantive law so that, applying the normal choice of law rule for matters of procedure, English law as the *lex fori* governed. Goulding J ultimately found it unnecessary to decide whether that argument was correct because he considered that the laws of England and New York were the same on the central facts before him so that it did not matter which law governed.

Goulding J: . . . The plaintiff's claim, viewed in the first place without reference to *any* system of positive law, raises problems to which the answers, if not always difficult, are at any rate not obvious. If one party P pays money to another party D by reason of a factual mistake, either common to both parties or made by P alone, few conscientious persons would doubt that D ought to return it. But suppose that D is, or becomes, insolvent before repayment is made, so that P comes into competition with D's general creditors, what then? If the money can still be traced, either in its original form or through successive conversions, and is found among D's remaining assets, ought not P to be able to claim it, or what represents it, as his own? If he ought, and if in a particular case the money has been blended with other assets and is represented by a mixed fund, no longer as valuable as the sum total of its original constituents, what priorities or equalities should govern the distribution of the mixed fund? If the money can no longer be traced, either separate or in mixture, should P have any priority over ordinary creditors of D? In any of these cases, does it make any difference whether the mistake was inevitable, or was caused by P's carelessness, or was contributed to by some fault, short of dishonesty on the part of D?

At this stage I am asked to take only one step forward, and to answer the initial question of principle, whether the plaintiff is entitled in equity to trace the mistaken payment and to recover what now properly represents the money. The subsequent history of the payment and the rules for ascertaining what now represents it have not been proved or debated before me. They will have to be established in further proceedings if the plaintiff can clear the first hurdle today.

This initial question in the action appears not to be the subject of reported judicial decision in England. Let me read a few lines from *Goff and Jones, The Law of Restitution*, 2nd edn (1978), 89. The authors say:

'Whether a person who has paid money under a mistake of fact should be granted a restitutionary proprietary claim can arise in a number of contexts. It will be most important when the payee is insolvent and the payer seeks to gain priority over the payee's general creditors. The English courts have never had to consider this question. But in the United States it has arisen on a few occasions. A leading case is *In re Berry* (1906) 147 Fed. 208.'

That was a case decided in the Circuit Court of Appeals, Second Circuit. I shall read a passage from the judgment of the court, delivered by judge Coxe, at 210:

'Stripped of all complications and entanglements we have this naked fact that Raborg & Manice by mistake paid Berry & Co. $1,500, which they did not owe and which Berry & Co. could not have retained without losing the respect of every honourable business man. It is conceded on all hands that had not insolvency and bankruptcy intervened Raborg & Manice could have recovered the money on an implied assumpsit in the event that Berry & Co. declined to return it after knowledge of the facts—a highly improbable contingency. Of course such an action would lie. On no possible theory could the retention of the money by Berry & Co. be justified; it was paid to them and received by them under mistake, both parties believing that Raborg & Manice owed the amount. If $1,500 had been placed in a package by Raborg & Manice and delivered to a messenger with instructions to deposit it in their bank, and the messenger, by mistake, had delivered it to Berry & Co., it will hardly be pretended that the latter would acquire any title to the money, and yet the actual transaction in legal effect gave them no better right. It is urged that to compel restitution now will work injustice to the general creditors of the bankrupts, but this contention loses sight of the fact that the money in dispute never belonged to the bankrupts, and their creditors, upon broad principles of equity, have no more right to it than if the transaction of November 25 had never taken place. If the trustees succeed on this appeal the creditors will receive $1,500, the equitable title to which was never in the bankrupts. There can be no doubt of the fact that the payment to Berry & Co. was a mistake and that by reason of this mistake the trustees have in their possession $1,500 which, otherwise, they would not have. The proposition that Raborg & Manice who have done no wrong, shall be deprived of their property and that it shall be divided among creditors to whom it does not fairly belong, is not one that appeals to the conscience of a court of equity.'

...

The effect of the American case law, developed in a number of different states, as well as in the federal jurisdiction, is summarised as follows in the important book of Professor A. W. Scott, *The Law of Trusts*, 3rd edn (1967), vol. 5, 3428:

'Similarly where chattels are conveyed or money is paid by mistake, so that the person making the conveyance or payment is entitled to restitution, the transferee or payee holds the chattels or money upon a constructive trust. In such a case, it is true, the remedy at law for the value of the chattels or for the amount of money paid may be an adequate remedy, in which case a court of equity will not ordinarily give specific restitution. If the chattels are of a unique character, however, or if the person to whom the chattels are conveyed or to whom the money is paid is insolvent, the remedy at law is not adequate and a court of equity will enforce the constructive trust by decreeing specific restitution. The beneficial interest remains in the person who conveyed the chattel or who paid the money, since the conveyance or payment was made under a mistake.'

In my opinion, on the evidence that I have heard, to which I shall have to return later, the foregoing passages correctly represent the law of the State of New York. I believe they are also in accord with the general principles of equity as applied in England, and in the absence of direct English authority I should wish to follow them. Mr Stubbs for the defendant contends that I am not at liberty to do so, because of the judgment of the Court of Appeal in *In re Diplock* [1948] Ch 465, explaining and developing the earlier decision of the House of Lords in *Sinclair v Brougham* [1914] AC 398. *In re Diplock* itself went to the House of Lords, *sub nom. Ministry of Health v Simpson* [1951] AC 251, but the appeal did not relate to the question which is material in the present litigation. Mr Stubbs says that, as stated in *Snell's Principles of Equity* 27th edn (1973), 289, there is no equitable right to trace property unless some initial fiduciary relationship exists, the right being founded on the existence of a beneficial owner with an equitable proprietary interest in property in the hands of a trustee or other fiduciary agent. Mr Stubbs says further that the essential fiduciary relationship must initially arise from some consensual arrangement.

The facts and decisions in *Sinclair v Brougham* [1914] AC 398 and in *In re Diplock* [1948] Ch 465 are well known and I shall not take time to recite them. I summarise my view of the *Diplock* judgment as follows: (1) The Court of Appeal's interpretation of *Sinclair v Brougham* was an essential part of their decision and is binding on me. (2) The court thought that the majority of the House of Lords in *Sinclair v Brougham* had not accepted Lord Dunedin's opinion in that case, and themselves rejected it. (3) The court (as stated in *Snell*, loc. cit.) held that an initial fiduciary relationship is a necessary foundation of the equitable right of tracing. (4) They also held that the relationship between the building society directors and depositors in *Sinclair v Brougham* was a sufficient fiduciary relationship for the purpose: [1948] Ch 465, 529, 540. The latter passage reads, at 540: 'A sufficient fiduciary relationship was found to exist between the depositors and the directors by reason of the fact that the purposes for which the depositors had handed their money to the directors were by law incapable of fulfilment.' It is founded, I think, on the observations of Lord Parker of Waddington at [1914] AC 398, 441.

This fourth point shows that the fund to be traced need not (as was the case in *In re Diplock* itself) have been the subject of fiduciary obligations before it got into the wrong hands. It is enough that, as in *Sinclair v Brougham* [1914] AC 398, the payment into wrong hands itself gave rise to a fiduciary relationship. The same point also throws considerable doubt on Mr Stubbs's submission that the necessary fiduciary relationship must originate in a consensual transaction. It was not the intention of the depositors and the directors in *Sinclair v Brougham* to create any relationship at all between the depositors and the directors as principals. Their object, which unfortunately disregarded the statutory limitations of the building society's powers, was to establish contractual relationships between the depositors and the society. In the circumstances, however, the depositors retained an equitable property in the funds they parted with, and fiduciary relationships arose between them and the directors. In the same way, I would suppose, a person who pays money to another under a factual mistake retains an equitable property in it and the conscience of that other is subjected to a fiduciary duty to respect his proprietary right. I am fortified in my opinion by the speech of Viscount Haldane LC in *Sinclair v Brougham* [1914] AC 398, 419, 420, who, unlike Lord Dunedin, was not suspected of heresy in *In re Diplock*. Lord Haldane (who spoke for Lord Atkinson as well as himself) includes money paid under mistake of fact among the cases where money could be followed at common law, and he proceeds, at 421, to the auxiliary tracing remedy, available (as he said) wherever money was held to belong in equity to the plaintiff, without making any relevant exception. Thus my problem over *In re Diplock* [1948] Ch 465 is in the end this: Can I adopt into English equity the passage I have quoted from Professor Scott without making the forbidden transition to the opinion of Lord Dunedin? I have carefully considered the passages, at 541 to 543, in *In re Diplock* where that opinion is criticised. In the end I believe that the whole subject of the Court of Appeal's condemnation was the suggestion that the tracing remedy could be applied wherever the defendant could be shown to have got an unjust enrichment, a superfluity as Lord Dunedin called it. The court insisted on the more precise test of a continuing right of property recognised in equity or of what I think to be its concomitant, 'a fiduciary or quasi-fiduciary relationship': [1948] Ch 465, 520. At the same time they recognised that exactly what relationships were sufficient for the purpose had not yet been precisely laid down: see 540.

Thus, in the belief that the point is not expressly covered by English authority and that *In re Diplock* does not conclude it by necessary implication, I hold that the equitable remedy of tracing is in principle available, on the ground of continuing proprietary interest, to a party who has paid money under a mistake of fact. On that prime question, I see no relevant difference between the law of England and the law of New York and there is no conflict of laws to be resolved.

It is important, however, to make clear the limits of what I have just said. I do not say, and I do not imply, that on the facts and figures of any particular case the courts of England and of New York, when tracing in equity a sum paid by mistake, will necessarily apply the same tracing rules or arrive at the same final result. For example, in *In re Berry* (1906) 147 Fed. 208, an extract from which I have read, the American court applied the rule in *In re Hallett's Estate* (1880) 13 Ch D 696, for the purpose of identifying the claimant's money in the bankrupt's bank account. Mr Stubbs, when discussing *In re Berry* (1906) 147 Fed. 208 before me, has argued that if, contrary to his contention, an English court allowed tracing at all on the facts of that case, it would apply a different rule. I decline to answer any question of that sort until actually raised on ascertained facts.

. . .

What I have said is enough to show that the plaintiff must succeed at this state in the action, but in case the matter goes further I ought to express my findings on New York law in greater detail than I did at the outset of my judgment. . . . The issue is whether the equitable right of a person who pays money by mistake to trace and claim such money under the law of New York is conferred by substantive law or is of a merely procedural character.

[*After citing conflicting opinions on whether a constructive trust is a substantive institution or a remedy in the United States, Goulding J suggested that rights and remedies are 'indissolubly connected and correlated' and continued:*] [T]he relevant municipal law of New York is not, in my view, in serious doubt. I find it, shortly stated in my own words, to be as follows:

(a) If one party P transfers property to another party D by reason of a mistake of fact, P has in general a right to recover it and D a duty to restore it. (b) P in general has a right to sue in equity for an order that D return the property, or its traceable proceeds, to P. Sometimes this requires actual transfer by D, sometimes the court can use the alternative remedy of reformation, i.e. rectification of instruments, to produce the same result. P is said to retain an equitable title to the property notwith-standing it may have been legally transferred to D, and D is treated as a constructive trustee thereof. (c) In many cases P has also a common law right of action in quasi-contract to recover damages in respect of his loss. (d) The court will not, in its equitable jurisdiction, order specific restitution under (b) above where common law damages under (c) furnish adequate relief. (e) Accordingly where the property in question is money, equitable relief is not available to restore the sum paid by mistake if the payee D is solvent. But when D is insolvent P is entitled to a decree in equity for the purpose of tracing the money paid and recovering it or the property representing it. (f) Modern analysis concentrates attention less on the protection of P than on preventing the unjust enrichment of D, thus bringing the law of mistake into a broad jurisprudence of restitutionary rights and remedies.

. . .

[T]he view I have formed on the American material as a whole [is] that the plaintiff is right in alleging that the defendant became a trustee for the plaintiff of the sum paid by mistake and that the plain-tiff's equitable interest as cestui que trust was given (so far as the distinction has any meaning within the confines of New York law itself) by a rule of substantive law and is not the mere result of a remedial or procedural rule. . . . I have held, after examining *In re Diplock* [1948] Ch 465, that under

English municipal law a party who pays money under a mistake of fact may claim to trace it in equity, and that this right depends on a continuing right of property recognised in equity. I have found, on the evidence presented by the parties, that a similar right to trace is conferred by New York municipal law, and that there too the party paying by mistake retains a beneficial interest in the assets. No doubt the two systems of law in this field are not in all respects identical, but if my conclusions are right no conflict has arisen between them in the present case, and there is no occasion to draw a line, on either side of the Atlantic, between provisions that belong to substantive law and provisions that belong to adjective law. . . .

Subject to any discussion of the wording, I will declare that on July 3, 1974, the defendant became trustee for the plaintiff of the $2,000,687.509 . . . and I will direct an inquiry what has become of that sum, and what assets (if any), in the possession or power of the defendant, now represent the said sum or any part thereof or any interest or income thereof.

NOTES AND QUESTIONS

1. As we saw in Chapter 3, in nearly all cases of mistaken payments personal restitution (through an action for money had and received) is in issue. The primary significance of recognizing a proprietary, as opposed to a personal, restitutionary right is where, as in *Chase Manhattan*, the payee is insolvent. Proprietary, but not personal, restitution will give the payor priority over unsecured creditors on the reasoning that property belonging to the payor cannot form part of the defendant's pool of assets for distribution among creditors.

2. Was equitable title created for, or retained by, the payor as a consequence of the mistaken payment? Was the trust better viewed as constructive or resulting? Was the effect of declaring that the defendant was a trustee confined to proprietary restitution (that is, would the defendant be personally liable to account as a fiduciary for gains and losses made)?

3. In *Westdeutsche Landesbank Girozentrale v Islington BC* (see below, 727), Lord Browne-Wilkinson, giving the leading speech of the majority, regarded the reasoning of Goulding J as wrong. Nevertheless he thought that the actual decision might be correct on the basis that the defendant knew of the mistake within two days of the receipt of the payment (Goulding J considered this fact to be irrelevant). Do you agree that the defendant's knowledge of the mistake should have been of central importance in determining whether or not the defendant held the payment on trust?

4. The reasoning and decision in *Chase Manhattan* were controversial from the outset, as is shown by the following extract from a note on the case by Tettenborn.

• A Tettenborn, 'Remedies for the Recovery of Money Paid by Mistake' [1980] CLJ 272

[Goulding J's] judgment involves considerable difficulty.

1. It is against authority. *Scott on Trusts* [cited by Goulding J at above, 728] is an American book and follows the American practice of regarding the constructive trust as a general remedy for unjust enrichment. (cf. 'Restatement of Restitution,' §§160, 163 (d) (5)). Though urged to do so (e.g., Scott (1955) 71 *LQR* 39), English authority has not yet adopted this approach. (See, e.g., Snell, *Equity*, 27th edn., 286). It is submitted that, however desirable a change may be, English courts should not change their approach without full discussion of the likely implications. No such discussion appears in *Chase Manhattan*, which simply uncritically espouses American authority. This is too crude a method for law reform.

2. The decision will cause unjustified uncertainty in bankruptcy law. The American view of the constructive trust, apparently accepted by Goulding J, gives the courts a discretion to apply this remedy whenever the defendant has been unjustly enriched at the plaintiff's expense. In other words, if it is to introduced into English law, the courts are to be given a general discretionary power

to dispense, in favour of those whose claims are based on unjust enrichment, with the fundamental principle of bankruptcy law that all unsecured obligations have equal priority. (Bankruptcy Act 1914, s. 33(7)). In effect, those alleging unjust enrichment are all potentially preferred creditors. It is suggested that such a remarkable power should be given, if at all, by statute and not by judicial intervention.

3. Injustice is caused to general creditors in bankruptcy. To make mistaken payers of money into preferred creditors is unjust to the payee's other creditors. It is submitted that good reason is required in the case of insolvency to treat any one class of obligations better than others, and that neither justification suggested in *Re Berry* and accepted by Goulding J in *Chase Manhattan* for doing so is acceptable. To take these justifications in turn:

First, it is argued, if A pays B by mistake, thinking he is C, no property passes in the money. Similarly no property should pass if A pays B forgetting that he has paid him already. The answer to this is old-fashioned but relevant: mistake as to person goes to intent, mistake as to circumstance goes to motive. If I pay the wrong person for the right reason I do not intend to pass property to the person whom I pay, and accordingly I do not; if I pay the right person for the wrong reason, I intend to pass title and therefore I do so—although I have, of course, a claim to recover what I have paid. This distinction is neither unreal nor disreputable; it appears, for instance, in the law of contract, where it explains the difference between rectification (failure of intent), and rescission for mistake, e.g., in *Solle v Butcher* [1950] 1 KB 671 (disappointment of motive). It is submitted, therefore, that there is ample justification for the distinction between mistake as to person and as to circumstances, and that property can pass in money paid by mistake.

Secondly, and more substantially, it is argued (147 F. 210) that where A pays B by mistake B has no moral claim to keep the money; B's creditors, who derive their rights through B, therefore equally have no right to pay themselves out of it. But this proves too much: for it applies not only to restitutionary claims but to most contractual claims as well. True, a man has no right to keep money paid to him by mistake: but he has no right to keep money lent without repaying it, goods sold without paying for them, or to break his contracts without paying damages. Yet lenders, sellers and contractors do not receive priority in bankruptcy—even if the bankrupt still has what he received from them.

This also disposes of the contention in *Scott on Trusts*, above, that remedies at law for unjust enrichment are 'inadequate' against insolvent defendants. For if 'adequacy' has any meaning here, it can only be as a function of fairness as between the plaintiff and the defendant's general creditors, and it is suggested that a mistaken payer should be refused priority in the bankruptcy of the payee precisely because to give him it is unfair to the general creditors.

It is therefore submitted that Goulding J was wrong to give a proprietary remedy against the payee. The moral, however, runs deeper. The Chancellor rightly has the power to protect his friends against the bankruptcy laws; no one suggests that a *cestui que trust* should suffer from his trustee's bankruptcy. Nevertheless, such a power is drastic and should be used sparingly. Its over-indulgence, as in *Chase Manhattan v Israel-British Bank*, may cause dangerous injustice. It might be hard, Maitland remarked, that a *cestui que trust* should not have 'his' property; he added, however, that it was equally hard that creditors should go unpaid.

• *Lord Napier & Ettrick v Hunter* [1993] AC 713, House of Lords

The defendants were 'stop loss insurers', who had paid out on stop loss policies issued to various names at Lloyd's ('the assureds'). The assureds had subsequently won a settlement of £116 million in an action for negligence (against Outhwaite) to recoup their losses. The first claimant, representing the assureds, and the second claimant, which was the firm of solicitors holding the £116M, brought proceedings to determine the respective rights to the £116M. One issue that does not directly concern us here, but was decided by the House of Lords unanimously in favour of the insurers, was that in determining the amount of the settlement to which the insurers were entitled, the assured must bear the excess agreed. On the proprietary interest point that does here concern us the House of Lords held that, applying the doctrine of subrogation, the insurers had an equitable proprietary right over the settlement moneys in the form of an equitable lien so as to recover the amount paid out under the policies.

Lord Templeman: . . . The second question is whether the stop loss insurers have an interest in the moneys held by Richards Butler. For this purpose it may be assumed by way of example that the moneys held by Richards Butler include £130,000 paid by Outhwaite as damages for negligence which inflicted a loss of £160,000 on a name in respect of the 1982 year of account; can the stop loss insurers assert an interest in that sum of £130,000 to the extent of the £95,000 which, as I have indicated, is due to them by way of subrogation?

When the hypothetical name suffered a loss of £160,000 as a result of the negligence of Outhwaite, the stop loss insurers were bound to pay and did pay £100,000 under the policy. The stop loss insurers immediately became entitled to be subrogated to the right of the name to sue and recover damages in an action against Outhwaite, albeit that the amount payable to the stop loss insurers by way of subrogation could not be quantified until the action had been concluded and the damages paid. Nevertheless in my opinion the stop loss insurers had an interest in the right of action possessed by the name against Outhwaite. That action, if brought by the name, would be an action for the benefit of the name and for the benefit of the stop loss insurers. Where an insurer has paid on the policy, the courts have recognised the interests of the insurer in any right of action possessed by the insured person which will enable the insurer to claim back the whole or part of the sum which he has paid under the policy. The courts recognise the interests of the insurer by allowing him to sue in the name of the insured person against the wrongdoer if the insured person refuses to pursue the action.

. . .

It may be that the common law invented and implied in contracts of insurance a promise by the insured person to take proceedings to reduce his loss, a promise by the insured person to account to the insurer for moneys recovered from a third party in respect of the insured loss and a promise by the insured person to allow the insurer to exercise in the name of the insured person rights of action vested in the insured person against third parties for the recovery of the insured loss if the insured person refuses or neglects to enforce those rights of action. There must also be implied a promise by the insured person that in exercising his rights of action against third parties he will act in good faith for the benefit of the insured person so far as he has borne the loss and for the benefit of the insurer so far as he has indemnified the insured person against the insured loss. My Lords, contractual promises may create equitable interests. An express promise by a vendor to convey land on payment of the purchase price confers on the purchaser an equitable interest in the land. In my opinion promises implied in a contract of insurance with regard to rights of action vested in the insured person for the recovery of an insured loss from a third party responsible for the loss confer on the insurer an equitable interest in those rights of action to the extent necessary to recoup the insurer who has indemnified the insured person against the insured loss.

. . .

If the stop loss insurers have no equitable remedy in connection with their rights and if a name becomes bankrupt then subrogation is a mockery. Suppose, for example, that a name receives £100,000 from an insurer under a policy, recovers judgment for £130,000 damages from the wrong-doer and the name goes bankrupt before he receives the damages owing £1m. and possessing no assets other than assets representing the £100,000 he has received from the insurer and the asset of £130,000 payable by the wrongdoer. In that case, if the argument on behalf of the names is correct, the unsecured creditors of the insured name will benefit by double payment. The stop loss insurers will be in a worse position than an unsecured creditor because the insurers could not resist payment under the policy whereas an unsecured creditor may choose whether to advance moneys or not. In the case of the bankruptcy of the name, the right of the insurer to subrogation will be useless unless equity protects that right.

Saville J and the Court of Appeal held that the stop loss insurers were confined to their remedy for money had and received. The damages must first be distributed to the names. The stop loss insurers must then agree or determine by application to the court the amount due to them respectively and must then bring proceedings for money had and received against each of the names. All the authorities which indicated that an insurer who pays on the policy and is entitled to recoupment by way of subrogation has an equitable interest in the right of action of the insured person against a wrongdoer and an equitable interest in the damages payable by the wrongdoer were said not to be binding on the courts. Those authorities which I have cited, and there are others, included *Randal v Cockran*, 1 Ves. Sen. 98 decided in 1748, *White v Dobinson*, 14 Sim. 273; 116 LTOS 233 decided in 1844, *Commercial Union Assurance Co. v Lister*, LR 9 Ch.App. 483 decided in 1874, and *In re Miller, Gibb & Co. Ltd* [1957] 1 WLR 703 decided in 1957. I am not prepared to treat authorities which span over two centuries in a cavalier fashion. The principles which dictated the decisions of our ancestors and inspired their references to the equitable obligations of an insured person towards an insurer entitled to subrogation are discernible and immutable. They establish that such an insurer has an enforceable equitable interest in the damages payable by the wrongdoer. The insured person is guilty of unconscionable conduct if he does not provide for the insurer to be recouped out of the damages awarded against the wrongdoer. Equity will not allow the insured person to insist on his legal rights to all the damages awarded against the wrongdoer and will restrain the insured person from receiving or dealing with those damages so far as they are required to recoup the insurer under the doctrine of subrogation.

Where the insured person has been paid policy moneys by the insurer for a loss in respect of which the insured person recovers damages from a wrongdoer the insured person is guilty of unconscionable conduct if he does not procure and direct that the sum due to the insurer shall by way of subrogation be paid out of the damages.

It is next necessary to consider how equity copes with such unconscionable conduct. Saville J and the Court of Appeal appear to have thought that equity can only interfere by creating a trust fund held in trust by trustees for different beneficiaries in different shares, the trustees being burdened with administrative and investment duties, the trustees being liable for all the duties imposed on trustees but being free from liability if the trust fund is lost without negligence. I agree that if this were the only method of protecting the rights of an insurer the practical disadvantages would be fearsome. Fortunately, equity is not so inflexible or powerless. In order to protect the rights of the insurer under the doctrine of subrogation equity considers that the damages payable by the wrongdoer to the insured person are subject to an equitable lien or charge in favour of the insurer. The charge is imposed by equity because the insurer, once he has paid under the policy, has an interest in the right of action against the wrongdoer and an interest in the establishment, quantification, recovery and distribution of the damages awarded against the wrongdoer. It would be unconscionable for the insured person, who has received £100,000 from the insurer, to put damages of £130,000 into his own pocket without providing for the recoupment of the insurer who only contracted to indemnify the insured person.

The insurer can give notice to the wrongdoer of his equitable charge. When the wrongdoer is ordered or agrees to pay £130,000 and has notice of the rights of the insurer to subrogation, the wrongdoer can either pay the damages into court or decline to pay without the consent of both the insured person and the insurer. It would be the duty of the insured person to direct the wrongdoer to pay £95,000 of the damages to the insurer in recoupment and to pay the balance of £35,000 to himself. The equitable charge in favour of the insurer is enforceable against the damages ordered to be paid; that charge can be enforced so long as the damages form an identifiable separate fund. If, in the present case, Richards Butler had distributed the damages to the names before the stop loss insurers issued proceedings or notified Richards Butler of their equitable charge, the stop loss insurers would have been reduced to exercising their rights to sue the names for money had and received.

In the present case damages of £116m are in a separate fund held by Richards Butler on behalf of the names albeit that the damages in the fund also include moneys held on behalf of other names and other insurers. For the reasons I have indicated it would be unconscionable for the names to take their shares of the damages without providing for the sums due to the stop loss insurers to be paid out of those damages. The equitable charge still affects the damages and affects Richards Butler who hold the damages with notice of the charge.

. . . .

Since drafting this speech I have read in draft the speech to be delivered by my noble and learned friend, Lord Goff of Chieveley. He agrees that the doctrine of subrogation confers on the insurer an equitable proprietary lien or charge on the moneys recovered by the insured person from a third party in respect of the insured loss. I agree that in the circumstances it is not now necessary to decide whether the equitable lien or charge attaches also to the rights of action vested in the insured person to recover from a third party. I have expressed the view that the doctrine of subrogation does apply in those circumstances but in any future case, if the point becomes material, that view may require reconsideration in the light of further research. . . .

Lord Goff of Chieveley: . . . I start with the common law. In *Yorkshire Insurance Co. Ltd v Nisbet Shipping Co. Ltd* [1962] 2 QB 330, a case concerned with marine insurance, Lord Diplock (then Diplock J) analysed the principle of subrogation in purely contractual terms. He said, at 339–40:

> 'The expression 'subrogation' in relation to a contract of marine insurance is thus no more than a convenient way of referring to those terms which are to be implied in the contract between the assured and the insurer to give business efficacy to an agreement whereby the assured in the case of a loss against which the policy has been made shall be fully indemnified, and never more than fully indemnified.'

He went on to say, at 340, that subrogation is concerned solely with the mutual rights and liabilities of the parties to the contract of insurance. The remedies of the insurer were, he said, essentially common law remedies; in particular, if the assured has, after payment of the loss by the insurer, received a sum from a third party in reduction of the loss, the insurer can recover the amount of the reduction as money had and received (for which Lord Diplock referred, at 341, to *Bullen and Leake, Precedents of Pleadings*, 3rd edn (1868), 187). The only role which Lord Diplock assigned to equity was to come to the aid of the common law by compelling the assured to allow his name to be used in proceedings against the third party: see also his judgment in *Hobbs v Marlowe* [1978] AC 16, 39.

Now there is no reason why, subject to the one matter to which Lord Diplock refers, the principle of subrogation in the field of insurance should not have developed as a purely common law principle. But as a matter of history it did not do so. It is true that our law of marine insurance was very largely established by Lord Mansfield, in a remarkable series of decisions during his tenure of office as Chief Justice at the Court of King's Bench, so much so that Park J dedicated the first edition of his treatise on the law of marine insurance (*Park, A System of the Law of Marine Insurances* (1786)) to Lord Mansfield, describing the subject in the dedication as one which 'must be admitted to be the exclusive property of your Lordship.' But in the early editions of the book there is little trace of the principle of subrogation, though there is much learning on the subject of abandonment. Lord Mansfield's decision in the leading case of *Mason v Sainsbury*, 3 Doug. 61 established that payment of a claim by an insurer did not preclude him from thereafter proceeding in the name of the assured against the wrongdoer who had caused the relevant damage, and recovering damages in full from him. The payment of the loss by the insurer to the assured did not affect the liability of the wrong-doer; the action against him was to be considered 'as if the insurers had not paid a farthing:' see at 64. However the [insurer] could not proceed against the third party in his own name; he had to proceed in the name of the assured: see *London Assurance Co. v Sainsbury* (1873) 3 Doug. 245.

It is of some interest that, in *Mason v Sainsbury*, the action against the wrongdoer was brought in the name of the assured with his consent, for the benefit of the insurer. Here we can see an early example of the fact that the insurer, upon payment to the assured of his loss, receives from him as a matter of course not merely a receipt for the money, but also what has for many years been called a letter of subrogation signed by the assured which authorises the insurer to proceed in this way, and indeed nowadays may assign the relevant rights of action to the insurer. It is very difficult to imagine an insurer paying a claim without taking this elementary precaution, especially as the assured can have little or no incentive to refuse to sign such a document. I strongly suspect that letters of subrogation have been a commonplace of insurance claims for a very long time; and that it is their regular use which explains what appears to be a dearth of authority on such matters as proceedings to compel the assured to allow the insurer to commence proceedings in his name, and actions for money had and received by insurers against assureds, because third parties would have settled direct with the insurer as expressly authorised by the assured (hence, pace Lord Diplock, the absence of any reference to such an action in *Bullen & Leake*, 3rd edn.). On the other hand, there is a substantial body of case law on the subject of the respective rights of insurer and assured in the institution, control and settlement of proceedings against wrongdoers who have caused the relevant loss (as to which see *MacGillivray and Parkington on Insurance Law*, 8th edn (1988), paras. 1191 ff.).

At all events, what appears to have happened is not simply that equity came to the aid of the common law by compelling an assured whose loss has been paid to allow the insurer to proceed in his name against a third party wrongdoer responsible for the loss, but that a principle of subrogation was the subject of separate development by courts of equity in a line of authority dating from *Randal v Cockran*, 1 Ves.Sen. 98, which was decided before Lord Mansfield was appointed Chief Justice of the Court of King's Bench. This line of authority is tracted in the speech of my noble and learned friend, Lord Templeman, and I am therefore spared the burden of setting it out in this opinion. Spasmodic but consistent, the cases assert that recoveries by the assured which reduce the loss paid by the insurer are held in trust for the insurer, so much so that by 1881 Sir George Jessel MT regarded this proposition as indisputable: see *Commercial Union Assurance Co. v Lister*, LR 9 Ch.App. 483, 484n. This principle was moreover recognised not only in courts of equity, but also in courts of common law: see the decision of the Court of Common Pleas in *Yates v White*, 1 Arn. 85; sub nom. *Yates v Whyte*, 4 Bing (NC) 272, subsequently approved by this House in *Simpson & Co. v Thomson* (1877) 3 App.Cas. 279, in which Lord Cairns LC, at 285–6, cited in extenso passages from the judgment in *Yates v Whyte*, 4 Bing. (NC) 272 in which reliance was placed on *Randal v Cockran*, and Lord Blackburn, at 293, relied on *Randal v Cockran* itself in a passage to which I shall refer later in this opinion. It is perhaps also relevant that in 1783 Lord Mansfield had justified his conclusion that the insurer could not proceed in his own name but must proceed in the name of the assured on the ground that 'trustee and cestui que trust cannot both have a right of action:' see *London Assurance Co. v Sainsbury*, 3 Doug. 245, 253.

I agree with my noble and learned friend, Lord Browne-Wilkinson, that the decisive case in the line of equity cases is *White v Dobinson*, 14 Sim. 273; 116 LTOS 233. The case was concerned with a collision at sea. The owner of one of the ships, after payment by his underwriter of £205, was awarded £600 damages in arbitration proceedings against the other shipowner. Sir Lancelot Shadwell V-C, relying upon *Randal v Cockran* and *Blaauwpot v Da Costa*, 1 Ed. 130, granted an interlocutory injunction which had the effect of retaining the fund, and not letting it pass into the hands of the assured. The injunction appears to have restrained both the assured from receiving, and the other shipowner from paying, the money without first paying or providing for the sum of £205 paid by the insurer:

see the report at 116 LTOS 233. Lord Lyndhurst LC discharged the injunction as against the other shipowner, but otherwise maintained it in force. The case is important for a number of reasons. First, the insurer's case was advanced on the basis that he had a lien on the sum awarded, and was resisted on the ground that the insurer's right, if it existed at all, was a right to proceed at law in an action for money had and received, and was not an equitable right. That argument was rejected. Second, the Lord Chancellor also rejected a claim by a bank as assignee from the assured, on the ground that the bank's security was taken subject to all the equities which would have affected the money received in the hands of the assured himself. Third, the Lord Chancellor held that the insurers had a claim upon the fund awarded, and were 'entitled in some shape or other to recover back the money they have paid.'

Now it is true that the case was concerned with an interlocutory injunction, a point which evidently concerned the Lord Chancellor himself. But he nevertheless upheld the injunction on the basis of the authority cited to him, in which, as he said:

'we have the clearly expressed opinions of Lord Hardwicke and Lord Northington, recognised by parke B., and more recently by Lord Abinger CB (*Brooks v MacDonnell* (1835) 1 Y. & C. 500), who at that time possessed considerable experience of the practice in equity, from having presided for several years on the equity side of the Court of Exchequer . . .'

Subsequent authorities to the same effect are *King v Victoria Insurance Co. Ltd* [1896] AC 250, 255–6, *per* Lord Hobhouse who (in a passage in which he appears to have placed no reliance upon the existence of an assignment by the assured of its rights and causes of action against the third party) expressed the opinion that the assured would have held any damages recovered from the third party as trustee for the insurer; and *In re Miller, Gibb & Co. Ltd* [1957] 1 WLR 703. The only case in equity which appears at first sight to be inconsistent with this line of authority is *Stearns v Village Main Reef Gold Mining Co. Ltd*, 10 Com.Cas. 89. However, as my noble and learned friend, Lord Browne-Wilkinson, has pointed out, that case was concerned with the recovery of an overpayment; indeed, it was upon that basis that it was distinguished by Wynn-Parry J in *In re Miller, Gibb & Co. Ltd* [1957] 1 WLR 703, 710–11.

Despite Saville J's reservations on this point, I can discern no inconsistency between the equitable proprietary right recognised by courts of equity in these cases and the personal rights and obligations embodied in the contract of insurance itself. No doubt our task nowadays is to see the two strands of authority, at law and in equity, moulded into a coherent whole; but for my part I cannot see why this amalgamation should lead to the rejection of the equitable pro-prictary right recognised in the line of cases to which I have referred. Of course, it is proper to start with the contract of insurance, and to see how the common law courts have worked out the mutual rights and obligations of the parties in contractual terms with recourse to implied terms where appropriate. But, with all respect, I am unable to agree with Lord Diplock that subrogation is in this context concerned *solely* with the mutual rights and obligations of the parties under the contract. In this connection, I observe from the report of *Yorkshire Insurance Co. Ltd v Nisbet Shipping Co. Ltd* [1962] 2 QB 330 that the important case of *White v Dobinson*, 14 Sim. 273; 116 LTOS 233 was not cited in argument, and indeed the existence of an equitable proprietary right was not in issue in that case. In these circumstances I cannot derive from Lord Diplock's judgment any justification for sweeping the line of equity cases under the carpet as though it did not exist. In my opinion, this line of authority must be recognised, and appropriate weight should be given to the views expressed in the cases by the distinguished judges who decided them. I wish to add that I do not read section 79 of the Marine Insurance Act 1906 (concerned with the right of subrogation) as in any way detracting from this conclusion.

Even so, an important feature of these cases is that the principle of subrogation in the law of insurance arises in a contractual context. It is true that in some cases at common law it has been described as arising as a matter of equity. Thus in *Burnand v Rodocanachi Sons & Co.*, 7 App. Cas. 333,

339, Lord Blackburn described it simply as 'an equity.' Furthermore, it has not been usual to express the principle of subrogation as arising from an implied term in the contract. Even so it has been regarded, both at law and in equity, as giving effect to the underlying nature of a contract of insurance, which is that it is intended to provide an indemnity but no more than an indemnity. Not only does this principle inform the judgments of the Court of Appeal in the leading case of *Castellain v Preston*, 11 QBD 380, but it underlies Lord Lyndhurst LC's judgment in *White v Dobinson*, 116 LTOS 233. In so far as the principle requires the payment of money, it could no doubt be formulated as an implied term, to which effect could have been given by the old action for money had and received. But I do not see why the mere fact that the purpose of subrogation in this context is to give effect to the principle of indemnity embodied in the contract should preclude recognition of the equitable proprietary right, if justice so requires. If I search for a parallel, the closest analogy is perhaps to be found in the law of agency in which, although the relationship between principal and agent is governed by a contract, nevertheless the agent may be held in certain circumstances to hold money, which he has received from a third party in his capacity as agent, as trustee for his principal. It is by no means easy to ascertain the circumstances in which a trusteeship exists; but, in a valuable discussion in *Bowstead on Agency*, 15th edn (1985), 162–3, Professor Francis Reynolds suggests that it is right to inquire

> 'whether the trust relationship is appropriate to the commercial relationship in which the parties find themselves; whether it was appropriate that money or property should be, and whether it was held separately, or whether it was contemplated that the agent should use the money, property or proceeds of the property as part of his normal cash flow in such a way that the relationship of debtor and creditor is more appropriate.'

He also suggests that

> 'a central question, perhaps too often overlooked (because not directly an issue), is whether the rights of the principal are sufficiently strong, and differentiable from other claims, for him to be entitled to a prior position in respect of them on the agent's bankruptcy.'

I have little doubt that the distinguished judges who decided the cases in the line of equity authority to which I have referred must have considered that money received by an assured from a third party in reduction of a loss paid by an insurer should not be treated as available for the assured's normal cash flow, and further that the rights of the insurer to such money were sufficiently strong to entitle the insurer to priority in the event of the assured's bankruptcy, as was indeed held by Wynn-Parry J in *In re Miller, Gibb & Co. Ltd* [1957] 1 WLR 703. I for my part can see no good reason to depart from this line of authority. However, since the constitution of the assured as trustee of such money may impose upon him obligations of too onerous a character (a point which troubled Saville J in the present case), I am very content that the equitable proprietary right of the insurer should be classified as a lien, as proposed by my noble and learned friend, Lord Templeman, and indeed as claimed by the insurer in *White v Dobinson*, 14 Sim. 273 itself. Indeed a lien is the more appropriate form of proprietary right in circumstances where, as here, its function is to protect the interest of the insurer in an asset only to the extent that its retention by the assured will have the effect that he is more than indemnified under the policy of insurance.

There is one particular problem to which I wish to refer, although, as I understand it, it does not fall to be decided in the present case. Does the equitable proprietary interest of the insurer attach only to a fund consisting of sums which come into the hands of the assured in reduction of the loss paid by the insurer? Or does it attach also to a right of action vested in the assured which, if enforced, would yield such a fund? The point is not altogether easy. I can see no reason in principle why such an interest should not be capable of attaching to property in the nature of a chose in action. Moreover that it should do so in the present context appears to have been the opinion of Lord Blackburn in

Simpson & Co. v Thomson, 3 App.Cas. 279, 292–3. On the other hand, cases such as *Morley v Moore* [1936] 2 KB 359 appear to point in the opposite direction, as perhaps does the decision of Lord Lyndhurst LC in *White v Dobinson*, 116 LTOS 233 to discharge the injunction as against the owner of the ship at fault in that case. However, since the point was not directly addressed in the argument before your Lordships, I am reluctant to reach any conclusion upon it without a full examination of the authorities relating to the respective rights and obligations of insurer and assured, especially with regard to the conduct and disposal of litigation relating to causes of action of the relevant kind. I therefore wish to reserve my opinion upon this question, the answer to which I do not regard as necessary for the resolution of the issue which has arisen in the present case.

Lord Browne-Wilkinson: ... What, then, was the basis on which equity enforced rights of subrogation? Was it merely a personal obligation of the assured to account to the insurers for benefits received from third party wrongdoers in diminution of the insured loss, or was it a proprietary right of the insurers in the damages recovered from third parties? In my judgment, the authorities show that it was a proprietary right in the damages recovered.

In my judgment therefore an insurer who has paid over the insurance moneys does have a proprietary interest in moneys subsequently recovered by an assured from a third party wrongdoer. Although many of the authorities refer to that right as arising under a trust, in my judgment the imposition of a trust is neither necessary nor desirable: to impose fiduciary liabilities on the assured is commercially undesirable and unnecessary to protect the insurers' interests. In my judgment, the correct analysis is as follows. The contract of insurance contains an implied term that the assured will pay to the insurer out of the moneys received in reduction of the loss the amount to which the insurer is entitled by way of subrogation. That contractual obligation is specifically enforceable in equity against the defined fund (i.e., the damages) in just the same way as are other contracts to assign or charge specific property e.g. equitable assignments and equitable charges. Since equity regards as done that which ought to be done under a contract, this specifically enforceable right gives rise to an immediate proprietary interest in the moneys recovered from the third party. In my judgment, this proprietary interest is adequately satisfied in the circumstances of subrogation under an insurance contract by granting the insurer a lien over the moneys recovered by the assured from the third party. This lien will be enforceable against the fund so long as it is traceable and has not been acquired by a bona fide purchaser for value without notive. In addition to the equitable lien, the insurer will have a personal right of action at law to recover the amount received by the assured as moneys had and received to the use of the insurer.

As to the question whether the insurers have a proprietary interest in the assured's cause of action against the third party (as contrasted with the damages actually recovered) I prefer to express no concluded view. I do not think that the proprietary interest in the damages necessarily postulates a pre-existing proprietary interest in the cause of action. The contrary view could be reached by an argument along the following lines. Any equitable proprietary right must be based on the contract between the insurers and the assured. The implied terms of such contract are established by the decided authorities. Some of those implied terms may be inconsistent with the insurers having any right of property in the cause of action as opposed to the damages recovered. Thus, the third party can compromise the claim with the assured alone, without requiring the concurrence of the insurers. Again, the third party will obtain a good discharge for a judgment only if he pays the assured as opposed to the insurers. If the insurers have a proprietary interest in the cause of action it could be argued that the assured alone could neither effect a valid compromise nor give a good discharge: the insurers also would have to be parties. Accordingly, it could be said that the implied terms of the contract between the insurers and the assured are such that equity would not be specifically enforcing the parties' bargain if it treated the insurers as having proprietary rights in the cause of action inconsistent with the rights of the assured and that accordingly the rights of the insurers are purely personal rights to require the assured either to pursue the cause of action against the third party or to permit the insurers to do so in his name. But there are plainly factors pointing the other way and since the question was not fully argued I prefer to express no view on the point.

Lord Jauncey and **Lord Steyn** concurred.

NOTES AND QUESTIONS

1. An indemnity insurer has two types of subrogation right. Both involve simple and not reviving subrogation (for this terminology see above, 194). The first type of right is where the insurer takes over the remedies of the assured against another party (e.g. a tortfeasor) in order to recover the sum paid out by the insurer and by which the assured would otherwise be overcompensated. The second type of right, with which the *Napier* case was concerned, entitles the insurer to recover from the assured, up to the amount paid to the assured, money that the assured has already received or subsequently receives from another party (e.g. a tortfeasor) and by which the assured is overcompensated.

2. Are an indemnity insurer's subrogation rights based on unjust enrichment? If so, what is the correct analysis of (i) the enrichment; (ii) at the claimant's expense; (iii) the unjust factor? See on this, Burrows, 107–12.

3. Charles Mitchell, *The Law of Subrogation* (1994), 83–4, has criticized the decision of the House of Lords in *Napier v Hunter*. In his view, the indemnity insurers should have been entitled merely to personal, and not proprietary, restitution.

> The insurers should not have been given a proprietary claim for the following reasons. First, they could not have been entitled to such a claim on the basis of 'proprietary base' reasoning, because the money to which they laid claim had never been in their possession and hence they could not have claimed to 'retain' a proprietary interest in it. Nor could they have been entitled to a proprietary remedy on the ground that they had not voluntarily assumed the risk of their insured's bankruptcy. This explanation of the insurers' entitlement to a proprietary claim was in fact advanced in the case by Lord Templeman, who felt it to be significant that 'the insurers could not resist payment whereas an unsecured creditor may choose whether to advance moneys or not'. With respect to Lord Templeman, though, this argument is unconvincing. An insurer chooses to enter into a contract of insurance with its insured in exactly the same way that an unsecured creditor chooses to enter a contract of loan with his debtor. Once either contract is entered into, neither the insurer nor the creditor can resist its legal obligation to pay. This strongly suggests that the element of compulsion underlying the insurer's payment referred to by Lord Templeman does not constitute a sufficient reason for elevating the insurer's claim above the claims of the insured's unsecured creditors. Since the insurer, like the unsecured creditors, does not stipulate for security in its contract with the insured, it should occupy the same position as they in the insured's insolvency.
>
> There is a further reason in principle why the insurers should not have been given a proprietary remedy in *Lord Napier*. If an insurer pays its insured after the insured's receipt of payment from a third party then . . . the claim which the insurer is thus allowed to bring against its insured is an action for money had and received to recover its overpayment, that is a personal claim. Why should the insurer be allowed a proprietary claim rather than a personal claim simply because the insurer happens to have paid its insured before rather than after the insured's receipt of payment from the third party? The effect of giving the insurer a proprietary claim in the latter, but not in the former, circumstances is to create an anomaly for which there is no justification.

Do you agree with Charles Mitchell that *proprietary* restitution was not justified in *Napier v Hunter*?

- *Boscawen v Bajwa* [1996] 1 WLR 328, Court of Appeal

Mr Bajwa was the owner of a house. The Halifax Building Society had a charge over the house. Bajwa contracted to sell the house to purchasers who were to obtain a mortgage from the Abbey National. Abbey National paid the purchase money to the purchasers' solicitors (B. Dave & Co.) pending completion of the sale. They in turn paid the money by cheque to Bajwa's solicitors (Hill Lawson) who then paid off the Halifax Building society's charge over the property. Hill Lawson had acted with undue haste in paying off the Halifax because B. Dave & Co.'s cheque was dishonoured and the only equity partner was insolvent. The sale then fell through. Judgment creditors of Bajwa with a charging order on the house brought a claim to enforce the charging order and the house was sold for £105,312 net. Abbey National counterclaimed that it was entitled to an equitable charge over the house (and hence the proceeds of sale) on the basis that it was subrogated to the charge of the Halifax Building Society which had been paid off with the Abbey National's money. At first instance Edward Nugee QC held for the Abbey National. The judgment creditors appealed but their appeal was dismissed by the Court of Appeal.

Millett LJ: . . .

TRACING AND SUBROGATION

The submission that the deputy judge illegitimately conflated two different causes of action, the equitable tracing claim and the claim to a right of subrogation, betrays a confusion of thought which arises from the admittedly misleading terminology which is traditionally used in the context of equitable claims for restitution. Equity lawyers habitually use the expressions 'the tracing claim' and 'the tracing remedy' to describe the proprietary claim and the proprietary remedy which equity makes available to the beneficial owner who seeks to recover his property in specie from those into whose hands it has come. Tracing properly so-called, however, is neither a claim nor a remedy but a process. Moreover, it is not confined to the case where the plaintiff seeks a proprietary remedy; it is equally necessary where he seeks a personal remedy against the knowing recipient or knowing assistant. It is the process by which the plaintiff traces what has happened to his property, identifies the persons who have handled or received it, and justifies his claim that the money which they handled or received (and, if necessary, which they still retain) can properly be regarded as representing his property. He needs to do this because his claim is based on the retention by him of a beneficial interest in the property which the defendant handled or received. Unless he can prove this he cannot (in the traditional language of equity) raise an equity against the defendant or (in the modern language of restitution) show that the defendant's unjust enrichment was at his expense.

In such a case the defendant will either challenge the plaintiff's claim that the property in question represents his property (i.e., he will challenge the validity of the tracing exercise) or he will raise a priority dispute (e.g., by claiming to be a bona fide purchaser without notice). If all else fails he will raise the defence of innocent change of position. This was not a defence which was recognised in England before 1991 but it was widely accepted throughout the common law world. In *Lipkin Gorman v Karpnale Ltd* [1991] 2 AC 548 the House of Lords acknowledge it to be part of English law also. The introduction of this defence not only provides the court with a means of doing justice in future, but allows a re-examination of many decisions of the past in which the absence of the defence may have led judges to distort basic principles in order to avoid injustice to the defendant.

If the plaintiff succeeds in tracing his property, whether in its original or in some changed form, into the hands of the defendant, and overcomes any defences which are put forward on the defendant's behalf, he is entitled to a remedy. The remedy will be fashioned to the circumstances. The plaintiff will generally be entitled to a personal remedy; if he seeks a proprietary remedy he must usually prove that the property to which he lays claim is still in the ownership of the defendant. If he succeeds in doing this the court will treat the defendant as holding the property on a constructive trust for the plaintiff and will order the defendant to transfer it in specie to the plaintiff. But this is only one of the proprietary remedies which are available to a court of equity. If the plaintiff's money has been applied by the defendant, for example, not in the acquisition of a landed property but in its improvement, then the court may treat the land as charged with the payment to the plaintiff of a sum representing the amount by which the value of the defendant's land has been enhanced by the use of the plaintiff's money. And if the plaintiff's money has been used to discharge a mortgage on the defendant's land, then the court may achieve a similar result by treating the land as subject to a charge by way of subrogation in favour of the plaintiff.

Subrogation, therefore, is a remedy, not a cause of action ... it is available in a wide variety of different factual situations in which it is required in order to reverse the defendant's unjust enrichment. Equity lawyers speak of a right of subrogation, or of an equity of subrogation, but this merely reflects the fact that it is not a remedy which the court has a general discretion to impose whenever it thinks it just to do so. The equity arises from the conduct of the parties on well settled principles and in defined circumstances which make it unconscionable for the defendant to deny the proprietary interest claimed by the plaintiff. A constructive trust arises in the same way. Once the equity is established the court satisfies it by declaring that the property in question is subject to a charge by way of subrogation in the one case or a constructive trust in the other.

Accordingly, there was nothing illegitimate in the deputy judge's invocation of the two doctrines of tracing and subrogation in the same case. They arose at different stages of the proceedings. Tracing was the process by which the Abbey National sought to establish that its money was applied in the discharge of the Halifax's charge; subrogation was the remedy which it sought in order to deprive Mr Bajwa (through whom the appellants claim) of the unjust enrichment which he would thereby otherwise obtain at the Abbey National's expense.

TRACING

It is still a prerequisite of the right to trace in equity that there must be a fiduciary relationship which calls the equitable jurisdiction into being: see *Agip (Africa) Ltd v Jackson* [1991] Ch 547, 566, *per* Fox LJ. That requirement is satisfied in the present case by the fact that from the first moment of its receipt by Dave in their general client account the £140,000 was trust money held in trust for the Abbey National. The appellants do not dispute that the Abbey National can successfully trace £137,405 of its money into Hill Lawson's client account. But they do dispute the judge's finding that it can trace the sum further into the payment to the Halifax.

The £137,405 was paid into Hill Lawson's general client account at the bank because it was only intended to be kept for a short time. Funds which were held for clients for any length of time were held in separate designated accounts. Hill Lawson's ledger cards showed Mr Bajwa as the relevant client. According to Mr Duckney [of Hill Lawson], Hill Lawson also hold other funds for Mr Bajwa which were the result of an inheritance which he had received. These were the source from which Hill Lawson made good the shortfall of £2,595 which arose when Dave's cheque was dishonoured. The amount of these other funds is unknown, though it was certainly nothing like £140,000. The evidence does not show whether they were held in Hill Lawson's general client account or whether they were held in a separate designated account. If they were held in the general client account the £137,405 received from Dave was (quite properly) mixed not only with moneys belonging to other clients but also with money belonging to Mr Bajwa. Hill Lawson can be presumed not to have committed a breach of trust by resorting to moneys belonging to other clients but they were perfectly entitled to use Mr Bajwa's own money to discharge the Halifax's charge on his property. Whether they did so or not cannot be determined in the absence of any evidence of the amount involved. Accordingly, it is submitted, the Abbey National has failed to establish how much of its money was applied in the discharge of the Halifax's charge and how much of the money which was applied for this purpose was Mr Bajwa's own money.

The Abbey National answers this submission in two ways. First, it submits that Hill Lawson's ledger cards show that Hill Lawson appropriated the £137,405, which they had received from Dave, towards the payment of the sum of £140,000 to the Halifax, and resorted to Mr Bajwa's other funds only when Dave's cheque for the balance was dishonoured. The ledger cards were, of course, made up after the event, though long before any litigation ensued, so they are not primary evidence of actual appropriation; but they are reliable evidence of the appropriation which Hill Lawson believed that they had made.

I accept this submission. It is not necessary to apply artificial tracing rules where there has been an actual appropriation. A trustee will not be allowed to defeat the claim of his beneficiary by saying that he has resorted to trust money when he could have made use of his own; but if the beneficiary asserts that the trustee has made use of the trust money there is no reason why he should not be allowed to prove it.

The second way in which the Abbey National answers the appellants' submission is by reliance on equity's ability to follow money through a bank account where it has been mixed with other moneys by treating the money in the account as charged with the repayment of his money. As against a wrongdoer the claimant is not obliged to appropriate debits to credits in order to ascertain where his money has gone. Equity's power to charge a mixed fund with the repayment of trust moneys enables the claimant to follow the money, not because it is his, but because it is derived from a fund which is treated as if it were subject to a charge in his favour: see *In re Hallett's Estate; Knatchbull v Hallett* (1880) 13 Ch D 696; *In re Oatway; Hertslet v Oatway* [1903] 2 Ch 356 and *El Ajou v Dollar Land Holdings Plc* [1993] 3 All ER 717.

[*Having considered the different tracing rules applicable to where the money was mixed by an innocent volunteer, citing* In re Diplock (*see above, 676*), *Millett LJ continued:*]

But the present case is very different. Neither Mr Bajwa nor his solicitors acted dishonestly, but nor were they innocent volunteers. Hill Lawson knew that the money was trust money held to Dave's order pending completion and that it would become available for use on behalf of their client only on completion. They were manifestly fiduciaries. Mr Bajwa, who was plainly intending to redeem the Halifax's mortgage out of the proceeds of sale of the property, must be taken to have known that any money which his solicitors might receive from the purchasers or their mortgagees would represent the balance of the proceeds of sale due on completion and that, since he had made no arrangement with the purchasers to be advanced any part of that amount before completion, it would be available to him only on completion. He cannot possibly have thought that he could keep both the property and the proceeds of sale. Had he thought about the matter at all, he would have realised that the money was not his to mix with his own and dispose of as he saw fit. The only reason that he and his solicitors can be acquitted of dishonesty is that he relied on his solicitors and they acted in the mistaken belief that, save for the tidying up of some loose ends, they were on the point of completing.

It follows that Mr Bajwa cannot avail himself of the more favourable tracing rules which are available to the innocent volunteer who unconsciously mixes trust money with his own.

SUBROGATION

The appellants submit that the mere fact that the claimant's money is used to discharge someone else's debt does not entitle him to be subrogated to the creditor whose debt is paid. There must be 'something more:' *Paul v Speirway Ltd* [1976] Ch 220, 230, *per* Oliver J; and see *Orakpo v Manson Investments Ltd* [1978] AC 95, 105, where Lord Diplock said:

> 'The mere fact that money lent has been expended upon discharging a secured liability of the borrower does not give rise to any implication of subrogation unless the contract under which the money was borrowed provides that the money is to be applied for this purpose: *Wylie v Carlyon* [1922] 1 Ch 51.'

From this the appellants derive the proposition that in order to be subrogated to the creditor's security the claimant must prove (i) that the claimant intended that his money should be used to discharge the security in question (that being the 'something more' required by Oliver J) and (ii) that he intended to obtain the benefit of the security by subrogation.

I cannot accept that formulation as a rule of general application, regardless of the circumstances in which the remedy of subrogation is sought. The cases relied on were all cases where the claimant intended to make an unsecured loan to a borrower who used the money to discharge a secured debt. In such a case the claimant is not entitled to be subrogated to the creditor's security since this would put him in a better position than he had bargained for. Oliver J in *Paul v Speirway Ltd* [1976] Ch 220, 232 was not prepared to say more than that:

> 'It is always dangerous to try to lay down general principles unnecessarily, but it does seem to me to be safe to say this: that where on all the facts the court is satisfied that the true nature of the transaction between the payer of the money and the person at whose instigation it is paid is simply the creation of an unsecured loan, this in itself will be sufficient to dispose of any question of subrogation. That really, as it seems to me, is to say no more than that the question of subrogation or no subrogation cannot be divorced from a review of the rights proved or presumed to be intended to be created between the payer of the money and the person requiring its payment.'

In that passage Oliver J was plainly limiting his observations to a claim to be subrogated to the creditor's security. The mere fact that the payer of the money intended to make an unsecured loan will not preclude his claim to be subrogated to the personal rights of the creditor whose debt is discharged if the contractual liability of the original borrower proves to be unenforceable: see, for example, *In re Wrexham, Mold and Connah's Quay Railway Co.* [1899] 1 Ch 440 (where the borrowing was ultra vires) and *B. Liggett (Liverpool) Ltd v Barclays Bank Ltd* [1928] 1 KB 48 (where the borrowing was unauthorised).

In *Orakpo v Manson Investments Ltd* Lord Diplock pointed out, at 104, that the remedy of subrogation was available in a whole variety of widely different circumstances, and that this made

> 'particularly perilous any attempt to rely upon analogy to justify applying to one set of circumstances which would otherwise result in unjust enrichment a remedy of subrogation which has been held to be available for that purpose in another and different set of circumstances.'

The converse is equally true. It is perilous to extrapolate from one set of circumstances where the court has required a particular precondition to be satisfied before the remedy of subrogation can be granted a general rule which makes that requirement a precondition which must be satisfied in other and different circumstances. In the present case there was no relevant transaction between Abbey National ('the payer of the money') and Mr Bajwa ('the person at whose instigation it was paid'). This does not mean that the test laid down by Oliver J in *Paul v Speirway Ltd* has not been satisfied; it means that the test is not applicable. In *Butler v Rice* [1910] 2 Ch 277 the fact that the debtor had not requested the claimant to make the payment and did not know of the transaction was held to be immaterial. This is not to say that intention is necessarily irrelevant in a case of the present kind; it is to say only that where the payment was made by a third party and the claimant had no intention to make any payment to or for the benefit of the recipient the relevant intention must be that of the third party.

In cases such as *Butler v Rice and Ghana Commercial Bank v Chandiram* [1960] AC 732, where the claimant paid the creditor direct and intended to discharge his security, the court took the claimant's intention to have been to keep the original security alive for his own benefit save in so far as it was replaced by an effective security in favour of himself. In the present case the Abbey National did not intend to discharge the Halifax's charge in the events which happened, that is to say, in the event that completion did not proceed. But it did not intend its money to be used at all in that event. If *Butler v Rice* and similar cases are relied upon to support the proposition that there can be no subrogation unless the claimant intended to keep the original security alive for its own benefit save in so far as it was replaced by a new and effective security, with the result that the remedy is not available where the claimant had no direct dealings with the creditor and did not intend his money to be used at all, then I respectfully dissent from that proposition. I prefer the view of Slade LJ in *In re T. H. Knitwear (Wholesale) Ltd* [1988] Ch 275 that in some situations the doctrine of subrogation is capable of applying even though it is impossible to infer a mutual intention to this effect on the part of the creditor and the person claiming to be subrogated to the creditor's security. In the present case the payment was made by Hill Lawson, and it is their intention which matters. As fiduciaries, they could not be heard to say that they had paid out their principal's money otherwise than for the benefit of their principal. Accordingly, their intention must be taken to have been to keep the Halifax's charge alive for the benefit of the Abbey National pending completion. In my judgment this is sufficient to bring the doctrine of subrogation into play.

The application of the doctrine in the present case does not create the problem which confronted Oliver J in *Paul v Speirway Ltd* [1976] Ch 220. The Abbey National did not intend to be an unsecured creditor of anyone. It intended to retain the beneficial interest in its money unless and until that interest was replaced by a first legal mortgage on the property. The factual context in which the claim to subrogation arises is a novel one which does not appear to have arisen before but the justice of its claim cannot be denied. The Abbey National's beneficial interest in the money can no longer be restored to it. If it is subrogated to the Halifax's charge its position will not be improved, nor will Mr Bajwa's position be adversely affected. Both parties will be restored as nearly as may be to the positions which they were respectively intended to occupy.

The appellants place much reliance on a passage in *In re Diplock* [1948] Ch 465, 549–50, where the court was dealing with the claim against the Leaf Homoeopathic Hospital. The hospital received a grant for the specific purpose of enabling it to pay off a secured bank loan. The passage in question reads:

'Here, too, we think that the effect of the payment to the bank was to extinguish the debt and the charge held by the bank ceased to exist. The case cannot, we think, be regarded as one of subrogation, and if the appellants were entitled to a charge it would have to be a new charge created by the court. The position in this respect does not appear to us to be affected by the fact that the payment off of this debt was one of the objects for which the grant was made. The effect of the payment off was that the charity, which had previously held only an equity of redemption, became the owners of unincumbered property. That unincumbered property derived from a combination of two things, the equity of redemption contributed by the charity and the effect of the Diplock money in getting rid of the incumbrance. If equity is now to create a charge (and we say 'create' because there is no survival of the original charge) in favour of the judicial trustee, it will be placing him in a position to insist upon a sale of what was contributed by the charity. The case, as it appears to us, is in effect analogous to the cases where Diplock money is expended on improvements on charity land. The money was in this case used to remove a blot on the title; to give the judicial trustee a charge in respect of the money so used would, we think, be equally unjust to the charity who, as the result of such a charge, would have to submit to a sale of the interest in the property which it brought in. We may point out that if the relief claimed were to be accepted as a correct application of the equitable principle, insoluble problems might arise in a case where in the meanwhile fresh charges on the property had been created or money had been expended upon it.'

The passage is not without its difficulties and is in need of reappraisal in the light of the significant developments in the law of restitution which have taken place in the last 50 years. The second sentence is puzzling. The discharge of the creditor's security at law is certainly not a bar to subrogation in equity; it is rather a precondition. But the court was probably doing no more than equate the remedy to the creation of a new charge for the purpose of considering whether this was justified.

It is also unclear what conclusion was thought to follow from the observation that the unincumbered property derived from two sources, the equity of redemption contributed by the charity and the money belonging to the next of kin which was used to redeem the mortgage. If the money had been used to buy the property without any contribution from the charity, the next of kin would have sought a declaration that they were solely and beneficially entitled to the property under a constructive trust. Their claim to be subrogated to the security which had been discharged with their money reflected the respective contributions which they and the charity had made, and did not encroach upon the charity's equity of redemption at all.

Nor is it clear to me why insoluble problems would arise in a case where there had been fresh charges created on the property in the meantime. The next of kin would obtain a charge by subroga-tion with the same priority as the charge which had been redeemed except that it would not enjoy the paramountcy of the legal estate. A subsequent incumbrancer who obtained a legal estate for value without notice of the interest of the next of kin would take free from it. It is not necessary to decide whether a subsequent incumbrancer who took an equitable charge only would take free from the interest of the next of kin; the question has not yet arisen for decision, but it is not insoluble.

Taken as a whole, however, the passage cited is an explanation of the reasons why, in the particular circumstances of that case, it was considered unjust to grant the remedy of subrogation. The hospital had changed its position to its detriment. It had in all innocence used the money to redeem a mortgage held by its bank, which, no doubt, was willing to allow its advance to remain outstanding indefinitely so long as it was well secured and the interest was paid punctually. The next of kin were seeking to be subrogated to the bank's security in order to enforce it and enable a proper distribution of the estate to be made. This would have been unjust to the hospital. It may be doubted whether in its anxiety to avoid injustice to the hospital the court may not have done an even greater injustice to the next of kin, who were denied even the interest on their money. Justice did not require the withholding of any remedy, but only that the charge by subrogation should not be enforceable until the hospital had had a reasonable opportunity to obtain a fresh advance on suitable terms from a willing lender, perhaps from the bank which had held the original security.

Today, considerations of this kind would be regarded as relevant to a change of position defence rather than as going to liability. They do not call for further consideration in the present case.

. . .

Nor, in my judgment, is there any justification for the proposition that the Abbey National's right to be subrogated to the Halifax's charge did not arise until the court made the necessary order. The order merely satisfied a pre-existing equity. The Abbey National's equity arose from the conduct of the parties. It arose at the very moment that the Halifax's charge was discharged, in whole or in part, with the Abbey National's money. It arose because, having regard to the circumstances in which the Halifax's charge was discharged it would have been unconscionable for Mr Bajwa to assert that it had been discharged for his benefit. At law, Mr Bajwa became the owner of an unincumbered freehold interest in the property; but he never did, even for an instant, in equity. . . .

Waite and **Stuart-Smith LJJ** concurred.

NOTES AND QUESTIONS

1. We have explained above (see 194) the distinction between simple and reviving subrogation. The importance of reviving subrogation, in a case like *Boscawen v Bajwa*, is that it comple-ments proprietary restitution following tracing. It can go where tracing cannot go. Where the defendant has been unjustly enriched at the claimant's expense by using money that was the claimant's to discharge a secured liability of the defendant, the claimant cannot trace into the discharged debt: the money has been dissipated. (This is subject to the possibility of 'backward tracing' i.e. that one can trace into the property that was previously acquired in return for incurring the debt, see Lionel Smith, 'Tracing into the Payment of a

Debt' [1995] *CLJ* 290; above, 700 note 2). But the claimant, by reviving subrogation, is entitled to take over the secured rights of the defendant's discharged creditor in order to secure restitution of the money paid. Reviving subrogation in this situation is therefore analogous to proprietary restitution following tracing. The analogy was very clearly illustrated by *Boscawen v Bajwa*: as the money had first been mixed before being used to discharge the defendant's liability, the claimant needed to be able to trace the money prior to the reviving subrogation.

2. While much of Millett LJ's judgment is to be warmly welcomed, particularly his analysis of the nature of tracing and of the relationship between tracing and subrogation, he does not attempt to articulate the precise injustice in play in the case. Rather he is content to say that 'the injustice of [Abbey National's] claim cannot be denied' and that 'it would have been unconscionable for Mr Bajwa to assert that [the Halifax's charge] had been discharged for his benefit'. The most obvious unjust factor was failure of consideration. Abbey National paid the purchasers' solicitors on the basis that the money would be used to finance the purchase of the house and that Abbey would take a charge over the house when purchased. Once the sale did not go ahead the basis for the payment totally failed. See Charles Mitchell's note on the case, 'Subrogation, Tracing and the *Quistclose* Principle' [1995] *LMCLQ* 451, 455–6.

3. For other examples of proprietary restitution through reviving subrogation, see *Butler v Rice* [1910] 2 Ch 277 and *Nottingham Permanent Benefit Building Soc. v Thurstan* [1903] AC 6 (although some doubt was cast on the latter by the House of Lords' reasoning in *Orakpo v Manson Investments Ltd* [1978] AC 95). See also a surety's reviving subrogation rights under section 5 of the Mercantile Law Amendment Act 1856 (above, 518–519).

- *Westdeutsche Landesbank Girozentrale v Islington London BC*
  [1996] AC 669, House of Lords

The claimant bank had entered into an interest rate swap transaction with the defendant local authority on 18 June 1987. (An interest rate swap transaction is an agreement under which each party agrees to pay to the other on specified dates the interest which would have accrued over a given period on the same notional principal sum assuming that each party agrees to pay a different rate of interest. Usually one party (the fixed rate payer) will agree to pay a fixed rate of interest while the other party (the floating rate payer) agrees to pay a rate of interest that is equivalent to, for example, the six month London Inter-bank Offered Rate (LIBOR).) Under that agreement the claimant bank was the fixed rate payer and the defendant local authority was the floating rate payer. Additionally the bank had agreed to pay, and had paid, £2.5 million to the local authority on the commencement of the contract. Interest rates had favoured the bank (that is, the floating rate had been higher than the fixed rate) so that the local authority had made four payments to the bank totalling £1,354,474. In November 1989 the Divisional Court of the Queen's Bench Division in *Hazell v Hammersmith and Fulham London BC* [1992] 2 WLR 17, in a decision subsequently upheld by the House of Lords [1992] 2 AC 1, held that interest rate swap transactions were *ultra vires* local authorities and void *ab initio*. The local authority refused to make any further payments under the agreement. The bank brought an action against the local authority claiming £1,145,526 (being the initial lump sum minus the four payments received from the local authority) plus interest from 18 June 1987. Hobhouse J held that, on the basis that the money had been paid for no consideration, the bank was entitled to restitution of the sum claimed. He also awarded compound interest on that sum from 1 April 1990. The Court of Appeal upheld that decision and, moreover, decided that, as the money was held by the defendant as a trustee, the compound interest should run from 18 June 1987. The local authority appealed to the House of Lords against the award of compound interest. The House of Lords, by a three to two majority (Lords Goff and Woolf dissenting), allowed the appeal, on the ground that the money was not held by the local authority as trustees or fiduciaries and that there was therefore no jurisdiction to award compound, rather than simple, interest.

Lord Browne-Wilkinson: . . .

COMPOUND INTEREST IN EQUITY

. . .

In the absence of fraud courts of equity have never awarded compound interest except against a trustee or other person owing fiduciary duties who is accountable for profits made from his position. Equity awarded simple interest at a time when courts of law had no right under common law or statute to award any interest. The award of compound interest was restricted to cases where the award was in lieu of an account of profits improperly made by the trustee. We were not referred to any case where compound interest had been awarded in the absence of fiduciary accountability for a profit. The principle is clearly stated by Lord Hatherley LC in *Burdick v Garrick*, LR 5 Ch.App. 233, 241:

'the court does not proceed against an accounting party by way of punishing him for making use of the plaintiff's money by directing rests, or payment of compound interest, but proceeds upon this principle, either that he has made, or has put himself into such a position as that he is to be presumed to have made, 5 per cent, or compound interest, as the case may be.'

The principle was more fully stated by Buckley LJ in *Wallersteiner v Moir (No 2)* [1975] QB 373, 397:

'Where a trustee has retained trust money in his own hands, he will be accountable for the profit which he has made or which he is assumed to have made from the use of the money. In *Attorney-General v Alford*, 4 De G M & G 843, 851 Lord Cranworth LC said: "What the court ought to do, I think, is to charge him only with the interest which he has received, or which it is justly entitled to say he ought to have received, or which it is so fairly to be presumed that he did receive that he is estopped from saying that he did not receive it." This is an application of the doctrine that the court will not allow a trustee to make any profit from his trust. The defaulting trustee is normally charged with simple interest only, but if it is established that he has used the money in trade he may be charged compound interest. . . . The justification for charging compound interest normally lies in the fact that profits earned in trade would be likely to be used as working capital for earning further profits. Precisely similar equitable principles apply to an agent who has retained moneys of his principal in his hands and used them for his own purposes: *Burdick v Garrick*.'

In *President of India v La Pintada Compania Navigacion SA* [1985] AC 104, 116 Lord Brandon of Oakbrook (with whose speech the rest of their Lordships agreed) considered the law as to the award of interest as at that date in four separate areas. His third area was equity, as to which he said:

Thirdly, the area of equity. The Chancery courts, again differing from the common law courts, had regularly awarded simple interest as ancillary relief in respect of equitable remedies, such as specific performance, rescission and the taking of an account. Chancery courts had further regularly awarded interest, including not only simple interest but also compound interest, when they thought that justice so demanded, that is to say in cases where money had been obtained and retained by fraud, or where it had been withheld or misapplied by a trustee or anyone else in a fiduciary position. . . . Courts of Chancery only in two special classes of case, awarded compound, as distinct from simple, interest.'

These authorities establish that in the absence of fraud equity only awards compound (as opposed to simple) interest against a defendant who is a trustee or otherwise in a fiduciary position by way of recouping from such a defendant an improper profit made by him. It is unnecessary to decide whether in such a case compound interest can only be paid where the defendant has used trust moneys in his own trade or (as I tend to think) extends to all cases where a fiduciary has improperly profited from his trust. Unless the local authority owed fiduciary duties to the bank in relation to the upfront payment, compound interest cannot be awarded.

WAS THERE A TRUST? THE ARGUMENT FOR THE BANK IN OUTLINE

The bank submitted that, since the contract was void, title did not pass at the date of payment either at law or in equity. The legal title of the bank was extinguished as soon as the money was paid into the mixed account, whereupon the legal title became vested in the local authority. But, it was argued, this did not affect the equitable interest, which remained vested in the bank ('the retention of title point'). It was submitted that whenever the legal interest in property is vested in one person and the equitable interest in another, the owner of the legal interest holds it on trust for the owner of the equitable title: 'the separation of the legal from the equitable interest necessarily imports a trust.' For this latter proposition ('the separation of title point') the bank, of course, relies on *Sinclair v Brougham* [1914] AC 398 and *Chase Manhattan Bank NA v Israel-British Bank (London) Ltd* [1981] Ch 105.

The generality of these submissions was narrowed by submitting that the trust which arose in this case was a resulting trust 'not of an active character:' see *per* Viscount Haldane LC in *Sinclair v Brougham* [1914] AC 398, 421. This submission was reinforced, after completion of the oral argument, by sending to your Lordships Professor Peter Birks' paper 'Restitution and Resulting Trusts:' see *Equity: Contemporary Legal Developments*, 335. Unfortunately your Lordships have not had the advantage of any submissions from the local authority on this paper, but an article by William Swadling 'A new role for resulting trusts?' 16 *Legal Studies* 133 puts forward counter-arguments which I have found persuasive.

It is to be noted that the bank did not found any argument on the basis that the local authority was liable to repay either as a constructive trustee or under the in personam liability of the wrongful recipient of the estate of a deceased person established by *In re Diplock; Diplock v Wintle* [1948] Ch 465. I therefore do not further consider those points.

THE BREADTH OF THE SUBMISSION

Although the actual question in issue on the appeal is a narrow one, on the arguments presented it is necessary to consider fundamental principles of trust law. Does the recipient of money under a contract subsequently found to be void for mistake or as being ultra vires hold the moneys received on trust even where he had no knowledge at any relevant time that the contract was void? If he does hold on trust, such trust must arise at the date of receipt or, at the latest, at the date the legal title of the payer is extinguished by mixing moneys in a bank account: in the present case it does not matter at which of those dates the legal title was extinguished. If there is a trust two consequences follow: (a) the recipient will be personally liable, regardless of fault, for any subsequent payment away of the moneys to third parties even though, at the date of such payment, the 'trustee' was still ignorant of the existence of any trust: see Burrows 'Swaps and the Friction between Common Law and Equity' [1995] *RLR* 15; (b) as from the date of the establishment of the trust (i.e. receipt or mixing of the moneys by the 'trustee') the original payer will have an equitable proprietary interest in the moneys so long as they are traceable into whomsoever's hands they come other than a purchaser for value of the legal interest without notice. Therefore, although in the present case the only question directly in issue is the personal liability of the local authority as a trustee, it is not possible to hold the local authority liable without imposing a trust which, in other cases, will create property rights affecting third parties because moneys received under a void contract are 'trust property.'

THE PRACTICAL CONSEQUENCES OF THE BANK'S ARGUMENT

Before considering the legal merits of the submission, it is important to appreciate the practical consequences which ensue if the bank's arguments are correct. Those who suggest that a resulting trust should arise in these circumstances accept that the creation of an equitable proprietary interest under the trust can have unfortunate, and adverse, effects if the original recipient of the moneys becomes insolvent: the moneys, if traceable in the hands of the recipient, are trust moneys and not available for the creditors of the recipient. However, the creation of an equitable proprietary interest in moneys received under a void contract is capable of having adverse effects quite apart from insolvency. The proprietary interest under the unknown trust will, quite apart from insolvency, be enforceable against any recipient of the property other than the purchaser for value of a legal interest without notice.

Take the following example. T (the transferor) has entered into a commercial contract with R1 (the first recipient). Both parties believe the contract to be valid but it is in fact void. Pursuant to that contract: (i) T pays £1m to R1 who pays it into a mixed bank account; (ii) T transfers 100 shares in X company to R1, who is registered as a shareholder. Thereafter R1 deals with the money and shares as follows; (iii) R1 pays £50,000 out of the mixed account to R2 otherwise than for value; R2 then becomes insolvent, having trade creditors who have paid for goods not delivered at the time of the insolvency; (iv) R1 charges the shares in X company to R3 by way of equitable security for a loan from R3.

If the bank's arguments are correct, R1 holds the £1m on trust for T once the money has become mixed in R1's bank account. Similarly R1 becomes the legal owner of the shares in X company as from the date of his registration as a shareholder but holds such shares on a resulting trust for T. T therefore has an equitable proprietary interest in the moneys in the mixed account and in the shares.

T's equitable interest will enjoy absolute priority as against the creditors in the insolvency of R2 (who was not a purchaser for value) provided that the £50,000 can be traced in the assets of R2 at the date of its insolvency. Moreover, if the separation of title argument is correct, since the equitable interest is in T and the legal interest is vested in R2, R2 also holds as trustee for T. In tracing the £50,000 in the bank account of R2, R2 as trustee will be treated as having drawn out 'his own' moneys first, thereby benefiting T at the expense of the secured and unsecured creditors of R2. Therefore in practice one may well reach the position where the moneys in the bank of R2 in reality reflect the price paid by creditors for goods not delivered by R2: yet, under the tracing rules, those moneys are to be treated as belonging in equity to T.

So far as the shares in the X company are concerned, T can trace his equitable interest into the shares and will take in priority to R3, whose equitable charge to secure his loan even though granted for value will pro tanto be defeated.

All this will have occurred when no one was aware, or could have been aware, of the supposed trust because no one knew that the contract was void.

I can see no moral or legal justification for giving such priority to the right of T to obtain restitution over third parties who have themselves not been enriched, in any real sense, at T's expense and indeed have had no dealings with T. T paid over his money and transferred the shares under a supposed valid contract. If the contract had been valid, he would have had purely personal rights against R1. Why should he be better off because the contract is void?

My Lords, wise judges have often warned against the wholesale importation into commercial law of equitable principles inconsistent with the certainty and speed which are essential requirements for the orderly conduct of business affairs: see *Barnes v Addy* (1874) LR 9 Ch.App. 244, 251 and 255; *Scandinavian Trading Tanker Co. A.B. v Flota Petrolera Ecuatoriana* [1983] 2 AC 694, 703–4. If the bank's arguments are correct, a businessman who has entered into transactions relating to or dependent upon property rights could find that assets which apparently belong to one person in fact belong to another; that there are 'off balance sheet' liabilities of which he cannot be aware; that these property rights and liabilities arise from circumstances unknown not only to himself but also to anyone else who has been involved in the transactions. A new area of unmanageable risk will be introduced into commercial dealings. If the due application of equitable principles forced a conclusion leading to these results, your Lordships would be presented with a formidable task in reconciling legal principle with commercial common sense. But in my judgment no such conflict occurs. The resulting trust for which the bank contends is inconsistent not only with the law as it stands but with any principled development of it.

THE RELEVANT PRINCIPLES OF TRUST LAW

(i) Equity operates on the conscience of the owner of the legal interest. In the case of a trust, the conscience of the legal owner requires him to carry out the purposes for which the property was vested in him (express or implied trust) or which the law imposes on him by reason of his unconscionable conduct (constructive trust).

(ii) Since the equitable jurisdiction to enforce trusts depends upon the conscience of the holder of the legal interest being affected, he cannot be a trustee of the property if and so long as he is ignorant of the facts alleged to affect his conscience, i.e. until he is aware that he is intended to hold the property for the benefit of others in the case of an express or implied trust, or, in the case of a constructive trust, of the factors which are alleged to affect his conscience.

(iii) In order to establish a trust there must be identifiable trust property. The only apparent exception to this rule is a constructive trust imposed on a person who dishonestly assists in a breach of trust who may come under fiduciary duties even if he does not receive identifiable trust property.

(iv) Once a trust is established, as from the date of its establishment the beneficiary has, in equity, a proprietary interest in the trust property, which proprietary interest will be enforceable in equity against any subsequent holder of the property (whether the original property or substituted property into which it can be traced) other than a purchaser for value of the legal interest without notice.

These propositions are fundamental to the law of trusts and I would have thought uncontroversial. However, proposition (ii) may call for some expansion. There are cases where property has been put into the name of X without X's knowledge but in circumstances where no gift to X was intended. It has been held that such property is recoverable under a resulting trust: *Birch v Blagrave* (1755) 1 Amb. 264; *Childers v Childers* (1857) 1 De G & J 482; *In re Vinogradoff, Allen v Jackson* [1935] WN 68; *In re Muller, Cassin v Mutual Cash Order Co. Ltd* [1953] NZLR 879. These cases are explicable on the ground that, by the time action was brought, X or his successors in title have become aware of the facts which gave rise to a resulting trust; his conscience was affected as from the time of such discovery and thereafter he held on a resulting trust under which the property was recovered from him. There is, so far as I am aware, no authority which decides that X was a trustee, and therefore accountable for his deeds, at any time before he was aware of the circumstances which gave rise to a resulting trust.

Those basic principles are inconsistent with the case being advanced by the bank. The latest time at which there was any possibility of identifying the 'trust property' was the date on which the moneys in the mixed bank account of the local authority ceased to be traceable when the local authority's account went into overdraft in June 1987. At that date, the local authority had no knowledge of the invalidity of the contract but regarded the moneys as its own to spend as it thought fit. There was therefore never a time at which both (a) there was defined trust property and (b) the conscience of the local authority in relation to such defined trust property was affected. The basic requirements of a trust were never satisfied.

I turn then to consider the bank's arguments in detail. They were based primarily on principle rather than on authority. I will deal first with the bank's argument from principle and then turn to the main authorities relied upon by the bank, *Sinclair v Brougham* [1914] AC 398 and *Chase Manhattan Bank NA v Israel-British Bank (London) Ltd* [1981] Ch 105.

THE RETENTION OF TITLE POINT

It is said that, since the bank only intended to part with its beneficial ownership of the moneys in performance of a valid contract, neither the legal nor the equitable title passed to the local authority at the date of payment. The legal title vested in the local authority by operation of law when the moneys became mixed in the bank account but, it is said, the bank 'retained' its equitable title.

I think this argument is fallacious. A person solely entitled to the full beneficial ownership of money or property, both at law and in equity, does not enjoy an equitable interest in that property. The legal title carries with it all rights. Unless and until there is a separation of the legal and equitable estates, there is no separate equitable title. Therefore to talk about the bank 'retaining' its equitable interest is meaningless. The only question is whether the circumstances under which the money was paid were such as, in equity, to impose a trust on the local authority. If so, an equitable interest arose for the first time under that trust.

This proposition is supported by *In re Cook*; *Beck v Grant* [1948] Ch 212; *Vandervell v Inland Revenue Commissioners* [1967] 2 AC 291, 311G, *per* Lord Upjohn, and 317F, *per* Lord Donovan; *Commissioner of Stamp Duties (Queensland) v Livingston* [1965] AC 694, 712B–E; *Underhill and Hayton, Law of Trusts and Trustees*, 15th edn (1995), 866.

THE SEPARATION OF TITLE POINT

The bank's submission, at its widest, is that if the legal title is in A but the equitable interest in B, A holds as trustee for B.

Again I think this argument is fallacious. There are many cases where B enjoys rights which, in equity, are enforceable against the legal owner A, without A being a trustee, e.g. an equitable right to redeem a mortgage, equitable easements, restrictive covenants, the right to rectification, an insurer's right by subrogation to receive damages subsequently recovered by the assured: *Lord Napier and Ettrick v Hunter* [1993] AC 713. Even in cases where the whole beneficial interest is vested in B and the bare legal interest is in A, A is not necessarily trustee, e.g. where title to land is acquired by estoppel as against the legal owner; a mortgagee who has fully discharged his indebtedness enforces his right to recover the mortgaged property in a redemption action, not an action for breach of trust.

The bank contended that where, *under a pre-existing trust*, B is entitled to an equitable interest in trust property, if the trust property comes into the hands of a third party, X (not being a purchaser for value of the legal interest without notice), B is entitled to enforce his equitable interest against the property in the hands of X because X is a trustee for B. In my view the third party, X, is not necessarily a trustee for B: B's equitable right is enforceable against the property in just the same way as any other specifically enforceable equitable right can be enforced against a third party. Even if the third party, X, is not aware that what he has received is trust property B is entitled to assert his title in that property. If X has the necessary degree of knowledge, X may himself become a constructive trustee for B on the basis of knowing receipt. But unless he has the requisite degree of knowledge he is not personally liable to account as trustee: *In re Diplock; Diplock v Wintle* [1948] Ch 465, 478; *In re Montagu's Settlement Trusts* [1987] Ch 264. Therefore, innocent receipt of property by X subject to an existing equitable interest does not by itself make X a trustee despite the severance of the legal and equitable titles. *Underhill and Hayton, Law of Trusts and Trustees*, 369–70, whilst accepting that X is under no personal liability to account unless and until he becomes aware of B's rights, does describe X as being a constructive trustee. This may only be a question of semantics: on either footing, in the present case the local authority could not have become accountable for profits until it knew that the contract was void.

RESULTING TRUST

This is not a case where the bank had any equitable interest which pre-dated receipt by the local authority of the upfront payment. Therefore, in order to show that the local authority became a trustee, the bank must demonstrate circumstances which raised a trust for the first time either at the date on which the local authority received the money or at the date on which payment into the mixed account was made. Counsel for the bank specifically disavowed any claim based on a constructive trust. This was plainly right because the local authority had no relevant knowledge sufficient to raise a constructive trust at any time before the moneys, upon the bank account going into overdraft, became untraceable. Once there ceased to be an identifiable trust fund, the local authority could not become a trustee: In re Goldcorp Exchange Ltd [1995] 1 AC 74. Therefore, as the argument for the bank recognised, the only possible trust which could be established was a resulting trust arising from the circumstances in which the local authority received the upfront payment.

Under existing law a resulting trust arises in two sets of circumstances: (A) where A makes a voluntary payment to B or pays (wholly or in part) for the purchase of property which is vested either in B alone or in the joint names of A and B, there is a presumption that A did not intend to make a gift to B: the money or property is held on trust for A (if he is the sole provider of the money) or in the case of a joint purchase by A and B in shares proportionate to their contributions. It is important to stress that this is only a *presumption* which presumption is easily rebutted either by the counter-presumption of advancement or by direct evidence of A's intention to make an outright transfer: see *Underhill and Hayton, Law of Trusts and Trustees*, 317 ff.; *Vandervell v Inland Revenue Commissioners* [1967] 2 AC 291, 312 ff.; *In re Vandervell's Trusts (No 2)* [1974] Ch 269, 288 ff. (B) Where A transfers property to B *on express trusts*, but the trusts declared do not exhaust the whole beneficial interest: *ibid.* and *Quistclose Investments Ltd v Rolls Razor Ltd (In Liquidation)* [1970] AC 567. Both types of resulting trust are traditionally regarded as examples of trusts giving effect to the common intention of the parties. A resulting trust is not imposed by law against the intentions of the trustee (as is a constructive trust) but gives effect to his presumed intention. Megarry J in *In re Vandervell's Trusts (No 2)* suggests that a resulting trust of type (B) does not depend on intention but operates automatically. I am not convinced that this is right. If the settlor has expressly, or by necessary implication, abandoned any beneficial interest in the trust property, there is in my view no resulting trust: the undisposed-of equitable interest vests in the Crown as bona vacantia: see *In re West Sussex Constabulary's Widows, Children and Benevolent (1930) Fund Trusts* [1971] Ch 1.

Applying these conventional principles of resulting trust to the present case, the bank's claim must fail. There was no transfer of money to the local authority on express trusts: therefore a resulting trust of type (B) above could not arise. As to type (A) above, any presumption of resulting trust is rebutted since it is demonstrated that the bank paid, and the local authority received, the upfront payment with the intention that the moneys so paid should become the absolute property of the local authority. It is true that the parties were under a misapprehension that the payment was made in pursuance of a valid contract. But that does not alter the actual intentions of the parties at the date the payment was made or the moneys were mixed in the bank account. As the article by William Swadling, 'A new role for resulting trusts?' 16 *Legal Studies* 133 demonstrates the presumption of resulting trust is rebutted by evidence of any intention inconsistent with such a trust, not only by evidence of an intention to make a gift.

Professor Birks, 'Restitution and Resulting Trusts:' see *Equity: Contemporary Legal Developments*, 335, 360, whilst accepting that the principles I have stated represent 'a very conservative form' of definition of a resulting trust, argues from restitutionary principles that the definition should be extended so as to cover a perceived gap in the law of 'subtractive unjust enrichment' (368) so as to give a plaintiff a proprietary remedy when he has transferred value under a mistake or under a contract the consideration for which wholly fails. He suggests that a resulting trust should arise wherever the money is paid under a mistake (because such mistake vitiates the actual intention) or when money is paid on a condition which is not subsequently satisfied.

As one would expect, the argument is tightly reasoned but I am not persuaded. The search for a perceived need to strengthen the remedies of a plaintiff claiming in restitution involves, to my mind, a distortion of trust principles. First, the argument elides rights in property (which is the only proper subject matter of a trust) into rights in 'the value transferred:' see 361. A trust can only arise where there is defined trust property: it is therefore not consistent with trust principles to say that a person is a trustee of property which cannot be defined. Second, Professor Birks's approach appears to assume (for example in the case of a transfer of value made under a contract the consideration for which subsequently fails) that the recipient will be deemed to have been a trustee from the date of his original receipt of money, i.e. the trust arises at a time when the 'trustee' does not, and cannot, know that there is going to be a total failure of consideration. This result is incompatible with the basic premise on which all trust law is built, viz. that the conscience of the trustee is affected. Unless and until the trustee is aware of the factors which give rise to the supposed trust, there is nothing which can affect his conscience. Thus neither in the case of a subsequent failure of consideration nor in the case of a payment under a contract subsequently found to be void for mistake or failure of condition will there be circumstances, at the date of receipt, which can impinge on the conscience of the recipient, thereby making him a trustee. Thirdly, Professor Birks has to impose on his wider view an arbitrary and admittedly unprincipled modification so as to ensure that a resulting trust does not arise when there has only been a failure to perform a contract, as opposed to total failure of consideration: see 356, 359 and 362. Such arbitrary exclusion is designed to preserve the rights of creditors in the insolvency of the recipient. The fact that it is necessary to exclude artificially one type of case which would logically fall within the wider concept casts doubt on the validity of the concept.

If adopted, Professor Birks's wider concepts would give rise to all the practical consequences and injustices to which I have referred. I do not think it right to make an unprincipled alteration to the law of property (i.e. the law of trusts) so as to produce in the law of unjust enrichment the injustices to third parties which I have mentioned and the consequential commercial uncertainty which any extension of proprietary interests in personal property is bound to produce.

THE AUTHORITIES

Three cases were principally relied upon in direct support of the proposition that a resulting trust arises where a payment is made under a void contract.

(A) Sinclair v Brougham

[*After considering the facts of* Sinclair v Brougham *and the personal claim for money had and received, see above, 40, Lord Browne-Wilkinson continued*:]

The claim in rem The House of Lords held that, the ordinary trade creditors having been paid in full by agreement, the assets remaining were to be divided between the ultra vires depositors and the members of the society pro rata according to their respective payments to the society. The difficulty is to identify any single ratio decidendi for that decision. Viscount Haldane LC (with whom Lord Atkinson agreed) and Lord Parker of Waddington gave fully reasoned judgments (considered below). Lord Dunedin apparently based himself on some 'super-eminent' equity (not a technical equity) in accordance with which the court could distribute the remaining assets of the society: see at 434 and 436. The members (by which presumably he means the society) were not in a fiduciary relationship with the depositors: it was the directors not the society which had mixed the moneys: 438. This indicates that he was adopting the approach of Lord Parker: yet he concurred in the judgment of Lord Haldane LC: 438. I can only understand his judgment as being based on some super-eminent jurisdiction in the court to do justice as between the remaining claimants in the course of a liquidation.

Lord Sumner plainly regarded the case as a matter of doing justice in administering the remaining assets in the liquidation, all other claims having been eliminated: 459. He said, at 458:

'The question is one of administration. The liquidator, an officer of the court, who has to discharge himself of the assets that have come to his hands, asks for directions, and, after hearing all parties concerned, the court has the right and the duty to direct him how to distribute all the assets. . . . In my opinion, if precedent fails, the most just distribution of the whole must be directed, so only that no recognised rule of law or equity be disregarded.'

Lord Haldane LC treated the case as a tracing claim: could the depositors follow and recover property with which, in equity, they had 'never really parted:' 418. After holding that the parties could not trace at law (418–20) he said that the moneys could be traced in equity 'based upon trust:' 420. The only passage in which he identifies the trust is at 421:

'The property was never converted into a debt, in equity at all events, and there has been throughout a resulting trust, not of an active character, but sufficient, in my opinion, to bring the transaction within the general principle.'

He treats the society itself (as opposed to its directors) as having mixed the depositors' money with its own money, but says, at 422, 423, that such mixing was not a breach of fiduciary duty by the society but authorised by the depositors: it was intended that 'the society should be entitled to deal with [the depositors' money] freely as its own.' On that ground he distinguished *In re Hallett's Estate* 13 Ch.D. 696 (a trustee is taken to have drawn his own money first) and held that the mixed moneys therefore belonged to the depositors and members pro rata.

Like others before me, I find Lord Haldane LC's reasoning difficult, if not impossible, to follow. The only equitable right which he identifies arises under 'a resulting trust, not of an active character' which, as I understand it, existed from the moment when the society received the money. Applying the conventional approach, the resulting trust could only have arisen because either the depositors were treated as contributors to a fund (a resulting trust of type (A) above) or because the 'trust' on which the moneys were paid to the society had failed (a resulting trust of type (B)). Yet the finding that the society was not in breach of fiduciary duty because it was the intention of the parties that the society should be free to deal with the money as its own (423) is inconsistent with either type of resulting trust. Such an intention would rebut the *presumption* of resulting trust of type (A) and is inconsistent with a payment on express trusts which fail, i.e. with a type (B) resulting trust. Therefore the inactive resulting trust which Lord Haldane LC was referring to was, as Professor Birks points out, not a conventional one: indeed there is no trace of any such trust in earlier or later authority. The question is whether the recognition of such a trust accords with principle and the demands of certainty in commercial dealings.

As to the latter, Lord Haldane LC's theory, if correct, gives rise to all the difficulties which I have noted above. Nor does the theory accord with principle. First, it postulates that the society became a trustee at a time when it was wholly ignorant of the circumstances giving rise to the trust. Second, since the depositors' money was *intended* to be mixed with that of the society, there was never any intention that there should be a separate identifiable trust fund, an essential feature of any trust. Third, and most important, if Lord Haldane LC's approach were to be applicable in an ordinary liquidation it is quite incapable of accommodating the rights of ordinary creditors. Lord Haldane LC's inactive resulting trust, if generally applicable, would give the depositors (and possibly the members) rights having priority not only to those of ordinary trade creditors but also to those of some secured creditors, e.g. the common form security for bank lending, a floating charge on the company's assets. The moneys of both depositors and members are, apparently, trust moneys and therefore form no part of the company's assets available to pay creditors, whether secured or unsecured. This seems to be an impossible conclusion. Lord Haldane LC appreciated the difficulty, but did not express any view as to what the position would be if there had been trade creditors in competition: see 421, 42 and 425–6.

Lord Parker analysed the matter differently. He held that the depositors had paid their money not to the society itself but to the directors, who apparently held the moneys on some form of *Quistclose* trust (*Quistclose Investments Ltd v Rolls Fazor Ltd (In Liquidation)* [1970] AC 567): the money had been paid by the depositors to the directors to be applied by them in making valid deposits with the society and, since such deposit was impossible, the directors held the moneys on a trust for the depositors: see at 441–2 and 444. It is to be noted that Lord Parker does not at any time spell out the nature of the trust. However, he held that the directors owed fiduciary duties both to the depositors and to the members of the society. Therefore it was not a case in which a trustee had mixed trust moneys with his own moneys (to which *In re Hallett's Estate* would apply) but of trustees (the directors) mixing the moneys of two innocent parties to both of whom they owed fiduciary duties: the depositors and members therefore ranked pari passu: 442.

I find the approach of Lord Parker much more intelligible than that of Lord Haldane LC: it avoids finding that the society held the money on a resulting trust at the same time as being authorised to mix the depositors' money with its own. In *In re Diplock; Diplock v Wintle* [1948] Ch 465 the Court of Appeal found the ratio of *Sinclair v Brougham* to lie in Lord Parker's analysis. But, quite apart from the fact that no other member of the House founded himself on Lord Parker's analysis, it is in some respects very unsatisfactory. First, the finding that the depositors' moneys were received by the directors, as opposed to the society itself, is artificial. Although it was ultra vires the society to enter into a contract to repay the moneys, it was not ultra vires the society to receive moneys. Second, Lord Parker's approach gives depositors and members alike the same priority over trade creditors as does that of Lord Haldane LC. The fact is that any analysis which confers an equitable proprietary interest as a result of a payment under a void contract necessarily gives priority in an insolvency to the recovery of the ultra vires payment. Lord Parker too was aware of this problem: but he left the problem to be solved in a case where the claims of trade creditors were still outstanding. Indeed he went further than Lord Haldane LC. He appears to have thought that the court had power in some cases to postpone trade creditors to ultra vires depositors and in other cases to give the trade creditors priority: which course was appropriate he held depended on the facts of each individual case: 444 and 445. There is much to be said for the view that Lord Parker, like Lord Haldane LC and Lord Summer, was dealing only with the question of the due administration of assets of a company in liquidation. Thus he says, at 449:

'nor, indeed, am I satisfied that the equity to which effect is being given in this case is necessarily confined to a liquidation. It is, however, unnecessary for your Lordships to decide these points.'

This makes it clear that he was not purporting to do more than decide how the assets of that society in that liquidation were to be dealt with.

As has been pointed out frequently over the 80 years since it was decided, *Sinclair v Brougham* is a bewildering authority: no single ratio decidendi can be detected; all the reasoning is open to serious objection; it was only intended to deal with cases where there were no trade creditors in competition and the reasoning is incapable of application where there are such creditors. In my view the decision as to rights in rem in *Sinclair v Brougham* should also be overruled. Although the case is one where property rights are involved, such overruling should not in practice disturb long-settled titles. However, your Lordships should not be taken to be casting any doubt on the principles of tracing as established in *In re Diplock*.

If *Sinclair v Brougham*, in both its aspects, is overruled the law can be established in accordance with principle and commercial common sense: a claimant for restitution of moneys paid under an ultra vires, and therefore void, contract has a personal action at law to recover the moneys paid as on a total failure of consideration; he will not have an equitable proprietary claim which gives him either rights against third parties or priority in an insolvency; not will he have a personal claim in equity, since the recipient is not a trustee.

(B) Chase Manhattan Bank NA v Israel-British Bank (London) Ltd [1981] Ch 105

In that case Chase Manhattan, a New York bank, had by mistake paid the same sum twice to the credit of the defendant, a London bank. Shortly thereafter, the defendant bank went into insolvent liquidation. The question was whether Chase Manhattan had a claim in rem against the assets of the defendant bank to recover the second payment.

Goulding J was asked to assume that the moneys paid under a mistake were capable of being traced in the assets of the recipient bank: he was only concerned with the question whether there was a proprietary base on which the tracing remedy could be founded: 116b. He held that, where money was paid under a mistake, the receipt of such money without more constituted the recipient a trustee: he said that the payer 'retains an equitable property in it and the conscience of [the recipient] is subjected to a fiduciary duty to respect his proprietary right:' 119.

It will be apparent from what I have already said that I cannot agree with this reasoning. First, it is based on a concept of retaining an equitable property in money where, prior to the payment to the recipient bank, there was no existing equitable interest. Further, I cannot understand how the recipient's 'conscience' can be affected at a time when he is not aware of any mistake. Finally, the judge found that the law of England and that of New York were in substance the same. I find this a surprising conclusion since the New York law of constructive trusts has for a long time been influenced by the concept of a *remedial* constructive trust, whereas hitherto English law has for the most part only recognised an institutional constructive trust: see *Metall und Rohstoff AG v Donaldson Lufkin & Jenrette Inc.* [1990] 1 QB 391, 478, 480. In the present context, that distinction is of fundamental importance. Under an institutional constructive trust, the trust arises by operation of law as from the date of the circumstances which give rise to it: the function of the court is merely to declare that such trust has arisen in the past. The consequences that flow from such trust having arisen (including the possibly unfair consequences to third parties who in the interim have received the trust property) are also determined by rules of law, not under a discretion. A remedial constructive trust, as I understand it, is different. It is a judicial remedy giving rise to an enforceable equitable obligation: the extent to which it operates retrospectively to the prejudice of third parties lies in the discretion of the court. Thus for the law of New York to hold that there is a remedial constructive trust where a payment has been made under a void contract gives rise to different consequences from holding that an institutional constructive trust arises in English law.

However, although I do not accept the reasoning of Goulding J, *Chase Manhattan* may well have been rightly decided. The defendant bank knew of the mistake made by the paying bank within two days of the receipt of the moneys: see at 115a. The judge treated this fact as irrelevant (114f) but in my judgment it may well provide a proper foundation for the decision. Although the mere receipt of the moneys, in ignorance of the mistake, gives rise to no trust, the retention of the moneys after the recipient bank learned of the mistake may well have given rise to a constructive trust: see *Snell's Equity*, 193; *Pettit, Equity and the Law of Trusts*, 7th edn (1993) 168; *Metall und Rohstoff AG v Donaldson Lufkin & Jenrette Inc.* [1990] 1 QB 391, 473–4.

(C) In re Ames' Settlement; Dinwiddy v Ames

In this case [1946] Ch 217 the father of the intended husband, in consideration of the son's intended marriage with Miss H., made a marriage settlement under which the income was payable to the husband for life and after his death to the wife for life or until her remarriage, with remainder to the issue of the intended marriage. There was an ultimate trust, introduced by the words 'If there should not be any child of the said intended marriage who attains a vested interest . . .' for an artificial class of the husband's next of kin. The marriage took place. Many years later a decree of nullity on the grounds of non-consummation had the effect of rendering the marriage void ab initio. The income was paid to the husband until his death which occurred 19 years after the decree of nullity. The question was whether the trust capital was held under the ultimate trust for the husband's next-of-kin or was payable to the settlor's estate. It was held that the settlor's estate was entitled.

The judgment is very confused. It is not clear whether the judge was holding (as I think correctly) that in any event the ultimate trust failed because it was only expressed to take effect in the event of the failure of the issue of a non-existent marriage (an impossible condition precedent) or whether he held that all the trusts of the settlement failed because the beneficial interests were conferred in consideration of the intended marriage and that there had been a total failure of consideration. In either event, the decision has no bearing on the present case. On either view, the fund was vested in trustees on trusts which had failed. Therefore the moneys were held on a resulting trust of type (B) above. The decision casts no light on the question whether, there being no express trust, moneys paid on a consideration which wholly fails are held on a resulting trust.

The stolen bag of coins The argument for a resulting trust was said to be supported by the case of a thief who steals a bag of coins. At law those coins remain traceable only so long as they are kept separate: as soon as they are mixed with other coins or paid into a mixed bank account they cease to be traceable at law. Can it really be the case, it is asked, that in such circumstances the thief cannot be required to disgorge the property which, in equity, represents the stolen coins? Moneys can only be traced in equity if there has been at some stage a breach of fiduciary duty, i.e. if either before the theft there was an equitable proprietary interest (e.g. the coins were stolen trust moneys) or such interest arises under a resulting trust at the time of the theft or the mixing of the moneys. Therefore, it is said, a resulting trust must arise either at the time of the theft or when the moneys are subsequently mixed. Unless this is the law, there will be no right to recover the assets representing the stolen moneys once the moneys have become mixed.

I agree that the stolen moneys are traceable in equity. But the proprietary interest which equity is enforcing in such circumstances arises under a constructive, not a resulting, trust. Although it is difficult to find clear authority for the proposition, when property is obtained by fraud equity imposes a constructive trust on the fraudulent recipient: the property is recoverable and traceable in equity. Thus, an infant who has obtained property by fraud is bound in equity to restore it: *Stocks v Wilson* [1913] 2 KB 235, 244; *R. Leslie Ltd v Sheill* [1914] 3 KB 607. Moneys stolen from a bank account can be traced in equity: *Bankers Trust Co. v Shapira* [1980] 1 WLR 1274, 1282C–E. See also *McCormick v Grogan* (1869) LR 4 HL 82, 97.

Restitution and equitable rights Those concerned with developing the law of restitution are anxious to ensure that, in certain circumstances, the plaintiff should have the right to recover property which he has unjustly lost. For that purpose they have sought to develop the law of resulting trusts so as to give the plaintiff a proprietary interest. For the reasons that I have given in my view such development is not based on sound principle and in the name of unjust enrichment is capable of producing most unjust results. The law of resulting trusts would confer on the plaintiff a right to recover property from, or at the expense of, those who have not been unjustly enriched at his expense at all, e.g. the lender whose debt is secured by a floating charge and all other third parties who have purchased an equitable interest only, albeit in all innocence and for value.

Although the resulting trust is an unsuitable basis for developing proprietary restitutionary remedies, the remedial constructive trust, if introduced into English law, may provide a more satisfactory road forward. The court by way of remedy might impose a constructive trust on a defendant who knowingly retains property of which the plaintiff has been unjustly deprived. Since the remedy can be tailored to the circumstances of the particular case, innocent third parties would not be prejudiced and restitutionary defences, such as change of position, are capable of being given effect. However, whether English law should follow the United States and Canada by adopting the remedial constructive trust will have to be decided in some future case when the point is directly in issue.

...

I would allow the appeal and vary the judgment of the Court of Appeal so as to order the payment of simple interest only as from 18 June 1987 on the balance from time to time between the sums paid by the bank to the local authority and the sums paid by the local authority to the bank.

Lord Goff (dissenting): . . . I have already stated that restitution in [this case] can be achieved by means of a personal claim in restitution. The question has however arisen whether the bank should also have the benefit of an equitable proprietary claim in the form of a resulting trust. The immediate reaction must be why should it? Take the present case. The parties have entered into a commercial transaction. The transaction has, for technical reasons, been held to be void from the beginning. Each party is entitled to recover its money, with the result that the balance must be repaid. But why should the plaintiff bank be given the additional benefits which flow from a proprietary claim, for example the benefit of achieving priority in the event of the defendant's insolvency? After all, it has entered into a commercial transaction, and has taken the risk of the defendant's insolvency, just like the defendant's other creditors who have contracted with it, not to mention other creditors to whom the defendant may be liable to pay damages in tort.

I feel bound to say that I would not at first sight have thought that an equitable proprietary claim in the form of a trust should be made available to the bank in the present case, but for two things. The first is the decision of this House in *Sinclair v Brougham* [1914] AC 398, which appears to provide authority that a resulting trust may indeed arise in a case such as the present. The second is that on the authorities there is an equitable jurisdiction to award the plaintiff compound interest in cases where the defendant is a trustee. It is the combination of those two factors which has provided the foundation for the principal arguments advanced on behalf of the bank in support of its submission that it was entitled to an award of compound interest.

[*After making some brief introductory remarks on the law on interest, Lord Goff continued:*]

EQUITABLE PROPRIETARY CLAIMS

I now turn to consider the question whether an equitable proprietary claim was available to the bank in the present case.

Ever since the law of restitution began, about the middle of this century, to be studied in depth, the role of equitable proprietary claims in the law of restitution has been found to be a matter of great difficulty. The legitimate ambition of restitution lawyers has been to establish a coherent law of restitution, founded upon the principle of unjust enrichment; and since certain equitable institutions, notably the constructive trust and the resulting trust, have been perceived to have the function of reversing unjust enrichment, they have sought to embrace those institutions within the law of restitution, if necessary moulding them to make them fit for that purpose. Equity lawyers, on the other hand, have displayed anxiety that in this process the equitable principles underlying these institutions may become illegitimately distorted; and though equity lawyers in this country are nowadays much more sympathetic than they have been in the past towards the need to develop a coherent law of restitution, and of identifying the proper role of the trust within that rubric of the law, they remain concerned that the trust concept should not be distorted, and also that the practical consequences of its imposition should be fully appreciated. There is therefore some tension between the aims and perceptions of these two groups of lawyers, which has manifested itself in relation to the matters under consideration in the present case.

In the present case, however, it is not the function of our Lordships' House to rewrite the agenda for the law of restitution, nor even to identify the role of equitable proprietary claims in that part of the law. The judicial process is neither designed for, nor properly directed towards, such objectives. The function of your Lordships' House is simply to decide the questions at issue before it in the present case; and the particular question now under consideration is whether, where money has been paid by a party to a contract which is ultra vires the other party and so void ab initio, he has the benefit of an equitable proprietary claim in respect of the money so paid. Moreover the manner in which this question has arisen before this House renders it by no means easy to address. First of all, the point was not debated in any depth in the courts below, because they understood that they were bound by *Sinclair v Brougham* [1914] AC 398 to hold that such a claim was here available. But second, the point has arisen only indirectly in this case, since it is relevant only to the question whether the court here has power to make an award of compound interest. It is a truism that, in deciding a question of law in any particular case, the courts are much influenced by considerations of practical justice, and especially by the results which would flow from the recognition of a particular claim on the facts of the case before the court. Here, however, an award of compound interest provides no such guidance, because it is no more than a consequence which is said to flow, for no more than historical reasons, from the availability of an equitable proprietary claim. It therefore provides no guidance on the question whether such a claim should here be available.

In these circumstances I regard it as particularly desirable that your Lordships should, so far as possible, restrict the inquiry to the actual questions at issue in this appeal, and not be tempted into formulating general principles of a broader nature. If restitution lawyers are hoping to find in your Lordships' speeches broad statements of principle which may definitively establish the future shape of this part of the law, I fear that they may be disappointed. I also regard it as important that your Lordships should, in the traditional manner, pay particular regard to the practical consequences which may flow from the decision of the House.

With these observations by way of preamble, I turn to the question of the availability of an equitable proprietary claim in a case such as the present. The argument advanced on behalf of the bank was that the money paid by it under the void contract was received by the council subject to a resulting trust. This approach was consistent with that of Dillon LJ in the Court of Appeal: see [1994] 1 WLR 938, 947. It is also consistent with the approach of Viscount Haldane LC (with whom Lord Atkinson agreed) in *Sinclair v Brougham* [1914] AC 398, 420–421.

I have already expressed the opinion that, at first sight, it is surprising that an equitable proprietary claim should be available in a case such as the present. However, before I examine the question as a matter of principle, I propose first to consider whether *Sinclair v Brougham* supports the argument now advanced on behalf of the bank.

SINCLAIR v BROUGHAM

The decision of this House in *Sinclair v Brougham* has loomed very large in both the judgments in the courts below and in the admirable arguments addressed to the Appellate Committee of this House. It has long been regarded as a controversial decision, and has been the subject of much consideration by scholars, especially those working in the field of restitution. I have however reached the conclusion that it is basically irrelevant to the decision of the present appeal. [*For Lord Goff's reasoning on* Sinclair v Brougham, *see the extract set out above, at 40. He then continued:*]

THE AVAILABILITY OF AN EQUITABLE PROPRIETARY CLAIM IN THE PRESENT CASE

Having put *Sinclair v Brougham* on one side as providing no authority that a resulting trust should be imposed in the facts of the present case, I turn to the question whether, as a matter of principle, such a trust should be imposed, the bank's submission being that such a trust arose at the time when the sum of £2.5m was received by the council from the bank.

As my noble and learned friend, Lord Browne-Wilkinson, observes, it is plain that the present case falls within neither of the situations which are traditionally regarded as giving rise to a resulting trust, viz. (1) voluntary payments by A to B, or for the purchase of property in the name of B or in his and A's joint names, where there is no presumption of advancement or evidence of intention to make an out-and-out gift; or (2) property transferred to B on an express trust which does not exhaust the whole beneficial interest. The question therefore arises whether resulting trusts should be extended beyond such cases to apply in the present case, which I shall treat as a case where money has been paid for a consideration which fails.

In a most interesting and challenging paper, 'Restitution and Resulting Trusts,' published in *Equity: Contemporary Legal Developments* (1992) (ed. Goldstein), 335, Professor Birks has argued for a wider role for the resulting trust in the field of restitution, and specifically for its availability in cases of mistake and failure of consideration. His thesis is avowedly experimental, written to test the temperature of the water. I feel bound to respond that the temperature of the water must be regarded as decidedly cold: see, e.g., Professor Burrows, 'Swaps and the Friction between Common Law and Equity' [1995] *RLR* 15, and Mr W. J. Swadling, 'A new role for resulting trusts?' (1996) 16 *Legal Studies* 133.

In the first place, as Lord Browne-Wilkinson points out, to impose a resulting trust in such cases is inconsistent with the traditional principles of trust law. For on receipt of the money by the payee it is to be presumed that (as in the present case) the identity of the money is immediately lost by mixing with other assets of the payee, and at that time the payee has no knowledge of the facts giving rise to the failure of consideration. By the time that those facts come to light, and the conscience of the payee may thereby be affected, there will therefore be no identifiable fund to which a trust can attach. But there are other difficulties. First, there is no general rule that the property in money paid under a void contract does not pass to the payee; and it is difficult to escape the conclusion that, as a general rule, the beneficial interest to the money likewise passes to the payee. This must certainly be the case where the consideration for the payment fails after the payment is made, as in cases of frustration or breach of contract; and there appears to be no good reason why the same should not apply in cases where, as in the present case, the contract under which the payment is made is void ab initio and the consideration for the payment therefore fails at the time of payment. It is true that the doctrine of mistake might be invoked where the mistake is fundamental in the orthodox sense of that word. But that is not the position in the present case; moreover the mistake in the present case must be classified as a mistake of law which, as at the law at present stands, creates its own special problems. No doubt that much criticised doctrine will fall to be reconsidered when an appropriate case occurs; but I cannot think that the present is such a case, since not only has the point not been argued but (as will appear) it is my opinion that there is any event jurisdiction to award compound interest in the present case. For all of these reasons I conclude, in agreement with my noble and learned friend, that there is no basis for holding that a resulting trust arises in cases where money has been paid under a contract which is ultra vires and therefore void ab initio. This conclusion has the effect that all the practical problems which would flow from the imposition of a resulting trust in a case such as the present, in particular the imposition upon the recipient of the normal duties of trustee, do not arise. The dramatic consequences which would occur are detailed by Professor Burrows in his article on 'Swaps and the Friction between Common Law and Equity' [1995] RLR 15, 27: the duty to account for profits accruing from the trust property; the inability of the payee to rely upon the defence of change of position; the absence of any limitation period; and so on. Professor Burrows even goes so far as to conclude that the action for money had and received would be rendered otiose in such cases, and indeed in all cases where the payer seeks restitution of mistaken payments. However, if no resulting trust arises, it also follows that the payer in a case such as the present cannot achieve priority over the payee's general creditors in the event of his insolvency— a conclusion which appears to me to be just.

For all these reasons I conclude that there is no basis for imposing a resulting trust in the present case, and I therefore reject the bank's submission that it was here entitled to proceed by way of an equitable proprietary claim. I need only add that, in reaching that conclusion, I do not find it necessary to review the decision of Goulding J in *Chase Manhattan Bank NA v Israel-British Bank (London) Ltd* [1981] Ch 105.

INTEREST

...

I wish to record that Hobhouse J was in no doubt that, if he had jurisdiction to do so, he should award compound interest in this case. He said [1994] 4 All ER 890, 955:

'Anyone who lends or borrows money on a commercial basis receives or pays interest periodically and if that interest is not paid it is compounded. . . . I see no reason why I should deny the plaintiff a complete remedy or allow the defendant arbitrarily to retain part of the enrichment which it has unjustly enjoyed.'

With that reasoning I find myself to be in entire agreement. The council has had the use of the bank's money over a period of years. It is plain on the evidence that, if it had not had the use of the bank's money, it would (if free to do so) have borrowed money elsewhere at compound interest. It has to that extent profited from the use of the bank's money. Moreover, if the bank had not advanced the money to the council, it would itself have employed the money on similar terms in its business. Full restitution requires that, on the facts of the present case, compound interest should be awarded, having regard to the commercial realities of the case. As the judge said, there is no reason why the bank should be denied a complete remedy.

It follows therefore that everything depends on the scope of the equitable jurisdiction. It also follows, in my opinion, that if that jurisdiction does not extend to apply in a case such as the present, English law will be revealed as incapable of doing full justice.

. . .

The question which arises in the present case is whether, in the exercise of equity's auxiliary jurisdiction, the equitable jurisdiction to award compound interest may be exercised to enable a plaintiff to obtain full justice in a personal action of restitution at common law.

I start with the position that the common law remedy is, in a case such as the present, plainly inadequate, in that there is no power to award compound interest at common law and that without that power the common law remedy is incomplete. . . . Fortunately, however, judges of equity have always been ready to address new problems, and to create new doctrines, where justice so requires. . . .

I therefore ask myself whether there is any reason why the equitable jurisdiction to award compound interest should not be exercised in a case such as the present. I can see none. Take, for example, the case of fraud. It is well established that the equitable jurisdiction may be exercised in cases of fraud. Indeed it is plain that, on the same facts, there may be a remedy both at law and in equity to recover money obtained by fraud: see *Johnson v The King* [1904] AC 817, 822, *per* Lord Macnaghten. Is it to be said that, if the plaintiff decides to proceed in equity, compound interest may be awarded; but that if he chooses to proceed in an action at law, no such auxiliary relief will be available to him? I find it difficult to believe that, at the end of the 20th century, our law should be so hidebound by forms of action as to be compelled to reach such a conclusion.

For these reasons I conclude that the equitable jurisdiction to award compound interest may be exercised in the case of personal claims at common law, as it is in equity. Furthermore I am satisfied that, in particular, the equitable jurisdiction may, where appropriate, be exercised in the case of a personal claim in restitution. . . .

I recognise that, in so holding, the courts would be breaking new ground, and would be extending the equitable jurisdiction to a field where it has not hitherto been exercised. But that cannot of itself be enough to prevent what I see to be a thoroughly desirable extension of the jurisdiction, consistent with its underlying basis that it exists to meet the demands of justice. An action of restitution appears to me to provide an almost classic case in which the jurisdiction should be available to enable the courts to do full justice. Claims in restitution are founded upon a principle of justice, being designed to prevent the unjust enrichment of the defendant: see *Lipkin Gorman v Karpnale Ltd* [1991] 2 AC 548. Long ago, in *Moses v Macferlan* (1760) 2 Burr. 1005, 1012, Lord Mansfield CJ said that the gist of the action for money had and received is that 'the defendant, upon the circumstances of the case, is obliged by the ties of natural justice and equity to refund the money.' It would be strange indeed if the courts lacked jurisdiction in such a case to ensure that justice could be fully achieved by means of an award of compound interest, where it is appropriate to make such an award, despite the fact that the jurisdiction to award such interest is itself said to rest upon the demands of justice I am glad not to be forced to hold that English law is so inadequate as to be incapable of achieving such a result. In my opinion the jurisdiction should now be made available, as justice requires, in cases of restitution, to ensure that full justice can be done. The seed is there, but the growth has hitherto been confined within a small area. That growth should now be permitted to spread naturally elsewhere within this newly recognised branch of the law. No genetic engineering is required, only that the warm sun of judicial creativity should exercise its benign influence rather than remain hidden behind the dark clouds of legal history.

. . .

It remains for me to say that I am satisfied, for the reason given by Hobhouse J, that this is a case in which it was appropriate that compound interest should be awarded. In particular, since the council had the free use of the bank's money in circumstances in which, if it had borrowed the money from some other financial institution, it would have had to pay compound interest for it, the council can properly be said to have profited from the bank's money so as to make an award of compound interest appropriate. However, for the reasons given by Dillon LJ [1994] 1 WLR 938, 947, 949, I agree with the Court of Appeal that the interest should run from the date of receipt of the money.

Lords Lloyd and **Slynn** gave speeches which largely agreed with **Lord Browne-Wilkinson's** reasoning. **Lord Woolf**, dissenting, largely agreed with **Lord Goff's** reasoning.

NOTES AND QUESTIONS

1. Parts of the articles by Birks and Swadling, referred to by the House of Lords, are set out below at 750–755. Chambers, *Resulting Trusts* (1997), 162 considers that the rejection of a trust in this case could only have been justified if the failure of consideration was subsequent rather than initial. Is that a possible interpretation of the decision?

2. Should compound interest be more readily awarded by the courts? Should it be a necessary pre-condition to the award of compound interest that the defendant was a defaulting fiduciary (as the majority thought)? See generally Law Commission Report No 287 *Pre-Judgment Interest on Debts and Damages* (2004).

3. Do you agree with Lord Browne-Wilkinson that the 'knowledge' of the recipient—and hence whether the recipient's conscience is affected—is crucial in determining whether equitable proprietary restitution through a trust should be imposed? Is there any link between that view and the debate we examined in Chapter 4 above as to whether *personal* restitutionary liability in equity for 'ignorance' requires *knowing* receipt rather than resting on strict liability?

4. Do you agree with Lord Browne-Wilkinson's suggestion that it may help to think in terms of a 'remedial constructive trust', rather than a resulting trust, as the means of effecting proprietary restitution in equity? This idea met with a frosty reception in *Re Polly Peck (No 2)* [1998] 3 All ER 812. It was there held that there was no seriously arguable case for (retrospectively) granting a remedial constructive trust, stripping gains made by an insolvent trespasser, because to do so would undermine the pari passu insolvency regime. In Mummery LJ's memorable phrase, at 827, 'The insolvency road is blocked off to remedial constructive trusts, at least when judge driven in a vehicle of discretion'. And Nourse LJ, at 831, clarified that the objection to the remedial constructive trust was that it gave the courts 'a discretion to vary proprietary rights'.

5. The House of Lords was concerned about various unsatisfactory consequences of finding that the payments had been held on a resulting trust. Is it correct that those unsatisfactory consequences would *necessarily* have followed the finding of a resulting trust? Or could one have imposed a resulting trust without imposing, for example, the normal personal consequences of trusteeship?

6. In *Napier v Hunter*, see above, 712, the House of Lords preferred to grant an equitable lien to effect proprietary restitution instead of a trust. Would the granting of an equitable lien for the balance of the money paid have been a more acceptable proprietary response than a trust in *Westdeutsche Landesbank*?

7. In *El Ajou v Dollar Land Holdings plc* [1993] 3 All ER 717 Millett J, in obiter dicta, considered that a person entitled to rescind a contract for fraud can establish the equitable proprietary interest necessary for equitable tracing because there is an 'old-fashioned institutional resulting trust'. He said, at page 734:

> [The plaintiff has no] difficulty in satisfying the precondition for equity's intervention. Mr Murad was the plaintiff's fiduciary, and he was bribed to purchase the shares. He committed a gross breach of his fiduciary obligations to the plaintiff, and that is sufficient to enable the plaintiff to invoke the assistance of equity. Other victims, however, were less fortunate. They employed no fiduciary. They were simply swindled. No breach of any fiduciary obligation was involved. It would, of course, be an intolerable reproach to our system of jurisprudence if the plaintiff were the only victim who could trace and recovery his money. Neither party before me suggested that this is the case; and I agree with them. But if the other victims of the fraud can trace their money in equity it must be because, having been induced to purchase the shares by false and fraudulent misrepresentations, they are entitled to rescind the transaction and revest the equitable title to the purchase money in themselves, at least to the extent necessary to support an equitable tracing claim: see *Daly v Sydney Stock Exchange Ltd* (1986) 160 CLR 371 at 387–90 *per* Brennan J. There is thus no distinction between their case and the plaintiff's. They can rescind the purchases for fraud, and he for the bribery of his agent; and each can then invoke the assistance of equity to follow property of which he is the equitable owner. But, if this is correct, as I think it is, then the trust which is operating in these cases is not some new model remedial constructive trust, but an old-fashioned institutional resulting trust.

It appears that, after *Westdeutsche Landesbank*, Millett J's dicta must be rejected. In so far as there is a trust in play following rescission, it would seem that it should be regarded as a constructive trust.

8. The question whether and when a trust arises to reverse an unjust enrichment may also have consequences for the law of theft and related criminal offences: see, for example, *Att.-Gen.'s Reference No 1 of 1985* [1986] QB 591; *R. v Shadrokh-Cigari* [1988] *Crim LR* 465; J Smith (1994) 110 *LQR* 180.

(2) ACADEMIC ANALYSES OF PROPRIETARY RESTITUTION

• A W Scott, 'Constructive Trusts' (1955) 71 *LQR* 39

It is, I think, coming to be recognised, particularly in the United States, that the constructive trust is a concept of a wide scope, of a scope which is gradually growing wider.

It is sometimes said that a constructive trust is imposed in case of fraud. It is sometimes said that it is imposed in case of a breach of fiduciary relation. It seems clear, however, that not only may a constructive trust be imposed in both of these cases, but it may be imposed in others too. How then shall we define a constructive trust? . . . I think that the best that we can do is to give a rough working description of it.

This we attempted to do in the *Restatement of Restitution* which was promulgated by The American Law Institute in 1936. It is there stated (§ 160):

'Where a person holding title to property is subject to an equitable duty to convey it to another on the ground that he would be unjustly enriched if he were permitted to retain it, a constructive trust arises.'

Certainly this is a pretty broad statement. It is not, perhaps, as broad as that which Judge Cardozo made when sitting on the Court of Appeals of New York, who said: 'A constructive trust is the formula through which the conscience of equity finds expression.'[1] The provision in the *Restatement* does not purport to define a constructive trust but purports to state the circumstances under which a constructive trust arises. It arises where the circumstances are such that the holder of the title to property would be unjustly enriched if he were permitted to retain it, and where, therefore, a court of equity (or a court having the powers of a court of equity) will compel him to convey the property to another.

Of course, we have not yet got very far in the development of the concept of constructive trust, since we have merely passed on to another concept, that of unjust enrichment. Here again, however, we are met with the difficulty, nay, the impossibility, of defining the concept. We are, nevertheless, at least one step nearer toward the end which we have in view, namely a statement of the situations in which a constructive trust will be imposed.

Before we consider affirmatively the situations in which a constructive trust will be imposed, let us approach the matter negatively and consider situations which are not included in the concept of constructive trust. . . .

An express trust is not a constructive trust. This, it would seem, is self-evident. But it is common in the books to assert that trusts are of two kinds, (1) express, (2) constructive; and this statement is followed or preceded by a suggested definition of a trust broad enough to include both an express trust and a constructive trust. It seems to me that this gets one nowhere. There is only a superficial resemblance between an express trust and a constructive trust. In both cases one person holds the title to property subject to a specifically enforceable equitable duty to hold it for or convey it to another, and in both cases a gratuitous transferee or a transferee with notice is subject to the same duty. There, however, the resemblance ceases. An express trust arises because of a manifestation of intention on the part of an owner of property to create it; a constructive trust is imposed regardless of intention. The express trustee is under a duty to administer the trust in accordance with its terms; a constructive trustee has no such duty. An express trust involves a very intensive fiduciary relation, which is lacking in the case of a constructive trust, unless, indeed, it arises, as it sometimes does, out of a breach of a fiduciary relation. It seems misleading to say, as Lord Westbury said in speaking of the jurisdiction to enforce a constructive trust: 'It is a jurisdiction by which a court of equity, proceeding on the ground of fraud, converts the party who has committed it into a trustee for the party who is injured by that fraud.'[2]

In such a case the court does not convert the fraudulent person into a trustee; it makes him surrender the property to his victim. In the meantime, before he surrenders it, he must not transfer it to someone else, and any transferee of the property, unless he is a bona fide purchaser, will also be compelled to surrender it. In other words, as Professor Pound has pointed out, a constructive trust, unlike an express trust, is a remedial and not a substantive institution.[3] The court does not give relief because a constructive trust has been created; but the court gives relief because otherwise the defendant would be unjustly enriched; and because the court gives this relief it declares that the defendant is chargeable as a constructive trustee.

There is the same relation between an express trust and a constructive trust that there is between a contract and a quasi-contractual obligation. It is, it seems to me, a foolish thing to attempt to

---

1 *Beatty v Guggenheim Exploration Co.* (1919) 225 NY 380, 386.

2 *McCormick v Grogan* (1869) LR 4 HL 82, 97.

3 Pound, 'The Progress of the Law,' 33 *Harvard Law Review* 420, 421 (1920).

include in one definition these two things. A contract arises from an agreement between the parties; a quasi-contractual obligation is imposed to prevent unjust enrichment. It is most misleading, I think, to speak of a quasi-contractual obligation as an implied contract, or even a contract implied in law. This involves the use of a fiction, and fictions, though they may be useful in the development of law in a primitive system, have no proper place among the sophisticated.

When, therefore, the *Restatement of Trusts* was in preparation, it was decided not to include constructive trusts, but to deal with them in a *Restatement of Restitution*. It is true that insofar as a constructive trust arises out of a breach of duty by an express trustee it was dealt with in the *Restatement of Trusts*; as, for example, where an express trustee in breach of trust transfers trust property to a third person who is not a bona fide purchaser. But the broader treatment of the constructive trust as a remedial device to prevent or redress unjust enrichment is the subject-matter of the second part of the *Restatement of Restitution*, the first part dealing with the general principles which govern both quasi-contract and constructive trust.

In the *Restatement of Restitution* we attempted to cover at least most of the situations in which a constructive trust is imposed in order to prevent unjust enrichment. There may, indeed, be other situations. There is certainly room for growth in this field of the law. We shall deal with the subject under the following heads: (1) Conveyance procured by fraud, duress, undue influence or mistake; (2) Acquisition of an interest in land under an oral agreement; (3) Acquisition of property on death; (4) Acquisition of property by a fiduciary; (5) Following property into a product; (6) Acquisition of property from a fiduciary who in breach of his duty transfers it to one who is not a bona fide purchaser.

(1) CONVEYANCE PROCURED BY FRAUD, DURESS, UNDUE INFLUENCE OR MISTAKE

Where the owner of property is induced by the fraud of another to transfer the title to property to him, he holds it upon a constructive trust for the transfer. In the case of land the defrauded person is entitled to compel specific restitution. In the case of chattels which are not unique and in the case of money the remedy at law for the recovery of damages is ordinarily adequate, and a court of equity will not ordinarily compel specific restitution. The fact, however, that the transferor has an equitable interest in the property and that the transferee is a constructive trustee is recognised in the cases which allow the transferor to reach the property in the hands of a third person to whom the fradulent person has transferred it, where he is not a bona fide purchaser. It is also recognised in the cases in which specific restitution is enforced because of the insolvency of the fraudulent person.

Similarly, a constructive trust arises where a transfer of property is induced by duress or undue influence or where it is made under a mistake. Thus where A paid money to B by mistake and B was later adjudicated a bankrupt, and the money which was paid was traceable to a bank account from which it had never been withdrawn, it was held that the payer could recover the money, and did not have a mere claim to recover *pro rata* with the other creditors of the bankrupt.[4]

A constructive trust will be imposed not only where a person wrongfully procures a conveyance to himself, but also where he procures a conveyance to a third person. Thus in *Bridgman v Green*[5] the plaintiff was induced by the fraud and undue influence of his valet to pay money to the valet and to his wife and to his brother and to an attorney in trust for his son. It was held that the plaintiff could recover the money, although the defendants other than the valet himself were not parties to the fraud. Wilmot CJ said: 'Let the hand receiving it be ever so chaste, yet if it come through a corrupt polluted channel, the obligation of restitution will follow it.'

[*After discussing his categories 2–3, Scott continues:*]

---

4 *Re Berry*, 147 Fed 208 (CCA 2d, 1906).   5 (1755) 2 Ves Sr 627, Wilm 58.

(4) ACQUISITION OF PROPERTY BY A FIDUCIARY

Here, perhaps, is the typical constructive trust. Indeed, in the books it is sometimes treated as the only situation in which a constructive trust arises. Thus, Mr Lewin says, 'A constructive trust is raised by a court of equity wherever a person, clothed with a fiduciary character, gains some personal advantage by availing himself of his situation as trustee.'[6]

The general principle covering this class of cases is stated in the *Restatement of Restitution*, § 190:

'Where a person in fiduciary relation to another acquires property, and the acquisition or retention of the property is in violation of his duty as fiduciary, he holds it upon a constructive trust for the other.'

This principle is applicable where a fiduciary purchases for himself property entrusted to him as fiduciary. It is applicable where he sells his individual property to himself as fiduciary. It is applicable where he purchases for himself property which he should purchase for the beneficiary. It is applicable where he renews for himself a lease held by him as fiduciary; indeed, in the English books they play up the *Romford Market* case[7] as though it were *the* constructive trust. It is applicable where a fiduciary purchases an incumbrance upon property held by him as fiduciary, and seeks to retain a profit which he makes thereby. It is applicable where he receives a bonus or commission in violation of his duty as fiduciary and seeks to retain it. It is applicable where he improperly competes with the beneficiary, as, for example, in *Re Thompson*,[8] where a testator bequeathed his business as a yacht agent to the defendant as trustee, who proceeded to establish a competing yacht agency of his own, in spite of the fact that the number of customers in such an agency is quite limited so that the business is highly competitive. It is applicable where a person makes an improper use of confidential information.

In all these situations the fiduciary would be unjustly enriched if he were permitted to profit through an abuse of the fiduciary relation, and he is chargeable as constructive trustee of the profit so made. This is true not only where he is an express trustee, but also where he is an executor, a guardian, a partner, a joint adventurer, a corporate officer or director, or an agent.

(5) FOLLOWING PROPERTY INTO ITS PRODUCT

We now come to the popular pastime of following the *res*, or, as they say in England, obtaining a tracing order. The principle is thus expressed in the *Restatement of Restitution*, § 202.

'Where a person wrongfully disposes of property of another knowing that the disposition is wrongful and acquires in exchange other property, the other is entitled at his option to enforce either (a) a constructive trust of the property so acquired, or (b) an equitable lien upon it to secure his claim for reimbursement from the wrongdoer.'

It will be noted that the principle thus laid down is applicable to conscious wrongdoers of all sorts. It is applicable although there is no fiduciary relation between the wrongdoer and the claimant. It is applicable where the wrongdoer obtains the property by fraud, and even where he is a converter, a person who has merely helped himself to the property of another and made a profit thereby. If a profit is made through the disposition of another's property, surely the other should have the profit and not the wrongdoer. The courts in the United States have so held. In England, it would seem, the doctrine has been confined to profits made by wrongdoers who are fiduciaries.

---

6 Lewin, *Trusts* (15th edn 1950) 155.   7 *Keech v Sandford* (1726) Sel Cas Ch 61.
8 [1930] 1 Ch 203.

(6) ACQUISITION OF PROPERTY FROM A FIDUCIARY

There is another class of cases where a person is chargeable as a constructive trustee, which was dealt with in the *Restatement of Trusts*. This is the situation where a trustee or other fiduciary wrongfully transfers property held by him as fiduciary. The transferee, unless he is in the position of a purchaser for value and without notice, holds the property upon a constructive trust for the beneficiary. This is true where he has notice of the breach of trust, or is a donee of the property. This is well settled both in England and in the United States.

WHERE THE ENRICHMENT IS NOT AT THE EXPENSE OF THE CLAIMANT

In many of the situations discussed above the defendant is unjustly enriched at the expense of the plaintiff. Recovery may be allowed, however, even though the enrichment is not at the plaintiff's expense. This is the case, for example, where a person by abusing his position as a fiduciary makes a profit, although not at the expense of his principal. Thus, in *Reading v Att.–Gen.*[9] where a British army sergeant, wearing his uniform, received some £20,000 as bribes for his services in accompanying civilian lorries transporting illicit drugs in Egypt, he was held accountable to the British Crown for the money so received. So also, where a person wrongfully makes a profit through the use of the property of another, he is chargeable as a constructive trustee of the profit so made, even though it was not made at the expense of the other, and in the United States, at least, even though there was not a fiduciary relation between the parties.

CHANGE OF POSITION AS A DEFENCE

Where a person receives property under such circumstances that he would be unjustly enriched if he were permitted to retain it, he may have a defence if without notice of the rights of the claimant he so changes his position that it would be inequitable to compel him to make restitution. The scope of this defence is somewhat indefinite, just as the scope of the doctrine of unjust enrichment is somewhat indefinite. There are situations in which it is clear enough that the defence is available, as in the case where a payment is made by mistake to an agent, who in ignorance of the mistake pays over or conveys the money or other property to his principal. There are other situations in which the result is not so clear, for example, where money received under a mistake is lost or stolen, or is expended in acquiring other property or in making improvements on the property of the person receiving it, or is given away by him. The recognition of the defence of change of position is much more limited in England than it is in the United States, the English courts applying rules as to the tracing of money paid by mistake,[10] which would be applied in the United States only where the claimant seeks to obtain priority over general creditors of the person receiving the money or where a profit is made by him through the use of the money.

CONCLUSION

It was Dean Ames who gave currency to the broad concept of unjust enrichment. He saw that this was the common denominator in all the situations which I have been discussing. It covers the situations in which, although there has been no tort or breach of contract, there is a duty to make restitution. It covers the situation where the plaintiff seeks to recover a money judgement, based on a quasi-contractual obligation, and it covers the situation where the plaintiff seeks to recover specific property, charging the defendant as a constructive trustee.

Perhaps the underlying generalisation may be thus stated: A person who has been unjustly enriched at the expense of another, or through the wrongful use of the property of another, or through the abuse of a fiduciary relation to another may be compelled to make restitution to the

---

9 [1951] AC 507.   10 *Ministry of Health v Simpson* [1951] AC 251, affg. *Re Diplock* [1948] Ch 465.

other. It is a principle rather than a rule. But the underlying concept is no more indefinite than many other concepts, like that of negligence, of prudence, of reasonableness, of unclean hands, or of equity.

In England, the latest judicial pronouncement on this matter is to be found in *Reading v Att.-Gen.,*[11] to which reference has already been made. The High Court, the Court of Appeal and the House of Lords all agreed that the unfaithful army sergeant was accountable for the profit which he made. Denning J (as he then was) said that 'The claim here is for restitution of moneys which, in justice, ought to be paid over.' Lord Porter said:

'It was suggested in argument that the learned judge founded his decision solely upon the doctrine of unjust enrichment and that that doctrine was not recognised by the law of England. My Lords, the exact status of the law of unjust enrichment is not yet assured. It holds a predominant place in the law of Scotland and, I think, of the United States, but I am content for the purposes of this case to accept that view that it forms no part of the law of England and that a right to restitution so described would be too widely stated.'

The English courts do, however, in this case and in many others, as we have seen, give relief against a defendant who would otherwise be unjustly enriched. Perhaps they will in due time accept the broader generalisation as the general principle underlying the many specific situations in which they do give relief. Perhaps they will ultimately regard a constructive trust as a remedial device, available whenever it is necessary to prevent unjust enrichment.

NOTES AND QUESTIONS

1. Scott, along with Seavey, was the reporter responsible for the Restatement of Restitution (see above, 9). His approach to constructive trusts has consequently been of immense importance. Scott's thesis may have been given renewed importance in England by Lord Browne-Wilkinson's suggestion in the *Westdeutsche Landesbank* case (see above, 727) that the 'remedial constructive trust' may be the way forward.

2. In our view, Scott's approach raises as many questions as it answers. For example: (i) which property is the constructive trustee required to convey to the claimant?; (ii) does a breach of the duty to convey the property to the claimant trigger personal liability and, if so, from which date (date of receipt or date of court judgment)?; (iii) why use the language of 'trust' if the defendant is not to have the normal duties associated with trusteeship?; (iv) what scope is left in Scott's scheme for purely personal restitutionary remedies (that is, Scott distinguishes quasi-contract from contract and constructive trusts from express trusts but leaves unclear the relationship between quasi-contract and constructive trusts); (v) where do resulting trusts belong on Scott's scheme?

3. Scott's thesis was adopted and developed by, for example, Donovan Waters *The Constructive Trust* (1962), who similarly argues that nearly all constructive trusts are remedies concerned to reverse unjust enrichment. See also the approach of the Canadian courts in cases such as *Rathwell v Rathwell* (see above, 138) and *LAC Minerals Ltd v International Corona Resources Ltd* (below, 1031). In a more recent paper, 'The Nature of the Remedial Constructive Trust' in P Birks (ed.), *The Frontiers of Liability* (1994), ii, 165, at 183, Waters writes: 'The constructive trust is the terminological vehicle for conferring specific property upon the [unjust enrichment] claimant. . . . [Canadian law should not] stipulate that the grant of a constructive trust by a court *recognises* in that property an interest of the claimant that arose at the time when the unjust enrichment . . . took place or commenced. Were the law so to provide, the claimant might effectively demand the recognition of the property interest when the court is of the view that the appropriate remedy would be damages or some other form of personal relief. Were

11 [1951] AC 507, 513.

that to be possible, the law would have found its way back to what Canadians see . . . as the barren state of the institutional constructive trust. . . . One can foresee increasing pressures . . . for the requirement of a direct and very obvious link between contribution and the property claimed. . . . Though the nature of that link will continue to be the subject-matter of argument in future litigation, linkage will be *the* criterion for the award of a remedial constructive trust.' For a sceptical view of the 'remedial constructive trust' approach, see Birks' paper 'Proprietary Rights as Remedies' in the same collection at 214. The theory that constructive trusts are remedies reversing unjust enrichment has been most carefully analysed by G Elias, *Explaining Constructive Trusts* (1990). In his view, constructive trusts are not always restitutionary (although they sometimes are). In certain circumstances, they are rather concerned to ensure that one who has chosen to dispose of his options in favour of another person should abide by the choice (the 'perfection aim'); and that one who has caused loss to another repairs the loss (the 'reparation aim').

- **P Birks, 'Restitution and Resulting Trusts' in *Equity and Contemporary Legal Developments* (ed Goldstein)** (1992) 335, 364–73

We set out here parts of the conclusion of Birks' essay.

The law of restitution is divided into two parts. In one part, identifiable as 'restitution for wrongs', the plaintiff seeks to establish that the defendant was enriched by *committing a wrong* to the plaintiff. The question which the law of restitution seeks to answer in this part is purely remedial: does the law allow restitution for the particular wrong on which the plaintiff relies? That question then divides according to the mode in which restitution might be allowed: if the law will allow restitution for the wrong, will it allow it only by way of a personal obligation to make over the enrichment, or will it also allow the plaintiff to assert a proprietary interest in the assets in which the enrichment subsists? The answer to the proprietary part of that question should generally be negative, since an affirmative answer carries with it the danger of surprising priorities in the event of the wrongdoer's insolvency. There has, therefore, to be a cogent justification for a conclusion that the victim of the wrong is not merely owed but actually owns the proceeds of the wrong held by the wrongdoer. But if an affirmative answer is given, the proprietary right will arise under a trust which can only be called 'constructive'. In no way can the proprietary interest be said to be carried back to the person from whom proceeded the value represented by the asset in which the interest subsists. For, *ex hypothesi* on this analysis, the connection between the plaintiff entitled to the interest and the value which is in question is only that that value was obtained, not from the plaintiff, but by committing a wrong against him. In other words, the analysis supposes a nexus between plaintiff and the asset in question which excludes the primary defining characteristic of a resulting trust.

The other part of the law of restitution, identifiable as 'subtractive unjust enrichment', is that in which the plaintiff seeks to establish and rely on the fact that the defendant was enriched by *subtraction from* him (i.e. in such a way that the plus to the defendant was a minus to the plaintiff) and that the circumstances were such that the defendant ought to make restitution (i.e. that the enrichment of the defendant would be 'unjust'). . . .

The proposition at the heart of this paper is that, within the field of subtractive unjust enrichment, if and so far as personal restitutionary claims—viewed from the other side, restitutionary obligations—are backed by equitable proprietary claims, we should learn to attribute those proprietary rights to the resulting trust, not the constructive trust. In the second section of this paper we reviewed the circumstances in which a trust arises when the consideration for a transfer fails. According to the definition of a resulting trust advanced in the third section, that trust should always be described as a resulting trust. Hence in the field of failure of consideration, which is one of the principal sub-divisions of subtractive enrichment, we can see the making of a close partnership between restitutionary obligations and resulting trusts.

Again, in the first section we saw how close and at present how contradictory an interaction there is between restitution of mistaken payments and resulting trusts arising in cases of apparent gift. We made some attempt to show how that contradiction can be minimized by integrating the presumption arising from apparent gift with the routine 'unjust' factors known to the law of restitution. The immediate role of the resulting trust in cases of subtractive unjust enrichment can perhaps be even more vividly illustrated if we suppose, merely for the sake of argument, that the element of contradiction were to be removed by eliminating the presumption. It would then always be a matter of proving, instead of presuming, that no beneficial gift was intended. And it would also then become true that resulting trusts could only arise in case of transfers proved by evidence not to have been intended to ensure to the benefit of the transferee and not to have made provision for the benefit to be held for any other person. . . . The most obvious way of doing that would be by proof of mistake. Where that approach was successfully used, the resulting trust thus established would provide, so to say, an independent proof of the correctness of *Chase Manhattan Bank NA v Israel-British Bank (London) Ltd* The plaintiffs' entitlement to a proprietary interest was recognized in that case without reference to resulting trust doctrine. But in fact that doctrine provides another path to the same conclusion. As in failure of consideration, a picture thus emerges in relation to mistake of a partnership between restitutionary obligations and resulting trusts.

. . .

The partnership between restitutionary obligations and the resulting trust may, it seems, turn out to operate over a considerable number of the causes of action within the field of subtractive unjust enrichment. In the great majority of cases within that sector the 'unjust' factors turns out to be, if the matter is stated at a rather high level of generality, that the plaintiff did not intend or did not fully and freely intend that the defendant should have the enrichment in question in the events which have happened. This is merely a different way of describing non-beneficial transfer: in the events which have happened the transfer was not intended to enure to the benefit of the recipient.

Within the action for money had and received to the use of the plaintiff, the common law developed the main principles of its law of restitution by asking itself the question: 'In what circumstances can it be said of a defendant that, even though he thought he was receiving for his own benefit ("to his own use" in the old language), the law should nevertheless hold that he received not for himself but for the plaintiff ("to the use of the plaintiff")'? If it is true that the resulting trust is equity's response to non-beneficial transfer, then, subject to the definitional limit that a resulting trust must carry the interest back whence it came and cannot therefore be concerned with capturing value obtained from others, the resulting trust rests on an inquiry of exactly the kind as the action for money had and received. . . .

If this is right, it cannot be far from the truth to say that the resulting trust, not the constructive trust, is equity's principal contribution to the independent law of unjust enrichment. If so, the map of the law of restitution can be redrawn, and more elegantly. If proprietary restitution in respect of subtractive unjust enrichment is seen to be both the work of and the definitive limit upon the resulting trust, both the law of restitution and the law of trusts will be more easily intelligible. Only more complex tasks—in particular the fulfilment of reasonable expectations, which is naturally the work of contract and is certainly quite beyond the scope of any law of unjust enrichment—will need to invoke the constructive trust, though in jurisdictions in which proprietary restitution for wrongs is encouraged the constructive trust will continue to have a role in that purely remedial sector of the subject.

On the other hand, if this view of the nature and mission of the resulting trust is wrong, it is important that the error should be exposed before a heresy takes root. It will not, I hope, seem to have been an abuse of the generosity of the benefactors who made this conference possible that I have used the occasion of the presence of so many distinguished equity lawyers to expound an experimental position in an attempt to discover where, if anywhere, its error lies.

• W Swadling, 'A New Role for Resulting Trusts?' (1996) 16 *Legal Studies* 110

INTRODUCTION

As Millett LJ recently remarked, there can be no doubt that 'the most difficult question' to be solved in the law of restitution is the exact circumstances in which a proprietary restitutionary remedy will be available to a restitutionary claimant.[1] The boundary between restitution and property is still largely unmapped and continues to generate controversy. What is needed is a comprehensive and systematic enquiry into the effects that the various restitutionary factors (mistake, duress, failure of consideration and so on) have on the passing of property between plaintiff and defendant. That, however, would require a whole book, or, at the very least, a series of articles. This article takes a modest step in that direction by concentrating on one specific topic within the area of restitution and property, *viz.* the inter-relationship between the law of restitution and resulting trusts.

The usual vehicle of proprietary restitution is the constructive trust. So, for example, in *AG for Hong Kong v Reid* the Privy Council held that the defendant, who in breach of fiduciary duty took bribes to drop prosecutions, held those bribes on constructive trust for his employer. And in *Chase Manhattan Bank NA v Israel-British Bank (London) Ltd* Goulding J held that $2 million mistakenly paid to the defendants was, subject to it being identified as still in their hands, held on constructive trust for the plaintiffs. But in a paper delivered in 1990 to the First International Conference on Equity, and later published in *Equity and Contemporary Legal Developments*, Professor Birks has put forward the novel suggestion that the resulting trust has been overlooked as a route to restitution and that, when not forgotten, equity could effect restitution via the resulting trust in most, though not all, of those situations in which the common law presently gives relief. Indeed, it is one of the themes of his paper that equity could go further than the common law does at present and effect restitution in situations in which it is presently doubtful or denied.

His argument centres around the fact that, at least in the area of autonomous unjust enrichment, the majority of enrichments received by restitutionary defendants will consist of transfers of wealth for which no reciprocal value has been given. Although the argument is directed specifically to mistaken gifts and failures of consideration, it can equally be applied to mistaken liability payments. Suppose a customer pays a gas bill twice. The customer will receive no value in respect of the second payment. According to Birks, the customer will have two claims. As well as having an undoubted restitutionary claim at common law in respect of the second payment, he argues that the second payment will be held on resulting trust for the customer by the Gas Board. A presumption of resulting trust arises because the payment amounts to a transfer of property without consideration between parties who are outside the range of any presumption of advancement. And since there is no positive evidence of an intention to make a gift, that presumption remains unrebutted. The same, he argues, can also be said for mistaken gifts, payments under duress and most failures of consideration. Indeed, it is only with some admitted artificiality that he manages to exclude from his analysis failures of consideration which result from the defendant's breach of contract. These apart, Birks claims that virtually all cases of common law restitution which involve a direct transfer of wealth from plaintiff to defendant will also give rise to claims in equity under a resulting trust.

But with his characteristic modesty Professor Birks does admit that he might be mistaken. Indeed, the last paragraph of his paper says that it expounds an 'experimental position' and that the occasion of the conference was used as an attempt to discover where, if anywhere, the error of his thesis lay. It is the thesis of this article that he is indeed wrong and that the resulting trust has little or no part to play in the law of restitution. Essentially, the argument which will be put is that Birks is wrong to admit of only one type of evidence which will rebut the presumption of resulting trust which arises in

---

1 (1995) 111 *LQR* 517, reviewing A Burrows, *The Law of Restitution* (London: 1993).

the case of a gratuitous transfer, *viz.* positive evidence of a donative intent. An examination of the historical origins of the resulting trust reveals that any evidence which is inconsistent with the presumption that the transferee is to be a trustee will suffice. And proof that the payment was made by mistake or for some other reason which makes its receipt unjust will always contradict that presumption of trust. In other words, proof of the unjust factor will itself be the evidence which rebuts the presumption of resulting trust.

RESULTING TRUSTS AND MISTAKEN GIFTS

The problem of mistaken gifts Professor Birks begins by pointing out that at common law a plaintiff who wants to recover a mistaken payment is still on difficult ground if he is unable to point to a liability mistake. The traditional view is that a mistaken payment is only recoverable if the mistake made by the plaintiff was as to a fact which, if true, would have rendered him liable to make the payment in question. It is obvious, he says, that in this state of the common law the recovery of a gift vitiated by mistake is bound to seem problematic.

But equity, he points out, takes a more generous view. In *Lady Hood of Avalon v Mackinnon*[2] a mother anxious to treat her daughters equally executed a deed giving a sum of £8,600 to her elder daughter. The mother had forgotten that she had already made an allocation to that daughter and, on the basis that her intention to transfer was vitiated by mistake, Eve J rescinded the second deed.

He then uses the case of *Fairhurst v Griffiths*,[3] a decision from the Isle of Man, as a bridge between his discussion of mistaken gifts and the attitude generally of equity to gifts. In *Fairhurst v Griffiths* a husband gave away £33,000 to a friend rather than see it go to his estranged wife. The husband and wife were later reconciled but the friend refused to give the money back. The husband's claim to recover it failed, the judge holding that the money was given as 'an absolute gift' and was not the 'subject of any class of trust'.

Birks says that it is not completely clear whether the judge:

'Conceived himself to be asking whether there was any affirmative evidence of intention that the money be held upon trust by the defendant or whether there was evidence to rebut a presumption of resulting trust. . . . The finding of evidence of an intention, however foolish in retrospect, to make an absolute gift can be understood in either sense.

Whichever way the [judge] intended to be understood, the facts before him were certainly suitable for a presumption of resulting trust. There was a transfer without consideration between parties who were outside the range of any presumption of advancement. Hence, unless there was positive evidence of an intention to make a gift, the defendant held on trust for the plaintiff. This is absolutely orthodox equity. Only a frontal assault on the very notion of the presumption of resulting trust could upset it.'

And later:

'equity approaches gifts with suspicion. Outside the relationships, few and narrow, within which gift-giving is to be expected—relationships, that is, which generate the presumption of advance-ment—it presumes that the "gift" is not one. In short the apparent donor gets his gift back unless, when the matter is double-checked, his intention to give is evident. It is simply not true . . . that in the absence of all circumstances of suspicion "a donor can *only* get back property which he has given away by showing that he was under some mistake of so serious a character as to render it unjust on the part of the donee to retain the property given to him." Mistake is quite unnecessary. He gets his property back, it jumps back to him under a resulting trust, unless there is affirmative proof that he intended it not to.'

---

2 [1909] 1 Ch 476.   3 High Ct. of the Isle of Man (His Honour the Deemster Corrin), 4 May 1989.

But, with the greatest respect, it is not 'orthodox equity' to say that a transfer of property without consideration will generate a presumption of resulting trust which can only be displaced by positive evidence of a donative intent. Such an approach would, it is submitted, contradict the true nature of this particular type of resulting trust.

The nature of resulting trusts We know from Megarry J's classic judgment in *Re Vandervell (No 2)*[4] that there are two types of resulting trusts, automatic and presumed. Since an automatic resulting trust cannot be rebutted by evidence of an intention to give, it is clearly a presumed resulting trust which Professor Birks has in mind. But it is misleading to label such a trust simply as a 'presumed resulting trust'. Since what is being 'presumed' is an intention on the part of the transferor to create a trust, it is more accurately called a 'presumed *intention* resulting trust'. That 'presumed intention resulting trust' is the correct description of the type of trust in operation here will be demonstrated through an historical examination of the origin of such trusts. [*Having examined the origin of such trusts and some more recent cases, Swadling continued:*] The point that the presumption of resulting trust is simply a device which shifts the burden of disproving a trust on to the transferee is crucial, for once we accept that the trust which arises in the case of a transfer made without consideration does so because of a presumption that this is what the parties actually intended, the Birks thesis can no longer be sustained. The reason for this is simple: the implication of a trust in favour of the donor in the case of a mistaken gift can hardly be said to reflect the true intentions of the parties to such a transaction.

[*Swadling goes on to criticize Birks' analysis of resulting trusts in the context of failure of consideration; and to offer general reasons for treating Birks' thesis with caution. He then concludes as follows:*]

CONCLUSION

Let us first recall Professor Birks's thesis. It is his contention that a transfer of property without consideration between parties who are outside the range of any presumption of advancement will, in the absence of positive evidence of an intention to make a gift, give rise to a resulting trust in favour of the transferor. He then applies it specifically to the case of a mistaken gift and to payments for which the consideration subsequently fails.

In the case of a mistaken gift made to a party to whom the donor does not stand in a relationship generating a presumption of advancement, Birks argues that because the transfer is made without consideration and (by reason of the mistake) with no positive evidence of an intention to give, the donee will hold on resulting trust for the donor. In the case of the payment made for a reason which later fails, he argues for a resulting trust on four grounds: first, that any other result would be inconsistent with his earlier conclusion in respect of mistaken gifts; second, that any other result would be inconsistent with the law relating to transfers on express trust which later fail; third, that the situation is covered by *Barclays Bank Ltd v Quistclose Investments Ltd*; and fourth, that the situation is covered by *Sinclair v Brougham*. I have argued that Professor Birks is wrong in his analysis both of mistaken gifts and payments made for a consideration which later fails.

In the case of mistaken gifts, my objection turns on the implication of a resulting trust in the teeth of evidence which shows that the donee was not intended by the parties to hold on trust for the donor. In the end, it boils down to a debate as to the type of evidence which will rebut the presumption of resulting trust in the case of a gratuitous transfer outside any relationship of advancement. For Professor Birks, only one type of evidence will do, *viz.* evidence of a positive intention to give. My argument has been that the presumed intention resulting trust which arises in the case of a gratuitous transfer is a presumption of actual intent and therefore any evidence that the parties

---

4 [1974] Ch 269; reversed on appeal ([1974] 3 WLR 256) but on grounds not affecting the analysis of resulting trusts.

intended something other than a transfer on trust will suffice. Evidence of a mistaken intent to give will therefore rebut the presumption of resulting trust in such a case.

If that is right, there would then be no inconsistency between mistaken gifts and failures of consideration. Professor Birks's first reason for finding a resulting trust where property is transferred on a basis which later fails would therefore fall away. As to the other three justifications, the authorities on transfers on express trusts which later fail were shown to be weak. *Quistclose* was shown to be confined to the specific area of fraudulent preferences in bankruptcy and laid down no principle of general application, and *Sinclair v Brougham* was no authority at all, since the question whether property passed was conceded by counsel in the House of Lords and not raised in the courts below.

The article then went on to discuss the implications of Professor Birks's thesis. It put forward three reasons why it must be treated with caution. First, it would elevate most restitutionary plaintiffs from mere claimants *in personam* at law to claimants *in rem* in equity. The essential point which should be borne in mind throughout is the far-reaching effect of Birks's thesis. Although applied by him to two specific areas, mistaken gifts and failures of consideration, if correct it would apply across virtually the whole spectrum of autonomous unjust enrichment. The second reason for caution was that it would destroy much of the substance of the present law since it has no room for the fine-tuning which currently takes place. It can, for example, draw no distinction between the types of pressure or mistake which should or should not give rise to a restitutionary claim. This leads on to the third and final reason for caution. If correct, Professor Birks's thesis would introduce a novel ground of claim, no consideration, and, as the example of the fully executed void contract shows, give restitution to a totally undeserving plaintiff. And at the same time, it would propel us into a system similar to that which prevails in civilian systems, which Professor Birks himself deprecates, where the focus is on the 'absence of juristic cause' for an enrichment rather than a 'down to earth' enquiry into the reasons for restitution. The argument is that this conclusion can and should be resisted and that the presumed intention resulting trust has little or no role to play in the English law of restitution.

- ## R Chambers, 'Tracing and Unjust Enrichment' in *Understanding Unjust Enrichment* (eds J Neyers, M McInnes, S Pitel, 2004), 263, 286–7.

It can be difficult to tell when a claimant is entitled to restitution of the actual enrichment, either instead of or in addition to a right to restitution of its value. . . . I believe there are two requirements for every property right to restitution of the unjust enrichment itself.

First, the enrichment must be an asset which is capable of being the subject matter of a property right. . . .

Secondly, if the enrichment consists of an asset that can be transferred to the claimant, property restitution is possible but will not be permitted if the defendant acquires full beneficial ownership of that asset before the right to restitution arises. In almost all of the cases in which the claimant had a property right to an unjust enrichment, that right arose immediately when an asset was transferred to the defendant. The defendant was unjustly enriched by receipt of that asset, possibly because it was transferred by mistake,[1] under duress,[2] or in response to undue influence.[3] The defendant may have obtained the asset by taking advantage of some factor which affected the claimant's ability to make decisions.[4] In some cases, the claimants were completely unaware of the unauthorised transfer of their assets to the defendants.[5] Also, resulting trusts can arise when it is proved or presumed that a

---

1 *Blacklocks v JB Developments (Godalming) Ltd* [1982] Ch 183.
2 *Barton v Armstrong* [1976] AC 104 (PC).   3 *Barclays Bank plc v O'Brien* [1994] 1 AC 180 (HL).
4 *Louth v Diprose* (1992) 175 CLR 621 (HCA).
5 *Malory Enterprises Ltd v Cheshire Homes (UK) Ltd* [2002] Ch 216 (CA).

transfer was not intended as a gift.[6] In some of these cases, a trust arose at the outset, returning beneficial ownership to the claimant immediately. In others, the claimant immediately acquired a power to recover beneficial ownership of the asset ... At no time did the defendant acquire unfettered beneficial ownership of the asset, free of the claimant's right to recover it.

NOTES

1. The above extract is a succinct summary of the Chambers thesis developed in *Resulting Trusts* (1997). See further R Chambers, 'Resulting Trusts' in *Mapping the Law: Essays in Memory of Peter Birks* (eds A Burrows and Lord Rodger, 2006), 247–64.

2. The Chambers thesis was endorsed by Birks, *Unjust Enrichment* (2nd edn, 2005), 181–2: '[T]he best interpretation of the English cases is that they should be divided between those in which there is no moment in which the enrichment is held free of any claim, and those in which for however short a time the enrichee holds the enrichment freely at his own disposition. This distinction almost exactly corresponds with the line between initial and subsequent failure of basis. In the former case, where the enrichment is never freely at the enrichee's disposition, there is always a proprietary response alongside the common or garden right *in personam*. In the latter case, where the value in question has been freely at the disposition of the defendant before the basis of the enrichment fails, there is no proprietary response'.

• E Sherwin, 'Constructive Trusts in Bankruptcy' (1989) *U of Illinois LR* 297

[A] constructive trust claim is supported by the restitutionary equation of loss and gain and by a tracing exercise that tends to show that the assets available for creditors have been increased at the claimant's expense. Still, these two elements do not fully explain the constructive trust claimant's priority over general creditors, because they do not distinguish her claim from the restitutionary claims of contract creditors. When a contract creditor has rendered performance to the debtor without payment, there is a corresponding gain and loss, and the contract creditor may be able to trace the benefit of her performance to specific assets. But the contract creditor generally is not entitled to priority by means of a constructive trust.

The final element in favor of the constructive trust claim, which separates it from ordinary contract claims, is that the claimant did not extend credit voluntarily to the debtor. At least in the simple case of conversion, the constructive trust claimant did not choose to deal with the debtor, and so did not voluntarily assume the risk of the debtor's insolvency. Further, unlike contract creditors, the constructive trust claimant had no opportunity to demand compensation for the risk of insolvency in the form of price or interest, or protection by means of collateral.

Under the present system of priorities in bankruptcy, the claimant's position as an involuntary creditor is not enough, in itself, to place her ahead of other creditors. Some writers, citing reasons of both fairness and efficiency, have proposed that tort creditors and others who did not bargain in a meaningful way for the risk of insolvency should have a special priority in bank-ruptcy. Neither state nor federal collection law, however, has made a general distinction in favor of involuntary creditors. A tort claimant who has suffered a loss but has no restitutionary claim to assets of the debtor is treated as a general creditor, even though she did not consent to be hit by the debtor's car.

Nevertheless, the involuntary nature of a constructive trust claim is a circumstance to be considered in combination with the others identified above. Unlike a contract creditor, the claimant did not agree to a risk of loss; and unlike an ordinary tort creditor, her loss corresponds to a gain she can locate among the debtor's assets. These elements together are the basis of the constructive trust claimant's priority over general creditors.

---

6 *Hodgson v Marks* [1971] Ch 892 (CA).

On the other hand, the characterization of a constructive trust claimant as an involuntary creditor does not hold true in all cases. When the basis of the claim shifts from theft to fraud or fiduciary misconduct or abuse of confidence, the distance between the constructive trust claimant and a voluntary contract creditor narrows. . . .

[To summarise,] it is wrong to begin analysis of a constructive trust claim in bankruptcy, as bankruptcy courts often do, with the assumption that the claimant is entitled to priority as the equitable owner of the property she claims. The claimant does not own the property unless the court grants the remedy. If the court places her ahead of general creditors, it must be because general creditors would be unjustly enriched by sharing in the property.

In a contest between the constructive trust claimant and other creditors, the claim of unjust enrichment depends on three facts: (1) the debtor obtained an unjust gain at the claimant's expense; (2) the claimant can identify the gain among the assets claimed by creditors; and (3) the claimant did not voluntarily extend credit to the debtor. These three elements of a constructive trust claim provide the basis for priority in bankruptcy. Deterrence is an important reason for constructive trusts outside bankruptcy, but it must be set aside when the claimant is competing for the property with other creditors. Occasionally, utility and other property concepts may weigh in favor of specific restitution, but they do not support a general assumption that the law should treat a constructive trust claimant as the owner of property traceable to her claim.

Whenever courts impose constructive trusts in bankruptcy, they will increase the costs of unsecured credit and interfere with the compensatory policies that support other involuntary claims. Further, proper application of the constructive trust remedy in bankruptcy, with reference to unjust enrichment of creditors, could involve the bankruptcy estate in difficult and costly litigation. Perhaps the reasons in favor of a constructive trust do not justify this added expense in any case. The answer depends on how much weight one gives to the 'rudimentary psychology' suggested by Professor Dawson: the intuition that a loss reflected in another's gain is doubly felt and should be corrected.

The intent of the present discussion is not to prove conclusively that a constructive trust claim should have priority over the claims of other creditors. The point is that the reasons identified above in support of constructive trust claims are the only justifications for priority. Equitable ownership justifies nothing, because it means nothing. Deterrence may be a justification for tracing remedies between the claimant and the defendant but not between the claimant and other creditors.

- **D Paciocco, 'The Remedial Constructive Trust: A Principled Basis for Priorities over Creditors'** (1989) 68 *Can BR* 315

We set out here the conclusion of this article.

There will be many cases where a plaintiff establishes a cause of action based upon the formula of unjust enrichment but where it will be unjust to remedy a breach of his rights with a remedial constructive trust order. The priority which the remedial constructive trust will give to a plaintiff over the unpaid general creditors of the defendant is warranted only where the plaintiff has a higher claim in equity to the specific property sought to be impressed with the constructive trust than do the general creditors of the constructive trustee. Where that priority is warranted, it should not be denied because of equitable principles culled from the historical recesses of equitable jurisdiction.

In general terms, before a claimant should be awarded a proprietary remedy there must be a causal connection or nexus between the plaintiff and the property. Yet, this alone is not enough. What distinguishes the meritorious constructive trust beneficiary from the general creditors of the defendant is that the general creditors can be taken to have accepted the risk of the defendant's insolvency in their dealings with him, while the constructive trust beneficiary cannot.

For a variety of compelling reasons, these considerations should produce a different approach in cases involving the division of spousal property than that used in purely commercial relationships.

NECESSARY CONDITION #1: THE CAUSAL CONNECTION REQUIREMENT

In spousal division of property cases, social policy reasons and the absence of a tradition of formalized property sharing arrangements have inspired a loose, but nonetheless important causal connection requirement. Before constructive trust relief is appropriate a court must be satisfied that the actions of the plaintiff spouse have contributed to the acquisition, maintenance or improvement of specific property, whether or not the specific property would have been acquired, maintained or improved in the absence of that contribution.

In commercial cases, the property, or, by the application of conventional tracing techniques, its proceeds, must be identifiable as the unjust enrichment of the defendant.

NECESSARY CONDITION #2: THE ABSENCE OF AN 'ACCEPTANCE OF RISK'

In spousal property division cases proprietary relief is justified because of the usual, implicit understanding that the plaintiff spouse has contributed money or money's worth in the reasonable expectation that, in return, he or she is contributing to the fruits of a partnership and that the partnership involves the joint benefit of acquisitions. Absent firm evidence that the contributing spouse did not have such expectations, constructive trust relief should be awarded.

In commercial cases proprietary relief will not be warranted where the plaintiff parted with the property or money which represents the defendant's enrichment, while accepting the role of a general creditor. This will occur where there is a valid contract between the parties which accounts for the defendant's enrichment, or a contract which has been avoided where the condition which rendered the contract ineffective does not vitiate the voluntariness of the plaintiff's decision to assume the role of a general creditor. This will also occur where the claim is quasi-contractual in nature and the plaintiff does not have a reasonable expectation that payment will be in the form of specific property.

MISCELLANEOUS CONSIDERATIONS

The wrongdoing of the defendant should be irrelevant to the provision of constructive trust relief to a plaintiff, but the wrongdoing or negligence of the plaintiff may be relevant where it has prejudiced third parties or the general creditors of the defendant.

At least in cases where the defendant is insolvent, constructive trust relief should attach only to so much of the unjust enrichment of the defendant as represents an actual deprivation to the plaintiff. Beyond the degree of his actual loss, the plaintiff has no higher claim to the defendant's profits than do the defendant's general creditors.

- • A Burrows, 'The English Law of Restitution: A Ten-Year Review' in *Understanding Unjust Enrichment* (eds J Neyers, M McInnes, S Pitel, 2004), 11, 24–7

The central question that we need to answer is when proprietary restitution, rather than the usual personal restitution, is, or should be, awarded to reverse unjust enrichment. One can now articulate two main views on this issue. The first, championed most notably by Virgo in *The Principles of the Law of Restitution*, is that proprietary restitution can never be awarded to reverse unjust enrichment. In Virgo's view, unjust enrichment has no role to play in explaining, for example, equitable proprietary remedies imposed after tracing or the conferment of secured rights through non-contractual subrogation. Just as someone whose bicycle has been stolen retains title to the bicycle and can recover it or its value from whoever has it without reference to the law of unjust enrichment, so too equitable proprietary remedies after tracing are concerned with the vindication of the claimant's proprietary rights. Unjust enrichment is not in play, and, logically, just as change of position is not a defence to a claim for delivery up or damages for conversion, so too it is not a defence to equitable proprietary remedies imposed after tracing. At a higher level of generality, the Virgo view sees unjust enrichment as purely being part of the law of obligations and as having no role within the law of property.

The counter-view, put forward by, for example, Birks and Chambers, is that the Virgo view is too simplistic and narrow. Proprietary rights *are* sometimes created to reverse unjust enrichment. The difficulty is not so much whether proprietary restitution exists to reverse unjust enrichment but rather in articulating a coherent theory as to when this is so. On this view, equitable proprietary remedies after tracing, for example, are significantly different from the recovery of one's stolen bicycle. They are significantly different precisely because a new proprietary right is created in the substitute traced asset that did not previously exist. The best explanation of that new proprietary right is that it is created to reverse the defendant's unjust enrichment at the claimant's expense. Like any other restitution reversing unjust enrichment, that proprietary restitution is subject to a defence of change of position.

. . .

A further aspect of the Birks and Chambers approach to proprietary restitution is their attempted articulation of a coherent theory as to *when* the cause of action of unjust enrichment triggers proprietary restitution, as well as the more usual personal restitution. According to their view, wherever an unjust enrichment at the claimant's expense triggers personal restitution, so too it should trigger proprietary restitution provided two additional conditions are satisfied. These conditions are: (i) the enrichment subtracted from the claimant exists, if necessary by applying tracing rules, in an asset to which the proprietary right can attach; and (ii) the injustice arose at the moment of the defendant's receipt, rather than subsequently, so that there was never a period of time when the defendant was entitled to the enrichment. Applying this approach, mistake, duress and undue influence, for example, should and do all trigger proprietary restitution, whether through a trust or a power to revest title by rescission. On the other hand, failure of consideration, which concerns a subsequent injustice, does not and should not trigger proprietary restitution.[1] So, according to Birks and Chambers, *Re Goldcorp*[2] and *Westdeutsche Landesbank*[3] were correct in denying proprietary restitution through a resulting or constructive trust precisely because the injustice was subsequent only: the ground for restitution was failure of consideration.

I essentially agree with Birks and Chambers' theory, although I do think it helps to add that, as a matter of policy, a good reason why one would not want to allow proprietary restitution for a subsequent failure of consideration is because, at least normally, this is the classic situation where we would say that the payor has taken the risk of the payee's insolvency. Allowing proprietary restitution would therefore unacceptably undermine our law of insolvency. So if a debtor fails to repay a loan to a creditor, the creditor is not, and should not be, entitled to proprietary restitution for failure of consideration even if the debtor retains the loaned money or its traceable substitute. The creditor is an unsecured creditor and has taken the risk of the debtor's insolvency. To allow the creditor proprietary restitution would eliminate the distinction between secured and unsecured creditors.

QUESTION

Do you agree with Sherwin, Paciocco, and Burrows that, in deciding whether *proprietary* restitution is justified, a relevant factor (along with others) is whether the claimant has taken the risk of the defendant's insolvency?

---

1 Unless the payment was 'ring-fenced' so that the defendant was not free to use it, as in *Barclays Bank Ltd v Quistclose Investments Ltd* [1970] AC 567.

2 [1995] 1 AC 74.   3 [1996] AC 669.

14

DEFENCES

In recent years defences have begun to play an increasingly important role in unjust enrichment claims. Until recently the courts kept liability within acceptable bounds by restricting the grounds on which a claim for unjust enrichment might be brought: thus, for example, until 1999, mistake of law was not a ground for restitution (see above, 167–187); mistakes of fact which generate a restitutionary claim were, until the 1980s confined to liability mistakes (see above, 147–162); and the courts still formally refuse to accept that a partial failure of consideration can constitute a ground for restitution, insisting that the failure must be *total* before a claim can arise (see above, 257–279). But in the more modern authorities the old restrictions on liability are being cast off. Cases such as *Lipkin Gorman v Karpnale Ltd* (see above, 28) and *Woolwich Equitable Building Society v Inland Revenue Commissioners* (see above, 626), exhibit a more expansionist approach to the scope of the law of restitution. And the wider the scope of the unjust factors, the greater is the role for the defences in keeping liability in check.

The clearest sign of this approach can be found in the judgment of Lord Goff in *Lipkin Gorman* when he said (see above, 35–39) that one beneficial effect of the recognition of the defence of change of position was that 'it will enable a more generous approach to be taken to the recognition of the right to restitution, in the knowledge that the defence is, in appropriate cases, available'. Yet there are problems with this approach because it is not clear that the defences are ready to play the role which has been allocated to them. In particular, the case law on change of position has developed without a clear rationale and there is a danger that some of the defences, particularly change of position, will degenerate into an unprincipled exercise of discretion. For reasons of space we have been unable to deal with the complex defences of *res judicata* and compromise or with the defence of limitation to claims for unjust enrichment (on which see Burrows, 542–52, H McLean, 'Limitation of Actions in Restitution' [1989] *CLJ* 472; J Edelman, 'Limitation Periods and the Theory of Unjust Enrichment' (2005) 68 *MLR* 848). We also do not deal in this chapter with what Goff and Jones describe as the defence of good consideration (see chapter 41). There is a view that such a defence is no different from change of position, as Waller LJ suggested in *Lloyds Bank plc v Independent Insurance Co. Ltd* (2000) QB 110, 127 (above, 164). Another view is that it is concerned with the proper claimant to bring the action (an issue concerning 'at the expense of', see above, 109). On either of these views, it may not be an independent defence (cf. J Edelman and E Bant, *Unjust Enrichment in Australia* (2006), chapter 15).

We should also emphasize that we are here concerned only with defences to the cause of action of unjust enrichment. We are not directly concerned with restitution for wrongs albeit that, in looking at the scope of change of position, it is convenient in this chapter to consider whether that defence applies to claims for restitution based upon a wrong (we think not). Defences to claims for wrongdoing essentially apply to all money remedies for the wrong (whether restitution or not) and are fully treated in the defences chapters of books dealing with torts, breach of contract, and equitable wrongs.

Before embarking upon a study of the leading cases, some profit may be gained by pausing to ask ourselves some questions which can then be kept in mind when reading the extracts from the cases.

1. How do the defences relate to the cause of action of unjust enrichment? It may be possible to link the defences up to the three principal stages of the restitutionary claim. Thus some defences (of which change of position may be an example) may go to the enrichment aspect of the claim so that the defendant is arguing, in effect, that as a result of his change of position he is no longer enriched. Or a defence may relate to the 'at the expense of' stage of the inquiry, as for example where the defendant argues that he was not enriched at the expense of the claimant because the claimant has passed on the loss which it suffered to a third party. Or, finally, the defence may go to the 'unjust' stage of the inquiry where the defendant argues that, in the light of some supervening event, it can no longer be regarded as 'just' to order him to restore the benefit to the claimant.

2. What is the scope of the defence of change of position? This is one of the most pressing problems in the defences. The defence was recognized for the first time by the House of Lords in *Lipkin Gorman*, but despite several important recent decisions its scope remains shrouded in uncertainty. Given the central importance of this defence, this is not a satisfactory position.

3. What is the relationship, if any, between the defences? A number of questions arise here. One is the effect of the recognition of change of position on existing defences. For example, there are suggestions in recent cases that estoppel will wither away now that change of position has been recognized. But are the defences based upon different principles? Are defences such as change of position, *bona fide* purchase, and payment over by an agent part of the same family or are they based upon different principles?

4. Are the defences really able to perform the role which has been given to them? Two doubts emerge here. The first relates to the uncertainty which surrounds the defences. Given the degree of doubt which exists, can they provide reliable tools for use by the judiciary? The second doubt is whether, on any view, the defences can keep liability within acceptable bounds. Mistake of law might provide a good example (on which, see above, 167–187). Can it be argued that it would have been a better way to keep liability within acceptable bounds by retaining the rule that mistake of law does not generate a claim in unjust enrichment?

General Reading

BURROWS, chapter 15 and 597–608; GOFF AND JONES, chapters 39–43; VIRGO, Part VI.

1. CHANGE OF POSITION

English law was slow to recognize the existence of a defence of change of position and, indeed, it was not until the decision of the House of Lords in *Lipkin Gorman v Karpnale Ltd.* (above, 28) that the step of recognizing the existence of the defence was taken. But the House of Lords has stated that the defence is to be developed on a case-by-case basis and so much work remains to be done in terms of establishing the basis and the scope of the defence. Thus our consideration of the defence is divided into two parts. The first is devoted to the recognition and basis of the defence and focuses on *Lipkin* itself. The second part considers the scope and application of the defence. It draws upon the decisions since

Lipkin Gorman, to consider the difficult issues that have arisen in relation to the basis and scope of the defence. Eight issues can be identified: (1) Does change of position require reliance by the defendant upon the receipt? (2) How much evidence is required? (3) Do changes of position which anticipate an enrichment count? (4) What is the relevance of fault to the defence? (5) Can a defendant change her position by purchasing something valuable which she still retains? (6) Does change of position apply to claims for propri-etary restitution? (7) Does change of position apply to claims where restitution or com-pensation is sought for a wrong? And when we consider the defence of estoppel we will also consider (8) What is the relationship between change of position and estoppel? Although all of these questions have been raised in cases subsequent to *Lipkin Gorman*, the answer to most of these questions remains unclear. Very useful discussions of these issues and many of the cases set out below are G Virgo, 'Change of Position: The Import-ance of Being Principled' [2005] *RLR* 34 and C Mitchell, 'Change of Position: the devel-oping law' [2005] *LMCLQ* 168.

(1) THE RECOGNITION AND BASIS OF CHANGE OF POSITION

- **Lipkin Gorman v Karpnale Ltd** [1991] 2 AC 548, House of Lords

See above, 28–39 and the discussion of the defence of change of position in the speeches of Lords Bridge, Templeman, and Goff.

NOTES AND QUESTIONS

1. Lord Goff said that the defence was 'likely to be available only on comparatively rare occasions' and that 'the recognition of change of position as a defence . . . will enable a more generous approach to be taken to the recognition of the right to restitution, in the knowledge that the defence is, in appropriate cases, available'. Can these statements be reconciled?

2. Lord Templeman (whose reasoning on the application of change of position to the facts was adopted by Lord Bridge) did not talk expressly in terms of a defence of change of position. Instead, he said that the claimant must show that 'the defendant was unjustly enriched *and remained unjustly enriched*' (emphasis added). Can these issues be resolved at the enrichment level of the inquiry without having to resort to the defence of change of position (see also note 1 at 762 above)? Echoing Lord Goff's statement (note 1 above), Birks' initial view of the rationale for change of position was that it 'is merely the necessary price of a more sensitive reconciliation between the demand for restitution and the interest in the security of receipts' (P Birks, 'Change of Position and Surviving Enrichment' in W Swadling (ed), *The Limits of Restitutionary Claims* (1997)). On this view, a relevant change of position would include not merely disenriching changes of position such as money spent on a party but also changes of position that do not directly affect the defendant's wealth (such as a decision to divorce). However, in the following extract from *Unjust Enrichment* (2005), Birks treated the rationale of change of position as both disenrichment and the security of receipts and suggested that non-disenriching changes of position must be treated as a different unjust-related defence. He said (at 208–9):

- **P Birks, *Unjust Enrichment* (2nd edn, 2005), 208–9**

1. DISENRICHMENT AND CHANGE OF POSITION

In *Lipkin Gorman v Karpnale Ltd* the House of Lords introduced, or revived, the defence of change of position. To the extent that restitution would no longer be equitable because of changed circumstances, the defendant must be relieved from liability.[1] This broad language, on its face, extends far beyond the single fact of disenrichment. Yet all known examples can be covered by a much narrower formulation in which the defence would be confined to disenrichment. The narrower formulation would be on the following lines. Unless the defendant is disqualified from the defence, his liability in unjust enrichment is extinguished to the extent that, by reason of an event which would not have happened but for the enrichment, his wealth is reduced.

It must be regarded as doubtful whether any non-disenriching changes of position will ever be found to give rise to a defence distinct from all the other unjust-related defences. There are two reasons. One is that it is part and parcel of the peculiar normativity of extant enrichment that it is difficult to come up with any argument for retaining a misplaced enrichment which one still has. The other is that such good arguments as can be found will probably turn out to be covered by a nominate unjust-related defence, as *res judicata* covers previous litigation and limitation covers delay. Nevertheless, recent dicta in the Court of Appeal in *Commerzbank AG v Gareth Price-Jones*[2] vigorously reject the suggestion that the broad defence should be cut down to disenrichment. The safe tactic is to divide the wide defence in two, between disenrichment and non-disenriching change of position. The latter, if it has any content, must clearly be an unjust-related defence. It will be revisited in the next chapter.

2. RATIONALE

The rationale of the defence of disenrichment can itself be divided into two. First, the defence draws a necessary line around the typically strict liability in unjust enrichment. That strict liability, triggered by relatively weak facts, is at first sight counter-intuitive, even repulsive. But we have seen that no other regime can be satisfactory in the business of relocating extant gains. The defence ensures that the defendant, unless disqualified, will be strictly liable only to the extent that his assets remain swollen. Only a recipient who is disqualified will remain liable despite disenrichment, but for him the liability will not be strict, since on all views disqualification supposes fault on the part of the recipient. Secondly, in the same breath the defence reconciles the interest in obtaining restitution of unjust enrichment with the competing interest in the security of receipts. There is a general interest in our being free to dispose of wealth which appears to be at our disposition. The defence avoids the need to sterilize funds against the danger of unsuspected unjust enrichment claims.

A consequential benefit, now that the defence is securely in place, is that it is not necessary to maintain the old restrictive posture in relation to the cause of action. The fragility of claims in unjust enrichment takes care of the fear of too much restitution. There is a price to pay. Deserving claimants will sometimes be defeated. The existence of the defence means that the claimants bear the ultimate risk of loss. Their plight must not narrow the interpretation of the defence. We cannot have the cake and eat it.

NOTE

The approach of Birks contrasts with that of Munby J in *Commerzbank AG v Gareth Price-Jones* [2004] 1 P & CR DG 15; [2003] EWCA Civ 1663 (below, 773). Although

---

1 [1991] 2 AC 548, 579–80 (HL); cf. *Restatement of the Law of Restitution* (American Law Institute St Paul Minn 1937) s. 142. The defence was already foreshadowed in *Moses v Macferlan*: 'This is equally beneficial to the defendant. It is the most favourable way in which he can be sued: he can be liable no further than the money he has received; and against that, may go into every equitable defence, upon the general issue; he may claim every equitable allowance; . . . in short, he may defend himself by every thing which shews that the plaintiff, ex aequo & bono, is not intitled to the whole of his demand, or to any part of it' (1760) 2 Burr 1005, 1010, 97 ER 676, 681.

2 [2003] EWCA Civ 1663, [65]–[66], [71]–[72] (Munby J).

Munby J considered that change of position should be a discretionary defence which is not constrained by 'black letter' law, he suggested that it should apply to non-pecuniary changes of position such as a decision to divorce. However, in support of Birks' approach is the statement by Potter LJ in *National Westminster Bank plc v Somer International (UK) Ltd* [2001] EWCA Civ 970; [2002] QB 1286 [47] (below, 814) that the defence of change of position 'only protects the actual reduction of the transferee's assets following receipt'.

(2) THE SCOPE AND APPLICATION OF CHANGE OF POSITION

We have seen that although Lord Goff identified a rationale for change of position as allowing a more generous approach to be taken to the primary claim (because the defence protects the security of receipts) it is unclear whether this is the exclusive rationale or whether change of position is also motivated by a rationale of disenrichment. In the cases which have considered the defence of change of position since *Lipkin Gorman*, eight central issues have arisen concerning the scope and application of the defence. Each of these questions is considered below, and we will see that the answer to most of the questions remains unclear. Much will depend upon what is ultimately identified as the rationale(s) underlying the defence.

(i) DOES CHANGE OF POSITION REQUIRE RELIANCE BY THE DEFENDANT UPON THE RECEIPT?

Writing after the decision in *Lipkin Gorman*, Burrows identified two possible versions of the change of position defence. The narrow version was like estoppel but with the representation struck out. In other words, it requires that the recipient has acted to his detriment on the faith of his receipt. The broad version does not require detrimental reliance, merely a causal link between the receipt and the change of position. Burrows later explained the difference between the two versions with the example of 'a defendant who is paid £100,000 by the mistake of his bank (perhaps even negligently) which is immediately stolen' (Burrows, 516). He argued that this result was 'grotesque', because the bank 'started the chain of events by first making the mistaken payment'. The broad view was adopted, obiter dicta, in the following case.

- *Scottish Equitable plc v Derby*
  [2001] EWCA Civ 369; [2001] 3 All ER 818, Court of Appeal

Upon being made redundant, Mr Derby made an investment of £90,000 in a single-premium pension policy with Scottish Equitable. Subsequently, in 1990, he exercised an option under the policy to take early retirement benefits. In 1995, Mr Derby received a print-out statement showing that his policy had a value of £201,938. The statement mistakenly ignored Mr Derby's retirement benefits. The correct amount was £29,486. Mr Derby exercised a payment option which resulted in an overpayment to him of £172,451. He used £41,671 to reduce (by two thirds) the mortgage on his home and spent £9,662 making modest improvements to his family's style of life. The remainder was paid to the Norwich Union which paid him a pension based on the sum advanced. In 1996 Scottish Equitable realized its mistake and brought proceedings for restitution of the overpayment. Norwich Union agreed to unwind the policy so that Mr Derby would receive the smaller pension to which he would have been entitled. Mr Derby relied on the defences of change of position and estoppel (which we will consider below, 804). The trial judge held that the change of position defence applied only to £9,662, and the Court of Appeal dismissed the appeal. The Court of Appeal held that the defence as to £9,662 did not fail merely because Mr Derby could not produce any detailed accounting for it. It failed because payment of his mortgage would have to have been made sooner or later and it was therefore not a change of position.

Robert Walker LJ:. . .[*After explaining that the carelessness of Scottish Equitable did not prevent its claim for restitution of its mistaken payment, continued*] . . .

Change of position

[26] The facts of the *Lipkin Gorman* case, in which the House of Lords recognised the defence of change of position, are well known. The gaming club had received large sums of money misappropriated by a solicitor who was addicted to gambling, but it had changed its position by paying out on his winning bets. Lord Goff (with whose speech Lord Bridge of Harwich, Lord Griffiths and Lord Ackner agreed) noted that in the past, where change of position had been relied by the defendant, it had been usual to treat the problem as one of estoppel (as in, for instance, the *R E Jones Ltd* case and *Avon CC v Howlett* [1983] 1 All ER 1073, [1983] 1 WLR 605).

[27] There were two main objections to that sort of approach. First, estoppel required there to have been a representation made by one party on which the other had placed reliance and had acted to his detriment: but in many cases involving a dishonest third party (such as the *Lipkin Gorman* case itself) the true owner had done nothing that could possibly be regarded as the making of a representation. (The *R E Jones Ltd* case was another case involving a fraudster, a confidence man whose plan might have been frustrated by an unexpected contact between the two innocent parties; the House of Lords were divided as to whether that equivocal contact amounted to a representation.) Second, estoppel was (as this court had held in the *Avon CC* case, a case to which it will be necessary to return) an inflexible all-or-nothing defence. Lord Goff observed ([1992] 4 All ER 512 at 533, [1991] 2 AC 548 at 579): 'Considerations such as these provide a strong indication that, in many cases, estoppel is not an appropriate concept to deal with the problem.'

[28] Lord Goff went on:

'In these circumstances, it is right that we should ask ourselves: why do we feel that it would be unjust to allow restitution in cases such as these? The answer must be that, where an innocent defendant's position is so changed that he will suffer an injustice if called upon to repay or to repay in full, the injustice of requiring him so to repay outweighs the injustice of denying the plaintiff restitution. If the plaintiff pays money to the defendant under a mistake of fact, and the defendant then, acting in good faith, pays the money or part of it to charity, it is unjust to require the defendant to make restitution to the extent that he has so changed his position.'

He noted the general acceptance of the defence in other common law jurisdictions (his citations could now be supplemented by reference to the decision of the High Court of Australia in *David Securities Pty. Ltd v Commonwealth Bank of Australia* (1992) 175 CLR 353).

[29] Lord Goff said:

'I am most anxious that, in recognising this defence to actions of restitution, nothing should be said at this stage to inhibit the development of the defence on a case by case basis, in the usual way . . . At present I do not wish to state the principle any less broadly than this: that the defence is available to a person whose position has so changed that it would be inequitable in all the circumstances to require him to make restitution, or alternatively to make restitution in full. I wish to stress, however, that the mere fact that the defendant has spent the money, in whole or in part, does not of itself render it inequitable that he should be called upon to repay, because the expenditure might in any event have been incurred by him in the ordinary course of things. I fear that the mistaken assumption that mere expenditure of money may be regarded as amounting to a change of position for present purposes has led in the past to opposition by some to recognition of a defence which in fact is likely to be available only on comparatively rare occasions. In this connection I have particularly in mind the speech of Lord Simonds in *Ministry of Health v Simpson* [1950] 2 All ER 1137 at 1147, [1951] AC 251 at 276.' (See [1992] 4 All ER 512 at 534, [1991] 2 AC 548 at 580.)

[30] The judge noted the view, put forward by Andrew Burrows (*The Law of Restitution* (1993) pp 425–428) that there is a narrow and a wide version of the defence of change of position, and that the wide view is to be preferred. The narrow view treats the defence as 'the same as estoppel minus the representation' (so that detrimental reliance is still a necessary ingredient). The wide view looks to a change of position, causally linked to the mistaken receipt, which makes it inequitable for the recipient to be required to make restitution. In many cases either test produces the same result, but the wide view extends protection to (for instance) an innocent recipient of a payment which is later stolen from him (see *Goff and Jones* p 822, also favouring the wide view).

[31] In this court Mr Stephen Moriarty QC (appearing with Mr Richard Handyside for Scottish Equitable) did not argue against the correctness of the wide view, provided that the need for a sufficient causal link is clearly recognised. The fact that the recipient may have suffered some misfortune (such as a breakdown in his health, or the loss of his job) is not a defence unless the misfortune is causally linked (at least on a 'but for' test) with the mistaken receipt. In my view Mr Moriarty was right to make that concession. Taking a wide view of the scope of the defence facilitates 'a more generous approach . . . to the recognition of the right to restitution' (Lord Goff in the *Lipkin Gorman* case [1992] 4 All ER 512 at 534, [1991] 2 AC 548 at 581; and compare Lord Goff's observations in *Kleinwort Benson Ltd v Lincoln City Council* [1998] 4 All ER 513 at 541, [1999] 2 AC 349 at 385).

[32] The criticisms of the judgment made by Mr Bernard Weatherill QC (appearing with Mr Paul Emerson for Mr Derby) were directed, not so much to the principles of law enunciated by the judge, as to the way in which he applied those principles to the facts as he found them. Before considering those criticisms in detail I think it may be useful to note that when a person receives a mistaken overpayment there are, even on the narrow view as to the scope of the defence, a variety of conscious decisions which may be made by the recipient in reliance on the overpayment. Some are simply decisions about expenditure of the receipt: the payee may decide to spend it on an asset which maintains its value, or on luxury goods with little second-hand value, or on a world cruise. He may use it to pay off debts. He may give it away. Or he may make some decision which involves no immediate expenditure, but is nevertheless causally linked to the receipt. Voluntarily giving up his job, at an age when it would not be easy to get new employment, is the most obvious example. Entering into a long-term financial commitment (such as taking a flat at a high rent on a ten-year lease which would not be easy to dispose of) would be another example. The wide view adds further possibilities which do not depend on deliberate choices by the recipient.

[33] Mr Weatherill criticised the judge for looking simply at particular items of expenditure (the £9,662 which was conceded, the sum used to pay off the mortgage and the sum paid to the Norwich Union) and for paying insufficient attention to Mr Derby's decision to slow down his work, and his omission to take alternative steps to provide for the future of himself and his family. I would readily accept that the defence is not limited (as it is, apparently, in Canada and some states of the United States: see *David Securities Pty. Ltd v Commonwealth Bank of Australia* (1992) 175 CLR 353 at 385, noted in *Goff and Jones* p 819) to specific identifiable items of expenditure. I would also accept that it may be right for the court not to apply too demanding a standard of proof when an honest defendant says that he has spent on overpayment by improving his lifestyle, but cannot produce any detailed accounting: see the observations of Jonathan Parker J in *Philip Collins Ltd v Davis* [2000] 3 All ER 808

at 827, with which I respectfully agree. The defendants in that case were professional musicians with a propensity to overspend their income, and Jonathan Parker J took a broad approach (at 830).

[34] In the present case, however, the judge made some clear findings of fact, set out in [13] above, to the effect that the improvements which Mr Derby was able to make in his family's lifestyle, between June 1995 and October 1996, were very modest and not irreversible, and that there was nothing that he could usefully have done to make provision for the future. Mr Weatherill has submitted that that seriously understates the devastating effect which the demand for repayment has had on Mr Derby, with his annual income after tax being reduced at a stroke from a sum of the order of £20,000 to a sum of the order of £12,000 (these figures do not include Mrs Derby's earned income). It is easy to accept that Scottish Equitable's demand for repayment must have come as a bitter disappointment to Mr Derby, and it is impossible not to feel sympathy for him, beset as he now is by financial problems, matrimonial problems and health problems. But the court must proceed on the basis of principle, not sympathy, in order that the defence of change of position should not (as *Burrows* puts it at p 426) 'disintegrate into a case by case discretionary analysis of the justice of individual facts, far removed from principle'. Mr Weatherill took the court to various passages in the transcript of Mr Derby's oral evidence but I am not persuaded that the judge erred in his findings of fact or that he failed to take advantage of seeing and hearing the witnesses.

[35] Mr Weatherill submitted that the payment-off of the mortgage was a change of position, but I cannot accept that submission. In general it is not a detriment to pay off a debt which will have to be paid off sooner or later: *RBC Dominion Securities Inc. v Dawson* (1994) 111 DLR (4th) 230. It might be if there were a long-term loan on advantageous terms, but it was not suggested that that was the case here; and as the judge said ([2000] 3 All ER 793 at 803) the evidence was that the house was to be sold in the near future.

[36] In relation to the Norwich Union policy it was argued below that Mrs Derby had certain rights or claims because of the impending divorce, and this argument is put forward again in para. 16 of the grounds of appeal and in oral argument. I found this argument rather surprising since it appears from the terms of the policy that Mrs Derby is named as a payee in respect of a reversionary annuity of £6,760 a year but that her right to the annuity ceases on divorce (although Mrs Derby may be able to take advantage of the new pension-sharing arrangements introduced by the Welfare Reform and Pensions Act 1999). However, it was only by reference to the impending divorce that Mr Weatherill attacked the judge's conclusion (at 798) that Mrs Derby's rights were no impediment to the unwinding of the policy to which Norwich Union is prepared to agree. Her potential rights on divorce do not depend on her having a power to veto the unwinding of the policy, nor do they have the effect of conferring such a power on her. They do not in my view assist Mr Derby's argument on change of position.

[37] For these reasons the judge was in my view correct to accept the defence of change of position only in relation to the sum of £9,662.

Keene LJ agreed and **Simon Brown LJ** also agreed in a short concurring judgment.

NOTES AND QUESTIONS

1. In adopting the wide view, Robert Walker LJ stressed that a sufficient causal link is still required. Misfortune, such as a breakdown in health or loss of a job, is not sufficient unless it is causally linked to the enrichment. Robert Walker LJ referred to the 'but for' test as the minimum causal connection. This 'but for' test is another way of explaining the requirement that expenditure that would have been made in any event (e.g. the weekly groceries or, as in *Scottish Equitable*, a debt which would have had to be paid off sooner or later) is not a relevant change of position. The same approach has been adopted by the Supreme Court of Canada (see *Regional Municipality of Storthoaks v Mobil Oil Canada Ltd* (1975) 55 DLR (3d) 1 where proof of expenditure of overpaid royalties was insufficient to establish change of position).

2. The strength of the case for the wide view may also depend upon the availability of proprietary restitution, particularly in claims consequent upon tracing (see below Chapter 13). Suppose A mistakenly pays money to B, who innocently invests it, making five-fold profits. If (as the law currently stands) A is entitled to the profits then there is a strong case for the wide view that has the effect that A bears any loss if, for example, the money is stolen from B.

3. In *Scottish Equitable*, several other issues are considered by the Court of Appeal: the relationship between change of position and estoppel and the level of evidence required to prove the defence. The relationship between change of position and estoppel will be considered when we turn to the defence of estoppel (below, 811–822) and the level of evidence required to satisfy the defence is considered next.

(ii) HOW MUCH EVIDENCE IS REQUIRED?

The next issue concerns the difficulty faced by defendants who claim that their change in position arises as the result of a general change in lifestyle or for some reason in which it would not usually be expected that they could produce receipts or precise details of the change in position.

- *Philip Collins Ltd v Davis* [2000] 3 All ER 808, Chancery Division

The claimant company, Philip Collins Ltd, was entitled to the services of the singer Phil Collins. As part of Phil Collins' world tour, the company engaged the services of professional backup musicians which included the two defendants. Clause 5.01 of the agreements with the backup musicians provided that they were entitled to royalties at a specified rate if live recordings were released for sale to the public which 'include an identifiable performance by artist'. For seven years the company paid the two defendants royalties on a live album sold to the public without any deduction for the fact that the defendants had performed on only five of the 15 tracks. The trial judge held that the true construction of clause 5.01 was that the defendants should only have been paid a pro-rated royalty for the number of tracks on which they had performed. By defence, the defendants argued that the company was estopped from denying their entitlement and that they had changed their position. The trial judge rejected the estoppel argument, finding that there had been no representation and that, in any event, estoppel is no longer apt where change of position is available. However, the defendants' change of position defence succeeded despite serious adverse findings by the trial judge about their credibility and despite a finding that the change of position had only been in relation to a 'vague and unspecific' alteration to their lifestyle.

Jonathan Parker J: . . .

As Mr Howe correctly observed in the course of argument, 'change of position' is what this case is really all about . . .

. . . Thus, if recovery of the overpayments is to be denied in the instant case, it must be denied not as a matter of discretion but of legal principle. What, then, are the relevant legal principles, in the context of the instant case?

For obvious reasons, it would not be appropriate for me to attempt to set out an exhaustive list of the legal principles applicable to the defence of change of position, but four principles in particular seem to me to be called into play in the instant case.

In the first place, the evidential burden is on the defendant to make good the defence of change of position. However, in applying this principle it seems to me that the court should beware of applying too strict a standard. Depending on the circumstances, it may well be unrealistic to expect a defendant to produce conclusive evidence of change of position, given that when he changed his position he can have had no expectation that he might thereafter have to prove that he did so, and the reason why he did so, in a court of law (see the observations of Slade LJ in *Avon CC v Howlett* [1983] 1 All ER 1073 at 1085–1086, [1983] 1 WLR 605 at 621–622, and Goff and Jones at p 827). In the second place, as Lord Goff stressed in the passage from his speech in the *Lipkin Gorman* case quoted above, to amount to a change of position there must be something more than mere expenditure of the money sought to be recovered, 'because the expenditure might in any event have been incurred . . . in the ordinary course of things'. In the third place, there must be a causal link between the change of position and the overpayment. In *South Tyneside Metropolitan BC v Svenska International plc* [1995] 1 All ER 545, Clarke J, following Hobhouse J in *Kleinwort Benson Ltd v South Tyneside Metropolitan BC* [1994] 4 All ER 972, held that, as a general principle, the change of position must have occurred after receipt of the overpayment, although in Goff & Jones the correctness of this decision is doubted (see pp 822–3). But whether or not a change of position may be anticipatory, it must (as I see it) have been made as a consequence of the receipt of, or (it may be) the prospect of receiving, the money sought to be recovered: in other words it must, on the evidence, be referable in some way to the payment of that money. In the fourth place, as Lord Goff also made clear in his speech in the *Lipkin Gorman* case, in contrast to the defence of estoppel the defence of change of position is not an 'all or nothing' defence: it is available only to the extent that the change of position renders recovery unjust.

With those basic principles in mind, I turn to the facts of the instant case.

At the outset, when considering the facts of the instant case, two matters are to be borne in mind. In the first place, the recovery which is sought relates only to the *excess* payments of royalty, since one-third of the sums actually paid was payable in any event. In consequence, any relevant change of position by the defendants must be referable to the receipt of such excess payments (or, it may be, the prospect of receiving such excess payments). In the second place, the fact that the defendants are currently in financial difficulties is not in itself indicative of a relevant change of position on their part. Although that fact might have been relevant in considering whether to order repayment of the sums overpaid, the claimant is not seeking an order which requires the defendants to make any payment to the claimant: as I explained earlier, it seeks only to set off the overpayments against future royalties.

In their witness statements, which formed the basis of their oral evidence-in-chief, the defendants addressed the issue of change of position in unequivocal terms. Mr Davis said this in his witness statement:

'Until the royalty payments were stopped, I had adjusted my day to day life according to the regular payments I had received over such a long period, and had become both accustomed to and dependent upon them. I had a few savings. However, with many different projects underway including a clothing business and my solo career, these were soon exhausted. I had relied on the royalties both for my living expenses and to enable me to carry on working. My elderly mother in Chicago and three dependants as well as my household in Los Angeles had all been supported with these payments. I could no longer financially assist them – indeed, I have had to borrow money from family and friends. Most of this remains unpaid . . . The unannounced withholding of funds has had a domino effect upon my life since most of my projects were predicated on the existence of these royalties.'

Mr Satterfield said this in his witness statement:

'I was heavily reliant upon these royalty payments. Over the period until they were stopped, I would estimate that on average they represented 80–90 per cent of my total income. I had, and have, no savings, and the money was used for the day to day living expenses of my family and myself. In particular, the payments were invaluable in assisting my wife with medical treatment . . . I sold my home in Chicago to assist with the care she required . . . The cutting of the royalty payments could not have come at a worse time. In addition, the stopping of the payments dramatically affected my ability to work. There was still a reasonable demand for me. However, the nature of my work involves a great deal of travel, hotels, etc. There were engagements offered to me which I had to decline because I had no money. The effect is a vicious circle . . .'

Had those factual accounts been true and accurate, they would undoubtedly have provided a strong foundation for a complete defence on grounds of change of position; particularly so in the case of Mr Davis. No doubt the statements were drafted with that very consideration in mind. In the event, however, the passages in the defendants' witness statements dealing with the question of change of position turned out to be seriously exaggerated. I do not entirely blame the defendants for this. It may well be that they did not sufficiently appreciate the need for precision in the framing of their witness statements. But whatever the reason, the fact remains that the defendants' oral evidence, coupled with such documentary evidence as they were able to produce relating to their financial affairs (I referred earlier to the fact that documents were disclosed on a piecemeal basis during the course of the trial), not only failed to approach the degree of particularity reflected in their witness statements, but actually demonstrated that statements of fact made in the passages quoted above were not true.

Thus, Mr Davis expressly accepted in cross-examination that there was no such 'domino effect' as is referred to in his witness statement. He also accepted that he was not 'dependent on' the royalty income. He frankly admitted that there is not, nor has there ever been, any reason why he cannot earn his living as a musician. It was also clear from his evidence that to the extent that he had not taken other jobs as a musician while the royalties were coming in, that was his choice. He acknowledged that at no stage did he have any savings to speak of, and that his present financial difficulties were due to some bad business decisions on his part. He was unable to point to any particular decision having been taken, or act done, whether by him or on his behalf, as being directly referable to the fact that he was in receipt of royalties calculated on a non-pro-rated basis. Rather, the true position (as revealed in cross-examination) was that he geared his expenditure to the level of his cash resources from time to time: he was content to enjoy the benefits of the royalty payments as and when they came in, and his outgoings increased accordingly. He was (as I find) fully aware at all material times that royalty income from a particular release tends to reduce over time to nil or a negligible sum. Consequently, he realised that his royalty income from the live album would not be maintained at the level of the payments received during the first year or so after its release. On the other hand, that realisation did not lead him to limit his outgoings to any significant extent.

So far as Mr Satterfield is concerned, I intend no criticism whatever of him when I describe him as having a somewhat relaxed and philosophical attitude to life in general, and in particular to financial and administrative matters. Like Mr Davis, Mr Satterfield accepted that there is nothing to prevent him continuing to earn his living as a musician, but, as he put it disarmingly in cross-examination, he earns money when he feels like it. He accepted that the assertion in his witness statement that he cannot work because he cannot afford the up-front hotel and travel costs is an overstatement. Further, it was apparent from his evidence, and I find, that such assets as he and his wife acquired post-1990 (including a number of properties in Chicago which his wife purchased with a view to refurbishment and letting) were not acquired in reliance on a future royalty stream but were purchased ad hoc, as and when they considered that they could afford it. At the conclusion of his cross-examination Mr Satterfield described his current financial position as follows (according to my note):

'I have no money left from my earnings. My lifestyle is hard to explain; you would not believe it. When I got the money in I spent it rather than saved it. A lot of the things I spent it on I am involved in now. I spent it for other people. I have done this throughout my career.'

In general, whilst it would plainly not be accurate to describe the defendants as having been careful with their money, I am satisfied that in gauging how much they could spend from time to time they had regard to their current cash resources, the principal source of which (at least in the first two years after the release of the live album) was their royalty income.

On the basis of the defendants' oral evidence, coupled with such documentary evidence as they were able to produce, I am unable to find that any particular item of expenditure was directly referable to the overpayments of royalties. Their evidence was simply too vague and unspecific to justify such a finding. On the other hand, in the particular circumstances of the instant case the absence of such a finding is not, in my judgment, fatal to the defence of the change of position. Given that the approach of the defendants to their respective financial affairs was, essentially, to gear their outgoings to their income from time to time (usually, it would seem, spending somewhat more than they received), and bearing in mind that the instant case involves not a single overpayment but a series of overpayments at periodic intervals over some six years, it is in my judgment open to the court to find, and I do find, that the overpayments caused a general change of position by the defendants in that they increased their level of outgoing by reference to the sums so paid. In particular, the fact that in the instant case the overpayments took the form of a series of periodical payments over an extended period seems to me to be significant in the context of a defence of change of position, in that it places the defendants in a stronger position to establish a general change of position such as I have described, consequent upon such overpayments.

Nor, on the evidence, can the defendants' increased level of expenditure be regarded as consisting exclusively of expenditure which (to use Lord Goff's words) 'might in any event have been incurred in the ordinary course of things'. I am satisfied that had the defendants been paid the correct sums by way of royalties their levels of expenditure would have been lower.

I accordingly conclude that each of the defendants has changed his position in consequence of the overpayments. The question then arises whether the defendants can rely on their change of position as a defence to the entirety of the claim, or only to some (and if so what) part of it.

In my judgment, the defence of change of position which I have found to be established cannot extend to the entirety of the claim, if only because had the correct amount of royalties been paid the defendants' level of outgoings might not have reduced proportionately. The defendants' propensity to overspend their income means that it is impossible to establish an exact correlation between their income and their outgoings.

So how far does the defence of change of position extend? I accept Mr Howe's submission that, on the particular facts of the instant case, the court should adopt a broad approach to this question; if only because, for reasons already given, the defendants' evidence as to their financial affairs does not admit of detailed analysis.

In all the circumstances as I have found them, I conclude that the defence of change of position extends to one-half of the overpayments: in other words, that (subject to the limitation issue) the claimant's recovery should be limited to $US 172,575.61 and £14,685.12. In my judgment that represents, on the evidence, a conservative assessment of extent to which the overpayments led to a change of position on the part of the defendants.

It is, however, to be observed that limiting the claim to half the overpayments will almost certainly have no practical effect, since on the evidence it is highly improbable, to put it no higher, that the defendants' future royalty entitlement from sales of the live album will amount to anything approaching that sum.

NOTES AND QUESTIONS

1. The same lenient approach to the evidence required of a claimant to prove that he has changed his position was taken in *Scottish Equitable v Derby* (above, 765). In that case Robert Walker LJ referred to *Phillip Collins Ltd* and said of the concession that Mr Derby had changed his position in relation to the £9,662 by modest improvements to his lifestyle: 'I would also accept that it may be right for the court not to apply too demanding a standard of proof when an

honest defendant says that he has spent an overpayment by improving his lifestyle, but cannot produce any detailed accounting'.

2. If it is right to take a lenient approach to the evidence required for changes of position relating to lifestyle, should such a lenient approach have been taken in this case where the trial judge had found that the defendants had 'seriously exaggerated' in their witness statements and made statements of fact that were not true?

3. In the following case, a stricter approach to the evidence required for change of position seems to have been taken.

- **Commerzbank AG v Gareth Price-Jones**
  [2004] 1 P & CR DG 15; [2003] EWCA Civ 1663, Court of Appeal

Mr Price-Jones worked as an investment banker for the claimant investment bank from April 2000 until November 2001 when he was made redundant. His initial written contract provided for guaranteed minimum annual bonuses of £250,000 for the years ended 31 December 2000 and 2001 (the performance years 2000 and 2001). On 29 June 2000 Mr Price Jones received a letter from the bank informing him that, in respect of the 2000 performance year he would receive a bonus of £265,000. On 15 December 2000 the bank paid Mr Price-Jones £250,000, and in March 2001, the bank paid him £265,000. The bank claimed that the first payment was a mistake because, in its letter of 29 June 2000 it had promised an increase in bonus of £15,000. Mr Price-Jones argued that the proper construction of the letter of 29 June 2000 was that he was promised an additional £265,000. The trial judge found that on the proper construction of the letter of 29 June 2000 the bank was obliged to make both payments. The Court of Appeal disagreed and held that the letter of 29 June 2000 only promised an increase in bonus of £15,000. However, Mr Price-Jones also argued that even if he was not entitled to both the payments, he had changed his position by staying at the bank after receiving the letter of 29 June 2000 and foregoing a good chance of obtaining similar employment elsewhere. The trial judge held that this was a relevant change of position notwithstanding that there was no actual reduction in Mr Price-Jones' assets. The Court of Appeal rejected this finding and held that Mr Price-Jones had not changed his position

Mummery LJ: [*After outlining the facts and trial judge's decision*] . . .

THREE POINTS DISCUSSED

A. CHRONOLOGY

36. The first point is chronological. The change of position proposed by Mr Price-Jones occurred *before* the overpayment of £250,000 was received by him on 15 December 2000. In general and in practice a relevant change of position is more likely to occur *after* receipt of the overpayment. For example, a person receives payment in good faith and then spends it, gives it away, or loses it. Depending on the particular circumstances it can be said that the recipient has, to borrow the expression used by Professor Birks and Professor Burrows, suffered disenrichment, so as to make it inequitable to require restitution.

37. In this case the change of position pleaded by Mr Price-Jones was his decision not to move from the Bank. His decision was made after the letter of 29 June 2000, but before he received the £250,000 in December 2000. He made the decision in the mistaken belief that he would be entitled to receive two guaranteed bonuses totalling £515,000 for the performance year 2000. The additional lock-in payment of £265,000 sent him a signal that he was a valued employee. If, however, he would only be entitled to an additional bonus of £15,000 paid three months later than was originally agreed, that would have sent a signal to him from the Bank that he was not well regarded and so he would not have stayed.

38. In my judgment, the mere reversal of the normal order of events does not affect the availability of the defence. As was held by the Judicial Committee of the Privy Council in the Dextra Bank case at p.204, the question whether it would be inequitable to require restitution can arise in cases of 'anticipatory reliance' where a recipient of an overpayment has already changed his position in good faith in the expectation of receiving a future benefit.

B. CHANGE

39. The second point is whether there was, on the findings of fact made by the Deputy Judge, any relevant disenrichment or change of position on the part of Mr Price-Jones. It was for him to establish that, in all the circumstances, it would be inequitable to require him to make restitution. The obvious cases occur where there has been a reduction in the assets of the recipient of the overpayment. In those cases he must prove that there has been a reduction of assets, although it is unnecessary for him to produce precise financial calculations quantifying the amount of the reduction. Lord Goff did not, however, restrict the scope of the defence to cases in which there has been a reduction of assets. The defence would also be available, in my view, in various employment situations in which the recipient has made a relevant change of position as a result of the mistaken payment to him: for example, by giving up his current job to lead a life of leisure in circumstances where it would be difficult to find another job, or by turning down a firm offer of a better paid job.

40. In my judgment, however, it is not inequitable to require Mr Price-Jones in his circumstances to make restitution to the Bank of the full amount of the overpayment. There has been no disenrichment. He has still got the money. He has not spent it, given it away, or lost it. The fact that, but for his expectation of a very large additional bonus, he would have decided to seek similar employment elsewhere is not sufficiently significant, precise or substantial in extent to be treated as a change of his position, which would make full restitution inequitable. Even though the Deputy Judge found that he had a 'very good chance of obtaining similar employment elsewhere', his decision not to seek such employment falls outside the scope of the defence

C. CAUSATION

41. On the facts of this case the defence runs into difficulties on another front. According to the cases the defence is not available to Mr Price-Jones unless he can show that there is a sufficient 'casual link' between the change of position by him and the actual or anticipated payment under a mistake.

42. Mr Price-Jones' case was that, but for his expectation of an additional bonus of £265,000 under the letter of 29 June, he would not have remained at the Bank and would have taken steps to seek employment with another investment bank. A bonus package of the kind intended by the Bank would have sent him a signal that he was not well regarded and so he would not have stayed. In those respects, it was contended, there was sufficient causal link entitling him to succeed in his defence.

43. There was discussion during oral argument about the approach to causation in cases of change of position. In my judgment, it is neither necessary nor desirable to carry across to the issue whether it is inequitable to require restitution and to impose on it all the mass of learning on causation questions generated by the cases on the recoverability of damages for tort. Change of position is based on a principle of justice. It is a broad defence to a claim for restitution, which is itself based on a broad principle of unjust enrichment. In deciding whether the particular circumstances render it inequitable to require the recipient of an overpayment to make full restitution, the need for a sufficient causal link should not be narrowly applied. The important point is that there should be a relevant connection between the change of position and the actual or anticipated payment. As was said by Jonathan Parker J in the Philip Collins case at p. 827 the change of position must in some way be 'referable to' the actual or anticipated payment of money by which the recipient is enriched.

44. On the facts of this case there was no relevant connection between Mr Price-Jones's decision to remain at the Bank and payment of the bonus actually promised by the Bank in the letter of 29 June

2000 for the performance year 2000. The true position is that Mr Price-Jones's decision to stay at the Bank was not connected with what the Bank actually promised to pay him. It was based on his erroneous belief, for which the Bank was not responsible, that he would in the future receive two guaranteed bonus payments for the performance year 2000 and on a belief that the bonus package, as intended by the Bank, would send him a signal that he was not well regarded by the Bank.

RESULT

45. To sum up, Mr Price-Jones was unjustly enriched. There can be no doubt about that. He received £250,000 to which he was not entitled. The payment was a mistake. He has still got the money. There is no obstacle to repaying it. He has not been disenriched. A just man would recognise that it was unjust to keep it and that he ought to repay it. He would not rely on his decision at the end of June 2000 to remain with the Bank as making it inequitable to repay. That decision did not have a significant, precise or substantial adverse impact on him nor was it connected in a relevant way with the payment actually promised by the Bank at that time. His decision did not stem from the actual payment of the bonus or from the actual promise of payment. It stemmed from his erroneous belief that the Bank was promising to make two very large minimum guaranteed bonus payments for one performance year and that, in the absence of the additional bonus, the Bank would have sent a signal that he was not well regarded. That belief and the circumstances in which he formed it do not make it inequitable to require him to repay the money. I would allow the appeal.

Sedley LJ agreed with **Mummery LJ**.

Munby J agreed with **Mummery LJ** and added: . . .

47. I agree with my Lord. I add some words of my own only because in one of its aspects this case raises important points of principle in relation to the still developing doctrine of change of position as a defence to a claim in restitution. I am emboldened to do so, in particular, because the very interesting arguments we have heard have tended at times to assume an approach as to how the law in this field should develop which I am not sure is either very helpful or indeed very desirable.

48. I start with a general point. Mr Hollander quite properly took us to Robert Walker LJ's endorsement in *Scottish Equitable plc v Derby* [2001] EWCA Civ 369, [2001] 3 All ER 818, at para [34], of the point made by Professor Burrows (see now *Burrows, The Law of Restitution* (ed 2, 2002) p 514) that the defence of change of position should not 'disintegrate into a case by case discretionary analysis of the justice of individual facts, far removed from principle'. In a field of law which has benefited more than most from much distinguished academic and other non-judicial writings it would be churlish not to acknowledge the huge debt we all owe to those whom Megarry J once described (*Cordell v Second Clanfield Properties Ltd* [1969] 2 Ch 9 at p 17A) as 'fertilisers of thought'. But if I may be permitted to say so, we need to be on our guard against over-refined analysis which may look all very well on the scholar's page but which may seem less convincing when exposed to 'the purifying ordeal of skilled argument on the specific facts of a contested case.' I agree entirely with Robert Walker LJ when he said that 'the court must proceed on the basis of principle, not sympathy'. But so long as we always keep the fundamental principles in mind this does not entail that we should allow ourselves to be beguiled into over subtle or over complicated attempts to refine or elaborate what is, after all, intended to be a broadly stated concept of practical justice. This is an area, it seems to me, in which technicality and black-letter law are to be avoided.

. . .

[after referring to the decisions in Lipkin Gorman, Munby J continued]

53. The focus of debate is accordingly to identify whether in the particular case it would in all the circumstances be an 'injustice' or 'inequitable' to require the overpaid recipient to make restitution of that which the payer is prima facie entitled to recover as of right. That is not, with all respect to those who might suggest otherwise, an exercise in judicial discretion. It is an exercise in judicial evaluation.

The judge is required to make a value judgment in the light of all the relevant circumstances. And there is nothing particularly difficult or unusual about this. It is an exercise of a type familiar in many different areas of both law and more particularly equity. The pages of *Snell's Equity* are replete with examples of situations where the essential question for the court is whether someone's conduct has been, or whether some outcome would be, equitable or inequitable.

54. Now there may be advantage in the courts identifying on a case by case basis matters which are *not* determinative of the question or identifying on a case by case basis matters which do *not* have to be established in order to make good the defence of change of position. An important and beneficial application of that approach can be seen in this court's acceptance in the *Scottish Equitable* case at paras [30]–[32] of the 'wide' in preference to the 'narrow' version of the defence (as to which see *Burrows* at pp 513–516). I respectfully agree that the wide version is to be preferred. The consequence is that, as a matter of law, the defence of change of position is *not* dependent upon proof of some representation by the payer, nor is it dependent upon proof of any detrimental reliance on the part of the payee. There will, no doubt, be certain factual circumstances where absent proof of detrimental reliance it will be unlikely, or perhaps even impossible, for the defence to be made out. But that is a long way from saying, and there is in law no warrant at all for saying, that proof of detrimental reliance is a prerequisite to making good a defence of change of position. Another example of this same approach can be seen in the rejection in the *Dextra Bank* case at para [45] of the concept of 'relative fault' in this branch of the law. In this context, as the Privy Council pointed out, good faith on the part of the recipient is sufficient.

55. What, though, is much more questionable, however tempting the exercise may seem, is to seek to define, in more qualified or restrictive terms than those used by Lord Goff, the requirements which, so it may be said, have to be established if the defence is to be made good. And there is, if I may say so, particular danger in seeking to elevate into general principles of law what are in truth no more than the particular factors which, in the particular circumstances of a specific case, have been judicially identified as more or less significant in leading to the conclusion that the defence in that case either is or is not made out.

56. We need, if I may say so, always to bear in mind that, at the end of the day, the simple question that has to be asked in every case, and in the final analysis it is the only potentially determinative question that ever has to be asked, is this: Has the position of the payee so changed that it would be inequitable in all the circumstances to require him to make restitution, or alternatively to make restitution in full? That is the test formulated by Lord Goff in the *Lipkin Gorman* case and reaffirmed by Lords Bingham and Goff in the *Dextra Bank* case. There is, in my judgment, no need to gloss or refine it. Indeed any attempt to do so is likely to be not merely unnecessary but fraught with potential difficulty.

57. This takes me to the first of the four specific points that I wish to make. It relates to the question of causation.

58. Our attention was drawn to the statement by Jonathan Parker J in *Philip Collins Ltd v Davis* [2000] 3 All ER 808 at p 827f that 'there must be a casual link between the change of position and the overpayment.' And some emphasis was placed on the fact that in the *Scottish Equitable* case Robert Walker LJ referred no fewer than three times (at paras [30]–[32]) to the need to show a sufficient casual link. I have no particular difficulty with the general principle that some such kind of causal link has to be shown, though I note that there is no reference to any such requirement in Lord Goff's statement of principle. But I should be very concerned to see this translated into a dogmatic legal rule, let alone into a legal analysis of the principles of causation of the kind that already bedevils too many areas of the common law or into a theoretical debate as to what particular test of cause and effect is appropriate or what particular kind of causal link has to be established.

59. For my own part I much prefer the way in which Jonathan Parker J put it in the *Philip Collins* case when, at p 827h, he said that the 'change of position . . . must, on the evidence, be referable in

some way to the payment of [the] money.' This is an approach familiar to any equity lawyer. It is the approach which we see in relation to the maxim that 'he who comes into equity must come with clean hands', where what has to be shown is misconduct which has 'an immediate and necessary relation to the equity sued for': see *Snell's Equity* (ed 30) para. 3–15 citing Eyre LCB in *Dering v Earl of Winchelsea* (1787) 1 Cox Eq 318 at p 319. And it is the approach which we see in the requirement of the doctrine of part performance that the acts of part performance relied upon must be 'referable' to the contract sued on: see *Snell* at para. 40–38 referring to the classic statement of principle by Lord Selborne LC in *Maddison v Alderson* (1883) 8 App Cas 467 at p 479. As my Lord has said (and the phrase captures the same essential concept) the important point is that there should be a relevant connection between the change of position and the actual or anticipated payment.

60. My second point relates to the much debated question of whether an anticipatory change of position can be a good defence to a restitutionary claim. In *South Tyneside Metropolitan BC v Svenska International plc* [1995] 1 All ER 545, Clarke J, following Hobhouse J in *Kleinwort Benson Ltd v South Tyneside Metropolitan BC* [1994] 4 All ER 972, said at p 565e that

'save perhaps in exceptional circumstances, the defence of change of position is in principle con- fined to changes which take place after receipt of the money . . . It does not however follow that the defence of change of position can never succeed where the alleged change occurs before the receipt of the money.'

Following on from this, Jonathan Parker J suggested in the *Philip Collins* case at p 827g that

'whether or not a change of position may be anticipatory, it must . . . have been made as a con- sequence of the receipt of, or (it may be) the prospect of receiving, the money sought to be recovered.'

61. Now with all respect this might be thought not to be particularly clear. And Clarke J's reference to 'exceptional circumstances' is potentially an invitation to the over-analytical to develop what is surely an entirely unnecessary jurisprudence of what can or cannot be an exceptional circumstance—a jurisprudence which, if allowed to flourish, would likely serve only to distract attention away from the true question identified by Lord Goff.

62. Clarke J's decision was criticised in *Goff & Jones, The Law of Restitution* (ed 5, 1998) pp 822–824, criticisms repeated in the following edition (ed 6, 2002) para. 40–004. By then, the Privy Council had decided the *Dextra Bank* case.

. . .

[after referring with approval to Dextra Bank *(below, 781) Munby J continued]*

65. My third point arises out of Mr Hollander's submission that there can be no change of position sufficient to found the defence in the absence of either *financial* detriment or, at the least, some detriment measurable in financial—by which I understood Mr Hollander really to mean *pecuniary*— terms. Perhaps not surprisingly, because in my judgment the point is completely unsound as a matter of principle, Mr Hollander was unable to point to any authority supportive of his submission. The passages in *Burrows* to which he directed our attention do not bear the weight of the argument any more than does the passage in Lord Goff's speech in the *Lipkin Gorman* case at p 580H to which he also directed our attention.

66. In the *Scottish Equitable* case, Robert Walker LJ at para [32] gave as 'the most obvious example' of the kind of decision made by a payee which, even though it involves no immediate expenditure, will nonetheless give rise to the defence of change of position, the voluntary giving up of a job at an age when it would not be easy to get new employment. Now if that decision can, as in appropriate circumstances it plainly can, give rise to the defence of change of position, why should not a decision for example to divorce? Can it really make any difference that in the first case it is possible to calculate the pecuniary cost to the payee of his decision to abandon his employment (that, after all, being the

kind of exercise conducted in personal injury and fatal accident cases every day of the week) whilst in the second case it may not be possible to measure in pecuniary terms the cost to the payee of his decision to divorce? Surely not. It is, in my judgment, a distinction without a difference. It is, as it seems to me, a distinction which lacks any justification when tested by reference to the 'broad approach based on practical justice' enshrined in Lord Goff's formulation of the principle. And it is, moreover, a distinction which is hardly consonant with the approach of equity in other more or less analogous situations.

67. Consider, for example, the kinds of detriment which have been held to give rise to a proprietary estoppel (see *Snell* at para. 39–14). Or consider, for example, *Sutton v Sutton* [1984] Ch 184, where a husband and his wife agreed that in consideration, *inter alia*, of the wife consenting to the husband divorcing her under section 1(2)(d) of the Matrimonial Causes Act 1973 (two years' separation and consent), he would transfer the matrimonial home to her. A decree absolute was made on the husband's petition but he refused to carry out his part of the bargain. It was held (at p 193C) that the wife's consenting to the divorce as agreed was an act of part performance, being an act referable to the contract. As the judge put it, 'her consent to the petition was in itself, in the circumstances, tied to the contract about the house'. The judge went on to say (at p 193F) that the husband 'stood by and let her perform that part of her bargain irretrievably, and that raised an equity' in her favour.

68. Thus the approach of equity. But consider the facts which I recently had to consider, albeit in a wholly different legal context, in *X v X (Y and Z intervening)* [2002] 1 FLR 508: an agreement under which the quid pro quo for the payment of a sum of money was a husband's agreement not to defend his wife's petition for divorce grounded on his behaviour (even though he believed that he had grounds for divorcing her for adultery) and his agreement also to give her a Jewish religious divorce—a get. Now if, as Robert Walker LJ tells us, giving up a job is capable of giving rise to the defence of change of position, then why should not the husband's actions in *X v X* equally be capable of giving rise to such a defence? And why should it make any difference that it is quite impossible to put any pecuniary value on what the husband did? For, as I remarked in *X v X* at paras [111]–[112]:

'[111] . . . A number of the factors in play are simply unquantifiable on any objective basis. How is a secular judge to evaluate the combination of the get and a decree based on the husband's conduct rather than the wife's adultery for a family apparently exercised by the possible religious and social ramifications? How am I to put a price on the cost to the husband of a divorce obtained by his wife against him on the ground of his behaviour rather than a divorce obtained by him on the ground of her adultery? . . .

[112] There are no means by which a secular judge, who may himself be an adherent of the same or a different faith or of no faith at all, can evaluate, let alone attribute some pecuniary value to, something as personal and of such religious significance as a get.'

69. As counsel submitted in that case, and I agreed, 'the husband has wholly fulfilled his side of the bargain and . . . it would be grotesquely unfair if the wife were able now to walk away with the two things she desired whilst wholly avoiding her obligations under the agreement.' True it is that the legal context in which I there had to consider the matter was wholly different from that with which we are here concerned, but surely it would be just as grotesquely unfair not to allow a husband to rely on such conduct were the question to arise in the context of an asserted defence of change of position.

70. I do not believe that anything I am saying is in any way inconsistent with anything Robert Walker LJ said in the *Scottish Equitable* case. But equally there is, in my judgment, no support to be found in that case for Mr Hollander's submissions. The point in *Scottish Equitable* at the end of the day was simply this: that if the circumstances do not otherwise justify a defence of change of position

it makes no difference that the demand for repayment will come as a bitter disappointment, or even as a devastating blow, to the payee.

71. My fourth and final point arises out of the assertions by *Fung & Ho, Change of Position and Estoppel* (2001) 117 LQR 14 at p 17 that:

'... the defence of change of position only protects *actual* reduction of the recipient's wealth. A recipient who acts upon a receipt (and representation) to forego a foreseeable and quantifiable opportunity to improve his wealth would not be protected. ... change of position seeks to undo the overpayment – and nothing more – by measuring the precise extent of the defendant's surviving enrichment ...'

That appears in what is in fact a case-note commenting on the decision at first instance in the *Scottish Equitable* case and thus ante-dates not merely the decision of this court in the *Scottish Equitable* case but also the decision of the Privy Council in the *Dextra Bank* case.

72. This article was mentioned in passing by Potter LJ giving the main judgment of this court in *National Westminster Bank plc v Somer International (UK) Ltd* [2001] EWCA Civ 970, [2002] QB 1286. At para [47] he said:

'... as pointed out by Fung and Ho ... "change of position" only protects actual reduction of the transferee's assets following receipt.'

It is to be noted that this observation, which I do not read as being any part of the ratio decidendi of the case, was made in the context not of a discussion of the defence of change of position but rather of a defence based on estoppel by representation. Moreover, as the editors of *Goff & Jones* bleakly comment at para. 40–013, 'The Lord Justice cites no authority for that statement, and we know of none.' In my judgment, and with all respect both to Potter LJ and to the learned authors he was citing, there is no authority for any of these propositions, and the assertions by Hung & Fo which I have quoted are not an accurate statement of the law.

73. So much for principle and law. I turn to the facts of the present case.

...

[after stating the facts, Munby J continued ...]

81. The Deputy Judge held that in these circumstances it would be inequitable to require the defendant to make restitution. With all respect to the Judge, as also to Mr Englehart's valiant attempts to persuade us that the Judge was correct, I profoundly disagree. Where is the justice, where is the equity, in allowing the defendant to retain, to the Bank's detriment, the fruits of what is simply his own mistake – and a mistake which, as I have said, was in no way caused or contributed to by the Bank? What is there in any way inequitable or unjust in the Bank seeking to recover its own money – and, as Lord Goff has pointed out, seeking to do so as a matter of right – when the only matter that can be prayed in aid in resisting that claim is the defendant's own mistake, a mistake which, to repeat, was not in any way caused or contributed to by the Bank and which, moreover, had nothing to do with anything either done or not done by the Bank? In my judgment, equity and justice are quite plainly in these circumstances on the side not of the defendant but rather of the Bank.

82. Mr Englehart says that Mr Hollander's argument is based on a fallacy, namely that the objective interpretation by the reasonable man which is used to answer the question as to what the letter means as a matter of construction has a part to play in assessing the merits of a defence of change of position to a restitution claim. With all respect to him I cannot accept Mr Englehart's submission. Why on earth, in an appropriate case, should Mr Hollander's point not have a part to play in assessing where the balance of justice and equity lies? And why on earth is this not precisely the kind of case where the point has a part – and, as it seems to me, a significant part – to play in striking the balance?

Mr Englehart further submits that Mr Hollander's approach is ruled out by the Privy Council's express condemnation in the *Dextra Bank* case of the concept of relative fault. I do not agree. I accept, as I have already said, that relative fault has no role to play in this branch of the law. But this does not mean that the court is required to blind itself to the fact, if fact it be, that someone seeking to make good the defence of change of position has only himself to blame for his predicament, having acted on a view which is not merely erroneous but which, moreover, fails to meet the standard of the reasonable man.

83. Mr Englehart submits that the inquiry here is simply whether or not the defendant bona fide believed that he was entitled to money he anticipated receiving and whether he changed his position in that belief. That, with respect to Mr Englehart, is not the relevant question. The relevant question is whether or not it is inequitable to deny the defendant a defence based on change of position when his decision to change his position was not in any way caused or contributed to by anything done or not done by the Bank but, on the contrary, was based entirely on his own erroneous understanding of what the Bank's letter meant. I can see nothing inequitable in denying the defendant such a defence. On the contrary, it would in my judgment be inequitable in the circumstances of this case to deny the Bank the right to recover its money.

84. I have not ignored the fact—and fact it is—that the Bank also made mistakes when it made the payments to the defendant on 15 December 2000 and 23 March 2001. The errors were thus not all on one side. But the Bank's errors, egregious though they may have been, are largely irrelevant for present purposes. For, as I have said, they long post-dated and therefore cannot have been operating on the defendant's mind at the time when, on his case, he changed his position.

85. Mr Hollander put forward various other arguments as to why, as he would have it, the defendant could not rely upon the defence of change of position. Those arguments were, in the final analysis, based upon propositions of law which, for the reasons I have already set out, I cannot accept. I say no more about his arguments. I should, however, make clear my agreement with Mr Englehart's submission that there is no material difference in substance in this kind of case between voluntarily giving up a job (the situation postulated by Robert Walker LJ in the *Scottish Equitable* case) and voluntarily choosing to stay in a job (what the defendant did here). Either may, in appropriate circumstances, suffice to found a defence of change of position; in other circumstances, neither may suffice. It all depends on the facts.

NOTES AND QUESTIONS

1. Mummery LJ accepted that in cases where there has been a reduction in the defendant's assets, it is unnecessary to prove precise financial calculations quantifying the amount of the reduction. But, on one view, the decision not to seek employment elsewhere after receipt of the 29 June 2000 letter reduced Mr Price-Jones' assets although by an unquantified amount. On the other hand, it might be said that unlike a case like *Philip Collins Ltd*, Mr Price-Jones had not even shown that his assets had been reduced (for example, by showing that it was likely that alternative employment would have been more lucrative) so the question of quantification was irrelevant.

2. Is it a harsh result that the defendants in *Philip Collins Ltd*, whose evidence was rejected in crucial respects by the trial judge, were allowed to rely on the defence despite absence of quantifiable evidence, but Mr Price-Jones, whose evidence was accepted by the trial judge, was not?

3. Do you agree with the suggestion by Mummery LJ that it is 'neither necessary nor desirable to carry across... all the mass of learning on causation questions generated by the cases on recoverability of damages for tort. Change of position is based on a principle of justice'? Surely, every legal rule is based on a principle of justice? Is the approach to causation advocated by Munby J, that the change of position be 'referable' to the payment of the money, any better?

4. Munby J (in his concurring judgment) suggested that in relation to all issues concerning change of position, 'technicality' and 'black letter law' are to be avoided and courts should adopt a discretionary assessment, case by case, into whether conduct is 'inequitable'. These comments were criticized by Virgo ([2005] *RLR* 34 at 36) who said that 'it was the fear that this defence would be too vague and unpredictable which was one of the main reasons why it had previously been rejected . . . If the defence is to succeed it must be interpreted by reference to principles rather than through the exercise of vague discretion'. Similarly, Burrows ([2004] *CLJ* 276, 280) has said that to accept 'without further articulation, that the change of position defence is simply a matter of whether the change means that it is inequitable or unconscionable or unjust to deny restitution would be to take us back to the dark ages of the subject'.

5. This case raises two other important issues for the scope of the change of position defence. First, both Mummery LJ and Munby J accepted, obiter dicta, that in the words of Mummery LJ 'the mere reversal of the normal order of events does not affect the availability of the defence.' The case they approved, which adopted this view was *Dextra Bank*, which is set out next. Second, their Lordships also seemed to suggest that the fault of the defendant was relevant to the defence. That issue is also considered below.

(iii) DO CHANGES OF POSITION WHICH ANTICIPATE AN ENRICHMENT COUNT?

In *Lipkin Gorman*, the defendants were entitled to bring into account the winnings which they had paid to Cass. Yet, in all probability, some of the winnings were paid to Cass *before* receiving some of the money that the claimants sought to recover. In *South Tyneside Metropolitan BC v Svenska International plc* [1995] 1 All ER 545, 566, Clarke J thought that *Lipkin Gorman* was an exceptional case in this regard, apparently because of 'Lord Goff's perception of the nature of gambling' and the fact that 'there was a series of transactions entered into by Cass at the casino'. He stated that the true rule was that 'save perhaps in exceptional circumstances, the defence of change of position is designed to protect a person who receives money in good faith and who *thereafter* changes his position in good faith so that it would be inequitable to require him to repay part or all of the money to its rightful owner' (emphasis added). This approach was confined to the facts of that case by the Privy Council in the following case.

- *Dextra Bank and Trust Co. Ltd v Bank of Jamaica*
  [2001] UKPC 50; [2002] 1 All ER (Comm) 193, Privy Council

The facts of this decision and the advice of the Privy Council (delivered by Lords Goff and Bingham) refusing Dextra's claim for mistake are set out above at 165. After refusing to allow the claim for mistake Lords Goff and Bingham turned to consider whether the Bank of Jamaica (BOJ) would have, in any event, had a defence of change of position.

Lords Goff and **Bingham** (delivering the advice of the Privy Council): . . . [34] Even so their Lordships propose to consider whether, against this background, the BOJ would, if necessary, have been able to rely on the defence of change of position. The submission of the BOJ has been that it would have been entitled to do so because the Dextra cheque was purchased by the BOJ's authorised agents on its behalf in good faith and the BOJ reimbursed their accounts in full, and that this rendered it inequitable for Dextra thereafter to recover the money so received by the BOJ as having been paid under a mistake of fact. Dextra has responded that the actions so relied on by the BOJ as constituting a change of position were performed by the BOJ before it received the benefit in question, and so amounted to what has been called 'anticipatory reliance' and as such could not amount to a change of position by the BOJ for the purposes of the law of restitution. Dextra's argument is that, for the act of the defendant to amount to a change of position, it must have been performed by the defendant in reliance on the plaintiff's payment, which cannot be the case if it was performed by him before he received the relevant benefit.

Anticipatory reliance

[35] The question whether anticipatory reliance of the kind just described can amount to an effective change of position has been much debated in the books. Their Lordships have studied the relevant material with interest and profit, and have also been much assisted by the arguments of counsel.

[36] Their Lordships start with the broad statement of principle by Lord Goff of Chieveley in *Lipkin Gorman (a firm) v Karpnale Ltd* [1992] 4 All ER 512 at 534, [1991] 2 AC 548 at 580 when he said:

'At present I do not wish to state the principle any less broadly than this: that the defence [of change of position] is available to a person whose position has so changed that it would be inequitable in all the circumstances to require him to make restitution, or alternatively to make restitution in full.'

Their Lordships add that, although the actual decision in that case does not provide any precise guidance on the question now under consideration, since it was based upon the peculiar nature of gaming transactions, nevertheless the Appellate Committee in that case appears to have adopted a broad approach based on practical justice and to have avoided technicality: see in particular [1992] 4 All ER 512 at 534–536, [1991] 2 AC 548 at 581–583 *per* Lord Goff.

[37] The response by the BOJ to Dextra's argument has been that it is no less inequitable to require a defendant to make restitution in full when he has bona fide changed his position in the expectation of receiving a benefit which he in fact receives than it is when he has done so after having received that benefit. Of course, in all these cases the defendant will ex hypothesi have received the benefit, because the context is an action by the plaintiff seeking restitution in respect of that benefit. For those who support the distinction, however, their reply appears to be that, whereas change of position on the faith of an actual receipt should be protected because of the importance of upholding the security of receipts, the same is not true of a change of position in reliance on an expected payment, which does not merit protection beyond that conferred by the law of contract (including promissory estoppel).

[38] Their Lordships confess that they find that reply unconvincing. Here what is in issue is the justice or injustice of enforcing a restitutionary claim in respect of a benefit conferred. In that context, it is difficult to see what relevant distinction can be drawn between (1) a case in which the defendant expends on some extraordinary expenditure all or part of a sum of money which he has received from the plaintiff, and (2) one in which the defendant incurs such expenditure in the expectation that he will receive the sum of money from the plaintiff, which he does in fact receive. Since ex hypothesi the defendant will in fact have received the expected payment, there is no question of the defendant using the defence of change of position to enforce, directly or indirectly, a claim to that money. It is surely no abuse of language to say, in the second case as in the first, that the defendant has incurred the expenditure in reliance on the plaintiff's payment or, as is sometimes said, on the faith of the payment. It is true that, in the second case, the defendant relied on the payment being made to him in the future (as well as relying on such payment, when made, being a valid payment); but, provided that his change of position was in good faith, it should provide, pro tanto at least, a good defence because it would be inequitable to require the defendant to make restitution, or to make restitution in full. In particular it does not, in their Lordships' opinion, assist to rationalise the defence of change of position as concerned to protect security of receipts and then to derive from that rationalisation a limitation on the defence. The defence should be regarded as founded on a principle of justice designed to protect the defendant from a claim to restitution in respect of a benefit received by him in circumstances in which it would be inequitable to pursue that claim, or to pursue it in full. In any

event, since (as previously stated) the context of a restitutionary action requires that the expected payment has in any event been received by the defendant, giving effect to 'anticipatory reliance' in that context will indeed operate to protect the security of an actual receipt.

[39] Before leaving this topic their Lordships think it right to refer to the decision of Clarke J in *South Tyneside Metropolitan BC v Svenska International plc* [1995] 1 All ER 545. There the defendant bank had entered into ultra vires swap transactions with the plaintiff local authority, but the bank had also entered into hedging transactions which would substantially cancel out its potential liability to the local authority under the swap transactions. In the result the local authority was the net payer under the void swap transactions, and claimed repayment of the money so paid by it. The bank was held liable to make restitution, but claimed to be entitled to set off the losses incurred by it under the hedging transactions on the ground that it had changed its position in good faith in reliance on the validity of the original swap contract by committing itself to the hedging transactions and by maintaining them thereafter. The local authority submitted that the bank should not be entitled to set off those losses, because it changed its position before receiving the payments in question. Clarke J's conclusion on this point was as follows (see 565):

'In my judgment in circumstances such as these the bank is not entitled to rely upon the underlying validity of the transaction either in support of a plea of estoppel or in support of a defence of change of position. That is because the transaction is ultra vires and void. It is for that reason that in a case of this kind, save perhaps in exceptional circumstances, the defence of change of position is in principle confined to changes which take place after receipt of the money. Otherwise the bank would in effect be relying upon the supposed validity of a void transaction . . . It does not however follow that the defence of change of position can never succeed where the alleged change occurs before the receipt of the money.'

It follows that the exclusion of anticipatory reliance in that case depended on the exceptional facts of the case; though it is right to record that the decision of Clarke J has been the subject of criticism—see, eg, Goff and Jones *The Law of Restitution* (5th edn, 1998) pp 823–824.

The relevance of fault to the defence of change of position

[40] It was a further submission of Dextra that, in cases in which the defendant invokes the defence of change of position, it is necessary to balance the respective faults of the two parties, because the object of the defence is to balance the equity of the party deprived with that of the party enriched.

[41] Their Lordships approach this submission as follows. First, they cannot help observing that the courts below appear to have formed the view that the fault of Dextra greatly outweighed the fault, if any, of the BOJ. If that is right, this submission will, if successful, do little to advance Dextra's case. Even so, their Lordships turn to consider the point as a matter of principle.

[42] They take as their starting point the statement of the law in the *Lipkin Gorman* case, where it was explained by Lord Goff that, for a defendant to be able to rely on his own conduct as giving rise to a change of position, he must have changed his position in good faith—see [1992] 4 All ER 512 at 533 and 534, [1991] 2 AC 548 at 579 and 580. No mention was made by him of the relevance of fault. On the other hand Lord Goff was careful to state (see [1992] 4 All ER 512 at 534, [1991] 2 AC 548 at 580) that 'nothing should be said at this stage to inhibit the development of the defence on a case by case basis, in the usual way', which left it open to the courts to consider matters such as the relevance of fault on a subsequent occasion. Their Lordships make the initial comment that, if fault is to be taken into account at all, it would surely be unjust to take into account the fault of one party (the defendant) but to ignore fault on the part of the other (the plaintiff). The question therefore is whether it should be relevant to take into account the relative fault of the two parties.

[43] In support of its submission, Dextra was able to invoke the law in two common law

jurisdictions. First, in the United States of America, the Restatement of Restitution provides, in para. 142(2), that:

'Change of circumstances may be a defense or a partial defense if the conduct of the recipient was not tortious and he was no more at fault for his receipt, retention or dealing with the subject matter than was the claimant.'

The Restatement of Restitution is a remarkable work, of which the reporters were two much respected jurists, Professor Warren A Seavey and Professor Austin W Scott. It was, however, a pioneering work, and much water has flowed under the bridge since its publication in 1937. In particular another much respected American expert in the law of restitution, Professor J P Dawson, was later to express his regret at the inclusion in para. 142(2) of the provision relating to relative fault: see (1981) 61 Boston UL Review 565 at 571 et seq, referred to by Professor Birks at p 41 of his account of 'Change of Position and Surviving Enrichment' in *The Limits of Restitutionary Claims: A Comparative Analysis* (1997) edited by William Swadling. Professor Dawson's comment on the relevant part of para. 142(2) of the restatement is as follows:

'The introduction of these complex themes would have been, I believe, a real disservice. Fortunately they have been disregarded in court decisions.'

[44] Second, in New Zealand a defence of change of position was introduced by statute, in s. 94B of the Judicature Act 1908, introduced into that statute in 1958. The statutory provision requires the court to have regard to all possible implications in respect of other persons when considering whether to deny relief, on the ground of change of position, in an action for the recovery of money paid under a mistake of law or fact. That provision was considered by the Court of Appeal of New Zealand in *Thomas v Houston Corbett & Co* [1969] NZLR 151, in which the court held that it was entitled to look at the equities from both sides (see 164, lines 13–14 *per* North P) and, taking a number of matters into account including, it appears, matters going beyond 'fault or neglect in the strict sense' on the part of the respondents (see 178, line 4 *per* McGregor J), held that the claim must be reduced. The quantum of the relief was treated as a matter of discretion on which opinions might differ (see 178, line 26, also *per* McGregor J). More recently, in *National Bank of New Zealand Ltd v Waitaki International Processing (NI) Ltd* [1999] 2 NZLR 211 (on which see the valuable note by Professor Grantham and Professor Rickett in [1999] RLR 158), the Court of Appeal of New Zealand has given further consideration to s. 94B. Following the decision of the Judicial Committee of the Privy Council in *Goss v Chilcott* [1997] 2 All ER 110, [1996] AC 788, the Court of Appeal concluded that s. 94B did not exclude the operation of the common law defence of change of position, but went on to conclude that the common law defence was, like the defence under s. 94B, an 'equitable' defence which required the court to undertake a 'balancing of the equities' by assessing the relative fault of the parties and apportioning the loss accordingly.

[45] Their Lordships are, however, most reluctant to recognise the propriety of introducing the concept of relative fault into this branch of the common law, and indeed decline to do so. They regard good faith on the part of the recipient as a sufficient requirement in this context. In forming this view, they are much influenced by the fact that, in actions for the recovery of money paid under a mistake of fact, which provide the usual context in which the defence of change of position is invoked, it has been well settled for over 150 years that the plaintiff may recover 'however careless [he] may have been, in omitting to use due diligence': see *Kelly v Solari* (1841) 9 M & W 54 at 59, [1835–42] All ER Rep 320 at 322 *per* Parke B. It seems very strange that, in such circumstances, the defendant should find his conduct examined to ascertain whether he had been negligent, and still more so that the plaintiff's conduct should likewise be examined for the purposes of assessing the relative fault of the parties. Their Lordships find themselves to be in agreement with Professor Peter Birks who, in his article already cited on 'Change of Position and Surviving Enrichment' at p 41, rejected the adoption

of the criterion of relative fault in forthright language. In particular he stated (citing *Thomas v Houston Corbett & Co* [1969] NZLR 151) that the New Zealand courts have shown how hopelessly unstable the defence (of change of position) becomes when it is used to reflect relative fault. Certainly, in the case of *Thomas*, the reader has the impression of judges struggling manfully to control and to contain an alien concept.

[46] For these reasons their Lordships are unable to accept the arguments advanced by Dextra in answer to the reliance by the BOJ on the defence of change of position.

NOTES AND QUESTIONS

1. The conclusion in this decision that change of position included cases of anticipatory reliance was referred to with approval in obiter dicta by all the judges in *Commerzbank AG v Gareth Price-Jones* [2004] 1 P & CR DG 15; [2003] EWCA Civ 1663 (above, 773). However, in *Commerzbank*, Mummery LJ considered that there was no 'relevant connection' between Mr Price-Jones's decision to stay at the bank (which was 'based on his erroneous belief, for which the bank is not responsible') and the bank's mistaken overpayment to him. But if this were correct, it would mean that a change of position could never occur in anticipation of a mistaken payment because, by definition, the future recipient will always be making a separate mistake about entitlement when he changes his position in good faith.

2. Mitchell, 'Change of Position: the developing law' [2005] *LMCLQ* 168 has observed that

    on their Lordships' formulation, the defence is available only where a defendant makes a conscious decision to change his position, and is not available where a third party decides to change his position for him, for example by taking his money in the expectation that the loss will be covered by a forthcoming payment by the claimant.

    Do you think that the Privy Council intended to confine anticipatory changes of position in this way? Is this consistent with the 'wide view' which the courts have taken of change of position (i.e. that it does not require that the claimant rely upon the receipt in changing his position, see above, 765)?

3. A separate issue considered by the Privy Council was whether relative fault could be considered in determining the availability and extent of the defence. The Privy Council rejected relative fault as 'hopelessly unstable'. However, as we will see in the next section, this conclusion is not yet settled law.

(iv) WHAT IS THE RELEVANCE OF FAULT TO THE DEFENCE?

In *Lipkin Gorman*, Lord Goff said that it is 'plain that the defence is not open to one who has changed his position in bad faith, as where the defendant has paid away the money with knowledge of the facts entitling the plaintiff to restitution; and it is commonly accepted that the defence should not be open to a wrongdoer. These are matters which can, in due course, be considered in depth in cases in which they arise for consideration'. The next two cases consider the meaning of first, 'bad faith' and 'knowledge' and, second, a 'wrongdoer'. As we saw in the previous case (*Dextra Bank*), the Privy Council rejected relative fault as 'hopelessly unstable'. It rejected the New Zealand approach (citing e.g. *Thomas v Houston Corbett & Co.* [1969] NZLR 151 and *National Bank of New Zealand Ltd v Waitaki International Processing (NI) Ltd* [1999] 2 NZLR 211) which had held that the defence should compare relative fault between the claimant and defendant. Instead, the Privy Council said that good faith is a sufficient requirement, especially as carelessness is irrelevant in establishing a *prima facie* claim in unjust enrichment for mistake. However, in subsequent cases, it is possible that notions of relative fault may be influencing an expansive meaning given by the courts to 'good faith' and 'wrongdoer'.

- ## *Niru Battery Manufacturing Co. v Milestone Trading Ltd*
  [2003] EWCA Civ 1446; [2004] QB 985, Court of Appeal

The first claimant, Niru Battery, entered into a contract with the first defendant, Milestone Trading, to purchase lead. Niru Battery was to pay for the lead with a letter of credit opened by Bank Sepah Iran which could be accessed once a bill of lading and quality inspection certificate had been presented. In order for Milestone Trading to obtain the inspection certificate it required warrants from the London Metal Exchange (which were documents of title to the lead) to enable the lead to be inspected. Mr Mahadavi, who controlled Milestone Trading, asked a financier, CAI, to finance the borrowing of warrants to enable the lead to be inspected. CAI was to pay for the warrants and it would be reimbursed when they were returned to the broker. CAI insisted upon holding the warrants until it was repaid. The problem for Milestone Trading was that in order to pay for the lead it needed the letter of credit, but in order to obtain the letter of credit it needed a bill of lading. A bill of lading would not be issued without the warrants (which would permit release of the lead from the warehouse). Mr Mahadavi's solution to this problem was to persuade the forwarding agent to issue a bill of lading without obtaining the warrants or possession of the lead. The bill of lading stated that the goods were in the charge of the forwarding agent. It was therefore a false document. The inspection certificate drawn up by SGS was also in some respects inaccurate. Unfortunately, Bank Sepah Iran did not pay promptly under the letter of credit (which would have enabled the purchase of the warrants from CAI). The price of lead then fell and CAI, concerned about the value of its security, sold the warrants and credited the amount to a company in Mr Mahadavi's group. Although Mr Mahadavi was aware of these actions, CAI did not inform Bank Sepah Iran or Niru Battery that the warrants had been sold. Unaware that the warrants had been sold, Bank Sepah Iran then told CAI that it was ready to pay for the warrants and Bank Sepah Iran paid CAI. Following instruction from Milestone Trading to Mr Francis, an officer of CAI, CAI then paid away the money to a company in Mr Mahadavi's group. No lead was ever delivered to Niru Battery but Bank Sepah Iran debited Niru Battery's account pursuant to a counter-indemnity. The trial judge held that CAI was liable to repay to Bank Sepah Iran and Niru Battery the amount mistakenly paid by Bank Sepah Iran under the letter of credit and that CAI did not have a defence of change of position because Mr Francis, whilst not dishonest, acted in a commercially unacceptable way knowing that he could be infringing the rights of others. The Court of Appeal upheld this finding.

Clarke LJ: [*after quoting from the speech of Lord Goff in* Lipkin Gorman *continued*] . . .

147. There is to my mind no indication in the speech of Lord Goff or of Lord Templeman to suggest that the defence of change of position is only lost where the defendant is guilty of dishonesty or other wrongdoing, although it would of course be lost in those circumstances. The underlying principles to be derived from the speech of Lord Goff seem to me to be these. (i) The question is whether it would be unjust to allow restitution, or restitution in full. (ii) It will be unjust to allow restitution where an innocent defendant's position has so changed that the injustice of requiring him to repay outweighs the injustice of denying the claimant restitution. (iii) The defence of change of position is not, for example, available to a defendant who has changed his position in bad faith, as where he has paid away the money with knowledge of the facts entitling the claimant to restitution. (iv) Nor is it available to a wrongdoer. (v) In general terms, the defence is available to a defendant whose position has so changed that it would be inequitable to require him to make restitution or to make restitution in full.

148. The emphasis in Lord Goff's speech is upon whether it would be unjust or inequitable to allow

restitution. It is not upon whether the defendant has been dishonest. Thus, for example, Lord Goff gave as an example of bad faith the case where the defendant had paid away the money with knowledge of the facts entitling the claimant to restitution. It seems to me that such a person may not be dishonest in the *Twinsectra Ltd v Yardley* [2002] 2 AC 164 sense. A similar approach can be seen in the speech of Lord Templeman. For example, he said [1991] 2 AC 548, 560, that the reason why the donee of money from a thief must return the money was that he could not 'in good conscience' rely on the bounty of the thief to deny restitution to the victim of the theft.

149. In short, as I read the speeches in the *Lipkin Gorman* case, the essential question is whether it would be inequitable or unconscionable, and thus unjust, to allow the recipient of money paid under a mistake of fact to deny restitution to the payer.

150. Mr Bloch submitted, by contrast, that the essential question is whether the recipient acts in good faith, that he acts in good faith unless he acts dishonestly and that the decision of this court in *Medforth v Blake* [2000] Ch 86 is authority for that proposition. In that case the question was whether a receiver and manager of a pig farm appointed by a mortgagee owed a duty to the mortgagor, over and above a duty of good faith. The plaintiff had alleged that the receiver was negligent in various respects. It was held that such a receiver owed duties in equity to the mortgagor and anyone else with an interest in the equity of redemption which included but were not necessarily confined to a duty of good faith.

151. The case was thus not directly concerned with the meaning of good or bad faith in that context but Mr Bloch relied upon the following dicta of Sir Richard Scott V-C, with whom Swinton Thomas and Tuckey LJJ agreed, at p 103:

'I do not think that the concept of good faith should be diluted by treating it as capable of being breached by conduct that is not dishonest or otherwise tainted by bad faith. It is sometimes said that recklessness is equivalent to intent. Shutting one's eyes deliberately to the consequences of what one is doing may make it impossible to deny an intention to bring about those consequences. Thereapart, however, the concepts of negligence on the one hand and fraud or bad faith on the other ought, in my view, to be kept strictly apart . . . In my judgment, the breach of a duty of good faith should, in this area as in all others, require some dishonesty or improper motive, some element of bad faith, to be established.'

That approach was followed by this court in the same context in *Starling v Lloyds TSB Bank plc* The Times, 12 November 1999; Court of Appeal (Civil Division) Transcript No 1835 of 1999, a decision to which Moore-Bick J was a party.

152. For my part, I would not apply that approach to the present class of case, where, as appears from *Lipkin Gorman v Karpnale Ltd* [1991] 2 AC 548, the question is whether it would be inequitable or unconscionable to deny restitution. Mr Bloch submitted that it cannot be considered equitable to allow a claimant to recover from an innocent recipient moneys which it has paid away on the directions of its customer or client with no dishonesty. I would not accept that submission. It appears to me that, where the recipient knows that the payer has paid the money to him as a result of a mistake of fact, or indeed a mistake of law, it will in general be unconscionable or inequitable to refuse restitution to the payer. In such a case I would not regard the recipient who has paid the money away as 'innocent' even though he was not guilty of dishonesty.

153. The principle identified in the *Lipkin Gorman* case seems to me to involve a balance between the interests of the payer and those of the payee and, in such a case, the balance of justice seems to me to fall on the side of the payer. If the payee who knows the facts which entitle the payer to repayment does not repay, perhaps, as here, because no proper advice is taken, justice requires that it repay the money. In my opinion, that approach is consistent with that in the *Lipkin Gorman* case and is not inconsistent with the principles stated in *Medforth v Blake* [2000] Ch 86, which was concerned with a very different situation.

154. It is an approach which seems to me to be consistent with the approach of this court to cases of knowing receipt in *Bank of Credit and Commerce International (Overseas) Ltd v Akindele* [2001] Ch 437. The court distinguished between cases of knowing receipt and cases of knowing or dishonest assistance. Nourse LJ, with whom Ward and Sedley LJJ agreed, set out the essential requirements of knowing receipt from the judgment of Hoffmann LJ in *El Ajou v Dollar Land Holdings plc* [1994] 2 All ER 685, 700 as follows [2001] Ch 437, 448:

'For this purpose the plaintiff must show, first, a disposal of his assets in breach of fiduciary duty; secondly, the beneficial receipt by the defendant of assets which are traceable as representing the assets of the plaintiff; and thirdly, knowledge on the part of the defendant that the assets he received are traceable to a breach of fiduciary duty.'

155. Following *Belmont Finance Corpn Ltd v Williams Furniture Ltd (No 2)* [1980] 1 All ER 393, the court held that dishonesty is not a necessary ingredient of liability in knowing receipt. Nourse LJ said [2001] Ch 437, 450 that the point was made most clearly by Vinelott J in *Eagle Trust plc v SBC Securities Ltd* [1993] 1 WLR 484, 497.

'What the decision in *Belmont (No 2)* [1980] 1 All ER 393 shows is that in a "knowing receipt" case it is only necessary to show that the defendant knew that the moneys paid to him were trust moneys and of circumstances which made the payment a misapplication of them. Unlike a "knowing assistance" case it is not necessary, and never has been necessary, to show that the defendant was in any sense a participator in a fraud.'

156. After a detailed analysis of the authorities, Nourse LJ asked and answered what seems to me to be a question which is directly relevant to the present problem. He said, at p 455:

'What then, in the context of knowing receipt, is the purpose to be served by a categorisation of knowledge? It can only be to enable the court to determine whether, in the words of Buckley LJ in *Belmont Finance Corpn Ltd v Williams Furniture Ltd (No 2)* [1980] 1 All ER 393, 405, the recipient can "conscientiously retain [the] funds against the company" or, in the words of Sir Robert Megarry V-C in *In re Montagu's Settlement Trusts* [1987] Ch 264, 273 "[the recipient's] conscience is sufficiently affected for it to be right to bind him by the obligations of a constructive trustee". But, if that is the purpose, there is no need for categorisation. All that is necessary is that the recipient's state of knowledge should be such as to make it unconscionable for him to retain the benefit of the receipt. For these reasons I have come to the view that, just as there is now a single test of dishonesty for knowing assistance, so ought there to be a single test of knowledge for knowing receipt. The recipient's state of knowledge must be such as to make it unconscionable for him to retain the benefit of the receipt.'

157. Although I recognise that there are differences between the problems associated with knowing receipt and those with which we are concerned, they seem to me to have significant similarities, as indeed Nourse LJ recognised in *Bank of Credit and Commerce International (Overseas) Ltd v Akindele* [2001] Ch 437, 455–456, where he referred to an essay by Lord Nicholls of Birkenhead entitled 'Knowing Receipt: The Need for a New Landmark' in *Restitution Past, Present and Future* (1998), p 231. In that article, at p 242, Lord Nicholls recognised the point made by Lord Goff in the *Lipkin Gorman* case [1991] 2 AC 548 that the change of position defence would be available to a person whose position had so changed that it would be inequitable in all the circumstances to make restitution or, alternatively, to make restitution in full and that the ingredients of the defence remained to be worked out. He added, at p 243, that as the law develops, it will be important never to lose sight of the underlying purpose of restitution in this field, which is confined to stripping the recipient of an enrichment he should not have received, an enrichment that it would be unjust to allow him to keep. Although Nourse LJ did not agree with all the views expressed by Lord Nicholls in

his article, he concluded his analysis in this way, after referring to the *Lipkin Gorman* case [2001] Ch 437, 456:

'Moreover, if the circumstances of the receipt are such as to make it unconscionable for the recipient to retain the benefit of it, there is an obvious difficulty in saying that it is equitable for a change of position to afford him a defence.'

I respectfully agree.

158. This approach seems to me also to derive support from that of the majority of the House of Lords in *Kleinwort Benson Ltd v Lincoln City Council* [1999] 2 AC 349 where it was held that money paid under a mistake of law should be recoverable on the same footing as money paid under a mistake of fact, subject in the same way to the defences available in the law of restitution, which of course include the defence of change of position. Some consideration was given to the nature of that defence.

159. One of the issues considered was called 'honest receipt'. It involved the consideration by the House of a principle proposed by Brennan J in *David Securities Pty. Ltd v Commonwealth Bank of Australia* (1992) 175 CLR 353, 399:

'It is a defence to a claim for restitution of money paid or property transferred under a mistake of law that the defendant honestly believed, when he learnt of the payment or transfer, that he was entitled to receive and retain the money or property.'

If the defence of change of position were put as widely as that, it would suggest that dishonesty was required to defeat it. However, the House of Lords unanimously held that the law should not recognise a defence put as widely as it was put by Brennan J: see especially *per* Lord Goff [1999] 2 AC 349, 384–385. That decision seems to me to suggest that Mr Bloch's submission also puts the defence too widely because, if correct, it would require dishonesty to defeat it.

160. We were also referred to the decision of the Privy Council in *Dextra Bank and Trust Co. Ltd v Bank of Jamaica* [2002] 1 All ER (Comm) 193, where the judgment of the Judicial Committee was given by Lord Bingham of Cornhill and Lord Goff. The Privy Council rejected the propriety of introducing a concept of relative fault into a determination of whether the recipient of money paid under a mistake of fact or law was obliged to repay it: see the discussion at pp 205–207, paras 40–46. No one suggested to us that it was sufficient to show that CAI was negligent in order to defeat a defence of change of position.

161. The view of the Judicial Committee can be seen at p 207, para. 45:

'Their Lordships are, however, most reluctant to recognise the propriety of introducing the concept of relative fault into this branch of the common law, and indeed decline to do so. They regard good faith on the part of the recipient as a sufficient requirement in this context.'

The reference to good faith must, as I see it, be read in the light of the underlying principle identified in the *Lipkin Gorman* case [1991] 2 AC 548 to which I have already referred and which was stated in much the same way by Lord Bingham and Lord Goff, at p 205, para. 38:

'The defence should be regarded as founded on a principle of justice designed to protect the defendant from a claim to restitution in respect of a benefit received by him in circumstances in which it would be inequitable to pursue that claim, or to pursue it in full.'

162. I have reached the conclusion that the authorities support the proposition already stated in para. 149 above that the essential question is whether on the facts of a particular case it would in all the circumstances be inequitable or unconscionable, and thus unjust, to allow the recipient of money paid under a mistake of fact to deny restitution to the payer. As I read his judgment, the judge reached the same conclusion and was, in my opinion, correct to do so.

163. It follows that I would accept Mr Bloch's submission (i) in para. 144 but would not accept his submission (ii) because I do not accept that a payment away is made in good faith in this context unless it is made dishonestly.

164. The question remains in what circumstances a bank will be held to have acted otherwise than in good faith. The answer is of course that all depends upon the circumstances so that it is not possible to lay down absolute principles. However, the judge addressed the problem in his judgment, which included the following [2002] 2 All ER (Comm) 705, 741, para. 135:

> 'I do not think that it is desirable to attempt to define the limits of good faith; it is a broad concept, the definition of which, in so far as it is capable of definition at all, will have to be worked out through the cases. In my view it is capable of embracing a failure to act in a commercially accept-able way and sharp practice of a kind that falls short of outright dishonesty as well as dishonesty itself. The factors which will determine whether it is inequitable to allow the claimant to obtain restitution in a case of mistaken payment will vary from case to case, but where the payee has voluntarily parted with the money much is likely to depend on the circumstances in which he did so and the extent of his knowledge about how the payment came to be made. Where he knows that the payment he has received was made by mistake, the position is quite straightforward: he must return it. This applies as much to a banker who receives a payment for the account of his customer as to any other person: see, for example, the comment of Lord Mersey in *Kerrison v Glyn Mills Currie & Co* (1912) 81 LJKB 465, 472. Greater difficulty may arise, however, in cases where the payee has grounds for believing that the payment may have been made by mistake, but cannot be sure. In such cases good faith may well dictate that an inquiry be made of the payer. The nature and extent of the inquiry called for will, of course, depend on the circumstances of the case, but I do not think that a person who has, or thinks he has, good reason to believe that the payment was made by mistake will often be found to have acted in good faith if he pays the money away without first making inquiries of the person from whom he received it.'

I agree. As appears below, this is a case in which Mr Francis thought he had good reason to believe that the payment was made by mistake.

165. The judge also expressed this principle in the context of a bank which thought or knew that the payment was made by mistake. He said, at p 742, para. 138:

> 'The need to make inquiries of Bank Sepah is not a matter to be viewed in terms of a duty owed by one banker to another; it is a matter to be viewed in terms of a duty of good faith which a person who has received a payment that he has good reason to think was made under a mistake owes to the person who made it. If under those circumstances the payee fails to make inquiry of the payer before disposing of the money he can properly be described as failing to act in good faith because he acts in the knowledge that he may be infringing the rights of another despite having the means of avoiding that consequence.'

Again, I agree.

The facts

166. It follows from the conclusions stated above that the fact that Mr Francis was not adjudged to be dishonest does not automatically afford CAI a defence to Bank Sepah's claim for repayment or restitution. The question remains whether the judge was right to hold CAI liable on the facts.

167. I set out the judge's findings of fact in this regard [2002] 2 All ER (Comm) 705, 735–737, paras 111–121, in para. 122 above. On those findings, especially those at pp 736–737, paras 120–121, Mr Francis did not know that a false bill of lading had been presented to Bank Sepah in order to obtain payment under the letter of credit but he knew that CAI had sold the warrants (and thus the lead) which formed the basis of the transaction and that the transaction could not therefore be completed.

He therefore realised that Bank Sepah must have paid by reason of a mistake. Moreover, as the judge put it, at p 737, para. 121, a moment's reflection would have led Mr Francis to appreciate that the reason given by Mr Mahdavi for wishing to retain the money did not justify the course he was asking the bank to take. In these circumstances the judge was entirely justified in saying, at the end of para. 121: 'Thus, on the facts as Mr Francis understood them, nothing said by Mr Mahdavi actually undermined Bank Sepah's right to repayment of the money.'

168. In these circumstances, having realised that Bank Sepah had paid by mistake, to my mind, good faith required Mr Francis to inquire of Bank Sepah before paying the money away in accordance with Mr Mahdavi's instructions and the judge was correct so to hold. As I read his judgment, the judge acquitted Mr Francis of dishonesty because he did not consciously act in disregard of the standards to be expected of the ordinary honest banker. The judge I think took the view that Mr Francis's state of mind was that CAI owed no duty to Bank Sepah, which could look after itself, but that CAI did owe a duty to its customer and in those circumstances paid the money away in accordance with Mr Mahdavi's instructions. The judge thought that that was misguided but not dishonest. As indicated earlier, it is my view that the judge was entitled to reach those conclusions.

169. On the other hand, the judge concluded that good faith required a person in Mr Francis's position who realised that the money had been paid by mistake to make inquiries of Bank Sepah to ascertain the position and not to pay the money away in the meantime. I have reached the clear conclusion that he was correct so to hold. This is, at the very least, an example of the case of the kind of bad faith expressly mentioned by Lord Goff in the *Lipkin Gorman* case [1991] 2 AC 548, 580 and quoted in para. 146 above, namely where a person 'has changed his position in bad faith, as where the defendant has paid away the money with knowledge of the facts entitling the plaintiff to restitution'. Here, on the judge's findings of fact, when the money was paid away, Mr Francis, and thus CAI, knew the facts which entitled Bank Sepah to restitution, namely that it had paid under a mistake of fact.

170. In all these circumstances the judge was in my opinion correct to hold that CAI did not act in good faith in paying the money away and that it would be inequitable or unconscionable to deny Bank Sepah a right to restitution by repayment of the moneys paid under the letter of credit. I would dismiss CAI's appeal under this head.

Sedley LJ: . . .

176. The judge having acquitted Mr Francis of dishonesty, Michael Bloch submits that nothing less can defeat the defence of change of position generated by CAI's payment away of the funds. *Twinsectra Ltd v Yardley* [2002] 2 AC 164, however, was a decision on the legal character of dishonest assistance. It has no direct bearing on the availability of the defence of change of position to a claim for restitution. Mr Bloch therefore seeks to link the two by the medium of bad faith.

177. Good faith and bad faith play no part either in their Lordships' reasoning in the *Twinsectra* case or in the reasoning of the Privy Council in *Royal Brunei Airlines Sdn Bhd v Tan* [1995] 2 AC 378 upon which the *Twinsectra* case builds. So it is from the decision of this court in *Medforth v Blake* [2000] Ch 86 that Mr Bloch seeks to derive a ubiquitous requirement of bad faith.

178. *Medforth's* case concerned a third kind of liability, that of a receiver of mortgaged property to persons with an interest in the equity of redemption. Sir Richard Scott V-C said, at pp 102–103:

'In my judgment, in principle and on the authorities, the following propositions can be stated. (1) A receiver managing mortgaged property owes duties to the mortgagor and anyone else with an interest in the equity of redemption. (2) The duties include, but are not necessarily confined to, a duty of good faith. (3) The extent and scope of any duty additional to that of good faith will depend on the facts and circumstances of the particular case. (4) In exercising his powers of management the primary duty of the receiver is to try and bring about a situation in which interest on the secured debt can be paid and the debt itself repaid. (5) Subject to that primary duty, the receiver owes a duty to manage the property with due diligence. (6) Due diligence does not oblige the receiver to continue to carry on a business on the mortgaged premises previously carried on by the mortgagor. (7) If the receiver does carry on a business on the mortgaged premises, due diligence requires reasonable steps to be taken in order to try to do so profitably . . . I do not think that the concept of good faith should be diluted by treating it as capable of being breached by conduct that is not dishonest or otherwise tainted by bad faith. It is sometimes said that recklessness is equivalent to intent. Shutting one's eyes deliberately to the consequences of what one is doing may make it impossible to deny an intention to bring about those consequences. Thereapart, however, the concepts of negligence on the one hand and fraud or bad faith on the other ought, in my view, to be kept strictly apart. Equity has not always done so. The equitable doctrine of 'fraud on a power' has little, if anything, to do with fraud. Lord Herschell in *Kennedy v De Trafford* [1897] AC 180 gave an explanation of a lack of good faith that would have allowed conduct that was grossly negligent to have qualified notwithstanding that the consequences of the conduct were not intended. In my judgment, the breach of a duty of good faith should, in this area as in all others, require some dishonesty or improper motive, some element of bad faith, to be established.'

179. Mr Bloch seeks to articulate this reasoning with that of the House of Lords in *Lipkin Gorman v Karpnale Ltd* [1991] 2 AC 548, 579G where in particular Lord Goff held that 'bona fide change of position should of itself be a good defence' to a claim for restitution. It follows, he submits, that bad faith is a necessary element both in establishing dishonest assistance and in rebutting the defence of change of position; so that nothing short of dishonesty will suffice to rebut the defence of change of position.

180. This syllogism in my view contains a series of fallacies. First, the *Lipkin Gorman* case is not predicated on a bad faith threshold for defeating a change of position defence: it posits a calculatedly intermediate threshold of inequitability. Secondly, *Medforth's* case [2000] Ch 86 does not assimilate bad faith to dishonesty. On the contrary, it explains bad faith as including both dishonesty and improper motive, without—it should be noted—limiting it to these. Thirdly, even if bad faith were of a piece with dishonesty, it would not follow, at least outside the law of dishonest assistance, that the judge, by acquitting Mr Francis of dishonesty, had acquitted him of bad faith. It would just as logically follow that by finding that he had acted in bad faith the judge had found him to have acted dishonestly.

181. To understand the first of these propositions it is necessary to consider with some care Lord Goff's speech in the *Lipkin Gorman* case [1991] 2 AC 548, 579–580 cited in its material part by Clarke LJ at para. 146 above.

182. It is simplistic to assume that by his reference to 'bona fide change of position' Lord Goff meant to set up a good faith/bad faith dichotomy for the change of position defence. The remainder of the passage makes it evident that he was using the phrase as it is often used, especially in the United States, to indicate an innocent change of position, which is the concept used by Lord Templeman in his assenting speech [1991] 2 AC 548, 560: he describes the donee to whom the defence of change of position may be available as an 'innocent recipient'. It also corresponds, as a bad faith limitation does not, with the test of inequitability at which Lord Goff arrives at the end of the cited passage.

183. The explicit purpose of this passage is to set nothing in stone but to point courts in the right direction for the future. The reference to 'one who has changed his position in bad faith' is therefore not a bright line but an illustration of the kind of case in which it would be inequitable to allow a change of position defence to succeed. As it happens, the example given by Lord Goff—'where the defendant has paid away the money with knowledge of the facts entitling the plaintiff to restitution'—is this case.

184. If, however, Lord Goff's reasoning is to be understood as limiting inequitability to bad faith, Mr Bloch's reliance on the strictures placed on the concept of good faith by this court in *Medforth's* case [2000] Ch 86 as a binding interpretation of inequitability is insecure. *Medforth's* case was argued and

decided without reference to the *Lipkin Gorman* case [1991] 2 AC 548. It is not that this casts any doubt on this court's conclusions, but that it is unsafe to carry its reasoning about good and bad faith back into an antecedent decision of the House of Lords which uses the same phrase without necessarily according it the same meaning.

185. The present facts are such that it would plainly be inequitable to allow CAI to rely on a change of position defence to the claim for restitution. On his own candid evidence Mr Francis was not merely negligent in checking the documentation he let a very large sum of money for which CAI had accepted responsibility be paid away when he had in his hands ample information to put CAI on its guard against doing so. 'Inequitable' is the right word for the idea that CAI should be protected by its own casualness from the ordinary consequences of what it did. If more—for example an improper motive—is needed, there was such a motive here: Mr Mahdavi was a profitable customer of CAI whose business Mr Francis was keen to keep, and who was now threatening a lawsuit. It is an almost irresistible inference that this was why the documents which revealed the critical gaps were treated by Mr Francis with an insouciance that no ordinary customer would encounter.

186. Such a situation sufficiently rebuts a defence of change of position. The common sense of this approach, without reference to authority, is demonstrated by the judgment of the Court of Appeal of New South Wales in *State Bank of New South Wales Ltd v Swiss Bank Corpn* (1995) 39 NSWLR 350, 356:

'A bank which receives a mistaken payment and disburses it can only bring itself within the change of position defence if it shows that at the time of disbursement it knew or thought it knew more than the fact of receipt standing alone. This must be information which, if true, would entitle the payee to deal with the receipt as it did and that information must have come from the payer . . . Looked at on its own terms State Bank of New South Wales' submission has an element of the fantastic about it. It says that it received this very large payment with a message from Swiss Bank saying: "Credit this to the account you keep for customers." Nothing more than that. State Bank of New South Wales' case involves the propositions: (a) that it was for it to decide which customer should be credited; and (b) that it credited Essington Ltd because Essington Ltd asked it to do so. On the judge's findings what State Bank of New South Wales did was not dishonest but on anybody's view it was not sensible and in our opinion it was not done on the faith of the receipt.'

187. This is an approach which rolls up the defence and the rebuttal. It requires the donee to show that it acted on real or reasonably supposed facts justifying payment away. Lord Goff's concept of a 'bona fide change of position' is similarly unitary. Whatever content is now worked out case by case for the phrase, it is clear from what Lord Goff subsequently held in *Kleinwort Benson Ltd v Lincoln City Council* [1999] 2 AC 349 that it is not only dishonest payment away which forfeits the defence. He said, at pp 384–385:

'Issue (IB): Honest receipt

'This issue arises from a principle proposed by Brennan CJ (then Brennan J) in *David Securities Pty. Ltd v Commonwealth Bank of Australia* (1992) 175 CLR 353, 399. It reads: 'It is a defence to a claim for restitution of money paid or property transferred under a mistake of law that the defendant honestly believed, when he learnt of the payment or transfer, that he was entitled to receive and retain the money or property.' This principle was expressly proposed in order to achieve a degree of certainty in past transactions. As Brennan J said, at p 398: 'Unless some limiting principle is introduced, the finality of any payment would be as uncertain as the governing law.' In this part of the law there has long been concern, among common law judges, about what is sometimes called the finality of transactions, and sometimes the security of receipts. This concern formed a significant part of the amalgam of concerns which led to the rule that money paid under a mistake of law was irrecoverable on that ground. Now that that rule has been abrogated throughout the common law world, attention has of course shifted to the formulation of appropriate defences to the right of recovery. The principle proposed by Brennan J is, I believe, the most far reaching of the defences to the right of recovery that has yet been proposed. Anything which falls from Brennan J is, of course, entitled to great respect. But I have to state at once that this proposal seems to have been stillborn. Of the judges who sat with Brennan J on the *David Securities* case, none supported this proposal. I know of no judicial support which the proposal has since received, nor of any support from any of the Law Commissions which have considered this part of the law. The reason for this lack of support is, I believe, that the proposal is generally regarded as being wider than is necessary to meet the perceived mischief. I start from the proposition that money paid under a mistake of law is recoverable on the ground that its receipt by the defendant will, prima facie, lead to his unjust enrichment, just as receipt of money paid under a mistake of fact will do so. There may of course be circumstances in which, despite the mistaken nature of the payment, it is not regarded as unjust for the defendant to retain the money so paid. One notable example is change of the defendant's position. Another is the somewhat undefined circumstance that the payment was made in settle-ment of an honest claim. Yet, Brennan J's proposed defence is so wide that, if it was accepted, these other defences would in practice cease to have any relevance in the case of money paid under a mistake of law. Moreover in many cases of this kind the mistake is shared by both parties, as for example in the case of the appeals now under consideration. In such cases, recovery by the plaintiff would automatically be barred by Brennan J's proposed defence. So sweeping is the effect of the defence that it is not perhaps surprising that it has not received support from the others. In my opinion, it would be most unwise for the common law, having recognised the right to recover money paid under a mistake of law on the ground of unjust enrichment, immediately to proceed to the recognition of so wide a defence as this which would exclude the right of recovery in a very large proportion of cases. The proper course is surely to identify particular sets of circumstances which, as matter of principle or policy, may lead to the conclusion that recovery should not be allowed; and in so doing to draw on the experience of the past, looking for guidance in particular from the analogous case of money paid under a mistake of fact, and also drawing upon the accumulated wisdom to be found in the writings of scholars on the law of restitution. However, before so novel and far-reaching defence as the one now proposed can be recognised, a very strong case for it has to be made out; and I can discover no evidence of a need for so wide a defence as this. In particular, experience since the recognition of the right of recovery of money paid under a mistake of law in the common law world does not appear to have revealed any such need. For these reasons with all respect to Brennan J, I am unable to accept that the defence proposed by him forms part of the common law.'

188. This is of a piece with the law of knowing receipt. In *Bank of Credit and Commerce Inter-national (Overseas) Ltd v Akindele* [2001] Ch 437, 448, 450 Nourse LJ, speaking for the court, said:

'So far as the law is concerned, the comprehensive arguments of Mr Sheldon and Mr Moss have demonstrated that there are two questions which, though closely related, are distinct: first, what, in this context, is meant by knowledge; second, is it necessary for the recipient to act dishonestly? Because the answer to it is the simpler, the convenient course is to deal with the second of those questions first.

Knowing receipt—dishonesty

'As appears from the penultimate sentence of his judgment, Carnwath J proceeded on an assump-tion that dishonesty in one form or another was the essential foundation of the claimants' case, whether in knowing assistance or knowing receipt. That was no doubt caused by the acceptance before him (though not at any higher level) by Mr Sheldon, recorded at [1999] BCC 669, 677F, that the thrust of the recent authorities at first instance was that the recipient's state of knowledge must fall into one of the first three categories listed by Peter Gibson J in *Baden v Société Générale pour*

Favoriser le Développement du Commerce et de l'Industrie en France SA (Note) [1993] 1 WLR 509, 575–576, on which basis, said Carnwath J, it was doubtful whether the test differed materially in practice from that for knowing assistance. However, the assumption on which the judge proceeded, derived as I believe from an omission to distinguish between the questions of knowledge and dishonesty, was incorrect in law. While a knowing recipient will often be found to have acted dishonestly, it has never been a prerequisite of the liability that he should.

Belmont Finance Corpn Ltd v Williams Furniture Ltd (No 2) [1980] 1 All ER 393 is clear authority for the proposition that dishonesty is not a necessary ingredient of liability in knowing receipt. There have been other, more recent, judicial pronouncements to the same effect. Thus in *Polly Peck International plc v Nadir (No 2)* [1992] 4 All ER 769, 777D Scott LJ said that liability in a knowing receipt case did not require that the misapplication of the trust funds should be fraudulent. While in theory it is possible for a misapplication not to be fraudulent and the recipient to be dishonest, in practice such a combination must be rare. Similarly, in *Agip (Africa) Ltd v Jackson* [1990] Ch 265, 292A Millett J said that in knowing receipt it was immaterial whether the breach of trust was fraudulent or not. The point was made most clearly by Vinelott J in *Eagle Trust plc v SBC Securities Ltd* [1993] 1 WLR 484, 497: "What the decision in *Belmont (No 2)* [1980] 1 All ER 393 shows is that in a "knowing receipt" case it is only necessary to show that the defendant knew that the moneys paid to him were trust moneys and of circumstances which made the payment a misapplication of them. Unlike a "knowing assistance" case it is not necessary, and never has been necessary, to show that the defendant was in any sense a participator in a fraud." '

189. It would, as Ali Malek suggests, be strange if the analogous doctrines of knowing receipt and unjust enrichment carried different defences, the former defeasible simply by proof of material knowledge, the latter only by proof of dishonesty.

190. One further alley has been authoritatively explored since the decision in the *Lipkin Gorman* case. In *Dextra Bank and Trust Co. Ltd v Bank of Jamaica* [2002] 1 All ER (Comm) 193 the Privy Council, in a joint opinion of Lord Bingham and Lord Goff, rejected a balance of fault test for change of position defences. We have not been asked to take a different course in the present appeal, no doubt because of the cogency of their Lordships' reasoning at pp 205–207, paras 40–46. It may fall for consideration on another occasion whether the balance of fault is to be ignored even where the claimant is blameless and the defendant solely at fault. For the present, it must be assumed that the defence depends on the quality of the defendant's fault, so that mere negligence is not enough to defeat the defence. If it were, an action in negligence, which was pleaded in the present case but not pursued, would make restitution redundant. But it may be observed that, if an action lay in negligence in such cases, there would be no obvious reason why the Law Reform (Contributory Negligence) Act 1945 should not reduce the entitlement of a claimant whose neglect has contributed to the loss.

191. What their Lordships said in the *Dextra* case, however, reinforces the view that it is not only dishonesty which will defeat a defence of change of position. They characterise, at p 204, para. 36, the decision taken in the *Lipkin Gorman* case [1991] 2 AC 548 as 'a broad approach based on practical justice' and one which 'avoided technicality'. They said [2002] 1 All ER (Comm) 193, 205, para. 38:

'The defence should be regarded as founded on a principle of justice designed to protect the defendant from a claim to restitution in respect of a benefit received by him in circumstances in which it would be inequitable to pursue that claim, or to pursue it in full.'

192. While this passage only echoes the coda, if one may call it that, of the key passage in the *Lipkin Gorman* case [1991] 2 AC 548, it has the effect of elevating the coda to a theme. As a theme, it tells the courts to which it now falls to elaborate the defence case by case that they are not tied to a single rigid standard in deciding whether a defence of change of position succeeds. They are to decide whether it is equitable to uphold the defence. Since the doctrine of restitution is centrally concerned

with the distribution of loss among parties whose rights are not met by some stronger doctrine of law, one is by definition looking for the least unjust solution to a residual problem. When Mr Mahdavi walks away, leaving the victims of his fraud to fight out who is to carry the loss he has caused them, it is a strange kind of equity which would make the innocent claimants bear their own loss because the defendant bank has paid away their money recklessly, venally and, as the judge has found, in bad faith, but not dishonestly.

Dame Elizabeth Butler-Sloss P agreed with both **Clarke** and **Sedley LJJ.**

NOTES AND QUESTIONS

1. In a passage not extracted from *Commerzbank* (above, 773) Munby J, in his concurring judgment, quoted with approval the comment of Clarke LJ in this case that 'the essential question' is whether on the facts it would 'be inequitable or unconscionable, and thus unjust, to allow the recipient of money paid under a mistake of fact to deny restitution to the payer.' Burrows 'Clouding the Issues on Change of Position' [2004] *CLJ* 276, 277 has said:

   > such broad tests tell us almost nothing. We need to know, for example, whether bad faith is wider than subjective dishonesty (as Moore Bick J [the trial judge] thought) and whether fault short of bad faith can ever bar change of position; and if the answer to the latter question is 'yes', we need to build up examples—so that in time one can clarify the underlying principle—of when this will be so. Clear answers to such questions are obscured if the courts resort to saying, without more, that everything turns on whether it is inequitable to allow change of position on the particular facts.

2. Both Clarke LJ and Sedley LJ emphasized that bad faith required more than negligence but they relied upon two analogies to reach their conclusion that it meant something less than dishonesty. The first analogy they relied upon was the unanimous rejection by the House of Lords in *Kleinwort Benson Ltd v Lincoln City Council* [1999] 2 AC 349 of a defence of 'honest receipt'. They argued that this rejection meant that something less than dishonesty must be able to defeat a claim for restitution. But it could equally be said that the Lords rejected a defence of honest receipt because they required some disenrichment in order to defeat a claim for restitution.

3. The other analogy relied upon by Clarke and Sedley LJJ was that dishonesty is not required for liability to be imposed for a claim for 'knowing' receipt. But it is a *non sequitur* to insist that the degree of fault required for the cause of action be mirrored in the defence, particularly when most claims in unjust enrichment are strict liability.

4. Arguably, the interpretation of 'bad faith' as involving a standard less than dishonesty was strained because of the reluctance by the trial judge and Court of Appeal to characterize the conduct of Mr Francis as dishonest. Clearly, disposing of an enrichment with actual knowledge of a lack of entitlement to it will be dishonest (see *Cressman v Coys of Kensington* above, 77). In the context of the wrong of dishonest assistance, the Privy Council has also held that a 'clear suspicion' can also amount to dishonesty or bad faith: *Barlow Clowes International Ltd v Eurotrust International Ltd* [2005] UKPC 37; [2006] 1 All ER 333 at 340 [28]. Should a similar approach have been taken to the conduct of Mr Francis in paying out the money received by Bank Sepah Iran whilst knowing that the warrants had been sold?

5. Why did CAI not raise the defence of payment over to a principal by an agent? Should the same test for knowledge or fault apply to that defence in the same way as change of position?

- ### *Barros Mattos Junior v Macdaniels Ltd*
  [2004] EWHC 1188 (Ch); [2004] 3 All ER 299, Chancery Divison

As part of a massive fraud involving forged SWIFT transfer documents, a Brazilian bank transferred $US 8.05 million to the defendants. The fraudsters (led by Chief Anajemba) instructed the defendants to receive the funds, convert them to Nigerian currency and pay them over. The defendants did this, taking a commission of $US 50,000. However, Nigerian law provided that such foreign exchange contracts were illegal. The claimants (who had taken an assignment of the bank's rights and stood in the shoes of the bank) sought summary judgment on their claim for restitution of unjust enrichment. It was not disputed that the bank credit received by the defendants from the Brazilian bank was to be treated as stolen. It was also conceded for the summary judgment application that the defendants were to be treated as innocent recipients. The central question on the summary judgment application was whether the defendants could claim change of position. Laddie J held that the Nigerian illegality was recognized by an English court and that such illegality barred a claim for change of position. Summary judgment was ordered.

Laddie J: . . .

[21] In the present case, I understand Mr Briggs to accept, at least for the purpose of this application, that there is an arguable case that these defendants were both innocent and changed position based on that innocence. The conversion of $US4,228,680.90 into naira and its transmission to General, the conversion of $US1,720,032 into naira and its transmission to MacDaniels Nigeria, the onward transmission of both those sums and the payment out of $US 2,085,528 in dollars to third party creditors all took place because these defendants thought it was Chief Anajemba's funds and therefore he had authority to do with them what he liked.

[22] Mr Briggs argues that this does not get the defendants home. He says that an innocent recipient cannot rely upon a plea of change of position where that change would be regarded by our courts as wrongful. This submission is based on the following passage in the speech of Lord Goff in the *Lipkin Gorman* case [1992] 4 All ER 512 at 534, [1991] 2 AC 548 at 580 (my emphasis):

'I am most anxious that, in recognising this defence to actions of restitution, nothing should be said at this stage to inhibit the development of the defence on a case by case basis, in the usual way. It is, of course, plain that the defence is not open to one who has changed his position in bad faith, as where the defendant has paid away the money with knowledge of the facts entitling the plaintiff to restitution; *and it is commonly accepted that the defence should not be open to a wrongdoer*. These are matters which can, in due course, be considered in depth in cases where they arise for consideration. They do not arise in the present case.'

[23] In this passage Lord Goff is considering two different classes of case. The first consists of those where the recipient has acted in bad faith or with knowledge of the claimant's entitlement to recovery of the funds. Those are cases where the defendant is not innocent of the claimant's rights. They are cases of knowing receipt or dishonest assistance. The second class consists of cases where the defendant is ignorant of the misappropriation from the claimant and, in respect of that part of the transaction, is innocent, but where his change of position is wrongful.

[24] Mr Briggs does not rely on any other authority for his proposition. It should be noted, and made clear by Lord Goff, that the principle had no application to the facts of *Lipkin Gorman*'s case itself since it was accepted that gambling was not illegal, even if gambling contracts are not enforceable. For that reason, the defendant could not be regarded as a wrongdoer.

[25] Mr Briggs explains this brief passage in the *Lipkin Gorman* case as follows. A court will not allow a party to plead or rely on activity which it regards as illegal or wrongful. Thus, if the change of position is wrongful, the court will decline to allow the recipient to rely on it. If, as he submits, the transactions entered into by these defendants were illegal under Nigerian law, they would be treated as illegal here as well. To adopt the approach of Lord Goff set out at [19], above, on the one hand there is the injustice inflicted on the victim in having his money taken from him and against that is the

position of the defendant who has engaged in illegal activities which the courts here will not recognise. In such a case, there is no injustice in letting the victim's claim prevail.

[26] He argues that this is consistent with the decision of the House of Lords in *Tinsley v Milligan* [1993] 3 All ER 65, [1994] 1 AC 340 which cited with approval ([1993] 3 All ER 65 at 72, [1994] 1 AC 340 at 354–355) the following passage from *Holman v Johnson* (1775) 1 Cowp 341 at 343, 98 ER 1120 at 1121:

> 'The objection, that a contract is immoral or illegal as between plaintiff and defendant, sounds at all times very ill in the mouth of the defendant. It is not for his sake, however, that the objection is ever allowed; but it is founded in general principles of policy, which the defendant has the advantage of, contrary to the real justice, as between him and the plaintiff, by accident, if I may so say. The principle of public policy is this; *ex dolo malo non oritur actio*. No court will lend its aid to a man who founds his cause of action upon an immoral or an illegal act. If, from the plaintiff's own stating or otherwise, the cause of action appears to arise *ex turpi causa*, or the transgression of a positive law of this country, there the court says he has not right to be assisted. It is upon that ground the court goes; not for the sake of the defendant, but because they will not lend their aid to such a plaintiff. So if the plaintiff and defendant were to change sides, and the defendant was to bring his action against the plaintiff, the latter would then have the advantage of it; for where both are equally in fault *potior est conditio defendentis*.'

[27] As Lord Goff explained in *Tinsley v Milligan* [1993] 3 All ER 65 at 72, [1994] AC 340 at 355:

> 'It is important to observe that, as Lord Mansfield CJ made clear, the principle is not a principle of justice: it is a principle of policy, whose application is indiscriminate and so can lead to unfair consequences as between the parties to litigation. Moreover the principle allows no room for the exercise of any discretion by the court in favour of one party or the other.'

[28] This principle applies as between conspirators in a wrongdoing. Neither can be heard to base his claim or his defence upon the wrongdoing. The court will not take notice of illegal activity. The result is indiscriminate in the sense that the party which benefits from the application of the principle does so not because of any merits on his side but simply because the other party is debarred from relying on the illegal activity for his claim or defence, as the case may be. Mr Briggs says that the same principle must apply not only as between parties to the wrongdoing but also, as here, where the claimant is not a party to the wrongdoing but the recipient of the stolen funds is. On public policy grounds, the court will not allow the recipient to hold onto the claimant's money if, to do so, he has to rely on a change of position which the court considers illegal.

[29] Mr Briggs says that the change of position relied on by the defendants here consists of the conversion of most of the $8.05m into naira and the distribution of all of it (less commission) to Chief Anajemba's order. All of that was done under and by reference to a foreign exchange contract which was illegal in Nigeria by virtue of that country's Foreign Exchange (Monitoring and Miscellaneous Provisions) Decree 1995 (the Decree). Since it was illegal in Nigeria, it is unenforceable and will not be recognised by the courts here.

[after considering the arguments relating to the illegality of the contracts, Laddie J continued]

[38] In my view, even at this stage, all the evidence points one way. All of the transactions entered into by these defendants in relation to the claimants' $US8.05m were illegal and any contracts entered into to effect such transactions were also illegal. There is no real or substantial case to the contrary.

[39] I should mention that during the course of argument I suggested to Mr Briggs that the conversion of the dollars to naira was covered by the Decree but that, perhaps, that was not so in respect of the $US2,085,528 which was passed on to Chief Anajemba's creditors without conversion. Mr Briggs said that even that sort of transaction would be caught by the provisions of s. 29(1)(c) of the Decree,

set out above. That is probably so. But in any event this point, if it is a point at all, was not taken by the defendants and it must be remembered in this context that Professor Collier's evidence was that 'the transactions' were illegal. By that he clearly meant all the relevant transactions. In their evidence in reply to this, the defendants did not seek to draw any distinction between the $US2,085,528 and the rest of the $US8.05m.

[40] It follows that I accept the submission that the transactions, save for the retention of the commission, were illegal as were the contracts providing for them and no real case to the contrary has been put forward.

IS THE NIGERIAN ILLEGALITY RECOGNISED AT COMMON LAW?

[41] Although Mr Briggs puts his case both at common law and under the Order, I did not understand Miss Roberts to dispute that, were he to succeed on the former, little point would be served by examining the strength of the latter. The nature of Mr Briggs' submission are set out at [30], above. In support of them he relies on *Foster v Driscoll, Lindsay v Attfield, Lindsay v Driscoll* [1929] 1 KB 470, [1928] All ER Rep 130, *Regazzoni v KC Sethia* (1944) Ltd [1957] 3 All ER 286, [1958] AC 301, *Kahler v Midland Bank Ltd* [1949] 2 All ER 621, [1950] AC 24 and *Ralli Bros v Cia Navieria Sota y Aznar* [1920] 2 KB 287, [1920] All ER Rep 427.

[42] I do not understand Miss Roberts to dispute Mr Briggs' general proposition. Her point is that this was an undeveloped area of law and that the courts have to decide on a case-by-case basis whether the wrongdoing is of sufficient significance to deprive the recipient of his defence of change of position. In each case the court needs to decide whether the recipient's actions are so heinous that it would be equitable to require restitution in full.

[43] I do not accept that submission. It would represent a return to the principle of the length of the Lord Chancellor's foot (or the foot of whosoever takes the Lord Chancellor's place). It seems to me that the approach of Lord Goff in *Tinsley v Milligan*, set out at [27], above, applies to this sort of case. There is no room for the exercise of any discretion by the court in favour of one party or the other. If the recipient's actions of changing position are treated here as illegal, the court cannot take them into account. The recipient cannot put up a tainted claim to retention against the victim's untainted claim for restitution. It may be, as Mr Briggs suggests, that in some cases the illegality will be so minor as to be ignored on the de minimis principle. This is not such a case.

[44] It follows that there is no defence to the claim. The claimants are entitled to recover all of the $US8.05m. I should add that, even were the commission of $US50,000 not illegal as being payment for carrying out illegal forex operations, it would be money retained by the defendants for no consideration (for none was asserted). It would have to be returned to the claimants for the same reasons as the $US155,000 had to be returned by the defendant in the *Lipkin Gorman* case.

NOTES AND QUESTIONS

1. Although Lord Goff also said that it is 'commonly accepted that the defence should not be open to a wrongdoer', he did not explain what was meant by the term 'wrongdoer'. One possibility was that Lord Goff had in mind the injunction from the United States *Restatement of Restitution* section 141(2) which states that change of position is not available to a tortfeasor. However, Laddie J treated a 'wrongdoer' in a wider sense by applying it to all illegal activity.

2. Although not mentioned by Laddie J, in *Garland v Consumers' Gas Co.* (2004) 237 DLR (4th) 385 (above, 140) the Supreme Court of Canada also denied the defence of change of position to the defendant who sold gas pursuant to regulations that turned out to be illegal. The Supreme Court quoted from Lord Goff and said that the illegality rendered the defendant a 'wrongdoer'.

3. In the following extract, Tettenborn levels three criticisms at the decision of Laddie J.

- **A Tettenborn, 'Bank Fraud, Change of Position and Illegality: The Case of the Innocent Money-Launderer'** [2005] *LMCLQ* 6, 7–8.

This decision will no doubt come as a very welcome windfall to harassed bank officials and their lawyers chasing after misapplied money, particularly as stolen money often ends up in third world states with strict foreign exchange laws, and the chances are that some recipient somewhere will have broken them in passing the funds on. Nevertheless, there are a number of difficulties with *Barros*, on both theoretical and practical grounds.

First, it is worth noting that Laddie J's reading of Lord Goff's opinion in *Lipkin Gorman v Karpnale* on the unavailability of change of position to a wrongdoer is, to say the least, novel. Most previous writers on restitution law have interpreted this reference as applying to the circumstances of the original unjust enrichment, thus (for example) preventing the defence being invoked in cases of enrichment by wrongdoing.[1] Laddie J, by contrast, reads it as referring to the circumstances of the alleged change of position itself. This seems, if one may say so, somewhat implausible. While literally we could regard someone who commits a crime in changing his position as a 'wrongdoer,' there is no indication that Lord Goff was thinking of a public policy rule precluding reliance on the defence in a situation of this sort.

Secondly, this brings us on to a further point that in *Barros* the *ex turpi causa* maxim was applied in a novel way, ie, to shut out a defence to an existing claim rather than to nullify a cause of action that would otherwise exist. Now, this certainly looks like a neat and logical step, albeit one for which there is no authority. Nevertheless, it is by no means clear that it is one the law ought to take. On the contrary: it is highly arguable that the effect of *ex turpi causa* in the law of obligations ought to be limited to the creation, or rather non-creation, of rights to sue. There is, it is suggested, a substantial difference between taking away a cause of action so as to give a defendant a possibly unjust escape from liability, and artificially disabling a defence so as to allow a claim to succeed on what is effectively a false basis (which was what *Barros* effectively did). The former can just be said to promote public policy, albeit in a rough and ready way. The latter is apt to lead to such wildly arbitrary results, especially if the claim—as here—is an enormous one, that it ought to make any lawyer think twice.

Thirdly, there are difficulties with Laddie J's strict approach to the maxim *ex turpi causa non oritur actio*. Whatever the position as regards illegal contracts, and even accepting that the *ex turpi causa* principle is not some head of discretionary relief to be to be applied or not in the same way as (say) an equitable remedy,[2] the tendency as regards non-contractual causes of action has previously been to apply the maxim with some degree of flexibility. With all respect to Laddie J, the practice has not been to operate the rule as a kind of rule of evidence arbitrarily barring any pleading of one's own illegal conduct in support of any part of one's case. On the contrary: even though entirely amorphous tests such as whether ignoring the illegality would 'shock the public conscience'[3] have been rejected[4] the degree of illegality and its interaction with the transaction concerned have continued to be regarded as highly relevant. Thus in the tort decision *Cross v Kirkby*,[5] concerning whether an attacker could sue for disproportionate force used in self-defence, Beldam LJ posited a more fluid test of whether the claim was 'so closely connected or inextricably bound up with his own criminal or illegal conduct' that the court could not permit recovery without appearing to condone that conduct. And

---

1 E.g. A Burrows, *Law of Restitution*, 2nd edn (2002), 526; Tettenborn, *Law of Restitution in England and Ireland*, 3rd edn (2002), 278.

2 See *Tinsley v Milligan* [1994] 1 AC 340, 355 (Lord Goff), cited by Laddie J at [27].

3 E.g. *Thackwell v Barclays Bank Ltd* [1986] 1 All ER 676, 687 (Hutchison J); *Euro-Diam Ltd v Bathurst* [1990] 1 QB 1, 35 (Kerr LJ).

4 See *Tinsley v Milligan* [1994] 1 AC 340, e.g., at 369 (Lord Browne-Wilkinson). All the Law Lords agreed in this.

5 [2000] TLR 268 (CA).

in the deceit case of *Standard Chartered Bank Ltd v Pakistan National Shipping Corp (No.2)*[6] Cresswell J said that, in order for *ex turpi causa* to bite, the claimant's conduct had to be so clearly reprehensible as to justify curial condemnation, and also to be so much part and parcel of his claim as to justify refusing relief.[7] Of course tort is not restitution: nevertheless, it would be odd, to say the least, if a different and more rigid rule applied in restitution cases.

So far we have been dealing with more or less theoretical points. But the proof of the pudding is in the eating, and it is suggested that the result in *Barros* is somewhat difficult to justify. Assuming that Nwandu was indeed the innocent dupe of the fraudsters who attacked Banco Noroeste, all the defendants had done was allow to pass through their hands monies that unknown to them were the proceeds of a fraud. Against this factor, which surely ought to have weighed heavily in their favour, was an offence that was not particularly heinous (a technical infraction of Nigerian exchange control laws). Furthermore, its connection with the defendant's change of position was fairly loose and incidental. On Laddie J's reasoning, it would apparently have made all the difference if the dollars had been passed on to the recipients as dollars, with the conversion to naira being done by them (since then no crime against the exchange would have been committed by the defendants). Even assuming that the commission of a crime by a defendant ought to be capable in principle of shutting out his right to defend, it is hard to avoid the conclusion that laying them open to an otherwise undeserving claim of $8 million was an entirely disproportionate response.

(v) CAN A DEFENDANT CHANGE HER POSITION BY PURCHASING SOMETHING VALUABLE WHICH SHE STILL RETAINS?

Although this issue has not yet been directly considered by an English Court, in an obiter dicta suggestion in *Lipkin Gorman* (above, 28), Lord Templeman suggested that a defendant that spent money received on a second hand motor car would not have a defence to the extent of the second hand value of the car. The following decision of the Newfoundland Court of Appeal reached the opposite conclusion.

- *RBC Dominion Securities Inc. v Dawson*
  (1992) 111 DLR (4th) 230, Newfoundland Court of Appeal

The appellant was a securities brokerage company that sold shares to a brother and sister, Mr and Ms Dawson. Years later the company mistakenly overstated to Mr and Ms Dawson the size of their share holdings and, upon sale, overpaid Ms Dawson by $4,919 and Mr Dawson by $3,206. Ms Dawson spent the money on (1) refurbishing a dining room table and chairs; (2) purchasing a video recorder; (3) purchasing a kitchen table and chairs; (4) purchasing a chesterfield; (5) purchasing a floor lamp and shades and drapes; and (6) purchasing clothing. Even though the Newfoundland Court of Appeal accepted that she remained enriched following her change of position, the change of position defence was applied in relation to all purchases except the chesterfield which she said she would have purchased in any event.

Cameron JA (delivering the judgment of the Court of Appeal): ... With the exception of the chesterfield, which Ms Dawson clearly stated she would have purchased anyway, there is no basis

---

6 [1998] 1 Lloyd's Rep. 684 (Cresswell J); varied [2000] 1 Lloyd's Rep 218 (CA); *rev'd* [2002] UKHL, 43; [2003] 1 AC 959.

7 [1998] 1 Lloyd's Rep 684, 705–706. Indeed, in that case the plaintiff successfully recovered in an action for deceit despite the fact that it had itself participated in a small deception.

upon which to overturn the trial judge's finding of fact that Ms Dawson would not have made the purchases had she not received the windfall from the sale of the stocks.

What are the equities of the situation where the defendant may have an asset which has some value though perhaps not equivalent to the money spent? If it is an asset, like the chesterfield, which the defendant would have purchased whether the mistake had been made or not, then clearly the defence of change of circumstances is not established to the extent of the money paid for that item. However, the more difficult questions arise with the refurbishing of the furniture and the purchase of items which would not have been bought except for the mistake but which continue to enrich the defendant.

The appellant submits that Ms Dawson has been enriched by the increase in value of her personal assets and should pay to the appellant an amount representing this enrichment. Of course, she has been enriched. These assets replace the money. That is not at issue. The question is should she now be called upon to return the money. The mere fact that she continues to benefit from the money does not defeat the defence of change of circumstances. Here, with one exception, the furniture acquisitions represent replacement of items Ms Dawson had in her possession when she would not have replaced the items except for the error. The trial judge found that Ms Dawson changed her standard of living when she would not have otherwise done so. The expenditures were not to meet ordinary expenses or pay existing debts. Equity favours Ms Dawson. Because of the actions of the appellant Ms Dawson exchanged less valuable items for more valuable items. Her position is not unlike the person who lives at a higher standard of living because more money is available but would not have done so were it not for the windfall.

NOTES AND QUESTIONS

1. Although this decision is contrary to the obiter dictum of Lord Templeman in *Lipkin Gorman*, it does have its supporters. Grantham and Rickett, *Enrichment and Restitution in New Zealand* (2000), 337 consider the rationale of the case to be that the court regarded the inconvenience to the defendant of having to make restitution as outweighing the claimant's right to restitution. In contrast, Nolan argues that the case is one of disenrichment by applying a notion of 'subjective revaluation': 'the new furniture is only valuable to her on the basis of her overall wealth that has turned out to be ill-founded': R Nolan, 'Change of Position' in P Birks (ed.) *Laundering and Tracing* (1995), 140.

2. Would the result of the case have been different if, instead of using the overpayment to purchase furniture and household items, she had used it to purchase different securities which were trading at the same price and could easily be sold? What if the hypothetical securities were trading at a *higher* price?

(vi) DOES CHANGE OF POSITION APPLY TO CLAIMS FOR PROPRIETARY RESTITUTION?

In principle (given that unjust enrichment is the ground of the claim) it must be the case that change of position operates as a defence to a *proprietary* restitutionary claim as well as a personal claim. In contrast, it is unlikely that change of position is a defence to a pure proprietary claim where the proprietary right is not created in response to an unjust enrichment: if this is so, it represents a crucial practical reason for recognizing a distinction between restitutionary proprietary claims and pure proprietary claims (see above, 704). This issue has been helpfully discussed in the following extract.

- **P Birks, 'Change of Position and Surviving Enrichment', in W Swadling (ed)** *The Limits of Restitutionary Claims* (1997)

Will the defence [of change of position] apply to a proprietary claim after a tracing exercise? Suppose that I pay you £1000 by mistake. Let it be given that the mistake is so fundamental as to prevent the property passing even at law. The circumstances are nevertheless such that you honestly and reasonably believe that you are entitled to the money. You put the money in a deposit account but, to celebrate the addition to your wealth, you spend £250 from your current account on a meal at the Ritz which you would never otherwise have bought. Some months later you take the £1,000 from the deposit account to buy a watercolour. That watercolour is now valued at £1,500.

My first thoughts are of a claim in the first measure of restitution, for the amount of the enrichment received. But I am warned that I shall be met by a defence of change of position which will reduce my recover to £750. I am therefore advised to go for the traceably surviving enrichment. I trace the £1,000 in and out of the deposit account and into the painting. I now claim to be entitled to the painting or, at least, to a charge over the plaintiff for £1,000.

This is very difficult. If we refuse to allow the defence of change of position to operate, we create a nonsense: the defence can be outflanked so long as (a) the enrichment received can be traced to specific assets and (b) the facts will support a proprietary claim. Goff and Jones cautiously say that a proprietary claim may in some cases be defeated by a change of position. They cite the Court of Appeal in *Re Diplock*, where the claim *in rem* was barred, as inequitable, in the case in which Guy's Hospital had used its Diplock money to improve a ward. If we construe the court as having said that the money was traceable into the building but that the proprietary claim would nevertheless be disallowed, that can indeed be understood as giving effect to a change of position. Unfortunately, the facts are somewhat less strong than those of our example, because in our example there is no doubt whatever that the value of the money received is traceable into the painting, while it could be said that when Guy's improved a ward it consumed the value altogether, so that it was no longer traceable at all. However, there is a strong need to avoid the nonsensical circumvention of the defence. Let us suppose therefore that we cling on to *Diplock* as authority for the proposition that it applies even to a proprietary claim.

There remain two questions. First, if we once accept the defence, we have to face the task of explaining how exactly it operates in relation to proprietary claims. With the lien, that task is relatively easy. The sum secured by the lien can simply be diminished. It is much less easy to see how the defence can bear on the claim to the ownership of the watercolour, whether at law or in equity. The only viable course would appear to be to put the plaintiff on terms, making his right to assert his property conditional upon a payment of money to make good the other's change of position.

The second question is if anything more difficult. Can the proprietary claim be said to arise from unjust enrichment? If not, it is altogether outside the scope of the defence. When a plaintiff traces value through substitutions and claims a proprietary right in the asset in which that value now resides, the right which he asserts is not the right which he had at the beginning of the story. The original right, the property which he had in the asset at the beginning of the story, may have arisen from, for example, a contract with and conveyance from a third party. The new right cannot be so explained. The plaintiff in our example never owned the water colour. The right acquired in the substitute in which the value of the original is invested is a right raised to reverse unjust enrichment. All proprietary rights which are contingent on a tracing exercise have that character. Having that character they are indeed vulnerable to the defence of change of position, since that defence is peculiar to claims arising from unjust enrichment. Furthermore, it is probably wrong to suppose that the tracing plaintiff has already acquired title immediately upon each substitution in the chain. What he has during the period of the substitutions is no more than a restitutionary power to vest in himself an asset into which he successfully traces his value, analogous to the power which the victim of a misrepresentation has to rescind and revest. If you use my mistaken payment to buy a sheep and then exchange the sheep for a goat, I cannot sue you for converting the goat, because, unless and until the power to vest the goat in me is exercised, I have no immediate right to possession of it.

The conclusion thus far must be that proprietary rights in substitute assets are restitutionary and that the defence applies no less to those proprietary restitutionary claims than to restitutionary personal claims in the first measure. Such claims being in the nature of powers, the power cannot be exercised without making good the recipient's change of position. In our example this means that the claim to the picture must one way or another be diminished to reflect the £250 change of position.

(vii) DOES CHANGE OF POSITION APPLY TO CLAIMS OTHER THAN UNJUST ENRICHMENT?

In *Lipkin Gorman* (above, 28) Lord Goff said that it is 'commonly accepted that the defence should not be open to a wrongdoer', although he did not explain what was meant by the term 'wrongdoer'. One possibility was that Lord Goff had in mind the injunction from the United States *Restatement of Restitution* section 141(2) which states that change of position is not available to a tortfeasor. We have seen that the Supreme Court of Canada in *Garland v Consumers' Gas Co.* (2004) 237 DLR (4th) 385 (above, 140), and Laddie J in *Barros Mattos Junior v Macdaniels Ltd* [2004] 3 All ER 299 (above, 796), interpreted 'wrongdoing' to mean any illegality that is not *de minimus*. This would also suggest (and is our preferred view) that the defence should not apply to claims for torts or other wrongs (whether the claim is for restitution for the wrong or for compensation for the wrong). Indeed, in *Lipkin Gorman* the defence of change of position was applied to the claim in unjust enrichment but in relation to the claim for conversion of the banker's draft it was denied. However, as the claim for conversion involved the same innocent defendant as the claim for unjust enrichment, some commentators have argued that this inconsistency should be eradicated (e.g. R Nolan, 'Change of Position' in P Birks (ed) *Laundering and Tracing* (1995) 135, 154; G Virgo 'What is the Law of Restitution About?' in W Cornish et al (eds) *Restitution: Past, Present and Future* (1999) 305, 321. Those that support the availability of change of position for claims in tort might derive some support from a cryptic obiter dictum of Lord Nicholls who, whilst speaking about the strict liability nature of a claim for conversion in *Kuwait Airways Corporation v Iraqi Airways Co. (Nos 4 and 5)* [2002] UKHL 19; [2002] 2 AC 883, 1093 [79], said this:

Some aspects of this rule have attracted criticism. Vindication of a plaintiff's proprietary interests requires that, in general, all those who convert his goods should be accountable for *benefits* they receive. They must make restitution to the extent they are unjustly enriched. The goods are his, and he is entitled to reclaim them and any benefits others have derived from them. Liability in this regard should be strict subject to defences available to restitutionary claims such as change of position: see *Lipkin Gorman v Karpnale Ltd* [1991] 2 AC 548. Additionally, those who act dishonestly should be liable to make good any *losses* caused by their wrongful conduct. Whether those who act innocently should also be liable to make good the plaintiff's losses is a different matter. A radical re-appraisal of the tort of conversion along these lines was not pursued on these appeals. So I shall say nothing more about it.

2. ESTOPPEL

Estoppel is a defence of considerable antiquity and has played a significant role in the early cases. But now its future is under a cloud. Indeed, it is strongly arguable that in unjust enrichment change of position will soon supplant estoppel completely. Given the doubts which currently surround the future of estoppel it is no longer appropriate to include a number of extracts from the old cases and so we shall focus attention on the leading modern case on the subject before turn to consider the future of the defence of estoppel in unjust enrichment and its relationship with the defence of change of position.

(1) THE TRADITIONAL POSITION

• *Avon County Council v Howlett* [1983] 1 WLR 605, Court of Appeal.

The claimants overpaid their employee, the defendant, when he was absent from work after suffering an injury during the course of his employment. It was held that the mistake which the claimants had made was one of fact rather than law, and that the claimants were *prima facie* entitled to recover the full amount of the over-payment which they had made (which was £1,007). The defendant argued that the claimants were estopped from recovering any part of the overpayment. The case was argued on a hypo-thetical basis because the trial judge found that all the money overpaid had been spent by the defendant. The court was asked to resolve the case on the following hypothetical state of facts, namely that the defendant had spent only £546.61 of the £1,007. The £546.61 was made up of £86.11 in social security benefits which the defendant did not claim, £53.50 spent on a suit, and £421 spent on the hire purchase of a motor car.

The Court of Appeal held that estoppel operated as a rule of evidence in an all or nothing fashion so that the claimants were not entitled to recover any part of the £1,007.

Cumming-Bruce LJ (after deploring the hypothetical nature of the question which the court had been asked to consider, continued): In argument before us upon this hypothetical question, it was contended on behalf of the defendant that where the defendant successfully proved that he had acted to his detriment upon a representation by the plaintiff which was inconsistent with the true facts, and that his detriment was proved to be substantial in the sense that it was not de minimis, he was entitled to keep all the money paid through the mistake which the plaintiff was estopped from alleging, even though the result was to leave him with a windfall profit. Alternatively, it was con-tended that if he was liable to repay any sum on the ground that it was inequitable for him to retain it (a) the onus lay upon the plaintiff to prove that the facts that made such retention inequitable, and (b) on the pleadings the plaintiffs had alleged no such facts or resulting inequity.

Having regard to the facts actually found by the judge, the whole of this argument was fanciful. The money had never been paid as a single sum to the defendant. £1,007 represented the total arrived at by adding together a large number of small sums received over a period of many months and paid as the remuneration on which he relied for discharge of his ordinary living expenses. By the date of trial nothing was left, and the judge found that it would be inequitable to require the defendant to repay anything. It would, in my view, be quite wrong in those circumstances for the court to indulge in speculation about where the onus might lie having regard to pleadings that were accepted by both parties to be a fiction. In other cases it may be a nice question whether on the pleaded facts the plaintiffs have established prima facie that it would be inequitable to retain some of the money had and received by a mistake which the plaintiffs are estopped from denying. If the defendant by his defence has raised estoppel, the plaintiff may be reply contend that it is inequitable to allow the defendant to retain part or all of the benefit of the mistake; the defendant may plead by rebuttal facts repelling the charge that retention is inequitable. At trial the evidential burden may shift. But none of this arises in this case because the facts found by the judge demonstrate that the case raised in grounds 2, 3 and 3A of the grounds of appeal is a fiction.

My conclusion is that once the judge had held that it would be inequitable to require the defendant to repay any part of the moneys overpaid, he should have refused to decide the case on a basis which was neither pleaded nor supported by evidence. If the plaintiffs wished to argue that it was inequitable that the defendant should retain some part of the £1,007, they should have pleaded the facts relied upon in support of that plea. It was submitted by Mr Fletcher [counsel for the plaintiffs] that only the defendant could know what had happened to the money, so to require the plaintiffs to plead facts giving rise to an equity in their favour is to place upon them a burden impossible to discharge. I disagree. The solution of their procedural problem may in the appropriate case lie in an application for discovery of documents and answers to interrogatories. But before the judge there was no reply by the plaintiffs alleging that it was inequitable for the defendant to retain any part of the money, and the evidence which the judge admitted proved that it was not inequitable. So on the case as pleaded, and on the evidence before him, there was no material on which he could hold that the defendant was liable to pay back any part of the money paid to him by the proved mistake of fact. . . .

Eveleigh LJ: . . . .

The judge was . . . asked to decide the case upon the basis that there had been an overpayment of £1,007 caused by a mistake of fact and that the defendant, relying upon a representation that he was entitled to the £1,007 spent £546.61 of it. The problem as thus posed contained no information as to whether or not it would be unconscionable for the defendant to retain the balance of the sum. It contained no information upon which the court could determine whether or not it would be unfair to make him repay. Having, in effect, been asked to ignore his finding of fact which was so favourable to the defendant I can readily understand the judge coming to the conclusion which he did. However, not without some hesitation, I have reached the same conclusion as Slade LJ, namely that once the defendant had shown detriment which prevented the plaintiffs from asserting the truth behind the payment that obstacle barred the whole of their claim for, pleaded simply as a case of mistake, evidence of the defendant's true entitlement was essential if the plaintiffs were to succeed. I think that this must follow from the speech of Lord Watson in *Ogilvie v West Australian Mortgage and Agency Corporation Ltd* [1896] AC 257, 270; and *Fung Kai Sun v Chan Fui Hing* [1951] AC 489 in which the former case was considered. Strictly speaking the words of Lord Watson were obiter, but as Slade LJ has pointed out, the decision of the Court of Appeal in *Greenwood v Martins Bank Ltd* [1932] 1 KB 371 was to the same effect. In that case Scrutton LJ said, at 383–4:

'If the claim of the bank were for damages for failure to disclose, it might be that the improbabilities of recovering anything in the action might be taken into account; but the authorities show that in a question of estoppel, where the question is whether the customer is estopped from alleging that certain bills are forgeries, if the bank has lost something, the value of that something is not the measure of its claim, but, the customer being estopped from proving the bills forgeries, the bank gains by the amount of the bills.'

I would not for myself regard *Skyring v Greenwood* (1825) 4 B & C 281 and *Holt v Markham* [1923] 1 KB 504 as determining the same question. Those cases may be explained upon the basis that the defendant's manner of living generally had been influenced by the payments made to them so that although they had not been able to point to specific items of expenditure amounting to the whole sum in question the money had nonetheless been spent. Alternatively such cases may be said to rest upon the basis that to compel the defendant to make any repayment would be to impose upon him an overall financial strain brought about only by his being misled as to his financial position by the representations of the plaintiffs.

However I am far from saying that whenever the recipient of money paid under a mistake has been led to think that it is his, then he will be entitled to retain the whole by demonstrating that he has spent part of it. The payment may involve no representation, as where a debtor presents an account to a creditor. Then while there might have been a representation there may be circumstances which would render it unconscionable for the defendant to retain a balance in his hands. There may also be circumstances which would make it unfair to allow the plaintiff to recover. It may be that it is important to determine whether or not the plaintiff making the representation owes a duty to the defendant as was the case in *Ogilvie v West Australian Mortgage and Agency Corporation Ltd* [1896] AC 257. I too am unhappy in being asked to decide a case in an unreal situation and I am content to say that the question we have been asked to determine is that already decided in *Greenwood v Martins Bank Ltd* by Scrutton LJ [1932] 1 KB 371.

Slade LJ: . . . .

ESTOPPEL

I now turn to the defence of estoppel. The following general propositions of law are to be found set out in *Goff and Jones, The Law of Restitution*, 2nd edn (1978), 554–5 (though I do not quote them verbatim). A plaintiff will be estopped from asserting his claim to restitution if the following conditions are satisfied: (a) the plaintiff must generally have made a representation of fact which led the defendant to believe that he was entitled to treat the money as his own; (b) the defendant must have, bona fide and without notice of the plaintiff's claim, consequently changed his position; (c) the payment must not have been primarily caused by the fault of the defendant.

In my opinion these propositions are entirely consistent with both the general principles which govern the doctrine of estoppel and with the authorities which have been cited to this court, illustrating the relevance of estoppel as a defence to claims to restitution. Examples of the more important of such authorities are *Skyring v Greenwood*, 4 B & C 281; *Holt v Markham* [1923] 1 KB 504 and *Lloyds Bank Ltd v Brooks* (1950) 6 Legal Decisions Affecting Bankers 161.

In the present case it is common ground that the plaintiffs made representations to the defendant which led him to believe that he was entitled to treat the entirety of the overpaid moneys as his own. This was conceded by the plaintiffs at the trial, so that the judge did not find it necessary in his judgment to give any particulars at all of the relevant representations. Certain authorities suggest that a plea of estoppel can afford a good defence to a claim for restitution only if the plaintiff owed a duty to the defendant to speak or act in a particular way: see, for example, *R. E. Jones Ltd v Waring and Gillow Ltd* [1926] AC 670, 693, per Lord Sumner; *Lloyds Bank Ltd v Brooks*, 6 Legal Decisions Affecting Bankers 161, 168 ff. However, this point causes no difficulty for the defendant in the present case since the plaintiffs, as the defendant's employers, in my opinion clearly owed him a duty not to misrepresent the amount of the pay to which he was entitled from time to time, unless the misrepresentations were caused by incorrect information given to them by the defendant. It has not been suggested that the misrepresentations were so caused or that the overpayments were brought about by the defendant's own fault.

The judge found as a fact that the defendant had, bona fide and without notice of the plaintiffs' claim, changed his position in reliance on the representations, by losing the claim for £86.11 social security benefit and expending the sum of £460.50 which I have already mentioned. In the circumstances and in accordance with the principles already stated, he was in my opinion clearly right to hold that the plaintiffs' claim was barred by estoppel to the extent of at least £546.61 and there is no challenge to this part of his decision. However, according to the defendant's case as specifically pleaded, the change of position which he has undergone in reliance on the plaintiffs' representations, has only deprived him of the opportunity to return £546.61 of the overpayment; it has not deprived him of the opportunity to return the outstanding balance of £460.39 which, so far as the pleading reveals, *may* be still in his possession.

The judge considered that the defence of estoppel was in effect capable of being applied pro tanto, in the sense that a payer who has overpaid a payee, even in circumstances where all of conditions (a), (b) and (c) above are satisfied, will be precluded from claiming restitution only to the extent that it would be inequitable to require the payee to repay the relevant sums or part of the relevant sums in question. The judge clearly regarded the doctrine of estoppel as being a flexible doctrine, as indeed

Lord Denning MR described it in *Amalgamated Investment & Property Co. Ltd v Texas Commerce International Bank Ltd* [1982] QB 84, 122.

If I may respectfully say so, I feel some sympathy with the judge's point of view. I also initially found unattractive the submission, placed before and rejected by him, that, if the defendant be treated as having spent in reliance on the plaintiff's representations some £546.61 of the £1,007 received, the plaintiffs could not recover the balance of £460.39, even if it were still sitting untouched in some deposit account. At first sight such a conclusion would seem to leave the defendant unjustly enriched.

On further reflection, however, I think that references to broad concepts of justice or equity in a context such as the present may be somewhat misleading, as well as uncertain in their application. The conclusion of the judge in the present case really involves the proposition that, if the defendant is successfully to resist a claim for repayment of the entire sum of £1,007, the onus falls on him to prove specifically that the pecuniary amount of the prejudice suffered by him as a result of relying on the relevant representations made by the plaintiffs equals or exceeds that sum. For present purposes, however, one has to postulate a situation in which the defendant was perfectly entitled to conduct his business affairs on the assumption that the relevant representations were true, until he was told otherwise. Meantime, a defendant in the situation of the defendant in the present case may, in reliance on the representation, have either altered his general mode of living or undertaken commitments or incurred expenditure or entered into other transactions which it may be very difficult for him subsequently to recall and identify retrospectively in complete detail; he may even have done so, while leaving some of the particular moneys paid to him by the plaintiff untouched. If the pecuniary amount of his prejudice has to be precisely quantified by a defendant in such circumstances, he may be faced with obvious difficulties of proof. Thus, though extreme hypothetical cases can be envisaged, and indeed were canvassed in argument, in which broad considerations of equity and justice might appear to require the barring of a plaintiff's claim only pro tanto, if this were legally possible, I would not expect many such cases to arise in practice. In any event I do not consider the present case to be one of them, even on the basis of the facts as pleaded. I prefer to approach it simply by what I regard as the established legal principles governing the doctrine of estoppel.

Estoppel by representation is a rule of evidence, the consequence of which is simply to preclude the representor from averring facts contrary to his own representation: see *Spencer Bower and Turner, Estoppel by Representation*, 3rd edn (1977), 112. It follows that a party who, as a result of being able to rely on an estoppel, succeeds on a cause of action on which, without being able to rely on it, he would necessarily have failed, may be able to recover more than the actual damage suffered by him as a result of the representation which gave rise to it. Thus if a bank's customer is estopped from asserting that a cheque with which he has been debited is a forgery because of his failure to inform the bank in due time, so that it could have had recourse to the forger, the debit will stand for the whole amount and not merely that which could have been recovered from the forger: see *Ogilvie v West Australian Mortgage and Agency Corporation Ltd* [1896] AC 257. In that case Lord Watson said, at 270:

'There are some obiter dicta favouring the suggestion that, in a case like the present, where the amount of the forged cheques is about £1,500, the estoppel against the customer ought to be restricted to the actual sum which the bank could have recovered from the forger. But these dicta seem to refer, not to the law as it was, but as it ought to be; and, in any view of them, they are contrary to all authority and practice.'

The decision of the Court of Appeal in *Greenwood v Martins Bank Ltd* [1932] 1 KB 371, affirmed in the House of Lords [1933] AC 51, is to the same effect.

So far as they go, the authorities suggest that in cases where estoppel by representation is available as a defence to a claim for money had and received, the courts similarly do not treat the operation of the estoppel as being restricted to the precise amount of the detriment which the representee proves he has suffered in reliance on the representation. In *Skyring v Greenwood*, 4 B & C 281, the paymasters of a military corps had given credit in account to an officer for a period from January 1817 to November 1820, for certain increased pay. They had mistakenly supposed that this had been granted by a general order of 1806 to an officer of his situation. But in fact the paymasters had been informed in 1816 that the Board of Ordnance would not allow the increased payments to persons in the officer's situation. A statement of that account was delivered to the officer early in 1821, giving him credit for the increased pay to which they supposed him to be entitled. After the officer's death in 1822, his personal representatives sought to recover the whole of the pay which had been credited to him. The defendants claimed the right to retain the overpaid sums. The Court of King's Bench rejected this claim, apparently without any inquiry as to the amount of the expenditure or financial commitments which the officer had incurred in reliance upon the erroneous credit. The basis of the court's decision is to be found in the following passage from the judgment of Abbott CJ, at 289:

> 'I think it was their duty to communicate to the deceased the information which they had received from the Board of Ordnance; but they forbore to do so, and they suffered him to suppose during all the intervening time that he was entitled to the increased allowances. It is of great importance to any man, and certainly not less to military men than others, that they should not be led to suppose that their annual income is greater than it really is. Every prudent man accommodates his mode of living to what he supposes to be his income; it therefore works a great prejudice to any man, if after having had credit given him in account for certain sums, and having been allowed to draw on his agent on the faith that those sums belonged to him, he may be called upon to pay them back.'

In *Holt v Markham* [1923] 1 KB 504 the defendant was a demobilised officer of the Royal Air Force. His name was on a list called the Emergency List. This meant that, under a certain military regulation, he was entitled to a gratuity at a lower rate than if he was not on that list. The plaintiffs acted as the government's agents for the payment of gratuities to demobilised officers. In ignorance of the fact that the defendant was on the Emergency List, but also in forgetfulness of the regulation, and not appreciating the materiality of an officer being on that list, they paid the defendant his gratuity at the higher rate to which he would have been entitled if he had not been on it. Subsequently they sought to recover this sum. But by then the defendant, thinking this matter was concluded, had sold his holding of War Savings certificates and invested a substantial sum in a company which subsequently went into liquidation: see p. 507 of the report of the facts. The Court of Appeal held that the plaintiffs' action failed on two grounds, first that the plaintiffs' mistake was one of law rather than of fact and secondly that, as their conduct had led the defendant to believe that he might treat the money as his own and he had altered his position in that belief, the plaintiffs were estopped from alleging that the money had been paid under a mistake. Scrutton LJ put the matter very simply, at 514:

> 'I think this is a simple case of estoppel. The plaintiffs represented to the defendant that he was entitled to a certain sum of money and paid it, and after a lapse of time sufficient to enable any mistake to be rectified he acted upon the representation and spent the money.'

However, the facts as set out in the report of the case do not indicate that the defendant had necessarily spent the whole of his gratuity and Bankes and Warrington LJJ were careful not to suggest that they did. They clearly regarded it as immaterial whether or not he had. Thus Bankes LJ said, at 511:

> 'it appears that for a considerable time he was left under the impression that, although there had been at one time a doubt about his title to the money, that doubt had been removed, and in consequence he parted with his War Savings certificates. Having done that, it seems to me that he altered his position for the worse, and consequently the plaintiffs are estopped from alleging that the payment was made under a mistake of fact.'

Warrington LJ, at 512, referred to the defendant as having spent 'the whole or a large part of the gratuity which had been paid him.'

If it were in every case possible for the doctrine of estoppel by representation to operate merely pro tanto in cases where it is being invoked as a defence to an action for money had and received, I think that the Court of King's Bench in *Skyring v Greenwood*, 4 B & C 281, and the Court of Appeal in *Holt v Markham* [1923] 1 KB 504 and indeed Lynskey J in *Lloyds Bank Ltd v Brooks*, 6 Legal Decisions Affecting Bankers 161, would have been bound to conduct a much more exact process of quantification of the alteration of the financial position of the recipients, which had occurred by reason of the representations. The courts, however, in those cases, manifestly regarded any such process as irrelevant and inappropriate. All the relevant conditions for the operation of an estoppel being satisfied in those cases, the plea operated as a rule of evidence which precluded the payers from recovering any part of the money mistakenly overpaid or from retaining any part of the moneys mistakenly over-credited.

I think that no authority has been cited, other than the judgment of the judge, which directly supports the proposition that estoppel is capable of operating merely pro tanto in a case such as the present, where it is otherwise capable of being invoked as a complete defence to an action for money had and received. For the reasons which I have given, I conclude that such a proposition is contrary to principle and authority. The authors of *Goff and Jones, The Law of Restitution*, 2nd edn (1978), do not assert any such proposition, but they do say, at 556:

'The effect of such an estoppel will generally be to defeat the claim altogether. But where the defendant's change of position has deprived him of the opportunity to return only part of the money he has received, to dismiss the plaintiff's claim in its entirety would enable the defendant to make a profit out of the transaction. This should not be allowed. In such circumstances the court may only give effect to the estoppel, subject to the defendant's undertaking to repay to the plaintiff any part of the sum received which he ought not to be entitled to keep.'

The suggestion of an undertaking stems from the speech of Viscount Cave LC in *R. E. Jones Ltd v Waring and Gillow Ltd* [1926] AC 670. In that case the majority of the House of Lords held that the plaintiffs were entitled to recover certain moneys on the principle of *Kelly v Solari*, 9 M & W 54. Viscount Cave LC who dissented and with whom Lord Atkinson agreed, considered that the plaintiffs were estopped from recovering the money. On the particular facts, however, the operation of an estoppel in this manner would have left the defendants with a profit. The defendants disclaimed any desire to make such a profit and offered an undertaking (in effect) to return it to the plaintiffs. Viscount Cave LC, at 685, expressed the view that such undertaking should be recited in the order to be made on the appeal, but said that, subject to the undertaking, he would dismiss it.

I recognise that in some circumstances the doctrine of estoppel could be said to give rise to injustice if it operated so as to defeat in its entirety an action which would otherwise lie for money had and received. This might be the case for example where the sums sought to be recovered were so large as to bear no relation to any detriment which the recipient could possibly have suffered. I would for my part prefer to leave open the question whether in such a case the court would have jurisdiction, in the exercise of its discretion, to exact an undertaking of the nature referred to by Viscount Cave LC, if it was not voluntarily proffered by the defendant.

On the particular facts of the present case as pleaded and proved, however, I could in any event see no sufficient ground for exacting any such undertaking from the defendant in the exercise of the court's discretion, even assuming that such discretion existed. The conditions for the operation of an estoppel have in my opinion all been satisfied. For the reasons which I have given, both on principle and in accordance with authority, I conclude that such estoppel bars the whole of the plaintiffs' claim.

NOTES AND QUESTIONS

1. Why was the purchase of a suit and the payment of money towards the hire-purchase of a car considered to be a detriment? Was this not ordinary everyday expenditure? In *Skyring v Greenwood* (1825) 4 B & C 281, Abbott CJ stated that 'every prudent man accommodates his mode of living to what he supposes to be his income' (cited in the judgment of Slade LJ). Does this suggest that normal, everyday expenditure does count as a detriment for the purposes of estoppel? Would these expenditures have sufficed for the purposes of the defence of change of position (see below)?

2. Why did the Court of Appeal not take account of the second-hand value of the suit or the car in assessing the extent to which the defendant was no longer enriched?

3. It seems clear that the substantive burden of proof of establishing a detriment is on the party asserting that he has so acted. But Cumming-Bruce LJ appeared to envisage that the evidential burden of establishing the extent of the detriment might lie upon the representor. Can this approach be justified?

4. There is some doubt in the cases about the basis of estoppel. In some cases there is an emphasis on the need for a representation of fact by the party alleged to be estopped, while in other cases, it is asserted that there must be a breach of duty by the party estopped. Both elements feature in the judgments in *Howlett* and it is suggested that the streams of authority can be reconciled by recognizing that these are alternative requirements: in other words, a party alleging estoppel must show *either* a breach of duty or a collateral representation.

5. Should estoppel provide a complete defence only when the claimant knows of the facts giving rise to the right to restitution and *subsequently* represents that the defendant is entitled to retain the benefit? Is estoppel synonymous with 'waiver'?

6. Should estoppel be available as a defence to a claim brought by a public authority against the recipient of an *ultra vires* payment (see *Commonwealth of Australia v Burns*, above, 621)?

(2) THE FUTURE OF ESTOPPEL AND ITS RELATIONSHIP WITH CHANGE OF POSITION

The Court of Appeal's decision in *Avon County Council v Howlett* has been widely criticised (see, for example, Paul Key 'Excising Estoppel by Representation as a Defence to Restitution' [1995] *CLJ* 525). In *Lipkin Gorman*, Lord Goff referred to *Avon* and the result in that case that estoppel did not operate *pro tanto*. He stated that considerations 'such as these provide a strong indication that, in many cases, estoppel is not an appropriate concept to deal with the problem.' The relationship between change of position and estoppel was subsequently considered in the next two cases.

- *Scottish Equitable plc v Derby*
  [2001] EWCA Civ 369; [2001] 3 All ER 818, Court of Appeal

For the facts, see above, 765.

Robert Walker LJ: . . .

Estoppel

[38] I have already quoted Lord Goff's observation in the *Lipkin Gorman* case [1992] 4 All ER 512 at 533, [1991] 2 AC 548 at 579 that estoppel is not an appropriate concept to deal with the problem, partly because of its 'all or nothing' operation. The same view has been widely expressed, both by academic writers and in the courts. The Newfoundland Court of Appeal (in the *RBC Dominion Securities* case) has flatly rejected it. Jonathan Parker J (in *Philip Collins Ltd v Davis* [2000] 3 All ER 808

at 825–826) has described it as no longer apt. In doing so he referred to the judgment now under appeal, in which the judge avoided a general statement of principle but (on the facts of this case) distinguished the *Avon CC* case and said ([2000] 3 All ER 808 at 807):

'In my judgment, the justice of the situation is met by the extent to which the defence of change of position has succeeded and it would be wholly unjust and inappropriate in those circumstances to allow estoppel to operate so as to provide a complete defence to the whole of the overpayment.'

[39] In considering this part of the case the judge proceeded on the footing that Scottish Equitable had made to Mr Derby a representation that he really was entitled to the payment made to him in June 1995. It is not entirely clear whether the judge (at 804) made a positive finding to that effect, or simply set out counsel's submission and assumed for the purposes of argument that it was correct; but on any view there was ample evidential material to justify such a finding.

[40] The decision of this court in the *Avon CC* case was discussed at length both below and in this court and it calls for detailed mention. Mr Howlett was a schoolteacher who had an accident at work and was off work (but still employed) for more than a year and a half. After his employment had been terminated the county council, his employer, found that during his time off work it had paid him for eight months (rather than six months) at the full rate of pay and for a further eleven months (rather than six months) at half-rate. It claimed £1,007 from him as money paid under a mistake of fact. In his defence Mr Howlett pleaded that he had spent £460 on a suit and a second-hand car and that he had refrained from claiming social security benefit of £86. He pleaded that this detrimental reliance estopped the employer from recovering any part of the £1,007.

[41] At trial Mr Howlett's evidence was that he had in fact spent all the money. But his counsel (who was instructed at a trade union's expense and wished to treat the matter as a test case) declined to apply for permission to amend his pleadings. Judgment was given against Mr Howlett for the balance sum of £460 (which was, by a confusing coincidence, the same sum as Mr Howlett had spent on the suit and the car). In this court Cumming-Bruce LJ took an adverse view of counsel's expedient. He was disinclined—

'to give a judgment founded on estoppel on facts which exist only in the mind of the pleader. The law does not and should not develop by such a device, and the ratio of such a decision is liable to be seriously misleading. I do not consider that the decision of this court in the instant appeal is authority for the proposition that, where on the facts it would be clearly inequitable to allow a party to make a profit by pleading estoppel, the court will necessarily be powerless to prevent it.' (See [1983] 1 All ER 1073 at 1075–1076, [1983] 1 WLR 605 at 608.)

Cumming-Bruce LJ thought that the judge should have refused to decide the case on a basis which was neither pleaded (that is, that it would be inequitable to allow the defendant to retain part or all of the benefit) nor supported by evidence.

[42] Eveleigh LJ gave a fairly short judgment agreeing, with some hesitation, with Slade LJ. Slade LJ gave a fairly long judgment, approaching the matter by the established legal principles governing estoppel. He emphasised that estoppel by representation is in origin a rule of evidence, and that that is what confers its 'all or nothing' character. He referred to some well-known cases including *Skyring v Greenwood* (1825) 4 B & C 281, [1824–34] All ER Rep 104 and *Holt v Markham* [1923] 1 KB 504, [1922] All ER Rep 134, commenting that if estoppel by representation could operate in a limited and pro-portionate way the courts which decided those cases ([1983] 1 All ER 1073 at 1088, [1983] 1 WLR 605 at 624):

'... would have been bound to conduct a much more exact process of quantification of the alteration of the financial position of the recipients which had occurred by reason of the representations.'

[43] However, Slade LJ also said ([1983] 1 All ER 1073 at 1089, [1983] 1 WLR 605 at 624–625):

'I recognise that in some circumstances the doctrine of estoppel could be said to give rise to injustice if it operated so as to defeat in its entirety an action which would otherwise lie for money had and received. This might be the case for example where the sums sought to be recovered were so large as to bear no relation to any detriment which the recipient could possibly have suffered.'

Eveleigh LJ had made similar observations ([1983] 1 All ER 1073 at 1078, [1983] 1 WLR 605 at 611), and I have already quoted the remarks of Cumming-Bruce LJ ([41] above). Harrison J ([2000] 3 All ER 793 at 807) treated the present case as—

'just the sort of situation that the Court of Appeal must have had in mind in *Avon CC v Howlett* when expressing reservations about the ambit of that decision.'

[44] I would be content to follow the judge in refraining from attempting any general statement of principle and treating this case as comfortably within the exception recognised by all three members of this court in the *Avon CC* case. We cannot overrule that case but we can note that it was not seen, even by the court which decided it, as a wholly satisfactory authority, because of its fictional element.

[45] I should record one further novel and ingenious argument addressed to us by Mr Moriarty (but generously attributed by him to his junior, Mr Handyside). That is that, since the *Lipkin Gorman* case, the defence of change of position pre-empts and disables the defence of estoppel by negativing detriment. Detriment must, it was correctly submitted, be judged at the time when the representor seeks to go back on his representation, since—

'the real detriment or harm from which the law seeks to give protection is that which would flow from the change of position if the assumption were deserted that led to it. So long as the assumption is adhered to, the party who altered his situation upon the faith of it cannot complain. His complaint is that when afterwards the other party makes a different state of affairs the basis of an assertion of right against him then, if it is allowed, his own original change of position will operate as a detriment.' (See Dixon J in *Grundt v Great Boulder Pty. Gold Mines Ltd* (1937) 59 CLR 641 at 674, quoted in Spencer Bower and Turner *The Law Relating to Estoppel by Representation* (3rd edn, 1977) pp 110–111.)

[46] The argument can be simply explained by an illustration in the form of a dialogue. A pays £1000 to B, representing to him 'I have carefully checked all the figures and this is all yours'. B spends £250 on a party and puts £750 in the bank. A discovers that he has made a mistake and owed B nothing. He learns that B has spent £250 and he asks B to repay £750. B: 'You are estopped by your representation on which I have acted to my detriment.' A: 'You have not acted to your detriment. You have had a good party, and at my expense, because I cannot recover the £250 back from you.' The facts that B has spent £250 in an enjoyable way, and that A readily limits his claim to £750, put the argument in its most attractive form. But it seems to have some validity even if B had lost £250 on a bad investment, and A began by suing him for £1000.

[47] I find this argument not only ingenious but also convincing. If I prefer to base my conclusion primarily on the grounds relied on by the judge it is partly because the argument is novel and appears not to have been considered by any of the distinguished commentators interested in this area of the law. But at present I do not see how the argument could be refuted.

[48] Will estoppel by representation wither away as a defence to a claim for restitution of money paid under a mistake of fact? It can be predicted with some confidence that with the emergence of the defence of change of position, the court will no longer feel constrained to find that a representation has been made, in a borderline case, in order to avoid an unjust result. It can also be predicted, rather less confidently, that development of the law on a case by case basis will have the effect of enlarging rather than narrowing the exception recognised by this court in the *Avon CC* case. That

process might be hastened (or simply overtaken) if the House of Lords were to move away from the evidential origin of estoppel by representation towards a more unified doctrine of estoppel, since proprietary estoppel is a highly flexible doctrine which, so far from operating as 'all or nothing', aims at 'the minimum equity to do justice' (*Crabb v Arun DC* [1975] 3 All ER 865 at 880, [1976] Ch 179 at 198). Paul Key has drawn attention ('Excising Estoppel by Representation as a Defence to Restitution' [1995] CLJ 525 at 533) to two decisions of the High Court of Australia (*Waltons Stores (Interstate) Ltd v Maher* (1988) 164 CLR 387 and *Commonwealth of Australia v Verwayen* (1990) 170 CLR 394) which he describes as a fundamental attack on the traditional perception of estoppel as a complete defence.

[49] The remarks in the last four paragraphs are no more than tentative observations on points which were not fully argued, as not being necessary for the determination of the appeal. For the reasons given earlier in this judgment—which are essentially the reasons given by the judge in his admirable judgment—I would dismiss this appeal.

Keene LJ agreed and **Simon Brown LJ** also agreed in a short concurring judgment.

- *National Westminster Bank plc v Somer International (UK) Ltd*
  [2001] EWCA Civ 970; [2002] QB 1286, Court of Appeal

Somer International was a client of the claimant bank. In April 1997, it informed the bank that it was expecting a deposit into its account of between $US 70,000 and 78,000 from a customer called Mentor. The next month the bank received $US 76,708 for a customer with a similar name and mistakenly credited the account of Somer International and notified Somer International that the amount had been received. Thinking that its customer had made the promised payment, Somer International sent two shipments of goods, worth £13,180 to the customer. Subsequently the bank notified Somer International of the error but the customer was no longer trading and had disappeared as a trading entity. The trial judge held that although the defence of estoppel had been made out, it only operated *pro tanto*, to the extent of the value of the goods sent to the customer. Somer International appealed to the Court of Appeal, contending that estoppel should operate as a complete defence. After considering *Avon County Council v Howlett* and *Scottish Equitable* in detail, the Court of Appeal dismissed the appeal, holding that the detriment suffered by Somer International was not proportionate to the size of the mistaken payment so that it would be unconscionable if Somer International were not required to make restitution of the difference.

Potter LJ [*after discussing the facts and judgments in Avon County Council and in Scottish Equitable*]

[29]. . . in a situation where A mistakenly transfers to B, or recognises his entitlement to a sum of money and B spends or loses some of it in a bad investment, but places the balance in the bank, if A then sues B but limits his claim to that balance, no detriment is demonstrable by B. Robert Walker LJ [in *Scottish Equitable*] stated that he found this argument, which appeared not to have been considered by commentators interested in this area of law, to be not only ingenious but convincing. However, he placed his decision upon the basis that recovery was in this case consistent with the decision in the *Avon CC* case. He concluded his judgment by predicting 'with some confidence' that with the emergence of the defence of change of position the court would no longer feel constrained to find that a representation has been made, in a borderline case, in order to avoid an unjust result, as appeared historically to be the position. He also predicted that the development of the law on a case by case basis would have the effect of enlarging rather than narrowing the exception recognised in the *Avon CC* case. Finally, he observed ([2001] 3 All ER 818 at [48]):

'That process might be hastened (or simply overtaken) if the House of Lords were to move away from the evidential origin of estoppel by representation towards a more unified doctrine of estoppel, since proprietary estoppel is a highly flexible doctrine which, so far from operating as "all or nothing", aims at "the minimum equity to do justice" (*Crabb v Arun DC* [1975] 3 All ER 865 at 880, [1976] Ch 179 at 198).'

[30] It seems to me that the facts of this case are such that, assuming the judge was correct in holding that a representation had been made by NatWest upon which Somer acted to its detriment in consigning further goods to Mentor to the value of some £13,000 but in no further respect, it involves this court in facing directly the questions raised by Robert Walker LJ. In the *Scottish Equitable* case the actual detriment found by the court, and which Scottish Equitable conceded it would not seek to recover, was some £9,660 out of a total overpayment of £172,451, a ratio of 1:17, giving rise to an overpayment of £162,790. While it could not be said that the detriment to Mr Derby was de minimis, it could readily be held that it was unconscionable and inequitable to allow him to retain the vast bulk of the overpayment, when his real detriment was limited to such a small proportion, and hence within the exception to the 'all or nothing' rule recognised in the *Avon CC* case. The instant case is, by reason of the sums involved, a somewhat less glaring illustration of an unjustifiable windfall to the defendant. That said, however, in cases of payments made under a mistake of fact, it is difficult to see why principles of equity and unconscionability should not apply to cover any case in which it appears a substantial windfall would otherwise be incurred by the transferee at the expense of the mistaken transferor.

. . . [*after discussing the facts, Potter LJ continued*]

[35] It is unattractive that, in a case of moneys paid over under a mistake of fact and sought to be recovered on the basis of unjust enrichment, the extent of the recovery should depend on whether or not, at the time of the transfer of the moneys, the transferor represented by words or conduct that the transferee was entitled to such payment. When the mistake occurs, particularly in the context of a banker/customer relationship, whether or not an actual representation as to entitlement was made or can be spelt out is largely fortuitous and ex hypothesi the result of accident rather than deliberate conduct. It also seems clear that, where there has been such a representation, the only substantial hurdle standing in the way of recovery, subject to an appropriate equitable adjustment in relation to the actual 'detriment' suffered, is the view that the historical origin and technical status of estoppel by representation as a rule of evidence dictates an 'all or nothing' solution the effect of which is that, once the representation has been acted on to the detriment of the transferee the contrary may not be asserted. This differs from the position in the case of so-called 'equitable' or 'promissory' estoppel in respect of which a specific promise to waive or refrain from enforcing rights may be withdrawn on reasonable notice and, in 'proprietary' estoppel, where when giving effect to the interest or right in property which the party raising the estoppel asserts, the court assumes a wide discretion as to the terms on which such relief is granted. In this respect estoppel by representation also differs in nature from the defence of 'change of position' which is only permitted to prevail to the extent that it would be inequitable to require the transferee to return the money.

[36] There is no doubt that the preponderance of legal authority and judicial dicta at the highest level favours the view that estoppel by representation is a rule of evidence rather than of substantive law: see *Low v Bouverie* [1891] 3 Ch 82 at 105, [1891–4] All ER Rep 348 at 355 *per* Bowen LJ:

'Estoppel is only a rule of evidence; you cannot found an action upon estoppel . . . [It] . . . is only important as being one step in the progress towards relief on the hypothesis that the defendant is estopped from denying the truth of something which he has said.'

And see to similar effect *Nippon Menkwa Kabushiki Kaisha* (*Japan Cotton Trading Co. Ltd*) *v Dawsons Bank Ltd* (1935) 51 Ll L Rep 147 at 150 *per* Lord Russell of Killowen, see also *London Joint Stock Bank Ltd v Macmillan* [1918] AC 777 at 818, [1918–19] All ER Rep 30 at 50 *per* Viscount Haldane: '. . . it is hardly a rule of what is called substantive law in the sense of declaring an immediate right or claim. It is rather a rule of evidence, capable not the less on that account of affecting gravely substantive rights.' Finally in *Evans v Bartlam* [1937] 2 All ER 646 at 653, [1937] AC 473 at 484 *per* Lord Wright: '. . . estoppel is a rule of evidence that prevents the person estopped from denying the existence of a fact . . .'

[37] None the less, because of the decisive impact which estoppel by representation may have upon the outcome of any individual case, whether as a step on the way to establishing a cause of action, or as defeating a prima facie valid claim based on facts which (absent the representation) would entitle the claimant to recover, such estoppel undoubtedly gives rise to substantive legal consequences. As Lord Wright later observed in *Canada and Dominion Sugar Co. Ltd v Canadian National (West Indies) Steamships Ltd* [1947] AC 46 at 56:

'Estoppel is a complex legal notion, involving a combination of several essential elements, the statement to be acted on, action on the face of it, resulting detriment to the actor. Estoppel is often described as a rule of evidence, as, indeed, it may be so described. But the whole concept is more correctly viewed as a substantive rule of law.'

It seems that the only judicial statement in unqualified form which classifies estoppel by representation as a rule of substantive law rather than a rule of evidence is the observation of Lord Denning MR in *Moorgate Mercantile Co. Ltd v Twitchings* [1975] 3 All ER 314 at 323, [1976] QB 225 at 241:

'Estoppel is not a rule of evidence. It is not a cause of action. It is a principle of justice and of equity. It comes to this. When a man, by this words or conduct, has led another to believe in a particular state of affairs, he will not be allowed to go back on it when it would be unjust or inequitable for him to do so.'

In the light of the state of the authorities and the clear statement in *Avon CC v Howlett* [1983] 1 All ER 1073, [1983] 1 WLR 605 on a matter integral to the court's decision, it does not seem to me that it is open to this court at least to depart from the traditional classification of estoppel by representation as a rule of evidence.

[38] I would only add in this connection that there are various dicta in terms which support the view that a single purpose underlies all forms of estoppel on the basis that all aspects of the rules developed are examples of general principle applied so as to prevent A from refusing to recognise, or seeking unjustly to deny or avoid, an assumption or belief which he has induced, permitted or encouraged in B and on the basis of which B has acted or regulated his affairs: see for instance the *Moorgate Mercantile* case [1975] 3 All ER 314 at 323–324, [1976] QB 225 at 241–242, see also the observations of Scarman LJ in *Crabb v Arun DC* [1975] 3 All ER 865 at 875, [1976] Ch 179 at 193 in relation to the distinction between promissory and proprietary estoppel. However, various particular difficulties in the manner in which, and the limitations subject to which, the various types of estoppel have been developed, have so far prevented a rationalisation of this kind. As stated by Millett LJ in *First National Bank plc v Thompson* [1996] 1 All ER 140 at 144, [1996] Ch 231 at 236:

'[An attempt] to demonstrate that all estoppels other than estoppel by record are now subsumed in the single and all-embracing estoppel by representation and that they are all governed by the same requirements has never won general acceptance. Historically unsound, it has been repudiated by academic writers and is unsupported by authority.'

[39] Despite some advances in this direction made in Commonwealth jurisdictions, it seems to me that the position remains unchanged in this country to date. Thus, faced with an invitation to formulate a single general principle to cover two types of estoppel with which he was called upon to deal in *The Indian Endurance* (*No 2*), *Republic of India v India Steamship Co. Ltd* [1997] 4 All ER 380 at 392, [1998] AC 878 at 914, Lord Steyn observed:

'The question was debated whether estoppel by convention and estoppel by acquiescence are but aspects of one overarching principle. I do not underestimate the importance in the continuing development of the law of the search for simplicity. I, also, accept that at a high level of abstraction such an overarching principle could be formulated. But ... to restate the law in terms of an overarching principle might tend to blur the necessarily separate requirements, and distinct terrain of application, of the two kinds of estoppel.'

[40] That said, and accepting estoppel by representation to be a rule of evidence, which *ordinarily* requires that a more than de minimis degree of detriment is definitive of the transferee's right to retain the entirety of a mistaken payment, it is plain that the court in the *Avon CC* case, and subsequently in the *Scottish Equitable* case, considered that there yet remained scope for the operation of equity to alleviate the position on grounds of unfairness or unconscionability, although in the latter case it failed to elucidate that conclusion by reference to authority other than the *Avon CC* case which in turn quoted no authority to that effect. It seems to me that authority in the form of a clear statement as to the underlying principles being those of equity is none the less available, whatever the appropriate juridical classification of estoppel by representation.

[41] Although the doctrine of estoppel by representation was developed in the field of commercial transactions by the common law in the early nineteenth century as a principle of broad application it had its origins in cases concerning the negotiation of marriage settlements which were principally heard in the Courts of Equity (see generally Cooke *The Modern Law of Estoppel* (2000) pp 19–22). In *Jorden v Money* (1854) 5 HL Cas 185 at 210, [1843–60] All ER Rep 350 at 354 estoppel by representation was described by Lord Cranworth LC as 'a principle well known in the law, founded upon good faith and equity, a principle equally of law and of equity'.

[42] Later he stated:

'The whole doctrine was very much considered at law, for it is a doctrine not confined to cases in equity, but one that prevails at law also; and there are, in fact, more cases upon the subject at law than in equity.' (See (1854) 5 HL Cas 185 at 212–213, [1843–60] All ER Rep 350 at 355.)

[43] Thus, whether or not the dicta of Lord Denning MR in the *Moorgate Mercantile* case (see [37] above) be correct in terms of classification, it is clear that the doctrine of estoppel by representation stems from and is governed by considerations of justice and equity. That being so, it is difficult to see why equity should, as between the parties, be impotent in an appropriate case or category of case to require a person relying upon the defence of estoppel by representation to rely upon it only to the extent of any detriment suffered.

[44] In the *Avon CC* case the court cited three cases which suggested that, where estoppel by representation is raised as a defence to a claim for money had and received, the courts do not treat the operation of estoppel as being restricted to the precise amount of the detriment which the representee proves he has suffered in reliance on the representation: *Skyring v Greenwood* (1825) 4 B & C 281 at 289, [1824–34] All ER Rep 104 at 106, citing a passage from the judgment of Abbott CJ, *Holt v Markham* [1923] 1 KB 504, [1922] All ER Rep 134, and *Lloyds Bank Ltd v Brooks* (1950) 6 Legal Decisions Affecting Bankers 161. The court also cited *Ogilvie v West Australian Mortgage and Agency Corp Ltd* [1896] AC 257 and *Greenwood v Martins Bank Ltd* [1932] 1 KB 371 (affirmed in the House of Lords [1933] AC 51, [1932] All ER Rep 318) as demonstrating that a claimant who, as a result of being able to rely on estoppel, succeeds on a cause of action on which, without being able to rely on it, he would necessarily have failed, may be able to recover more than the actual damage suffered by him as a result of the representation which gave rise to it.

[45] It is difficult to see how the last two cases support the principle for which they were cited. In each case a bank customer discovered that cheques drawn on his account had been forged, but failed to inform the bank until a substantial period had elapsed. In each case it was held that there was no

need to investigate whether the bank could in fact have recovered money from the forger had it acted immediately. The banks had not received benefit, but had suffered loss of any opportunity for recovery elsewhere, as to which the uncertainty of such recovery was resolved in favour of the representee. That point is made in Goff and Jones *The Law of Restitution* (5th edn, 1998) p 832.

[46] Similarly, the point is made that, albeit in *Skyring v Greenwood* and *Holt v Markham* there was no exact inquiry into the degree to which each defendant had altered his financial position, there was equally no judicial statement that estoppel by representation could not operate pro tanto in an appropriate case. In *Skyring v Greenwood*, indeed, it is not clear that there was evidence of any detrimental reliance, the court simply assuming that it had taken place. In *Holt v Markham*, while it is clear from the judgment of Warrington LJ ([1923] 1 KB 504 at 512, [1922] All ER Rep 134 at 140) that not all the money had been spent, there is no indication whether the balance which remained was substantial and it is clear that, in addition to mere spending, the defendant had parted with his war savings certificates (see [1923] 1 KB 504 at 511, [1922] All ER Rep 134 at 139 *per* Bankes LJ). It seems to me that those cases do no more than establish that the court will generally think it appropriate to treat the matter broadly and will not require the defendant to demonstrate in detail the precise degree or value of the detriment which he has suffered in circumstances where, as Slade LJ pointed out (*Avon CC v Howlett* [1983] 1 All ER 1073 at 1086, [1983] 1 WLR 605 at 622), he may find it difficult subsequently to recall and identify retrospectively the nature and extent of commitments undertaken or expenditure incurred as a result of an alteration in his general mode of living. However, it is open to the court, acting on equitable principles, to take the view that some restitution is necessary, albeit the burden upon the defendant of proving the precise extent of his detriment should be a light one. In these circumstances, the court may well have broad regard to, without being bound to follow, the developing lines of the courts' approach in 'change of position' cases. However, the two defences will remain distinct, unless or until the House of Lords rules otherwise.

[47] There may indeed be good reasons why this should be so and why the issue is not simply one of jurisprudential 'tidiness'. First, in considering the equities between the parties, there are plainly arguments for holding that the fact that a representation was made (albeit mistakenly) may in particular circumstances affect the court's view as to whether and how far, detriment having been established, it should order a restitutionary payment. Second, as pointed out by Fung and Ho in their article 'Change of Position and Estoppel' (2001) 117 LQR 14 at 17, the defence of 'change of position' only protects actual reduction of the transferee's assets following receipt. A transferee who, in reliance upon a receipt, forgoes a realistic and quantifiable opportunity to increase his assets is not apparently protected. It has also been held in *South Tyneside Metropolitan BC v Svenska International plc* [1995] 1 All ER 545, following Hobhouse J in *Kleinwort Benson Ltd v South Tyneside Metropolitan BC* [1994] 4 All ER 972 that, in order to be successful, a change of position defence must be based on a change *after* the receipt of the mistaken payment, the facts of *Lipkin Gorman (a firm) v Karpnale Ltd* [1992] 4 All ER 512, [1991] 2 AC 548 having been exceptional. The *South Tyneside* decision has been the subject of some criticism (see *Goff and Jones* pp 822–824). However, assuming its correctness (and we have heard no submissions in that regard), it marks a further difference between the defence of 'change of position' and of estoppel in any case where a representation as to the entitlement of the payee has been communicated to him and relied on in anticipation of actual receipt.

[48] Thus, the question to be decided on this appeal is whether, in the light the judge's findings that Somer had suffered detriment and/or changed its position only to the extent of £13,180.57, it should be obliged to repay the balance of the sum received from NatWest on the basis of the exception recognised in the *Avon CC* case. This was a case where the mistake of the bank would have been detected early had Somer kept close account of its dealings with Mentor. Although the judge found that Mr Richardson had continued to rely upon the information first communicated to him that the payment from Mentor had now been received, NatWest shortly afterwards forwarded a credit advice which made the position clear at a time when Somer had forwarded goods worth only

£5,221.99. The judge rejected the case for Somer that it had incurred any detriment other than despatch of goods worth £13,180.57 in reliance upon the representation, being satisfied that Somer's chance of pursuing Mentor successfully for payment was nil. In those circumstances, it seems to me that the judge was fully entitled to hold that the payment sought was of such a size that it bore no relation to the detriment which Somer could possibly have suffered and that it would be unconscionable for Somer to retain the balance over and above the value of the goods shipped.

CONCLUSION

[49] For the reasons above stated, I would dismiss this appeal.

Clarke LJ . . .

[50] I agree that this appeal should be dismissed for the reasons given by Peter Gibson and Potter LJJ, whose judgments I have seen in draft.

[54] In the interesting article by Fung and Ho on 'Change of Position and Estoppel' (2001) 117 LQR 14 which is referred to by Potter LJ, the authors criticise that approach and say (at p 19) that it is high time that estoppel was regarded as a substantive (as opposed to an evidential) defence and that it can operate pro tanto. There seems to me to be much to be said for that point of view, but I do not think that it is open to this court to develop the law in that way in the light of the decisions in the *Avon CC* case and the *Scottish Equitable* case. However, as I see it, much the same result has been achieved by an application of the second proposition to be derived from the *Avon CC* case.

[55] All three members of the court in the *Avon CC* case recognised that the application of the first proposition might lead to injustice. So they concluded that there was or might be an exception to it, although they did not all express the exception in the same terms. Potter LJ has quoted the relevant passages from the judgments. Slade LJ gave as an example ([1983] 1 All ER 1073 at 1089, [1983] 1 WLR 605 at 625) a case where the sums sought to be recovered were so large as to bear no relation to any detriment which the recipient could possibly have suffered. Cumming-Bruce LJ, who was particularly concerned by the hypothetical nature of the exercise upon which (as Peter Gibson LJ explains) the court was engaged, said ([1983] 1 All ER 1073 at 1076, [1983] 1 WLR 605 at 608) that he did not consider the decision as authority for the proposition that where, on the facts, it would be clearly inequitable to allow a party to make a profit by pleading estoppel, the court will necessarily be powerless to prevent it.

[56] Eveleigh LJ to my mind most clearly pointed the way to the future. He said:

'However, I am far from saying that, whenever the recipient of money paid under a mistake has been led to think that it is his, then he will be entitled to retain the whole by demonstrating that he has spent part of it. The payment may involve no representation, as where a debtor presents an account to a creditor. Then while there might have been a representation there may be circum-stances which would render it unconscionable for the defendant to retain a balance in his hands. There may also be circumstances which would make it unfair to allow the plaintiff to recover.' (See [1983] 1 All ER 1073 at 1078, [1983] 1 WLR 605 at 611–612.)

Eveleigh LJ thus appears to have regarded a relevant test, if not the relevant test, as unconscionability.

[57] The exception was further considered in the *Scottish Equitable* case [2001] 3 All ER 818, although the court did not attempt to formulate the nature of the exception. Robert Walker LJ, who gave the leading judgment, did not attempt a formulation of his own but (at [43]) was content to adopt the view of the judge that the case was 'just the sort of situation that the Court of Appeal must have had in mind in . . . *Avon CC v Howlett* when expressing reservations about the ambit of the decision'. He added ([2001] 3 All ER 818 at [44]) that it can be predicted (albeit with some reservation) that development of the law on a case by case basis will have the effect of enlarging rather than narrowing the exception.

[58] It seems to me that the exception recognised in both the *Avon CC* case and the *Scottish Equitable* case can best be formulated as suggested by Cumming-Bruce and Eveleigh LJJ, namely that the estoppel should not operate in full where it would be clearly inequitable or unconscionable for the defendant to retain a balance in his hands. Whether it would or not of course depends upon all the circumstances of the particular case, which may include the nature of the representation and (as Peter Gibson LJ observes) will certainly include the steps taken by the recipient in reliance upon the representation.

[59] I recognise that there is a tension between the first proposition in the *Avon CC* case and the exception because, as I see it, even after making all allowances in favour of the recipient, it will very often be unconscionable to permit him to keep the whole of the sums paid to him. However, I do not think that it is appropriate to allow a defendant to rely upon an estoppel, whether at common law or in equity, to achieve a result which can fairly be regarded as unconscionable. I am conscious of recent cases in which it has been said that it is not appropriate to try to identify a common principle applicable to all estoppels. However, I observe that in *Johnson v Gore Wood & Co (a firm)* [2001] 1 All ER 481, [2001] 2 WLR 72, which was admittedly not concerned with estoppel by representation, Lord Goff of Chieveley said:

> 'In the end, I am inclined to think that the many circumstances capable of giving rise to an estoppel cannot be accommodated within a single formula, and that it is unconscionability which provides the link between them.' (See [2001] 1 All ER 481 at 508, [2001] 2 WLR 72 at 100.)

[60] This is perhaps an example of the principles of equity being employed to mitigate the rigours of the common law. However that may be, it seems to me to follow from the *Avon CC* case and the *Scottish Equitable* case that there are exceptions to the strict rule of evidence that an estoppel by representation cannot operate pro tanto and that those exceptions are or include cases where it would be unconscionable or wholly inequitable to permit the recipient of money to retain the whole of it.

[61] I am not sure that this approach is markedly different from that described by Robert Walker LJ in the *Scottish Equitable* case [2001] 3 All ER 818 at [45]–[47] and referred to as a 'novel and ingenious point'. If, as Dixon J put it in *Grundt v Great Boulder Pty. Gold Mines Ltd* (1937) 59 CLR 641 at 674, and as Robert Walker LJ said was correct ([2001] 3 All ER 818 at [45]), detriment must be judged when the representee seeks to go back on his representation, the recipient will not have acted to his detriment if he is entitled to keep the part of the money that he has spent but not the rest. Provided that he is entitled to keep the amount spent, it is likely (subject to the circumstances of the particular case) to be unconscionable to allow him to keep the rest, in which event he should not in principle be entitled to do so. As I see it, the application of what may be called the unconscionability test does not involve the exercise of a discretion but provides a principled approach to the problem in a case of this kind.

[62] For the reasons given by both Peter Gibson and Potter LJJ I agree that on the facts found by the judge it would be unconscionable and inequitable for Somer International (UK) Ltd to be permitted to retain the balance paid to it in error by National Westminster Bank plc. It follows that I too would dismiss the appeal.

Peter Gibson LJ . . .

[66] The *Avon CC* case is a procedural oddity. The trial judge found as a fact that the defendant had spent all the money overpaid to him but decided the case on the artificial basis pleaded in the defence that he had only spent a little over half the money overpaid. The judge held that the payers were entitled to recover the balance, but they undertook not to execute the judgment without leave of the court. The defendant appealed, although, as Cumming-Bruce LJ put it ([1983] 1 All ER 1073, [1983] 1 WLR 605 at 608), he had no practical reason for objecting to the order, and the appeal was

brought in order to obtain the decision of this court upon a purely hypothetical question of detriment in its relevance to the law of estoppel. It was decided at a time when the defence of change of position was not recognised. But it was not expressly overruled by the House of Lords in the *Lipkin Gorman* case. In Goff and Jones *The Law of Restitution* (5th edn, 1998) p 829, it is said that 'the House of Lords may conclude that *Avon County Court v Howlett* cannot stand with *Lipkin Gorman (a firm) v Karpnale Ltd* and should be overruled'. The caution of the editor should be noted: he is suggesting the possibility that the *Avon CC* case will be overruled by the House of Lords. I doubt if this court is free to treat the *Avon CC* case as overruled.

[67] In my judgment in the present case this court should follow the approach adopted in *Scottish Equitable plc v Derby*, both by Harrison J at first instance ([2000] 3 All ER 793) and by this court on appeal from him ([2001] EWCA Civ 369, [2001] 3 All ER 818), and should consider whether the circumstances are such that the case falls within the exception recognised as a possibility by each of the members of this court in the *Avon CC* case (see [1983] 1 All ER 1073 at 1076, 1078, 1089, [1983] 1 WLR 605 at 608–609, 611–612, 624–625 *per* Cumming-Bruce, Eveleigh and Slade LJJ respectively). (See also *Chitty on Contracts* (28th edn, 1999) vol 1, p 1527 (para. 30–113).) When Slade LJ posited the case where the sums sought to be recovered were so large as to bear no relation to any detriment which the recipient could possibly have suffered, he did so expressly by way of an example of circumstances where the doctrine of estoppel could be said to give rise to injustice were it to defeat in its entirety an action in restitution. The test is whether it would be unconscionable and inequitable for the recipient of the moneys mistakenly paid to retain the moneys having regard to what the recipient did in reliance on the representation made to him.

[68] I fully accept that the court, when assessing detriment, should not apply too demanding a standard of proof because of the practical difficulties faced by a defendant conducting a business who has been led to believe that the moneys paid by mistake are his (see the remarks of Slade LJ in the *Avon CC* case [1983] 1 All ER 1073 at 1086–1087, [1983] 1 WLR 605 at 621–622). But in view of the clear findings of fact made by the judge as to the extent of the detriment suffered by Somer and in particular his outright rejection of the argument that Somer was induced to forgo the opportunity to pursue Mentor for payment, I am not able to accede to Mr Virgo's submission that this is a case where it would be unjust not to give full effect to the estoppel. On the contrary, the circumstances here, as found by the judge, are such that the disparity between the $US76,708.57 mistakenly credited to Somer and £13,180.57, being the value of the goods despatched by Somer in reliance on the bank's representation, makes it unconscionable and inequitable for Somer to retain the balance.

[69] For these as well as the reasons given by Potter LJ I would dismiss the appeal. I also agree with him in rejecting the bank's challenges by the respondent's notice to the judge's findings of fact.

NOTES AND QUESTIONS

1. Although all of the judgments in *National Westminster Bank plc v Somer International (UK) Ltd* refer to estoppel as a 'rule of evidence' this reveals little about the nature of the defence. In other words, it does not explain what evidence it is for which the rule denies proof nor does it reveal why proof of that evidence is denied. In a note, to which the judgments referred (Fung and Ho, 'Change of Position and Estoppel' (2001) 117 *LQR* 14, 17) the authors say that 'despite its historical origin and technical status as a rule of evidence . . . the substantive effect of estoppel is to recognise an obligation in certain circumstances to make good a representation that has been acted on'.

2. Potter and Clarke LJJ both referred to the 'novel and ingenious' argument of junior counsel in *Scottish Equitable v Derby* that the 'defence of change of position pre-empts and disables the defence of estoppel by negativing detriment'. Do you agree with this argument? Can estoppel,

which is a defence of general application, be expelled from the law of unjust enrichment while, presumably, retaining its traditional role as a defence in other areas of the law?

3. Why did the Court of Appeal reject the argument of Somer International that, as a result of the bank's representation that the money had arrived, it suffered detriment because it lost the opportunity to obtain payment of the entire sum from its customer (Mentor)?

4. *In Phillip Collins Ltd v Davis* (above, 769), although decided two years earlier, the decisions in *Scottish Equitable v Derby* and *National Westminster Bank plc v Somer International (UK) Ltd* were, to some extent, anticipated. After rejecting an argument based on estoppel, Jonathan Parker J said that 'the law has now developed to the point where a defence of estoppel by representation is no longer apt in restitutionary claims where the most flexible change of position is in principle available.' The same approach was taken by the Newfoundland Court of Appeal in *RBC Dominion Securities Inc. v Dawson* (1994) 111 DLR (4th) 230, 237 (above, 801) where, in rejecting the defence of estoppel on the facts, Cameron JA stated '[w]e conclude that estoppel is no longer an appropriate method of dealing with the problem. The change of circumstances defence is the one which most fairly balances the equities'.

3. *BONA FIDE* PURCHASE

This is a defence which traditionally belongs within the law of property. But, even within the law of property, there is no general defence of *bona fide* purchase. On the contrary, the general rule is *nemo dat quod non habet* and *bona fide* purchase acts as a limited exception to that rule at common law in the case of, for example, money (see *Miller v Race* (1758) 1 Burr. 454) and rather more generally in equity (*Cave v Cave* (1880) 15 ChD 639; *Pilcher v Rawlins* (1872) 7 Ch App. 259). The proposition that *bona fide* purchase can act as a defence to a restitutionary proprietary claim is generally accepted (see Goff and Jones, 857), but the proposition that *bona fide* purchase has a role to play as a defence to a personal restitutionary claim is a much more controversial one, as is the theoretical basis of the defence and its relationship with the defence of change of position.

- • *Lipkin Gorman v Karpnale Ltd* [1991] 2 AC 548, House of Lords

See above, 28–40, in particular the section of Lord Goff's speech headed, 'Whether the respondents gave consideration for the money'.

NOTES AND QUESTIONS

1. The application of the *bona fide* purchase for value defence to the facts of *Lipkin* is discussed by E McKendrick, 'Restitution, Misdirected Funds and Change of Position', above, 219–225.

2. Why did the provision of gambling services not constitute the provision of value?

3. Why, according to Lord Goff, does a shop which uses chips have a defence of *bona fide* purchase, when a casino does not? Why did Lord Goff choose to apply 'common sense' in the case of the shop, but not in the case of the casino?

4. What is the function of the defence of *bona fide* purchase? Is it to protect detrimental reliance by the defendant or is its function to protect the security of the transactions entered into in good faith by the defendant?

5. What is the relationship between *bona fide* purchase and change of position? Writing extra-judicially ('Tracing the Proceeds of Fraud' (1991) 107 *LQR* 71, 82), Lord Millett once argued that:

it may come to be recognised that the defence of bona fide purchaser for value is simply the paradigm change of position defence, and that the true rule, embracing both volunteers and those who have given consideration, is that equity will not permit a defendant to set up title to property in which the plaintiff has a beneficial interest unless he has given value or otherwise changed his position to his detriment without notice, actual or constructive, of the plaintiff's interest.

On the other hand, K Barker maintains that the two defences are functionally distinct ('After Change of Position: Good Faith Exchange in the Modern Law of Restitution' in P Birks (ed.), *Laundering and Tracing* (1995), 191), see also Burrows, 585–91). Barker asserts (at 192) that change of position 'aims to protect individual recipients against unfair losses caused by a given receipt' while *bona fide* purchase 'deploys a broad policy of transactional security in exchange dealings, with the primary (economic) objective of facilitating the free transfer of wealth'. On this view change of position is an 'individualistic defence with moral foundations' whereas *bona fide* purchase seeks to 'meet instrumentalist concerns about the facilitation of trade' and is not 'concerned with the individual position of the purchaser at all' (196). He points out the following differences between the defences:

> The defences have very different features. Change of position operates *pro tanto*, investigating the extent of the value lost by a defendant and diminishing the plaintiff's claim only in this sum. The point at which the defendant loses value must, it is thought, postdate the receipt. Moreover, the defendant's change of position protects only the defendant and does not shield subsequent recipients of property which the plaintiff is able to trace. None of these points is true of bona fide purchase which: bars the plaintiff's claim entirely (thereby fully protecting the defendant's contractual expectation); is unconcerned by the chronology of receipt and payment; and protects not only the initial (bona fide) purchaser, but also his successors in title, including those with notice of the plaintiff's rights. In effect, bona fide purchase protects the full expectation interests of both defendant and of those who derive property from him. Change of position protects only the defendant, and then only against post-receipt diminutions in his wealth (out-of-pocket losses).

Barker maintains this approach in a more recent article, 'Bona fide Purchase as a Defence to Unjust Enrichment Claims: A concise Restatement' [1999] *RLR* 75.

6. A thief steals £1,000 from the claimant. He purchases a meal at the Ritz with the money stolen. The meal costs £1,000 but its objective value is £200. Does the Ritz have a defence of (a) *bona fide* purchase or (b) change of position? If both of these defences are available, do they reach the same result?

7. Given that the claimant's claim in *Lipkin Gorman* was a personal one, why was the defence of *bona fide* purchase in play at all? Paul Key argues ('Bona Fide Purchase as a Defence in the Law of Restitution' [1994] *LMCLQ* 421, 425–6) that *bona fide* purchase is confined to proprietary claims and that there is no need for the defence in personal claims after the recognition of change of position. Abandoning his earlier extrajudicial view (above, note 5), in *Foskett v McKeown* (above, 678) Lord Millett took a similar approach to Paul Key and said that a 'claim in unjust enrichment is subject to a change of position defence, which usually operates by reducing or extinguishing the element of enrichment. An action like the present [to vindicate a proprietary right] is subject to the bona fide purchaser for value defence, which operates to clear the defendant's title'. On the other hand, K Barker argues (above) that the policy of transactional security applies with equal force to personal claims as it does to proprietary claims. Which view is the better one?

8. Is *bona fide* purchase an enrichment-related defence, a defence which relates to the alleged unjustness of the enrichment or is it part of the claim which the claimant himself must establish (see on this the extract from Birks, above, 239)? The view that *bona fide* purchase should be viewed as a defence is supported by *Lipkin Gorman* itself and by *Re Nisbet and Potts Contract* [1905] 1 Ch 391, 402, where Farwell J stated that 'the plea of purchaser for value without notice is a single plea, to be proved by the person pleading it; it is not to be regarded as a plea of purchaser for value, to be met by a reply of notice.'

9. Does *bona fide* purchase have a role to play in two-party cases? K Barker (above, at 823) maintains that the *bona fide* purchase defence 'need only be invoked where the defendant has received a benefit *by way of exchange with a party other than the plaintiff*. . . . Where, as in the typical two—party case, the receipt occurs as part of an agreement with the plaintiff himself (or with one on whose behalf he is acting), no defence of bona fide purchase is needed. A valid contract for the receipt and retention of the benefit remains in being, thereby ousting the plaintiff's restitutionary rights. The defendant's good faith is relevant, not because it fits into the defence of bona fide purchase, but because it is a precondition of his entitlement to invoke the 'objective' principle of contract law' (emphasis in the original). The next case raises this issue.

- ***Dextra Bank and Trust Co. Ltd v Bank of Jamaica*** [2001] UKPC 50; [2002] 1 All ER (Comm) 193, Privy Council

The facts of this case are discussed above at 165. In a passage not extracted, Lords Goff and Bingham said that even if Dextra's claim had succeeded, the Bank of Jamaica would have had a defence of bona fide purchase:

It is commonly accepted that the defence of bona fide purchaser is only available to a third party, which includes an indirect recipient, i.e. a person who received the benefit from someone other than the plaintiff or his authorised agent. Here the BoJ received the cheque from Beckford, who was acting without authority from Dextra in selling the cheque to the BOJ, so that the BOJ can properly be described as an indirect recipient; and the BOJ through its agents Jones and Mitchell, paid for the cheque in accordance with the directions of Beckford. In so doing, the agents of BOJ acted in good faith.

NOTES AND QUESTIONS

Assuming that the Privy Council is correct to say that the defence only applied to third parties, was it correct to treat the Bank of Jamaica as an indirect recipient? Although the mistake claim failed because the Privy Council controversially held that Dextra had made a misprediction rather than a mistake (as to which see above, 165), for the purposes of that claim the Privy Council had treated the case as if it were a two party case: the payment being made from Dextra, via its agents, to the Bank of Jamaica. Does it make sense to treat the case as a two party transaction for the purpose of the primary claim but a three party transaction for the purposes of the defence of bona fide purchase?

4. AGENCY

English law has accepted for some considerable time that a defence may be available to an agent who receives money which was not due to his principal and who, before learning of that fact, pays the money over to his principal. The exact scope of the defence (sometimes rather unhelpfully termed the defence of 'ministerial receipt') is unclear but is commonly said to consist of three elements. The first is that the defendant must have received the benefit as an agent and not as a principal (see *Baylis v Bishop of London* [1913] 1 Ch 127), the second is that the agent must have paid the benefit over to his principal before he had notice of the claim (*Buller v Harrison* (1777) 2 Cowp 565, but contrast *Sadler v Evans* (1766) 4 Burr 1984), and the third is that the agent must not be a wrongdoer (*Snowden v Davis* (1808) 1 Taunt 359: this requirement has been doubted by W Swadling, 'The Nature of Ministerial Receipt' (below, 831), but is supported by Goff and Jones,

(6th edn, 847–8). It appears that the defence is available to an agent who was acting for a disclosed principal but not in the case where the principal is undisclosed (*Agip (Africa) Ltd v Jackson* [1990] Ch 265, 288, the facts of which are set out above, 209), although the occasional case can be found in which it is assumed that the defence can be invoked where the principal has not been disclosed (see, for example, *Transvaal and Delegoa Bay Investment Co. v Atkinson* [1944] 1 All ER 579). The operation of the defence can be seen in the following case.

- *Australia and New Zealand Banking Group Ltd v Westpac Banking Corporation* (1987) 164 CLR 662, High Court of Australia

The ANZ bank, as a result of a clerical error, paid $114,158 instead of $14,158 to Westpac bank for the credit of Jakes Meats Pty Ltd. Immediately prior to the overpayment Jakes' account showed a debit balance of $67,000 with an effective overdraft limit of $90,000. Westpac was notified by ANZ of the overpayment three days after it had been made, but by that time they had already credited Jakes' account with the overpayment, so paying off the overdraft and had then honoured a number of cheques drawn by Jakes. Jakes then went into liquidation and ANZ sought to recover the $100,000 from Westpac. It was held that, while ANZ had a *prima facie* right to recover the $100,000, Westpac had a defence to the extent of $82,978.32 which represented the sums which they had irretrievably paid out on the instructions of Jakes.

Mason CJ, Wilson, Deane, Toohey and Gaudron JJ: . . . [In short, the issue] is whether the fact that an agent has paid over money received by him as an agent to, or on behalf of, his principal will of itself constitute a good defence to an action against him for recovery of money paid under a fundamental mistake.

It was submitted on behalf of ANZ that the fact that Westpac had applied most of the over-payment in payments made on behalf of Jakes did not of itself constitute any defence in relation to the moneys so applied. The basis of that submission was the contention that the fact that an agent has applied funds received by him on behalf of a principal by payment to, or on behalf of, the principal does not, of itself, constitute a defence to an action for money paid under fundamental mistake of fact unless it appears that the agent would have suffered overall detriment if it had repaid the money at the time when it first received notice of the claim for repayment The fact that Westpac had paid out most of the funds received on behalf of Jakes would not so it was said, constitute such a detriment unless it appeared that Westpac would have been worse off by reason of the overpayment if it had, when it received notice of the mistake, repaid the $100,000 to ANZ, debited Jakes' account with that amount (on the basis that it was entitled to claim indemnity from Jakes), and dishonoured all of the cheques which it might then have dishonoured. The measure of whether Westpac would have been worse off appears, upon analysis, to be whether Jakes would have owed it more in the situation which would have existed if, at the time it received notice of the mistake, Westpac had taken the above steps than Jakes would have owed it in the hypothetical situation which would have existed at that time if the overpayment had never been made and the cheques which it would probably have dishonoured but for the overpayment had in fact been dishonoured.

There are several points at which this submission of ANZ is susceptible of legitimate criticism. For example, the proposition that a financial institution which makes profits by lending money at interest is better off whenever a corporate customer, which is not known to be insolvent, reduces its use of an overdraft facility which has been made available on commercial terms sounds somewhat strangely in modern ears. The complete answer to the overall submission is however, that its legal basis is mistaken for the reason that, on balance, both authority and principle support the conclusion that an agent who has received money on his principal's behalf will, without more, have a good defence if, before learning that the money was paid under fundamental mistake, he has 'paid it to the principal or done something equivalent' thereto (see *Rahimtoola v Nizam of Hyderabad* [1958] AC 379 at 396, 406; Goff and Jones, *The Law of Restitution*, at 707). The rationale of such a general rule can be identified in terms of the law of agency and of notions of unjust enrichment. If money is paid to an agent on behalf of a principal and the agent receives it in his capacity as such and, without notice of any mistake or irregularity in the payment, applies the money for the purpose for which it was paid to him, he has applied it in accordance with the mandate of the payer who must look to the principal for recovery (see *per* Palles CB, *Fitzpatrick v M'Glone* [1897] 2 IR 542 at 551 and *per* Cockburn CJ, *Holland v Russell* (1861) 1 B & S 424 at 434; [121 ER 773 at 777]). In those circumstances, the benefit of the payment has been effectively passed on to the principal who will be prima facie liable to make restitution if the payment was made under a fundamental mistake of fact. If the matter needs to be expressed in terms of detriment or change of position, the payment by the agent to the principal of the money which he has received on the principal's behalf, of itself constitutes the relevant detriment or change of position. In that regard, no relevant distinction can be drawn between payment to the principal or payment to another or others on behalf of the principal (cf. *Gowers v Lloyds and National Provincial Foreign Bank Ltd*, at 773G–H).

In support of the submission that an agent who has paid out the money to, or on behalf of his principal will have no defence to a claim for repayment by the payer unless he can show some overall detriment which would result from his receipt of the payment if he, as distinct from his principal, were required to make restitution, ANZ placed particular reliance upon *Buller v Harrison* and *Kleinwort, Sons and Co. v Dunlop Rubber Company* (1907) 97 LT 263. *Buller v Harrison*, like *Cox v Prentice*, was a case where money paid under a fundamental mistake was recovered from an agent notwithstanding that he had made a reversible entry in his own books crediting the amount to his principal. In neither case however, had there been any subsequent transaction which would be affected if the book entry were reversed. Thus, in *Buller v Harrison*, Lord Mansfield was at pains to stress (at 568; 1245 [ER]):

'In this case, there was no new credit, no acceptance of new bills, no fresh goods bought or money advanced. In short, no alteration in the situation which the defendant and his principals stood in towards each other . . .'

In so far as general principle was concerned, Lord Mansfield was emphatic (at 568: 1244–5 [ER]):

'The whole question at the trial was, whether the defendant, who was an agent, had paid the money over. Now, the law is clear, that if an agent pay over money which has been paid to him by mistake, he does no wrong; and the plaintiff must call on the principal . . .'

In that regard, we do not read Lord Mansfield's subsequent comment that if 'there had been *any* new credit given, it would have been proper to have left it to the jury to say, whether any prejudice had happened to the defendant by means of this payment' (at 568; 1245 [ER], italics added) as intended to qualify his earlier statement that payment over of the money paid would constitute a good defence. If that subsequent comment is, however, properly to be read as imposing a separate requirement of overall prejudice in a case where the money received has been paid over, it should not be accepted as correctly stating the law.

Similarly, *Cox v Prentice* was a case where it was stressed that 'things remained unaltered between the agent and his principal' (*per* Dampier J, at 351; 643 [ER]) and no 'new credit' had been 'given' (*per* Le Blanc J, at 349; 643 [ER]). Again, there was no doubt about the general rule which was stated by Lord Ellenborough CJ in plain terms (at 348; 642 [ER]):

'I take it to be clear, that an agent who receives money for his principal is liable as a principal so long as he stands in his original situation; and until there has been a change of circumstances by his having paid over the money to his principal, or done something equivalent to it.'

The case of *Kleinwort, Sons and Co. v Dunlop Rubber Co.* is not really in point since, as Robert Goff J pointed out in *Barclays Bank Ltd v W. J. Simms Son & Cooke (Southern) Ltd* (at 690), the appellant's defence based on payment had been conclusively negatived by the jury's finding that they had received the money as 'principals, and in their own right' (see *Kleinwort*, at 264, 265). It is true that, in the course of his judgment, Lord Loreburn LC commented (at 264) that

> 'if money is paid under a mistake of fact and is redemanded from the person who received it before his position has been altered to his disadvantage, the money must be repaid in whatever character it was received.'.

There is, however, nothing in Lord Loreburn's judgment that would indicate that he would not have regarded payment by the agent to, or at the direction of, the principal as not of itself representing an alteration of the agent's position to his disadvantage. Lord Atkinson left no doubt that payment to, or at the direction of, the principal would suffice as a good defence. He said (at 265):

> 'Whether he would be liable if he dealt as agent with such a person will depend upon this, whether, before the mistake was discovered, he had paid over the money which he received to the principal, *or* settled such an account with the principal as amounts to payment, *or* did something which so prejudiced his position that it would be inequitable to require him to refund' [italics added].

If further authority is required for that proposition, one need do no more than go back to the judgment of Erle CJ (in which Pollock CB, Williams, Willes, and Keating JJ and Bramwell and Channell BB all concurred) in *Holland v Russell* when that case reached the Exchequer Chamber (1863) 4 B & S 14 at 16; [122 ER 365 at 366]) then forward to the judgment of Farwell LJ in *Baylis v Bishop of London* [1913] 1 Ch 127 at 137–8, the judgment of Bankes LJ, Warrington LJ and Scrutton LJ in *British American Continental Bank v British Bank for Foreign Trade*, at 337, 341 and 343, the judgment of Greene MR in *Gowers v Lloyds and National Provincial Foreign Bank Ltd*, at 773 and the speeches of Viscount Simonds and Lord Cohen in *Rahimtoola v Nizam of Hyderabad*, at 396 and 406.

It follows that Westpac has a good defence to ANZ's claim to the extent that it had, on behalf of Jakes, paid out the proceeds of the telegraphic transfer before it first received notice of ANZ's mistake. Acting on the basis of the concessions made by Westpac in ANZ's favour, Westpac had, by that time, irretrievably paid out $82,978.32 of the overpayment of $100,000 in honouring cheques drawn on it by ANZ. That being so, ANZ's appeal must be dismissed and Westpac's cross appeal seeking that the judgment against it should be reduced to an amount of $17,021.68, plus interest, must be sustained.

NOTES AND QUESTIONS

1. Why is the defence not available to an agent who pays the money over to his principal with notice of the claim?

2. The High Court rejected the submission of ANZ that an overall detriment to the agent needed to be shown before a defence of payment over could succeed and said that 'if the matter needs to be expressed in terms of detriment or change of position, the payment by the agent to the principal, of the money which he has received on the principal's behalf, of itself constitutes the relevant detriment or change of position'. The suggestion seemed to be that the defence would apply if the money remained in the account of the principal and could be easily reversed by a mere book entry. Is this different from a defence of change of position?

3. Before the High Court, Westpac had conceded that it was liable to ANZ from the time of the mistaken payment so that it should have dishonoured all cheques drawn by Jakes on the account from that date. The issue before the court was therefore solely whether Westpac had a

defence for money which it had paid out to on Jakes' instructions. However, the High Court pointed out the difficulty associated with that concession (at 671–2):

> one is led to speculate about what Westpac's position vis-à-vis Jakes would have been if it had, of its own initiative, dishonoured those cheques. . . . Certainly, its position would have been a somewhat difficult one if it had subsequently turned out that ANZ's claim for repayment could be met by a good defence on the part of Jakes.

In other words, the court considered whether the defence should apply even if the agent still retains the money. The concern is that the agent could find itself at the centre of a claim by the payer for restitution of benefits transferred pursuant to a mistake, as well as a claim from its principal to account for those benefits. The agent does not know which claim will succeed. What is the agent to do? One solution is that the common law should take the same approach as in equity cases where knowing receipt claims are brought against agents: the agent should 'drop out'. In the next decision, Millett LJ suggests, obiter dicta, a different solution.

- *Portman Building Society v Hamlyn Taylor Neck (a firm)*
  [1998] 4 All ER 202, Court of Appeal

The defendants were a firm of solicitors who acted for the purchaser of a property and also for the claimant building society to which the purchaser had applied for a mortgage to finance part of the purchase price. In his mortgage application and in a later letter to the building society the purchaser stated that it was his intention to use the property exclusively for residential purposes. The building society agreed to a mortgage on the condition that it was only used for residential purposes. In fact, the property was used, and was intended to be used, as a guest house. The solicitors were aware of this prior to completion but did not advise the building society of this in their report. The building society advanced £92,100 to the solicitors which they paid into the client account where it was held until it was paid to the vendor's solicitor at completion of the purchase. The purchaser later defaulted and after selling the property for a loss, the building society sued the solicitors seeking £92,100 as money had and received and also claims for breach of contract, tort, breach of trust and breach of fiduciary duty. The Master struck out the claims for breach of contract, tort and breach of trust as statute barred and struck out the claims for breach of fiduciary duty and money had and received as disclosing no cause of action. The building society appealed only in relation to the dismissal of its claim for money had and received arguing that the money was paid to the solicitors as a result of a mistake of fact. Sir Richard Scott V-C dismissed the appeal and the Court of Appeal dismissed a further appeal.

Millett LJ: . . . any claim to restitution raises the questions. (1) Has the defendant been enriched? (2) If so, is his enrichment unjust? (3) Is his enrichment at the expense of the plaintiff? There are several factors which make it unjust for a defendant to retain the benefit of his enrichment; mistake is one of them. But a person cannot be unjustly enriched if he has not been enriched at all. That is why it is necessary to ask all three questions and why the fact that a payment may have been made, e.g. by mistake, is not by itself sufficient to justify a restitutionary remedy.

In the present case the firm was not enriched by the receipt of the £92,100. The money was trust money, which belonged in equity to the society, and was properly paid by the firm into its client account. The firm never made any claim to the money. It acknowledged that it was the society's money, held to the order of the society and it was applied in accordance with the society's instructions in exchange for a mortgage in favour of the society. The firm did not receive the money for its own use and benefit, but to the society's use. Given that the money was held to the order of the society, the only question is whether the firm obtained a good discharge for the money. It is conceded that it did.

In its argument before us the society relies on three lines of authority. The first is the line of cases which establish that an action lies to recover payments made under a mistake of fact: see for example *Barclays Bank Ltd v WJ Simms Son & Cooke (Southern) Ltd* [1979] 3 All ER 522 at 535, [1980] QB 677 at 695. So it does. In such cases the money is (mistakenly) paid to the defendant for his own use and benefit, or at least for the use and benefit of a third party and not for the use and benefit of the plaintiff himself. But for the mistake, there would be no injustice in the defendant or the third party retaining the benefit of the payment, for that is the common intention of the parties. The effect of the plaintiff's mistake, however, is to make it unjust for the defendant or the third party to retain the benefit of the payment. The action for restitution reverses the unjust enrichment.

But in the present case the society paid the money to the firm to hold to the society's order, that is to say for the society's own use and benefit. The society was entitled to give the firm directions as to the application of the money, and to revoke those directions and demand the repayment of the money if not previously applied in accordance with its unrevoked directions. The society did not need to plead mistake or any other ground of restitution. The firm received the money on terms which made it an accounting party and has never denied its liability to account. The society's difficulty is not in establishing the firm's liability to account, but in showing that anything is due from the firm after it applied the money in accordance with the society's instructions.

Secondly, the society relies on those cases which show that the cause of action for money had and received is complete when the plaintiff's money is received by the defendant. It does not depend on the continued retention of the money by the defendant. Save in strictly limited circumstances it is no defence that the defendant has parted with the money. All that is true. But it is, of course, a defence that he has parted with it by paying it *to the plaintiff or to the plaintiff's order*: see *Holland v Russell* (1863) 4 B & S 14, 122 ER 365; *affg* (1861) 1 B & S 424, 121 ER 773. That is what the firm did in the present case.

Thirdly, the society relies on the doctrine described in art 113 of *Bowstead and Reynolds on Agency* (16th edn, 1996) and Goff and Jones *The Law of Restitution* (4th edn, 1993) pp 750–751. The general rule is that money paid (e.g. by mistake) to an agent who has accounted to his principal without notice of the claim cannot be recovered from the agent but only from the principal. The society submits that the agent's defence in such a case is a particular species of the change of position defence and does not avail the agent who has notice, actual or constructive, of the mistake which founds the plaintiff's claim.

I myself do not regard the agent's defence in such a case as a particular instance of the change of position defence, nor is it generally so regarded. At common law the agent recipient is regarded as a mere conduit for the money, which is treated as paid to the principal, not to the agent. The doctrine is therefore not so much a defence as a means of identifying the proper party to be sued. It does not, for example, avail the agent of an undisclosed principal; though today such an agent would be able to rely on a change of position defence.

The true rule is that where the plaintiff has paid money under (for example) a mistake to the agent of a third party, he may sue the principal whether or not the agent has accounted to him, for in contemplation of law the payment is made to the principal and not to his agent. If the agent still retains the money, however, the plaintiff may elect to sue either the principal or the agent, and the agent remains liable if he pays the money over to his principal after notice of the claim. If he wishes to protect himself, he should interplead. But once the agent has paid the money to his principal or to his order without notice of the claim, the plaintiff must sue the principal.

But all this is by the way, because the doctrine is concerned with the receipt of money by an agent from a third party and his subsequent payment of the money to his own principal without the authority of the third party. Where the agent remains liable, it is not because a change of position defence is not available. It is because neither he nor his own principal was entitled to retain the money as against the third party who made the payment. The agent is liable to make restitution to the third party because he knew that his principal was no more entitled to the money than he was himself: see *Ex p Edwards, re Chapman* (1884) 13 QBD 747.

But in the present case, while the society's mandate remained unrevoked, the firm was entitled and bound to deal with the money in accordance with the mandate. In the present case there is no third party plaintiff. The firm was the agent of the society. It received the payment from its principal, held it to the order of its principal and applied it in accordance with its principal's instructions. The firm's defence is not that it has paid the money away to a third party but that it has dealt with it in accordance with the society's instructions, and thereby obtained a good discharge.

In the course of argument counsel submitted that the society's mistake, induced by the firm, rendered the money repayable and the mandate revocable. In fact, of course, the mandate was revocable in any case. The problem is that it was never revoked. The continuing validity of the transaction under which the money was paid to the firm is, in my judgment, fatal to the society's claim. The obligation to make restitution must flow from the ineffectiveness of the transaction under which the money was paid and not from a mistake or misrepresentation which induced it. It is fundamental that, where money is paid under a legally effective transaction, neither misrepresentation nor mistake vocates consent or gives rise by itself to an obligation to make restitution. The recipient obtains a defeasible right to the money, which is divested if the payer rescinds or otherwise withdraws from the transaction. If the payer exercises his right of rescission in time and before the recipient deals with the money in accordance with his instructions, the obligation to make restitution may follow.

This court explained the effect of a defeasible payment in the recent case of *Bristol and West Building Society v Mothew* (t/a Stapley & Co) [1996] 4 All ER 698 at 716, [1998] Ch 1 at 22, where I said:

> '. . . it would appear that the judge was of opinion that the defendant's authority to deal with the money was automatically vitiated by the fact that it (and the cheque itself) was obtained by misrepresentation. But that is contrary to principle. Misrepresentation makes a transaction voidable not void. It gives the representee the right to elect whether to rescind or affirm the transaction. The representor cannot anticipate his decision. Unless and until the representee elects to rescind the representor remains fully bound. the defendant's misrepresentations merely gave the society the right to elect to withdraw from the transaction on discovering the truth. Since its instructions to the defendant were revocable in any case, this did not materially alter the position so far as he was concerned, though it may have strengthened the society's position in relation to the purchasers.'

That, in my judgment, is the position in the present case.

The society brings a claim for money had and received. The firm does not deny that it is an accounting party. It is an accounting party irrespective of the existence of any mistake on the part of the society. But it has dealt with the whole of the money which it received from the society in accordance with the society's instructions, which have never been revoked. Accordingly, although the firm is accountable for the money it received, it is plain that there is nothing due to the society on the taking of the account. The whole of the money has been expended on the society's behalf. The court does not order an account to be taken where it is plain that there is nothing due.

In my judgment the action is entirely misconceived and the appeal must be dismissed.

Morritt and Brooke LJJ agreed.

NOTES AND QUESTIONS

1. Millett LJ's solution to the 'agent's dilemma', discussed above (828), is that the agent should interplead in any litigation. This solution imposes a heavy burden on a bank because whenever a payer suggests to a bank that a payment might have been made by mistake the bank cannot allow either the customer or the payer access to the money and must pay it into court in any litigation. Further, this solution hardly seems satisfactory from the point of view of the customer whose outstanding cheques will be dishonoured as soon as the bank is notified of a possible claim by the payer (see further J Moore, 'Restitution from Banks' (DPhil thesis, 2000, available at http://www.ucc.ielaw/restitution/archive/articles/ 262–77)).

2. Millett LJ dismissed the claim because the solicitors had parted with the money on the instructions of their principal, the building society, as they were bound to do. The solicitors had 'thereby obtained a good discharge'. Millett LJ denied that this is an example of the defence of payment over by an agent because he said the defence operated only where the agent receives a payment from a third party and accounts for it to the principal. Here, the solicitors had received the payment from their principal and accounted for it to a third party (in accordance with the principal's instructions). If the agent's defence of payment over is just an example of the change of position defence, it is difficult to see why the change in parties should make a difference. But although Millett LJ denies that the defence of payment over is an example of change of position, he does not give any other reason for why the defence exists. The next two extracts offer two different theories to explain the nature of the defence.

- **W Swadling 'The Nature of Ministerial Receipt' in P Birks (ed), *Laundering and Tracing* (1995), 253–9**

4 EXPLANATIONS GIVEN FOR THE DEFENCE OF MINISTERIAL RECEIPT

...

4.1. Agent's Duty to Account to his Principal

In a number of cases it is suggested that the reason why the agent escapes liability is because by paying over to his principal he is merely doing what he is bound to do by the terms of his agency. It is, in other words, a defence of superior orders. Thus, in *East India Co. v Tritton*,[1] Abbott CJ said that the agent was not liable to a restitutionary claim because,

> As soon as the defendants received the money [their principals] might have maintained an action against them for it; they were therefore bound to pay it over . . . The plaintiffs, therefore, cannot now call upon them to restore money which is not in their hands, and which they had no right to withhold from their principals.[2]

This explanation is unsatisfactory for a number of reasons. First, it is not consistent with the rule that the defence only operates in the event of a payment over. If it is the fact of the agent's duty to account to his principal which bars the plaintiff's claim then, since the duty to account arises at the moment the payment is received, there should be no further requirement of a subsequent payment over. Secondly, the explanation is not consistent with the rule that the payment must be made to a known agent, for an undisclosed agent is just as much liable to account to his principal as is a disclosed agent. But the most telling criticism is that it is not consistent with the approach adopted by the law of torts where . . . the fact that a defendant was performing a duty owed to another has never provided him with a defence.

---

1 (1824) 3 B & C 280.   2 *Ibid.* 289.

4.2. Receipt of the Agent is the Receipt of the Principal

One question which has arisen in the context of payments to agents is whether a restitutionary claim can be brought against the principal in the absence of any payment over to him by the agent. The courts have consistently held that there is no need to prove a payment over in such circumstances, on the ground that the receipt of the agent is to be treated as the receipt of the principal. This, in fact, is the true *ratio* of *Duke of Norfolk v Worthy*.[3] . . . The fiction that the agent's receipt is his principal's receipt operates to give the plaintiff a choice between two possible restitutionary defendants.

But though the fiction can be used to explain why a principal can be sued from the moment of the agent's receipt, it cannot likewise explain the operation of the defence of ministerial receipt. First, it too would be inconsistent with the payment over requirement, for if the receipt of the agent is from the start the receipt of the principal then it follows that the agent can never be sued because he is never enriched. Yet we know that this is not the case. Secondly, it would mean that even undisclosed agents could take advantage of the defence, for the fiction draws no distinction between the two types of agency. And finally, it would not explain the absence of an agent's immunity in the law of tort, for it could equally be said that the agent's act of conversion when acting under the authority of his principal is the conversion of his principal.[4] Yet . . . the agent will still be personally liable. Thus, the rule that the receipt of the agent is the receipt of the principal is nothing more than a rule which gives the plaintiff a choice of restitutionary defendants: it does not provide any justification for the agent's defence of ministerial receipt.

4.3. Agent assumed a duty to no-one but his principal

This is probably the weakest explanation for the operation of the defence. It does, however, have some judicial support. In *Owen v Cronk*[5] the manager of a company extracted moneys by duress from the plaintiff, which the plaintiff alleged to be an extortionate sum for work which the company had done for him. The manager paid the money over to the defendant, a receiver who had been appointed under a debenture deed to manage the company, the terms of the appointment being that he was to act throughout as the agent of the company. The defendant paid the money into the company's bank account. In an *ex tempore* judgment the Court of Appeal held that the plaintiff's restitutionary claim against the defendant receiver failed. The plaintiff's main line of argument seems to have been that the defendant stood in the same position as a receiver appointed by the court. Lord Esher MR disagreed. He said that:

> When . . . a man is appointed by the Court receiver and to manage a business he knows that he is appointed, and he accepts the appointment, upon the terms that he is to be personally liable to the creditors of that business, and that he will have to account to the Court, while at the same time he will be entitled to an indemnity out of the business. If a man accepts liability on those terms there is no difficulty in holding that he is personally liable to the creditors. In the present case, however, the defendant did not accept the appointment of receiver on any such terms; he accepted it upon the terms contained in the debenture deed.[6]

His lordship then examined the contents of the deed and, finding no undertaking by the defendant of any personal liability, held that he could not be liable to the plaintiff. The reasoning is difficult to support . . . liability in restitution is imposed by law; it does not arise as the result of any assumption of responsibility on the part of the defendant. However, at the time this case was decided, the implied-contract theory of restitution was rife. The decision is probably best explained as a misguided application of that now discredited approach. It provides no general authority on the operation of the defence of ministerial receipt.

---

3 (1808) 1 Camp 342.   4 *Embank v Nutting* (1849) 7 CB 797.   5 [1895] 1 QB 265.
6 *Ibid*. 271.

4.4. Change of Position

The most plausible explanation offered is that the defence of ministerial receipt is an early manifest-ation of the defence of change of position. It is, for instance, the only explanation which is consistent with the payment over requirement. But for a number of reasons this rationale will not suffice.

First, if the defence was truly a sub-species of change of position then it should logically avail both a disclosed and an undisclosed agent, for a payment over by an undisclosed agent is just as much a change of position as is a payment over by a disclosed agent. Secondly, the defence of change of position requires that the defendant somehow act to his detriment, yet in paying over to his principal the agent may be doing no such thing. Indeed, by performing his duty to his principal he thereby avoids the possibility of an action for account being brought against him. For that reason the High Court of Australia in *Australia & New Zealand Banking Group Ltd v Westpac Banking Corporation*[7] said that the defence was not to be considered in terms of detriment suffered by the agent. Instead,

> The rationale of . . . [the] rule can be identified in terms of the law of agency and of notions of unjust enrichment. If money is paid to an agent on behalf of a principal and the agent receives it in his capacity as such and, without notice of any mistake or irregularity in the payment, applies the money for the purpose for which it was paid to him, he has applied it in accordance with the mandate of the payer who must look to the principal for recovery.[8]

A third and final reason is that even were the defence to be considered a sub-species of change of position, we would still not have a satisfactory explanation of why an agent who passes on the plaintiff's property to his principal has no similar defence to a claim in conversion.

5. A BETTER EXPLANATION FOR THE DEFENCE OF MINISTERIAL RECEIPT?

It is submitted that there is a better explanation for the defence which is both consistent with the case law in the area of restitution and with the lack of a similar defence in tort. The explanation is one which focuses on the fact that in all the cases in which the defence has succeeded the agent can be said to have received and passed on the benefit concerned to his principal *on the instructions of the restitutionary plaintiff*. The consequence of this is that the plaintiff cannot say that his opponent was wrong in doing that which he himself invited him to do. For want of a better word, this will be called the 'estoppel' theory of ministerial receipt.

The idea that the plaintiff is somehow estopped from complaining of the very action which he has requested the agent to do, namely, make a payment over to his principal, or that he does no 'wrong'[9] in doing so, is supported by dicta in a number of cases. Thus, in *Buller v Harrison*,[10] Lord Mansfield said that 'if an agent pay over money which has been paid to him by mistake, he does no wrong; and the plaintiff must call on the principal . . .',[11] while in *Chappels v Poles*[12] Parke B said that the defence failed because there was no intention on the part of the payer that the agent pay the money over to another. And, in the passage quoted above from *Australia & New Zealand Banking Ltd v Westpac Banking Corporation*, the agent is described as acting with the 'mandate' of the payer.

More importantly, however, the estoppel theory of ministerial receipt is both consistent with and even explains the various constituents of the defence. . . . Take first the payment over requirement. We saw that only change of position came close to explaining this undoubted requirement of the defence, but that it was flawed in other respects. An estoppel theory, however, gives us an

---

7 (1988) 164 CLR 662.   8 *Ibid.* 682.

9 The term 'wrong' is used here in a very loose sense and is not meant to refer to that category of restitutionary actions known as 'Restitution for Wrongs'.

10 (1777) 2 Cowp. 565.   11 *Ibid.* 568.   12 (1837) 2 M & W 867.

explanation as to why the agent escapes liability on payment over which does not depend on proof of detriment. The agent escapes liability on the ground that in paying over to his principal he simply does what the payer has asked him to do. And is also explains why he remains liable before payment over, because until then the payer is free to countermand his authority and thereby remove the justification for the transfer.

Consider next the rule that the payer must know that he is dealing with an agent. This requirement could not be explained by any of the alternative theories put forward. But with an estopped theory as the underlying rationale, the requirement makes perfect sense, for it is only in the case where the payer knows that he is dealing with an agent that he can be said to authorize the payment over to the principal. In the case of an undisclosed agent there is nothing in the payer's conduct to preclude him from treating the agent as a principal.

An estoppel theory also explains the supposed rule that the defence is not available to 'wrong-doers', a rule which . . . struggled to explain the case law which caught agents who were not strictly speaking wrongdoers. The 'estoppel' theory explains the 'wrongdoer' cases because where an agent extracts money from the payer in circumstances involving the commission of a wrong against the payer which the agent has paid over that money to his principal it can hardly be said that the payer mandated the agent's subsequent payment over. In the circumstances, there will be nothing in the payer's conduct which will prevent him from suing an agent who has made such a payment over, since it will have been done without the payer's authority. And this will also be so in cases such as *Miller v Aris*,[13] where the agent's conduct, though not amounting to an actionable wrong, never the less results in the payment being non-consensual. This, it is submitted, is the real reason underlying the 'wrongdoer' cases. Thus, . . . in *Snowden v Davis*,[14] Lord Mansfield denied the agent the defence because it could not be said that the money was paid 'for the purpose of paying it to the [principal]'. And in *Oatesa v Hudson*[15] Parke B allowed the claim because 'the money was not paid to the defendant in his character of agent, so as to prevent the plaintiff from having a remedy against him.' The defence would only apply, he said, where the money was paid to the agent 'expressly for the use of the person to whom he has so paid it over'.

Finally, using an estoppel theory as the basis of the operation of the defence in the law of restitution at the same time explains why no comparable defence is available in the law of torts, for where a tort is committed there will by definition have been no consent given by the plaintiff to the agent's actions.

6. CONCLUSION

What are the implications of the conclusion that the defence of ministerial receipt in the law of restitution rests on the mandate given by the restitutionary plaintiff to the agent to pay the money over to his principal? The most obvious is that it operates to limit the types of restitutionary claim to which the defence can apply. Since a consensual transfer will be a prerequisite it would seem to be confined to claims based on such unjust factors as mistake or failure of consideration. It can, for example, have no application to restitution for wrongs or to payments made under duress. And if it has no application to payments made under duress then *a fortiori* it will have no application to the case where wealth is transferred from the plaintiff without any consent on his part at all, the so-called 'ignorance' cases. This would have the added advantage of bringing the law of restitution into line with the law of tort where, as we have seen, a claim for conversion (which is also an example of wealth moving from the plaintiff in 'ignorance') cannot be met by a defence of ministerial receipt. And for that reason, the one case where the defence has succeeded in such circumstances, *Transvaal and Delegoa Bay Investment Co. v Atkinson*,[16] must be said to have been wrongly decided.

---

13 (1800) 3 Esp 231.   14 (1808) 1 Taunt 359.   15 (1851) 6 Ex 346.
16 [1944] 1 All ER 579.

NOTES AND QUESTIONS

1. Swadling argues that the basis of the defence is a valid mandate by the payor to the payee. This explains why the law insists on payment over (because this is what the payor has mandated), why the agent must be disclosed (because the payor must want the payment to go to someone other than the payee), and why the defence does not apply, for example, to cases of duress (because the necessary consensual basis for the mandate does not exist). But if this theory is correct, ought it not also to follow that the defence rarely applies to a restitutionary claim because most of such claims are 'non-consensual'? In particular, where the payor pays by mistake, there would appear to be no valid mandate for the 'agent' to pay the money over to its 'principal'.

2. Why, as a matter of principle, should the defence be confined to cases in which the claimant has given instructions to the agent as to the way in which he is to deal with the money? If the defence is to be explained in terms of an 'estoppel' theory, as Swadling would have us believe, why is there no requirement that the agent act to his detriment?

3. In contrast with the view of Swadling, in the next extract Stevens argues that there is no independent defence at all. He says that there is nothing unique about the position of an agent in the law of unjust enrichment and there is no reason why agents should be given any special protection and allowed to 'drop out'.

- ● R Stevens, 'Why do agents "drop out"?' [2005] *LMCLQ* 101, 109–18

Where an agent receives money for a principal, should and does a claim in unjust enrichment lie against the agent, the principal or both? Several commentators have argued that the agent should 'drop out'. For this proposition they rely upon the general law of agency. For example Professor Burrows argues:[1]

> The standard effect of agency in contract law is that the agent, having concluded the contract, drops out of the picture. It is strongly arguable that, by analogy, the same should apply in relation to restitution of an unjust enrichment by subtraction.

To similar effect, Birks and Mitchell have written:

An agent is no more than an extension of his principal[2]

. . .

> The rule of equity is that an action in unjust enrichment lies only against the principal and not the agent. The claimant must sue the principal. This does not touch the case in which the claimant can show that the agent has committed some wrong against him. Civilian countries follow the same rule. The agent drops out. This accords with fundamental principles of agency. It is unrelated to change of position. It might nonetheless be related to enrichment, in amounting to an assertion that the agent is never enriched. But it is more properly explained as based on the nature and utility of the institution of agency.[3]

This position has led commentators to denounce the differences they discern between approaches in law and equity. For some, this is an(other) anomaly generated by the historical accident of the common law's division into law and equity.

---

1 A. Burrows, *The Law of Restitution*, 2nd edn (London 2002), 602.

2 P. Birks and C. Mitchell, *Unjust Enrichment*, ch 15 of P. Birks (ed), *English Private Law* (Oxford, 2000). para. 15.310.

3 *Ibid*, para. 15.259. The fullest defence of this position is the unpublished DPhil thesis of Dr Jonathon Moore, *Restitution from Banks* (2000). C Mitchell in P Birks and A Pretto, *Breach of Trust* (Oxford 2002), 184–187 and in C Mitchell, 'Banks, Dishonesty and Negligence' in *Meredith Lectures 2002—Dirty Money: Civil and Criminal Aspects of Money-Laundering* (Cowansville, Quebec, 2003), 126–133 adopts the thesis and summarizes it.

Hopefully, enough has now been done to demonstrate that an agent does (or does not) drop out in the situations set out above, not because of any principle specific to the law of agency but, rather, due to the operation of more general rules of law. The alternative view, that agents drop out because of the independent operation of agency doctrine, gives no guidance as to when the agent will or will not drop out.

One of several reasons why a recipient of a payment is *prima facie* liable to make restitution is that the payment was made by mistake[4] Where money is mistakenly paid to an agent, it is submitted that there may be two reasons why an agent may not be liable to make restitution of the money received. First, the receipt of money may not be an enrichment, as the defendant may not have received it for his own benefit. Secondly, although initially enriched, the recipient has changed his position, usually by paying over to someone else. Neither reason is (any longer) specific to agents.

Authority for the first proposition is less common than for the second. An extreme example of the first is provided by the Post Office. If A mistakenly believes that he owes B £100 and pays by putting ten £10 notes in the post, A cannot sue either the Post Office or the individual postman in unjust enrichment. This result is not reached through the application of principles specific to the law of agency. The Post Office is not an agent except in a colloquial sense. Rather, it is submitted that the Post Office is never enriched. The Post Office is a mere bailee of the notes. It should not be required that the Post Office demonstrates that it has changed its position by delivering the notes to the consignee. If an individual postman appropriated the notes to his own use, an action should lie against him.

That someone who receives notes as a mere bailee should not be liable is not specific to agency law. The claim should fail, not because of any defence, but because an essential element of the cause of action, enrichment, cannot be made out. The essential requirement is that the defendant 'receives the property for his own use and benefit'.[5]

A modern example of the operation of this rule is *Agip (Africa) Ltd v Jackson*.[6] The defendants were chartered accountants who had received the proceeds of a fraud committed by the plaintiff's accountant. The money had been received into the partnership's client account before being paid out to other parties. One of the partners, Bowers, was not a party to the fraud; the others were held liable for knowing assistance. Millett J (as he then was) held that Bowers could not be liable in equity for the money received, as he 'did not take it for his own benefit'[7] It is submitted that this is correct. One advantage of this analysis is that it provides a possible explanation for a requirement of fault before holding a recipient liable to make restitution where the recipient is not beneficially entitled to the money received.

Unfortunately, Millett J confined his remarks to the equitable claim, adopting a different rule in relation to the action at common law.[8] The rationale for different approaches at law and in equity is unclear. However, in *Portman Building Society v Hamlyn Taylor Neck*[9] he departed from his earlier approach. A building society alleged that it had made a mistake in lending money to a Mr Biggins. The money was paid to Mr Biggins' solicitors, the defendants, who had paid it on to Mr Biggins. The claim was an action for money had and received (at common law). Millett LJ rejected the claim in the following terms:[10]

In the present case the firm was not enriched by the receipt of the [money]. The money was trust money, which belonged in equity to the Society, and was properly paid by the firm into its client

---

4 *Kelly v Solari* (1841) 9 M & W 54; *Kleinwort Benson v Lincoln City Council* [1999] 2 AC 349.

5 P Millett, 'Tracing the Proceeds of Fraud' (1991) 107 LQR 71, 83; *cf. Agip (Africa) Ltd v Jackson* [1990] Ch 265, 291; *International Sales Agencies Ltd v Marcus* [1982] 3 All ER 551, 557; *Westpac Banking Corp v Savin* [1985] 2 NZLR 41, 69; *El Ajou v Dollar Land Holdings Plc* [1994] 2 All ER 685, 700; *Eagle Trust v SBC Securities* [1993] 1 WLR 484, 490.

6 [1990] Ch 265.   7 [1990] Ch 265, 292.   8 [1990] Ch 265, 288.

9 [1998] 4 All ER 202.   10 *Ibid*, 206g–h.

account. The firm never made any claim to the money. It acknowledged that it was the Society's money, held to the order of the Society and it was applied in accordance with the Society's instructions in exchange for a mortgage in favour of the Society. The firm did not receive the money for its own use and benefit, but to the Society's use.

Proof of payment over to someone else is unnecessary on this reasoning. It should be noted that it cannot be said that this is a purely equitable rule, as the claim was at common law for money had and received.

Millett LJ's reasoning is an interesting example of the 'fusion' of rules of equity and the common law. If the decision had been taken by a judge sitting in the Court of King's Bench before the Judicature Acts,[11] it may be queried whether the court would have taken off its common law blinkers and looked at the existence of the trust.[12] It is arguable that the court was wrong to remove these blinkers even today. Take an example: A owes £100 to B who holds the debt on trust for several beneficiaries. After repaying this sum, A mistakenly pays B a second time. It would be inconvenient if A was forced to seek recovery from each of the beneficiaries under the trust. Two alternative solutions may be tentatively suggested. The first option is that the second payment is not held on trust at all, in which case B is beneficially enriched. It cannot be sufficient for the sum to be held on trust by B that A expected that it would be. Even if the sum was paid into a trust account, it should be capable of withdrawal by B on proof that it did not belong there. Alternatively, the court should decide the case at common law, ignoring the existence of the trust.

What is the position where the defendant is initially beneficially entitled to the money received but is obliged to account to another for its value? It would be possible for the law to take the view that the beneficial recipient of money is not enriched if he is obliged to account for the same sum to another. On a balance sheet test, the increment in assets is matched by an increase in liabilities. Such a rule would not be limited to those who receive as agents. For example, it would apply to banks which receive money paid in by their customers where a claim is made against them by a third party. Such a rule is not the approach of English law.[13]

If the recipient has changed his position, usually by payment over to another, he should have a defence.[14] Today we would call the defence change of position[15] but the defence was originally confined to agents.[16] Initially, however, the recipient agent is enriched and is liable absent change of position. Millett LJ (as he then was) correctly stated the principle in *Portman BS v Hamlyn Taylor Neck*[17]

> [W]here the plaintiff has paid the money under (for example) a mistake to the agent of a third party, he may sue the principal whether or not the agent has accounted to him . . . If the agent still retains the money, however, the plaintiff may elect to sue either the principal or the agent, and the agent remains liable if he pays the money over to his principal after notice of the claim. If he wishes to protect himself he should interplead. But once the agent has paid the money to his principal or to his order without notice of the claim, the plaintiff must sue the principal.

---

11 Supreme Court of Judicature Act 1873; Supreme Court of Judicature Act 1875.

12 See, eg. *Re Diplock* [1948] Ch 465, 519; *cf. Taylor v Plumer* (1815) 3 M & S 562; L Smith, '*Tracing in Taylor v Plumer*: Equity in the Court of King's Bench' [1995] LMCLQ 240.

13 M Bryan, 'Recovering Misdirected Money From Banks', ch 10 of F Rose (ed), *Restitution and Banking Law* (Oxford 1998), 181–187; L Smith, 'Property, Unjust Enrichment and the Structure of Trusts' (2000) LQR 412, 433; S Gleeson 'The Involuntary Launderer: the Banker's Liability for Deposits of the Proceeds of Crime', ch 5 of P Birks (ed), *Laundering and Tracing* (Oxford 1995), 126–127.

14 *Holland v Russell* (1861) 1 B & S 424; *aff'd* (1863) 4 B & S 114.

15 *Lipkin Gorman v Karpnale Ltd* [1991] 2 AC 548.

16 G Jones, *Goff & Jones: The Law of Restitution*, 6th edn (London 2002), 844–848.

17 [1998] 4 All ER 202, 207.

That this is the law in relation to mistaken payments is decided by a long line of authority.[18] *Cox v Prentice*[19] is authority for the proposition that the agent will not drop out unless there has been payment over. An agent for the sale of a silver bar was mistakenly paid too much. He resisted a claim for restitution of the amount overpaid on the basis that he had sent an account to his principal, which included an allowance for the full price received. The agent remained liable until there had been a payment over.[20] By contrast, in *Holland v Russell*[21] a payment was made in error by an insurer to an agent of the insured. The agent paid over to his principal most of the money received but retained two amounts. One of the amounts was retained by the agent to satisfy a debt owed to him by the principal. The other amount was used by the agent to pay a third party at the principal's direction.[22] It was held that the agent had a complete defence to the insurer's claim.

This approach is as applicable to banks as it is to other intermediaries. The old case of *Sadler v Evans*[23] provides some authority for providing the agent with a defence even where there has been no payment over but this cannot be considered to be good authority in the light of subsequent case law.

It is submitted that the rule suggested applies in equity as well as law.[24] Three difficulties arise in analysing the equitable decisions concerning what we would today call 'knowing receipt'. First, as is well known, the earlier decisions fail to differentiate adequately between accessory liability (dishonest assistance) and receipt based liability.[25] Secondly, the decisions rarely use the language of unjust enrichment,[26] although this may be explicable by the relatively recent recognition of a coherent body of English law which can be organized under this principle.[27] Thirdly, knowing receipt may not be concerned with unjust enrichment at all. Some have argued that knowing receipt is an equitable wrong: the analogue of the common law tort of conversion.[28] Others have argued that the

---

18 *Buller v Harrison* (1777) 2 Cowp. 565; *Cox v Prentice* (1815) 3 M & S 344; *Shand v Grant* [1863] 15 CB (NS) 324; *Owen v Cronk* [1895] 1 QB 265 (duress); *Colonial Bank v Exchange Bank of Yarmouth Nova Scotia* (1885) 11 App Cas 84; *Continental Caoutchoc & Gutta Percha Co. v Kleinwort Sons & Co* (1904) 90 LTR 474; *Kleinwort Sons & Co. v Dunlop Rubber Co* (1907) 97 LT 263; 23 TLR 696; *Kerrison v Glyn Mills, Currie & Co* (1911) 81 LJKB 465; *Admiralty Commissioners v National Provincial and Union Bank* (1922) 127 LT 452; *British American Continental Bank v British Bank for Continental Trade* [1926] 1 KB 328; *Gowers v Lloyds and National Provincial Foreign Bank Ltd* [1938] 1 All ER 766; *Traansvaal & Delagou Investment Co. Ltd v Atkinson* [1944] 1 All ER 579; *Rahimtoola v Nizam of Hyderabad* [1958] AC 379; *Australia and New Zealand Banking Group Ltd v Westpac Banking Corp* (1988) 78 ALR 157; *Standard Bank London Ltd v Canara Bank* [2002] EWHC 1032; *Papamichael v National Westminster Bank Plc* [2003] EWHC 164 (Comm); [2003] 1 Lloyd's Rep 341.

19 (1815) 3 M & S 344.

20 *Cox v Prentice* (1815) 3 M & S 344, 348, *per* Lord Ellenborough.

21 (1863) 4 B & S 14.

22 Unlike the credit to an overdrawn account, this amounted to a contractual settlement of the debts between agent and principal and could not be unilaterally reversed by the agent. *Cf. Buller v Harrison* (1777) 2 Cowp. 565.

23 (1766) 4 Burr. 1984.

24 *Gray v Johnston* (1868) LR 3 HL 1; *Foxton v Manchester and Liverpool District Banking Co* (1881) 44 LT 406; *Thompson v Clydesdale Bank Ltd* [1893] AC 282; *Coleman v Bucks & Oxon Union Bank* [1897] 2 Ch 243; *Stephens Travel Services International v Qantas Airways* (1988) 13 NSWLR 31, 365; *Agip (Africa) Ltd v Jackson* [1990] Ch 265; *Cigna Life Insurance New Zealand Ltd v Westpac Securities Ltd* [1996] 1 NZLR 80; *Macmillan Inc. v Bishopsgate Investment Trust plc (No 3)* [1996] 1 WLR 387, 409, *per* Auld LJ; *Citadel General Assurance Co. v Lloyds Bank Canada* [1997] 3 SCR 805.

25 *Cf. Royal Brunei Airlines Sdn Bhd v Tan* [1995] 2 AC 378, 386, *per* Lord Nicholls.

26 *Cf. Powell v Thompson* [1991] 1 NZLR 597, 607, *per* Thomas J; *Equiticorp Industries Group Ltd v R.* [1998] 2 NZLR 481, 604, *per* Smellie J; *Kooratang Nominees Pty. Ltd v Australia and New Zealand Banking Group Ltd* [1998] 3 VR 16.

27 *Lipkin Gorman v Karpnale* [1991] AC 548.

28 L Smith [1995] LMCLQ 240; L Smith, 'W(h)ither Knowing Receipt' (1998) 114 LQR 394; *cf. Twinsectra Ltd v Yardley* [2002] 2 AC 164, [105], *per* Lord Millett; A Burrows, *The Law of Restitution*, 2nd edn (London 2002), 202–203.

single entity 'knowing receipt' actually contains two different kinds of claim, one wrong based and the other based on unjust enrichment.[29]

Despite these difficulties, it is submitted that the weight of authority discloses a similar pattern to the common law: the claim against the agent will succeed to the extent that there has not been an innocent payment over to the principal. For example, in *Foxton v Manchester and Liverpool District Banking Co*[30] a trustee arranged for funds to be transferred from a trust account into his overdrawn personal account. The bank was held liable as constructive trustee to make good the shortfall. A similar result was reached in *Citadel General Assurance Co. v Lloyds Bank Canada*.[31] The defendant bank's customer carried on business as an insurance agent. The balance of premiums after deductions for losses and fees was held on trust for their principals. In breach of trust, these sums were transferred into the overdrawn account at the same bank of the insurance agent's parent company. The bank was held liable to the insurers on the basis of knowing receipt.

Where there has been payment over, an equitable claim based upon unjust enrichment should fail. In *Nimmo v Westpac Banking Corp*[32] a rogue director of an investment company arranged for approximately Aus$250,000 to be transferred to an account in credit with the defendant bank which he then withdrew using a cheque which he had tricked his co-director into signing. The claim based upon knowing receipt failed:

> [The] credit only existed for a short time because Westpac immediately put Mr Eaton in possession of bank cheques and travellers cheques and debited its books accordingly. The net result disregarding the fees, was that Westpac was in no better position as a result of the transaction. It had not been enriched.[33]

There are judicial statements supporting the proposition that the bank should not be liable in equity where the account into which the funds are deposited is in credit and those funds have not been withdrawn.[34] It may be queried whether this is correct and it is not the position adopted at common law. The decision of the Court of Appeal in *Polly Peck International v Nadir (No 2)*[35] provides some authority for such an equitable rule. The defendant, Central Bank, received £45 million from another bank, IBK, in exchange for which it credited IBK with an equivalent sum in Turkish lire. IBK also made nine transfers to Central Bank which were credited in sterling. All of the sums deposited belonged in equity to the plaintiff company. The Court of Appeal held that the bank did not beneficially receive the sums credited in sterling but did beneficially receive the sum credited in Turkish lire. It could, therefore, only be liable in relation to the latter sum. It is submitted that no such distinction can be drawn. As Bryan argues:[36]

> The Central Bank received all money from IBK for its own commercial purposes. It was liable as debtor, to pay IBK an equivalent sum on demand. Whether the payment is made in sterling or Turkish lire was a simple matter of customer preference.

---

29 Lord Nicholls, 'Knowing Receipt: The Need for a New Landmark', ch 15 of W Cornish, R Nolan, J O'Sullivan and G Virgo (eds), *Restitution Past, Present and Future* (Oxford 1998), 231–246; P Birks, 'Receipt', ch 7 of P Birks and A Pretto (eds), *Breach of Trust* (Oxford 2002), 224.

30 (1881) 44 LT 406.

31 [1997] 3 SCR 805.   32 [1993] 3 NZLR 218.   33 *Ibid*, 220.

34 *Agip (Africa) Ltd v Jackson* [1990] Ch 265, 292; *Citadel General Assurance Co. v Lloyds Bank Canada*, *ibid*, at 422–423; P Millett, 'Tracing the Proceeds of Fraud' (1991) 107 LQR 71, 82–83.

35 [1992] 4 All ER 769; powerfully criticized by M. Bryan, *supra*, fn 13, see also *Lankshear v ANZ Banking Group* [1993] 1 NZLR 481; *Compagnie Commercial Andre v Artibell Shipping* [2001] SC 653, 661–662; *cf. Nimmo v Westpac Banking Corp* [1993] 3 NZLR 218, 225; *Cigna Life Insurance New Zealand v Westpac* [1996] 1 NZLR 80, 86.

36 Bryan, *supra*, fn 13, at 83.

The recognition of the defence of change of position frees the law from enquiring as to whether the defendant who has paid over is properly described as an agent. Where a bank receives money into an account from an account holder, it cannot be argued that it is acting as an agent. If this is an agency relationship, every loan or repayment gives rise to a relationship of agency. By contrast, it is arguable that, whilst a bank which receives money into an account from its account holder is not acting as agent, it is so acting where the funds are deposited by a third party.[37] It is difficult to see why it should be thought that the bank should have a defence in the latter situation but not in the former.[38] Where the bank's position has changed subsequent to the deposit, usually due to payment over to the account holder, the bank should possess a defence to a claim based upon unjust enrichment. Similarly, in the notorious case of *Baylis v Bishop of London*[39] a bishop received mistakenly paid tithe rent charges. After meeting certain expenses of the parish, he paid the surplus to the rector's trustee in bankruptcy. It was held that, as he had received as principal rather than as agent, he was afforded no defence. It must be very doubtful whether this case would be followed today. Furthermore, there seems no reason to believe that it should any longer matter whether the agency was disclosed.[40] Whether the defence is called change of position or ministerial receipt should no longer be of significance.[41]

The mere fact of a payment over by the agent should not be decisive for the operation of this defence. For example: A mistakenly pays £100 into B's account with C bank leaving a credit balance of £200. B withdraws £200. If C bank would not have permitted B to withdraw £200 if it would have left the account overdrawn, C bank has changed its position in reliance upon A's payment. If, however, C bank would have allowed the withdrawal in any event, C bank's position has not changed because of the deposit and it should remain liable to A.

The analysis suggested here has most significance for banks. Where a bank receives money for the account of its customer, whether from the account holder or a third party, the bank is beneficially entitled to the funds deposited. This is so regardless of whether the account is in credit or overdrawn. The method of payment—cash, cheque or electronic transfer—is irrelevant. Where the account is in credit, the bank's obligation to pay to its account holder is increased by the sum deposited.[42] Where the account is overdrawn, the customer's obligation to pay the bank is reduced by the sum deposited. The change in the nature of the obligation is not, however, irrevocable. All that has taken place is a book entry. If the bank is immediately notified of the error, it remains free to reverse the book entry.[43] If the book entry can no longer be reversed, because the account holder has drawn down on the account or in some other way relied upon his honest belief as to the true state of the account in a way which he would not have done had the funds not been deposited,[44] the bank should have a defence of change of position.

It may be objected that the bank may be placed in an invidious position. Its customer may demand payment on the account whilst the third party demands return of the funds. The solution is, as Millett LJ suggests, that the bank should interplead.

---

37 *Cf* G Treitel, *The Law of Contract*, 11th edn (London 2003), 707.

38 *Cf* L Smith 'Unjust Enrichment, Property and the Structure of Trusts' (2001) 116 LQR 412, 433–434.

39 [1913] 1 Ch 127; *cf. Newall v Tomlinson* (1871) LR 6 CP 405.

40 *Cf. USA v Steele* (1959) 175 F Supp 24.

41 *Portman Building Society v Hamlyn Taylor Neck* [1998] 4 All ER 202 207, *per* Millett LJ.

42 *Foley v Hill* (1848) 2 HL Cas 28.

43 *Commercial Bank of Scotland v Rhind* (1860) 3 Macq. HL 643; *British and North European Bank Ltd v Zalzstein* [1927] 2 KB 92; *United Overseas Bank v Jiwani* [1976] 1 WLR 964.

44 *Skyring v Greenwood and Cox* (1825) 4 B & C 281; *Holland v Manchester and Liverpool District Banking Co* (1909) 14 Com Cas 241; *Holt v Markham* [1923] 1 KB 504; *Lloyds Bank Ltd v Brooks* (1950) 6 LDAB 161.

That the bank should not have a blanket 'agency' defence is also commercially useful in the context of misdirected funds. The account holder may be domiciled outside of the jurisdiction. Persuading an English court to take jurisdiction over a defendant domiciled in, say, Venezuela may not be easy and the law that the English court should apply, to a claim in unjust enrichment is, to say the least, obscure. If the money has been deposited in, say, the National Westminster Bank, Chancery Lane, obtaining jurisdiction should pose no difficulty, the applicable law appears obvious and the bank's contract with its account holder will permit it to correct the book entry.

If correct, the analysis suggested will mean that it will in many instances be unnecessary to decide whether the claimant has a proprietary claim against an account holder. Where the misdirected funds are paid to a bank and there has been no change of position, the claim against the bank should succeed regardless of the solvency of the eustomer. It will be unnecessary to establish a proprietary claim against the customer in order to be protected upon his insolvency. It is, relatively, rare for banks to be unable to pay.

The bank's customer is liable to a claimant in unjust enrichment from the moment of receipt by his bank, regardless of whether the customer has withdrawn the funds.[45] This is correct in principle. Assuming the bank's solvency, a credit to a bank account is as good as cash. The majority of the wealth we hold takes the form of a claim against another party. Double recovery from bank and customer should not, of course, be allowed, but joint liability for the same sum raises few difficulties. This result seems to show that the English law of unjust enrichment is not a 'zero sum game': the payment of a single sum can enrich more than one party.[46] That an account-holder is enriched by the receipt of a sum of money does not lead to the converse proposition that the bank is not enriched.

Where a principal is initially enriched as well as his agent, it is important to know when the principal will drop out. If A mistakenly pays £100 into B's account with C bank, B is enriched. What if the bank goes into insolvent liquidation before B has withdrawn the sum deposited? Should B have a defence of change of position?

If B had withdrawn the money and, before learning of A's error, spent it on an expensive meal he would not otherwise have purchased, it seems that he would now have a defence to the claim for restitution. The insolvency of the bank is no more B's fault than his liking of good food. In both examples his initial enrichment has disappeared. Although there is no clear authority,[47] the better view seems to be that change of position may take the form either of reliance expenditure or, as with the bank failure, any disenrichment causally related to the initial receipt.[48]

What if A mistakenly pays money to B's agent who deliberately absconds with the money? Should B be entitled to rely upon change of position in these circumstances? Again, the position is unclear. The defence of change of position is excluded if the defendant has changed his position with knowledge that the money received was not due, regardless of whether he can be described as dishonest.[49] If the agent's knowledge is to be attributed to B, eg, because B is a company and the agent is the managing director, it seems clear that the defence should be excluded in this case. If, however, the agent's knowledge is not attributable to his principal, should the principal's carelessness in entrusting his affairs to a dishonest agent exclude the defence? If the recipient of money carelessly loses it, it is unclear whether his fault should bar the defence of change of position.

45 *National Westminster Bank Ltd v Barclays Bank Ltd* [1975] QB 654; *Chase Manhattan Bank NA v Israel British Bank (London) Ltd* [1981] Ch 105; *Australia and New Zealand Banking Group Ltd v Westpac Banking Corp* (1988) 78 ALR 157; *Portman Building Society v Hamlyn Taylor Neck* [1998] 4 All ER 202.

46 *Cf* L Smith 'Three-Party Restitution: A Critique of Birk's Theory of Interceptive Subtraction' (1991) 11 OJLS 481, 483.

47 *Cf. National Bank of New Zealand Ltd v Waitaki International Processing (NI) Ltd* [1999] 2 NZLR 211.

48 A Burrows, *The Law of Restitution*, 2nd edn (London 2002), 514–517.

49 *Niru Battery Manufacturing Co. v Milestone Trading Ltd* [2003] EWCA Civ 1446; [2004] 1 Lloyd's Rep 344; noted A Tettenborn [2004] *Restitution Law Review* 155.

AN EXCEPTION?: THE RECOVERY OF DEPOSITS

In a long line of cases, where the unjust enrichment arises from a failure of consideration, the action against the recipient agent fails even where no payment over to the principal has been made.[50] Some commentators have relied upon these cases as authority for a more general rule that 'agents drop out' where a claim in unjust enrichment is made.[51] These commentators argue that, not only is the common law inconsistent with the approach in equity, but the common law is itself internally incoherent.

Bowstead & Reynolds argue that the result in these cases is correct and that 'the principal should alone be liable, for the agent may not be in a position to know whether the money is returnable, and the matter should be disputed between the principal and the third party'.[52] This is unpersuasive as a basis for distinguishing these cases from those where the money has been paid to the agent by mistake. Where the money is paid by mistake, the agent may be wholly ignorant of the error and will equally not be in a position to know whether the money is returnable.

It is submitted that these cases are correctly decided on the basis that the ground of recovery relied upon, failure of consideration, cannot normally be made out as against a disclosed agent.[53] They are not, therefore, correctly seen as an exception to the general rule. An example: A agrees to paint B's house for £100 payable in advance. B deposits a cheque for this amount into A's account with C bank. A now refuses to carry out the work. B clearly has an action against A to recover the money paid based upon a total failure of consideration. It is submitted that a total failure of consideration cannot be made out as against C bank. Failure of consideration is probably best seen as the common law's equivalent of the civilian notion of *causa data causa non secuta*: a thing given on a basis which fails. For this to be made out it is necessary for the conditionality of the transfer to be objectively apparent to and shared by the recipient.[54] This is obviously satisfied where the benefit is conferred under a contract but it is also required for non-contractual transfers. In the example given, C bank may have no notion of the basis of the payment. So far as the bank is concerned, no condition has been attached and the claim in unjust enrichment against it must fail.

Mere knowledge of the condition under which the payment has been made is insufficient. The conditionality of the payment must be the shared basis for the payment. For example, in *Ellis v Goulton*[55] a purchaser of premises paid a deposit to the vendor's solicitor as agent for the vendor. The sale went off through the default of the vendor and the action to recover the deposit from the solicitor failed. The solicitor was not a party to the agreement of sale. The solicitor's knowledge that the payment was conditional so far as the purchaser and vendor were concerned did not make it conditional so far as he was concerned: '[i]t is impossible to treat money paid under these circumstances and remaining in the hands of the agent as there under any condition . . . in relation to the payer'.[56]

---

50 *Duke of Norfolk v Worthy* (1880) 1 Camp. 337; *Ellis v Goulton* [1893] 1 QB 350; *Bamford v Shuttleworth* (1840) 11 A & E 926; *Edgell v Day* (1865) LR 1 CP 80; *North Eastern Timber Importers v Ch Arendt & Sons* [1952] 2 Lloyd's Rep 513; *Burt v Claude Cousins & Co. Ltd* [1971] 2 QB 426, 435; *Goodey v Garriock* [1972] 2 Lloyd's Rep 369; *Arnhem Technology Ltd v Dudley Joiner* (31 January 2001) Unreported (Ch D); *cf. Wilder v Pilkington* [1956] JPL 739.

51 A Burrows, *The Law of Restitution*, 2nd edn (London 2002), 600–601.

52 *Bowstead & Reynolds*, 521.

53 Swadling, in an elegant argument, states that ministerial receipt is in fact a species of estoppel: see *supra*. However, the deposit cases are inconsistent with his theory and he is forced to argue that they are all incorrectly decided.

54 *Guardian Ocean Cargoes v Banco de Brasil SA* [1991] 2 Lloyd's Rep 68. Mere mispredictions which are not made objectively apparent to the counter-party will not, at least usually, render an enrichment unjust: *Dextra Bank & Trust Co. Ltd v Bank of Jamaica* [2001] UKPC 50; [2002] 1 All ER (Comm) 193.

55 [1893] 1 QB 350.   56 *Ibid*, 353 *per* Bowen LJ.

It is possible for the third party to make it objectively apparent to the agent that the payment in his favour is also to be treated as conditional so far as the agent is concerned. The agent is in these circumstances termed a 'stakeholder' and is concurrently obliged with his principal to make restitution upon failure of the condition.[57]

Where the ground for recovery is mistake, there is no requirement that the mistake be known or shared, and so recovery against the recipient agent is successful unless there has been payment over. Similarly, where the payer has been the subject of duress, the recipient agent will be obliged to make restitution of any payments made which he has not paid over, even though he did not apply the duress and had no knowledge of it.[58] The claimant's vitiation of consent is sufficient.

A further important difference is that the defence of change of position should rarely, if ever, succeed where the ground of recovery is failure of consideration. If we take again the example of the defaulting housepainter, if he has spent the money, however innocently, he should not be relieved from liability. He knew that the payment was conditional and if, in the meantime, he has spent the money, he has done so in the knowledge that he must repay if the condition is unfulfilled. The failure of the defence is not dependent upon the defendant's being in breach of contract.[59] More difficult is the case where the disenrichment has occurred not because of the defendant's deliberate expenditure but for some other reason—for example, because of the failure of the bank into which the funds were deposited or the defendant's agent absconding with the money. In *Martin v Pont*[60] the clients of an accountant entrusted him with NZ $600,000 for investment in a particular way. The accountant's daughter misappropriated most of the funds. Although the defendant was not in any way implicated in the misappropriation, he remained liable. It was argued that the claim should fail on the basis that the plaintiff could no longer establish that the defendant remained enriched. This was correctly rejected: it is only necessary to show that the enrichment was received not that it persists in the defendant's hands.[61] The court also rejected the application of any defence of change of position. On balance it is submitted that they were right to do so. Unless there are contrary indications, the normal basis upon which money will have been paid is that the defendant must take the risk of the enrichment being dissipated. The principal should not, therefore, drop out.

NOTES AND QUESTIONS

1. Stevens adopts Millett LJ's suggestion that the solution to the 'agent's dilemma' (above, 831) is to interplead and he argues that 'whether the defence is called change of position or ministerial receipt should no longer be of significance'. But he does not answer the criticisms of Swadling (831) that the agent's defence operates differently from the defence of change of position. On the other hand, as Stevens observes, Swadling's theory is inconsistent with the deposit cases and Swadling is forced to argue that those cases are wrong.

2. Stevens argues that the denial of a failure of consideration claim against an agent in a case involving a deposit is not anomalous because it is not a case of application of an agent's defence. Rather, the primary claim against the agent is not satisfied because the agent rarely receives the payment subject to a condition or basis. In cases where the agent does receive subject to conditions, the agent is treated as a 'stakeholder' and is liable, concurrently with its principal. Stevens therefore assumes that failure of consideration (basis) requires a shared basis, see above, 253.

---

57 Eg, *Hastingwood Property Ltd v Saunders Bearman Anselm* [1991] Ch 114, esp. 123–124; See *Bowstead & Reynolds* 475–476.

58 *Owen v Cronk* [1895] 1 QB 265.

59 *Cf. Goss v Chilcott* [1996] AC 788.   60 [1993] 3 NZLR 25.

61 *Lipkin Gorman v Karpnale Ltd* [1991] 2 AC 548; *cf. Roxburgh v Rothmans of Pall Mall Australia Ltd* [2001] HCA 68; 208 CLR 516.

3. Suppose a bank (agent) receives money from a third party for the account of its customer (principal). The bank credits the customer's account and the customer spends the money. Before the bank credits the customer's account it had received a facsimile from the payer alleging that the payment was a mistake. Carelessly, the facsimile had not been read. If the defence were treated as part of change of position as Stevens suggests, would the bank have a defence? Should older cases allowing recovery against a bank in such a case (e.g. *Edwards v Hodding* (1814) 5 Taunt 815) be overruled?

5. COUNTER-RESTITUTION IMPOSSIBLE

A claimant who wishes to reverse an unjust enrichment that the defendant has obtained at his expense must be prepared to recompense the defendant for any benefit that he has received at the expense of the defendant. In other words, a claimant cannot both get back what he has parted with and keep what he has received in return. The requirement that the claimant must make counter-restitution is directed to ensuring that the claimant is not unjustly enriched: it does not have as its aim the avoidance of loss on the part of the defendant (*Armstrong v Jackson*, below, 847).

While it is clear that a claimant who seeks restitution must give counter-restitution, the proposition that it should be a defence for a defendant to show that counter-restitution is 'impossible' is much more controversial. In the first place as a matter of terminology, the phrase 'counter-restitution impossible' is not part of the language of all restitution lawyers. It was first coined by Birks but, for example, it finds no place in the terminology of Goff and Jones. They prefer the more traditional language that a claimant who is seeking to rescind a contract must make *restitutio in integrum* and their discussion can be found not in the section of the book on defences but at various points throughout the book (89–90, 262–3, 355–8, 507). The second and more substantial difficulty is that it is not easy to explain why the need to make counter-restitution has been transformed into a bar where counter-restitution is 'impossible' because 'it is a nonsense to suggest that restitution may be impossible. Personal restitution is always possible' (Burrows, 541). Counter-restitution may be difficult to assess, but it is never impossible because a monetary value can always be put on the value of non-money benefits received by the claimant who seeks restitution. The defence 'counter-restitution impossible' appears to be a reflection of the traditional unwillingness of the courts (especially at common law) to enter into complex issues of valuation. At common law the courts insisted upon precise restitution but, as we shall see, the harshness of this rule has been mitigated by the intervention of equity. In equity a party who can make substantial, but not precise restitution can rescind the contract if he returns the subject-matter of the contract in its altered form and gives an account of the value obtained through his use of the product together with an allowance for any deterioration in the product.

• *Clarke v Dickson* (1858) EB & E 148, Court of Queen's Bench

In 1853 the claimant was induced to pay deposits for shares in a a company called The Welsh Potosi Lead and Copper Mining Company which was formed to work a mine on the cost-book principle and of which the defendants were directors. The mine was worked by the company between 1854 and 1856 and dividends were declared in each year. In 1857 the company was in a bad way and, with the claimant's assent, it was registered as a company with limited liability. It was later wound up. When the claimant discovered that the representations which had been made to him were false, he brought an action to recover back the deposits which he had paid for the shares. His action failed because he could not restore the parties to their pre-contractual position: his remedy lay in an action for deceit.

Crompton J: When once it is settled that a contract induced by fraud is not void, but voidable at the option of the party defrauded, it seems to me to follow that, when that party exercises his option to rescind the contract, he must be in a state to rescind; that is, he must be in such a situation as to be able to put the parties into their original state before the contract. Now here I will assume, what is not clear to me, that the plaintiff bought his shares from the defendants and not from the Company, and that he might at one time have had a right to restore the shares to the defendants if he could, and demand the price from them. But then what did he buy? Shares in a partnership with others. He cannot return those; he has become bound to those others. Still stronger, he has changed their nature: what he now has and offers to restore are shares in a quasi corporation now in process of being wound up. That is quite enough to decide this case. The plaintiff must rescind in toto or not at all; he cannot both keep the shares and recover the whole price. That is founded on the plainest principles of justice. If he cannot return the article he must keep it, and sue for his real damage in an action on the deceit. Take the case I put in the argument, of a butcher buying live cattle, killing them, and even selling the meat to his customers. If the rule of law were as the plaintiff contends, that butcher might, upon discovering a fraud on the part of the grazier who sold him the cattle, rescind the contract and get back the whole price: but how could that be consistently with justice? The true doctrine is, that a party can never repudiate a contract after, by his own act, it has become out of his power to restore the parties to their original condition.

Erle J and Lord Campbell CJ delivered concurring judgments.

NOTES AND QUESTIONS

1. *Clarke* is often cited as one of the cases in which the courts insisted on precise counter-restitution (for example, by Lord Blackburn in *Erlanger v New Sombrero Phosphate Co.*, below, 845). Other frequently cited examples of the same restrictive approach are *Blackburn v Smith* (1848) 2 Ex 783 and *Hunt v Silk* above, 257).

2. In the light of the more flexible approach subsequently adopted in equity (see *Erlanger v New Sombrero Phosphate Co.*, below, 845), would *Clarke* be decided the same way today? How did McCardie J analyse the case in *Armstrong v Jackson* (below 847)?

3. In the example given by Crompton J why can the butcher not rescind the contract by offering to make an allowance in money for the change in condition of the cattle?

4. Is the requirement that the claimant make counter-restitution a recognition of the fact that the defendant has a counter-claim or set-off against the claimant or is it a defence (that operates even though the defendant does not have a valid counter-claim or set-off against the claimant)? The distinction between the two views can have significant practical consequences (an illustration of which is provided by *Kleinwort Benson Ltd v South Tyneside MBC* [1994] 4 All ER 972, 978–81, where Hobhouse J, in the context of his analysis of the law relating to limitation of actions, effectively treated counter-restitution as a defence rather than a separate claim (see further A Burrows, 'Swaps and the Friction Between Common Law and Equity' [1995] *RLR* 15, 22)).

- *Erlanger v New Sombrero Phosphate Co.* (1878) 3 App Cas 1218, House of Lords

The defendants, who were promoters of the claimant company, sold a phosphate mine to the claimant for £110,000. After it had worked the mine for a period of time, the claimant sought to rescind the contract of sale on the ground that the defendants had breached the fiduciary duty which they owed to the claimant by failing to disclose that they had bought the mine a few days before the sale to the claimant for £55,000. The defendants argued that the claimant was not entitled to rescission because the parties could not be restored to their pre-contractual position. It was held that the claimant was entitled to rescind the contract and recover the purchase price on terms of giving up possession of the mine and accounting to the defendants for any profits made from working the mine.

Lord Blackburn: . . . The contract was not void, but only voidable at the election of the company.

In *Clough v The London and North Western Railway Company*,[1] in the judgment of the Exchequer Chamber, it is said, 'We agree that the contract continues valid till the party defrauded has determined his election by avoiding it. In such cases, (i.e., of fraud) the question is, Has the person on whom the fraud was practised, having notice of the fraud, elected not to avoid the contract? Or, Has he elected to avoid it? Or, Has he made no election? We think that so long as he has made no election he retains the right to determine it either way; subject to this, that if, in the interval whilst he is deliberating, an innocent third party has acquired an interest in the property, or if, *in consequence of his delay the position even of the wrongdoer is affected*, it will preclude him from exercising his right to rescind.' It is, I think, clear on principles of general justice, that as a condition to a rescission there must be a *restitutio in integrum*. The parties must be put *in statu quo*. See *per* Lord Cranworth in *Addie v The Western Bank*.[2] It is a doctrine which has often been acted upon both at law and in equity. But there is a considerable difference in the mode in which it is applied in Courts of Law and Equity, owing, as I think, to the difference of the machinery which the Courts have at command. I speak of these Courts as they were at the time when this suit commenced, without inquiring whether the Judicature Acts make any, or if any, what difference.

It would be obviously unjust that a person who has been in possession of property under the contract which he seeks to repudiate should be allowed to throw that back on the other party's hands without accounting for any benefit he may have derived from the use of the property, or if the property, though not destroyed, has been in the interval deteriorated, without making compensation for that deterioration. But as a Court of Law has no machinery at its command for taking an account of such matters, the defrauded party, if he sought his remedy at law, must in such cases keep the property and sue in an action for deceit, in which the jury, if properly directed, can do complete justice by giving as damages a full indemnity for all that the party has lost: see *Clarke v Dickson*,[3] and the cases there cited.

But a Court of Equity could not give damages, and, unless it can rescind the contract, can give no relief. And, on the other hand, it can take accounts of profits, and make allowance for deterioration. And I think the practice has always been for a Court of Equity to give this relief whenever, by the exercise of its powers, it can do what is practically just, though it cannot restore the parties precisely to the state they were in before the contract. And a Court of Equity requires that those who come to it to ask its active interposition to give them relief, should use due diligence, after there has been such notice or knowledge as to make it inequitable to lie by. And any change which occurs in the position of the parties or the state of the property after such notice or knowledge should tell much more against the party *in morâ*, than a similar change before he was *in morâ* should do. . . .

Lord Penzance, Lord Hatherley, Lord O'Hagan, Lord Selborne and **Lord Gordon** delivered concurring speeches. **Lord Cairns LC** delivered a speech in which he stated that laches operated to deny the claimant the relief to which it was otherwise entitled.

1 Law Rep 7 Ex 34, 35. 2 Law Rep 1 HL, Sc 165. 3 E B & E 148.

QUESTION

Can the difference in approach between equity and the common law be justified? Should we not be able to formulate a uniform set of rules?

- *Armstrong v Jackson* [1917] 2 KB 822, King's Bench Division

In 1910 the claimant instructed the defendant to purchase 600 shares in the Champion Gold Reefs of West Africa Ltd The defendant informed him that the order had been executed and debited the claimant with £1760. The claimant later discovered that the defendant had not purchased any shares in the company but had in fact sold the claimant his (the defendant's) own shares in the company, which he had acquired as a promoter of the company. The claimant brought an action to set aside the transaction on the ground of the defendant's fraud in issuing false documentation to the claimant, which the defendant resisted, *inter alia*, on the basis that it was no longer possible to restore the parties to their pre-contractual position because the shares had since decreased in value. It was held that this was no defence to the claim and that the claimant was entitled to set aside the contract and recover the sum which he had paid to the defendant, together with interest, less £45 in respect of the dividends which the claimant had received on the shares. The claimant was also ordered to transfer the 600 shares to the defendant upon payment of the sum due from the defendant.

McCardie J: . . . [Counsel for the defendant] argued that no decree should be granted inasmuch as the circumstances had changed through the lapse of time and that the plaintiff could not restore in 1917 that which he had received from the defendant in 1910. The shares in 1910 stood at nearly 3*l.* for each 5*s.* share. They are now worth 5*s.* only, or slightly less, and at such a price they have been standing at and since the issue of the writ. But in my view this second contention fails also, although, of course, it is clear law that restitutio in integrum is essential to a claim for rescission. The plaintiff still holds the shares he bought in 1910. He can hand them back to the defendant. The company is the same as in 1910. Its name only has been changed. The objects of the company have not changed though the assets of the company may have varied. The market valuation of the shares has greatly dropped, but the shares are the same shares. In my view the words of Lord Blackburn in *Erlanger v New Sombrero Phosphate Co.*,[1] quoting *Clough v London and North-Western Ry. Co.*,[2] have no application to the present case. In the *Erlanger Case* Lord Blackburn says this: ' "We think that so long as he has made no election he retains the right to determine it either way; subject to this, that if, in the interval whilst he is deliberating, an innocent third party has acquired an interest in the property, or if, in consequence of his delay, the position even of the wrongdoer is affected, it will preclude him from exercising his right to rescind." It is, I think, clear on principles of general justice, that as a condition to a rescission there must be a restitutio in integrum. The parties must be put in statu quo. See *per* Lord Cranworth in *Western Bank of Scotland v Addie*.[3] It is a doctrine which has often been acted upon both at law and in equity.' I think that such words refer to a delay which occurs after a plaintiff has ascertained his right to rescind and whereby the position of a defendant is substantially altered and prejudiced. No such delay has here occurred, inasmuch as the plaintiff acted with promptitude in issuing his writ when he became suspicious of the defendant's conduct. The phrase 'restitutio in integrum' is somewhat vague. It must be applied with care. It must be considered with respect to the facts of each case. Deterioration of the subject-matter does not, I think, destroy the right to rescind nor prevent a restitutio in integrum. Indeed, it is only in cases where the plaintiff has sustained loss by the inferiority of the subject-matter or a substantial fall in its value that he will desire to exert his

---

1 (1878) 3 App Cas 1218, 1278.   2 (1871) LR 7 Ex 26, 35.   3 LR 1 HL Sc 145, 165.

power of rescission. Such was the state of things in *Rothschild v Brookman*.[4] Such, I infer, was the state of things in *Gillett v Peppercorne*,[5] where the plaintiff alleged that he had paid extravagant prices for the shares. Such too, I infer, was the state of things in *Oelkers v Ellis*.[6] If mere deterioration of the subject-matter negatived the right to rescind, the doctrine of rescission would become a vain thing. Rescission was refused in *Clarke v Dickson*[7] because the plaintiff had there changed the shares in a company on the cost-book principle into shares in a joint-stock corporation. Upon that ground the decision in *Clarke v Dickson* is correct. The dicta in that case, so far as they go beyond that ground, are not, I think, consistent with the various decisions already cited in this judgment. Rescission was impossible in *Western Bank of Scotland v Addie*,[8] inasmuch as the shares purchased by the plaintiff, namely, shares in an unincorporated company, had been changed into shares of a company registered under the then existing Companies Acts. But Lord Cranworth in his opinion[9] used the following words: 'I agree with the learned judges below, that the circumstance that the shares, from mismanagement or otherwise, had become depreciated in value subsequently to the purchase by the pursuer, would of itself have been of no importance. He might still have been able to restore that which he was fraudulently induced to purchase.' Those words are directly applicable to the present case: see also the American decision of *Conkey v Bond*,[10] cited in Story on Agency, notes to s. 211. The fall of the shares here is serious. Had, indeed, the plaintiff discovered the fraud at an early date he could have repudiated the transaction whilst the price was still high, and the loss to the defendant would then not have been so great in view of his power to dispose of them on the market. But the plaintiff is in no way to blame, and the considerations of hardship urged before me by Mr Disturnal were similarly urged in 1856 before Sir John Romilly in a somewhat analogous case. Yet the plea of hardship fails here as it failed sixty years ago. In rejecting the plea of hardship in *Blake v Mowatt*[11] the then Master of the Rolls said: 'It is the leading principle of the equity administration in this Court, that truth shall govern all transactions, and that one who deludes another in a contract, or permits him to be deluded, and takes advantage of that delusion, cannot afterwards complain, that, if the contract be set aside, he will be in a worse situation than if the contract had never been entered into.'

The extent to which the requirement of restitutio in integrum may be limited in its application is strikingly illustrated by the decision in *Adam v Newbigging*.[12]

I may point out that mere lapse of time is no answer to a plea of rescission. Here some six years elapsed before the plaintiff claimed to rescind. ... In cases like the present the right of the party defrauded is not affected by the mere lapse of time so long as he remains in ignorance of the fraud. ... If, however, he delays his claim to rescission until after the lapse of six years from his discovery of the fraud, then the Court will (apart from any other point) act by analogy to the Statute of Limitations and refuse to grant relief: see *Oelkers v Ellis*.[13] ...

NOTES

1. The decision of the Court of Appeal in *Newbigging v Adam* is set out above, 196.

2. This case demonstrates that the fact that the defendant has suffered a detriment and so cannot be restored to his pre-contractual position is not in itself a bar to rescission (see also *Mackenzie v Royal Bank of Canada* [1934] AC 468) Thus Professor Treitel has stated (*The Law of Contract* (11th edn), 380) that 'it is sometimes said that the object of rescission is to restore the parties to the situation in which they would have been if the contract had never been made, but ... such statements are not quite accurate. The essential point is that the representee should not be unjustly enriched at the representor's expense; that the representor should not be prejudiced is a secondary consideration, which is only taken into account when some benefit has been received by the representee.'

---

4 5 Bli. (NS) 165.   5 3 Beav 78.   6 [1914] 2 KB 139.   7 E B & E 148.
8 LR 1 HL Sc. 145, 165.   9 LR 1 HI Sc 166.   10 (1861) 34 Barbour 276.
11 (1856) 21 Beav 603, 613.   12 (1888) 13 App Cas 308.   13 [1914] 2 KB 139, 151.

• *Spence v Crawford* [1939] 3 All ER 271, House of Lords

The appellant was induced by the fraudulent misrepresentation of the respondent to sell him his shares in a company. The respondent in turn agreed to relieve the appellant of his liability to a bank under a guarantee in respect of the company's overdraft and also to procure the release within two years of securities which the appellant had deposited with the bank. Both parties performed their side of the agreement and the respondent obtained the release of the appellant's securities by giving the bank a personal guarantee. When the appellant sought to set aside the contract on the ground of misrepresentation the respondent maintained that he was not entitled to rescind because he had obtained a benefit which he could not restore, namely the release of his securities from the bank and his release from the guarantee. It was held that the appellant was entitled to rescind the agreement because he could make substantial, if not precise restitution.

Lord Wright: . . . On the basis that the fraud is established, I think that this is a case where the remedy of rescission, accompanied by *restitutio in integrum*, is proper to be given. The principles governing that form of relief are the same in Scotland as in England. The remedy is equitable. Its application is discretionary, and, where the remedy is applied, it must be moulded in accordance with the exigencies of the particular case. The general principle is authoritatively stated in a few words by Lord Blackburn in *Erlanger v New Sombrero Phosphate Co.* [(1878) 3 App. Cas. 1218] where, after referring to the common law remedy of damages, he went on to say, at 1278:

> But a court of equity could not give damages, and, unless it can rescind the contract, can give no relief. And on the other hand, it can take accounts of profits, and make allowance for deterioration. And I think the practice has always been for a court of equity to give this relief whenever, by the exercise of its powers, it can do what is practically just, though it cannot restore the parties precisely to the state they were in before the contract.

In that case, Lord Blackburn is careful not to seek to tie the hands of the court by attempting to form any rigid rules. The court must fix its eyes on the goal of doing 'what is practically just.' How that goal may be reached must depend on the circumstances of the case, but the court will be more drastic in exercising its discretionary powers in a case of fraud than in a case of innocent misrepresentation. This is clearly recognised by Lindley, MR, in *Lagunas Nitrate Co. v Lagunas Syndicate* [1899] 2 Ch 392. There is no doubt good reason for the distinction. A case of innocent misrepresentation may be regarded rather as one of misfortune than as one of moral obliquity. There is no deceit or intention to defraud. The court will be less ready to pull a transaction to pieces where the defendant is innocent, whereas in the case of fraud the court will exercise its jurisdiction to the full in order, if possible, to prevent the defendant from enjoying the benefit of his fraud at the expense of the innocent plaintiff. Restoration, however, is essential to the idea of restitution. To take the simplest case, if a plaintiff who has been defrauded seeks to have the contract annulled and his money or property restored to him, it would be inequitable if he did not also restore what he had got under the contract from the defendant. Though the defendant has been fraudulent, he must not be robbed, nor must the plaintiff be unjustly enriched, as he would be if he both got back what he had parted with and kept what he had received in return. The purpose of the relief is not punishment, but compensation. The rule is stated as requiring the restoration of both parties to the *status quo ante*, but it is generally the defendant who complains that restitution is impossible. The plaintiff who seeks to set aside the contract will generally be reasonable in the standard of restitution which he requires. However, the court can go a long way in ordering restitution if the substantial identity of the subject-matter of the contract remains. Thus, in the *Lagunas* case, though the mine had been largely worked under the contract, the court held that, at least if the case had been one of fraud, it could have ordered an account of profits or compensation to make good the change in the position. In *Adam v Newbigging*, where the transaction related to the sale of a share in a partnership, which had become insolvent since the contract, the court ordered the rescission and mutual restitution, though the misrepresentation was not fraudulent, and gave ancillary directions so as to work out the equities. These are merely instances. Certainly in a case of fraud the court will do its best to unravel the complexities of any particular case, which may in some cases involve adjustments on both sides.

In the vast majority of cases of the transfer of property, it is a purchaser who is seeking to reduce the contract, on the terms, on the one hand, of restoring what he has purchased, and, on the other hand, of being repaid the purchase price with all proper allowances and accounts. The present case is peculiar in that it is a vendor who seeks rescission. Nevertheless, the principles must be the same. The appellant is content to take back 2,925 shares in the company, though the constitution of the company has been changed by a reconstruction and enlargement of the share capital. He is willing to pay back what he received with interest. He is also willing to pay any further compensation which the court thinks is due. So far the position might seem to be clear. The difficulties which have been raised have reference to the collateral terms of the contract. Of these I need only refer to cll. 5 and 6. These clauses were primarily due to the fact that completion of the transaction was deferred for the benefit of the respondent for 2 years, but they also involved relieving the appellant of the obligations which he had assumed while a shareholder and director. When he sold all his shares and interest in the company, it was natural, that he should be relieved of these liabilities, in particular of his guarantee to the bank, and of the deposit of his shares with the bank. When, however, the *status quo ante* is restored and he again becomes holder of 2,925 shares, it might seem equitable that he should reassume the liabilities to which he was subject when he made the contract. However, during the years since the sale, during which the respondent has been conducting the affairs of the company on his own responsibility and in his own interest, the financial position of the company has been so changed that it is not clear to me that anything further is necessary to restitution than the retransfer of 2,925 shares and repayment of the purchase price with interest. The appellant's claim for inter-mediate profits or dividends was not originally brought into the action. I cannot see how the fact that for the 2 years between the contract and its completion the respondent relieved, under cl. 6, the appellant of his liability can affect the position. If the respondent had been compelled to pay moneys, or was still under the liabilities under which the appellant had been, it would be different. However, the whole financial position of the company changed. It is not suggested that an indemnity for the past liabilities would be of any use. Though there is a further point on which I feel more difficulty, I am not satisfied that the sale which the bank required of the respondent's shares held by it as security would ever have been necessary, even to secure the release of the appellant's shares, except for the manner in which the respondent conducted the affairs of the company, in particular in regard to the understatement of stock and suppression of sales in the balance sheets. However, it is unnecessary to decide finally how these matters should be dealt with, because, as my noble and learned friend Lord Thankerton stated, the parties have agreed upon a form of order which is to be made in the event of this House holding that the contract should be rescinded and that there should be restitution.

I should, however, refer shortly to *Hunt v Silk*, which was quoted by Lord Carmont [in the court below]. With all respect, I do not think that that decision affords any assistance here. That was an action at common law for money had and received. The plaintiff had paid £10 under an agreement for a lease of premises which contained certain conditions. The plaintiff entered into possession of the premises, and continued in possession after the conditions had to his knowledge been broken. It was held that he could not claim to rescind and recover the money he had paid, but that his action was in damages. It appears from the judgment of Lawrence, J, that he failed because there had been no total failure of consideration, so that the money could not be recovered in that form of action. Nor could he claim to rescind the contract, because he had held possession after he knew of the breach of condition, and had thereby waived any right to rescind. The contract could not be rescinded *in toto* and the parties replaced *in statu quo*, because there had been a part execution of the agreement. It is clear that the form of action at law in that case was different from the equitable jurisdiction which the appellant invokes in these proceedings.

Lord Thankerton delivered a concurring speech. **Lord Atkin** and **Lord Russell of Killowen** agreed with **Lord Thankerton** and **Lord Macmillan** agreed with both **Lord Thankerton** and **Lord Wright**.

QUESTIONS

1. What should have been the outcome of the case if the defendant had made the misrepresentations (a) innocently and (b) negligently?
2. On what ground did Lord Wright distinguish *Hunt v Silk* (above, 257)? What is the relationship between the requirement that a failure of consideration must be total and the requirement that a claimant must make counter-restitution (see further E McKendrick, 'Total Failure of Consideration and Counter-Restitution: Two Issues or One?' in P Birks (ed.), *Laundering and Tracing* (1995), 217)? Does the more flexible approach to counter-restitution taken in the present case suggest that we should also take a more flexible approach to voluation issues when considering whether a failure of consideration need be total to ground a restitutionary claim?

• *O'Sullivan v Management Agency and Music Ltd* [1985] QB 428, Court of Appeal

The claimant songwriter entered into a series of disadvantageous transactions with a group of companies controlled by the defendant, Mills. The plaintiff succeeded in establishing that the transactions had been procured by undue influence and in restraint of trade. The defendant sought to resist the plaintiff's attempt to rescind the transactions and recover, *inter alia*, the copyright in his songs and the master tapes of them on the ground that the agreements had been performed so that if was no longer possible to restore the parties to their pre-contractual position. The Court of Appeal rejected this argument and, adopting a flexible approach to the giving back of value, it allowed the claimant to set aside the transactions. It ordered the defendants to account for their profits under the agreements but they were given credit (including a small profit element) for their skill and labour in promoting the claimant and making a significant contribution to his success.

Dunn LJ [*having considered* Erlanger *(above, 845)* Lagunas Nitrate Co. v Lagunas Syndicate *[1899] 2 Ch 392,* Armstrong v Jackson *(above, 847),* Spence v Crawford *(above, 849),* Regal (Hastings) Ltd v Gulliver *(below, 1002),* and Phipps v Boardman *(below, 1007) and continued): The distinction between the remedies at law and in equity was explained by Dixon CJ in* Alati v Kruger *(1955) 94 CLR 216, 223*]

'If the case had to be decided according to the principles of the common law, it might have been argued that at the date when the respondent issued his writ he was not entitled to rescind the purchase, because he was not then in a position to return to the appellant in specie that which he had received under the contract, in the same slight as that in which he had received it: *Clarke v Dickson*, EB & E 148. But it is necessary here to apply the doctrine of equity, and equity has always regarded as valid the disaffirmance of a contract induced by fraud even though precise restitutio in integrum is not possible, if the situation is such that, by the exercise of its powers, including the power to take accounts of profits and to direct inquiries as to allowances proper to be made for deterioration, it can do what is practically just between the parties, and by so doing restore them substantially to the status quo: *Erlanger v New Sombrero Phosphate Co.*, 3 App. Cas. 1218, at 1278, 1279, *Brown v Smith* (1924) 34 CLR 160, 165, 169; *Spence v Crawford* [1939] 3 All ER 271, 279, 280. It is not that equity asserts a power by its decree to avoid a contract which the defrauded party himself has no right to disaffirm, and to revest property the title to which the party cannot affect.

Rescission for misrepresentation is always the act of the party himself: *Reese River Silver Mining Co. Ltd (Directors of the) v Smith* (1869) LR 4 HL 64, 73. The function of a court in which proceedings for recission are taken is to adjudicate upon the validity of a purported disaffirmance as an act avoiding the transaction ab initio, and, if it is valid, to give effect to it and make appropriate consequential orders: see *Abram Steamship Co. Ltd v Westville Shipping Co. Ltd* [1923] A.C. 773. The difference between the legal and the equitable rules on the subject simply was that equity, having means which the common law lacked to ascertain and provide for the adjustments necessary to be made between the parties in cases where a simple handing back of property or repayment of money would not put them in as good a position as before they entered into their transaction, was able to see the possibility of restitutio in integrum, and therefore to concede the right of a defrauded party to rescind, in a much wider variety of cases than those which the common law could recognise as admitting of rescission. Of course, a rescission which the common law courts would not accept as valid cannot of its own force revest the legal title to property which had passed, but if a court of equity would treat it as effectual the equitable title to such property revests upon the rescission.'

. . .

This analysis of the cases shows that the principles of restitutio in integrum is not applied with its full rigour in equity in relation to transactions entered into by persons in breach of a fiduciary relationship, and that such transactions may be set aside even though it is impossible to place the parties precisely in the position in which they were before, provided that the court can achieve practical justice between the parties by obliging the wrongdoer to give up his profits and advantages, while at the same time compensating him for any work that he has actually performed pursuant to the transaction. *Erlanger v New Sombrero Phosphate Co.*, 3 App.Cas. 1218 is a striking example of the application of this principle.

Mr Bateson [counsel for the plaintiff] submitted that the defendants had gained the following advantages: (1) profits from the agreements; and (2) the copyrights in the songs and master tapes for the life of O'Sullivan and 50 years thereafter. He pointed out that none of the agreements obliged the defendants to do any work on behalf of O'Sullivan whether by promoting or exploiting him or his works or at all, although he conceded that the defendants had in fact done such work gratuitously. He accepted that the defendants in accounting for their profits were entitled to credit in respect of their proper and reasonable expenses for the work done, including work done gratuitously, but that they were not entitled to credit for any profit element in such work. He submitted that the exception made in *Phipps v Boardman* [1967] 2 AC 46, where the trustees were morally blameless should not become the rule.

I do not think that equity requires such a narrow approach. It is true that in this case moral blame does lie upon the defendants as the judge's findings of fact show. On the other hand it is significant that until O'Sullivan met Mills he had achieved no success, and that after he effectively parted company with Mills in 1976 he achieved no success either. During the years that he was working with Mills his success was phenomenal. Although equity looks at the advantage gained by the wrongdoer rather than the loss to the victim, the cases show that in assessing the advantage gained the court will look at the whole situation in the round. And it is relevant that if Mr Bateson's approach is applied O'Sullivan would be much better off than if he had received separate legal advice and signed agreements negotiated at arm's length on reasonable terms current in the trade at the time. This point was made forcibly by Mr Miller at the conclusion of his address in reply, when he relied on the maxim 'He who seeks equity must do equity' and submitted that equity required that the position of O'Sullivan was relevant in considering the appropriate remedy.

In my judgment the judge was right to set the agreements aside and to order an account of the profits and payment of the sums found due on the taking of the account. But in taking the account the defendants are entitled to an allowance as proposed by Fox LJ, whose judgment I have read in draft, for reasonable remuneration including a profit element for all work done in promoting and exploiting O'Sullivan and his compositions, whether such work was done pursuant to a contractual obligation or gratuitously. What constitutes 'reasonable remuneration' will depend on evidence on the taking of the account, but not the evidence of Mr Levison who approached the question on a different basis.

The assignments of the copyrights were made pursuant to the agreements. It was said on behalf of the defendants that each separate assignment was made for good consideration, and consequently that the copyrights cannot be re-assigned. Mr Bateson submitted that the individual assignments were made for no consideration and that the only consideration was contained in the agreements themselves. However that may be I accept that the validity of the individual assignments depends on the validity of the agreements themselves, and if the agreements are set aside I see no reason why the copyrights should not be re-assigned to O'Sullivan.

The same consideration applies to the delivery up of the master tapes. . . .

Fox LJ: . . . In cases where a plaintiff was seeking to obtain rescission for breach of contract the requirement of restitutio in integrum seems to have been strictly enforced at common law: see for example *Hunt v Silk* (1804) 5 East 449 and *Blackburn v Smith* (1848) 2 Ex. 783. But the equitable rules were, or became, more flexible. The position is stated in the dissenting judgment of Rigby LJ in *Lagunas Nitrate Co. v Lagunas Syndicate* [1899] 2 Ch 392 (and was approved by the House of Lords in *Spence v Crawford* [1939] 3 All ER 271, 279 and 285), at 456:

'Now, no doubt it is a general rule that in order to entitle beneficiaries to rescind a voidable contract of purchase against the vendor, they must be in a position to offer back the subject-matter of the contract. But this rule has no application to the case of the subject-matter having been reduced by the mere fault of the vendors themselves; and the rule itself is, in equity, modified by another rule, that where compensation can be made for any deterioration of the property, such deterioration shall be no bar to rescission, but only a ground for compensation. I adopt the reasoning in *Erlanger's* case, 3 App.Cas. 1218, 1278 of Lord Blackburn as to allowances for depreciation and permanent improvement. The noble Lord, after pointing out that a court of law had no machinery for taking accounts or estimating compensation, says: "But a court of equity could not give damages, and, unless it can rescind a contract, can give no relief. And, on the other hand, it can take accounts of profits, and make allowances for deterioration. And I think the practice has always been for a court of equity to give this relief whenever, by the exercise of its powers, it can do what is practically just, though it cannot restore the parties precisely to the state they were in before the contract." This important passage is, in my judgment, fully supported by the allowance for deterioration and permanent improvements made by Lord Eldon and other great equity judges in similar cases.'

The result, I think, is that the doctrine is not to be applied too literally and that the court will do what is practically just in the individual case even though restitutio in integrum is impossible. *Spence v Crawford* [1939] 3 All ER 271 was itself concerned with misrepresentation. But the principles states by Rigby LJ are, I think, equally applicable in cases of abuse of fiduciary relationship and indeed Rigby LJ regarded *Lagunas* [1899] 2 Ch 392 as such a case: see 442.

It is said on behalf of the plaintiffs that, if the principle of equity is that the fiduciary must account for profits obtained through the abuse of the fiduciary relationship there is no scope for the operation of anything resembling restitutio in integrum. The profits must simply be given up. I think that goes too far and that the law has for long had regard to the justice of the matter. If, for example, a person is by undue influence persuaded to make a gift of a house to another and that other spent money on improving the house, I apprehend that credit could be given for the improvements. That, I think, is recognised by Lord Blackburn in *Erlanger v New Sombrero Phosphate Co.*, 3 App. Cas. 1278 and by Rigby LJ in *Lagunas* in the reference to allowance for permanent improvements in the passage which I have cited.

Accordingly, it seems to me that the principle that the court will do what is practically just as between the parties is applicable to a case of undue influence even though the parties cannot be restored to their original position. That is, in my view, applicable to the present case. The question is not whether the parties can be restored to their original position; it is what does the justice of the case require? That approach is quite wide enough, if it be necessary in the individual case, to accommodate the protection of third parties. The rights of a bona fide purchaser for value without notice would not in any event be affected.

The next question is, it seems to me, the recompensing of the defendants. The rules of equity against the retention of benefits by fiduciaries have been applied with severity. In *Phipps v Boardman* [1967] 2 AC 46, where the fiduciaries though in breach of the equitable rules, acted with complete honesty throughout, only succeeded in obtaining an allowance 'on a liberal scale' for their work and skill. They were allowed that in the High Court by Wilberforce J [1964] 1 WLR 993, 1018 on the ground that it would be inequitable for the beneficiaries to take the profit without paying for the skill and labour which produced it. The point does not seem to have been disputed thereafter. In the Court of Appeal [1965] Ch 992 Pearson LJ said, at 1030;

> 'It is to my mind a regrettable feature of this case that the plaintiff seems likely to recover an unreasonably large amount from the defendants'—the fiduciaries—'even when under the judgment [1964] 1 W.L.R. 993, 1018 the defendants have been credited with an allowance on a liberal scale for their work and skill. The rule of equity is rigid. The agent who has made a profit from his agency, without having obtained informed consent from his principal, has to account for the whole of the profit.'

Russell LJ, at 1032, said that, without intending to throw doubt on the defendants' right to the liberal allowance, he preferred to express no view on the law, the matter not having been argued. Lord Denning MR said, at 1020:

> 'Ought Boardman and Tom Phipps to be allowed remuneration for their work and skill in these negotiations? The plaintiff is ready to concede it, but in case the other beneficiaries are interested in the account, I think we should determine it on principle. This species of action is an action for restitution such as Lord Wright described in the *Fibrosa* case [1943] A.C. 32, 61. The gist of it is that the defendant has unjustly enriched himself, and it is against conscience that he should be allowed to keep the money. The claim for repayment cannot, however, be allowed to extend further than the justice of the case demands. If the defendant has done valuable work in making the profit, then the court in its discretion may allow him a recompense. It depends on the circumstances. If the agent has been guilty of any dishonesty or bad faith, or surreptitious dealing, he might not be allowed any remuneration or reward.'

In the House of Lords [1967] 2 AC 46, Lord Cohen, at 104, and Lord Hodson, at 112, agreed with Wilberforce J that the allowance should be on a 'liberal scale.'

These latter observations (and those of Lord Denning MR and the judgment of Wilberforce J at first instance) accept the existence of a power in the court to make an allowance to the fiduciary. And I think it is clearly necessary that such a power should exist. Substantial injustice may result without it. A hard and fast rule that the beneficiary can demand the whole profit without an allowance for the work without which it could not have been created is unduly severe. Nor do I think that the principle is only applicable in cases where the personal conduct of the fiduciary cannot be criticised. I think that the justice of the individual case must be considered on the facts of that case. Accordingly, where there has been dishonesty or surreptitious dealing or other improper conduct then, as indicated by

Lord Denning MR, it might be appropriate to refuse relief; but that will depend upon the circumstances.

What the first five defendants in substance are seeking is that the parties should be put in a position in which they would have been if the agreements had been on the basis which Mr Levison, an expert witness, thought might reasonably have been negotiated if Mr O'Sullivan had received independent advice from experienced persons. I do not feel able to accept that. In the first place, Mr Levison's evidence was really only directed to the question of what might reasonably have been negotiated. The question what recompense in the circumstances of this case it would be reasonable to allow was not investigated. If, for example, there was any failure by the M.A.M. companies or Mr Mills to promote Mr O'Sullivan's interests as vigorously or competently as they might have been expected to do, with the result that Mr O'Sullivan suffered loss that might affect the position. Secondly, an order which, in effect, would involve substantial division of the profits between the beneficiary on the one hand and the fiduciary (and persons for whom he procured benefits) on the other, goes far beyond anything hitherto permitted.

Once it is accepted that the court can make an appropriate allowance to a fiduciary for his skill and labour I do not see why, in principle, it should not be able to give him some part of the profit of the venture if it was thought that justice as between the parties demanded that. To give the fiduciary any allowance for his skill and labour involves some reduction of the profits otherwise payable to the beneficiary. And the business reality may be that the profits could never have been earned at all, as between fully independent persons, except on a profit sharing basis. But be that as it may, it would be one thing to permit a substantial sharing of profits in a case such as *Phipps v Boardman* [1967] 2 AC 46 where the conduct of the fiduciaries could not be criticised and quite another to permit it in a case such as the present where, though fraud was not alleged, there was an abuse of personal trust and confidence. I am not satisfied that it would be proper to exclude Mr Mills and the M.A.M. companies from all reward for their efforts. I find it impossible to believe that they did not make a significant contribution to Mr O'Sullivan's success. It would be unjust to deny them a recompense for that. I would, therefore, be prepared as was done in *Phipps v Boardman* to authorise the payment (over and above out of pocket expenses) of an allowance for the skill and labour of the first five defendants in promoting the compositions and performances and managing the business affairs of Mr O'Sullivan, and that an inquiry (the terms of which would need to be considered with counsel) should be ordered for that purpose. Such an allowance could include a profit element in the way that solicitors' costs do.

In my view this would achieve substantial justice between the parties because it would take account of the contribution made by the defendants to Mr O'Sullivan's success. It would not take full account of it in that the allowance would not be at all as much as the defendants might have obtained if the contracts had been properly negotiated between fully advised parties. But the defendants must suffer that because of the circumstances in which the contracts were procured. On the basis that the first five defendants are remunerated as I have mentioned I see no reason in equity why the agreements and the assignments of copyright should not be set aside, the master recordings transferred to Mr O'Sullivan and an account of profits ordered. . . .

Waller LJ: . . . The important words of Lord Blackburn are that equity should give relief 'whenever, by the exercise of its powers, it can do what is practically just.' In my judgment this court is not concerned with punishing the defendants for their behaviour. We are concerned to see that the plaintiff gets the profit to which he is entitled and at the same time see that the defendants receive fair remuneration, but no more, for all the work that they have done in pursuance of this joint project. Although the trustee authorities indicate that trustees should retain no profit secretly made and only reasonable remuneration for their work as trustees, and although the present case is a fiduciary situation it is a case where the defendants, as the plaintiff knew, were doing a considerable amount of work. They are entitled to reasonable remuneration for that work. To apply the words of Lord Wright in *Regal (Hastings) Ltd v Gulliver (Note)* [1967] 2 AC 134, 154, the defendants here did make some profit with the knowledge and assent of the plaintiff. This the defendants are entitled to keep and would be reasonable remuneration. On the other hand it is clear that the profit which the defendants kept was excessive. The excess profit was retained without the knowledge of the plaintiff. The defendants must account for this profit. It will be for the official referee to decide what would be reasonable remuneration. It must include all expenses and a fair profit.

In the present case the publishing agreement for overseas is different from the other contracts. In that case there were deductions made and part of the overseas receipts was transferred before any account was made to the plaintiff. When this account is taken it will require very careful inquiry to see that only legitimate costs are deducted.

It was part of the defendants' argument that the decision of this court should be confined to compensation and should not include the transfer of all copyrights back to the plaintiff. Since I would adopt Lord Blackburn's approach of doing what is practically just, I have come to the conclusion that restitution requires that the court order should include the transfer of all the plaintiff's copyrights back to him and, disagreeing on this point with Dunn and Fox LJJ, that only the master recording in which the copyright would be in the maker should remain with the maker. Since all, or nearly all, the master recordings have been transferred to third parties for good consideration this question is probably academic and I do not further discuss it. . . .

NOTES AND QUESTIONS

1. The expert witness, Mr Levison, to whom Fox LJ referred, gave evidence for the defendants of the price that would reasonably have been negotiated if Mr O'Sullivan had received independent advice. Their argument was that this should be the measure of restitution made, because this was the value of the benefit they had obtained but for the undue influence they had over O'Sullivan and his lack of independent advice. Fox LJ's (contradictory) reasons for rejecting this award were that it was an award of compensation and also that courts had not previously apportioned a defendant's profits in such a way. However, an award disgorging all the profits made by the defendants (less an allowance) arguably goes beyond the usual measure of the enrichment obtained at the expense of the claimant. Compare the award of restitution sought by Mr Ward in the next case, *Guinness plc v Saunders* (below, 857).

2. Does the decision of the Court of Appeal effectively empty the counter-restitution impossible bar of all content?

3. Could the defendants have successfully counterclaimed for restitution for the value of the work which they had done on the basis of total failure of consideration once the claimant had set aside the transaction? Is this the basis of the counter-restitution requirement?

4. In *Vadasz v Pioneer Concrete (SA) Pty. Ltd* (1995) 184 CLR 102 the defendant was induced to enter into a guarantee by a misrepresentation that the guarantee was limited to the future indebtedness of the company, when in fact it extended to past indebtedness as well. The High Court of Australia held that the guarantee should be rescinded in so far as it related to the past indebtedness of the company. 'Practical justice' required that the defendant should be held liable for the debts incurred after he entered into the guarantee on the ground that 'to enforce the guarantee to the extent of future indebtedness is to do no more than hold the [appellant] to what he was prepared to undertake independently of any misrepresentation' The courts in England have refused to embrace the idea that a transaction can be partially set aside or set aside on terms: rescission is an all-or-nothing process (see *T.S.B. Bank plc v Camfield* [1995] 1 WLR 430). See further L Proksch, 'Rescission on Terms' [1996] *RLR* 71 and D O'Sullivan, 'Partial Rescission for Misrepresentation in Australia' (1997) 113 *LQR* 16.

- *Guinness plc v Saunders* [1990] 2 AC 663, House of Lords

A committee of the board of directors of the claimant company agreed to pay one of their number, Mr Ward, the sum of £5.2 million for services rendered to the claimant company during a take-over battle. The claimant company later sought repayment of the sum so paid on the ground that the agreement had been made in breach of the company's articles of association and that Mr Ward had been in breach of his fiduciary duty to the company. Its claim succeeded. Mr Ward then sought to recover a reasonable sum for the services which he had rendered to the company but his claim was rejected by the House of Lords.

Lord Templeman: . . . Since, for the purposes of this application, Guinness concede that Mr Ward performed valuable services for Guinness in connection with the bid, counsel on behalf of Mr Ward submits that Mr Ward, if not entitled to remuneration pursuant to the articles, is, nevertheless, entitled to be awarded by the court a sum by way of quantum meruit or equitable allowance for his services. Counsel submits that the sum awarded by the court might amount to £5.2m. or a substantial proportion of that sum; therefore Mr Ward should be allowed to retain the sum of £5.2m. which he has received until, at the trial of the action, the court determines whether he acted with propriety and, if so, how much of the sum of £5.2m. he should be permitted to retain; Mr Ward is anxious for an opportunity to prove at a trial that he acted with propriety throughout the bid. It is common ground that, for the purposes of this appeal, it must be assumed that Mr Ward and the other members of the committee acted in good faith and that the sum of £5.2m. was a proper reward for the services rendered by Mr Ward to Guinness.

My Lords, the short answer to a quantum meruit claim based on an implied contract by Guinness to pay reasonable remuneration for services rendered is that there can be no contract by Guinness to pay special remuneration for the services of a director unless that contract is entered into by the board pursuant to article 91. The short answer to the claim for an equitable allowance is the equitable principle which forbids a trustee to make a profit out of his trust unless the trust instrument, in this case the articles of association of Guinness, so provides. The law cannot and equity will not amend the articles of Guinness. The court is not entitled to usurp the functions conferred on the board by the articles.

The 28th edition (1982) of *Snell's Principles of Equity*, first published in 1868, contains the distilled wisdom of the author and subsequent editors, including Sir Robert Megarry, on the law applicable to trusts and trustees. It is said, at 244, that:

'With certain exceptions, neither directly nor indirectly may a trustee make a profit from his trust. . . . The rule depends not on fraud or mala fides, but on the mere fact of a profit made.'

Equity forbids a trustee to make a profit out of his trust. The articles of association of Guinness relax the strict rule of equity to the extent of enabling a director to make a profit provided that the board of directors contracts on behalf of Guinness for the payment of special remuneration or decides to award special remuneration. Mr Ward did not obtain a contract or a grant from the board of directors. Equity has no power to relax its own strict rule further than and inconsistently with the express relaxation contained in the articles of association. A shareholder is entitled to compliance with the articles. A director accepts office subject to and with the benefit of the provisions of the articles relating to directors. No one is obliged to accept appointment as a director. No director can be obliged to serve on a committee. A director of Guinness who contemplates or accepts service on a committee or has performed outstanding services for the company as a member of a committee may apply to the board of directors for a contract or an award of special remuneration. A director who does not read the articles or a director who misconstrues the articles is nevertheless bound by the articles. Article 91 provides clearly enough for the authority of the board of directors to be obtained for the payment of special remuneration and the submissions made on behalf of Mr Ward, based on articles 2, 100(D) and 110, are more ingenious than plausible and more legalistic than convincing. At the board meeting held on 19 January 1986, Mr Ward was present but he did not seek then or thereafter to obtain the necessary authority of the board of directors for payment of special remuneration. In these circumstances there are no grounds for equity to relax its rules further than the articles of association provide. Similarly, the law will not imply a contract between Guinness and Mr Ward for remuneration on a quantum meruit basis awarded by the court when the articles of association of Guinness stipulate that special remuneration for a director can only be awarded by the board.

It was submitted on behalf of Mr Ward that Guinness, by the committee consisting of Mr Saunders, Mr Ward and Mr Roux, entered into a voidable contract to pay remuneration to Mr Ward and that since Mr Ward performed the services he agreed to perform under this voidable contract there could be no restitutio integrum and the contract cannot be avoided. This submission would enable a director to claim and retain remuneration under a contract which a committee purported to conclude with him, notwithstanding that the committee had no power to enter into the contract. The fact is that Guinness never did contract to pay anything to Mr Ward. The contract on which Mr Ward relies is not voidable but non-existent. In support of a quantum meruit claim, counsel for Mr Ward relied on the decision of Buckley J in *In re Duomatic Ltd* [1969] 2 Ch 365. In that case a company sought and failed to recover remuneration received by a director when the shareholders or a voting majority of the shareholders had sanctioned or ratified the payment. In the present case there has been no such sanction or ratification either by the board of directors or by the shareholders. Mr Ward also relied on the decision in *Craven-Ellis v Canons Ltd* [1936] 2 KB 403. In that case the plaintiff was appointed managing director of a company by an agreement under the company's seal which also provided for his remuneration. By the articles of association each director was required to obtain qualification shares within two months of his appointment. Neither the plaintiff nor the other directors obtained their qualification shares within two months or at all and the agreement with the managing director was entered into after they had ceased to be directors. The plaintiff having done work for the company pursuant to the terms of the agreement was held to be entitled to the remuneration provided for in the agreement on the basis of a quantum meruit. In *Craven-Ellis* the plaintiff was not a director, there was no conflict between his claim to remuneration and the equitable doctrine which debars a director from profiting from his fiduciary duty, and there was no obstacle to the implication of a contract between the company and the plaintiff entitling the plaintiff to claim reasonable remuneration as of right by an action in law. Moreover, as in *In re Duomatic Ltd*, the agreement was sanctioned by all the directors, two of whom were beneficially entitled to the share capital of the company. In the present case Mr Ward was a director, there was a conflict between his interest and his duties, there could be no contract by Guinness for the payment of remuneration pursuant to article 91 unless the board made the contract on behalf of Guinness and there was no question of approval by directors or shareholders.

In support of a claim for an equitable allowance, reference was made to the decision of Wilberforce J in *Phipps v Boardman* [1964] 1 WLR 993. His decision was upheld by the Court of Appeal [1965] Ch 992 and ultimately by this House under the name of *Boardman v Phipps* [1967] 2 AC 46. In that case a trust estate included a minority holding in a private company which fell on lean times. The trustees declined to attempt to acquire a controlling interest in the company in order to improve its performance. The solicitor to the trust and one of the beneficiaries, with the knowledge and approval of the trustees, purchased the controlling interest from outside shareholders for themselves with the help of information about the shareholders acquired by the solicitor in the course of acting for the trust. The company's position was improved and the shares bought by the solicitor and the purchasing beneficiary were ultimately sold at a profit. A complaining beneficiary was held to be entitled to a share of the profits on the resale on the grounds that the solicitor and the purchasing beneficiary were assisted in the original purchase by the information derived from the trust. The purchase of a controlling interest might have turned out badly and in that case the solicitor and the purchasing beneficiary would have made irrecoverable personal losses. In these circumstances it is not surprising that Wilberforce J decided that in calculating the undeserved profit which accrued to the trust estate there should be deducted a generous allowance for the work and trouble of the solicitor and purchasing beneficiary in acquiring the controlling shares and restoring the company to prosperity. *Phipps v Boardman* decides that in exceptional circumstances a court of equity may award remuneration to the trustee. Therefore, it is argued, a court of equity may award remuneration to a director. As at present advised, I am unable to envisage circumstances in which a court of equity would exercise a power to award remuneration to a director when the relevant articles of association confided that power to the board of directors. Certainly, the circumstances do not exist in the present case. . . .

Lord Goff of Chieveley: . . . As a matter of general law, to the extent that there was failure by Mr Ward to comply with his duty of disclosure under the relevant article of Guinness (article 100(A), the contract (if any) between him and Guinness was no doubt voidable under the ordinary principles of law. . . . But it has long been the law that, as a condition of rescission of a voidable contract, the parties must be put in statu quo; for this purpose a court of equity can do what is practically just, even though it cannot restore the parties precisely to the state they were in before the contract. The most familiar statement of the law is perhaps that of Lord Blackburn in *Erlanger v New Sombrero Phosphate Co.* (1878) 3 App.Cas. 1218, when he said, at 1278:

> 'It is, I think, clear on principles of general justice, that as a condition to a rescission there must be a restitutio in integrum. The parties must be put in statu quo. . . . It is a doctrine which has often been acted upon both at law and in equity.'

However on that basis Guinness could not simply claim to be entitled to the £5.2m. received by Mr Ward. The contract had to be rescinded, and as a condition of the rescission Mr Ward had to be placed in statu quo. No doubt this could be done by a court of equity making a just allowance for the services he had rendered; but no such allowance has been considered, let alone made, in the present case.

. . .

Let it be accepted that the contract under which Mr Ward claims to have rendered valuable services to Guinness was . . . void for want of authority. I understand it to be suggested that articles 90 and 91 provide (article 100 apart) not only a code of the circumstances in which a director of Guinness may receive recompense for services to the company, but an exclusive code. This is said to derive from the equitable doctrine whereby directors, though not trustees, are held to act in a fiduciary capacity, and as such are not entitled to receive remuneration for services rendered to the company except as provided under the articles of association, which are treated as equivalent to a trust deed constituting a trust. It was suggested that, if Mr Ward wishes to receive remuneration for the services he has rendered, his proper course is now to approach the board of directors and invite them to award him remuneration by the exercise of the power vested in them by article 91.

The leading authorities on the doctrine have been rehearsed in the opinion of my noble and learned friend, Lord Templeman. These indeed demonstrate that the directors of a company, like other fiduciaries, must not put themselves in a position where there is a conflict between their personal interests and their duties as fiduciaries, and are for that reason precluded from contracting with the company for their services except in circumstances authorised by the articles of association. Similarly, just as trustees are not entitled, in the absence of an appropriate provision in the trust deed, to remuneration for their services as trustees, so directors are not entitled to remuneration for their services as directors except as provided by the articles of association.

Plainly, it would be inconsistent with this long-established principle to award remuneration in such circumstances as of right on the basis of a quantum meruit claim. But the principle does not altogether exclude the possibility that an equitable allowance might be made in respect of services rendered. That such an allowance may be made to a trustee for work performed by him for the benefit of the trust, even though he was not in the circumstances entitled to remuneration under the terms of the trust deed, is now well established. In *Phipps v Boardman* [1964] 1 WLR 993, the solicitor to a trust and one of the beneficiaries were held accountable to another beneficiary for a proportion of the profits made by them from the sale of shares bought by them with the aid of information gained by the solicitor when acting for the trust. Wilberforce J directed that, when accounting for such profits, not merely should a deduction be made for expenditure which was necessary to enable the profit to be realised, but also a liberal allowance or credit should be made for their work and skill. His reasoning was, at 1018:

'Moreover, account must naturally be taken of the expenditure which was necessary to enable the profit to be realised. But, in addition to expenditure, should not the defendants be given an allowance or credit for their work and skill? This is a subject on which authority is scanty; but Cohen J, in *In re Macadam* [1946] Ch 73, 82, gave his support to an allowance of this kind to trustees for their services in acting as directors of a company. It seems to me that this transaction, i.e., the acquisition of a controlling interest in the company, was one of a special character calling for the exercise of a particular kind of professional skill. If Boardman had not assumed the role of seeing it through, the beneficiaries would have had to employ (and would, had they been well advised, have employed) an expert to do it for them. If the trustees had come to the court asking for liberty to employ such a person, they would in all probability have been authorised to do so, and to remunerate the person in question. It seems to me that it would be inequitable now for the beneficiaries to step in and take the profit without paying for the skill and labour which has produced it.'

Wilberforce J's decision, including his decision to make such an allowance, was later to be affirmed by the House of Lords: *sub nom. Boardman v Phipps* [1967] 2 AC 46.

It will be observed that the decision to make the allowance was founded upon the simple proposition that 'it would be inequitable now for the beneficiaries to step in and take the profit without paying for the skill and labour which has produced it.' Ex hypothesi, such an allowance was not in the circumstances authorised by the terms of the trust deed; furthermore it was held that there had not been full and proper disclosure by the two defendants to the successful plaintiff beneficiary. The inequity was found in the simple proposition that the beneficiaries were taking the profit although, if Mr Boardman (the solicitor) had not done the work, they would have had to employ an expert to do the work for them in order to earn that profit.

The decision has to be reconciled with the fundamental principle that a trustee is not entitled to remuneration for services rendered by him to the trust except as expressly provided in the trust deed. Strictly speaking, it is irreconcilable with the rule as so stated. It seems to me therefore that it can only be reconciled with it to the extent that the exercise of the equitable jurisdiction does not conflict with the policy underlying the rule. And, as I see it, such a conflict will only be avoided if the exercise of the jurisdiction is restricted to those cases where it cannot have the effect of encouraging trustees in any way to put themselves in a position where their interests conflict with their duties as trustees.

Not only was the equity underlying Mr Boardman's claim in *Phipps v Boardman* clear and, indeed, overwhelming; but the exercise of the jurisdiction to award an allowance in the unusual circumstances of that case could not provide any encouragement to trustees to put themselves in a position where their duties as trustees conflicted with their interests. The present case is, however, very different. Whether any such allowance might ever be granted by a court of equity in the case of a director of a company, as opposed to a trustee, is a point which has yet to be decided; and I must reserve the question whether the jurisdiction could be exercised in such a case, which may be said to involve interference by the court in the administration of a company's affairs when the company is not being wound up. In any event, however, like my noble and learned friend, Lord Templeman, I cannot see any possibility of such jurisdiction being exercised in the present case. I proceed, of course, on the basis that Mr Ward acted throughout in complete good faith. But the simple fact remains that, by agreeing to provide his services in return for a substantial fee the size of which was dependent upon the amount of a successful bid by Guinness, Mr Ward was most plainly putting himself in a position in which his interests were in stark conflict with his duty as a director. Furthermore, for such services as he rendered, it is still open to the board of Guinness (if it thinks fit, having had a full opportunity to investigate the circumstances of the case) to award Mr Ward appropriate remuneration. In all the circumstances of the case, I cannot think that this is a case in which a court of equity (assuming that it has jurisdiction to do so in the case of a director of a company) would order the repayment of the £5.2m. by Mr Ward to Guinness subject to a condition that an equitable allowance be made to Mr Ward for his services. . . .

Lord Keith and **Lord Brandon** agreed with the speech of **Lord Templeman**. **Lord Griffiths** agreed with the speeches of **Lord Templeman** and **Lord Goff**.

NOTES AND QUESTIONS

1. The case is discussed in more detail by P Birks in 'Restitution Without Counter-Restitution' [1990] *LMCLQ* 330.

2. Was Lord Templeman correct to conclude that, because the claimant could not have entered into a contract to pay for the services rendered, the law could not imply a contract to pay for these same services? Was the basis for Mr Ward's claim an 'implied contract'?

3. Why did Mr Ward's claim for remuneration fail?

4. On what basis did Lord Templeman distinguish *Craven-Ellis v Canons Ltd* (above, 356)? Is the distinction which he draws a convincing one?

5. How can this case be reconciled with *Boardman v Phipps* (below, 1007)? Can the decision to award the defendants a profit element in *O'Sullivan v Management Agency and Music Ltd* (above, 851) be reconciled with the approach of the House of Lords in the present case?

- *Cheese v Thomas* [1994] 1 WLR 129, Court of Appeal

The claimant contributed £43,000 to the purchase price of a house. The house was bought by the defendant, who was the claimant's great nephew. The basis upon which the parties entered into the transaction was that the defendant would buy the house in his own name and the claimant would be entitled to live in the property rent-free for the rest of his life. The house was purchased by the defendant in 1990 for £83,000, and he took out a mortgage of £40,000 to finance his contribution to the purchase price. The defendant failed to pay his mortgage instalments. The claimant sought to withdraw from the transaction on the ground of undue influence, and to recover his £43,000. The house was eventually sold in 1993 for £55,400. It was held that the presumption of undue influence had been raised and that the transaction was manifestly disadvantageous to the claimant, so that he was entitled to have the contract set aside on the ground of undue influence. But he was not entitled to recover the full £43,000 which he had paid to the claimant: he was entitled to recover only a proportionate share of the net proceeds of the sale of the house. The trial judge had therefore been correct in ordering that the proceeds of the sale be divided between the parties in the proportions 43:40.

Sir Donald Nicholls V-C: . . .

MANIFEST DISADVANTAGE

The necessity for a plaintiff to prove that the transaction was manifestly disadvantageous to him before he can succeed in a claim to set it aside for undue influence finds recent expression in *National Westminster Bank plc v Morgan* [1985] AC 686 and *Bank of Credit and Commerce International SA v Aboody* [1990] 1 QB 923. Here, Mr Cheese paid £43,000, and in return he had the right to live rent-free for the rest of his life in a house approved by him, and which he himself could not afford to buy, in an area where he wished to live. But there were drawbacks in the transaction so far as he was concerned.

The principal drawbacks were threefold. First, he paid over all his capital. The £43,000 represented the major part of the proceeds of his flat at Peacehaven. He had no other money of his own. Second, if in future he needed or wished to live elsewhere, there was no way he could compel Mr Thomas to sell the house or return his money or even some of it. At the time Mr Cheese was 85 years old. He might become less robust and need to live in sheltered accommodation. He had moved house in 1985 and in 1986, and in 1990 he had in mind that he might wish to move again and not be confined to Jonson Close for the rest of his days. Third, and importantly, Mr Cheese would be in jeopardy if Mr Thomas failed to keep up the mortgage payments to the building society. When the house was acquired both Mr Thomas and his company were finacially embarrassed. If Mr Thomas defaulted, Mr Cheese had no money of his own with which to keep up the mortgage payments. If Mr Cheese were evicted by the building society, he would have a claim against Mr Thomas for damages for breach of contract. But that, for what it might be worth, would be poor consolation for all the upset and worry and possible loss involved. Indeed, these proceedings were prompted by Mr Cheese's concern when he opened a letter from the building society in October 1990 and learned that Mr Thomas was four months in arrears with the mortgage payments. He became fearful and anxious and disillusioned.

I agree with the judge that the transaction is properly to be described as manifestly, that is, clearly and obviously, disadvantageous to Mr Cheese. He used all his money, and it was not an insignificant amount, in buying a right which was seriously insecure and which tied him to this particular house.

I add two points. First, their Lordships in the House of Lords are currently considering their judgments on two appeals where one of the issues is whether manifest disadvantage is an essential ingredient of an undue influence claim. Having regard to the view I have reached, it is not necessary to postpone giving judgment on this appeal until the outcome in those two cases is known.[1] Mr Cheese has established manifest disadvantage whether or not, as remains to be seen, this is a necessary prerequisite to success on this claim. Second, a feature of importance is that before the trial judge Mr Thomas conceded that the presumption of undue influence applied on the facts of this case. Mr Thomas did not seek to rebut the application of the presumption, for instance, by showing that Mr Cheese received independent advice. So the only issue the judge was called upon to decide on this part of the claim was whether or not the transaction was clearly disadvantageous to Mr Cheese. I mention this in fairness to Mr Thomas. Otherwise one might think Mr Thomas had behaved improperly, and sought to trick or take advantage of his aged uncle. No conduct of this sort occurred. This point is also relevant on the next issue.

SETTING ASIDE THE TRANSACTION

If, then, the transaction is to be set aside, the next step is the restoration of the parties to their original positions. Achieving this would mean sale of the house and repayment of what each had paid over.

---

1 *Reporter's note.* See now *Barclays Bank v O'Brien* [1993] 3 WLR 786 and *C.I.B.C. Mortgages plc v Pitt* [1993] 3 WLR 802. Discussed in *Royal Bank of Scotland v Etridge (No 2)* [2001] UK HL 44; [2002] 2 AC 773, above, 457.

Mr Cheese should get back his £43,000, and Mr Thomas should get back and repay to the building society the money he borrowed for the purchase.

The house has now been sold. Unhappily, as already mentioned, although £83,000 was spent in buying the house, only £55,400 came from the sale. By the time of the sale the amount outstanding on the mortgage was about £37,700. On the sale the building society had to be repaid first. It had a mortgage over the house. The effect of paying back the building society was, in substance, to restore Mr Thomas to his original position, although he had paid some mortgage instalments. The net balance remaining from the sale proceeds was only £17,667. Clearly, this sum has to be paid to Mr Cheese, but that will still leave him more than £25,000 out of pocket. The shortfall represents, in round figures, the amount by which the house declined in value after its purchase in June 1990.

The question therefore arises: on whom should this loss fall? Mr Cheese contends he is entitled to look to Mr Thomas personally to make good the whole of the shortfall. He paid £43,000 to Mr Thomas, and on the transaction being set aside he can look to Mr Thomas for repayment of a like sum. The judge did not accept this. He held that the loss brought about by the fall in the market value of the house should be shared between the two of them in the same proportions (43:40) as they had contributed to the price. He said that the parties went into a joint venture, investing approximately similar sums in it: they should bear the loss equally. In short, this would mean that Mr Cheese could look to Mr Thomas for a further £11,000 Mr Cheese would then recover altogether about £28,700, leaving him £14,300 out of pocket compared with his original contribution of £43,000. For his part Mr Thomas would be out of pocket by a similar but proportionately smaller amount. He would be out of pocket to the extent of £13,300, made up of the £11,000 he would have to pay Mr Cheese and £2,300 he had paid to the building society, before the sale, in reduction of the principal owing on the mortgage. From that decision Mr Cheese has appealed.

RESTORING THE PARTIES TO THEIR ORIGINAL POSITIONS

I can summarise the thrust of Mr Hamer's argument as follows. When the court sets aside the transaction between Mr Cheese and Mr Thomas, the inflexible rule of equity which comes into play is that Mr Cheese is entitled to have restored to him the benefits he passed to Mr Thomas under the impugned transaction. It matters not if, for reasons unconnected with Mr Cheese, the property being returned to the defendant has declined in value: that is irrelevant.

I approach the matter in this way. Restitution has to be made, not damages paid. Damages look at the plaintiff's loss, whereas restitution is concerned with the recovery back from the defendant of what he received under the transaction. If the transaction is set aside, the plaintiff also must return what he received. Each party must hand back what he obtained under the contract. There has to be a giving back and a taking back on both sides, as Bowen LJ observed in *Newbigging v Adam* (1886) 34 ChD 582, 595. If, for this purpose, the transaction in this case is analysed simply as a payment of £43,000 by Mr Cheese to Mr Thomas in return for the right to live in Mr Thomas's house, there is a strong case for ordering repayment of £43,000, the benefit received by Mr Thomas, regardless of the subsequent fall in the value of the house. In the ordinary way, if a plaintiff is able to return to the defendant the property received from him under the impugned transaction, it matters not that the property has meanwhile fallen in value. This is not surprising. A defendant cannot be heard to protest that such an outcome is unfair when he is receiving back the very thing he persuaded the plaintiff, by undue influence or misrepresentation, to buy from him.

In my view the present case stands differently. Mr Cheese paid Mr Thomas £43,000, not utright, but as part of the purchase price of a house in which both would have rights: Mr Cheese was to have sole use of the house for his life, and then the house would be Mr Thomas's. Mr Thomas was not free to dispose of the house, or use it, until then. In fact the money was handed over by Mr Cheese in the form of a bankers' draft, made payable to the solicitors acting for Mr Thomas in the purchase of 4, Jonson Close. For his part Mr Thomas also contributed to the purchase of the house. He contributed £40,000, by obtaining a building society loan of this amount. In other words, the transaction was that each would contribute a sum of money to buying a house in which each was to have an interest. This is the transaction which has to be reversed. Doing so requires, first, that the house should be sold and, second, that each party should receive back his contribution to the price. There is no difficulty over the first requirement. Mr Cheese sought an order for sale, the judge so directed, and the sale has taken place. The second requirement is more difficult. Indeed, it cannot be achieved, because under the transaction the money each contributed was spent in buying a house which then lost one third of its value.

This difficulty, rightly in my view, has not been allowed to stand in the way of setting aside the transaction. It is well established that a court of equity grants this type of relief even when it cannot restore the parties precisely to the state they were in before the contract. The court will grant relief whenever, by directing accounts and making allowances, it can do what is practically just: see *Erlanger v New Sombrero Phosphate Co.* (1878) 3 App.Cas. 1218, 1278–9, *per* Lord Blackburn. Here justice requires that each party should be returned as near to his original position as is now possible. Each should get back a proportionate share of the net proceeds of the house, before deducting the amount paid to the building society. Thus the £55,400 should be divided between Mr Cheese and Mr Thomas in the proportions of 43:40. Mr Cheese should receive about £28,700 and Mr Thomas £26,700. To achieve this result Mr Thomas should pay £11,033 on top of the net proceeds, of £17,667, remaining after discharging the mortgage. This was the view of the judge, and I see no occasion to disturb his conclusion. On the contrary, I agree with him. It is interesting to note that this result accords with the primary relief sought by Mr Cheese in the action. His primary claim was that the house belonged to them both in the proportions of 43:40. Had the claim succeeded, Mr Cheese would have borne a proportionate share of the loss on the sale of the house.

RESTITUTION FOR BOTH PARTIES

We were much pressed with an argument that there is no decided case in which a court has ever directed a sharing of the loss in this way. This is a principle unknown to English law. The court has no discretion in this regard. I have two observations on this argument.

First, when considering what was the original position of the parties it is important to identify, and properly characterise, the transaction being set aside. In a simple case of a purchase of property there is no difficulty. Before the transaction the plaintiff had a sum of money and the defendant owned the property. By the transaction the money passed to the defendant, and the property was transferred to the plaintiff. That is the transaction which has to be reversed. Likewise there is no difficulty with a simple case of a gift. The present case, as already noted, is not so straightforward. Here the transaction involved *both* parties making a financial contribution to the acquisition of a new asset from which both were intended to benefit. This was so even though Mr Cheese's only interest in the house was as a contractual licensee, and even though Mr Thomas regarded the house as an investment. It is axiomatic that, when reversing this transaction, the court is concerned to achieve practical justice for both parties, not the plaintiff alone. The plaintiff is seeking the assistance of a court of equity, and he who seeks equity must do equity. Under the transaction Mr Thomas parted with money, albeit borrowed, as well as Mr Cheese.

This situation is to be contrasted with the facts in *Newbigging v Adam*, 34 ChD 582; (1888) 13 App.Cas. 308. There the plaintiff was induced to enter into a partnership with the defendant by misrepresentations about the state of the business. The business foundered. On having the transaction set aside, the court held the plaintiff was entitled to the return of the capital introduced by him and to an indemnity against the liabilities he had assumed as a partner. In that case the transaction was akin to a sale of property, there a share in a partnership. The defendant had to return the capital sum introduced and reassume the burden of partnership debts which under the contract the plaintiff had taken upon himself.

My second observation is this. The basic objective of the court is to restore the parties to their original positions, as nearly as may be, consequent upon cancelling a transaction which the law will not permit to stand. That is the basic objective. Achieving a practically just outcome in that regard requires the court to look at all the circumstances, while keeping the basic objective firmly in mind. In carrying out this exercise the court is, of necessity, exercising a measure of discretion in the sense that it is determining what are the requirements of practical justice in the particular case. It is important not to lose sight of the very foundation of the jurisdiction being invoked. As Lord Scarman observed in the *Morgan* case [1985] AC 686, a court in the exercise of this jurisdiction is a court of conscience. He noted, at 709:

> 'There is no precisely defined law setting limits to the equitable jurisdiction of a court to relieve against undue influence . . . Definition is a poor instrument when used to determine whether a transaction is or is not unconscionable: this is a question which depends upon the particular facts of the case.'

As with the jurisdiction to grant relief, so with the precise form of the relief to be granted, equity as a court of conscience will look at all the circumstances and do what fairness requires. Lord Wright adverted to this in *Spence v Crawford* [1939] 3 All ER 271, which was a misrepresentation case. He said regarding rescission and restitution, at 288:

> 'The remedy is equitable. Its application is discretionary, and, where the remedy is applied, it must be moulded in accordance with the exigencies of the particular case.'

The law reports are replete with examples of the way courts have applied this principle. These, and the reasoning underlying them, afford valuable guidance when fairly comparable situations arise in the future. They are not immutable rules of law which must be applied irrespective of whether in the particular case they will assist in achieving an outcome which is practically just. A few examples will suffice. If the defendant has improved the property he is ordered to return, the plaintiff may be required to compensate him. On the other hand, if the plaintiff has improved the property he seeks to return, he will not necessarily be entitled to a further payment from the defendant; it may not be just to require the defendant to pay for improvements he does not want. If the plaintiff has permitted the property to deteriorate, he may be required to make an allowance to the defendant for this when seeking an order compelling him to retake the property. If a joint business venture is involved, such as an agreement between a pop star and a manager, and the agreement is set aside and an account directed of the profits received by the defendant under the agreement, the court in its discretion may permit the defendant to retain some profits, if it would be inequitable for the plaintiff to take the profits without paying for the expertise and work which produced them. In *O'Sullivan v Management Agency and Music Ltd* [1985] QB 428, 468 Fox LJ observed it was clearly necessary that the court should have power to make an allowance to a fiduciary. He continued:

> 'Substantial injustice may result without it. A hard and fast rule that the beneficiary can demand the whole profit without an allowance for the work without which it could not have been created is unduly severe. Nor do I think that the principle is only applicable in cases where the personal conduct of the fiduciary cannot be criticised. I think that the justice of the individual case must be considered on the facts of that case. Accordingly, where there has been dishonesty or surreptitious dealing or other improper conduct then, as indicated by Lord Denning MR, it might be appropriate to refuse relief; but that will depend upon the circumstances.'

What is true of profits must also be true of losses. In the ordinary way, when a sum of money is paid to a defendant under a transaction which is set aside, the defendant will be required to repay the whole sum. There may be exceptional cases where that would be unjust. This may the more readily be so where the personal conduct of the defendant was not open to criticism. Here, having heard the parties give evidence, the judge acquitted Mr Thomas of acting in a morally reprehensible way towards Mr Cheese. He described Mr Thomas as an innocent fiduciary. Here also, and I return to this feature because on any view it was an integral element of the transaction, each party applied money in buying the house. In all the circumstances, to require Mr Thomas to shoulder the whole of the loss flowing from the problems which have beset the residential property market for the last year or two would be harsh. That is not an outcome a court of conscience should countenance. . . .

Butler-Sloss and **Peter Gibson LJJ** concurred.

NOTES AND QUESTIONS

1. The decision of the Court of Appeal appears to contain a fundamental flaw in that the court seemed to regard the claimant as a licensee for the purpose of assessing manifest disadvantage but a co-owner for the purpose of rescinding the transaction (see J Martin, 'Elderly Relatives, Estoppel and Undue Influence' (1994) 144 *NLJ* 264, 265).

2. Did the claimant receive a benefit as a result of the actions of the defendant? If not, can this possibly be an example of counter-restitution?

3. How would the defence of change of position have applied to the facts of the case? Is it a more appropriate justification for the award made? (see M Chen-Wishart, 'Loss Sharing, Undue Influence and Manifest Disadvantage' (1994) 110 *LQR* 173, 176, and P Birks, 'Change of Position and Surviving Enrichment' in W Swadling (ed), *The Limits of Restitutionary Claims* (1997)).

4. What is the relationship between change of position and counter-restitution? Is counter-restitution no more than a species of change of position where the change of position takes the form of exchange value given to the claimant (Birks, *Restitution – The Future*, 128)?

- • *Smith New Court Securities Ltd v Scrimgeour Vickers (Asset Management) Ltd*
  [1994] 1 WLR 1271, Court of Appeal

The claimants were induced by the fraudulent misrepresentations of the second defendants to purchase shares in Ferranti International Signal plc for 82.5 pence *per* share. Ferranti had been the victim of a massive fraud which was only disclosed after the claimants had bought the shares. The effect of the revelation of the fraud was to cause the price of Ferranti shares to collapse. The claimants sought to minimize their loss by selling the shares in small parcels over a period of time and they realized prices between 49 pence and 30 pence *per* share. The claimants abandoned their restitutionary claim for the return of the purchase price of the shares at trial, and before the Court of Appeal the issue was the assessment of damages in the tort of deceit. It was held that damages should be assessed by reference to the price of Ferranti shares on the open market at the time of the misrepresentation and not by reference to the price of the shares had the existence of the fraud been known.

Nourse LJ [delivering the judgment of the court]: The remedies available to a party who has been induced to enter into a contract by a fraudulent misrepresentation are rescission and damages. Rescission is a restitutionary remedy which allows the defrauded party to recover the property with which he has parted under the contract and return the benefit which he received. It is however a necessary condition of this remedy in English law that the plaintiff should be able to make substantial restitution in specie of the property which he has received. If S.N.C. had retained the shares, it would have been able to return them and claim repayment of the full price, even though the value of the shares had fallen. But, no doubt after weighing the commercial risks of winning the action against the possibility of a further decline in the Ferranti share price, it decided to sell. Thereby it lost the right to rescission. In the case of a fungible asset like quoted shares, the rule which requires restitution in specie is a hard one. Not every legal system would insist upon it, particularly in a case of fraud. But S.N.C. accepted that it could not pursue the claim to restitution and abandoned it at the trial.

NOTES AND QUESTIONS

1. The House of Lords subsequently allowed the claimants' appeal and held that the correct measure of damages was the difference between the price paid for the shares and the amount subsequently realised on their sale ([1997] AC 254) Lord Browne-Wilkinson stated (at 262) that 'the reasons why Smith abandoned their claim to rescind were not explored before your Lordships. I will therefore say nothing about the point save that if the current law in fact provides (as the Court of Appeal thought) that there is no right to rescind the contract for the sale of quoted shares once the specific shares have been sold, the law will need to be closely looked at hereafter. Since in such a case other, identical, shares can be purchased on the market, the defrauded purchaser can offer substantial restitutio in integrum which is normally sufficient.'

2. Was counsel for the claimants correct in accepting that he could not pursue a restitutionary claim?

3. Had the claimants retained the shares, they could have returned them and claimed repayment of the price which they had paid. Why did their eminently reasonable decision to sell have the effect of removing their entitlement to bring a restitutionary claim?

4. Could the claimants have gone out into the market and bought fresh Ferranti shares, tendered them to the defendants and then claimed restitution of the price they had paid for the shares?

5. Should the claimants have been allowed to make counter-restitution in money, at least in the case where the defendants were guilty of fraud? Does Spence v Crawford (above, 849) go this far? If so, at what date would the shares fall to be valued for the purpose of making counter-restitution?

• Mahoney v Purnell [1996] 3 All ER 61, Queen's Bench Division

The claimant, Mr Mahoney operated a hotel in partnership with his nephew, the defendant, Mr Purnell. In 1982 the partnership was incorporated with Mahoney and Purnell each taking 50 per cent of the shares. Mahoney had little or no sense of financial details and relied heavily on the judgment of Purnell. In 1987, Purnell wanted to run the business on his own. He asked Mahoney to sell his shares but Mahoney was reluctant to do so even though he needed the money. Without independent legal advice, Mahoney eventually agreed to sell and, in agreements executed in March 1988, Purnell agreed to pay Mahoney an annuity of £20,000 a year for 10 years. The annuity was in exchange for cancellation of Mahoney's shares and included an accelerated repayment of a loan by Mahoney to the company. The sale was greatly to Mahoney's disadvantage. The present value difference between what Mahoney gave up and that which he received was £202,131. In 1989, Purnell sold the hotel for £3.275 million and Mahoney sought to set aside the 1988 sale of his shares to Purnell on the ground of undue influence. The trial judge held that Mahoney had been acting under undue influence when he agreed to sell his shares and ordered that Purnell pay £202,131 to Mahoney.

May J: . . . The normal remedy where a claim based upon undue influence succeeds is for the transaction to be set aside with, in appropriate circumstances, an account of profits. In this case, it is agreed and obvious that the parties cannot be restored to their former positions. Among other impediments, the hotel has been sold, the company has been wound up and Mr Mahoney plainly cannot have his shares back, let alone in the circumstances which pertained in 1988. No point is taken on delay.

The Court of Appeal considered the appropriate equitable remedy in circumstances such as these in *O'Sullivan v Management Agency and Music Ltd* [1985] 3 All ER 351, [1985] QB 428, where agreements entered into by an inexperienced musician with defendants with whom he was held to have been in fiduciary relationship were presumed to have been induced by undue influence.

[*after quoting from O'Sullivan at length, May J continued . . .*]

In my judgment, what in summary emerges from the passages in *O'Sullivan* which I have quoted is that where an agreement is made as a result of undue influence in circumstances where the court will in equity intervene, the normal remedy is for the agreement to be set aside and for the defendant to account for profits obtained from the improper agreements. The court is not deflected from this course because the parties cannot be restored to their former positions. The remedy is not to leave the agreement as it is and simply compensate the plaintiff for loss upon the principle in *Nocton v Lord Ashburton* [1914] AC 932, [1914–15] All ER Rep 45. Allowance must be made to the defendant for improvements or benefits which he has made and which accrue to the plaintiff upon the setting aside of the agreement. Where the facts do not fit neatly into this scheme, the court has to achieve practical justice between the parties. The question is what does the justice of the case require.

In this case, the commonsense and, if I may say so, fair remedy for Mr Mahoney is for him to receive in compensation the March 1988 value of what he surrendered under the agreements, appropriate credit being given for what he received under the agreements. The question is whether the law permits that result. Both Mr Wilson-Smith and Mr Russell were inclined to submit that *O'Sullivan* required the taking of an account. This was indeed Mr Russell's eventual submission with reference to *Target Holdings Ltd v Redferns (a firm)* [1995] 3 All ER 785, [1995] 3 WLR 352 and the dissenting judgment of McLachlin J in *Canson Enterprises Ltd v Boughton & Co* (1991) 85 DLR (4th) 129. But taking an account in this case would not, in my view, do practical justice since, on the evidence, the value of what Mr Mahoney surrendered has been lost through no fault or action of his. The company is in liquidation and there is no presently quantifiable profit in the hands of Mr Purnell personally. The fact that at times between 1988 and now profits might have been calculated does not help, since there is no reason in principle for choosing any moment in time other than the present for the taking of an account. Practical justice in this case requires an award which is akin to damages. It might be said that the court cannot do that since in other circumstances not applicable to this case equity appeared to be so inflexible that statutes were required to enable the court to award damages—s 2 of the Chancery Amendment Act 1858 (Lord Cairns' Act) (damages instead of an injunction) and s. 2(2) of the Misrepresentation Act 1967 (damages instead of rescission for misrepresentation). But I am loath to reach that conclusion if the result would be, as I think it would be, that Mr Mahoney was denied commonsense and fair compensation.

In my view, the law is not so constrained. *O'Sullivan* recognises that transactions may be set aside provided that the court can achieve practical justice by obliging the defendant to give up advantages while at the same time compensating him for value which he has contributed. No doubt that balance will usually be achieved by taking an account. But where that precise route will not achieve practical justice, an analogous permissible route to that end may be to balance the value which the plaintiff surrendered against any value which he has received and to award him the difference. That is not, I think, to award him damages, but fair compensation in equity as an adjunct to setting aside the agreement.

I consider that *Nocton v Lord Ashburton* may be seen as authority supporting—or at least strongly encouraging—the conclusion that the court does have power to award fair compensation in equity where a plaintiff who has trusted a defendant succeeds in persuading the court to set aside an unfair agreement induced by reliance on that trust. In that case, the plaintiff claimed to be indemnified against loss which he had sustained by having been improperly advised and induced by the defendant, acting as his confidential solicitor, to release a part of a mortgage security, whereby the security became insufficient. The trial judge found that fraud had not been proved and dismissed the action.

The Court of Appeal reversed this finding and granted relief on the basis of fraud. The House of Lords reversed the Court of Appeal's finding of fraud, but held that the plaintiff was not precluded from claiming relief on the footing of breach of duty arising from fiduciary relationship. Viscount Haldane LC said ([1914] AC 932 at 945–946, [1914–15] All ER Rep 45 at 48):

'I cannot, therefore, treat the case, so far based on intention to deceive, as made out. But where I differ from the learned judges in the Courts below is as to their view that, if they did not regard deceit as proved, the only alternative was to treat the action as one of mere negligence at law unconnected with misconduct. This alternative they thought was precluded by the way the case had been conducted. I am not sure that, on the pleadings and on the facts proved, they were right even in this. The question might well have been treated as in their discretion and as properly one of costs only, having regard to the unsatisfactory evidence of the appellant. But I do not take the view that they were shut up within the dilemma they supposed. There is a third form of procedure to which the statement of claim approximated very closely, and that is the old bill in Chancery to enforce compensation for breach of a fiduciary obligation.'

Viscount Haldane LC observed that, in cases of actual fraud, the remedies in early days available to the Court of Chancery were more elastic than those of the courts of common law ([1914] AC 932 at 952, [1914–15] All ER Rep 45 at 51):

'Operating in personam as a Court of conscience it could order the defendant, not, indeed, in those days, to pay damages as such, but to make restitution, or to compensate the plaintiff by putting him in as good a position pecuniarily as that in which he was before the injury.'

And he said ([1914] AC 932 at 956–957, [1914–15] All ER Rep 45 at 54):

'When, as in the case before us, a solicitor has had financial transactions with his client, and has handled his money to the extent of using it to pay off a mortgage made to himself, or of getting the client to release from his mortgage a property over which the solicitor by such release has obtained further security for a mortgage of his own, a Court of Equity has always assumed jurisdiction to scrutinize his action. It did not matter that the client would have had a remedy in damages for breach of contract. Courts of Equity had jurisdiction to direct accounts to be taken, and in proper cases to order the solicitor to replace property improperly acquired from the client, or to make compensation if he had lost it by acting in breach of a duty which arose out of his confidential relationship to the man who had trusted him.'

Lord Dunedin concluded his opinion as follows ([1914] AC 932 at 965, [1914–15] All ER Rep 45 at 58):

'But apart from that, for the reasons given by my noble friend the Lord Chancellor, I think there was here a remedy in equity for breach of duty. I agree that the form that remedy would have taken would not have been damages, but, looking to the course the case has taken, I do not think it is incumbent on us to alter the remedy to another which would practically come to much the same.'

In other words, the Court of Appeal had awarded damages for fraud. Fraud was not to be found. But there was an alternative equitable remedy of compensation producing much the same result and there was no point in changing its name.

I do not read the opinions of Lord Shaw and Lord Parmoor in *Nocton v Lord Ashburton* as disagreeing with what Viscount Haldane LC and Lord Dunedin said about equitable remedy. Accordingly, a plaintiff who suffers loss as a result of breach of a fiduciary duty by a defendant may claim relief in equity which need not be limited to the taking of an account of profit, and can take the form of compensation if the defendant has lost the property acquired from the plaintiff by a transaction which arose out of his confidential relationship with the man who had trusted him. This analysis is supported by what McLachlin J said in *Canson Enterprises Ltd v Boughton & Co* (1991) 85 DLR (4th) 129 esp at 157 and explicitly at 163, where he said:

'In summary, compensation is an equitable monetary remedy which is available when the equitable remedies of restitution and account are not appropriate. By analogy with restitution, it attempts to restore to the plaintiff what has been lost as a result of the breach, *i.e.*, the plaintiff's lost opportunity.'

In *Target Holdings Ltd v Redferns (a firm)* [1995] 3 All ER 785 at 799, [1995] 3 WLR 352 at 366 Lord Browne-Wilkinson contrasted a claim for an account of profits made by a fiduciary with a claim for compensation for breach of trust, but I do not read his opinion as necessarily requiring the former remedy where it is not appropriate or fair.

The relationship which existed in this case between Mr Mahoney and Mr Purnell from which undue influence is presumed is based upon trust and may be described as fiduciary. Although Mr Mahoney's claim is not conventionally framed in the language of breach of duty, his ground for equitable relief is founded on abuse of trust. For present purposes the difference may be seen as semantic only. In *Nocton v Lord Ashburton* the breach of duty was that which lost the property. In this case, the abuse of the fiduciary relationship induced the agreements and the property was lost later. I do not consider that this is a distinction material to the search for a remedy, since in each case the plaintiff seeks equitable relief for an abuse of (or breach of) trust. Nor do I consider that what Fox LJ said with reference to *Nocton v Lord Ashburton* in *O'Sullivan v Management Agency and Music Ltd* [1985] 3 All ER 351 at 371, [1985] QB 428 at 465, which I have quoted earlier in this judgment, should be read as saying that compensation in equity other than by means of an account is not available where an agreement is set aside for undue influence. Rather was he rejecting the submission, critical on the facts of that case, that the agreements could not, and therefore should not, be set aside leaving the plaintiff with equitable compensation only.

I consider therefore, that the court is able to give the commonsense and fair remedy suitable for the peculiar circumstances of this case, so that Mr Mahoney may receive in compensation the March 1988 value of what he surrendered under the agreements, appropriate credit being given for what he received under the agreements.

NOTES AND QUESTIONS

May J seemed to conflate two different approaches. The first, was to treat the award as one of the money value of rescission (which was impossible in specie because the shares could not be restored). The second approach, seen in his reference to undue influence as a 'wrong' and references to the award as 'compensation', is to treat the award as compensation for a wrong of, in the words of May J, 'abuse of trust'. The first approach is supported by P Birks, 'Unjust Factors and Wrongs: Pecuniary Restitution for Undue Influence' [1997] *RLR* 72 and N Nahan, 'Rescission: A case for rejecting the classical model' (1997) 27 *UWAL Rev* 66. The second view is supported by JD Heydon, 'Equitable Compensation for Undue Influence' (1997) 113 *LQR* 8. Which do you prefer? Are both analyses possible?

6. PASSING ON

The status of passing on as a defence, at common law, to a restitutionary claim was, until recently, the subject of some controversy in English law. In *Woolwich Equitable Building Society v Inland Revenue Commissioners*, above, 626 Lord Goff left the point open, but the Court of Appeal has since concluded that English law knows of no general defence of passing on (see *Kleinwort Benson Ltd v Birmingham City Council*, below). In reaching its conclusion the Court of Appeal placed considerable reliance on the judgment of Mason

CJ in the High Court of Australia in *Commissioner of State Revenue v Royal Insurance Australia Ltd.* (below, 879), which has subsequently been confirmed in *Roxborough v Rothmans of Pall Mall Ltd* (2001) 208 CLR 516.

- ## *Kleinwort Benson Ltd v Birmingham City Council*
  [1996] 3 WLR 1139, Court of Appeal

The claimant bank sought to recover the payments which it had made to the defendant local authority pursuant to a swaps agreement which was *ultra vires* the local authority, and hence void. The defendant argued that it was not liable to repay the money because the claimant bank had not suffered any loss as it had passed any loss it had suffered on to third parties through its hedging transactions. It was held that passing on was not a defence to the claimant's claim so that the claimant was entitled to recover the sums which it had paid to the defendant.

Evans LJ: ...

'PASSING ON' OR 'WINDFALL GAIN'

This defence has been considered by the Supreme Court of Canada in *Air Canada v British Columbia* (1989) 59 DLR (4th) 161 and twice by the High Court of Australia in *Mason v New South Wales* (1959) 102 CLR 108 and *Commissioner of State Revenue v Royal Insurance Australia Ltd* (1994) 126 ALR 1. In these as in numerous United States authorities the claim was for repayment of over-paid tax (in *Mason*'s case, statutory dues paid as fees). In such cases, the defence is raised when the plaintiff taxpayer has passed on the burden of the tax to his own customers and he will be under no obligation to reimburse them if he succeeds in recovering the tax which he has paid. Then it can be said that repayment will result in a windfall gain for him or, conversely, that the benefit to the taxing authority even if it is properly regarded as 'unjust enrichment' has not been at the tax-payer's expense.

Whether the defence is available in taxation cases under English law must be regarded as uncertain. The taxpayer's right to recover tax paid under a void statutory instrument was upheld in the *Woolwich Equitable Building Society v Inland Revenue Commissioners* [1993] AC 70, where Lord Goff said with regard to a passing on defence at 177–8:

> 'It will be a matter for consideration whether the fact that the plaintiff has passed on the tax or levy so that the burden has fallen on another should provide a defence to his claim. Although this is contemplated by the European Court of Justice in the *San Georgio* case [1983] ECR 3595, it is evident from *Air Canada v British Columbia* that the point is not without its difficulties and the availability of such defence may depend upon the nature of the tax or other levy.'

Lord Goff then referred to pending consultations by the Law Commission. Its Report has now been published (*Restitution: Mistakes of Law and Ultra Vires Public Authority Receipts and Payments* (1994) (Law Com. No 227) (Cm. 2731) and its recommendations include at 192 '(20) it should be a defence to claims for the repayment of taxes overpaid [as a result of mistake] that repayment will unjustly enrich the claimant' (cf. (21) dealing with *ultra vires* claims). A statutory scheme has this effect with regard to V.A.T.: see the Value Added Tax Act 1994, section 80(3). But the Law Commission expressly excluded questions arising under swaps contracts from its consideration (para. 1.11) and so there is nothing in its report of direct relevance to the present case.

Apparently there is no reported authority from Canada, Australia or the United States where the defence has been raised, except to a claim for overpaid tax and apart from an anti-trust suit in the United States where the defence was rejected by the Supreme Court: *United Shoe Machinery Corporation v Hanover Shoe Inc.* (1968) 392 US 481.

In my judgment, the taxation cases are of limited assistance in addressing the question of general principle which is raised by the present appeal. There is a public law element involved in them (see *Air Canada v British Columbia*, 59 DLR (4th) 161, 170, *per* Wilson J) and a further question, akin to agency, which is whether the taxpayer should be regarded as having collected tax from his customers on behalf of the taxing authority. Conversely, it may appear that any tax recovered by him will be held by him as a fiduciary for his customers: *123 East Fifty-Fourth Street Inc. v United States* (1946) 157 F Rep. (2d) 68 *per* Learned Hand J. Statements of principle in the *Air Canada* case are favourable to the authority in the present case, but the converse is true so far as the Australian cases are concerned. These judgments are most relevant for present purposes, in my respectful view, for what they say with regard to the private law of restitution, and in particular the full survey of the common law position by Mason CJ in *Commissioner of State Revenue v Royal Insurance Australia Ltd* 126 ALR 1. His conclusion in that case was that 'the Commissioner would have no defence to a restitutionary claim by Royal to recover the mistaken payments of duty' and that even if it was established that Royal charged the tax as a separate item on the policy holders it would be entitled to recover the moneys which it would then hold as a constructive trustee (see 18). In relation to restitutionary relief, which he distinguished from the public law aspects, he quoted with approval what Windeyer J said in *Mason v New South Wales*, 102 CLR 108, 146:

'If the defendant be improperly enriched on what legal principle can it claim to retain its ill-gotten gains merely because the plaintiffs have not, it is said, been correspondingly impoverished? The concept of improverishment as a correlative of enrichment may have some place in some fields of continental law. It is foreign to our law. Even if there were any equity in favour of third parties attaching to the fruits of any judgment the plaintiffs might recover . . . this circumstance would be quite irrelevant to the present proceedings. Certainly it would not enable the defendant to refuse to return moneys which it was not in law entitled to collect and which ex hypothesi it got by extortion.'

He then said, 126 ALR 1, 15:

'Restitutionary relief, as it has developed to this point in our law, does not seek to provide compensation for loss. Instead, it operates to restore to the plaintiff what has been transferred from the plaintiff to the defendant whereby the defendant has been unjustly enriched. As in the action for money had and received, the defendant comes under an obligation to account to the plaintiff for money which the defendant has received for the use of the plaintiff. The substraction from the plaintiff's wealth enables one to say that the defendant's unjust enrichment has been "at the expense of the plaintiff", notwithstanding that the plaintiff may recoup the outgoing by means of transactions with third parties. On this approach, it would not matter that the plaintiff is or will be overcompensated because he or she has passed on the tax or charge to someone else. And it seems that there is no recorded instance of a court engaging in the daunting exercise of working out the actual loss sustained by the plaintiff and restricting the amount of an award to that measure.'

There are also judgments of the Court of Justice of the European Communities, including *Amministrazione delle Finanze Stato v San Giorgio* (Case 199/82) [1983] ECR 3595 to which Lord Goff referred in *Woolwich Equitable Building Society v Inland Revenue Commissioners* [1993] AC 70, 177–8 (quoted above). This too was a claim to recover overpaid statutory charges. Italian law required the taxpayer to prove that he had not passed them on to his customers and it imposed a burden of proof upon him which it might be virtually impossible to discharge. The European Court held that this provision of Italian law was contrary to European law, but the judgment and the opinion of Advocate General G. F. Mancini were in terms which can be regarded as supporting the lawfulness of a passing on defence. This approach was re-affirmed in *Les Fils de Jules Bianco SA and J. Girard Fils SA v*

Directeur Général des Douanes et Droits Indirects (Joined Cases 331/85, 376/85) [1988] ECR 1099, and in *Commission of the European Communities v Italian Republic (Case 104/86)* [1988] ECR 1799 the court held that Community law does not require (but neither does it prohibit) an order for such repayment to be made in circumstances which would involve an 'unjust enrichment' of the taxpayer, including the passing on to other traders or to consumers of the burden of the charge. The opinion of the Advocate General, Sir Gordon Slynn, in the former case shows the difficulties that can arise when it becomes necessary to inquire whether the burden of the over payment has been passed on to customers in the form of increased charges for the taxpayer's goods or services. Economic factors come into play: has the taxpayer by raising his prices reduced the demand for what he supplies, so that he has not benefited overall? This prompts a further question: why should it be assumed that a repayment of tax will not be passed on to future customers in the form of reduced prices?

The present case is far removed from the taxation authorities. No element of public law is involved. No question of a constructive trust or of any obligation to account to customers can arise. This follows from the admitted fact that the hedge contracts, even if they were perfect matches, were market transactions independent of the swaps contract which were and remained binding on the bank and third parties notwithstanding that the swaps contract was void. This also means that the bank paid its own money to the authority and for its own account: no question of agency or any third party interest can arise.

SOUTH TYNESIDE

The relevant part of the judgment of Hobhouse J in *Kleinwort Benson Ltd v South Tyneside Metropolitan Borough Council* [1994] 4 All ER 972 is 984–7. He held, first, that the defendants were seeking to invoke 'some unspecific principle which derives not from the law of restitution but from some concept of causation' (984–5). He continued: 'Even in the simplest cases where parties are dealing on a market, other individual contracts are in principle too remote to be taken into account' and he held as a second ground of his decision that the hedge contracts were too remote to be taken into account, in any event (987). But the primary answer was that such considerations were not relevant to restitution. 'What contracts or other transactions or engagements the plaintiffs may have entered into with third parties have nothing to do with the principle of restitution. Therefore is suffices in the present case for the plaintiffs to show that they were the payers of the relevant money, that the defendants were unjustly enriched by the payments and that there is no obstacle to restitution' (985). He held that in the law of taxation special considerations may apply (987D) and that there was no place in the law of restitution 'for some principle borrowed from the law of compensation' (987F).

SUBMISSIONS

Mr Underhill [counsel for the authority] submits that, the law of compensation apart, there is a relevant restriction on the right to restitution, and that it is found in the express words of section 1 of the *American Law Institute Restatement of the Law, Restitution* (1937): the plaintiff must show that the defendant is unjustly enriched at his (the plaintiff's) expense. He relies upon the following passage from Birks *Introduction to the Law of Restitution* (1985, 132) under the heading 'At the plaintiff's expense':

> 'The plaintiff must bring himself within these words. If he cannot he has not even a prima facie entitlement to sue. For the defendant may have been enriched, and unjustly, yet unless it happened at the plaintiff's expense it will seem to be no business of his. That is what Goulding, J, [*in Chase Manhattan Bank NA v Israel-British Bank Ltd* [1981] Ch 105, 125E] meant when he said that the words "unjust enrichment" fail on their own to identify any plaintiff.'

He submits further that there is no justification for interpreting this requirement by reference to the relationship between the payer and the payee alone. Regard should also be had to related transactions, including in the present case any hedges which were entered into in order to protect the bank from suffering losses under the swaps contract. The area of inquiry should be limited, he concedes, by what he calls the normal rules of remoteness; but within those limits, the plaintiff cannot show that the defendant was enriched 'at his expense' if after taking account of all the relevant transactions he suffered no or only a smaller loss than the amount which he seeks to recover from the defendant.

Mr Rhodri Davies for the bank submits that the law of restitution as it is now established does not recognize the claimed defence of passing on, except possibly in the special case where the plaintiff seeks to recover over-paid tax. He carefully analysed the authorities to show that there is no support, as he submits, for Mr Underhill's contention, and he pointed to practical difficulties and certain anomalies which might result if the defence was one of general application. Among these anomalies was the possible conflict between a judgement in the present case which recognized hedge contacts as providing a passing-on defence, though not as increasing the amount of the claim, and the judgements in *Kleinwort Benson Ltd v South Tyneside Metropolitan Borough Council* [1994] 4 All ER 972 and *South Tyneside Metropolitan Borough Council v Svenska International plc* [1995] 1 All ER 545 which have held, as he submits, that market transactions with third parties do not enable the defendant to rely upon the 'change of position' defence, which logically he ought to be able to do if the passing on defence was recognized.

CONCLUSION

I can accept Mr Underhill's submission that the phrase 'at the expense of' forms part of the definition of a restitutionary claim, and that the central issue is whether that has to be interpreted by reference to the payer/payee relationship alone, as distinct from other parts of what he calls the overall transaction. But I have no doubt that the former interpretation is correct. This is because the payee's obligation, which is correlative to the payer's right to restitution is to refund or repay the amount which he has received and which it is unjust that he should keep. 'At his expense', in my judgement, serves to identify the person by or on whose behalf the payment was made and to whom repayment is due: compare *Chase Manhattan Bank N.A. v Israel British Bank (London) Ltd* [1981] Ch 105, 125 E, *per* Goulding, J and see *Birds Introduction to the Law of Restitution* 132. That person, having made the payment, is necessarily out of pocket to that extent, and the defendant's obligation is to replenish his pocket when the circumstances are such that the money should be returned.

If the payment was made for valuable consideration, then the payer did not suffer 'loss' even though the payment was made by him. But if it appears, as it did in the present case, that in law there was no consideration for it, then in that sense the payer has suffered loss. His pocket is emptier than it would have been if the money, or its value, was still there. But I would not give 'loss' any wider meaning than that. In particular, it seems to me that it would be inconsistent with the principle of repayment that 'loss' should be given some wider meaning equivalent to 'overall losses on the transaction', even if 'the transaction' could be sufficiently identified, or that the right to recover restitution should be limited to the amount of 'loss' in that sense, though never increased above the amount of the payment.

I therefore agree with the first of Hobhouse J's two reasons for holding that no 'passing on' defence arises in the present case. I agree with the second reason also. If the claim is treated as limited to compensation for loss in fact suffered, taking account of related transactions which are not too remote from it, then in my judgement such hedge contracts as were entered into by the bank in the normal course of its business were 'too remote' to be taken into account. Market rates are taken into account when assessing damages because the plaintiff comes under a duty to mitigate his loss and it is presumed that he has done so by entering the market for that purpose. It is only in special cases that actual transactions are taken in to account: *R. Pagnan & Fratelli v Corbisa Industrial Agropacuaria Limitada* [1970] 1 WLR 1306. But here, there was no duty on the bank to hedge the risks to which it was exposed under the swaps contract, and its claim for restitution is not based on any wrongdoing or breach of contract by the authority.

For these reasons, I would hold that the alleged passing on defence does not arise in the present case. Out of deference to the through and well-researched submissions which were so attractively presented to us I would add just the following. (1) This is not a proprietary claim, and Mr Underhill accepted that there could be no scope for a passing on defence, if it was. It is a claim for restitution precisely because the plaintiff can only claim repayment of an equivalent amount of money to what he paid. That is a further reason, in my judgement, for defining the right to recovery in terms of that amount of money, and nothing else. (2) If it was necessary to have regard to the status of the 'change of position' defence, which in my judgement it is not, then I would agree with Mr Underhill's submission (in reply) that the existing authorities of *Kleinwort Benson Ltd v South Tyneside Metropolitan Borough Council* [1994] 4 All ER 972 and *South Tyneside Metropolitan Borough Council v Svenska International plc* [1995] 1 All ER 545 do not establish a clear rule that no such defence can be raised. The *Svenska* case in particular turned on special facts, and I prefer to express no view as to whether that defence, which was recognized in *Lipkin Gorman v Karpnale Ltd* [1991] 2 AC 548, could ever be established by reference to market transactions. (3) This is not a case where the payment which it is sought to recover was made to the defendant by a third party, not by the plaintiff. Again, it is unnecessary in my view to deal further with this different aspect of the problem. . . . I would dismiss the appeal.

Saville LJ: I agree. I also agree with the Judgment of Morritt LJ, which I have had the advantage of reading in draft.

. . . The payee has been unjustly enriched by receiving and retaining money he has received from the payer and to which he has no right. He does not cease to be unjustly enriched because the payer for one reason or another is not out of pocket. His obligation to return the money is not based on any loss the payer may have sustained, but on the simple ground that it is unjust that he should keep something to which he has no right and which he only received through the payer's performance of an obligation which did not in fact exist.

The expression 'at the payer's expense' is a convenient way of describing the need for the payer to show that his money was used to pay the payee. Thus there may well be cases where this cannot be shown, but where in truth, for example, the payer was only the conduit through which the funds of others passed to the payee. What this expression does not justify is the importation of concepts of loss or damage with their attendant concepts of mitigation, for these have nothing whatever to do with the reason why our law imposes an obligation on the payee to repay to the payer what he has no right to retain. I too would dismiss this appeal.

Morritt LJ: . . .

The case for the authority depends on extending and applying to the facts of this case the propositions enunciated by La Forest J in *Air Canada v British Columbia* (1989) 59 DLR (4th) 161, 193–4 where he said:

'The law of restitution is not intended to provide windfalls to plaintiffs who have suffered no loss. Its function is to ensure that where a plaintiff has been deprived of wealth that is either in his possession or would have accrued for his benefit, it is restored to him. The measure of restitutionary recovery is the gain the province made at the airlines' expense. If the airlines have not shown that they bore the burden of the tax, then they have not made out their claim. What the province received is relevant only in so far as it was received at the airlines' expense.'

The application in England of the principle referred to in that passage was considered and rejected by Hobhouse J in *Kleinwort Benson Ltd v South Tyneside Metropolitan Borough Council* [1994] 4 All ER 972. He considered the principle and said (at 984–5):

'What is the legal principle which the defendants invoke? It can only be some unspecific principle which derives not from the law of restitution but from some concept of compensation. The essential features in what the defendants here are asking the court to do (and other defendants in similar actions) is to make an assessment of the loss suffered by the relevant plaintiff as if one were investigating a right to compensation. The argument involves problems of remoteness. Even in the simplest cases where parties are dealing on a market, other individual contracts are in principle too remote to be taken into account. Compensation is assessed by reference to the market, not by reference to individual contracts. Where the position is more complex and it is not a question of looking at individual contracts but at the overall position of the plaintiff which may change from time to time, the problems of remoteness become self-evident and the risk of entering into an infinite regress likewise become apparent. But the primary answer is that such considerations may be relevant to compensation but are not relevant to restitution. Here there is no problem about recognising a restitutionary remedy in personam against the defendants in favour of the plaintiffs. What contracts or other transactions or engagements the plaintiffs may have entered into with third parties have nothing to do with the principle of restitution. Therefore it suffices in the present case for the plaintiffs to show that they were the payers of the relevant money, that the defendants were unjustly enriched by the payments and that there is no obstacle to restitution. The problems which arise in different classes of case and are referred to in the textbooks, where the defendant has enjoyed some less tangible benefit and it does not derive from a payment made by the plaintiff to the defendant, do not arise for consideration in this case.'

Later, he concluded (at 987):

'In the present case I am concerned with payments made under void transactions where there is no question but that the relevant plaintiff made the payment on his own account and out of his own money. If the plaintiff is to be denied his remedy in respect of the sum which he has paid to the defendant and which it is unjust that the defendant should retain, it must be upon a basis that is relevant to the law of restitution and not some principle borrowed from the law of compensation. Further the application of the principle, if it is to be adopted, must respect the principles of remoteness recognised in the law of compensation.'

Counsel for the authority contends that the propositions advanced by La Forest J in *Air Canada v British Columbia* 59 DLR (4th) 161 are consistent with the principles of the law of restitution in England, that Hobhouse J was wrong to have concluded otherwise, and that such propositions should be applied in this case if the facts as established at trial warrant it. He submits that restitution does involve the concept of loss and hence compensation, for they are inherent in the consideration of whether the enrichment of the defendant was 'at the expense of the plaintiff'. He accepts that the recognition of the defence may give rise to considerable problems of knowing where to draw the line and suggests that suitable control mechanisms may be found in the application of two well-established principles. The first is the burden of proof. It is suggested that once the plaintiff has shown that he had paid the sum claimed to the defendant then the burden would shift to the defendant to establish if he could that the loss had been passed on by the plaintiff. The second is that in seeking to do so the court should apply principles well-recognized in the assessment of damages for breach of contract or tort which require that the innocent party bring into account benefits derived from connected transactions. For my part I do not accept any of these propositions.

I will consider first the suggested control mechanisms. The principle which requires a plaintiff to bring into account in the assessment of damages benefits derived from connected transactions was established in *British Westinghouse Electric and Manufacturing Co. Ltd v Underground Electric Railways Co. of London Ltd* [1912] AC 673 and has been considered in a number of cases since, including *Hussey v Eels* [1990] 2 QB 227. The principle is one aspect of the requirement that the plaintiff should mitigate his loss. Thus a benefit derived from a subsequent transaction arising out of the consequences of the original wrong and entered into by the plaintiff in the ordinary course of his business must be brought into account in assessing the loss sustained by virtue of the wrong.

But this principle can have no application to a claim to restitution such as is made in this case. First the claim is not founded on a wrong inflicted on the bank, but is for restitution of money paid by the bank to the authority as money had and received to the use of the bank. In such circumstances there is no duty to mitigate anything. But even if there were the principle on which the authority seeks to rely would not apply. Let it be assumed that there are two precisely matching equal but opposite interest rate swaps only one of which is made with a local authority and therefore void. In such a case the valid transaction which the City Council contends should be brought into account would have been concluded in reliance on the validity of the other not on or as a consequence of its invalidity. Thus even if the restitutionary claim were to depend on loss the usual rules as to mitigation would treat the matching swap transaction as unconnected. In consequence any gain made as a result of it would not diminish the loss sustained as a result of the wrong. I can see no reason why the defendant to a claim for restitution based on the invalidity of a contract should be put in a better position than he would have been in if the claim had been for damages for the breach of a valid contract.

The idea that the evidential burden of proof of passing on might switch to the defendant when the plaintiff has produced evidence sufficient to establish his initial payment to the defendant is supported by the opinion of Sir Gordon Slynn as Advocate General in *Les Fils Jules Bianco S A and J Girard Fils SA v Directeur Général des Douanes et Droits Indirects* (Joined Cases 331/85, 376/85, 378/85) [1988] ECR 1099. But Sir Gordon was not suggesting that such a principle somehow mitigated any perceived injustice in the suggested defence; he was concerned with whether the requirement of Italian law for documentary evidence was a material restriction. The switch of the onus of proof could do little to ameliorate the wide-ranging practical consequences of a defence of passing on. It would be little consolation to a claimant required to disclose on discovery all its books and other records relevant to a defence of passing on to be told that the onus of proof rested on its adversary.

Accordingly I reject the suggestion that either of the control mechanisms relied on could have the effects for which the authority contends. It must follow that in the consideration of the suggested defence, to which I now return, it is necessary to face the practical consequences referred to by Hobhouse J down to and including the infinite regression. As I have already indicated I would reject the argument of the authority.

First, there is no doubt that in this case the bank was legally, and, if it is material, beneficially, entitled to the money it paid to the authority. This is not a case in which the claimant held the money claimed as a bare trustee or tax collector such as, arguably, in *Air Canada v British Columbia* (1989) 59 DLR 161 (4th) or *123 East Fifty-Fourth Street Inc. v United States* 157 F 2d 68. It is true, as shown in *Friends Provident Life Office v Hillier Parker May & Rowden* [1996] 2 WLR 123, 125, on which the authority relied, that in certain statutory contexts compensation for damage may include restitution for unjust enrichment; but that cannot alter the fact that the claim of the bank is for restitution of the money it paid to the authority. The bank does not seek compensation for loss.

Second, the words 'at the expense of the plaintiff' on which the authority place such reliance do not appear in a statute and should not be construed or applied as if they did. In my view they do no more than point to the requirement that the immediate source of the unjust enrichment must be the plaintiff. Were it otherwise the decision of this court in *Banque Belge pour l'Etranger v Hambrouck* [1921] 1 KB 321 would have been different. Some commentaries equate the phrase 'at the expense of' with a subtraction from the wealth of the plaintiff. No doubt this is a useful description. But the type of restitutionary claim with which this appeal is concerned relates to a subtraction from the plaintiff's gross wealth. The suggested defence of passing on would involve the different concept of a reduction in the net worth of the plaintiff.

Third, if the authority were permitted to retain that which the bank paid under the void swap it would have the result of giving effect to that which was ultra vires and void. Whilst the theory of restitution no longer involves the implication of any promise to repay, all those factors which go to establish the case for restitution would be nullified or undermined by a defence of passing on.

Fourth, I do not accept the proposition that if the loss has been passed on it is necessarily unjust for the claimant to recover what La Forest J in *Air Canada v British Columbia*, 59 DLR (4th) 161, 193 described as 'a windfall'. The concept of relative titles is not unfamiliar, for example in the case of trespass to land. If in accordance with the relevant principles the defendant has been unjustly enriched by the payment by the plaintiff it seems to me that the plaintiff has a better title than the defendant to any 'windfall' available, not least so as to be in a position to satisfy any claim made against him by those from whom 'the windfall' was ultimately derived. I do not suggest that this is a proprietary claim, merely that proprietary principles are applicable by analogy to claims *in personam:* cf. *Lipkin Gorman v Karpnale Ltd* [1991] 2 AC 548, 572.

Fifthly, if the defence is recognized it will place at the disposal of an unjustly enriched defendant a powerful weapon with which to postpone the entry of judgment against him. I do not think that the fact that the recovery might in some cases represent a 'windfall' in the hands of the plaintiff is sufficient reason to enable an unjustly enriched defendant to delay recovery from him in the many cases where it would not.

Finally there is the overwhelming weight of authority against the contentions of the authority. Apart from the cases to which I have already referred, the defence of passing on has been referred to in two other recent cases, namely *Amministrazione delle Finanze dello Stato v SpA San Giorgio* (Case 199/82) [1983] ECR 3595 and *Woolwich Equitable Building Society v Inland Revenue Commissioners* [1993] AC 70. In the first the European Court concluded that Community law did not prevent a national legal system from disallowing the repayment of charges which had been unduly levied on the ground that they had been passed on to the ultimate purchaser by incorporation in the price of goods. In the second Lord Goff of Chieveley recognized that it would be a matter for consideration whether the fact that the plaintiff has passed on the tax or levy so that the burden has fallen on another should provide a defence to his claim. Neither of those cases throws any light on the answer to the question posed by this appeal.

In my view, and in agreement with Evans and Saville LJJ, the relevant principles and precedents require the dismissal of this appeal.

NOTES AND QUESTIONS

1. The defence is discussed in more detail by F Rose in 'Passing On' in P Birks (ed.), *Laundering and Tracing* (1995), 261 and by B Rudden and W Bishop, 'Gritz and Quellmehl: Pass It On' (1981) 6 *ELR* 243. It is now the subject of a monograph by Michael Rush, *The Defence of Passing On* (2006), which concludes that there is no place for such a defence in unjust enrichment. He therefore applauds the decision in *Kleinwort Benson v Birmingham City Council* and argues that the statutes embodying the defence should be reformed.

2. Some scholars (e.g. Birks, *Unjust Enrichment* (2005), 219–21; Rush, *The Defence of Passing On* (2006)) treat the defence of passing on as related to the inquiry of whether the enrichment is 'at the expense of' the claimant. As Rush, who describes the defence as 'disimpoverishment', explains (at 91):

    Before a claimant's 'disimpoverishment' can be considered relevant, the claimant must first be required to show that he incurred an initial 'impoverishment'. In other words, before the defence of disimpoverishment is accepted as part of the law of unjust enrichment the claimant must, as condition of the defendant's liability, be obliged to prove that he suffered a loss. That is what Mason CJ meant when he stated in *Comr State Revenue (Victoria) v Royal Insurance Australia Ltd* that the defence cannot be established if 'the defendant's enrichment has not been at the expense of the plaintiff' ((1994)

182 CLR 51, 75). It is by no means certain, however, that the claimant is and should be obliged to show that he incurred a loss when establishing *a prima facie* claim for restitution. That is because the requirement that the defendant's unjust enrichment must have come 'at the expense of' the claimant need not be interpreted to mean that the claimant must have suffered a 'loss'... An alternative interpretation of the phrase 'at the expense of' exists. That is, the claimant need merely show that the defendant's enrichment came 'from' him.

3. The decision of the Court of Appeal was given prior to the decision of the House of Lords in *Westdeutsche Landesbank Girozentrale v Islington London Borough Council* (above, 40, 362), and so it was assumed that the Court of Appeal in *Westdeutsche Landesbank* had been correct in concluding that the ground of restitution was 'no consideration'. That assumption may no longer hold good after the decision of the House of Lords (see above, 368–383).

4. Section 80(3) of the Value Added Tax Act 1994 states that 'It shall be a defence, in relation to a claim under this section, that repayment of an amount would unjustly enrich the claimant.' Is this a recognition of the defence of passing on? Is an indirect tax, such as VAT, an example of a case in which the enrichment of Customs and Excise is not 'at the expense of' the retailer but rather at the expense of the customer?

5. Apart from the Value Added Tax Act 1994, the defence of passing on has also been recognized in the Finance Act (UK) 1994, sch. 7 para. 8(3) (relating to insurance premium tax), Finance Act (UK) 1996, sch. 5 para. 14(3) (relating to landfill tax), Customs & Excise Management Act (UK) 1979 s. 137A(3) (relating to excise tax inserted by the Finance Act (UK) 1997, ch 16, sch. 5); Finance Act (UK) 2000, ch 17, sch. 6 (relating to a climate change levy); and Finance Act (UK) 2001, ch 9, sch. 8 (relating to an aggregates levy). Can it be rational for the defence to be rejected at common law but accepted in statutes dealing with tax?

6. Was Morritt LJ correct to conclude that the duty to mitigate can have no application to a claim in restitution?

• *Commissioner of State Revenue v Royal Insurance Australia Ltd*   (1995) 182 CLR 51

Royal overpaid stamp duty of $1,907,908 over a period of four years. The Commissioner admitted that there had been such an overpayment but refused to return the money in the exercise of her discretion under section 111 of the Stamp Duty Act 1958 which stated that the Commissioner 'may refund . . . the amount of the duty found to be overpaid'. One of the reasons offered by the Commissioner for her refusal to return the money was that it would amount to a windfall to Royal because it had passed the cost on to its policy holders. The High Court of Australia upheld Royal's claim and made an order by way of mandamus directing the Commissioner to refund the overpayment. In so concluding, the court stated that the Commissioner was not entitled to rely on the defence of passing on. The central passage in the reasoning of Mason CJ has already been set out in the judgment of Evans LJ above. But, after concluding that there was no recorded instance of a court engaging in the daunting exercise of working out the actual loss sustained by the claimant and restricting the amount of an award to that measure, he continued in the following terms:

Mason CJ . . . Nonetheless, in the United States, relief has been denied, on equitable amongst other grounds, to a plaintiff who has passed on the tax or charge, reference being made to coming to court with unclean hands.[1] Why, as between the plaintiff and the defendant, the passing on of the tax to customers of the plaintiff results in conduct which should disentitle the plaintiff in equity from

---

1 *Standard Oil Co. v Bollinger* (1929) 169 NE 236; see also *Richardson Lubricating Co. v Kinney* (1929) 168 NE 886.

recovery is difficult to understand. The better view is that, if passing on of the tax disentitles the plaintiff, it is because, in the particular circumstances, the defendant's enrichment has not been at the expense of the plaintiff.

That was the way in which the problem was approached by Learned Hand J in his dissenting opinion in *123 East Fifty-Fourth Street v United States*.[2] There the Court rejected the defence of passing on in circumstances where a restaurant owner, in accordance with advice received from revenue authorities that it was liable to cabaret tax, paid amounts as and for that tax. The Court held that the tax was not payable because the restaurant was not a cabaret. The restaurant owner had charged the tax to its patrons so that items on the patrons' bills were actually part of the price paid by them and the money became that of the restaurant owner. The majority considered that this was no bar to recovery by the restaurant owner because the money, when paid to the government, belonged to and was the property of the restaurant owner. However, Learned Hand J was prepared to infer that the owner had added the tax as a separate item to the bills and described it as a tax which it must pay and was collecting it from patrons in order to pay it to the Treasury. His Honour regarded as crucial the distinction between passing on the tax in this form and merely including in the bills the amount of the tax without saying anything about it.

Learned Hand J went on to say:[3]

'If it said nothing, I should agree ... that the guests had no legally recognisable interest in the money collected, which gave them any claim to it superior to the plaintiff's ... On the other hand, if the plaintiff collected the money under what the guests must have understood to be a statement that it was obliged to pay it as a tax and that it meant to do so, the money was charged with a constructive trust certainly so long as it remained in the plaintiff's hands.'

According to his Honour, the constructive trust attached to the claim for recovery of the money so that if the plaintiff recovered the payments it would hold as trustee for the patrons. That would be no answer to the claim if the plaintiff could and would distribute the recovery to the patrons. But that did not appear to be the case so that in the result, the equities being equal, the legal title should prevail.

In *Decorative Carpets Inc. v State Board of Equalization*,[4] the Supreme Court of California followed the dissenting opinion of Learned Hand J. In that case, the plaintiff had overpaid sales tax with respect to transactions combining sales and installation. The plaintiff had collected for each transaction giving rise to a liability to pay sales tax a separately stated amount to cover the tax imposed on it, and had charged to its customers the amounts computed to be payable as sales tax on those transactions. The Court held that the plaintiff's mistake of law gave rise to an involuntary trust in favour of the customers and that the plaintiff could recover only if it submitted proof that the refund would be returned to the customers from whom the payments were erroneously collected. Traynor J, with whom Gibson CJ, Peters and White JJ concurred, said:[5]

'To allow the plaintiff a refund without requiring it to repay its customers the amounts erroneously collected from them would sanction a misuse of the sales tax by a retailer for his private gain.'

The Court considered that, although the defendant would ordinarily, like the plaintiff, become a constructive trustee of the moneys for the plaintiff's customers, adherence to statutory procedures precluded the imposition on the defendant of an obligation to make refunds to the customers. The Court did not discuss the question whether the defendant would be unjustly enriched if the plaintiff were unable to offer proof that it could and would refund the sums to its customers.

---

2 (1946) 157 F Rep. (2d) 68.   3 (1946) 157 F Rep (2d) 70.   4 (1962) 373 P 2d 637.
5 *Ibid*. 638.

On the other hand, in *Favor v State Board of Equalization*[6] car purchasers sought to recover amounts of sales tax which had been passed on to them by retailers. The amount paid was excessive because of the repeal, with retrospective effect, of a federal manufacturers' excise tax which had been included in the sales tax base. The overpaid tax was in excess of $10,000,000; however, each customer was owed only a very small amount.[7] Only a retailer could apply for a refund, which was required to be paid over to the customer. Accordingly, a retailer had no particular incentive to request the refund. Sullivan J, with whom Wright CJ, Tobriner, Mosk and Burke JJ concurred, considered that:[8]

> 'the Board is very likely to become enriched at the expense of the customer to whom the amount of the excessive tax actually belongs.
> . . . The integrity of the sales tax requires not only that retailers not be unjustly enriched, but also that the state not be similarly unjustly enriched.'

The Court found that the customers could compel the retailers to make refund applications, and require the refunded sales tax to be paid into court.

I would accept so much of Learned Hand J's analysis in *123 East Fifty-Fourth Street* as leads to the conclusion that the restaurant owner was a constructive trustee of the amount of the tax received from its patrons if the owner charged the separate amount of the tax to its patrons. The tax so received was received by the owner as a fiduciary on the footing that it would apply the money in payment of the tax. If that purpose failed or could not be effected because the tax was not payable then the owner held the moneys for the benefit of the patrons who paid the moneys. The same result would ensue if the owner recovered payments from the revenue authority made as and for tax which was not payable. And, in my view, the patrons who paid the tax to the owner would have a right of recovery, as Learned Hand J makes clear, against the revenue authority so long as it retained the payments which it was not entitled to retain.

But does all this require the further conclusion that in the circumstances predicated by Learned Hand J—the addition of the tax as a separate item to the bills—the restaurant owner could not recover? I would answer the question in the negative on the footing that the restaurant owner had a legal title to the money immediately before it was paid to the revenue authority. In that respect, the money belonged to the plaintiff even though, if it recovered the money, it would hold as trustee for the patrons. But, in such a case, the plaintiff should be required to satisfy the court, by the giving of an undertaking or other means, that it will distribute the moneys to the patrons from whom they were collected, thereby recognising their beneficial ownership of those moneys.

If, however, the plaintiff did not become the constructive trustee of the moneys by separately charging them as tax to the patrons, I do not see why the plaintiff's claim should be defeated simply because the plaintiff has recouped the outgoing from others. As between the plaintiff and the defendant, the plaintiff having paid away *its* money by mistake in circumstances in which the defendant has no title to retain the moneys, the plaintiff has the superior claim. The plaintiff's inability to distribute the proceeds to those who recoup the plaintiff was, in my view, an immaterial consideration, as Windeyer J suggested it was in *Mason v New South Wales*. There was in that case the additional element of an unlawful demand but the absence of that element does not mean that, in the situation under consideration, unjust enrichment was otherwise than at the plaintiff's expense.

In the present case, that reasoning leads me to the conclusion that the Commissioner would have no defence to a restitutionary claim by Royal to recover the mistaken payments of duty. Even if it had

---

6 (1974) 527 P 2d 1153.

7 For example, the plaintiff, who had purchased a Rolls Royce, was owed $65.72.

8 (1974) 527 P 2d, at 1160–1.

been established that Royal charged the tax as a separate item to its policy holders so that it was a constructive trustee of the moneys representing that separate charge when it made the payments to the Commissioner, it would have been entitled to recover from the Commissioner, provided that it satisfied the court that it will account to its policy holders. The Courts below, unlike Learned Hand J in *123 East Fifty-Fourth Street*, did not draw an inference that the tax was charged as a separate item to the policy holders. And, in any event, it has not been suggested that the Court should draw such an inference.

It then follows, in the light of my earlier conclusion that the discretion under s. 111 is to be exercised in accordance with the principles of the law of restitution, that the discretion was exercised erroneously. On the basis on which the case was fought in the courts below, . . . Royal was entitled to recover the overpayments in conformity with the law of restitution.

Brennan J (with whom **Toohey** and **McHugh JJ** agreed) and **Dawson J** both delivered concurring judgments.

NOTES AND QUESTIONS

1. In his concurring judgment, Brennan J said that 'it may be that, if Royal recovers the overpayments it made, the policy holders will be entitled themselves to claim a refund from Royal . . . of so much of the overpayments made by Royal to the Commissioner as represents the amount paid to Royal by the policy holder'. If the policy-holders have such a claim what is the unjust factor upon which they would rely?

2. In *Roxborough v Rothmans of Pall Mall Ltd* (2001) 208 CLR 516 (above, 252) the High Court of Australia (Kirby J dissenting) approved the result in *Royal Insurance* and rejected the common law defence of passing on. Gleeson CJ, Gaudron and Hayne JJ said that there was no reason to depart from the decision in *Royal Insurance* 'and every reason in principle to support it'. Kirby J, in dissent, argued as follows:

   > as to the law of restitution outside the context of public law, Mason CJ noted that an accurate determination of the effects of an attempt to pass on an expense to others could be 'a very complex undertaking'.[1] Sometimes a taxpayer will indeed have been able to effect a transmission of its statutory obligation to consumers. As Professor Birks has pointed out, its capacity to do so will depend upon many factors, including the 'elasticity of demand' for its product.[2] This too is a consideration addressed in recent United States authority and in academic commentary on the application of the law of restitution in this context.[3]
   >
   > It can therefore safely be said that, in Australia, no general legal 'defence' to recovery of a tax found to have been unlawful is established merely by proof that the taxpayer has 'passed on' the tax in question to unknown and unidentifiable consumers. There are special reasons, in proceedings for recovery from a State authority, as to why such a 'defence' may not apply. In every case the suggested 'passing on', so far as it is said to be relevant, should be subjected to factual analysis. However, where, as in the present case, the demand for recovery is addressed not to a government or government party but to a private corporation the 'important constitutional value'[4] of upholding recovery of the unlawful tax from the State is absent. In such a case, in my view, Australian law (as in the law of the United States, Canada and the European Union) is free to, and does, take into account the fact (if it be established) that the plaintiff taxpayer, seeking recovery, has already passed on the tax in question to third party consumers and has not done, or will not do, anything to reimburse those consumers but instead seeks only to make a private gain

---

1 (1994) 182 CLR 51, 71.

2 Birks, *Restitution—The Future*, (1992) at 126.

3 e.g. Bryan, 'Mistaken Payments and the Law of Unjust Enrichment: *David Securities Pty. Ltd v Commonwealth Bank of Australia*', (1993) 15 *Sydney Law Review* 461 at 471; cf. Rose, 'Passing On', in Birks (ed.), *Laundering and Tracing*, (1995) 261 at 284; see *Royal Insurance* (1994) 182 CLR 51 at 73 *per* Mason CJ.

4 *Royal Insurance* (1994) 182 CLR 51, 69.

for itself. In such a case the fact of 'passing on' is certainly relevant. In a given case, it may mean that the taxpayer has, in fact, suffered no loss and is entitled to no legal recovery.

Do you think that the decision in *Royal Insurance* was intended to be confined to recovery from the government as Kirby J suggests? The other point made by Kirby J relates to the relevance of the claimant's 'loss'. As observed above (878, note 2) this raises the issue of whether 'at the expense of' requires that the claimant suffer a loss.

7. ILLEGALITY

We have already noted in Chapter 10 the difficulties involved in classifying the cases in which it is sought to recover benefits which have been conferred in the performance of an illegal contract. The view which we took was that, in many cases, the illegality does not act as a ground of restitution, but that it operates as a defence to a restitutionary claim brought on one of the standard grounds, such as mistake, duress, total failure of consideration, etc. It is at this point that this claim is put to the test. In the cases which follow, is the ground of restitution the fact that the parties were not *in pari delicto* or is it one of the abovementioned unjust factors?

(1) MISTAKE

• *Oom v Bruce* (1810) 12 East 225, Court of King's Bench

The claimants, acting as agents of a Russian subject, entered into a contract of insurance with the defendants in connection with the transportation of goods by ship from St Petersburg to London. The contract was entered into the day after hostilities broke out between Russia and Great Britain (although this fact was unknown to the claimants), and so the contract was void and unenforceable. The vessel was seized by the Russian authorities. The Russian assured recovered his goods upon payment of a certain sum, and in the present action the claimants sought to recover the premium which they had paid to the defendants. It was held that the claimants were entitled to recover the premium so paid.

Lord Ellenborough CJ: [The assured cannot recover back the premium] if the party making the insurance know it to be illegal at the time: but here the plaintiffs had no knowledge of the commencement of hostilities by Russia, when they effected this insurance; and, therefore, no fault is imputable to them for entering into the contract; and there is no reason why they should not recover back the premiums which they have paid for an insurance from which, without any fault imputable to themselves, they could never have derived any benefit. . . .

Le Blanc J delivered a concurring judgment. **Grose** and **Bayley JJ** concurred.

NOTES AND QUESTIONS

1. It is unclear from the judgments whether or not the defendants were also mistaken. What is the relevance, if any, of the state of mind of the defendant? Goff and Jones, 618 cite the case as an example of a situation in which the parties were not *in pari delicto*. But can it be said that the parties were not *in pari delicto* if the defendants shared the claimants' mistake?

2. The mistake must have the effect of concealing the illegality from the claimant. Where the claimant is mistaken, but the effect of the mistake is not to hide the illegality from the claimant, then the illegality is likely to provide the defendant with a defence to the claimant's

restitutionary claim (see, for example, *Morgan v Ashcroft*, above, 150, where, although the claimant bookmaker mistakenly overpaid the defendant, the mistake did not mask from the claimant the unenforceable nature of the wagering contract).

3. The leading case involving illegality and mistake of law is *Kiriri Cotton Co. v Dewani* [1960] AC 192. Mr Dewani made an illegal 'key money' payment to his landlord, the Kiriri Cotton Co. Neither party knew that the payment was illegal. The Privy Council held that the payment could be recovered. One difficulty was the mistake of law bar which still existed in 1960. Lord Denning acknowledged that mistake of law would not 'by itself' allow recovery but said that (at 204) 'If there is something more in addition to a mistake of law—if there is something in the defendant's conduct which shows that, of the two of them, he is the one primarily responsible for the mistake—then it may be recovered back.' The 'something more' in that case was that the legislation was enacted for the protection of tenants such as Mr Dewani.

4. Birks approached the question of illegality in a different way. In the following extract, he argued that the same approach should underlie every case in which illegality is considered as a defence: does allowing the defence stultify the purpose underlying the illegality?

• P Birks, *Unjust Enrichment* (2nd edn, 2005), 247–8

LEVER AND SAFETY-NET

..., if the enrichee turns out to have a good defence, his victory is rather to be attributed to the danger of stultifying the law's refusal to enforce an illegal contract made between the parties. In this context the risk of such stultification is endemic in allowing an action in unjust enrichment. The same risk attaches to allowing any other non-contractual action, as, for example, conversion. All non-contractual actions, and especially actions in unjust enrichment, routinely provide a lever to compel performance and a safety-net in case that indirect compulsion fails. Suppose *C* makes a charitable donation to *D* and in return *D* undertakes to secure an honour for him, and then no honour is forthcoming.[1] Or, again, suppose that *C* deposits a share certificate with *D* as security for a foreign currency loan, in breach of exchange control legislation, and no loan is made.[2] In such cases the very availability to *C* of an action to recover that which he transferred will both reduce the risks of the illegal transaction and provide a threat which will indirectly compel performance.

The question in any one case must be whether the danger inherent in the lever and the safety-net should prevail, with the result that the action will be denied. Stultification is contradiction without a reason, here contradiction without reason of the law's refusal to enforce the contract. In the particular case there may on closer inspection be no contradiction, or there may be a reason for allowing the non-contractual action which weighs heavier than the fear of the lever and the safety-net. If the contradiction is real and there is no good reason to override it, the defendant will win. He himself may be very unattractive. All the same, in order to save the law being made a fool of, he has to be allowed his defence. That is the spirit in which we should understand the second maxim recurrent in this field: *in pari delicto potior est conditio defendentis* (when the parties are as bad as each other, the defendant has the stronger position). There is no doubt that the trend of the modern law has been to try to avoid arriving at the point at which that maxim has to be applied, but the ride has been very bumpy and the case law is in a mess.

---

1 *Parkinson v College of Ambulance* [1925] 2 KB 1.
2 *Bigos v Bousted* [1951] 1 All ER 92.

(2) DURESS AND EXPLOITATION OF WEAKNESS

- **Smith v Bromley** (1760) 2 Doug 696n, Court of King's Bench

The claimant's brother committed an act of bankruptcy. The defendant, his chief creditor, refused to sign the certificate of discharge unless he was paid £40 and given a note for a further £20. The claimant paid over £40 to an agent of the defendant, who, in turn, paid it over to the defendant. The defendant signed the discharge and the claimant's brother was discharged. The claimant then brought an action to recover the £40 which she had paid to the defendant. The defendant maintained that she was not entitled to recover because, *inter alia*, she had paid the money aware of the nature of the transaction into which she was entering. The claimant's action succeeded.

Lord Mansfield: . . . It is argued, that, as the plaintiff founds her claim on an illegal act, she shall not have relief in a Court of Justice. But she did not apply to the defendant or his agent to sign the certificate on an improper or illegal consideration: but, as the defendant insulted upon it, she, in compassion to her brother, paid what he required. If the act is in itself immoral or a violation of the general laws of public policy, there, the party paying shall not have this action; for where both parties are equally criminal against such general laws, the rule is, potier est conditio defendentis. But there are other laws, which are calculated for the protection of the subject against oppression, extortion, deceit, &c. If such laws are violated, and the defendant takes advantage of the plaintiff's condition or situation, there the plaintiff shall recover, and it is astonishing that the reports do not distinguish between the violation of the one sort and the other. . . . [T]he present is the case of a transgression of a law made to prevent oppression, either on the bankrupt, or his family, and the plaintiff is in the case of a person oppressed, from whom money has been extorted, and advantage taken of her situation and concern for her brother. This does not depend on general reasoning only, but there are analogous cases; as that of *Astley v Reynolds* (B R M 5 Geo. 2, 2 Str. 915). There, the plaintiff having pawned some goods with the defendant for £20, he refused to deliver them up, unless the plaintiff would pay him £10. The plaintiff had tendered £4 which was more than the legal interest amounted to; but, finding that he could not otherwise get his goods back, he at last paid the whole demand, and brought an action for the surplus beyond legal interest, as money had and received to his use, and recovered. It is absurd to say, that any one transgresses a law made for his own advantage, willingly. . . . Upon the whole, I am persuaded it is necessary, for the better support and maintenance of the law, to allow this action; for no man will venture to take, if he knows he is liable to refund. Where there is no temptation to the contrary, men will always act right. . . .

- **Smith v Cuff** (1817) 6 M & S 169, Court of King's Bench

The defendant, one of the claimant's creditors, agreed to enter into a composition agreement with the claimant's other creditors only in return for being paid the balance of the debt which was owed to him. The claimant gave the defendant promissory notes for the balance of the debt and the defendant negotiated the notes to a third party who enforced payment against the claimant. The claimant successfully brought an action to recover the amount so paid from the defendant.

Lord Ellenborough CJ: This is not a case of par delictum: it is oppression on one side, and submission on the other: it never can be predicated as par delictum, when one holds the rod, and the other bows to it. There was an inequality of situation between these parties: one was creditor, the other debtor, who was driven to comply with the terms which the former chose to enforce. And is there any case where money having been obtained extorsively, and by oppression, and in fraud of the party's own act as it regards the other creditors, it has been held that it may not be recovered back? On the contrary, I believe it has been uniformly decided that an action lies.

Bayley J: The reason assigned in *Smith v Bromley* for that decision was, that the party who insisted on payment was acting with extortion and oppressively, and in the teeth of that which he had agreed to accept. And does not this reason apply to the present case? The conduct of the defendant here, is that of one taking undue advantage of the plaintiff's situation, and endeavouring to extort from him by oppression that which he stipulated not to demand.

Holroyd J delivered a concurring judgment.

NOTES AND QUESTIONS

1. Was there duress on the part of the defendant in either of the above two cases? Was the defendant in each case not entitled to demand that he be paid the sum which was owed to him?

2. An alternative way to analyse these cases is that the unjust factor is the exploitation of the claimant's weakness or vulnerability. The illegality is created for the protection of the class of vulnerable persons of whom the claimant is a member and is part of the claim for restitution of unjust enrichment based on exploitation of weakness.

(3) TOTAL FAILURE OF CONSIDERATION

- *Parkinson v College of Ambulance Ltd* [1925] 2 KB 1, King's Bench Division

The claimant paid £3,000 to the defendant charity, after the defendant's secretary, Harrison, had fraudulently represented to the claimant that he would be able to obtain a knighthood for the claimant if he made a large donation to the charity. When no knighthood was forthcoming after the payment was made, the claimant sought to recover the sum which he had paid. His claim for damages or for return of the money paid was dismissed.

Lush J [*after concluding that the contract was, indeed, contrary to public policy*]: The contract being against public policy, and being of the character that I have described, can the plaintiff still rely upon the fraud of Harrison and recover damages against him; and can he, as against the college, recover the 3000*l*. which the college has received through that fraud, as money had and received to his use? I am not prepared to hold—it is not necessary that I should decide the question—that in every case where a contract is against public policy, where one of the parties to it is defrauded by the other, he is prevented from recovering. It may be that whenever one party to a contract which is not improper in itself is unaware that it is illegal and is defrauded, the parties may not be in pari delicto. However that may be, I am of opinion that if the contract has any element of turpitude in it the parties are in pari delicto and no action for damages can be maintained by the party defrauded. It is not correct to say, as was contended before me, that it is only if the contract is of a criminal nature that the plaintiff is precluded from recovering. . . . It was also contended that fraud has the same effect as duress, and that it would be contrary to public policy to allow a party who has defrauded another to retain the fruits of his fraud. I cannot agree with that contention. The case of *Hughes v Liverpool Victoria Legal Friendly Society*,[1] which appears to support it, does not do so when the facts are considered. The fraud there was committed by an agent of the defendants who deceived the plaintiff into believing

---

1 [1916] 2 KB 482.

that an insurance could be properly effected and would be valid, although there was no insurable interest. The fraud there related to the validity of the contract. The agent of the insurance company, who knew that the contract was illegal, deceived the policy holder as to its validity. It was held that the parties were not in pari delicto, and that an action would lie to recover the premiums which the plaintiff had paid. The decision of the Court of Appeal in *Kettlewell v Refuge Assurance Co.*[2] is another illustration of the same principle. These cases are very different from the present case. In the present case the plaintiff knew that he was entering into an illegal and improper contract. He was not deceived as to the legality of the contract he was making. How then can he say that he is excused? How can he say that he has suffered a loss through being defrauded into making a contract which he knew he ought never to have made? The answer is that he ought not to have made it. Where he was deceived was that he thought he would make a profit, derive a benefit from his unlawful act. He cannot be heard to say that. He has himself to blame for the loss that he has incurred. It is no excuse to say that Harrison was more blame-worthy than he, which is all that he really can say. That being the position, the plaintiff is in this difficulty. He cannot recover damages either against Harrison or the college, because he is disclosing or setting up a contract which is unlawful, and which he had no right to make. For the same reason he cannot recover the 3000*l.* from the college as money had and received.

. . .

• Re Cavalier Insurance Co. Ltd [1989] 2 Lloyd's Rep 430, Chancery Division

Cavalier Insurance Co. Ltd underwrote extended warranty insurance policies and received premiums from the claimant policy-holders over a period of time. Cavalier was authorized under the Insurance Companies Act 1974 to carry on business in relation to certain classes of insurance, but it was held that this authorization did not extend to writing extended warranty insurance cover. It was further held that this lack of authorization rendered the policies so written unenforceable by the policy holders. But it was held that the policy-holders who had not submitted claims which had been satisfied by Cavalier were entitled to the return of the premiums which they had paid. However policy-holders who had submitted claims which were satisfied by Cavalier were not entitled to the return of their premiums.

Knox J: . . . I turn now to the last issue argued before me namely whether Mr Carey and others in his position can recover the premiums they paid on the basis that they were paid for a consideration which wholly failed. Mr Pickering made the following submissions on this aspect of the matter which I accept.

The assured had no knowledge or notice of any illegality nor were they personally involved in the commission of any offence or moral turpitude of any sort. If the contracts are not enforceable at all through illegality the assured received no benefit whatever from them. This needs some qualification with regard to those few cases where Cavalier did satisfy claims and I shall return to deal with that aspect later. In seeking a return of premiums the assured are in no sense seeking to enforce what Parliament has prohibited but rather to undo the prohibited transaction. Finally if an unauthorized insurer is permitted to keep the premiums he has taken in breach of the unilateral prohibition laid upon him he succeeds in doing rather better than that which Parliament has said he shall not do, namely carry on the relevant insurance business, because he not only receives and keeps the premium but does not have to underwrite the risk.

2 [1908] 1 KB 545.

In general the test applied to determine whether a plaintiff is prevented from recovering money or property paid or transferred pursuant to a transaction affected by illegality is to ask whether the plaintiff has to set up the illegal transaction to establish his cause of action for recovery. Thus in *Taylor v Chester* (1869) LR 4 QB 309 at 314 Mr Justice Mellor said:

> The true test for determining whether or not the plaintiff and the defendant were in pari delicto is by considering whether the plaintiff could make out his case otherwise than through the medium and by the aid of the illegal transaction to which he was himself a party.

If that was a universal limit to a plaintiff's right to recovery the insured here would fail because it would be necessary for them to plead the insurance contracts in order to establish their right to recovery of the premiums. There is however an exception to the general rule which applies where the parties are treated as not being in pari delicto so that the innocent can recover notwithstanding that the illegal transaction has to be pleaded to establish his cause of action. The relevant line of authority for present purposes is that dealing with statutory illegality where the statute in question was passed to protect one class of persons from the undesirable activities of another class. Thus it was said by Lord Mansfield in *Browning v Morris* (1778) 2 Cowp. 790 at 792:

> When contracts or transactions are prohibited by positive statutes, for the sake of protecting one set of men from another set of men: the one, from their situation and condition, being liable to be oppressed or imposed upon by the other: then the parties are not in pari delicto: and in furtherance of those statutes the person injured after the transaction is finished and completed may bring his action and defeat the contract.

The oppressor or imposers in that case were lottery office keepers. Ironically it emerged that the plaintiff himself was a lottery office keeper so that he failed and a non suit was entered but Lord Mansfield's statement of principle has often been applied. A modern illustration of the principle is *Kiriri Cotton Co. Ltd v Dewani* [1960] AC 192 where an illegal premium was held by the Privy Council to be recoverable because the duty of observing the law was placed on the shoulders of the landlord rather than the tenant, the two were therefore not in pari delicto and the money could be recovered back. Mr Leigh-Jones submitted that it was not enough to establish this exception to show that the statute in question was passed for the protection of the persons of this class but that there also had to be oppression or exploitation by one class of persons of another including the plaintiffs, and that there was no exploitation discernible in an extended warranty insurance contract. I do not accept that the doctrine is so narrow as this, nor do I accept that there is not a significant measure of exploitation in the activities of an unauthorised insurer who takes premiums and does not underwrite the risk. In a sense the transaction is even less advantageous than the eighteenth century lottery where there must have been some chance of winning. In my judgment the circumstances of this case where the statutory duty was laid exclusively on the shoulders of the insurer for the protection of insured persons and the insured had no reason to suspect that he was being asked to enter into a void contract amply justify treating the insured as not equally delictual as the insurer and therefore entitled to recover the premiums.

It was also submitted that *Green v Portsmouth Stadium* [1953] 2 QB 190 established a principle that for there to be a right of recovery of money paid in the course of a transaction made illegal by Parliament the statute must positively contemplate the bringing of a civil action to recover the money. Doubtless that is true where the statute in question was not passed to protect the class of persons of whom the plaintiff is one. In *Green v Portsmouth Stadium* it was held, not surprisingly, that the Betting and Lotteries Act, 1934, the Act in question, was not passed for the protection of book-makers. As *Kiriri Cotton Co. Ltd v Dewani, sup.*, shows where the Act is passed for the protection of a class of persons of whom the plaintiff is one it is not necessary for the Act in question to provide for recovery. It was in fact Lord Denning who as Lord Justice Denning gave the leading judgment in *Green v Portsmouth Stadium* and the opinion of the Privy Council in *Kiriri Cotton Co. Ltd v Dewani* and it seems to me plain that he did not intend to lay down a rule of universal application in the former case.

Accordingly I conclude that the insured are entitled to recover the premiums paid by them. There remain those who submitted claims which were satisfied by Cavalier. In my judgment it is not possible to say to those contracts that the consideration wholly failed and that does constitute a bar against recovery of the premiums.

I have deliberately refrained from expressing a view upon the validity of an alternative claim put forward by Mr Pickering that premiums could be recovered on the basis of a mistake of fact, that is to say that Cavalier had a relevant authorization. In the circumstances it is not necessary for me to decide that issue and I prefer to express no view upon it.

Another question upon which no decision is called for is whether the rule in *Ex parte James* [1874] LR 9 Ch App. 609 can have any application in the circumstances of this case. The argument that it could was confined to the situation that would have arisen had I held that Mr Carey and other assured persons under extended warranty policies could neither enforce contractual rights nor recover the premiums they had paid. In those circumstances it would have been at least possible that Cavalier's liabilities could all be met and a surplus would have been available for contributories. That problem does not arise on the view I have taken of the matter and here too I prefer to say nothing about it.

NOTES AND QUESTIONS

1. The claimant in *Parkinson* could establish that there had been a total failure of consideration but the illegal nature of the transaction prevented him from recovering that which he had paid. Lush J stated that it was no excuse for the claimant to say that the secretary was more blameworthy than he was. Why was this so?

2. What was the unjust factor in *Cavalier*? Was it (a) total failure of consideration; (b) mistake of fact; (c) mistake of law; or (d) the fact that the claimant was a member of a vulnerable class which the illegality was designed to protect (see above, 500–503)? If it was the latter, why were claimants whose claims had been satisfied by Cavalier not entitled to recover their premiums?

3. Was the wrong which the claimant had committed in *Parkinson* so heinous as to prevent a court from coming to his aid and enforcing rights which he otherwise would have enjoyed? Would the dignity of the court really have been offended by intervention on behalf of the claimant? In cases such as *St John Shipping Corporation v Joseph Rank Ltd* [1957] 1 QB 267 and *Shaw v Groom* [1970] 2 QB 504, the courts have adopted a more flexible approach to the enforcement of contracts which are tainted by illegality. Should the same approach be adopted in cases in which the claimant's claim is a restitutionary one? If so, how should such a flexible approach be applied on the facts of *Parkinson*? Alternatively, could it be said that a greater willingness to grant restitution would send the wrong message to the commercial community (see *Taylor v Bhail* [1996] CLC 377, especially the judgment of Sir Stephen Brown P).

4. In *Berg v Sadler and Moore* [1937] 2 KB 158, the claimant was placed on the stop list of the Tobacco Trade Association as a result of his breach of the Association's rules. He persuaded a friend of his, Rees, to order cigarettes in his own name but in reality for the claimant. The defendants accepted the order on the basis that the cigarettes were for Rees, but when they discovered that the cigarettes were in fact for the claimant they refused to supply the cigarettes or to return the purchase price. The claimant's action to recover the purchase money was dismissed on the ground that he could bring his claim only by disclosing the illegal nature of the transaction and that the court would not allow him to do.

• *Mohamed v Alaga & Co. (a firm)* [1999] 3 All ER 699, Court of Appeal

The claimant, Mr Mohamed, alleged that he had entered into an agreement with the defendant firm of solicitors by which the claimant would introduce Somali asylum seekers to the defendant and assist with translation and preparation of their cases. In return the solicitors promised half of the fees received from Legal Aid. Mr Mohamed claimed the solicitors had breached their agreement and brought claims for breach of contract and for a *quantum meruit* for the services he performed for the firm. On a trial of a preliminary issue, it was assumed that an agreement had been made and that Mr Mohamed was unaware that the agreement might be unenforceable under the Solicitors' Practice Rules 1990. The Court of Appeal held that the agreement was illegal and although the prohibition was only expressed to apply to solicitors, the policy behind the rule required that such contracts could not be enforced by a member of the public either. However, Mr Mohamed was entitled to pursue a claim for a *quantum meruit*.

Lord Bingham of Cornhill CJ: [*After stating the facts and dismissing the contractual claim, continued* . . .] Reference has already been made to the pleaded allegation in para. 8 of the statement of claim that the plaintiff carried out translations and interpretations, wrote letters and attended meetings. In para. 15 a claim in quasi contract was made for remuneration for those services, which also featured as the fourth head of claim at the end of the pleading as a quantum meruit claim for services rendered. It is further a matter of agreement between the parties that the plaintiff has been paid what the defendant says were fees for interpretation and translation. Mr McCombe accordingly claims that, even if the alleged agreement is discarded as illegal and unenforceable, and, without making any reference to that agreement at all, the plaintiff is entitled to be paid a reasonable sum for professional services rendered by him to the defendant on behalf of the defendant's clients, the surrounding circumstances being such as to show that such services were not rendered gratuitously.

Sir Godfray Le Quesne QC, representing the defendant, resisted that argument. It was, he submitted, only because of the unlawful fee-sharing agreement that the introductions were made by the plaintiff to the defendant at all. Accordingly, he suggested that the plaintiff was in effect seeking to recover part of the consideration payable under an illegal and unenforceable agreement.

That is, I think, a possible view of the case. But the preferable view in my judgment is that the plaintiff is not seeking to recover any part of the consideration payable under the unlawful contract, but simply a reasonable reward for professional services rendered. I accept that as an accurate description of what on this limited basis the plaintiff is, in truth, seeking. It is furthermore in my judgment relevant that the parties are not in a situation in which their blameworthiness is equal. The defendant is a solicitors' firm and bound by the rules. It should reasonably be assumed to know what the rules are and to comply with them. If, in truth, it made the agreement as alleged, then it would seem very probable that it acted in knowing disregard of professional rules binding upon it. By contrast the plaintiff, on the assumption made (which I have no difficulty in accepting), was ignorant that there was any reason why the defendant should not make the agreement which he says was made. In other commercial fields, after all, such agreements are common.

It appears to me that the present case is readily distinguishable from *Taylor v Bhail* [1996] CLC 377. In that case there was a criminal conspiracy to defraud an insurance company. The plaintiff was obliged to rely on the illegal contract to maintain his claim and both parties were equally culpable. These conditions are not satisfied in this case.

The judge and the defendant relied on the dictum of Lord Radcliffe already referred to in *Boissevain v Weil*. There may be some doubt whether that dictum is fully reconcilable with observations of the House of Lords in *Westdeutsche Landesbank Girozentrale v Islington London BC, Kleinwort Benson Ltd v Sandwell BC* [1996] 2 All ER 961 at 972, 992, 1000, 1017, 1018, [1996] AC 669 at 688, 710, 718, 736 and 738. In any event, however, there is a crucial distinction between a case in which a plaintiff is in effect suing on a contract of loan and a case in which the plaintiff is not suing on any contract but simply for the value of work done. On that limited basis I would for my part allow the appeal and reinstate the action to the extent of permitting the plaintiff to pursue a quantum meruit claim for reasonable remuneration for professional services rendered.

Robert Walker LJ: I also agree that this appeal should be allowed to the extent and for the reasons stated by Lord Bingham of Cornhill CJ. I add a few comments of my own on what Lord Radcliffe said in *Boissevain v Weil* [1950] 1 All ER 728 at 734–735, [1950] AC 327 at 341, in a passage cited and relied on by Lightman J. In that passage Lord Radcliffe gave two reasons why the claimant could not have obtained a restitutionary remedy, even if the point had been properly pleaded. The first was that the very act of borrowing was prohibited by the Defence (Finance) Regulations 1939, SR & O 1939/950, and was a criminal offence. Therefore, as Lord Radcliffe put it, 'the matter passes beyond the field in which the requirements of the individual conscience are the determining consideration.'

The other reason given by Lord Radcliffe was wider. Until recently it was generally thought that in every case where some statute or common law rule made a contract or supposed contract unenforceable or ineffective, the court would not grant a restitutionary remedy if to do so would have the substantial effect of enforcing the void or unenforceable contract. That principle (the rejection of what Lord Bingham CJ referred to as 'relabelling') depended on public policy but was by no means limited to cases of illegality. Lord Summer's observations in *Sinclair v Brougham* [1914] AC 398 at 452, cited by Lord Radcliffe in *Boissevain v Weil*, were directed to ultra vires borrowing by a building society.

In *Westdeutsche Landesbank Girozentrale v Islington London BC, Kleinwort Benson Ltd v Sandwell BC* [1996] 2 All ER 961, [1996] AC 669 the House of Lords has departed from *Sinclair v Brougham* on this point, as well as on the resulting trust point (see especially the speech of Lord Browne-Wilkinson [1996] 2 All ER 961 at 992, [1996] AC 669 at 710, and compare the observations of Lord Goff [1996] 2 All ER 961 at 972, [1996] AC 669 at 688; Lord Goff would have preferred to see *Sinclair v Brougham* simply wither away). Lord Radcliffe may have far-sightedly anticipated this development because he added, after the citation from Lord Summer's speech: 'His principle is surely right whether the action for money had and received does or does not depend on an imputed promise to pay.' (See [1950] 1 All ER 728 at 735, [1950] AC 327 at 341.)

In my view nothing in the *Westdeutsche* case casts any doubt on the correctness of the result in *Boissevain v Weil*, which was concerned with a credit transaction expressly prohibited, and indeed made a criminal offence, by regulations with statutory force. It was not a case in which either party to the transaction contended that he or she had a lower level of culpability than the other. The same is true of the decision in this court in *Taylor v Bhail* [1996] CLC 377, the case of the headmaster and the builder who conspired together to concoct a fraudulent insurance claim.

In the present case, by contrast, it was common ground that the judge should approach the summons under RSC Ord 14A on the footing that the claimant was innocent in the sense of being unaware of the prohibition on fee-sharing contained in r 7 of the Solicitors' Practice Rules 1990. Rule 7 was not of course made for the purpose of protecting persons in the position of the claimant. It was made for the benefit and the protection of the general public, as the judge clearly explained in a passage already read by Lord Bingham. Nevertheless, the claimant may be able to establish at trial that he was not culpable, or was significantly less culpable than the defendant solicitors, and that they should not be unjustly enriched as the result of unremunerated services such as interpreting and translating actually performed by the claimant for the solicitors' clients. Remuneration which the claimant received on that basis would be a proper disbursement and would not, it seems to me, involve either a payment for introductions or the sharing of part of the solicitors' own profit costs.

Otton LJ agreed with **Lord Bingham** of **Cornhill CJ**

NOTES AND QUESTIONS

1. This case was distinguished in *Awwad v Geraghty & Co. (a firm)* [2000] 1 All ER 608 in which the claimant was a solicitor.

2. A helpful note on this case is N Enonchong, 'Restitution following Illegal Fee-Sharing Agreement with Solicitor' [2000] *RLR* 241. Enonchong observes that there are four strands to the reasoning in the Court of Appeal as to why the restitutionary claim was allowed to proceed: (1) the claim was not one for part of the consideration under the illegal contract; (2) the claimant did not need to rely upon the illegal contract; (3) the claimant was less blameworthy; (4) the decision in *Boissevain v Weill* (above, 891) has been undermined by the decision of the House of Lords in *Westdeutsche* (above, 368).

3. Although not affecting the principle in *Mohamed v Alaga*, the Access to Justice Act 1999 has abolished the prohibition, in the Solicitors' Practice Rules, against contingency fees.

4. The judgments referred to the decision in *Taylor v Bhail* [1996] CLC 377. In that decision the defendant headmaster conspired with a builder to inflate the price for repairing storm damage so that the extra sum could be claimed from the insurer. The Court of Appeal held that the effect of the illegality was that that the builder could not claim from the headmaster for the value of his work (although, fortuitously, the builder had already received £7,400). The decision was distinguished on the basis that the parties were equally culpable. Is this basis for distinction consistent with the decision of Lush J in *Parkinson* (above, 886)?

(4) TITLE CLAIMS

• *Bowmakers Ltd v Barnet Instruments Ltd* [1945] 1 KB 65, Court of Appeal

The claimants entered into three hire-purchase transactions with the defendants. The subject-matter of each transaction was machine-tools. All three agreements were illegal because they had not complied with statutory requirements. The defendants paid for some of the goods and then sold the goods which were the subject-matter of the first and third transactions, while they refused to deliver up on demand the goods which were the subject-matter of the second transaction. The claimants brought an action in conversion against the defendants and their claim succeeded in relation to all three transactions.

Du Parcq LJ (delivered the judgment of the court): . . . The question, then, is whether in the circumstances the plaintiffs are without a remedy. So far as their claim in conversation in concerned, they are not relying on the hiring agreements at all. On the contrary, they are willing to admit for this purpose that they cannot rely on them. They simply say that the machines were their property, and this, we think, cannot be denied. We understood Mr Gallop to concede that the property had passed from Smith to the plaintiffs, and still remained in the plaintiffs at the date of the conversion. At any rate, we have no doubt that this is the legal result of the transaction and we find support for this view in the dicta of Parke B in *Scarfe v Morgan*.[1]

Why then should not the plaintiffs have what is their own? No question of the defendants' rights arises. They do not, and cannot, pretend to have had any legal right to possession of the goods at the date of the conversion. Their counsel has to rely, not on any alleged right of theirs, but on the requirements of public policy. He was entitled, and bound, to do so, although, as Lord Mansfield long ago observed, 'The objection, that a contract is immoral or illegal as between plaintiff and defendant, sounds at all times very ill in the mouth of the defendant.' 'No court,' Lord Mansfield added, 'will lend its aid to a man who founds his cause of action upon an immoral or an illegal act:' *Holman v Johnson*.[2]

---

1 (1838) 4 M & W 270, 281.   2 (1775) 1 Cowp 341, 343.

This principle, long firmly established, has probably even been extended since Lord Mansfield's day. Mr Gallop is, we think, right in his submission that, if the sale by Smith to the plaintiffs was illegal, then the first and second hiring agreements were tainted with the illegality, since they were brought into being to make that illegal sale possible, but, as we have said, the plaintiffs are not now relying on these agreements or on the third hiring agreement. Prima facie, a man is entitled to his own property, and it is not a general principle of our law (as was suggested) that when one man's goods have got into another's possession in consequence of some unlawful dealings between them, the true owner can never be allowed to recover those goods by an action. The necessity of such a principle to the interests and advancement of public policy is certainly not obvious. The suggestion that it exists is not, in our opinion, supported by authority. It would, indeed, be astonishing if (to take one instance) a person in the position of the defendant in *Pearce v Brooks*,[3] supposing that she had converted the plaintiff's brougham to her own use, were to be permitted, in the supposed interests of public policy, to keep it or the proceeds of its sale for her own benefit. The principle which is, in truth, followed by the courts is that stated by Lord Mansfield, that no claim founded on an illegal contract will be enforced, and for this purpose the words 'illegal contract must now be understood in the wide sense which we have already indicated and no technical meaning must be ascribed to the words 'founded on an illegal contract.' The form of the pleadings is by no means conclusive. More modern illustrations of the principle on which the courts act are *Scott v Brown, Doering, McNab & Co.*[4] and *Alexander v Rayson*,[5] but as Lindley LJ said in the former of the cases just cited:[6] 'Any rights which [a plaintiff] may have irrespective of his illegal contract will, of course, be recognized and enforced.'

In our opinion, a man's right to possess his own chattels will as a general rule be enforced against one who, without any claim of right, is detaining them, or has converted them to his own use, even though it may appear either from the pleadings, or in the course of the trial, that the chattels in question came into the defendant's possession by reason of an illegal contract between himself and the plaintiff, provided that the plaintiff does not seek, and is not forced, either to found his claim on the illegal contract or to plead its illegality in order to support his claim.

Mr Gallop sought to derive assistance from the decision of the Court of Queen's Bench in *Taylor v Chester*.[7] The decision there was, however, entirely consonant with the view which we have expressed. It differed from the present case in one essential respect, since in that case the defendant had prima facie a right to possession of the half-note which the plaintiff claimed. She was holding it as a pledge to secure the payment of money which remained due. The plaintiff could only defeat her plea by showing that the money due had been lent for an immoral purpose, and this could not avail him since he was in pari delicto with her. The judgment of the court, delivered by Mellor J, makes it plain that this was the ratio of the decision. 'The plaintiff,' said Mellor J,[8] 'no doubt, was the owner of the note, but he pledged it by way of security for the price of meat and drink provided for, and money advanced to, him by the defendant. Had the case rested there, and no pleading raised the question of illegality, a valid pledge would have been created, and a special property conferred upon the defendant in the half-note, and the plaintiff could only have recovered by showing payment or a tender of the amount due. In order to get rid of the defence arising from the plea, which set up an existing pledge of the half-note, the plaintiff had recourse to the special replication, in which he was obliged to set forth the immoral and illegal character of the contract upon which the half-note had been deposited. It was, therefore, impossible for him to recover except through the medium and by the aid of an illegal transaction to which he was himself a party. Under such circumstances, the maxim "in pari delicto potior est conditio possidentis" clearly applies, and is decisive of the case.' The Latin maxim which Mellor J cited must not be understood as meaning that where a transaction is vitiated

---

3 (1866) LR 1 Ex 213.   4 [1892] 2 QB 724.   5 [1936] 1 KB 169.   6 [1892] 2 QB 729.
7 (1869) LR 4 QB 309.   8 *Ibid.* 314.

by illegality the person left in possession of goods after its completion is always and of necessity entitled to keep them. Its true meaning is that, where the circumstances are such that the court will refuse to assist either party, the consequence must, in fact, follow that the party in possession will not be disturbed. As Lord Mansfield said in the case already cited, the defendant then obtains an advantage 'contrary to the real justice,' and, so to say, by accident.'

It must not be supposed that the general rule which we have stated is subject to no exception. Indeed, there is one obvious exception, namely, that class of cases in which the goods claimed are of such a kind that it is unlawful to deal in them at all, as for example, obscene books. No doubt, there are others, but it is unnecessary, and would we think be unwise, to seek to name them all or to forecast the decisions which would be given in a variety of circumstances which may hereafter arise. We are satisfied that no rule of law, and no considerations of public policy, compel the court to dismiss the plaintiffs' claim in the case before us, and to do so would be, in our opinion, a manifest injustice. The appeal will be dismissed, with costs.

NOTES AND QUESTIONS

1. Does this case properly fall within the law of unjust enrichment at all? All that the claimant is doing is asserting his own pre-existing property rights. See above, 704–5 for the distinction between pure proprietary claims and restitutionary proprietary claims. However, it is included here because it is an important case in the development of the 'pleading test' for illegality in title claims.

2. Although the Court of Appeal emphasized that the claimant was not 'forced to found his claim on the illegal contract or to plead its illegality', this sits ill with the court's statement that the words 'founded on an illegal contract' are not to be given a technical meaning and that 'the form of the pleading is by no means conclusive'.

3. Can it be said that the claimants were able to establish title to the goods without relying on the illegal contract? This problem is particularly evident in relation to the second hire-purchase transaction, where the claimants must have relied on the transaction for the purpose of showing that they were entitled to terminate future performance of the contract on account of the breach which had occurred. Indeed, N Enonchong has argued ('Title Claims and Illegal Transactions' (1995) 111 *LQR* 135) that it was only by relying on the contract that the claimant could establish that the possessory title which was transferred to the defendants had expired. He suggests (at 136) that the true principle is one which 'allows a party to recover property or money transferred under an illegal contract if he can establish his right or title to it *by relying on the contract or its illegality*' (emphasis in the original). Is this a better explanation for *Bowmakers*? What is its underlying rationale?

4. Why does illegality not affect property rights in the same way as contractual rights?

5. Coote has stated ('Another Look at Bowmakers v Barnet Instruments' (1972) 35 *MLR* 38, 51) that 'the real difficulty lies in the arbitrary, all-or-nothing character of the common law governing illegal contracts'. Do you agree?

6. Hamson ('Illegal Contracts and Limited Interests' [1949] *CLJ* 249, 259) states that the Court of Appeal 'appears to come very close, under cover of an action in tort, to enforcing the terms of the illegal bailment against the defendants' Is this correct and, if so, does it present a problem?

• *Tinsley v Milligan* [1994] 1 AC 340, House of Lords

The claimant and defendant jointly purchased a house which was registered in the sole name of the claimant in order to enable the defendant, with the knowledge of the claimant, to make false benefit claims from the Department of Social Security. The defendant later repented of her fraud and informed the DSS of what she had done. The parties subsequently quarrelled and the claimant moved out. She then brought an action seeking possession of the house, asserting that she was the sole owner. The defendant replied that she had an equitable interest in the house by virtue of her contributions to the purchase price. The claimant argued that the defendant was not entitled to assert any such equitable interest because of her participation in the fraud. By a majority (Lord Keith and Lord Goff dissenting), it was held that the defendant was entitled to succeed in her counterclaim because she did not have to rely on the illegality to establish her equitable interest.

Lord Goff (dissenting): . . . The reason why the court of equity will not assist the claimant to recover his property or to assert his interest in it has been variously stated. It is sometimes said that it is because he has not come to equity with clean hands. This was the reason given by the Lord Chief Baron Sir William Alexander in *Groves v Groves*, 3 Y & J 163, 174 and by Salmon LJ (with whom Cross LJ agreed) in *Tinker v Tinker* [1970] P 136, 143. Sometimes it is said that the claimant cannot be heard or allowed to assert his claim to an equitable interest, as in *Curtis v Perry*, 6 Ves. 739, 746, *per* Lord Eldon LC; *Childers v Childers* (1857) 3 K & J 310, 315, *per* Page Wood V-C and *Cantor v Cox*, 239 EG 121, 122, *per* Plowman V-C. But this is, as I see it, another way of saying that the claimant must fail because he has not come to the court with clean hands. It follows that in these cases the requirements necessary to give rise to an equitable interest are present; it is simply that the claimant is precluded from asserting them. This explains why, in cases where the unlawful purpose has not been carried into effect, the court is able to hold that, despite the illegality, there is an equitable interest to which the claimant is entitled.

Another conclusion follows from the identification of the basis upon which equity refuses its assistance in these cases. This is that the circumstances in which the court refuses to assist the claimant in asserting his equitable interest are not limited to cases in which there is a presumption of advancement in favour of the transferee. If that was the case, the principle could be said to be limited to those cases in which the transferor has to rely upon the illegal transaction in order to rebut the presumption; in other words the cases could be said to fall within what is sometimes called the *Bowmakers* rule, under which a claimant's claim is unenforceable when he has either to found his claim on an illegal transaction, or to plead its illegality in order to support his claim: *Bowmakers Ltd v Barnet Instruments Ltd* [1945] KB 65. Of course, in a number of cases of this kind, especially in modern times, the presumption of advancement does apply, because many cases are concerned with a man hiding away his assets in order to escape his creditors or for some other similar purpose, by transferring them to his wife or to one of his children. But there are cases in which the principle has been applied, or has been recognised, where there was no presumption of advancement. Examples are *Curtis v Perry*, 6 Ves. 739; *Ex parte Yallop*, 15 Ves. 60; *Roberts v Roberts*, Dan. 143; *Groves v Groves*, 3 Y & J 163; *Haigh v Kaye*, LR 7 Ch.App. 469; *In re Great Berlin Steamboat Co.*, 26 ChD 616 and *Cantor v Cox*, 239 EG 121. Of course, where the presumption of advancement does apply, and the illegality is not established from another source, for example by the defendant, the claimant will be in the particular difficulty that, in order to rebut the presumption, he will have to rely upon the underlying transaction and so will of necessity have to disclose his own illegality. This is what happened in *Palaniappa Chettiar v Arunasalam Chettiar* [1962] AC 294 where the property in question had been transferred by the claimant to his son who, having fallen ill, took no part in the hearing and so himself gave no evidence of the illegality; even so, the father's claim failed because he was unable to rebut the presumption of advancement without relying upon the illegal transaction. But the case does not decide that the principle only applies where it is necessary to rebut the presumption of advancement; and, as I have already stated, there are many cases in which the principle has been recognised or applied where there was no such presumption. Furthermore, if for example the defendant proves that the property was transferred to him for a fraudulent or illegal purpose, a court of equity will refuse to assist the claimant when asserting his interest in it, even though the claimant's case can be, and was, advanced, without reference to the underlying legal purpose, for example on the simple basis that the transfer of the property to the defendant was without consideration. This conclusion follows inevitably from the nature of the principle, and the grounds upon which equity refuses its assistance; it is at least implicit in a number of cases, such as *Platamone v Staple*, Coop. 250, *Groves v Groves*, 3 Y & J 163; and *Haigh v Kaye*, LR 7 Ch.App. 469. It follows that the so-called *Bowmakers* rule [1945] KB 65 does not apply in cases concerned with the principle under discussion, because once it comes to the attention of a court of equity that the claimant has not come to the court with clean hands, the court will refuse to assist the claimant, even though the claimant can prima facie establish his claim without recourse to the underlying fraudulent or illegal purpose. . . .

It is against the background of these established principles that I turn to consider the judgments of the majority of the Court of Appeal. As I have recorded, Nicholls LJ in particular invoked a line of recent cases, largely developed in the Court of Appeal, from which he deduced the proposition that, in cases of illegality, the underlying principle is the so-called public conscience test, under which the court must weigh, or balance, the adverse consequences of respectively granting or refusing relief. This is little different, if at all, from stating that the court has a discretion whether to grant or refuse relief. It is very difficult to reconcile such a test with the principle of policy stated by Lord Mansfield CJ in *Holman v Johnson*, 1 Cowp. 341, 343, or with the established principles to which I have referred. [*He considered the line of recent cases relied on by Nicholls LJ and continued:*] It is sufficient for present purposes to say, with the greatest respect, that to apply the public conscience test as qualifying the principle established for nearly 200 years as applicable in cases such as the present is, for reasons I have already stated, inconsistent with numerous authorities binding on the Court of Appeal. . . .

I have already expressed my respectful disagreement with the view expressed by my noble and learned friend, Lord Browne-Wilkinson, that the law has already developed at least in the direction of the conclusion which he favours. I have nevertheless considered whether your Lordships' House should in the present case develop the law, with a view to qualifying the principle by the application to it of the *Bowmakers* rule. I can see the temptation of doing so, if one focuses only on the facts of the present case in which it seems particularly harsh not to assist the respondent to establish her equitable interest in the house where not only was the appellant implicated in precisely the same fraud on the Department of Social Security, but the fraud in question can be regarded as relatively minor and indeed all too prevalent, and the respondent has readily confessed her wrongdoing to the Department and has made amends to them. Furthermore it is probable that, if the appeal should be allowed, the effect will be that she will lose all her capital. But it is not to be forgotten that other cases in this category will not evoke the same sympathy on the part of the court. There may be cases in which the fraud is far more serious than that in the present case, and is uncovered not as a result of a confession but only after a lengthy police investigation and a prolonged criminal trial. Again there may be cases in which a group of terrorists, or armed robbers, secure a base for their criminal activities by buying a house in the name of a third party not directly implicated in those activities. In cases such as these there will almost certainly be no presumption of advancement. Is it really to be said that criminals such as these, or their personal representatives, are entitled to invoke the assistance of a court of equity in order to establish an equitable interest in property? It may be said that these are extreme cases; but I find it difficult to see how, in this context at least, it is possible to distinguish between degrees of iniquity. At all events, I cannot think that the harsh consequences which will arise from the application of the established principle in a case such as the present provide a satisfactory basis for developing the law in a manner which will open the door to far more unmeritorious cases, especially as the proposed development in the law appears to me to be contrary to the established principle underlying the authorities.

Finally, I wish to revert to the public conscience test favoured by Nicholls LJ in the Court of Appeal. Despite the fact that I have concluded that on the authorities it was not open to the Court of Appeal to apply the public conscience test to a case such as the present, I have considered whether it is open to your Lordships' House to do so and, if so, whether it would be desirable to take this course. Among the authorities cited to your Lordships, there was no decision of this House; technically, therefore, it may be said that this House is free to depart from the line of authority to which I have referred. But the fact remains that the principle invoked by the appellant has been consistently applied for about two centuries. Furthermore the adoption of the public conscience test, as stated by Nicholls LJ, would constitute a revolution in this branch of the law, under which what is in effect a discretion would become vested in the court to deal with the matter by the process of a balancing operation, in place of a system of rules, ultimately derived from the principle of public policy enunciated by Lord Mansfield CJ in *Holman v Johnson*, 1 Cowp. 341, which lies at the root of the law relating to claims which are, in one way or another, tainted by illegality. Furthermore, the principle of public policy so stated by Lord Mansfield cannot be disregarded as having no basis in principle. In his dissenting judgment in the present case Ralph Gibson LJ pointed out [1992] Ch 310, 334:

> 'In so far as the basis of the ex turpi causa defence, as founded on public policy, is directed at deterrence it seems to me that the force of the deterrent effect is in the existence of the known rule and in its stern application. Lawyers have long known of the rule and must have advised many people of its existence. It does not stop people making arrangements to defraud creditors, or the revenue, or the D.S.S. Such arrangements as are under consideration in this case are usually made between married couples as in *Tinker v Tinker*, or between unmarried lovers as in this case or in *Cantor v Cox*, 239 E.G. 121. If they do not fall out, no one will know. If they do fall out, one side may reveal the fraud. It is an ugly situation when that is done. I think that the law has upheld the principle on the simple ground that, ugly though its working may be, it is better than permitting the fraudulent an avenue of escape if the fraud is revealed.'

I recognise, of course, the hardship which the application of the present law imposes upon the respondent in this case; and I do not disguise my own unhappiness at the result But, bearing in mind the passage from the judgment of Ralph Gibson LJ which I have just quoted, I have to say that it is by no means self-evident that the public conscience text is preferable to the pressent strict rules. Certainly, I do not feel able to say that it would be appropriate for your Lordships House, in the face of a long line of unbroken authority stretching back over 200 years, now by judicial decision to replace the principles established in those authorities by a wholly different discretionary system.

In saying this, I have well in mind the reform introduced in New Zealand by the New Zealand Illegal Contracts Act 1970, which in section 6 provides that 'every illegal contract shall be of no effect and no person shall become entitled to any property under a disposition made by or pursuant to any such contract . . .' and in section 7 confers on the court the power to grant relief:

> 'by way of restitution, compensation, variation of the contract, validation of the contract in whole or part or for any particular purpose, or otherwise howsoever as the court in its discretion thinks just.'

These provisions of the Act demonstrate how sweeping a reform was considered necessary by the New Zealand legislature in order to substitute a system of discretionary relief for the present system of rules founded upon the in pari delicto principle; and even then the Act is restricted to cases concerned with illegal contracts. Your Lordships have no means of ascertaining how successful the Act has proved to be in practice; or whether, for example, it is considered that the scope of the Act should be extended to embrace other types of illegality. In truth, everything points to the conclusion that, if there is to be a reform aimed at substituting a system of discretionary relief for the present rules, the reform is one which should only be instituted by the legislature, after a full inquiry into the matter by the Law Commission, such inquiry to embrace not only the perceived advantages and disadvantages of the present law, but also the likely advantages and disadvantages of a system of discretionary relief, no doubt with particular reference to the New Zealand experience. The real criticism of the present rules is not that they are unprincipled, but rather that they are indiscriminate in their effect, and are capable therefore of producing injustice. It is this effect which no doubt prompted the reform of the law in New Zealand, embodied in the Act of 1970; and it prompts me to say that, speaking for myself, I would welcome an investigation by the Law Commission, if this is considered desirable and practicable by the authorities concerned; and that I would be more than happy if a new system could be evolved which was both satisfactory in its effect and capable of avoiding the kind of result which flows from the established rules of law in cases such as the present.

For these reasons, which are substantially the same as those expressed by Ralph Gibson LJ in his dissenting judgment in the Court of Appeal, I would allow the appeal.

Lord Browne-Wilkinson: My Lords, I agree with the speech of my noble and learned friend, Lord Goff of Chieveley, that the consequences of being a party to an illegal transaction cannot depend, as the majority in the Court of Appeal held, on such an imponderable factor as the extent to which the public conscience would be affronted by recognising rights created by illegal transactions. However, I have the misfortune to disagree with him as to the correct principle to be applied in a case where equitable property rights are acquired as a result of an illegal transaction.

Neither at law nor in equity will the court enforce an illegal contract which has been partially, but not fully, performed. However, it does not follow that all acts done under a partially performed contract are of no effect. In particular it is now clearly established that at law (as opposed to in equity), property in goods or land can pass under, or pursuant to, such a contract. If so, the rights of the owner of the legal title thereby acquired will be enforced, provided that the plaintiff can establish such title without pleading or leading evidence of the illegality. It is said that the property lies where it falls, even though legal title to the property was acquired as a result of the property passing under the illegal contract itself. I will first consider the modern authorities laying down the circumstances under which an illegal transaction will be enforced by the courts. I will then consider whether the courts adopt a different attitude to equitable proprietary interests so acquired.

The position at law is well illustrated by the decision in *Bowmakers Ltd v Barnet Instruments Ltd* [1945] KB 65. In that case Barnet acquired three parcels of machine tools which had previously belonged to Smith. The transaction was carried through by three hire-purchase agreements under which Smith sold the goods to Bowmakers who then hired them to Barnet. All three agreements were unlawful as being in breach of Defence Regulations: it is important to note that in the case of at least two of the parcels the illegality lay in the contract under which Bowmakers acquired the machine tools from Smith: see 69. Bowmakers succeeded in an action for conversion against Barnet. Even though it appeared from the pleadings and the evidence that the contract under which Bowmakers acquired the goods was illegal, such contract was effective to pass the property in the goods to Bowmakers who could therefore found their claim on the property right so acquired.

The position at law is further illustrated by *Ferret v Hill* (1854) 15 CB 207 where A, with intent to use premises as a brothel, took a lease from B. B, having discovered that the premises were being used as a brothel, ejected A. A was held entitled to maintain ejectment against B notwithstanding that A entered into the lease for an illegal purpose.

In *Taylor v Chester*, LR 4 QB 309 the plaintiff had deposited with the defendant half a £50 note as security for payment due under an illegal contract with the defendant. The plaintiff was held unable to recover the half note as a special property in it (i.e. the security interest) had passed to the defendant.

In *Alexander v Rayson* [1936] 1 KB 169 the plaintiff had leased a property to the defendant. For the purpose of defrauding the rating authorities, the plaintiff had carried through the transaction by two documents, one a lease which expressed a low rent the other a service agreement providing for additional payments sufficient to bring up the annual payment to the actual rent agreed. The plaintiff failed in an action to recover rent due under the agreements but the Court of Appeal, at 186, said that if the plaintiff had let the flat to be used for an illegal purpose, the leasehold interest in the flat would have vested in the defendant who would have been entitled to remain in possession of the flat until and unless the plaintiff could eject her without relying on the unlawful agreement.

From these authorities the following propositions emerge: (1) property in chattels and land can pass under a contract which is illegal and therefore would have been unenforceable as a contract; (2) a plaintiff can at law enforce property rights so acquired provided that he does not need to rely on the illegal contract for any purpose other than providing the basis of his claim to a property right; (3) it is irrelevant that the illegality of the underlying agreement was either pleaded or emerged in evidence: if the plaintiff has acquired legal title under the illegal contract that is enough.

I have stressed the common law rules as to the impact of illegality on the acquisition and enforcement of property rights because it is the appellant's contention that different principles apply in equity. In particular it is said that equity will not aid Miss Milligan to assert, establish or enforce an equitable, as opposed to a legal, proprietary interest since she was a party to the fraud on the D.S.S. The house was put in the name of Miss Tinsley alone (instead of joint names) to facilitate the fraud. Therefore, it is said, Miss Milligan does not come to equity with clean hands: consequently, equity will not aid her.

Most authorities to which we were referred deal with enforcing proprietary rights under a trust: I will deal with them in due course. But before turning to them, I must point out that if Miss Tinsley's argument is correct, the results would be far reaching and, I suggest, very surprising. There are many proprietary rights, apart from trusts, which are only enforceable in equity. For example, an agreement for a lease under which the tenant has entered is normally said to be as good as a lease, since under such an agreement equity treats the lease as having been granted and the 'lessee' as having a proprietary interest enforceable against the whole world except the bona fide purchaser for value without notice. Would the result in *Ferret v Hill*, 15 CB 207 have been different if there had only been an agreement for a lease? Say that in *Taylor v Chester*, LR 4 QB 309 the plaintiff had deposited by way of security share certificates instead of half a bank note (thereby producing only an equitable security): would the outcome have been different? Similarly, if the plaintiff were relying on an assignment of a chose in action would he succeed if the assignment was a legal assignment but fail if it were equitable?

In my judgment to draw such distinctions between property rights enforceable at law and those which require the intervention of equity would be surprising. More than 100 years has elapsed since law and equity became fused. The reality of the matter is that, in 1993, English law has one single law of property made up of legal and equitable interests. Although for historical reasons legal estates and equitable estates have differing incidents, the person owning either type of estate has a right of property, a right in rem not merely a right in personam. If the law is that a party is entitled to enforce a property right acquired under an illegal transaction, in my judgment the same rule ought to apply to any property right so acquired, whether such right is legal or equitable.

In the present case, Miss Milligan claims under a resulting or implied trust. The court below have found, and it is not now disputed, that apart from the question of illegality Miss Milligan would have been entitled in equity to a half share in the house in accordance with the principles exemplified in *Gissing v Gissing* [1971] 1 AC 886; *Grant v Edwards* [1986] Ch 638 and *Lloyds Bank plc v Rosset* [1991] AC 107. The creation of such an equitable interest does not depend upon a contractual obligation but on a common intention acted upon by the parties to their detriment. It is a development of the old law of resulting trust under which, where two parties have provided the purchase money to buy a property which is conveyed into the name of one of them alone, the latter is presumed to hold the property on a resulting trust for both parties in shares proportionate to their contributions to the purchase price. In argument, no distinction was drawn between strict resulting trusts and a *Gissing v Gissing* type of trust.

A presumption of resulting trust also arises in equity when A transfers personalty or money to B: see *Snell's Equity*, 29th edn (1990), 183–4; *Standing v Bowring* (1885) 31 ChD 282, 287, *per* Cotton LJ; *Dewar v Dewar* [1975] 1 WLR 1532, 1537. Before 1925, there was also a presumption of resulting trust when land was voluntarily transferred by A to B: it is arguable, however, that the position has been altered by the 1925 property legislation: see *Snell's Equity*, 182. The presumption of a resulting trust is, in my view, crucial in considering the authorities. On that presumption (and on the contrary presumption of advancement) hinges the answer to the crucial question 'does a plaintiff claiming under a resulting trust have to rely on the underlying illegality?' Where the presumption of resulting trust applies, the plaintiff does not have to rely on the illegality. If he proves that the property is vested in the defendant alone but that the plaintiff provided part of the purchase money, or voluntarily transferred the property to the defendant, the plaintiff establishes his claim under a resulting trust unless either the contrary presumption of advancement displaces the presumption of resulting trust or the defendant leads evidence to rebut the presumption of resulting trust. Therefore, in cases where the presumption of advancement does not apply, a plaintiff can establish his equitable interest in the property without relying in any way on the underlying illegal transaction. In this case Miss Milligan as defendant simply pleaded the common intention that the property should belong to both of them and that she contributed to the purchase price: she claimed that in consequence the property belonged to them equally. To the same effect was her evidence in chief. Therefore Miss Milligan was not forced to rely on the illegality to prove her equitable interest. Only in the reply and the course of Miss Milligan's cross-examination did such illegality emerge: it was Miss Tinsley who had to rely on that illegality.

Although the presumption of advancement does not directly arise for consideration in this case, it is important when considering the decided cases to understand its operation. On a transfer from a man to his wife, children or others to whom he stands in loco parentis, equity presumes an intention to make a gift. Therefore in such a case, unlike the case where the presumption of resulting trust applies, in order to establish any claim the plaintiff has himself to lead evidence sufficient to rebut the presumption of gift and in so doing will normally have to plead, and give evidence of, the underlying illegal purpose.

Against this background, I turn to consider the authorities dealing with the position in equity where A transferred property to B for an illegal purpose. The earlier authorities, primarily Lord Eldon, support the appellant's proposition that equity will not aid a plaintiff who has transferred property to another for an illegal purpose. [*Having discussed the early authorities, he continued:*]

However, in my view, the law was not so firmly established as at first sight it appears to have been. The law on the effect of illegality was developing throughout the 19th century. [*He then considered the development of the law during the nineteenth century and continued:*] Although in the cases decided during the last 100 years there are frequent references to Lord Eldon's wide principle, with one exception (*Cantor v Cox*, 239 EG 121) none of the English decisions are decided by simply applying that principle. They are all cases where the unsuccessful party was held to be precluded from leading evidence of an illegal situation in order to rebut the presumption of advancement. Lord Eldon's rule would have provided a complete answer whether the transfer was made to a wife or child (where the presumption of advancement would apply) or to a stranger. Yet with one exception none of the cases in this century has been decided on that simple basis.

The majority of cases have been those in which the presumption of advancement applied: in those authorities the rule has been stated as being that a plaintiff cannot rely on evidence of his own illegality to rebut the presumption applicable in such cases that the plaintiff intended to make a gift of the property to the transferee. Thus in *Gascoigne v Gascoigne* [1918] 1 KB 223; *McEvoy v Belfast Banking Co. Ltd* [1934] NI 67; *In re Emery's Investments Trusts* [1959] Ch 410; *Palaniappa Chettiar v Arunsalam Chettiar* [1962] AC 294 and *Tinker v Tinker* [1970] P 136, 141h, 142c the crucial point was said to be the inability of the plaintiff to lead evidence rebutting the presumption of advancement.

In each case the plaintiff was claiming to recover property voluntarily transferred to, or purchased in the name of, a wife or child, for an illegal purpose. Although reference was made to Lord Eldon's principle, none of those cases was decided on the simple ground (if it were good law) that equity would not in any circumstances enforce a resulting trust in such circumstances. On the contrary in each case the rule was stated to be that the plaintiff could not recover because he had to rely on the illegality to rebut the presumption of advancement.

In my judgment, the explanation for this departure from Lord Eldon's absolute rule is that the fusion of law and equity has led the courts to adopt a single rule (application both at law and in equity) as to the circumstances in which the court will enforce property interests acquired in pursuance of an illegal transaction, viz., the *Bowmakers* rule [1945] KB 65. A party to an illegality can recover by virtue of a legal or equitable property interest if, but only if, he can establish his title without relying on his own illegality. In cases where the presumption of advancement applies, the plaintiff is faced with the presumption of gift and therefore cannot claim under a resulting trust unless and until he has rebutted that presumption of gift: for those purposes the plaintiff does have to rely on the underlying illegality and therefore fails.

The position is well illustrated by two decisions in the Privy Council. In the first, *Singh v Ali* [1960] AC 167 a plaintiff who had acquired legal title to a lorry under an illegal transaction was held entitled to succeed against the other party to the illegality in detinue and trespass. The Board approved the *Bowmakers* test. Two years later in *Palaniappa Chettiar v Annasalam Chettiar* [1962] AC 294 the Board had to consider the case where a father, who had transferred land to his son for an illegal purpose, sought to recover it under a resulting trust. It was held that he could not, since he had to rely on his illegal purpose in order to rebut the presumption of advancement. The Board distinguished, at 301, the decision in *Haigh v Kaye*, LR 7 Ch 469 on the following grounds:

> 'It appears to their Lordships, however, that there is a clear distinction between *Haigh v Kaye* and the present case. In *Haigh v Kaye* the plaintiff conveyed a freehold estate to the defendant. In the conveyance it was stated that a sum of £850 had been paid by the defendant for it. The plaintiff proved that no such sum was paid and claimed that the defendant was a trustee for him. Now in that case the plaintiff had no reason to disclose any illegality and did not do so. It was the defendant who suggested that the transaction was entered into for a fraudulent purpose. He sought to drag it in without pleading it distinctly and he was not allowed to do so. But in the present case the plaintiff had of necessity to disclose his own illegality to the court and for this reason: He had not only to get over the fact that the transfer stated that the son paid $7,000 for the land. He had also to get over the presumption of advancement, for, whenever a father transfers property to his son, there is a presumption that he intended it as a gift to his son; and if he wishes to rebut that presumption and to say that his son took as trustee for him, he must prove the trust clearly and distinctly, by evidence properly admissible for the purposes, and not leave it to be inferred from slight circumstances: see *Shepherd v Cartwright* [1955] AC 431, 445.'

Further, the Board distinguished *Singh v Ali* [1960] AC 167. It was pointed out that in *Singh v Ali* the plaintiff founded his claim on a right of property in the lorry and his possession of it. The Board continued [1962] AC 294, 303:

> '[The plaintiff] did not have to found his cause of action on an immoral or illegal act. He was held entitled to recover. But in the present case the father has of necessity to put forward, and indeed, assert, his own fraudulent purpose, which he has fully achieved. He is met therefore by the principle stated long ago by Lord Mansfield "No court will lend its aid to a man who founds his cause of action upon an immoral or an illegal act," see *Holman v Johnson*, 1 Cowp. 341, 343.'

In my judgment these two cases show that the Privy Council was applying exactly the same principle in both cases although in one case the plaintiff's claim rested on a legal title and in the other on an equitable title. The claim based on the equitable title did not fail simply because the plaintiff was a party to the illegal transaction; it only failed because the plaintiff was bound to disclose and rely upon his own illegal purpose in order to rebut the presumption of advancement. The Privy Council was plainly treating the principle applicable both at law and in equity as being that a man can recover property provided that he is not forced to rely on his own illegality.

I therefore reach the conclusion that, although there is no case overruling the wide principle stated by Lord Eldon, as the law has developed the equitable principle has become elided into the common law rule. In my judgment the time has come to decide clearly that the rule is the same whether a plaintiff founds himself on a legal or equitable title: he is entitled to recover if he is not forced to plead or rely on the illegality, even if it emerges that the title on which he relied was acquired in the course of carrying through an illegal transaction.

As applied in the present case, that principle would operate as follows. Miss Milligan established a resulting trust by showing that she had contributed to the purchase price of the house and that there was common understanding between her and Miss Tinsley that they owned the house equally. She had no need to allege or prove *why* the house was conveyed into the name of Miss Tinsley alone, since that fact was irrelevant to her claim: it was enough to show that the house was in fact vested in Miss Tinsley alone. The illegality only emerged at all because Miss Tinsley sought to raise it. Having proved these facts, Miss Milligan had raised a presumption of resulting trust. There was no evidence to rebut that presumption. Therefore Miss Milligan should succeed. This is exactly the process of reasoning adopted by the Ontario Court of Appeal in *Gorog v Kiss* (1977) 78 DLR (3d) 690 which in my judgment was rightly decided.

Finally, I should mention a further point which was relied on by Miss Tinsley. It is said that once the illegality of the transaction emerges, the court must refuse to enforce the transaction and all claims under it whether pleaded or not: see *Scott v Brown, Doering, McNab & Co.* [1892] 2 QB 724. Therefore, it is said, it does not matter whether a plaintiff relies on or gives evidence of the illegality: the court will not enforce the plaintiff's rights. In my judgment, this submission is plainly ill founded. There are many cases where a plaintiff has succeeded, notwithstanding that the illegality of the transaction under which she acquired the property has emerged: see, for example, *Bowmakers Ltd v Burnet Instruments Ltd* [1945] KB 65 and *Singh v Ali* [1960] AC 167. In my judgment the court is only entitled and bound to dismiss a claim on the basis that it is founded on an illegality in those cases where the illegality is of a kind which would have provided a good defence if raised by the defendant. In a case where the plaintiff is not seeking to enforce an unlawful contract but founds his case on collateral rights acquired under the contract (such as a right of property) the court is neither bound nor entitled to reject the claim unless the illegality of necessity forms part of the plaintiff's case.

I would therefore dismiss the appeal.

Lord Jauncey of Tullichettle and Lord Lowry gave speeches concurring with **Lord Browne-Wilkinson**. **Lord Keith of Kinkel** gave a dissenting speech.

NOTES AND QUESTIONS

1. Was the defendant's claim for restitution of an unjust enrichment? If it was, what was the unjust factor?

2. What would have been the result in *Tinsley* if the parties had been husband and wife?

3. Lord Browne-Wilkinson could also have assimilated the position at law and in equity by overruling *Bowmakers*. Why did he not do so?

4. Even if Lord Browne-Wilkinson's approach were adopted, there could still be cases where the claimant's conduct, *turpi causa*, is so atrocious that even though a claim can be made out without pleading the illegality the claim will be denied. Birks gave an example of a contract to

procure a child for sexual abuse (*Unjust Enrichment* (2nd edn), 261). Even if this contract did not, on its face, disclose the true purpose, a defence of illegality would surely not be avoided by application of a 'pleading test'. But such cases are likely to be rare. In *Bowmakers* (above, 892) the illegality of the contract by which the claimants acquired the machine tools did not bar their claim and, applying this decision, the Court of Appeal in *Costello v Chief Constable of Derbyshire* [2001] 1 WLR 1437 held that even a thief is not barred from bringing an action for conversion.

5. Why did the claimant fail in *Chettiar v Chettiar* (discussed by both Lord Goff and Lord Browne-Wilkinson)? Could the claimant not have established his claim without relying upon the illegality by relying instead on his transfer of the land and the parties' common understanding that the son was to hold the land as a trustee for the claimant? Can a distinction be drawn between *Chettiar* and *Tinsley* (a) as a matter of principle or (b) as a matter of policy?

6. Should English law adopt a discretionary approach of the type enacted in New Zealand? A broader, discretionary approach has its academic supporters (see, for example, B Dickson 'Restitution and Illegal Transactions' in A Burrows (ed), *Essays on the Law of Restitution* (1991), 171), but it is open to the criticism that it is productive of uncertainty and tends towards palm tree justice.

7. We saw earlier (884, note 4) the proposed solution of Birks' to the confusion in the cases concerning the defence of illegality. A different approach, based upon a 'structured discretion', was suggested in the Law Commission's *Illegal Transactions: The effect of Illegality on Contracts and Trusts* (1999 Consultation Paper No 154) para. 7.43:

> The proposed discretion should be structured so that the court shuld be required to take into account specific factors in reaching its decision; and that those factors should be: (1) the seriousness of the illegality involved; (2) the knowledge and intention of the plaintiff; (3) whether denying relief will act as a deterrent; (4) whether denying relief will further the purpose of the rule which renders the conduct illegal; and (5) whether denying relief is proportionate to the illegality involved.

• *Tribe v Tribe* [1996] Ch 107, Court of Appeal

The claimant, David Tribe, held 459 of the 500 shares in the family company. He transferred these shares to his son, Kim Tribe, the defendant, for a consideration of £78,000 which was never paid. The trial judge found that the transfer was entered into for an illegal purpose, namely to defeat the claimant's creditors. At the time of the transfer the claimant feared that his liability for dilapidations to premises used by the family company would force him into selling his shareholding in the company. So, in an attempt to safeguard his interests, he transferred his shares to the defendant. The illegal purpose was never carried into effect because the claimant reached an agreement with his creditors, and so he asked the defendant to retransfer the shares to him. The defendant refused. The claimant brought an action seeking a declaration that he was entitled to the entire beneficial interest in the 459 shares and an order for delivery to him of the share certificates and the transfer of them into his name. The defendant argued that this was a case in which the presumption of advancement arose, and that the claimant could not rely on the illegality for the purpose of rebutting the presumption. It was held that the claimant was entitled to the declaration which he sought on the ground that the claimant was entitled to rely on the illegal purpose to rebut the presumption of advancement where the illegal purpose had not been carried into effect.

Nourse LJ: In *Tinsley v Milligan* [1994] 1 AC 340 it was held by a majority of the House of Lords that where, in order to achieve an illegal purpose, property is transferred by one person into the name of another, being persons between whom the presumption of advancement does not apply, the transferor can recover the property, on the ground that he is not forced to rely on the illegality but only on the resulting trust that arose in his favour on the transfer. It is inherent in that decision that it makes no difference whether or not the illegal purpose has been carried into effect, as it clearly had been in that case. Here the question is whether, where the presumption of advancement applies, the transferor can still recover the property, on the ground that, although he is forced to rely on the illegality in order to rebut the presumption, the illegal purpose has not been carried into effect in any way.

. . .

In both *Tinsley v Milligan* [1994] 1 AC 340 and the present case A transferred property into the name of B with the mutual intention of concealing A's interest in the property for a fraudulent or illegal purpose. Before *Tinsley v Milligan* the general rule that A could not recover the property was consistently applied irrespective of whether the presumption of advancement arose between A and B or not: see *per* Lord Goff, at 356 and the authorities there cited. But now the majority of their Lordships have made a clear distinction between the two cases. In holding that the general rule does not apply where there is no presumption of advancement, they have necessarily affirmed its application to cases where there is. Thus Lord Browne-Wilkinson pointed out, at 372, that, in a case where the presumption of advancement applies in order to establish any claim, the plaintiff has himself to lead evidence sufficient to rebut the presumption of gift and in so doing will normally have to plead, and give evidence of, the underlying illegal purpose: see also at 375c.

At the end of his judgment in the court below, Judge Weeks QC said:

> 'Finally, it is not for me to criticise their Lordships' reasoning, but with the greatest respect I find it difficult to see why the outcome in cases such as the present one should depend to such a large extent on arbitrary factors, such as whether the claim is brought by a father against a son, or a mother against a son, or a grandfather against a grandson.'

I see much force in those observations. If the defendant had been his brother, grandson, nephew or son-in-law, the plaintiff would have succeeded without further inquiry. Moreover, in times when the presumption of advancement has for other purposes fallen into disfavour (see, for example, the observations of Lord Reid, Lord Hodson and Lord Diplock in *Pettit v Pettit* [1970] AC 777, 793, 811, 824) there seems to be some perversity in its elevation to a decisive status in the context of illegality. Be that as it may, we are bound by *Tinsley v Milligan* [1994] 1 AC 340 for what it decided. It decided that where the presumption of advancement arises the general rule applies. It did not decide that there is no exception where the illegal purpose has not been carried into effect. If anything, it may be said to support the existence of the exception in such a case: see in particular Lord Goff's reference, at 356H, to *Perpetual Executors and Trustees Association of Australia Ltd v Wright* (1917) 23 CLR 185.

I turn then to the authorities in which the presumption of advancement has arisen, seeking primarily to establish what light they throw on the applicability of the exception [he considered the cases and continued].

There is one authority in which it has been distinctly held that the exception can apply to a case where the presumption of advancement arises: see *Perpetual Executors and Trustees Association of Australia Ltd v Wright* (1917) 23 CLR 185, which does not appear to have been cited in any English case before *Tinsley v Milligan* [1994] 1 AC 340. In that case the plaintiff in about 1906 and out of his own moneys and savings, had purchased a piece of land and erected thereon a house and premises. He said in evidence at the trial that the property had been put in his wife's name at her request, and for convenience, and not as a gift, but for the purpose of securing a home for himself and his family in the event of his failing in business. The wife died in 1915. The administrators of her estate having refused to recognise his claim to the property, the plaintiff brought an action against them claiming a declaration that he was beneficially and absolutely entitled there to and an order that the defendants should transfer it to him.

The defendants argued that, because of the illegal purpose to defeat his creditors, the plaintiff could not set up the arrangement under which he said that the property had been put into his wife's name, and that there was therefore no evidence to rebut the presumption of advancement. The High Court of Australia rejected that argument and gave judgement for the plaintiff, on the ground that the illegal purpose had not in any respect been carried into effect. Barton ACJ said, at 193:

'Had there been creditors to hoodwink or, at any rate, had there been any attempt at such an act, the case would probably have been different. But, so far as we know, there were no creditors to hoodwink, and the whole thing rested on what might happen but never did happen. That such a state of things, carried no further, is not a bar to the respondent's claim to what is beneficially his own is to me apparent, and I need only mention three cases, namely, *Symes v Hughes* (1870) LR 9 Eq. 475; *Taylor v Bowers* (1876) 1 QBD 291 and *Payne v McDonald* (1908) 6 CLR 208.'

The other three members of the court, Isaacs, Gavan Duffy and Rich JJ, gave a joint judgment They said, 23 CLR 185, 196:

'The test appears to be, not whether the plaintiff in such a case relies on the illegal agreement, because in one sense he always does so, but whether the illegal purpose from which the plaintiff insists on retiring still rests in intention only. If either he is seeking to carry out the illegal purpose, or has already carried it out in whole or in part, then he fails.'

Having then referred to *Payne v McDonald*, 6 CLR 208 and having read at some length from the judgment of the Privy Council in *Petherpermal Chetty v Muniandi Servai*, LR 35 Ind. App. 98, 103, they said, 23 CLR 185, 198:

'In this case no creditors have been defrauded, the illegal purpose has never been in any respect carried into effect, and therefore the respondent was entitled to succeed, and is now entitled to a dismissal of this appeal.'

On this state of the authorities I decline to hold that the exception does not apply to a case where the presumption of advancement arises but the illegal purpose has not been carried into effect in any way. *Wright's* case, 23 CLR 185, supported by the observations of the Privy Council in *Palaniappa Chettiar v Arunasalam Chettiar* [1962] AC 294, is clear authority for its application and no decision to the contrary has been cited. In the circumstances I do not propose to distinguish between law and equity, or to become embroiled in the many irreconcilable authorities which deal with the exception in its application to executory contrack, on even to speculate as to the significance, if any, of calling it a locus poenitentiae, a name I have avoided as tending to mislead. In a property transfer case the exception applies if the illegal purpose has not been carried into effect in any way.

I return to the facts of this case. The judge found that the illegal purpose was to deceive the plaintiff's creditors by creating an appearance that he no longer owned any shares in the company. He also found that it was not carried into effect in any way. Mr Tunkel, for the defendant, attacked the latter finding on grounds which appeared to me to confuse the purpose with the transaction. Certainly the transaction was carried into effect by the execution and registration of the transfer. But *Wright's* case, 23 CLR 185 shows that that is immaterial. It is the purpose which has to be carried into effect and that would only have happened if and when a creditor or creditors of the plaintiff had been deceived by the transaction. The judge said there was no evidence of that and clearly he did not think it appropriate to infer it. Nor is it any objection to the plaintiff's right to recover the shares that he did not demand their return until after the danger had passed and it was no longer necessary to conceal the transfer from his creditors. All that matters is that no deception was practised on them. For these reasons the judge was right to hold that the exception applied.

...

Millett LJ: . . .

The judge held that, because the illegal purpose had not been carried out, the plaintiff was entitled to withdraw from the transaction and to rely on his evidence of the reason why he transferred the shares to the defendant in order to rebut the presumption of advancement. According to the judge he had what is called a locus poenitentiae. It is submitted on behalf of the defendant that the judge was in error. First, it is said, the doctrine of the locus poenitentiae allows a party to an illegal contract to withdraw while the contract is still executory, but it has no application to a transfer of property. In such a case the illegal purpose is partly carried into effect as soon as the property is transferred. Secondly, and in the alternative, a transferor cannot rely on his illegal purpose to rebut the presumption of advancement, and it makes no difference that the illegal purpose has not been carried into effect. Thirdly, there was no true repentance in the present case. The plaintiff never abandoned his illegal purpose; he did not demand the return of his shares until the danger had passed and it was no longer necessary to conceal them from his creditors.

There are, in my opinion, two questions of some importance which fall for decision in the present case. The first is whether, once property has been transferred to a transferee for an illegal purpose in circumstances which give rise to the presumption of advancement, it is still open to the transferor to withdraw from the transaction before the purpose has been carried out and, having done so, give evidence of the illegal purpose in order to rebut the presumption of advancement. The second is whether, if so, it is sufficient for him to withdraw from the transaction because it is no longer necessary and without repenting of his illegal purpose. I shall deal with these two questions in turn.

THE PRESUMPTION OF ADVANCEMENT AND THE LOCUS POENITENTIAE

In *Tinsley v Milligan* [1994] 1 AC 340, 370 Lord Browne-Wilkinson summarised the common law rules which govern the effect of illegality on the acquisition and enforcement of property rights in three propositions:

'(1) property in chattels and land can pass under a contract which is illegal and therefore would have been unenforceable as a contract; (2) a plaintiff can at law enforce property rights so acquired provided that he does not need to rely on the illegal contract for any purpose other than providing the basis of his claim to a property right; (3) it is irrelevant that the illegality of the underlying agreement was either pleaded or emerged in evidence: if the plaintiff has acquired legal title under the illegal contract that is enough.'

The decision of the majority of their Lordships in that case was that the same principles applied in equity. It is, therefore, now settled that neither at law nor in equity may a party rely on his own fraud or illegality in order to found a claim or rebut a presumption, but that the common law and equity a like will assist him to protect and enforce his property rights if he can do so without relying on the fraud or illegality. This is the primary rule.

It is, however, also settled both at law and in equity that a person who has transferred property for an illegal purpose can nevertheless recover his property provided that the withdraws from the transaction before the illegal purpose has been wholly or partly performed. This is the doctrine of the locus poenitentiae and it applies in equity as well as at law: see *Symes v Hughes* (1870) LR 9 Eq. 475 for the former and *Taylor v Bowers* (1876) 1 QBD 291 for the latter. The availability of the doctrine in a restitutionary context was expressly confirmed by Lord Browne-Wilkinson in *Tinsley v Milligan* [1994] 1 AC 340, 374.

While both principles are well established, the nature of the relationship between them is unclear. Is the doctrine of the locus poenitentiae coextensive with and by way of general exception to the primary rule? The question in the present case is whether a plaintiff who has made a gratuitous transfer of property to a person in whose favour the presumption of advancement arises can withdraw from the transaction before the illegal purpose has been carried into effect and then recover the property by leading evidence of his illegal purpose in order to rebut the presumption. Closely connected with this question is its converse: is a plaintiff who has made such a transfer in circumstances which give rise to a resulting trust so that he has no need to rely on the illegal purpose, as in *Tinsley v Milligan* itself, barred from recovering if the illegal purpose has been carried out? If both questions are answered in the negative, then either the locus poenitentiae is a common law doctrine which has no counterpart in equity or it is a contractual doctrine which has no place in the law of restitution.

It is convenient to consider first the position at common law. It is important to bear in mind that the common law starts from the opposite premise from that on which equity bases the presumption of resulting trust. In an action for money had and received, for example, whatever the relationship between the parties, the burden lies on the plaintiff to prove that the money was not paid by way of gift or pursuant to an enforceable contract. Absence of consideration is not of itself a ground of restitution: it is for the transferor to show that no gift was intended.

The leading case is *Taylor v Bowers*, 1 QBD 291. In order to prevent his creditors seizing his goods the plaintiff transferred all is stock-in-trade to one Alcock in exchange for fictitious bills of exchange. At first instance Cockburn CJ held, at 295:

'where money has been paid, or goods delivered, under an unlawful agreement, but there has been no further performance of it, the party paying the money or delivering the goods may repudiate the transaction, and recover back his money or goods.'

The decision was affirmed in the Court of Appeal. All four members of the court held that the plaintiff could prove his title without having to rely on the fraud. Significantly, however Mellish LJ (with whom Baggallay JA agreed) laid stress on the fact that the illegal purpose had not been carried out and made it clear that, even though the plaintiff did not need to rely on the illegality in order to prove title, he could not have recovered the goods if the illegal purpose had been carried out.

The case is described as controversial and criticised in *Goff & Jones, The Law of Restitution* 4th edn (1993), 513 partly on the ground that the contract was not wholly executory because the goods had been handed over to Alcock. But the principle has been applied in subsequent cases and the case itself is cited without disapproval in *Tinsley v Milligan* [1994] 1 AC 340, 374. It is too late now to hold that it was an illegitimate application of a contractual doctrine to a claim for restitution. But the proposition that the plaintiff did not need to rely on the illegality could not be supported today. It is explicable only on the basis that the rule that title can pass under an illegal contract had not yet been clearly established. Nowadays we would say that Alcock, or his successor in title, did not need to rely on the illegal nature of the contract pursuant to which the goods were delivered because the title passed to him despite the illegality and want of consideration; but the plaintiff did. In order to recover the goods as goods received and held to his own use he had to show that they had not been delivered by way of gift or pursuant to an enforceable contract. This required him to show that they had been delivered pursuant to an illegal contract which he had repudiated; and he could not repudiate the contract once the illegal purpose had been wholly or partly achieved.

In *Taylor v Bowers*, 1 QBD 291 the goods were delivered for an illegal purpose but the delivery itself was not illegal. In *Bowmakers Ltd v Barnet Instruments Ltd* [1945] KB 65 the transfers were assumed to be illegal and it was obviously too late for the transferor to invoke the locus poenitentiae. (In any case the transferor did not bring a claim in restitution but contented itself with pleading illegality as a defence to a claim in conversion.) In *Singh v Ali* [1960] AC 167 Lord Denning, giving the opinion of the Board, confirmed the rule that title passes at law notwithstanding the illegal purpose for which the transfer was made. But he was clearly of the opinion that the transferor's claim to restitution was barred only where the illegal purpose had been carried out. He explained, at 176:

'The reason is because the transferor, *having fully achieved his unworthy end*, cannot be allowed to turn round and repudiate the means by which he did it—he cannot throw over the transfer.' (Emphasis added.)

Lord Denning clearly intended it to be understood that the converse applies: the transferor is allowed to repudiate the transfer provided that the illegal purpose has not been achieved. This has not been displaced by anything in *Tinsley v Milligan* [1994] 1 AC 340. Lord Browne-Wilkinson, at 374, expressly confirmed the existence of the doctrine of the locus poenitentiae and its application in a restitutionary context; indeed, he founded part of his reasoning upon it. Moreover, it is in accordance with ordinary restitutionary principles. The fact that title has passed is no bar to a claim for restitution; on the contrary, this is the normal case. But to succeed at law it is necessary for the transferor to repudiate the transaction which gave rise to its passing, and this is what the locus poenitentiae allows him to do.

The locus poenitentiae is not therefore an exclusively contractual doctrine with no place in the law of restitution. It follows that it cannot be excluded by the mere fact that the legal ownership of the property has become lawfully vested in the transferee. It would be unfortunate if the rule in equity were different. It would constitute a further obstacle to the development of a coherent and unified law of restitution. Most of the cases in equity have been concerned with gratuitous transfers made with the intention of defrauding creditors and often for a pretended consideration. It is not easy to discern any difference in principle between a transfer of property against fictitious bills of exchange and a transfer of shares for a stated consideration which it is not intended shall be paid.

The leading cases on illegality and resulting trusts prior to *Tinsley v Milligan* are *Curtis v Perry* (1802), 6 Ves. 739; *Ex parte Yallop* (1808), 15 Ves. 60; *Groves v Groves* (1829) 3 Y & J 163; *Coultwas v Swan* (1870) 18 WR 746; *Symes v Hughes*, LR 9 Eq. 475; *In re Great Berlin Steamboat Co.* (1884) 26 ChD 616; *Petherpermal Chetty v Muniandi Servai* (1809) LR 35 Ind.App. 98 and *Rowan v Dann* (1991) 64 P & CR 202.

. . .

In his dissenting speech [in *Tinsley*] Lord Goff of Chieveley refused to draw any distinction between cases where the presumption of advancement applied and cases in which the plaintiff could rely on a resulting trust. From the authorities he derived a single principle: that if one party puts property in the name of another for a fraudulent or illegal purpose neither law nor equity will allow him to recover the property: see 356. Even if he can establish a resulting trust in his favour he cannot enforce it. Given Lord Goff's opinion that there was but one principle in play, it was natural for him to describe the doctrine of the locus poenitentiae as an exception to that principle. Since the defendant could not bring herself within the exception, he would have allowed the appeal. This was not, however, the view of the majority. Lord Browne-Wilkinson expressly held, at 371, that the rule was the same whether the plaintiff founded himself on a legal or an equitable title; he was entitled to succeed if he was not forced to rely on his own illegality, even if it emerged that the title on which he relied was acquired in the course of carrying through an illegal transaction. The defendant had established a resulting trust by showing that she had contributed to the purchase price and that there was a common understanding between her and the plaintiff that they should own the house equally. She had no need to allege or prove why she had allowed the house to be conveyed into the sole name of the plaintiff, since that fact was irrelevant to her claim.

The necessary consequence of this is that where he can rely on a resulting trust the transferor will normally be able to recover his property if the illegal purpose has not been carried out. In *Tinsley v Milligan* she recovered even though the illegal purpose had been carried out. It does not, however, follow that the transferor will invariably succeed in such circumstances, so that the presence or absence of a locus poenitentiae is irrelevant where the transfer gives rise to a resulting trust. A resulting trust, like the presumption of advancement, rests on a presumption which is rebuttable by evidence: see *Standing v Bowring* (1885) 31 ChD 282, 287. The transferor does not need to allege or prove the purpose for which property was transferred into the name of the transferee; in equity he can rely on the presumption that no gift was intended. But the transferee cannot be prevented from rebutting the presumption by leading evidence of the transferor's subsequent conduct to show that it was inconsistent with any intention to retain a beneficial interest. Suppose, for example, that a man transfers property to his nephew in order to conceal it from his creditors, and suppose that he afterwards settles with his creditors on the footing that he has no interest in the property. Is it seriously suggested that he can recover the property? I think not. The transferor's own conduct would be inconsistent with the retention of any beneficial interest in the property. I can see no reason why the nephew should not give evidence of the transferor's dealings with his creditors to rebut the presumption of a resulting trust and show that a gift was intended. He would not be relying on any illegal arrangement but implicitly denying it. The transferor would have to give positive evidence of his intention to retain a beneficial interest and dishonestly conceal it from his creditors, evidence which he would not be allowed to give once the illegal purpose had been carried out.

This analysis is not, in my view, inconsistent with a passage in Lord Browne-Wilkinson's speech [1994] 1 AC 340, 374, where he said:

> 'The equitable right, if any, must arise at the time at which the property was voluntarily transferred to the third party or purchased in the name of the third party. The existence of the equitable interest cannot depend upon events occurring after that date. Therefore if, under the principle of locus poenitentiae, the courts recognise that an equitable interest did arise out of the underlying transaction, the same must be true where the illegal purpose was carried through. The carrying out of the illegal purpose cannot, by itself, destroy the pre-existing equitable interest.'

But it does not follow that subsequent conduct is necessarily irrelevant. Where the existence of an equitable interest depends upon a rebuttable presumption or inference of the transferor's intention, evidence may be given of his subsequent conduct in order to rebut the presumption or inference which would otherwise be drawn.

Tinsley v Milligan [1994] 1 AC 340 is, in my opinion, not authority for the proposition that a party who transfers property for an illegal purpose in circumstances which give rise to a resulting trust can invariably enforce the trust and recover the property even though the illegal purpose has been carried into effect. I do not accept the suggestion that cases such as *In re Great Berlin Steamboat Co.*, 26 ChD 616 have been impliedly overruled or that the dicta in the many cases, including *Taylor v Bowers*, 1 QBD 291 and *Singh v Ali* [1960] AC 167, indicating that the result would have been otherwise if the illegal purpose had or had not been carried out must be taken to have been overruled.

The question in the present case is the converse: whether the transferor can rebut the presumption of advancement by giving evidence of his illegal purpose so long as the illegal purpose has not been carried into effect. The leading cases on illegality and the presumption of advancement are *Childers v Childers* (1857) 3 K & J 310; *Crichton v Crichton* (1895) 13 R 770; *Perpetual Executors and Trustees Association of Australia Ltd v Wright* (1917) 23 CLR 185; *Gascoigne v Gascoigne* [1918] 1 KB 223; *McEvoy v Belfast Banking Co. Ltd* [1935] AC 24; *In re Emery's Investments Trusts* [1959] Ch 410; *Palaniappa Chettiar v Arunasalam Chettiar* [1962] AC 294 and *Tinker v Tinker* [1970] P 136. [He considered these cases and continued].

There is no modern case in which restitution has been denied in circumstances comparable to those of the present case where the illegal purpose has not been carried out. In *Tinsley v Milligan* Lord Browne-Wilkinson expressly recognized, at 374, the availability of the doctrine of the locus poenitentiae in a restitutionary context, and cited *Taylor v Bowers*, 1 QBD 291 as well as *Symes v Hughes*, LR 9 Eq. 475 without disapproval. In my opinion the weight of the authorities supports the view that a person who seeks to recover property transferred by him for an illegal purpose can lead evidence of his dishonest intention whenever it is necessary for him to do so provided that he has withdrawn from the transaction if he can rely on an express or resulting trust in his favour; but it is necessary (i) if he brings an action at law and (ii) if he brings proceedings in equity and needs to rebut the presumption of advancement. The availability of the locus poenitentiae is well documented in the former case. I would not willingly adopt a rule which differentiated between the rule of the common law and that of equity in a restitutionary context.

It is of course true that equity judges are fond of saying that a party 'cannot be heard to say' that his purpose was dishonest, and that this approach represents a mainspring of equitable jurisprudence. A man who puts himself in a position where his interest conflicts with his duty, for example, 'cannot be heard to say' that he acted in accordance with his interest; he is treated as having acted in accordance with his duty: see for example *In re Biss* [1903] 2 Ch 40, 45 and *Attorney-General for Hong Kong v Reid* [1994] 1 AC 324. But this is a substantive rule of equity, not a merely procedural rule as the primary rule appears to be, and it does not preclude the court from taking cognisance of an uneffectuated intention from which the party in question has resiled. I would hold that Sir William Page Wood V-C's first thoughts in *Childers v Childers*, 3 K & J 310, 315–16 are to be preferred to his second. I would also hold that there was no 'inescapable dilemma' in *Tinker v Tinker* [1970] P 136, where it was said by Salmon LJ in the course of the argument at 139 that the transferor was either an honest man, in which case the property belonged to his wife, or he would have to give evidence of his dishonesty, it being implicit that this was something which he could not do. Such statements are due to an instinctive feeling that a dishonest man should not succeed where an honest man would fail, but this is to misrepresent the effect of allowing a locus poenitentiae. The dishonest man is not treated more favourably than the honest man; provided that the illegal purpose has not been carried out they are treated in the same way. The outcome is different because their intentions were different. The honest man intended a gift; the dishonest man did not.

At heart the question for decision in the present case is one of legal policy. The primary rule which precludes the court from lending its assistance to a man who founds his cause of action on an illegal or immoral act often leads to a denial of justice. The justification for this is that the rule is not a principle of justice but a principle of policy: see the much quoted statement of Lord Mansfield CJ in *Holman v Johnson* (1775) 1 Cowp. 341, 343. The doctrine of the locus poenitentiae is an exception which operates to mitigate the harshness of the primary rule. It enables the court to do justice between the parties even though, in order to do so, it must allow a plaintiff to give evidence of his own dishonest intent. But he must have withdrawn from the transaction while his dishonesty still lay in intention only. The law draws the line once the intention has been wholly or partly carried into effect.

Seen in this light the doctrine of the locus poenitentiae, although an exception of the primary rule, is not inconsistent with the policy which underlies it. It is, of course, artificial to think that anyone would be dissuaded by the primary rule from entering into a proposed fraud, if only because such a person would be unlikely to be a studious reader of the law reports or to seek advice from a lawyer whom he has taken fully into his confidence. But, if the policy which underlies the primary rule is to discourage fraud, the policy which underlies the exception must be taken to be to encourage withdrawal from a proposed fraud before it is implemented, an end which is no less desirable. And, if the former objective is of such overriding importance that the primary rule must be given effect even where it leads to a denial of justice, then in my opinion the latter objective justifies the adoption of the exception where this enables justice to be done.

To my mind these considerations are even more compelling since the decision in *Tinsley v Milligan* [1994] 1 AC 340. One might hesitate before allowing a novel exception to a rule of legal policy, particularly a rule based on moral principles. But the primary rule, as it has emerged from that decision, does not conform to any discernible moral principle. It is procedural in nature and depends on the adventitious location of the burden of proof in any given case. Had the plaintiff transferred the shares to a stranger or distant relative whom he trusted, albeit for the same dishonest purpose, it cannot be doubted that he would have succeeded in his claim. He would also have succeeded if he had given them to the defendant and procured him to sign a declaration of trust in his favour. But he chose to transfer them to a son whom he trusted to the extent of dispensing with the precaution of obtaining a declaration of trust. If that is fatal to his claim, then the greater the betrayal, the less the power of equity to give a remedy.

In my opinion the following propositions represent the present state of the law. (1) Title to property passes both at law and in equity even if the transfer is made for an illegal purpose. The fact that title has passed to the transferee does not preclude the transferor from bringing an action for restitution. (2) The transferor's action will fail if it would be illegal for him to retain any interest in the property. (3) Subject to (2) the transferor can recover the property if he can do so without relying on the illegal purpose. This will normally be the case where the property was transferred without consideration in circumstances where the transferor can rely on an express declaration of trust or a resulting trust in his favour. (4) It will almost invariably be so where the illegal purpose has not been carried out. It may be otherwise where the illegal purpose has been carried out and the transferee can rely on the transferor's conduct as inconsistent with his retention of a beneficial interest. (5) The transferor can lead evidence of the illegal purpose whenever it is necessary for him to do so provided that he has withdrawn from the transaction before the illegal purpose has been wholly or partly carried into effect. It will be necessary for him to do so (i) if he brings an action at law or (ii) if he brings proceedings in equity and needs to rebut the presumption of advancement. (6) The only way in which a man can protect his property from his creditors is by divesting himself of all beneficial interest in it. Evidence that he transferred the property in order to protect it from his creditors, therefore, does nothing by itself to rebut the presumption of advancement; it reinforces it. To rebut the presumption it is necessary to show that he intended to retain a beneficial interest and conceal it from his creditors. (7) The court should not conclude that this was his intention without compelling circumstantial evidence to this effect. The identity of the transferee and the circumstances in which the transfer was made would be highly relevant. It is unlikely that the court would reach such a conclusion where the transfer was made in the absence of an imminent and perceived threat from known creditors.

THE DOCTRINE OF THE LOCUS POENITENTIAE

It is impossible to reconcile all the authorities on the circumstances in which a party to an illegal contract is permitted to withdraw from it. At one time he was allowed to withdraw so long as the contract had not been completely performed; but later it was held that recovery was barred once it had been partly performed: see *Kearley v Thomson* (1890) 24 QBD 742. It is clear that he must withdraw voluntarily, and that it is not sufficient that he is forced to do so because his plan has been discovered. In *Bigos v Bousted* [1951] 1 All ER 92 this was, perhaps, dubiously, extended to prevent withdrawal where the scheme has been frustrated by the refusal of the other party to carry out his part.

The academic articles Grodecki, 'In Pari Delicto Potior Est Conditio Defendentis' (1955) 71 *LQR* 254, Beatson, 'Repudiation of Illegal Purpose as a Ground for Repudiation' (1975) 91 *LQR* 313 and Merkin, 'Restitution by Withdrawal from Executory Illegal Contracts' (1981) 97 *LQR* 420 are required reading for anyone who attempts the difficult task of defining the precise limits of the doctrine. I would draw back from any such attempt. But I would hold that genuine repentance is not required. Justice is not a reward for merit; restitution should not be confined to the penitent. I would also hold that voluntary withdrawal from an illegal transaction when it has ceased to be needed is sufficient. It is true that this is not necessary to encourage withdrawal, but a rule to the opposite effect could lead to bizarre results. Suppose, for example, that in *Bigos v Bousted* [1951] 1 All ER 92 exchange control had been abolished before the foreign currency was made available: it is absurd to suppose that the plaintiff should have been denied restitution. I do not agree that it was correct in *Groves v Groves*, 3 Y & J 163, 174, and similar cases for the court to withhold its assistance from the plaintiff because 'if the crime has not been completed, the merit was not his.'

CONCLUSION

On the facts found by the judge the plaintiff was entitled to judgment. I would dismiss the appeal.

Otton LJ concurred.

NOTES AND QUESTIONS

1. We have chosen to include *Tribe* at this point in the book largely because the reasoning of the court is heavily dependent upon the decision of the House of Lords in *Tinsley v Milligan* so that it is more convenient for the reader to consider *Tribe* after reading *Tinsley*. However it can be argued that, as a matter of principle, *Tribe* should have been located in Chapter 10 as an example of the operation of illegality as the ground for restitution. Assuming that the resulting trust in this case is a proprietary restitutionary response to unjust enrichment, an alternative to seeing illegality as the ground for restitution is the absence of basis approach favoured by Birks in his last book (above, 137). At one point Millett LJ seems to endorse that approach when he says: 'the burden lies on the plaintiff to prove that the money was not paid by way of gift or pursuant to an enforceable contract'. If this is correct then the emphasis by all of the judges, including Millett LJ, on the withdrawal doctrine (*locus poenitentiae*) must have been concerned with rejecting illegality as a defence.

2. An alternative analysis of the case is that it does not belong within the law of unjust enrichment at all. W Swadling has argued ([1995] *All ER Rev.* 442), that rights acquired under 'a presumption of express trust' are consent-based so that the claim in *Tribe* was not a claim in unjust enrichment. Do you agree?

3. The judgment of Millett LJ, in so far as it deals with the claimant's *locus poenitentiae*, is discussed in more detail in Chapter 10 above (see in particular 605–606).

4. Is the decision of the Court of Appeal consistent with *Tinsley v Milligan* (above, 894)? Does it leave the law in a satisfactory state?

5. This decision was reluctantly applied by the Court of Appeal in *Collier v Collier* [2002] EWCA Civ 1095. Mr Collier gave his daughter a lease and option to purchase properties in an attempt to defraud his creditors and mortgagees. With his assistance his daughter exercised the option. Whether his case was analysed as seeking to rebut a presumption of advancement or a claim that she held the properties on express trust (as agreed), Mr Collier needed to rely upon his illegal agreement with his daughter. He could not rely upon the *locus poenitentiae* or withdrawal doctrine because he had successfully carried through the illegality. Although compelled to reach this conclusion, Mance LJ said (at [106]) that he strongly sympathized with the criticisms of the *Tinsley v Milligan* approach by the Law Commission (see above) and High Court of Australia in *Nelson v Nelson* (immediately below).

- *Nelson v Nelson* (1995) 184 CLR 538, High Court of Australia

Mrs Nelson provided funds for the purchase of a house, the title to which was registered in the names of her son and daughter. Her purpose in doing so was to preserve her entitlement, under the Defence Service Homes Act 1918, to subsidized finance on the purchase of another home. Shortly afterwards she obtained the subsidy on another property after having falsely declared that she had no interest in any house other than the one for which the subsidy was sought. The house which was registered in the names of her son and daughter was then sold, but the daughter refused to pay over her share of the proceeds. She maintained that the presumption of advancement was applicable to the transaction so that she had a beneficial interest in the property, and that her mother could not defeat that interest by leading evidence of her illegal purpose. It was held that the presumption of advancement was applicable to the transaction but that Mrs Nelson was entitled to lead evidence of her illegal purpose in order to rebut that presumption. In so concluding four justices of the court (Deane, Gummow, Toohey, and McHugh JJ) paid careful attention to the policy pursued by the legislation (Dawson J reached the same conclusion, but was of the view that the illegality was not a breach of the Act but the fraud in obtaining the advance) and the penalties which it provided for its infringement. They concluded that Mrs Nelson was entitled to a declaration that the property and the proceeds of its sale were held on trust for her. We set out here extracts from the judgments of Dawson and McHugh JJ in so far as they deal with restitutionary issues which go beyond the particular policies which underpinned the legislation.

Dawson J: ... Agreeing, as I do, that disconformity is undesirable in the rules relating to illegality at law and in equity, I find difficulty in accepting the distinction drawn in *Tinsley v Milligan* between a resulting trust established without the need to rebut the presumption of advancement and a resulting trust that can only be established by rebutting that presumption. In the former case, according to the decision, an illegal purpose does not preclude relief because the resulting trust will be presumed upon proof that the purchase price was paid by the party asserting the trust without any need for that party to place reliance upon the illegal purpose. In the latter case, however, where the presumption of advancement cannot be rebutted without revealing the illegal purpose, there can be no assertion of a resulting trust. The distinction can hardly be based upon a policy of discouraging the transfer of property for an illegal purpose because a knowledgable transferor would choose a transferee other than one who could take advantage of the presumption of advancement. Moreover, where a presumption of advancement applied, the distinction would be such as to lead the transferee to encourage the carrying out of the illegal purpose so as to acquire a benefit for himself. And, if the presumption of advancement cannot be rebutted because of the revelation of an illegal purpose, the result is a windfall gain to the transferee who may in fact share the illegal purpose.

Once it is recognised that Lord Eldon's broad rule exceeds the true scope of the equitable maxim that he who comes to equity must come with clean hands and that a party who the evidence reveals is tainted with illegality may nevertheless succeed, as in *Tinsley v Milligan*, in establishing a resulting trust, it seems to me to be unacceptable that a party, tainted by a similar illegality, cannot establish a resulting trust merely because evidence advanced to rebut the presumption of advancement reveals the illegality. The different result is entirely fortuitous being dependent upon the relationship between the parties and is wholly unjustifiable upon any policy ground. That the transfer of property by a husband to his wife for an illegal purpose and not intended as a gift should not give rise to a resulting trust whereas a similar transfer of property by a man to his de facto wife[1] for a similar illegal purpose should do so, because in the former instance the husband is required to rebut the presumption of advancement and cannot do so merely because he would reveal the illegal purpose, cannot, in my view, have any basis in principle. If, as it does, a locus poenitentiae exists, then there is an existing equitable interest in each instance.[2] It is simply that in the former instance the husband will not be heard to assert its existence. In the words of Lord Browne-Wilkinson in *Tinsley v Milligan*[3] in each instance:

'The effect of illegality is not substantive but procedural. The question therefore is, "In what circumstances will equity refuse to enforce equitable rights which undoubtedly exist."'

Nor, in my view, can it be said that a party seeking to rebut the presumption of advancement in the case of a transaction for an illegal purpose is forced to rely upon his own illegality. What must be established in order to rebut the presumption is that no gift was intended. There may be an illegal purpose for the transfer of the property and that may bear upon the question of intention,[4] but it

---

1 See *Culverley v Green* (1984) 155 CLR 242.   2 See *Tinsley v Milligan* [1994] 1 AC 340 at 374.
3 [1994] 1 AC 340 at 374.   4 See *Martin v Martin* (1959) 110 CLR 297 at 305.

is the absence of any intention to make a gift upon which reliance must be placed to rebut the presumption of advancement. Intention is something different from a reason or motive. The illegal purpose may thus be evidentiary, but it is not the foundation of a claim to rebut the presumption of advancement.[5] Both the presumption of a resulting trust and the presumption of advancement may be rebutted by showing the actual intention of the parties.[6] Each presumption dictates where the evidentiary burden of doing so lies. But that affords no basis for drawing a distinction between the effect of an illegal purpose where the presumption of advancement applies and where it does not. Reliance is placed in each case upon the intention of the parties, whether aided by a presumption or not, and not upon the illegality.

Justification for the view that the presumption of advancement may be rebutted so as to allow a resulting trust to arise, notwithstanding that the rebuttal reveals that the transaction involved was for an illegal purpose, is to be found in the principle that illegal conduct on the part of a person claiming equitable relief does not in every instance disentitle that person to the relief. The illegality must have 'an immediate and necessary relation to the equity sued for'.[7] Where reliance is not placed upon the illegality—where the court is not asked to effectuate the illegal purpose but merely to recognise an interest admittedly in existence—there is not, in my view, an immediate and necessary relation between the illegality and the claim. The illegal purpose in those circumstances has been effectuated without any intervention by the court and the property right has passed. If there is to be a correspondence between the rules at common law and in equity, then the property right ought to be recognised notwithstanding that it is the result of an illegal transaction. The relevance of the illegal transaction is confined to explaining how the property right arose; to 'providing the basis of [a] claim to a property right'.[8]

In the present case, the purchase of the first house by the mother and the placing of it in the names of the son and daughter took place a considerable time before the failure of the mother to disclose her interest in her application for an advance. During the whole of that time the mother was in a position to rebut the presumption of advancement and to claim the beneficial interest in the house which had passed to her. Given the existence of that interest and the fact that, had it been a legal interest, it would have been recoverable notwithstanding the maxim ex turpi causa, I do not think that it should be concluded that the mother in her claim for equitable relief placed reliance upon her fraudulent conduct in any direct or necessary way. The purchase of the house did not of itself involve any fraud and the relevance of the illegal purpose, which was at the time of the purchase yet to be carried into effect, was at most to explain why the purchase did not constitute a gift to the children. The amount of the subsidy paid as a result of the mother's fraud is recoverable by the Commonwealth so that the mother cannot, without qualification, be said to be entitled to the benefit of having carried out her illegal purpose.

I would allow the appeal and make the declarations and order sought by the mother and son. The mother is, on the view which I have expressed, entitled to the relief which she seeks and I see no reason to place conditions upon granting it. . . .

McHugh J: . . .

THE WIDE PRINCIPLE AND THE BOWMAKERS RULE

I think that the majority speeches in the House of Lords in *Tinsley* were correct in denying the existence of the 'wide principle'. I doubt that Lord Eldon intended to lay down a rule to the effect

---

5 See *Donaldson v Freeson* (1934) 51 CLR 598 at 617, *per* McTiernan J.
6 See *Martin v Martin* (1959) 110 CLR 297 at 303–4.
7 See *Deering v Earl of Winchelsea* (1787) 1 Cox Eq. 318 at 319 [29 ER 1184 at 1185].
8 See *Tinsley v Milligan* [1994] 1 AC 340 at 370, *per* Lord Browne-Wilkinson.

that, if the purpose of a transaction was to defeat the operation of an Act of Parliament equity would always refuse its remedies to a person who had participated in that transaction, is true that, in *Muckleston v Brown*,[9] *Curtis v Perry*,[10] *Cottington v Fletcher*[11] and other cases the judges of the Court of Chancery were dealing with trusts and agreements whose objects were to defeat the operation of Acts of Parliament and that they concluded that those trusts and agreements were not enforceable in equity. But that was obviously because, in the circumstances of those cases, the policy of the Acts required the courts to firmly suppress the use of trusts and agreements to avoid the operation of the legislation. Those decisions say nothing about legislation whose policy does not require such drastic remedies. Nor do they require a court of equity to disregard a circumstance that affects the real justice of the case and calls for the assistance of equitable remedies. It would be out of character for a court of equity to do so. In Lord Stowell's words: 'A Court of Equity . . . looks to every connected circumstance that ought to influence its determination upon the real justice of the case.'[12]

With great respect to the view expressed by Lord Goff in *Tinsley*, I do not think that the clean hands doctrine constitutes or provides a sound basis for a special rule in equity. The illegality principle is one of general application; it is not limited to proceedings in equity. To say that in the equitable context it derives from the clean hands doctrine is to wrongly deny its conceptual links to the rule as it is applied in other areas. Further, it fails to recognise that the rationale for the two doctrines is distinct: the clean hands doctrine arises from the relationship between the parties to the proceedings, the illegality doctrine derives from public policy considerations. Accordingly, the majority of the House of Lords in *Tinsley* were correct in rejecting the 'wide principle' as governing cases of illegality in equity. But that said, I do not think that this Court should adopt the majority's rule that a claimant cannot obtain relief in any court if that person must plead or rely on illegal conduct (the *Bowmakers* rule).

THE BOWMAKERS RULE

A doctrine of illegality that depends upon the state of the pleadings or the need to rely on a transaction that has an unlawful purpose is neither satisfactory nor soundly based in legal policy. The results produced by such a doctrine are essentially random and produce windfall gains as well as losses, even when the parties are in pari delicto. To demonstrate the random nature of the assignment of substantive relief under the *Bowmakers* rule approved by the majority in *Tinsley* one has only to consider the application of that rule to the circumstances of the present case. If the rule were applied in this case, the determining factor would be whether a presumption of advancement arose. Only if it did, would Mrs Nelson need to answer the presumption of a resulting trust and rely on her illegal purpose. If the presumption of advancement did not arise, there would be no need to rely on the illegal purpose to rebut the presumption and the result would be the reverse. Thus, if Mrs Nelson had had the property placed in the name of a friend or relative—or anybody other than her children—she could recover the proceeds of the sale of the Bent Street property, notwithstanding her illegal purpose.

The *Bowmakers* rule has no regard to the legal and equitable rights of the parties, the merits of the case, the effect of the transaction in undermining the policy of the relevant legislation or the question whether the sanctions imposed by the legislation sufficiently protect the purpose of the legislation. Regard is had only to the procedural issue; and it is that issue and not the policy of the legislation or the merits of the parties which determines the outcome. Basing the grant of legal remedies on an essentially procedural criterion which has nothing to do with the equitable positions of the parties or the policy of the legislation is unsatisfactory, particularly when implementing a doctrine that is

9 (1801) 6 Ves Jun 52 [31 ER 934].   10 (1802) 6 Ves Jun 739 [31 ER 1285].
11 (1740) 2 Atk 155 [26 ER 498].   12 *The 'Juliana'* (1822) 2 Dods 504 at 521 [165 ER 1560 at 1567].

founded on public policy. In *Tinsley*, Lord Goff recognised the perverse nature of the rule adopted by the minority in that case in words that apply equally to the *Bowmakers* rule adopted by the majority judges. Lord Goff said:[13]

> 'It is important to observe that . . . the principle is not a principle of justice; it is a principle of policy, whose application is indiscriminate and so can lead to unfair consequences as between the parties to litigation.'

At least the position of the minority in *Tinsley* had the virtue that the indiscriminate nature of the rule which they adopted did not depend on procedural issues.

The policy justification for the rule adopted in the minority speeches in *Tinsley* is that the harsh and indiscriminate nature of the rule will deter people from entering into unlawful agreements and trusts because they know that the courts will not provide them with equitable relief. Whether the rule adopted by the minority would be an effective deterrent is debatable. However, the notion of deterrence seems a weak argument to justify the *Bowmakers* rule adopted by the majority in *Tinsley*. The defendant in *Tinsley*, for example, succeeded in recovering her property notwithstanding the unlawful purpose for which she transferred the property. Moreover, while the *Bowmakers* rule may impose severe losses on those who are forced to rely on the illegality, it also gives windfall gains to those who rely on the defence of illegality. In so far as the *Bowmakers* rule is a deterrent, it is also an incentive to illegality because it encourages those to whom property is conveyed to encourage transferors to carry out their unlawful purpose.

Furthermore, even if this random process of assigning losses and gains without regard to the substantive equities of a dispute is a disincentive to those who might enter illegal transactions, it does not follow that the *Bowmakers* rule is the most efficient rule to protect the community against the making of trusts and agreements for unlawful purposes. There are other rules that could achieve the same goals of legal policy through a less extreme and a more just process.

A final criticism of the *Bowmakers* rule adopted by the majority in *Tinsley* is that it may often defeat the intention of the legislature. Parliament almost invariably provides mechanisms for dealing with breaches of its laws. Those mechanisms sometimes include a provision that makes unlawful and unenforceable an agreement that defeats or evades the operation of the relevant law. If a particular enactment does not contain such a provision, the prima facie conclusion to be drawn is that Parliament regarded the sanctions and remedies contained in the enactment as sufficient to deter illegal conduct and saw no need to take the drastic step of making unenforceable an agreement or trust that defeats the purpose of the enactment.[14]

THE PRESENT NEED FOR THE DOCTRINE OF ILLEGALITY

The doctrine of illegality expounded in *Holman* was formulated in a society that was vastly different from that which exists today. It was a society that was much less regulated. With the rapid expansion of regulation, it is undeniable that the legal environment in which the doctrine of illegality operates has changed. The underlying policy of *Holman* is still valid today—the courts must not condone or assist a breach of statute, nor must they help to frustrate the operation of a statute. As Mason J put it in *Yango Pastoral Co. Pty. Ltd v First Chicago Australia Ltd*,[15] the courts must not 'be instrumental in offering an inducement to crime or removing a restraint to crime'. However, the *Holman* rule, stated in the bald dictum: 'No court will lend its aid to a man who founds his cause of action upon an

---

13 *Tinsley* [1994] 1 AC 340 at 355.
14 Cf. *Yango Pastoral Co. Pty. Ltd v First Chicago Australia Ltd* (1978) 139 CLR 410 at 429.
15 (1978) 139 CLR 410 at 429.

immoral or an illegal act'[16] is too extreme and inflexible to represent sound legal policy in the late 20th century even when account is taken of the recognised exceptions to this dictum.

One of the most significant reasons for adopting a less rigid approach to illegality that the bald dictum in *Holman* or, for that matter, the *Bowmakers* rule adopted in *Tinsley* is that statutory illegality can arise in a number of different ways.[17] First, the statute may directly prohibit the contract or trust. Second, while the statute may not prohibit making the contract or trust, it may prohibit the doing of some particular act that is essential for carrying it out. Third, the statute may not expressly prohibit the contract or trust but the contract or trust may be associated with or made in furtherance of a purpose of frustrating the operation of the statute. Fourth, the statute may make unlawful the manner in which an otherwise lawful contract or trust is carried out. It would be surprising if sound legal policy required each of these forms of illegality to be treated in the same way. There is, for example, a vast difference between the performance of a contract for carriage of goods by ship that is overloaded in breach of the law and the making of a contract for the carriage of goods where the making of the contract is specifically prohibited.[18]

It is worth noting the approach in the cases in the English Court of Appeal which preceded, and were rejected by, the decision in *Tinsley v Milligan* and which sought a less rigid and dogmatic approach to illegality than is found in the *Holman* dictum. Those cases included cases in equity,[19] contract[20] and tort.[21] The effect of the approach developed by the Court of Appeal in those cases was summarised in the decision of that Court in *Tinsley* by Nicholls LJ who said:[22]

'These authorities seem to me to establish that when applying the "ex turpi causa" maxim in a case in which a defence of illegality has been raised, the court should keep in mind that the underlying principle is the so-called public conscience test. The court must weigh, or balance, the adverse consequences of granting relief against the adverse consequences of refusing relief. The ultimate decision calls for a value judgment. The detailed principles summarised by Kerr LJ in the *Euro-Diam* case,[23] and distinctions such as that between causes of action which arise directly ex turpi causa and causes of action to which the unlawful conduct is incidental, are valuable as guidelines. But they are no more than guidelines. Their value and justification lie in the practical assistance they give to the courts by focusing attention on particular features which are material in carrying out the balancing exercise in different types of cases.'

This approach confers a broad judicial discretion upon the judge to determine whether the grant of relief would affront 'the public conscience'. While it provides a ready means for a judge to do what he or she thinks is just in the circumstances of the particular case, it does so by means of an unstructured discretion. The so called 'public conscience' test, although providing a flexible approach, leaves the matter at large. Greater certainty in the application of the illegality doctrine will be achieved if the courts apply principles instead of a vague standard such as the 'public conscience'. But what principles, consistent with the public policy underpinnings of the doctrine of illegality, should the courts apply?

If courts withhold relief because of an illegal transaction, they necessarily impose a sanction on one of the parties to that transaction, a sanction that will deprive one party of his or her property rights

---

16 *Holman* (1775) 1 Cowp 341 at 343 [98 ER 1120 at 1121].

17 See *Yango* (1978) 139 CLR 410 at 413.

18 Cf. *St John Shipping Corporation v Joseph Rank Ltd* [1957] 1 QB 267.

19 *Tinsley v Milligan* [1992] Ch 310.

20 *Saunders v Edwards* [1987] 1 WLR 1116; *Howard v Shirlstar Ltd* [1990] 1 WLR 1292; *Euro-Diam Ltd v Bathurst* [1990] 1 QB 1.

21 *Pitts v Hunt* [1991] 1 QB 24.

22 *Tinsley v Milligan* [1992] Ch 310 at 319–20.   23 [1990] 1 QB 1.

and effectively vest them in another person who will almost always be a willing participant in the illegality. Leaving aside cases where the statute makes rights arising out of the transaction unenforceable in all circumstances, such a sanction can only be justified if two conditions are met.

First, the sanction imposed should be proportionate to the seriousness[24] of the illegality involved. It is not in accord with contemporary notions of justice that the penalty for breaching a law or frustrating its policy should be disproportionate to the seriousness of the breach.[25] The seriousness of the illegality must be judged by reference to the statute whose terms or policy is contravened. It cannot be assessed in a vacuum. The statute must always be the reference point for determining the seriousness of the illegality; otherwise the courts would embark on an assessment of moral turpitude independently of and potentially in conflict with the assessment made by the legislature.

Second, the imposition of the civil sanction must further the purpose of the statute and must not impose a further sanction for the unlawful conduct if Parliament has indicated that the sanctions imposed by the statute are sufficient to deal with conduct that breaches or evades the operation of the statute and its policies. In most cases, the statute will provide some guidance, express or inferred, as to the policy of the legislature in respect of a transaction that contravenes the statute or its purpose. It is this policy that must guide the courts in determining, consistent with their duty not to condone or encourage breaches of the statute, what the consequences of the illegality will be. Thus, the statute may disclose an intention, explicitly or implicitly, that a transaction contrary to its terms or its policy should be unenforceable. On the other hand, the statute may inferentially disclose an intention that the only sanctions for breach of the statute or its policy are to be those specifically provided for in the legislation.[26]

Accordingly, in my opinion, even if a case does not come within one of the four exceptions to the *Holman* dictum to which I have referred, courts should not refuse to enforce legal or equitable rights simply because they arose out of or were associated with an unlawful purpose unless:

(a) the statute discloses an intention that those rights should be unenforceable in all circumstances; or

(b) (i)   the sanction of refusing to enforce those rights is not disproportionate to the seriousness of the unlawful conduct;

    (ii) the imposition of the sanction is necessary, having regard to the terms of the statute, to protect its objects or policies; and

    (iii) the statute does not disclose an intention that the sanctions and remedies contained in the statute are to be the only legal consequences of a breach of the statute or the frustration of its policies.[27]

[*He concluded that Mrs Nelson was entitled to the relief which she sought, although a condition was appended to her right to relief that she must first repay to the Commonwealth the benefit which she obtained as a result of her unlawful conduct.*]

Deane and Gummow JJ delivered a joint judgment reaching the same conclusion. **Toohey J** agreed that the claimant was entitled to the relief which she sought but would not have appended a condition that the claimant first repay to the Commonwealth the benefit which she had obtained.

NOTES AND QUESTIONS

1. Are the criticisms levelled against both the majority and the minority approaches in *Tinsley v Milligan* convincing?

---

24 See, however, the reservations about the use of 'seriousness' as the test for granting or withholding relief in *Pitts* [1991] 1 QB 24 at 56 (a tort case) quoting *Jackson v Harrison* (1978) 138 CLR 438 at 455.

25 *In re Torrez* (1987) 827 F 2d 1299 at 1301–2.

26 Cf. *Yango* (1978) 139 CLR 410 at 429.   27 Elements (ii) and (iii) may often overlap.

2. What alternative has the High Court put forward in place of the approaches adopted in *Tinsley*? Is it any more satisfactory?

3. The majority of the court (Deane, Gummow, and McHugh JJ) granted relief on terms. Can this restriction upon the claimant's entitlement to relief be justified?

4. In their joint judgment, Deane and Gummow JJ approved comments of Professor Scott concerning the relationship between the resulting trust and illegality generally:

> Although a resulting trust ordinarily arises where A purchases property and takes title in the name of B, A may be precluded from enforcing the resulting trust because of the illegality of his purpose. If A cannot recover the property, B keeps it and is thereby enriched. The question in each case is whether the policy against unjust enrichment of the grantee is outweighed by the policy against giving relief to the payor who has entered an illegal transaction.

5. *Nelson* and *Tribe* are discussed in more detail by N Enonchong [1996] *RLR* 78.

8. INCAPACITY

(1) MINORS

We have already discussed a number of cases in which minors have sought to recover benefits conferred upon adults, using their minority as the ground of restitution (see Chapter 11 above). In the cases which follow, the minor appears as a *defendant* seeking to rely upon his or her minority as a defence to a restitutionary claim which is being brought against him or her. Minors have limited contractual capacity and so, in certain circumstances (for example, in the case of contracts for necessaries) may incur contractual liability (see generally G. Treitel, *The Law of Contract* (11th edn, 2003), 539–50). We are not concerned with such contractual liability here, except to note that minors do have limited contractual capacity, and one might expect the law of restitution to be wary of undermining the rules of the law of contract by recognising a wide liability on the part of the minor in the law of restitution.

Minors may incur liability in restitution in one of two ways. The first is liability at common law (including equity) and the second is as a result of the intervention of statute, in the form of the Minors' Contracts Act 1987.

(i) LIABILITY AT COMMON LAW AND IN EQUITY

The position at common law and in equity was (and still is) a confused one. The general picture which emerges is that the courts have been prepared to recognize that a minor may incur liability where he had committed a wrong, but they have been extremely reluctant to admit liability where no wrong had been committed. But the cases are not at all satisfactory: they are tied up with the now discredited 'implied contract' theory of restitution and, further, are not at all easy to reconcile. We shall consider the cases in chronological order.

- *Cowern v Nield* [1912] 2 KB 419, King's Bench Division

The claimant paid the defendant minor £35 19s for clover and hay. The defendant failed to deliver the hay and the clover which he delivered was found to be rotten. The claimant rejected the clover and sought to recover his prepayment. It was held that his claim could not succeed unless he could show that the defendant had obtained the money by fraud.

Phillimore J: ... I am satisfied from the authorities which have been cited to us that the only contracts which, if for the infant's benefit, are enforceable against him are contracts relating to the infant's person, such as contracts for necessaries, food, clothing, and lodging, contracts of marriage, and contracts of apprenticeship and service. In my opinion a trading contract does not come within that category. ... Infants ... are not liable ex contractu, except in the cases I have mentioned, but they always have been liable ex delicto. If an infant has acquired personal property to which he has no title an action of trover or detinue will lie against him, and in *Bristow v Eastman*,[1] which was an action against an infant for money had and received which he had embezzled, and which has, I think, an important bearing on the present case, Lord Kenyon said that 'he was of opinion that infancy was no defence to the action; that infants were liable to actions ex delicto, though not ex contractu; and though the present action was in its form an action of the latter description, yet is was of the former in point of substance.' That proposition ... shews that an action for money had and received can be maintained against an infant if the substance of the action is that the infant has obtained the money ex delicto. If, therefore, the plaintiff can prove in the present case that the defendant obtained his money by fraud the action can be maintained. ...

NOTES AND QUESTIONS

1. The claimant clearly had a claim for the return of the money paid on the ground of total failure of consideration. Why did the court refuse to recognize the claim?
2. Would the defendant have been liable to make restitution to the claimant if the claimant had paid the money to the defendant under a mistake of fact?
3. The defendant having received money, there was no difficulty in establishing that he had been enriched. But what would have been the position if the defendant had received a non-money benefit? Is incontrovertible benefit the only test which can be applied in determining whether the minor has been enriched, or is there any room for the 'bargained-for' test for enrichment, or any other test?
4. Professor Treitel (*The Law of Contract* (11th edn, 2003), 557) maintains that the claimant in *Cowern* should not have been able to succeed merely by proving that the defendant had been fraudulent. He argues that the 'minor should have been liable only to the extent that the money or its identifiable proceeds were still in his hands' (see further the discussion of *R. Leslie Ltd v Sheill*, below, 922).

- *Stocks v Wilson* [1913] 2 KB 235, King's Bench Division

The infant defendant, by fraudulently misrepresenting his age, induced the claimant to sell and deliver to him some furniture and other goods from her house. The sale price was £300. The defendant promised to repay the value of the goods at a later date and gave the claimant a licence to repossess the goods in the event of his failure to pay. The defendant sold some of the goods for £30 and, with the consent of the claimant, granted a bill of sale of the remainder as security for an advance of £100. The defendant failed to pay the claimant on the appointed day, and so an action was brought in equity to recover the reasonable value of the goods supplied. It was held that the defendant was not liable in conversion because property in the goods had vested in the defendant, but that the defendant was liable to account for the £30 and the £100 advance which he had obtained as a result of the transactions which he had entered into. But the defendant was not liable on the contract for the reasonable value of the goods obtained.

---

1 1 Esp 172.

Lush J: . . . The next question, which is the one that has caused me some difficulty, is whether under the peculiar circumstances of this case the plaintiff has a claim for equitable relief, and if so to what amount. That an infant who appears to be of full age, and who has made an express representation that he is of full age fraudulently and to deceive some other person, incurs an equitable liability under some circumstances is clear enough. He cannot be sued for damages although he is generally speaking liable for a tort; the reason being that a temptation would be offered both to the infant himself and to other persons to enter into contracts if the other party were able by obtaining a representation of majority by the infant to make the contract practically effective. For the more complete protection of the infant, the law prevents the other contracting party not only from suing on the contract, but also from suing for damages, if the fraud is connected with and forms the inducement to the contract. Nor is the infant estopped from proving the true facts, which again, if such an estoppel were permitted, would deprive the infant of the protection necessary for his security. What the Court of Equity has done in cases of this kind is to prevent the infant from retaining the benefit of what he has obtained by reason of his fraud. It has done no more than this, and this is a very different thing from making him liable to pay damages or compensation for the loss of the other party's bargain. If the infant has obtained property by fraud he can be compelled to restore it; if he has obtained money he can be compelled to refund it. If he has not obtained either, but has only purported to bind himself by an obligation to transfer property or to pay money, neither in a Court of law nor a Court of Equity can he be compelled to make good his promise or to make satisfaction for its breach

[*He then considered whether the plaintiff was entitled to a remedy and continued:*]

Now I am of opinion that she has a remedy. The jurisdiction which the Court exercises is not only a jurisdiction over the property which the infant has acquired by his fraud, but also over the infant himself to compel him to make satisfaction. . . . In my opinion it follows that, if an infant has wrongfully sold the property which he acquired by a fraudulent misrepresentation as to his age, he must at all events account for the proceeds to the party he has defrauded. I can see no logical ground on which he can be allowed to resist such a claim in that case, if he is accountable for the money itself in a case where he has obtained money and not goods by means of a like fraud. It is not necessary for me to decide more than this in the present case because, assuming that an infant, who has wrongfully obtained goods in the way in which this defendant obtained them, and who wrongfully parts with them either as a gift or at an undervalue, must account for their real value, I must hold on the facts of this case that the defendant is only bound to account for what he actually received, for the following reason: Some of the goods, as I have said, he sold for 300*l.*, and I have no evidence to lead me to say that they were sold for too little. As to the remainder he gave a bill of sale over them which was assented to and even arranged by the plaintiff acting through Arthur St. Claire Stocks, her agent. It was, I think, known to all the parties to be very problematical whether the defendant would be able, and in fact he has been unable, to redeem the goods. The advance made by the bill of sale holder was of course much less than the value of the goods, (the jury found that the value of the whole collection was 30*l.*); but I do not think that under these circumstances the plaintiff ought to be permitted to say that the defendant should account for the actual value or to say that the defendant obtained any other benefit from his fraud than the moneys he actually received. The defendant did not, except as to the 30*l.* worth of goods, wrongfully part with the goods at all; on the contrary, the plaintiff through her agent assented to his putting it out of his power to restore them, and she cannot therefore complain that he is not in a position to do so. There was a dispute as to whether the plaintiff's agent, Arthur St. Claire Stocks received some of the moneys advanced to the defendant by the bill of the sale holder. It has been left to me to decide the amount for which the defendant is liable, and I accept, as the jury accepted, the evidence of Arthur St. Claire Stocks in preference to that of the defendant, and find that he did not receive any part of the money as alleged. The defendant received the benefit of the whole of the advance, the plaintiff herself providing part of the money, namely, 50*l.* What the total advance was I am not clear and, if necessary, I must take an account in order to ascertain it, but no doubt the parties will be able to agree the figures. For this sum, to which the 30*l.* for what was sold must be added, I hold the defendant liable.

QUESTIONS

1. Was the equity recognized by Lush J of a personal or a proprietary nature?
2. Did Lush J inquire whether the proceeds were still in the hands of the defendant?
3. Can the decision be criticized on the ground that it indirectly enforced a contract which was void at law?

● *R Leslie Ltd v Sheill* [1914] 3 KB 607, Court of Appeal

The infant defendant induced the claimant moneylenders to lend him £400 by fraudulently misrepresenting that he was an adult. When they discovered the true position, the claimants sought to recover their advances. Their claim was brought on the ground that the money had been obtained by means of the defendant's fraudulent misrepresentation and in the alternative for money had and received by the defendant to the use of the claimants. The claimants failed in their attempt to recover the £400. The Court of Appeal held that the defendant's minority provided him with a good defence to the claims brought.

Lord Sumner: . . . To the claim for return of the principal moneys paid to the infant under the contract that failed, as money had and received to the plaintiffs' use, there are at least two answers: the infancy itself was an answer before 1874 at common law, and the Infants' Relief Act, 1874, is an answer now. An action for money had and received against an infant has been sustained, where in substance the cause of action was ex delicto: *Bristow v Eastman*,[1] approved before 1874 in *In re Seager*,[2] and cited without disapproval in *Cowern v Nield*.[3] Even this has been doubted, but where the substance of the cause of action is contractual, it is certainly otherwise. To money had and received and other indebitatus counts infancy was a defence just as to any other action in contract: *Alton v Midland Ry. Co.*, per Willes J;[4] *In re Jones*, per Jessel Mr.[5] Dicey on Parties, 284; Bullen and Leake's Precedents of Pleadings, 3rd edn, 605. Further, under the statute the principle, which at common law relieved an infant from liability for a tort directly connected with a voidable contract, namely, that it was impossible to enforce in a roundabout way an unenforceable contract, equally forbids Courts of law to allow, under the name of an implied contract or in the form of an action quasi ex contractu, a proceeding to enforce part of a contract, which the statute declares to be wholly void. This has been recently illustrated in the closely analogous case of a claim on the footing of money had and received for moneys paid but irrecoverable under what in law was a lending and borrowing ultra vires: *Sinclair v Brougham*.[6]

The ground on which Horridge J held the appellant liable was that by reason of his fraud he was compellable in equity to repay the money, actually received and professedly borrowed, and compellable too by a judgment in personam for the amount, not by any mere proprietary remedy. [*He then considered the development of the rule in equity and continued:*] I think that the whole current of decisions down to 1913, apart from dicta which are inconclusive, went to shew that, when an infant obtained an advantage by falsely stating himself to be of full age, equity required him to restore his ill-gotten gains, or to release the party deceived from obligations or acts in law induced by the fraud, but scrupulously stopped short of enforcing against him a contractual obligation, entered into while he was an infant, even by means of a fraud. This applies even to *In re King, Ex parte Unity*

---

1 1 Esp 172.   2 60 LT 665.   3 [1912] 2 KB 419.   4 (1865) 34 LJ (CP) 292, at 297, 298.
5 18 ChD at 118.   6 [1914] AC 398.

Joint Stock Mutual Banking Association.[7] Restitution stopped where repayment began; as Kindersley V-C puts it in *Vaughan v Vanderstegen*,[8] an analogous case, 'you take the property to pay the debt.'

Last year, in *Stocks v Wilson*,[9] an infant, who had obtained furniture from the plaintiff by falsely stating that he was of age and had sold part of it for 30*l.*, was personally adjudged by Lush J to pay this 30*l.* as part of the relief granted to the plaintiff. This is the case which more than any other influenced Horridge J in the Court below. I think it is plain that Lush J conceived himself to be merely applying the equitable principle of restitution. The form of the claim was that, by way of equitable relief, the infant should be ordered to pay the reasonable value of the goods, which he could not restore because he had sold them. The argument was that equity would not allow him to keep the goods and not pay for them, that if he kept the property he must discharge the burthen, and that he could not better his position by having put it out of his power to give up the property, Lush J expressly says 'it is a jurisdiction to compel the infant to make satisfaction,' and, at 246, 'the remedy is not on the contract.' At 242–3 he says 'what the Court of Equity has done in cases of this kind is to prevent the infant from retaining the benefit of what he has obtained by reason of his fraud. It has done no more than this, and this is a very different thing from making him liable to pay damages and compensation for the loss of the other party's bargain. If the infant has obtained property by fraud he can be compelled to restore it'; but now comes the proposition, which applies to the present case and is open to challenge, 'if he has obtained money he can be compelled to refund it.' The learned judge thought that the fundamental principle in *In re King, Ex parte Unity Joint Stock Mutual Banking Association* was a liability to account for the money obtained by the fraudulent representation, and that in the case before him there must be a similar liability to account for the proceeds of the sale of the goods obtained by this fraud. If this be his ratio decidendi, though I have difficulty in seeing what liability to account there can be (and certainly none is named in *In re King, Ex parte Unity Joint Stock Mutual Banking Association*), the decision in *Stocks v Wilson* is distinguishable from the present case and is independent of the above dictum, and I need express no opinion about it. In the present case there is clearly no accounting. There is no fiduciary relation: the money was paid over in order to be used as the defendant's own and he has so used it and, I suppose, spent it. There is no question of tracing it, no possibility of restoring the very thing got by the fraud, nothing but compulsion through a personal judgment to pay an equivalent sum out of his present or future resources, in a word nothing but a judgment in debt to repay the loan. I think this would be nothing but enforcing a void contract. So far as I can find, the Court of Chancery never would have enforced any liability under circumstances like the present, any more than a Court of law would have done so, and I think that no ground can be found for the present judgment, which would be an answer to the Infants' Relief Act.

. . .

A. T. Lawrence J: . . .

It has been the policy of the law to protect infants; they have been held incapable of binding themselves by their contracts—with certain exceptions not material to this case. That this is the law was admitted. But it was argued for the plaintiffs that these considerations do not affect the claim for 'money had and received.' Horridge J was induced to take the view (following a decision of Lush J in *Stocks v Wilson* that there was in equity a right to relief to the extent of the money actually received. It was said for the plaintiffs that the action for money had and received was not founded upon a promise implied by law, but rested upon what was called by counsel a 'doctrine of equity.' I do not think this argument is well founded. There are no doubt many cases in which equity will give relief against frauds perpetrated by infants. Wherever the infant requires as a plaintiff the assistance of any Court, it will be refused until he has made good his fraudulent representation. Wherever the infant is still in possession of any property which he has obtained by his fraud he will be made to restore it to

7 3 De G & J 63.   8 (1854) 2 Drew 363.   9 [1913] 2 KB 235.

its former owner. But I think that it is incorrect to say that he can be made to repay money which he has spent, merely because he received it under a contract induced by his fraud.

The contracts of an infant, which were formerly voidable only, are now by the Infants' Relief Act, 1874, made absolutely void. He is further protected in respect of loans by 55 & 56 Vict. c. 4, ss. 3, 4, 5. These statutes are as binding upon the equitable, as they are upon the common law, jurisdiction of the Court. I do not think that it is correct to say that the action for money had and received is wholly independent of contract. It arises wherever money has been received which ex æquo et bono belongs to the plaintiff. In such case the law implies a promise to pay it to the plaintiff, but where the express promise to repay the money is by statute 'absolutely void' it is impossible to imply a promise to repay the same money . . . To do so would be to (in large part) defeat the policy of the statute, and would violate the well-established principle that where there is an express promise no other like promise can be implied.

. . . .

The judgment in *Stocks v Wilson* seems to treat the subsequent sale of the property by the infant as wrongful, and as affording a foundation for treating the money obtained thereby as received to the plaintiff's use. If this had been so, if it had been a wrong independent of contract, it would no doubt have made a case in which the plaintiff could, by waiving the tort, have afforded a consideration for the implied promise to pay over the proceeds, and he could have recovered on the common count for 'money had and received.' But this is rendered impossible by the judge's finding that the property in the goods had passed to the infant before he disposed of them (and as to the major portion thereof that he did so with the concurrence of the plaintiff in the action). The really wrongful act was the obtaining the goods under the contract of purchase by the pretence that he was of full age; as to that, it was admitted that he could not be sued in tort for the fraud. There was therefore no actionable tort independent of contract which could be waived to form a consideration for the implied promise.

In the case of *Watts v Cresmell*,[10] which was relied upon the fraudulent infant was in possession of the lands as to which he had misrepresented the title, and was setting up a former settlement upon himself to defeat the mortgagee under that title. It was held that he could not do so in equity without making satisfaction for the fraud. This is a long way from establishing anything like an equity to sue as for 'money had and received.' If when the action is brought both the property and the proceeds are gone, I see no ground upon which a Court of Equity could have founded its jurisdiction. . . .

Kennedy LJ gave a concurring judgment.

NOTES AND QUESTIONS

1. Can *Stocks v Wilson* be reconciled with *Leslie v Sheill* or has it effectively been overruled?

2. If the court had recognized the existence of a restitutionary claim, would the effect of its decision have been indirectly to enforce a contract of loan which was not binding on the minor at law? Would the contractual measure of recovery and the restitution measure always be the same, given that interest cannot be recovered on a restitutionary claim except under statute? What impact does the recognition of change of position in *Lipkin Gorman* have on your answer to the latter question?

3. Birks argued (*Unjust Enrichment*, 255) that 'the crucial proposition is that the protection of the minor is not subverted by making him give up still surviving enrichment'. Does this case support his view? Would it not be better to recognize a claim to the value received subject to the defence of change of position?

---

10 9 Vin Abr 415.

4. In the light of the fact that *Sinclair v Brougham* (above, 6) was over-ruled by the House of Lords in *Westdeutsche Landesbank Girozentrale v Islington London Borough Council* (above 40, 368) can the reasoning of Lord Summer still be regarded as good law?

(ii) STATUTORY LIABILITY

• Minors' Contracts Act 1987, section 3

3.—(1) Where—

(a) a person ('the plaintiff') has after the commencement of this Act entered into a contract with another ('the defendant'), and

(b) the contract is unenforceable against the defendant (or he repudiates it) because he was a minor when the contract was made,

the court may, if it is just and equitable to do so, require the defendant to transfer to the plaintiff any property acquired by the defendant under the contract, or any property representing it.

(2) Nothing in this section shall be taken to prejudice any other remedy available to the plaintiff.

NOTES AND QUESTIONS

1. The right of recovery created by section 3 appears to be wider than the liability of the minor at common law, and it may therefore be that the common law rules have been rendered virtually redundant. But section 3(2) expressly preserves existing rights of action against the minor.

2. What is meant by 'any property acquired by the defendant under the contract, or any property representing it'? How will the courts work out whether or not any property 'represents' the property which he or she received?

3. Does 'property' acquired by the defendant or 'property representing it' include money?

4. Brian agrees to sell his computer to Arnold, aged 15, for £1,000, payment to be made two weeks after delivery of the computer. Brian delivers the computer, but Arnold fails to make any payment. Instead he sells the computer for £750 and pays £500 into his bank account (which at the time had a credit balance of £60) and uses the remaining £250 to purchase a second-hand motorbike. Arnold now has £450 in his bank account but refuses to make any payment to Brian. Advise Brian.

5. Has the Act introduced a coherent set of rules or is further reform still required?

6. Legislation has also been introduced in Australia in an effort to provide a more satisfactory solution to these problems. The solution has generally taken the form of entrusting the court with a broad discretion to order restitution on such terms and conditions as it thinks just. An example of this approach is provided by section 37 of the New South Wales Minors (Property and Contracts) Act 1970. Section 37(1) provides that, where a 'civil act' is repudiated by a minor in accordance with the terms of the Act, a court may, on the application of any person interested in the civil act, make orders

(a) for the confirmation, wholly or in part, of the civil act or of anything done under the civil act; or

(b) for the adjustment of rights arising out of the civil act or out of the repudiation or out of anything done under the civil act.

The section continues in the following terms:

(2) Without limiting the generality of paragraph (a) of subsection (1) of this section, where, on an application under this section, it appears to the court that any party to the civil act was induced to participate in the civil act by a misrepresentation made by a minor participant in the civil act, being a fraudulent misrepresentation as to the age of the minor participant or as to any other matter affecting the capacity of the minor participant to participate in the civil act, the court may confirm the civil act and anything done under the civil act.

(3) Where a civil act is presumptively binding in favour of any person, the court shall not make any order under this section adversely affecting his rights except with his consent.

(4) Subject to subsection (3) of this section, and except so far as the court confirms the civil act or anything done under the civil act, the court shall make such orders as are authorised by this section and as the court thinks fit for the purpose of securing so far as practicable that—

(a) each minor participant in the civil act makes just compensation for all property, services and other things derived by him by or under the civil act to the extent that the derivation of that property or of those services or things is for his benefit;

(b) each other participant in the civil act makes just compensation for all property, services and other things derived by him by or under the civil act; and

(c) subject to paragraphs (a) and (b) of this subsection, the parties to the civil act and those claiming under them are restored to their positions before the time of the civil act.

(5) Any court having jurisdiction under this section may, for the purposes of this section, make orders—

(a) for the delivery of goods; and

(b) for the payment of money.

(6) In addition to its jurisdiction under subsection (5) of this section, the Supreme Court may, for the purposes of this section, make orders for—

(a) the making of any disposition of property;

(b) the sale or other realisation of property;

(c) the disposal of the proceeds of sale or other realisation of property;

(d) the creation of a charge on property in favour of any person;

(e) the enforcement of a charge so created;

(f) the appointment and regulation of the proceedings of a receiver of property;

(g) the vesting of property in any person; and

(h) the rescission or variation of any order of the Supreme Court under this section.

(7) A court may make an order under this section on such terms and conditions as the court thinks fit.

Does this approach constitute an improvement upon the Minors' Contracts Act? If so, in what respects?

7. Should minority ever be a defence to a claim for restitution of an unjust enrichment?

(2) LOCAL AUTHORITIES AND COMPANIES

The role of ultra vires as a defence to a claim brought against a company has been virtually eliminated by section 35(1) of the Companies Act 1985 which states that 'The validity of an act done by a company shall not be called into question on the ground of lack of capacity by reason of anything in the company's memorandum.' The position at common law was, however, rather more uncertain and this uncertainty has proved to be of considerable significance recently in the context of local authorities acting *ultra vires* in entering into swap transactions.

There was some authority to support the proposition that ultra vires did not provide a company with a defence to a restitutionary claim brought by the other party to the *ultra vires* transaction. Thus in *Re Phoenix Life Assurance Co.* (1862) 2J & H 441 the defendant company acted ultra vires in issuing marine insurance policies when under its objects it was entitled to issue only life assurance policies. It was held that the claimant policy holders were not entitled to enforce their policies on the winding up of the company, but that they were entitled to recover the premiums which they had paid on the ground that they had been paid for a consideration which had wholly failed. However the decision in *Phoenix Life* was soon put under a cloud as a result of the decision of the House of Lords in *Sinclair v Brougham* (above, 6) in which it was held that the depositors could not recover the payments which they had made to the society in an action for money had and received. Although the decision was the subject of considerable academic criticism in the intervening eighty years, it was not until the case of *Westdeutsche Landesbank Girozentrale v Islington London Borough Council* (above, 40) that the House of Lords was given the opportunity to reconsider *Sinclair v Brougham*. Lord Browne-Wilkinson, with whom Lords Slynn and Lloyd agreed, held that the depositors should have had a personal claim to recover the moneys at law based on a total failure of consideration.

QUESTION

In the light of the decision of the House of Lords in *Westdeutsche Landesbank* can incapacity ever provide a local authority with a defence to an otherwise valid claim for restitution of an unjust enrichment?

15

RESTITUTION FOR WRONGS

At the start (above, 2–3) it was explained that this book is largely concerned with restitution of unjust enrichments, where the cause of action (or event) to which restitution responds is an unjust enrichment of the defendant at the claimant's expense. But in this final chapter we cross over into a fundamentally distinct part of the law of restitution where the cause of action (or event) to which restitution responds is the commission of a (civil) wrong by the defendant against the claimant. As the structure of this chapter makes clear the primary common law wrongs are torts and breach of contract; and the primary equitable wrongs are breach of fiduciary duty and breach of confidence.

Apart from having to establish different criteria for the two different causes of action (unjust enrichment and the wrong), secondary legal rules (e.g. as regards limitation of actions and conflict of laws) may differ as between those two causes of action. Moreover, some of the defences applicable are different: most importantly, change of position applies to the restitution of unjust enrichment but not, it appears, to restitution for wrongs (see above, 804).

In many cases—but not all—a further distinguishing feature of restitution for wrongs, as against restitution of unjust enrichments, will be the measure of restitution. In relation to restitution for wrongs, it is clear that the claimant can recover more than its loss. This will often be the primary reason why the claimant seeks restitution rather than the standard remedy of compensation for the wrong. In contrast, the cause of action of unjust enrichment requires that the defendant's gain was at the expense of the claimant in the sense that it was subtracted from the claimant's wealth (see above, 109–110). And normally, albeit not always, there will be an equivalence between the defendant's gain and the claimant's loss.

A further possible difference concerns the establishing and valuing of the benefit. We have seen that in relation to restitution of unjust enrichments, establishing that the defendant was benefited can be problematic (above, 71–109) In particular, the law respects a defendant's subjective devaluation of an objective benefit albeit that that may be overcome by the claimant showing, for example, that the defendant was incontrovertibly benefited. But subject to a rare exception (see *Ministry of Defence v Ashman*, below, 964) 'subjective devaluation' has no role to play in respect of restitution for wrongs precisely because the defendant has made the gain by committing a wrong. Admittedly, one could say that particular tests overcoming subjective devaluation are in play (e.g. that the defendant 'reprehensibly sought out the benefit'). But it may be better to recognize that, because the policies in play in respect of the different causes of action are different, objective identification and valuation of the benefit is almost invariably straightforwardly applicable in the context of restitution for wrongs.

At a deeper level, all these differences may reflect different moral ideas underpinning restitution for wrongs and restitution of unjust enrichments. Nevertheless, we include extracts here from Barker (937) and Weinrib (938) who seek to defend the idea that restitution for wrongs, like restitution of unjust enrichments, rests on corrective justice.

There are two main linked legal uncertainties in this area. First, it is unclear when restitution is available for wrongs. Features that appear to have been important in some past cases include whether the wrong is a proprietary (rather than a personal) wrong; whether the wrong was committed cynically/intentionally: and whether compensation is inadequate. We here include extracts by Jackman, Birks, and Edelman who have grappled with these ideas in attempting to present a coherent picture of the law.

Secondly, there is uncertainty as to the correct measure of restitution for a wrong. Edelman's central thesis (below, 936) is that so-called restitution for wrongs in fact embodies two different remedial measures which should be kept distinct. The first is the reversal of a wrongful transfer of value from a claimant to a defendant. He terms this measure 'restitutionary damages'. The second is the stripping away of profits made by the defendant committing a wrong to the claimant. He calls this measure 'disgorgement damages'.

Four further complications are as follows. First, a host of different remedies, including an award of money had and received, damages and an account of profits, have all been used to effect personal restitution for wrongs. Secondly, in respect of equitable wrongs, the courts have been willing to grant proprietary restitution by making the wrongdoer a constructive trustee of the gains (see, for example, *LAC Minerals Ltd v International Corona Resources Ltd, Attorney General for Hong Kong v Reid*, and *Daraydon Holdings Ltd v Solland International Ltd*, below, 1031, 1018, 1023). It is controversial as to whether this creation of proprietary rights to effect restitution for a wrong is justified. Thirdly, in some of the damages cases (e.g. *Jaggard v Sawyer* below, 967) it is a matter of dispute whether the courts were compensating the claimant's wrongful loss (albeit by taking an unconventional view of the relevant loss) or were awarding restitution to remove some (or all) of the defendant's wrongful gain. Finally, some commentators, for example Lionel Smith, 'The Province of the Law of Restitution' (1992) 71 *Can BR* 672, have argued that the term 'restitution' should be confined to the cause of action of unjust enrichment where one is concerned with the gain being a loss to, or a subtraction from, the claimant. The gain-based response to a wrong, because it is not linked to loss/subtraction, is better termed 'disgorgement' rather than 'restitution'. While we do not think such a terminological switch would be helpful, not least because restitution can equally well refer to a giving up as well as a giving back, we have indicated at the start of this chapter (see also above, 2–3) that we accept that there is a fundamental difference between restitution of unjust enrichments and restitution for wrongs.

General Reading

Burrows, chapter 14; Goff and Jones, 20-024–20-034, chapters 33, 34, 36; Virgo, Part IV.

1. THREE ACADEMIC ANALYSES OF WHEN THERE SHOULD BE RESTITUTION FOR WRONGS

- I Jackman, 'Restitution for Wrongs' (1989) 48 *CLJ* 302

In what circumstances can a person be liable to a pecuniary remedy for conduct which has not caused the plaintiff any harm? This question lies at the heart of the present topic, in which the plaintiff seeks to disgorge a benefit acquired by the defendant through the latter's wrongful act, even though the wrong has not actually caused him loss or injury. Consider, for example, a trespasser who has benefited by using a track across the plaintiff's land without reducing the value of the land; the plaintiff, who might never have been willing to consent to such use of his land, now seeks payment as if his permission for that user had been sought at a price. In terms of 'unjust enrichment,' the plaintiff's claim is that the defendant's enrichment is 'unjust' by virtue of the wrong committed, without showing that the enrichment is at his expense.

The concept of 'unjust enrichment,' however, begs the question of identifying the precise concept of injustice at stake in the defendant's gain. In the context of restitution for wrongs, the injustice cannot lie in causing harm or loss to the plaintiff, for the remedy is available without proof that the wrong has made him worse off. But some kind of harm or loss other than to the plaintiff personally might still arise. The basis of the present article is that the rationale for the right to restitution for wrongs is the protection of a variety of private legal facilities, or facilitative institutions, namely private property, relationships of trust and confidence, and (with some qualification) contracts. Such facilities require protection against those who seek to take the benefits of an institution without submitting to the burden thereof, and in this way the right to restitution for a wrong is triggered not by harm to a person as such, but by harm to an institution. The catalogue of wrongs which give rise to restitution can thus be seen to fall into a coherent pattern, ranging across the law of obligations, both at common law and in equity.

. . .

It is often suggested that no one shall be allowed to profit from his own wrong. That maxim mis-leadingly implies the universal availability of restitution for benefits made by any legal wrong, and there are many breaches of legal duty (for example, breach of contract and certain torts such as defamation) which do not give rise to restitutionary remedies. Hence, as Lord Goff said recently, the maxim 'does not of itself provide any sure guidance to the solution of a problem in any particular case.'[1] We require instead a criterion to determine which wrongs do, and which do not, trigger the right to restitution.

As a starting-point, it is instructive to consider the 'harm principle' of J. S. Mill, that 'the only purpose for which power can be rightfully exercised over any member of a civilised community, against his will, is to prevent harm to others.'[2] Read narrowly in the context of private law, with 'harm to others' interpreted as a reference to harm to the plaintiff, Mill's harm principle seems hostile to the very possibility of liability where the plaintiff has not personally suffered loss or injury through the defendant's acquisitive wrong. But there are grounds for a broader interpretation, based on the width of the expression 'harm to others,' which prompts inquiry as to who those others might be and how their concern with acquisitive wrongs might arise.

To this end, it should be noted that Mill prefaces the harm principle with the remark that the principle is 'to govern absolutely the dealings of society with the individual *in the way of compulsion and control.*'[3] There are, however, functions of a legal system other than those designed to control human behaviour by means of coercion. In particular, the law provides power-conferring facilities for the creation of private arrangements between individuals, such as contracts, trusts and private prop-erty;[4] and it is these facilitative institutions, it is submitted, which provide the context for the present topic. We are not concerned here with the rules for the creation of such private legal orders or institutions, but with the remedies available under them. As Raz points out, the provision of facilities for private arrangements between individuals is not solely concerned with rights and powers; for the

---

1 *Attorney-General v Guardian Newspapers Ltd (No 2)* [1988] 3 All ER 545, at 662 (the *'Spycatcher'* case).

2 J Mill, *Utilitarianism, Liberty. Representative Government* (Everyman edn, London, 1910), 73.

3 *Ibid.* 72 (emphasis added).

4 See H Hart, *The Concept of Law* (Oxford, 1961), 27, 40–1; Joseph Raz, *The Authority of Law* (Oxford, 1979), 169–70.

'[r]ights and powers to conclude contracts, acquire and dispose of property, establish corporations, marry etc., would be pointless and without effect but for the duties to perform contracts, respect property rights, etc.'[5] It is at this remedial point that coercive control arises. Just as the law protects people directly from harm, so must the law protect the integrity of these facilitative legal institutions, and the structure of civil remedies thus reflects the need to guard against not only personal harm, but also institutional harm.[6] In stitutional harm may not be a form of immediate 'harm to others,' but will be in a mediate way, by depriving a community of the integrity (and thus the utility) of its facilitative institutions. Further, these two kinds of protection from harm operate independently, so that even if no one personally and immediately has suffered harm, a remedy might still be attracted to protect a particular facilitative institution. The central questions are to identify first, which facilitative institution is at stake in any given case, and secondly, what is required to fulfil the rights and duties which exist by virtue of it. The subject-matter falls into three categories: private property, relationships of trust and confidence, and contract. And subject to the qualification to be made below in respect of contractual remedies, the characteristic pecuniary remedy for institutional harm is restitutionary, while the remedial counterpart for personal harm lies in compensation.

[*Jackman then examines in detail the cases awarding restitution in order to protect property (through restitutionary damages, an account of profits, or waiver of tort, for proprietary torts) and in order to protect relationships of trust and confidence (through an account of profits for breach of fiduciary duty or through an account of profits or restitutionary damages for breach of confidence). He also explains that 'once the infringement of a private legal facility is shown, there may be scope for applying different measures of relief according to different degrees of wrongfulness.' He then goes on to examine cases on breach of contract*:]

It is submitted . . . that on present authority restitution (in the form of an account of profits or constructive trust) is not available for breach of contract, unless the breach involves a concurrent infringement of proprietary rights or fiduciary obligations, which institutions represent irreducibly distinct categories of legal thought.

Why, then, has the law taken such an absolute stance against regarding breach of contract as a restitution-yielding wrong? The answer may lie in the nature of the pecuniary remedies already available for breach of contract. The aim of compensatory damages in contract is to place the innocent party 'so far as money can do it . . . in the same situation . . . as if the contract had been performed,'[7] which typically involves compensating the plaintiff for the gains which he expected to receive from the performance of the other party's obligations.[8] Atiyah has argued that, contrary to this orthodoxy, contractual expectations are relatively unworthy of legal protection, for 'a disappointed expectation is a psychological rather than a pecuniary injury, and the law is generally sparing in its willingness to award compensation for injuries or losses which are neither physical nor pecuniary.'[9] This argument, however, does not conclude the matter. It may be that any personal harm caused by disappointed expectations is a weak ground for protecting those expectations, but there remains the problem of institutional harm. On this basis, expectation damages may be seen as aimed at preserving the integrity and stability of contractual obligations, by making good the underlying promises. As Raz argues:

---

5 Joseph Raz, *The Authority of Law*, 170.

6 Joseph Raz, 'Promises in Morality and Law' (1982) 95 *Harv. LR* 916 at 937; C Ten, *Mill On Liberty* (Oxford, 1980), 57.

7 *Robinson v Harman* (1848) 1 Exch. 850 at 855.

8 Charles Fried, *Contract as Promise* (Cambridge, Mass., 1981), 17–21. This is not to deny that there are other sources of compensation, such as the plaintiff's detrimental reliance, as I Fuller and W Perdue showed: 'The Reliance Interest in Contract Damages' (1936) 46 *Yale LJ* 52, 373.

9 P Atiyah, *Essays in Contract* (Oxford, 1986), 34–5; 'Contracts, Promises and the Law of Obligations' (1978) 94 *LQR* 193 at 215–16; cf. *The Rise and Fall of Freedom of Contract* (Oxford, 1979), 3–5.

'Harm' includes institutional harm. Preventing the erosion or debasement of the practice of undertaking voluntary obligations is therefore a fit object for the law to pursue.[10]

Herein lies an asymmetry, though not an anomaly, in the availability of restitution for wrongs. The analysis of proprietary torts and relationships of trust and confidence suggests a simple dichotomy whereby restitutionary remedies are directed against institutional harm whereas compensatory remedies operate to redress personal harm. But the rationale for awarding compensation for lost expectations in contract is to give contracts sufficient institution protection to maintain that degree of stability which is essential to any practice of promise-making Hence, the compensatory remedy provides protection from institutional harm, without the intervention of restitution.

English law, at present, is content to leave the matter there. The common law does not take a censorious attitude to breach of contract, consistently with the view that a party to a contract, unlike a fiduciary, operates at arm's length and holds his powers for his own benefit. He is thus free to change his mind about the wisdom of a particular contract which he has entered into and, in the absence of specific performance or an injunction, then on payment of compensation for the other party's reliance or lost expectations, he may deploy his resources more profitably elsewhere. Once expectation damages are awarded, the argument might run, there is no institutional harm left to be redressed.

Elsewhere in this topic, however, the availability of particular measures of restitutionary relief indicates that the flatness and moral bluntness of a rule based solely on the nature of the facilitative institution may need to be supplemented by the infusion of a hierarchy of moral fault, although this has not been achieved systematically in our law. In the same way, the person who makes 'deliberate recourse to breach of contract for the sake of making a gain'[11] threatens the integrity of contracts in a way which might demand additional institutional protection, in the form of an account of profits in equity. The availability of such a remedy would then enable the court to consider the full range of features of each case, particularly the moral quality of the breach, which should, but cannot at present, influence the measure of pecuniary relief.

CONCLUSION

By enriching Mill's harm principle, so as to include institutional as well as personal harm, the question posed at the outset may be answered thus. Even where the defendant's conduct has not caused the plaintiff any harm, the plaintiff can disgorge the defendant's gain if he can show that such restitution is necessary to protect one of the facilitative institutions: property, relationships of trust and confidence, or contract. The basic principles are thus drawn in terms of the type of facility at stake, but the appropriate flexibility can be achieved only by fortifying that strategy with considerations of the moral calibre of the defendant's conduct.

NOTES AND QUESTIONS

1. Jackman's article was written before *Attorney-General v Blake*, (below, 981), which laid down that an account of profits can, exceptionally, be awarded for breach of contract. That case may be regarded as supporting his general thesis for, in the above extract, he clearly had some difficulty in explaining why, on the then state of the law, restitution could not be awarded to protect the 'facilitative institution' of contract.

2. Jackman's thesis may provide a coherent explanation for the present law on when restitution is available. But is it sufficiently convincing as a prescriptive rather than a descriptive account? In particular, can it be sensible to award restitution to the victim of a proprietary tort but

---

10 Joseph Raz, 'Promises in Morality and Law' (1982) 95 *Harv. LR* 916 at 937.
11 Peter Birks, 'Restitutionary Damages for Breach of Contract' (1987) *LMCLQ* 421.

not to the victim who is personally injured or defamed by someone who makes a huge gain out of the tort?

- **P Birks, 'Civil Wrongs: A New World'** (Butterworth Lectures 1990–1), 94–8

JUSTIFYING RESTITUTIONARY DAMAGES

First, a distinction should be taken between deliberate recourse to wrongdoing as a means of profit and other cases. Generally, the need in the former case to suppress that kind of gainful activity is obvious and in itself provides a strong justification of the windfall to the plaintiff. Restitutionary damages should always be allowed, unless in rare cases (. . . deliberate breach of contract may be [an example]) where the court is willing to say that suppression of that form of intentionally unlawful profit is not necessary or desirable. Here the goals of exmplary and restitutionary damages coincide, for this is one of the cases in which the use of exemplary damages has been preserved.[1]

(i) *The Blunt Instrument and the Sharp.* The coalescence of punitive damages under the head of deliberate recourse to unlawful means of profit and what I am here calling restitutionary damages has been foreshadowed in judicial dicta. Lord Diplock described punitive damages under this head as a blunt instrument against unjust enrichment intended to demonstrate that tort does not pay, and he likened what was done to 'the civil law concept of *enrichessment indue*'.[2] In America, in *Douglass v Hustler Magazine, Inc.*,[3] where the actress Robyn Douglass recovered a punitive award for a deliberate unauthorised publication of nude photographs, Judge Richard Posner said that the profit made should supply the ceiling for the quantification. In the case in which it was impossible to know what profits had been made, the award should, he thought, still be profit-related: the ceiling could be the total profit from the sales of the offending issues.[4] Hence, it must be a question whether both the blunt instrument of exemplary damages and the sharp instrument of restitutionary damages need to be kept in play.

There are two arguments in favour of keeping both. First, the blunt instrument does provide one way of covering the case in which profits are indubitable but the amount is impossible to calculate. Secondly, some cases of deliberate wrongdoing for profit seem to require more than restitution of the profit made. In *Macmillan v Singh*,[5] for example, a tenant was literally thrown out of his rooms by his landlord so that they could be let at a higher rent. In the seven weeks which ensued before the courts put the tenant back in possession, the landlord had managed to make an extra £70 from another tenant. But the Court of Appeal thought that the award of punitive damages, though it must subsume the profits actually made 'as a sort of accounting',[6] must also go a good deal further. The Court therefore awarded £250 under this head, still the tiniest of sums by American standards.

If punitive damages can overcome their negative image in this country and be seen instead as socially useful, subject to the need for determinate standards to be applied by the judges, the best solution will be to allow restitutionary damages to take care of the profit actually made and, separately, to add punitive damages in an appropriate case on the ground of the wanton and malicious character of the wrong. That will involve enlarging the English categories of exemplary damages, bringing the English rules into line with the Australian.[7] McGregor sees the law as being in a transitional phase in which penal damages under this head will give way to 'direct, and more appropriate, remedies as the means for ensuring that tortfeasors are not permitted to retain profits made by them

---

1 *Rookes v Barnard* [1964] AC 1129 at 1227.
2 *Cassell and Co. Ltd v Broome* [1972] AC 1027 at 1129, 1130C–D.   3 769 F 2d 1128 (1985).
4 At 1144.   5 (1985) 17 HLR 120.   6 At 125.
7 Australia never accepted the *Rookes v Barnard* restrictions and was not compelled to do so by the Privy Council: *Uren v John Fairfax and Sons Pty. Ltd* (1966) 117 CLR 118; *Australian Consolidated Press v Uren* [1969] AC 590.

through their tortious conduct.'[8] This development will certainly be best fostered if restitutionary damages and punitive damages are allowed to work in tandem, the former taking the profits, the latter punishing the malice.

(ii) *Prophylactic Interventions*. The next case is *Keech v Sandford*[9] prophylaxis. Lord Chancellor King there took the view, and it has been taken ever since, that there must be absolutely no room for argument between a cestui que trust and a trustee as to whether a given acquisition by the trustee had or had not entailed a sacrifice of the cestui que trust's interests. There must be no argument, and there must be no temptation to argue. The only way to achieve these goals was for the law to intervene against the trustee without looking for or waiting for proof of loss to the cestui que trust. The law's inquiry had to be pitched at the level of hypothesis: might the trustee have been tempted to sacrifice the interests which he should have protected? The commitment to this prophylactic approach, which is the basis of fiduciary discipline, itself necessitates and explains the availability of gain-based remedies. We should want to stamp out the fiduciary's pursuit of gains at the beneficiary's expense, and also want to do it in a manner that leaves no room for the fiduciary to argue the toss. Then to explain why we tolerate windfall profits to plaintiffs, even windfalls to rather sharp plaintiffs at the expense of honest and industrious defendants as in *Boardman v Phipps*.[10]

(iii) *Other Cases*. For the rest, outside these two cases of deliberate recourse and prophylaxis, there is no hope of certainty in the pursuit of a purely conceptual line. It is not helpful, for example, to say that restitutionary damages should always be available for a 'proprietary' tort.[11] The difficult questions will merely be transferred to the defintion of property. It is not helpful, either, to ask whether the wrong is designed to suppress a particular means of enrichment, an 'anti-enrichment wrong'.[12] The difficult questions will merely be transferred to the discussion of the orientation of every particular wrong. And it is not helpful, though it may be nearer the mark, to channel the problems through the question whether 'facilitative institutions' require to be reinforced by the availability of restitutionary remedies.[13] Again, there is intermediate clutter.

The only viable alternative to the universal answer preferred by Goff and Jones is to confront the problem directly. There is no objection to restitutionary damages except only their tendency to give the plaintiff a windfall and to negative and suppress economic activity without regard to harm done. Hence, on the model of the two categories already discussed, we have to ask whether we see a sufficient justification for doing the latter and tolerating the former. Ex hypothesi we are at this point talking of conduct . . . which is innocent at least in the sense that it does not consist in knowing recourse to unlawful means of gain. I suspect that, beyond the need for the prophylactic interventions of the second category, when the matter is put in this direct way it will turn out that the number of cases in which restitutionary damages are justified will not be large. Moreover, it may be that, even in the cases in which they are justified, they will only be justified at a lower level. That is to say, the cut-off point, or in other words the rule as to remoteness of gain, will confine the plaintiff to claiming only the defendant's immediate enrichment, not his consequential profits—the reasonable rental . . . not the . . . profits.

NOTE AND QUESTION

In this passage, Birks espoused two main tests for whether restitution should be available for a wrong: (i) was the wrong committed cynically in order to make a profit? and (ii) is special

---

8 *McGregor on Damages*, para. 423, 267–8.

9 (1726) Sel Cas temp King 61; *White and Tudor LC*, 648.   10 [1967] 2 AC 46.

11 Favoured by D Friedmann, 'Restitution of Benefits Obtained through the Appropriation of Property or the Commission of a Wrong' (1980) 80 *Col. LR* 504.

12 Birks, 328–32.   13 I Jackman, 'Restitution for Wrongs' [1989] *CLJ* 302.

deterrence justified? Beyond those two tests, Birks gave up the quest for a third conceptual test in favour of asking, case by case, whether there is a sufficient justification for giving the claimant a windfall and suppressing economic activity. Do you agree with this approach?

• J Edelman, *Gain-Based Damages* (2002), 1–4

This book is an examination of two particular remedies given in response to wrongdoing, both of them gain-based—that is to say, measured by the gain or benefit to the defendant wrongdoer—rather than the loss to the claimant victim. It is argued that these two distinct measures are legitimate responses for torts, breach of contract, equitable wrongs and intellectual property wrongs. Further, the circumstances in which each of these remedies are available are rationalised and explained, providing a coherent framework within which this recognition of gain-based damages can operate.

The two monetary remedies for wrongdoing considered in this book are entitled 'restitutionary damages' and 'disgorgement damages'.

. . .

The first of these two forms of gain-based damages, restitutionary damages, is explained as concerned with reversing wrongful transfers of value from a claimant to a defendant. Once a transfer of value is found to be wrongful a natural monetary response should be to reverse that transfer and restitutionary damages should be generally available. Restitutionary damages are measured by the objective value received by a defendant which has been transferred from the claimant's wealth. Restitutionary damages could therefore be said to focus upon an objective 'enrichment' of a defendant and a requirement that the 'enrichment' come 'at the expense' of the claimant. These requirements are also two essential characteristics of an action in unjust enrichment. Thus there is a powerful parallel between restitutionary damages for wrongs and restitution for unjust enrichment. However, although it is now well established that an action for restitution is available to reverse illegitimate (but non-wrongful) transfers in unjust enrichment it is not yet as well accepted that a corresponding action for restitutionary damages exists where that transfer is wrongful. . . .

The other gain-based damages remedy explained in chapter three is disgorgement damages. The remedy of disgorgement damages is explained as a remedy which operates to disgorge profits made by a wrongdoer as a result of a wrong. It is a remedy which operates, irrespective of any transfer of value, to provide deterrence where compensatory damages cannot adequately deter wrongdoing. This is in two circumstances. First, where a wrong is committed with a view to material gain and the profit made exceeds the compensation payable. In such a case it is only possible to deter such deliberate wrongdoing by showing that any profit made will be disgorged. Secondly, in cases of breach of fiduciary duty, even profit made by innocent commission of that wrong must be stripped as there is a need for such a high level of deterrence to protect the institution of trust inherent in the fiduciary relationship.

Two schools of argument oppose the recognition of a remedy entitled 'disgorgement damages'. The first lies in the view of many commentators that a single term should encompass both gain-based remedies of restitutionary damages and disgorgement damages. The second is the view that disgorgement damages is solely an equitable remedy and should simply be referred to as an 'account of profits'. [This book] rejects both these views. In relation to the first view, it is shown that the two different remedies have entirely different rationales and great difficulty and confusion is created in the cases by the conflation of two different remedies under the same name. The second argument is rejected by showing that the 'account of profits' is not the only remedy used by the law to perform this function of disgorging profits. The same function is performed by common law awards and sometimes simply referred to as 'damages' or as 'money had and received'.

. . .

Throughout this book a key principle constantly employed is that like events and responses should be treated alike. This requires that language and nomenclature should not obscure the true nature of particular events or the law's response to them. This is the reason that the protean descriptions given to different awards which effect reversal of wrongful transfers are collected together as 'restitutionary damages' and those descriptions given to awards which effect profit-stripping for wrongs are assimilated as 'disgorgement damages'. The converse to this principle is also true. Just as like responses should be treated alike, so too should different responses be treated differently. And this is the reason that this book insists upon separation of restitutionary damages and disgorgement damages.

NOTES AND QUESTIONS

1. When you are reading the cases extracted in this chapter, consider whether Edelman's thesis is consistent with them. He would argue that, for example, *Bracewell v Appleby* (below, 955) *Wrotham Park Estate Co. Ltd v Parkside Homes Ltd* (below, 978) and *Experience Hendrix LLC v PPX Enterprises Inc* (below, 990) are examples of 'restitutionary damages'; whereas *Attorney-General v Blake*, (below, 981), *Boardman v Phipps* (below, 1007) and *Reading v Attorney-General* (below, 1016) are examples of 'disgorgement damages'.

2. According to Edelman, 'restitutionary damages' rest on corrective justice, are analogous to unjust enrichment by subtraction, are relatively uncontroversial and should always be available for a wrong. In contrast, 'disgorgement damages' are designed to deter a wrong where compensatory damages are inadequate to do so. Disgorgement damages are, and should therefore be, restricted to two main circumstances. First, where the profit made exceeds the compensation payable; and, secondly, for breach of fiduciary duty in order to protect the institution of trust inherent in the fiduciary relationship.

3. Applying Edelman's thesis, does disgorgement require all profits to be given up? If so, how would he explain the generous allowance for time and skill given in *Boardman v Phipps*?

4. Is there a clear distinction between Edelman's restitutionary damages for a wrong and (i) restitution for the cause of action of unjust enrichment and (ii) compensation for a wrong?

5. See further J Edelman, 'Gain-Based Damages and Compensation' in *Mapping the Law: Essays in Memory of Peter Birks* (eds A Burrows and Lord Rodger, 2006), 141–60.

2. CORRECTIVE JUSTICE AND RESTITUTION FOR WRONGS

- **K Barker, 'Unjust Enrichment: Containing the Beast'** (1995) 15 *OJLS* 457

We have extracted above (48) some of the earlier part of this article where Barker argues that corrective justice can explain restitution of unjust enrichments despite there being no wrong. He now turns more briefly to whether corrective justice can explain restitution for wrongs despite there being no loss.

My own view is that it may still be possible to justify a restitutionary response by reference to corrective justice, even when the plaintiff has suffered no loss by virtue of the defendant's wrong. On this view, 'correcting' wrongs can mean stripping defendants of the profits which they make via the infringement of a plaintiff's right, even where the infringement has caused the latter no harm and even where the consequence is to enhance the plaintiff's prior economic position. 'Correcting' the imbalance which occurs by virtue of the defendant's infringement is part and parcel of the desire to fully protect the plaintiff's enjoyment of a right. This still requires us, of course, to identify those rights which deserve such a high degree of protection. It comes to us as no surprise, perhaps, that property (and analogous) rights currently feature at the head of this list. But there is no reason why the list should not lengthen over time to include more controversial cases such as rights to reputation and to privacy.

The point is a relatively simple one. Whilst it is easy to be tempted towards instrumentalist models of restitution for wrongdoing, on the basis that corrective-justice claims have to be loss-based, this is not in fact the case. This is not to say that we are never justified in using restitutionary remedies for instrumentalist purposes, but we should not be blind to the explanations which corrective justice can supply, particularly when the ideological premises of corrective justice models are more consistent with the two-party structure of our system of private litigation.

NOTE

See the note to the extract from Barker (above, 50). In 'Understanding the Unjust Enrichment Principle in Private Law: A Study of the Concept and its Reasons' in *Understanding Unjust Enrichment* (eds J Neyers, M McInnes and S Pitel, 2004); 79 at 100–1, Barker succinctly summarizes his view (drawing on Weinrib's notion of a normative loss) as to why corrective justice can explain restitution of gains that exceed the claimant's loss. He writes, '[C]orrective justice restores prior legal *entitlements*, not simply prior *factual positions*. Forcing the infringer of the copyright or seller of the property to hand over his or her profits to its owner sets right the injustice done in each case because it makes good the owner's *normative* loss. It restores his or her right. Although the owner is *factually* better off at the end of the story than at the beginning, he or she is no better off than he or she was *entitled* to be at that time'.

- **E Weinrib, 'Restitutionary Damages as Corrective Justice'** (2000) 1 *Theoretical Inquiries in Law* 1

On what basis can damages for tortious conduct be measured by the defendant's gain rather than the plaintiff's loss? This question recently has received increasing attention with the revival of interest in restitution throughout the common law world. The reason for this interest is not hard to see. Restitutionary damages for torts implicate fundamental issues in our conception of private law. On the one hand, they open up the possibility of a more nuanced assessment of damages both by extending the long-established jurisprudence of waiver of tort and by linking tortious liability with the appealing and newly invigorated principle of unjust enrichment. On the other hand, they present an intellectual puzzle. If tort law is concerned with wrongful injury to the plaintiff, special arguments are required to explain why, as a matter of justice, the remedy should refer to the gains of the defendant. The reparation of injury seems satisfied by compensating the plaintiff for his or her loss. To place into the plaintiff's hands the defendant's gain in excess of that loss seems to confer a windfall.

My immediate excuse for revisiting this topic is to draw attention to the relevance of inquiring into the *plaintiff's* entitlement to damages measured by the defendant's gain. Many of the current treatments of restitutionary damages for torts focus on the defendant's desert in the aftermath of wrongdoing or on the social good that can be achieved by compelling the disgorgement of the wrongdoer's gain. Hence commentators appeal to the idea that one should not profit from a wrong,[1] that disgorgement of wrongful gain is an effective deterrence for potential wrongdoers,[2] or that restitutionary damages are directed toward the protection of legal facilities in whose integrity the community has an interest.[3] However, the injustice or social inexpediency of the defendant's retention of the gain indicates only the party from whom the gain should be taken, not the party to whom it should be

---

1 Andrew Burrows, *The Law of Restitution*, 376, 395–6 (1993).

2 Peter Cane, 'Exceptional Measures of Damages: In Search of a Principle', in Peter Birks (ed.), *Wrongs and Remedies in the Twenty-First Century* (1996), 301.

3 I Jackman, *Restitution for Wrongs*, 48 Cambridge L. J. 302 (1989). By 'legal facilities' Jackman means 'private property, relations of trust and confidence, and (with some qualification) contracts,' which 'require protection against those who seek to take the benefits of an institution without the burdens thereof.' *Id.* at 302.

awarded. Thus, such accounts fail to provide a reason for the law to transfer the defendant's gain to the plaintiff, of all people. If the basic difficulty with an award of gain-based damages is the supposed windfall of the plaintiff, an adequate treatment must show either that the award is justified despite being a windfall or that the award, where appropriate, is not really a windfall but damages that the plaintiff may of right demand from the defendant. The latter is the strategy that I will essay here.

More broadly, my aim in this article is to situate restitutionary damages within the theoretical framework of corrective justice. [*Weinrib then summarizes his theory of corrective justice as elaborated in Weinrib,* The Idea of Private Law *(1995). For a useful summary, see the extract from Lionel Smith, above, 50.*]

When we think of wrongful gains for restitutionary purposes, precisely how are the ideas of wrongfulness and gain connected? One possibility is that a gain is wrongful because of its history; that is, a gain is wrongful if it is the consequence of a wrongful act. Rather than pointing to a feature of the gain itself, 'wrongful' is used to indicate that wrongful conduct by the defendant is an historical antecedent of the defendant's gain. The wrongdoing that underlies ascription of wrongfulness stands to the gain as cause to effect. 'Wrongful gain,' then, could be understood as a shorthand for the more accurate description 'gain resulting from a wrongful act.'

The other and more restrictive possibility is that we call a gain 'wrongful' by virtue of its inherent normative quality. Here the significane of the wrongfulness is not merely that it produces the gain, but that it survives into the gain and informs it. The gain's origin in wrong is a necessary condition for the gain's having this normative quality, but something further is required. For the gain to take on the normative quality of wrongfulness, it must be the materialization of a possibility—the opportunity to gain—that rightfully belonged to the plaintiff. Because it is an incident of the plaintiff's entitlement that the defendant has wrongfully infringed, the gain is not merely the result of a wrongful act, but is the continuing embodiment of the injustice between the parties.

. . .

The corrective justice analysis of compensation for wrongful loss applies, *mutatis mutandis*, to restitution for wrongful gain. If the wrongfulness consists in creating the prospect of a loss (as, let us assume for the moment, is the case with negligence), the fact that the defendant has realized a gain as well adds nothing to the plaintiff's case. Because the gain lies beyond the wrong done to the plaintiff, the plaintiff suffers no injustice through the existence of the gain. The parties do and suffer injustice only with respect to the loss, not the gain; the gain remains external to their relationship. Accordingly, from the standpoint of corrective justice, factual causation no more suffices for liability on the gain side than it does on the loss side. What matters is not the historical connection of gain to wrong, but rather the nature of the wrong and whether the gain partakes of the wrong's normative quality. Gain-based damages are justified when the defendant's gain is of something that lies within the right of the plaintiff and is therefore integral to the continuing relationship of the parties as the doer and sufferer of an injustice. Then the gain stands not merely as the sequel to the wrong but as its present embodiment, and the plaintiff is as entitled to the gain as he or she was to the defendant's abstention from the wrong that produced it. A gain that thus embodies the injustice done by the defendant to the plaintiff carries with it the immediate implication of disgorgement.

. . .

As has often been noted, the misappropriation of another's property is the paradigmatic example of a tort that gives rise to resitutionary damages.[4] Because property rights give proprietors the

---

4 *See especially* Daniel Friedmann, 'Restitution of Benefits Obtained Through the Appropriation of Property or the Commission of a Wrong', (1980) *Colum. L Rev* 504.

exclusive right to deal with the thing owned, including the right to profit from such dealings, any gains resulting from the misappropriation of property are necessarily subject to restitution. Gains from dealings in property are as much within the entitlement of the proprietor as the property itself.

The disgorgement of these proprietary gains fits readily within the correlativity of corrective justice. Property consists simultaneously in a right of the proprietor and in a correlative duty on others to respect that right. Just as the owner's right to set the terms on which property is used or transferred implies a correlative duty on others to abstain from using or selling it, so the owner's right to the profits from the use or transfer of the property imports a correlative duty on others to abstain from such profits. This correlativity of the proprietor's right and the wrongdoer's duty means that the realization of an unauthorized gain is an injustice as between them. The gain is the continuing embodiment of this injustice, and the injustice is undone when the gain is restored to the owner of the object from which the gain accrued.

Gain-based damages for dealing with another's property mirror the wrong and illuminate its nature. The law's focus on the benefits of ownership at the remedial stage presupposes the defendant's intention to act on the owned object at the stage of wrongdoing. In appropriating the benefits from using or alienating the object, the defendant implicitly asserts the ownership that alone would entitle the defendant to those benefits. Restitutionary damages reverse the wrong by showing, through the return of the benefits, that the law considers the defendant's implicit assertion of ownership to be a nullity whose consequences are to be undone. The remedy is conditioned, therefore, not merely on the defendant's realization of a benefit but on the defendant's having treated the object as if it were his or her own. One treats an object in this way when one so directs one's attention to the object, that its use or alienation can be regarded as an execution of one's purposes. In contrast, action that inadvertently produces an effect on the object does not qualify as an expression of one's will with respect to the object, and so is not the basis for restitutionary damages. Thus, restitutionary damages are available for intentional torts against property and not for harm to property that results from negligence.

. . .

So far I have emphasized the significance of property for a corrective justice approach to restitutionary damages for tort. Since such an approach highlights the correlativity of the injustice done by the defendant and the injustice suffered by the plaintiff, it conditions liability on the requirement that the defendant's conduct be wrongful with respect to the plaintiff's right. If the plaintiff is to recover gain-based damages, that right must include an entitlement to the profit from whatever embodies the right. Proprietary rights contain this entitlement.

Strictly speaking, a proprietary right has two features. First, a proprietary right can be asserted against the world, and therefore the right carries with it a correlative duty, incumbent on everyone else, not to interfere. The proprietor's entitlement to the profit from what is owned derives from the power to determine the object's use, including the conditions under which it can be alienated, to the exclusion of everyone else. Since the proprietor must agree to the terms on which the object can enter the stream of commerce, the proprietor also owns whatever can be realized through use or alienation.

Second, the subject matter of a proprietary right has to be morally capable of being acquired and alienated. For example an incident of a person's bodily integrity is not the subject of a proprietary right. One's body is not what one owns but what one is; it is the organism through which humans as self-conscious and purposive beings express themselves in the world. One does not come to be entitled to one's body by any act of acquisition, and one cannot morally alienate it to someone else. The right to one's body is so intimately connected to the person whose body it is that it lacks the moral possibility of being externalized and passing into the possession of someone else. Similar considerations apply to other aspects of one's dignity—to what Hegel compendiously termed 'those goods, or rather substantive characteristics, which constitute my own private personality and the universal essence of my self-consciousness.'[5] Such interests in physical integrity and dignity are, of course, legally protected with the status of rights, but they are not considered to be rights of a proprietary kind.

Under certain circumstances, restitutionary damages are justified even if either or both of these features are absent. Although restitutionary damages do not then respond to the violation of what is strictly speaking a proprietary right, the relationship between the parties can give rise to an interest sufficiently property-like to allow this kind of award.[6] These relational property-like wrongs can be grouped into two broad categories. In the first category, a gain-based remedy emerges from the pre-existing relationship between the parties, so that the remedy is available only against the defendant and not against the whole world. In the second, the remedy emerges as a response to the defendant's particular conduct.

The violation of a fiduciary duty is the paradigmatic example of the situation in which a gain-based remedy can emerge from the objective nature of the relationship. From the perspective of corrective justice, a fiduciary relationship reflects the Kantian idea that private law as a system of rights supposes persons to be ends in themselves rather than means to the ends of others.[7] Accordingly, a relationship such as that between fiduciary and beneficiary, the legal structure of which makes one person's interests entirely subject to another's discretion, must have as one of its incidents the duty of loyalty owed by the latter to the former. The fiduciary's duty of loyalty then becomes for purposes of this relationship an entitlement of the beneficiary. Since the meaning of this duty of loyalty is that the fiduciary cannot profit from the relationship, gains can be regarded as the material embodiment of the breach of duty—what the fiduciary has, as it were, sold out the duty for—and the beneficiary is as entitled to these profits as he or she was to the duty for which they were exchanged. Courts occasionally refer to the opportunity to profit from the relationship as the beneficiary's 'property'[8] though, since it entails the right to exclude only the fiduciary and not the whole world, it 'is not property in the strict sense.'[9] Seen in this light, the fiduciary's liability to disgorge profits is not an example of a policy of deterrence impacting the relationship from the outside, but is rather the remedial consequence that reflects the nature of the obligation owed by the fiduciary to the beneficiary.

The other property-like wrongs are those characterized by action of the defendant that implicitly or explicitly treats the plaintiff's right as an asset whose value the defendant can appropriate.[10] For things that can be acquired and alienated, value belongs to the owner as an aspect of property; as noted above . . ., the wrongdoer who deals with such things can be liable for the market value or for

---

5 Hegel, *Philosophy of Right* (Knox trans., 1952) at § 66 *Cf.* Immanuel Kant, The Metaphysics of Morals 63 (Gregor trans., 1991) (describing innate right as something 'belonging to every man by virtue of his humanity').

6 The danger, of course, is that the possibility of calling something 'property-like' may appear to provide a convenient black box into which to stuff the residual instances that do not fit what a property-based approach requires. However, I think that the property-like aspects of these situations are salient enough to bring them within the approach I have suggested. Peter Birks writes that '[i]t is not helpful . . . to say that restitutionary damages should always be available for a "proprietary" tort. The difficult questions will merely be transferred to the definition of property.' *Civil Wrongs: A New World* 98 (Butterworth Lectures 1990–1). While the fear is well-founded, the truth is that, as with every interesting legal issue, difficult questions are unavoidable. The basic issue is whether property is the appropriate concept, not whether the concept is completely determinate in its application . . . In any case, property seems to be a more manageable criterion than the one Birks proposes, namely that one ask whether there is sufficient justification for giving the plaintiff a windfall and for tolerating the suppression of economic activity.

7 Kant, *supra* note 5, at 62.

8 See, e.g., *Boardman v Phipps* [1967] 2 AC 46, 107, 115 (HL).

9 *Ibid.* at 102.

10 See Peter Benson, 'The Basis for Excluding Liability for Economic Loss in Tort Law', in David Owen, *Philosophical Founations of Tort Law* (1995), 427, 457.

the realized gains. In the case of property-like wrongs, the same liability is available for wrongs done with respect to things, like physical integrity, that cannot be acquired and alienated. Compared to the victim of a true proprietary wrong, the plaintiff is not placed in a worse position by virtue of the fact that the right was too intimately connected with the plaintiff's being and dignity even to rank as proprietary. Because the defendant acted with knowledge of the plaintiff's right and with the intent to appropriate its value, the law ascribes a proprietary quality to the right so far as the relationship between the defendant and the plaintiff is concerned. In doing this, the law merely holds the defendant to the implications of his or her own conduct. Since the plaintiff's right was treated as a commodity whose value was available to the defendant, the plaintiff is allowed to recapture the gain that was realized through it. Thus, once the wrong is construed as a property-like one for purposes of the parties' relationship, the plaintiff has available the restitutionary damages that attend a dealing with another's property.

. . .

NOTE

For criticism of Weinrib's article, see J Gordley, 'The Purpose of Awarding Restitutionary Damages: A Reply to Professor Weinrib' (2000) 1 *Theoretical Inquiries in Law* 39; H Dagan, *The Law and Ethics of Restitution* (2004), ch 7. See also the articles referred to, above, 54, note 1, criticizing corrective justice in relation to restitution of unjust enrichments.

3. RESTITUTION FOR TORTS

(1) PROPRIETARY TORTS (OTHER THAN PROTECTING INTELLECTUAL PROPERTY)

• *United Australia Ltd v Barclays Bank Ltd* [1941] AC 1, House of Lords

A cheque for £1,900 in favour of United Australia Ltd (the claimant) was indorsed, without the claimant's authority, by its secretary Emons so as to make the cheque payable to M. F. G. Trust Ltd, of which Emons was a director. The defendant bank collected the proceeds of the cheque for M. F. G. and credited its account. The claimant first brought an action for money had and received against M. F. G. for the £1,900 but, before that action proceeded to trial, M. F. G. went into liquidation. The action was thereupon automatically stayed and no judgment was ever obtained. The claimant therefore brought the present action against the defendant bank, claiming damages of £1,900 for conversion of the cheque. The central question at issue, decided in favour of the claimant, was whether the first action barred the second action in tort; that is, whether the claimant had 'waived the tort' (in the sense of extinguishing the tort) by bringing the action for money had and received.

Viscount Simon LC: . . . The question to be decided in this appeal is whether the proceedings against M. F. G., carried on up to the point that they in fact reached, constitute a valid ground of defence for the respondent bank and so relieve it in the present action from a liability, which would otherwise certainly attach to it, to repay to the appellant company the sum of 1900*l*. of which they had been deprived and which they have not received from any other source.

   The view taken by the Courts below is that the appellant company, by bringing their action against M. F. G., elected to 'waive the tort' and thereby became irrevocably committed, even against a different defendant, to the view that Emons was, as he professed to be, duly authorised rised as the appellant company's agent to deal with the cheque as he did. If so, the Bank's dealing with the cheque was not tortious and the present action would fail.

. . .

The House has now to decide whether the Courts below are right in holding that the appellants are barred from recovering judgment against the bank because they previously instituted proceedings, on the basis of 'waiving the tort' against M. F. G., when those proceedings never produced any judgment or satisfaction in the plaintiff's favour. This question may be conveniently dissected by first asking whether there would be any such bar even if the present action was an action in tort against M. F. G. If a remedy in tort would remain open against the same defendant, then there certainly cannot have been any conclusive election which could prevent an action against a different defendant who had previously not been sued at all.

[*After reviewing several authorities, he continued*:] There is, as far as I can discover, no reported case which has ever laid it down as matter of decision that when the plaintiff 'waives the tort' and starts an action in assumpsit, he then and there debars himself from a future proceeding based on the tort. It would be very remarkable if it were so. 'The fallacy of the argument,' as Lord Ellenborough said in *Hunter v Prinsep*,[1] 'appears to us to consist in attributing more effect to the mere form of this action than really belongs to it. In bringing an action for money had and received, instead of trover, the plaintiff does no more than waive any complaint, with a view to damages, of the tortious act by which the goods were converted into money, and takes to the neat proceeds of the sale as the value of the goods.' When the plaintiff 'waived the tort' and brought assumpsit, he did not thereby elect to be treated from that time forward on the basis that no tort had been committed; indeed, if it were to be understood that no tort had been committed, how could an action in assumpsit lie? It lies only because the acquisition of the defendant is wrongful and there is thus an obligation to make restitution.

The true proposition is well formulated in the Restatement of the Law of Restitution promulgated by the American Law Institute, 525, as follows: 'A person upon whom a tort has been committed and who brings an action for the benefits received by the tortfeasor is sometimes said to 'waive the tort.' The election to bring an action of assumpsit is not, however, a waiver of tort but is the choice of one of two alternative remedies.' Contrast with this, instances of true waiver of rights, e.g., waiver of forfeiture by receiving rent.

If, under the old forms of procedure, the mere bringing of an action while waiving the tort did not constitute a bar to a further action based on the tort, still less could such a result be held to follow after the Common Law Procedure Act, 1852, and the Judicature Act, 1875. For it is now possible to combine in a single writ a claim based on tort with a claim based on assumpsit, and it follows inevitably that the making of the one claim cannot amount to an election which bars the making of the other. No doubt, if the plaintiff proved the necessary facts, he could be required to elect on which of his alternative causes of action he would take judgment, but that has nothing to do with the unfounded contention that election arises when the writ is issued. There is nothing conclusive about the form in which the writ is issued, or about the claims made in the statement of claim. A plaintiff may at any time before judgment be permitted to amend. The substance of the matter is that on certain facts he is claiming redress either in the form of compensation, i.e., damages as for a tort, or in the form of restitution of money to which he is entitled, but which the defendant has wrongfully received. The same set of facts entitles the plaintiff to claim either form of redress. At some stage of the proceedings the plaintiff must elect which remedy he will have. There is, however, no reason of principle or convenience why that stage should be deemed to be reached until the plaintiff applies for judgment.

---

1 10 East 378, 391.

So far, I have been discussing what is the true proposition of law when the second action is brought against the same defendant. In the present case, however, the action which is said to be barred by former proceedings against M. F. G. is not an action against M. F. G. at all, but an action against Barclays Bank. I am quite unable to see why this second action should be barred by the plaintiff's earlier proceedings against M. F. G. In the first place, the tort of conversion of which the bank was guilty is quite a separate tort from that done by M. F. G. M. F. G.'s tort consisted in taking the cheque away from the appellants without the appellants' authority; that tort would have equally existed if M. F. G., instead of getting the cheque cleared through the bank, had kept it in its own possession. The bank's tort, on the other hand, consisted in taking a cheque, which was the property of the appellants, and without their authority using it to collect money which rightly belonged to the appellants. M.F.G. and the bank were not joint tortfeasors, for two persons are not joint tortfeasors because their independent acts cause the same damage.

. . .

[I]t follows that the earlier proceedings against M. F. G. could provide the present respondents with no defence, unless as a result of them the plaintiffs had received satisfaction for their loss. . . .

Lord Atkin: . . . I do not propose to discuss at any length the history of the claim in indebitatus assumpsit, and the cases through which that history has been traced. Very much learning has been devoted to this subject, and lawyers are indebted to Professor Ames, Sir William Holdsworth, and Professor Winfield for the light they have thrown upon the subject in well known works; and I should not like to omit the work of Mr. R. M. Jackson on 'The History of Quasi-Contract in English Law,' published in 1936 in the Cambridge Studies in English Legal History, from which I have derived assistance. There is also what I hope I may respectfully call a valuable contribution to the discussion in the articles recently published by my noble and learned friend Lord Wright on *Sinclair v Brougham*,[2] and a review of the American Restatement of the Law of Restitution at 1 to 65 of Legal Essays and Addresses published in 1939. I have myself consulted most of the cases referred to in these works with the exception of the cases from the Year Books which I have accepted from the authors.

The story starts with the action of debt which was not necessarily based upon the existence of a contract, for it covered claims to recover sums due for customary dues, penalties for breaches of by-laws, and the like. The action of debt had its drawbacks, the chief being that the defendant could wage his law. There followed the application of the action on the case of assumpsit to debt. 'The defendant being indebted then promised.' At first there must be an express promise; then the Courts implied a promise from an executory contract: *Slade's* case.[3] *Slade's* case was not a claim in indebitatus assumpsit, but the principle was applied, and it became unnecessary to prove an express promise in those cases. Then the action was allowed in respect of cases where there was no contract, executory or otherwise, as in the cases where debt would have lain for customary fees and the like; and by a final and somewhat forced application to cases where the defendant had received money of the plaintiff to which he was not entitled. These included cases where the plaintiff had intentionally paid money to the defendant, e.g., claims for money paid on a consideration that wholly failed and money paid under a mistake: cases where the plaintiff had been deceived into paying money, cases where money had been extorted from the plaintiff by threats or duress of goods. They also included cases where money had not been paid by the plaintiff at all but had been received from third persons, as where the defendant had received fees under colour of holding an office which in fact was held by the plaintiff: and finally cases like the present where the defendant had been wrongfully in possession of the plaintiff's goods, had sold them and was in possession of the proceeds. Now to find a basis for the actions in any actual contract whether express or to be implied from the conduct of the parties

2 [1914] AC 398.   3 (1602) 4 Coke 92(b).

was in many of the instances given obviously impossible. The cheat or the blackmailer does not promise to repay to the person he has wronged the money which he has unlawfully taken: nor does the thief promise to repay the owner of the goods stolen the money which he has gained from selling the goods. Nevertheless, if a man so wronged was to recover the money in the hands of the wrongdoer, and it was obviously just that he should be able to do so, it was necessary to create a fictitious contract: for there was no action possible other than debt or assumpsit on the one side and action for damages for tort on the other. The action of indebitatus assumpsit for money had and received to the use of the plaintiff in the cases I have enumerated was therefore supported by the imputation by the Court to the defendant of a promise to repay. The fiction was so obvious that in some cases the judge created a fanciful relation between the plaintiff and the defendant. Thus in cases where the defendant had wrongly sold the plaintiff's goods and received the proceeds it was suggested in some cases, not in all, that the plaintiff chose to treat the wrongdoer as having sold the goods as his agent and so being under an implied contract to his principal to repay. Even here in the relatively more recent cases where this explanation is given by Grose J in *King v Leith*[4] and *Marsh v Keating*[5] by Park J in delivering the opinion of the judges in the House of Lords the wrongdoer had in fact in both cases purported to sell the goods as the agent of his principal. But the fiction is too transparent. The alleged contract by the blackmailer and the robber never was made and never could be made. The law, in order to do justice, imputed to the wrongdoer a promise which alone as forms of action then existed could give the injured person a reasonable remedy. But while it was just that the plaintiff in such cases should be able to recover the money in the possession of the other party, he was not bound to exercise this remedy: in cases where the money had been received as the result of a wrong he still had the remedy of claiming damages for tort in action for trespass, deceit, trover, and the like. But he obviously could not compel the wrongdoer to recoup him his losses twice over. Hence he was restricted to one of the two remedies: and herein as I think arose the doctrine of 'waiver of the tort.' Having recovered in contract it is plain that the plaintiff cannot go on to recover in tort. Transit in rem judicatam. The doctrine has thus alternatively been said to be based on election: i.e., election between two remedies and the stage at which this election takes place was the subject of discussion in the argument in the present case. I will treat of election later. But at present I wish to deal with the waiver of the tort which is said to arise whenever the injured person sues in contract for money received. If the plaintiff in truth treats the wrongdoer as having acted as his agent, overlooks the wrong, and by consent of both parties is content to receive the proceeds this will be a true waiver. It will arise necessarily where the plaintiff ratifies in the true sense an unauthorized act of an agent: in that case the lack of authority disappears, and the correct view is not that the tort is waived, but by retroaction of the ratification has never existed. But in the ordinary case the plaintiff has never the slightest intention of waiving, excusing or in any kind of way palliating the tort. If I find that a thief has stolen my securities and is in possession of the proceeds, when I sue him for them I am not excusing him. I am protesting violently that he is a thief and because of his theft I am suing him: indeed he may be in prison upon my prosecution. Similarly with the blackmailer: in such a case I do not understand what can be said to be waived. The man has my money which I have not delivered to him with any real intention of passing to him the property. I sue him because he has the actual property taken: and I suggest that it can make no difference if he extorted a chattel which he afterwards sold. I protest that a man cannot waive a wrong unless he either has a real intention to waive it, or can fairly have imputed to him such an intention, and in the cases which we have been considering there can be no such intention either actual or imputed. These fantastic resemblances of contracts invented in order to meet requirements of the law as to forms of action which have now disappeared should not in these days be allowed to affect actual rights. When these ghosts of the past stand in the path of

---

4 (1787) 2 Term Rep 141, 145.   5 (1834) 1 Bing NC 198, 215.

justice clanking their mediæval chains the proper cause for the judge is to pass through them undeterred.

Concurrently with the decisions as to waiver of tort there is to be found a supposed application of election: and the allegation is sometimes to be found that the plaintiff elected to waive the tort. It seems to me that in this respect it is essential to bear in mind the distinction between choosing one of two alternative remedies, and choosing one of two inconsistent rights. As far as remedies were concerned, from the oldest time the only restriction was on the choice between real and personal actions. If you chose the one you could not claim on the other. Real actions have long disappeared: and, subject to the difficulty of including two causes of action in one writ which has also now disappeared, there has not been and there certainly is not now any compulsion to choose between alternative remedies. You may put them in the same writ: or you may put one in first, and then amend and add or substitute another. . . .

On the other hand, if a man is entitled to one of two inconsistent rights it is fitting that when with full knowledge he has done an unequivocal act showing that he has chosen the one he cannot afterwards pursue the other, which after the first choice is by reason of the inconsistency no longer his to choose. . . . I therefore think that on a question of alternative remedies no question of election arises until one or other claim has been brought to judgment. Up to that stage the plaintiff may pursue both remedies together, or pursuing one may amend and pursue the other: but he can take judgment only for the one, and his cause of action on both will then the merged in the one. This seems to me to be the decision of both Lord Russell of Killowen CJ and of Vaughan Williams LJ in *Rice v Reed*:[6] and I cannot agree with the dictum of A. L. Smith LJ[7] that to bring an action for money had and received waives the tort. . . .

In the present case, therefore, I find that the plaintiffs were at no stage in the proceedings they took against M. F. G. Trust called to make an election, and, if it were necessary so to hold, in fact made no election, to claim in contract and not to claim in tort: and the foundation of the defendant's defence disappears. But I think it necessary to add that even if the tort had been waived, or the plaintiff had made any final election against M. F. G. Trust, Ld., I fail to see why that should have any effect upon their claims against the bank. If a thief steals the plaintiff's goods worth 500*l*. and sells them to a receiver for 50*l*. who sells them to a fourth party for 400*l*., if I find the thief and he hands over to me the 50*l*. or I sue him for it and recover judgment I can no longer sue him for damages for the value of the goods, but why should that preclude me from suing the two receivers for damages. . . .

Lord Romer: . . . A person whose goods have been wrongfully converted by another has the choice of two remedies against the wrongdoer. He may sue for the proceeds of the conversion as money had and received to his use, or he may sue for the damages that he has sustained by the conversion. If he obtains judgment for the proceeds, it is certain that he is precluded from thereafter claiming damages for the conversion. But, in my opinion, this is not due to his having waived the tort but to his having finally elected to pursue one of his two alternative remedies. The phrase 'waive the tort' is a picturesque one. It has a pleasing sound. Perhaps it was for these reasons that it was regarded with so much affection by the old Common Lawyers, one of whom, indeed, was moved to break into verse upon the subject. But with all respect to their memories, I firmly believe that the phrase was an inaccurate one if and so far as it meant that the tortious act was affirmed. What was waived by the judgment was not the tort, but the right to recover damages for the tort. As was said by Lord Ellenborough in the case of *Hunter v Prinsep*[8] 'in bringing an action for money had and received, instead of trover, the plaintiff does no more than waive any complaint, with a view to damages, of the tortious act by which the goods were converted into money, and takes to the neat proceeds

---

6   [1900] 1 QB 54.   7   *Ibid.*, 65, 66.   8   10 East 378, 391.

of the sale as the value of the goods.' The plaintiff in no way affirms the tortious act so as to treat it as having been a rightful one. As has been pointed out by the Lord Chancellor the action of assumpsit would not lie if it were to be understood that no tort had been committed. . . .

Lord Porter delivered a concurring speech. **Lord Thankerton** concurred.

NOTES AND QUESTIONS

1. The primary importance of this case lies in its clarification of the point that, in 'waiving a tort' by claiming a restitutionary remedy for the gains made by a tortfeasor, a claimant does not normally extinguish the tort but on the contrary claims one of two alternative remedies for the tort (the other being compensatory damages). The Lords were anxious to contrast this with true waiver where a claimant does excuse an infringement of his rights (for example, a tort may be extinguished where a principal ratifies an agent's tort against him in order to recover gains made by the agent as in *Verschures Creameries Ltd v Hull and Netherlands SS Co. Ltd* [1921] 2 KB 608).

2. Although no mention is made of this in their Lordships' reasoning, there is a third possible meaning of 'waiver of tort' which could have been made out on the facts. This is where the claimant ignores the tort by founding the claim on the cause of action of unjust enrichment. That is, although their Lordships treated the claim for money had and received against M. F. G. as dependent on M. F. G.'s *wrongful* acquisition (i.e. by tortious conversion), the claimant might have alternatively grounded its restitutionary claim on the the defendant's gain of the £1,900, at the claimant's expense, without the claimant's knowledge (the unjust factor being ignorance, as discussed in Chapter 4).

3. Implicit in the Lords' clarification of 'waiver of tort' was the recognition that a claimant can choose to bring an action for money had and received to recover the gains made by the tort of conversion. See also, for example, *Oughton v Seppings* (1830) 1 B & Ad. 241 (trespass to goods); *Lamine v Dorrell* (1701) 2 Ld. Ray. 1216 (conversion); *Chesworth v Farrar* [1967] 1 QB 407. In this last case, a deceased landlord had wrongfully converted, by selling off, property belonging to his tenant. The tenant successfully recovered the sale price of the goods from the deceased's administrators in an action for money had and received. The main issue in the case was whether the claim was time barred by the (then) six-month time limit for an action in tort where the tortfeasor had died. Edmund Davies J reasoned that the action was not so time barred, because in claiming restitution he was not bringing 'an action in tort'. This reasoning is not easy to accept because it appears that Edmund Davies J did regard the restitutionary claim as dependent on the tort. Hence in an important passage, at 417, he said: 'A person upon whom a tort has been committed has at times a choice of alternative remedies, even though it is a *sine qua non* regarding each that he must establish that a tort has been committed. He may sue to recover damages for the tort, or he may waive the tort and sue in quasi-contract to recover the benefits received by the wrongdoer'. Does Edmund Davies J's reasoning illustrate a policy decision to circumvent an unwarranted short limitation period? See on this case, Burrows, 553.

4. The *United Australia* case also establishes that, in relation to alternative remedies, the claimant must elect which remedy to pursue at the time of judgment. For an excellent analysis of the judgments in the *United Australia* case, which relies on the important distinction between alternative and cumulative remedies, see the breach of trust case of *Tang Min Sit v Capacious Investments Ltd* [1996] 1 AC 514, Privy Council. This makes clear that an account of profits and compensatory damages for a wrong are alternative and inconsistent remedies. Lord Nicholls said, at 197, 'The law frequently affords an injured person more than one remedy for the wrong he has suffered. Sometimes the two remedies are alternative and inconsistent. The classic example, indeed, is (1) an account of the profits made by a defendant in breach of his fiduciary obligations and (2) damages for the loss suffered by the plaintiff by reason of the same breach. The former is measured by the wrongdoer's gain, the latter by the injured party's

loss ... Faced with alternative and inconsistent remedies a plaintiff must choose, or elect, between them. He cannot have both.' See also on these alternative remedies, *Neilson v Betts* ((1871) LR 5 HL 1; *De Vitre v Betts* (1873) LR 6 HL 319; *Mahesan v Malaysia Government Officers' Co-op Housing Society Ltd* [1979] AC 374; *Island Records Ltd v Tring International plc* [1996] 1 WLR 1256; *Spring Form Inc. v Toy Brokers Ltd* [2002] FSR 276; and see below, 696 (the *Colbeam Palmer* case), 971 (Patents Act 1977, section 61(2)) and 964 (*Ministry of Defence v Ashman*). In his case-note on the *Tang Ming Sit* case, 'Inconsistency between Compensation and Restitution' (1996) 112 *LQR* 375, Peter Birks suggests that it may be incorrect to regard compensation and restitution for a wrong as inconsistent. 'If a plaintiff is entitled to recover the defendant's gains when he has suffered no loss at all, it is not clear why there should be any inconsistency in his asking, where he has suffered loss, that the defendant should both disgorge his own gains and make good the plaintiff's loss' (at 378). See further S Watterson, 'Alternative and Cumulative Remedies: What is the Difference?' [2003] RLR 7.

• *Phillips v Homfray* (1883) 24 ChD 439, Court of Appeal

The deceased had, committed the tort of trespass by using roads and passages under the claimants' land for the purpose of transporting coal. In an earlier action (1871) 6 Ch App 770) the claimants won a judgment for inquiries as to the quantities of minerals transported under the claimants' land (the second inquiry) and what ought to be paid as wayleave for user of the roads and passages by the then living tortfeasor (the third inquiry). The tortfeasor died before those inquiries. The question at issue in the present proceedings was whether the *actio personalis* bar to tort claims meant that the judgment for the inquiries relating to wayleave could not be enforced against the deceased's executors. The majority of the Court of Appeal, reversing Pearson J, held that the inquiries should be stayed.

Bowen and Cotton L JJ: ... The Plaintiffs' claim out of which the 2nd and 3rd inquiries spring is a claim to be compensated for the secret and tortious use made by the deceased R. *Fothergill* and others during his lifetime of the underground ways and passages under the Plaintiffs' farm for the purpose of conveying the coal and ironstone of R. *Fothergill* and his cotrespassers. The judgment of Mr Justice *Pearson* as to these two inquiries is based upon the view that this description of claim did not abate upon R. *Fothergill's* death, but was capable of being prosecuted against the assets in the hands of his executrix. That it is in form a clause of the nature of a claim for trespass, the damages for which were to be measured by the areas of wayleave which the Defendants would have had to pay for permission to use the Plaintiff's ways and passages, cannot be disputed. But Mr Justice *Pearson* was of opinion that this was one of the class of cases in which a deceased man's estate remained liable for a profit derived by it out of his wrongful acts during his lifetime. The learned Judge founded his opinion upon certain language of Lord *Mansfield* in the case of *Hambly v Trott*,[1] to the effect that, so far as the act of the offender had been beneficial to himself, his assets ought to be answerable. We have therefore to consider, in the first place, what is the true limit and meaning of the rule that a personal action dies upon a defendant's death, and whether there is, or can be, in the circumstances raised by the case, a profit received by his assets, which the Plaintiffs can follow.

The only cases in which, apart from questions of breach of contract, express or implied, a remedy for a wrongful act can be pursued against the estate of a deceased person who has done the act, appear to us to be those in which property, or the proceeds or value of property, belonging to another, have been appropriated by the deceased person and added to his own estate or moneys. In such cases, whatever the original form of action, it is in substance brought to recover property, or its proceeds or value, and by amendment could be made such in form as well as in substance. In such

---

1 Cowp 374.

cases the action, though arising out of a wrongful act, does not die with the person. The property or the proceeds or value which, in the lifetime of the wrongdoer, could have been recovered from him, can be traced after his death to his assets, and recaptured by the rightful owner there. But it is not every wrongful act by which a wrongdoer indirectly benefits that falls under this head, if the benefit does not consist in the acquisition of property, or its proceeds or value. Where there is nothing among the assets of the deceased that in law or in equity belongs to the plaintiff, and the damages which have been done to him are unliquidated and uncertain, the executors of a wrongdoer cannot be sued merely because it was worth the wrongdoer's while to commit the act which is complained of, and an indirect benefit may have been reaped thereby. . . . It seems to us that Lord *Mansfield* [in *Hambly v Trott*] does no more than indicate that there is a class of cases in which assumpsit can be brought against a wrongdoer to recover the property he has taken or its proceeds or value, and that in such cases the action will survive against the executor. In the illustration given by him of the horse, he does not mean that an action for the use and hire of a horse wrongfully taken will always lie against an executor, but that it will lie whenever a similar action would have lain against the wrongdoer himself. The case he puts is the case of a horse taken and restored, not of a horse taken and held under an adverse claim, and we are not prepared to say that, if absolutely nothing appeared in evidence except that a horse was taken and was afterwards brought back again, the owner might not recover for the use and hire of the horse on the hypothesis of an implied contract to pay for him. . . . [T]he true test to be applied in the present case is whether the Plaintiffs' claim against the deceased *R. Fothergill*, in respect of which inquiries 2 and 3 were directed in his lifetime, belongs to the category of actions *ex delicto*, or whether any form of action against the executors of the deceased, or the deceased man in his lifetime, can be based upon any implied contract or duty. In other words, could the Plaintiffs have sued the deceased at law in any form of action in which 'Not guilty' would not be the proper plea? If such alternative form of action could be conceived it must be either an action for the use, by the Plaintiff's permission, of the Plaintiff's roads and passages, similar in principle, though not identical, with an action for the use and occupation of the Plaintiffs' land. Or it must be in the shape of an action for money had and received, based upon the supposition that funds are in the hands of the executors which properly belong in law or in equity to the Plaintiffs. . . .

[A]ctions in which the owners of goods wrongfully sold were held entitled to waive the tort, and to recover in assumpsit for the proceeds, had become familiar to the common law as far back as towards the end of the 17th century: see *Lamine v Dorrell*.[2]

The difficulties of extending the above principle to the present case appear to us insuperable. The deceased, *R. Fothergill*, by carrying his coal and ironstone in secret over the Plaintiffs' roads took nothing from the Plaintiffs. The circumstances under which he used the road appear to us to negative the idea that he meant to pay for it. Nor have the assets of the deceased Defendant been necessarily swollen by what he has done. He saved his estate expense, but he did not bring into it any additional property or value belonging to another person. . . .

It remains to be considered whether there is any equitable doctrine which can extend or vary the above rules of the common law. We can see none. An action for account will only, under such circumstances, lie where the defendant has something in his hands representing the plaintiffs' property or the proceeds or value of it. But if there were any such it could be recovered at law as well as in equity. . . .

Baggallay LJ (dissenting): It has hardly been disputed on the present appeal that a remedy for a wrongful act can be pursued against the estate of a deceased person by whom the act has been committed, when property, or the proceeds of property, belonging to another have been appropriated by the deceased person, in other words that the action in such cases, though arising out of a

---

2 L.d. Raym 1216.

wrongful act, does not die with the person; but it has been urged that the principle thus enunciated is limited to cases in which property, or the proceeds of property, have been appropriated by the deceased person, and that it does not apply to a case in which the deceased person has derived any other benefit from his wrongdoing than property or the proceeds of property, and in particular that it does not apply to a case in which the benefit derived has not been in the form of an actual acquisition of property, but of a saving of expenditure which must otherwise have been incurred by the wrongdoer, as in the present case, in which, for the purpose of the present argument, it must be assumed that by the use by the Defendants, for the carriage of their minerals, of the roads and passages under the Plaintiffs' farm, there was a saving to them of an expenditure which they must otherwise have incurred.

Speaking with much diffidence, as my views in this respect differ from those of my colleagues, I feel bound to say that I cannot appreciate the reasons upon which it is insisted that although executors are bound to account for any accretions to the property of their testator derived directly from his wrongful act, they are not liable for the amount or value of any other benefit which may be derived by his estate from or by reason of such wrongful act. I can find nothing in the language used by Lord *Mansfield* [in *Hambly v Trott*] that can support this view. On the contrary, when classifying the actions which survive against an executor by reason of the causes of action, he includes among such causes of action 'gain or acquisition by the testator by the work and labour or property of another,' and he in no respect limits or qualifies the nature or character of the 'gain' referred to. A gain or acquisition to the wrongdoer by the work and labour of another does not necessarily, if it does at all, imply a diminution of the property of such other person. . . . Upon the whole, I have come to the conclusion that the causes of action which were the foundation of the decree made in the present suit, and to which I deem it unnecessary to more particularly refer, were such as, within the rule in *Hambly v Trott*, to entitle the Plaintiffs to maintain their suit against Mrs *Fothergill* as the executrix of the deceased Defendant *R. Fothergill* in respect of the subject-matter of the second and third inquiries directed by the decree. Whether the proceedings which the Plaintiffs have adopted for the purpose of enforcing their rights are in form such as to entitle Mrs *Fothergill* to succeed in her appeal is a question the consideration of which I will postpone until after I have referred to some cases in equity which appear to me to have an important bearing upon it, but as to some of which the views formed by me in some respects differ from those expressed in the judgment of my colleagues.

[*After referring to cases in equity. Baggallay LJ continued*:] a Court of Equity will give effect to the demand against the estate of a deceased person in respect of a wrongful act done by him, if the wrongful act has resulted in a benefit capable of being measured pecuniarily, and if the demand is of such a nature as can be properly entertained by the Court. The principles thus acted upon by Courts of Equity are in accordance with the conclusions enunciated by Lord *Mansfield* with reference to actions at common law which survive or die on account of the cause of action; but as regards those actions which at common law survive or die on account of the form of action, Courts of Equity will not permit the justice of the case to be defeated by reason of the technicalities of particular procedure. That the demand of the Plaintiffs in this suit was one proper to be made in a Court of Equity cannot be disputed; the decree is conclusive on this point. Upon the question whether the wrongful act resulted in a benefit to the estate of the wrongdoer I think the proper inquiry is that suggested by Sir *Thomas Plumer* in *Marquis of Lansdowne v Dowager of Lansdowne*,[3] 'Did the wrongdoer derive any benefit from the wrong done by him, or was it a naked injury by which his estate was in no way benefited?' My answer to that inquiry, as applied to the circumstances of the present case, is that the estate of the Defendant *R. Fothergill* was benefited by the wrongful user by the Defendants of the roads and passages under the Plaintiffs' farm. . . .

3 1 Madd 116.

NOTES AND QUESTIONS

1. Had the deceased been enriched by committing the tort of trespass? If so, what was the enrichment?

2. The majority's judgment is commonly treated as laying down that restitutionary remedies (whether common law or equitable) cannot be awarded for a tort unless the gain made by the tortfeasor comprises the claimant's property or its proceeds. Is this an accurate interpretation? If so: (a) is such a restriction on restitution intelligible?; (b) consider, after reading the other cases in this section, whether such a restriction has been applied or ignored in subsequent cases.

3. Swadling, 'The Myth of *Phillips v Homfray*' in *The Search for Principle* (eds Swadling and Jones, 1999), 277–94 argues that, although this decision is dealing with restitution for wrongs, it should be regarded as posing no difficulty for the modern law because of the abolition of the *actio personalis* rule. Taking into account the earlier 1871 decision, this 1883 decision was accepting, not denying, that a court can award restitution of the value of negative benefits against a living trespasser. For other interpretations of the case, see Burrows, 473–5.

4. Baggallay LJ relied on Lord Mansfield's obiter dicta in *Hambly v Trott* (1776) 1 Cowp. 371 as supporting his wider approach to restitution. But the majority thought that what Lord Mansfield said did not conflict with their restrictive view. Lord Mansfield said the following, at 375–7:

> '[W]e have carefully looked into all the cases upon the subject. To state and go through them all would be tedious, and tend rather to confound than elucidate. Upon the whole, I think these conclusions may be drawn from them.
>
> First, as to actions which survive against an executor, or die with the person, on account of the cause of action. Secondly, as to actions which survive against an executor, or die with the person, on account of the form of action.
>
> As to the first; where the cause of action is money due, or a contract to be performed, gain or acquisition of the testator, by the work and labour, or property of another, or a promise of the testator express or implied; whether these are the causes of action, the action survives against the executor. But where the cause of action is a tort, or arises ex delicto . . . supposed to be by force and against the King's peace, there the action dies; as battery, false imprisonment, trespass, words, nuisance, obstructing lights, diverting a water course, escape against the sheriff, and many other cases of the like kind.
>
> Secondly, as to those which survive or die, in respect of the form of action. In some actions the defendant could have waged his law; and therefore, no action in that form lies against an executor. But now, other actions are substituted in their room upon the very same cause, which do survive and lie against the executor. No action where in form the declaration must be quare vi et armis, et contra pacem, or where the plea must be, as in this case, that the testator was not guilty, can lie against the executor. Upon the face of the record, the cause of action arises ex delicto: and all private criminal injuries or wrongs, as well as all public crimes, are buried with the offender.
>
> But in most, if not in all the cases, where trover lies against the testator, another action might be brought against the executor, which would answer the purpose. An action on the custom of the realm against a common carrier, is for a tort and supposed crime: the plea is not guilty; therefore, it will not lie against an executor. But assumpsit, which is another action for the same cause, will lie. So if a man take a horse from another, and bring him back again; an action of trespass will not lie against his executor, though it would against him, but an action for the use and hire of the horse will lie against the executor. . . .
>
> Here therefore is a fundamental distinction. If it is a sort of injury by which the offender acquires no gain to himself at the expense of the sufferer, as beating or imprisoning a man, &c. there, the person injured has only a reparation for the delictum in damages to be assessed by a jury. But where, besides the crime, property is acquired which benefits the testator, there an action for the value of the property shall survive against the executor. As for instance, the executor shall not be chargeable for the injury done by his testator in cutting down another man's trees, but for the benefit arising to his testator for the value or sale of the trees he shall.

So far as the tort itself goes, an executor shall not be liable; and therefore it is, that all public and all private crimes die with the offender, and the executor is not chargeable; but so far as the act of the offender is beneficial, his assets ought to be answerable; and his executor therefore shall be charged.'

• *Edwards v Lee's Administrators, 96 SW 2d 1028*
(1936), Court of Appeals of Kentucky

The defendant (Edwards) discovered a cave (the 'Great Onyx Cave') under his land. The entrance to the cave was on his land but about one third of it ran under land belonging to the claimant (Lee). The defendant developed the cave, which contained beautiful rock crystal formations. It became a well-known tourist attraction. The claimant brought an action in trespass claiming damages, an accounting of profits, and an injunction preventing further trespass. At first instance, the injunction was granted and it was held that the claimant was entitled to one third of the net profits made from the cave. On appeal by the defendant the judgment was upheld, subject to correcting an error in the calculation of the profits.

Stites J: . . . [T]he case is sui generis, and counsel have been unable to give us much assistance in the way of previous decisions of this or other courts. We are left to fundamental principles and analogies.

We may begin our consideration of the proper measure of damages to be applied with the postulate that appellees held legal title to a definite segment of the cave and that they were possessed, therefore, of a right which it is the policy of the law to protect. We may assume that the appellants were guilty of repeated trespasses upon the property of appellees. . . . The proof likewise clearly indicates that the trespasses were willful, and not innocent.

Appellees brought this suit in equity, and seek an accounting of the profits realized from the operation of the cave, as well as an injunction against future trespass. In substance, therefore, their action is ex contractu and not, as appellants contend, simply an action for damages arising from a tort. Ordinarily, the measure of recovery in assumpsit for the taking and selling of personal property is the value received by the wrongdoer. On the other hand, where the action is based upon a trespass to land, the recovery has almost invariably been measured by the reasonable rental value of the property. . . . Strictly speaking, a count for 'use and occupation' does not fit the facts before us because, while there has been a recurring use, there has been no continuous occupation of the cave such as might arise from the planting of a crop or the tenancy of a house. Each trespass was a distinct usurpation of the appellees' title and interruption of their right to undisturbed possession. But, even if we apply the analogy of the crop cases or the wayleave cases (*Phillips v Homfray*, 24 Ch Div. 439; *Whithem v Westminster Co.*, 12 Times LR 318; *Carmichael v Old Straight Creek Coal Corporation*, 232 Ky. 133, 22 SW (2d) 572), it is apparent that rental value has been adopted, either consciously or unconsciously, as a convenient yardstick by which to measure the proportion of profit derived by the trespasser directly from the use of the land itself. In other words, rental value ordinarily indicates the amount of profit realized directly from the land as land, aside from all collateral contracts.

That profits rather than rent form the basis of recovery is illustrated by the cases involving the question of when an action of this character survives against the personal representative of a wrong-doer. If rent alone were the basis of recovery, we would expect to find that an action would survive against the estate of the trespasser. It would certainly be reasonable to assume that a simple action for debt would lie and that this would survive. The rule, however, has been established to the contrary. [*Stites J considered Lord Mansfield's judgment in Hambly v Trott and 'the leading case' of Phillips v Homfray and continued*:]

Other English cases in harmony with *Hambly v Trott* and *Phillips v Homfray* might be cited, but we deem these two to be sufficient to illustrate the principle. Clearly, the unjust enrichment of the wrongdoer is the gist of the right to bring an action ex contractu. Rental value is merely the most convenient and logical means for ascertaining what proportion of the benefits received may be attributed to the use of the real estate. In the final analysis, therefore, the distinction made between assumpsit concerning real and personal property thus disappears. In other words, in both situations the real criterion is the value received for the property, or for the use of the property, by the tortfeasor.

Similarly, in illumination of this conclusion, there is a line of cases holding that the plaintiff may at common law bring an action against a trespasser for the recovery of 'mesne profits' following the successful termination of an action of ejectment. . . .

Finally, in the current proposed final draft of the Restatement of Restitution and Unjust Enrichment (March 4, 1936), Part I, § 136, it is stated:

'A person who tortiously uses a trade name, trade secret, profit a prendre, or other similar interest of another, is under a duty of restitution for the value of the benefit thereby received.'

The analogy between the right to protection which the law gives a trade-name or trade secret and the right of the appellees here to protection of their legal rights in the cave seems to us to be very close. In all of the mineral and timber cases, there is an actual physical loss suffered by the plaintiff, as well as a benefit received by the defendant. In other words, there is both a plus and a minus quantity. In the trade-name and similar cases, as in the case at bar, there may be no tangible loss other than the violation of a right. The law, in seeking an adequate remedy for the wrong, has been forced to adopt profits received, rather than damages sustained, as a basis of recovery. . . .

Whether we consider the similarity of the case at bar to (1) the ordinary actions in assumpsit to recover for the use and occupation of real estate, or (2) the common-law action for mesne profits, or (3) the action to recover for the tortious use of a trade-name or other similar right, we are led inevitably to the conclusion that the measure of recovery in this case must be the benefits, or net profits, received by the appellants from the use of the property of the appellees. The philosophy of all these decisions is that a wrongdoer shall not be permitted to make a profit from his own wrong. . . .

Clay CJ and **Perry, Ratcliff** and **Rees JJ** concurred. **Thomas J** delivered a separate judgment concurring but on different reasoning based on regarding the cave as jointly owned.

NOTES AND QUESTIONS

1. We have included this case because it is one of the best-known and memorable of the many United States cases on restitution for torts. See also, for example, *Federal Sugar Refining Co. v United States Sugar Equalization Board*, 268 F 575 (1920) (profits from tort of inducing breach of contract); *Raven Red Ash Coal Co. v Ball*, 39 SE 2d 231 (1946) (value of use of land awarded against trespasser); *Olwell v Nye and Nissen Co.*, 26 Wash. 2d 282 (1946) (reasonable value of use / expense saved by conversion of egg-washing machine). Cf. *Hart v E. P. Dutton & Co. Inc.*, 93 NYS 2d 871 (1949) (restitution for libel refused).

2. In the extract set out above at 113, Birks used this case to illustrate that, once one recognizes that (the cause of action of) unjust enrichment does not require a correspondence of loss and gain, it becomes possible to 'alternatively analyse' many restitution for wrongs cases as awarding restitution of an unjust enrichment at the claimant's expense. But how precisely could one establish that Edwards was enriched *at the expense of* Lee?

- *Penarth Dock Engineering Co. Ltd v Pounds*
  [1963] 1 Lloyd's Rep 359, Queen's Bench Division

On 9 August 1961, the claimant sold a floating pontoon to the defendant. The pontoon was occupying part of dock premises leased by the claimant from the British Transport

Commission. As the claimant wished to shut down its ship-repairing business, and as the British Transport Commission wished to close the dock, the claimant and defendant agreed as an express term of the contract of sale that the defendant would remove the pontoon as soon as possible. Despite requests and demands by the claimant the defendant failed to remove the pontoon until 25 March 1963. The claimant sought damages from the defendant for breach of contract or trespass. That claim succeeded.

Lord Denning MR (sitting as an additional judge of the Queen's Bench Division): . . .

The question which remains is, what are the damages? True it is that the Penarth company themselves would not seem to have suffered any damage to speak of. They have not to pay any extra rent to the British Transport Commission. The dock is no use to them; they would not have made any money out of it. But, nevertheless, in a case of this kind, as I read the law, starting with *Whitwham v Westminster Brymbo Coal and Coke Company* [1896] 2 Ch 538, on which I commented myself in the case of *Strand Electric and Engineering Company, Ltd v Brisford Entertainments, Ltd* [1952] 2 QB 246, at 253 to 254, the test of the measure of damages is not what the plaintiffs have lost, but what benefit the defendant obtained by having the use of the berth; and he has been a trespasser, in my judgment, since Aug. 9, 1962. What benefit has the defendant obtained by having the use of it for this time? If he had moved it elsewhere, he would have had to pay, on the evidence, £37 10s. a week for a berth for a dock of this kind. But the damages are not put as high as that, and the damages are to be assessed in accordance with the law as I have stated it at the rate of £32 5s. a week for a period commencing from Aug. 9, 1962, which I would let run to Mar. 25, 1963, because the dock has now been removed. . . .

There will be judgment for the sum to be calculated on the above basis, with costs.

NOTES AND QUESTIONS

1. Although this is not made entirely clear, it would appear (and is generally assumed) that Lord Denning was awarding the damages, assessed on a restitutionary basis, for the tort of trespass and not for the breach of contract.

2. Lord Denning relied on his own judgment in *Strand Electric and Engineerin Co. Ltd v Brisford Entertainments Ltd* [1952] 2 QB 246, where he said the following (see also, below, 958):

   If a wrongdoer has made use of goods for his own purposes, then he must pay a reasonable hire for them, even though the owner has in fact suffered no loss. It may be that the owner would not have used the goods himself or that he had a substitute readily available which he used without extra cost to himself. Nevertheless the owner is entitled to a reasonable hire. . . . The claim for a hiring charge is therefore not based on loss to the plaintiff but on the fact that the defendant has used the goods for his own, purposes. It is an action against him because he has had the benefit of the goods. It resembles therefore an action for restitution, rather than an action for tort.

   But the majority of the Court of Appeal in *Strand Electric* clearly regarded the damages as compensatory.

3. The claimant had also sought a mandatory injunction requiring the defendant to remove the pontoon. Although there is no reference to this in the judgment, it may be that the damages were being awarded in equity under Lord Cairns's Act 1858 (see now section 50 of the Supreme Court Act 1981).

4. It is unclear why the damages were assessed at £32 5s a week rather than £37 10s. Perhaps this is all that the claimant sought.

5. It has sometimes been suggested (see, e.g., Robert Sharpe and S Waddams, below, 956) that, contrary to Lord Denning's express reasoning, the damages could be viewed as compensating the claimant for loss of the opportunity to bargain (that is, for what the claimant would have accepted for releasing the defendant from his obligation to remove the pontoon). Do you agree?

• *Bracewell v Appleby* [1975] Ch 408, Chancery Division

The defendant built a house on land to which the only access was along a private road owned by the claimants. The claimants sought an interim injunction restraining the defendant from trespassing by using the road to gain access to the house. The injunction was refused by Graham J because the claimants had stood by and allowed the building to be completed before seeking the injunction and the effect of the injunction would be to make the house uninhabitable. But damages in lieu of the injunction were awarded.

Graham J: . . . I come now to the question of relief. As already stated, I am unwilling in the circumstances to grant an injunction, but as, in my judgment, the plaintiffs have established their legal right, and by reason of the Chancery Amendment Act 1858 (Lord Cairns' Act) they can ask for, and the court can grant, damages in lieu of an injunction. The defendant accepted that such was the position if I was thus far in the plaintiffs' favour. After consideration I propose to approach the question of damages and assess the amount, which I was requested to do by both parties, along the same lines as those followed by Brightman J in *Wrotham Park Estate Co. Ltd v Parkside Homes Ltd* [1974] 1 WLR 798, 812 ff. It seems to me that the defendant must be liable to pay an amount of damages which in so far as it can be estimated is equivalent to a proper and fair price which would be payable for the acquisition of the right of way in question. In dealing with the case before him, Brightman J said, at 815:

> 'In my judgment a just substitute for a mandatory injunction would be such a sum of money as might reasonably have been demanded by the plaintiffs from Parkside as a quid pro quo for relaxing the covenant.'

Then, after rejecting the approach which aimed at obtaining half or a third of the development value, he went on:

> 'I think that in a case such as the present a landowner faced with a request from a developer which, it must be assumed, he feels reluctantly obliged to grant, would have first asked the developer what profit he expected to make from his operations.'

The profit in that case was large, being of the order of £50,000 and in the end the damages were assessed at £2,500, being 5 per cent of the profit.

In the present case, the plaintiffs, for amenity reasons, did not want an extra house built in the cul-de-sac and I think it is right to regard them also as 'reluctant,' just as Brightman J did in the case of the plaintiffs before him. On the other hand, in all the circumstances, I think that for the purpose of estimating damages they and the other servient owners in Hill Road, albeit reluctant, must be treated as being willing to accept a fair price for the right of way in question and must not be treated as if they were in the extremely powerful bargaining position which an interlocutory injunction would have given them if it had been obtained before the defendant started operations and incurred expense. Such is to my mind the penalty of standing by until the house is built.

On the evidence here the probable figure of notional profit which the defendant has made, being the difference between the overall cost of the new house and its present-day value seems to be somewhere between £4,000 and £6,000 and I think it is fair to take £5,000 as about as accurate a figure as one can get. The circumstances here are very different from those in the *Wrotham Park* case and I think that the proper approach is to endeavour to arrive at a fair figure which, on the assumption made, the parties would have arrived at as one which the plaintiffs would accept as compensating them for loss of amenity and increased user, and which at the same time, whilst making the blue land a viable building plot would not be so high as to deter the defendant from building at all. The defendant was not a speculative builder and in fact wanted to live in, and does now live in, 2A himself and I think he would have been prepared to pay what is relatively to his notional profit quite a large sum for the right of way in question and to achieve the building of his new home. This was a time of rising property values and I think he would have been prepared to pay £2,000 to get his right of way and if he had made such an offer, I think the other five owners in Hill Road ought also to have been prepared to accept it. The plaintiffs are, of course, only entitled to their appropriate share of this figure, namely, 1/5th each and I therefore award them £400 each by way of damages for the exercise of a right of way over their respective pieces of land.

QUESTION
Were the damages awarded in this case compensatory or restitutionary?

In the following extract, R Sharpe and S Waddams argue that the damages awarded for the wrongful use of another's property in, for example, *Penarth Dock v Pounds* and *Bracewell v Appleby* can be viewed as compensation for a lost opportunity to bargain rather than as being restitutionary.

- ● **R Sharpe and S Waddams, 'Damages for Lost Opportunity to Bargain'**
  (1982) 2 *OJLS* 290

Where wrongful use is made of another's property without diminishing its ultimate value, courts have faced a difficulty in assessing damages. The compensatory principle seems to suggest that no loss is suffered by the property owner. But there is a widespread and deeply felt appreciation that the defendant, having saved himself the expense of buying the right to use the property, ought to pay for it. As Lord Shaw put it in a Scottish case, if the defendant wrongfully borrows a horse from the plaintiff's stable he ought not to be allowed to say 'Against what loss do you want to be restored? I restore the horse. There is no loss. The horse is none the worse; it is the better for the exercise'. *(Watson, Laidlaw & Co. Ltd v Pott, Cassels & Williamson* (1914) 31 RPC 104, 119).

    As commonly happens when legal principle seems to depart from common sense, a variety of devices has evolved to justify the imposition of liability. These include punitive damages, restitution, accounting, awards of damages in lieu of an injunction, and a neglected line of cases (often called the 'wayleave' cases) awarding damages in the amount of a reasonable licence fee for the defendant's conduct. It is our purpose to suggest that all these cases can be explained on a simple and rational basis that is fully consistent with the compensatory theory of damages. That is that the plaintiff does suffer a real loss, namely, the opportunity to sell to the defendant the right to use the plaintiff's property. If this view is accepted, the instances referred to where damages have been awarded will be seen not as anomalous exceptions to the compensatory principle, hedged around with peculiar and archaic restrictions, but as applications of that principle fully in accord with the requirements of just compensation.

    Where the defendant has profited by his violation of the plaintiff's property right, a damage award based upon the extent of the defendant's gain does reflect something the plaintiff has lost. The defendant's wrongful conduct has deprived the plaintiff of the opportunity to bargain with the defendant, and to set his own price on his consent. The legal position can be explained by saying that the defendant should be prevented from circumventing the bargaining process, and where prevention fails, damages should be awarded to compensate the plaintiff for this lost opportunity.

    Injunctive relief is the most effective method of protecting the right to bargain. . . .

    Where an injunction is refused, the plaintiff's loss of his opportunity to bargain can still be given substantial protection through an award of damages in lieu of the injunction, sometimes called 'equitable damages', and originally made possible by Lord Cairns' Act (Chancery Law Amendment Act, 1858). In such cases, explicit reference has been made to the bargain which might have been made at the outset. Thus, in *Wrotham Park Estate Co. Ltd v Parkside Homes Ltd* ([1974] 1 WLR 798) it was held that rather than require the demolition of houses constructed in violation of a restrictive covenant, a preferable remedy was to award damages as a substitute. The plaintiffs had been unable to demonstrate a diminution in the value of their property caused by the violation of the restrictive covenant, yet, the court felt, it was hardly just 'that the plaintiffs should receive no compensation and that the defendants should be left in undisturbed possession of the fruits of their wrongdoing' (812). Brightman J concluded that 'a just substitute for a mandatory injunction would be such a sum of money as might reasonably have been demanded by the plaintiffs from Parkside as a quid pro quo for relaxing the covenant' (815). This he calculated on the basis of a percentage of the profit gained by the defendant in developing the site in violation of the covenant. Similarly in a Canadian case (*Arbutus Park Estates Ltd v Fuller* (1977) 74 DLR (3d) 257), the defendant had built a garage in violation of a covenant requiring him to have plans approved by the plaintiffs. Although the defendant made no direct profit, he did save the cost of having such plans prepared, and the court awarded that amount in the form of damages on the ground that the plaintiffs could easily have insisted that the defendant retain an architect to prepare aesthetically appropriate plans for the garage.

Equitable damages can be measured, where appropriate, to adjust recovery for loss of opportunity to bargain to suit particular circumstances where the plaintiff is entitled to something but not all. In *Bracewell v Appleby* ([1975] Ch 408) the plaintiffs had delayed in asserting their rights and allowed the defendants to build in violation of a restriction. They were 'treated as being willing to accept a fair price' and not 'as if they were in the extremely powerful bargaining position which an interlocutory injunction would have given them'. The award was made reflecting the amount 'which the plaintiffs would accept as compensating them for loss of amenity and increased user, and which at the same time, whilst making the . . . land a viable building plot would not be so high as to deter the defendant from building at all' (419–20).

Although the award of equitable damages is an effective way to compensate the plaintiff for loss of opportunity to bargain, for technical reasons it formerly was not always available. Because such awards are made as a substitute for an injunction which might be given, it was possible to take the view that damages in this measure could not be justified where an injunction was out of the question. If the defendant had ceased his unlawful activity, and the inquiry was entirely retrospective, damages could, it seemed, hardly be awarded in lieu of an injunction which the court could not possibly give. In *Price v Strange* ([1978] Ch 337), however, it was held that the court could award damages in lieu of specific performance, even though a decree of specific performance would not have been granted in the circumstances. This case suggests a distinction that would be rather difficult to apply between cases where specific relief was 'absolutely out of the question' (in which case no damages could be awarded in lieu) and cases where specific relief was contrary to settled principles but not 'absolutely impossible' (in which case damages could be available). *Johnson v Agnew* ([1980] AC 367) however, strongly suggests that no such distinctions are tenable, for there the House of Lords held, while approving the result of an earlier case awarding equitable damages, that there can be no difference in result between equitable damages and damages at law. So, if justice requires an award of damages according to a certain measure, such a measure should be used, whether or not it is possible to bring the case under Lord Cairns' Act or to describe the award as 'equitable damages'. This suggests a most welcome reconciliation between cases where damages are awarded 'in lieu of an injunction' and cases where damages are awarded simply as just compensation. In both kinds of case, we suggest, damages should compensate the plaintiff for loss of his opportunity to bargain. . . .

[T]he 1883 decision in *Phillips v Homfray* prevented the use of waiver of tort to avoid the rule *actio personalis moritur cum persona*, but left intact the earlier decision on the wayleavclaim. Whether or not one can waive the tort no longer determines the right to substantial damages. Thus *Phillips v Homfray*, far from establishing that damages measured by the wrongdoer's profits are not available in the case of trespass to land, actually established almost the contrary: damages are available, measured by the reasonable licence fee that the plaintiff could have charged. It is suggested that this principle is readily explained as compensation for lost opportunity to bargain.

Lord Denning relied on the wayleave cases in *Strand Electric and Engineering Co. Ltd v Brisford Entertainments Ltd* ([1952] 2 QB 246), and once again, the language he used suggests protection of the plaintiff's opportunity to bargain. There, property belonging to the plaintiff had been used without payment by the defendants. The defendants argued that the plaintiffs had in fact suffered no loss as they had not shown that the equipment would have been rented out had it been in their possession. The Court of Appeal rejected the argument on the basis that the wrongdoer 'must pay a reasonable hire . . . even though the owner had in fact suffered no loss . . . if the wrongdoer had asked the owner for permission to use the goods, the owner would be entitled to ask him for a reasonable remuncration as the price of his permission. The wrongdoer cannot be better off because he did not ask permission. He cannot be better off by doing wrong than he would be by doing right' (254).

Similarly, the Court of Appeal decision in *Seager v Copydex Ltd (No 2)* ([1969] 2 All ER 718) also fits this pattern. There, an inquiry had been ordered into damages assessed on the basis of reasonable compensation for use of confidential information in the manufacture of a device. In order to assess the value of information taken by the defendant, it was held that a lump sum based on a capitalization of the royalty for such information should be assessed, on the basis of the price the plaintiff would claim for the use of such information.

There are many other cases in which recovery has been based on the reasonable fee that the plaintiff might have charged—where the defendant has refused to remove his goods from the plaintiff's property (*Penarth Dock Engineering Co. v Pounds* [1963] 1 Lloyd's Rep. 359), refused to vacate rented premises on expiration of the lease (*Swordheath Properties Ltd v Tabet* [1979] 1 WLR 285), or made unauthorized use of the plaintiff's sewage system (*Daniel v O'Leary* (1976) 14 NBR (2d) 564). Similarly, recovery has been allowed for wrongful appropriation of personality where the plaintiff could have turned permission for its use to commercial advantage (*Athans v Canadian Adventure Camps Ltd* (1977) 17 OR (2d) 425). In all of these cases, recovery has been based on the amount the plaintiff might reasonably have charged for permission, and thus is consistent with the concept of compensation for loss of opportunity to bargain.

Yet another line of authority stemming from equity may also be seen as protecting a lost opportunity to bargain—the remedy of account. This technique is most frequently encountered in the industrial property area where the infringer is required to account to the owner for the benefit gained from the unauthorized use of confidential information, patent, or copyright. (*Peter Pan Manufacturing Corporation v Corsets Silhouette Ltd* [1963] 3 All ER 402).

At first sight it appears that a restitutionary approach to these problems is bound to lead to a more generous measure of damages than a purely compensatory approach. The defendant gains from his wrong, but the plaintiff appears to lose nothing. But if attention is focused on the question of what the defendant would have had to pay for the right to act as he did, had he sought to purchase it, it will be seen only that the plaintiff has suffered a loss, but also that the amount of the loss can realistically be measured at an amount equal to the defendant's net gain.

Where substitutes for the property in question are available to the defendant, as in the case of residential premises (*Swordheath*), theatrical lighting equipment (*Strand Electric*) or storage facilities for floating docks (*Penarth*) the appropriate measure of the value of the right to the defendant will be what the defendant would have had to pay in the marketplace for a substitute. The justification for this measure is not that the plaintiff would have sold his property right on the market, but that the defendant would have had to buy it in the market, and so would presumably have paid the market price to the plaintiff had he sought to buy the right to use the plaintiff's property.

Where there are no substitutes available to the defendant, as in the case of rights over the plaintiff's land, the court must construct a hypothetical bargain in order to value the plaintiff's right to sell his property. Although the plaintiff would probably not, in an actual bargain, have succeeded in extracting the defendant's full profit, here is a situation where the defendant, by his own misconduct, has prevented anyone from knowing how much in fact would have been paid for the right taken. Plainly it would be unfair to the defendant to allow proof by the plaintiff that he would only have sold the right for an enormous sum. Equally it would be unfair to the plaintiff to allow proof that the defendant would, by dint of hard bargaining, have acquired the property at a very low price. On balance it seems not unfair to assume that the defendant would have paid up to the full value to him of the right in question, i.e. the full amount of his net gain from acquiring the right.

It is true that this approach allows the plaintiff the benefit of a presumption that he would have demanded the greatest sum that the defendant would rationally have paid, and a critic might say, therefore, that the presumption is used as a fictitious justification for what should preferably be viewed as a restitutionary measure. Our purpose, however, is not to displace restitution, but rather to offer a new explanation and justification of results, widely agreed to be just, that formerly had been thought only to be defensible on restitutionary and other exceptional grounds. It is our suggestion that these results can often be justified on a compensatory basis.

QUESTIONS

Do you agree with Sharpe and Waddams' analysis? Can it be accurate to regard even an account of profits awarded for the intellectual property torts (see below, 969–973) as compensatory?

- ### *Stoke-on-Trent City Council v W & J Wass Ltd*
  [1988] 1 WLR 1406, Court of Appeal

The defendant company had committed the tort of nuisance by operating a Thursday market from 12 April 1984 within a distance infringing the claimant council's proprietary market right (that is, within 6 2/3 miles of the claimant's same day market). At first instance, Peter Gibson J granted the claimant, from 4 March 1987, a permanent injunction to restrain further infringement of its right. He also awarded substantial damages, not on the basis that the claimant had suffered any loss of custom, but on the basis of an appropriate licence fee that the claimant could have charged the defendant for lawful operation of its market from 12 April 1984 to 4 March 1987. The defendant company successfully appealed against the award of substantial damages, the Court of Appeal holding that the claimant was entitled merely to £2 nominal damages.

Nourse LJ: . . . The levying of an unlawful rival market is a tort. Whether it should properly be categorised as a nuisance or a trespass is probably not a question of importance. The better view must be that it is a nuisance. The general rule is that a successful plaintiff in an action in tort recovers damages equivalent to the loss which he has suffered, no more and no less. If he has suffered no loss, the most he can recover are nominal damages. A second general rule is that where the plaintiff has suffered loss to his property or some proprietary right, he recovers damages equivalent to the diminution in value of the property or right. The authorities establish that both these rules are subject to exceptions. These must be closely examined, in order to see whether a further exception ought to be made in this case.

[*Nourse LJ considered the 'way-leave' trespass cases, such as* Whitwham v Westminster Brymbo Coal and Coke Co. *[1896] 2 Ch 538, the detinue cases of* Strand Electric and Engineering Co. Ltd v Brisford Entertainments Ltd *[1952] 2 QB 246, infringement of patent cases*, Wrotham Park Estate Co. Ltd v Parkside Homes Ltd, *see below, 978 and* Bracewell v Appleby, *see above, 955, and continued*:]

As I understand these authorities, their broad effect is this. In cases of trespass to land and patent infringement and in some cases of detinue and nuisance the court will award damages in accordance with what Nicholls LJ has aptly termed 'the user principle.' On an analogous principle, in a case where there was a breach of a restrictive covenant the court has, in lieu of a permanent mandatory injunction to restore the breach, awarded damages equivalent to those which the plaintiffs might reasonably have demanded for a relaxation of the convenant. But it is only in the last-mentioned case and in the trespass cases that damages have been awarded in accordance with either principle without proof of loss to the plaintiff. In all the other cases, the plaintiff having established his loss, the real question has not been whether substantial damages should be awarded at all, but whether they should be assessed in accordance with the user principle or by reference to the diminution in value of the property or right. In other words, those other cases are exceptions to the second, but not to the first, of the general rules stated above.

Do the authorities support an award of damages in accordance with the user principle where an unlawful rival market has caused no loss to the market owner? In other words, is this case to be governed by the principle of the trespass cases and that of the *Wrotham Park* case?

The latter decision is in my opinion one which stands very much on its own. The conclusion of Brightman J may, I think, be more fully explained as follows. An injunction is frequently, granted to enforce an express negative covenant, especially a restrictive covenant affecting land, without proof of loss to the plaintiff. Injunctions could therefore and would have been granted in that case but for the social and economic reasons against ordering the demolition of 14 houses. If injunctions had been granted, the loss to the defendant purchasers would have been enormous. If, on the other hand, injunctions were not granted and no damages were awarded, the purchasers would have been left in undisturbed possession of the correspondingly enormous fruits of their wrongdoing. Accordingly, if the plaintiffs had not been awarded substantial damages, justice manifestly would not have been done. If this analysis is correct, the practical result of the *Wrotham Park* decision was something akin to an award of exemplary damages for breach of contract, albeit that their amount bore no relation to the loss which would have been suffered by the defendant purchasers if they had had to demolish their houses. In saying this, I do not wish to suggest that that case was wrongly decided. Indeed, I regard the result as having been entirely appropriate and I see no reason why it should not serve as a precedent for other cases of the same kind. I merely wish to emphasise that it stands a long way away from the present problem and does not assist in its solution.

On a superficial view, the trespass cases present a greater difficulty. In trespass the defendant makes an unlawful use of the plaintiff's land. Similarly, it can be said that in levying an unlawful rival market the defendant makes an unlawful use of the plaintiff's right to hold his own market, which, at any rate in the case of a franchise market, is an incorporeal hereditament. Ought it to make all the difference that in the first case the unlawful use is a physical one? This is a formidable line of argument, but I think that it is unsound. If the way-leave cases are put on one side, it seems to me that the trespass cases really depend on the fact that the defendant's use of the plaintiff's land deprives the plaintiff of *any* opportunity of using it himself. And even on the assumption, which may be correct, that the broad view of Denning LJ in the *Strand Electric* case [1952] 2 QB 246 is a correct view of the law, the same can be said of an unlawful detention of the plaintiff's chattel. On the other hand, an unlawful use of the plaintiff's right to hold his own market does not deprive him of the opportunity of holding one himself. Such indeed has been the state of affairs in the present case. If of course the plaintiff can show that he has thereby suffered loss, nobody would suggest that he ought not to receive substantial damages. But why should he receive them when he has been able to hold his own market and has suffered no loss from the defendant's?

It is characteristic of the development of the common law that the invention and increasingly extended application of the user principle should appear to have come about by accident rather than by design. Thus it seems from the interlocutory observations of the members of this court in *Whitwham's* case [1896] 2 Ch 538, 539, 540, 541 that they were initially resistant to the principle of the way-leave cases. But they saw in it a basis for the just decision of that case, and once it had been so decided the application of the principle to analogous states of affairs, for example the wrongful detention of chattels, seems to have been a perfectly natural development. However, in a process of development it is sometimes necessary to stand back from the authorities and to ask not simply where they have come to, but where, if a further extension is made, they may go next.

Although I would accept that there may be a logical difficulty in making a distinction between the present case and the way-leave cases, I think that if the user principle were to be applied here there would be an equal difficulty in distinguishing other cases of more common occurrence, particularly in nuisance. Suppose a case where a right to light or a right of way had been obstructed to the profit of the servient owner but at no loss to the dominant owner. It would be difficult, in the application of the user principle, to make a logical distinction between such an obstruction and the infringement of a right to hold a market. And yet the application of that principle to such cases would not only give a right to substantial damages where no loss had been suffered but would revolutionise the tort of nuisance by making it unnecessary to prove loss. Moreover, if the principle were to be applied in nuisance, why not in other torts where the defendant's wrong can work to his own profit, for example in defamation? As progenitors of the rule in trespass and some other areas, the way-leave cases have done good service. But just as their genus is peculiar, so ought their procreative powers to be exhausted.

These considerations have led me to conclude that the user principle ought not to be applied to the infringement of a right to hold a market where no loss has been suffered by the market owner. If loss caused by the diversion of custom from one market to the other had been proved, I would have agreed with Nicholls LJ that the general rule ought to apply, so that the council would have recovered damages equivalent to the diminution in value of their right through the loss of stallage, tolls and so forth. But I rest my decision in this case on the simple ground that where no loss has been suffered no substantial damages of any kind can be recovered. Otherwise we would have to allow that the right to recover nominal damages for disturbance of a same day market without proof of loss had become one to receive substantial damages on top. If we had to allow that, why not also in the case of an other day market where no loss had been proved? It is possible that the English law of tort, more especially of the so-called 'proprietary torts,' will in due course make a more deliberate move towards recovery based not on loss suffered by the plaintiff but on the unjust enrichment of the defendant: see *Goff and Jones, The Law of Restitution*, 3rd edn (1986), 612–14. But I do not think that that process can begin in this case and I doubt whether it can begin at all at this level of decision. . . .

Nicholls LJ: It is an established principle concerning the assessment of damages that a person who has wrongfully used another's property without causing the latter any pecuniary loss may still be liable to that other for more than nominal damages. In general, he is liable to pay, as damages, a reasonable sum for the wrongful use he has made of the other's property. The law has reached this conclusion by giving to the concept of loss or damage in such a case a wider meaning than merely financial loss calculated by comparing the property owner's financial position after the wrongdoing with what it would have been had the wrongdoing never occurred. Furthermore, in such a case it is no answer for the wrongdoer to show that the property owner would probably not have used the property himself had the wrongdoer not done so. In *The Mediana* [1900] AC 113, 117, Earl of Halsbury LC made the famous observation that a defendant who had deprived the plaintiff of one of the chairs in his room for 12 months could not diminish the damages by showing that the plaintiff did not usually sit upon that chair or that there were plenty of other chairs in the room.

What is in issue on this appeal is a novel application of this principle (which, for convenience, I shall call 'the user principle'). Heretofore that principle has been applied to the use of land. In 1896 Lindley LJ in *Whitwham v Westminster Brymbo Coal and Coke Co.* [1896] 2 Ch 538, 542, observed that if one man trucks on rails over another man's land it does not do any harm whatever, and there is no pecuniary damage, but that the law was 'now settled.' He stated the principle thus, at 541–2; 'if one person has without leave of another been using that other's land for his own purposes, he ought to pay for such user.'

. . .

The user principle has also been applied to chattels: *Strand Electric and Engineering Co. Ltd v Brisford Entertainments Ltd* [1952] 2 QB 246. But the principle is not confined to the physical use of another's property. The same principle has been applied in relation to incorporeal property, in particular patents. [*Nicholls LJ referred to patent infringement cases such as* Watson, Laidlaw & Co. Ltd v Pott, Cassels and Williamson *(1914) 31 RPC 104 and continued*:]

In the present case the council seeks to extend the user principle by applying it to a case of disturbance of market rights. . .

The common law . . . is constantly being developed and adapted as social conditions change, and novelty by itself is not an answer to the present claim. Indeed, for some time I was attracted by the analogy between infringement of a patent and infringement of a market right. The argument is to the following effect. The owner of a market right has a legal monopoly in respect of the holding of a market within a certain area. If, for the purpose of assessment of damages on the user principle, infringement of a patent is to be regarded as the invasion and abstraction by the infringer of the property which consists of the monopoly of the patented articles granted to the patentee, as Lord Shaw observed in the passage I have cited from the *Watson, Laidlaw* case, so also is the disturbance of a market right to be regarded as the invasion and abstraction of the property which consists of the monopoly of the holding of a market in the place in question. In other words, if the infringement of a patent is to be regarded as the wrongful user of the property comprised in the patent, then by parity of reasoning the disturbance of a market right may properly be regarded as the wrongful user of the property comprised in the market right. If, in the one instance, damages may be awarded on the user principle in a suitable case, so may they be in the other instance.

I have, however, concluded that the analogy is unsound and that the application of the user principle in the case of the disturbance of a market right would not accord with the basic principles applicable to that cause of action. A market right confers a monopoly, as does a patent, but the protection which the law affords to the owner of a market right is limited to protecting him against being disturbed in the enjoyment of his right. If an unauthorised market is held without disturbing the lawful market, the owner of the lawful market has no remedy, either for damages or otherwise. In such an event there is no place for an award of damages to be assessed on the user principle. Thus, for example, if and so long as the owner of the market right is currently not exercising or seeking to exercise his right, and is not holding a market at all, he has no cause of action against a person holding an unauthorised market, for in such a case he is not being disturbed in the enjoyment of his market right. . . .

Disturbance may exist in fact or, in the case of a 'same day' market, be presumed as a matter of law. In the case of an 'other day' market, where disturbance exists in fact the remedies which the law provides are (a) an injunction and (b) damages to compensate for the disturbance. Again I can see no scope for the application of the user principle. If, on the one hand, the unauthorised, other day market has caused and is causing no loss, either of stallage or of tolls or under any of the other heads of loss which may affect the owner of a market right, there is no cause of action. There is, in that event, no question of applying the user principle. If, on the other hand, the owner of the market right does sustain loss under one or more of those heads, damages must surely be commensurate with the quantum of the loss so sustained. The damages will correspond, so far as the court can fairly assess them, to the amount of the loss flowing to the owner of the market right from the respects in which he has in fact been damnified in his enjoyment of that right by the holding of the unauthorised, other day market. Again, there would be no place for awarding, by application of the user principle, damages in a sum greater than the amount of that loss.

If I am right so far, and the user principle does not fit into the scheme of things thus far, it would be curious in the extreme if nonetheless the user principle could be invoked in the case of a same day market where in fact no loss exists under any of the recognised heads of loss.

I can see no justification for introducing such an anomaly into the law. The owner of a market right has a cause of action in the case of a same day market even though the unauthorised market has not in fact caused him any loss. Despite the absence of loss, an injunction may be granted. . . . Indeed . . . the remedy of an injunction may be peculiarly appropriate in such a case precisely because damages will not be an adequate remedy. But, in my view, to award damages on the user principle in such a case in respect of the period prior to the grant of an injunction would lead to the owner of the market right obtaining a greater measure of relief than would be justified by the nature of his right.

For the future injunctive relief would, rightly, prevent the unauthorised market from being held, but as to the past he would obtain, under the guise of damages, a sum to compensate him for disturbance when, in fact, there had been none. It may be anomalous today that, in the case of a same day market, the owner of the market right has a cause of action at all in respect of an unauthorised market which in fact causes no disturbance to the lawful market. But, whether this is anomalous or not, I see no justification for departing from what hitherto has long been accepted at the law, namely, that where there is in fact no loss sustained under any of the recognised heads, of stallage and so forth, the owner of the market right has a cause of action in respect of a same day market but his claim for damages is confined to nominal damages.

I say nothing about a claim for exemplary damages or whether, if such a claim had been made in this case, it would have been well-founded. Certainly the defendants' conduct in persisting in holding their market despite the plaintiffs' objections, is not conduct calculated to attract much sympathy. But for the reasons I have sought to state, I have to part company from the judge's conclusion that, although the plaintiffs had suffered no loss under any of the normal heads of loss, damages should be assessed by reference to a notional licence fee for the period from April 1984 to 4 March 1987, being the date of his order.

The plaintiffs also placed some reliance on the decision of Brightman J in *Wrotham Park Estate Co. Ltd v Parkside Homes Ltd* [1974] 1 WLR 798. I do not think that decision takes the matter any further so far as the present case is concerned. That case concerned an award of damages for breach of a restrictive covenant in lieu of a mandatory injunction. It is far removed from the present case. Wherever precisely the boundary, separating causes of action in which the user principle will be applied from those in which it will not, is to be drawn, for the reasons I have sought to state above that principle, in my view, has no application to a cause of action for disturbance of a market where, for the pre-injunction period during which the unauthorised market was held, the unauthorised market did not in fact disturb the lawful market.

Mann LJ agreed.

NOTES AND QUESTIONS

1. Do you agree with Nourse LJ's suggestion that a deliberate move to granting restitution for a tort would require a new beginning by the House of Lords? Was Lord Denning of the same view in the *Strand Electric* or *Penarth Docks* cases? For a sustained attack on what he terms 'the *Wass* illusion' (that is, that a gain-based remedy would have been a troubling innovation) see P Birks, *Civil Wrongs: A New World* (Butterworths Lectures, 1990–1), 55–112, especially 57–77.

2. Would exemplary damages have been awarded had they been pleaded?

3. In his leading speech in the *Blake* case (below, 981), Lord Nicholls returned to damages based on the 'user principle' and appeared to treat such damages as an example of restitution for a wrong. Subsequent to *Blake*, he made reference to 'user principle' damages in the context of the tort of conversion in *Kuwait Airways Corporation v Iraqi Airways Co. (Nos 4 and 5)* [2002] 2 AC 1066. This case arose from the actions of the Iraqi Airways Company (IAC) following the invasion of Kuwait by Iraq on 2 August 1990. From the date of the invasion until the commencement of the Gulf War in 1991, IAC removed aircraft from the Kuwait International Airport and transported them to Baghdad. An action for recovery of the aircraft and/or

damages was brought and appealed on various issues to the House of Lords. In the leading speech, Lord Nicholls (with whom Lords Steyn, Hoffmann and Hope agreed, Lord Scott dissenting) examined aspects of the tort of conversion from first principles. His Lordship observed that, in relation to six of the planes which had been returned, a separate claim, in addition to compensation for any loss suffered, could have been brought by the Kuwait Airways Corporation (KAC) to recover the value of the benefit that IAC had obtained from the use of those six aircraft. Although he held that it was too late to advance such a claim for the first time in the House of Lords, Lord Nicholls said (at [2002] 2 AC 1094 [87])

> Sometimes, when the goods or their equivalent are returned, the owner suffers no financial loss. But the wrongdoer may well have benefited from his temporary use of the owner's goods. It would not be right that he should be able to keep this benefit. The court may order him to pay damages assessed by reference to the value of the benefit he derived from his wrongdoing. I considered this principle in *A-G v Blake* (below, 982–984). In an appropriate case the court may award damages on this 'user principle' in addition to compensation for loss suffered. For instance, if the goods are returned damaged, the court may award damages assessed by reference to the benefit obtained by the wrongdoer as well as the cost of repair.

• *Ministry of Defence v Ashman* (1993) 66 P & CR 195, Court of Appeal

After her husband left her, the defendant tenant wrongly ignored notices from the Ministry of Defence to quit RAF accommodation because she and her children had nowhere else to go. In the Ministry's action for damages for trespass to land ('mesne profits') the county court awarded damages based on the subsidized rent that the defendant's former husband had been paying. The Ministry appealed. The Court of Appeal allowed the appeal and remitted the case to the county court for assessment, but on the basis that the claimant was entitled to restitutionary damages for the trespass (i.e. the benefit to the defendant of the accommodation) and not on the basis that the Ministry was entitled to the market rental value of the property.

Kennedy LJ: . . . The second defendant was at all material times a Flight Sergeant in the Royal Air Force and the first defendant was his wife. After they separated she stayed on in the married quarters which they had occupied together. The issue raised by this appeal is the way in which, in such a situation, mesne profits should be calculated. Should they be calculated by reference to the market rent, by reference to the subsidised rent paid by the serviceman so long as he and his family remained in lawful occupation or in some other way?

[*After setting out the facts in greater detail, together with the reasoning of the county court judge, he continued:*] [How should] the judge have approached the problem of quantifying damages in this case[?] In my judgment it is helpful to start, as Megaw LJ did in *Swordheath Properties v Tabet*[1] with the statement of principle to be found in *Halsbury's Laws of England*. The paragraph begins:[2]

> Particular rules have been evolved in cases of trespass to land. A plaintiff is entitled to nominal damages for trespass even if no damage or loss is caused; if damage or loss is caused, he is entitled to recover in respect of his loss according to general principles.

A little later there is a passage cited by Megaw LJ which reads thus:

> Where the defendant has by trespass made use of the plaintiff's land the plaintiff is entitled to receive by way of damages such sum as should reasonably be paid for the use. It is immaterial that the plaintiff was not in fact thereby impeded or prevented from himself using his own land either because he did not wish to do so or for any other reason.

---

1 [1979] 1 WLR 285.   2 4th edn, Vol. 12, at para. 1170.

In further support of that passage Megaw LJ referred to *Penarth Dock Engineering Co. Ltd v Pounds*. There the defendant failed to recover a pontoon he had purchased from the plaintiff company which could not of itself point to any loss. Lord Denning MR said,[3]

> The test of the measure of damages is not what the plaintiffs have lost, but what benefit the defendant obtained by having the use of the berth . . . If he had moved it elsewhere, he would have had to pay on the evidence £37–10s a week for a berth for a dock of this kind.

Damages were claimed in that case at a lower rate. That rate was awarded. As Megaw LJ later explained, damages in the *Penarth Dock* case were calculated by reference to 'the proper value to the trespassers of use of the property.'

In the *Swordheath Properties* case the Court of Appeal was able to apply that approach, which may be somewhat analogous to quasi-contractual restitution, to a claim by a landlord against occupants of residential property who had remained in unlawful possession. The landlord was held entitled to recover 'the proper letting value of the property' for the relevant period, that being in an ordinary case, in a free market, the value to the trespassers of its use.

But where, as in the present case, the property is not normally let on the open market, and the trespasser only remains in possession because she is in no position to move anywhere else, it seems to me that more assistance as to the proper value to Mrs. Ashman of the use of the property might be gained by looking at what she would have had to pay for suitable local authority accommodation, had any been available, than by focusing on evidence given on behalf of the Ministry as to market rent.

. . .

Accordingly I would allow the appeal and remit the matter to the County Court judge so that he may decide what was in that relevant period the value to Mrs. Ashman of the use of the property. For the purposes of that hearing Mrs. Ashman might be wise to obtain from the local authority information as to what rent she would have had to pay for three bedroom accommodation for the period from May 16, 1991, to April 4, 1992, had such accommodation been available.

Hoffmann LJ: A person entitled to possession of land can make a claim against a person who has been in occupation without his consent on two alternative bases. The first is for the loss which he has suffered in consequence of the defendant's trespass. This is the normal measure of damages in the law of tort. The second is the value of the benefit which the occupier has received. This is a claim for restitution. The two bases of claim are mutually exclusive and the plaintiff must elect before judgment which of them he wishes to pursue. These principles are not only fair but, as Kennedy LJ demonstrated, well established by authority.

It is true that in the earlier cases it has not been expressly stated that a claim for mesne profit for trespass can be a claim for restitution. Nowadays I do not see why we should not call a spade a spade. In this case the Ministry of Defence elected for the restitutionary remedy. It adduced no evidence of what it would have done with the house if the Ashmans had vacated. In my judgment such matters are irrelevant to a restitution claim. All that matters is the value of benefit which the defendant has received. . . .

That leaves . . . the question of how one values the benefit which Mr. and Mrs. Ashman received. In *Swordheath Properties Limited v Tabet* Megaw LJ said, 'in the absence of anything special in the particular case' it will ordinarily be the rating value of the property in the open market. This the judge found to be £472 a month as against the concessionary licence fee of £95 a month which Mr. Ashman had previously been charged. As the only special feature found by the judge was the estoppel we

---

3 [1963] 1 Lloyd's Rep. 359 at 362.

have held to be unsustainable, the Ministry asks that we substitute a figure of £472 a month for that ordered by the judge.

In my judgment, however, the law of restitution is not so inflexible. The open market value will ordinarily be appropriate because the defendant has chosen to stay in the premises rather than pay for equivalent premises somewhere else. But such benefits may in special circumstances be subject to what Professor Birks, in his *Introduction to the Law of Restitution* has conveniently called subjective devaluation. This means a benefit may not be worth as much to the particular defendant as to someone else. In particular, it may be worth less to a defendant who has not been free to reject it. Mr. and Mrs. Ashman would probably have never occupied the premises in the first place if they had to pay £472 a month instead of the concessionary licence fee of £95. Mrs. Ashman would certainly not have stayed in the premises at the market rate if she had any choice in the matter. She stayed because she could not establish priority need to be rehoused by the local authority until the eviction order had been made against her. Once the necessary proceedings had been taken she was able to obtain local authority housing at £145 a month.

In my judgment, therefore, the special circumstances in this case are created by the combination of two factors. First, the fact that the Ashmans were occupying at a concessionary licence fee. Secondly, the fact that Mrs. Ashman had, in practice, no choice but to stay in the premises until the local authority were willing to rehouse her. The first factor is important because I think if the Ashmans had voluntarily paid the ordinary market rate, they could not claim the premises had become worth less to them because they could not find anywhere else to go.

The second factor is important because I do not think the defendant can say the premises were worth less to him than suitable accommodation he could realistically obtain. In the circumstances of this case the value to Mrs. Ashman was no more than she would have had to pay for suitable local authority housing, if she could have been immediately rehoused. Allowing subjective devaluation in circumstances like this case will not cause any injustice to a landlord. If he has suffered greater loss, (for example, because there would have been a re-letting at market value) it is always open to him to elect for the alternative tort measure of damages. Although Mrs. Ashman produced an agreement of the local authority showing the rent she now pays, there was no evidence on this point before the judge. The action must therefore be remitted to the County Court.

Lloyd LJ would have remitted the case for an assessment of damages on a compensatory, not a restitutionary, basis but was content to go along with the basis proposed by **Kennedy** and **Hoffmann LJJ**.

NOTES AND QUESTIONS

1. Was the benefit to Mrs Ashman of staying on in the RAF accommodation: (i) the expense saved of equivalent accommodation in the open market?; or (ii) the expense saved of suitable local authority housing (had any been available)?

2. See also the similar case of *Ministry of Defence v Thompson* [1993] 40 EG 148. See generally on these cases, E Cooke, 'Trespass, Mesne Profits and Restitution' (1994) 110 *LQR* 420. For two further cases in which the courts appeared to take a restitutionary analysis of the damages awarded against a trespasser, see *Gondall v Dillon Newspapers Ltd* [2001] RLR 221, CA; and *Horsford v Bird* [2006] UKPC 3.

3. In *Inverugie Investments v Hackett* [1995] 1 WLR 713 the Privy Council had to decide what 'mesne profits' a tenant of hotel apartments was entitled to for trespass committed by the landlord over a period of fifteen years. Lord Lloyd said that no issue of principle arose in assessing the damages, as the agreed problem was how a reasonable rent should be calculated. In line with this, the amount awarded, and the method of computation adopted, by the Privy Council did not seem to rest on either a compensatory or a restitutionary basis. Indeed Lord

Lloyd's view (at 718) was that 'The [user] principle need not be characterised as exclusively compensatory, or exclusively restitutionary; it combines elements of both.' With respect, we find this lack of principled reasoning both confusing and disappointing. For a (strained) restitutionary interpretation of the reasoning, see Charles Mitchell, 'Mesne Profits and Restitutionary Damages' [1995] *LMCLQ* 343.

- ● *Jaggard v Sawyer* [1995] 1 WLR 269, Court of Appeal

The claimant and the defendants owned houses on a small residential estate served by a private road. The defendants bought and built a house on a plot of land adjoining their own. The only access from the new house was along the private road. But use of it as a means of access to the new house constituted a breach of the defendants' restrictive covenant with the claimant (as with the other owners of houses in the estate) and a trespass over the claimant's part of the road. The claimant had threatened to bring proceedings for an injunction before the defendants had begun building the new house but had only actually brought proceedings when the building of the house was at an advanced stage. The claimant was refused an injunction to prevent the continuing trespass and breach of restrictive covenant but she was awarded damages of £694.44, in lieu of the injunction, which the Court of Appeal explicitly regarded as compensating her for her loss.

Sir Thomas Bingham MR (with whom **Kennedy LJ** agreed): . . . Instead of injunctions, [Judge Jack QC] awarded the plaintiff damages. He asked himself what the defendants might reasonably have paid for a right of way and the release of the covenant. . . . He held that the defendant would have been prepared to pay not less than £6,250. Split among the nine residents (excluding those in No 5), that total yielded £694.44 *per* resident. That is the sum (with interest) which he awarded the plaintiff.

[*After referring to a number of cases, including* Wrotham Park Estate v Parkside Homes Ltd, Bracewell v Appleby *and* Surrey CC v Bredero Homes Ltd, *the Master of the Rolls continued:*]

The court's approach to restitutionary damages in [the Bredero] case has provoked some regretful comment (see Professor Birks, 'Profits of Breach of Contract' (1993) 109 *LQR* 518), and it may be, as suggested (see 520) that these judgments will not be the last word on that subject. But the court plainly treated the case as one not falling under the principles derived from Lord Cairns's Act. I cannot, however accept that Brightman J's assessment of damages in the *Wrotham Park* case was based on other than compensatory principles. The defendants had committed a breach of covenant, the effects of which continued. The judge was not willing to order the defendants to undo the continuing effects of that breach. He had therefore to assess the damages necessary to compensate the plaintiffs for this continuing invasion of their right. He paid attention to the profits earned by the defendants, as it seems to me, not in order to strip the defendants of their unjust gains, but because of the obvious relationship between the profits earned by the defendants and the sum which the defendants would reasonably have been willing to pay to secure release from the covenant. I am reassured to find that this is the view taken of the *Wrotham Park* case by Sir Robert Megarry V-C in *Tito v Waddell (No 2)* [1977] Ch 106, 335, when he said:

'Brightman J resolved the difficult question of the appropriate quantum of damages by holding that the plaintiffs should recover 5 per cent of the defendants' expected profit from their venture. In *Bracewell v Appleby*, Graham J applied the same principle where the right in question was not a consent under a restrictive covenant, but an easement of way. I find great difficulty in seeing how these cases help Mr Macdonald. If the plaintiff has the right to prevent some act being done without his consent, and the defendant does the act without seeking that consent, the plaintiff has suffered a loss in that the defendant has taken without paying for it something for which the plaintiff could have required payment, namely, the right to do the act. The court therefore makes the defendant pay what he ought to have paid the plaintiff, for that is what the plaintiff has lost. The basis of computation is not, it will be observed, in any way directly related to wasted expenditure or other loss that the defendant is escaping by reason of an injunction being refused: it is the loss that the plaintiff has suffered by the defendant not having observed the obligation to obtain the plaintiff's consent. Where the obligation is contractual, that loss is the loss caused to the plaintiff by the breach of contract.'

I can see no reason why a judge should not assess damages on the *Wrotham Park* basis when he declines to prevent commission of a future wrong.

. . .

The judge [in the present case] considered the value of the injury to the plaintiff's right a capable of being estimated in money. He based himself on the *Wrotham Park* approach. In my view he was justified. He valued the right at what a reasonable seller would sell it for. In situations of this kind a plaintiff should not be treated as eager to sell, which he very probably is not. But the court will not value the right at the ransom price which a very reluctant plaintiff might put on it. I see no error in the judge's approach to this aspect.

. . .

The only argument pressed on damages was that the only damages properly awardable on compensatory principles would have been nominal and that therefore an injunction should have been granted. As already indicated, I think that the *Wrotham Park* approach was appropriate even on pure compensatory principles and the judge followed it correctly.

Millett LJ: . . . It is . . . necessary to notice the observations of Steyn LJ in *Surrey County Council v Bredero Homes Ltd* [1993] 1 WLR 1361, 1369:

'In my view *Wrotham Park Estate Co. Ltd v Parkside Homes Ltd* [1974] 1 WLR 798 is only defensible on the basis of the third or restitutionary principle . . . The plaintiffs' argument that the *Wrotham Park* case can be justified on the basis of a loss of bargaining opportunity is a fiction.'

I find these remarks puzzling. It is plain from his judgment in the *Wrotham Park* case that Brightman J's approach was compensatory, not restitutionary. He sought to measure the damages by reference to what the plaintiff had lost, not by reference to what the defendant had gained. He did not award the plaintiff the profit which the defendant had made by the breach, but the amount which he judged the plaintiff might have obtained as the price of giving its consent. The amount of the profit which the defendant expected to make was a relevant factor in that assessment, but that was all.

Both the *Wrotham Park* and *Bredero Homes* cases (unlike the present) were concerned with a single past breach of covenant, so that the measure of damages at common law and under the Act was the same. Prima facie the measure of damages in either case for breach of a covenant not to build a house on neighbouring land is the diminution in the value of the plaintiff's land occasioned by the breach. One element in the value of the plaintiff's land immediately before the breach is attributable to his ability to obtain an injunction to prevent the building. Clearly a defendant who wished to build would pay for the release of the covenant, but only so long as the court could still protect it by the grant of an injunction. The proviso is important. It is the ability to claim an injunction which gives the benefit of the covenant much of its value. If the plaintiff delays proceedings until it is no longer possible for him to obtain an injunction, he destroys his own bargaining position and devalues his right. The unavailability of the remedy of injunction at one and the same time deprives the court of jurisdiction to award damages under the Act and removes the basis for awarding substantial damages at common law. For this reason, I take the view that damages can be awarded at common law in accordance with the approach adopted in the *Wrotham Park* case, but in practice only in the circumstances in which they could also be awarded under the Act.

This may be what Steyn LJ had in mind when he said that the loss of bargaining opportunity was a fiction. If he meant it generally or in relation to the facts which obtained in the *Wrotham Park* case, then I respectfully disagree. But it was true in the circumstances of the case before him, and not merely for the reason given by Rose LJ (that the plaintiffs did not object to the extra houses and would have waived the breach for a nominal sum). The plaintiffs did not bring the proceedings until after the defendant had sold the houses and was no longer susceptible to an injunction. The plaintiffs had thereby deprived themselves of any bargaining position. Unable to obtain an injunction, they were equally unable to invoke the jurisdiction to award damages under Lord Cairns's Act. No longer exposed to the risk of an injunction, and having successfully disposed of the houses, the defendant had no reason to pay anything for the release of the covenant. Unless they were able to recover damages in accordance with restitutionary principles, neither at common law nor in equity could the plaintiffs recover more than nominal damages.

In the present case the plaintiff brought proceedings at a time when her rights were still capable of being protected by injunction. She has accordingly been able to invoke the court's jurisdiction to award in substitution for an injunction damages which take account of the future as well as the past. In my view there is no reason why compensatory damages for future trespasses and continuing breaches of covenant should not reflect the value of the rights which she has lost, or why such damages should not be measured by the amount which she could reasonably have expected to receive for their release.

In my judgment the judge's approach to the assessment of damages was correct on the facts and in accordance with principle.

NOTE

For another trespass to land case in which the damages were analysed as compensating for the loss of the reasonable fee that could have been negotiated for the right in question, see *Severn Trent Water Ltd v Barnes* [2004] EWCA Civ 570.

(2) INTELLECTUAL PROPERTY TORTS

- *Colbeam Palmer Ltd v Stock Affiliates Pty. Ltd*
  (1968) 122 CLR 25, High Court of Australia

From 1961 the claimant was the registered owner of a word trade mark 'Craftmaster' for painting sets. The defendant sold painting sets under that name not knowing that the claimant had registered the mark. The claimant did not inform the defendant of its registration until 30 August 1965. The claimant sought, *inter alia*, an account of the profits made by the defendant from selling the sets after 1961. Windeyer J ordered that an account of profits be taken from 30 August 1965.

Windeyer J: . . . The plaintiff whose mark has been infringed can choose between damages or an account of profits. He cannot have both. They are alternative remedies. . . .

The distinction between an account of profits and damages is that by the former the infringer is required to give up his ill-gotten gains to the party whose rights he has infringed: by the latter he is required to compensate the party wronged for the loss he has suffered. The two computations can obviously yield different results, for a plaintiff's loss is not to be measured by the defendant's gain, nor a defendant's gain by the plaintiff's loss. Either may be greater, or less, than the other. If a plaintiff elects to take an inquiry as to damages the loss to him of profits which he might have made may be a substantial element of his claim: see *Mayne on Damages*, 11th edn (1946), 71 note. But what a plaintiff might have made had the defendant not invaded his rights is by no means the same thing as what the defendant did make by doing so.

I need not elaborate the distinction between a defendant's profits and a plaintiff's loss. It has been explained often enough—very clearly in the article 'Equity' by Professor Hanbury in *Halsbury's Laws of England*, 3rd edn, vol. 14, 524–5. The aspect which is significant for the present case, in which the plaintiff has chosen an account of profits in lieu of damages, is the extent to which the amount recoverable by the plaintiff depends upon whether the account is to be taken from the date when the defendant became aware of the plaintiff's registered trade mark, or from some earlier date when the defendant was in fact infringing it.

As to the facts, I am satisfied that the defendant did not know before 30th August 1965 that the plaintiff was the proprietor of the name *Craftmaster* as a registered trade mark in Australia. I accept the evidence of Mr Winstock. He was, I thought, a truthful, but cautious and somewhat reticent, witness. It may be that he did not before August 1965 make all the inquiries that a more prudent person in his position might have made, and that he was, as he says, in that sense remiss. But a lack of diligence in inquiry does not turn ignorance into knowledge. Dishonesty is not to be inferred from lack of care. This is not a case of 'wilful blindness', the expression used in another context to describe a deliberate abstaining from inquiry from fear of what inquiry might reveal. Moreover for the defendant's ignorance before the end of August 1965 of the plaintiff's registered trade mark the plaintiff must take some responsibility, because it did not earlier assert its rights. I reject the defendant's contention that the plaintiff's dilatoriness amounts to laches altogether barring its right to an account. Nevertheless I think it is a circumstance to be considered with the rest of the evidence to determine when it was that the defendant first became aware of the trademark.

. . .

It was suggested that the defendant's profit should be measured by the difference between the amount it received for painting sets bearing the trade mark and the amount it had paid to obtain them . . . . But in the case of a registered trade mark, infringement consists in the unauthorized use of the mark in the course of trade in relation to goods in respect of which it is registered. The profit for which the infringer of a trade mark must account is thus not the profit he made from selling the article itself but, as the ordinary form of order shews, the profit made in selling it under the trade mark . . . . [T]he account of profits retains the characteristics of its origin in the Court of Chancery. By it a defendant is made to account for, and is then stripped of, profits he has made which it would be unconscionable that he retain. These are profits made by him dishonestly, that is by his knowingly infringing the rights of the proprietor of the trade mark. This explains why the liability to account is still not necessarily coextensive with acts of infringement. The account is limited to the profits made by the defendant during the period when he knew of the plaintiff's rights. So it was in respect of common law trade marks. So it still is in respect of registered trade marks: *Edelsten v Edelsten* (1863) 1 De GJ & S 185 *Slazenger & Sons v Spalding & Bros.* [1910] 1 Ch 257; *Moet v Couston* (1864) 33 Beav 578. I think that it follows that it lies upon a plaintiff who seeks an account of profits to establish that profits were made by the defendant knowing that he was transgressing the plaintiff's right. . . .

For the reasons I have given, I consider that the account of profits for which the plaintiff asked ought not to go further back than 30th August 1965. . . .

No case was cited which supported the claim made for the plaintiffs that the defendant must account for the whole of the profit which it made by selling painting sets in fact marked Craftmaster and there is much to the contrary. Using the words of the common order for an account, the defendant must account for profits made in selling painting sets under the name Craftmaster—that means such profit as was attributable to the wrongful use of the mark. And that is not necessarily at all the same as the profit made by the sale of goods bearing the mark. The reason for that is clear enough. A trade mark is in its nature something apart and distinct from the goods in relation to which it is to be used. . . .

What the defendant must account for is what it made by its wrongful use of the plaintiffs' property. The plaintiffs' property is in the mark, not in the painting sets. The true rule, I consider, is that a person who wrongly uses another man's industrial property—patent, copyright, trade mark—is accountable for any profits which he makes which are attributable to his use of the property which was not his. . . .

NOTES AND QUESTIONS

1. What is the rationale for requiring a claimant to choose between an account of profits and (compensatory) damages? Why should a claimant not be entitled to both? (See also above, 947, note 4).

2. In similar vein to Windeyer J's approach in the *Colbeam Palmer* case is the following statement of principle by the High Court of Australia (Mason CJ, Deane, Dawson, and Toohey JJ) in *Dart Industries Inc. v Decor Corp. Pty. Ltd* (1993) 179 CLR 101, 111 (which concerned the calculation of an account of profits for a patent infringement): '[A]n account of profits retains its equitable characteristics in that a defendant is made to account for, and is then stripped of, profits which it has dishonestly made by the infringement and which it would be unconscionable for it to retain. An account of profits is confined to profits actually made, its purpose being not to punish the defendant but to prevent its unjust enrichment. The ordinary requirement of the principles of unjust enrichment that regard be paid to matters of substance rather than technical form is applicable. But it is notoriously difficult in some cases, particularly cases involving the manufacture or sale of a range of products, to isolate those costs which are attributable to the infringement from those which are not so attributable'. (See similarly McHugh J at 123).

3. In England, the classic statement of the purpose of an account of profits was made by Slade J in *My Kinda Town Ltd v Soll* [1982] FSR 147, 156 (reversed on liability by the Court of Appeal [1983] RPC 407) in which the claimants argued, that the defendants were passing off their chain of restaurants as the claimants. Slade J said, 'The purpose of ordering an account of profits in favour of a successful plaintiff in a passing off case is not to inflict punishment on the defendants. It is to prevent an unjust enrichment of the defendant by compelling him to surrender those . . . parts of the profits, actually made by him which were improperly made and nothing beyond this.' It followed that, as the alleged tort comprised confusing the public into thinking the defendants' restaurants were the claimants', the profits to be accounted for were only those additional profits caused by that confusion, and not all the profits made by the defendants from those restaurants. See also *Potton Ltd v Yorkclose Ltd* [1990] FSR 11 (infringement of copyright).

4. There has been some conflict of authority as to whether, in contrast to an account of profits, (compensatory) damages for infringement of a trade mark or passing off can be awarded where the defendant was innocent. In *Gillette UK Ltd v Edenwest Ltd* [1994] RPC 279 Blackburne J held that, while different considerations might apply to an account of profits, damages could be awarded even though the defendant (who, on the facts, sold counterfeit razor blades) did not know that it was infringing the claimant's trade mark or was passing off the claimant's goods. As regards infringement of trade mark, the decision to the contrary in *Slazenger & Sons v Spalding & Bros.* [1910] 1 Ch 257 and the dicta to the contrary in *Edelsten v Edelsten* (1863) 1 De GJ & S 185 were regarded as incorrect.

• Patents Act 1977, section 61(1) and (2) and section 62(1)

61.—(1) Subject to the following provisions of this Part of this Act, civil proceedings may be brought in the court by the proprietor of a patent in respect of any act alleged to infringe the patent and (without prejudice to any other jurisdiction of the court) in those proceedings a claim may be made—

(*a*) for an injunction or interdict restraining the defendant or defender from any apprehended act of infringement;

(*b*) for an order for him to deliver up or destroy any patented product in relation to which the patent is infringed or any article in which that product is inextricably comprised;

(*c*) for damages in respect of the infringement;

(*d*) for an account of the profits derived by him from the infringement;

(*e*) for a declaration or declarator that the patent is valid and has been infringed by him.

(2) The court shall not, in respect of the same infringement, both award the proprietor of a patent damages and order that he shall be given an account of the profits.

. . .

62.—(1) In proceedings for infringement of a patent damages shall not be awarded, and no order shall be made for an account of profits, against a defendant or defender who proves that at the date of the infringement he was not aware, and had no reasonable grounds for supposing, that the patent existed. . . .

- **Copyright, Designs and Patents Act 1988, sections 96(1) and (2), 97(1), 191I(1) and (2), 191J(1), 229(1) and (2), 233(1)–(3)**

96—(1) An infringement of copyright is actionable by the copyright owner.

(2) In an action for infringement of copyright all such relief by way of damages, injunctions, accounts or otherwise is available to the plaintiff as is available in respect of the infringement of any other property right.

. . .

97—(1) Where in an action for infringement of copyright it is shown that at the time of the infringement the defendant did not know, and had no reason to believe, that copyright subsisted in the work to which the action relates, the plaintiff is not entitled to damages against him, but without prejudice to any other remedy.

. . .

191I—(1) An infringement of a performer's property rights is actionable by the rights owner.

(2) In an action for infringement of a performer's property rights all such relief by way of damages, injunctions, accounts or otherwise is available to the plaintiff as is available in respect of the infringement of any other property right.

191J—(1) Where in an action for infringement of a performer's property rights it is shown that at the time of the infringement the defendant did not know and had no reason to believe, that the rights subsisted in the recording to which the action relates, the plaintiff is not entitled to damages against him, but without prejudice to any other remedy.

229—(1) An infringement of design right is actionable by the design right owner.

(2) In an action for infringement of design right all such relief by way of damages, injunctions, accounts or otherwise is available to the plaintiff as is available in respect of the infringement of any other property right.

. . .

233—(1) Where in an action for infringement of design right brought by virtue of section 226 (primary infringement) it is shown that at the time of the infringement the defendant did not know, and had no reason to believe that design right subsisted in the design to which the action relates, the plaintiff is not entitled to damages against him, but without prejudice to any other remedy.

(2) Where in an action for infringement of design right brought by virtue of section 227 (secondary infringement) a defendant shows that the infringing article was innocently acquired by him or a predecessor in title of his, the only remedy available against him in respect of the infringement is damages not exceeding a reasonable royalty in respect of the act complained of.

(3) In subsection (2) 'innocently acquired' means that the person acquiring the article did not know and had no reason to believe that it was an infringing article.

NOTES AND QUESTIONS

The relevant statutory provisions above lay down that the standard of fault required to trigger an account of profits (or damages) for patent infringement differs from that for an account of profits (but not damages) for infringement of copyright, infringement of a performer's property right, and the primary infringement of a design right. Is there any good reason for that statutory difference? We have also seen that dishonesty was the standard for an account of profits for infringement of trade mark in the *Colbeam Palmer* case (and this also appears to be required for an account of profits for passing off). Does all this constitute irrational inconsistency which, within this limited area of intellectual property torts, encapsulates the root difficulty across the whole range of torts, and indeed other wrongs, of articulating a single convincing justification for restitution for wrongs?

(3) NON-PROPRIETARY TORTS

While the clearest examples of restitution being awarded for torts have been in respect of proprietary torts, including intellectual property torts, it has been argued by, for example, Birks (see above, 934), that other torts should trigger restitution especially where intentionally committed. In this respect the second category of punitive (or exemplary) damages recognized by the House of Lords in *Rookes v Barnard* [1964] AC 1129 is closely linked to restitutionary damages.

In that case the House of Lords held that punitive damages should only be available in English law in three categories of case: (i) 'Oppressive, arbitrary or unconstitutional actions by servants of government'; (ii) '[Where] the defendant's conduct has been calculated by him to make a profit for himself which may well exceed the compensation payable to the plaintiff'; (iii) express authorization by statute. A new trial on damages was ordered on the basis that the jury should have been directed that, on the facts, punitive damages could not be awarded for the tort of intimidation. Lord Devlin, giving the leading speech on punitive damages, said of the second category, at 1226–7:

Cases in the second category are those in which the defendant's conduct has been calculated by him to make a profit for himself which may well exceed the compensation payable to the plaintiff . . . Where a defendant with a cynical disregard for a plaintiff's rights has calculated that the money to be made out of his wrongdoing will probably exceed the damages at risk, it is necessary for the law to show that it cannot be broken with impunity. This category is not confined to moneymaking in the strict sense. It extends to cases in which the defendant is seeking to gain at the expense of the plaintiff some object—perhaps some property which he covets—which either he could not obtain at all or not obtain except at a price greater than he wants to put down. Exemplary damages can properly be awarded whenever it is necessary to teach a wrongdoer that tort does not pay.

In *Cassell & Co. v Broome* [1972] AC 1027 in which the House of Lords upheld an award of punitive damages for libel, on the basis that the jury could have found that the facts fell within Lord Devlin's second category, Lord Diplock said the following, at 1130:

[The second category] may be a blunt instrument to prevent unjust enrichment by unlawful acts. But to restrict the damages recoverable to the gain made by the defendant if it exceeded the loss caused to the plaintiff, would leave a defendant contemplating an unlawful act with the certainty has he had nothing to lose to balance against the chance that the plaintiff might never sue him or, if he did, might fail in the hazards of litigation. It is only if there is a prospect that the damages may exceed the defendant's gains that the social purpose of this category is achieved—to teach a wrongdoer that tort does not pay.

Apart from libel, the main type of case in which punitive damages have been awarded in this second category has been in actions by tenants against landlords for wrongful harassment or eviction founded on the torts of trespass or nuisance. See for example, *Drane v Evangelou* [1978] 2 All ER 437; *Guppys (Bridport) Ltd v Brooking and James* (1983) 269 EG 846; and, analogously, *Design Progression Ltd v Thurloe Properties Ltd* [2004] EWHC 324 (Ch).

In thinking about the relationship between punitive and restitutionary damages consider the following questions. Does an award of punitive damages within the second of Lord Devlin's categories mean that restitutionary damages must inevitably have been available in that situation? Can restitutionary damages fulfil all the functions of punitive damages awarded within the second category; if not, wherein would lie the lacunae if punitive damages were abolished?

Connected with its recommendations for widening the availability of punitive damages, the Law Commission (below) recommended that (without prejudice to any other power to award restitution for civil wrongs) statute should permit the courts to award restitutionary damages for any tort or equitable wrong if the defendant's conduct showed a deliberate and outrageous disregard of the claimant's rights.

- **Aggravated, Exemplary and Restitutionary Damages, Law Commission Report No 247 (1997) Draft Bill, clauses 12(1), (5), 15(6).**

12(1) Restitutionary damages may be awarded if—

  (a) a tort or an equitable wrong is committed, and
  (b) the defendant's conduct shows a deliberate and outrageous disregard of the plaintiff's rights.

...

  (5) [Subsection 1 does] not prejudice any power to award restitutionary damages in other cases.

...

15(6) Restitutionary damages are damages designed to remove a benefit derived by a person from his tort or other wrong.

The idea that restitution should be awarded to strip away gains made by a deliberately committed tort was dealt a blow by *Halifax Building Society v Thomas* (below) in which a restitutionary claim for the tort of deceit was rejected by the Court of Appeal.

- **Halifax Building Society v Thomas** [1996] 2 WLR 63, Court of Appeal

By fraudulently misrepresenting his identity and creditworthiness, Thomas obtained a 100 per cent mortgage advance from the plaintiff to finance the purchase of a flat. When Thomas defaulted on the mortgage repayments, the plaintiff exercised its rights to sell off the flat. The proceeds of sale exceeded the mortgage advance. In the claimant's application for a declaration of rights, the question at issue was whether the claimant was entitled to retain the surplus (£10,504.90 plus accrued interest) on the basis that it had a personal restitutionary claim (secured by the mortgage) or a proprietary restitutionary claim (through a constructive trust) to the gains made by Thomas from his deceit. If made out, those claims would have defeated the competing claims of the Crown

Prosecution Service to confiscate the surplus in execution of a criminal confiscation order made when Thomas was found guilty of conspiracy to obtain mortgage advances by deception. The Court of Appeal held that the restitutionary claims failed.

Peter Gibson LJ: This appeal gives rise to an interesting point of law. Where there has been a mortgage fraud, can the mortgagee, misled by fraudulent misrepresentations into making mortgage advance, not only enforce its rights as a secured creditor to sell the mortgaged property and recover what it is owed but also, having recovered in full, take any surplus on the sale after the discharge of the mortgage? . . .

Mr Waters for the society has argued on this appeal, as he did before the judge, that the society is entitled as against Mr Thomas to retain the surplus for its own benefit on the principle of unjust enrichment. That principle was defined in the *American Law Institute, Restatement of the Law, Restitution* (1937), section 1 as being that 'A person who has been unjustly enriched at the expense of another is required to make restitution to the other.' An overview of the law in this area is to be found in the statement of Lord Goff of Chieveley in *Attorney-General v Guardian Newspapers Ltd (No 2)* [1990] 1 AC 109, 286:

> 'That there are groups of cases in which a man is not allowed to profit from his own wrong, is certainly true. An important section of the law of restitution is concerned with cases in which a defendant is required to make restitution in respect of benefits acquired through his own wrongful act—notably cases of waiver of tort; of benefits acquired by certain criminal acts; of benefits acquired in breach of a fiduciary relationship; and, of course, of benefits acquired in breach of confidence. The plaintiff's claim to restitution is usually enforced by an account of profits made by the defendant through his wrong at the plaintiff's expense.'

Mr Waters accepts, as he must, that the surplus does not represent property which the society has lost. Accordingly it cannot rely on the principle of subtractive unjust enrichment, to use the language of Professor Peter Birks QC in his influential work, *An Introduction to the Law of Restitution* (1985). Instead it relies on the broad principle of restitution for wrongs: Mr Thomas has been enriched at the society's expense in the sense that he has gained by committing a wrong against the society. Thereby the society seeks a remedy enabling it 'to obtain restitution of a benefit gained by the tortfeasor from a tortious act in circumstances where he has suffered little or no loss:' *Goff & Jones, The Law of Restitution*, 4th edn (1993), 715.

Mr Waters puts the society's case in each of two ways: that Mr Thomas should be required to account to the society on the basis of the application of the doctrine of waiver of tort, alternatively as the beneficiary of a constructive trust of the surplus, and that, if entitled to retain the surplus for its own benefit as against Mr Thomas, it need not pay it over to the CPS. He lays emphasis on the fact that the surplus represents a profit from a fraud. He submits that it would be offensive to basic concepts of justice if a fraudster were to be allowed to take that profit and, whilst he accepts that in the present case the confiscation order has avoided that offensive result, he submits that the respective entitlements of the society and Mr Thomas must be looked at in the first place without regard to the confiscation order.

[*Having dismissed the argument that a liability to account would be secured by the mortgage, Peter Gibson LJ continued:*] But in any event is the claim for an account in the circumstances of the present case a valid one? Mr Waters frankly acknowledges that there is no English authority that goes so far. Indeed he accepts that there is no English authority to support the proposition that a wrongdoing defendant will be required to account for a profit which is not based on the use of the property of the wronged plaintiff. Cases where a fiduciary is required to account for a profit are plainly distinguishable from the facts of the present case. So too is the one authority citied by Mr Waters of an action for an account which was not based on the use of the property of the plaintiff, the decision of the US

District Court for the Southern District of New York, *Federal Sugar Refining Co. v United States Sugar Equalization Board* (1920) 268 F 575. In that case a buyer contracted to purchase from the plaintiff, the defendant procured the buyer to break that contract and purchase from itself instead, and the plaintiff's claim to recover from the defendant the profit made on the sale was upheld on demurrer.

Mr Water's difficulty is that the society's only interest was that of a secured creditor who has fully recovered all that it was entitled to recover under the mortgage . . .

Attractively though Mr Waters has argued the point, I remain wholly unpersuaded that in the circumstances of the present case the law should accord a restitutionary remedy to a secured creditor who has elected not to avoid the mortgage but to affirm it and has received full satisfaction there-under. To my mind there is an inconsistency between a person being such a creditor and yet claim-ing more than that to which he is contractually entitled and which he has already fully recovered. Once the creditor has so elected and recovered in full, I do not see why the law should come to his aid to allow him to make a further claim. In *In re Simms; Ex parte Trustee* [1934] Ch 1 this court refused to allow a trustee in bankruptcy, who had elected to treat a receiver as a tortfeasor for converting to his own use the chattels of a bankrupt, to recover the profits made by the receiver as money had and received. The authority of that case is weakened by the reliance by this court on the now exploded implied promise theory, but I note that it is still cited in textbooks: see, for example, *Chitty on Contracts*, 27th edn (1994), vol. 1, 1437, para. 29-052, and it serves to illustrate that not every action for an account of profits from a wrongdoer, even where there has been use of the plaintiff's property, will be allowed, and that it may be barred when there has been an election for another remedy.

Further I am not satisfied that in the circumstances of the present case it would be right to treat the unjust enrichment of Mr Thomas as having been gained 'at the expense of' the society, even allowing for the possibility of an extended meaning for those words to apply to cases of non-subtractive restitution for a wrong. There is no decided authority that comes anywhere near to covering the present circumstances. I do not overlook the fact that the policy of law is to view with disfavour a wrongdoer benefiting from his wrong, the more so when the wrong amounts to fraud, but it cannot be suggested that there is a universally applicable principle that in every case there will be restitution of benefit from a wrong. As Professor Birks says (*An Introduction to the Law of Restitution*, 24): 'there are some circumstances in which enrichment by wrongdoing has to be given up. That is, the wrong itself is not always in itself a sufficient factor to call for restitution.' On the facts of the present case, in my judgment, the fraud is not in itself a sufficient factor to allow the society to require Mr Thomas to account to it.

[*Peter Gibson LJ then moved on to consider the constructive trust argument:*] Again in the present case there is the difficulty that the society, having affirmed the mortgage, remained only a secured creditor. I cannot accept that the wrongdoing of the mortgagor can translate the mortgagee into the owner of the entire beneficial interest in the property when the mortgage has not been set aside. That appears to have been the view too of Hoffmann J in another case of mortgage fraud, *Chief Constable of Leicestershire v M* [1989] 1 WLR 20, 21, where he said:

> 'None of the lenders have made any claim by way of constructive trust or otherwise to the profits made on the houses bought with their money. They have preferred to affirm the advances and enforce their rights under the mortgages.'

In *Lister & Co. v Stubbs* (1890) 45 Ch D 1 this court considered the case of a servant who received a bribe. Lindley LJ said, at 15, that the relationship between the plaintiff employers and the defendant servant in respect of that bribe

> 'is that of debtor and creditor, it is not that of trustee and cestui que trust. We are asked to hold that it is—which would involve consequences which, I confess, startle me.'

That decision has been subjected to much criticism and was disapproved by the Privy Council in *Attorney-General for Hong Kong v Reid* [1994] 1 AC 324 on the basis that it was inconsistent with basic principles of equity affecting the conduct of a fiduciary. In *Daly v Sydney Stock Exchange Ltd* (1986) 160 CLR 371, 379 Gibbs CJ refused to accept that money lent by an investor to a firm in a fiduciary relationship with him should be treated as subject to a constructive trust. He said that the reasons of Lindley LJ in the *Lister* case, 45 Ch D 1 appeared to him to be 'impeccable when applied to the case in which the person claiming the money has simply made an outright loan to the defendant.' In the present case there was no fiduciary relationship between Mr Thomas and the society in respect of the mortgage but merely that of debtor and secured creditor.

English law has not followed other jurisdictions where the constructive trust has become a remedy for unjust enrichment. As is said in *Snell's Equity*, 29th edn (1990), 197:

'In England the constructive trust has in general remained essentially a substantive institution; ownership must not be confused with obligation, nor must the relationship of debtor and creditor be converted into one of trustee and cestui que trust.'

In considering whether to extend the law of constructive trusts in order to prevent a fraudster benefiting from his wrong, it is also appropriate to bear in mind that Parliament has acted in recent years (notably in Part VI of the Criminal Justice Act 1988) on the footing that without statutory intervention the criminal might keep the benefit of his crime. Moreover, Parliament has given the courts the power in specific circumstances to confiscate the benefit rather than reward the person against whom the crime has been committed. I bear in mind the wise comment of Hoffmann J in *Chief Constable of Leicestershire v M* [1989] 1 WLR 20, 23:

'The recent and detailed interventions of Parliament in this field suggest that the courts should not indulge in parallel creativity by the extension of general common law principles.'

Accordingly I would reject the argument based on constructive trust.

No other argument is put forward by the society for defeating the title of Mr Thomas to the surplus immediately before the confiscation and charging orders made by the C.P.S. or for defeating those orders. For these reasons I would dismiss this appeal.

Simon Brown LJ agreed. **Glidewell LJ** gave a short judgment agreeing with **Peter Gibson LJ**.

NOTES AND QUESTIONS

1. Should restitutionary damages for the tort of deceit have been awarded in this case?

2. Would punitive damages have been awarded in this case had they been pleaded?

3. Instead of denying the validity of a personal restitutionary remedy, would it have been preferable for the Court of Appeal to have said simply that the criminal confiscation order was sufficient to reverse Thomas' wrongful gains? (Cf. the problem of double jeopardy in respect of punitive damages and criminal prosecutions: it was held in, for example, *Archer v Brown* [1985] QB 401, that the courts will not award punitive damages where the defendant has already been punished by the criminal law in respect of the facts upon which the claimant founds his tortious action). In particular, had there been no prosecution for criminal fraud and no confiscation order would it have been right to have left Thomas with the profits of his fraud?

4. For notes on this case, see P Birks (1996) 10 *Trusts Law International* 2; C Mitchell [1996] *LMCLQ* 314.

4. RESTITUTION FOR BREACH OF CONTRACT

- ● *Wrotham Park Estate Co. Ltd v Parkside Homes Ltd*
  [1974] 1 WLR 798, Chancery Division

Land belonging to the defendants was subject to a restrictive covenant, registered as a land charge, forbidding development of the land except with the approval of the owners for the time being of the Wrotham Park Estate (the claimants). The defendants built fourteen houses without seeking the approval of the claimants, and hence in breach of that restrictive covenant. The claimants sought a mandatory injunction seeking demolition of the houses. That injunction was refused by Brightman J because demolition would constitute a waste of much needed housing. But damages in lieu were awarded.

Brightman J: . . . I turn to the consideration of the quantum of damages. I was asked by the parties to assess the damages myself, should the question arise, rather than to direct an inquiry. The basic rule in contract is to measure damages by that sum of money which will put the plaintiff in the same position as he would have been in if the contract had not been broken. From that basis, the defendants argue that the damages are nil or purely nominal, because the value of the Wrotham Park Estate as the plaintiffs concede is not diminished by one farthing in consequence of the construction of a road and the erection of 14 houses on the allotment site. If, therefore, the defendants submit, I refuse an injunction I ought to award no damages in lieu. That would seem, on the face of it, a result of questionable fairness on the facts of this case. Had the offending development been the erection of an advertisement hoarding in defiance of protest and writ, I apprehend (assuming my conclusions on other points to be correct) that the court would not have hesitated to grant a mandatory injunction for its removal. If for social and economic reasons, the court does not see fit in the exercise of its discretion, to order demolition of the 14 houses, is it just that the plaintiffs should receive no compensation and that the defendants should be left in undisturbed possession of the fruits of their wrongdoing? Common sense would seem to demand a negative answer to this question. A comparable problem arose in wayleave cases where the defendant had trespassed by making use of the plaintiff's underground ways to the defendant's profit but without diminishing the value of the plaintiff's property. The plaintiff, in such cases, received damages assessed by reference to a reasonable wayleave rent. This principle was considered and extended in *Whitwham v Westminster Brymbo Coal and Coke Co.* [1896] 2 Ch 538. For six years the defendant wrongfully tipped colliery waste onto the plaintiff's land. At the trial the defendant was directed to cease tipping and give up possession. The question then arose what damages should be awarded for the wrongful act done to the plaintiff during the period of the defendant's unauthorised user of the land. The official referee found that the diminution in the value of the plaintiff's land was only £200, but that the value of the plaintiff's land to the defendant in 1888 for tipping purposes for six years was some £900. It was held that the proper scale of damages was the higher sum on the ground that a trespasser should not be allowed to make use of another person's land without in some way compensating that other person for the user.

A like principle was applied by the House of Lords in a Scottish case, *Watson, Laidlaw & Co. Ltd v Pott, Cassels and Williamson* (1914) 31 RPC 104. A patentee elected to sue an infringer for damages rather than for an account of profits. Part of the infringement had taken place in Java. There was evidence that the patentee could not have competed successfully in that island. It was submitted that no damages ought to be awarded in respect of the Java infringement. Lord Shaw said at 119–120:

'It is at this stage of the case, . . . that a second principle comes into play. It is not exactly the principle of restoration, either directly or expressed through compensation, but it is the principle underlying price or hire. It plainly extends—and I am inclined to think not infrequently extends—to patent cases. But, indeed, it is not confined to them. For wherever an abstraction or invasion of property has occurred, then, unless such abstraction or invasion were to be sanctioned by law, the law ought to yield a recompense under the category or principle, as I say, either of price or of hire. If A, being a Everyman, keeps his horse standing idle in the stable, and B, against his wish or without his knowledge, rides or drives it out, it is no answer to A for B to say: "Against what loss do you want to be restored? I restore the horse. There is no loss. The horse is none the worse; it is the better for the exercise." I confess to your Lordships that this seems to me to be precisely in principle the kind of question and retort which underlay the argument of the learned counsel for the appellants about the Java trade. . . . in such cases it appears to me that the correct and full measure is only reached by adding that a patentee is also entitled, on the principle of price or hire, to a royalty for the unauthorised sale or use of every one of the infringing machines in a market which the infringer, if left to himself, might not have reached. Otherwise, that property which consists in the monopoly of the patented articles granted to the patentee has been invaded, and indeed abstracted, and the law, when appealed to, would be standing by and allowing the invader or abstractor to go free.'

The same principle was applied in detinue in *Strand Electric and Engineering Co. Ltd v Brisford Entertainment Ltd* [1952] 2 QB 246. The defendant came into possession of portable switchboards which were part of the stock-in-trade of the plaintiff. The defendant used them for its own profit for 43 weeks. The trial judge, Pilcher J, ordered the return of the switchboards and awarded damages. The damages took into account the fact that if the defendant had not wrongfully retained the switchboards the plaintiff would be unlikely to have hired out every one for the full period of 43 weeks. It was held by the Court of Appeal that the plaintiff was entitled to recover as damages the full market rate of hire for the whole period of detention. It will be sufficient to read these extracts from the judgment of Denning LJ, at 253:

'In assessing damages, whether for a breach of contract or for a tort, the general rule is that the plaintiff recovers the loss he has suffered, no more and no less. This rule is, however, often departed from.'

He then gave examples and continued:

'The question in this case is: What is the proper measure of damages for the wrongful detention of goods? Does it fall within the general rule that the plaintiff only recovers for the loss he has suffered or within some other, and if so what, rule? It is strange that there is no authority upon this point in English law; but there is plenty on the analogous case of detention of land. The rule is that a wrongdoer, who keeps the owner out of his land, must pay a fair rental value for it, even though the owner would not have been able to use it himself or to let it to anyone else. So also a wrongdoer who uses land for his own purposes without the owner's consent, as, for instance, for a fair ground, or as a wayleave, must pay a reasonable hire for it, even though he has done no damage to the land at all: *Whitwham v Westminster Brymbo Coal and Coke Co.* [1896] 2 Ch 538. I see no reason why the same principle should not apply to detention of goods. If a wrongdoer has made use of goods for his own purposes, then he must pay a reasonable hire for them, even though the owner has in fact suffered no loss. It may be that the owner would not have used the goods himself, or that he has a substitute readily available, which he used without extra cost to himself. Nevertheless the owner is entitled to a reasonable hire. If the wrongdoer had asked the owner for permission to use the goods, the owner would be entitled to ask for a reasonable remuneration as the price of his permission. The wrongdoer cannot be better off because he did not ask permission. He cannot be better off by doing wrong than he would be by doing right. He must therefore pay a reasonable hire.'

The point was further considered in *Penarth Dock Engineering Co. Ltd v Pounds* [1963] 1 Lloyd's Rep. 359 by Lord Denning MR sitting as a judge of the Queen's Bench Division. The defendant had contracted to buy a floating dock and to remove it from the plaintiff's dock premises. The defendant defaulted in the removal of the purchase. The plaintiff, however, had suffered no damage, since the dock premises had become disused. The plaintiff claimed a mandatory injunction and damages. It was held that the plaintiff was entitled to damages at a rate *per* week representing a reasonable berthing charge.

The facts of the cases I have mentioned are a long way from the facts of the case before me. Should I, as invited by the plaintiffs, apply a like principle to a case where the defendant Parkside, in defiance of protest and writ, has invaded the plaintiffs' rights in order to reap a financial profit for itself? In *Leeds Industrial Co-operative Society Ltd v Slack* [1924] AC 851 Lord Sumner said, at 870:

'no money awarded in substitution can be justly awarded, unless it is at any rate designed to be a preferable equivalent for an injunction and therefore an adequate substitute for it.'

This was said in a dissenting speech but his dissent did not arise in the context of that observation.

In the present case I am faced with the problem what damages ought to be awarded to the plaintiffs in the place of mandatory injunctions which would have restored the plaintiffs' rights. If the plaintiffs are merely given a nominal sum, or no sum, in substitution for injunctions, it seems to me that justice will manifestly not have been done.

As I have said, the general rule would be to measure damages by reference to that sum which would place the plaintiffs in the same position as if the covenant had not been broken. Parkside and the individual purchasers could have avoided breaking the covenant in two ways. One course would have been not to develop the allotment site. The other course would have been for Parkside to have sought from the plaintiffs a relaxation of the covenant. On the facts of this particular case the plaintiffs, rightly conscious of their obligations towards existing residents, would clearly not have granted any relaxation, but for present purposes I must assume they could have been induced to do so. In my judgment a just substitute for a mandatory injunction would be such a sum of money as might reasonably have been demanded by the plaintiffs from Parkside as a quid pro quo for relaxing the covenant. The plaintiffs submitted that that sum should be a substantial proportion of the development value of the land. This is currently put at no less than £10,000 *per* plot, i.e. £140,000 on the assumption that the plots are undeveloped. Mr Parker gave evidence that a half or a third of the development value was commonly demanded by a landowner whose property stood in the way of a development. I do not agree with that approach to damages in this type of case. I bear in mind the following factors:

(1) The lay-out covenant is not an asset which the estate owner ever contemplated he would have either the opportunity or the desire to turn to account. It has no commercial or even nuisance value. For it cannot be turned to account except to the detriment of the existing residents who are people the estate owner professes to protect.

(2) The breach of covenant which has actually taken place is over a very small area and the impact of this particular breach on the Wrotham Park Estate is insignificant. The validity of the covenant over the rest of [the area to which it relates] is unaffected.

I think that in a case such as the present a landowner faced with a request from a developer which, it must be assumed, he feels reluctantly obliged to grant, would have first asked the developer what profit he expected to make from his operations. With the benefit of foresight the developer would, in the present case, have said about £50,000 for that is the profit which Parkside concedes it made from the development. I think that the landowner would then reasonably have required a certain percentage of that anticipated profit as a price for the relaxation of the covenant, assuming, as I must, that he feels obliged to relax it. In assessing what would be a fair percentage I think that the court ought, on the particular facts of this case, to act with great moderation. For it is to be borne in mind that the plaintiffs were aware, before the auction took place, that the land was being offered for sale as a freehold building land for 13 houses, and they knew that they were not going to consent to any such development. They could have informed the Potters Bar Urban District Council of their attitude in advance of the auction, or could have given the like information to Parkside prior to completion of the contract for sale. In either event it seems highly unlikely that Parkside would have parted with its £90,000, at any rate unconditionally. I think that damages must be assessed in such a case on a basis which is fair and, in all the circumstances in my judgment a sum equal to five per cent of Parkside's anticipated profit is the most that is fair. I accordingly award the sum of £2,500 in substitution for mandatory injunctions. I think that this amount should be treated as apportioned between the 14 respective owners or joint owners of the plots and Parkside (as the owner of the road) in 1/15th shares, so that the damages awarded will be £166 odd in each case. In fact, I apprehend that by virtue of the arrangement between Parkside and the insurance office the entirety of the £2,500 will ultimately be recoverable from Parkside, so that the apportionment does not have any real significance.

NOTES AND QUESTIONS

1. Were the damages awarded in this case compensatory or restitutionary? Compare, for example, the view of the Court of Appeal in *Jaggard v Sawyer* (above, 967) with the following view of Steyn LJ in *Surrey CC v Bredero Homes Ltd* [1993] 1 WLR 1361, 1369: 'The plaintiffs' argument that the *Wrotham Park* case can be justified on the basis of a loss of bargaining opportunity is a fiction. The object of an award in the *Wrotham Park* case was not to compensate the plaintiffs for financial injury, but to deprive the defendants of an unjustly acquired gain.' The facts and decision in *Surrey CC v Bredero* are set out below in Lord Nicholls' speech in *Att-Gen v Blake*, 986.

2. Does restitution of the price paid after termination for breach illustrate restitution for breach of contract? Or is it rather a claim for the cause of action of unjust enrichment grounded on failure of consideration?

● *Attorney General v Blake* [2001] 1 AC 268, House of Lords

The notorious spy, George Blake, had written his autobiography in 1989. The publishers had agreed to pay him, as an advance against royalties, three sums of £50,000 on signing the contract, delivery of the manuscript and on publication. They had paid him £60,000 so that £90,000 was still owing. The Crown sought to stop him being paid that £90,000 and for that sum, instead, to be paid to the Crown. Their claims were brought in both public and private law. The Court of Appeal had upheld Sir Richard Scott V-C's decision at first instance that Blake was not acting in breach of fiduciary duty in publishing the book because there was no fiduciary duty owed by an ex-employee to the Crown. There was also no question of a breach of confidence claim succeeding because, by the time of publication, the information in the book was in the public domain and no longer confidential. But the Court of Appeal had decided that a public law claim should succeed: the Attorney General, as an extension of his power to obtain injunctions in aid of the criminal law in furtherance of the public interest, was entitled to an order for payment so as to prevent Blake receiving money from his breach of the Official Secrets Act 1989.

The House of Lords firmly rejected that novel public law order on the ground that, without any established private law claim, it constituted a criminal confiscatory order that had not been expressly authorised by Parliament. Nevertheless the House of Lords (Lord Hobhouse dissenting) found in favour of the Crown not in public law but by revisiting obiter dicta of the Court of Appeal in relation to whether the Crown was entitled to the private law remedy of 'restitutionary damages' for breach of contract.

Lord Nicholls of Birkenhead: . . . .

The private law claim

In the course of his judgment [1998] Ch 439, 455–459 Lord Woolf MR made some interesting observations on a matter which had not been the subject of argument either in the Court of Appeal or before Sir Richard Scott V-C. The point arose out of the amendments made to the statement of claim in the course of the proceedings in the Court of Appeal. On 16 August 1944 Blake signed an Official Secrets Act declaration. This declaration included an undertaking:

> '. . . I undertake not to divulge any official information gained by me as a result of my employment, either in the press or in book form. I also understand that these provisions apply not only during the period of service but also after employment has ceased.'

This undertaking was contractually binding. Had Blake not signed it he would not have been employed. By submitting his manuscript for publication without first obtaining clearance Blake committed a breach of this undertaking. The Court of Appeal suggested that the Crown might have a private law claim to 'restitutionary damages for breach of contract', and invited submissions on this issue. The Attorney General decided that the Crown did not wish to advance argument on this point in the Court of Appeal. The Attorney General, however, wished to keep the point open for a higher court. The Court of Appeal expressed the view, necessarily tentative in the circumstances, that the law of contract would be seriously defective if the court were unable to award restitutionary damages for breach of contract. The law is now sufficiently mature to recognise a restitutionary claim for profits made from a breach of contract in appropriate situations. These include cases of 'skimped' performance, and cases where the defendant obtained his profit by doing 'the very thing' he contracted not to do. The present case fell into the latter category: Blake earned his profit by doing the very thing he had promised not to do.

This matter was pursued in your Lordships' House. Prompted by an invitation from your Lordships, the Attorney General advanced an argument that restitutionary principles ought to operate to enable the Crown to recover from Blake his profits arising from his breach of contract. It will be convenient to consider this private law claim first.

. . .

Interference with rights of property . . .

I shall first set the scene by noting how the court approaches the question of financial recompense for interference with rights of property. As with breaches of contract, so with tort, the general principle regarding assessment of damages is that they are compensatory for loss or injury. The general rule is that, in the oft quoted words of Lord Blackburn, the measure of damages is to be, as far as possible, that amount of money which will put the injured party in the same position he would have been in had he not sustained the wrong: *Livingstone v Rawyards Coal Co* (1880) 5 App Cas 25, 39. Damages are measured by the plaintiff's loss, not the defendant's gain. But the common law, pragmatic as ever, has long recognised that there are many commonplace situations where a strict application of this principle would not do justice between the parties. Then compensation for the wrong done to the plaintiff is measured by a different yardstick. A trespasser who enters another's land may cause the landowner no financial loss. In such a case damages are measured by the benefit received by the trespasser, namely, by his use of the land. The same principle is applied where the wrong consists of use of another's land for depositing waste, or by using a path across the land or using passages in an underground mine. In this type of case the damages recoverable will be, in short, the price a reasonable person would pay for the right of user: see *Whitwham v Westminster Brymbo Coal and Coke Co* [1896] 2 Ch 538, and the 'wayleave' cases such as *Martin v Porter* (1839) 5 M & W 351 and *Jegon v Vivian* (1871) LR 6 Ch App 742. A more recent example was the non-removal of a floating dock, in *Penarth Dock Engineering Co. Ltd v Pounds* [1963] 1 Lloyd's Rep 359.

The same principle is applied to the wrongful detention of goods. An instance is the much cited decision of the Court of Appeal in *Strand Electric and Engineering Co. Ltd v Brisford Entertainments Ltd* [1952] 2 QB 246, concerning portable switchboards. But the principle has a distinguished ancestry. The Earl of Halsbury LC famously asked in *The Mediana* [1900] AC 113, 117, that if a person took away a chair from his room and kept it for 12 months, could anybody say you had a right to diminish the damages by showing that I did not usually sit in that chair, or that there were plenty of other chairs in the room? To the same effect was Lord Shaw's telling example in *Watson, Laidlaw & Co. Ltd v Pott, Cassels and Williamson* (1914) 31 RPC 104, 119. It bears repetition:

'If A, being a liveryman, keeps his horse standing idle in the stable, and B, against his wish or without his knowledge, rides or drives it out, it is no answer to A for B to say: "Against what loss do you want to be restored? I restore the horse. There is no loss. The horse is none the worse; it is the better for the exercise." '

Lord Shaw prefaced this observation with a statement of general principle:

'wherever an abstraction or invasion of property has occurred, then, unless such abstraction or invasion were to be sanctioned by law, the law ought to yield a recompense under the category or principle . . . either of price or of hire.'

That was a patent infringement case. The House of Lords held that damages should be assessed on the footing of a royalty for every infringing article.

This principle is established and not controversial. More difficult is the alignment of this measure of damages within the basic compensatory measure. Recently there has been a move towards applying the label of restitution to awards of this character: see, for instance, *Ministry of Defence v Ashman* [1993] 2 EGLR 102, 105 and *Ministry of Defence v Thompson* [1993] 2 EGLR 107. However that may be, these awards cannot be regarded as conforming to the strictly compensatory measure of damage for the injured person's loss unless loss is given a strained and artificial meaning. The reality is that the injured person's rights were invaded but, in financial terms, he suffered no loss. Nevertheless the common law has found a means to award him a sensibly calculated amount of money. Such awards are probably best regarded as an exception to the general rule.

Courts of equity went further than the common law courts. In some cases equity required the wrongdoer to yield up all his gains. In respect of certain wrongs which originally or ordinarily were the subject of proceedings in the Court of Chancery, the standard remedies were injunction and, incidental thereto, an account of profits. These wrongs included passing off, infringement of trade marks, copyrights and patents, and breach of confidence. Some of these subjects are now embodied in statutory codes. An injunction restrained the continuance of the wrong, and the wrongdoer was required to account for the profits or benefits he had obtained from breaches or infringements which had already occurred. The court always had a discretion regarding the grant of the remedy of an account of profits, and this remains the position. Further, the circumstances in which an account of profits is available under the statutes vary. For instance, an account of profits may not be ordered against a defendant in a patent infringement action who proves that at the date of the infringement he was not aware, and had no reasonable grounds for supposing, that the patent existed: Patents Act 1977, section 62(1).

In these cases the courts of equity appear to have regarded an injunction and account of profits as more appropriate remedies than damages because of the difficulty of assessing the extent of the loss. Thus, in 1803 Lord Eldon LC stated, in *Hogg v Kirby*, 8 Ves 215, 223, a passing off case:

'what is the consequence in law and in equity? . . . a court of equity in these cases is not content with an action for damages; for it is nearly impossible to know the extent of the damage; and therefore the remedy here, though not compensating the pecuniary damage except by an account of profits, is the best: the remedy by an injunction and account.'

Whether this justification for ordering an account of profits holds good factually in every case must be doubtful. Be that as it may, in these types of case equity considered that the appropriate response to the violation of the plaintiff's right was that the defendant should surrender all his gains, and that he should do so irrespective of whether the violation had caused the plaintiff any financially measurable loss. Gains were to be disgorged even though they could not be shown to correspond with any disadvantage suffered by the other party. This lack of correspondence was openly acknowledged. In *Lever v Goodwin* (1887) 36 Ch D 1, 7, Cotton LJ stated it was 'well known' that in trade mark and patent cases the plaintiff was entitled, if he succeeded in getting an injunction, to take either of two forms of relief: he might claim from the defendant either the damage he had sustained from the defendant's wrongful act or the profit made by the defendant from the defendant's wrongful act.

Considered as a matter of principle, it is difficult to see why equity required the wrongdoer to account for all his profits in these cases, whereas the common law's response was to require a wrongdoer merely to pay a reasonable fee for use of another's land or goods. In all these cases rights of property were infringed. This difference in remedial response appears to have arisen simply as an accident of history.

In some instances the common law itself afforded a wronged party a choice of remedies. A notable example is the wrong of conversion. A person whose goods were wrongfully converted by another had a choice of two remedies against the wrongdoer. He could recover damages, in respect of the loss he had sustained by the conversion. Or he could recover the proceeds of the conversion obtained by the defendant: see *United Australia Ltd v Barclays Bank Ltd* [1941] AC 1, 34, *per* Lord Romer. Historically, the latter alternative was achieved by recourse to an element of legal fiction, whereby the innocent party 'waived the tort'. The innocent party could suppose that the wrongful sale had been made with his consent and bring an action for money 'had and received to his use': see *Lamine v Dorrell* (1705) 2 Ld Raym 1216, 1217. Holt CJ observed that these actions had 'crept in by degrees'.

Breach of trust and fiduciary duty

I should refer briefly to breach of trust and breach of fiduciary duty. Equity reinforces the duty of fidelity owed by a trustee or fiduciary by requiring him to account for any profits he derives from his office or position. This ensures that trustees and fiduciaries are financially disinterested in carrying out their duties. They may not put themselves in a position where their duty and interest conflict. To this end they must not make any unauthorised profit. If they do, they are accountable. Whether the beneficiaries or persons to whom the fiduciary duty is owed suffered any loss by the impugned transaction is altogether irrelevant. The accountability of the army sergeant in *Reading v Attorney General* [1951] AC 507 is a familiar application of this principle to a servant of the Crown.

Damages under Lord Cairns's Act

. . . [I]n the same way as damages at common law for violations of a property right may by measured by reference to the benefits wrongfully obtained by a defendant, so under Lord Cairns' Act damages may include damages measured by reference to the benefits likely to be obtained in future by the defendant. This approach has been adopted on many occasions. Recent examples are *Bracewell v Appleby* [1975] Ch 408 and *Jaggard v Sawyer* [1995] 1 WLR 269, both cases concerned with access to a newly-built house over another's land.

The measure of damages awarded in this type of case is often analysed as damages for loss of a bargaining opportunity or, which comes to the same, the price payable for the compulsory acquisition of a right. This analysis is correct. The court's refusal to grant an injunction means that in practice the defendant is thereby permitted to perpetuate the wrongful state of affairs he has brought about. But this analysis takes the matter now under discussion no further forward. A property right has value to the extent only that the court will enforce it or award damages for its infringement. The question under discussion is whether the court will award substantial damages for an infringement when no financial loss flows from the infringement and, moreover, in a suitable case will assess the damages by reference to the defendant's profit obtained from the infringement. The cases mentioned above show that the courts habitually do that very thing.

Breach of contract

Against this background I turn to consider the remedies available for breaches of contract. The basic remedy is an award of damages. In the much quoted words of Baron Parke, the rule of the common law is that where a party sustains a loss by reason of a breach of contract, he is, so far as money can do it, to be placed in the same position as if the contract had been performed: *Robinson v Harman* (1848) 1 Exch 850, 855. Leaving aside the anomalous exception of punitive damages, damages are compensatory. That is axiomatic. It is equally well established that an award of damages, assessed by reference to financial loss, is not always 'adequate' as a remedy for a breach of contract. The law recognises that a party to a contract may have an interest in performance which is not readily measurable in terms of money. On breach the innocent party suffers a loss. He fails to obtain the benefit promised by the other party to the contract. To him the loss may be as important as financially measurable loss, or more so. An award of damages, assessed by reference to financial loss, will not recompense him properly. For him a financially assessed measure of damages is inadequate.

The classic example of this type of case, as every law student knows, is a contract for the sale of land. The buyer of a house may be attracted by features which have little or no impact on the value of the house. An award of damages, based on strictly financial criteria, would fail to recompense a disappointed buyer for this head of loss. The primary response of the law to this type of case is to ensure, if possible, that the contract is performed in accordance with its terms. The court may make orders compelling the party who has committed a breach of contract, or is threatening to do so, to carry out his contractual obligations. To this end the court has wide powers to grant injunctive relief. The court will, for instance, readily make orders for the specific performance of contracts for the sale of land, and sometimes it will do so in respect of contracts for the sale of goods. In *Beswick v Beswick* [1968] AC 58 the court made an order for the specific performance of a contract to make payments of money to a third party. The law recognised that the innocent party to the breach of contract had a legitimate interest in having the contract performed even though he himself would suffer no financial loss from its breach. Likewise, the court will compel the observance of negative obligations by granting injunctions. This may include a mandatory order to undo an existing breach, as where the court orders the defendant to pull down building works carried out in breach of covenant.

All this is trite law. In practice, these specific remedies go a long way towards providing suitable protection for innocent parties who will suffer loss from breaches of contract which are not adequately remediable by an award of damages. But these remedies are not always available. For instance, confidential information may be published in breach of a non-disclosure agreement before the innocent party has time to apply to the court for urgent relief. Then the breach is irreversible. Further, these specific remedies are discretionary. Contractual obligations vary infinitely. So do the circumstances in which breaches occur, and the circumstances in which remedies are sought. The court may, for instance, decline to grant specific relief on the ground that this would be oppressive.

An instance of this nature occurred in *Wrotham Park Estate Co. Ltd v Parkside Homes Ltd* [1974] 1 WLR 798.

. . .

In reaching his conclusion the judge applied by analogy the cases mentioned above concerning the assessment of damages when a defendant has invaded another's property rights but without diminishing the value of the property. I consider he was right to do so. Property rights are superior to contractual rights in that, unlike contractual rights, property rights may survive against an indefinite class of persons. However, it is not easy to see why, as between the parties to a contract, a violation of a party's contractual rights should attract a lesser degree of remedy than a violation of his property rights. As Lionel D Smith has pointed out in his article 'Disgorgement of the profits of Breach of Contract: Property, Contract and "Efficient Breach" ' (1995) 24 Can BLJ 121, it is not clear why it should be any more permissible to expropriate personal rights than it is permissible to expropriate property rights.

I turn to the decision of the Court of Appeal in *Surrey County Council v Bredero Homes Ltd* [1993] 1 WLR 1361. A local authority had sold surplus land to a developer and obtained a covenant that the developer would develop the land in accordance with an existing planning permission. The sole purpose of the local authority in imposing the covenant was to enable it to share in the planning gain if, as happened, planning permission was subsequently granted for the erection of a larger number of houses. The purpose was that the developer would have to apply and pay for a relaxation of the covenant if it wanted to build more houses. In breach of covenant the developer completed the development in accordance with the later planning permission, and the local authority brought a claim for damages. The erection of the larger number of houses had not caused any financial loss to the local authority. The judge awarded nominal damages of £2, and the Court of Appeal dismissed the local authority's appeal.

This is a difficult decision. It has attracted criticism from academic commentators and also in judgments of Sir Thomas Bingham MR and Millett LJ in *Jaggard v Sawyer* [1995] 1 WLR 269. I need not pursue the detailed criticisms. In the *Bredero* case Dillon LJ himself noted, at p 1364, that had the covenant been worded differently, there could have been provision for payment of an increased price if a further planning permission were forthcoming. That would have been enforceable. But, according to the *Bredero* decision, a covenant not to erect any further houses without permission, intended to achieve the same result, may be breached with impunity. That would be a sorry reflection on the law. Suffice to say, in so far as the *Bredero* decision is inconsistent with the approach adopted in the *Wrotham Park* case, the latter approach is to be preferred.

The *Wrotham Park* case, therefore, still shines, rather as a solitary beacon, showing that in contract as well as tort damages are not always narrowly confined to recoupment of financial loss. In a suitable case damages for breach of contract may be measured by the benefit gained by the wrongdoer from the breach. The defendant must make a reasonable payment in respect of the benefit he has gained. In the present case the Crown seeks to go further. The claim is for all the profits of Blake's book which the publisher has not yet paid him. This raises the question whether an account of profits can ever be given as a remedy for breach of contract. The researches of counsel have been unable to discover any case where the court has made such an order on a claim for breach of contract. In *Tito v Waddell (No 2)* [1977] Ch 106, 332, a decision which has proved controversial, Sir Robert Megarry V-C said that, as a matter of fundamental principle, the question of damages was 'not one of making the defendant disgorge' his gains, in that case what he had saved by committing the wrong, but 'one of compensating the plaintiff'. In *Occidental Worldwide Investment Corporation v Skibs A/S Avanti* [1976] 1 Lloyd's Rep 293, 337, Kerr J summarily rejected a claim for an account of profits when ship owners withdrew ships on a rising market.

There is a light sprinkling of cases where courts have made orders having the same effect as an order for an account of profits, but the courts seem always to have attached a different label. A person who, in breach of contract, sells land twice over must surrender his profits on the second sale to the original buyer. Since courts regularly make orders for the specific performance of contracts for the sale of land, a seller of land is, to an extent, regarded as holding the land on trust for the buyer: *Lake v Bayliss* [1974] 1 WLR 1073. In *Reid-Newfoundland Co. v Anglo-American Telegraph Co. Ltd* [1912] AC 555 a railway company agreed not to transmit any commercial messages over a particular telegraph wire except for the benefit and account of the telegraph company. The Privy Council held that the railway company was liable to account as a trustee for the profits it wrongfully made from its use of the wire for commercial purposes. In *British Motor Trade Association v Gilbert* [1951] 2 All ER 641 the plaintiff suffered no financial loss but the award of damages for breach of contract effectively stripped the wrongdoer of the profit he had made from his wrongful venture into the black market for new cars.

These cases illustrate that circumstances do arise when the just response to a breach of contract is that the wrongdoer should not be permitted to retain any profit from the breach. In these cases the courts have reached the desired result by straining existing concepts. Professor Peter Birks has deplored the 'failure of jurisprudence when the law is forced into this kind of abusive instrumental-ism'; see 'Profits of Breach of Contract' (1993) 109 LQR 518, 520. Some years ago Professor Dawson suggested there is no inherent reason why the technique of equity courts in land contracts should not be more widely employed, not by granting remedies as the by-product of a phantom 'trust' created by the contract, but as an alternative form of money judgment remedy. That well known ailment of lawyers, a hardening of the categories, ought not to be an obstacle: see 'Restitution or Damages' (1959) 20 Ohio SLJ 175.

My conclusion is that there seems to be no reason, *in principle*, why the court must in all circum-stances rule out an account of profits as a remedy for breach of contract. I prefer to avoid the unhappy expression 'restitutionary damages'. Remedies are the law's response to a wrong (or, more precisely, to a cause of action). When, exceptionally, a just response to a breach of contract so requires, the court should be able to grant the discretionary remedy of requiring a defendant to account to the plaintiff for the benefits he has received from his breach of contract. In the same way as a plaintiff's interest in performance of a contract may render it just and equitable for the court to make an order for specific performance or grant an injunction, so the plaintiff's interest in performance may make it just and equitable that the defendant should retain no benefit from his breach of contract.

The state of the authorities encourages me to reach this conclusion, rather than the reverse. The law recognises that damages are not always sufficient remedy for breach of contract. This is the foundation of the court's jurisdiction to grant the remedies of specific performance and injunction. Even when awarding damages, the law does not adhere slavishly to the concept of compensation for financially measurable loss. When the circumstances require, damages are measured by reference to the benefit obtained by the wrongdoer. This applies to interference with property rights. Recently, the like approach has been adopted to breach of contract. Further, in certain circumstances an account of profits is ordered in preference to an award of damages. Sometimes the injured party is given the choice: either compensatory damages or an account of the wrongdoer's profits. Breach of confidence is an instance of this. If confidential information is wrongfully divulged in breach of a non-disclosure agreement, it would be nothing short of sophistry to say that an account of profits may be ordered in respect of the equitable wrong but not in respect of the breach of contract which governs the relationship between the parties. With the established authorities going thus far, I consider it would be only a modest step for the law to recognise openly that, exceptionally, an account of profits may be the most appropriate remedy for breach of contract. It is not as though this step would contradict some recognised principle applied consistently throughout the law to the grant or withholding of the remedy of an account of profits. No such principle is discernible.

The main argument against the availability of an account of profits as a remedy for breach of contract is that the circumstances where this remedy may be granted will be uncertain. This will have an unsettling effect on commercial contracts where certainty is important. I do not think these fears are well founded. I see no reason why, *in practice*, the availability of the remedy of an account of profits need disturb settled expectations in the commercial or consumer world. An account of profits will be appropriate only in exceptional circumstances. Normally the remedies of damages, specific performance and injunction, coupled with the characterisation of some contractual obligations as fiduciary, will provide an adequate response to a breach of contract. It will be only in exceptional cases, where those remedies are inadequate, that any question of accounting for profits will arise. No fixed rules can be prescribed. The court will have regard to all the circumstances, including the subject matter of the contract, the purpose of the contractual provision which has been breached, the circumstances in which the breach occurred, the consequences of the breach and the circumstances in which relief is being sought. A useful general guide, although not exhaustive, is whether the plaintiff had a legitimate interest in preventing the defendant's profit-making activity and, hence, in depriving him of his profit.

It would be difficult, and unwise, to attempt to be more specific. In the Court of Appeal [1998] Ch 439 Lord Woolf MR suggested there are at least two situations in which justice requires the award of restitutionary damages where compensatory damages would be inadequate: see p 458. Lord Woolf MR was not there addressing the question of when an account of profits, in the conventional sense, should be available. But I should add that, so far as an account of profits is concerned, the suggested categorisation would not assist. The first suggested category was the case of 'skimped' performance, where the defendant fails to provide the full extent of services he has contracted to provide. He should be liable to pay back the amount of expenditure he saved by the breach. This is a much discussed problem. But a part refund of the price agreed for services would not fall within the scope of an account of profits as ordinarily understood. Nor does an account of profits seem to be needed in this context. The resolution of the problem of cases of skimped performance, where the plaintiff does not get what was agreed, may best be found elsewhere. If a shopkeeper supplies inferior and cheaper goods than those ordered and paid for, he has to refund the difference in price. That would be the outcome of a claim for damages for breach of contract. That would be so, irrespective of whether the goods in fact served the intended purpose. There must be scope for a similar approach, without any straining of principle, in cases where the defendant provided inferior and cheaper services than those contracted for.

The second suggested category was where the defendant has obtained his profit by doing the very thing he contracted not to do. This category is defined too widely to assist. The category is apt to embrace all express negative obligations. But something more is required than mere breach of such an obligation before an account of profits will be the appropriate remedy.

Lord Woolf MR [1998] Ch 439, 457, 458, also suggested three facts which should not be a sufficient ground for departing from the normal basis on which damages are awarded: the fact that the breach was cynical and deliberate; the fact that the breach enabled the defendant to enter into a more profitable contract elsewhere; and the fact that by entering into a new and more profitable contract the defendant put it out of his power to perform his contract with the plaintiff. I agree that none of these facts would be, by itself, a good reason for ordering an account of profits.

The present case

The present case is exceptional. The context is employment as a member of the security and intelligence services.

. . . .

In considering what would be a just response to a breach of Blake's undertaking the court has to take these considerations into account. The undertaking, if not a fiduciary obligation, was closely akin to a fiduciary obligation, where an account of profits is a standard remedy in the event of breach. Had the information which Blake has now disclosed still been confidential, an account of profits would have been ordered, almost as a matter of course. In the special circumstances of the intelligence services, the same conclusion should follow even though the information is no longer confidential. That would be a just response to the breach. I am reinforced in this view by noting that most of the profits from the book derive indirectly from the extremely serious and damaging breaches of the same undertaking committed by Blake in the 1950s. As already mentioned, but for his notoriety as an infamous spy his autobiography would not have commanded royalties of the magnitude Jonathan Cape agreed to pay.

. . . .

Lord Steyn gave a concurring speech and **Lord Goff of Chieveley** and **Lord Browne-Wilkinson** concurred with Lord Nicholls. **Lord Hobhouse** gave a dissenting speech.

NOTES AND QUESTIONS

1. Did Lord Nicholls lay down any clear guide as to when an account of profits will be awarded for breach of contract?

2. Would *Surrey County Council v Bredero Homes Ltd* (above, 986), be decided differently after *Blake*? In *Lane v O'Brien Homes Ltd* [2004] EWHC 303 (QB) a defendant developer built four houses, instead of three, in breach of a collateral contract with the claimant seller of the land. David Clarke J upheld an award of damages of £150,000 based on the defendant's estimated profit from building the extra house of £280,000. The *Wrotham Park* case was applied and the damages were treated as compensating the claimant's loss of opportunity to bargain.

3. A breaks his contract with B in order to make a much more lucrative contract with C. Can B recover from A, the profits made by A on the contract with C? See, e.g., *AB Corpn v CD Company, The Sine Nomine* [2002] 1 Lloyd's Rep 805 in which an account of profits was refused by arbitrators for the withdrawal, and use of, a ship in breach of a charterparty.

4. Did Lord Nicholls regard the decisions in *Wrotham Park Estate Co. Ltd v Parkside Homes Ltd* (above, 978), and *Bracewell v Appleby* (above, 955), as governed by the same principle as that applying in *Blake*? In *Commercial Remedies* (2003, eds Burrows and Peel), 129, it is reported that, in extra-judicial discussion, Lord Nicholls thought that, 'Once one had crossed the threshold for being able to recover an account of profits for breach of contract, rather than compensatory damages or specific relief . . . the measure of recovery could extend from expense saved through to stripping a proportion of the profits made through to stripping all of the profits made from the breach. The *Wrotham Park Estate* case (where 5 per cent of the [anticipated] profits had been stripped) was therefore based on the same principle as *Att-General v Blake* (where all the profits had been stripped)'.

5. Lord Nicholls said that he preferred 'to avoid the unhappy expression "restitutionary damages".' In *Commercial Remedies* (2003, eds Burrows and Peel), 129, it is reported that, in extra-judicial discussion, 'Lord Nicholls explained that the reason why he preferred to avoid the term "restitutionary damages" in *A-G v Blake* was because, for many, damages are virtually synonymous with compensation. If one could therefore use terminology that avoided alienating or confusing such people that was preferable. In other words, the terminology of "restitutionary damages" was an unnecessary additional complication to the acceptance of the new development in *A-G v Blake*'. Do you agree that if one is talking about a 'gain-based monetary remedy' an 'account of profits' is less problematic terminology than 'restitutionary damages'?

6. Lord Nicholls referred, in what he termed a footnote, to the US case of *Snepp v US* (1980) 444 US 507 in which, on very similar facts (concerning a book published by a former employee of the CIA) the Supreme Court held that a constructive trust should be imposed on Snepp's profits.

7. As part of his reasoning, Lord Nicholls referred to the straining of the distinction in some cases between breach of fiduciary duty and breach of contract. The thinness of that distinction is well-illustrated by the Australian case of *Hospital Products Ltd v United States Surgical Corp* (1984) 156 CLR 41. By a 3–2 majority the High Court of Australia overturned the lower courts' decisions declaring a constructive trust of the profits made in breach of fiduciary duty and instead held that, because in the majority's view there was no fiduciary relationship, the claimant was merely entitled to compensatory damages for breach of contract.

8. For useful analyses of *Blake* see D Fox, 'Restitutionary Damages to Deter Breach of Contract' [2001] *CLJ* 33; E McKendrick, 'Breach of Contract, Restitution for Wrongs, and Punishment' in *Commercial Remedies* (2003, eds A Burrows and E Peel), ch 10. For a very hostile view of restitutionary damages for breach of contract, see D Campbell and D Harris, 'In Defence of Breach: a Critique of Restitution and the Performance Interact' (2002) 22 *Legal Studies* 208 and D Campbell and P Wylie, 'Ain't No Telling (Which Circumstances are Exceptional)' [2003] *CLJ* 605.

- *Experience Hendrix LLC v PPX Enterprises Inc*
  [2003] EWCA Civ 323; [2003] 1 All ER (Comm) 830, Court of Appeal

This case followed from a settlement in 1973 of a dispute between the rock star Jimi Hendrix and the defendant record company. By the terms of that contractual settlement, it was agreed that certain master tapes could be used for recording purposes by the defendant but that the rest ('non-Schedule A material') should be delivered up to Jimi Hendrix. In breach of that contract, the defendant used master tapes that should have been delivered up. The claimant, the estate of Jimi Hendrix, sought damages or an account of profits for that breach of contract. The Court of Appeal, allowing the claimant's appeal, held that substantial damages, albeit not an account of profits, should be awarded.

Mance LJ: . . .

[14] At the outset of the trial before Buckley J, Mr Jones representing the appellant made clear that he had no evidence, and he said that he did not imagine that he could ever possibly get any evidence, to show or quantify and financial loss suffered by the appellant as a result of PPX's breaches. So it was accepted that, if this was the only available measure, then no (or perhaps strictly only a nominal) award of damages could be made. However, Mr Jones obtained leave to amend to introduce claims for (i) damages consisting of such sums as could reasonably have been demanded by the appellant for relaxing the prohibitions contained in cl 3(b) of the settlement agreement or, alternatively, (ii) the entire profit attributable to PPX's exploitation of the non-Sch A material. It was agreed that the trial should concern itself with the points of principle raised by this claim, and that the quantification of any such claims for damages and/or profit should be stood over. . . .

[16] The inspiration for the appellant's amendment of its case was the House of Lords decision in *A-G v Blake* (*Jonathan Cape Ltd, third party*) [2000] 2 All ER (Comm) 487, [2001] 1 AC 268. This marks a new start in this area of law. The exposition by counsel before us of prior authority threw light on considerations which may still be relevant to its future development. But, as I see the decision in *Blake*'s case, it freed us from some constraints that prior authority in this court (particularly *Surrey CC v Bredero Homes Ltd* [1993] 3 All ER 705, [1993] 1 WLR 1361 and some of the reasoning in *Jaggard v Sawyer* [1995] 2 All ER 189, [1995] 1 WLR 269) would have imposed. To apply Lord Steyn's words, *Blake*'s case leaves future courts with the task of 'hammering out on the anvil of decided cases when and how far remedies such as the appellant now seeks should be available. The original Nibelungen produced a powerful image of restitution. The appellant invites us to fashion a modern and more deliberate equivalent on Jimi Hendrix's legacy.

. . .

[26] Whether the adoption of a standard measure of damages represents a departure from a compensatory approach depends upon what one understands by compensation and whether the term is only apt in circumstances where an injured party's financial position, viewed subjectively, is being precisely restored. The law frequently introduces objective measures (e g the available market rules in sale of goods) or limitations (e g remoteness). The former may increase or limit a claimant's ability to recover loss actually suffered. Another situation where damages do not necessarily depend upon precisely what would have occurred but for the wrong is where there has been a conversion (cf *Kuwait Airways Corp v Iraqi Airways Co* (*No 3*) [2002] UKHL 19, [2002] 1 All ER (Comm) 843, [2002] 2 AC 883, especially at [82], [83]). In a case such as the *Wrotham Park* case the law gives effect to the instinctive reaction that, whether or not the appellant would have been better off if the wrong had not been committed, the wrongdoer ought not to gain an advantage for free, and should make some reasonable recompense. In such a context it is natural to pay regard to any profit made by the wrongdoer (although a wrongdoer surely cannot always rely on avoiding having to make reasonable recompense by showing that despite his wrong he failed, perhaps simply due to his own incompetence, to make any profit). The law can in such cases act either by ordering payment over of a

percentage of any profit or, in some cases, by taking the cost which the wrongdoer would have had to incur to obtain (if feasible) equivalent benefit from another source.

[31] As to subsequent authority, we were referred to *Esso Petroleum Co. Ltd v Niad Ltd* [2001] All ER (D) 324 (Nov), where Sir Andrew Morritt V-C ordered an account of profits as a remedy for breach of a contractual scheme called 'Pricewatch' operated by Esso with its dealers. Dealers agreed to report competitors' prices and to abide by prices set daily by Esso which were intended to match the competition. Dealers received financial support by Esso to assist them to do this. The defendant failed to maintain prices as agreed on four occasions, despite giving repeated assurances that he would do so. Damages were an inadequate remedy, since it was impossible for Esso to attribute lost sales to breach by one dealer. Yet the obligation to observe Pricewatch was fundamental to its operation, and failure to do so gave the lie to Esso's advertising campaign to support it. Account was also taken of the defendant's repetition of its breaches, and of Esso's legitimate interest in preventing the defendant profiting. Sir Andrew Morritt V-C regarded an account of profits as particularly appropriate when the defendant had been receiving financial support from Esso to maintain Pricewatch.

[34] It was argued before us by Mr Englehart that any order for the payment of damages or a fortiori an account of profits must in a case such as the present be precluded by the judge's grant of an injunction. . . . The decision in *Blake's* case in my view avoids the need to consider Mr Englehart's submissions on these points at length. . . .

[35] I can take the example put in argument of breach of a restrictive covenant not to use land for a pop concert, committed in circumstances where the beneficiary was out of the country and suffered no discomfort at all. Why should he not obtain an injunction to restrain repetition and a reasonable sum having regard to the financial benefit obtained by the neighbouring landowner from the infringement? Likewise, if a breach of contract occurs in such circumstances that there is no possibility at all of obtaining an injunction (eg because the interests of a third party have intervened), I see no reason why that should, since *Blake's* case, present any insuperable bar, in appropriate circumstances, to an order for payment of a reasonable sum having regard to any benefit made by the infringement, even though the appellant cannot prove any financial loss (cf *Jaggard v Sawyer* [1995] 2 All ER 189 at 211–212, [1995] 1 WLR 269 at 291 *per* Millett LJ). Lord Nicholls in *Blake's* case [2000] 2 All ER (Comm) 487 at 500, [2001] 1 AC 268 at 285 took as 'A useful general guide, although not exhaustive' of circumstances in which an account of profit might be appropriate, 'whether the plaintiff had a legitimate interest in preventing the defendant's profit-making activity'. Those are precisely the circumstances in which an injunction for the future is likely to be granted. It would be paradoxical if its granting in the light of a continuing future risk were at the same time to deprive the appellant of any claim to strip, or seek a reasonable sum taking account of, the defendant's profit from past infringement. And if Lord Nicholls' general guide is a useful starting point in respect of an account of profits, it must be all the more so in respect of the lesser claim to a reasonable sum taking account of the defendant's profitable infringement.

[36] I turn to apply these principles to the present facts. As in *Blake's* case, we are concerned with a breach of a negative obligation, and PPX did do the very thing it had contracted not to do. Further, as in *Blake's* case so here on the judge's findings, PPX through Mr Chalpin knew that it was doing something which it had contracted not to do, and in 1995 and 1999 well knew that the appellant would not consent thereto. Further, as in *Wrotham Park Estate Co. v Parkside Homes Ltd* [1974] 2 All ER 321, [1974] 1 WLR 798, it can be said that the restriction against use of PPX's property of which PPX was in breach was imposed to protect the appellant's property, although there is the distinction that PPX's property did not ever belong to the appellant or appellant's predecessor. Finally, the grant of an injunction for the future shows that the appellants had a legitimate interest in

preventing PPX's profit-making activity (cf Lord Nicholls in *Blake*'s case [2000] 2 All ER (Comm) 487 at 500, [2001] 1 AC 268 at 285). But, since we are concerned with past profits, it is too late for either specific performance or an injunction to offer any effective remedy, and it is not suggested that this was or is the appellant's fault.

[37] On the other hand, there are also obvious distinctions from *Blake*'s case. First, we are not concerned with a subject anything like as special or sensitive as national security. The state's special interest in preventing a spy benefiting by reaches of his contractual duty of secrecy, and so removing at least part of the financial attraction of such breaches, has no parallel in this case. Second, the notoriety which accounted for the magnitude of Blake's royalty-earning capacity derived from his prior breaches of secrecy, and that too has no present parallel. Third, there is no direct analogy between PPX's position and that of a fiduciary.

[38] The case of *Esso Petroleum Co. Ltd v Niad Ltd* presents a similar feature to the present, in so far as damages may be said to be an inadequate remedy, because of the practical impossibility in each case of demonstrating the effect of a defendant's undoubted breaches on the appellant's general programme of promoting their product. But, despite Mr McDermott's evidence, it is not shown that the present defendants' breaches went to the root of the appellant's programme or gave the lie to its integrity. Nor is the present a case where the defendant can be said to have profited directly, by receipt under the agreement which it broke of monies that it ought in fairness to restore.

[39] The present case does, however, arise out of a particular background, which has no direct parallel in these prior cases. . . .

[42] In the light of this background and in the light of the terms of the settlement agreement itself, I consider that any reasonable observer of the situation would conclude that, as a matter of practical justice. PPX should make (at the least) reasonable payment for its use of masters in breach of the settlement agreement. The intention of the agreement is clear. Consent to extensions or renewals was only contemplated in the case of existing licences. Even then, if it was given at all, it would no doubt only be given on terms requiring payment of a royalty. In relation to masters not on Sch A and not subject to any existing licences, the appellant's dominant interest was to remove them from the market. Mr McDermott's evidence indicates at least some of the reasons and risks why this is likely to have been so.

CONCLUSIONS

[43] It would in these circumstances be anomalous and unjust if PPX could, by simply breaching the agreement, avoid paying royalties or any sum, when they have to pay royalties in respect of Sch A masters and they would have expected that, even if consent to the extension or renewal of existing licences of non-Sch A masters was forthcoming at all, it would only be on terms as to payment of further royalties. As it is, this case is concerned with fresh licences of non-Sch A masters to different licensees, so that the incongruity of allowing PPX free user to its own profit is yet more obvious.

[44] However, I do not regard this case as exceptional to the point where the court should order a full account of all profits which have been or may be made by PPX by its breaches. I have already drawn attention to significant features of *Blake*'s case which have no counterpart in this case (see [37], above). Here, the breaches, though deliberate, took place in a commercial context. PPX, though knowingly and deliberately breaching its contract, acted as it did in the course of a business, to which it no doubt gave some expenditure of time and effort and probably the use of connections and some skill (although how much is evidently in issue, and is not a matter on which we can at this stage reach any view). An account of profits would involve a detailed assessment of such matters, which, as is very clear from *Blake*'s case, should not lightly be ordered.

[45] We are furthermore concerned with material falling within cl 3(b) of the agreement. Although the 1995 and 1999 licences were not by way of extension or renewal of licences existing in 1973, the

reference to consent in cl 3(b) proviso (A) of the settlement agreement is some indication that the parties contemplated that commercial considerations might make the appellant willing to contemplate further utilisation of material within that clause on suitable terms. The appellant now of course resists any utilisation or marketing of material outside Sch A. The injunction that it has obtained will protect it for the future. For the past, in the absence of any proven loss, I would confine any financial remedy to an order that PPX pay a reasonable sum for its use of material in breach of the settlement agreement. That sum can properly be described as being 'such sum as might reasonably have been demanded' by Jimi Hendrix's estate 'as a quid pro quo for agreeing to permit the two licences into which PPX entered in breach of the settlement agreement', which was the approach adopted by Brightman J in the *Wrotham Park* case (see [22], above). This involves an element of artificiality, if, as in the *Wrotham Park* case, no permission would ever have been given on any terms. And, where no injunction is possible, even the value of a bargaining opportunity depends on the value which the court puts on the right infringed (see [19], above, citing Lord Nicholls in *Blake's* case). That said, the approach adopted by Brightman J has the merit of directing the court's attention to the commercial value of the right infringed and of enabling it to assess the sum payable by reference to the fees that might in other contexts be demanded and paid between willing parties. It points in the present case towards orders that PPX pay over, by way of damages, a proportion of each of the advances received to date and (subject to deduction of such proportion) an appropriate royalty rate on retail selling prices. I would therefore allow the appeal against the judge's decision on the first point and declare accordingly.

[46] Counsel were also agreed that we should in that event go as far as we could to give guidance to the parties regarding the appropriate proportion. I do not consider that it is possible on the present state of information to reach any final conclusions as the appropriate sum(s) or the appropriate royalty rate(s) on retail selling prices which might be used to arrive at such sums. However, whatever retail sales may or may not have been made, I consider, as I have said, that PPX should pay to the appellant a proportion of the advances that it has received from CBH and Crown. That proportion can only be assessed after excluding such proportions of such advances as must be taken to have been attributable to Sch A masters, since they attract a royalty of 2 per cent (or 1 per cent) on retail sales. Further, since the breaches related to masters which PPX was under an absolute commitment not to use, I consider that any royalty rate used as the basis for calculating any further sums due to the appellant should be significantly in excess of 2 per cent (or of 1 per cent if PPX's own entitlement was to a royalty of 6 per cent or less). The settlement agreement was, as I have said at [7], above, designed to give Jimi Hendrix's estate not less than about one-sixth of PPX's royalties in respect of Sch A masters, itself a considerable improvement on the original agreement. In respect of non-Sch A masters, in respect of which PPX was not intended to have any marketing rights at all as matters stood in the 1990s, any rate must be significantly higher. I do not wish to fetter any future court in any way. But it may assist if I express my present view (albeit one reached without the benefit of any expert evidence that might be available hereafter) that I would be surprised if the appropriate rate in respect of non-Sch A masters was less than twice that agreed in respect of Sch A masters, or was in other words less than one-third of PPX's royalties on the retail selling price of records.

...

Peter Gibson LJ ...

...

[53] *Blake's* case builds on the recognition in one case on compensation for a breach of a contractual obligation as well as on authorities in other areas of the law that financial loss to the claimant is not always the appropriate or just measure of damages to compensate the claimant for the wrong done to him. A claimant's interest in the performance of a contract may render it just and equitable

that the defendant should not benefit from his breach but should account for the profits made by that breach. But it is made abundantly clear in *Blake's* case that this is a remedy to be granted only in exceptional circumstances.

. . .

[55] However, like Mance LJ, I do not think the present case an appropriate one for ordering an account of profits. He has drawn attention at [37], above, to the features of the present case which distinguish it from the circumstances in *Blake's* case. No doubt deliberate breaches of contract occur frequently in the commercial world; yet something more is needed to make the circumstances exceptional enough to justify ordering an account of profits, particularly when another remedy is available.

[56] It is apparent from Lord Nicholls' speech that he regarded the decision of Brightman J in *Wrotham Park Estate Co. v Parkside Homes Ltd* [1974] 2 All ER 321, [1974] 1 WLR 798 as a crucial stepping-stone in his reasoning as to why the absence of financially measurable loss flowing from a breach of contract was not necessarily fatal to a claimant's claim for compensation. . . .

[57] Lord Nicholls was clearly of the view that Brightman J was right not to decide the case on the basis that the breach of covenant did not diminish the value of the houses in the estate at all. As Lord Nicholls said ([2000] 2 All ER (Comm) 487 at 497, [2001] 1 AC 268 at 283), if the estate company was given a nominal or no sum by way of compensation, justice would manifestly not have been done. The same in my judgment applies to the present case. Buckley J thought it relevant that the claimant would never have agreed to PPX's exploitation of the non-Sch A masters, and he rejected a wholly fictional approach. But the *Wrotham Park* case itself demonstrated that it is irrelevant, in assessing compensation on the basis adopted by Brightman J, that in reality there would have been no relaxation of the relevant obligation because of the opposition of the person entitled to the benefit of that obligation. As Brightman J said:

'On the facts of this particular case the plaintiffs, rightly conscious of their obligations towards existing residents, would clearly not have granted any relaxation, but for present purposes I must assume that they would have been induced to do so.' (See [1974] 2 All ER 321 at 341, [1974] 1 WLR 798 at 815.)

[58] In my judgment, because (1) there has been a deliberate breach by PPX of its contractual obligations for its own reward, (2) the claimant would have difficulty in establishing financial loss therefrom, and (3) the claimant has a legitimate interest in preventing PPX's profit-making activity carried out in breach of PPX's contractual obligations, the present case is a suitable one (as envisaged by Lord Nicholls: [2000] 2 All ER (Comm) 487 at 498, [2001] 1 AC 268 at 283–284) in which damages for breach of contract may be measured by the benefits gained by the wrongdoer from the breach. To avoid injustice I would require PPX to make a reasonable payment in respect of the benefit it has gained. I agree with the guidance suggested by Mance LJ for the court assessing the damages.

. . .

[60] For these as well as the reasons given by Mance LJ I too would allow the appeal.

Hooper J concurred.

NOTES AND QUESTIONS

1. The Court of Appeal was not required to assess the reasonable sum to be awarded as damages but, at 993 above, Mance LJ thought that one-third of the defendant's royalties on the retail selling price of records made from the forbidden tapes would probably be an appropriate reasonable sum. Were these damages compensatory or restitutionary?

2. Was Sir Andrew Morritt V-C correct to order an account of profits in *Esso Petroleum Co. Ltd v Niad* [2001] All ER (D) 324, a case referred to by Mance LJ (at 991–92)?

3. Did the Court of Appeal in part apply *Blake* and in part distinguish *Blake*? See A Burrows, *Remedies for Torts and Breach of Contract* (3rd edn, 2004), 406–7.

4. Is it correct to say that two factors that were influential in the decisions in *Blake* and *Experience Hendrix* were that the breach of contract was cynical and that normal compensatory damages were inadequate?

5. For a helpful case-note, see M Graham, 'Restitutionary Damages: The Anvil Struck' (2004) 120 *LQR* 26.

6. For Edelman's view that this case exemplifies an award of 'restitutionary damages' but not 'disgorgement damages' for breach of contract (see above, 936), see his case-note '*Attorney-General v Blake* Revisited' [2003] *RLR* 101.

- • *World Wide Fund for Nature (formerly World Wildlife Fund) v World Wrestling Federation Entertainment Inc*
  [2006] EWHC 184 (Ch), Chancery Division

The claimant is a well-known environment conservation charity and its name and initials, WWF, are internationally recognized. The defendant, a US company, started to use a logo comprising a version of the letters WWF. The claimant objected and, after legal proceedings were begun, a settlement was reached whereby the defendant agreed to substantial restrictions on the use of the initials. The defendant then broke that agreement. At an earlier hearing, it was held by Jacob J, [2002] FSR 32, distinguishing *Att-General v Blake*, that awarding an account of profits for that breach of contract would not be appropriate. But the question then arose, as a preliminary issue, of whether damages could be awarded, following the *Wrotham Park* case, as a reasonable payment for the release by the claimant of its rights under the agreement. In a wide-ranging judgment in which he carefully examined the *Wrotham Park*, *Blake* and *Experience Hendrix* cases, as well as academic works, Peter Smith J decided that such damages could be awarded albeit that it would be for the court hearing the inquiry as to damages to determine whether they should, on the facts, be awarded.

Peter Smith J: . . .

119. It is important to appreciate that damages under the *Wrotham* principle are not the same as an account. The judgments in the House of Lords [in *Blake*] must be read in the light of their primary decision that Blake was liable to account exceptionally. There is a close affinity in my view between damages under the *Wrotham* principle and an account. That closeness becomes marked when a Claimant seeks damages under the *Wrotham* principle by reference to the Defendant's profits especially when as in the the present case the Fund seeks a percentage of all profits whether derived from the use of the Initials (and thus in breach of contract) or whether as a result of the Federation's separate and independent efforts to make profit.

120. One can see this blurring by considering the following. In the *Wrotham* case the judge rejected the argument based upon the development value of the land but instead awarded it as a percentage of the profits. In so doing he makes inferentially allowances for the expenditure that the wrongdoer commits in making the profits.

121. An accounting party can sometimes obtain a reduction of the principle that there should be an account of the profits gross by obtaining a deduction for his own efforts in making the profits. The extent to which allowance can be made for the effort of the wrongdoer is a matter of controversy: see my decision *Crown Dilmun v Sutton* [2004] 1 BCLC 468 at paragraphs 211–213. Another example is to be derived from the law of partnership. A partner on a dissolution maybe required to account for profits he has made using the partnership assets after dissolution: see for example *Sandhu v Gill*

[2006] 2 WLR 8. In requiring such a partner to account he is often entitled to 'just allowances' i.e. recompense for his efforts in generating the profits.

122. On that analysis the difference in some cases between a claim for damages on the Wrotham principle and account of profits can be very fine.

. . .

137. What I derive from the judgments [in *Blake*] is that the *Wrotham* remedy is of general application in appropriate cases for any breach of contract. It is also compensation based and not resitutionary based. It appears to be an exceptional discretionary remedy when the more traditional bases for compensating an innocent person for breach of contract would provide no or an illusory result. It is not therefore a basis for damages that can be claimed as of right but is a remedy designed to fill what would otherwise be a gap and lead to an innocent person having a justified belief that the laws had failed him in dealing properly with a breach of contract i.e. in colloquial words the wrong-doer had 'got away with it'.

. . .

168. There are observations (as appears from the judgments in the Court of Appeal in *Blake* and in the House of Lords and *Hendrix* p875) that a deliberate breach is a factor that can be borne in mind when deciding whether to grant a *Wrotham Park* type remedy for breach of contract.

169. I have difficulty with that as a matter of fundamental principle. First as the *Blake* case establishes the award of damages under this principle is compensatory not restitutionary. It is in this context a remedy for breach of contract. Before *Blake* an account was traditionally not considered to be available for a breach of contract because it was punishment rather than compensation

170. It seems to me whilst the decision in *Blake* may have changed that in relation to an account it cannot have intended to have changed the principle that damages for breach of contract are compensation not punishment. Nor can it have been the case that the House of Lords in *Blake* intended without discussion to reverse the *Addis* case in respect of contractual damages.

. . .

173. [I]t seems to me that it might be of advantage to the parties of this action and generally to indicate what in my view is the way in which the court should approach the assessment of damages under [the *Wrotham* principle]

174. I set [the principles] out in numerical order as follows:—

1. The primary basis of assessment is in my view that identified by Mr Mann in the *Amec* case [*Amec Developments v Jury's Hotel* [2001] 1 EGLR 81, 83] namely 'is to consider the sum that would have been arrived at in negotiations between the parties had each been making reasonable use of their respective bargaining positions without holding out for unreasonable amounts'.

2. The outcome of that hypothetical negotiation, must be determined by reference to the parties' actual knowledge at the time that negotiations would have taken place. This would normally be on the date of the breach.

3. The fact that the innocent party would never have agreed to any such sale or relaxation is irrelevant.

4. The conduct of the wrongdoer is also irrelevant as to the breach of contract.

5. The decision to award damages under this head is discretionary according to the circumstances of the case but the decision should be taken when damages would be an inadequate remedy and without an award under this basis the innocent party would obtain no just recompense for the breach by the wrongdoer in doing what he agreed not to do.

6. The decision whether or not to award damages on this basis can take into account factors such as delay in intimating the claim and prosecuting the action, if appropriate. Those factors also could be taken into account at a later stage in quantifying the claim. Thus it may be

possible to argue that where a wrongdoer was led to believe that no claim would be forth-coming on this head and acted to its detriment in reliance upon that that may bar the claim completely. Equally part of a claim may be disallowed by reason of delay if the delay caused prejudice: see . . . *Shaw v Applegate* [1997] 1 WLR 970 and *Gafford v Graham* [1997] 77 P & CR 73. The assessment of those damages involves a number of possibilities:—

7 As one is assessing the amount by reference to hypothetical negotiations, each party is entitled as part of that exercise to adduce evidence that it would have deployed in such hypothetical negotiations. Those can include (but this is not exhaustive as it is fact based):—

7.1 Evidence that it (in this case the Fund) had a reputation which it would have tarnished or diminished by association with the Federation and what would consequentially be a reasonable payment for compensating it for that tarnishment.

7.2 Evidence from the Federation to show that they would have persuaded the Fund by reference to material available to it at the time that its profits would be to some degree attributable to its efforts as opposed to the use of the Initials and that that should be taken into account in assessing the price.

7.3 Evidence from the Federation would be able to show that their costings and assumptions would have involved them in expenditure in incurring the profits that they have made (irrespective of the breach of contract).

175. The damages that can be awarded are to reflect the case. It is possible that the damages could reflect a diminishment or tarnishment of the Claimant's reputation and a reasonable price represent-ing that, or a reasonable sum for the relaxation of the covenant or a negotiation of a reasonable sum that the parties would have agreed as being payable for the breach of the covenant by reference to the subsequent profits in percentage terms (or a combination of all three).

176. In considering all of those the court can take into account the factors relating to the potential for earning profits without committing a breach of contract and the cost of making such profits.

177. The overriding principle is that the damages are compensatory and not to be punitive. That should reflect the nature of the negotiations that take place hypothetically. Ordinarily where a claim is based on subsequent profits the Claimant must show there was a reasonable prospect of connection between the breach of contract and the subsequent profits.

NOTES AND QUESTIONS

1. Peter Smith J took the clear view that 'damages under the *Wrotham* principle' are compensa-tory not restitutionary; and that they are available, exceptionally and as a matter of discretion, where compensatory damages assessed in the normal way would be inadequate. On the other hand, he regarded those damages as not being as exceptional as is an account of profits awarded under *Blake*.

2. Is the judge's acceptance that 'damages under the *Wrotham* principle' are more widely avail-able than an account of profits consistent with his reasoning that there may be a very fine line between the two awards?

3. In treating the defendant's conduct in breaking the contract as irrelevant in assessing damages, the judge thought that one would otherwise be undermining the principle that damages are not awarded to punish a contract-breaker. Do you agree with that reasoning?

Although written many years before *Blake*, the following article by Gareth Jones repays careful attention. In it, he argues that restitution should be available to strip gains made by a breach of contract provided the claimant can establish that the gains would not have been made but for the breach (i.e. that causation is satisfied) and subject to an overall discretion in the court to refuse restitution.

- G Jones, 'The Recovery of Benefits Gained From A Breach of Contract' (1983) 99 *LQR* 442

[Having examined cases including *Wrotham Park Estate* and *Penarth Dock*, Jones continues:] A bold court could find, therefore, respectably attractive precedents for a conclusion that the law is now sufficiently mature to recognise a restitutionary claim for profits made from a breach of contract. But the critical and hard question is whether it is really desirable to recognise a new restitutionary claim based on the defendant's breach of contract.

Some very distinguished judges have implicitly concluded that the common law's reticence to recognise any claim to recover the defendant's profits from a breach of contract is wise. In *Bromage v Gunning*[1] Coke CJ is reported to have said that if a covenantee could compel a convenator to execute a lease as he had agreed to do, this 'would subvert the intention of the covenantor [the lessor] when he intends it to be at his election either to lose the damages or make the lease.' In *The Common Law*,[2] Oliver Wendell Holmes Jr elaborated the reasoning underlying that rather cryptic sentence in the following way:

'If, when a man promised to labour for another, the law made him do it, his relation to his promisee might be called a servitude ad hoc with some truth. But that is what the law never does. It never interferes until a promise has been broken, and therefore cannot possibly be performed according to its tenor. It is true that in some instances equity does what is called compelling specific performance. . . . This remedy is an exceptional one. The only universal consequence of a legally binding promise is, that the law makes the promisor pay damages if the promised event does not come to pass. In every case it leaves him free from interference until the time for fulfilment has gone by, and therefore free to break his contract if he chooses.'

Some economists have applauded these words as yet another illustration of the intuitive efficiency of the common law. Richard Posner, in his *Economic Analysis of Law*,[3] justifies the Holmes' 'bad man' theory[4] in the following way:

'But in some cases a party would be tempted to breach the contract simply because his profit from breach would exceed his expected profit from completion of the contract. If his profit from breach would also exceed the expected profit to the other party from completion of the contract, and if damages are limited to loss of expected profit, there will be an incentive to commit a breach. There should be. The opportunity cost of completion to the breaching party is the profit that he would make from a breach, and if it is greater than his profit from completion, then completion will involve a loss to him. If that loss is greater than the gain to the other party from completion, breach would be value-maximizing and should be encouraged. And because the victim of the breach is made whole for his loss, he is indifferent; hence encouraging breaches in these circumstances will not deter people from entering into contracts in the future.'

It is a truism that at common law a person cannot be compelled to carry out his promise to the letter. But it is not a necessary consequence of that proposition that contractual performance and the payment of damages should be regarded in all respects as alternative obligations. As Pollock recognised, that conclusion would mean that it would not be a wrong to induce a man to break his contract and a court would never grant specific performance.[5] More important, such a conclusion

---

1 (1617) 1 Rolle 368.

2 *The Common Law* (ed. by Mark de Wolfe Howe), 235–6.

3 *Economic Analysis of Law* (2nd edn, 1977), 89–90. Cf. R Birmingham, 'Breach of Contract, Damage Measures, and Economic Efficiency' (1970) 24 *Rutgers LRev.* 273.

4 *The Common Law* (ed. by Mark de Wolfe Howe), 227 ff.

5 *The Pollock-Holmes Letters*, Vol. 1, 79–80; Vol. II, 201, 233–4.

would frustrate the natural and reasonable commercial expectations of the contracting parties. In Buckland's graphic sentence: 'One does not buy a right to damages, one buys a horse.'[6] Judge Posner would not deny that. But, in his view, an award of damages would equally be consistent with those commercial expectations. The innocent party is said to be 'indifferent' because an award of damages makes him whole. But the promisee will often prefer performance; and the promisor did, after all, promise to perform. Moreover, Judge Posner's argument assumes that the innocent party can always discharge the burden of proving his precise loss; and every student of the law of contract knows that this is not always true. It also ignories the transaction costs imposed on the innocent party as a result of the breach, for example, in attempting to resolve the contractual dispute or to mitigate loss.

The other dependent limb of Judge Posner's argument is more seductive: breaches are value-maximising and should be encouraged. A restitutionary clam for profits gained is therefore objectionable because it would persuade a promisor to carry out his promise when it would be inefficient to do so. It would give a promisee a 'windfall' for which he has not bargained; and it would dissuade the promisee from mitigating his loss. It is doubtful whether these objections are in themselves conclusive against the recognition of a restitutionary claim. Given the uncertainty of litigation, the simple existence of a restitutionary claim will rarely deter a promisor from breaking his promise if he were minded to do so. Moreover Judge Posner's argument discounts the facts that the promisor has failed to do what he promised to do; that the promisee paid for that promise; and, to add insult to injury, that the promisor profited from his breach. These considerations must be appealing to those who believe that promises should be kept and who could fairly claim that the promisee would have made a different bargain for a different consideration if the promisor had not made the promise which he has not performed. So in *Groves v John Wunder Co.*[7] the plaintiff could argue that it is not open to the defendant to deny that but for the defendant's promise to level the land, the plaintiff would have demanded $105,000 *plus* the cost of levelling the land.

One decision, from a civilian jurisdiction, is a particularly striking illustration of a situation where the defendant saved himself considerable expense by failing to provide a particular service and where the plaintiff was properly deemed to have suffered no loss.[8] In *City of New Orleans v Fireman's Charitable Association*[9] the defendants had agreed for a consideration to provide the plaintiff with a fire-fighting service for a number of years. Under the contract they promised to keep available a certain number of men and horses and a particular footage of fire-fighting hosepipe. The plaintiff paid the consideration which was due under the contract. After the contract period had expired, the plaintiff discovered that during that time the defendants had available neither the number of men and horses nor the footage of hosepipe which had been promised under the contract. The defendants had thereby saved themselves over $40,000. There was no averment that the defendants had failed to extinguish any fire because of this breach of contract or that the plaintiff had suffered any other loss. The Supreme Court of Louisiana held that the plaintiff's claim for relief must fail. The city could not claim substantial damages because it had suffered no loss. Moreover, it could not recover the consideration which it had paid to the defendants; it had not paid the money under mistake and the main purpose of the contract had been fulfilled. Yet the defendants had undoubtedly made a gain, for they had saved over $40,000, and that gain had been made at the plaintiff's expense. The city would certainly have paid considerably less for the promise of a less adequate service.

It is one thing to admit the desirability of some kind of restitutionary claim, it is another to define its limits. For example, should the nature of the particular contract be at all relevant? If the courts were to recognise only claims for profits gained from a breach of a contract which was specifically enforceable, then they would simply confirm existing precedent; for a vendor is known to be a constructive

---

6 'The Nature of Contractual Obligations' (1944) 8 *CLJ* 247.

7 286 NW 235 (1939).

8 See also *Tito v Waddel (No 2)* [1977] Ch 106. 9 9 So. 486 (1891).

trustee of the land (and the proceeds from any resale) between contract and conveyance. But equity has always been prepared to strip a fiduciary of profits gained by him from a breach of contract which is not specifically enforceable, such as a contract of employment, if his breach of contract also amounts to a breach of his fiduciary duty to his principal. So in *Hunter v Shell Oil Co.*[10] the Federal Court of Appeals for the Fifth Circuit held that a company controlled by an employee of Shell Oil, Hunter, held certain oil and gas interests on trust for Shell Oil; for they had been acquired as a result of Hunter's wrongful disclosure of confidential geological information. In principle there is much to be said for the view that the scope of this restitutionary claim should similarly not depend on the kind of contract which is breached. Some writers have suggested that an exception should be made if the contract is one of personal services, seemingly on the ground that the existence of the restitutionary claim would induce an employee to continue in an employment which he found odious—and that is a particularly bad thing. This argument assumes that the restitutionary claim would effectively deter an employee from leaving his employment which is (*ex hypothesis* undesirable. But gentlemen like Mr Hunter who are both promisors and fiduciaries have never in the past been deterred by the long shadow of the rule in *Keech v Sandford.*[11] Moreover to be deprived of what you have gained can never be a penal liability and may be less severe than the existing sanction—to compensate another for the loss he has suffered. It may be persuasive to conclude, therefore, that the courts should accept the existence of a restitutionary claim for benefits gained from a breach of any contract, whether it is specifically enforceable or not, and whether it does or does not involve the performance of personal services. This is the restitutionary claim in its broadest form and is not dependent on any notion that the contractual right of performance is a right of property.

There is another and less radical conclusion, namely, that a restitutionary claim should only lie if the defendant has saved himself expense by failing to perform a collateral term of a contract which he has substantially performed; conversely there should be no restitutionary claim if he fails to perform at all. So if this limit is accepted, a plaintiff could recover the expense which a defendant saved from failing to leave the demised property in good repair or land levelled to a uniform grade but not the profits gained by an owner who, in breach of the terms of the charter, withdraws a ship and hires her to another at a higher freight rate. This distinction is pragmatically attractive to those who share Judge Posner's economic philosophy since it does not deter a defendant from non-performance when it would be profitable to do so.

The novelty of a restitutionary claim for profits might otherwise tempt judges to restrict its breadth, in particular to say that it should lie only if the defendant's breach was wilful. The English common law has consistently denied the relevance of the inquiry, why did the defendant fail to carry out his promise? In the United States the distinction between wilful and non-wilful breach assumed for a time importance in the context of a claim brought by a party in breach for the value of the benefits conferred on the innocent party. The first *Restatement of Contracts*[12] admitted such a claim only if the breach was wilful. But Corbin, who was with Cardozo responsible for this distinction, soon repudiated it[13] and concluded that in many cases it would be impossible to characterise a particular 'breach' as either wilful or non-wilful. Certainly there are cases where it will be possible to do so—as the facts of *British Motor Trade Association v Gilbert*[14] demonstrate. But there are other situations where it is not at all clear whether a promisor honestly but erroneously thought that he was entitled to repudiate or that he well knew that he was tearing up his contract in acting as he did. On balance, it is preferable to reject a bald distinction between wilful and non-wilful breach but to affirm that the remedy of an account of profits from a breach of contract is a remedy which it is in the discretion of

---

10 198 F 2d 485 (5th Cir. 1952).   11 (1726) Sel Cas in Ch 61.   12 s. 357.
13 *Contracts*, Vol. 5A, s. 1123.   14 [1951] 2 All ER 641.

the court to grant or refuse. The nature of the promisor's conduct may be a factor for the court in determining whether to grant an accounting but it should not be a decisive one.

The burden will be on the promisee to prove that the promisor could not have gained the profits in question except by breaking his contract with the promise. The promisor, having repudiated his contract with the promisee, enters into an incompatible and more profitable contract with a third party. Can these profits be deemed to have been gained from his breach of contract? This question will of course only arise if the courts recognise a broad restitutionary claim. The advisers of the *Restatement of Restitution*[15] were divided when they were asked to decide whether a plaintiff, a contracting party, should recover the profits made by a tortfeasor who had induced the other contracting party to repudiate his contract with the plaintiff and contract with him. There were some who thought that there was no causal connection between inducing the breach of the original contract and the profits gained by the tortfeasor through the performance of the new contract. The United States District Court in *Federal Sugar Refining Co. v United States Sugar Equalisation Board*[16] had correctly rejected that argument; if the tortfeasor could not have made his profit but for his tortious act, then it is proper to hold that the profit was the product of the tort and gained at the expense of the injured party. Similarly if the plaintiff can prove that the defendant could not have performed the new contract unless he had previously repudiated the original contract, then the plaintiff has demonstrated that the profits were gained from the breach of contract and at his expense. On occasion this burden will be easily discharged; for example, when the defendant has, in breach of contract, sold his own goods, rather than the plaintiff's in a particular geographical locality. Conversely, the plaintiff will fail if it is evident that the defendant has the economic resources to perform both contracts and has repudiated simply because he discovered that the contract was a disastrously losing one. There will be difficult intermediate cases. The promisee demonstrates that the new contract requires a greater deployment of services and goods but could not be performed without the services and goods committed to the original contract; then the burden may shift to the promisor to apportion the profit, taking into account the resources which he has and has not committed to the performance of the original contract.

. . .

It is difficult to accept the justice of the result of such cases as *Tito v Waddell (No 2)*[17] where the defendant had saved himself considerable expense from failing to execute his promise but where the plaintiff's damages were trivial because he had suffered no 'loss'; a restitutionary claim whose object is to deprive the defendant of the unjust enrichment gained at the plaintiff's expense will not be defeated by a plea that he has suffered no loss. Such a restitutionary claim is not wholly novel. But it is novel enough that an English court will require much persuasion even to accept a limited restitutionary claim to deprive a defendant of a gain made in the performance of a contract which he has substantially performed. Such claims will be rare; for a plaintiff will generally be content with a claim for damages; the loss which the plaintiff has suffered from going into the market to mitigate will generally not be significantly different from the gain which the defendant has made from his breach of contract. Moreover the court should always retain a discretion to refuse an accounting if it thinks proper to do so.

Finally it should be emphasised that a defendant who is required to account for profits made from a breach of contract is not necessarily a constructive trustee of those profits for the innocent party. He will be if he is in a fiduciary relationship to the plaintiff. If there is no subsisting fiduciary relationship then it would appear from the English authorities that a constructive trust will not be imposed.

15 S. 133, caveat.   16 268 F 575 (SDNY 1920).   17 [1977] Ch 106.

NOTES

1. What is the relevance to restitution for breach of contract of the 'efficient breach' theory referred to by Jones?

2. The Louisiana case of *City of New Orleans v Fireman's Charitable Association* 9 So. 486 (1891), referred to by Jones above, 999, is a particularly graphic illustration of the normal principle that there shall be no restitution of benefits gained by a breach of contract. McEnery J said, at 487–8:

> The petition of the plaintiff avers that by the contract the contractor was required to keep employees in its service aggregating 124 men, and that instead of this number the defendant association had in its employ during the continuance of its contract not more than 70, thus avoiding an outlay of $25,920; that there was a failure on the part of the defendant to keep at Milnerburg the number of men and horses required by the contract, and an expenditure of $8,800 was thus avoided; that the defendant failed to keep the required amount of hose, there being a deficiency of 4,750 feet, worth $4,275.
>
> The mere statement of the case is sufficient to show that the dismissal of the suit by the district court on the exception of no cause of action was proper. . . . There is no averment in the petition that the fires were not extinguished as required by the contract, or that the fire department, under the control of the management of the defendant association, was not efficient. The city of New Orleans, during the existence of the contract, made regular payments as they fell due. The petition does not disclose any damage suffered by the city in consequence of any violation of the contract. It had nothing to do with the payments made to the employees, or for payments of money for equipments. These expenses were borne by the association, and the money paid on the contract was not destined for any particular purpose except for the extinguishment of fires. The action brought by the city is one of repetition, by which a person demands and seeks to recover what he has paid by mistake, or delivered on a condition which has not been performed. In order to entitle a party to recover back money paid by mistake, it must have been paid by him to a person to whom he did not owe it. There is no averment in the petition of plaintiff to maintain the action. There is no averment that the money was paid through error in law or fact, or that it was delivered on a condition which has not been performed. The condition was the extinguishment of fires in certain districts of the city. From the absence of any averment in the petition that the fires were not extinguished, and from the documents annexed to the petition particularly affirming that this condition was performed, we are of opinion that the main purpose of the contract was faithfully executed. The complaint is to the deficiencies in the minor parts of the contract, relating to the employment of a certain number of men and the use of equipments. During the execution of the contract the city accepted the fire department tendered by the association with the alleged deficiencies. The city, therefore, has no just cause of complaint, unless it can show some damage from the failure of the association to carry out its contract by reason of the alleged deficiencies.

5. RESTITUTION FOR BREACH OF FIDUCIARY DUTY

(1) UNAUTHORIZED PROFIT

• *Regal (Hastings) Ltd v Gulliver* [1942] 1 All ER 378, House of Lords

The claimant company, Regal (the appellants), owned a cinema in Hastings and wanted to acquire two other cinemas. The directors found that Regal could not itself afford to buy the cinemas so they put up much of the money themselves by creating a subsidiary company (Amalgamated) in which they themselves (with the exception of the chairman of directors, Mr Garton) took 2,000 £1 shares, the company's solicitor (Mr Gulliver) took 500 £1 shares, outside purchasers took 500 £1 shares, and Regal took 2,000 £1 shares. The two cinemas were bought and subsequently the shares in the subsidiary company were sold at a considerable profit (£2 16s 1d profit *per* share). Regal, now under new directors, sought to recover the profits made by the former directors (the respondents) from the sale of the shares in the subsidiary company. The claim failed at first instance and before the Court of Appeal but (except as against Garton and Gulliver) succeeded in the House of Lords.

Viscount Sankey: . . . The appellants say they are entitled to succeed: (i) because the respondents secured for themselves the profits upon the acquisition and sale of the shares in Amalgamated by using the knowledge acquired as directors and solicitors respectively of Regal and by using their said respective positions and without the knowledge or consent of Regal; (ii) because the doctrine laid down with regard to trustees is equally applicable to directors and solicitors. . . . In my view, the respondents were in a fiduciary position and their liability to account does not depend upon proof of *mala fides*. The general rule of equity is that no one who has duties of a fiduciary nature to perform is allowed to enter into engagements in which he has or can have a personal interest conflicting with the interests of those whom he is bound to protect. If he holds any property so acquired as trustee, he is bound to account for it to his *Cestui que trust*. The earlier cases are concerned with trusts of specific property: *Keech v Sandford*,[1] *per* Lord King, LC. The rule, however, applies to agents, as, for example, solicitors and directors, when acting in a fiduciary capacity. . . .

I will deal first with the respondents, other than Gulliver and Garton. . . .

It was . . . argued that it would have been a breach of trust for the respondents, as directors of Regal, to have invested more than £2,000 of Regal's money in Amalgamated, and that the transaction would never have been carried through if they had not themselves put up the other £3,000. Be it so, but it is impossible to maintain that, because it would have been a breach of trust to advance more than £2,000 from Regal and that the only way to finance the matter was for the directors to advance the balance themselves, a situation arose which brought the respondents outside the general rule and permitted them to retain the profits which accrued to them from the action they took. At all material times they were directors and in a fiduciary position, and they used and acted upon their exclusive knowledge acquired as such directors. They framed resolutions by which they made a profit for themselves. They sought no authority from the company to do so, and, by reason of their position and actions, they made large profits for which, in my view, they are liable to account to the company.

I now pass to the cases of Gulliver and Garton. Their liability depends upon a careful examination of the evidence. Gulliver's case is that he did not take any shares and did not make any profit by selling them. . . . In these circumstances, and bearing in mind that Gulliver's evidence was accepted, it is clear that he made no profits for which he is liable to account. The case made against him rightly fails, and the appeal against the decision in favour should be dismissed.

Garton's case is that in taking the shares he acted with the knowledge and consent of Regal, and that consequently he comes within the exception to the general rules as to the liability of the person acting in a fiduciary position to account for profits. . . .

[*After reviewing the evidence concerning Garton*] In these circumstances, and bearing in mind that this evidence was accepted, it is clear that he took the shares with the full knowledge and consent of Regal and that he is not liable to account for profits made on their sale. The appeal against the decision in his favour should be dismissed.

The appeal against the decision in favour of the respondents other than Gulliver and Garton should be allowed.

---

1 (1726) Sel Cas t King 61.

Lord Russell: . . . The rule of equity which insists on those, who by use of a fiduciary position make a profit, being liable to account for that profit, in no way depends on fraud, or absence of *bona fides*; or upon such questions or considerations as whether the profit would or should otherwise have gone to the plaintiff, or whether the profiteer was under a duty to obtain the source of the profit for the plaintiff, or whether he took a risk or acted as he did for the benefit of the plaintiff, or whether the plaintiff has in fact been damaged or benefited by his action. The liability arises from the mere fact of a profit having, in the stated circumstances, been made. The profiteer, however honest and well-intentioned, cannot escape the risk of being called upon to account.

The leading case of *Keech v Sandford* is an illustration of the strictness of this rule of equity in this regard, and of how far the rule is independent of these outside considerations. A lease of the profits of a market had been devised to a trustee for the benefit of an infant. A renewal on behalf of the infant was refused. It was absolutely unobtainable. The trustee, finding that it was impossible to get a renewal for the benefit of the infant, took a lease for his own benefit. Though his duty to obtain it for the infant was incapable of performance, nevertheless he was ordered to assign the lease to the infant, upon the bare ground that, if a trustee on the refusal to renew might have a lease for himself, few renewals would be made for the benefit of *cestuis que trust*. Lord King, LC, said, at 62:

> This may seem hard, that the trustee is the only person of all mankind who might not have the lease: but it is very proper that the rule should be strictly pursued, and not in the least relaxed . . .

One other case in equity may be referred to in this connection, viz., *Ex p. James*,[2] decided by Lord Eldon, LC. That was a case of a purchase of a bankrupt's estate by the solicitor to the commission, and Lord Eldon, LC, refers to the doctrine thus, at 345:

> This doctrine as to purchases by trustees, assignees, and persons having a confidential character, stands much more upon general principles than upon the circumstances of any individual case. It rests upon this: that the purchase is not permitted in any case however honest the circumstances; the general interests of justice requiring it to be destroyed in every instance; as no court is equal to the examination and ascertainment of the truth in much the greater number of cases.

Let me now consider whether the essential matters, which the plaintiff must prove, have been established in the present case. As to the profit being in fact made there can be no doubt. The shares were acquired at par and were sold three weeks later at a profit of £2 16s. 1d. per share. Did such of the first five respondents as acquired these very profitable shares acquire them by reason and in course of their office of directors of Regal? In my opinion, when the facts are examined and appreciated, the answer can only be that they did. . . .

In the result, I am of opinion that the directors standing in a fiduciary relationship to Regal in regard to the exercise of their powers as directors, and having obtained these shares by reason and only by reason of the fact that they were directors of Regal and in the course of the execution of that office, are accountable for the profits which they have made out of them. The equitable rule laid down in *Keech v Sandford* and *Ex p. James*, and similar authorities applies to them in full force. It was contended that these cases were distinguishable by reason of the fact that it was impossible for Regal to get the shares owing to lack of funds, and that the directors in taking the shares were really acting as members of the public. I cannot accept this argument. It was impossible for the *cestui que trust* in *Keech v Sandford* to obtain the lease, nevertheless the trustee was accountable. The suggestion that the directors were applying simply as members of the public is a travesty of the facts. They could, had they wished, have protected themselves by a resolution (either antecedent or subsequent) of the Regal shareholders in general meeting. In default of such approval, the liability to account must

---

2 (1803) 8 Ves 337.

remain. The result is that, in my opinion, each of the respondents Bobby, Griffiths, Bassett and Bentley is liable to account for the profit which he made on the sale of his 500 shares in Amalgamated.

The case of the respondent Gulliver, however, requires some further consideration, for he has raised a separate and distinct answer to the claim, he says: 'I never promised to subscribe for shares in Amalgamated. I never did so subscribe. I only promised to find others who would be willing to subscribe. I only found others who did subscribe. The shares were theirs. They were never mine. They received the profit. I received none of it.' If these are the true facts, his answer seems complete. The evidence in my opinion establishes his contention. . . .

There remains to consider the case of Garton. He stands on a different footing from the other respondents in that he was not a director of Regal. He was Regal's legal adviser; but, in my opinion, he has a short but effective answer to the plaintiffs' claim. He was requested by the Regal directors to apply for 500 shares. They arranged that they themselves should each be responsible for £500 of the Amalgmated capital, and they appealed, by their chairman, to Garton to subscribe the balance of £500 which was required to make up the £3,000. In law his action, which has resulted in a profit, was taken at the request of Regal, and I know of no principle or authority which would justify a decision that a solicitor must account for profit resulting from a transaction which he has entered into on his own behalf, not merely with the consent, but at the request of his client. . . .

Lord Wright: . . . [T]he important question of principle brought into issue by the decisions of Wrottesley, J, and the Court of Appeal call for determination. That question can be briefly stated to be whether an agent, a director, a trustee or other person in an analogous fiduciary position, when a demand is made upon him by the person to whom he stands in the fiduciary relationship to account for profits acquired by him by reason of his fiduciary position, and by reason of the opportunity and the knowledge, or either, resulting from it, is entitled to defeat the claim upon any ground save that he made profits with the knowledge and assent of the other person. The most usual and typical case of this nature is that of principal and agent. The rule in such cases is compendiously expressed to be that an agent must account for net profits secretly (that is, without the knowledge of his principal) acquired by him in the course of his agency. The authorities show how manifold and various are the applications of the rule. It does not depend on fraud or corruption.

The courts below have held that it does not apply in the present case, for the reason that the purchase of the shares by the respondents, though made for their own advantage, and though the knowledge and opportunity which enabled them to take the advantage came to them solely by reason of their being directors of the appellant company, was a purchase which, in the circumstances, the respondents were under no duty to the appellant to make, and was a purchase which it was beyond the appellant's ability to make, so that, if the respondents had not made it, the appellant would have been no better off by reason of the respondents abstaining from reaping the advantage for themselves. With the question so stated, it was said that any other decision than that of the courts below would involve a dog-in-the-manger policy. What the respondents did, it was said, caused no damage to the appellant and involved no neglect of the appellant's interests or similar breach of duty. However, I think the answer to this reasoning is that, both in law and equity, it has been held that, if a person in a fiduciary relationship makes a secret profit out of the relationship, the court will not inquire whether the other person is damnified or has lost a profit which otherwise he would have got. The fact is in itself a fundamental breach of the fiduciary relationship. Nor can the court adequately investigate the matter in most cases. The facts are generally difficult to ascertain or are solely in the knowledge of the person who is being charged. They are matters of surmise; they are hypothetical because the inquiry is as to what would have been the position if that party had not acted as he did, or what he might have done if there had not been the temptation to seek his own advantage, if, in short, interest had not conflicted with duty. Thus, in *Keech v Sandford*, a case in which the fiduciary relationship was that of trustee and *cestui que trust*, the trustee was held liable to assign a lease to the infant *cestui que trust*, though the lessor had refused to renew to the infant. Lord King, LC, said, at 62:

> This may seem hard, that the trustee is the only person of all mankind who might not have the lease. . . .

It did not matter that the infant could not himself have got it and that he was not damaged by the trustee taking it for himself. One reason why the rule is strictly pursued is given by Lord Eldon in *Ex p. James*, at 345:

> . . . no court is equal to the examination and ascertainment of the trust in much the greater number of cases.

In *Parker v McKenna*[3] a most instructive case, the rule is so admirably stated by James LJ, that I cannot resist repeating his language, though my noble and learned friend Lord Russell of Killowen, in his speech just delivered, which I have had the opportunity of reading in print and with which I agree completely, has already quoted it to your Lordships. The words of James LJ, which I emphasise, are [124, 125]:

> . . . that the rule is an inflexible rule and must be applied inexorably by this court which is not entitled, in my judgment, to receive evidence, or suggestion, or argument as to whether the principal did or did not suffer any injury in fact by reason of the dealing of the agent; *for the safety of mankind requires that no agent shall be able to put his principal to the danger of such an inquiry as that.*

The italics are mine. I need not multiply citations to the same effect or illustrations of the different circumstances in which the rule has been applied. . . .

The analysis of the facts in the present case which has been made by Lord Russell of Killowen shows clearly enough that the opportunity and the knowledge which enabled the four respondents to purchase the shares came to them simply in their position as directors of the appellant company. Wrottesley, J, clearly so held. He said at the outset of his judgment:

> There is no doubt they (the respondents) did take up in their own names shares which only after a few days and certainly only after a week or two they were able to sell at a very large profit indeed. There is no doubt that it was only because they were directors and solicitor respectively of the plaintiff company that this stroke of fortune came in their way.

He decided against the appellant company because he fixed his attention on his view that the appellant suffered no loss by the respondents' conduct, instead of fixing attention on the crucial fact that the respondents made a secret profit out of their agency. I do not think that any different view was taken on this aspect of the case by the Court of Appeal, or that it was questioned by that court that the opportunity of making the profits came to the four respondents by reason of their fiduciary position as directors. The Court of Appeal held that, in the absence of any dishonest intention, or negligence, or breach of a specific duty to acquire the shares for the appellant company, the respondents as directors were entitled to buy the shares themselves. Once, it was said, they came to a *bona fide* decision that the appellant company could not provide the money to take up the shares, their obligation to refrain from acquiring those shares for themselves came to an end. With the greatest respect, I feel bound to regard such a conclusion as dead in the teeth of the wise and salutary rule so stringently enforced in the authorities. It is suggested that it would have been mere quixotic folly for the four respondents to let such an occasion pass when the appellant company could not avail itself of it; but Lord King, LC, faced that very position when he accepted that the person in the

---

3 (1874) 10 Ch App 96.

fiduciary position might be the only person in the world who could not avail himself of the opportunity. It is, however, not true that such a person is absolutely barred, because he could by obtaining the assent of the shareholders have secured his freedom to make the profit for himself. Failing that, the only course open is to let the opportunity pass. To admit of any other alternative would be to expose the principal to the dangers against which James LJ, in the passage I have quoted uttered his solemn warning. The rule is stringent and absolute, because 'the safety of mankind' requires it to be absolutely observed in the fiduciary relationship. In my opinion, the appeal should be allowed in the case of the four respondents.

In the case of the other two respondents, I agree with Lord Russell of Killowen that the appeal should be dismissed for the several reasons which he has given in regard to each of them. These appeals turn on issues of evidence and fact, and I do not desire to add to what has fallen from my noble and learned friend.

Lords Macmillan and **Porter** delivered concurring judgments.

- *Boardman v Phipps* [1967] 2 AC 46, House of Lords

The claimant (the respondent) was a beneficiary with a 5/18ths beneficial interest in the Phipps trust. The trust property, *inter alia*, comprised shares in a company (Lester & Harris Ltd). The defendants (the appellants), who were another beneficiary (Tom Phipps) and the solicitor to the trustees (Mr Boardman), sought to improve the value of the shares. Using information acquired while acting as agents for the trustees (the active trustee being a Mr Fox), the defendants embarked on a skilful operation whereby they acquired for themselves the majority of shares in the company. The value of the shares in the company rose sharply so that the defendants' operations were profitable for themselves personally and for the trust holding. The claimant beneficiary nevertheless brought an action claiming a declaration that the defendants held 5/18ths of their shares on constructive trust for him and that they should account to him for 5/18ths of the profit they had personally made. The House of Lords by a three to two majority upheld the decisions of Wilberforce J and the Court of Appeal to the effect that the declaration sought should be granted and that the defendants were personally liable to account as constructive trustees for the profit they had made.

Lord Cohen: .... The respondent became critical of the action of the appellants, and on March 1, 1962, issued the writ in this action claiming (1) that the appellants held 5/18ths of the above-mentioned 21,986 shares as constructive trustees for the respondent and (2) an account of the profits made by the appellants out of the said shares.

He based his claim on an allegation that the information as to the said shares and the opportunity to purchase the same and the shares when purchased were assets of the testator's estate and that the appellants were accountable to him for 5/18ths of the profit made by them in breach of their fiduciary duty. The appellants denied any breach of duty and alleged that the purchase of the shares personally and for their own benefit was made with the knowledge and consent of the plaintiff.

The action was tried by Wilberforce J and on March 25, 1964, he made an order declaring that the appellants held 5/18ths of the 21,986 ordinary shares in the company as constructive trustees for the plaintiff and directed an account of the profits which had come to the hands of the appellants and each of them from the said shares and an inquiry as to what sum is proper to be allowed to the appellants or either of them in respect of their or his work and skill in obtaining the shares and the said profits. From this order the appellants appealed to the Court of Appeal, who dismissed the appeal.

The ratio decidendi of the trial judge is conveniently summed up in the following passage from the judgment in the Court of Appeal of Pearson LJ, where he said:[1]

'... the defendants were acting with the authority of the trustees and were making ample and effective use of their position as representing the trustees and wielding the power of the trustees, who were substantial minority shareholders, to extract from the directors of the company a great deal of information as to the assets and resources of the company; and ... this information enabled the defendants to appreciate the true potential value of the company's shares and to decide that a purchase of the shares held by the director's group at the price offered would be a very promising venture. The defendants made their very large profit, not only by their own skill and persistence and risk-taking, but also by making use of their position as agents for the trustees. The principles stated in *Regal (Hastings) Ltd v Gulliver* are applicable in this case.'

. . .

In the present case had the company been a public company and had the appellants bought the shares on the market, they would not, I think, have been accountable. But the company is a private company and not only the information but the opportunity to purchase these shares came to them through the introduction which Mr Fox gave them to the board of the company and in the second phase when the discussions related to the proposed split-up of the company's undertaking it was solely on behalf of the trustees that Mr Boardman was purporting to negotiate with the board of the company. The question is this: when in the third phase the negotiations turned to the purchase of the shares at £4 10s. a share, were the appellants debarred by their fiduciary position from purchasing on their own behalf the 21,986 shares in the company without the informed consent of the trustees and the beneficiaries?

Wilberforce J and, in the Court of Appeal, both Lord Denning MR and Pearson LJ based their decision in favour of the respondent on the decision of your Lordships' House in *Regal (Hastings) Ltd v Gulliver*. [*He considered the case and continued*:] [Counsel for the appellants] argued that the present case is distinguishable. He puts his argument thus. The question you ask is whether the information could have been used by the principal for the purpose for which it was used by his agents? If the answer to that question is no, the information was not used in the course of their duty as agents. In the present case the information could never have been used by the trustees for the purpose of purchasing shares in the company; therefore purchase of shares was outside the scope of the appellant's agency and they are not accountable.

This is an attractive argument, but it does not seem to me to give due weight to the fact that the appellants obtained both the information which satisfied them that the purchase of the shares would be a good investment and the opportunity of acquiring them as a result of acting for certain purposes on behalf of the trustees. Information is, of course, not property in the strict sense of that word and, ... it does not necessarily follow that because an agent acquired information and opportunity while acting in a fiduciary capacity he is accountable to his principals for any profit that comes his way as the result of the use he makes of that information and opportunity. His liability to account must depend on the facts of the case. In the present case much of the information came the appellants' way when Mr Boardman was acting on behalf of the trustees on the instructions of Mr Fox and the opportunity of bidding for the shares came because he purported for all purposes except for making the bid to be acting on behalf of the owners of the 8,000 shares in the company. In these circumstances it seems to me that the principle of the *Regal* case applies and that the courts below came to the right conclusion.

---

1 [1965] Ch 992, 1022.

That is enough to dispose of the case but I would add that an agent is, in my opinion, liable to account for profits he makes out of trust property if there is a possibility of conflict between his interest and his duty to his principal. ... Mr Boardman would not have been able to give unprejudiced advice if he had been consulted by the trustees and was at the same time negotiating for the purchase of the shares on behalf of himself and Tom Phipps. In other words, there was, in my opinion ... a possibility of conflict between his interest and his duty.

...

I desire to repeat that the integrity of the appellants is not in doubt. They acted with complete honesty throughout and the respondent is a fortunate man in that the rigour of equity enables him to participate in the profits which have accrued as the result of the action taken by the appellants in March, 1959, in purchasing the shares at their own risk. As the last paragraph of his judgment clearly shows, the trial judge evidently shared this view. He directed an inquiry as to what sum is proper to be allowed to the appellants or either of them in respect of his work and skill in obtaining the said shares and the profits in respect thereof. The trial judge concluded by expressing the opinion that payment should be on a liberal scale. With that observation I respectfully agree.

Lord Hodson: ... The proposition of law involved in this case is that no person standing in a fiduciary position, when a demand is made upon him by the person to whom he stands in the fiduciary relationship to account for profits acquired by him by reason of his fiduciary position and by reason of the opportunity and the knowledge, or either, resulting from it, is entitled to defeat the claim upon any ground save that he made profits with the knowledge and assent of the other person.

...

This information was obtained on behalf of the trustees, most of it at a time during the history of the negotiations when the proposition was to divide the assets of the company between two groups of shareholders. This object could not have been effected without a reconstruction of the company and Mr Boardman used the strong minority shareholding which the trusteees held, that is to say, 8,000 shares in the company, wielding his holding as a weapon to enable him to obtain the information of which he subsequently made use.

As to this it is said on behalf of the appellants that information as such is not necessarily property and it is only trust property which is relevant. I agree, but it is nothing to the point to say that in these times corporate trustees, e.g., the Public Trustee and others, necessarily acquire a mass of information in their capacity of trustees for a particular trust and cannot be held liable to account if knowledge so acquired enables them to operate to their own advantage, or to that of other trusts. Each case must depend on its own facts and I dissent from the view that information is of its nature something which is not properly to be described as property. We are aware that what is called 'know-how' in the commercial sense is property which may be very valuable as an asset. I agree with the learned judge and with the Court of Appeal that the confidential information acquired in this case which was capable of being and was turned to account can be properly regarded as the property of the trust. It was obtained by Mr Boardman by reason of the opportunity which he was given as solicitor acting for the trustees in the negotiations with the chairman of the company, as the correspondence demonstrates. The end result was that out of the special position in which they were standing in the course of the negotiations the appellants got the opportunity to make a profit and the knowledge that it was there to be made.

...

Regal (Hastings) Ltd v Gulliver differs from this case mainly in that the directors took up shares and made a profit thereby, it having been originally intended that the company should buy these shares. Here there was no such intention on the part of the trustees. There is no indication that they either had the money or would have been ready to apply to the court for sanction enabling them to do so. On the contrary, Mr Fox, the active trustee and an accountant who concerned himself with the details of the trust property, was not prepared to agree to the trustees buying the shares and encouraged the appellants to make the purchase. This does not affect the position. As *Keech v Sandford* shows, the inability of the trust to purchase makes no difference to the liability of the appellants, if liability otherwise exists. The distinction on the facts as to intention to purchase shares between this case and *Regal (Hastings) Ltd v Gulliver* is not relevant. The company (Regal) had not the money to apply for the shares upon which the profit was made. The directors took the opportunity which they had presented to them to buy the shares with their own money and were held accountable. Mr Fox's refusal as one of the trustees to take any part in the matter on behalf of the trust, so far as he was concerned, can make no difference. Nothing short of fully informed consent which the learned judge found not to have been obtained could enable the appellants in the position which they occupied having taken the opportunity provided by that position to make a profit for themselves.

The confidential information which the appellants obtained at a time when Mr Boardman was admittedly holding himself out as solicitor for the trustees was obtained by him as representing the trustees, the holders of 8,000 shares of Lester & Harris. As Russell LJ put it:[2]

> 'The substantial trust shareholding was an asset of which one aspect was its potential use as a means of acquiring knowledge of the company's affairs, or of negotiating allocations of the company's assets, or of inducing other shareholders to part with their shares.'

Whether this aspect is properly to be regarded as part of the trust assets is, in my judgment immaterial. The appellants obtained knowledge by reason of their fiduciary position and they cannot escape liability by saying that they were acting for themselves and not as agents of the trustees. Whether or not the trust or the beneficiaries in their stead could have taken advantage of the information is immaterial, as the authorities clearly show. No doubt it was but a remote possibility that Mr Boardman would ever be asked by the trustees to advise on the desirability of an application to the court in order that the trustees might avail themselves of the information obtained. Nevertheless, even if the possibility of conflict is present between personal interest and the fiduciary position the rule of equity must be applied. . . .

I agree with the decision of the learned judge and with that of the Court of Appeal which, in my opinion, involves a finding that there was a potential conflict between Boardman's position as solicitor to the trustees and his own interest in applying for the shares. He was in a fiduciary position vis-à-vis the trustees and through them vis-à-vis the beneficiaries. For these reasons in my opinion the appeal should be dismissed; but I should add that I am in agreement with the learned judge that payment should be allowed on a liberal scale in respect of the work and skill employed in obtaining the shares and the profits therefrom.

Lord Guest: . . . I take the view that from first to last Boardman was acting in a fiduciary capacity to the trustees. . . . In saying this I do not for one moment suggest that there was anything dishonest or underhand in what Boardman did. He has obtained a clean certificate below and I do not wish to sully it. But the law has a strict regard for principle in ensuring that a person in a fiduciary capacity is not allowed to benefit from any transactions into which he has entered with trust property. If Boardman was acting on behalf of the trust, then all the information he obtained . . . became trust property. The weapon which he used to obtain this information was the trust holding. And I see no reason why information and knowledge cannot be trust property. . . .

Applying [the] principles [of *Regal (Hastings) Ltd v Gulliver*] to the present case I have no hesitation in coming to the conclusion that the appellants hold the Lester & Harris shares as constructive trustees and are bound to account to the respondent. It is irrelevant that the trustees themselves

---

2 [1965] Ch 992, 1031.

could not have profited by the transaction. . . . In the present case the knowledge and information obtained by Boardman was obtained in the course of the fiduciary position in which he had placed himself. The only defence available to a person in such a fiduciary position is that he made the profits with the knowledge and assent of the trustees. It is not contended that the trustees had such knowledge or gave such consent.

. . . Boardman and Tom Phipps . . . placed themselves in a special position which was of a fiduciary character in relation to the negotiations with the directors of Lester & Harris relating to the trust shares. Out of such special position and in the course of such negotiations they obtained the opportunity to make a profit out of the shares and knowledge that the profit was there to be made. A profit was made and they are accountable accordingly.

Viscount Dilhorne (dissenting): . . . In my opinion, . . . the unanimous opinion of the Court of Appeal and of Wilberforce J that the [appellants'] relationship to the trust was fiduciary is correct. In my opinion that relationship arose from their being employed as agents of the trust on the occasions I have mentioned and continued throughout.

It does not, however, necessarily follow that they are liable to account for the profit they made. If they had entered into engagements in which they had or could have had a personal interest conflicting with the interests of those they were bound to protect, clearly they would be liable to do so. On the facts of this case there was not, in my opinion, any conflict or possibility of a conflict between the personal interests of the appellants and those of the trust. There was no possibility so long as Mr Fox was opposed to the trust buying any of the shares of any conflict of interest arising through the purchase of the shares by the appellants.

. . . .

I do not think that my conclusion involves any departure from the principles so often and firmly laid down as to the liability of agents to account if there has been a conflict or possibility of conflict between their interests and duties, and in breach of their fiduciary duty they have made profits out of their agency without the knowledge and consent of their principals. In this case, as Lord Macmillan said in the *Regal* case, the result depends on issues of fact. Liability to account must depend on there being some breach of duty, some impropriety of conduct on the part of those in a fiduciary position. On the facts of this case I do not consider that there was any breach of duty or impropriety of conduct on the part of the appellants.

Lord Upjohn (dissenting): . . . The relevant rule for the decision of this case is the fundamental rule of equity that a person in a fiduciary capacity must not make a profit out of this trust which is part of the wider rule that a trustee must not place himself in a position where his duty and his interest may conflict. . . . It is perhaps stated most highly against trustees or directors in the celebrated speech of Lord Cranworth LC in *Aberdeen Railway v Blaikie*,[3] where he said:

'And it is a rule of universal application, that no one, having such duties to discharge, shall be allowed to enter into engagements in which he has, or can have, a personal interest conflicting, or which possibly may conflict, with the interests of those whom he is bound to protect.'

The phrase 'possibly may conflict' requires consideration. In my view it means that the reasonable man looking at the relevant facts and circumstances of the particular case would think that there was a real sensible possibility of conflict; not that you could imagine some situation arising which might, in some conceivable possibility in events not contemplated as real sensible possibilities by any reasonable person, result in a conflict.

. . .

3 1 Macq 461, 471.

The trustees were not willing to buy more shares in the company. The active trustees were very willing that the appellants should do so themselves for the benefit of their large minority holding. The trustees, so to speak, lent their name to the appellants in the course of prolonged and difficult negotiations and, of course, the appellants thereby learnt much which would have otherwise been denied to them. The negotiations were in the end brilliantly successful.

And how successful Tom [Phipps] was in his reorganisation of the company is apparent to all. They ought to be very grateful.

In the long run the appellants have bought for themselves at entirely their own risk with their own money shares which the trustees never contemplated buying and they did so in circumstances fully known and approved of by the trustees.

To extend the doctrines of equity to make the appellants accountable in such circumstances is, in my judgment, to make unreasonable and unequitable applications of such doctrines.

NOTES AND QUESTIONS

1. The remedies granted were (i) a declaration that 5/18ths of the shares were held by the defendants on constructive trust for the claimant; (ii) an account of the profits made by the defendants from the shares (that is, on the assumption that the shares would be transferred to the claimant, the capital distributions from the shares that had been paid); subject to (iii) a generous allowance for the work and skill involved in obtaining the shares and the profits therefrom. As regards (iii), cf. *Guinness plc v Saunders*, below, 835.

2. Which of these statements most accurately describes the ratio of *Boardman v Phipps*?

   (i) The defendants were held liable because they had used confidential information belonging to the trust for their own benefit without the beneficiaries' consent.
   (ii) The defendants had made gains out of their position as fiduciaries without the beneficiaries' consent.
   (iii) The defendants had made gains in a situation where there might possibly have been a conflict between their own interests and their fiduciary duty.

3. For criticism of *Regal Hastings Ltd v Gulliver* and *Boardman v Phipps*, as imposing too strict a duty, see Gareth Jones, 'Unjust Enrichment and the Fiduciary's Duty of Loyalty' (1968) 84 LQR 472. See also obiter dicta of the Court of Appeal in *Murad v Al-Saraj* (below).

4. There are many other decisions in which an account of profits, has been ordered, or a declaration that a constructive trust exists has been granted, in respect of unauthorized profits made in breach of fiduciary duty. See, for example, *Parker v McKenna* (1874) LR 10 Ch App 96; *English v Dedham Vale Properties Ltd* [1978] 1 WLR 93; *Chan v Zacharia* (1984) 154 CLR 178; *Warman v Dwyer* (1995) 128 ALR 201.

• Murad v Al-Saraj [2005] EWCA Civ 959, Court of Appeal

Mr Al-Saraj and the Murad sisters entered into a joint venture to purchase a hotel. They agreed that they would split the profits (including from any subsequent resale of the hotel) between them. The hotel was purchased but then the Murads discovered that Al-Saraj had deceived them because he had come to a deal with the vendor of the hotel whereby his supposed contribution of £500,000 cash to the purchase was largely illusory (comprising, e.g., a bribe to Al Saraj and the discharge of debts the vendor owed him). It was clear that there had been a breach of fiduciary duty constituted by Al-Saraj's non-disclosure to the Murads of the true nature of his contribution. In the Murads' claim for an account of profits for that breach of fiduciary duty, the trial judge found that, even if there had been full disclosure, the Murads would have continued with the transaction albeit with an altered profit-sharing ratio. This was the basis for Al-Saraj's argument that he should not be stripped of all his profits in the venture. The majority (Arden and Jonathan Parker LJJ) rejected that argument in relation to the facts of this case where the fiduciary was acting in bad faith. Clarke LJ dissented and would have reduced the profits for which Al-Saraj was accountable.

Arden LJ: . . .

76. For policy reasons, the courts decline to investigate hypothetical situations as to what would have happened if the fiduciary had performed his duty. In *Regal* case at page 154G, Lord Wright made the following point, to which I shall have to return below:

'Nor can the court adequately investigate the matter in most cases. The facts are generally difficult to ascertain or are solely in the knowledge of the person being charged. They are matters of surmise; they are hypothetical because the inquiry is as to what would have been the position if that party had not acted as he did, or what he might have done if there had not been the temptation to seek his own advantage, if, in short, interest had not conflicted with duty.'

77. Again, for the policy reasons, on the taking of an account, the court lays the burden on the defaulting fiduciary to show that the profit is not one for which he should account: see, for example, *Manley v Sartori* [1927] Ch 157. This shifting of the onus of proof is consistent with the deterrent nature of the fiduciary's liability. The liability of the fiduciary becomes the default rule.

78. This principle was applied by the High Court of Australia in the *Warman* case:

'It is for the defendant to establish that it is inequitable to order an account of the entire profits. If the defendant does not establish that that would be so, then the defendant must bear the consequences of mingling the profits attributable to those earned by the defendant's efforts and investment, in the same way that a trustee of a mixed fund bears the onus of distinguishing what is his own.'

79. In the *Warman* case, the defaulting fiduciary was able to show that some of the profit was not attributable to his wrongful act, but to his own skill and effort. The Court limited the account accordingly. On the facts, the court was satisfied that the period of time for which profits were to be accounted should be limited to two years. I will come back to this point below.

. . .

82. . . . Under the rule of equity applied in [the *Regal Hastings* case] . . . cases can be found where the fiduciary or trustee acted in all good faith believing that he was acting in the interests of his beneficiary but yet has been made to account for the profits obtained as a result of the breach of trust without limitation. Now, in a case like the *Regal* case, if the rule of equity under which the defendants were held liable to account for secret profits were not inflexible, the crucial issue of fact would be: what the company would have done if the opportunity to subscribe for shares in its subsidiary had been offered to it? In the passage just cited, as I have said, Lord Wright makes the point that it is very difficult to investigate that issue. However, while that may have been so in the past in the days of Lord Eldon and Lord King, that would not be the case today. The court has very extensive powers under the Civil Procedure Rules for instance to require information to be given as to a party's case. If the witness cannot attend the hearing, it may be possible for his evidence to be given by way of a witness statement or it may be possible for him to give evidence by video-link. The reasons for the rule of equity are many and complex (for a recent discussion, see Conaglen, 'The Nature and Function of Fiduciary Loyalty' [2005] LQR 452). There have been calls for its re-examination (see, for example, the articles cited at [2005] LQR 452, 478 at footnote 151). It may be that the time has come when the court should revisit the operation of the inflexible rule of equity in harsh circumstances, as where the trustee has acted in perfect good faith and without any deception or concealment, and in the belief that he was acting in the best interests of the beneficiary. I need only say this: it would not be in the least impossible for a court in a future case, to determine as a question of fact whether the

beneficiary would not have wanted to exploit the profit himself, or would have wanted the trustee to have acted other than in the way that the trustee in fact did act. Moreover, it would not be impossible for a modern court to conclude as a matter of policy that, without losing the deterrent effect of the rule, the harshness of it should be tempered in some circumstances. In addition, in such cases, the courts can provide a significant measure of protection for the beneficiaries by imposing on the defaulting trustee the affirmative burden of showing that those circumstances prevailed . . .

83. In short, it may be appropriate for a higher court one day to revisit the rule on secret profits and to make it less inflexible in appropriate circumstances, where the unqualified operation of the rule operates particularly harshly and where the result is not compatible with the desire of modern courts to ensure that remedies are proportionate to the justice of the case where this does not conflict with some other overriding policy objective of the rule in question.

84. However that is not this case. Mr Al-Saraj was found to have made a fraudulent misrepresentation to the Murads who had placed their trust in him. I do not consider that, even if we were free to revisit the *Regal* case, this would be an appropriate case in which to do so. The appropriate remedy is that he should disgorge all the profits, whether of a revenue or capital nature, that he made from inducing the Murads by his fraudulent representations from entering into the Parkside Hotel venture, subject to any allowances permitted by the court on the taking of the account.

85. The imposition of liability to account for secret profits and the placing of the burden of proof on the defaulting trustee are not, however, quite the end of the matter. The kind of account ordered in this case is an account of profits, that is a procedure to ensure the restitution of profits which ought to have been made for the beneficiary and not a procedure for the forfeiture of profits to which the defaulting trustee was always entitled for his own account. . . . Even when the fiduciary is not fraudulent, the profit obtained from the breach of trust has to be defined. It may indeed be derivative, as where a trustee misappropriates trust property and then sells it and make a profit out of something else. But equity does not take the view that simply because a profit was made as part of the same transaction the fiduciary must account for it. . . .

86. In the present case, any recognisable contribution made by Mr. Al-Saraj was to the business of the joint venture. As the *Warman* case shows, there can be particular difficulty applying the above principles where the trustee mixes trust property with his own business. The profit which belongs to the trust has to be disentangled from that which belongs to the defaulting trustee because it is a profit of his business. I have explained above how these difficulties were resolved in the *Warman* case by limiting the account to two years' profits. The problem in the *Warman* case has also faced courts within our own jurisdiction.

[*After referring to* Vyse v Foster *(1872) 9 Ch App 309, Arden LJ continued:*]

87. Does this line of authority help Mr Al-Saraj in this case? I think not. The hypothetical share, which the Murads would have given him if he had disclosed the set off arrangement, is not relevant to this argument because it was never actually agreed or put up as his contribution. Mr Al-Saraj under this approach would have to say that the £500,000 which he actually put up by way of set off should be treated as his investment in the joint venture. But that was the very sum that he lied to the Murads about. It was not a cash sum as they had been led to believe and accordingly I do not consider that he can say that he is entitled to an order which treats the £500,000 as his contribution to the profits made by the venture.

88. It would, however, be open to Mr Al-Saraj to apply to the court for an allowance for his services and disbursements, as indeed he did. The order of 12 July 2004 makes an allowance for his remuneration for managing the hotel. It is well established that, on the taking of an account, the court may make an allowance for the skill and efforts of the defaulting trustee: see, for example, *Re Jarvis, dec'd* [1958] 1 WLR 815, *Boardman v Phipps* [1967] 2 AC 46. This is common ground. The grant of an allowance is discretionary . . .

Jonathan Parker LJ: . . .

121. [T]here can be little doubt that the inflexibility of the 'no conflict' rule may, depending on the facts of any given case, work harshly so far as the fiduciary is concerned. It may be said with force that that is the inevitable and intended consequence of the deterrent nature of the rule. On the other hand, it may be said that commercial conduct which in 1874 was thought to imperil the safety of mankind may not necessarily be regarded nowadays with the same depth of concern. So, like Arden LJ (see paragraph 82 above), I can envisage the possibility that at some time in the future the House of Lords may consider that the time has come to relax the severity of the 'no conflict' rule to some extent in appropriate cases.

122. In my judgment, however, that day has not yet arrived. Nor, in any event, would I regard the instant case as being an appropriate case for any such relaxation. In the instant case, after all, Mr Al-Saraj acted in bad faith. It follows, in my judgment, that in contrast to cases such as *Regal* and *Boardman v Phipps*, where the fiduciaries acted out of the best of motives, the instant case would not be a candidate for any relaxation of the 'no conflict' rule. As I see it, only the complete abolition of the rule could assist Mr Al-Saraj, and that must be out of the question.

Clarke LJ (dissenting):

124. With one important exception, I agree with the conclusions reached by Arden LJ. That exception relates to the principles applicable to the taking of an account in a case of this kind. I have reached the conclusion that the principles applicable to the correct approach to the amount of the profits in respect of which an account should be ordered are more flexible than Arden LJ suggests.

. . .

141. . . . [I]f the matter were free from authority I would hold that a person who makes a profit in the course of a fiduciary relationship must account for the profits he makes, that prima facie he must account for all the profits but that it should be open to him to show that it was always intended that he would make a profit from the transaction and to persuade the court if he can that, in the exercise of its equitable jurisdiction to order an account, in the circumstances of the particular case, he should not be ordered to account for the whole of the profits. Thus I would hold that, while the question what the claimant would have done if told the true facts, is irrelevant to the question whether the fiduciary should be ordered to account, it is or may be relevant to the extent of the account.

. . .

158. . . . Arden LJ expresses the view that it may be that the time has come when the court should revisit the inflexible rule of equity in what she describes as harsh circumstances. I agree. . . .

159. Moreover, I do not think that the court is prevented from applying [the principles identified in the *Warman* case] on the facts of this case. I recognise that the judge has made findings of fraud against Mr Al-Saraj and that his fraud is a very important factor in deciding whether Mr Al-Saraj has discharged the burden of showing that it would be inequitable to order him to account for all the profits. Nevertheless, while of great importance, the finding of fraud does not seem to me to be conclusive. In the end the question for the judge should be whether the court is persuaded by Mr Al-Saraj that it would be inequitable to order an account of all the profits having regard to all the circumstances of the case.

160. Here there was an antecedent arrangement for profit sharing. But for the fraudulent breach of fiduciary duty, the profit sharing agreement would have been different but there would still have been a profit sharing agreement and the court might hold that, given the resources provided by Mr Al-Saraj, it would be inequitable not to allow him some share of the profits and not merely to make an allowance for his skill, expertise and expenditure, albeit that the amount of any such share must take full account of his fraudulent breach of duty.

161. I do not think that the authorities, taken as a whole, lead to the conclusion that it is not open to the court to adopt that approach. As stated above, the approach is in my opinion consistent with

that in *Warman*, which is not to my mind inconsistent with the English cases, none of which addresses the scope of the permissible account of profits on the facts of a case of this kind.

162. In all these circumstances I have reached a different conclusion from Arden LJ. I would hold that the finding that the Murads would have entered into this joint venture in any event is relevant to the scope of the account which should be ordered. The judge did not so hold because he regarded the finding as irrelevant because of equity's inflexible rule. In these circumstances, subject to hearing submissions as to the precise scope of the remission, I would remit the matter to the judge in order to give Mr Al-Saraj the opportunity to seek to persuade him that it would be inequitable to order him to account for all the profits of the joint venture, subject only to his expenses and skill. I would therefore allow the appeal to that extent.

. . .

NOTES AND QUESTIONS

1. Did Arden LJ accept the need for a causal link between the breach of fiduciary duty and the profits for which the fiduciary is accountable? If so, what test for that causal link did she apply? How did she distinguish the *Warman* case?
2. For a helpful note on this case, see M McInnes, 'Account of Profits for Breach of Fiduciary Duty' (2006) 122 *LQR* 11.

(2) BRIBES

- *Reading v Attorney-General* [1951] AC 507, House of Lords

The claimant was a sergeant in the British Army serving in Egypt. In return for bribes totalling £20,000, he sat on several occasions in his military uniform on lorries illegally transporting alcohol, thereby avoiding their inspection by the police. Ultimately he was found out and court-martialled. The Crown seized the bribe money. The claimant brought this action to recover it. In the Court of Appeal it was held that the Crown was entitled to it either as money had and received or because the claimant was accountable as a fiduciary. The House of Lords dismissed the claimant's appeal.

Lord Porter (with whom **Viscount Jowitt LC** concurred): . . . Denning, J, held that the Crown was entitled to the money in question. It was, in his view, immaterial to consider whether the method of seizure was justified or not. Even if it was not, the Crown had a valid counterclaim and, avoiding a circuity of action, could thus defeat the appellant's claim. 'The claim here is', he says,[1] 'for restitution of moneys which, in justice, ought to be paid over.' It was suggested in argument that the learned judge founded his decision solely upon the doctrine of unjust enrichment and that that doctrine was not recognized by the law of England. My Lords, the exact status of the law of unjust enrichment is not yet assured. It holds a predominant place in the law of Scotland and, I think, of the United States, but I am content for the purposes of this case to accept the view that it forms no part of the law of England and that a right to restitution so described would be too widely stated.

But, indeed, this doctrine is not of the essence of Denning, J's my judgment. His reasoning is to be found in the passage which succeds that quoted. He says: 'In my judgment, it is a principle of law that if a servant, in violation of his duty of honesty and good faith, takes advantage of his service to make a profit for himself, in this sense, that the assets of which he has control, or the facilities which he enjoys, or the position which he occupies, are the real cause of his obtaining the money, as distinct

---

1 [1948] 2 KB 268, 275.

from being the mere opportunity for getting it, that is to say, if they play the predominant part in his obtaining the money, then he is accountable for it to the master. It matters not that the master has not lost any profit, nor suffered any damage. Nor does it matter that the master could not have done the act himself. It is a case where the servant has unjustly enriched himself by virtue of his service without his master's sanction. It is money which the servant ought not to be allowed to keep, and the law says it shall be taken from him and given to his master, because he got it solely by reason of the position which he occupied as a servant of his master'. And again:[2] 'The uniform of the Crown, and the position of the man as a servant of the Crown were the sole reasons why he was able to get this money, and that is sufficient to make him liable to hand it over to the Crown'. The learned judge, however, also says: 'This man Reading was not acting in the course of his employment: and there was no fiduciary relationship in respect of these long journeys nor, indeed, in respect of his uniform'. If this means, as I think it does, that the appellant was neither a trustee nor in possession of some profit-earning chattel, and that it was contrary to his duty to escort unwarranted traffic or possibly any traffic through the streets of Cairo, it is true, but, in my view, irrelevant. He nevertheless was using his position as a sergeant in His Majesty's Army and the uniform to which his rank entitled him to obtain the money which he received. In my opinion any official position, whether marked by a uniform or not, which enables the holder to earn money by its use gives his master a right to receive the money so earned even though it was earned by a criminal act. 'You have earned', the master can say, 'money by the use of your position as my servant. It is not for you, who have gained this advantage, to set up your own wrong as a defence to my claim'.

Asquith LJ, in the Court of Appeal, points out[3] that there is a well-established class of cases in which a master can recover whether or not he has suffered any detriment in fact, e.g., those in which a servant or agent has realized a secret profit, commission or bribe in the course of his employment, and that the sum recoverable is the amount of such profit. . . .

But it is said that this right to recover is subject to two qualifications: (1.) the sum obtained must have been obtained in the course of the servant's employment, and (2.) there must exist in the matter in question a fiduciary relationship between employer and employee.

It is often convenient to speak of money obtained as received in the course of the servant's employment, but strictly speaking I do not think that expression accurately describes the position where a servant receives money by reason of his employment but in dereliction of his duty. . . .

As to the assertion that there must be a fiduciary relationship, the existence of such a connexion is, in my opinion, not an additional necessity in order to substantiate the claim; but another ground for succeeding where a claim for money had and received would fail. In any case, I agree with Asquith LJ,[4] in thinking that the words 'fiduciary relationship' in this setting are used in a wide and loose sense and include, inter alia, a case where the servant gains from his employment a position of authority which enables him to obtain the sum which he receives.

My Lords, the fact that the Crown in this case, or that any master, has lost no profits or suffered no damage is, of course, immaterial and the principle so well known that it is unnecessary to cite the cases illustrating and supporting it. It is the receipt and possession of the money that matters, not the loss or prejudice to the master. . . .

Lord Normand: My Lords, I agree with the Court of Appeal with the single reservation that I have not found it necessary to consider whether the Crown would have been entitled to succeed in an action at law for money had and received. On that question I would have desired to hear further argument had it been necessary to decide it.

Though the relation of a member of His Majesty's forces to the Crown is not accurately described as that of a servant under a contract of service or as that of an agent under a contract of agency, the

---

2 *Ibid.* 276.   3 [1949] 2 KB 232, 236.   4 [1949] 2 KB 232, 236.

Court of Appeal has held that he owes to the Crown a duty as fully fiduciary as the duty of a servant to his master or of an agent to his principal, and in consequence that all profits and advantages gained by the use or abuse of his military status are to be for the benefit of the Crown. I respectfully think that these are unassailable propositions, and further that the appellant cannot be allowed to propone as a defence to the Crown's claim his own criminal conduct either in accepting a bribe in breach of military discipline or in participating in an offence against the municipal law of Egypt.

Lords Oaksey and **Radcliffe** agreed that the plaintiff was liable in an action for money had and received and to account as a fiduciary.

NOTES AND QUESTIONS

1. With the exception of Lord Normand, their Lordships did not consider it necessary to hold that Reading was acting in breach of fiduciary duty. What then was the wrong which was in question?

2. What do you understand Lord Porter to have meant when he rejected the view that Denning J's decision was based on the doctrine of unjust enrichment?

- *Attorney-General for Hong Kong v Reid* [1994] 1 AC 324, Privy Council

Mr Reid, a Crown Prosecutor and ultimately acting Director of Public Prosecution in Hong Kong, had accepted bribes so as to obstruct the prosecution of certain criminals. He was convicted of offences under the Prevention of Bribery Ordinance and imprisoned. He was also made subject to a confiscation order to pay the Crown $HK12.4M, being the value of his assets that could only have been derived from the bribes. None of that sum was paid. In the present action the Hong Kong Government sought to establish that three properties in New Zealand, bought by Mr Reid using the bribes, were held on constructive trust for it so that its registration of caveats on the title of the three properties was valid. That claim was successful before the Privy Council who allowed the Government's appeal from the Court of Appeal of New Zealand.

Lord Templeman: . . . A bribe is a gift accepted by a fiduciary as an inducement to him to betray his trust. A secret benefit, which may or may not constitute a bribe, is a benefit which the fiduciary derives from trust property or obtains from knowledge which he acquires in the course of acting as a fiduciary. A fiduciary is not always accountable for a secret benefit but he is undoubtedly accountable for a secret benefit which consists of a bribe. In addition a person who provides the bribe and the fiduciary who accepts the bribe may each be guilty of a criminal offence. In the present case the first respondent was clearly guilty of a criminal offence.

Bribery is an evil practice which threatens the foundations of any civilised society. In particular bribery of policeman and prosecutors bring the administration of justice into disrepute. Where bribes are accepted by a trustee, servant, agent or other fiduciary, loss and damage are caused to the beneficiaries, master or principal whose interests have been betrayed. The amount of loss or damage resulting from the acceptance of a bribe may or may not be quantifiable. In the present case the amount of harm caused to the administration of justice in Hong Kong by the first respondent in return for bribes cannot be quantified.

When a bribe is offered and accepted in money or in kind, the money or property constituting the bribe belongs in law to the recipient. Money paid to the false fiduciary belongs to him. The legal estate in freehold property conveyed to the false fiduciary by way of bribe vests in him. Equity, however, which acts in personam, insists that it is unconscionable for a ficuciary to obtain and retain a benefit in breach of duty. The provider of a bribe cannot recover it because he committed a criminal offence when he paid the bribe. The false fiduciary who received the bribe in breach of duty must pay and account for the bribe to the person to whom that duty was owed. In the present case, as soon as

[Mr Reid] received a bribe in breach of the duties he owed to the Government of Hong Kong, he became a debtor in equity to the Crown for the amount of that bribe. So much is admitted. But if the bribe consists of property which increases in value or if a cash bribe is invested advantageously, the false fiduciary will receive a benefit from his breach of duty unless he is accountable not only for the original amount or value of the bribe but also for the increased value of the property representing the bribe. As soon as the bribe was received it should have been paid or transferred instanter to the person who suffered from the breach of duty. Equity considers as done that which ought to have been done. As soon as the bribe was received, whether in cash or in kind, the false fiduciary held the bribe on a constructive trust for the person injured. Two objections have been raised to this analysis. First it is said that if the fiduciary is in equity a debtor to the person injured, he cannot also be a trustee of the bribe. But there is no reason why equity should not provide two remedies, so long as they do not result in double recovery. If the property representing the bribe exceeds the original bribe in value, the fiduciary cannot retain the benefit of the increase in value which he obtained solely as a result of his breach of duty. Secondly, it is said that if the false fiduciary holds property representing the bribe in trust for the person injured, and if the false fiduciary is or becomes insolvent, the unsecured creditors of the false fiduciary will be deprived of their right to share in the proceeds of that property. But the unsecured creditors cannot be in a better position than their debtor. The authorities show that property acquired by a trustee innocently but in breach of trust and the property from time to time representing the same belong in equity to the cestui que trust and not to the trustee personally whether he is solvent or insolvent. Property acquired by a trustee as a result of a criminal breach of trust and the property from time to time representing the same must also belong in equity to his cestui que trust and not to the trustee whether he is solvent or insolvent.

When a bribe is accepted by a fiduciary in breach of his duty then he holds that bribe in trust for the person to whom the duty was owed. If the property representing the bribe decreases in value the fiduciary must pay the difference between that value and the initial amount of the bribe because he should not have accepted the bribe or incurred the risk of loss. If the property increases in value, the fiduciary is not entitled to any surplus in excess of the initial value of the bribe because he is not allowed by any means to make a profit out of a breach of duty.

The courts of New Zealand were constrained by a number of precedents of the New Zealand, English and other common law courts which established a settled principle of law inconsistent with the foregoing analysis. That settled principle is open to review by the Board in the light of the foregoing analysis of the consequences in equity of the receipt of a bribe by a fiduciary. In *Keech v Sandford* (1726) Sel.Cas.Ch. 61 a landlord refused to renew a lease to a trustee for the benefit of an infant. The trustee then took a new lease for his own benefit. The new lease had not formed part of the original trust property, the infant could not have acquired the new lease from the landlord and the trustee acted innocently, believing that he committed no breach of trust and that the new lease did not belong in equity to his cestui que trust. Lord King LC held nevertheless, at 62, that 'the trustee is the only person of all mankind who might not have the lease;' the trustee was obliged to assign the new lease to the infant and account for the profits he had received. The rule must be that property which a trustee obtains by use of knowledge acquired as trustee becomes trust property. The rule must, a fortiori, apply to a bribe accepted by a trustee for a guilty criminal purpose which injures the cestui que trust. The trustee is only one example of a fiduciary and the same rule applies to all other fiduciaries who accept bribes. . . .

[*After considering a number of less well-known cases Lord Templeman continued:*] *Metropolitan Bank v Heiron* (1880) 5 Ex.D 319 was a decision of a distinguished Court of Appeal heard and determined on one day, 5 August 1880, perilously close to the long vacation without citation of any of the relevant authorities. An allegation of the receipt of a bribe by a director was considered in 1872 by the board of directors of the company and they decided to take no action. In 1879 the company sued to recover the bribe of £250 and it was held that the action was barred by the Statute of Limitations (3 & 4 Will. 4, c. 27). James LJ said, at 323:

'The ground of this suit is concealed fraud. If a man receives money by way of a bribe for misconduct against a company or cestui que trust, or any person or body towards whom he stands in a fiduciary position, he is liable to have that money taken from him by his principal or cestui que trust. But it must be borne in mind that the liability is a debt differing from ordinary debts in the fact that it is merely equitable, and in dealing with equitable, and in dealing with equitable debts of such a nature Courts of Equity have always followed by analogy the provisions of the Statute of Limitations, in cases in which there is the same reason for making the length of time a bar as in the case of ordinary legal demands.'

This judgment denies that any proprietary interest exists in the bribe. Brett LJ said, at 324:

'It seems to me that the only action which could be maintained by the company or by the liquidator of the company against this defendant would be an action in equity founded upon the alleged fraud of the defendant. Neither at law nor in equity could this sum of £250 be treated as the money of the company, until the court, in an action by the company, had decreed it to belong to them on the ground that it had been received fraudulently as against them by the defendant.'

This is a puzzling passage which appears to mean that a proprietary interest in the bribe arises as soon as a court has found that a bribe has been accepted. Cotton LJ said, at 325:

'Here the money sought to be recovered was in no sense the money of the company, unless it was made so by a decree founded on the act by which the trustee got the money into his hands. It is a suit founded on breach of duty or fraud by a person who was in the position of trustee, his position making the receipt of the money a breach of duty or fraud. It is very different from the case of a cestui que trust seeking to recover money which was his own before any act wrongfully done by the trustee.'

This observation does draw a distinction between moneys which are held on trust and are taken out by the trustee and moneys which are not held on trust but which the trustee receives in circumstances which oblige him to pay the money into the trust. The distinction appears to be inconsistent with *Keech v Sandford* and with those authorities which make the recipient of the bribe liable for any increase in value. The decision in *Metropolitan Bank v Heiron* is understandable given the finding that the fraud was made known to the company more than six years before the action was instituted. But the same result could have been achieved by denying an equitable remedy on the grounds of delay or ratification.

It has always been assumed and asserted that the law on the subject of bribes was definitively settled by the decision of the Court of Appeal in *Lister & Co. v Stubbs* (1890) 45 ChD 1.

In that case the plaintiffs, Lister & Co., employed the defendant, Stubbs, as their servant to purchase goods for the firm. Stubbs, on behalf of the firm, bought goods from Varley & Co. and received from Varley & Co. bribes amounting to £5,541. The bribes were invested by Stubbs in freehold properties and investments. His masters, the from Lister & Co., sought and failed to obtain an interlocutory injunction restraining Stubbs from disposing of these assets pending the trial of the action in which they sought, inter alia, £5,541 and damages. In the Court of Appeal the first judgment was given by Cotton LJ who had been party to the decision in *Metropolitan Bank v Heiron*. He was powerfully supported by the judgment of Lindley LJ and by the equally powerful concurrence of Bowen LJ. Cotton LJ said, at 12, that the bribe could not be said to be the money of the plaintiffs. He seemed to be reluctant to grant an interlocutory judgment which would provide security for a debt before that debt had been established. Lindley LJ said, at 15, that the relationship between the plaintiffs, Lister &

Co., as masters and the defendant, Stubbs, as servant who had betrayed his trust and received a bribe:

'is that of debtor and creditor; it is not that of trustee and cestui que trust. We are asked to hold that it is—which would involve consequences which, I confess, startle me. One consequence, of course, would be that, if Stubbs were to become bankrupt, this property acquired by him with the money paid to him by Messrs. Varley would be withdrawn from the mass of his creditors and be handed over bodily to Lister & Co. Can that be right? Another consequence would be that, if the appellants are right, Lister & Co. could compel Stubbs to account to them, not only for the money with interest, but for all the profits which he might have made by embarking in trade with it. Can that be right?'

For the reasons which have already been advanced their Lordships would respectfully answer both these questions in the affirmative. If a trustee mistakenly invests moneys which he ought to pay over to his cestui que trust and then becomes bankrupt, the moneys together with any profit which has accrued from the investment are withdrawn from the unsecured creditors as soon as the mistake is discovered. A fortiori if a trustee commits a crime by accepting a bribe which he ought to pay over to his cestui que trust, the bribe and any profit made therefrom should be withdrawn from the unsecured creditors as soon as the crime is discovered.

The decision in *Lister & Co. v Stubbs* is not consistent with the principles that a fiduciary must not be allowed to benefit from his own breach of duty, that the fuduciary should account for the bribe as soon as he receives it and that equity regards as done that which ought to be done. From these principles it would appear to follow that the bribe and the property from time to time representing the bribe are held on a constructive trust for the person injured. A fiduciary remains personally liable for the amount of the bribe if, in the event, the value of the property then recovered by the injured person proved to be less than that amount.

The decisions of the Court of Appeal in *Metropolitan Bank v Heiron* and *Lister & Co. v Stubbs* are inconsistent with earlier authorities which were not cited. Although over 100 years has passed since *Lister & Co. v Stubbs*, no one can be allowed to say that he has ordered his affairs in reliance on the two decisions of the Court of Appeal now in question. Thus no harm can result if those decisions are not followed.

. . . .

The authorities which followed *Lister & Co. v Stubbs* do not cast any new light on that decision. Their Lordships are more impressed with the decision of Lai Kew Chai J in *Sumitomo Bank Ltd v Kartika Ratna Thahir* [1993] 1 SLR 735. In that case General Thahir who was at one time general assistant to the president director of the Indonesian state enterprise named Pertamina opened 17 bank accounts in Singapore and deposited DM.54m. in those accounts. The money was said to be bribes paid by two German contractors tendering for the construction of steel works in West Java. General Thahir having died, the moneys were claimed by his widow, by the estate of the deceased general and by Pertamina. After considering in detail all the relevant authorities Lai Kew Chai J determined robustly, at 810, that *Lister & Co. v Stubbs* was wrong and that its 'undesirable and unjust consequences should not be imported and perpetuated as part of' the law of Singapore. Their Lordships are also much indebted for the fruits of research and the careful discussion of the present topic in the address entitled 'Bribes and Secret Commissions' [1993] RLR 7 delivered by Sir Peter Millett to a meeting of the Society of Public Teachers of Law at Oxford in 1993. The following passage, at 20, elegantly sums up the views of Sir Peter Millett:

'[The fiduciary] must not place himself in a position where his interest may conflict with his duty. If he has done so, equity insists on treating him as having acted in accordance with his duty; he will not be allowed to say that he preferred his own interest to that of his principal. He must not obtain a profit for himself out of his fiduciary position. If he has done so, equity insists on treating him as having obtained it for his principal; he will not be allowed to say that he obtained it for himself. He must not accept a bribe. If he has done so, equity insists on treating it as a legitimate payment intended for the benefit of the principal; he will not be allowed to say that it was a bribe.'

The conclusions reached by Lai Kew Chai J in *Sumitomo Bank Ltd v Kartika Ratna Thahir* and the views expressed by Sir Peter Millett were influenced by the decision of the House of Lords in *Phipps v Boardman* [1967] 2 AC 46 which demonstrates the strictness with which equity regards the conduct of a fiduciary and the extent to which equity is willing to impose a constructive trust on property obtained by a fiduciary by virtue of his office. In that case a solicitor acting for trustees rescued the interests of the trust in a private company by negotiating for a takeover bid in which he himself took an interest. He acted in good faith throughout and the information which the solicitor obtained about the company in the takeover bid could never have been used by the trustees. Nevertheless the solicitor was held to be a constructive trustee by a majority in the House of Lords because the solicitor obtained the information which satisfied him that the purchase of the shares in the takeover company would be a good investment and the opportunity of acquiring the shares as a result of acting for certain purposes on behalf of the trustees; see *per* Lord Cohen, at 103. If a fiduciary acting honestly and in good faith and making a profit which his principal could not make for himself becomes a constructive trustee of that profit then it seems to their Lordships that a fiduciary acting dishonestly and criminally who accepts a bribe and thereby causes loss and damage to his principal must also be a constructive trustee and must not be allowed by any means to make any profit from his wrongdoing.

. . . .

The Attorney-General for Hong Kong has registered caveats against the title of the three New Zealand properties. He seeks to renew the caveats to prevent any dealing with the property pending the hearing of proceedings which, their Lordships are informed, have been initiated for the purpose of claiming the properties on a constructive trust. [Mr and Mrs Reid] oppose the renewal of the caveats on the grounds that the Crown had no equitable interest in the three New Zealand properties. For the reasons indicated their Lordships consider that the three properties so far as they represent bribes accepted by [Mr Reid] are held in trust for the Crown. . . .

Their Lordships will therefore humbly advise Her Majesty that this appeal should be allowed. Since an unfulfilled order has been made against [Mr Reid] in the courts of Hong Kong to pay H.K. $12.4m., his only purpose in opposing the relief sought by the Crown in New Zealand must reflect that the properties, in the absence of a caveat, can be sold and the proceeds whisked away to some Shangri La which hides bribes and other corrupt moneys in numbers bank accounts. In these circumstances Mr and Mrs Reid must pay the costs of the Attorney General before the Board and in the lower courts.

NOTES AND QUESTIONS

1. Lord Templeman makes it clear that, in his view, the constructive trust arose at the date that the bribes were received. Has that observation any bearing on whether one describes the constructive trust as a remedy? Is it any less a response to the defendant's wrongful enrichment if the constructive trust is regarded as arising prior to any claim or court action?

2. Although technically of only persuasive authority, the very firm opinion of the Privy Council that a fiduciary is not merely personally liable to account for bribes, but holds them on constructive trust, effectively put an end to the debate as to whether *Lister v Stubbs* (1890) 45 Ch D 1 was rightly decided: and see further *Daraydon Holdings Ltd v Solland International Ltd* (below, 1023). It is now clear that for breach of fiduciary duty (*quaere* breach of confidence) the courts will be willing not merely to award restitution for the wrong but to do so by imposing a constructive trust. The impact of this is that (i) subject to a possible allowance for time and

skill involved in making the profit the claimant will be entitled to all profits made by the wrongdoer from the wrong (including gains made from using the initial gains); (ii) the claimant is equitable owner of the profits so as to be able to trace through to, and assert priority over, identifiable products of the profits on the wrongdoer's insolvency. This widens the gulf between the treatment of the victims of equitable wrongs and the victims of common law wrongs (torts and breach of contract)—the latter group being rarely entitled even to personal restitution as opposed to compensation.

3. For case notes or short articles on the *Reid* case see, for example, R Pearce, 'Personal and Proprietary Claims against Bribes' [1994] *LMCLQ* 189; D Crilley, 'A Case of Proprietary Overkill' [1994] *RLR* 57; P Birks, 'Property in the Profits of Wrongdoing' (1994) 24 *Univ of W Aust LR* 8.

4. For a robust defence of *Lister v Stubbs*, see Birks, *An Introduction to the Law of Restitution* (rvsd edn 1989) 387–9. Roy Goode also strongly disapproves of granting proprietary restitution in respect of bribes. In 'Ownership and Obligation in Commercial Transactions' (1987) 103 *LQR* 433, 444 he writes:

> It is when the opponents of *Lister v Stubbs* . . . argue for a proprietary right when there is no proprietary base that the line is crossed between what is fair and what is not, for it is the defendant's unsecured creditors who are then at risk. If the court wishes to show its disapproval of the defendant's conduct by making a personal restitutionary order, no harm is done. If the defendant is not in bankruptcy the order will be complied with and enforced for the plaintiff's benefit; if the defendant does become bankrupt before then, the plaintiff is properly required to compete with other unsecured creditors. To accord the plaintiff a proprietary right to the benefit obtained by the defendant, and to any profits or gains resulting from it, at the expense of the defendant's unsecured bankruptcy creditors seems completely wrong, both in principle and in policy, because the wrong done to the plaintiff by the defendant's improper receipt is no different in kind from that done to creditors who have supplied goods and services without receiving the bargained-for payment, so that the debtor's default has swelled his assets at their expense. Indeed, it is strongly arguable that they should be in a better position, for they have parted with property against a promised payment, whereas our plaintiff has not parted with anything and may not have lost anything. The court should exercise particular care before recognising a proprietary claim in proceedings potentially affecting unsecured bankruptcy creditors whose interests are not represented in the litigation.

See also Goode, 'Property and Unjust Enrichment' in *Essays on the Law of Restitution* (ed. Burrows, 1991), 215, 230–1; Goode, 'Proprietary Restitutionary Claims' in *Restitution: Past, Present and Future* (ed. Cornish, 1998), 63, 69.

- ***Daraydon Holdings Ltd v Solland International Ltd*** [2004] EWHC 622 (Ch), [2005] Ch 119, Chancery Division

The defendant, Mr Khalid, worked for the Deputy Prime Minister of Qatar and his companies (the claimants) as a properties and administration manager. Between 1997 and 2001, in breach of fiduciary duty to the claimants, he extracted bribes totalling £1.8M from Mr and Mrs Solland and their companies. The bribes represented a 10 per cent commission paid to Mr Khalid on contracts he organized on behalf of the claimants for the luxurious refurbishment by Mr and Mrs Solland's companies of properties in London and Qatar. The 10 per cent was added on to the cost charged to the claimants by Mr and Mrs Solland and then paid back to the defendant by Mr and Mrs Solland. The claimants sought a declaration that the bribes were held on trust by Mr Khalid because they wished to trace the proceeds of bribes into the hands of recipients. Their claim succeeded.

Lawrence Collins J: . . .

1. This case is concerned with an allegation of bribes or secret commissions. 'Bribery is an evil practice which threatens the foundations of any civilised society': Lord Templeman in *Attorney General for Hong Kong v Reid* [1994] 1 AC 324, 330. It corrupts not only the recipient but the giver of the bribe.

2. Mr Khalid, the fifth defendant, extracted from Mr and Mrs Solland and their companies (the first to fourth defendants) about £1.8m between 1997 and 2001, which represented a 10 per cent commission on receipts from contracts with the claimants for the luxurious refurbishment of properties in London and Qatar.

3. The proceedings against Mr and Mrs Solland and their companies have now been settled, and the issues for decisions are whether Mr Khalid is accountable to the claimants, and in particular whether the claimants are entitled to an order that he holds the payments on constructive trust. That question in turn depends on whether the controversial decision in *Lister & Co. v Stubbs* (1890) 45 Ch D 1 continues to have any life after the decision of the Privy Council in *Attorney General for Hong Kong v Reid* [1994] 1 AC 324, and (if so) whether it applies in the present case.

. . .

77. It has been held by the Privy Council that *Lister & Co. v Stubbs* was wrongly decided: *Attorney General for Hong Kong v Reid* [1994] 1 AC 324, in which the Board consisted of Lord Templeman, Lord Goff of Chieveley, Lord Lowry, Lord Lloyd of Berwick and Sir Thomas Eichelbaum. Lord Templeman said, at p 336:

> 'The decision in *Lister & Co. v Stubbs* is not consistent with the principles that a fiduciary must not be allowed to benefit from his own breach of duty, that the fiduciary should account for the bribe as soon as he receives it and that equity regards as done that which ought to be done. From these principles it would appear to follow that the bribe and the property from time to time representing the bribe are held on a constructive trust for the person injured.'

78. Those who have supported *Lister & Co. v Stubbs* rely on the policy that proprietary restitution is only justified where there has been a substraction from the claimant's ownership or where the claimant has a proprietary basis for the claim. The general creditors have given value, and there is no reason why the agent's principal should have a preferred position. The policy against bribery is sufficiently vindicated through a personal remedy. Thus, according to Professor Roy Goode, proprietary remedies should only be available where the defendant receives gains which derive from the claimant's property, or where they stem from activity which the defendant was under an equitable obligation to undertake (if at all) for the plaintiff: the decision in *Lister & Co. v Stubbs* was correct, because the bribe resulted from conduct in which the defendant should not have engaged at all: Goode, 'Property and Unjust Enrichment', in *Essays on the Law of Restitution*, ed. Burrows (1991), pp 215, 230–231 and Goode, 'Proprietary Restitutionary Claims', in *Restitution: Past, Present and Future*, ed. Cornish (1998), pp 63, 69. So also Professor Birks considers that proprietary restitution is only justified where the claimant has a proprietary base to his claim, i.e. where the defendant's breach of duty consists of misapplication of property belonging to the claimant; but in the case of bribery, the money paid to the agent comes from the third party, and not from the principal: *Birks, Introduction to the Law of Restitution*, 2nd ed. (1989), p 386. See also *Virgo, The Principles of the Law of Restitution* (1999), p 543, *Burrows, The Law of Restitution*, 2nd ed. (2002), p 500 and *Tettenborn, Law of Restitution in England and Ireland*, 2nd ed. (1996), pp 231–233.

79. But the Privy Council preferred the views of Sir Peter Millett, in 'Bribes and Secret Commissions' [1993] RLR 7, 20:

> '[The fiduciary] must not place himself in a position where his interest may conflict with his duty. If he has done so, equity insists on treating him as having acted in accordance with his duty; he will

not be allowed to say that he preferred his own interest to that of his principal. He must not obtain a profit for himself out of his fiduciary position. If he has done so, equity insists on treating him as having obtained it for his principal; he will not be allowed to say that he obtained it for himself. He must not accept a bribe. If he has done so, equity insists on treating it as a legitimate payment intended for the benefit for the principal; he will not be allowed to say that it was a bribe.'

80. The decision of the Privy Council is regarded as black-letter law by *Bowstead & Reynolds on Agency*, para 6–082. It is also treated as representing the law by *Lewin on Trusts*, 17th ed. (2000), para 20–34 and by *Snell's Equity*, 30th ed. (2000), para 9–53. *Goff & Jones, The Law of Restitution*, 6th ed. (2002), para 33–025, prefer *Attoney General for Hong Kong v Reid* [1994] 1 AC 324 but consider that *Lister & Co. v Stubbs* 45 Ch D 1 is a decision which is still technically binding.

81. *Attorney General for Hong Kong v Reid* has been preferred at first instance to *Lister & Co. v Stubbs* by Laddie J in *Ocular Sciences Ltd v Aspect Vision Care Ltd* [1997] RPC 289, 412–413 (a breach of confidence case) and by Toulson J (obiter) in *Fyffes Group Ltd v Templeman* [2000] 2 Lloyd's Rep 643. But Sir Richard Scott V-C in *Attorney General v Blake* [1997] Ch 84, 96 and the Court of Appeal in *Halifax Building Society v Thomas* [1996] Ch 217, 229 treated *Lister & Co. v Stubbs* as still binding, although neither of those cases was a case involving bribery of an agent.

82. The House of Lords forcefully reaffirmed the rules of stare decisis in *Davis v Johnson* [1979] AC 264, but nothing was said about the decisions both in the Court of Appeal (eg *Doughty v Turner Manufacturing Co. Ltd* [1964] 1 QB 518 and *Worcester Works Finance Ltd v Cooden Engineering Co. Ltd* [1972] 1 QB 210) and at first instance which suggest that both a judge of first instance and the Court of Appeal are free to follow decisions of the Privy Council on common law principles which depart, after full argument, from earlier decisions of the Court of Appeal.

. . .

85. The system of precedent would be shown in a most unfavourable light if a litigant in such a case were forced by the doctrine of binding precedent to go to the House of Lords (perhaps through a leap-frog appeal under the Administration of Justice Act 1969, section 12) in order to have the decision of the Privy Council affirmed. That would be particularly so where the decision of the Privy Council is recent, where it was a decision on the English common law, where the Board consisted mainly of serving Law Lords, and where the decision had been made after full argument on the correctness of the earlier decision.

86. Accordingly, if this case were not distinguishable from *Lister & Co. v Stubbs* 45 Ch D 1, I would have applied *Attorney General for Hong Kong v Reid* [1994] 1 AC 324. There are powerful policy reasons for ensuring that a fiduciary does not retain gains acquired in violation of fiduciary duty, and I do not consider that it should make any difference whether the fiduciary is insolvent. There is no injustice to the creditors in their not sharing in an asset for which the fiduciary has not given value, and which the fiduciary should not have had.

87. But even if I were bound by *Lister & Co. v Stubbs*, in my judgment there are two very significant differences between this case and that decision which in any event justify the restitutionary remedy. First, the facts of this case make it a case where there is a proprietary basis for the claim and where the bribe derives directly from the claimants' property. This is not a case where the price is presumed (for the purposes of the personal remedy) to have been increased by the amount of the bribe. Rather it is a case where the evidence is that the price was actually increased by the amount of the bribe, and where the bribe was paid out of the money paid by the claimants for what they thought was the price. These factors make the claim one for the restitution of money extracted from the claimants.

88. Secondly (and independently), the portion representing the bribe was paid as a result of a fraudulent misrepresentation of the Sollands, to which Mr Khalid was a party, that the true price was the invoice price, when it fact the price had been inflated to pay the bribes. I do not consider that *Halifax Building Society v Thomas* [1996] Ch 217 rules out a proprietary claim to the proceeds of

fraud. In that case the defendant fraudulently obtained a loan from the building society, and it sought a declaration that it could keep the proceeds of sale as against the Crown's competing claim to confiscate the surplus in execution of a criminal confiscation order. The Court of Appeal refused to make the declaration on the grounds that the fraudster was not a fiduciary, that there was no universal principle that wherever there was a personal fraud the fraudster would become a trustee for the defrauded party, and that the building society had, with knowledge of the fraud, affirmed the mortgage, and was therefore only a secured creditor. The decision is controversial: see e g *Goff & Jones, The Law of Restitution*, para 36–017, *Essays on the Law of Restitution*, ed. Burrows (1991), p 476 and *Virgo, The Principles of the Law of Restitution* (1999), pp 494–496. But in the present case Mr Khalid was a fiduciary, and the claimants had not affirmed any of the contracts, and had rescinded the only contracts still to be performed.

. . .

95. . . . I consider that the claimants are entitled to judgment against Mr Khalid and to the proprietary remedy which they seek.

NOTE AND QUESTION

Although he thought it unnecessary to do so, Lawrence Collins J distinguished *Lister v Stubbs* on two grounds. First, the bribe in this case was previously owned by the claimants (i.e. the claimants were here paying the bribe ultimately received by the defendant). Secondly, there was a fraudulent misrepresentation made to the claimants which induced the payment. Are these valid reasons for preferring proprietary, rather than personal, restitution of a bribe?

6. RESTITUTION FOR BREACH OF CONFIDENCE

- *Attorney-General v Guardian Newspapers (No 2)* [1990] 1 AC 109, House of Lords

Peter Wright, a former member of M15 (a branch of the British Secret Service), had written a book entitled 'Spycatcher' about his experiences in the service. The publication of that book constituted a breach of his obligation of confidence to the Crown. The book subsequently became widely available, so that the information in it entered the public domain and could no longer be classed as confidential. One of the many questions at issue was whether *The Sunday Times*, in publishing extracts of the book at an early stage before the information had reached the public domain, was liable to an account of profits for breach of confidence. The House of Lords held that it was. (Extracts containing wide ranging dicta of Lord Goff on the issue of whether an injunction should be granted to restrain publication of the book are also included here because of his Lordship's general examination of restitution for breach of confidence.)

Lord Keith of Kinkel: . . . It is a general rule of law that a third party who comes into possession of confidential information which he knows to be such, may come under a duty not to pass it on to anyone else. . . .

The next issue for examination is conveniently the one as to whether 'The Sunday Times' was in breach of an obligation of confidentiality when it published the first serialised extract from *Spycatcher* on 12 July 1987. I have no hesitation in holding that it was. Those responsible for the publication well knew that the material was confidential in character and had not as a whole been previously published anywhere. . . .

This leads on to consideration of the question whether 'The Sunday Times' should be held liable to account to the Crown for profits made from past and future serialisation of *Spycatcher*. An account of profits made through breach of confidence is a recognised form of remedy available to a claimant:

Peter Pan Manufacturing Corporation v Corsets Silhouette Ltd [1964] 1 WLR 96; cf. *Reading v Attorney-General* [1951] AC 507. In cases where the information disclosed is of a commercial character an account of profits may provide some compensation to the claimant for loss which he has suffered through the disclosure, but damages are the main remedy for such loss. The remedy is, in my opinion, more satisfactorily to be attributed to the principle that no one should be permitted to gain from his own wrongdoing. Its availability may also, in general, serve a useful purpose in lessening the temptation for recipients of confidential information to misuse it for financial gain. In the present case 'The Sunday Times' did misuse confidential information and it would be naive to suppose that the prospect of financial gain was not one of the reasons why it did so. I can perceive no good ground why the remedy should not be made available to the Crown in the circumstances of this case, and I would therefore hold the Crown entitled to an account of profits in respect of the publication on 12 July 1987. . . .

In relation to future serialisation of further parts of the book, however, it must be kept in mind that the proposed subject matter of it has now become generally available and that 'The Sunday Times' is not responsible for this having happened. In the circumstances 'The Sunday Times' will not be committing any wrong against the Crown by publishing that subject matter and should not therefore be liable to account for any resultant profits. It is in no different position from anyone else who now might choose to publish the book by serialisation or otherwise.

. . .

Lord Brightman: . . .
FIRST INSTALMENT (12 JULY 1987) OF THE INTENDED SERIALISATION BY 'THE SUNDAY TIMES'
I am in complete agreement with your Lordships, as with the courts below, that this serialisation, which shortly preceded the entry of the contents of *Spycatcher* into the public domain, constituted a breach of confidence on the part of 'The Sunday Times.' The only remedy available to the Crown is the inadequate remedy of an account of profits, on the basis that 'The Sunday Times' unjustly enriched itself and should therefore be stripped of the riches wrongfully acquired: cf. *Reading v Attorney-General* [1951] AC 507. I see no reason why 'The Sunday Times' should not account for a due proportion of the entirety of the total net profits of the issue of 12 July 1987, with possibly an allowance for those copies of the paper which omitted the offending instalment as part of a deceit to hoodwink the Government.

. . .

Lord Goff: . . . [I]t has been held by the learned judge, and by all members of the Court of Appeal in the present case, that Peter Wright cannot be released from his duty of confidence by his own publication of the confidential information, apparently on the basis that he cannot be allowed to profit from his own wrong. I feel bound to say that, in my opinion, this proposition calls for careful examination.

The statement that a man shall not be allowed to profit from his own wrong is in very general terms, and does not of itself provide any sure guidance to the solution of a problem in any particular case. That there are groups of cases in which a man is not allowed to profit from his own wrong, is certainly true. An important section of the law of restitution is concerned with cases in which a defendant is required to make restitution in respect of benefits acquired through his own wrongful act—notably cases of waiver of tort; of benefits acquired by certain criminal acts; of benefits acquired in breach of a fiduciary relationship; and, of course, of benefits acquired in breach of confidence. The plaintiff's claim to restitution is usually enforced by an account of profits made by the defendant through his wrong at the plaintiff's expense. This remedy of an account is alternative to the remedy of damages, which in cases of breach of confidence is now available, despite the equitable nature of the wrong, through a beneficent interpretation of the Chancery Amendment Act 1858 (Lord Cairns' Act), and which by reason of the difficulties attending the taking of an account is often regarded as a more satisfactory remedy, at least in cases where the confidential information is of a commercial nature, and quantifiable damage may therefore have been suffered.

I have to say, however, that I know of no case (apart from the present) in which the maxim has been invoked in order to hold that a person under an obligation is not released from that obligation by the destruction of the subject matter of the obligation, on the ground that that destruction was the result of his own wrongful act. To take an obvious case, a bailee who by his own wrongful, even deliberately wrongful, act destroys the goods entrusted to him, is obviously relieved of his obligation as bailee, though he is of course liable in damages for his tort. Likewise a nightwatchman who deliberately sets fire to and destroys the building he is employed to watch; and likewise also the keeper at a zoo who turns out to be an animal rights campaigner and releases rare birds or animals which escape irretrievably into the countryside. On this approach, it is difficult to see how a confidant who publishes the relevant confidential information to the whole world can be under any further obligation not to disclose the information, simply because it was he who wrongfully destroyed its confidentiality. The information has, after all, already been so fully disclosed that it is in the public domain: how, therefore, can he thereafter be sensibly restrained from disclosing it? Is he not even to be permitted to mention in public what is now common knowledge? For his wrongful act, he may be held liable in damages, or may be required to make restitution; but . . . the confidential information, as confidential information has ceased to exist, and with it should go, as a matter of principle, the obligation of confidence. In truth, when a person entrusts something to another—whether that thing be a physical thing such as a chattel, or some intangible thing such as confidential information—he relies upon that other to fulfil his obligation. If he discovers that the other is about to commit a breach, he may be able to impose an added sanction against his doing so by persuading the court to grant an injunction; but if the other simply commits a breach and destroys the thing, then the injured party is left with his remedy in damages or in restitution. The subject matter is gone: the obligation is therefore also gone: all that is left is the remedy or remedies for breach of the obligation. This approach appears to be consistent with the view expressed by the Law Commission in their Report on Breach of Confidence (Cmnd. 8388), paragraph 4.30 (see also the Law Commission's Working Paper No 58, paragraphs 100–1). It is right to say, however, that they may have had commercial cases in mind, rather than a case such as the present. It is however also of interest that, in *Commonwealth of Australia v John Fairfax & Sons Ltd*, 147 CLR 39, 54, Mason J (as he then was) was not prepared to grant an injunction to restrain further publication of a book by the defendants on the ground of breach of confidence, because the limited publication which had taken place was sufficient to cause the detriment which the plaintiffs, the Commonwealth of Australia, apprehended. If however the defendants had published the book in breach of confidence, it is difficult to see why, on the approach so far accepted in the present case, the defendants should not have remained under a duty of confidence despite the publication and so liable to be restrained by injunction.

It is not to be forgotten that wrongful acts can be inadvertent, as well as deliberate; and yet it is apparently suggested that, irrespective of the character of his wrongdoing, the confidant will be held not to be released from his obligation of confidence. Furthermore, the artificial perpetuation of the obligation, despite the destruction of the subject matter, leads to unacceptable consequences. Take the case of confidential information with which we are here concerned. If the confidant who has wrongfully published the information so that it has entered the public domain remains under a duty of confidence, so logically must also be anybody who, deriving the information from him, publishes the information with knowledge that it was made available to him in breach of a duty of confidence. If Peter Wright is not released from his obligation of confidence neither, in my opinion, are Heinemann Publishers Pty. Ltd, nor Viking Penguin Inc., nor anybody who may hereafter publish or sell the book in this country in the knowledge that it derived from Peter Wright—even booksellers who have in the past, or may hereafter, put the book on sale in their shops, would likewise be in breach of duty. If it is suggested that this is carrying the point to absurd lengths, then some principle has to be enunciated which explains why the continuing duty of confidence applies to some, but not to others, who have wrongfully put the book in circulation. Such a distinction cannot however be explained by reliance upon the general statement that a man may not profit from his own wrong.

I have naturally been concerned by the fact that so far in this case it appears to have been accepted on all sides that Peter Wright should not be released from his obligation of confidence. I cannot help thinking that this assumption may have been induced, in part at least, by three factors—first, the fact that Peter Wright himself is not a party to the litigation, with the result that no representations have been made on his behalf; second, the wholly unacceptable nature of his conduct; and third, the fact that he appears now to be able, with impunity, to reap vast sums from his disloyalty. Certainly, the prospect of Peter Wright, safe in his Australian haven, reaping further profits from the sale of his book in this country is most unattractive. The purpose of perpetuating Peter Wright's duty of confidence appears to be, in part to deter others and in part to ensure that a man who has committed so flagrant a breach of his duty should not be enabled freely to exploit the formerly confidential information, placed by him in the public domain, with impunity. Yet the real reason why he is able to exploit it is because he has found a safe place to do so. If within the jurisdiction of the English courts, he would be held liable to account for any profits made by him from his wrongful disclosure, which might properly include profits accruing to him from any subsequent exploitation of the confidential information after its disclosure: and, in cases where damages were regarded as the appropriate remedy, the confidant would be liable to compensate the confider for any damage, present or future, suffered by him by reason of his wrong. So far as I can see, the confider must be content with remedies such as these.

I have considered whether the confidant who, in breach of duty, places confidential information in the public domain, might remain at least under a duty thereafter not to exploit the information, so disclosed, for his own benefit. Suppose that the confidant in question was a man who, unwisely, has remained in this country, and has written a book containing confidential information and has disposed of the rights to publication to an American publishing house, whose publication results in the information in the book entering the public domain. The question might at least arise whether he is free thereafter to dispose of the film rights to the book. To me, however, it is doubtful whether the answer to this question lies in artificially prolonging the duty of confidence in information which is no longer confidential. Indeed, there is some ground for saying that the true answer is that the copyright in the book, including the film rights, are held by him on constructive trust for the confider—so that the remedy lies not in breach of confidence, but in restitution or in property, whichever way you care to look at it. . . .

At all events, since the point was not argued before us, I wish to reserve the question whether, in a case such as the present, some limited obligation (analogous to the springboard doctrine) may continue to rest upon a confidant who, in breach of confidence, destroys the confidential nature of the information entrusted to him. It must not however be forgotten that cases of breach of confidence may well involve questions of property (in particular, copyright) as well as questions of personal liability; and that, in a case involving national security rather than a personal or commercial secret, where disclosure in breach of confidence may be damaging to the whole community rather than to an individual or a corporation, the guilty confidant may be liable to criminal prosecution. It is only if we take all these matters into account that we can see such a case in the round. Even so, let us not forget that we have in the past seen convicted criminals, on release from prison, being invited by newspapers to give an account of their experiences, no doubt for substantial sums. This is highly offensive to many people, but I doubt whether the mere fact that such activities are offensive provides of itself an appropriate basis for defining the scope of a confidant's civil obligations at common law. And let us not forget that, in the present case, it is Peter Wright's absence from this country which renders him immune from prosecution, and, in Australia, it now appears, also immune from a claim to restitution, founded upon his unjust enrichment from his undoubted wrong at the expense of the whole community. It is perhaps this immunity from process which prompts a temptation to continue his duty of confidence, despite the destruction of the subject matter of that duty.

I fear that I have dealt at too great length with this point, which has troubled me very much. I need not, however, decide it in the present case (and I stress that, in the absence of argument, I am most reluctant to do so) for a very simple reason. Even if my provisional view on the point is wrong, and Peter Wright remains under a continuing duty of confidence, so that those who derive the information in the book from him would prima facie also be under a duty of confidence, I nevertheless take the view in the present case that to prevent the publication of the book in this country would, in the present circumstances, not be in the public interest. It seems to me to be an absurd state of affairs that copies of the book, all of course originating from Peter Wright—imported perhaps from the United States should now be widely circulating in this country, and that at the same time other sales of the book should be restrained. To me, this simply does not make sense. I do not see why those who succeed in obtaining a copy of the book in the present circumstances should be able to read it, while others should not be able to do so simply by obtaining a copy from their local bookshop or library. In my opinion, artificially to restrict the readership of a widely accessible book in this way is unacceptable: if the information in the book is in the public domain and many people in this country are already able to read it, I do not see why anybody else in this country who wants to read it should be prevented from doing so.

. . .

'THE SUNDAY TIMES'

Publication on 12 July 1987

. . . The simple fact is that, on 12 July, publication in the United States had not taken place; certainly, on 12 July, the information in *Spycatcher* was not yet in the public domain. The substantial extract from *Spycatcher* published in 'The Sunday Times' included, as the learned judge held, a good deal of material in respect of which the public interest to be served by disclosure would not be thought not outweigh the interests of national security. I have no doubt that it was in this sense that the judge described the extract as 'indiscriminate,' whatever exercise the editor may himself have undertaken in making his choice. In my opinion, therefore, the publication in 'The Sunday Times' was plainly in breach of confidence; so, if discovered in time, it could have been restrained by injunction. I can see no reason why 'The Sunday Times' should not be liable to account for profits flowing from their wrong, subject however to all the difficulties attendant on this remedy and its (perhaps excessively) technical nature. . . .

Lords Griffiths and **Jauncey** agreed that *The Sunday Times* should account for the profits made from the publication on 12 July 1987.

NOTES AND QUESTIONS

1. See on this case, P Birks, 'A Lifelong Obligation of Confidence' (1989) 105 *LQR* 501; and G Jones, 'Breach of Confidence—after *Spycatcher*' [1989] *CLP* 49.

2. For an earlier case in which an account of profits was awarded for breach of confidence, see *Peter Pan Manufacturing Corp. v Corsets Silhouette Ltd* [1963] 3 All ER 402 (where the defendants had manufactured and sold brassieres knowingly using confidential information obtained from the claimants).

3. Lord Goff, above, 1027, expressed the conventional view that breach of confidence is an equitable wrong. See also *Wainwright v Home Office* [2003] UKHL 53, [2003] 3 WLR 1137 at para. 18. Cf. Lord Nicholls (dissenting) in *Campbell v Mirror Group Newspapers Ltd* [2004] UKHL 22, [2004] 2 AC 457 at paras 14–15 who seemed to envisage there as being a tort of misuse of private information that has grown from the equitable cause of action of breach of confidence.

4. For cases arguably awarding, or recognizing, restitutionary damages for breach of confidence, see *Seager v Copydex (No 1)* and *(No 2)* [1967] 1 WLR 293 and [1969] 1 WLR 809 (Court of Appeal). (See also *Universal Thermosensors Ltd v Hibben* [1992] 1 WLR 840, 856, 858–9, *per* Sir Donald Nicholls V-C.) In *Seager v Copydex (No 1)*, where the defendants had manufactured a carpet grip, honestly and unconsciously making use of confidential information given to them by the claimant, the Court of Appeal ordered damages to be assessed. Lord Denning MR said, at 932, 'It may not be a case for an injunction or even for an account, but only for damages, depending on the worth of the confidential information to him in saving him time and trouble.' In *Seager v Copydex (No 2)*, in which the case came back to the Court of Appeal in relation to the assessment of the damages, Lord Denning said the following, at 813:

> The difficulty is to assess the value of the information taken by the defendants. We have had a most helpful discussion about it. The value of the confidential information depends on the nature of it. If there was nothing very special about it, that is, if it involved no particular inventive step, but was the sort of information which could be obtained by employing any competent consultant, then the value of it was the fee which a consultant would charge for it: because in that case the defendants, by taking the information, would only have saved themselves the time and trouble of employing a consultant. But, on the other hand, if the information was something special, as, for instance, if it involved an inventive step or something so unusual that it could not be obtained by just going to a consultant, then the value of it is much higher. It is not merely a consultant's fee, but the price which a willing buyer—desirous of obtaining it—would pay for it. It is the value as between a willing seller and a willing buyer.

• *LAC Minerals Ltd v International Corona Resources Ltd* (1989) 61 DLR (4th) 14, Supreme Court of Canada

In negotiations for a joint venture between them, the defendants acquired from the claimant information about the mineral potential of some land (the Williams property). The defendants subsequently outbid the claimant in buying that land and set up a successful gold-mine on it. All the judges in the Supreme Court held the defendants liable for breach of confidence. The majority (La Forest, Lamer, and Wilson JJ), upholding the trial judge and Ontario Court of Appeal, decided that the appropriate remedy for breach of confidence here was a constructive trust, subject to an allowance to the defendants, secured by a lien, for expenses in developing the mine that the claimant itself would have necessarily had to incur. The minority (Sopinka and McIntyre JJ) preferred to award compensatory damages. La Forest and Wilson JJ would alternatively have found the defendants liable for breach of fiduciary duty.

Wilson J: . . .

THE REMEDY

It seems to me that when the same conduct gives rise to alternate causes of action, one at common law and the other in equity, *and the available remedies are different*, the court should consider which will provide the more appropriate remedy to the innocent party and give the innocent party the benefit of that remedy. Since the result of LAC's breach of confidence or breach of fiduciary duty was its unjust enrichment through the acquisition of the Williams property at Corona's expense, it seems to me that the only sure way in which Corona can be fully compensated for the breach in this case is by the imposition of a constructive trust on LAC in favour of Corona with respect to the property. Full compensation may or may not be achieved through an award of common law damages depending upon the accuracy of valuation techniques. It can most surely be achieved in this case through the award of an *in rem* remedy. I would therefore award such a remedy. The imposition of a constructive trust also ensures, of course, that the wrongdoer does not benefit from his wrongdoing, an important consideration in equity which may not be achieved by a damage award.

It is, however, my view that this is not a case in which the available remedies are different. I believe that the remedy of constructive trust is available for breach of confidence as well as for breach of fiduciary duty. The distinction between the two causes of action as they arise on the facts of this case is a very fine one. Inherent in both causes of action are concepts of good conscience and vulnerability. It would be strange indeed if the law accorded them widely disparate remedies. In his article on 'The Role of Proprietary Relief in the Modern Law of Restitution', John D. McCamus, Cambridge Lecture (1987) 141 at 150, Professor McCamus poses the rhetorical question:

> Would it not be anomalous to allow more sophisticated forms of relief for breach of fiduciary duty than for those forms of wrongdoing recognized by the law of torts, some of which, at least, would commonly be more offensive from the point of view of either public policy or our moral sensibilities than some breaches of fiduciary duty?

I believe that where the consequence of the breach of either duty is the acquisition by the wrong-doer of property which rightfully belongs to the plaintiff or, as in this case, ought to belong to the plaintiff if no agreement is reached between the negotiating parties, then the *in rem* remedy is appropriate to either cause of action.

La Forest J: . . . It is convenient to set forth my conclusions at the outset. I agree with Sopinka J that LAC misused confidential information confided to it by Corona in breach of a duty of confidence. With respect, however, I do not agree with him about the nature and scope of that duty. Nor do I agree that in the circumstances of this case it is appropriate for this court to substitute an award of damages for the constructive trust imposed by the courts below. Moreover, while it is not strictly necessary for the disposition of the case, I have a conception of fiduciary duties different from that of my colleague, and I would hold that a fiduciary duty, albeit of limited scope, arose in this case. . . .

REMEDY

The appropriate remedy in this case can not be divorced from the findings of fact. . . . [T]here is no doubt in my mind that but for the actions of LAC in misusing confidential information and thereby acquiring the Williams property, that property would have been acquired by Corona. That finding is fundamental to the determination of the appropriate remedy. Both courts below awarded the Williams property to Corona on payment to LAC of the value to Corona of the improvements LAC had made to the property. The trial judge dealt only with the remedy available for a breach of a fiduciary duty, but the Court of Appeal would have awarded the same remedy on the claim for breach of confidence, even though it was of the view that it was artificial and difficult to consider the relief available for that claim on the hypothesis that there was no fiduciary obligation.

The issue then is this. If it is established that one party (here LAC) has been enriched by the acquisition of an asset, the Williams property, that would have, but for the actions of that party been acquired by the plaintiff (here Corona), and if the acquisition of that asset amounts to a breach of duty to the plaintiff, here either a breach of fiduciary obligation or a breach of a duty of confidence, what remedy is available to the party deprived of the benefit? In my view the constructive trust is one available remedy, and in this case it is the only appropriate remedy.

In my view the facts present in this case make out a restitutionary claim, or what is the same thing, a claim for unjust enrichment. When one talks of restitution, one normally talks of giving back to someone something that has been taken from them (a restitutionary proprietary award), or its equivalent value (a personal restitutionary award). As the Court of Appeal noted in this case, Corona never in fact owned the Williams property, and so it cannot be 'given back' to them. However, there are concurrent findings below that but for its interception by LAC, Corona would have acquired the property. In *Air Canada v British Columbia* (judgment pronounced May 4, 1989 [now reported at 59 DLR (4th) 161 at 193–4]), I said that the function of the law of restitution 'is to ensure that where a plaintiff has been deprived of wealth that is either in his possession *or would have accrued for his benefit*, it is restored to him. The measure of restitutionary recovery is the gain the [defendant] made at the [plaintiff's] expense'. In my view the fact that Corona never owned the property should not preclude it from the pursuing a restitutionary claim: see Birks, *An Introduction to the Law of Restitution* (1985), at 133–9. LAC has therefore been enriched at the expense of Corona.

That enrichment is also unjust, or unjustified, so that the plaintiff is entitled to a remedy. There is, in the words of Dickson J in *Pettkus v Becker* (1980), 117 DLR (3d) 257 at 274, 'an absence of any juristic reason for the enrichment'. The determination that the enrichment is 'unjust' does not refer to abstract notions of morality and justice, but flows directly from the finding that there was a breach of a legally recognized duty for which the courts will grant relief. Restitution is a distinct body of law governed by its own developing system of rules. Breaches of fiduciary duties and breaches of confidence are both wrongs for which restitutionary relief is often appropriate. . . .

I noted earlier that the jurisdictional base for the law of confidence is a matter of some dispute. In the case at bar however, it is not suggested that either the contractual or property origins of the doctrine can be used to found the remedy. Thus while there can be considerable remedial flexibility for such claims, it was not argued that the court may not have jurisdiction to award damages as compensation and not merely in lieu of an injunction in the exercise of its equitable jurisdiction, and since I am of the view that a constructive trust is in any event the appropriate remedy, I need not consider the question of jurisdiction further.

In view of this remedial flexibility, detailed consideration must be given to the reasons a remedy measured by LAC's gain at Corona's expense is more appropriate than a remedy compensating the plaintiff for the loss suffered. In this case, the Court of Appeal found that if compensatory damages were to be awarded, those damages in fact equalled the value of the property. This was premised on the finding that but for LAC's breach, Corona would have acquired the property. Neither at this point nor any other did either of the courts below find Corona would only acquire one half or less of the Williams property. While I agree that, if they could in fact be adequately assessed, compensation and restitution in this case would be equivalent measures, even if they would not, a restitutionary measure would be appropriate.

The essence of the imposition of fiduciary obligations is its utility in the promotion and preservation of desired social behaviour and institutions. Likewise with the protection of confidences. In the modern world the exchange of confidential information is both necessary and expected. Evidence of an accepted business morality in the mining industry was given by the defendant, and the Court of Appeal found that the practice was not only reasonable, but that it would foster the exploration and development of our natural resources. The institution of bargaining in good faith is one that is worthy of legal protection in those circumstances where that protection accords with the expectations of the parties. The approach taken by my colleague, Sopinka J, would, in my view, have the effect not of encouraging bargaining in good faith, but of encouraging the contrary. If by breaching an obligation of confidence one party is able to acquire an asset entirely for itself, at a risk of only having to compensate the other for what the other would have received if a formal relationship between them were concluded, the former would be given a strong incentive to breach the obligation and acquire the asset. In the present case, it is true that had negotiations been concluded, LAC could also have acquired an interest in the Corona land, but that is only an expectation and not a certainty. Had Corona acquired the Williams property, as they would have but for LAC's breach, it seems probable that negotiations with LAC would have resulted in a concluded agreement. However, if LAC, during the negotiations, breached a duty of confidence owed to Corona, it seems certain that Corona would have broken off negotiations and LAC would be left with nothing. In such circumstances, many business people, weighing the risks, would breach the obligation and acquire the asset. This does nothing for the preservation of the institution of good faith bargaining or relationships of trust and confidence. The imposition of a remedy which restores an asset to the party who would have acquired it but for a breach of fiduciary duties or duties of confidence acts as a deterrent to the breach of duty and strengthens the social fabric those duties are imposed to protect. The elements of a claim in unjust enrichment having been made out, I have found no reason why the imposition of a restitutionary remedy should not be granted.

This court has recently had occasion to address the circumstances in which a constructive trust will be imposed in *Hunter Engineering Co. v Syncrude Canada Ltd* (judgment pronounced March 23, 1989 [now reported at 57 DLR (4th) 321]). There, the Chief Justice discussed the development of the constructive trust over 200 years from its original use in the context of fiduciary relationships, through to *Pettks v Becker, supra*, where the court moved to the modern approach with the constructive trust as a remedy for unjust enrichment. He identified that *Pettkus v Becker*, set out a two-step approach. First, the court determines whether a claim for unjust enrichment is established, and then, secondly, examines whether in the circumstances a constructive trust is the appropriate remedy to redress that unjust enrichment. In *Hunter v Syncrude*, a constructive trust was refused, not on the basis that it would not have been available between the parties (though in my view it may not have been appropriate), but rather on the basis that the claim for unjust enrichment had not been made out, so no remedial question arose.

In the case at hand, the restitutionary claim has been made out. The court can award either a proprietary remedy, namely that LAC hand over the Williams property, or award a personal remedy, namely a monetary award. While, as the Chief Justice observed, 'the principle of unjust enrichment lies at the heart of the constructive trust': see *Pettkus v Becker*, at 273, the converse is not true. The constructive trust does not lie at the heart of the law of restitution. It is but one remedy, and will only be imposed in appropriate circumstances. Where it could be more appropriate than in the present case, however, it is difficult to imagine.

The trial judge assessed damages in this case at $700,000,000 in the event that the order that LAC deliver up the property was not upheld on appeal. In doing so he had to assess the damages in the face of evidence that the Williams property would be valued by the market at up to 1.95 billion dollars. Before us there is a cross-appeal that damages be reassessed at $1.5 billion. The trial judge found that no one could predict future gold prices, exchange rates or inflation with any certainty, or even on the balance of probabilities. Likewise he noted that the property had not been fully explored and that further reserves may be found. The Court of Appeal made the following comment, at 651 DLR, with which I am in entire agreement:

> ... there is no question but that gold properties of significance are unique and rare. There are almost insurmountable difficulties in assessing the value of such a property in the open market. The actual damage which has been sustained by Corona is virtually impossible to determine with any degree of accuracy. The profitability of the mine, and accordingly its value, will depend on the ore reserves of the mine, the future price of gold from time to time, which in turn depends on the rate of exchange between the U.S. dollar and Canadian dollar, inflationary trends, together with myriad other matters, all of which are virtua. impossible to predict.

To award only a monetary remedy in such circumstances when an alternative remedy is both available and appropriate would, in my view, be unfair and unjust.

There is no unanimous agreement on the circumstances in which a constructive trust will be imposed. Some guidelines can, however, be suggested. First, no special relationship between the parties is necessary. I agree with this comment of Wilson J in *Hunter v Syncrude, supra*, at [383 DLR]:

> Although both *Pettkus v Becker* and *Sorochan v Sorochan* (1986) 29 DLR (4th) 1 were 'family' cases, unjust enrichment giving rise to a constructive trust is by no means confined to such cases: see *Deglman v Guaranty Trust Co. of Canada* [1954] 3 DLR 785, [1954] SCR 725. Indeed, to do so

would be to impede the growth and impair the flexibility crucial to the development of equitable principles.

As I noted earlier, the constructive trust was refused in *Hunter v Syncrude*, not because the parties did not stand in any special relationship to one another, but because the claim for unjust enrichment was not made out.... In *Chase Manhattan Bank NA v Israel-British Bank (London) Ltd* [1981] Ch 105 a constructive trust was imposed, but to describe the banks as standing in a special relationship one to the other would be as much of a fiction as describing them as fiduciaries. Insistence on a special relationship would undoubtedly lead to that same sort of reasoning from conclusions. Courts, coming to the conclusion that a proprietary remedy is the only appropriate result will be forced to manufacture 'special relationships' out of thin air, so as to justify their conclusions. In my view that result can and should be avoided.

Secondly, it is not the case that a constructive trust should be reserved for situations where a right of property is recognized. That would limit the constructive trust to its institutional function, and deny to it the status of a remedy, its more important role. Thus, it is not in all cases that a pre-existing right of property will exist when a constructive trust is ordered. The imposition of a constructive trust can both recognize and create a right of property. When a constructive trust is imposed as a result of successfully tracing a plaintiff's asset into another asset, it is indeed debatable which the court is doing. Goff and Jones, *The Law of Restitution*, 3rd edn (1986) at 78, take the position that:

... the question whether a restitutionary proprietary claim should be granted should depend on whether it is just, in the particular circumstances of the case, to impose a constructive trust on, or an equitable lien over, particular assets, or to allow subrogation to a lien over such assets.

It is the nature of the plaintiff's claim itself which is critical in determining whether a restitutionary proprietary claim should be granted; the extent of that claim is a different matter, which should be dependent upon the defendant's knowledge of the true facts. There are certain claims which must always be personal. Such are claims for services rendered under an ineffective contract; the plaintiff is then in no different position from any unsecured creditor. In contrast there are other claims, for example, those arising from payments made under mistake, compulsion or another's wrongful act, where a restitutionary proprietary claim should presumptively be granted, although the court should always retain a discretion whether to do so or not.

In their view, a proprietary claim should be granted when it is just to grant the plaintiff the additional benefits that flow from the recognition of a right of property. It is not the recognition of a right of property that leads to a constructive trust. It is not necessary, therefore, to determine whether confidential information is property, though a finding that it was would only strengthen the conclusion that a constructive trust is appropriate. This is the view of Fridman and McLeod, *Restitution* (1982), at 539, where they say:

... there appears to be no doubt that a fiduciary who has consciously, made use of confidential information for private gain will be forced to account for the entire profits by holding such profits made from the use of the confidential information on a constructive trust for the bene-ficiary-estate. The proprietary remedy flows naturally from the conclusion that the information itself belonged to the beneficiary, and there has been no transaction effective to divest his rights over the property.

I do not countenance the view that a proprietary remedy can be imposed whenever it is 'just' to do so, unless further guidance can be given as to what those situations may be. To allow such a result would be to leave the determination of proprietary rights to 'some mix of judicial discretion ... subjective views about which party "ought to win" ... and "the formless void of individual moral opinion" ', *per* Deane J in *Muschinski v Dodds* (1985), 160 CLR 583 at 616.

As Deane J further noted, at 616:

Long before Lord Seldon's anachronism identifying the Chancellor's foot as the measure of Chancery relief, undefined notions of 'justice' and what was 'fair' had given way in the law of equity to the rule of ordered principle which is of the essence of any coherent system of rational law. The mere fact that it would be unjust or unfair in a situation of discord for the owner of a legal estate to assert his ownership against another provides, of itself, no mandate for a judicial declaration that the ownership in whole or in part lies, in equity, in that other.

Much of the difficulty disappears if it is recognized that in this context the issue of the appropriate remedy only arises once a valid restitutionary claim has been made out. The constructive trust awards a right in property, but that right can only arise once a right to relief has been established. In the vast majority of cases a constructive trust will not be the appropriate remedy. Thus, in *Hunter, supra*, had the restitutionary claim been made out, there would have been no reason to award a constructive trust, as the plaintiff's claim could have been satisfied simply by a personal monetary award; a constructive trust should only be awarded if there is reason to grant to the plaintiff the additional rights that flow from recognition of a right of property. Among the most important of these will be that it is appropriate that the plaintiff receive the priority accorded to the holder of a right of property in a bankruptcy. More important in this case is the right of the property holder to have changes in value accrue to his account rather than to the account of the wrongdoer. Here as well it is justified to grant a right of property since the concurrent findings below are that the defendant intercepted the plaintiff and thereby frustrated its efforts to obtain a specific and unique property that the courts below held would otherwise have been acquired. The recognition of a constructive trust simply redirects the title of the Williams property to its original course. The moral quality of the defendants' act may also be another consideration in determining whether a proprietary remedy is appropriate. Allowing the defendant to retain a specific asset when it was obtained through conscious wrongdoing may so offend a court that it would deny to the defendant the right to retain the property. This situation will be more rare since the focus of the inquiry should be upon the reasons for recognizing a right of property in the plaintiff, not on the reasons for denying it to the defendant.

Having specific regard to the uniqueness of the Williams property, to the fact that but for LAC's breaches of duty Corona would have acquired it, and recognizing the virtual impossibility of accurately valuing the property, I am of the view that it is appropriate to award Corona a constructive trust over that land.

. . .

Sopinka J (dissenting): . . . Although unjust enrichment has been recognized as having an existence apart from contract or tort under a heading referred to as the law of restitution, a constructive trust is not the appropriate remedy in most cases. As pointed out by Professor Waters in *Law of Trusts in Canada*, (2nd edn, 1984), at 394, although unjust enrichment gives rise to a number of possible remedies:

. . . the best remedy in the particular circumstances is that which corrects the unjust enrichment without contravening other established legal doctrines. In most cases, as in *Deglman v Guar. Trust Co. of Can. and Constantineau* itself, a personal action will accomplish that end, whether its source is the common law or equity, providing as it often will monetary compensation.

While the remedy of the constructive trust may continue to be employed in situations where other remedies would be inappropriate or injustice would result, there is no reason to extend it to this case.

The conventional remedies for breach of confidence are an accounting of profits or damages. An injunction may be coupled with either of these remedies in appropriate circumstances. A restitutionary remedy is appropriate in cases involving fiduciaries because they are required to disgorge any benefits derived from the breach of trust. In a breach of confidence case, the focus is on the loss to the plaintiff and, as in tort actions, the particular position of the plaintiff must be examined. The object is to restore the plaintiff monetarily to the position he would have been in if no wrong had been committed; see *Dowson & Mason Ltd v Potter*, [1986] 2 All ER 418 (CA), and *Talbot v General Television Corp. Pty. Ltd* [1980] 2 VR 224. Accordingly, this object is generally achieved by an award of damages, and a restitutionary remedy is inappropriate.

The Williams property was acquired as a result of information which was in part public and in part private. It would be impossible to assess the role of each. The trial judge went no further than to find that the confidential information was 'of value' to Lac and

> ... of assistance to Lac not only in assessing the Corona property but also in assessing other property in the area and in making an offer to Mrs Williams.

The Court of Appeal went further and stated that 'but for the confidential information LAC received from Corona, it is not likely that it would have acquired the Williams property'. The reasons do not disclose any factual basis for extending the finding of the trial judge and I see no basis for so doing. The best that can therefore be said is that it played a part. When the extent of the connection between the confidential information and the acquisition of the property is uncertain, it would be unjust to impress the whole of the property with a constructive trust.

The case has been presented on the basis that either a transfer of the property or damages is the appropriate remedy. The respondent contends that the former is appropriate and the appellant the latter. No submissions were made in oral argument for or against an accounting of profits. Moreover, damages were assessed in the alternative in the event that on appeal this was considered the appropriate remedy. In all the circumstances, therefore, I have concluded that of the two alternatives presented, damages is the proper remedy.

. . .

NOTES AND QUESTIONS

1. Wilson J appeared to regard the constructive trust as a compensatory rather than a restitutionary remedy.

2. Are the reasons given by La Forest J good reasons for imposing a proprietary restitutionary remedy?

3. What does La Forest J mean when he describes the constructive trust as being a remedy rather than having an 'institutional function'? (For help on this, see above, 744–750.)

4. Did the imposition of the constructive trust in itself constitute a court order requiring the defendants to transfer the land? Or would that require further proceedings?

5. In *Cadbury Schweppes Inc. v FBI Foods Ltd* (1999) 167 DLR (4th) 577 the Supreme Court of Canada has subsequently stressed that, in Canada, the imposition of a constructive trust is discretionary and dependent on the particular facts of a case. It was there held that compensation for breach of confidence, and not a proprietary remedy, was appropriate (the claimants not having sought an account of profits). See A Abdullah and T Hang, 'To Make the Remedy Fit the Wrong' (1999) 115 *LQR* 376.

6. Might a constructive trust be imposed as the appropriate remedy in those cases where restitution is awarded for a tort?

INDEX

absence of basis
  unjust factors 137–8, 149
account of profits
  intellectual property torts
      995–6
advancement
  locus poenitentiae and 911
  presumption of 906–11
agency
  agent's duty to account to
      principle 831
  change of position and
      824–44, 833
  receipt of agent is receipt of
      principle 832
  undue influence 467
agency of necessity 573–81
  bailment 577–80
  principles 576–7
American Law Institute
  Restatement of the Law of
      Restitution 9–10, 17,
      21, 36, 47, 165, 799,
      943
anticipated enrichment
  change of position 781–5
apportionment
  on dissolution of partnership
      14, 17
Aristotle
  contemplation of corrective
      justice duty of
      rectification 49–51,
      53
assumpsit
  action of 10–13, 15, 26–7
  writ of 16
Australia
  acceptance of law of restitution
      in 22
  legislation on frustration of
      contract in 331–2
  restitution 2

bailment 577–80
bank
  obligation of 160–1
bankruptcy
  constructive trusts in 756–7
benefit
  academic analysis
      Beatson, J. 90–3

Birks, P. 93–100, 113–14,
  119–21
Burrows, A. 84–6
Garner, M. 86–9
McInnes, M. 110–13
Muir, G. 103–6
Smith, L. 117–18
Stoljar, S. 101–3
  acceptance of 24, 93–6
  bargained for 87–8
  claimant's expense *see* expense
      of claimant
  damages for 964
  definition of 71–2
  freedom of choice 75
  judicial analysis 72–84
  part performance 99–101
  recovery of gained from breach
      of contract 998–1002
  recovery of value of 17
  saving of expenditure as
      104–6
  services, receipt of 104
  subjective benefit 86–9
    areas of operation 88–90
  subjective revaluation 87–8
  test for 75, 93
  use as 104
  use of in restitution 57–8
benefits in kind
  rendered by mistake 187–95
bona fide **purchase** 222–3
  change of position and
      224
  defence of 822–4
Bowmakers **rule** 915–16
breach of confidence
  restitution for 1026–37
breach of contract 107, 109
  failure of consideration
      257–79
  liability 352–5
  interference with rights of
      property 982–4
  private law claim 982
  recovery of benefits gained
      from 998–1002
  remedies available for
      985–1002
  restitution as alternative
      remedy for 11
  restitution for 978–1002

breach of duty
  in tort 66
breach of fiduciary duty
  984
  restitution for 1002–26
    bribes 1016–26
    unauthorised profit
      1002–16
breach of statutory duty 12
breach of trust 984
bribes
  breach of fiduciary duty
      1016–26
building work 24
burden of proof
  undue influence 459–60
burial expenses
  right to recovery, recognition
      of 565–9

Canada
  law of restitution 74–5
  legislation on frustration of
      contract in 329–30
  restitution 2
  unjust enrichment 18–9, 113,
      138–44
capacity
  restriction on 7
causes of action 16
  triggering restitution 2
  unjust enrichment 41–7
change of position
  agency defence 824–44
  anticipated enrichment 781–5
  bona fide purchase and 224,
      822–4
  defence of 748, 762–804
  disenrichment and 763–4
  estoppel and 811–22
  evidence required to prove
      769–81
    causation 774–5
    chronology 773–4
  honest receipt 793–4
  knowing receipt 794–801
  proprietary claims, application
      to 802–4
  purchasing something of value
      while retaining, by
      801–2
  rationale of 764–5

change of position – *Contd.*
   recognition of 35–8, 763–5
      United States 36
   relevance of fault to defence of
        783–801
   reliance by claimant on
        receipt 765–9
   scope and application of
        765–804
chattels
   user principle applied to
        962–3
class protection 500–1
common interests 66
Commonwealth 329–32
companies
   ultra vires defence
        926–7
compensation
   right to 25
completed transactions
   mistake of law 177–9
compound interest 728–9,
        742–4
compulsion *see* duress
confidence
   restitution for breach of
        1026–37
consideration 33–5
   absence of 364–7
   executed 25–6
   failure of 13, 15, 17
      Scots law 17
   meaning of 251–6
   total failure of 368–82
constructive trusts
   bankruptcy, in 756–7
   proprietary restitution
        729
   remedial 757–8
contract
   anticipated
      failure of consideration
        332–48
   de certo corpore 14
   enforceable 14
   failure of performance 13
   initially valid 120, 122–8
   oral 24–5, 28
   part performance 89
   quantum meruit as means of
      enforcing 24
   rescission *see* rescission of
        contract
   subsisting
      failure of consideration
        386–91
   void 13

contribution 551–3
   assessment of 553
   entitlement to 552–3
   recovery of 553
conveyance
   fraud, duress, undue influence
      or mistake, procured
      by 746
corrective justice
   Aristotelian contemplation of
      duty of rectification
      49–51, 53
   restitution for wrongs
      937–42
   unjust enrichment 48–53
counter-restitution impossible
      844–70
   manifest disadvantage 862
   restitution for both parties
      864–6
   restoring parties to original
      positions 863–4
   setting aside transaction
      862–3
Court of Admiralty
   claims in 19
Court of Conscience 4

damages *see also* restitutionary
      damages
   compensatory not
      restitutionary 997
   exemplary 963
   lost opportunity to bargain
      956–9
debt *see* payment of debt
defaulting fiduciary 237–9
defences 36–7, 145, 761–927
   agency 824–44
   bona fide purchase 222–4,
      822–4
   change of position 748
      honest receipt 793–4
      knowing receipt 794–801
      relevance of fault to
        783–801
   counter-restitution
      impossible 844–70
   estoppel 804–22
   illegality 150–3, 883–919
   incapacity 919–27
      local authorities and
        companies 926–7
      minors 919–24
      statutory liability 925–6
   passing on 870–83
   strict liability subject to
      204–10, 237–9

deposits
   recovery of 842–3
detention of goods 188
detinue 959
deviation
   failure of consideration 311–3
difficult circumstances
   exploitation of 498–500
discharge of another's legal
      liability *see* legal
      compulsion
disenrichment
   change of position and
      763–4
dishonesty
   knowing receipt and dealing
      225–31
duress
   conveyance procured by 746
   economic duress 405–35
   illegality, defence of 885–6
   rescission for 1
duress of goods
   illegitimate pressure 404–5
duress of the person
   illegitimate pressure 399–403

economic duress 405–35
economic weakness
   exploitation of 494–8
empowering legislation
   ultra vires 74
equitable tracing *see* tracing
estoppel 804–22
   change of position and
      811–22
   defence of 807
   general principles of 807
   traditional position 805–6
evidence
   required to prove change of
      position 769–81
      causation 774–5
      chronology 773–4
executory contracts 17
exhaustion of the fund rule
      687–700
expense of the claimant, at the
      109–10, 130–3, 220–1
exploitation of disadvantage
      482
exploitation of weakness
      447–501 *see also*
      undue influence
   illegality, defence of 885–6

failure of consideration 13, 15,
      17, 249–395

anticipated contract which
does not materialise
332–7, 339–48
breach, contracts discharged
for 257–79
contract-breaker claiming
for recovery of money
paid 287–97
contract-breaker claiming
for value of work
done 297–307
innocent party claiming for
recovery of money
paid 257–79
innocent party claiming for
value of work done
279–87
liability 352–5
deviation 310–3
free acceptance and 392–4
frustration, contracts
discharged by 313–32
illegality, defence of 886–92
mistake of fact 360
money had and received
363–8
quantum meruit 360–2
Scots law 17
subsisting contracts 386–91
unconscionability 309–10
unenforceable contracts
want of formality 355–6
unjust factors 307–9
void contracts 356–86
fault
relevance of to defence of
change of position
783–801
fiduciary
acquisition of property by
747
acquisition of property from
748
defaulting 237–9
fiduciary duty
restitution for breach of
1002–26
bribes 1016–26
unauthorised profit
1002–16
fiduciary's liability 1
France
unjust enrichment in 2
fraud
conveyance procured by 746
free acceptance 307, 392–4
freedom of choice
benefit 75

frustration of contract 17–18,
67
failure of consideration
313–32
Australian developments
331–2
Canadian developments
329–30
Commonwealth
developments
329–32
Law Reform (Frustrated
Contracts) Act 1943
314–29
adjustment of rights and
liabilities of parties
314–16
claims under 316–17
claims under s 1(2)
318–19
claims under s 1(3)(a)
319–23
cross-claims 324
effect of s 2(3) 323–4
recovery, principle of
317–18
recovery and expenses
327–9
relevance to claim under of
prior breach by
claimant 324–6

general average 19
Germany
unjust enrichment in 2

Holdsworth, Sir William Searle
[1871–1944] 9
honest receipt
change of position 793–4
mistake of law 177

ignorance 203–48
mistake and 167
strict liability and 239–48
illegality 66, 597–606,
883–919
class protection 500–1
duress and exploitation of
weakness 885–6
mistake 883–4
present need for doctrine of
916–18
title claims 892–919
total failure of consideration
886–92
withdrawal in *locus
poenitentiae* 597–605

illegitimate pressure 397–445
duress of goods 404–5
duress of the person 399–403
economic duress 405–35
threats to prosecute, sue, or
publish information
435–45
implied contract theory 6–8
advance of 21
historical aspects 20
implied promise 1
improvement of goods 188
incapacity 607–23
defence of 919–27
ground for restitution, as
607–23
infants 607–12
local authorities and
companies 926–7
mental illness 612–20
minors 919
provision of necessaries
581–4
incorporeal hereditament 960
*indebitatus assumpsit see
assumpsit*
independent advice
undue influence 460–1, 466–7
inducement 14
infancy *see minors*
intellectual property torts
account of profits 995–6
restitution for 969–73
interference with rights of
property 982–4
interceptive subtraction
unjust enrichment 116–19
intermediate balance rule
687–700

joint liability
debt or damage, for 553
judicial decision
declaratory theory of 174–5
judicial review
ultra vires demands by public
authorities 642
justifiable sacrifice 76, 78

Kant, Immanuel [1724–1804]
51, 53
knowing receipt
change of position 794–801
dealing and 225–31
dishonesty 225–31
negligence 232–3
unconscionability test
233–7

legal advice
   undue influence 465–6
legal compulsion 503
   common liability
      claimant's liability
         secondary 507–23
   contribution, restitution by
      551–3
   discharge of another's legal
      liability 504–6
   no restitution because no
      liability discharged
      523–34
   payment of another's debt,
      effect of 534–51
   rejection of unjust enrichment
      as ground for
      restitution 554–6
liability
   fiduciary's 1
   giving rise to obligation
      65–6
   in unjust enrichment 77–83
local authorities
   ultra vires defence 926–7
locus poenitentiae
   doctrine of 911
   withdrawal in 597–605
Lord Cairn's Act
   restitutionary damages 984–5
loss of opportunity
   bargain, to
      damages for 956–9

manifest disadvantage 862
   requirement for
      undue influence 461–2
Mansfield, Earl of William
      Murray [1705–93]
   contribution of 4–5, 8, 10,
      15–6, 21
maritime liens 570
mental illness
   ground for restitution
      612–20
mental inadequacy
   exploitation of 486–90
mesne profits 964–9
ministerial receipt, defence of
      see **agency**
minors
   contractual capacity 919
   contractual incapacity 607–12
   liability in restitution
      common law and equity
      919–24
      statutory liability 925–6
misdirection of funds 239–45

misrepresentation
   rescission for 1
mistake 115–6
   benefits in kind rendered by
      187–91, 193–5
   conveyance procured by 746
   fact, of 147–67, 360
   gifts
      resulting trusts and 753–4
   illegality, defence of 883–4
   law, of 167–87
      completed transactions
      177–9
      criticism of rule 171, 173
      honest receipt 177
      Law Commission's
         recommendations on
         170–3, 175–6
      recommendations for
         changes to law on 168
      rejection of rule in common
         law 171
   payments *see* **mistaken**
      payments
   rescission of contract for
      195–202
   unjust enrichment and 180–2
mistaken payments 147–87
   causes of action 179–80
   completed transactions 177–9
   honest receipts 177
   innocent recipients of 68–9
   Law Commission's
      recommendations on
      170–3, 175–6
   law, of criticism of rule 171
   mistakes of fact 147–67,
      162–4
   mistakes of law 167–87
      recommendations for
         changes to law on 168
   proprietary restitution 711–21
mixed fund
   tracing *see* **tracing**
money had and received
   217–19, 363–8

necessity 559–99
   agency of 573–81
   burial expenses 565–9
   European law, principles of
      593–5
   necessaries provided for the
      incapacitated 581–4
   right of recovery, recognition
      of 565–9
   future development of law
      591–5

   traditional analysis: no right
      of 561–5
   salvage 569–73
   traditional analysis 561–5
negligence
   knowing receipt and dealing
      323
Nicomachean Ethics 50
non-proprietary torts
   restitution for 973–7
nuisance of trespass 959–63

obligation
   bank 160–1
   creation of law of 15
   liability giving rise to 65–6
obligationes quasi ex
      contractu 11
officious intervener
   unjust sacrifice 103–6
oral contract 24–5, 28

part performance
   contract 89, 99–101
partnership
   apportionment on dissolution
      14, 17
passing on 870–83
patent infringement 959
payment of another's debt
   alternative remedies 548–51
   creditor, restitution from
      547
   debtor, restitution from 547
   non-volunteers 539–41
   power of stranger to discharge
      another's debt 544
   volunteers 539–40
payment of debt 5, 128–9
   barred by Statute of
      Limitations 5
performance
   failure of 13
personal remedies 3–4
   unjustifiable enrichment 9
possession of land
   entitlement to 965–6
precedents
   doctrine of 16
prepayment 14–16
private law
   breach of contract 982
   unjust enrichment 46
promise
   implied 15
property
   acquisition by fiduciary 747
   acquisition from fiduciary 748

proprietary connection
  unjust enrichment 119–20
proprietary estoppel 66
proprietary restitution
      704–59
  academic analyses
    Birks, P. 750–1
    Burrows, A. 758–9
    Chambers, R. 755–6
    Paciocco, D. 757–8
    Scott, A.W. 744–50
    Sherwin, E. 756–7
    Swadling, W. 752–5
  acquisition of property from
      fiduciary 748
  acquisition of property by
      fiduciary 747
  breadth of submission
      729–31
  change of position, application
      of 802–4
  compound interest 742–4
  constructive trusts 729
    bankruptcy, in 756–7
  conveyance 746
  equitable proprietary claims
      739–41
  mistaken payments 711–21
  remedial constructive trusts
      757–8
  resulting trusts 732–4, 750–2,
      754–5
  retention of title 732
  scope 707–11
  separation of title 732
  subrogation 723–8
  tracing 721–3
  trust law and 731
proprietary theory
  restitution 54–5
proprietary torts
  restitution for 942–69
prosecute
  threat to 435, 437–45
public authorities
  ultra vires actions 621–3
  ultra vires demands 625–45
publish information
  threat to 435–45

quantum meruit 18–9, 22, 66,
      92, 100, 106, 345–9
  as means of enforcing
      contract 24
  failure of consideration
      360–2
  right to recovery 23
quantum valebat 19

quasi ex contractu 15
quasi-contract 1, 11, 15, 19–20,
      89
  remedy in 13, 40, 441
quasi-contractual relief 66

receipt
  reliance by claimant on
      765–9
relational undue influence
      448–80
remedies
  personal 3–4
  quasi-contract 13, 40–1
remoteness 57
rescission of contract
  executed contract 1
  mistake, for 195–202
Restatement of the Law of
     Restitution
    (American Law
    Institute) 9–10, 17,
    21, 36, 47, 165, 799,
    943
restitution
  acceptance of law of in
     Australia 22
  alternative remedy for breach
     of contract 11
  Australia 2
  Canada 2
  Canadian law of 74–5
  classification of concepts
     within 57–8
  common law of 15
  consent based 44–5
  defences for 36–7
  defining and analysing event
     41–8
  defining law of 1
  for wrongs 2
  free acceptance of law of
     84–6
  future of 61–4
  grounds for 215–16
  law of based on unjust
     enrichment 219–20
  new theory of 60–1
  no recognised right to
     22
  not to be confused with
     reversing unjust
     enrichment 3
  proprietary theory 54–5
  proprietary torts 942–69
  quasi-contract and 19–20
  recent recognition of law of in
     England 2

  rejection of unjust enrichment
     as ground for 554–6
  scholarship of 3
  structure of law of 631
  unjust enrichment basis of
     claim for 55
  unjust enrichment used to
     define subject matter
     of 56–7
  use of unjust enrichment to
     rationalise law of 58
  whether generalised right for
     unjust enrichment
     should be
     introduced 58–9
restitutionary damages 938–42
  assessment of 961
  breach of confidence 1026–37
  breach of contract 978–1002
    interference with rights of
     property 982–4
    private law claim 982
  compensatory 997
  trespass to land 964–9
  under Lord Cairn's Act
     984–5
restitutionary defences *see*
     defences
restoring parties to original
     positions 863–4
resulting trusts 752–5
  arising from void contracts
     734–9
  mistaken gifts and 753–4
  proprietary restitution and
     732–4, 750–1
retention of title
  proprietary restitution 732
right to recovery
  quantum meruit 23
right to sue 210–12
Roman law 11
  implied promise in 15

sale of goods 16
salvage 19, 569–73
  elements of law of 570–3
saving of expenditure
  benefit as 104–6
separation of title
  proprietary restitution 732
services
  benefit as 104
  receipt of as benefit 91
  unjust enrichment 96–8
setting aside transaction 862–3
sexual relationships
  undue influence 468

Statute of Limitations
debt barred by 5
statutory duty
breach of 12
statutory societies
capacity of 7
strict liability
defences, subject to 204–10,
237–9
exhausting remedies against
defaulting fiduciary
237–9
ignorance and 239–48
subjective benefit
areas of operation 88–90
unjust enrichment 86, 88–9
subrogation 2
proprietary restitution
723–8
simple 556
subsisting contracts
failure of consideration
386–91
subtraction
unjust enrichment by 116–18
sue
right to 210–12
threat to 435–45
title to 213–15
suretyship transactions
undue influence 462–4

three party factors
unjust enrichment 119–21
thresholds
undue influence 464–5
title
retention of 732
separation of 732
title claims
illegality, defence of 892–919
title to money 31–3
title to sue 213–15
tortious liability 65–6
torts
formalisation of law of 11
restitution for 942–69
intellectual property torts
969–73
non-proprietary torts
973–6
proprietary torts 942–69
total failure of consideration *see*
failure of
consideration
tracing 647–87, 689–704
academic analyses
Birks, P. 701–3

Evans, S. 703
Smith, L. 700–1
bank account, into and
through 682
cause of action 683–6
common law 212–13, 216–17,
648–55
definition of 647
equity 656–700
"exhaustion of the fund"
rule 687–700
"intermediate balance" rule
687–700
mixed fund comprising
money of beneficiary
and fiduciary 672–87
mixed fund comprising
money of two
innocent parties
657–71
following and 681–2, 747
proprietary restitution 721–3
unjust enrichment and 755–6
trespass
nuisance of 959–63
trespass to land 959–60, 964–9
trusts
proprietary restitution and
731

ultra vires 1, 7
banking facilities 6
empowering legislation 74
ultra vires contracts 7
public authorities 621–3
ultra vires defence
local authorities and
companies 926–7
ultra vires demands by public
authorities 625–45
absence of consideration 629
colore officii 628
developments in Canadian
law 633
duress 626, 628
German law on 633
implied compulsion 628–30
judicial review 641–2
Law Commission report
(1994) 627–8, 635
mistake of law bar 628
overpaid taxes, recovery of
627–8
statutory rights of recovery
631
unconstitutional statutes 633
unauthorised profit
accounting for 1

breach of fiduciary duty
1002–16
unconscionable conduct
undue influence 480–6
unconscionability
failure of consideration
309–10
unconscionability test
knowing receipt and dealing
233–7
unconstitutional statute
recovery of payments under
633
undue influence 447–501
agency 467
burden of proof 459–60
conveyance procured by
746
difficult circumstances,
exploitation of
498–500
economic weakness,
exploitation of 494–8
independent advice 460–1,
466–7
legal advice 465–6
manifest disadvantage
requirement 461–2
mental inadequacy,
exploitation of
486–92
rescission for 1
relational 448–80
fiduciary 472–3
husband and wife 472
presumed 455–80, 469–70
sexual relationships 468
suretyship transactions
462–4
thresholds 464–5
unconscionable conduct
480–6
unenforceable contracts 25–8,
66
want of formality 355–6
United States
Restatement of the Law of
Restitution (American
Law Institute) 9–10,
17, 21, 36, 47, 165,
799, 943
unjust enrichment in 2
unjust enrichment
abuse of 90–3
at the expense of the claimant
109–12, 130–3
autonomous action 112
basis of restitution claim 55

Canada 18–19, 113
Canadian approach to
        138–44
causes of action 41–7
corrective justice 48–53,
        937–42
defences 762–927
enrichments conferred by one
        but procured by
        another 120
establishing 93–4
France 2
from own property 113–14
future as legal doctrine
        61–4
future of law on 114
Germany 2
initially valid contract 120,
        122–8
law of restitution based on
        219–20
liability in 77–83
mistake and 180–2
no initial contract 121
prevention of 72–3
principle of 20–41
private law and 46
problems with jurisprudence
        65
proprietary connection
        119–20
receipt of services 91
recognition of 71
recognition of principle of
        9–41
rejection of as ground for
        restitution
        554–6

remedies for 15
reversal of 758–9
reversing 1–3
services 96–8
structure of claims 230
subtraction, by 116–18
test for 92
three party factors 119–21
tracing and 755–6
United States 2
used to define subject matter
        of restitution 56–7
used to rationalise law of
        restitution 58
whether generalised right of
        restitution for
        should be introduced
        58–9
wrongdoing, by 28–39,
        43–4
unjust factors 133–8, 221–2,
        307–14, 382–6 *see also*
        failure of
        consideration;
        ignorance; illegality;
        incapacity; legal compulsion;
        mistake; *ultra vires*
        demands by public
        authorities; undue
        influence
Birks' and Chambers'
        structuring 135–6
Birks' new "absence of basis"
        scheme 137–8,
        149
failure of consideration
        307–9
free acceptance 307

incremental development
        from them 134–5
unjust sacrifice 54–5
officious intervener 103–6
unsolicited services 101–3
unsolicited services
unjust sacrifice 101–3
use
benefit as 104
user principle 959–61
application to chattels 962–3

void contracts 13
absence of consideration
        364–7
failure of consideration
        356–86
resulting trusts arising from
        734–9
total failure of consideration
        368–82

way-leave 959, 961
windfall gain *see* **passing on**
wrongdoing
unjust enrichment by 28–39,
        43–4
**wrongful interference with
        goods**
defined 188
wrongs
restitution for 2, 929–1037
        academic analyses
                Birks, P. 934–6
                Edelman 936
                Jackman, I. 930–3
        corrective justice and
                937–42